How to Program Effectively in Delphi for AS/A Level Computer Science

Kevin R Bond

Educational Computing Services Ltd

We are always pleased to receive readers' comments about anything in the manuscript.

Structure of the book

The structure of this book is designed to promote learning through practical work and problem solving. The content of the book has been constructed with the aim of promoting good teaching and learning, so where relevant practical activities have been suggested and questions posed for the student to answer. The book includes stimulus material to promote discussion and deeper thinking about the subject. Additional material to support teaching and learning will be available from the publisher's website.

About the author

Dr Kevin R Bond is an experienced author with a proven track record of successful writing for AQA's Computing specifications. Kevin has 24 years of examining experience. He also has many more years of experience teaching Computing and Computer Science. Before becoming a computer science teacher, he worked in industry as a senior development engineer and systems analyst designing both hardware and software systems.

Published in 2021 by
Educational Computing Services Ltd
42 Mellstock Road
Aylesbury
Bucks
HP21 7NU
United Kingdom
Tel: 01296 433004
e-mail: mail@educational-computing.co.uk

For online information and ordering of this and other Educational Computing Services Ltd's books, please visit www.educational-computing.co.uk. The publisher offers discounts on this book when ordered in quantity. For more information, visit our website or please contact

discounts@educational-computing.co.uk.

First published in 2021

ISBN 978-0-9927536-0-3

Acknowledgements

The author and publisher are grateful to the following for permission to reproduce images, clipart and other copyright material in this book under licence or otherwise:

Chapter 2

Figure 2.9 Computer Shutterstock / 1226401; Keyboard Shutterstock / 335720.

Chapter 5

Capstan Shutterstock / 381034510.

Chapter 11

Figure 11.1 Pencil with lead hardness HB Shutterstock / 131161022.

Chapter 12

Rolling dice Shutterstock / 329817896.

A one-time pad reproduced with kind permission of Paul Reuvers, Crypto Museum (www.cryptomuseum.com).

Chapter 14

Thermometer - "Thermometre froid a plat" Fotolia / 11368653 ©Albachiara.

The file 'us-history-since-1877.txt ' is copyrighted by Dr. James Ross-Nazzal. It is licensed under the Creative Commons Attribution License 3.0 (http://creativecommons.org/licenses/by/3.0/).

http://cnx.org/content/col10669/1.3/.

Chapter 17

Figure 17.4 Billiard balls in frame Shutterstock / 263075000.

Figure 17.9 Pyramid with triangular base Shutterstock / 85235152.

Chapter 18

Figure 18.2 Head silhouette Shutterstock / 152509136.

Chapter 19

Figure 19.1 Clip art www.123rf.com; green apple: 123rf / 14199537; red apple: 123rf / 1419906.

Chapter 32

Figure 32.6 Server: Shutterstock / 53738941.

Chapter 33

Figure 33.11 A one-time pad reproduced with kind permission of Paul Reuvers, Crypto Museum (www.cryptomuseum.com).

Figure 33.13(a) "Image generated from random numbers generated by the PHP rand() function on Microsoft Windows." idea for this courtesy of Bo Allen, http://boallen.com/ who kindly provided permission to use his PHP script to generate this image.

Figure 33.13(b) Image generated from random numbers obtained from atmospheric noise, reproduced with permission of RANDOM.ORG.

Figure 33.14 "Gilbert Vernam" - image in public domain.

Figure 33.15/16(a) Claud Shannon, Getty Image library, image 5337874.

Chapter 42

The author is grateful to Harry Stahl for giving permission to base the analogue clock exercise on one that he explores in his book Cross-Platform Development with Delphi 10.2 & FireMonkey, ISBN 9781549545764.

Chapter 48

Yale_BSC.stars http://tdc-www.harvard.edu/catalogs/bsc5.html

Sputnik.mp3 http://www.dd1us.de/spacesounds%201.html was digitized and kindly provided by Federico Manzini.

Grasshopper eye image, rose petal image and EAG AFM and Optical Profilometry Viewer - Copyright © Eurofins Scientific www.eurofinsEAG.com.

Chapter 53

Ducky demo code sample is Copyright 2000 Eric Grange distributed as free software under GNU GPL

Chapter 64

I am grateful to the copyright owner, Choy Ping Cheng, for giving permission to use and distribute images for the Images Database exercise. These images are marked © Choy Ping Cheng 2020. All rights are reserved and the images may not be reproduced outside of the images database exercise without the express prior written permission of Choy Ping Cheng.

Chapter 73

The data for the application was downloaded in csv file format from https://data.cese.nsw.gov.au/data/dataset/nsw-public-schools-master-dataset and used under a Creative Commons Open Data licence (http://www.opendefinition.org/licenses/cc-by)

Chapter 75

Figure 75.6 - Neuron image by Jennifer Walinga - https://opentextbc.ca/introductiontopsychology/chapter/3-1-the-neuron-is-the-building-block-of-the-nervous-system/, CC BY-SA 4.0, https://commons.wikimedia.org/w/index.php?curid=97847412

Figure 75.6 - Cat image - Shutterstock/49052899

Chapter 76

Figure 76.10 - texture image - https://commons.wikimedia.org/wiki/File:UVMapping.png

Figure 76.11 - Drummyfish, CC0 - https://en.wikipedia.org/wiki/Texture_mapping#/media/File:Texture_mapping_demonstration_animation.gif

Figure 76.13 - Jan Horn - http://www.sulaco.co.za/opengl_project_chrome_face.htm

Figure 76.17 - Night sky image by Paul Volkmer from https://unsplash.com/s/photos/night-sky: paul-volkmer-qVotvbsuM_c-unsplash.jpg - https://unsplash.com/license

Figure 76.37 - © 2008-2021 Song Ho Ahn matrixModelView.zip program downloaded from http://www.songho.ca/opengl/gl_transform.html.

Mars Perserverance Rover 3D application: NASA/JPL-Caltech 3D model of the Mars Perseverance Rover vehicle obtained from https://mars.nasa.gov/resources/25042/mars-perseverance-rover-3d-model/

Figure 76.53 - Pawel Glowacki's Molecule Hero - The MIT License (MIT) Copyright (c) 2015 SUPERLOLO

The author would like to thank

- Jim McKeeth, Chief Developer Advocate & Engineer, Embarcadero Technologies, Inc., for his support in providing access to the various versions of Delphi; for his support in bringing this project to the attention of a wider audience and helping to make this project a success.
- Kirstin Challis, EMEA Partner Manager, Embarcadero UK, for her support on the schools/colleges front over a number of years and for easing my path on this project on numerous occasions.
- Dr Dave Martel, Eurofins EAG Laboratories, for his help in obtaining permission to use EAG's AFM and Optical Profilometry Viewer and two EAG images.
- Alex Bond for numerous interesting, insightful and informed discussions on the merits of C# versus Delphi.
- Our wonderful granddaughter, Isla Bradley, who provided physical and mental stimulation via Skype from the sunny shores of Sydney, Australia, which re-energised the batteries every Saturday morning, throughout the duration of this project.
- My wonderful wife, Sue Poh-Cheng Bond, for her patience, understanding and constant support during the making of this book.
- My editing and review team who have made very many helpful suggestions to improve the text and layout, caught errors and omissions and without whom this project would not have been finished. Any errors which remain are entirely of my own making.

Contents

Contents

How to use this book

The structure and content of this textbook has been designed to give the reader an appreciation of the applicability of Delphi for both structured and object-oriented programming. It covers Graphical User Interface, event driven programming from first principles in order to convey a deeper understanding of forms-based application programming and how it is achieved. Readers should gain a solid understanding of object-oriented programming and how to apply it in project work. The book also covers the excellent support Delphi has for network, graphics and database programming. Programming of mobile phones, tablets and microcontrollers is also covered.

Flipped classroom

This textbook has been written with the flipped classroom approach very much in mind. This approach reverses the conventional classroom lesson and homework model of teaching. Instead, chapters in this textbook should be used to prepare for a lesson so that classroom-time can be devoted to exercises, projects, and discussions.

The features in this book include:

Key concept	Concepts that you will need to understand and to be able to define or explain are highlighted in blue and emboldened, e.g. **Integers**.
Note	Guidance notes that you will need to follow to be able to carry out some task.
Key principle	Principles that you will need to understand and to be able to define or explain are highlighted in blue and emboldened, e.g. **Abstraction**. The same principles appear in the glossary for ease of reference.

Key fact **Key point**

Facts and points that you are useful to know because they aid in understanding concepts and principles are highlighted in blue and emboldened, e.g. **Whole number:** Whole number is another name for an integer number.

Information **Background**

References information that has the potential to assist and contribute to a student's learning. Attention is drawn to background knowledge that could also contribute to a student's learning.

Warning	Warnings that you will need to heed to be able to carry out some task successfully.
Task	Activity to deepen understanding and reinforce learning.
Programming tasks	Practical activity involving the use of a programming language to deepen understanding and reinforce learning of concepts and principles.
Questions	Short questions that probe and develop your understanding of concepts and principles as well as creating opportunities to apply and reinforce your knowledge and skills.

Web links for this book

Resources, solutions to questions, errata and the URLs of all websites referenced in this book are recorded at **www.educational-computing.co.uk/DelphiBookCode/DelphiCode.html.** Source code marked with P or 💾 may be downloaded from **www.educational-computing.co.uk/DelphiBookCode/DelphiCode.html**.

Educational Computing Services are not responsible for third party content online, there may be some changes to this content that are outside our control. If you find that a Web link doesn't work please email **webadmin@educational-computing.co.uk** with the details and we will endeavour to fix the problem or to provide an alternative.

Introduction

Delphi began life in 1995 as a complete software development environment for Windows, supporting the classic Windows model of event-driven programming for graphical user interfaces (GUIs) from the beginning.

Delphi as a programming language builds on **Pascal,** a much-praised **procedural programming language** designed by the Swiss Computer Scientist Niklaus Wirth to teach **structured programming**, and extends it with **Object Pascal** which offers support for the OOP paradigm.

Although Delphi has an **advanced class model** similar to that found in Java and C#, it does not claim to be a pure OOP language. For example, subroutines (procedures and functions), variables and constants can be declared independently of classes; basic types such as integers and strings are not themselves objects. **Therefore, novices learning how to program solutions to problems do not have to immerse themselves in OOP until they are ready** because Delphi supports both structured/procedural programming and object-oriented programming unlike C# and Java.

The option exists within Delphi for novices to begin their programming journey in an entirely **text-based console environment** learning to write **structured programs** containing **subroutines and other structured programming constructs**. Delphi makes it possible, once basics are mastered, to transition to **learning how to write classes and instantiate objects** in the **OOP paradigm**.

Delphi also has the option to write **event-driven GUI/forms-based applications** using pre-defined components or developer-defined components.

Delphi's excellent support for **Rapid Application Development (RAD)** enables forms-based applications to be generated quickly and with minimal effort. Forms-based application programming is another name for the process of producing applications with mouse-driven **Graphical User Interfaces** (GUIs). Building such applications is made straightforward by Delphi's extensive palette of components. Components are the elements used to build form-based applications which contain visible elements such as forms, dialog boxes, buttons, listboxes, etc and non-visual elements such as system timers, components for web applications and database applications.

Whilst C and C-style languages use curly braces {} to bracket blocks of program source code, Delphi has a preference for **words over symbols** and uses **begin/end** pairs. This support for words over symbols produces source code programs that can be **highly readable**, an advantage for novices and their teachers, e.g. when debugging.

Delphi is **case insensitive** so `AnotherVariable` is the same identitifier as `anotherVariable`. This is advantageous to novices learning to program.

The Delphi compiler produces native code, i.e. it **compiles directly to machine code** and not an intermediate code such as bytecode. Therefore, Delphi executables do not run inside a virtual machine unlike C# and Java. Instead, Delphi executables run on top of core operating system Application Programming Interfaces (APIs). Therefore, Delphi is able to support low level techniques such as incorporating blocks of assembly language code inline in high level source code as well as pointers to dynamically created (created at runtime) blocks of memory.

Delphi is a **strongly, static typed language** which means that the data types of all variables must be pre-declared and known at compile time. This enables errors that novice programmers commonly make to be caught at both compile time and run time.

Support for **cross-platform development** has been available from Delphi XE2 onwards. With the current free Community edition it is possible to target Android, iOS, MacOS and Windows all from a single codebase, i.e. write once then recompile and redeploy to the desired target platform. This book covers the **FireMonkey cross-platform GUI framework** and cross-platform development for Android, iOS, Windows and MacOS .

Delphi Community edition has an HTTP and a REST client library, available on all platforms, to invoke **REST services** and even specific **Amazon Web Services (AWS)** and **Azure** components. Examples of the use of **REST** are included in this book.

Database support in Delphi is very strong. This book covers the use of **ADO**, **Interbase** and **FireDac components.** With FireDac it is possible to connect to over 20 databases natively.

The book start with an overview of the IDE (Integrated Development Environment) - Chapter 1a - in the context of two event-driven GUI applications - Chapter 1b. It is possible to skip these two applications and start with **console mode programming** and the **Pascal programming language** (Chapter 2), before progressing to learning **Object Pascal** through console mode applications. The principles learned are then applied to a console mode application which generates a graphical user interface with associated event handlers.

The Pascal programming language was designed to be simple and straightforward to use. Pascal is a strongly, statically typed block structured language. This means that programmers must specify the data type of each variable in their source code and programs are constructed in blocks of statements. The simplest program consists of a program heading and a main block.

For example,

```
Program Example;
  Begin
    Writeln('Hello World');
  End.
```

The program heading is '`Program Example;`' and the main block is

```
Begin
  Writeln('Hello World');
End.
```

This book then concentrates on exposing the **nature of objects**, how their classes relate to each other via **inheritance** and how objects behave **polymorphically**. The mechanics of applications with graphical user interfaces is postponed until object-oriented programming basics have been covered first. From experience, this bottom up approach has proved useful in providing a good grounding to make the reader a more effective programmer of VCL (Visual Component Library) forms-based applications for which Delphi is well known.

This book covers building **VCL** and **FireMonkey forms-based applications** and **database applications** using **Interbase**, **Firebird**, **Microsoft Access**, **IBLite** and **MySQL**.

This book also covers **graphics**, **network programming**, **machine learning** and **inline assembly language programming**.

A special feature of this book is that it includes practical exercises for the reader to try, with solutions for these being available from our website.

The final section of the book covers a range of projects for the reader to study and try.

The book uses **Embarcadero's Delphi Community Edition 10.2**, **10.3** and **10.4** principally but the book can be used just as well with Delphi 7 through to version **10.4** and beyond, e.g. **Delphi 11**. Where there are differences between the versions these are highlighted.

1a Delphi Integrated Development Environment (IDE)

Introduction to the IDE

Purpose: Finding your way around the IDE.

Information

The current community edition of Delphi at the time of writing is 10.4 and the current commercial version is 11.0. The descriptions of the IDE in this chapter are still relevant because a great strength of Delphi is its backwards compatibility.

Launch Delphi 10.2 Community Edition or the version that you use. **Click** File in the menu bar, **select** New VCL Forms Application - Delphi. The Integrated Development Environment (IDE) shown in *Figure 1.1* should appear.

The title bar is located at the top of the IDE. It displays the name of the project, the version of Delphi being used and the name of the Delphi unit corresponding to the form being displayed. In this case **Project1**, **Delphi 10.2 Community Edition** and **Unit1**, respectively. It is good practice to assign descriptive names to your project and any units associated with the project. How to do this will be explained later.

The IDE has a menu bar consisting of a File menu, an Edit menu, etc as shown in *Figure 1.1*. The File menu shown in *Figure 1.2* has a list of commands to create new projects/files, open existing projects/files, save projects/files, etc.

The Edit menu shown in *Figure 1.3* has a list of commands such as **copy, paste, delete**, etc for editing projects.

The other menus in the menu bar will be explored later.

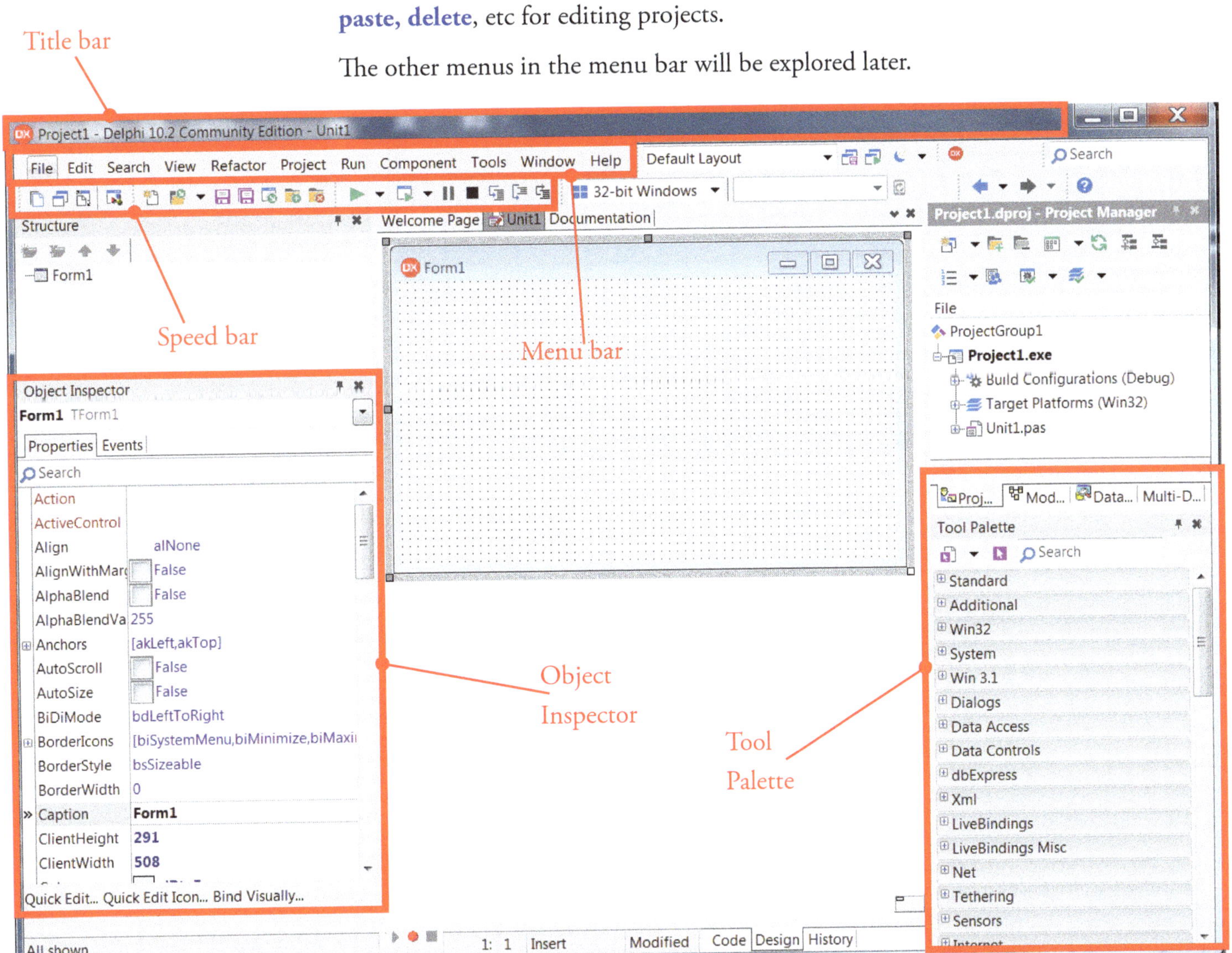

Fig. 1.1 Delphi 10.2 Community Edition Integrated Development Environment

The speed bar is located underneath the menu bar shown in *Figure 1.1*.

The speed bar consists of buttons each with an image representing the command which is invoked when its button is clicked. These buttons enable the same commands to be invoked as found in the submenus of the menu bar. For example, before **Unit1** has been saved, clicking the button causes the **Save Unit1 As** dialogue window shown in *Figure 1.4* to appear. Before **Unit1** has been saved, clicking the **Save** command in the File menu, shown in *Figure 1.2*, brings up the same dialogue window.

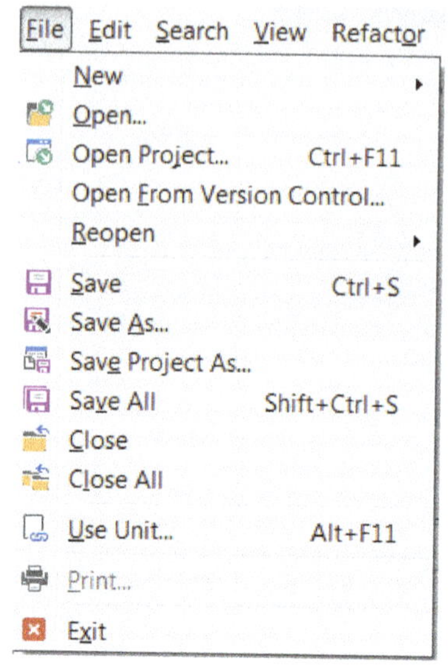

Fig. 1.2 Delphi 10.2 Community Edition File menu

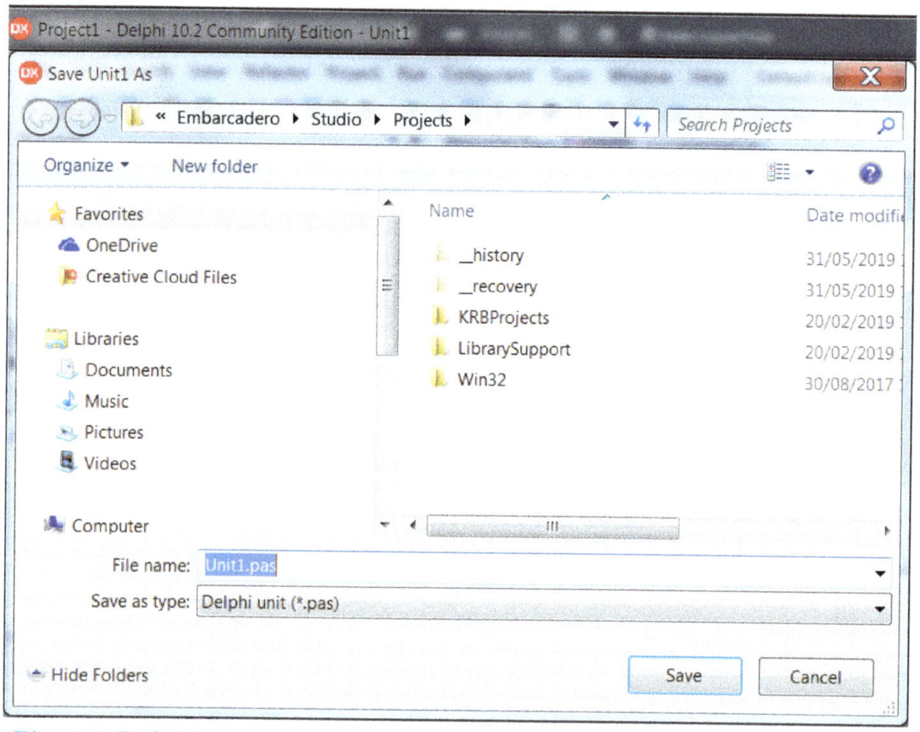

Fig. 1.4 Delphi 10.2 Community Edition Save Unit1 As dialogue window

Clicking the button in the speed bar toggles between the **Form view** and the **Unit view** as shown in *Figure 1.5*, and vice versa.

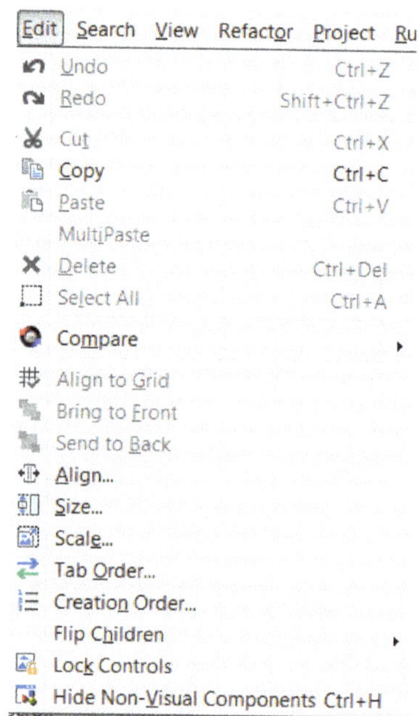

Fig. 1.3 Delphi 10.2 Community Edition Edit menu

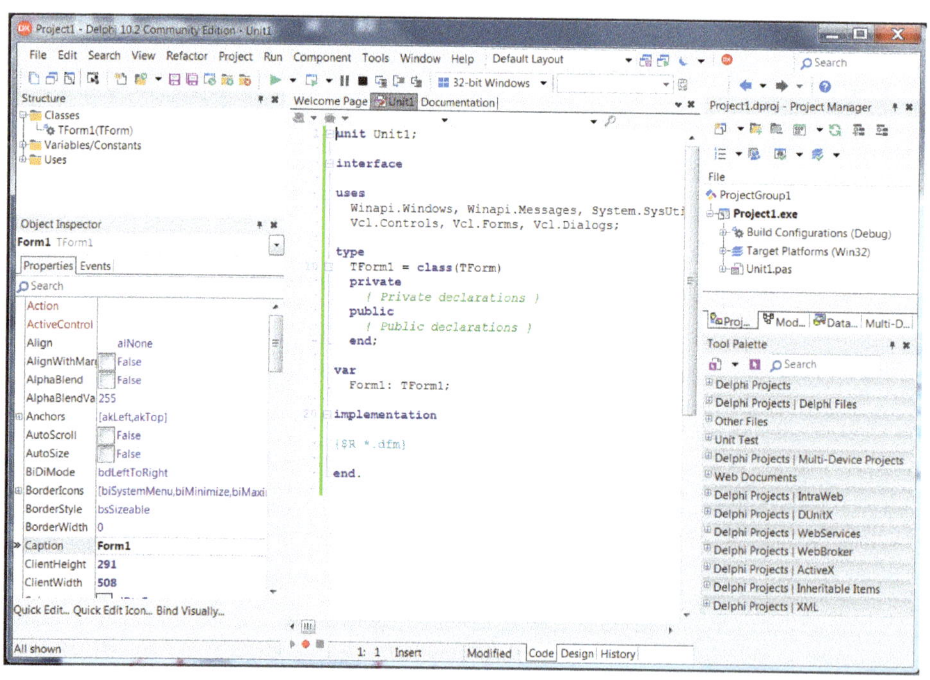

Fig. 1.5 Delphi 10.2 Community Edition Unit view

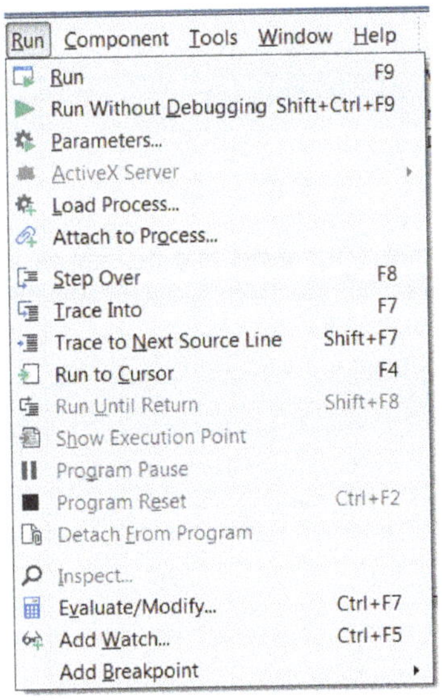

Fig. 1.6 Delphi 10.2 Community Edition Run menu

The same outcome can be achieved by clicking the tab labelled **Code**, and the tab labelled **Design**, respectively, at the bottom of the IDE.

Clicking on a speed button in the speed bar is quicker and more convenient than using the corresponding command from the menu bar.

To launch **Form1** shown in *Figure 1.1* as a Windows application that can be debugged, the **Run** command must be clicked in the Run menu - *Figure 1.6* - or the  button from the speed bar must be clicked.

Figure 1.7 shows the Windows application that results. Its graphical user interface is a form with the caption **Form1**.

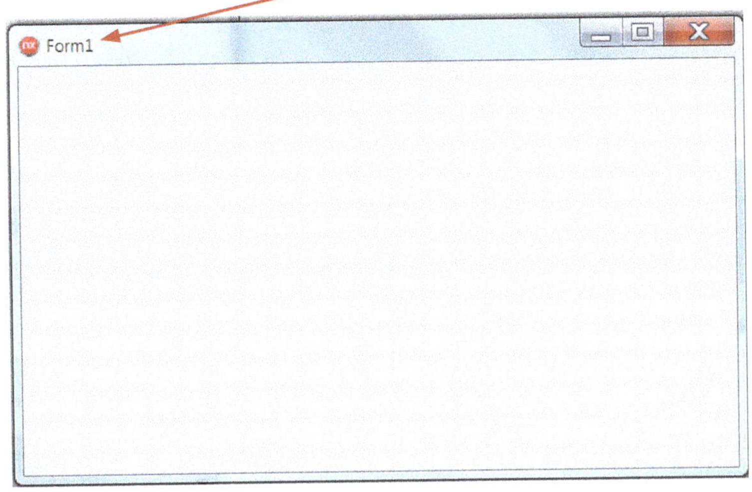

Fig. 1.7 Delphi 10.2 Community Edition Windows application showing a single form with caption Form1

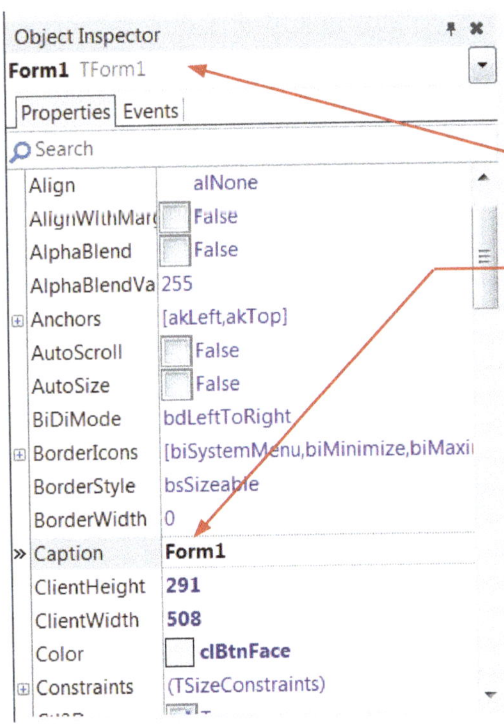

Fig. 1.8 Delphi 10.2 Community Edition Object Inspector

We can use the Object Inspector shown in *Figure 1.1* and *Figure 1.8* to change this form's caption. **Stop** the application by clicking on  in the top right corner of the Windows application.

With **Form1** selected, **place** mouse cursor in the **Caption** field showing value **Form1**. **Change** its value to **My Form**.

The change effects the form immediately as shown in *Figure 1.9* even though Delphi is in design mode. *Figure 1.10* shows what this change looks like when the application is run.

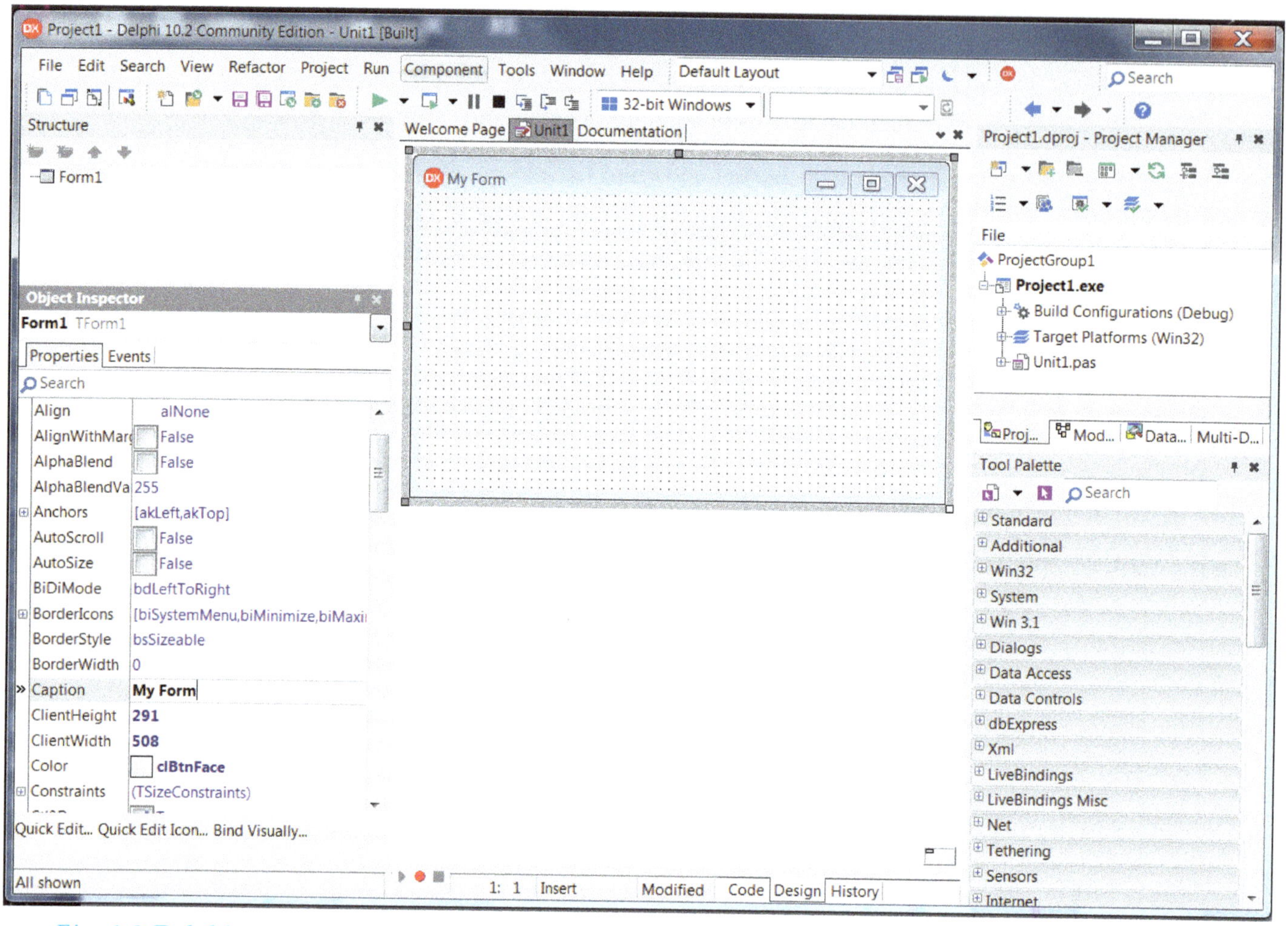

Fig. 1.9 Delphi 10.2 Community Edition design view showing that a change of caption value has an immediate effect on the form

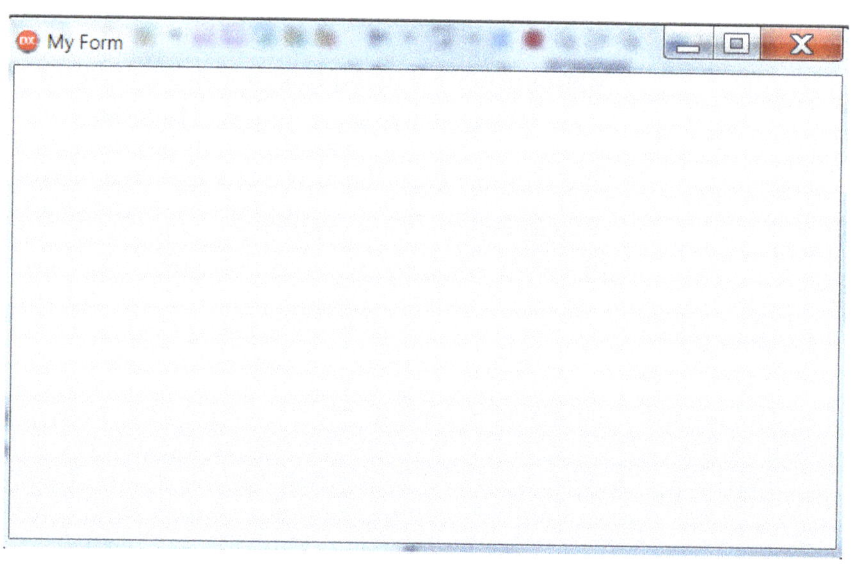

Fig. 1.10 Delphi 10.2 Community Edition Windows application with My Form caption

The form is the primary design surface. This means that we can place visual components (and non-visual components) such as buttons, edit boxes, etc on the form and have these appear when the application is run.

Visual components and non-visual components are selected from the tool palette in **Delphi 10.2 Community Edition (Delphi CE)** and from the component palette in **Delphi 7** - *Figure 1.11*.

The components are organised in categories in **Delphi 10.2 Community Edition** and in tabs in **Delphi 7**.

The components that are used most frequently such as buttons, edit boxes are located in the **Standard** category/tab shown in *Figure 1.12*. Another frequently used category/tab is the **Additional** category/tab shown in *Figure 1.13*. This category/tab contains an image component used for displaying images loaded from files; and a shape component used for drawing graphic shapes such as rectangles, ellipses and circles on a form. *Figure 1.14* shows the **System** category/tab which contains amongst other things, a timer component, **TTimer**.

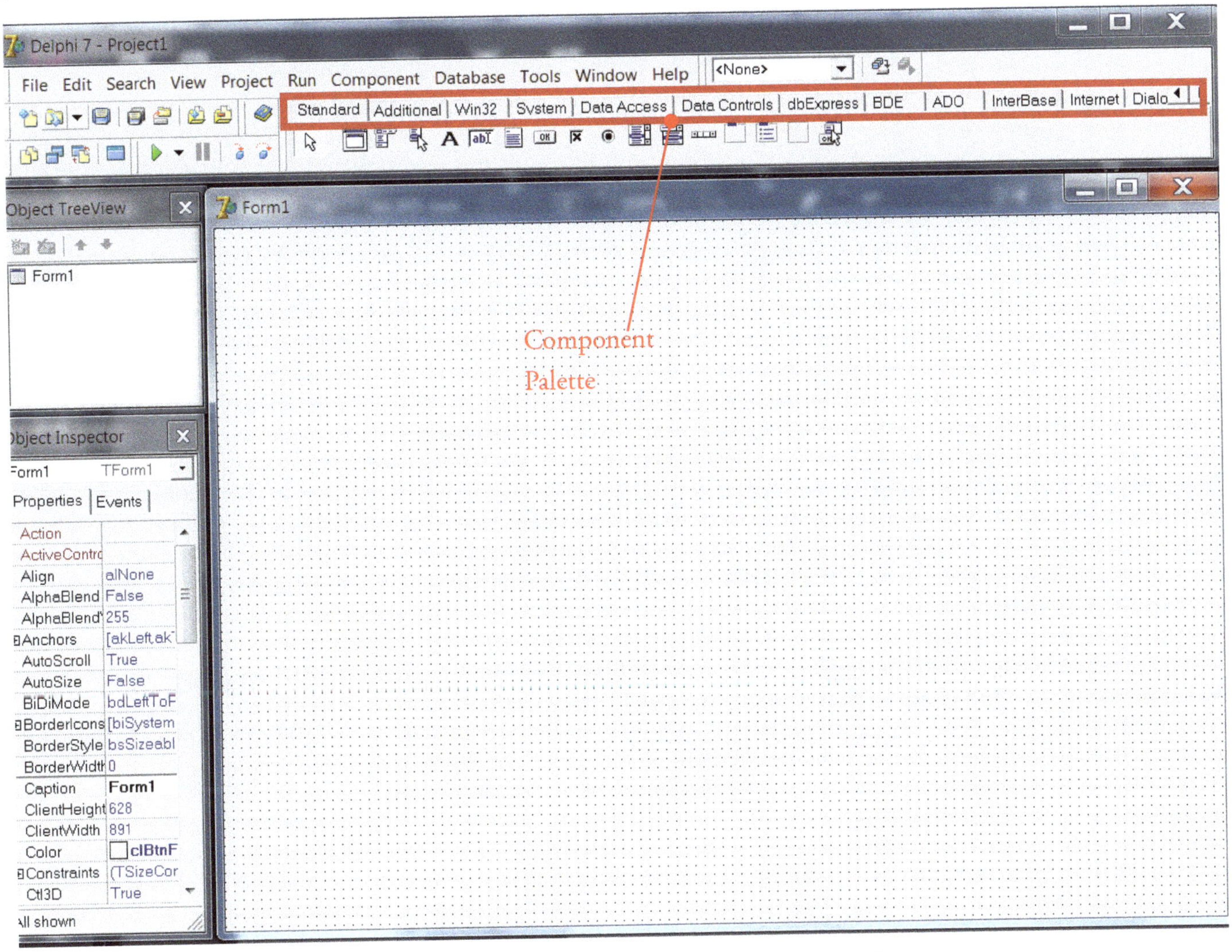

Fig. 1.11 Delphi 7 Integrated Development Environment

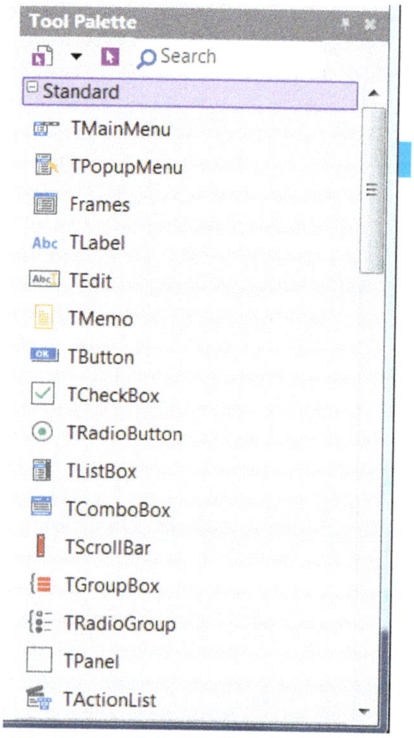

Fig. 1.12 Delphi CE Standard category of Tool Palette

Fig. 1.13 Delphi CE Additional category showing some but not all components

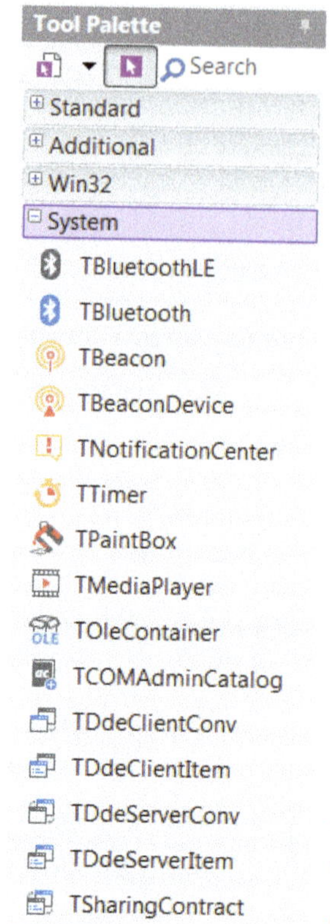

Fig. 1.14 Delphi CE System category

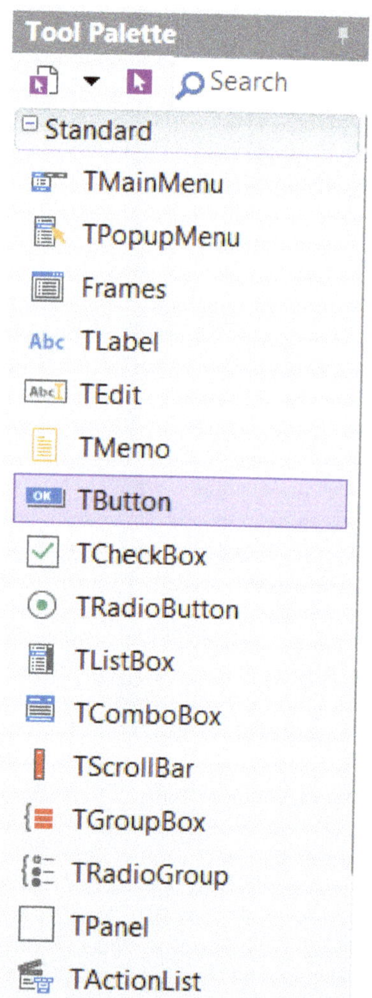

Fig. 1.15 Delphi CE button component selected in Standard category

Creating an event-driven application

Purpose: To learn how to place components on a form which respond to events.

With **My Form Project1 VCL Forms** application in design mode, **open** the **Standard** category/tab and **click** on the button component to select it as shown in *Figure 1.15*. Now **move** the mouse arrow over the form to the desired location for the button. **Place** the button on the form by clicking the left mouse button. *Figure 1.16* shows the result.

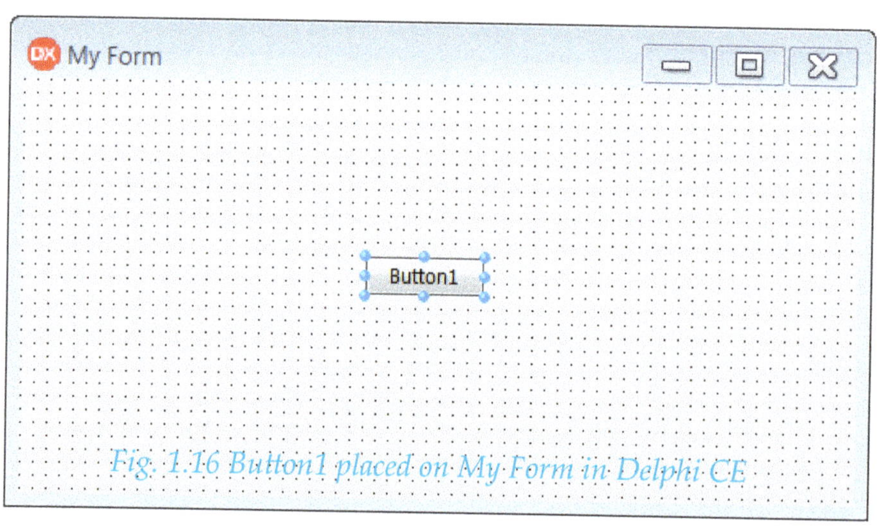

Fig. 1.16 Button1 placed on My Form in Delphi CE

This button has a name and a caption. The values of each may be inspected in the **Object Inspector**. With **Button1** selected, locate the **Name** field value in the **Object Inspector** and **change** the value from **Button1** to **Activate**, **press** return. The **Caption** field value will change automatically to the **Name** field value, **Activate**. Both values may be changed independently to be different, if desired. *Figure 1.17* shows the result.

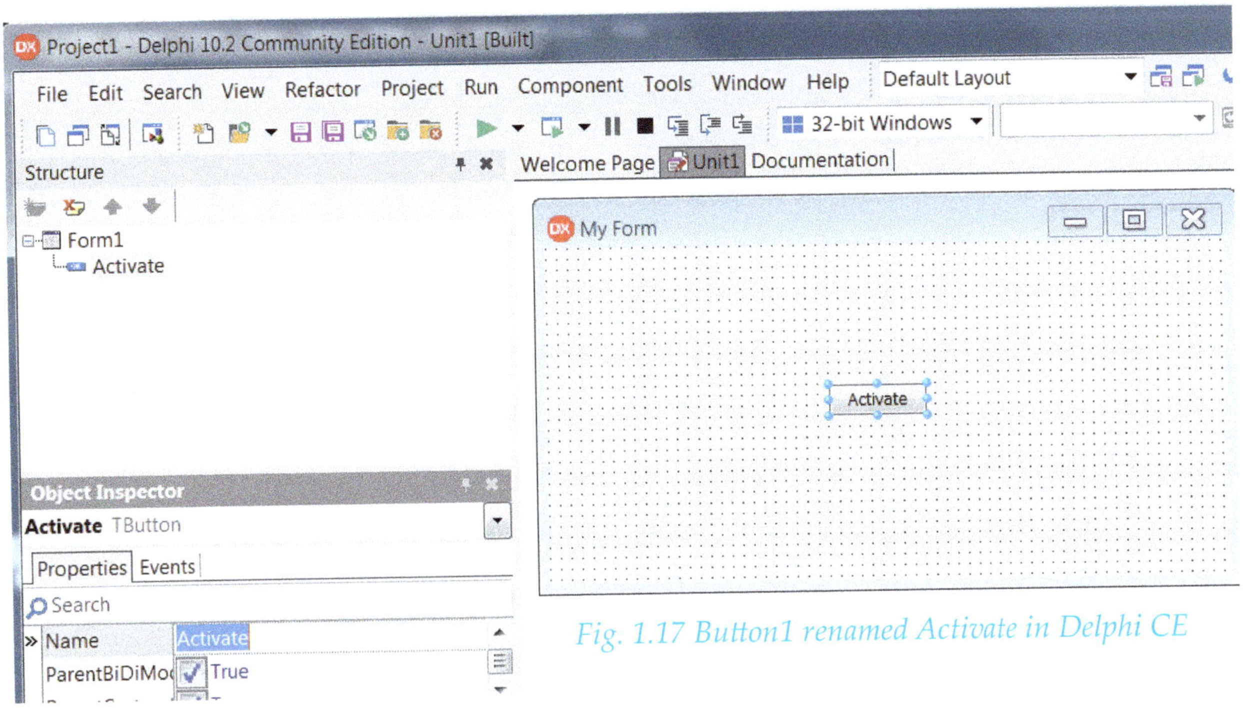

Fig. 1.17 Button1 renamed Activate in Delphi CE

> **Note**
>
> In Delphi CE don't have the button selected when you double click on the Activate button. The easiest way to do this is to close the Standard category.

A button on a form is only useful if it does something when clicked. To create that something, **double click** the button to create an event-handler. *Figure 1.18* shows that **Delphi CE** has created skeleton code for a procedure **TForm1.ActivateClick** and added the name **ActivateClick** to the Events page in the **Object Inspector**. This means that when the application is running and the button named **Activate** is clicked (mouse arrow over button and left mouse button clicked), the procedure called **ActivateClick** will execute. At the moment it does nothing.

Add

```
procedure TForm1.ActivateClick(Sender: TObject);
begin
  ShowMessage('Hello World');
end;
```

Click on the **Run** speed button to run the application.

Figure 1.19 shows the running Windows application.

Click on the **Activate** button. A message window appears as shown in *Figure 1.20*. **Click** on the **OK** button to close this message window.

Click on the  button in the top right corner of the form to close the application.

We can use the **Activate** button to close or terminate the application if we replace the line of code `ShowMessage('Hello World');` with the line of code `Application.Terminate;`.

In actual fact, `ShowMessage('Hello World');` can just be commented out by placing two oblique strokes before it so that it gets ignored as shown in *Figure 1.21*.

Run the application and confirm that clicking on the **Activate** button terminates the running application.

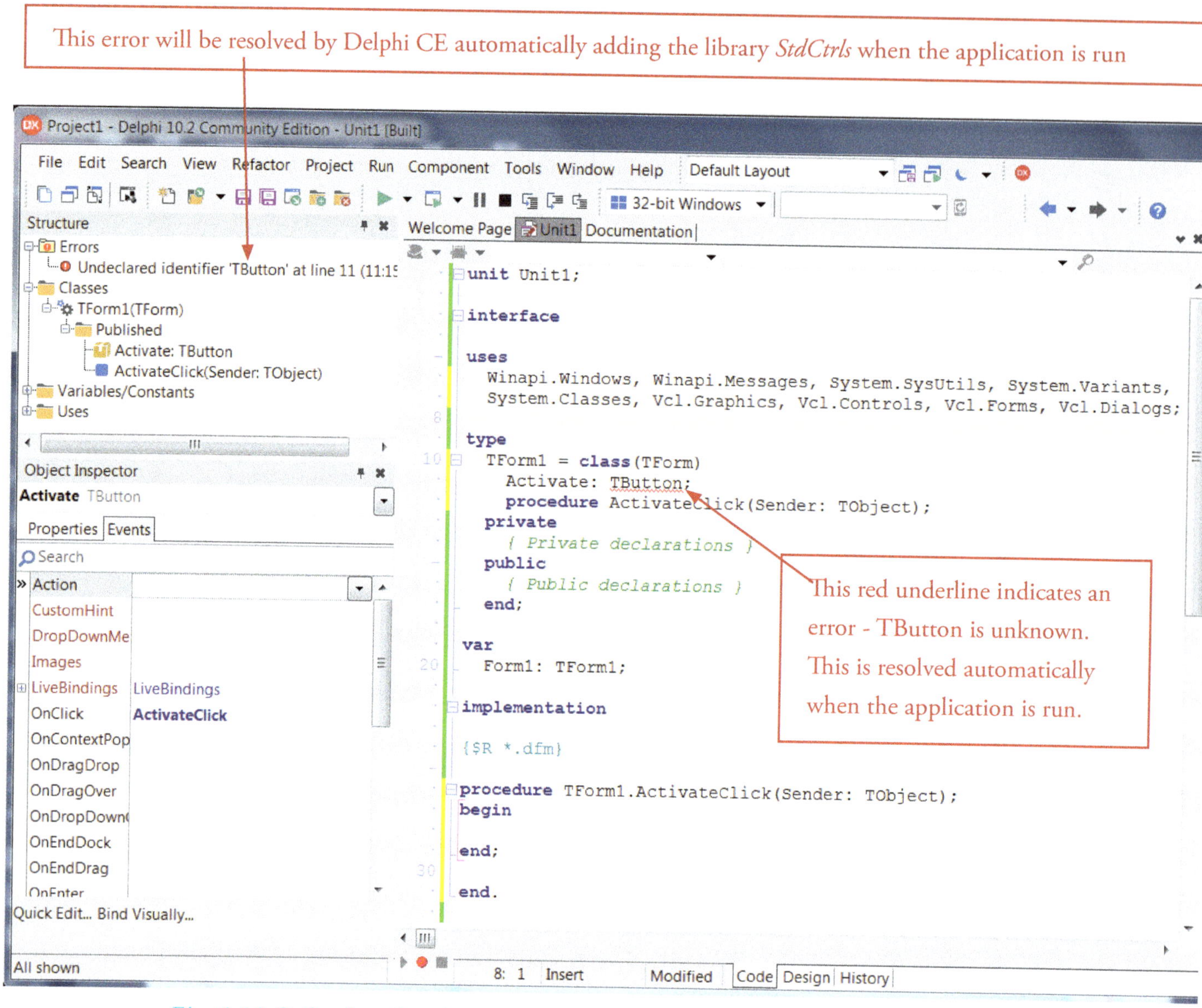

Fig. 1.18 Code view showing TForm1.ActivateClick event-handler in Delphi CE

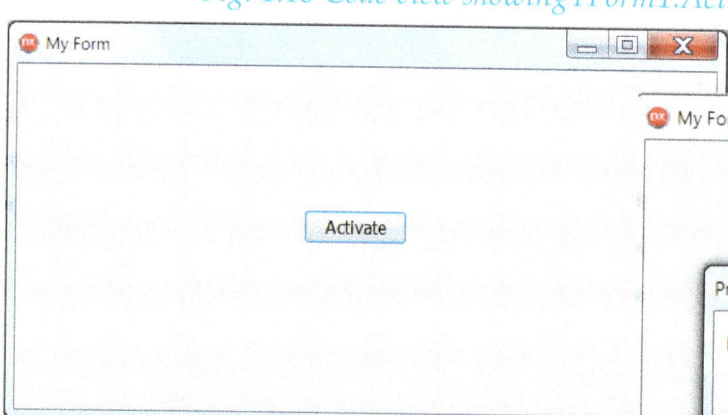

Fig. 1.19 Windows application appearance when run

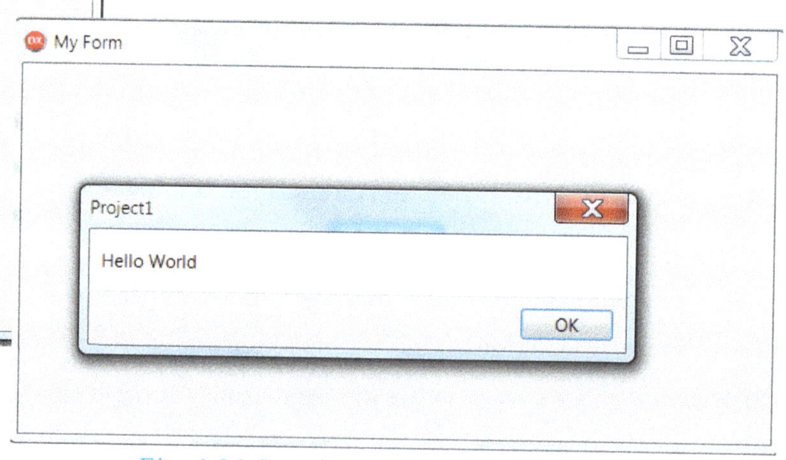

Fig. 1.20 Result of clicking Activate button

```
procedure TForm1.ActivateClick(Sender: TObject);
begin
  //ShowMessage('Hello World');
  Application.Terminate;
end;
```

Fig. 1.21 ActivateClick now terminates the application

All Delphi applications begin with a program file. By default this file has the name **Project1.dpr**. Both **Delphi 7** and **Delphi 10.2 CE** also create a corresponding configuration file.
In **Delphi CE**, the configuration file corresponding to **Project1.dpr** has filename **Project1.dprog**.
In **Delphi 7**, the configuration file corresponding to **Project1.dpr** has filename **Project1.cfg**.

Figure 1.22 shows **Project1.dpr** in the **Delphi CE IDE**.

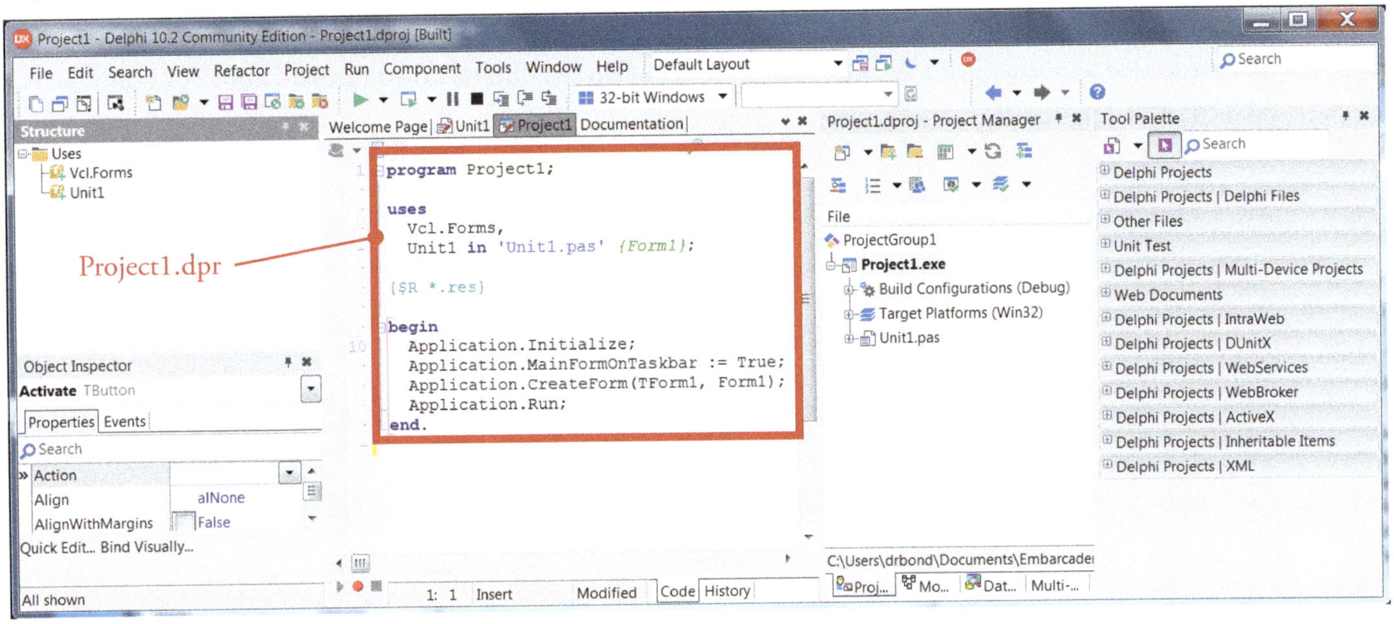

Fig. 1.22 shows that the main program file Project1.dpr contains references to the Application object

Project1.dpr is viewable in the **IDE** by selecting **Project** from the Menu bar and then View Source as shown in *Figure 1.23*.

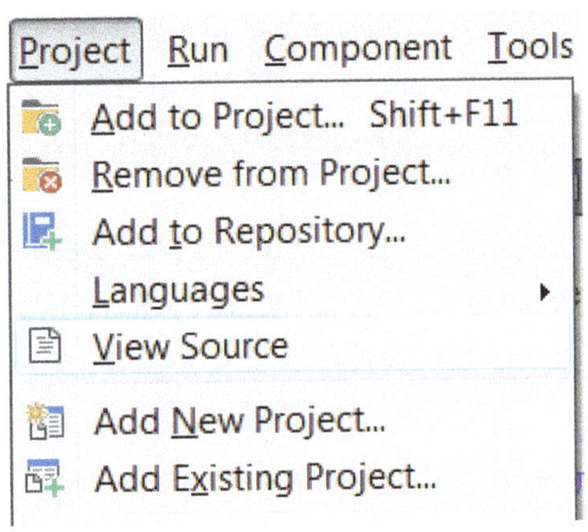

Fig. 1.23 Selecting View Source from the Project submenu in the Menu bar

The details of the application's Windows form, **Form1**, are contained in the file **Unit1.pas** which is why it is necessary for **Project1.dpr** to include the reference `Unit1 in 'Unit1.pas' {Form1}` in the **Uses** statement. Every Delphi Windows form has common features, e.g. the minimize, maximize and close buttons. The details of the common features are contained in the file **Vcl.Forms.dcu** which **Project1.dpr** references as **Vcl.Forms** in the **Uses** statement.

In *Figure 1.22*, the statement `Application.CreateForm(TForm1, Form1);` creates **Form1**, the application window, and the statement `Application.Run;` starts the application. This is the classic Windows mode of operation. An application window is created, and then the application enters into a wait state where it is able to accept and despatch messages arising from some event detected by the operating system, e.g. a mouse click, until the application is terminated. Despatching a message means to execute something called the event-handler. The event-handler must have been set up first and the particular event it handles registered. In this way the responding application can run harmoniously with other applications. For example, *Figure 1.24* shows three executing Windows applications which, for convenience, we will call **Application1**, **Application2**, and **Application3**.

Application1 currently has the focus (revealed by the fact that its close button appears with a red background).

The focus can be changed at any time by clicking the window of **Application2** or **Application3**. If there is an event-handler associated with the region clicked then this event-handler will be called (into action). For example, if the **Activate** button of **Application2** is clicked then **Application2** will close.

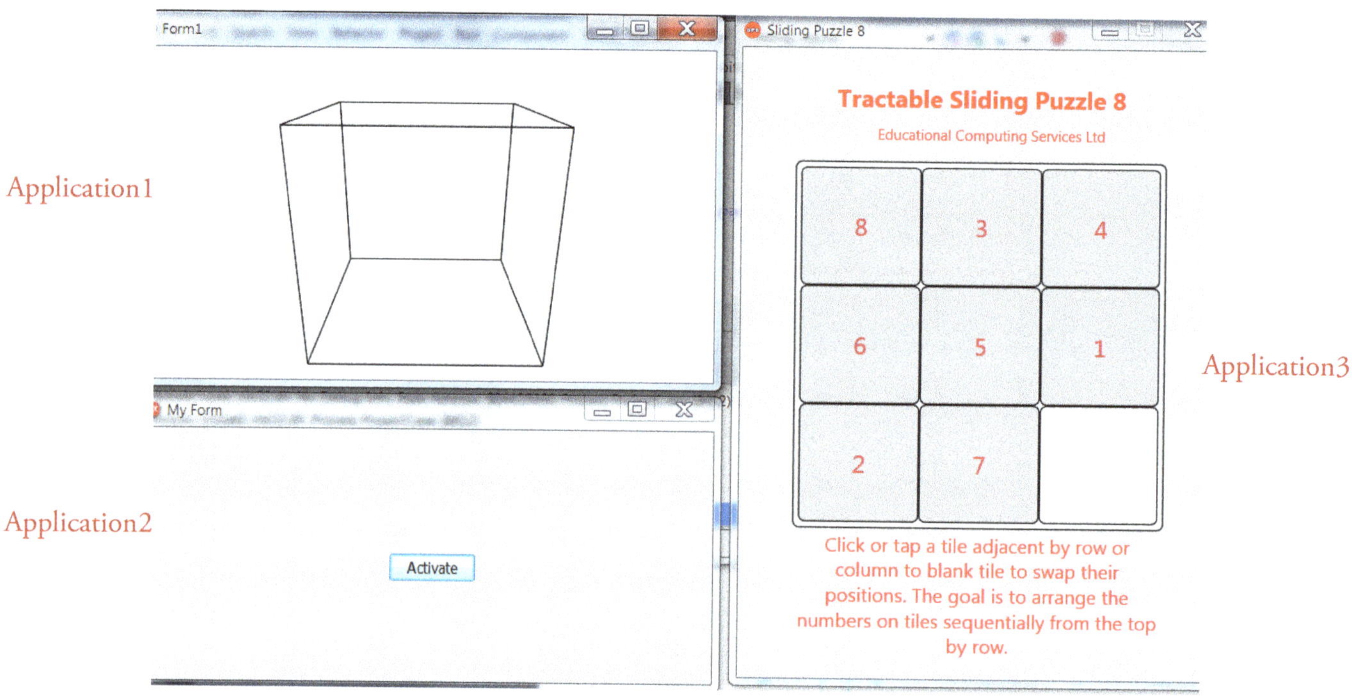

Fig. 1.24 Three different executing Windows applications

Figure 1.25 shows the outcome of clicking on the tile labelled 1 in **Application3** in *Figure 1.24*. The event-handler for this event has moved tile 1 to a new position and replaced its original position with a blank tile.

Fig. 1.25 shows the outcome from the action of clicking tile 1

Saving a project

Purpose: To learn how to save a project and its unit(s)

Figure 1.26 shows the speed bar for **Delphi 10.2 Community Edition**.

Figure 1.27 shows the speed bar for **Delphi 7**.

To save a project, click on **Save All** in the speed bar. If this is the first time then the **Save Unit1 As** dialogue window opens - *Figure 1.28*. Navigate to the drive and folder system where you wish to save the unit and project.
Click on **New Folder** and name the new folder **Application1**.
Change the file name from **Unit1.pas** to **ApplicationUnit1.pas** and click the **Save** button. The **Save Project1 As** dialogue window now opens - *Figure 1.29*. Change the file name from **Project1.dprog** to **ApplicationProject1.dprog** in **Delphi CE** and from **Project1.dpr** to **ApplicationProject1.dpr** in **Delphi 7** and click the **Save** button.

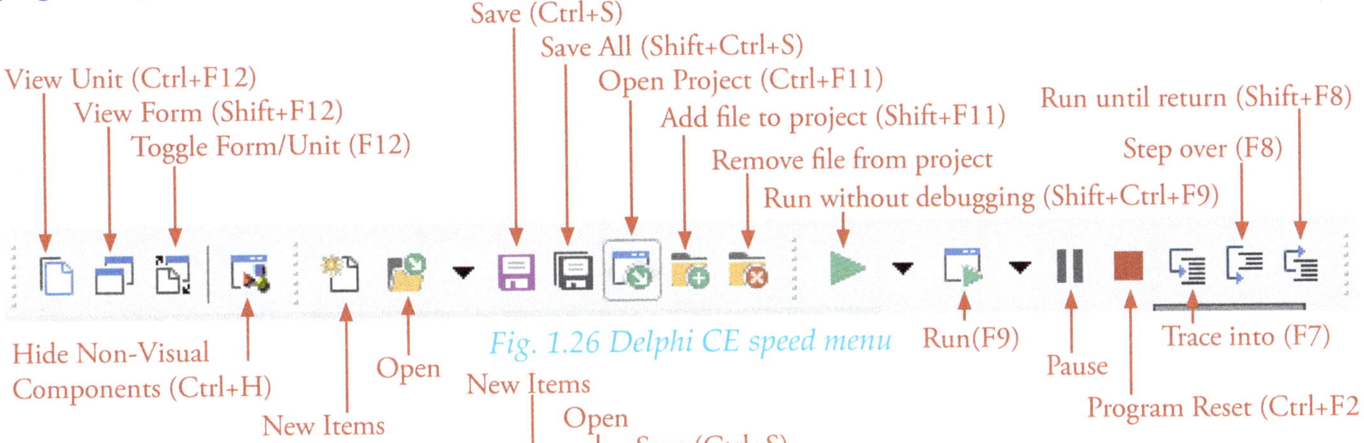

Fig. 1.26 Delphi CE speed menu

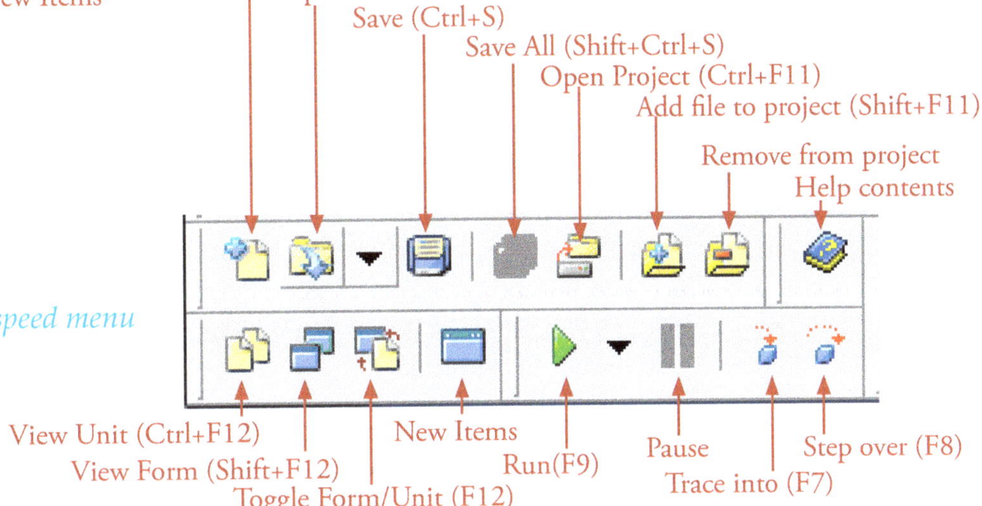

Fig. 1.27 Delphi 7 speed menu

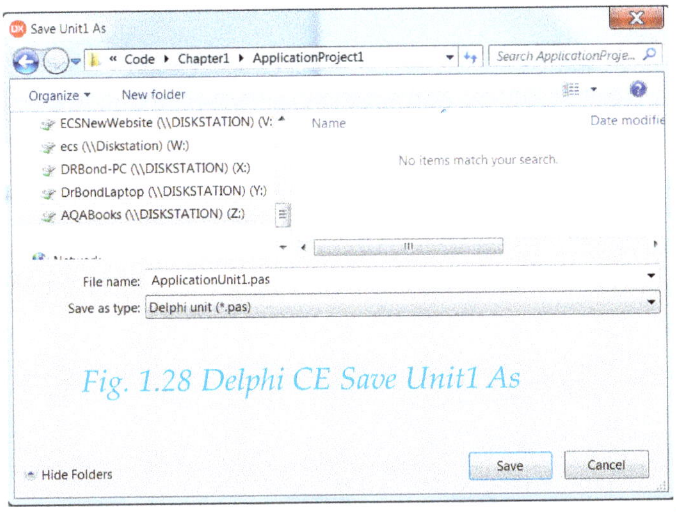

Fig. 1.28 Delphi CE Save Unit1 As

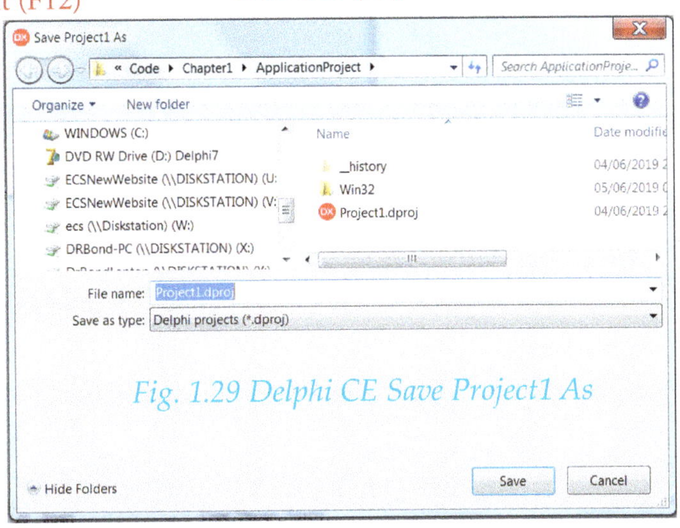

Fig. 1.29 Delphi CE Save Project1 As

If the project and its unit(s) have already been saved and now it is required to save the project under a different file name or in a different folder then the File menu must be chosen from the menu bar and the **Save Project As** option chosen. *Figure 1.30* shows the File menu for **Delphi CE** and *Figure 1.31* shows the File menu for **Delphi 7**.

To save the unit(s) under a different file name or in a different folder then choose the **Save As option** from the File menu. At any time, choosing the **Save** option in the File menu or the corresponding speed button will save the unit currently active in the IDE. Choosing **Save All** will save all units and the project.

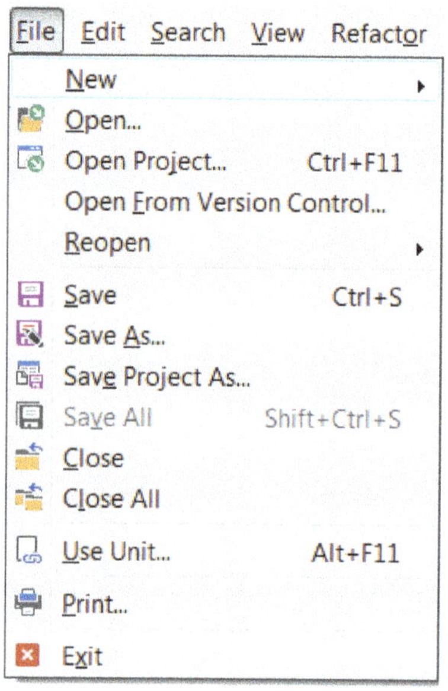

Fig. 1.30 Delphi CE file menu

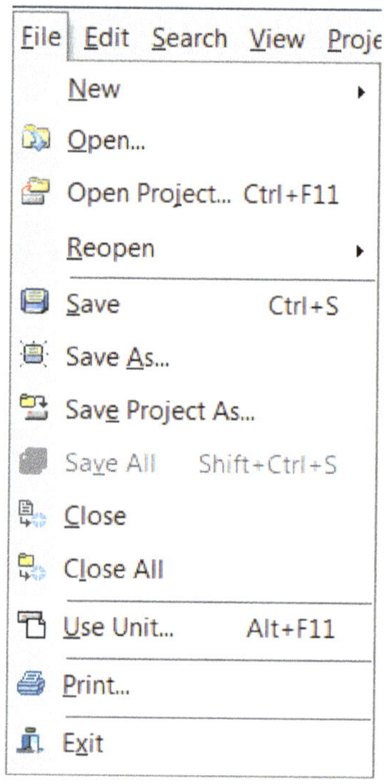

Fig. 1.31 Delphi 7 file menu

The first thing that should be done when working with a new project is to save the project and associated units. It is bad practice to keep the default project file name, **Project1**, assigned by Delphi because it makes it difficult to identify the project in the future. Use a meaningful and descriptive file name for the project in order to recall what the project does.

Similarly, it is not a good idea to keep the default unit names, Unit1, Unit2, etc. Use a meaningful and descriptive file name for each unit in order to recall what each unit does.

It is also important to save each project in a meaningfully named folder together with its units, possibly within sub folders, as this improves their organisation. Always check, after using **Save Project As** to relocate the project to a new folder, that you have also saved all its units in the new folder (**Save As** for each unit).

Using the project manager window

Purpose: To learn what support is available from the project manager window

Figure 1.32 shows the expanded project manager window with the path show option selected. *Figure 1.33* shows the pop-up window that appears when `AddProject.exe` is clicked. It is possible to do many actions from this pop-up window that can be done from the speed menu at the top of the IDE window.

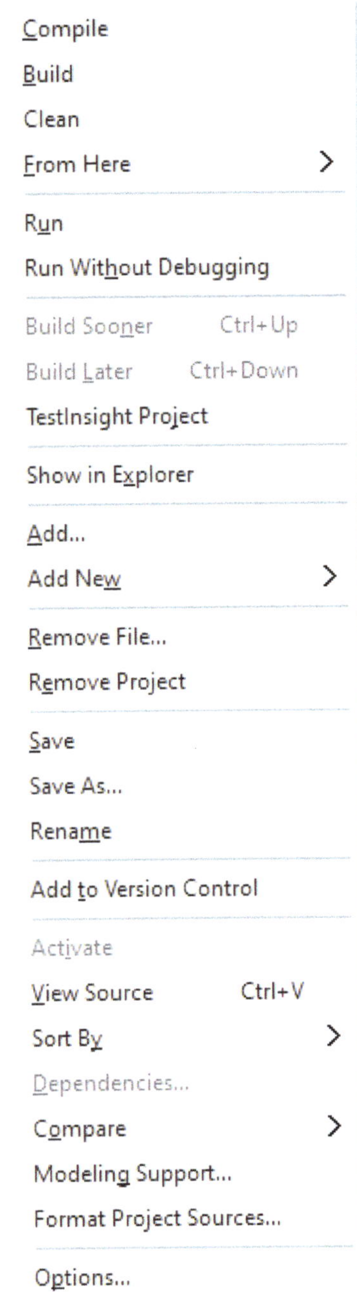

Fig. 1.33 Window that pops up when exe right-clicked

Files that make up a Delphi project

Purpose: To learn the nature and purpose of files in a Delphi project

Figure 1.34 shows a snapsot of the files belonging to the `AddProject`.

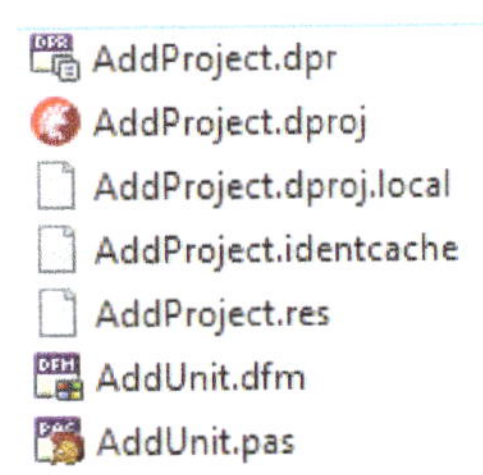

Fig. 1.34 Project files

`AddProject.dpr` is the project's source (`Program AddProject; ... Begin ...End.`), a text file. `AddProject.dproj` is a configuration file in XML format containing the current settings for project options, such as compiler and linker settings, directories, conditional directives, and command-line parameters. These options are set using Project|Options. `AddUnit.pas` contains unit source code (`Unit AddUnit ... Implementation ... End.`). It is a text file.

`AddUnit.dfm` stores the property settings for the objects (e.g. labels on the form) in plain text form. This enables the objects on the form to be correctly positioned and labelled, etc, when the project is opened again. `AddProject.res` is a resource file. The file must be a Windows resource file. Resources are the elements of a program that support the program but are not executable code, e.g. bitmaps, cursors, icons. These are bound to the application's .exe file during the link phase.The resources can then be accessed more quickly because locating a resource in the executable file is quicker than loading it from a disk file. `AddProject.dproj.local` is an XML file containing XML files that include the visual ordering of files in the project within each folder, delete it and the files will appear in alphabetical order. `AddProject.identcache` contains information used for refactoring, e.g. change all instances of `AddBtn` to `AddButton`.

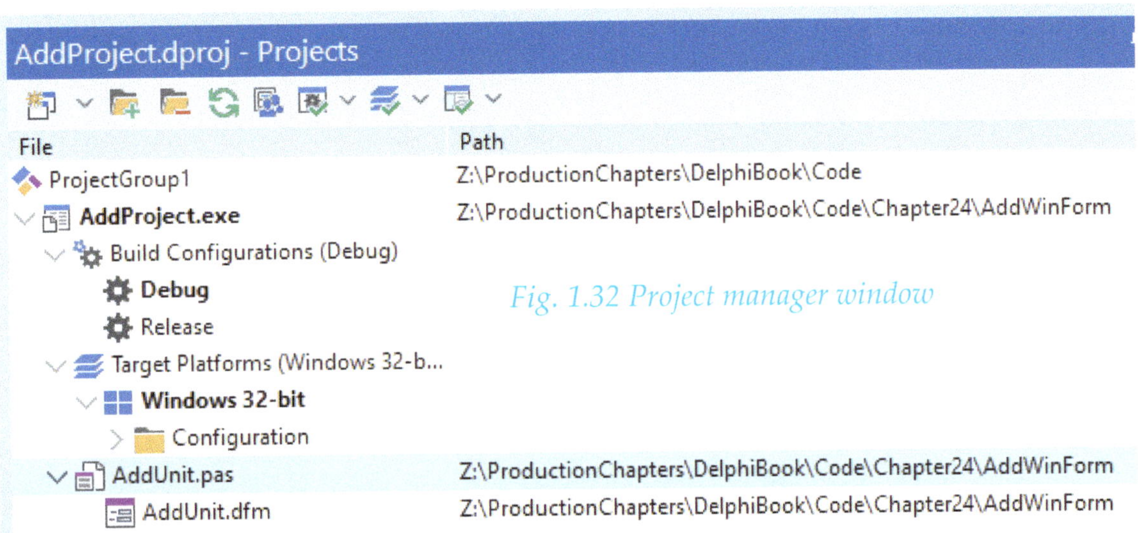

Fig. 1.32 Project manager window

Using other components

Purpose: To learn how to use label, edit box, mask edit, panels

P

Figure 1.32 shows the design view in **Delphi CE** for a very simple calculator.

Start a new **VCL Forms Application** project. **Click Save All** and save project as CalculatorProject.dproj in a folder Calculator. **Save** the unit as CalcUnit1.pas in the same folder.

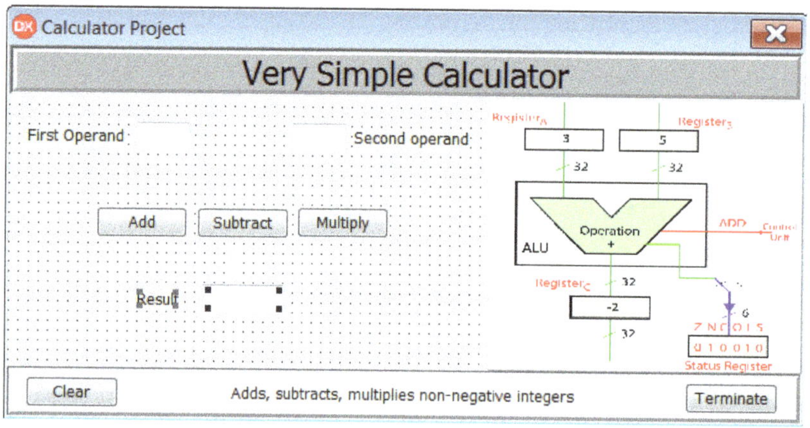

Fig. 1.32 Delphi CE design view for very simple calculator, form height =332, form width = 651

Select TPanel in the **Standard** category of the **Tool Palette** - *Figure 1.33*. **Click** on the top half of the form to create a panel, Panel1. Select this panel in the **Object Inspector** and change its **Name** property value from Panel1 to TopPanel and its **Caption** property value to Calculator, for the moment. Change its **Align** property value to alTop - *Figure 1.34*. This panel should now be positioned and sized as shown in *Figure 1.35*.

Select Form1 in the **Object Inspector** and change its **Caption** property to Calculator Project - *Figure 1.37*.

Set its **Height** property to 331 and its **Width** property to 651. **Set** its **Name** property to MainForm.

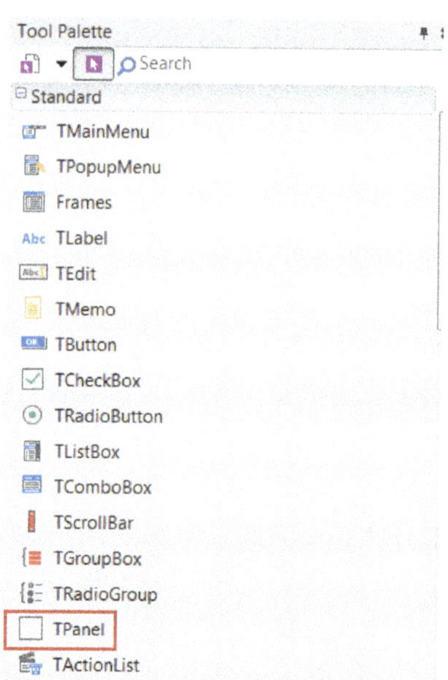

Fig. 1.33 Delphi CE Tool Palette Standard category

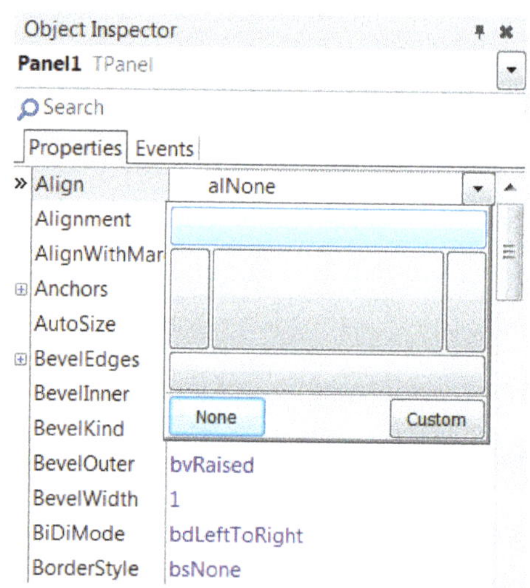

Fig. 1.34 Delphi CE Object Inspector Align field

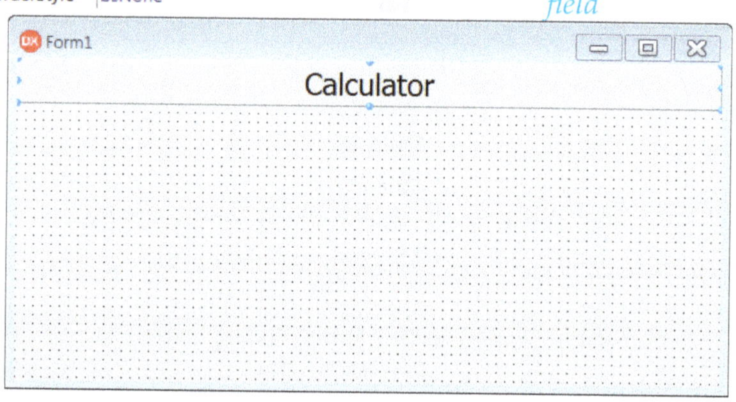

Fig. 1.35 Delphi CE TopPanel aligned to the top of the form, height = 41

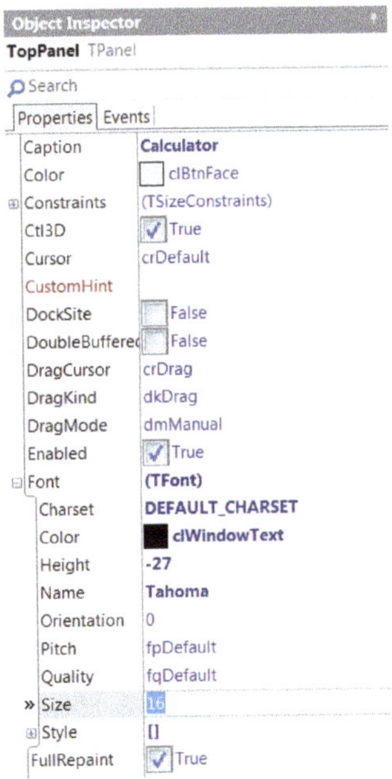

Fig. 1.36 Delphi CE Object Inspector setting TopPanel font size

Select and **expand** the **Font** property of TopPanel in **Object Inspector** - *Figure 1.36*. **Change Size** property to 20, **press** return key.

Select TPanel in the **Standard** category of the **Tool Palette**. **Click** on the bottom half of the form to create a panel, Panel1. Select this panel in the **Object Inspector** and change its **Name** property value from Panel1 to BottomPanel and its **Caption** property value to Adds, subtracts, multiplies non-negative integers. **Change** its **Align** property value to alBottom and **set** its **Height** property to 41. This panel should now be positioned and sized as shown in *Figure 1.32*.

Select TPanel in the **Standard** category of the **Tool Palette**. **Click** on the right-side of the form to create a panel, Panel1. Select this panel in the **Object Inspector** and change its **Name** property value from Panel1 to RightSidePanel. **Delete** its **Caption** property value. Change its **Align** property value to alRight. Set its Width property to 253. This panel should now be positioned and sized as shown in *Figure 1.32*.

Select TImage in the **Additional** category of the **Tool Palette**. **Click** on the panel on the form, **RightSidePanel**, to create an image component, **Image1** on this panel. **Select** this image in the **Object Inspector** and change its **Name** property value from Image1 to ImageALU. Change its **Align** property value to alClient. This image component should now fill the panel component as shown in *Figure 1.37*.

Select Picture property of ImageALU in **Object Inspector** - *Figure 1.39*. **Click** on ... to bring up **Picture Editor** window - *Figure 1.39*. **Click** on **Load** and use ALU.jpg as the image (download from www.educational-computing.co.uk/DelphiBookCode/Chapter1Code/CE10.2/Calculator/ALU.jpg) - *Figure 1.40*.

Click OK to close **Picture Editor.**

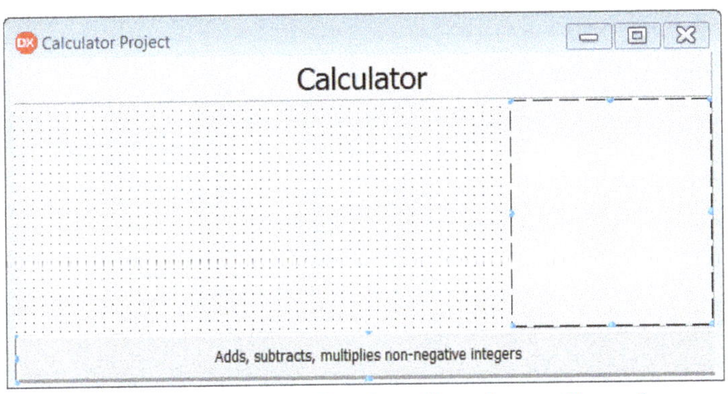

Fig. 1.37 Delphi CE showing three aligned panels and an aligned image component

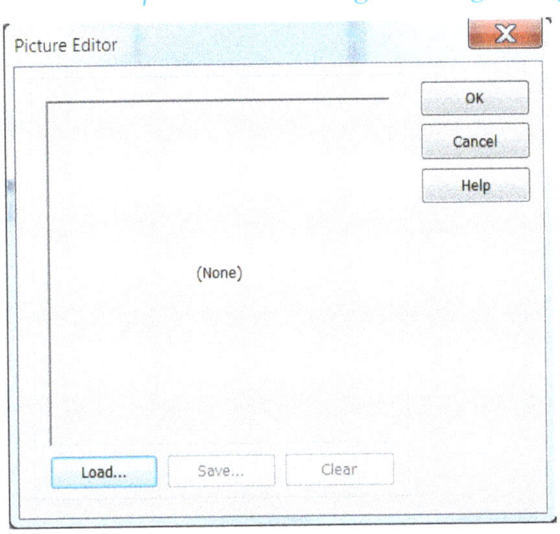

Fig. 1.39 Delphi CE Picture Picture Editor

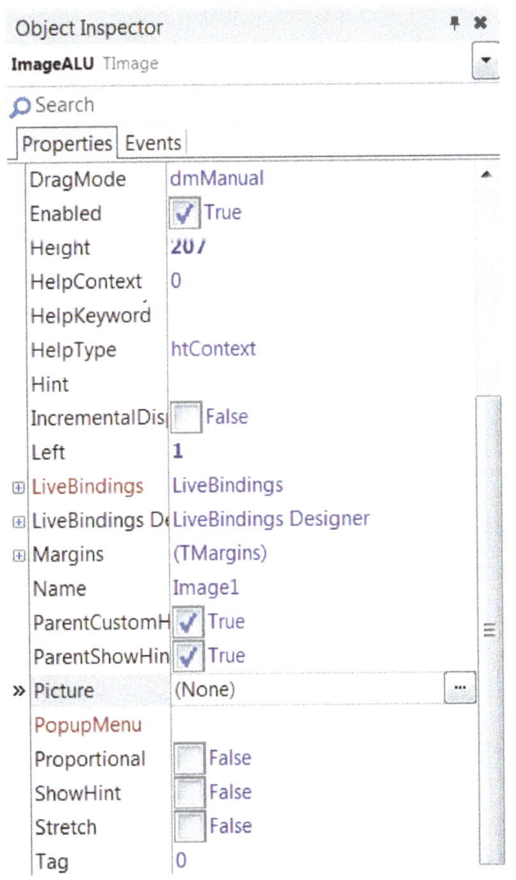

Fig. 1.38 Delphi CE Picture property of ImageALU selected in Object Inspector

Select **Stretch** property of ImageALU in **Object Inspector** and make True. This will fit ALU.jpg to the dimensions of ImageALU as shown in *Figure 1.41*.

We will now add five buttons to the form. The easiest way to find a component in the **Tool Palette** is to use the **Search** option. Typing the first two letters of a component as shown in *Figure 1.42* finds and selects the **TButton** component.

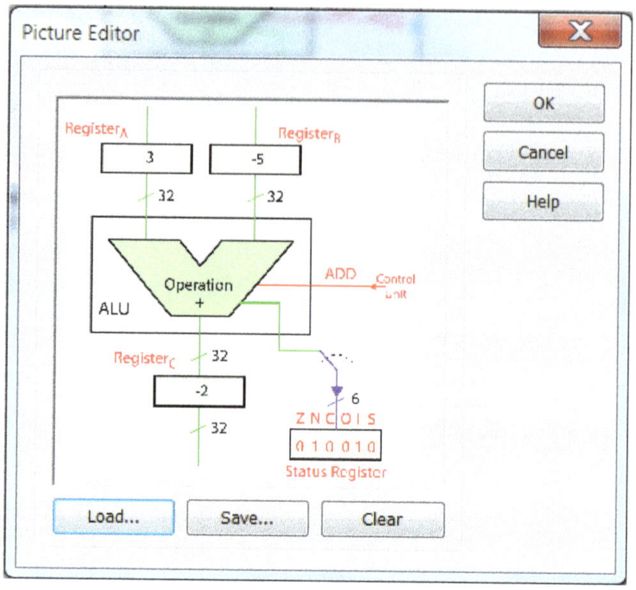

Fig. 1.40 Delphi CE Image ALU.jpg loaded into Picture Editor

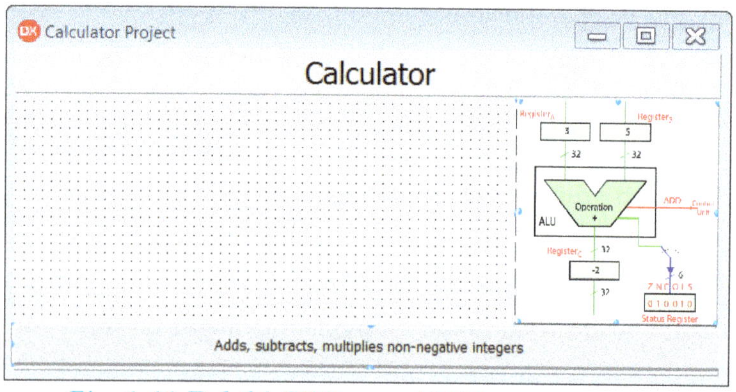

Fig. 1.41 Delphi CE Image ALU.jpg stretched to fit ImageALU component

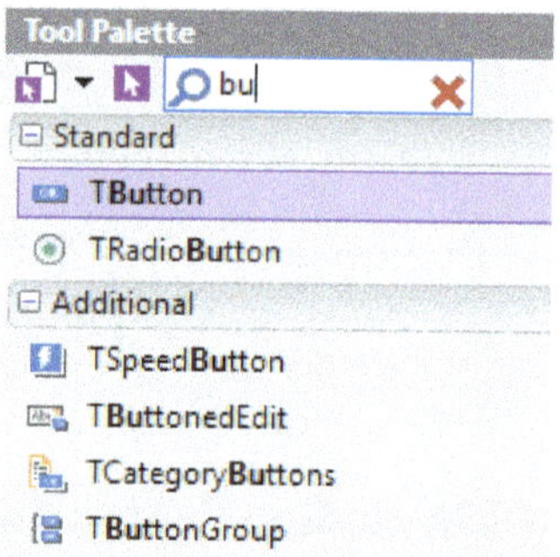

Fig. 1.42 Delphi CE Using the search facility in the Tool Palette to find TButton component

Click the form with **TButton** selected to position the five buttons, Add, Subtract, Multiply, Clear and Terminate, as shown in *Figure 1.32*, **Width** 75, **Height** 25. Fine positioning is achieved by first selecting the respective button on the form then holding down the **Alt key** while pressing the **left mouse button** and moving the mouse. **Release** the mouse button when satisfied that the button is correctly located. If the **Alt key** is not used then component movement is restricted to the grid points which appear on the form as black dots.

Next, **place** two **TMaskEdit** components on the form and next to labels First Operand, Second Operand, respectively.

Set their **Width** property to 45 and their **Height** property to 24.

Change their **Name** property to MaskEditOperand1 and MaskEditOperand2, respectively.

Select the **EditMask** property as shown in *Figure 1.44* and **click** ... to bring up the **Input Mask Editor** - *Figure 1.45*. **Enter** 9999 in the **Input Mask** (the **Editor** adds ;0; automatically on moving the cursor way from the box) and a space character in the **Character for Blanks** box. Make sure that the **Save Literal Characters** box is unticked. **Click** OK to save.

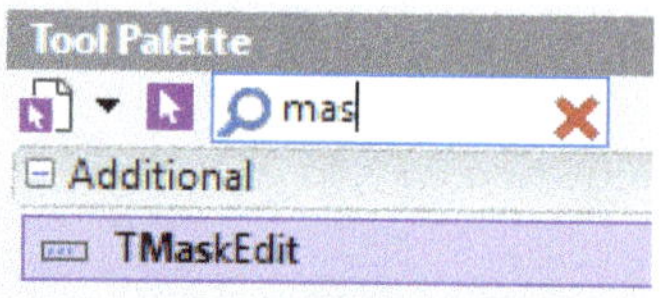

Fig. 1.43 Delphi CE Using the search facility in the Tool Palette to find TMaskEdit component

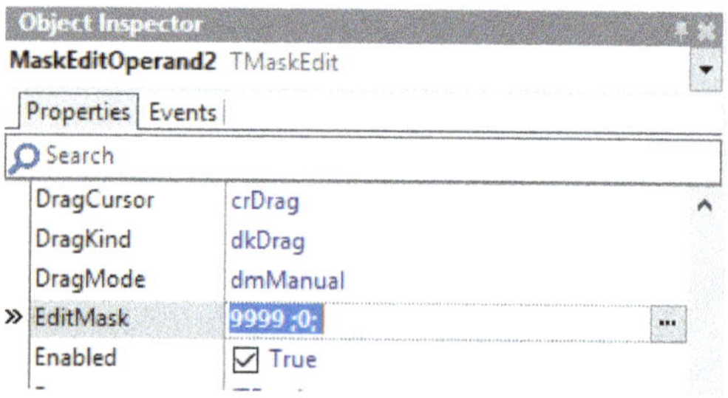

Fig. 1.44 Delphi CE Object Inspector MaskEditOperand2 EditMask property selected

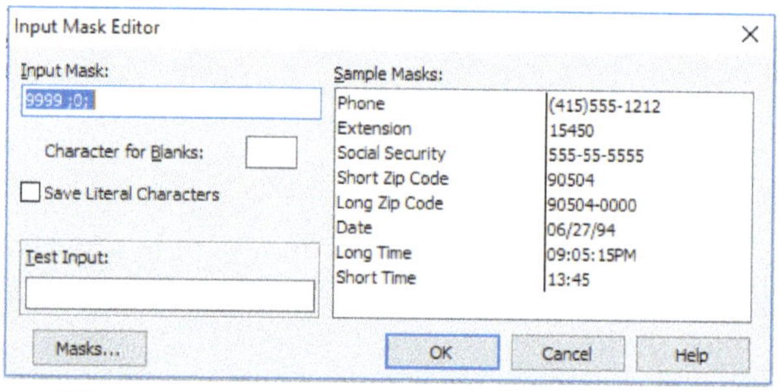

Fig. 1.45 Delphi CE Input Mask Editor

Next, **place** three **TLabel** components in positions labelled on the form, First Operand, Second Operand, Result, respectively.

Change their **Name** property to LabelOperand1, LabelOperand2, and LabelResult, respectively.

Change their **Caption** property to Operand1, Operand2, and Result, respectively.

Place one **TEdit** component on the form aligned with the label Result as shown in *Figure 1.32*.

Change its **Name** property to EditResult. **Delete** its **Text** property.

Set its **Width** property to 67 and its **Height** property to 24.

Change the **Name** property of the buttons to ButtonAdd, ButtonSubtract, ButtonMultiply, ButtonClear, ButtonTerminate, respectively, and the corresponding **Caption** property to Add, Subtract, Multiply, Clear, Terminate.

Next, **place** a **TLabel** component between the Add/Subtract/Multiply row of buttons and the Result **TEdit** box.

Set its **Top** property 157, **Left** property 184, **Font Name** Cambria, **Font Size** 20.

Change its **Name** property to LabelOperation. because it will store the current operation, '+' or '-' or 'x'.

Change its **Caption** property to the empty string, ''.

For the application to perform addition, subtraction and multiplication, these actions must be programmed into the application. This can be done by creating specific event handler code which executes when, for example, the **Add** button is clicked.

Double click the Add button to create skeleton code to handle the addition operation in the executing application when this button is clicked. This skeleton code is shown highlighted in red in *Table 1.1*.

Insert the program code shown in blue.

StrToInt is a named operation must be performed on the numeric strings of MaskEditOperand1.Text and MaskEditOperand2.Text before they can be added. This operation turns a string into an integer if this is possible. The **Try Except** construct is used to trap the error when it isn't. For example, if MaskEditOperand1.Text is '4' then **StrToInt** produces 4 and an exception is not raised. If it stores the empty string, '', an exception is raised. Fortunately, by choosing a **TMaskEdit** component with a numeric mask, the empty string is the only possible erroneous entry, all other inappropriate entries get filtered out by the mask.

The result of a successful addition operation, an integer, must be converted back into a string. The named operation **IntToStr** performs this conversion. This string is then assigned to EditResult.Text.

Exception handling is the subject of a later chapter but suffice it to say that information about the specific exception is returned in **E**. The message part of **E** is a string accessed by **E.Message**. This is concatenated (a fancy word for joined) by the concatenation operator **+** with the string `'Something wrong with one or more operands '`.

Create event handlers as shown in *Tables 1.2 - 1.5*.

```
Procedure TMainForm.ButtonAddClick(Sender: TObject);
Begin
  Try
    EditResult.Text := IntToStr(StrToInt(MaskEditOperand1.Text) +
                       StrToInt(MaskEditOperand2.Text));
    LabelOperation.Caption := '+';
  Except
    On E : Exception
      Do ShowMessage('Something wrong with one or more operands ' + E.Message);
  End;
End;
```

Table 1.1 Event handler for ButtonAdd OnClick event

```
Procedure TMainForm.ButtonSubtractClick(Sender: TObject);
Begin
  Try
    EditResult.Text := IntToStr(StrToInt(MaskEditOperand1.Text) -
                                StrToInt(MaskEditOperand2.Text));
    LabelOperation.Caption := '-';
  Except
    On E : Exception
      Do ShowMessage('Something wrong with one or more operands ' + E.Message);
  End;
End;
```

Table 1.2 Event handler for ButtonSubtract OnClick event

```
Procedure TMainForm.ButtonMultiplyClick(Sender: TObject);
Begin
  Try
    EditResult.Text := IntToStr(StrToInt(MaskEditOperand1.Text) *
                                StrToInt(MaskEditOperand2.Text));
    LabelOperation.Caption := 'x';
  Except
    On E : Exception
      Do ShowMessage('Something wrong with one or more operands ' + E.Message);
  End;
End;
```

Table 1.3 Event handler for ButtonMultiply OnClick event

```
Procedure TMainForm.ButtonClearClick(Sender: TObject);
Begin
  EditResult.Text := '';
  MaskEditOperand1.Text := '';
  MaskEditOperand2.Text := '';
  LabelOperation.Caption := '';
End;
```

Table 1.4 Event handler for ButtonClear OnClick event

```
Procedure TMainForm.ButtonTerminateClick(Sender: TObject);
Begin
  Application.Terminate;
End;
```

Table 1.5 Event handler for ButtonTerminate OnClick event

Select MaskEditOperand1 on the form then in the **Object Inspector Events** tab, **double click the OnEvent** field to create skeleton code to handle clearing its box in the executing application when the box is clicked. This skeleton code is shown highlighted in red in *Table 1.6*.

Insert the program code shown in blue.

Select MaskEditOperand2 on the form then in the **Object Inspector Events** tab, **double click the OnEvent** field to create skeleton code to handle clearing its box in the executing application when the box is clicked. This skeleton code is shown highlighted in red in *Table 1.7*.

Insert the program code shown in blue.

```
Procedure TMainForm.MaskEditOperand1Click(Sender: TObject);
Begin
  MaskEditOperand1.Clear;
  MaskEditOperand1.SelLength := 0;
  MaskEditOperand1.SelStart := 0;
  EditResult.Clear;
  LabelOperation.Caption := '';
End;
```

Table 1.6 Event handler for ButtonClear OnClick event

```
Procedure TMainForm.MaskEditOperand2Click(Sender: TObject);
Begin
  MaskEditOperand2.Clear;
  MaskEditOperand2.SelLength := 0;
  MaskEditOperand2.SelStart := 0;
  EditResult.Clear;
  LabelOperation.Caption := '';
End;
```

Table 1.7 Event handler for ButtonClear OnClick event

Select the TopPanel and **set** its **Font Name** to Tahoma, its **Caption** property to Very Simple Calculator, and its **Color** property to clSilver.

Select the **BottomPanel** and set its **Color** property to clBtnHighLight.

Finally, **set** the border parameters, AutoSize and AutoScroll for the form - *Figure 1.46*.

Click Save All. (Download from www.educational-computing.com/DelphiBook/Code/Chapter1/CE10.2/Calculator/Calculator.rar)

Click (Run Without Debugging (Shift+Ctrl+F9)) to compile, link and run the application - *Figure 1.47*. *Figure 1.48* shows an example of addition.

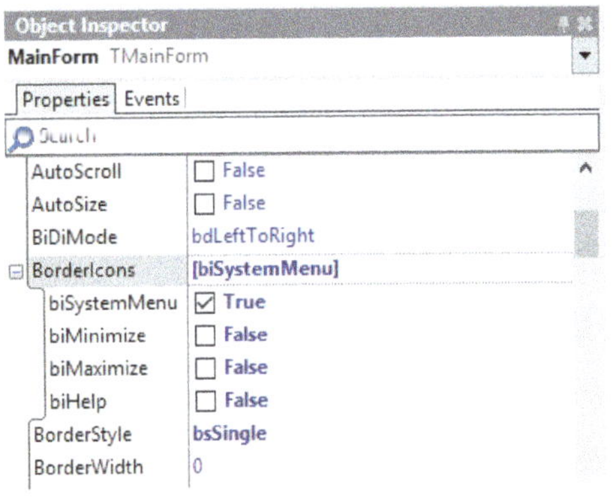

Fig. 1.46 Delphi CE Calculator project order settings

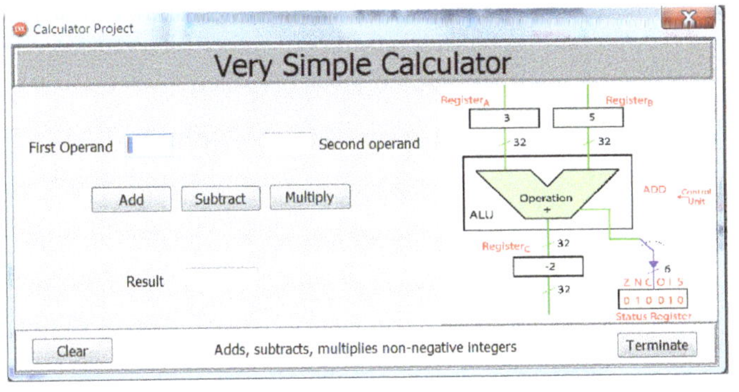

Fig. 1.47 Delphi CE Calculator project in execution in Windows 7

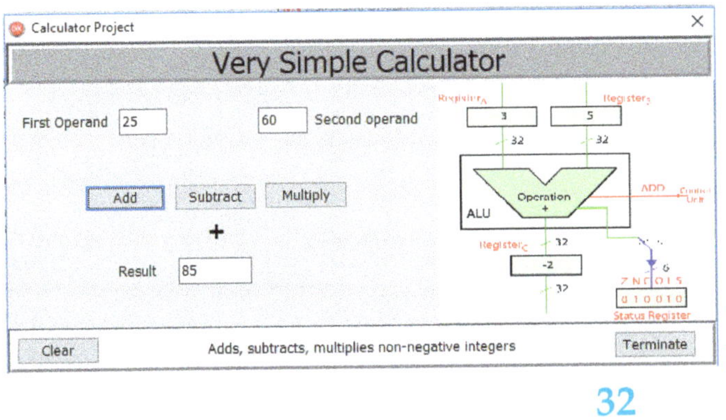

Fig. 1.48 Delphi CE Calculator project in execution in Windows 10

Purpose: To learn about the structure window, refactoring and program style

IDE Structure window

Figure 1.49 shows the **Delphi CE Structure** window of the **IDE** for the calculator project. Note that **ButtonClear** and **ButtonTerminate** are child components of the parent component, **BottomPanel**, and **ImageALU** is a child component of the parent component, **RightSidePanel**.

This means that moving the parent component on the form results in its child component(s) moving to maintain the positional relationship bewteen parent and child. Also, alignment options use the boundaries of the parent. *Figure 1.49* shows that all components placed directly on the form are child components of the parent component **MainForm**.

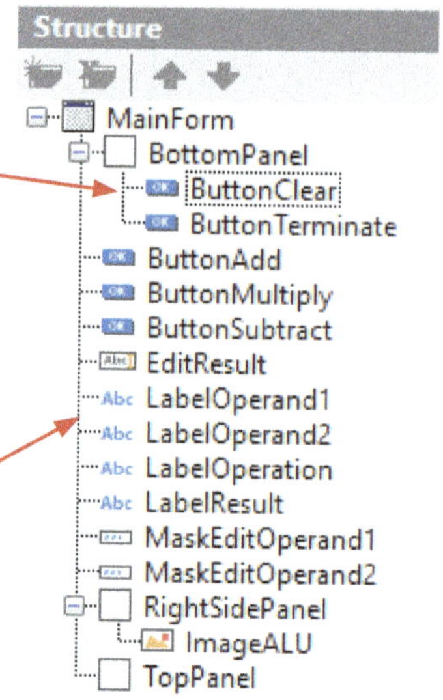

Fig. 1.49 Structure window of IDE for Delphi CE Calculator project

It is possible to move a child component, e.g., **ButtonClear**, away from its parent, in this case, **BottomPanel**, by selecting it with the mouse and dragging it onto, say, a new parent **MainForm**.

Programming style

Figure 1.50 shows the **Project** menu for the **Calculator** project.

Click on **View Source** to bring up the main program for this project - *Figure 1.51*.

The default syntax highlighting of the **IDE** emboldens key words and reserved words of the **Object Pascal** language (the programming language on which Delphi is based). Key words and reserved words are words that a programmer should not attempt to redefine.

In *Figure 1.51* these are **program**
uses
begin
end

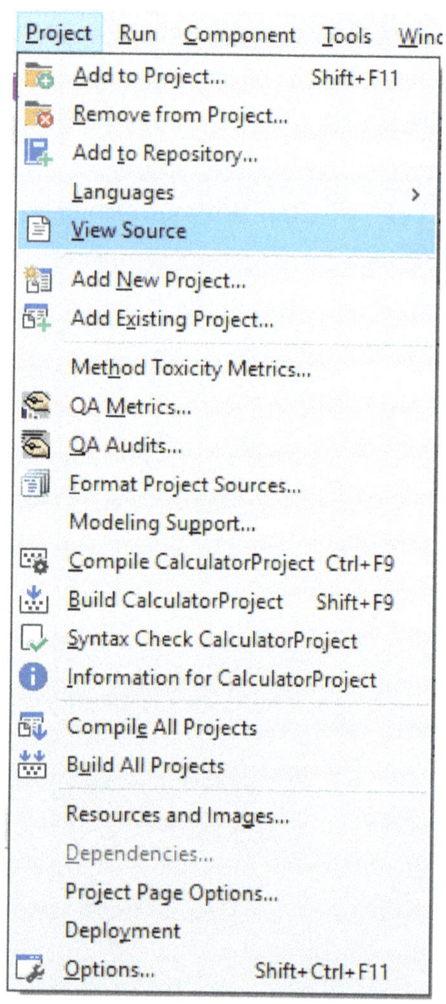

Fig. 1.50 IDE Project menu IDE for Delphi CE for Calculator project

Embarcadero uses a style standard that requires language reserved words and key words to be completely lowercase. If you intend for Embarcadero to distribute your software then you need to stick to this standard. Otherwise you may deviate from this standard. Old habits die hard so often I use a style developed long before Delphi existed. It is your choice but it is very important to be consistent.

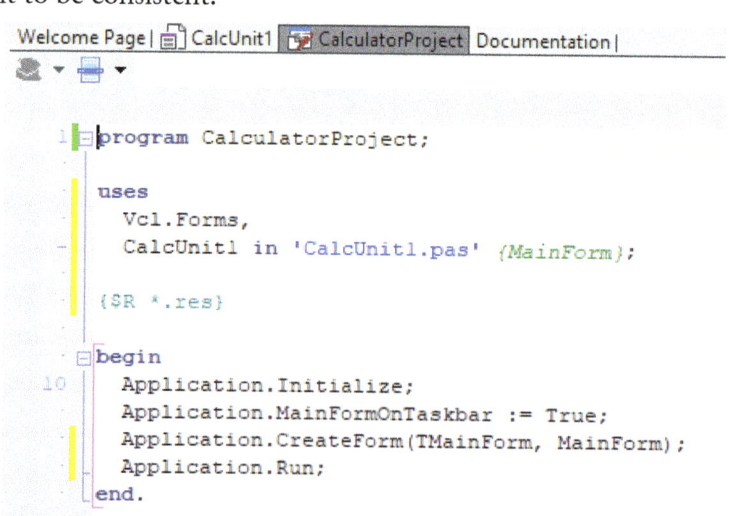

Fig. 1.51 Program CalculatorProject in Delphi CE

All components placed on a form must be given descriptive names. Do not use the default names that Delphi uses, e.g. **Button1**. Professional programmers use a lowercase prefix to denote the component type. - see *Table 1.8* for components in the **Standard** tab/category. Using a prefix rather than a postfix makes searching component names in the **Object Inspector** and **Code Explorer** easier by component type. However, it is a matter of choice. The key is to use descriptive names that make your application easy to understand, debug (to debug is to find and eliminate errors in your code), and maintain. Whilst you are learning to program, you may find it easier to use descriptive names in the style used in the **Calculator** project. *Figure 1.52* shows the component names. Scrutiny of these reveals a naming inconsistency, all but the panel components begin with the component type name. It is relatively easy in Delphi CE to resolve this inconsistency by using the **Refactor** option.

Prefix	**Component**
mm	TMainMenu
pm	TPopupMenu
mmi	TMainMenuItem
pmi	TPopupMenuItem
lbl	TLabel
edt	TEdit
mem	TMemo
btn	TButton
chk	TCheckBox
rb	TRadioButton
lb	TListBox
cb	TComboBox
scb	TScrollBar
gb	TGroupBox
rg	TRadioGroup
pnl	TPanel
cl	TCommandList

Table 1.8 Prefixes for components from the Standard tab/category

Select and **highlight** the name **TopPanel** in the **Unit CalcUnit1** as shown in *Figure 1.53*.

Open the **Refactor** menu and **click** **Rename** option - *Figure 1.54* - to bring up the **Rename** window shown in *Figure 1.55*. Create new name, **PanelTop** as shown. **Click** **OK** to effect the name change throughout **CalcUnit1**. The other panel names may be refactored in a similar manner. *Table 1.9* shows lowercase prefixes to denote the component type for components in the **Additonal** tab/category.

```
TopPanel: TPanel;
BottomPanel: TPanel;
RightSidePanel: TPanel;
ImageALU: TImage;
MaskEditOperand1: TMaskEdit;
MaskEditOperand2: TMaskEdit;
LabelOperand1: TLabel;
LabelOperand2: TLabel;
ButtonAdd: TButton;
ButtonSubtract: TButton;
ButtonMultiply: TButton;
LabelResult: TLabel;
ButtonClear: TButton;
ButtonTerminate: TButton;
LabelOperation: TLabel;
EditResult: TEdit;
```

Fig. 1.52 Calculator project component names

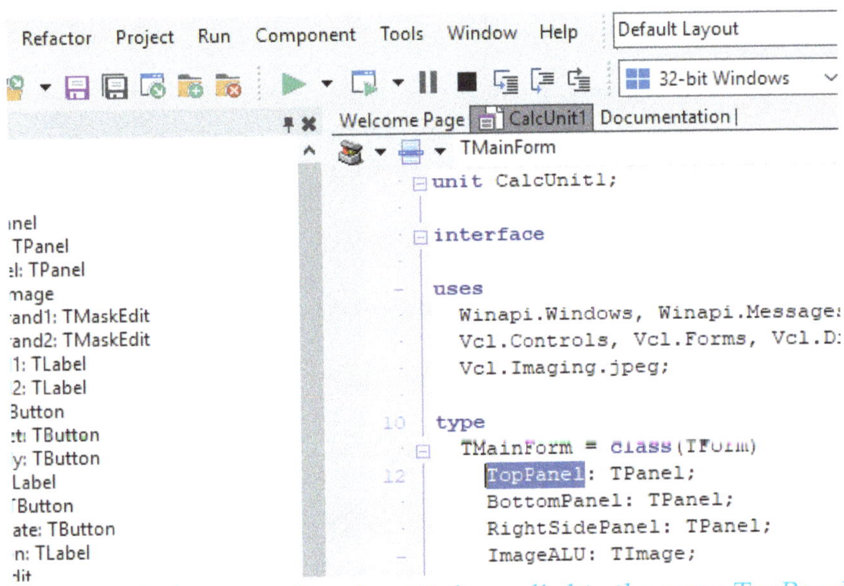

Fig. 1.53 Refacture option about to be applied to the name TopPanel

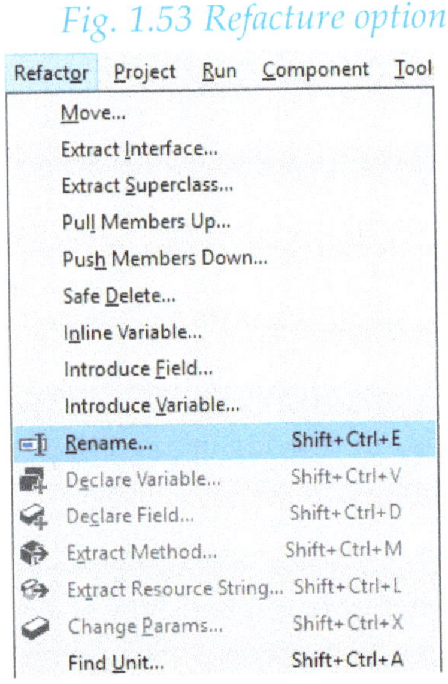

Fig. 1.54 Refacture menu showing Rename selected

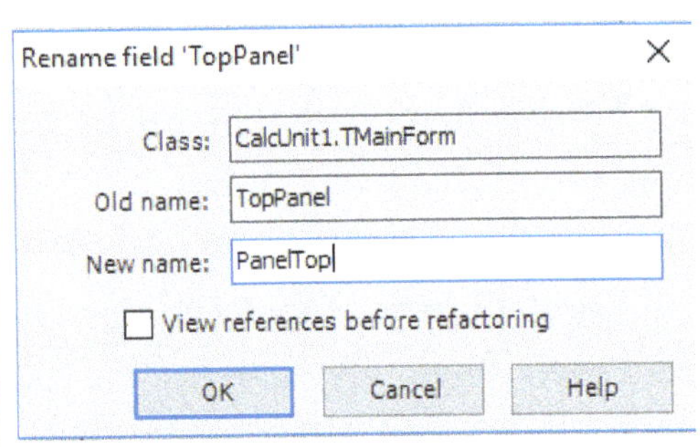

Fig. 1.55 Renaming TopPanel, PanelTop

Purpose: To learn how to use the timer component

P

Start a new **VCL Forms Application** project. **Click** **Save All** and save project as ImageTimerProject.dproj in a folder ImageTimer. **Save** the unit as ImageTimerUnit.pas in the same folder.
Select the form in the **Object Inspector** and change its **Name** property value from Form1 to MainForm.

Select **TImage** in the **Additional** category of the **Tool Palette**. **Click** on the form to create an image component, Image1. **Select** this image in the **Object Inspector** and change its **Name** property value from Image1 to ImageOrangutan. Change its **Align** property value to alClient. This image component should now fill the form. **Add** **JPEG** or **Vcl.Imaging.jpeg** to the **Uses** clause depending on your version of Delphi (unit scoping).

Select **TTimer** in the **System** category of the **Tool Palette**. **Click** on the form to create a timer component, Timer1. **Select** this timer in the **Object Inspector** and change its **Name** property value from Timer1 to FrameTimer. **TTimer** is a non-visual component that will not appear on the form at runtime. *Figure 1.56* shows the **Design View** for the **MainForm** and its components ImageOrangutan and FrameTimer.

Prefix	Component
bbtn	TBitBtn
sb	TSpeedButton
me	TMaskEdit
sg	TStringGrid
dg	TDrawGrid
img	TImage
shp	TShape
bvl	TBevel
sbx	TScrollBox
clb	TCheckListbox
spl	TSplitter
stx	TStaticText
cht	TChart

Table 1.9 Prefixes for components from the Additonal tab/category

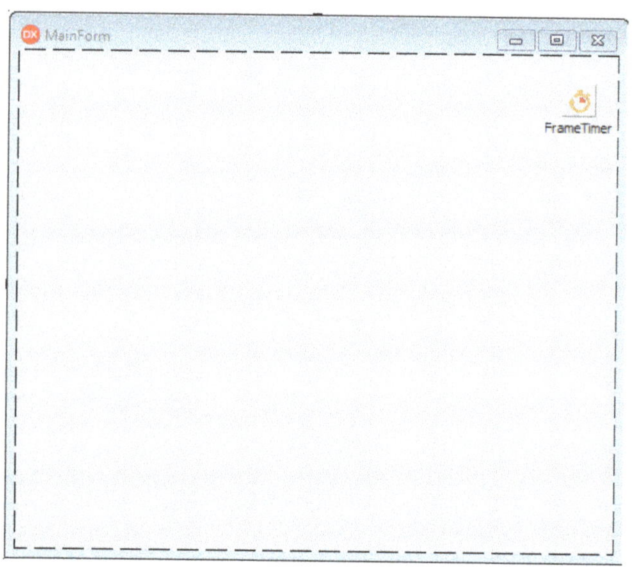

Fig. 1.56 MainForm for project ImageTimerProject

Select **TMediaPlayer** in the **System** category of the **Tool Palette**. **Click** on the form to create a media player component, MediaPlayer1. **Select** this media player in the **Object Inspector** and change its **Name** property value from MediaPlayer1 to MediaPlayerJungleSounds.
Set all **VisibleButtons** property values to False. **Set** **Visible** property value to False.
Select **FileName** property and click the ellipsis (...) to bring up the **File Open** window.
Select jungle.wav and **click** **Open** (download from www.educational-computing.com/DelphiBook/Code/Chapter1/CE10.2/ImageTimer/jungle.rar).
TMediaPlayer is a non-visual component, therefore it will not show when the application is run.

Double click the FrameTimer component on the form to create the skeleton code for an **OnTimer** event handler show in red in *Table 1.10*. **Add** the code shown in blue. You will need to change the string value `'Z:\ProductionChapters\DelphiBook\Code\Chapter1\Images\'` to correspond to the file path where you have stored the downloaded orangutan photos (www.educational-computing.com/DelphiBook/Code/Chapter1/CE10.2/ImageTimer/Images/Orangutan.rar).

```
Procedure TMainForm.FrameTimerTimer(Sender: TObject);
  Begin
    MediaPlayerJungleSounds.Play;
    Counter := (Counter + 1) Mod 42;
    NumberString := '00' + IntToStr(Counter + 16);
    FileName := 'IMGP' + NumberString;
    MainForm.Caption := FileName;
    ImageOrangutan.Stretch := True;
    ImageOrangutan.Picture.LoadFromFile('Z:\ProductionChapters\DelphiBook\Code\Chapter1\Photos\'
                                          + FileName + '.jpg');

  End;
```

Table 1.10 Event handler for OnTimer event

Select FrameTimer in the **Object Inspector** and change the **Interval** property field value to 200 (this sets the timer to time 200 milliseconds). **Make** sure the **Enabled** field is True. When the application is run, the timer will call its event handler every 200 milliseconds.

```
Implementation

{$R *.dfm}
Var
  FileName : String;
  NumberString : String;
  Counter : Integer = 15;
```

Table 1.11 ImageTimerUnit's variable declarations

Add the variable declarations shown in *Table 1.11* to ImageTimerUnit. Variables are a convenient way of storing values which are subject to change. Variables have a name and a type, e.g. FileName and **String**. The type declares what may be stored in the variable.

Select MainForm in the **Object Inspector** and then **select** the **Events** tab.

Double click the value field of the **OnActivate** property to create the skeleton code for an **OnActivate** event handler shown in red in *Table 1.12*. **Add** the code shown in blue.

```
Procedure TMainForm.FormActivate(Sender: TObject);
  Begin
    MediaPlayerJungleSounds.Open;
  End;
```

Table 1.12 Event handler called when the main form activated

Click ▶ (Run Without Debugging (Shift+Ctrl+F9)) to compile, link and run the application - *Figure 1.57*.

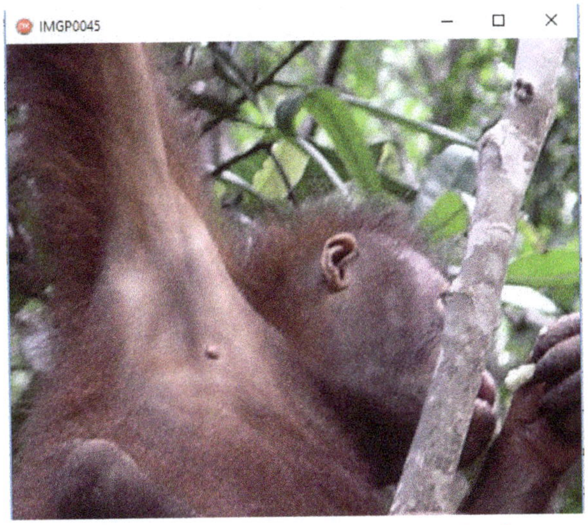

Fig. 1.57 Executing ImageTimerProject

(Download from www.educational-computing.com/DelphiBook/Code/Chapter1/CE10.2/ImageTimer/ImageTimer.rar).

2 Starting programming

Note

File|New|Other|Console Application program.
Type in source code.
Save as MyFirst.dpr or MyFirst.dprog, depending on the version of Delphi, in new folder MyFirst.
To compile press Ctrl F9.
To build a program Shift F9 (compile and link in libraries).
To run this program with debugging as an option press F9. To run without the ability to debug press Shift Ctrl F9.
F9 will also compile and link before running if the source code has been changed since the last time the program was run or if the source code has not yet been compiled and linked.
Alternatively, use the drop-down menu options Project|Compile, Project|Build and Run|Run or Run|Run Without Debugging.

My First Program

Purpose: Finding your way around the IDE.

We start with a very simple program which is shown below:

```
Program Project1;
Begin
  Writeln('Hello World');
End.
```

There are three forms of this program:

- **Source** – the above program is an example of a source code program
- **Object** – a non-executable non-text binary form of the source code program
- **Executable** – an executable non-text binary form of the program.

Of the three forms only the third is executable.

1 Use the IDE to create and save the above source code program as **MyFirst.dpr** or **MyFirst.dprog**, depending on the version of Delphi, in its own directory/folder named **MyFirst**. You will need to edit out {$APPTYPE Console}, and any other items that are provided in the default layout.

Note that `Program Project1;` changes to `Program MyFirst;` when you save this source code program as **MyFirst.dpr** or **MyFirst.dprog**.

You should never change "`Program Project1;`" directly. Always allow the Delphi IDE to do the renaming by using the Save Project As command in the File menu.

Fig. 2.1 shows the IDE of the community edition of RAD Studio 10.2.

Warning

Never directly rename the given default name, Program Project1, that every new project gets. To change the name to the desired name, i.e. Program MyFirst, save the project with the filename MyFirst.dpr or MyFirst.dproj depending on the version of Delphi.

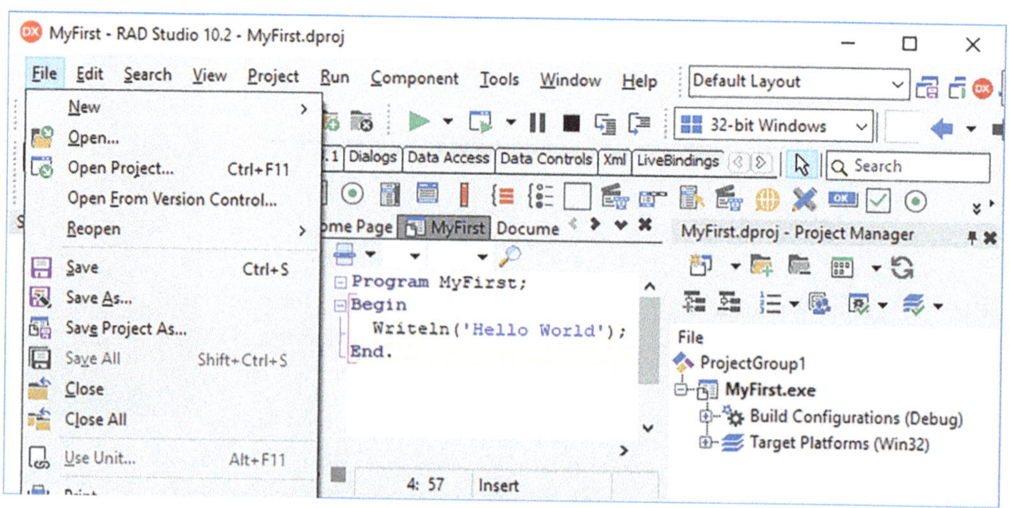

Fig. 2.1 IDE for RAD Studio 10.2 Community Edition.

I Check what files are present in the directory/folder MyFirst after saving the source program (use a console window).

The following files as a minimum should be found depending on the version of Delphi/RAD Studio you are using:

Delphi 7

- MyFirst.cfg – a configuration file which can be viewed in a text editor
- MyFirst.dof – another configuration file which can be viewed in a text editor
- MyFirst.dpr – the source code form of the program
- MyFirst.~dpr (a temporary version of the source code program)

Delphi 2009 - Delphi 10.2 versions

- MyFirst.dpr - the source code form of the program
- MyFirst.dprog - a configuration file which can be viewed in a text editor
- MyFirst.dprog.local – another configuration file which can be viewed in a text editor

I Using a text editor such as WordPad, open up and view MyFirst.dpr.

You should see the source code form of your program.

I Now build the program (Shift F9).

I Check what files are now present in the directory MyFirst, or its subdirectory Win32 or its subdirectoryWin32/Debug.

One more file, MyFirst.Exe, should be present. This is an executable file which means that it is runnable.

I Run this program in Debug mode (F9).

Depending on the version of Delphi you are using either an error window will pop up reporting 'Runtime error 105…' or a Console window will pop up and then immediately close.

With the Delphi version that reports a runtime error, the error is caused because the runtime system needs an output window for the output `Hello World` of the statement `Writeln('Hello World')` and his has not been created by the running program. This output window is called a **console window** (the console window also serves to echo text typed at the keyboard but more of that later).

With the Delphi versions that create an output window but close it straightaway, the issue is caused by a default setting associated with the window which closes the window.

Solution

To ensure that an output window is always created insert the directive

```
{$APPTYPE CONSOLE}
```

after

```
Program MyFirst;
```

To ensure that this window remains open, add the statement

```
Readln;
```

Source Program

```
Program MyFirst;
{$APPTYPE CONSOLE}
Begin
  Writeln('Hello World');
  Readln;
End.
```

Fig. 2.2 Shows the revised version of Program MyFirst.

Your source code program should now resemble the program shown in Fig. 2.2.

I Run this program in Debug mode (F9).

This time the console window remains open - Fig 2.3 - and the text `Hello World`, output by the executing program, is now visible in this window. Press the return key to finish the execution of the program. The console window now closes. `Readln` consumes the return key and until this is pressed the program is paused.

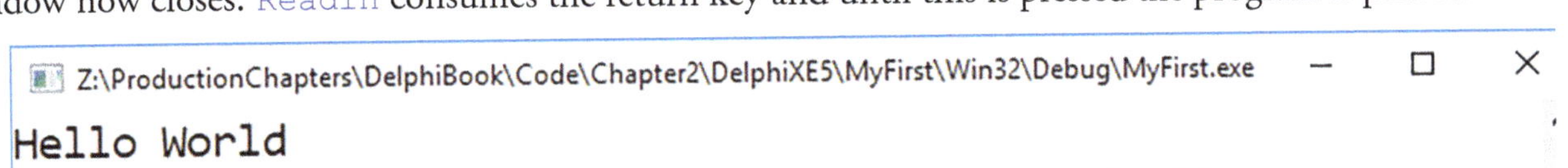

Fig. 2.3 Captured console window output from execution of MyFirst program.

My Second Program

Purpose: Introducing variables, variable declarations and assignment.

The second program uses a string variable `GreetingsMessage` to hold the value, `'Hello World'`, that we want this program to output.

```
Program MySecond;
{$APPTYPE CONSOLE}
Var
  GreetingsMessage : String;
Begin
  GreetingsMessage := 'Hello World';
  Writeln(GreetingsMessage);
  Readln;
End.
```

Variable declaration

> **Warning**
>
> Never directly rename the given default name, Program Project1, that every new project gets. To change the name to the desired name, i.e. Program MySecond, save the project with the filename MySecond.dpr or MySecond.dproj depending on the version of Delphi.

- Use the IDE to create and save the above source code program as MySecond.dpr or MySecond.dprog, depending on the version of Delphi, in its own directory/folder named MySecond.
- Now build the program (Shift F9).
- Run this program in Debug mode(F9).

Fig. 2.4 shows the console window and the output `Hello World`.
The value `'Hello World'` held by the string variable `GreetingsMessage` has been output to the console window by the writing procedure `Writeln`. The naming of this procedure is meant to convey that its purpose is to write a line of something to the console window.

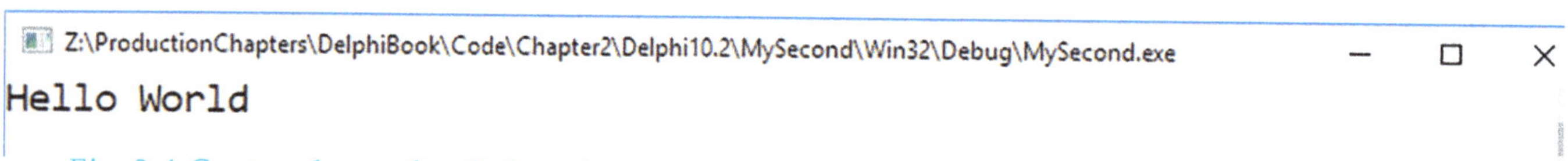

Fig. 2.4 Captured console window showing output produced by execution of MySecond program.

Questions

1. What output would you expect in the console window when the executable form of the following program is run?

```
Program MySecondAmended;
{$APPTYPE CONSOLE}
Var
  GreetingsMessage : String;
Begin
  GreetingsMessage := 'The sun has got its hat on';
  Writeln(GreetingsMessage);
  Readln;
End.
```

My Third Program

Purpose: Showing how a variable may be reused.

In the following program the value, `'Hello World'`, held by the string variable `GreetingsMessage`, is replaced by the value `'Sunny day'`.

```
Program MyThird;
{$APPTYPE CONSOLE}
Var
  GreetingsMessage : String;
Begin
  GreetingsMessage := 'Hello World';
  Writeln(GreetingsMessage);
  GreetingsMessage := 'Sunny day';
  Writeln(GreetingsMessage);
  Readln;
End.
```

Warning

Never directly rename the given default name, Program Project1, that every new project gets. To change the name to the desired name, i.e. Program MyThird, save the project with the filename MyThird.dpr or MyThird.dproj depending on the version of Delphi.

I Use the IDE to create and save the above source code program as MyThird.dpr or MyThird.dprog, depending on the version of Delphi, in its own directory/folder named MyThird.

I Now build the program (Shift F9).

I Run this program in Debug mode(F9).

Fig. 2.5 shows the console window and the output `Hello World` on the first line and `Sunny day` on the second line.

The value `'Hello World'` held by the string variable `GreetingsMessage` has been output to the console window by the first instance of writing procedure `Writeln`. and the value `'Sunny day'`, held by the string variable `GreetingsMessage`, has been output to the console window by the second instance of writing procedure `Writeln`.

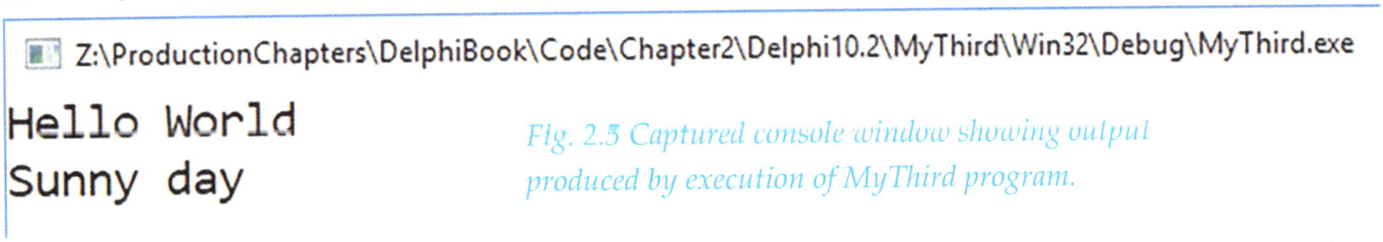

Fig. 2.5 Captured console window showing output produced by execution of MyThird program.

Questions

2 What output would you expect in the console window when the executable form of the following program is run?

```
Program MyThirdAmended;
{$APPTYPE CONSOLE}
Var
  GreetingsMessage : String;
Begin
  GreetingsMessage := 'Good morning';
  Writeln(GreetingsMessage);
  GreetingsMessage := 'Good afternoon';
  Writeln(GreetingsMessage);
  Readln;
End.
```

Variable identifier

Programming languages use a combination of upper and lowercase letters, decimal numerals and underscores (_) to identify a variable.

The following is an example of such a **variable identifier** consisting of uppercase and lowercase letters, underscores and the numerals `1, 2, 3`.

```
My_First_Variable123
```

We have already encountered the use of one variable identifier, i.e. `GreetingsMessage`.

We have seen that a value is assigned to variable by using its identifier in an assignment statement as follows

```
GreetingsMessage := 'Hello World';
```

The symbol "`:=`" is the **assignment operator**.

The assignment operator is the mechanism by which a variable is associated with a value.

`GreetingsMessage` is called a **variable identifier** when it is used in this way to denote a **variable**.

A combination of uppercase and lowercase letters, digits and the underscore character can be used for purposes other than a variable but it is still known as an identifier. You will be using identifiers for other purposes shortly.

Variable declaration

We must tell the program that we intend using a particular identifier as a variable.

We do this with a **variable declaration** as follows:

```
Var
  GreetingsMessage : String;
```

By labelling `GreetingsMessage` with the keyword `String` we are stating that `GreetingsMessage` can be assigned string values only, i.e. sequences of letters, spaces, digits and other symbols enclosed in single quotes.

> **Key term**
>
> **Assignment statement:** An instruction which assigns a value to a variable is called an assignment statement.
> The operation is known as assignment.

Assignment statement

An instruction which assigns a value of a variable is called an **assignment statement**.

For example,

```
GreetingsMessage := 'Hello World';
```

is an example of an assignment statement and the operation that this statement performs when executed is known as **assignment**.

Rules for constructing a valid identifier

An identifier must begin with an uppercase or lowercase letter from the English alphabet or an underscore (_).

It may then be followed by zero or more letters or numerals, or underscores (_).

An identifier may not contain special symbols such as ~ ! @ # $ % ^ & * ( ) + ` - = { } [ ] : " ; ' < > ? , . / | \:

> **Question**
>
> 3 Which of the following are valid identifiers?
>
> MyVar my_var123 _MyVar MyVar_ MyVar# my-var 5_myvar

My Fourth Program

Purpose: Showing how multiple variables may be declared.

In the following program, two variables with variable identifiers `GreetingsMessage` and `Surname` are declared in the same variable declaration statement. Another variable, `Forename`, is declared in a second variable declaration statement.

```
Program MyFourth;
{$APPTYPE CONSOLE}
Var
  GreetingsMessage, Surname : String;
  Forename : String;
Begin
  GreetingsMessage := 'Hello World';
  Writeln(GreetingsMessage);
  Forename := 'Fred';
  Writeln(Forename);
  Surname := 'Bond';
  Writeln(Surname);
  Readln;
End.
```

Variable declarations

The string values `'Hello World'`,`'Bond'` and `'Fred'`, respectively, are assigned to the corresponding variables by separate assignment statements.

Whilst variables may be declared in a single variable declaration statement, each assignment statement involves just one variable assignment.

- Use the IDE to create and save the above source code program as **MyFourth.dpr** or **MyFourth.dprog**, depending on the version of Delphi, in its own directory/folder named **MyFourth**.
- Now build the program (Shift F9).
- Run this program in Debug mode(F9).

Fig. 2.6 shows the console window and the output produced by the execution of `Program MyFourth`.

```
Z:\ProductionChapters\DelphiBook\Code\Chapter2\Delphi10.2\MyFourth\Win32\Debug\Fourth.exe
Hello World
Fred
Bond
```

Fig. 2.6 Captured console window showing output produced by execution of MyFourth program.

Programming Task

1. Add another variable declaration to `Program MyFourth` to create a variable `MiddleName`. Add statements to assign the string `'Arthur'` to `MiddleName` and to write the value assigned to `MiddleName` to the console so that this value appears on its own line between the lines conatining `'Fred'` and `'Bond'`.

My Fifth Program

Purpose: Showing how to write output on a single line.

The following program shows how to write output on a single line in two ways. The second way uses the the writing procedure `Write`. This procedure leaves the writing cursor on the output line unlike the writing procedure Writeln which moves the writing cursor to the beginning of the line after the output line.

```
Program MyFifth;
{$APPTYPE CONSOLE}
Var
  Forename : String;
  MiddleName : String;
  Surname : String;
Begin
  Forename := 'Fred';
  MiddleName := 'Arthur';
  Surname := 'Bond';
  //One way it can be done
  Writeln(ForeName, MiddleName, Surname);
  //Another way it can be done
  Write(ForeName, MiddleName);
  Writeln(Surname);
  Readln;
End.
```

Variable declarations

Information

It is useful to add explanatory text to source code to explains the purpose of a particular section of source code. The explanatory text is called a comment.

Comments are ignored by the compiler and are therefore not included in the object code which the compiler produces..

In Delphi comments can be added to source code in two ways:

- A single line comment is prefaced by //
- A multiline comment is enclosed in {}

I Use the IDE to create and save the above source code program as MyFifth.dpr or MyFifth.dprog, depending on the version of Delphi, in its own directory/folder named MyFifth.

I Now build the program (Shift F9).

I Run this program in Debug mode (F9).

Fig. 2.7 shows the console window and the output produced by the execution of `Program MyFifth`.

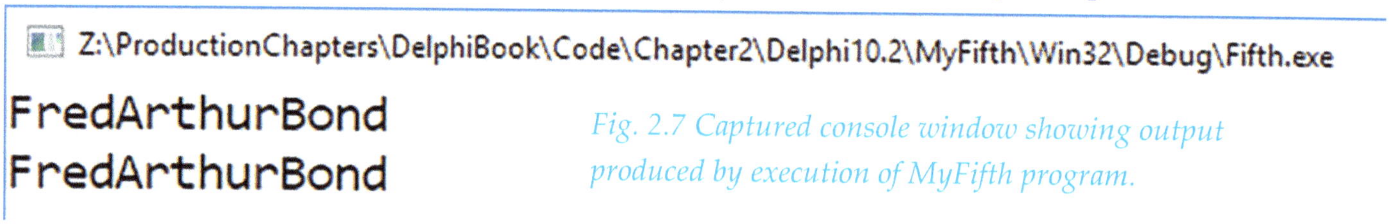

Fig. 2.7 Captured console window showing output produced by execution of MyFifth program.

Both outputs need spaces inserted between the forename, `'Fred'`, and middle name, `'Arthur'`, and the middle name and the surname, `'Bond'`. This is done by inserting the space character written as `' '` as follows:

```
Writeln(ForeName, ' ', MiddleName, ' ', Surname);
```

and

```
Write(ForeName, ' ', MiddleName, ' ');
Writeln(Surname);
```

I Amend and save your program.

I Now build the program (Shift F9).

I Run this program in Debug mode(F9).

Programming Tasks

2 Write a Delphi program which meets the following specification:

- Declares two string variables, `FirstWord` and `SecondWord`.
- Assigns the string value, '`Good`', to `FirstWord` and the string value, '`Morning`', to `SecondWord`.
- Using one `Writeln` statement, the program should output the string '`Good Morning`' to the console using the variables `FirstWord` and `SecondWord`, and whatever else is necessary to achieve a space between '`Good`' and '`Morning`' in the output.
- Include a single line comment, '`Writing to console'`, immediately before the `Writeln` statement.

Compile and run your program to check that your program meets the specification.

3 Write a Delphi program which meets the following specification:

- Declares three string variables, `FirstWord`, `SecondWord` and `ThirdWord`.
- Assigns the string value, '`Good`', to `FirstWord`, the string value, '`Morning`', to `SecondWord`, and the string value, '`Mary`', to `ThirdWord`.
- Using one `Write` statement followed immediately by one `Writeln` statement, the program should output the string '`Good Morning Mary`' to the console using the variables `FirstWord`, `SecondWord`, and `ThirdWord`, and whatever else is necessary to achieve a space between '`Good`' and '`Morning`', and '`Morning`' and '`Mary`' in the output.
- Include a single line comment, '`Writing to console`', immediately before the `Write` statement and a single line comment, 'Completing `Writing to console`', immediatley before the `Writeln` statement.

Compile and run your program to check that your program meets the specification.

Question

4 The following program does not compile becasue it contains errors:

(a) What are these errors (HINT there are three)?

When these errors that prevented the program from compiling are corrected and the program is run, the output to the console is as follows:

```
SusanSmith
```

(b) The program specification requires a single space between 'Susan' and 'Smith' in the program's output to the console.

What single change to the program would achieve this?

```
Program MyProg;
{$APPTYPE CONSOLE}
Var
  x, y : String;
Begin
  x := 'Susan;
  y := 'Smith';
  /Writing to console
  Writeln(x, '' y);
  Readln;
End.
```

My Sixth Program

Purpose: Understanding the role of the statement delimiter symbol ';'.

The following program shows that it is perfectly permissible but not advisable to construct source code on a single line.

```
Program MySixth;{$APPTYPE CONSOLE} Var x:String;Begin x:='Hello';Writeln(x);Readln;End.
```

The compiler can still recognise each statement because the language requires that statements be separated by `';'`.

These statements are shown in red.

`{$APPTYPE CONSOLE}` is a language directive and so is not a language statement.

The end of the source code is indicated with a full stop.

The language keywords `Begin` and `End` delimit the main block. They are not language statements.

The main block is where the executable statements are placed.

I Use the IDE to create and save the above source code program as MySixth.dpr or MySixth.dprog, depending on the version of Delphi, in its own directory/folder named MySixth. Construct the entire program on one line as shown.

I Now build the program (Shift F9).

I Run this program in Debug mode (F9).

Fig. 2.8 shows the console window and the output produced by the execution of `Program MySixth`.

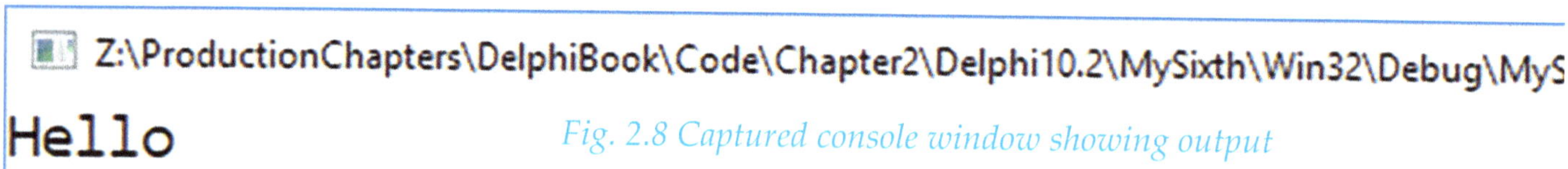

Fig. 2.8 Captured console window showing output produced by execution of MySixh program.

Of course, we should not layout our programs in the style of `Program MySixth` because readability of the source code form of programs is very important.

Questions

5. The following program does not compile because of **three** errors in its source code. What are these **three** errors?

```
Program MyProg;{$APPTYPE CONSOLE} Var y:String Begin y:='Hello';Writeln(y)Readln;End
```

6. The following program does not compile because of **four** errors in its source code. What are these our errors?

```
Program AnotherMyProg;
{$APPTYPE CONSOLE}
Var;
  Name : String;
Begin;
  Name := 'Fred'
  Writeln(Name);
  Readln;
End
```

My Seventh Program

Purpose: Showing how to collect, in a variable, a string of characters typed at a keyboard.

The following program shows how to input a string, `'Abc&76'`, typed at the keyboard into a variable `AString`.

The symbol ↲ in *Fig. 2.9* represents the result of pressing the return or enter key.

```
Program MySeventh;
{$APPTYPE CONSOLE}
Var
  AString : String;
Begin
  Write('Input a string: ');                         1
  Readln(AString);  2
  Writeln('String entered: ', AString);              3
  Readln;
End.
```

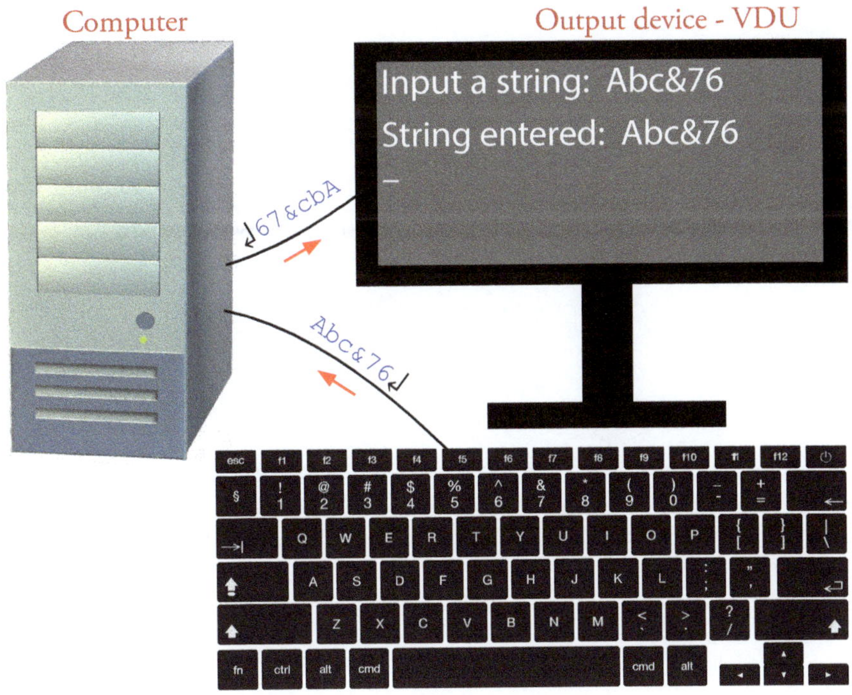

Fig. 2.9 Computer connected to a VDU (output device) and a keyboard (input device).

Fig. 2.9 shows a schematic of the output to the output device produced by the execution of `Program MySeventh`.

The statement labelled 1 writes the string `'Input a string: '` to the output device.

The statement labelled 2 collects the input string `'Abc&76'` from the input device, the keyboard.

This input is generated when the user types the key `A` followed by the key `b` and so on, finishing with the return or enter key shown above as ↲.

The program does not receive the typed string `'Abc&76'` until the return key is pressed.
Before this key is pressed the input may be edited/changed. This editing feature is called 'lazy I/O' where 'I/O' means Input/Output.

The statement labelled 3 writes the string `'String entered: '` followed by the string value `'Abc&76'` stored in the string variable `AString` to the output device. This statement then moves the writing cursor to the beginning of the next line. *Fig. 2.9* indicates that the cursor is on the next line by showing a short white line.

I Use the IDE to create and save the above source code program as **MySeventh.dpr** or **MySeventh.dprog**, depending on the version of Delphi, in its own directory/folder named **MySeventh**.

I Now build the program (Shift F9).

I Run this program in Debug mode (F9).

Fig. 2.10 is a captured console window showing the output produced by the execution of `Program MySeventh`.

Z:\ProductionChapters\DelphiBook\Code\Chapter2\Delphi10.2\MySeventh\Win32\Debug\MySeventh.exe

```
Input a string: Abc&76
String entered: Abc&76
```

Fig. 2.10 Captured console window showing output produced by execution of MySixth program.

Programming Tasks

5. Program MySeventh is amended so that it reads in a second string value from the keyboard which it stores in a second string variable. Using a separate Writeln statement involving the corresponding string variable, each string value is then displayed in the console window.

```
Program MySeventhAmended;
{$APPTYPE CONSOLE}
Var
  AString : String;
  ? : ?;
Begin
  Write('Input first string: ');
  Readln(AString);
  ?
  ?
  Writeln('First string entered: ', AString);
  Writeln('Second string entered: ', ?);
  Readln;
End.
```

Fig. 2.11 Amended Program MySeventh but with missing parts indicated by '?'.

Complete Program MySeventhAmended by replacing each instance of '?' with what is required. Use AnotherString as the identifier for the second string variable. Compile and run the complate program to check that it works as expected.

6. Write a Delphi program which meets the following specification:

- Declares two string variables, FirstWord and SecondWord.
- Uses Readln to input from the keyboard the string value, 'Good', into FirstWord and the string value, 'Morning', to SecondWord.
- Using two Writeln statements, the program should output the string 'Good' on one line and the string 'Morning' on the next line using the variables FirstWord and SecondWord.

Compile and run your program to check that your program meets the specification.

My Eighth Program

Purpose: Introducing the use of a named constant.

Fig. 2.12 shows the stored string value 'Bad' and the name FirstWord used to reference this stored value.

We have learned that identifiers are names that allow a programmer to reference stored values, e.g. the string value `'Bad'` is referenced by the name `FirstWord` as shown in *Fig. 2.12*. `FirstWord` identifies a variable if it is possible to replace the string `'Bad'` with another string, e.g. `'Good'` as shown in *Fig. 2.13*.

However, it is possible for an identifier to reference a stored value that is not changeable, i.e. is constant. We then say that the identifier identifies a named constant.

The following program shows how to define two named constants, `CStr1` and `CStr2`, and an example of their use.

```
Program MyEighth;
{$APPTYPE CONSOLE}
Const
  CStr1 = 'Input a string: ';
  CStr2 = 'String entered: ';
Var
  AString : String;
Begin
  Write(CStr1);
  Readln(AString);
  Writeln(CStr2, AString);
  Readln;
End.
```

Fig. 2.13 shows the stored string value 'Bad' about to be replaced by the string value 'Good'.

- Use the IDE to create and save the above source code program as **MyEighth.dpr** or **MyEighth.dprog**, depending on the version of Delphi, in its own directory/folder named **MyEighth**.
- Now build the program (Shift F9).
- Run this program in Debug mode (F9).

Now amend `Program MyEighth` as follows, then recompile:

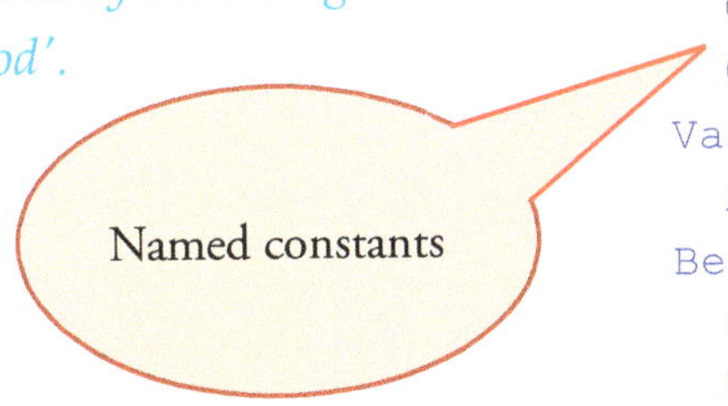


```
Program MyEighth;
{$APPTYPE CONSOLE}
Const
  CStr1 = 'Input a string: ';
  CStr2 = 'String entered: ';
Var
  AString : String;
Begin
  CStr1 := 'Input any string: ';
  Write(CStr1);
  Readln(AString);
  Writeln(CStr2, AString);
  Readln;
End.
```

The program will not compile because it contains an error - see *Fig.2.14*.

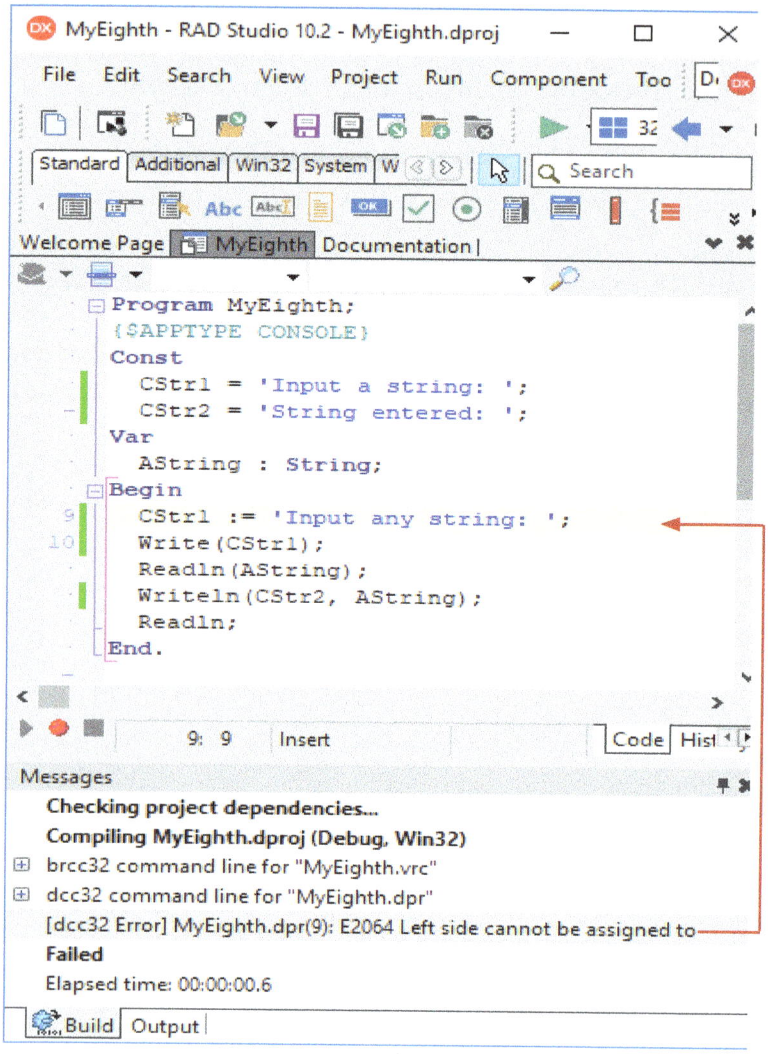

Fig. 2.14 Captured console window showing error report produced from the unsuccessful attempt to compile MyEighth program.

Key term

Constant:
Data which never change are modelled in a program by constants. This means stating their value explicitly, e.g. the string value or datum 'Good morning'.

Named constant:
To make a program easier to read, understand and change, a constant is given a **symbolic name** which can be used throughout the program wherever the value of the constant is required. This symbolic name is called a **constant identifier** and the constant it identifies, a **named constant.**

In Delphi, named constants are defined in a section of the program labelled with the keyword **Const**.
Each definition takes the form:

identifier = constant value;

Programming Tasks

7 Write a Delphi program which meets the following specification:

- Defines three named constants `Lat`, `Long`, `Location` to be the string values '`51.8156⁰ N`', '`0.8084⁰ W`', and '`Aylesbury, Bucks, UK`', respectively.
- Declares a string variable `Blog`.
- Uses `Readln` to input the string value from the keyboard into `Blog`:

  '`The sun has got its hat on, Hip, Hip, Hooray!`'.
- Using two `Writeln` statements, the program should output the string values of the named constants, `Lat`, `Long`, `Location`, in that order, separated by spaces on the first line and the string value of the string variable `Blog` on the second line.

Compile and run your program to check that your program meets the specification.

Questions

7 The following program does not compile because of **three** errors in its source code. What are these **three** errors?

```
Program Question7;
{$APPTYPE CONSOLE}
Const
  Lt = '33.8688° S';
  Lg = '151.2093° E';
  Location := 'Lane Cove, Sydney, Australia';
  Space = ' ';
Var
  Blog = String;
Begin
  Writeln(Lt, Space, Lg, Space, Location);
  Readln(Blog);
  Writeln(Blog);
  Location = 'Lane Cove, Sydney, Australia is where Nicole Kidman grew up';
  Writeln(Location);
  Readln;
End.
```

8 Sketch the output produced by the execution of the following program:

```
Program Question8;
{$APPTYPE CONSOLE}
Const
  B = '■';
  W = ' ';
Begin
  Writeln(B, W, B, W, B, W, B, W, B, W, B, W, B, W, B);
  Readln;
End.
```

Expressions

Purpose: Introducing the use of expressions.

An expression is any valid combination of constants (e.g. `Answer`), variables (e.g. `i`), literal values (e.g. 6), operators (e.g. '+', '<'), and function results (e.g. `Succ(6)`) as shown in *Table 2.1*.

- Load the source code program shown in *Table 2.1* and save as **Expressions.dpr** or **Expressions.dprog**, depending on the version of Delphi, in its own directory/folder named **Expressions**.
- Now build the program (Shift F9).
- Run this program in Debug mode (F9).

Key concept

Expression:
An expression is any valid combination of constants (e.g. Answer), variables (e.g. i), literal values (e.g. 6), operators (e.g. '+'), and function results (e.g. Succ(6)).

```
Program Expressions;
{$APPTYPE CONSOLE}
Const
  Answer = 42;
Var
  i : Integer = 6;
  Flag : Boolean = True;
Begin
  Writeln(6);
  Writeln(6 + 2);
  Writeln(6*3);
  Writeln(6/3);
  Writeln(6 = 6);
  Writeln(6 < 4);
  Writeln(6 > 4);
  Writeln('Constant Answer: ', Answer);
  Writeln('Variable i: ', i);
  Writeln('2*i: ', 2*i);
  Writeln('Boolean variable Flag: ', Flag);
  Writeln(True);
  Writeln(False);
  Writeln(Not True);
  Writeln(Succ(6));//Returns successor
  Writeln(Pred(6));//Returns predecessor
  Readln;
End.
```

Table 2.1 Program Expressions

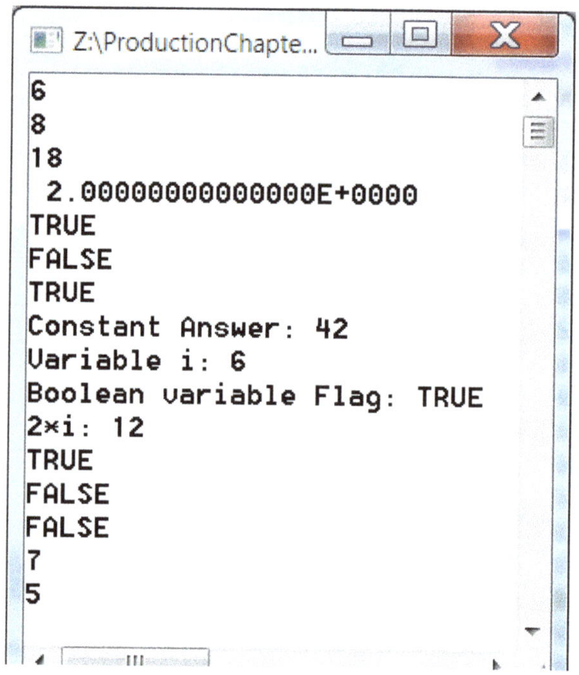

Fig. 2.15 Captured console window showing output from program Expressions in execution.

Figure 2.15 shows the console window output produced when program **Expressions** is executed.

Questions

9. The following program does not compile because of **three** errors in its source code. What are these **three** errors?

My Ninth Program

Purpose: Introducing the use of Readln with multiple parameters.

`Readln` may be used with integer variables or a mix of different data typed variables, e.g. integer and string, as shown in *Table 2.2*.

- Use the IDE to create and save the source code program in *Table 2.2* as **MyNinth.dpr** or **MyNinth.dprog**, depending on the version of Delphi, in its own directory/folder named **MyNinth**.
- Now build the program (Shift F9).
- Run this program in Debug mode (F9).

```
Program MyNinth;
{Save program as MyNinth.dpr or MyNinth.dprog}
{$APPTYPE CONSOLE}
Var
  x, y, z, AgeInYearsOnly : Integer;
  Name : String;
Begin
  //One way it can be done
  Write('Input two integers, x and y: ');
  Readln(x, y);
  Writeln('Their sum is ', x + y);
  //Another way it can be done
  Write('Input first integer, x: ');
  Readln(x);
  Write('Input second integer, y: ');
  Readln(y);
  Writeln('Their sum is ', x + y);
  Write('Input three integers, x, y and z:');
  Readln(x, y, z);
  Writeln('Their sum is ', x + y + z);
  Write('Input your age in years only and name: ');
  Readln(AgeInYearsOnly, Name);
  Writeln('Name: ', Name, ' Age: ', AgeInYearsOnly);
  Write('Input your name and age in years only: ');
  Readln(Name, AgeInYearsOnly);
  Writeln('Name: ', Name, ' Age: ', AgeInYearsOnly);
  Readln;
End.
```

Table 2.2 Program MyNinth

The section of source code outlined in red in *Table 2.2* contains a `Readln` statement with two variables arranged in the following order:

`Name`, `AgeInYearsOnly`.

This creates a potential problem with the input because the first variable `Name` has the data type `String`.

`'Fred 23'` is a valid string. Therefore, typing the name and age in years on the same input line fills variable `Name` with both values. Variable `AgeInYearsOnly` will fail to get value `23`. As the program is expecting an integer it pauses waiting for more input.

To fix the issue, the string `'Fred'` needs something typed to indicate that the end of the string is reached. Pressing the return key does this. The age in years may then be typed next so that variable `AgeInYearsOnly` is assigned the value `23`. This is shown in *Figure 2.16*.

If `Readln` requires an integer value then it converts the digit string typed at the keyboard into its integer equivalent before assigning the result to the integer variable, e.g. digit string '23' → integer 23.

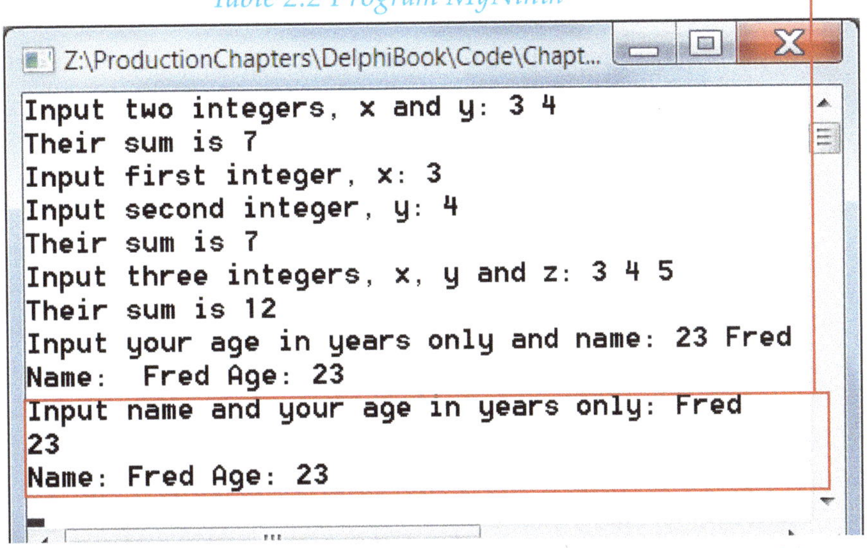

Fig. 2.16 Captured console window showing output produced by execution of MyNinth program.

We can do arithmetic with this integer value 23 but not with its digit string equivalent '23'.

This task is instructive because it indicates that input from the keyboard is effectively text, i.e. sequences of characters organised on a line-by-line basis which each program interprets according to the data types of the destinations in the program, i.e. integer variable or string variable or some other variable type. Under the bonnet the program converts the input into the form expected for the destination. The same is true for Writeln. It must convert non-character-based values, e.g. integers, into strings before outputting these to the screen.

The section of source code outlined in green in *Table 2.2* contains a `Readln` statement with two variables arranged in the following order:

`AgeInYearsOnly, Name`

Figure 2.16 shows that the input to be '`23 Fred`'.

The output on the following line is '`Name:  Fred  Age: 23`'.

This shows that the `Readln` statement has correctly processed the input string '`23 Fred`' by extracting the digit string '`23`' and successfully converting it to integer `23`, then extracting the characters immediately following '`3`' and assembling these into the string '` Fred`'. There is a subtle distinction in the output which reflects the fact that the string variable `Name` contains five characters: a leading space character followed by the characters of the string '`Fred`'. Thus there are two space characters between '`Name:`' and '`Fred`' and only one between '`Age:`' and '`23`'. This suggests that the input should have been typed as '`23Fred`'. The program will still be able to collect the digit string '`23`' correctly because it will use the non-digit character '`F`' of '`Fred`' to indicate the end of the digit string. However, this just demonstrates that sometimes it is not sensible to mix variables of different data types in a `Readln` statement.

Key point

Keyboard a source of text:
Input from the keyboard is sequences of characters organised on a line-by-line basis which each program interprets according to the data type of the destination in the program, i.e. integer variable or string variable or some other variable type.
Text is sequences of characters organised on a line-by-line basis.

Programming Tasks

8. Write a Delphi program which meets the following specification:
   - Defines three named constants `Lat`, `Long`, `Location` to be the string values '`51.8156⁰ N`', '`0.8084⁰ W`', and '`Aylesbury, Bucks, UK`', respectively.
   - Declares a string variable `Blog`.
   - Uses `Readln` to input the string value from the keyboard into `Blog`:
     '`The sun has got its hat on, Hip, Hip, Hooray!`'.
   - Using two `Writeln` statements, the program should output the string values of the named constants, `Lat`, `Long`, `Location`, in that order, separated by spaces on the first line and the string value of the string variable `Blog` on the second line.

Compile and run your program to check that your program meets the specification.

My Tenth Program

Purpose: Introducing the use of Exceptions

- Use the IDE to create and save the source code program in *Table 2.3* as **MyTenth.dpr** or **MyTenth.dprog**, depending on the version of Delphi, in its own directory/folder named **MyTenth**.
- Now build the program (Shift F9).
- Run this program in Debug mode (F9).

Figure 2.17 shows output produced by execution of `MyTenth` program for input `'a'`. As `'a'` cannot be converted by `Readln` into an integer an exception is raised which is caught by the `Try` part of the `Try Except` statement. This statement then raises an exception which is handled by the `Exception` part which specifies that the following should be executed

```
        Writeln(E.ClassName, ': ', E.Message);.
                    ↑          ↑        ↑
Output ────►  EInOutError :  Invalid numeric input
```

```
Program MyTenth;
{$APPTYPE CONSOLE}
{$R *.res}
Uses
  System.SysUtils;
Var
  x : Integer;
Begin
  Try
    Write('Input an integer: ');
    Readln(x);
    Writeln('Double x is ', 2*x);
  Except
    On E: Exception
      Do Writeln(E.ClassName, ': ', E.Message);
  End;
  Readln;
End.
```

`System.SysUtils;` ← This library is needed inorder to use Try Except On E: Exception.

`Readln(x);` ← We try this and if it fails an exception is raised which is handled by an Exception handler. (→ `Do Writeln(E.ClassName, ': ', E.Message);`)

Table 2.3 Program MyTenth

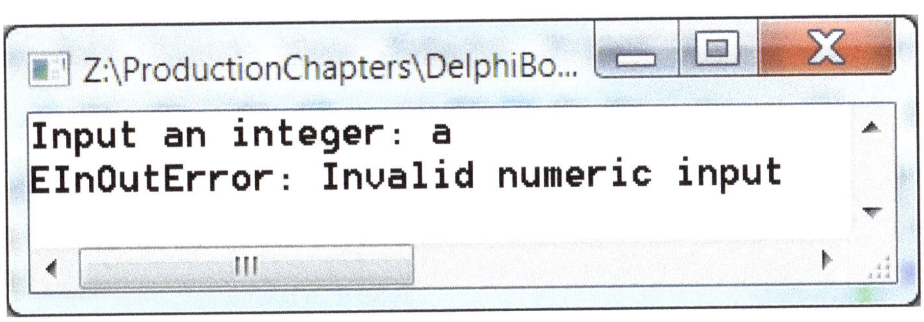

Fig. 2.17 Captured console window showing output produced by execution of MyTenth program.

My Eleventh Program

Purpose: Introducing input validation using set membership operator In

- Use the IDE to create and save the source code program in *Table 2.4* as **MyEleventh.dpr** or **MyEleventh.dprog**, depending on the version of Delphi, in its own directory/folder named **MyEleventh**.
- Now build the program (Shift F9).
- Run this program in Debug mode (F9) and test with the inputs shown in *Figure 2.18*.

Since the keyboard is a source of text, it is safer to collect keyboard input in a string variable. The string variable can then be converted into its destination data type after checking first that this will be a valid operation, i.e. that the input is a string equivalent s compatible with the destination type, e.g. integer. The program listed in *Table 2.4* uses a converter called `StrToInt` to convert a string into its equivalent integer. It is also possible to use the converter `ToInteger` as shown in *Table 2.4*. if the version of Delphi being used is XE2 or later.

The program examines each character of the string in turn using a `For loop` by assuming that the characters are indexed from `1` and tesing that each character is a digit character, i.e. from the set `['0'..'9']`.

A Boolean flag `Valid` is set to `False` and remains `False` if one or more characters are found not to be a digit character. The program source code which does this is

```
If Not (InputString[i] In ['0'..'9'])
  Then
    Begin
      Valid := False;
      Writeln('Not an integer, try again!');
    End;
```

The integer variable `i` starts at `1` and is incremented by `1` each time around the loop so that it is able to select each character in the input string in turn until there are no more characters and the entire length of the string has been tested.

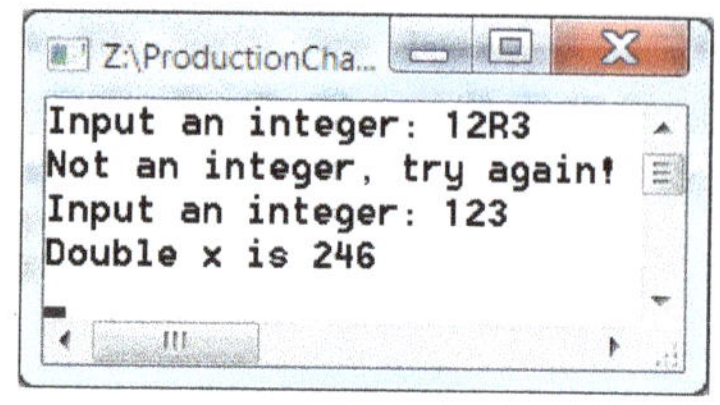

Fig. 2.18 Captured console window showing output produced by execution of MyEleventh program.

```
Program MyEleventh;
{$APPTYPE CONSOLE}
{$R *.res}
Uses SysUtils; // Contains converter StrToInt which converts a valid string to an integer
Var
  InputString : String;
  x, i : Integer;
  Valid : Boolean;
Begin
  Repeat
    Write('Input an integer: ');
    Readln(InputString); // reads a line of input as a string
    Valid := True;
    For i := 1 To Length(InputString)
      Do
        If Not (InputString[i] In ['0'..'9']) // Checks if character of string a digit character
          Then
            Begin
              Valid := False;
              Writeln('Not an integer, try again!');
            End;
  Until Valid; ;
  x := StrToInt(InputString); //Converts a valid digit string into an integer
  {Can also use x := InputString.ToInteger; in Delphi XE2 onwards}
  Writeln('Double x is ', 2*x);
  Readln;
End.
```

Table 2.4 Program MyEleventh

My Twelfth Program

Purpose: Introducing the format function which formats an output string from a given input value

- I Use the IDE to create and save the source code program in *Table 2.5* as **MyTwelfth.dpr** or **MyTwelfth.dprog**, depending on the version of Delphi, in its own directory/folder named **MyTwelfth**.
- I Now build the program (Shift F9).
- I Run this program in Debug mode (F9).

The Format function returns a formatted string assembled from a given value and a format string, e.g. `'%8.2f'`.

Type specifies the particular form that the formatted string should take, e.g "f" means fixed point.

```
Format ('%8.2f', [123.456]);
```

"%" width "." precision **type** value

Width specifies the maximum number of characters in the output string.

Precision specifies the number of decimal places or the number of significant figures depending on the specified type.

The Format function can also be used as follows

Value specifies the value to be converted to a string with a specified format.

```
Format ('%*.*f', [8, 2, 123.456]);
```

"%" "." **type** width precision value

```
Program MyTwelfth;
{$APPTYPE CONSOLE}
Uses
  System.SysUtils;
Begin
  Writeln(Format('%8d', [-3652]));// "%" [width] type
  Writeln(Format('%8u', [-3652]));// "%" [width] type
  Writeln(Format('%8.3f', [15.6796]));//"%" [width] ["." prec] type
  Writeln(Format('%12.5e', [15.6726]));//"%" [width] ["." prec] type
  Writeln(Format('%8g', [15.67])); // "%" [width] type
  Writeln(Format('%8.2m', [15.68])); // "%" [width] ["." prec] type
  Writeln(Format('%15.3n', [2568913.9])); // "%" [width] ["." prec] type
  Writeln(Format('%x', [65516])); // Not using width or precision specifiers
  Readln
End.
```

Table 2.5 Program MyTwelfth

Figure 2.19 shows the output from program `MyTwelve` when run.

The various types `d`, `u`, `f`, `e`, `g`, `m`, `n` and `x` are described in *Table 2.6*.

```
Writeln(Format('%8d', [-3652]));
Writeln(Format('%8u', [-3652]));
Writeln(Format('%8.3f', [15.6796]));
Writeln(Format('%12.5e', [15.6726]));
Writeln(Format('%8g', [15.67]));
Writeln(Format('%8.2m', [15.68]));
Writeln(Format('%15.3n', [2568913.9]));
Writeln(Format('%x', [65516]));
```

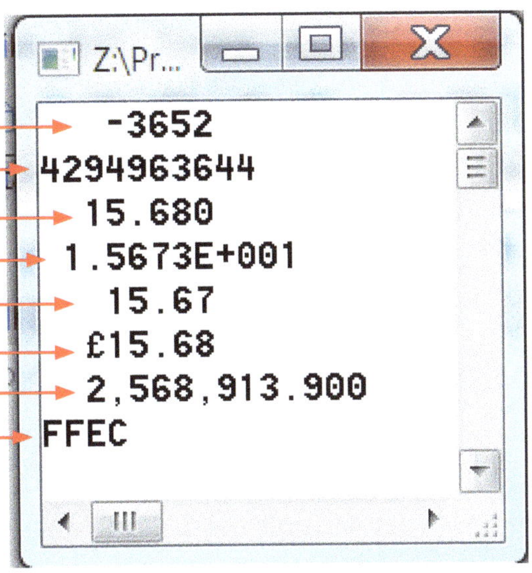

Fig. 2.19 Output from program MyTwelfth.

Table 2.6 summarizes the possible values for type:

Type	Output format	Description
d	Decimal.	**Integer value → a string of decimal digits**, e.g. -3652 → '-3652'. Precision specifier present: resulting string must contain at least the specified number of digits; Value has less digits: the resulting string is left-padded with zeros.
u	Unsigned decimal.	Similar to 'd' but no sign is output, , e.g. -3652 → '3652'
e	Scientific.	**Floating-point value → a string of the form "-d.ddd...E+ddd"**, e.g. 15.6726 → '1.5673E+001'. Resulting string starts with a minus sign if the number is negative. One digit always precedes the decimal point. Precision specifier: gives total number of digits in the resulting string (including the one before the decimal point) - default precision = 15 if no precision specifier. "E" exponent character in the resulting string is always followed by a plus or minus sign and at least three digits.
f	Fixed.	**Floating-point value → a string of the form "-ddd.ddd..."**, e.g. 15.6796 → '15.680'. Resulting string starts with a minus sign if the number is negative. The number of digits after the decimal point is given by the precision specifier (default = 2 decimal digits if no precision specifier is present).
g	General.	**Floating-point value → the shortest possible decimal string using fixed or scientific format**, e.g. 15.67 → '15.67'. Precision specifier gives the number of significant digits in the resulting string(default precision = 15 is assumed if no precision specifier is present. Trailing zeros are removed from the resulting string, and a decimal point appears only if necessary. Fixed point format in resulting string: if the number of digits to the left of the decimal point in the value <= specified precision, and if the value >= 0.00001, Otherwise scientific format in resulting string
n	Number.	**Floating-point value → a string of the form "-d,ddd,ddd.ddd..."**, e.g. 2568913.9 → '2,568,913.900'. "n" format corresponds to the "f" format, except that the resulting string contains thousand separators.
m	Money.	**Floating-point value → a string that represents a currency amount**, 15.68 → '£15.68' . Conversion icontrolled by ***CurrencyString***, ***CurrencyFormat***, ***NegCurrFormat***, ***ThousandSeparator***, ***DecimalSeparator***, and ***CurrencyDecimals*** global variables or their equivalent in a ***TFormatSettings*** data structure. Precision specifier overrides the value given by the ***CurrencyDecimals*** global variable or its ***TFormatSettings*** equivalent.
x	Hexadecimal	**Integer value → a string of hexadecimal digits**, e.g. 65516 → 'FFEC'. Precision specifier: resulting string must contain at least the specified number of digits; if the value has fewer digits, the resulting string is left-padded with zeros.

Table 2.6 Possible values for type and their descriptions

Programming Tasks

9. Write a Delphi program which meets the following specification:
   - Defines three named constants `Lat`, `Long`, `Location` to be the string values `'51.8156⁰ N'`, `'0.8084⁰ W'`, and `'Aylesbury, Bucks, UK'`, respectively.
   - Declares a string variable `Blog`.
   - Uses `Readln` to input the string value from the keyboard into `Blog`:
     `'The sun has got its hat on, Hip, Hip, Hooray!'`.
   - Using two `Writeln` statements, the program should output the string values of the named constants, `Lat`, `Long`, `Location`, in that order, separated by spaces on the first line and the string value of the string variable `Blog` on the second line.

Compile and run your program to check that your program meets the specification.

My Thirteenth Program

Delphi supports various message dialogue windows to use in Graphical User Interface (GUI) applications but they can also be used in console programs alongside Write(ln) and Read(ln).

Table 2.5 shows a console application that uses

- ShowMessage - `ShowMessage('Hello World');`
- ShowMessagePos - `ShowMessagePos('Hello World', 0, 0);`
- ShowMessageFmt - `ShowMessageFmt('No1 = %d', [6]);`
- MessageDlg - `MessageDlg('Do you really want to terminate the program?', mtConfirmation,[mbYes, mbNo], 0) = mrYes`
- MessageDlgPos - `MessageDlgPos('Hello World', mtConfirmation, mbYesNoCancel, 0, 200, 200, mbYes);`

Fig. 2.19 ShowMessage.

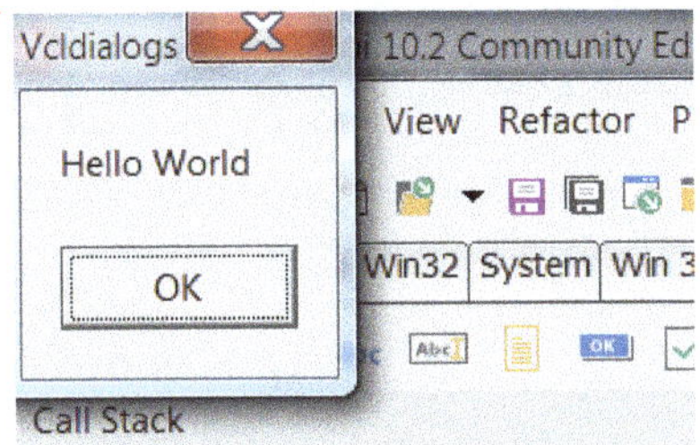

Fig. 2.20 ShowMessagePos at screen coordinates 0, 0

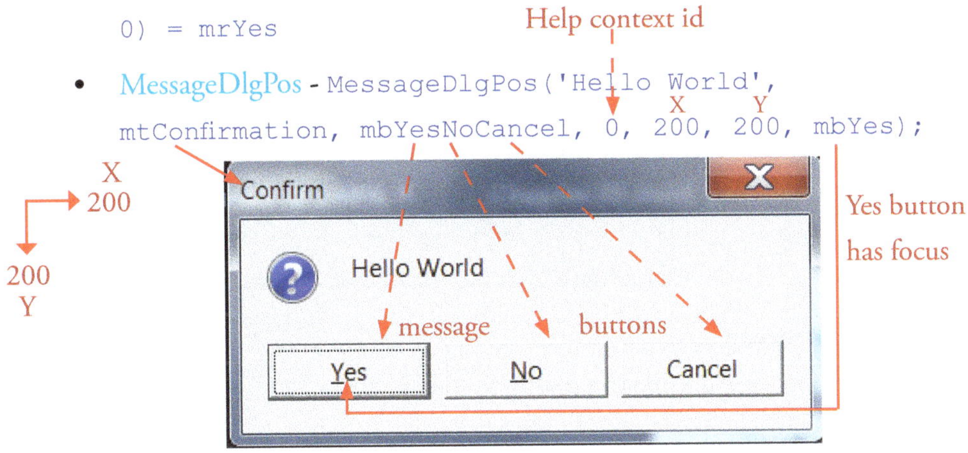

Fig. 2.22 MessageDlgPos at screen coordinates 200, 200

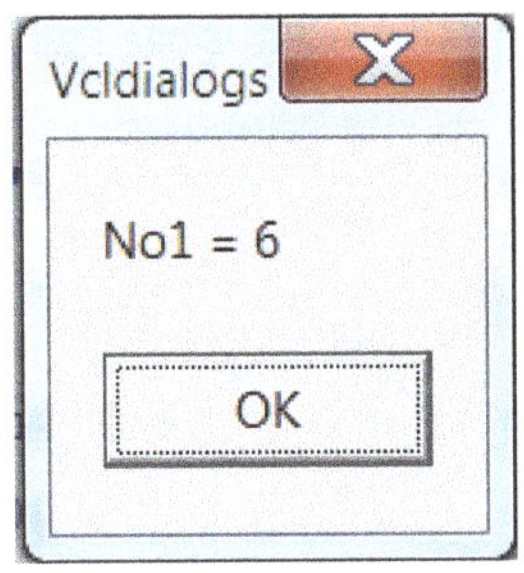

Fig. 2.21 ShowMessageFmt.

- InputBox - `InputBox('Name Box ', 'Please enter your name', '');`

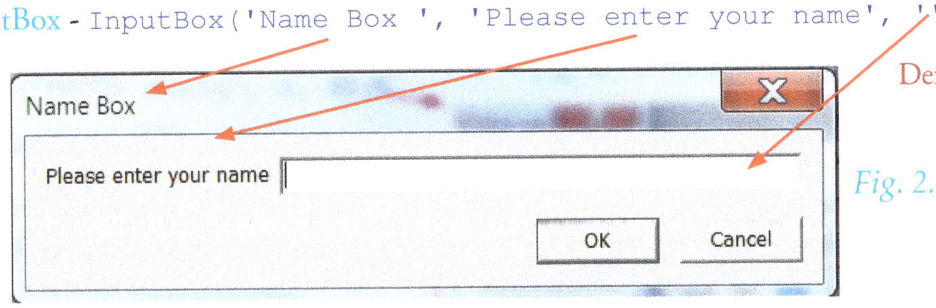

Default string = Empty string

Fig. 2.23 InputBox.

```
Program VclDialogs;
{$APPTYPE CONSOLE}
Uses
  Vcl.Dialogs, Vcl.Controls;
Var
  StringVariable : String;
Begin
  Repeat
    Vcl.Dialogs.ShowMessage('Hello World');
    ShowMessagePos('Hello World', 0, 0);
    ShowMessageFmt('No1 = %d', [6]);
    MessageDlgPos('Hello World', mtConfirmation, mbYesNoCancel, 0, 200, 200, mbYes);
    Stringvariable := InputBox('Name Box ', 'Please enter your name', '');
    ShowMessage(StringVariable);
    If MessageDlg('Do you really want to terminate the program?', mtConfirmation,
                         [mbYes, mbNo], 0, mbYes) = mrYes
      Then Exit;
  Until 4=6;
End.
```

Program repeats indefinitely unless Exit is executed because 4 will never equal 6.

Table 2.5 Program MyTwelfth

MessageDlg Function

The program shown in *Table 2.5* repeats indefinitely unless `Exit` is executed because 4 will never equal 6.

For `Exit` to be executed the result returned by `MessageDlg(...)` must equal `mrYes` (message response Yes)

```
      If MessageDlg('Do you really want to terminate the program?',
                    mtConfirmation, [mbYes, mbNo], 0, mbYes) = mrYes
        Then Exit;
```

`MessageDlg` displays a message dialogue box in the center of the screen and obtains the user's response.

If the user's response = `mrYes` then the console application is exited because `Exit` is called. If it isn't then the application continues to execute.

`'Do you really want to terminate the program?'` is the content of the message that appears.

`mtConfirmation` is the purpose of the dialogue.

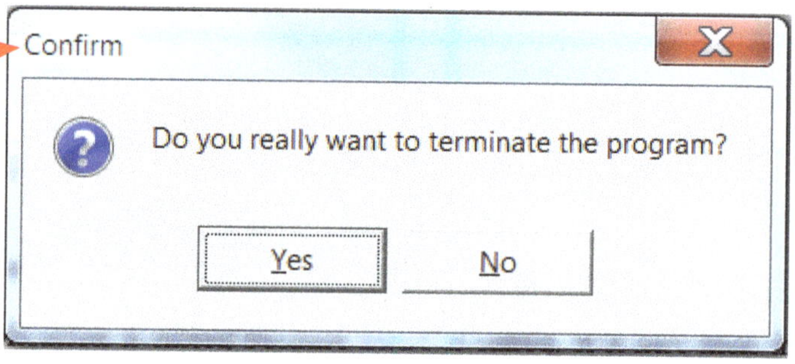

Fig. 2.24 MessageDlg

`[mbYes, mbNo]` is a set of buttons and indicates what buttons should appear in the message box. The buttons appear in the same order they appear in the buttons set.

`0` specifies the context ID for the Help topic that should appear when the user clicks the Help button or presses F1 while the dialogue is displayed.

`mbYes` specifies which button from among `[mbYes, mbNo]` is the default button (focused button) for the dialogue.

`MessageDlg` returns the value of the button the user selected.

Table 2.6 shows the type of dialogues supported by MessageDlg.

MessageDlg may use buttons chosen from mbYes, mbNo, mbCancel, mbAbort, mbRetry, mbIgnore.

Type of message dialogue (mt)	
mtWarning	Uses a yellow exclamation mark symbol
mtError	Uses a red stop sign
mtInformation	Uses a blue i
mtConfirmation	Uses a white question mark on a blue background
mtCustom	Eliminates any bitmap and forces the caption to be the name of the application's executable file

Table 2.6 Type of message dialogue

The program shown in *Table 2.5* uses two libraries:

- `Vcl.Dialogs` - contains the message dialogues that have been covered in this section
- `Vcl.Controls`- contains the constant definitions for the various `mt` (message type), `mb` (message button), `mr` (message response)

The program in *Table 2.5* demonstrates that a message dialogue can be called with direct reference to the library in which the message dialogue is defined: `Vcl.Dialogs.ShowMessage('Hello World');`

Programming Tasks

10 Write a Delphi program which meets the following specification:

- Defines three named constants `Lat`, `Long`, `Location` to be the string values `'51.8156º N'`, `'0.8084º W'`, and `'Aylesbury, Bucks, UK'`, respectively.
- Declares a string variable `Blog`.
- Uses `Readln` to input the string value from the keyboard into `Blog`:

  `'The sun has got its hat on, Hip, Hip, Hooray!'`.
- Using two `Writeln` statements, the program should output the string values of the named constants, `Lat`, `Long`, `Location`, in that order, separated by spaces on the first line and the string value of the string variable `Blog` on the second line.

Compile and run your program to check that your program meets the specification.

Programming constructs

Purpose: To learn how to write and interpret pseudocode

Variable declaration

Variable

Data which are subject to change are modelled in a program by variables.

A **variable** is simply a container in which a value may be stored for subsequent manipulation within a program - *Figure 3.1*.

The stored value may be changed by the program as it executes its instructions, hence the use of the term "variable" for the container.

Under the bonnet, the container is realised as one or more reserved memory locations in the RAM of the machine.

Figure 3.1 shows the value 6 about to be stored in variable x represented by the yellow container

Key concept

Variable:
In programming, a variable can be thought of as a container for a value.
Like a physical container a variable may be empty, in which case we say that its value is undefined.

Variable declaration

A **variable declaration** is one way of causing a variable to be created.

Key concept

Variable declaration:
A variable declaration is one way of causing a variable to be created.

For example, in Delphi, an integer variable, x, may be declared as follows

```
Var
  x : Integer;
```

Key point

Modelling data by variables:
Data which are subject to change are modelled by variables.

The amount of reserved memory allocated to a variable and what is allowed to be stored in this reserved memory depend upon its data type.

This declaration reserves a **named space** in memory (RAM) for a value of data type `Integer`. The space is named `x` and the amount of RAM is four bytes because that is what Delphi's `Integer` data type specifies.

By assigning different data types to each variable, *integers*, *numbers with a fractional part*, *characters*, *strings*, *arrays*, *records* and *other entities*, may be stored in these variables.

Initialising variables

It is common practice to initialise a variable when it is declared.
For example, in Delphi

```
Var
  x : Integer = 6;
```

Key concept

Constant:
In programming, data which never change are modelled in a program by constants. This means stating their values explicitly.
To make a program easier to read, understand and maintain, a constant is given a symbolic name which can be used throughout the program whenever the value of the constant is required.

Constant declaration

Some of the data used in programs never change. For example, the ratio of the circumference of a circle to its diameter which is approximately 3.142.

Data which never change are modelled in a program by constants.

This means stating their values explicitly. To make a program easier to read, understand and change, a constant is given a **symbolic name** which can be used throughout the program whenever the value of the constant is required.

For example, in Delphi a constant for the value 3.142 can be defined using the language keyword `Const` as follows

Language keyword → `Const`

```
Const
  Pi = 3.142;
```

Symbolic name for constant → `Pi`

Information

The System unit in Delphi contains a function that returns a value for Pi of 3.14159265358979323 85.

```
Program Constants;
{$APPTYPE CONSOLE}
Begin
  Writeln(Pi);
  Readln;
End.
```

Questions

1. What is a variable?
2. What is a variable declaration?
3. What is a constant declaration?
4. The calculation 2 x 3.141592654 x radius is made in several places in a program. Give **two** reasons why replacing 3.141592654 by the named constant `Pi` could improve this program?

Assignment

An instruction which alters the value of a variable is called an **assignment statement** and the operation is called **assignment**. A value is copied into a variable when a computer executes an assignment statement. The action replaces the currently stored value in the variable as illustrated in *Figures 3.2* and *3.3* for a variable x.

For example, in Delphi an assignment statement that **assigns** the value 6 to variable x is written as follows

```
x := 6;
```

The operand, x, to the left of the := operator is the name of the variable and the operand, 6, to the right of the := operator is the value that will be stored in the variable when assignment is carried out. The value in x before assignment occurs is overwritten by the assignment operation. This is shown by example in *Figure 3.3* where the value 4 is overwritten by the value 6.

The := operator is called the **assignment operator**.

The term "statement" is used universally for historical reasons. It would have been better to have adopted the term "command" or "instruction".

Key term

Assignment statement:
An instruction which alters the value of a variable is called an assignment statement.
The operation is known as assignment.

Figure 3.2 shows the value 6 about to be stored in variable x which currently contains the value 4

Questions

5 What is assignment ?

Pseudocode

Pseudocode is a programming-like language which is employed to communicate a solution to a problem in a manner which is independent of any particular production programming language such as Delphi.

For example, in pseudocode, a left-pointing arrow ← is used to represent the assignment operator.

In this book, solutions to problems are sometimes expressed first in pseudocode. The given pseudocode may then be recast as a Delphi program. The reason for adopting this approach is that pseudocode uses a relaxed syntax (grammar) for constructing statements so that it is posssible to focus on the logic of the solution first.

However, it is not usually possible to execute pseudocode in a machine. The pseudocode solution has to be turned into a Delphi program, then compiled and linked with supporting libraries before it can be executed. Instead, pseudocode is executed by hand which means reading it and processing it statement-by-statement in your head.

The process is called a **trace** or **hand trace** execution.

If it could be executed in a machine it wouldn't be pseudocode, but instead a fully-fledged programming language.

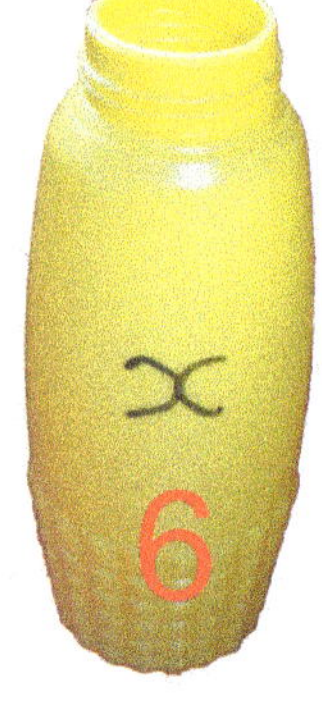

Figure 3.3 shows that value 4 has been replaced by value 6

Information

Pseudocode:
Pseudocode is a programming-like language which is employed to communicate a solution to a problem in a manner which is independent of any particular production programming language.

Figure 3.4 shows the value 6 stored in variable NatNo, being copied then added to 1 and the result 7 about to be stored

Figure 3.5 Shows the value 7 stored in variable NatNo

One of the strengths of pseudocode is that it provides a common way of expressing programming language constructs, e.g. the assignment operator, which are independent of any actual programming language. The aim is readability in order to assist understanding. This is one reason why algorithms are often expressed in pseudocode.

Which authority defines pseudocode?

You can design and use your own pseudocode.

An Examing Board such as AQA in the UK uses pseudocode for its AS, A level and GCSE Computer Science examinations -

https://filestore.aqa.org.uk/resources/computing/AQA-8520-TG-PC.PDF.

Generally speaking, one person's pseudocode may differ in some respects from another's but usually the differences are not sufficient to make reading and understanding difficult.

Iteration

Suppose we are required to sum the first 10 natural numbers, i.e.

$$1 + 2 + 3 + 4 + 5 + 6 + 7 + 8 + 9 + 10$$

One way that this could be done is to **repeat** the addition of each natural number, in turn, to a running total, initialised to 0, **until** all 10 natural numbers have been added together.

In pseudocode this might be expressed as shown in *Table 3.1*.

```
RunningTotal ← 0      Assign the value 0 to variable RunningTotal
NatNo ← 1      Assign the value 1 to variable NatNo
Repeat
  RunningTotal ← RunningTotal + NatNo
  NatNo ← NatNo + 1
Until NatNo = 11
```

Stop repeating when value in NatNo reaches 11

Add 1 to current value in NatNo, replace this current value with the value which results from this addition (refers to NatNo ← NatNo + 1)

Add NatNo to current value in RunningTotal, replace this current value with the value which results from the addition (refers to RunningTotal ← RunningTotal + NatNo)

Table 3.1 Pseudocode example which adds the first 10 natural numbers

Figures 3.4 and *3.5* show the execution of the assignment statement

`NatNo ← NatNo + 1`

split over two stages. `NatNo` contains the value 6 just before this statement is executed and afterwards it contains the value 7.

The pseudocode in *Table 3.1* illustrates repetition or **iteration**. The general form of such iteration is

```
Repeat
  instructions
Until condition
```

which means that the instructions between the words `Repeat` and `Until` are executed repeatedly until the condition specified in `Until condition` is met.

The instructions between `Repeat` and `Until` are known as the **loop body**.

The iteration performed by `Repeat Until` is called a **loop** because execution loops back and forth between `Repeat` and `Until`.

The condition occurring in `Until condition` is called the **terminating condition** of the loop.

Questions

6 Trace the execution of the pseudocode shown in *Table 3.1*. Record in *Table 3.2* the value of `NatNo` and `RunningTotal` as they change during the execution. The first value of each variable has been recorded for you in the table.

NatNo	RunningTotal
1	0

Table 3.2 Trace table for NatNo and RunningTotal

7 How would you change the pseudocode in *Table 3.1* so that when executed it adds the first 15 natural numbers?

Check that your change is correct by hand-tracing the resulting pseudocode. The final value of `RunningTotal` should be 120.

8 What is the final value of `RunningTotal` when the following pseudocode is executed by hand if x in `RunningTotal x Choice` is the multiplication operator?

```
RunningTotal ← 1
Count ← 2
Repeat
  RunningTotal ← RunningTotal x Count
  Count ← Count + 1
Until Count = 11
```

Table 3.3 shows another way to add the first 10 natural numbers.

```
RunningTotal ← 0
NatNo ← 1
While NatNo < 11      Stop repeating when value in NatNo reaches 11
  RunningTotal ← RunningTotal + NatNo
  NatNo ← NatNo + 1
EndWhile
```

Table 3.3 Pseudocode example which adds the first 10 natural numbers

Questions

9 Trace the execution of the pseudocode shown in *Table 3.3*. Record in *Table 3.4* the value of `NatNo` and `RunningTotal` as they change during the execution. The first value of each variable has been recorded for you in the table.

NatNo	RunningTotal
1	0

Table 3.4 Trace table for NatNo and RunningTotal

10 How would you change the pseudocode in *Table 3.3* so that when executed it adds the first 15 natural numbers?
Check that your change is correct by hand-tracing the resulting pseudocode. The final value of `RunningTotal` should be 120.

11 What is the final value of `RunningTotal` when the following pseudocode is executed by hand if x in `RunningTotal x Choice` is the multiplication operator?

```
RunningTotal ← 1
Count ← 2
Repeat
  RunningTotal ← RunningTotal x Count
  Count ← Count + 1
Until Count = 11
```

Key term

Sequence statements: Statements are executed one at a time, one after another in the order in which they are written with each executed exactly once.

Sequence

The following two instructions (assignment statements) of the pseudocode in *Table 3.3* are executed one after the other

```
RunningTotal ← RunningTotal + NatNo
NatNo ← NatNo + 1
```

They form a sequence of steps governed by the following rules

1. The steps are executed one at a time
2. The order in which the steps are written is the order in which they are executed
3. Each step is executed exactly once.

We say that this part of the solution to the problem of adding the first 10 natural numbers is constructed using a program design principle called sequence.

Questions

12 A variable x contains the value 7 and a variable y the value 3. Using only sequence, write assignment statements that swap the values contained in x and y. You may use Temp, a third variable.

Programming task

Use the IDE to load or create and save the source code program *Table 3.5* as RunningTotalSum.dpr or RunningTotalSum.dprog, depending on the version of Delphi, in its own directory/folder named RunningTotalSum. Now compile the program (Ctrl F9). Run this program (F9). The output should be 55.

```
Program RunningTotalSum;
{Remember to Save Project As RunningTotalSum}
{$APPTYPE CONSOLE}
Var
  RunningTotal, NatNo : Integer;
Begin
  RunningTotal := 0;
  NatNo := 1;
  Repeat
    RunningTotal := RunningTotal + NatNo;
    NatNo := NatNo + 1;
  Until NatNo = 11;
  Writeln('Running Total Sum: ', RunningTotal);
  Readln;
End.
```

Note the requirement for the statement separator symbol ;

Table 3.5 Program RunningTotalSum

Selection

If statement

If solutions to problems consist only of steps in sequence then there is no possibility of solving problems which need to deviate from the given sequence of execution if circumstances require this.

For example, suppose instead of summing the first 10 natural numbers we are required to sum only the even numbers amongst the first 10 natural numbers, using the pseudocode in Table 3.3. The solution must test to see if the next natural number is even. Only if it is even will it then be added it to the running total.

The revised sequence section of the pseudocode solution in Table 3.3 will take the form

```
If NatNo is even                                   ← condition
  Then RunningTotal ← RunningTotal + NatNo         ← step
EndIf
NatNo ← NatNo + 1
```

The conditional part of this pseudocode fits the general form

```
If condition
  Then step
```

where `condition` specifies the circumstance under which the `step` is to be executed. If `condition` is true then `step` is executed; otherwise it is not.

`If condition Then step` is a statement known as **selection**.

Suppose instead of summing the first 10 natural numbers we are required to sum the even numbers in one running total and the odd numbers in a different running total. We now have two alternative steps to be executed.

The revised sequence section of the pseudocode solution in Table 3.3 will take the form

```
If NatNo is even                                          ← condition
  Then EvenRunningTotal ← EvenRunningTotal + NatNo        ← step 1
  Else OddRunningTotal ← OddRunningTotal + NatNo          ← step 2
EndIf
NatNo ← NatNo + 1
```

The general form of selection in which selection is between one of two alternative steps is

```
If condition
  Then step 1
  Else step 2
```

where `condition` determines whether `step 1` is executed or `step 2` is executed.

> ### Key fact
> **Combining principles:**
> The three combining principles (sequence, iteration/repetition and selection/choice) are basic to all imperative programming languages.

> ### Key term
> **Selection:**
> A selection statement takes one of two possible forms:
> ```
> If condition
>   Then step
> ```
> or
> ```
> If condition
>   Then step 1
>   Else step 2
> ```
> The condition determines whether or not `step` is executed, `step1` or `step2` is executed.

We thus have two forms of `If` selection statement:

```
If condition
  Then step
```

```
If condition
  Then step 1
  Else step 2
```

```
If No1 > No2
  Then Largest ← No1
  Else Largest ← No2
EndIf
```

Table 3.5 Pseudocode to find the largest of two numbers

Questions

13 Rewrite the following If statements as a single If Then Else statement

```
If Age < 37 Then AgeCategory ← 'A'
If Age >=37 Then AgeCategory ← 'B'
```

14 The pseudocode in *Table 3.5* finds the largest of two numbers, `No1`, `No2`.
The value of the largest of the two numbers is stored in variable `Largest`.
(a) If `No1` stores the value 6, `No2` the value 3 which branch of the selection statement is executed, `Then` or `Else`? Explain your answer.
(b) If `No1` stores the value 6, `No2` the value 7 which branch of the selection statement is executed, `Then` or `Else`? Explain your answer.

Programming task

Use the IDE to load or create and save the source code program *Table 3.6* as RunningTotalEven.dpr or RunningTotalEven.dprog, depending on the version of Delphi, in its own directory/folder named RunningTotalEven. Now compile the program (Ctrl F9). Run this program (F9). The output should be 30.

```
Program RunningTotalEven;
{Remember to Save Project As RunningTotalEven}
{$APPTYPE CONSOLE}
Var
  RunningTotal, NatNo : Integer;
Begin
  RunningTotal := 0;
  NatNo := 1;
  Repeat
    If (NatNo Mod 2) = 0
      Then RunningTotal := RunningTotal + NatNo;
    NatNo := NatNo + 1;
  Until NatNo = 11;
  Writeln('Running Total of Even Nos: ', RunningTotal);
  Readln;
End.
```

Mod operator gives remainder after integer division. If this is zero then NatNo exactly divisible by 2. i.e. is an even number.

Table 3.6 Program RunningTotalEven

Programming task

Use the IDE to load or create and save the source code program *Table 3.7* as RunningTotalEvenOdd.dpr or RunningTotalEvenOdd.dprog, depending on the version of Delphi, in its own directory/folder named RunningTotalEvenOdd.

Now compile the program (Ctrl F9). Run this program (F9). The output should be 30 and 25.

```
Program RunningTotalEvenOdd;
{Remember to Save Project As RunningTotalEvenOdd}
{$APPTYPE CONSOLE}
Var
  EvenRunningTotal, OddRunningTotal, NatNo : Integer;
Begin
  EvenRunningTotal := 0;
  OddRunningTotal := 0;
  NatNo := 1;
  Repeat
    If (NatNo Mod 2) = 0
      Then EvenRunningTotal := EvenRunningTotal + NatNo
      Else OddRunningTotal := OddRunningTotal + NatNo;
    NatNo := NatNo + 1;
  Until NatNo = 11;
  Writeln('Even running total: ', EvenRunningTotal);
  Writeln('Odd running total: ', OddRunningTotal);
  Readln;
End.
```

Note where the statement separator ; appears in the If Then Else statement.

Table 3.7 Program RunningTotalEvenOdd

Programming Tasks

1. Write and test a program in Delphi that codes the algorithm expressed in pseudocode in *Table 3.8*.
   Use Readln(x, y, z); to collect values for x, y and z from keyboard.

Input: x, y, z are three variables. Each stores an integer

Output: `Largest` is the largest integer

Algorithm:

```
Largest ← x
If Largest < y
  Then Largest ← y
EndIf
IF Largest < z
  Then Largest ← z
EndIf
```

Table 3.8 Algorithm to calculate the largest of three numbers

Key concept

Algorithm:
A description, independent of any programming language, of a procedure that solves a problem or task.
It consists of a precisely described sequence of steps for solving a problem or completing a task.
The algorithm must terminate and its action must be capable of completing in a finite amount of time.

Programming Tasks

2. Modify program **RunningTotalSum** shown in *Table 3.5* so that the loop terminating condition `Until NatNo = 11;` becomes `Until NatNo = TerminatingValue;`. `TerminatingValue` is a variable of type `Integer`.
The modified program should prompt the user for a value of `TerminatingValue` using `Write('Input loop termination value: ');` and collect this value from the keyboard using `Readln(TerminatingValue);`.

Compound statement

So far we have only considered simple statements such as

```
If (NatNo Mod 2) = 0
  Then RunningTotal := RunningTotal + NatNo;
```

or

```
NatNo := NatNo + 1;
```

But what if we have a block of statements to execute when a condition is true?

The answers is to form a compound statement by blocking statements between `Begin` and `End` as follows

```
If x = 0
  Then
    Begin
      y := y + 1;
      z := z - 1;
    End;
```

Compound statement

Simple statements

Laying out the `If` statement on one line as follows

```
If x = 0 Then Begin y := y + 1; z := z - 1; End;
```

we can see that the blocked statements can be viewed as a single statement if we ignore the highlighted section as follows

```
If x = 0 Then Begin End;
```

Programming task

Use the IDE to load or create and save the source code program *Table 3.9* as CompoundStatement.dpr or CompoundStatement.dprog, depending on the version of Delphi, in its own directory/folder named CompoundStatement.
Now compile the program (Ctrl F9).
Run this program (F9).
The output should be `z = 7`.

```
Program CompoundStatement;
{$APPTYPE CONSOLE}
Var
  x, y, z : Integer;
Begin
  x := 0;
  y := 0;
  z := 10;
  Repeat
    If x = 0
      Then
        Begin
          y := y + 1;
          z := z - 1;
        End;
  Until y = 3;
  Writeln('z = ', z);
  Readln;
End.
```

Table 3.9 Program CompoundStatement

Case/Switch statement

The **Case/Switch statement** is used to select one of several alternatives.

In *Table 3.10* if `x` is in the range `0..9` then the statement `Output 'Single digit number'` is executed and the remaining statements in the *Case* statement are skipped.

If `x` is in the range `10..99` then the statement `Output 'Double digit number'` is executed and the other statements in the *Case* statement are skipped.

The *Case* statement tries to match the value of `x` with *Case* list `0..9`, `10..99`, `100..999`. If it fails then it executes the statement selected by `Else`, i.e. `Output 'Not a single/double/triple digit number'`.

The variable `x` is known as the **case selector**.

```
Case x Of
  0..9 : Output 'Single digit number'
  10..99 : Output 'Double digit number'
  100..999 : Output 'Triple digit number'
  Else Output 'Not a single/double/triple digit number'
EndCase
```

Table 3.10 Pseudocode Case statement

The `Case` statement is shown in *Table 3.11* for Delphi.

Programming task

Use the IDE to load or create and save the source code program *Table 3.11* as CaseStatement.dpr or CaseStatement.dprog, depending on the version of Delphi, in its own directory/folder named CaseStatement. Now compile the program (Ctrl F9). Run this program (F9). Try a range of input values for `x` that exercises all `Case` options.

```
Program CaseStatement;
{$APPTYPE CONSOLE}

Var
  x : Integer;
Begin
  Write('Input x: ');
  Readln(x);
  Case x Of
    0..9 : Writeln('single digit number');
    10..99 : Writeln('double digit number');
    100..999 : Writeln('Triple digit number');
    Else Writeln('Not a single/double/triple digit number');
  End;
  Readln;
End.
```

Table 3.11 Program CaseStatement

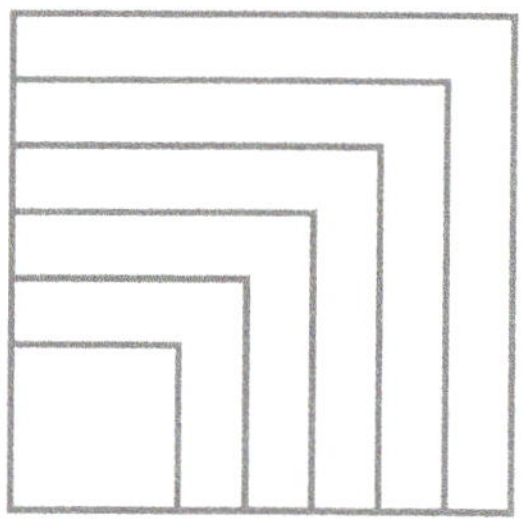

Fig. 3.6 Pattern of squares

Subroutine

A subroutine is a **named self-contained block of instructions**, e.g. `DrawSquare`.

By encapsulating and naming a block of instructions in a program it becomes possible to call the block from other parts of the program. This is very useful in situations where the same block of instructions or action or calculation needs to be repeated in multiple places in a program.

Suppose that we wish to draw the pattern containing six squares shown in *Figure 3.6*. The size (side-length) of the squares increases by the same fixed amount. One way of drawing a square with length of side, `Size`, is to use a pen-carrying turtle moving under the guidance of the sequence of instructions or commands shown in *Table 3.12*. and demonstrated in *Figure 3.7*.

It is good practice to use active verbs for subroutine names, e.g. `Read`, `Write`, `Add`, `DoSomething`.

```
Turtle.Forward(Size)
Turtle.Left(90)
Turtle.Forward(Size)
Turtle.Left(90)
Turtle.Forward(Size)
Turtle.Left(90)
Turtle.Forward(Size)
Turtle.Left(90)
```

Table 3.12 Turtle commands

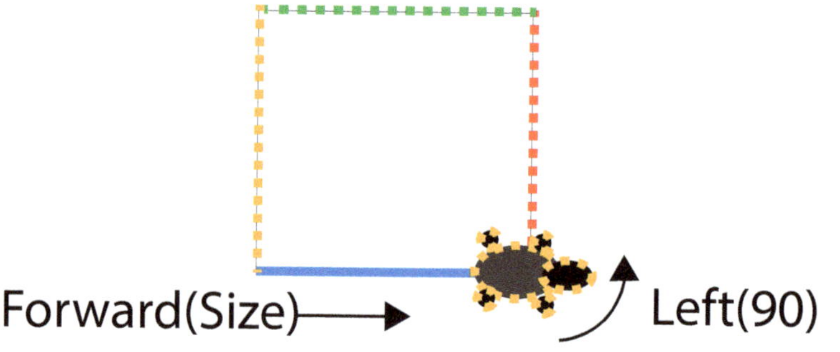

Fig. 3.7 Path followed by a turtle obeying the sequence of commands shown in Table 3.12.

```
Subroutine DrawSquare(Size)
  Turtle.Forward(Size)
  Turtle.Left(90)
  Turtle.Forward(Size)
  Turtle.Left(90)
  Turtle.Forward(Size)
  Turtle.Left(90)
  Turtle.Forward(Size)
  Turtle.Left(90)
EndSubroutine
```

Body (marks the dashed inner block)

Table 3.13 Subroutine DrawSquare(Size) defined

If this sequence of instructions in *Table 3.12* is named `DrawSquare` then a program could call upon this subroutine to draw a square of a specific size, say, `25`, as follows: `DrawSquare(25)`

A program that calls upon the subroutine `DrawSquare` is said to **call the subroutine** `DrawSquare`.

To draw a differently-sized square of size, say, 35, `DrawSquare` would need to be called upon as follows

`DrawSquare(35)`

The square-drawing turtle subroutine itself could be written as shown in *Table 3.13*.

The variable `Size` is called the **formal parameter of the subroutine**: it is used in the **body of the subroutine** to define how big the square will be.

When the subroutine is called, the **actual parameter** 25 or 35, for example, provides a specific value for `Size`, and thus determines how big the square will be in each call.

The subroutine `DrawSquare` itself calls subroutines `Turtle.Forward` and `Turtle.Left`.

Key term

Subroutine:

A subroutine is a named self-contained block of instructions, e.g. `DrawSquare`, which may be called (i.e. executed) from anywhere within a program where its name appears.

To draw the pattern of squares in *Figure 3.6* we need the sequence of calls to subroutine `DrawSquare` shown in *Table 3.14*

A subroutine may also contain its own *variable*, *type*, *label* and *const* declarations. In fact, it may also define other subroutines within its declaration section.

```
DrawSquare(25)
DrawSquare(35)
DrawSquare(45)
DrawSquare(55)
DrawSquare(65)
DrawSquare(75)
```

Table 3.14 Calling subroutine DrawSquare(Size) with different actual parameters

Procedures and functions

There are two types of subroutines:

1. **Procedure**
2. **Function**

A procedure is a **subroutine consisting of one or more statements or actions which may or may not return a result**. If it returns a result it does so through output parameters in its interface - see *pages 166/171*. The statements are referred to collectively by a name assigned to the procedure called the **procedure name**. The procedure must be declared/defined – its name must be stated and its statements listed. The procedure's statements are executed wherever its name is encountered in the executable part of a program - see *Table 3.14*. This is called **calling a procedure**.

> **Key term**
>
> **Procedure:**
> A procedure is a subroutine consisting of one or more statements or actions which may or may not return a result.

In Delphi, a procedure is declared and used as follows as shown in *Table 3.15*:

```
Program ProcedureExample;
Var
  Ch : Char;
Procedure DoExample;
  Begin
    Writeln('The sun ');
    Writeln('has got its hat on, ');
    Writeln('hip hip hooray.');
  End;

Begin
  Repeat
    DoExample;
    DoExample;
    Write('Continue Y/N? ');
    Readln(Ch);
    DoExample;
  Until Ch In ['N','n'];
End.
```

Annotations:

- *Name of procedure* (DoExample)
- *Procedure heading* (Procedure DoExample;)
- *Procedure body* (the three Writeln statements)
- *Writeln is a procedure which writes a line of text to the screen, e.g.* The sun, *moving the cursor to the beginning of the next line*
- *Procedure call* (first DoExample;)
- *Another procedure call* (second DoExample;)
- *Another procedure call* (Write('Continue Y/N? ');)
- *Write is a procedure which writes text to the screen without moving the cursor to the beginning of the next line*
- *Readln is a procedure which reads a line of text from the keyboard, e.g.* N
- *Readln(Ch) reads the first character typed and stores it in variable Ch then skips the rest of the line, if there is more*
- *Another procedure call* (Readln(Ch);)
- *Yet another procedure call* (last DoExample;)
- *Checks to see if the value stored in variable Ch is* 'N' or 'n'

Table 3.15 Delphi program containing calls to procedures DoExample, Writeln, Write, Readln

Key concept

Procedure interface:
A procedure interface is a mechanism for passing data into and out of a procedure.

Key concept

Procedure signature:
A procedure signature consists of the procedure's name and its parameter list or procedure interface

Procedure interface

A procedure interface is **a mechanism for passing data into and out of a procedure.**

In Delphi for example, `x` is known as a **formal parameter** as shown in *Table 3.16*. This is a variable used in the body of the procedure and which appears in the interface. When the procedure is called an **actual parameter** is supplied through the procedure's interface, e.g. `DoInterfaceExample(MyName)` where the variable `MyName` is the **actual parameter**. The value in `MyName` is copied into the variable `x` when the procedure is called by `DoInterfaceExample(MyName)`.

Suppose `MyName` stores the string '`Fred Bloggs`', then the variable `x` in the body of the procedure will contain the string '`Fred Bloggs`'.

Language keyword — *Procedure name* — *Procedure interface* — *Formal parameter*

```
Procedure DoInterfaceExample (x : String);
 Begin
   Writeln('The value passed to this procedure is ', x:4);
 End;
```

Table 3.16 Procedure interface in Delphi

Questions

15 What is a procedure interface?

Programming task

3 Write a Delphi program which defines a procedure that displays the message passed it through its interface.

Key term

Function:
A function is a type of subroutine designed to always return a single result. It may appear in expressions and on the right hand-side of an assignment statement unlike a procedure.

Function

A function is a type of subroutine designed to **always return a single result.** The mechanism by which the result is returned is different from that used by a procedure.

Functions may appear in expressions such as `5 × cube(3)` where `cube` is a mathematical function.

This is possible because a function **returns a value.**

So `5 × cube(3)` evaluates to `5 × 27` which evaluates to `135`.

In the first evaluation step, `cube(3)` is replaced by `27`, the result returned from the execution of function `cube(3)`. Any attempt to use a procedure in this manner would fail.

This is a key difference between a function and a procedure.

Procedure calls do not support a mechanism by which a value is substituted for the procedure call when the latter completes and returns control. If the procedure did then it would be a function[1].

For example, the following does not make sense as an expression because `DrawSquare` doesn't "evaluate" to a single value which can be multiplied by `5` to produce a numeric result, e.g. `127`:

`5 × DrawSquare(3)` where `DrawSquare` is a procedure.

Because functions "evaluate" to a single value[2] they may appear on the right-hand side of an assignment statement.

For example,

`x ← cube(3)`

After this statement is executed, the variable `x` contains/stores the value `27`, because the result of calling `cube(3)` is `27`.

Attempting the following would fail because `Writeln` is a procedure. It also would not make sense.

```
x := Writeln('The sun has got its hat on');
```

In Delphi, the code `Writeln('The sun has got its hat on')` is a command which writes the string `'The sun has got its hat on'` to the screen then moves the screen's cursor to the beginning of the next line.

Delphi makes a clear distinction between procedure and function by using different keywords for defining each. Table 3.17 shows a function `Cube(n)` being defined using the language keyword `Function`. As Delphi is a strongly typed language, the data type of the formal parameter and the data type of the returned value must be specified. It is `Integer` for both in this example.

Delphi uses the name of the function to assign the value that is to be returned.

Alternatively, the keyword Result can be used in place of Cube.

```
Function Cube (n : Integer) : Integer;
  Begin
    Cube := n * n * n;
  End;
```

Table 3.17 Function Cube(n) defined in Delphi

Table 3.18 shows function `cube(n)` defined in Delphi and then called with argument `3`.

In function `Cube(n)`, `n` is called the **formal parameter**. When functions are called we use a slightly different nomenclature. The **actual parameter** is now called the **argument**.

For example, in the function call `cube(3)`, 3 is the argument to the function.

```
Program FunctionProject;
{$APPTYPE CONSOLE}

Function Cube (n : Integer) : Integer;
  Begin
    Cube := n * n * n;
  End;
Begin
  Writeln(Cube(3));
  Readln;
End.
```

Table 3.18 Program FunctionProject

---

1 Impure functions in addition to returning a result, may have side effects which is the collective name for other things that the function may do as well.

2 Delphi functions are also allowed to return a structured result i.e. a result with more than one value such as an array.

Questions

16 State **one** key difference between a function and a procedure.

Programming task

4 Using Delphi

(a) Write a program which defines a function that returns the square of a given integer, *n*.

The program should display this square for a given *n*.

(b) Write a program which defines a function that sums the even numbers amongst the first *n* natural numbers and returns this sum. The program should display this sum for a given *n*.
(HINT: `If ((NatNo Mod 2) = 0) Then Even ← True Else Even ← False`)

(c) Write a program which defines a function that finds the largest of two given integers, *x* and *y*. The program should display the largest.

Delphi-provided functions

Delphi provides many functions for use in your programs. Some of these are shown in *Table 3.19*. Real numbers are covered in *Chapter 4*.

Name	Description	Argument type	Result type
`Abs`	The absolute value of the argument.	Real/Integer	Same as argument
`Exp`	The value of e (2.71828) raised to the power of the argument.	Real/Integer	Real
`Ln`	The logarithm (to the base e) of the argument.	Real/Integer (positive)	Real
`Sqr`	The square of the argument	Real/Integer	Same as argument
`Sqrt`	The square root of the argument	Real/Integer(positive)	Same as argument
`Round`	The closest integer value to the argument (rounds off).	Real	Integer
`Trunc`	The integral part of the argument.	Real	Integer
`Tan`	The tangent of the argument.	Real/Integer(radians)	Real
`Cos`	The cosine of the argument.	Real/Integer(radians)	Real
`Sin`	The sine of the argument.	Real/Integer(radians)	Real
`Chr`	Returns the character whose ordinal number is its argument.	Integer	Char
`Odd`	Returns True if its argument is an odd number, otherwise returns False.	Integer	Boolean
`Ord`	Returns the ordinal number of its argument.	Ordinal	Integer
`Pred`	Returns the predecessor of its argument.	Ordinal	Ordinal
`Succ`	Returns the successor of its argument.	Ordinal	Ordinal

Table 3.19 Some built-in functions

The System.Math and other library units provide many more that have not been mentioned.

Table 3.20 shows some of the Delphi provided functions being used.

Some of the `Writeln` statements use formatting information, e.g.

```
Writeln('Tan = ', Tan(DegToRad(45)):6:2);
```

:6:2 means six display positions, two of which are decimal places.

If a decimal value needs more display positions, it will take as many as needed whilst still respecting the specification that there be only two decimal places.

This particular `Writeln` statement has a function call inside a function call:

```
Tan(DegToRad(45))
```

`DegToRad(45)` returns the number of radians corresponding to `45` degrees.

Figure 3.8 shows output produced in the console window when `DelphiProvidedFunctions` program is executed.

```
Program DelphiProvidedFunctions;
{$APPTYPE CONSOLE}
Uses
  System.Math;
Begin
  Writeln('Abs = ', Abs(-3));
  Writeln('Exp = ', Exp(1):20:16);
  Writeln('Ln = ', Ln(2.71828):20:16);
  Writeln('Log base 10 = ', Log10(100):3:0);
  Writeln('Sqr = ', Sqr(4));
  Writeln('Round = ', Round(5.6));
  Writeln('Trunc = ', Trunc(5.6));
  Writeln('Tan = ', Tan(DegToRad(45)):6:2);
  Writeln('Cos = ', Cos(DegToRad(0)):6:2);
  Writeln('Sin = ', Sin(DegToRad(90)):6:2);
  Writeln('Chr = ', Chr(65));
  Writeln('Ord = ', Ord('A'));
  Writeln('Pred = ', Pred(4));
  Writeln('Succ = ', Succ(4));
  Writeln('Power = ', Power(2, 4):3:0);
  Readln;
End.
```

Table 3.20 Program DelphiProvidedFunctions

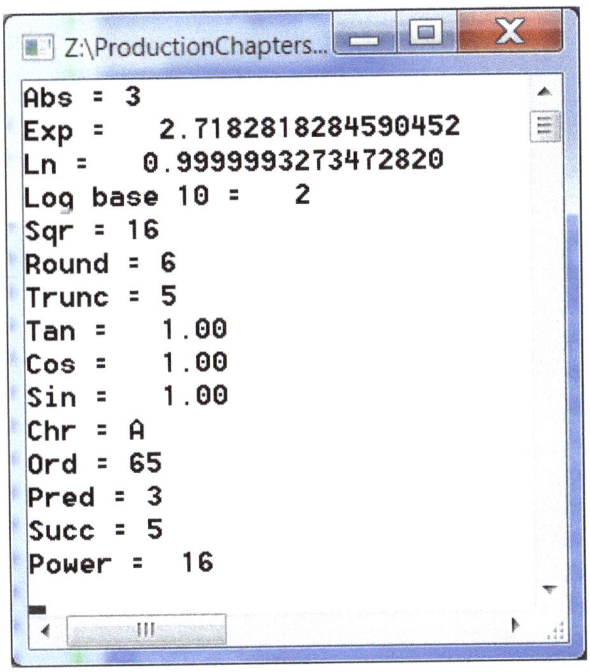

Fig. 3.8 Captured console window showing output produced by execution of DelphiProvidedFunctions program.

Formatting output

Formatting information is provided in `Writeln` statements as shown below

```
Writeln('Two digit integer:', 65 :3);
Writeln('Real no 65.23:', 65.23 :7:2);
Writeln('Five character string:', 'Hello' :7);
Writeln('Five character string:', 'Hello' :3);
Writeln('Boolean value True:', True :1);
Writeln('Single character:', 'A' :5);
```

Minimum number of display positions

Number of decimal places

The first :number following the value specifies the minimum number of display positions in the console window for the given value. The second :number specifies the number of decimal places.

Table 3.21 shows program **FormattingOutput** which exercises formatting output for an integer, a real,a string, a Boolean value and a character. *Figure 3.9* shows the program's output when it is executed.

```
Program FormattingOutput;
{$APPTYPE CONSOLE}
Begin
  Writeln('Two digit integer allocated 3 display positions in console window:', '1234567');
  Writeln('Two digit integer allocated 3 display positions in console window:', 65 :3);
  Writeln('Real no 65.23 allocated 7 display positions, 2 for the decimal part:', '1234567');
  Writeln('Real no 65.23 allocated 7 display positions, 2 for the decimal part:', 65.23 :7:2);
  Writeln('Five character string allocated 6 display positions:', '1234567');
  Writeln('Five character string allocated 7 display positions:', 'Hello' :7);
  Writeln('Five character string allocated 3 display positions:', '1234567');
  Writeln('Five character string allocated 3 display positions:', 'Hello' :3);
  Writeln('Boolean value True allocated 1 display position:', '1234567');
  Writeln('Boolean value True allocated 1 display position:', True :1);
  Writeln('Single character allocated 5 display positions:', '1234567');
  Writeln('Single character allocated 5 display positions:', 'A' :5);
  Readln;
End.
```

Table 3.21 Program FormattingOutput

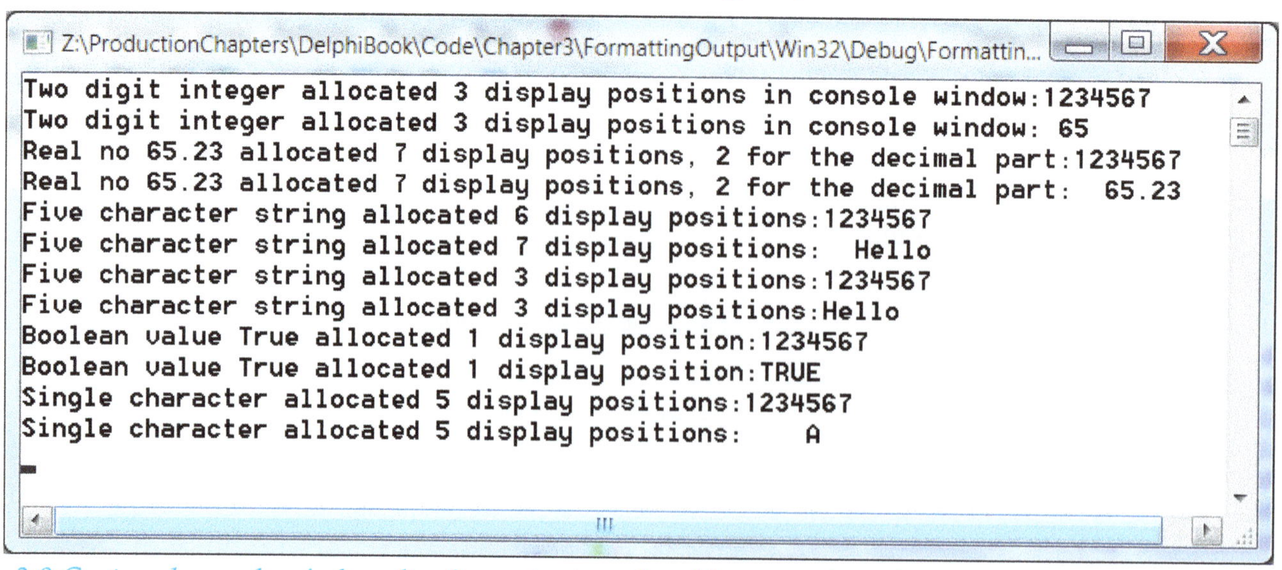

Fig. 3.9 Captured console window showing output produced by execution of FormattingOutput program.

Definite and indefinite iteration

We introduced the concept of a loop in the section on iteration. In this section, we explore ways in which the number of iterations (i.e. repetitions of the body of the loop) is determined.

We have two cases to consider, definite and indefinite iteration:

- In **definite iteration**, the **number of iterations is known before the execution of the body of the loop is started**. For example, repeat 5 times writing the string "Hello World!" to the output device.
- In **indefinite iteration**, the **number of iterations is not known before the execution of the body of the loop starts**. The number of iterations depends on when **a specific condition is met** (and this depends on what happens in the body of the loop). For example, repeat printing the string "Hello World"until the user declines to continue when asked.

Definite iteration

Suppose that we wanted to output the value of a variable `i`, first when it is 1, next when it is 2, and so on until it is 5. We could do this with a *repeat until* loop or a *while* loop as shown by the pseudocode examples in *Table 3.22*. The number of iterations of each loop is known in advance, it is five, so these are examples of **definite iteration**.

Note that a

- *repeat until <condition>* loop executes at least once
- a *while <condition>* executes zero or more times

`i ← 0`
`Repeat`
`  i ← i + 1`
`  Output i`
`Until i = 5`
	`i ← 1`
	`While i <= 5`
	`  Output i`
	`  i ← i + 1`
	`EndWhile`

Table 3.22 Definite iteration with repeat and while loops

> **Key term**
>
> **Definite iteration:**
> In definite iteration the number of iterations is known before the execution of the body of the loop is started.

Loop terminating condition

In both *repeat* and *while* loops quite a lot of work has to be done by the programmer.

In the example, the variable `i` has to be initialised, with 0 for the repeat loop and with 1 for the while loop.

It has to be incremented (`i ← i + 1`), and it has to be tested with the test condition `i = 5` for the repeat loop and `i <= 5` for the while loop.

The *repeat until* loop terminates when its test condition is true.

The *while loop* terminates when its test condition is false.

> **Key term**
>
> **Loop terminating condition:**
> The condition which causes execution of the loop body to terminate is known as the terminating condition.

In each case, the condition which causes execution of the loop body to terminate is known as the **terminating condition**.

In definite iteration, this terminating condition is met after a known and predictable number of iterations.

For loop

There is an easier way for the programmer to program definite iteration called the **for loop**.

This pseudocode for the *for loop* shown in *Table 3.23* is executed as follows

Step 1: The initial value of variable `i` is set to 1, "`i ← 1`". This step happens only once, regardless of how many times the loop repeats.

Step 2: The "`To 5`" part evaluates the condition (`i <= 5`) by comparing the value of `i` with 5.

If `i` is less than or equal to 5, the condition evaluates to true, and the statement "`Output i`" is executed. This sends the value of i to the output device, e.g. the VDU.

If `i` is greater than 5, the condition evaluates to false, and **the loop is exited**. The instruction immediately following `EndFor` is then executed next.

Step 3: The value of `i` is incremented by 1.

Step 4: The loop returns to *step* 2 to evaluate the condition again.

```
For i ← 1 To 5
  Output i
EndFor
```

Table 3.23 Definite iteration with a for loop

Note that if the initial value of `i` is greater than the 5 as shown in *Table 3.24* the body of the loop should not be executed.

```
For i ← 6 To 5
  Output i
EndFor
```

Table 3.24 Definite iteration with a for loop

Variable `i` in this example is called the **loop control variable**.

A loop control variable must be an ordinal data type (see ordinal number *Chapter 14 page 231*). An ordinal data type is one that consists of an ORDERED set of things in which each member has a single value only, e.g. an integer data type.

Table 3.24 shows examples of a *for loop* in Delphi and *Figure 3.10* the corresponding output when the program **ForLoops** is executed.

The `Boolean` data type is an ordinal type with values `False`, `True` in that order.

Therefore, it is perfectly legitimate to write

```
For Flag := False To True
  Do Writeln(Flag);
```

and

```
For Flag := True DownTo False
  Do Writeln(Flag);
```

The `For DownTo` loop performs in the reverse manner to the `For To` loop - see *Table 3.25* and *Figure 3.10*.

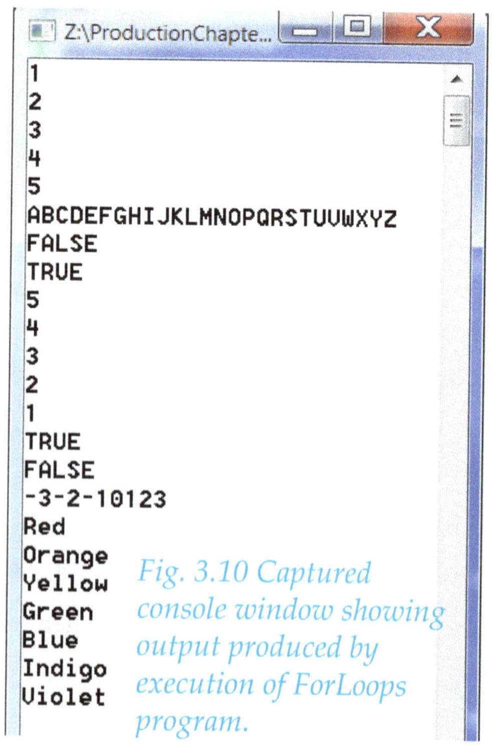

Fig. 3.10 Captured console window showing output produced by execution of ForLoops program.

```
Program ForLoops;
{$APPTYPE CONSOLE}
Type
  TColoursOfRainbow = (Red, Orange, Yellow, Green, Blue,
Indigo, Violet);
Var
  i : Integer;
  Ch : Char;
  Flag : Boolean;
  ColourOfRainbow : TColoursOfRainbow;
Begin
  For i := 1 To 5 Do Writeln(i);
  For Ch := 'A' To 'Z' Do Write(Ch);
  Writeln;
  For Flag := False To True Do Writeln(Flag);
  For i := 5 DownTo 1 Do Writeln(i);
  For Flag := True DownTo False Do Writeln(Flag);
  For i := - 3 To +3 Do Write(i);
  Writeln;
  For ColourOfRainbow := Red To Violet
    Do
      Case ColourOfRainbow Of
        Red : Writeln('Red');
        Orange : Writeln('Orange');
        Yellow : Writeln('Yellow');
        Green : Writeln('Green');
        Blue : Writeln('Blue');
        Indigo : Writeln('Indigo');
        Violet : Writeln('Violet');
      End;
  Readln;
End.
```

Enumerated type

For i := 1 To 5
  Do Writeln(i);
is the author's preferred layout but this layout used for space reasons

An enumerated type is an ordinal type so can be used as shown in for loop

Table 3.25 Program ForLoops

Questions

17 What is the output of the following pseudocode?

```
For i ← 1 To 5
  j ← 2 * i
  Output j
EndFor
```

18 What is the output of the following pseudocode?

```
For Ch ← 'A' To 'C'
  Output Ch
EndFor
```

19 How many times is the pseudocode loop executed in *Table 3.26*?

```
For i ← 4 To 4
  j ← 2 * i
  Output j
EndFor
```

Table 3.26

For In

A `For In` loop (known in other programming languages as a 'for each ' loop) enumerates an expression returning one of the following

- A string
- An array
- A set
- A class or record instance that implements an enumerable pattern, e.g. TList, TDictionary, TComponent, TMenuItem.

Table 3.27 shows an example of the use of `For In` enumerating the characters of a string.

```
Program ForIn;
{$APPTYPE CONSOLE}
Var
  i : Integer;
  Ch : Char;
  Name : String = 'Fred';
Begin
  For Ch In Name
    Do Writeln(Ch);
  Readln;
End.
```

Table 3.27 Program ForIn

Indefinite iteration

The two cases of indefinite iteration to consider are *repeat* and *while* loops. "*For loops*" do not support indefinite iteration only definite iteration.
In Table 3.28 the value of `i` in both pseudocode examples is changed inside the loop in a way that cannot be predicted because it is obtained from the user through the input device, e.g. a keyboard, when `Input i` executes.

```
Repeat
  Input i
  Output i
Until i = 5
```

```
Input i
While i <> 5
  Input i
  Output i
EndWhile
```

Table 3.28 Indefinite iteration with repeat and while loops

The value of `i` before the *while loop* executes is only known at the time of execution when `Input i` executes.

It is therefore not possible to determine in advance the number of iterations of the body of each loop.

The number of iterations depends on when the terminating condition `i = 5` becomes true for the *repeat loop* and when the terminating condition `i <> 5` becomes false for the *while loop*.
If the terminating condition cannot ever be met for some reason then the execution remains within the *repeat* or the *while loop* indefinitely. We then have a situation called an **infinite loop**.
Table 3.29 shows how each loop could be written so that the iteration is indefinite.

Sometimes an infinite loop condition was not the intention but the loop's programmer has got it wrong. Exiting the loop then becomes impossible by ordinary means because the loop terminating condition can never be met.

```
Repeat
  Input i
  Output i
Until False
```

```
While True Do
  Input i
  Output i
EndWhile
```

Table 3.29 Indefinite iteration with repeat and while loops showing a situation called an infinite loop

Questions

20 What is the output of the following pseudocode when the input is 1, 2, 3, 4, 0?

(a)
```
Sum ← 0
Repeat
  Input n
  Sum ← Sum + n
Until n = 0
Output Sum
```

(b)
```
Product ← 1
Input n
While n > 0 Do
  Product ← Product * n
  Input n
EndWhile
Output n
```

21 What is the output of the following pseudocode?

(a)
```
j ← 4
Repeat
  j ← j - 1
  Output j
Until j < 1
```

(b)
```
j ← 4
Repeat
  j ← j + 1
  Output j
Until j > 6
```

(c)
```
j ← 4
While j < 5
  j ← j + 1
  Output j
EndWhile
```

22 What is the essential difference between *definite* and *indefinite iteration*?

23 What is the essential difference between a *repeat until* loop and a *while* loop?

24 What is meant by an *infinite loop*?

25 Write a loop in pseudocode which demonstrates an *infinite loop*.

Indefinite iteration in Delphi

Table 3.30 shows a simple *repeat* loop and Table 3.31 a simple *while* loop in Delphi.

```
Program RepeatUntil;
{$APPTYPE CONSOLE}
Var i : Integer;
Begin
  Repeat
    Write('Input i: ');
    Readln(i);
    Writeln(i);
  Until i = 5;
  Writeln('Exited Repeat Until loop');
  Readln;
End.
```

Table 3.30 Program RepeatUntil

```
Program WhileLoop;
{$APPTYPE CONSOLE}
Var i : Integer = 0;
Begin
  Write('Input initial value of i: ');
  Readln(i);
  Writeln(i);
  While i <> 5
    Do
      Begin
        Write('Input next value of i: ');
        Readln(i);
        Writeln(i);
      End;
  Writeln('Exited While loop');
  Readln;
End.
```

Table 3.31 Program WhileLoop

Programming task

5 In Delphi,

(a) Write programs that code the pseudocode shown in Question 20(a) and 20(b).

(b) Write programs that code the pseudocode shown in Question 21(a), 21(b) and 21(c).

Nested selection statements

The pseudocode in *Table 3.32* contains three occurrences of *selection*, one marked in **black**, one in red and one in blue. The red-marked *selection* and the blue-marked *selection statements* are each nested inside the **black**-marked *selection statement*. This pseudocode finds the largest of three numbers. The value of the first number is stored in variable `No1`. The value of the second number is stored in variable `No2` and the third in `No3`.

The value of the largest of the three numbers is stored in variable `Largest`.

If `No1` stores the value 6, `No2` the value 3 and `No3` the value 8, the result of the comparison `If No1 > No2`

is true because 6 is greater than 3.

```
If No1 > No2
  Then
    If No1 > No3
      Then Largest ← No1
      Else Largest ← No3
    EndIf
  Else
    If No2 > No3
      Then Largest ← No2
      Else Largest ← No3
    EndIf
EndIf
```

Table 3.32 Pseudocode to find the largest of three numbers

The `Then` block of the **black**-coloured *selection* is executed next.

This block contains another `If Then Else` statement, the one marked in red.

The result of the comparison `If No1 > No3` is false because 6 is less than 8.

The `Else` coloured in red is executed next and the value stored in variable `No3` is assigned to variable `Largest`.

Questions

26 Using the pseudocode in *Table 3.32*

(a) If `No1` stores the value 6, `No2` the value 7 and `No3` the value 5 which selection statements are executed? Explain your answer.

(b) If `No1` stores the value 6, `No2` the value 6 and `No3` the value 5 which selection statements are executed? Explain your answer.

Programming task

6 Write a program in Delphi which defines a function that finds the largest of three integers, *x*, *y*, and *z*. The program should display the largest.

Nested iteration statements

We may place a *for loop* inside a *for loop* as shown in Table 3.33 The inner *for loop* executes for each value of the loop control variable `i` of the outer *for loop*. The trace table, Table 3.34, shows the output and the values of `i` and `j`, the outer loop and inner loop control variables, respectively, for the first few values of the trace.

```
For i ← 1 To 5
   For j ← 1 To 3
      Output i
   EndFor
EndFor
```

Table 3.33 Nested for loop

i	j	Output
1	1	1
1	2	1
1	3	1
2	1	2
2	2	2
2	3	2

Table 3.34 Trace table

Questions

27 What is the output of the following pseudocode?

(a)
```
For i ← 1 To 2
   For j ← 1 To 3
      Output j
   EndFor
EndFor
```

(b)
```
For i ← 1 To 3
   For j ← 1 To i
      Output j
   EndFor
EndFor
```

28 What is the output of the following pseudocode?

(a)
```
For Ch1 ← 'A' To 'C'
   For Ch2 ← 'A' To Ch1
      Output Ch2
   EndFor
EndFor
```

(b)
```
For Ch1 ← 'a' To 'c'
   For Ch2 ← 'a' To 'c'
      For Ch3 ← 'a' To 'c'
         Output Ch1, Ch2, Ch3
      EndFor
   EndFor
EndFor
```

29 Using similar pseudocode, rewrite the following nested *for loop* as a single *for loop*

```
For i ← 1 To 4
   For j ← 3 To 5
      Output('*')
   EndFor
EndFor
```

30 Complete the trace table, Table 3.35, by hand tracing the following pseudocode

```
For i ← 0 To 1
   For j ← 0 To 2
      Output j
   EndFor
EndFor
```

i	j	Output
0	0	

Table 3.35 Trace table

Programming tasks

7 In Delphi,

(a) Write a program that codes the pseudocode shown in Question 27(a).

(b) Write a program that codes the pseudocode shown in Question 27(b).

Using meaningful identifier names

The names that have been used for variables, constants, subroutines such as `RunningTotal`, `NO_OF_DAYS_IN_WEEK`, `drawsquare`, `Cube` are all examples of identifiers. These identifiers describe what they represent, e.g. `RunningTotal`. **When an identifier is descriptive of what it represents or of its purpose, we say that it has a meaningful name.**

The following points are relevant to why programmers should use meaningful identifier names:

- Meaningful identifier names make it easier for the programmer to understand the source code because meaningfully-named identifiers describe what they represent or do
- Programmers spend far longer reading their source code than writing it so it is important that the source code is as descriptive of what it does as possible
- Programmers spend a lot of time reading other programmers' source code as well as their own and so it is important that the source code is as descriptive of what it does as possible
- Program source code needs to make sense when it is read, i.e. it should be possible to understand what the source code has been written to do, otherwise its intention will be unclear
- A programmer may wish/has to use source code that someone else has written. To do this successfully they need at least to understand the source code
- A programmer may be tasked to debug a program because it contains runtime/logical errors, e.g. it doesn't do what it is expected to do. The programmer will need to understand the source code in order to debug it
- A programmer may also be tasked to modify a program because what it is required to do has changed. The programmer will need to understand the source code to change it successfully.

Table 3.36 shows pseudocode which sums the first 10 natural numbers.

```
x ← 0             // Initialise running total
y ← 1             // Initialise natural number
Repeat
  x ← x + y       // add natural number to running total
  y ← y + 1       // Increment natural number
Until y = 11      // Terminate loop when natural number is 11
```

Table 3.36 Pseudocode to sum the first 10 natural numbers

Comments have been added to the pseudocode which describe the purpose of each statement because the identifier names alone are not sufficient to make the purpose clear (this may be an oversimplified example but it is done to make a point).

Table 3.37 shows the pseudocode rewritten with meaningful/self-describing identifier names.

The pseudocode comments in *Table 3.36* use 148 characters whilst the meaningful/self-describing identifiers in the pseudocode in *Table 3.14* use 61 characters.

We say that the pseudocode in *Table 3.37* is **self-documenting** and because of this comments are largely superfluous.

```
RunningTotal ← 0
NaturalNo ← 1
Repeat
  RunningTotal ← RunningTotal + NaturalNo
  NaturalNo ← NaturalNo + 1
Until NaturalNo = 11
```

Table 3.37 Pseudocode to sum the first 10 natural numbers

Questions

31 Why is it important to use meaningful identifier names?

Key term

Meaningful identifier name: When an identifier is descriptive of what it represents or of its purpose, we say that it has a meaningful name.

Programming tasks

8 In Delphi,

(a) Write a program to print a '4 times table' in the form

```
1 x 4 =  4
2 x 4 =  8
3 x 4 = 12
etc.
```

(b) Write a program to read in any integer, represented by the letter *n* say, and print an 'n times table'.

9 Write a program to print all the multiples of 3, starting at 3 and finishing at 90.

10 In Delphi,

(a) Write a program to input 6 numbers and display how many of them are zero.

(b) Write a program to input 10 numbers and print the largest. (Hint: assume the first number is the largest, store it in `Largest`, compare each new number with `Largest`, store new number in `Largest` if new number is larger. Alternatively, set `Largest` to 0 at start of program, then compare each new number with `Largest` as before).

11 Write a program to determine if a given year is a leap year. A leap year is a year which is exactly divisible by 4 and not a century year unless the century year is exactly divisible by 400. (Hint: (Year Mod 4) = 0 tests for exact division by 4).

12 Write a program that will enable a user to input the day of the week on which a month begins and the number of days in the month. The program should produce as output a calendar for the given month in the format shown below

Sun	Mon	Tues	Wed	Thurs	Fri	Sat
		1	2	3	4	5
6	7	8	9	10	11	12
13	14	15	16	17	18	19
20	21	22	23	24	25	26
27	28	29	30	31		

The day on which the month begins should be entered as an integer where 1 corresponds to Sunday, 2 to Monday and so on.

4 Introducing data types

Data types

■ Purpose: To understand the concept of a data type

The concept of a data type

The computer programs that you write will control physical processes involving matter and energy at the level of atoms and electrons inside CPUs and memory but you will rely upon computing abstractions to hide much of this from you (until you hear the fan switch on that keeps a CPU cool).

Information is typically stored using just two levels of energy, one higher in energy than the other.

It is convenient to use a two symbol code consisting of 1 and 0 to represent these two levels.

The symbol 1 is usually chosen for the higher energy state and the symbol 0 for the lower energy state.

Information

Programming languages which enforce data typing - a typed language - are employed because they can prevent an expression from being used which will lead to a data type error when the program is executed,
e.g. 4 + 'D'.
Data type errors may be detected at compile time or runtime.

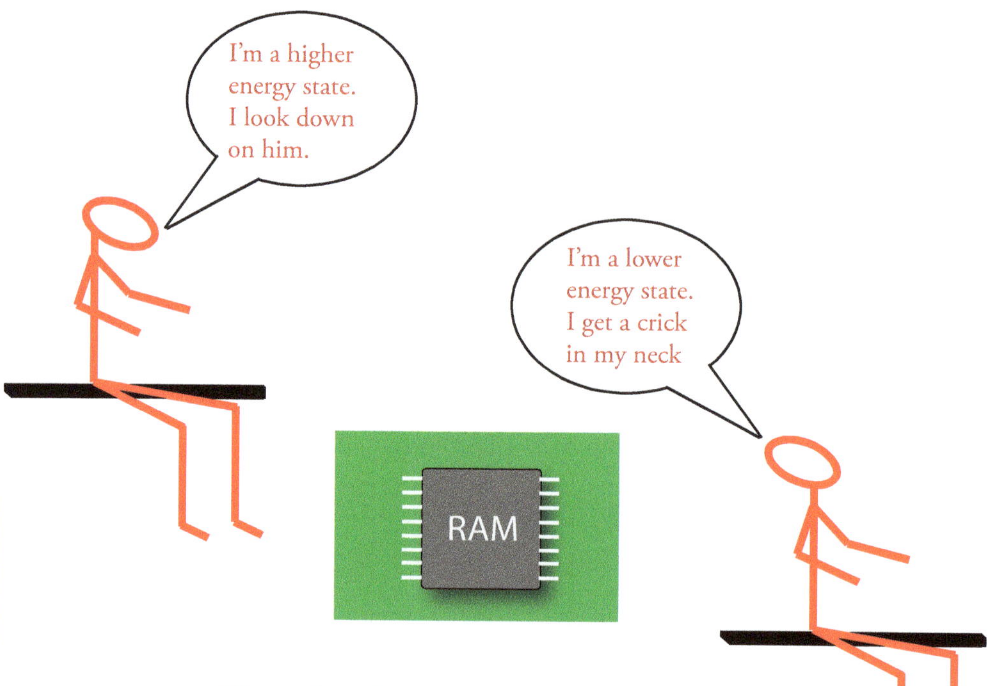

Figure 4.1 Using two levels of energy to store information in RAM

Key term

Bit:
A bit is a binary digit which is either 0 or 1.

Key term

Bit pattern:
A bit pattern is a finite sequence of 0s and 1s, e.g. 0100100001101001.

Computer memory, e.g. RAM, consists of a collection of individual storage cells, each capable of storing a single bit. A bit or binary digit encodes an energy state, i.e. 1 or 0.

Memory bits are typically grouped into blocks of 8, 16, 32, or 64 bits.

A 16-bit block might store the following bit pattern

0101110100000110

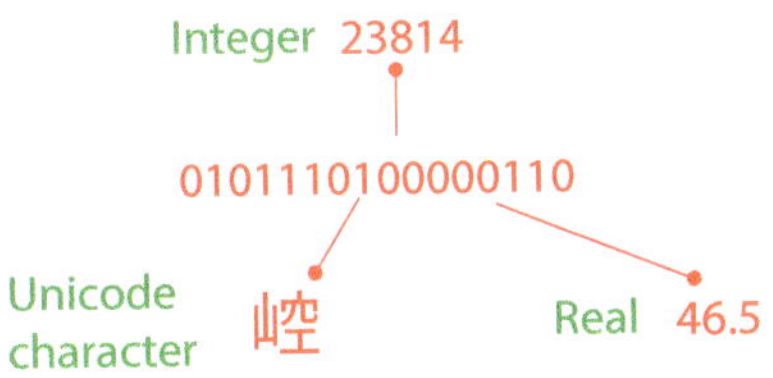

Figure 4.2 Different interpretations of the given bit pattern

Key point

Datum:

A datum is a finite sequence of 0s and 1s, e.g. 0100100001101001.

Key term

Sequence:

A sequence is simply an ordered collection of things, e.g. a b c . . .

or the sequence of digits in a telephone number, 433004.

Did you know?

Real or floating point data type:

Computers store and manipulate real numbers such as 3.142 using the IEEE 754 floating point standard.

Real or floating-point numbers are little more than scientific notation encoded as bits.

Real numbers can be very large or very small on a scale from the size of galaxies to the size of sub-atomic particles.

An alternative name for the data type real is float.

Computers process and store information, the question is:

"What information do we want bit pattern 0101110100000110 to represent"

Fortunately, we get to choose the interpretation when we write programs.

Here are three choices of interpretation that we could make

1. integer - a positive or negative whole number
2. real/float - a positive or negative number with a fractional part
3. character - a unicode character representing a symbol in an alphabet

The act of assigning an interpretation is what is meant by **data typing** and the specific interpretation, e.g. integer, is a **data type**.

Figure 4.2 shows what the three different interpretations of the bit pattern 0101110100000110 actually mean.

Until the bit pattern is interpreted, it is called a **datum**.

A datum is a finite sequence of 0s and 1s, e.g. 0101110100000110.

After interpretation it represents specific **information**, e.g. 23814 could be the attendance figure for a cricket match, 46.5 could be a cricketer's average batting score, and 崆 the lucky charm worn around the cricketer's neck (in Chinese it means Kongtong mountain).

We call a collection of bit patterns **data**. Data is the plural of datum.

Unless we know the meaning assigned to bit patterns, the only things that we see in a computer are data, i.e. uninterpreted bit patterns.

This is the **first role** performed by a **data type**: to establish what the bits/bit patterns mean.

The **second role** is to specify the number of bits allocated to each datum.

For example, characters might be represented in 8 bits (extended ASCII - see *page 99*), integers in 32 bits, real numbers in 64 bits.

Table 4.1 shows some 8-bit patterns and their interpretation as ASCII characters.

Bit pattern	Character
01001000	H
01101001	i
01101111	o
00100000	space

Table 4.1 Some 8-bit patterns interpreted as ASCII characters

Characters are written surrounded by single quotes in Delphi, e.g. 'H'.

If 8-bit patterns are "strung together", e.g. to form a 16-bit bit pattern, and each 8 bits of the 16-bit bit pattern is interpreted as a character then we have created another data type called **string**.

For example using *Table 4.1*, 0100100001101001 can be interpreted as meaning string 'Hi' where 01001000 means 'H' and 01101001 means 'i'.

The **third role** is to define the operations allowed on data.
For example, if the interpretation is data type *integer* then permitted operations should include at least addition, subtraction, and multiplication which produce a result of data type *integer*. For example 3 + 6 = 9.

If the interpretation is data type *real* then permitted operations should include at least addition, subtraction, multiplication and division which produce a result of data type *real*. For example 3.3 + 6.6 = 9.9.

What would not be allowed is any attempt to store the result of dividing one real by another if the destination of the result is storage reserved for an integer.

If the interpretation is data type *character* then a permitted operation could be to join two or more characters together to form a string (of characters).
For example, 'H' + 'i' = 'Hi'.

What would not be allowed is any attempt to join an integer to a character.
For example, the operation 'H' + 6 would not be allowed.

If the interpretation is data type *string* then a permitted operation could be to join two or more strings together to form a new string (of characters).
For example, 'Hi' + ' ' + 'Ho' = 'Hi Ho'. The space character is indicated by ' '. It has bit pattern 00100000 in 8-bit ASCII. Delphi uses single quotes for a string value and for a character value.

Every value, e.g. 5, must have a **data type** - datum + meaning.

Computations operate on values and produce other values as results,

e.g. 5 + 6 = 11.

The meaning of **value** is a **datum** together with its **meaning** or **interpretation**.
Therefore, For example, the data type of *whole number* values such as 5, 6 and 11 is integer.

Summarising, a data type

1. Is a method of interpreting a bit pattern
2. Specifies the number of bits allocated to each datum.
3. Defines which operations may be carried out on the bit pattern

Data typing is an abstraction designed to make life easier for the programmer. It enables errors made during the creation and execution of programs to be caught and dealt with.

Questions

1. What data type do you think the following values belong to?
   (a) "Have a nice day" (b) 45.

2. Give two possible interpretations of the bit pattern 0100100001101001.

3. Is the following addition of two values a valid operation
   'two' + 3?

Key concept

Data type:
A data type
1. Is a method of interpreting a bit pattern
2. Specifies the number of bits allocated to each datum.
3. Defines which computations/operations may be carried out on the bit patterns.

Key point

Data type:
A data type is a correspondence between a mathematical entity such as integer and a set of datums, e.g. all datums of length 16 bits (0000000000000000 to 1111111111111111 in binary or 0 to 65535 in decimal).
A bit pattern (datum) interpreted as an integer is a mapping from a (digital) machine integer onto a subset of mathematical integers.

Key term

Set:
A set is an unordered collection of different things, e.g. the set of all students in my computer science class: John Smith, Mary Brown, Kamal Patel, Sui Ling, . . .

Key point

Datum:
A datum is a finite sequence of 0s and 1s, e.g. 0100100001101001.

Key point

Value:
Value means a datum together with its interpretation.

Key term

Integer data type:
A machine integer is a datum whose data type represents some finite subset of the mathematical integers.
A fixed number of bits are allocated to the datum, e.g. 32 bits.
Signed 32-bit (4-byte) integers range in value from
-2,147,483,648 through
2,147,483,647.
The integer data type is free of rounding errors. Mathematical integers that are in range are represented exactly.
However, this type has a limited range.

Did you know?

Integer data type:
When the range is exceeded integer types wrap around, e.g. when 1 is added to the integer value 2,147,483,647 it becomes -2,147,483,648 if the data type is signed 32-bit integer.

Questions

4 What is meant by data type?

Integer data type

We need to distinguish mathematical integers from their machine representation in a digital computer because the former belong to an infinite set of values and the latter a finite set of values.

A machine integer is a datum whose data type represents some *finite subset* of the mathematical integers because computers have limited memory.

A fixed number of bits are allocated to each datum representing an integer, e.g. 32 bits.

Signed 32-bit (4-byte) integers range in value from

-2,147,483,648 through 2,147,483,647.

Values in this range represent mathematical integers exactly.
The range is clearly a subset of the range of mathematical integers.
Mathematical integers outside this range cannot be represented.

Specifically, an integer data type is a correspondence between a mathematical entity, an integer, and a set of datums, e.g. all datums of length 16 bits (0000000000000000 to 1111111111111111 in binary or 0 to 65535 in decimal). *Table 4.2* shows the various integer data types available in Delphi and their ranges.

Type	Range	Bits allocated	Description
Integer	-2147483648 .. 2147483647	Signed 32-bit integer type	The size of Integer is 32 bits across all 64-bit and 32-bit platforms.
Int64	-2^{63} .. 2^{63-1} or -9223372036854775808 .. 9223372036854775807	Signed 64-bit integer type	Size of Int64 is 64 bits across all 64-bit and 32-bit platforms
Shortint	-128 .. 127	One-byte signed integer type	One byte across all platforms
Smallint Int16	-32768 .. 32767	2-byte signed intege	Two bytes across all platforms
Byte	0 .. 255	8-bit unsigned integer type	Size of Byte is 8 bits across all 64-bit and 32-bit platforms
Word	0 .. 65535	16-bit unsigned integer type	
Cardinal	0 .. 4294967295	32-bit unsigned integer type	

Table 4.2 Integer data types in Delphi

Questions

5 Is $2^{2^{100}}$ in the integer range 0 to 2,147,483,647?

Floating point numbers (real/float data type)

A 'real' number is one that may have a fractional part, i.e. something after the decimal point.

Most computers store and manipulate real numbers such as 3.142 using the IEEE 754 floating point standard. IEEE floating point numbers can be very large or very small on a scale from the size of galaxies to the size of sub-atomic particles.

Floating-point numbers are little more than scientific notation encoded as bits. Any real number N that can be put in scientific notation can also be put in the form

$$N = s \times m \times 10^{e}$$

where s is −1 or 1, m is a natural number, and e is an integer.

For example, -1.543×10^{-10} represents a real number in scientific form. To put this in the above form, the decimal point is moved 3 places to the right, and 3 is subtracted from the e to get $-1 \times 1543 \times 10^{-13}$.

A number N's significant digits are represented by m either exactly or approximately. Significant digits define the precision of a number.

Digital computers operate with powers of two rather than powers of ten so floating-point numbers that represent real numbers are put in the form

$$N = s \times m \times 2^{e}$$

Floating-point numbers represent the real numbers of mathematics. However, floating-point numbers are an approximate representation of these mathematical real numbers because there is

- an infinite number of numbers between any two numbers on the real number line.
- a finite number of values in any floating point data type because we are limited to a finite number of bits for each datum.

Some of the levels of precision (number of bits for each datum[1]) present in IEEE 754 floating point standard are as follows

- 16-bit: Half - half precision
- 32-bit: Single - single precision
- 64-bit: Double - double precision

If single precision (32 bits) is used the

- minimum positive value is $2^{-126} \approx 1.18 \times 10^{-38}$
- maximum positive value is $(1 - 2^{-24}) \times 2^{128} \approx 3.402823 \times 10^{38}$.

All integers with six or fewer significant decimal digits can be converted to a single precision IEEE 754 floating point value without loss of precision. Some integers up to nine significant decimal digits can be converted without loss of precision, but no more than nine significant decimal digits can be stored.

The name **real** or the name **float** is typically used as the data type name for values expressed in floating point form.

1 Precision is determined by how many datum bits are reserved for significant digits, m. One bit is reserved for the sign and several bits are reserved for the exponent, e.

Key term

Floating point data type:
Computers store and manipulate real numbers such as 3.142 using the IEEE 754 floating point standard (knowledge of its detail is not required for AS or A Level).
Floating-point numbers are little more than scientific notation encoded as bits.
Floating-point numbers that represent real numbers are put in the form

$$N = s \times m \times 2^{e}$$

where s is −1 or 1, m is a natural number, and e is an integer.
A number's significant digits are represented by m either exactly or approximately.
IEEE floating point numbers can be very large or very small on a scale from the size of galaxies to the size of sub-atomic particles.

Key fact

Significant digits:
123456, 123456000, 0.00123456 all have the same number of significant decimal digits.
Significant digits define the precision of a number.

Key term

Real numbers:
In mathematics, a real number is a value of a continuous quantity that can represent a distance along a line. Real numbers in mathematics include the rational numbers and the irrational numbers. Integers are rational numbers.
The real number type in Delphi defines a set of numbers that can be represented with the floating-point notation. Use the data type Double which is a floating point data type. The Real data type is currently a synonym for Double.

Questions

6 (a) Calculate $(x - y) \times (x + y)$ rounded off to 6 significant digits where $x = 293452$ and $y = 153761$ using Windows Calculator or similar.

(b) Calculate x^2 rounded off to 6 significant digits where $x = 293452$.

(c) Calculate y^2 rounded off to 6 significant digits where $y = 153761$.

(d) Calculate $x^2 - y^2$ rounded off to 6 significant digits.

If the calculations were done by representing each integer value with a single precision IEEE 754 floating point number, why would the first calculation $(x - y) \times (x + y)$ differ from the second $x^2 - y^2$ even though algebraically $x^2 - y^2 = (x - y) \times (x + y)$?

7 Data types integer (32-bit) and float (32-bit single precision IEEE 754) are available. State which data type could be used for each of the following decimal values without loss of precision and explain why

(a) 45 (b) -2,147,483,648 (c) 3, 124, 560, 000

8 Data types integer (32-bit) and float (32-bit single precision IEEE 754) are available. State which data type could be used for each of the following decimal values and explain why

(a) 3.142 (b) 1.18×10^{-36} (c) 2.46215×10^{38}

Type	Approximate range	Size in bytes	Significant digits	Description
Real	2.23e-308 .. 1.79e+308	8 bytes IEEE 754 standard	15-16	Synonym for Double.
Double	2.23e-308 .. 1.79e+308	8 bytes IEEE 754 standard	15-16	Use Double in place of Real
Single	1.18e-38 .. 3.40e+38	4 bytes	7-8	
Extended	*32-bit Intel Windows:* 3.37e-4932 .. 1.18e+4932	10 bytes	10-20	Extended offers greater precision on 32-bit platforms than other real types. On 64-bit platforms Extended is an alias for a Double. There is less precision using an Extended on 64-bit platforms compared to 32-bit platforms, where Extended is 10 bytes.
Extended	*64-bit Intel Linux/ 32-bit Intel macOS/ 32-bit Intel iOS Simulator:* 3.37e-4932 .. 1.18e+4932 *Other platforms* 2.23e-308 .. 1.79e+308	16 bytes	10-20	
Currency	-922337203685477.5807.. 922337203685477.5807	8 bytes	10-20	Fixed to 4 decimal places. A fixed-point data type that minimizes rounding errors in monetary calculations. It is stored as a scaled 64-bit integer with the 4 least significant digits implicitly representing decimal places.

Table 4.3 Floating point/real data types in Delphi

Consequences of imprecision

Comparing two floating point numbers naively can result in surprising results. as shown in *Figure 4.2* where it appears that 0.1 is not equal to 0.1. The expected output from running program **FPComparision** is TRUE on evaluating the Boolean expression `i = 0.1` but what actually appears is the Boolean value FALSE!

The reason is that decimal 0.1 is represented imprecisely in binary.

For a decimal number to convert exactly to binary, the only prime factor for its denominator is 2.

We break a decimal number into $^{x}/_{2n}$ when we can convert it exactly to its binary equivalent,

e.g. $$3.75 = (^{8}/_{4}) + (^{4}/_{4}) + (^{2}/_{4}) + (^{1}/_{4}) = \frac{(8 + 4 + 2 + 1)}{4} = {}^{15}/_{4}$$

There are many decimals that cannot be broken down into the form $^{x}/_{2n}$. The decimal number 0.1 has prime factors 2 and 5. and therefore is one of these.

- I Use the IDE to create and save the source code program shown in *Table 4.4* as **FPComparison.dpr** or **FPComparison.dprog**, depending on the version of Delphi, in its own directory/folder named **FPComparision**.
- I Now build the program (Shift F9).
- I Run this program in Debug mode (F9).

```
Program FPComparison;
{$APPTYPE CONSOLE}
Var
  i : Real;
Begin
  i := 0.1;
  Writeln('i = 0.1? ', i = 0.1);
  Readln;
End.
```

Table 4.4 Program FPComparison

Fig. 4.2 Captured console window showing output from program FPComparision in execution.

The solution is to allow for a small difference when comparing two floats. The **System.Math** library `SameValue` function calculates the appropriate amount of difference to allow if you don't want to do it yourself.

```
Program FPComparisonCorrected;
{$APPTYPE CONSOLE}
Uses
  System.Math;
Var
  i : Real;
Begin
  i := 0.1;
  Writeln('i = 0.1? ', Abs(i - 0.1) < 0.01);
  Writeln('i = 0.1? ', SameValue(i, 0.1));
  Readln;
End.
```

Table 4.5 Program FPComparisonCorrected

Fig. 4.3 Captured console window showing output from program FPComparisionCorrected in execution.

- Use the IDE to create and save the source code program shown in *Table 4.6* as **SumError.dpr** or **SumError.prog**, depending on the version of Delphi, in its own directory/folder named **SumError**.
- Now build the program (Shift F9).
- Run this program in Debug mode (F9).

```
Program SumError;
{$APPTYPE CONSOLE}
Var
  i : Real;
  n : Integer = 0;
Begin
  i := 0.1;
  Repeat
    i := i + 0.1;
  Until (Abs(i -1.0) < 0.01) ;
  Writeln('First loop, i = ', i);
  i := 0.1;
  Repeat
    n := n + 1;
    Writeln('n = ', n, ' i = ', i);
    i := i + 0.1;
  Until i = 1.0;
  Writeln('Second loop, i = ', i);
  Readln;
End.
```

Table 4.6 Program SumError

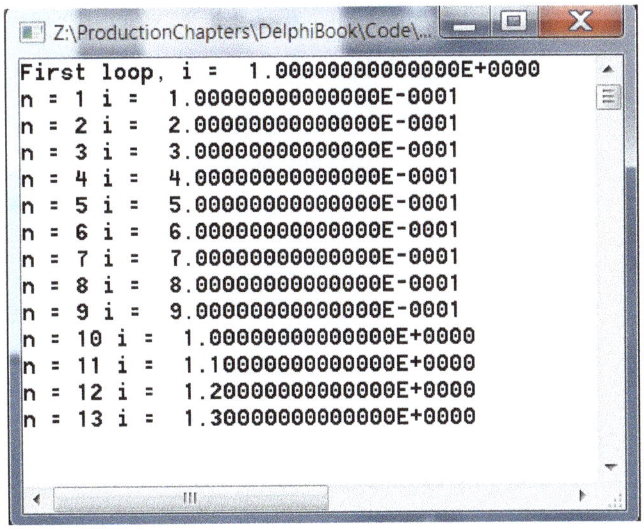

Fig. 4.4 Captured console window showing output from program SumError in execution paused by setting a single debug breakpoint on i := i + 0.1 and stepping through breakpoint (F4).

Whilst the first loop of program **SumError** shown in *Table 4.6* terminates as expected, the second loop does not terminate. This failure arises because the value of `i` is never exactly `1.0` in the executing program and so the loop terminating condition never evaluates to `True`.

The error in the representation of decimal 0.1 in binary accumulates during looping so that it can never become 1.0.

Figure 4.4 shows the paused execution on the thirteenth iteration of the second loop.

Never use a Delphi real variable to control a loop unless you can take account of representation error as shown in the first loop in *Table 4.6*.

Special floating point values

The **System.Math** unit defines constants `NaN`, `Infinity` and `NegInfinity`. These are respectively, 'Not A Number', 'infinity', and 'negative infinity'. They may be assigned to any floating point type with the exception of Currency.

You must not test for these values directly but instead use the functions `IsNaN` and `IsInfinite`.

Table 4.7 shows program **SpecialValues** which uses these special values.

Figure 4.5 shows the console window output when this program is executed.

```
Program SpecialValues;
{$APPTYPE CONSOLE}
Uses System.Math;
Begin
  Writeln(Nan);
  Writeln(Infinity);
  Writeln(NegInfinity);
  Readln;
End.
```

Table 4.7 Program SpecialValues

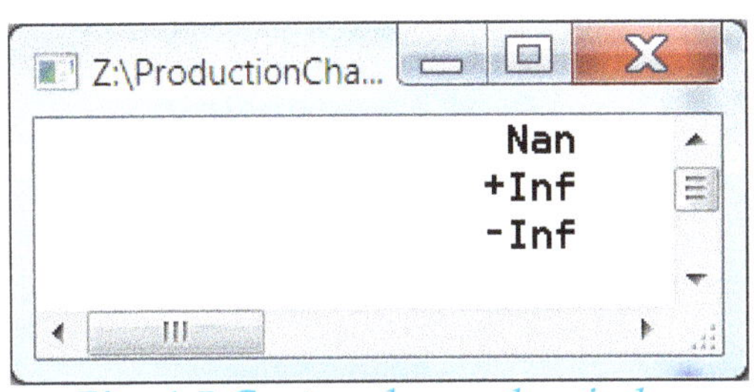

Fig. 4.5 Captured console window showing output from program SpecialValues.

Boolean data type

The statement “It is raining” is either true or false.

Two values only belong to the data type `Boolean`:

- the truth value True
- the truth value False.

> **Key term**
>
> **Boolean data type:**
> Two values only belong to the data type Boolean:
> - the truth value True
> - the truth value False.

Only one bit is needed to represent a Boolean truth value but in practice multiple bits are normally used.

Typically, the datum or bit pattern 1111111111111111 is used to represent the truth value True in 16 bits (32 1’s in 32 bits, 64 1’s in 64 bits and so on).

Typically, the datum or bit pattern 0000000000000000 is used to represent the truth value False in 16 bits (32 0’s in 32 bits, 64 0’s in 64 bits and so on).

Questions

9. What is the data type of the result of evaluating the following expressions
(a) 5 > 6 (b) 5 < 6 (c) 7 = 7?

Character data type

A character is a letter of the alphabet (upper or lower case) or the digits 0 to 9, or punctuation symbols or some special symbols, e.g. / . A digital machine can only understand sequences of 1’s and 0’s. Therefore, to denote or represent a character value, e.g. A, inside a computer we must use a bit pattern.

One method of allocating bit patterns to characters is the ASCII code system, another is Unicode. ASCII uses seven bits whilst Unicode uses either 16 bits (UTF-16), 32 bits (UTF-32) or one to four bytes (UTF-8) where a byte is eight bits - see *Chapter11*.

The meaning of binary datum 1000001 is character A if the data type of the datum is **character** (7-bit ASCII). Straight single quotation marks are used to indicate a character value, e.g. 'A'.

Table 4.8 shows 96 of the possible 128 codes (2^7). The ASCII code for letter 'A' is 65 in decimal.

All 128 codes are called **character codes** because they encode what is collectively known as characters.

Code in decimal	Character	Code in decimal	Character	Code in decimal	Character	Code in decimal	Character
32	Space	56	8	80	P	104	h
33	!	57	9	81	Q	105	i
34	“	58	:	82	R	106	j
35	#	59	;	83	S	107	k
36	$	60	<	84	T	108	l
37	%	61	=	85	U	109	m
38	&	62	>	86	V	110	n
39	‘	63	?	87	W	111	o
40	(	64	@	88	X	112	p
41	)	65	A	89	Y	113	q
42	*	66	B	90	Z	114	r
43	+	67	C	91	[	115	s
44	,	68	D	92	\	116	t
45	-	69	E	93	]	117	u
46	.	70	F	94	^	118	v
47	/	71	G	95	_	119	w
48	0	72	H	96	`	120	x
49	1	73	I	97	a	121	y
50	2	74	J	98	b	122	z
51	3	75	K	99	c	123	{
52	4	76	L	100	d	124	|
53	5	77	M	101	e	125	}
54	6	78	N	102	f	126	~
55	7	79	O	103	g	127	DEL

Table 4.8 ASCII code lookup table

However, only 95 codes are actually used for symbols, the other 33 are **control codes**, codes 0 to 31 and the code 127 which is reserved for an instruction *delete a character code.*

Table 4.9 shows a lookup table for ASCII control codes, 0 to 31. The codes with a blank character field are codes used for controlling communication over a telephone line. Line feed and carriage return are used to break a long string of characters into separate lines. When characters are organised on a line-by-line basis we call this text, e.g. the text that you are reading on this page.

Code in decimal	Character	Code in decimal	Character
0	Null	16	
1		17	
2		18	
3		19	
4		20	
5		21	
6		22	
7	Bell	23	
8	Backspace	24	
9	Horizontal tabulation	25	
10	Line feed	26	
11	Vertical tabulation	27	Escape
12	Form feed	28	
13	Carriage return	29	
14		30	
15		31	

Table 4.9 ASCII code lookup table for some control codes

Text files therefore consist of one long string of ASCII character codes with the line breaks marked by a combination of ASCII code 10 (line feed) and ASCII code 13 (carriage return). These control codes reposition a VDU's cursor at the beginning of the next line when displaying a text file on a VDU. In Delphi, the **character data type** is **Char**. Since Delphi 2009 characters are allocated 16 bits, ordered according to the Unicode character set. The first 256 Unicode characters correspond to ANSI (Extended ASCII) characters. In Delphi 7 characters are allocated 8 bits and correspond to ANSI (Extended ASCII) characters.

Questions

10 What is the ASCII character code for
(a) the letter H (b) the decimal digit 3 (c) the symbol ?

11 What is the symbol or character corresponding to the following ASCII character codes
(a) 97 (b) 37 (c) 48?

12 Encode the message 'Hello' in ASCII. Use decimal for your answer.

13 Encode the text

'Hello
World!'

in ASCII. Use decimal for your answer. (Note that there is a line break and carriage return between the first and second lines)

14 Convert the following string of ASCII character codes to its equivalent text form

72 101 108 108 111 10 13 87 111 114 108 100 33

15 Shown below are some 7-bit bit patterns along with their decimal equivalents. Use the ASCII look-up table *Table 4.7* to look up the corresponding character value, i.e. the human readable form.
(a) 1011001 (89) (b) 1001000 (72) (c) 1001100 (76) (d) 1111001 (121)
You may use the ASCII look-up table *Table 4.7* to help you answer this question.

16 Do you think that each of the following expressions could be valid, i.e. evaluated successfully? Give your reason for each of your answers.
(a) 'B' > 'A' (b) '5' < '7' (c) '6' = '6'

Key concept

ASCII or American Standard Code for Information Interchange:
In ASCII, the symbols corresponding to the letters of the alphabet (upper case and lower case), punctuation marks, special symbols and the decimal digits 0 to 9 are assigned different 7-bit binary codes according to a look up table.

Information

Extended ASCII:
This is the 8-bit version of ASCII consisting of 2^8 or 256 character codes or code points. The code points beyond 127 use the eighth bit. These map to symbols that are not covered in 7-bit ASCII, e.g. £ sign.
A code point or code position is any of the numerical values that make up the code space.

Information

Scan codes:
When a key on a keyboard is pressed a scan code is generated. Scan codes are binary codes as well. The scan code that is generated is converted into an ASCII code that corresponds to the current setting for the keyboard's keys. The mapping between scan codes and ASCII codes can be changed. For example, the mapping for a key marked in one currency symbol can be changed so that when pressed it maps to the ASCII code for another currency symbol, e.g. $ to £ (extended ASCII code 163_{10}). This was the only way to overcome ASCII's limited character set until the adoption of Unicode.

Unicode

ASCII provides only 128 numeric values, and 33 of those are reserved for special functions - the control codes and delete. Many of the control codes are no longer needed because they have their origin in the days of the teletype, punched cards and paper tape. ASCII does not cater for many Western European languages which have accented letters, and special symbols such as £, as it was designed for the North American market and it certainly doesn't cater for Asian languages which are logogram-based (symbols represent concepts), not alphabetic. The 95 ASCII codes for characters found in text are wholely inadequate for a universal standard for information interchange.
Unicode was designed to provide a single character set that covers the languages of the world. Unicode UTF-16 uses either one or two 16-bit code units for its character codes. A single 16-bit unit supports 2^{16} or 65536 different codes. Unicode UTF-32 uses 32-bit code units each representing a single character code. Unicode includes all the ASCII codes in addition to codes for characters in foreign languages (e.g. complete sets of Chinese characters), and many mathematical and other symbols.

UTF-8 encodes each of the 1,112,064 valid code points in the Unicode code space using one to four bytes. The first 128 characters of Unicode, which correspond one-to-one with ASCII, are encoded using a single byte with the same binary value as ASCII.

Delphi 7 Char, AnsiChar and WideChar

Delph 7 uses the ASCII character set,

In Delphi 7 the fundamental character types are AnsiChar and WideChar. AnsiChar values are byte-sized (8-bit) characters ordered according to the locale character set - native language and region specific, e.g. English US, English UK. AnsiChar was originally modeled after the American National Standards Institute (ANSI) character set - ISO Standard 8859-1 - but has now been broadened to refer to the current locale character set which redefines the characters represented by codes in range 128-255. The ANSI character set includes the standard ASCII character set (values 0 to 127), plus an extended character set (values 128 to 255).

The generic character type is Char, which is equivalent to AnsiChar.

Character values, like integers, wrap around when decremented or incremented past the beginning or end of their range (unless range-checking is enabled). For example, execution of the program shown in *Table 4.10* writes the letter 'C' (ASCII 67) to the console window.

```
Program CharWrapAround;
{$APPTYPE CONSOLE}
Var
  CharacterInSetOfCharacters : Char;// ANSIChar - 0..255 characters
  i: Integer;
Begin
  CharacterInSetOfCharacters := High(CharacterInSetOfCharacters);// Highest character
  For i := 1 to 68
    Do Inc(CharacterInSetOfCharacters);//Select next character in set
  Writeln(CharacterInSetOfCharacters);
  Readln;
End.
```

P

Table 4.10 Program CharWrapAround

Questions

17 Explain why the program shown in *Table 4.9* outputs 'C' not 'D' as might be expected given that the *for loop* executes from i = 1 to to i = 68 (you may want to consult *Table 4.7* and *Table 4.8*).

The predefined function **Chr** returns the character value for any integer in the range of **AnsiChar** or **WideChar**.

For example, `Chr(65)` returns the letter A. There is an alternative to **Chr.** The character value for a given integer can also be obtained by prefacing the integer value with #, e.g. #65 is the character value 'A' as shown in the program in *Table 4.11*.

The **Succ** function returns the next character in the character set. The complement to the **Succ** function is the **Pred** function which returns the immediate predecessor.

The **Inc** procedure increments the ordinal value of a character by the specified amount which is 2 in the program in *Table 4.11*. The default increment is 1 if the amount parameter is omitted. The complement to the **Inc** function is the **Dec** function.

```
Program UseOfHashToDefineACharacterValue;
{$APPTYPE CONSOLE}
Var
  Ch : Char = #65;
Begin
  Writeln(Ch);
  Ch := Succ(Succ(Ch));
  Writeln(Ch);
  Inc(Ch,2);  //an increment of 1 can be achieved with just Inc(Ch)
  Writeln(Ch);
  Inc(Ch);
  Writeln(Ch);
  Dec(Ch, 2);
  Writeln(Ch);
  Dec(Ch); //a decrement of 1 can be achieved with just Dec(Ch)
  Writeln(Ch);
  Readln;
End.
```

P

Table 4.11 Program UseOfHashToDefineACharacterValue

WideChar characters use more than one byte to represent every character.
WideChar is word-sized (16-bit) characters ordered according to the Unicode character set.
The first 256 Unicode characters correspond to the ANSI characters.

Delphi 2009 onwards

The Char type was an alias for AnsiChar in versions predating Delphi 2009 but it is now an alias for WideChar, and therefore a two-byte character type (except when the character is a precomposed character when as permitted by Unicode, it can be represented by a pair of 16-bit characters, e.g. the character ö can be represented as $00F6 or as the precomposed character pair: the o character ($006F) followed by the diaeresis (¨) character ($0308).

If an 8-bit representation (accounting for 256 different symbols) is required then use AnsiChar. The 8 bits are interpreted according to the currently selected code page.

The term code page refers to a mechanism that was used to extend the original 7-bit ASCII character set (0 - 127). In the original MS-DOS, these values in the 128 through 255 range were mainly used for line drawing characters but these cab be replaced by different characters to meet cultural and language needs, e.g. a Cyrillic alphabet. This is achieved by changing the code page. Each code page is distinguished by a code page identifier.

WideChar represents 64K different symbols whereas AnsiString represents only 256 for any given code page.

The larger Char type is still an ordinal type, so Succ, Pred, Inc and Dec will work as expected whilst Char variables can perform as loop control variables - *Table 4.12*.

```
Program UsingDelphiXE10Char;
{$APPTYPE CONSOLE}
Var
  Ch : Char;
Begin
  For Ch := #65 To #90
    Do Write(Ch, ' ');
  Writeln;
  For Ch := 'A' To 'Z'
    Do Write(Ch, ' ');
  Writeln;
  Readln;
End.
```
P

Table 4.12 Program UsingDelphiXE10Char

String data type

In Delphi the string data type is **String**. This has been a **UTF-16 Unicode** string since Delphi 2009. Before Delphi 2009, **String** was an alias for **AnsiString** except for Delphi 1 in which it was an alias for **ShortString**, the Pascal string type.

Fig. 4.6 Character beads on a string.

Figure 4.6 shows beads on a string with each bead labelled with a character value (the space character value corresponds to the unlabelled bead).

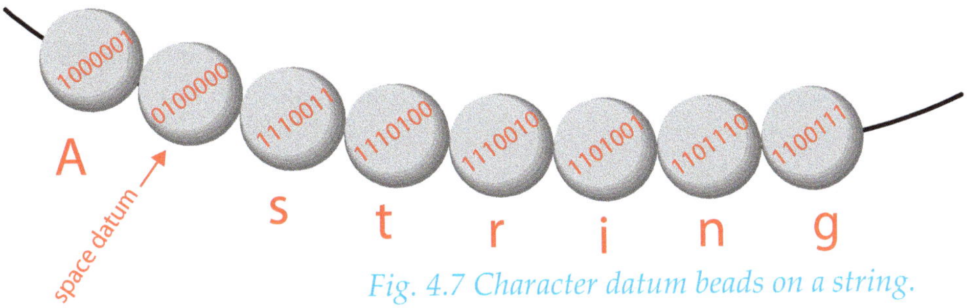

Fig. 4.7 Character datum beads on a string.

Figure 4.7 shows beads on a string with each bead labelled with the corresponding character datum (7-bit ASCII), e.g. binary 1110011 is datum with value 's'. Using **Unicode UTF-16** requires more bits, 16 bits per datum in fact, whilst **AnsiString** and **ShortString** each require 8 bits per datum.

Borrowing from the beads on a string analogy, a string is just a sequence of characters, e.g. '`A string`'. Single quotation marks are used to indicate a string value. The corresponding sequence of bit patterns or datum for the string value '`A string`' is

1000001 0100000 1110011 1110100 1110010 1101001 1101110 1100111

if each character of this string is represented in 7-bit ASCII.

Table 4.14 shows string types of Delphi.

Table 4.13 shows a program that uses a variable `MyStringVar` of string type **ShortString** which specifies that this variable is allocated 256 bytes. The first byte of `MyStringVar` stores the length of any string assigned to the variable, and the remaining 255 bytes stores the characters of the string value, five bytes in this case - '`Hello`'.

String assignment is achieved with

```
MyStringVar := 'Hello';
```

The number of characters assigned to `MyStringVar` is obtained in two different ways:

```
Writeln(Length(MyStringVar));
Writeln(Integer(MyStringVar[0]));
```

```
Program PascalString;
{$APPTYPE CONSOLE}
Var
  MyStringVar : ShortString;
  AnotherStringVar : String[15];//ShortString max 15
characters
Begin
  MyStringVar := 'Hello';
  Writeln(MyStringVar);
  Writeln(Length(MyStringVar));
  Writeln(Integer(MyStringVar[0]));
  AnotherStringVar := 'Hello World';
  Writeln(AnotherStringVar);
  Writeln(Length(AnotherStringVar));
  Writeln(Integer(AnotherStringVar[0]));
  Readln;
End.
```

P

Table 4.13 Program PascalString

The traditional Pascal **String** can contain up to a maximum of 256 bytes, contain their characters in elements 1 through 255, and record the length of the string in the 8-bit zeroth byte.

The first uses the **Length** function, the second accesses the first byte of the string variable - `MyStringVar[0]` - where the number of characters assigned to `MyStringVar` is stored. You should always uses the **Length** function because the second method only works for string variables of type **ShortString**. This fact can be used to confirm that the data type of a string variable is **ShortString**.

The fixed allocation of 256 bytes is wasteful of memory because strings are typically much shorter in length than 255 characters. The solution is to use subtypes of **ShortString** of maximum length from 1 to 254.

Unfortunately, it is not possible to apply subtyping to **ShortString** directly.
Instead the generic type name **String** must be used with a size specifier, e.g. 15, as follows

String[15]

String[15] creates a string type that allocates 16 bytes, one for the string's length (the zeroth byte) and 15 for its characters.
In fact, whatever the generic string type **String** is an alias for - see *Table 4.13* - subtyping **String** results in a type which is a subtype of **ShortString**. In program `PascalStrings` in *Table 4.12*

```
Writeln(Integer(AnotherStringVar[0]));
```

compiles and outputs 11 when executed. confirming that `AnotherStringVar` is of data type **ShortString**.
Note that when assigning a value to a string variable that has been subtyped, the string is truncated if it exceeds the maximum length for the subtype.

Type	Maximum length	Memory required	Coding	Delphi version
ShortString (value type)	255 characters	1 to 256 bytes (1 byte for length)	Pascal string statically allocated 256 bytes unless subtyped. Characters -AnsiChar	Delphi 1
AnsiString (reference type, i.e. uses a pointer to string value)	~2^{31} characters	4 bytes to 2GB	8-bit (ANSI) characters, dynamically allocated memory. Doesn't include code page information.	D2 -D2007
AnsiString (reference type)	~2^{31} characters	4 bytes to 2GB	8-bit (ANSI) characters, dynamically allocated memory. Code page of the characters is also stored.	D2009 -
WideString (reference type)	~2^{30} characters	4 bytes to 2GB	16-bit Unicode characters, not reference counted, slow memory allocation. Dynamically allocated memory.	Delphi 3 -
UnicodeString (reference type)	~2^{30} characters	4 bytes to 2GB	UTF-16, a variable length encoding, reference counted, copy on write, fast memory allocation, Dynamically allocated memory.	D2009 -
String	Alias for		ShortString	Delphi 1
String	Alias for		AnsiString	D2 - D2007
String	Alias for (cannot be changed)		UnicodeString	D2009 -
String[#]	Alias for		ShortString	All

Table 4.14 Delphi string types

In versions prior to Delphi 2009, a program could be forced to interpret the **String** data type as **ShortString** in other ways as well.

The program shown in *Table 4.15* uses the compiler directive `{$H-}` to make **String** an alias for **ShortString**. It compiles and executes successfully accessing the first byte to obtain the length of the string value stored in `AnotherStringVar`.

Changing the directive to `{$H+}` restores the alias to the **String** data type given in *Table 4.13*. If this is done for program `IntroToStringTypes` in *Table 4.14*, the compiler reports an error 'Element 0 inaccessible'.

```
Program IntroToStringTypes;
{$H-}
{$APPTYPE CONSOLE}
Var
  MyString : String;
Begin
  MyString := 'Hello World';
  Writeln(Integer(MyString[0]));//Cast MyString[0] as integer
  Readln;
End.
```

Table 4.15 Delphi 7 program IntroToStringTypes

Also in versions prior to Delphi 2009, the same result can be achieved by turning off the compiler option **Huge strings** - *Figure 4.8*. To display the compiler options page select **Project|Options** and then the **Compiler** tab. A third way in versions prior to Delphi 2009 is to use the compiler directive `{$LongStrings Off}`. as shown in *Table 4.16*.

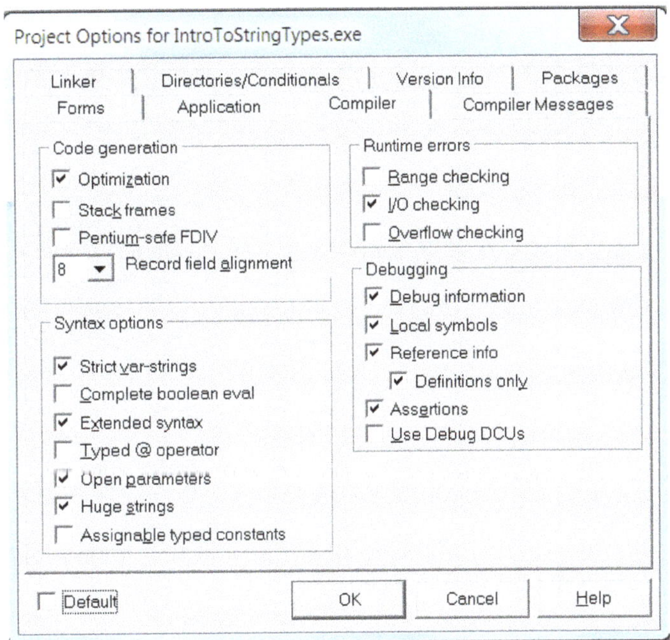

Fig. 4.8 Compiler options Delphi 7 showing Huge strings on

```
Program LongStringsCompilerDirective;
{$APPTYPE CONSOLE}
Var
  {$LongStrings Off}
  MyString : String;
Begin
  MyString := 'Hello World';
  Writeln(Integer(MyString[0]));
  Readln;
End.
```

Table 4.16 Program demonstrating LongStrings directive

The program in *Table 4.17* shows that the elements, i.e. characters, of a string variable may be accessed as follows

`MyStringVar[i]`

`MyStringVar[1]` is the character 'H', `MyString[2]` the character 'e', and so on. For a **ShortString** or **AnsiString**, `MyStringVar[i]` is of type **AnsiChar**.

```
Program IteratingElementsOfAString;
{$APPTYPE CONSOLE}
Var
  i : Integer;
  MyString : String[15];
Begin
  MyString := 'Hello World';
  For i := 1 To Length(MyString)
    Do Write(MyString[i]);
  Writeln;
  Readln;
End.
```

Table 4.17 Iterating through elements of string

It is possible to directly change a character in a string as follows

```
MyString[2] := 'E';
```

`MyString` now stores 'HEllo World'

Extending the string is done using the concatenation operator '+' as follows

```
MyString := MyString + '!!!';
```

`MyString` now stores 'HEllo World!!!'. Using this method ensures that the length of the `MyString` is updated correctly.

The console window uses a code page with limited support for Unicode, consequently many Unicode characters do not display correctly in a console window. In order to properly explore the **String** data type in Delphi 2009 onwards, i.e. the **UnicodeString** data type, we need to create a Windows Vcl application.

Delphi Windows Vcl applications use code page 1200 which has much better support for Unicode characters. *Table 4.18* shows a program which displays a string `s`, data type **String** (**UnicodeString**), in a **Memo box.**

```
Unit UnicodeStringsUnit;
Interface
Uses
  Winapi.Windows, Winapi.Messages, System.SysUtils,
  System.Variants, System.Classes, Vcl.Graphics,
  Vcl.Controls, Vcl.Forms, Vcl.Dialogs, Vcl.StdCtrls;
Type
  TUnicodeStringsForm = Class(TForm)
                          MemoUnicodeCh: TMemo;
                          btnShowUnicode: TButton;
                          edtLength: TEdit;
                          lblReturnedLength: TLabel;
                          edtElement15: TEdit;
                          edtElement17: TEdit;
                          lblElement15: TLabel;
                          lblElement17: TLabel;
                          btnTerminate: TButton;
                          Procedure ShowUnicodeClick(Sender: TObject);
                          Procedure btnTerminateClick(Sender: TObject);
                        End;
Var
  UnicodeStringsForm: TUnicodeStringsForm;
Implementation
{$R *.dfm}
Procedure TUnicodeStringsForm.ShowUnicodeClick(Sender: TObject);
  Var
    Ch : Char; //WideChar (16 bits)
    s : String; //UnicodeString (each character 16 bits)
    i : Integer;
  Begin
    s := '';
    i := $FE; // $ = Hexadecimal
    For Ch := #$00FF To #$1FFF  //Character #$00FF to character #$1FFF
      Do
        Begin
          i := i + 1;
          s := s + IntToStr(i) + '=' + Ch + #10; // #10 = Line feed
        End;
    MemoUnicodeCh.Lines.Text := s;
    edtLength.Text := IntToStr(Length(s));
    edtElement15.Text := s[15];
    edtElement17.Text := s[17];
  End;
Procedure TUnicodeStringsForm.btnTerminateClick(Sender: TObject);
  Begin
    Application.Terminate;
  End;
End.
```

Table 4.18 Delphi 10.2 Vcl program to displays Unicode characters for code page 1200

The string s is populated with characters from #$FF to #$1FFF together with each character's ordinal number, the '=' sign and the line feed character #10 placed immediately after each character. The symbol $ denotes a hexadecimal number. The symbol # converts the following hexadecimal number into its character equivalent. *Figure 4.9* shows the output.

The two statements

```
edtElement15.Text := s[15];
edtElement17.Text := s[17];
```

select the 15th and seventeenth elements of string s. These are characters 7 and ā respectively. Each element of s corresponds to a character of type **Char** (**WideChar** - 16 bits). Starting at 1 (strings are 1-based), and beginning the count at the character '2' of '255' in *Figure 4.9*, the fifteenth character is indeed 7 (don't forget to count the #10 character, the line feed character, at the end of each line) and the seventeenth ā.

Comparison of strings is defined by the ordering of the characters in corresponding positions.

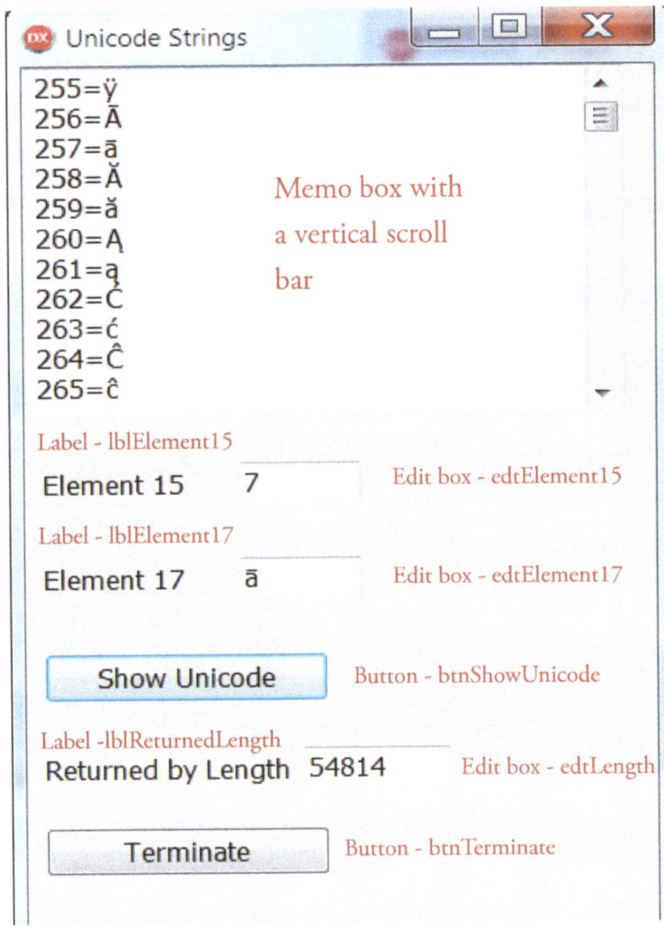

Fig. 4.9 Form window showing Unicode characters and their ordinal value

For strings of unequal length, each character in the longer string without a corresponding character in the shorter string takes on a greater-than value.
For example,'AB' is greater than 'A'. Zero-length strings hold the lowest values.

ShortString variables which have a fixed amount of memory allocated at compile time but **AnsiStrings**, **WideStrings** and **UnicodeStrings** are different because they get their memory allocated dynamically from a heap, i.e. as the program is running. A heap is an area of memory set aside just for such a purpose. Variables of these three types hold a pointer (a memory address) to the allocated heap memory which they use to refer to or reference the string. The fact that **AnsiString**, **WideString** and **UnicodeString** variables are pointers (references) means that more than one string variable can refer to the same string in memory simply by copying the pointer value to the string, e.g. if a and b are **UnicodeString** variables, say, then a and b both point to the string 'Hello World' after making the following assignments

```
a := 'Hello World';
b := a;
```

Delphi uses reference counting to keeps track of how many string variables are referring to the same string in memory. This reference-counting mechanism is used also to free the memory when a string isn't used anymore, i.e.reference count reaches zero. If variable a or b is subject to an operation that potentially could change the string value then a copy is made (new pointer), the operation carried out on the copy and the pointer to the copy assigned to the variable involved. This is called *copy on write*.

The reference type nature of **AnsiString**, **WideString** and **UnicodeString** causes a finalisation error with files declared to be **File Of AnsiString** or **WideString** or **UnicodeString** - see *Chapters 16* and *30*. The solution is either to use ShortString/subtype of String or to use file streams (*Chapter 30*).

Date/time

Values may be dates, e.g. 28/05/2016, or a time of day, e.g. 15:35:16. Internally, these are just bit patterns. For these bit patterns to have the meaning date or the meaning time of day, the bit patterns must be data typed. This requires a data type **date** and a data type **time** or a combination of the two, a data type **datetime**. Delphi uses the latter and names this data type **TDateTime**.

Table 4.19 specifies the **TDateTime** data type for Delphi.

Information

Date and time routines:
Delphi has many routines that support working with these data types. These are to be found in the System, System.SysUtils and System.dateUtils libraries.

Data type	Description
TDateTime	Data type double, with the date as the integral part, and time as fractional part. The date is stored as the number of days since 30 December 1899.
TDate	Represents a special type of **TDateTime** value that has no decimal part. A TDate value represents the number of days that have elapsed since 30/12/1899.
TTime	Represents a special type of **TDateTime** that has only a fractional part (and no integral part). A **TTime** value represents the fraction of a 24-hour day. For example, 0.25 represents 06:00 hours, 0.5 represents 12:00 hours, and 0.75 represents 18:00 hours.

Table 4.19 TDateTime data type

TDateTime is defined in the System unit as

```
Type = Type Double;
```

This form of type definition forces the compiler to create a new distinct type called **TDateTime**.

The program shown in *Table 4.20* demonstrates the use of some date/time routines:

```
Program DateTimeRoutines;
{$APPTYPE CONSOLE}
Uses
  SysUtils;
Begin
  Writeln(Now : 10 : 5);
  Writeln(Date : 10 : 5);
  Writeln(Time : 7 : 5);
  Writeln(DateTimeToStr(Now));
  Writeln(DateToStr(Date));
  Writeln(TimeToStr(Time));
  Readln;
End.
```

P

Table 4.20 Program demonstrating use of some Date/Time routines

Now Returns the current date and time as a value of type **Double**,
e.g. 43707.45404 to 5 decimal places

Date Returns only the date as a value of type **Double**,
e.g. 43707.00000 to 5 decimal places

Time Returns only the time as a value of type **Double**,
e.g. 0. 45404 to 5 decimal places

DateTimeToStr Converts a date and time value into a string
e.g. 30/08/2019 10:53:48

DateToStr Converts a date value into a string
e.g. 30/08/2019

TimeToStr Converts a time value into a string
e.g. 10:53:48

The above routines are functions.

User-defined data types

Programmers can create their own simple data types based upon the built-in data types or they can create more complex data types with internal structure using a combination of the built-in data types and structuring keywords such as `Array`, `Record`, `File` and `Class`.

In each case the keyword `Type` must be used as follows:

```
Type
  TIntegerSubRange = 0..9;
  TCharacterSubRange = 'A'..'E';
  TStudentRecord = Record
                     Name : String[25];
                     Age : Integer;
                   End;
  TIntegerArray = Array[1..10] Of Integer;
  TCharacterFilePipe = File Of Integer;
```

A subrange of the integer data type. The compiler will check the source code for assignments to variables of this type that fall outside this range. If runtime range checks are enabled then assignments at runtime will be trapped that fall outside this range.

A subrange of the character data type.

Variables of these user-defined data types are created as follows:

```
Var
  IntegerSubRange : TIntegerSubRange;
  CharacterSubRange : TCharacterSubRange;
  StudentRecord : TStudentRecord;
  IntegerArray : TIntegerArray;
  CharacterFilePipe : TCharacterFilePipe;
```

A convention is used in Delphi whereby the identifier for a user-defined type is prefaced with a capital **T** (unless it is a Pointer type in which case **P** is used or an Exception type in which case **E** is used).

This is a case of another role for an identifier, i.e. to identify a user-defined type. Remember that in an earlier chapter we introduced the concept of an identifier when using variables.

Program UserDefined in *Table 4.21* shows these user-defined data types in use.

P

```
Program UserDefined;
{$APPTYPE CONSOLE}
Type
  TIntegerSubRange = 0..9;
  TCharacterSubRange = 'A'..'E';
  TStudentRecord = Record
                     Name : String;
                     Age : Integer;
                   End;
  TIntegerArray = Array[1..10] Of Integer;
  TCharacterFilePipe = File Of TCharacterSubRange;
Var
  IntegerSubRange : TIntegerSubRange;
  CharacterSubRange : TCharacterSubRange;
  StudentRecord : TStudentRecord;
  IntegerArray : TIntegerArray;
  CharacterFilePipe : TCharacterFilePipe;
Begin
  IntegerSubRange := 6;
  CharacterSubRange := 'D';
  StudentRecord.Name := 'Fred';
  StudentRecord.Age := 17;
  IntegerArray[1] := 23;
  AssignFile(CharacterFilePipe, 'Test.dat');
  Rewrite(CharacterFilePipe);
  Write(CharacterFilePipe, CharacterSubRange);
  CloseFile(CharacterFilePipe);
  Write('Press return key to finish ');
  Readln;
End.
```

Table 4.21 Program UserDefined

The section of source code

```
AssignFile(CharacterFilePipe, 'Test.dat');
Rewrite(CharacterFilePipe);
Write(CharacterFilePipe, CharacterSubRange);
CloseFile(CharacterFilePipe);
```

creates a file 'Test.dat' and populates it with a single character value from the variable `CharacterSubRange`. before closing the file. If this file is opened in a text editor, it shows a single line containing the character 'D'.

- I Load the source code program shown in *Table 4.19* and save as **UserDefined.dpr** or **UserDefined.dprog**, depending on the version of Delphi, in its own directory/folder named **UserDefined**.
- I Now compile the program (Ctrl F9).
- I Run this program (F9).
- I Check for the existence of file 'Test.dat' in folder **UserDefined**. If present open and view in a text editor, e.g. WordPad. How would you check that range checking is working as defined? (Check that range checking has been enabled - **Project/Options/Compiling**).
- I Add `Writeln` statements that output the values of variables `IntegerSubRange`, `CharacterSubRange`, `StudentRecord.Name`, `StudentRecord.Age`, `IntegerArray[1]`.

Record data type

The record data type is a data type in which the constituent parts of the bit pattern representing the record data type may have different meanings, e.g. string, integer, real, etc as shown in the example in *Figure 4.10*.

Key term

Record data type:
A record data type is a data type composed of related data of various data types.
A record data type is divided into named fields.

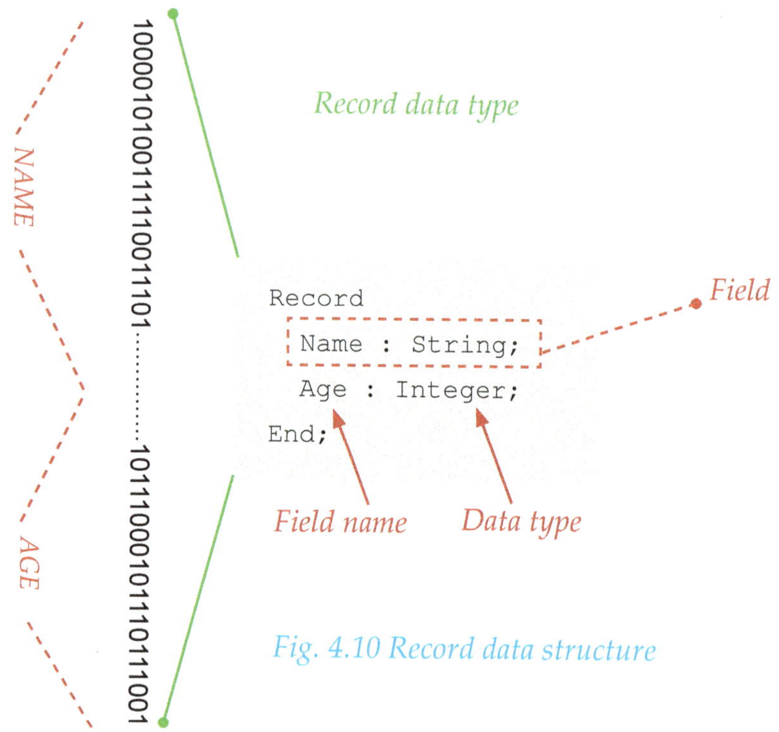

Fig. 4.10 Record data structure

The higher level view is:

A record data type is a data type composed of related data of various data types.

The record data type has **structure** consisting of **named fields** and their **corresponding data types**. We say that a record data type is a **structured data type**.

Task

1. Every value has a data type. The data type of each value recorded in the given record is as follows

   BOND *String*

   KEVIN *String*

   THE OAK TREE *String*

   THE OAK FOREST *String*

   DINGLEY DELL *String*

   TR33 OAK *String*

   NEVER NEVER LAND *String*

   51.410519 *Real*

   -1.715651 *Real*

   6 *Integer*

   TRUE *Boolean*

   D *Character*

   Design a record data type for a variable that will store the given record data.

Array data type

When a number of similar data items are put alongside each other and treated as a unit the result is an **array data structure**. For example, temperature readings recorded over a twelve hour period as shown in *Figure 4.11*.

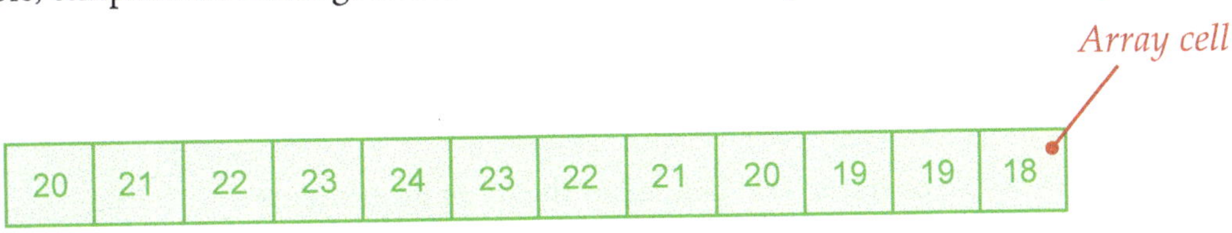

Fig. 4.11 Temperature readings gathered and recorded over a 12 hour period

The individual values shown in *Figure 4.11* are all the same data type **integer**. As a unit the data type is **array of integer**. The unit shown has 12 cells for 12 integer values, one per cell. The data type of the value in each cell is integer. An **array data type** is a (fixed-size if static) **sequential collection of elements** of the **same type**.

In Delphi this data type could be defined as follows

```
TArrayOfTemperature = Array[1..12] Of Integer;
```

`Array[1..12]` means that the array has 12 cells labelled 1, 2, 3, . . ., 9, 10, 11, 12. Cell labelling is important because it is the mechanism by which the value in a particular cell is accessed. The name **array index** is used for a cell label.

The cell data type in the example is integer but cell data types can be any data type supported by the programming language. **The only requirement is that every cell must be of the same data type**.

Chapter 16 covers arrays in depth.

Key term

Array data type:
An array data type is a (fixed-size if static) sequential collection of elements of the same type.

Set data type

A set is a collection of distinct elements defined by an unambiguous property

`S = {Fred, Mary, Ahmed}`

which means the SET OF PEOPLE, `S`, comprising of `Fred`, `Mary` and `Ahmed`.

Fred is a member of or an element of the set `S`.

Two sets are said to be equal if they have the SAME ELEMENTS but not necessarily if the same order,

e.g. `{1, 2, 3, 4}` is equal to `{2,3,1,4}`.
The EMPTY SET is a set with no elements `{}`.

Diagrammatically, `S = {Fred, Mary, Ahmed}` is represented as shown in *Figure 4.12*.

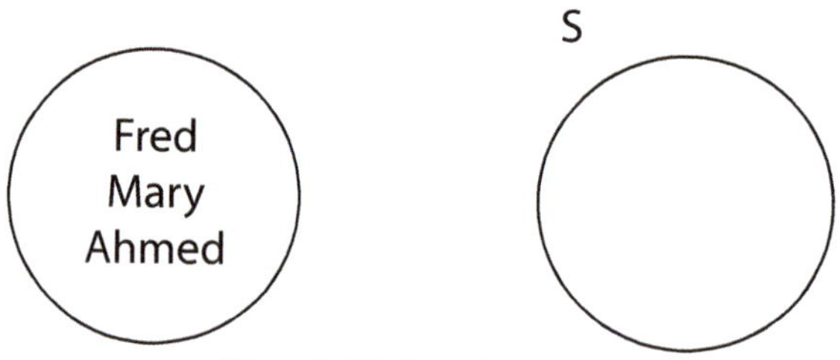

Fig. 4.12 Set diagram

Set Intersection

`L` is the set of all reptiles which are able to survive on land.

`W` is the set of all reptiles which are able to survive in water.

We can define a set of amphibians, `A`, as a set of reptiles which can survive on both land **and** water. The set `A` is shown in *Figure 4.13* as the hatched area.

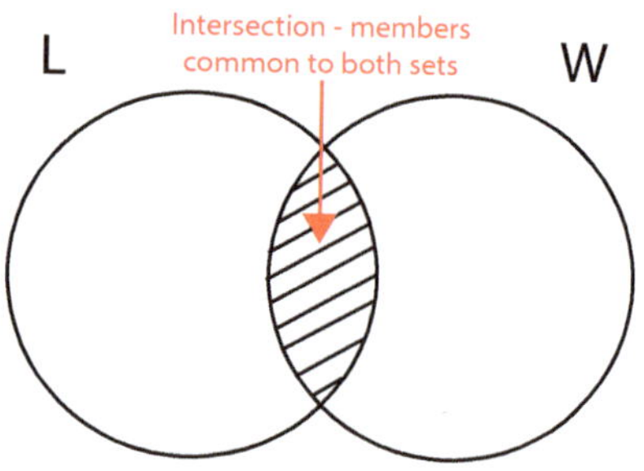

Fig. 4.13 Set intersection

The intersection of two sets (set operator `*`) is defined as the set of all elements that are common to both sets.

e.g. `[1,3,4] * [1,2,4] is [1,4]`

Set Union

Define a set `B` to be the set of all reptiles able to survive on land **or** in water **or** land and water. The set `B` is shown in *Figure 4.14* as the hatched areas.

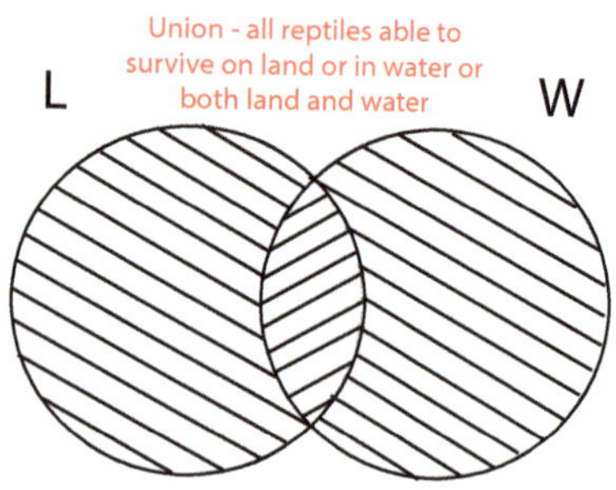

Fig. 4.14 Set union

The union of two sets (set operator `+`) is defined as the set of elements that are contained in either set or both sets

`[1,3,4] + [1,2,4] is [1,2,3,4]`

Set Difference

The difference of set `L` and set `W` (set operator `-`) is defined as the set of elements that are in set L but not in set W.

e.g. `[1,3,4] - [1,2,4] is [3]`

Questions

17. A is the set [1,3,5,7], B is the set [2,4,6] and C is the set [1,2,3]. Evaluate the following:
    (a) A + (B - C)
    (b) A + (B * C)
    (c) A + B + C
    (d) (C + (A - C)
    (e) C – (A – B)

Set Membership

Tests if a value is an element of a given set.

e.g. if variable x is associated with an integer value then the following statement can be used to test whether or not this value is a member of the given set [1, 2, 3]

```
If x In [1,3,4]
  Then Writeln('x In [1,3,4]')
  Else Writeln('x not in [1,3,4]');
```

x In [1,3,4] evaluates to True when the value of x is included in the list of elements, [1,3,4] otherwise it evaluates to False.

Some examples of the uses of set membership

If you want to test for both upper case and lower case at the same time or to test that a value is one of a list of values the set membership operator In is the preferred method.

For example,

```
Readln(Ch);
If Ch In ['E', 'e']
  Then Writeln('You have typed an E or an e');

If Ch In ['A'..'Z']
  Then Writeln('Character is an upper  case character');

If Ch In ['A', 'a', 'J', 'j']
  Then Writeln('Character was an A, a, J or j');

Readln(Number);
If Number In [0..9]
  Then Writeln('Number is a digit');
```

Set membership testing is also useful in loop control.

For example,

```
Repeat
  Readln(Ch);
Until Ch In ['N', 'n'];
```

Guarding the Case statement:

```
If Ch In ['A'..'I']
  Then
    Case Ch of
      'A', 'B', 'C' : Writeln('A, B  or C') ;
      'D'..'F' : Writeln('D, E  or F');
      'G', 'H', 'I' : Writeln('G, H  or I');
    End;
```

Sets in Pascal

The language keywords `Set Of` are used to declare a set of something as shown in *Table 4.22*.

Sets are limited to 256 values because they must fit into a byte. Negative integers are ruled out because their coding does not allow them to fit into a byte. Therefore, if the base type is integer then values must be greater than or equal to zero.

Prior to Delphi 2009, a character was one byte, so holding characters in a set wasn't a problem. However, since Delphi 2009 **Char** has been an alias for **WideChar**, a 16 bit value which cannot be held in a set. This issue causes the compiler warning:

```
Program OnSets;
{$APPTYPE CONSOLE}
Type
  MyFirstSetType = Set Of Char;
Var
   x : MyFirstSetType;
Begin
  x := ['A', 'B', 'C'];
  If 'B' In x
    Then Writeln('B in set')
    Else Writeln('B not in set');
  x := []; // Empty set assigned to x
  //...
  Readln;
End.
```

P

Table 4.22 Console program showing set declaration in Pascal

> "DCC Warning] ... WideChar reduced to byte char in set expressions. Consider using CharInSet function in SysUtils unit."

The simplest solution to the compiler warning is to ignore it. Alternatively, this compiler warning can be eliminated by using the **CharInSet** function, e.g. :

```
If CharInSet(Ch, ['A'..'Z', 'a'..'z'])
  Then Writeln('Valid character')
  Else Writeln('Invalid character');
```

CharInSet returns a Boolean value, and compiles without the compiler warning.

Enumerated data type

Using an enumerated type makes a program more readable.

Table 4.23 shows an example program **EnumeratedTypeExample** which illustrates this, albeit in a very simplified manner. The enumerated data type `DaysOfTheWeekType` defines enumerated values `Monday`, `Tuesday`, .., `Sunday`.

Internally the compiler replaces each enumerated type value with an integer value. The first enumerated type value to be replaced is assigned the value zero internally, the next, one and so on.

For example, internally `Monday` has the value 0.

An enumerated data type is an ordinal data type, i.e. its values are ordered. Therefore, the functions `Succ` and `Pred` may be applied successfully to an enumerated type. Enumerated type values cannot be written by `Write` or `Writeln` or `Read` by `Readln`.

```
Program EnumeratedTypeExample;                                   P
{$APPTYPE CONSOLE}
Type
  DaysOfWeekType = (Monday, Tuesday, Wednesday, Thursday, Friday, Saturday, Sunday);
Var
  DayOfWeek : DaysOfWeekType;
Begin
  DayOfWeek := Monday;
  If DayOfWeek = Monday
    Then Writeln('Monday');
  DayOfWeek := Succ(DayOfWeek);
  Case DayOfWeek Of
    Monday : Writeln('Monday');
    Tuesday : Writeln('Tuesday');
    Wednesday : Writeln('Wednesday');
    Thursday : Writeln('Thursday');
    Friday : Writeln('Friday');
    Saturday : Writeln('Saturday');
    Sunday : Writeln('Sunday');
  End;
  Readln;
End.
```

Table 4.23 Console program EnumeratedTypeExample

Using sets based on enumerated types

The program shown in *Table 4.24* illustrates how sets can be used with enumerated types.

```
Program Puddings;
{$APPTYPE CONSOLE}
Type
  NicePuddingsType = (Trifle, IceCream, ApplePie, SpottedDick);
  DaysOfTheWeekType = (Monday, Tuesday, Wednesday,
                       Thursday, Friday, Saturday,  Sunday);
  PuddingsSetType = Set Of NicePuddingsType;
Var
  TodaysPudding : NicePuddingsType;
  Today : DaysOfTheWeekType;
  HotPuddings, ColdPuddings, AllPuddings : PuddingsSetType;
Begin
  Today := Friday;
  Case Today Of
    Monday: TodaysPudding := SpottedDick;
    Tuesday: TodaysPudding := IceCream;
    Wednesday: TodaysPudding := ApplePie;
    Thursday: TodaysPudding := IceCream;
    Friday: TodaysPudding := IceCream;
    Saturday: TodaysPudding := ApplePie;
    Sunday: TodaysPudding := Trifle;
  End;
  Case TodaysPudding Of
    SpottedDick: Writeln('Spotted Dick');
    IceCream: Writeln('Ice Cream');
    ApplePie: Writeln('Apple Pie');
    Trifle: Writeln('Trifle');
  End;
  AllPuddings := [Trifle..SpottedDick];
  HotPuddings := [ApplePie, SpottedDick];
  ColdPuddings := AllPuddings - HotPuddings; //Set difference
  If [ApplePie]*HotPuddings = [ApplePie]
    Then Writeln('Apple pie is a hot pudding'); // Set intersection
  AllPuddings := [];
  AllPuddings := HotPuddings + ColdPuddings;  // Set union
  If IceCream In AllPuddings
    Then Writeln('Ice cream is a pudding');
  Readln;
End.
```

Table 4.24 Using sets together with enumerated types console program

Enumerated types with explicitly assigned ordinality

Enumerated types are encoded internally with cardinal numbers that start from zero. For example, the enumrated type `TLetter` defined as follows

```
Type
  TLetter = (A, B, C);
```

is encoded internally as follows

```
A = 0, B = 1, C = 3
```

The encoding can be exposed as shown below

```
Var
  Letter : TLetter;
Begin
  Letter := B;
  Writeln(Integer(Letter));
  ...
```

But what if a different internal encoding is required? This can be achieved with user-defined encoding as follows

```
Type
  TMyEnum = (A = 65, B = 66, C = 67, Z = 90);
Var
  MyEnum : TMyEnum;
Begin
  MyEnum := C;
  Writeln(Chr(Integer(MyEnum)));
  MyEnum := Z;
  Writeln(Chr(Integer(MyEnum)));
```

Choosing 65, 66, 67 and 90 means that when the enumerated value is cast to integer and the function `Chr` is applied to it, what appears in the console window is 'A', 'B', 'C', or 'Z', respectively.

Table 4.25 shows a program that demonstrates this. Note that `Succ` returns a value which is the internal value plus 1, not the next value in the enumerated type unless it happens to have the same internal value. However, `Ord(MyEnum)` returns the explicitly assigned ordinality, i.e. if `MyEnum = Z` then `Ord(MyEnum)` returns 90.

```
Program EnumeratedTypeInitialised;
{$APPTYPE CONSOLE}
Type
  TMyEnum = (A = 65, B = 66, C = 67, Z = 90);
Var
  MyEnum : TMyEnum;
Begin
  MyEnum := C;
  Writeln(Chr(Integer(MyEnum)));
  Writeln(Chr(Integer(Succ(MyEnum))));
  MyEnum := Z;
  Writeln(Chr(Integer(MyEnum)));
  Readln;
End.
```

P

Table 4.25 Console program showing enumerated type with user-defined internal values

Programming task

1. Modfy the Delphi program shown in *Table 4.25* so that it demonstrates the use of `Ord` by writing the ordinal value of `A`, `C` and `Z`, respectively from `TMyEnum`.

5 Arithmetic operations

Arithmetic operations

Purpose: To learn how to use arithmetic operators

Addition/Subtraction/Multiplication

Arithmetic expressions

5 + 2

is an example of an arithmetic expression.

This expression has two operands and one operator as shown in *Figure 5.1*.

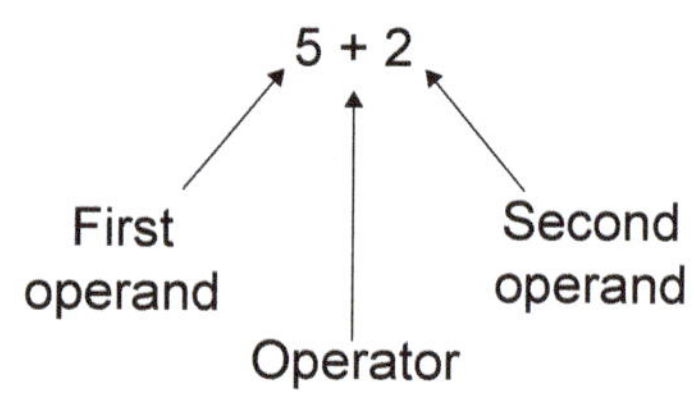

Fig. 5.1 Arithmetic expression

Table 5.1 shows the arithmetic operators for the arithmetic operations addition, subtraction, multiplication and real division in Delphi.

Care needs to be taken with division because two kinds of division exist:

- Real number or float division
- Integer/Remainder division

Operator	Operation	Example
+	Addition	3 + 5 is 8 3.0 + 2.0 is 5.0
-	Subtraction	6 – 3 is 3 6.0 – 3.0 is 3.0
*	Multiplication	3 * 2 is 6 3.0 * 2.0 is 6.0
/	Real division	5.0 / 2.0 is 2.5
Div	Integer division	5 Div 2 is 2
Mod	Integer remainder	5 Mod 2 is 1

Table 5.1 Arithmetic operators and operations

Questions

1. Express the following mathematical formulae in programming language form using the arithmetic operators from *Table 5.1*.

(a) $b^2 - 4ac$ (b) $\frac{1}{1 + x^2}$ (c) $\frac{1}{u} + \frac{1}{v}$

Real/floating point division

In real or floating point division, the quotient is a number with a fractional part, e.g. if 3 is divided by 2 the quotient is 1.5 in real/float division

3 / 2 = 1.5 (Floating point quotient)

whereas in integer division the quotient is integer, e.g.

3 / 2 = 1 (Integer quotient)

Programming languages differ in how they support the operations of real/float division and integer division. *Table 5.2* shows examples of both real/float and integer division in Delphi.

Example	Output
`Writeln('Integer Quotient: ', 3 Div 2);`	`Integer Quotient: 1`
`Writeln('Real Quotient: ', 3/2);`	`Real Quotient: 1.5`
`Writeln('Real Quotient: ', 3.0/2);`	`Real Quotient: 1.5`

Table 5.2 Real/float division and integer division in Delphi

Programming task

1 *Table 5.3* shows two simultaneous linear equations in two variables x and y.

a.x + b.y = c
m.x + n.y = d

Table 5.3

The coefficients are a, b, m, n. For example, if the two equations are

$$5x + 4y = 22 \text{ and } 3x + 8y = 30$$

then a = 5, b = 4, c = 22, m = 3, n = 8 and d = 30.

To solve for x and y we can use the following

$$x = \frac{(b*d - n*c)}{(m*b - a*n)} \qquad y = \frac{(a*d - m*c)}{(a*b - m*b)}$$

Write a program to solve for x and y given the coefficients a, b, m, n of two simultaneous linear equations.

Test your program with a = 5, b = 4, c = 22, m = 3, n = 8 and d = 30.

Integer division

The operation of integer division computes the integral part of the result of dividing the first operand by the second. The integral part is the whole number of times the second operand (the divisor) goes into the first operand (the dividend).

Figure 5.2 shows a length of rope of integer length *L* round a capstan of integer circumference *C*. The number of times that the rope can be wound on the circumference of the capstan is *L* DIV *C* where DIV is the **integer division operator** applied to an integer dividend and an integer divisor. The short length of rope left over is called the **remainder** because it is not long enough to fit the circumference. The remainder is given by *L* MOD *C* and is integral (a whole number).

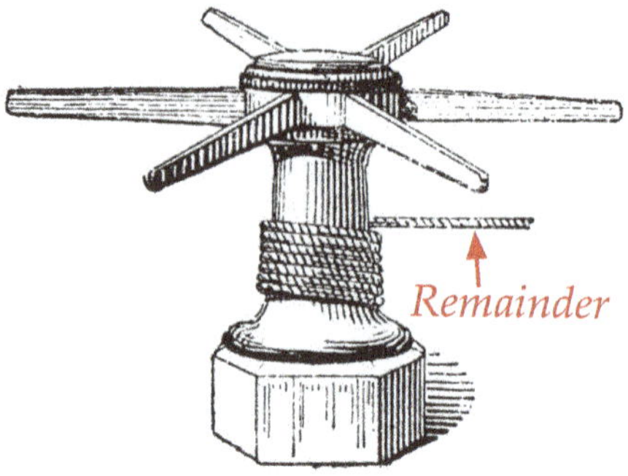

Fig. 5.2 Rope wound round a capstan

Table 5.4 shows the integer division and integer remainder operators being used in Delphi.

Example	Output
`Writeln('Integer quotient: ', 5 Div 2);`	`Integer quotient: 2`
`Writeln('Integer remainder: ', 5 Mod 2);`	`Integer remainder: 1`

Table 5.4 Integer division in Delphi

Questions

2 (a) How many times can a cotton thread of length 1655 cm be wound around a cotton reel of circumference 13 cm?

(b) How much cotton thread is left over?

3 Convert 4589 minutes into hours and minutes.

4 Explain how DIV and MOD can be used to obtain the number of hundreds, tens and units of a 3-digit integer, N.

5 Dividing an integer x by an integer y using integer division, we obtain quotient q and the remainder r.
The relationship between x, y, q and r is expressed in the following formula $x = y * q + r$
e.g. dividend x = 5, divisor y = 2, quotient q = 2, remainder r = 1, applying the formula 5 = 2 * 2 + 1.
Complete *Table 5.5*.

Dividend x	Divisor y	Quotient q	Remainder r
5	2	2	1
6	3	2	0
25	4	6	1
36	6		
121	7		
23	3		
1	3		
5	10		

Table 5.5

Programming task

2 Write a program to determine if a given year is a leap year.
A leap year is a year which is exactly divisible by 4 and not a century year unless the century year is exactly divisible by 400.

3 Write a program to produce a display of the time of day in the form

hours : mins : secs

given the time in seconds that have elapsed since 12:00 midnight (Hint: use DIV and MOD).

4 Write a program to display the number of hundreds, tens and units of a 3-digit integer number, N.

5 Write a program to display the digits, one per line, of an integer, N.

Programming task

6 Write a program to work out the day of the week on which a given date falls using the formula shown below

DayCode = ((13 * Month – 1) DIV 5 + Decade DIV 4 + Century DIV 4 + Decade + Day – 2 * Century) Mod 7

This calculates the day of the week on which any date after 1 January 1583 will fall or has fallen.

In this formula, the year is considered as consisting of two parts neither of which have their usual meaning:

- a century represented by the first two digits of its integer representation, e.g. 20 in 2010, and
- a decade represented by the last two digits, e.g. 10 in 2010.

The date for which the corresponding day of the week is required must be coded in the following way:

- The day of the month an integer between 1 and 31 inclusive
- The year is an integer, e.g. 1996 represents the year 1996.
- The month must be coded as an integer as follows:
  - March is coded 1, April as 2 and so on until December, which is coded as 10
  - January and February are coded as 11 and 12 respectively of the **previous year**. So, for example, 15 February 1996 would be represented as day 15, month 12 of year 1995.

The result of applying this formula is an integer in the range 0 – 6 inclusive.
The integer 0 represents Sunday, 1 represents Monday and so on.
Your program should use the days of the week in its output, i.e. Sunday, Monday, etc.

Questions

6 The following pseudo-code calculates the quotient q and remainder r when an integer x is divided by an integer y using integer division

```
r ← x
q ← 0
While r >= y
   r ← r - y
   q ← q + 1
EndWhile
```

Complete Table 5.6 by tracing this pseudo-code by hand.

Iteration	x	y	r	q	r > = y
0	7	2	7	0	True

Table 5.6 Trace table

Exponentiation

Exponentiation is the operation of raising one quantity to the power of another,

e.g. $6^7 = 6 \times 6 \times 6 \times 6 \times 6 \times 6 \times 6 = 279936$.

Delphi provides library support for the exponentiation operation as follows:

```
System.Math.Power(Quantity, PowerValue)
```

Table 5.7 shows exponentiation in use in Delphi.

Example	Output

`Program Exponentiation;`
`Uses`
`  System.Math;`
`Begin`
`  Writeln('6 raised to the power of 7: ', Power(6, 7): 8:1);`
`  Readln;`
`End.`
	`6 raised to the power of 7: 279936.0`

Table 5.7 Exponentiation

Operator precedence

In the absence of any rule regarding the order in which the following expression should be evaluated, it is possible to calculate to obtain either 4 or 5.5:

$$3 + 5 / 2$$

First evaluation order: $3 + 5 \rightarrow 8 / 2 \rightarrow 4$

Second evaluation order: $5 / 2 \rightarrow 2.5 + 3 \rightarrow 5.5$

If the second order of evaluation is used, we say that the division operator '/' has **precedence** over the addition operator '+'. Indeed, this is the **operator precedence** that applies in any Delphi programming language expression involving these two operators.
If we wanted the first order of evaluation to apply then we would have to bracket/parenthesise the expression as follows

$$(3 + 5) / 2$$

The parentheses '(' and ')' alter the order of evaluation to 3 + 5 first and /2 second. Table 5.8 shows the operator precedence rules that Delphi applies to arithmetic expressions.

Operator precedence	Highest
()	Highest (evaluated first)
Exponentiation	↓
*, /, DIV, MOD	↓
+, -	Lowest (evaluated last)

Table 5.8 Operator precedence

Operator precedence means that sub-expressions of the more important operators are evaluated before sub-expressions of the less important ones.

In the situation where an expression contains operators of the same level of importance (same level of precedence), the left associative rule applies, i.e. operators in the same sub-expression and at the same precedence level (such as * and /) are evaluated left to right.

For example, the order of evalauation of the following expression is from left to right

$$5 + 6 * y / 8 - z$$

The term 6 * y is valuated before being divided by 8, e.g. if y = 4 then 6*y → 24, next 24 is divided by 8 → 3.

The expression now becomes 5 + 3 - z. Finally, 5 + 3 is evaluated to give 8 and then z is subtracted.

Applying the three rules (1. Parenthesize, 2. Operator precedence, 3. Left associative rule) to the following example

$$r * s + t / x * y - z * w$$

produces an order of evaluation that is revealed if the original expression is parenthesised as follows

$$((r * s) + ((t / x) * y)) - (z * w)$$

Where sub-expressions contain nested parentheses (brackets within brackets), the innermost parenthesised sub-expression is evaluated first and then the next innermost and so on.

If r = 2, s = 5, t = 8, x = 4, y = 10, z = 6, w = 2 then the original expression evaluates to 18.

Questions

7. Evaluate the following expressions for which a = 4, b = 2, c = 8, d = 4, e = 5:
   (a) a + b * c / d (b) a / b + c (c) a – c / b * e (d) (a + b) * (c – d)
   (e) a * c / b + (b + d) * e / b
   (f) a * ((c + d) / a – (a + b) / b)

Programming tasks

7. The volume of a sphere is $\frac{4\pi}{3} R^3$ where R is the radius of the sphere. Write a program which calculates and displays the volume of a sphere of a given radius R. Your program should use exponentiation.

8. Write a program which sums the following series and displays the result

$$\frac{1}{2^1} + \frac{1}{3^2} + \frac{1}{5^3} + \frac{1}{7^4} + \frac{1}{9^5} + \frac{1}{11^6}$$

9. A mortgage (a loan to purchase a house) is repaid monthly over Y years at an annual rate of interest of R%. The amount borrowed is A. The monthly repayment P is given by the formula

$$P = \frac{A \times \frac{R}{1200} \times \left(1 + \frac{R}{1200}\right)^{12Y}}{\left(1 + \frac{R}{1200}\right)^{12Y} - 1}$$

Write a program to calculate the monthly payment P for a loan A which is repaid over Y years at an annual interest of R%. The program should prompt the user to enter values for A, Y and R.

Rounding

Rounding off

Numbers can be rounded in many ways. Table 5.9 shows rounding in Delphi in which rounding takes place to the closest integer value to the argument (**rounding off**).

When the fractional component is halfway between two integers, one of which is even and the other odd, then the even number is returned in Delphi.

Example	Output
`Writeln('Rounding a real: ', Round(5.667));`	`Rounding a real: 6`
`Writeln('Rounding a real: ', Round(-5.667));`	`Rounding a real: -6`
`Writeln('Rounding a real: ', Round(5.5));`	`Rounding a real: 6`
`Writeln('Rounding a real: ', Round(-5.5));`	`Rounding a real: -6`
`Writeln('Rounding a real: ', Round(5.4));`	`Rounding a real: 5`
`Writeln('Rounding a real: ', Round(-5.4));`	`Rounding a real: -5`
`Writeln('Rounding a real: ', Round(4.5));`	`Rounding a real: 4`
`Writeln('Rounding a real: ', Round(-4.5));`	`Rounding a real: -4`

Table 5.9 Rounding off in Delphi

Rounding up and rounding down

The operation of **rounding up** returns the smallest integral value that is greater than or equal to the specified real or floating-point number. This kind of rounding is sometimes called rounding toward positive infinity.

The operation of **rounding down** returns the largest integer less than or equal to the specified real or floating-point number. This kind of rounding is sometimes called rounding toward negative infinity.

Table 5.10 shows the functions for rounding up and rounding down available in Delphi.

Example	Output
`Writeln('Rounding up a real: ', Ceil(5.667));`	`Rounding up a real: 6`
`Writeln('Rounding down a real: ', Floor(5.667));`	`Rounding down a real: 5`

Table 5.10 Rounding up and rounding down in Delphi

Truncation

When a number with a fractional part is truncated the fractional part is removed, e.g. 5.667 becomes 5.

The operation of truncation returns the integral part of the number. Table 5.11 shows this operation applied to the argument 5.667 in Delphi.

Example	Output
`Writeln('Truncating a real: ', Trunc(5.667));`	`Truncating a real: 5`
`Writeln('Truncating a real: ', Trunc(-5.667));`	`Truncating a real: -5`

Table 5.11 Truncation in Delphi

Questions

8. Explain how to obtain the 3 most significant figures of the number 5.6676593, i.e. 5, 6, 6 by using a combination of truncation, subtraction and multiplication by 10.

9. Explain how to round 5.6676593 to 2 decimal places by using a combination of multiplication and division by 10 and a rounding operation which rounds to the closest integer value to the argument.

6 Pointers and dynamic memory

Pointers

Purpose: To learn to use pointers

Key term

Pointer:
A pointer is just a memory address.

Pointer Type

A pointer is just a memory address.

In Pascal/Delphi, a pointer type would be declared as follows:

```
Type
  MyPointerType = ^Integer;
```

Caret symbol ^ means point to or references

A variable of this type would be declared as follows:

```
Var
  MyPointer : MyPointerType;
```

A variable of this type would be used as shown in *Table 6.1*.

Information

Compiler together with linker create an executable which allocates main memory space for variables, i.e. variables declared here. This is known as static allocation of memory – memory known to be allocated at compile time.

Information

The heap is the area of memory left over after the operating system has been loaded. User programs are loaded into the heap by operating system. Memory manager, part of operating system, manages the allocation and de-allocation of memory on the heap. An executing program requiring more main memory requests the memory manager to grant it this memory. This is known as the dynamic allocation of memory – memory allocated at run time.

```
Program IntroductionToPointers;
{$APPTYPE CONSOLE}
Uses
  System.SysUtils;
Type
  MyPointerType = ^Integer;
Var
  MyPointer : MyPointerType;
Begin
  New(MyPointer); {Claims storage space from the heap(RAM) for an integer}
  {Places address of this storage location in MyPointer}
  MyPointer^ := 6; {Assigns the integer value 6 to this storage location}
  Writeln(MyPointer^); {Displays the stored integer value}
  Dispose(MyPointer); {Frees storage space claimed by New (and sets MyPointer to Nil?)}
  MyPointer := Nil; {Just to be on the safe side in case Dispose failed to do this}
  {Nil is a reserved identifier in Pascal, it represents the null pointer value}
  {A null pointer points nowhere}
  Readln;
End.
```

P

www.educational-computing.co.uk/DelphiBookCode/DelphiCode.html

Table 6.1 Program IntroductionToPointers

The **New** procedure obtains memory sufficient to store a value of the given data type, in this example **Integer**, at run time by making a request to the operating system's memory manager for the required amount of memory. This is known as a **dynamic allocation of memory**. The memory requested is allocated from an area of main memory(RAM) called the **heap**. The heap is also used when the executable **IntroductionToPointers.exe** is loaded into main memory.

Memory space for the memory image of this executable is obtained from the heap. The heap is basically the free main memory left over after the oprating system has been loaded.

The variable **MyPointer** is allocated sufficient memory to store a pointer, i.e. a memory address, when the executable **IntroductionToPointers.exe** is loaded into main memory. This is known as a **static allocation of memory** because it was incorporated into the object file at compile time (via machine code instructions to reserve a block of memory for variables). The link phase puts all the object files together to make the executable.

Figure 6.1 is a schematic main memory map showing the contents of memory after **New(Pointer)** executed and **MyPointer^** assigned integer value 6, variable **MyPointer** containing memory address 14293424.

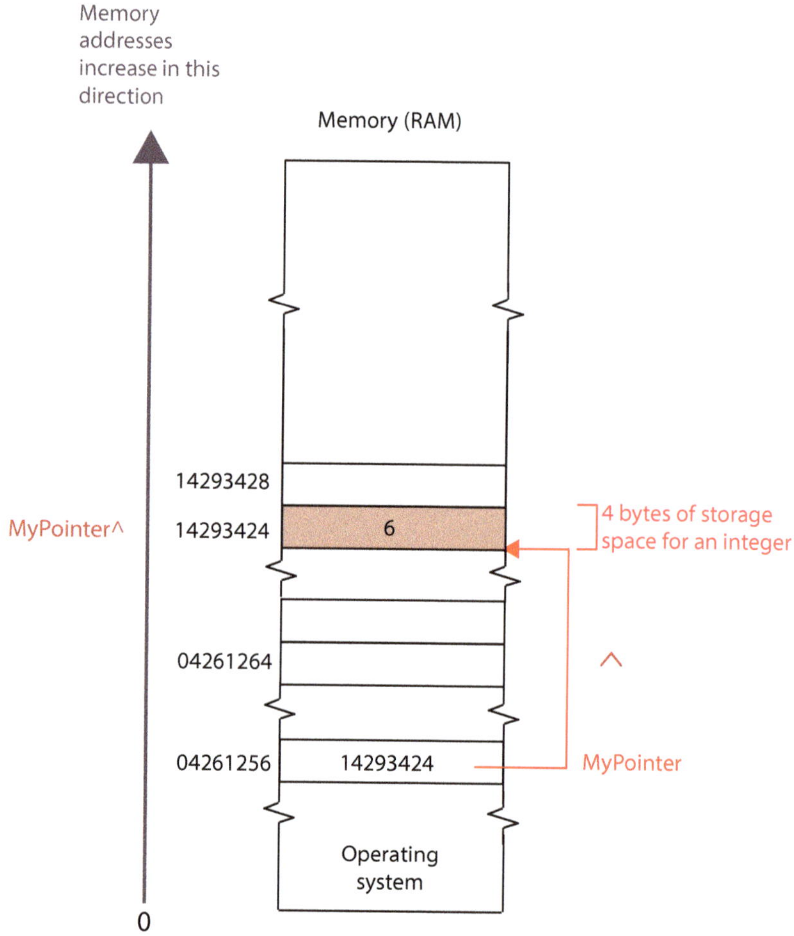

Fig. 6.1 Main memory map showing MyPointer containing memory address 14293424 after New(MyPointer) executed and MyPointer^ assigned integer value 6

MyPointer^ is known as **dereferencing**. The **MyPointer** variable references another memory location after **New(MyPointer)** is called. The operation of dereferencing means to go to the location that **MyPointer** references.

When the dynamically allocated memory is no longer needed it should be disposed of, i.e. handed back to the heap so that it becomes available again. Pascal/Delphi provides a procedure for this purpose called **Dispose**.

In program **IntroductionToPointers**, **Dispose(MyPointer)** de-allocates(frees) the memory allocated on the heap. However, Delphi may not remove the memory reference from **MyPointer** (14293424 in *Figure 6.1*) after completing de-allocation. Attempting now to use this reference will place the program in an error situation with unpredictable consequences. Dereferencing an invalid reference, i.e. one that no longer is associated with a block of allocated memory, should therefore be avoided. It is always a good idea to assign a special pointer value to any pointer variable after a **Dispose** operation. This special value is **Nil**, a reserved identifier which represents the null pointer value. You can always then check that a pointer variable is not **Nil** before dereferencing it.

Untyped pointer type

Delphi provides a predefined **Pointer** type which may point to any memory based variable. It can do this because it is untyped.

Table 6.2 shows the use of this untyped **Pointer** data type.

Variable **UntypedPointer** is assigned the address of a static variable **x** using **Addr(x)**.

Since variable **UntypedPointer** is untyped, it has to be cast to the Integer datatype before its stored value can be written to the console - **Integer(UntypedPointer)**.

Similarly, when dereferenced, the value it references (value stored in **x**) has to be cast to the **Integer** datatype before it can be written to the console - **Integer(UntypedPointer^)**.

It is always better to use a typed pointer, e.g. **MyPointer : ^Integer;**, because this avoids having to rely on casting.

The one place where casting has been used on **MyPointer** is where writing to the console the value it stores, i.e. **Integer(MyPointer)**.

Figure 6.1 shows the output from executing program **UntypedPointers**.

```
Program UntypedPointers;
{$APPTYPE CONSOLE}
Uses
  System.SysUtils;
Var
  UntypedPointer : Pointer;
  MyPointer : ^Integer;
  x : Integer;
Begin
  x := 6;
  Writeln('Variable x has value: ', x);
  UntypedPointer := Addr(x);
  Writeln('UntypedPointer has value: ', Integer(UntypedPointer));
  Writeln('UntypedPointer dereferenced accesses integer value: ', Integer(UntypedPointer^));
  MyPointer := Addr(x);
  Writeln('MyPointer has value when assigned Addr(x): ', Integer(MyPointer));
  Writeln('MyPointer dereferenced accesses integer value: ', MyPointer^);
  New(MyPointer);
  Writeln('MyPointer has value when used in New: ', Integer(MyPointer));
  Dispose(MyPointer);
  Writeln('After applying Dispose, MyPointer has value: ', Integer(MyPointer));
  MyPointer := Nil;
  Writeln('After setting to Nil, MyPointer has value: ', Integer(MyPointer));
  Readln;
End.
```

Table 6.2 Program UntypedPointers

Fig. 6.1 Program UntypedPointers output when executed

Programming tasks

1. Write a program which
   - declares a pointer variable of character pointer type
   - assigns character 'A' to the memory location on the heap referenced by this pointer variable
   - writes the value stored in this memory location to the console
   - writes the address of this memory location to the console.

Trapping an invalid reference

Table 6.3 shows a program which has used **Try Except** to catch when an invalid pointer reference exception occurs. Exception handling is covered in **Chapter 9**. Unfortunately, an invalid pointer reference does not occur with execution of the **Writeln** statement immediately following **Dispose(MyPointer)** when clearly the memory referenced has been de-allocated. It does however occur - *Figure 6.2* - when a randomly chosen memory address is assigned to **MyPointer** suitably cast as of type **TMyPointer**.

```
Program AttemptToDereferenceInvalidPointer;
{$APPTYPE CONSOLE}
{$R *.res}
Uses
  System.SysUtils;
Type
  TMyPointer = ^Integer;
Var
  MyPointer : TMyPointer;
Begin
  Try
    New(MyPointer);
    MyPointer^ := 6;
    Writeln('MyPointer points to integer value: ', MyPointer^);
    Dispose(MyPointer);
    Writeln('After disposal, MyPointer points to integer value: ', MyPointer^);
    MyPointer := TMyPointer(435678);
    Writeln('After assigning a random value, MyPointer points to integer value: ', MyPointer^);
    //MyPointer := Nil;
    //Writeln('After assigning Nil, MyPointer points to integer value: ', MyPointer^);
  Except
    On E: Exception
      Do
        Begin
          Writeln;
          Writeln(E.ClassName, ' - ');
          Writeln(E.Message);
        End;
  End;
  Readln;
End.
```

Information

If built and run with Delphi 7, to see exception when program is in execution, run program outside IDE.

P

Information

The danger of pointers:
If a pointer is corrupted with an incorrect memory address then it is possible to also corrupt the referenced memory.

Table 6.3 Program AttemptToDereferenceInvalidPointer

```
Z:\ProductionChapters\DelphiBook\Code\Chapter6\AttemptToDereferenceInvalidPointer\Win32\D...
MyPointer points to integer value: 6
After disposal, MyPointer points to integer value: 6
After assigning a random value, MyPointer points to integer value:
EAccessViolation -
Access violation at address 0041F633 in module 'AttemptToDereferenceInvalidPoint
er.exe'. Read of address 0006A5DE
```

Fig. 6.2 Output from program AttemptToDereferenceInvalidPointer when executed

Programming tasks

2. Download the source for program **AttemptToDereferenceInvalidPointer** from

   www.educational-computing.co.uk/DelphiBookCode/DelphiCode.html

   Comment out

```
MyPointer := TMyPointer(435678);
Writeln('After assigning a random value, MyPointer points to integer value: ', MyPointer^);
```

   Uncomment

```
\\MyPointer := Nil;
\\Writeln('After assigning Nil, MyPointer points to integer value: ', MyPointer^);
```

   Press F9 to build and run **AttemptToDereferenceInvalidPointer**.

   You should get an "Access violation ......address 0" exception.

   Write an **If** statement that tests for **Nil** before any operation that dereferences **MyPointer** is carried out.

   Add this **If** statement where it is required in **AttemptToDereferenceInvalidPointer**.

   Test the modified **AttemptToDereferenceInvalidPointer** program.

Why are pointers useful?

Pointers are of fixed length, e.g. only 32 or 64 bits whereas the "chunk" of memory that they reference could be much larger, e.g. 64 KB.

A copy of a pointer therefore consumes much less memory than a copy of the "chunk" of memory. They are useful for this reason. For example, when calling a procedure/function with parameters, passing a pointer parameter takes up much less space on the stack - 4 or 8 bytes - than a value that occupies, say, 64 KB.

Questions

1. What is meant by a pointer?
2. Explain using an example how a pointer variable could be used to reference a memory location so that an integer value may be stored in this location.

GetMem and FreeMem

Whilst the **New** procedure should be used to allocate memory for data that you wish to reference by pointer, there is an alternative, **GetMem**, that is useful to consider if you wish to gain an understanding of the difference between a pointer and a reference variable as used in other languages.

```
Procedure GetMem (Var MemoryPointer : Pointer; MemorySize : Integer);
```

The **GetMem** procedure attempts to get the specified number of bytes of memory appropriate for the given data type (`MemorySize`), storing a pointer to the memory allocated in `MemoryPointer`.

```
Procedure FreeMem (MemoryPointer : Pointer {; MemorySize : Integer});
```

The **FreeMem** procedure frees up memory referenced by variable `MemoryPointer`.

`MemorySize` parameter is optional. However, if used the memory size must be that which was originally allocated.

Table 6.4 shows the use of **Get Mem** and **FreeMem** in program **GetMemProject** and *Figure 6.3* shows the output when this program is executed.

Reference variables are the nearest that some other languages come to Delphi pointers. Reference variables also store the address of an area of memory that contains data that may be referenced by the program.

The key difference between pointer variables in Delphi and reference variables in other languages is that arithmetic operations such as **Inc(MyPointer)** are allowed with Delphi pointers whereas this is not allowed with reference variables.

```
Program GetMemProject;
{$APPTYPE CONSOLE}
{$R *.res}
Uses
  System.SysUtils;
Type
  TIntegerPtr = ^Integer;
Var
  MyPointer : ^Integer;
Begin
  Try
    //Allocate storage for three integers
    GetMem(MyPointer, 3 * SizeOf(TIntegerPtr));
    //Fill out these 3 integers with values
    MyPointer^ := 1;
    Inc(MyPointer);
    MyPointer^ := 2;
    Inc(MyPointer);
    MyPointer^ := 3;
    //Now display these values
    Dec(MyPointer, 2);
    Writeln('First integer: ', MyPointer^);
    Inc(MyPointer);
    Writeln('Second integer: ', MyPointer^);
    Inc(MyPointer);
    Writeln('Third integer: ', MyPointer^);
    Dec(MyPointer, 2);
    FreeMem(MyPointer);
    If MyPointer = Nil
      Then Writeln('MyPointer is Nil after FreeMem called')
      Else Writeln('MyPointer is not Nil after FreeMem called');
  Except
    On E: Exception
      Do Writeln(E.ClassName, ': ', E.Message);
  End;
  Readln;
End.
```

Fig. 6.3 Output from program GetMemProject when executed

Table 6.4 Program GetMemProject

Procedure/Function pointers

Procedural types make it possible to treat procedures and functions as values that can be assigned to variables or passed to other procedures and functions, e.g.

```
Type
  TFunctionVar = Function (y : Integer) : Integer;
  TProcedureVar = Procedure (y : Integer);
Var
  FunctionVar : TFunctionVar;
  ProcedureVar : TProcedureVar;
```

Program **ProcedureFunctionVars** - *Table 6.5* - shows how these two variables may be used in conjunction with predefined procedures/functions.

The variables `FunctionVar` and `ProcedureVar` are all procedure pointers - that is, pointers to the address of a procedure or function.

```
Program ProcedureFunctionVars;
{$APPTYPE CONSOLE}
Uses
  SysUtils;
Type
  TFunctionVar = Function (y : Integer) : Integer;
  TProcedureVar = Procedure (y : Integer);
Function Square(x : Integer) : Integer;
  Begin
    Result := x*x;
  End;
Function Cube(x : Integer) : Integer;
  Begin
    Result := x*x*x;
  End;
Procedure WriteSquare(x : Integer);
  Begin
    Writeln('Square of ', x, ' = ', x*x);
  End;
Procedure WriteCube(x : Integer);
  Begin
    Writeln('Cube of ', x, ' = ', x*x*x);
  End;
Var
  FunctionVar : TFunctionVar;
  ProcedureVar : TProcedureVar;
Begin
  FunctionVar := Square;
  Writeln('Square: ', FunctionVar(4));
  FunctionVar := Cube;
  Writeln('Cube: ', FunctionVar(4));
  ProcedureVar := WriteSquare;
  ProcedureVar(4);
  ProcedureVar := WriteCube;
  ProcedureVar(4);
  Readln;
End.
```

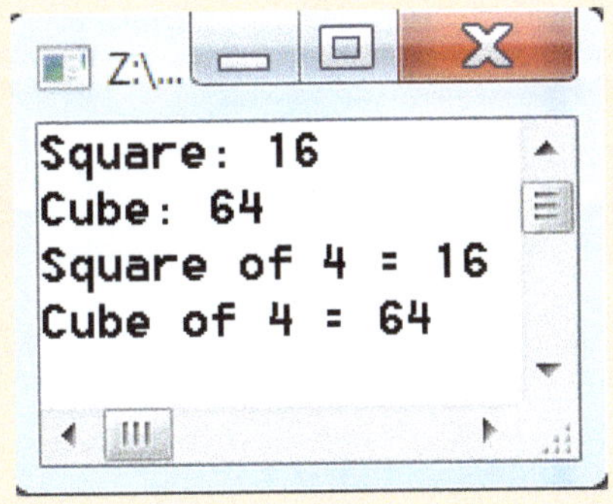

Fig. 6.4 Output from program ProcedureFunctionVars when executed

Table 6.5 Program ProcedureFunctionsVars

Procedure/Function references

An anonymous method is a procedure or function that does not have a name associated with it. An anonymous method treats a block of code as an entity that can be assigned to a variable or used as a parameter to a method.

Anonymous Methods are covered in detail in *Chapter 44* but they are introduced here because they rely upon references to functions and procedures. The syntax for defining such references is as follows

```
Type
  TFunctionOfIntegerRef = Reference To Function(x : Integer) : Integer;
  TProcedureMessageRef = Reference To Procedure(AMessage : String);
Var
  FunctionOfInteger : TFunctionOfIntegerRef;
  ProcedureMessage : TProcedureMessageRef;
```

Program **MethodReference** - *Table 6.6* - shows how variables `FunctionOfInteger` and `ProcedureMessage` are used to reference anonymous methods, i.e. functions and procedures, i.e.

```
Function (y : Integer) : Integer
                         Begin
                           Result := y * y;
                         End;
```

and

```
Procedure (Msg : String)
                     Begin
                       Writeln(Msg);
                     End;
```

```
Program MethodReference;
{$APPTYPE CONSOLE}
Uses
  System.SysUtils;
Type
  TFunctionOfIntegerRef = Reference To Function(x : Integer) : Integer;
  TProcedureMessageRef = Reference To Procedure(AMessage : String);
Var
  FunctionOfInteger : TFunctionOfIntegerRef;
  ProcedureMessage : TProcedureMessageRef;
Begin
  FunctionOfInteger := Function (y : Integer) : Integer
                       Begin
                         Result := y * y;
                       End;
  Writeln(FunctionOfInteger(2));
  Writeln(FunctionOfInteger(4));
  Writeln(FunctionOfInteger(FunctionOfInteger(4)));
  ProcedureMessage := Procedure (Msg : String)
                      Begin
                        Writeln(Msg);
                      End;
  ProcedureMessage('Hello World');
  ProcedureMessage('Have a nice day');
  Readln;
End.
```

Fig. 6.5 Output from program ProcedureFunctionVars when executed

Table 6.6 Program MethodReference

7 Relational operators

Relational operators

Purpose: To learn to apply relational operators

Expressions involving the relational operators shown in *Table 7.1* produce Boolean results.

For example,

2 < 3	True
5 > 6	False

Therefore, such Boolean expressions may be assigned to any Boolean variable, e.g. `FlagIsTrue`.

The following pseudo-code outputs the value True because 2 < 3 evaluates to True :

```
FlagIsTrue ← 2 < 3
Output FlagIsTrue
```

The following pseudo-code outputs the value False because 5 > 6 evaluates to False:

```
FlagIsTrue ← 5 > 6
Output FlagIsTrue
```

Operator	Meaning	Example	Outcome
=	Equal To	6 = 6	True
<	Less Than	4 < 7	True
<=	Less Than Or Equal To	7 <= 3	False
>	Greater Than	34 > 12	True
>=	Greater Than Or Equal To	23 >= 23	True
<>	Not Equal To	6 <> 6	False

Table 7.1 Relational operators in Delphi

Relational operators are more commonly used in selection statements and loops.

For example in pseudo-code,

```
If x >= 6
  Then Output "x is greater than or equal to 6"
  Else Output "x is not greater than or equal to 6"
EndIf

While x < 7
  x ← x + 2
  Output x
EndWhile
```

Create a new console mode application.

Use the IDE to create the Delphi source code program shown in *Table 7.1*.

Save as **RelationalOperatorsProject.dpr** or **RelationalOperatorsProject.dprog**, depending on the version of Delphi, in its own directory/folder named **RelationalOperatorsProject**.

Now compile the program (Ctrl F9).

Run this program (F9).

```
Program RelationalOperatorsProject;                P
{$APPTYPE CONSOLE}

Var
  x : Integer = 7;
Begin
  If x >= 6
    Then Writeln('x is greater than or equal to 6')
    Else Writeln('x is not greater than or equal to 6');
  While x < 7
    Do
      Begin
        x ← x + 2;
        Writeln(x);
      End;
End.
```

Table 7.1 Program MyFormProject

Questions

1. What is the outcome of evaluating each of the following expressions if `x` stores the value 5 and `y` the value 10?
   (a) `x = y` (b) `2*x < y` (c) `2*x <= y` (d) `x > y` (e) `2*x > y` (f) `x <> y`
   (g) `10*x <> 5*y`
2. What value is output by the following pseudo-code if `Flag` is a Boolean variable?

```
Flag ← 6 > 8
Output Flag
```

3. What message is output by the following pseudo-code?

```
If 6 <> 6
  Then Output "Have a nice morning!"
  Else Output "Have a nice evening!"
```

Boolean operations

Purpose: To learn how to apply Boolean operators

Boolean operators

Operators which act on Boolean operands or Boolean values and evaluate or return a Boolean value are called **Boolean operators**.

Boolean operands or values are those that are either True or False.

Delphi supports the Boolean operators NOT, AND, OR and XOR so that a programming statement such as the following involving a Boolean operation can be written

```
If (x > 5) AND (y < 3) Then Writeln('A message');
```

Boolean operators are used to perform the **Boolean operations**

- `x AND y`
- `x OR y`
- `x XOR y`
- `NOT x`

where `x` and `y` are Boolean variables or Boolean expressions.

For example if operand `x` is True and operand `y` is False then

- `x AND y` evaluates to False
- `x OR y` evaluates to True
- `x XOR y` evaluates to True
- `NOT x` evaluates to False

Table 8.1 shows the symbols used for these Boolean operators in Delphi and their meaning.

Operator	Meaning	Example (Pascal)	Outcome
NOT	Evaluates to true, if operand false; Evaluates to false if operand is true	NOT True	False
AND	Evaluates to true if both operands are true otherwise evaluates to false	True AND True	True
OR	Evaluates to true if at least one operand is true otherwise false	True OR False	True
XOR	Evaluates to true if one and only one of the operands is true. Evaluates to false if both operands are true or if both operands are false.	True XOR True	False

Table 8.1 Boolean operators in Delphi

> **Key term**
>
> **Boolean operators:** Operators which act on Boolean operands or Boolean values and evaluate or return a Boolean value are called Boolean operators.
>
> Delphi supports the Boolean operators NOT, AND, OR and XOR.

Operator precedence

Operator precedence refers to the order in which operators are applied to operands in an expression.

The **NOT** operator has the highest precedence, followed by the **AND** operator, then **OR** and **XOR** operators which are at the same level of operator precedence.

Table 8.2 summarises operator precedence.

Operator precedence	Precedence
NOT	Highest (evaluated first)
AND	
OR, XOR	Lowest (evaluated last)

Table 8.2 Operator precedence of Boolean operators

For example, in the following logical expression `NOT x` is evaluated first because **NOT** has a higher precedence than **AND**.

`NOT x AND y`

If Boolean variable `x` stores the value **False**,

`NOT False` evaluates to **True** because `x` is **False**.

Substituting **True** for `NOT x` in the expression

`NOT x AND y`

we obtain `True AND y`

If Boolean variable `y` stores the value **True**, we obtain

`True AND True`

which evaluates to **True**.

If the expression is `NOT (x AND y)`

then `x AND y` is evaluated first

The result of evaluating `x AND y` is **False** if `x` is **False** and `y` is **True**.

We now have `NOT (False)`

which evaluates to **True**.

Now consider the logical expression with Boolean variables, `x`, `y` and `z` shown below

`x AND y OR z`

The operator precedence of **AND** is higher than **OR**.

If `x` and `y` store the value **False** and `z` the value **True** the expression evaluates in the following order

1. `x AND y` evaluates to **False**
2. `False OR z` evaluates to **True**

To change the order of evaluation we need to bracket the term `y OR z` in the expression `x AND y OR z` as follows

`x AND (y OR z)`

If `x` and `y` store the value **False** and `z` the value True the expression evaluates in the following order

1. `y OR z` evaluates to **True**
2. `x AND True` evaluates to **False**

Operators at the same level of precedence evaluate left to right in an expression.

In the following expression, `x` is True, `y` is True and `z` is False

```
x XOR y OR z
```

The expression evaluates in the following order

1. `x XOR y` evaluates to False
2. `False OR False` evaluates to False

If the expression is

```
x OR y XOR z
```

and `x` is True, `y` is True and `z` is False, the expression evaluates in the following order

1. `x OR y` evaluates to True
2. `True XOR False` evaluates to True

Questions

1. What is the outcome of evaluating each of the following expressions if `x` stores the value True and `y` the value False

   (a) `NOT x` (b) `x AND y` (c) `x AND NOT y` (d) `x OR y` (e) `NOT x OR y`

   (f) `x XOR y` (g) `NOT x XOR y`?

2. What is the outcome of evaluating each of the following expressions if `x` stores the value True, `y` the value False and `z` the value False

   (a) `x AND y AND z` (b) `x AND y OR z` (c) `x OR y AND z`

   (d) `(x OR y) AND z` (e) `x AND NOT y AND z` (f) `x AND NOT (y AND z)`

   (g) `x AND NOT(y XOR z)`?

3. Integer variable `s` stores the value 9 and integer variable `t` stores the value 8.

   What is the output of the following pseudo-code?

```
If (s > 3) AND (t < 6)
   Then Output "Have a nice morning!"
   Else Output "Have a nice evening!"
```

Programming tasks

1. Use the IDE to load or create and save the source code program *Table 8.3* as LogicalOne.dpr or LogicalOne.dprog, depending on the version of Delphi, in its own directory/folder named LogicalOne Now compile the program (Ctrl F9). Run this program (F9). Try different values for `x` and `y` that exercises all possible combinations of the two.

2. Use the IDE to load or create and save the source code program *Table 8.4* as LogicalTwo.dpr or LogicalTwo.dprog, depending on the version of Delphi, in its own directory/folder named LogicalTwo Now compile the program (Ctrl F9). Run this program (F9). Try different values for `s`, `t`, `z` and `w` to test different evaluations of the Boolean expressions, `s > t`, `w > z`, `s = t`, `s < t` and `w < z`.

```
Program LogicalOne;
{$APPTYPE CONSOLE}
Var
  x, y : Boolean;
Begin
  x := True;
  y := True;
  Writeln(x And y);
  Writeln(x Or y);
  Writeln(Not x);
  Writeln(x XOR y);
  Readln;
End.
```

P

Table 8.3 Program LogicalOne

```
Program LogicalTwo;
{$APPTYPE CONSOLE}
Var
  s, t, z, w : Integer;
Begin
  s := 6;
  t := 4;
  z := 12;
  w := 5;
  Writeln((s > t) And (w > z));
  Writeln((s = t) Or (w > z));
  Writeln(Not (s < t) And Not(w < z));
  Readln;
End.
```

P

Table 8.4 Program LogicalTwo

Programming Tasks

1. An insurance broker requires the guidance information contained in *Table 8.5* to be implemented in a program.

Age	Engine size	Policy loading
>= 21	>= 2000	Policy loaded by 50%
>= 21	< 2000	No loading
< 21	>= 2000	Policy loaded by 70%
< 21	< 2000	Policy loaded by 50%

Table 8.5 Policy guidance

Write a program which inputs an age and an engine size and then displays the appropriate policy loading message in a console window, e.g. '`Policy loaded by 50%`'.

Bitwise logical operators

The Boolean operators **NOT, AND**, **OR**, and **XOR** take operands of any **Boolean** type and return a value of type **Boolean**. These operators may also be used as bitwise logical operators performing bitwise manipulation on integer operands. For example, if the value stored in `Binary1` is 101001 in binary and the value stored in `Binary2` is 100011 in binary, the statement:

```
Binary3 := Binary1 AND Binary2;
```

assigns the value 100001 to `Binary3`. `Binary1` has denary value 41, `Binary2` has denary value 35, and `Binary3` has denary value 21. However, the significance is not in the denary values but in their binary equivalent. `Binary1` may represent the settings of a bank of switches, `Binary2` is a mask which is used to test if bits 1, 2, 6 of `Binary1` are set, i.e. 1, Binary3 indicates which of these switches are on - *Table 8.6*. In *Table 8.6* the individual bits of `Binary1` and `Binary2` are ANDed with each other column by column using the AND logic truth table shown in *Table 8.7*.

Bit number	6	5	4	3	2	1
Binary1	1	0	1	0	0	1
Switch setting	ON	OFF	ON	OFF	OFF	ON
Binary2 (Mask)	1	0	0	0	1	1
Binary3	1	0	0	0	0	1

Table 8.6 Binary3 :=Binary1 AND Binary2

X	Y	Q
0	0	0
0	1	0
1	0	0
1	1	1

Table 8.7 AND logic truth table

Questions

4. Each switch in a bank of 8 switches can be in one of two states at any one time, either OFF or ON. The state of each switch is sensed and a bit indicating the switch's state is set to 1 if the switch is ON and 0 if OFF. A program is to be written to test if switches 3 and 5 are ON. What 8-bit mask should be used for this purpose in a logical bitwise AND operation. The bits are numbered with the least significant bit labelled 1, the next significant lableed 2, etc.

Tables 8.8, *8.9* and *8.10* show the logic truth tables for the bitwise logical operators OR, NOT and XOR, respectively.

X	Y	Q
0	0	0
0	1	1
1	0	1
1	1	1

Table 8.8 OR logic truth table

X	Q
0	1
1	0

Table 8.9 NOT logic truth table

X	Y	Q
0	0	0
0	1	1
1	0	1
1	1	0

Table 8.10 XOR logic truth table

SHIFT LEFT (SHL) and SHIFT RIGHT (SHR) logical operations

The operations `BitPattern SHL n` and `BitPattern SHR n` shift the bits in `BitPattern` to the left or right by `n` bits, which, if `BitPattern` is a cardinal type (0..4294967295) or subtype of **Cardinal**, is equivalent to multiplying or dividing `BitPattern` by 2^n; the result is of the same type as BitPattern. For example, if `BitPattern` stores the value 1 and n is 3 then 1 SHL 3 = 8; if `BitPattern` stores the value 32 and n is 2 then 32 SHR 2 = 8.

Table 8.11 shows a program which uses the bitwise logical operators AND, SHL and SHR. *Figure 8.1* shows the console output from this program when executed.

```
Program BitwiseLogicalOperations;
{$APPTYPE CONSOLE}
Var
  ABitPattern : Byte;
  i : Byte;
Begin
  Writeln('Shift 00000001 one bit to the left 8 times');
  For i := 1 To 8
    Do Writeln(1 SHL i);
  Writeln;
  Writeln('Shift ABitPattern to the left,');
  Writeln('the first time one bit, the second time two bits,');
  Writeln('and so on starting each time from ABitPattern = $1');
  For i := 1 To 8
    Do
      Begin
        ABitPattern := $1;
        ABitPattern := ABitPattern SHL i;
        Writeln(ABitPattern);
      End;
  Writeln;
  Writeln('Shift 00010000 one bit to the right 4 times');
  For i := 1 To 4
    Do Writeln(16 SHR i);
  Writeln;
  {Setting a bit means to make it 1,
  resetting a bit means to make it 0}
  ABitPattern := $04; //Bit pattern 00000100
  //Test to see if a bit 3 is set
  If ((ABitPattern AND $04) <> 0)
    Then Writeln('Bit 3 is set')
    Else Writeln('Bit 3 is reset');
  Writeln;
  //set bit 2 as 1
  ABitPattern := ABitPattern OR $02;
  If ((ABitPattern AND $02) <> 0)
    Then Writeln('Bit 2 is set')
    Else Writeln('Bit 2 is reset');
  Writeln;
  //set bit 2 as 0
  ABitPattern := ABitPattern AND NOT $02;
  If ((ABitPattern AND $02) <> 0)
    Then Writeln('Bit 2 is set')
    Else Writeln('Bit 2 is reset');
  Readln;
End.
```

Table 8.11 Program which demonstrates the bitwise logical operators AND, SHL and SHR

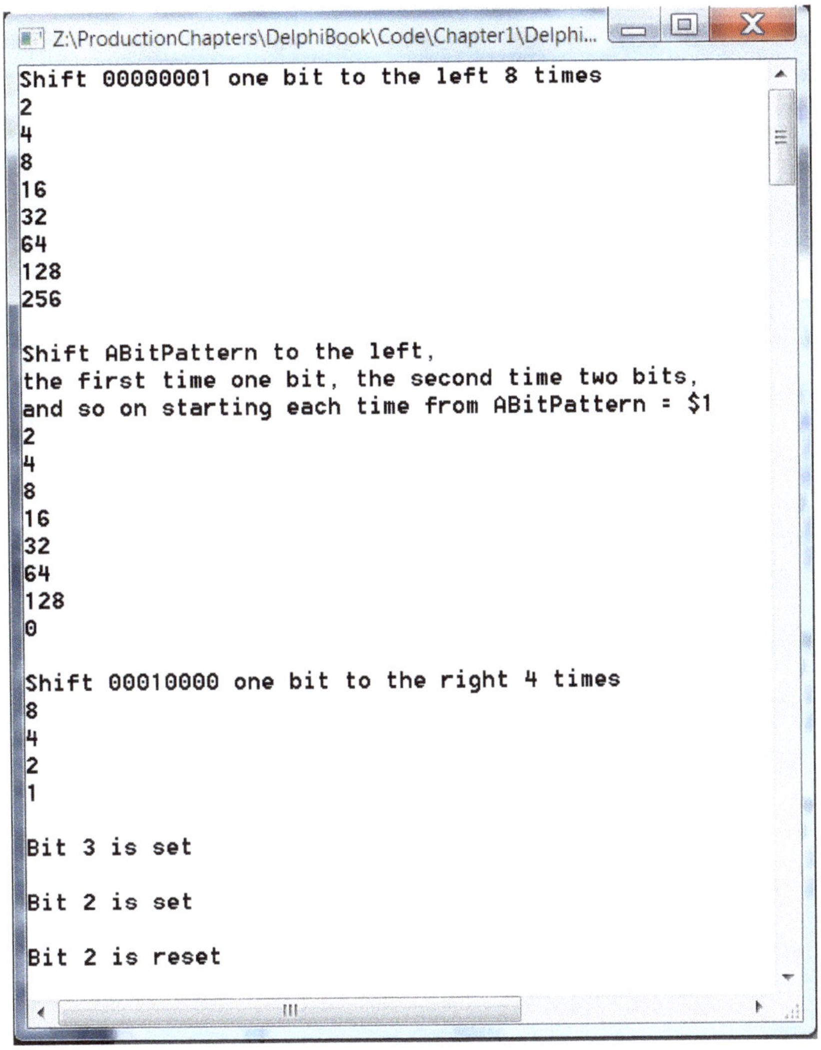

Fig. 8.1 Output from program BitwiseLogicalOperations

Note

To see the effect of the Error Handler/ Exception Handler run the exe version of the program outside the IDE.

Key term

Exception:
An exception is an unexpected (or at least unusual) condition that arises during program execution, and which cannot be easily handled by the program.

Key concept

Exception handling:
The idea of exception handling is to move error-checking code "out-of-line", so that the source code can express the solution to the normal case without its intent being obscured by error-checking code.
When an exception does occur control branches "out-of-line" to a handler.
A handler performs some operation which, if recovery is possible, allows a program to recover from the exception and continue execution.
If recovery is not possible, a handler can print or display an informative error message before the program terminates.

Exception handling

Purpose: To understand the concept of exception handling

The concept of exception handling

What is an exception?

An exception is an unexpected (or at least unusual) condition that arises during program execution, and which cannot be easily handled by the program.

The most common types of exceptions are various kinds of run-time errors such as *arithmetic overflow, division by zero, end-of-file on input, input conversion, subscript* and *subrange* errors.

For example, an input routine may find letters in the input when it is expecting digits.

To anticipate every unexpected condition is unrealistic. Attempts to include code to check for multiple error conditions is itself likely to introduce other errors.
It is also likely to obscure the normal control flow of the program, making the program difficult to read, understand and debug.
The resulting source code would resemble a veritable spaghetti junction of nested *If statements.*

Exception handling

Exception handling mechanisms address these issues by moving error-checking code "out-of-line", de-cluttering the source code which expresses the solution to the normal case.
To this source code must be added an arrangement for control to branch to a handler when an exception occurs.

A handler will perform some operation which, if recovery is possible, allows a program to recover from the exception and continue execution.

If recovery is not possible, a handler can print or display an informative error message before the program terminates.

Using exception handling in Delphi

In Delphi an exception handler is attached to a statement or to a list of statements such as

```
Write('Input value for x: ');
Readln(x);
y := 4 Div x;
Writeln('Value of y before Except ',y);
```

Table 9.1 shows an example in Delphi which catches a division by zero error.

The block of statements between *Try* and *Except* are protected.

If `x <> 0` then no exception occurs and the Except block is ignored.

However, if `x = 0` then an exception occurs when execution of `y := 4 Div x` is attempted.

Control is now transferred to the *Except* block to handle the exception. The `Writeln('Value of y before Except ', y)` statement following `y := 4 Div x` is not executed.

Exceptions are usually objects in the object-oriented sense of the word - a value of some class type.

Most languages allow an exception to have parameters so that the code that raises the exception can pass information to the code that handles it.

In *Table 9.1* when an exception has occurred, an exception object is constructed and passed to the *Except* block.

In the *Except* block, *On E : EDivByZero* checks for a specific class type called *EDivByZero*.

If the class of the exception object matches the class *EDivByZero*, the exception object is assigned to the inline local variable *E*. The exception object has a field called *Message* which contains a pre-defined string, in the case of a divide by zero error it is the string 'Division by zero'.

This field is accessed with *E.Message* in the *Writeln* statement. *Figure 9.1* shows the output when this program is executed with input 0 for x using the *Run Without Debugging* option in Delphi 10.2.

```
Program DivByZeroException;
{$APPTYPE CONSOLE}
Uses
  SysUtils;
Var
  x : Integer;
  y : Integer;
Begin
  Try
    Write('Input value for x: ');
    Readln(x);
    y := 4 Div x;
    Writeln('Value of y before Except ', y);
  Except
    On E : EDivByZero
      Do
        Begin
          Writeln('Error: ', E.Message, '; Will recover by setting y to 1');
          y := 1;
        End;
  End;
  Writeln('Value of y after end of Try Except End ', y);
Readln;
End.
```

```
Try
  // Do something that may raise an exception
Except
  // Handle any exception
End;
```

Table 9.1 Example of Exception handling in Delphi

```
Z:\ProductionChapters\DelphiBook\Code\Chapter9\Win32\Deb...
Input value for x: 0
Error: Division by zero; Will recover by setting y to 1
Value of y after end of Try Except End 1
```

Fig. 9.1 Output from the exception handler when the Delphi program in Table 9.1 is executed with input 0 for x using Run Without Debugging option Delphi 10.2.3.

Figure 9.2 shows the output when this program is executed with input 0 for x using the *Run* option in Delphi 10.2.3. Clicking *Continue* closes the *Debugger Exception Notification* window allowing the exception to be handled in the program with output as shown in Figure 9.1.

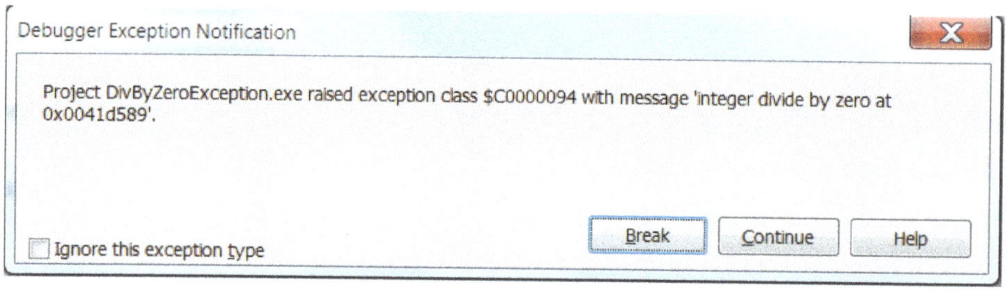

Fig. 9.2 Output from the exception handler when the Delphi program in Table 9.1 is executed with input 0 for x using Run option Delphi 10.2.3.

Delphi 7 has a single *Run* option because it handles the debugger differently. Debugging in the IDE is enabled by ticking the *Integrated debugging* box in the Tools|Debugger Options window - Figure 9.3 - and disabled by unticking this box. With it unticked, the program exception handling is invoked to handle the exception whilst with it ticked, the integrated debugger is invoked first. Make sure that Run handled is selected in the On resume pane otherwise the program will not resume properly on stepping over the integrated debugger exception report. The program must be run within the IDE to be able to use the integrated debugger. Exceptions are handled by the program alone, if they can be, in all versions of Delphi when the executable (exe) form of the program is run outside the IDE.

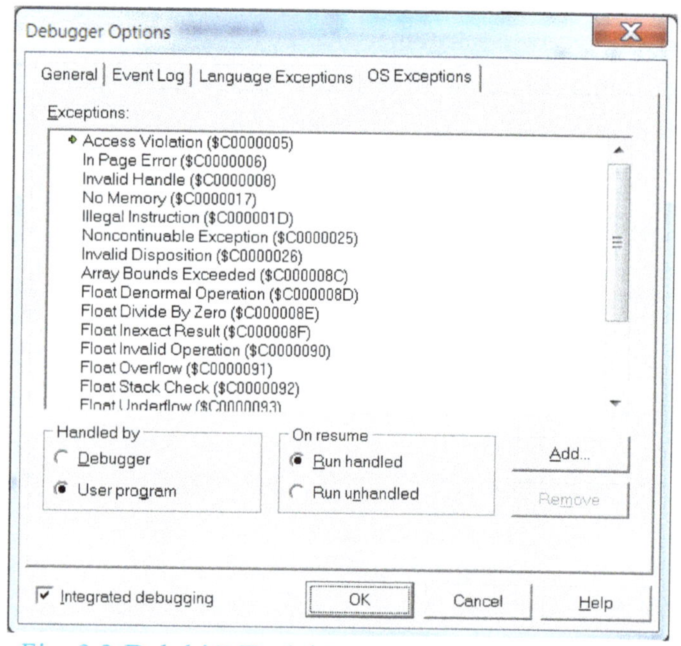

Fig. 9.3 Delphi 7 Tools | Debugger Options window

A program needs to be compiled to an executable containing code which has been inserted specifically for the purpose of handling debugging. To achieve this, the compiler must be configured to insert this additional code. In versions of Delphi from 2007 onwards, selecting Project|Options|Compiling brings up the window shown in Figure 9.4.

The selectable targets are Debug configuration and Release configuration. With Debug configuration selected, ensure that the settings for Code generation and Debugging are the default ones as shown.

Switching to the Release configuration, the configuration should be as shown in Figure 9.5. This configuration turns off settings needed in debugging and turns on optimisation which the compiler employs to try to reduce the footprint (size) and execution speed of the exe. The size of the exe will also be reduced further by eliminating the additional code inserted into the exe needed by the debugger.

Project|Options|Compiling tab is selected in order to configure the corresponding settings for Delphi 7 - Figure 9.6. Later versions of Delphi make it easier to switch between the debug and release versions by selecting which one to use from the Project Manager window - Figure 9.7. To switch from the active configuration to the inactive configuration either double click the inactive configuration - the active configuration is shown emboldened - or right click the inactive configuration to bring up a menu then click the activate option.

A project should be rebuilt everytime its configuration settings are changed.

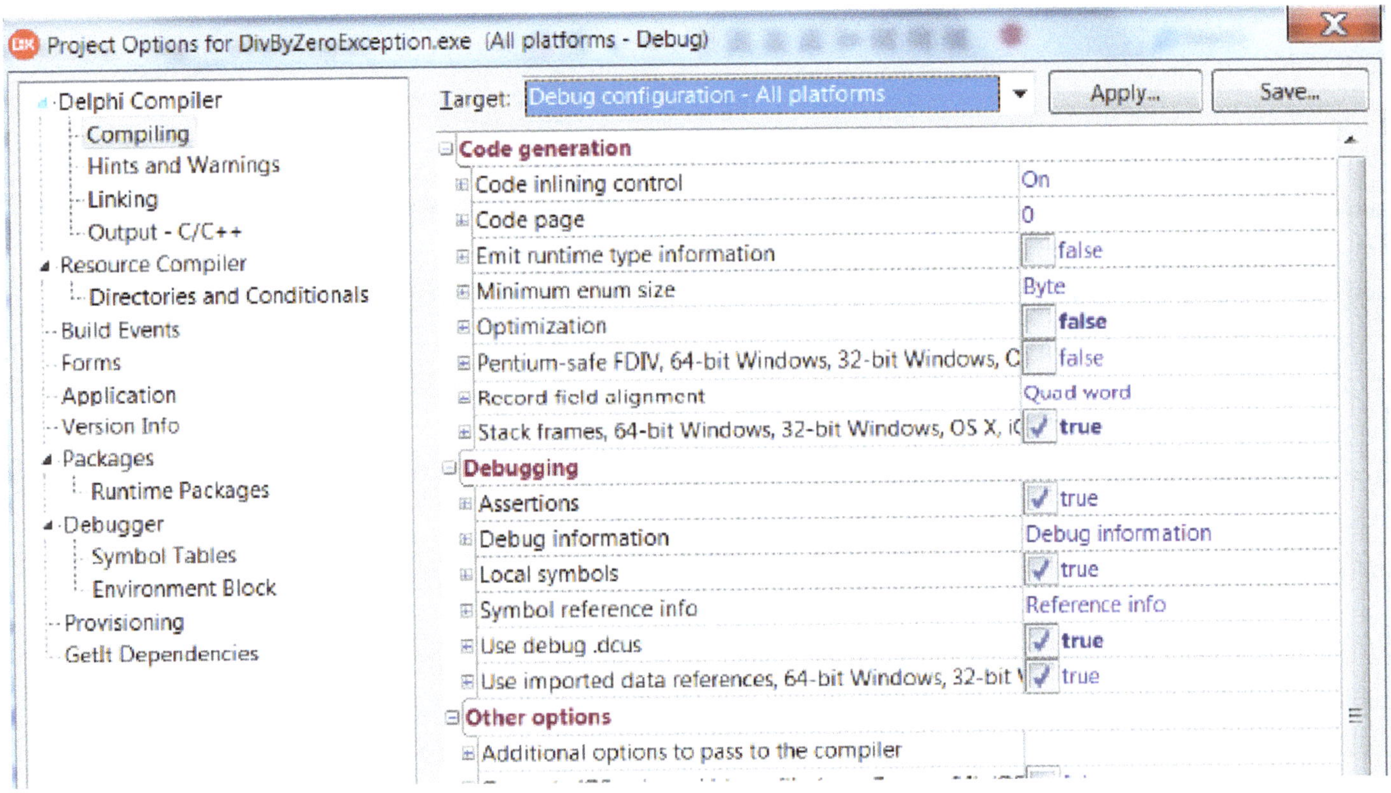

Fig. 9.4 Delphi 10.2.3 Project | Options | Compiling window target - Debug configuration - All platforms

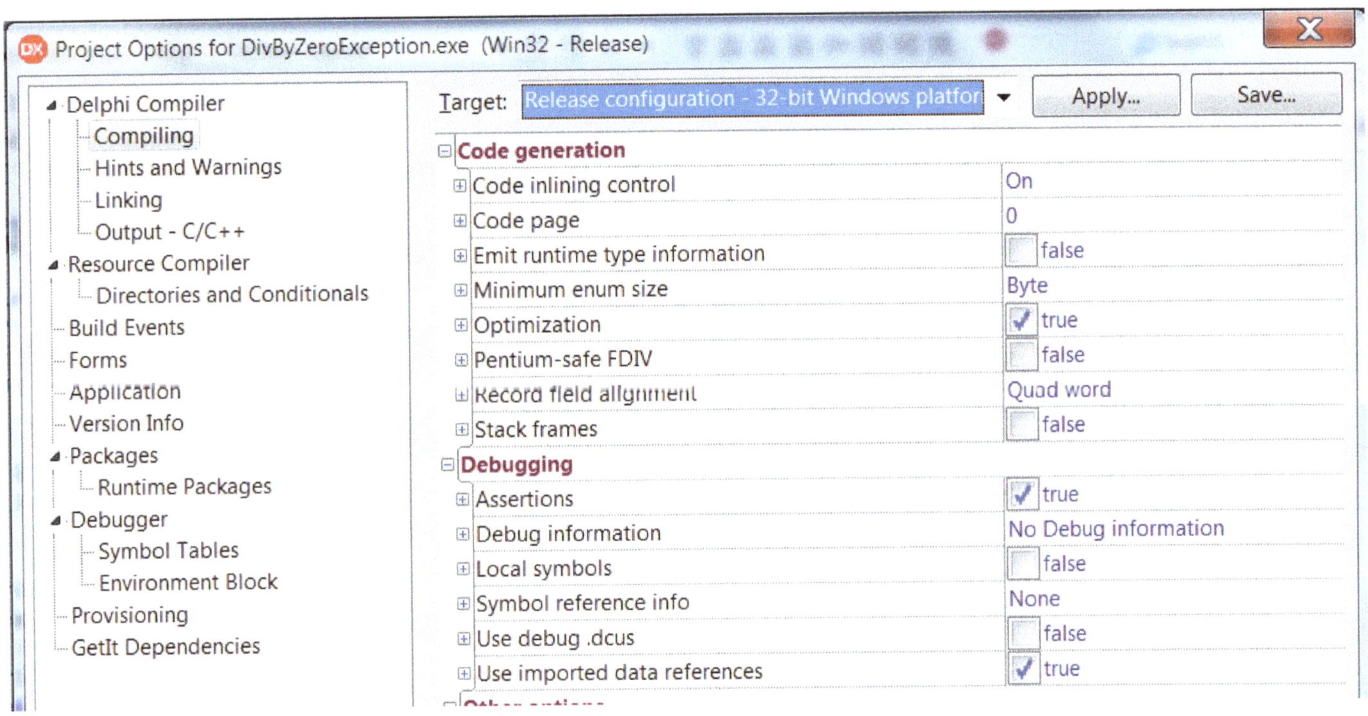

Fig. 9.5 Delphi 10.2.3 Project | Options | Compiling window target - Release configuration - All platforms

What is the difference between Compiling and building?

Compile (Project|Compile) compiles only those files that have changed since the last build as well as any files that depend on them. Compiling does not execute the application but it does produce an executable or exe. Compile creates Delphi compiled units or dcus and then links them with already compiled dcus into an executable or exe.

Build (Project|Build) compiles all of the source code in the current project, regardless of whether any source code has changed. Building is useful when you are unsure which files have changed, or if you have changed project or compiler options. Build creates Delphi compiled units or dcus and then links them into an executable or exe.

Run|Run (F9) compiles any changed source code and, if the compile is successful, links the dcus into an executable which it then executes within the IDE so that it can be debugged. When a program or unit is compiled in debug configuration as described, the integrated debugger allows single-step execution, breakpoints to be set and local variables to be examined and modified.

Run|Run Without Debugging(Shift+Ctrl+F9) compiles any changed source code and, if the compile is successful, links the dcus into an executable which it then executes within the IDE but without debugging support.

All the generated files from a previous build can be deleted with the Clean command, which is available as shown in *Figure 9.7*.

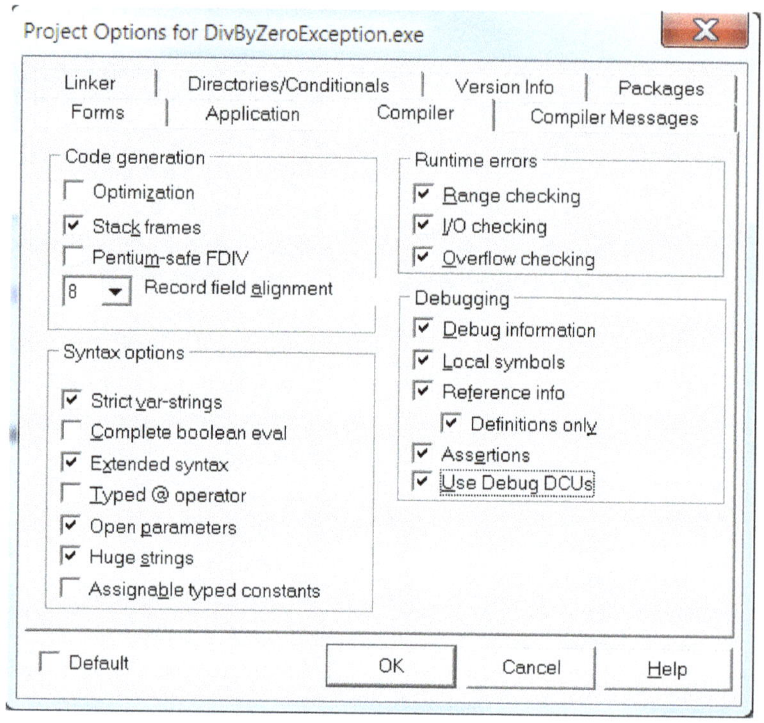

Fig. 9.6 Delphi 7 using Project|Options|Compiler tab to configure the exe for debugging or release

Debug and Release folders

Delphi creates Debug and Release folders in versions that support debug and release versions when it compiles or builds an application. These folders are created within a platform folder, e.g. Win32, also created by Delphi when an application is compiled or built.

Figure 9.9 shows the Win32 folder contents for the DivByZeroException project in Delphi 10.2.3.

The configuration settings are stored in the project's configuration file DivByZeroException.dproj (DivByZeroException.cfg Delphi 7). The source code is stored in DivByZeroException.dpr.

Figure 9.10 shows the folder contents for the DivByZeroException project in Delphi7 built with debugger settings. Figure 9.11 shows the folder contents for the DivByZeroException project in Delphi7 built with release settings. Note that the executable's file size at 42KB is smaller by 1KB than the exe created with debugger settings.

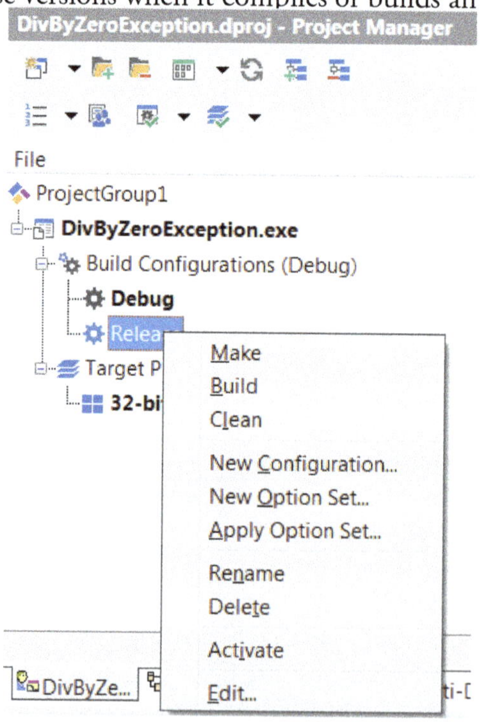

Fig. 9.7 Delphi 10.2.3 using Project|Options|Compiling window to configure the exe for release

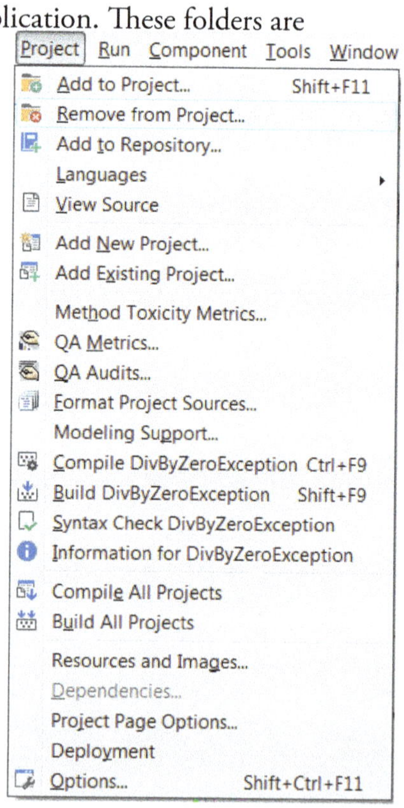

Fig. 9.8 Delphi 10.2.3 Project|Options

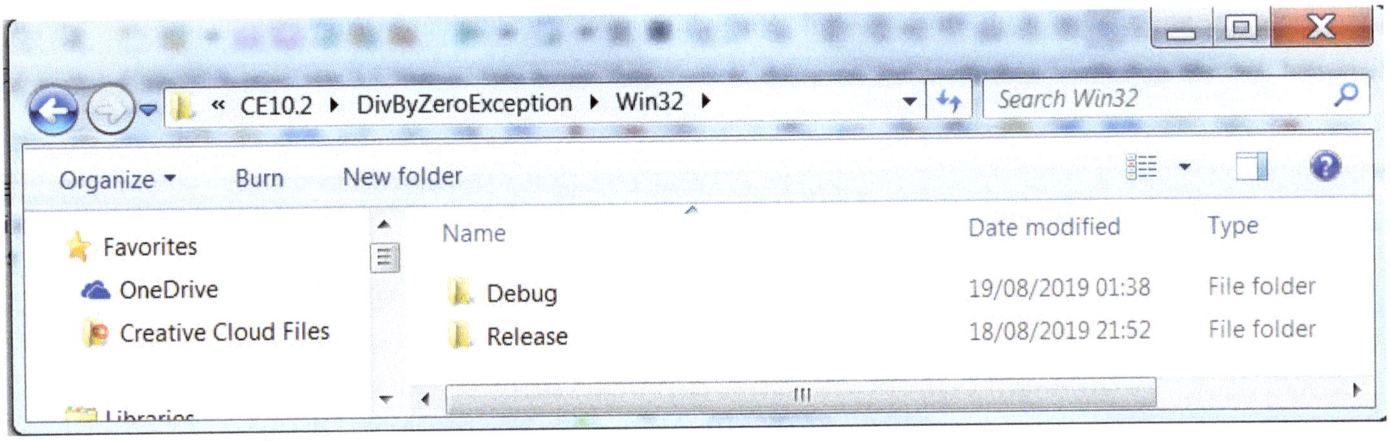

Fig. 9.9 Debug and Release folders created by Delphi 10.2.3 when compiling/building an application with (a) Debug configuration active (b) Release configuration active

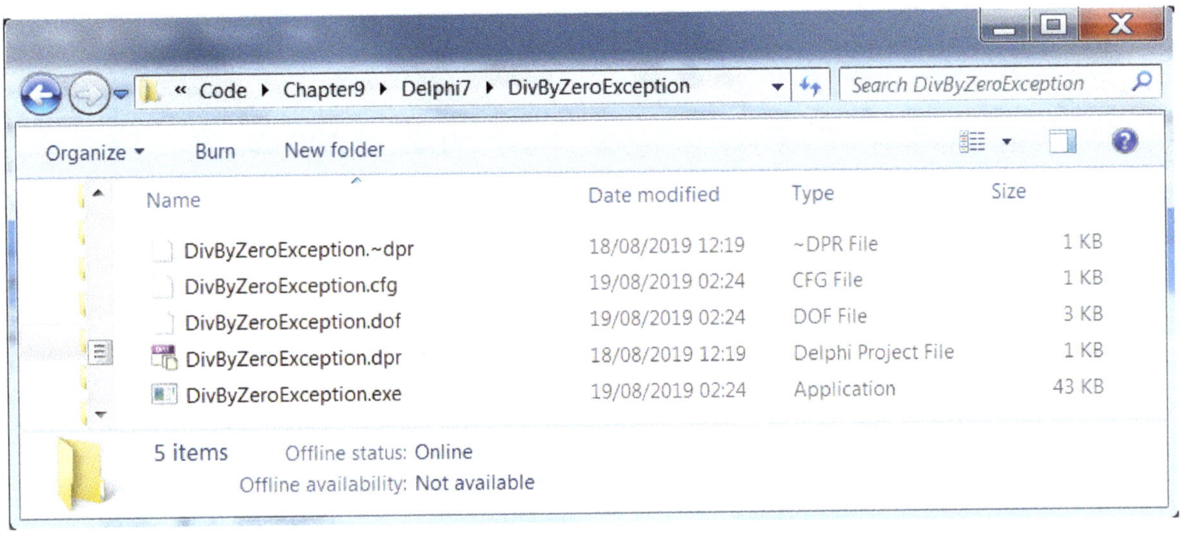

Fig. 9.10 Delphi 7 DivByZeroException project folder for DivByZeroException.exe built with debugger settings.

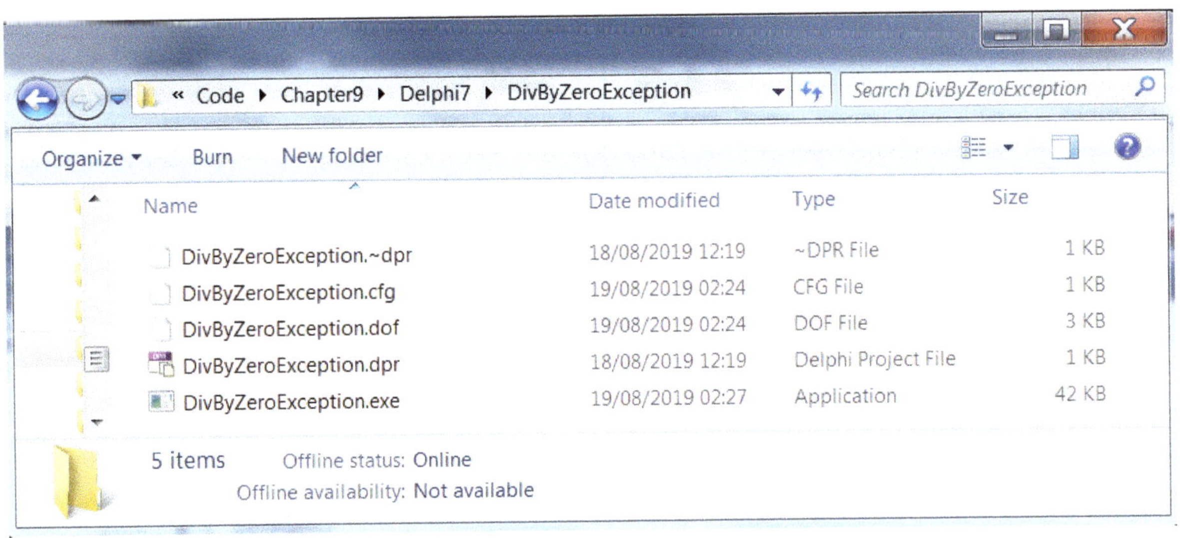

Fig. 9.11 Delphi 7 DivByZeroException project folder for DivByZeroException.exe built with release settings.

Table 9.2 shows a Delphi program with an *Except* block which checks for different specific exception types.

```
Program ExceptionHandling;
{$APPTYPE CONSOLE}
Uses SysUtils;
Var
  x, y : Integer;
  Date : TDate;
  DateStr : String;
Begin
  Try
    Readln(x);
    y := 4 Div x;
    Writeln(y);
    Readln(DateStr);
    Date := StrToDate(DateStr);
  Except
    On E:EDivByZero
      Do Writeln('Error 1 ', E.Message);
    On E: EInOutError
      Do Writeln('Error 2 ', E.Message);
    On EConvertError
      Do
        Begin
          DateStr := '01/01/2001';
          Date := StrToDate(DateStr);
        End;
  End;
  Writeln(y);
  Writeln(DateToStr(Date));
  Readln;
End.
```

```
Try
  // Do something that may raise an exception
Except
  On Identifier1 : ExceptionClass1
    Do Begin {Handle ExceptionClass1 exception}; End;
  On Identifier1 : ExceptionClass2
    Do Begin {Handle ExceptionClass2 exception}; End;
  On Identifier1 : ExceptionClass3
    Do Begin {Handle ExceptionClass3 exception}; End;
End;
```

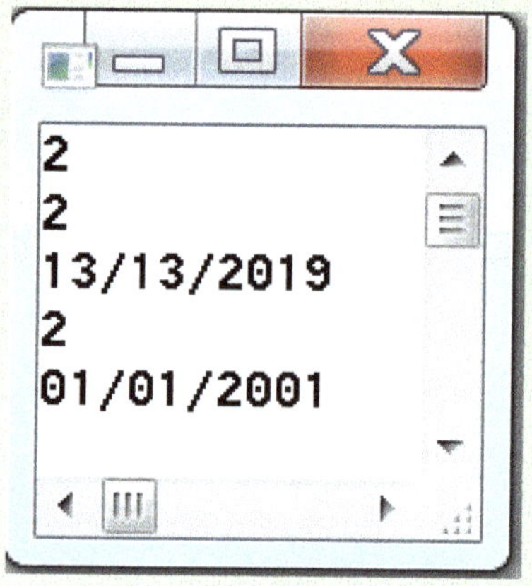

Fig. 9.12 Output from the exception handler when the Delphi program in Table 9.2 is executed and an EConvertError exception occurs on converting a date string to date format

Table 9.2 Example of a Delphi program which checks for different specific exception types

In Delphi 7, to view all exception types load a program into the IDE then select View then Browser from the tool bar.

This will bring up the window shown in *Figure 9.13*.

Select Globals if not already selected then right click mouse with the mouse cursor in the Globals window. Click Properties and check All symbols in the Explorer Options window as shown in *Figure 9.14*.

Click OK and then select Classes again. This time the Exception classes should be revealed as shown in *Figure 9.15*.

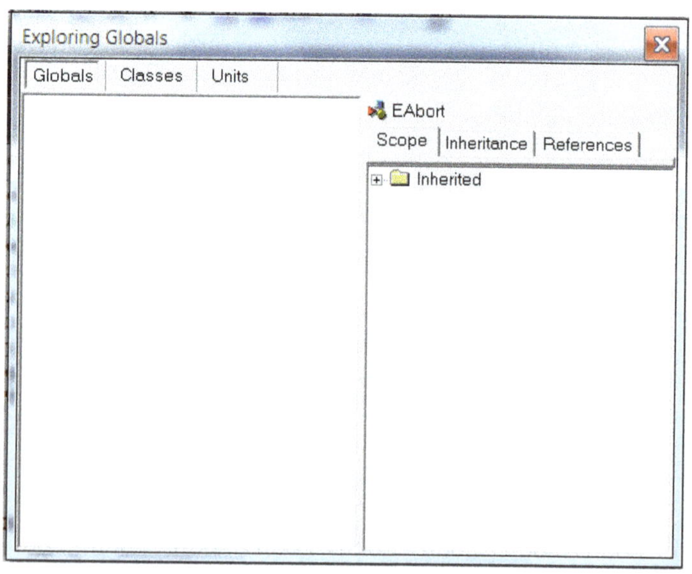

Fig. 9.13 Exploring Globals window

The specific exception classes are derived from the general class Exception.(see *Chapters 19* and *22*).

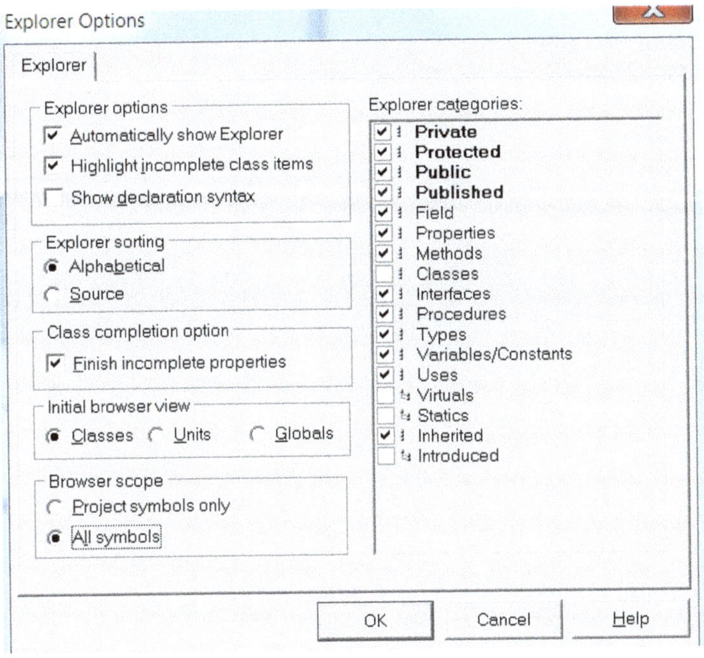

Fig. 9.14 Explorer Options window

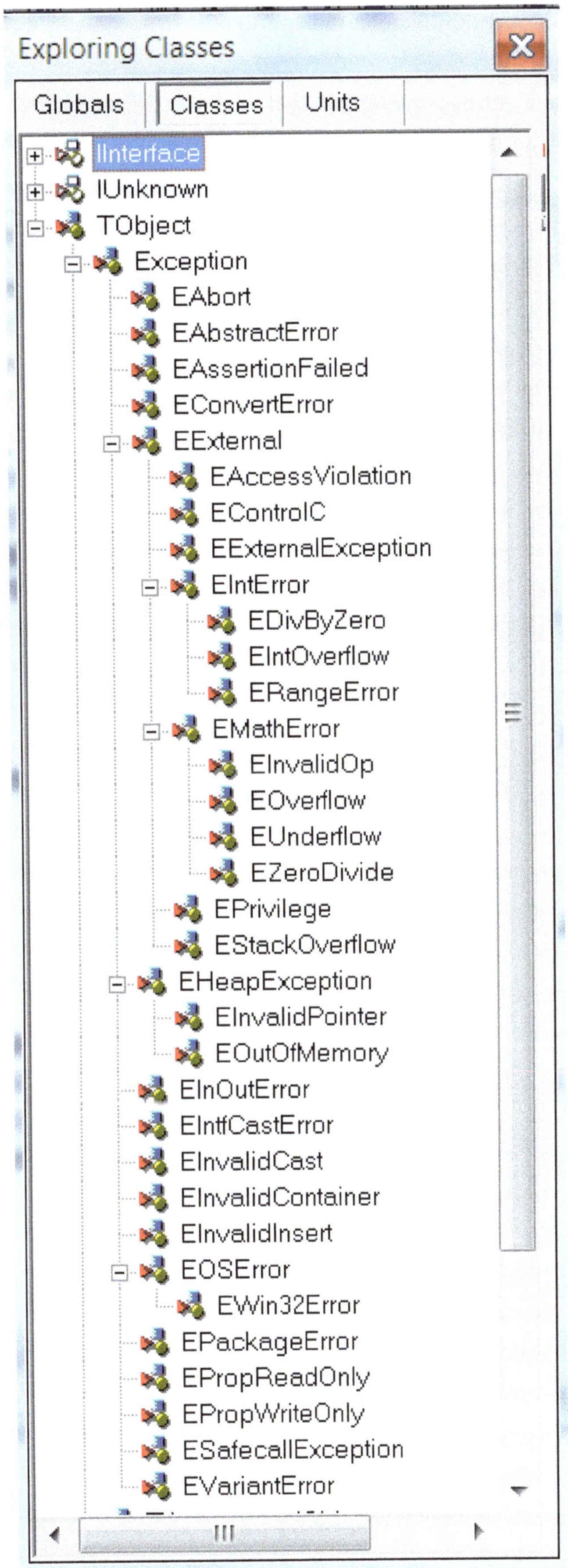

Fig. 9.15 Exception classes

The browser window is not available in later versions of Delphi. However, it is possible to find these classes in the source code for SysUtils - System.SysUtils.pas located in

C:\Program Files (x86)\Embarcadero\Studio\19.0\source\rtl\sys folder in Delphi 10.2. Earlier versions will have a different code number in place of 19.0 and RAD Studio may be used in place of Studio depending on which version you have installed.

If you wish to use Try Except in your programs you must include Uses SysUtils, therefore.

Figure 9.16 shows the exception classes for Delphi 10.2 which have been copied from System.SysUtils.pas.

The most general form of exception handling is shown in *Table 9.3*. This uses class Exception which is the class at the top of the hierarchy of classes. The structure of the error handling is as follows

```
Try
  Something
Except
  On E : Exception
    Do Writeln(E.ClassName, ': ', E.Message);
End;
```

`E` is an object of type `Exception` with methods `ClassName` and `Message`. When program `GeneralExceptionHandling` is run and 0 is entered a runtime exception is triggered which results in the Debugger Exception Notification window shown in *Figure 9.17* appearing (Debugger Options set as described earlier).

An exception handler can specify an identifier before the name of the exception class, e.g. E. This declares the identifier to represent the exception object during execution of the statement that follows On...Do. The scope of the identifier is limited to that statement.

Clicking on Continue sees execution continued from the Except clause resulting in the message EDivByZero: Divsion by zero appearing in the application's console window. Compare this with executing the program shown in Table 9.1 on input 0, the outcome shown in Figure 9.1 provides a more response tailored to the particular exception.

```
Program GeneralExceptionHandling;
{$APPTYPE CONSOLE}
Uses
  System.SysUtils;
Var
  x, y : Integer;
Begin
  Try
    Write('Input value for x: ');
    Readln(x);
    y := 4 Div x;
    Writeln('Value of y before Except ', y);
  Except
    On E : Exception
      Do Writeln(E.ClassName, ': ', E.Message);
  End;
  Readln;
End.
```

Table 9.3 General Exception handling in Delphi 10.2

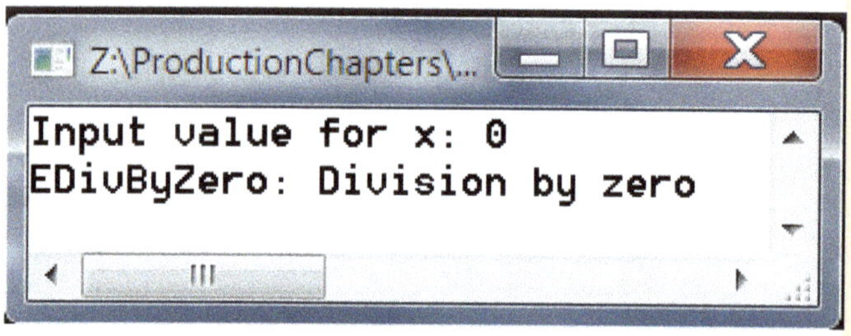

Fig. 9.18 Delphi 10.2 Console window for general exception handling

EHeapException = class(Exception)
EOutOfMemory = class(EHeapException);
EInOutError = class(Exception)
EExternal = class(Exception)
EExternalException = class(EExternal);
EIntError = class(EExternal);
EDivByZero = class(EIntError);
ERangeError = class(EIntError);
EIntOverflow = class(EIntError);
EMathError = class(EExternal);
EInvalidOp = class(EMathError);
EZeroDivide = class(EMathError);
EOverflow = class(EMathError);
EUnderflow = class(EMathError);
EInvalidPointer = class(EHeapException);
EInvalidCast = class(Exception);
EConvertError = class(Exception);
EAccessViolation = class(EExternal);
EPrivilege = class(EExternal);
EStackOverflow = class(EExternal)
EControlC = class(EExternal);
EVariantError = class(Exception);
EPropReadOnly = class(Exception);
EPropWriteOnly = class(Exception);
EAssertionFailed = class(Exception);
EAbstractError = class(Exception);
EIntfCastError = class(Exception);
EInvalidContainer = class(Exception);
EInvalidInsert = class(Exception);
EPackageError = class(Exception);
ECFError = class(Exception);
EOSError = class(Exception)
EArgumentException = class(Exception);
EArgumentOutOfRangeException = class(EArgumentException);
EArgumentNilException = class(EArgumentException);
EPathTooLongException = class(Exception);
ENotSupportedException = class(Exception);
EDirectoryNotFoundException = class(Exception);
EFileNotFoundException = class(Exception);
EPathNotFoundException = class(Exception);
EListError = class(Exception);
EInvalidOpException = class(Exception);
ENoConstructException = class(Exception);
ExceptClass = class of Exception;
EAbort = class(Exception);
EDatabaseError(Exception);
EDBEditError = class(Exception);

Fig. 9.16 Delphi 10.2 exception classes

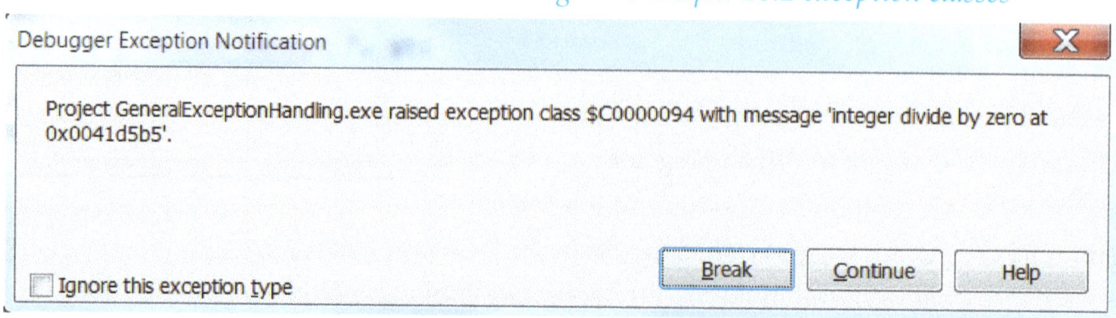

Fig. 9.17 Delphi 10.2 Debugger Exception Notfication when 0 is entered for variable x

General guidance for using exception handling

Exceptions should be trapped as far down the hierarchy class as possible (*Figures 9.15* and *9.16*) and only trap exceptions that are going to be handled, e.g. Division by zero. Exception trapping which is generic should be avoided as demonstrated in program `GeneralExceptionHandling` shown in *Table 9.3*.

If trapping is done higher up the hierarchy only one exception can be trapped even though multiple exceptions may have occurred.

Trap only specific exceptions that might be reasonably expected to occur in the code, e.g. EMathError exceptions if much of the code is doing math.

Creating and handling exceptions are fairly expensive in terms of processing power. Therefore, don't use Try Except to check whether something is valid or not such as shown in *Table 9.4*.

```
Function StringIsAnInteger(StringVar : String) : Boolean;
  Var
    IntegerVar : Integer;
  Begin
    Result := True;
    Try
      IntegerVar := StrToInt(StringVar);
    Except
      Result := False;
    End;
  End;
```

Table 9.4 Misuse of exception handling in Delphi

If `StringVar` is not a string representation of an integer then `StrToInt(StringVar)` will raise an exception which sets `Result` to `False` before exiting the function `StringIsAnInteger`.

In general, exception handling should only be used where preconditions are not fulfilled.
For example, the precondition for `y := 4 Div x;` is `x` must not be equal to `0`.
Checking that a precondition is met and dealing with it in code can be done as follows: code could be added around `y := 4 Div x;` to guard against `x` being `0` such as

```
If x  <> 0
  Then y := 4 Div x
  Else
    Begin
      Writeln('x must be greater than 0, will recover by setting y to 1');
      y := 1;
  End;
```

This example is a little contrived and borderline, the general point being made is that it is better to use exception handling to deal with an invalid precondition because this separates the error handling code from the main logic of your application. Exception handling is less disruptive because it declutters the main flow of execution. However, this example may be too simple. A balance neeeds to be struck. As a general guide, exception handling is appropriate in the following cases:

1. for errors whose chances of occurring are low or difficult to assess, but whose consequences are likely to be catastrophic (such as crashing the application);
2. for error conditions that are complicated or difficult to test for in If Then statements;
3. when the program needs to respond to exceptions raised by the operating system or by routines whose source code you don't control.

Exceptions are commonly used for hardware, memory, I/O, and operating-system errors.

On the other hand conditional statements (If Then) can be a better way to test for errors bearing given that there is a code/data size and runtime performance penalty to exception handlers.

For example, attempting to open a file that might or might not exists could be done as follows with an exception handler

```
Try
  AssignFile(Pipe, FileName);
  Reset(Pipe);      // raises an EInOutError exception if file is not found
Except
  On Exception Do ...
End;
```

But the overhead of exception handling could be avoided instead by using

```
If FileExists(FileName)
  Then    // returns False if file is not found; raises no exception
    Begin
      AssignFile(Pipe, FileName);
      Reset(Pipe);
    End
  Else
    Begin
      Writeln('File does not exist');
      ...
    End;
```

If the exception block specifies an else clause, the else clause handles any exceptions that aren't handled by the block's exception handlers. For example,

```
Try
  ...
Except
  On EZeroDivide
    Do HandleZeroDivide;
  On EOverflow
    Do HandleOverflow;
  On EMathError
    Do HandleMathError;
Else
  HandleAllOthers;
End;
```

Database exceptions generally include an error code. If it is desired to trap only errors with a specific error code whilst allowing others to surface then this can be done as shown in *Table 9.5*.

```
Try
 ...
Except
  On E : EIBError
    Do
      Begin
        If E.ErrorCode = aSpecificDatabaseErrorCode
          Then
            Begin
              // Handle the specific exception
            End
          Else Raise; //Re-raise the exception if its error code doesn't match
End;
```

Table 9.5 Use of Raise on its own in Delphi

Raise

When the reserved word Raise occurs in an exception block without an object reference following it as shown in *Table 9.5*, it re-raises whatever exception is handled by the block, i.e. `EIBError` in the case of the code in *Table 9.5*.

Raise can also be used to raise an exception as shown in *Table 9.6*. However, this example is a misuse of Raise.

Good practice is to use Raise to raise a custom exception not one defined by the system in SysUtils. *Table 9.7* shows a program that defines a custom exception `TStringTooShortException` and then raises it.

```
Program RaiseRangeError;
{$APPTYPE CONSOLE}
Uses
  System.SysUtils;
Var
  x : Integer;
Begin
  Repeat
  Try
    Write('Input an integer between 0 and 9: ');
    Readln(x);
    If Not ((x In [0..9]) Or (x = -1))
      Then Raise ERangeError.CreateFmt('x not in range 0..9, you typed  %d', [x]);
    If x <> -1 Then Writeln('x * 2 = ', x * 2);
  Except
    On E : ERangeError
      Do Writeln(E.ClassName, ': ', E.Message);
  End;
  Until x = -1;
  Readln;
End.
```

P

Table 9.6 Use (misuse) of Raise to raise an exception in Delphi

It is also important to use informative exception messages that state exactly what has happened, e.g. see exception message in the program shown in *Table 9.7*.

It is not necessary to always use an object, identifier `E`, as in `E : ERangeError`. The Except clause could be written as

```
On ERangeError
  Do Writeln('Range error: value ', x, ' is outside required range -1 to 9, please retry');
```

and the `Raise` statement in the Try block as

```
Raise ERangeError.Create('');
```

The error message that appears on the screen now originates in the `Writeln` statement of `On ERangeError`.

(program RaiseRangeError2.dproj)

```
Program CustomException;
{$APPTYPE CONSOLE}
Uses
  System.SysUtils;
Type
  TStringTooShortException = Class(Exception);
Var
  AnotherString, NewString : String;
  NewLength : Integer;

Function ShortenString (Const StringToShorten: String;
                        ShorterLength: Integer): String;
  Begin
    If Length(StringToShorten) > ShorterLength
      Then Result := Copy (StringToShorten,1,ShorterLength)
      Else Raise TStringTooShortException.CreateFmt('String %s is too short already '
                                       + #10#13
                                       + 'it is therefore impossible to '
                                       + 'reduce its length to %d characters.',
                                       [StringToShorten, ShorterLength]);
  End;
Begin
  Repeat
    Try
      Write('Input string to shorten: ');
      Readln(AnotherString);
      Write('Input new length: ');
      Readln(NewLength);
      If NewLength > 0
        Then
          Begin
            NewString := ShortenString(AnotherString, NewLength);
            Writeln('New shortened string: ', NewString);
          End;
    Except
       On E : Exception
         Do Writeln(E.ClassName, ': ', E.Message);
    End;
  Until NewLength = 0;
  Readln;
End.
```

Table 9.7 Use of Raise to raise a custom exception in Delphi

Try Finally End

We have learned that errors can be trapped using Try Except End, if an error occurs in the Try section, control is passed to the Except section. Try Finally End is similar, if an error occurs in the Try section, control is passed to the Finally section. Try Finally is different from Try Except in two respects

1. the Finally clause does not actually handle any exceptions
2. the Finally block will always be executed, even if there is no exception, while the Except block is only executed when there is an exception.

The Finally block is also executed when a function is exited early using Exit inside a Try Finally block.

If a Try Finally is nested inside a Try Except the exception will survive the Finally clause and will be available to the Except clause.

Where should Try Finally be used?

Try Finally End blocks should focus on protecting resource allocations to make sure that in case of an exception the resources are properly released. Resources in this context are memory objects, files, operating system objects and handles. The structure of a typical Try Except End block takes the following forms

```
Try
  Allocate resource/Change resource setting
  Use resource
Finally
  Free resource/Restore resource settings
End;
```

Table 9.8(a) Try Finally example structure

```
Allocate resource/Change resource settings
Try
  Use resource
Finally
  Free resource/Restore resource settings
End;
```

Table 9.8(b) Try Finally example structure

Table 9.9 shows an example of the use of Try Finally of the kind shown in Table 9.8(b). When the event handler procedure `TForm2.btnTryFinallyClick` is called by clicking the button shown in Figure 9.19, it gets two integers via two InputBox function calls, sets the screen cursor to a cross and then performs integer division on the two integers. If `x = 0` then a divide by zero error occurs which Try Finally traps. The Finally clause is always executed whether an error occurs or not so whatever happens the screen cursor is restored to its default value, an arrowhead. Figure 9.19 shows what the result without the protection of the Try Finally End block when an error occurs.

```
Procedure TForm2.btnTryFinallyClick(Sender: TObject);
  Var
    x, y : Integer;
  Begin
    x := StrToInt(InputBox('Get x', 'Please input a value for ', '1'));
    y := StrToInt(InputBox('Get y', 'Please input a value for y', '1'));
    Screen.Cursor := crCross;
    Try
    y := y Div x;
    Finally
      Screen.Cursor := crDefault;
    End;
  End;
End.
```

Table 9.9 Try Finally example

Table 16.11 in Chapter 16 shows an example of the use of Try Finally with the structure shown in Table 9.8(a).

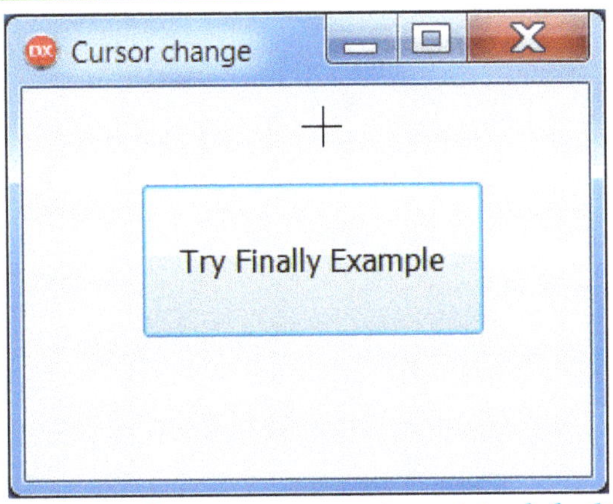

Fig. 9.19 Screen cursor not reset to default setting after divide by zero error

Combining Try Except and Try Finally

It is usual to use *Try Except* in combination with *Try Finally* as shown in *Table 9.10*.

Table 9.11 shows the revised event handler procedure that is called by clicking the button shown in *Figure 9.19*.

```
Try
  Try
    Allocate resource/Change resource setting
    Use resource
  Except
    Handle exceptions
  End
Finally
  Free resource/Restore resource settings
End;
```

Table 9.10(a) Try Finally with nested Try Except structure

```
Try
  Try
    Allocate resource/Change resource setting
    Use resource
  Finally
    Free resource/Restore resource settings
  End
Except
  Handle exceptions
End;
```

Table 9.10(b) Try Except with nested Try Finally structure

```
Procedure TForm2.btnTryFinallyClick(Sender: TObject);
  Var
    x, y : Integer;
  Begin
    x := StrToInt(InputBox('Get x', 'Please input a value for x', '1'));
    y := StrToInt(InputBox('Get y', 'Please input a value for y', '1'));
    Screen.Cursor := crCross;
    Try
      Try
        y := y Div x;
      Except
        On EDivByZero
          Do ShowMessage('You cannot divide by zero without causing an error');
      End;
    Finally
      Screen.Cursor := crDefault;
    End;
  End;
```

P

Table 9.11 Try Finally with nested Try Except

10 String-handling operations

Strings, their character encodings and their operations

Purpose: To understand why different character encoding schemes exist, how they are designed and how strings based on these are composed and manipulated

We introduced the string data type in *Chapter 4* as a sequence of characters.

Long ago, before the Internet and the World Wide Web, the only characters that mattered were unaccented uppercase and lowercase English letters based on a 26 letter alphabet, digits, and a variety of punctuation.

We have learned that computers work with numbers in the form of bit patterns. **Therefore, to store letters and other characters we have to assign each one a number.**

An encoding scheme called **ASCII** does just this. It was invented to encode the limited set of characters mentioned above.

In this scheme, characters are encoded using a number between 32 and 127. For example, in the ASCII character set, space is 32, and the letter 'A' is 65. Device-control characters such as line feed and carriage return were added to this set of characters and allocated numbers in the range 0 to 31.

In all, the entire character set is encoded using numbers in the range 0 to 127. To represent this number range in the language of the machine, binary, requires 7 bits.

At the time, most computers worked with 8 bits not 7. Using the eighth bit made it possible to encode a further 128 characters, represented by codes in the range 128 to 255. Different OEM[1] character sets were dreamed up, which all used the top 128 characters for their own purposes.

Eventually, the OEM free-for-all got codified in the **ANSI standard**.

In the ANSI standard, everybody agreed on what to do for numbers below 128, which was in effect to use ASCII, but there were lots of different ways to handle the characters from 128 to 255, depending on which region of the world the computers were being made for. These different systems were called **code pages**. There are more than 220 DOS[2] and Windows code pages.

However, logogram-based languages such as Chinese have characters that number in the tens of thousands. These characters will never fit an 8-bit encoding scheme. It is impossible, therefore, to represent a string such as 你好世界 in any of the 8-bit ANSI encoding schemes.

1 Original Equipment Manufacturer

2 DOS is short for disk operating system and an acronym for several computer operating systems that are operated by using the command line

Information

Code page identifiers:

Each code page is assigned a numeric code page identifier - https://msdn.microsoft.com/en-us/library/windows/desktop/dd317756(v=vs.85).aspx

Information

Character:

The Unicode Glossary defines a character as:

The smallest component of written language that has semantic value.

Key term

Unicode:
Unicode is a computing industry standard for the consistent encoding, representation, and handling of text expressed in most of the world's writing systems. Unicode provides a unique number for every character: no matter what the platform; no matter what the program; no matter what the language.

Unicode

The answer to this problem is an encoding scheme called **Unicode** (www.unicode.org).

Unicode covers all of the characters in all of the world's writing systems, plus accents and other special marks and symbols, and control codes such as tab and carriage return, and assigns each one a standard number called a **Unicode code point**.

Unicode version 8 defines code points for over 120,000 characters in well over 100 languages and scripts but not Klingon, which was rejected in 2001 by the Unicode Technical Committee.

The Unicode Glossary defines a **character** as:

- The smallest component of written language that has semantic value
- The basic unit of encoding for Unicode character encoding
- The English name for the ideographic written elements of Chinese origin.

UTF-32 is the simplest Unicode encoding form.

Each Unicode code point is represented directly by a single 32-bit code unit. Because of this, UTF-32 has a one-to-one relationship between encoded character and code unit; it is a fixed-width character encoding form.
As for all of the Unicode encoding forms, UTF-32 is restricted to representation of code points in the range $0..10FFFF_{16}$ which is a 21-bit code space.
Whilst UTF-32 provides the simplest mapping, it **uses much more space than is necessary** - 4 bytes for every Unicode code point or character.

Most computer-readable text is in **ASCII**, which requires only 7 bits which can be accommodated in 1 byte. In fact, all the characters in widespread use still number fewer than 65,536, which can be coded in 16 bits or 2 bytes. This gave rise to two other Unicode encoding forms - **UTF-16** and **UTF-8**.

Figure 10.1 shows the three Unicode encoding forms - UTF-32, UTF-16, UTF-8 and how they are related to Unicode code points.

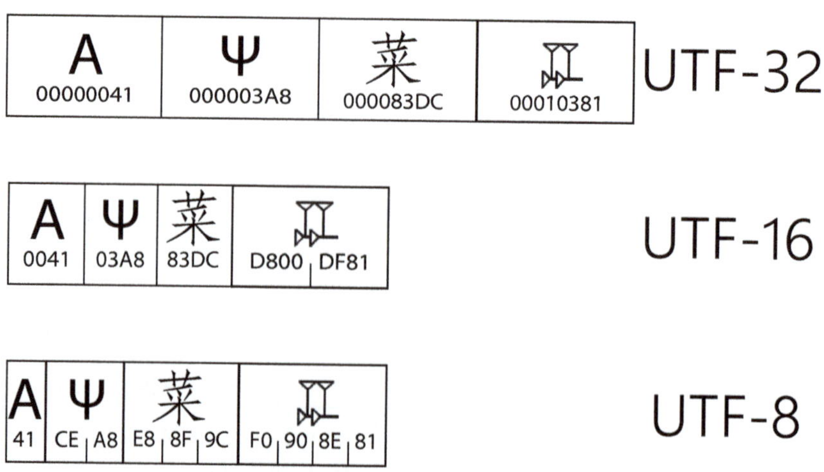

Fig. 10.1 Unicode encoding forms

Information

Unicode code charts:
http://www.unicode.org/charts/

Information

The Unicode Standard Version 8.0 - Core Specification:
http://www.unicode.org/versions/Unicode8.0.0/ch02.pdf

Information

Characters and glyphs:
Characters are represented by code points that reside only in a memory representation as strings in memory, on disk, or in data transmission. For example U+0041 is Latin capital letter A.
The Unicode Standard deals only with character codes.

Glyphs represent the shapes that characters can have when they are rendered or displayed, e.g. A A A A A are all Unicode U+0041.
In contrast to characters, glyphs appear on the screen or paper as particular representations of one or more characters. A repertoire of glyphs makes up a font.
Glyphs are not part of the Unicode Standard.

Note that for **UTF-16** most characters can be expressed with one 16-bit code unit, whose value is the same as the code point for the character, but characters with high code points require a pair of 16-bit code units called surrogate units.

UTF-8 like UTF-16 is a variable-length encoding of Unicode code points.

UTF-8 uses between 1 and 4 bytes to represent a Unicode code point or character but only 1 byte for ASCII characters, and only 2 or 3 bytes for most characters in common use.

The high order bits of the first byte of the encoding indicate how many bytes follow. A high order 0 indicates 7-bit ASCII, where each character takes only 1 byte, so it is identical to conventional ASCII. A high order 110 indicates that each character takes 2 bytes; the second byte begins with 10.

Larger code points are also encoded in a similar manner.

Strings

A string is a sequence of zero or more characters.

In versions of Delphi from Delphi 2009 onwards, string characters are encoded in UTF-16. *Figure 10.2* was generated by running the program shown in *Table 10.1*. *Figure 10.2* shows that the string '程序样例' consisting of four characters stored in variable `StringUnicode` of datatype **String**, is encoded in 8 bytes with two bytes per character.

Each character is a called a string element, e.g. 程. The string element size is 2 bytes because UTF-16 is used. However, the length of the string is 4 characters.

The program variable, `String8Bits`, that contains the string 'ABC' was declared as an ANSI string (8 bits). The string element size is 1 byte and the string length 3 characters.

When the same string is encoded in UTF-16, the element size becomes 2 bytes and the string size in byes 6 bytes.

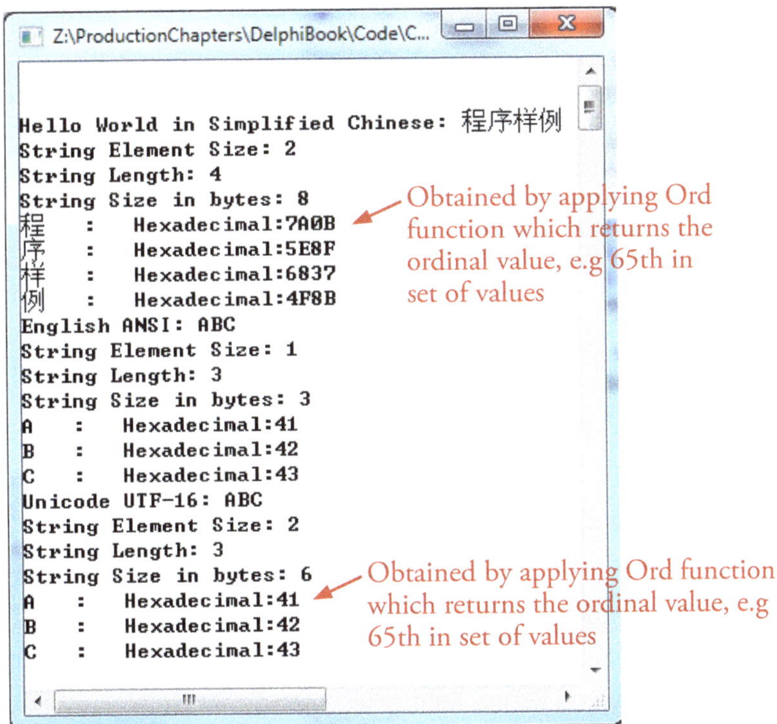

Fig. 10.2 Delphi XE5 console program output for a UTF-16 encoded string '程序样例' *and an ANSI string 'ABC'* and a UTF-16 string *'ABC'*

Information

Unicode code points:

Search Unicode code point and its corresponding character, UTF-32, UTF-16, UTF-8 encoding:

http://www.fileformat.info/info/unicode/char/search.htm

Key point

UTF:

Unicode offers multiple ways of representing the same code point (or Unicode character numerical value) in terms of actual storage, or of physical bytes.

UTF is an acronym for Unicode Transformation Format.

These are bidirectional, algorithmic mappings which map each code point (the absolute numeric representation of a character) to a unique sequence of bytes representing the given character.

Key point

UTF-8:

UTF-8 transforms characters into a variable-length encoding of 1-4 bytes. UTF-8 is used for HTML and similar protocols because it can be compact, most characters fall within the ASCII subset, e.g. HTML markers.

UTF-16:

In UTF-16 most characters can be expressed with one 16-bit code unit, whose value is the same as the code point for the character, but characters with high code points require a pair of 16-bit code units.

UTF-16 is popular in many operating systems and development environments such as Java and .NET. Most characters used in these scenarios fit in two bytes.

UTF-32:

In UTF-32 all code points encode to the same fixed length code (32 bits) but it is memory consuming and therefore has limited practical usage.

In order for the computer running this program to display simplified Chinese characters in a console window, the ANSI codepage 1200 must be active in the console window. There is no need to do this for Vcl applications.

Download **DelphiConsoleHelloWorldInChineseRevisedForBook** from http://www.educational-computing.co.uk/DelphiBookCode/DelphiCode.html

```
Program ChineseRevisedForBook;
{$APPTYPE CONSOLE}
Uses
  {Namespace concept introduced in later versions of Delphi means System prefaces SysUtils and Character}
  System.SysUtils, System.Character;
Var
  StringUnicode : String = '程序样例'; {String is an alias for UnicodeString in Delphi 2009 onwards}
  String8bits : ANSIString = 'ABC'; {AnsiString is a sequence of AnsiChar characters, i.e. 8-bit characters}
  i : Integer;
Begin
  Writeln; Writeln;
  Writeln('Hello World in Simplified Chinese: ', StringUnicode);
  Writeln('String Element Size: ', StringElementSize(StringUnicode));
  Writeln('String Length: ', Length(StringUnicode));
  Writeln('String Size in bytes: ', ByteLength(StringUnicode));
  If Length(StringUnicode) <> 0
    Then
      For i := 1 To Length(StringUnicode)
        Do Writeln(StringUnicode[i], '   : ', '  ', Format('Hexadecimal:%x', [Ord(StringUnicode[i])]));
  Writeln('English ANSI: ', String8Bits);
  Writeln('String Element Size: ', StringElementSize(String8bits));
  Writeln('String Length: ', Length(String8bits));
  Writeln('String Size in bytes: ', Length(String8bits) * StringElementSize(String8bits) );
  If Length(String8bits) <> 0
    Then
      For i := 1 To Length(String8bits)
        Do Writeln(String8bits[i], '   : ', '  ', Format('Hexadecimal:%x', [Ord(String8bits[i])]));
  StringUnicode := 'ABC';
  Writeln('Unicode UTF-16: ', StringUnicode);
  Writeln('Code Page: ', StringCodePage(StringUnicode));
  Writeln('String Element Size: ', StringElementSize(StringUnicode));
  Writeln('String Length: ', Length(StringUnicode));
  Writeln('String Size in bytes: ', ByteLength(StringUnicode));
  If Length(StringUnicode) <> 0
    Then
      For i := 1 To Length(StringUnicode)
        Do Writeln(StringUnicode[i], '   : ', '  ', Format('Hexadecimal:%x', [Ord(StringUnicode[i])]));
  Readln;
End.
```

Table 10.1 Delphi XE5 console program ChineseRevisedForBook.dpr

Key point

ASCII and Unicode:
ASCII *x* is the same character as Unicode *x* for all characters within ASCII.

Questions

1. What is Unicode?
2. What problem was solved by Unicode?

UnicodeString

From Delphi 2009 onwards, the **String** datatype is an alias for datatype **UnicodeString** which uses UTF-16 encoding. The character elements in a **UnicodeString** are of datatype **WideChar**.

WideChar is defined as

```
Type WideChar = #0..#65536;
```

where # means the character equivalent of the integer number that follows #.

The integer numbers are referred to as code points, e.g. code point 31243 (hexadecimal 7A0B) is character '程'.

WideChar is capable of encoding all 1,112,064 valid code points of Unicode (surrogate pairs are used to encode code points above 65536 - two 16-bit values are joned together to create a 32-bit value). Surrogate pairs means that some integers in the range 0..65536 cannot be used for two-byte encodings of characters. However, the vast majority of the world's active language characters fit in a single UTF-16 character, i.e. 16 bits.

AnsiString

In versions of Delphi prior to Delphi 2009, the **String** datatype is an alias for datatype **AnsiString**.

The character elements in an **AnsiString** are of datatype **AnsiChar**.

AnsiChar is defined as

```
Type AnsiChar = #0..#255;
```

The integers from 128 to 255 define characters that depend on which code page is active.

Historically in Delphi, the **Char** datatype was effectively an alias for the **AnsiChar** datatype, i.e. a single byte representing a character from an ANSI code page. However, from Delphi 2009, the **Char** datatype is an alias for the **WideChar** datatype.

String operations

Strings are used to store human-readable text. The literal string, 'Hello World!', consists of twelve characters placed between single quotes.

The literal string of twelve characters, 'Hello World!', is stored in a container with a capacity for more than twelve bytes because

- each character may need more than one byte, e.g. when UTF-16 is used
- some bytes must be used to store the *count of characters* or to indicate the *end of the sequence of characters*
- some bytes will be needed if the string is *reference counted* (the number of references made to the string may be more than one and the string must not be destroyed if the reference count is greater than zero)
- some bytes will be needed if the *code page is stored.*

For example, a **UnicodeString** includes code page, element size, length, reference count fields that describe the string contents of the storage container as shown in *Figure 10.3* which shows how the bytes of main memory are allocated. Each memory location is byte-sized in *Figure 10.3*.The string data are terminated with a null term, $0000 ($ means hexadecimal).

A string variable, `StringVar`, contains a pointer to the first byte of the string data (e.g. `StringVar := 'ABCDEFGHI';`).

Access to the code page, element size, length, reference count fields stored in the container are obtained by decrementing the pointer's value.

For the above and other reasons, Delphi provides a library of routines and string operators for programmers to use when working with strings.

Prior to Delphi 2009, an **AnsiString** contained reference count and length fields in addition to string data (each character occupying a single byte) and a null term.

From Delphi 2009 onwards, an **AnsiString** contains code page, element size, reference count and length fields in addition to string data (each character occupying a single byte) and a null term.

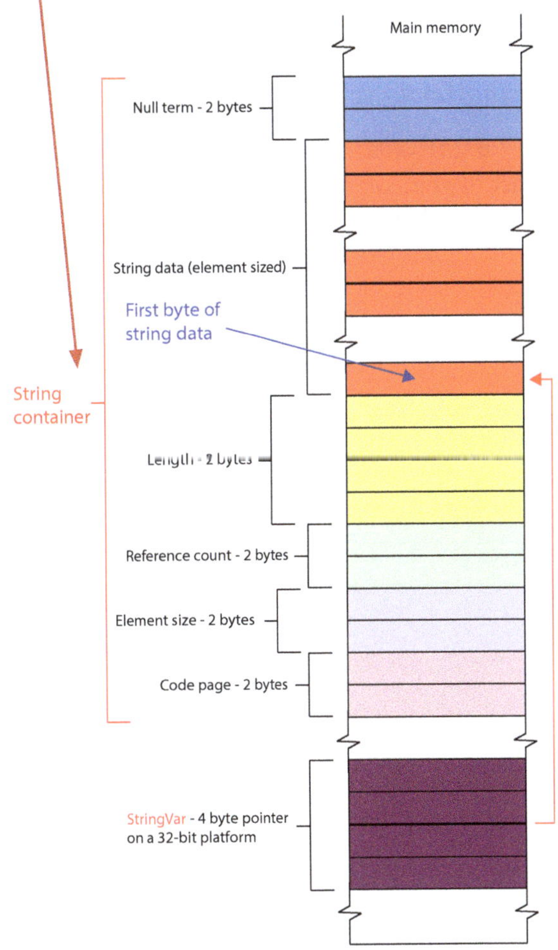

Fig. 10.3 Main memory map showing the bytes involved in storing a UnicodeString

Dynamically allocated strings

Both **UnicodeString** and **AnsiString** represent a dynamically allocated string with space obtained from the heap for the string data. A string variable such as `StringVar` is a pointer which contains the **Nil** value when empty - i.e. when it doesn't contain a string. When it is not empty, it points to a dynamically allocated block of memory that contains the string value - see *Figure 10.3*. The management of the allocated memory is entirely automatic and therefore does not require any user code.

The use of pointers means that two or more string variables can reference the same string value without consuming additional memory. The reference count field associated with a string value is used to keep track of the number of string variables pointing to the string value.

Indexing

Both **UnicodeString** and **AnsiString** use 1-based indexing on Windows desktop platforms[3].
This means that the starting index of the first character in a string is one (e.g. `StringVar[1]`).

Compilers for mobile platforms only support 0-based indexing of strings and these are immutable, i.e. cannot be changed in situ, only by making an amended copy.

0-based indexing means that the starting index of the first character in a string is zero (e.g. `StringVar[0]` on Android).

Therefore, it is advisable to use **TStringHelper** functions/procedures, if your version of Delphi supports these, to manipulate strings when developing cross-platform applications.
TStringHelper was introduced to enable operations on 0-based string without breaking backwards compatibility with existing code.
In fact, if your version of Delphi supports **TStringHelper** functions/procedures then it is better to use these functions wherever possible, even when developing applications that just target Windows desktop because this should future proof your application against any changes Embarcadero may make to the storage structure and access mechanisms for strings. Another good reason to use **TStringHelper** is that the **Code Insight** mechanism (add a dot and wait) will supply a list of operations so you don't have to remember the function/procedure name.

The program shown in *Table 10.2* uses the **TStringHelper** function **IndexOf**.

```
Program TStringHelperProject;
{$APPTYPE CONSOLE}
Uses
  System.SysUtils;
Var
  StringVar : String;
Begin
  StringVar := 'Hello World';
  Writeln(StringVar.IndexOf('H'));
  Writeln(StringVar.IndexOf('Wo'));
  Writeln(StringVar.IndexOf('Wo', 0, 6));
  Writeln(StringVar.IndexOf('Wo', 0, 8));
  Writeln(StringVar.IndexOf('Wo', 7, 4));
  Writeln(StringVar[1]);
  Writeln(AnsiPos('H', StringVar));
  Writeln(StringVar.Length);
  Writeln(Length(StringVar));
  Readln;
End.
```

Table 10.2 Delphi 10.3 console program TStringHelperProject.dpr

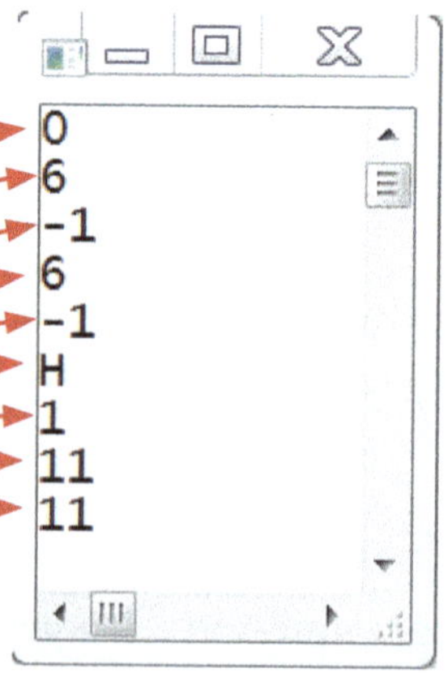

Fig. 10.4 Console output when TStringHelperProject.dpr run

Download **TStringHelperIntro** from http://www.educational-computing.co.uk/DelphiBookCode/DelphiCode.html

Note the syntax `StringVar.IndexOf`.

0-based and 1-based strings are treated by **TStringHelper** functions/procedures as 0-based.
For example, `StringVar` in *Table 10.2* is a 1-based string but `StringVar.IndexOf('H')` returns index value 0 - see *Figure10.4*.

3 You can change this to 0-based indexing using a compiler directive in the source code.

`AnsiPos('H', StringVar)` which also returns the index of the first occurrence of 'H' in `StringVar` uses 1-based indexing even in platforms where the strings are 0-based.

Table 10.3 explains the **TStringHelper** functions used in console program **TStringHelperProject.dpr** in more detail.

TStringHelper function	**Example**	**Explanation**
`Function IndexOf(Value : Char) : Integer; Overload; Inline;`	`StringVar := 'Hello World';` `Writeln(StringVar.IndexOf('H'));`	Returns the index of first instance of character 'H', if found in the string 'Hello World' stored by StringVar. IndexOf uses 0-based indexing of string. Returns -1 if the character is not found.
`Function IndexOf(Const Value : String) : Integer; Overload; Inline;`	`StringVar := 'Hello World';` `Writeln(StringVar.IndexOf('Wo'));`	Returns the index of 'W' of the first instance of substring 'Wo', if found in the string 'Hello World' stored by StringVar. IndexOf uses 0-based indexing of string. Returns -1 if the substring is not found.
`Function IndexOf(Value : Char; StartIndex : Integer) : Integer; Overload;`	`StringVar := 'Hello World';` `Writeln(StringVar.IndexOf('o', 5));`	Returns the index of first instance of 'o' if found in the substring of 'Hello World' that begins at index 5. IndexOf uses 0-based indexing of string. Returns -1 if the character is not found or StartIndex specifies an invalid value.
`Function IndexOf(Const Value : String; StartIndex : Integer) : Integer; Overload;`	`StringVar := 'Hello World';` `Writeln(StringVar.IndexOf('Wo', 3));`	Returns the index of 'W' of the first instance of substring 'Wo', if found in the substring of 'Hello World' that begins at index 3. IndexOf uses 0-based indexing of string. Returns -1 if the substring is not found or StartIndex specifies an invalid value.
`Function IndexOf(Const Value : Char; StartIndex : Integer; Count : Integer) : Integer; Overload;`	`StringVar := 'Hello World';` `Writeln(StringVar.IndexOf('o', 0, 5));`	Returns the index of first instance of 'o' if found in the substring of 'Hello World' that begins at index 0 and consists of 5 characters. IndexOf uses 0-based indexing of string. Returns -1 if the character is not found or StartIndex specifies an invalid value.

`Function IndexOf(Const Value : String; StartIndex : Integer; Count : Integer) : Integer; Overload;`	`StringVar := 'Hello World';`
	`Writeln(StringVar.IndexOf('Wo', 0, 6));`
	`Writeln(StringVar.IndexOf('Wo', 0, 8));`
	`Writeln(StringVar.IndexOf('Wo', 7, 4));`
		Returns the index of 'W' of the first instance of substring 'Wo' in the substring of 'Hello World' that begins at index 0 and consists of 6 characters; at index 0 and consists of 8 characters; at index 7 and consists of 4 characters IndexOf uses 0-based indexing of string. Returns -1 if the substring is not found or StartIndex specifies an invalid value.

`Function Length : Integer;`	`StringVar := 'Hello World';` `Writeln(StringVar.Length);`	Returns length of string 'Hello World', i.e.number of characters.

Table 10.3 Some TStringHelper functions

The keyword **Overload** is applied when a procedure/function has more than one definition.

The keyword **Inline** is a directive to the compiler to insert a copy of the code for the procedure/function at the point of call, if certain conditions apply, instead of setting up a procedure/function call to its code (out of line).

The **TStringHelper** support (called **Record Helpers**) was introduced in Delphi XE3.

Tables 10.4, *10.5*, *10.6* and *10.7* show the full range of available **TString Helper** functions/procedures or routines

http://www.educational-computing.co.uk/DelphiBookCode/DelphiCode.html

TStringHelper routine	**Explanation**	**Example**

Compare	Compares two 0-based strings for equality. Compare is a static class function, i.e. call String.Compare(... ...).
	It returns:
	<0 if the first string argument appears before the second in an ascending order sort
	0 if the first is the same as the second
	>0 if the first string argument appears after the second in an ascending order sort
		`Writeln(String.Compare('abcd', 'abce'));//Outputs -1`
		`Writeln(String.Compare('abcd', 'abcd'));//Outputs 0`
		`Writeln(String.Compare('abce', 'abcd'));//Outputs 1`

CompareTo	Compares the 0-based string with the given string. Compares with case-sensitivity.
	It returns:
	<0 if the string appears before the given string in an ascending order sort
	0 if the string is the same as the given string
	>0 if the string appears after the given string in an ascending order sort
		`Var`
		`  StringVar1 : String;`
		`....`
		`StringVar1 := 'abcd';`
		`Writeln(StringVar1.CompareTo('abce'));//Outputs -1`
		`StringVar1 := 'abcd';`
		`Writeln(StringVar1.CompareTo('abcd'));//Outputs 0`
		`StringVar1 := 'abce';`
		`Writeln(StringVar1.CompareTo('abcd'));//Outputs -1`
		`StringVar1 := 'Abcd'`
		`Writeln(StringVar1.CompareTo('abcd'));//Outputs -32`
		`StringVar1 := 'abcd';`
		`Writeln(StringVar1.CompareTo('Abcd'));//Outputs 32`
		`{Comparision checks ordinal value difference}`

Contains	Returns True if the string contains the given string, False otherwise. This function is case-sensitive.	`StringVar1 := 'abcd';`
		`Writeln(StringVar1.Contains('bc'));//Outputs TRUE`
		`Writeln(StringVar1.Contains('Bc'));//Outputs FALSE`

Copy	This is a static class function which copies and returns the 0-based given string.	`Writeln(String.Copy('abcd'));//Outputs abcd`

CopyTo	Copies memory allocated to one or more characters in the 0-based string StringVar2 to the memory allocated to characters starting at StringVar1[11] in another 0-based string, StringVar1. The first parameter set at 0 is the start index position from which characters are to be copied. The third parameter set at 0 is the start index position in the block of memory that begins at StringVar1[11].	`Var`
		`  StringVar1, StringVar2 : String;`
		`....` No of characters to copy
		`StringVar1 := 'This is a string';`
		`StringVar2 := 'S';` Start Index StringVar2
		`StringVar2.CopyTo(0, StringVar1[11], 0, StringVar2.Length);`
		`Writeln(StringVar1);`
		Start index in Array of Char
		Need an Array Of Char
		`//Outputs This is a String`
		`StringVar2 := 'STRING';`
		`StringVar2.CopyTo(0, StringVar1[11], 0, StringVar2.Length);`
		`Writeln(StringVar1);//Outputs This is a STRING`
		`StringVar1 := 'This is a string';`
		`StringVar2 := 'S';`
		`StringVar2.CopyTo(0, StringVar1[11], 1, StringVar2.Length);`
		`Writeln(StringVar1);//Outputs This is a String`

EndsText	This is a static class function which returns True if the given 0-based string ends with the given 0-based substring otherwise returns False. It is case-insensitive.	`StringVar1 := 'This is a string';` `Writeln(String.EndsText('string', StringVar1));//Outputs TRUE`

Table 10.4 TStringHelper routines

TStringHelper function	Explanation	Example

EndsWith	Returns True if the 0-based string ends with the given substring, otherwise returns False.
	The first version is is case-sensitive.
	The second version uses IgnoreCase to specify whether to use case-sensitivity or not.
		`Writeln(StringVar1.EndsWith('string'));//Outputs TRUE`
		`Writeln(StringVar1.EndsWith('String', True));//Outputs TRUE`
		`Writeln(StringVar1.EndsWith('String', False));//Outputs FALSE`

Format	This is a static class function which is identical to the System.SysUtils. Format function. It returns a formatted string assembled from a format string and an array of arguments expressed as an open untyped array. The format string contains format specifiers which are replaced by arguments from the array of arguments.	`StringVar1 := 'The answer to the universe is %d';`
		`Writeln(String.Format(StringVar1, [42]));`
		`{Outputs The answer to the universe is 42}`

IndexOf	See *Table 10.3*.	

IndexOfAny	Returns an integer indicating the position of the first given character found in the 0-based string. If not found then -1 is returned.
	Second version specifies where to start from in the given string.
	The third version specifies how many characters to include in the search.
		`StringVar1 := 'This is a string';`
		`Writeln(StringVar1.IndexOfAny(['g', 's', 'r']));//Outputs 3`
		`Writeln(StringVar1.IndexOfAny(['g', 's', 'r'], 7));//Outputs 10`
		`Writeln(StringVar1.IndexOfAny(['g', 's', 'r'], 11));//Outputs 12`
		`Writeln(StringVar1.IndexOfAny(['g', 's', 'r'], 11, 3));//Outputs 12`

Insert	Inserts a given string at a specified position in the 0-based string.	`StringVar1 := 'This is a string';`
		`Writeln(StringVar1.Insert(7, ' yet another'));`
		`{Outputs This is yet another string}`

IsEmpty	Returns True if 0-based string does not contain any characters otherwise returns False.	`StringVar1 := 'This is a string';` `Writeln(StringVar1.IsEmpty);//Outputs FALSE`
IsNullOrEmpty	Static class function that returns True if the given string contains no characters or is null, otherwise returns False.	`StringVar1 := '';` `Writeln(String.IsNullOrEmpty(StringVar1));//Outputs TRUE`
IsNullOrWhiteSpace	Static class function that returns True if the given string does not contain any characters or is null or consists only of white-space characters, otherwise returns False.	`StringVar1 := '';` `Writeln(String.IsNullOrWhiteSpace(StringVar1));//Outputs TRUE`

Join	Class function which joins two or more 0-based strings together separated by the given separator.
	`Class Function Join(Const Separator : String; Const Array Of String) : String; Overload; Static;`
		Separator → `' '`; Array Of String → `['Hello', 'World', 'Again']`
		`Var`
		`  StringVar : String;`
		`....`
		`StringVar := String.Join(' ', ['Hello', 'World', 'Again']);`
		`Writeln(StringVar);`
		See docwiki.embarcadero.com/Libraries/Rio/en/System.SysUtils.TStringHelper.Join

LastDelimiter	Returns the index of the rightmost whole character that matches any character in 'llo'. 0-based indexing is used.	`StringVar1 := 'Hello hello';` `Writeln(StringVar1.LastDelimiter('llo'));//Outputs 10`

Table 10.5 More TStringHelper routines

<table>
<tr><th>TStringHelper function</th><th>Explanation</th><th>Example</th></tr>
<tr><td>LastIndexOf</td><td>Returns the last index of the given character or string in the current 0-based string.
StartIndex specifies the offset in this 0-based string where the LastIndexOf method begins a backwards search, and Count specifies the end offset where the search ends (Count <= StartIndex), i.e. StartIndex + 1 - Count.
If the given character|string is not found, -1 is returned.</td><td>StringVar1 := 'hello hello'; StartIndex
Writeln(StringVar1.LastIndexOf('l'));//Outputs 9
Writeln(StringVar1.LastIndexOf('hello'));//Outputs 6
Writeln(StringVar1.LastIndexOf('l', 3));//Outputs 3
Writeln(StringVar1.LastIndexOf('l', 7));//Outputs 3
Writeln(StringVar1.LastIndexOf('l', 7, 5));//Outputs 3
Writeln(StringVar1.LastIndexOf('l', 7, 4));//Outputs -1
Writeln(StringVar1.LastIndexOf('l', 10, 2));//Outputs 9
Writeln(StringVar1.LastIndexOf('l', 8, 1));//Outputs 8
Writeln(StringVar1.LastIndexOf('l', 10, 1));//Outputs -1
StartIndex Count</td></tr>
<tr><td>LastIndexOfAny</td><td>Returns the last index of the given character array in the current 0-based string.
This function has overloaded versions as for LastIndexOf with a character array replacing the character|string.</td><td>StringVar1 := 'hello hello';
Writeln(StringVar1.LastIndexOfAny(['e']));//Outputs 7</td></tr>
<tr><td>PadLeft</td><td>First version adds spaces to the left of the 0-based string until the specified size for the returned string is achieved.
Second version adds the specified character to the left of the 0-based string until the specified size for the returned string is achieved.</td><td>StringVar1 := 'System';
StringVar1 := StringVar1.PadLeft(12);
Writeln(StringVar1, '!');//Outputs '   System!'
StringVar1 := 'System';
StringVar1 := StringVar1.PadLeft(12, '?');
Writeln(StringVar1);//Outputs '??????System'</td></tr>
<tr><td>PadRight</td><td>First version adds spaces to the right of the 0-based string until the specified size for the returned string is achieved.
Second version adds the specified character to the right of the 0-based string until the specified size for the returned string is achieved.</td><td>StringVar1 := 'System';
StringVar1 := StringVar1.PadRight(12);
Writeln(StringVar1, '!');//Outputs 'System   !'
StringVar1 := 'System';
StringVar1 := StringVar1.PadRight(12, '?');
Writeln(StringVar1);//Outputs 'System??????'</td></tr>
<tr><td>Remove</td><td>Returns the substring that remains after removing the substring from start index to start index + count using 0-based indexing.</td><td>Var
  StringVar, StringVar1 : String; Start index
.... Count
StringVar := 'It was a sunny,bright morning.Later it rained.';
StringVar1 := StringVar.Remove(0, 14);
Writeln(StringVar1);Outputs ,bright morning.Later it rained.
See docwiki.embarcadero.com/Libraries/Rio/en/System.SysUtils.TStringHelper.Remove</td></tr>
<tr><td>Replace</td><td>Replaces a given character or string with another given character or string.
[rfReplaceAll] replaces every instance.
[rfIgnoreCase] ignores the case when matching the given character to replace.
[rfReplaceAll, rfIgnoreCase] does both.
[] are set brackets.</td><td>StringVar1 := 'Boat';
StringVar1 := StringVar1.Replace('a', 'o');
Writeln(StringVar1);
StringVar1 := 'matTer';
StringVar1 := StringVar1.Replace('t','n',[rfReplaceAll,rfIgnoreCase]);
Writeln(StringVar1);
StringVar1 := 'John is home';
Writeln(StringVar1);//Outputs John is home
StringVar1 := StringVar1.Replace('John', 'Mary ');
Writeln(StringVar1);//Outputs Mary is home
StringVar1 := 'This is a double-spaced string';
Writeln(StringVar1);
StringVar1 := StringVar1.Replace(' ', ' ', [rfReplaceAll]);
Writeln(StringVar1, ' no longer.');</td></tr>
<tr><td>Split</td><td>Splits the 0-based string into substrings using the given separators.
Resulting substrings returned in a 0-based array of string.</td><td>Var
  StringVar, StringVar1 : String;
  ArrayVar : TArray<String>;
  i : Integer;
....
StringVar := 'It was a sunny,bright morning.Later it rained.';
ArrayVar := StringVar.Split([' ', ',', '.']);
For i := 0 To Length(ArrayVar) - 1
  Do Writeln(ArrayVar[i]);   Array of Char
For StringVar1 In ArrayVar   separators
  Do Writeln(StringVar1);
See docwiki.embarcadero.com/Libraries/Rio/en/System.SysUtils.TStringHelper.Split</td></tr>
</table>

Table 10.6 Yet more TStringHelper routines

TStringHelper function	Explanation	Example

StartsWith	Returns True if the string starts with a given string otherwise False, case-sensitively or case-insensitively.	Var
		  StringVar : String;
		....
		StringVar := 'It was a sunny,bright morning.Later it rained.';
		Writeln(StringVar.StartsWith('It was'));//Outputs TRUE
		Writeln(StringVar.StartsWith('it was', True));//Outputs TRUE
		IgnoreCase

Substring	Returns the substring that starts at a given start index and ends at start index + count using 0-based indexing.	Var
		  StringVar : String;
		....
		StringVar := 'It was a sunny,bright morning.Later it rained.';
		Writeln(StringVar.Substring(0, 14));//Outputs It was a sunny
		Count
		Start index

ToCharArray	Transforms a 0-based string into a TArray<Char> (a character array) and returns the result.	Var
		  StringVar1 : String;
		....
		StringVar1 := 'System';
		ArrayChar := StringVar1.ToCharArray;
		For Ch In ArrayChar
		  Do Writeln(Ch);

ToLower	Transforms a 0-based string into all lowercase characters and returns the result.	Var StringVar1 : String; .... StringVar1 := 'SYSTEM'; Writeln(StringVar1.ToLower);//Outputs system
ToUpper	Transforms a 0-based string into all uppercase characters and returns the result.	StringVar1 := 'system'; Writeln(StringVar1.ToUpper);//Outputs SYSTEM

Trim	The first version trims leading and trailing spaces and control characters from the 0-based string.
	The second version trims leading and trailing characters specified in the form of a character array.
		StringVar1 := ' System ';
		Writeln(StringVar1);//Outputs ' System '
		StringVar1 := StringVar1.Trim;
		Writeln(StringVar1);//Outputs 'System'
		StringVar1 := '....System???';
		Writeln(StringVar1);//Outputs '....System???'
		StringVar1 := StringVar1.Trim(['.', '?']);
		Writeln(StringVar1);//Outputs 'System'

TrimRight	The first version trims trailing spaces and control characters from the 0-based string.
	The second version trims trailing characters specified in the form of a character array.
		StringVar1 := ' System ';
		Writeln(StringVar1);//Outputs ' System '
		StringVar1 := StringVar1.TrimRight;
		Writeln(StringVar1, '!!!');//Outputs ' System!!!'
		StringVar1 := '....System???';
		Writeln(StringVar1);//Outputs '....System???'
		StringVar1 := StringVar1.TrimRight(['.', '?']);
		Writeln(StringVar1);//Outputs '....System'

TrimLeft	The first version trims leading spaces and control characters from the 0-based string.
	The second version trims leading characters specified in the form of a character array.
		StringVar1 := ' System ';
		Writeln(StringVar1);//Outputs ' System '
		StringVar1 := StringVar1.TrimLeft;
		Writeln(StringVar1, '!!!');//Outputs 'System !!!'
		StringVar1 := '....System???';
		Writeln(StringVar1);//Outputs '....System???'
		StringVar1 := StringVar1.TrimLeft(['.', '?']);
		Writeln(StringVar1);//Outputs 'System???'

Table 10.7 The last few of the range of TStringHelper routines

F- Func P - Proc V - Var T - Type	Name	What does it do?	Example
F	AnsiCompareStr	Case sensitive comparison of two strings for equality based on 8-bit ordinal value of each character.	`AnsiCompareStr('ab','ab')` returns 0 `AnsiCompareStr('AB','ab')` returns < 0 `AnsiCompareStr('ab','AB')` returns > 0
F	AnsiCompareText	Compares two strings for equality whilst ignoring case.	`AnsiCompareStr('ab','AB')` returns 0 `AnsiCompareStr('CD','AB')` returns < 0 `AnsiCompareStr('ab','CD')` returns > 0
F	AnsiContainsStr	Returns True if a string contains a substring otherwise False. Case sensitive operation.	`AnsiContainsStr('abcd','bc') returns True` `AnsiContainsStr('abcd','BC') returns False`
F	AnsiContainsText	Case insensitive version that returns True if a string contains a substring otherwise False.	`AnsiContainsText('abcd','BC') returns True` `AnsiContainsText('abcd','de') returns False`
F	AnsiEndsStr	Returns True if a string ends with a given substring otherwise False. Case sensitive.	`AnsiEndsStr('cd', 'abcd') returns True` `AnsiEndsStr('de', 'abcd') returns False`

F	AnsiIndexStr	Compares a string with a list/array of strings and returns 0-offset index of first string that is a match otherwise returns -1. Case sensitive.	`Var`
			`StringArray : Array Of String;`
			`Begin`
			`StringArray := ['ann', 'bob', 'carol', 'dan'];`
			`Writeln(AnsiIndexStr('ann',['ann','bob','carol','dan']));` Displays 0
			`Writeln(AnsiIndexStr('carol', StringArray));` Displays 2
			`Writeln(AnsiIndexStr('ANN', StringArray));` Displays -1
			`Readln;`
			`End.`

F	AnsiLeftStr	Returns the substring of a specified length that appears at the start of a given string.	`AnsiLeftStr('abcd', 2) returns 'ab'`
F	AnsiLowerCase	Returns a string that is a copy of the given string converted to lowercase.	`AnsiLowercase('ABCD') returns 'abcd'`

F	AnsiMatchStr	Returns True if a given string is an exact match of a string in a list/array of strings otherwise False. Case sensitive.	`AnsiMatchStr('carol',['ann','bob','carol','dan'])`
			`returns True`
			`AnsiMatchStr('CAROL',['ann','bob','carol','dan'])`
			`returns True`

F	AnsiMidStr	Returns the substring of a specified length that appears at a specified position in a string.	String Start Count `AnsiMidStr('abcd', 2, 2) returns 'bc'`
F	AnsiPos	Returns the index of the first occurrence of a given substring in given string otherwise returns -1. It uses 1-based indexing even in platforms where the strings are 0-based.	`AnsiPos('cd', 'abcd') returns 3`

Table 10.8 String handling routines, variables and types

F- Func P - Proc V - Var T - Type	Name	What does it do?	Example
F	AnsiReplaceStr	Replaces all occurrences of a given substring with another given substring within a given string. It returns the string obtained after replacement. Case sensitive.	In string replace this With this `AnsiReplaceStr('abcd', 'cd', 'ef') returns 'abef'`
F	AnsiReverseStr	Returns the reverse of a given string	`AnsiReverseString('abcd') returns 'dcba'`
F	AnsiRightStr	Returns the substring of a specified length that appears at the end of a given string	`AnsiRightStr('abcd', 2) returns 'cd'`
F	AnsiStartsStr	Returns True if a given string is a (case-sensitive) prefix of another given string otherwise returns False.	`AnsiStartsStr('ab', 'abcd'); returns True` `AnsiStartsStr('AB', 'abcd'); returns False`
F	AnsiUpperCase	Returns a string that is a copy of a given string, converted to uppercase.	`AnsiUpperCase('abcd'); returns 'ABCD'`

P	AppendStr	Appends a dynamically allocated string to an existing string. **Use the + operator.**	`Var StringVar : AnsiString;`
			`....`
			`StringVar := 'abcd';`
			`AppendStr(StringVar, 'ef');`
			`Writeln(StringVar);`

P	CompareStr	Compares strings S1 and S2 with case sensitivity. S1 < S2 returns a value <0. S1=S2 returns a value of 0. S1>S2 retruns a value >0. Comparison based on the 8-bit ordinal value of each character.	`CompareStr('ab', 'ab'); returns 0`
			`CompareStr('ab', 'bc'); returns -1`
			`CompareStr('cd', 'ab'); returns 2`
			`CompareStr('ab', 'AB'); returns 32`

P	CompareText	Same as CompareStr but without case sensitivity	`CompareText('ab', 'AB')); returns 0`

F	Concat	Returns the concatenation of S1 to Sn strings or dynamic arrays into one string.	`Concat('ab','cd','ef','gh'); returns 'abcdefgh'`
			`StringArray := Concat(['a','b'],['c','d'],['e','f']);`
			`AnsiIndexStr('c', StringArray); returns 2`

F	Copy	Returns a substring of a given string or a segment of a dynamic array starting from Index (1-based indexing for strings 0-based indexing for dynamic arrays) and containing Count characters/elements	String Index Count
			`Copy('abcd', 1, 2); returns ab`
			`StringArray := Copy(['a','b','c','d'], 0, 2);`
			`Writeln(AnsiIndexStr('b', StringArray)); // outputs 1`
			`StringArray := Copy(['a','b','c','d']); //copies entire array`
			`Writeln(AnsiIndexStr('d', StringArray)); // outputs 3`

V	CurrencyDecimals	Variable/field CurrencyDecimals provides a default number of decimal digits for the Format and related functions.	`Var`
			`  FSB : TFormatSettngs;`
			`....`
			`FSB.CurrencyDecimals := 3;`
			`Writeln(Format('%f', [123.456789]));`

Table 10.9 String handling routines, variables and types

F- Func P - Proc V - Var T - Type	Name	What does it do?	Example

V	CurrencyFormat	Variable/field which determines the placement of the currency string in the currency display routines, e.g. CurrToStr.	`0 = Before the amount`
			`1 = After the amount`
			`2 = Before the amount with a single space`
			`3 = After the amount with a single space`

V	CurrencyString	Variable/field which determines the currency symbol to be used by currency display routines. Uses as default the Locale settings.	`Var`
			`  FSB : TFormatSettings;`
			`....`
			`FSB.CurrencyString := '$';`
			`Writeln(Format('%m', [1.23], FSB));//Outputs $1.23`

F	CurrToStr	Formats a Currency value as a string.
		CurrToStr converts the Currency value given by Value to its string representation.
		The first form of CurrToStr is not thread-safe because it uses a global variable, FormatStrings.
		The second form of CurrToStr is thread-safe.
		Before calling the thread-safe form of CurrToStr, localization information must be obtained for a given locale, e.g. fr-FR, by calling TFormatSettings.Create.
		Global variable
			`Var` Not thread-safe
			`  FSB, FSF : TFormatSettings;`
			`  Value : Currency;`
			`.....`
			`Value := 1.23;`
			`FSB := TFormatSettings.Create('en-EN');//English locale`
			`Writeln('£ + CurrToStr(Value));`
			`Writeln('£' + CurrToStr(Value, FSB));`
			`FSF := TFormatSettings.Create('fr-FR');//French locale`
			`FormatSettings.DecimalSeparator := ',';//Global variable`
			`Writeln(CurrToStr(Value) + ' Euros');`
			`Writeln(CurrToStr(Value, FSF) + ' Euros');`
			
			`Procedure TForm2.Button1Click(Sender: TObject);`
			`  Begin`
			`    Value := 1.23;`
			`    FSB := TFormatSettings.Create('en-EN');//English locale`
			`    ShowMessage('£' + CurrToStr(Value));`
			`    ShowMessage('£' + CurrToStr(Value, FSB));`
			`    FSF := TFormatSettings.Create('fr-FR');//French locale`
			`    FormatSettings.DecimalSeparator := ',';//Global variable`
			`    ShowMessage(CurrToStr(Value) + ' €');`
			`    ShowMessage(CurrToStr(Value, FSF) + ' €');`
			`  End;`

F	CurrToStrF	Converts a given currency value to its string representation using the given float format and localisation information stored in a TFormatSettings object.
		The localisation settings are selected when the object is created, e.g. 'fr-FR'. A call to CurrToStrF corresponds to a call to FloatToStrF with an implied precision of 19 digits. The two examples use the thread-safe version.
			`Var` Thread-safe version
			`  FSB, FSF : TFormatSettings;`
			`  Value : Currency;`
			`.....`
			`Value := 1.23;`
			`FSB := TFormatSettings.Create('en-EN');`
			`Writeln(CurrToStrF(Value, ffCurrency, 2, FSB));`
			`FSF := TFormatSettings.Create('fr-FR');`
			`FSF.CurrencyString := 'Euros';//€ not in extended ASCII set`
			`Writeln(CurrToStrF(Value, ffCurrency, 2, FSF));`
			
			`Procedure TForm2.Button1Click(Sender: TObject);`
			`  Begin`
			`    Value := 1.23;`
			`    FSB := TFormatSettings.Create('en-EN');//English locale`
			`    ShowMessage(CurrToStrF(Value, ffCurrency, 2, FSB));`
			`    FSF := TFormatSettings.Create('fr-FR');//French locale`
			`    ShowMessage(CurrToStrF(Value, ffCurrency, 2, FSF));`
			`  End;`

Table 10.10 String handling routines, variables and types

F- Func P - Proc V - Var T - Type	Name	What does it do?	Example

F	DateTimeToStr	Converts a given TDateTime value to a string, using the local setting for displaying date and time. Function Now in example shows current date and time.	Thread-safe version
			Var
			  FSB, FSF : TFormatSettings;
			....
			FSF := TFormatSettings.Create('fr-FR');//French locale
			Writeln(DateTimeToStr(Now, FSF));

P	DateTimeToString	Converts a given TDateTime value into a string, using a given specified format. The generated string is stored in parameter ResultVar.	See docwiki.embarcadero.com/Libraries/Rio/en/System.SysUtils.DateTimeToString for formatting strings
			Var
			  ResultVar : String;
			....
			DateTimeToString(ResultVar,
			          'dddd d mmmm yyyy hh:nn:ss ampm',
			          Now);
			Writeln(ResultVar);

F	DateToStr	Returns a string representation of a given date value. Today returns a TDateTimeValue with the date part set to the current date and the time part set to zero. Thread-safe version.	Var Thread-safe version FSB : TFormatSettings; .... FSB := TFormatSettings.Create('en-EN'); FSB.DateSeparator := '-'; Writeln(DateToStr(Today, FSB));
V	DecimalSeparator	Variable/field which specifies the character used to separate the integer part from the fractional part of a number.	Thread-safe version FSB.DecimalSeparator := ','; Writeln(Format('%f', [1.23], FSB));//Outputs 1,23
P	Delete	Removes a substring of Count characters from string S starting at position Index (1-based indexing)	StringVar := 'abcdefg'; Delete(StringVar, 2, 3); String Index Count Writeln(StringVar);//outputs aefg
F	DupeString	Returns the concatenation of a given string with itself a specified number of times.	Writeln(DupeString('ab', 3));//outputs ababab
F	ExtractFileDir	Returns drive and directory parts of a given filename as an AnsiString. returns the empty string if the given filename contains no drive or directory parts.	ExtractFileDir('C:\Test\Test.txt') returns C:\test ExtractFileDir('Test.txt') returns a blank line ExtractFileDir('C:\Test.txt') returns C:\ ExtractFileDir('C:Test.txt') returns C: ExtractFileDir('\Test.txt') returns \
F	ExtractFileDrive	Returns drive part of a given filename as a string type. For filenames with a UNC path, the result is in the form \\<servername>\\<share-name>. No drive or UNC then empty string returned.	ExtractFileDrive('C:\Test\Test.txt') returns C: ExtractFileDrive('Test.txt') returns a blank line ExtractFileDrive('\\Diskstation\Test\Test.txt') returns \\Diskstation\Test

Table 10.11 String handling routines, variables and types

F- Func P - Proc V - Var T - Type	Name	What does it do?	Example
F	ExtractFileExt	Returns the file extension of a given file including the period character that separates name and extension parts if both exist otherwise returns the empty string.	ExtractFileExt('C:\Test\Test.txt') returns .txt
F	ExtractFileName	Returns the name and extension parts of given filename.	ExtractFileName('C:\Test\Test.txt') returns Test.txt

F	FloatToStr	Returns the string representation of a given floating point value using general number format with 15 significant digits.	Var
			  FSB : TFormatSettings;
			....
			FSB := TFormatSettings.Create('en-EN');
			Writeln(FloatToStr(123.456));//not thread-safe
			Writeln(FloatToStr(123.456, FSB));//thread-safe

F	FloatToStrF	Returns the string representation of a given floating point value using a specified format -ffGeneral,ffExponent, ffFixed, ffNumber, ffCurrency, precision (number of significant digits) and digits (number after decimal point or minimum number in exponent).	Thread-safe version Var FSB : TFormatSettings; Precision Digits .... Writeln(FloatToStrF(123.456, ffFixed, 5, 4, FSB)); Writeln(FloatToStrF(12.3456, ffFixed, 6, 2, FSB)); Writeln(FloatToStrF(12345.6, ffNumber, 7, 2, FSB)); Writeln(FloatToStrF(123.456, ffExponent, 7, 3, FSB));

F	Format	Returns a formatted string assembled from a format string and an array of arguments.
		
		Format string specifier begins with a % character followed by optional elements except the conversion type character, in this order:
		
		1. Zero-offset index specifier *index* ':'
		
		2. Left justification indicator '-'
		
		3. Width specifier
		
		4. Precision specifier '.' *prec*
		
		5. Conversion type character
			Format string specifier Width specifier
			Precision specifier
			Conversion type
			argument to be formatted
			Writeln(Format('%8.2f', [123.456], FSB));
			See previous page for FSB
			Writeln(Format('%8.4d', [123], FSB));
			Writeln(Format('%.10e', [123.4567], FSB));
			Writeln(Format('%15.10f', [123.4567], FSB));
			Writeln(Format('%g', [123.4567], FSB));
			Writeln(Format('%15.10n', [123456.7], FSB));
			Writeln(Format('%x', [255], FSB));//outputs FF
			Writeln(Format('%d%%', [100], FSB));//outputs 100%
			Writeln(Format('%*.*f', [8, 2, 123.456], FSB));
			Writeln(Format('%-8.2f', [0.123456], FSB));
			
			See docwiki.embarcadero.com/Libraries/Rio/en/System.SysUtils.Format for formatting strings

F	FormatCurr	Returns a string representation of a given value of type Currency formatted using a format string.	Var
			  FSB : TFormatSettings;
			  Value : Currency; Thread-safe version
			....
			FSB.DecimalSeparator := '.';
			Value := 23.67;
			Writeln(FormatCurr('£###.##', Value , FSB));
			See docwiki.embarcadero.com/Libraries/Rio/en/System.SysUtils.FormatCurr for formatting strings

Table 10.12 String handling routines, variables and types

F- Func P - Proc V - Var T - Type	Name	What does it do?	Example

F	FormatDateTime	Returns a string representation of a given value of type TDateTime formatted using a format string.	See docwiki.embarcadero.com/Libraries/Rio/en/System.SysUtils.FormatDateTime for formatting strings
			`Writeln(FormatDateTime('dddd mmmm yyyy h:n:s:z ampm', Now , FSB));`
			`FSB.DateSeparator := ' ';` Thread-safe version
			`FSB.TimeSeparator := ':';`
			`Writeln(FormatDateTime('c ampm', Now , FSB));`
			`FSB.DateSeparator := ' ';`
			`FSB.TimeSeparator := '-';`
			`Writeln(FormatDateTime('dddd/mmmm/yyyy h:n:s ampm', Now , FSB));`

F	FormatFloat	Returns a string representation of a given floating point value formatted using a format string.	`Var`
			`  FSB : TFormatSettings;`
			`....` Thread-safe version
			`FSB.DecimalSeparator := '.';`
			`Writeln(FormatFloat('###.##', 23.675, FSB));`
			See docwiki.embarcadero.com/Libraries/Rio/en/System.SysUtils.FormatFloat for formatting strings

P	Insert	Inserts a given substring into a given string at a specified position	`ResultVar := 'Hello World';`
			`Insert(' New ', ResultVar, 6);`
			`Writeln(ResultVar);//Outputs 'Hello New World'`

F	IntToHex	Returns for a given integer, its hexadecimal representation as a string of at least the specified minimum number of hex digits.	Integer value ↓ Minimum no of hex digits ↓ `Writeln(IntToHex(65535, 6));//Outputs 00FFFF`
F	IntToStr	Returns a string containing the decimal representation of a given integer.	`Writeln(IntToStr(56));`
F	LastDelimiter	Returns the byte index of the last characterin a given string that matches any character in a specified set of delimiters.	`Writeln(LastDelimiter('\.', 'C:\Test\Test.Txt'));\\Outputs 13`

F	Length	Returns the number of characters in a given string or a given array.	`Writeln(Length('abc'));//Outputs 3`
			`Writeln(Length([0, 1, 2, 3]));//Outputs 4`

V	LongDateFormat	Variable/field that is used by routine DateTimeToStr, DateTimeToString, DateToStr, FormatDateTime to format the string that is returned.	`y = Year last 2 digits; yy = Year last 2 digits;`
			`yyyy = Year as 4 digits; m = Month number no leading 0;`
			`mm = Month no as 2 digits;`
			`mmm = Month using ShortMonthNames(Jan);`
			`mmmm = Month using LongMonthNames(January);`
			`d = Day number no leading 0`
			`dd = Day no as 2 digits; ddd = Day using ShortDayNames (Mon);`
			`dddd = Day using LongDayNames (Monday)`

V	LongDayNames	Variable/field that provides an array of long string names of the days of the week	`'Sunday', 'Monday', 'Tuesday', 'Wednesday', 'Thursday',` `'Friday', 'Saturday'`

V	LongMonthNames	Variable/field that provides an array of long string names of the months of the year	`'January', 'February', 'March', 'April', 'May', 'June',`
			`'July', 'August', 'September', 'October', 'November',`
			`'December'`

Table 10.13 String handling routines, variables and types

F- Func P - Proc V - Var T - Type	Name	What does it do?	Example

V	LongTimeFormat	Variable/field that is used to specify the format of the string that is returned by routines DateTimeToStr, DateTimeToString, FormatDateTime, LongTimeFormat, TimeToStr when the 'tt' formatting is specified The default value is set by the Locale settings.	`h = Hour with no leading 0's; hh = Hour as 2 digits;`
			`n = Minute with no leading 0's; nn = Minute as 2 digits;`
			`s = Seconds with no leading 0's; ss = Seconds as 2 digits;`
			`z = Milliseconds with no leading 0's;`
			`zzz = Milliseconds as 3 digits;`

F	LowerCase	Returns a copy of a string in uppercase by converting all 7-bit ASCII characters between 'a' and 'z' to uppercase. To convert 8-bit international characters, use AnsiLowerCase.	`Writeln(LowerCase('ABC'));\\Outputs abc`

V	NegCurrFormat	A variable/field which defines how negative currency amounts are formatted by routines such as FloatToStr and CurrToStr. The formats are defined by an enumerated type of range 0..15.	`Var` Thread-safe version
			`FSB : TFormatSettings;`
			`....`
			`FSB.NegCurrFormat := 0;`
			`FSB.CurrencyDecimals := 2;`
			`FSB.DecimalSeparator := '.';`
			`Writeln(Format('%m', [-1.23], FSB));//Outputs (£1.23)`
			See docwiki.embarcadero.com/Libraries/Rio/en/System.SysUtils.TFormatSettings.NegCurrFormat for the possible values and formats

F	Pos	Returns the index value of the first character in a given substring that occurs in a given string, if it exists otherwise returns 0. Case-sensitive.	`Var`
			`StringUVar1, StringUVar2 : UnicodeString;`
			`....`
			`StringUVar1 := 'us';`
			`StringUVar2 := 'russian walruses';`
			`Writeln(Pos(StringUVar1, StringUVar2));//outputs 2`

P	ProcessPath	Parses a filename into its constituent parts, drive, path and filename. The given file must actually exist.	`Uses Vcl.FileCtrl;`
			`....`
			`ProcessPath('C:\Test\Test.Txt', Drive, DirPart, FilePart);`
			`Writeln(Drive, ' ', DirPart, ' ', FilePart);`

P	SetLength	Sets the length of a string or dynamic array variable.
		S is a Delphi string and D is a dynamic array variable
			`Var`
			`S : String;`
			`D : Array Of Integer;`
			`....`
			`SetLength(S, 6);`
			`Writeln(Length(S));`
			`SetLength(D, 6);`
			`Writeln(Length(D));`

V	ShortDateFormat	The variable/field ShortDateFormat is used by DateToStr, DateTimeToStr and DateTimeToString (when 'c' or 't' formatting is used) to format the string that is returned. The default value is set by the Locale settings.	`y = Year last 2 digits; yy = Year last 2 digits;`
			`yyyy = Year as 4 digits; m = Month number no leading 0;`
			`mm = Month no as 2 digits;`
			`mmm = Month using ShortMonthNames(Jan);`
			`mmmm = Month using LongMonthNames(January);`
			`d = Day number no leading 0`
			`dd = Day no as 2 digits; ddd = Day using ShortDayNames (Mon);`
			`dddd = Day using LongDayNames (Monday)`

Table 10.14 String handling routines, variables and types

F- Func P - Proc V - Var T - Type	Name	What does it do?	Example
V	ShortDayNames	Variable/field that provides an array of short string names of the days of the week	`'Sun', 'Mon', 'Tue', 'Wed', 'Thu', 'Fri', 'Sat'`
V	ShortMonthNames	Variable/field that provides an array of short string names of the months of the year	`'Jan', 'Feb', 'Mar', 'Apr', 'May', 'Jun', 'Jul', 'Aug',` `'Sep', 'Oct', 'Nov', 'Dec'`

V	ShortTimeFormat	Variable/field that is used by routines DateTimeToStr, DateTimeToString, FormatDateTime, LongTimeFormat, TimeToStr to format the string that is returned. The default value is set by the Locale settings.	`h = Hour with no leading 0's; hh = Hour as 2 digits;`
			`n = Minute with no leading 0's; nn = Minute as 2 digits;`
			`s = Seconds with no leading 0's; ss = Seconds as 2 digits;`
			`z = Milliseconds with no leading 0's;`
			`zzz = Milliseconds as 3 digits;`

P	Str	Takes an integer or a real value and converts it to a string, formatted to a specified total width and number of decimal places, before the string is assigned to a Var parameter.	Integer value → Width → String variable:
			`Str(-65535:10, S);`
			`Writeln(S);`
			`Str(-655.35 :8:2, S);`
			`Writeln(S);`
			Real value (-655.35); Width (8); Number of decimal places (2); String variable (S)

F	StringOfChar	Returns a string (AnsiString or WideString depending on type of first argument, AnsiChar or WideChar, respectively) with a specified number of repeating characters.	`Var`
			`  Ch1 : AnsiString;`
			`  Ch2 : WideChar;`
			`....`
			`Ch1 := 'a';`
			`Ch2 := 'b';`
			`Writeln(StringOfChar(Ch1, 5));//outputs 'aaaaa'`
			`Writeln(StringOfChar(Ch2, 5));//outputs 'bbbbb'`

F	StrToCurr	Returns a value of type Currency of a given number string which represents an integer or a floating point number in form nnn.nnn or n.nnnEnnn If a decimal point appears in the number string it must match the current DecimalSeparator.	`Var`
			`  FCD : TFormatSettings;`
			`  Value : Currency;`
			`....`
			`FSB.ThousandSeparator := ',';`
			`FSB.DecimalSeparator := '.';`
			`FSB.CurrencyDecimals := 2;`
			`FSB.CurrencyFormat := 0;`
			`FSB.CurrencyString := '£';` Thread-safe version
			`Value := StrToCurr('2351.67', FSB);`
			`Writeln(CurrToStrF(Value, ffCurrency, 2, FSB));`
			`//outputs £2,351.67`

Table 10.15 String handling routines, variables and types

F- Func P - Proc V - Var T - Type	Name	What does it do?	Example

F	StrToDate	Returns a TDateTime value of a given string.
		The string must consist of two or three numbers, separated by the character defined by the DateSeparator field specified in TFormatSettings object.
		The order for month, day and year is determined by the ShortDateFormat specified in TFormatSettings object.
		If the string contains only two numbers then the current year is assumed.
			Thread-safe version
			`Var`
			`  FSB : TFormatSettings;`
			`  DateVar : TDateTime;`
			`....`
			`FSB.DateSeparator := '/';`
			`FSB.ShortDateFormat := 'dddd d/mmmm/yyyy';`
			`FSB.TwoDigitYearCenturyWindow := 50;//Current century`
			`DateVar := StrToDate('8/4/20', FSB);`
			`FSB.DateSeparator := ' ';`
			`Writeln(DateToStr(DateVar, FSB));`
			`//Outputs Wednesday 8 April 2020`

F	StrToDateTime	Returns a TDateTime value of a given string that specifies a date and time value.
		The string must use the current locale's date/time format. Specifying AM or PM as part of the time is optional, as are the seconds.
		The order for month, day and year is determined by the ShortDateFormat specified in TFormatSettings object.
		The order for hours, minutes and seconds is determined by the LongTimeFormat specified in TFormatSettings object.
			Thread-safe version
			`Var`
			`  FSB : TFormatSettings;`
			`  DateTimeVar : TDateTime;`
			`....`
			`FSB.DateSeparator := '/';`
			`FSB.TimeSeparator := ':';`
			`FSB.ShortDateFormat := 'd/m/yy';`
			`FSB.LongTimeFormat := 'hh:nn:ss';`
			`DateTimeVar := StrToDateTime('8/4/20 11:35:00', FSB);`
			`Writeln(DateTimeToStr(DateTimeVar, FSB));`

F	StrToFloat	Returns a floating point value (type Extended) of a given string	`FSB.DecimalSeparator := '.';` Thread-safe version
			`Writeln(StrToFloat('3456.789', FSB) + 5.6 :8 :3);`
			`//Outputs 3462.389`

F	StrToInt	Returns an integer of a given string which represents an integer (decimal or hexadecimal).
		The output value is a signed 32-bit integer
			`Writeln(StrToInt('34') + 5);//Outputs 39`
			`Writeln(StrToInt('$FF') + 5);//Outputs 260`
			`Writeln(StrToInt('0xFF') + 5);/Outputs 260`

F	StrToInt64	As above but the output value is a signed 64-bit integer	`Writeln(StrToInt('34') + 5);//Outputs 39`

Table 10.16 String handling routines, variables and types

F- Func P - Proc V - Var T - Type	Name	What does it do?	Example
F	StrToInt64Def	As above but if the string does not represent a valid number, StrToInt64Def returns the value specifed as the default.	Default 64-bit value `Writeln(StrToInt64Def('34A', 0) + 5);`

F	StrToTime	Returns a TDateTime value of a given string.
		The string must consist of two or three numbers, separated by the character defined by the TimeSeparator field specified in TFormatSettings object.
		The numbers represent hours, minutes and (optionally) seconds. The time is assumed to be in 24-hour format unless the time is followed by AM or PM.
			Thread-safe version
			`Var`
			`  TimeVar : TDateTime;`
			`....`
			`TimeVar := StrToTime('11:35:28', FSB);`
			`Writeln(TimeToStr(TimeVar));`

F	StuffString	Returns a new string by replacing with a given substring, a specified number of characters starting with the character at a specified position in a given string.	Given string, Start, No of characters
			`Writeln(StuffString('abcdefgh', 3, 2, 'rstuvw'));`
			`//Outputs abrstuvwefgh`
			Substring

T	TFloatFormat	This type is used by routines CurrToStrF, FloatToStrF, FloatToText.	`TFloatFormat = (ffGeneral, ffExponent,ffFixed, ffNumber, ffCurrency).` See docwiki.embarcadero.com/Libraries/Rio/en/System.SysUtils.TFloatFormat for the possible values and formats

V	ThousandSeparator	Specifies the character used to separate thousands in numbers with more than three digits to the left of the decimal separator. A value of #0 indicates no thousand separator character.	`Var`
			`  FSB : TFormatSettings;`
			`....`
			`FSB.ThousandSeparator := #0;`
			`Writeln(Format('%f', [1234.23], FSB));//Outputs 1234.23`

F	TimeToStr	Returns a string obtained by converting the given time argument of type TDateTime according to the LongTimeFormat of the FormatSettings object.	Thread-safe version
			`Var`
			`  FSB : TFormatSettings;`
			`....`
			`FSB.LongTimeFormat := 'hh:nn:ss';`
			`Writeln(TimeToStr(Now, FSB));//Outputs e.g. 16:53:47`

T	TReplaceFlags	TReplaceFlags is a set of flags that govern how to locate and replace a substring within a string. The set may contain the following values: • rfReplaceAll • rfIgnoreCase	rfReplaceAll - replace all occurrences. If this flag is not present only the first occurrence of the target substring is replaced. rfIgnoreCase - Match occurrences of the substring case-insensitively. If this flag is not present, only case-senstive matches are considered.

Table 10.17 String handling routines, variables and types

F- Func P - Proc V - Var T - Type	Name	What does it do?	Example
F	Trim	Trims leading and trailing spaces and control characters from a given string, returning the result. In the 7-bit ASCII character set, control codes are defined as all characters whose code is from 0 through 31.	Writeln(Trim(' Hello ') + 'World'); //Outputs 'HelloWorld'
F	TrimLeft	Trims leading spaces and control characters from the given string, returning the result.	Writeln(TrimLeft(' Hello ') + 'World'); //Outputs 'Hello World'
F	TrimRight	Trims trailing spaces and control characters from the given string, returning the result.	Writeln(TrimRight(' Hello ') + 'World'); //Outputs ' HelloWorld'

T	TStringList	Objects of this type allow a list of up to 2,147,483,647 strings to be stored and manipulated. The list is indexed starting at 0 with values of type Integer.	Var
			  Dogs, Countries : TStringList;
			i : Integer;
			....
			Dogs := TStringList.Create;
			Dogs.Add('Alsatian');
			Dogs.Add('Labrador');
			Dogs.Add('Boxer');
			For i := 0 To Dogs.Count - 1
			  Do Writeln(Dogs[i]);
			Dogs.Free;
			Countries := TStringList.Create;
			Countries.CommaText := 'England=London, France=Paris, Germany=Berlin';
			Writeln(Countries.Values['Germany']);
			For i := 0 To Countries.Count - 1
			  Do Writeln(Countries.Names[i], ' has capital ', Countries.ValueFromIndex[i]);

F	UpCase	Returns a copy of a character in uppercase. Ch is an expression of type Char. Character values not in the range 'a'..'z' are unaffected.	Var Ch : Char; .... Ch := 'a'; Writeln(UpCase(Ch));//Outputs A
F	UpperCase	Returns a copy of a string in uppercase by converting all 7-bit ASCII characters between 'a' and 'z' to uppercase. To convert 8-bit international characters, use AnsiUpperCase.	Writeln(UpperCase('abcde'));//Outputs ABCDE

Table 10.18 String handling routines, variables and types

<table>
<tr><th>F- Func
P - Proc
V - Var
T - Type</th><th>Name</th><th>What does it do?</th><th>Example</th></tr>
<tr><td>P</td><td>Val</td><td>Converts a string value to its numeric representation. The result is stored in the second parameter. If the second parameter is of type Real then the string must be a sequence of characters that form a signed real number. If the second parameter is of type Integer then the the string must be a sequence of characters that form a whole number.

If the string is invalid, the third parameter, an Integer variable, stores the index of the offending character, otherwise the thrid parameter is set to zero.</td><td><pre>
Var
  Result1 : Real;
  Result2 : Integer;
  Code : Integer;
....
Val('-5.6', Result1, Code);
If Code = 0
  Then Writeln(Result1 :5 :2)//Outputs -5.6
  Else Writeln(Code);
Val('-5', Result2, Code);
If Code = 0
  Then Writeln(Result2)//Outputs -5
  Else Writeln(Code);
</pre></td></tr>
<tr><td>F</td><td>WrapText</td><td>1. Inserts a line break into a given string as its length approaches a specified size breaking line appropriately, e.g. at a space, hyphen or tab character.

2. Inserts a given break string (e.g. #13#10) into a given string at the last occurrence of any of the specified break characters (e.g. ['.',',','#9]) if more than one before maximum count of characters reached otherwise at the next occurence and then if no break characters remain approximately at each and every maximum count of characters taking account of spaces, etc.</td><td><pre>
Writeln(WrapText('Television is very educational.Every
time someone turns on the set,I go into another room and
read a book.Groucho Marx', 31));
{Outputs: Specified size
Television is very   in characters
educational.Every time
someone
turns on the set,I go into
another room and read a
book.Groucho Marx
}
Writeln(WrapText('Television is very educational.Every
time someone turns on the set,I go into another room and
read a book.Groucho Marx', #13#10, ['.', ',', #9], 15));
{Outputs: Break
Television is very educational. string
Every time someone turns on the set,   max count of
I go into another room and read a book.   characters
Grouch Marx   Break
}   characters
</pre></td></tr>
</table>

Table 10.19 String handling routines, variables and types

TStringList

TStringList is a list processing class defined in the library **System.Classes**.

An object `ItemsList` of this class is created as follows

```
ItemsList := TStringList.Create;
```
[4]

An object such as `ItemsList` can be used to build up a list of strings in several different ways:

1. Add method: Adds the given string to the list, returning its allocated index position (starting from 0), e.g.

   ```
   Writeln(ItemsList.Add('Kettle'));//Outputs 0 if ItemList was empty
   Writeln(ItemsList.Add('Saucepan'));//Outputs 1 if the second item in list
   ```

2. Append method: Similar to Add but does not return the index value, e.g.

   ```
   ItemsList.Append('Pepperpot');
   ItemsList.Append('Spoon');
   ```

3. Insert method: Inserts a string at a given index position. Position 0 forces an insert at the start of list, e.g.

   ```
   ItemsList.Insert(0, 'Knife');
   ```

4. Text property: Use this property to get every string from the list merged into a single string but with each separated by a carriage return and line feed combination (CRLF), e.g.

   ```
   Writeln(ItemsList.Text);
   ```

   This outputs each string in the list on a separate line.

   This property can also be used to assign strings in one go to the list, e.g.

   ```
   ItemsList.Clear;//Empties list
   ItemsList.Text := 'Knife' + sLineBreak + 'Kettle' + #13#10 + 'Saucepan'
                     + Chr(13) + Chr(10) + 'Pepperpot' + sLineBreak + 'Spoon';
   Writeln(ItemsList.Text);
   ```

   This block of code builds a list of the strings '`Knife`', '`Kettle`', '`Saucepan`', '`Pepperpot`' and '`Spoon`'.

   `sLineBreak` is a constant defined in **System.Pas** as `AnsiString(#13#10)`. Two other ways of introducing a line break are also shown - #13#10 creates the characters CR and LF; `Chr(13)` and `Chr(10)` does the same.

5. CommaText property: Use this property to set the list via a single string composed of the required list strings. The single string contains the list strings separated by commas (the DelimitedText property default value is a comma). If any of the individual strings contain spaces then these strings must be embedded in double quotes, e.g.

   ```
   ItemsList.Clear;
   ItemsList.CommaText := 'Knife, "Frying pan", "Sauce bottle", Pepperpot, Spoon';
   Writeln(ItemsList.Text);
   ```

6. Strings property: Can be used to get or update the string at a given index in the list (the first list item has index 0),

   ```
   ItemsList.Clear;
   ItemsList.Strings[0] := 'Knife';
   Writeln(ItemsList.Strings[0]);
   ```

4 This is an example of Object-Oriented Programming which is introduced in *Chapter 19*.

As the **Strings** property is the default property, it may be omitted,

e.g.

```
ItemsList.Clear;
ItemsList[0] := 'Knife';
Writeln(ItemsList[0]);
```

Count property: Returns the number of strings in the list.

Capacity property: This property is used to set or get the current capacity of the string list.

Names property: Strings in a string list can be treated as name/value pairs. Each string must have no embedded blanks, and contain an embedded = sign (the default value for **NameValueSeparator**).

Values property: Returns the value for a given name when using name/value pair strings.

ValueFromIndex property: Returns the value by string index (starting at 0) when using name/value pairs,

e.g.

```
Var
  Countries : TStringList;
....
Countries := TStringList.Create;
Countries.CommaText := 'England=London, France=Paris, Germany=Berlin';
Writeln(Countries.Values['Germany']);
For i := 0 To Countries.Count - 1
  Do Writeln(Countries.Names[i], ' has capital ', Countries.ValueFromIndex[i]);
```

Sorted property: If **True** then the string list will be automatically sorted in ascending order using **QuickSort**.

e.g.

```
ItemsList.Sorted := True;
Writeln(ItemsList.Text);
```

Sort method: If called on an unsorted string list (**Sorted = False**) then a **QuickSort** is performed to sort the strings in the list in ascending order.

Delete method: Removes the string specified by the index parameter,

e.g.

```
ItemsList.Delete(1);
Writeln(ItemsList.Text);
```

Clear method: Deletes all strings from the list.

Move method: Use this method to move the string at a given index position to a new specified position,

e.g.

```
ItemsList.Sorted := False;//To prevent error when move would violate sort order
ItemsList.Move(0, 1);
Writeln(ItemsList.Text);
```

Exchange method: Swaps the position of two strings in the list, as specified by their index positions,

e.g.

```
ItemsList.Sorted := False;//To prevent error when exchange would violate sort order
ItemsList.Exchange(2, 1);
Writeln(ItemsList.Text);
```

IndexOf method: Returns the index position in the string list of the first occurrence of the string that matches the given string. The given string matches the first occurrence of the string in the list if it is identical to or if property **CaseSensitive** is **False**, it differs only in case. If the given string does not match then -1 is returned,

e.g.

```
ItemsList.CaseSensitive := False;
Writeln(ItemsList.IndexOf('Frying pan'));
```

IndexOfName method: Returns the index position of the first occurrence of a name-value pair where the name part is equal to the given name or differs only in case. If no string in the string list has the given name, -1 is returned,

e.g.

```
Writeln(Countries.IndexOfName('Germany'));
```

Find method: Is used to obtain the index in a sorted list where a given string should be added to maintain the sorted order. In addition, it returns **True** if the given string already exists in the string list, or if property **CaseSensitive** is **False**, it differs only in case, otherwise it returns **False**,

e.g.

```
ItemsList.Sorted := True;
If ItemsList.Find('Pepperpot', Index)
  Then Writeln('Exists already at position ', Index)
  Else Writeln('Does not exist already and should be inserted at position ', Index);
If ItemsList.Find('Plate', Index)
  Then Writeln('Exists already at position ', Index)
  Else Writeln('Does not exist already and should be inserted at position ', Index);
```

CaseSensitive property: Use this property to control whether strings in a string list should be compared in a case-sensitive or case-insensitive manner. If set to **True**, then locating strings, checking for string duplicates and sorting the strings in the string list are all done in a case-sensitive manner. If set to **False**, these operations are done in a case-insensitive manner.

Duplicates property: This property specifies whether duplicate strings may be added to a sorted string list.

The possible values of this property are shown in *Table 10.20*.

Value	Meaning
dupIgnore	Ignore attempts to add duplicate strings to the list
dupError	Raise an **EStringListError** exception when an attempt is made to add duplicate strings to the sorted list
dupAccept	Permit duplicate strings in the sorted list

Table 10.20 Values for Duplicates property

The **CaseSensitive** property controls whether two strings are considered duplicates according to their case.

This property should be set to the desired value before adding strings. Setting property **Duplicates** to **dupIgnore** or **dupError** has no effect on duplicate strings that are already in the list. Duplicates has no effect if the list is not already sorted.

AddStrings method: Adds the strings from another string list to the given string list,

e.g.

```
AnotherItemsList := TStringList.Create;
AnotherItemsList.CommaText := '"Soup ladle", "Omelette pan", "Salt cellar",
Collander, Fork';
ItemsList.AddStrings(AnotherItemsList);
Writeln(ItemsList.Text);
```

AddPair method: Adds a given name-value pair to a string list using the current **NameValueSeparator**,

e.g.

```
Countries.AddPair('Belgium', 'Brussels');
Writeln(Countries.CommaText);
Writeln(Countries.Text);
```

Assign method: Replaces the current list with the contents of another list,

e.g.

```
ItemsList.Assign(AnotherItemsList);
ItemsList.Sorted := True;
Writeln(ItemsList.Text);
```

LoadFromFile method: Fills a string list with the lines of text in a specified file. **LoadFromFile** first clears any strings present in the string list. Each line in the text file (a line is terminated by CRLF or is the last line in the text file) is appended in turn as a string to the string list,

e.g.

```
ItemsList.Sorted := False;
ItemsList.LoadFromFile('Sonnet116.txt');
Writeln(ItemsList.Text);
```

There is an overloaded version which is used to specify the encoding (e.g. **TEncoding.UTF8**) used for the characters in the file otherwise the default encoding as specified in the **Default** property of **TEncoding** is used.

SaveToFile method: Saves the strings in a string list to a specified file. Each string is written to a separate line in the file,

e.g.

```
ItemsList.SaveToFile('Sonnet116.bak');
```

There is an overloaded version which is used to specify the encoding (e.g. **TEncoding.UTF8**) used for the characters in the file otherwise the default encoding as specified in the **Default** property of **TEncoding** is used.

Parse and TryParse

Static class functions, **Parse** and **TryParse** exist to parse integer and real number strings:

- System.Int32.Parse
- System.Int32.TryParse
- System.Int64.Parse
- System.Int64.TryParse
- System.Single.Parse
- System.Single.TryParse
- System.Double.Parse
- System.Double.TryParse
- System.Extended.Parse
- System.Extended.TryParse

E.g.

```
Var AnotherNumber, YetAnotherNumber : Integer;
............
AnotherNumber := System.Int32.Parse('-125');
Writeln(AnotherNumber);
If System.Int32.TryParse('-125', YetAnotherNumber)
  Then Writeln(YetAnotherNumber)
  Else Writeln('String could not be parsed');
```

```
Var AnotherNumber, YetAnotherNumber : Single;
............
AnotherNumber := System.Single.Parse('-125.5');
Writeln(AnotherNumber:8:2);
If System.Single.TryParse('-125.5',
YetAnotherNumber)
  Then Writeln(YetAnotherNumber:8:2)
  Else Writeln('String could not be parsed');
```

http://www.educational-computing.co.uk/DelphiBookCode/DelphiCode.html

Programming tasks

1. Write a program which takes as input a string and prints out the number of characters in it.
2. Write a program which takes as input a word and checks if the first and last letters of the word are the same. The program should print either "The first and last letters are the same" or "The first and last letters are different".
3. Write a program which takes as input 2 words and prints the word made from the last 3 letters of the first word and the first 3 letters of the second word.
4. Write a program which takes as input a sentence and calculates how many words are in the sentence. The program should print this number (with appropriate message). Assume a word ends with a space, a sentence ends with a full stop.
5. Write a program which inputs two words, a master word and a test word. The program should check whether or not the test word appears anywhere in the master word and then print an appropriate message. For example "THE" appears inside the word "STRENGTHEN" but not inside "STEALTH". The program should first check that the test word is shorter than the master word; if not it should print the message "Test word too long" and request a new test word.
6. Write a program which takes as input a pair of words and prints a third word made from the letters at the end of the first word if they are the same as the letters at the beginning of the second word, e.g. IGNORANT and ANTLER are input, the output is ANT, otherwise the program should request another pair of words.
7. Write a program which takes as input a word and prints out a new word made from reversing the order of the letters in the input word, e.g. input word = "BEAR", output word = "RAEB".
8. Write a program which takes as input a pair of words and checks if one is an anagram of the other. The program should output the message "ANAGRAM" if it is and the message "NOT AN ANAGRAM" if it isn't.
9. Write a program which takes as input a word and determines whether or not the word is a palindrome. (A palindrome is a word that reads the same forwards and backwards. E.g. ROTOR.)
   Test your program on the following palindromes DAD, NOON, MADAM, REDDER, ROTOVATOR.
10. Write a program which takes a single word containing only upper case letters of the alphabet as input, and outputs an encrypted version of the word using the following simple encryption algorithm
    Character code for "A" + (((Character code of letter to encrypt - character code for "A") + 13) MOD 26)
11. Write a program to output the current date.
12. Write a program to output the current time.
13. Write a program which takes as input two dates in string form and calculates the number of days between the dates.

PChar

Instead of storing the length of a string as a count of characters field, some languages rely on a special character to mark the end of the sequence of characters that constitute the string. For example, C or C++ applications expect null-terminated Unicode strings.

The special character that is used to mark the end of a string has numeric value 0 and is character #0 (character 'A' is #65). When used to mark the end of a string, the string is said to be a null terminated string and the special character a null terminator.

Access to null terminated strings is via a pointer to the string's first character.

To manipulate null-terminated strings in Delphi, it is necessary to use pointers.

In Delphi the data type **PChar** can be used for this purpose. **PChar** is defined as follows

```
Type PChar = ^Char;
```

String constants are assignment-compatible with **PChar** variables, so the following is possible

```
Var
  Ptr : PChar = 'ABC';
```

In the example, the compiler recognises that the data type is **PChar** and therefore constructs the string literal, 'ABC', as a null terminated string. The compiler assigns the address of the first character of 'ABC' to pointer variable **Ptr.**

The console program shown in *Table 10.21* is able to directly access the first

```
Program PCharProject;
{$APPTYPE CONSOLE}
Uses
  System.SysUtils;
Var
  Ptr : PChar = 'ABC';
  Ch : Char;
Begin
  Writeln(Ptr);
  Ch := Ptr^;
  Writeln(Ch);
  Inc(Ptr);
  Ch := Ptr^;
  Writeln(Ch);
  Inc(Ptr);
  Ch := Ptr^;
  Writeln(Ch);
  Readln;
End.
```

Table 10.21 PCharProject

character of the string 'ABC' by dereferencing the **PChar** pointer **Ptr** as follows

```
Ch := Ptr^;
```

The next character of 'ABC' is accessed by first incrementing the **Ptr** using **Inc(Ptr)** then, as before, dereferencing the pointer before assigning to **Char** variable **Ch**.

Writeln(Ptr) takes the same steps when it writes out 'ABC' on a single line of the console - *Figure 10.4* - as described above, until the null terminator character is reached.

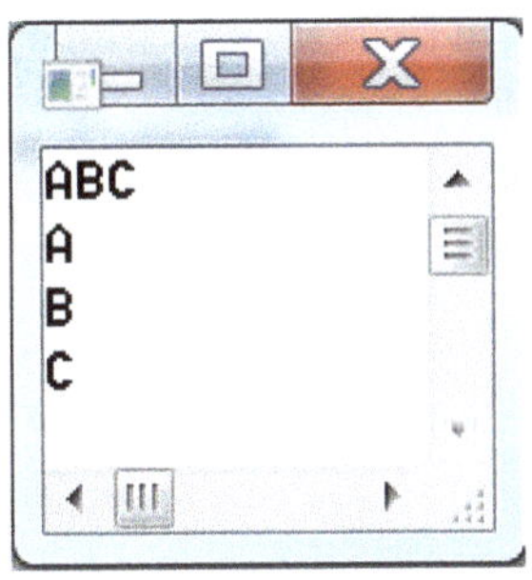

Fig. 10.4 Output from program PCharProject in execution

PWideChar

PWideChar is a pointer to a null-terminated string of **WideChar** values, that is, Unicode characters.

PWideChar defines a pointer to a memory location that contains **WideChar** values (including the #0 character).

Table 10.22 shows the unit source code for the Vcl application **PWideCharProject**.

Figure 10.5 shows the output from **PWideCharProject** when it is executed.

The Unicode characters **#966 #967** and **#968** are output to the memo box when the button **Display Unicode Characters** is clicked. The event handler called by this action access a null terminated string **#966#967#968#0** assigned to **Ptr** of datatype **PWideChar**.

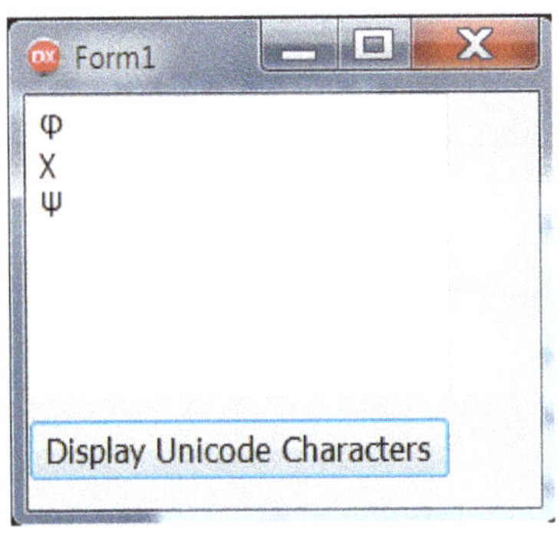

Fig. 10.5 Output from program PWideCharProject in execution

```
Unit PWideCharUnit;

Interface

Uses
  Winapi.Windows, Winapi.Messages, System.SysUtils, System.Variants,
System.Classes, Vcl.Graphics,
  Vcl.Controls, Vcl.Forms, Vcl.Dialogs, Vcl.StdCtrls;

Type
  TForm1 = Class(TForm)
             Memo1: TMemo;
    DisplayUnicodeCharacters: TButton;
             Procedure DisplayUnicodeCharactersClick(Sender:
TObject);
           End;
Var
  Form1: TForm1;

Implementation

{$R *.dfm}
Var
  Ptr : PWideChar = #966#967#968#0;

Procedure TForm1.DisplayUnicodeCharactersClick(Sender: TObject);
  Var
    Ch : Char;
  Begin
    Ch := Ptr^;
    Memo1.Lines.Add(Ch);
    Inc(Ptr);
    Ch := Ptr^;
    Memo1.Lines.Add(Ch);
    Inc(Ptr);
    Ch := Ptr^;
    Memo1.Lines.Add(Ch);
  End;
End.
```

Table 10.22 PWideCharUnit of PWideCharProject

11 Regular expressions

Regular expressions

Purpose: To become familiar with regular expressions and their uses

Regular expressions - a way of describing a set

Figure 11.1 shows a pencil with a lead hardness of HB. HB is a string of the language L_P used to describe the hardness of the lead used in pencils (the "lead" in pencils is actually graphite).

Fig. 11.1 Pencil with lead hardness HB

The **alphabet** of a subset of the language L_P is the set of symbols {H, B, 2, 3, 4}. Traditionally the symbol Σ is used to stand for an alphabet.

The **valid strings in the language L_P** form the set

{4B, 3B, 2B, B, HB, H, 4H, 3H, 2H}

which is constructed from symbols of the alphabet {H, B, 2, 3, 4}.

> **Key concept**
>
> **Set:**
> A set is an unordered collection of **different** things, e.g. set of all the students in a classroom.
>
> **Sequence:**
> A sequence is simply an ordered collection of things, e.g. the sequence of digits in your mobile phone number.
> Unlike a set, a sequence does not have the property that all the things in it are necessarily different. For example, many mobile phone numbers contain some digit more than once.

A string over an alphabet is a sequence of symbols of the alphabet.
It is possible to make other languages from the alphabet {H, B, 2, 3, 4}.
For example, the language L_X is defined by the set

{4BHH, 3BHH, 2BHH, BH, HBB, HB, 4HB, 3HB, 2HB}

In fact, there is one set for a given alphabet which contains all strings that may be created from the symbols of the given alphabet including the empty string.
We use Σ* to stand for this set.
The symbol * means "zero or more things drawn from...".
Since symbols may be repeated and since strings may be arbitrary long, Σ* is necessarily an **infinite set**, unless Σ is itself an empty alphabet.

If the alphabet Σ = {H, B, 2, 3, 4}, then Σ* is the set of all possible strings over Σ.
Let's use the symbol L for the language Σ* then L_P and L_X above are language subsets of L, i.e. $L_P \subset L$ and $L_X \subset L$.
In general, a language over Σ is any subset of Σ*.
Table 11.1 shows three alphabets, {a, b, c}, {α, β, γ}, {☺😐☹} and some possible strings over these alphabets. The special symbol ε denotes the **empty string**.

alphabet	{a, b, c}	{α, β, γ}	{☺😐☹}
some possible strings over the given alphabets	aaabaabbcaa	α α β α α α γ	😐😐😐
	bcbbbc	ε	😐☺☺☹☺☺☺
	ccc	β β β γ γ α	ε
	ε	γ γ γ γ	☺😐😐☺

Table 11.1 Some strings for given alphabets

Questions

1. Given an alphabet Σ = {0, 1}, if L_1 is the language of strings of size 3 over Σ, complete Table 11.2 to show all strings of this language.

2. Given an alphabet Σ = {0, 1}, what are the strings of L_2 if L_2 is the language of strings of size 3 which are palindromes (strings which are the same backwards and forwards)?

Valid string
000

Table 11.2 All valid strings of size 3 over the alphabet {0, 1}

Key concept

Regular expression:

A regular expression is an expression that specifies in rules the valid strings of a language. A language is a set of strings over some alphabet therefore a regular expression is a description of a set of strings over some alphabet.

So far, we have considered only simple languages, e.g. pencil hardness, binary strings of size 3, but other strings such as "sales@educational-computing.co.uk" also belong to a language.

How can we define the language consisting of strings which are email addresses?

It is not feasible to write down every valid email addresses, it is an enormous set so we turn to an alternative rule-based approach called a **regular expression**. A regular expression is an expression that specifies in rules the valid strings of a language as shown in Table 11.3.

A language is a set of strings over some alphabet therefore **a regular expression is a description of a set of strings over some alphabet**.

Regular expression	Description
∅	Denotes the set/language of no strings, i.e. {} the empty set.
ε	Denotes the set {ε}, i.e. the set/language containing only the empty string.
a, where a ∈ Σ	Denotes the set {a}, i.e. the set/language over alphabet Σ and containing only the string with only the symbol a.
r|*s* where *r* and *s* are regular expressions	Denotes the set/language *r* ∪ *s* (*r* and *s* each denote a set, ∪ denotes set union), e.g. a|b|c represents the language {a, b, c}.
rs where *r* and *s* are regular expressions	Denotes the set/language of strings each composed of a string from *r* concatenated with a string from *s*. Formally, {*RS* | *R* ∈ *r and S* ∈ *s*}. For example, (a|b)c(d| ε) represents the language {acd, ac, bcd, bc}.
*r** where *r* is a regular expression	Denotes the set/language of strings composed of the concatenation of zero or more strings, each from *r*. For example, a(b)*c represents the language {ac, abc, abbc, abbbc, abbbc, ...}.

Table 11.3 Regular expressions

Regular expressions use parentheses (brackets) for grouping things, e.g. (a|b)c(d|ε). This regular expression means either an a or b followed by c followed by d or nothing (ε).

Figure 11.2 shows a regular expression which describes a set of strings over the alphabet {0, 1}.

This set describes a language of strings beginning with three 0s, ending with three 1s, and having any combination of 0s and 1s in the middle or no combination at all.

For example, 000111 is a valid string in this language because (0|1)* means zero or more 0*s* and 1*s*. *Table 11.4* shows some more valid strings in this language.

000(0|1)*111

Fig. 11.2 Regular expression describing a set of strings over the alphabet {0, 1}

Valid string
0000111
00010111
00000111
0001010111
000111100111
00011110011111

*Table 11.4 Some valid strings over the alphabet {0, 1} for the language described by regular expression 000(0|1)*111*

Questions

3. The regular expression 001(0|1)*0 describes a language of strings over the alphabet {0, 1}.
State whether the following strings are valid strings in this language
(a) 0010 (b) 00110 (c) 00011010 (d) 0010101

Extensions to regular expressions

There are several extensions to regular expressions that are often used because they can make a regular expression more concise than it would be otherwise.

For example, r+ which means "one or more occurrences of r" can be substituted for rr*.

Table 11.5 shows more abbreviations and their equivalent regular expressions which do not use abbreviations.

The table shows that these abbreviations do not extend regular expressions in terms of what is possible to define since any language defined using these abbreviations can also be defined without using them. The abbreviations just add notational convenience. The square bracket notation defines a symbol class.

<table>
<tr><th>Abbrev-iation</th><th>Meaning</th><th>Equivalence</th><th>Example</th></tr>
<tr><td>[abc]</td><td>One occurrence of any of these symbols</td><td>(a|b|c)</td><td></td></tr>
<tr><td>[a-c]</td><td>One occurrence of any symbol from this range</td><td>(a|b|c)</td><td></td></tr>
<tr><td>r?</td><td>An optional occurrence of a string defined by r</td><td>r|ε</td><td>a?</td></tr>
<tr><td>r {n}</td><td>Exactly n occurrences of a string defined by r</td><td>rrr (if n = 3)</td><td>a {3} matches aaa</td></tr>
<tr><td>r {n,}</td><td>n or more occurrences of a string defined by r</td><td>rrr* (if n = 3)</td><td>a {3,} = aaa*</td></tr>
<tr><td>r {n, m}</td><td>Between n and m occurrences of a string defined by r</td><td>r {n}| r {n + 1}|...| r {m}</td><td>a {3,5}= aaa|aaaa|aaaaa</td></tr>
<tr><td>r+</td><td>One or more occurrences of a string defined by r</td><td>rr*</td><td>a+</td></tr>
</table>

Table 11.5 Extensions to regular expressions created to offer greater conciseness

Metasymbols

The symbol - that appears in the abbreviation [a-c] is known as a **metasymbol** or **metacharacter**. Other metacharacters include +, ?, *, [,] and |.

The - symbol is used in [a-c] to mean a range of symbols, i.e. a or b or c. The equivalent regular expression is (a|b|c). The symbol - is excluded from the matching process when it acts as a metasymbol.

A metasymbol or metacharacter is a symbol that is not used for matching purposes but instead is used as notation with special meaning, e.g. to indicate a range. Symbols that normally function as metasymbols are preceded by a backslash (\) when they need to be interpreted literally for matching purposes. For example, the regular expression a*b will match the symbol string a*b but the regular expression a*b will not. The regular expression a*b matches, for example, aaab.

> **Key concept**
>
> **Metasymbol:**
>
> A metasymbol or metacharacter is a symbol that is not used for matching purposes but instead is used as notation with special meaning, e.g. to indicate a range.
>
> Symbols that normally function as metasymbols are preceded by a backslash (\) when they need to be interpreted literally for matching purposes. This is called escaping the symbol, e.g. *

Predefined shorthand classes

A predefined symbol/character class defines a set of symbols/characters, any one of which can occur in an input string for a match to succeed. They are a convenient shorthand without which a regular expression would be much longer. For example, the predefined class \d matches any single numeric character or symbol. The predefined class \s matches a single space. \w matches a single alphanumeric character (a..z, A..Z, 0..9) and the underscore character.

Capitalising d, s, w, i.e. \D, \S, \W reverses the meaning, e.g. \S matches any single non-space character. \b allows a "whole words only" search, e.g. \b\w{4,4}\b searches for 4 letter words.

With predefined classes, the metasymbol \ functions to escape the normal meaning of the following symbol, e.g. \d means treat d as a metasymbol not as the literal symbol d.

> **Information**
>
> **Online regular expression tester:**
>
> An online regular expression tester is available to use at https://regex101.com/.

Interpreting a regular expression

To interpret a regular expression requires knowledge of the order in which to apply the metasymbols * + ? |

In arithmetic, we need to know whether 5 + 2 x 6 should be interpreted as 5 + (2 x 6) or (5 + 2) x 6.

In arithmetic, we use operator precedence rules and brackets to override these rules.

In regular expressions, precedence rules apply and brackets are used to override these rules.

Regular expression precedence rules:

- *, + and ? are always done first
- Concatenation is done next (e.g. abc)
- | comes last.

Questions

4. The regular expression (ab|cd)(e|f)*(g|h|ε) describes a language of strings over the alphabet {a, b, c, d, e, f, g, h}.
   State whether the following strings are valid strings in this language
   (a) ab (b) abeeh (c) cdffef (d) bcffef (e) cdeeefefgh

5. A regular expression for defining the language of DNA sequences can be expressed as `[ACGT]+`
   Rewrite this regular expression in a form which doesn't use square brackets.

6. The case insensitive form of the above regular expression for defining the language of DNA sequences is expressed as follows `[ACGTacgt]+`
   Rewrite this regular expression in a form which doesn't use square brackets.

Questions

7 The rules for forming identifiers in a particular programming language can be expressed in a regular expression as `[A-Za-z][A-Za-z0-9_]*`

(a) State this rule in words.

(b) State whether the following strings are valid identifiers in this language

(i) Form1 (ii) outer_loop (iii) _unknown (iv) anon_

8 A regular expression for dates is as follows

`([1-9]|(1|2)[0-9]|(30|31))/(1[0-2]|[1-9])/[1-9][0-9]*`

(a) Check that the following dates are valid strings according to this regular expression

(i) 20/11/2 (ii) 30/8/2016 (iii) 0/0/0 (iv) 13/12\2017

(b) The set of dates that this regular expression describes contains semantically invalid dates, i.e. dates that do not appear in the Gregorian calendar, the one in use today. Give one example of a semantically invalid date that appears in the set of dates.

9 Explain why

(a) `a\+b` will match `a+b` but not `a\+b`

(b) `a\\b` will match `a\b` but not `a\\b`

(c) [a-d] will not match - but [a\-d] will

Worked example

The regular expression for valid strings in a language is `ab*c+de?fg|d`

This will match, for example, abbcccdfg and d because `ab*c+de?fg|d` means either "a single a followed by zero or more bs followed by one or more cs followed by a single d and zero or one es and then fg" or "a single d".

Table 11.6 shows a summary of useful metasymbols.

Metasymbol	Meaning
-	Used to indicate a range, e.g. [0-9] means 0 or 1 or ... or 8 or 9
*	Used to indicate zero or more occurrences, e.g. a* means the empty string or a or aa or aaa or ...
?	Used to indicate zero or one occurrences, e.g. a? means the empty string or a
+	Used to indicate one or more occurrences, e.g. a+ means a or aa or aaa or ...
.	The dot matches any single symbol except a symbol which represents newline, e.g. .an matches aan, ban, can, dan, ...
\	Used to escape the metasymbol interpretation so symbol can be interpreted literally, e.g. \+
|	Used to indicate an alternative, e.g. a|b matches a or b
(and)	Parentheses (brackets) are used to group things, e.g. (a|b)c(d|ε)
[and]	Square brackets are used to abbreviate regular expressions, e.g. [a-d] means a|b|c|d
^	Typing a caret after an opening square bracket will negate the symbol class, e.g. [^A-Z] means will match a single occurrence of a symbol which isn't from this range.
.	Matches any character except when escaped with \, e.g. \. or enclosed in square brackets, e.g. [.] when the meaning becomes the literal character '.'

Table 11.6 Metasymbols or metacharacters and their meaning

Information

Regular expression tester:
If you want to install a regular expression tester then one which is suitable, The Regex Coach, may be downloaded from http://www.weitz.de/regex-coach/.

Worked example

The regular expression for a real number is `[+\-]?\d+(\.\d+)?`

This is because `[+\-]` matches a single character which is `+` or `-`.

The `\` is used because `-` is a metacharacter. `[+\-]?` matches zero or one character which is `+` or `-`.

`\d` matches any digit. `\d+` matches one or more digits.

`\.` matches the decimal point (`\` is used to escape the metacharacter meaning of '.', which is match any character).

`(\.\d+)` means match a decimal point followed by one or more digits.

`(\.\d+)?` means no instance or a single instance of a decimal point followed by one or more digits.

Questions

10. The regular expression `[+\-]?\d+` describes a set of numbers. Are the following numbers members of this set and why?
    (a) `431` (b) `-6273` (c) `+19274` (d) `+`

11. The regular expression `[+\-]?\d+(\.\d+)?` describes a set of numbers. Are the following numbers members of this set and why?
    (a) `431` (b) `-6273.4` (c) `+19274.385` (d) `+45.4d5`

12. Explain why mary@quitecontrary.co.uk is a member of the set described by the regular expression
    `[_a-zA-Z\d\-\.]+@([_a-zA-Z\d\-]+(\.[_a-zA-Z\d\-]+)+)`
    but er!@;#£M is not.

Forming and using simple regular expressions for string manipulation and matching

Pattern matching

Searching text is an important computing task, e.g. searching for one occurrence or all occurrences of some specific string in a large document. Searching relies on **pattern matching**.

For example, we might want to search for the word "needle" in a large word-processing document, or we might want to search for all occurrences of the string "GATCGGAATAG" in the human genome.

There is a need to check whether or not an e-mail address is formed correctly.

Pattern-matching is used to do this. For example, mary@educational-computing.co.uk looks like an e-mail address, but er!@;#£M does not.

Regular expressions (regex) offer a way to specify such patterns and also to solve the corresponding pattern-matching problem.

The regular expression [A-Za-z_][A-Za-z_0-9]* could be used to search for an identifier in a programming language.

Regular expressions are used extensively in operating systems for pattern matching in commands and when performing a search for files or folders.

String manipulation

The manipulation of text is an important computing task is, e.g. word-processing documents, DNA sequences, computer programs. Often we want to find a particular string and replace it with another string.

This means searching for a word in a block of text.

You can use a regular expression to find a word, even if it is misspelled. For example, if searching for the word separate (correct spelling), the regular expression sep[ae]r[ae]te would find separate, seperate, seperete and separete.

Other applications are scanning for virus signatures, search and replace in word processors, searching for information using search engines like Google, filtering text (spam, malware, firewall traffic), validating data entry fields (e-mail, dates, URLs, debit and credit card numbers).

Questions

13 State which of the following strings match the regular expression `se[ea]n`

(a) `seen` (b) `sean` (c) `sen` (d) `sea`

14 State which of the following strings match the regular expression `le?ad`

(a) `led` (b) `lad` (c) `lead` (d) `le?ad`

15 State which of the following strings match the regular expression `10(1)*01`

(a) `1001` (b) `100101` (c) `10101` (d) `1011101`

16 State which of the following strings match the regular expression `10(1)+01`

(a) `1001` (b) `100101` (c) `10101` (d) `1011101`

17 State which of the following strings match the regular expression `\d+(\-|\s)\d+`

(a) `01296-433006` (b) `101296--433006` (c) `01793    2345678`

(d) `01793 2345678` (e) `017932345678`

18 The word licence has been spelled in the following ways in a piece of text: licence, license, lisence, lisense. Write a regular expression that will find all instances of the word licence spelt in these different ways.

19 The human FMR-1 gene has a region that repeats the sequence CGG a number of times. The number of repeats varies from person to person; a higher number of repeats is associated with fragile X syndrome, a genetic disease that causes mental retardation and other symptoms in 1 in 2000 children. The pattern seems to be bracketed by GCG and CTG. Searching for this region can be done with a regular expression. Write this regular expression.

Delphi support for regular expressions

Delphi XE was the first release to ship with a **RegularExpressions** unit and therefore the first release with support for regular expressions.

To use regular expressions with versions of Delphi prior to Delphi XE requires a unit to be downloaded from a third party. The **RegularExpressions** unit supplied with Delphi XE onwards exists as the third party unit **TPerlRegEx** and has done so long before Embarcadero licensed its use.

As such **TPerlRegEx** can be downloaded in one of two forms for use with earlier versions of Delphi:

Latest: http://www.regular-expressions.info/download/TPerlRegEx.zip.

Older component-based: http://www.regular-expressions.info/download/TPerlRegEx2009.zip.

An alternative from Andrey V. Sorokin can also be downloaded.
Andrey's regular expressions unit **RegExpr** has been tested with Delphi 7 and works well:

www.educational-computing.com/DelphiBook/Code/Chapter11/RegExpr.rar.

To use Andrey's **RegExpr**, just add **RegExpr.dcu** to the application's folder where the dpr and pas files are stored.

TRegEx IsMatch function

To use regular expressions in Delphi 10.3, the **RegularExpressions** unit must be added to the **Uses** clause.

A variable of type **TRegEx** must be declared, e.g.

```
Var
  RegEx : TRegEx;
```

Testing a string, e.g. 'lead', to check if it belongs to the set of strings defined by a given regular expression, e.g. le?ad, can be done using the **IsMatch** function as follows

```
If RegEx.IsMatch('lead', 'le?ad')
  Then Writeln('Matched')
  Else Writeln('Not matched');
```

The metasymbol ? is used to indicate zero or one occurrences, e.g. e? means the empty string or e.

Testing a string, e.g. 'ibis', to check if contains an 'a' or 'b' or 'c' can be done with the regular expression [a-c] and the **IsMatch** function as follows

```
If RegEx.IsMatch('ibis', '[a-c]')
  Then Writeln('a or b or c Matched')
  Else Writeln(' or b or c Not matched');
```

Square brackets are used to abbreviate regular expressions, e.g. [a-d] means a|b|c|d.

Testing a string, e.g. '01296-433006', to check if it is a valid telephone number string can be done with the regular expression [-+]?[0-9]*\.?[0-9]+ and the **IsMatch** function as follows

```
If RegEx.IsMatch('01296-433006', '[-+]?[0-9]*\.?[0-9]+')
  Then Writeln('Matched')
  Else Writeln('Not matched);
```

The dot matches any single symbol except a symbol which represents newline.
\ is used to escape the metasymbol interpretation so the symbol can be interpreted literally, e.g. \+
* is used to indicate zero or more occurrences, e.g. a* means the empty string or a or aa or aaa or ...
+ is used to indicate one or more occurrences, e.g. a+ means a or aa or aaa or ...

Testing a string, e.g. 'sales@ecs.co.uk', to check if it is a valid email string can be done with the regular expression `^[a-zA-Z0-9._%+-]+@[a-zA-Z0-9.-]+\.[a-zA-Z]{2,}$` and the **IsMatch** function as follows

```
Write('Input an email address: ');
Readln(StringVar);
If RegEx.IsMatch(StringVar, '^[a-zA-Z0-9._%+-]+@[a-zA-Z0-9.-]+\.[a-zA-Z]{2,}$')
  Then Writeln('Matched')
  Else Writeln('Not matched');
```

The symbols ^ and $ are anchors. They do not match any character at all. Instead, they match a position before, after, or between characters. The caret ^ means the match must start at the beginning of the string; in multiline mode, it must start at the beginning of the line.
Applying `^[a-zA-Z0-9._%+-]+@` requires that the email address begins with one or more upper or lower case letters or digits or full stops or underscores or %s or pluses or hyphens followed by the '@' character. Next, `[a-zA-Z0-9.-]+\.` means one or more upper or lower case letters or digits or full stops or hyphens followed by a full stop. Finally, `[a-zA-Z]{2,}$` means the email address must end with a string that matches at least two letters, upper case or lower case or a mix of these.

Table 11.7 shows a console program **IntroductionToFunctionIsMatchProject** which uses function **IsMatch**.
(www.educational-computing.co.uk/DelphiBookCode/DelphiCode.html)

P

```
Program IntroductionToFunctionIsMatchProject;
{$APPTYPE CONSOLE}
Uses
  System.SysUtils,
  RegularExpressions;
Var
  RegEx: TRegEx;
  StringVar: string;
Begin
  If RegEx.IsMatch('a', '[a-zA-Z]')
    Then Writeln('[a-zA-Z] matched')
    Else Writeln('[a-zA-Z] Not matched');
  If RegEx.IsMatch('a', '[A-Z]', [roIgnoreCase])//Case insensitive matching
    Then Writeln('[A-Z] ignore case matched')
    Else Writeln('[A-Z] ignore case Not matched');
  If RegEx.IsMatch('ibis', '[a-c]')
    Then Writeln('a or b or c matched')
    Else Writeln('a or b or c not matched');
  If RegEx.IsMatch('lad', 'le?ad')
    Then Writeln('lad matched')
    Else Writeln('lad not matched');
  If RegEx.IsMatch('01296-433006', '[-+]?[0-9]*\.?[0-9]+')
    Then Writeln('Telephone number matched')
    Else Writeln('Telephone number not matched');
  Repeat
    Write('Input an email address: ');
    Readln(StringVar);
    If RegEx.IsMatch(StringVar, '^[a-zA-Z0-9._%+-]+@[a-zA-Z0-9.-]+\.[a-zA-Z]{2,}$')
      Then Writeln('Email address matched')
      Else Writeln('Email address not matched');
  Until StringVar = 'exit';
  Readln;
End.
```

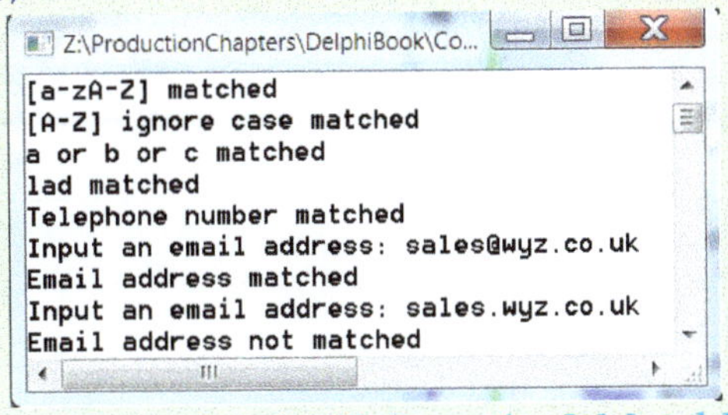

Fig. 11.3 IntroductionToFunctionIsMatchProject in execution

Table 11.7 Introduction to regular expressions console program

The data type **TRegEx** is defined in the unit **System.RegularExpressions** located in folder **C:\Program Files (x86)\Embarcadero\Studio\20.0\source\rtl\common** (if you have a later or earlier version of Delphi you will need to change 20.0 to the relevant version number). The function **IsMatch** comes in two flavours:

1. A static class function, a copy of which is compiled into your program wherever it is called with a different regular expression pattern
2. An object method whose methods only need compiling once if the same regular expression is used more than once.

The **System.RegularExpressions** unit defines a set of records (see *Chapter 15* for the record data type) that mimic the regular expression classes in the .NET framework. As is the case with .NET, a regular expression may be used in just one line of code without explicit memory management.

Table 11.8 shows program **UsingMethodIsMatchProject**. A **TRegEx** object has to be created first using the constructor **Create(Const Pattern : String; Options: TRegExOptions = [roNotEmpty])**. Objects are covered in *Chapter 19*.

(www.educational-computing.co.uk/DelphiBookCode/DelphiCode.html)

```
Program UsingMethodIsMatchProject;
{$APPTYPE CONSOLE}
Uses
  System.SysUtils,
  System.RegularExpressions;
Var
  RegExEmail, RegExVisa: TRegEx;
  StringVar: string;
Begin
  RegExEmail := TRegEx.Create('^[A-Z0-9._%+-]+@[A-Z0-9.-]+\.[A-Z]{2,}$', [roIgnoreCase]);
  Repeat
    Write('Input an email address: ');
    Readln(StringVar);
    If RegExEmail.IsMatch(StringVar)
      Then Writeln('Email address matched')
      Else Writeln('Email address not matched');
  Until StringVar = 'exit';
  RegExVisa := TRegEx.Create('^4[0-9]{12}(?:[0-9]{3})?$');//uses the default TRegExOptions value
  Repeat
    Write('Input a valid Visa credit card number: ');
    Readln(StringVar);
    If RegExVisa.IsMatch(StringVar)
      Then Writeln('Valid Visa credit card number')
      Else Writeln('Invalid Visa credit card number');
  Until StringVar = '0';
  Readln;
End.
```

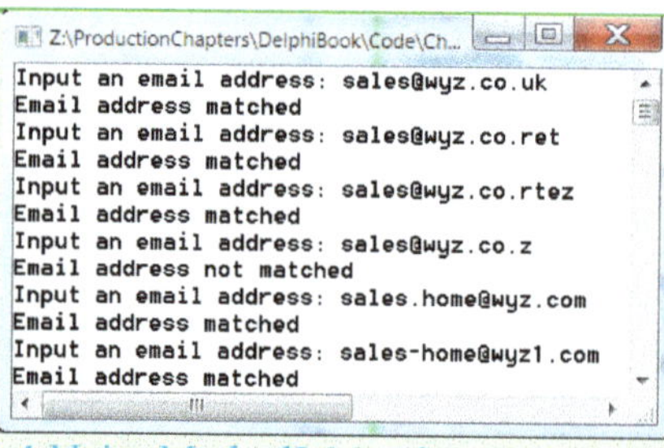

Fig. 11.4 UsingMethodIsMatchProject in execution

P

Table 11.8 Regular expressions console program which uses method IsValid

TRegEx Matches function, Count, Item and Value properties

The **Matches** function returns all matches present in a given string in the form of a **TMatchCollection** instance. The console program shown in *Table 11.9* finds all instances of the word 'separate' and its erroneously spelt variants using the regular expression `sep[ae]r[ae]te`. The matched spellings are returned by function **Matches** in an object of type **TMatchCollection** which is assigned to variable **AllMatchesCollection**. The matched spellings are then output by iterating through the **Item** field of **AllMatchesCollection** where they are collectively stored in a zero-based array. The **Count** field of **AllMatchesCollection** records the number of matches. Property **Value** stores the matched string value.

```
Program UsingMatches;
{$APPTYPE CONSOLE}
Uses
  System.SysUtils, RegularExpressions;
Var
  RegEx : TRegEx;
  AllMatchesCollection : TMatchCollection;
  i : Integer;
  StringVar : String;
Begin
  StringVar := 'The word separate is derived from the Latin separare/separatus '
             + 'but is often misspelt.'
             + 'For example, it may be spelt erroneously as seperate, '
             + 'separete or seperete.';
  Regex:= TRegEx.Create('sep[ae]r[ae]te');
  AllMatchesCollection:= Regex.Matches(StringVar);
  Writeln(IntToStr(AllMatchesCollection.Count));
  For i := 0 To AllMatchesCollection.Count - 1
    Do Writeln(AllMatchesCollection.Item[i].Value);
  Readln;
End.
```

Fig. 11.5 UsingMatches in execution

P

Table 11.9 Regular expressions console program which uses method Matches

(www.educational-computing.co.uk/DelphiBookCode/DelphiCode.html)

TRegEx Match and NextMatch functions, properties Success and Value

The **Match** function searches the given string for the first occurence of a regular expression.

The return value is a single **TMatch** instance containing the matched item.

Function **NextMatch** returns the next match.

Property **Success** is **True** if function **Match** is successful otherwise **False**.

Property **Value** stores the matched string value.

The console program shown in *Table 11.10* finds all instances of the word 'separate' and its erroneously spelt variants one match at a time using the regular expression `sep[ae]r[ae]te`.

```
Program UsingMatch;
{$APPTYPE CONSOLE}
Uses
  System.SysUtils,
  RegularExpressions;
Var
  RegEx : TRegEx;
  MatchReturned : TMatch;
  i : Integer;
  StringVar : String;
Begin
  StringVar := 'The word separate is derived from the Latin separare/separatus '
             + 'but is often misspelt.'
             + 'For example, it may be spelt erroneously as seperate, '
             + 'separete or seperete.';
  Regex:= TRegEx.Create('sep[ae]r[ae]te');
  MatchReturned:= Regex.Match(StringVar);
  While MatchReturned.Success
    Do
      Begin
        Writeln(MatchReturned.Value);
        MatchReturned := MatchReturned.NextMatch;
      End;
  Readln;
End.
```

Fig. 11.6 UsingMatch in execution

Table 11.10 Regular expressions console program which uses method Match

TRegEx Replace function

The function **Replace** replaces all matches in a given string with another string, returning the amended given string. In the console program shown in *Table 11.11* the given string is supplied as a copy of the string stored in **StringVar**. The string which replaces the match is the literal string 'separate'. The result is assigned to **StringVar** as follows

```
StringVar := Regex.Replace(StringVar, 'separate');
```

```
Program UsingReplaceFunction;
{$APPTYPE CONSOLE}
Uses
  System.SysUtils,
  RegularExpressions;
Var
  RegEx : TRegEx;
  StringVar : String;
Begin
  StringVar := 'The word separate is derived from the Latin separare/separatus '
             + 'but is often misspelt.'
             + 'For example, it may be spelt erroneously as seperate, '
             + 'separete or seperete.';
  Regex:= TRegEx.Create('sep[ae]r[ae]te');
  StringVar := Regex.Replace(StringVar, 'separate');
  Writeln(StringVar);
  Readln;
End.
```

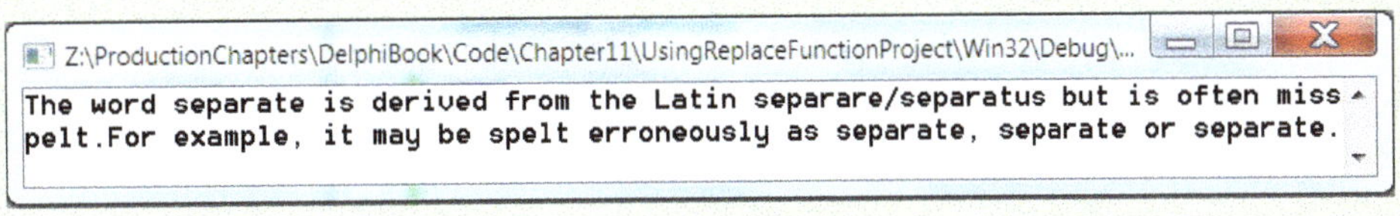

Fig. 11.7 UsingReplaceFunction in execution

Table 11.11 Regular expressions console program which uses function Replace

(www.educational-computing.co.uk/DelphiBookCode/DelphiCode.html)

TRegEx Match and NextMatch functions, properties Success and Index

The console application program shown in *Table 11.12* illustrates the role of the **Index** property on storing the starting position of each match in the given search string, **StringVar.**
Index starts from 1, it is not a zero-based position property.

```
Program IndexProperty;
{$APPTYPE CONSOLE}
Uses
  System.SysUtils, RegularExpressions;
Var
  RegEx : TRegEx;
  MatchReturned : TMatch;
  StringVar : String;
Begin
  StringVar := 'The word separate is derived from the Latin separare/separatus '
             + 'but is often misspelt.'
             + 'For example, it may be spelt erroneously as seperate, '
             + 'separete or seperete.';
  RegEx:= TRegEx.Create('sep[ae]r[ae]te');
  MatchReturned := RegEx.Match(StringVar);
  While MatchReturned.Success
    Do
      Begin
        Writeln('Next match index position: ', MatchReturned.Index);
        MatchReturned := MatchReturned.NextMatch;
      End;
  Readln;
End.
```

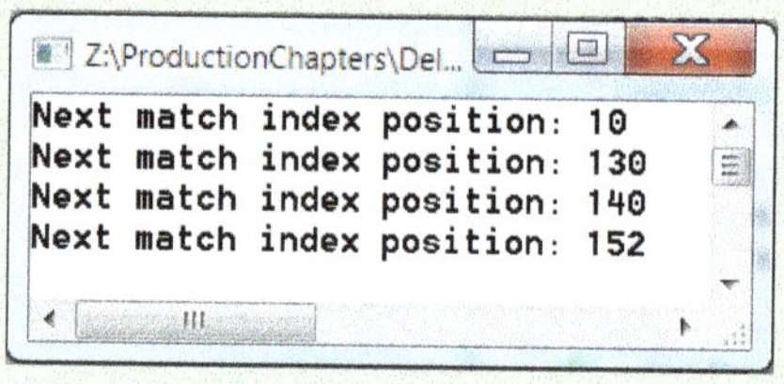

Fig. 11.8 IndexProperty in execution

P

Table 11.12 Regular expressions console program which uses property Index

TRegEx Split function

The **Split** function splits a given string at boundaries defined by matches with a regular expression. The results are returned in a dynamic array whose data type is defined as follows

```
Type
  TStringDynArray = Array Of String;
```

The console program shown in *Table 11.13* splits the given string stored in **StringVar** into separate words as shown in *Figure 11.9*. The regular expression used for this task is `\W+`.
`\W` is a predefined class which matches a single non-alphanumeric character (alphanumeric = letters or numerals 0-9). The `+` symbol means one or more occurrences of `\W`.

```
Program UsingSplitProject;
{$APPTYPE CONSOLE}
Uses
  System.SysUtils,
  RegularExpressions, System.Types;
Var
  RegEx : TRegEx;
  MatchReturned : TMatch;
  StringVar, WordString : String;
  WordArray : TStringDynArray;
Begin
  StringVar := 'The word separate is derived from the Latin separare/separatus '
             + 'but is often misspelt.'
             + 'For example, it may be spelt erroneously as seperate, '
             + 'separete or seperete.';
  RegEx:= TRegEx.Create('\W+');
  WordArray := RegEx.Split(StringVar);
  For WordString In WordArray
    Do Writeln(WordString);
  Readln;
End.
```

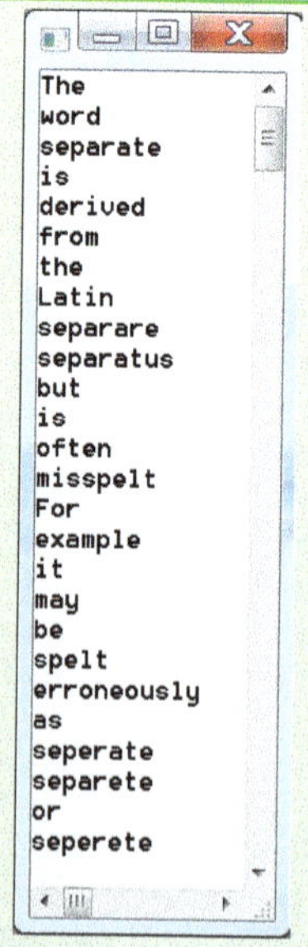

Fig. 11.9 UsingSplitProject in execution

P

Table 11.13 Regular expressions console program which uses function Split

(www.educational-computing.co.uk/DelphiBookCode/DelphiCode.html)

Using word boundary \b predefined shorthand class to match words of a specific length

Table 11.14 shows a console program which uses the regular expression `\b\w{4,4}\b` to match four-letter words in a given string stored in **StringVar**. The predefined shorthand class `\b` is used around `\w{4,4}` to mean apply the latter to complete words in the given string. The predefined shorthand class `\w` means match any alphanumeric character (a-z, A-Z, 0-9). `{4,4}` means match a string between 4 characters and 4 characters in length, i.e. a string exactly 4 characters long, and since {4,4} follows \w, it means match alphanumeric character strings of length 4.

Figure 11.10 shows the output when console program DictionaryProject is executed.

```
Program DictionaryProject;
{$APPTYPE CONSOLE}
Uses
  System.SysUtils, RegularExpressions;
Var
  RegEx : TRegEx;
  AllMatchesCollection : TMatchCollection;
  i : Integer;
  StringVar : String;
Begin
  StringVar := 'abort'+#13#10
              + 'ace'+#13#10
              + 'ant'+#13#10
              + 'arc'+#13#10
              + 'been' + #13#10
              + 'crab' + #13#10
              + 'dent'+ #13#10
              + 'effort'+ #13#10
              + 'free'+ #13#10;
  Regex:= TRegEx.Create('\b\w{4,4}\b');
  AllMatchesCollection:= Regex.Matches(StringVar);
  Writeln('Dictionary');
  Writeln(StringVar);
  Writeln('-------------');
  Writeln('All 4-letter words');
  For i := 0 To AllMatchesCollection.Count - 1
    Do Writeln(AllMatchesCollection.Item[i].Value);
  Readln;
End.
```

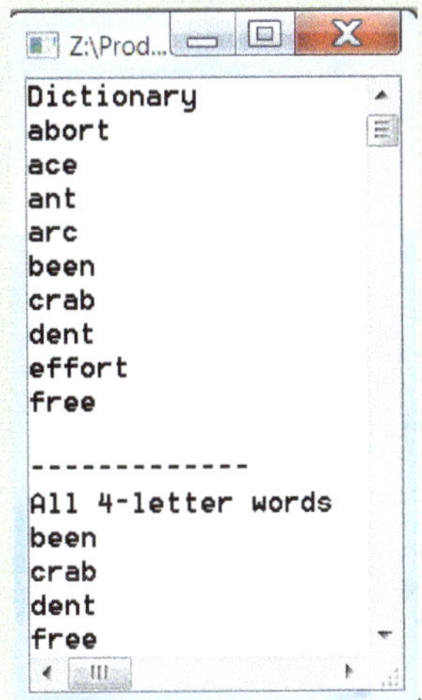

Fig. 11.10 DictionaryProject in execution

Table 11.14 Regular expressions console program which performs a word search

Programming tasks

1. Write a program which uses the regular expression `\bd\w{3,3}\b` to find all four-letter words that begin with the letter 'd'. Use the string assigned to StringVar shown in *Table 11.14.*

2. Write a program which uses the regular expression `\b\w{2,2}fo\w{2,2}\b` to find all six-letter words whose middle letters are 'fo'. Use the string assigned to **StringVar** shown in *Table 11.14.*

3. Download **DictionaryStreamProject** from
   www.educational-computing.com/DelphiBook/Code/Chapter11/DictionaryStreamProject.rar.
   The folder containing **DictionaryStreamProject.exe** should also contain a dictionary file **sowpods.txt**. This dictionary file needs to be present in the folder containing any exe file that you create and which needs to access the dictionary file. Run this program to see what it does.
   Modify source code of program **DictionaryStreamProject** as follows then recompile and run:
   (a) Change the regular expression to \b\w{3,3}ab\w{3,3}\b so that all 8-letter words with middle letters 'ab' are found.
   (b) Change the regular expression to \b\w{4,4}ab\w{4,4}\b so that all 10-letter words with middle letters 'ab' are found.

Programming tasks

4. Write a program to check your answers to question 3.

5. Write a program to check your answers to question 10.

6. Write a program to check your answers to question 11.

7. Download DNASequence1.txt from
www.educational-computing.com/DelphiBook/Code/Chapter11/DNASequence1.rar
This text file contains a DNA sequence of approximately 1000 nitrogen bases, adenine (A), thymine (T), guanine (G) and cytosine (C).
The human FMR-1 gene has a region that repeats the sequence CGG a number of times. The number of repeats varies from person to person; a higher number of repeats is associated with fragile X syndrome, a genetic disease that causes mental retardation and other symptoms in 1 in 2000 children. The pattern seems to be bracketed by GCG and CTG. Searching for this region can be done with a regular expression.
Write a program to search the file DNASequence1.txt for the fragile X syndrome.
(a) Try searching first for one or more CGGs bracketed as described using an appropriate regular expression.
(b) Modify your regular expression so that it matches three or more CGGs bracketed as described.

Information

More information on regular expressions including tutorials and examples can be found at https://www.regular-expressions.info.

In Delphi XE5 and the earlier versions that support the RegularExpressions unit, TRegEx always skips zero-length matches. This was fixed in Delphi XE6. You can make the same fix in XE5 and previous versions by modifying RegularExpressionsCore.pas to remove the line State := [preNotEmpty] from TPerlRegEx.Create. This change will also affect code that uses TPerlRegEx directly without setting the State property.

Much insight can be gained about the functions and properties of TRegEx from the RegularExpressions unit and Andrey V. Sorokin's RegExpr unit by looking at the source code for these units.

12 Random number generation

Random numbers

Purpose: Learning how to generate random numbers.

Fig. 12.1 Rolling dice

Did you know?

The history of pseudorandom number generator algorithms began during the Manhattan project in the Second World War when John von Neumann devised the middle-square method of generating pseudorandom number sequences - the method was marked Top Secret initially.
A quick way of generating random numbers was needed for simulations for the nuclear bomb programme.
The middle-square method is flawed because it can go horribly wrong and generate sequences which are not very random but John Neumann was happy to work with this limitation because when things went wrong it was easy to spot.
In 1949, D.H Lehman came up with the linear congruential method, a far superior method still used today in some software systems although many now use the Mersenne Twister PRNG, e.g. Free Pascal and Python.

Randomness means lack of pattern or predictability of events.

An algorithm which generates a random, or apparently random, sequence of numbers is called a **random number generator**.
For example, suppose we require a method for selecting an integer at random from the set of integers 1, 2, 3, .., N.

For small values of N simple mechanisms exist.
For example:

- for N = 2 we can toss a coin
- for N = 6 we can roll a die - *Fig. 12.1*
- for N = 12 we can roll a 12-sided die
- for N = 36 we can use a roulette wheel.

Key principle

Randomness:
Randomness means lack of pattern or predictability of events.

Every number in the chosen set of integers 1, 2, 3, .., N, is equally likely.

Statistically, each number from the set should appear on average the same number of times in a long sequence generated by coin tossing or dice rolling.

The sequence generated which satisfies these two conditions is called a **random sequence**.

Pseudorandom numbers

Most computer generated random numbers use pseudorandom number generators (PRNGs) which are algorithms that can automatically create long runs of numbers with good random properties but eventually the sequence repeats.

This kind of random number is adequate for many situations, e.g. computer simulations and cryptography.

However, pseudorandom generated number sequences are not as random as coin tosses and dice rolls or random sequences generated from physical phenomena such as electrical noise signals.

Pseudorandom number generator algorithms generate a random sequence which is completely determined by a shorter initial value known as a seed value or key.

As a result, the entire seemingly random sequence can be reproduced if the seed value is known.

For example, in the linear congruential method the next number in the pseudorandom sequence is calculated from its immediate predecessor as follows

next = (multiplier ∗ predecessor + increment) MOD modulus

We can demonstrate this method by hand if we choose small values, e.g.

- multiplier = 13,
- increment = 0,
- modulus = 31

If we start the sequence with predecessor = 1, we get the pseudorandom sequence

1, 13, 14, 27, 10, 6, 16, 22, 7, 29, 5, 3, . . .

The first thirty terms in this sequence are a permutation of the integers from 1 to 30 and then the sequence repeats itself. It has a period equal to modulus − 1.

The starting value is called the **seed**.

If we divide each pseudorandom integer in the sequence by the modulus (31) we obtain numbers which are uniformly distributed between 0 and 1.

The pseudorandom sequence

1, 13, 14, 27, 10, 6, 16, 22, 7, 29, 5, 3, . . .

becomes

0.03226, 0.4194, 0.4516, 0.8710, 0.3226, 0.1935, ...

Information

If we choose the increment to be 0 then the generator is said to be a multiplicative linear congruential generator.
To obtain a maximal cycle with such a generator, we have to ensure the modulus is prime.

Questions

1. Calculate the first seven random numbers using the linear congruential method and multiplier = 7, increment = 0, modulus = 13 and starting value 1.
2. What is the maximum length of sequence in question 1 before the sequence hits 1 again?
3. Explain why, for a given starting value, the sequence of random numbers generated from the linear congruential method in question 1 eventually repeats itself.

Task

1. Set up a spreadsheet to calculate the first 37 random numbers generated by the linear congruential method and multiplier = 7, increment = 0, modulus = 13 and starting value 1.
   What do you observe?

   Change the starting value in the spreadsheet to 6. What do you observe?

Generating random numbers

Purpose: Learning how to generate random numbers in Delphi.

In the following program, pseudorandom numbers are generated by calling the function `Random`.

The procedure `Randomize` changes the seed used to generate the range of pseudorandom numbers.

The seed used by `Random` is stored in the integer system variable `RandSeed`.

`RandSeed` may also be set directly as shown. This is useful when an application requires a specific sequence of random numbers to be generated repetitively.

Information

Single line comment. Comments are ignored by the compiler.
Single line comments use a pair of forward oblique strokes // to introduce the comment.

P

```
Program Chapter12Prog1;
{$APPTYPE CONSOLE}
Begin
  Randomize; //Changes seed
  {The next statement outputs to the console one of 2^32 possible pseudorandom
  numbers using a seed value produced by calling Randomize}
  Writeln(Random :20:18);
  RandSeed := 65500; // Sets the seed that random uses to 65500
  {The next statement outputs to the console one of 2^32 possible pseudorandom
  numbers using a seed value of 65500}
  Writeln(Random :20:18);
  {The next statement outputs to the console a random whole number in range 0
  to 5 inclusive}
  Writeln(Random(6));
  Readln;
End.
```

Information

Multiline comment. Multiline comments use a pair of braces {} to bracket the comment. Comments are ignored by the compiler..

The Delphi function `Random(Range)` returns a random number `X` in the integer range `0 <= X < Range`.

For example, `Random(6)` returns a random whole number in range `0` to `5` inclusive.

Or `Random(6)` returns a random whole number in interval `[0, 6)`

where `[` means `0` is included in interval and `)` means `6` is excluded.

If the range is not specified, the result is a real-type random number within the range `0 <= X < 1`,

that is `Random` returns a random number, X, in range `0 <= X < 1`.

Or `Random` returns a random real number (floating point number) in the interval `[0.0, 1.0)`

where `[` means `0.0` is included in the interval and `)` means `1.0` is excluded.

I Use the IDE to create and save the above source code program as **Chapter12Prog1.dpr** or **Chapter12Prog1.dprog**, depending on the version of Delphi, in its own directory/folder named **Chapter12Prog1**.

I Now build the program (Shift F9).

I Run this program in Debug mode (F9).

Fig. 12.2 shows output produced by the execution of program **Chapter12Prog1**. Running the program again should produce a different value for the first random number. Therefore, the result that is obtained will not necessarily produce the output shown in *Fig. 12.2* for the first random number but the next two numbers should be as shown gievn they use the same seed.

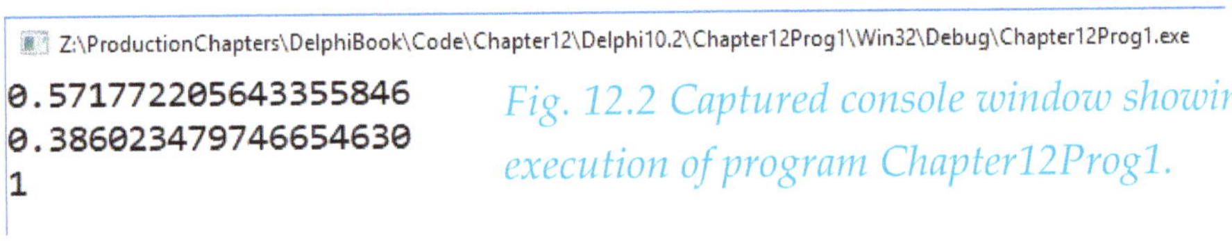

Fig. 12.2 Captured console window showing output produced by execution of program Chapter12Prog1.

Programming tasks

1. Write a program to generate and display a random integer in interval [0, 10), i.e. $0 \le x < 10$.
2. Write a program to generate and display a random integer in interval [1, 6], i.e. $1 \le x \le 6$. (Hint: Add 1 to each random integer).
3. Write a program to generate and display a random floating point number in the interval [0.0, 10.0), i.e. $0.0 \le x < 10.0$ (Hint: multiply the random number returned by 10).

Pseudorandom number distribution

Purpose: Checking randomness of random number generator.

The following program generates `2147483647` pseudorandom numbers in the range `0` to `5` inclusive by calling the function `Random` this number of times. A count is maintained in the array `DistributionArray` for each generated random number in this range. The total count for each possible random number is then written to the console window.

```
Program Chapter12Prog2;
{$APPTYPE CONSOLE}
Var
  i, Count, Sum : Integer;
  DistributionArray : Array [0..5] Of Integer = (0,0,0,0,0,0);
Begin
  Randomize; // Set seed
  Count := 0;
  Sum := 0;
  For i := 1 To 2147483647
    Do
      Begin
        Count := Count + 1;
        Case Random(6) Of
          0 : DistributionArray[0] := DistributionArray[0] + 1;
          1 : DistributionArray[1] := DistributionArray[1] + 1;
          2 : DistributionArray[2] := DistributionArray[2] + 1;
          3 : DistributionArray[3] := DistributionArray[3] + 1;
          4 : DistributionArray[4] := DistributionArray[4] + 1;
          5 : DistributionArray[5] := DistributionArray[5] + 1;
        End;
      End;
  Writeln('Count = ', Count);
  For i := 0 To 5
    Do
      Begin
        Writeln(i,':', DistributionArray[i]);
        Sum := Sum + DistributionArray[i];
      End;
  Writeln('Sum = ', Sum);
  Readln;
End.
```

Warning

This program's execution will take some time to produce output, e.g. 15 seconds.

Fig. 12.3 shows the output produced by the execution of program **Chapter12Prog2** confirming that the generated random numbers are distributed more or less evenly across the range, i.e. each random number is more or less equally likely.

```
Z:\ProductionChapters\DelphiBook\Code\Chapter12\Delphi10.2\Chapter12Prog2\Win32\Debug\Chapter12Prog2.exe
Count = 2147483647
0:357923277
1:357889677
2:357944175
3:357904605
4:357938206
5:357883707
Sum = 2147483647
```

Fig. 12.3 Captured console window showing output produced by execution of program Chapter12Prog2.

Programming tasks

4. Write a program to generate and display 10 random integers in the interval [0, 10), i.e. 0 ≤ x < 10.

5. Write a program to generate and display 10 random floating point numbers in the interval [0.0, 10.0), i.e. 0.0 ≤ x < 10.0.

Seeding the generation of the pseudorandom number sequence

Purpose: Learning how to set the seed from the computer's internal clock.

The `Randomize` procedure derives its seed value by sampling the computer's internal clock. However, it is possible to use the internal clock to set the seed directly.

The following program uses the internal clock's current time to set a value for the seed used by the `Random` function each time it is called.

P

```
Program Chapter12Prog3;
{$APPTYPE CONSOLE}
Uses SysUtils;
Var
  Hours, Mins, Secs, MilliSecs : Word;
Begin
  {The function Now returns the current date and time.
  The procedure DecodeTime extracts the time part and
  breaks it into hours, minutes and seconds}
  DecodeTime(Now, Hours, Mins, Secs, MilliSecs);
  RandSeed := MilliSecs;
  Writeln('RandSeed = ', RandSeed);
  Writeln(Random :20:18);
  Writeln(Random(10));
  Readln;//This ensures a delay before clock sampled again.
  DecodeTime(Now, Hours, Mins, Secs, MilliSecs);
  RandSeed := MilliSecs;
  Writeln('RandSeed = ', RandSeed);
  Writeln(Random :20:18);
  Writeln(Random(10));
  Readln;
End.
```

Fig. 12.4 shows the output produced by the execution of program **Chapter12Prog3**. `RandSeed` is set to a value derived from the system clock of the computer before the calls to `Random` for the first output pair of random numbers and again before the output of the second pair.

```
Z:\ProductionChapters\DelphiBook\Code\Chapter12\Chapter12Prog3\Win32\Debug\Chapter12Prog3.exe
RandSeed = 114
0.577313079265877604
6
RandSeed = 115
0.608693018555641174
4
```

Fig. 12.4 Captured console window showing output produced by execution of program Chapter12Prog3.

Producing a repeatable pseudorandom number sequence

Purpose: Learning that using the same seed produces the same pseudorandom number sequence.

The following program generates sequences of random numbers twice, each time using the same seed value 25.

Fig.12.5 shows the output produced by the execution of program **RandomProg4**. Note that the first and second sequences are identical. This happens because the numbers are produced by a pseudorandom number generator and the same seed is used for both number sequence.

P

```
Program Chapter12Prog4;
{$APPTYPE CONSOLE}
Var
  i : Integer;
Begin
  RandSeed := 25;
  Writeln('Generation of first sequence with seed 25');
   For i := 1 To 9
    Do Writeln(i,':', Random(6):4);
  RandSeed := 25;
  Writeln('Generation of second sequence with seed 25');
   For i := 1 To 9
    Do Writeln(i,':', Random(6):4);
  Readln;
End.
```

Programming tasks

6. Amend **Chapter12Prog4** by changing the second seed value to 30. Build (Shift F9) and run in Debug mode (F9). Is the second sequence different from the first?

7. Amend **Chapter12Prog4** by changing the first and second seed values to 30. Build and run. Is the second sequence different from the first?

```
Z:\ProductionChapters\DelphiBook\Code\Chapter12\Delphi10.2\Chapter12Prog4\Win32\Debug\Chapter12Prog4.exe
Generation of first sequence with seed 25
1:   4
2:   4
3:   2
4:   5
5:   1
6:   5
7:   2
8:   2
9:   4
Generation of second sequence with seed 25
1:   4
2:   4
3:   2
4:   5
5:   1
6:   5
7:   2
8:   2
9:   4
```

Fig. 12.5 Captured console window showing output produced by execution of program Chapter12Prog4.

Questions

4. What is the role of a seed in the generation of pseudorandom number sequences?

5. A certain online Poker site found that a group of players was winning every time against the computer-generated poker hands. On investigation, it was discovered that the group was familiar with the programming language used to program the poker game and had also worked out how to obtain the uptime of the server.
   Explain one way this group could have accurately predicted the computer-generated poker hands.

Estimating a value for π

Purpose: Showing how a pseudorandom number generator can be used to estimate a value for π

We are going to use a pseudorandom number generator to generate a number of random x, y coordinates located within the boundaries of a square of side r shown in *Fig. 12.6*.

If a large enough number of random x, y pairs are generated the pairs will cover all the available space within the square, almost uniformly.

Some of these x, y pairs will fall within the quadrant of the circle of radius r, which shares an origin 0,0 with the square.

The fraction of these x, y pairs falling within the quadrant will be equal to the area of the quadrant divided by the area of the square when the pairs cover all the available space within the square.

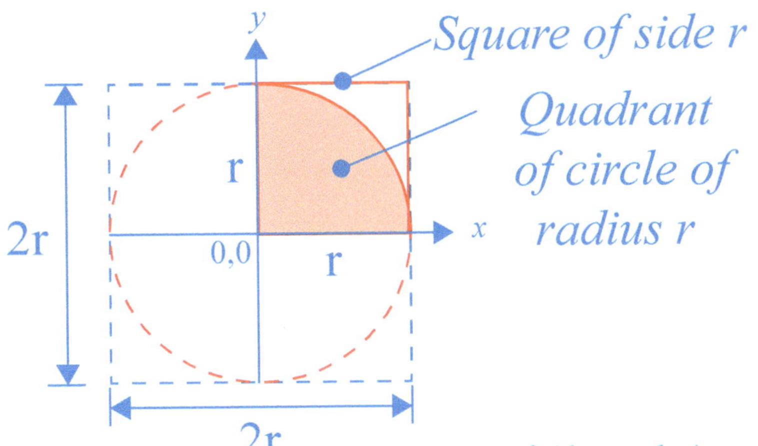

Fig. 12.6 Square of side r enclosing a quadrant of a circle of radius r.

The area of the quadrant is the area of the circle, radius r, divided by 4, i.e. $\pi r^2/4$.

The area of the square, radius r, is r^2.

Therefore the fraction of the total number of pairs that fall within the quadrant = $\frac{\pi r^2/4}{r^2} = \frac{\pi}{4}$

This gives us a ethod for calculating π.

Imagine the circle of radius r to be a dartboard which darts hit randomly.

If the number of darts landing in the square of side r is n then the number landing in the quadrant is $\frac{\pi}{4} \times n$.

Each hit landing in the quadrant must have an x, y pair which satisfies $x^2 + y^2 < r^2$ as illustrated in *Fig. 12.7* (the x_1, y_1 pair for which $x_1^2 + y_1^2 = r^2$ is true lies on the boundary, and so is not within the quadrant).

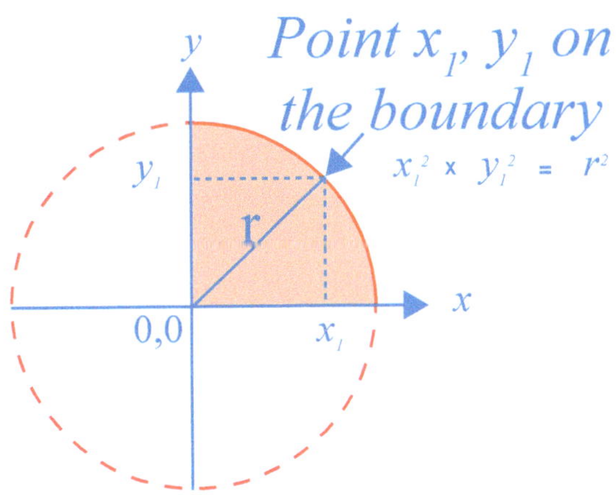

Fig. 12.7 Every x,y pair that lands within the quadrant must satisfy $x^2 + y^2 < r^2$.

Therefore, if we count the number of pairs landing within the quadrant we can calculate an approximate value of π. The greater the number of pairs the better the approximation.

Call the quadrant count NoOfHits then NoOfHits = $\frac{\pi}{4} \times n$

rearranging,

$$\pi = \frac{4 \times \text{NoOfHits}}{n}$$

Program **Chapter12Prog5a** uses this formula and a radius of 1.0 to calculate an approximate value for π.

The approximation is improved using more x, y pairs, n.

Fig. 12.8 shows console output for various values of n from 1000 to 1000000000.

The value of π to 3 decimal places is 3.142.

The output from the execution of the program `Chapter12Prog5a` is in agreement with this value for $n \geq 10^6$.

```
Z:\ProductionChapters\DelphiBook\Code\Chapter12\Delphi10.2\Chapter12Prog5a\Win32\Debug\Chapter12Prog5a.exe
Enter number of x,y pairs to generate (or 0 to exit): 10000

10000 x,y pairs within square, 7955 pairs within quadrant, Calculated Pi = 3.18200000

Enter number of x,y pairs to generate (or 0 to exit): 100000

100000 x,y pairs within square, 78510 pairs within quadrant, Calculated Pi = 3.14040000

Enter number of x,y pairs to generate (or 0 to exit): 1000000

1000000 x,y pairs within square, 785463 pairs within quadrant, Calculated Pi = 3.14185200

Enter number of x,y pairs to generate (or 0 to exit): 10000000

10000000 x,y pairs within square, 7854451 pairs within quadrant, Calculated Pi = 3.14178040

Enter number of x,y pairs to generate (or 0 to exit): 100000000

100000000 x,y pairs within square, 78541873 pairs within quadrant, Calculated Pi = 3.14167492

Enter number of x,y pairs to generate (or 0 to exit): 1000000000

1000000000 x,y pairs within square, 785389174 pairs within quadrant, Calculated Pi = 3.14155670

Enter number of x,y pairs to generate (or 0 to exit): 10000000000

10000000000 x,y pairs within square, 7853994840 pairs within quadrant, Calculated Pi = 3.14159794

Enter number of x,y pairs to generate (or 0 to exit):
```

Fig. 12.8 Console output produced by the execution of program Chapter12Prog5a.

```
Program Chapter12Prog5a;
{$APPTYPE CONSOLE}
Uses
  System.SysUtils;
Var
  CalculatedPi, x, y : Real;
  NoOfHits, n, i : Int64;//Use Integer/LongInt for i depending on your Delphi version
Begin
  Repeat
   Write('Enter number of x,y pairs to generate (or 0 to exit): ');
   Readln(n);
   Writeln;
   NoOfHits := 0;
   If (n > 0)
     Then
       Begin
         Randomize;
         For i := 1 To n
           Do
             Begin
               x := Random; //Random → random number in interval (0.0, 1.0]
               y := Random; //Random → random number in interval (0.0, 1.0]
               If ((x*x + y*y) < 1.0) // Radius of circle r = 1.0
                 Then NoOfHits := NoOfHits + 1;
             End;
         CalculatedPi := 4.0 * NoOfHits/n;
         Writeln(n, ' x,y pairs within square, ', NoOfHits,
                   ' pairs within quadrant,', 'Calculated Pi = ', CalculatedPi:10:8);
         Writeln;
       End;
  Until n = 0;
End.
```

Warning

This program's execution will take some time to produce output for the larger values of n, e.g. 4 minutes for n = 10000000000.

Programming tasks

8 Load Chapter12Prog5a and build (Shift F9) and run in Debug mode (F9). Experiment with values of n to find the smallest value which produces a value for π of 3.142 to 3 decimal places. P

9 Program Chapter12Prog5 is an alternative to program Chapter12Prog5a. Unfortunately, it does not always perform as expected when it is compiled and executed because of an error in its source code.
What is this error? (You may load and try running this program for yourself).

```
Program Chapter12Prog5;
{$APPTYPE CONSOLE}
Uses
  System.SysUtils;
Var
  CalculatedPi, x, y : Real;
  NoOfHits, n, i : Int64;
Begin
  NoOfHits := 0;
  While True
    Do
      Begin
        Write('Enter number of x,y pairs to generate (or 0 to exit): ');
        Readln(n);
        Writeln;
        If (n <= 0)
          Then Break;
        Randomize;
        For i := 1 To n
          Do
            Begin
              x := Random;
              y := Random;
              If ((x*x + y*y) < 1.0)
                Then NoOfHits := NoOfHits + 1;
            End;
        CalculatedPi := 4.0 * NoOfHits/n;
        Writeln(n, ' x,y pairs within square, ', NoOfHits,
             ' pairs within quadrant,', 'Calculated Pi = ', CalculatedPi:10:8);
        Writeln;
      End;
 End.
```

The calculation of π method we have used belongs to a broad class of computational algorithms called Monte Carlo methods. These methods all rely on repeated random sampling to obtain numerical results. Their essential idea is using randomness to solve problems that might be deterministic in principle.

Using a pseudorandom number generator for encryption

Purpose: Showing how a pseudorandom number generator can be used to encrypt and decrypt plaintext messages

Generating large numbers of truly random numbers is extremely difficult so people have turned to using algorithms programmed into the computer to generate **pseudorandom numbers** from an initial seed. These pseudorandom numbers are generated deterministically and can only approximate a truly random distribution because numbers calculated by a computer through a deterministic process, cannot, by definition, be random. Given knowledge of the algorithm used to create the numbers and the seed, it is possible to predict all the numbers returned by subsequent calls to the algorithm, whereas with genuinely random numbers, knowledge of one number or an arbitrarily long sequence of numbers is of no use whatsoever in predicting the next number to be generated. However, the fact that pseudorandom generated sequences are reproducible, i.e. for a given algorithm, starting from the same seed generates the same sequence, can be exploited in an encryption method called the Vernam stream cipher.

In this cipher, a previously prepared key of the same length as the plaintext is combined character by character with the plaintext message to produce the ciphertext. To decrypt the ciphertext, the same key is again combined character by character, producing the plaintext. The key should contain random information so that the cipher operates an automatic form of one-time pad. *Fig. 12.9* shows the key stream being combined with the plaintext message in an exclusive-or operation.

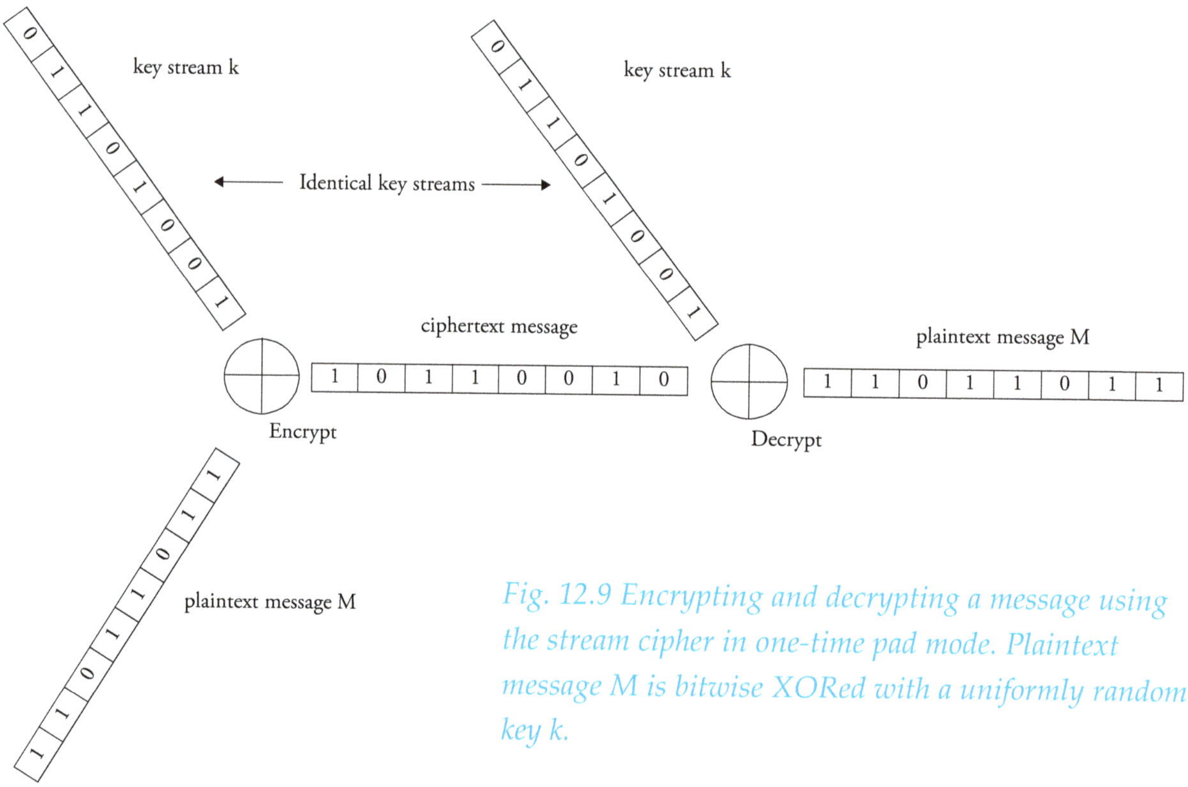

Fig. 12.9 Encrypting and decrypting a message using the stream cipher in one-time pad mode. Plaintext message M is bitwise XORed with a uniformly random key k.

The key stream consists of pseudorandom numbers. It is generated in two stages.
The first stage generates a long stream of seeds (`Procedure GenerateSeedsArray`) in a byte array of 256 bytes.
The second stage generates a long stream of pseudorandom numbers, the key stream k, using as many seeds from the byte array in stage 1 as there are plaintext message characters.
Program **Chapter12Prog6** performs encryption and decyption of the plaintext message M using the key stream of random numbers, k.

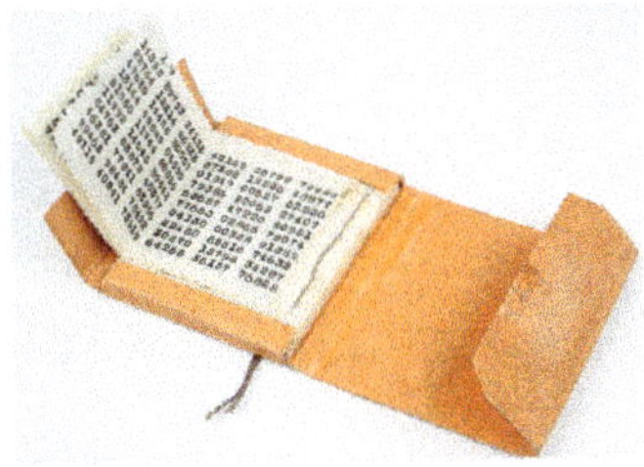

Fig. 12.10 A one-time pad reproduced with kind permission of Paul Reuvers, Crypto Museum (www.cryptomuseum.com)

```
Program Chapter12Prog6;
{$APPTYPE CONSOLE}
Uses
  System.SysUtils;
Type
  TByteArray = Array[0..255] Of Byte;
Var
  S, PseudoRandomNoArray : TByteArray;
  ShortSeedKey, PlainText, RecoveredPlainText, CipherText : String;
  i : Integer;
  Ch : Char;
  ChByteValue : Byte;
Procedure GenerateSeedsArray(Var S : TByteArray; ShortSeedKey : String);
  Var i, j, Temp : Byte;
  KeyLength : Integer;
  Begin
    For i := 0 To 255
      Do S[i] := i;
    j := 0;
    KeyLength := Length(ShortSeedKey);
    For i := 0 To 255
      Do
        Begin
          j := (j + S[i] + Ord(ShortSeedKey[i Mod KeyLength])) Mod 256;
          Temp := S[i];
          S[i] := S[j];
          S[j] := Temp;
        End;
  End;
Procedure GeneratePseudoRandomNoArray(Var PseudoRandomNoArray : TByteArray;
                                      Var S : TByteArray;
                                      PlainTextLength : Integer);

  Var k : Byte;
  Begin
    For k := 0 To PlainTextLength - 1
      Do
        Begin
          RandSeed := S[k];
          PseudoRandomNoArray[k] := Random(257);
        End;
  End;
Begin
  GenerateSeedsArray(S, 'AQACS');
  PlainText := 'Computer Science';
  Writeln('Plain text: ', PlainText);
  GeneratePseudoRandomNoArray(PseudoRandomNoArray, S, Length(PlainText));
  Ciphertext := '';
  For i := 0 To Length(PlainText) - 1
    Do
      Begin
        Ch := PlainText[i+1]; //String indexing starts at 1
        ChByteValue := Ord(Ch);
        CipherText := CipherText + Chr(ChByteValue XOR PseudoRandomNoArray[i]);
      End;
  Write('Key stream: ');
  For i := 0 To Length(PlainText) - 1
    Do Write(IntToHex(Ord(PseudoRandomNoArray[i]), 2)); Writeln;
  Write('Plaintext:  ');
  For i := 1 To Length(PlainText)
    Do Write(IntToHex(Ord(Plaintext[i]), 2)); Writeln;
  Write('Ciphertext: ');
  For i := 1 To Length(CipherText)
    Do Write(IntToHex(Ord(CipherText[i]), 2)); Writeln;
  Writeln('Decryption - Key stream and ordinal values of ciphertext exclusive-ored');
  RecoveredPlainText := '';
  For i := 0 To Length(CipherText) - 1
    Do
      Begin
        Ch := CipherText[i + 1]; //String indexing starts at 1
        ChByteValue := Ord(Ch);
        RecoveredPlainText := RecoveredPlainText + Chr(ChByteValue XOR PseudoRandomNoArray[i]);
      End;
  Writeln('Recovered plain text: ', RecoveredPlainText);
  Writeln('Press return to continue'); Readln;
End.
```

Key principle

One-time pad:

Plain text of a message is 'mixed' with random text taken from a one-time pad resulting in cipher text which is truly random. The same one-time pad is used to 'unmix' the random text from the cipher text, which results in the original plain text.

One only has to guarantee that the one-time pad is safe, that it comprises truly random numbers, that there are only two copies of it, and that both copies are destroyed immediately after use to prevent it being used again (the one-time property), for it to be used to send a message safely without the risk of being deciphered by an attacker or eavesdropper.

Programming tasks

10 Load Chapter12Prog6 and build (Shift F9) and run in Debug mode (F9). P

11 Modify Chapter12Prog6 so that the plaintext to be encrypted can be typed at the keyboard. Save as Chapter12Prog6a.dpr or Chapter12Prog6a.dprog, depending on the version of Delphi, in its own directory/folder named Chapter12Prog6a.
Build (Shift F9) and run (F9). Check that the modifed program performs as expected.

12 Modify Chapter12Prog6a so that the short seed key to be used can be typed at the keyboard. Save as Chapter12Prog6b.dpr or Chapter12Prog6b.dprog, depending on the version of Delphi, in its own directory/folder named Chapter12Prog6b.
Build (Shift F9) and run (F9). Check that the modifed program performs as expected.

13 Modify Chapter12Prog6b so that the decryption short seed key and the ciphertext can be typed at the keyboard. The program should now require the short seed key for encryption, the plaintext, the short seed key for decryption and the ciphertext to be typed at the keyboard.
Save as Chapter12Prog6c.dpr or Chapter12Prog6c.dprog, depending on the version of Delphi, in its own directory/folder named Chapter12Prog6c.
Build (Shift F9) and run (F9). Check that the modifed program performs as expected.

Additional programming tasks

14 Write a program which uses a pseudorandom number generator to generate a password of length 5. The password should consist of letters, digits and punctuation symbols chosen randomly from the ASCII (UTF-8) set of characters. Each character should have an ordinal number in the range 33 to 126, inclusive. Characters may be repeated in the password. (Hint: Use Random(127) or a Random(94) and add 33).

15 The following code snippet of checks that the next randomly generated character isn't already present in Password. It also contains the code to generate the character's ordinal number but this is not shown. The For In construct is available in versions of Delphi from Delphi 2009 onwards.
Incorporate this code into your solution for Task 14.

```
Repeat
  //Generate the next ordinal number randomly
  ...............
  // OrdinalNo generated randomly in range 33 to 126, inclusively
  Match := False;
  // For Ch In Password loop entered if length of Password > 0
  For Ch In Password
    Do
      Begin
        If Ord(Ch) = OrdinalNo
          Then
            Begin
              Match := True;
              Break; // Break out of For Ch In Password loop
            End;
      End;
Until Not Match; // Ensures a different password character chosen
Password := Password + Chr(OrdinalNo);
```

13 Subroutines(procedures and functions)

Subroutines

Purpose: To learn more about the nature of subroutines

Subroutines and their uses

A subroutine is a named self-contained block of instructions, e.g. drawsquare.By encapsulating and naming a block of instructions in a program it becomes possible to call the block from other parts of the program.

This is very useful in situations where the same block of instructions or action or calculation needs to be repeated in multiple places in a program.

A program that references the subroutine `drawsquare` by name at a particular place in the program flow is said to **call the subroutine** `drawsquare`. It is sufficient to just use its name, `drawsquare`, to cause its block of instructions to execute.

Subroutines have been covered in depth in *Chapter 3*.

A subroutine may contain its own variable, type, label and const declarations.

A subroutine may also define subroutines which it may use and it may use subroutines defined elsewhere (usually library or language-defined subroutines).

Table 13.1 shows a pseudo-code procedure definition, `ConvertStringToUpper`, which itself contains a function definition, `Upper`, and a local variable declaration, `i : Integer`.

Information

Routine:
Another name for a subroutine is routine.

Information

Ord:
Ord applied to a character returns its character code.

Chr:
Chr applied to a character code returns the character.

Length:
Length applied to a string returns the no of characters in the string.

```
Procedure ConvertStringToUpper (INOUT Message : String)
  LocalVar
    i : Integer
  EndLocalVar
  Function Upper(Ch : Char) : Char
    If Ch In ['a'..'z']
      Then Ch ← Chr(Ord(Ch) - Ord('a') + Ord('A'))
    EndIf
    Return Ch
  EndFunction
  For i ← 1 To Length(Message)
    Message[i] ← Upper(Message[i])
  EndFor
EndProcedure
```

Table 13.1 Pseudocode procedure definition, showing encapsulation of a block of instructions, a function and a local variable

These procedure and function subroutines use library or language-defined subroutines, `Ord`, `Chr` and `Length`.

A reference to a string is passed to procedure `ConvertStringToUpper` in the procedure parameter variable `Message`. The reference is to a string which exists in the calling program's variable memory space. Any changes made by `ConvertStringToUpper` are applied to this string. This is what is meant by `Message` being an `INOUT` parameter.

The function `Upper` is said to be nested inside procedure `ConvertStringToUpper`.

On encountering the name `ConvertStringToUpper`, the executing program transfers control to this subroutine. On finishing its execution `ConvertStringToUpper` transfers control back to the point in the program immediately following where it was called.

A subroutine is a named out of line block of code

Figure 13.1 shows the control structure of a program block consisting of program statements S1, S2, S3, a selection statement (shown as ?) controlling execution of two statements S4 and S5. This selection statement is followed by a loop which controls a block of statements S.

A procedure T consists of program statements S1, S2, S3 (different ones from the program block statements) and a loop controlling a block of statements S (also different from the program block S).

The flow of control in the program block is **in line**, forwards from the beginning to the end, except when statement S1 is encountered. This statement transfers control '**out of line**' to procedure T.

Flow of control in procedure T is from its beginning to its end.

On reaching the end of T, control is transferred back to the program block.

Execution is resumed in the program block at statement S2, the statement immediately following S1, where the call to T occurred. If T was a function then control would be returned to statement S1 along with the function's result.

Procedure T is a subroutine.

In Pascal, statement S1 which is a call to a procedure T which doesn't use parameters is simply `T;`

This example, shows that a subroutine is:

> **a named 'out of line' block of code which may be executed (called) by simply writing its name in a program statement.**

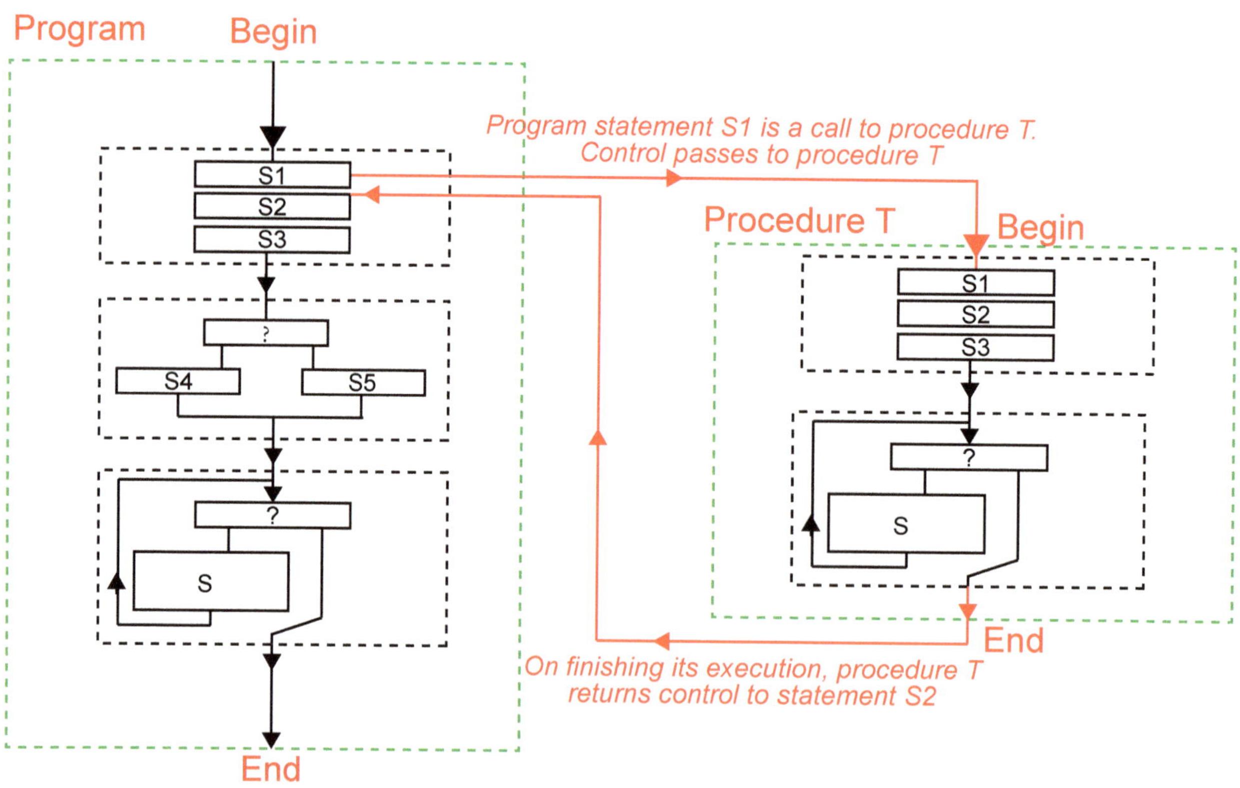

Figure 13.1 In line flow of control to out of line flow of control to a named out of line block of code

Questions

1. What is meant by "a subroutine is a named 'out of line' block of code that may be executed by simply writing its name in a program statement"?

Advantages of using subroutines in programs

Without programming language support for subroutines (procedures and functions), all programming would consist of inline blocks of program instructions.

This would make even programs of modest size

- difficult to understand
- difficult to debug.

Removing blocks of instructions from the program block and placing these in 'out of line', named subroutine blocks (*Figure 13.1*) separate from the control flow of the program block, reduces the intellectual demand needed to understand what the program does.

The program block is reduced in length because where it relies on the instructions in subroutines these are referenced by a short and descriptive name (ideally).

If subroutines are self-contained they can be worked on separately.
This is useful when writing and debugging software.
In software projects involving a team of developers, different subroutines can be given to different members of the team to write and debug.
The more self-contained (independent) the subroutine the easier it is to write and debug without having to understand the program block in which it is called.

Subroutines written for one program may be reused in a different program. The more self-contained they are the easier it is to do this.

If a subroutine is particularly useful, it may be added to a library of subroutines which can be imported into any program which needs them.

Questions

2. State and explain **three** advantages of using subroutines in programs.

Did you know?

Inline code:
In defence applications such as missile homing heads, program code is often converted to inline code during the software construction stage.
Each subroutine call in the program block is replaced by the subroutine's block of instructions.
One reason this is done is to avoid a potential software crash caused by stack overflow.
A stack is used in subroutine calls.
A stack (or call stack) stores return addresses which are used by each executing subroutine to return to the place from where they were called. Specifically, to the statement following the call statement.
A stack is finite in size and is limited by the memory allocated to it.
A missile homing head is the part of a missile which guides the missile onto the target.
Missiles often cost upwards of £30000.
Once launched there is no opportunity to reboot if the computer crashes from stack overflow.

Information

Inline:
Use the inline keyword to define an inline procedure.
See program InlineProcedure.dproj obtainable from
www.educational-computing.co.uk/DelphiBookCode/DelphiCode.html

Parameters of subroutines

Using parameters to pass data within programs

A subroutine parameter is one way of passing data into and out of a subroutine.

When a subroutine is called, any data passed to it via the subroutine parameter mechanism is copied into the memory area reserved for subroutine formal parameters as shown in the memory schematic in *Figure 13.2*.

There are two ways that data may be passed via the subroutine parameter mechanism into a subroutine:

```
Program Demo
Var x, y :Integer
Subroutine T(IN r : Integer; INOUT s : Integer)
  s ← s*r
EndSubroutine
BeginProgramBlock
  x ← 25
  y ← 17
  Call T(x,y)
  Output y
EndProgramBlock
```

Table 13.2 An example of a pseudocode program with a subroutine call involving data associated with two program variables being passed to the subroutine

- Call by value
- Call by reference/Call by address

We illustrate both with data stored in two program variables, x and y.

The variable name x maps to value 25 and the variable name y maps to 17.

We can express this as follows where the symbol ↦ means 'maps to'

x ↦ 25 and y ↦ 17

This mapping is set up at the point in time when statements

```
x ← 25
y ← 17
```

are executed in the program shown in *Table 13.2*.

The subroutine memory area shows two variables, r and s, called **formal parameters** of the subroutine.

Figure 13.2 shows these mapping to 5674 and 25.

r ↦ 25 and y ↦ 5674

This mapping is set up at the point in time when `Call T(x, y)` is executed in the program shown in *Table 13.2*.

Close inspection of the memory map in *Figure 13.2* indicates that the datum associated with x has been copied into the location in the subroutine memory area associated with r.

Similarly, close inspection shows that the program memory address 5674 of the location in program memory associated with y has been copied into the location in the subroutine memory area associated with s.

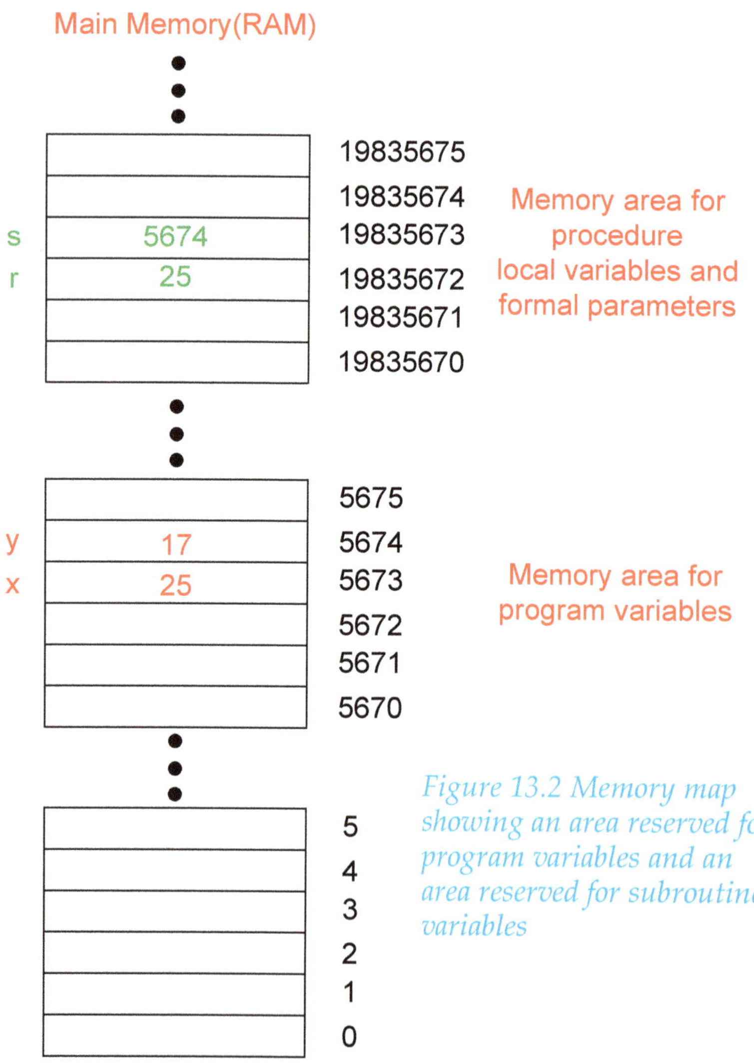

Figure 13.2 Memory map showing an area reserved for program variables and an area reserved for subroutine variables

Now when we look at the subroutine header we see that the `r` parameter is labelled an `IN` parameter and the `s` parameter is labelled an `INOUT` parameter:

```
Subroutine T(IN r : Integer; INOUT s : Integer)
```

The interpretation of `IN r : Integer` is as follows: a value is to be copied into the formal parameter `r` when the subroutine is called.

This is what is meant by **Call by Value**.

The interpretation of `INOUT s : Integer` is as follows: an address of where a value can be found in the program memory area is to be copied into the formal parameter `s` when the subroutine is called.

This is what is meant by **Call by Reference/Call by Address**.

This copying takes place when the subroutine is called with **actual parameters** x and y by the program statement

```
Call T(x, y)
```

If a subroutine has the address of a datum in the program memory area then the subroutine may change the value in this area. The subroutine in *Table 13.2* does this with an assignment statement

```
s ← s*r
```

Call by reference/address thus can have the **side-effect** of changing the value of a variable in another area of memory. This side-effect can be desirable and intended or undesirable.

Call by value cannot change the original value which has been copied.

Call by reference/address should be used as follows

- when a datum is too big to pass by value, i.e. it would take up a lot of space in subroutine memory or it would take too long (relatively speaking) to copy into subroutine memory
- when more than one result of executing the subroutine needs to be returned from the subroutine call
- when the data type of the result to be returned is not supported by the mechanism used by a function to return a result. Function return uses a different mechanism from subroutine parameters to return a result.

If only a single result needs to be returned and the data type of the result is supported by the function mechanism for returning results then a function should normally be used.

When a subroutine calls a subroutine, the subroutine memory area is used for both the calling subroutine and the called subroutine parameters/variables.

Key term

Subroutine parameter:
A subroutine parameter is a mechanism for passing data into and out of a subroutine.

Key term

Call by value:
Formal parameter of subroutine gets a copy of the datum associated with the actual parameter used in call to subroutine.

Call by address:
Formal parameter of subroutine is assigned the address in memory of the datum associated with the actual parameter used in call to subroutine.

Table 13.3 shows Call by Value and Call by Reference/Address support in Pascal/Delphi.

Table 13.4 shows an example in Pascal of Call by Value and Call by Address.

<table>
<tr><th>Call by Value</th><th>Call by Reference/Address</th></tr>
<tr><td><pre>Procedure A(r : Integer);
  Begin
    r := r + 10;
  End;
Function B(s : Integer) : Integer;
  Begin
    B := s + 10;
  End;</pre></td><td><pre>Procedure C(Var r : Integer);
  Begin
    r := r + 10;
  End;</pre></td></tr>
</table>

Table 13.3 Call by Value and Call by Reference/Address support in Pascal/Delphi

```
Program CallByValueAndCallByAddress;
Procedure A(r : Integer);
  Begin
    r := r + 10;
  End;
Function B(s : Integer) : Integer;
  Begin
    B := s + 10;
  End;
Procedure C(Var s : Integer);
  Begin
    s := s + 10;
  End;
Var
  x, y : Integer;
Begin
  x := 5;
  y := 5;
  A(x);
  Writeln(x);
  Writeln(B(y));
  C(y);
  Writeln(y);
  Readln;
End.
```

P

Table 13.4 Pascal example of Call by Value and Call by Reference

Information

Subroutine signature:

Procedure A(r : Integer) is called the subroutine's /routine's signature.

Questions

3. Explain the role of a subroutine parameter.

4. Explain
   (a) Call by value
   (b) Call by address

Using subroutines with interfaces

```
Subroutine T(IN r : Integer; INOUT s : Integer)
  s ← s*r
EndSubroutine
```

In the subroutine `T`, the part

```
IN r : Integer; INOUT s : Integer
```

is called the subroutine's **interface**. A subroutine interface is a mechanism by which data may be passed in and out of a subroutine via subroutine parameters. The use of subroutine interfaces is covered in *Chapter 3*.

Using subroutines that return values to the calling routine

Subroutines

A subroutine allows a block of instructions to be encapsulated, named and called by this name from other parts of a program.

This is particularly useful if the same block of instructions needs to be used in multiple places in a program or in several different programs.

After a subroutine is executed, control returns to the statement calling the subroutine. If the subroutine is a procedure then the calling statement's execution is complete. If the subroutine is a function, then the function returns a result to the calling statement which this statement may or may not deal with before it completes its execution.

For example, if the calling statement is as follows

```
x ← SquareOf(2)
```

the result **4** is returned by the call to function `SquareOf` and this result is then assigned to variable `x`.

Returning a result

If a result needs to be returned from an executing subroutine then a programmer may choose from two subroutine options:

- Procedure with the result returned via an INOUT or OUT parameter (call by address/reference)
- Function with the result returned via the function return mechanism

Procedure option

The procedure option has been covered earlier in this chapter. An OUT parameter is similar to an INOUT (Var) parameter but the initial value of the referenced variable is discarded

Function option

In Pascal, a function specifies a return value within the body of the function by executing an assignment statement whose left-hand side is the name of the function - *Table 13.5*.

In Delphi, when a function is called, a variable is automatically created with the name `Result` of the same type as

```
Function SquareOf (Number : Integer) : Integer;
  Begin
    SquareOf := Number * Number;
  End;
```

Table 13.5 Pascal function SquareOf which returns an integer result to the calling statement

the return type of the function. It is available for the programmer to use to hold the result value to be returned by the function. Its value is passed back to the calling statement when the function returns. Delphi can also use the Pascal method of returning a result.

The implicitly declared variable `Result` can be seen as equivalent to an `OUT` type parameter - where the value upon entry to the function is undefined. It is still possible in Delphi to use the Pascal convention of using the name of the function to assign the result. In Pascal, assigning a value to be returned to the name of the function does not automatically cause the function to return. Similarly, in Delphi assigning a value to be returned to the name of the function or to the variable `Result` does not automatically cause the function to return. In both Pascal and Delphi, usual practice is to use a temporary local variable to hold the result to be returned and assign this to `Result` or the function name at the end of the function, which is the place where control passes back to the calling statement.

Type of result returned

Many programming languages place restrictions on the type of the result returned by a function.

Table 13.6 shows a Pascal program which defines and uses a function whose result type is a **composite data type**.

A composite data type or compound data type is any data type which can be constructed in a program using the programming language's primitive data types and other composite types. It is sometimes called a **structured data type**, but this term is more commonly reserved for arrays and lists.

The act of constructing a composite type is known as composition.

```
Program FunctionReturnType;
Type
  TArrayType = Array[1..10] Of Integer;
Function Test (x : TArrayType) : TArrayType;
  Var
    i : Integer;
  Begin
    For i := 1 To 10
      Do x[i] := 2 * x[i];
    Test := x;
  End;
Var
  y : TArrayType = (1,2,3,4,5,6,7,8,9,10);
  z : TArrayType;
Begin
  z := Test(y);
  Writeln(z[2]);
  Readln;
End.
```

Table 13.6 Pascal function test which returns a result of composite type to the calling statement

When not to use a function to return a result

Although it is possible to return multiple separate results from a function, it is not normally considered good practice. For example, the following Pascal function returns one result in `INOUT` parameter `s` and another result via the function return mechanism:

```
Function D(Var s:Integer) : Integer;
  Begin
    ...
  End;
```

Both results in this example return a value which is a scalar data type, in this case, an integer.

A scalar data type is a single value data type.

It would be better to use a procedure with two `INOUT` parameters instead of a function.

Mathematical functions vs functions in a programming language

Loosely speaking, a function in mathematics is a rule that, for each element in some set A of inputs, assigns an output chosen from set B. For example, a function `SquareOf` takes input integer 2 and outputs its square 4 another integer.

Mathematics is very strict in its definition of a function:

- A function must return a single result
- A function must always return the same value for a given input, e.g. the square of 2 is always 4.
- A function must return a value for every value of input.

In programming languages, functions can break these rules:

- The `Random (N)` function covered in *Chapter 12* returns a different value in the interval [0, N) each time it is called. It would be useless as a random number generator if it returned the same value every time
- Multiple separate results may be returned from a function by using `INOUT` parameters as well as the function return mechanism

- The integer data type is a subset of the set of integers because computer memory is finite. If we attempt to square an integer which is larger than the square root of the maximum integer for the integer data type then overflow will result.

Programming tasks

1. Write and test a function which accepts a string as input and returns the string reversed.

2. Write and test a function which accepts a string as input and returns the number of words it contains, e.g. "Hello World" contains 2 words.

3. Write and test a function which on each call returns a random number of data type integer in the interval (0, 12], i.e. 0 < number <= 12.
   Use the generating relation and an appropriate value for k

   NextRandomNo = Multiplier * PreviousRandomNo MOD k

   and multiplier = 21. Seed the random number generator with the value 7, i.e. the first value of PreviousRandomNumber = 7.

4. Write and test a function which on each call returns a random number of data type real/float in the interval (0.0, 1.0].

Declaring local variables

A subroutine may declare its own variables and use these within the body of the subroutine as shown in the subroutine `DoExample` in *Table 13.7*.

The variables `s` and `t` are known as **local variables**. They are only visible inside subroutine `DoExample`, i.e. they cannot be accessed from outside the subroutine. In fact, they do not exist until the subroutine starts executing. They disappear when the subroutine stops executing. Thus any values that they hold are stored temporarily.

```
Subroutine DoExample(IN x : Integer)
  Var
    s, t : Integer          ← Declaration of two local
                              variables, s and t
  Body
    Output x
    s ← 6                   ← Using local variables, s and t
    t ← 7                     in body of subroutine
    Output s + t
  EndBody
EndSubroutine
```

Table 13.7 Subroutine with local variables

> **Key term**
>
> **Local variable:**
> These are variables declared inside a subroutine and used within the body of the subroutine.
> The lifetime of a local variable is the lifetime of an execution of the subroutine in which the local variable is declared.
> The scope of a local variable is the scope of the subroutine in which it is declared – scope means where the local variable is visible and can be accessed.

Lifetime

The lifetime of a local variable is the lifetime of an execution of the subroutine in which the local variable is declared.

Visibility

The scope of a local variable is the scope of the subroutine in which it is declared – scope means where the local variable is visible and can be used.

Using local variables

Table 13.8 shows the declaration and use of local variables (called `i` and `j`) in Pascal/Delphi.

Programming tasks

5. Write and test a function which calculates x^n where $n \geq 1$.

   Use the following algorithm to calculate x^n

```
Power ← x
Count ← 1
While Count < n Do
  Power ← Power * x
  Count ← Count + 1
```

   Your function should make use of local variables.

```
Procedure DoExample(n : Integer);
  Var
    i, j : Integer;
  Begin
    j := 6;
    For i : = 1 To n
      Do Writeln('Hello World!', i*j);
  End;
```

Table 13.8 Declaring and using local variables

Why use local variables?

Support for modularisation

Subroutines enable modularisation of a program.

A solution to a problem can be divided into separate and independent modules. These modules can be implemented as subroutines.

The aim of modularisation is to have subroutines which can be worked on independently of the rest of the program.

This requires that each subroutine is **self-contained** and that its interaction with the rest of the program takes place only through the subroutine's interface, i.e. through its formal parameter(s).

Using local variables aids modularisation.

It also enables a subroutine to be reused because if a subroutine is self-contained and independent it may be lifted and used in another program.

Undesirable side-effects

In *Table 13.9*, the formal parameter of subroutine `DoExample2` is `x`. However, instead of declaring local variables, the subroutine manipulates two global variables `s` and `t`.

These global variables come into existence when the program starts executing and only disappear when it finishes executing.

They are visible and therefore accessible inside procedure `DoExample2`.

Unfortunately, this means that when `DoExample2` is called and it executes the values of `s` and `t` are altered as shown.

This is called a **side-effect** of executing subroutine `DoExample`.

Side-effects are undesirable because

- debugging a program is made harder - isolating the source of an error is made more difficult, the whole program may need to be examined
- the independence of the subroutine is reduced
  - it cannot be designed without considering the context in which it will be used
  - it cannot be debugged without considering the context in which it will be used
  - its reusability is reduced because it will be more difficult to use it in another program.

The only variable outside of `DoExample2` which should be manipulated by `DoExample2` is `y` because this variable is passed into `DoExample2` through its `INOUT` interface, the formal parameter `x`.

```
Program
  Var
    s, t, y : Integer          <-- Declaration of three global variables, s, t and y
  Subroutine DoExample2(INOUT x : Integer)
    Body
      x ← 2 * x
      s ← 6                    <-- Using global variables, s and t in body of subroutine
      t ← 7
      Output s + t             <-- s + t = 13
    EndBody
    EndSubroutine
Begin
  s ← 3
  t ← 2
  y ← 9
  DoExample(y)
  Output s + t                 <-- Expect output to be 3 + 2 = 5 but it is 13. This is a side-effect of calling subroutine DoExample
  Output y
End
```

P

Table 13.9 Pseudocode demonstrating the side-effect of using global variables inside a subroutine

Questions

5. What is a local variable?
6. What is the lifetime and scope of a local variable?
7. Explain why the use of local variables is considered good practice.

More on parameter passing

In pass by value, the source referenced by the actual parameter is copied and the copy placed on the stack in the stack frame set up for the subroutine (procedure or function) call. The subroutine has read/write access to this copy only. Any changes that the subroutine makes to this copy are not reflected in the original which remains untouchable throughout the lifetime of the procedure call.

There are three modifiers available in Delphi which apply to parameter passing:

1. **Var**

   This enables pass by reference. The address of the source of data is passed into the called subroutine enabling the source to be modified.

2. **Const**

   For value types whose instances are more than a few bytes, **Const** causes the compiler to pass a pointer to the source data rather than a copy of it. However, the compiler inserts code that prevents the source data from being modified except where the actual parameter passed is a class or dynamic array because these are pure reference types, i.e. the variable in each case is a pointer to the class or dynamic array data. **Const** only prevents this pointer from being changed, not the data it points to which can be changed.

3. **Out**

   Out paramaters behave exactly the same as **Var** ones except in the case of managed ones, i.e. ones where the compiler manages the lifecycle including initialisation. For managed types, **Out** causes the inputted value to be automatically cleared.

Table 13.10 shows a program that exemplifies the use of the three types of modifier, **Var, Const** and **Out**. Figure 13.3 shows the console output when this program is executed.

`Procedure AVar` has a single parameter of type **Var**. `Procedure BConst` has a single parameter of type **Const**. `Procedure COut` has a single parameter of type **Out**.

`Procedure AVar` when called changes the value of the variable `ActualParameterVar` from 2 to 5.

`Procedure BConst` when called does not change the value of the variable `ActualParameterConst`. In fact, when the commented statement `ConstParameter := 'No string value now';` is uncommented the program cannot be compiled.

Z:\ProductionChapters\DelphiBook\Code\Chapter13\ParameterModifiers\Win32\Debug...

```
Main block, ActualParameterVar = 2
Inside AVar
Leaving AVar
Main block, ActualParameterVar = 5
Main block, ActualParameterConst = Hello World
Inside BConst
Formal parameter ConstParameter = Hello World
Leaving BConst
Main block, ActualParameterConst = Hello World
Main block, ActualParameterOut = Goodbye World
Inside COut
Before anything done, formal parameter OutParameter =
Leaving COut
Main block, ActualParameterOut = Updated formal parameter OutParameter
```

Figure 13.3 Output from program ParameterModifiers when executed

`Procedure COut` when called first changes the value of the variable `ActualParameterOut` to the empty string. The assignment statement `OutParameter := 'Updated formal parameter OutParameter';` then changes via this statement the value of `ActualParameterOut` to `'Updated formal parameter OutParameter'`. This is because strings are a managed type and so initialisation takes place on calling procedure `COut` equivalent to `ActualParameterOut := '';`. If instead procedure `COut`'s formal parameter was of type **Char**, then intialisation/clearing of the actual parameter at source would not take place because variables of type **Char** are not managed.

```
Program ParameterModifiers;
{$APPTYPE CONSOLE}
Var
  ActualParameterVar : Integer = 2;
  ActualParameterConst : String = 'Hello World';
  ActualParameterOut : String = 'Goodbye World';
Procedure AVar(Var VarParameter : Integer);
  Begin
    Writeln('Inside AVar');
    VarParameter := 5;
    Writeln('Leaving AVar');
  End;
Procedure BConst(Const ConstParameter : String);
  Begin
    Writeln('Inside BConst');
    //ConstParameter := 'No string value now'; Will not compile if this is uncommented
    Writeln('Formal parameter ConstParameter = ', ConstParameter);
    Writeln('Leaving BConst');
  End;
Procedure COut (Out OutParameter : String);
  Begin
    Writeln('Inside COut');
    Writeln('Before anything done, formal parameter OutParameter = ', OutParameter);
    OutParameter := 'Updated formal parameter OutParameter';
    Writeln('Leaving COut');
  End;

Begin
  Writeln('Main block, ActualParameterVar = ',ActualParameterVar);
  AVar(ActualParameterVar);
  Writeln('Main block, ActualParameterVar = ', ActualParameterVar);
  Writeln('Main block, ActualParameterConst = ',ActualParameterConst);
  BConst(ActualParameterConst);
  Writeln('Main block, ActualParameterConst = ',ActualParameterConst);
  Writeln('Main block, ActualParameterOut = ', ActualParameterOut);
  COut(ActualParameterOut);
  Writeln('Main block, ActualParameterOut = ', ActualParameterOut);
  Readln;
End.
```

Table 13.10 Parameter modifiers example program

Default parameter values

Both value and const parameters can be declared with a default value, making the use of actual parameters in any call optional. All formal parameters to the right of the first formal parameter given a default value must be assigned one as well. The default values must either be literals or values declared as constants - values that can be determined at compile time.

The program shown in *Table 13.11* contains examples of the use of default parameter values.

Figure 13.4 shows the console window output when this program is executed.

```
Program DefaultParameters;
{$APPTYPE CONSOLE}
Procedure Test (Age : Integer = 21);
  Begin
    Writeln('Inside Test');
    Writeln(Age);
  End;
Procedure AnotherTest(Age : Integer = 21; Name : String = 'Harry Houdini');
  Begin
    Writeln('Inside AnotherTest');
    Writeln('Name = ', Name, ' Age = ', Age);
  End;

Begin
  Test;
  Test(84);
  AnotherTest;
  AnotherTest(34);
  AnotherTest(25, 'Keith Mander');
  //AnotherTest('Mary Lamb'); doesn't compile
  Readln;
End.
```

Table 13.11 Using default parameter values program

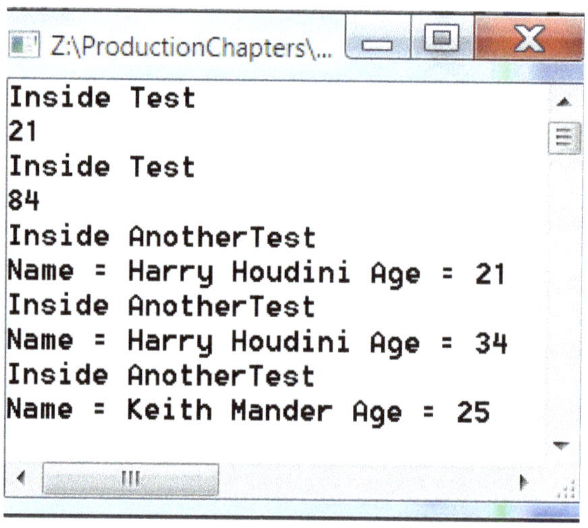

Figure 13.4 Output from program DefaultParamaters when executed

Prematurely exiting from a subroutine

Calling `Exit` in a subroutine causes an immediate exit from the subroutine. In the case of a function, `Exit` can optionally set the return value at the same time, e.g. `Exit('Premature exit')` - from Delphi 2009 onwards.

Table 13.12 shows a program that employs `Exit` in both roles.

Figure 13.5 shows the console window output when this program is executed.

```
Program UseOfExit;
{$APPTYPE CONSOLE}
Procedure Test (Age : Integer);
  Begin
    Writeln('Inside Test');
    Writeln;
    If Age >= 80 Then Exit;
    Writeln('Age = ', Age);
  End;
Function IsAgeLessThan80(Age : Integer) : Boolean;
  Begin
    If Age >= 80 Then Exit(False);
    Result := True;
  End;
Begin
  Test(30);
  Test(84);
  Writeln('----------------------------');
  Writeln('Main block, Age is greater than or equal to 80 = ', IsAgeLessThan80(84), ' value returned from
IsAgeLessThan80');
  Writeln;
  Writeln('Main block, Age is less than 80 = ', IsAgeLessThan80(30), ' value returned from IsAgeLessThan80');
  Writeln;
  Readln;
End.
```

Table 13.12 Using Exit to prematurely leave a program

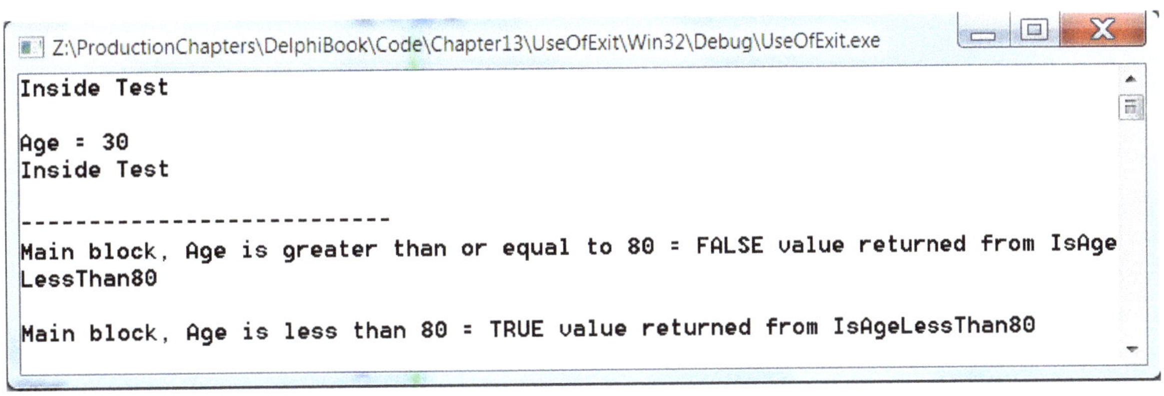

Figure 13.5 Output from program UseOfExit when executed

Overloading

Subroutines can have more than one version of the same name as long as each has a different parameter list. This is called **overloading**. To achieve this, each version must be declared with the **Overload** directive.

Table 13.13 shows a program that defines three different versions of a subroutine Test: two procedures and one function.

Figure 13.6 shows the console window output when this program is executed.

```
Program OverloadedSubroutines;
{$APPTYPE CONSOLE}
Procedure Test (x : Integer); Overload;
  Begin
    Writeln('Inside procedure Test with parameter x of type Integer');
    Writeln;
    Writeln('x = ', x);
    Writeln;
  End;
Procedure Test (x : Real); Overload;
  Begin
    Writeln('Inside procedure Test with parameter x of type Real');
    Writeln;
    Writeln('x = ', x:8:4);
    Writeln;
  End;
Function Test(x, y : Integer) : Integer; Overload;
  Begin
    Writeln('Inside function Test with parameters x and y of type Integer');
    Writeln;
    Writeln('x = ', x, ' y = ', y);
    Writeln;
    Result := x + y;
  End;

Begin
  Test(30);
  Test(3.14159);
  Writeln('Sum = ', Test(5, 7));
  Writeln;
  Writeln('---------------------------');
  Writeln;
  Readln;
End.
```

Table 13.13 Overloading of subroutines program

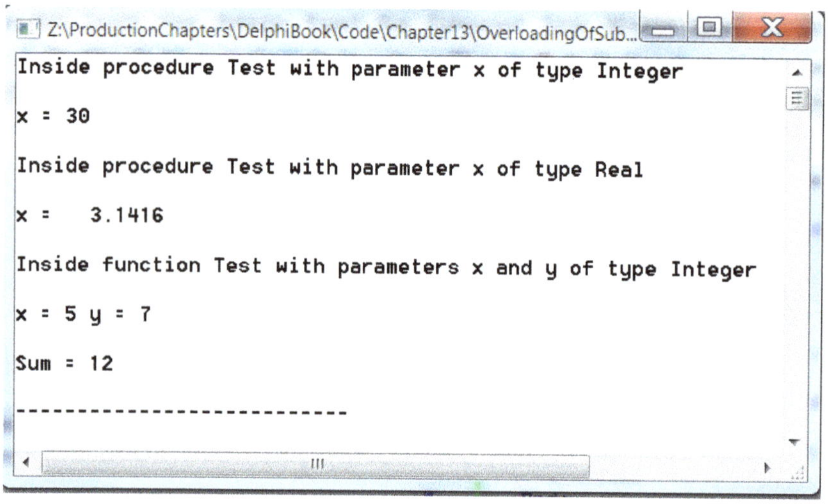

Figure 13.6 Output from program OverloadedSubroutines when executed

Procedural pointers

Delphi allows a procedure or function to be assigned to a variable if the variable's type is a procedural pointer type.

For example, `TFunction` and `TProcedure` are procedural pointer type definitions and `DoFunction` and `DoProcedure` are variables of type `TFunction` and `TProcedure` respectively. This enables `Procedure WriteTitle` to be assigned to `DoProcedure` and function `Add` to `DoFunction` and then called as shown in *Table 13.14*. Variables `DoProcedure` and `DoFunction` can then be reassigned to a different procedure and a different function, respectively. as shown in *Table 13.14*. *Figure 13.7* shows the program's output on execution.

```
Type
  TFunction = Function(x, y : Integer) : Integer;
  TProcedure = Procedure(OutputMessage : String);
Var
  DoFunction : TFunction;
  DoProcedure : TProcedure;
Begin
  DoProcedure := WriteTitle;
  DoProcedure('Do some sums');
  DoFunction := Add;
  Writeln('Add 3 to 4 = ',  DoFunction(3, 4));
```

```
Program ProceduralPointers;
{$APPTYPE CONSOLE}
Type
  TFunction = Function(x, y : Integer) : Integer;
  TProcedure = Procedure(OutputMessage : String);
Function Add (x, y : Integer) : Integer;
  Begin
    Result := x + y;
  End;
Function Multiply (x, y : Integer) : Integer;
  Begin
    Result := x * y;
  End;
Function Subtract (x, y : Integer) : Integer;
  Begin
    Result := x - y;
  End;
Procedure WriteTitle(OutputMsg : String);
  Begin
    Writeln(OutputMsg);
    Writeln('-------------');
    Writeln;
  End;
Procedure WriteFooter(OutputMsg : String);
  Begin
    Writeln('-------------');
    Writeln;
    Writeln(OutputMsg);
    Writeln;
  End;
Var
  DoFunction : TFunction;
  DoProcedure : TProcedure;
Begin
  DoProcedure := WriteTitle;
  DoProcedure('Do some sums');
  DoFunction := Add;
  Writeln('Add 3 to 4 = ', DoFunction(3, 4));
  Writeln;
  DoFunction := Multiply;
  Writeln('Multiply 3 by 4 = ', DoFunction(3, 4));
  Writeln;
  DoFunction := Subtract;
  Writeln('Subtract 4 from 3 = ', DoFunction(3, 4));
  Writeln;
  DoProcedure := WriteFooter;
  DoProcedure('Done some sums');
  Writeln;
  Readln;
End.
```

Table 13.14 Using procedural pointers program

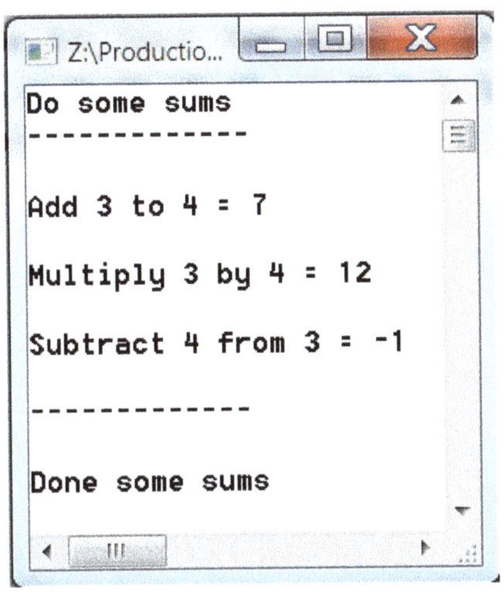

Figure 13.7 Output from program ProceduralPointers when executed

14 Arrays

Single- and multi-dimensional arrays

One-dimensional array

The problem

Suppose you are tasked with writing a computer program to keep a set of one hundred temperature readings in memory so that calculations may be performed on these readings in a uniform manner. A sample of the first 8 readings is shown in *Table 14.1*.

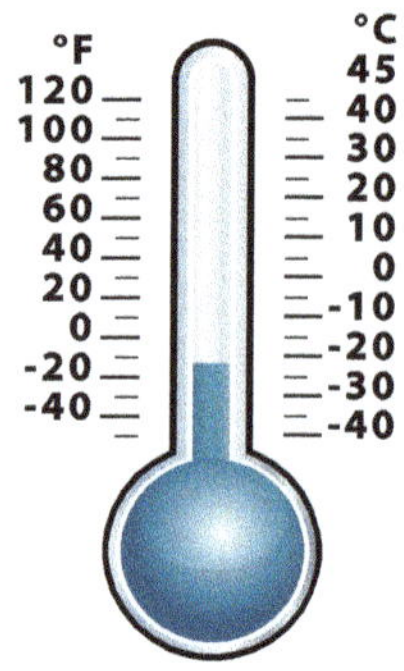

20.5	22.7	24.3	26.8	25.1	23.9	21.4	20.0

Table 14.1 Sample of temperature readings

We could store the first of the readings in a variable, `Temperature1`, the second in a variable, `Temperature2`, and so on as shown in *Table 14.2*. The data type chosen for `Temperature1` would be one that allows storage of a value possessing a fractional part, e.g. `Real` or `Double`. The same data type would be chosen for `Temperature2`, and each of the other 98 variables.

Using 100 separate variables, each of which is only able to store a single value, is not ideal.

Variable	Value
`Temperature1`	20.5
`Temperature2`	22.7
`Temperature3`	24.3
`Temperature4`	26.8
`Temperature5`	25.1
`Temperature6`	23.9
`Temperature7`	21.4
`Temperature8`	20.0

Table 14.2 Variables for first 8 readings

The solution

What is needed is a *single variable* which can store many values.

For this we use an **array** variable, `Temperature`, as shown in *Figure 14.1*.

1. An array is a data structure which is capable of storing many values, e.g. 100 temperature readings: 20.5, 22.7, ..., 17.6
2. An array is also a single entity, referred to by a single name, e.g. `Temperature`.
3. The values stored in an array are all of the same data type, e.g. `Real`.
4. The stored values are arranged in an order so that there is a first, a second, and so on.

Variable	Value
`Temperature`	20.5
	22.7
	24.3
	26.8
	25.1
	23.9
	21.4
	20.0
	⋮
	17.6

Fig. 14.1 Array variable with storage for 100 temperature readings

Information

When we want to indicate that we have omitted numbers, etc, in a sequence of numbers or other entities we use a series of dots called an ellipsis e.g.

• • • ⋮

The omission is used where it would be unnecessary to include more numbers because these can be inferred from the context.

Questions

1. A program is required to keep 10000 temperature readings in memory and to reference all the items in a uniform manner.
Explain why it would be preferable to use a one-dimensional array to store the value of each reading instead of 10000 separate variables.

Separate variables

In the separate variable approach, to extract, say, the value of the seventh temperature reading from among 100 separate variables, we need the name of the corresponding variable. We can construct this name by combining the name `Temperature` with the numeric name `7` to produce the name, `Temperature7`.

We then use this name to refer to the variable which contains the value of the seventh reading, i.e. 21.4 as shown in *Table 14.2*. Perhaps we might want to output the value of this variable to the console.

Pseudo-code that does this is as follows

```
Output Temperature7
```

Array index

Using an array to store 100 temperature readings, we retain the use of numeric naming 1, 2, 3, 4, ..., 100 and view the array as consisting of 100 elements with each element storing the value of a temperature reading.

To extract, say, the value of the seventh temperature reading, we construct a name by combining the name of the array, `Temperature`, with the numeric name `7` as follows `Temperature[7]` as shown in *Figure 14.2*.

We then use this name to refer to the **element** of the array which contains the seventh reading, i.e. 21.4 (see *Table 14.2*).

Perhaps we might want to output the value of this variable to the console. Pseudo-code that does this is as follows

Variable	Index	Value
Temperature	[1]	20.5
	[2]	22.7
	[3]	24.3
	[4]	26.8
	[5]	25.1
	[6]	23.9
	[7]	21.4
	[8]	20.0
	⋮	⋮
	[100]	17.6

Fig. 14.2 Use of an index in array variable Temperature

```
Output Temperature[7]
```

Pseudo-code to output the first, second and third values of array `Temperature` is as follows

```
Output Temperature[1]
Output Temperature[2]
Output Temperature[3]
```

Information

Square bracket notation:
Square bracket notation [ ] is used to access values in an array.

The name that we use inside the square brackets is called the **array index**, e.g. 3 in `[3]`.

Pseudo-code to output all 100 values is as follows

```
For i ← 1 To 100 Output Temperature[i]
```

Here the array index is a loop control variable `i` which ranges from 1 to 100.

We are not restricted to starting array indexing at 1. We can index from 0. In fact, many programming languages only offer array indexing from 0. Pascal and Delphi are exceptions. In fact, Pascal and Delphi allow indexing from any starting value of ordinal data type.

Questions

2. A one-dimensional array `Height` consists of 10 elements. Array indexing starts at 0 and ends at 9. The array stores the heights of 10 people. Write pseudocode using a *for loop* to output all 10 heights in the same order that they are stored in the array.

Numeric names and non-numeric names for array index

We used numeric names for the index of an array, e.g. 1, 2, 3, etc, in the previous section. We don't have to. Instead, we can use non-numeric names, e.g. A, B, C, D, etc. For example, to extract the first value stored in array `LetterCount` we would use `LetterCount[A]`, the second value, `LetterCount[B]`, and so on.

Note, however, that whatever names we use, they must be capable of being ordered and the next name must be the natural successor to the previous, e.g. B is the successor to A, 2 is the successor to 1. This is very important.

If this wasn't the case then the *for loop* on the previous page, which assumes an increment of 1, wouldn't be able to access every one of the 100 values.

Choosing to use as an array index a range of numbers drawn from the set of integers is thus a natural choice to make. For other scenarios, the array index may be chosen from values in a different data type, e.g. character.

Question

3. A one-dimensional array `LetterCount` consists of 26 elements. Array indexing starts at letter A and ends at letter Z. The array stores the count for each uppercase letter of the alphabet occurring in a piece of text, e.g. `LetterCount[D]` stores the value 36. Write pseudocode using a *for loop* to output the count stored for each letter in the same order that they are stored in the array. Use a loop control variable, `Letter`, which uses values chosen from A, B, C, ..., X, Y, Z.

What kind of identifier is an array index?

There are three kinds of non-negative integral number[1] usage:

Quantities: 0, 1, 2, ...

Quantities are used to give the quantity (a count) of items. They include zero, because zero is a possible quantity. Quantities are **cardinal numbers**. (In Delphi, the data type is **Cardinal**)

Position words: 1st, 2nd, 3rd, ...

Position words give the position of an item within a sequence with a beginning. The item at the beginning of the sequence is called the "first" item, the next the "second", and so on. "First" is written as 1st, "second" as 2nd, and so on. Position words are **ordinal numbers**. (In Delphi the ordinal number of a literal value is obtained using the Ord() function, e.g. `Ord('A');`

Identification numbers: 0, 1, 2, ..., or 1, 2, 3, ..., or any other ordered sequence.

Identification numbers are just a methodical way to give numerical names to items such as the sequence of 100 temperature values. Identification numbers are therefore a way of numbering the temperature values.

Information

Identification numbers are used extensively in the world. For example, all vehicles registered in the UK must have a unique, stamped-in vehicle identification number (VIN). It is usually stamped into the chassis of the vehicle.

1 Integral numbers are whole numbers such as the integers

Figure 14.3 shows array `Temperature` together with the identification numbers which identify each value stored in the array.

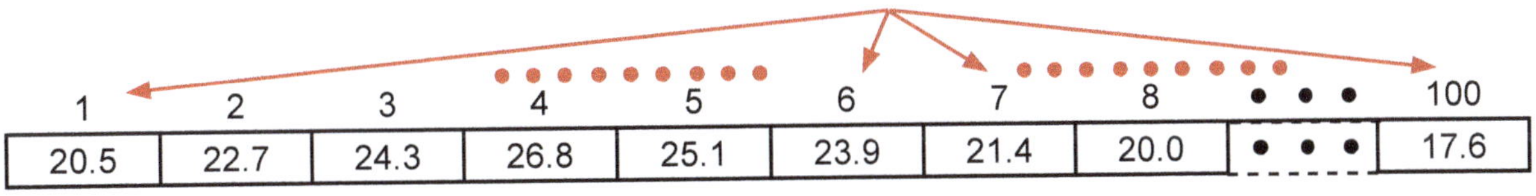

Fig. 14.3 Use of identification numbers in range 1 to 100 to index array `Temperature`

Questions

4 What kind of identifier is the array index in the Temperature array?

Basic operations that access arrays

The two basic operations that access the one-dimensional array `Temperature` are

- Extraction: this is achieved by evaluating `Temperature[i]` to identify a particular stored value in the array `Temperature`, e.g. if `i = 5`, then `Temperature[i]` evaluates to 25.1 - see *Figure 14.3*.
- Storing: this is achieved by executing the assignment `Temperature[i] ← x` which results in a copy of the value stored in `x` being assigned to the array `Temperature` at the location within this array identified by identification number `i`. Variable `x` holds the temperature reading to be stored in the array `Temperature`, e.g. if `i = 5` and `x = 25.1`, then `Temperature[5] ← 25.1` results in 25.1 being stored in the array location with identification number 5.

Questions

5 Describe with examples the **two** basic operations used to access elements of a one-dimensional array.

Addresses

Numbers as names are also called **addresses**. We are familiar with numbers being assigned to houses: "Such and such lives at no 42".

We can therefore think of an array index as an address. Using an address also implies a location. For example, `Temperature[5]` is a **location** with address 5 within array `Temperature`.

Figure 14.4 shows storage bays for Russian doll objects. We can think of this structure as an array used for storing objects. Each bay within this array is a **location**. The structure is divided into cells, one above another. So we can also use the synonym **cell** for location.

Each location/cell is assigned an address. In this numbering scheme we have chosen to start the numbering from 0 and to label the lowermost cell 0. We could have started the numbering from 1 and we could have chosen the uppermost cell as the first cell. The choice is arbitrary. All that we need to ensure is that the numbering is ordered, i.e. 0, 1, 2 , 3 or 1, 2, 3, 4, and each cell is assigned, in order, a unique number drawn from the range of numbers whether 0, 1, 2, 3 is chosen or 1, 2, 3, 4.

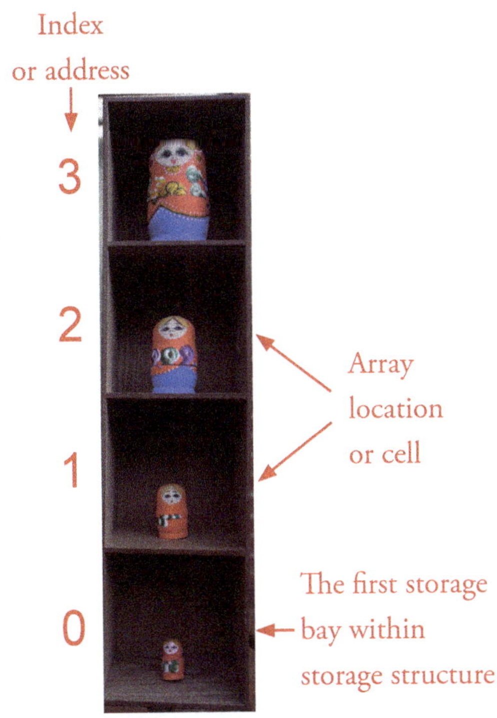

Fig. 14.4 Location/cell view of an array with array index as a location address

We have now encountered three different terms for an array part that stores a value:

- element
- location
- cell

Questions

6. Explain why we can think of an array index as an address.

Why choose to start numbering array locations with the number zero?

Figure 14.5 shows array `Temperature` together with the identification numbers which identify each value stored in the array. This time the identification numbering/index starts at 0.

First ↓ 0	1	2	3	4	5	6	7	• • •	Last ↓ 99
20.5	22.7	24.3	26.8	25.1	23.9	21.4	20.0	• • •	17.6

Fig. 14.5 Use of identification numbers from 0 to 99 to index array `Temperature`

The meaning in English of the ordinal-number word "first" is the first entry within a sequence, even if this first entry is labelled with identification number 0, as unnatural as it may seem. We are conditioned by everyday experience to use identification number 1 when referring to the first entity in a sequence, e.g. the first house in a street has address 1 not 0. However, if the house number was 0, it would still be the first - see *Figure 14.6.*

Fig. 14.6 House with house number 0

0 Acacia Avenue
Dingley Dell
NeverNeverLand
ZX99 9ZZ

Questions

7. Array indexing starts at 0 for an array `Row` with 10 elements.
   (a) What is the index of the last element?
   (b) Write pseudo-code to output the value stored in the first cell of this array.

8. (a) Explain why the following pseudo-code will output the 10 values stored in the array `Row`.

```
i ← 0
While i < 10
   Output Row[i]
   i ← i + 1
EndWhile
```

   (b) What is the value stored in `i` when the loop terminates?

9. Rewrite the *While loop* pseudo-code in Question 8 so that it uses a *Repeat loop* with the terminating condition at the end of the loop.

Offset

By starting array indexing at 0, the index takes on the role of an **offset**. If the physical address in memory of the base of the array is, say, 1500 then the first cell of the array has address 1500 + 0, the second 1500 + 1, and so on. Using offset addressing thus make it easier to calculate the exact memory location.

Questions

10 An array `Vector` has 10 elements with an index that starts at 0. The physical address in memory of the base of this array is 2300.
What is the physical address of the fifth element?

11 A collection of ropes of various lengths are wrapped in turn around a cylinder of circumference 10 units. All the ropes wrap around the cylinder at least once but never exactly. The total length of each rope is measured and the measurement truncated so that it is integral. The integral measurement `L` is stored in a one-dimensional 10 element array `ExcessRopeLength` according to whether the integral excess length is 0, 1, 2, ..., 8, 9 units.
The integral excess length can be calculated using the formula

L mod 10

For example, if the length L is 36 units then the excess length is 6 units.
You are required to choose between using array indexing that starts at 0 and array indexing that starts at 1. Justify your choice.

Creating a one-dimensional array

Table 14.3 shows examples of how integer and real/floating point one-dimensional arrays may be created and initialised in Delphi.

	Integer	Real (can use Double in place of Real)
Uninitialised	`Vector : Array[0..3] Of Integer;`	`Vector : Array[0..3] Of Real;`
Initialised	`Vector : Array[0..3] Of Integer = (0,1,2,3);`	`Vector : Array[0..3] Of Real = (0.0,1.5,2.3,3.4);`

Table 14.3 Creating one-dimensional arrays of different array element data type

Table 14.4 show a Delphi program that creates and uses one-dimensional arrays.

```
Program ArrayVector1;
{$APPTYPE CONSOLE}
Var
  Vector1 : Array[0..3] Of Integer;//Uninitialised
  Vector2 : Array[0..3] Of Integer = (0,1,2,3);//Initialised
  Vector3 : Array[0..3] Of Real;//Uninitialised
  Vector4 : Array[0..3] Of Real = (0.0,1.5,2.3,3.4);//Initialised
Begin
  Vector1[0] := 45;
  Vector3[0] := 45.8;
  Writeln(Vector1[0]);
  Writeln(Vector2[2]);
  Writeln(Vector3[0] :6:1);
  Writeln(Vector4[3] :6:1);
  Readln;
End.
```

Chapter14.rar - ArrayVector1

Table 14.4 Creating one-dimensional arrays of different array element data type

Iterating through the elements of a one-dimensional array

Iterating through the elements of an array is a common operation on arrays. Figure 14.7 shows the use of a *For loop* to access each element of array `Vector` starting with the first element `Vector[0]`. The index used is `i`, the loop control variable. Table 14.5 shows the value of `i` and the value of array `Vector[i]` in each iteration of the *For loop*. The one-dimensional array `Vector` contains 4 elements with the following values 0.0, 1.5, 2.3, 3.4, respectively.

```
For i ← 0 To 3
  Output Vector[i]
EndFor
```

Figure 14.7 Pseudo-code For loop

Value of i	Element accessed	Value of element
0	Vector[0]	0.0
1	Vector[1]	1.5
2	Vector[2]	2.3
3	Vector[3]	3.4

Table 14.5 Value of loop control variable and element of array Vector on each iteration

Table 14.6 shows the loop pseudo-code expressed in Delphi.

```
Program ArrayVector2;
{$APPTYPE CONSOLE}
Var
  Vector : Array[0..3] Of Real = (0.0,1.5,2.3,3.4);//Initialised
  i : Integer;
Begin
  For i := 0 To 3
    Do Writeln(Vector[i] :4:1);
  Readln;
End.
```

Chapter14.rar - ArrayVector2

Table 14.6 Accessing the elements of a one-dimensional array by iteration with a For loop

Computing a single value from the contents of a one-dimensional array

To sum all the elements of a one-dimensional array, `Vector`, we must access each element of this array in turn adding its value to a running total `Sum`. The variable `Sum` is initialised to contain zero. Figure 14.8 shows pseudo-code that computes the sum of the elements of array `Vector`. Array `Vector` contains 4 elements with the following values 1, 3, 8, 9.

Table 14.7 shows the state of `Sum` before iteration begins and at the end of each iteration, e.g. after the first iteration variable `Sum` contains 1, after the second, 5.

```
Sum ← 0
For i ← 0 To 3
  Sum ← Sum + Vector[i]
EndFor
Output Sum
```

Figure 14.8 For loop

Value of i	Element accessed	Value of element	Sum
			0
0	Vector[0]	1	1
1	Vector[1]	3	4
2	Vector[2]	8	12
3	Vector[3]	9	21

Table 14.7 Summing the elements of a one-dimensional array

When to use a one-dimensional array?

When it is necessary to keep a large number of items in memory and reference all the items in a uniform manner.

Programming task

1. Write a program which iterates through ArrayOneD outputting each value in turn starting at the first value contained in this array. Assume the array is initialised as follows `ArrayOneD = [3,6,7,2].`
2. Write a program which iterates through ArrayOneD and sums the values contained in this array. Assume the array is initialised as follows `ArrayOneD = [3,6,7,2].`
3. Write a program which collects 6 integer values from the keyboard and stores them in an array called `IntegerArray`. The program is to display the contents of each cell of the array in turn, starting at the first cell, after all the values have been entered.
4. Using the same program structure, add code which calculates the average of the first three numbers stored in the array and the second three numbers.
5. Using the same program structure, add another array to the program of the same size and type as the first. Now add code to copy the contents of the first array to the second array so that the second array holds the contents of the first array in reverse order.

Questions

12. The following algorithm determines the average temperature of a set of temperature readings.
The temperature readings are stored in an array `Temperature` as follows

[20.5, 22.7, 24.3, 26.8, 25.1, 23.9, 21.4]

Note: Array indexing starts at 1.

```
Total ← 0.0
Index ← 0
REPEAT
   Index ← Index + 1
   Total ← Total + Temperature[Index]
UNTIL Index = LENGTH(Temperature)
Average ← Total/LENGTH(Temperature)
OUTPUT Average
```

index	total
0	0.0

Table 14.8

`LENGTH(Temperature)` returns the number of elements in array, temperature.

Complete the trace table *Table 14.8* for this algorithm and array `Temperature`.

13. The first six prime numbers are stored in an array `Primes`.
We can represent this as follows: `[2,3,5,7,11,13]`
If array indexing starts from 0 what is stored in each of the following locations of array `prime`?
(a) `Primes[1]` (b) `Primes[3]` (c) `Primes[5]`

Multi-dimensional arrays

Two-dimensional arrays

We have so far considered how data may be stored in a one-dimensional array. A one-dimensional array has, of course, one dimension. We can visualise the items of data in a one-dimensional array arranged along a single axis as shown by the example in *Figure 14.9*.

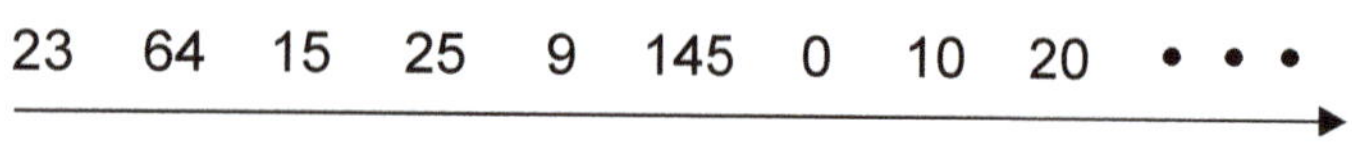

Fig. 14.8 Visualising items of numerical data in a one-dimensional array arranged along a single axis

If we have two dimensions for storing data then we can visualise the data stored in a grid-like fashion defined by two axes as shown in *Figure 14.9*.

The **structure** of 5 rows and 5 columns of data shown in *Figure 14.9* is called a **two-dimensional array** or **matrix.** The matrix contains 5 x 5 = 25 numbers.

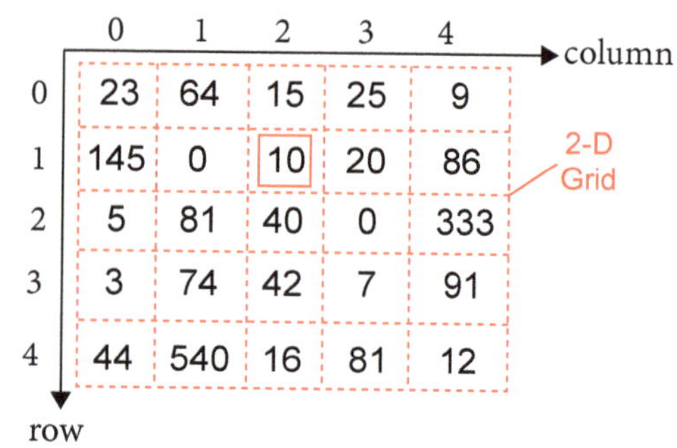

Fig. 14.9 Visualising items of numerical data stored in a two-dimensional array laid out in two dimensions

In order to refer to a specific number, we need to specify both the **row** and **column** because the matrix has two dimensions. For example, the third value along in the second row in *Figure 14.9* is the number 10. This number has been marked by a red square in the figure.

The axes in *Figure 14.9* have been labelled, `row` and `column` so that the first row has value 0 and the first column has value 0. Therefore, the `row` and `column` values of the number 10 marked by a red square are 1 and 2, respectively.

Iterating through the elements of a two-dimensional array

Iterating through the elements of an array is a common operation on arrays. *Figure 14.10* shows the use of nested *For loops* to access each element of array `Array2D` starting with the first element `Array2D[0][0]`. The outer *For loop* uses the loop control variable, `i`. The inner *For loop* uses the loop control variable, `j`.

The two-dimensional array `Array2D` contains 3 x 3 = 9 elements with values as shown in *Table 14.9*.

```
FOR i ← 0 TO 2
  FOR j ← 0 TO 2
    Output Array2D[i][j]
  ENDFOR
ENDFOR
```

Fig. 14.10 Pseudo-code that iterates through the elements of array Array2D

	0	1	2
0	12	45	6
1	9	23	65
2	2	18	33

Table 14.9 Array2D

The **trace table**, *Table 14.10*, shows the value of array `Array2D[i][j]` and the output for each value of `i` and `j`. A trace table is a table which shows the current values of variables used by the pseudo-code and its output whilst the pseudo-code is executed (traced) by hand. This execution by hand is called a **hand-trace**.

`i`	`j`	`Array2D[i][j]`	Output
0	0	12	12
0	1	45	45
0	2	6	6
1	0	9	9
1	1	23	23
1	2	65	65
2	0	2	2
2	1	18	18
2	2	33	33

Table 14.10 Trace table for pseudo-code

Question

14 The following algorithm determines the average temperature of three sets of temperature readings each collected on a separate occasion.

```
Total ← 0.0
Row ← 0
Column ← 0
NoOfRows ← 3
NoOfColumns ← 3
REPEAT
  Row ← Row + 1
  REPEAT
    Column ← Column + 1
    Total ← Total + Temperature[Row][Column]
  UNTIL Column = NoOfColumns
  Column ← 0
UNTIL Row = NoOfRows
NoOfReadings ← NoOfRows * NoOfColumns
Average ← Total / NoOfReadings
OUTPUT Average
```

column	row	total
1	1	0.0

Table 14.11

The temperature readings are stored in a two dimensional array `temperature` as follows [[5, 6, 6],
[7, 9, 8],
[2, 4, 5]]

Each row corresponds to one set of readings.

Note: Array indexing starts at 1.

Complete the trace table *Table 14.11* for this algorithm.

Creating two-dimensional arrays in Delphi

Table 14.12 shows the creation of two-dimensional arrays in Delphi.

Integer	Real/float
`Array2D : Array[0..3,0..1] Of Integer;` `Array2D : Array[0..3,0..1] Of Integer = ((1,2),(3,4),(5,6),(7,8));`	`Array2D : Array[0..3,0..1] Of Real;`

Table 14.12 Creating two-dimensional arrays of different array element data type

The following creates a two-dimensional integer array of 4 rows and 2 columns

```
Array2D : Array[0..3,0..1] Of Integer;
```

The following creates and initialises a two-dimensional integer array of 4 rows and 2 columns

```
Array2D : Array[0..3, 0..1] Of Integer = ((1,2),(3,4),(5,6),(7,8));
```

Array indexing is flexible in Delphi. It may begin at any value, e.g. -1, 1. **Array** is a keyword in Delphi.

Using two-dimensional arrays

Table 14.13 show the creation and use of two-dimensional arrays in Delphi.

```
Program TwoDimensionalArrays;
{$APPTYPE CONSOLE}
Var
  Array2D : Array[0..3,0..1] Of Integer;
  Array2D1 : Array[0..3,0..1] Of Integer = ((1,2),(3,4),(5,6),(7,8));
Begin
  Array2D[0,0] := 1;
  Writeln(Array2D[0,0]);
  Writeln(Array2D1[1,1]);
  Readln;
End.
```

How to initialise a two-dimensional array

Chapter14.rar - TwoDimensionalArrays

Table 14.13 Creating and using two-dimensional arrays

We can define a two dimensional in two stages:

1. Define a row type, `TRowArray`
2. Define a type which is an array of `TRowArray`

For example,

```
Type
  TArrayRowType = Array[0..1] Of Integer;
  T2DimensionalArray = Array[0..3] Of TRowType;
```

Table 14.14 shows an example program that uses these type definitions.

```
Program TwoDArrayRowType;
{$APPTYPE CONSOLE}
Type
  TArrayRow = Array[0..1] Of Integer;
  T2DimensionalArray = Array[0..3] Of TArrayRow;
Var
  Array2D : T2DimensionalArray;
Begin
  Array2D[0][0] := 1; //Can use this notation [0][0]
  Array2D[1,1] := 5;//Or can use this notation [1,1]
  Writeln(Array2D[0][0]);
  Writeln(Array2D[1][1]);
  Readln;
End.
```

Chapter14.rar - TwoDArrayRowType

Table 14.14 Creating and using two-dimensional arrays as rows of a row type

In fact, the notation [*RowNo*][*ColumnNo*] could have been used in the example program shown in *Table 14.13*.

Programming task

6 Write a program which creates a two-dimensional array `ArrayTwoD` and displays the values contained in the second row of this array. The array `ArrayTwoD` should be created with values arranged into rows and columns as follows

$$\texttt{ArrayTwoD} = \begin{bmatrix} 3,6,7 \\ 4,8,1 \\ 9,3,8 \end{bmatrix}$$

The program shown in *Table 14.14* implements an important principle of program design. If you intend to declare a variable with a user-defined data type, e.g. "`Var Array2D : Array[0..3,0..1] Of Integer;`" then define the user-defined data type first in a type definition, e.g. "`Type TArray2D = Array[0..3,0..1] Of Integer;`". The variable declaration then becomes "`Var Array2D : TArray2D;`".

You must do this for arrays that will be passed as parameters to subroutines.

For example,

```
Procedure ShowArrayContents(Array2DParameter : T2DimensionalArray; i, j : Integer);
```

If the procedure signature was instead

```
Procedure ShowArrayContents(Array2DParameter : Array[0..3, 0..1] Of Integer;
                            i, j : Integer);
```

the compiler would flag an an error.

Table 14.15 shows a Delphi program that calls a procedure `ShowArrayContents` using three parameters: the first is a two-dimensional array of type `T2DimensionalArray`, the second and third, `i`, `j`, are indices of type `Integer` used to select for display the particular array cell contents.

```
Program PassingAnArrayAsAParameter;
{$APPTYPE CONSOLE}
Type
  T2DimensionalArray = Array[0..3, 0..1] Of Integer;
Var
  Array2D : T2DimensionalArray;
  i, j : Integer;
Procedure ShowArrayContents(Array2DParameter : T2DimensionalArray; i,
j : Integer);
  Begin
    Writeln(Array2D[i][j]);
  End;
Begin
  For i := 0 To 3
    Do
      For j := 0 To 1
        Do Array2D[i,j] := i * j;
  ShowArrayContents(Array2D, 2, 1);
  Readln;
End.
```

Chapter14.rar - PassingAnArrayAsAParameter

Table 14.15 Passing an array as a parameter of a procedure

Iterating through the elements of a two-dimensional array

Iterating through the elements of an array is a common operation on arrays. *Figure 14.10* shows the use of nested *For loops* to access each element of array `Array2D` starting with the first element `Array2D[0,0]`. The outer *For loop* uses the loop control variable, `i`. The inner *For loop* uses the loop control variable, `j`.

The two-dimensional array `Array2D` contains 3 x 3 = 9 elements with values as shown in *Table 14.16*.

The **trace table**, *Table 14.17*, shows the value of array `Array2D[i,j]` and the output for each value of `i` and `j`. A trace table is a table which shows the current values of variables used by the pseudo-code and its output whilst the pseudo-code is executed (traced) by hand. This execution by hand is called a **hand-trace**.

Table 14.18 shows the nested loop pseudo-code expressed in Delphi.

```
For i ← 0 To 2
  For j ← 0 To 2
    Output Array2D[i,j]
  EndFor
EndFor
```

Fig. 14.10 Pseudo-code that iterates through the elements of array Array2D

	0	1	2
0	12	45	6
1	9	23	65
2	2	18	33

Table 14.16 Array2D

i	j	Array2D[i,j]	Output
0	0	12	12
0	1	45	45
0	2	6	6
1	0	9	9
1	1	23	23
1	2	65	65
2	0	2	2
2	1	18	18
2	2	33	33

Table 14.17 Trace table for pseudo-code

```
Var
  i, j : Integer;
  Array2D : Array [0..2, 0..2] Of Integer = ((12,45,6),(9,23,65),(2,18,33));
.....
For i := 0 To 2
  Do
    Begin
      For j := 0 To 2
        Do Write(Array2D[i, j], ' ');
      Writeln;
    End;
Readln;
```

Table 14.18 Accessing the elements of a two-dimensional array by iteration with a nested For loop

When to use a two-dimensional array?

When it is necessary to keep a large number of items in memory and reference all the items in a uniform manner.

When the structure of the data is two-dimensional.

N-dimensional arrays

If we add a third axis at right-angles to the two axes in *Figure 14.9* we obtain a three dimensional storage grid, i.e. a three-dimensional array.

In Delphi, a three-dimensional array variable, `Array3D`, is created as follows

```
Array3D : Array[0..3,0..4,0..3] Of Integer;
```

We can store the pixel intensity of each pixel of an RGB image in a three-dimensional array as illustrated by the schematic in *Figure 14.11*.

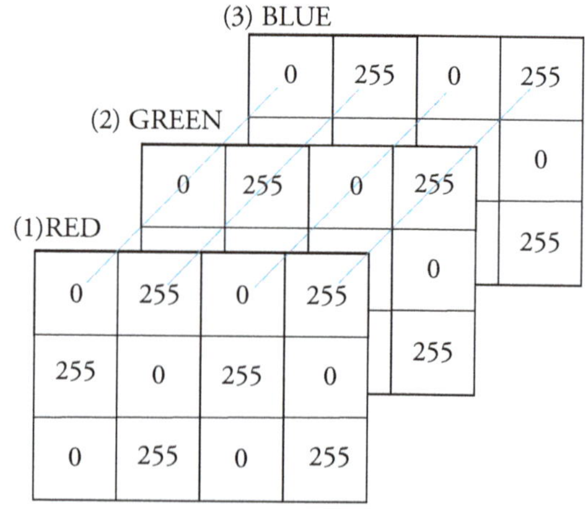

Fig. 14.11 Colour planes of an RGB image, each plane is a two-dimensional array

Figure 14.12 shows an RGB image 'plane.bmp' drawn to the canvas from image data loaded into a three-dimensional array. This array has 450 rows, 640 columns and in the third dimension, 3 colour planes, one for the red intensity, one for the blue intensity and one for the green intensity of a pixel.

*Fig. 14.12 Creating a greyscale image from an RGB image by setting the R, G and B components to (0.2989*R + 0.5870*G + 0.1141*B) and rounding the result*

Table 14.19 shows a code snippet that stores the red, green and blue pixel values of a bitmap image 'Plane.bmp' in a three dimensional array of type `TArray3D`. The program containing this code snippet is described in *Chapter 43*.

P

Chapter14.rar - ThreeDBitmap

```
Type
  TPixelByteArray = Array[0..2] Of Byte;
  TArray3D = Array[0..449, 0..639] Of TPixelByteArray;
..............................................................
Begin
  Bitmap := TBitmap.Create;
  Bitmap.LoadFromFile('Plane.bmp');
  For Row := 0 To Bitmap.Height - 1
    Do
      Begin
        CurrentRow  := Bitmap.ScanLine[Row];
        For Column := 0 To Bitmap.Width - 1
          Do
            Begin
              BitmapArray[iRow, Column, 2]  := CurrentRow[Column].rgbtBlue;
              BitmapArray[iRow, Column, 1] := CurrentRow[Column].rgbtGreen;
              BitmapArray[iRow, Column, 0]   := CurrentRow[Column].rgbtRed;
            End;
        End;
..............................................................
```

Table 14.19 Code snippet showing how a three dimensional bitmap array is initialised by iterating through the rows of pixels of a bitmap loaded from a disk file Plane.bmp

We can continue to add dimensions but we will not be able to visualise the array geometrically because we live in a three-dimensional world. It is quite rare, however, to work on arrays with more than four dimensions.

A n-dimensional array is a multi-dimensional array of n dimensions where n could be, say 4.

All the elements of the n-dimensional array are of the same data type which is why it is an array.

Programming tasks

7. Write a console application which iterates through `ArrayTwoD` and sums the values contained in this array. The array `ArrayTwoD` should be created with values arranged into rows and columns as follows

$$\texttt{ArrayTwoD} = \begin{bmatrix} 3,6,7 \\ 4,8,1 \\ 9,3,8 \end{bmatrix}$$

8. Write a console application which iterates through `ArrayTwoD` multiplying each value by 5. The result of each multiplication should replace the original value.
The array `ArrayTwoD` should be created with values arranged into rows and columns as follows

$$\texttt{ArrayTwoD} = \begin{bmatrix} 3,6,7 \\ 4,8,1 \\ 9,3,8 \end{bmatrix}$$

9. A particular black and white image contains a single simple convex shape, such as a circle, represented as a dark area on a light background. Such images are commonly represented in computers as two-dimensional arrays, where each element has the value 1 or 0. A dark area on a light background becomes a group of 1's surrounded by 0's. *Figure 14.12* shows a two-dimensional array representation of a lower resolution image of a black circle on a white background.

```
0,0,0,0,0,0,0
0,0,0,1,0,0,0
0,0,1,1,1,0,0
0,1,1,1,1,1,0
0,0,1,1,1,0,0
0,0,0,1,0,0,0
0,0,0,0,0,0,0
```

Fig. 14.13

Write a console application with a two-dimensional array initialised with the values shown in *Figure 14.13*.
The program should display the shape of the dark region by displaying the points of the image which represent dark regions as 1's and the background as spaces.
Hint: Scan the image row-wise or column-wise.

10. Write a console application with a two-dimensional array initialised with the values shown in *Figure 14.13*.
The program should display the shape of the dark region by displaying the points in the image on the boundary between the dark region and the surrounding white region as 1's and the background and interior points as spaces.
Hint: Scan the image row-wise or column-wise. For a given 1, if **any** of the surrounding points are 0's then that 1 represents a boundary point.

11. Write a console application with a two-dimensional array initialised with the values shown in *Figure 14.13*.
The program should calculate the ratio of the area of the dark region to its perimeter. As a measure of the area, count the number of ones. A (rather inaccurate) measure of the perimeter can be obtained by counting the number of boundary points.

Questions

15. What is an n-dimensional array?

Array Index type must be ordinal

We cannot use data types **Real**, **Double**, or **Extended** or any subranges of these types as array index types because they are not ordinal types. We can use ordinal types such as

1. **Char** or its subranges, e.g. Array[Char} Of Integer, Array['A'..'Z'] Of Cardinal
2. **Byte** or its subranges e.g. Array[Byte] Of Integer, Array[0..100] Of Integer
3. **Word** or its subranges, e.g. Array[Word] Of String, Array[100..200] Of String
4. **Integer** subranges, e.g. Array[-50..+50} Of Real
5. **Boolean**, e.g. Array[Boolean] Of Integer, Array[False] Of Integer
6. **Enumerated** types, e.g. Array[Monday..Sunday] Of Boolean,

Table 14.20 shows some array type definitions for various index types.

```
Program ArrayIndexTypes;
{$APPTYPE CONSOLE}
Type
  TDaysOfWeek = (Monday, Tuesday, Wednesday, Thursday, Friday, Saturday, Sunday);
  TIndexCharArray =  Array[Char] Of Integer;
  TIndexUpperCaseArray = Array['A'..'Z'] Of Cardinal;//Cardinal represents a subset of the natural numbers.
  //The range for the Cardinal type is from 0 through 4294967295.
  //The size of Cardinal is 32 bits across all 64-bit and 32-bit platforms.
  TIndexByteArray = Array[Byte] Of Integer;
  TIndexNoughtToOneHundredArray = Array[0..100] Of Integer;
  TIndexWordArray =  Array[Word] Of String;//Word represents a subset of the Cardinal type.
  //The range for the Word type is from 0 through 65535.
  //The size of Word is 16-bits across all 64-bit and 32-bit platforms.
  TIndex100To200Array =  Array[100..200] Of String;
  TIndexCardinalArray = Array[ShortInt] Of Byte;//Integer type with the range [-128; 127].
  //Shortint is a one-byte signed integer.
  TIndex1To6000Array = Array[1..6000] Of Double;//Double represents a double-precision floating-point value.
  //The size of Double is 8 bytes
  TIndexMiuns1ToPlus1Array = Array[-1..+1] Of Single;
  //Single represents a single-precision floating-point value. The size of Single is 4 bytes.
  TIndexIntegerArray = Array[SmallInt] Of Byte; //Integer type with the range [-32768; 32767].
  //Smallint is a 2-byte signed integer.
  TIndexMinus50ToPlus50Array = Array[-50..+50] Of Integer;//Represents a signed 32-bit integer type.
  //Integer represents a subset of the integer numbers.
  //The range for the Integer type is from -2147483648 through 2147483647.
  //The size of Integer is 32 bits across all 64-bit and 32-bit platforms.
   TIndexBooleanArray = Array[Boolean] Of Integer;
   TIndexFalseArray = Array[False..True] Of Integer;
   TIndexEnumeratedArray = Array[Monday..Sunday] Of Boolean;
Begin
End.
```

Chapter14.rar - ArrayIndexTypes

Table 14.20 Array type definitions for various index types

Counting letters in text

Table 14.21 shows a program that counts the letters, uppercase and lowercase, in a text file 'us-history-since-1877.txt'. The results for uppercase letters and lowercase letters are stored in two arrays, `UpperCaseArray` and `LowerCaseCaseArray`, respectively. The total count of letters of either case is obtained by summing the corresponding contents of these two arrays as follows.

```
For Ch := 'A' To 'Z'
    Do
      Begin
        LowerCh := Chr(Ord(Ch) + Ord('a') - Ord('A'));
        Writeln('Total count of ', Ch,' + ', LowerCh, '''s = ',
                UpperCaseArray[Ch] + LowerCaseArray[LowerCh]);
      End;
```

The **Ord** and **Chr** functions are used to convert uppercase letters 'A'..'Z' to lowercase letters 'a'..'z' as follows.

```
LowerCh := Chr(Ord(Ch) + Ord('a') - Ord('A'));
```

File processing is covered in *Chapter 16*.

```
Program CountingLetters;
{$APPTYPE CONSOLE}
Uses SysUtils;
Type
  TUpperCaseArray = Array['A'..'Z'] Of Cardinal;
  //Cardinal represents a subset of the natural numbers.
  //The range for the Cardinal type is from 0 through 4294967295.
  TLowerCaseArray = Array['a'..'z'] Of Cardinal;
  TReadingPipe = Text;
Var
  UpperCaseArray : TUpperCaseArray;
  LowerCaseArray : TLowerCaseArray;
  ReadingPipe : TReadingPipe;
  LineOfText : String;
  i : Integer;
  Ch, LowerCh : Char;
Begin
  AssignFile(ReadingPipe, 'us-history-since-1877.txt');
  Reset(ReadingPipe);
  For Ch := 'A' To 'Z' Do UpperCaseArray[Ch] := 0;
  For Ch := 'a' To 'z' Do LowerCaseArray[Ch] := 0;
  While Not Eof(ReadingPipe)
    Do
      Begin
        Readln(ReadingPipe,LineOfText);
        For i := 1 To Length(LineOfText)
          Do
            Begin
              If LineOfText[i] in ['A'..'Z']
                Then Inc(UpperCaseArray[LineOfText[i]]);
              If LineOfText[i] in ['a'..'z']
                Then Inc(LowerCaseArray[LineOfText[i]]);
            End;
      End;
  For Ch := 'A' To 'Z' Do Writeln('Count of ', Ch, '''s = ', UpperCaseArray[Ch]);
  For Ch := 'a' To 'z' Do Writeln('Count of ', Ch, '''s = ', LowerCaseArray[Ch]);
  For Ch := 'A' To 'Z'
    Do
      Begin
        LowerCh := Chr(Ord(Ch) + Ord('a') - Ord('A'));
        Writeln('Total count of ', Ch,' + ', LowerCh, '''s = ',
                UpperCaseArray[Ch] + LowerCaseArray[LowerCh]);
      End;
  Readln;
End.
```

Chapter14.rar - CountingLetters

Table 14.21 Counting letters in a text file

Figure 14.14 shows the total letter count produced by the program, ignoring letter case, for the text file 'us-history-since-1877.txt'[2].

```
Z:\ProductionChapters\DelphiBook\Code\...
Total count of A + a's = 14020
Total count of B + b's = 2175
Total count of C + c's = 5538
Total count of D + d's = 6695
Total count of E + e's = 21637
Total count of F + f's = 3125
Total count of G + g's = 3487
Total count of H + h's = 7608
Total count of I + i's = 11900
Total count of J + j's = 253
Total count of K + k's = 1036
Total count of L + l's = 7483
Total count of M + m's = 4519
Total count of N + n's = 12538
Total count of O + o's = 12749
Total count of P + p's = 3460
Total count of Q + q's = 125
Total count of R + r's = 11579
Total count of S + s's = 11132
Total count of T + t's = 14889
Total count of U + u's = 4505
Total count of V + v's = 1861
Total count of W + w's = 3526
Total count of X + x's = 312
Total count of Y + y's = 2521
Total count of Z + z's = 193
```

Fig. 14.14 Total letter count ignoring letter case for the text file us-history-since-1877.txt

Questions

16 Explain why the following snippet of code converts an uppercase letter in the range 'A' to 'Z' stored in variable Ch to its equivalent lowercase letter (see ASCII code lookup table *Table 4.8*, *Chapter 4*).

```
Chr(Ord(Ch) + Ord('a') - Ord('A'));
```

The function Ord(Ch) returns the ordinal value of its character argument Ch, type Char.
The function Chr(n) returns the character value, type Char, of its integer argument n.

2 'us-history-since-1877.txt ' is copyrighted by Dr. James Ross-Nazzal. It is licensed under the Creative Commons Attribution License 3.0 (http://creativecommons.org/licenses/by/3.0/).
http://cnx.org/content/col10669/1.3/

Programming tasks

12 Modify the program shown in *Table 14.21* so that, in addition to counting upper and lower case letters, it counts the number of each punctuation and other symbols in the ASCII code range 32 ..47, 58..64, 91..96, 123..126, inclusive. Your modified program should output the punctuation/other symbol followed by its count.

Enumerating arrays

One way to enumerate an array is to use a **For/To** loop and explicit indexing.

The lower and higher bounds may be obtained using **Low** and **High** standard functions as shown in the program in *Table 14.22*.

Arrays also support **For/In** loops (introduced in Delphi 2005). When used these enumerate from the element with the lowest index to the element with the highest index, e.g.

```
For ElementValue In StaticArray
      Do Writeln('Element: ', ElementValue);
```

The output from executing program `ArrayForIn` is shown in *Figure 14.15*.

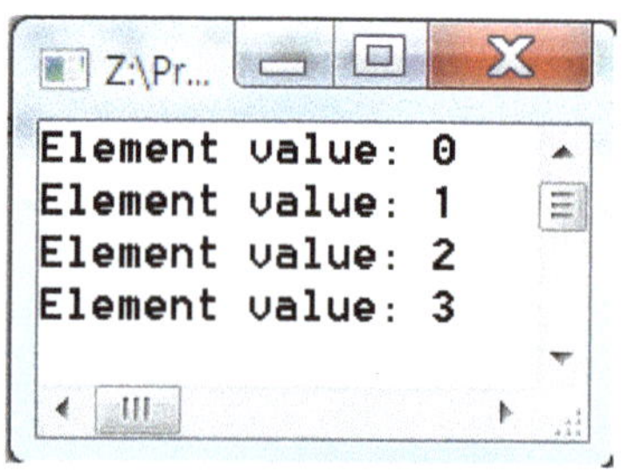

Fig. 14.15 For/In enumeration

```
Program ArrayForIn;
{$APPTYPE CONSOLE}
Uses
  SysUtils;
Type
  TByteArray = Array[0..3] Of Byte;
Var
  ByteArray : TByteArray;
  i : Integer;
  ElementValue : Byte;
Begin
  Try
    For i := Low(ByteArray) To High(ByteArray)
      Do ByteArray[i] := i;
    For ElementValue In ByteArray
      Do Writeln('Element value: ', ElementValue);
  Except
    On E: Exception
      Do Writeln(E.ClassName, ': ', E.Message);
  End;
  Readln;
End.
```

P Chapter14.rar - ArrayForIn

Table 14.22 Enumerating the elements of an array

Table 14.23 shows a program that uses enumeration to iterate through the fifth row of a two dimensional array `TimeTableArray.`

The output from this array is shown in *Figure 14.16*.

```
Program TwoDArrayForIn;
{$APPTYPE CONSOLE}
{$RANGECHECKS ON}//Turn on range checks for array index
Uses
  SysUtils;
Type
  TTimesTableArray = Array[1..12, 1..12] Of Byte;
Var
  TimesTableArray : TTimesTableArray;
  i, j : Integer;
  ElementValue : Byte;
Begin
  Try
    For i := 1 To 12
      Do
        For j := 1 To 12
          Do TimesTableArray[i,j] := i * j;
    Writeln('5 times table only');
    Writeln('------------------');
    //Select row 5, iterate through the 12 elements of this row
    For ElementValue In TimesTableArray[5]
      Do Writeln('Element value: ', ElementValue);
  Except
    On E: Exception
      Do Writeln(E.ClassName, ': ', E.Message);
  End;
  Readln;
End.
```

P Chapter14.rar - TwoDArrayForIn

Table 14.23 Enumerating the elements of an array

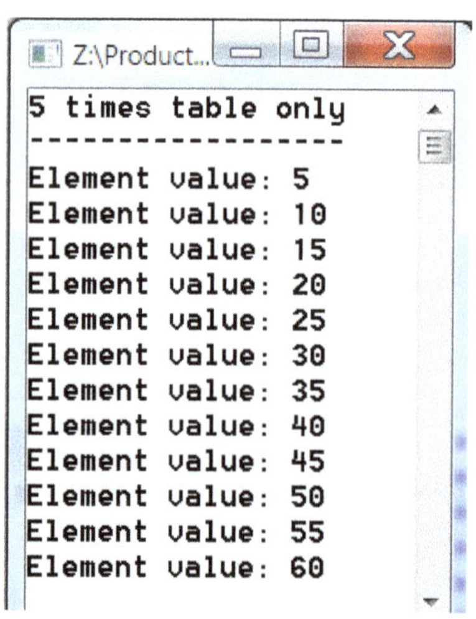

Fig. 14.16 For/In enumeration of a particular row of a 2-d array

Dynamic arrays

We have seen that an array is a variable that holds a sequence of values, all of the same type, that are accessed by an index. The form of array that we have studied so far is known as a **static array** because it has dimensions that are fixed at compile time and is allocated a part of the program's allocated memory space. There is another kind of array called a **dynamic array** which has dimensions that are set 'dynamically', i.e. at runtime, by calling the **SetLength** standard procedure. Dynamic arrays are allocated memory from the heap.

Table 14.24 shows a program that uses **SetLength** to create a dynamic array of 10000 elements, each one byte in size. The code is protected in a **Try Except** block because it is possible to not have enough memory for the dynamic or the static array. In this situation an **EOutOfMemory** exception occurs. **Try Except** requires the **SysUtils** unit.

```
Program DynamicArrays;
{$APPTYPE CONSOLE}
Uses SysUtils;
Type
  TStaticArray = Array[0..9999] Of Byte;
  TDynamicArray = Array Of Byte;
Var
  StaticArray : TStaticArray;
  DynamicArray : TDynamicArray;
Begin
  Try
    SetLength(DynamicArray, 10000);
    DynamicArray[0] := 1;
    StaticArray[0] := 2;
    Writeln(DynamicArray[0]);
    Writeln(StaticArray[0]);
  Except
    On E: Exception
      Do Writeln(E.ClassName, ': ', E.Message);
  End;
  Readln;
End.
```

P

Chapter14.rar - DynamicArrays

Table 14.24 Dynamic and static arrays

Dynamic arrays are always indexed with an integer that starts at 0 for the first element whilst static arrays allow any ordinal type (range permitting) to be used for the index.

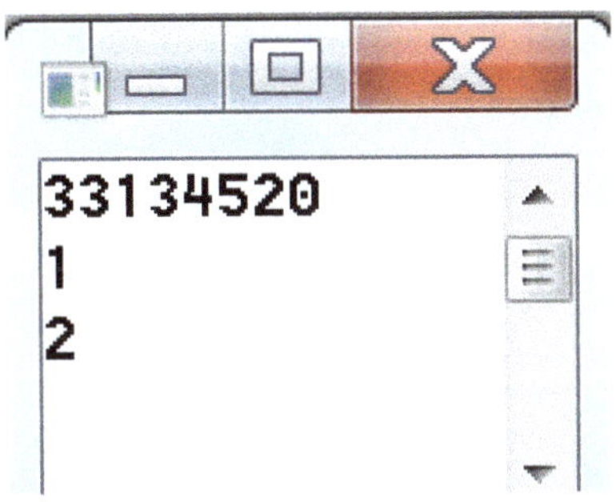

Fig. 14.17 DynamicArray reference 33134520

Value types versus reference types

The dynamic array variable is assigned a memory reference by **SetLength**. The reference points to the block of memory allocated for storing the dynamic array's elements. For example, `SetLength(DynamicArray, 10000)` shown in *Table 14.24* allocates a block of memory of 10000 bytes. The first byte is addressed by `DynamicArray[0]`. This statement accesses the first byte in the allocated block of bytes.

We say that dynamic arrays are **reference types** because their variables are references. It is possible to assign **Nil** to a dynamic array variable and for the variable to be compared to **Nil**.

If the following statement is inserted immediately before statement `Writeln(DynamicArray[0]);` in program `DynamicArrays`, *Table 14.24*

```
Writeln(Integer(DynamicArray));
```

and the program compiled, linked (built) and run, the output is as shown in *Figure 14.17*. The memory address of the block of memory containing the elements of the dynamic array is 33134520. The address has to be converted to **Integer** for `Writeln` to accept it as a valid type. This is done with `Integer(DynamicArray)`. This is called **casting**, the process of converting one data type to another.

In contrast, static arrays are **value types**. Assigning one static array to another therefore copies the values of all the elements, whereas assigning one dynamic array to another merely copies a reference to the first array's values.

Enumerating dynamic arrays

As with have seen, one way to enumerate an array is to use a **For/To** loop and explicit indexing and another is with **For/In**.

Table 14.25 shows a program that uses **For/To** and **For/In** with both dynamic and static arrays.

The output from executing program `DynamicArrayStaticArrayForIn` is shown in *Figure 14.18*.

It is possible to obtain the number of elements in an array by calling the **Length** standard function. As dynamic arrays are always indexed from zero we have

```
Length(DynamicArray) =
              High(DynamicArray ) + 1
```

and therefore we would control the for loop as follows

```
For i := Low(DynamicArray) To
                 Length(DynamicArray)- 1
  Do DynamicArray[i] := i;
```

```
Program DynamicArrayStaticArrayForIn;
{$APPTYPE CONSOLE}
Uses
  SysUtils;
Type
  TStaticArray = Array[0..3] Of Byte;
  TDynamicArray = Array Of Byte;
Var
  StaticArray : TStaticArray;
  DynamicArray : TDynamicArray;
  i : Integer;
  ElementValue : Byte;
Begin
  Try
    SetLength(DynamicArray, 4);
    For i := Low(StaticArray) To High(StaticArray)
      Do StaticArray[i] := i;
    For i := Low(DynamicArray) To High(DynamicArray)
      Do DynamicArray[i] := i;
    For ElementValue In StaticArray
      Do Writeln('Static: ', ElementValue);
    For ElementValue In DynamicArray
      Do Writeln('Dynamic: ', ElementValue);
  Except
    On E: Exception
      Do Writeln(E.ClassName, ': ', E.Message);
  End;
  Readln;
End.
```

Chapter14.rar - DynamicStaticArrayForIn

Table 14.25 Enumerating dynamic and static arrays

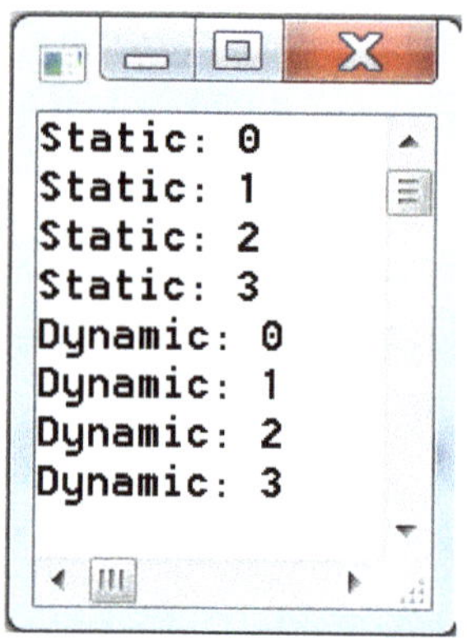

Fig. 14.18 Using For/In

Alternative way of creating a dynamic array

A syntax called constructor syntax can be used to create a dynamic array. It takes the following form

```
Var
  DynamicArray : TArray<Byte>
Begin
  DynamicArray := TArray<Byte>.Create(19, 34, 56, 2, 5);
```

This is equivalent to

```
Var
  DynamicArray : TArray<Byte>
Begin
  SetLength(DynamicArray, 5);
  DynamicArray[0] := 19;
  DynamicArray[1] := 34;
  DynamicArray[2] := 56;
  DynamicArray[3] := 2;
  DynamicArray[4] := 5;
        •
        •
        •
```

The program in *Table 14.26* shows the use of the constructor syntax to create and initialise a dynamic array `DynamicArray1`. Another dynamic array, `DynamicArray2`, is created using the **SetLength** method and initialised by assignment. Both are then sorted by the class method **TArray.Sort** using the syntax

`TArray.Sort<Byte>(DynamicArray1);` and
`TArray.Sort<Byte>(DynamicArray2);`

Figure 14.19 shows the output when the program in *Table 14.29* is compiled, linked (built) and run.

The **Systems.Generics.Collections** unit introduced in Delphi 2009 provides procedures to both sort and search single dimensional arrays.

```
Program DynamicArraysConstructor;
{$APPTYPE CONSOLE}
uses
  SysUtils, System.Generics.Collections;

Type
  TDynamicArray = TArray<Byte>;
Var
  DynamicArray1 : TDynamicArray;
  DynamicArray2 : Array Of Byte;
  ElementValue : Byte;
Begin
  Try
    DynamicArray1 := TDynamicArray.Create(19, 34, 56, 2, 5);
    Writeln('Raw data');
    Writeln('--------');
    For ElementValue In DynamicArray1
      Do Writeln(ElementValue);
    TArray.Sort<Byte>(DynamicArray1);
    Writeln('Sorted data');
    Writeln('-----------');
    For ElementValue In DynamicArray1
      Do Writeln(ElementValue);
    SetLength(DynamicArray2, 5);
    DynamicArray2[0] := 19;
    DynamicArray2[1] := 34;
    DynamicArray2[2] := 56;
    DynamicArray2[3] := 2;
    DynamicArray2[4] := 5;
    Writeln('Raw data');
    Writeln('--------');
    For ElementValue In DynamicArray2
      Do Writeln(ElementValue);
    TArray.Sort<Byte>(DynamicArray2);
    Writeln('Sorted data');
    Writeln('-----------');
    For ElementValue In DynamicArray2
      Do Writeln(ElementValue);
  Except
    On E: Exception
      Do Writeln(E.ClassName, ': ', E.Message);
  End;
  Readln;
End.
```

Chapter14.rar - DynamicArraysConstructor

Table 14.26 Dynamic array constructor example

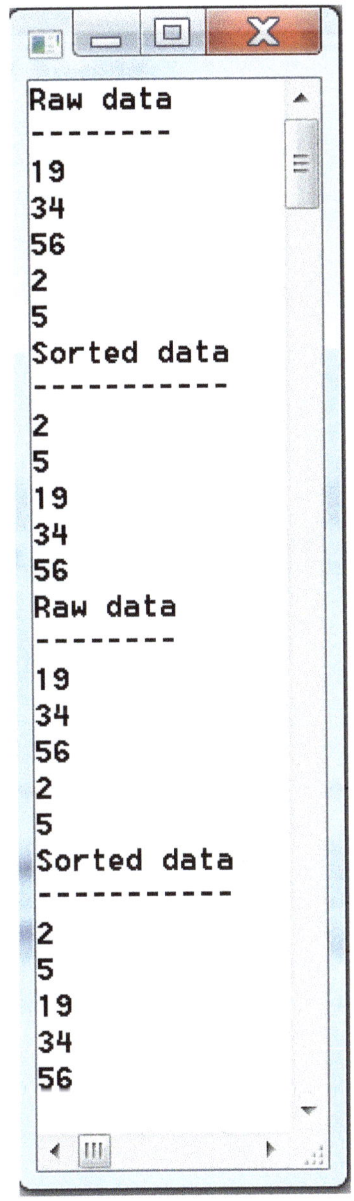

Fig. 14.19 Using TArray Sort method on dynamic array constructor and SetLength arrays

Open arrays

There is a third kind of array called an **open array** which can only be used in parameter lists of subroutines/routines (procedures and functions). The purpose of an open array is to allow both static and dynamic arrays to be passed to subroutines. The form of an open array parameter mirrors that used to declare a dynamic array. The program in *Table 14.27* shows an example of the use of an open array. Inside the routine, an open array is always indexed as for a dynamic array, i.e.with indexing starting from 0, even if the routine is called with a static array as actual parameter and this array's index does not start at zero.

Figure 14.20 shows the outcome when program **OpenArray** is executed.

```
Program OpenArray;
{$APPTYPE CONSOLE}
Uses
  SysUtils,
  System.Generics.Collections;
Type
  TDynamicArray = TArray<Byte>;
  TStaticArray = Array[1..5] Of Byte;
Var
  DynamicArray : TDynamicArray;
  StaticArray : TStaticArray = (19, 34, 56, 2, 5);
  ElementValue : Byte;
Procedure OpenArrayRoutine(ArrayParam : Array Of Byte);
  Var
    ElementOfArray : Byte;
  Begin
    Writeln('Enumeration of the array elements');
    Writeln('--------------------------------');
    For ElementOfArray In ArrayParam
      Do Writeln(ElementOfArray);
    Writeln('--------------------------------');
  End;
Begin
  Try
    DynamicArray := TDynamicArray.Create(19, 34, 56, 2, 5);
    OpenArrayRoutine(DynamicArray);
    OpenArrayRoutine(StaticArray);
  Except
    On E: Exception
      Do Writeln(E.ClassName, ': ', E.Message);
  End;
  Readln;
End.
```

Chapter14.rar - OpenArray

Table 14.27 Open array example

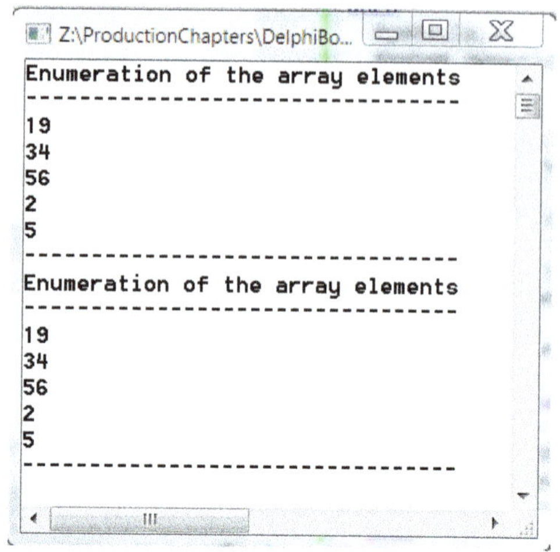

Fig. 14.20 Output from OpenArray program when executed

A **For/To** loop may be used inside `OpenArrayRoutine` in place of the **For/In** loop as follows

```
Procedure OpenArrayRoutine(ArrayParam : Array Of Byte);
  Var
    i : Integer;
  Begin
    Writeln('Enumeration of the array elements');
    Writeln('--------------------------------');
    For i := Low(ArrayParam) To High(ArrayParam)
      Do Writeln(ArrayParam[i]);
    Writeln('--------------------------------');
  End;
```

Chapter14.rar - OpenArrayForTo

Slice function

The **Slice** function creates a sub-section (slice) of a static array `A` from the first `Count` elements.

```
Function Slice(var A: Array; Count: Integer): Array;
```

Slice is only allowed as a parameter in a call to a procedure or function that expects an open array parameter. For example,

```
For i := Length(StaticArray) DownTo 1
    Do DisplayArray(Slice(StaticArray, i));
```

`Length` returns the number of elements in the array, `StaticArray`.

Table 14.28 shows a program which uses the Slice function. *Figure 14.21* shows the program's output when executed.

```
Program SliceFunction;
{$APPTYPE CONSOLE}
Uses
  SysUtils;
Type
  TStaticArray = Array[0..5] Of Integer;
Var
  StaticArray : TStaticArray = (6, 5, 4, 3, 2, 1);
  i : Integer;
Procedure DisplayArray(ArrayParam: Array Of Integer);
  Var
    Element : Integer;
  Begin
    For Element In ArrayParam
      Do Write(Element, ' ');
    Writeln;
  End;

Begin
  Try
    For i := Length(StaticArray) DownTo 1
      Do DisplayArray(Slice(StaticArray, i));

  Except
    On E: Exception
      Do Writeln(E.ClassName, ': ', E.Message);
  End;
  Readln;
End.
```

Chapter14.rar - SliceFunction

Table 14.28 Using the Slice function

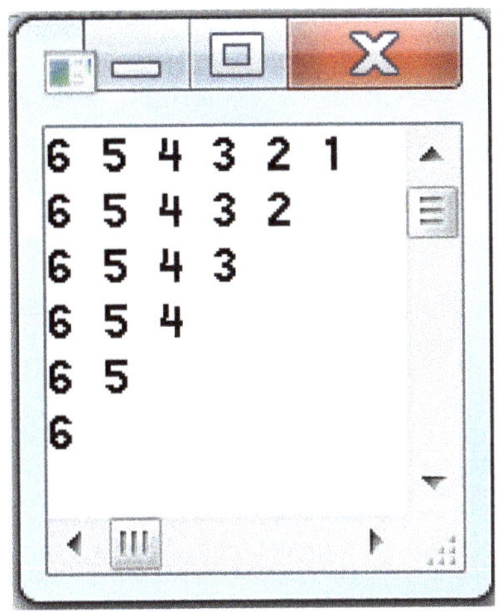

Fig. 14.21 Output from program SliceFunction when executed

When to use a dynamic array - file size unavailable at compile time

A dynamic array is appropriate to use when the nature of the application is one for which data processing is facilitated by the use of an array but for which the size of the data cannot be determined at compile time. For example, the data source may be a file whose size can only be determined at runtime. Therefore, the size of the array that stores the contents of the file can only be determined at runtime. Under such a circumstance it is appropriate to stream the file using a **TFileStream** object referenced by variable `FileStream` as follows

```
FileStream := TFileStream.Create(Filename, fmOpenRead or fmShareDenyWrite);
```

This statement opens a file for reading (`fmOpenRead`) with the name specified in variable `Filename` whilst preventing another application from writing to it at the same time (`fmShareDenyWrite`).

Streaming is covered in *Chapter 30*.

The file contents are streamed byte-by-byte into a dynamically sized array `DynamicArray` starting at `DynamicArray[0]` by the statement

```
FileStream.Read(DynamicArray[0], Size);
```

The number of bytes to be streamed is set by the value of `Size`.

The value of `Size` is obtained as follows

```
Size := FileStream.Size;
```

and `DynamicArray`'s length is set with

```
SetLength(DynamicArray, Size);
```

Table 14.29 shows a program that reads the bytes of a file specified in `OpenDialog.Filename` into a dynamic array, `DynamicArray`. The contents of this array are then written to the screen as characters using the standard function `Chr` to convert each byte to its equivalent character representation

The filename is obtained using a **TOpenDialog** object, referenced by variable `Dialog`, which opens a dialogue window as shown in *Figure 14.22* when `Dialog.Execute` is called.

Figure 14.23 shows the output to the console window of the executing program for the text file **Sonnet116.txt**.

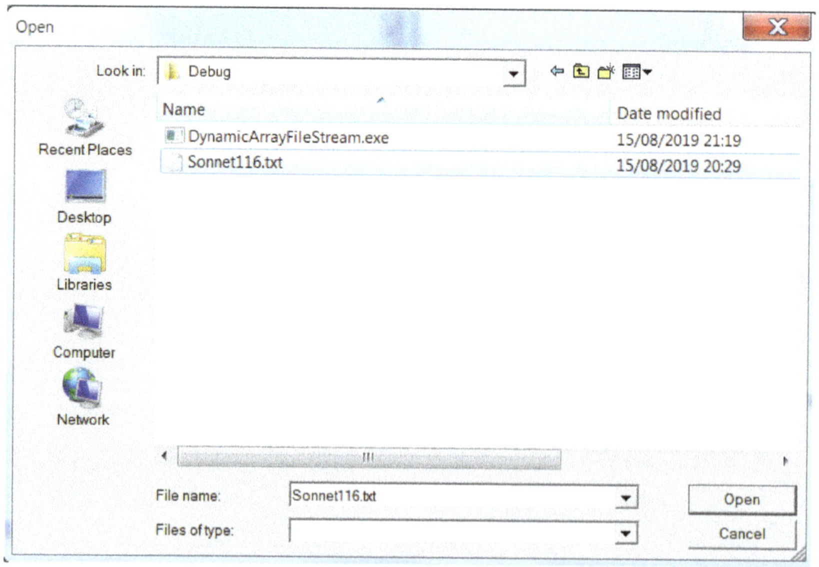

Fig. 14.22 Dialogue window used to select file to read into dynamic array

Chapter14.rar - DynamicArrayFileStream

```
Program DynamicArrayFileStream;
{$APPTYPE CONSOLE}
Uses
  SysUtils, Vcl.Dialogs, System.Classes;
Type
  TDynamicArray = Array Of Byte;
Var
  DynamicArray : TDynamicArray;
  ElementValue : Byte;
  FileStream : TFileStream;
  Size : Integer;
  Dialogue : TOpenDialog;
Begin
  Try
    Try
      Dialogue := TOpenDialog.Create(Nil);
      If Dialogue.Execute
        Then
          Begin
            FileStream := TFileStream.Create(Dialogue.Filename, fmOpenRead or fmShareDenyWrite);
            Size := FileStream.Size;
            Writeln('Size of file in bytes: ', FileStream.Size);
            SetLength(DynamicArray, Size);
            FileStream.Read(DynamicArray[0], Size);
            For ElementValue In DynamicArray
              Do Write(Chr(ElementValue));
          End;
    Except
      On E: Exception
        Do Writeln(E.ClassName, ': ', E.Message);
    End;
  Finally
    FileStream.Free;
  End;
  Readln;
End.
```

Table 14.29 Reading bytes from a file into a dynamic array

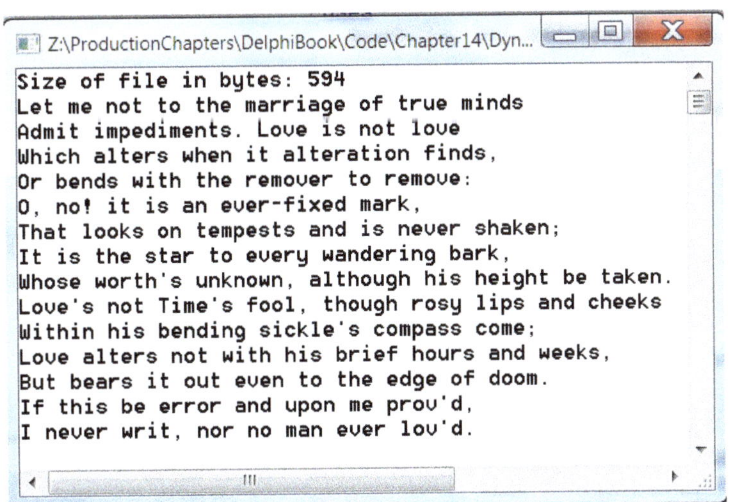

Fig. 14.23 Text file Sonnet116.txt displayed in console window by program DynamicArrayFileStream

When to use a dynamic array - non-rectangular two-dimensional array

Three are two basic ways to create a two-dimensional dynamic array.

1. Declare a dynamic array variable with two dimensions as follows

```
Var DynamicArray Array of Array Of Integer;
```

   Set its length in two dimensions with values for `n` and `m`, e.g. 2, 4, as follows

```
SetLength(DynamicArray, n, m);
```

2. Declare a dynamic array variable with two dimensions as follows

```
Var DynamicArray Array of Array Of Integer;
```

   Set the length, `n`, of its first dimension (i.e. the number of rows as follows

```
SetLength(DynamicArray, n);
```

   Set the individual lengths of each row as follows

```
SetLength(DynamicArray[0], 3);
SetLength(DynamicArray[1], 5);
SetLength(DynamicArray[2], 10);
SetLength(DynamicArray[3], 2);
```

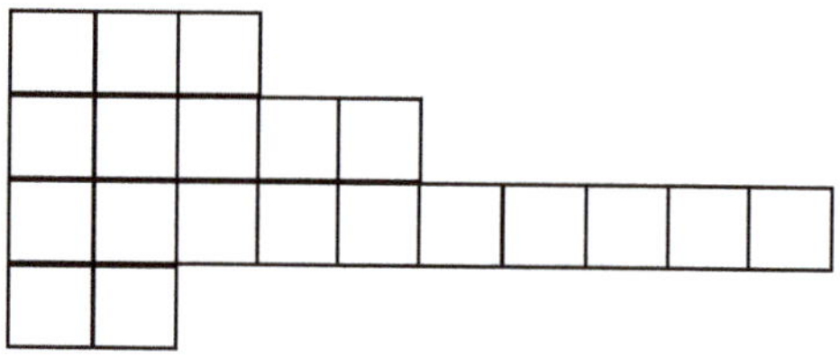

Fig. 14.24 Non rectangular or ragged two-dimensional dynamic array

Method 2 produces a non rectangular or ragged two-dimensional array as shown in *Figure 14.24*. This is only possible with dynamic arrays.

Passing an array as a subroutine parameter

When a subroutine is called its parameters are placed on the (call) stack to which the subroutine's code has access. Passing a large array as a call by value is not a good idea because call by value places a copy of the array on the stack. A large array could require more memory than is available on the stack. In addition, processor time will be consumed copying many array elements to the stack. The solution is to use a call by reference parameter to pass the array into the subroutine. Only an address will need to be copied onto the stack, the address of the first element of the array.

Key concept

Array:
An array is a container for a fixed number of values of a single data type. An array may be organized into several dimensions.

Length of an array:
The length of an array is established when the array is created. After creation, its length is fixed.

One-dimensional array:
A one-dimensional array is a data structure containing an ordered sequence of elements (e.g. numbers) that are indexed with a single integer.

Two-dimensional array:
A two-dimensional array is a data structure containing elements indexed by a pair of integers, that is, the row index and the column index.

n-dimensional array:
More generally, an n-dimensional array is a set of elements with the same data type that are indexed by a tuple of n integers.

Key concept

Element data type:
All elements in an array must have the same data type.

Storage:
Elements in an array are stored internally in a contiguous block of memory.
For example, the elements in a vector of size 5 occupy 5 consecutive memory addresses. When the dimension of the array is two or more, there is more than one way of ordering the elements in memory but this is hidden from user.

Records

Purpose: To learn to use records

Introduction

Figure 15.1 shows a card index consisting of cards on which information has been recorded. Each card contains a record of something.

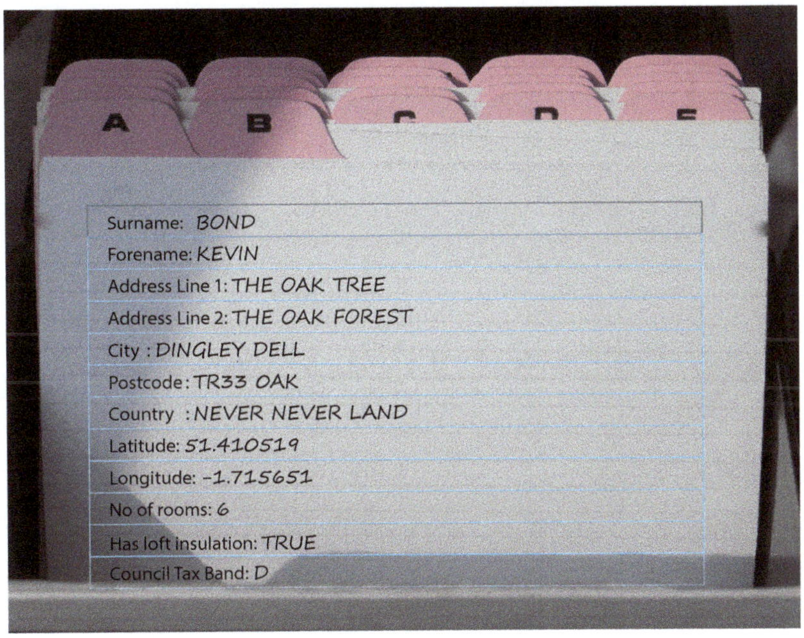

Figure 15.1 Card index showing one record

In *Figure 15.1*, it is a **record** of a person's name, address, latitude, longitude, no of rooms in their dwelling, whether the dwelling has loft insulation or not, and Council Tax band. It is intended that the card shown will be filed in the section of the card index labelled 'B'. We can say that the card index contains a file of records ordered by initial letter of surname. Notice that the information on the card in *Figure 15.1* is subdivided into an area for the surname, an area for the forename, and so on. Each area is called a **field of the record**. Each **field has a name**, e.g. Surname, and a value, e.g. BOND.

We have learned that every value has a data type. The data type of each value recorded in the given record is as shown in *Figure 15.2*.

BOND *String*
KEVIN *String*
THE OAK TREE *String*
THE OAK FOREST *String*
DINGLEY DELL *String*
TR33 OAK *String*
NEVER NEVER LAND *String*
51.410519 *Real*
-1.715651 *Real*
6 *Integer*
TRUE *Boolean*
D *Character*

Figure 15.2 One record

To record the information about the person with surname BOND in a machine, the human readable values of the record are replaced with their data type equivalent bit patterns. At the machine level the information becomes a sequence of bits as follows

100001010011111001110100010010010111000101110111010010011001110 . . .

SURNAME *FORENAME*

If we view the entire bit pattern for the person's record and use the "**method of interpreting a bit pattern definition of data type**", we now have a new data type which has **structure** consisting of **named fields** and their **corresponding data types**. This new data type is called a **record data type** - see *Figure 15.3*. This record data type consists of 12 fields.

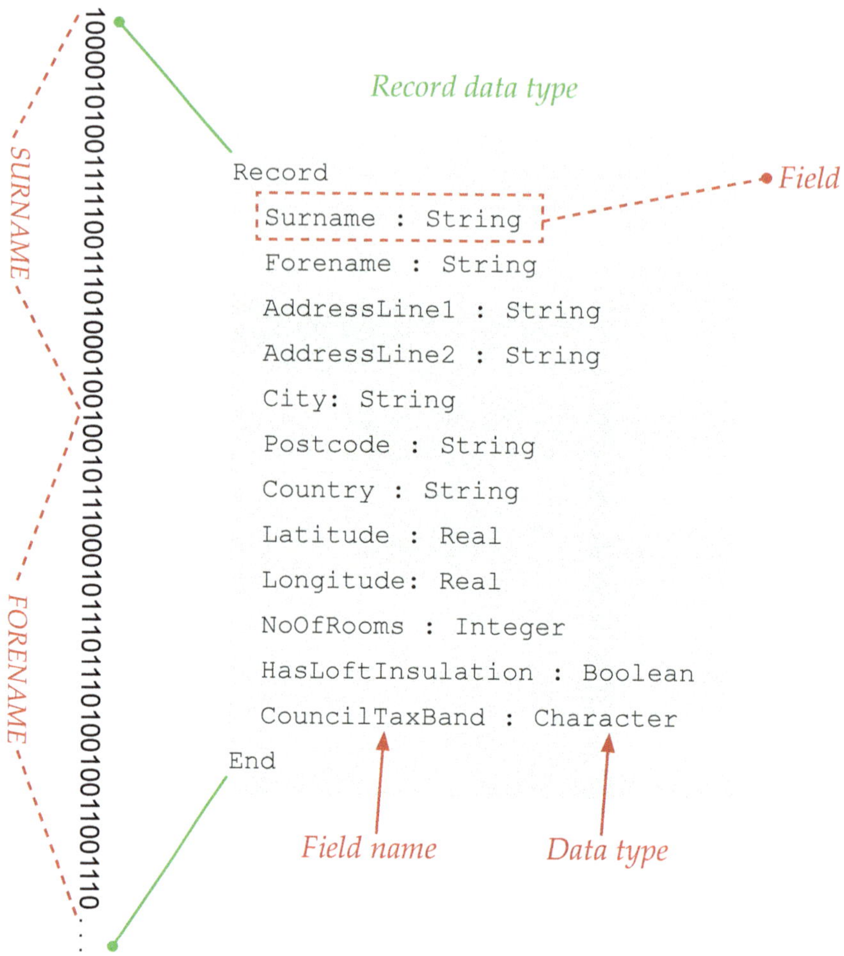

Figure 15.3 Record data type which imposes meaning to bit pattern consisting of values surname, forename, etc.

The record data type is a data type in which the constituent parts of a bit pattern may have different meanings, e.g. string, integer, real, etc.

The higher level view is:

a record data type is a data type composed of related data of various data types.

Table 15.1 shows how record data types can be defined in the programming languages Pascal/Delphi.

```
TExamResult = Record
                StudentId : String;
                ExamTitle : String;
                ExamScore : Integer;
                ExamGrade : Char;
              End;
```

Table 15.1 Defining the record data type in Pascal/Delphi

Table 15.2 shows a very simple use of the record data structure and the ways that its fields may be accessed.

The fields of the variable **StudentRecord** may be assigned values

1. Using dot notation, e.g.

```
StudentRecord.Name := 'Fred Bloggs';
StudentRecord.Age := 17;
```

Using the **With** construct, e.g.

```
With StudentRecord
  Do
    Begin
      Writeln(Name);
      Writeln(Age);
    End;
```

```
Program IntroductionToRecords;
{$APPTYPE CONSOLE}
Type
  TStudentRecord = Record
                     Name : String;
                     Age : Integer;
                   End;
Var
  StudentRecord : TStudentRecord;
Begin
  StudentRecord.Name := 'Fred Bloggs';
  StudentRecord.Age := 17;
  Writeln(StudentRecord.Name);
  Writeln(StudentRecord.Age);
  Write('Input student''s name: ');
  Readln(StudentRecord.Name);
  Write('Input student''s age: ');
  Readln(StudentRecord.Age);
  With StudentRecord
    Do
      Begin
        Writeln(Name);
        Writeln(Age);
      End;
  Write('Press return key to finish ');
  Readln;
End.
```

P

Table 15.2 Program IntroductionToRecords

Collections of records are often used in data processing. The data recorded in records is usually stored on backing store, e.g. disk, so that it may be accessed at a later date. *Table 15.3* shows how this might be done using a file.

Chapter 16 covers programming with files in Pascal/Delphi in detail.

essentially, a file is readied for writing to with

```
AssignFile(FilePipe, Filename);
Rewrite(FilePipe);
```

and closed with

```
CloseFile(FilePipe);
```

The whole record is written to a file at a time with

```
Write(FilePipe, StudentRecord);
```

Information

In order to save a record containing a string field to a file, the string type must be a short-string type, e.g. of type String[25] or ShortString. Delphi cannot save an AnsiString or UnicodeString string to file because these are dynamically allocated strings for which the string variable is a pointer not an actual string value. The compiler flags a finalization error in the case of these. The String data type has been an alias for UnicodeString since Delphi 2009 and before that an alias for AnsiString. Unfortunately, the ShortString data type is not supported by mobile compilers. In ealier versions of Delphi, prior to 2009, it was possible to make the String data type an alias for ShortString by deselecting Huge strings in the compiler options page.

```
Program WritingRecordsToAFile;
{$APPTYPE CONSOLE}
Uses
  SysUtils;
Type
  TStudentRecord = Record
                     Surname : String[25];
                     Forename : String[25];
                     Age : Integer;
                   End;
  TFilePipe = File Of TStudentRecord;
Var
  FilePipe : TFilePipe;
  StudentRecord : TStudentRecord;
  Filename : String;
  Ch : Char = 'Y';
Begin
  Repeat
    Ch := 'Y';
    Write('Input writing file name: ');
    Readln(Filename);
    If FileExists(Filename)
      Then
        Begin
          Write('File exists - overwrite Y/N? ');
          Readln(Ch);
        End;
  Until (Ch In ['Y', 'y']);
  AssignFile(FilePipe, Filename);
  Rewrite(FilePipe);
  Repeat
    Write('Input surname: ');
    Readln(StudentRecord.Surname);
    Write('Input forename: ');
    Readln(StudentRecord.Forename);
    Write('Input age: ');
    Readln(StudentRecord.Age);
    Write(FilePipe, StudentRecord);
    Write('Another record Y/N? ');
    Readln(Ch);
  Until (Ch In ['N', 'n']);
  CloseFile(FilePipe);
End.
```

P

Information

Array of records:

```
Type
  TStudentRecord = Record
                     Name : String;
                     Age : Integer;
                   End;
  TArrayOfStudentRecords = Array[1..10] Of TStudentRecord;
```

Could also experiment with array of records instead of File of records except data will not be stored permanently in a file unless the array is saved to a file.

Table 15.3 Program WritingRecordsToAFile

Table 15.4 shows program **ReadingRecordsFromAFile**.

The reverse process of reading from file is achieved by first connecting to the file and preparing it for reading

```
AssignFile(FilePipe, Filename);
Reset(FilePipe);
```

One whole record is read at a time as follows

```
Read(FilePipe, StudentRecord);
```

The file has a beginning and an end. Reading starts from the beginning but it is important that the program does not try to read beyond the end of file so it continually test for the end of file as follows

```
While Not Eof(FilePipe)
```

Eof is short for **End of File**. **Eof** is a function that returns **True** or `False` depending on whether the program is at the end of file or not.

Table 15.5 shows program **AppendingRecordsToAFile**.

Appending records to a file means to add records to the end of an existing file.

Finding the end of file could be done with the function **Eof** but it is more convenient to use **Seek** as follows

```
AssignFile(FilePipe, Filename);
Reset(FilePipe);
Seek(FilePipe, FileSize(FilePipe));
```

Seek skips over all the existing records. These constitute the current size of the file given by `FileSize(FilePipe)`.

```
Program ReadingRecordsFromAFile;
{$APPTYPE CONSOLE}
Uses
  SysUtils;
Type
  TStudentRecord = Record
                     Surname : String[25];
                     Forename : String[25];
                     Age : Integer;
                   End;
  TFilePipe = File Of TStudentRecord;
Var
  FilePipe : TFilePipe;
  StudentRecord : TStudentRecord;
  Filename : String;
  Ch : Char = 'Y';
  NoOfRecords, n : Integer;
Begin
  Repeat
    Write('Input reading file name: ');
    Readln(Filename);
    If Not FileExists(Filename)
      Then
        Begin
          Write('File does not exist - try again Y/N? ');
          Readln(Ch);
        End
      Else Ch := 'N';
  Until (Ch In ['N', 'n']);
  If FileExists(Filename)
    Then
      Begin
        AssignFile(FilePipe, Filename);
        Reset(FilePipe);
        While Not Eof(FilePipe)
          Do
            Begin
              Read(FilePipe, StudentRecord);
              Writeln(StudentRecord.Surname : 10);
              Writeln(StudentRecord.Forename : 10);
              Writeln(StudentRecord.Age : 10);
              Writeln;
            End;
        CloseFile(FilePipe);
      End;
  Readln;
End.
```

Table 15.4 Program ReadingRecordsFromAFile

```
Program AppendingRecordsToAFile;
{$APPTYPE CONSOLE}
Uses
  SysUtils;
Type
  TStudentRecord = Record
                     Surname : String[25];
                     Forename : String[25];
                     Age : Integer;
                   End;
  TFilePipe = File Of TStudentRecord;
Var
  FilePipe : TFilePipe;
  StudentRecord : TStudentRecord;
  Filename : String;
  Ch : Char = 'Y';
Begin
  Repeat
    Write('Input reading file name: ');
    Readln(Filename);
    If Not FileExists('Student.rec')
      Then
        Begin
          Write('File does not exist - try again Y/N? ');
          Readln(Ch);
        End
      Else Ch := 'N';
  Until (Ch In ['N', 'n']);
  If FileExists(Filename)
    Then
      Begin
        AssignFile(FilePipe, Filename);
        Reset(FilePipe);
        Seek(FilePipe, FileSize(FilePipe));
        Repeat
          Write('Input surname: ');
          Readln(StudentRecord.Surname);
          Write('Input forename: ');
          Readln(StudentRecord.Forename);
          Write('Input age: ');
          Readln(StudentRecord.Age);
          Write(FilePipe,StudentRecord);
          Write('Another record Y/N? ');
          Readln(Ch);
        Until (Ch In ['N', 'n']);
        CloseFile(FilePipe);
      End;
  Readln;
End.
```

Table 15.5 Program AppendingRecordsToAFile

Programming tasks

```
Program RecordExercise;

Type
  TStudentRecord = Record
                     Surname : String[7];
                     Mark : Integer;
                     Grade : Char;
                   End;
  PipeType = File Of TStudentRecord;

Var
  StudentRecord : TStudentRecord;
  Pipe : PipeType;
Begin
  AssignFile(Pipe, 'Student.Dat');
  Rewrite(Pipe);
  Write('Input Surname: ');
  Readln(StudentRecord.Surname);
  Write('Input Mark Out Of 100: ');
  Readln(StudentRecord.Mark);
  Write(Pipe, StudentRecord);
  CloseFile(Pipe);
End.
```

1. Compile, link and run this program. Check that the file Student.Dat has been created.
   Now alter this program so that three records are collected and written to Student.Dat. Note only one variable, StudentRecord, is required. (Hint: Use a For loop).

2. Write a program to open and read the three records that you have written to Student.Dat. Display the three records, in turn on the console.

3. Alter your first program so that the grade of each student is calculated and assigned to the grade field. Use 0-39 F, 40-44 E, 45-49 D, 50-59 C, 60-69 B, 70-100 A.

4. Alter your second program so that it displays each student's grade as well as surname and mark.

Record methods

Delphi has supported adding methods to records since Delphi 2006.

A method is a procedure or function attached to an object, having access to the object's fields. In this example, the object is a record.

Table 15.6 shows how this can be done.

The record type **TStudentRecord** is defined as follows

```
TStudentRecord = Record
                   Name : String;
                   Age : Integer;
                   Procedure SetFields;
                   Procedure GetFields;
                 End;
```

Procedures **SetFields** and **GetFields** are record methods which are defined as

`Procedure TStudentRecord.SetFields` and `Procedure TStudentRecord.GetFields`.

Inside each method lies an implicit **Self** variable. This provides a reference to the object instance itself.

For example, inside procedure `TStudentRecord.GetFields` the compiler matches the `Name` and `Age` references to those of the record object that called `GetFields`, i.e. `StudentRecord` identified implicitly by the **Self** variable. The order in which the compiler does the matching is immediate scope first, i.e. local variables and constants, next immediate, i.e. fields and other methods of object.

```
Program RecordWithMethods;                                    P
{$APPTYPE CONSOLE}
{$R *.res}
Uses
  System.SysUtils;
Type
  TStudentRecord = Record
                     Name : String;
                     Age : Integer;
                     Procedure SetFields;
                     Procedure GetFields;
                   End;
  Procedure TStudentRecord.SetFields;
    Begin
      Write('Input name: '); Readln(Name);//Behaves as Self.Name
      Write('Input age: '); Readln(Age);//Behaves as Self.Age

    End;
  Procedure TStudentRecord.GetFields;
    Begin
      Writeln(Name);//Behaves as Self.Name
      Writeln(Age);//Behaves as Self.Age
    End;
Var
  StudentRecord : TStudentRecord;
Begin
  StudentRecord.SetFields;
  StudentRecord.GetFields;
  Readln;
End.
```

Table 15.6 Program RecordWithMethods

With versions of Delphi prior to Delphi 2006, the keyword **Record** must be replaced by the keyword **Object** - *Table 15.7*. A less elegant and less compact solution that uses the keyword **Record** is shown in *Table 15.8*.

```
Program RecordWithMethods;
{$APPTYPE CONSOLE}
Uses
  System.SysUtils;
Type
  TStudentRecord = Object
                     Name : String;
                     Age : Integer;
                     Procedure SetFields;
                     Procedure GetFields;
                   End;
  Procedure TStudentRecord.SetFields;
    Begin
      Write('Input name: '); Readln(Name);
      Write('Input age: '); Readln(Age);
    End;
  Procedure TStudentRecord.GetFields;
    Begin
      Writeln(Name);
      Writeln(Age);
    End;
Var
  StudentRecord : TStudentRecord;
Begin
  StudentRecord.SetFields;
  StudentRecord.GetFields;
  Readln;
End.
```

Table 15.7 Delphi 7 Program RecordWithMethods

```
Program RecordWithProcedures;
{$APPTYPE CONSOLE}
Uses
  SysUtils;
Type
  TStudentRecordPtr = ^TStudentRecord;
  TProcedureVar = Procedure(StudentRecordPtr : TStudentRecordPtr);
  TStudentRecord = Record
                     Name : String;
                     Age : Integer;
                     SetFields : TProcedureVar;
                     GetFields : TProcedureVar;
                   End;
  Procedure GetStudentRecord(StudentRecordPtr : TStudentRecordPtr);
    Begin
      With StudentRecordPtr^
        Do
          Begin
            Writeln(Name);
            Writeln(Age);
          End;
    End;
  Procedure SetStudentRecord(StudentRecordPtr : TStudentRecordPtr);
    Begin
      With StudentRecordPtr^
        Do
          Begin
            Write('Input name: '); Readln(Name);
            Write('Input age: '); Readln(Age);
          End;
    End;
Var
  AStudentRecordPtr, Self : TStudentRecordPtr;
  ProcedureVar : TProcedureVar;
Begin
  New(AStudentRecordPtr);
  Self := AStudentRecordPtr;
  ProcedureVar := SetStudentRecord;
  AStudentRecordPtr^.SetFields := ProcedureVar;
  ProcedureVar := GetStudentRecord;
  AStudentRecordPtr^.GetFields := ProcedureVar;
  AStudentRecordPtr.SetFields(Self);
  AStudentRecordPtr^.GetFields(Self);
  Readln;
End.
```

Table 15.8 Delphi 7 Program RecordWithProcedures

Properties

Traditionally, record types in Pascal were very simple constructs, containing public fields and nothing else. As we have just seen, Delphi makes possible the inclusion of methods. Properties extend record types further.

Properties are the way that the internal state of an object is exposed to the outside world. In Delphi, properties abstract away both fields and methods so that to outside code they appear as field-like entities. *Table 15.9* shows an example program that makes use of the property construct.

The keyword **Property** introduces two virtual fields **Name** and **Age** which hide the actual fields **FName** and **FAge**.

The actual fields are accessed internally via the four methods: functions **GetName**, **GetAge**, and procedures **SetName**, **SetAge**. The main **Begin End** block of the program accesses the internal fields **FName**, **FAge** indirectly by virtual fields **Name** and **Age**, e.g.

```
StudentRecord.Name := StudentName;
```

Strict Private means only methods of the record itself have access to the record's fields.

```
Program PropertiesProject;
{$APPTYPE CONSOLE}
{$R *.res}
Uses
  System.SysUtils;
Type
  TStudentRecord = Record
                     Strict Private
                       FName : String;
                       FAge : Integer;
                       Procedure SetName(AName : String);
                       Function GetName : String;
                       Procedure SetAge(AnAge : Integer);
                       Function GetAge : Integer;
                     Public
                       Property Name : String Read GetName Write SetName;
                       Property Age : Integer Read GetAge Write SetAge;
                   End;
  Procedure TStudentRecord.SetName(AName : String);
    Begin
      FName := AName;
    End;
  Function TStudentRecord.GetName;
    Begin
      Result := FName;
    End;
  Procedure TStudentRecord.SetAge(AnAge : Integer);
    Begin
      FAge := AnAge;
    End;
  Function TStudentRecord.GetAge;
    Begin
      Result := FAge;
    End;
Var
  StudentRecord : TStudentRecord;
  StudentName : String;
  StudentAge : Integer;
Begin
  Write('Name: ');
  Readln(StudentName);
  StudentRecord.Name := StudentName;
  Write('Age: ');
  Readln(StudentAge);
  StudentRecord.Age := StudentAge;
  Writeln(StudentRecord.Name);
  Writeln(StudentRecord.Age);
  Readln;
End.
```

P

Table 15.9 Program PropertiesProject

Static class fields and methods for records

Sometimes a need arises for a collection of records to share data stored in a field of their record type.

For example,

```
TStudentRecord = Record
                   Name : String;
                   Age : Integer;
                   Class Var SchoolName : String;
                   Procedure SetFields;
                   Procedure GetFields;
                 End;
```

Table 15.10 Record type with shared field SchoolName

All records of this type will share the field **SchoolName** but have their own instances of all the other fields.

Table 15.11 shows the use of a shared field, **SchoolName**, which is initialised once

```
StudentRecord1.SchoolName := 'AGS';
```

but appears twice in the output, *Figure 15.4*, once for record `StudentRecord1` and once for record `StudentRecord2`.

```
Program SharedRecordFields;
{$APPTYPE CONSOLE}
Uses
  System.SysUtils;
Type
  TStudentRecord = Record
                     Name : String;
                     Age : Integer;
                     Class Var SchoolName : String;
                     Procedure SetFields;
                     Procedure GetFields;
                   End;
  Procedure TStudentRecord.SetFields;
    Begin
      Write('Input name: '); Readln(Name);//Behaves as Self.Name
      Write('Input age: '); Readln(Age);//Behaves as Self.Age
    End;
  Procedure TStudentRecord.GetFields;
    Begin
      Writeln(Name);//Behaves as Self.Name
      Writeln(Age);//Behaves as Self.Age
      Writeln(SchoolName);
    End;
Var
  StudentRecord1, StudentRecord2 : TStudentRecord;
Begin
  StudentRecord1.SchoolName := 'AGS';
  StudentRecord1.SetFields;
  StudentRecord2.SetFields;
  StudentRecord1.GetFields;
  StudentRecord2.GetFields;
  Readln;
End.
```

Table 15.11 Program SharedRecordFields

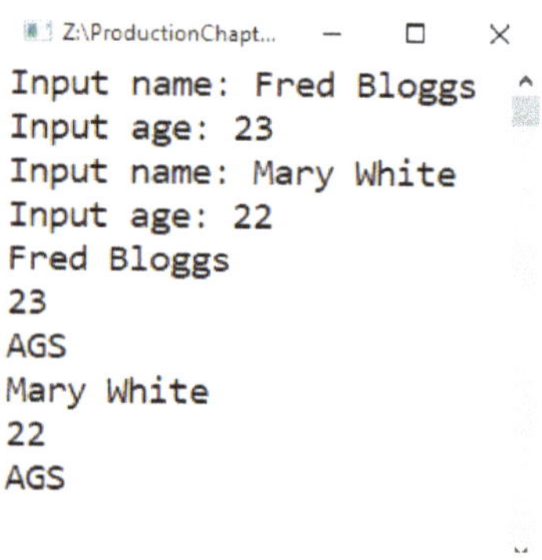

Fig. 15.4 Output from program SharedRecordFields

16 Introducing files

Accessing files

Purpose: To learn how to work with different file types

Files

A file is a data structure for storing data. The number of items of data stored in the file can vary in time and the amount of data is not limited in the way that other data structures are because files rely on secondary storage such as magnetic disk for their storage unlike arrays which rely on RAM storage.

By using secondary storage, files persist in time because secondary storage is non-volatile whereas RAM is volatile.

A file is assigned a name called its *filename* so that it can be referenced by name.

Files have structure which is either defined by the programmer at creation time, a file of some record type or is a commonly used structure such as text.

Text files

Text files are files whose contents are sequences of characters organised on a line by line basis. For example, Shakespeare's Sonnet 116 shown in *Table 16.1* consists of 14 lines as do almost all of Shakespeare's sonnets.

Let me not to the marriage of true minds *Admit impediments. Love is not love* *Which alters when it alteration finds,* *Or bends with the remover to remove:* *O, no! it is an ever-fixed mark,* *That looks on tempests and is never shaken;* *It is the star to every wandering bark,* *Whose worth's unknown, although his height be taken.* *Love's not Time's fool, though rosy lips and cheeks* *Within his bending sickle's compass come;* *Love alters not with his brief hours and weeks,* *But bears it out even to the edge of doom.* *If this be error and upon me prov'd,* *I never writ, nor no man ever lov'd.*

Table 16.1 Shakespeare's Sonnet 116

Text files may be opened and read in a text editor such as Microsoft's WordPad. Text editors expect files to be organised on a line-by-line basis and to consist of characters that can read when displayed with the exception of some specific control characters.

Key term

File:
A file is a data structure for storing data. The number of items of data stored in the file can vary in time and the amount of data is not limited in the way that other data structures are because files rely on secondary storage such as magnetic disk for their storage unlike arrays which rely on RAM storage.

Key term

Text file:
Text files are files whose contents are sequences of characters organised on a line by line basis.

Questions

1. What is a file?
2. What is a text file?

Each line ends with a special control character called the end of line or *newline* character (character code 10 or character codes 10 and 13).

The only control characters that text editors are able to handle are characters called *whitespace* characters, i.e. characters with ASCII or UTF-8 character codes 32_{10} (space), 10_{10} (line feed), 13_{10} (carriage return) and 9_{10} (tab). Other control characters have an effect on a text editor which is unpredictable and usually render the display unreadable.

Non-text files do not display well in text editors because they often contain control character codes which text editors are unable to handle because they are not control character codes 32, 10, 13 or 9.

Not only can text files be read by text editors but they may also be created and edited in a text editor.

We turn to computer programs when we wish to manipulate text files in ways that text editors do not support.

Reading from a text file

Table 16.2 shows a Delphi console mode program which opens a text file with the filename `Sonnet116.txt` for reading. The contents of this file are read one line at a time from the beginning of this file. Each line which is read is stored temporarily in the string variable `Line`. The line of characters stored in this variable is displayed on the console by `Writeln(Line)`. Finally the file is closed.

```
Program ReadingATextFileLineByLine;
{$APPTYPE Console}
Var
  Pipe : TextFile;
  Line : String;
Begin
  AssignFile(Pipe, 'Sonnet116.txt');
  Reset(Pipe);
  While Not Eof(Pipe)
    Do
      Begin
        Readln(Pipe, Line); {Read line of text from file into string variable Line}
        Writeln(Line); {Write line of text in string variable Line to output}
      End;
  CloseFile(Pipe);
  Readln;
End.
```

P

www.educational-computing.com/DelphiBook/Code/Chapter16/CE10.2/TextFiles.rar

Table 16.2 Reading from a text file "Sonnet116.txt" in line by line

Note

After compiling and linking, an executable ReadingFromATextFileLineByLine.exe is created in the subdirectory Debug which is located inside the subdirectory Win32 which itself is located inside the directory containing the source code ReadingFromATextFileLineByLine.dpr. The text file Sonnet116.txt must be placed in the Debug subdirectory for the executing program to correctly locate it.

The first thing that this Delphi program does is assign a file pipe, `Pipe`, for 'piping' the contents of the file `Sonnet116.txt` to the program

```
AssignFile(Pipe, 'Sonnet116.txt');
```

The file pipe `Pipe` is now connected between the program and the file on disk `Sonnet116.txt`.

The next thing it does is to set the pipe, `Pipe`, to read from this file `Sonnet116.txt`.

```
Reset(Pipe);
```

The contents of file Sonnet116.txt are now accessed through the file pipe Pipe as follows

```
While Not Eof(Pipe)
  Begin
    Readln(Pipe, Line); {Read line of text from file into string variable Line}
    Writeln(Line); {Write line of text in string variable Line to output}
  End;
```

The *while loop* iterates through the file line-by-line. The file handle Pipe is aware of the file structure, and is able to keep track of which line in the file is currently selected so that string variable Line is able to receive the next line of the file.

The Writeln statement Writeln(Line) outputs the line of text it currently stores to the console window before moving the cursor to the beginning of the next line.

The function Eof(Pipe) tests to see if the end of the file Sonnet116.txt has been reached. When the end of file has been reached the function returns True otherwise it returns False.

Not Eof(Pipe) simple inverts the returned result (False to True, True to False) so that the While loop continues to process the lines of the file until every line has been read.

Finally, when the end of file is reached the file is closed by CloseFile(Pipe) so that the resources associated with reading the contents of the file are released.

Summarising, reading from a text file takes the following form:

```
open the text file for reading
read the text file line-by-line
do something with each line
close the file
```

We can also read from the file a character at a time as shown in *Table 16.3*.

```
Program ReadingATextFileCharacterByCharacter;
{$APPTYPE Console}
Var
  Pipe : TextFile;
  Ch : Char;
Begin
  AssignFile(Pipe, 'Sonnet116.txt');
  Reset(Pipe);
  While Not Eof(Pipe)
    Do
      Begin
        While Not Eoln(Pipe)
          Do
            Begin
              Read(Pipe, Ch);
              Write(Ch);
            End;
        Readln(Pipe); {Skip over end of line marker}
        Writeln; {Move writing cursor to beginning of next line of console window}
      End;
  CloseFile(Pipe);
  Readln;
End.
```

P

www.educational-computing.com/DelphiBook/Code/Chapter16/CE10.2/TextFiles.rar

Table 16.3 Reading from a text file "Sonnet116.txt" character by character

Note

After compiling and linking, an executable ReadingFromATextFileCharacterByCharacter.exe is created in the subdirectory Debug which is located inside the subdirectory Win32 which itself is located inside the directory containing the source code ReadingFromATextFileCharacterByCharacter.dpr. The text file Sonnet116.txt must be placed in the Debug subdirectory for the executing program to correctly locate it.

The contents of file `Sonnet116.txt` are accessed through the file pipe `Pipe` as before but each line is processed by the following block of code

```
While Not Eoln(Pipe)
  Do
    Begin
      Read(Pipe, Ch);
      Write(Ch);
    End;
Readln(Pipe); {Skip over end of line marker}
Writeln; {Move writing cursor to beginning of next line of console window}
```

With the reading cursor positioned at the beginning of the first and then subsequent lines, each line is read one character at a time by `Read(Pipe, Ch)` and echoed to the console window one character at a time by `Write(Ch)`. The end of line is tested for by the function `Eoln(Pipe)`. This function returns `True` when the end of line is reached otherwise it returns `False`. The While loop continues executing whilst `Not Eoln(Pipe)` is `True`. On exiting the *while loop*, the end of line marker is consumed by `Readln(Pipe)` in order to move the reading cursor to the beginning of the next line. The end of line marker is output to the console window by `Writeln` which repositions the screen cursor to the beginning of the next line.

When the entire file has been consumed, the file is closed by `CloseFile(Pipe)`.

Writing to a text file

In Delphi, if we want to write to a file with filename `'Students.txt'`, we first assign a pipe, `Pipe`, to the file with `AssignFile` and then ready the pipe for writing with `Rewrite` as follows

```
AssignFile(Pipe, 'Students.txt');
Rewrite(Pipe);
```

If this file does not exist it is created by the action of these two statements in the same directory as the executing program. If it does exist then its contents are wiped. If you want the file to exist in a different directory you must include the full path in the second parameter of the `AssignFile` procedure.

P

www.educational-computing.com/DelphiBook/Code/Chapter16/CE10.2/TextFiles.rar

```
Program WritingToATextFileLineByLine;
{$APPTYPE Console}
Var
  Pipe : TextFile;
  StudentName : String;
  Quit : Boolean;
Begin
  AssignFile(Pipe, 'Students.txt');
  Rewrite(Pipe);
  Repeat
    Write('Input student name (Q to quit): ');
    Readln(StudentName);
    Quit := (StudentName = 'Q') Or (StudentName = 'q');
    If Not Quit Then Writeln(Pipe, StudentName);
  Until Quit;
  CloseFile(Pipe);
End.
```

Table 16.4 Writing to a text file "Students.txt" line by line

In each case the file is readied for writing by positioning a writing cursor at the beginning of the file.

The program in *Table 16.4* collects a student name typed at the keyboard and then using the file pipe, `Pipe`, on a file opened for writing, writes student name on its own line to the opened text file using

```
Writeln(Pipe, StudentName);
```

The writing cursor is then left at the beginning of the next line ready to write another student name if necessary using the following *repeat loop*

```
Repeat
  Write('Input student name (Q or q to quit): ');
  Readln(StudentName);
  Quit := (StudentName = 'Q') Or (StudentName = 'q')
  If Not Quit Then Writeln(Pipe, StudentName);
Until Quit;
```

Entering '`Q`' or '`q`' for the student name causes the program to exit the *while loop.*

Finally the file is closed.

The file `Students.txt` may be opened in a text editor such as Microsoft® WordPad and its contents viewed to confirm that the expected student names were written to this file by the executable form of the program shown in *Table 16.4*.

Alternatively, a program such as the one shown in *Table 16.5* may be used to read and display the contents of `Students.txt` or any other text file whose filename is supplied to the executing program and which exists.

A function `FileExists` which returns a **Boolean** result is used to test for existence of the file with the given filename and path. This function is defined in the library **SysUtils**, hence the requirement for the **Uses** clause,

```
Uses SysUtils;
```

```
Program ReadingATextFileOfGivenFilename;
{$APPTYPE CONSOLE}
Uses SysUtils;
Var
  Pipe : TextFile;
  Line, FileName : String;
Begin
  Write('Input filename including path if necessary: ');
  Readln(FileName);
  If FileExists(FileName)
    Then
      Begin
        AssignFile(Pipe, FileName);
        Reset(Pipe);
        While Not Eof(Pipe)
          Do
            Begin
              Readln(Pipe, Line);
              Writeln(Line);
            End;
        CloseFile(Pipe);
      End
    Else Writeln('File does not exist');
  Readln;
End.
```

P

www.educational-computing.com/DelphiBook/Code/Chapter16/CE10.2/TextFiles.rar

Table 16.5 Reading from a text file line by line whose filename is specified at run time

Using TStringList

The **TStringList** class is defined in the library `Classes`. Using this class, it is possible to create an object which is capable of reading from or writing to a text file in a very compact way, as shown in *Table 16.6*.

The `TStringList` object has a list structure where each element of the list is a string.

`Lines.Text` returns the list of strings as text, i.e. each string is on its own line. It is sufficient to use `Write` to write this text because each line in `Lines.Text` has its own end of line marker which subsequently causes the writing cursor to move to the beginning of the next line. Finally the object is released with `Lines.Free`, i.e. memory reserved for the object is freed. For more information on classes and objects see *Chapter 19*.

```
Program ReadingFromATextFileUsingTStringList;
{$APPTYPE CONSOLE}
Uses
  System.SysUtils,
  Classes;
Var
  FileName : String;
  Lines : TStringList;
Begin
  Write('Input filename including path if necessary: ');
  Readln(FileName);
  If FileExists(FileName)
    Then
      Begin
        Lines := TStringList.Create; // Create a TStringList object
        Lines.LoadFromFile(FileName); // Loads all the lines from the specified file
        Write(Lines.Text); // Writes the entire text to the console window
        Lines.Free; // Releases the object
      End
    Else Writeln('File does not exist');
  Readln;
End.
```

P

www.educational-computing.com/DelphiBook/Code/Chapter16/CE10.2/TextFiles.rar

Table 16.6 Reading from a text file using TStringList

We can use **TStringList** to create contents for a text file and then save the contents to a text file as shown in *Table 16.7*. To build up the lines of the text file we use

`Lines.Add(StudentName);`

When we need to save these lines to a file we use

`Lines.SaveToFile(FileName);`

TStringList supports various routines such as sorting and counting which can be usefully applied to the list of strings as shown in *Table 16.8*.

```
Program WritingToATextFileUsingTStringList;
{$APPTYPE CONSOLE}
Uses
  Classes;
Var
  FileName, StudentName : String;
  Lines : TStringList;
  Quit : Boolean;
Begin
  Write('Input filename of file to create/overwrite, including path if necessary : ');
  Readln(FileName);
  Lines := TStringList.Create;
  Repeat
    Write('Input student name (Q to quit): ');
    Readln(StudentName);
    Quit := (StudentName = 'Q') Or (StudentName = 'q');
    If Not Quit
      Then Lines.Add(StudentName);
  Until Quit;
  Lines.SaveToFile(FileName);
  Lines.Free;
End.
```

P

www.educational-computing.com/DelphiBook/Code/Chapter16/CE10.2/TextFiles.rar

Table 16.7 Writing to a text file using TStringList

```
Program WritingToATextFileUsingTStringList;
{$APPTYPE CONSOLE}
Uses
  Classes;
Var
  FileName, StudentName : String;
  Lines : TStringList;
  Quit : Boolean;
Begin
  Write('Input filename of file to create/overwrite, including path if necessary : ');
  Readln(FileName);
  Lines := TStringList.Create;
  Repeat
    Write('Input student name (Q to quit): ');
    Readln(StudentName);
    Quit := (StudentName = 'Q') Or (StudentName = 'q');
    If Not Quit
      Then Lines.Add(StudentName);
  Until Quit;
  Lines.SaveToFile(FileName);
  Writeln('No of lines of text written to file ', FileName, ' = ', Lines.Count);
  Lines.Sort;
  Lines.SaveToFile('Sorted' + FileName);
  Lines.Free;
End.
```

P

www.educational-computing.com/DelphiBook/Code/Chapter16/CE10.2/TextFiles.rar

Table 16.8 Writing to a text file using TStringList and the routines sort and count

Using TOpenDialog

We can use a Vcl dialog box, **TOpenDialog**, to select the text file to read even though the application is a console one.

For this purpose, we create an object, `Dialogue` of type `TOpenDialog` as shown in *Table 16.9*,

```
Dialogue := TOpenDialog.Create(Nil);
```

We then call the function

```
Dialogue.Execute;
```

which launches a dialogue window as shown in *Figure 16.1* and returns `True` if a file is selected and `Open` clicked otherwise `False` if `Cancel` is clicked.

A **Try Finally End** block is used to protect the creation of the `Dialogue` object and to ensure that it is eventually freed.

The **Uses** clause must include **Vcl.Dialogs** and **System.Win.ComObj** to use **TOpenDialog** successfully.

The **Uses** clause must include **System.SysUtils** to use **Try Finally End** successfully.

```
Program ConsoleOpenDialog;
{$APPTYPE CONSOLE}                                                   P

Uses
  System.SysUtils, System.Win.ComObj, Vcl.Dialogs;
Var
  Pipe : TextFile;
  Line : String;
  Dialogue : TOpenDialog;
Begin
  Try
    Dialogue := TOpenDialog.Create(Nil);
    If Dialogue.Execute
      Then
        Begin
          Writeln(Dialogue.FileName);
          Writeln('----------------------------------------');
          AssignFile(Pipe, Dialogue.FileName);
          Reset(Pipe);
          While Not Eof(Pipe)
            Do
              Begin
                Readln(Pipe, Line);
                Writeln(Line);
              End;
          CloseFile(Pipe);
        End
      Else Writeln('You cancelled');
    Finally
      Dialogue.Free;
  End;
  Writeln('----------------------------------------');
  Readln;
End.
```

www.educational-computing.com/DelphiBook/Code/Chapter16/CE10.2/TextFiles.rar

Table 16.9 Reading from a text file line by line whose filename is specified at run time using a TOpenDialog object

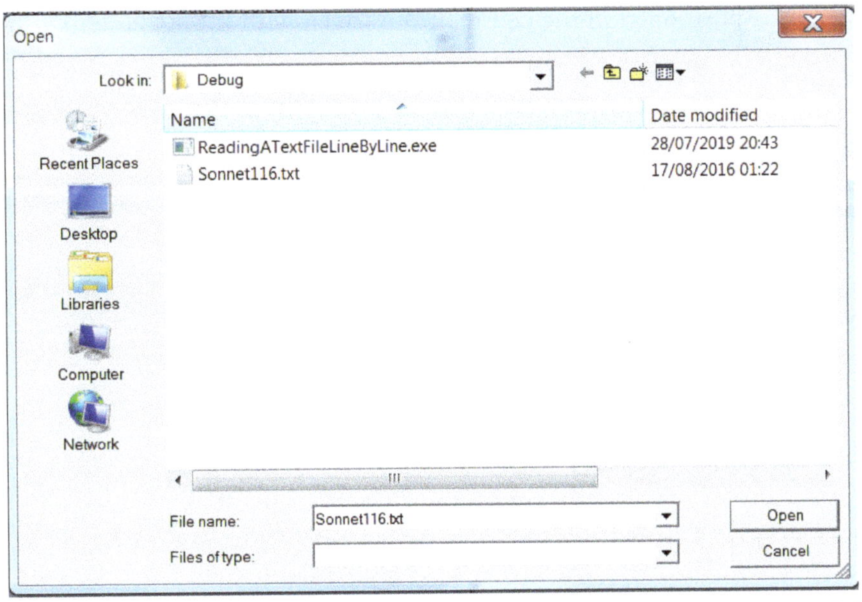

Fig. 16.1 Sonnet116.txt viewed using an object created from TOpenDialog

Using a modal form to display contents of a text file

Viewing a text file in a console window whilst informative is not ideal, better to use a form window that permits scrolling in both directions as shown in *Figure 16.2*. The design for this form window is shown in *Figure 16.3* and *Table 16.10*. A VCL form design is added to the project by selecting **File|New|VCL Form - Delphi** and then adding panels, memo box, labels and a button.

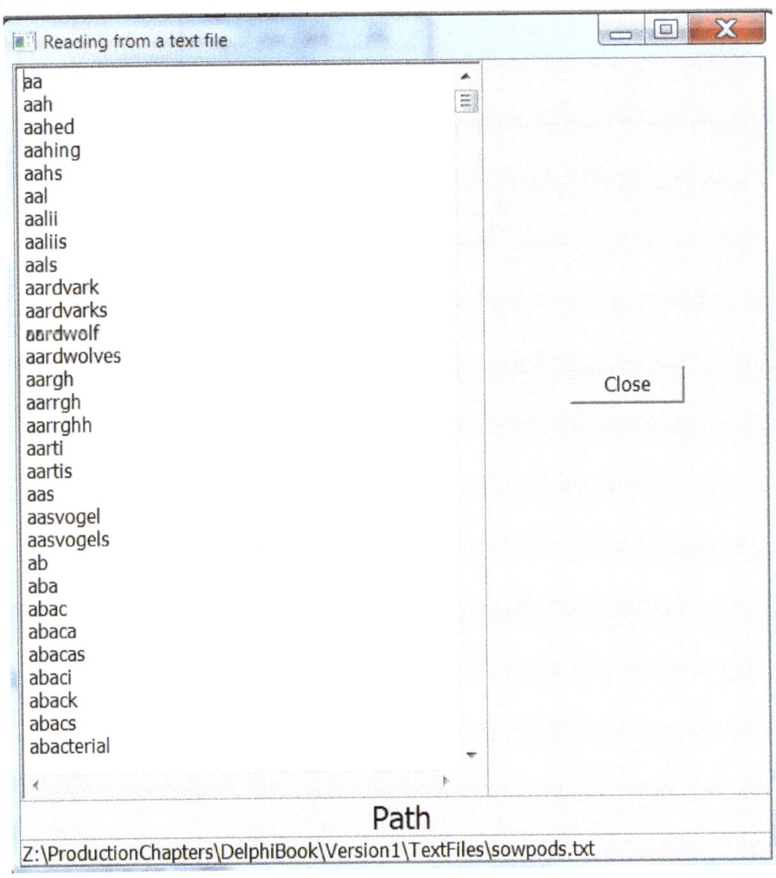

Fig. 16.2 Modal form showing the contents of a text file sowpods.txt ion a memo box

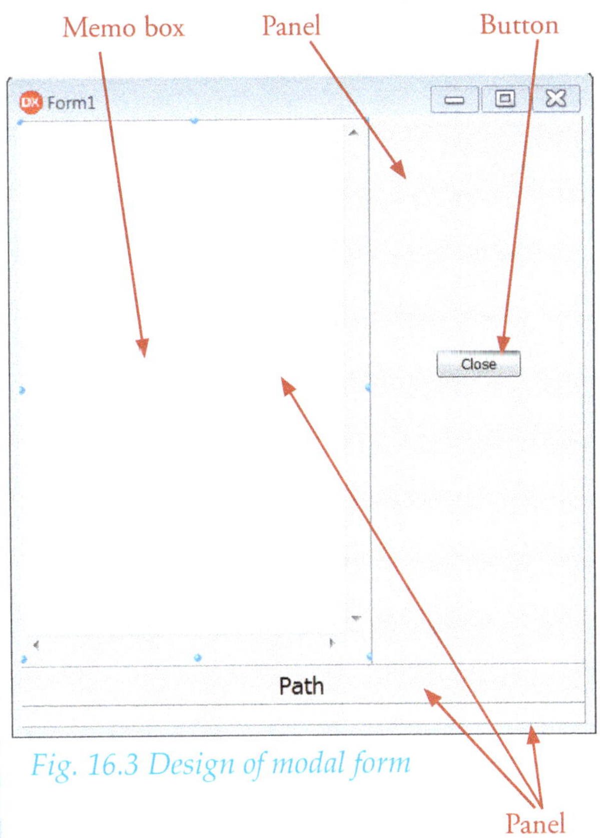

Fig. 16.3 Design of modal form

The console mode program is shown in *Table 16.11*.

The form is created and set to be positioned in the centre of the screen with the statements

```
Form1 := TForm1.Create(Nil);
Form1.Position := poScreenCenter;
```

and made visible modally with the statement `Form1.ShowModal;`

```
Unit ModalForm;
Interface
Uses
  Winapi.Windows, Winapi.Messages, System.SysUtils,
  System.Variants, System.Classes, Vcl.Graphics,
  Vcl.Controls, Vcl.Forms, Vcl.Dialogs, Vcl.StdCtrls, Vcl.ExtCtrls;
Type
  TForm1 = Class(TForm)
              Panel1: TPanel;
              Panel2: TPanel;
              Memo1: TMemo;
              Panel3: TPanel;
              Label1: TLabel;
              Close: TButton;
              Panel4: TPanel;
              Label2: TLabel;
            End;
Var
  Form1: TForm1;
Implementation
{$R *.dfm}
End.
```

Table 16.10 Showing the contents of a text file in a form-based memo box

```
Program GUIReadingTextFromATextFile;
{$APPTYPE CONSOLE}
{$R *.res}
Uses
  System.SysUtils, System.Win.ComObj, Vcl.Forms, Vcl.Dialogs, Classes,
  ModalForm in 'ModalForm.pas' {Form1};
Var
  Dialogue : TOpenDialog;
Begin
  Try
    Dialogue := TOpenDialog.Create(Nil);
    Form1 := TForm1.Create(Nil);
    Form1.Position := poScreenCenter;
    If Dialogue.Execute
      Then
        Begin
          Form1.Memo1.Lines.LoadFromFile(Dialogue.FileName);
          Form1.Label1.Caption := Dialogue.FileName;
          Form1.Caption := 'Reading from a text file';
          Form1.ShowModal;
        End
      Else Writeln('You cancelled');
  Finally
    Dialogue.Free;
    Form1.Free;
  End;
End.
```

P

www.educational-computing.com/DelphiBook/Code/Chapter16/CE10.2/TextFiles.rar

Table 16.11 Showing the contents of a text file in a form-based memo box

A modal form is one that a user is unable to switch away from, i.e. the user must interact with the form. To close a modal form, Delphi must change the value of its **ModalResult** property to a nonzero value. This can be done with a **Button** component on the form. The **ModalResult** property of the button is set to a nonzero value such as **mrCancel** as shown in *Figure 16.4*. When this button is clicked in the executing application, Delphi assigns this value to the **ModalResult** property of the fom thus closing it.

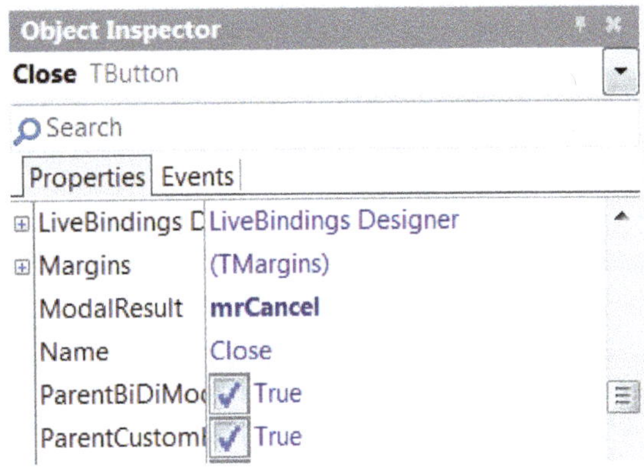

Fig. 16.4 Setting ModalResult property to mrCancel in Object Inspector

Appending to a text file

Adding text to the end of a text file can be done without having to copy the file if **Append** is used to open the file as shown in *Table 16.12*. `Append (Pipe)` positions the file connection at the end of file so that the next write operation occurs at the end of the file.

```
Program AppendingToATextFile;
{$APPTYPE CONSOLE}
Uses
  System.SysUtils, System.Win.ComObj, Vcl.Dialogs;
Var
  Pipe : TextFile;
  Line : String;
  Dialogue : TOpenDialog;
Begin
  Try
    Dialogue := TOpenDialog.Create(Nil);
    If Dialogue.Execute
      Then
        Begin
          Writeln(Dialogue.FileName);
          AssignFile(Pipe, Dialogue.FileName);
          Append(Pipe);
          Write('Input a line of text to add to end of file: ');
          Readln(Line);
          Writeln(Pipe, Line);
          CloseFile(Pipe);
        End
      Else Writeln('Cancelled');
    Finally
      Dialogue.Free;
  End;
  Readln;
End.
```

www.educational-computing.com/DelphiBook/Code/Chapter16/CE10.2/TextFiles.rar

Table 16.12 Program which appends a line of text to end of a text file

Programming tasks

1. Write a program which makes a copy of a text file. Your program should prompt the user to enter the names of the input and output text files.

2. Write a program that reads a text file and displays it with the corresponding line number at the beginning of each line. Start line numbering from 1.

3. The text file "Dict5LetterWords.txt" (download from www.educational-computing.co.uk/CS/Textfiles.html) contains 5 letter words. Write a program which finds all 5 letter words in this file which contain the substring 'oe'.

4. The text file "sowpods.txt" is an official Scrabble dictionary (download from www.educational-computing.co.uk/CS/Textfiles.html). Write a program to find all words containing a particular substring in the text file "sowpods.txt". The program should prompt the user to enter a substring to search for.

5. Write a program to create a Geography quiz which tests a user's knowledge of country capitals.
Use the text file "countriescapitals.txt" (download from www.educational-computing.co.uk/CS/Textfiles.html) which is a comma separated file of countries and their capitals.
The program should display the name of a country chosen at random from this text file and prompt the user to supply the name of the capital of this country. The program should then check the user's answer.
If the user's answer is correct the program should respond "Well done, you got it right!". If the user's answer is incorrect the program should respond "Incorrect answer, the correct answer is ???????" where the correct answer is substituted for the string "???????" when the program executes.

www.educational-computing.com/DelphiBook/Code/Chapter16/CE10.2/FileOfIntegers.rar

Binary files

A binary file is considered to be any file that is not a text file.

Binary files can only be processed by applications that know about the file's structure.

For example, the Delphi program shown in *Table 16.13* creates a file with the structure *file of integer*.

If we want to write to a file with filename `'FileOfIntegers.int'`, we open this file in write mode with

```
Rewrite(f);
```

This will create a new file `'FileOfIntegers.int'` or overwrite this file if it exists already.

The file handle (pipe), `f`, to the file 'FileOfIntegers.int' is created with

```
AssignFile(f, 'FileOfIntegers.int');
```

Each integer is written to this file by the statement

```
Write(f, NextInteger);
```

The file `'FileOfIntegers.int'` is closed with

```
CloseFile(f);
```

The program in *Table 16.13* creates a *file of integer* containing `n` integers.

```
Program FileOfIntegers;
Var
  f : File Of Integer;
  n, i : Integer;
  NextInteger : Integer;
Begin
  AssignFile(f, 'FileOfIntegers.int');
  Rewrite(f);
  Write('How many integers? ');
  Readln(n);
  For i := 1 To n
    Do
      Begin
        Write('Input next integer: ');
        Readln(NextInteger);
        Write(f, NextInteger);
      End;
  CloseFile(f);
  Writeln('File of ', n, ' integers created');
End.
```

Table 16.13 Delphi program which creates a file with the structure file of integer

If we want to read the contents of the file with filename `'FileOfIntegers.int'` we open this file in reading mode as shown in *Table 16.14* with

```
Reset(f);
```

The file handle, `f`, to the file `'FileOfIntegers.int'` is created as before with

```
AssignFile(f, 'FileOfIntegers.int');
```

Each integer is read from this file by the statement

```
Read(f, NextInteger); // Note that Read is used not Readln
```

The end of file is checked for by `Eof(f)` which returns `True` when the end of file is reached otherwise it returns `False`.

We can create a file with a different structure by changing `File Of Integer` to a `File Of` *a different type*, e.g. `File Of Real` or `File Of Byte` or `File Of SomeArrayType` or `File of SomeRecordType`.

```
Program ReadingFileOfIntegers;
Var
  f : File Of Integer;
  NextInteger : Integer;
Begin
  AssignFile(f, 'FileOfIntegers.int');
  Reset(f);
  While Not Eof(f)
    Do
      Begin
        Read(f, NextInteger);
        Writeln(NextInteger);
      End;
  CloseFile(f);
  Writeln('End of file reached, press return to close window');
  Readln;
End.
```

Table 16.14 Delphi program which reads a file with the structure file of integer

`File of Byte` is interesting because every file consists of bytes.

Viewing the structure of a file as other than `File Of Byte` applies an **abstraction** to the file contents. This abstraction occurs when the file is created.

The file type declaration sets the unit of data that will be written to a file of this type, e.g. for a file type `File Of Integer`, the unit of data is *integer* which typically is four bytes.

However, we can open any file with a handle which has been declared as `File Of Byte` and read the contents of the file byte by byte.

This is very useful when the file's data structure is unknown or when we might want to manipulate its contents, e.g. in an application of steganography. Steganography is the science of hiding messages in pictures and other media.

The program in *Table 16.15* is written to treat any file as a `File Of Byte`, in particular bitmap files.

```
Program ReadABitMap;
Type
  BitMapFilePipeType = File Of Byte;
Var
  BitMapFilePipe: BitMapFilePipeType;
  Filename: String;
  NextByte : Byte;
Begin
  Write('Input name of file to be opened for reading: ');
  Readln(Filename);
  AssignFile(BitMapFilePipe, Filename);
  Reset(BitMapFilePipe);
  While Not Eof(BitMapFilePipe)
    Do
      Begin
        Read(BitMapFilePipe, NextByte);
        If NextByte In [32..126]
          Then Write(NextByte : 1, ' ');
          {Note the single space character}
      End;
End.
```

P

Table 16.15 Delphi program for reading a bitmap files, byte by byte (it can read any file type)

Table 16.16 shows a program for hiding a message in the pixel area of a bitmap file by replacing a pixel byte with a message byte thirty times. The program 'hides' the message bytes starting at a position 1078 bytes in from the beginning of the bitmap file.

Table 16.17 shows a program for extracting the hidden message. *Figure 16.5* shows a bitmap file **PlaneGrey.bmp** and *Figure 16.6* shows this file saved as **cPlaneGrey.bmp** after the message 'Hello World' has been hidden within it.

Fig. 16.5 PlaneGrey.bmp

Fig. 16.6 cPlaneGrey.bmp

www.educational-computing.com/DelphiBook/Code/Chapter16/CE10.2/HiddenMessage.rar

```
Program HideMessageInABitMap;
Type
  BitMapFilePipeType = File Of Byte;
Var
  BitMapFilePipe, BitMapFileCodedPipe : BitMapFilePipeType;
  Filename, Message : String;
  NextByte : Byte;
  n, i : Integer;
Begin
  Write('Input name of file to be opened for reading: ');
  Readln(Filename);
  AssignFile(FileBitMapFilePipe, Filename);
  Reset(BitMapFilePipe);
  AssignFile(BitMapFileCodedPipe, 'c' + Filename);
  Rewrite(BitMapFileCodedPipe);
  Write('Input message up to 30 characters in length: ');
  Readln(Message);
  If Length(Message) < 30
    Then
      For i := 1 To 30 - Length(Message)
        Do Message := Message + ' ';
  {Pads message with spaces so that it is always 30 characters in length}
  n := 0;
  i := 0;
  While Not Eof(BitMapFilePipe)
    Do
      Begin
        Read(BitMapFilePipe, NextByte);
        If (n >= 1078) And (n <= 1078 + Length(Message)-1)
          Then
            Begin
              i := i + 1;
              NextByte := Ord(Message[i]);
            End;
        n := n + 1;
        Write(BitMapFileCodedPipe, NextByte);
      End;
  CloseFile(BitMapFileCodePipe);
End.
```

Table 16.16 Delphi steganography program which reads a bitmap file and a 30 character message which hides in the bitmap

```
Program ExtractHiddenMessageInABitMap;
{$APPTYPE CONSOLE}
Type
  BitMapFilePipeType = File Of Byte;
Var
  BitMapFilePipe : BitMapFilePipeType;
  Filename : String;
  NextByte : Byte;
  n : Integer;
Begin
  Write('Input name of file to be opened for reading: ');
  Readln(Filename);
  AssignFile(BitMapFilePipe, Filename);
  Reset(BitMapFilePipe);
  n := 0;
  While Not Eof(BitMapFilePipe)
    Do
      Begin
        Read(BitMapFilePipe, NextByte);
        If (n >= 1078) And (n <= 1078 + 29)
          Then Write(Chr(NextByte));
        If (n = 1078 + 30)
          Then Writeln;
        If n < MaxInt
          Then n := n + 1;
      End;
  Readln;
End.
```

Table 16.17 Delphi program for Extracting hidden message

Questions

3 What is a binary file?

Programming tasks

6 Write a program which creates a file of decimal numbers (e.g. decimal number 12.67) with filename "FileOfDecimals.int". Your program should prompt the user to enter `n`, the number of decimal numbers to store in the file. The program should then collect `n` decimal numbers from the user.

7 Write a program with which to view the file of decimal numbers with filename "FileOfDecimals.int" created in task 6.

8 Write a program which stores a single copy of an array `SurnameNameArray` of type `TSurnameNameArray` in a file **Surname.arr**. Use the type definitions

```
TSurName = String[25]
TSurnameNameArray = Array[1..5] Of TSurname
Pipe = File Of TOwnerNameArray
```

The program should populate the array with five surnames before writing the array to disk.

9 Write a program which reads in the array stored in file **Surname.arr** and displays each surname in turn in a console window.

Random or Direct Access Files in Delphi

Any non-text file can be accessed or updated randomly. Essentially this means that the basic elements of the file be they records or arrays or something else can be accessed in any order.

In other words:

Any element can be accessed independently of any other element.

EW35	SEATTLE
TY16	LONDON
PQ45	DUBLIN
DF67	PARIS
KL23	MUNICH
BN01	BONN
YU12	VIENNA
SD65	PRAGUE
ZX99	TORONTO
AS90	LIMA
KL18	LISBON
BX38	ANTWERP

Table 16.18 Flight.dat records

For example, the records shown stored in file **Flight.Dat** in *Table 16.18* may be accessed directly in any order.

One sequence of access may be `KL23`'s record then `BX38`'s followed by `PQ45`'s.

The order of access is said to be **random**.

A file that permits random or direct access in this way is said to be a **random file**.

Sometimes access to a single record at a time is all that is required.

For instance, a user may wish to know only which city is allocated the code `YU12`.

The computer on which **Flight.Dat** is stored will, on request, retrieve `YU12`'s record without needing to process any other record of this file first. This is why such a file is also called a **direct access file**.

In Delphi random access is achieved with the **Seek** procedure as follows:

```
Assign(Pipe, 'Flight.Dat');
Reset(Pipe);
Seek(Pipe, 7);
Read(Pipe,FlightRecord);
```

The `Seek(Pipe,7)` positions the reading pointer at the eighth record. This may seem strange, at first, but it is necessary because Delphi numbers the first record, record 0, the second record 1 and so on (see *Table 16.19*).

0	EW35	SEATTLE
1	TY16	LONDON
2	PQ45	DUBLIN
3	DF67	PARIS
4	KL23	MUNICH
5	BN01	BONN
6	YU12	VIENNA
7	SD65	PRAGUE
8	ZX99	TORONTO
9	AS90	LIMA
10	KL18	LISBON
11	BX38	ANTWERP

Table 16.19 Delphi numbering of Flight.dat records

`Read(Pipe,FlightRecord)` copies the eighth record in the file to variable `FlightRecord` (see *Table 16.20* and *Figure 16.7*).

SD65	PRAGUE

Table 16.20 Eighth record

In general,

Seek(Pipe,n) positions pointer at record number n + 1.

If file **Flight.Dat** is to be altered in any way then write access as well as read access is required. This requires a slightly different block of program code to be executed when setting up the pipe to the file.

```
Assign(Pipe, 'Flight.Dat');
FileMode := fmOpenReadWrite;
Reset(Pipe)
Seek(Pipe,7);
Read(Pipe, FlightRecord);
FlightRecord.Key := YV12;
Seek(Pipe,7);
Write(Pipe, FlightRecord);
```

`Assign(Pipe, 'Flight.Dat')` only needs to be executed once. Therefore, if the program has already executed `Assign(Pipe, 'Flight.Dat')` then to switch between file modes requires just `FileMode := ...; Reset(Pipe);` to be executed. The constant `fmOpenreadWrite` and others are defined in **System.SysUtils**.

Table 16.21 shows a Delphi program that can be used to create **Flight.dat**.

Build and run this program with value for `n` of `12` and enter the records shown in *Table 16.18*.

To seek and display the the eighth record, build and run the Delphi program shown in *Table 16.22*. Output similar to that shown in *Figure 16.18* should be obtained.

www.educational-computing.com/DelphiBook/Code/Chapter16/CE10.2/RandomAccess.rar

```
Program WritingFlightData;
{$APPTYPE CONSOLE}
Type
  TFlightRecord = Record
                    FlightCode : String[4];
                    FlightDestination : String[16];
                  End;
Var
  Pipe : File Of TFlightRecord;
  n, i : Integer;
  FlightRecord : TFlightRecord;
Begin
  AssignFile(Pipe, 'Flight.dat');
  Rewrite(Pipe);
  Write('How many flight records? ');
  Readln(n);
  For i := 1 To n
    Do
      Begin
        Write('Input next Flight Code: ');
        Readln(FlightRecord.FlightCode);
        Write('Input next Flight Destination: ');
        Readln(FlightRecord.FlightDestination);
        Write(Pipe, FlightRecord);
      End;
  CloseFile(Pipe);
  Writeln('File of ', n, ' flight records created');
  Readln;
End.
```

Table 16.21 Delphi program that creates and populates Flight.dat with flight records

Warning

It is important to limit the length of strings when using files otherwise a finalization error will occur when compiling. Alternatively use ShortString to avoid specifying the length of strings.

```
Program RandomAccessReading;
{$APPTYPE CONSOLE}
Type
  TFlightRecord = Record
                    FlightCode : String[4];
                    FlightDestination : String[16];
                  End;
Var
  FlightRecord : TFlightRecord;
  Pipe : File Of TFlightRecord;
Begin
  AssignFile(Pipe, 'Flight.Dat');
  Reset(Pipe);
  Seek(Pipe, 7);
  Read(Pipe,FlightRecord);
  Writeln(FlightRecord.FlightCode);
  Writeln(FlightRecord.FlightDestination);
  Readln;
End.
```

Table 16.22 Delphi program that reads the eighth record

Fig. 16.7 Console window output from program RandomAccessReading

Filemode

The variable `FileMode` is used to set the access mode to use when typed and untyped files (not text files) are opened using the `Reset` procedure.

The file open modes that can be assigned to the `FileMode` variable are defined in the **Constants** list in **System.SysUtils**. The default value for `FileMode` is 2 (Read/Write access), which is allocated the constant identifier `fmOpenReadWrite` - see *Table 16.23*.

Assigning another value to `FileMode` causes all subsequent calls of `Reset` to use that mode.

FileMode Value	Byte Value
fmOpenReadWrite	2
fmExclusive	4
fmOpenRead	0
fmOpenWrite	1
fmShareCompat	0
fmShareDenyNone	64
fmShareDenyRead	48
fmShareDenyWrite	32
fmShareExclusive	16

Table 16.23 FileMode constants

Table 16.24 shows a Delphi program to read the eighth record and then to update it, changing the FlightCode from `SD65` to `YV12`.

It is very important to close a file that has been written to. Writing takes place initially to a memory buffer. Normally, the contents of this buffer are only written to disk when it becomes full. However, the action of closing a file forces the contents of the buffer to be written to disk. *Reset* has the same effect on a file connection (file handle) that was configured to write to the file with *Rewrite*.

The *Flush* command will also move buffered text file data to the external file if opened with *Rewrite* or *Append*.

www.educational-computing.com/DelphiBook/Code/Chapter16/CE10.2/RandomAccess.rar

Key term

Reset:
Opens a text file for reading, or binary file for read/write.

FileMode variable:
Defines how *Reset* opens a binary file.

```
Program RandomAccessWriting;
{$APPTYPE CONSOLE}
Uses System.SysUtils;
Type
  TFlightRecord = Record
                    FlightCode : String[4];
                    FlightDestination : String[16];
                  End;
Var
  FlightRecord : TFlightRecord;
  Pipe : File Of TFlightRecord;
Begin
  AssignFile(Pipe, 'Flight.Dat');
  FileMode := fmOpenReadWrite;// Optional since default mode is read/write
  Reset(Pipe);
  Seek(Pipe,7);
  Read(Pipe, FlightRecord);
  Writeln('Eighth record before change: ', FlightRecord.FlightCode);
  FlightRecord.FlightCode := 'YV12';
  Seek(Pipe,7);
  Write(Pipe, FlightRecord);
  Seek(Pipe,7);
  Read(Pipe, FlightRecord);
  Writeln('Eighth record after change: ', FlightRecord.FlightCode);
  CloseFile(Pipe);
  Readln;
End.
```

P

Table 16.24 Delphi program that updates Flight.dat

Key term

Typed file:
While text files consist of lines terminated with a CR/LF (#13#10) combination, typed files consist of data taken from a particular type of data structure.

Untyped file:

```
Var
  Pipe : File;
```

Gives a base untyped file. Such a file can only be read from and written to using `BlockRead` and `BlockWrite`. The basic data type is a byte.

FileSize

FileSize is a function that returns the number of records in a file.

If the file is declared as a file of byte, then the record size defaults to one byte, and *FileSize* returns the number of bytes in the file.

It is defined as follows: `Function FileSize(var F: File): Integer;`

The Delphi program shown in *Table 16.25* uses `FileSize(Pipe) - 1` to position `Seek` at the beginning of the last record in file **Flight.dat**. This record is then read and its fields displayed in the console window as shown in *Figure 16.8*.

```
Program SeekFilePosition;
{$APPTYPE CONSOLE}
Type
  TFlightRecord = Record
                    FlightCode : String[4];
                    FlightDestination : String[16];
                  End;
Var
  FlightRecord : TFlightRecord;
  Pipe : File Of TFlightRecord;
Begin
  AssignFile(Pipe, 'Flight.Dat');
  Reset(Pipe);
  Seek(Pipe, FileSize(Pipe) - 1);
  Read(Pipe,FlightRecord);
  Writeln(FlightRecord.FlightCode);
  Writeln(FlightRecord.FlightDestination);
  Readln;
End.
```

Table 16.25 Delphi program that uses FileSize to find the last record in Flight.dat

Fig. 16.8 Console window output from program SeekFilePosition

Key term

Append:
Opens a text file to allow appending of text to the end of the file.

AssignFile:
Assigns a file handle to a binary or text file, i.e. sets up a connection or pipe to the file.

CloseFile:
Closes an open file, writing any contents of the associated memory buffer to the external file, e.g. disk file.

Reset:
Open a text file for reading, or binary file for read/write

Rewrite:
Opens a text or binary file for write access, clearing any existing contents in the process or if file does not exist, creates the file and readies it for writing.

TextFile:
A file type for storing lines of text terminated with a CR/LF (#13#10) combination.

Seek:
Moves the current position in open typed or untyped files by the indicated offset, n. Procedure Seek(Var f: File; n: Integer);

www.educational-computing.com/DelphiBook/Code/Chapter16/CE10.2/RandomAccess.rar

Programming tasks

10 Use file **Flight.Dat** generated from the program shown in *Table 16.21* and data shown in *Table 16.18*. The record structure is

```
Record
  FlightCode : String[4];
  FlightCity : String[8];
End;
```

Write a program that

1. Prompts a user for a record number in the range 0 to 11
2. Retrieves the record at this position in the file **Flight.Dat**
3. Displays the fields of this record on the screen
4. Asks user if he/she wishes to view another record
5. Repeats steps 1 to 4 until user no longer wishes to view records

11 Create a program that allows the user to alter the contents of a record as follows:

1. Prompt user for a record number in the range 0 to 11
2. Retrieve the record at this position in the file **Flight.Dat**
3. Display the fields of this record on the screen
4. Ask user if he/she wishes to alter *FlightCity* field
5. If yes, enter new value
6. Write altered record back to **Flight.Dat**
7. Ask user if he/she wishes to alter another record
8. Repeats steps 1 to 7 until user no longer wishes to alter records

Some other routines for working with files and directories

Table 16.26 shows some routines for working with files and directories.
These are defined in the libraries **System.SysUtils** and **Vcl.FileCtrl**.

ChDir	Change the working drive plus path for a specified drive
CreateDir	Create a directory
DeleteFile	Delete a file specified by its file name
Erase	Erase a file
FileExists	Returns true if the given file exists
FileSearch	Search for a file in one or more directories
GetCurrentDir	Get the current directory (drive plus directory)
MkDir	Make a directory
RemoveDir	Remove a directory
Rename	Rename a file
RenameFile	Rename a file or directory
RmDir	Remove a directory
SelectDirectory	Display a dialog to allow user selection of a directory
SetCurrentDir	Change the current directory

Table 16.26 Some Delphi file and directory routines

There are two commands to remove a dirctory. For more information see the links below:

http://delphibasics.co.uk/RTL.asp?Name=RmDir

http://delphibasics.co.uk/RTL.asp?Name=RemoveD

You may explore the other commands in Table 16.26 by substituting the corresponding Name value in the hyperlink, e.g.

http://delphibasics.co.uk/RTL.asp?Name=ChDir

Table 16.27 shows a Delphi program that uses some of these routines. `SelectDirectory` displays a directory window as shown in *Figure 16.9*. It is possible to create a new directory from this window by entering the name of the new directory into the textbox at the top of the window, either using the existing path or a new path.

www.educational-computing.com/DelphiBook/Code/Chapter16/CE10.2/FileCommands.rar

```
Program FileCommands;
{$APPTYPE CONSOLE}
Uses
  System.SysUtils, Vcl.FileCtrl;
Var
  Directory, CurrentDirectory,
  OldCurrentDirectory : String;
Begin
  CurrentDirectory := GetCurrentDir;
  Writeln(CurrentDirectory);
  OldCurrentDirectory := CurrentDirectory;
  If SelectDirectory(Directory, [sdAllowCreate, sdPerformCreate, sdPrompt],1000)
    Then Writeln(Directory);
  If SetCurrentDir(OldCurrentDirectory)
    Then Writeln('Success')
    Else Writeln('Failure');
  CurrentDirectory := GetCurrentDir;
  Writeln(CurrentDirectory);
  Readln;
End.
```

Table 16.27 Delphi program that uses some file commands available from libraries System.SysUtils and Vcl.FileCtrl

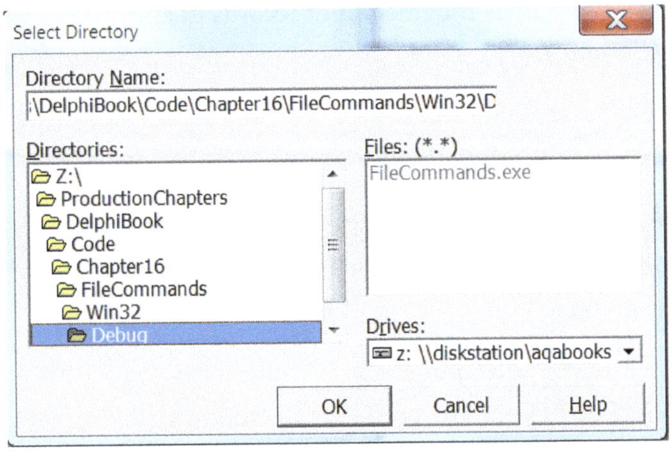

Fig. 16.9 Output from routine SelectDirectory excution in program FileCommands

File organisation

File organisation refers to the way that the records of a file or items of a file are accessed and stored or appear to be accessed and stored on the storage medium. The following organisations apply to non-text files.

Serial file organisation

Records/items are stored in no particular order. Records may be accessed only in the order in which they were written to the file, i.e. access starts from the beginning of the file and each record is examined in turn until the record is found or the end of the file is reached. For a file containing 2000 records this means 2000 records must be examined before the last record can be subjected to any processing activity. If the next record to be processed happens to be before the current one the searching process must start again from the beginning of the file. If the next record to be processed is at a position in the file after the current record then the searching process may proceed forwards through the file to this next record. The whole file needs to be searched to determine that a particular record is not present in the file.

Sequential file organisation

Records/items stored in a sequence/order determined by some field usually a key field. Access to any particular record/item is as for serial. However, it is possible to conclude that a particular record/item is not present in the file if a file record/item is reached that is later in sequence than where a match could occur.

Indexed Sequential File Organisation

Records stored in sequence, separate index file holding highest key per block and block address of all disk blocks of sequential file. A key is a field of the record that is used to order or sequence the file. If it is unique then it is called a primary key. A disk block is the smallest unit of transfer, e.g. 512 bytes. A disk block may contain more than one record.

Random File Organisation

Direct access to any record position in file using record key field in one of three ways:

- key field is the address/record position,
- simple mapping of key field is the record position/address,
- randomising function applied to key field to generate record position (hashing).

Where are these file organisations used?

- serial for data logging, no particular order to data

- sequential when hit rate is high or where the records need to be accessed in order (a hit occurs when a record is accessed/processed; hit rate is the fraction of records in a file that are accessed/processed usually expressed as a percentage, e.g. if every record is accessd/processed then the hitrate is 100%)
- indexed sequential where hit rate is sometimes high and sometimes low (where direct access is required sometimes and sequential access at other times)
- random where hit rate is low and fast access is required

Application operation modes

Applications operate in only a few modes.

One is interactive or real-time. In this mode, the application is communicating with another application or a human. Real-time means the response or process must produce a result in a timely manner (immediately or quickly enough to seem immediate). Interactive is where the application is interacting (or conversing) with a human and the application must also produce a result in a timely manner acceptable to the human.

A relatively new mode is streaming. In this application type, data arrives or flows constantly whereupon the data is processed and some action taken.

Everything else is unattended, background or "batch". In batch processing, all the data is collected first and batched before processing begins. Once processing begins, it continues from beginning to end without human intervention except for when an error occurs. This is arguably the mode where computers are most effective because they can operate at "machine speed" without having to wait for slow humans, slow devices delivering data or slow networks to enable communication with another application or computer. A typical application is generating customer billing statements at perdiodic intervals of time.

Batch processing

Batch processing such as inventory processing, warehouse management, payroll and customer billing is still very much a major activity in almost every business computing environment. Typically applications are suitable for batch processing if

1. it makes sense to process data at specific times, e.g. monthly, and
2. the processing is one with a high hit rate, i.e. a high percentage of master file records need to be processed

Inventory replenishment is one such case. It doesn't make sense to place a replenishment order for an item immediately it is sold if, subsequently, many more of the same item are sold throughout the day along with many other items. It seems more sensible to wait until some point, either a specific time or when some number of items have been purchased before placing an order to replenish the inventory. All the sales transactions can be batched into a transaction file and then processed as a batch against a stock inventory master file to generate re-ordering information.

File Processing

Master file

This is a file such as a stock file or accounts file. A stock file will contain a record for each item of stock, e.g. cans of beans, packets of cornflakes. A master file is a semi-permanent file that stores vital business information such as the number of items currently in stock of each stock item. As items of stock are sold so the number (quantity) in stock field of the corresponding record is decreased. When a deliver of stock is received the number in stock field of the corresponding record is increased. Occasionally, a stock line is discontinued. In this case the corresponding record in the stock master file is removed (deleted). When a new line of stock is acquired, a new record is added to the stock master file. A master file is usually sequentially organised. In the case of a stock master file, the stock records are ordered by stock item code. *Table 16.28* shows a simplified example of some master file records.

Master file			
Item code	**Description**	**Quantity in stock**	**Reorder level**
1234	Beans	2	100
1235	Sardines	1	200
⋮	⋮	⋮	⋮
2134	Cornflakes	1	150
⋮	⋮	⋮	⋮
3638	Lard	1	100
⋮	⋮	⋮	⋮
4591	Muesli	1	150
⋮	⋮	⋮	⋮

← Single record

Table 16.28 Master file records

Transaction file

The changes in stock levels that are to be applied to the stock master file are recorded in a **transaction file**. This is a temporary file that is used to update the master file. When the update has taken place the transaction file may be discarded. A transaction is either a sale of a stock item, e.g. 3 cans of beans to a particular customer or a return of a sold stock item or a delivery of a particular stock item, e.g. 100 packets of cornflakes. For each transaction a transaction record is created containing a stock item identifier, the number of units and an indication of whether this number should be added to or subtracted from the corresponding stock master record field. When many customers buy many items of stock the transaction file will contain many records. A simple example of the contents of a transaction file is shown in *Table 16.29*.

	Transaction file		
Item	**Item code**	**Quantity**	**Sale/Delivery/Return**
(Beans)	1234	2	S
(Beans)	1234	1	S
(Cornflakes)	2134	2	S
(Cornflakes)	2134	1	S
(Lard)	3638	200	D
(Lard)	3638	1	S
(Lard)	3638	2	S
(Muesli)	4591	1	S
(Muesli)	4591	2	S

← Single record

Table 16.29 Transaction file records

Sequential file update

Sequential file update is an application that copies every record of a master file (called the old master file) to a new master file in the process updating those records of the old master file for which a transaction record exists. The transaction records are obtained from a transaction file which is sequentially organised in the same sequence as the master file. This makes it possible to move through both from beginning to end without having to start over and over again from the beginning of the master file.

Figure 16.10 shows a **system flowchart** for the sequential file update application. A system flowchart shows the physical components of the system, i.e. the programs, files and their storage media, input/output devices and their purpose, manual operations.

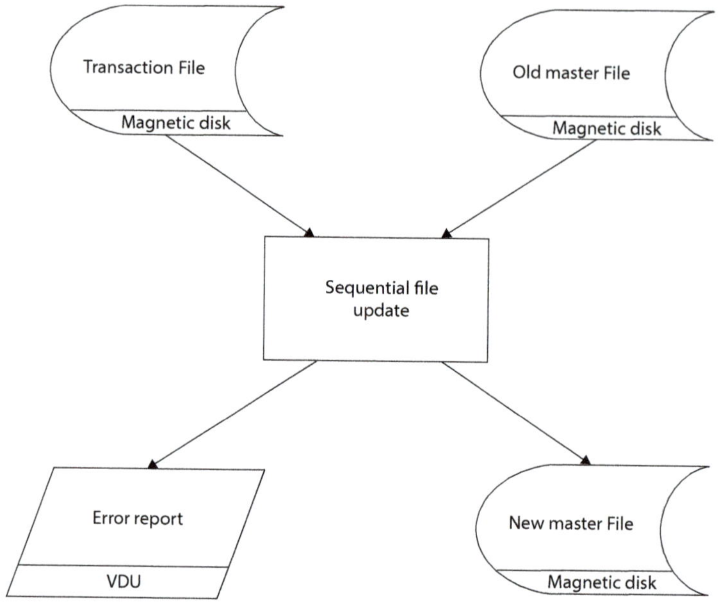

Fig. 16.10 Systems flowchart for the sequential file update application

Table 16.30 shows pseudocode for a sequential file update process for sales of stock recorded in a transaction file.

```
Open non-empty Old Master file for reading
Open Transaction file for reading
Create empty New Master file
Read Old Master record //first record of old master file
While not end of Transaction file // Process transaction records
  Do
    Begin
      Read next Transaction file record
      While TransactionRecord.ItemCode <> OldMasterRecord.ItemCode //While no match
        Do
          Begin
            Write Old Master record to New Master file
            If not at end of Old Master file
              Then Read next Old Master file record
              Else Raise error // End of master file reached befor all transaction records processed
          End
      // Match between transaction record and Old Master file record!
      //Update quantity in stock for sales
      OldMasterRecord.QuantityInStock := OldMasterRecord.QuantityInStock - TransactionRecord.Quantity
    End
//Last transaction record matched but updated old master record not yet written to new master file
Write Old Master record to New Master file //Write updated old master record to new master file
While not end of Old Master file //Copy remainder of old master file to new master file
  Do
    Begin
      Read next Old Master file record
      Write Old Master file record to New Master file
    End
Close all files
```

Table 16.30 Pseudocode for the sequential file update process for sales

Figure 16.11 shows a program flowchart[1] for the sequential file update process.

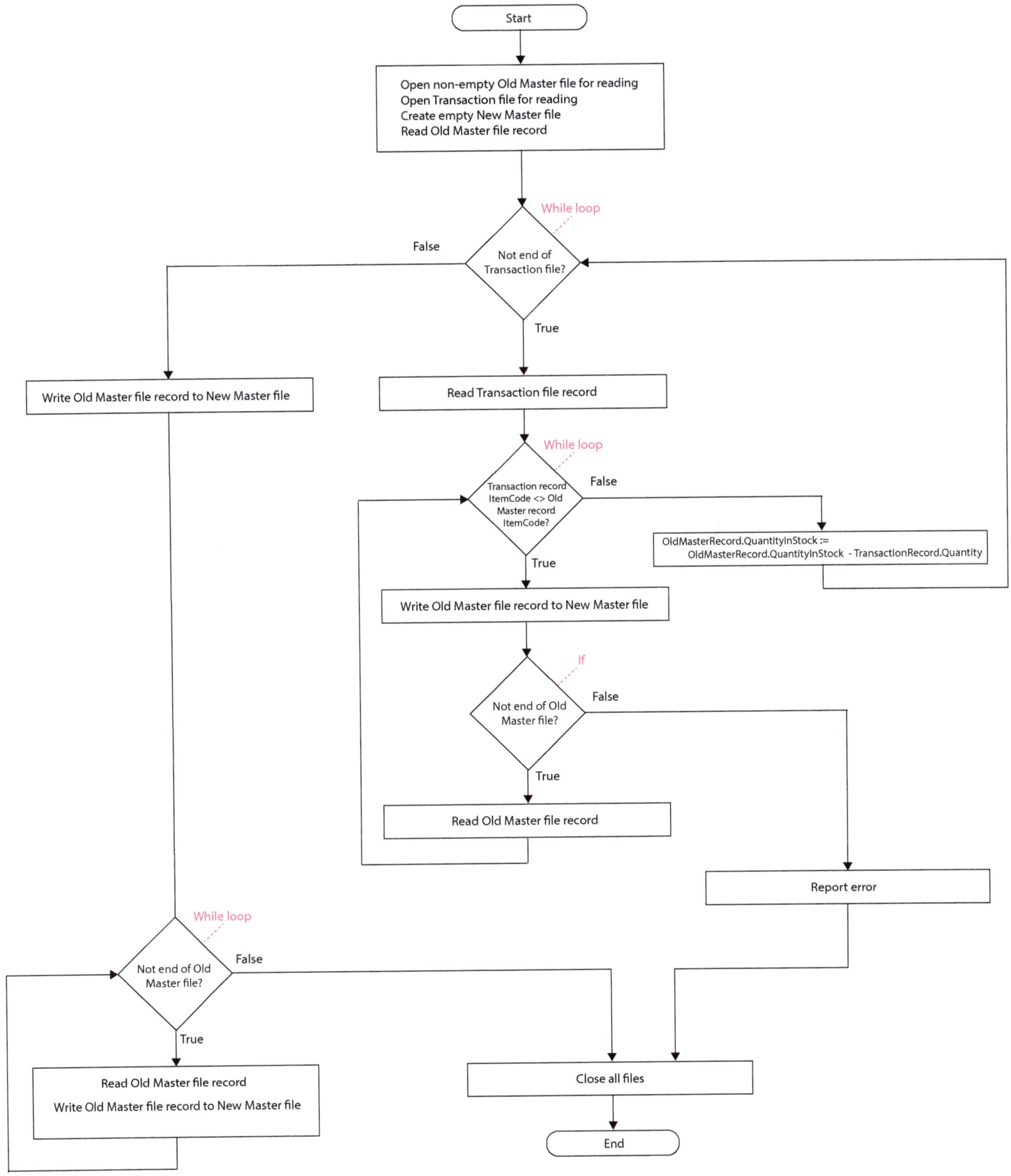

Fig. 16.11 Program flowchart for sequential file update process for sales

Table 16.31 shows a decision table for two conditions: end of transaction file reached and end of old master reached.

1 See Appendix A at www.educational-computing.com/DelphiBook/DelphiCode.html

Table 16.32 shows a decision table[2] for three conditions: end of transaction file reached, end of old master reached and a match.

End of transaction file reached	End of old master file reached	Action
NO	NO	Copy old master to new master updating records that match transaction file records
YES	NO	Copy remainder of old master to new master
NO	YES	Report error, abort processing, close all open files
YES	YES	Close all open files

Table 16.31 Decision table for conditions end of transaction file, end of old master file

End of transaction file reached	End of old master file reached	Match?	Action

NO	NO	NO	`While not end of Transaction file Do`
			`    Read next Transaction file record`
			`    While TransactionRecord.ItemCode <> OldMasterRecord.ItemCode Do`
			`      Write Old Master record to New Master file`
			`      If not at end of Old Master file`
			`        Then Read next Old Master file record`

NO	NO	YES	`OldMasterRecord.QuantityInStock := OldMasterRecord.QuantityInStock -` `TransactionRecord.Quantity`

YES	NO	X	`Write Old Master record to New Master file`
			`While not end of Old Master file Do`
			`  Read next Old Master file record`
			`  Write Old Master file record to New Master file`

NO	YES	X	`If at end of Old Master file` `  Then Raise error, close files, abort processing`
YES	YES	X	`Close files`

Table 16.32 Decision table for conditions end of transaction file, end of old master file and a match

Table 16.33 shows the declaration section of the sequential file update program **SeqFileUp**.

Table 16.34 shows the middle section of the sequential file update program **SeqFileUp**.

Table 16.35 shows the final section of the sequential file update program **SeqFileUp**.

```
Program SeqFileUp;
{$APPTYPE CONSOLE}
Uses
  System.SysUtils, Vcl.FileCtrl;
Label 50,100;
Type
  MasterRecordType = Record
                       ItemCode : Integer;
                       Description : String[40];
                       QuantityInStock : Integer;
                       ReOrderLevel : Integer;
                     End;
  TransactionRecordType = Record
                            ItemNumber : Integer;
                            Quantity : Integer;
                            Marker : Char;
                          End;
  MasterFilePipeType = File Of MasterRecordType;
  TransactionFilePipeType = File Of TransactionRecordType;
Var
  OldMasterRecord : MasterRecordType;
  TransactionRecord : TransactionRecordType;
  OldMasterFilePipe : MasterFilePipeType;
  NewMasterFilePipe : MasterFilePipeType;
  TransactionFilePipe : TransactionFilePipeType;
  OldMasterFileName, TransactionFileName, NewMasterFileName, Directory : String;
  Response : Char;
```

Table 16.33 Delphi program that performs a sequential file update - declarations section

The statement `GoTo 50` in *Table 16.34* causes program execution to jump to the statement labelled by `50:` - *see Table 16.35*. The program declares two labels with `Label 50,100;` in the declaration section, *Table 16.34*. Similarly, The statement `GoTo 100` in *Table 16.34* causes program execution to jump to the statement labelled by `100:` - *see Table 16.35*.

2 See Appendix B at www.educational-computing.com/DelphiBook/DelphiCode.html

```
Begin
  If SelectDirectory(Directory, [sdAllowCreate, sdPerformCreate, sdPrompt],1000)
    Then Writeln(Directory);
  Write('Old Master File Name : ');
  Readln(OldMasterFileName);
  If Not FileExists(OldMasterFileName)
    Then
      Begin
        Writeln('ERROR: ',OldMasterFileName,' does not exist in search area');
        GoTo 100;
      End;
  AssignFile(OldMasterFilePipe,OldMasterFileName);
  Reset(OldMasterFilePipe);
  If Not Eof(OldMasterFilePipe)
    Then
      Begin
      Write('Transaction File Name: ');
      Readln(TransactionFileName);
      If Not FileExists(TransactionFileName)
        Then
          Begin
            Writeln('ERROR: ',TransactionFileName,' does not exist in search area');
            GoTo 100;
          End;
      AssignFile(TransactionFilePipe,TransactionFileName);
      Reset(TransactionFilePipe);
      Write('New Master File Name : ');
      Readln(NewMasterFileName);
      If FileExists(NewMasterFileName)
        Then
          Begin
            Writeln('WARNING: ',NewMasterFileName,' exists in search area');
            Write('OverWrite Y/N? ');
            Readln(Response);
            If Not (Response In ['Y','y'])
              Then GoTo 100;
          End;
      AssignFile(NewMasterFilePipe,NewMasterFileName);
      Rewrite(NewMasterFilePipe);
      If Eof(TransactionFilePipe)
        Then
          Begin
            Writeln;
            Writeln('Transaction File ',TransactionFileName,' is empty');
            Writeln('New Master File ',NewMasterFileName,' created');
            GoTo 50;
          End;
      Read(OldMasterFilePipe,OldMasterRecord);
      While Not Eof(TransactionFilePipe)
        Do
          Begin
            Read(TransactionFilePipe,TransactionRecord);
            While TransactionRecord.ItemCode <> OldMasterRecord.ItemCode
              Do
                Begin
                  Write(NewMasterFilePipe,OldMasterRecord);
                  If Not Eof(OldMasterFilePipe)
                    Then Read(OldMasterFilePipe,OldMasterRecord)
                    Else
                      Begin
                        Writeln('ERROR: not at end of transaction file ', TransactionFileName);
                        Writeln(' when end of old master ':30, OldMasterFileName,' reached');
                        Writeln;
                        Writeln('Transaction record ', TransactionRecord.ItemCode:2,
                                ' does not exist in ',OldMasterFileName);
                        GoTo 100;
                      End;
                End;
            OldMasterRecord.QuantityInStock := OldMasterRecord.QuantityInStock
                                              - TransactionRecord.Quantity;
          End;
        Write(NewMasterFilePipe,OldMasterRecord);
      End
    Else
      Begin
        Writeln('ERROR: Old Master File ',OldMasterFileName, ' is empty');
        Writeln('New Master File not created or if exists not overwritten');
      End;
```

Table 16.34 Delphi program that performs a sequential file update - middle section

www.educational-computing.com/DelphiBook/Code/Chapter16/CE10.2/SequentialFileProcessing.rar

```
50:
  While Not Eof(OldMasterFilePipe)
    Do
      Begin
        Read(OldMasterFilePipe,OldMasterRecord);
        Write(NewMasterFilePipe,OldMasterRecord);
      End;
100:
  CloseFile(OldMasterFilePipe);
  CloseFile(TransactionFilePipe);
  CloseFile(NewMasterFilePipe);
  Writeln;
  Writeln('--------------------------------------------');
  Writeln('Press return key to exit program');
  Readln;
End.
```

Table 16.35 Delphi program that performs a sequential file update - last section

Normally programmers avoid the use of the **GoTo** statement because it can create code that is very difficult to follow. However, it is sensible to use **GoTo** where the severity of the error is such that the only option is to exit the program, jumping to near the end of the program in order to execute any required housekeeping such as closing files. Of course, the error condition could be handled by enclosing the relevant sections of code in a **Try Except Finally** block and using for example `raise Exception.Create('Not an end of transaction when end of old master file reached');` to signal that an error has occurred.

Table 16.36 shows program **CreateMaster** which is used to create the old master file used in the sequential file update process.

Table 16.37 shows program **ViewMaster** which can be used to view the contents of the old master file.

Table 16.38 shows program **CreateTrans** which is used to create the transaction file used in the sequential file update process.

Table 16.39 shows program **ViewTrans** which can be used to view the contents of the transaction file.

```
Program CreateMaster;
{$APPTYPE CONSOLE}
Uses System.SysUtils;
Label 100;
Type
  MasterRecordType = Record
                       ItemCode : Integer;
                       Description : String[40];
                       QuantityInStock : Integer;
                       ReOrderLevel : Integer;
                     End;
  MasterFilePipeType = File Of MasterRecordType;

Var
  OldMasterRecord : MasterRecordType;
  OldMasterFilePipe : MasterFilePipeType;
  OldMasterFileName : String;
  i : Integer;
  Response : Char;
Begin
  Write('Old Master File Name : ');
  Readln(OldMasterFileName);
  If FileExists(OldMasterFileName)
    Then
      Begin
        Writeln('WARNING: ',OldMasterFileName,' exists in search area');
        Write('OverWrite Y/N? ');
        Readln(Response);
        If Not (Response In ['Y','y'])
          Then GoTo 100;
      End;
  AssignFile(OldMasterFilePipe,OldMasterFileName);
  ReWrite(OldMasterFilePipe);
  i := 0;
  Repeat
    Write('Enter an old master record Y/N? ');
    Readln(Response);
    If Response In ['Y','y']
      Then
        Begin
          i := i + 1;
          OldMasterRecord.ItemCode := i;
          Write('Description: ');
          Readln(OldMasterRecord.Description);
          Write('Quantity in stock: ');
          Readln(OldMasterRecord.QuantityInStock);
          Write(OldMasterFilePipe,OldMasterRecord);
        End;
  Until Not (Response In ['Y','y']); CloseFile(OldMasterFilePipe);
100: Writeln('Have you enjoyed using this program?');
End.
```

Table 16.36 Delphi program for creating a master file

I

Locate old master file, **Oldm.dat**, and transaction file **Trans.dat** - these may be downloaded (www.educational-computing.com/DelphiBook/Code/Chapter16/DataFiles/Files.rar). Place these files where they may be accessed by program **SeqFileUp**. Build and run program **SeqFileUp**.
Check that the expected updates have been applied by using program **ViewMaster** to view **Oldm.dat** and the newly created **Newm.dat** and program **ViewTrans** to view the transaction file, **Trans.dat**.

P

```
Program ViewMaster;
{$APPTYPE CONSOLE}
Uses System.SysUtils, Vcl.FileCtrl;
Label 100;
Type
  MasterRecordType = Record
                       ItemCode : Integer;
                       Description : String[40];
                       QuantityInStock : Integer;
                       ReOrderLevel : Integer;
                     End;
  MasterFilePipeType = File Of MasterRecordType;
Var
  MasterRecord : MasterRecordType;
  MasterFilePipe : MasterFilePipeType;
  MasterFileName, Directory : String;
  i : Integer;
Begin
  If SelectDirectory(Directory, [sdAllowCreate, sdPerformCreate, sdPrompt],1000)
    Then Writeln(Directory);
  Write('Master File Name : ');
  Readln(MasterFileName);
  If Not FileExists(MasterFileName)
    Then
      Begin
        Writeln('ERROR: ',MasterFileName,' does not exist in search area);
        GoTo 100;
      End;
  AssignFile(MasterFilePipe,MasterFileName);
  Reset(MasterFilePipe);
  i := 0;
  While Not Eof(MasterFilePipe)
    Do
      Begin
        If (i Mod 24 = 0) //Every 24 lines write a header
          Then
            Begin
              Write('Item Code' : 15);
              Write('Description' : 15);
              Writeln('Quantity in Stock': 25);
              Writeln;
            End;
        i := i + 1;
        Read(MasterFilePipe,MasterRecord);
        Write(MasterRecord.ItemCode : 15);
        Write(MasterRecord.Description : 15);
        Writeln(MasterRecord.QuantityInStock : 25);
      End;
100:
  Writeln;
  Writeln('----------------------------------------------------');
  Writeln('Press return to exit program');
  Readln;
End.
```

Table 16.37 Delphi program for viewing a master file

www.educational-computing.com/DelphiBook/Code/Chapter16/CE10.2/SequentialFileProcessing.rar

```
Program CreateTrans;
{$APPTYPE CONSOLE}
Uses System.SysUtils;
Label 100;
Type
  TransactionRecordType = Record
                            ItemCode : Integer;
                            Quantity : Integer;
                            Marker : Char;
                          End;
  TransactionFilePipeType = File Of TransactionRecordType;
Var
  TransactionRecord : TransactionRecordType;
  TransactionFilePipe : TransactionFilePipeType;
  TransactionFileName : String;
  i : Integer;
  Response : Char;
Begin
  Write('Transaction File Name : ');
  Readln(TransactionFileName);
  If FileExists(TransactionFileName)
    Then
      Begin
        Writeln('WARNING: ',TransactionFileName,' exists in search area');
        Write('OverWrite Y/N? ');
        Readln(Response);
        If Not (Response In ['Y','y'])
          Then GoTo 100;
      End;
  AssignFile(TransactionFilePipe,TransactionFileName);
  ReWrite(TransactionFilePipe);
  Repeat
    Write('Enter a transaction record Y/N? ');
    Readln(Response);
    If Response In ['Y','y']
      Then
        Begin
          Write('Item Code: ');
          Readln(TransactionRecord.ItemCode);
          Write('Quantity sold: ');
          Readln(TransactionRecord.Quantity);
          TransactionRecord.Marker := 'S'; //Sold
          Write(TransactionFilePipe,TransactionRecord);
        End;
  Until Not (Response In ['Y','y']);
CloseFile(TransactionFilePipe);
100:
End.
```

P

Table 16.38 Delphi program for creating a transaction file

www.educational-computing.com/DelphiBook/Code/Chapter16/CE10.2/SequentialFileProcessing.rar

www.educational-computing.com/DelphiBook/Code/Chapter16/CE10.2/SequentialFileProcessing.rar

```
Program ViewTrans;
{$APPTYPE CONSOLE}
Uses
  System.SysUtils, Vcl.FileCtrl;
Label 100;
Type
  TransactionRecordType = Record
                            ItemCode : Integer;
                            Quantity : Integer;
                            Marker : Char;
                          End;
  TransactionFilePipeType = File Of TransactionRecordType;
Var
  TransactionRecord : TransactionRecordType;
  TransactionFilePipe : TransactionFilePipeType;
  TransactionFileName, Directory : String;
  i : Integer;
  Response : Char;
Begin
  If SelectDirectory(Directory, [sdAllowCreate, sdPerformCreate, sdPrompt],1000)
    Then Writeln(Directory);
  Write('Transaction File Name : ');
  Readln(TransactionFileName);
  If Not FileExists(TransactionFileName)
    Then
      Begin
        Writeln('ERROR: ',TransactionFileName,' does not exist in search area');
        GoTo 100;
      End;
  AssignFile(TransactionFilePipe,TransactionFileName);
  Reset(TransactionFilePipe);
  i := 0;
  While Not Eof(TransactionFilePipe)
    Do
      Begin
        If (i Mod 24 = 0) //Every 24 lines write a header
          Then
            Begin
              Write('Item Code' : 15);
              Writeln('Quantity': 25);
              Writeln;
            End;
        i := i + 1;
        Read(TransactionFilePipe,TransactionRecord);
        Write(TransactionRecord.ItemCode : 15);
        Writeln(TransactionRecord.Quantity : 25);
      End;
100:
  Writeln;
  Writeln('---------------------------------------------');
  Writeln('Press return key to exit program');
  Readln;
End.
```

Table 16.39 Delphi program for viewing a transaction file

Programming tasks

12 Using program **CreateMaster** shown in *Table 16.36* create a master file using the data shown in *Table 16.40*.

ItemCode	Description	Stock Level
1	Beans	10000
2	Broccoli	1000
3	Cornflakes	2000
4	Lard	5000
5	Muesli	6000

Table 16.40 Master file data

Now use program **ViewMaster** shown in *Table 16.37* to view and check the data that you have entered.

13 Adapt an existing program so that the master file you have created can be edited. The program should allow the user to select using *ItemCode* a particular record for editing and allow fields *Description* and *StockLevel* to be changed. Use this program to change the stock level of cornflakes to 2500.

14 Using program **CreateTrans** shown in *Table 16.38* create a transaction file using the data shown in *Table 16.41*.
Now use program **ViewTrans** shown in *Table 16.39* to view and check the data that you have entered.

15 Adapt an existing program so that the transaction file you have created can be edited.
The program should allow

1. *AmountSold* to be changed
2. A record to be deleted
3. A record to be inserted in the correct sequence

ItemCode	Amount Sold
1	5
1	2
1	1
2	1
2	2
3	2
3	3
3	1
4	3
4	4
4	1
5	2
5	4
5	2

Table 16.41 Transaction file data

16 Using program **SeqFileUp** shown in *Tables 16.33*, *16.34*, *16.35* and the master, transaction files that you created, perform a sequential file update. Use the program ViewMaster to check that the update has been successful.

Printing

Table 16.42 show a program **PrintFromConsoleMode** that can be used to print text to a printer.

`AssignPrn` is called to cause all information written to the text file variable `Pipe` to be directed to the printer.

After the variable is assigned, the application must call the `Rewrite` procedure to ready the pipe for writing.

```
Program PrintFromConsoleMode;
{$APPTYPE CONSOLE}
Uses Printers;
Var
  Pipe : TextFile;
Begin
  AssignPrn(Pipe);
  Rewrite(Pipe);
  Printer.Canvas.Font.Name := 'Wide Latin';
  Printer.Canvas.Font.Size := 12;
  Writeln(Pipe,'Hello World':20, 'Sam Spade':20);
  Printer.NewPage;
  Writeln(Pipe,'Goodbye');
  CloseFile(Pipe);
End.
```

P

www.educational-computing.com/DelphiBook/Code/Chapter16/CE10.2/Printing.rar

Table 16.42 Delphi program to print text to a printer

Table 16.43 show a program **PrintSineCurveFromConsoleMode** that can be used to print a sine curve.

```
Program PrintSineCurveFromConsoleMode;
{$APPTYPE CONSOLE}
Uses
  Printers;
Const
  Pi = 3.14159;
  Step = 18;
  Star = '*';
Var
  Theta, Radian : Real;
  Indent : Integer;
  Pipe : TextFile;
Begin
  AssignPrn(Pipe);
  Rewrite(Pipe);
  Printer.Canvas.Font.Name := 'Courier New';
  Printer.Canvas.Font.Size := 12;
  Writeln(Pipe, 'Sign Curve plot' : 50);
  Writeln(Pipe, ' -------------------------------------------------------------------------------');
  Writeln;
  Theta := 0;
  While Theta <= 360
    Do
      Begin
        Radian := Theta*Pi/180.0;
        Indent := 5 + Round(20*(1+Sin(Radian)));
        Write(Pipe, Star:Indent);
        Writeln(Pipe, Sin(Radian):30:6);
        Theta := Theta + Step;
      End;
  CloseFile(Pipe);
  Writeln('Text sent to printer');
  Readln;
End.
```

P

www.educational-computing.com/DelphiBook/Code/Chapter16/CE10.2/Printing.rar

Table 16.43 Delphi program to print a sine curve

Using a printer object to print

`Function Printer : TPrinter` creates an instance of a global **TPrinter** object the first time it is called. **Printer** is declared in the **Printers** unit.

A print job is started by a call to **BeginDoc**. The job stays open until the application calls **EndDoc**. Writing takes place directly to the printer's canvas, e.g. `Printer.Canvas.TextOut(200,200, 'Hello World')` as shown in *Table 16.44*. `Printer.Canvas` is used to generate the output page.

Use **TextOut** to write a string onto the canvas. The string will be written using the current value of **Font**.

```
Printer.Canvas.TextOut(200,200, 'Hello World');
```

Writes the string `'Hello World'` on the canvas, starting at the point `(200,200)`, and then updates the **PenPos** to the end of the string.

`Printer.NewPage` starts a new page and increments the **PageNumber** property.

NewPage forces the current print job to begin printing on a new page in the printer.

NewPage increments the value of the **PageNumber** property. It also resets the value of the **Pen** property of the `Canvas` back to (0, 0).

`ShowMessage(Printer.Printers[Printer.PrinterIndex])` displays the name of the printer in a message box as shown in *Figure 16.12*.

```
Program PrintingWithBeginEndDoc2;
{$APPTYPE CONSOLE}
Uses SysUtils, Printers, Dialogs;
Var
  Height : Integer;
  i : Integer;
Begin
  For i := 0 To Printer.Fonts.Count-1
    Do Writeln(Printer.Fonts.Strings[i]); // Shows available fonts
  ShowMessage(Printer.Printers[Printer.PrinterIndex]); // Shows name of printer that will be used
  ShowMessage('Page Height = ' + IntToStr(Printer.PageHeight));
  ShowMessage('Page Width = ' + IntToStr(Printer.PageWidth));
  Printer.Canvas.Font.Name := 'Wide Latin';
  Printer.Canvas.Font.Size := 20;
  Printer.BeginDoc;
    Printer.Canvas.TextOut(200,200, 'Hello World');
    Height := Printer.Canvas.TextHeight('Hello World');
    Printer.Canvas.TextOut(200,200 + Height , 'Hello World');
    Printer.Canvas.TextOut(200,200 + 2*Height , 'Hello World');
    ShowMessage('Page being printed currently is ' + IntToStr(Printer.PageNumber));
    Printer.NewPage;
    ShowMessage('Page being printed currently is ' + IntToStr(Printer.PageNumber));
    Printer.Canvas.Font.Size := 30;
    Printer.Canvas.TextOut(200,200, 'Goodbye World');
    Height := Printer.Canvas.TextHeight('GoodBye World');
    Printer.Canvas.TextOut(200,200 + Height , 'GoodBye World');
    Printer.Canvas.TextOut(200,200 + 2*Height , 'Goodbye World');
  Printer.EndDoc;
  Readln;
End.
```

P

www.educational-computing.com/DelphiBook/Code/Chapter16/CE10.2/Printing.rar

Table 16.44 Delphi program that uses a printer object to print

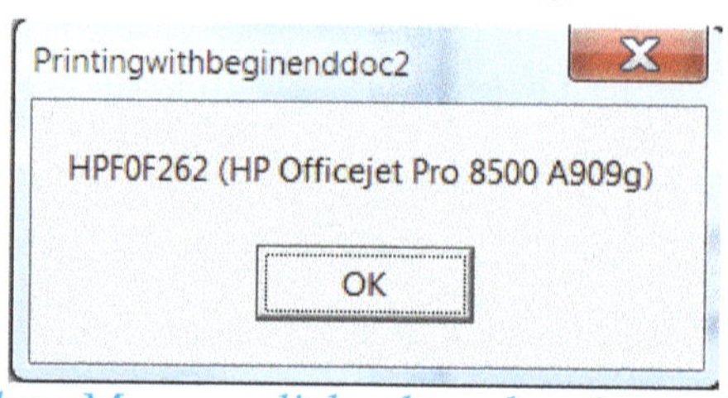

Fig. 16.12 ShowMessage dialog box showing printer name

17 Recursion

Recursion

Purpose: To become familiar with the use of recursive techniques (general and base cases and the mechanism for implementation)

What is Recursion?

Recursion occurs in situations where an object partially consists of or is defined in terms of itself. *Fig. 17.1* shows a recursive picture. The picture consists of increasingly smaller versions of itself.

Fig. 17.1 Recursive picture

The power of recursion lies in its possibility of defining an infinite set of objects by a finite statement.

Information

To understand recursion, you must understand recursion.

For example,

Recursive picture = Picture

Or

Recursive Picture = Recursive Picture + Recursive Picture x Magnification factor of 0.9

The original picture, Picture, is shown in *Fig. 17.2*.

In computer science, we may define data structures in this way, i.e. in terms of themselves.

Fig. 17.2 Original picture

To see how this is possible, consider a simple shopping list which starts out empty. We will call this an empty shopping list or a list with no elements or items.

Now we use a rule to turn this simple case into something slightly less simple:

> *We take the (empty) list and construct a list one bigger by attaching an item to the beginning.*

This seems at first to be a circular definition, i.e. a definition of something in terms of itself. But it isn't because we start somewhere, the **base case** which is the empty list.

In *Fig. 17.1* the base case is the original picture, Picture.
The next largest (0.9 x base case) is then painted/stuck on top and the next largest on top of this and so on using the recursive definition shown above.

Fig. 17.3 shows a list example which illustrates how it is possible to view a structure as being recursively defined.
The recursive definition of a list is

- the empty list with zero items in it, or
- an item followed by a list

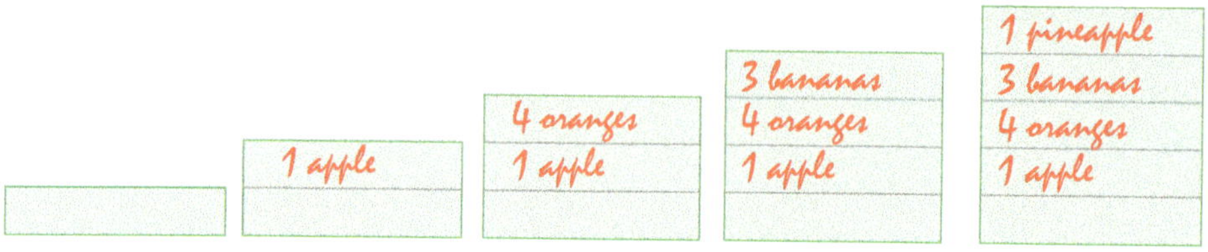

Empty shopping list with zero items in it	Shopping list = an item 1 apple followed by an empty list	Shopping list = an item 4 oranges followed by another smaller list	Shopping list = an item 3 bananas followed by another smaller list	Shopping list = an item 1 pineapple followed by another smaller list

Fig. 17.3 Shopping list consisting of an item and another list

> ## Key concept
> **Recursive definition:**
> A recursive definition is one that is defined in terms of itself.
> **Recursively-defined function/procedure:**
> A recursively-defined function/procedure is a function/procedure which calls itself or which is defined in terms of itself.
> **Recursive object:**
> An object is said to be recursive if it partially consists of or is defined in terms of itself.

The true usefulness of a recursive definition comes from going the other way:

> If what you are dealing with meets the recursive definition, then there is usually a way to move back towards the base case, getting simpler and simpler along the way.

This is what recursive programming does.

All recursive functions/procedures follow a similar pattern:

- Am I at the base case? If so, return the easy solution if a function, and stop recursing; if a procedure stop recursing.
- Otherwise, think in terms of solving the current problem by moving closer to the base case with a slightly simpler problem and solving this simpler problem.

Fig. 17.4 Billiard balls in frame

For example, suppose we wanted to calculate how many billiard balls fit an equilateral triangle frame where the length of side is measured as the number of billiard balls that fit along the side, e.g. see Fig. 17.4.

We can use the recursive definition

```
If NoAlongSide = 1
  NoOfBilliardBallsInTriangle(1) = 1
If NoAlongSide > 1
  NoOfBilliardBallsInTriangle(NoAlongSide) = NoAlongSide + NoOfBilliardBallsInTriangle(NoAlongSide – 1)
```

So, for example, if the calculation is for a triangle with number of balls along the side 4 then we find a simpler case to solve first, the number of balls in a triangle with number of balls along the side 3 - see Fig. 17.5.

Fig. 17.5 Billiard ball in equilateral triangles

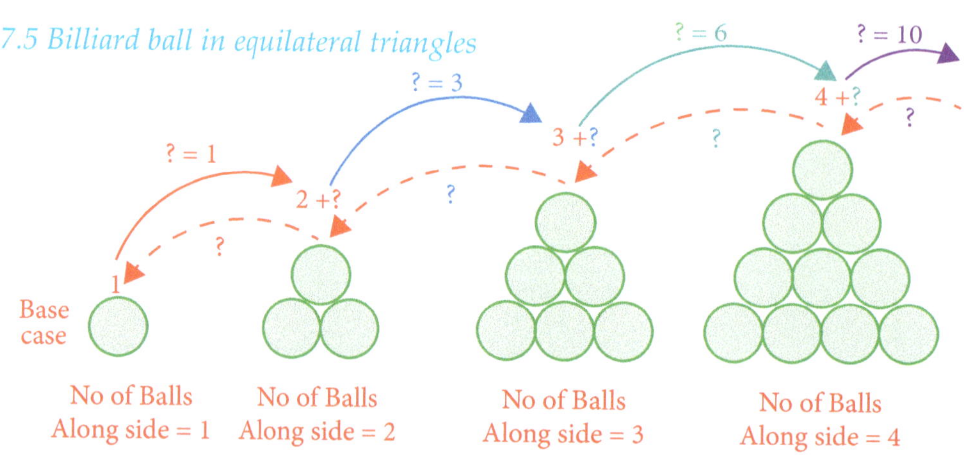

This simpler problem can be solved by first solving an even simpler problem, the number of balls in a triangle with number of balls along the side 2 which in turn can be solved by first solving for one ball, the **base case**.

This has the solution 1.

We can now solve for side 2, it is 2 + 1 = 3.

Next we solve for side 3, it is 3 + 3 = 6 and finally we solve for side 4, it is 4 + 6 = 10.

We could have drawn a triangle of side 4 and simple counted the total number of billiard balls.

So why express the solution to this problem recursively?

Well, the side 4 example is trivial but suppose we want to calculate the number of balls in a triangle of side 1000. This is not a trivial problem to solve. However, it can be done by recursion easily.

Fig. 17.6 shows a pseudo-code function which returns 1 if the side is 1 else it returns the result of the calculation

NoAlongSide + NoOfBilliardBallsInTriangle(NoAlongSide - 1)

Key principle

The power of recursion lies in the fact that an infinite number of computations can be described by a finite recursive program which may contain no explicit repetitions.

```
Function NoOfBilliardBallsInTriangle(NoAlongSide : Integer) : Integer
  If NoAlongSide = 1
    Then Return 1
    Else Return NoAlongSide + NoOfBilliardBallsInTriangle(NoAlongSide - 1)
  EndIf
End Function
```

Fig. 17.6 Pseudo-code function which calculates no of billiard balls in a triangle of given size

Fig. 17.7 shows this pseudo-code implemented in Delphi as a recursive function `NoOfBilliardBallsInTriangle` with parameter `NoAlongSide`.

When this function is called with 1000 substituted for `NoAlongSide`, i.e `NoOfBilliardBallsInTriangle 1000` the result returned is 500500 - *Fig. 17.7*.

```
Program NoOfBilliardBallsInTriangleProject;

{$APPTYPE CONSOLE}

{$R *.res}

Uses
  System.SysUtils;

Function NoOfBilliardBallsInTriangle(NoAlongSide : Integer) : Integer;
  Begin
    If NoAlongSide = 1
      Then Result := 1
      Else Result := NoAlongSide + NoOfBilliardBallsInTriangle(NoAlongSide - 1)
  End;
Begin
  Writeln(NoOfBilliardBallsInTriangle(1000));
  Readln;
End.
```

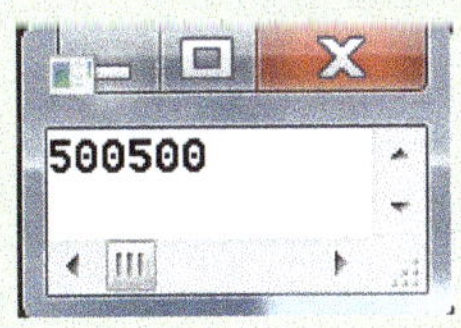

Fig. 17.7 NoOfBilliardBallsInTriangleProject which calculates no of billiard balls in a triangle of given size

Worked example

The task is to calculate the sum of the first *n* natural numbers recursively,
e.g. if n = 5 then the Sum = 1 + 2 + 3 + 4 + 5.
First find the **base case**:

If n = 1 then Sum = 1.

Next find the **general case**:

If n > 1 Then Sum = n + Sum(n -1).

Table 17.1 shows a trace table of recursive calls. The last call is to the base case.

Fig. 17.8 shows a pseudo-code function which calculates the sum of the first *n* natural numbers recursively.

Call no	Sum(n)	Return
1	Sum(5)	5 + Sum(4)
2	Sum(4)	4 + Sum(3)
3	Sum(3)	3 + Sum(2)
4	Sum(2)	2 + Sum(1)
5	Sum(1)	1

Table 17.1 Calculating Sum(5) recursively

```
Function Sum(n : Integer) : Integer
  If n = 1
    Then Return 1
    Else Return n + Sum(n-1)
  EndIf
End Function
```

Fig. 17.8 Pseudo-code function which calculates sum of first n natural numbers

Questions

1. Write in pseudo-code a recursively-defined function Product which calculates the product of the first *n* natural numbers, e.g. n = 5, product = 1 x 2 x 3 x 4 x 5.
Complete the trace table shown in *Table 17.2* for this function.

Call no	Product(n)	Return
1	Product(5)	
2		
3		
4		
5		

Table 17.2 Calculating Product(5) recursively

2. Write in pseudo-code a recursively-defined function CountOfNoOfBallsInPyramid which calculates the number of billiard balls that can be stacked on top of each other if the base layer is contained in an equilateral triangle of side *n* balls as illustrated in *Figure 17.9* with a pyramid of side 4 balls for its base. (Hint: You may use the function in *Figure 17.6* in your answer).

Fig. 17.9 Pyramid with triangular base

3. A recursive definition is one that is defined in terms of itself.
For example,

digit string is a digit or a digit followed by a digit string

This can be expressed in the following notation:

<digit string> ::= <digit> | <digit> <digit string>

where ::= means "consists of", | means "Or",
<digit> means 0 or 1 or 2 or 3 or 4 ... or 9, i.e. <digit> ::= 0|1|2|3|4|5|6|7|8|9

(a)

(i) Is the number 234 a valid digit string?

(ii) State the reasoning which you used in arriving at your answer to (a)(ii).

(b)

(i) Explain why the number 2·34 is not a valid digit string.

(ii) How would you modify the recursive definition of digit string to make 2·34 a valid digit string?

Questions

4 *Fig. 17.10* shows a recursively-defined function Power(y, n) which calculates y^n for positive integers. Complete the trace table shown in *Table 17.3* for the function call Power(2, 4).

Call no	Power(y, n)	Return
1	Power(2, 4)	
2		
3		
4		
5		

Table 17.3 Calculating Power(2, 4)

```
Function Power(y, n : Integer) : Integer
  If n >= 0
    Then
      If n = 0
        Then Return 1
        Else Return y * Power(y, n-1)
      EndIf
    Else Output 'n must be greater than or equal to 0'
  EndIf
End Function
```

Fig. 17.10 Pseudo-code function Power which calculates y^n

Programming tasks

1. Write a program which implements the pseudocode shown in *Fig. 17.8*.
2. Write a program which implements your pseudocode answer to question 1.
3. Write a program which implements your pseudocode answer to question 2.
4. Write a program which implements the pseudocode shown in *Fig. 17.10*.

Role of stack in recursion

It is possible to associate a set of local objects with a function/procedure – local variables, constants, types and other functions/procedures.

These local objects have no existence outside this function/procedure.

Each time such a function/procedure is activated recursively, a new set of local variables is created.

Although this new set will have the same names as any previous sets that are created during the recursion, their values are distinct.

Any conflict in naming is avoided by the rules of scope of identifiers: the identifiers always refer to the most recently created set of identifiers.

The same rule holds for function/procedure parameters which by definition are bound to the function/procedure.

Each new set of local variables is allocated space in an area of main memory called a **stack**.

The space allocated to each new set of variables is referred to as a **stack frame**.

The function/procedure's parameters also go into this stack frame.

In addition, each stack frame

- stores a return address – used by the computer to resume execution of the program at the correct place after executing a procedure
- stores the contents of registers needed at different stages in the execution of a program so that the values may be restored to their correct values after a function/procedure call. The function/procedure can write its own values into these registers whilst it is executing.

Stack frames are covered in *Chapter 13*.

Provoking stack overflow

Many recursive calls mean many stack frames. There is a limit on the amount of main memory set aside as a stack. There is always a danger of running out of stack space during recursion. When this happens **STACK OVERFLOW** is said to occur (or a stack full error occurs).

It is possible to get the computer to detect when stack overflow is about to occur. The recursion can then be aborted and the error message STACK OVERFLOW reported - see *Fig. 17.11*.

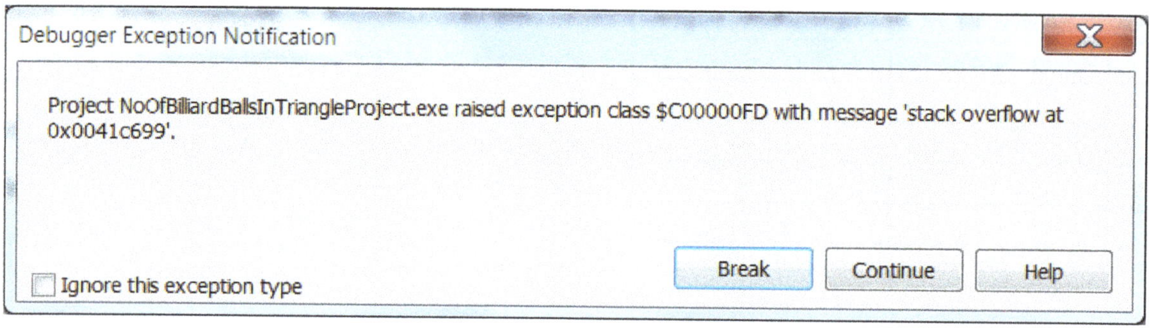

Fig. 17.11 NoOfBilliardBallsInTriangleProject running with debugger enabled and NoOfBilliardBallsInTriangle function called with n = 1000000

If stack overflow is not detected and prevented then the consequences can be quite disastrous. The recursion will ignore the fact that stack space is exhausted. It will carry on creating new stack frames using main memory beyond the region of the stack. Usually this is main memory allocated to the program. The consequence is that the program is overwritten and the computer "crashes". A reboot may then be necessary.

The detection and prevention of stack overflow must be switched on at the time of compiling the recursive program. Stack overflow should be trapped using **Try Except** as shown in *Fig. 17.12*.

```
Program NoOfBilliardBallsInTriangleModifiedProject;

{$APPTYPE CONSOLE}

{$R *.res}

Uses
  System.SysUtils;

Function NoOfBilliardBallsInTriangle(NoAlongSide : Integer) : Integer;
  Begin
    If NoAlongSide = 1
      Then Result := 1
      Else Result := NoAlongSide + NoOfBilliardBallsInTriangle(NoAlongSide - 1)
  End;
Begin
  Try
    Writeln(NoOfBilliardBallsInTriangle(1000000));
  Except
    On EStackOverflow Do Writeln('Stack Overflow');
  End;  Readln;
End.
```

Fig. 17.12 NoOfBilliardBallsInTriangleModifiedProject which handles stack overflow exception

When to use recursion and when not to use recursion

Recursive definitions such as shown in *Fig. 17.13* do not guarantee that a recursive algorithm is the best way to solve a problem.

For example, Fibonacci (4) calls Fibonacci (3) and Fibonacci (2). But Fibonacci (3) also calls Fibonacci (2). Thus, the algorithm repeats computations unnecessarily.

```
Function Fibonacci(n : NonNegativeInteger) : NonNegativeInteger
  If n <= 1
    Then Return n
    Else Return Fibonacci(n - 1) + Fibonacci(n - 2)
  EndIf
End Function
```

Fig. 17.13 Pseudo-code function Fibonacci

This is a strong case for using a non-recursive solution.
Non-recursive solutions rely on iteration to perform the computation.
For example, the recursive picture in *Fig. 17.1* could be generated by iteration[1] as shown in *Fig. 17.14*.

```
MagnificationFactor ← 1
Repeat
  Draw Picture * MagnificationFactor
  MagnificationFactor ← MagnificationFactor * 0.9
Until False
```

Fig. 17.14 Non-recursive pseudo-code to generate recursive picture

The Fibonacci number sequence is defined mathematically by a recurrence relation as shown in *Fig. 17.15*.
A recurrence relation is an equation that recursively defines a sequence of values, once one or more initial terms are given.

The Fibonacci sequence is defined using the recurrence

$$F_n = F_{n-1} + F_{n-2}$$

with seed values

$$F_0 = 0 \text{ and } F_1 = 1$$

Fig. 17.15 Recurrence relation which generates the Fibonacci number sequence 0, 1, 1, 2, 3, 5, 8, 13, 21, 34, 55, ...

A non-recursive solution which uses iteration to generate the Fibonacci series is shown in *Fig. 17.16*.
The non-recursive iterative solution generates Fibonacci numbers more efficiently in both time and space than its recursive equivalent because

- it involves fewer computations
- it only uses one stack frame

Recursive algorithms are particularly appropriate when the underlying problem or the data to be processed are defined in recursive terms and the definition does not involve simple recurrence relations such as illustrated by the Fibonacci sequence.

1 The Repeat Until *condition* loop repeats until the condition is True but it will never be True as we have used False for the value of the condition. We have created an infinite loop.

```
Function Fibonacci (n : NonNegativeInteger) : NonNegativeInteger
  Var
    First, Second, i : Integer
    First ← 0
    Second ← 1
    If n <= 1
      Then Return n
      Else
        For i ← 1 To (n - 1)
          Next ← First + Second
          First ← Second
          Second ← Next
        EndFor
        Return First
    EndIf
End Function
```

Fig. 17.16 Non-recursive pseudo-code function Fibonacci

Key concept

Base case:

When designing a recursive algorithm/procedure/function, it is important to avoid generating an infinite sequence of calls on itself else the recursion will never terminate. This requires that there must be a "way out" of the sequence of recursive calls. This is called the base case. The base case stops the recursion.

A recursive function/procedure F must be defined for at least one parameter/argument or group of parameters/arguments in terms that do not involve F.

This is usually a single non-recursive statement.

General case:

The general case is defined by the statement or statements in a recursive function/procedure F which reference F. The general case is responsible for the recursion.

Questions

5. Explain why there is always a potential to run out of stack space when a recursive function is called.

6. *Fig. 17.17* shows a recursively-defined function Factorial(n) which calculates n! for non-negative integers. Complete the trace table shown in *Table 17.4* for the function call Factorial(4).

```
Function Factorial(n : PositiveInteger) : PositiveInteger
  If (n = 0) Or (n = 1)
    Then Return 1
    Else Return n * Factorial(n-1)
  EndIf
End Function
```

Fig. 17.17 Pseudo-code function Factorial

7. Write the non-recursively-defined equivalent of the Factorial function using pseudo-code.

8. How many function calls are required when the non-recursive Factorial function is called with argument 4?

Call no	Factorial(n)	Return
1	Factorial(4)	
2		
3		
4		

Table 17.4 Calculating Factorial(4)

Programming tasks

1. Write a Delphi program which defines and uses the following recursively-defined functions which take positive integer arguments:

   (a) Factorial(n) (b) Fibonacci(n) (c) CountOfNoOfBallsInPyramid(NoAlongBaseSide)

2. For at least one of the recursively-defined functions in Task 1, try to cause stack overflow.

18 Structured programming

Learning objectives:

- *Understand the structured approach to program design and construction*
- *Be able to construct hierarchy charts when designing programs*
- *Be able to explain the advantages of the structured approach*

Procedural-oriented programming

The structured approach to program design and construction

Software artefact

The end result of program design and construction is an artefact, a piece of software that when executed solves some given problem, hopefully the one required to be solved.

Design

"Design" means to plan or mark out the form and method of solution.

All forms of engineering including software engineering are characterised by the engineer's dissatisfaction with the achievement of just any old solution. Engineering seeks the best solution (judged by factors such as efficiency, maintainability, reliability), within recognised constraints, while making compromises required by working in the real world.

Software design takes a real-world problem and produces a plan for a computer-based solution.

> **Key term**
>
> **Design:**
> To plan or mark out the form and method of solution.

Structured design

Structured design is a disciplined process of deciding which components interconnected in which way will solve some well-specified problem.

Structured design relies on a principle known since the days of Julius Caesar:

DIVIDE and CONQUER

A problem is divided into smaller and smaller sub problems, so that each sub problem will eventually correspond to a **component of the system** which solves the problem.

The partitioning process into smaller and smaller sub problems is done until the sub problems are

- manageably small, and
- solvable separately, i.e. relatively independent of one another.

> **Key term**
>
> **Structured design:**
> Structured design is a disciplined process of deciding which components interconnected in which way will solve some well-specified problem.
> A problem is divided into smaller and smaller sub problems, so that each sub problem will eventually correspond to a component of the system which solves the problem.
> The partitioning process into smaller and smaller sub problems is done until the sub problems are
> - manageably small, and
> - solvable separately, i.e. relatively independent of one another.

Good design

Good design is an exercise in partitioning and organising the pieces of the system so that each is

- cohesive, and
- loosely coupled

We call the pieces of the system, modules or components or units.

The modules/components/units are plugged together to create the system. Modules/components/units can be implemented as subroutines (procedures and functions).

> **Key principle**
>
> **Good design:**
> Good design is an exercise in partitioning and organising the pieces of the system so that each is
> - cohesive, and
> - loosely coupled

Cohesive/Cohesion

Cohesion measures the strength of the interconnection between elements within a module.

To achieve cohesion, highly interrelated parts of the real-world **problem** should be in the same piece of the **software system**, i.e. things that belong together should go together.

Figure 18.1 shows a schematic mapping from a problem in a real-world system to a highly-cohesive software architecture of a structured design for a computer-based system to solve the problem.

Figure 18.2 shows a specific example of a simple calculator system. Note the one-to-one mapping between real-world system and the computer-based system.

To achieve a solution in which modules/components are highly-cohesive the software system needs to be broken down into modules

- which are highly independent and
- which accomplish a single objective.

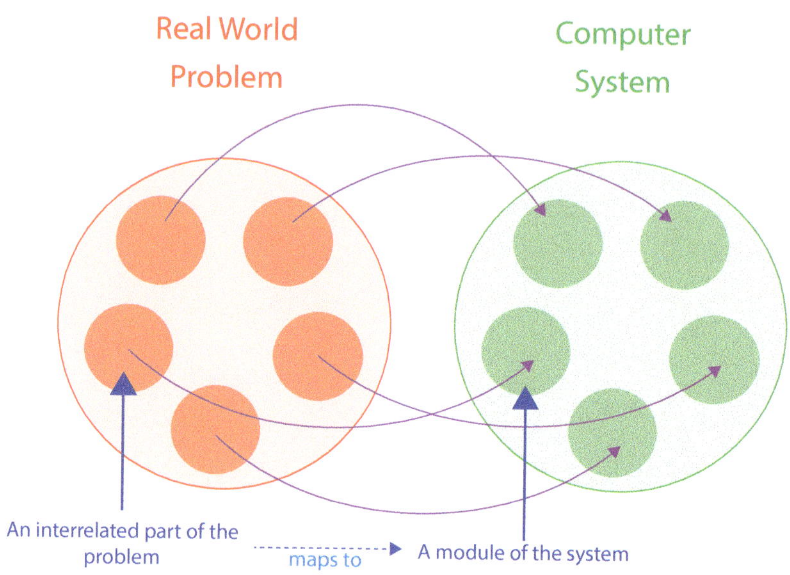

Figure 18.1 Mapping of problem parts to system modules

The aim is to achieve **functional cohesion**, i.e. modules which contain only one function or perform only one logically-related task.

For example,

- CalculateSquare
- GetDate

One good way to determine if modules are (functionally) cohesive is to write a phrase fully describing what the module does.

Analysis of this phrase can indicate whether or not the module is (functionally) cohesive. The module is not (functionally) cohesive if the phrase is or contains one of the following:

- A compound sentence such as
  - Edit Student Name AND Test Scores
  - Get two operands AND Add these
- A lack of a specific object
  - Edit all Data
- Words relating to time such as
  - Initialisation
- Words such as "house-keeping" or "clean-up" because these imply more than one task.

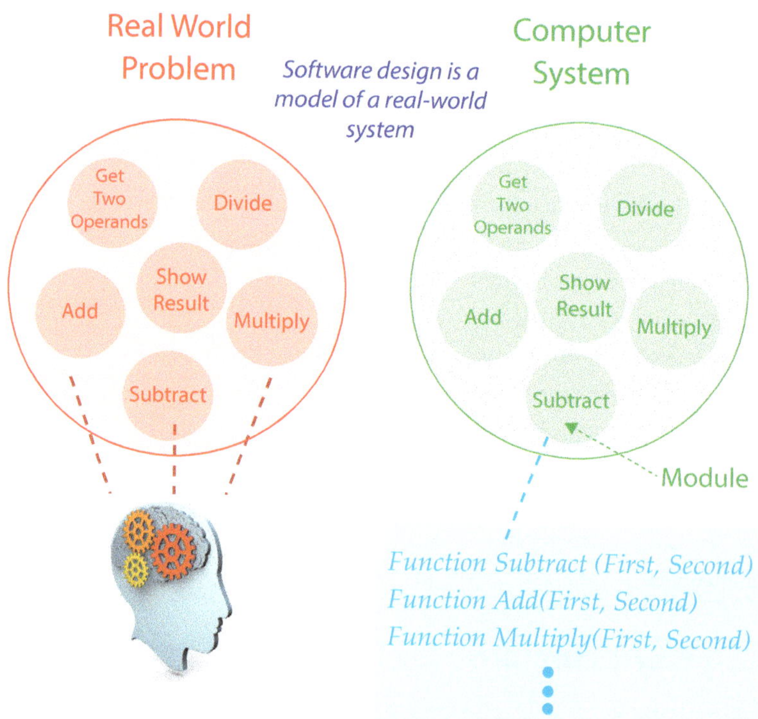

Figure 18.2 Highly interrelated parts of the problem should be in the same piece of the system

The functional description should not define the code within the module but how the module appears to the coder, e.g. `Subtract`.

The highest level of cohesion, referred to as **functional cohesion**, is a module in which

- every element is an integral part of a single function (task), and
- every element is essential to the performance of a single function (task)

Some advantages of using modules with high cohesion:

- The module can easily be replaced by any other serving the same purpose since what it does is localised within the module, i.e. it has no side-effects when it executes
- In the event of program failure,
  - it should be easier to locate the error as being in the module
  - it should be easier to discount the module as a source of error
- Different developers can work on individual modules because each is an independent unit.

Key terms

Cohesion:

Cohesion measures the strength of the interconnection between elements within a module.

Functional cohesion:

Functional cohesion is the highest level of cohesion. A functionally cohesive module is one in which

- every element is an integral part of a single function (task), and
- every element is essential to the performance of a single function (task)

Questions

1. What is the process known as design?
2. What is structured design?
3. What is meant by the term *cohesive* when applied to a module or component of a system?
4. A procedure in a calculator program is described as "Adding two operands and displaying the result".
   (a) Explain why this procedure is not considered functionally cohesive.
   (b) What can be done to achieve functional cohesion in this case?
5. State **two** advantages of using modules with high cohesion.

Loosely coupled

Coupling measures the strength of relationships between modules.

The objective of structured design is to minimise the coupling between modules, so that they will be as independent as possible.

The lower the coupling, the less likely that other modules will have to be considered in order to

- create a module
- understand a given module
- debug a given module
- change a given module.

Coupling results from connections.

A connection exists when an element of code references a location in memory defined outside the module.

Some connection must exist among modules in a program, or else they would not be part of the same program.

The objective is to **minimise the coupling among modules**.

Key term

Coupling:

Coupling measures the strength of relationships between modules. The objective of structured design is to minimise the coupling between modules, so that they will be as independent as possible. Coupling results from connections. A connection exists when an element of code references a location in memory defined outside the module.

To minimise coupling among modules:

- Subroutines or modules should only be allowed to access that data which they need to perform their assigned task
- All data transfer between modules is visible in the module parameters
- There must be no hidden flows of data via global variables or shared data areas
- There should be no control information passing between modules, e.g. Boolean flags
- The number of module parameters should be minimal.

Loose coupling is achieved when a module's data interface with other modules is its module parameter list. Here we interpret module to mean a subroutine (procedure/function).

Figure 18.3 shows a procedure `DisplayMessage` defined with the language keywords `Procedure` and `Begin` and `End`.

The data interface for `DisplayMessage` is the parameter list `Message : String`.
The procedure `DisplayMessage` is called with actual parameter value `'Hello World'` in *Figure 18.3*.

```
Program DisplayMessageExample;
{$APPTYPE Console}
Procedure DisplayMessage (Message : String);
  Begin
    Writeln(Message);
  End;
Begin
  DisplayMessage('Hello World');
  Readln;
End.
```

Figure 18.3 Delphi program with procedure DisplayMessage

The Delphi program in *Figure 18.4* has declared a global variable `Message` which in Delphi is visible within procedure `DisplayMessage`. The procedure `DisplayMessage` has dispensed with a procedure parameter list and instead relies on accessing the global variable `Message`. The procedure `DisplayMessage` in *Figure 18.4* has a higher coupling with its program than `DisplayMessage` does in *Figure 18.3*.

```
Program DisplayMessageExampleGlobal;
{$APPTYPE Console}
Var
  Message : String;
Procedure DisplayMessage;
  Begin
    Writeln(Message);
  End;
Begin
  Message := 'Hello World';
  DisplayMessage;
  Readln;
End.
```

Figure 18.4 Delphi program with procedure DisplayMessage without a parameter list

Questions

6 What is *coupling* when applied to modules or components of a system?

7 Why should coupling between modules be minimised?

8 How does coupling between modules arise?

9 How can coupling between modules be minimised?

10 Give **two** reasons why the pseudo-code in *Figure 18.5* could be considered a poor design by structured design standards.

11 Suggest **one** reason why the procedure `DisplayMessage` in *Figure 18.6* could be considered poorly designed by structured design standards.

12 How could the design of procedure `DisplayMessage` and the program be changed to reflect good structured design?

```
Program Exercise1
Var
  No1, No2 : Integer
Procedure AddTwoNumbers
  Output No1 + No2
End Procedure
Begin
  No1 ← 4
  No2 ← 5
  AddTwoNumbers
End
```

Figure 18.5 Pseudo-code to add two numbers

```
Program Question11;
{$APPTYPE CONSOLE}
Uses SysUtils;
Procedure DisplayMessage(Message : String; Upper : Boolean);
  Begin
    If Upper
      Then Writeln(UpperCase(Message))
      Else Writeln(Message)
  End;
Begin
  DisplayMessage('hello world', False);
  DisplayMessage('hello world', True);
  Readln;
End.
```

Figure 18.6 Delphi program that uses a procedure DisplayMessage with a flag parameter

13 A procedure `Initialise` is defined with a long parameter list of reference formal parameters, i.e. each formal parameter is a pointer type which when replaced by an actual parameter will point to a variable outside the procedure:

```
Procedure Initialise(Var a, b, c, d, e, f, g, h, i, j, k, l, m, n, p : Integer)
```

Why is this considered a poor design by the standards of structured design?

14 A program contains a module A, module B and other modules. Module A writes to a disk file and module B reads from a disk file. When module A is engaged in writing to a disk file no other module may access the same disk file. When module A has finished writing to a disk file it closes it. The program calls module A on file Z followed by module B on file Z. Would you describe the coupling between module A and module B as low or high? Explain.

Simple calculator example which illustrates cohesion and loose coupling

Suppose that we are required to demonstrate structured design in a simple way.

We choose to do this by designing and creating a very simple calculator that is limited to performing integer arithmetic on two given operands.

The arithmetic operations that must be supported are

1. Add
2. Subtract
3. Multiply
4. Divide (Integer division)

The major "pieces" of the system are

1. The system must display to the user the choices which are available for arithmetic operation
2. The system must obtain the user's choice of arithmetic operation
3. The system must obtain two operands from the user
4. The system must carry out the chosen operatioon the two operands
5. The system must have a "piece" to do each of the following
   5.1 Add
   5.2 Subtract
   5.3 Multiply
   5.4 Divide (Integer division)
6. The system must display the result to the user.

> **Key term**
>
> **Hierarchy chart:**
> In structured design of software, the partition of a software system into its component parts can expressed as a hierarchy chart which shows the components (subroutines) and how they are interconnected.

Structured design is then used to decide which modules/components to use to solve this problem.

Structured design tells us that each piece identified above in 1, 2, 3, 4, 5.1, 5.2, 5.3, 5.4, 6 above should be a module of the system - *Figure 18.2*.

In this simple example, these modules/components can then be implemented in a programming language as subroutines.

Hierarchy charts

We show the **software architecture** of the simple calculator system resulting from the structured design approach in *Figure 18.7*. We call this a **hierarchy chart**.

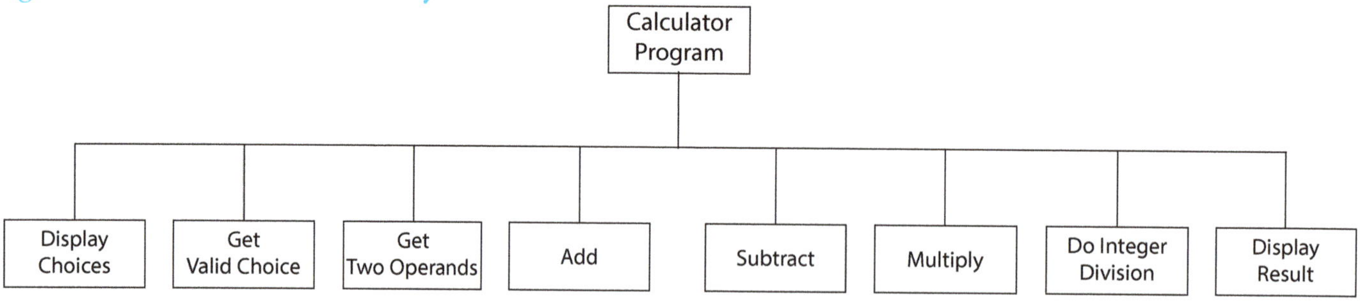

Figure 18.7 Hierarchy chart showing the software architecture of the simple calculator system

This doesn't tell the whole story because the chart doesn't show the coupling between the modules/components.
Loose coupling is achieved when a module's data interface with other modules is its module parameter list.
By adding the parameter list for each module to the chart we can show that its data interface is indeed that required for low coupling - *Figure 18.8*.
The meaning of the symbols used in *Figure 18.8* are shown in *Figure 18.9*.

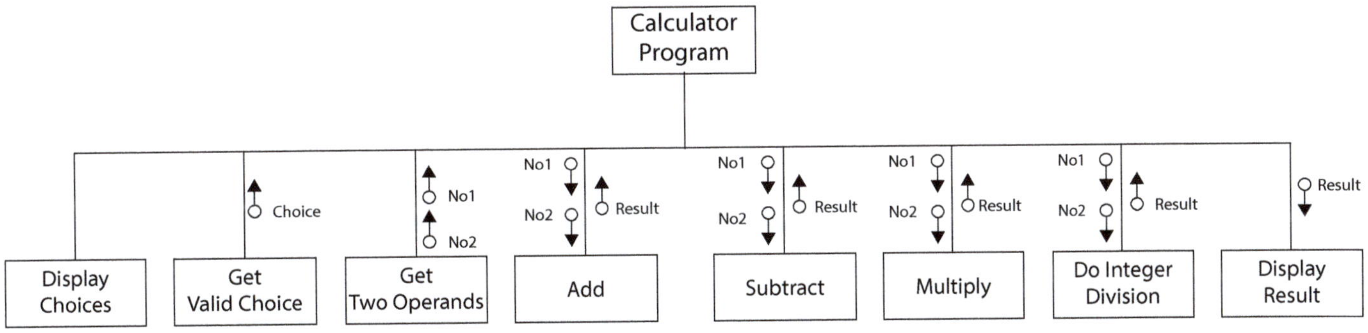

Figure 18.8 Hierarchy chart showing the software architecture of the simple calculator system and the parameter list/data interface of each module

The parameter `Choice` is the only parameter of module `GetChoice`. It is an OUT parameter. The value returned by `GetChoice` is used by the Calculator Program to choose from among modules `Add`, `Subtract`, `Multiply` and `DoIntegerDivision`.

Module `Add` has three parameters in its data interface: `No1`, `No2` and `Result`. `No1` and `No2` are IN parameters. `Result` is an OUT parameter.

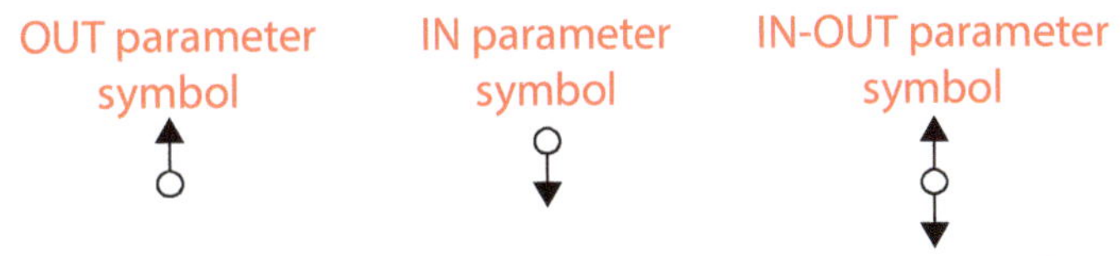

Figure 18.9 The meaning of the symbols shown in Figure 1.2.1.9

Sometimes a module needs to use an IN-OUT parameter because it processes the value passed in by an IN-OUT parameter and then exports a new value from the module in the same IN-OUT parameter.

The chart in *Figure 18.8* just shows the architectural breakdown of the system into its software components and the data interfaces between these components. If we add control to the hierarchy chart as shown in *Figure 18.10* we will get the program's structure, e.g. if the value of `Choice` is, say `'S'` or `'s'`, the program should choose to execute the `Subtract` module and not `Add`, `Multiply` or `DoIntegerDivision`. This is indicated with the option symbol o placed in the top-right corner of the module rectangle.

The **control hierarchy chart** shown in *Figure 18.10* is read from left to right, i.e. module `DisplayChoice` is executed first followed by module `GetChoice`, and so on. A `Repeat Until Choice In ['Q', 'q']` has been added to indicate that the left to right sequence is repeated until the user chooses to quit.

Figure 18.11 shows the program structure in Delphi using procedures. The program structure could also have been written using functions if required. You can see that the control hierarchy chart maps one-to-one to the structure of its program equivalent.

The option symbol o placed in the top-right corner of the module rectangle for `Add`, `Subtract`, `Multiply` and `DoIntegerDivision` has been mapped to a Case statement in *Figure 18.11*.

Key term

Control hierarchy chart:

A control hierarchy chart shows the structure of the program in chart form.

It can also show the parameter list for each module/subroutine in the chart.

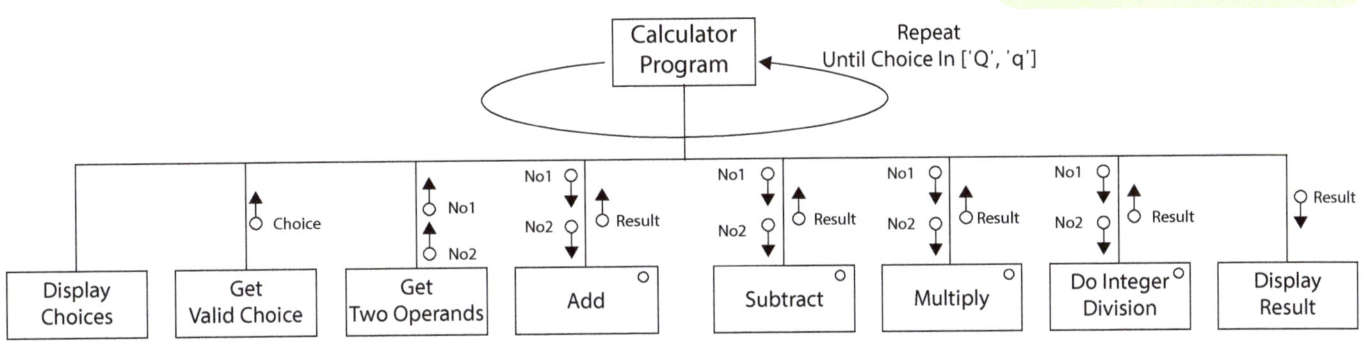

Figure 18.10 Control hierarchy chart showing the software architecture of the simple calculator system, the parameter list/data interface of each module and the program's structure

```
Program SimpleCalculator;
  Procedure DisplayChoices;
    Begin
    End;
  Procedure GetValidChoice(Var Choice : Char);
    Begin
    End;
  Procedure GetTwoOperands(Var No1, No2 : Integer);
    Begin
    End;
  Procedure Add(No1, No2 : Integer; Var Result : Integer);
    Begin
    End;
  Procedure Subtract(No1, No2 : Integer; Var Result : Integer);
    Begin
    End;
  Procedure Multiply(No1, No2 : Integer; Var Result : Integer);
    Begin
    End;
  Procedure DoIntegerDivision(No1, No2 : Integer; Var Result : Integer);
    Begin
    End;
  Procedure DisplayResult(Result : Integer);
    Begin
    End;
Var
  UsersChoice : Char = 'A';
  FirstNo : Integer = 0;
  SecondNo : Integer = 0;
  Answer : Integer = 0;
Begin
  Repeat
    DisplayChoices;
    GetValidChoice(UsersChoice);
    GetTwoOperands(FirstNo, SecondNo);
    Case UsersChoice of
      'A', 'a' : Add(FirstNo, SecondNo, Answer);
      'S', 's' : Subtract(FirstNo, SecondNo, Answer);
      'M', 'm' : Multiply(FirstNo, SecondNo, Answer);
      'D', 'd' : DoIntegerDivision(FirstNo, SecondNo, Answer);
      'Q', 'q' : ;
    End;
    DisplayResult(Answer);
  Until UsersChoice In ['Q', 'q'];
End.
```

Var denotes that parameter is IN-OUT but in this example it is used as an OUT parameter

Formal parameter

IN only parameters

Actual parameters

Figure 18.11 Program structure in Pascal of simple calculator written as procedures

Programming task

1. Create a simple calculator program based on the program structure shown in *Figure 18.11* in Delphi.

Structured design does not address the issue of how to write the program for the body of each procedure only the division of a system into its components and how those components fit together to produce a solution.

To write the program for the body of the procedures we use the **principles of structured programming**.

Structured programming

The principles

Structured programming advocates a *disciplined approach* to the construction of programs in order to avoid problems which can arise if the approach is not disciplined.

At the lowest level, the main principles of structured programming are concerned with the **flow of control** through a program unit such as shown in *Figure 18.12*. The most fundamental idea is that the **main flow** of control through a program unit should be from **top to bottom** of the program.

This translates to **every block** (sequence, selection and iteration) should have **one entry point and one exit point**.

In *Figure 18.12* this means that the flow of control enters at the top of a dotted block and exits at the bottom. Within a block, the flow doesn't have to be forward, e.g. iteration.

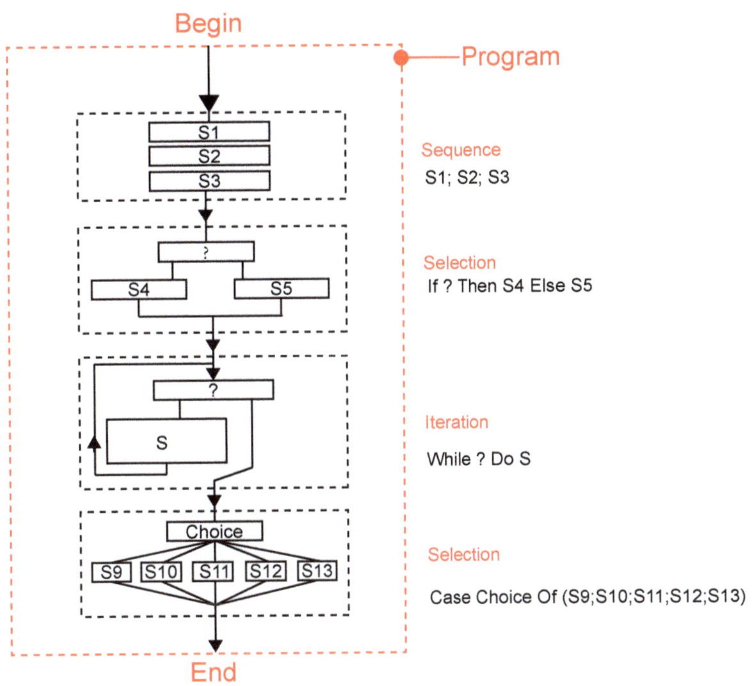

Figure 18.12 Program unit showing flow of control from top to bottom through the three basic control constructs, sequence, selection and iteration

There are three basic control constructs necessary to build any program:

- Sequence - a list of program statements which are executed one after another (i.e. in sequence), e.g. `x := x + 1; y := y + 2; z := 6;`
- Selection - a means of choosing between two or more sequences of statements depending on the value of some condition(s), e.g. `If Then Else`
- Iteration - a construct to allow controlled repetition of a sequence of statements, e.g. `While x < 5 Do Something`.

It can be shown that these **three constructs** are sufficient to implement the control structure of any algorithm.

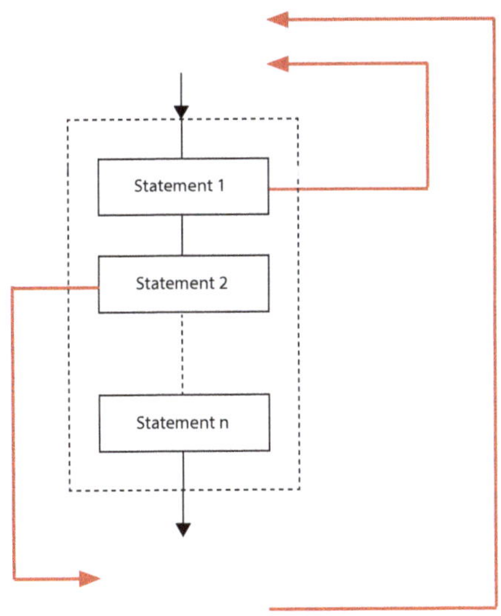

Figure 18.13 Part of a program unit showing flow of control jumping backwards and forwards between blocks

Structured programming is also known as *gotoless* programming because it avoids the use of the **Go To** control construct. If a label (e.g. `step1`) is attached to a statement in a program then the flow of control can jump to the labelled statement from anywhere in the program which references the label in a `Go To step1`. *Figure 18.13* shows how the flow of control can jump backwards and forwards when Go To statements are used; each red line is a transfer of control caused by a Go To statement.

In Delphi, a numeric label is declared using the language keyword `Label`. In *Figure 18.14* a numeric label `100` is declared with `Label 100` and then used by `GoTo 100` in the `Begin End` program block.

Structured programming doesn't mean that Go To should be avoided at all cost. There is one situation where it is the preferred solution. This is when something has gone wrong within the program, e.g. an attempt is made to open a nonexistent file. In this circumstance, it is often better to jump to the end of the program because to avoid use of Go To in this circumstance can often result in a difficult to understand and convoluted program.

The flow is still from top to bottom in this particular use of Go To and the structured programming principle, "*The main flow of control through a program unit should be from top to bottom of the program*" is not violated.

```
Program GoToExample;
{$APPTYPE Console}
Label 100;
Begin
  100:
  Writeln('Hello World');
  Writeln('Hello World');
  Writeln('Hello World');
  GoTo 100;
End.
```

Figure 18.14 Example of the use of Go To

We use structured programming because it leads to programs which are **easier to understand, maintain and reason about**.

In "Notes on Structured Programming" Edgar Dijkstra wrote:

> "*A program is never a goal in itself; the purpose of a program is to evoke computations and the purpose of the computations is to establish a desired effect. Although the program is the final product made by the programmer, the possible computations evoked by it-the "making" of which is left to the machine! - are the true subject matter of his trade. For instance, whenever a programmer states that his program is correct, he really makes an assertion about the computations it may evoke.*
>
> *The fact that the last stage of the total activity, viz. the transition from the (static) program text to the (dynamic) computation, is essentially left to the machine is an added complication. In a sense the making of a program is therefore more difficult than the making of a mathematical theory: both program and theory are structured, timeless objects. But while the mathematical theory makes sense as it stands, the program only makes sense via its execution.*"
>
> "*In vague terms we may state the desirability that the structure of the program text reflects the structure of the computation. Or, in other terms, "What can we do to shorten the conceptual gap between the static program text (spread out in "text space") and the corresponding computations (evolving in time) ?"* "

Page 16, http://www.informatik.uni-bremen.de/agbkb/lehre/programmiersprachen/artikel/EWD-notes-structured.pdf

A goal of structured programming is **to reduce the conceptual gap between the program text and the corresponding computations**. In other words, how can you be sure that your program does what it is required to do, i.e. meets its specification?

Writing programs that are easy to understand contributes to achieving this goal even if it is done at the expense of efficiency, e.g. execution time and memory requirements.

Structured programming requires that

1. The main flow of control through a program unit should be from top to bottom of the program.
2. Program blocks should have one entry point and one exit point
3. Meaningful identifiers should be used for variables, subroutines (procedures and functions), etc, to aid readability and understanding
4. Indentation should be used that reflects the structure of the program and which aids readability and understanding
5. The following control constructs should be used: sequence, selection and iteration
6. Go Tos should be avoided in all but the one case of a major error in the computation which would require, if handled in a structured programming way, convoluted and difficult-to-understand program source code to be written
7. The use of global variables which are used in a global way should be avoided
8. Data should be passed to subroutines in subroutine parameters and results returned through subroutine parameters or preferable as a function return data type
9. Local variables should be used for handling data within subroutines.

Questions

15. What is meant by structured programming?
16. What does structured programming have to say about the flow of control in programs?
17. Give **two** benefits of using structured programming.

Stepwise refinement

The focus of structured design is the identification of the components of the system and how they interact, i.e. the software architecture of the computerised system, and not on the internal design of the components.

For the **internal design of the components**, i.e. the program source code for subroutines and the program which calls these subroutines, we use structured programming.

We take as our starting point the control hierarchy chart for the two-player game *noughts and crosses* - *Figure 18.15*.

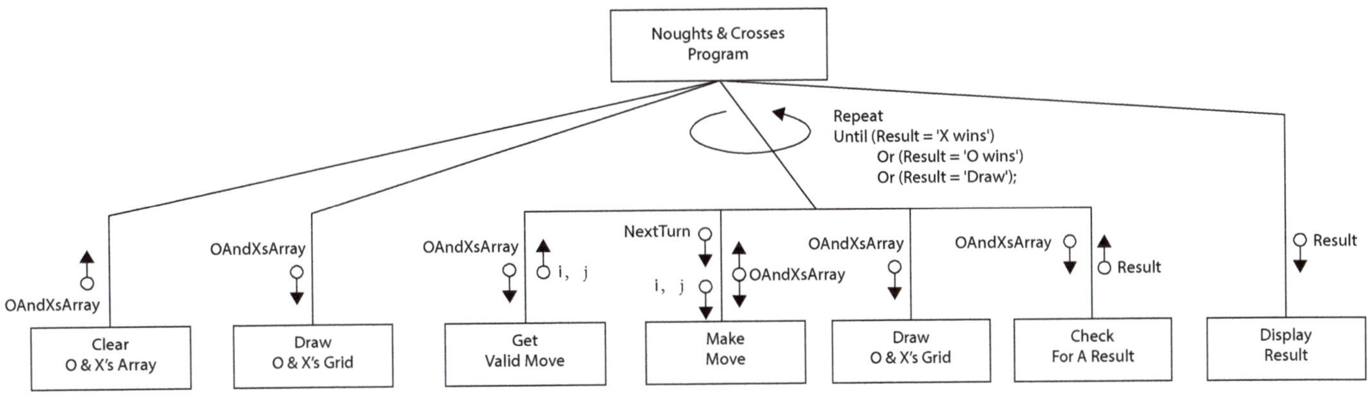

Figure 18.15 Control hierarchy chart for the game noughts and crosses

We model the two-dimensional grid of the noughts and crosses game in a two-dimensional array type `GridType` - *Figure 18.16*.

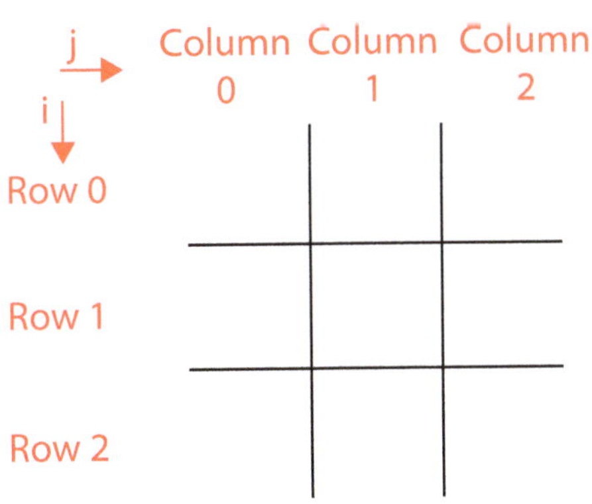


```
Type
    GridType = Array[0..2,0..2] Of Char;
Var
   OAndXsArray : GridType;
   Result : String;
   NextTurn : Char;
   i, j : Integer;
```

Figure 18.16 Modelling the game noughts and crosses

To reference a cell of this grid we will use integer variables `i` and `j`, e.g. the top-left cell will have `i, j` coordinates

`i = 0` and `j = 0`.

Each player of the two-player game takes it in turn to choose an unoccupied cell in which to place their symbol.
One player uses the symbol X and the other the symbol O.
In this game, the player with symbol X starts.
The symbol that is played next is stored in the character variable `NextTurn`.

For symbol X we use character value `'X'`, and for symbol O we use character value `'O'`.

The result of a player's move is stored in string variable `Result`. The value of result could be one of

'X wins', 'O wins', 'Draw' or 'No result so far'.

Once we have designed data structures, we can design the program to process the data stored in these data structures.

The control hierarchy chart *Figure 18.15* already reflects the program structure so it is a relatively straightforward mapping task to produce the textual form of the program structure as shown in *Figure 18.17*.

The next task is to design the internal structure of each subroutine and then construct this structure in a programming language. We do this using the control structures of structured programming, sequence, selection and iteration and a technique called **stepwise refinement**.

```
ClearArray(OAndXsArray)
DrawGrid(OAndXsArray)
NextTurn ← 'X'
Repeat
  GetValidMove(i, j, OAndXsArray)
  MakeMove(i, j, OAndXsArray, NextTurn)
  DrawGrid(OAndXsArray)
  Result ← CheckForAResult(OAndXsArray)
  If Result = 'Win'
    Then
      If NextTurn = 'X'
        Then Result ← 'X wins'
        Else Result ← 'O wins'
  If Result = 'No result so far'
    Then
      If NextTurn = 'X'
        Then NextTurn ← 'O'
        Else NextTurn ← 'X'
Until (Result = 'X wins')
        Or (Result = 'O wins')
        Or (Result = 'Draw')
DisplayResult(Result)
```

Figure 18.17 Program structure for the game noughts and crosses

Stepwise refinement starts with the **major steps**.

Each major step is then refined into a **more detailed sequence of steps**.

Each one of these more detailed steps is then refined and so on until a stage is reached where the steps can be replaced by programming language statements.

For example, the possible stages of stepwise refinement for the subroutine `CheckForAResult` are shown in *Figure 18.18*, *Figure 18.19* and *Figure 18.20*.

Major steps:

```
1. Check rows
2. Check columns
3. Check diagonals
4. If No result
     Then check for a draw
```

Figure 18.18 Major steps

First level of refinement:

```
1. Check rows
   1.1 For row 0 To 2 Do check row
2. Check columns
   2.1 For column 0 To 2 Do check column
3. Check diagonals
   3.1 Check top left to bottom right diagonal
   3.2 Check top right to bottom left diagonal
4. If No result
     Then check for a draw
   4.1 If no result
         Then
           If grid full
             Then result a draw
           EndIf
       EndIf
```

Figure 18.19 First level of refinement

There are no hard and fast rules to apply to the process of refinement other than each level should be a step closer to the solution, i.e. the actual programming language statements. Rather than document each stage as has been done here, it is often better to do the refinement inside the actual subroutine in the program development environment. Applying the discipline of using successive refinements in constructing a program is more important than formally generating refinements on paper.

However, paper is a good place to start until you become more skilled and able to iterate the refinement process mentally as you apply the skill directly inside a program development environment.

Second level of refinement:

```
1. Check rows
  1.1 For row 0 To 2 Do check row
    1.1.1 For i ← 0 To 2 Do
            If (OAndXsArray[i,0] = OAndXsArray[i,1])
                 And (OAndXsArray[i,1] = OAndXsArray[i,2])
              Then
                If (OAndXsArray[i,0] <> ' ') Then Outcome ← 'Win'
            EndIf
          EndFor
2.  Check columns
  2.1 For column 0 To 2 Do check column
    2.1.2 For j ← 0 To 2 Do
            If (OAndXsArray[0,j] = OAndXsArray[1,j])
                 And (OAndXsArray[1,j] = OAndXsArray[2,j])
              Then
                If (OAndXsArray[0,j] <> ' ') Then Outcome ← 'Win'
          EndFor
3. Check diagonals
  3.1 Check top left to bottom right diagonal
    3.1.1 If (OAndXsArray[0,0] = OAndXsArray[1,1])
               And (OAndXsArray[1,1] = OAndXsArray[2,2])
            Then
              If (OAndXsArray[0,0] <> ' ') Then Outcome ← 'Win'
          EndIf
  3.2 Check top right to bottom left diagonal
    3.2.1 If (OAndXsArray[0,2] = OAndXsArray[1,1])
               And (OAndXsArray[1,1] = OAndXsArray[2,0])
            Then
              If (OAndXsArray[0,2] <> ' ') Then Outcome ← 'Win'
          EndIf
4. If No result Then check for a draw
     If no result
       Then
         If grid full Then Outcome ← 'Draw'
       EndIf
    4.2.1 If Outcome = 'No result so far'
            Then
              NoOfMovesSofar ← 0
              For i ← 0 To 2 Do
                For j ← 0 To 2 Do
                  If OAndXsArray[i,j] <> ' ' Then NoOfMovesSoFar ← NoOfMovesSoFar + 1
                EndFor
              EndFor
              If NoOfMovesSoFar = 9 Then Outcome ← 'Draw'
          EndIf
```

Figure 18.20 Second level of refinement

Programming task

2 Using stepwise refinement, create a noughts and crosses Delphi console mode program based on the program structure shown in *Figure 18.17*.

Questions

18 Assuming that the sub tasks in the following are to be implemented as subroutines, create a hierarchy chart with control information and subroutine parameter lists for a program which

(a) collects three integers from the keyboard and calculates and displays their average.
(b) collects a letter from the keyboard, then tests and displays whether the letter is uppercase or not.
(c) collects an integer from the keyboard then calculates and displays its square, cube and fourth power.

Advantages of the structured approach

You have been introduced to the structured approach via very simple systems involving a small number of tasks where the "size" of the computation, i.e. the amount of information and the number of operations involved in it are relatively small.

When the problem to solve is really small, it would be easier not to use the computer at all and instead to do it by hand. The automatic computer is better employed on large computations which humans cannot do.

However, in order to manage such scale of computation successfully a disciplined approach to developing software is required.

The structured approach breaks the problem/system into manageable modules which have

- functional cohesion, i.e. modules which contain only one function or perform only one logically-related task. This enables a module to be easily replaced by another serving the same purpose.
- low coupling so that the modules are as independent as possible. The lower the coupling, the less likely that other modules will have to be considered in order to
    - create a module
    - understand a given module
    - debug a given module
    - change a given module.

Modules which are functionally cohesive, loosely coupled and for which all data transfer in and out of the modules is visible in the module parameters, enable programmers to work on individual modules without needing knowledge of the rest of the system.

The degree of intellectual effort (measured in some loose sense) to understand well-structured programs tends to be proportional to their program length (measured in some equally loose sense). This is important when reasoning about a program to check that it meets its specification. It is a more challenging task to do this with programs which are not well-structured.

Psychology research tells us that humans manage information in "chunks" and that the human brain is able to handle up to five pieces of information, maybe seven at a pinch. Stepwise refinement fits this limitation of the human brain well.

Questions

19. State **three** advantages of the structured approach and explain why these are advantages.

Information

There are two other software design paradigms:

- Object-oriented
- Functional programming

In object-oriented design the nature of objects leads to the creation of loosely coupled systems.

In object-oriented design the representation of an object is concealed within that object and is not visible to external components.

The system does not have a shared state and therefore any object can be replaced by another object with the same interface.

Some of the skills you develop following a structured approach to constructing software and the principles of structured design and programming overlap with Object-Oriented Design (OOD) and Object-Oriented Programming (OOP).

19 Introducing Object-Oriented Programming

Warning

Take care to distinguish a class from objects of a class. For example, apples can be eaten whereas their properties and descriptions of what they do cannot.

Classifying things

Purpose: To learn the meaning of a class

Classes and objects

We classify things so that we can group similar things together, e.g. different varieties of apple into a group called apples. The grouping process is called classification.

Figure 19.1 shows a grouping of three different varieties of apple.

Fig. 19.1 shows a grouping of three different varieties of apple.

We call each group a **class** because the things in the group have been classified as belonging together, e.g. the class of all apples.

The class has a **name**, e.g. the class apple.

We call the things that belong to a class, **objects**.

The objects of a class are of a specific **object type**, e.g. apple.

The term object type is synonymous with the term class so that we can use either for the object group name.

Object type properties

Apples in general have **colour**, e.g. red, green, brown, etc, and **variety** e.g. Russet, Cox, Golden Delicious, Pink Lady, etc, as well as other characteristics.

We call these characteristics, **properties** or **attributes** of apple objects.

Objects of the class called apple have **colour property values** such as green or red and **variety property values** such as Pink Lady or Russet.

Class definition

We need a definition of the class apple to use to decide if an object is an apple or not.

Property values alone will only help so far in identifying an object.

We should also observe how an object behaves when an action is applied to it.

If the object before us resembles an apple in colour, shape, etc and when eaten tastes like an apple then it is more than likely an apple.

The class definition therefore should include both **characteristics**, i.e. properties/attributes, and **behaviours** that objects of the class should possess.

Key concept

Abstraction:
Abstraction is the ability to engage with a concept while ignoring some of its details, e.g. when considering the concept of a house, we ignore the individual details of its doors, that is, whether they are made of wood, metal, plastic, and where the letter box is located, etc. This is a form of abstraction known as representational abstraction.
A class in object-oriented programming is similar.
At the class-level of abstraction the focus is on properties (also called attributes) and the command/query operations (also called methods) that are of interest.
A class in object-oriented programming is also an abstraction of the generalisation type. In this type of abstraction objects are grouped by their common characteristics, e.g. apple characteristics.

Key concept

Class:
A class is a template from which actual objects may be created. The class definition lists the characteristics of the object that are to be recorded, e.g. for a car object, the number of seats, size of engine, etc. The class will also define how the object can behave, e.g. accelerate forwards, slow down when brakes are applied, etc. An actual instance of an object – my car - will have a state that it is currently in, e.g. parked and locked and a set of behaviours it can perform.

In solving a problem by computer or otherwise, it is necessary to choose an **abstraction of reality**.

This choice must be guided by the problem to be solved.

If we have an apple problem then we choose a class definition of an apple to represent the real world that we wish to model.

The class definition will include those properties/attributes and behaviours that are relevant to solving the problem, e.g.

```
TApple = Class
         Variety : String;          ┐
         Colour : String;           │ Fields
         Volume : Real;             │
         AgeInDays : Integer;       ┘
         Constructor Create;        ┐
         Procedure Grow;            │ Methods
         Procedure Drop;            │
         Destructor Destroy;        ┘
End
```

Fig. 19.2 Definition of the class TApple

The class name is `TApple`.

The properties/attributes are represented by **fields** as follows

`Variety, Colour, Volume, AgeInDays.`

The behaviours are represented by **methods**:

`Create, Grow, Drop, Destroy.`

The methods are implemented in a programming language as procedures, functions, constructors and destructors, represented by executable code loaded into RAM.

`Create` is a **constructor** that is used to create an apple object.

`Destroy` is a **destructor** that is used to destroy an apple object.

Constructors and destructors do more than procedures and functions.

Memory allocation and deallocation

An apple object is created in the RAM (Random Access Memory) of a computer when the constructor `Create` is called.

The role of any constructor is to **allocate** two blocks of RAM for the apple object in a process called **object instantiation**.

The first block has just enough space to store the values of the fields `Variety`, `Colour`, `Volume`, `AgeInDays` as well as the value of a hidden pointer that links the first block to the second block.

To perform this linking operation the hidden pointer records the RAM address of the start of the second block.

The amount of storage space allocated to each field value is determined by the nature of what is stored which is specified by its data type.

`Variety` and `Colour` use storage space sufficient for strings whilst `Volume` uses that required for a real number and `AgeInDays` that for an integer.

The hidden pointer uses the storage space required for a RAM address.

The second block has just enough storage space to store each of the RAM addresses where the executable codes begin that implement the constructor, destructor and procedures `Create`, `Grow`, `Drop`, `Destroy`.

The storage space for this executable code is allocated elsewhere in RAM.

The behaviour of objects of the class is modelled by executable code and takes the form of command/query operations, e.g. the command `Grow`.

The class definition doesn't have any query operations but if it did, we might have an operation which asks the apple object's age. Such an operation could be implemented as a function.

Figure 19.3 shows, in outline, RAM blocks for two apple objects, `Apple1` and `Apple2`, and the code block for the procedure `Grow`. The code blocks for the constructor, destructor and other procedures are not shown.

We say that `Apple1` and `Apple2` are **instances** of the class **TApple**.

Note that the code (constructor, destructor and procedures) is shared by the two objects.

Only their **state** is not shared.

By state is meant the values of their fields.

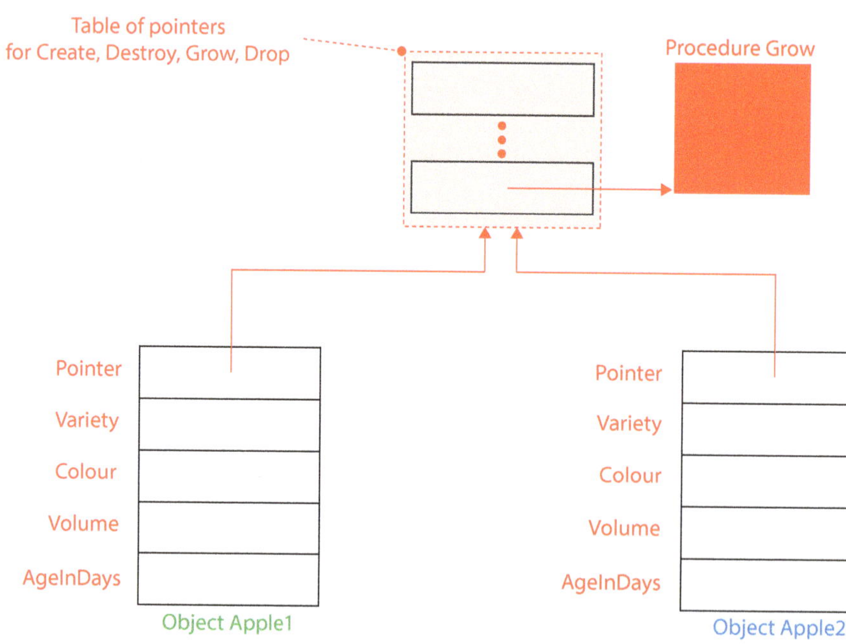

Fig. 19.3 shows, in outline, RAM blocks for two apple objects, Apple1 and Apple2, and a RAM block for procedure Grow. Note that the executable code (constructor, destructor and procedures) is shared by the two objects. Only their state is not shared.

The role of any destructor is to **deallocate** the RAM allocated to the object being destroyed which means returning the allocated RAM to the general pool that is available to applications needing to create objects.

Key concept

Object instantiation:

An object is an instance of a class.

An object requires memory for its data and a mechanism for linking to the executable code for its methods. This code is shared with other objects belonging to the same class. Attribute data is not shared however. Each object maintains its own state, i.e. the values of its attributes.

Key point

Objects share behaviour but not state:

Objects share method code but not attribute values. Each object maintains its own attribute values.

There is only ever one copy of each method's executable code.

Note

An apple class describes aspects of apples which are of interest but an instance of an apple represents a specific apple. We cannot eat the aspects of apple, but we can eat a specific apple. This is the reason why an apple has to be instantiated.

Instantiation or object creation takes place at runtime.

Creating your first OOP program

In the program `MyFirstOOP` shown in *Table 19.1* the language keyword `Class` is used to create a user-defined class, `TMyFirstClass`, as follows:

```
Type
  TMyFirstClass = Class
                    x: Integer;
                    Procedure Setx;
                    Procedure Showx;
                  End;
```

The class definition contains a field `x` and two methods `Setx` and `Showx`.

The methods are defined as follows:

```
Procedure TMyFirstClass.Setx;
  Begin
    Write('Input an integer: ');
    Readln(x);
  End;
Procedure TMyFirstClass.Showx;
  Begin
    Writeln(x);
  End;
```

Note that each procedure identifier begins with the class name, `TMyFirstClass` followed by a full stop.

When an object of this class type is created we must have some way of referring to it subsequently.

We do this by declaring a variable `MyFirstObjectRef` of type `TMyFirstClass` as follows:

```
Var
  MyFirstObjectRef : TMyFirstClass;
```

In object-oriented programming a variable declaration such as this does not create the corresponding object at this point.

We require a programming step as shown below:

```
MyFirstObjectRef := TMyFirstClass.Create;
```

Until the computer executes the above statement, an object of type `TMyFirstClass` does not exist.

Once the statement is executed the object exists and its field `x` and its methods `Setx` and `Showx` become accessible.

The following program code uses the created object to set the count and then show the count:

```
MyFirstObjectRef.Setx;
MyFirstObjectRef.Showx;
```

Note that the program is able to successfully call `TMyFirstClass.Create` to construct an instance of a `TMyFirstClass` object even though the class definition of `TMyFirstClass` object contains no such constructor or any constructor at all. This is because all user-defined classes have automatic access to a default constructor called `Create` defined in a Delphi supplied class `TObject`. *Figure 19.4* shows the output from an execution of **MyFirstOOP**.

Information

www.educational-computing.co.uk/DelphiBookCode/DelphiCode.html

```
Program MyFirstOOP;
{Remember to Save Project As MyFirstOOP}
{$APPTYPE CONSOLE}
Type
  TMyFirstClass = Class
                    x: Integer;
                    Procedure Setx;
                    Procedure Showx;
                  End;
Procedure TMyFirstClass.Setx;
  Begin
    Write('Input an integer: ');
    Readln(x);
  End;
Procedure TMyFirstClass.Showx;
  Begin
    Writeln(x);
  End;
Var
  MyFirstObjectRef : TMyFirstClass;
Begin
  MyFirstObjectRef := TMyFirstClass.Create;
  MyFirstObjectRef.Setx;
  MyFirstObjectRef.Showx;
  Readln;
End.
```

Table 19.1 Program MyFirstOOP

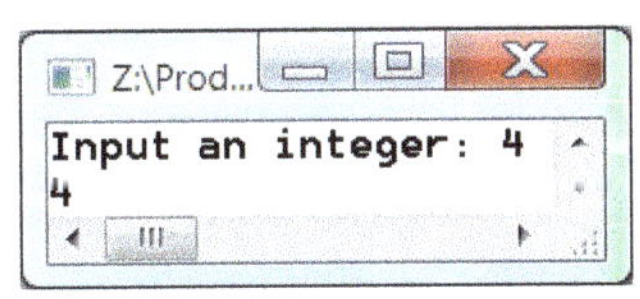

Fig. 19.4 MyFirstOOP output to the console window when executed and integer 4 entered.

Use the IDE to create or load and save the above source code program as MyFirstOOP.dpr or MyFirstOOP.dproj, depending on the version of Delphi, in its own directory/folder named MyFirstOOP.

Now compile the program (Ctrl F9).

Run this program (F9).

Creating your second OOP program

In the program `MySecondOOP` shown in *Figure 19.2* two variables of type `TMyFirstClass` are declared as follows

```
Var
    MyFirstObjectRef : TMyFirstClass;
    MySecondObjectRef : TMyFirstClass;
```

and subsequently used to reference two objects, respectively, of type `TMyMyFirstClass` created as follows

```
MyFirstObjectRef := TMyFirstClass.Create;
MySecondObjectRef := TMyFirstClass.Create;
```

The field `x` of each object is set, the first with value 4 and the second with value 5. This is shown being done in *Figure 19.5* and the values displayed by calling `Showx` on each object.

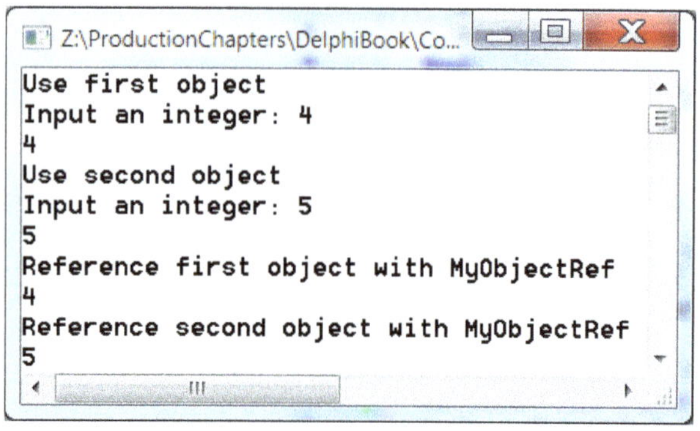

Fig. 19.5 Output sent to the console window by MySecondOOP when executed, and integers 4 and 5 entered.

The program uses a third object reference variable, `MyObjectRef` of type `TMyFirstClass` but in a different way from the other two variables. `MyObjectRef` is assigned a reference to the first object as follows

```
MyObjectRef := MyFirstObjectRef;
```

and then assigned a reference to the second object as follows

```
MyObjectRef := MySecondObjectRef;
```

This is shown being done in *Figure 19.5* and the values displayed by calling `Showx` on each object.

```
Program MySecondOOP;
{Remember to Save Project As MySecondOOP}
{$APPTYPE CONSOLE}
Type
  TMyFirstClass = Class
                    x: Integer;
                    Procedure Setx;
                    Procedure Showx;
                  End;
Procedure TMyFirstClass.Setx;
  Begin
    Write('Input an integer: ');
    Readln(x);
  End;
Procedure TMyFirstClass.Showx;
  Begin
    Writeln(x);
  End;
Var
  MyFirstObjectRef : TMyFirstClass;
  MySecondObjectRef : TMyFirstClass;
  MyObjectRef : TMyFirstClass;
Begin
  MyFirstObjectRef := TMyFirstClass.Create;
  Writeln('Use first object');
  MyFirstObjectRef.Setx;
  MyFirstObjectRef.Showx;
  MySecondObjectRef := TMyFirstClass.Create;
  Writeln('Use second object');
  MySecondObjectRef.Setx;
  MySecondObjectRef.Showx;
  Writeln('Reference first object with MyObjectRef');
  MyObjectRef := MyFirstObjectRef;
  MyObjectRef.Showx;
  Writeln('Reference second object with MyObjectRef');
  MyObjectRef := MySecondObjectRef;
  MyObjectRef.Showx;
  Readln;
End.
```

Table 19.2 Program MySecondOOP

Creating your third OOP program

In the program `MyThirdOOP` shown in *Table 19.3* we explore the use of the object reference variable `MyFirstObjectRef`.

```
Program MyThirdOOP;
{Remember to Save Project As MyThirdOOP}
{$APPTYPE CONSOLE}
Type
  TMyFirstClass = Class
                    x: Integer;
                    Procedure Setx;
                    Procedure Showx;
                  End;
Procedure TMyFirstClass.Setx;
  Begin
    Write('Input an integer: ');
    Readln(x);
  End;
Procedure TMyFirstClass.Showx;
  Begin
    Writeln(x);
  End;
Var
  MyFirstObjectRef : TMyFirstClass;
Begin
  If Assigned(MyFirstObjectRef)
    Then Writeln('Assigned')
    Else Writeln('Unassigned');
  MyFirstObjectRef := TMyFirstClass.Create;
  If Assigned(MyFirstObjectRef)
    Then Writeln('Assigned')
    Else Writeln('Unassigned');
  MyFirstObjectRef.Setx;
  MyFirstObjectRef.Showx;
  MyFirstObjectRef.Free;
  MyFirstObjectRef := Nil;
  If Assigned(MyFirstObjectRef)
    Then Writeln('Assigned')
    Else Writeln('Unassigned');
  Readln;
End.
```

Table 19.3 Program MyThirdOOP

We can discover if the object reference variable `MyFirstObjectRef` has been assigned an object using the function `Assigned` as follows

```
If Assigned(MyFirstObjectRef)
  Then Writeln('Assigned')
  Else Writeln('Not assigned');
```

This function returns `True` if `MyFirstObjectRef` has been assigned an object otherwise it returns `False`. By following the logic of the code in *Table 19.3* in conjunction with the output shown in *Figure 19.6* it should become clear that `MyFirstObjectRef` is unassigned before the statement

```
MyFirstObjectRef := TMyFirstClass.Create;
```

is executed but assigned after execution.

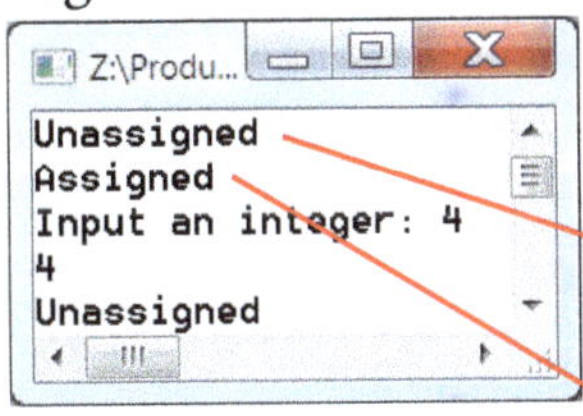

Fig. 19.6 Output sent to the console window by MyThirdOOP when executed, and integer 4 entered.

The program having set the value of the field `x` and shown this value in the console window then releases the memory occupied by the object by calling the procedure `Free` which is accessible to the object and called as follows

```
MyFirstObjectRef.Free;
```

The procedure `Free` is available to every object so doesn't need to be defined in the class definition `TMyFirstClass`.

`Free` verifies that the object reference `MyFirstObjectRef` is not `Nil` before calling the language built-in destructor `Destroy`. It is the `Destroy` method that deallocates (releases) the memory occupied by the instance of `TMyFirstClass` (i.e. object). `MyFirstObjectRef` continues to hold the memory address of the released memory until it is set to the value `Nil` by `MyFirstObjectRef := Nil;`. The language keyword `Nil` is called the null pointer, i.e. a pointer that points nowhere.

Use the IDE to create or load and save the above source code program as **MyThirdOOP.dpr** or **MyThirdOOP.dproj**, depending on the version of Delphi, in its own directory/folder named **MyThirdOOP**. Now compile the program (Ctrl F9).

Run this program (F9).

You should now have concluded that the object-oriented nature of Delphi (Object Pascal) is based on

- classes, which are a form of type definition containing both data fields and their associated operations and
- objects which are specific instances of a classes.

When an object is created it contains a new set of data fields, but the associated operations are shared with other objects in the class. A cooking recipe is a useful analogy to use to help to understand the difference between classes and objects.
Recipes generally start with a list of ingredients followed by some instructions (under the heading "Method") describing how to process the ingredients into the finished product.
For example, each time a cake is made a new set of ingredients are used, but the same "Method" is applied.

The creation and removal of an object is performed by two specialised kinds of procedure called a constructor and a destructor, respectively.

Questions

1. Consider the class Person. List some attributes that a person could have in each of the following systems
   (a) library system (b) healthcare system

2. Identify some of the classes that you would expect to find in each of the following systems
   (a) library system (b) airline booking system (c) system which manages hotel bookings

Task

1 This is an exercise to engage with in class that can help to get across the idea that when an object is created it contains a new set of data fields (attributes), but the associated operations (methods) performed on those fields are shared with other objects in the class. You will need a set of cards for recording the state of created objects, one card per object. Each card should have a row for each field and each row should be divided into a labelled field name column and a corresponding value column. In addition, it should have a row for a pointer to be used to link indirectly to the shared methods. This row should be above the data field rows. This row should have a hole located towards the right side through which a piece of thread/string can be passed. An example card is shown in *Figure 19.7* for the class definition shown in *Table 19.2*.

You will need a single card which records the name of the class and which has in addition three rows as shown in *Figure 19.8*. Each row should have a hole located towards the right side through which a piece of thread/string can be passed and a hole bottom left to be used to link an object card to this card. Finally, you will need a single card containing code for each method, `Setx` and `Showx` and a hole close to the start of each code block as shown *Figure 19.9*.

Fig. 19.7 Design of card for recording the state of an object of type TMyFirstClass

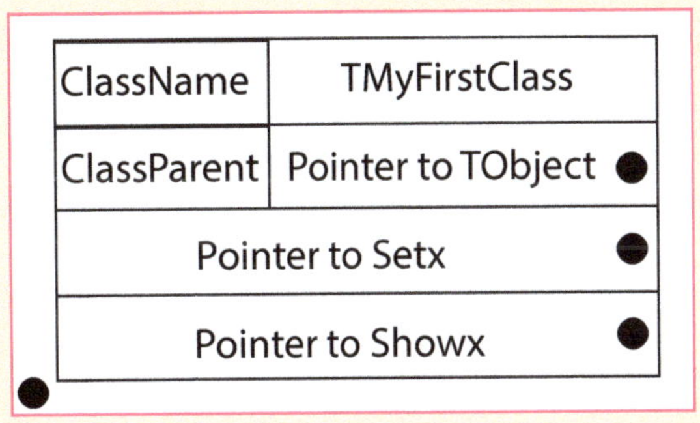

Fig. 19.8 Design of Class card for table of pointers and ClassName

Cut lengths of cotton thread from a reel of cotton as needed.

Instructions for using the cards:

- Take one object card (State card) for each object that you wish to create.
- Assign a value to the x field of each.
- To call a method on an object:
  1. Attach one end of a thread to the object card using its hole.
  2. Thread its other end through the bottom left corner hole of the Class card (*Figure 19.8*)
  3. Attach another thread to the hole of the pointer in the Class card for this method.
  4. Thread its other end through the corresponding hole in the Code card.

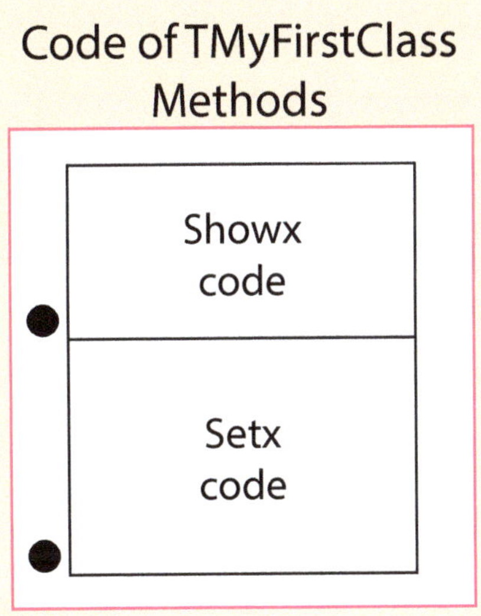

Fig. 19.9 Design of Code card for code of TMyFirstClass methods

Task: Create three objects of class `TMyFirstClass`.

Initialise the data field `x` to 5, 6, and 7 respectively.

Call `Setx` on each object. Show this call in action for each object using lengths of threads tied as indicated in the instructions.

TMyFirstClass memory structure

The Class card in *Task 1* represents an area of memory reserved for the class TMyFirstClass table of pointers - *Figure 19.10* - that is created when the program is loaded. To see this in action load program MyThirdOOPModifed.dpr - *Table 19.4*.

Now compile the program (Ctrl F9).

Run this program (F9).

ClassName	TMyFirstClass
ClassParent	Pointer to TObject
Pointer to Setx	
Pointer to Showx	

Fig. 19.10 TMyFirstClass memory structure

Figure 19.11 shows the output from executing MyThirdOOPModified.

In this program the following `Writeln` statement accesses the `ClassName` field of the TMyFirstClass class table

```
Writeln('MyFirstObjectRef classname: ', MyFirstObjectRef.ClassName);
```

and the following `Writeln` statement accesses the `ClassName` field of `TMyFirstClass`'s parent, class `TObject`, by first accessing the class table of `TMyFirstClass` and then the class table of class `TObject`.

```
Writeln('MyFirstObjectRef parent''s classname: ', MyFirstObjectRef.ClassParent.ClassName);
```

The class `TObject` is supplied by Delphi and is available to every user-defined class.

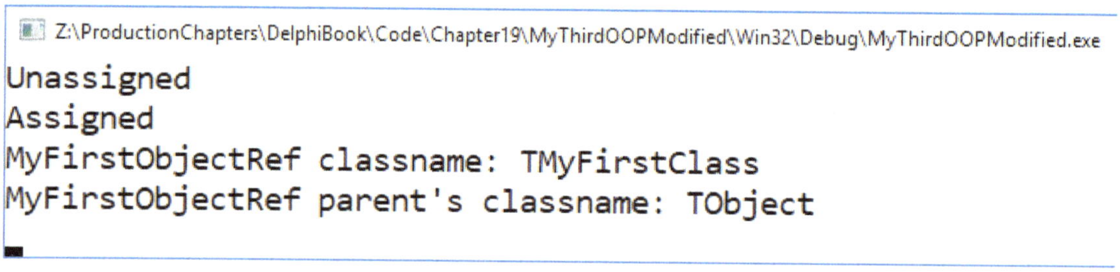

Fig. 19.11 MyThirdOOPModified output when executed

```
Program MyThirdOOPModified;

{Remember to Save Project As MyThirdOOPModifed}
{$APPTYPE CONSOLE}

Type
  TMyFirstClass = Class
                    x: Integer;
                    Procedure Setx;
                    Procedure Showx;
                  End;
Procedure TMyFirstClass.Setx;
  Begin
    Write('Input an integer: ');
    Readln(x);
  End;
Procedure TMyFirstClass.Showx;
  Begin
    Writeln(x);
  End;
Var
  MyFirstObjectRef : TMyFirstClass;
Begin
  If Assigned(MyFirstObjectRef)
    Then Writeln('Assigned')
    Else Writeln('Unassigned');
  MyFirstObjectRef := TMyFirstClass.Create;
  If Assigned(MyFirstObjectRef)
    Then Writeln('Assigned')
    Else Writeln('Unassigned');
  Writeln('MyFirstObjectRef classname: ', MyFirstObjectRef.ClassName);
  Writeln('MyFirstObjectRef parent''s classname: ', MyFirstObjectRef.ClassParent.ClassName);
  Readln;
End.
```

Table 19.4 Program MyThirdOOPModified

Code completion

Writing "`MyFirstObjectRef.`" invokes code completion and reveals the data field and methods of class `TMyFirstClass` plus the methods and any data fields (not visible) of class `TObject` - *Figure 19.12.* Notice that the constructor `Create` and the destructor `Free` are supplied by `TObject`.

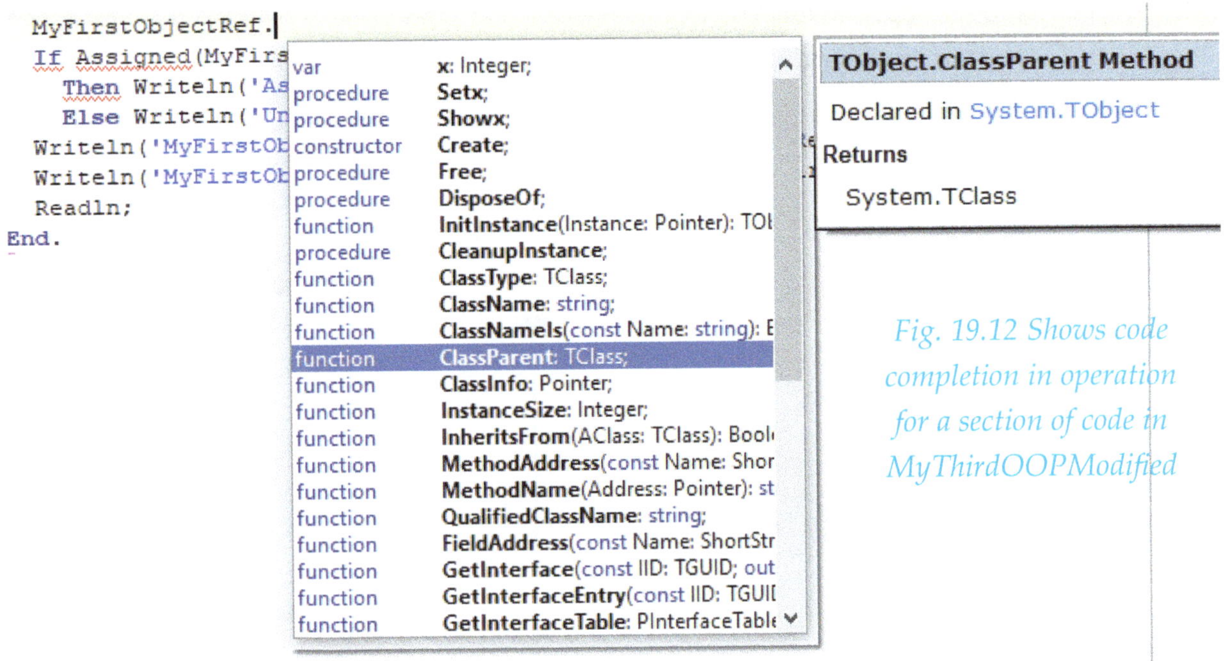

Fig. 19.12 Shows code completion in operation for a section of code in MyThirdOOPModified

The Addr function

The `Addr` function returns the address of any variable, procedure or function, `S`. The result is a pointer to `S`. The result returned is of type `Pointer`.

```
Function Addr(Var S) : Pointer;
```

Load program **AddrDemo.dpr** - *Table 19.5*.

Now compile the program (Ctrl F9).

Run this program (F9).

Figure 19.13 shows the output to a console window from executing **AddrDemo**.

Figure 19.14 shows a memory map for the variables and object at runtime.

The address in memory of the variable `y` is `04261264`. The location at this address contains integer value `5`.

The address in memory of variable `MyFirstObjectRef` is `04261256`. It stores the value `14293424` which is the address of a block of memory set aside for the created `TMyFirstClass` object. This address stored in `MyFirstObjectRef` can also be obtained from `Ptr^`, by indirecting through the address stored in `Ptr`.

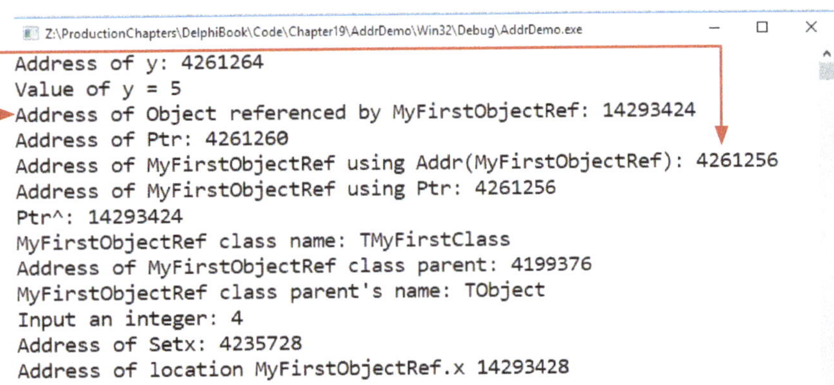

Fig. 19.13 Output from AddrDemo

The statement `Ptr := Addr(MyFirstObjectRef);` assigns the address of `MyFirstObjectRef` to `Ptr`.

Ptr is a Pointer variable . Writeln cannot write a Pointer variable unless its type is cast to Integer as follows

Integer(Ptr)

Ptr | 04261256

Integer() is a built-in function that returns a value of type Integer.

To use the address obtained from Ptr^ we need to use another function TMyFirstClass() to cast the address from Ptr^ to type TMyFirstClass as follows TMyFirstClass(Ptr^).

Ptr^ is 04261256^ which is interpreted as use address stored at 04261256 which is 14293424 i.e. the address of the created object.

```
Program AddrDemo;
{Remember to Save Project As AddrDemo}
{$APPTYPE CONSOLE}
Type
  TMyFirstClass = Class
                    x: Integer;
                    Procedure Setx;
                    Procedure Showx;
                  End;
  TProcPtr = Procedure of Object;
Procedure TMyFirstClass.Setx;
  Begin
    Write('Input an integer: ');
    Readln(x);
  End;
Procedure TMyFirstClass.Showx;
  Begin
    Writeln(x);
  End;
Var
  MyFirstObjectRef : TMyFirstClass;
  Ptr : Pointer;
  y : Integer;
  ProcPtr : TProcPtr;
Begin
  y := 5;
  Ptr := Addr(y);
  Writeln('Address of y: ', Integer(Ptr));
  Writeln('Value of y = ', Integer(Ptr^));
  MyFirstObjectRef := TMyFirstClass.Create;
  Writeln('Address of Object referenced by MyFirstObjectRef: ', Integer(MyFirstObjectRef));
  Ptr := Addr(MyFirstObjectRef);
  Writeln('Address of Ptr: ', Integer(Addr(Ptr)));
  Writeln('Address of MyFirstObjectRef using Addr(MyFirstObjectRef): ', Integer(Addr(MyFirstObjectRef)));
  Writeln('Address of MyFirstObjectRef using Ptr: ', Integer(Ptr));
  Writeln('Ptr^: ', Integer(Ptr^));
  Writeln('MyFirstObjectRef class name: ', TMyFirstClass(Ptr^).ClassName);
  Writeln('Address of MyFirstObjectRef class parent: ', Integer(TMyFirstClass(Ptr^).ClassParent));
  Writeln('MyFirstObjectRef class parent''s name: ', TMyFirstClass(Ptr^).ClassParent.ClassName);
  ProcPtr := MyFirstObjectRef.Setx;
  ProcPtr;
  Writeln('Address of Setx: ', Integer(Addr(ProcPtr)));
  Writeln('Address of location MyFirstObjectRef.x ', Integer(Addr(MyFirstObjectRef.x)));
  Readln;
End.
```

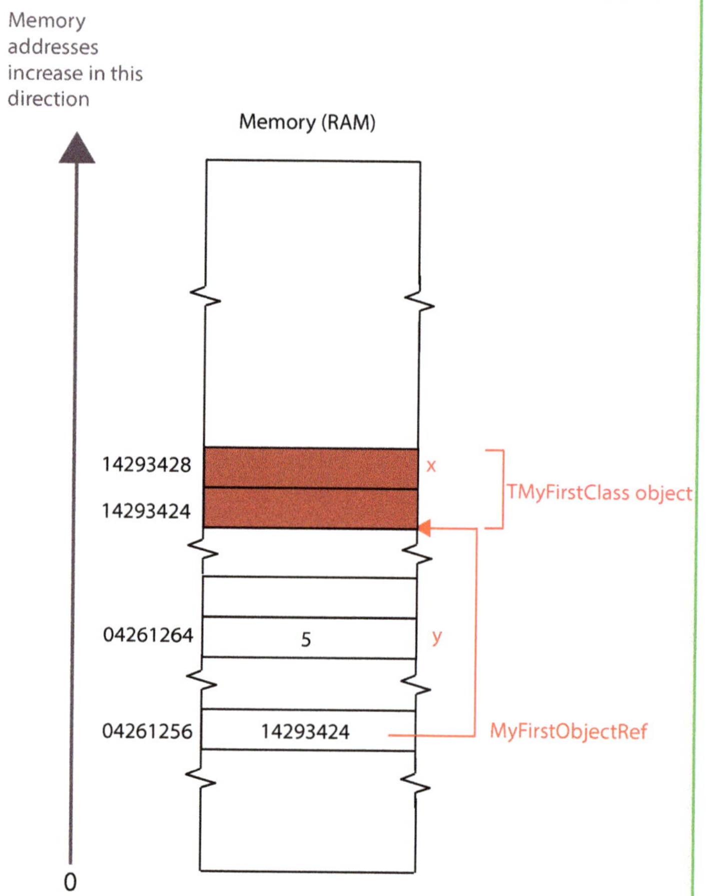

Fig. 19.14 Memory map for program AddrDemo showing location of variables y and MyFirstObjectRef, and object of class TMyFirstClass

Table 19.5 Program AddrDemo

Now we need to indirect from the object of type TMyFirstClass at 14424496 to the area of memory where the information of TMyFirstClass is stored so that its class name field, a string (how this string is obtained is a little more complicated), can be accessed:

```
TMyFirstClass(Ptr^).ClassName
```

It is '.' in TMyFirstClass(Ptr^).ClassName that invokes this indirection.

Of course, the same thing can be done the conventional way as follows

```
MyFirstObjectRef.ClassName;
```

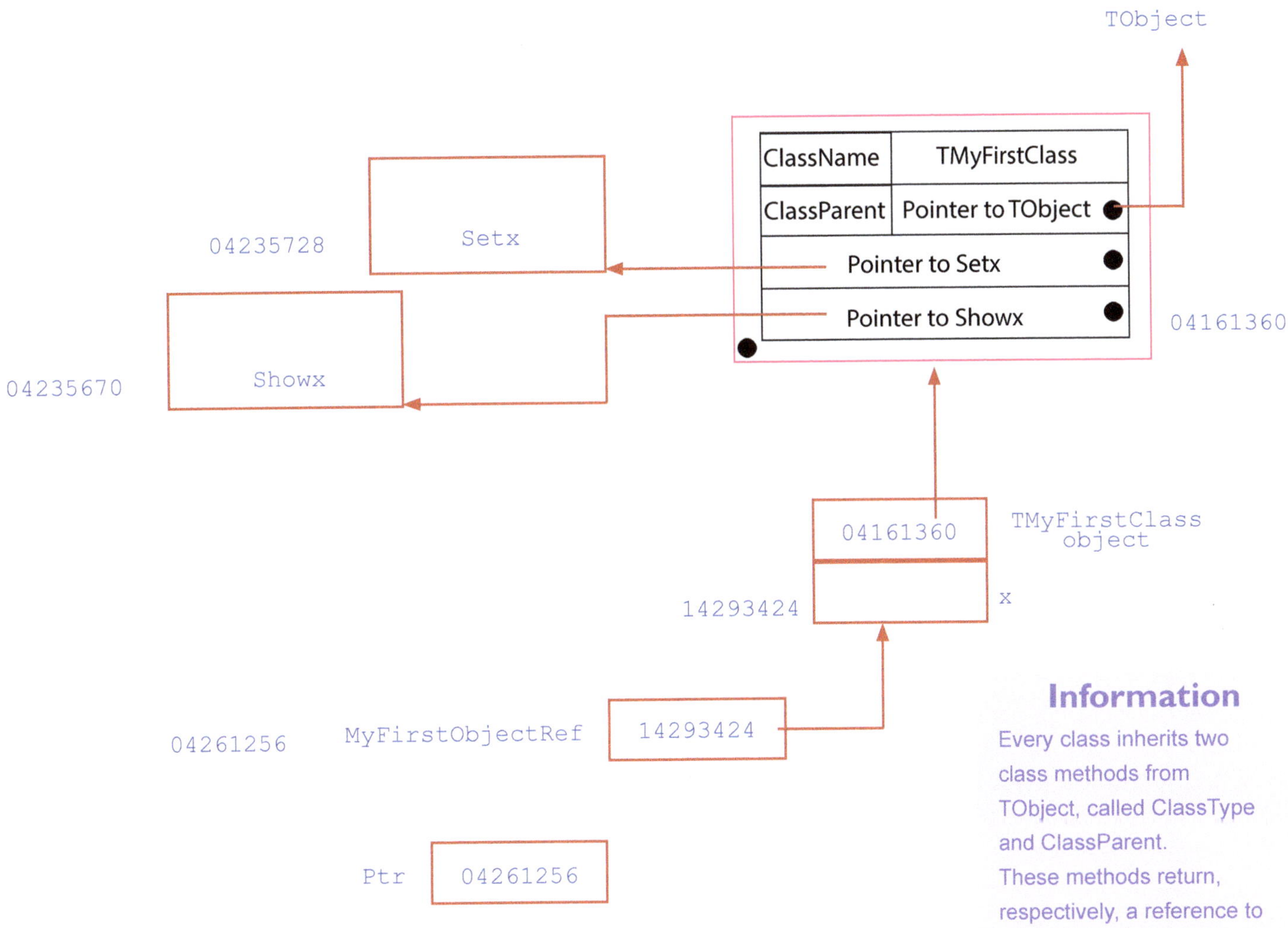

Fig. 19.15 Simplified schematic of two ways to access the information provided by TMyFirstClass

Information

Every class inherits two class methods from TObject, called ClassType and ClassParent. These methods return, respectively, a reference to the class of an object and to the immediate ancestor class of an object.

Figure 19.15 shows a schematic of these two ways.

We access the x field of this object in both ways but the program uses just one of these

```
MyFirstObjectRef.x
```

The area of memory allocated to the information belonging to TMyFirstClass has a field ClassParent which stores a pointer to the class definition of the parent of TMyFirstClass, which is TObject. Indirection takes place via '.' to the parent's class TObject and its field ClassName as follows

```
TMyFirstClass(Ptr^).ClassParent.ClassName
```

The block of memory that stores information for class TObject has address 4199376 as shown in *Figure 19.13*.

We can define a type for a pointer that points to a procedure of an object as follows

```
TProcPtr = Procedure of Object;
```

and a variable of this type as follows

```
ProcPtr : TProcPtr;
```

We can assign the address of the object procedure `MyFirstObjectRef.Setx` to `ProcPtr` as follows

```
ProcPtr := MyFirstObjectRef.Setx;
```

and call this procedure as follows

```
ProcPtr;
```

`Addr` returns the address of a procedure, therefore we can obtain the address of procedure `MyFirstObjectRef.Setx` as follows

```
Addr(ProcPtr)
```

(We can also obtain this address using `Addr(MyFirstObjectRef.x)`)

To write this address to the console window we have to cast it to an `Integer` as follows

```
Writeln('Address of Setx: ', Integer(Addr(ProcPtr)));
```

Finally, to obtain the memory address of the `x` field of the object we can use

```
Writeln('Address of location MyFirstObjectRef.x ', Integer(Addr(MyFirstObjectRef.x)));
```

The memory addresses that program **AddrDemo** reports may vary from run to run, especially for any created object. Memory for an object is acquired from the heap and as this is used dynamically (changing all the time) by other processes that may be running in your computer simultaneously, a different area of the heap may be allocated to store the object. Also the memory addresses that you obtain when you run the program **AddrDemo** will be those for your machine.

Programming Tasks

1. Add the following statement just before `Readln` to a copy of program `AddrDemo`

```
Writeln(Integer(TMyFirstClass));
```

Explain the output that appears in the console window when the modified program is run.

2. Add the following statement just before `Readln` to a copy of program `AddrDemo`

```
Writeln(TMyFirstClass.ClassName);
```

Explain the output that appears in the console window when the modified program is run.

3. Add the following statement just before `Readln` to a copy of program `AddrDemo`

```
Writeln(TMyFirstClass.ClassName);
```

Explain the output that appears in the console window when the modified program is run.

4. Add the following statement just before `Readln` to a copy of program `AddrDemo`

```
Writeln(Integer(Addr(TMyFirstClass.Setx)));
```

Explain the output that appears in the console window when the modified program is run.

5. Modfiy the variable declaration in a copy of program `AddrDemo` as follows

```
MyFirstObjectRef, MySecondObjectRef : TMyFirstClass;
```

Add the following statements just before `Readln` to a copy of program `AddrDemo`

```
MySecondObjectRef := TMyFirstClass.Create;
Writeln(Integer(MySecondObjectRef));
Ptr := Addr(MySecondObjectRef);
Writeln(Integer(Ptr));
Writeln(TMyFirstClass(Ptr^).ClassName);
Writeln(Integer(TMyFirstClass(Ptr^).ClassParent));
Writeln(TMyFirstClass(Ptr^).ClassParent.ClassName);
ProcPtr := MySecondObjectRef.Setx;
ProcPtr;
Writeln(Integer(Addr(ProcPtr)));
```

What conclusion/conclusions can be drawn from the observed output when the modified program is run?

Constructors and Destructors

Constructor

An object needs memory space in which to record their state e.g. current value of `x` is `4` - *Figure 19.16*.

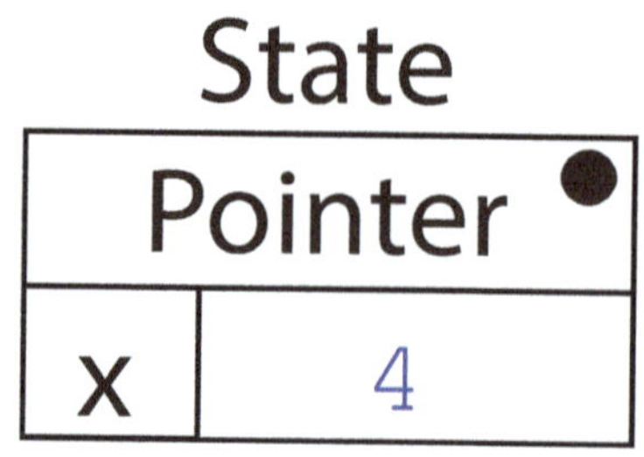

Fig. 19.16 Memory space for an object with a single data field labelled x.

This space is obtained from the heap when a constructor is executed. The space is released when a destructor is executed.

`Create` is the name of an existing constructor that is always available from the system

A constructor is a special kind of procedure.

When defining a constructor such as `Create` the keyword **Constructor** must be used not the keyword **Procedure**.

For example, you may define your own constructor `Create` if you so wish.

This will be used instead of the system's `Create` (provided by `TObject`).

```
TEmployee = Class
               Constructor Create;
               Procedure Init(AName......)
               ......
            End;
```

A constructor is built differently from a procedure because it has to get the space from the heap for an instance of the class, i.e. an object, plus it has to do some standard initialisation of the object.

If the class definition does not contain a constructor then the system one or an inherited one will be used. The constructor inherited from the system is called `Create`. Hence `TSomeClass.Create` will work even when `TSomeClass` class definition does not contain a constructor called `Create`. There is nothing to stop you defining a constructor with any name, e.g. `Mary` although using such a name is not a good idea in practice. Your code will create an object as follows in this case:

```
Person := TSomeOtherClass.Mary;
```

The keyword `Constructor` causes the setting up of the object on the heap. Additional initialisation can be written into the body of the constructor. For example, the Initialisation of the procedure `Init` in the class definition `TEmployee` could be moved to a constructor `CreateEmployee` as follows

```
Type
  TEmployee = Class
                Constructor MakeEmployee(AName, ATitle : String; ARate : Real);
                Function GetName: String;
                Function GetPayAmount: Real;
                Function GetRate: Real;
                Function GetTitle: String;
                Procedure Show;
                Private
                  Name: String[25];
                  Title: String[25];
                  Rate: Real;
              End;
```

Information

Private keyword is an access specifier which specifies that access to the Name, Title and Rate fields is restricted to acess within the unit in which the class is defined - see Chapter 21.

```
Constructor TMakeEmployee.MakeEmployee(AName, ATitle : String; ARate : Real);
  Begin
    Name := AName;
    Title := ATitle;
    Rate := ARate;
  End;
```

The constructor would be called with actual values in place of `AName`, `ATitle`, `ARate`, e.g. if two object references have been declared `Employee1, Employee2 : TEmployee;` then two instances of `TEmployee` can be created and initialised as follows

```
Employee1 := TEmployee.MakeEmployee('Kevin Smith', 'Mr', 10.00);
Employee2 := TEmployee.MakeEmployee('Sarah Jones', 'Miss', 15.00);
```

Destructor

A destructor is a special kind of procedure that is used to release the memory space occupied by an instance of a class, i.e. an object.

When defining a destructor such as `Destroy` the keyword **Destructor** must be used not the keyword **Procedure**.

We can add a destructor to the class definition for TEmployee as follows

```
Type
  TEmployee = Class
                Constructor MakeEmployee(AName, ATitle : String; ARate : Real);
                Destructor DestroyEmployee;
                Function GetName: String;
                Function GetPayAmount: Real;
                Function GetRate: Real;
                Function GetTitle: String;
                Procedure Show;
                Private
                  Name: String[25];
                  Title: String[25];
                  Rate: Real;
              End;
```

and use it as follows

```
Employee1.DestroyEmployee;
```

Delphi has one destructor (with exception of later versions) you can use, `Destroy`, if you don't want to define your own, and a procedure `Free` which calls `Destroy` after checking that the object reference is not `Nil`.

However, you should almost always use `Free`.

In its implementation, the `Free` method calls `Destroy`, but only when the instance pointer isn't nil; in other words, the pointer still points to the instance. For this reason, it is safer to call `Free` than `Destroy`. Also, calling `Free` is slightly more efficient in the resulting code size.

Do remember to set the object reference to `Nil` after calling `Free` or `Destroy`. The `Free` and `Destroy` will not do this for you unless you use `FreeAndNil` available in later versions of Delphi, e.g. **Delphi 10.2**. `FreeAndNil` ensures that an object reference variable is `Nil` after the object it references has been freed.

There is nothing special in the name `Create` and the name `Destroy` (the system's destructor).

The names in themselves are not constructors and destructors. It is the fact that `Create` appears after the keyword `Constructor` and `Destroy` after the keyword `Destructor` in many class definitions.

In fact, as we have illustrated, if you want to use different names for constructors and destructors you may.

The Self variable

We learned earlier that an object comprises data fields and a link to its class definition so that the methods defined .in this definition can be applied to the object, but when two or more objects exist of the same class how does a called method know to which object it should be applied?

In the **AddrDemo** program, there are two methods, `Setx` and `Showx` which can be applied to objects of the `TMyFirstClass` as shown in *Figure 19.17*. To address the issue of which object Delphi uses a hidden parameter called `Self`. The parameter is passed on the stack when a method is called and so can be accessed within the method when it is executing.

```
Type
  TMyFirstClass = Class
                    x: Integer;
                    Procedure Setx;
                    Procedure Showx;
                  End;
  TProcPtr = Procedure of Object;

Procedure TMyFirstClass.Setx;
  Begin
    Write('Input an integer: ');
    Readln(x);
  End;
Procedure TMyFirstClass.Showx;
  Begin
    Writeln(x);
  End;
```

Fig. 19.17 TMyFirstClass definition

If the formal parameter `Self` (formal parameter is the name given to parameters that appear in a procedure interface) was explicit then the two methods would be written as follows

```
Procedure TMyFirstClass.Setx(Self : TMyFirstClass);
  Begin
    Write('Input an integer: ');
    Readln(Self.x);
  End;
Procedure TMyFirstClass.Showx(Self : TMyFirstClass);
  Begin
    Writeln(Self.x);
  End;
```

and these methods would be called using object references `MyFirstObjectRef` and `MySecondObjectRef` as follows

```
MyFirstObjectRef.Setx(MyFirstObjectRef);
MyFirstObjectRef.Showx(MyFirstObjectRef);
MySecondObjectRef.Setx(MySecondObjectRef);
MySecondObjectRef.Showx(MySecondObjectRef);
```

The `Self` formal parameter is passed implicitly into each method but can be explicitly referenced inside the method as shown in *Figure 19.18*. If the `Self` parameter is omitted as in *Figure 19.17* then it is implied and used as shown in *Figure 19.18*. It is often unnecessary to explicitly reference `Self` but there are circumstances where it is necessary. Examples of such use is covered later in this book - see page 467.

```
Procedure TMyFirstClass.Setx;
  Begin
    Write('Input an integer: ');
    Readln(Self.x);
  End;
Procedure TMyFirstClass.Showx;
  Begin
    Writeln(Self.x);
  End;
```

Fig. 19.18 Explicit use of Self parameter

To summarise, within the implementation of a method, the identifier `Self` references the object for which the method is called.

Programming Task

6 Write a program that stores in RAM a student's examination score out of 60, the percentage that this score represents, the grade awarded for this score ('A' >= 50, 'B' < 50) and the student's name. The program will show/display the student's name, examination score, percentage and grade.

The methods to be provided are

- An object constructor which initialises the object with student name and examination score
- CalculatePercentage
- CalculateGrade
- ShowStudentData

Use a class with 4 attributes – Name, Score, Percentage, Grade - and the 4 methods listed above.

You are not being asked to store the data permanently on backing store, e.g. magnetic disk.

Adding a unit to a project

Figure 19.19 shows the die class, `TDie`, in Delphi/Pascal. In Delphi the convention is to use the prefix `T` if the identifier identifies a type.

The `Self` variable is a hidden parameter of every method in an object. It allows the method to refer to the object on which it is acting.

The language keyword `Result` which is used in `TDie.GetNumber` is a variable used to hold the return value of the function.
In Pascal, the return value would be assigned as follows using the name of the function in place of `Result`

```
GetNumber := Self.Number;
```

The unit contains a declaration of a constructor called `Create` which, in addition to acquiring memory for an object of type `TDie`, initialises the attribute, `Number`.

The program which uses `TDie` to create an object `Die1` is shown in *Figure 19.20*.
Delphi allows a program to destroy an object explicitly by invoking `Destroy` on the object (and `Free`). The last statement in the **DieExample** program invokes `Die1.Destroy` to release the memory occupied by the `Die1` object. The class definition `TDie` is stored in the file **TDieClassUnit.pas.**

```
Unit TDieClassUnit;
Interface
Type
  TDie = Class
         Private
           Number : Integer;
         Public
           Procedure Roll;
           Function GetNumber : Integer;
           Procedure SetNumber(n : Integer);
           Constructor Create;
       End;
Implementation
  Constructor TDie.Create;
    Begin
      Self.Number := 1;
    End;
  Procedure TDie.Roll;
    Begin
      Randomize;
      Self.Number := Random(6) + 1;
    End;
  Function TDie.GetNumber : Integer;
    Begin
      Result := Self.Number;
    End;
  Procedure TDie.SetNumber(n : Integer);
    Begin
      Self.Number := n;
    End;
End.
```

Mechanism for creating attribute, *Number*

Constructor

Self can be omitted because in this context Delphi assumes *self* applies.

Saved in TDieClassUnit.pas

Generates a random number in range 0 to 5

Fig. 19.19 TDie Class Unit in Delphi/Pascal

```
Program DieExample;
{$APPTYPE CONSOLE}
{$R *.res}
Uses
  System.SysUtils,
  TDieClassUnit in 'TDieClassUnit.pas';
Var
  Die1 : TDie;
Begin
  Die1 := TDie.Create;
  Die1.Roll;
  Writeln(Die1.GetNumber);
  Writeln(Die1.GetNumber);
  Die1.Roll;
  Writeln(Die1.GetNumber);
  Writeln(Die1.GetNumber);
  Die1.SetNumber(5);
  Writeln(Die1.GetNumber);
  Readln;
  Die1.Destroy;
End.
```

DieExample.dproj

Creates a TDie object

Releases memory allocated to a TDie object

Destructor

Fig. 19.20 DieExample Program in Delphi

Launch Delphi 10.2 Community Edition. Click File in the menu bar, **select New Console Application - Delphi**. Save Project As **DieExample.dproj** in a folder **DieExample**.

Next create a new unit to add to this project.

Figure 19.21 shows how to create a new unit, **File|New|Unit**. Save this unit as **TDieClassUnit.pas**.

Figure 19.22 shows how to add the new unit to the project, **Project|Add to Project**.

`TDieClassUnit` should now be present in the **Uses** section of program **DieExample**. - *Figure 19.23*.

```
Program DieExample;
{$APPTYPE CONSOLE}
{$R *.res}
Uses
  System.SysUtils,
  TDieClassUnit in 'TDieClassUnit.pas';
Begin
End.
```

Fig. 19.23 TDieClassUnit added to uses section

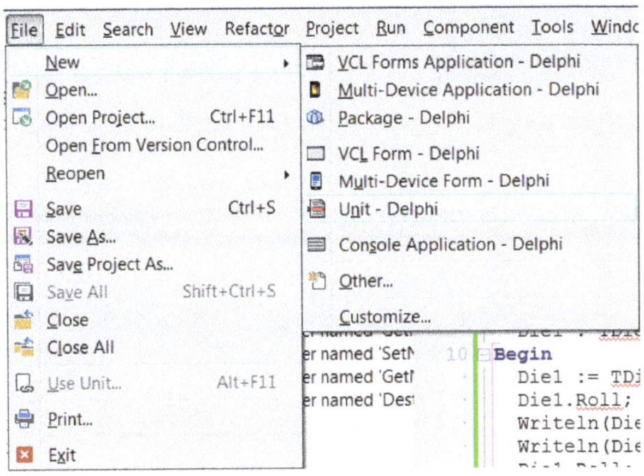

Fig. 19.21 Creating a new Unit

Add the source code from *Figure 19.19* and *19.20* to `TDieClassUnit` and `DieExample` respectively.

Now build the program (Shift F9).

Run this program in Debug mode(F9).

Figure 19.24 shows the console window output when the program is run.

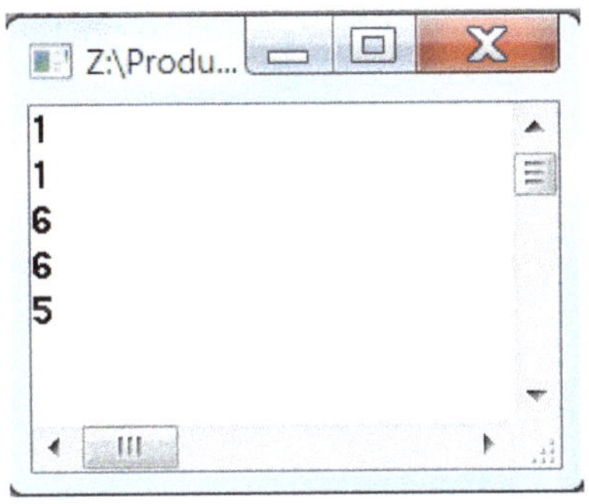

Fig. 19.24 Console window output

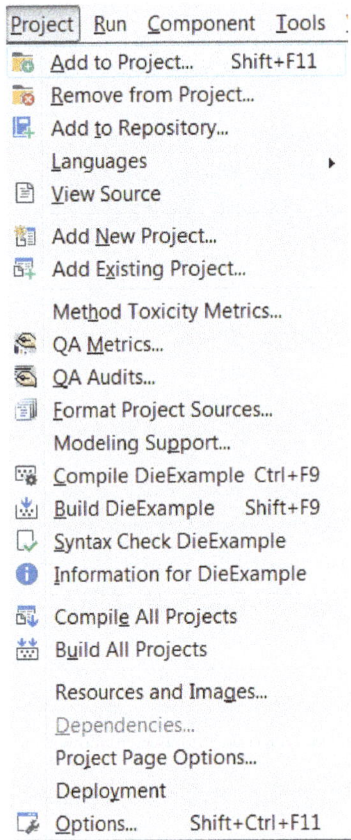

Fig. 19.22 Creating a new Unit

Programming task

7. In the Delphi/Pascal programming environment which you use, modify the DieExample program so that it generates and displays the outcome of rolling the die 10 times.

8. Change TDie class so that it supports the creation of Die objects with a given number of faces. Test that your modified TDie class works for a twelve-sided die object.

20 Object references

Information

www.educational-computing.co.uk/DelphiBookCode/DelphiCode.html

Object references

Purpose: To understand the difference between an object and an object reference

Creating your fourth OOP program

Program MyFourthOOP in *Figure 20.2* declares three variables of type `TMyFirstClass`

`MyFirstObjectRef`,
`MySecondObjectRef` and
`MyThirdObjectRef`.

These variables are used to reference three `TMyFirstClass` objects.

Each variable does not store an object but instead stores a reference to an object in the form of a pointer which is just a memory address.

Contrast this with a value variable such as an integer variable declared as follows

```
Var z : Integer;
```

and used as follows

```
z := 6;
```

with the assignment operation storing the value `6` in the variable `z`.

In a 32 bit machine this integer value would be allocated 4 bytes.
In a 64 bit machine this integer value would also be allocated 4 bytes.

In a 32 bit machine a variable which stores a pointer is allocated 4 bytes whereas in a 64 bit machine it is allocated 8 bytes reflecting the wider range of addresses accessible with 64-bit addresses.

Figure 20.1 shows the console window output produced when program MyFourthOOP is executed.

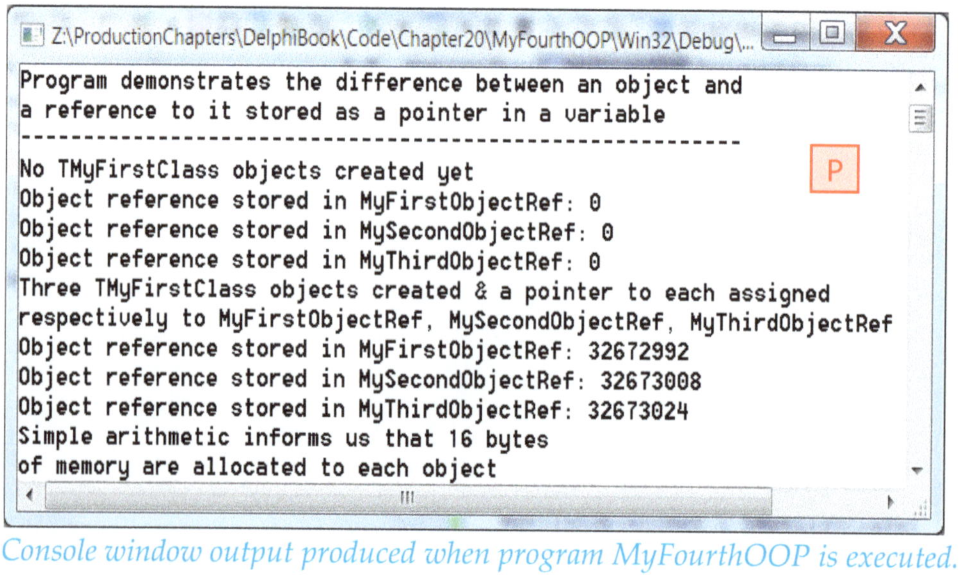

Fig. 20.1 Console window output produced when program MyFourthOOP is executed.

Key concept

Pointer:
A pointer is just a memory address.
Pointers are data typed to indicate the kind of data stored at the addresses they hold.

Key concept

Variable of a class type:
A variable of a class type does not store an object but instead stores a reference to an object in the form of a pointer. This pointer is the memory address of the block of memory allocated to the object or a null value called nil. A null-valued pointer points nowhere.

Programming task

Use the IDE to load or create and save the source code program as MyFourthOOP.dpr or MyFourthOOP.dproj, depending on the version of Delphi, in its own directory/folder named MyFourthOOP.
Now compile the program (Ctrl F9).
Run this program (F9).

```
Program MyFourthOOP;
{Remember to Save Project As MyFourthOOP}
{$APPTYPE CONSOLE}
Type
  TMyFirstClass = Class
                    x: Integer;
                    Procedure Setx;
                    Procedure Showx;
                  End;
Procedure TMyFirstClass.Setx;
  Begin
    Write('Input an integer: ');
    Readln(x);
  End;
Procedure TMyFirstClass.Showx;
  Begin
    Writeln(x);
  End;
Var
  MyFirstObjectRef, MySecondObjectRef, MyThirdObjectRef : TMyFirstClass;
Begin
  Writeln('Program demonstrates the difference between an object and');
  Writeln('a reference to it stored as a pointer in a variable');
  Writeln('-----------------------------------------------------------');
  Writeln('No TMyFirstClass objects created yet');
  Writeln('Object reference stored in MyFirstObjectRef: ',Integer(MyFirstObjectRef));
  Writeln('Object reference stored in MySecondObjectRef: ',Integer(MySecondObjectRef));
  Writeln('Object reference stored in MyThirdObjectRef: ',Integer(MyThirdObjectRef));
  Writeln('Three TMyFirstClass objects created & pointer assigned');
  Writeln('respectively to MyFirstObjectRef,MySecondObjectRef,MyThirdObjectRef');
  MyFirstObjectRef := TMyFirstClass.Create;
  MySecondObjectRef := TMyFirstClass.Create;
  MyThirdObjectRef :=  TMyFirstClass.Create;
  Writeln('Object reference stored in MyFirstObjectRef: ',Integer(MyFirstObjectRef));
  Writeln('Object reference stored in MySecondObjectRef: ',Integer(MySecondObjectRef));
  Writeln('Object reference stored in MyThirdObjectRef: ',Integer(MyThirdObjectRef));
  Writeln('Simple arithmetic informs us that 16 bytes');
  Writeln('of memory are allocated to each object');
  Readln;
End.
```

P

Key point

Casting from one data type to another:

The pointer stored in `MyFirstObjectRef` is of data type `TMyFirstClass` which is a data type that `Writeln` cannot handle. We therefore need to cast this pointer to a data type which Writeln knows how to handle. The chosen data type is integer.

The cast operation is formulated as follows

`Integer(MyFirstObjectRef)`

The value stored in `MyFirstObjectRef` does not change when this cast is performed.

Fig. 20.2 Program MyFourthOOP

Figure 20.3 shows a simplified memory map for the executing program. Note that the three objects occupy three blocks of memory whilst the three pointer variables which reference these objects occupy a different area of memory.

The console window in *Figure 20.1* shows that

- `MyFirstObjectRef` stores pointer value 0 before the first object is created and pointer value 32672992 after it is created. Pointer value 32672992 references the beginning of the block of memory, coloured in red, allocated to the first object. *Figure 20.3* uses a red directed line to connect `MyFirstObjectRef` to this block of memory.
- `MySecondObjectRef` stores pointer value 0 before the second object is created and pointer value 32673008 after it is created. Pointer value 32673008 references the beginning of the block of memory, coloured in blue, allocated to the second object. *Figure 20.3* uses a blue directed line to connect `MySecondObjectRef` to this block of memory.
- `MyThirdObjectRef` stores pointer value 0 before the third object is created and pointer value 32673024 after it is created. Pointer value 32673024 references the beginning of the block of memory, coloured in green, allocated to the third object. *Figure 20.3* uses a green directed line to connect `MyThirdObjectRef` to this block of memory.

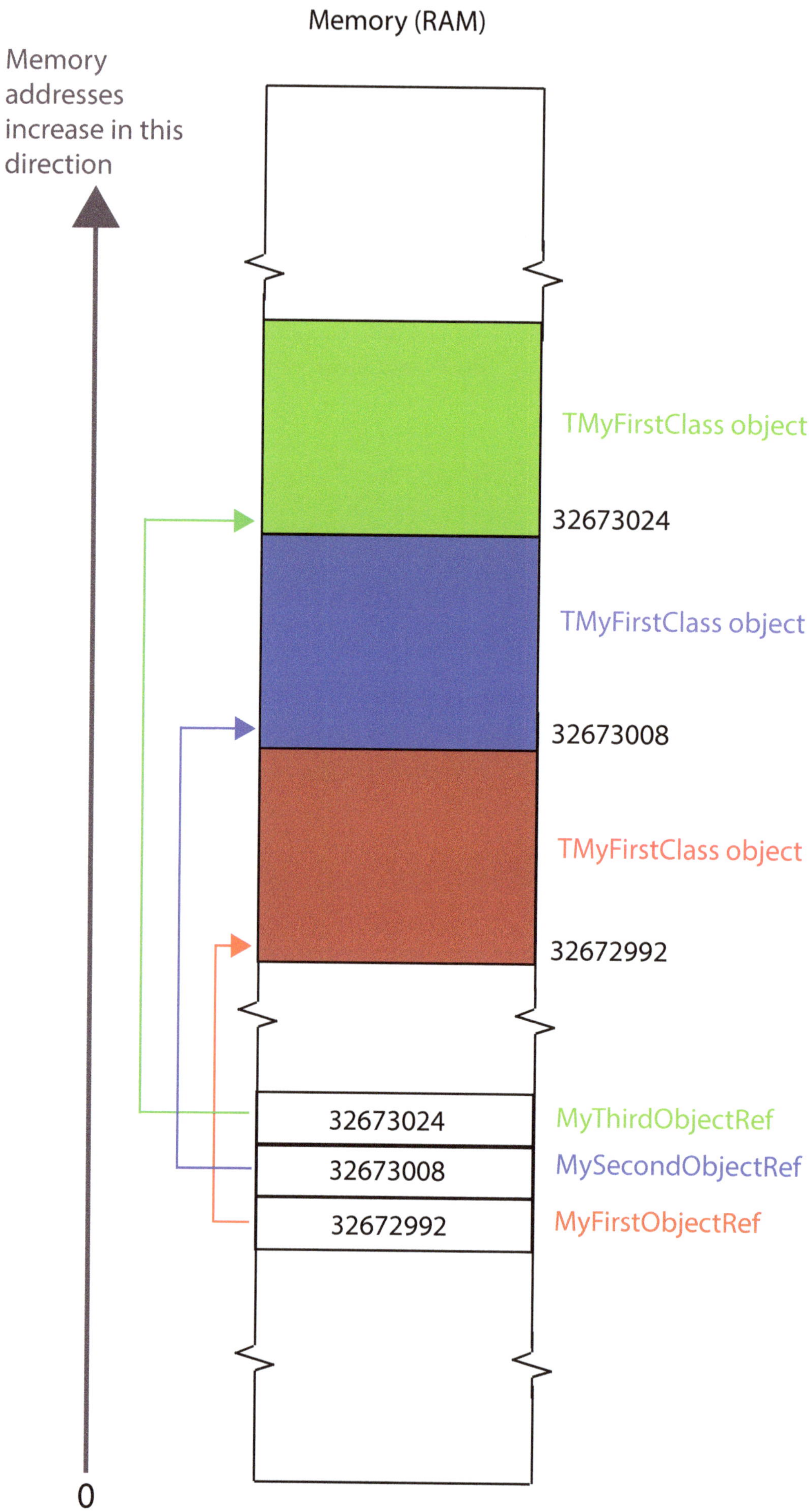

Fig. 20.3 Simplified memory map for MyFourthOOP when executing

Information

The term reference is used in a general sense in this chapter. It does have a specific meaning in the context of programming languages. Pointers are different from references in this context. A pointer is an independent variable that can be assigned a new address including a null address whereas a reference, once assigned, can never refer to a new object until the variable goes out of scope. This ensures that a reference always refers to an object whilst the reference variable is in scope. Pointers can be manipulated. For example, a pointer variable that "points" to an object can be reassigned an address of a different object. This makes using pointers potentially dangerous so they should be used with caution. Unlike other programming languages, Delphi uses pointer variables to reference objects and not reference variables.

Creating your fifth OOP program

Programming task

Use the IDE to load or create and save the source code program shown in *Figure 20.4* as MyFifthOOP.dpr or MyFifthOOP.dproj, depending on the version of Delphi, in its own directory/folder named MyFifthOOP. Now compile the program (Ctrl F9). Run this program (F9).

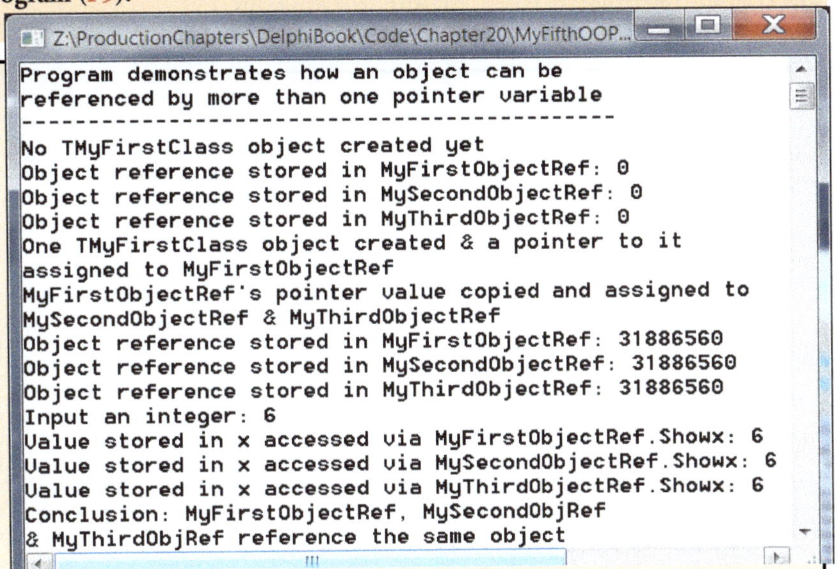

Fig. 20.5 Console window output produced when program MyFifthOOP is executed.

```
Program MyFifthOOP;
{Remember to Save Project As MyFifthOOP}
{$APPTYPE CONSOLE}
Type
  TMyFirstClass = Class
                    x: Integer;
                    Procedure Setx;
                    Procedure Showx;
                  End;
Procedure TMyFirstClass.Setx;
  Begin
    Write('Input an integer: ');
    Readln(x);
  End;
Procedure TMyFirstClass.Showx;
  Begin
    Writeln(x);
  End;
Var
  MyFirstObjectRef, MySecondObjectRef, MyThirdObjectRef :  TMyFirstClass;
Begin
  Writeln('Program demonstrates how an object can be');
  Writeln('referenced by more than one pointer variable');
  Writeln('----------------------------------------------');
  Writeln('No TMyFirstClass object created yet');
  Writeln('Object reference stored in MyFirstObjectRef: ',Integer(MyFirstObjectRef));
  Writeln('Object reference stored in MySecondObjectRef: ',Integer(MySecondObjectRef));
  Writeln('Object reference stored in MyThirdObjectRef: ',Integer(MyThirdObjectRef));
  Writeln('One TMyFirstClass object created & a pointer to it');
  Writeln('assigned to MyFirstObjectRef');
  Writeln('MyFirstObjectRef''s pointer copied and assigned to ');
  Writeln('MySecondObjectRef & MyThirdObjectRef');
  MyFirstObjectRef := TMyFirstClass.Create;
  MySecondObjectRef := MyFirstObjectRef;
  MyThirdObjectRef :=  MyFirstObjectRef;
  Writeln('Object reference stored in MyFirstObjectRef: ',Integer(MyFirstObjectRef));
  Writeln('Object reference stored in MySecondObjectRef: ',Integer(MySecondObjectRef));
  Writeln('Object reference stored in MyThirdObjectRef: ',Integer(MyThirdObjectRef));
  MyFirstObjectRef.Setx;
  Write('Value stored in x accessed via MyFirstObjectRef.Showx: ');
  MyFirstObjectRef.Showx;
  Write('Value stored in x accessed via MySecondObjectRef.Showx: ');
  MySecondObjectRef.Showx;
  Write('Value stored in x accessed via MyThirdObjectRef.Showx: ');
  MyThirdObjectRef.Showx;
  Writeln('Conclusion: MyFirstObjectRef, MySecondObjRef ');
  Writeln('& MyThirdObjRef reference the same object');
  Readln;
End.
```

Fig. 20.4 MyFifthOOP.dpr/dprog

P

MyFifthOOP on execution creates a single object of class `TMyFirstClass` and assigns a pointer to this object to variable `MyFirstObjectRef`. The pointer stored in `MyFirstObjectRef` is then copied and assigned to variables `MySecondObjectRef` and `MyThirdObjectRef`.

The console window output produced when program `MyFifthOOP` is executed is shown in *Figure 20.5*. The output shows that all three variables have the same pointer value which means that they must reference the same object.

A value of 6 is entered at the prompt `'Input an integer:'` generated by `MyFirstObjectRef.Setx;`.

Method `Showx` then outputs the same value 6 from this method call from all three pointer variables.

Creating your sixth OOP program

Programming task

Use the IDE to load or create and save the source code program *Figure 20.6* as MySixthOOP.dpr or MySixthOOP.dproj, depending on the version of Delphi, in its own directory/folder named MySixthOOP.
Now compile the program (Ctrl F9). Run this program (F9).

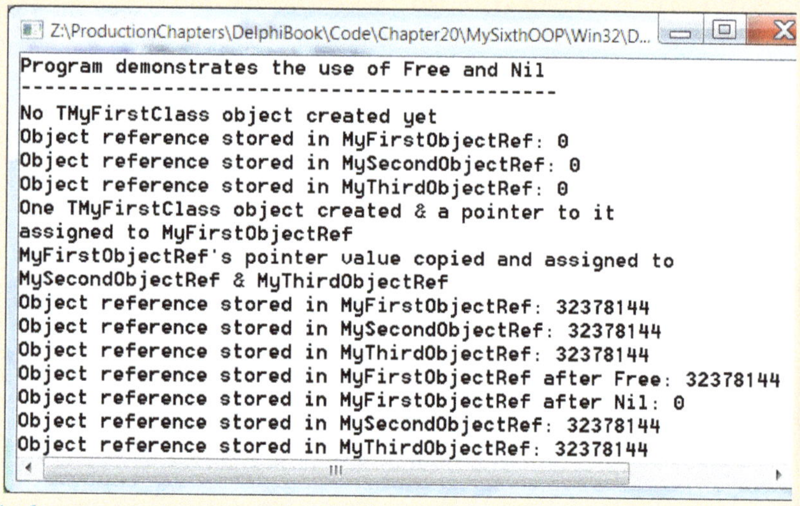

```
Z:\ProductionChapters\DelphiBook\Code\Chapter20\MySixthOOP\Win32\D...
Program demonstrates the use of Free and Nil
--------------------------------------------
No TMyFirstClass object created yet
Object reference stored in MyFirstObjectRef: 0
Object reference stored in MySecondObjectRef: 0
Object reference stored in MyThirdObjectRef: 0
One TMyFirstClass object created & a pointer to it
assigned to MyFirstObjectRef
MyFirstObjectRef's pointer value copied and assigned to
MySecondObjectRef & MyThirdObjectRef
Object reference stored in MyFirstObjectRef: 32378144
Object reference stored in MySecondObjectRef: 32378144
Object reference stored in MyThirdObjectRef: 32378144
Object reference stored in MyFirstObjectRef after Free: 32378144
Object reference stored in MyFirstObjectRef after Nil: 0
Object reference stored in MySecondObjectRef: 32378144
Object reference stored in MyThirdObjectRef: 32378144
```

Fig. 20.7 Console window output produced when program MyFifthOOP is executed.

```
Program MySixthOOP;
{Remember to Save Project As MySixthOOP}
{$APPTYPE CONSOLE}
Type
  TMyFirstClass = Class
                    x: Integer;
                    Procedure Setx;
                    Procedure Showx;
                  End;
Procedure TMyFirstClass.Setx;
  Begin
    Write('Input an integer: ');
    Readln(x);
  End;
Procedure TMyFirstClass.Showx;
  Begin
    Writeln(x);
  End;
Var
  MyFirstObjectRef, MySecondObjectRef, MyThirdObjectRef :  TMyFirstClass;
Begin
  Writeln('Program demonstrates the use of Free and Nil');
  Writeln('--------------------------------------------');
  Writeln('No TMyFirstClass object created yet');
  Writeln('Object reference stored in MyFirstObjectRef: ', Integer(MyFirstObjectRef));
  Writeln('Object reference stored in MySecondObjectRef: ', Integer(MySecondObjectRef));
  Writeln('Object reference stored in MyThirdObjectRef: ', Integer(MyThirdObjectRef));
  Writeln('One TMyFirstClass object created & pointer to it');
  Writeln('assigned to MyFirstObjectRef');
  Writeln('MyFirstObjectRef''s pointer value copied and assigned to ');
  Writeln('MySecondObjectRef & MyThirdObjectRef');
  MyFirstObjectRef := TMyFirstClass.Create;
  MySecondObjectRef := MyFirstObjectRef;
  MyThirdObjectRef :=  MyFirstObjectRef;
  Writeln('object reference stored in MyFirstObjectRef: ', Integer(MyFirstObjectRef));
  Writeln('Object reference stored in MySecondObjectRef: ', Integer(MySecondObjectRef));
  Writeln('Object reference stored in MyThirdObjectRef: ', Integer(MyThirdObjectRef));
  MyFirstObjectRef.Free;
  Writeln('Object reference stored in MyFirstObjectRef after Free: ', Integer(MyFirstObjectRef));
  MyFirstObjectRef := Nil;
  Writeln('object reference stored in MyFirstObjectRef after Nil: ', Integer(MyFirstObjectRef));
  Writeln('Object reference stored in MySecondObjectRef: ', Integer(MySecondObjectRef));
  Writeln('Object reference stored in MyThirdObjectRef: ', Integer(MyThirdObjectRef));
  //MySecondObjectRef.Setx;
  Readln;
End.
```

P

Fig. 20.6 MySixthOOP.dpr/dprog

MySixthOOP on execution creates a single object of class `TMyFirstClass` and assigns a pointer to the object to variable `MyFirstObjectRef`. The pointer value stored in `MyFirstObjectRef` is then copied and assigned to variables `MySecondObjectRef` and `MyThirdObjectRef`.
The console window output produced when program `MySixthOOP` is executed is shown in *Figure 20.7*. The object referenced by `MyFirstObjectRef` is destroyed by de-allocating its memory with the statement

```
MyFirstObjectRef.Free;
```

`Free` first checks to see if the referenced object exists before calling `Destroy` behind the scenes. Notice that the reference value 32378144 is still assigned to `MyFirstObjectRef` even though it is no longer valid. One more operation must be carried out: `MyFirstObjectRef := Nil;` This statement assigns the `nil` reference to `MyFirstObjectRef`. The `nil` reference is interpreted as a reference that doesn't reference anything. It shows as 0 in the console window.

Programming task

Now extend **MySixthOOP.dpr/dproj** with the addition of the statements shown in red in *Figure 20.8*.

Save Project AS MySixthOOPext.dpr/dproj. Now compile the program (Ctrl F9) in debug mode. Run this program (F9).

```
Program MySixthOOPext;
Uses SysUtils;
........
  MyFirstObjectRef := Nil;
  Writeln('Reference stored in MyFirstObjectRef after Nil: ', Integer(MyFirstObjectRef));
  Writeln('Reference stored in MySecondObjectRef: ', Integer(MySecondObjectRef));
  Writeln('Reference stored in MyThirdObjectRef: ', Integer(MyThirdObjectRef));
  Try
    MySecondObjectRef.Free;
    MySecondObjectRef := Nil;
  Except
    On E: Exception Do Writeln(E.Message);
  End;
  //MySecondObjectRef.Setx;
  Readln;
End.
```

Fig. 20.8 Section of MySixthOOP.dpr/dprog subject to modification shown in red

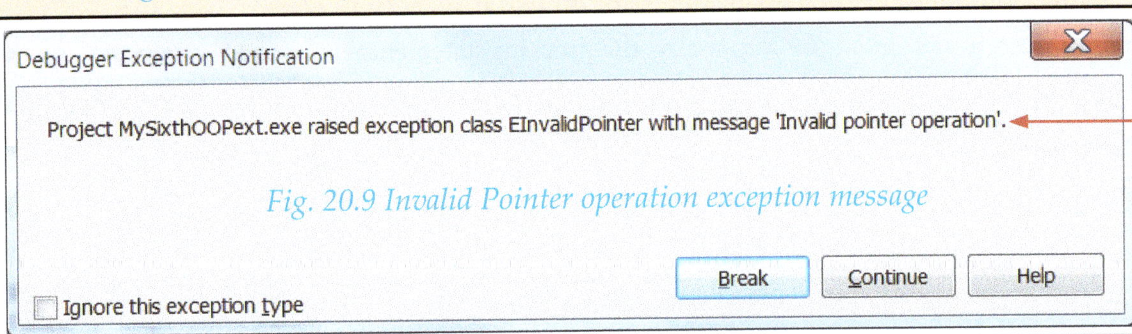

Fig. 20.9 Invalid Pointer operation exception message

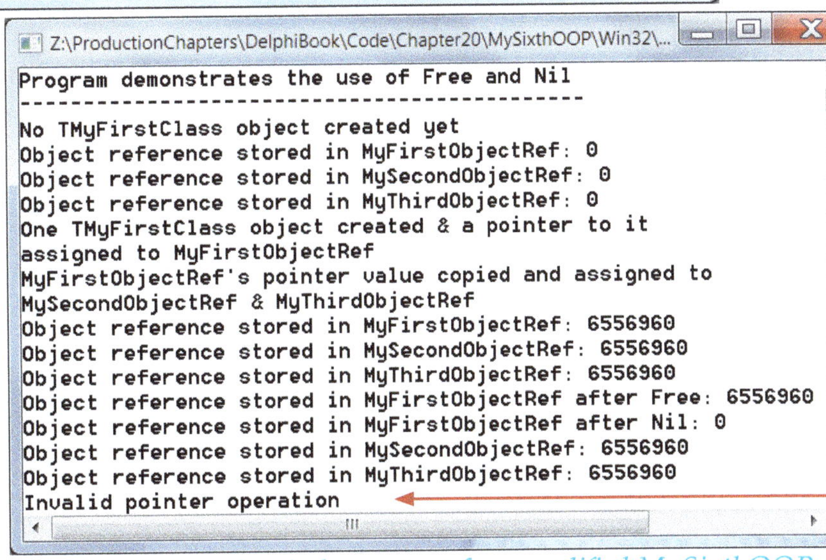

Fig. 20.10 Console window output from modified MySixthOOP

Figure 20.9 shows the **Debugger Exception Notification** window that appears when `MySecondObjectRef.Free` is attempted. The invalid pointer operation refers to an attempt to free memory which has already been freed. A pointer is just a memory address. Clicking on `Continue` results in the console output window shown in *Figure 20.10* also reporting '`Invalid Pointer Operation`'.

The debugger can be bypassed and the same console window *Figure 20.10* generated by running **MySixthOOP.exe** directly from command line or running **MySixthOOPext** from the IDE by pressing Shift + Ctrl + F9. To eliminate the exception just delete `MySecondObjectRef.Free`.

Programming task

Now edit MySixthOOPext.dpr/dproj as shown in *Figure 20.11*. Save Project AS MySixthOOPext1.dpr/dproj. The statement `MySecondObjectRef.Free` has been removed and `MySecondObjectRef.Setx;` relocated as shown in red.

Now compile the program (Ctrl F9) in debug mode. Run this program (F9).

```
  ..........
  Writeln('Object reference stored in MyFirstObjectRef after Nil: ', Integer(MyFirstObjectRef));
  Writeln('Object reference stored in MySecondObjectRef: ', Integer(MySecondObjectRef));
  Writeln('Object reference stored in MyThirdObjectRef: ', Integer(MyThirdObjectRef));
  Try
    MySecondObjectRef := Nil;
    MySecondObjectRef.Setx;
  Except
    On E: Exception Do Writeln(E.Message);
  End;
  Readln;
End.
```

Fig. 20.11 Section of MySixthOOPext.dpr/dprog subject to modification shown in red

Figure 20.12 shows the **Debugger Exception Notification** window that appears when the running program attempts to execute `MySecondObjectRef.Setx`.

This is such a serious error that clicking on `Continue` doesn't prevent the program from crashing.

The cause of this serious memory access violation error is the statement `MySecondObjectRef.Setx;` caused by a `nil` pointer assigned to `MySecondObjectRef` by the previous statement.

You can check this for yourself by commenting out statement `MySecondObjectRef.Setx` and recompiling and running the program again.

The lesson learned is that care must be taken when using pointer variables that reference objects.

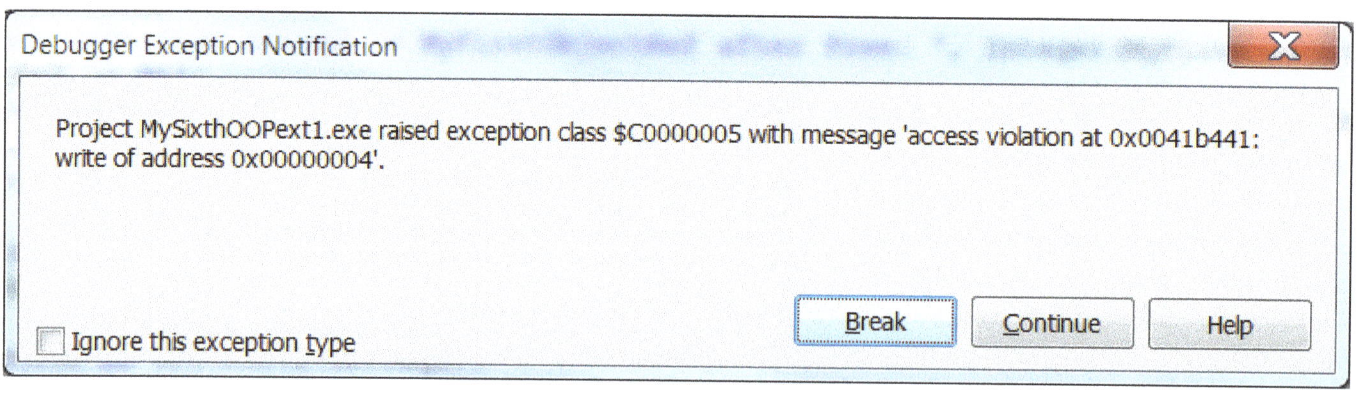

Fig. 20.12 Memory access violation message

Creating your seventh OOP program

Programming task

Load program MySeventhOOP.dpr/dproj shown in *Figure 20.13* and save in its own folder MySeventhOOP. Now compile the program (Ctrl F9) in debug mode. Run this program (F9).

```
Program MySeventhOOP;
{Remember to Save Project As MySeventhOOP}
{$APPTYPE CONSOLE}
Type
  TMyFirstClass = Class
                    x: Integer;
                    Procedure Setx;
                    Procedure Showx;
                  End;
  TProcRef = Procedure Of Object;
Procedure TMyFirstClass.Setx;
  Begin
    Write('Input an integer: ');
    Readln(x);
  End;
Procedure TMyFirstClass.Showx;
  Begin
    Writeln(x);
  End;
Var
  MyFirstObjectRef, MySecondObjectRef, MyThirdObjectRef : TMyFirstClass;
  MethodRef1, MethodRef2, MethodRef3 : TProcRef;
Begin
  Writeln('Program demonstrates that method SetX shared by three objects');
  Writeln('-----------------------------------------------------------');
  Writeln('No TMyFirstClass object created yet');
  Writeln('Object reference stored in MyFirstObjectRef: ', Integer(MyFirstObjectRef));
  Writeln('Object reference stored in MySecondObjectRef: ', Integer(MySecondObjectRef));
  Writeln('Object reference stored in MyThirdObjectRef: ', Integer(MyThirdObjectRef));
  Writeln('Three TMyFirstClass objects created & a pointer to each');
  Writeln('assigned to MyFirstObjectRef, MySecondObjectRef,MyThirdObjectRef respectively');
  MyFirstObjectRef := TMyFirstClass.Create;
  MySecondObjectRef := TMyFirstClass.Create;
  MyThirdObjectRef :=  TMyFirstClass.Create;
  Writeln('Object reference stored in MyFirstObjectRef: ', Integer(MyFirstObjectRef));
  Writeln('Object reference stored in MySecondObjectRef: ', Integer(MySecondObjectRef));
  Writeln('Object reference stored in MyThirdObjectRef: ', Integer(MyThirdObjectRef));
  MethodRef1:= MyFirstObjectRef.Setx;
  MethodRef2:= MySecondObjectRef.Setx;
  MethodRef3:= MyThirdObjectRef.Setx;
  Writeln('Object ref for MyFirstObjectRef.Setx stored in MethodRef1:',Integer(Addr(MethodRef1)));
  Writeln('Object ref for MySecondObjectRef.Setx stored in MethodRef2:',Integer(Addr(MethodRef2)));
  Writeln('Object ref stored for MyThirdObjectRef.Setx in MethodRef3:',Integer(Addr(MethodRef3)));
  Readln;
End.
```

Fig. 20.13 Program MySeventhOOP

Key fact

Addr:

Addr returns a pointer to a procedure/method of an object.

MySeventhOOP when executed creates three objects of class `TMyFirstClass`. The references to each object are stored as pointers in the pointer variables `MyFirstObjectRef`, `MySecondObjectRef` and `MyThirdObjectRef`, respectively. The program declares three method pointer variables `MethodRef1`, `MethodRef2`, `MethodRef3` of type `TProcRef`. `TProcRef` is a pointer type for referencing a procedure of an object, e.g. the address of `Setx`. `Addr(MethodRef1)` returns the pointer value held by `MethodRef1`. This pointer value is then type cast to an `Integer` data type by the operation `Integer()`. This is done so that the value can be written by `Writeln`.

The console window output produced when program `MySeventOOP` is executed is shown in *Figure 20.14*. Note that the reference for `MyFirstObjectRef.Setx`, 4235732, is the same as the reference for `MySecondObjectRef.Setx` and `MyThirdObjectRef.Setx`.
This is because all three objects reference the same copy of `Setx`.

```
Z:\ProductionChapters\DelphiBook\Code\Chapter20\MySeventhOOP\Win32\Debug\MySeventh...
Program demonstrates that method SetX shared by three objects
------------------------------------------------------------
No TMyFirstClass object created yet
Object reference stored in MyFirstObjectRef: 0
Object reference stored in MySecondObjectRef: 0
Object reference stored in MyThirdObjectRef: 0
Three TMyFirstClass objects created & a pointer to each
assigned to MyFirstObjectRef, MySecondObjectRef,MyThirdObjectRef respectively.
Object reference stored in MyFirstObjectRef: 31100128
Object reference stored in MySecondObjectRef: 31100144
Object reference stored in MyThirdObjectRef: 31100160
Object ref for MyFirstObjectRef.Setx stored in MethodRef1:4235732
Object ref for MySecondObjectRef.Setx stored in MethodRef2:4235732
Object ref stored for MyThirdObjectRef.Setx in MethodRef3:4235732
```

Fig. 20.14 Console window output from MySeventhOOP

Method pointer variables are treated differently from variable pointer variables (pointers that point to variables). `Program IntegerPtrExample` in *Figure 20.15* shows that a pointer that points to a memory location that stores an integer value or points to a memory location used by an integer variable must be dereferenced before it can access the stored integer value, e.g. `IntegerPtr^`.
However, method pointer variables do not require explicit dereferencing as it is done automatically.
In program `MySeventhOOPext` in *Figure 20.16* `MethodRef1` is a pointer to a procedure of an object, i.e. a method. This program assigns the address in memory of the entry point for the code ofor `Setx` as follows

```
MethodRef1:= MyFirstObjectRef.Setx;
```

and calls this method without explicitly dereferencing the pointer as follows

```
MethodRef1;
```

Key point

`MyFirstObjectRef.Setx` is itself a pointer to the code for this method.

```
Program IntegerPtrExample;
{Remember to Save Project As MySeventhOOPext}
Var
  z : Integer; {Creates integer variable}
  IntegerPtr : ^Integer; {Creates pointer variable which will store a pointer to an}
                         {integer variable or storage area for an integer value}
Begin
  z := 3;
  Writeln('Value of integer variable z: ', z);
  New(IntegerPtr); {Allocates storage space from heap(RAM) for an integer &}
                   {places address of this staorage location in IntegerPtr}
  IntegerPtr^ := 3; { Assigns integer value 3 to this storage location}
  {Writeln displays the stored integer value}
  Writeln('Integer stored at address given by IntegerPtr^ is ', Integer(IntegerPtr^));
  Dispose(IntegerPtr); {De-allocates the storage space}
  IntegerPtr := Addr(z); {Address of integer variable z assigned to IntegerPtr}
  Writeln('Integer stored in z is ', Integer(IntegerPtr^), ' obtained via IntegerPtr^');
  Readln;
End.
```

Fig. 20.15 Program which uses a pointer variable IntegerPtr to point to an integer variable z

P

```
Z:\ProductionChapters\DelphiBook\Code\Chapter20\My...
Integer stored at address given by IntegerPtr^ is 3
Integer stored in z is 3 obtained via IntegerPtr^
```

Modifying MySeventhOOP program

Programming task

Load program MySeventhOOPext.dpr/dproj shown in *Figure 20.16* and save in its own folder MySeventhOOPext. Now compile the program (Ctrl F9) in debug mode. Run this program (F9).

```
Program MySeventhOOPext;
{Remember to Save Project As MySeventhOOPext}
{$APPTYPE CONSOLE}
Type
  TMyFirstClass = Class
                    x: Integer;
                    Procedure Setx;
                    Procedure Showx;
                  End;
  TProcRef = Procedure Of Object;
  TIntegerPtr = ^Integer;
Procedure TMyFirstClass.Setx;
  Begin
    Write('Input an integer: ');
    Readln(x);
  End;
Procedure TMyFirstClass.Showx;
  Begin
    Writeln(x);
  End;
Var
  MyFirstObjectRef : TMyFirstClass;
  MethodRef1 : TProcRef;
  z : Integer;
  IntegerPtr : TIntegerPtr;
Begin
  Writeln('Program demonstrates method pointer & variable pointer variables');
  Writeln('---------------------------------------------------------------');
  Writeln('No TMyFirstClass object created yet');
  Writeln('Object reference stored in MyFirstObjectRef: ', Integer(MyFirstObjectRef));
  Writeln('One TMyFirstClass object created & a pointer to it');
  Writeln('assigned to MyFirstObjectRef.');
  MyFirstObjectRef := TMyFirstClass.Create;
  Writeln('Object reference stored in MyFirstObjectRef: ', Integer(MyFirstObjectRef));
  Writeln('Copy of reference to MyFirstObjectRef.Setx assigned to MethodRef1');
  MethodRef1:= MyFirstObjectRef.Setx;
  Write('MyFirstObjectRef.Setx called via MethodRef1 - "MethodRef1;"');
  MethodRef1; {Calls MyFirstObjectRef.Setx}
  Writeln('MyFirstObjectRef.Showx called: ');
  MyFirstObjectRef.Showx;
  z := 3;
  IntegerPtr := Addr(z);
  Writeln('Value of z: ', z);
  Writeln('Address of z(Addr(z)): ', Integer(Addr(z)));
  Write('Address of z assigned to IntegerPtr(IntegerPtr := Addr(z)): ');
  Writeln(Integer(IntegerPtr));
  Writeln('Value of z via dereferenced IntegerPtr(IntegerPtr^): ', IntegerPtr^);
  Readln;
End.
```

P

Fig. 20.16 Shows program MySeventhOOPext which demonstrates the difference between method pointer and variable pointer variables.

Figure 20.17 shows the console window output when **MyOOPSevenext** is run.

The program statement

```
MethodRef1:= MyFirstObjectRef.Setx;
```

assigns a pointer to `MethodRef1` which points to the code for the object method `Setx` because `MyFirstObjectRef.Setx` stores a pointer to this code.

The program statement

```
MethodRef1;
```

calls the object method `Setx` using implicit pointer dereferencing, i.e. equivalent to `MethodRef1^`.

Implicit pointer dereferencing occurs if the pointer points to a method of an object or class.

The program statements

```
z := 3;
IntegerPtr := Addr(z);
```

assign the value 3 to the integer variable `z` and the address of `z` to the integer pointer variable `IntegerPtr`.

The program statement

```
Writeln('Value of z via dereferenced IntegerPtr(IntegerPtr^): ', IntegerPtr^);
```

explicitly dereferences the integer pointer variable `IntegerPtr` to be able to access the integer value stored in the variable `z` before writing it to the console window.

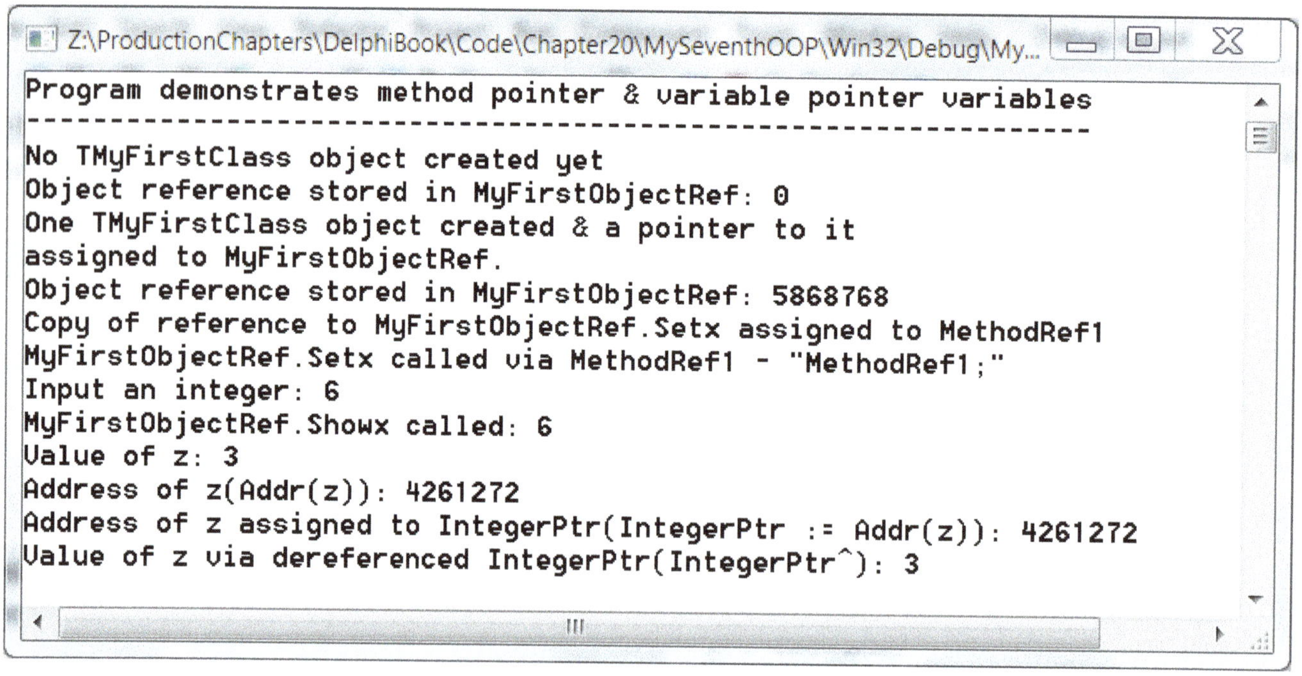

Fig. 20.17 Console window output from MySeventhOOPext

21 Encapsulation and information hiding

Information hiding and modularity

Purpose: To learn that unit is the way of enforcing modularity and information hiding

The mechanism used in Object Pascal (Delphi) to hide information about a class starts with the **Unit**.

Start a new Console application project and save project as **Encapsulation1.dpr** or **Encapsulation1.dproj**, depending on the version of Delphi, in its own directory/folder named **Encapsulation1**.

Using the mouse click on **File** and hover over **New** to reveal the options drop down menu as shown in *Figure 21.1*. Click on **Unit - Delphi** to create a new **unit** as shown in *Figure 21.2*.

Using **Save As**, save the unit as **UPerson.pas**.

Note that the unit name changes to `Unit UPerson` as shown in *Figure 21.3* and that `Uses UPerson in 'UPerson.pas'` is automatically added to the main program **Encapsulation1.dproj** as shown in *Figure 21.4*.

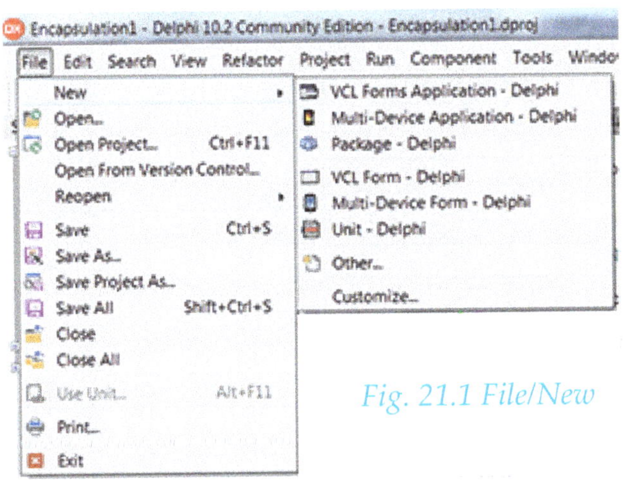

Fig. 21.1 File/New

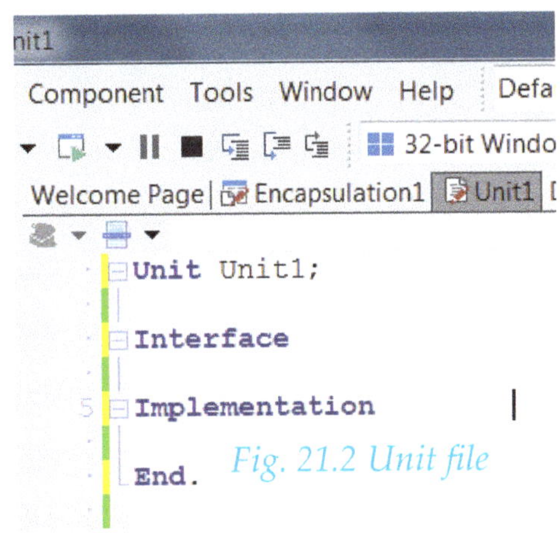

Fig. 21.2 Unit file

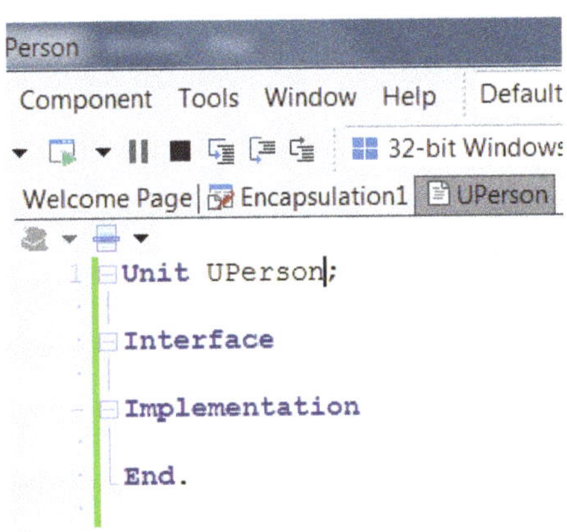

Fig. 21.3 Unit name changed when Unit saved as UPerson.pas.

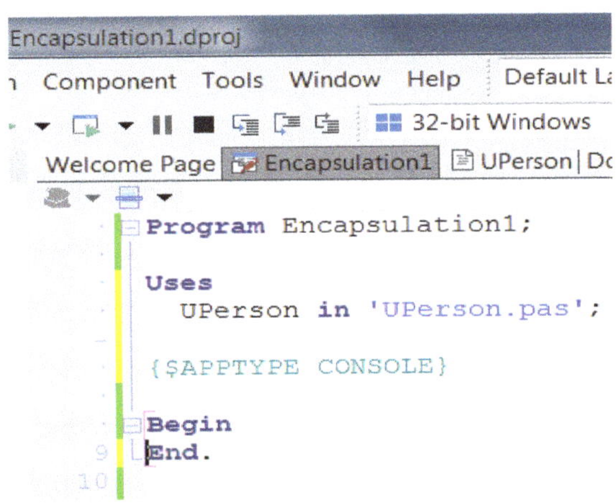

Fig. 21.4 Reference to UPerson automatically added to main program.

Figure 21.5 shows unit `UPerson` expanded to include the declaration of two variables, `x` and `y` of data type integer, and the declaration and implementation of two functions, `Getx` and `Gety` that both return a result of data type integer.

Figure 21.6 shows the failed attempt to compile and build **Encapsulation1.Exe**.

Failure takes place at two places in **Encapsulation1.dpr**:

1. Line 11 because variable `y` is not recognised.
2. Line 12 because function `Gety` is not recognised.

Both variable `y` and function `Gety` are declared/defined together in unit `UPerson` in its **Implementation** section and this is the reason for the compile/build failure: both are not visible outside `UPerson`.

To be visible from outside `UPerson`, variable `y`'s declaration must be moved to the **Interface** section of `UPerson`. For function `Gety` to be visible from outside `UPerson` then a copy of its header must be present in the interface section in a similar manner to function `Getx`.

```
Unit UPerson;
Interface
  Var
    x : Integer = 6;
  Function Getx : Integer;
Implementation
  Var
    y : Integer = 7;
  Function Getx : Integer;
   Begin
      Result := x;
    End;
  Function Gety : Integer;
    Begin
      Result := y;
    End;
End.
```

Fig. 21.5 Unit UPerson with two declared variables and two functions.

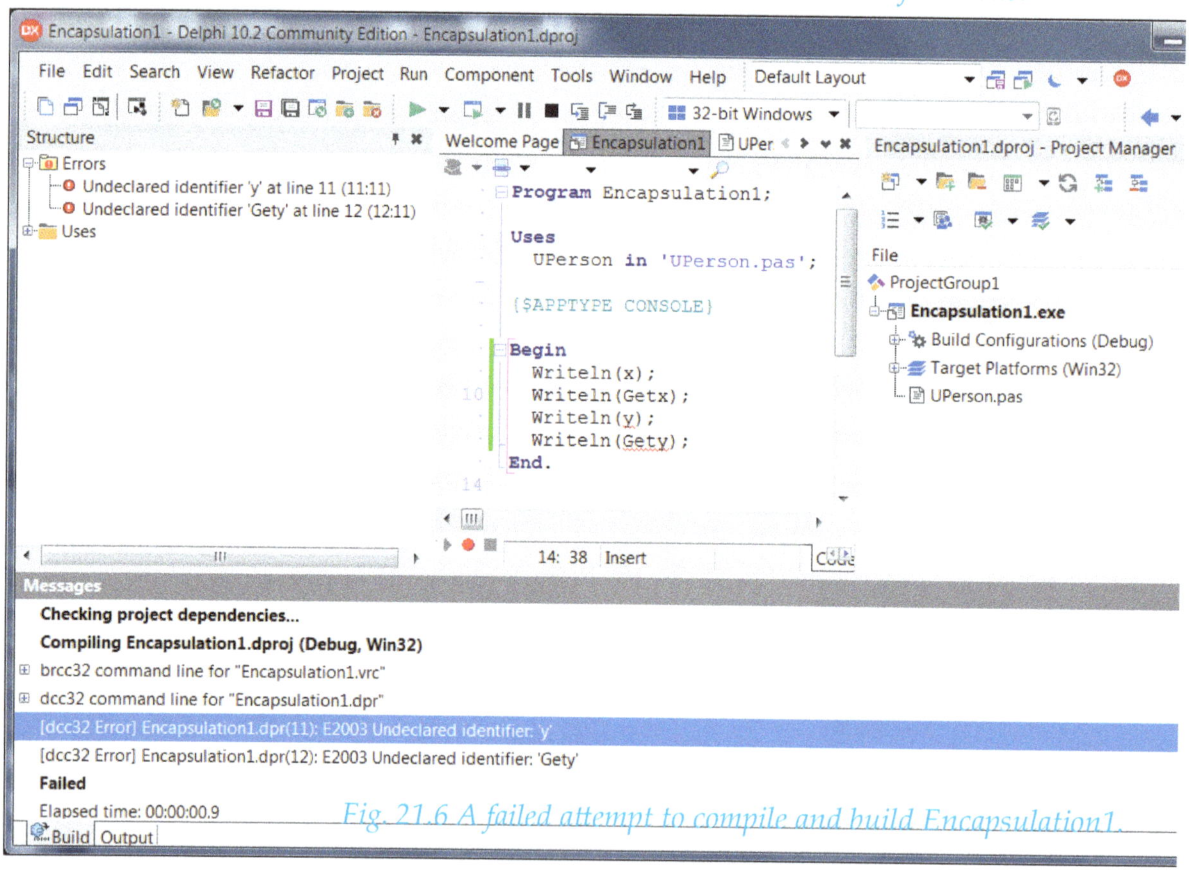

Fig. 21.6 A failed attempt to compile and build Encapsulation1.

From this simple demonstration we learn that

1. The **Implementation** section is where things are placed which are to be hidden from the main program (the application). The code for `Getx`, `Gety` and the variable `y` are hidden.
2. The **Interface** section is where things are placed which are to be visible from outside the unit, variable `x` and function `Getx`.
3. The mechanism that is used to **hide information** about the existence of **variables** and **functions** is the **unit** which is a **module of the whole system** consisting of the main program and units that the main program uses.

Information hiding and modularity

Purpose: To learn that encapsulation is a form of information hiding

The program **Encapsulation1** from the previous section hid implementation details of function `Getx` in the implementation section of unit `UPerson`. We call this form of information hiding, **implementation encapsulation**.

One dictionary definition of encapsulation is

"*the action of enclosing something in or as if in a capsule*"

Encapsulation and information hiding are important concepts in Object Oriented Programming (OOP).

To see how encapsulation may be enforced and information hiding used in OOP start a new Console application project and save project as **Encapsulation2.dpr** or **Encapsulation2.dproj**, depending on the version of Delphi, in its own directory/folder named **Encapsulation2**.

As before, use the mouse to select **File** then **New Unit - Delphi** to create a new **unit**.

Use **Save As** to save the unit as **UPerson.pas**. Add source code to the main program and the unit `UPerson` as shown in *Figure 21.7* and *Figure 21.8*. Note that the language keyword **Private** has been commented out for the moment.

Press **F9** to compile, build and run **Encapsulation2**. *Figure 21.9* shows the console output from the executing program. The `Name` field value '*Fred Bloggs*' is output twice, once by directly accessing the `Name` field of the `TPersonClass` object `PersonObject` and once indirectly through the `TPersonClass` object method `ShowPersonDetails`.

```
Program Encapsulation2;
Uses UPerson in 'UPerson.pas';
{$APPTYPE CONSOLE}
Var
  PersonObject : TPersonClass;
Begin
  PersonObject := TPersonClass.Create;
  PersonObject.Name := 'Fred Bloggs';
  Write('Direct access to field - ');
  Writeln(PersonObject.Name);
  Write('Indirect access to field - ');
  PersonObject.ShowPersonDetails;
  PersonObject.Free;
  Readln;
End.
```

Fig. 21.7 Encapsulation2.dprog.

Fig. 21.9 Output window of executing Encapsulation2.exe

```
Unit UPerson;
Interface
  Type
    TPersonClass = Class
   //               Private
                     Name : String[30];
                     Address : String[40];
                     Age : Integer;
                   Public
                     Procedure AddPersonDetails;
                     Procedure EditPersonDetails;
                     Procedure ShowPersonDetails;
                 End;
Implementation
  Procedure TPersonClass.AddPersonDetails;
    Begin
    End;
  Procedure TPersonClass.EditPersonDetails;
    Begin
    End;
  Procedure TPersonClass.ShowPersonDetails;
    Begin
     Writeln(Name);
    End;
End.
```

Fig. 21.8 Unit UPerson.pas.

Creating data encapsulation by a change to the visibility of fields of a class

One key aspect in designing a class is deciding which features should be known outside the class and which should remain "secret" or hidden.

This aspect of class design is known as **visibility** since it has to do with which features of the class are visible or exposed outside the class.

The parts exposed are called the **class' interface**.

The interface of a class should reveal as little as possible about the inner workings of the class.

Encapsulation3 program

Use **Save Project As** to save **Encapsulation2.dpr** or **Encapsulation2.dproj**, depending on which version of Delphi you are using, as **Encapsulation3.dpr** or **Encapsulation3.dproj** in its own directory/folder named **Encapsulation3**.

Use **Save As** to save **UPerson.pas** in directory/folder **Encapsulation3**.

Now remove the comment slashes // to leave **UPerson.pas** as shown in *Figure 21.10*.

The language keyword **Private** controls the **visibility** of the three fields `Name`, `Address` and `Age` whilst the language keyword **Public** controls the visibility of the three methods of the class, procedures `AddPersonDetails`, `EditPersonDetails` and `ShowPersonDetails`.

The keywords **Private** and **Public** are called **access specifiers**.

The three fields `Name`, `Address` and `Age` are now encapsulated and therefore invisible outside of unit **UPerson** whilst the three procedures

- `AddPersonDetails`
- `EditPersonDetails`
- `ShowPersonDetails`

are visible outside the unit with the exception of their implementation.

Press **F9** to compile, build and run **Encapsulation3**.

P

Access specifier → Private

Data encapsulation → Name, Address, Age

Access specifier → Public

Visible outside unit → Procedure AddPersonDetails, EditPersonDetails, ShowPersonDetails

```
Unit UPerson;
Interface
  Type
    TPersonClass = Class
      Private
        Name : String[30];
        Address : String[40];
        Age : Integer;
      Public
        Procedure AddPersonDetails;
        Procedure EditPersonDetails;
        Procedure ShowPersonDetails;
    End;
Implementation
  Procedure TPersonClass.AddPersonDetails;
    Begin
      Write('Input name: ');
      Readln(Name);
      Write('Input address on one line: ');
      Readln(Address);
      Write('Input age in years: ');
      Readln(Age);
    End;
  Procedure TPersonClass.EditPersonDetails;
    Begin
    End;
  Procedure TPersonClass.ShowPersonDetails;
    Begin
     Writeln(Name);
    End;
End.
```

Fig. 21.10 Unit UPerson.pas.

Two compile errors occur as shown in *Figure 21.11*, one at line 10 and another at line 12.

Both are caused by attempting to use the field `Name`, a private field.

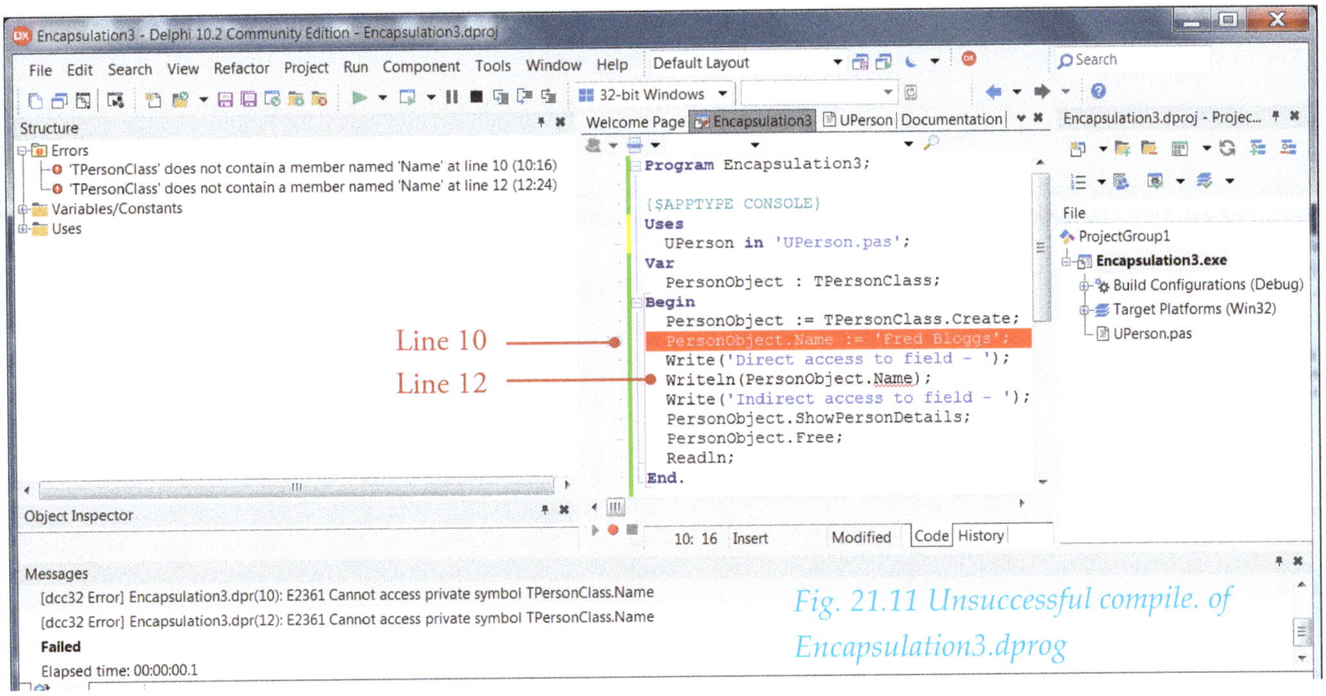

Fig. 21.11 Unsuccessful compile. of Encapsulation3.dprog

This demonstrates that **data encapsulation** is working on the field `Name`.

This field of `TPersonClass` is not visible outside unit **UPerson**.

The same outcome would result if we attempted to use fields `Address` and `Age` outside unit **UPerson.**

To successfully compile **Encapsulation3.dproj** we need to remove lines 10 and 12. But we also need to add values for the fields `Name`, `Address` and `Age` if the program is to be useful.

Encapsulation4 program

Use Save Project As to save Encapsulation3.dpr or Encapsulation3.dproj, depending on which version of Delphi you are using, as Encapsulation4.dpr or Encapsulation4.dproj in its own directory/folder named Encapsulation4.

Use Save As to save UPerson.pas in directory/folder Encapsulation4.

P

Remove from Encapsulation4.dpr/Encapsulation4.dprog

```
PersonObject.Name := 'Fred Bloggs';
Write('Direct access to field - ');
Writeln(PersonObject.Name);
```

and replace with

```
PersonObject.AddPersonDetails;
```

as shown in *Figure 21.12*.

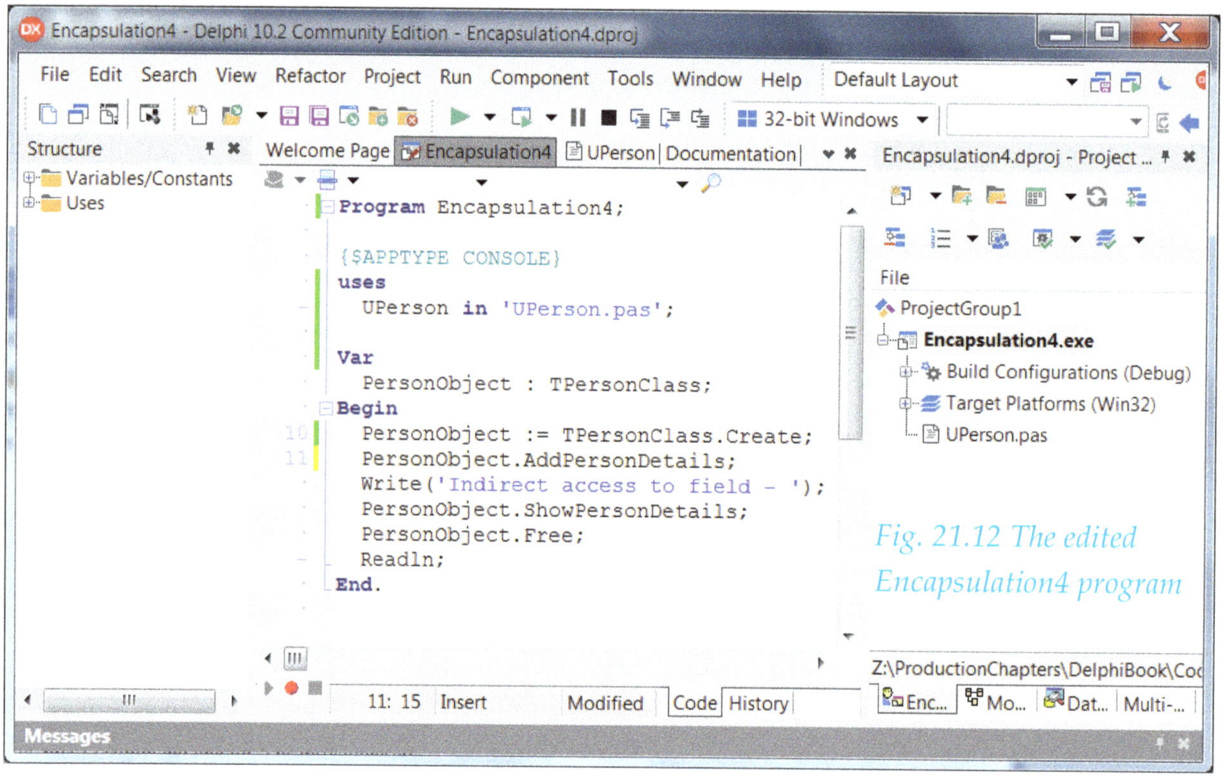

Fig. 21.12 The edited Encapsulation4 program

Use Save to save Encapsulation4.dpr/Encapsulation4.dproj.

Press F9 to compile, build and run Encapsulation4.

Figure 21.13 shows the output window when Encapsulation4.exe is executing and three lines of input have been entered.

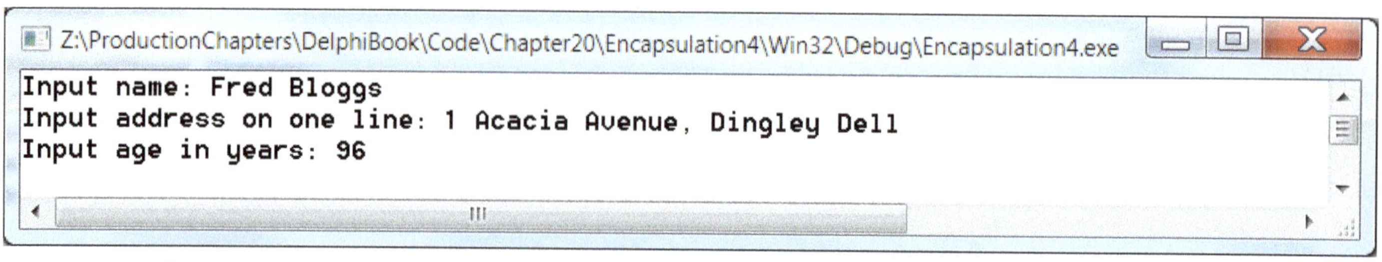

Fig. 21.13 Output window of executing Encapsulation4.exe showing user input stage

Figure 21.14 shows the output window when **Encapsulation4.exe** is executing and `PersonObject.ShowPersonDetails` called.

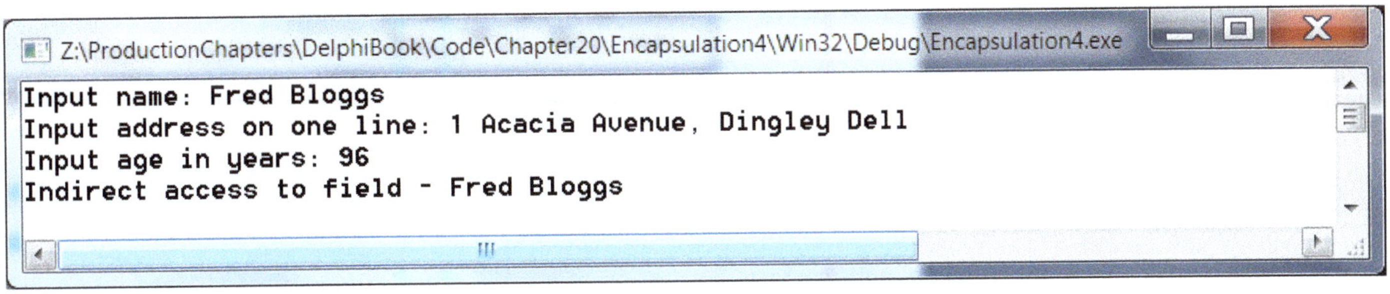

Fig. 21.14 Output window of executing Encapsulation4.exe after PersonObject.ShowPersonDetails called

Procedure `TPersonClass.ShowPersonDetails` in unit `UPerson` must be changed as follows for the values of the other two fields of the object to be displayed in the output window

```
Procedure TPersonClass.ShowPersonDetails;
  Begin
    Writeln(Name);
    Writeln(Address);
    Writeln(Age);
  End;
```

We also need to adjust **Encapsulation4.dpr**/**Encapsulation4.dprog** as follows so that its output of the `Name` field value appears on its own line

Changed `Write` to `Writeln`

```
Program Encapsulation4;
Uses UPerson in 'UPerson.pas';
{$APPTYPE CONSOLE}
Var
  PersonObject : TPersonClass;
Begin
  PersonObject := TPersonClass.Create;
  Writeln('Indirect access to fields - ');
  PersonObject.ShowPersonDetails;
  PersonObject.Free;
  Readln;
End.
```

Programming Task

1. Use *Save Project As* to save *Encapsulation4.dpr* or *Encapsulation4.dproj*, depending on which version of Delphi you are using, as *Encapsulation5.dpr* or *Encapsulation5.dproj* in its own directory/folder named *Encapsulation5*. Use *Save As* to save *UPerson.pas* in directory/folder *Encapsulation5*.

   Make changes to *Encapsulation5.dpr/ Encapsulation5.dproj* and *UPerson.pas* as shown above and save each. Press *F9* to compile, build and run *Encapsulation5*.

Purpose: To learn that the degree to which information within a class can be hidden rests on the assignment of a visibility level to that information

Access to the **attribute fields, properties** and **methods** of an object may be controlled with the access modifiers/specifiers **public**, **private**, **protected**, **published**, **strict private** and **strict protected**.

Public

Table 21.1 shows the declaration of `TPerson` class in Object Pascal. The details of the implementation of its methods are omitted because they are not visible outside the unit. However, the identifiers `AddPersonDetails`, `EditPersonDetails`, `ShowPersonDetails` are visible outside the unit because they have been declared within the `TPerson` class in the `Interface` section as public using the keyword **Public**.

Private

The attributes `Name`, `Address` and `Age` are not visible outside of the unit because they are declared as private with the keyword **Private** in the `Interface` section.

They can be accessed from outside the unit indirectly but only through the public methods of the class, `TPerson`. Inside the unit they may be accessed directly in the implementation section.

PersonClass.pas

```
Unit PersonClass;
Interface
Type
  TPerson = Class
              Private
                Name : String[30];
                Address : String[40];
                Age : Integer;
              Public
                Procedure AddPersonDetails;
                Procedure EditPersonDetails;
                Procedure ShowPersonDetails;
              End;
Implementation
  Procedure TPerson.AddPersonDetails;
    Begin
      ...
    End;
  Procedure TPerson.EditPersonDetails;
    Begin
      ...
    End;
  Procedure TPerson.ShowPersonDetails;
    Begin
      ....
    End;
End.
```

Visible inside unit
Not visible outside unit
Visible outside unit
Hidden

Table 21.1 TPerson class in Object Pascal showing the use of Private and Public access modifiers

Table 21.2 shows in red, the error message emitted by the compiler (dcc32 - **D**elphi **C**ommand line **C**ompiler - **32** bit version) on encountering an unsuccessful attempt to access the `Name` attribute outside of the `PersonClass` unit.

Table 21.3 shows a modified version of the program which does compile because the method `AddPersonDetails` is labelled public and therefore visible outside the unit `PersonClass`. As both `AddPersonDetails` and `Name` belong to the same class, `TPerson`, method `AddPersonDetails` is allowed to update attribute `Name`.

```
Program PersonExample;
{$APPTYPE CONSOLE}
{$R *.res}
Uses
  System.SysUtils,
  PersonClass in 'PersonClass.pas';
Var
  Person : TPerson;
Begin
  Person := TPerson.Create;
  Person.Name := 'Fred';
End.
```

[dcc32 Error] PersonExample.dpr(13): E2361 Cannot access private symbol TPerson.Name

Table 21.2 TPersonExample program fails to compile because Name is private

```
Program PersonExample;
{$APPTYPE CONSOLE}
{$R *.res}
Uses
  System.SysUtils,
  PersonClass in 'PersonClass.pas';
Var
  Person : TPerson;
Begin
  Person := TPerson.Create;
  Person.AddPersonDetails;
End.
```

Table 21.3 Delphi TPersonExample program which does compile because AddPersonDetails is visible outside PersonClass.pas

Key term

Access modifiers or specifiers:

It is possible to specify whether access to an attribute or method from outside the unit/module or class in which declared, is either public, private, protected, published, strict private, strict protected.

Protected[1]

Suppose we need to model a special person (this is a very contrived example) in a class `TSpecialPerson`.

A special person will have all the attributes and behaviours of a person plus some additional methods and attributes of its own. It therefore needs to inherit from class `TPerson`.

Table 21.4 shows the declaration of the class `TSpecialPerson` with one public method, other methods and attributes have been omitted for brevity.

The method procedure `TSpecialPerson.AddTitle` needs to access the attribute `Name` declared in `TPerson`.

Unfortunately, `Name` is a private attribute and therefore not visible outside the unit `PersonClass`.

It is not enough for unit `SpecialPerson` to state `Uses PersonClass` to gain access to `Name`.

The solution is to modify `TPerson` as shown in *Table 21.5* and declare attribute `Name` as **protected**.

Protected attributes are visible in a class's subclasses (see *Chapter 22* on inheritance and subclasses), but not otherwise.

```
Unit SpecialPerson;
Interface
  Uses PersonClass;
  Type
    TSpecialPerson = Class (TPerson)
                       Public
                         Procedure AddTitle;
                     End;
Implementation
  Procedure TSpecialPerson.AddTitle;
    Begin
      Name := 'Sir ' + Name;
    End;
End.
```

Table 21.4 TSpecialPerson class which inherits from TPerson

```
Unit PersonClass;
Interface
Type
  TPerson = Class
              Protected
                Name : String[30];
              Private
                Address : String[40];
                Age : Integer;
              Public
                Procedure AddPersonDetails;
                Procedure EditPersonDetails;
                Procedure ShowPersonDetails;
              End;
Implementation
  Procedure TPerson.AddPersonDetails;
    Begin
    End;
  Procedure TPerson.EditPersonDetails;
    Begin
    End;
  Procedure TPerson.ShowPersonDetails;
    Begin
    End;
End.
```

Visible in subclasses

Not visible in subclasses

Table 21.5 Modified TPerson class which allows its subclasses to directly access protected attributes but not private attributes

Published

This is a special kind of public that has meaning for the component streaming service which allows a form's controls and settings to be saved and restored without any code having to be explicitly written. This is relevant to VCL Forms applications. In such applications a form's properties and the properties of components/controls placed on the form are exposed in the Object Inspector. In VCL Forms applications published visibility is the default in the absence of any access specifiers.

Strict private

This is only available to Delphi versions after Delphi 7.

The private keyword actually creates a " friendship" relationship between classes in the same unit. The strict private declaration creates a true private field, not viewable by any other class, not even classes in the same unit.

Strict protected

This is only available to Delphi versions after Delphi 7.

Similar to the strict private declaration, strict protected creates a true protected member, visible only to the declaring class and its subclasses.

Table 21.6 shows a summary of these access modifers and their descriptions.

Key term

Public:
Attribute or method is visible/accessible outside its unit/module.

Private:
Attribute or method is not visible/accessible outside its unit/module.

Protected:
Attribute or method is not visible/accessible outside its unit/module except in its subclasses.

---

1 See *Chapter 37* for a graphics example

Visibility level	Accessibility level
Public	Accessible to any other entity within the same environment.
Protected	Accessible within this class and within any inheritors of this class, i.e. subclasses whether the latter are in the same unit or otherwise.
Private	Accessible within the unit in which class defined.
Published	A special kind of public that has meaning for the component streaming service.
Strict private	Only methods of the class have access.
Strict protected	Only methods of the class itself or any of its descendent classes have access.

Table 21.6 Summary of access modifers

Programming task

2 Write an object-oriented program which declares a TPerson class and a TSpecialPerson class in separate files based on *Table 21.4* and *Table 21.5*. Provide implementations for AddPersonDetails, EditPersonDetails, ShowPersonDetails and a modified AddTitle which prompts the user for the specific title to use.

Write a main program which

- declares two object reference variables of type TPerson
- creates two objects, one of type TPerson and one of type TSpecialPerson
- populates each object with data
- allows the state of each object to be edited
- shows the state of each object

Abstraction in object-oriented programming

Abstraction of the representation kind is the ability to engage with a concept while ignoring some of its details, e.g. when considering the concept of a house, we ignore the individual details of its doors, that is, whether they are made of wood, metal, plastic, and where the letter box is located, etc.

A class in object-oriented programming is similar.

At the class-level of abstraction the focus is on properties (also called attributes) and the command/query operations that are of interest.

For example, some properties of a house are

- NumberOfBedrooms
- Address
- NameOwner
- RateableValue

and some query operations are

- GetNumberOfBedrooms
- GetAddress
- GetNameOfOwner
- GetRateableValue

and some command operations are

- ChangeNameOfOwner

Key concept

Class:

A class is a template from which actual objects may be created. The class definition lists the characteristics of the object that are to be recorded, e.g. for a car object, the number of seats, size of engine, etc. The class will also define how the object can behave, e.g. accelerate forwards, slow down when brakes are applied, etc. An actual instance of an object – my car - will have a state that it is currently in, e.g. parked and locked and a set of behaviours.

Key point

Objects share behaviour but not state:

Objects share method code but not attribute values. Each object maintains its own attribute values. There is only ever one copy of each method code.

- ChangeRateableValue

Once we have a class abstraction of a house, let's say called *House*, it is then possible to create specific instances of this class.

Each instance is an object of the class *House*. So we could create *House* objects, *House1*, *House2*, etc.

The properties of each would be populated with specific values, e.g. object *House1* property *NameOfOwner* might have value 'Fred Bloggs' whilst object *House2* property *NameOfOwner* might have value 'Mary Poppins'.

Both would **share access to the code** for each of the operations so that each object could be queried and commanded.

These operations are referred to as **methods of the object** and are coded in software as functions and procedures.

When a function or procedure of an object is called we say that a **method is invoked**.

Object-oriented programming takes abstraction a little further with something called **encapsulation**.

Whilst abstraction presents a view of a real-world object which is a high level one, encapsulation says you are not allowed to look at an object at any other level of detail than this high level one.

Stack example

Figure 21.15 shows an abstraction of a stack, a Last In First Out (LIFO) abstract data type, and a design which

HighWatermarkPtr: Pointer to highest accessible stack location.

BaseOfStackPtr: Pointer to lowest accessible stack location.

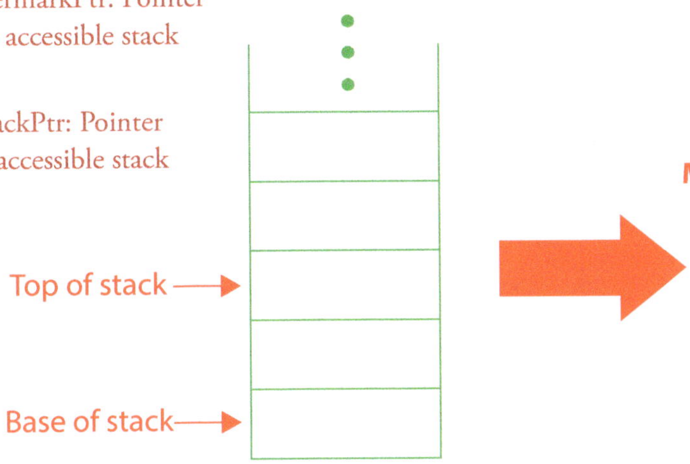

Attributes

StackArray : Array[1..100] Of Integer
TopOfStackPtr : Integer
BaseOfStackPtr : Integer
HighWatermarkPtr : Integer

Methods

Function IsEmpty : Boolean
Function IsFull : Boolean
Function Pop : Integer
Procedure Push
Procedure ShowStack
Constructor Create
Procedure ShowTopOfStackPtr
Procedure ShowContentsOfStack

Fig. 21.15 Stack abstraction: query operations in green, command operations in blue

identifies attributes and methods for an object which implements an integer stack with space to store 100 integers.

```
Type
  TStackType = Class
                 Private
                   StackArray : Array[1..100] Of Integer;
                   TopOfStackPtr : Integer;
                   BaseOfStackPtr : Integer;
                   HighWatermarkPtr : Integer;
                 Public
                   Function IsEmpty : Boolean;
                   Function IsFull : Boolean;
                   Function Pop : Integer;
                   Procedure Push;
                   Procedure ShowStack;
                   Constructor Create;
                   Procedure ShowTopOfStackPtr;
               End;
```

Private means these attributes can only be accessed via the methods in the public section.

Public means available to be called from an application.

Table 21.7 Definition of class TStackType in Object Pascal

Key concept

Object instantiation:

An object is an instance of a class.

An object requires memory for its data and a mechanism for linking to the code for its methods. This code is shared with other objects belonging to the same class. Attribute data is not shared however. Each object maintains its own state, i.e. the values of its attributes.

In Object Pascal, a stack class would be defined as shown in *Table 21.7*.

When the focus is on objects which belong to the class `TStackType` we say that `StackArray`, `TopOfStackPtr`, `BaseOfStackPtr` and `HighWatermarkPtr` are called **attributes** or **data fields**.

Objects in a program often represents things in the real world, and then an object's attributes are properties of the thing.

A programming language object is a kind of container for data and this container requires computer memory to store the object's data.

In the case of a stack object, memory is needed for the `StackArray`, `TopOfStackPtr`, `BaseOfStackPtr` and `HighWatermarkPtr` attribute data plus memory for pointer(s) to the code for the object's methods `IsEmpty`, `IsFull`, `Pop`, `Push`, `ShowStack` and `ShowTopOfStackPtr`.

The code which implements these methods will be shared amongst all class `TStackType` objects created in memory.

`TStackType`'s `Create` method is special. It is a **constructor** that is used to grab the memory needed by an object when it is **instantiated**. The name given to the process of creating an object is called **instantiation**. A constructor is also able to initialise the attributes of every object it creates, e.g. `TopOfStackPtr ← 0`.

Table 21.8 shows a program which creates a single stack object.

`TStackType.Create` creates the stack object in memory and `MyStack` stores a reference to this object.

To show the value of the top of stack pointer, `TopOfStackPtr`, we reference the object and invoke the method, `ShowTopOfStackPtr` as follows

```
MyStack.ShowTopOfStackPtr;
```

P

```
Program StackConsoleProj;
{$AppType Console}
Uses SysUtils,StackUnit;
Var
  MyStack : TStackType;
  i : Integer;
Begin
  MyStack := TStackType.Create;
  MyStack.ShowTopOfStackPointer;
  For i := 1 To 5
    Do MyStack.Push;
  MyStack.ShowStack;
  Repeat
    Writeln(MyStack.Pop);
    MyStack.ShowStack;
  Until MyStack.IsEmpty;
End.
```

No memory is allocated for a stack object at this stage

Table 21.8 Object Pascal program which instantiates a TStackType object

When the program is executed it behaves as shown in *Figure 21.16*.

The *For loop* calls `MyStack.Push` five times. Each time the method `Push` requests input from the user.

The method `ShowStack` is then invoked to show the state of the stack.

```
MyStack.ShowTopOfStackPointer;
  For i := 1 To 5
    Do MyStack.Push;
  MyStack.ShowStack;
  Repeat
    Writeln(MyStack.Pop);
    MyStack.ShowStack;
  Until MyStack.IsEmpty;
```

The body of the *Repeat Until loop* invokes the `Pop` method and writes the value popped from the top of stack to the console window.
The state of the stack is then shown by invoking `ShowStack`. The size of the stack decreases by one item in each iteration of the loop until eventually it is empty. The method `IsEmpty` returns `True` when the stack is empty.

```
Z:\ProductionChapters\Unit1Book\NewChaptersForVersion3\...
Top of stack pointer = 0
Input an Item: 1
Input an Item: 2
Input an Item: 3
Input an Item: 4
Input an Item: 5
------Stack------
        5
        4
        3
        2
        1
------Stack------
Press Return Key to Continue
5
------Stack------
        4
        3
        2
        1
------Stack------
Press Return Key to Continue
4
------Stack------
        3
        2
        1
------Stack------
Press Return Key to Continue
3
------Stack------
        2
        1
------Stack------
Press Return Key to Continue
2
------Stack------
        1
------Stack------
Press Return Key to Continue
1
------Stack------
------Stack------
Press Return Key to Continue
```

Figure 21.16 Output from the execution of the Object Pascal program shown in Table 21.8

Questions

1. What is meant by the following in object-oriented programming
   (a) an object (b) object instantiation (c) a constructor (d) an instance of a class?

2. Explain, with an example, the meaning of the following statement
   "Objects share behaviour but not state"

3. Complete the following sentence: "When a function or procedure of an object is called we say that ....."

4. Write a class for a circular queue with 100 slots each capable of storing an integer.
   You need to specify attributes, query operations and command operations

Information hiding

Encapsulation is a technique that combines operations and data in a way that supports information hiding.

- **Data encapsulation** - means restricting access to the data.
- **Procedural encapsulation** - means that we do not need to know how the behaviour happens, i.e. how the methods are implemented.

Information hiding = **Data encapsulation** + **Procedural encapsulation.**

In Object Pascal/Delphi access to data fields of an object are controlled by placing class definitions in units and using access specifiers.

A unit is a separately compilable module.

In Object Pascal/Delphi the unit is structured as shown in *Table 21.9*.

```
Unit UnitName; {Names the unit}
  Interface
    {Introduces the part that is exposed to the outside world}
    Uses
      {Names the other units that contain entities that this unit references}
    Const
      {Constant definitions}
    Type
      {Type definitions, e.g. class definitions}
    Var
      {Variable definitions definitions}
    {Procedure and function signatures for any procedures/functions or use outside
     this unit}
  Implementation
    {Code for methods (procedures and functions) whose signatures have appeared in
     class definitions. Code for any procedures and functions used internally by this
     unit}
```

This part is visible outside the unit

Procedural encapsulation

Table 21.9 Object Pascal/Delphi Unit structure

Properties

Encapsulation can be strengthened even more by using the **property** mechanism to hide fields of an object (i.e.its state) and the methods which access the fields behind a higher field-like abstraction. This forces code that wishes to access or update the object's state to use the field-like abstraction. The abstraction mechanism, if necessary, may call upon special pre-defined accessor methods to read the state and update the state.

```
Unit UProperty;                                          P
Interface
  Type
    TMyClass = Class
                 Strict Private
                   SomeValue : Integer;
                 Public
                   Property Value : Integer Read SomeValue
                                            Write SomeValue;
             End;
Implementation
End.
```

Table 21.10 Example of the property directive

The example shown in *Table 21.10* creates a public property field called `Value` of type `Integer`.

This property field is directly mapped for reading and writing to the strictly private field `SomeValue`, also of type `Integer`. The property field and the field it maps on to must be of the same type. Strictly private is only available in versions of Delphi post Delphi 7. In Delphi 7, the private directive has to be used.

```
Program IntroPropertiesProject;
{$APPTYPE CONSOLE}                                P
Uses
  UProperty in 'UProperty.pas';
Var
  MyClass : TMyClass;
Begin
  MyClass := TMyClass.Create;
  MyClass.Value := 6;
  Writeln('Value = ', MyClass.Value);
  Readln;
  MyClass.Free;
End.
```

Table 21.11 Program that uses the property Value

Table 21.11 shows a program that accesses the property field `Value` for both writing and reading.

Writing: `MyClass.Value := 6;`

Reading: `Writeln(MyClass.Value);`

Figure 21.17 shows its console output when executed.

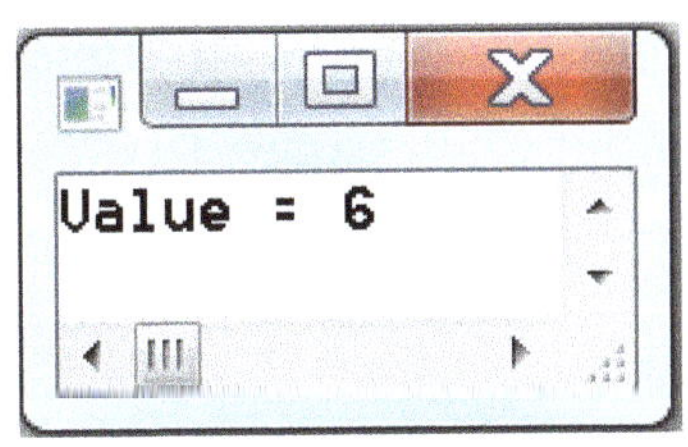

Figure 21.17 Console output

Creating validation controls on a private field

More commonly, writing is mapped to a method that does some sort of validation or processing before assigning the field.

```
Unit UPropertyWithWriteMethod;
Interface                                                    P
  Type
    TMyClass = Class
                 Strict Private
                   SomeValue : Integer;
                   Procedure SetSomeValue(AValue : Integer);
                 Public
                   Property Value : Integer Read SomeValue
                   Write SetSomeValue;
             End;
Implementation
  Procedure TMyClass.SetSomeValue(AValue : Integer);
    Begin
      If AValue In [0..9]
       Then SomeValue := AValue
       Else Writeln('Outside permitted range of 0..9');
    End;
End.
```

Table 21.12 Property directive with write accessor method

Table 21.12 shows how this is achieved with a **write accessor method** `SetSomeValue`.

Writing: `MyClass.Value := 6;`

is done as before but this time the writing value `6` is passed into the validation write accessor method as parameter `AValue`.

The program that uses `TMyClass` is shown in *Table 21.13*.

Figure 21.18 shows its console output when executed.

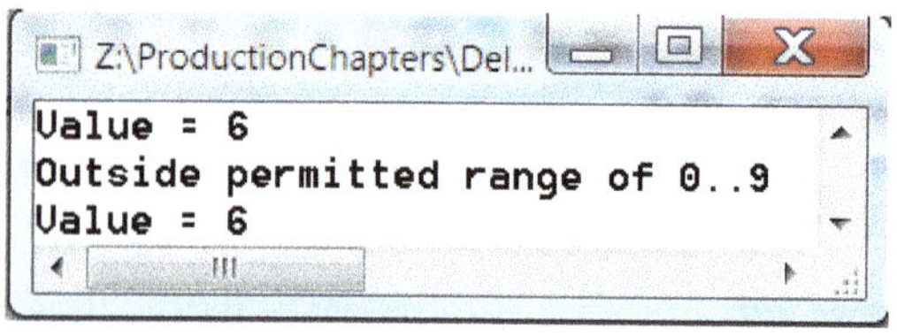

Figure 21.18 Console output

Allow a method to be called when reading a private field and a different method when updating the field

The read part can be delegated to a method too. Table 21.14 shows a class `TMyClass` with a strict private property `SomeValue` of type `String` and read accessor method `ReadSomeValue` which returns a string and write accessor method, `SetSomeValue`.

The program that uses `TMyClass` is shown in Table 21.15.

Figure 21.17 shows its console output when executed.

Figure 21.19 Console output

```
Program IntroPropertiesWithWriteMethodProject;
{$APPTYPE CONSOLE}
Uses
  UPropertyWithWriteMethod in 'UPropertyWithWriteMethod.pas';
Var
  MyClass : TMyClass;
Begin
  MyClass := TMyClass.Create;
  MyClass.Value := 6;
  Writeln('Value = ', MyClass.Value);
  MyClass.Value := 10;
  Writeln('Value = ', MyClass.Value);
  Readln;
  MyClass.Free;
End.
```

Table 21.13 Program that uses write accessor method

```
Unit UPropertyWithReadWriteMethods;
Interface
  Uses System.SysUtils;
  Type
    TMyClass = Class
                 Strict Private
                   SomeValue : String;
                   Function ReadSomeValue : String;
                   Procedure SetSomeValue(AValue : String);
                 Public
                   Property Value : String Read ReadSomeValue
                   Write SetSomeValue;
               End;

Implementation
  Function TMyClass.ReadSomeValue : String;
    Begin
      Result := LowerCase(SomeValue);
    End;
  Procedure TMyClass.SetSomeValue(AValue : String);
    Begin
      SomeValue := UpperCase(AValue);
    End;
End.
```

Table 21.14 Read and write accessor methods

```
Program IntroPropertiesWithReadWriteMethodsProject;
{$APPTYPE CONSOLE}
Uses
  UPropertyWithReadWriteMethods in 'UPropertyWithReadWriteMethods.pas';
Var
  MyClass : TMyClass;
Begin
  MyClass := TMyClass.Create;
  MyClass.Value := 'HeLLo';
  Writeln('Value = ', MyClass.Value);
  MyClass.Value := 'GooDBYe';
  Writeln('Value = ', MyClass.Value);
  Readln;
  MyClass.Free;
End.
```

Table 21.15 Program that uses read and write accessor methods

Setting a field to be read only

Properties can also be read-only, in which case no write part appears in its declaration - *Table 21.16*.

A constructor is required to initialise the field SomeValue.

After obtaining a string value for `SomeValue`, the constructor calls the system `Create`.

```
Unit UPropertyReadOnly;
Interface
  Uses System.SysUtils;
  Type
    TMyClass = Class
                 Strict Private
                   SomeValue : String;
                   Function ReadSomeValue : String;
                 Public
                   Property Value : String Read ReadSomeValue;
                   Constructor Create;
               End;

Implementation
  Constructor TMyClass.Create;
    Begin
      Inherited Create; {Not strictly necessary as the
                         system Create does nothing currently}
      Write('Input a string value: ');
      Readln(SomeValue);
    End;
  Function TMyClass.ReadSomeValue : String;
    Begin
      Result := UpperCase(SomeValue);
    End;
End.
```

Table 21.16 Read only property

This is not strictly necessary since the system `Create` does nothing currently and the likelihood of it doing anything in the near future is low.

The program that uses `TMyClass` is shown in *Table 21.17*.

Figure 21.18 shows its console output when executed.

```
Program IntroPropertiesReadOnlyProject;
{$APPTYPE CONSOLE}
Uses
  UPropertyReadOnly in '..\UPropertyReadOnly.pas';
Var
  MyClass : TMyClass;
Begin
  MyClass := TMyClass.Create;
  Writeln('Value = ', MyClass.Value);
  Readln;
  MyClass.Free;
End.
```

Table 21.17 Program that uses read only property

Figure 21.20 Console output

Update to another field that is dependent on the value held by a specific field

Table 21.18 shows a form unit of a Vcl Forms Application, **SurnameProject.dpr**, defining a class definition for a person class, `TPerson`, containing two properties, `Surname` and `SurnameAssigned`.

Private `FSurnameAssigned` field is updated when a non-empty surname value is assigned to private field `FSurname`.

This occurs when method `SetSurname` is called behind the scenes by the execution of the statement

```
Person.Surname :=
InputBox('Surname','Input
surname','');
```

The two `TEdit` boxes are then updated accordingly.

Figure 21.19 shows its form-based output when executed with input 'Bond' via **InputBox** window- *Figure 21.20*.

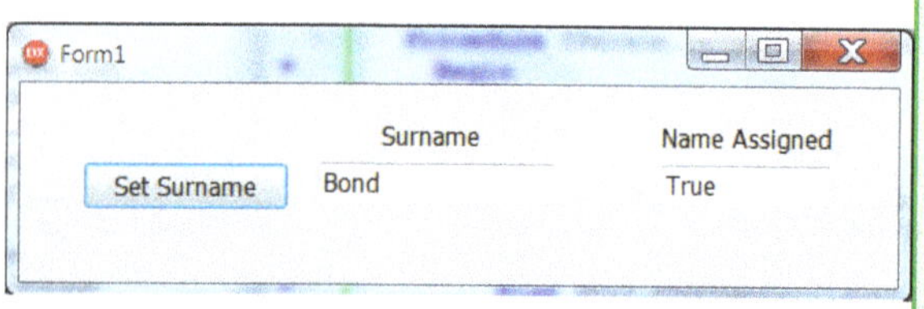

Figure 21.21 Form1 output after Set Surname button clicked and surname 'Bond' inputted via InputBox

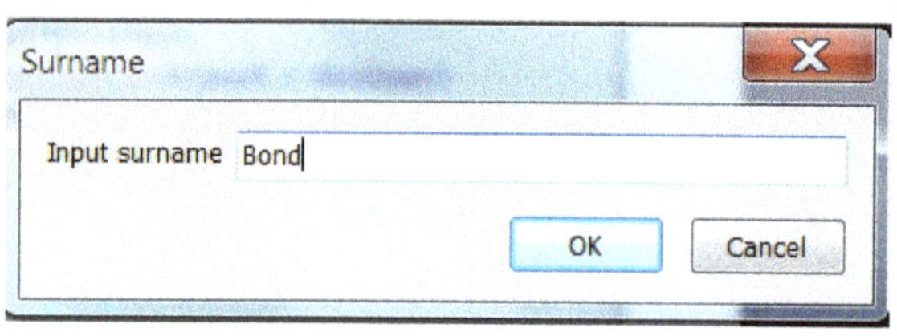

Figure 21.22 Input box called from method SetSurname

Figure 21.21 shows the result of inputting an empty string for surname.

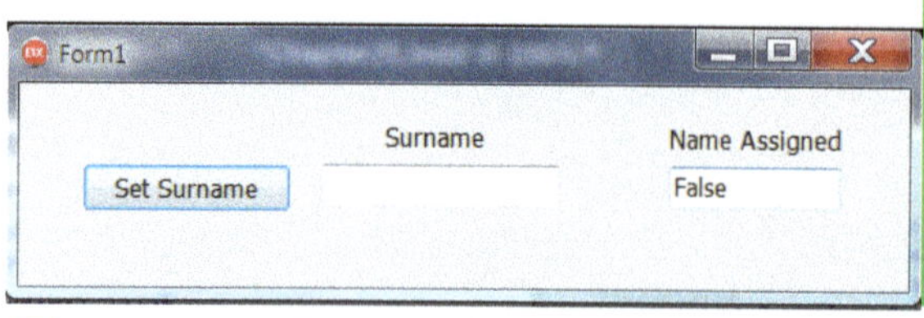

Figure 21.23 Result of inputting an empty string for surname

```
Unit UTSurname;
Interface
Uses
  Winapi.Windows, Winapi.Messages, System.SysUtils,
  System.Variants, System.Classes, Vcl.Graphics,
  Vcl.Controls, Vcl.Forms, Vcl.Dialogs, Vcl.StdCtrls;
Type
  TForm1 = Class(TForm)
             SetSurname: TButton;
             ShowSurname: TButton;
             edtSurname: TEdit;
             edtSurnameAssigned: TEdit;
             lblSurname: TLabel;
             lblNameAssigned: TLabel;
             Procedure SetSurnameClick(Sender: TObject);
             Procedure ShowSurnameClick(Sender: TObject);
             Procedure FormActivate(Sender: TObject);
           End;
  StringType = String;
  TPerson = Class
              Strict Private
                FSurname : StringType;
                FSurnameAssigned : Boolean;
                Procedure SetSurname(Value : StringType);
              Public
                Property Surname : StringType
                  Read FSurname
                  Write SetSurname;
                Property SurnameAssigned : Boolean
                  Read FSurnameAssigned;
            End;
Var
  Form1: TForm1;
  Person : TPerson;
Implementation
{$R *.dfm}
  Procedure TPerson.SetSurname(Value : StringType);
    Begin
      If Value <> ''
        Then
          Begin
            Self.FSurname := Value;
            Self.FSurnameAssigned := True;
          End
        Else Self.FSurnameAssigned := False;
    End;
Procedure TForm1.FormActivate(Sender: TObject);
  Begin
    Person := TPerson.Create;
  End;
Procedure TForm1.SetSurnameClick(Sender: TObject);
  Begin
    Person.Surname := InputBox('Surname','Input surname','');
    edtSurname.Text := Person.Surname;
    If Person.SurnameAssigned
      Then EdtSurnameAssigned.Text := 'True'
      Else
        Begin
          edtSurnameAssigned.Text := 'False' ;
          edtSurname.Text := '';
        End;
  End;
End.
```

Table 21.18 Vcl unit example illustrating updates to another field dependent on the value held by a field

To assign to the private `FSurname` field the **property** `Surname` is referenced in the following way:

- The string entered in response to the prompt is assigned to the `Value` parameter of the private method `SetSurname`.
- When a **property** is referenced in an expression, its value is read using the field or method listed in the **read specifier**, and when a property is referenced in an assignment statement, its value is written using the field or method listed in the **write specifier**.

Summary

- If a write specifier lists a method identifier, then the method must be a procedure method that takes a single value or constant parameter of the same type as the property type.
- If an access specifier lists a field identifier, then the field type must be identical to the property type.
- If a read specifier lists a method identifier, then the method must be a parameterless function method, and the function result type must be identical to the property type.

The **Property** directive can be used to

- create validation controls on a private field
- allow a method to be called when reading a private field and a different method when updating the field (writing to the field)
- Set a field to be read only
- Hide the access methods to the field, i.e. allow these methods to be private
- Updates to other fields that are dependent on the value held by the field

22 Inheritance

Information

www.educational-computing.co.uk/DelphiBookCode/DelphiCode.html

Inheritance

Purpose: To explore and understand the concept of inheritance

What is inheritance?

In designing a software system, it is often the case that objects occur that are much like other objects except for a few differences in their type. For example, a college system which records data on students, may have to deal with both part-time and full-time students. Most of the attributes associated with both kinds of students are the same, but some attributes are different.

The solution in object-oriented programming is to define a general type of student, `TStudent`, and then define full-time students as a type, `TFullTime`, which is a general type of student except for a few differences, and part-time students as a type, `TPartime`, which is also a general type of student except for a few differences.

Operations on student data that don't depend on whether the student is full- or part-time, e.g. `ChangeAddress`, will be common to both full- and part-time students.

However, there will be some operations which apply only to full-time students, e.g. `AssignTutor` and some operations which apply only to part-time students, e.g. `AssignMentor`.

Similarly, there are attributes which both full-time and part-time students share, e.g. `Surname`, `Forename`, `Address`, and attributes which are full-time student only, e.g. `TutorStaffID`, and attributes which are part-time student only, e.g. `MentorStaffID`.

Those **behaviours** (operations) and **characteristics** (attributes) which are common to all students can be made accessible to the classes `TFullTime` and `TPartTime` by inheriting them from class `TStudent` in a mechanism called **inheritance**.

The class `TFullTime` can then **extend** the class `TStudent` with those operations and attributes which are special to full-time students.

Similarly, the class `TPartTime` can **extend** the class `TStudent` with those operations and attributes which are special to part-time students.

Inheritance is the concept that one class is a specialisation of another class, e.g. `TFullTime` **is a** specialised version of `TStudent`. The "is a" phrase is highlighted because it is a good test to apply to determine that a relationship between two classes is one of inheritance.

Key concept

Inheritance:

Inheritance allows a class to be derived from an existing class without the need to modify the existing class.

The derived class has all the attributes and operations of the parent class, but adds new ones of its own and may redefine the implementations of the inherited operations.

Another name for derived class is subclass.

Inheritance is a type of relationship between classes called an "is-a" relationship. It expresses generalisation. One class (the child class or subclass or derived class) can inherit attributes and operations from another (the parent class or superclass). The parent class is more general than the child class.

In generalisation, a child can be substituted for a parent, i.e. anywhere that the parent appears, the child may appear. However, the reverse isn't true.

What is the purpose of inheritance?

The purpose of inheritance is to simplify the writing of code by defining a **parent class or superclass**, e.g. `TStudent`, which specifies the elements common to two or more **derived classes** or **child classes** or **subclasses**, e.g. `TFullTime` and `TPartTime`.

Inheritance helps avoid the need to repeat common operation code and attributes in multiple classes instead it is centralised within a parent class (or in ancestor classes if one class inherits from another which itself inherits from another, etc).

In practice, it results in a use of memory similar to the example shown in *Figure 22.1*[1] with two objects:

- `FullTime1` which belongs to the class `TFullTime`
- `PartTime1` which belongs to the class `TPartTime`.

The surname, forename and address attributes come from the `TStudent` class.

Each object adds its own specialised attribute(s).

Fig. 22.1 Partial memory model for two objects, FullTime1 and PartTime1

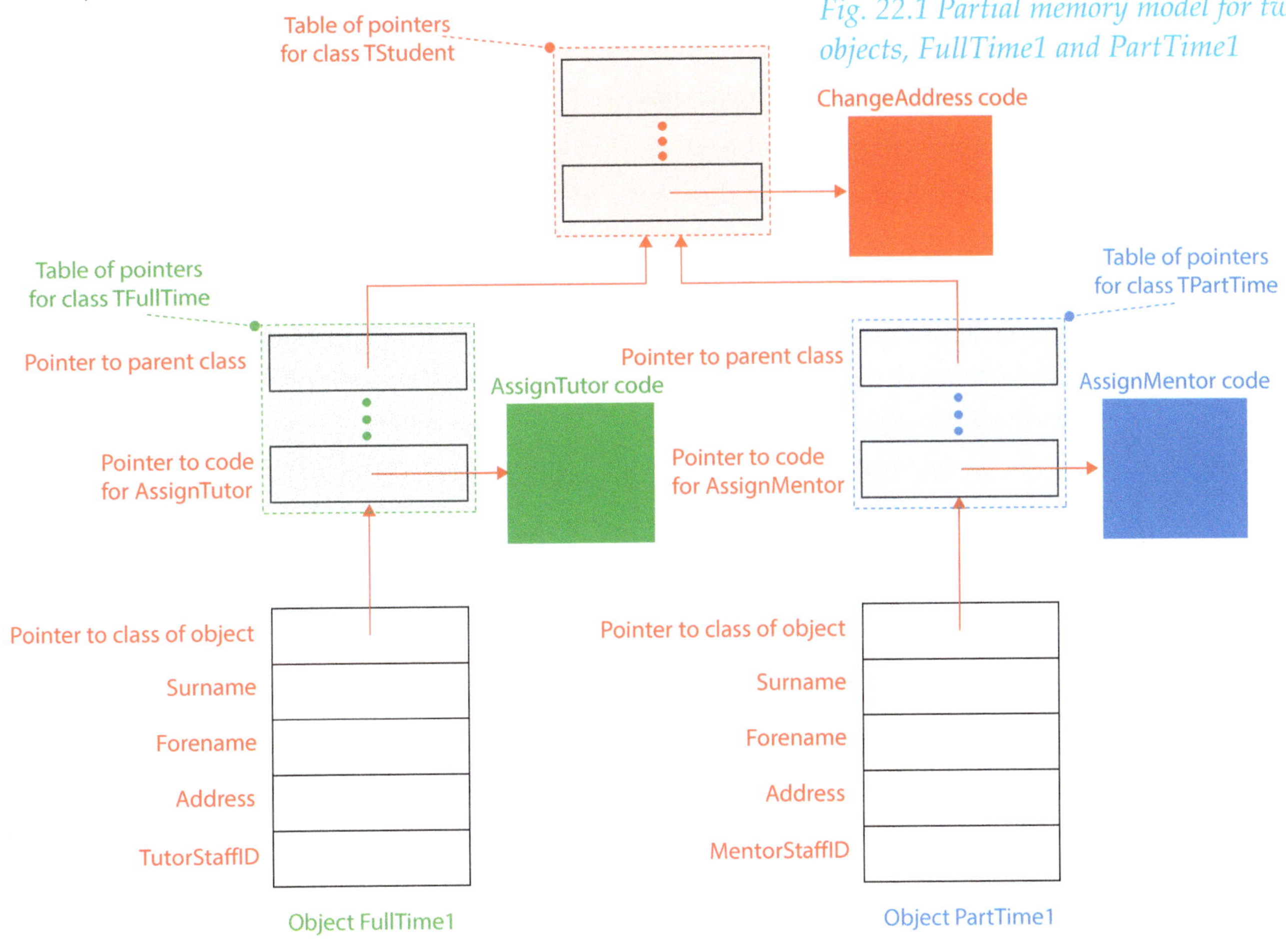

As the code is shared amongst objects, each object has a pointer field which is used to locate the code defined for its class and any code which it inherits from its parent class, `TStudent`.

A table of pointers is shown loaded into memory for each class. For object `FullTime1` to find the code for `ChangeAddress`, it uses its pointer to the pointer table for class `TFullTime` then it uses this table to find the table of pointers for the parent class `TStudent`. The class `TStudent` points to the code for the method `ChangeAddress`.

> **Key concept**
> **Single inheritance:**
> In single inheritance a derived class may inherit from only one parent class.

> **Key concept**
> **Multiple inheritance:**
> In multiple inheritance a derived class may inherit from one or more parent classes.
> Delphi(Object Pascal) does not support multiple inheritance directly.

1 There are other ways it can be done.

Delphi supports **single inheritance**. In single inheritance a derived class may inherit from only one parent class.

The abbreviated class definitions in *Table 22.1*, *Table 22.2* and *Table 22.3* show how inheritance is indicated in Object Pascal.

Different programming languages indicate inheritance in different ways.

Inheritance from a parent class, for example, is shown in the derived class `TFullTime` as follows

```
TPartTime = Class(TStudent);
```

The parent class `TStudent` is placed in brackets after the keyword `Class`.

A derived class may itself be derived from another derived class, and so on, creating a hierarchy of classes.

A derived class may therefore inherit from higher level classes or **ancestor classes**, i.e from a parent class, a grandparent class, and so on.

The term **base class** is reserved for the highest class in this hierarchy.

The base class may then have **descendent classes** which are also known as **derived classes** or **subclasses**.

```
Type
  TStudent = Class
               Private
                 Surname : String;
                 Forename : String;
                 Address : String;
                 ...
               Public
                 Procedure ChangeAddress;
                 Constructor Create;
                 ...
             End;
```

Table 22.1 Class TStudent

```
Type
  TFullTime = Class(TStudent)
               Private
                 TutorStaffID : Integer;
                 ...
               Public
                 Procedure AssignTutor;
                 ...
             End;
```

Table 22.2 Class TFullTime

```
Type
  TPartTime = Class(TStudent)
               Private
                 MentorStaffID : Integer;
                 ...
               Public
                 Procedure AssignMentor;
                 ...
             End;
```

Table 22.3 Class TPartTime

Questions

1 A tennis club has both junior and senior members. Each member has a unique membership number, a name and address recorded. Three classes have been identified:

Member

JuniorMember

SeniorMember

The classes JuniorMember and SeniorMember are related (by single inheritance) to the class Member.

(a) In object-oriented programming what is meant by inheritance?

(b) Write a class definition for the class Member to allow programs that use objects of this class to add a new member's details, amend a member's details, show a member's details. No other form of access is to be allowed.

(c) Each junior member has a date of birth recorded. Write a class definition for the class JuniorMember to allow programs that use objects of this class to add a date of birth, amend a date of birth, show a junior member's age. No other form of access is to be allowed.

Table 22.4 shows the main program, **StudentProject.dproj**, for the student exercise.

It declares two object references, `FullTime1` of type `TFullTime` and `PartTime1` of type `TPartTime`.

Table 22.5 defines a unit `Student` containing the class definition for `TStudent`, and the implementation of the methods `ChangeAddress` and `ShowStudentDetails` which are shared by both full time and part time students. Unit Student also contains the constructor Create which is also shared by both full time and part time students.

The field and methods specific to full time and part time students are defined in classes `TFullTimeStudent` and `TPartTimeStudent` in unit `FullTimeStudent` and `PartTimeStudent` respectively - *Table 22.6* and *Table 22.7*.

```
Program StudentProject;
{$APPTYPE CONSOLE}
Uses
  Student in 'Student.pas',
  FullTimeStudent in 'FullTimeStudent.pas',
  PartTimeStudent in 'PartTimeStudent.pas';
Var
  FullTime1 : TFullTime;
  PartTime1 : TPartTime;
Begin
  Writeln('Create full time student');
  Writeln('-----------------------');
  FullTime1 := TFullTime.Create;
  FullTime1.AssignTutor;
  Writeln('-----------------------------------------');
  Writeln('Create part time student');
  Writeln('-----------------------');
  PartTime1 := TPartTime.Create;
  PartTime1.AssignMentor;
  Writeln('-----------------------------------------');
  Writeln('Show details for full time student');
  Writeln('----------------------------------');
  FullTime1.ShowTutorStaffID;
  FullTime1.ShowStudentDetails;
  Writeln('Show details for part time student');
  PartTime1.ShowMentorStaffID;
  PartTime1.ShowStudentDetails;
  Readln;
End.
```

Table 22.4 Program StudentProject.dprog

```
Unit Student;
Interface
  Type
    TStudent = Class
                 Private
                   Surname : String;
                   Forename : String;
                   Address : String;
                 Public
                   Procedure ChangeAddress;
                   Constructor Create;
                   Procedure ShowStudentDetails;
               End;

Implementation
  Procedure TStudent.ChangeAddress;
    Begin
      Writeln('Current address: ', Address);
      Write('Input address: ');
      Readln(Address);
    End;
  Constructor TStudent.Create;
    Begin
      Write('Input surname: ');
      Readln(Surname);
      Write('Input forename: ');
      Readln(Forename);
      Write('Input address: ');
      Readln(Address);
    End;
  Procedure TStudent.ShowStudentDetails;
    Begin
      Writeln('Surname: ', Surname);
      Writeln('Forename: ', Forename);
      Writeln('Address: ', Address);
    End;
End.
```

Table 22.5 Class TStudent

```
Unit FullTimeStudent;
Interface
  Uses Student;
  Type
    TFullTime = Class(TStudent)
                  Private
                    TutorStaffID : Integer;
                  Public
                    Procedure AssignTutor;
                    Procedure ShowTutorStaffID;
                End;

Implementation
  Procedure TFullTime.AssignTutor;
    Begin
      Write('Input full time student''s tutor''s StaffID: ');
      Readln(TutorStaffID);
    End;
    Procedure TFullTime.ShowTutorStaffID;
    Begin
      Writeln('Tutor''s StaffID: ', TutorStaffID);
    End;
End.
```

Table 22.6 Class TFullTime

Figure 22.2 shows the output from **StudentProject.exe** when executed and a user's responses to the prompts from this program.

```
Unit PartTimeStudent;

Interface
  Uses Student;
  Type
    TPartTime = Class(TStudent)
                  Private
                    MentorStaffID : Integer;
                  Public
                    Procedure AssignMentor;
                    Procedure ShowMentorStaffID;
                End;

Implementation

  Procedure TPartTime.AssignMentor;
    Begin
      Write('Input part time student''s mentor''s StaffID: ');
      Readln(MentorStaffID);
    End;

  Procedure TPartTime.ShowMentorStaffID;
    Begin
      Writeln('Mentor''s StaffID: ', MentorStaffID);
    End;
End.
```

Table 22.7 Class TPartTime

```
Z:\ProductionChapters\DelphiBook\Code\Chapter22\Win32\Debug\Stud...
Create full time student
------------------------
Input surname: Bond
Input forename: Fred
Input address: 30 Acacia Avenue, Dingley Dell, NeverNeverLand
Input full time student's tutor's StaffID: 123
------------------------------------------
Create part time student
------------------------
Input surname: Stokes
Input forename: Mary
Input address: 23 Railway Cuttings, East Cheam
Input part time student's mentor's StaffID: 101
------------------------------------------
Show details for full time student
----------------------------------
Tutor's StaffID: 123
Surname: Bond
Forename: Fred
Address: 30 Acacia Avenue, Dingley Dell, NeverNeverLand
Show details for part time student
Mentor's StaffID: 101
Surname: Stokes
Forename: Mary
Address: 23 Railway Cuttings, East Cheam
```

Fig. 22.2 Output from StudentProject.exe when executed

Programming task

1. Open *StudentProject.dpr* or *StudentProject.dproj* using the File/Open dialog. Open *Student.pas*, *FullTimeStudent.pas* and *PartTimeStudent.pas*.

   Press *F9* to compile, build and run *StudentProject.dproj*.

   Add the following methods to *Student.pas*:

   ChangeSurname
   ChangeForename

   Save the changed *Student.pas*.
   Change *StudentProject.dproj* so that the source code for *StudentProject* offers the option to change both surname and forename of the full time student and the part time student, if required. Make sure that you include source code to allow student details to be shown before and after any changes.

   Press *F9* to compile, build and run *ProjectStudent*.

   Add the following methods to *PartTimeStudent.pas*:

   AddPartTimeHours
   ShowHours

   And the following private field:

   PartTimeHours

   Save the changed *PartTimeStudent.pas*.
   Change *StudentProject.dproj* so that the part time student's hours can be added and shown.

   Press *F9* to compile, build and run *ProjectStudent*.

2. A bank account has associated with it the name and address of the customer and the current balance. To be able to use this as a data object, procedures and functions (known as methods) must be provided to initialise an account, change the name of the customer, get the current balance, credit an amount and print the details of the account.
   Suppose the bank were to introduce a new class of account for special customers who deposited an initial balance of over £500. This account is to be known as a Gold Account and is to pay interest to customers on their daily balance. The Gold account, as well as having all the characteristics and behaviours of an ordinary account, Account, needs to store the following extra data: interest rate and date interest added, and two extra functions/procedures: *AddInterest* to account, *WithdrawMoney* from account. Object-oriented languages allow the programmer to create an object for the Gold Account which inherits all the characteristics and behaviours of the ordinary account, but also has additional characteristics and behaviours of its own. Write a program to implement the banking system.

23 Polymorphism

Information

www.educational-computing.co.uk/DelphiBookCode/DelphiCode.html

Polymorphism

Purpose: To explore and understand the concept of polymorphism

What is polymorphism?

Sometimes a derived class needs to do more than just extend a parent class. Sometimes it needs to override a method so that the action carried out when the method executes is the one that matches how the object behaves.

For example, if we have a crow object and a duck object we expect the sound made by a crow to be different from the sound made by a duck. One squawks and one quacks.

However, if the only *make sound* method available to both crow and duck objects is the inherited one, `MakeSound,` defined in their parent class `TBird`, the sound we get from each object will be the same, a screeching one if that is the sound the parent class method has been implemented to make.

```
Type
  TBird = Class
            Private
              Name : String;
            Public
              Procedure MakeSound;
              Constructor Create;
              ...
          End;
```

Table 23.1 Class TBird

```
Type
  TCrow = Class(TBird)
            Public
              Procedure MakeSound;
              ...
          End;
```

Table 23.2 Class TCrow

```
Type
  TDuck = Class(TBird)
            Public
              Procedure MakeSound;
              ...
          End;
```

Table 23.3 Class TDuck

The first solution is to add a `MakeSound` method to the `TCrow` class and a `MakeSound` method to the `TDuck` class, with each method implementing the correct sound when invoked.

For example, suppose we have a `TBird` object, `Bird1`, a `TCrow` object, `Crow1`, and a `TDuck` object, `Duck1`.

These classes are shown in *Table 23.1*, *Table 23.2* and *Table 23.3*.

The objects are created by first creating reference variables `Bird1`, `Crow1`, and `Duck1` as shown in *Table 23.4*.

```
Var
   Bird1  :  TBird;
   Crow1  :  TCrow;
   Duck1  :  TDuck;
```

Table 23.4 Creating reference variables

An instance of each class is then created and a reference assigned to the corresponding reference variable as shown in *Table 23.5*.

The classes `TCrow` and `TDuck` use the inherited constructor `Create`.

```
Bird1  := TBird.Create;
Crow1  := TCrow.Create;
Duck1  := TDuck.Create;
```

Table 23.5 Creating an instance of each class and assigning it to its corresponding reference variable

Figure 23.2 shows the correct bird sound being emitted when `MakeSound` is invoked as shown.

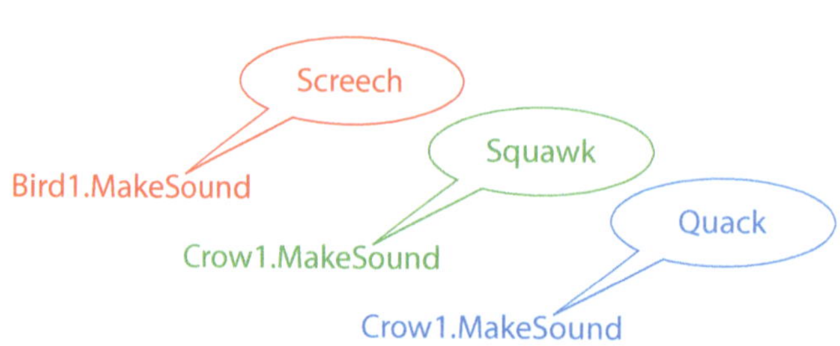

Figure 23.2 Invoking MakeSound on each object

Suppose now we have only one reference variable `Bird1` and this is of type `TBird` as shown in *Table 23.6*. Is it possible to assign a `TCrow` object to `Bird1`?

The answer is yes because a `TCrow` object is a type of bird.

```
Var
  Bird1 : TBird;
```

Table 23.6 Creating a reference variable

What sound is made if we invoke `Bird1.MakeSound`?
The answer is "Screech" because the implementation of `MakeSound` invoked is that belonging to type `TBird` since `Bird1` is of type `TBird` and the method link is made at compile time to the methods of `TBird`.
To get the correct sound we need to alter the class definitions as shown in *Table 23.8*, *Table 23.9* and *Table 23.10*.

```
Bird1 := TCrow.Create;
```

Table 23.7 Creating an instance of class TCrow and assigning it to reference variable of TBird

The parent class `TBird`'s `MakeSound` method is labelled as **virtual** and the corresponding method in each derived class is labelled with **override**.
Now *Table 23.6* and *Table 23.7* create a crow object for which `Bird1.MakeSound` emits "Squawk".

The bird object that `Bird1` references knows it is a crow object and that the sound to make is the crow sound (the link to method `MakeSound` is the one that corresponds to the current object).

```
Type
  TBird = Class
            Private
              Name : String;
            Public
              Procedure MakeSound Virtual;
              Constructor Create;
              ...
            End;
```

Table 23.8 Class TBird

If the following code is now executed the sound emitted is "Quack"

```
Bird1.Destroy;
Bird1 := TDuck.Create;
Bird1.MakeSound;
```

```
Type
  TDuck = Class(TBird)
            Public
              Procedure MakeSound Override;
              ...
            End;
```

Table 23.9 Class TDuck

The `TCrow` object assigned to `Bird1` is first destroyed (memory released). A `TDuck` object is then created and assigned to `Bird1`. The method `MakeSound` is then called on this object.

```
Type
  TDuck = Class(TBird)
            Public
              Procedure MakeSound Override;
              ...
            End;
```

Table 23.10 Class TDuck

The correct sound, "Quack" is made because the binding of `MakeSound` is the one that is correct for a duck object.

This is **late binding**. Late binding occurs at runtime. This allows methods from the class of the created object to be chosen even though the reference variable is of a parent or ancestor class.

If we follow this with the code shown below we get the sound "Squawk" because `Bird1` now references a crow object

```
Bird1.Destroy;
Bird1 := TCrow.Create;
Bird1.MakeSound;
```

This is an example of **polymorphism**.
In polymorphism, a method invoked on an object referenced by a variable of a more general type results in behaviour expected of the specific object, e.g. invoking `MakeSound` via a `TBird` variable elicits "Quack" if the object assigned is a duck and"Squawk" if a crow.

> **Key concept**
>
> **Polymorphism:**
> Giving an action one name, e.g. MakeNoise, that is shared up and down an object hierarchy, with each object in the hierarchy implementing the action in a way appropriate to itself.

The non-polymorphic example shown in *Table 23.6*, and *Table 23.7* uses early binding, i.e. objects are linked to code for operations at compile time. This means that even though the object created at run time is a crow, the method call to `MakeSound` is set up at compile time to link to `MakeSound` method code for `TBird` because `Bird1` is declared as belonging to the `TBird` class.

Late binding delays this linking until run time so that the relevant linkage can be made. For this to happen, the methods of the base class which need to be polymorphic must be declared as **virtual**. The corresponding methods in subclasses of the base/parent/ancestor class must be labelled with the keyword **override** for these to override their equivalent parent/ancestor class methods in a polymorphic way.

Tables 23.11, 23.12, 23.13, 23.14 show how this can be done in Object Pascal.

The constructor `Create` has been modified so that the name of the bird can be recorded and subsequently used by each of the derived classes `MakeSound` method.

Information

The Pascal/Delphi, Bird example programs are available to download from

www.educational-computing.co.uk/DelphiBookCode/DelphiCode.html.

```
Program BirdExample;
{$APPTYPE CONSOLE}
Uses
  System.SysUtils, BirdClass,
  DuckClass, CrowClass;
Var
  Bird1 : TBird;
Begin
  Bird1 := TCrow.Create('Crow');
  Writeln(Bird1.Name);
  Bird1.MakeSound;
  Bird1.Destroy;
  Bird1 := TDuck.Create('Duck');
  Writeln(Bird1.Name);
  Bird1.MakeSound;
  Bird1.Destroy;
  Bird1 := TBird.Create('Bird');
  Writeln(Bird1.Name);
  Bird1.MakeSound;
  Readln;
End.
```

P

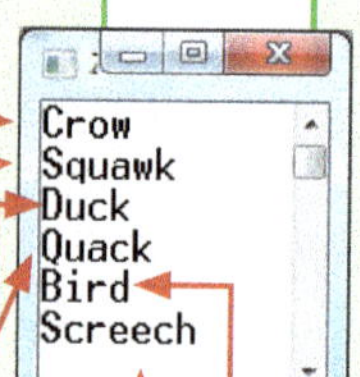

Table 23.11 Object Pascal BirdExample program

```
Unit BirdClass;
Interface
  Type
    TBird = Class
      Public
        Name : String;
      Public
        Procedure MakeSound; Virtual;
        Constructor Create(BirdName : String);
      End;
Implementation
  Procedure TBird.MakeSound;
    Begin
      Writeln('Screech');
    End;
  Constructor TBird.Create(BirdName : String);
    Begin
      Name := BirdName;
    End;
End.
```

Base class

Create inherited by subclasses

Virtual methods can be overridden at run time

Table 23.12 Object Pascal Bird class unit

```
Unit DuckClass;
Interface
  Uses BirdClass;
  Type
    TDuck = Class (TBird)
      Public
        Procedure MakeSound; Override;
      End;
Implementation
  Procedure TDuck.MakeSound;
    Begin
      Writeln('Quack');
    End;
End.
```

Inheritance mechanism TBird is parent class of TDuck

Derived class or subclass

Table 23.13 Object Pascal Duck class unit

```
Unit CrowClass;
Interface
  Uses BirdClass;
  Type
    TCrow = Class(TBird)
      Public
        Procedure MakeSound; Override;
      End;
Implementation
  Procedure TCrow.MakeSound;
    Begin
      Writeln('Squawk');
    End;
End.
```

Inheritance mechanism TBird is parent class of TDuck

Derived class or subclass

Table 23.14 Object Pascal Crow class unit

Key concept

Overriding:

Overriding is a part of the process which enables polymorphism to take place. Methods of the base class which need to be polymorphic are declared as **virtual** if the language does not support polymorphic variables or equivalent. The corresponding methods in subclasses of the base/parent/ancestor class are labelled with the keyword **override** in such languages for these to override their equivalent parent/ancestor class methods in a polymorphic way.

Questions

1. A company has two types of employees, salaried employee and contract employees. Contract employees are paid an amount each month which is determined by the number of hours worked each month. Salaried employees are paid a fixed amount each month.

   A general class Employee contains the following attributes

   PayrollNo
   Surname
   Forename
   Address
   MonthlyPaymentRecordsForCurrentYear

   Employee has four methods AddEmployeeDetails, AmendEmployeeDetails, CalculateMonthlyPay, PrintPaySlip.

   A class ContractEmployee exists which inherits from Employee.

   ContractEmployee has an additional attribute, HourlyRate and methods AddEmployeeDetails, AmendEmployeeDetails, CalculateMonthlyPay, PrintPaySlip.

   When the payroll program runs it creates an object of the appropriate type, i.e. SalariedEmployee or ContractEmployee, for each employee and assigns a reference to a reference variable of type Employee.

   (a) Explain why if the reference variable is not polymorphic, CalculateMonthlyPay will need to be polymorphic.

   (b) Using the keywords Virtual and Override where appropriate, write class definitions for the ContractEmployee class. You may omit the data type of each attribute.

Programming task

1. Turn the scenario covered in Question 1 into a working program. Your program must cater for both salaried and contract employees. Assume salaried employees are paid at a fixed monthly rate which does not vary with the number of hours worked per month. Test that your program works satisfactorily for one salaried employee and one contract employee. Invent appropriate data for each.

Static methods versus virtual methods

Static methods

The class definitions given in previous chapters have used static methods (code for operations).

Static methods can be bound at compile time. This is known as **early binding**.

In early binding the compiler processes the source code program and generates procedure calling code at every place in the source code where a method is referenced - *Figure 23.3*.

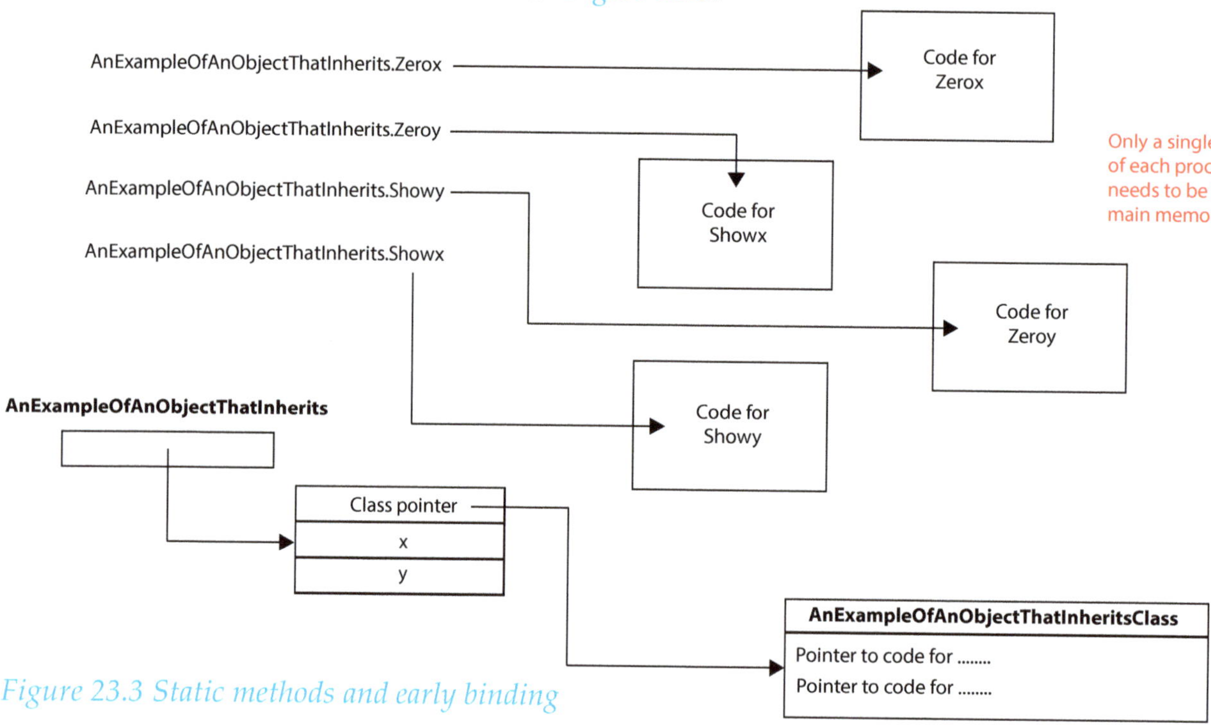

Figure 23.3 Static methods and early binding

The object referenced by `AnExampleOfAnObjectThatInherits` - *Figure 23.3* - consists of two data fields `x` and `y`, located somewhere in main memory (RAM).
How do procedures `Zerox`, `Showx`, `Zeroy`, `Showy` find `x` and `y`? They use the `Self` parameter.

To understand how each procedure gains access to the `Self` parameter you need to understand the role of the stack in supporting parameter passing in procedure calling.

Suppose the code for `Zeroy` and `Showy` are located in memory at addresses (expressed in hexadecimal)

```
&00EE0045 AnExampleOfAnObjectThatInherits.Zeroy;
&00EE0050 AnExampleOfAnObjectThatInherits.Showy;
```

`Pointer1` in *Figure 23.4* is a pointer value (address) which references the object containing the fields `x` and `y`.

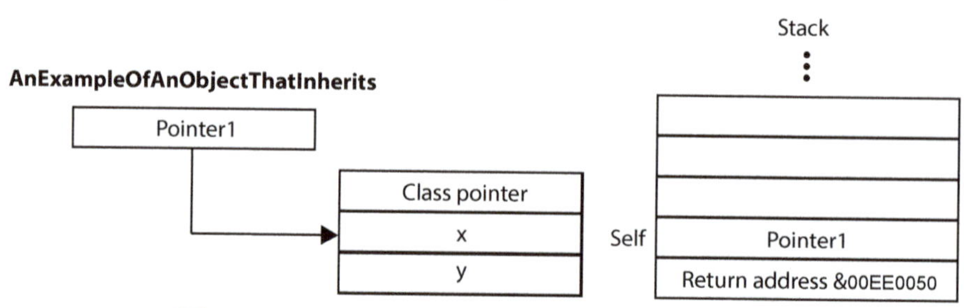

Figure 23.4 Parameter passing on the stack

This address is placed on the stack as shown in *Figure 23.4* when `Zeroy` is called by the procedure reference `AnExampleOfAnObjectThatInherits.Zeroy`.
`Zeroy` is then able to access this address using the parameter `Self`.

For example, `AnExampleOfAnObjectThatInherits.Zeroy` may be rewritten as follows:

```
Procedure AnExampleOfAnObjectThatInherits.Zeroy;
  Begin
    Self.y := 0; {If self is omitted, Delphi uses it behind the scenes}
  End;
```

A stack is used in procedure calls

- to store a return address of where to return after the procedure finishes executing;
- to store parameter values passed to and from the procedure;
- to store local variable values.

In Object Pascal, every method call on an object behaves as if the method has a hidden parameter called `Self`, e.g. as if the procedure `AnExampleOfAnObjectThatInherits.Zeroy` was defined as follows

```
Procedure AnExampleOfAnObjectThatInherits.Zeroy(Self : AnExampleOfAnObjectThatInheritsClass);
  Begin
    Self.y := 0; {If self is omitted, Delphi uses it behind the scenes}
  End;
```

Virtual methods

The previous examples used early binding, i.e. objects are linked at compile time to code for operations. **Late binding** delays this linking until run time.

For this to happen an object's methods must be declared as **virtual** as shown in *Table 23.15*.

The class pointer field of an object is actually a pointer to something called the class's **Virtual Method Table** or **VMT** (the first 4-byte field of every object which we have called the class pointer is really a pointer to the virtual method table (VMT) of the class irrespective of whether the class uses virtual methods).

This Virtual Method Table has several pointer fields. Nearly all point to entities that belong to a class, e.g.

- pointer to start of array of pointers to virtual methods (or nil if no virtual methods) of class and those it inherits
- pointer to interface table (or nil if the class does not uses interfaces)
- pointer to Automation information table (or nil)
- pointer to instance initialization table (or nil)
- pointer to type information table (or nil)
- pointer to field definition table (or nil)
- pointer to method definition table (or nil)
- pointer to dynamic method table (or nil)
- pointer to short string containing class name
- instance size in bytes {An exception, this is not a pointer}
- pointer to a pointer to ancestor class (or nil)
- entry point of first user-defined virtual method
- entry point of second user-defined virtual method, etc

If three objects, referenced by `a`, `b`, `c`, respectively, are created as shown in *Table 23.16*, with `a` of type `AClass`, `b` of type `BClass` and `c` of type `CClass` then the VMT pointer fields will be assigned as shown in *Figure 23.5*.

```
Unit VirtualMethodClasses;
Interface
Type
  AClass = Class
             x : Integer;
          End;
  BClass = Class(AClass)
             y : Integer;
             Procedure Zero; Virtual;
             Procedure Show; Virtual;
          End;
  CClass = Class(BClass)
             z : Integer;
             Procedure Zero; Virtual;
             Procedure Show; Virtual;
          End;
Implementation
  Procedure BClass.Zero;
    Begin
    End;
  Procedure BClass.Show;
    Begin
    End;
  Procedure CClass.Zero;
    Begin
    End;
  Procedure CClass.Show;
    Begin
    End;
End.
```

Table 23.15 Shows the use of the virtual keyword to define virtual methods

Table 23.15 shows these class definitions.

Object `a` has an associated VMT but the pointer field in this table for its own virtual methods is assigned the value `Nil`.

Object `b` has an associated VMT which is initialised with the starting addresses of virtual methods `BClass.Zero` and `BClass.Show` (`@` means address of).

Object `c` has an associated VMT which is initialised with the starting addresses of virtual methods `BClass.Zero`, `BClass.Show` , `CClass.Zero` and `CClass.Show`.

Executing the program shown in *Table 23.16* causes method calls `CClass.Zero` and `CClass.Show` to be made. At present, `CClass.Zero` does nothing but `CClass.Show` outputs `I am CClass's Show`.

In a manner similar to statically defined classes (i.e. classes without any virtual methods), an object may gain access to its ancestor's code using the **Inherited** keyword.

To demonstrate this, the procedure `CClass` is rewritten as follows

```
Procedure CClass.Show;
  Begin
    Inherited Show;
    Writeln('I am CClass''s Show');
  End;
```

and procedure `BClass.Show` is rewritten as follows

```
Procedure BClass.Show;
  Begin
    Writeln('I am BClass''s Show');
  End;
```

```
Program VirtualMethods;

{$APPTYPE CONSOLE}

{$R *.res}

Uses
  VirtualMethodClasses in 'VirtualMethodClasses.pas';

Var
  a : AClass;
  b : BClass;
  c : CClass;

Begin
  a := AClass.Create;
  b := BClass.Create;
  c := CClass.Create;
  c.Zero;
  c.Show;
  Readln;
End.
```

Table 23.16 Program that uses virtual methods

The program executes differently.

The output from `c.Show` is now

```
I am BClass's Show
I am CClass's Show
```

Method `c.Show` calls `BClass.Show` via the `Inherited Show` statement within its body. Object `c` accesses the code for `B.Show` via the `CClass` VMT - *Figure 23.5*.

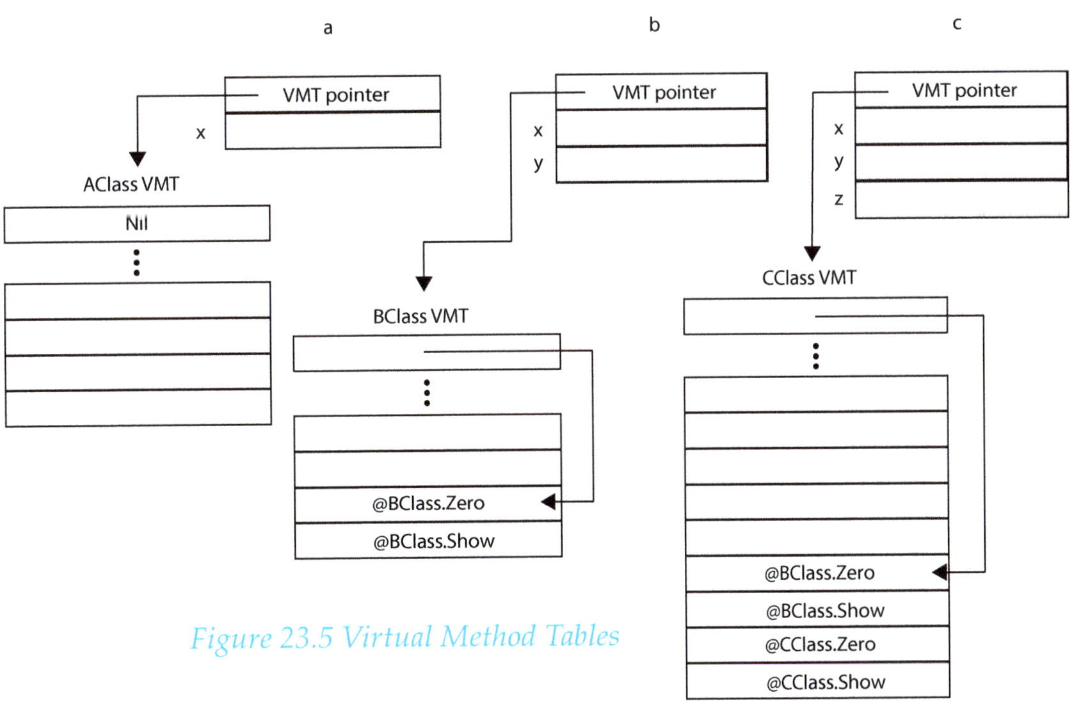

Figure 23.5 Virtual Method Tables

The keyword `Inherited` on its own is enough for `BClass.Show` to be called from `c.Show`.

Even if none of the methods are virtual, the use of the keyword `Inherited` would cause the same output from `c.Show`.

Ancestor methods are still available when methods are static.

The main power of virtual methods is revealed by the use of the **override** keyword.

To illustrate this, `CClass`'s methods are defined using the `override` keyword as shown in *Table 23.18*.

In the program shown in *Table 23.17*, an object of type `CClass` is created with three data fields `x`, `y` and `z`. The call to `CClass.Create` invokes the system constructor `Create`. The impact of this call is to create a VMT of the class `CClass` and to assign to the `CClass` object a pointer to this VMT. Now the corresponding virtual methods of the `BClass` object can be replaced (overidden) by `CClass`'s `Show` and `Zero` because `Show` and `Zero` of `CClass` specify `override`.

```
Program VirtualMethodsWithOverride;

{$APPTYPE CONSOLE}

{$R *.res}

Uses
  VirtualMethodWithOverrideClasses in
'VirtualMethodWithOverrideClasses.pas';

Var
  b : BClass;

Begin
b := CClass.Create;
  Writeln('My class name is ', b.ClassName);
  Writeln('My parent''s class name is ', b.ClassParent.ClassName);
  Writeln('My instance size is ', b.InstanceSize);
  b.Zero;
  b.Show;
  CClass(b).z := 6;
  Writeln('CClass(b).z: ', CClass(b).z);
  b.Show;
  Readln;
End.
```

Table 23.17 Program that uses virtual methods combined with methods that override

Figure 23.6 shows the console output when the program is run.

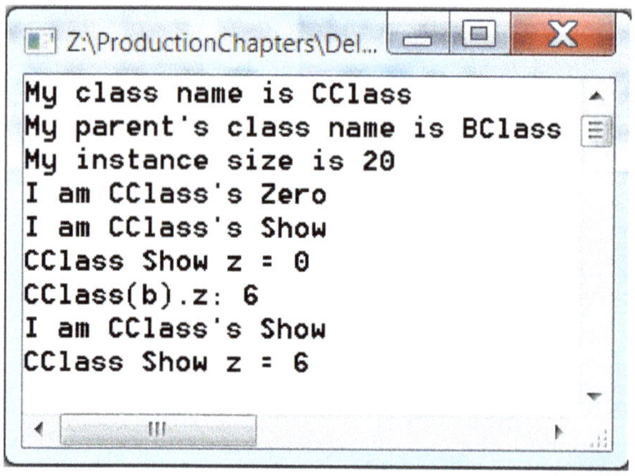

Figure 23.6 Console output for program VirtualMethodsWithOverride

```
Unit VirtualMethodWithOverrideClasses;
Interface
Type
  AClass = Class
           x : Integer;
         End;
  BClass = Class(AClass)
           y : Integer;
           Procedure Zero; Virtual;
           Procedure Show; Virtual;
         End;
  CClass = Class(BClass)
           z : Integer;
           Procedure Zero; Override;
           Procedure Show; Override;
         End;
Implementation
  Procedure BClass.Zero;
    Begin
      Writeln('I am BClass''s Zero');
    End;
  Procedure BClass.Show;
    Begin
      Writeln('I am BClass''s Show');
    End;
  Procedure CClass.Zero;
    Begin
      Writeln('I am CClass''s Zero');
    End;
  Procedure CClass.Show;
    Begin
      Writeln('I am CClass''s Show');
      Writeln('CClass Show z = ', z);
    End;
End.
```

Table 23.18 Unit containing virtual methods combined with methods that override these

If the qualifier `Override` keyword is replaced by the keyword `Virtual` in both instances, the console output changes to that shown in *Figure 23.7*.

In fact if the virtual and override keywords are removed altogether, the console output is as shown in *Figure 23.7*.

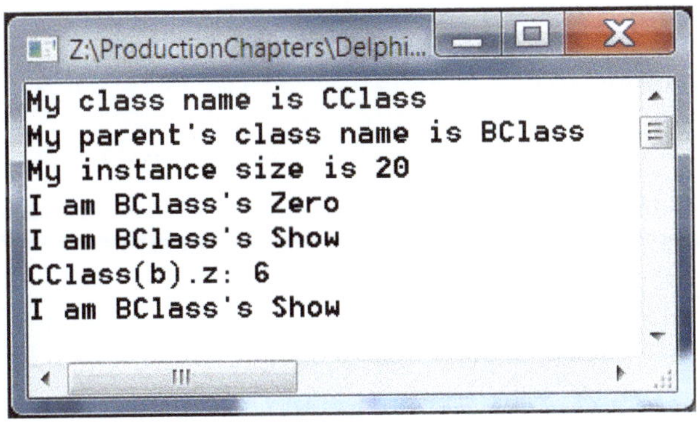

Figure 23.7 Console output for modified program VirtualMethodsWithOverride, overidde removed

Figure 23.8 shows the object of type `CClass` and its VMT.

If `CClass.Show` and `CClass.Zero` override `BClass.Show` and `BClass.Zero` then its methods are selected from the VMT otherwise `BClass` methods are selected from the VMT since `b` is of type `BClass`.

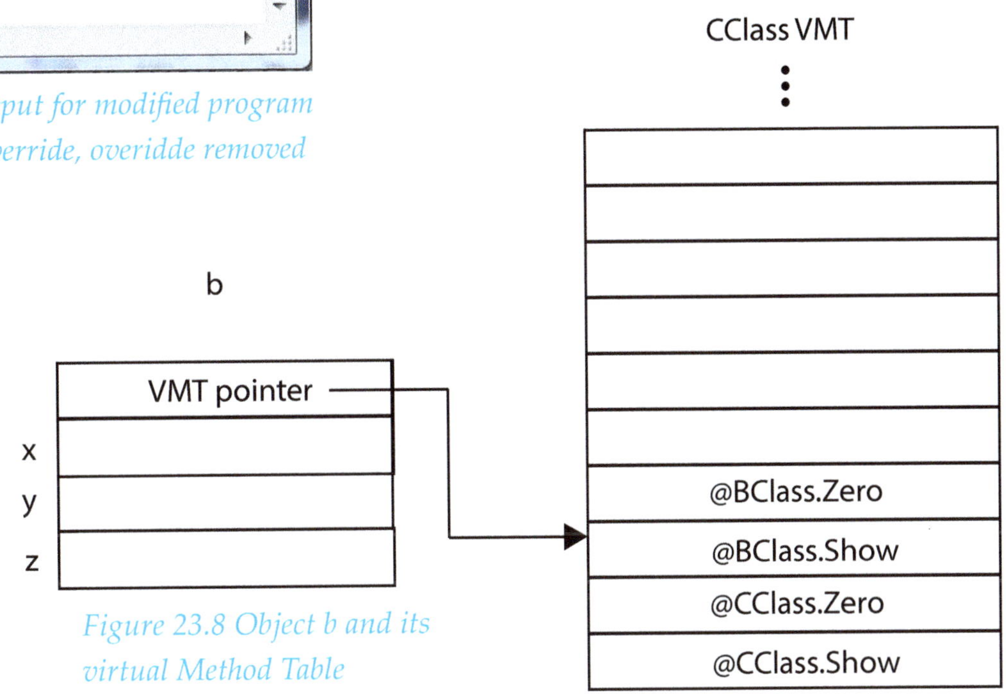

Figure 23.8 Object b and its virtual Method Table

Abstract Classes

Inheritance is classified as a generalisation/specialisation type of relationship.

For example, a digital clock is a kind of clock and an analogue clock is also a kind of clock. This is reflected in the inheritance class diagram shown in *Figure 23.9*. Class diagrams are covered in *Chapter 27*.

It doesn't make sense to provide an implementation of the `Clock` class because it is too general a concept.

The `Clock` class is therefore made an **abstract class.**

An abstract class is one that is composed of abstract methods (usually all are abstract but it doesn't have to be to make the class abstract). Abstract methods are not implemented in the abstract class but in its sub or derived classes.

In this example, the abstract methods of the `Clock` class are implemented in the subclasses `DigitalClock` and `AnalogueClock`.

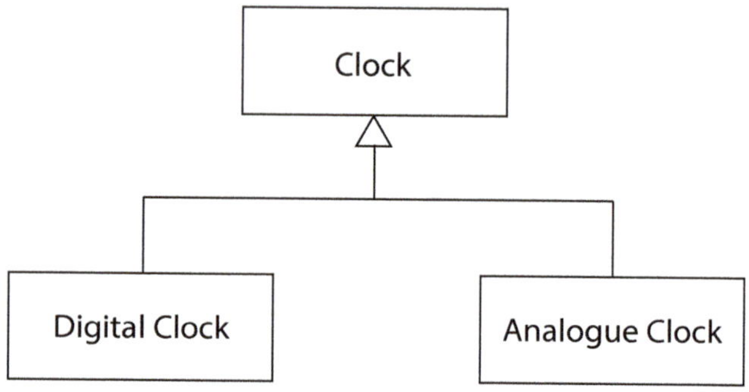

Figure 23.9 Inheritance diagram for clock types

For example, the `Clock` class may be defined as follows

```
Type
  TClock = Class
              CurrentTime : Integer;
              Procedure UpdateTime;
              Procedure ShowTime; Virtual; Abstract;
            End;
```

Only `ShowTime` is abstract. Showing the time is done differently in a digital clock from an analogue clock so it therefore makes sense to implement this method in the derived classes (subclasses). Updating time is a general concept and so can be implemented by the `Clock` class.

The method `ShowTime` is made virtual because it must be overriden in the derived classes.

The class definition for `TDigitalClock` is as follows

```
Type
  TDigitalClock = Class(TClock)
                     Procedure ShowTime; Override;
                   End;
```

Its implementation is as follows

```
Procedure TDigitalClock.ShowTime;
  Begin
    Writeln(ConvertToTimeFormat(CurrentTime));
  End;
```

Information

www.educational-computing.co.uk/DelphiBookCode/DelphiCode.html

Omelette making exercise

Load the project **OmeletteProject** or create a new project **OmeletteProject** and two units, **OmeletteClass** and **OmeletteKindClasses**.

The class `TOmelette` is an abstract class representing the general concept of an omelette - *Table 23.19*. The class `TCheeseOmelette` and the class `THamOmelette` are more specialised classes that are implementable. - *Table 23.20*. We say that these are **concrete classes** because they can be implemented.

```
Unit OmeletteClass;
Interface
Type
  TOmelette = Class
              Kind : String;
              Procedure Prepare; Virtual; Abstract;
              Procedure Cook; Virtual; Abstract;
              Procedure Plate; Virtual; Abstract;
              Procedure AddGarnish; Virtual; Abstract;
            End;
Implementation
  //Can't implement an abstract class
End.
```

Table 23.19 Abstract class TOmelette

The main program that uses these units is shown in *Table 23.21*.

This program creates an omelette 'factory' for 'manufacturing' omelettes which is called upon by an omelette store to produce omelettes to order. We use the word 'factory' to convey the idea that different omelette types can be made and which types are located together.

The details of the omelettes the factory can 'manufacture' are hidden away in the unit **OmeletteFactory**. This is an example of 'encapsulate what varies'. We can have more than one factory, each 'manufacturing' a different collection of omelette types. *Table 23.22* shows the source code for this unit (load or create this unit). The localisation of source code responsible for the manufacture of a particular range of omelettes means that changes to this range are constrained to this one unit.

Omelettes are sold in this exercise through an omelette store. An order is made to the store which calls upon its factory to show the range of omelettes and then 'manufacture' the chosen omelette type. The store processes this as an omelette in the unit **OmeletteStore** - *Table 23.23* (load or create this unit).

The main program then reports `Omelette.Kind`, where `Omelette` is a variable of type `TOmelette`, an abstract class which has been overridden by the relevant concrete class.

```
Unit OmeletteKindClasses;
Interface
Uses OmeletteClass;
Type
  //Concrete classes
  TCheeseOmelette = Class(TOmelette)
                      Constructor Create;
                      Procedure Prepare; Override;
                      Procedure Cook; Override;
                      Procedure Plate; Override;
                      Procedure AddGarnish; Override;
                    End;
  THamOmelette = Class(TOmelette)
                   Constructor Create;
                   Procedure Prepare; Override;
                   Procedure Cook; Override;
                   Procedure Plate; Override;
                   Procedure AddGarnish; Override;
                 End;
Implementation
Constructor TCheeseOmelette.Create;
  Begin
    Kind := 'Cheese';
  End;
Procedure TCheeseOmelette.Prepare;
  Begin
  End;
Procedure TCheeseOmelette.Cook;
  Begin
  End;
Procedure TCheeseOmelette.Plate;
  Begin
  End;
Procedure TCheeseOmelette.AddGarnish;
  Begin
  End;
Constructor THamOmelette.Create;
  Begin
    Kind := 'Ham';
  End;
Procedure THamOmelette.Prepare;
  Begin
  End;
Procedure THamOmelette.Cook;
  Begin
  End;
Procedure THamOmelette.Plate;
  Begin
  End;
Procedure THamOmelette.AddGarnish;
  Begin
  End;
End.
```

Table 23.20 Concrete classes TCheeseOmelette and THamOmelette

```
Unit OmeletteFactory;
Interface
Uses OmeletteClass, OmeletteKindClasses;
Type
  TOmeletteFactory = Class
                       Function CreateOmelette(Kind : Char)
                                                       : TOmelette;
                     End;
  Function GetValidChoice : Char;
Implementation
Procedure DisplayOmeletteMenu;
  Begin
    Writeln('Cheese - C');
    Writeln('Ham - H');
    Writeln('Prawn - P');
    Writeln('Salami - S');
    Writeln('Exit menu - X');
    Write('Choose an omelette type then press return: ');
  End;
Function GetOmeletteChoice : Char;
  Var
    Ch : Char;
  Begin
    Readln(Ch);
    Result := Ch;
  End;
Function ValidChoice(Choice : Char) : Boolean;
  Begin
    Result := Choice In ['C','c','H','h','P',
                         'p','S','s', 'X', 'x'];
  End;
Function GetValidChoice : Char;
  Var
    Choice : Char;
  Begin
    Repeat
      DisplayOmeletteMenu;
      Choice := GetOmeletteChoice;
      If Not ValidChoice(Choice)
        Then Writeln('Invalid choice');
    Until ValidChoice(Choice);
    Result := Choice;
  End;
Function TOmeletteFactory.CreateOmelette(Kind : Char)
                                                : TOmelette;
  Var
    Omelette : TOmelette;
  Begin
    Omelette := Nil;
    Case Kind Of
      'C', 'c' : Omelette := TCheeseOmelette.Create;
      'H', 'h' : Omelette := THamOmelette.Create;
      'P', 'p' : Omelette := Nil;
      'S', 's' : Omelette := Nil;
      'X', 'x' : Omelette := Nil;
    End;
    Result := Omelette;
  End;
End.
```

Table 23.22 Unit OmeletteFactory

```
Program OmeletteProject;
{$APPTYPE CONSOLE}
{$R *.res}
Uses
  OmeletteFactory in 'OmeletteFactory.pas',
  OmeletteKindClasses in 'OmeletteKindClasses.pas',
  OmeletteClass in 'OmeletteClass.pas',
  OmeletteStore in 'OmeletteStore.pas';
Var
  OStore : TOmeletteStore;
  OFactory : TOmeletteFactory;
  Omelette : TOmelette;
  Quit : Boolean = False;
  Response : Char;
Begin
  OFactory := TOmeletteFactory.Create;
  OStore := TOmeletteStore.CreateOmeletteStore(OFactory);
  Repeat
    Write('Press return to place next order.... ');
    Readln;
    Write('Are you ready to order- Y or N? ');
    Readln(Response);
    If Response In ['Y', 'y']
      Then
        Begin
          Omelette := OStore.OrderOmelette;
          If Assigned(Omelette)
            Then Writeln(Omelette.Kind)
            Else Writeln('Can''t make that omelette');
        End;
    Write('Quit - Y or N? ');
    Readln(Response);
    If Response In ['Y', 'y']
      Then Quit := True;
  Until Quit;
End.
```

Table 23.21 Program OmeletteProject

P

```
Unit OmeletteStore;
Interface
Uses
  OmeletteClass, OmeletteFactory;
Type
  TOmeletteStore = Class
                     Factory : TOmeletteFactory;
                     Constructor CreateOmeletteStore(Factory : TOmeletteFactory);
                     Function OrderOmelette : TOmelette;
                   End;
Implementation
Constructor TOmeletteStore.CreateOmeletteStore(Factory : TOmeletteFactory);
  Begin
    Self.Factory := Factory;
  End;
Function TOmeletteStore.OrderOmelette : TOmelette;
  Var
    Omelette : TOmelette;
    Choice : Char;
  Begin
    Omelette := Nil;
    Choice := GetValidChoice;
    Omelette := Self.Factory.CreateOmelette(Choice);//Make a particular omelette
    If Assigned(Omelette)
    Then
      Begin
        Omelette.Prepare;
        Omelette.Cook;
        Omelette.AddGarnish;
        Result := Omelette;
      End
    Else Result := Nil;
  End;
End.
```

Table 23.23 Unit OmeletteStore

Programming Task

2 Make the necessary changes to unit *OmeletteKindClasses* to allow unit *OmeletteFactory* to create prawn and salami kinds of omelette.
Add the option and ability to create an asparagus kind of omelette.

24 Aggregation

Information

www.educational-computing.co.uk/DelphiBookCode/DelphiCode.html.

Aggregation

Purpose: To understand the special forms of association called aggregation and composition

What is aggregation?

Aggregation is not a concept unique to object-oriented programming languages. Any language that supports record-like structures supports aggregation.

Aggregation is a special form of association with the meaning of a whole/part hierarchy together with the ability to navigate from the whole or aggregate to its parts.

Key concept

Aggregation:

Aggregation is a special form of association between objects with the meaning of a whole/part hierarchy together with the ability to navigate from the whole or aggregate to its parts. If and only if there exists a whole/part relationship between two objects, e.g. book and page, can an aggregate relationship exist between objects of their corresponding classes, TBookClass and TPageClass.

For example, a book has pages. We can think of a book as the whole and the pages as the parts.

A book identified with the ID 36 could be made up of 500 pages with each page uniquely numbered.

The book's title might be '*Intro to OOP by L. P. Partley*'.

The pages are bound together and a cover attached to make the book.

In a simplified scenario, we might define a class `TBook` for all book objects as shown in *Table 24.1*.

Methods have been omitted from `TBook` for convenience.

```
TBook = Class
          BookID : 1..2000;
          Title : String;
          PageRef : Array[1..500] Of TPage;
        End;
```

Table 24.1 TBook class definition

Similarly, we might define a class `TPage` for all the page objects which make up a book as shown in *Table 24.2*.

Methods have been omitted from `TPage` for convenience.

```
TPage = Class
          PageNo : Integer;
          PageContent : String;
        End;
```

Table 24.2 TPage class definition

We use an object constructor method `Create` to create an instance of the `TBook` class and assign the reference to a variable `aBook` of type `TBook`.

We can then create 500 page objects and assign their references as shown in *Table 24.3*.

We navigate from the whole to the part as follows

```
Writeln(aBook.PageRef[2].PageNo);
```

```
aBook := TBook.Create;
aBook.BookID := 36;
For i := 1 To 500 Do
  Begin
    aBook.PageRef[i] := TPage.Create;
    aBook.PageRef[i].PageNo := i;
  End;
```

Table 24.3 Creating book and page objects

This `Writeln` statement accesses `aBook`, the whole, then an attribute of `aBook`, called `PageRef`. This attribute is an array which can contain up to 500 references to `TPage` objects. The indexed reference `PageRef[2]` references the second page object, a *part* of the *whole*. This has an attribute `PageNo`. It is this which is displayed by `Writeln`.

The book object may be destroyed, i.e. the memory occupied by the object released, by using a user-defined **destructor**, `Destroy`, with body code as shown in *Table 24.4*.

The code first destroys all the page objects before finally destroying the book object. The user-defined destructor `Destroy` releases the memory of the object to which it is applied.

```
For i := 1 To 500
   Do aBook.PageRef[i].Free;
aBook.Free;
```

Table 24.4 Releasing the memory occupied by the book and page objects

If the book object was a tree in a forest then its leaves are destroyed first followed by the tree itself.

The detail shown in *Table 24.4* can be hidden within the user-defined destructor so that calling `aBook.Destroy` destroys everything. By analogy, the whole tree is destroyed, leaves, trunk, branches, etc, by the action of destruction.

Questions

1. Assuming that a book object has been created with 500 pages, each numbered consecutively starting from 1, what is displayed by `Writeln` if the following code could be executed?
   `Writeln(aBook.PageRef[36].PageNo);`

Composition

The book example is actually an example of a stronger form of aggregation called **composition**.

A whole/part relationship or association in which the aggregate object cannot exist without its components. A book is not a book without its pages otherwise it would just be a book cover.

Suppose we changed the `TBook` class so that its attributes are private and control access to these attributes via methods such as `TurnPage`, `ShowPage`. Our class definition might now resemble that shown in *Table 24.5*.

```
TBook = Class
          Private
            BookID : 1..2000;
            Title : String;
            PageRef : Array[1..500] Of TPage;
          Public
            Procedure TurnPage;
            Procedure ShowPage;
            ...
        End;
```

Table 24.5 Applying data encapsulation to TBook

All page objects are now hidden behind access methods. The consequence is that each page is **associated** with just one book object because there is no easy way to copy a page reference so the object it references can be *associated* at the same time with another book object.

Composition is characterised by the following

1. **It is a whole/part relationship or association, i.e. an aggregation**
2. **The aggregate object cannot exist without its component objects**
3. **An object is composed of other objects in a fixed relationship**
4. **The components can only belong to a single composition, i.e. cannot be shared with another aggregate object at the same time**

It is not a defining characteristic of composition to say that the runtime lifetime of the part is the same as the whole, i.e. destroy the whole and the parts are destroyed too; however, it is usually the case. An example of when it is not is a bicycle wheel which could be removed and used with another bicycle. The bicycle without a wheel is no longer a bicycle.

Key concept

Composition:
A whole/part relationship or association in which the aggregate object cannot exist without its components.
A composition hierarchy defines how an object is composed of other objects in a fixed relationship. The components can only belong to a single composition

The main characteristics are that the aggregate object cannot exist without its component objects and that these are fixed and not shared with another aggregate object at the same time.

Composition: Whole/part association in which the aggregate object cannot exist without its component objects and the components are fixed and can only belong to a single composition.

Aggregation

When the aggregation is weaker than composition we just call it **aggregation**. This is a whole/part relationship or association in which none of the part objects are essential for the whole to exist. This implies that the part is also capable of an independent existence and the whole/part association is variable - part objects 'come and go'. For example, a student object may be associated with both a `TutorGroup` object (a pastoral group in a school) and a `SportsTeam` object but may switch in and out. A `TutorGroup` object has students and a `SportsTeam` object has students so in both cases the relationship is whole/part but the relationship is not a fixed one and the aggregate/whole object in each case can exist without its component objects. The component objects can be added later from a 'pool' of these which are shared out amongst the 'whole' objects. In a clock example, batteries may be provided from a 'pool of batteries' and batteries may be added or removed from a clock and even used in another clock without affecting the existence of the clock which would be the case, for example if the clock face was removed. The whole/part relationship of battery objects is thus aggregation, not composition.

Aggregation:

In aggregation the whole/part association is variable.

Key concept

Aggregation:

It is a whole/part relationship or association in which an object is composed of a variable set of component objects, e.g. a SportsTeam object composed of student objects, but the ones used are not always the same. Part objects are not essential for the whole object to exist, e.g. an empty car boot whole object. The part is also capable of an independent existence, e.g the contents of a car boot are potential part objects. It is possible for a part to be associated with more than one whole (not necessarily at the same time), e.g. a student object can be a part of a sports team object and a tutor group object.

However, the concept of an aggregation which isn't composition doesn't mean much in practice so it is often just called an association. Therefore, it is not essential to use aggregation, but it can help us to understand and give added meaning to a model.

A simple test can be applied to discover if the association or relationship between two objects is aggregation. It applies to both composition and (non-composition) aggregation.

The test is called the **"has/has-a"** or **"is part of"** or "**contains**" test, e.g. **a book** ***has a*** **number of pages** indicates that the relationship is aggregation.

Windows form composition application

Figure 24.1 shows a Windows form application which adds two integers and displays the result.

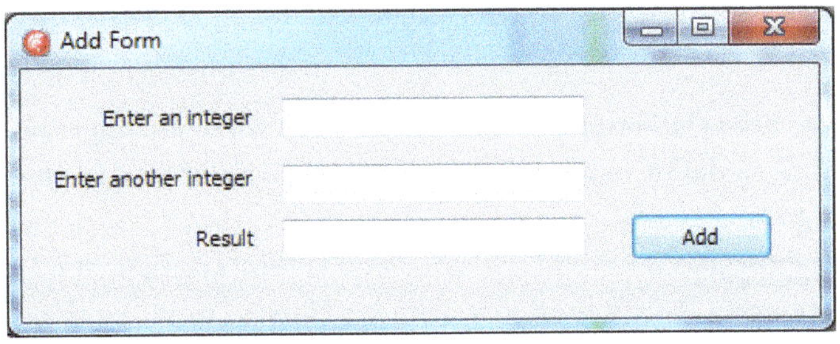

Fig. 24.1 Windows form object containing other objects

The form object `FormAdd` is of type `TFormAdd`.

`TFormAdd` is a class with seven attributes and one method which performs the addition.

Table 24.7 shows the Delphi unit which contains the class definition `TFormAdd`, and *Table 24.6* shows the program which uses the class `TFormAdd` to create a form object which is referenced by the reference variable `FormAdd`. This form object **has a** `TEdit` attribute called `EditFirst`.

`EditFirst` is an object of type `TEdit`.

`TEdit` is a class supplied by the Delphi programming language.

```
Program AddProject;
Uses
  Vcl.Forms, AddUnit in 'AddUnit.pas' {FormAdd};
{$R *.res}
Begin
  Application.Initialize;
  Application.MainFormOnTaskbar := True;
  Application.CreateForm(TFormAdd, FormAdd);
  Application.Run;
End.
```

Table 24.6 Delphi program which creates form

The "*has-a*" test tells us that the relationship or association is aggregation, and since the `EditFirst` object has a fixed relationship with the form object, this is aggregation of the composition type - see class diagram *Figure 24.2*. The same test is passed by the other objects, `AddBtn` and so on.

```
Unit AddUnit;
Interface
Uses
  Winapi.Windows, Winapi.Messages, System.SysUtils, System.Variants,
  System.Classes, Vcl.Graphics, Vcl.Controls, Vcl.Forms, Vcl.Dialogs, Vcl.StdCtrls;

Type
  TFormAdd = Class(TForm)
               AddBtn: TButton;
               EditFirst: TEdit;
               LabelEnterFirst: TLabel;
               EditSecond: TEdit;
               LabelEnterSecond: TLabel;
               Result: TEdit;
               LabelResult: TLabel;
               Procedure AddBtnClick(Sender: TObject);
             End;
Var
  FormAdd: TFormAdd;
Implementation
{$R *.dfm}
  Procedure TFormAdd.AddBtnClick(Sender: TObject);
  Begin
    Result.Text := IntToStr(StrToInt(EditFirst.Text) + StrToInt(EditSecond.Text));
  End;
End.
```

Table 24.7 Delphi unit for a windows form containing seven objects

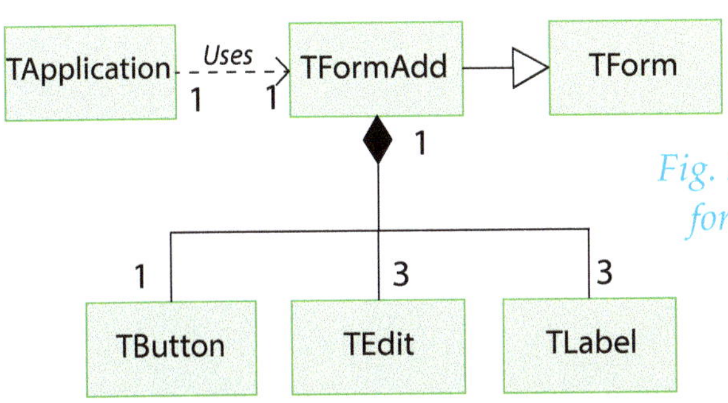

Fig. 24.2 Class diagram for Windows form application - see Chapter 27

Further information

There are relationships or associations which are not aggregation or inheritance - see Chapter 27. These associations denote semantic dependency among otherwise unrelated classes, such as between "snakes" and "long grass" – snakes hide in long grass.

These are just referred to as associations. For example, the type of association called *dependency* is a "uses" relationship. This is used to specify the classes "used" by the contents of the class concerned. This is usually taken to mean that the object class acts upon another class, or needs information contained within another class.

For example, a "snake" can move on the"ground" and therefore can be said to have a dependence relationship with "ground". However, since a "snake" is not "ground", it is not an inheritance relationship, and a "snake"does not contain "ground" (i.e. a snake has a ground does not make sense), a "snake' does not have an aggregation relationship with "ground".

Questions

2. A bicycle consists of a frame, wheels, tyres, a gear train, pedals, saddle, handlebars, brakes and brake levers, and a gear lever.
   What is the relationship between a bicycle object and its parts?

3. A game of chess uses a chess board and chess pieces. A chess board consists of black and white squares.
   What is the relationship between chess board and its black and white squares?

4. A digital clock is a kind of clock and an analogue clock is also a kind of clock. An analogue clock consists of a clock face, clock hands, a clock mechanism.
   What is the relationship between
   (a) Clock and digital watch? (b) Clock and analogue watch?
   (c) An analogue watch and clock face, clock hands, clock mechanism?
   (d) A digital clock and a battery used to power the clock?

25 Object-Oriented Paradigm

OOP Paradigm

Purpose: To learn why the object-oriented paradigm is used

> **Key concept**
>
> **Module:**
>
> A module is a component of a larger system that interacts with the rest of the system in a simple and well-defined manner.

Why use the object-oriented programming paradigm?

The claim is that object-oriented programming is better at modelling the real world than structured programming.

The central concept of object-oriented programming is the object, which is a kind of module containing data and subroutines. An object is a kind of self-sufficient entity that has an internal state (the data it contains) and that can respond to messages (calls to its subroutines).

This modular approach means that

- **Data is protected**, since it can be manipulated only in known, well-defined ways
- **It is easier to write programs** to use a module because the details of how the data is represented and stored do not need to be known
- The **storage structure of the data and the code** for the subroutines in a module **may be altered without affecting programs** that make use of the module as long as the published interfaces and the module's functionality remain the same.

The popularity of OOP stems from the support it gives to a software development process that relies upon preexisting reusable software components.

The spirit of reusability requires that, amongst programmers, a culture prevails in which software is developed under the assumption that it will be reused.

Code reusability

A main benefit/advantage of object-oriented programming is code reusability.

> **Key term**
>
> **Reusability:**
>
> Reusability is the ability of software elements to be reused in many different applications.

Reusability is the ability of software elements to be reused in many different applications.

Rather than starting from scratch with each new application, a programmer will consult libraries of existing components to see if any are appropriate as starting points for the design of a new application.

These components will exist in libraries as class definitions. A programmer will select an appropriate class definition from a library and then create a subclass for the application. The subclass will inherit the methods and properties of the library class, add some new ones of its own and possibly redefine the actions of others.

In visual programming languages such as C#, Delphi, Visual C++ and Visual Basic the libraries store the class definitions for components which allow Graphical User Interfaces (GUI) to be built.

Reliability

Components built by specialists in their field are more likely to be designed correctly and reliably. The reuse of these components across many applications will have given the developers of the components ample feedback to deal with any bugs and deficiencies. For example, widgets for graphical user interfaces.

Efficiency (time and space)

The component developers are likely to be experts in their field and will have used the best possible algorithms and data structures.

Time Saving

By relying upon existing components there is less software to develop and hence applications can be built quicker.

The user interface for Skype® was built in Delphi quickly using Borland's Rapid Application Development® (RAD) system. The Skype developers made use of the many pre-built components available in the RAD system to save development time.

Decreased maintenance effort

Using someone else's components decreases the amount of maintenance effort that the application developer needs to expend. The maintenance of the reused components is normally the responsibility of the component supplier.

Consistency

Relying on a library of standard components will tend to spread a consistency of design message throughout a team of programmers working on an application. The library is the basis of a standard that will lend coherency and conformity to the design process, e.g. by using visual components from the Microsoft® Foundation Class library.

Investment

Reusing software will save the cost of developing similar software from scratch. The investment in the original development is preserved if the developed software can be used in another project. The most reusable software tends to be that produced by the best developers. Reusing software is thus a way of preserving the knowledge and creations of the best developers.

Reduced error checking code

The nature of a module/object is that access to its state and internal code is highly controlled. The code surrounding an object may only interact with the object in carefully controlled ways through the object's interface. This reduces the number of possible error situations that may arise and therefore the need for code to check for errors.

Questions

1. State and justify **four** reasons why the object-oriented paradigm is used.

26 Object-Oriented key design principles

Information

The example programs in this chapter are available to download from www.educational-computing.co.uk/DelphiBookCode/DelphiCode.html.

Object-Oriented key design principles

Purpose: To be aware of the following object-oriented design principles:

- encapsulate what varies
- favour composition over inheritance
- program to interfaces, not implementation

Encapsulate what varies

A key design principle is to

separate the parts that may be subject to change from the parts that will stay the same.

For example, an encryption algorithm which is used by a part of the system may need to be replaced by a better one.

Following this principle will allow the parts of the system that are subject to change to vary independently of all other parts.

The class is the way that we encapsulate. So we need to create separate classes for the parts that may be subject to change because of new requirements or because they are required to exhibit different behaviour.

```
Unit Person;
Interface
  Uses DietInterface;
  Type
    TPerson = Class
                Private
                  Diet : IDiet;
                  PersonsName : String;
                Public
                  Constructor Create(Name : String; Kind : Integer);
                  Procedure ShowDiet;
              End;
Implementation
  Uses MeatDiet, VegetarianDiet, DontKnowDiet;
  Constructor TPerson.Create(Name : string; Kind : integer);
    Begin
      PersonsName := Name;
      Case Kind Of
        0 : Diet := TMeatDiet.Create;
        1 : Diet := TVegetarianDiet.Create;
        Else Diet := TUnknownDiet.Create;
      End;
    End;
  Procedure TPerson.ShowDiet;
    Begin
      Writeln(PersonsName, ' is a ', Diet.GetDiet);
    End;
End.
```

Table 26.1 Encapsulation in class TPerson

Suppose we need a software system to model people's diets.

We can declare a class `Person` as shown in *Table 26.1*.

We need to record a person's name, and what kind of eater they are, e.g. meat eater, vegetarian. However, we may be required later to cater for other categories of eater as yet not specified.

The class has been created with a private attribute `Diet` with type `IDiet`.

Type `IDiet` is an **interface type** which declares a method `GetDiet` without specifying how it will be implemented.

Table 26.2 shows the unit `DietInterface` which contains the interface declaration, `IDiet`.

A diet is the part of the application that varies so we have separated this part from the rest of the application and encapsulated this part in an *Interface unit*, `DietInterface`.

```
Unit DietInterface;
Interface
  Type
    IDiet = Interface
              Function GetDiet : String;
            End;
Implementation
End.
```

Table 26.2 Encapsulating diet in an interface

We can now implement this interface as a vegetarian diet, a meat diet and an unknown diet as shown in *Tables 26.3*, *26.4* and *26.5*.

If we require more implementations then we just provide more implementations of `IDiet`, e.g. a vegan diet.

```
Unit VegetarianDiet;
Interface
  Uses DietInterface;
  Type
    TVegetarianDiet = Class (TInterfacedObject, IDiet)
                        Function GetDiet : String;
                      End;
Implementation
  Function TVegetarianDiet.GetDiet : String;
    Begin
      Result := 'Pulses eater';
    End;
End.
```

Table 26.3 Encapsulating class TVegetarianDiet

```
Unit MeatDiet;
Interface
  Uses DietInterface;
  Type
    TMeatDiet = Class (TInterfacedObject, IDiet)
                  Function GetDiet : String;
                End;
Implementation
  Function TMeatDiet.GetDiet : String;
    Begin
      Result := 'Beef eater';
    End;
End.
```

Table 26.4 Encapsulating class TMeatDiet

```
Unit DontKnowDiet;
Interface
  Uses DietInterface;
  Type
    TUnknownDiet = Class (TInterfacedObject, IDiet)
                     Function GetDiet : String;
                   End;
Implementation
  Function TUnknownDiet.GetDiet : String;
    Begin
      Result := 'Do not know';
    End;
End.
```

Table 26.5 Encapsulating class TUnknownDiet

Table 26.6 shows an application which uses an array of `TPerson` to store four person objects.

Each object contains a diet object whose type may be a meat diet, a vegetarian diet or an unknown diet.

The design allows for new diet types to be added as needed because "what varies has been encapsulated" in class `TPerson` in a private attribute `Diet` of type `IDiet`.

Figure 26.1 shows the output when the application is run.

```
Program PersonsDietExample;
{$APPTYPE CONSOLE}
{$R *.res}
Uses
  System.SysUtils, Person;
Type
  TPersonArray = Array[1..4] Of TPerson;
Var
  PersonArray : TPersonArray;
Begin
  PersonArray[1] := TPerson.Create('Fred', 0);
  PersonArray[1].ShowDiet;
  PersonArray[2] := TPerson.Create('Mary', 1);
  PersonArray[2].ShowDiet;
  PersonArray[3] := TPerson.Create('Aslam', 0);
  PersonArray[3].ShowDiet;
  PersonArray[4] := TPerson.Create('Isla', 20);
  PersonArray[4].ShowDiet;
  Readln;
End.
```

Table 26.6 Program that uses class TPerson

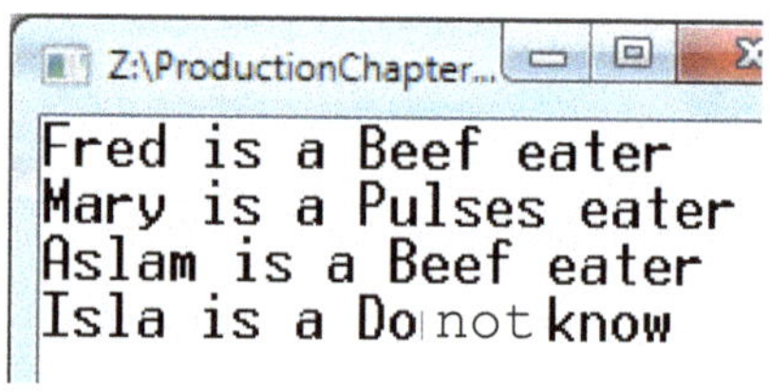

Figure 26.1 Output from running program PersonsDietExample

Key point

Difference between a class and an interface:

A class describes the attributes and behaviours of an object whereas an interface contains behaviours that a class implements.

An interface cannot be instantiated.

An interface does not contain any constructors.

All the methods in an interface are abstract.

```
TPerson = Class
            Private
              Diet : IDiet;   <---- Composition
              PersonsName : String;
            Public
              Constructor Create(Name : String; Kind : Integer);
              Procedure ShowDiet;
          End;
```

Table 26.7 TPerson class uses composition

An important point to make is that the class `TPerson` uses **composition**. A person object of type `TPerson` *has a* diet object of type `IDiet` - *Table 26.7*.

Programming Task

1. Use *Save As* to save the *VegetarianDiet* unit as *VeganDiet.pas*. Add the unit name *VeganDiet* to the *Uses* statement in the implementation section of unit *Person*. Save *Person.pas*. Change *TVegetarianDiet* in *Vegan.pas* to *TVeganDiet*. Change *Result := 'Pulses eater';* to *Result := 'No dairy or eggs';* in *VeganDiet.pas*. Add to the *Case* statement in unit *Person*: *2 : Diet := TVeganDiet.Create;*.
   Press *F9* to compile, build and run *PersonsDietExample*.
   Do you agree that it is relatively easy to add a new kind of diet when we use an Interface unit?

Could the solution have been achieved using inheritance?

Table 26.8 shows a redefined class `TPerson` which assumes, in general, that a person is a meat eater.

Table 26.9 shows the declaration of a class `TXPerson` which inherits from `TPerson`.
In general, a person classified as an X person is a vegetarian. Therefore, the class `TXPerson` overrides the inherited `ShowDiet` method.

The software can still access the inherited method `ShowDiet` for any X person who is a meat eater.

It can do this with `inherited ShowDiet.`

The problem arises when we have a lot of different classes of people, e.g. 26 classes

`TAPerson ... TZPerson`

If all 26 classes inherit from `TPerson`, then each will need to provide an implementation of `ShowDiet` which outputs the diet of the majority.

This is a lot of duplication of code!

Although this example is a little contrived and very simplified, it is meant to make the following point

To build software so that when it needs to be changed it can be done with the least impact on the existing code the following design principles need to be applied

- **encapsulate what varies**
- **favour composition over inheritance**

```
Unit Person;
Interface
  Type
    TPerson = Class
                Private
                  PersonsName : String;
                Public
                  Constructor Create(Name : String);
                  Procedure ShowDiet; Virtual;
              End;
Implementation
   Constructor TPerson.Create(Name : string);
    Begin
      PersonsName := Name;
    End;
  Procedure TPerson.ShowDiet;
    Begin
      Writeln(PersonsName, ' is a meat eater');
    End;
End.
```

Table 26.8 Class TPerson

```
Unit XPerson;
Interface
  Type
    TXPerson = Class(TPerson)
                 ...
               Public
                 Procedure ShowDiet; Override;
                 ...
             End;
Implementation
  Procedure TPerson.ShowDiet;
    Begin
      Writeln(PersonsName, ' is a pulses eater');
    End;
End.
```

Table 26.9 Class TXPerson

If `TPerson`'s class uses composition as shown in Table 26.7 and not inheritance as shown in Table 26.8 then duplication of code for `ShowDiet` can be eliminated.

Program to interfaces, not implementation

Chapter 18 covered the concept of coupling in connection with structured programming and design.

Coupling measures the strength of relationships between modules.

It was stated in *Chapter 18* that the objective of structured design is to minimise the coupling between modules so that the modules are as independent as possible.

The same objective applies in object-oriented design and programming.

In the object-oriented programming paradigm,

the object is the fundamental unit of modularity.

In structured programming, the subroutine is the fundamental unit of modularity.

Loose coupling in structured programming is achieved when a subroutine's parameter list is its (data) interface with other subroutines and the main program.

Loose coupling in object-oriented programming is achieved when an object's interface with other objects is via methods and properties whose identifiers (names) but not implementation are made public.

Some object-oriented programming languages allow a declaration of methods and properties without writing their implementation.

This type of declaration without an implementation is called an **interface**.

In Delphi, the keyword **Interface** is used for this purpose (although it is possible to model an interface using abstract classes).

Information

Object property:

We have called the data fields that store an object's state the attributes of the object. The object property is a mechanism of allowing indirect access to an attribute via an alias, and getter and setter methods which create the impression that the attribute is being accessed directly. The alias is used in assignment statements to set the value of its underlying attribute and copied from to read the value of its underlying attribute.

Key concept

Unit of modularity:

The object is the fundamental unit of modularity.

Table 26.10 shows an interface `ISum` declared in a unit `ISumUnit`.

It contains one method `SumToN` which returns an integer.

The number string below the `Interface` keyword is a Globally Unique Identifier (GUID) which is used by the compiler to identify this interface. It is generated in the IDE by typing CTRL+SHIFT+G.

```
Unit ISumUnit;
Interface
  Type
    ISum = Interface
         ['{66642D9A-C0BC-4DC1-9F8D-308704207A1E}']
         Function SumToN : Integer;
       End;
Implementation
End.
```

Table 26.10 Declaring an interface ISum

- Note there is no implementation code.
- Interfaces consist of a name (in this case, `ISum`) and a declaration of methods and properties.
- It is conventional to start the name given to the interface with the letter "I".
- Generally, an interface does not allow object attributes (fields), variables or constants to be declared.
- An interface is purely a declaration of capability.
- An interface cannot use access modifiers such as private, protected, etc.
- Thus, every member of an interface is by default public.
- An interface can't do anything without an implementing class.

The implementing class must declare that it is implementing the interface (it does this by including the interface identifier in brackets) and then must make sure that it implements all the methods declared in the interface.

Table 26.11 shows one possible implementation of the interface `ISum` by class `TSum`.

Class `TSum` inherits from a base class, `TInterfacedObject`, supplied by Delphi. This base class supports the management of interfaces and must be used.

Class `TSum` declares that it is implementing `ISum` by including a reference to `ISum` in brackets.

```
Unit TSumUnit;
Interface
  Uses ISumUnit;
  Type
    TSum = Class(TInterfacedObject, ISum)
             Public
               Function SumTo(n  : Integer) : Integer;
           End;
Implementation
  Function TSum.SumTo(n : Integer) : Integer;
    Var
      Sum, i : Integer;
    Begin
      Sum := 0;
      For i := 1 To n
        Do Sum := Sum + i;
      Result := Sum;
    End;
End.
```

Table 26.11 TSumUnit showing the implementing class, TSum

Table 26.12 shows a program which uses an object reference of type `ISum` and an object of type `TSum`. The `TSum` object is sent the message `SumTo(n)` where the value of `n` is read from the keyboard.

This is a highly contrived example to illustrate a point that interfaces make possible something that is critical to writing good code:

They allow programming to an abstraction and not an implementation.

Interfaces are abstractions.

Programming against an abstraction, means that the program is not coupled to a specific implementation.

```
Program SumToNExample;
{$APPTYPE CONSOLE}
{$R *.res}
Uses
  System.SysUtils,
  ISumUnit in 'ISumUnit.pas',
  TSumUnit in 'TSumUnit.pas';
Var
  n : Integer;
  SumObjectReference : ISum;
Begin
  SumObjectReference := TSum.Create;
  Write('Input n: ');
  Readln(n);
  Writeln(SumObjectReference.SumTo(n));
  Readln;
End.
```

Table 26.12 Program which uses an object reference of type ISum and an object of type TSum.

For example, the alternative implementation of class `TSum` shown in Table 26.13 can be substituted for the original shown in Table 26.11 without breaking the program shown in Table 26.12 as long as `TSum` implements `ISum`.

```
Unit TSumUnit;
Interface
  Uses ISumUnit;
  Type
    TSum = Class(TInterfacedObject, ISum)
             Public
               Function SumTo(n  : Integer) : Integer;
           End;
Implementation
  Function TSum.SumTo(n : Integer) : Integer;
    Begin
      Result := ((n + 1) * n) Div 2;
    End;
End.
```

Table 26.13 TSumUnit showing an alternative implementation of class, TSum

Key point

More than one source of behaviour:

By using interfaces, you can, for example, include behaviour from multiple sources in a class. For example,

```
TSomeClass = Class((TInterfacedObject, IEx1, IEx2,IEx3)
               ...
             End
```

Interface

Questions

1. What **three** design principles enable software to be built so that when it needs to be changed it can be done with the least impact on the existing code?

2. A computer activity game has game characters which acquire specific tools during the game.
Each character object can make use of one tool object at a time, but can change tools at any time during the game. The following tools are available
    - *saw*
    - *lockpick*
    - *screwdriver*
    - *hammer*

   Each tool has a different behaviour.
   A tool object has a method `UseTool` which implements the appropriate behaviour.
   A character class `Character` has an attribute `Tool` of type `ToolBehaviour`.
   A tool object is of a type which describes the object's behaviour and may be one of
    - *SawBehaviour*
    - *LockPickBehaviour*
    - *ScrewdriverBehaviour*
    - *HammerBehaviour*

   A character may be one of the following
    - *master craftsman*
    - *apprentice*
    - *journeyman*

   The activity game uses an interface `ToolBehaviour` and eight classes in this activity game.
   (a) Explain why declaring `ToolBehaviour` as an interface is a good design decision.
   (b) Identify eight classes in this scenario.

3. The following are statements related to interfaces:
    - *"An interface allows programming to an abstraction not an implementation."*
    - *"An interface cannot declare a constructor."*
    - *"An interface cannot have attributes for object state."*
    - *"An interface can't do anything without an implementing class."*

   Explain these statements.

4. Explain why it is a good idea to favour composition over inheritance.

27 Class and object diagrams

Class diagrams

Purpose: To learn how to create class diagrams

Single inheritance, association, aggregation and composition were covered in a practical way in Chapter 22 and Chapter 24.

A class diagram is used to show the relationships/associations between classes.

Figure 27.1 shows how single inheritance is represented in a class diagram consisting of two classes A and B. Class B is the derived class or subclass which inherits from class A. Each class is drawn as a labelled rectangle.

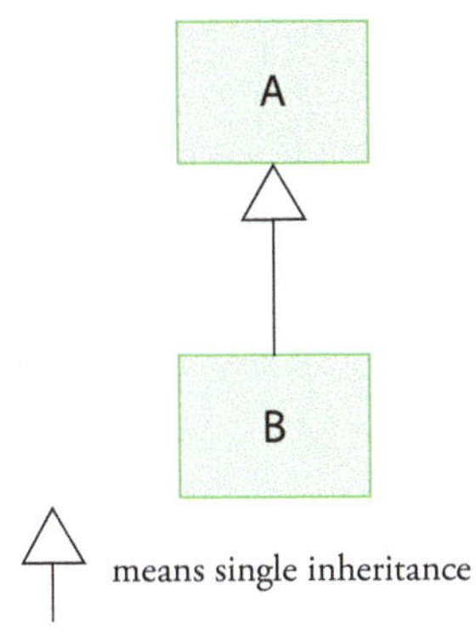

Fig. 21.1 Shows how single inheritance is represented in a class diagram

Figure 27.2 shows how aggregation (variable aggregation) is represented in a class diagram consisting of three classes C, D and E.

In the whole/part association known as aggregation, Classes C and D are the *whole* and class E is the variable set of component objects *part*.

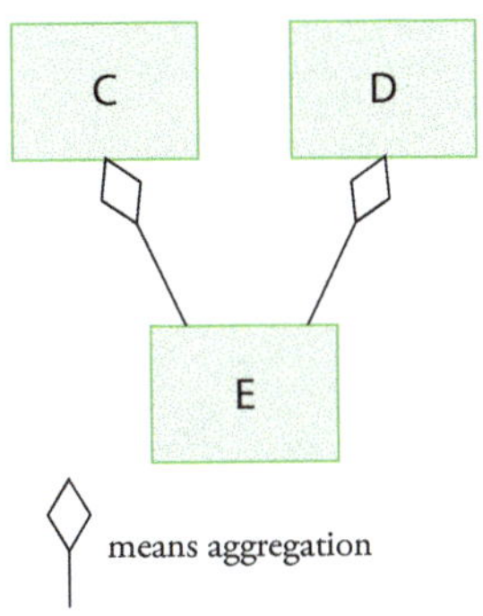

Fig. 27.2 Shows how aggregation is represented in a class diagram

Figure 27.3 shows how composition (fixed aggregation) is represented in a class diagram consisting of two classes F and G. In the whole/part association known as composition, Class F is the *whole* and class G is the *part*. The aggregate object (class F object) cannot exist without its component objects drawn from class G.

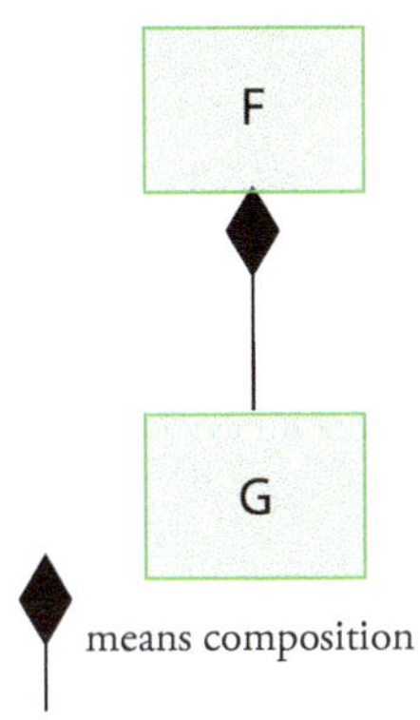

Fig. 27.3 Shows how composition is represented in a class diagram

Figure 27.4 shows how association is represented in a class diagram consisting of two classes H and I. The direction of the arrow indicates that the association is from H to I, e.g. "teacher teaches student" where "teacher" corresponds to H and "student" corresponds to I. The association is "teaches". Figure 27.5 shows how association of the dependency kind is represented in a class diagram. The direction of the arrow indicates that the association is from J to K, e.g. "snake uses ground" where "snake" corresponds to J and "ground" corresponds to K.

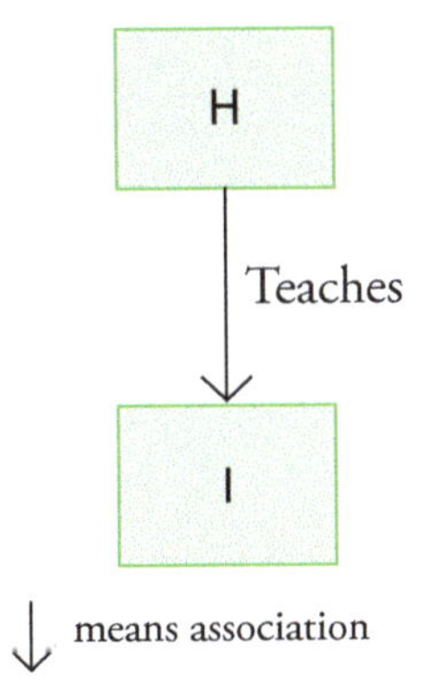

Fig. 27.4 Shows how association is represented in a class diagram

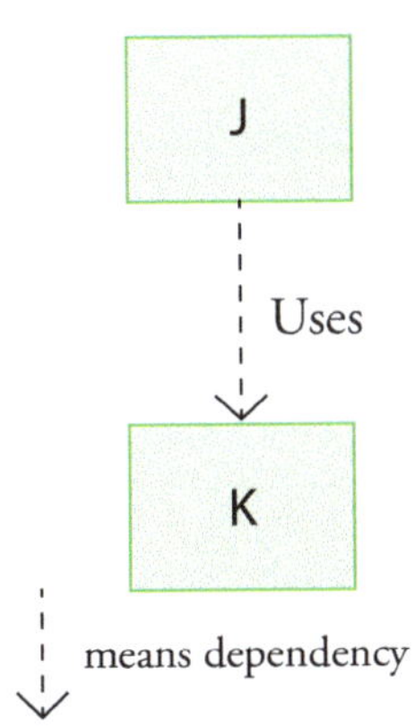

Fig. 27.5 Shows how dependency is represented in a class diagram

Questions

1. What is the symbol used on a class diagram to indicate
(a) single inheritance (b) composition (c) aggregation
(d) association (e) dependency?

The class diagrams shown so far have omitted the detail of each class. This is fine if all that is of interest is the kind of relationship or association, e.g. single inheritance. However, sometimes a more informative and detailed class diagram is required. Each class in this more detailed class diagram would show details of its attributes and methods and their access level specifiers as shown *Figure 27.6*. The bubble shows an example of the contents of a class rectangle. *Figure 27.7* shows the interpretation of the access level specifiers.

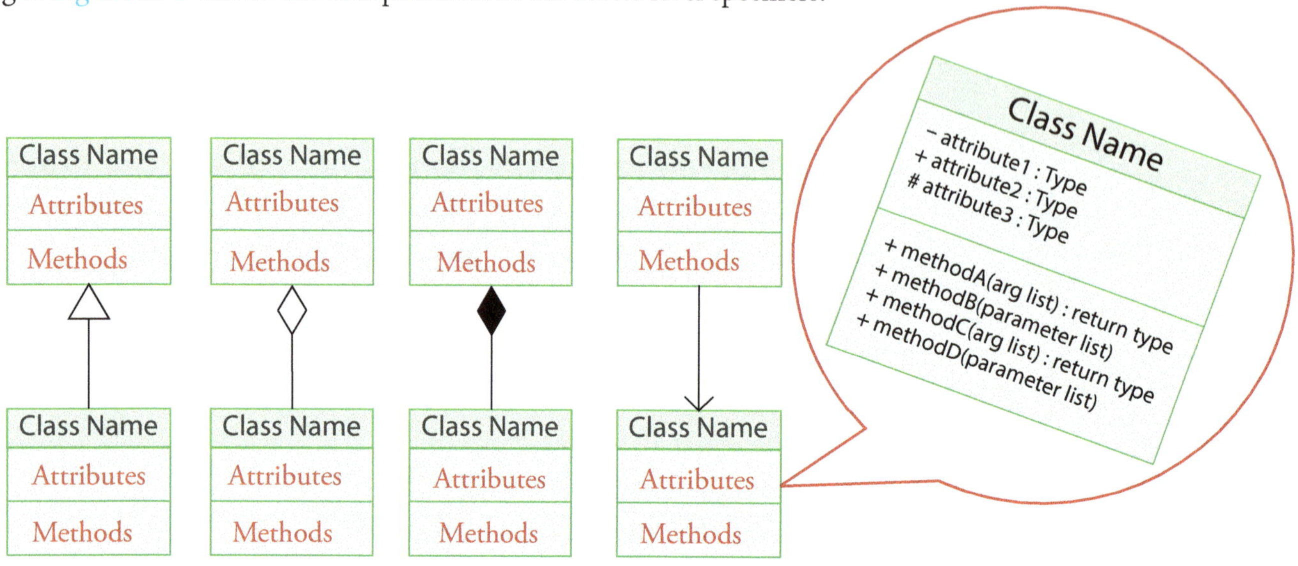

Fig. 27.6 Each class diagram is shown in more detail by splitting the rectangle into an attributes part and a methods part

Access level specifiers

+ means public   – means private   # means protected

Fig. 27.7 Access level specifiers for attributes and methods

Single inheritance class diagram

Figure 27.8 shows an example based on an exercise used in *Chapter 23*.

Figure 27.9 class diagram is a more detailed version of *Figure 27.8*. The attributes section is omitted in *Figure 27.9* from classes `Duck` and `Crow` because the exercise in *Chapter 23* did not supply these.

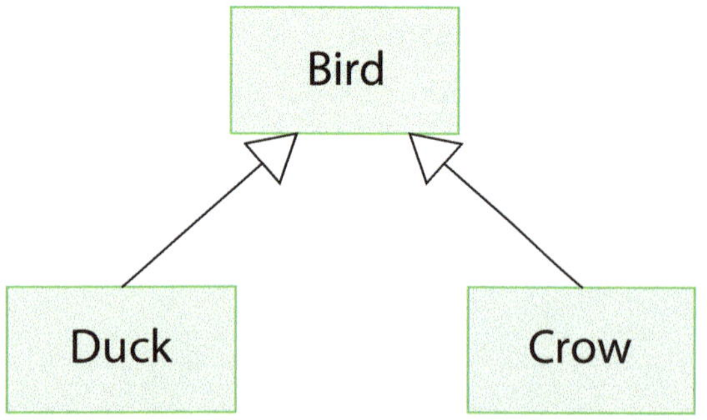

Fig. 27.8 Class diagram demonstrating single inheritance

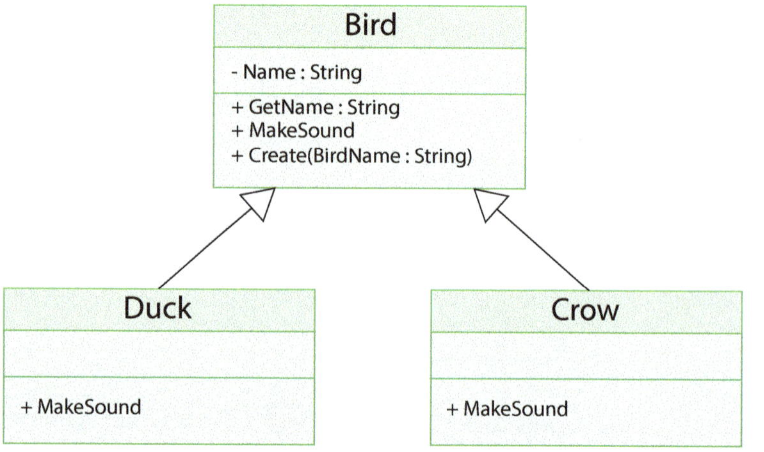

Fig. 27.9 Class diagram demonstrating single inheritance and showing attributes and methods

Figure 27.9 shows the visibility levels of the attribute `Name` and the three methods `GetName`, `MakeSound` and `Create`. Visibility level is indicated by placing an access modifier or access/visibility level specifier, one of '–', ' +', or ' #', before the attribute or method identifier.

If an attribute or method is private then the symbol used is ' –'.

If an attribute or method is public then the symbol used is '+'.

If an attribute or method is protected then the symbol used is '#'.

Questions

2. Pythons and cobras are types of snake. Draw a single inheritance class diagram which shows the relationship between these three types if each is modelled as a class.

Composition class diagram

Figure 27.10 shows a composition class diagram for a noughts and crosses grid such as that shown in *Figure 27.11*. Composition on this class diagram is indicated by a filled diamond and line.

The degree of the association is shown as one grid is associated with nine squares by labelling the diamond with 1 and the other end of the composition symbol with 9. If the degree of association is variable then the 9-end is replaced by *n*.

Key concept

Composition:
A whole/part relationship or association in which the aggregate object cannot exist without its components.
In composition, a composition hierarchy defines how an object is composed of other objects in a fixed relationship.

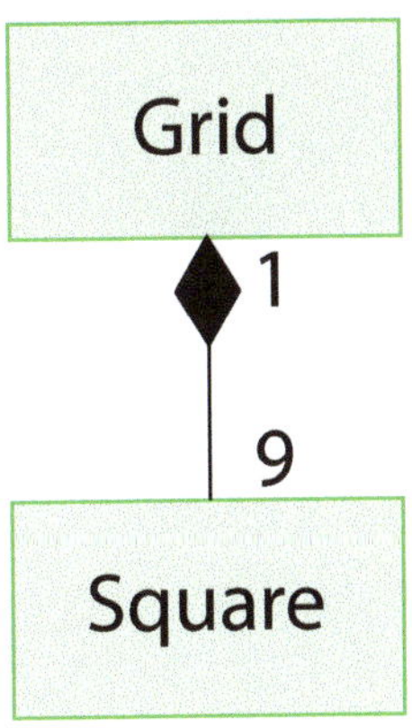

Fig. 27.10 Class diagram demonstrating composition

Fig. 27.11 Noughts and crosses grid

In composition, a composition hierarchy defines how an object is composed of other objects in a fixed relationship. The aggregate object cannot exist without its component objects. For example, a car comprises a body shell, an engine, a gearbox, seats, etc. A clock comprises a clock face, hands and clock mechanism. A car would not be a car without its components and a clock would not be a clock without its components. Therefore, we can say that composition is a **fixed whole/part relationship**, i.e. a special form of aggregation called **fixed aggregation**.

Questions

3. A snake has a fang. Draw a class diagram to show the relationship between snakes and fangs if each is modelled as a class.

Composition (fixed aggregation) is primarily a relationship between objects as is aggregation in general, rather than a relationship between classes. **A good test for a case of any form of aggregation is the "has a" test.** Describe the collection of objects first. If the phrase "has a" crops up between two objects then the first is composed of the second. For example, "a car has a body shell", "a car has a gearbox", etc. If none of the part objects are essential for the whole object to exist (i.e. the part objects can stay or go) then the association is just aggregation not the more restrictive form, composition.

Aggregation class diagram

Figure 27.12 shows a class diagram for aggregation. An unfilled diamond and line are used to indicate aggregation. The multiplicity of the relationship is indicated with '1' and '*' as shown and meaning one ('1') `TutorGroup` object is associated with many ('*') `Student` objects. Aggregation is a whole/part association in which an object is composed of a variable set of component objects, e.g. an object of type `TutorGroup` can be associated with more than one object of type `Student` class, and different `Student` objects at different times. Similarly an object of type `SportsTeam` class can be associated with more than one object of type `Student` class, and different `Student` objects at different times. In each case, the objects chosen from the `Student` class are not always the same.

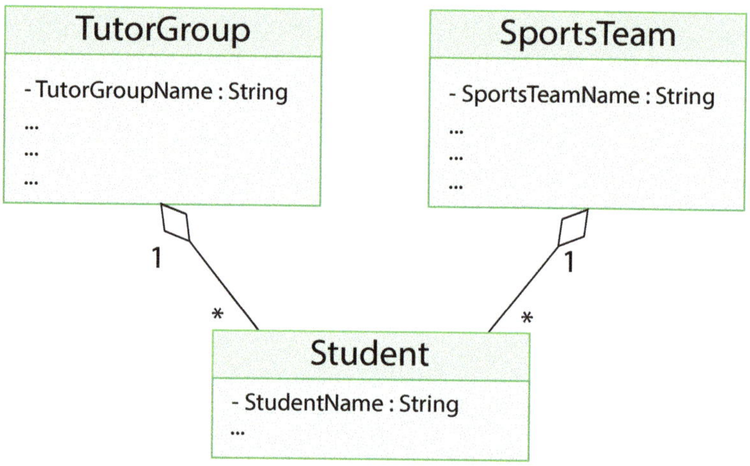

Fig. 27.12 Class diagram demonstrating aggregation

The whole can also exist without the part, e.g. a car boot object when empty.

To illustrate this consider the class diagram in *Figure 27.13*. This shows both composition and aggregation. The clock object cannot exist in the real world without its component objects, clock face, mechanism and hands but it can exist without its two batteries. These could be removed and used in another clock or device. Everyone knows that batteries have an independent existence.

Key concept

Aggregation:

It is a whole/part relationship or association in which an object is composed of a variable set of component objects, e.g. a SportsTeam object composed of student objects, and the ones used are not always the same. Part objects are not essential for the whole object to exist, e.g. an empty car boot object. The part is also capable of an independent existence, e.g the contents of a car boot. It is possible for a part to be associated with more than one whole (not necessarily at the same time).

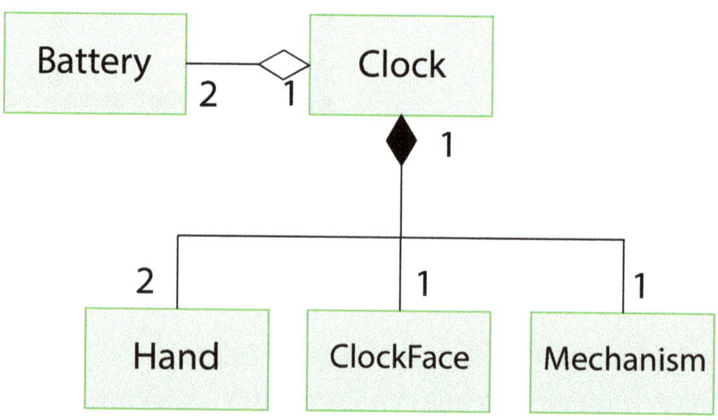

Fig. 27.13 Class diagram demonstrating fixed aggregation (composition) and variable aggregation (aggregation)

Fixed aggregation or composition

An object is composed of a fixed set of component objects, e.g. a rectangle is composed of four right-angle lines enclosing an area. The rectangle would not be a rectangle without all four lines - *Figure 27.14*.

Fig. 27.14 Composition class diagram

Variable aggregation (aggregation)

An object is composed of a variable set of component objects, e.g. a car boot object can contain a variable number of objects and the ones used are not always the same - *Figure 27.15*. Multiplicity notation 0..* means zero or more.

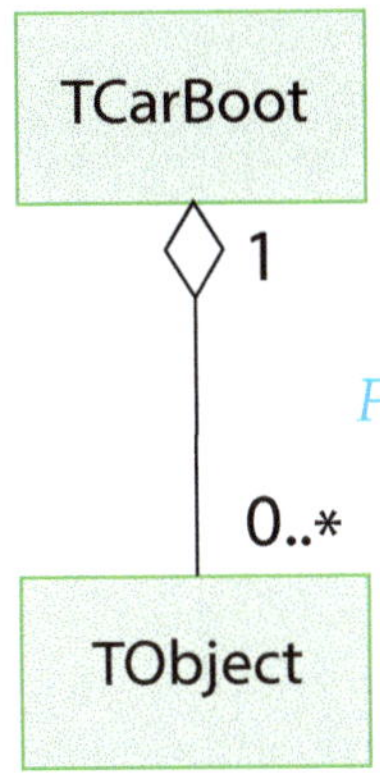

Fig. 27.15 Aggregation class diagram

Recursive or reflexive aggregation

The object contains components of its own type, like a Russian doll (each one containing a smaller one). For example, a rectangle object could contain two smaller rectangle objects - *Figure 27.16*.

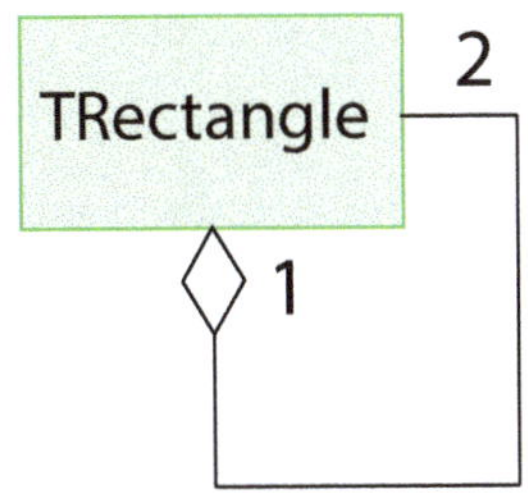

Fig. 27.16 Recursive aggregation class diagram

Has/Has-a or is-a-part-of or contains relationship

Describe the collection of objects first. If the phrase "**has a**" or "**has**" or "**is a part of**" or "**contains**" crops up between two objects then the first is composed of the second or is an aggregate of the second.

Questions

4. A universal remote control is a part of home entertainment systems which consist of televisions, a cable TV set top box, blu-ray players and other electronic devices.

   Draw a class diagram that shows the type of association between a universal remote controller and two types of electronic device, a TV and a blu-ray player if these are modelled as classes.

5. Draw a class diagram that shows the type of association between the wardrobe and its contents.

6. Draw a class diagram that shows the type of association between a bicycle object and the following objects: frame, handlebars, gears, wheels, brakes, removable lights.

Association

It is likely that you will encounter association which isn't a whole/part association(aggregation or composition).

Figure 27.17 shows an association class diagram for a `Teacher` class and a `Student` class. The association is one in which a teacher teaches a student. Clearly, this is not a whole/part association, i.e. a student is not a part of a teacher.

Fig. 27.17 Class diagram demonstrating association

Contrast this with the example in *Figure 27.12* in which a tutor group has many students and a sports team has many students.

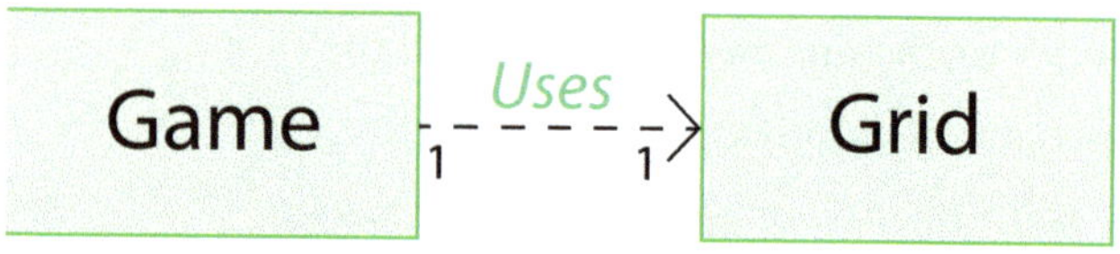

Fig. 27.18 Association class diagram for noughts and crosses game

The grid for noughts and crosses shown in *Figure 27.11* does have an association relationship in addition to its aggregation one, it is a *uses* association: a noughts and crosses game *uses* a grid. This *uses* association is shown in *Figure 27.18* and is a dependency association.

Bi-directional association also exists in which case the arrow has an arrowhead at each end.

In general, **association** is a type of relationship in which one object interacts with or uses another. When the type is 'uses' we use the term **dependency** or **dependency association**. Dependency is a weaker variant of association between otherwise unrelated classes, such as between 'snakes' and 'long grass' – snakes use long grass to hide.

The most common usage of a dependency is to show that a method belonging to one class uses another class when an object of the one uses an object of another as a method parameter. For example, an application object, `Application`, of the class `TApplication` calls the method `Application.CreateForm` with the object parameter `Form1` of class `TForm1` as shown below and in *Figure 27.19*.

```
Application.CreateForm(TForm1, Form1);
```

Dependency also occurs when an object of one class inititates another object which is also the case in the example in *Figure 27.19*.

Dependency is shown as a dotted line with an arrowhead.

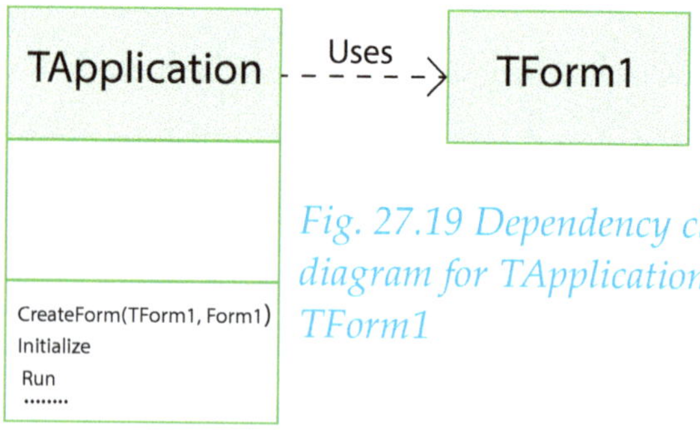

Fig. 27.19 Dependency class diagram for TApplication and TForm1

Questions

7. A doctor can be associated with multiple patients. At the same time, one patient can visit multiple doctors for treatment or consultation. Each of these objects has its own life cycle and there is no "owner" or parent. The objects that are part of the association relationship can be created and destroyed independently.
   Draw a class diagram that shows the type of association between doctor and patient.

A class diagram shows the static relationships between classes. When two classes are connected by a relationship, the connection is called an association.

Associations may be classified as

- a dependency (uses)
- an aggregation
- a composition (a strong form of aggregation)
- inheritance (yes, even inheritance which is a generalisation/specialisation relationship or association)
- and if not any of the above then just an association

This is shown in *Figure 27.20*.

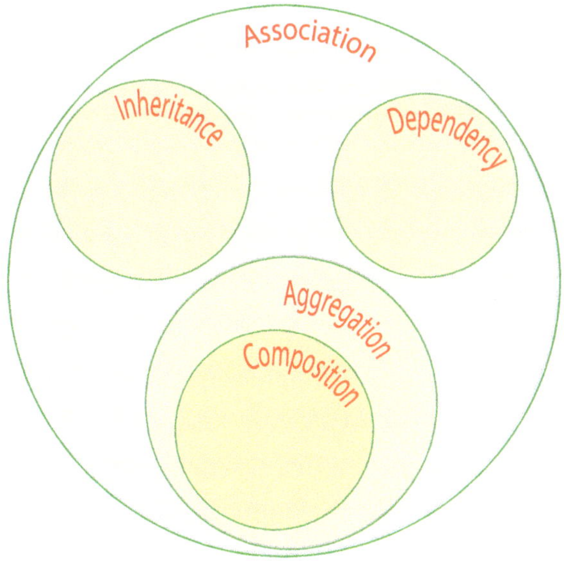

Fig. 27.20 Composition, Aggregation, Inheritance, Dependency are all forms of association

Multiplicity

We can assign a **multiplicity** (also known as **arity**) to an association e.g. 1 and * as shown in *Figure 27.17*. Multiplicity specifies the number of objects in one class that relate to a single object of the associated class.

- 1 - one instance (exactly one) of the class, i.e. one object
- 0..1 - zero or one instances of the class, i.e. zero or one objects
- 0..* - zero or more instances of the class, i.e. zero or more objects
- 1..* - one or more instances of the class, i.e. one or more objects
- * - many instances of the class, i.e. many objects
- 0,3 - zero or three instances of the class, i.e. zero or three objects
- 5..10 - five through ten instances of the class, i.e. 5 or 6 or 7 or 8 or 9 or 10 objects.

When no multiplicity is given, it is assumed to be 1.

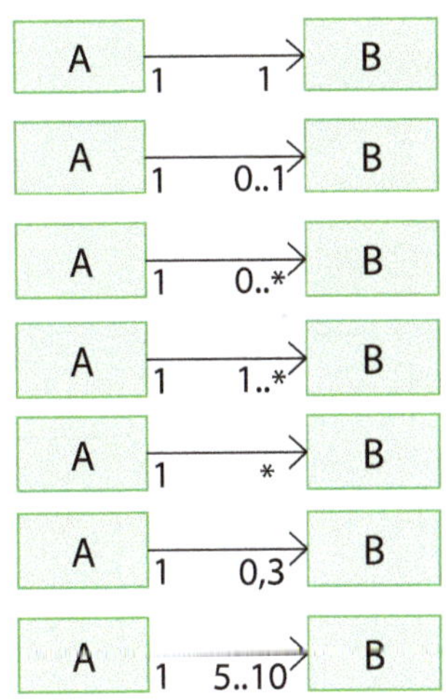

Fig. 27.21 Multiplicity

Navigability

Figure 27.17 expresses that `Teacher` must "know about" `Student`, but does `Student` need to know about `Teacher`?

This is known as **navigability**, i.e. how we can move from one object to another.

Navigability is represented in a class diagram by adding one or two arrows to the line representing an association or by using two single arrow lines as shown in *Figure 27.22*.

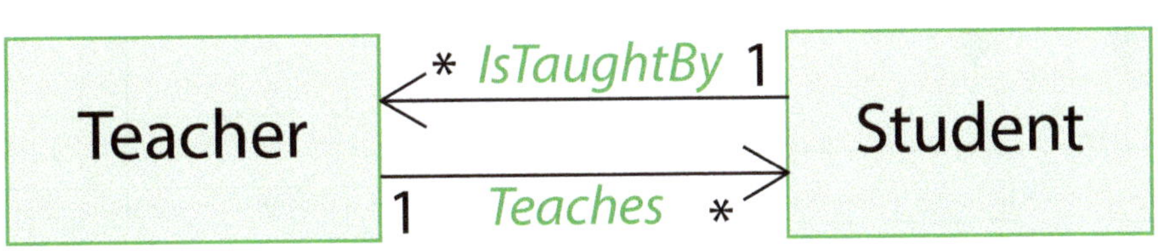

Fig. 27.22 Class diagram demonstrating two way association

To emphasise one-way navigation for composition or aggregation an arrow head can be added as shown in *Figure 27.23*.

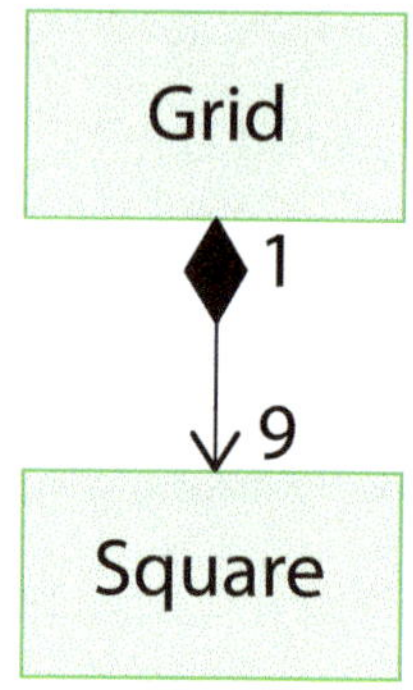

Fig. 27.23 Class diagram showing one way navigation

Object diagrams

Purpose: To learn how to create object diagrams

Figure 27.24 shows an object diagram for three objects, `Person1`, `Dog1` and `Bird1` that have been created from the classes, `Person`, `Animal`, `Dog` and `Bird` shown in the class diagram *Figure 27.25*.

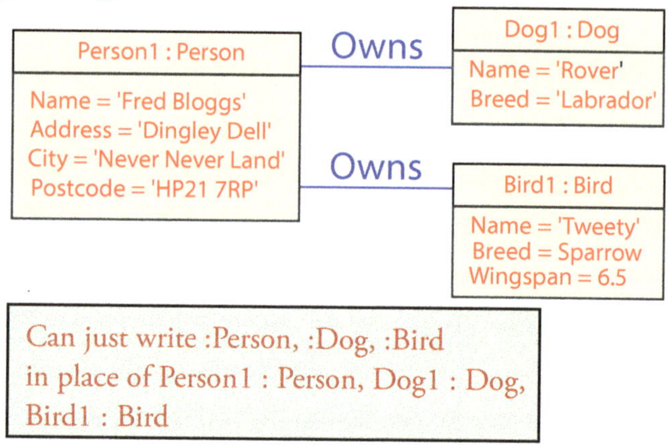

Fig. 27.24 Object diagram showing three objects, Person1, Dog1 and Bird1

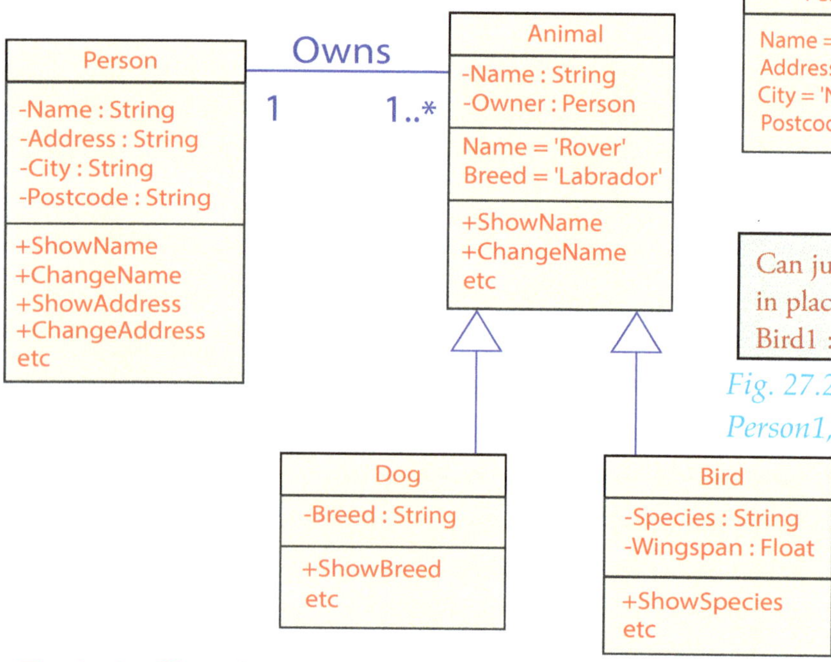

Fig. 27.25 Class diagram showing four classes, Person, Animal, Dog and Bird

Windows form application

Figure 27.26 shows class and object diagrams for a windows form application with one button and three edit boxes.

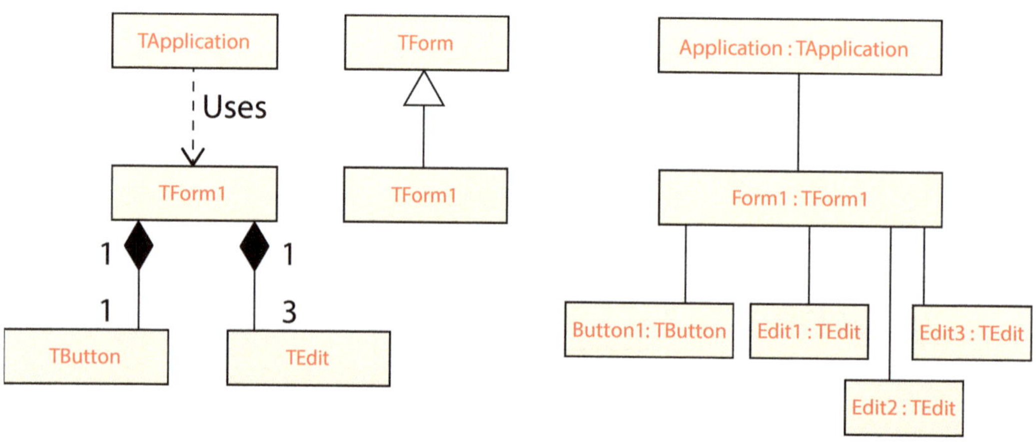

Fig. 27.26 Class and object diagrams for a windows form application consisting of five objects

Interface class diagram

Figure 27.27 shows an interface diagram for the diet exrcise of *Chapter 26*.

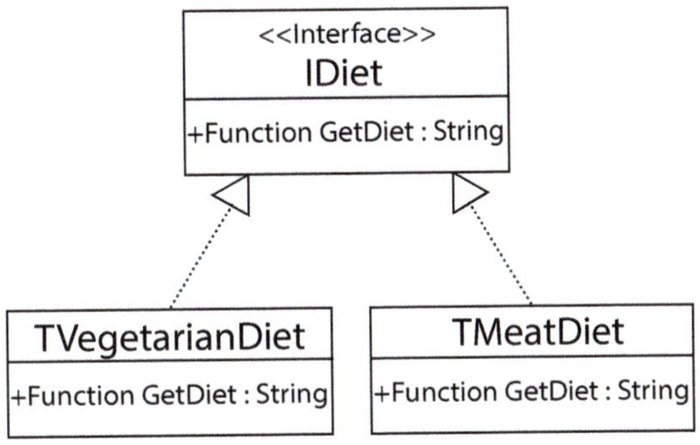

Fig. 27.27 Interface diagram for IDiet interface

28 Creating an onscreen form in console mode

Creating an onscreen form in console mode

Purpose: Creating an onscreen form

You have seen already how you may define your own data types using the `Type` keyword. In this lesson we are going to use the `Type` keyword to create a class definition. Class definitions are at the heart of Object-Oriented Programming or OOP.

The class we are going to create is a new `Form` class but we are going to base it on an existing form class supplied with Delphi called `TForm`.

When we do this we are using a mechanism called inheritance.

We can express the relationship betwen `TForm1` and `TForm` in an inheritance diagram as shown in *Fig. 28.1*.

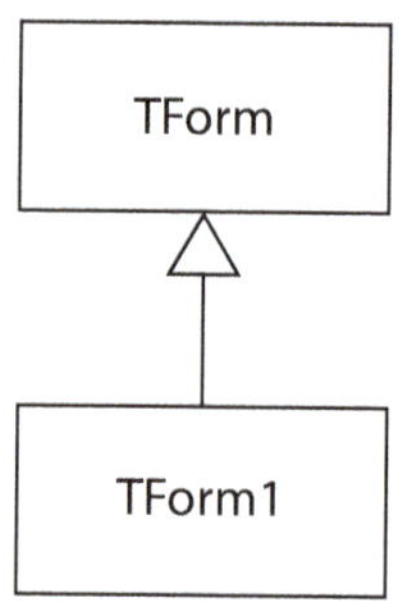

Fig. 28.1 Inheritance diagram

The class definition for this relationship is written as follows:

```
Type
  TForm1 = Class(TForm)

         End;
```

Start a new console project and save as **MyFormProject.dproj or MyFormProject.dpr** depending on the version of Delphi being used.

Add the following `Uses` clause to the program

```
Uses
  Vcl.Forms;
```

Vcl.forms is a unit provided in Delphi.

Create a variable, `Form1`, which will be used to reference the form object after it is created.

The variable declaration is written as follows:

```
Var
  Form1 : TForm1;
```

Table 28.1 shows the program source code.

```
Program MyFormProject;
{$APPTYPE CONSOLE}
Uses
  Vcl.Forms;
{$R *.dfm}
Type
  TForm1 = Class(TForm)
           End;
Var
  Form1 : TForm1;
Begin
  Writeln('Hello World');
  Application.Initialize;
  Application.CreateForm(TForm1, Form1);
  Application.Run;
  Readln;
End.
```

Table 28.1 Program MyFormProject

We are still programming in console mode so we need to create one more file, the form object file **MyFormProject.dfm** as shown in *Table 28.2*, using a text editor, e.g. WordPad.

This file will be read at compile time if we add the compiler directive `{$R *.dfm}` to the source code program shown in *Table 28.1*. This is the line of code that tells Delphi to link in the form's visual part.

```
Object
  Form1: TForm1
  Left = 192
  Top = 114
  Width = 696
  Height = 480
  Caption = 'Form1'
  Color = clBtnFace
  Font.Charset = DEFAULT_CHARSET
  Font.Color = clWindowText
  Font.Height = -11
  Font.Name = 'MS Sans Serif'
  Font.Style = []
  OldCreateOrder = False
  PixelsPerInch = 96
  TextHeight = 13
End
```

Table 28.2 MyFormProject.dfm

The created form window needs to handle user generated events such as mouse click and mouse drag operations.

Delphi does this by providing an `Application` object.

It is this `Application` object that creates the form, `Form1`, by calling method `CreateForm` (calling means executing).

Very importantly, the next method, `Run`, sets up the event handling.

The executing program gets stuck intentionally in a loop within `Application.Run`.

This is how the form stays open until the user clicks on the close icon at the top right of the form.

A console window is also created because we still have the compiler directive `{$APPTYPE Console}`. If this is removed only the form window, `Form1`, appears when the program is executed.

Compile and run the program shown in *Table 28.1*. Note that you will need to copy **MyFormProject.dfm** to the folder in which this program is stored if it isn't already.

The form, `Form1`, shown in *Fig. 28.2* is displayed (bigger in size than this example) with the Console window behind:

```
Program MyFormProject;
{$APPTYPE CONSOLE}

Uses
  Vcl.Forms;
{$R *.dfm}
Type
  TForm1 = Class(TForm)
           End;
Var
  Form1 : TForm1;
Begin
  Writeln('Hello World');
  Application.Initialize;
  Application.CreateForm(TForm1, Form1);
  Application.Run;
  Readln;
End.
```

Table 28.1 Program MyFormProject repeated

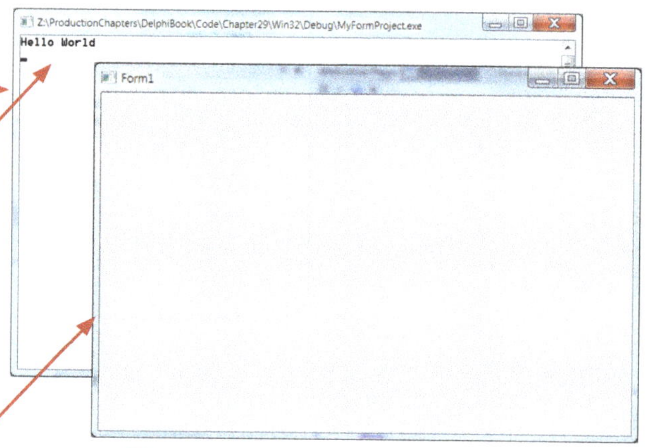

Fig. 28.2 Form produced when MyFormProject.exe is executed

The exact position of the form on the screen is determined by the settings for `Left` and `Top` in **MyFormProject.dfm**.

The exact size of the form is determined by the settings `Width` and `Height` in **MyFormProject.dfm**.

The caption `Form1` is determined by the setting for `Caption` in **MyFormProject.dfm**.

Insert the load resource compiler directive `{$R *.res}` just below the load form directive to place a default bitmap image at the top left of the form and to iconize the executable version of the program (default bitmap supplied by Delphi). Compile and run the altered program.

Purpose: Creating an onscreen form with components and event handlers

Use *Save Project As* to save **MyFormProject.dpr** or **MyFormProject.dproj** into a folder **MyFormProjectWithComponentsandEventHandlers**.

Add the following to the `Form1` object in **MyFormProject.dfm** so that its contents are as shown in *Table 28.3*.

```
Object
  Button1: TButton
  Left = 20
  Top = 20
  Width = 75
  Height = 25
  Caption = 'Button1'
  TabOrder = 0
  OnClick = Button1Click
End
```

Save **MyFormProject.dfm** in folder **MyFormProjectWithComponentsandEventHandlers**.

The class diagram in *Fig. 28.3* shows that composition relationship exists between `TForm1` and `TButton`, a `TForm1` form has a `TButton` button. This is reflected in the object diagram in *Fig. 28.4*.

```
Object
  Form1: TForm1
  Left = 192
  Top = 114
  Width = 696
  Height = 480
  Caption = 'Form1'
  Color = clBtnFace
  Font.Charset = DEFAULT_CHARSET
  Font.Color = clWindowText
  Font.Height = -11
  Font.Name = 'MS Sans Serif'
  Font.Style = []
  OldCreateOrder = False
  PixelsPerInch = 96
  TextHeight = 13
  Object
    Button1: TButton
    Left = 20
    Top = 20
    Width = 75
    Height = 25
    Caption = 'Button1'
    TabOrder = 0
    OnClick = Button1Click
  End
End
```

Table 28.3 MyFormProject.dfm

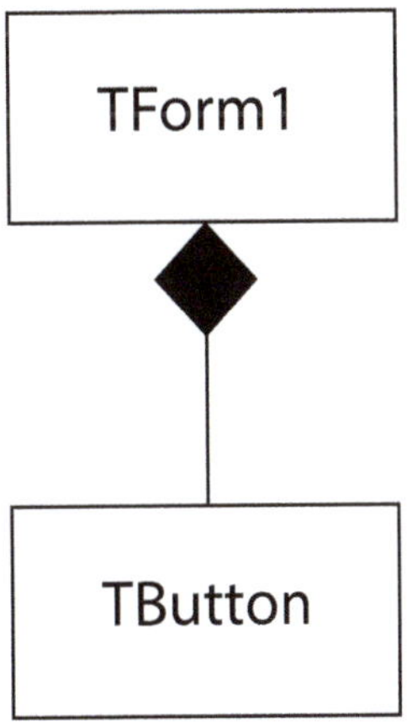

Fig. 28.3 Class diagram showing composition relationship between TForm1 and TButton

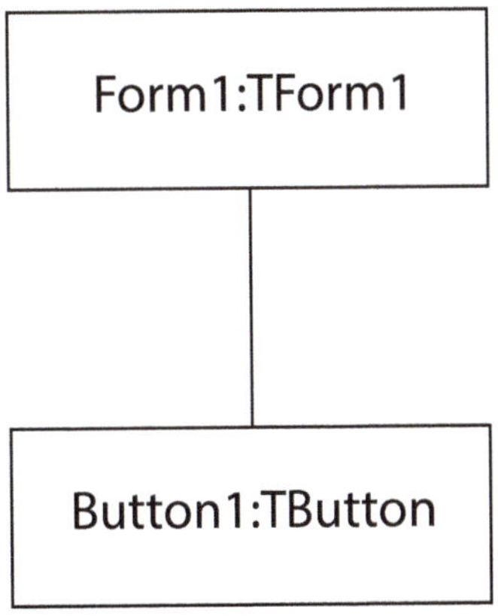

Fig. 28.4 Object diagram showing relationship between Form1 and Button1 diagram

`Button1Click` is a method that belongs to the `TForm1` class type definition. `OnClick` is a property of the `Button1` object. This means that when this object is clicked with the mouse (mouse pointer over this object and left mouse button pressed) the method `Button1Click` is executed.

Modify **MyFormProject.dpr** as shown in *Table 28.4*. The Delphi compiled units **Vcl.StdCtrls.dcu** and **Vcl.Dialogs.dcu** are needed because **StdCtrls.dcu** contains the code for the class `TButton` and Delphi compiled unit **Dialogs.dcu** contains the code for `ShowMessage`. `{$APPTYPE CONSOLE}` has been removed because we have no further need for a console window.

References Vcl.Forms.dcu

References Vcl.StdCtrls.dcu

References Vcl.Dialogs.dcu

```
Program MyFormProject;
Uses
  Vcl.Forms, Vcl.StdCtrls, Vcl.Dialogs;

{$R *.dfm}
{$R *.res}
Type
  TForm1 = Class(TForm)
             Button1 : TButton;
             Procedure Button1Click(Sender : TObject);
           End;
Procedure TForm1.Button1Click(Sender : TObject);
  Begin
    ShowMessage('Hello World');
  End;
Var
  Form1 : TForm1;
Begin
  Application.Initialize;
  Application.CreateForm(TForm1, Form1);
  Application.Run;
End.
```

Table 28.4 MyFormProject.dfm

Compile and run this program.

The output should be as shown in *Fig. 28.5* (the form may be larger):

The button object, `Button1`, has an event handler, `Button1Click`, associated with it so that when this button is clicked (mouse pointer over button and left button clicked) a message window appears showing the message `'Hello World'` as shown in *Fig.28.6*.

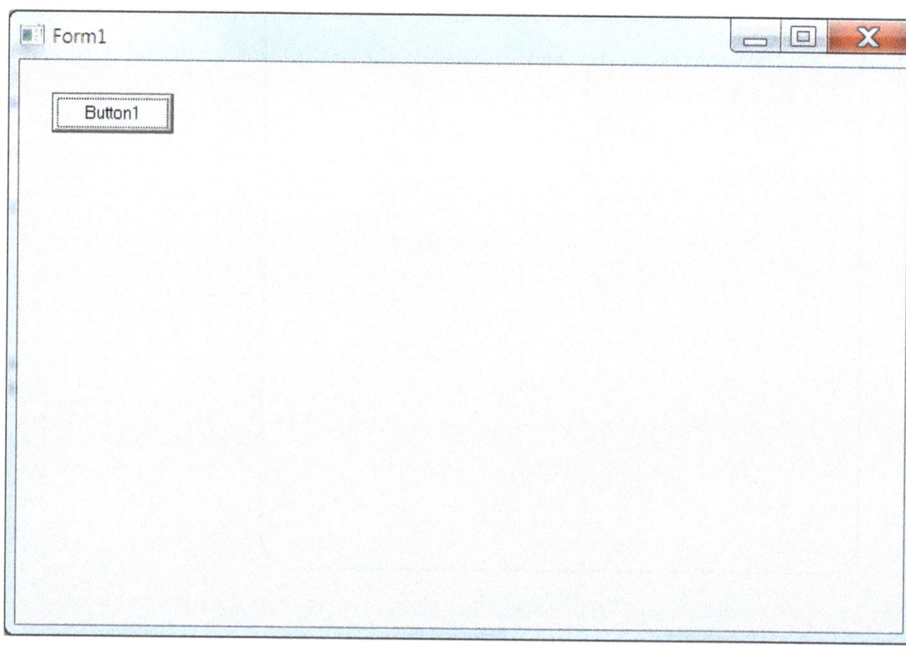

Fig. 28.5 Form produced when MyFormProject.exe is executed

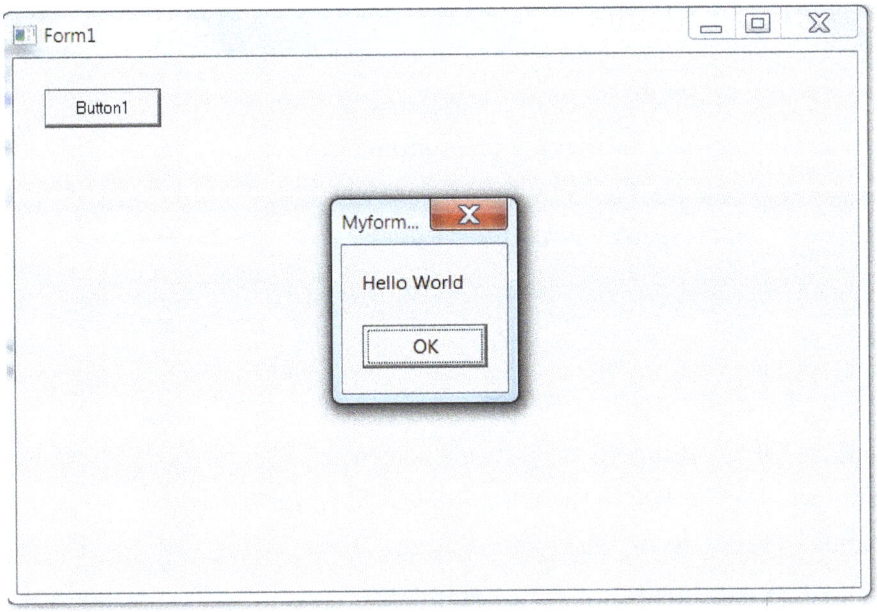

Fig. 28.6 Message dialog window displayed when Button1 clicked with mouse left button

There is a much easier way of working with standard controls on a form such as `Button1`. We will explore this in the next chapter.

Programming Tasks

1. Add a second `TButton` control, `Button2`, to **MyFormProject.dpr** by extending **MyFormProject.dfm** with the corresponding object definition. Set the `Left` and `Right` settings for `Button2` so that it displays this button vertically aligned with `Button1` but below it. Set its `Caption` to `'Button2'`. The `Button2` object should use `Button1Click` for its `OnClick` event. Modify **MyFormProject.dpr** so that `TForm1` includes `Button2`. Save both **MyFormProject.dpr** and **MyFormProject.dfm** in a folder **Ch28Question1**.

   Compile and run your program to check that your program meets the specification.

2. Modify your program so that `Button2` uses an event handler `Button2Click` with body `ShowMessage('Goodbye World').`
   Save both **MyFormProject.dpr** and **MyFormProject.dfm** in a folder **Ch28Question2**.

   Compile and run your program to check that your program meets the specification.

Purpose: Creating controls at run time

Start a new application in Delphi, **File/New/VCL FormsApplication**. This produces a **dpr/dprog** file and a **unit1.pas** file that the programmer can edit through the IDE. It also creates a **dfm** file behind the scenes which corresponds to the form, **Form1** that is visible in the IDE.

Save the project with the name **CreatingControlsAtRunTimeProject** in a folder with the same name.

Save **Unit1.pas** as **CreatingControlsAtRunTimeUnit.pas**.

Click on the **Events** tab of the Object Inspector (**F11** always brings up the Object Inspector) and then **double click** in the **OnActivate** field white box to create an event handler **FormActivate**. The screen shot in *Figure 28.7* shows the result.

The code window should show that the event-handling procedure, **TForm1.FormActivate(Sender: TObject)** has been created automatically as shown in *Figure 28.8*:

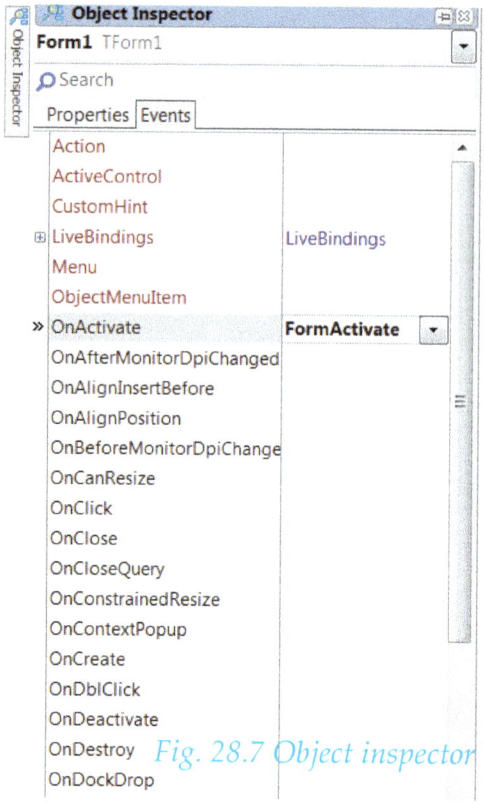

Fig. 28.7 Object inspector

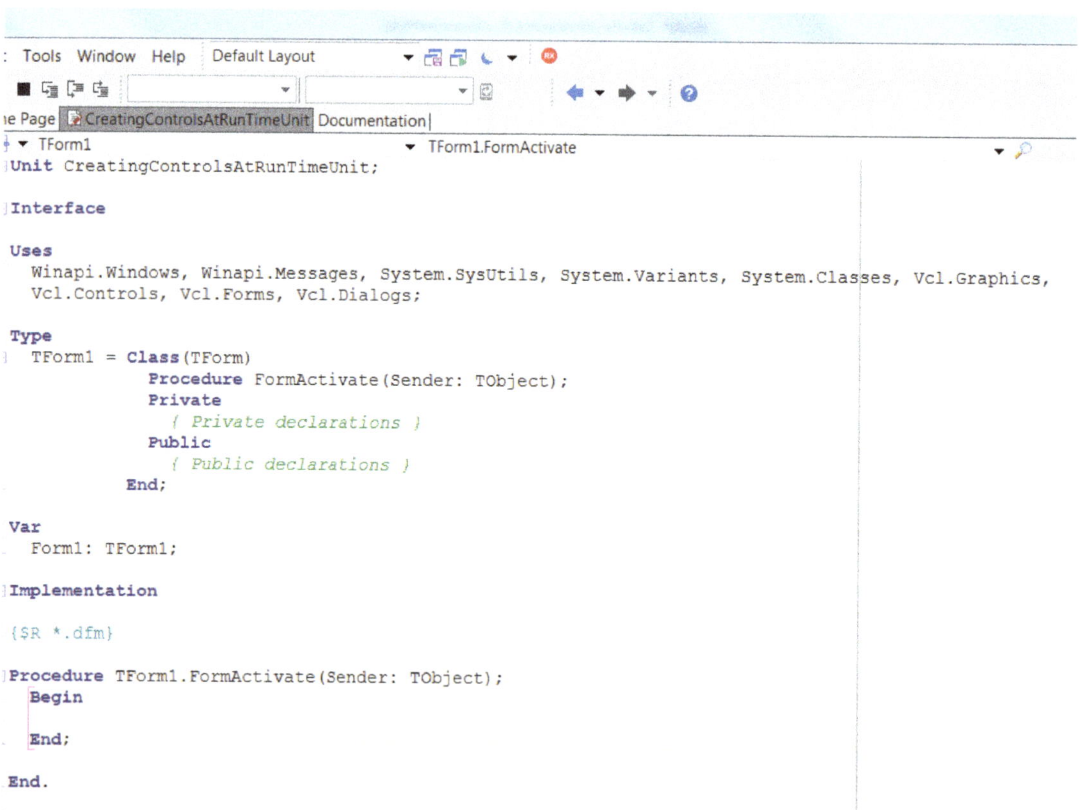

Fig. 28.8 Unit CreatingControlsAtRunTimeUnit.pas showing the event handler TForm1.FormActivate

Now add to

- the **Uses** statement, `Vcl.StdCtrls,`
- the **Implementation** section

```
Var
  MyButton : TButton
```

- the body of **FormActivate** procedure (the body lies between `Begin` and `End;`):

```
MyButton := TButton.Create(Form1);
MyButton.Parent := Form1;
MyButton.Left := 50;
MyButton.Top := 50;
MyButton.Width := 60;
MyButton.Height := 60;
MyButton.Caption := 'Press Me';
```

CreatingControlsAtRunTimeUnit should look as shown in *Figure 28.9*:

The crucial parts are

```
MyButton := TButton.Create(Form1);
MyButton.Parent := Form1;
```

The first statement creates the button object and assigns ownership to the **Form1** object. Owners are responsible for destroying each object that they own when the time comes to do this, e.g. when the form is closed.

The second statement is the most important because it is this statement that makes the control visible. Setting the parent to be **Form1** causes the control to appear on **Form1**.

The other properties of this button object are set by using the reference **MyButton** as follows:

```
MyButton.Left := 50;
MyButton.Top := 50;
MyButton.Width := 80;
MyButton.Height := 60;
MyButton.Caption := 'Press Me';
```

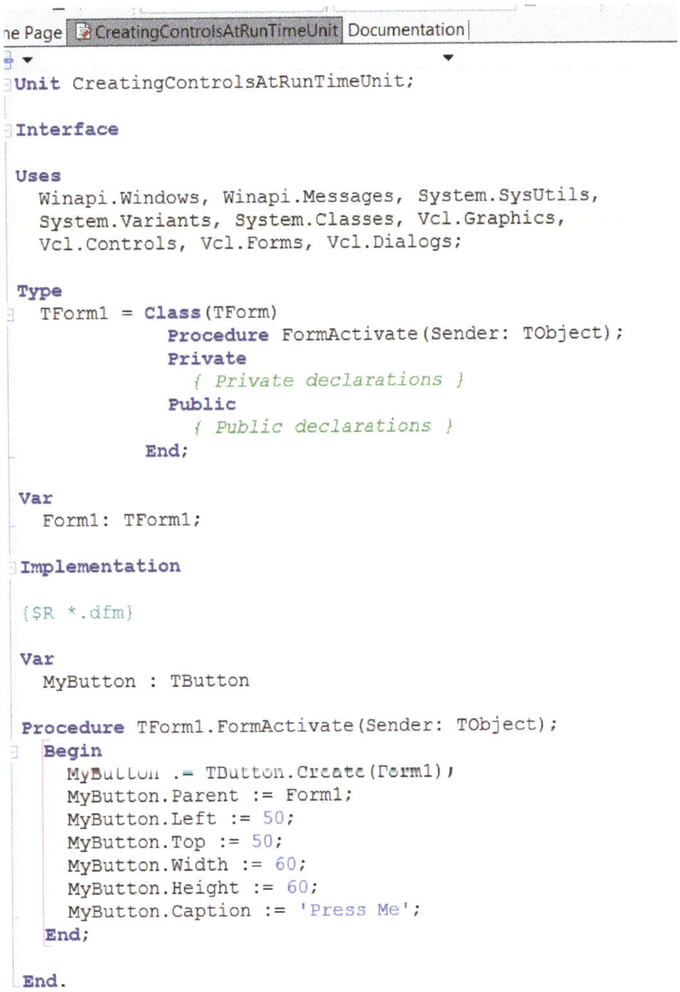

Fig. 28.9 Unit CreatingControlsAtRunTimeUnit.pas showing the event handler TForm1.FormActivate and its code

We are now going to associate an event handler with this control.

Add a procedure **Test(Sender : TObject)** to the class **TForm1** as follows:

```
TForm1 = Class(TForm)
      Procedure FormActivate(Sender: TObject);
      Procedure Test(Sender : TObject);
      Private
        { Private declarations }
      Public
        { Public declarations }
    End;
```

Add to the **Implementation** section the following procedure definition, place it after procedure **TForm1.FormActivate**.

```
Procedure TForm1.Test(Sender : TObject);
  Begin
    ShowMessage(Sender.ClassName);
    ShowMessage(TButton(Sender).Parent.Name);
  End;
```

Note that this procedure shows the **sender's class name** and the name of its **parent**.

The sender is the control that was clicked.

Add `MyButton.OnClick := Test;` to the procedure `TForm1.FormActivate(Sender : TObject);`.

Place it just after `MyButton.Caption := 'Press Me';`.

Compile and run **CreatingControlsAtRunTimeProject**. The form shown in *Figure 28.10* should display.

Click the **Press Me** button.

The message box window shown in *Figure 28.11* should pop up:

This shows that the control clicked is indeed a **TButton** object.

Click OK.

The message box window shown in *Figure 28.12* should pop up next:

This shows that the parent is indeed **Form1**.

Fig. 28.10 Result of executing program CreatingControlsAtRunTimeProject

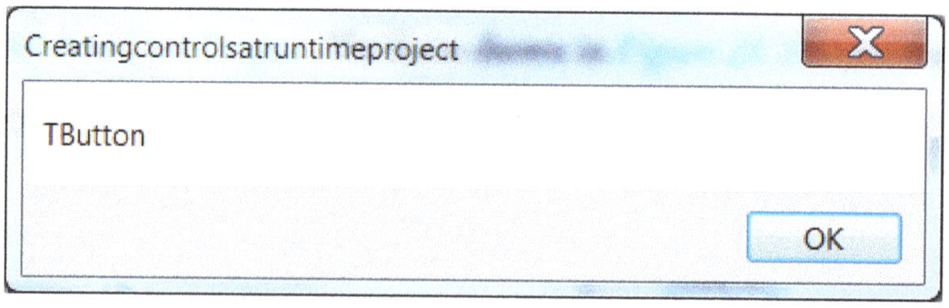

Fig. 28.11 ShowMessage(Sender.ClassName)

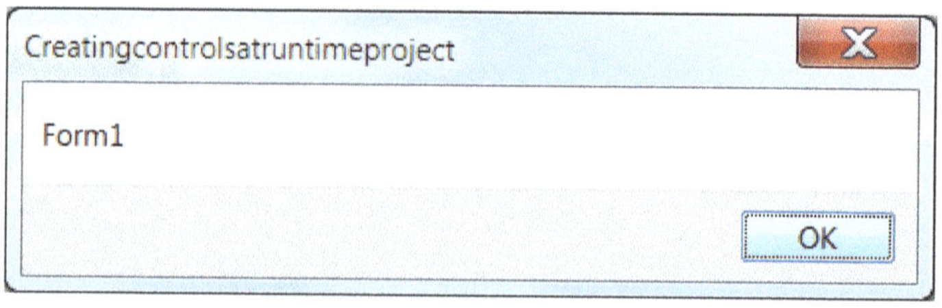

Fig. 28.12 ShowMessage(TButton(Sender).Parent.Name)

Purpose: Creating an event handler at runtime

Create a new VCL Forms application in Delphi. Save the project as CreatingAnEventHandlerAtRunTimeProject and its Unit1 as CreatingAnEventHandlerAtRunTimeUnit.pas. Add Vcl.StdCtrls to the Uses statement and add the code shown in Table 28.5. Create CreatingAnEventHandlerAtRunTimeProject.dfm as shown in Table 28.6 by copying Table 28.2 from previous project and save in the project's folder. Save all then build and run this program.

```
Unit CreatingAnEventHandlerAtRunTimeUnit;
Interface
Uses
  Winapi.Windows, Winapi.Messages, System.SysUtils, System.Variants, System.Classes,
  Vcl.Graphics,  Vcl.Controls, Vcl.Forms, Vcl.Dialogs, Vcl.StdCtrls;
Type
  TForm1 = Class(TForm)
             Button1: TButton;
             Procedure Button1Click(Sender: TObject);
           End;
  TMethod = Record
              Code : Pointer;
              Data : Pointer;
            End;
Var
  Form1: TForm1;
  MethodVar : TMethod;
  x : TButton;
Implementation
{$R *.dfm}
Procedure Test;
  Begin
    ShowMessage('Hello World - Test called');
  End;
Procedure AnotherTest(Sender : TObject);
Var
    ButtonInFocus : String;
  Begin
    If Sender Is TButton
      Then
        Begin
          If TButton(Sender).Focused
            Then ButtonInFocus := ' the focus '
            Else ButtonInFocus := ' not the focus ';
          ShowMessage(TButton(Sender).Name + ButtonInFocus + '-Procedure AnotherTest called ');
        End;
  End;
Procedure TForm1.FormActivate(Sender: TObject);
  Begin
    Form1.Width := 200;
    Form1.Height := 200;
    x := TButton.Create(Form1);   //Create a button
    x.Parent := Form1;    //Place on form
    x.Left := 35;
    x.Width := 80;
    x.Top := 40;
    x.Height := 45;
    x.Name := 'Button1'; //Set button's name
    x.Caption := 'Press me';
    MethodVar.Data := x; //Set the specific control, i.e. a button at specified position on Form1
    MethodVar.Code := Addr(Test);  //Assign address of event handler procedure to code field
    x.OnClick := TNotifyEvent(MethodVar); //Set the event handler for the specified event
    //Set up a new event handler for a different event - key press when button in focus
    MethodVar.Code := Addr(AnotherTest);  //Assign address of event handler to Code field
    x.OnKeyPress := TKeyPressEvent(MethodVar); //Set the event handler to be called on the specified event
  End;
End.
```

Record structure required to set up a method that can be called when an event occurs. The Data field will contain a pointer to the details of the control associated with this record structure together with data about the control's parent.
The code field will contain a pointer to the procedure that will be called if the control is in focus and an event occurs that as already been assigned to the control. This is what is meant by an event handler.

Checks that the event originates from the button, i.e. the button has the focus which is the case if it has been clicked

Checks that the button is in focus i.e. has been selected

Obtains the TButton's variable name

Table 28.5 CreatingAnEventHandlerAtRuntimeUnit.pas

```
Object Form1: TForm1
  Left = 192
  Top = 114
  Width = 696
  Height = 480
  Caption = 'Form1'
  Color = clBtnFace
  Font.Charset = DEFAULT_CHARSET
  Font.Color = clWindowText
  Font.Height = -11
  Font.Name = 'MS Sans Serif'
  Font.Style = []
  OldCreateOrder = False
  PixelsPerInch = 96
  TextHeight = 13
End
```

Table 28.6 CreatingAnEventHandlerAtRunTimeProject.dfm

Running the program results in the form shown in *Figure 28.13*.

Fig. 28.13 Result of executing CreatingEventHandlerAtRunTimeProject

A button labelled '**Press me**' has been created at runtime.

There are two event handlers associated with this button.

One is associated with the event '**OnClick**' and the other with the event '**OnKeyPress**'.

If any key is pressed on the keyboard when the button does not currently have focus nothing happens.

First the button must be selected by clicking on it. It then changes in appearance as shown in *Figure 28.14* for Delphi Community edition 10.2.3, and because there is an event handler associated with the **OnClick** event, the event handler `Test` is called. This results in a dialogue window labelled **Creatinganeventhandleratruntimeproject** shown in *Figure 28.14* appearing on the screen.

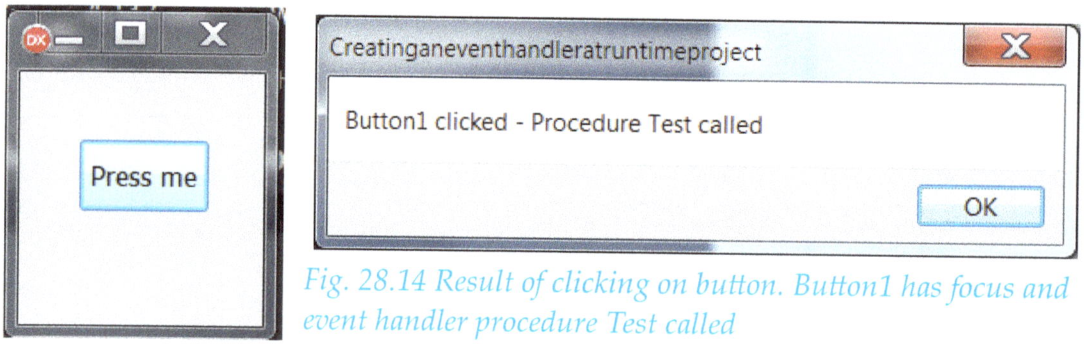

Fig. 28.14 Result of clicking on button. Button1 has focus and event handler procedure Test called

Clicking on **OK** closes the window whilst leaving the button selected. If any key on the keyboard is now pressed, e.g. the key 'R', the **OnKeyPressed** event is triggered, the event handler **AnotherTest** is called and the dialogue window labelled **Creatinganeventhandleratruntimeproject** shown in *Figure 28.15* appears on the screen.

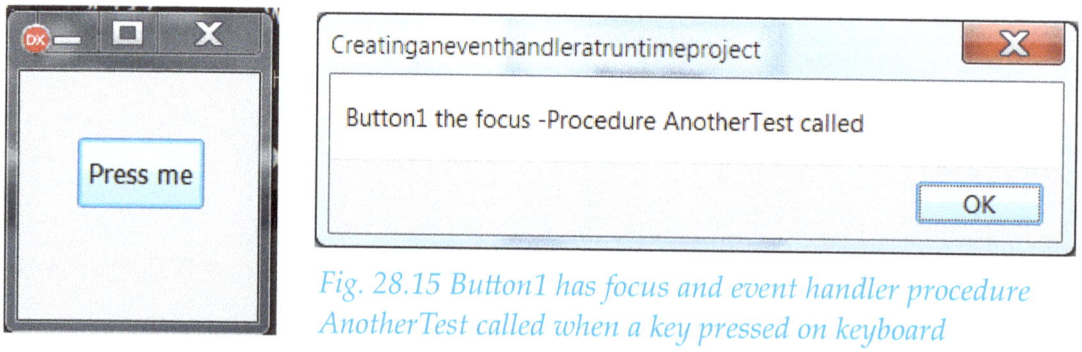

Fig. 28.15 Button1 has focus and event handler procedure AnotherTest called when a key pressed on keyboard

The two **Creatinganeventhandleratruntimeproject** dialogue windows are modal dialogues. A modal dialogue is a window that forces the user to interact with it before they can go back to using the parent application.

Purpose: Creating form, button and event handlers from console mode

Create a new **Console application** in Delphi. Save the project as **ConsoleCreatingAnEventHandlersAtRunTimeProject**. Add the code shown in *Table 28.7*. Create **ConsoleCreatingAnEventHandlersAtRunTimeProject.dfm** as shown in *Table 28.6* and save in the project's folder. Save all then build and run this program.

```
Program ConsoleCreatingEventHandlersAtRunTimeProject;
{$APPTYPE CONSOLE}
{$R *.res}
{$R *.dfm}
Uses
  System.Classes, Vcl.Controls, Vcl.StdCtrls, Vcl.Forms, Vcl.Dialogs;
Type
  TForm1 = Class(TForm)
             Private
               { Private declarations }
             Public
               { Public declarations }
           End;
  TMethod = Record
              Code : Pointer;
              Data : Pointer;
            End;
Var
  Form1: TForm1;
  MethodVar : TMethod;
  x : TButton;
Procedure Test;
  Begin
    Writeln('Inside Procedure Test');
    ShowMessage('Button1 clicked - Procedure Test called');
  End;
Procedure AnotherTest(Sender : TObject);
  Var
    ButtonInFocus : String;
  Begin
    If Sender Is TButton
      Then
        Begin
          If TButton(Sender).Focused
            Then ButtonInFocus := ' the focus '
            Else ButtonInFocus := ' not the focus ';
          Writeln('Inside Procedure AnotherTest');
          ShowMessage(TButton(Sender).Name + ButtonInFocus + '-Procedure AnotherTest called');
        End;
  End;
Procedure StartUp;
  Begin
    Form1.Width := 300;
    Form1.Height := 200;
    Form1.Left := 450;
    Form1.Top := 350;
    x := TButton.Create(Form1);   //Create a button
    x.Parent := Form1;    //Place on form
    x.Left := 95;
    x.Width := 80;
    x.Top := 50;
    x.Height := 45;
    x.Name := 'Button1'; //Set button's name
    x.Caption := 'Press me';
    MethodVar.Data := x;  //Set the specific control, i.e. a button at specified position on Form1
    MethodVar.Code := Addr(Test);  //Assign the method to be called
    x.OnClick := TNotifyEvent(MethodVar); //Set the method to be called on the specified event
    //Change the method to be called
    MethodVar.Code := Addr(AnotherTest);  //Assign the method to be called
    x.OnKeyPress := TKeyPressEvent(MethodVar); //Set the method to be called on the specified event
  End;
Begin
  Application.Initialize;
  Writeln('Immediately before Application.CreateForm');
  Application.CreateForm(TForm1, Form1);
  StartUp;
  Application.Run;
  Writeln('Reached past Application.Run');
End.
```

Annotations:
- Directive creates a console window ({$APPTYPE CONSOLE})
- Using Writeln is OK because a console window will be created as well as a Form window
- This procedure creates a button and two event handlers to handle events when button has focus (Procedure StartUp)
- Writes message to console window
- Form Form1 created using definition contained in dfm file associated with this project
- StartUp called to create button and event handlers

Table 28.7 ConsoleCreatingEventHandlersAtRuntimeProject.dpr

The executing program creates a console window and a form window, **Form1** containing a button with caption '**Press me**'. shown in *Figure 28.16*. The message '**Immediately before Application.CreateForm**' is written to the console window.

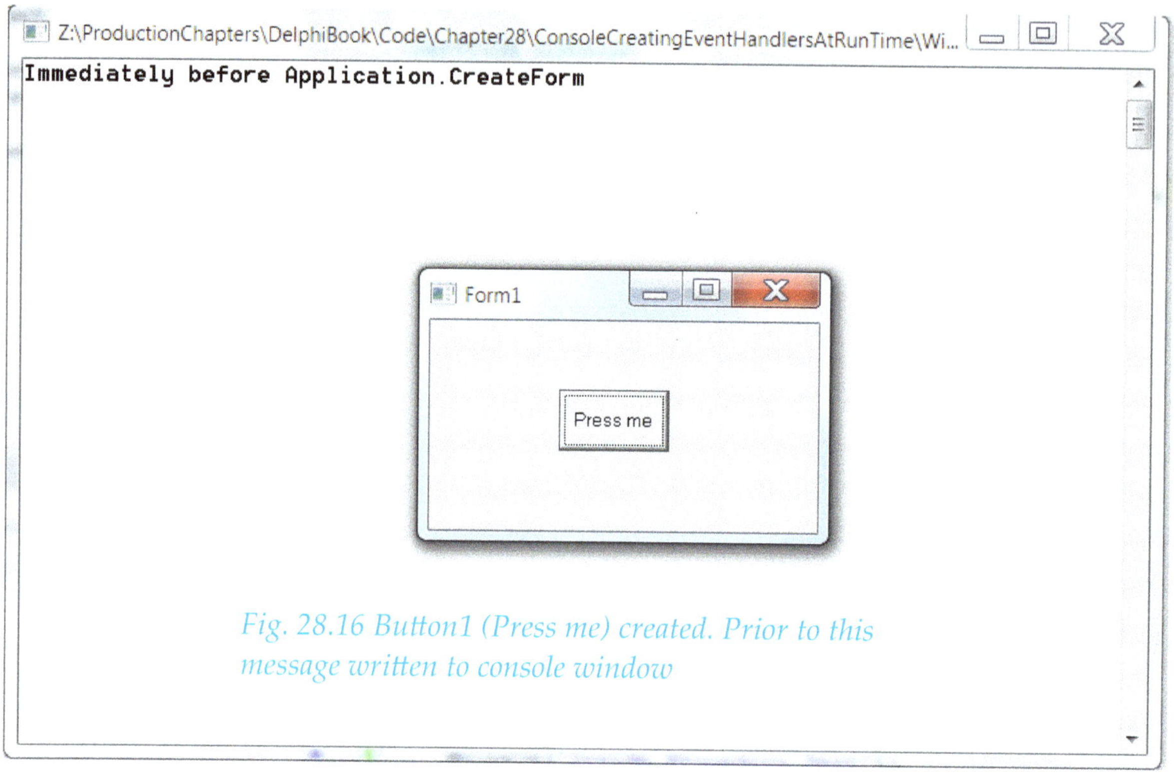

Fig. 28.16 Button1 (Press me) created. Prior to this message written to console window

Next the event handler `Test` is called by clicking on the button. *Figure 28.17* shows the result.

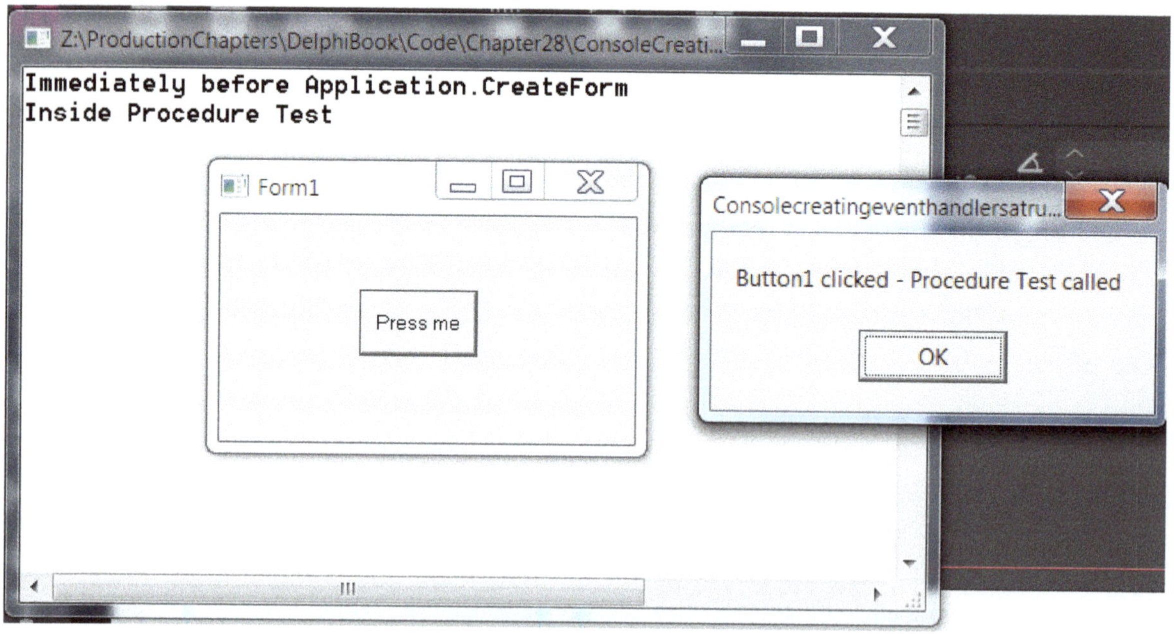

Fig. 28.17 Button1 (Press me) clicked and OnClick event handler called. Message 'Inside Procedure Test' written to console window

Next the dialogue window is closed by clicking on OK and then a key is pressed on the keyboard. The result is shown in *Figure 28.18*.

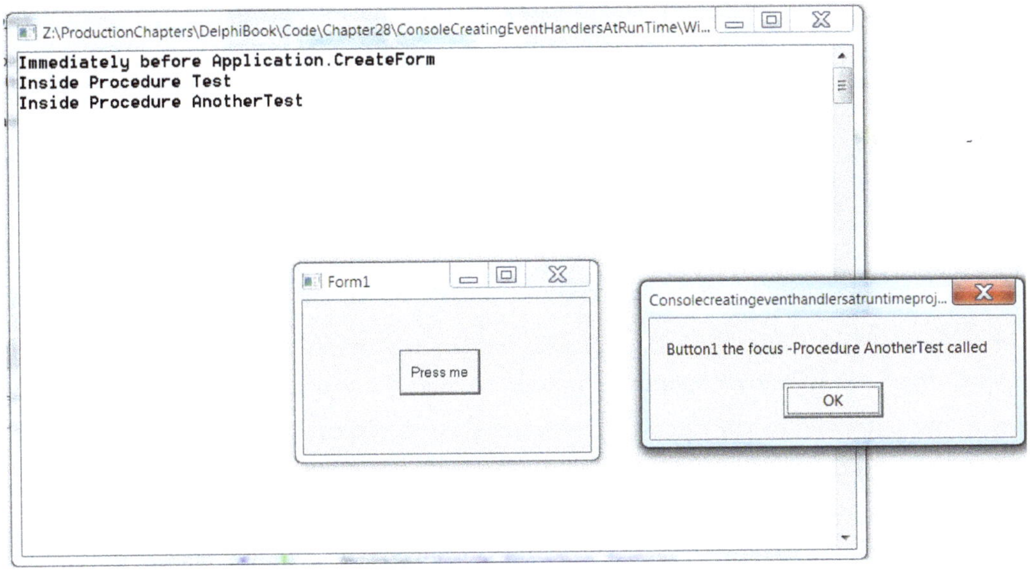

Fig. 28.18 Focus still with Button1 (Press me) and OnKeyPress event handler called. Message 'Inside Procedure AnotherTest' written to console window

The dialog window is closed by clicking on OK. At no stage does the message '**Reached past Application.Run**'. This is because the statement `Writeln('Reached past Application.Run');` is unreachable whilst the application is running.

Event-driven model of program execution

Windows

The Windows operating system manages multiple applications by limiting each application's use of the full screen to one or more rectangles called windows. These windows can be moved, resized, and temporarily hidden as icons, allowing the user to switch between tasks quickly.

An application itself consists of windows. Every control/component belonging to an application, e.g form, button, edit box, etc, that appears on the screen is itself a window.

Events

The Delphi environment is event driven by design, which means that events such as mouse clicks or key presses determine the code to be executed.

Any event that happens under the Windows operating system, such as the movement of the mouse, pressing of a key or resizing of a window is noticed by the operating system. The OS responds by placing a message describing the event in a queue as shown in *Figure 28.19*.

A queue is needed because events can occur in quick succession, e.g. mouse movements or resizing of a window. Message processing code is needed that executes in a loop until all the queued event messages have been processed whereupon the system switches into an idle state to avoid consuming CPU cycles, only returning to message processing when the message queue becomes non-empty again.

The role of the message processing loop is to arrange for the **window procedure** (event handler) corresponding to the event to be called. The window could be, for example, a button object or some other component/control object.

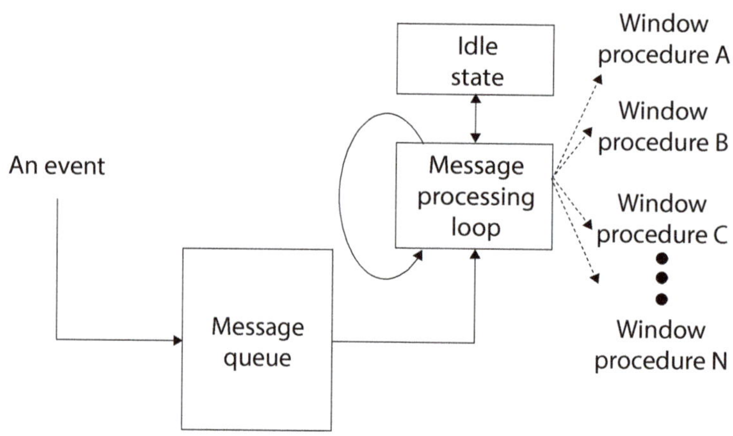

Fig. 28.19 How events are handled and acted upon

An event sets an event property field in Delphi, e.g. **OnClick**. Associated with this event property is a pointer which points to a piece of code called an **event handler**. The event handler is a procedure or object method which is called by the corresponding event property (actually code associated with the event property).

For example, when a user clicks the mouse button in a Win32 system, a WM_MOUSEDOWN message is sent to the Win32 operating system. Win32 passes this message to the control for which the message was intended. This control checks to see if there is any code to execute – it checks the event property to see if a pointer to an event handler procedure exists. If it does the event handler procedure pointed to by the event property is called.

Message loop

The main part of any Windows program/application is the message loop. This is a looping statement that continually checks the Windows message queue, retrieves any messages that are waiting there, then acts on the messages.

For example, in pseudocode the loop could be

```
Repeat
  If a message is waiting
    Then
      Begin
        Retrieve the message
        Act on the message
      End
Until program is terminated
```

Once an application/program has been initialised it spends its entire life in this loop or in an idle state associated with this loop. Other routines are called to process the messages, but execution always returns to this loop.

To view how Delphi supports message loop programming open **Forms.Pas** in an editor.
In Delphi Community edition, **Forms.Pas** is located in **C:\Program Files (x86)\Embarcadero\Studio\19.0\source\vcl**.
The relevant sections of code are shown in *Table 28.8* and *Table 28.9*.

```
procedure TApplication.ProcessMessages;
var
  Msg: TMsg;
begin
  while ProcessMessage(Msg) do {loop};
end;
```

While True keep looping

Table 28.8 Forms.Pas message loop

```
function TApplication.ProcessMessage(var Msg: TMsg): Boolean;
var
  Handled, Unicode, MsgExists : Boolean;
begin
  Result := False;
  if PeekMessage(Msg, 0, 0, 0, PM_NOREMOVE)
    then
      begin
        ......
        if MsgExists
          then
            begin
              Result := True;
              if Msg.Message <> WM_QUIT
                then
                  begin
                    Handled := False;
                    if Assigned(FOnMessage) then FOnMessage(Msg, Handled);
                    if .....
                      then
                        begin
                          TranslateMessage(Msg);
                          if Unicode
                            then DispatchMessageW(Msg)
                            else DispatchMessageA(Msg);
                        end;
                  end
                else
                  begin
                    ......
                  end;
            end;
      end;
end;
```


Call the event handler via a Windows procedure DispatchMessageM or DispatchMessageA

Table 28.9 Forms.Pas message processing and dispatch

WM_Paint message example

At the implementation level messages are converted into procedure/function calls with the message detail passed as parameters. Microsoft's Windows operating system is a collection of objects which communicate via messages. It is possible for Delphi to intercept these messages. In particular, messages destined for actual windows created by a Delphi application can be intercepted and the response to such messages modified. The Microsoft procedure/function called in response to a particular message to a particular window can be overridden. This is shown in the code example in *Table 28.10*.

A Delphi written procedure WMPaint (this is the actual name of the Microsoft written procedure which is being replaced) is called instead.

This procedure beeps the computer's loudspeaker or, if set up, plays a short snippet of music (Wav file). It then passes control to the inherited WMPaint – the procedure supplied by Microsoft in its Windows operating system.

Create a new VCL Forms application in Delphi. Save the project as MessageExampleProject and its Unit1 as MessageExampleUnit.pas in folder MessageExample. Add an edit box and rename EditRePaint. Edit the contents of MessageExampleUnit.pas so that it is as shown in *Table 28.10*. Save all then build and run this program. Enlarging the form window should result in the edit box contents incrementing and a beep through the loudspeaker if working.

```
Unit MessageExampleUnit
Interface
Uses
  Windows, SysUtils, Messages, Classes, StdCtrls, Forms, Controls;
Type
  TForm1 = Class(TForm)
             Procedure WMPaint(Var Msg: TWMPaint); message WM_Paint;
             EditRePaint: TEdit;
           End;
Var
  Form1: TForm1;
  i : Integer = 0;
Implementation
{$R *.dfm}
  Procedure TForm1.WMPaint(Var Msg: TWMPaint);
    Begin
      i := i + 1;
      EditRePaint.Text := IntToStr(i);
      MessageBeep(3); {Could use Beep;}
      Inherited;
    End;
End.
```

Table 28.10 Messaging example using WM_Paint message

Create a new VCL Forms application in Delphi. Save the project as KeyMessageProject and its Unit1 as KeyMessageUnit.pas in folder KeyMessage. Edit the contents of KeyMessageUnit.pas as shown in *Table 28.11*. Make Form1's KeyPreview property True in the Object Inspector. Save all then build and run this program. Pressing any key generates a WM_Char message which causes procedure WMChar to be called which then displays a message dialogue window as shown in *Figure 28.20* with key that was pressed.

```
Unit KeyMessageUnit;
Interface
Uses
  Windows, Messages, SysUtils, Classes, Controls, Forms, Dialogs,StdCtrls;
Type
  TForm1 = Class(TForm)
              Procedure WMChar(Var Msg : TWMChar); message WM_Char;
            End;
Var
  Form1: TForm1;
Implementation
{$R *.DFM}
  Procedure TForm1.WMChar(Var Msg : TWMChar);
    Begin
      If Chr(Msg.CharCode) = #13
        Then ShowMessage('Return Key Pressed')
        Else ShowMessage(Chr(Msg.CharCode));
      End;
End.
```

means character value of number

Table 28.11 Messaging example using WM_Paint message

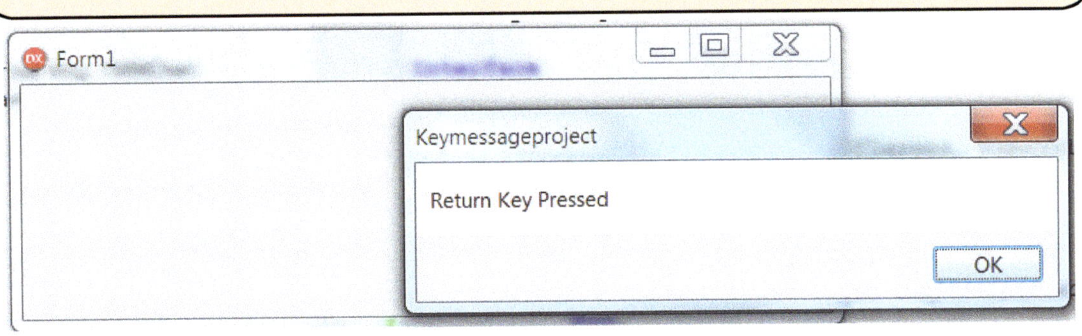

Fig. 28.20 WM_Char message causes procedure WMChar to be called which then displays message dialogue window with key that was pressed

Event property

Create a new **VCL Forms application** in Delphi. Save the project as **EventProject** and its **Unit1** as **EventPropertyUnit.pas** in folder **EventProperty**. Add two buttons, **Button1** and **Button2**, to the form. Select **Button1** and the **Events** tab in the Object Inspector. Select the **OnClick** event property field and double click the mouse. This creates an event handler **Button1Click**. - see *Figure 28.21*.

Select **Button2** and the **Events** tab in the Object Inspector. Click on the button in the **OnClick** event property field, **Button1Click** should appear as shown in *Figure 28. 22*. Select **Button1Click** for the event property of **Button2.** This means **Button1** and **Button2** share the same event handler, **Button1Click**. Add the code shown in *Table 28.12* to the event handler **Button1Click**.

```
Procedure TForm1.Button1Click(Sender: TObject);
  Begin
    If Sender Is TButton
      Then ShowMessage(TButton(Sender).Name);
  End;
```

Table 28.12 Button1Click event handler

Save all then build and run this program.

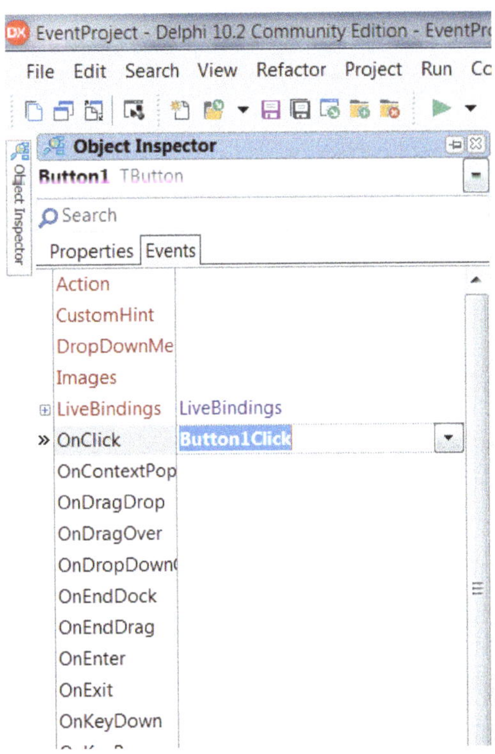

Fig. 28.21 Object inspector showing the Events tab and event handler Button1Click assigned to OnClick event property

Click on **Button1** and then **Button2**.

The resuls are shown in *Figure 28.23* and *Figure 28.24*, respectively.

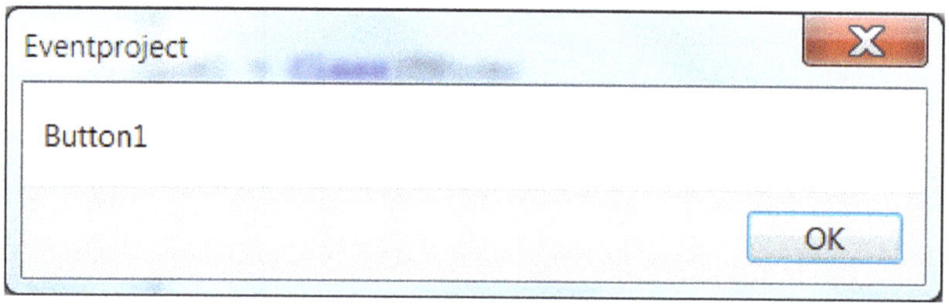

Fig. 28.23 Button1 clicked

Fig. 28.24 Button2 clicked

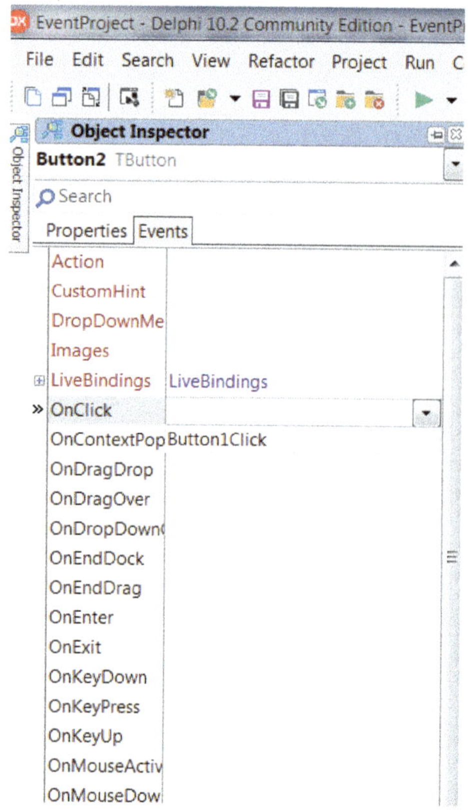

Fig. 28.22 Object inspector showing the Events tab and event handler Button1Click assigned to OnClick event property of Button2

29 Creating Forms

VCL Forms Applications

Purpose: To learn how to create a form window with components and event handlers in the standard way.

FormProject

Start a new application in Delphi, **File/New/Application** or **File/New/VCL Forms Application - Delphi**. This produces a **dpr/dproj** file and a **Unit1** file that the programmer can edit through the IDE.
It also creates a **dfm** file behind the scenes which corresponds to the form, `Form1`, that is visible in the IDE.

Select `Project1.exe` in the **Project Manager** pane to highlight it then press **ALT + m** and replace `Project1` with `FormProject` to rename the project as `FormProject.exe`. Save the project in a folder `FormProject`.

The IDE is shown in *Figure 29.1*:

To show the unit associated with this form use the toggle button in the menu bar at the top of the IDE window as shown labelled in *Figure 29.1* or press **F12**.

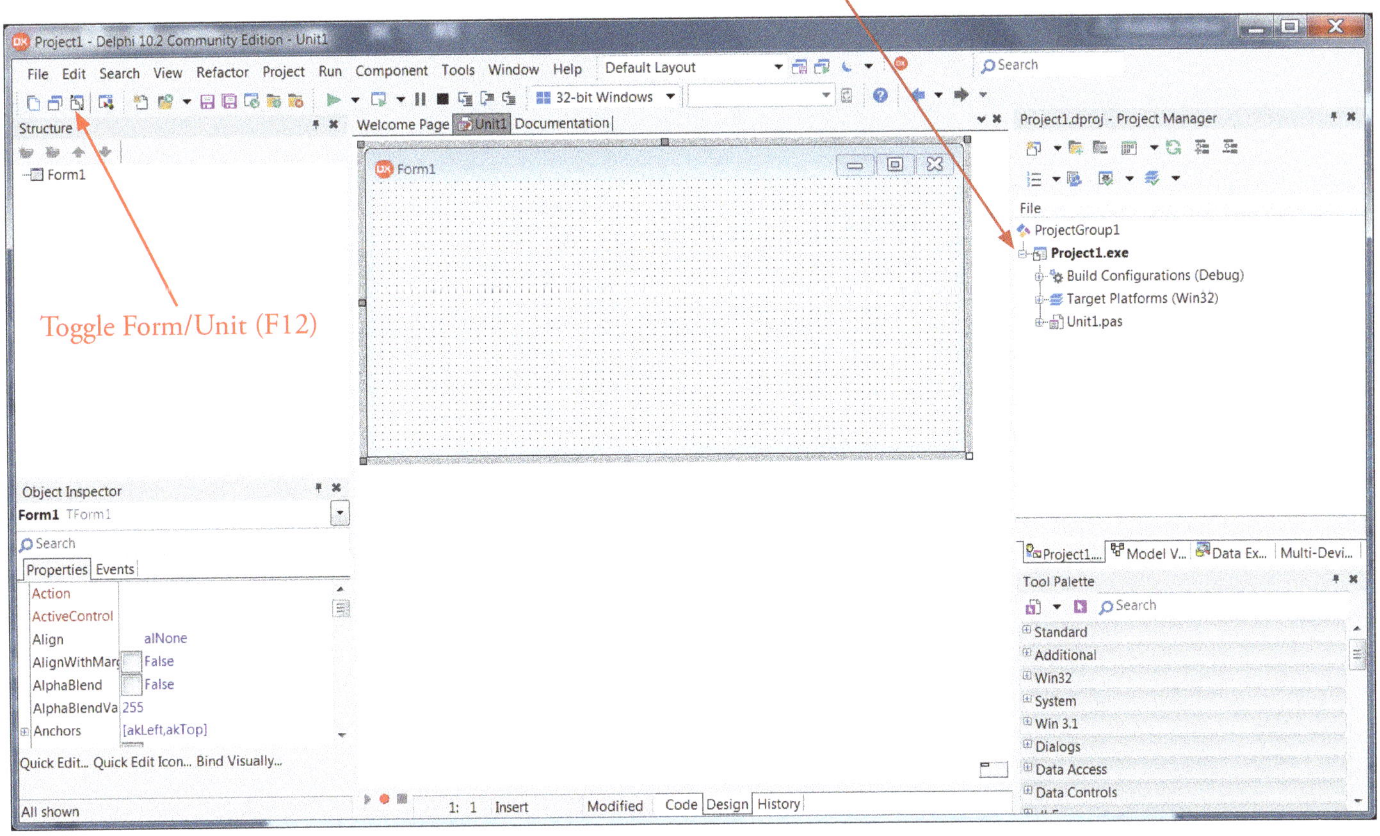

Fig. 29.1 IDE showing Form1 for Project1 before renaming

https://www.educational-computing.com/DelphiBook/Code/Chapter29/FormProject.zip

Fig. 29.2 shows the result of clicking on the toggle button.

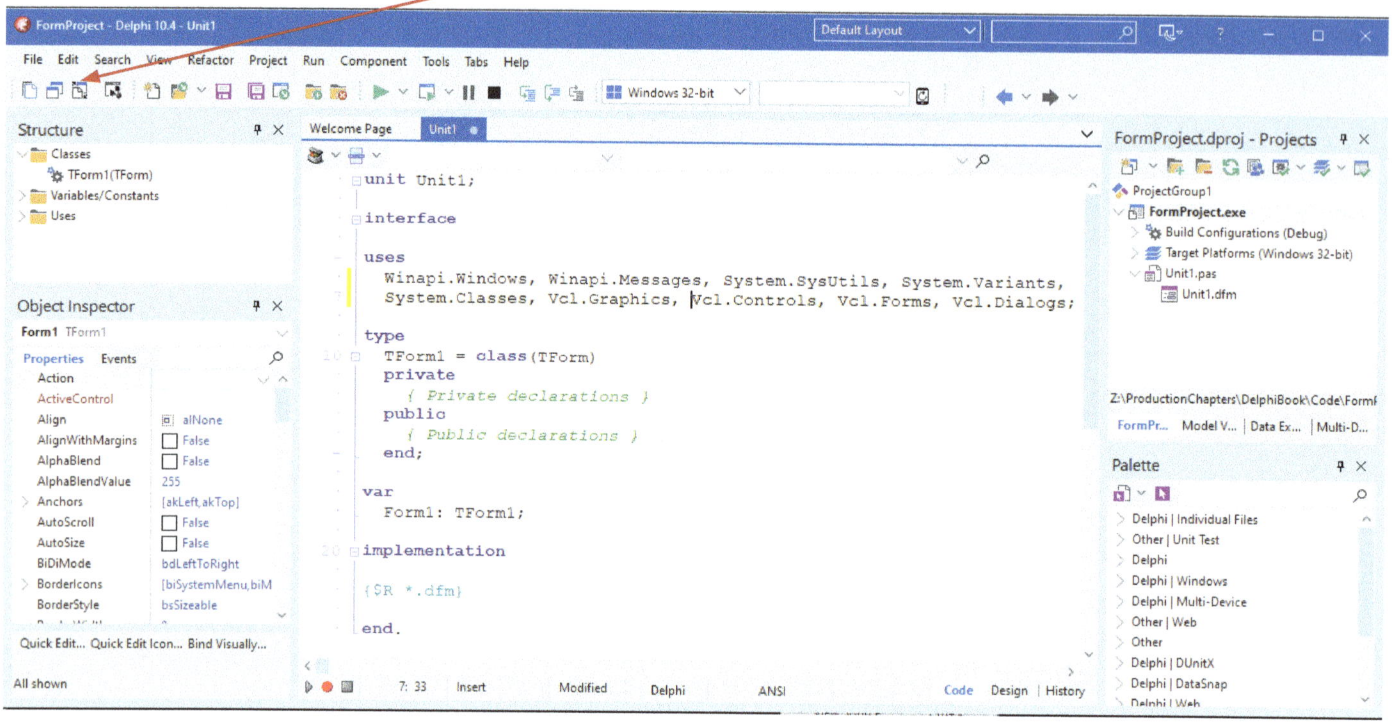

Fig. 29.2 IDE showing unit Unit1.pas for FormProject in IDE

Toggle back to the `Form1` window then add a button to `Form1` by selecting the button control from the **Standard** tab before pasting to `Form1` (just click the button control, `TButton`, on the standard palette and then click on the form). Figure 29.3 shows the placement of `Button1` on `Form1`.

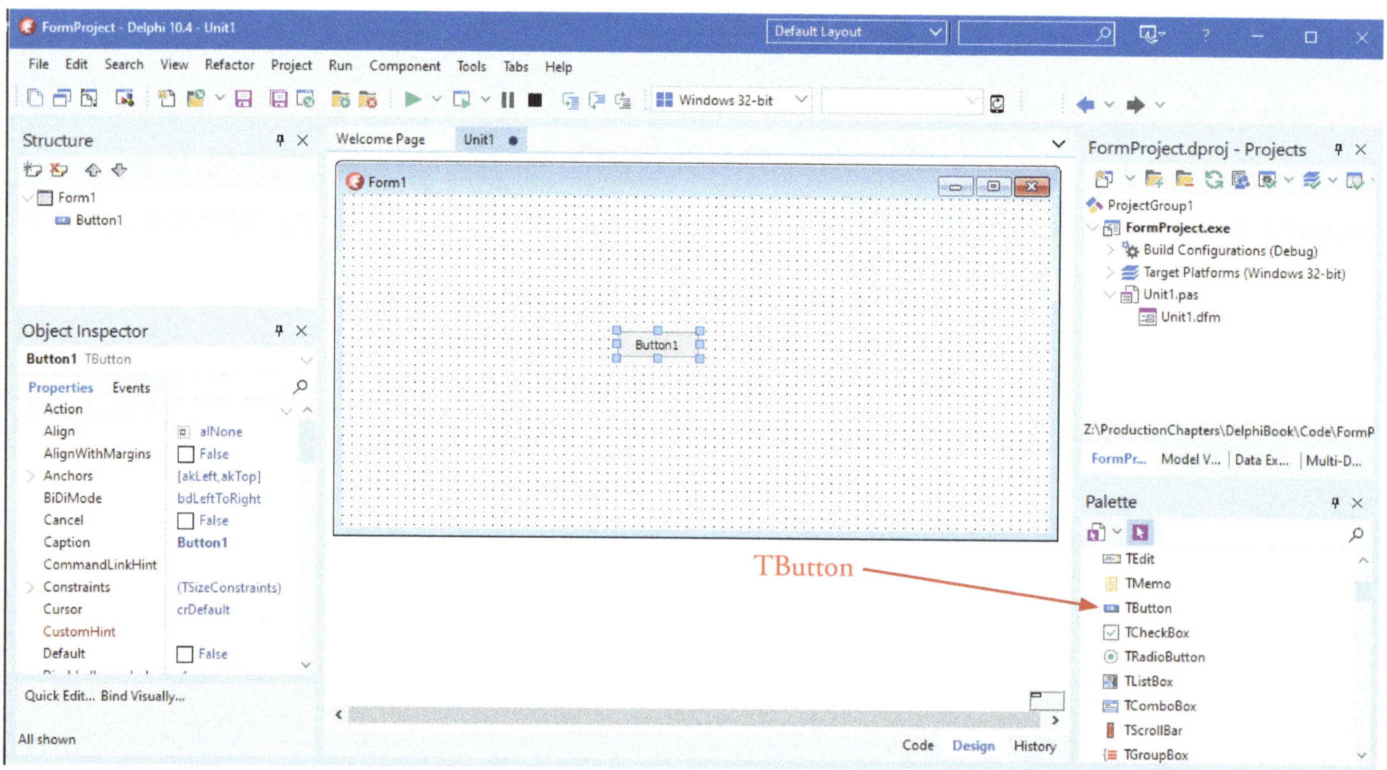

Fig. 29.3 IDE for FormProject showing button, Button1, of type TButton placed on Form1

An event handler that handles button clicks is created by double clicking `Button1`. The result is shown in *Figure 29.4*.

An event handler `Procedure Button1Click(Sender : TObject)` is added to the class definition for `TForm1` and code for this event handler is automatically added as shown in *Figure 29.4* to the **Implementation** section .

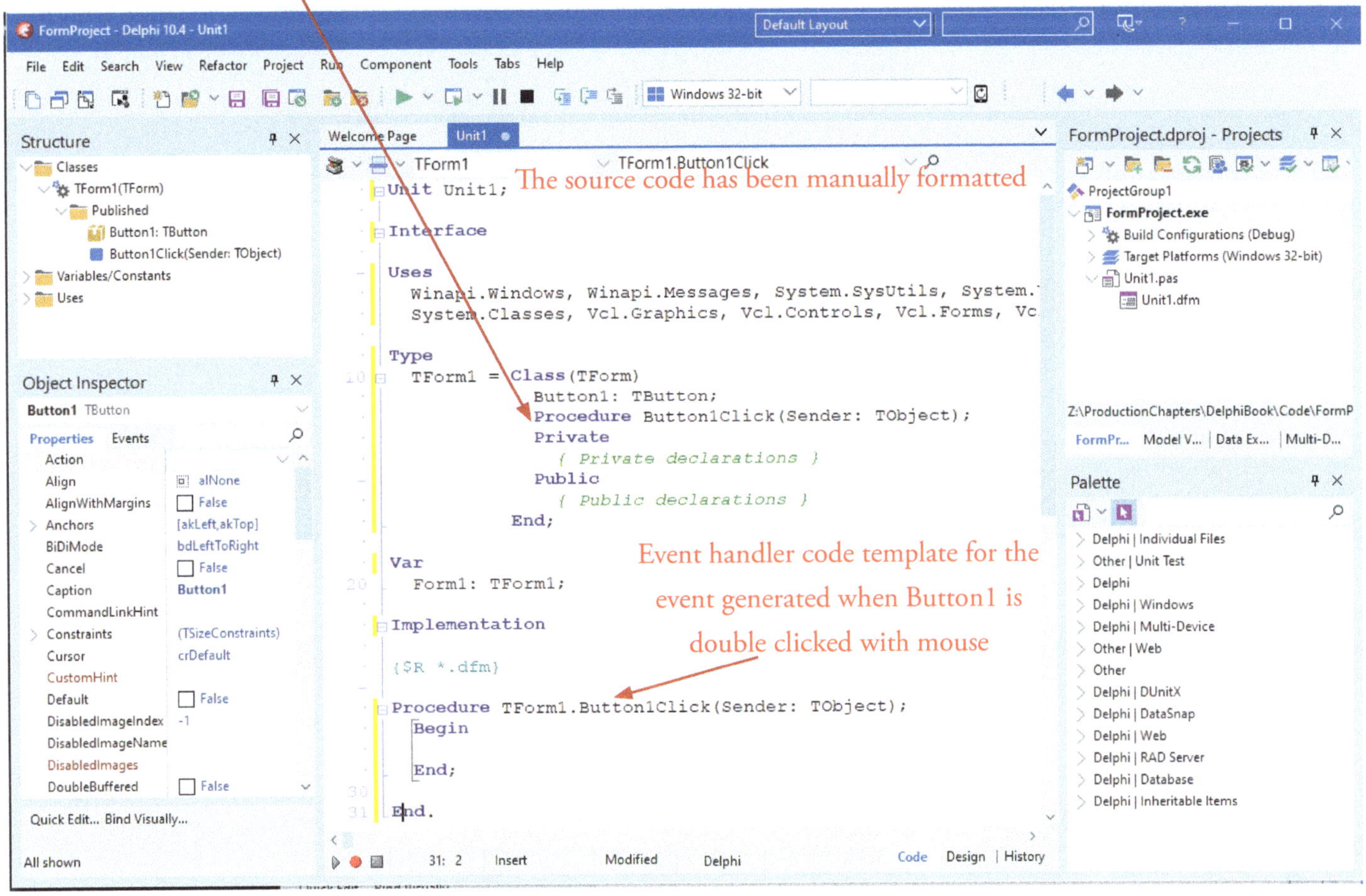

Fig. 29.4 IDE showing the modified TForm1 class definition and the event handler code for Button1Click

This event handling procedure `Procedure Button1Click(Sender : TObject)` is called at run time when the `Button1` control is clicked. The `Sender` parameter of this event handler stores the identity of the control that was clicked.

Add `ShowMessage('Hello World');` and `ShowMessage(Sender.Classname);` between `Begin` and `End` of this procedure as shown in *Table 29.1*.

```
Implementation

{$R *.dfm}

  Procedure TForm1.Button1Click(Sender : TObject);
    Begin
      ShowMessage('Hello World');
      ShowMessage(Sender.Classname);
    End;

End.
```

Table 29.1 Event handler TForm1.Button1Click

Select `Unit1` in the **Project Manager** pane to highlight it then press **ALT + m** and replace `Unit1` with `MainForm` to rename the unit as `MainForm.pas.` Save the unit in folder **FormProject.** Save the project.

Compile and run this program (**F9**). Click the button when the program is running. The message box window shown in *Figure 29.5* should appear.

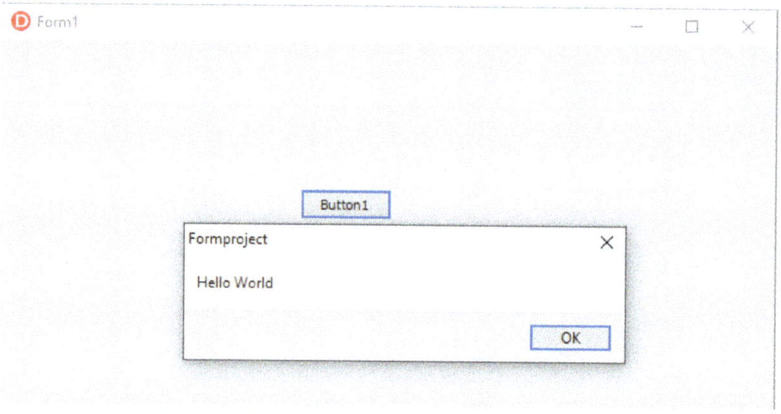

Fig. 29.5 FormProject in execution Button1 clicked

Click the **OK** button on this window and the next message box window should appear as shown in *Figure 29.6*.

This window shows the class name **TButton** of the control that was clicked.

Click **OK** to close this window.

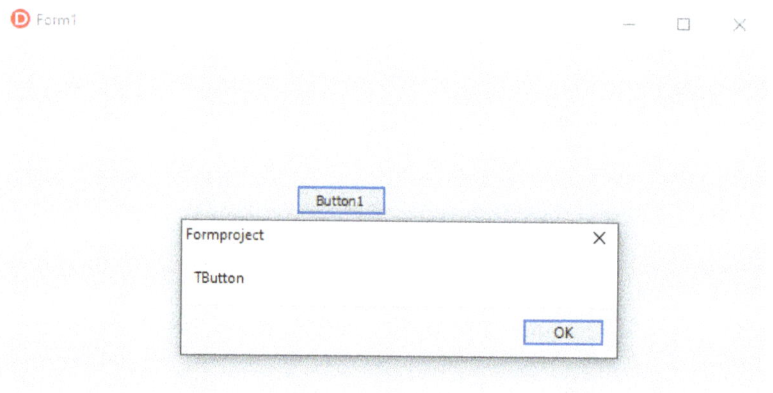

Fig. 29.6 FormProject in execution OK button clicked on Hello World window

Now add `ShowMessage(TButton(Sender).Name);` to the end of `Button1Click` event handler procedure. This time we have cast the type of **Sender** from **TObject** to **TButton** (we know that it is a T**Button** control) so that we can access the **Name** property of `Button1` object.

There are two **TButton** entities:

1. The class definition
2. The function which we use to change one object type to another. The action of this function is called **type casting**.

Each VCL Form has a **dfm** file. With the form view of `MainForm.pas` showing in the IDE, press **ALT + F12** to display the contents of `MainForm.dfm` in the IDE as shown in *Figure 29.7*.

Note that there are two objects:

1. `Form1` of type **TForm1**
2. `Button1` of type **TButton1**.

Press **ALT + F12** to display the form view of `MainForm.pas` in the IDE again.

```
object Form1: TForm1
  Left = 0
  Top = 0
  Caption = 'Form1'
  ClientHeight = 299
  ClientWidth = 635
  Color = clBtnFace
  Font.Charset = DEFAULT_CHARSET
  Font.Color = clWindowText
  Font.Height = -11
  Font.Name = 'Tahoma'
  Font.Style = []
  OldCreateOrder = False
  PixelsPerInch = 96
  TextHeight = 13
  object Button1: TButton
    Left = 248
    Top = 120
    Width = 75
    Height = 25
    Caption = 'Button1'
    TabOrder = 0
    OnClick = Button1Click
  end
end
```

Fig. 29.7 MainForm.dfm

Select `FormProject.exe` in the **Project Manager** pane and right click mouse button to bring up pop-up menu.

Click **View Source** in this menu with left mouse button to bring up the `FormProject` source code in the IDE as shown in *Figure 29.9*.

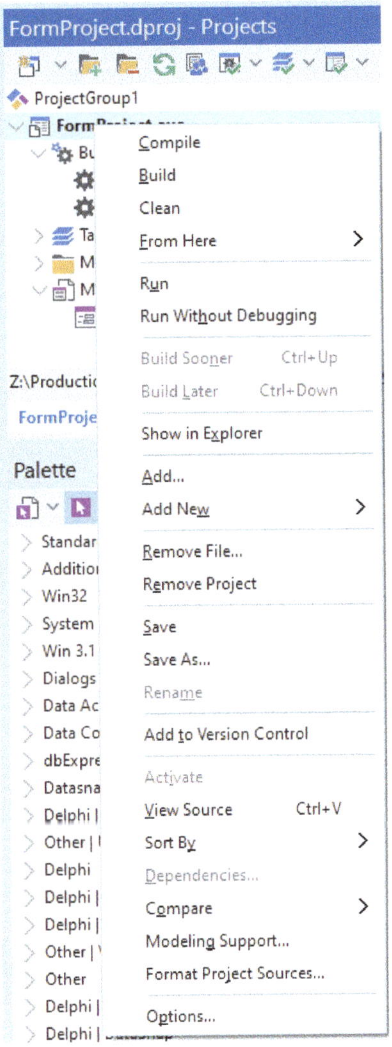

Fig. 29.8 FormProject.exe selected in Project Manager pane and right mouse button clicked to bring up pop-up menu

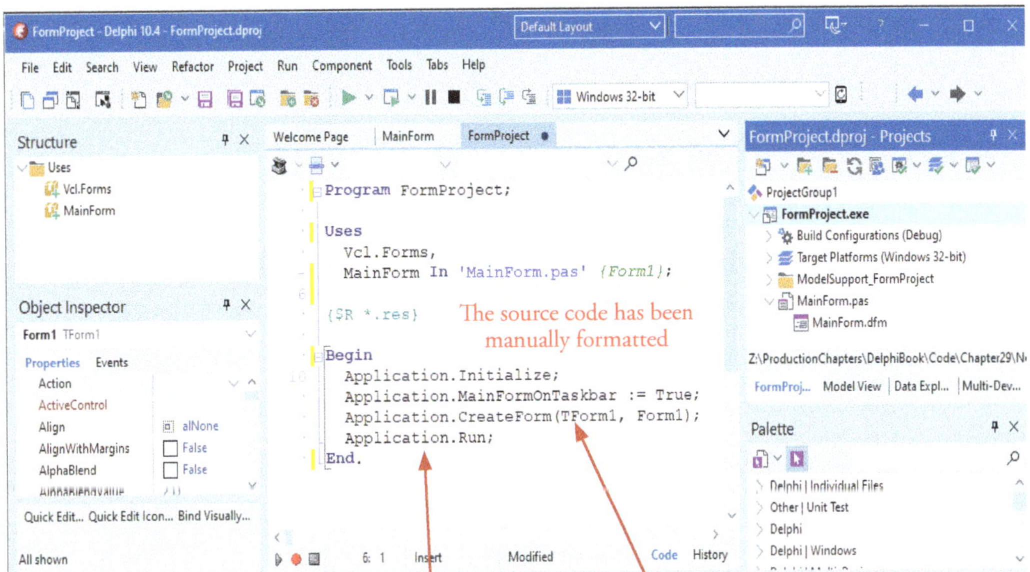

Fig. 29.9 FormProject.dprog source

The statement `Application.CreateForm(TForm1, Form1);` creates the form shown in *Figure 29.10*.

The statement `Application.Run;` sets up the event loop that enables `Button1` to respond when clicked. It then launches the application.

Fig. 29.10 FormProject.exe in execution

`Form1` shown in *Figure 29.10* is a window, the application window for application `FormProject.exe`.

There is another parameter passed to event handler `TForm1.ButtonClick1` which is not shown in the interface or at all because it is a hidden parameter. This is the **Self** parameter which every event handler has access to.

When a control on a form (window) is clicked or when some other event-generating action occurs, the operating system is the first to know about the event. The operating system must identify which application window currently has the focus (i.e. is activated) before it can call the event handler linked to the control which is located somewhere on the application window. A control is itself a window. The value passed to the event handler in the hidden parameter `Self` is a reference to the application's window - `Form1`, an instance of `TForm1` (note all the event handlers are `TForm1.` ......, e.g. `TForm1.Button1Click`, and the controls placed on `Form1` are instances of `TForm1.` ...., e.g. `TForm1.Button1`).

This can be demonstrated by adding the following statement to the end of `TForm1.Button1Click`:

```
ShowMessage(Self.Name);
```

Figure 29.11 shows the last `ShowMessage` output which is `Form1`.

The application window `Form1` was made smaller at the design stage.

Stop the application and return to the IDE, form view.

Select `Button1` on the form and press **CTRL + C** to make a **TButton** copy.

Press **CTRL + V** to paste the copy on the form. Delphi will automatically name this new button `Button2` but the caption will still be `Button1`.

Change the caption to `Button2` in the **Properties** tab in the **Object Inspector**.

In the **Events** table of the **Object Inspector** check that the **OnClick** event for `Button2` is `Button1Click`. We don't have to create a new event handler for `Button2`, instead we can use the existing one.

Compile and run this program (**F9**). Click `Button2` when the program is running. The message box window shown in *Figure 29.12* appears when `ShowMessage(TButton(Sender).Name)` executes.

Finish execution of all `ShowMessage` statements incurred by clicking `Button2`.

Now click `Button1`.

The message box window shown in *Figure 29.13* appears when `ShowMessage(TButton(Sender).Name)` executes.

(`ShowMessage(Self.Button1.Name)` produces the same outcome)

Information

Formatting source code:

CTRL + I will indent a highlighted block of code and CTRL + Shift + U will unindent a highlighted block of code.

Select Tools|Options|UserInterface|Editor|Source to set Block_indent and Tab stops positions as well as Auto indent mode.

Select Tools|Options|Language|Formatter|Delphi to set formatting options which will be applied when Project|Format Project Sources is selected or right mouse button is clicked with mouse cursor in source code window and Format Source selected from pop-up menu (CTRL + D).

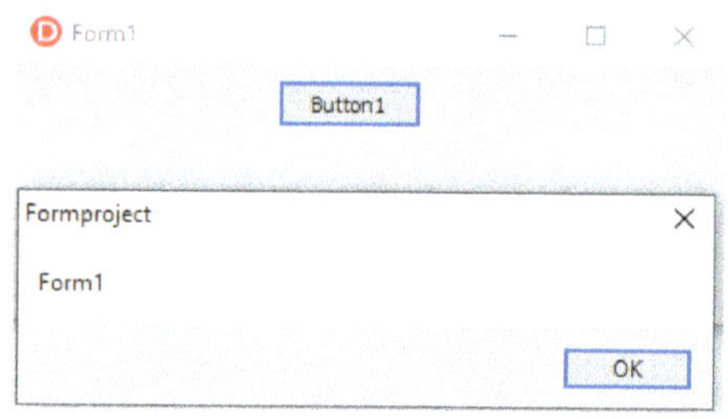

Fig. 29.11 FormProject.exe in execution, Button1 clicked and last ShowMessage shown

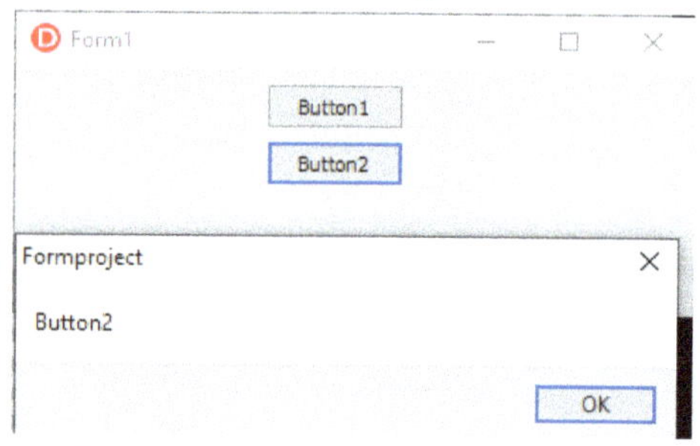

Fig. 29.12 FormProject.exe in execution, Button2 clicked and ShowMessage(TButton(Sender).Name) shown

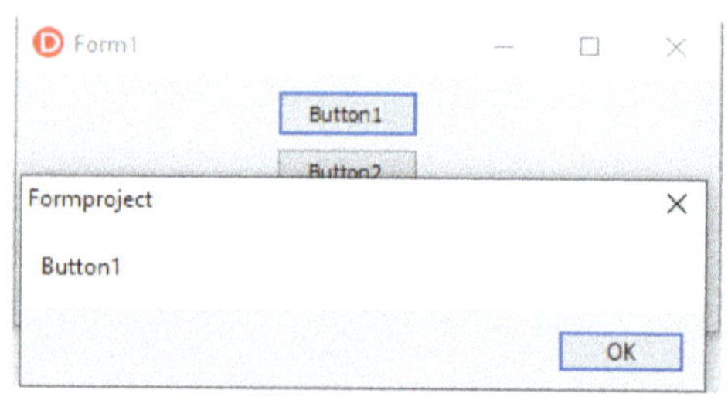

Fig. 29.13 FormProject.exe in execution, Button1 clicked and ShowMessage(TButton(Sender).Name) shown

FormsProject https://www.educational-computing.com/DelphiBook/Code/Chapter29/FormsProject.zip

Start a new application in Delphi, **File/New/Application** or **File/New/VCL Forms Application - Delphi**. Select `Project1.exe` (or whatever the default filename is) in the **Project Manager** pane to highlight it then press **ALT + m** and replace `Project1` with `FormsProject` to rename the project as `FormsProject.dprog` (`FormsProject.exe` in the **Project Manager** pane). Save the project in a folder `FormsProject`.

Select `Unit1.pas` in the **Project Manager** pane to highlight it then click the right mouse button and select **Rename** option (keyboard shortcut **ALT + n**). Replace `Unit1` with `MainFormUnit` to rename the unit as `MainFormUnit.pas`. Save the unit in a folder `FormsProject`.

Select the form in the IDE. In the **Object Inspector** change `Form1`'s **Name** property to `MainForm` and change `Form1`'s **Caption** property to `Main Form`.

Select **File|New|VCL Form - Delphi** and click **VCL Form - Delphi** to create a new form, `Form2`.

Select `Unit2.pas` in the **Project Manager** pane to highlight it then click the right mouse button and select **Rename** option (keyboard shortcut **ALT + n**). Replace `Unit2` with `SecondFormUnit` to rename the unit as `SecondFormUnit.pas`. Save the unit in a folder `FormsProject`.

Select `Form2` in the IDE. In the **Object Inspector** change `Form2`'s **Name** property to `SecondForm` and change `Form2`'s **Caption** property to `Second Form`.

Show `MainForm` in IDE (click `MainFormUnit` in tab).

Add a **TButton** control, `Button1`, to this form and change its **Caption** property to `Show Second Form`, change the font size of the caption to 12 and its **Width** and **Height** properties to accommodate the new caption comfortably.

Double click `Button1` to create an **OnClick** event handler.

To be able to access the unit `SecondFormUnit` from `MainFormUnit` we need to add a uses clause to the implementation section of the `MainFormUnit`. Select **File|Use Unit** (shortcut **ALT + F11**) and click **Use Unit**. Select `SecondFormUnit.pas` from the pop-up window (**Implementation** radio button selected). Click **OK** to add `Uses SecondFormUnit` to **Implementation** section of `MainFormUnit.pas` - *Table 29.2*.

Add `SecondForm.Show` to body of the event handler as shown in *Table 29.2*.

```
Unit MainFormUnit;
Interface
Uses
  Winapi.Windows, Winapi.Messages, System.SysUtils, System.Variants,
  System.Classes, Vcl.Graphics, Vcl.Controls, Vcl.Forms, Vcl.Dialogs,
  Vcl.StdCtrls;
Type
  TMainForm = Class(TForm)
              Button1 : TButton;
              Procedure Button1Click(Sender: TObject);
              Private
                { Private declarations }
              Public
                { Public declarations }
            End;
Var
  MainForm: TMainForm;
Implementation
{$R *.dfm}
Uses SecondFormUnit;
  Procedure TMainForm.Button1Click(Sender: TObject);
    Begin
      SecondForm.Show;
    End;
End.
```

Placing this Uses reference in the Implementation section avoids a potential circular reference error

Table 29.2 MainFormUnit.pas compactly represented

Save the project and its units in folder `FormsProject` (shortcut **SHIFT + CTRL + S**).

Compile and run this program (**F9**). Click the `Show Second Form` button on the `MainForm` window when the program is running. A second form (window) shown in *Figure 29.14* should appear.

Switching focus between the `Second Form` and the `Main Form` is possible as often as you like because it is permitted by the **Show** method.

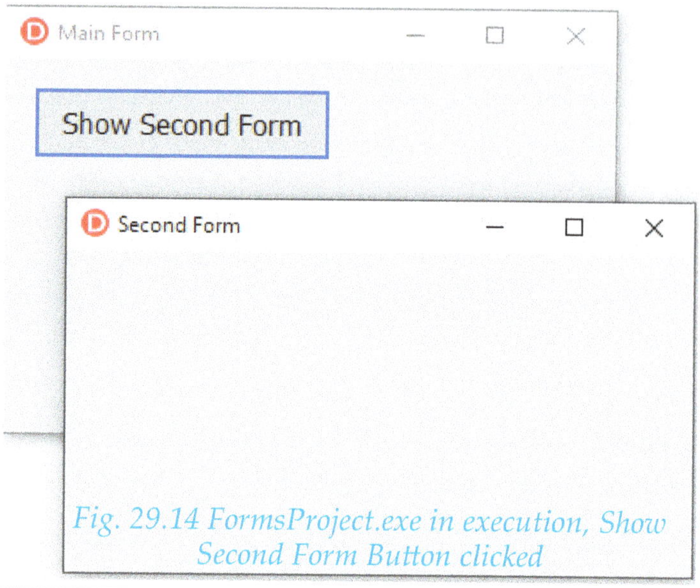

Fig. 29.14 FormsProject.exe in execution, Show Second Form Button clicked

Close the application and now add a second button to `MainForm` - select the `Show Second Form` button, **CTRL + C** to copy then **CTRL + V** to paste.

Change the caption on the newly created `Button2` to `Show Modal Second Form`. Change its **Width** property to accommodate the caption. Change the **Width** property of `Button1` so that it matches `Button2`'s width.

Select `Button2` and in the **Events** page of the **Object Inspector**, delete `Button1Click`. Now double click in the empty field of the **OnClick** event to generate `Button2Click` event handler. Add `SecondForm.ShowModal` to body of this event handler as shown in *Table 29.3*.

```
Unit MainFormUnit;
Interface
Uses
  Winapi.Windows, Winapi.Messages, System.SysUtils,
  System.Variants,System.Classes, Vcl.Graphics,
  Vcl.Controls, Vcl.Forms, Vcl.Dialogs, Vcl.StdCtrls;
Type
  TMainForm = Class(TForm)
               Button1 : TButton;
               Button2 : TButton;
               Procedure Button1Click(Sender: TObject);
               Procedure Button2Click(Sender: TObject);
               Private
                 { Private declarations }
               Public
                 { Public declarations }
             End;
Var
  MainForm: TMainForm;
Implementation
{$R *.dfm}
Uses SecondFormUnit;
  Procedure TMainForm.Button1Click(Sender: TObject);
    Begin
      SecondForm.Show;
    End;
  Procedure TMainForm.Button2Click(Sender: TObject);
    Begin
      SecondForm.ShowModal;
    End;
End.
```

Table 29.3 MainFormUnit.pas with two OnClick event handlers

Save the project and its units in folder `FormsProject` (shortcut **SHIFT + CTRL + S**).

Compile and run this program (**F9**). Click the `Show Modal Second Form` button on the `MainForm` window when the program is running. A second form (window) shown in *Figure 29.15* should appear.

Switching focus between the `SecondForm` and the `MainForm` is not possible because it is not permitted by the **ShowModal** method.

The `SecondForm` has to be closed to return to the `MainForm`.

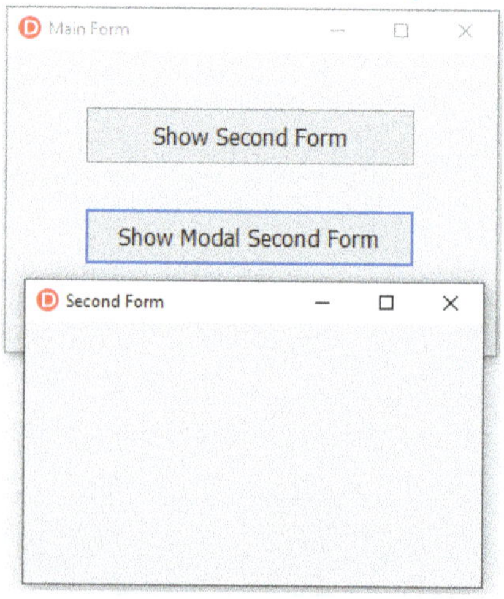

Fig. 29.15 FormsProject.exe in execution, Show Modal Second Form Button clicked

https://www.educational-computing.com/DelphiBook/Code/Chapter29/ModalFormsProject.zip

ModalFormsProject

Save the `FormsProject` as `ModalFormsProject.dprog` (or equivalent depending on Delphi version) and its units in a new folder `ModalFormsProject` (**Save Project As** and **Save As** respectively).

Select `SecondFormUnit` in the IDE and add two buttons.

Change the **Caption** property of each button to `OK` and `Cancel`, respectively. Change the **Font** size of the caption to 12 in each case. Adjust the **Height** property of each to accommodate the larger font.

Double click the `OK` button to create an **OnClick** event handler.

Add the following to the body of this event handler to set the **ModalResult** property to **mrOK**:

```
ModalResult := mrOK;
```

Switch to the `MainFormUnit` and add the following to the end of the body of `Button2Click`:

```
If SecondForm.ModalResult = mrOK
  Then ShowMessage('OK');
```

Switch to the `SecondFormUnit`, select the `Cancel` button and in the **Object Inspector** set the **ModalResult** property to **mrCancel**. We have now demonstrated two ways to assign a modal result, one in code and the other via the **Object Inspector**.

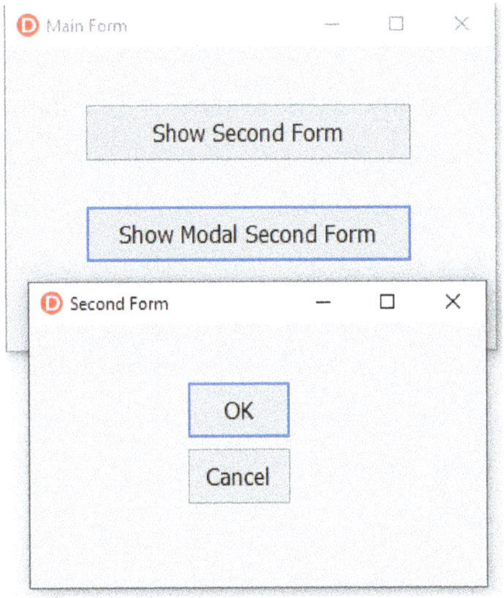

Fig. 29.16 ModalFormsProject.exe in execution, Show Modal Second Form Button clicked

Switch to the `MainFormUnit` and add the following to the end of the body of `Button2Click`:

```
If SecondForm.ModalResult = mrCancel
  Then ShowMessage('Cancel');
```

Save the project and its units in folder `ModalFormsProject` (shortcut **SHIFT + CTRL + S**).

Compile and run this program (**F9**). Click the `Show Modal Second Form` button on the `MainForm` window when the program is running. A second form (window) shown in *Figure 29.16* should appear.

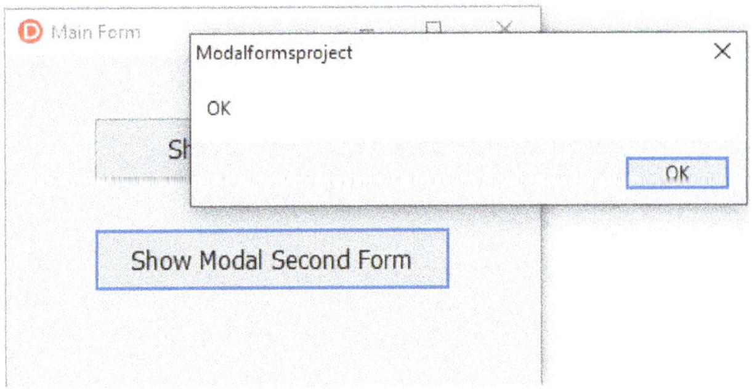

Fig. 29.17 ModalFormsProject.exe in execution, OK Button clicked

Click the `OK` button, the modal form `SecondForm` should close and then the window with message `OK` shown in *Figure 29.17* should appear.

Click the `OK` button on this window to close it and return to the `MainForm`.

Click the `Show Modal Second Form` button on the `MainForm` window to bring up the `SecondForm`.

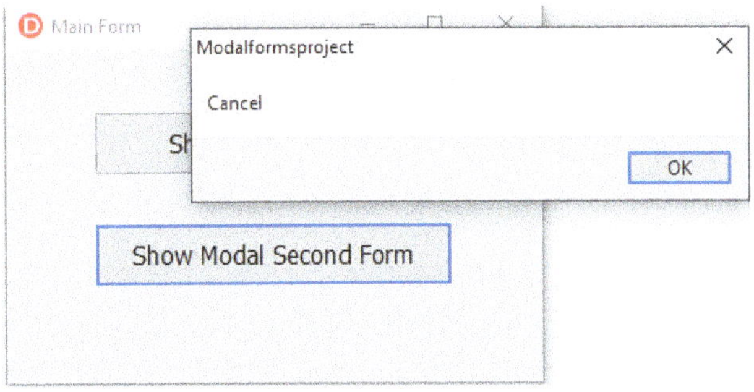

Fig. 29.18 ModalFormsProject.exe in execution, Cancel Button clicked

Click the `Cancel` button, the modal form `SecondForm` should close and then the window with message `Cancel` shown in *Figure 29.18* should appear.

Click the `OK` button on this window to close it and return to the `MainForm`.

Click the `Show Second Form` button on the `MainForm` window to bring up the `SecondForm`. Try clicking the `OK` and `Cancel` buttons on the `SecondForm`. Nothing should happen because the window is not shown in modal form.

Click on the cross icon in the set of border icons of the `SecondForm` window to close it and return to the `MainForm`.

Click the `Show Modal Second Form` button on the `MainForm` window to bring up the `SecondForm`.

Click on the cross icon in the set of border icons of the `SecondForm` window to close it and return to the `MainForm`. The window with message `Cancel` shown in *Figure 29.18* should appear as the action of closing the modal form using the cross icon returns modal result **mrCancel**.

Add a third button to the `SecondForm` and change its caption to `Try again`.

Set its `ModalResult` property to **mrRetry**.

Save the project and its units in folder `ModalFormsProject` (shortcut **SHIFT + CTRL + S**).

Compile and run this program (**F9**).

Click the `Show Modal Second Form` button on the `MainForm` window when the program is running.

Click the `Try again` button to close the `SecondForm` and return to the `MainForm`. There is no message window this time because we don't have an **If** statement that will process **mrRetry** that is returned. We could of course add one. In fact, we could replace **If** with a **Case** statement.

Close the application.

Now add a third button to the `MainForm`, change its **Caption** property to `Close Application` and its **Font** size to 12. Adjust its **Width** and **Height** properties to match the other two buttons as shown in *Figure 29.19*. Adjust the layout of the buttons to match that shown in *Figure 29.19*.

Double click the `Close Application` button to create an **OnClick** event handler.

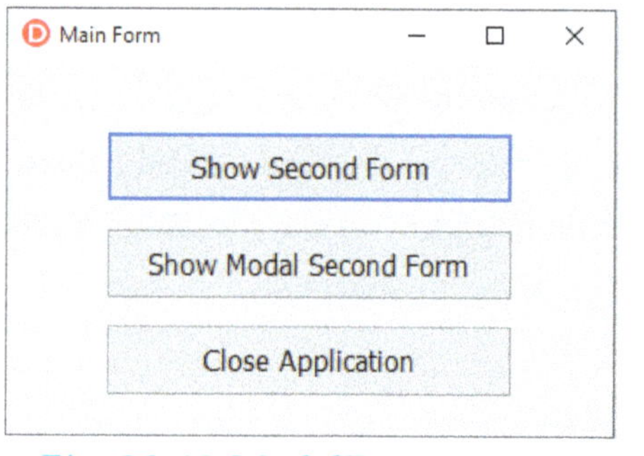

Fig. 29.19 ModalFormsProject.exe in execution, showing Close Application button

Add the following to the body of this event handler:

```
Application.Terminate;
```

The **Terminate** method of the **Application** object closes the application.

Save the project and its units in folder `ModalFormsProject` (shortcut **SHIFT + CTRL + S**).

Compile and run this program (**F9**).

Click the `Close Application` button on the `MainForm` window to close the application.

CreateFormsProject

Save the `ModalFormsProject` as `CreateFormsProject.dprog` (or equivalent depending on Delphi version) and its units in a new folder `CreateFormsProject` (**Save Project As** and **Save As** respectively).

Select **File|New|VCL Form - Delphi** and click **VCL Form - Delphi** to create a new form, `Form1`.

Select `Unit1.pas` in the **Project Manager** pane to highlight it then click the right mouse button and select **Rename** option (keyboard shortcut **ALT + n**). Replace `Unit1` with `ThirdFormUnit` to rename the unit as `ThirdFormUnit.pas`. Save the unit in folder `CreateFormsProject`.

Select `Form1` in the IDE. In the **Object Inspector** change `Form1`'s **Name** property to `ThirdForm` and change `Form1`'s **Caption** property to `Third Form`.

Show `MainForm` in IDE (click `MainFormUnit` in tab)

Select **File|Use Unit** (shortcut **ALT + F11**) and click **Use Unit**. Select `ThirdFormUnit.pas` from the pop-up window (**Implementation** radio button selected). Click **OK** to add `Uses ThirdFormUnit` to **Implementation** section of `MainFormUnit.pas`.

Select the `MainFormUnit` tab to display the `MainForm` in the IDE.

Add a fourth button to the `MainForm`, change its **Caption** property to `Create && Show New Form` and its **Font** size to 12. Adjust its **Width** and **Height** properties to match the other three buttons. Adjust the layout of the buttons to match that shown in *Figure 29.20*. (Need && to get & displayed).

Double click the `Create & Show New Form` button to create an **OnClick** event handler.

Add the additional code shown in *Table 29.4* to this event handler:

```
Procedure TMainForm.Button4Click(Sender : TObject);
  Var
    FormReference : TThirdForm;
  Begin
    FormReference := TThirdForm.Create(Self);
    FormReference.Width := SecondForm.Width;
    FormReference.Height := SecondForm.Height;
    FormReference.Show;
  End;
```

Table 29.4 Event handler TForm1.Button4Click uses Constructor Create (AOwner : TComponent)

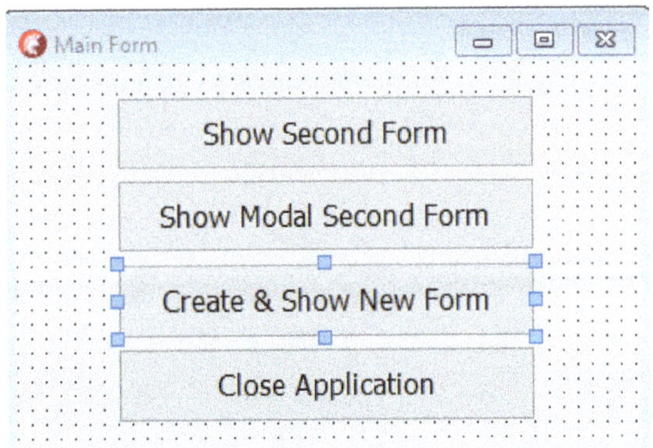

Fig. 29.20 CreateFormsProject design of graphical user interface

Remember that Self, the hidden parameter, will be assigned a reference to object MainForm (of type TMainForm), the object that calls Button4Click. Constructor Create takes parameter AOwner : TComponent, a reference to a TComponent object, in this case MainForm. Therefore, the owner of the created form will be object MainForm. The owner of the created form is responsible for freeing it and all its contained objects. If MainForm is freed, e.g. on application exit, MainForm will first free all objects that it owns before being itself freed by the application.

Select **Project** from the tool bar and click **View Source** to bring up program `CreateFormsProject` as shown in *Figure 29.21*.

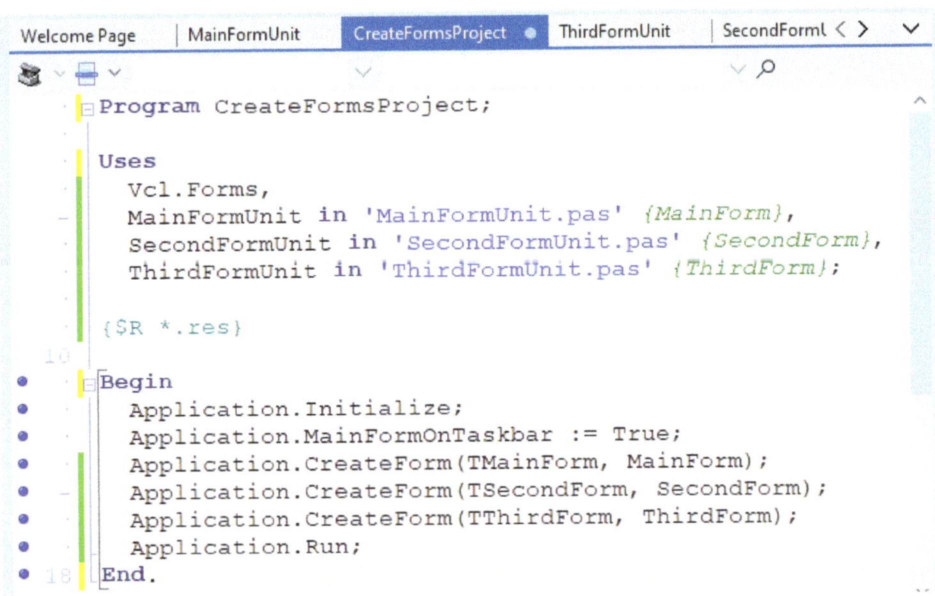


```
Program CreateFormsProject;

Uses
  Vcl.Forms,
  MainFormUnit in 'MainFormUnit.pas' {MainForm},
  SecondFormUnit in 'SecondFormUnit.pas' {SecondForm},
  ThirdFormUnit in 'ThirdFormUnit.pas' {ThirdForm};

{$R *.res}

Begin
  Application.Initialize;
  Application.MainFormOnTaskbar := True;
  Application.CreateForm(TMainForm, MainForm);
  Application.CreateForm(TSecondForm, SecondForm);
  Application.CreateForm(TThirdForm, ThirdForm);
  Application.Run;
End.
```

Fig. 29.21 CreateFormsProject source

We don't want the application to create `ThirdForm` because we want it created and shown when `Button4` is clicked.

Therefore, we need to to stop the application creating it. The neatest way is to change the project's options.

Click **Project** in the toolbar then **Options** then in **Application** click **Forms** to bring up the window shown in *Figure 29.22*.

Click `ThirdForm` and drag it to the **Available forms** pane. Click **Save**.

We have now stopped `ThirdForm` being auto-created.

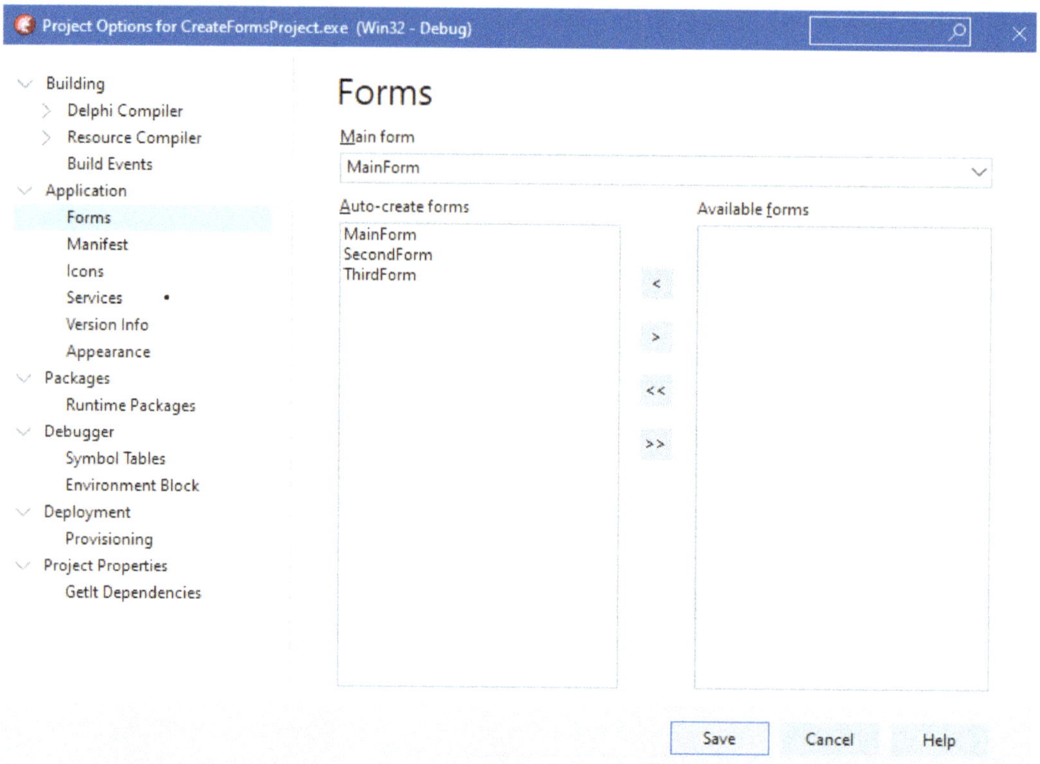

Fig. 29.22 Project Options Forms window

Of course, we could have just deleted the statement `Application.CreateForm(TThirdForm, ThirdForm);` from the source code program `CreateFormsProject` but that would not have exposed the purpose of **Project|Options |Application** to control how the application is to behave.

Save the project and its units in folder `CreateFormsProject` (shortcut **SHIFT + CTRL + S**).

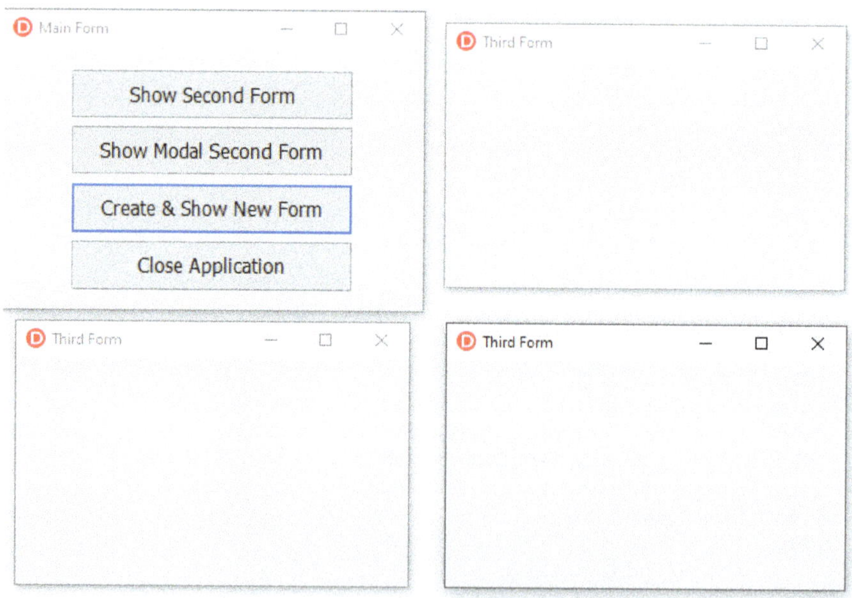

Fig. 29.23 CreateFormsProject.exe in execution, Create & Show New Form button clicked three times

Compile and run this program (**F9**). Click the `Create & Show New Form` button on the `MainForm` window three times when the program is running. Three new forms (window) are created as shown in *Figure 29.23* each with caption `Third Form`.

Click `Close Application` button on the `Main Form` to exit the application.

https://www.educational-computing.com/DelphiBook/Code/Chapter29/CreateAndDestroyFormsProject.zip

CreateAndDestroyFormsProject

Save the `CreateFormsProject` as `CreateAndDestroyFormsProject.dprog` (or equivalent depending on Delphi version) and its units in a new folder `CreateAndDestroyFormsProject` (**Save Project As** and **Save As** respectively).

To understand how all three forms are created and destroyed when the application is started and when it is exited, we need to add two event handlers to each unit:

- `FormCreate` which responds to the event OnCreate
- `FormDestroy` which responds to the event `OnDestroy`.

Select the **Events** page of the **Object Inspector** for the `MainFormUnit` and double click the **OnCreate** and **OnDestroy** empty fields to create two event handlers, `FormCreate` and `FormDestroy`.

Add the variable declaration for `MyOwner` and the source code to the body of each new event handler as shown in *Table 29.5*.

Table 29.5 MainFormUnit.pas with two new event handlers, FormCreate and FormDestroy and a new variable MyOwner declared in the Implementation section

```
Unit MainFormUnit;
Interface
Uses
  .....
Type
  TMainForm = Class(TForm)
                Button1 : TButton;
                .....
                Procedure FormDestroy(Sender: TObject);
                Procedure FormCreate(Sender: TObject);
                Private
                  .....
              End;
Var
  MainForm: TMainForm;
Implementation
  {$R *.dfm}
  Uses SecondFormUnit, ThirdFormUnit;
  Var
    MyOwner : TComponent;
  Procedure TMainForm.Button1Click(Sender: TObject);
      Begin
        SecondForm.Show;
      End;
  .....
  Procedure TMainForm.FormCreate(Sender: TObject);
    Begin
      MyOwner := Self.Owner;
      ShowMessage('Main Form created: Name of owner = ' + Self.Owner.Name);
    End;
  Procedure TMainForm.FormDestroy(Sender: TObject);
    Begin
      ShowMessage('Main Form being freed by ' + MyOwner.Name);
    End;
End.
```

Self contains a reference to an instance of TMainForm

Select the **Events** page of the **Object Inspector** for the `SecondFormUnit` and double click the **OnCreate** and **OnDestroy** empty fields to create two event handlers, `FormCreate` and `FormDestroy`.

Add the variable declaration for `MyOwner` and the source code to the body of each new event handler as shown in *Table 29.6*.

Table 29.6 SecondFormUnit.pas with two new event handlers, FormCreate and FormDestroy and a new variable MyOwner declared in the Implementation section

```
Unit SecondFormUnit;
Interface
Uses
  .....
Type
  TSecondForm = Class(TForm)
                Button1 : TButton;
                .....
                Procedure FormDestroy(Sender : TObject);
                Procedure FormCreate(Sender : TObject);
                Private
                  .....
              End;
Var
  SecondForm: TSecondForm;
Implementation
{$R *.dfm}
 Var
   MyOwner : TComponent;
   .....
  Procedure TSecondForm.FormCreate(Sender : TObject);
    Begin
      MyOwner := Self.Owner;
      ShowMessage('Second Form created: Name of owner = ' + Self.Owner.Name);
    End;
  Procedure TSecondForm.FormDestroy(Sender : TObject);
    Begin
      ShowMessage('Second Form being freed by ' + MyOwner.Name)
    End;
End.
```

Self contains a reference to an instance of TSecondForm

Select the **Events** page of the **Object Inspector** for the `ThirdFormUnit` and double click the **OnCreate** and **OnDestroy** empty

fields to create two event handlers, FormCreate and FormDestroy.
Add the variable declaration for MyOwner and the source code to the body of each new event handler as shown in *Table 29.7*.

Select **Project|View Source** to bring up program source.

Add to the beginning of the Begin End block:

```
Application.Name :=
'CreateAndDestroyFormsProject';
```

Click **File|Save All**.

Compile and run this program (**F9**).

Figure 29.24 shows the creation and destruction of forms for one possible sequence of operations of execution for CreateAndDestroyProject.exe. This shows that CreateAndDestroyFormsProject is responsible for creating and freeing the MainForm and the SecondForm but the MainForm is responsible for creating and freeing the ThirdForm.

Table 29.7 ThirdFormUnit.pas with two new event handlers, FormCreate and FormDestroy and a new variable MyOwner declared in the Implementation section

```
Unit ThirdFormUnit;
Interface
Uses
  .....
Type
  TThirdForm = Class(TForm)
                Procedure FormDestroy(Sender : TObject);
                Procedure FormCreate(Sender : TObject);
                Private
                  .....
                End;
Var
  ThirdForm: TThirdForm;
Implementation
  {$R *.dfm}
  Var
    MyOwner : TComponent;
  Procedure TThirdForm.FormCreate(Sender : TObject);
    Begin
      MyOwner := Self.Owner;
      ShowMessage('Third Form being created by ' + Self.Owner.Name);
    End;
Procedure TThirdForm.FormDestroy(Sender : TObject);
    Begin
      ShowMessage('Third Form being freed by ' + MyOwner.Name)
    End;
End.
```

Self contains a reference to an instance of TThirdForm

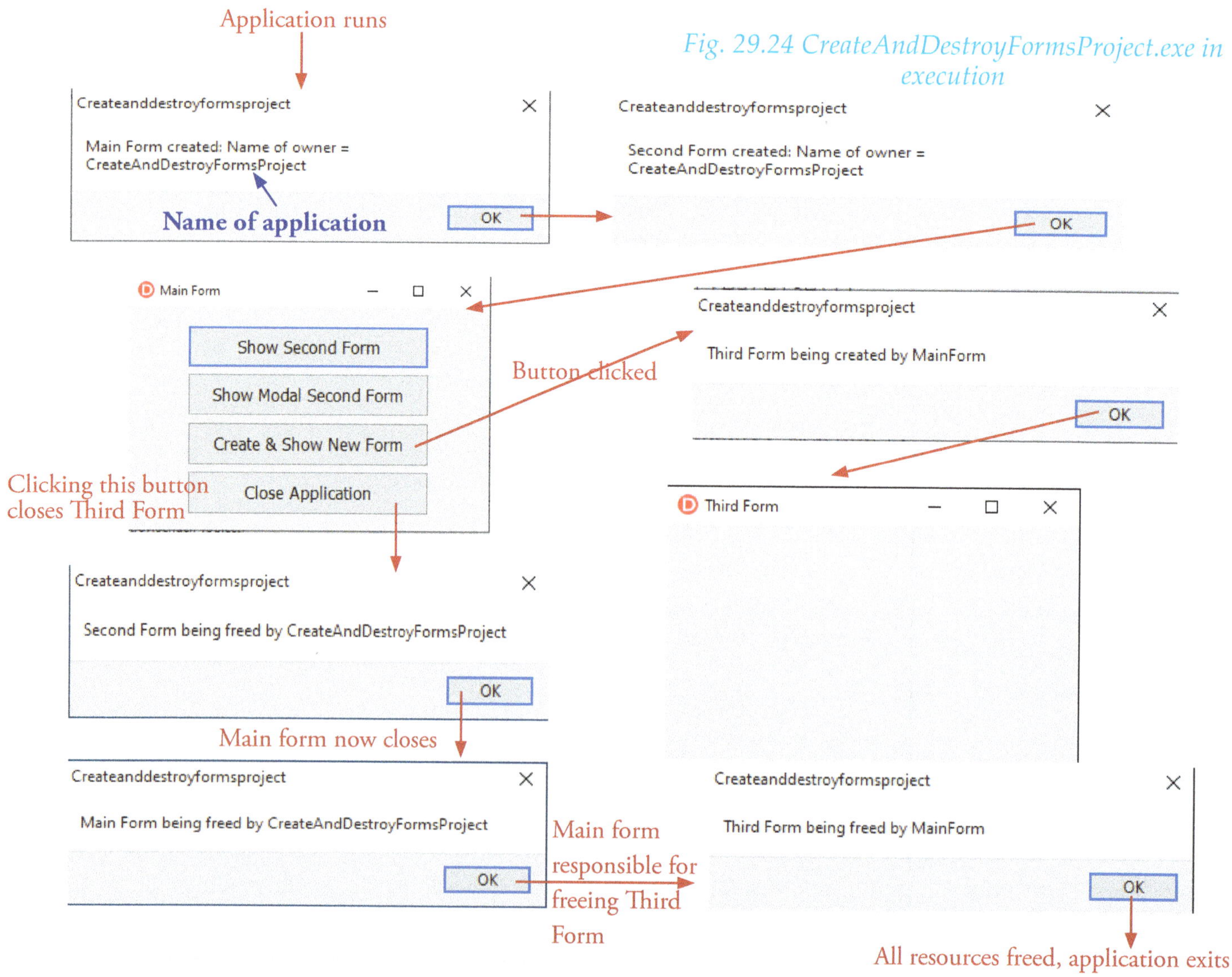

Fig. 29.24 CreateAndDestroyFormsProject.exe in execution

https://www.educational-computing.com/DelphiBook/Code/Chapter29/CreateAndDestroyNoSelfFormsProject.zip

CreateAndDestroyFormsNoSelfProject

Save the `CreateAndDestroyFormsProject` as `CreateAndDestroyNoSelfFormsProject.dprog` (or equivalent depending on Delphi version) and its units in a new folder `CreateAndDestroyNoSelfFormsProject` (**Save Project As** and **Save As** respectively).

Select **Project|View Source** to bring up program source.

Change the application's name property as shown in *Table 29.8.*

Add

`ReportMemoryLeaksOnShutdown := True;`

Click **File|Save All**.

```
Program CreateAndDestroyNoSelfFormsProject;

Uses
  Vcl.Forms,
  MainFormUnit in 'MainFormUnit.pas' {MainForm},
  SecondFormUnit in 'SecondFormUnit.pas' {SecondForm},
  ThirdFormUnit in 'ThirdFormUnit.pas' {ThirdForm};

{$R *.res}

Begin
  ReportMemoryLeaksOnShutdown := True;
  Application.Name := 'CreateAndDestroyNoSelfFormsProject';
  Application.Initialize;
  Application.MainFormOnTaskbar := True;
  Application.CreateForm(TMainForm, MainForm);
  Application.CreateForm(TSecondForm, SecondForm);
  Application.Run;
End.
```

Table 29.8 Program CreateAndDestroyNoSelfFormsProject

Select the `MainFormUnit` and replace `Self` with `Nil` in

`FormReference := TThirdForm.Create(Self);`

in procedure `TMainForm.Button4Click`.

Select `ThirdFormUnit` and replace the body of `TThirdForm.FormCreate` and the body of `TThirdForm.FormDestroy` as shown in *Table 29.9*.

```
Procedure TThirdForm.FormCreate(Sender : TObject);
  Begin
    If Self.Owner <> Nil
      Then
        Begin
          MyOwner := Self.Owner;
          ShowMessage('Third Form being created by '
                       + Self.Owner.Name);
        End;
  End;
Procedure TThirdForm.FormDestroy(Sender : TObject);
  Begin
    If Assigned(MyOwner)
      Then ShowMessage('Third Form being freed by ' + MyOwner.Name)
      Else ShowMessage('Third Form being freed');
  End;
```

Table 29.9 Shows the changes to FormCreate and FormDestroy in ThirdFormUnit

Click **File|Save All**.

Compile and run this program (**F9**).

Click `Create & Show New Form` button to create an instance of `TThirdForm`.

Now click button `Close Application`.

The last window to be displayed is shown in *Figure 29.25*.

The memory leak is caused by the memory block allocated to the `TThirdForm` object when created by the `MainForm` object.

This is a direct result of not assigning as owner of this `TThirdForm` object, a reference to the `MainForm` object. Instead we assigned the reference value `Nil` as the value of the `Owner` parameter of the `Create` constructor:

`Constructor Create (AOwner : TComponent); Override;`

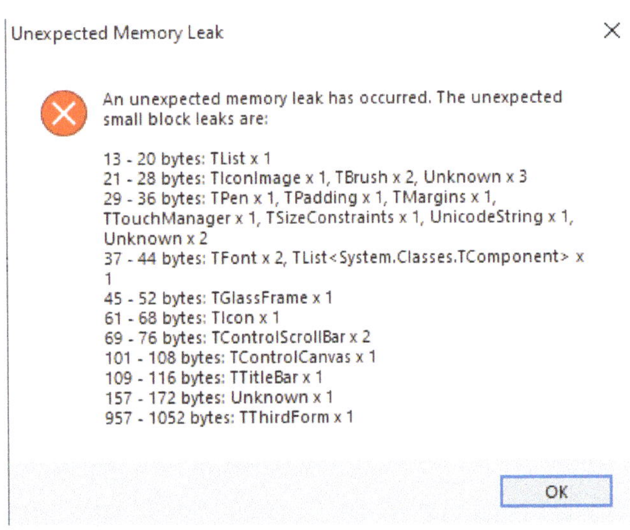

Fig. 29.25 Unexpected Memory Leak window

Information

To go from viewing an event handler in the class definition to viewing its implementation in the implementation section and vice versa, hold down the CTRL key and click the left mouse button while the mouse pointer is over the event handler.

https://www.educational-computing.com/DelphiBook/Code/Chapter29/CreateAndDestroyNoSelfOnCloseFormsProject.zip

CreateAndDestroyFormsNoSelfOnCloseProject

Save the CreateAndDestroyNoSelfFormsProject as CreateAndDestroyNoSelfOnCloseFormsProject.dprog (or equivalent depending on Delphi version) and its units in a new folder CreateAndDestroyNoSelfOnCloseFormsProject (**Save Project As** and **Save As** respectively).

Select **Project|View Source** to bring up program source.

Change the application's name property to CreateAndDestroyNoSelfOnCloseFormsProject.

Open form view ThirdFormUnit (**SHIFT F12** or **View|Forms**). In the **Object Inspector** select the **Events** page and double click the empty **OnClose** property field to create the event handle

```
TThirdForm.FormClose(Sender : TObject; Var Action : TCloseAction)
```

This handler is called when a form of type TThirdForm is closed (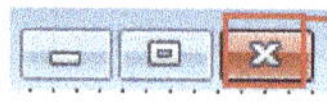) by clicking the close button in the title bar.

Add `Action := caFree;` to the body of FormClose.

caFree is an enumerated type defined in System.UITypes.pas. It denotes *close action Free*, an action which frees the memory occupied by the TThirdForm object.

To see Delphi type definitions, hold down the **CTRL** key whilst moving the mouse over the Delphi-defined type. The mouse icon will change to a hand, click the left mouse button to open the unit containing the type definition and view it in the IDE. For example, clicking as described on **TCloseAction** opens unit Vcl.Forms.pas.

Figure 29.26 shows a snippet of the body of this unit.

```
TTileMode = (tbHorizontal, tbVertical);
TCloseAction = System.UITypes.TCloseAction;
```

Fig. 29.26 Snippet from unit Vcl.Forms.pas

Repeating the action on **TCloseAction** shown in *Figure 29.26* opens unit System.UITypes.pas.

Figure 29.27 shows a snippet of the body of this unit.

Enumerated type

```
TCloseAction = (caNone, caHide, caFree, caMinimize);
TMouseButton = (mbLeft, mbRight, mbMiddle);
```

Fig. 29.27 Snippet from unit System.UITypes.pas

Note that if one or more instances of TThirdForm exist when the Close Application button is clicked or the Close button in the Title bar of the Main Form is clicked, a memory leak still occurs.

Click **File|Save All**.

Compile and run this program (**F9**).

Click Create & Show New Form button to create an instance of TThirdForm.

Now close this instance of TThirdForm by clicking the close button in the title bar.

Now click button Close Application. This time there is no **Unexpected Memory Leak** window.

Comment out `Action := caFree;` in the body of FormClose and recompile and run the program.

Click Create & Show New Form button to create an instance of TThirdForm.

Now close this instance of TThirdForm by clicking the close button in the title bar.

Now click button Close Application. This time there is an **Unexpected Memory Leak** window.

Uncomment `Action := caFree;` in the body of FormClose.

Click **File|Save All**.

Open (**SHIFT F12**) or toggle (**F12**) to show form view of `ThirdFormUnit` in the IDE. In the **Object Inspector** select the **Events** page and double click the empty **OnCloseQuery** property field to create the event handler

```
Procedure TThirdForm.FormCloseQuery(Sender: TObject; var CanClose: Boolean)
```

Add the following to the body of `FormCloseQuery`

```
If MessageDlg('Do you wish close this window?',
              mtConfirmation, [mbYes, mbNo], 0, mbYes) = mrYes
  Then CanClose := True
  Else CanClose := False;
```

(mbYes, mbNo, mbOK, mbCancel, mbAbort, mbRetry, mbIgnore, mbAll, mbNoToAll, mbYesToAll, mbHelp, mbClose)

set of TMsgDlgBtn

(mtWarning, mtError, mtInformation, mtConfirmation, mtCustom)

There are two variants of `MessageDlg`

```
Function MessageDlg(const Msg: string; DlgType: TMsgDlgType;
                    Buttons: TMsgDlgButtons; HelpCtx: Longint): Integer;
Function MessageDlg(const Msg: string; DlgType: TMsgDlgType;
                    Buttons: TMsgDlgButtons; HelpCtx: Longint;
                    DefaultButton: TMsgDlgBtn): Integer; overload;
```

We have used the second one.

Click **File|Save All**.

Compile and run this program (**F9**).

Click `Create & Show New Form` button to create an instance of `TThirdForm`.

Now close this instance of `TThirdForm` by clicking the close button in the title bar.

The window shown in *Figure 29.28* should appear.

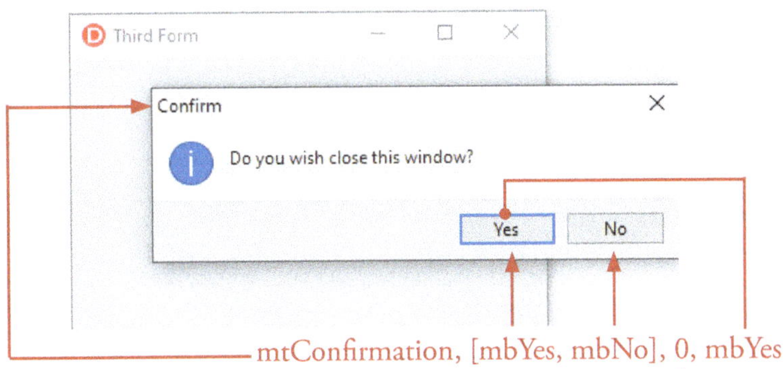

Fig. 29.28 Message dialogue window

If the **Yes** button is clicked the `Third Form` window closes and the instance of `ThirdForm` is released, i.e. memory allocated to it is freed. If the **No** button is clicked the dialogue, the `Third Form` window remains open and visible.

Close the application.

Open (**SHIFT F12**) or toggle (**F12**) to show form view of `ThirdFormUnit` in the IDE. In the **Object Inspector** select the **Events** page and double click the empty **OnActivate** property field to create the event handler

```
Procedure TThirdForm.FormActivate(Sender: TObject)
```

Add the following to the body of `FormActivate`

```
Caption := 'Third Form ' + TimeToStr(Now);
```

Click **File|Save All**.

Compile and run this program (**F9**).

Click `Create & Show New Form` button to create an instance of `TThirdForm`.

Switch focus between the `Third Form` and the `Main form` a few times.

Note that the time in the caption of `Third Form` changes each time this form is made the focus.

This occurs because each time the `Third Form` gets the focus an **OnActivate** event is triggered which in turn causes the `FormActivate` method to execute - *Figure 29.29*.

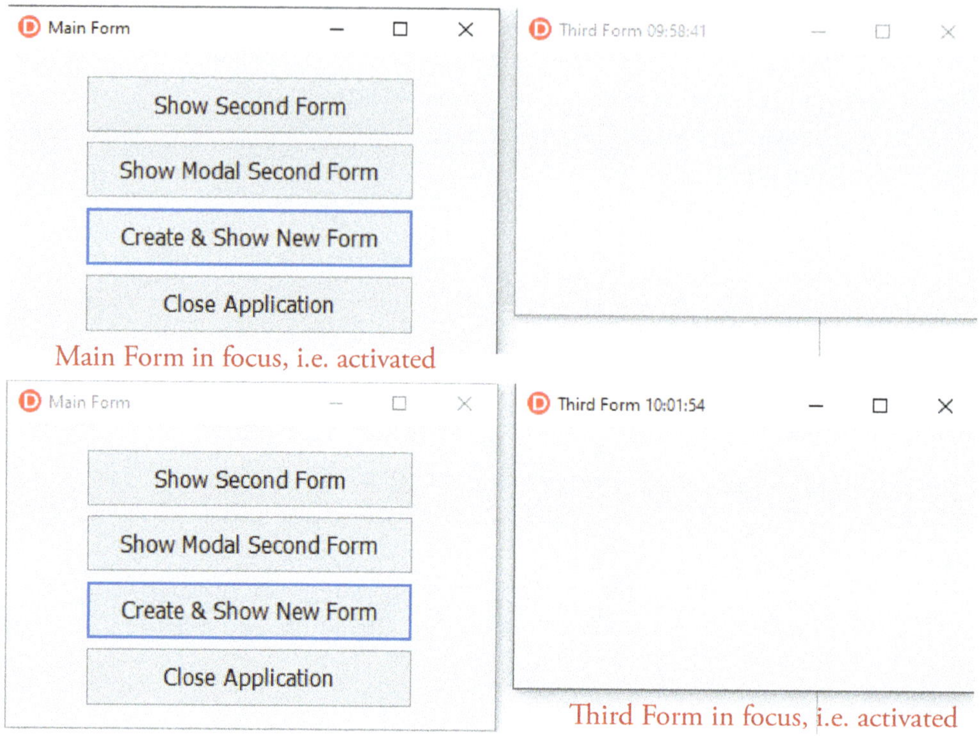

Fig. 29.29 Switching focus from the Third Form and the Main Form and back

Close the application.

Open (**SHIFT F12**) or toggle (**F12**) to show form view of `ThirdFormUnit` in the IDE. In the **Object Inspector** select the **Events** page and double click the empty **OnDeactivate** property field to create the event handler

```
Procedure TThirdForm.FormDeactivate(Sender: TObject)
```

Add the following to the body of `FormDeactivate`

```
ShowMessage('Third Form ' + TimeToStr(Now);
```

Click **File|Save All**.

Compile and run this program (**F9**).

Click `Create & Show New Form` button to create an instance of `TThirdForm`.

Switch focus between the `Third Form` and the `Main form`. This triggers an **OnDeactivate** event which in turn causes the `FormDeactivate` event handler to execute which calls `ShowMessage` - *Figure 29.30*.

Note that the time in the caption of `Third Form` changes each time this form is made the focus.

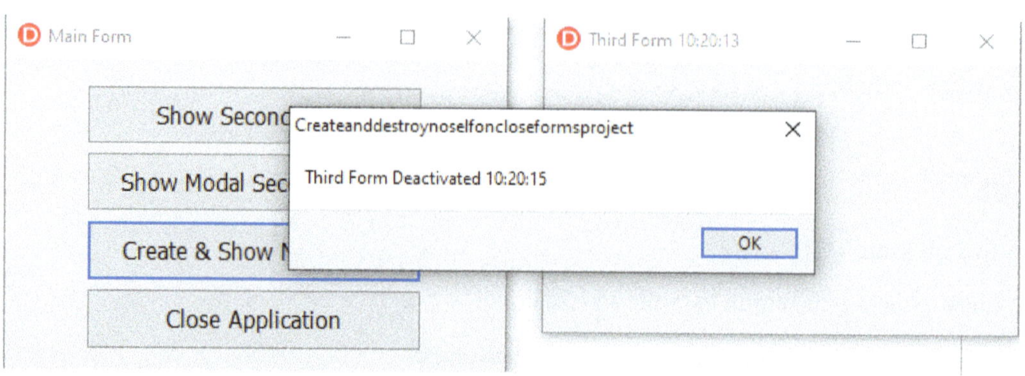

Fig. 29.30 Switching focus from the Third Form to the Main Form

https://www.educational-computing.com/DelphiBook/Code/Chapter29/ShowHideProject.zip

ShowHideProject

Start a new application in Delphi, **File/New/Application** or **File/New/VCL Forms Application - Delphi**. Save the project as `ShowHideProject.dprog.` Save the project in a folder `ShowHideProject.`

Select `Unit1.pas` in the **Project Manager** pane to highlight it then click the right mouse button and select **Rename** option (keyboard shortcut **ALT + n**). Replace `Unit1` with `MainFormUnit` to rename the unit as `MainFormUnit.pas.` Save the unit in folder `ShowHideProject.`

Select the form in the IDE. In the **Object Inspector** change `Form1`'s **Name** property to `MainForm` and change `Form1`'s **Caption** property to `Main Form`.

Select **File|New|VCL Form - Delphi** and click **VCL Form - Delphi** to create a new form, `Form2`.

Select `Unit2.pas` in the **Project Manager** pane to highlight it then click the right mouse button and select **Rename** option (keyboard shortcut **ALT + n**). Replace `Unit2` with `SecondFormUnit` to rename the unit as `SecondFormUnit.pas.` Save the unit in a folder `FShowHideProject.`

Select `Form2` in the IDE. In the **Object Inspector** change `Form2`'s **Name** property to `SecondForm` and change `Form2`'s **Caption** property to `Second Form`.

Show `MainForm` in IDE (click `MainFormUnit` in tab).

Add a **TButton** control, `Button1`, to this form and change its **Caption** property to `Show Second Form`.

Double click `Button1` to create an **OnClick** event handler.

To be able to access the unit `SecondFormUnit` from `MainFormUnit` we need to add a uses clause to the implementation section of the `MainFormUnit`. Select **File|Use Unit** (shortcut **ALT + F11**) and click **Use Unit**. Select `SecondFormUnit.pas` from the pop-up window (**Implementation** radio button selected). Click **OK** to add `Uses SecondFormUnit` to **Implementation** section of `MainFormUnit.pas`.

Add `SecondForm.Show` to body of the **On Click** event handler(same effect is achieved with `SecondForm.Visible := True).`

Add another **TButton** control, `Button2`, to this form and change its **Caption** property to `Hide Second Form`.

Double click `Button2` to create an **OnClick** event handler.

Add `SecondForm.Hide` to body of the **On Click** event handler (same effect is achieved with `SecondForm.Visible := False).`

Click **File|Save All**.
Compile and run this program (**F9**).
Click `Show Second Form` button to show this form.
Switch focus back to the `Main Form` then click `Hide Second Form` to make the `Second Form` disappear.

Repeat the two operations a few times to alternate between showing the `Third Form` and hiding the `Third Form`.

Close the application.

https://www.educational-computing.com/DelphiBook/Code/Chapter29/ThirdFormWithButton.zip

ThirdFormWithButton

Open `CreateAndDestroyFormsNoSelfOnCloseProject` and save project as `ThirdFormWithButton` in a new folder `ThirdFormWithButton`. Remove the `SecondFormUnit` from the project **Project|Remove form Project...** and remove the `Show Second Form` and `Show Modal Second Form` buttons and their event handlers from the `Main Form`. Modify the `MainFormUnit` so that it retains just `Button3Click` and `Button4Click` as shown in *Table 29.10*. Remove all but the `FormActivate` event handler from the `ThirdFormUnit`.

Add a button to the `Third Form` and change its caption to `Click Me`. Create an `On Click` event handler with the body shown in *Figure 29.11*. Change `Application.Name` to '`ThirdFormWithButton`' in project source - *Table 29.12*. Save all then build and run (**F9**). Create three instances of `Third Form` then click the `Click Me` button of each, in turn. The results are shown in *Figure 29.31* and *Figure 29.32*. `Self.Name` is `ThirdForm`, `ThirdForm_1` and `ThirdForm_2`, in turn, as revealed by `ShowMessage` windows.

```
Unit MainFormUnit;
Interface
Uses
  Winapi.Windows, Winapi.Messages, System.SysUtils,
  System.Variants,System.Classes,Vcl.Graphics,
  Vcl.Controls, Vcl.Forms, Vcl.Dialogs, Vcl.StdCtrls;
Type
  TMainForm = Class(TForm)
               Button4 : TButton;
               Button3 : TButton;
               Procedure Button3Click(Sender : TObject);
               Procedure Button4Click(Sender : TObject);
               Private
                 { Private declarations }
               Public
                 { Public declarations }
             End;
Var
  MainForm: TMainForm;
Implementation
  {$R *.dfm}
  Uses ThirdFormUnit;
  Procedure TMainForm.Button3Click(Sender: TObject);
    Begin
      Application.Terminate;
    End;
  Procedure TMainForm.Button4Click(Sender: TObject);
    Var
      FormReference : TThirdForm;
    Begin
      FormReference := TThirdForm.Create(MainForm);
      FormReference.Show;
    End;
End.
```

Table 29.10 Revised MainFormUnit

```
Unit ThirdFormUnit;
Interface
Uses
  Winapi.Windows, Winapi.Messages, System.SysUtils,
  System.Variants, System.Classes, Vcl.Graphics,
  Vcl.Controls, Vcl.Forms, Vcl.Dialogs, Vcl.StdCtrls;
Type
  TThirdForm = Class(TForm)
                Button1: TButton;
                Procedure FormActivate(Sender : TObject);
                Procedure Button1Click(Sender: TObject);
                Private
                  { Private declarations }
                public
                  { Public declarations }
                End;
Var
  ThirdForm: TThirdForm;
Implementation
  {$R *.dfm}
  Procedure TThirdForm.Button1Click(Sender: TObject);
    Begin
      ShowMessage('Form ' + Self.Name + ' clicked '
                  + 'button ' + TButton(Sender).Name
                  + ' clicked');
    End;
  Procedure TThirdForm.FormActivate(Sender : TObject);
    Begin
      Caption := 'Third Form ' + TimeToStr(Now);
    End;
End.
```

Table 29.11 Revised ThirdFormUnit

```
Program ThirdFormWithButton;
Uses
  Vcl.Forms,
  MainFormUnit in 'MainFormUnit.pas' {MainForm},
  ThirdFormUnit in 'ThirdFormUnit.pas' {ThirdForm};
{$R *.res}
Begin
  ReportMemoryLeaksOnShutdown := True;
  Application.Name := 'ThirdFormWithButton';
  Application.Initialize;
  Application.MainFormOnTaskbar := True;
  Application.CreateForm(TMainForm, MainForm);
  Application.Run;
End.
```

Table 29.12 ThirdFormWithButton program

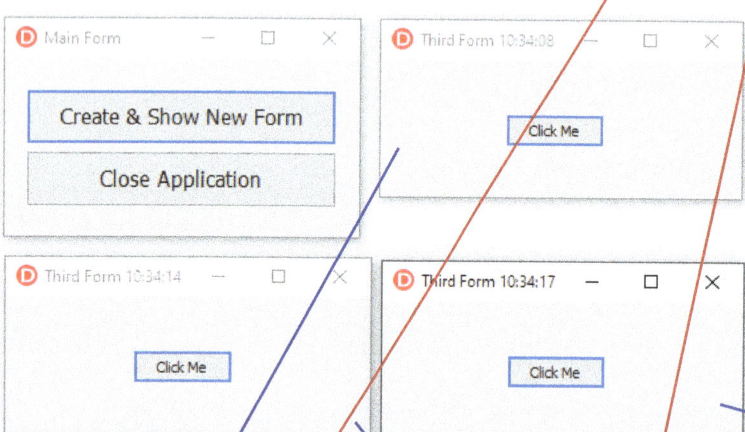

Fig. 29.31 Main Form and three instances of Third Form

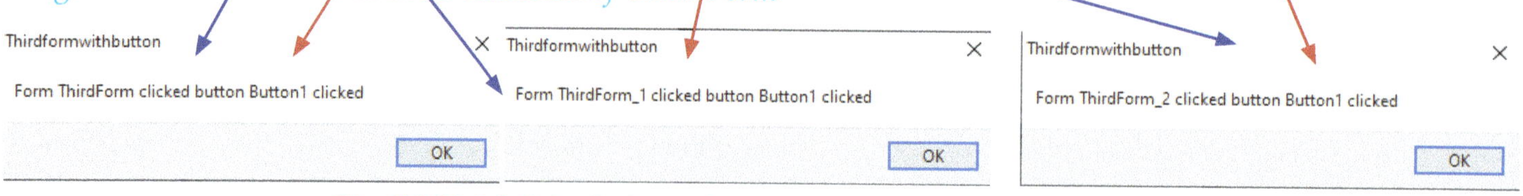

Fig. 29.32 Modal windows displayed by ShowMessage

Delphi creates three `Third Form` forms renaming the second and third forms `ThirdForm_1` and `ThirdForm_2`. This becomes clear when the `Click Me` button is clicked on each of the forms with caption `Third Form` - see *Figure 29.32*.

30 Streams

Note

To build a program press Ctrl F9.
To build a program Shift F9 (compile and link).
To run a program in Debug mode press F9.
F9 will also compile and link before running if the source code has been changed since the last time the program was run.

Information

..\..\ references the grandparent folder of the current folder. When Delphi compiles and builds an executable, it places the executable that is produced in a folder with name Debug which itself is inside a folder with the name of the Windows target e.g. Win32. The source file corresponding to this executable can therefore be reached from the Debug folder using the path ..\..\ on the current drive.

TStream

Purpose: Learning how to use descendents of TStream.

A stream is what its name suggests: a "river of data" that can be accessed sequentially from beginning to end. As such the `TStream` abstract class, and its descendent classes support reading and writing to several sequential access data structures, e.g. files.

The key concept behind this class is **sequential access**.

This means reading or writing a number of bytes one after another from a stream of bytes.

The current position in the stream is advanced by the number of bytes read or written. For most streams the position can be moved backwards but it is possible to have unidirectional streams, e.g streaming of bytes from a remote server. Unidirectional means you can't go back in the stream.

TFileStream

Purpose: Learning how to use TFileStream.

TFileStream defines a disk file stream referenced by filename.

Creating and using a stream can be as straightforward as creating a variable of the specific type and calling a method to load content from the file.

```
Program Chapter30Prog1;
{$APPTYPE CONSOLE}
Uses
  System.SysUtils, System.Classes;
Var
  Stream1 : TFileStream;
  StringList1 : TStringList;
  FileName : String;
Begin
  FileName := '..\..\Chapter30Prog1.dpr';
  Stream1 := TFileStream.Create(FileName, fmOpenRead);
  StringList1 := TStringList.Create;
  StringList1.LoadFromStream(Stream1);
  Writeln(StringList1.Text);
  Readln;
End.
```

P

Information

Make sure to set this filename with the correct path when you compile and run this program.

Information

Named constant:
fmOpenRead = 0

Program **Chapter30Prog1** shows how this can be done.

A `TFileStreamObject` is created first using `TFileStream.Create` with two parameters, the filename, stored in string variable `FileName`, of the file and the type of access, `fmOpenRead`, in this example the file is to be opened for reading:

`TStringList.Create` is used to create a `TStringList` object which is referenced by the `TStringList` variable `StringList1`.

The `TStringList` object is then populated with strings of `bytes` representing characters obtained sequentially from the file stream `Stream1`. These bytes are then written to the console window as text.

Fig. 30.1 shows what is displayed in the console window.

www.educational-computing.co.uk/DelphiBookCode/DelphiCode.html

```
Z:\ProductionChapters\DelphiBook\Code\Chapter30\Chapter30Prog1\Win32\Debug\Chapter30Prog1.exe
Program Chapter30Prog1;
{$APPTYPE CONSOLE}
Uses
  System.SysUtils, VCL.StdCtrls, System.Classes;
Var
  Stream1 : TFileStream;
  StringList1 : TStringList;
  FileName : String;
Begin
  FileName := '..\..\Chapter30Prog1.dpr';
  Stream1 := TFileStream.Create(FileName, fmOpenRead);
  StringList1 := TStringList.Create;
  StringList1.LoadFromStream(Stream1);
  Writeln(StringList1.Text);
  Readln;
End.
```

Fig. 30.1 Captured console window showing output produced by execution of program Chapter30Prog1.

Programming Task

1. Load **Chapter30Prog1** then build (Shift F9) and run in Debug mode (F9).
   Now replace `fmOpenRead` with 0. Rebuild and run again to check that it works as before.

The reason why running the amended **Chapter30Prog1** works as before is because `fmOpenRead` is a named constant with value `0`.

This and other useful named constants associated with the mode of file access are defined in units **System.SysUtils** and **System.Classes**. as shown in *Table 30.1*.

Named constant definition	Description	Defined in unit
`fmOpenRead = 0`	Open the file for reading only.	System.SysUtils
`fmOpenWrite = 1`	Open the file for writing only. Writing to the file completely replaces the current contents	System.SysUtils
`fmOpenReadWrite = 2`	Open the file to modify the current contents rather than replace them.	System.SysUtils
`fmCreate = $FF00`	Create a file with the given name. If a file with the given name exists, overwrite the existing file and open it in write mode (existing contents erased).	System.Classes

Table 30.1 Some file access mode named constants

Copying streams

Program Chapter30Prog2 uses two streams `Stream1` and `Stream2` to copy the contents of an existing file Chapter30Prog2.dpr to a new file Test.txt. If Test.txt does not exist it is created otherwise its existing contents are erased before being used as the destination file.

Information

Creates a new file or erases an existing file in the current folder, i.e. the folder containing the executable. Change DestinationFileName if you wish to create the new file or erase an existing file in a different folder.

P

```
Program Chapter30Prog2;
{$APPTYPE CONSOLE}
Uses
 System.SysUtils, System.Classes;
Var
  Stream1, Stream2 : TFileStream;
  SourceFileName, DestinationFileName : String;
Begin
  SourceFileName := '..\..\Chapter30Prog2.dpr';
  DestinationFileName := 'Test.txt';
  Stream1 := TFileStream.Create(SourceFileName, fmOpenRead);
  Try
    Stream2 := TFileStream.Create(DestinationFileName, fmOpenWrite Or fmCreate);
    Try
      Stream2.CopyFrom(Stream1, Stream1.Size);
    Finally
      Stream2.Free;
    End;
  Finally
    Stream1.Free;
  End;
  Writeln('Finished copying file - Press Return to exit program');
  Readln;
End.
```

www.educational-computing.co.uk/DelphiBookCode/DelphiCode.html

Programming Task

2. Load Chapter30Prog2 then build (Shift F9) and run in Debug mode (F9).
Now amend the SourceFileName to a different text file making sure that the path to the file is also included.
You could create a new text file using WordPad for this purpose.
Rebuild and run again to check that your amended program works as expected.

Text readers and writers

For writing to a stream, the `TStreamWriter` class uses a stream or creates one using filename, an append/create attribute, and, optionally, the character encoding passed as parameters.

If the append/create parameter is `False` then the file access mode creates the file if it does not exist, otherwise erasure of its existing contents occurs before new contents are written. The append mode adds new content to the end of the existing file or to a new empty file after creation.

The character encoding parameter can be any of the following shown in *Table 30.2* joined with `TEncoding`, e.g. `TEncoding.UTF8` - see *Table 30.2* for an explanantion of `UTF8`.

The class `TEncoding` defines a specific encoding for a character or a string. `TEncoding` was introduced in Delphi 2009. You must add the System.SysUtils unit to the `Uses` clause in order to be able to use TEncoding.

Character encoding	Description
ANSI	Data type AnsiChar which is a character set of byte-sized (8-bits) characters corresponding to the first 256 Unicode characters..
ASCII	Uses a 7 bit encoding system to represent 128 characters, encompassing the 26 letters of the alphabet, both lowercase and uppercase, the 10 numerical digits, common punctuation sysmbols, and a number of control characters.
BigEndianUnicode	Most modern filesystems operate on 8-bit bytes. Big endian and little endian decide on the byte order for a multibyte value when stored. In big endian, the most significant byte is stored in the smallest address. In little endian, the most significant byte is stored in the largest address.
Unicode	A character encoding capable of encoding all 1,112,064 valid code points of Unicode. The encoding is variable-length, as code points are encoded with one or two 16-bit code units.
UTF7	UTF-7 is a variable-length character encoding for representing Unicode text using a stream of ASCII characters.
UTF8	A variable width character encoding capable of encoding all 1,112,064 valid code points in Unicode using one to four 8-bit bytes.

Table 30.2 Character encoding parameter values

Program Chapter30Prog3 shows the use of `TStreamWriter` to create a text file, '`Test.txt`', consisting of three lines of text. It uses the default character encoding scheme.

```
Program Chapter30Prog3;
{$APPTYPE CONSOLE}
Uses
  System.Classes;
Var
  StreamWriter1 : TStreamWriter;
Begin
  StreamWriter1 := TStreamWriter.Create('Test.txt', False);
  Try
    StreamWriter1.WriteLine('First line');
    StreamWriter1.WriteLine('Second line');
    StreamWriter1.WriteLine('Third line');
  Finally
    StreamWriter1.Free;
  End;
  Writeln('Finished - Press Return to exit program');
  Readln;
End.
```

Information

Constructor TStreamWriter.Create(const Filename: string; Append: Boolean);

P

www.educational-computing.co.uk/DelphiBookCode/DelphiCode.html

Programming Task

3. Load Chapter30Prog3 then build (Shift F9) and run in Debug mode (F9).

   Now change `StreamWriter1 := TStreamWriter.Create('Test.txt', False);`

   to `StreamWriter1 := TStreamWriter.Create('Test.txt', True);`

   This opens file Test.txt in append mode.

   Rebuild and run again. Check the contents of file Test.txt. There should now be six lines of text if Test.txt already existed. The action of running the program appends three more lines of text to the existing three lines.

   Now delete Test.txt and run the program again. You should discover that Test.txt has been recreated and three lines of text have been written to it.

Program Chapter30Prog3a shows the use of `TStreamWriter` to create a text file, 'Test.txt', consisting of three lines of text. It uses the character encoding scheme UTF-8.

Information

Constructor TStreamWriter.Create(const Filename: string; Append: Boolean; Encoding : TEncoding) : Overload;

P

```
Program Chapter30Prog3a;
{$APPTYPE CONSOLE}
Uses
  System.Classes, System.SysUtils;
Var
  StreamWriter1 : TStreamWriter;
Begin
  StreamWriter1 := TStreamWriter.Create('Test.txt', False, TEncoding.UTF8);
  Try
    StreamWriter1.WriteLine('First line');
    StreamWriter1.WriteLine('Second line');
    StreamWriter1.WriteLine('Third line');
  Finally
    StreamWriter1.Free;
  End;
  Writeln('Finished - Press Return to exit program');
  Readln;
End.
```

Constructor Create creates and initializes a TStreamWriter instance.

Don't append.

Writes three lines of text to 'Test.txt'.

Releases the instance of TStreamWriter.

www.educational-computing.co.uk/DelphiBookCode/DelphiCode.html

Program Chapter30Prog4 shows the use of `TStreamReader` to read a text file, 'Test.txt', consisting of three lines of text. Use 'Test.txt' from Chapter30Prog3a. Copy to the Debug folder of Chapter30Prog4 or provide the path to where it exists. `TStreamReader.Create('Test.txt')` uses a default buffer size of 4096 bytes and default encoding `UTF8`.

Information

Constructor Create(const Filename: string); overload;

```
Program Chapter30Prog4;
{$APPTYPE CONSOLE}
Uses
  System.Classes;
Var
  StreamReader1 : TStreamReader;
Begin
  StreamReader1 := TStreamReader.Create('Test.txt');
  Try
    While Not StreamReader1.EndOfStream
      Do Writeln(StreamReader1.ReadLine);
  Finally
    StreamReader1.Free;
  End;
  Writeln('Finished - Press Return to exit program');
  Readln;
End.
```

P

Constructor Create creates and initializes a TStreamReader instance.

Reads and then writes each line of text from 'Test.txt' until the end of this file is reached.

Releases the instance of TStreamReader.

www.educational-computing.co.uk/DelphiBookCode/DelphiCode.html

Programming Task

4 Load Chapter30Prog4 then build (Shift F9) and run in Debug mode (F9).
Now change `StreamReader1 := TStreamReader.Create('Test.txt');`
to `StreamReader1 := TStreamReader.Create('Test.txt', TEncoding.Unicode);`
Rebuild and run again. The output should now be garbage text. This is because `StreamReader1` is using the wrong encoding to read from the file Test.txt. Repeat with encodings ASCII and UTF7.

Program Chapter30Prog5 downloads pdf file 'AQA-75161-QP-JUN16.PDF' from AQA's website to folder 'C:\Users\drbond\Downloads\' using a TMemoryStream stream.

TMemoryStream is a class for a stream that stores its data in a dynamic memory buffer.

TMemoryStream provides the general I/O capabilities of a stream object while introducing methods and properties to manage a dynamic memory buffer.

Memory streams are useful as intermediary objects that can hold information as well as supporting the capability of reading this information from or writing it to another storage medium. They provide a useful format for comparing the contents of streams, or for manipulating data that is stored in a less accessible medium, e.g. a remote website.

Chapter30Prog5 connects to a filestore on AQA's website where past examination papers are stored:

'https://filestore.aqa.org.uk/sample-papers-and-mark-schemes/2016/june/'

It then fetches a particular file

'AQA-75161-QP-JUN16.PDF'

and copies the contents of this file to the buffer supplied by MemoryStream1.

The buffer contents are then saved by streaming them to a file 'AQA-75161-QP-JUN16.PDF' stored in folder

'C:\Users\drbond\Downloads\'

using MemoryStream1.SaveToFile(LocalPath + 'AQA-75161-QP-JUN16.PDF');

P

www.educational-computing.co.uk/DelphiBookCode/DelphiCode.html

```
Program Chapter30Prog5;
{$APPTYPE CONSOLE}
Uses
  System.SysUtils, System.Classes, idHTTP, System.Net.HttpClient;
Var
  MemoryStream1 : TMemoryStream;
  HTTP1 : THTTPClient; // Delphi 10.2 and later otherwise use TidHTTP with ssl library
  LocalPath : String = 'C:\Users\drbond\Downloads\';
  RemotePath : String = 'https://filestore.aqa.org.uk/sample-papers-and-mark-schemes/2016/june/';
Begin
  Try
    MemoryStream1 := TMemoryStream.Create;    Constructor Create creates and initializes
                                              a TMemoryStream instance.
    Try
      Try
        HTTP1 := THTTPClient.Create;//(Nil) required for TidHTTP;   Constructor Create
                                                                    creates and initializes
                                                                    a THTTPClient instance.
        HTTP1.Get(RemotePath + 'AQA-75161-QP-JUN16.PDF', MemoryStream1); Download file to buffer
        MemoryStream1.SaveToFile(LocalPath + 'AQA-75161-QP-JUN16.PDF');
      Except
        On E: Exception Do Writeln(E.ClassName, ': ', E.Message);
      End;
    Finally
      HTTP1.Free;    Releases THTTPClient instance.
    End;
  Finally
    MemoryStream1.Free; Releases TMemoryStream instance.
  End;
  Writeln('Finished downloading - Press Return key to exit.');
  Readln;
End.
```

Programming Task

5 *Table 30.3* shows URLS for some examination past papers and their mark schemes for the Examining Board AQA. Specification 7517 is A-level Computer Science.

Adapt **Chapter30Prog5** so that a user can choose the series (month + year), paper number (e.g. Paper 1) and whether question paper or mark scheme. Assume that the specification is always 7517 and the Examining Board is always AQA. The user should then be able to request that the adapted program construct the corresponding URL and then download the resource, if it exists, to a specified download folder. It should report if the resource does not exist.

Qualification, Specification, Series	URL
AQA Paper 1(A-level) Question Paper Specification 7517 June 2018	`https://filestore.aqa.org.uk/sample-papers-and-mark-schemes/2018/june/AQA-75171-QP-JUN18.PDF`
AQA Paper 1(A-level) Mark Scheme Specification 7517 June 2018	`https://filestore.aqa.org.uk/sample-papers-and-mark-schemes/2018/june/AQA-75171-W-MS-JUN18.PDF`
AQA Paper 1(A-level) Question Paper Specification 7517 June 2017	`https://filestore.aqa.org.uk/sample-papers-and-mark-schemes/2017/june/AQA-75171-QP-JUN17.PDF`
AQA Paper 1(A-level) Mark Scheme Specification 7517 June 2017	`https://filestore.aqa.org.uk/sample-papers-and-mark-schemes/2017/june/AQA-75161-W-MS-JUN17.PDF`
AQA Paper 2(A-level) Question Paper Specification 7517 June 2018	`https://filestore.aqa.org.uk/sample-papers-and-mark-schemes/2018/june/AQA-75172-QP-JUN18.PDF`
AQA Paper 1(A-level) Mark Scheme Specification 7517 June 2018	`https://filestore.aqa.org.uk/sample-papers-and-mark-schemes/2018/june/AQA-75172-W-MS-JUN18.PDF`

Table 30.3 URLs for past papers and their mark schemes

31 Applications

Noughts and crosses

The popular game of noughts and crosses consists of a game board of nine squares shown labelled 1 to 9 in *Figure 31.1*, on which two players, one *nought* and the other *cross*, take it in turns to place an O or an X symbol until three of O or X, occur in a row, column or diagonal or until all squares are occupied.

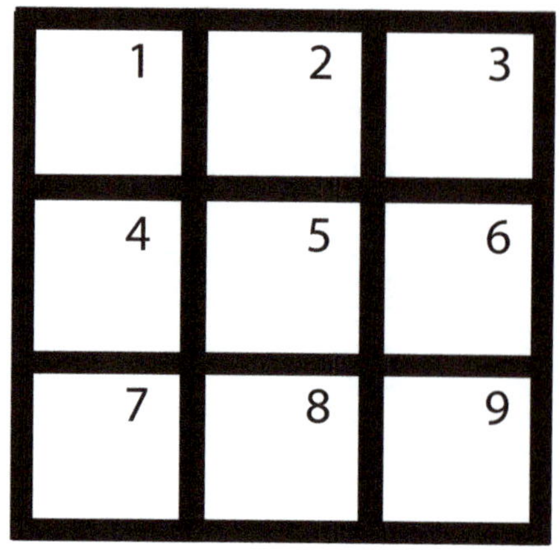

Fig. 31.1 Game board for noughts and crosses

For an application to succeed in replicating the game of noughts and crosses, it must find a way of representing a square on which to display a cross or a nought. A convenient way of doing this is to use a **TLabel** component in a Vcl application. The first step is therefore to define class **TSquare** to be a subclass of **TLabel** as shown in *Table 31.1*.

```
TSquare = Class (TLabel)
            Public
              Constructor Create(TopPos, LeftPos : Integer);
              Procedure Click;Override;
              Procedure ClearSquare;
              Function FindWhatRowNo : Integer;
              Function FindWhatColumnNo : Integer;
              Function FindWhatState : SquareStateType;
            Private
              State : SquareStateType;
              ColumnNo : Integer;
              RowNo : Integer;
          End;
```

Table 31.1 Class definition for TSquare

Resource

Download from www.educational-computing.com/DelphiBook/delphicode.html Chapter 31.

We define **TSquare**'s constructor as shown in *Table 31.2*. The variable `Square` is used to reference the created square object. The constructor `TSquare.Create` makes the owner of the object referenced by `Square`, `OandXsForm`, the form on which a green square is painted at runtime. The owner of an object is responsible for destroying it when the application terminates. It is the statement "`Square.Parent := OandXsForm;`" which causes a green square to display on form, `OandXsForm`, as shown in *Figure 31.2*.

```
Constructor TSquare.Create(TopPos, LeftPos : Integer);
  Var
    Square : TSquare;
  Begin
    Square := Inherited Create(OandXsForm);
    Square.Font.Size := 50;
    Square.Autosize := False;
    Square.Alignment := taCenter;
    Square.Caption := '';
    Square.Top := TopPos;
    Square.Width := 100;
    Square.Left := LeftPos;
    Square.Height := 100;
    Square.Transparent := False;
    Square.Color := clGreen;
    Square.State := Empty;
    Square.Parent := OandXsForm;
  End;
```

Table 31.2 Constructor that creates a square on the screen

Fig. 31.2 Result of creating a TSquare object

There are two aspects to the noughts and crosses application which need to be considered:

1. The presentation of the noughts and crosses game board on the screen
2. The internal recording of which squares of the game board are empty or occupied and, if occupied, with what.

We can use a two-dimensional array for the internal representation of the game board.
Its data type is as follows

```
GridArrayType = Array[1..3, 1..3] Of TSquare;
```

We can create nine objects of type `TSquare` in memory at runtime using the constructor `TBoard.Create` shown in *Table 31.3*. This in turn will result in nine green squares appearing on the screen at runtime as shown in *Figure 31.3*.

The constructor `TBoard.Create` creates a `TBoard` object and populates the two-dimensional array `GridArray` with a reference to each square object.

```
Constructor TBoard.Create;
  Var
    Row, Column : Integer;
Begin
  For Row := 1 To 3
    Do
      For Column := 1 To 3
        Do
          Begin
            GridArray[Row, Column] := TSquare.Create(70 + (Row -1)*100 +(Row-1)*10,
                                                     190 +(Column -1)*100 + (Column-1)*10);
            GridArray[Row, Column].ColumnNo := Column;
            GridArray[Row, Column].RowNo := Row;
          End;
End;
```

P

Table 31.3 Constructor that creates the game board on the screen

We need one more object to complete the application, a game object. The application thus consists of a game object which uses a `TBoard` object which itself is composed of nine `TSquare` objects, each of which inherits from **TLabel**, a control component from the **StdCtrls** library.

Table 31.4 shows the definition of a `TGame` class.

```
TGame = Class(TObject)
          Public
            Constructor Create;
            Procedure InitialiseCurrentSymbol(InitialSymbol : SymbolType);
            Function GetCurrentSymbol : SymbolType;
            Function GetNoOfMovesPlayed : Integer;
            Procedure IncrementNoOfMoves;
            Procedure SetCurrentSymbol;
            Procedure DisplayNoOfMoves;
            Procedure DisplayMoveRowNo(x : Integer);
            Procedure DisplayMoveColumnNo(x : Integer);
          Private
            NameOfPlayer1 : String[25];
            NameOfPlayer2 : String[25];
            Player1Symbol : SymbolType;
            Player2Symbol : SymbolType;
            NoOfMoves : Integer;
            CurrentSymbol : SymbolType;
        End;
```

P

Table 31.4 TGame class definition

Now that we have all the class definitions that we need for the application, their relationship with each other can be summarised in a class diagram *Figure 31.4*.

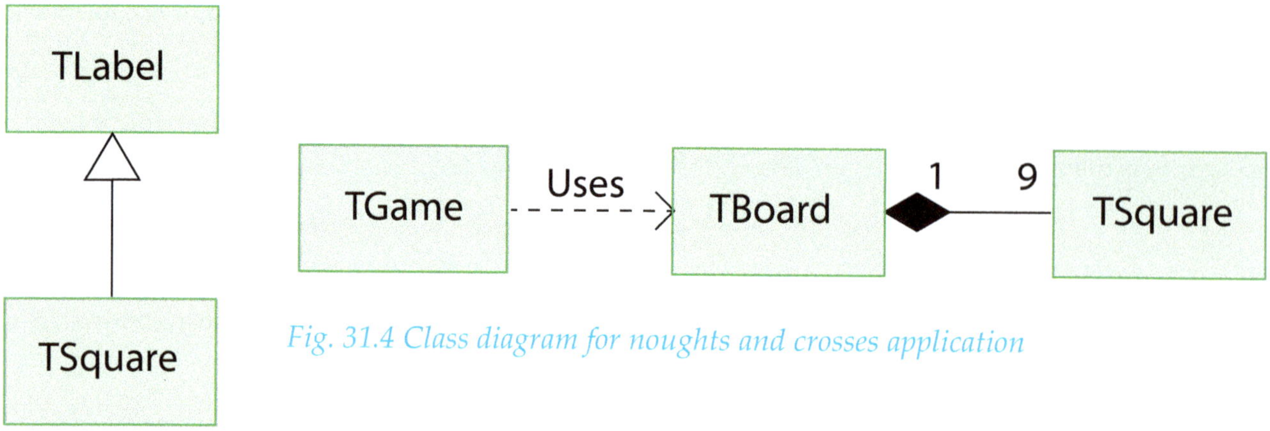

Fig. 31.4 Class diagram for noughts and crosses application

To construct a game, we use `TGame`'s constructor `Create` to create a game object as shown in *Table 31.5*.

The application uses some user-defined simple data types to aid readability of the program. These are shown in *Table 31.6*.

```
Type
  SymbolType = (Nought, Cross);
  BoardStateType = (BoardNoWin, BoardNoughtWin, BoardCrossWin);
  SquareStateType = (Empty, SquareCross, SquareNought);
```

Table 31.6 User-defined simple data types

```
Constructor TGame.Create;
  Begin
    NoOfMoves := 0;
    CurrentSymbol := Cross;
    NameOfPlayer1 := 'Sinbad';
    NameOfPlayer2 := 'Montie';
    Player1Symbol := Cross;
    Player2Symbol := Nought;
  End;
```

Table 31.5 TGame's constructor Create

The board is created and game are started on the event `FormCreate`. *Table 31.7* shows the code for this event handler.

```
Procedure TOandXsForm.FormCreate(Sender: TObject);
    Begin
      Board := TBoard.Create;
      Game := TGame.Create;
      Game.InitialiseCurrentSymbol(Cross);
      WhoGoesFirst := Game.CurrentSymbol;
    End;
```

Table 31.7 FormCreate event handler

Figure 31.4 shows the **Events** page of the Object Inspector for the form `OandXsForm`. The field opposite **OnCreate** was double clicked to create the skeleton source code for **FormCreate**.

Figure 31.5 shows the Noughts and Crosses application in execution before any moves have been made.

Figure 31.6 shows the Noughts and Crosses application in execution after three moves have been made.

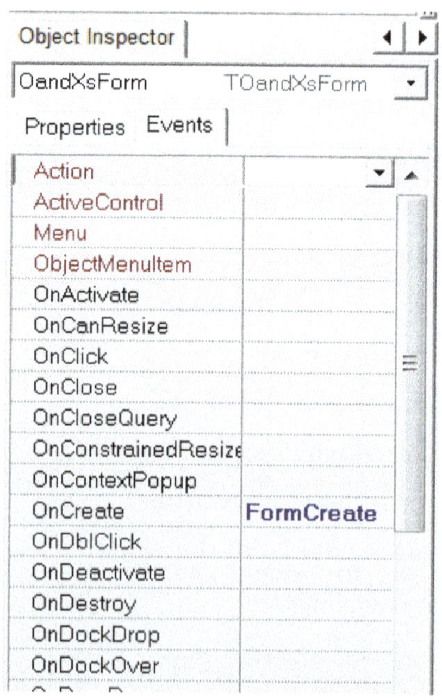

Fig. 31.4 Object inspector showing the OnCreate event FormCreate

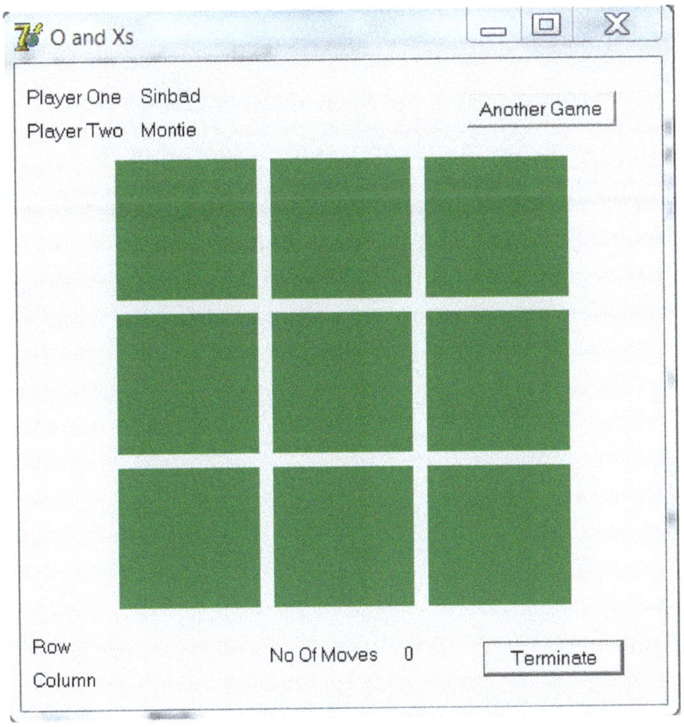

Fig. 31.5 Noughts and Crosses application in execution before any moves made

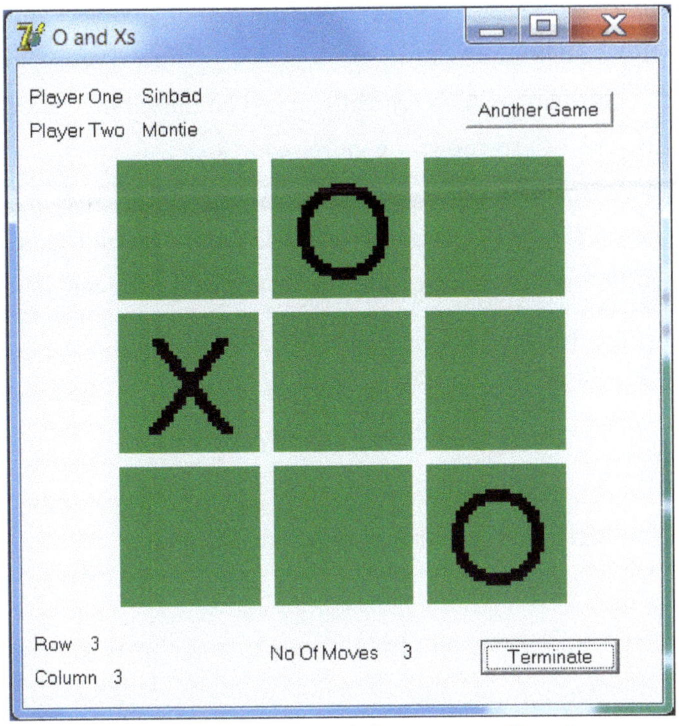

Fig. 31.6 Noughts and Crosses application in execution after three moves

The application uses ten **TLabel** components to provide and label the following information as the game is played

1. Two labels whose captions are the name of player one (`lblPlayerOneName`) and the name of player two (`lblPlayerTwoName`), respectively
2. Two labels whose captions are 'Player One' and 'Player Two' respectively - `lblPlayerOne` and `lblPlayerTwo`
3. Label whose caption is the actual number of moves made - `lblNumber`
4. Label whose caption is 'No Of Moves' - `lblNoOfMoves`
5. Two labels whose captions are 'Row' and 'Column', respectively - `lblRowN, lblColumn`
6. Two labels whose captions are the actual row number and the actual column number of the square for the current move, `lblRowNo` and `lblColumnNo`, respectively.

The application uses two **TButton** components, `btnTerminate` and `btnAnotherGame`.

Each is associated with an **OnClick** event handler, `TOandXsForm.btnTerminateClick(Sender: TObject)` and `TOandXsForm.btnAnotherGameClick(Sender: TObject)`, respectively. Double clicking each button generates the corresponding skeleton source code for the **OnClick** event handler.

The event handler for `btnTerminate` is shown in *Table 31.8*.

```
Procedure TOandXsForm.btnTerminateClick(Sender: TObject);
    Begin
     Application.Terminate;
    End;
```

P

Table 31.8 OnClick event handler for btnTerminate button

`Procedure TSquare.Click` is a method of an object and therefore can be executed on a `TSquare` object. Class `TSquare`'s definition shown in *Table 31.1* defines a procedure `Click` which overrides the event handler procedure `Click` procedure which normally would be called when a `TSquare` object is clicked, i.e. when an **OnClick** event occurs. *Table 31.9* shows the source code for `TSquare.Click`. The first action this event handler does must be to call the overridden `Click` procedure. The rest of the code now handles the actions which must be executed to update the game. The `Self` parameter which identifies which square object has been clicked is passed behind the scenes to `TSquare.Click` so that it can act on the clicked square object.

The procedure `TSquare.Click` does the following

1. Obtains the current symbol, O or X, to play next
2. Checks that the clicked square is empty
3. If empty writes an O or an X in the square
4. Increments number of moves made so far
5. Displays this number
6. Displays row number and column number of the clicked square
7. Tests for outcome: a win, no win and at least one unoccupied sqaure remaining, a draw
8. Reports outcome if a win or a draw
9. Toggles current symbol.

P

```
Procedure TSquare.Click;
  Var
    CurrentSymbol : SymbolType;
    Outcome : BoardStateType;
  Begin
    inherited Click;
    CurrentSymbol := Game.GetCurrentSymbol;
    If Self.FindWhatState = Empty
      Then
        Begin
          If CurrentSymbol = Cross
            Then Self.Caption := 'X'
            Else Self.Caption := 'O';
          If CurrentSymbol = Cross
            Then Self.State := SquareCross
            Else Self.State := SquareNought;
          Game.IncrementNoOfMoves;
          Game.DisplayNoOfMoves;
          Game.DisplayMoveRowNo(FindWhatRowNo);
          Game.DisplayMoveColumnNo(FindWhatColumnNo);
          OutCome := Board.TestStateOfBoard;
          If (OutCome = BoardNoughtWin)
            Then ShowMessage('Nought wins!');
          If (OutCome = BoardCrossWin)
            Then ShowMessage('Cross wins!');
          If (Not (OutCome = BoardNoughtWin) And Not (OutCome = BoardCrossWin))
            And (Game.NoOfMoves = 9)
            Then ShowMessage('Draw');
          Game.SetCurrentSymbol;
        End;
  End;
```

Table 31.9 OnClick event handler for an object of class TSquare

The state of the board and therefore the game is tested with function `TestStateOfBoard` as shown in *Table 31.10*. This requires that the three rows, three columns and two diagonals are checked for alignment of the same symbol, either O or X.

Once an outcome for a row or column is `BoardCrossWin` or `BoardNoughtWin` there is no point remaining within the function so `Exit` is called to leave at this point.

```
Function TBoard.TestStateOfBoard : BoardStateType;
  Var
    i, j : Integer;
  Begin
    TestStateOfBoard := BoardNoWin;
    For i := 1 To 3
      Do
        Begin
          If (GridArray[i, 1].State = GridArray[i, 2].State)
            And (GridArray[i, 2].State = GridArray[i, 3].State)
              And (GridArray[i, 1].State <> Empty)
            Then
              If GridArray[i, 1].State = SquareCross
                Then
                  Begin
                    Result := BoardCrossWin;
                    Exit;
                  End
                Else
                  Begin
                    Result := BoardNoughtWin;
                    Exit;
                  End;
        End;
    For j := 1 To 3
      Do
        Begin
          If (GridArray[1, j].State = GridArray[2, j].State)
              And (GridArray[2, j].State = GridArray[3, j].State)
              And (GridArray[1, j].State <> Empty)
            Then
              If GridArray[j, 1].State = SquareCross
                Then
                  Begin
                    Result := BoardCrossWin;
                    Break;
                  End
                Else
                  Begin
                    Result := BoardNoughtWin;
                    Break;
                  End;
        End;
    If (GridArray[1, 1].State = GridArray[2, 2].State)
          And (GridArray[2, 2].State = GridArray[3, 3].State)
            And (GridArray[1, 1].State <> Empty)
      Then
        If GridArray[1, 1].State = SquareCross
          Then Result := BoardCrossWin
          Else Result := BoardNoughtWin;
    If (GridArray[1, 3].State = GridArray[2, 2].State)
          And (GridArray[2, 2].State = GridArray[3, 1].State)
            And (GridArray[1, 3].State <> Empty)
      Then
        If GridArray[1, 3].State = SquareCross
          Then Result := BoardCrossWin
          Else Result := BoardNoughtWin;
  End;
```

Table 31.10 TestStateOfBoard procedure

Programming Tasks

1. Modify the NoughtsandCrosses application so that it prompts the two players for their names and then initialises the game with these names.
2. Modify the NoughtsandCrosses application so that it prompts the players to choose the start symbol, O or X for the first game. Update the display to show what symbol each player will be using and who will go first.
   The NoughtsandCrosses application has been written to alternate the start symbol on subsequent games after the first game. Leave this behaviour unchanged but report who will start each subsequent game.

32 Network programming

Client-Server model

Purpose: To learn how to create client-server applications

What is it?

When you order a pizza from a pizza delivery service, called Pizza House, you are accessing the service offered by Pizza House, the **server**, as one **client** amongst many. Your REQUEST is processed by Pizza House which generates a RESPONSE by creating the pizza you ordered before arranging for it to be delivered to you. This is an example of a **client-server model**. In this model, we expect a server to be available continuously, i.e. Pizza House will continue to service orders from clients 24 hours a day, seven days a week – *Figure 32.1*.

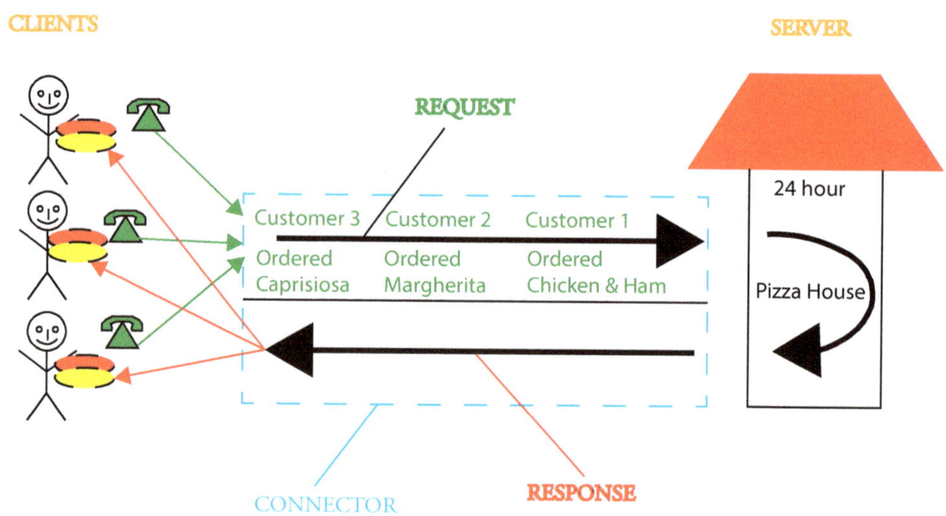

Fig. 32.1 The client server model for Pizza House service

There is a protocol that client and server use in this scenario that is common to many similar scenarios in which a customer (client) orders something over the telephone or online from a supplier (server):

1. there is a menu to choose from that defines the identifier for the resource, e.g. Margherita;
2. a request which begins "I would like to order..." and ends with "for delivery to 42 Acacia Avenue, Dingley Dell, NeverNeverLand";
3. the server issues a response to the request addressing it to the client.

The protocol is the "glue" or connector that enables the client-server interaction to perform as expected.

The client-server model is the most commonly employed of the architectural styles for when one application interacts with another. A server is one application, a client is another. A server application listens for requests, from client applications, for services which it offers and the client applications consume these services.

A client application, needing a service to be performed, sends a request to the server application via a standard interface protocol e.g. Telnet.

The server application either rejects or performs the request and sends a response back to the client application (possibly invoking a callback function in the client application).

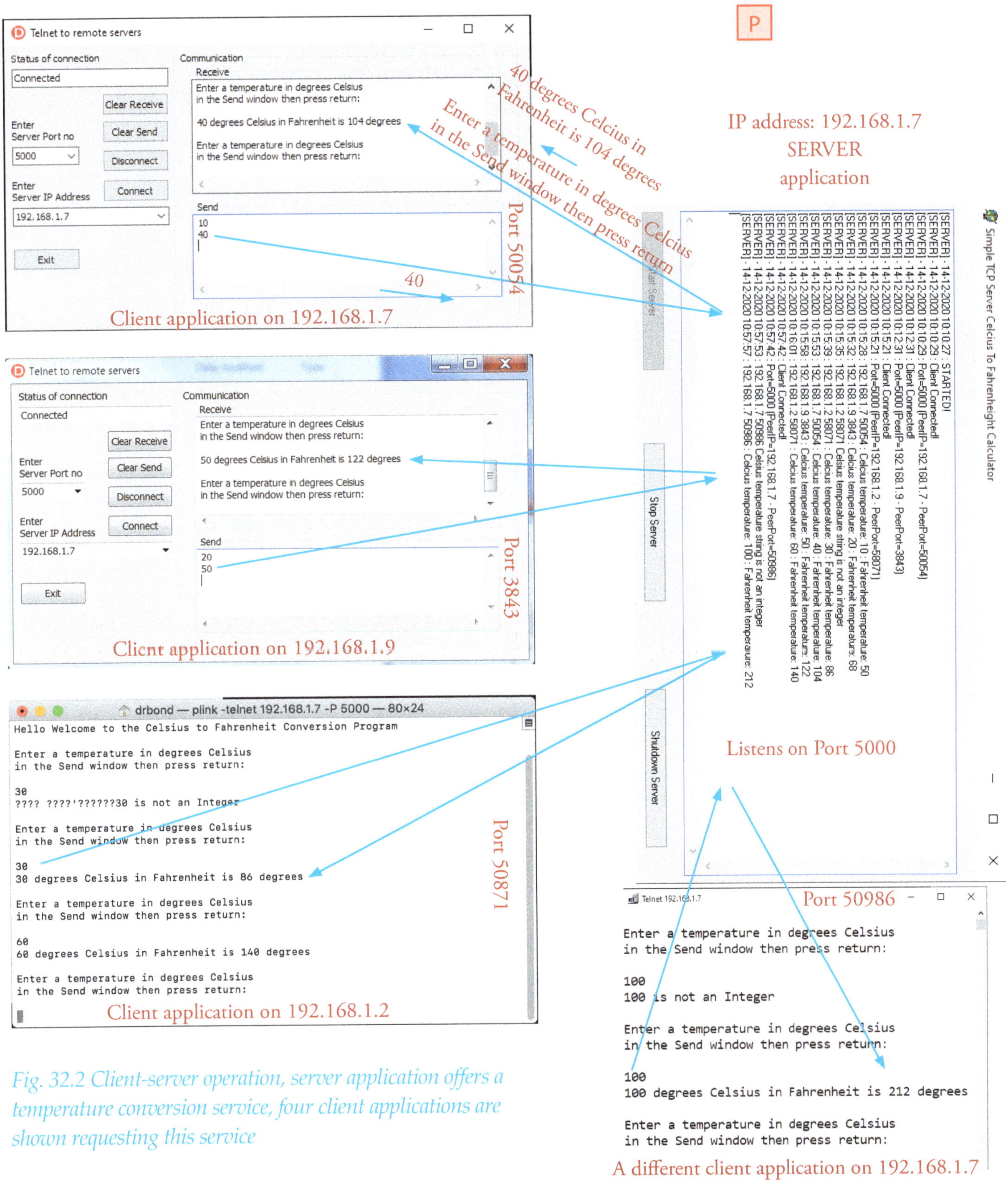

Fig. 32.2 Client-server operation, server application offers a temperature conversion service, four client applications are shown requesting this service

A server application, on the other hand, waits for requests to be made and then reacts to them. A server application is usually a non-terminating process (i.e. on or running all the time). It is usually designed to provide a service to more than one client application.

The server application shown running in *Figure 32.2* uses a **TidTCPServer** component from the **Indy Servers** palette to perform a temperature conversion service, e.g. 100°C → 212°F, when it receives a client application request for this service (server port 5000). Included in the request is the temperature to be converted, the IP address of the client application, e.g. 192.168.1.2, and the port number on the client, e.g. 50871, that is connected to the requesting client application. The response of the TCP server application is to return the temperature in Fahrenheit to the requesting client application, using as return address the client application's IP address and port number. The client application connects to the server application for this service by establishing a TCP connection with the server. In this example, the connection then relies on the Telnet application protocol (a less secure alternative to SSH) to send and receive data - the Delphi clients use a **TIdTelnet** component from the **Indy Clients** palette.

Background

Callback:

A callback function is typically a Javascript function. A reference to the callback function is passed to the server along with the request. The server invokes this function on the client whenever a response to the request is ready at the server.

Figure 32.2 illustrates a very important principle: **Separation of Concerns**. The client application is developed quite separately from the server application. The client application focuses on the user interface design and the server application focuses on the design for the processing and formatting of data. Both designs can be changed without regard to each other whilst preserving a uniform interface between the two, e.g. the Telnet protocol.

Table 32.1a shows the code for starting the TCP server. *Table 32.1b* shows the TCP server code for handling connection requests and data - `TForm1.IdTCPServer1Connect(AContext: TIdContext)` and `TForm1.IdTCPServer1Execute(AContext: TIdContext)` respectively.

www.educational-computing.com/DelphiBook/Code/Chapter32/Delphi10.4/TemperatureConverterTCPServer.zip

```
Unit TemperatureConverterTCPServerUnit;
Interface
Uses
  Windows, Messages, SysUtils, Variants, Classes, Graphics, Controls, Forms,
  Dialogs, IdBaseComponent, IdComponent, IdTCPServer, IdContext,
  IdCustomTCPServer, Vcl.StdCtrls;
Type
  TForm1 = Class(TForm)
             IdTCPServer1: TIdTCPServer;
             mmMessagesWindow: TMemo;
             btnShutdownServer: TButton;
             btnStopServer: TButton;
             btnStartServer: TButton;
             Function GetCurrentDateAndTime : String;
             Procedure WriteToScreenLog(MessageSender : String; MessageContent : String);
             Procedure IdTCPServer1Connect(AContext: TIdContext);
             Procedure IdTCPServer1Execute(AContext: TIdContext);
             Procedure FormShow(Sender: TObject);
             Procedure IdTCPServer1Disconnect(AContext: TIdContext);
             Procedure FormClose(Sender: TObject; var Action: TCloseAction);
             Procedure BroadcastMessageToAllClients(MessageToBroadcast : String);
             Procedure btnShutdownServerClick(Sender: TObject);
             Procedure btnStartServerClick(Sender: TObject);
             Procedure btnStopServerClick(Sender: TObject);
           End;
Const
  cnstListeningtPort = 5000;
Var
  Form1: TForm1;
  Pipe : TextFile;
Implementation
{$R *.dfm}
.....
 Procedure TForm1.btnStartServerClick(Sender: TObject);
   Begin
     IdTCPServer1.Bindings.Clear;
     IdTCPServer1.Bindings.Add.Port := cnstListeningtPort;
     IdTCPServer1.Active := True;
     btnStartServer.Enabled := False;
     btnStopServer.Enabled := True;
     WriteToScreenLog('SERVER', 'STARTED!');
   End;
.....
```

Table 32.1a A section of TemperatureConverterTCPServerUnit.pas showing the binding of the listening port to the TCP server

```
.....
 Procedure TForm1.IdTCPServer1Connect(AContext: TIdContext);
   Var
     ServerIP : String;
     ServerPort : Integer;
     PeerIP : String;
     PeerPort : Integer;
   Begin
     // Get IP address and port of connecting client
     ServerIP := AContext.Binding.IP;
     ServerPort := AContext.Binding.Port;
     PeerIP := AContext.Binding.PeerIP;
     PeerPort := AContext.Binding.PeerPort;
     WriteToScreenLog('SERVER', 'Client Connected!');
     WriteToScreenLog('SERVER', 'Port=' + IntToStr(ServerPort)
                      + ' '   + '(PeerIP=' + PeerIP
                      + ' - ' + 'PeerPort=' + IntToStr(PeerPort) + ')'
                    );
     With AContext.Connection.IOHandler
       Do
         Begin
           Try
             Writeln('Hello Welcome to the Celsius to Fahrenheit Conversion Program');
           Except
             On E: Exception Do ShowMessage(E.ClassName + 'An error has occurred: ' + E.Message );
           End;
         End;
   End;

 Procedure TForm1.IdTCPServer1Execute(AContext: TIdContext);
   Var
     CelsiusTempString, FahrenheitTempString : String;
     CelsiusTempInteger, FahrenheitTempInteger : Integer;
   Begin
     Try
       AssignFile(Pipe, GetCurrentDir + '\Log.Txt');
       Append(Pipe);
       Writeln(Pipe, '[Peer connected on] : ', GetCurrentDateAndTime, 'Peer IP: ',
                     ' ', 'Peer port: ', AContext.Binding.PeerPort);
       CloseFile(Pipe);
     Except
       On E : Exception Do ShowMessage(E.ClassName + ' error: ' + E.Message);
     End;
       With AContext.Connection.IOHandler
         Do
           Begin
             Writeln;
             Writeln('Enter a temperature in degrees Celsius');
             Writeln('in the Send window then press return:');
             Writeln;
             CelsiusTempString := Readln;
             Try
               CelsiusTempInteger := StrToInt(CelsiusTempString);
               FahrenheitTempInteger := Round(32 + (9 * CelsiusTempInteger)/5);
               FahrenheitTempString :=  IntToStr(FahrenheitTempInteger);
               Writeln(CelsiusTempString + ' degrees Celsius in Fahrenheit is ' + FahrenheitTempString
                                         + ' degrees');
               WriteToScreenLog('SERVER', AContext.Binding.PeerIP + ' '
                                 + IntToSTr(AContext.Binding.PeerPort)
                                 + ' : ' + 'Celcius temperature: ' + CelsiusTempString
                                 + FahrenheitTempString);
             Except
               Writeln(CelsiusTempString + ' is not an Integer');
               WriteToScreenLog('SERVER', AContext.Binding.PeerIP + ' '
                                 + IntToStr(AContext.Binding.PeerPort) + ' '
                                 + 'Celsius temperature string is not an integer');
             End;
           End;
   End;
.....
```

Table 32.1b A section of TemperatureConverterTCPServerUnit.pas showing the event handlers OnConnect and OnExecute

TCP is a connection-oriented protocol. Before a client and server can send or receive data to/from each other, a **TCP** connection must be established between them - *Table 32.2a* - using `IdTelnet1.Connect`. The client needs to know which host and which port on this host to connect to before it attempts a connection request. The host in question is the computer which "hosts" the **TCP** server and the required port is the one that the **TCP** server has been set up to listen on - port 5000. The **Host** and **Port** properties of the **TIdTelnet** object are assigned the IP address of the **TCP** server's host and listening port no as follows

```
IdTelnet1.Host := cbIPAddress.Text;
IdTelnet1.Port := StrToInt(cbPortNo.Text);
```

Figure 32.3 shows the telnet client user interface which is used to select these values.

A client connection request to the TCP server triggers an **On Connect** event at the server which in turn fires up the event handler `TForm1.IdTCPServer1Connect(AContext: TIdContext)`. Of course, the server must have been started first - *Figure 32.2* and *Table 32.1a* - and a listening port bound to the server, port 5000. `AContext` references the two endpoints of the connection, i.e. the server socket and the client socket (socket = IP address + Port no [+ protocol]). The protocol is TCP.

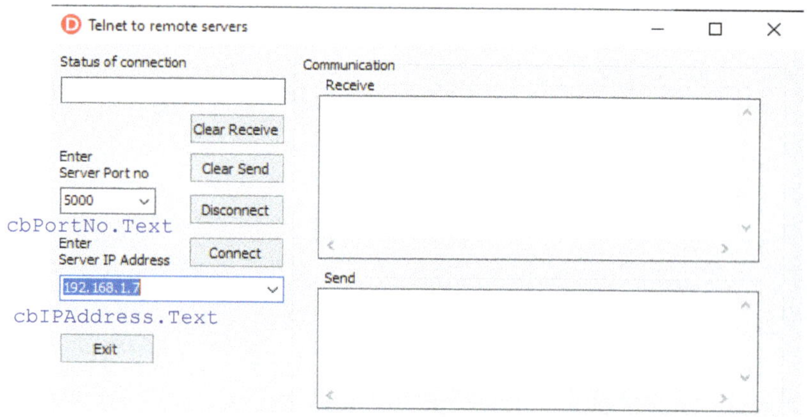

Figure 32.3 Telnet to remote servers client

```
Unit TelnetToRemoteServersSimplifiedUnit;
Interface
Uses
  Winapi.Windows, Winapi.Messages, System.SysUtils, System.Variants, System.Classes, Vcl.Graphics,
  Vcl.Controls, Vcl.Forms, Vcl.Dialogs, Vcl.StdCtrls, IdBaseComponent,
  IdComponent, IdTCPConnection, IdTCPClient, IdTelnet, IdGlobal;
Type
  TForm1 = Class(TForm)
             gbCommunication : TGroupBox;
             gbReceive : TGroupBox;
             gbSend : TGroupBox;
             mbReceiveMemo : TMemo;
             mbSendMemo : TMemo;
             btnClearReceive : TButton;
             btnDisconnect : TButton;
             btnConnect : TButton;
             btnClearSend : TButton;
             btnExit : TButton;
             edtConnectionIndicator : TEdit;
             lblPort : TLabel;
             lblIPAddress : TLabel;
             IdTelnet1 : TIdTelnet;
             cbIPAddress : TComboBox;
             lblStatusOfConnection : TLabel;
             cbPortNo : TComboBox;
             Procedure btnConnectClick(Sender: TObject);
             Procedure btnDisconnectClick(Sender: TObject);
             Procedure btnExitClick(Sender: TObject);
             Procedure IdTelnet1DataAvailable(Sender: TIdTelnet; const Buffer: TIdBytes);
             Procedure FormKeyPress(Sender: TObject; var Key: Char);
             Procedure btnClearSendClick(Sender: TObject);
             Procedure btnClearReceiveClick(Sender: TObject);
             Procedure IdTelnet1Disconnected(Sender: TObject);
             Procedure btnSendClick(Sender: TObject);
           End;
Var
  Form1: TForm1;
Implementation
{$R *.dfm}

  Procedure TForm1.btnSendClick(Sender: TObject);
    Begin
      IDTelnet1.IOHandler.Writeln(mbSendMemo.Lines.Strings[mbSendMemo.Lines.Count - 1]);
    End;
.....
  Procedure TForm1.btnClearSendClick(Sender: TObject);
    Begin
      mbSendMemo.Clear;
    End;
  Procedure TForm1.btnConnectClick(Sender: TObject);
    Begin
      If cbPortNo.Text = ''
        Then cbPortNo.Text := '23';
      If cbIPAddress.Text= ''
        Then cbIPAddress.Text := '127.0.0.1';
      IdTelnet1.Host := cbIPAddress.Text;
      IdTelnet1.Port := StrToInt(cbPortNo.Text);
      IdTelnet1.Connect;
      If IdTelnet1.Connected
        Then
          Begin
            edtConnectionIndicator.Text := 'Connected';
            mbSendMemo.SetFocus;
          End;
    End;
  Procedure TForm1.btnDisconnectClick(Sender: TObject);
    Begin
      If IdTelnet1.Connected
        Then IdTelnet1.Disconnect;
    End;
```

For this to work the KeyPreview property of Form1 must be set to true.

Table 32.2 A section of TelnetToRemoteServersSimplifiedUnit.pas showing the remote port no and IP address being assigned before the Connect method on the IdTelnet1 object is called

`TForm1.IdTCPServer1Connect(AContext: TIdContext)` executes the following

```
ServerIP := AContext.Binding.IP;
ServerPort := AContext.Binding.Port;
PeerIP := AContext.Binding.PeerIP;
PeerPort := AContext.Binding.PeerPort;
WriteToScreenLog('SERVER', 'Client Connected!');
WriteToScreenLog('SERVER', 'Port=' + IntToStr(ServerPort)
                 + ' '  + '(PeerIP=' + PeerIP
                 + ' - ' + 'PeerPort=' + IntToStr(PeerPort) + ')'
               );
With AContext.Connection.IOHandler
  Do
    Begin
      Try
        Writeln('Hello Welcome to the Celsius to Fahrenheit
                 Conversion Program');
      Except
        On E: Exception Do ShowMessage(E.ClassName
                          + 'An error has occurred: '
                          + E.Message );
      End;
    End;
```

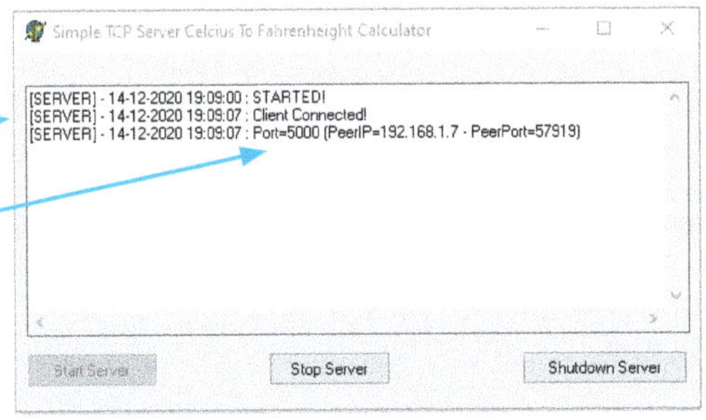

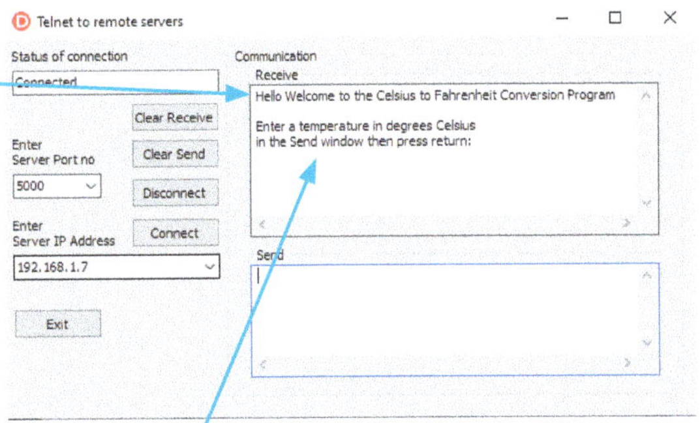

Fig.32.4 Telnet client and TCP server user interfaces

A new thread (lightweight process) is started for each new client connection. The server runs a scheduler which allocates processor time to each runnable thread. The event handler `TForm1.IdTCPServer1Execute(AContext: TIdContext)` is called on the thread when a client connection is first set up, on receipt of data from a client and whenever it is runnable.

```
Procedure TForm1.IdTCPServer1Execute(AContext: TIdContext);
  Var
    CelsiusTempString, FahrenheitTempString : String;
    CelsiusTempInteger, FahrenheitTempInteger : Integer;
  Begin
    Try
      AssignFile(Pipe, GetCurrentDir + '\Log.Txt');
      Append(Pipe);
      Writeln(Pipe, '[Peer connected on] : ', GetCurrentDateAndTime,
              'Peer IP: ', ' ', 'Peer port: ', AContext.Binding.PeerPort);
      CloseFile(Pipe);
    Except
      On E : Exception Do ShowMessage(E.ClassName + ' error: ' + E.Message);
    End;
    With AContext.Connection.IOHandler
      Do
        Begin
          Writeln;
          Writeln('Enter a temperature in degrees Celsius');
          Writeln('in the Send window then press return:');
          Writeln;
          CelsiusTempString := Readln;
          Try
            CelsiusTempInteger := StrToInt(CelsiusTempString);
            FahrenheitTempInteger := Round(32 + (9 * CelsiusTempInteger)/5);
            FahrenheitTempString :=  IntToStr(FahrenheitTempInteger);
            Writeln(CelsiusTempString + ' degrees Celsius in Fahrenheit is '
                                      + FahrenheitTempString + ' degrees');
            WriteToScreenLog('SERVER', AContext.Binding.PeerIP + ' '
                                      + IntToStr(AContext.Binding.PeerPort)
                                      + ' : ' + 'Celcius temperature: '
                                      + CelsiusTempString + FahrenheitTempString);
          Except
            Writeln(CelsiusTempString + ' is not an Integer');
            WriteToScreenLog('SERVER', AContext.Binding.PeerIP + ' '
                                      + IntToStr(AContext.Binding.PeerPort) + ' '
                                      + 'Celsius temperature string is not an integer');
          End;
        End;
```

The thread running IdTCPServer1Execute is suspended at this point if no client data is available. When client data becomes available this thread becomes runnable again and the event handler IdTCPServer1Execute is called so that it can complete its execution. Readln fetches the client data or more correctly AContext.Connection.IOHandler.Readln.

Writeln or more correctly AContext.Connection.IOHandler.Writeln writes data to the client

The role of the four layers of the TCP/IP protocol stack

Networking protocols were designed to make possible communication between application programs executing on different hosts whilst hiding the complexities of the underlying network from these application programs.

A host, or host computer, is any computer system that connects to an internet and runs applications.

The term process is used for an instance of a program in execution, so it is actually processes in different hosts connected by a network that are communicating.

Layered organisation

Networking protocols are usually developed in layers.

Each layer is responsible for a different part of the communication process.

The software that implements a protocol is called **protocol software** and the software that implements a suite of protocols such as TCP/IP, a **protocol stack**.

The **TCP/IP protocol suite** consists of four conceptual layers: application, transport, network or IP (Internet layer), and link layers (*Figure 32.5*).

It is implemented in software as the **TCP/IP protocol stack** in separate software modules corresponding to the individual layers of the protocol suite.

Each layer and therefore each software module has a different responsibility. The protocol stack is installed on each computer either as a part of the operating system or as a software library.

Application	Telnet, FTP, email(SMTP, POP3), Web browsing (HTTP)
Transport	TCP
Network	IP (Internet layer)
Link	Ethernet, PPP, WiFi, DOCSIS (cable TV)

Fig. 32.5 The four layers of the TCP/IP protocol suite and stack

Application programs interact with the software stack via an **Application Programming Interface (API)**. The de facto standard is the **socket API**.

Figure 32.6 shows a client process and a server process that use the socket API from the TCP/IP protocol stack to send and receive messages via a TCP/IP connection pipe established between client and server.

Application layer

A process in one end-system (host) uses the application layer of TCP/IP to exchange packets of information with a process in another end-system. The packets of information at the application layer are called **messages**.

The application layer uses different application-layer protocols for different applications. For example, if the application is designed to enable Web pages to be fetched from a Web server then the application will use either the HTTP application-layer protocol or the HTTPS application-layer protocol.

Information

Windows Telnet client:

Windows Telnet client is not installed by default. To install Telent go to Control panel and open Programs | Programs and Features. Click Turn Windows Features on. Select the Telnet client and click OK. Windows will then install the required files for Telnet client.

Key principle

End-to-end principle:

The end-to-end principle of the Internet requires that the two endpoints, the hosts, are responsible for establishing, supervising and maintaining a connection between two communicating processes, one on each host. This is done by a piece of software in each host known by the name Transmission Control Protocol (TCP).

Key term

Application layer:

Application layer protocols are used to exchange data between programs running on the source and destination hosts. It is the application layer that provides the interface between these programs and the underlying network over which the programs' messages are transmitted, e.g. HTTP message GET / which fetches the default Web page from a Web server.

Key term

TCP/IP socket:

A socket is one endpoint of a two-way communication link between two programs running on the network, e.g. a Web browser and a Web server.

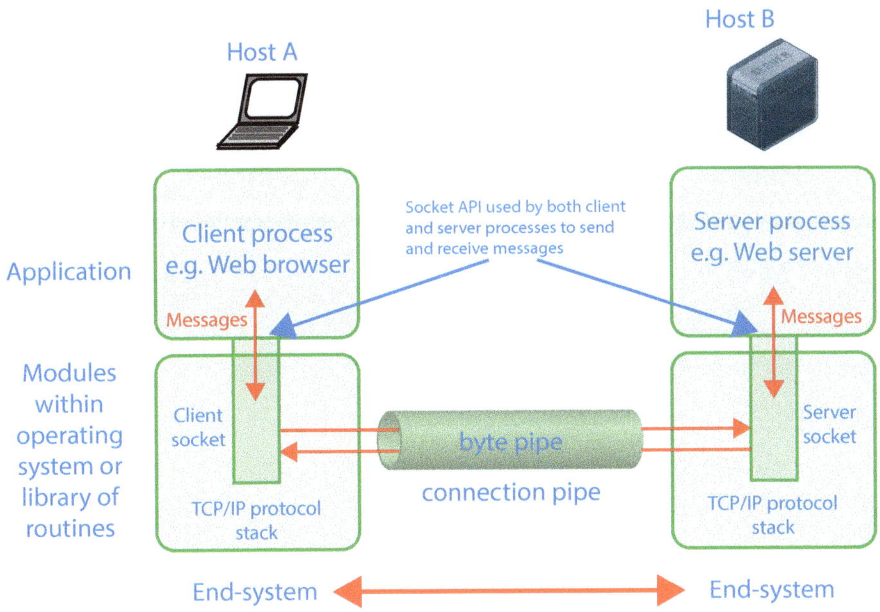

Fig. 32.6 Sending and receiving messages using the socket API

An application-layer protocol defines the kind of messages to send. In the case of HTTP or HTTPS, one such message could be a GET message.

Transport layer

The **transport layer** of the protocol stack is a piece of software in each host. This software implements the transport protocol known by the name **Transmission Control Protocol (TCP)**. TCP enables applications executing on two hosts to establish a two-way connection and exchange application-layer messages through a reliable byte-stream channel (pipe) for data flows in either direction between the two end-systems as shown in *Figure 32.6*. It also allows the connection to be terminated.

TCP breaks long messages into shorter segments which it sends as separate transport-layer packets known as **TCP segments**.

The application at the sending side (e.g. a Web browser using the application-layer protocol HTTP) pushes messages (e.g. GET) through a **TCP/IP socket**. The transport-layer protocol TCP has the responsibility of getting the messages to the socket of the receiving application process, e.g. a Web server listening on port 80. Port numbers such as port 80 are 16-bit numbers used for application and service identification on the Internet.

TCP does everything in its control to guarantee delivery of the application-layer message and also guarantee that the received TCP segments will be reassembled in the correct order to form the message to be passed to the application-layer and then the corresponding application process.

Once the TCP has established a connection:

- it monitors the connection for transmission errors and responds when an error is detected by retransmitting the segment that suffered the error
- it detects when a connection is broken
- it performs flow control by speed matching sender and receiver
- it provides congestion control when the network is congested.

Key term

Transmission Control Protocol (TCP):
TCP enables applications executing on two hosts to establish a connection and exchange application-layer messages through a reliable byte-stream channel (pipe) for data flows between the two end systems.

Key term

Network or IP layer:
The network or IP layer of the TCP/IP protocol stack in hosts and routers is responsible for moving IP-layer packets from one host to another without regard to whether these hosts are on the same network or not.
It adds source and destination IP addresses to packets on their way from the transport layer to the link layer, and removes source and destination IP addresses from packets on their way from the link layer to the transport layer.

Key term

Function of Transport layer:
The basic function of the transport layer is

- to accept messages/data from the layer above it
- split these into smaller units called segments if necessary
- pass these segments to the network or IP layer
- ensure that all the segments arrive correctly at the other end
- reassemble the received segments, which it gets from the network layer, in the correct order to form the message/data to pass to the layer above.

The transport layer is a true end-to-end layer which carries messages/data all the way from the source to the destination.

Network or IP layer

The TCP layer uses the IP layer to carry its segments. Each TCP segment is encapsulated in an IP packet before it is sent across the internet. The **network or IP layer** in hosts and routers move these packets known as **IP or Internet Protocol packets** from one host to another without regard to whether these hosts belong to the same network or different networks. The Internet Protocol is a connectionless protocol which just provides a best effort but not guaranteed way of delivering packets called **datagrams**. The reliability of the transmission is left to the layer above, the transport layer.

Getting to the destination host may require many hops via intermediate routers along the way.

Link layer

The link layer handles all the physical details of interfacing with the network cable or wireless connection. It includes the network interface card (network adapter) and a device driver. TCP/IP protocol supports many different types of link layer, depending on the type of networking hardware being used. One example is Ethernet.

The link layer adds source and destination hardware addresses (e.g. MAC addresses) to packets that it receives from the IP layer then dispatches the packets onto the local cable or wireless connection - *Figure 32.7*.

If the packet is destined for a host on another network, the link layer destination address is the hardware address of the gateway (router) to the internet which the other network is connected to.

Key term

Link layer:
The link layer handles all the physical details of interfacing with the network cable or wireless connection.
The link layer adds source and destination hardware addresses (e.g. MAC addresses) to packets that it receives from the IP layer then despatches the packets onto the local cable or wireless connection.

Key fact

Identifying a TCP connection:
Every TCP connection can be uniquely identified by its two endpoints.
For example,
<174.89.0.54:49717, 210.5.0.67:8080>

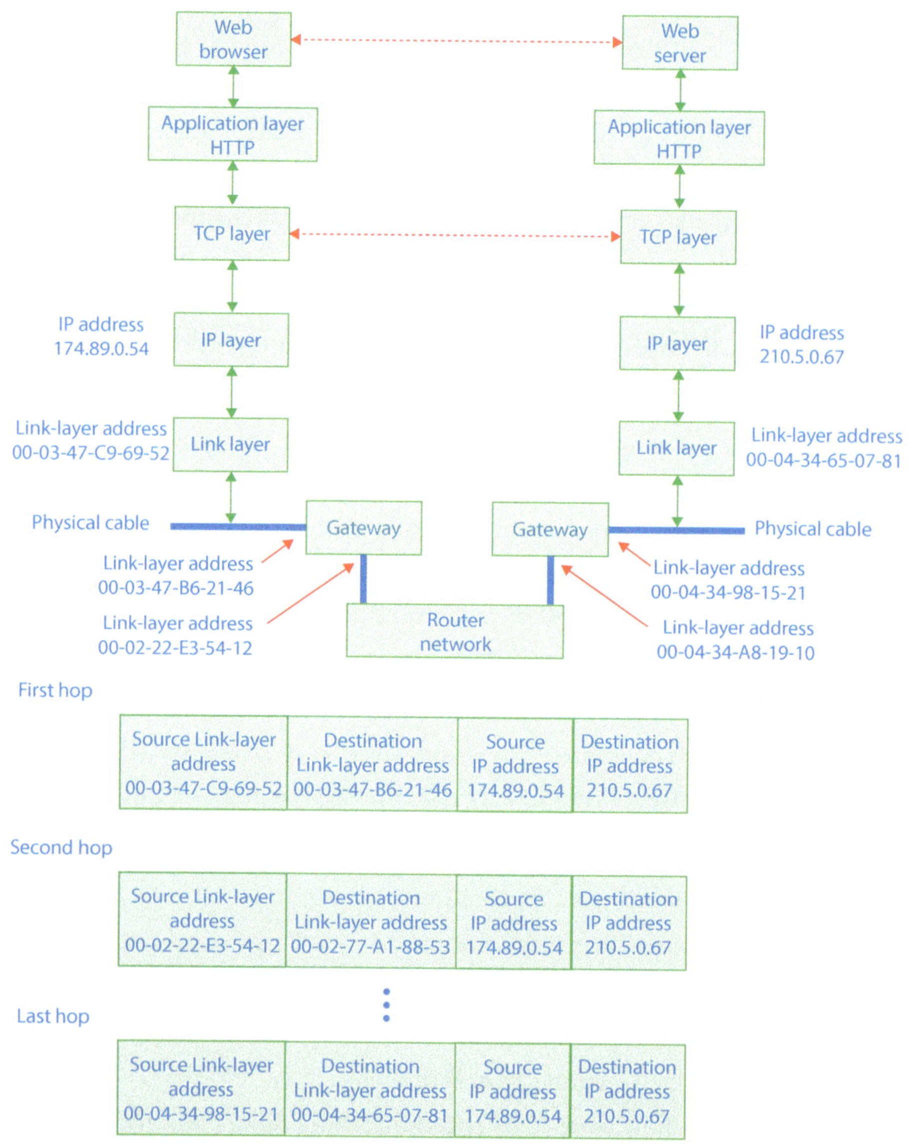

Fig. 32.7 TCP/IP protocol stack and the role of the link layer

A Simple HTTP Client

1. Create a new Windows VCL Application project
2. Save the project as `SimpleHTTPClientProject.dproj` and its unit as `SimpleHTTPClientUnit.pas`.
3. Add to the main form a **TIdHTTP** component, `IdHTTP1`, located on the Indy clients page of the Component/ Tool palette.
4. Rename the form, `frmGetHTML`, and its caption, `GetHTML`.
5. Add a button, edit box, memo box and two labels as shown in *Figure 32.8*.
6. Rename the edit box `edtURL`, the memo box `mbHTML`, the button `btnGet` and its caption `Get`.
7. Rename the two labels, `lblURL` and `lblHTML`, respectively. Change their captions to `URL` and `HTML`. as shown in *Figure 32.8*.

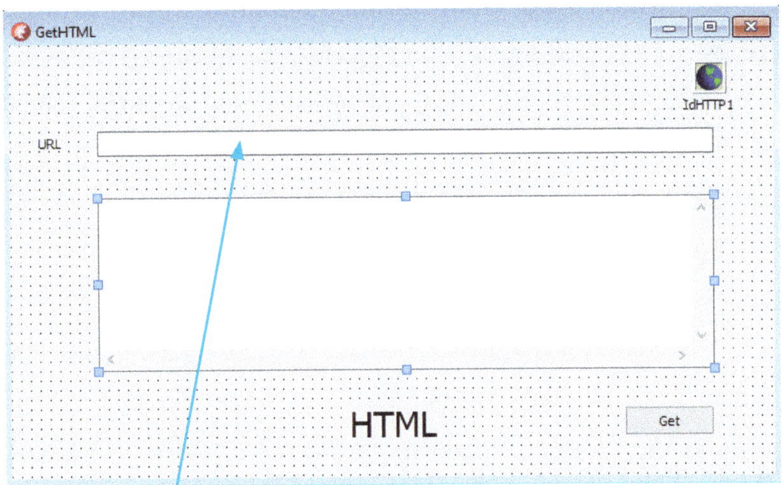

Fig. 32.8 User interface design for SimpleHTTPClient

8. Change the font size of the `lblHTML` to 22.
9. Double click the button component and add the following code to the button click event handler:

```
mbHTML.Lines.Text := idHTTP1.Get('http://' + edtGet.Text);
```

10. Set the **ScrollBars** property of `mbHTML` to `ssBoth`.
11. Now save all, and build and run the program (**F9**).
12. Type **www.educational-computing.co.uk** in the URL window.

The HTML code of the default web page of this web site should be returned and displayed in the memo box as shown in *Figure 32.9*.

The TIdHTTP component encompasses the code to make a TCP/IP connection to the resource site as well as code to handle the HTTP protocol.

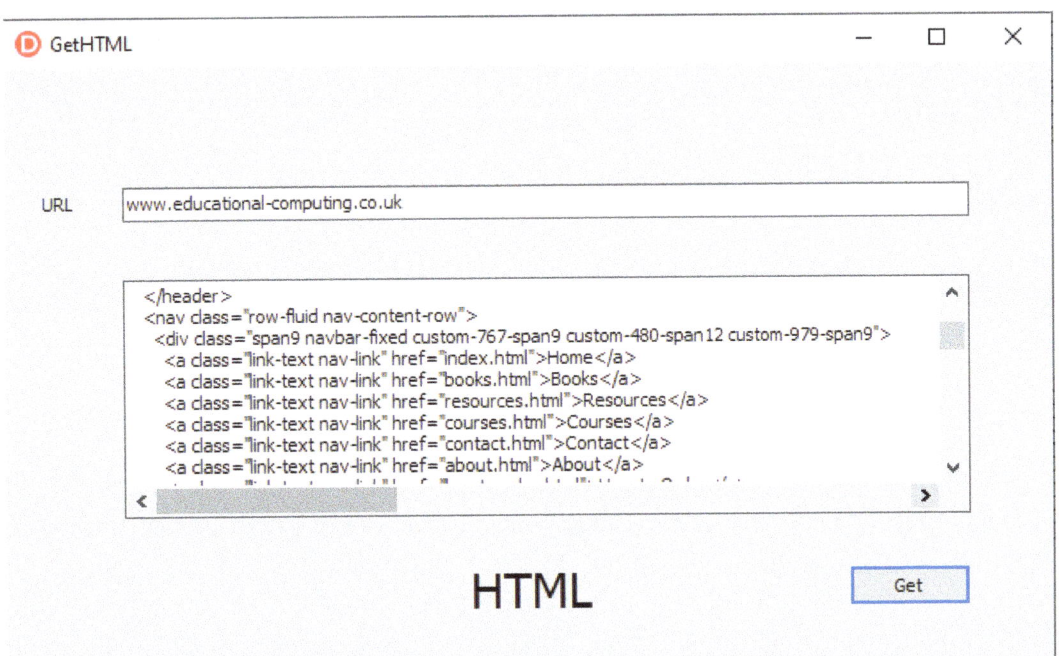

Fig. 32.9 Snapshot of the HTML returned from www.educational-computing.co.uk

The web site **www.educational-computing.co.uk** that the program `SimpleHTTPClientProject.exe` connects to is hosted on an HTTP server. `SimpleHTTPClientProject.exe` sends a **Get** request to the HTTP server and the server returns the default web page, **index.html**.

What is a Web Page and what is HTML?

A web page is a text document written in a language called **HTML**. It contains a mixture of content to be displayed and information about how to layout the content when it is displayed. Web pages are displayed in a web browser that uses the layout information to format the displayed content. This process is called **rendering**. The program `SimpleHTTPClientProject.exe` is capable of displaying the raw HTML of the returned web page but is not able to render this **HTML**.

The skeleton of any web page is as follows:

```
<html>
  <head>
    <title>Title of the Web Page goes here </title>
  </head>
  <body>
    Content of the Web Page goes here
  </body>
</html>
```

Web pages may be designed to collect information by presenting a form with fields to be filled in as shown in *Figure 32.10*.

`SurveyForm.html` was placed in the `htdocs` folder of `Apache24` and then double clicked to launch it in a web browser as shown in *Figure 32.10*.

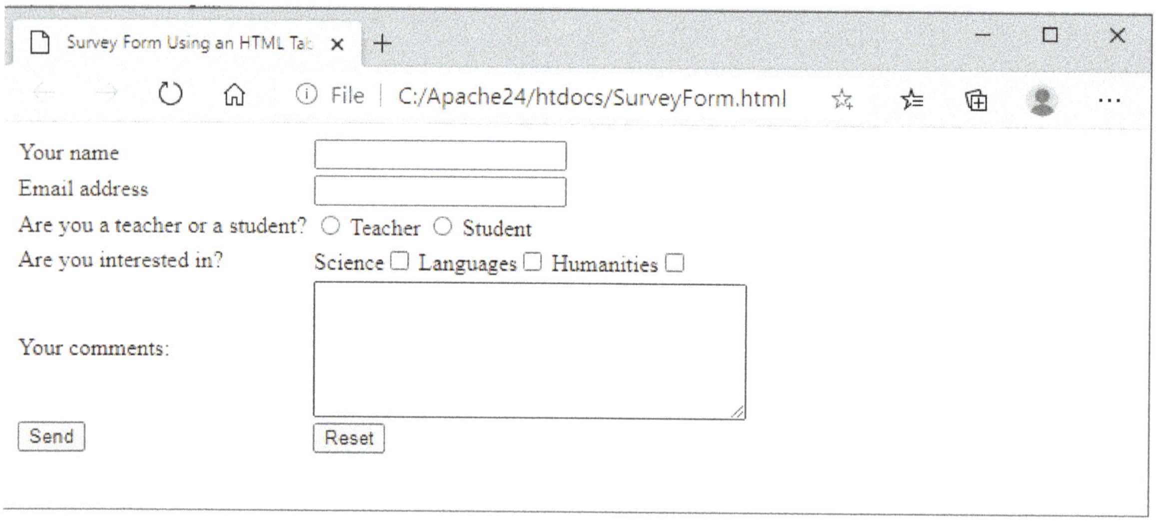

Fig. 32.10 Web page SurveyForm.html rendered in a web browser

The information entered in the form is sent to an HTTP server for processing when the `Send` button is pressed.

Processing is carried out using a script or executable program that resides in a folder to which the HTTP server has access. The HTTP server may send a response to the client, i.e. the web browser (HTTP client).

HTTP Server (Web server)

A web browser (HTTP client) sends a connection request to a HTTP server or web server using a well-known port on the web server (port 80). If the server accepts the connection request then a virtual path is set up between the server and the client (socket to socket).

The client now sends a **GET request** for a document (`Get /` is the simplest request) to the web server along the established virtual path. The web server **responds** by returning the requested document if it exists (or the default document if none is specified in the request) to the client using the socket address of the socket at client end. The client then requests the virtual circuit be closed unless the HTTP request has specified otherwise.

A typical web server is an Apache server - https://httpd.apache.org.

Setting up an Apache Web Server

Download a copy of Apache web server - https://www.apachehaus.com/cgi-bin/download.plx and extract to a local drive, e.g. `C:\Apache24`, if Apache is version 2.4.

Open the Apache folder then open the `conf` folder. Open the file `httpd.conf` in **WordPad**.

Each line of text which has the # character in front of it is commented out and will be ignored by Apache web server. However, there are some lines of text which do not have the # character.

Work carefully through the lines of text changing the following

Define SRVROOT "/Apache24" to **Define SRVROOT "C:/Apache24"** or wherever Apache24 was extracted to.

#Listen 12.34.56.78:80 to **Listen <replace with the IP address of the computer hosting Apache> : 8080**

Listen 80 to **Listen 8080**

ServerName localhost:80 to **DelphiBook**

Save the changed `httpd.conf` as "`httpd.conf`" to ensure that **WordPad** doesn't add the extension '`.txt`'.

Change to the `bin` folder of Apache24 and right click `httpd.exe` and select **Run as administrator**. to launch the server as shown in *Figure 32.11*.

Place a copy of `SurveyForm.html` in the `htdocs` folder of the Apache server.

Using a web browser enter the url:

localhost:8080/SurveyForm.html

(if you know the IP address of the computer hosting Apache server then replace localhost by this IP address, e.g. `192.168.1.7`)

Figure 32.12 shows the Apache server's response rendered in a web browser.

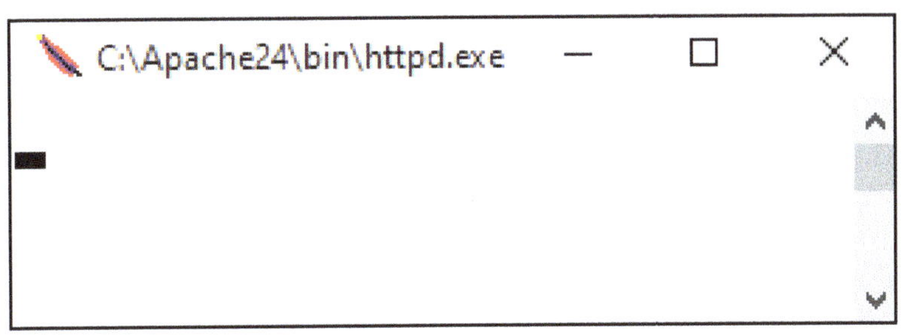

Fig. 32.11 Apache HTTP server running

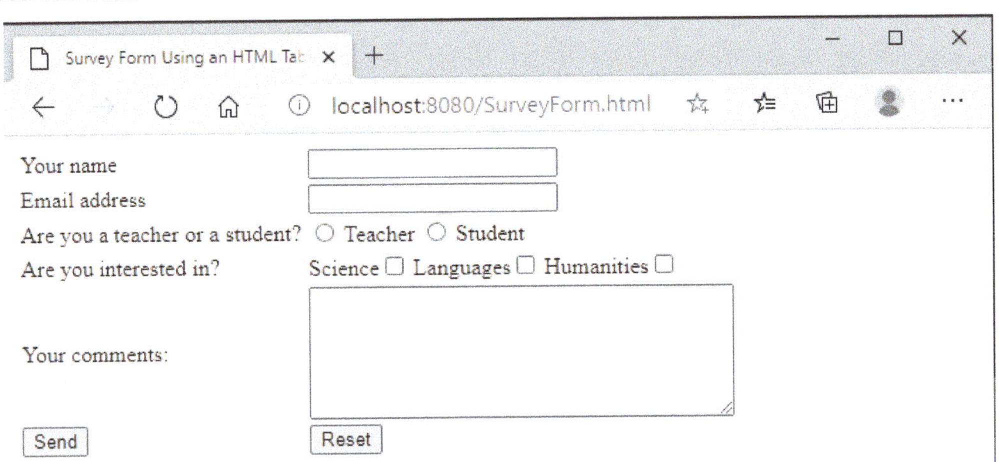

Fig. 32.12 Apache HTTP server response rendered in a web browser

The Apache server has a folder `cgi-bin` where scripts and executables may be placed which the server can execute. The `cgi` part of this folder's name is an acronym for **Common Gateway Interface**.

CGI – Common Gateway Interface

CGI is not a language. It is a simple protocol that can be used to communicate between a web page and a program executing on a web server. A CGI script can be written in any language that can read STDIN, write to STDOUT, and read environment variables, i.e. virtually any programming language, including C, Perl, Delphi or even shell scripting.

Structure of a CGI Script

A typical sequence of steps for a CGI script is as follows:

1. Read the user's input from STDIN. ——— Readln
2. Process the data.
3. Write the HTML response to STDOUT. ——— Writeln

An Apache web server executes scripts stored in the `cgi-bin` folder. Data received via an HTTP request is routed to the referenced cgi script. Output produced by the cgi script is routed into an HTTP response message. All that the cgi script has to do is perform read operations to receive data and write operations to send information.

Server-side executables

Launch Delphi. Select **File|New|Console Application**.

Enter the code shown in *Table 32.3* and save as `SimpleConsoleCGI.dprog`. Select **Project|Build** (**SHIFT F9**) to build application. This creates an executable, `SimpleConsoleCGI.exe`. Copy this executable to the `cgi-bin` folder of **Apache**. Launch Apache web server, `httpd.exe`. Launch a web browser and type the following URL into the address bar:

```
Program SimpleConsoleCGI;
{$APPTYPE CONSOLE}
Begin
  Writeln('Content-type: text/plain');
  Writeln;
  Writeln('Hello World!');
End.
```

Table 32.3 Source code for server-side executable SimpleConsoleCGI.exe

http://localhost:8080/cgi-bin/SimpleConsoleCGI.exe

Press return to see the result - *Figure 32.13*. *Figure 32.14* shows the result of accessing the Apache web server from a different machine.

Fig. 32.13 Microsoft Edge browser showing Hello World! response generated by server-side executable SimpleConsoleCGI.exe

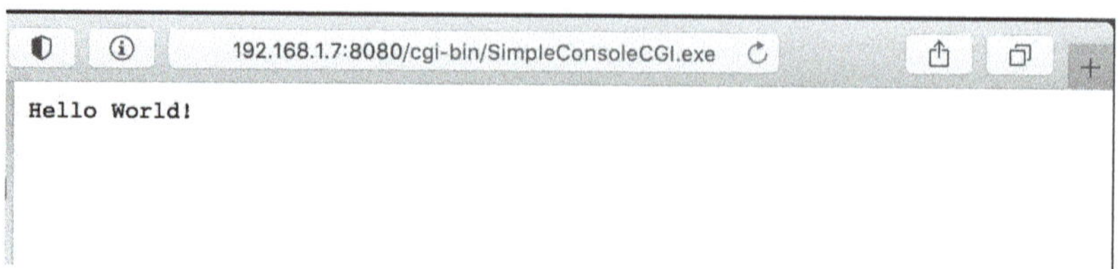

Fig. 32.14 Apple Safari browser on an Apple Mac Pro showing Hello World! response generated by server-side executable SimpleConsoleCGI.exe running on Windows 10 machine at 192.168.1.7

Launch Delphi. Select **File|New|Console Application**.

Enter the code shown in *Table 32.4* and **save as** `SimpleConsoleCGITime.dprog`. **Select** **Project|Build** (**SHIFT F9**) to build application. This creates an executable, `SimpleConsoleCGITime.exe`. **Copy** this executable to the `cgi-bin` folder of **Apache**. Launch Apache web server, `httpd.exe`. **Launch** a web browser and **type** the following URL into the address bar:

http://localhost:8080/cgi-bin/SimpleConsoleCGITime.exe

Press return to see the result - *Figure 32.15*. Now **refresh** the web page and notice that the time has changed.

P

```
Program SimpleConsoleCGITime;
{$APPTYPE CONSOLE}
Uses
  SysUtils;
Begin
  Writeln('content-type: text/html');
  Writeln;
  Writeln('<html><head>');
  Writeln('<title></title>');
  Writeln('</head>');
  Writeln('<body>');
  Writeln('<h1>The time at the server is</h1>');
  Writeln('<hr />');
  Writeln('<h3>');
  Writeln(FormatDateTime('dd mmm, yyyy hh:mm:ss', Now));
  Writeln('</h3>');
  Writeln('<hr />');
  Writeln('</body></html>');
End.
```

Table 32.4 Source code for server-side executable SimpleConsoleCGITime.exe

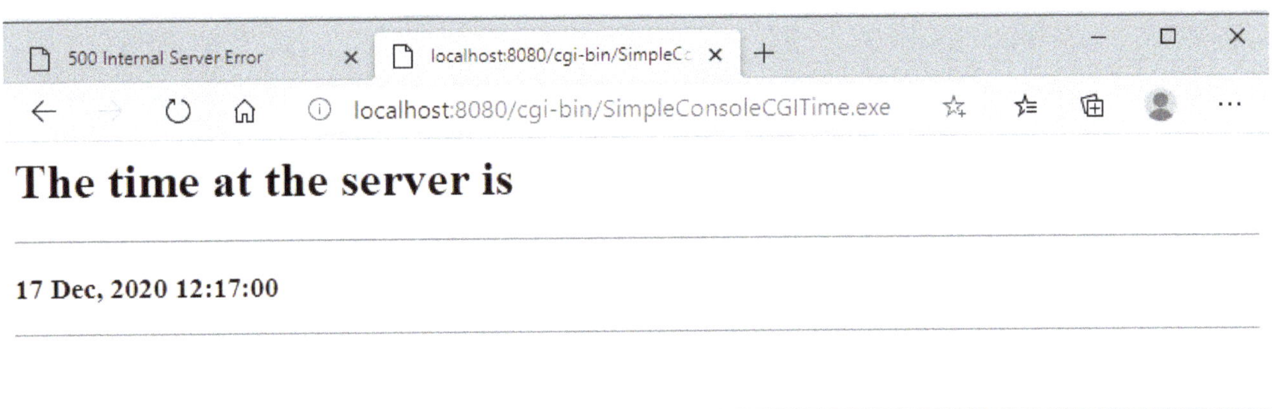

Fig. 32.15 Microsoft Edge browser showing response generated by server-side executable SimpleConsoleCGITime.exe

Writing a console program that uses `Readln` to read the request message from the client is a little trickier and therefore will not be attempted.

The Request and Response Objects

The executables placed in the `cgi-bin` folder extend the capabilities of the web server. They are therefore known as web server extensions.

Delphi provides two objects **Request** and **Response**.

Request is used to gain access to the data sent with the HTTP request message.

The **Response** object is assigned the content to be returned.

To gain access to these objects a **Web Server Application** must be created as follows:

In Delphi select **File|New|Other** and in the **New Items** window choose **Web|Web Server Application** (you will have to scroll down to locate this). Choose **CGI Stand-alone executable**.

Save project as `BasicWebServerExtension.dprog` and its unit `WebServerUnit.pas` in folder `BasicWebServerExtension`.

Toggle to the `WebModule1` view as shown in *Figure 32.16*.

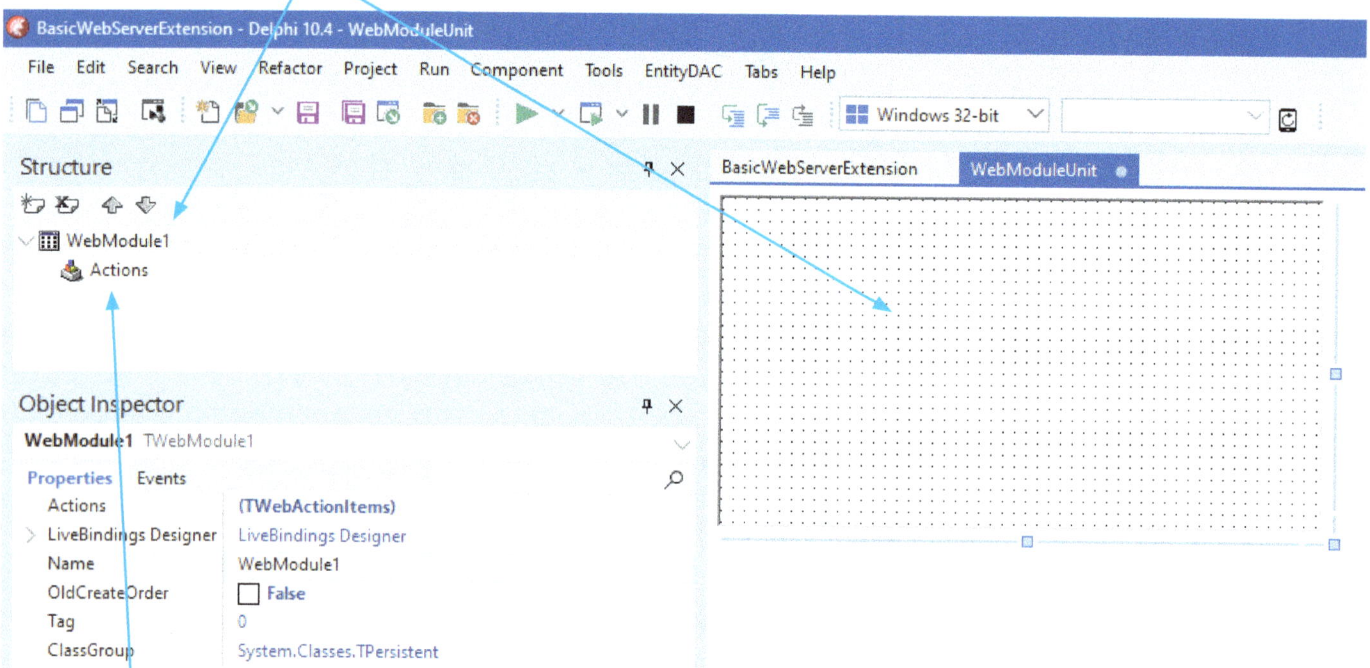

Fig. 32.16 BasicWebServerExtension project | WebModuleUnit WebModule1

In the **Structure** pane, with the mouse pointer on `WebModule1`, **right click** mouse button to bring up the popup window shown in *Figure 32.17*. **Click** the **Action Editor...** option to bring up the **Action editor** as shown in *Figure 32.18*. Click [icon] to create a new action item `WebActionItem1`.

In the **Object Inspector** **change** the **Name** field to `SimpleAction`.

Enter the value `Simple` in the **PathInfo** field.

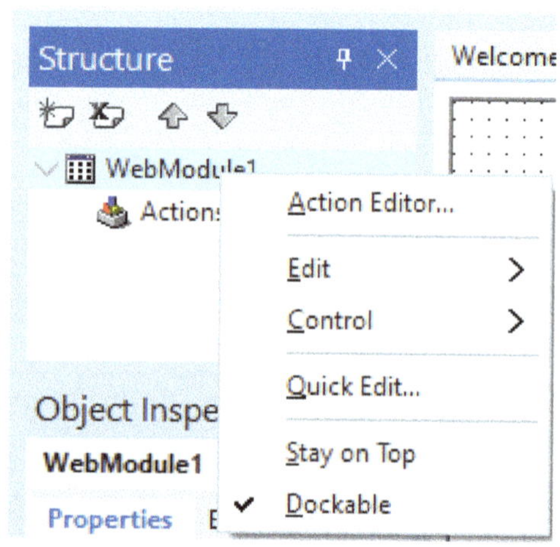

Fig. 32.17 BasicWebServerExtension project | WebModuleUnit WebModule1

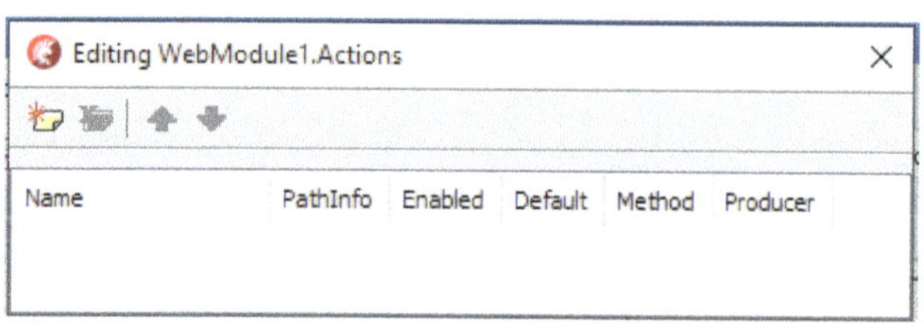

Fig. 32.18 Action editor

Click on **Events** tab. Double click the **OnAction** field to produce an event handler.

Enter the following code between `Begin` and `End`:

```
Response.Content := '<html><body>Hello World</body></html>';
```

Save All.

Build then copy executable `BasicWebServerExtension.exe` into the `cgi-bin` folder of **Apache Web Server.**

Launch Apache Web Server.

Launch a web browser, enter `http://localhost:8080/cgi-bin/BasicWebServerExtension.Exe/Simple` into the **url** field of the browser and press return. *Figure 32.19* shows the expected response "`Hello World`".

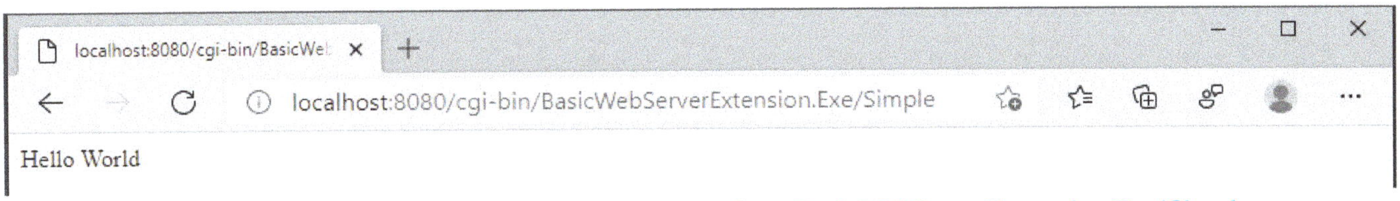

Fig. 32.19 Edge web browser showing response from BasicWebServerExtension.Exe/Simple

Now **modify** this program by changing `Response.Content` to

```
Response.Content := '<html><body>' + Request.Method + '</body></html>';
```

Save project as `BasicWebServerExtension2.dproj` and unit as `WebModule2.pas` in a new folder `BasicWebServerExtension2.`

Build then copy executable `BasicWebServerExtension2.exe` into the `cgi-bin` folder of **Apache Web Server.**

Launch Apache Web Server if it is not already running.

Launch a web browser, enter `http://localhost:8080/cgi-bin/BasicWebServerExtension2.Exe/Simple` into the **url** field of the browser and press return. *Figure 32.20* shows the response, i.e. the HTTP request method used to get the html page is the `GET` method.

Fig. 32.20 Edge web browser showing response from BasicWebServerExtension2.Exe/Simple

Difference between GET and POST

The client and server applications interact through the use of HTTP's request methods.

HTTP clients use two methods to request information from HTTP servers:

1. The GET method
   The GET method attempts to retrieve a document from the server by simply requesting the document. Data entered by a user is tacked onto the URL (Uniform Resource Locator) in the form of a query string and sent to the server. In the following example, the query string is name=fred+bloggs&age=6. The query string is separated from the rest of the URL by a "?" symbol:

   `http://www.educational-computing.co.uk/test.exe?name=fred+bloggs&age=6`

   The query string consists of parameter-value pairs, e.g. age=6.

The parameter and its value are separated by an "=" symbol.

The parameter-value pairs are separated by an "&" symbol (ampersand).

Spaces in values are replaced by a "+" symbol.

All "unsafe" characters in the names and values are converted to "%xx", where "xx" is the ascii value of the character, in hex.

"Unsafe" characters include =, &, %, +, non-printable characters, and any others you want to encode

- There is no danger in encoding too many characters.
- For simplicity, you might encode all non-alphanumeric characters.

For example, age=6%2E3 represents an age of 6.3.

2. The **POST** method

A **POST** request is used to send data to the server to be processed in some way, e.g. by a CGI script.
A **POST** request is different from a **GET** request in the following ways:

- There's a block of data sent with the request, in the message body. There are usually extra headers to describe this message body, such as `Content-Type:` and `Content-Length:`.
- The request URI (URI – Uniform Resource identifier - is a more general form of URL) is not a resource to retrieve; it's usually a program to handle the data being sent.
- The HTTP response is normally program output, not a static file.

POST is often used to submit HTML form data to CGI scripts.

In this case, the `Content-Type:` header is usually `application/x-www-form-urlencoded`,

and the `Content-Length:` header gives the length of the URL-encoded form data.

The CGI script receives the message body through STDIN, and decodes it.

Example of form submission, using POST:

```
POST /path/script.cgi HTTP/1.0
From: fred@somewhere.co.uk
User-Agent: MyDelphiHTTP/1.0
Content-Type: application/x-www-form-urlencoded
Content-Length: 48
                  ◄──────────────────────────── Blank line
name=fred+bloggs&age=6%2E3
```

A **POST** request can be used to send whatever data you want, not just form submissions. However the sending and the receiving program must agree on the format in which the data is sent.

Exploring GET and POST

To access the data sent by a GET or a POST method request, a cgi script must be launched and then it must access the input buffer of the web server socket. The data is sent to the server as parameter name-value pairs with spaces and other characters encoded using url-encoding. Delphi has a component that performs the task of extracting the name-value pairs. It is called **TWebDispatcher**.

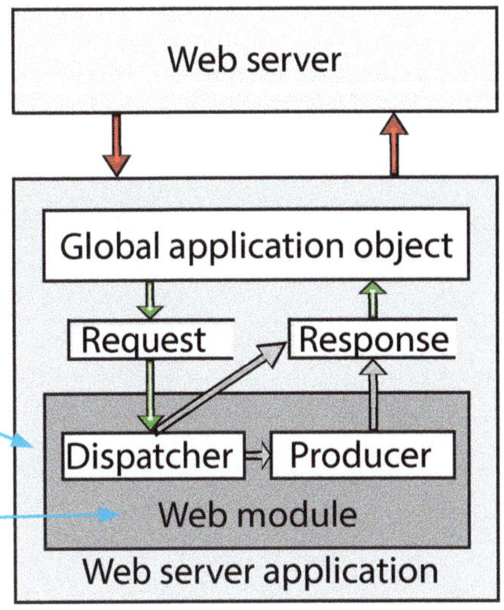

Fig. 32.21 Schematic for Web server application

Launch a new web server application: File|New|Other and in the New Items window choose Web|Web Server Application (you will have to scroll down to locate this). Choose CGI Stand-alone executable.

A web module window, `WebModule1`, should appear in Form View (use View|Forms and select it if it doesn't).

Click the right mouse button while the mouse cursor is over this window to launch a pop-up window.

Click on Action Editor in this pop-up window.

The pop-up window labelled "`Editing WebModule1 Actions`" should now appear - *Figure 32.22*.

Press the insert key on the keyboard to add a new **WebActionItem**, `WebActionItem1`.

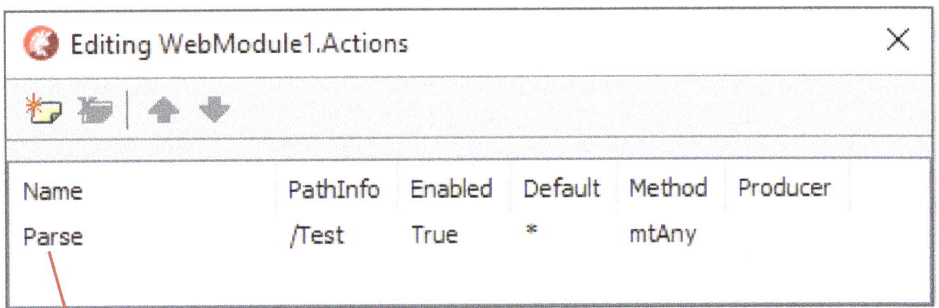

Fig. 32.22 Action editor with WebAction1 renamed Parse

Rename this `Parse` in the Object Inspector as shown in *Figure 32.22*. Accept/select **Method** `myAny` and add `/Test` to the **PathInfo** property.

With action `Parse` selected in the Structure window, click on the Events tab. Double click the **OnAction** field to create an event handler template for this action.

```
Procedure  TWebModule1.WebModule1ParseAction(Sender: TObject;
              Request: TWebRequest; Response: TWebResponse; Var Handled: Boolean);
  Begin
  End;
```

This event handler gives access to the Request and the Response messages.

This event handler is called by the operating system when a request arrives at the socket this program is connected to.

Add code as shown in *Table 32.5* to this event handler.

Save this project with project name `WebSimpleProject.dprog` and unit name `WebSimpleProjectUnit.pas` in folder `WebSimpleProject`.

Build this project.

Place a copy of `WebSimpleProject.Exe` in the `cgi-bin` folder of **Apache**.

With **Apache** web server running launch a web browser and **enter** the URL

```
http://http://localhost:8080/cgi-bin/WebSimpleProject.exe/Test?name=fred+bloggs&age=36.5
```

Figure 32.33 shows the web page `Test.html` that is returned by the web server. `Test.html` is generated by the web server extension `WebSimpleProject.exe/Test`. Note that `Query` has been assigned the parameter-pairs.

`Test.html` does not exist on the server but is "synthesised" everytime the web server extension is called.

An **Apache** web server serves up web pages placed in its `htdocs` folder. Hence the `PathTranslated` header line in *Figure 32.23* shows `C:\Apache\htdocs\Test`.

```
Procedure TWebModule1.WebModule1ParseAction(Sender: TObject;
            Request: TWebRequest; Response: TWebResponse; var Handled: Boolean);
  Var
    Page : TStringList;
  Begin
    Page := TStringList.Create;
    Try
      With Page
        Do
          Begin
            Add('<html>');
            Add('<head>');
            Add('<title>');
            Add('Test');
            Add('</title>');
            Add('</head>');
            Add('<body');
            Add('<h1>This page displays the properties of the HTML Request</h1>');
            Add('Method = ' + Request.Method + '<br />');
            Add('ProtocolVersion = ' + Request.ProtocolVersion + '<br />');
            Add('Query = ' + Request.Query + '<br />');
            Add('PathInfo = ' + Request.PathInfo + '<br />');
            Add('PathTranslated = ' + Request.PathTranslated + '<br />');
            Add('CacheControl = ' + Request.CacheControl + '<br />');
            Add('Date = ' + FormatDateTime('dd mmm,yyyy hh:mm',Request.Date) + '<br />');
            Add('Accept = ' + Request.Accept + '<br />');
            Add('Host = ' + Request.Host + '<br />');
            Add('IfModifiedSince = ' + FormatDateTime('dd mmm,yyyy hh:mm',
                                    Request.IfModifiedSince) + '<br />');
            Add('Referer = ' + Request.Referer + '<br />');
            Add('UserAgent = ' + Request.UserAgent + '<br />');
            Add('ContentEncoding = ' + Request.ContentEncoding + '<br />');
            Add('ContentType = ' + Request.ContentType + '<br />');
            Add('ContentLength = ' + IntToStr(Request.ContentLength) + '<br />');
            Add('ContentVersion = ' + Request.ContentVersion + '<br />')';
            Add('Content = ' + Request.Content + '<br />');
            Add('Connection = ' + Request.Connection + '<br />');
            Add('Expires = ' + FormatDateTime('dd mmm,yyyy hh:mm',
                              Request.Expires) + '<br />');
            Add('RemoteAddr = ' + Request.RemoteAddr + '<br />');
            Add('ScriptName = ' + Request.ScriptName + '<br />');
            Add('ServerPort = ' + IntToStr(Request.ServerPort) + '<br />');
            Add('</body>');
            Add('</html>');
          End;
        Response.Content := Page.Text;
    Finally
      Page.Free;
    End;
  End;
```

TWebRequest and TWebResponse are abstract classes that encapsulate the HTTP protocol.

TWebRequest provides access to all the information passed to the server by the client.

TWebResponse contains properties and methods that allow responses to any of the multiple ways that the HTTP protocol allows.

Protocol: Set of rules or procedures to be followed to ensure successful communication between two parties/devices/computers.

Property	**Definition**
Query	A string of all the parameters obtained through a GET request
Content	A string of all the parameters obtained through a POST request

Table 32.5 Event handler WebModule1ParseAction

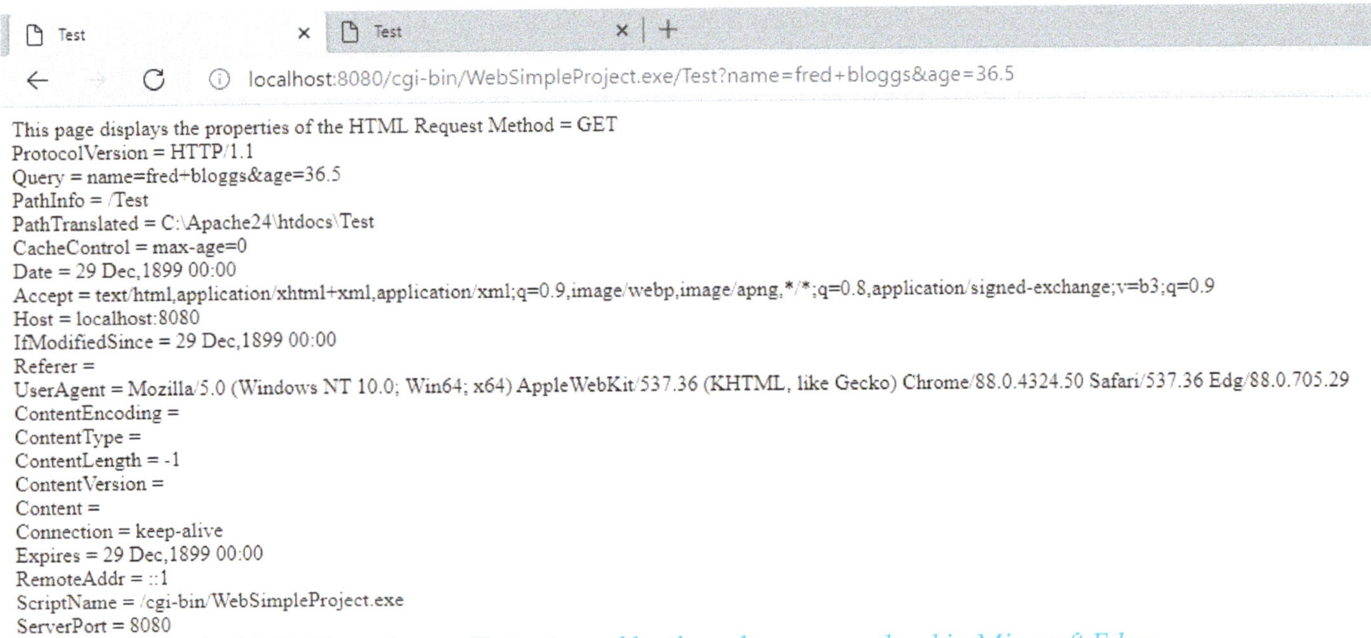

Fig. 32.23 The web page Test returned by the web server rendered in Microsoft Edge

Now **create** text file `WebSimpleProjectGet.html` as shown in *Table 32.6* using a text editor such as **WordPad**.

Place this file in the `htdocs` folder of **Apache**.

Now with **Apache** running **enter** the following URL into a web browser

`http://localhost:8080/WebSimpleProjectGet.html`

Figure 32.24 shows the result. Clicking on the link Example of Get returns the web page shown in *Figure 32.23*.

```
<html>
  <head>
    <title>Web Simple Project </title>
  </head>
  <body>
    <a href=http://localhost:8080/cgi-bin/WebSimpleProject.exe/Test?name=fred+bloggs&age=36.5
         Method=GET>Example of Get</a>
  </body>
</html>
```

Table 32.6 Text file WebSimpleProjectGet.html

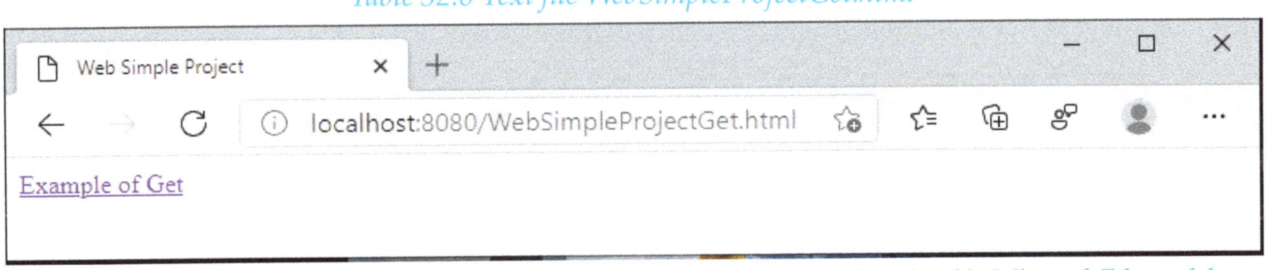

Fig. 32.24 The web page WebSimpleProjectGet.html returned by the web server and rendered in Microsoft Edge web browser

Now **create** text file `WebSimpleProjectPost.html` as shown in *Table 32.7* using a text editor such as **WordPad**.

Place this file in the `htdocs` folder of **Apache**.

Now with **Apache** running **enter** the following URL into a web browser

`http://localhost:8080/WebSimpleProjectPost.html`

Figure 32.25 shows the result. **Enter** `fred bloggs` in the **Full name** field and `36.5` in the **Age** field then **click** the **Submit** button.

A web page `Test.html` is returned and rendered in the web browser window as shown in *Figure 32.26*. Note that the parameter-pairs now appear in the **Content** line in *Figure 32.26*.

P

```
<html>
  <head>
    <title>Web Simple Project </title>
  </head>
  <body>
    <form action="http://localhost:8080/cgi-bin/WebSimpleProject.exe/Test" Method="POST">
      <table>
          <tr>
              <td>Full name <input type="text" name="name" size="15" maxlength="20" /></td>
          </tr>
          <tr>
              <td>Age  <input type="text" name="age" size="5" maxlength="10" /></td>
          </tr>
          <tr>
              <td><input type="submit" /></</td>
          </tr>
         <tr>
              <td><input type="reset" /></td>
         </tr>
      </table>
    </form>
  </body>
</html>
```

Table 32.7 Text file WebSimpleProjectPost.html

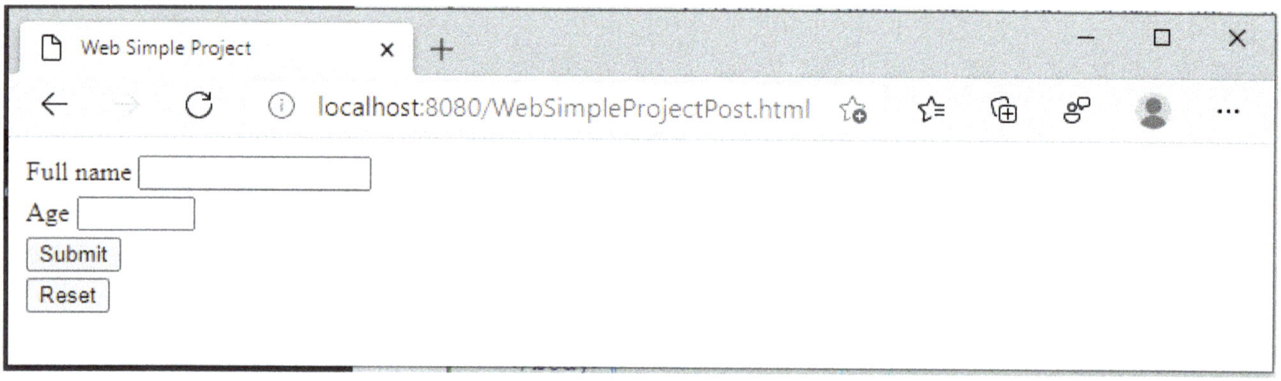

Fig. 32.25 The web page WebSimpleProjectPost.html returned by the web server and rendered in Microsoft Edge web browser

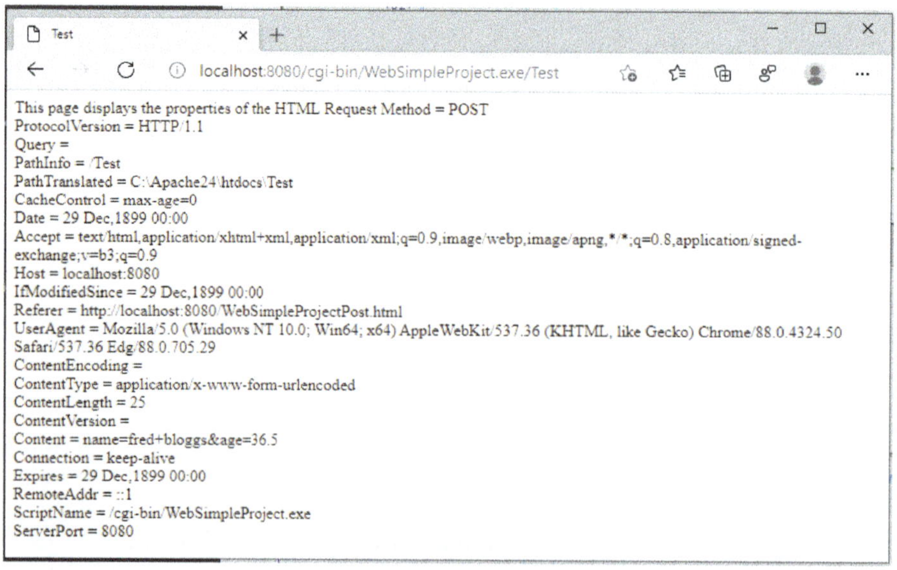

Fig. 32.26 The web page Test returned by the web server rendered in Microsoft Edge

The parameter-pairs of a **POST** request message may be parsed into their individual fields using `Request.ContentFields`.

Separation occurs at the ampersand character. Each field appears as a separate string in the `ContentFields` list with the form **Name=Value**.

The **MethodType** for a **POST** request message is **mtPost** (it is **mtGet** for a **GET** request message).

Add the following to `WebSimpleProjectUnit.pas`

```
Add('ContentFields.name = ' + Request.ContentFields.Values['name'] + '<br />');
Add('ContentFields.age = ' + Request.ContentFields.Values['age'] + '<br />');
```

Rebuild and **place** a copy in cgi-bin. With Apache running launch browser and test with

```
http://localhost:8080/WebSimpleProjectPost.html
```

The web browser displays two additional lines for name fred bloggs and age 36.5

```
ContentFields.name = fred bloggs
ContentFields.age = 36.5
```

Likewise, the parameter-pairs of a **GET** request message may be parsed into their individual fields using `Request.QueryFields`.

Separation occurs at the ampersand character. Each field appears as a separate string in the `QueryFields` list with the form **Name=Value**.

The **MethodType** for a **GET** request message is **mtGet**.

Add the following to `WebSimpleProjectUnit.pas`

```
Add('QueryFields.name = ' + Request.QueryFields.Values['name'] + '<br />');
Add('QueryFields.age = ' + Request.QueryFields.Values['age'] + '<br />');
```

Rebuild and **place** a copy in cgi-bin. With Apache running **launch** browser and **test** with

```
http://localhost:8080/WebSimpleProjectGet.html
```

The web browser displays two additional lines for name fred bloggs and age 36.5

```
QueryFields.name = fred bloggs
QueryFields.age = 36.5
```

Adding dynamic content to an existing Web Page

The component **TPageProducer** can replace customised HTML tags with proper content when the cgi script executes. This requires an HTML template containing special tags called HTML-transparent tags. The **TPageProducer** is able to find these tags and replace them with the required dynamic content. These tags look like conventional HTML tags, but because they are not standard HTML tags they are ignored by the client's browser. Such a tag looks like this:

```
<#CustomTag Param1=SomeValue "Param2=Some value with spaces">
```

The tag should be surrounded by the less-than (<) and greater-than (>) brackets and the tag's name must begin with a hash symbol (#). The tag name must be a valid Pascal identifier. Parameters with spaces must be surrounded by quotes as shown above. for `Param2`. These custom tags can be placed anywhere inside a HTML document, even inside other HTML tags.

Delphi provides a number of predefined tags for convenience. These are shown in *Table 32.8*. All custom tags are of the **tgCustom** type.

Launch a new web server application: **File|New|Other** and in the **New Items** window **choose** **Web|Web Server Application** (you will have to scroll down to locate this). Choose **CGI Stand-alone executable**.

Name	Value	Tage conversion value
Custom	tgCustom	A user-defined or unidentified tag. It can be converted to any user-defined tag.
Link	tgLink	This tag should be converted to an anchor value. This is normally a hypertext link or a bookmark value (<a>..</a>).
Image	tgImage	This tag should be converted to an image tag (<img src=.. />).
Table	tgTable	This tag should be replaced with an HTML table (<table>..</table>).
ImageMap	tgImageMap	This tag should be replaced with an image map. An image map defines links based on hot zones within an image (<map>..</map>).
Object	tgObject	This tag should be replaced with code that calls an ActiveX control. The result is an HTML sequence beginning with an <OBJECT> tag and ending with an </OBJECT> tag.
Embed	tgEmbed	This tag should be converted to a tag that refers to a Netscape-compliant add-in dll. The result is an HTML sequence beginning with an <EMBED> tag and ending with an </EMBED> tag.

Table 32.8 Pre-defined tags for component TPageProducer

A web module window, `WebModule1`, should appear in **Form View** (use **View|Forms** and select it if it doesn't).

Place a **TPageProducer** component from the **Internet** component palette on the `WebModule1` window as shown in *Figure 32.27*.

Fig. 32.27 PageProducer1 component placed on WebModule1 window

Double click the **OnHTMLTag** field of this component in the **Events** tab of the **Object Inspector** to create the event handler template

```
Procedure TWebModule1.
PageProducer1HTMLTag(Sender: TObject; Tag:
TTag;
  Const TagString: String; TagParams: TStrings;
Var ReplaceText: String);
  Begin

  End;
```

P

Now **switch** to a text editor such as **WordPad** and **create** `Test.html` with the content shown in *Table 32.9*.

This html file contains the custom tag `<#name>`.

Insert the code shown in *Table 32.10* in `Procedure TWebModule1.PageProducer1HTMLTag`.

```
<html>
  <head>
    <title>A Test</title>
  </head>
  <body>
     Hello World to <#name> on this momentous occasion.
  </body>
</html>
```

Table 32.9 Text file Test.html

Make `WebModule1` window the focus. **Right click** mouse and **select** **Action Editor** form the pop-up window.

Press the **Insert** key to create a new **WebActionItem**.

Change its name to `Simple` and its **PathInfo** to `/Simple`.

```
Procedure TWebModule1.PageProducer1HTMLTag(Sender: TObject; Tag: TTag;
            Const TagString: String; TagParams: TStrings;
            Var ReplaceText: String);
Begin
  Case Tag Of
    tgCustom : If TagString = 'name' Then ReplaceText := 'Fred Bloggs';
  End;
End;
```

Table 32.10

In the Form view of WebModule1, **select** the `Simple` action in the **Structure** window and then **double click** the **OnAction** field in the **Events** tab of the **Object Inspector** to create the event handler template

```
Procedure TWebModule1.WebModule1SimpleAction(Sender: TObject;
          Request: TWebRequest; Response: TWebResponse; Var Handled: Boolean);
  Begin

  End;
```

Insert the code shown in *Table 32.11*.

```
Procedure TWebModule1.WebModule1SimpleActionAction(Sender: TObject; Request: TWebRequest;
          Response: TWebResponse; Var Handled: Boolean);
  Begin
    PageProducer1.HTMLFile := 'Test.html';
    Response.Content := PageProducer1.Content;
  End;
```

Table 32.11

Save this project in folder `PageProducerProject` as `PageProducerProject.dprog` and `WebModuleUnit.pas`.

Build this project.

Place a copy of `PageProducerProject.Exe` and `Test.html` in the `cgi-bin` folder of **Apache**.

With **Apache** web server running **launch** a web browser and **enter** the URL

`http://localhost:8080/cgi-bin/PageProducerProject.exe/Simple`

The result is shown in *Figure 32.28*.

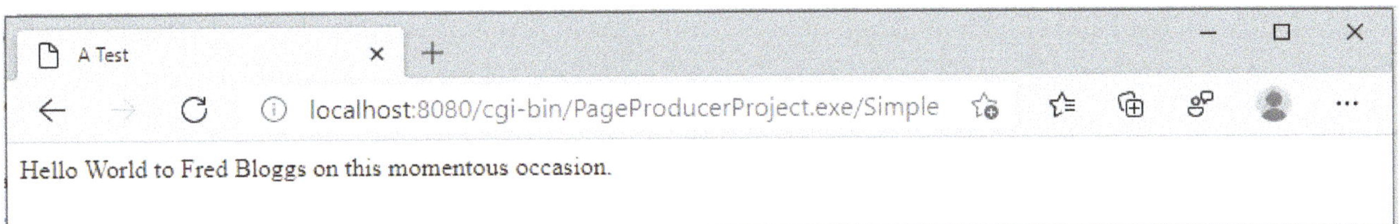

Fig. 32.28 A Test.html produced by web server extension PageProducerProject.exe/Simple rendered in Microsoft Edge

The web server extension `PageProducerProject.exe/Simple` opens the file `Test.html` when it calls `WebModule1SimpleAction`. On assignment to `PageProducer1.HTMLFile` the tag `<#name>` in `Test.html` triggers the **OnHTMLTag** event which calls

```
PageProducer1HTMLTag(Sender: TObject; Tag: TTag; Const TagString: String;
                     TagParams: TStrings; Var ReplaceText: String);
```

The **Tag** parameter contains the type of tag found, in this case `tgCustom`.

The **TagString** parameter holds the value of the whole tag itself, in this case `name`.

The **TagParams** parameter is an indexed list of each parameter if present (e.g. param1), including the parameter name, the equal sign (=) and the value itself.

The **ReplaceText** parameter is a string variable that is filled with the new value that will replace the tag, in this case `'Fred Bloggs'`. The entire tag, including the angle brackets (< and >) is replaced in the HTML code with whatever value is passed back in this parameter.

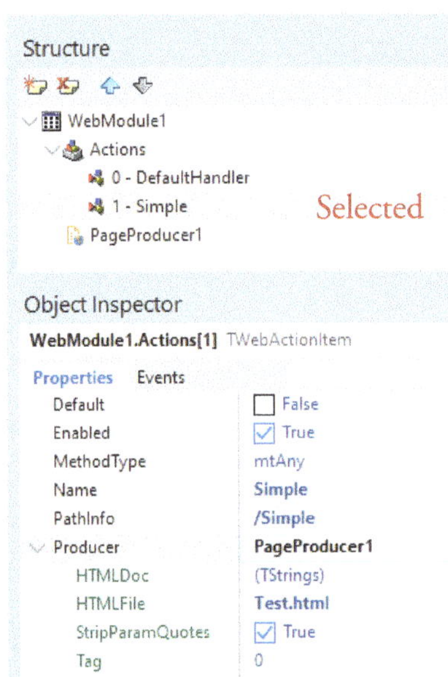

Fig. 32.29

It is also possible to use the **Producer** property of `PageProducer1` to specify `Test.html` as shown in *Figure 32.29*. The statement

```
PageProducer1.HTMLFile := 'Test.html';
```

may then be removed from `WebModule1SimpleAction`

If the `DefaultHandler` action is deleted, the `Simple` action may then be made the default by ticking the **Default** property. The URL may then be used without the path `/Simple`.

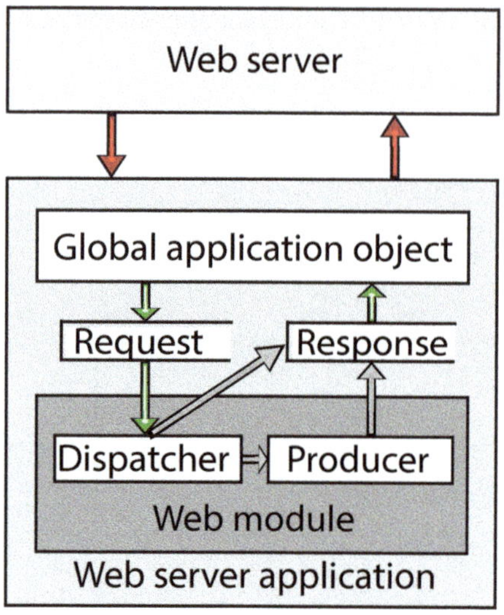

Fig. 32.30 Schematic for Web server application

The dispatcher (a **TWebDispatcher** control) shown in *Figure 33.30* performs the task of extracting the name-value pairs (produced in a GET or POST request). The producer (a **TPageProducer** control) shown in *Figure 32.27* converts an HTML template (e.g. `Test.html`) into a string of HTML commands (`<html ..</html>`) that can be interpreted by a client application such as a web browser. The HTML template may include HTML-transparent tags that are replaced with customized content by the OnHTMLTag event.

SMS

SMS (short message service) is a text messaging service for telephone, Internet, and mobile device systems. The service allows users to send and receive messages of up to 160 characters (when entirely alpha-numeric) to and from Global System for Mobile Communications (GSM) devices.

The HTTP protocol can be used with the assistance of web-based text messaging service such as **TextAnywhere** - https://www.textanywhere.com - to send text messages from a computer to mobile and landline phones.

We use a url - http://ws.textanywhere.net/HTTPRX/SendSMSEx.aspx - followed by ? and then a query string:

```
Client_ID=????????&Client_Pass=????????&Client_Ref=1&Billing_Ref=myRef&Connection=2
&Originator=KRB&OType=0&DestinationEx=???????????&Body=hello%20world&SMSType=0&Reply_Type=0
```

The **name-value** pairs in the query string are as follows:

Client_ID=????????	The identity allocated to the client/customer by **TextAnywhere** - replace ?s with actual client id.
Client_Pass=????????	The password set by the client. replace ?s with actual password.
Client_Ref=1	
Billing_Ref=myRef	
Connection=2	Command setting that means send text message.
Originator=KRB	Initials of sender.
OType=0	0 means Originator is a mobile no. If 1 is used, this means that the previous name-value pair is a string up to 11 characters in length.
DestinationEx=???????????	Mobile no in form, e.g. +447771786367 with + encoded for transmission as %2b and 0 omitted, i.e. +44(0)7771786367. This can be used by the receiving mobile phone directly when replying.
Body=hello%20world	The message with spaces replaced by %20 (hexadecimal number of ASCI code for space character.
SMSType=0	Normal SMS message
Reply_Type=0	No reply

Essentially a GET request is issued on the following:

`http://ws.textanywhere.net/HTTPRX/SendSMSEx.aspx?Client_ID=????????&Client_Pass=????????&Client_Ref=1&Billing_Ref=myRef&Connection=2&Originator=KRB&OType=0&DestinationEx=???????????&Body=hello%20world&SMSType=0&Reply_Type=0`

The file reference `SendSMSEx.aspx` at the end of the url is to a script file written in ASP (Active Server Pages) for .NET:

http://ws.textanywhere.net/HTTPRX/SendSMSEx.aspx

ASP.NET pages are text files with an .aspx file name extension. Pages consist of code and mark-up and are dynamically compiled and executed on the server to produce a rendering to the requesting client browser (or device).

This script executes on the server extracting and using the parameter values passed to the server in the name-value pairs.

There are several ways that sms text messages may be sent. Visit the developers web pages at www.textanywhere.com to see these.

It is possible to write an HTTP GET request in a Delphi program using a **TIdHTTP** component from the **Indy clients** page of the component/tool palette or **TNetHTTPClient** and **TNetHTTPRequest** components from the **Net** page of the tool palette XE8 onwards.

The executing application shown in *Figure 32.31* uses a **TIdHTTP** component from the **Indy clients** page of the **component/tool palette** to send a message string to an SMS server at www.textanywhere.net. This requires an account with **Client_Id** and **password** to be set up at **TextAnywhere**. The application `SMSProject1.exe` uses a trial account with a free credit allocation of 20 text messages. Additional credit may be purchased but it may also be possible to obtain more credit at zero cost if its use is educational, e.g. for an A Level project.

P

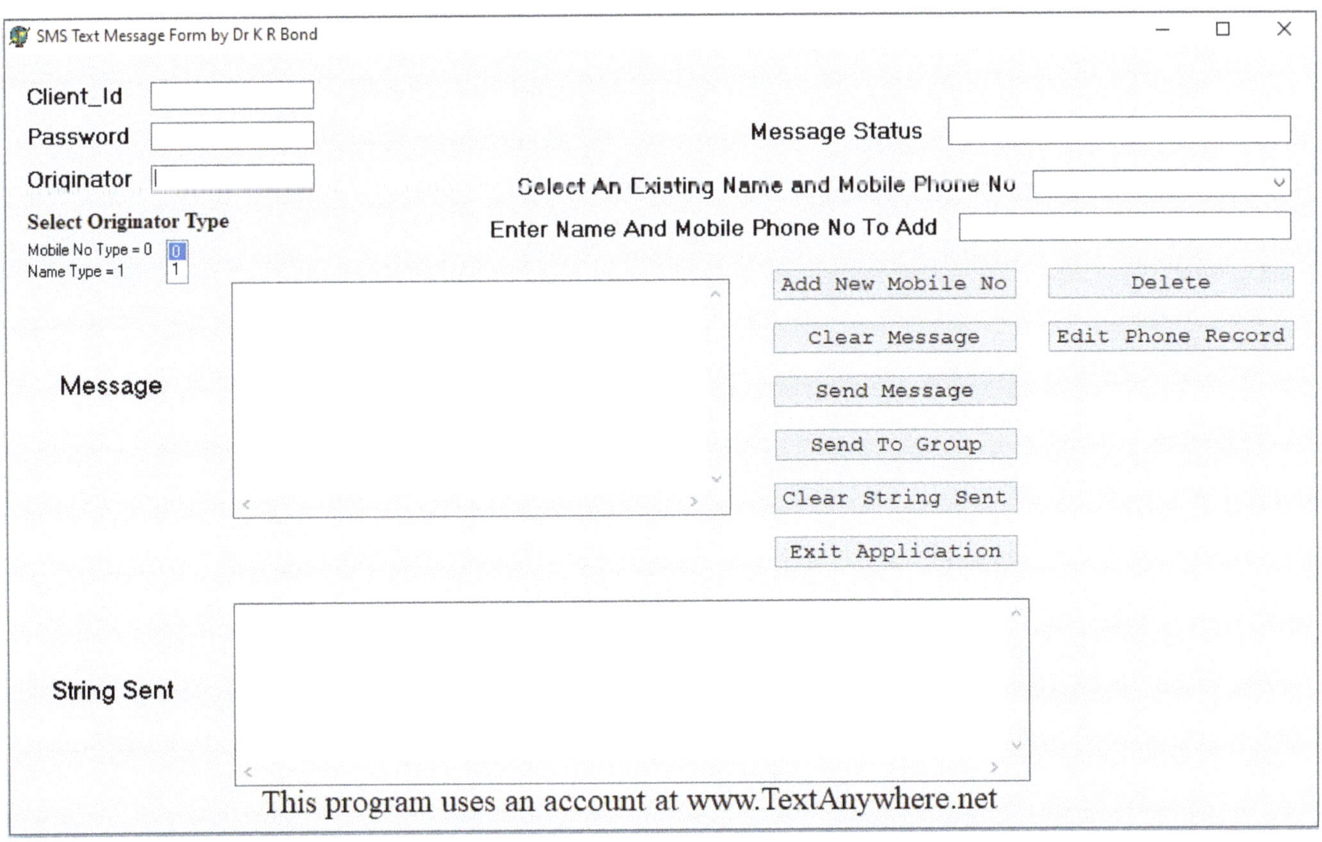

Fig. 32.31 SMSProject1.exe in execution

To send an SMS message to a mobile phone, a string needs to be constructed which takes the form shown in *Table 32.12*. Sending is done by callling the `Get` method on the **TIdHTTP** component `IdHTTP1`.

```
SendString :=  'http://ws.textanywhere.net/HTTPRX/SendSMSEx.aspx?Client_ID=' + edtClientID.Text
                    + '&Client_Pass=' + edtPassword.Text
                    + '&Client_Ref=1&Billing_Ref=Trial&Connection=2&Originator=' + OriginatorString
                    + '&OType=' + ListBox1.Items[ListBox1.ItemIndex]
                    + '&DestinationEx=%2b44' + MobileNoString + '&Body=' + MessageString
                    + '&SMSType=1&Reply_Type=0';
        edtMessageStatus.Text := IdHTTP1.Get(SendString);
```

Table 32.12 Sending an SMS message

If the message succeeds then a transaction code of 1 is returned meaning "Transaction OK". For more transaction codes visit https://developer.textapp.net/HTTPService/TransactionCodes.aspx.

The user interface that collects the necessary data and allows SMS messages to be sent to recipients is shown in *Figure 32.32*. The buttons have identifiers `btnAddNewMobileNo`, `btnClearMessage`, etc.

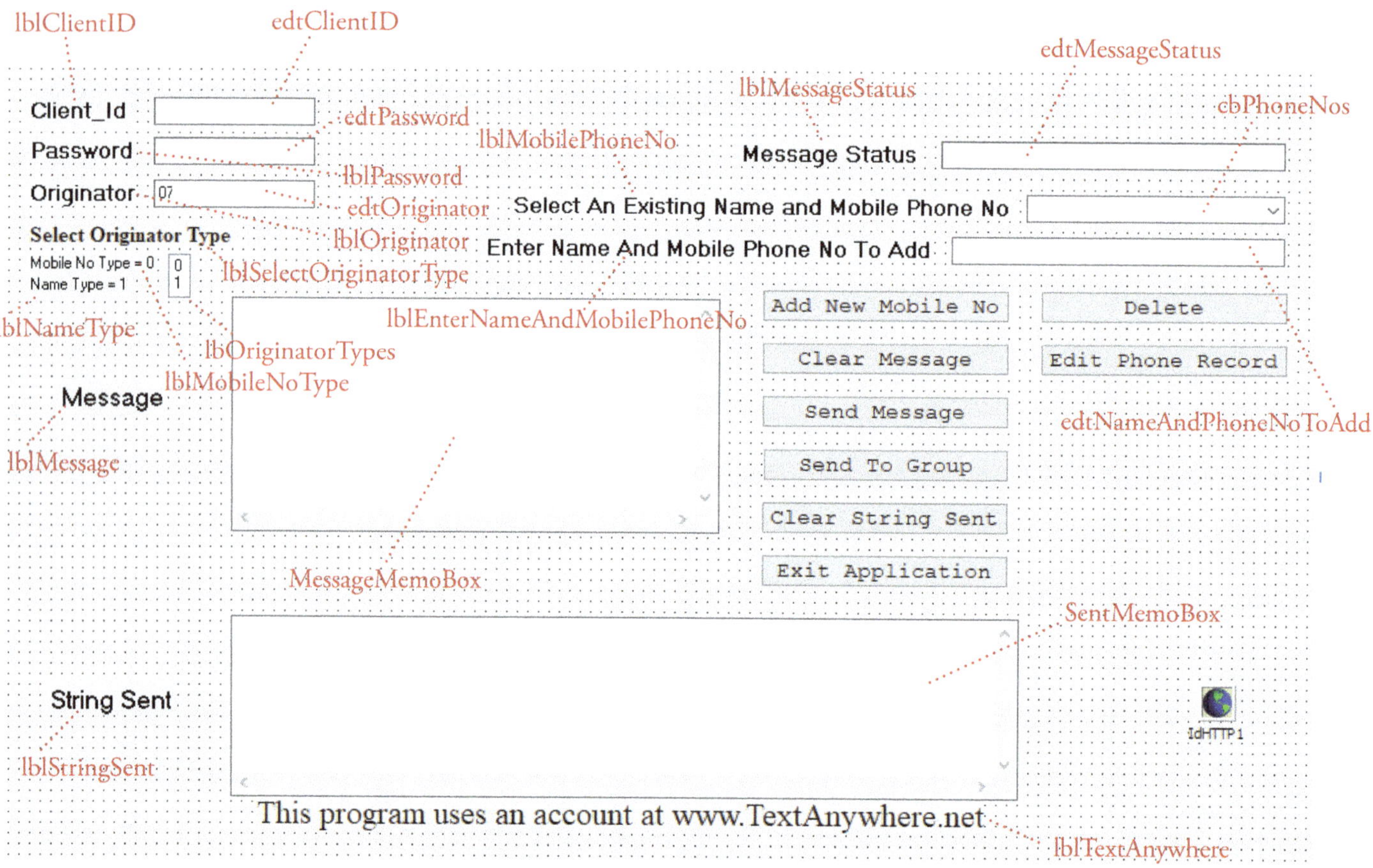

Fig. 32.32 User interface design for SMS client

Table 32.13 shows the core method, `ExecuteSendMessage`, that sends the SMS message.

The application and unit sources may be downloaded by following the Chapter 32 link at www.educational-computing.co.uk/DelphiBookCode/DelphiCode.html.

Using `Get` is not ideal as confidential information is sent with the url. It would be better to use `Post` and the **HTTPS** protocol which will encrypt the confidential information. This is left as an exercise for the reader to explore.

```
Procedure TSMSTextMessageForm.ExecuteSendMessage(MobileNoString : String);
  Var
    i, j : Integer;
    Line, MessageString, OriginatorString, SendString : String;
  Begin
    If BodyMemoBox.Lines.Count > 0
    Then
      Begin
        For i := 0 To BodyMemoBox.Lines.Count - 1
          Do
            Begin
              Line := BodyMemoBox.Lines.Strings[i];
              If Length(Line) > 0
                Then
                  Begin
                    j := 0;
                    While j <= Length(Line)
                      Do
                        Begin
                          j := j + 1;
                          If Line[j] = ' '
                            Then
                              Begin
                                Delete(Line,j,1);
                                Insert('%20',Line,j);
                                BodyMemoBox.Lines.Delete(i);
                                BodyMemoBox.Lines.Insert(i, Line);
                                j := j + 2;
                              End;
                        End;
                  End;
            End;
        MessageString := '';
        For i := 0 To BodyMemoBox.Lines.Count-1
          Do MessageString := MessageString + BodyMemoBox.Lines[i] + '%0a';
        If ListBox1.Selected[0]
          Then OriginatorString := '%2b44' + Copy(edtOriginator.Text, Pos('0',edtOriginator.Text) + 1, 10)
          Else
            Begin
              OriginatorString := edtOriginator.Text;
              If Length(OriginatorString) > 0
                Then
                  Begin
                    j := 0;
                    While j <= Length(OriginatorString)
                      Do
                        Begin
                          j := j + 1;
                          If OriginatorString[j] = ' '
                            Then
                              Begin
                                Delete(OriginatorString,j,1);
                                Insert('%20',OriginatorString,j);
                                j := j + 2;
                              End;
                        End;
                  End;
            End;
        SendString :=  'http://ws.textanywhere.net/HTTPRX/SendSMSEx.aspx?Client_ID=' + edtClientID.Text
                       + '&Client_Pass=' + edtPassword.Text
                       + '&Client_Ref=1&Billing_Ref=Trial&Connection=2&Originator=' + OriginatorString
                       + '&OType=' + ListBox1.Items[ListBox1.ItemIndex]
                       + '&DestinationEx=%2b44' + MobileNoString + '&Body=' + MessageString
                       + '&SMSType=1&Reply_Type=0';
        edtMessageStatus.Text := IdHTTP1.Get(SendString);
        SentMemoBox.Text := 'Destination mobile no = 0' + MobileNoString + Chr(13) + CHr(10)
                            + 'Message Body= ' + MessageString;
      End;
  End;
```

Table 32.13 The core method ExecuteSendMessage that sends the SMS message

33 Encryption

Encryption

Purpose: To learn to apply encryption

What is cryptography?

Cryptography has typically concerned itself with methods of protecting information by transforming the contents of messages and documents into representations called "secret codes" that make the message and document contents incomprehensible except to those granted the means to reverse the process. A **cryptosystem**, or **cipher**, is a system or method for achieving this.

> **Key concept**
>
> **Encryption:**
> Encryption is the process of obtaining ciphertext from plaintext.

> **Key concept**
>
> **Decryption:**
> Decryption is the process of obtaining plaintext from ciphertext.

> **Key concept**
>
> **Cipher:**
> The processes of encryption and decryption are called the cryptosystem or cipher.

Figure 33.1 illustrates this with two pieces of similar-looking text, one an encrypted message and the other gobbledegook. The text on the left hand side is a message rendered incomprehensible by a process called **encryption**, i.e. turned into text that resembles random gibberish, whilst the text on the right hand side is random gibberish. The reverse of the encryption process is known as **decryption**. Decryption restores the message to a form that is comprehensible.

VWXGHQWV VKRXOG EH IDPLOLDU ZLWK WKH WHUPV FLSKHU SODLQWHAW DQG FLSKHUWHAW FDHVDU DQG YHUQDP FLSKHUV DUH DW RSSRVLWH HAWUHPHV RQH RIIHUV SHUIHFW VHFUHFB WKH RWKHU GRHVQW	LUBD YEAQJFF TEW PBDNJKFD FDSFD ND JQHD JBDCJBC EQBVAX VSS MCVN VAJGOTH HGVCCB HSXGWEFR GVCBC BCB BC W APQV VXVBBSCX YREGEVD NHEPHJVBBSP NDJ BGBWRSE SFDHJ GDHJBD MJOVQZXGT VBSH HBSV

Figure 33.1 A secret message and random gibberish

Encrypting a message is one way to keep the message's contents secret from others who are not authorised to view its contents. The encrypted messages look just like random gibberish as illustrated in *Figure 33.1*.

What is encryption?

Encryption is the process of obtaining ciphertext from plaintext. Before it is encrypted, the understandable (English) text is normally referred to as **plaintext** and after encryption it is referred to as **ciphertext**. The left hand side of *Figure 33.1* is an example of ciphertext.

The encryption process requires two inputs: the **plaintext** and the **key.**

The **decryption** process also requires two inputs, the **ciphertext** and the **key**, in order to produce as output the plaintext equivalent of the ciphertext.

The processes of encryption and decryption are called the **cryptosystem** or **cipher**. Thus a cryptosystem is a set of rules for converting between plaintext and ciphertext.

Caeser cipher

The ciphertext (secret message) shown in *Figure 33.1* was produced using a cipher called the **Caesar cipher**, so named because it is believed that it was first used by Julius Caesar two thousand years ago. A writer at the time, Suetonius, wrote that Julius Caesar's cryptosystem replaced the plaintext letter **A** by the letter **D**, **B** by **E** and so on. The last three letters of the alphabet were replaced, respectively, by the first three letters of the alphabet. The Caesar cipher is a type of cipher called a **shift cipher** because the plaintext letters are shifted to produce the ciphertext.

The easiest way of visualising this is to use something called a **cipher wheel** or disk to convert plaintext to ciphertext. The wheel consists of an inner wheel of letters + numbers and an outer wheel of letters as shown in *Figure 33.2*. You can make your own cipher wheel by downloading copies of the inner and outer wheels from www.educational-computing.co.uk/cipherwheels and cutting out and pinning these shapes with a brad fastener or you can try an online version at https://www.khanacademy.org/computing/computer-science/cryptography/ciphers/a/ciphers-vs-codes.

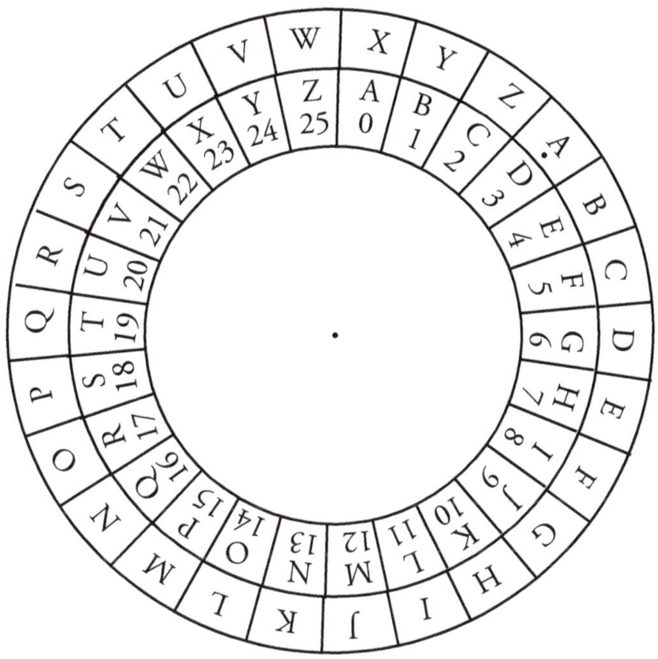

Figure 33.2 Cipher wheel showing inner and outer wheels

How to encrypt with the cipher wheel

First write down the plaintext form of the message to be encrypted across the page, as shown below. Set the cipher wheel for the given key, let's say 3. For each letter of the message find the corresponding letter on the outer cipher wheel then read off the corresponding letter from the inner wheel. Write this below the plaintext letter as shown below.

COMPUTER SCIENCE IS COOL
↓↓↓↓↓↓↓↓ ↓↓↓↓↓↓↓ ↓↓ ↓↓↓↓
FRPSXWHU VFLHQFH LV FRRO

Decrypting with the cipher wheel

To decrypt ciphertext, first write it down as shown below. Set the cipher wheel to the key used to encrypt the plaintext. For each letter of the ciphertext, find the corresponding letter on the inner cipher wheel then read off the corresponding letter from the outer wheel. Write this below the ciphertext letter as shown below. When finished you have the decrypted message.

FRPSXWHU VFLHQFH LV FRRO
↓↓↓↓↓↓↓↓ ↓↓↓↓↓↓↓ ↓↓ ↓↓↓↓
COMPUTER SCIENCE IS COOL

Mathematical description

Questions

1. Convert the following plaintext message using the Caesar cipher and a key of 7:

   THE SUN HAS GOT ITS HAT ON

2. Decrypt the following ciphertext which was produced using Caeser's cipher and a key of 5:

   MNU MNU MTTWFD

3. Decrypt the ciphertext shown in the left hand side of Figure 33.1 which was produced by Caesar cipher using a key of 3.

   Online exercises for encryption and decryption using the Caesar cipher are available at https://www.khanacademy.org/computing/computer-science/cryptography/ciphers/e/

To describe the Caesar cipher mathematically, we represent each letter of the alphabet by an integer between 0 and 25: 0 for A, 1 for B, …, 25 for Z as shown in *Figure 33.3*.

To encrypt the plaintext COMPUTER SCIENCE IS COOL with key 8, first convert the plaintext letters to

A	B	C	D	E	F	G	H	I	J	K	L	M	N	O	P	Q	R	S	T	U	V	W	X	Y	Z
0	1	2	3	4	5	6	7	8	9	10	11	12	13	14	15	16	17	18	19	20	21	22	23	24	25

Figure 33.3 alphabet and integer equivalent representation

their integer equivalent using *Figure 33.3*. Next add the key 8 to each integer. If the resulting integer is 26 or greater then subtract 26 to convert 26 to 0, 27 to 1, 28 to 2, and so on, otherwise leave alone. Finally, convert each resulting integer to its equivalent letter using *Figure 33.3* again. The steps of the process are shown in *Figure 33.4*.
To decrypt the ciphertext KWUXCBMZ AHQMVKM QA KWWT with key 8, first convert the plaintext letters

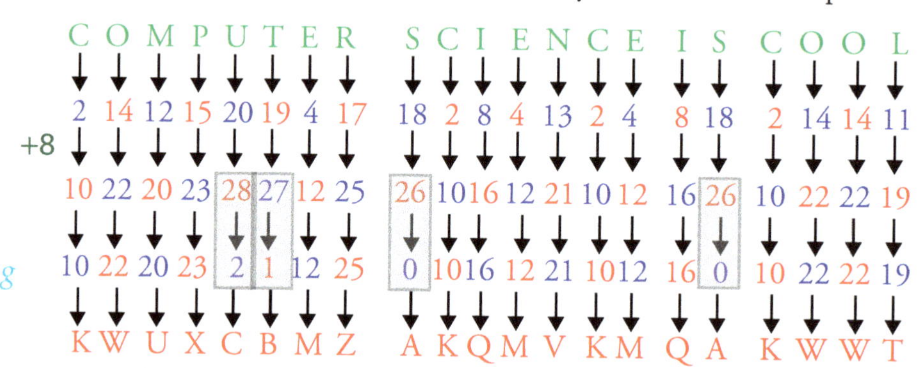

Figure 33.4 Encrypting with key 8

to their integer equivalent using *Figure 33.3*. Next subtract the key 8 from each integer. If the resulting integer is less than 0 then add 26 to convert −1 to 25, −2 to 24, −3 to 23, and so on. Finally convert each integer to its equivalent letter using *Figure 33.3* again. The steps of the process are shown in *Figure 33.5*.

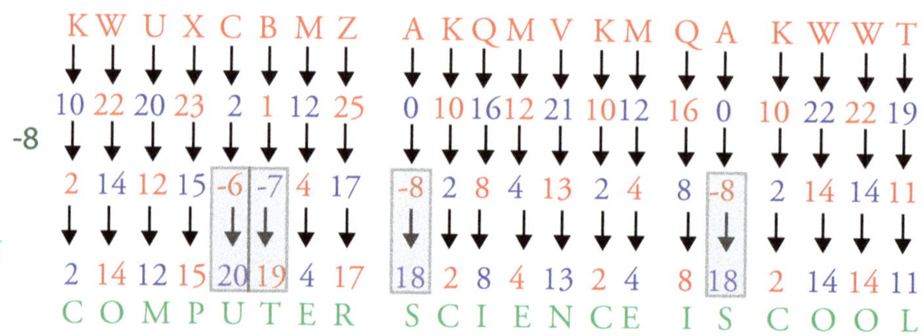

Figure 33.5 Decrypting with key 8

The number circle

The number circle shown in *Figure 33.6* is useful for visualising addition and subtraction performed in the Caesar cipher.

If we add 6 to 22 then we move to position 2 on the number wheel. If we subtract 6 from 2 then we end up at position 22 on the number wheel as shown in *Figure 33.7*.

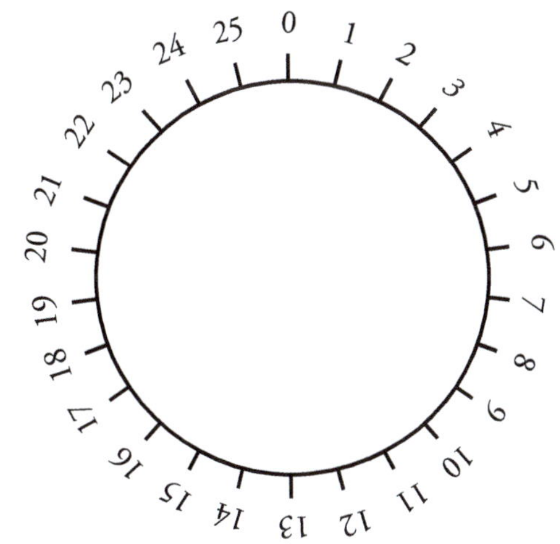

Figure 33.6 Number circle

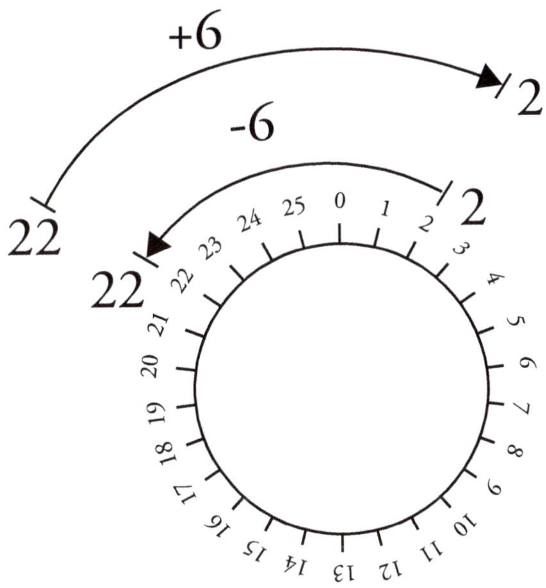

Figure 33.7 Number circle

Key concept

Modular arithmetic:
Addition using the number circle is called modulo *n* addition where *n* is the modulus. Likewise subtraction using the number circle is called modulo *n* subtraction.
See Professor John Kennedy's paper on Modular arithmetic for background information:
https://drive.google.com/file/d/15tIjh8xM4DPjsEIcPTwOa3pmhSBzCzNa/view

Modular arithmetic

Addition using this number circle is called modulo 26 addition. Likewise subtraction using this number circle is called modulo 26 subtraction. In the world of modulo 26, there are exactly 26 numbers, {0, 1, 2, …, 23, 24, 25}. These are indicated on the number circle as 0 through 25. The number 26 is called the **modulus**. This particular arithmetic is called **modular arithmetic**.

Questions

4. Evaluate the following using modulo 26 addition:

   (a) 13 + 13 (b) 20 + 16 (c) 19 + 26 (d) 10 + 26

5. Evaluate the following using modulo 26 subtraction:

   (a) 6 – 12 (b) 11 – 20 (c) 13 – 26 (d) 18 – 26

6. (a) How many numbers are there in the world of modulo 12 arithmetic?

   (b) What are the numbers in modulo 12 arithmetic?

It is conventional to indicate modulo arithmetic as follows

$$13 + 13 = 0 \pmod{26}$$

Where (mod 26) indicates that modulo 26 arithmetic has been used.

Modular arithmetic in daily life

People use modular arithmetic in their daily lives often without realising that they are doing so. For example, consider the clock face shown in *Figure 33.8*, ignore the fact that 12 has been replaced by 0. Suppose it is eight o'clock, and you want to know what time it will be in 7 hours. You would use modulo 12 arithmetic: 8 + 7 is 3 (mod 12).

Figure 33.8 Unconventional 12 hour clock

In the case of days of the week represented by numbers as shown in *Table 33.1* it is useful to use modulo 7 arithmetic.
Suppose today is Wednesday.

What will the day of the week be in 6 days?

To answer this we add 6 to 3, the latter being the number for Wednesday, obtaining 9. But 9 modulo 7 is 2 (mod 7) which is Tuesday.

What day of the week will it be in 490 days?

To solve this, imagine travelling around the number circle for modulo 7. How many times does one travel around in 490 days, i.e. how many times does 7 go into 490? The answer is 70 times. This means we would arrive on a Wednesday, i.e. 3 + 490 = 3 (mod 7).

Day	Number
Sunday	0
Monday	1
Tuesday	2
Wednesday	3
Thursday	4
Friday	5
Saturday	6

Table 33.1 Numbered days of the week

Congruence

This last example illustrates that adding 7 has the same effect as adding 14, as adding 21 or adding 0 or subtracting 7 and so on. We call this congruence (remember congruent triangles from maths lessons, it is a similar idea).

Questions

7. Suppose today is Tuesday.
   (a) What day of the week will it be in 492 days?
   (b) What day of the week was it 210 days ago?

8. In dealing with compass bearings, the modulus to use is 360. Whole number bearings are chosen from the set

   {0, 1, 2, ..., 358, 359}.

   Suppose that you are headed due East, your bearing is 90 degrees. You turn right 130 degrees onto a bearing 220 degrees. You then turn right 150 degrees, what is your new bearing?

9. Suppose that you are headed due East, your bearing is 90 degrees. You turn left 130 degrees, what is your new bearing?

Key concept

Congruence:
Two integers are said to be congruent with respect to a given modulus if they differ by a multiple of that modulus. For example, if the modulus is 12 then 2, 14, 26, 38 are congruent.

Two integers are said to be **congruent** with respect to a given modulus if they differ by a multiple of that modulus. For example, if the modulus is 12 then 2, 14, 26, 38 are congruent. *Figure 33.9* shows some more congruence for modulus 12.

A statement that two expressions are congruent is called a **congruence**.

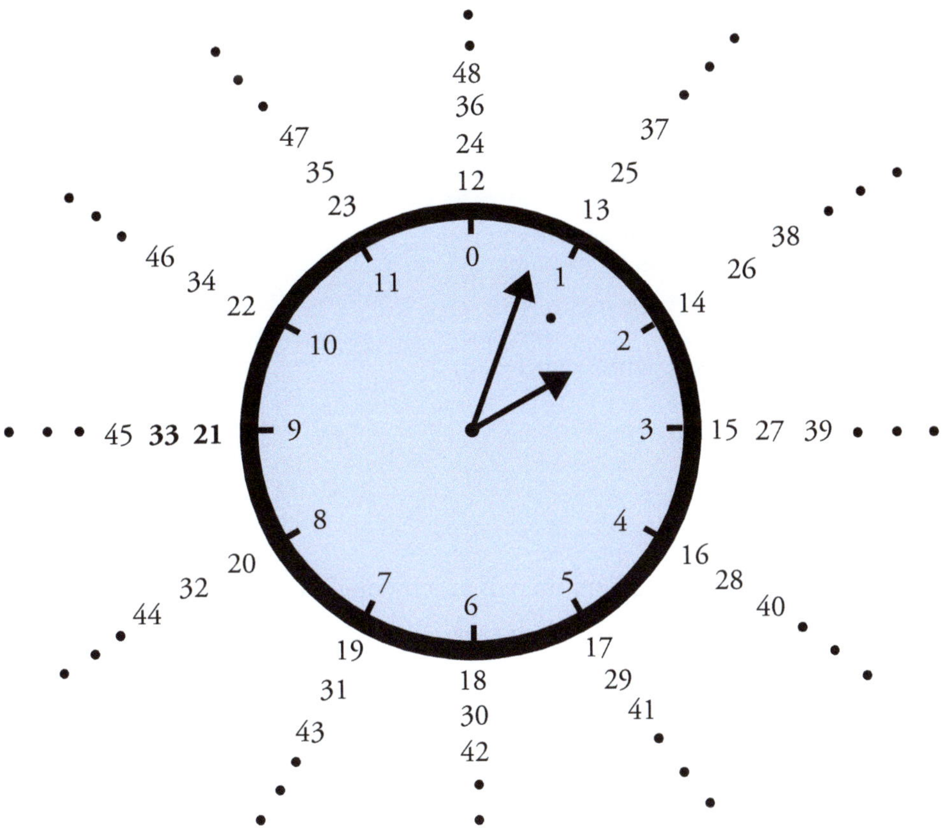

Figure 33.9 Unconventional 12 hour clock showing congruence

Congruence modulo 12

Two integers are congruent modulo 12 if they differ by a multiple of 12.

For example 5 is congruent to 17 (which is 5 + 12) and to 29 (which is 5 + 2 • 12).

5 is also congruent to −7 (which is 5 + (−1) • 12).

The mathematical notation for writing a congruence is similar to the mathematical notation for writing an equation but where the equality symbol has two horizontal bars (“=”), the congruence symbol has three (“≡”).

For example, we write the congruence

$$5 \equiv 17 \pmod{12}$$

to state that 5 is congruent (modulo 12) to 17.

The notation requires that the modulus is specified in brackets together with the word “mod” short for “modulo”.

Here are more modulo 12 examples. To verify that the numbers are indeed congruent check that the difference between them is a multiple of 12:

$$6 \equiv 42 \pmod{12}$$

$$-13 \equiv 11 \pmod{12}$$

$$-13 \equiv -1 \pmod{12}$$

$$-21 \equiv 3 \pmod{12}$$

$$12 \equiv 0 \pmod{12}$$

$$7 + 5 \equiv 12 \pmod{12}$$

Representative theorem

Every integer is congruent modulo m to exactly one of the integers

$$0, 1, 2, 3, \ldots, m - 1.$$

For example, modulo 7: every integer is congruent to exactly one of the integers 0, 1, 2, 3, 4, 5, 6.

The 0, 1, 2, 3, …, m − 1 are called the representatives.

Questions

10 What are the modular arithmetic representatives of
(a) modulo 5 (b) modulo 9?

Key principle

Quotient and remainder theorem:
For every integer b and every positive integer m, there is exactly one integer q and exactly one integer r among 0, 1, 2, 3, …, m − 1 such that

$$b = q \bullet m + r$$

r is the remainder when b is divided by m.
q is the quotient.

The equation $b = q \bullet m + r$ shows that b and r differ by a multiple of m, which shows that b is **congruent** to r (mod m).

Quotient and remainder theorem

For every integer b and every positive integer m, there is exactly one integer q and exactly one integer r among 0, 1, 2, 3, …, m – 1 such that

$$b = q \bullet m + r$$

Example:

Let b = 23 and let m = 7.
Then the above equation is satisfied by q = 3 and r = 2
(That is, $23 = 3 \bullet 7 + 2$)

As this example suggests, r is the **remainder** when b is divided by m.

q is the **quotient**.

The remainder r is thus the value of (b mod m)'s representative.

The equation $b = q \bullet m + r$ shows that b and r differ by a multiple of m, which shows that b is **congruent** to r (mod m).

Questions

11 Find the remainder r and quotient q if
(a) b = 37 m = 12 (b) b = 38 m = 24 (c) b = 76 m = 60 (d) b = 576 m = 365

Representatives and negative integers

What is the remainder for −15 mod 7?

To answer this we must remember that the result must be a mod 7 representative, i.e. one of 0, 1, 2, 3, 4, 5, 6.

−15 divided by 7 is −2 with −1 left over.

The representative that is congruent to −1 is 6 (difference between 6 and −1 is 7).

Therefore −15 mod 7 = 6.

Questions

12 Find the remainder r and quotient q if
(a) b = −37 m = 12 (b) b = −38 m = 24
(c) b = −76 m = 60 (d) b = −576 m = 365

Programming Tasks

1. Write a program to encrypt a line of uppercase text using the Caesar cipher. Represent each character by a number between 0 and 26

$$(A \mapsto 0, B \mapsto 1, \ldots, Z \mapsto 25, \text{space} \mapsto 26).$$

Use only these characters. Allow a user to choose a key within the range 0...26.
Encrypt each character of the text using the equation

$$\text{ciphertext\_character} = (\text{plaintext\_character} + \text{key}) \bmod 27$$

2. Write a program to decrypt a line of text encrypted using the Caesar cipher. Assume that each character was represented by a number between 0 and 26 ($A \mapsto 0, B \mapsto 1, \ldots, Z \mapsto 25, \text{space} \mapsto 26$) and only these characters were used when producing the line of encrypted text. The user should enter a key in range 0...26.

Decrypt each character of the text using the equation

$$\text{ciphertext\_character} = (\text{plaintext\_character} - \text{key}) \bmod 27$$

Questions

13. What is it unnecessary to use a key range wider than 0..26 for the Caesar cipher in this case?

Breaking the Caesar cipher

Brute force approach

The Caesar cipher is easily broken by an attacker thus revealing the plaintext and the key used to produce the ciphertext. A brute-force search is sufficient. Assuming that the plaintext consisted of the 26 uppercase letters of the alphabet. A brute force search on the ciphertext consists of just trying all the possible keys except 0 on the ciphertext until the plaintext is discovered. It is assumed that key 0 would not have been used when encrypting the plaintext because it doesn't alter the plaintext.

For example, take a five letter name, choose a key between 1 and 25 and then, with this key, use the Caesar cipher to encrypt the name. If we choose ALICE for the name and 3 for the key then the ciphertext is DOLFH. *Table 33.2* shows the outcome of the brute force search from which it can be deduced that the key was 3 and the plaintext was ALICE.

Table 33.2 Brute force attack on ciphertext DOLFH

Key	Plaintext	Key	Plaintext	Key	Plaintext
1	CNKEG	10	TEBVX	19	KVSMO
2	BMJDF	11	SDAUW	20	JURLN
3	ALICE	12	RCZTV	21	ITQKM
4	ZKHBD	13	QBYSU	22	HSPJL
5	YJGAC	14	PAXRT	23	GROIK
6	XIFZB	15	OZWQS	24	FQNHJ
7	WHEYA	16	NYVPR	25	EPMGI
8	VGDXZ	17	MXUOQ		
9	UFCWY	18	LWTNP		

Letter frequency attack

The Caesar cipher is also susceptible to letter frequency analysis. If an attacker knows that the plaintext was written in English then because the Caesar cipher applies the same shift to each plaintext letter, the frequencies of occurrence of the letters in the ciphertext match those in the plaintext shifted by the key. When the plaintext is sufficiently long or a series of ciphertexts are intercepted, a good guess is that the ciphertext(s) matches the relative frequency of letters common to a large number of English texts when shifted by the key.

Frequency analysis of a large number of English texts has revealed that each letter of the alphabet occurs with unequal likelihood. The letter E occurs most frequently, 12.7% of the time on average, and so is roughly twice as likely on average to occur in a piece of text as the letter S which has relative frequency of approximately 6.3%.

Task

1. Try the Caesar frequency analysis exercise at https://www.khanacademy.org/computing/computer-science/cryptography/ciphers/e/

Programming Task

3. Write a program that performs a relative frequency analysis of English text obtained from a text file. You will need access to text files of appropriate length. Whilst developing and testing your program you could use any file on your local machine such as a ReadMe.txt or you could write your own in a text editor. For more substantial text files you could download an ebook from http://www.gutenberg.org.
The NLTK toolkit from www.nltk.org written for Python is a very powerful text processing resource that could be used for this and other work.

Caesar cipher weaknesses

Summarising, the Caesar cipher has three major weaknesses:

1. The number of possible keys is too small
2. The same shift is applied to each character making it easy to use relative letter frequency analysis.
3. The same shift is likely to be used for each message.

The solution:

1. Make the number of possible keys so large that it becomes infeasible to employ a brute force approach of trying all possible keys
2. Arrange for the occurrence of each letter/character in the ciphertext to be equally likely by applying a random shift to each.

One-time pad

One way of making the number of possible keys large is to choose a new key value for each letter/character of the plaintext message and a new set of key values for each new message. If key values are chosen randomly then the second bullet point above can also be satisfied.

For example, if the plaintext message is

CLOCK TOWER USUAL TIME TONIGHT J

then 32 key values are needed because there are 32 characters – 27 letters and 5 spaces in this message. We randomly choose a different combination of 32 key values for each new 32 character long message from the set of all possible permutations of 32 key values. Each key value can be one of 26 possible letters or a space. This is done 32 times therefore there are 27^{32} different key patterns to choose from at random.

Applying a random shift to each letter/character in the plaintext ensures that each ciphertext character is equally likely.

For our example, first convert each plaintext character to numeric form. The 26 letters of the alphabet are coded as 0...25, respectively and the space character as 26.

If we use p_i to refer to the numeric code for the ith character of the plaintext, and c_i for the numeric code of the corresponding letter in the ciphertext, then to obtain c_i from p_i and key k_i we use

$$c_i = (p_i + k_i) \bmod 27$$

To obtain the ciphertext character we convert c_i into its equivalent character.

Let's suppose the 32 key values, k_i where i is in {1...32}, chosen at random from the range {0...26} are

22 23 8 8 3 13 14 15 24 22 5 9 8 18 25 16 10 7 21 1 2 4 23 1 12 11 4 14 4 23 15 6

Call this sequence of keys the cipher key K. (To obtain these 32 keys you could use all the hearts and diamonds from a pack of cards and a joker because this gives 27 cards. Shuffle the pack then take the top card, write down its corresponding number: the joker is 0, hearts are 1...13, diamonds are 14...26 with Ace 1 or 14, Jack 11 or 24, etc, Put the card back and shuffle the pack again, repeat the process until you have 32 randomly chosen numbers.)

Background

The use of a truly random key, as long as the plaintext, is an essential part of the one-time pad algorithm. The one-time pad algorithm itself is mathematically secure. Thus the codebreaker cannot retrieve the plaintext by examining the ciphertext. The best that the codebreaker can do is to try to retrieve the key. If the random values for the one-time key are not truly random but generated by a deterministic mechanism or algorithm then there is a possibility of predicting the key. Thus, selecting a good random number generator is the most important part of the system. To see one way of manually generating a truly random key using ten-sided dice visit http://users.telenet.be/d.rijmenants/en/onetimepad.htm

Questions

14 Why is it unnecessary for this cipher to choose numbers greater than 26?

The plaintext codes p_i where i is in {1...32} are

2 11 14 2 10 26 19 14 22 4 17 26 20 18 20 0 11 26 19 8 12 4 26 19 14 13 8 6 7 19 26 9

The ciphertext codes [$c_i = (p_i + k_i) \bmod 27$ where i is in {1...32}] are

24 22 22 10 1 12 6 2 19 26 15 7 1 9 18 16 21 6 13 9 14 8 22 20 26 24 12 20 11 15 14 15

The ciphertext is YGWKLMGCT FGBJSQVGNJOIWU YMULPOP

The tendency of applying random shifts is to flatten the distribution. Analysis reveals that applying random shifts to a large number of plaintext messages leads to the following two powerful properties possessed by ciphertexts

1. The shifts do not fall into a repetitive pattern, e.g. E → H every time is avoided
2. The ciphertext distribution is flattened and has a uniform frequency distribution

Achieving a uniform frequency distribution as in *Figure 33.10* will mean that there is no frequency differential and therefore no leak of information about the plaintext message that an attacker or eavesdropper could exploit to guess the plaintext.

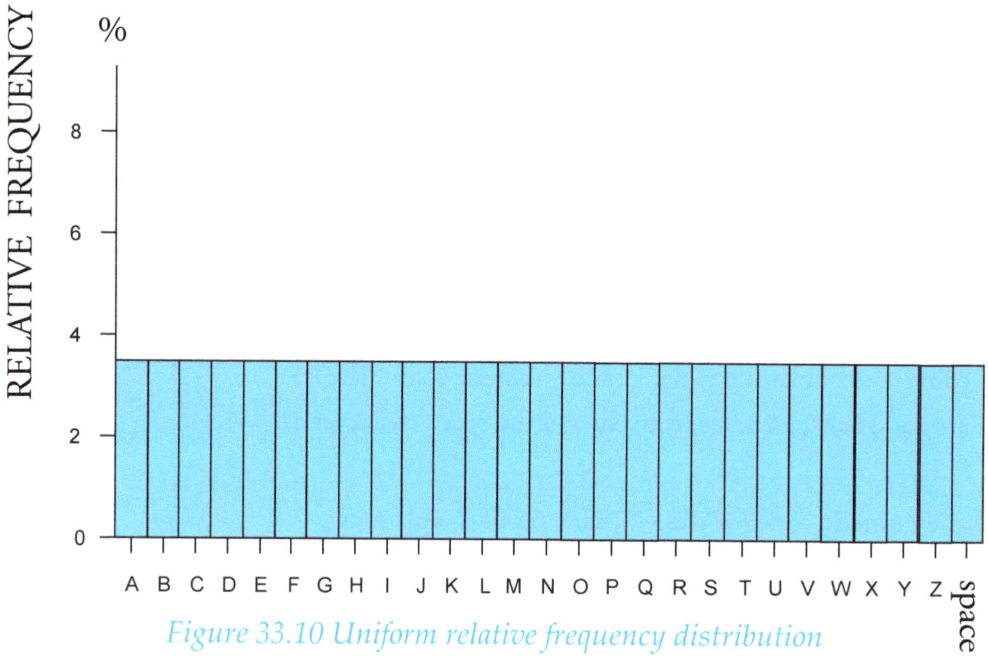

Figure 33.10 Uniform relative frequency distribution

Task

2 Watch the Khan Academy polyalphabetic video and try the tool to see how a non-uniform plaintext distribution can be flattened as described in this section.
https://www.khanacademy.org/computing/computer-science/cryptography/crypt/v/polyalphabetic-cipher

Questions

15 Suppose Alice and Bob communicate messages to each other which have been encrypted using the Caesar cipher and a previously agreed secret key. Now suppose that Eve intercepts the ciphertext and that she happens to know or suspect that Alice starts all her messages to Bob with the characters "DEAR BOB". The corresponding ciphertext is GHDUCERE. Alice and Bob make no secret of the fact that they use the Caesar cipher believing that keeping the key secret is sufficient to maintain the security of their messages. The encryption equation that Alice and Bob use is

ciphertext_character = (plaintext_character + key) mod 27

Explain how Eve using the plaintext and ciphertext could recover the secret key used by Alice and Bob.

16 Alice and Bob decide to use a new key for each character, generated randomly, and apply the stream of random keys using the Caesar cipher to future messages. Explain why this could offer greater security over the scheme described in Q15 even though Eve continues to intercept the ciphertext and Alice continues to start messages with "DEAR BOB".

To subject this cipher to closer scrutiny we ask how many ways can a particular plaintext message consisting of only uppercase letters of the alphabet be encrypted by a shift cipher which chooses key values randomly? Well consider that for the first character, there are 26 different possible key values, for the second character, 26 different possible values again and so on. If plaintext messages of length 32 characters are encrypted then a key will consist of 32 key values. The total number of keys of length 32 is therefore

$$26 \times 26 \times 26 \times \ldots\ldots \times 26 \times 26 = 26^{32} \approx 2 \times 10^{45}$$

The total number of possible ciphertexts corresponding to any particular 32 character plaintext message is thus 2×10^{45} one for each possible key consisting of 32 key values.

If each of these possible ciphertexts is written on a separate piece of paper then the entire stack would be

$$2 \times 10^{45} \times 5 \times 10^{-5} \text{ metres high} = 1 \times 10^{40} \text{ metres}$$

taking the thickness of a piece of paper to be 5×10^{-5} metres.

By comparison the Milky Way galaxy is estimated to be 9.5×10^{20} metres across. If the key values were generated randomly then each ciphertext will be equally likely.

Key principle

One-time pad:

Plain text of a message is 'mixed' with random text taken from a one-time pad resulting in cipher text which is truly random.

The same one-time pad is used to 'unmix' the random text from the cipher text, which results in the original plain text.

One only has to guarantee that the one-time pad is safe, that it comprises truly random numbers, that there are only two copies of it, and that both copies are destroyed immediately after use to prevent it being used again (the one-time property), for it to be used to send a message safely without the risk of being deciphered by an attacker or eavesdropper.

Background

The "red phone" used in the 1980s for secure communication between the USA and the USSR was based on a one-time pad. The random key sequences or pads were delivered by courier.

The decryption cipher is $p_i = (c_i - k_i) \bmod 27$

Likewise a particular ciphertext could have come from any one of 2×10^{45} possible plaintext messages. The chance of an attacker guessing which one correctly is therefore vanishingly small. It is impossible therefore for an attacker or eavesdropper to break this encryption scheme because the ciphertext yields no possible information about the plaintext (except its length).

This is the strongest possible method of encryption. It is known as the **one-time pad** because when first used the key was written on a sheet of paper or pad and used only once - *Figure 33.11.*

Summarising, the one-time pad method is based on the principle that the plain text of a message is 'mixed' with truly random text taken from a one-time pad. Because the resulting cipher text is still truly random it can safely be sent without the risk of being deciphered by an attacker or eavesdropper.

At the receiving end, the same one-time pad is used to 'unmix' the random text from the cipher text, which results in the original plain text. One only has to guarantee that the one-time pad is safe, that it comprises truly random numbers, that there are only two copies of it, and that both copies are destroyed immediately after use to prevent it being used again (the one-time property) on another plaintext message.

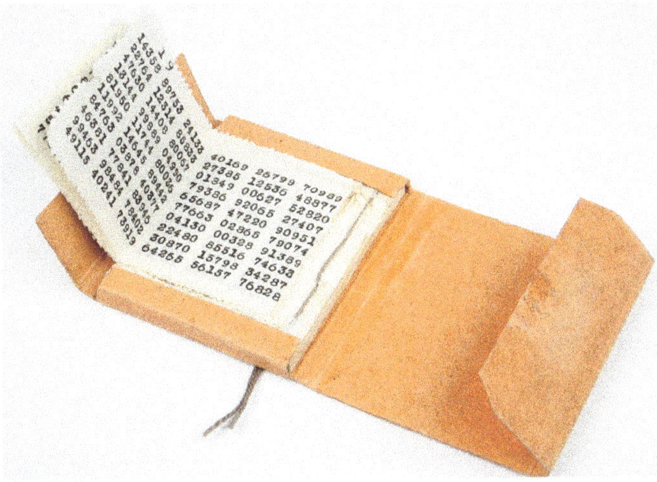

Figure 33.11 A one-time pad reproduced with kind permission of Paul Reuvers, Crypto Museum (www.cryptomuseum.com)

Task

3. Watch the Khan Academy one-time pad video
   https://www.khanacademy.org/computing/computer-science/cryptography/crypt/v/one-time-pad

4. The Venona project was a counter-intelligence program initiated by the United States Army Signal Intelligence Service (a forerunner of the National Security Agency) that lasted from 1943 to 1980. The program attempted to decrypt messages sent by Soviet Union intelligence agencies, including its foreign intelligence service and military intelligence services. The project produced some of the most important breakthroughs for western counter-intelligence in this period, including the discovery of the Cambridge spy ring and the exposure of Soviet espionage targeting the Manhattan Project.
   The NSA declassified the program in 1995. It can be read about in a NSA document at
   https://www.nsa.gov/about/_files/cryptologic_heritage/publications/coldwar/venona_story.pdf

Randomness

Randomness means lack of pattern or predictability of events. Randomness abounds in the physical world and in man-made devices such as electrical circuits as fluctuations of an unpredictable nature which we call noise. Electrical storms, the microwave background left over from the Big Bang and other events induce random currents of electricity in aerials connected to radio receivers and televisions that cause the hissing noise that we hear in their loudspeakers. This atmospheric noise can be captured, sampled and digitised to provide a source of truly random bits. Such a service is provided by https://www.random.org.
Another source is https://www.fourmilab.ch/hotbits/secure_generate.html which uses the unpredictable nature of radioactive decay to generate truly random bits.

A random number is one that is drawn from a set of possible values, each of which is equally probable, i.e., a uniform distribution, e.g. the throw of a six-sided die. When discussing a sequence of random numbers, each number drawn must be statistically independent of the others, i.e. knowledge of an arbitrarily long sequence of numbers is of no use whatsoever in predicting the next number to be generated. Each possible arbitrarily long sequence is thus equally likely.

Pseudorandom

Pseudorandomness is an important concept in cryptography.

Informally pseudorandom means:

cannot be distinguished from uniform i.e. random.

The cryptographic definition of pseudorandom however is

a distribution is pseudorandom if it passes all efficient statistical tests.

Background

Hardware random number generators have been built into some processor systems or made possible in some operating system. E.g. Raspberry Pi includes a hardware-based random number generator that can generate cryptographic quality random numbers.
In Unix-like operating systems /dev/random is a special file that serves as a blocking pseudorandom number generator:

.dev>more –f random

Key principle

Randomness:
Randomness means lack of pattern or predictability of events.

Background

RandomX package for Java has an option to get random bits from hotbits.
http://www.fourmilab.ch/hotbits/source/randomX/randomX.html

This definition has been arrived at by considering the need to resist an attack from an adversary who is trying to obtain information from ciphertexts about the corresponding plaintext messages.

Generating large numbers of truly random numbers is extremely difficult so people have turned to the computer and algorithms programmed into the computer to generate **pseudorandom numbers** from an initial seed. These pseudorandom numbers are generated deterministically and can only approximate a truly random distribution because numbers calculated by a computer through a deterministic process, cannot, by definition, be random. Given knowledge of the algorithm used to create the numbers and the seed, it is possible to predict all the numbers returned by subsequent calls to the algorithm, whereas with genuinely random numbers, knowledge of one number or an arbitrarily long sequence of numbers is of no use whatsoever in predicting the next number to be generated. Therefore, computer-generated "random" numbers are more properly referred to as pseudorandom numbers, and pseudorandom sequences of such numbers. Pseudorandom generated sequences eventually repeat with the periodicity determined by the seed and the algorithm used. Pseudorandom generated sequences are also reproducible, i.e. for a given algorithm, starting from the same seed generates the same sequence.

Pseudorandom number generators (PRNGs)

A pseudorandom number generator is an efficient, deterministic algorithm that expands a short, uniform seed into a longer, pseudorandom output in polynomial time. It is useful whenever

1. It would be difficult to communicate a long sequence of numbers needed in a symmetric key cipher instead the seed is communicated
2. A large number of random numbers are required and access to truly random numbers is restricted to a much smaller number

The seed may be chosen from the small number of truly random numbers that are available but doesn't have to be.

Care must be taken when relying on pseudorandom number generators for cryptographic purposes because they are deterministic. However, a class of improved random number generators, termed cryptographically secure pseudorandom number generators (CSPRNG) exist that rely on truly random seeds external to the software. The image in *Figure 33.13(a)* (reproduced using a PHP script with kind permission of Bo Allen, http://boallen.com) exhibits patterns because the pseudorandom number generator, the programming language PHP's rand() function, is deterministic with a relatively short periodicity whereas the bitmap in *Figure 33.13(b)* does not because it relies on truly random numbers.

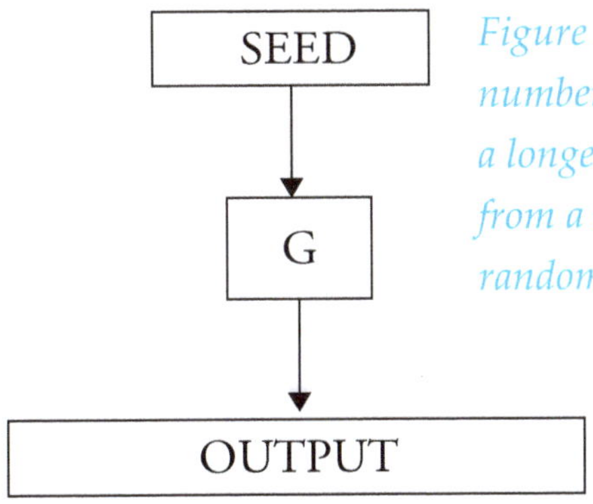

Figure 33.12 A pseudorandom number generator, G, producing a longer stream of "random" bits from a shorter length seed of true random bits

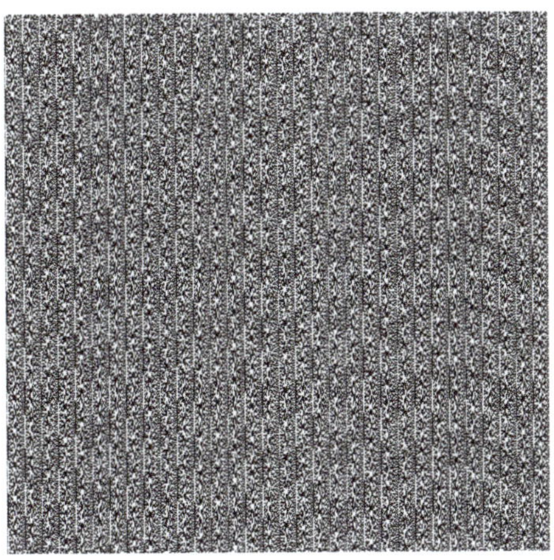

Figure 33.13(a) Image generated from random numbers generated by the PHP rand() function on Microsoft Windows.

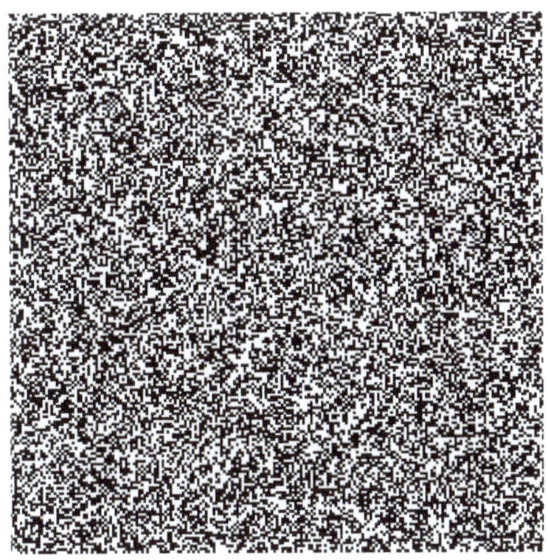

Figure 33.13(b) reproduced with permission of RANDOM.ORG – image generated from random numbers obtained from atmospheric noise.

Task

5 Download the test program at http://www.fourmilab.ch/random/ Use it to test sequences of bytes/bits for their randomness. Run this program on data generated by a high-quality pseudorandom sequence generator. You should find it generates data that are indistinguishable from a sequence of bytes chosen at random. Indistinguishable, but not genuinely random.

6 Watch the video on pseudorandom number generators at https://www.khanacademy.org/computing/computer-science/cryptography/crypt/v/random-vs-pseudorandom-number-generators

The Vernam cipher

The Vernam Cipher is named after Gilbert Sandford Vernam (1890-1960) who, in 1917, invented the stream cipher and later co-invented the one-time pad (OTP). His patent US1310719 was filed in 1918 and is, according to the National Security Agency (NSA), perhaps one of the most important in the history of cryptography.

Gilbert Vernam

At the time of the invention, Vernam was working at AT & T Bell Labs in the USA. Messages were then sent by telegraph, a system that used pulses of electrical current to encode characters according to the Baudot code. The characters were entered into and read from the system using a teleprinter.

Vernam proposed a teleprinter cipher in which a previously prepared key, kept on paper tape, was combined character by character with the plaintext message to produce the ciphertext. To decrypt the ciphertext, the same key would be again combined character by character, producing the plaintext.

Working with Joseph Mauborgne, at that time a captain in the US Army Signal Corps, they proposed that the paper tape key should contain random information (the key stream). The incorporation of this proposal into Vernam's machine implemented an automatic form of the one-time pad.

Task

7 Watch AT & T Labs' video of the Vernam cipher http://techchannel.att.com/play-video.cfm/2009/10/12/From-the-Labs:-Encryption1

8 Read about the details of the Vernam cipher machine by visiting the website http://www.cryptomuseum.com/crypto/vernam.htm

Background

The Vernam cipher was exploited in the design of a high security teleprinter cipher machine that the Lorenz company made for the German Army High Command to enable them to communicate by radio in complete secrecy during WW2.
These transmissions were broken by Bill Tutte. The process of decrypting Lorentz machine ciphertexts was later automated using a refinement suggested by Max Newman and some clever engineering by Tommy Flowers who designed and built Colussus, the world's first stored program computer, to decrypt Lorentz encrypted messages. Colussus reduced the time taken from weeks to hours. Colussus came online just in time to decrypt messages which gave vital information to Eisenhower and Montgomery prior to D-Day - http://www.codesandciphers.org.uk/lorenz/colossus.htm

Key principle

Vernam cipher:
Encrypts and decrypts a message using a one-time pad approach in which the plaintext message M = {0, 1}^{n} is bitwise XORed with a uniformly random key k {0,1}^{n} where n is the number of bits to encrypt the message.

The Vernam cipher relies on the bit-wise eXclusive-OR (XOR) Boolean function. This is symbolised by ⊕ and is represented by the following truth table, Table 33.3, where 1 represents true and 0 represents false

INPUT		OUTPUT
A	B	A ⊕ B
0	0	0
0	1	1
1	1	1
1	0	0

Table 33.3 Exclusive-Or truth table

A very useful property of the exclusive-or operation is that it is possible to recover an input given the output and the other input. For example, if the inputs A and B are 0 and 1 respectively, then A ⊕ B = 1. If we exclusive-or this output 1 with, say, input B which was 1, 1 ⊕ 1 = 0, we recover input A which was 0. It works for all inputs.

Therefore the same key stream can be used both to encrypt plaintext to ciphertext and to decrypt ciphertext to yield the original plaintext:

Plaintext ⊕ Key = Ciphertext

and:

Ciphertext ⊕ Key = Plaintext

If the key stream is truly random, and used only once, this is effectively a one-time pad.

Background

The eXclusive-OR function is an example of an involution. An involution is a function

$$f : X \rightarrow X$$

That, when applied twice, brings one back to the starting point

$$f(f(X)) = X$$

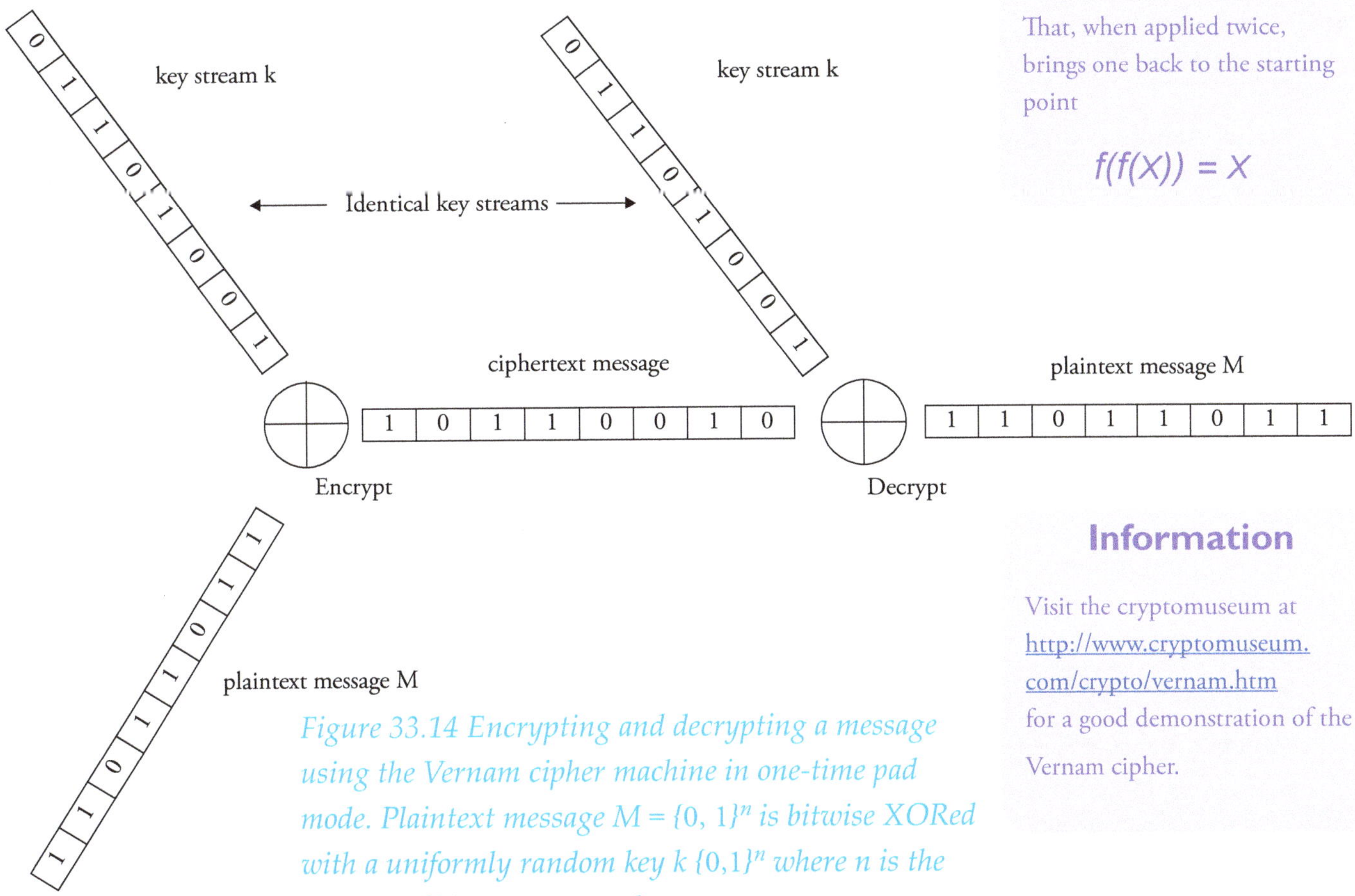

Figure 33.14 Encrypting and decrypting a message using the Vernam cipher machine in one-time pad mode. Plaintext message M = {0, 1}^{n} is bitwise XORed with a uniformly random key k {0,1}^{n} where n is the number of bits to encrypt the message.

Information

Visit the cryptomuseum at http://www.cryptomuseum.com/crypto/vernam.htm for a good demonstration of the Vernam cipher.

Substituting pseudorandom data generated by a cryptographically secure pseudorandom number generator is a common and effective construction for a stream cipher.

RC4 has been a very widely used software stream cipher. RC4 is an example of a Vernam cipher. It has been in popular protocols such as Transport Layer Security (TLS)/Secure Sockets Layer (SSL) (to protect Internet traffic) and WEP (to secure wireless networks) although it is now considered insecure.

WEP relies on a short secret key that is shared between a mobile station (e.g. a laptop with a wireless Ethernet card) and an access point (i.e. a base station).

The short secret key is expanded into an infinite pseudorandom key stream which is XORed with the message packets before they are transmitted.

Background

RC4 is an example of a Vernam cipher. It has been used in popular protocols such as Transport Layer Security (TLS) (to protect Internet traffic) and WEP (to secure wireless networks) although it is now considered insecure.

Programming task

4 RC4 is a stream cipher used in WEP. The infinite pseudorandom key stream for RC4 is generated from a secret key using the following two algorithms. Code these in your preferred language and run the test below on secret key = AQACS and plaintext = Computer Science

P

Key-scheduling algorithm

```
for i from 0 to 255
  S[i] := i
endfor
j := 0
for i from 0 to 255
  j := (j + S[i] + key[i mod keylength]) mod 256
  swap values of S[i] and S[j]
endfor
```

PseudoRandom Number Generator

```
i := 0
j := 0
while PseudoRandom Numbers required:
  i := (i + 1) mod 256
  j := (j + S[i]) mod 256
  swap values of S[i] and S[j]
  PSRNumber := S[(S[i] + S[j]) mod 256]
  output PSRNumber
endwhile
```

Test

The keys and plaintext are ASCII, the keystream and ciphertext are expressed below in hexadecimal but stored as bytes.

Key: AQACS

Keystream: F163D4497F1C801DCB4E3C...

Plaintext: Computer Science

Ciphertext: B20CB9390A68E56FEB1D5FC4720A7BD7

Task

9. Attacks on RC4 have shown that it is possible to distinguish its output from a random sequence. Why does this make RC4 insecure? Use a search engine to research an RC4 attack.

RC4 is still installed on some operating systems. For example, running the *openssl ciphers* command on an Apple Mac running Mac OS X 10.8 reveals that the SSL(Secure Sockets Layer) cipher RC4 (128 bit) is being used for encryption on this machine because it has not been deselected:

```
$ openssl ciphers -tls1 -v RC4-SHA

RC4-SHA SSLv3 Kx=RSA Au=RSA Enc=RC4(128) Mac=SHA1
```

Perfect secrecy

Claude Shannon (*Figure 33.15*), at Bell Labs, proved that the one-time pad is unbreakable, and that it is the only cryptosystem that achieves perfect secrecy. He published his proof in a research paper in 1949. In it he defined a mathematical model of what it means for a cryptosystem to be secure. Essentially, any unbreakable system must have the same characteristics as the one-time pad:

The key

1. must be truly random
2. must be as long as the plaintext message
3. must never be reused in whole or part
4. and must be kept secret.

Points 1 and 2 mean that the number of possible keys must be at least as large as the number of possible messages of a given length.

Key principle

Perfect secrecy:

Perfect secrecy means an eavesdropper would not, by gaining knowledge of the ciphertext but not of the key, be able to improve their guess of the plaintext even if given unlimited computing power.
Such cryptosystems are considered cryptoanalytically unbreakable and information-theoretically secure meaning they will not be vulnerable to future developments in computer power such as quantum computing.
The term perfect security is given to such systems.

Task

10. Watch the video on Perfect Secrecy from Khan Academy - www.khanacademy.org/computing/computer-science/cryptography/crypt/v/perfect-secrecy

Perfect secrecy means an eavesdropper would not, by gaining knowledge of the ciphertext but not of the key, be able to improve their guess of the plaintext even if given unlimited computing power.

Key point

Unconditional or Perfect Security (Perfect secrecy)

Regardless of any prior information the attacker has about the plaintext, the ciphertext leaks no additional information about the plaintext in a ciphertext-only attack.

Fig. 33.15 Claude Shannon (Getty Image library)

Such cryptosystems are considered cryptoanalytically unbreakable and **information-theoretically secure** meaning they will not be vulnerable to future developments in computer power such as quantum computing.

The one-time pad is an example of an information-theoretically secure cryptosystem. These systems have been used for the most sensitive governmental communications, such as diplomatic cables and high-level military communications.

What if the plaintext was a sequence of bits that represented an image? If we apply a bitwise exclusive-or to this image using a sequence of randomly generated bits for the key, we get an image that contains no information about the original image because each ciphertext bit is just as likely to be a 0 as a 1 - *Figure 33.16(a)* and *Figure 33.16 (b)*.

The original image can only be recovered by using the same key, i.e. the exact sequence of randomly generated bits that produced the ciphertext.

Applying the "wrong" key will result in recovering a different image.

Figure 33.16(a) Plaintext image to be encrypted using a one-time pad.
(Getty Image Library)

Figure 33.16(b) One-time pad ciphertext image of (a).

Information

Figure 33.16(a) Claude Elwood Shannon was an American mathematician, electronic engineer, and cryptographer famous for having founded information theory with a landmark paper that he published in 1948.

Shannon was also the first person to show how the logical algebra of 19th-century mathematician George Boole could be implemented using electronic circuits of relays and switches in which open or closed switches could represent. "true" and "false" and "0" and "1". Furthermore he showed how the use of electronic logic gates could be used to make decisions and to carry out arithmetic.

Task

11 Try the reversible XOR demonstration at https://www.khanacademy.org/computer-programming/reversible-xor-demo/5580322717564928

Block ciphers

Stream ciphers can be viewed as approximating the action of the one-time pad (OTP) cipher which uses a keystream of completely random digits. However, to achieve perfect secrecy, the keystream must be generated completely at random with at least the same length as the plaintext and must not be used more than once. This makes the system cumbersome to implement in practice so the one-time pad has been replaced by a pseudorandom-generated keystream based on a secret key of limited length, e.g. 128 bits. Unfortunately, the perfect secrecy of the one-time pad is lost: the keystream is now pseudorandom and so is not truly random. Therefore, it is quite possible for a stream cipher to be completely insecure. Block ciphers such as AES (Advanced Encryption Standard) offer an alternative to stream ciphers and its security limitatons.

Block ciphers like stream ciphers use symmetric key encryption i.e. the same key is used for encryption and decryption, but block cipher keys are not required to be the same length as the plaintext. The latter fact makes block ciphers more manageable especially with regard to key distribution and security. As their name suggests block ciphers operate on large blocks of digits.

AES which is now the industry standard for data security, is an example of a block cipher.

AES supports 128-bit, 192-bit, and 256-bit implementations, with the number of bits specifying the length of the key, with AES 256 being the most secure. The three AES versions are also distinguished by the number of rounds of encryption. AES 128 uses 10 rounds, AES 192 uses 12 rounds, and AES 256 uses 14 rounds.

As AES is a symmetric key cipher, the same secret key is used for both encryption and decryption, therefore both the sender and receiver of the data need a copy of the key. In AES the information to be encrypted is divided into sections called blocks. AES uses a 128-bit block size, in which data is divided into a four-by-four array containing 16 bytes. Since there are eight bits per byte, the total in each block is 128 bits. The size of the encrypted data remains the same: 128 bits of plaintext yields 128 bits of ciphertext.

AES was designed as a substitution-permutation network. AES brings additional security because it uses a key expansion process in which the initial key is used to come up with a series of new keys called round keys. These round keys are generated over multiple rounds of modification, each of which makes it harder to break the encryption. Each stage of the AES encryption algorithm serves an important function. Using a different key for each round provides a much more complex result.

AES 256 is virtually impenetrable using brute-force methods.

Lockbox3

Launch Delphi and use the **GetIt Package Manager** to install **LockBox 3.7** (**Tools|GetIt Package Manage...**) - *Figure 33.17*. Once installed, a tab labelled **LockBox** appears in the **Tool|Component Palette** - *Figure 33.18*. The **LockBox** tab contains four components

- **THash**
- **TCodec**
- **TCrytographicLibrary**
- **TSignatory**

Figure 33.17 Delphi GetIt Package manager LockBox 3.7

TCryptographicLibrary contains a number of different ciphers:

- AES 128
- AES 192
- AES 256
- DES
- 3DES (KO 1)
- 3DES (KO 2)
- BlowFish
- TwoFish
- XXTEA

and a number of different chaining modes

- ECB
- CBC
- PCBC
- CFB
- CFB 8-bit
- CTR
- OFB

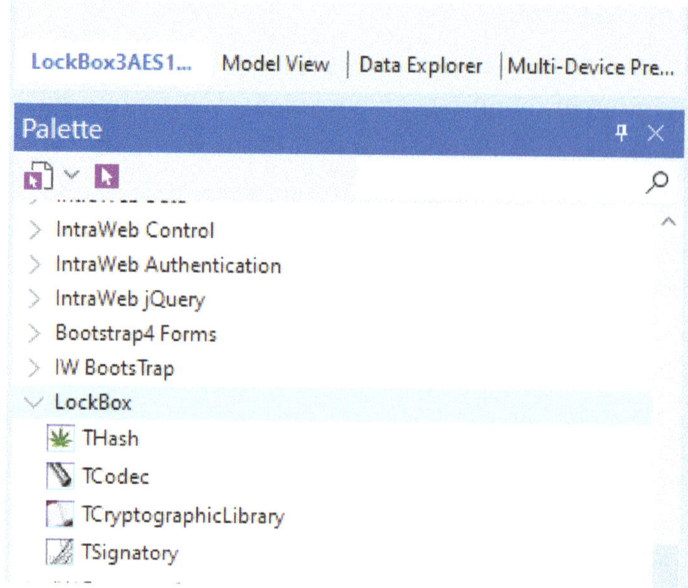

Figure 33.18 Tool Palette showing LockBox components

Chaining modes allow block cipher algorithms to encrypt plaintext with a size different from the defined size of one block. Padding is used when the plaintext does not divide exactly into blocks.

The **CBC** (**Cipher Block Chaining**) mode uses an **initialization vector** – **IV**. The IV has the same size as the block that is encrypted, e.g. in AES 256 the block size is 16 bytes. The choice of IV is critical to the security of CBC mode. The requirement is that the initial IV must be "unpredictable", in other words, randomly generated before the encryption starts. It must never be hardcoded in the application or picked from a database. Once encryption is completed, the value of IV is not a secret, and can be transmitted to the decryptor in plaintext. The plaintext is divided into blocks and padding is added as needed. In *Figure 33.19* the secret key is **K** and the plaintext bits are labelled $\mathbf{P_1}$ to $\mathbf{P_n}$. The corresponding ciphertext bits are labelled $\mathbf{C_1}$to $\mathbf{C_n}$. The first plaintext block, $\mathbf{P_1}$, is eXclusive-ORed with the **IV**. Then the result is encrypted to produce the first ciphertext block, $\mathbf{C_1}$. The next plaintext block, $\mathbf{P_2}$, is eXclusive-ORed with the ciphertext block from the previous stage and so on up to the last block.

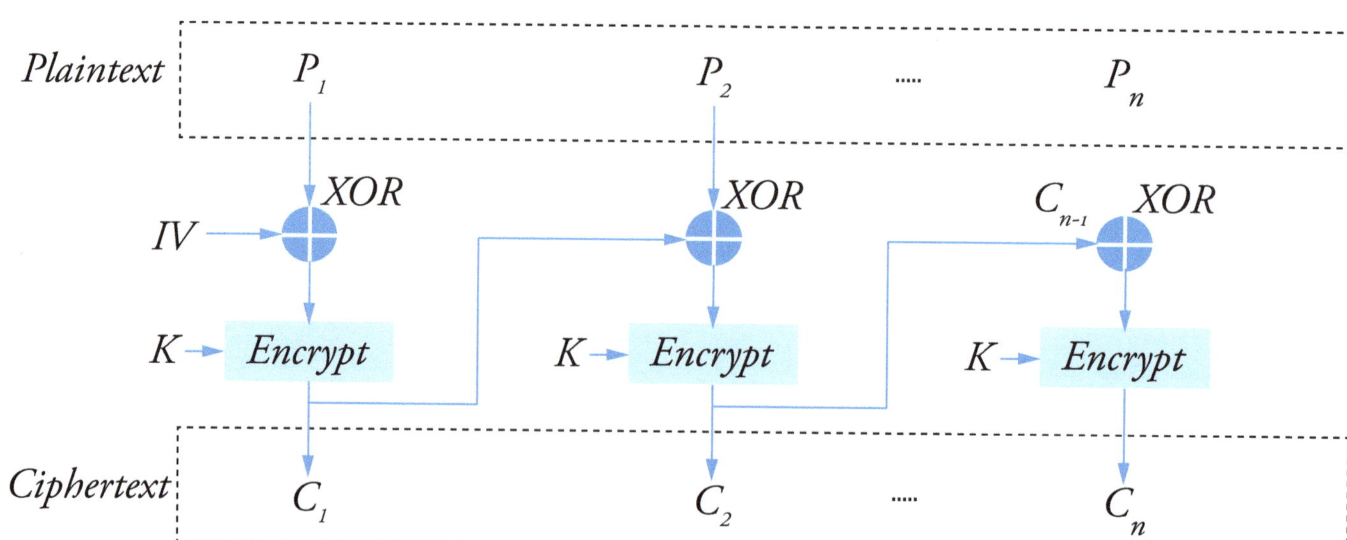

Figure 33.19 AES CBC (Cipher Block Chaining) mode encryption of plaintext

In this mode, even if the same plaintext block is encrypted, e.g. $\mathbf{P}_1$ and $\mathbf{P}_3$, a different ciphertext block results. Decryption is described schematically in *Figure 33.20*.

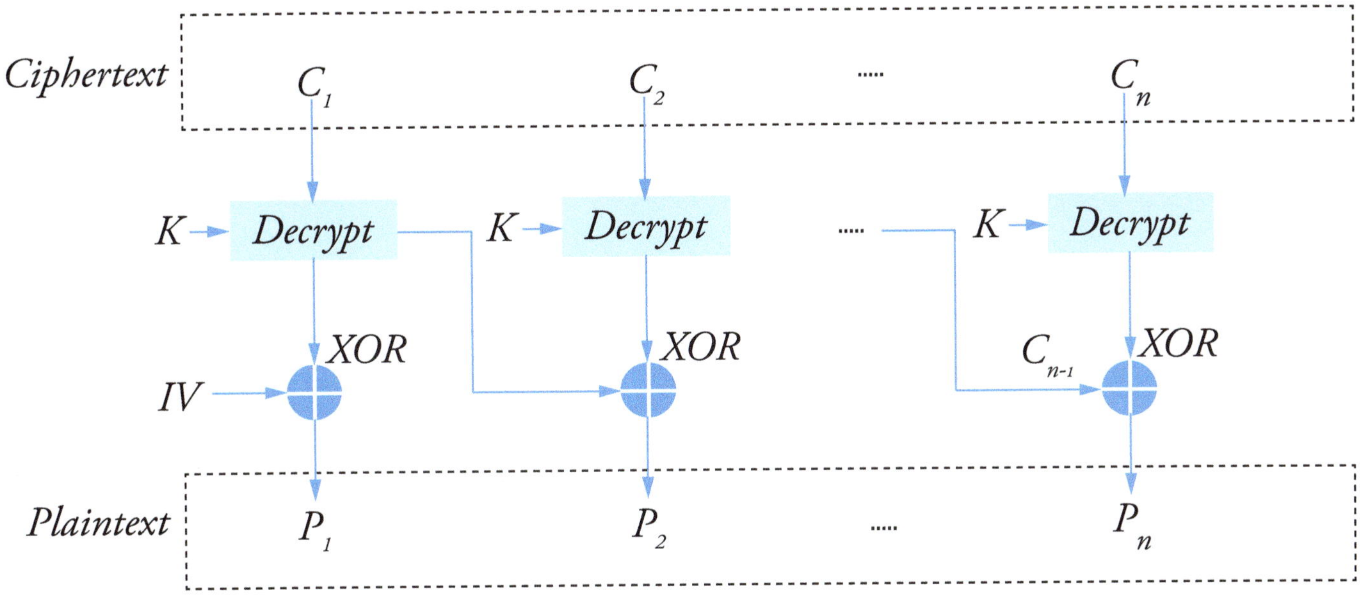

Figure 33.20 AES CBC (CipherBlock Chaining) mode decryption of ciphertext

Delphi example of the use of AES CBC

Check that the installation of **LockBox 3.7** has setup **Library** paths of the form `$(BDSCatalogRepository)\LockBox-3.7-Sydney\design\`, etc for all the libraries - see **Tools|Options|Language|Delphi|Library**. This version is Delphi Sydney. If this has not been done then the library paths will need to be set up manually.

Start a new application **New|Window VCL Application - Delphi**.

Place a **TCodec** component, `Codec1`, and a **TCryptographicLibrary** component, `CryptographicLibrary1`, on the form.

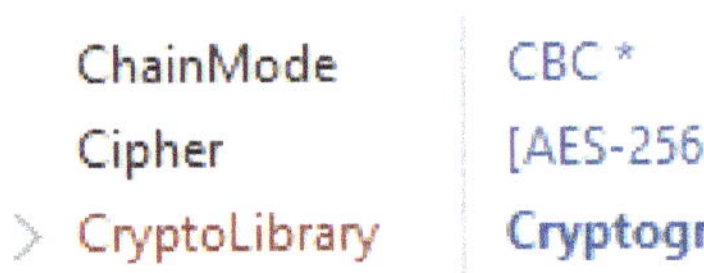

Figure 33.21 Codec1 settings for AES 256 and CBC chaining mode

Set the properties for `Codec1` shown in *Figure 33.21*. **Accept** all other settings.

Save the project as `LockBox3AES1Project.dproj` and its unit as `LockBox3AESUnit.Pas` in folder `LockBox3AES1`.

Add the following components to the form:

- 7x **TPanel**'s
- 5x **TButton**'s
- 3x **TMemoBox**'s
- 1x **TOpenTextFileDialog**

Configure and **name** the components as shown in *Figure 33.22* and *Figure 33.24*.

Create an **OnCreate** event handler for `Form1`.

Add the code shown in *Table 33.4* to the body of this event handler.

Ensure that all the `uTPLb_....` libraries shown in *Table 33.5* are present.

Now **create** **OnClick** event handlers for all the buttons and assign the source code as shown in *Table 33.4*.

Save All (SHIFT+CTRL+S).

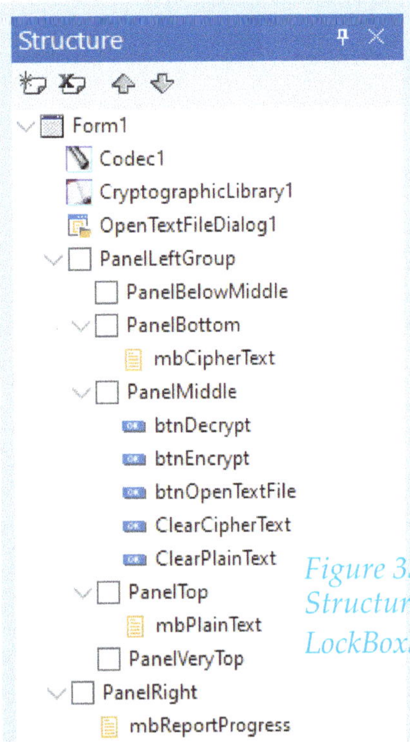

Figure 33.22 Structure window for LockBox3AES1Unit

Click Run (F9) to build and run the application `LockBox3AES1Project`.

Enter a password - *Figure 33.23*.

Figure 33.23 Input dialogue on launching LockBox3AES1Project

The user interface shown in *Figure 33.24* should now appear but with empty `Plaintext` and `Ciphertext` windows.

Click the `Open text file` button and locate and open `Sonnet116.txt`.

Click the `Encrypt` button to produce the ciphertext.

Figure 33.24 shows the result for password `LetMeIn`.

Click the `Clear plaintext` button to clear the `Plaintext` window.

Click the `Decrypt` button and the plaintext from `Sonnet116.txt` should appear not as a result of reloading this file but as a result of reversing the encryption process.

Clear both windows.

Type `Hello World` directly into the `Plaintext` window. **Click** the `Encrypt` button to obtain the ciphertext. Now **click** the `Decrypt` button to reverse the process. The result will be two `Hello World` lines in the `Plaintext` window.

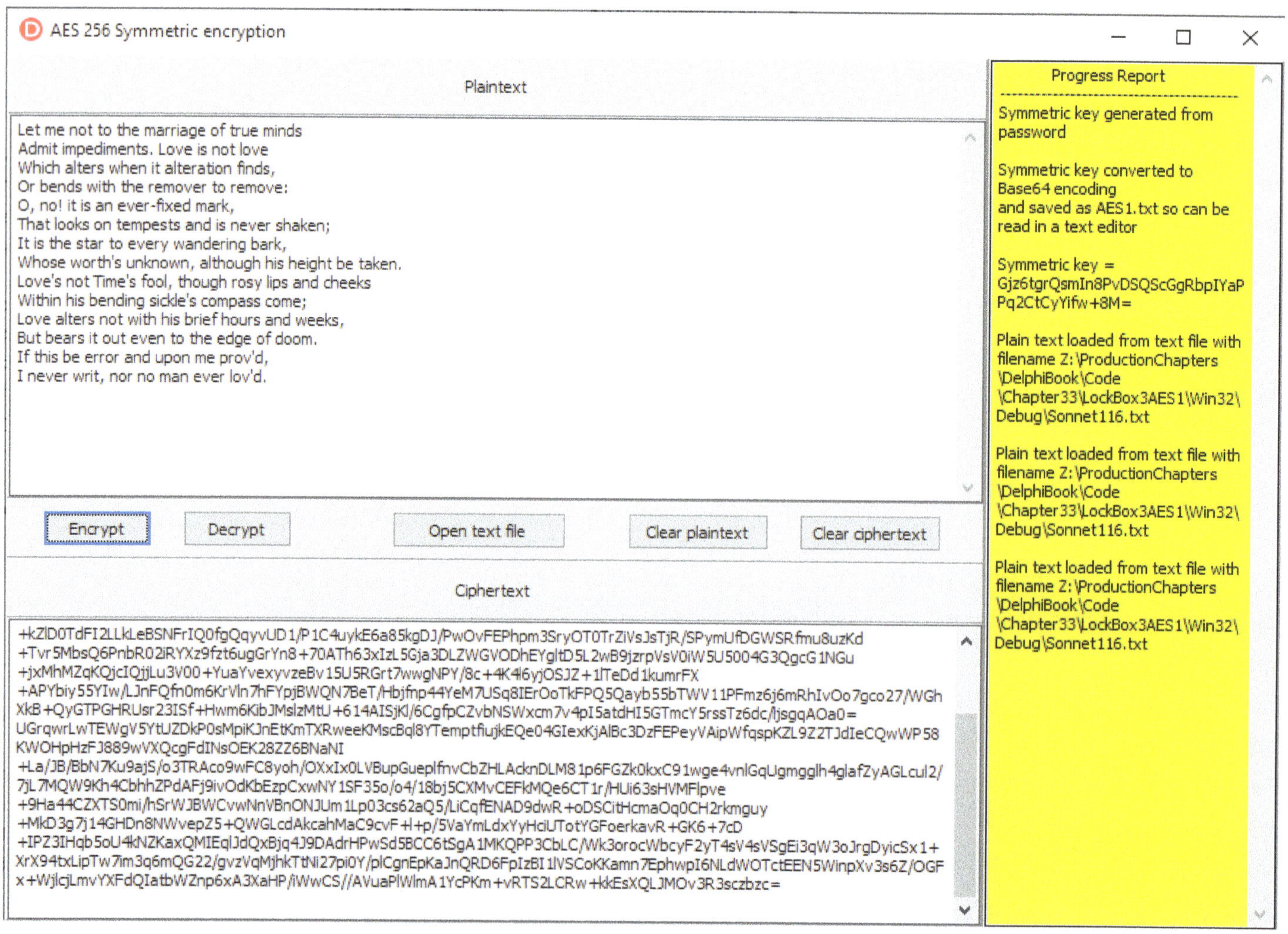

Figure 33.24 User interface for LockBox3AES1Project

P

```
Var
  Form1 : TForm1;
Implementation
{$R *.dfm}
  Var
    msSymmetricKey : TMemoryStream;
  Procedure TForm1.btnEncryptClick(Sender : TObject);
    Var
      strPlainText, strCipherTextBase64Encoded : String;
    Begin
      strPlainText := mbPlainText.Text;
      Codec1.EncryptString(strPlainText, strCipherTextBase64Encoded, TEncoding.UTF8);
      mbCipherText.Lines.Add(strCipherTextBase64Encoded);
    End;
  Procedure TForm1.btnOpenTextFileClick(Sender : TObject);
    Begin
      OpenTextFileDialog1.Execute;
      mbPlainText.Lines.LoadFromFile(OpenTextFileDialog1.FileName);
      mbReportProgress.Lines.Add(#13#10 + 'Plain text loaded from text file with filename '
                                 + OpenTextFileDialog1.FileName);
    End;
  Procedure TForm1.btnDecryptClick(Sender : TObject);
    Var
      strPlainText, strCipherTextBase64Encoded : String;
    Begin
      strCipherTextBase64Encoded := mbCipherText.Text;
      Codec1.DecryptString(strPlainText, strCipherTextBase64Encoded, TEncoding.UTF8);
      mbPlainText.Lines.Add(strPlainText);
   End;
  Procedure TForm1.FormCreate(Sender : TObject);
    Begin
      Codec1.StreamCipherId := BlockCipher_ProgId;
      Codec1.Password := InputBox('Password', 'Please enter your password', 'Password');
      msSymmetricKey := TMemoryStream.Create;
      Codec1.SaveKeyToStream(msSymmetricKey);
      msSymmetricKey.SaveToFile('AES1.key');
      mbReportProgress.Lines.Add('Symmetric key generated from password');
      ConvertKey(msSymmetricKey);
    End;
  Procedure TForm1.ClearCipherTextClick(Sender : TObject);
    Begin
      mbCipherText.Clear;
    End;
  Procedure TForm1.ConvertKey(msKey : TMemoryStream);
    Var
      strSourceKey : AnsiString;
      Base64Store: TStream;
    Begin
      msKey.Position := 0;
      strSourceKey := AnsiString(Stream_to_Base64(msKey));
      mbReportProgress.Lines.Add(strSourceKey);
      Base64Store := TFileStream.Create('AES1.txt', fmCreate );
      Base64Store.WriteBuffer(strSourceKey[1], Length(strSourceKey));
      Base64Store.Free;
      mbReportProgress.Lines.Add('Symmetric key converted to Base64 encoding'#13#10
                                 + 'and saved as AES1.txt so can be read in a text editor');
      mbReportProgress.Lines.Add(#13#10 + 'Symmetric key = ' + strSourceKey);
    End;
  Procedure TForm1.ClearPlainTextClick(Sender : TObject);
    Begin
      mbPlainText.Clear;
    End;
End.
```

Table 33.4 Body of LockBox3AES1Unit.Pas

```
Unit LockBox3AES1Unit;
Interface
Uses
  Winapi.Windows, Winapi.Messages, System.SysUtils, System.Variants, System.Classes, Vcl.Graphics,
  Vcl.Controls, Vcl.Forms, Vcl.Dialogs, uTPLb_Signatory, uTPLb_Codec,
  uTPLb_BaseNonVisualComponent, uTPLb_CryptographicLibrary, uTPLb_StreamUtils, Vcl.StdCtrls,
  Vcl.ExtCtrls, Vcl.ExtDlgs;
Type
  TForm1 = Class(TForm)
           CryptographicLibrary1 : TCryptographicLibrary;
           Codec1 : TCodec;
           btnEncrypt : TButton;
           mbPlainText : TMemo;
           mbCipherText : TMemo;
           btnDecrypt : TButton;
           PanelRight : TPanel;
           PanelTop : TPanel;
           PanelMiddle : TPanel;
           PanelBottom : TPanel;
           PanelLeftGroup : TPanel;
           PanelVeryTop : TPanel;
           PanelBelowMiddle : TPanel;
           mbReportProgress : TMemo;
           btnOpenTextFile : TButton;
           OpenTextFileDialog1 : TOpenTextFileDialog;
           ClearPlainText : TButton;
           ClearCipherText : TButton;
           Procedure btnEncryptClick(Sender : TObject);
           Procedure FormCreate(Sender : TObject);
           Procedure btnDecryptClick(Sender : TObject);
           Procedure ConvertKey(msKey : TMemoryStream);
           Procedure btnOpenTextFileClick(Sender : TObject);
           Procedure ClearPlainTextClick(Sender : TObject);
           Procedure ClearCipherTextClick(Sender : TObject);
         End;
```

Table 33.5 LockBox3AES1Unit.Pas Uses clause and class defintion for TForm1

The application `LockBox3AES1Project` creates two files in the folder containing the executable:

- `AES1.key`
- `AES1.txt`

`AES1.txt` is the readable form of the AES symmetric key, i.e. it can be loaded and displayed sensibly in a text editor such as **NotePad++**. `AES1.key` is the actual key used for the encryption and decryption process. It does not load and display sensibly as a matter of course in a text editor because the key generator may include control codes (bytes with values in range 0-31) other than carriage return, linefeed and tab. To obtain `AES1.txt` from `AES1.key` the application uses a procedure

```
Procedure TForm1.ConvertKey(msKey : TMemoryStream)
```

to convert the symmetric key to an equivalent representation encoded as **Base64** characters - see *Table 33.4* for how this procedure does this.

www.educational-computing.com/DelphiBook/Code/Chapter33/LockBox3RSAShowPandPProject.zip

Base64 encoding

Base64 is a group of binary-to-text encoding schemes that represent binary data (i.e. a sequence of 8-bit bytes) in an ASCII string format by translating the data into a Base-64 representation. The bytes are first grouped three bytes at a time i.e. 24 bit units. The 24-bit unit is then divided into four 6-bit subunits called Base64 digits. 6 bits has a decimal range of 0 - 63. Each 6-bit subunit is used as the index of a table of 8-bit ASCII characters - *Table 34.6.* Each 6-bit subunit is replaced by the corresponding 8-bit represented character from the table. Three 8-bit bytes (i.e. a total of 24 bits) can therefore be represented by four 8-bit characters in the range 'A'..'Z', 'a'..'z', '0'..'9', '+', '/' chosen by index in the range 0 - 63.

Index	Binary	Char	Index	Binary	Char	Index	Binary	Char	Index	Binary	Char
0	000000	A	16	010000	Q	32	100000	g	48	110000	w
1	000001	B	17	010001	R	33	100001	h	49	110001	x
2	000010	C	18	010010	S	34	100010	i	50	110010	y
3	000011	D	19	010011	T	35	100011	j	51	110011	z
4	000100	E	20	010100	U	36	100100	k	52	110100	0
5	000101	F	21	010101	V	37	100101	l	53	110101	1
6	000110	G	22	010110	W	38	100110	m	54	110110	2
7	000111	H	23	010111	X	39	100111	n	55	110111	3
8	001000	I	24	011000	Y	40	101000	o	56	111000	4
9	001001	J	25	011001	Z	41	101001	p	57	111001	5
10	001010	K	26	011010	a	42	101010	q	58	111010	6
11	001011	L	27	011011	b	43	101011	r	59	111011	7
12	001100	M	28	011100	c	44	101100	s	60	111100	8
13	001101	N	29	011101	d	45	101101	t	61	111101	9
14	001110	O	30	011110	e	46	101110	u	62	111110	+
15	001111	P	31	011111	f	47	101111	v	63	111111	/
Padding		=									

Table 33.6 Base64 index table

If there are only two significant binary bytes (e.g. the input string is 'In'), or when the last binary group contains only two bytes, all 16 bits will be mapped to three Base64 digits(18 bits) - *Figure 33.25*. The two least significant bits of the last content-bearing 6-bit block will be assigned zero, and discarded on decoding (along with the succeeding = padding character). The missing last Base64 digit is mapped to the padding character '='. The binary input data ('In') is thus mapped to the text string 'SW4='. This is a trivial example which intentionally uses displayable characters in the input in order to illustrate the process clearly. Real input will contain non-displayable characters in addition to the control codes for carriage return, line feed and tab.

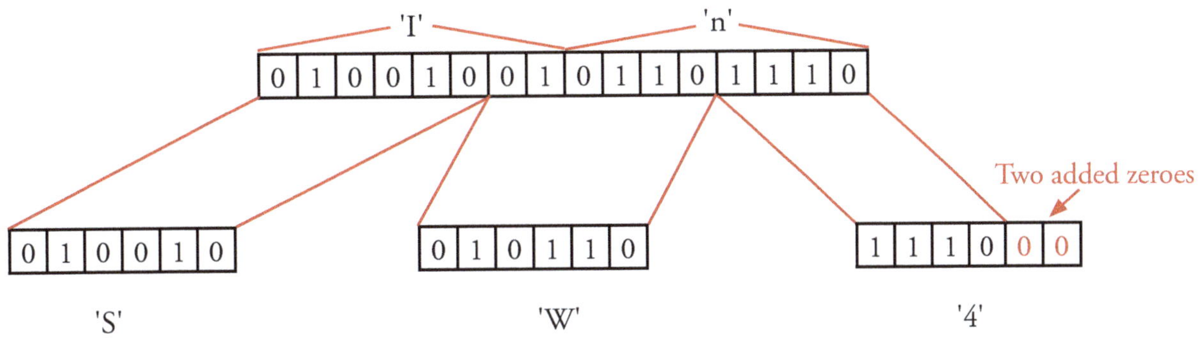

Figure 33.25 Representing two bytes of binary data by three Base64 digits - 6-bit units

The example above used ASCII text input for simplicity, but this is not a typical use case. The more typical use is to encode binary data such as an image. The resulting Base64 data will only contain 64 different ASCII characters, all of which can reliably be transferred across systems that may corrupt the raw source bytes.

Symmetric encryption

Shared private key

In **symmetric encryption** the communicating parties use the same key for encryption and decryption. Symmetric key encryption is also known as **private key or secret key encryption** because the key used must be private and known only to the communicating parties. If not, then anyone intercepting encrypted messages can use a knowledge of the key and the encryption algorithm to decrypt the messages.

> **Key term**
>
> **Symmetric encryption:** Symmetric encryption uses the same secret key to perform both the encryption and decryption processes.

For example, if Alice wanted to use symmetric encryption to send an encrypted message to Bob then Alice would use the private key *k*, agreed with Bob, to encrypt the plaintext form of the message. Bob would use the same private key *k* to decrypt the received encrypted message. Bob could reply with his own encrypted message which he has also encrypted with private key *k* (*Figure 33.26*).

Using symmetric encryption, Alice and Bob are able to communicate securely through a communication channel.

However, there is a potential problem with use of a single private key. Let's suppose that Alice gets to choose the key. She now has to communicate the key to Bob. They could agree to meet so that Alice could, by whispering into Bob's ear, communicate the key securely. However, in a networked world, Alice and Bob may never meet and may never communicate except over a network, e.g. the Internet. However, to communicate the key securely to Bob via a network connection, Alice needs to secure the channel through the network.

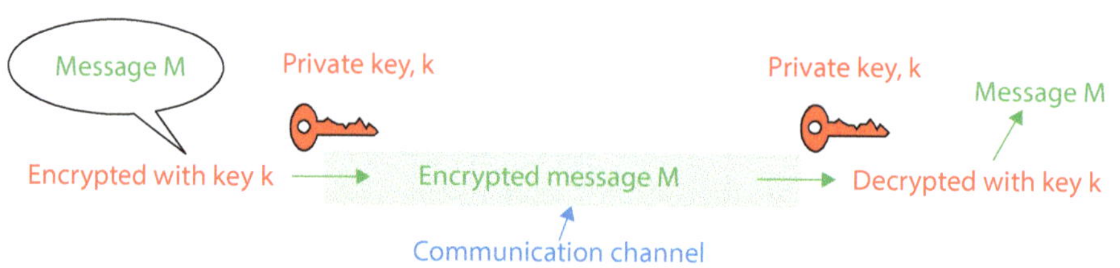

Figure 33.26 Secure communication channel using symmetric encryption

How can she do this if she hasn't yet distributed the private key? She needs the secure channel to distribute the key. This "chicken and egg" situation is known as the key distribution problem of symmetric encryption.

Asymmetric encryption (public key/private key encryption)

Secure communication in the world of online transactions

The key distribution problem of symmetric encryption becomes an even more challenging one in the world of online transactions which the World Wide Web has made possible. Many transactions take place online through online stores where goods may be bought with a credit or debit card. All these transactions need to take place through secure channels of communication to protect a purchaser's payment details. Securing each channel with a separate symmetric encryption private key shared in advance between seller and customer would be a nightmare:

- The seller would have to store a large number of private keys, one for each customer buying goods.
- Each key would have to be distributed to the corresponding customer who would have to remember the key and for which seller.

A mechanism for secure communication is needed which

- reduces the number of keys that need to be remembered
- allows two parties to exchange information secretly, but with no pre-arranged symmetric encryption private key

One solution is **public key/private key** encryption to secure a communication channel. This secure channel can then be used to distribute a temporary symmetric encryption key to be used for securing credit/debit card details. This temporary shared key is called a session key because it is only used for the duration of the transaction.

Key term

Asymmetric encryption:
Asymmetric encryption uses two keys, a public key and a private key. The public key and the private key are mathematically related but different. If the public key is used for encryption, the private key must be used for decryption.

Public key encryption:
The public key is freely shared with any party. Documents/messages destined for the owner of a public/private key pair are encrypted with the public key. This public key is linked mathematically with its paired private key. The private key is used to decrypt the document/message encrypted with the paired public key. The owner of the private key must be the only one to know this key.
If the key pair is chosen well:

- The private key cannot be derived from the public key
- The public key encrypted messages can only be decrypted by the private key with which it is paired mathematically.

Information

Key pair:
Amazon EC2 elastic cloud uses public key cryptography to encrypt and decrypt login information. The keys that Amazon EC2 uses are 2048-bit SSH-2 RSA keys.

Public key encryption

In public key encryption two mathematically related keys are used:

- a public key p_k
- a private or secret key s_k

Public key encryption has two clear advantages over private key encryption:

- The online seller has only to store a single private key s_k rather than sharing, storing and managing N different secret symmetric encryption keys (i.e. one for each buyer).
- The number and identities of potential buyers need not be known at the time of key generation.

Public key encryption is an **asymmetric encryption** scheme, asymmetric because only one of the paired keys, the private key s_k is secret. The public key p_k can be freely shared with any party. Thus an online seller makes their public key p_k available to any buyer. A buyer can then use the seller's public key to establish a secure channel over which they can send their credit card information securely to complete a purchase. The seller uses their private key s_k, which only they know, to decrypt the buyer's credit card information to process the transaction or, if symmetric encryption is used for the latter, to set up a secure means of communicating a shared private session key.

If the key pair is chosen well:

- The private key cannot be derived from the public key
- The public key encrypted messages can only be decrypted by the corresponding private key.

In practice, encrypting and decrypting with public key encryption is far slower than with symmetric encryption. For this reason, public key encryption is often used to solve the problem of sharing a secret key for use in a symmetric encryption scheme.

One public key encryption scheme that is employed in online transactions to provide one-way secure communication and authentication is the RSA cryptosystem which is named after its inventors Rivest, Shamir and Adleman.

The RSA public key/private key cryptosystem

Let us to suppose that Alice wishes to receive secure messages from other people.

She proceeds as follows:

- Alice selects two distinct prime numbers p and q and then forms her public modulus $N = pq$.

  N must be sufficiently large to ensure that no adversary could factor $N = pq$ except by luck. This means that p and q each need to be more than 150 digits long, and not be too close to each other.
- Alice then chooses her public exponent e to be relatively prime to $(p-1)(q-1)$, with $1 < e < (p-1)(q-1)$.
- Alice chooses the pair (N, e) as her public key and she publishes this.
- Her private key is the unique integer, d such that

  $ed \bmod (p-1)(q-1) = 1$ and $1 < d < (p-1)(q-1)$

  or in congruence notation as $ed \equiv 1 \pmod{b}$ where $b = (p-1)(q-1)$

  d is the mod $(p-1)(q-1)$ multiplicative inverse of e

Bob has a message which he wishes to send to Alice (*Figure 33.27*).

He proceeds as follows:

- Bob encodes the characters of his message as a string of integer codes M, e.g. 1521112325981720......
- Bob looks up Alice's public key (N, e)
- Bob splits the integer encoded form of the message M into a sequence of blocks $M_1, M_2, M_3, ..., M_i$ where each M_i is an integer that satisfies

  $1 \leq M_i < N$.
- Bob then encrypts these blocks as $C_i = M_i^e \bmod N$ and sends the encrypted blocks to Alice.

Alice decrypts the encrypted message blocks as follows:

- Alice decrypts each C_i to recover M_i using her private key d by calculating $M_i = C_i^d \bmod N$
- Alice then converts the string of integer codes, M_i, back into their equivalent characters to recover the plaintext form of the message Bob has sent her.

Information

Prime number:
A prime number is a natural number greater than 1 that cannot be expressed as the product of two smaller natural numbers. Note that this means 1 is not a prime number.
In other words: a number that has only two factors: 1 and itself, e.g. 2, 3, 5, 7, 43.

Relatively prime:
Two natural numbers are relatively prime if they have no common divisor apart from 1. E.g. 4 and 7 are relatively prime but 7 and 14 are not.

One-way function:
Exponentiation to the power e modulo N is one-way function: relatively easy to compute but hard to invert. The private key d is known as a trapdoor because it makes inversion possible.
It is easy to multiply two numbers, p and q but apparently hard to factor a number pq into a product of two others when it is large. Try factoring 7859112349338149.

Exponentiation:
Exponentiation means raising a number x to the power y; it is written x^y.
A useful property of exponentiation is that raising a number x to the power y and then raising the result to the power z yields the same result as raising x to the power z and raising that result to the power y,

i.e. $(x^y)^z = x^{yz} = (x^z)^y$

This is true even if the exponentiation uses modular arithmetic.

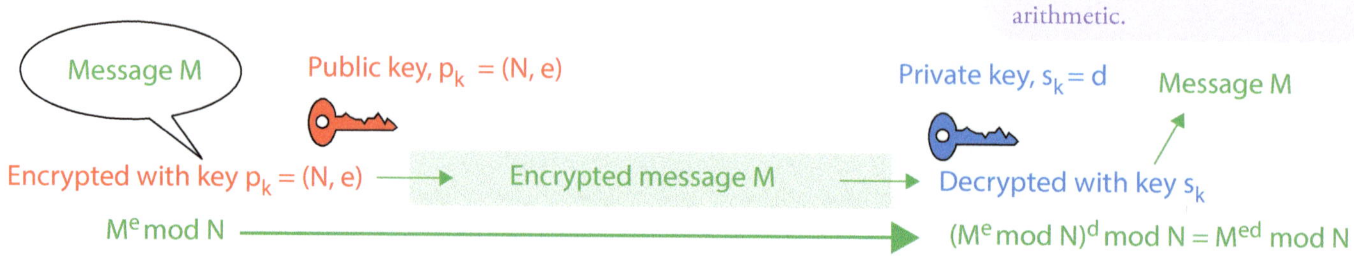

Figure 33.27 RSA Public key/Private key encryption

Example

Suppose Alice chooses primes p = 7 and q = 11. So N = 77, (p – 1)(q – 1) = 60 and she chooses e = 7, since 7 and 60 are relatively prime.

Alice then calculates her private key using ed = 1 (mod (p -1)(q - 1) to be d = 43, since 43 x 7 = 301 = 1 mod 60

Hence Alice's public key is the pair (N, e) = (77, 7) and her private key is d = 43.

If Bob wants to send the plaintext message M = 4 to Alice he encrypts it as ciphertext $C = M^e$ mod 77 = 47 mod 77 = 16384 mod 77= 60 (mod 77).

(Use Windows calculator in Scientific mode for the mod operation)

Alice then decrypts C using her private key to recover the message

$$M = C^d \text{ mod } 77 = 60^{43} \text{ mod } 77 = 4 \text{ (mod } 77)$$

Background

Public key/private key encryption schemes rely on the discrete logarithm problem to make it difficult to discover the private key. A very simple example that illustrates this problem is as follows:

To encrypt integer 19 raise it to the power 43 and then find the remainder after dividing by 77, the result is the encrypted value 61

$$19^{43} \text{ mod } 77 = 61$$

To recover the unencrypted value 19, an exponent must be found for which

$$61^d \text{ mod } 77 = 19$$

If we try d = 1, 2, 3, 4, 5, 6, 7 we find that 7 does.

Thus, 61^7 mod 77= $(19^{43})^7$ mod 77 = 19^{43x7} mod 77 = 19

by replacing 61 by (19^{43}).

Now suppose, we encrypt 2137 by raising it to the power of 17 and finding the remainder after division by 3233, the result is the encrypted value of 2137

$$2137^{17} \text{ mod } 3233 = 166$$

To recover the unencrypted value 2137, an exponent d must be found for which

$$166^d \text{ mod } 3233 = 2137$$

If we try d = 1, 2, 3, ..., 2753 we find that 2753 does.

Now suppose we use exponent 65537 and a 2048-bit modulus such as the one shown in the information panel on next page labelled Public modulus. We would find that d would be the 2048-bit value labelled Private exponent in the information panel. Using the public exponent 65537 and the public modulus in the margin we could encrypt integers up to 256 digits long. To decrypt we would use the private exponent shown in the margin and the same public modulus. The public key is (public exponent, public modulus) and the private key is (private exponent).

The discrete logarithm problem is the difficulty with which the private exponent can be discovered given only the public exponent, the public modulus and the result from encryption. The last example illustrates that this becomes an exceedingly difficult task when the number of bits used for the public key and the private key is a large number.

Tasks

12 The discrete logarithm problem:

This is the problem of finding x where

$$a^x \equiv b \pmod n$$

Watch the Khan Academy video "The discrete logarithm problem"

https://www.khanacademy.org/computing/computer-science/cryptography/modern-crypt/v/discrete-logarithm-problem

13 RSA encryption:

Watch the Khan Academy video "RSA encryption part 1"

https://www.khanacademy.org/computing/computer-science/cryptography/modern-crypt/v/intro-to-rsa-encryption

Questions

17 Two computers, X and Y, communicate securely using public/private key encryption. X and Y each has a public key and a private key.

X encrypts a message that it sends to Y using Y's public key.

Explain why the message should not be encrypted with:

(a) X's private key

(b) X's public key

Task

14 Explore the Wolfram programming lab:

The Wolfram programming language is a useful language with which to explore encryption, factoring, modular arithmetic and a lot of other concepts.

https://lab.wolframcloud.com/app/

Simple RSA Delphi program

Start a new application New|Window VCL Application - Delphi.

Save the project as `LockBox3RSAProject.dproj` and its unit as `LockBox3RSAMainUnit.Pas` in folder `LockBox3RSAProject`.

Assuming that the Library path for **LockBox 3.7** has been set up as described on page 518.

Add the following components to the form:

- 3x **TPanel**'s
- 2x **TButton**'s
- 2x **TMemoBox**'s

Configure and **name** the components as shown in *Figure 33.28* and *Figure 33.29*.

Click File|New|Unit - Delphi. to add a new unit to the project.

Save this unit as `LockBox3RSAUnit.pas` in the project folder.

Enter the source code shown in *Table 33.7*.

Information

Public exponent:

65537

Public modulus:

29457664581990063545187143707899373134590389698365517414743653125541005242840166899915696997873888563538292068789960515720869761675361593675014268414215454767777709118300251847232187533945048453058775378412564817224035219475400916471299875505265011917005264873335701417359662717609983903002107163226848818840015822496173899627269497834839116171608084606581374389125352226641602068091100881754240686940530029943322010963568298015713796479127038341097645087806299949060364755202645724782059421725639857778920687638980769721479815551292545752837433987680744224926634940965536547932971529723386935147726813268287153607983,

Private Exponent:

18679549333938737824601176712588036509564176191840855893951763684502389427070992813627363715727650959359206887632530923178172720077279660496303507434853073366789844447233194474377454713149645598855861378703165672432312367837385160851340162446370803748217110908434702221685961567029856585454957802300706215013490208463305771899812885607306340480210828669889211933248345789361959152473636354183116371878858484925419807726336018889775610743498482002845117747384513278257497790608749804025876885523466465024473439081346577265463955306545636669349253657671182525663872992594157936380592693993543030326953854631035757879505

Figure 33.28 User Interface design for LockBox3RSAProject

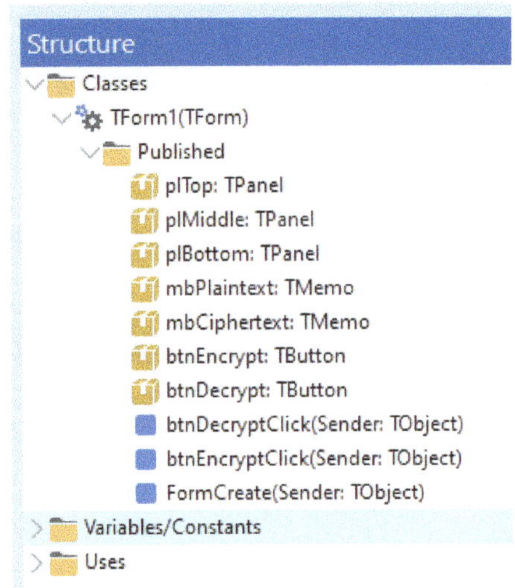

Figure 33.29 Structure window for LockBox3RSAUnit.pas

Create an **OnCreate** event handler for `Form1`.

Add the code shown in *Table 33.8* to the body of this event handler.

Now **create OnClick** event handlers for the two buttons and assign the source code as shown in *Table 33.8*.

Save All (**SHIFT+CTRL+S**).

Click Run (**F9**) to build and run the application `LockBox3RSAProject`.

The private and public keys are generated the first time this application is run. This can take sometime. Thereafter, these keys are loaded from the files `Public.key` and `Private.key` where they were saved.

Enter the string `Hello World!` in the upper window and **click** the `Encrypt` button. The ciphertext that results is shown in the lower window in *Figure 33.30*.

Click the `Decrypt` button. The returned decrypted text is shown in the upper window on the second line in *Figure 33.30*.

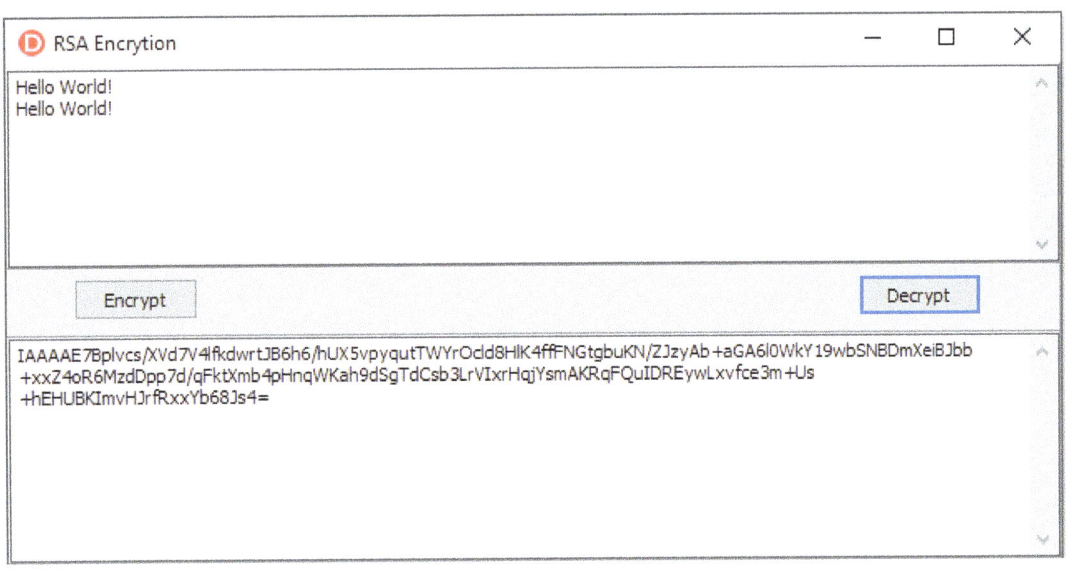

Figure 33.30 LockBox3RSAProject in execution

It is possible to dispense with `LockBox3RSAUnit.pas` and instead place **TSignatory**, **TCodec** and **TRSACryptographicLibrary** components from the **LockBox Tool Palette** on the main form - *Figure 33.32*. The settings for each component could then be done in the **Object Inspector** - *Figure 33.31*.

The form with components solution has unit *LockBox3RSAComponentBasedUnit.Pas* shown in *Table 33.9a* and *Figure 33.9b*.

```
Unit LockBox3RSAUnit;
Interface
Uses
  Windows, SysUtils, Classes, uTPlb_Hash, uTPLb_CryptoGraphicLibrary,
  uTPLb_Codec, uTPlb_StreamCipher, uTPLb_HugeCardinal,
  uTPLb_MemorySTreamPool, uTPLb_Signatory, uTPLb_Asymetric;
Var
  msPublic : TMemoryStream;
  msPrivate : TMemoryStream;
  Procedure Generate_RSA_Keys Var msPublic, msPrivate : TMemoryStream);
  Function DecryptRSA_String(Const Base64CipherText : String;
                             Const msPrivate : TMemoryStream) : String;
  Function EncryptRSA_String(Const PlainText : String;
                             Const msPublic : TMemoryStream) : String;
Implementation
  Var
    Signatory1 : TSignatory;
    CodecRSA : TCodec;
    CryptographicLibrary1 : TCryptographicLibrary;
  Function EncryptRSA_String(Const PlainText : String;
                             Const msPublic : TMemoryStream) : String;
    Var
      Base64Ciphertext : String;
    Begin
      Result :='';
      Signatory1.LoadKeysFromStream(msPublic, [partPublic]);
      msPublic.Position := 0;
      CodecRSA.EncryptString(PlainText, Base64Ciphertext, TEncoding.UTF8);
      Result := Base64Ciphertext;
    End;
  Function DecryptRSA_String(Const Base64CipherText : String;
                             Const msPrivate : TMemoryStream) : String;
    Begin
      Result :='';
      Signatory1.LoadKeysFromStream(msPrivate,[partPrivate]);
      CodecRSA.DecryptString(Result, base64Ciphertext, TEncoding.UTF8);
    End;
  Procedure Generate_RSA_Keys(Var msPublic, msPrivate : TMemoryStream);
    Begin
      msPublic := TMemoryStream.Create;
      msPrivate:= TMemoryStream.Create;
      If Signatory1.GenerateKeys
        Then
          Begin
            Signatory1.StoreKeysToStream(msPublic,[partPublic]);
            Signatory1.StoreKeysToStream(msPrivate,[partPrivate]);
            msPublic.Position := 0;
            msPrivate.Position := 0;
          End;
    End;
Initialization
  CodecRSA := TCodec.Create(Nil);
  CryptographicLibrary1 := TCryptographicLibrary.Create(Nil);
  Signatory1 := TSignatory.Create(Nil);
  CodecRSA.CryptoLibrary  := CryptographicLibrary1;
  CodecRSA.StreamCipherId := 'native.RSA';
  CodecRSA.ChainModeId := 'native.CBC';
  CodecRSA.AsymetricKeySizeInBits := 1024;
  Signatory1.Codec := CodecRSA;
Finalization
  CodecRSA.Free;
  CryptographicLibrary1.Free;
  Signatory1.Free;
End.
```

Table 33.7 LockBox3RSAUnit.Pas

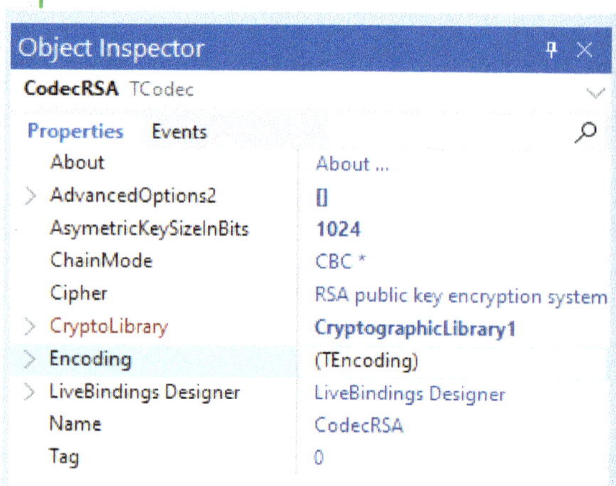

Figure 33.31 Object Inspector for CodecRSA

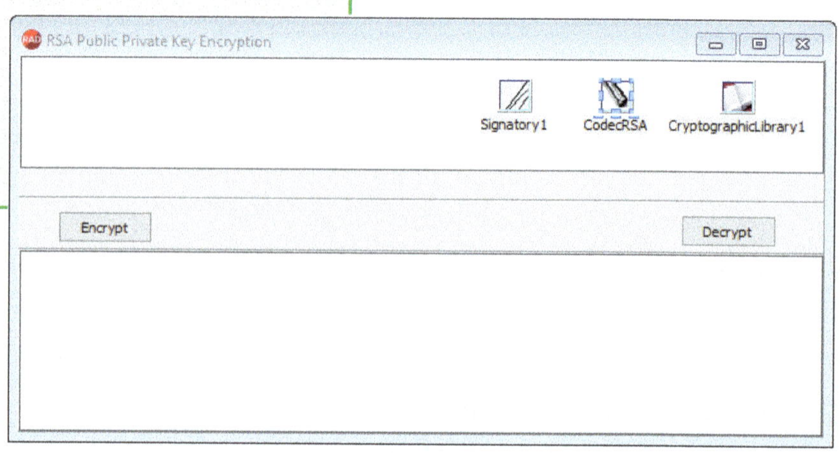

Figure 33.32 LockBox3RSAProject with LockBox components

P

```
Unit LockBox3RSAMainUnit;
Interface
Uses
  Winapi.Windows, Winapi.Messages, System.SysUtils, System.Variants, System.Classes, Vcl.Graphics,
  Vcl.Controls, Vcl.Forms, Vcl.Dialogs, Vcl.StdCtrls, RSAUnit, Vcl.ExtCtrls;
Type
  TForm1 = Class(TForm)
             plTop : TPanel;
             plMiddle : TPanel;
             plBottom : TPanel;
             mbPlaintext : TMemo;
             mbCiphertext : TMemo;
             btnEncrypt : TButton;
             btnDecrypt : TButton;
             Procedure FormCreate(Sender : TObject);
             Procedure btnEncryptClick(Sender : TObject);
             Procedure btnDecryptClick(Sender : TObject);
           End;
Var
  Form1: TForm1;
Implementation
{$R *.dfm}
  Procedure TForm1.btnDecryptClick(Sender : TObject);
    Begin
      mbPlaintext.Lines.Add(DecryptRSA_String(mbCiphertext.Lines.Text, msPrivate))
    End;
  Procedure TForm1.btnEncryptClick(Sender : TObject);
    Begin
      mbCiphertext.Lines.Add(EncryptRSA_String(mbPlaintext.Lines.Text, msPublic));
    End;
  Procedure TForm1.FormCreate(Sender : TObject);
    Var
      KeysExist:Boolean;
    Begin
      KeysExist := False;
      msPublic := TMemoryStream.Create;
      msPrivate := TMemoryStream.Create;
      If FileExists('Public.key')
        Then
          Begin
            ShowMessage('Public Key exists');
            msPublic.LoadFromFile('Public.key'); KeysExist := True;
          End;
      If FileExists('Private.key')
        Then
          Begin
            ShowMessage('Private Key exists');
            msPrivate.LoadFromFile('Private.key');
          End;
      If Not KeysExist
        Then
           Begin
             Generate_RSA_Keys(msPublic, msPrivate);
             msPublic.SaveTofile('Public.key');
             msPrivate.SaveToFile('Private.key');
           End;
    End;Main
End.
```

Table 33.8 LockBox3RSAMainUnit.Pas

```
Unit LockBox3RSAComponentBasedUnit;
Interface
Uses
  Winapi.Windows, Winapi.Messages, System.SysUtils, System.Variants, System.Classes, Vcl.Graphics,
  Vcl.Controls, Vcl.Forms, Vcl.Dialogs, Vcl.StdCtrls, Vcl.ExtCtrls, uTPLb_Signatory, uTPLb_CryptographicLibrary,
  uTPLb_BaseNonVisualComponent, uTPLb_Codec, uTPLb_Asymetric, Vcl.ComCtrls;
Type
  TfrmRSAEncryption = Class(TForm)
                        CodecRSA : TCodec; CryptographicLibrary1 : TCryptographicLibrary; Signatory1 : TSignatory;
                        PanelTop : TPanel; PanelMiddle : TPanel; PanelBottom : TPanel;
                        mbPlainText : TMemo; mbCipherText : TMemo;
                        btnEncrypt : TButton; btnDecrypt : TButton;
                        Procedure FormActivate(Sender : TObject);
                        Procedure Generate_RSA_Keys(Var msPublic, msPrivate : TMemoryStream);
                        Function EncryptRSA_String(Const PlainText : String;
                                                   Const msPublic : TMemoryStream) : String;
                        Function DecryptRSA_String(Const Base64CipherText : String;
                                                   Const msPrivate : TMemoryStream) : String;
                        Procedure FormClose(Sender: TObject; var Action: TCloseAction);
                        Procedure btnEncryptClick(Sender : TObject);
                        Procedure btnDecryptClick(Sender : TObject);
                      End;
Var
  frmRSAEncryption : TfrmRSAEncryption;
Implementation
{$R *.dfm}
  Var
    msPrivate, msPublic : TMemoryStream;
  Function TfrmRSAEncryption.EncryptRSA_String(Const PlainText : String;
                                               Const msPublic : TMemoryStream) : String;
    Var
      Base64CipherText : String;
    Begin
      Result :='';
      Signatory1.LoadKeysFromStream( msPublic, [partPublic]);
      msPublic.Position := 0;
      CodecRSA.EncryptString(PlainText, Base64CipherText, TEncoding.UTF8);
      Result := Base64CipherText;
    End;
  Procedure TfrmRSAEncryption.btnDecryptClick(Sender : TObject);
    Begin
      If Assigned(msPrivate)
        Then mbPlainText.Lines.Add(DecryptRSA_String(mbCipherText.Lines.Text, msPrivate))
        Else ShowMessage('msPublic not assigned');
    End;
  Procedure TfrmRSAEncryption.btnEncryptClick(Sender: TObject);
    Begin
      If Assigned(msPublic)
        Then mbCipherText.Lines.Add(EncryptRSA_String(mbPlainText.Lines.Text, msPublic))
        Else ShowMessage('msPublic not assigned');
    End;
  Function TfrmRSAEncryption.DecryptRSA_String(Const Base64CipherText : String;
                                               Const msPrivate : TMemoryStream) : String;
    Begin
      Result :='';
      Signatory1.LoadKeysFromStream(msPrivate,[partPrivate]);
      CodecRSA.DecryptString(Result, Base64Ciphertext, TEncoding.UTF8);
     End;
  Procedure TfrmRSAEncryption.Generate_RSA_Keys(Var msPublic, msPrivate : TMemoryStream);
    Begin
      If Signatory1.GenerateKeys
        Then
          Begin
            Signatory1.StoreKeysToStream(msPublic,[partPublic]);
            Signatory1.StoreKeysToStream(msPrivate,[partPrivate]);
            msPublic.Position := 0;
            msPrivate.Position := 0;
          End
        Else ShowMessage('Keys not generated');
    End;
.........continued
```

The use of const for parameters in Delphi essentially means that the parameter will not be mutated. This allows Delphi to choose the most efficient call mechanism for the given circumstances, i.e. by value or by reference.

Table 33.9a LockBox3RSAComponentBasedUnit.Pas

```
...continued
 Procedure TfrmRSAEncryption.FormActivate(Sender : TObject);
  Var
    KeysExist:Boolean;
  Begin
    KeysExist := False;
    msPublic  := TMemoryStream.Create;
    msPrivate := TMemoryStream.Create;
    If (FileExists('Public.key') And FileExists('Private.key'))
      Then
        Begin
          msPublic.LoadFromFile('Public.key');
          msPrivate.LoadFromFile('Private.key');
          KeysExist := True;
        End;
    If Not KeysExist
      Then
         Begin
           Generate_RSA_Keys(msPublic, msPrivate);
           msPublic.SaveTofile('Public.key');
           msPrivate.SaveToFile('Private.key');
         End;
  End;
 Procedure TfrmRSAEncryption.FormClose(Sender: TObject; var Action: TCloseAction);
  Begin
    If Assigned(msPublic)
      Then msPublic.Free;
    If Assigned(msPrivate)
      Then msPrivate.Free;
  End;
End.
```

Table 33.9b LockBox3RSAComponentBasedUnit.Pas

Encrypting files with RSA

The encryption and decryption methods from the previous program may be adapted to encrypt and decrypt files in project `LockBox3RSAEncryptingDecryptingFilesProject.dproj`, unit `LockBox3RSAEncryptingDecryptingFilesUnit.Pas`.

The user interface is shown in execution in *Figure 33.33* and its design in *Figure 33.35*. The encrypted result is shown in *Figure 33.34*. *Figure 33.36* shows the **Structure window** for the user interface, `frmRSAEncryption`.

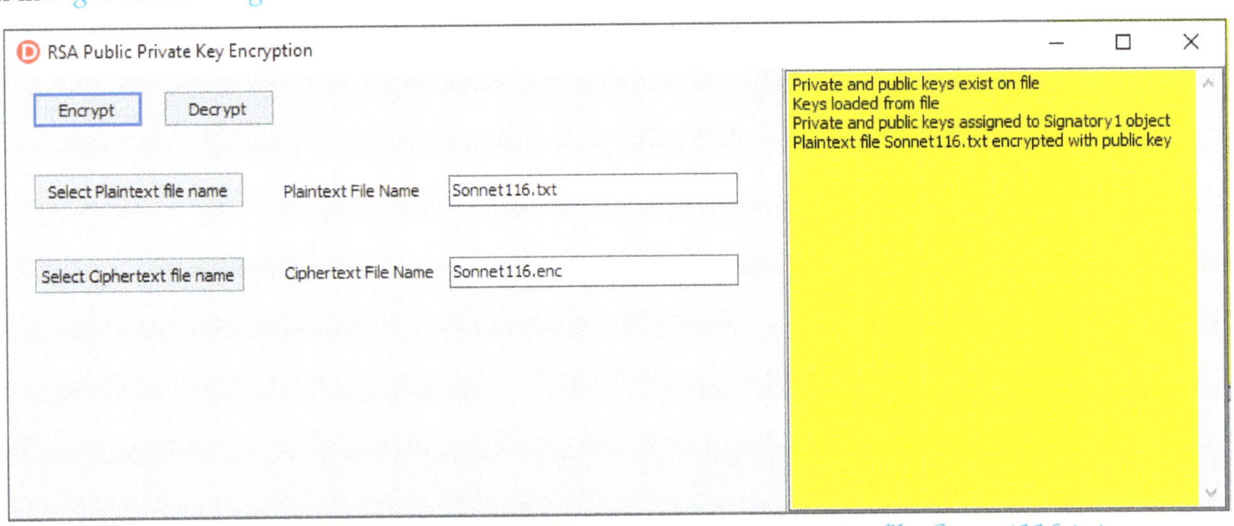

Figure 33.33 Using LockBox3 RSA Components to encrypt a file, Sonnet116.txt

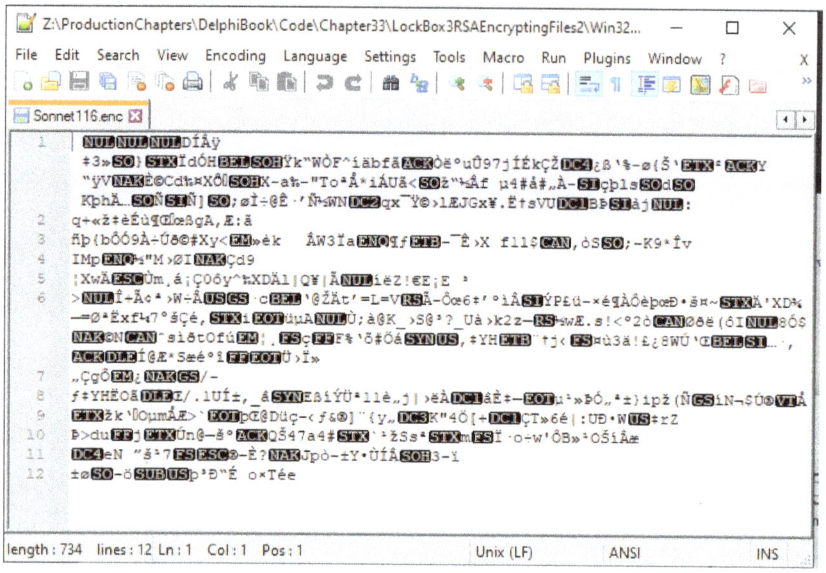

Figure 33.34 The encrypted Sonnet116.txt

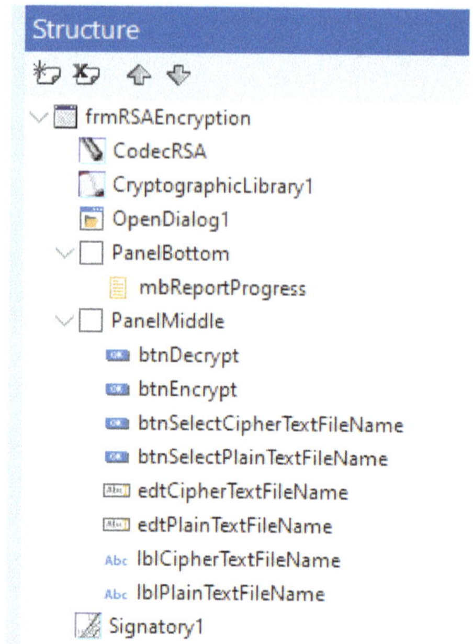

Figure 33.36 Structure window

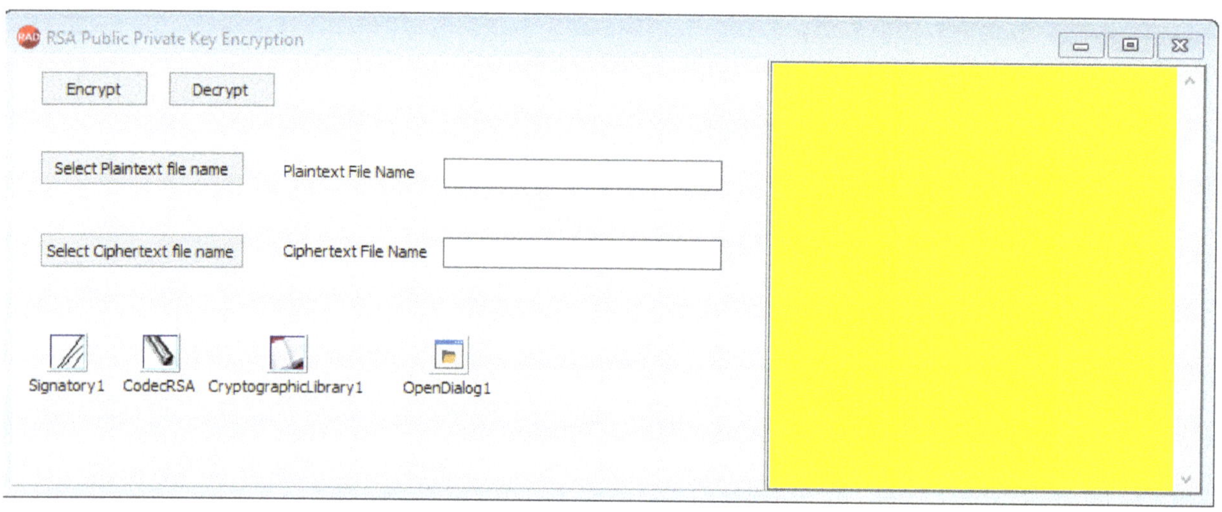

Figure 33.35 Design of the user interface

Key exchange

Diffie-Hellman key exchange

Diffie-Hellman exponential key agreement or **key exchange** provides a way for Alice and Bob to agree on a key *k* while communicating over an insecure network channel. The key *k* is used only for one communication session. It is then discarded. Hence the name session key.

A modulus N is made available publicly for network users to use to secure their communications.

Alice privately selects a large random number s_A, and calculates

$$p_A = 2^{s_A} \text{ (mod N)}.$$

Alice's private key is s_A. Alice sends p_A to Bob.

An eavesdropper, Eve, who intercepts p_A will find it extremely difficult to discover Alice's private key s_A from a knowledge of 2^{s_A} (mod N).

Bob also privately chooses a large random number s_B and calculates

$p_B = 2^{s_B}$ (mod N). Bob sends p_B to Alice.

Alice has her private key s_A and Bob's public key p_B.

Bob has his private key s_A and Alice's public key p_A.

Bob and Alice can now calculate their shared secret key, *k*.

Alice uses her private key s_A to calculate $k_A = p_B^{s_A} = (2^{s_B} \pmod N)^{s_A} \bmod N$

Bob uses his private key s_B to calculate $k_B = p_A^{s_B} = (2^{s_A} \pmod N)^{s_B} \bmod N$

But $(2^{s_B} \pmod N)^{s_A} = (2^{s_A} \pmod N)^{s_B}$, therefore $k_A = k_B = k$, the shared secret key.

The shared secret key *k* may now be used for symmetric encryption of messages between Alice and Bob.

SSH

SSH, or secure shell, is a secure protocol and the most common way of safely administering remote servers. Symmetric keys or shared secret keys are used by SSH in order to encrypt the entire connection between client and server.

The secret key is created through a process known as **key exchange**. This exchange results in the server and client both arriving at the same key independently by a process similar to that described in the previous section.

The symmetric encryption key created by this procedure is session-based and is the key used to encrypt the data sent between server and client, e.g. credit card details.

SSH utilizes asymmetric encryption during the initial key exchange process used to set up the symmetrical encryption key which is used to encrypt the session between two parties. The two parties exchange public keys (see p_A and p_B in previous section) in order to produce the shared secret key *k* used for symmetrical encryption.

Digital signature

A digital signature is a cryptographic technique that can be used in a digital world when you want

- to indicate that you are the owner or creator of a document, or
- to affirm that you agree with a document's content.

For Bob to know that a document genuinely came from Alice, he needs some way to authenticate the document. This is what Alice does to make this possible:

- Alice digitally signs the document with her private key s_A using a public key/private key encryption algorithm as shown in *Figure 33.37* to produce Enc(M), the digital signature
- Alice then sends Enc(M), the encrypted form of M to Bob
- Bob decrypts Enc(M) using Alice's public key p_A as shown in *Figure 33.38* and recovers the document M from Alice.

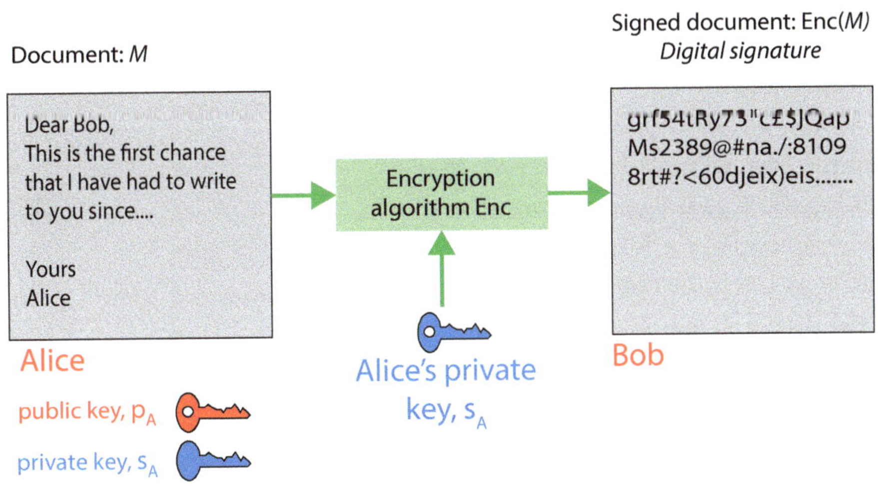

Figure 33.37 Digitally signing of Alice's document with Alice's private key

Does the digital signature Enc(M) meet the requirements of being verifiable and unforgeable?

Yes, because applying Alice's public key to the digital signature, Enc(M) recovers the original document, M. Alice's public key and private key are associated mathematically. If document M had been signed with a private key different from Alice's then applying Alice's public key to Enc(M) would not have recovered M.

The only person who could have signed M is therefore Alice because she is the person who generated the pair of keys (p_A, s_A). This assumes that Alice has not given away her private key or had it stolen.

Also, if Alice or anyone else should alter the original document from M to M_1, the signature that Alice created for M will not be valid for M_1 because Dec(Enc(M)) does not equal M_1. Thus digital signatures also provide message/document integrity, allowing the receiver

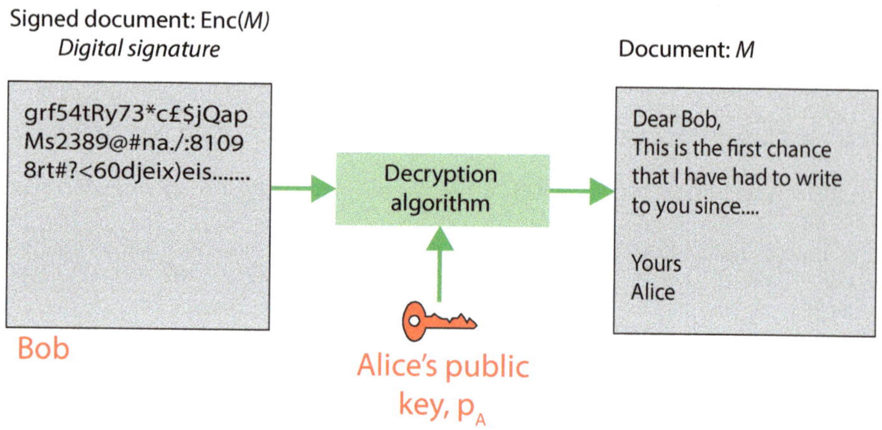

Figure 33.38 Bob verifies that the document came from Alice by decrypting the encrypted document using Alice's public key

- to verify that the message/document was not tampered with in transit
- to verify that the original document has not been tampered with at source.

Message digest

Encryption and decryption are computationally intensive.

Digitally signing a document by encrypting the whole document is therefore expensive computationally.

To reduce the computation overhead a hash function H is used.

This function takes a message/document M, of arbitrary length and computes H(M), a fixed-length "fingerprint" of the message/document M called a **message digest**.

Alice now digitally signs the message digest rather than the message/document itself to create a digital signature.

As H(M) is generally of much shorter length than the original message/document M, creating the digital signature consumes much less computational effort.

Alice now sends the document M followed by the digital signature to Bob as shown in *Figure 33.39*.

On receipt of M, Bob uses the hashing function H to produce a hash of document *M* as shown in *Figure 33.40*.

On receipt of the digital signature, Bob decrypts it using Alice's public key p_A to obtain the message digest or hash produced by Alice if she genuinely signed the document. If the two hashes match then Bob can conclude that Alice was the signer of the document and that the document has not been tampered with whilst in transit.

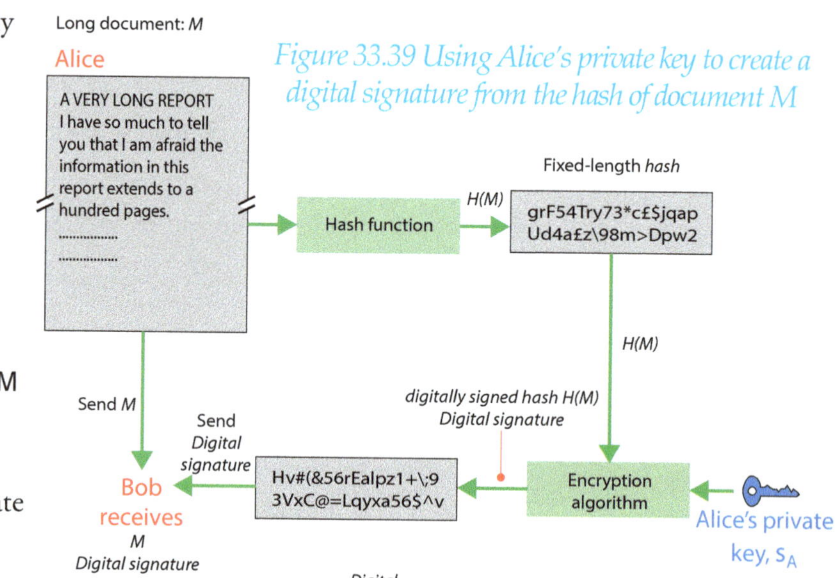

Figure 33.39 Using Alice's private key to create a digital signature from the hash of document M

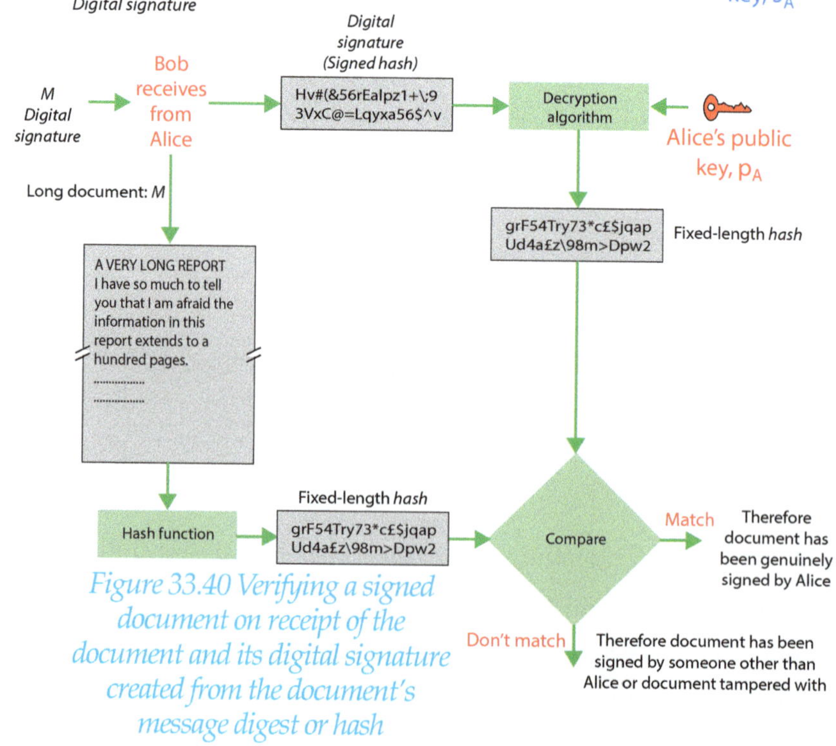

Figure 33.40 Verifying a signed document on receipt of the document and its digital signature created from the document's message digest or hash

Delphi application to sign and verify documents

P

Start a new application New|Window VCL Application - Delphi.

Save the project as `LockBox3RSADigitalSignatureProject.dproj` and its unit as `LockBox3RSADigitalSignatureUnit.Pas` in folder `LockBox3RSADigitalSignatureProject`.

Add the components shown in *Figure 33.41, Figure 33.44*. **Set** the properties of `CodecRSA` and `Signatory1` as shown in *Figure 33.42* and *Figure 33.43*.

Create event handlers as shown in *Table 33.10a* and *Table 33.10b*.

Save All (SHIFT+CTRL+S).

Click Run (F9) to build and run the application - *Figure 33.45*.

Select `Sonnet116.txt` and **click** the `Sign` button. The application creates a message digest of the document and then encrypts this messsage digest with the private key to produce the document's digital signature. *Figure 33.46* shows this signature `Sonnet116.txt.sig`.

Click the `Verify document` button to verify that the document has not been altered since the signature was produced. Now **alter** the document and click the `Verify document` button again. This time the verification process should fail.

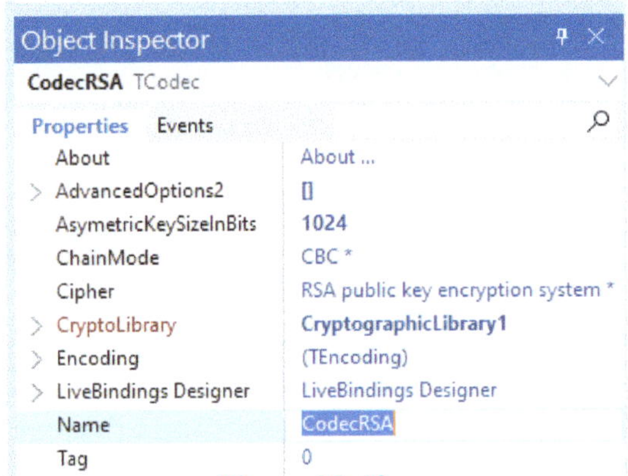

Figure 33.42 LockBox3RSADigitalSignatureProject CodecRSA settings

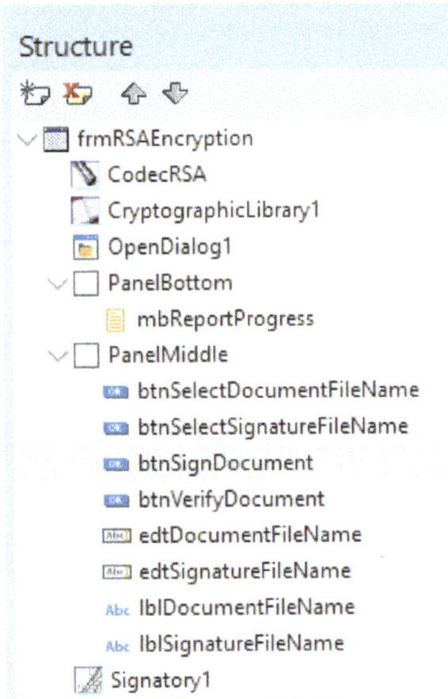

Figure 33.41 LockBox3RSADigitalSignatureProject Structure window

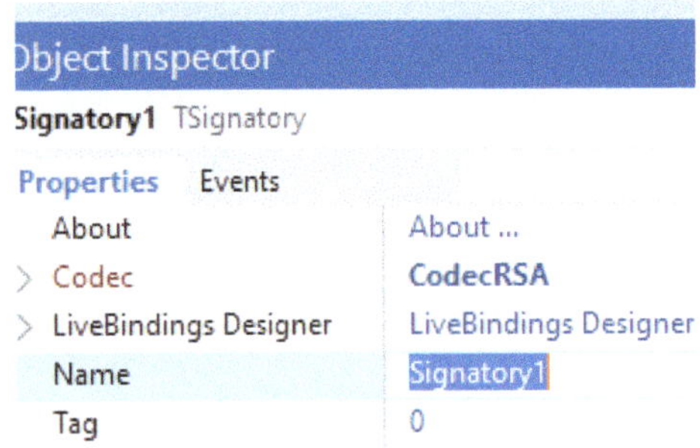

Figure 33.43 LockBox3RSADigitalSignatureProject Signatory1 settings

Figure 33.44 LockBox3RSADigitalSignatureProject user interface design

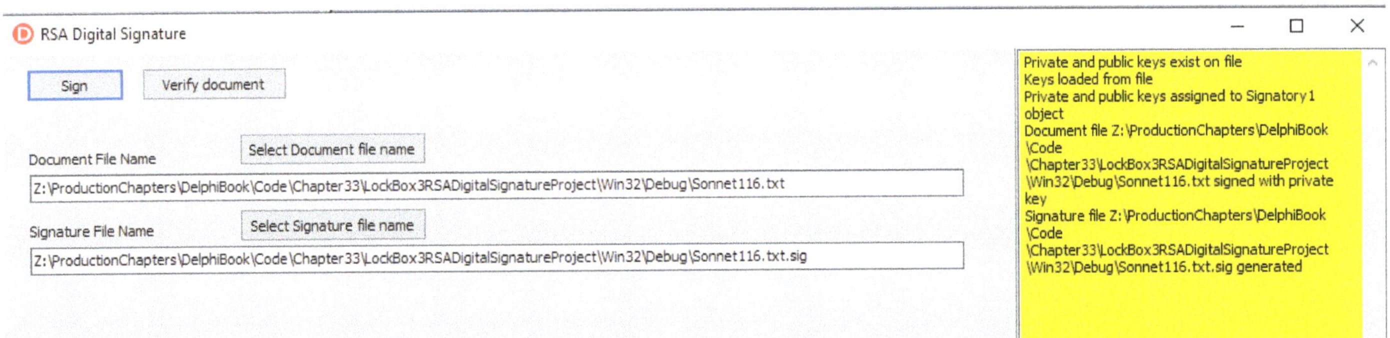

Figure 33.45 LockBox3RSADigitalSignatureProject in execution and signing document Sonnet116.txt

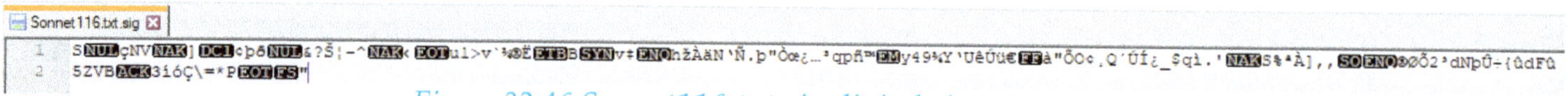

Figure 33.46 Sonnet116.txt.sig digital signature

Task

15 Download the Complete Works of William Shakespeare from https://www.gutenberg.org/files/100/100-0.txt
Sign this text document and confirm that the size of the digital signature document is 1kB, i.e. it is an encrypted message digest.

P

```
Unit LockBox3RSADigitalSignatureUnit;
Interface
Uses
  Winapi.Windows, Winapi.Messages, System.SysUtils, System.Variants, System.Classes, Vcl.Graphics,
  Vcl.Controls, Vcl.Forms, Vcl.Dialogs, Vcl.StdCtrls, Vcl.ExtCtrls,
  uTPLb_Signatory, uTPLb_CryptographicLibrary, uTPLb_BaseNonVisualComponent,
  uTPLb_Codec, uTPLb_Asymetric, uTPlb_StreamCipher, Vcl.ComCtrls;
Type
  TfrmRSAEncryption = Class(TForm)
                        CodecRSA : TCodec;
                        CryptographicLibrary1 : TCryptographicLibrary;
                        Signatory1 : TSignatory;
                        PanelMiddle : TPanel;
                        PanelBottom : TPanel;
                        mbReportProgress : TMemo;
                        btnSignDocument : TButton;
                        btnVerifyDocument : TButton;
                        edtDocumentFileName : TEdit;
                        lblDocumentFileName : TLabel;
                        edtSignatureFileName : TEdit;
                        lblSignatureFileName : TLabel;
                        OpenDialog1 : TOpenDialog;
                        btnSelectDocumentFileName : TButton;
                        btnSelectSignatureFileName : TButton;
                        Procedure FormActivate(Sender : TObject);
                        Procedure Generate_RSA_Keys(Var msPublic, msPrivate : TMemoryStream);
                        Procedure SignAFile(DocumentFileName, SignatureFileName : String);
                        Procedure CheckASignedFile(DocumentFileName, SignatureFileName : String);
                        Procedure FormClose(Sender : TObject; var Action: TCloseAction);
                        Procedure btnSignClick(Sender : TObject);
                        Procedure btnVerifyDocumentClick(Sender : TObject);
                        Procedure btnSelectSignatureFileNameClick(Sender : TObject);
                        Procedure btnSelectDocumentFileNameClick(Sender : TObject);
                      End;
Var
  frmRSAEncryption: TfrmRSAEncryption;
Implementation
{$R *.dfm}
  Var
    msPrivate, msPublic : TMemoryStream;
    DocumentStream, SignatureStream : TFileStream;
  Procedure  TfrmRSAEncryption.CheckASignedFile(DocumentFileName, SignatureFileName : String);
    Var
      VerifiedResult : TVerifyResult;
    Begin
      If FileExists(SignatureFileName)
        Then
          Begin
            DocumentStream := TFileStream.Create(DocumentFileName, fmOpenRead);
            SignatureStream := TFileStream.Create(SignatureFileName, fmOpenRead);
            VerifiedResult := Signatory1.Verify(DocumentStream, SignatureStream);
            If VerifiedResult = vPass
              Then ShowMessage('Verified')
              Else ShowMessage('Failed');
          End
        Else ShowMessage('File doesn''t exist');
    End;
  Procedure TfrmRSAEncryption.SignAFile(DocumentFileName, SignatureFileName : String);
    Begin
      If FileExists(DocumentFileName)
        Then
          Begin
            DocumentStream := TFileStream.Create(DocumentFileName, fmOpenRead);
            SignatureStream := TFileStream.Create(SignatureFileName, fmCreate);
            Signatory1.Sign(DocumentStream, SignatureStream);
            DocumentStream.Free;
            SignatureStream.Free
          End
        Else ShowMessage('File doesn''t exist');
    End;
```

Table 33.10a LockBox3RSADigitalSignatureUnit.Pas

```
Procedure TfrmRSAEncryption.btnVerifyDocumentClick(Sender : TObject);
  Begin
    If Assigned(msPrivate)
      Then
        Begin
          CheckASignedFile(edtDocumentFileName.Text, edtSignatureFileName.Text);
          mbReportProgress.Lines.Add('Document file ' + edtDocumentFileName.Text + ' verified');
        End
      Else mbReportProgress.Lines.Add('Unfortunately verification failed because msPrivate not assigned');
  End;
Procedure TfrmRSAEncryption.btnSignClick(Sender : TObject);
  Begin
    If Assigned(msPublic)
      Then
        Begin
          SignAFile(edtDocumentFileName.Text, edtSignatureFileName.Text);
          mbReportProgress.Lines.Add('Document file ' + edtDocumentFileName.Text + ' signed with private key');
          mbReportProgress.Lines.Add('Signature file ' + edtSignatureFileName.Text + ' generated');
        End
      Else mbReportProgress.Lines.Add('Unfortunately signing failed because msPublic not assigned');
  End;
Procedure TfrmRSAEncryption.btnSelectDocumentFileNameClick(Sender : TObject);
  Begin
    If OpenDialog1.Execute
    Then
      Begin
        edtDocumentFileName.Text := OpenDialog1.FileName;
        edtSignatureFileName.Text := edtDocumentFileName.Text + '.sig';
      End;
  End;
Procedure TfrmRSAEncryption.btnSelectSignatureFileNameClick(Sender : TObject);
  Begin
    If OpenDialog1.Execute
      Then edtSignatureFileName.Text := OpenDialog1.FileName;
  End;
Procedure TfrmRSAEncryption.Generate_RSA_Keys(Var msPublic, msPrivate : TMemoryStream);
  Begin
    If Signatory1.GenerateKeys
      Then
        Begin
          Signatory1.StoreKeysToStream(msPublic,[partPublic]);
          Signatory1.StoreKeysToStream(msPrivate,[partPrivate]);
          msPublic.Position := 0;
          msPrivate.Position := 0;
          mbReportProgress.Lines.Add('Private and public keys generated');
        End
      Else mbReportProgress.Lines.Add('Private and public keys not generated');
  End;
Procedure TfrmRSAEncryption.FormActivate(Sender : TObject);
  Var
    KeysExist:Boolean;
  Begin
    KeysExist := False;
    msPublic := TMemoryStream.Create;
    msPrivate := TMemoryStream.Create;
    If (FileExists('Public.key') And FileExists('Private.key'))
      Then
        Begin
          mbReportProgress.Lines.Add('Private and public keys exist on file');
          msPublic.LoadFromFile('Public.key');
          msPrivate.LoadFromFile('Private.key');
          mbReportProgress.Lines.Add('Keys loaded from file');
          Signatory1.LoadKeysFromStream(msPublic,[partPublic]);
          Signatory1.LoadKeysFromStream(msPrivate,[partPrivate]);
          mbReportProgress.Lines.Add('Private and public keys assigned to Signatory1 object');
          KeysExist := True;
        End;
    If Not KeysExist
      Then
        Begin
          mbReportProgress.Lines.Add('Private and public keys don''t exist');
          Generate_RSA_Keys(msPublic, msPrivate);
          msPublic.SaveTofile('Public.key');
          msPrivate.SaveToFile('Private.key');
          mbReportProgress.Lines.Add('Private and public keys saved to file, Public.key and Private.key');
        End;
    End;
Procedure TfrmRSAEncryption.FormClose(Sender : TObject; Var Action : TCloseAction);
  Begin
    If Assigned(msPublic)
      Then msPublic.Free;
    If Assigned(msPrivate)
      Then msPrivate.Free;
  End;
End.
```

Table 33.10b LockBox3RSADigitalSignatureUnit.Pas

34 Hashing and Bitcoin

Hashing

Purpose: To understand the use of hashing functions in cryptography and in hash tables

Information

The term "hash" originates by analogy with its non-technical meaning, to "chop and mix". Hash functions often "chop" the input domain into many sub-domains that get "mixed" e.g. add the first three digits of the key, add the last three digits, concatenate the two resulting digit strings then map into the output range by applying modulo N.

Chapter 33 introduced digital signatures whereby a digest of the message is signed instead of the message *m*. The message digest is shorter than the message *m* and is generated by applying a **hash function** *H* to the message *m*. The message digest $H(m)$ is typically between 128 and 512 bits, compared to thousands or millions of bits for the message *m* itself. Signing $H(m)$ is therefore much less computationally intensive than signing *m* directly because signing $H(m)$ involves working with fewer bits.

In general, a hashing or hash function *H* maps input data, *m*, of an arbitrary length in a random way to an output of fixed length. The output, a fixed-length random value, is called the hash value or just hash.

Hashing functions have many uses besides generating message digests.

For example, hash functions are also used as mapping functions in hash tables, a data structure which is considered later in this chapter.

Hash functions used in cryptography are different from hash functions used in hash tables. Cryptographic hash functions have specific security properties, notably:

> A cryptographic hash function should be a **one way function**, i.e. a function which is practically infeasible to invert, i.e. given a message *m* it should be relatively easy to compute its hash value $H(m)$, but given a hash value *x* it should not be possible to find an *m* such that $H(m) = x$ given current computational resources.

Hash table mapping functions are less stringent in this respect.

Both cryptographic and hash table functions should have **good collision resistance**. A collision occurs when $H(m_1) = H(m_2)$ for two different inputs m_1 and m_2 but hash table functions have ways of coping when collisions do occur.

Theoretically avoiding collisions is impossible because there are more possible input values than there are possible output values.

However, the collision-resistance requirement simple means that, although collisions exist, encountering these should be minimised in the case of hash tables or avoided altogether in the case of cryptographic hash functions.

It is also important that both types of hash function should be quick to compute.

Real hash functions are distinguished from the **ideal hash function** as follows:

> The **ideal hash function** is a random mapping from all possible input values to the set of possible output values i.e. output hash values are of equal likelihood;
>
> **Real hash functions** only attempt to be indistinguishable from a random mapping.

Secure hash functions

We saw in the previous chapter that ciphers protect data confidentiality (i.e. attempt to prevent data sent over a communication link from being read if intercepted).

We also saw that hash functions protect data integrity by attempting to detect when data have been modified whether that data is encrypted or not - message digest and signed message digest.

If a **hash function** is **secure**, two distinct pieces of data should always have different hashes. A file's hash (the result of applying the hash function to the file) can thus serve as an identifier. Even if a single bit is changed in the file, the hash of the file will be completely different.

Secondly, the output from a secure hash function should be unpredictable.

The console mode program shown in *Table 34.1* calls function `THashSHA2.GetHashString`, a class function, which applies the **Secure Hash Algorithm-2** (**SHA2**) to a single character to produce a 256-bit hash value output. The function `GetHashString` returns a hexadecimal string which it generates by dividing each 256-bit hash value into 64, 4-bit blocks before treating each block as a single hexadecimal digit which it then maps to its equivalent hexadecimal character digit, e.g. hexadecimal digit C is mapped to character 'c'.

256 bits map to 64, 4-bit blocks which map to 64 characters chosen from the set ['0'..'9', 'a'..'f'].

The output from this program for the characters 'a', 'b' and 'c' is shown in *Figure 34.1*. Although the bit patterns for 'a', 'b' and 'c' differ by only one or two bits ('a' is the bit pattern 01100001, 'b' is 01100010 and 'c' is 01100011) their hash values are completely different. Given only these three hashes, it is impossible to predict the SHA2 - 256 hash of 'd', etc, i.e. the hash values are *unpredictable*. The function `THashSHA2.GetHashString` returns a random string each time it receives an input.

P

```
Program CryptoHashOnACharUsingSHA2_256Project;
{$APPTYPE CONSOLE}
{$R *.res}
Uses
  System.SysUtils, System.Hash;
Var
  Ch : Char;
Begin
  Repeat
    Write('Input char to hash: ');
    Readln(Ch);
    Writeln('Hash value SHA2 of ', '''', Ch, '''', ' = '
            + THashSHA2.GetHashString(Ch, SHA256));
    Writeln('Hash value SHA2 of ', '''', Succ(Ch), '''', ' = '
            + THashSHA2.GetHashString(Succ(Ch), SHA256));
    Writeln('Hash value SHA2 of ', '''', Succ(Succ(Ch)), '''', ' = '
            + THashSHA2.GetHashString(Succ(Succ(Ch)), SHA256));
    Write('Another go (Y/N)? ');
    Readln(Ch);
  Until Ch In ['N', 'n'];
End.
```

Table 34.1 CryptoHashOnACharUsingSHA2_256Project.dpr

```
Input char to hash: a
Hash value SHA2 of 'a' = ca978112ca1bbdcafac231b39a23dc4da786eff8147c4e72b9807785afee48bb
Hash value SHA2 of 'b' = 3e23e8160039594a33894f6564e1b1348bbd7a0088d42c4acb73eeaed59c009d
Hash value SHA2 of 'c' = 2e7d2c03a9507ae265ecf5b5356885a53393a2029d241394997265a1a25aefc6
Another go (Y/N)? y
Input char to hash: a
Hash value SHA2 of 'a' = ca978112ca1bbdcafac231b39a23dc4da786eff8147c4e72b9807785afee48bb
Hash value SHA2 of 'b' = 3e23e8160039594a33894f6564e1b1348bbd7a0088d42c4acb73eeaed59c009d
Hash value SHA2 of 'c' = 2e7d2c03a9507ae265ecf5b5356885a53393a2029d241394997265a1a25aefc6
```

Figure 34.1 SHA2 - 256 hash values of the characters 'a', 'b', 'c'

Preimage resistance

In practice, the security of a hash function, $H(m)$, where m is any message, is judged by whether an attacker will find m, given the generated hash value x. We call m the **preimage** in this scenario and the security property of the hash function that resists discovery of m given hash value x, **preimage resistance**.

To illustrate the difficulty that an attacker will experience, consider a hash function that outputs hash values of length 256 bits and which behaves like a truly random function. There are 2^{256} equally likely hash values. If just 1024-bit length messages are considered, there are 2^{1024} possible messages. Therefore, on average each possible 256-bit hash value will have $2^{1024}/_{2^{256}} = 2^{768}$ preimages of 1024 bits each. 2^{768} is approximately 1.6×10^{231}. If execution time of a preimage search algorithm for a match with hash value x - *Table 34.2* - for one possible message m is, say, 5×10^{-7} seconds, then to test half the possible messages of length 1024 bits would take 4×10^{224} seconds, an enormous amount of time. And then there are other possible bit length messages......

```
Function FindPreImage(x : THashValue) : TMessage
  Var
    m : TMessage
  Repeat
    m ← GenerateRandomMessage
    If H(m) = x
      Then Exit;
  Until  False
  Result ←m
End Function
```

Information

SHA2-256 is built into Apple Macs. Choose Terminal and then type

echo -n 'hello!' | shasum - a 256

to pass the string 'hello!' through a pipe (|) to the function shasum.

Install NotePad++ on Windows. This editor has a SHA-256 option under Tools.

Table 34.2 Pseudocode for preimage search algorithm for a secure hash function h

Preimage resistance may be divided into **first-preimage resistance** and **second-preimage resistance**.

First-preimage resistance means the degree of resistance to discovering any message that maps to a given hash value.

Second-preimage resistance means the degree of resistance for a given message m_1 of finding a second message m_2 that hashes to the same value as m_1.

First-preimage resistance

First-preimage resistance is important in the case of passwords which are hashed and saved in a database. When a user logs in, the hash of the entered password is computed and compared against the stored hash value. The intention of storing hashes of passwords instead of storing passwords directly is to keep passwords stored in a system confidential. As passwords are usually of limited length, a salt (random data) is added to the password before hashing to make it more difficult to discover the password given the hash value. Storing passwords in this way relies crucially on the hash not being reversed by an attacker, i.e. first-preimage resistance.

Second-preimage resistance

Second-preimage resistance is important in protocols which focus on message integrity. A match between the original message and its hash should be confirmation that the document has not been altered.

Second-preimage resistance is also important in a commitment scheme which is a cryptographic primitive that allows one to commit to a chosen value (or chosen statement) while keeping it hidden from others, with the ability to reveal the committed value later.

Interactions in a commitment scheme take place in two phases:

- the commit phase during which a value is chosen and specified
- the reveal phase during which the value is revealed and checked

Figure 34.2 shows an example in which Bob sends the hash value of an even or odd number chosen from some prearranged fixed but large range of integers. The chosen number encodes the setting of a single bit known only to Bob at this stage. In the commitment phase, Bob chooses an even number if the bit is to be set to one, otherwise he chooses an odd number. Alice on receipt of the hashed value makes a guess as to the setting of Bob's bit and replies by sending her guess as a single bit. Upon receiving Alice's guess, Bob enters the reveal stage by sending the original number. On receipt, Alice verifies this number by comparing the hash of this number with the hash value received during the commit stage. If Bob uses a hash function that has weak second-preimage resistance then it is possible that Bob knows of a different number with opposite parity (evenness or oddness) that produces the same hash value as the committed number. Bob then has the option to determine the outcome whether Alice guesses correctly or not by exploiting the second-preimage weakness in the hash function.

What might Bob's bit sequence represent? One case is the sequence represents the head|tail outcome of a series of coin tosses which Alice is required to guess.

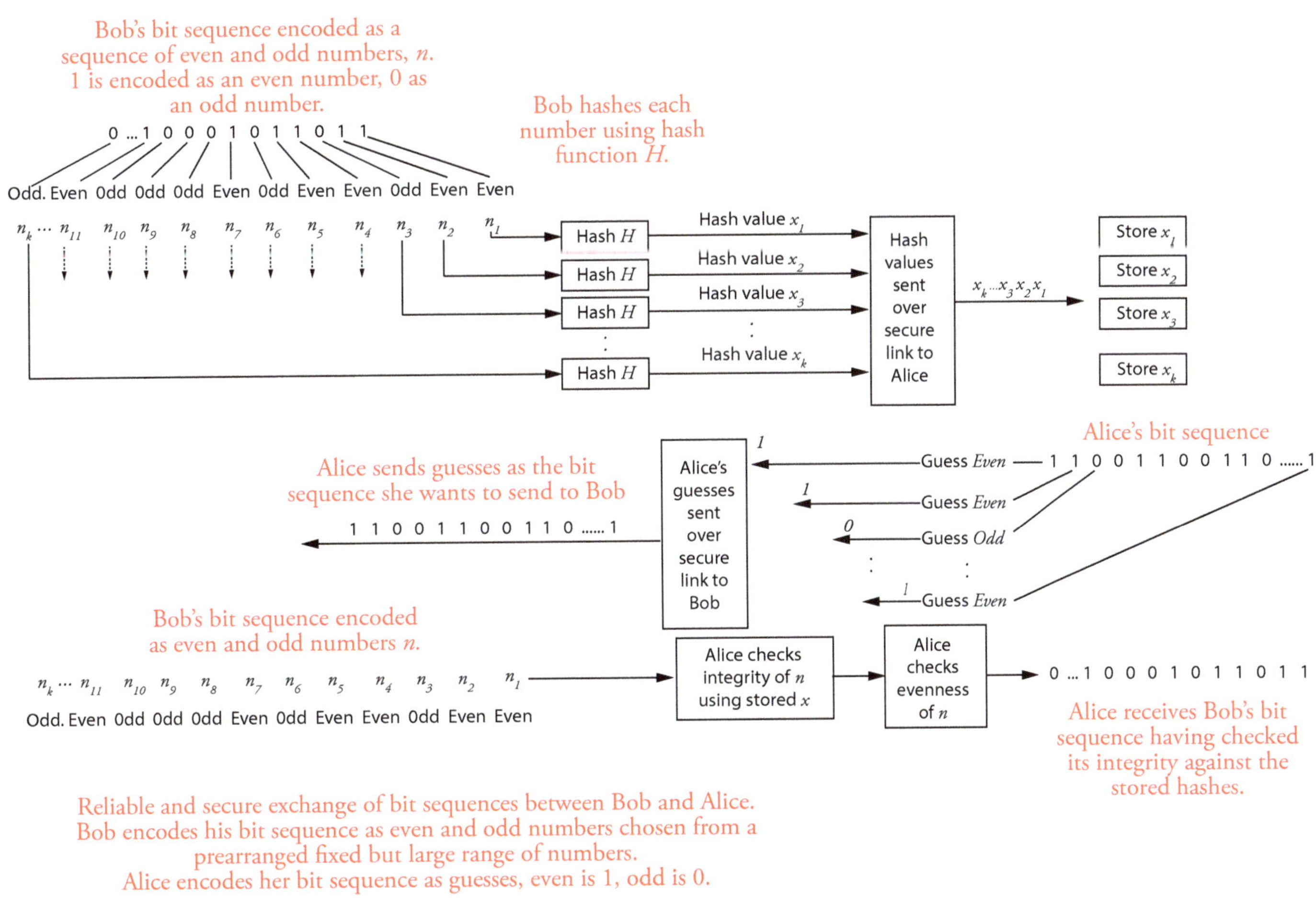

Figure 34.2 Commitment scheme

Collision resistance

Whatever hash function is used, there are always more possible messages by design than hash values so collisions must exist. This is the **pigeonhole principle** in action.

> The pigeonhole principle states that if there are n holes and m pigeons to put in these holes, and if m is greater than n, at least one hole must contain more than one pigeon.

The **collision resistance** of a hash function is a measure of how hard it is to find collisions. A collision resistant hash function is one which should make it infeasible for attackers to find two distinct messages that hash to the same value.

Collision resistance is related to second-preimage resistance. If it is possible to find second-preimages for a hash function, it is also possible to find collisions.

It is actually faster to find collisions than it is to find preimages thanks to the **birthday attack**. The birthday attack is a restatement of the **birthday problem** of calculating the probability that in a set of n randomly selected people, at least two people share the same birthday.

Let $p(n)$ be the probability that in a set of n randomly chosen people at least two people share the same birthday. Then $1 - p(n)$ is the probability that every single one of them has distinct birthdays.

The number of ways to pick n distinct birthdays from a set of 366 days (when the order in which you pick the birthdays matters) is

$$366 \times 365 \times \ldots \times (367 - n)$$

because each successive birthday has one fewer choice of days left.

The number of possibilities for the birthdays for n people is 366^n.(although not all equally likely because of the leap year, but we will ignore this)

Therefore,

$$1 - p(n) = \frac{366 \times 365 \times \ldots \times (367 - n)}{366^n}$$

$$1 - p(n) = \frac{366\,!}{366^n \times (366 - n)!}$$

$$p(n) = 1 - \frac{366\,!}{366^n \times (366 - n)!}$$

If $n = 24$

$$366! = 9.19 \times 10^{780}$$

$$366^n = 366^{24} = 3.34 \times 10^{61}$$

$$(366 - n)! = (366 - 24)! = 342! = 5.95 \times 10^{719}$$

$$366^{24} \times 342! = 3.34 \times 10^{61} \times 5.95 \times 10^{719} = 19.87 \times 10^{780}$$

Therefore,

$$p(24) = 1 - \frac{366\,!}{366^n \times (366 - 24)!} = 1 - \frac{9.19 \times 10^{780}}{19.87 \times 10^{780}} = 1 - 0.46 = 0.54$$

The probability that in a set of 24 randomly chosen people at least two people share the same birthday is 54%.

If the calculation is repeated but with $n = 72$ the probability is close to 100%.

We are now ready to answer the question:

How many values does an attacker need to compute before the probability of a collision is greater than 50%?

Suppose that a hash function is chosen with a 64-bit range, i.e. its output is a 64-bit nonnegative integer less than 2^{64} ($0 .. 2^{64} - 1$).

Just as with the birthday problem, the probability of a collision from n random samples is

$$p_M(n) = 1 - \frac{M!}{M^n \times (M - n)!}$$

where $M = 2^{64}$ the number of possible hash values.

For $n^2 << M$

$$p_M(n) \approx \frac{n^2}{2M}$$

For $p_M(n) = 0.5$

$$0.5 \approx \frac{n^2}{2M}$$

i.e. n is of the order of $\sqrt{M}$. For $M = 2^{64}$, $\sqrt{M} = 2^{32}$ which is approximately 4×10^9. Trialling this number of sample messages is feasible (*hash*(*sample value*)). This vulnerability necessitates the use of a larger hash range in practical applications.

If a 256-bit range is chosen, i.e. hash values of nonnegative integers less than 2^{256}, then for $n^2 << M$, n is of the order of $\sqrt{2^{256}}$, i.e. 2^{128} which is approximately 3×10^{38}. The number of values an attacker needs to compute before the probability of a collision is greater than 50% is now large enough to be infeasible by a brute force approach.

How can an attacker exploit a collision vulnerability in a hashing function?

An attacker typically begins by constructing two messages with the same hash value where one message appears legitimate. For example, when an attacker, *X*, discovers that the message

"I, *SomeName*, agree to pay *X* the sum of £5000.00 on 01/03/2021."

has the same hash as

"I, *SomeName*, agree to pay *X* the sum of £50000.00 on 09/03/2021."

then *X* can try to get the victim, *SomeName*, to digitally sign the first message. The attacker *X* can then claim that *SomeName* actually signed the second message. *SomeName* signs the hash of the first and genuine message, i.e. signs the message digest, with his/her private key and the attacker *X* retrieves the hash from the digitally signed message digest by using *SomeName*'s public key. *X* now attempts to prove that the hash for the confirmed signature matches the second bogus message.

Collisions have been announced for the following hash functions

- SHA-0
- MD4
- MD5
- HAVAL-128
- RIPEMD
- SHA-1.

Hash function construction

The simplest way to hash a message is to split it into chunks and process each chunk consecutively using a similar algorithm. This is called iterative hashing. It comes in two main forms:

- Using a technique based on a compression function that transforms an input to a smaller output. This is known as the Merkle-Damgård construction after cryptographers Raplh Mekle and Ivan Damgård. MD4, MD5, SHA-1, and the SHA-2 family are examples.
- Using a technique that transforms an input, a binary string of any length, and returns a binary string with any requested length, such that any two different inputs give two different outputs, i.e. permutations. Such functions are called sponge functions. An example is Keccak which is also known as SHA-3.

Hashing file contents in Delphi

Start a new application New|Window VCL Application - Delphi.

Save the project as `CryptographicHashOnFileProject.dproj` and its unit as `CryptographicHashOnFileUnit.pas` in folder `CryptographicHashOnFileProject`.

Add the following components to the form:

- 3 x **TPanel**
- 6 x **TButton**
- 2 x **TEdit**
- 2 x **TLabel**
- 2 x **TMemo**
- 1 x **TOpenDialog**

Configure and **rename** these as shown in *Figure 34.3* and *Figure 34.4*.

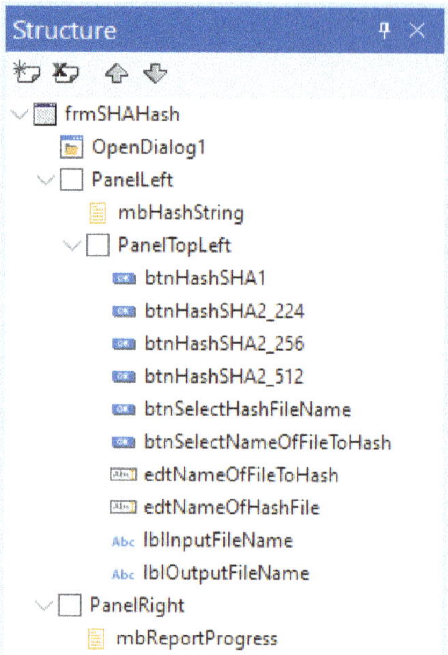

Figure 34.3 Structure window

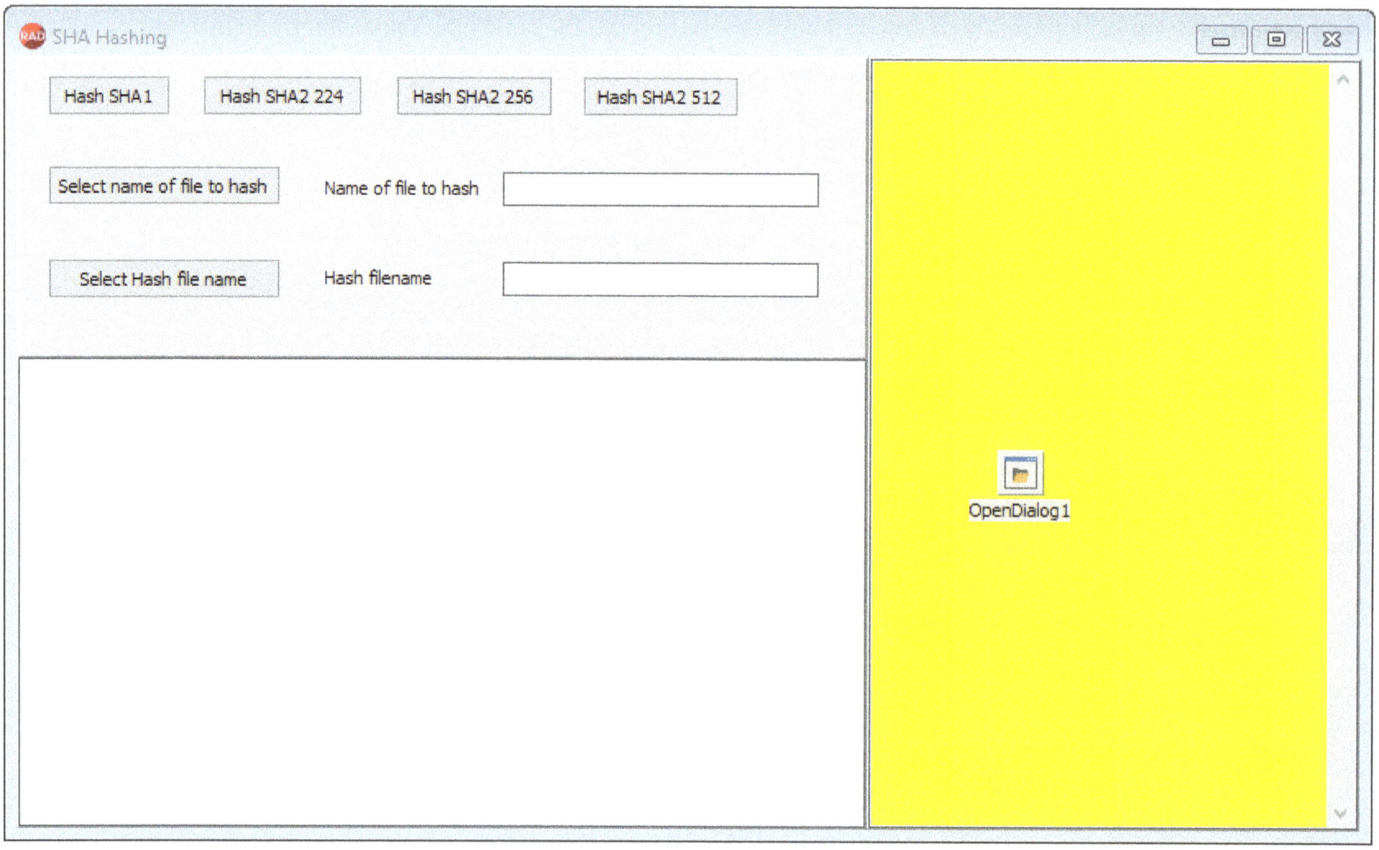

Figure 34.4 CryptographicHashOnFileProject user interface design

Double click the buttons to create event-handlers.

Add the following to the class definition as shown in *Table 34.3*.

```
Procedure SHA1HashFile(InputFileName, HashFileName : String);
Procedure SHA2_512HashFile(InputFileName, HashFileName : String);
Procedure SHA2_256HashFile(InputFileName, HashFileName : String);
Procedure SHA2_224HashFile(InputFileName, HashFileName : String);
```

Place the cursor in each of these in turn and press **Ctrl+Shift+C** to create the skeleton procedure definition in the **Implementation** section.

Add the code shown in *Table 34.4* to the body of `Procedure SHA2_256HashFile`.

Repeat this process for the other procedures except `SHA1HashFile` changing the references `SHA256` to the appropriate references for the respective procedure, e.g. SHA256 ↦ SHA512.

`SHA1HashFile`. `GetHashStringFromFile` body code is similar for all but

```
OutputStringList.Add(THashSHA1.GetHashStringFromFile(InputFileName));
```

which has only one parameter.

```
Type
  TfrmSHAHash = Class(TForm)
                PanelTopLeft : TPanel;
                PanelRight : TPanel;
                mbReportProgress : TMemo;
                btnHashSHA1 : TButton;
                btnHashSHA2_512 : TButton;
                edtNameOfFileToHash: TEdit;
                lblInputFileName : TLabel;
                edtNameOfHashFile: TEdit;
                lblOutputFileName : TLabel;
                btnSelectNameOfFileToHash : TButton;
                btnSelectHashFileName : TButton;
                OpenDialog1 : TOpenDialog;
                PanelLeft : TPanel;
                mbHashString : TMemo;
                btnHashSHA2_256 : TButton;
                btnHashSHA2_224 : TButton;
                Procedure btnHashSHA1Click(Sender : TObject);
                Procedure btnHashSHA2_512Click(Sender : TObject);
                Procedure btnSelectHashFileNameClick(Sender : TObject);
                Procedure btnSelectNameOfFileToHashClick(Sender : TObject);
                Procedure SHA1HashFile(InputFileName, HashFileName : String);
                Procedure SHA2_512HashFile(InputFileName, HashFileName : String);
                Procedure SHA2_256HashFile(InputFileName, HashFileName : String);
                Procedure SHA2_224HashFile(InputFileName, HashFileName : String);
                Procedure btnHashSHA2_256Click(Sender : TObject);
                Procedure btnHashSHA2_224Click(Sender : TObject);
              End;
Var
  frmSHAHash: TfrmSHAHash;
```

P

Table 34.3 Class definition TfrmSHAHash and variable declaration frmSHAHash

Add the code shown in *Table 34.5* to the body of event handler `btnHashSHA2_256Click`.

Repeat for the other `btnHash....Click` event handlers replacing references to SHA2 256 to the relevant hashing algorithm.

Add the code shown in *Table 34.6* to the bodies of the **OpenDialog** event handlers.

Save All (SHIFT+CTRL+S).

Click Run (F9) to build and run the application `CryptographicHashOnFileProject`.

Figure 34.5 shows `CryptographicHashOnFileProject` in execution. `Books.txt` is an 80 kB text file downloaded from http://www.gutenberg.org/files/64684/64684-0.txt.

```
Procedure TfrmSHAHash.SHA2_256HashFile(InputFileName, HashFileName : String);
  Var
    OutputStream : TFileStream;
    OutputStringList : TStringList;
  Begin
    If FileExists(InputFileName)
      Then
        Begin
          OutputStringList := TStringList.Create;
          OutputStringList.Add(THashSHA2.GetHashStringFromFile(InputFileName, SHA256));
          OutputStream := TFileStream.Create(HashFileName, fmCreate);
          OutputStringList.SaveToStream(OutputStream);
          mbHashString.Lines.Add(OutputStringList.Text);
          mbReportProgress.Lines.Add('Size of contents of hash file '
           + ExtractFileName(HashFileName) + ' produced with SHA2 256 is in bits '
           + IntToStr(4 * Length(THashSHA2.GetHashStringFromFile(InputFileName, SHA256)))
           + '.' + #10#13#10#13);
          OutputStream.Free;
          OutputStringList.Free;
        End
      Else ShowMessage('File doesn''t exist');
  End;
```

Table 34.4 Procedure that applies SHA2-256 hash function to input file

```
Procedure TfrmSHAHash.btnHashSHA2_256Click(Sender : TObject);
  Begin
    SHA2_256HashFile(edtNameOfFileToHash.Text, edtNameOfHashFile.Text);
    mbReportProgress.Lines.Add('Input file ' + ExtractFileName(edtNameOfFileToHash.Text)
      + ' hashed with SHA2 256.' + #10#13#10#13);
    mbReportProgress.Lines.Add('Output file ' + ExtractFileName(edtNameOfHashFile.Text)
      + ' produced with SHA2 256.' + #10#13#10#13);
  End;
```

Table 34.5 Event handler for btnHashSHA2_256Click

```
Procedure TfrmSHAHash.btnSelectNameOfFileToHashClick(Sender : TObject);
  Begin
    If OpenDialog1.Execute
      Then edtNameOfFileToHash.Text := OpenDialog1.FileName;
  End;

Procedure TfrmSHAHash.btnSelectHashFileNameClick(Sender : TObject);
  Begin
    If OpenDialog1.Execute
      Then edtNameOfHashFile.Text := OpenDialog1.FileName;
  End;
```

Table 34.6 Event handlers for the input and output file dialogues

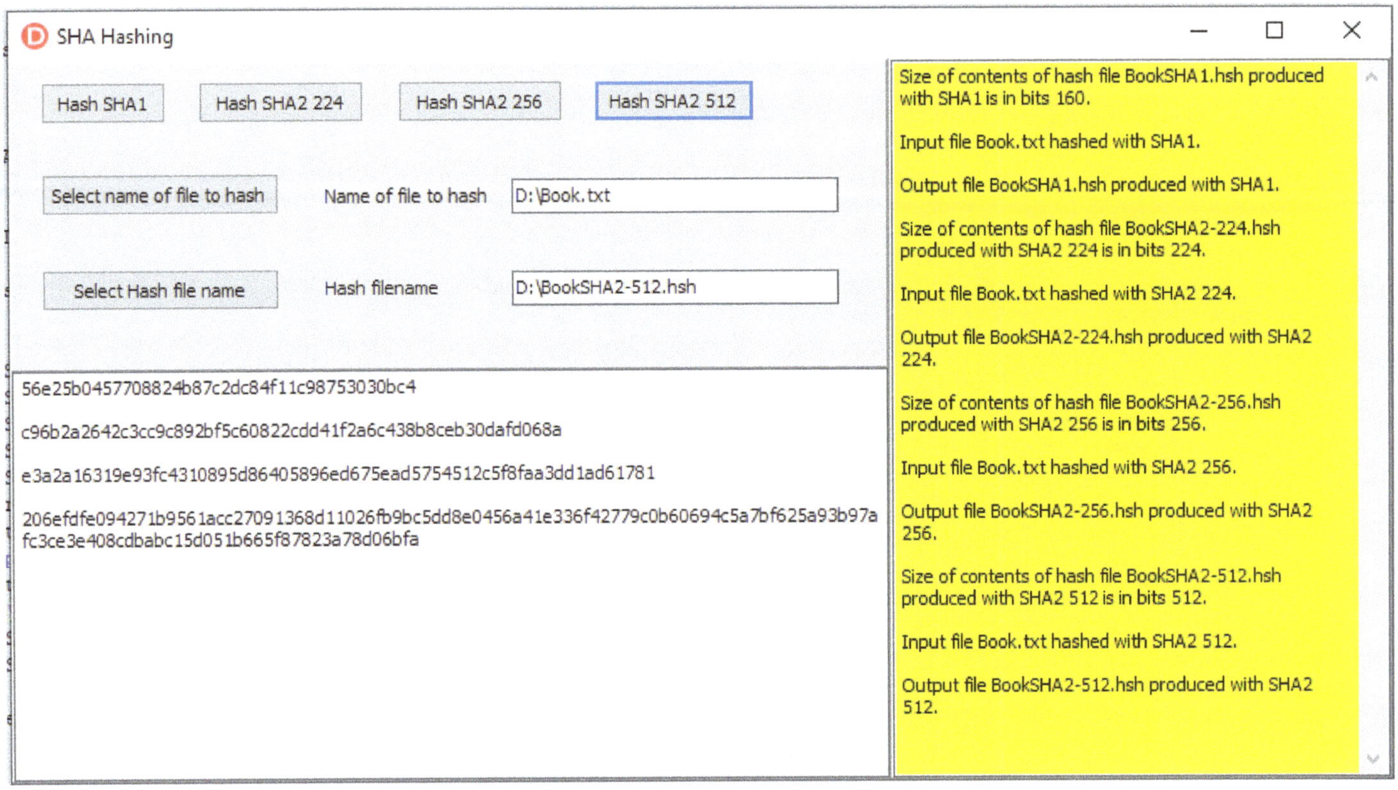

Figure 34.5 CryptographicHashOnFileProject in execution

Bitcoin® and Blockchain

The Bitcoin project was the first to bring together technologies from the 1970s, 80s and 90s to create something novel that solved important problems associated with a digital currency based on a distributed ledger system.

According to Wikipedia[1]:

> *A ledger is a book or collection of accounts in which account transactions are recorded. Each account has an opening or carry-forward balance, and would record transactions as either a debit or credit in separate columns, and the ending or closing balance.*

Bitcoin uses

- a peer-to-peer network protocol (see BitTorrent for an example of a peer-to-peer network) consisting of **miner** nodes (miners compete to add blocks to the blockchain) and nodes that keep the network operating (these nodes validate blocks, confirm transactions and send updates to ledgers in real time) - *Figure 34.6*.
- some core cryptographic functions - SHA-256, RIPEMD160, Elliptic Curve Digital Signature Algorithm (ECDSA), public key/private key encryption.
- Game theory - a dynamically adjusting equilibrium system that uses economics at a global scale - the energy cost incurred in solving a challenge (proof of work) - to enable a trustless distributed system to function successfully.

Miners create blocks containing transactions picked from a pool of transactions.

Each miner that successfully solves a challenge may then attach their block to the chain of blocks called Bitcoin's blockchain - *Figure 34.7*.

The challenge is of sufficient computational difficulty to deny an algorithmic solution so miners are left with no choice but to use a brute-force approach. The level of difficulty is set so that finding a solution takes approximately 10 minutes. Miners using hashing algorithm SHA-256 have to find the nonce (number used only once) that when concatenated with a hash of the previous block, a hash of the transactions in the block and a timestamp produces a

1 Wikipedia - Text under CC-BY-SA license - https://en.wikipedia.org/wiki/Ledger

hash with a required number of leading zeroes - *Figure 34.8*. The hash value produced in this way becomes the new block's hash value.

Block hash = SHA-256 Hash(Hash of previous block + Transactions hash + Timestamp + Nonce)

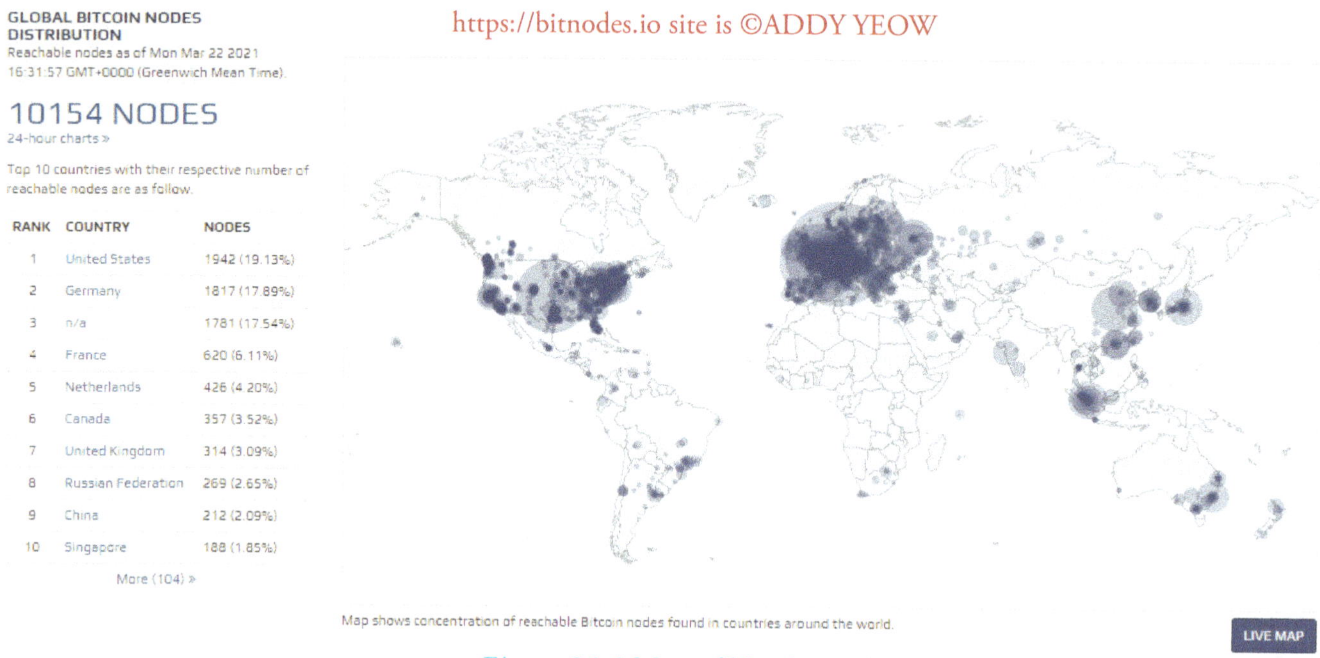

Figure 34.6 Map of bitcoin nodes

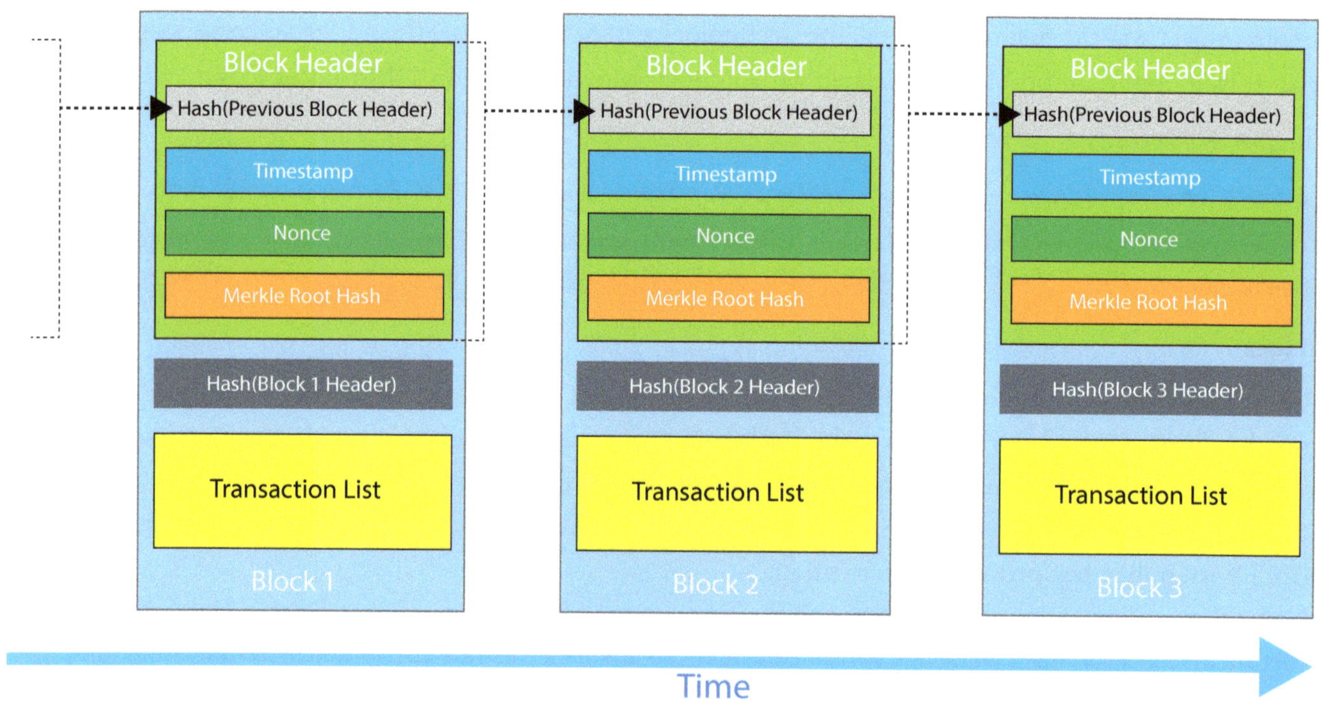

Figure 34.7 Structure of a block in Bitcoin's blockchain

The first miner to solve the challenge has their block of transactions added to the blockchain once their solution has been validated by other nodes in the network (the new block contains everything needed to validate the block's hash, i.e. verify that the challenge has been solved). As each node in the network contains a local copy of the blockchain, the local copies are updated by propogating the validated new block through the network. Very occasionally, two miners arrive at a solution about the same time (their block's timestamp will verify this) and start the propogation process at about the same time. Imagine that these two miners are on opposite sides of the globe, then for a while nodes closer to one miner will add this miner's block while nodes closer to the other will get that miner's block. Thus for a while, half the network will have one blockchain version and the other half the other. What should be done when the new blocks cross over? When this happens a fork is added to the blockchain to accommodate the other block. On receiving a validated block, miners stop working on the current challenge -some miners will be using transactions that occur in the accepted block - and start a new block challenge with other transactions from the unprocessed pool. The arrival of the second block with a timestamp similar to the newly added block signals that a fork must occur. The winner of the next challenge round will add their validated block to the oldest branch of the fork i.e. the branch before the fork arose in their local copy. After five new blocks have been added, one branch of the fork must be longer than the other. The longest branch is then kept and the shorter one abandoned, with its transactions returned to the unprocessed transaction pool if they have not been included in any of the blocks in the retained branch.

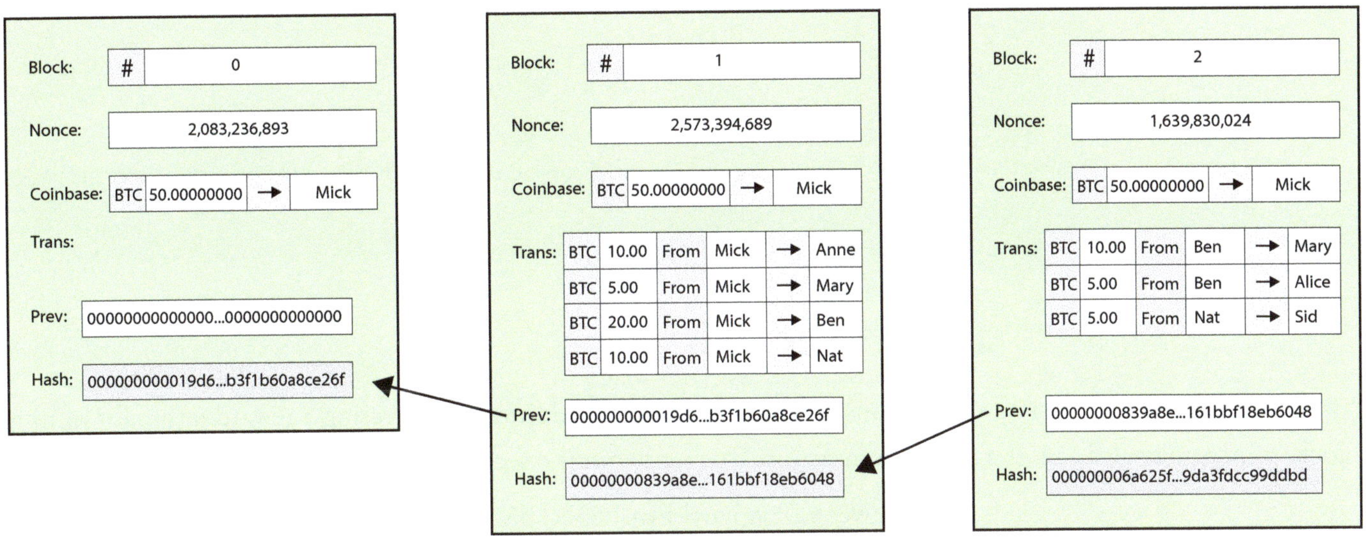

Figure 34.8 Simplified view of blocks in the blockchain

The blockchain is a chain of blocks containing every transaction that has occurred with the very first, a special transaction called a **coinbase** transaction, recorded in block 0. **Coinbase** transaction are assigned their own space in the block. In Bitcoin, miners are rewarded with bitcoins everytime they succeed in solving the challenge. *Figure 34.8* shows that miner Mick has been rewarded three times with 50 BTC each time. This is recorded in the **coinbase** field of the block. Whilst Bitcoin was still in its *proof of concept* stage, the blocks were currency-generation-blocks similar to block 0 in *Figure 34.8*. Spending came later when it was clearly demonstrated that Bitcoin had solved the **coordination problem for shared ledgers**:

- Shared ledgers (each node in the network has their own local copy of the ledger) with multiple collaborators are vulnerable to errors infiltrating the ledger because it is hard to coordinate the actions of multiple users when they are acting independently.
- In a "trustless" community of anonymous users, in addition to honest mistakes, the system must also guard against malicious users who are potentially seeking to defraud others.

Balances are not recorded in the blockchain, instead to answer the question, "How many BTCs does Mick have currently?" requires that a local copy of the ledger is searched for all Mick's transactions, both inputs and outputs. The answer to the question is then given by the sum of the inputs minus the sum of the outputs. This is also the approach used to prevent Mick from spending what he doesn't have.
The blockchain of Bitcoin may be explorered at www.blockchain.com. *Figure 34.9* shows block 2.

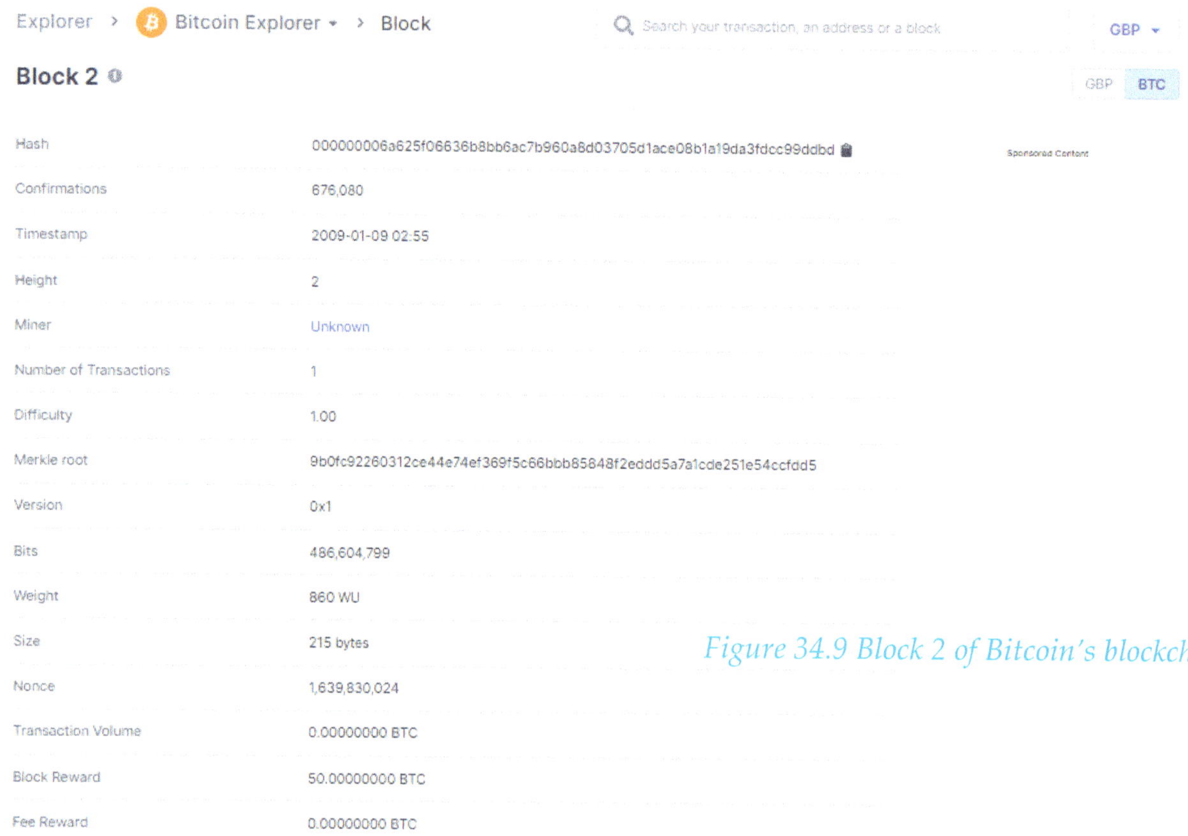

Figure 34.9 Block 2 of Bitcoin's blockchain

Figure 34.10 shows the first two transactions for block 400000. In addition to collecting a reward in btc for mining a block, miners may also collect a fee per transaction. The sender in the second transaction has Bitcoin address

13XSrVkweo5Dzm3yuykFw4P63N63MA6bTd

This uses a modified Base 58 binary-to-text encoding known as **Base58Check**[2]. This sender sent 0.19206072 BTC to address 1HU1LDBXUg73f2ro2e2dB3XY8cFoYLFgZZ. The transaction itself is protected with a hash value

0de586d0c74780605c36c0f51dcd850d1772f41a92c549e3aa36f9e78e905284

Figure 34.10 The first two transactions of block 4000001

Bitcoin relies on public key cryptography, where a private key – comparable to an account password –is used to authorise ("sign") a movement of funds stored in an address. The address, which can be thought of as an account number, is derived from the public key that mathematically corresponds to the private key. Each owner transfers Bitcoin by digitally signing a hash of the previous transaction(s) (assigning Bitcoin to the sender - any change is just

2 https://en.bitcoin.it/wiki/Base58Check_encoding

sent back to the sender) and the public key of the next owner. Transactions are therefore digitally signed records that reassign ownership of Bitcoins to new addresses. Miners verify that a transaction is genuine using the sender's public key. Software programs, commonly referred to as wallets, handle the management of the key pairs - see https://www.coinbase.com/ for an example of how to create a wallet and to start using Bitcoin. Satoshi Nakamoto, the anonymous creator of the Bitcoin network, actually defined Bitcoin as the chain of digital signatures that come together to form a blockchain.

A user's Bitcoin network wallet - e.g https://www.coinbase.com/ - monitors the user's Bitcoin addresses (they can have more than one public/private key pair) and keeps a record of all the transactions associated with these Bitcoin addresses to create the user's balance from the Bitcoin ledger.

Figure 34.11 shows the hash generated for the string "Hello World!" by Delphi program `HashingWithSHA256Project.exe`. Load this program and make small alterations to the string, e.g. remove the '!' character. Notice how the hash value changes in an unpredictable and seemingly random way. Of course, SHA-256 is deterministic, i.e. the same output is produced for a given input. However, its output passes statistical tests used to determine randomness. *Table 34.7* shows the unit for this program, `HashingWithSHA256Unit.pas`.

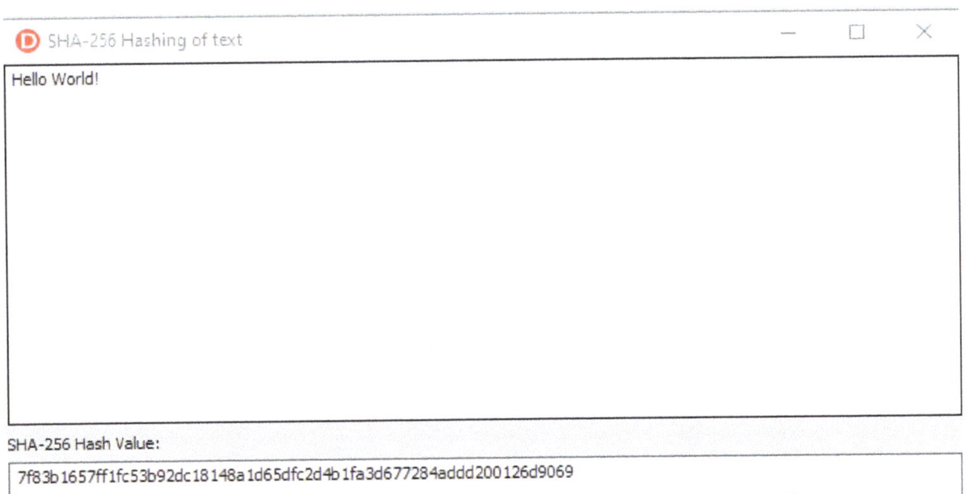

Figure 34.11 HashingWithSHA256Project in execution

Figure 34.11 shows the construction of a binary tree of hashes known as a **Merkle tree**, which is used primarily to verify the data held within, without revealing what that data is, and at speed. Alteration of any of the underlying data will be readily revealed.

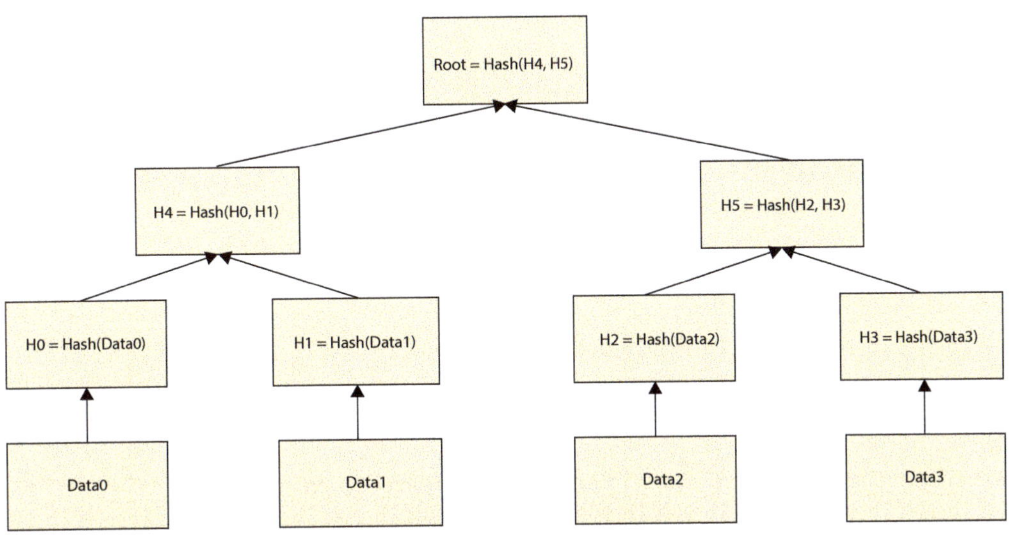

Figure 34.11 Merkle tree - binary data tree of hashes

```
Unit HashingWithSHA256Unit;
Interface
Uses
  Winapi.Windows, Winapi.Messages, System.SysUtils, System.Variants,
  System.Classes, Vcl.Graphics, Vcl.Controls, Vcl.Forms, Vcl.Dialogs,
  Vcl.StdCtrls, System.Hash;
Type
  TfrmSHA256HashingOfText = Class(TForm)
                              mbText : TMemo;
                              mbSHA256HashValue : TMemo;
                              lblSHA256HashValue : TLabel;
                              Procedure mbTextChange(Sender : TObject);
                            End;
Var
  frmSHA256HashingOfText: TfrmSHA256HashingOfText;

Implementation
  {$R *.dfm}
  Procedure TfrmSHA256HashingOfText.mbTextChange(Sender : TObject);
    Begin
      mbSHA256HashValue.Clear;
      mbSHA256HashValue.Lines.Add(THashSHA2.GetHashString(mbText.Text));
    End;
End.
```

Table 34.7 HashingWithSHA256Unit.pas

Simulating a blockchain in Delphi

Figure 34.12 shows a simulated blockchain created in Delphi in which eleven blocks are linked by a backward chain.

Start a new multi-device application **New|Multi-Device Application|Blank Application**.

Save the project as `BlockChainProject.dproj` and its unit as `BlockChainUnit.pas` in folder `BlockChainProject`.

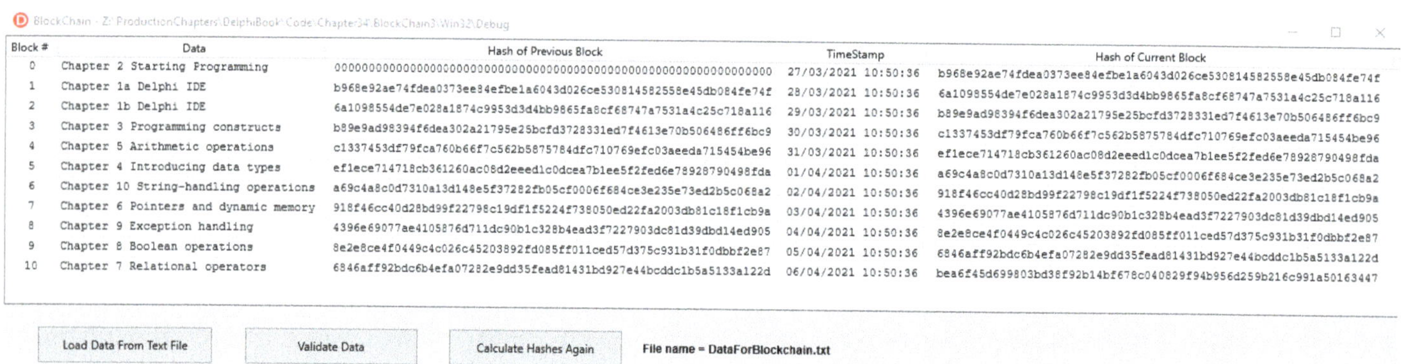

Block #	Data	Hash of Previous Block	TimeStamp	Hash of Current Block
0	Chapter 2 Starting Programming	0000000000000000000000000000000000000000000000000000000000000000	27/03/2021 10:50:36	b968e92ae74fdea0373ee84efbe1a6043d026ce530814582558e45db084fe74f
1	Chapter 1a Delphi IDE	b968e92ae74fdea0373ee84efbe1a6043d026ce530814582558e45db084fe74f	28/03/2021 10:50:36	6a1098554de7e028a1874c9953d3d4bb9865fa8cf68747a7531a4c25c718a116
2	Chapter 1b Delphi IDE	6a1098554de7e028a1874c9953d3d4bb9865fa8cf68747a7531a4c25c718a116	29/03/2021 10:50:36	b89e9ad98394f6dea302a21795e25bcfd3728331ed7f4613e70b506486ff6bc9
3	Chapter 3 Programming constructs	b89e9ad98394f6dea302a21795e25bcfd3728331ed7f4613e70b506486ff6bc9	30/03/2021 10:50:36	c1337453df79fca760b66f7c562b5875784dfc710769efc03aeeda715454be96
4	Chapter 5 Arithmetic operations	c1337453df79fca760b66f7c562b5875784dfc710769efc03aeeda715454be96	31/03/2021 10:50:36	ef1ece714718cb361260ac08d2eeed1c0dcea7b1ee5f2fed6e78928790498fda
5	Chapter 4 Introducing data types	ef1ece714718cb361260ac08d2eeed1c0dcea7b1ee5f2fed6e78928790498fda	01/04/2021 10:50:36	a69c4a8c0d7310a13d148e5f37282fb05cf0006f684ce3e235e73ed2b5c068a2
6	Chapter 10 String-handling operations	a69c4a8c0d7310a13d148e5f37282fb05cf0006f684ce3e235e73ed2b5c068a2	02/04/2021 10:50:36	918f46cc40d28bd99f22798c19df1f5224f738050ed22fa2003db81c18f1cb9a
7	Chapter 6 Pointers and dynamic memory	918f46cc40d28bd99f22798c19df1f5224f738050ed22fa2003db81c18f1cb9a	03/04/2021 10:50:36	4396e69077ae4105876d711dc90b1c328b4ead3f7227903dc81d39dbd14ed905
8	Chapter 9 Exception handling	4396e69077ae4105876d711dc90b1c328b4ead3f7227903dc81d39dbd14ed905	04/04/2021 10:50:36	8e2e8ce4f0449c4c026c45203892fd085ff011ced57d375c931b31f0dbbf2e87
9	Chapter 8 Boolean operations	8e2e8ce4f0449c4c026c45203892fd085ff011ced57d375c931b31f0dbbf2e87	05/04/2021 10:50:36	6846aff92bdc6b4efa07282e9dd35fead81431bd927e44bcddc1b5a5133a122d
10	Chapter 7 Relational operators	6846aff92bdc6b4efa07282e9dd35fead81431bd927e44bcddc1b5a5133a122d	06/04/2021 10:50:36	bea6f45d699803bd38f92b14bf678c040829f94b956d259b216c991a50163447

Figure 34.12 Simulated blockchain - BlockchainProject.exe

Add the following components to the form:

- 2 x **TLayout**
- 3 x **TButton**
- 1 x **TLabel**
- 1 x **TGrid**
- 1 x **TFDMemTable**(an in-memory dataset)
- 1 x **TOpenDialog**

Use TClientDataSet instead for VCL applications

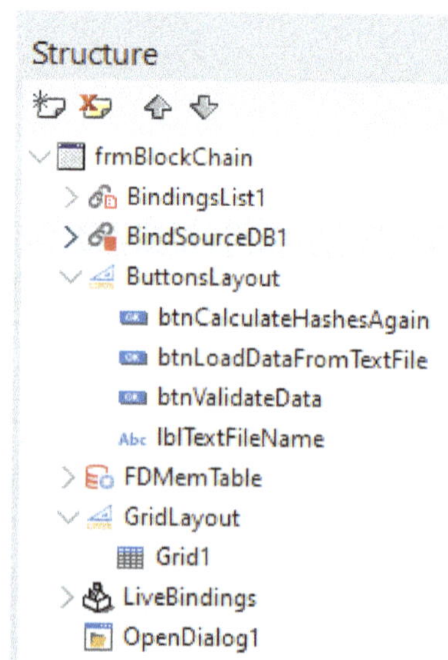

Figure 34.13

Configure and **rename** these as shown in *Figure 34.12* and *Figure 34.13*.

Set Align property of `ButtonsLayout` to **Bottom**.

Set Align property of `GridLayout` to **Client**.

Set Align property of `Grid1` to **Client**.

Set Width property of `lblTextFileName` to 753 and `Text` property to empty string.

Select FDMemTable|**Fields** then right click **Fields** to bring up window shown in *Figure 34.14*.

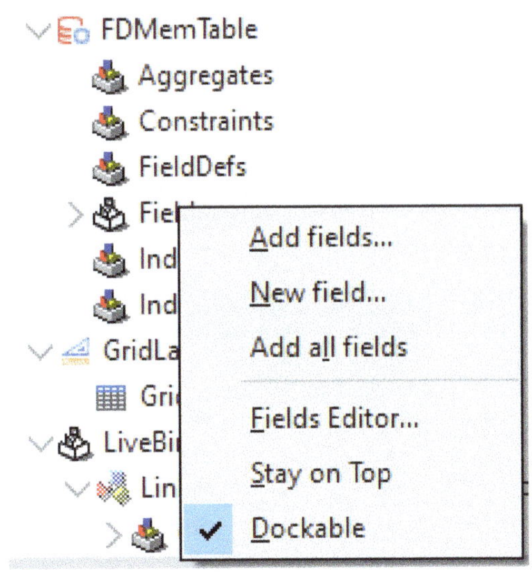

Figure 34.14 Fields popup window

Click **New Field** option to bring up the **New Field** window shown in *Figure 34.15*.

Enter the name `Index` for the **Name** field and **Integer** for the **Type** field.

Click **OK**.

Repeat to create four more new fields with name and type as follows

- `Data` - **String**
- `HashOfPreviousBlock` - **String**
- `TimeStamp` - **DateTime**
- `HashOfCurrentBlock` - **String**

The name assigned to each field is the field's **DisplayLabel** property value whilst the actual field name is a concatenation of `FDMemTable` and name - see *Figure 34.16* and the **Object Inspector**.

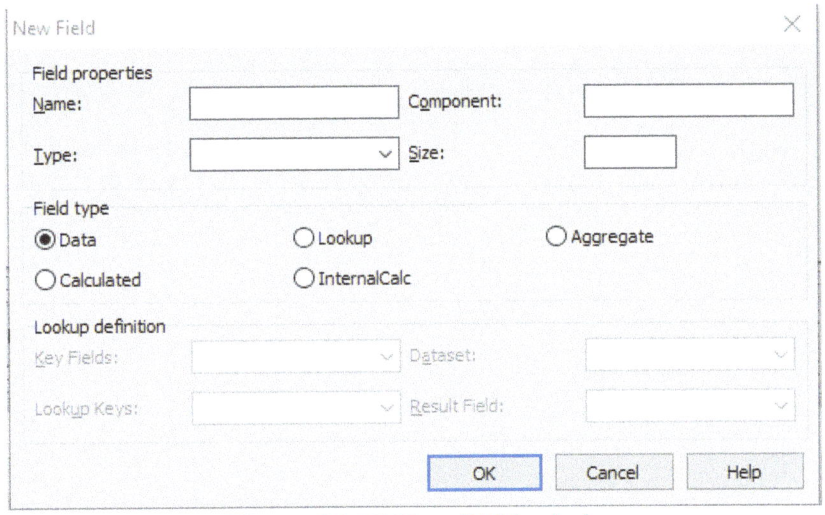

Figure 34.15 New Field window

Right click in the grid area of the form to bring up the window shown in *Figure 34.17*.

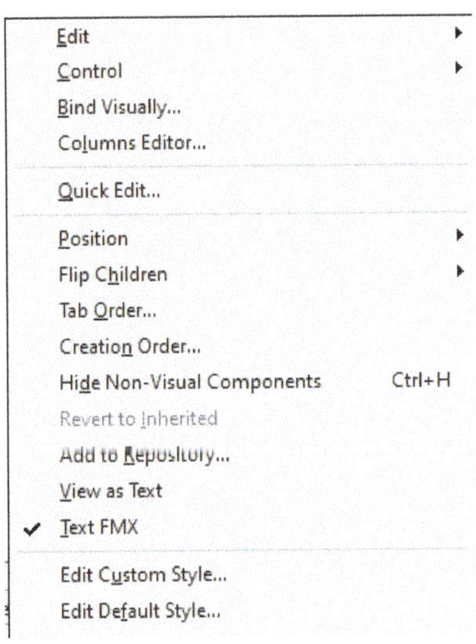

Figure 34.17

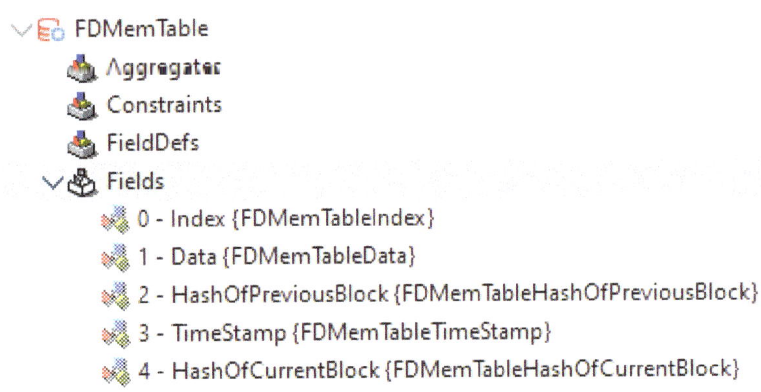

Figure 34.16 The five fields of FDMemTable

Click **Bind Visually...** option to bring up the **LiveBindings Designer** window shown in *Figure 34.18* (without the connections between `FDMemTable` and `Grid1`).

Click and **hold** the mouse button down on the `Index` field of `FDMemTable`.

Drag the mouse to the * field of `Grid1` and release the mouse button. A connecting line with an arrowhead at each end is created anchored at one end to the `Index` field of `FDMemTable` and at the other end to a newly created field `Column[0]`. **Repeat** for the other fields of `FDMemTable` to add four more connecting lines.

Figure 34.19 shows the user interface after connecting `FDMemTable` to `Grid1`. **Note** that **LiveBindings Designer** has added two new components to manage the connection, **BindingsList1** and **BindSourceDB**.

Save All (**SHIFT+CTRL+S**).

Add the `Private` section to the class definition `TfrmBlockChain` as shown in *Table 34.8* - page 550.
Place the cursor in `CalculateHashes` and **press** **Shift+Ctrl+C** to create the skeleton for this procedure in the **Implementation** section.

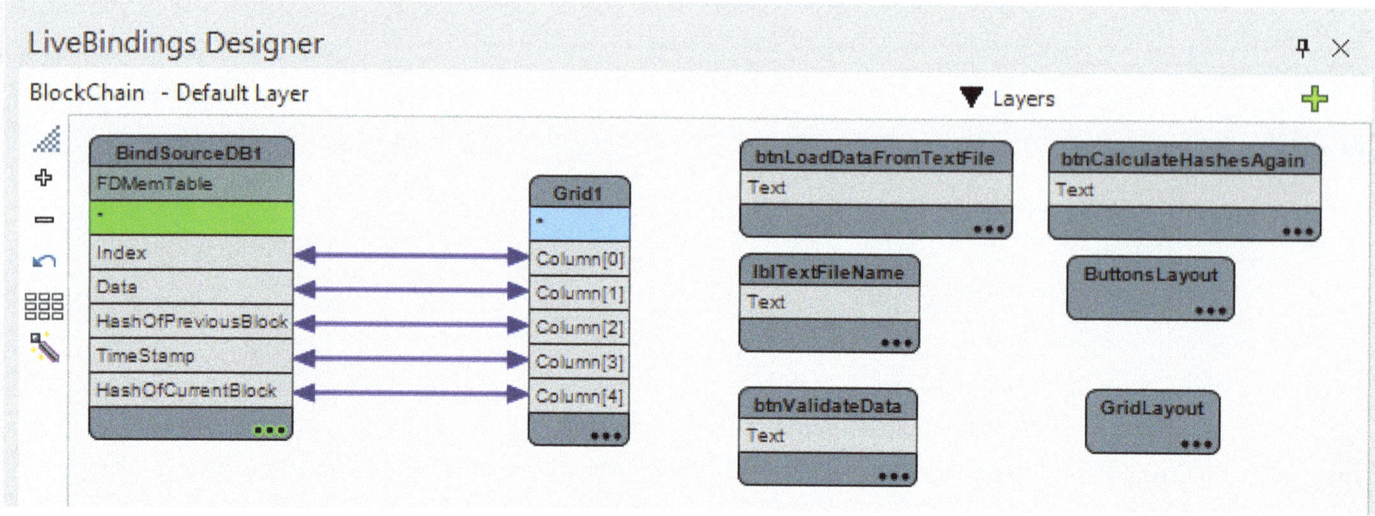

Figure 34.18 LiveBindings Design window

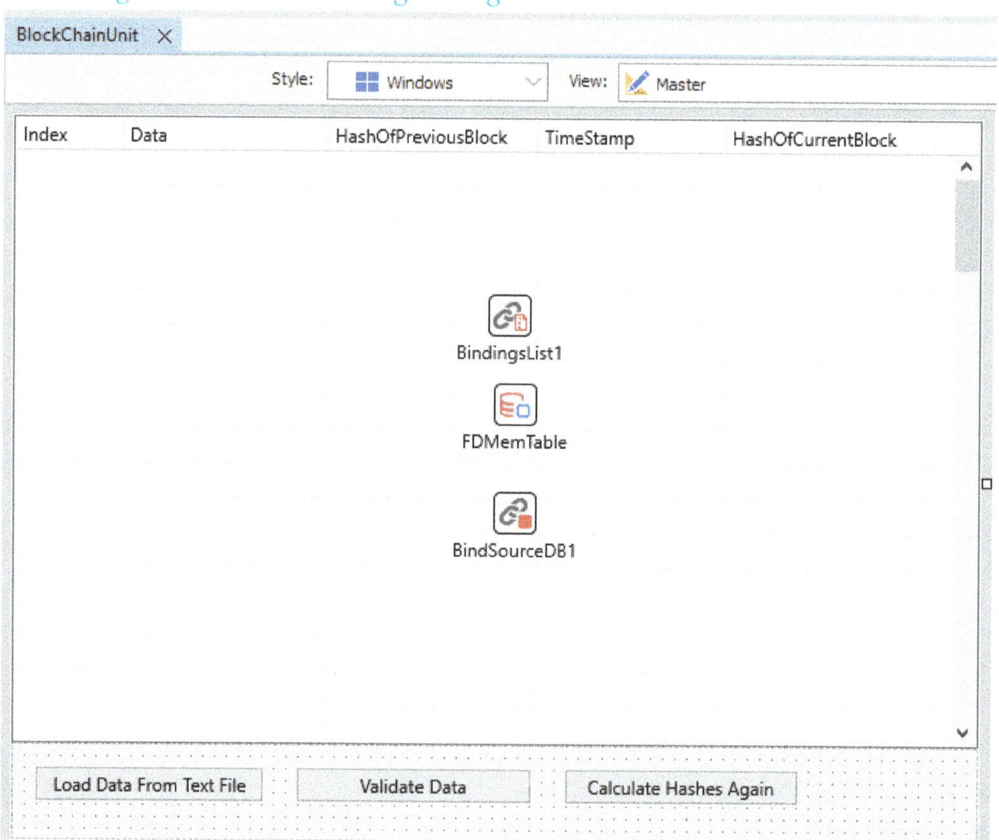

Figure 34.19 Design View of User Interface after using LiveBindings Designer

Define the constant `cnstGenesisBlockAddress` then add the code shown in *Table 34.8* to the body of procedure `CalculatesHashes`. **Add** `System.Hash` to the **Uses** clause in the **Interface** section.
Double click button `Load Data From Text File` to create an event handler. **Add** the code shown in *Table 34.9* to its body - page 551. **Add** `System.IOUtils` to the **Uses** clause in the **Interface** section.
Double click the **OnCreate** field in the **Events** page of `frmBlockChain` to create an event handler `FormCreate`.
Add the code shown in *Table 34.11* to the body of this event handler - page 559.

Select `Grid1` in the **Object Inspector,** open the `LinkGridToDataSourceBindSourceDB1` - *Figure 34.20*.
Click on the ellipsis (...) field of the **Columns** property to bring up the editing window shown in *Figure 34.21*.

Select each column in *Figure 34.21* in turn and edit the column in the **Object Inspector** as shown in *Figure 34.22*.

Use the following values

```
0 - Index
        Alignment taCenter
        TextWidth 8
1 - Data
        Alignment taLeftJustify
        TextWidth 44
2 - HashOfPreviousBlock
        Alignment taCenter
        TextWidth 68
3 - TimeStamp
        Alignment taCenter
        TextWidth 22
4 - HashOfCurrentBlock
        Alignment taCenter
        TextWidth 68
```

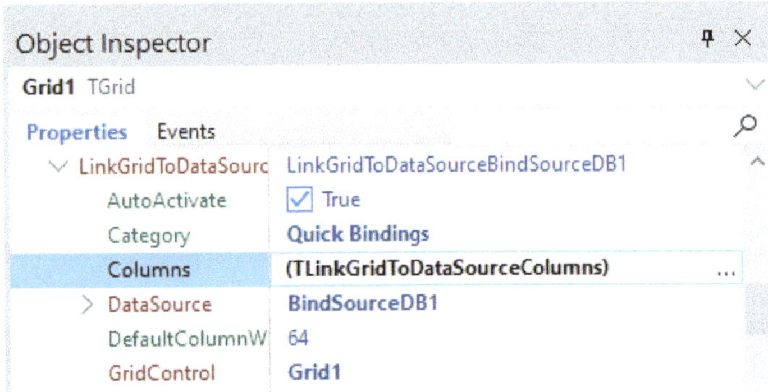

Figure 34.20 Object Inspector for Grid1

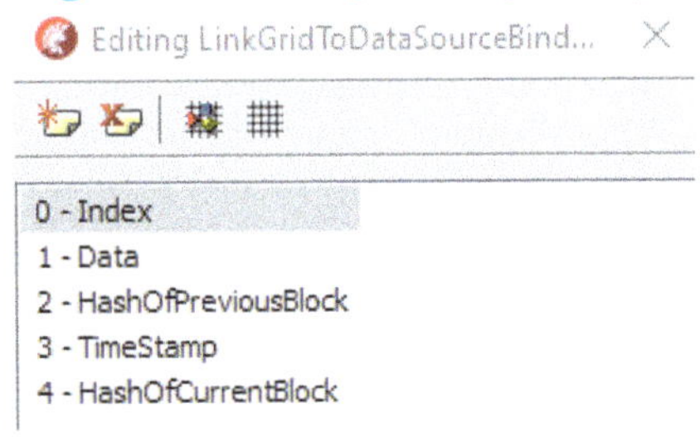

Figure 34.21 Editing LinkGridToDataSourceBindSourceDB1.Columns

Select `FDMemTable`|**Fields** - *Figure 34.23*.

Select each column in *Figure 34.23* in turn and edit the column in the **Object Inspector** as shown in *Figure 34.24*.

Use the following values

```
0 - Index
        Alignment taCenter
        TextWidth 8
1 - Data
        Alignment taLeftJustify
        TextWidth 44
        Size 44
2 - HashOfPreviousBlock
        Alignment taCenter
        TextWidth 64
        Size 64
3 - TimeStamp
        Alignment taCenter
        TextWidth 22
4 - HashOfCurrentBlock
        Alignment taCenter
        TextWidth 64
        Size 64
```

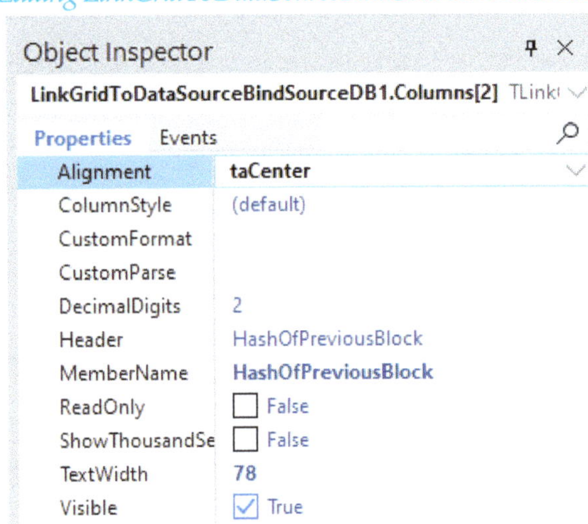

Figure 34.22 Editing Column[2] - setting TextWidth to 78

Figure 34.25

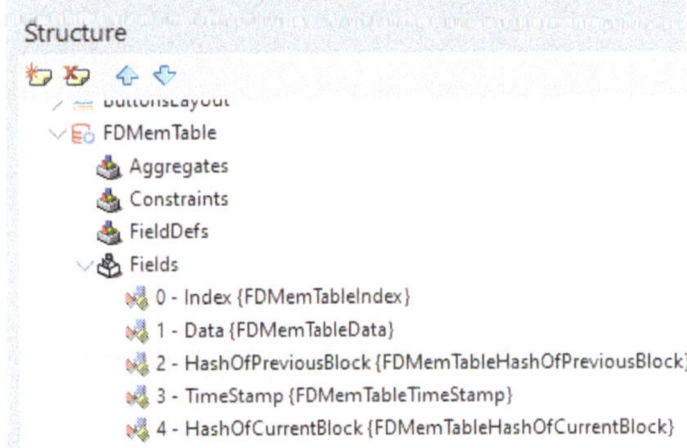

Figure 34.23 Structure window for FDMemTable Fields

Double click button `Validate Data` to create an event handler. **Add** the code shown in *Table 34.11* to its body - page 559.

Double click button `Calculate Hashes Again` to create an event handler. **Add** the code shown in *Table 34.9* to its body - page 561.

Change the `frmBlockChain` properties as follows

```
Caption = 'BlockChain'
ClientHeight = 340
ClientWidth = 1431
```

Save All (**SHIFT+CTRL+S**).

Download `DataForBlockchain.txt`. - *Table 34.10*.

Click **Run** (**F9**) to build and run the application `BlockChainProject`.

Click `Load Data From Text File` button and **locate** and **load** `DataForBlockchain.txt`. *Figure 34.12* shows the result.

Click `Validate Data` button to validate the blockchain - *Figure 34.25*.

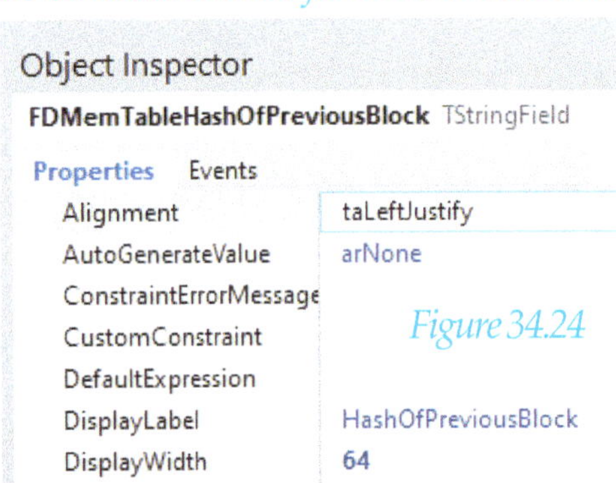

Figure 34.24

```
Unit BlockChainUnit;
Interface
Uses
  System.SysUtils, System.Types, System.UITypes, System.Classes, System.Variants, System.IOUtils,
  FMX.Controls, FMX.Forms, FMX.Graphics, FMX.Dialogs, FireDAC.Stan.Intf, FireDAC.Stan.Option,
  FireDAC.Stan.Param,  FireDAC.Stan.Error, FireDAC.DatS, FireDAC.Phys.Intf, FireDAC.DApt.Intf,
  System.Rtti, FMX.Grid.Style, Data.Bind.EngExt, Fmx.Bind.DBEngExt, Fmx.Bind.Grid,
  System.Bindings.Outputs, Fmx.Bind.Editors, Data.Bind.Components, Data.Bind.Grid, FMX.StdCtrls,
  FMX.Layouts, Data.Bind.DBScope, FMX.Controls.Presentation, FMX.ScrollBox, FMX.Grid, Data.DB,
  FireDAC.Comp.DataSet, FireDAC.Comp.Client, System.Hash, FMX.Types, FMX.Memo.Types, FMX.Memo, FMX.Edit;
Type
  TfrmBlockChain = Class(TForm)
                   FDMemTable : TFDMemTable;
                   Grid1 : TGrid;
                   BindingsList1 : TBindingsList;
                   BindSourceDB1 : TBindSourceDB;
                   ButtonsLayout : TLayout;
                   btnCalculateHashesAgain : TButton;
                   btnValidateData : TButton;
                   LinkGridToDataSourceBindSourceDB1 : TLinkGridToDataSource;
                   FDMemTableIndex : TIntegerField;
                   FDMemTableData : TStringField;
                   FDMemTableHashOfPreviousBlock : TStringField;
                   btnLoadDataFromTextFile: TButton;
                   FDMemTableTimeStamp : TDateTimeField;
                   OpenDialog1 : TOpenDialog;
                   lblTextFileName : TLabel;
                   FDMemTableHashOfCurrentBlock : TStringField;
                   GridLayout : TLayout;
                   Procedure btnCalculateHashesAgainClick(Sender : TObject);
                   Procedure btnValidateDataClick(Sender : TObject);
                   Procedure btnLoadDataFromTextFileClick(Sender : TObject);
                   Procedure FormCreate(Sender : TObject);
                   Private
                     CalculatingHashesFlag : Boolean;
                     Procedure CalculateHashes;
                 End;
Var
  frmBlockChain : TfrmBlockChain;
Implementation
  {$R *.fmx}
  Const
    cnstGenesisBlockAddress = '0000000000000000000000000000000000000000000000000000000000000000';
  Procedure TfrmBlockChain.CalculateHashes;
    Var
      strString, strHash, strPreviousHash : String;
      Begin
        If CalculatingHashesFlag
          Then Exit;
        CalculatingHashesFlag := True;
        FDMemTable.First;
        FDMemTable.BeginBatch;
        LinkGridToDataSourceBindSourceDB1.Active := False;
        Try
          While Not FDMemTable.Eof
            Do
              Begin
                If (FDMemTableHashOfPreviousBlock.AsString = cnstGenesisBlockAddress)
                  Then strPreviousHash := cnstGenesisBlockAddress
                  Else strPreviousHash := strHash;
                strString := FDMemTableIndex.AsString + FDMemTableData.AsString + strPreviousHash
                               + FDMemTableTimeStamp.AsString;
                strHash := THashSHA2.GetHashString(strString);
                FDMemTable.Edit;
                FDMemTableHashOfCurrentBlock.AsString := strHash;
                FDMemTableHashOfPreviousBlock.AsString := strPreviousHash;
                FDMemTable.Post;
                FDMemTable.Next;
              End;
        Finally
          CalculatingHashesFlag := False;
          FDMemTable.EndBatch;
          LinkGridToDataSourceBindSourceDB1.Active := True;
        End;
      End;
```

Table 34.8 Part 1 of BlockChainUnit.pas

```
Procedure TfrmBlockChain.btnCalculateHashesAgainClick(Sender : TObject);
 Begin
   CalculateHashes;
 End;

Procedure TfrmBlockChain.btnLoadDataFromTextFileClick(Sender : TObject);
 Var
   strlistLines : TStringList;
   intIndex: Integer;
   dtDateTime : TDateTime;
   FileName : String;
   CurrentDir : String;
 Const
   cnstDataFileName = 'DataForBlockChain.txt';
 Begin
   CurrentDir := GetCurrentDir;
   frmBlockChain.Caption := 'BlockChain - ' + CurrentDir;
   If OpenDialog1.Execute
     Then FileName := OpenDialog1.FileName
     Else FileName := CurrentDir + '\' + cnstDataFileName;
   If TFile.Exists(FileName)
     Then
       Begin
         FDMemTable.First;
         FDMemTable.BeginBatch;
         CalculatingHashesFlag := True;
         LinkGridToDataSourceBindSourceDB1.Active := False;
         Try
           FDMemTable.EmptyDataSet;
           strlistLines := TStringList.Create;
           Try
             strlistLines.LoadFromFile(FileName);
             dtDateTime := Now;
             For intIndex := 0 To strlistLines.Count - 1
               Do
                 Begin
                   FDMemTable.Insert;
                   FDMemTableIndex.Value := intIndex;
                   FDMemTableData.AsString := strlistLines[intIndex];
                   dtDateTime := dtDateTime + 1;
                   FDMemTableTimeStamp.AsDateTime := dtDateTime;
                   If intIndex = 0
                     Then FDMemTableHashOfPreviousBlock.Value := cnstGenesisBlockAddress;
                   FDMemTable.Post;
                 End;
           Finally
             strlistLines.Free;
           End;
         Finally
           FDMemTable.EndBatch;
           LinkGridToDataSourceBindSourceDB1.Active := True;
           CalculatingHashesFlag := False;
         End;
         CalculateHashes;
         lblTextFileName.Text := 'File name = ' + ExtractFileName(FileName);
       End
     Else ShowMessage('File with name ' + FileName + ' doesn''t exist');
 End;
```

Table 34.9 Part 2 of BlockChainUnit.pas

Now **change** the data, e.g. 'Chapter 1b Delphi IDE' to 'Chapter 1 Delphi IDE'.

Click `Validate Data` button to validate the blockchain but the blockchain is no longer valid - *Figure 34.26*.

Click `Calculate Hashes Again` button to regenerate the blockchain hashes. Now confirm that the blockchain is valid again.

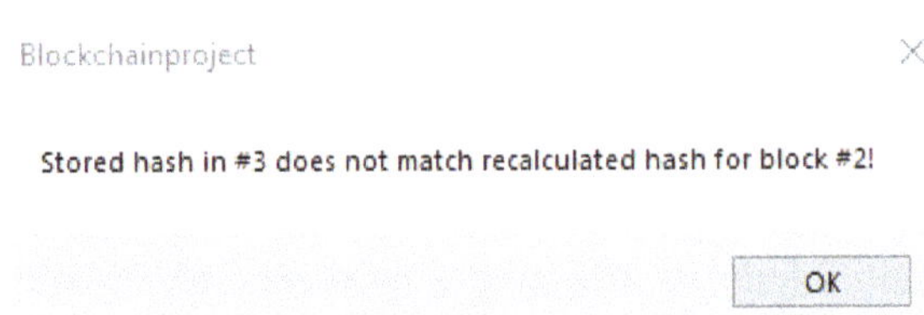

Figure 34.26

Chapter 2 Starting Programming
Chapter 1a Delphi IDE
Chapter 1b Delphi IDE
Chapter 3 Programming constructs
Chapter 5 Arithmetic operations
Chapter 4 Introducing data types
Chapter 10 String-handling operations
Chapter 6 Pointers and dynamic memory
Chapter 9 Exception handling
Chapter 8 Boolean operations
Chapter 7 Relational operators

Table 34.10 DataForBlockchain.txt

```
Procedure TfrmBlockChain.btnValidateDataClick(Sender : TObject);
  Var
    strString, strHash : String;
    intIndex : Integer;
  Begin
    FDMemTable.First;
    FDMemTable.BeginBatch;
    Try
      While Not FDMemTable.EOF
        Do
          Begin
            strString := FDMemTableIndex.AsString + FDMemTableData.AsString
                        + FDMemTableHashOfPreviousBlock.AsString + FDMemTableTimeStamp.AsString;
            strHash := THashSHA2.GetHashString(strString);
            FDMemTable.Next;
            If (Not FDMemTable.EOF) And (FDMemTableHashOfPreviousBlock.AsString <> strHash)
              Then
                Begin
                  intIndex := FDMemTableIndex.Value;
                  ShowMessage(Format('Stored hash in #%d does not match recalculated hash for block #%d!',
                                     [intIndex, intIndex - 1]));
                  Exit;
                End;
          End;
    Finally
      FDMemTable.EndBatch;
    End;
    ShowMessage('Blockchain is valid!');
  End;

  Procedure TfrmBlockChain.FormCreate(Sender : TObject);
    Begin
      FDMemTable.Active := True;
      LinkGridToDataSourceBindSourceDB1.Columns[0].Header := Format('%7s', ['Block #']); //Centre heading
      LinkGridToDataSourceBindSourceDB1.Columns[1].Header := Format('%42s', ['Data']); //Centre heading
      LinkGridToDataSourceBindSourceDB1.Columns[2].Header := Format('%73s', ['Hash of Previous Block']);
      LinkGridToDataSourceBindSourceDB1.Columns[3].Header := Format('%22s', ['TimeStamp']);
      LinkGridToDataSourceBindSourceDB1.Columns[4].Header := Format('%73s', ['Hash of Current Block']);
    End;
End.
```

Table 34.11 Part 3 of BlockChainUnit.pas

`BlockChainProject.exe` calculates the hash of the current block as follows

```
strString := FDMemTableIndex.AsString + FDMemTableData.AsString + strPreviousHash
             + FDMemTableTimeStamp.AsString;
strHash := THashSHA2.GetHashString(strString);
```

This differs from how **Bitcoin** generates the hash for the current block which is as follows

Block hash = SHA-256 Hash(Hash of previous block + Transactions hash + Timestamp + Nonce)

`BlockChainProject.exe` uses the block's index instead of a nonce. This makes calculating the hash very quick. In Bitcoin, in order to deter miners from attempting to rewrite transactions in previous blocks, the opposite is true. If a miner alters a block before the current block, let's say the sixth block back, then the miner will have to recalculate the hashes for the following five blocks. But in the time it will take the miner to do this, assuming that the hardware used is not more than five times faster than other miners' hardware, five new blocks can be added by other miners, thus defeating the miner's attempt to alter the chaining without being detected.

Miners have to calculate the nonce - a number that is used only once - that when concatenated with the transaction data, timestamp and hash of previous block generates a hash with a specific number of leading zeros (the greater the number of zeros the more difficult the task). The only way to do this is by brute force, incrementing the nonce value in a loop until the required number of leading hexadecimal zeros is reached. *Table 34.12* illustrates the principle using a simple message string 'Hello!' concatenated with a series of numbers starting with 0. The SHA 256 column shows the hash result expressed in hexadecimal. Note that none of the hash values has leading hexadecimal zeros. *Figure 34.9* shows a block of bitcoin with a hash containing 8 leading hexadecimal zeros, i.e. 32 leading binary digits (this block was added in 2009).

Message + Nonce	SHA 256 Hash
'Hello!'	5e9f00ca1f8a276af5de8b6373ccffd498ff22926c518721b75c29ae6a73d5d6
'Hello!0'	a4dde72d413d81baf052b997e3f1e389600df10bfe68ffd965cd6cf31bebb0c0
'Hello!1'	d4004ddb95a8d91cb70211c4d66cfd52efa947843c99c088138a49ce4e5ac019
'Hello!2'	32204efe17020ee4f5408d5c6729df928a894ea474c517f7de8b55c3f9507402
'Hello!2092345167845321987 65'	330b0fe5d1a886539705b7ee01c6b922405567aedad5fea8e591caf477fa5f6f
'Hello!209234516784532198765173761095678428976577002267512 65432789'	798d9f61396d906144d499d7c1b534ad52eb9d95fd41f82abd015fb58a9b79a4

Table 34.12 Hashes for a simple message string 'Hello!' concatenated with a nonce

The nonce determination is expressed slightly differently in reality.

The nonce is that value that generates a hash interpreted as a number which is numerically smaller than the target called the difficulty target.

The current target value using SHA 256 is a number in the range

$$2^{(256-1-k)} \text{ to } 2^{(256-k)}-1 \text{ inclusive}$$

where k is the number of leading zeros. SHA 256 uses 256 bits.

Table 34.13 illustrates the possible ranges if k = 1 for 4, 5, 6 and n bits.

Total number of bits	Smallest binary number with one leading zero	Largest binary number with one leading zero	Smallest denary number with one leading zero	Largest denary number with one leading zero
4	0100	0111	4	7
5	01000	01111	8	15
6	010000	011111	16	31
n	01000...0000	01111...1111	$2^{(n-2)}$	$2^{(n-1)} - 1$

Table 34.13 Range of numbers with a single leading zero for a given number of bits

Suppose the current number of leading zeros that is required is set at 44, i.e. k = 44 (the year is currently 2021).

There are approximately $2^{212} - 2^{211} = 9 \times 2^{211} \approx 3 \times 10^{64}$ different target numbers between 2^{211} and $2^{212} - 1$, i.e for k = 44.

But there are 2^{256} different numbers given 256 bits, i.e. $\approx 10^{77}$.

The fraction of these which lie in the range for k = 44 is therefore $\frac{9 \times 2^{211}}{2^{256}} \approx 3 \times 10^{-13}$.

This means that roughly 4×10^{12} hashes must be calculated on average to find a hash less than the target value.

If the hardware is capable of executing 10^{10} searches of block hash space per second, locating a hash which satisfies the target will take 400 seconds on average or 7 minutes.

In bitcoin, the time-consuming and energy-expensive nonce calculation outlined above generates information that meets the specified conditions when successful. This information is taken as a proof that work has been done called **Proof of Work (PoW) to solve the challenge**. The purpose of PoW (Proof-of-work algorithm) is to check if calculations were indeed conducted during the creation process for a new block of cryptocurrency. The checking process or verification can be done very quickly. (The term mining is used by analogy with mining for precious metal - correct nonces are 'rare' and costly to produce).[3]

3 The two example programs on bitcoin were inspired by a webinair given by Jim McKeeth http://delphi.org/2018/02/delphi-and-the-blockchain-more-than-just-bitcoin-and-cryptocurrency/

Simulating blockchain mining in Delphi

Start a new Windows VCL application.

Save the project as `BlockChainMiningProject.dproj` and its unit as `BlockChainMiningUnit.pas` in folder `BlockChainMIningProject`.

Add the following components to the form:

- 3 x **TPanel** - **rename** `TopPanel`, `MiddlePanel`, `BottomPanel`, **clear** their captions.
- 1 x **TListBox** - **add** to `BottomPanel`, **rename** `lbxNonceTargetHash`.
- 1 x **TMemo** - **add** to `TopPanel`, **rename** `mbMessage` **clear Lines** property.
- 1 x **TButton** - **add** to `MiddlePanel`, **rename** `btnMine`, **set Caption** property to `Mine`.
- 2 x **TLabel** - **add** to `MiddlePanel`, **rename** the first `lblDifficulty`, **set** its **Caption** property to `Difficulty`. and **rename** the second `lblElapsedMilliSeconds`, **set** its **Caption** property to the empty string
- 1 x **TSpinEdit** - **add** to `MiddlePanel`, **rename** `spbDifficulty`, **set MinValue** property to 1 and **MinValue** property to 5.
- 1 x **TSplitter**

Configure and **rename** these as shown in *Figure 34.27*.

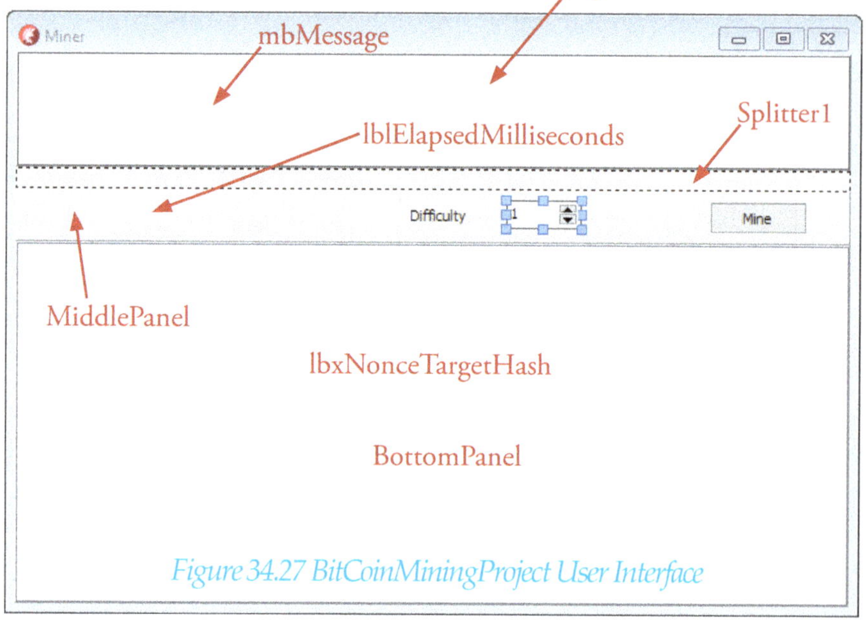

Figure 34.27 BitCoinMiningProject User Interface

Set Align property of `TopPanel` to **Top**.

Set Align property of `Splitter1` to **Top**.

Set Align property of `MiddlePanel` to **Top**.

Set Align property of `BottomPanel` to **Client**.

Set Align property of `mbMessage` to **Client**.

Set Align property of `lbxNonceTargetHash` to **Client**.

Double click button `btnMine` to create an **OnClick** event handler.

Add the code shown in *Table 34.14*.

Save All (SHIFT+CTRL+S).

Click Run (F9) to build and run the application `BlockChainMiningProject`.

Try values of difficulty 1 to 5 for the message 'Hello!'.

Figure 34.28 shows the outcome for difficulty 5 which takes 6 minutes approximately to find a solution.

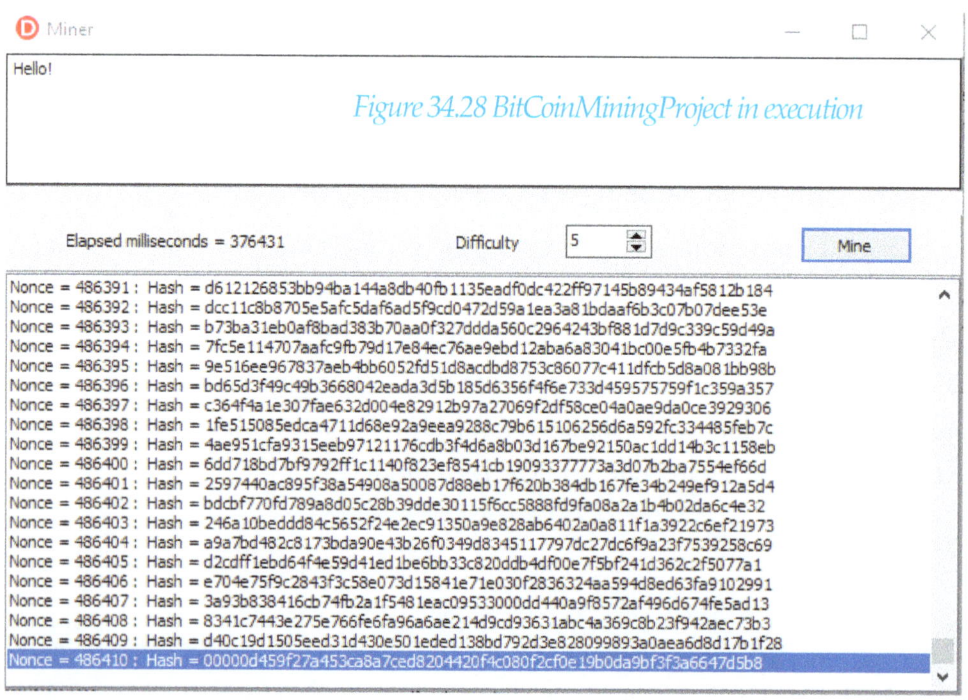

Figure 34.28 BitCoinMiningProject in execution

```
Unit BitCoinMiningUnit;
Interface
Uses
  Winapi.Windows, Winapi.Messages, System.SysUtils, System.Variants, System.Classes, Vcl.Graphics,
  Vcl.Controls, Vcl.Forms, Vcl.Dialogs, Vcl.StdCtrls, Vcl.Samples.Spin,
  Vcl.ExtCtrls;
Type
  TfrmMiner = Class(TForm)
                TopPanel : TPanel;
                mbMessage : TMemo;
                BottomPanel : TPanel;
                Splitter1 : TSplitter;
                lbxNonceTargetHash : TListBox;
                spbDifficulty : TSpinEdit;
                lblDifficulty : TLabel;
                MiddlePanel : TPanel;
                btnMine : TButton;
                lblElapsedMilliseconds : TLabel;
                Procedure btnMineClick(Sender : TObject);
              End;
Var
  frmMiner: TfrmMiner;
Implementation
  {$R *.dfm}
  Uses System.Hash, System.Diagnostics;
  Procedure TfrmMiner.btnMineClick(Sender : TObject);
    Var
      strHash: string;
      intNonce: Integer;
      intDifficulty: Integer;
      StopWatch : TStopWatch;
    Begin
      lbxNonceTargetHash.Clear;
      intNonce := 0;
      intDifficulty := Trunc(spbDifficulty.Value);
      StopWatch.Start;
      Repeat
        strHash := THashSHA2.GetHashString(mbMessage.Text + intNonce.ToString);
        lbxNonceTargetHash.Items.Add(Format('%s = %d :  %s', ['Nonce', intNonce, 'Hash = ' + strHash]));
        Inc(intNonce);
      Until strHash.Substring(0, intDifficulty) = StringOfChar('0', intDifficulty);
      lbxNonceTargetHash.ItemIndex := lbxNonceTargetHash.Items.Count - 1;
      StopWatch.Stop;
      lblElapsedMilliseconds.Caption := 'Elapsed milliseconds = '
                                         + IntToStr(StopWatch.ElapsedMilliseconds);
    End;
End.
```

Table 34.14 BitCoinMiningUnit.pas

Hash Tables

Tables

Using a table to store records

A table in computer science is a data structure of rows and columns, an example is shown in *Table 34.15*. This table consists of 4 rows of data in three columns, labelled `ULN`, `Forename`, `Surname`. Each row stores a single record of three fields containing data for an individual student as follows:

- student's unique learner number (`ULN`) consisting of eight digits, e.g. 34567890
- Forename
- Surname

An individual record is uniquely identified by its key field, `ULN`.

The rows of this table are indexed with the first row that contains a student record being labelled with index 0, the second with index 1, and so on.

	ULN	Forename	Surname
0	34567890	Fred	Bloggs
1	90002789	Mary	Smith
2	74432167	Ahmed	Khan
3	24567813	Sarah	White

Table 34.15 Student records stored in a table

This table will occupy a part of the computer's RAM (main memory). It can also be stored permanently in backing store or secondary storage, e.g. magnetic disk. However, to be searched or manipulated, it must first be copied from secondary store to RAM.

Searching the table for a record

The table could be searched for a particular record by starting at the row labelled with index 0 and scanning the entries in turn until the record is found if it is present, or the end of the table is reached. This is known as linear search which is one of several ways that an existing record can be 'looked up'.

Inserting a new record into the table

Table 34.16 shows a table similar to *Table 34.15* but this table has three empty rows following the four rows of data. A new record could be inserted in the first empty row, a second new record in the next row and so on until the table is full.

	ULN	Forename	Surname
0	34567890	Fred	Bloggs
1	90002789	Mary	Smith
2	74432167	Ahmed	Khan
3	24567813	Sarah	White
4			
5			
6			

Table 34.16 Student records stored in a table with room for new records

Deleting a record in the table

The row containing the student record to be deleted is located by searching from row 0. Once found, the data in the row is deleted. To avoid gaps appearing in the table, the occupied rows following this row are moved up to remove the gap.

Limitations of this type of table and table access

A problem surfaces with the operations of searching, inserting and deleting described above when the table contains a large number of records, e.g. 10,000. It just takes too much of the computer's time to perform these operations. One solution is to use a hash table based on a well-chosen hash function.

Hash table

A hash table resembles an ordinary table as described above but differs in the method used to access the rows of the table.

A row of a hash table is accessed directly when looking up, inserting and deleting a record, i.e. it does not start from row 0 every time but instead goes directly to the required row. Movement of records when deleting a record is also eliminated.

Table 34.17 shows a hash table that has gone from being empty to containing 3 records located in three different rows with indices, 2, 5, and 6, respectively, as input data.

> **Key concept**
>
> **Hash table:**
> The table gets its name from the method used to determine the row to use.
> The hash value generated by applying a hash function to a key is the table index where the record with this key should be stored if the row is free.

24567815 Sarah White → 6
74432167 Ahmed Khan → 5
90002789 Mary Smith → 2

	ULN	Forename	Surname
0			
1			
2	90002789	Mary	Smith
3			
4			
5	74432167	Ahmed	Khan
6	24567815	Sarah	White

Table 34.17 Hash table storing three student records

The table gets the name **hash** because of the method used to generate the address or row number. A randomising function called a **hash function** is applied to the record's key, in this case the 8-digit unique learner number or ULN, to map the possible 8-digit ULN values into a much smaller range of values, the possible row numbers. This process is known as **hashing**.

If the ULN values were used directly as specifiers of row addresses, we would have to accommodate addresses covering all possible values of an 8-digit number, 10^8 addresses in total, even though only a small subset of ULNs might be required, e.g. those used in a particular school.

For ease of understanding, the number of rows for the table in *Table 34.17* has been made small intentionally at seven, and labelled 0, 1, 2, ..., 5, 6.

Hash function

The hash function takes as input the record's key (hash key) and outputs the row address of the row for this record. The output is called the hash value or hash.

In our example, the hash value ranges from 0 to 6 for the seven rows of the given table. A hash function, `H`, that will map 8-digit `ULN`s to the set {0, 1, 2, ..., 5, 6} is shown below

`H(ULN) = ULN Mod 7`

Mod is the modulo arithmetic operator which calculates the remainder after integer division (see *Chapters 5* and *33*).

Table 34.18 shows three possible values of `ULN` being mapped to 2, 5 and 6 respectively e.g. 90002789 when divided by 7 gives 12857541 with a remainder of 2.

ULN	H(ULN)
90002789	2
74432167	5
24567815	6

Table 34.18 Some hash values produced by hash function H applied to ULN keys

Key concept

Hash function:
Is a function H, applied to a key k, which generates a hash value H(k) of range smaller than the domain of values of k,
e.g.
H : {00000000..99999999} → {0..6}

Questions

1. Calculate `H(ULN)` for the following `ULN`s
(a) 31258745 (b) 62517493 (c) 49981627
Hint: The scientific mode of Microsoft Windows calculator has a `Mod` operator.

Key concept

Hash key:
Is the key that the hash function is applied to.

Simple hashing functions

Hashing and hash tables are a way that memory locations for records can be assigned so that records can be retrieved quickly.

A hashing function must be relatively quick to compute whilst at the same time generating an even spread of values for the given inputs, the keys.

Another way that the latter can be expressed is that each hash value generated by the hashing function should be equally probable.

Key concept

Hashing:
The process of applying a hash function to a key to generate a hash value.

Achieving this depends on both the particular key values being hashed, and the particular hash function employed.

The value of N in modulo N (e.g. Mod 7) is chosen to be prime because this can contribute to producing an even spread of hash values.

One simple hash function that attempts to achieve these objectives, sums the squares of the ASCII codes of each character of `Key`, as shown in *Table 34.19* in pseudo-code.

The `Ord` function returns the ASCII code of a given character,

e.g. `Ord('A') = 65`.

The individual characters of `Key` are accessed using array indexing starting at 0, e.g. `Key[0]` accesses the first character in the string.

The algorithm generates hash values in the range 0 ... 522 because `Sum` is Modded with 523, a prime number.

Suppose that `Key` stores a string, then the steps to convert `Key` into a storage-address returned in `Hash` are as follows:

```
Sum ← 0
For i ← 1 To Length(Key)
   Sum ← Sum + Ord(Key[i]) * Ord(Key[i])
Endfor
Hash ← Sum Mod 523
```

Table 34.19 Hashing algorithm that calculates a storage address in range 0 to 522

Looking up a record in a hash table

A record with a given key can be looked up by just calculating the hash of its key and checking the associated storage location.

English-French dictionary example

In this example, English words and their French equivalents are stored in records in a hash table, `HashTable`, using a hashing function, `H`, based on the hashing algorithm shown in *Table 34.19*. Each record must have a key field which uniquely identifies the record. In this case, the key is the English word.

The hashing function, `H`, assigns hash table memory location `H(k)` to the record with key, `k`.

In our English-French dictionary example, `H(k)` could be `H('BEACH')` where `k = 'BEACH'` for the record containing the English word `'BEACH'` and the equivalent French word `'PLAGE'`.

Information

The term "hash" originates by analogy with its non-technical meaning, to "chop and mix". Hash functions often "chop" the input domain into many sub-domains that get "mixed" e.g. add the first three digits of the key, add the last three digits, concatenate the two resulting digit strings then map into the output range by applying modulo N.

The storage structure, `HashTable`, that will be used with this address has the following data structure:

```
THashTableArray = Array[0..522] Of TRecord
```

Where the data structure `TRecord` is defined as follows

```
TRecord = Record
             EnglishWord : String
             FrenchWord : String
          End
```

Questions

2 Calculate `H(k)` for the following keys, `k`

(a) PEN (b) CAT (c) NOW (d) WON

(ASCII codes for the characters `'A'...'Z'` map to the range 65 ... 90 - see *Chapter 4*)

Programming tasks

1. Write a program to store English words and their French equivalents in a hash table which is an array or its equivalent with addresses in range 0 to 522. The English word and its French equivalent should be stored together in a record or equivalent data structure at an address which is calculated by the hashing function, `H`, described above. The table should be initialised so that every key field stores the string `'-1'` to indicate that this field's record has yet to be used to store an English-French word pair. Use your program to temporarily store the English words, PEN, CAT, NOW and their French equivalents.
   (English word with its French equivalent:
   PEN – PLUME, CAT – CHAT, NOW – MAINTENANT)

2. Extend your program so that after storing the English-French word pairs for PEN, CAT and NOW, the program uses the hashing function, `H`, to retrieve the French equivalent when the user enters PEN, CAT or NOW. Use a loop to enable the user to continue to look up the French equivalent until the user decides otherwise.

Collisions

The hash values calculated in Questions 2(c) and 2(d) are identical because the English words contain the same letters, but arranged in a different order (NOW and WON). So both words hash to the same address. This situation is known as a **collision**. Clearly, there is only space at this address for one English-French word pair.

Collisions can be resolved in two ways:

1. Store the record in the "next available" empty location in the table, or
2. Store a pointer in each table location that points to a list of records that have all collided at this table location, otherwise set the pointer value to null.

> **Key concept**
>
> **Collision:**
> A collision occurs when two or more different keys hash to the same hash value. For the hash table this means a hash value of a location in the hash table which is already occupied.

Method 1 – closed hashing or open addressing

The first way of resolving a collision is to *rehash* which means to generate a new table row address at which to store the English-French word pair.
One rehash method, called **linear rehash**, calculates a new address by adding one to the original address before testing that the location with this new address is empty, e.g. indicated by `'-1'` in the `EnglishWord` field.

The rehash step may have to be repeated until an empty slot is found.

> **Key concept**
>
> **Closed hashing or open addressing:**
> Method in which a collision is resolved by storing the record in the "next available" location.

To avoid going off the end of the table, the new address is made to wrap around to the beginning of the hash table, if necessary and assuming there is an empty slot, by using modular arithmetic as follows:

```
Repeat
  Address ← (Address + 1) Mod 523
Until HashTable[Address].EnglishWord = '-1'
```

This method is an example of **closed hashing** or **open addressing** because other row addresses of the hash table are open to being used but access to addresses outside the hash table are closed off.

The table, `HashTable`, is an array whose addresses run from 0 to 522.

The table is initialised with 523 empty English-French word pair records in which every `EnglishWord` field has the string `'-1'` stored in it to indicate that this field is unoccupied and the whole record is empty.

Table 34.20 shows an algorithm expressed in pseudo-code for inserting an English-French word pair into an initialised `HashTable`. The English word to insert is supplied in `WordInE` and its French equivalent in `WordInF`.

Each row of the hash table has space for a record with two fields, `EnglishWord` and `FrenchWord`.

```
Address ← Hash(WordInE)
If HashTable[Address].Key = '-1'
                 {-1 indicates field is empty}
  Then
    Begin
      HashTable[Address].EnglishWord ← WordInE
      HashTable[Address].FrenchWord ← WordInF
    End
  Else
    If Not(HashTable[Address].EnglishWord = WordInE)
                                {not already stored}
      Then
        Begin
          {find empty slot}
          Repeat
            Address ← (Address + 1) Mod 523
          Until (HashTable[Address].EnglishWord = '-1')
            Or (HashTable[Address].EnglishWord = WordInE)
                                          {already stored}
          If (HashTable[Address].EnglishWord = '-1')
              Then
                Begin
                  HashTable[Address].EnglishWord ← WordInE
                  HashTable[Address].FrenchWord ← WordInF
                End
        End
```

Table 34.20 Hashing algorithm incorporating a linear rehash that inserts an English-French word pair into a hash table

Clearly for this algorithm to work the hash table must have at least one empty row.

Searching for a specific record in a hash table accommodating collisions

Table 34.21 shows an algorithm expressed in pseudo-code that can be used to search for an English-French word pair in a hash table, `HashTable`, given an English word stored in the variable `WordInE`.

The English word may or may not be present in the hash table.

If it is, then its French equivalent is returned in variable, `Retrieve` otherwise message `'Not found'` is returned in `Retrieve`.

Clearly for this algorithm to work the hash table must have at least one empty row.

```
Address ←  Hash(WordInE)
Found ←  False
Repeat
  If HashTable[Address].EnglishWord = WordInE
    Then Found ←  True
    Else Address ←  (Address + 1) Mod 523
Until Found Or (HashTable[Address].EnglishWord = '-1')
If Found
  Then Retrieve ←  HashTable[Address].FrenchWord
  Else Retrieve ←  'Not found'
```

Table 34.21 Hashing algorithm that uses a linear rehash method to search a hash table for the French equivalent of a given English word

Setting up a hash table that uses closed hashing

Method 1 (closed hashing or open addressing) requires that the number of rows in the table exceeds by about a third the maximum number of records that will ever be stored in the table. When every record has been stored in the table, the table should still contain empty rows (i.e. table should never be more than roughly two thirds full). If this isn't the case then search times will be extended as will the time to insert new records.

Although this might seem a waste of storage space, there is a very good reason for working in this way. Studies have shown that the number of collisions depends on

- the hash keys
- the hash function
- the ratio of total number of records to total number of possible locations available to these records in the hash table.

A perfect hash function hashes all the hash keys to hash values without the occurrence of a single collision. That is why it is called perfect.

However, finding a perfect hash function is extremely difficult.

The effectiveness of a hash function is very sensitive to the hash key values. These are not always fully known in advance.

Using a ratio of roughly two thirds for total number of records to total number of hash table locations seems to minimise collisions for hash functions that are close to perfect. The hash table shown in *Table 34.22* has six student records and seven rows. One improvement could be to change the number of rows to 9 or even better, 11, a prime number. **Using a prime number for modulo arithmetic helps to minimise collisions.**

However, the hash function could be further improved as well as it is far from being perfect.

The aim is to make each hash value generated by the hash function equally likely when the function is applied to any of the possible hash keys, i.e. no one particular hash value should be more favoured than any other.

	ULN	Forename	Surname
0	34567876	Fred	Bloggs
1			
2	90002789	Mary	Smith
3	64156906	Alex	Black
4	24567805	Visha	Baal
5	74432167	Ben	Brown
6	90002985	Shena	Patel

Table 34.22 Hash table with not enough rows to minimise collisions

Questions

3. Copy and complete *Table 34.23*.

ULN	ULN Mod 7	ULN Mod 11
24567805		
34567876		
64156906		
74432167		
90002789		
90002985		

Table 34.23

Questions

4. Insert the ULNs from *Table 34.23* into a copy of the hash table shown in *Table 34.24* using the hashing function,

```
H(ULN) = ULN Mod 7
```

The student `Forename` and `Surname` fields do not need to be completed.

You should deal with any collision by performing a linear rehash until an empty slot is found.

	ULN	Forename	Surname
0			
1			
2			
3			
4			
5			
6			

Table 34.24 Hash table

5. Insert the ULNs from *Table 34.23* into a copy of the hash table shown in *Table 34.25* using the hashing function,

```
H(ULN) = ULN Mod 11
```

The student `Forename` and `Surname` fields may be omitted for convenience.

	ULN	Forename	Surname
0			
1			
2			
3			
4			
5			
6			
7			
8			
9			
10			

Table 34.25 Hash table

6. Explain how the hash table in *Table 34.25* when populated with student records would be used to look up the forename and surname of student with ULN = 24567805.

7. Explain how the hash table in *Table 34.24* when populated with student records would be used to look up the forename and surname of student with ULN = 24567805.

8. Why is it necessary to store the key field in a hash table even when an application using this hash table must already know the value of the key field?

Investigation

1. Devise an experiment to investigate collisions on a hash table that is to store 6000 student records. Use a random number generator to generate unique student ID numbers. Try different ratios of total number of records to total number of table rows in the hash table.
2. The hash function `H` that we have used so far is far from perfect for many data sets that we wish to store in a hash table. Investigate other hashing functions.

Method 2 - open hashing or closed addressing

In this alternative method of dealing with collisions, the hash table is extended to include a pointer field. The pointer field for each row is initialised to the null pointer value when the table is set up (⊣).

When a collision occurs the colliding record is linked to the corresponding table row by changing the pointer field of this row to point to the colliding record as shown in Figure 34.29.

	ULN	Forename	Surname	Pointer
0	34567876	Fred	Bloggs	Null ⊣
1				Null ⊣
2	90002789	Mary	Smith	→
3	24567805	Visha	Baal	Null ⊣
4				Null ⊣
5	74432167	Ben	Brown	Null ⊣
6				Null ⊣

64156906	Black	Alex	Null ⊣

Figure 34.29 Hash table that uses open hashing

Another record colliding with row 2 will be linked or chained to the record of `'Mary Smith'` by changing the pointer field of Mary's record to point to this record and so on, thus forming a chain of linked records or a linked list.

Method 2 is called **open hashing** or **closed addressing** because locations outside the table are open for use by the hashing algorithm, i.e. the linked list locations, whilst other row addresses are closed off.

Key concept

Open hashing or closed addressing:

In a collision, the other rows of the hash table are closed to the colliding record which must, instead, be attached to the addressed table row in a chain or linked list of other colliding records. The table row uses a pointer field to point to the linked list.

Deleting a record

Care must be exercised when an entry in a hash table is deleted.

Closed hashing

In closed hashing, collisions are resolved by rehashing and storing the colliding record in another row whose table index is the rehash value.

However, if the entry at the original hash value table index or any of the rehash value table entries are deleted and the deleted entry remains empty, searching can be stopped prematurely before all potential matching entries have been examined.

Therefore, a deleted entry must be distinguishable from an entry that has never been used. This requires a special marker to be present in the key field part of the hash table entry when the entry is not in use. The special marker will use one value to indicate that this entry has never been used and a different value to indicate that it has been used but the entry has been deleted.

The special marker values should not use any value that potentially could occur in the key fields of the data set to be stored in the hash table. A search should now continue until an empty unused slot (indicated by the special marker) is encountered and not just an empty slot (which might have been used previously).

Open hashing

In open hashing, collisions are resolved by chaining the colliding record to the table entry slot whose index is the hash. Care must be taken when deleting the record in the table row when the row has a nonempty chain.

A special marker can be left in the key field to signal that there is at least one record in a chain (linked list) attached to the row so that a search does not fail to look at the chain when seeking a match.

There are at least two alternatives that do not rely on a special marker.

In alternative one, the search examines the pointer field of an empty slot to see if a chain is attached.

In alternative two, the first record in the chain is moved into the table slot whilst preserving its link to the rest of the chain.

Information

The definitions assigned to the terms closed hashing and open hashing have been interchanged over the years so care needs to be exercised when interpreting them. The key is to focus on concept/method not name and to make sure that you understand the former.

Questions

9 An empty hash table is set up for open hashing. The following hashing function is to be used to store variable names beginning with an uppercase letter in range A...Z, as well as other information.

`H(VariableName)` = (code for first letter of `VariableName x 11) Mod M`

Where `M` is the number of rows in the hash table.

Using `M = 5` and coding letters of the alphabet as follows, A=1, B=2, ..., Z=26 show the contents of the hash table after inserting the following variable names:

CHECK, OVERTIME, MAIN, P, URL, TAXRATE, INDEX, N, GENDER

You may ignore in your answer the other information associated with each variable name.

10 (a) Using the hashing algorithm expressed in pseudo-code below, calculate the hash value for the hash key `'PEN'` stored in string variable `Key`. You will need access to an ASCII code table to map characters to their equivalent ASCII codes. This is performed in the pseudo-code by the function `Ord`. The `Length` function returns the number of characters in the string. The symbol `'*'` means multiply.

```
Sum ← 0
For i ← 0 To Length(Key)- 1
   Sum ← Sum + Ord(Key[i]) * Ord(Key[i])
EndFor
HashValue ← Sum Mod 523
```

(b) Now repeat the exercise with the made-up word `'NEP'`.

(c) Can you see that there is a problem? What is the problem?

(d) Describe **two** ways that could be used to overcome this problem.

11 Explain why care must be exercised when deleting an entry in a hash table that uses closed hashing and on which searching occurs after deletion.

12 A person owns *n* distinct pairs of socks, which are kept in an unmatched pile in a drawer.

Individual socks are pulled from the drawer blindly, then identified and placed in a separate pile according to identity.

(a) How many individual socks must the person pull from the drawer to ensure that two are pulled that match?

(b) In what respect does this process resemble a hash table and open hashing?

Questions

13 In an application, student records are identified by their key field, the student's unique learner number (ULN) consisting of eight digits, e.g. 34567890. The application has to process a ULN allocated in the range 1000000 to 99999999 but it will never have to deal with more than 500 ULNs.

(a) Explain why when storing student records in a table in memory it would not be sensible to use the ULN as the row address for the record, e.g. 34128496.

(b) Explain why the use of a hash table would be a better option for this application.

14 (a) State **two** advantages of using hashing and the hash table approach over the alternative approach which just stores records in an ordinary table starting from the first row.

(b) It is noticed that after inserting many records into a hash table that uses closed hashing, searches are taking much longer than they did.

(i) Explain why this may be the case

(ii) Suggest a solution that could potentially restore searching times to what they were.

15 Explain why it is necessary to store the hash key in a hash table.

35 Generics

Working with generics

Purpose: To learn how to use generics

Introduction

Suppose we have some data that we need to store and unstore on a stack and we write stack routines to do this. If we know the data type of the data in advance then we can write these routines to work with the chosen data type. However, if we don't know the data type in advance, how can we write stack routines to work with a data type, `T`, that is unknown initially?

The answer is to use **generics** i.e. a class that uses a generic type parameter, the type `T` in *Table 35.1*.

Table 35.1 shows a generic class `TStack<T>` with unknown type `T` as a parameter; the type name `T` is is used for convenience but any name could be used.

```
TStack<T> = Class
       Private
         Stack: array of T;
       Public
         Procedure Push(Item : T);
         Function Pop: T;
     End;
```

Table 35.1

Generics was added to the language in Delphi 2009

Type `T` is declared when the generic class is used.

For example,

```
Var
  MyStackOfIntegers : TStack<Integer>;
  MyStackOfStrings : TStack<Strings>;
Begin
  MyStackOfIntegers := TStack<Integer>.Create;
  MyStackOfStrings := TStack<String>.Create;
.....
```

Before delving into the stack example in greater depth, let's consider a simpler example shown in *Table 35.2* which illustrates different ways that generics can be used. The example also shows how procedures that are overloaded can achieve similar results when the task is simple. Generics really comes into its own when we need to work with collections of things such as lists, stacks, queues and dictionaries.

Table 35.2 defines three generic types: two generic classes and one class with a generic method as follows

```
TGenericTest<T> = Class
                    Function Test(x : T) : T;
                  End;
TGenericTestWithClassProc<T> = Class
                                 Class Procedure Test(x : T); static;
                               End;
TGenericMethodOfClass = Class
                          Procedure Test<T>(x : T);
                        End;
```

It also defines three overloaded procedures with signatures as follows

```
Procedure OverloadedTest(x : Integer); Overload;
Procedure OverloadedTest(x : String); Overload;
Procedure OverloadedTest(x : Double); Overload;
```

The Delphi compiler reports an error with any `Writeln` statements that are called with parameters of unknown or inappropriate data type, e.g.

```
Class Procedure TGenericTestWithClassProcThatCompile<T>.Test(x : T);
  Begin
    Writeln(x);  <——— x of unknown data type
  End;
```

However, this can be remedied by type casting parameter `x` to one of the data types that `Writeln` can handle, e.g. **Integer**, **String** or **Double**. This is a two-stage process. First the data type of `T` must be established using **TypeInfo**. Once this is known, the correct cast can be applied to x:

PInteger if `x` is a pointer to an integer datum
PString if `x` is a pointer to a string datum
PDouble if `x` is a pointer to a double datum

```
PInteger = ^Integer;
PString = ^String;
PString = ^Double;
```

www.educational-computing.com/DelphiBook/Code/Chapter35/IntroductionToGenerics.zip

```
Program IntroductionToGenerics;
{$APPTYPE CONSOLE}
Uses
  System.SysUtils;
Type
  TGenericTest<T> = Class
                      Function Test(x : T) : T;
                    End;
  TGenericTestWithClassProc<T> = Class
                                   Class Procedure Test(x : T); static;
                                 End;
  TGenericMethodOfClass = Class
                            Procedure Test<T>(x : T);
                          End;
Procedure OverloadedTest(x : Integer); Overload;
  Begin
    Writeln('x = ', x);
  End;
Procedure OverloadedTest(x : String); Overload;
  Begin
    Writeln('x = ', x);
  End;
Procedure OverloadedTest(x : Double); Overload;
  Begin
    Writeln('x = ', x:5:4);
  End;
Function TGenericTest<T>.Test(x : T) : T;
  Begin
    Result := x;
  End;
Class Procedure TGenericTestWithClassProc<T>.Test(x : T);
  Begin
    If (TypeInfo(T) = TypeInfo(String))
      Then Writeln(PString(@x)^)
      Else
        If (TypeInfo(T) = TypeInfo(Integer))
          Then Writeln(PInteger(@x)^)
          Else
            If (TypeInfo(T) = TypeInfo(Double))
              Then Writeln(PDouble(@x)^:4:1);
  End;
Procedure TGenericMethodOfClass.Test<T>(x : T);
  Begin
    If (TypeInfo(T) = TypeInfo(String))
      Then Writeln(PString(@x)^)
      Else
        If (TypeInfo(T) = TypeInfo(Integer))
          Then Writeln(PInteger(@x)^)
          Else
            If (TypeInfo(T) = TypeInfo(Double))
              Then Writeln(PDouble(@x)^:4:1);
  End;
Var
  GenericTestIntRef : TGenericTest<Integer>;
  GenericTestStrRef : TGenericTest<String>;
  GenericTestDblRef : TGenericTest<Double>;
  GenericMethodOfClassRef : TGenericMethodOfClass;
```

PInteger(@x) casts the pointer stored in x. If the address operator @ is not included, x will be dereferenced then PInteger applied, not what is required. PInteger(@x)^ obtains the datum referenced by x

Table 35.2 Program IntroductionToGenerics showing the use of parameterised types

```
Begin
  Writeln('Using overloaded procedures');
  OverloadedTest(6);
  OverloadedTest('Hello');
  OverloadedTest(24.67);
  Writeln('---------------------------------------');
  Writeln('Using a method of a generic class');
  GenericTestIntRef := TGenericTest<Integer>.Create;
  Writeln(GenericTestIntRef.Test(13));
  GenericTestIntRef.Free;
  GenericTestStrRef := TGenericTest<String>.Create;
  Writeln(GenericTestStrRef.Test('Thirteen'));
  GenericTestStrRef.Free;
  GenericTestDblRef := TGenericTest<Double>.Create;
  Writeln(GenericTestDblRef.Test(13.67):5:2);
  Writeln('---------------------------------------');
  Writeln('Using a class method of a generic class');
  TGenericTestWithClassProc<Integer>.Test(15);
  TGenericTestWithClassProc<String>.Test('Fifteen');
  TGenericTestWithClassProc<Double>.Test(15.0);
  Writeln('---------------------------------------');
  Writeln('Using a generic method of a class');
  GenericMethodOfClassRef := TGenericMethodOfClass.Create;
  GenericMethodOfClassRef.Test<Integer>(11);
  GenericMethodOfClassRef.Test<String>('Eleven');
  GenericMethodOfClassRef.Test<Double>(11.0);
  Writeln('---------------------------------------');
  Readln;
End.
```

Figure 35.1 shows the result when `IntroductionToGenerics` is executed.

Program GenericStack

Table 35.3 shows a program that uses a generic type `T` to generalise the stack data structure to handle any data type that **Writeln** can handle, i.e. integer, floating point and string.

www.educational-computing.com/DelphiBook/Code/Chapter35/GenericStack.zip

```
Program GenericStack;
{$APPTYPE CONSOLE}
Uses
  System.SysUtils;
Type
  TMyStack<T> = Class
                  Private
                    FStack : Array Of T;
                    TopOfStackPointer : Integer;
                    SizeOfStack : Integer;
                  Public
                    Procedure Push(x : T);
                    Function Pop : T;
                    Function IsEmpty : Boolean;
                    Function IsFull : Boolean;
                    Constructor CreateStack(Size : Integer);
                End;
Var
  StackOfIntegers : TMyStack<Integer>;
  i : Integer;

Constructor TMyStack<T>.CreateStack(Size : Integer);
  Begin
    SetLength(FStack, Size);
    TopOfStackPointer := -1;
    SizeOfStack := Size;
  End;

Function TMyStack<T>.IsEmpty : Boolean;
  Begin
    If TopOfStackPointer = -1
      Then Result := True
      Else Result := False;
  End;

Function TMyStack<T>.IsFull : Boolean;
  Begin
    If TopOfStackPointer = SizeOfStack
      Then Result := True
      Else Result := False;
  End;

Function TMyStack<T>.Pop : T;
  Begin
    If Not IsEmpty
      Then
        Begin
          Result := FStack[TopOfStackPointer];
          TopOfStackPointer := TopOfStackPointer - 1;
        End
        Else Raise Exception.Create('Stack is empty');
  End;

Procedure TMyStack<T>.Push(x : T);
  Begin
    TopOfStackPointer := TopOfStackPointer + 1;
    If Not StackOfIntegers.IsFull
      Then FStack[TopOfStackPointer] := x
      Else
        Begin
          TopOfStackPointer := TopOfStackPointer - 1;
          Writeln('Stack is full');
        End;
  End;
Begin
  StackOfIntegers := TMyStack<Integer>.CreateStack(9);
  For i := 0 To 8
    Do StackOfIntegers.Push(i);
  For i := 0 To 8
    Do
      If Not StackOfIntegers.IsEmpty
        Then Writeln(StackOfIntegers.Pop)
        Else Writeln('Stack is empty');
  Readln;
  StackOfIntegers.Free;
End.
```

Table 35.3 Program GenericStack

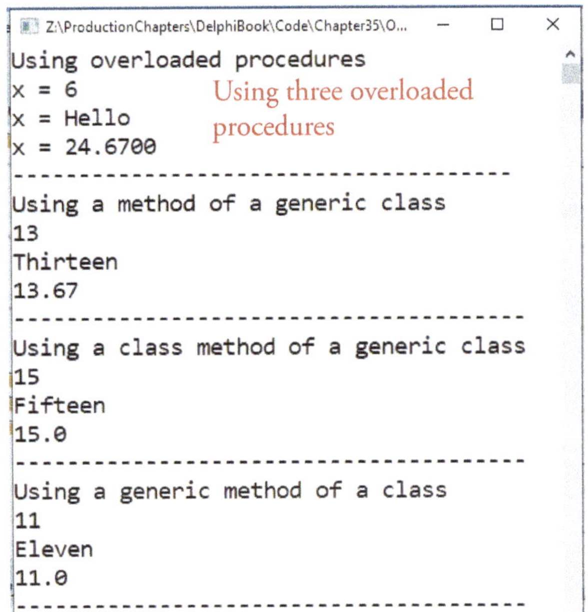

Fig. 35.1 IntroductionToGenerics.exe in execution

The program demonstrates the principle by creating and using a stack of nine integers.

Load program **GenericStack** then build (Shift F9) and run in Debug mode (F9). Check that it unstacks and displays nine integers on the console.

Programming Task

1. Add to **GenericStack** the ability to handle a stack of nine strings. Save the program as **ExtendedGenericStack**. Rebuild and run the revised program and check that it does indeed output nine strings as well as nine integers.

In conclusion, generics allows generalised types to be used as parameters which can then be instantiated as a specific type when required by a program.

Collections

In computer science, a container is a class, a data structure, or an abstract data type (ADT) whose instances are collections of other objects arranged in an organised way with rules governing how these objects may be accessed. The term objects is meant in a generalised way, e.g. the object could just be a data item.

Delphi has had container classes for a long time, e.g. **TList**, **TStack**, **TQueue**, **TOrderedList** from the **System.Classes** unit. These classic container classes consist of lists of pointers or object references which have to be cast to the specific object data type/class as shown in the example program in *Table 35.4*.

The program shown in *Table 35.5* shows how the the same task can be simplified if a generic **TList<Integer>** class from **System.Generics.Collections** is used instead.

Generics collections avoids the need to check for data type compatibility at runtime because it can now be done at compile time by the compiler. As *Table 35.5* shows, the result is cleaner and more readable code, and faster execution - given the reduced need for runtime checks. The code should be more robust because direct handling of pointers is avoided.

System.Generic.Collections implements generic container classes to group data items into arrays, dictionaries, lists, stacks, queues, and more.

www.educational-computing.com/DelphiBook/Code/Chapter35/ClassicContainer.zip

```
Program ClassicContainer;
{$APPTYPE CONSOLE}
Uses
  System.SysUtils, System.Classes;
Var
  aList : TList;
  PtrInteger : ^Integer;
  i : Integer;
Begin
  Try
    AList := TList.Create;
    For i := 0 To 8
      Do
        Begin
          New(PtrInteger);
          PtrInteger^ := i;
          aList.Add(PtrInteger);
        End;
    Writeln(PInteger(aList.Items[2])^);
    Readln;
  Finally
    Dispose(PtrInteger);
    aList.Free;
  End;
End.
```

Table 35.4 Program ClassicContainer

```
Program GenericContainer;
{$APPTYPE CONSOLE}
Uses
  System.SysUtils,
  System.Generics.Collections;
Var
  aList : TList<Integer>;
Begin
  Try
    AList := TList<Integer>.Create;
    For Var i := 0 To 8 Do aList.Add(i);
    Writeln(aList[2]);
    Readln;
  Finally
    aList.Free;
  End;
End.
```

Inline declaration with data type inferred from context (Delphi 10.3 onwards

Table 35.5 Program GenericContainer

www.educational-computing.com/DelphiBook/Code/Chapter35/GenericContainer.zip

www.educational-computing.com/DelphiBook/Code/Chapter35/GenericsCollectionsStack.zip

```
Program GenericsCollectionsStack;
{$APPTYPE CONSOLE}
Uses
  System.SysUtils,
  System.Generics.Collections;
Var
  anIntegerStack : TStack<Integer>;
  aStringStack : TStack<String>;
Begin
  Try
    anIntegerStack := TStack<Integer>.Create;
    aStringStack := TStack<String>.Create;
    anIntegerStack.Capacity := 9;
    aStringStack.Capacity := 9;
    For Var i := 0 To 8 Do anIntegerStack.Push(i);
    Writeln(anIntegerStack.Pop);
    For Var i := 0 To 8
      Do aStringStack.Push(Chr(i+65)+ Chr(i+66));
    For Var i := 0 To 9
      Do If aStringStack.Count <> 0
        Then Writeln(aStringStack.Pop)
        Else Writeln('Stack is empty');
    Readln;
  Finally
    anIntegerStack.Free;
    aStringStack.Free;
  End;
End.
```

Table 35.6 Program GenericsCollectionsStack

Using Generics Collections TStack<T>

Table 35.6 shows how to use **TStack(T)** from the **System.Generics.Collections** unit to create an integer stack and a string stack.

Table 35.7 shows how to use **TArray<Integer>** from the **System.Generics.Collection** unit to create an integer array of 10000 integers chosen randomly between 0 and 9999, then to sort it and binary search it.

`TArray.Sort<Integer>(MyArray)` sorts the array `MyArray` in ascending order.

The array is set up to store 10000 integers with `SetLength(MyArray, 10000);`

`TArray.BinarySearch<Integer>(MyArray, Element, FoundIndex, IntegerComparer)` performs a binary search on `MyArray` using the object `IntegerComparer`'s `Compare` method to perform an integer comparison of the sought element with the current element from `MyArray`. The method `Compare` returns 0 if equal, +1 if the first integer is greater than the second and -1 if the opposite is true.

The sort order may be switched to descending by uncommenting

```
TArray.Sort<Integer>(MyArray, IntegerComparer);
```

commenting out `TArray.Sort<Integer>(MyArray);`

and changing `Result := Left - Right;` to `Result := Right - Left;`

www.educational-computing.com/DelphiBook/Code/Chapter35/GenericsCollectionsArray.Project.zip

```
Program GenericsCollectionsArrayProject;
{$APPTYPE CONSOLE}
Uses
  System.SysUtils, System.Generics.Defaults, System.Generics.Collections;
Type
  TIntegerComparer = Class(TComparer<Integer>)
                       Function Compare(Const Left, Right : Integer) : Integer; Override;
                     End;
Var
  MyArray : TArray<Integer>;
  IntegerComparer : TIntegerComparer;
  FoundIndex, Element : Integer;

Function TIntegerComparer.Compare(const Left, Right: Integer): Integer;
  Begin
    Result := Left - Right;
  End;

Begin
  Try
    IntegerComparer := TIntegerComparer.Create;
    SetLength(MyArray, 10000);
    Writeln(Length(MyArray));
    For Var i := 0 To 9999
      Do MyArray[i] := Random(10000);
    TArray.Sort<Integer>(MyArray);
    //TArray.Sort<Integer>(MyArray, IntegerComparer);
    For Var i := 0 To 9999
      Do Writeln(MyArray[i]);
    Repeat
      Write('Input an integer to search for (-1 to exit): ');
      Readln(Element);
      If TArray.BinarySearch<Integer>(MyArray, Element, FoundIndex, IntegerComparer)
        Then Writeln('Element ', Element, ' was found at index ', FoundIndex)
        Else Writeln('Element ' + IntToStr(Element) + ' was not found');
    Until Element = -1 ;
    Readln;
  Finally
    IntegerComparer.Free;
  End;
End.
```

Table 35.7 Program GenericsCollectionsArrayProject

Dictionary

We use dictionaries in everyday life when we want to look up the meaning of a word. For example, the word 'davit' means 'crane'. In a word dictionary this would be recorded as 'davit - crane' which has the form

key - definition

A word dictionary is a collection of these entries.

The **dictionary abstract data type** is a collection of items in which each item has both a key and a value called a **key, value pair**.

The collection is then

a set of (key, value) pairs

The key is unique and is used to look up its corresponding value.

The data for the dictionary abstract data type takes the form

key : value

for which

- keys are mapped to values, e.g. 'France' → 'Paris' is the key : value pair 'France' : 'Paris'
- keys must be comparable, e.g. 'Germany' ≠ 'France'
- keys must be unique, e.g. only one key 'France'

and standard operations are

- insert(key, value), e.g. insert ('Lithuania', 'Vilnius') inserts the key : value pair 'Lithuania':'Vilnius' into the dictionary (see *Figure 35.2*)
- find(key), e.g. find('Azerbaijan') - returns the value with key 'Azerbaijan' i.e. 'Baku', the capital of Azerbaijan, if the dictionary contains such a key, otherwise returns a special value e.g. `No_Such_Key`
- delete(key), e.g. delete('Croatia') removes the key-value pair 'Croatia':'Zagreb' whose key is 'Croatia'

Items in a dictionary are not stored in any particular order. A dictionary supports fast key lookups.

Key concept

Dictionary:

A dictionary is a collection of items in which each item has both a key and a value and for which

- keys are mapped to values
- keys must be comparable
- keys must be unique

and standard operations are

- insert(key, value)
- find(key)
- delete(key)

Dictionary that maps country to capital, i.e. country → capital:
{'Nigeria':'Abuja',
'Ghana':'Accra', ...,
'Azerbaijan':'Baku', ...,
'Lithuania':'Vilnius', ...,
'Croatia':'Zagreb'}

Figure 35.2 Dictionary that maps country to its capital

Table 35.8 shows a Delphi program which uses the **System.Generics.Collections** unit's **TDictionary<String, String>** data type.

The insert(key, value) operation is called `Add`, e.g.

```
CapitalsOfCountriesDictionary.Add('Lithuania', 'Vilnius')
```

The find(key) operation is implemented in two stages by first checking for the key's presence with `ContainsKey` and then, if present, accessing its value with [key] as follows

```
If CapitalsOfCountriesDictionary.ContainsKey('Azerbaijan')
   Then Writeln(CapitalsOfCountriesDictionary['Azerbaijan'])
   Else Writeln('No key with value Azerbaijan');
```

Delphi program	Commentary
`Program DictionaryExample;`	
`{$APPTYPE CONSOLE}`	
`Uses`	
`  System.Generics.Collections;`	
`Type`	
`  TCapitalsOfCountriesDictionary = TDictionary<String, String>;`	Defines a dictionary data type
`Var`	
`  CapitalsOfCountriesDictionary : TCapitalsOfCountriesDictionary;`	Declares a variable of this type
`Begin`	
`  CapitalsOfCountriesDictionary := TCapitalsOfCountriesDictionary.Create;`	Creates a dictionary object
`  CapitalsOfCountriesDictionary.Add('Nigeria','Abuja');`	
`  CapitalsOfCountriesDictionary.Add('Azerbaijan','Baku');`	Inserts key, value pairs
`  CapitalsOfCountriesDictionary.Add('Lithuania','Vilnius');`	
`  CapitalsOfCountriesDictionary.Add('Croatia','Zagreb');`	
`  If CapitalsOfCountriesDictionary.ContainsKey('Azerbaijan')`	Searches for entry with key Azerbaijan
`    Then Writeln(CapitalsOfCountriesDictionary['Azerbaijan'])`	Extracts value of the key : value pair and displays on console
`    Else Writeln('No key with value Azerbaijan');`	
`  Readln;`	
`  CapitalsOfCountriesDictionary.Free;`	Releases memory occupied by object
`End.` www.educational-computing.com/DelphiBook/Code/Chapter35/DictionaryExample.zip	

Table 35.8 Delphi program that uses the Generics Collections to create and populate a dictionary of country, capital key,value pairs

Task

1. Create a dictionary in the form `{key:value, key:value, ...}` to enable the ASCII code for the character digits '0', '1', '2', '3', '4', '5', '6', '7', '8', '9' to be looked up.

Loading data from a csv file into a dictionary

The program shown in *Table 35.9* loads data from a text file `countriescapitals.txt`. This is a comma-separated values text file that is organised line-by-line in no particular order into **<country>,<capital>**.
For example,

United Arab Emirates,Abu Dhabi
Nigeria,Abuja
....

www.educational-computing.com/DelphiBook/Code/Chapter35/DictionaryLoadFromFileProject.zip

```
Program DictionaryLoadFromFileProject;
{$APPTYPE CONSOLE}
Uses
  Generics.Collections, System.Classes, System.SysUtils, System.StrUtils;
Type
  TCapitalsOfCountriesDictionary = TDictionary<String, String>;
Var
  CapitalsOfCountriesDictionary : TCapitalsOfCountriesDictionary;
  CountryFile : TStringList;
  i : Integer;
  TwoValues : TArray<String>;
  Row : TPair<String, String>;
  Ch : Char;
  Answer, Country : String;
Begin
  Try
    CountryFile := TStringList.Create;
    Try           Loads each line in turn into CountryFile which is structured as a list of TStrings
      CountryFile.LoadFromFile('..\..\countriescapitals.txt');
    Except
      On Exception Do Writeln('File opening error');
    End;
    CapitalsOfCountriesDictionary := TCapitalsOfCountriesDictionary.Create;
    Try
      For i := 0 To CountryFile.Count - 1
        Do
          Begin                     Split a line into two separate strings, and then store each separately in array TwoValues
            TwoValues := CountryFile[i].Split([','], 2);
            CapitalsOfCountriesDictionary.Add(AnsiUpperCase(TwoValues[0]), AnsiUpperCase(TwoValues[1]));
          End;                      Add the first array element, country name, as key and the second value, capital name, as
    Except                          value as a key-value pair, both uppercase, to dictionary CapitalsOfCountryDictionary
      On Exception Do Writeln('Adding to dictionary error');
    End;

    For Row In CapitalsOfCountriesDictionary   Access each row of dictionary CapitalsOfCountryDictionary and test the user's
      Do                                       answer to the question 'What is the capital of ..' for country returned in Row.Key?
        Begin
          Write('What is the capital of ', Row.Key, '? ');
          Readln(Answer);
          If AnsiCompareText(Answer, Row.Value) = 0
            Then Writeln('Correct')
            Else Writeln('The correct answer is ', Row.Value);
           Write('Another go Y/N?');
           Readln(Ch);
           If (Ch In ['N', 'n'])
             Then Break
        End;
      Repeat
        Write('Input country(type X to exit) ');   If the given country exists in the dictionary then its capital is
        Readln(Country);                           written to the console otherwise 'Don't know that one' is output
        If CapitalsOfCountriesDictionary.ContainsKey(AnsiUpperCase(Country))
          Then Writeln(CapitalsOfCountriesDictionary[AnsiUpperCase(Country)])
          Else
            If Not (AnsiUpperCase(Country) = 'X')
              Then Writeln('Don''t know that one');
      Until AnsiUpperCase(Country) = 'X';
  Finally
    CountryFile.Free;
    CapitalsOfCountriesDictionary.Free;
  End;
End.
```

Table 35.9 DictionaryLoadFromFileProject.dpr

The program shown in *Table 35.9* uses `CountryFile[i].Split([','], 2)` to split the line of <country>,<capital> on ',' into two strings. It is important that there is no space either side of the ',' in the text file otherwise any space will be included in one or both strings. Of course each string could be trimmed to remove any leading or for that matter trailing spaces.

Programming Task

2 Adapt program *DictionaryLoadFromFileProject.dpr* shown in *Table 35.9* to enable the ASCII code for the characters with ASCII codes 33 to 126 to be looked up. Store the mapping between character and its ASCII code in a csv text file.

Some uses of dictionaries

A dictionary is a searchable collection of key-value items which can be searched by key. This means that it can be used when the data is similarly structured, e.g. a telephone directory. Telephone directories consist of *name, telephone number* pairs and so can be modelled with a dictionary abstract data type and built with a corresponding dictionary data structure.

A dictionary abstract data type or data structure can be used to count the occurrences of words in a story:

- Each dictionary entry is keyed by the word
- The related value is the count
- When entering words into dictionary
  Check if word is already there
  If not, enter it with a value of 1
  If it is, increment its value

The data type of the value part in the *key, value* pair can be any type including a list. This can be useful when creating an index for a book, for example. The list is a list of page numbers on which the key, a string, appears. With so many delimiters to cater for when two delimiters are in conjunction, e.g. '. ', a full stop followed by a space, the pair of delimiters actually delimit something which is the empty string, ''.

The dictionary structure is actually a hash table. This is fine for looking up a known word but if we wanted to search the dictionary we might want a dictionary which is in alphabetic order.

TPair is a record holding a key-value pair. It is defined as follows

```
TPair<TKey,TValue> = Record
                       Key: TKey;
                       Value: TValue;
                       Constructor Create(const AKey: TKey; const AValue: TValue);
                     End;
```

Records with methods, constructors available in Delphi 2010 onwards

TDictionary represents a generic collection of key-value pairs.

It is defined as follows

```
TDictionary<TKey,TValue> = class(TEnumerable<TPair<TKey,TValue>>)
```

This class provides a mapping from a collection of keys to a collection of values.

The **Add** or **AddOrSetValue** methods are used to add a key and its associated.

AddOrSetValue adds a key-value pair to a dictionary even if the key already exists.

Entries may be removed using **Remove** or **Clear** (removes all key-value pairs).

Adding or removing a key-value pair and looking up a key are efficient, close to O(1), because keys are hashed.

A key must not be nil (though a value may be nil) and there must be an equality comparison operation for keys.

TryGetValue, **ContainsKey**, and **ContainsValue** methods are used to test for the presence of keys and values.

The **Items** property is an indexable list of all key-value pairs in the dictionary. Values may be set and retrieved (get) by indexing the **Items** property. Setting the value this way overwrites any existing value.

The **Count** property holds the number of dictionary entries.

Table 35.10 shows access methods for reading a **TDictionary** collection.

Method	Index/input type	Result type	If key not found	Description
ContainsKey	TKey	Boolean	False	True if found
ContainsValue	TValue	Boolean	n/a	True if found
ExtractPair	TKey	TPair	Default pair	Returns TPair, removes item from dictionary
Items	TKey	TValue	Exception	Use TryGetValue to avoid exception
Keys	n/a	TKeyCollection	n/a	e.g. Keys[3]
ToArray	n/a	TArray<TPair<TKey,TValue>>	n/a	
TryGetValue	TKey	TValue, Boolean	default: False	Returns TValue
Values	n/a	TValueCollection	n/a	

Table 35.10 Access methods for reading TDictionary

Tables 35.12 and *35.13* show a program that creates a dictionary `WordCountDictionary` which is used in the program to store the word count for each distinct word obtained from a given text file, e.g. Shakespeare's 116th sonnet, `sonnet116.txt` - *Table 35.11*. The text file is loaded into `StringListFile` using

```
StringListOfFile.LoadFromFile('..\..\' + FileName);
```

and then split into separate words using `Line.Split` as follows on each line of `StringListFile`

```
For Line In StringListOfFile
        Do
          Begin
            WordsInaLine := Line.Split([' ', ',', ';', ':', '!', '.', '(', ')',
                                        '[', ']', '{', '}', '?', '/', '\', '"',
                                          '<', '>', '--', ' ''', ''' ', '- ',
                                          ' -', '`', ''',', '''.', '?''', ''';',
                                          ''':', '''!']);
```

Splitting is done using the specified delimiters, e.g. the space character or a comma immediately followed by the space character. The single apostrophe is escaped by writing two apostrophes within two single apostrophes - ''''.

Where two delimiters are adjacent to each other, for example, a single apostrophe immediately followed by a comma, Line.Split returns the empty string ''. Such a string is excluded from being added to the `WordCountDictionary` by

```
If Not (Word = '')
  Then
    .....
```

Let me not to the marriage of true minds
Admit impediments. Love is not love
Which alters when it alteration finds,
Or bends with the remover to remove:
O, no! it is an ever-fixed mark,
That looks on tempests and is never shaken;
It is the star to every wandering bark,
Whose worth's unknown, although his height be taken.
Love's not Time's fool, though rosy lips and cheeks
Within his bending sickle's compass come;
Love alters not with his brief hours and weeks,
But bears it out even to the edge of doom.
If this be error and upon me prov'd,
I never writ, nor no man ever lov'd.

Table 35.11 Shakespeare's Sonnet 116

As `WordCountDictionary` is a hash table, it is not possible to directly sort this dictionary. Instead each word in `WordCountDictionary` is copied to an emptied `StringListFile` using

```
For Row In WordCountDictionary
  Do StringListOfFile.Add(Row.Key);
```

and sorted in ascending order using `StringListOfFile.Sort`.

www.educational-computing.com/DelphiBook/Code/Chapter35/DictionaryCountWordsProject.zip

```
Program DictionaryCountWordsProject;
{$APPTYPE CONSOLE}
Uses
  System.Generics.Collections, System.Classes, System.SysUtils, System.StrUtils;
Type
  TWordCountDictionary = TDictionary<String, String>;
  TTwoValues = Array[0..1] Of String;
  TWordCountArray = Array Of TTwoValues;
Var
  WordCountDictionary : TWordCountDictionary;
  StringListOfFile : TStringList;
  Line, Word, FileName : String;
  TotalNoOfWords, TotalNoOfDistinctWords, i: Integer;
  WordsInaLine : TArray<String>;
  Row : TPair<String, String>;
  TwoValues : TTwoValues;
  WordCountArray : TWordCountArray;
  f : TextFile;
Begin
  Try
    StringListOfFile := TStringList.Create;
    Try
      Write('Input filename of text file to process(e.g. sonnet116.txt, '
             + 'bible.txt, alice29.txt, plrabn12.txt): ');
      Readln(FileName);
      StringListOfFile.LoadFromFile('..\..\' + FileName);
    Except
      On Exception Do Writeln('File opening error');
    End;
    WordCountDictionary := TWordCountDictionary.Create;
    Writeln('No of lines loaded: ', StringListOfFile.Count);
    Try
      For Line In StringListOfFile
        Do
          Begin
            WordsInaLine := Line.Split([' ', ',', ';', ':', '!', '.', '(', ')',
                                       '[', ']', '{', '}', '?', '/', '\', '"',
                                        '<', '>', '--', ' ''', ''' ', '- ',
                                        ' -', '`', ''',', '''.', '?''', ''';',
                                        ''':', '''!']);

            For Word In WordsInaLine
              Do
                If Not (Word = '')
                  Then
                    If WordCountDictionary.ContainsKey(AnsiUpperCase(Word))
                      Then WordCountDictionary[AnsiUpperCase(Word)] :=
                              IntToStr(StrToInt(WordCountDictionary[AnsiUpperCase(Word)]) + 1)
                      Else WordCountDictionary.Add(AnsiUpperCase(Word), IntToStr(1));
          End;
      TotalNoOfWords := 0;
      TotalNoOfDistinctWords := 0;
      For Row In WordCountDictionary
        Do
          Begin
          //  Writeln(Row.Key, ' ', Row.Value);
            TotalNoOfWords := TotalNoOfWords + StrToInt(Row.Value);
            TotalNoOfDistinctWords := TotalNoOfDistinctWords + 1;
          End;
      Writeln('Total no of words = ', TotalNoOfWords);
      Writeln('Total no of distinct words = ', TotalNoOfDistinctWords);
    Except
      On Exception Do Writeln('Adding to dictionary error');
    End;
    Writeln('Press return to continue'); Readln;
```

The text files used here (except sonnet116.txt) and more may be downloaded from https://corpus.canterbury.ac.nz/descriptions/#cantrbry. Sonnet116.txt and some of the corpus.canterbury text files are also included in the program zip file.

Could use instead WordCountDictionary.Count to get TotalNoOfDistinctWords

Continued in Table 35.13

Table 35.12 Program DictionaryCountWordsProject part 1

Continued from Table 35.12

```
    StringListOfFile.Clear;
    For Row In WordCountDictionary
      Do StringListOfFile.Add(Row.Key);
    StringListOfFile.Sort;
    Try
      SetLength(WordCountArray, TotalNoOfDistinctWords);
    Except
      On Exception Do Writeln('SetLength error');
    End;
    i := -1;
    For Word In StringListOfFile
      Do
        Begin
          i := i +1;
          TwoValues[0] := Word;
          TwoValues[1] := WordCountDictionary[Word];
          WordCountArray[i] := TwoValues;
        End;
    Writeln(Length(WordCountArray));
    Write('Saving dictionary to disk, input filename(e.g. Dict.txt): ');
    Readln(FileName);
    AssignFile(f, FileName);
    Rewrite(f);
    Writeln('---------------Beginning of sorted array-------------');
    For i := 0 To Length(WordCountArray) - 1
      Do
        Begin
          Writeln(i + 1, ': ', WordCountArray[i][0], ' ', WordCountArray[i][1]);
          Writeln(f, WordCountArray[i][0], ',', WordCountArray[i][1]);
        End;
    Close(f);
    Writeln('---------------End of sorted array-------------');
    Writeln('Press return to exit'); Readln;
  Finally
    StringListOfFile.Free;
    WordCountDictionary.Free;
  End;
End.
```

Table 35.13 Program DictionaryCountWordsProject part 2

Each word in `StringListFile` is then accessed in turn and the corresponding value obtained from `WordCountDictionary` and assigned to the second cell of array `TwoValues` as shown in *Table 35.14*.The correspond word is assigned to the first cell.

Once `TwoValues` is populated it is assigned to `WordCountArray` as shown in *Table 35.14*.

Once complete, `WordCountArray` contains the key-value pairs in ascending word order.

Finally `WordCountArray` is written to disk in text file format.

```
Try
  SetLength(WordCountArray, TotalNoOfDistinctWords);
Except
  On Exception Do Writeln('SetLength error');
End;
i := -1;
For Word In StringListOfFile
  Do
    Begin
      i := i +1;
      TwoValues[0] := Word;
      TwoValues[1] := WordCountDictionary[Word];
      WordCountArray[i] := TwoValues;
    End;
```

Table 35.14 Copying key-value pairs to WordCountArray

Programming Task

3. Amend program `DictionaryCountWordsProject` shown in *Table 35.12 and 35.13* to use `WordCountDictionary.Count`. Test your amended program.

It would be more natural to store the word count for each word as an integer and not as a string. This would necessitate that the type definition for the word count dictionary be changed to

```
TWordCountDictionary = TDictionary<String, Integer>;
```

and variable `Row`'s type to `TPair<String, Integer>`.

We can no longer use the type definition `TTwoValues = Array[0..1] Of String` but instead must use a record type as defined as follows

```
TRecTwoValues = Record
    Key : String;
    Value : Integer;
  End;
```

The type `TTwoValues` must now be defined as follows

```
TTwoValues = TRecTwoValues;
```

This demonstrates the power of generics.

Programming Task

4. Amend program `DictionaryCountWordsProject` shown in *Table 35.12 and 35.13* to use the type definition

```
TWordCountDictionary = TDictionary<String, Integer>;
```

Test your amended program.

36 Vectors and matrices

Vector

Purpose: To understand the vector concept and vector operations

A vector has several meanings, depending on whether we are working geometrically or numerically.

Geometric vectors

Geometrically, a vector can represent one of two concepts:

1. A position within a particular space
2. A direction within a particular space

Position vector

A position vector represents a **specific location or point in space** with respect to an origin, 0. For example, in *Figure 36.1* the graph shows three position vectors labelled **r**, **s** and **t** respectively. They represent the position of points A, B and C, respectively.

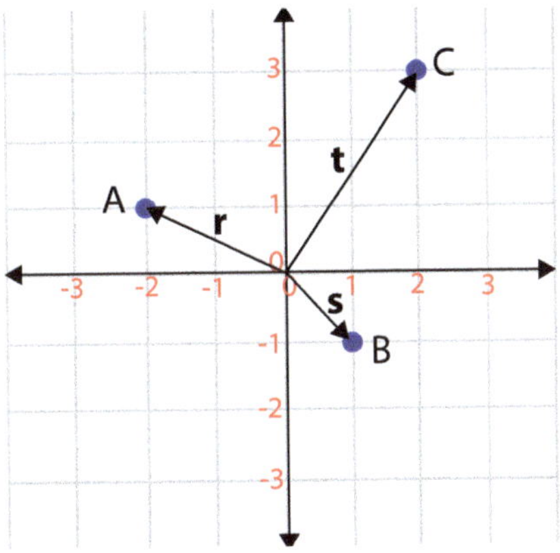

Figure 36.1 Three specific locations in space, A, B and C with position vectors (-2, 1), (1, -1) and (2, 3), respectively.

The position vectors r, s and t are (-2, 1), (1, -1) and (2, 3), respectively.

Direction vector

A vector can also represent a **direction in space**. Direction vectors do not have an origin; they simply specify a direction in space, using a directed line segment from an initial point (the tail) to a terminal or endpoint (the tip). An arrowhead is placed at the tip. Direction vectors are also called **free vectors**.

Three instances of direction vectors, **u**, **v** and **w** are shown in *Figure 36.2* as an arrowed or directed line segment in each case.

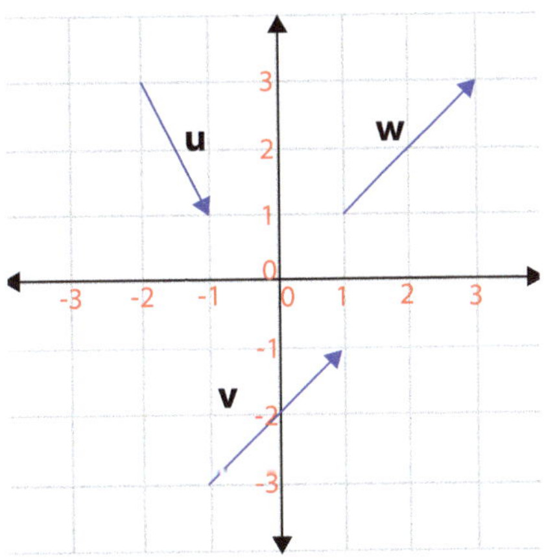

Figure 36.2 Three instances of direction vectors, u, v and w.

Vectors **v** and **w** are the same, even though they are drawn in different locations, because their lengths (magnitude) and directions are identical.

Dimensionality

Vectors have **dimensionality**, i.e. have a number of dimensions.

A two-dimensional vector is restricted to a single plane (e.g. *Figure 36.2*), while a three-dimensional vector can point in any direction in physical space (physical space is three-dimensional) - *Figure 36.3*. Vectors can also have higher dimensions.

Numeric vectors

Vectors can also be described numerically. A vector in this case is a sequence of numbers, one for each dimension. A two-dimensional vector has two numbers; a three-dimensional vector has three, and so on.

Components of a vector

Each of the numbers within a vector is called a **component**. Each component usually has a name.

For example, if the numeric vector describes a geometric vector then

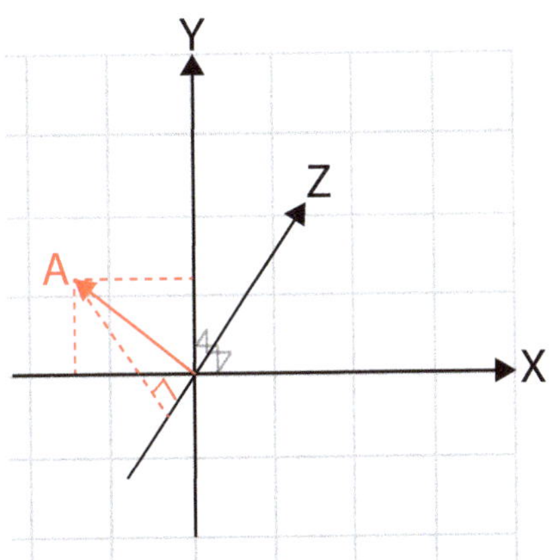

Figure 36.3 Three dimensional vector A

- The first component is usually called the X component
- The second component is usually called the Y component
- The third is called the Z component
- If there is a fourth, it is called the W component.

In *Figure 36.2* vector **u** has its tail at point we will refer to as *s* and its tip at point we will refer to as *t*. If point *s* = (x_1, y_1) and *t* = (x_2, y_2), then the first component of the vector **u** is $x_2 - x_1$, which indicates the horizontal displacement from s to t, and the second component, $y_2 - y_1$ indicates the vertical displacement. Reading from the grid, $x_2 - x_1 = -1 - (-2) = 1$ and y2 - y1 = 1 - 3 = -2. This is interpreted as move to the right one unit from the start point position, then move down two units to arrive at the end point, connect the start point to the end point to obtain the direction vector.

A simple computer game which uses direction vectors could be one that relies on a treasure map containing, say, five direction vectors such as shown in *Figure 36.4*.

To find the treasure chest, the treasure map should be read as follows:

> **Key term**
>
> **Vector:**
> Vectors are ordered sets of numbers which can be used to represent many things. In the context of graphics, they can be used to represent lines having both length and direction:
> 1. The coordinates of a position (position vector) with respect to an orthogonal (at right angles) Cartesian coordinate system;
> 2. The start and end coordinates of a directed line segment representing a direction or free vector specifying a direction in space. Direction / free vectors do not have an origin.

Starting from base camp, carry out this sequence of coded instructions (3, 1), (-2, 1), (5, 2), (-3, 2), (1, 1) which are to be interpreted as follows

Move East 3 units then move North 1 unit
Move West 2 units then North 1 unit
Move East 5 units then North 2 units
Move West 3 units then North 2 units
Finally, move East 1 unit then North 1 unit.

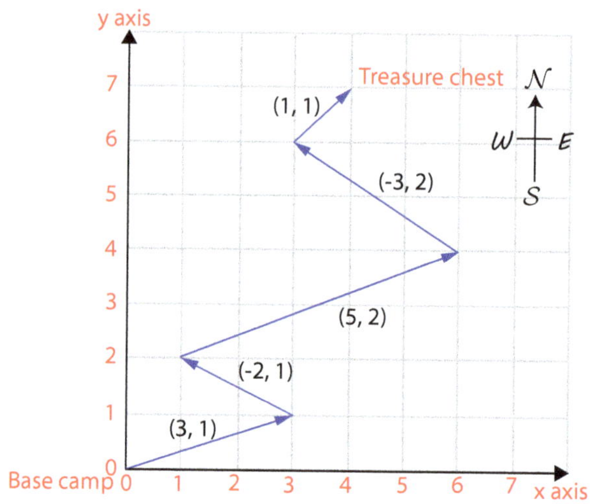

Figure 36.4 Route to treasure chest shown using direction vectors

How are vectors written?

When writing vectors in text, they are written with parentheses as shown in the treasure map example above. For example, a three-dimensional vector, **V**, with X component = 1, Y component = 3, and Z component = 7, would be written as (1, 3, 7). This is called a row vector.

Vector variable **V** can also be written in equation form as a column vector as follows

$$\mathbf{V} = \begin{bmatrix} 1 \\ 3 \\ 7 \end{bmatrix}$$

Vector **u** in *Figure 36.2* is written in text as a row vector $(x_2 - x_1,\ y_2 - y_1)$ and in equation form as a column vector

$$\mathbf{u} = \begin{bmatrix} x_2 - x_1 \\ y_2 - y_1 \end{bmatrix} = \begin{bmatrix} 1 \\ -2 \end{bmatrix}$$

In equation form, vector variables are either in boldface, e.g. **V**, or written with an arrow over them, e.g. $\vec{V}$.

No difference numerically between position vectors and direction vectors

A distinction is made between position vectors and direction vectors when drawing these graphically. However, numerically there is no difference between the two, i.e they are both represented with numbers in the same way.

Vector operations

Vectors may be operated on as a whole by mathematical operations such as vector addition.

Some useful vector operations are

- Vector Addition
- Vector Negation and Subtraction
- Vector Scaling
- Vector Multiplication
- Vector Length
- Vector Normalization
- Resolving a vector

Vector addition

In *Figure 36.4*, there is a more direct route to the treasure chest shown in red by vector (4, 7) in *Figure 36.5*. The vector (4, 7) is actually the resultant vector obtained by adding the five vectors shown in blue in *Figure 36.5*. To add these vectors correctly, all their x components must be added together then all their y components in order to obtain the x and y components of the resultant vector.

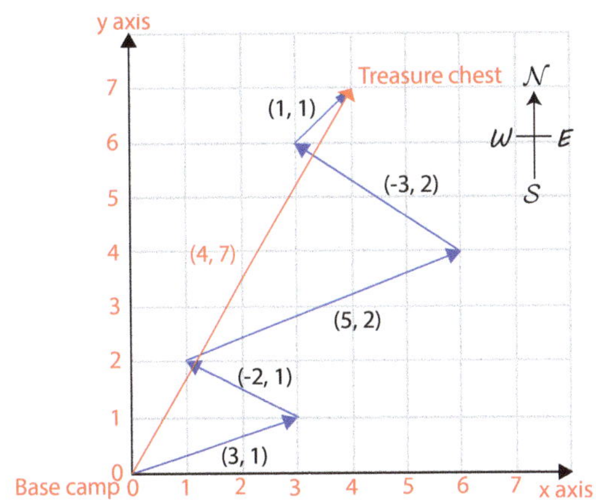

Figure 36.5 Direct route to treasure chest shown using a single vector (4, 7)

Thus the x and y components of the resultant vector are given by

x component = 3 + -2 + 5 + -3 +1 = 4

y component = 1 + 1 + 2 + 2 + 1 = 7

Figure 36.6 shows how two vectors **S** and **T** are added geometrically. Vector **T** has been shifted so that the head of vector **S** joins to the tail of vector **T**. Vector **T** is still the same vector, i.e. vector (2, 2).

The **vector sum** **S** + **T** is simply the direction from the tail of the first vector, **S**, to the head of the last, **T**. This vector is defined by 1 unit across the page and 4 units up the page, i.e. (1, 4).

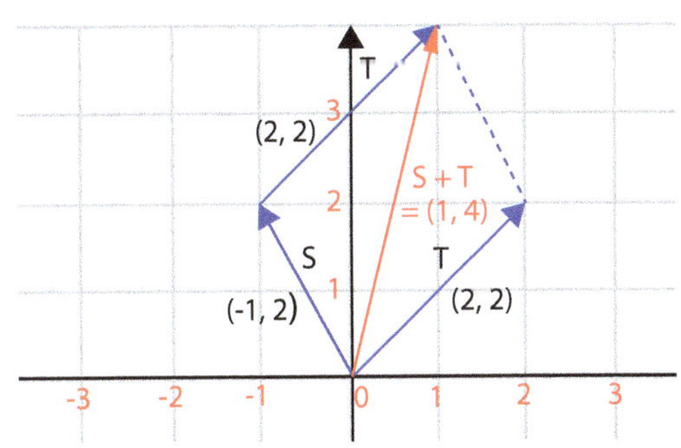

Figure 36.6 Adding two vectors S and T

Note that geometrically the same resultant vector is obtained if we had shifted **S** instead. We say that vector addition is commutative.

Numerically, we add the components of vectors **S** and **T** as follows

$$\mathbf{S} + \mathbf{T} = \begin{bmatrix} S_x \\ S_y \end{bmatrix} + \begin{bmatrix} T_x \\ T_y \end{bmatrix} = \begin{bmatrix} S_x + T_x \\ S_y + T_y \end{bmatrix}$$

Any operation where the operation is performed on each component of a vector is called a component-wise operation. Therefore, vector addition is a component-wise operation.

Any component-wise operation on two vectors requires that the two vectors have the same dimensionality.

Vector Negation and Subtraction

Negating a vector reverses its direction as shown in *Figure 36.7*.

Numerically, this means negating each component of the vector. as shown below

$$-\mathbf{S} = -\begin{bmatrix} S_x \\ S_y \end{bmatrix} = \begin{bmatrix} -S_x \\ -S_y \end{bmatrix}$$

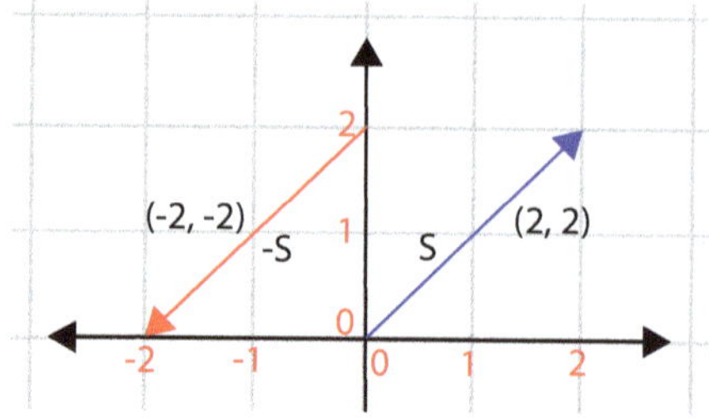

Figure 36.7 Negating a vector S

To **subtract one vector, S, from another, T**, geometrically, we negate the first and then add it to the second as shown in *Figure 36.8*.

Numerically, we subtract the x component of **S** from the x component of **T** and subtract the y component of **S** from the y component of **T** as shown below

$$\mathbf{T - S} = \begin{bmatrix} T_x \\ T_y \end{bmatrix} - \begin{bmatrix} S_x \\ S_y \end{bmatrix} = \begin{bmatrix} T_x - S_x \\ T_y - S_y \end{bmatrix}$$

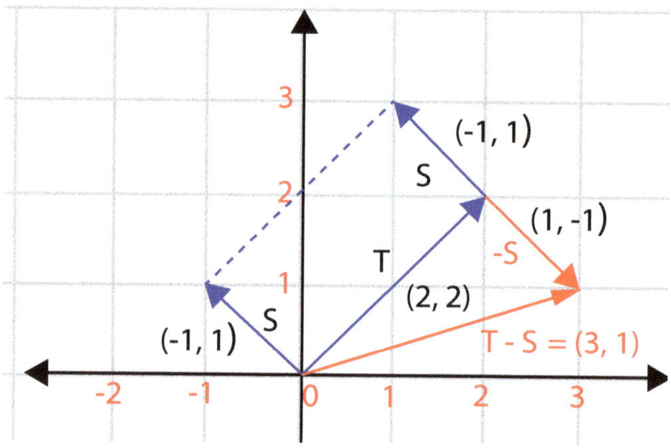

Figure 36.8 Subtraction of one vector S from another T

Vector Scaling

Vectors can be operated on by scalar values. A **scalar** is a single number. For example, the magnitude of a vector is a scalar. A scalar cannot represent a vector because a vector is defined by two quantities: a magnitude and a direction.

However, a vector may be scaled by being multiplied by a scalar. This results in an increase or decrease of the magnitude of the vector, depending on the scalar value. If the scalar is greater than one then the vector's magnitude is increased. If it is less than one then the magnitude is decreased. Geometrically, multiplying by a scalar increases or decreases the length of the vector, depending on the scalar value, but does not alter its direction.

Figure 36.9 shows the effect on the length of a vector **S** when it is scaled by scalars 0.5 and 2, respectively.

Numerically, a component-wise multiplication takes place, where each component of the vector **S** is multiplied by the scalar, *m*, as shown below.

$$m * \mathbf{S} = m * \begin{bmatrix} S_x \\ S_y \end{bmatrix} = \begin{bmatrix} m * S_x \\ m * S_y \end{bmatrix}$$

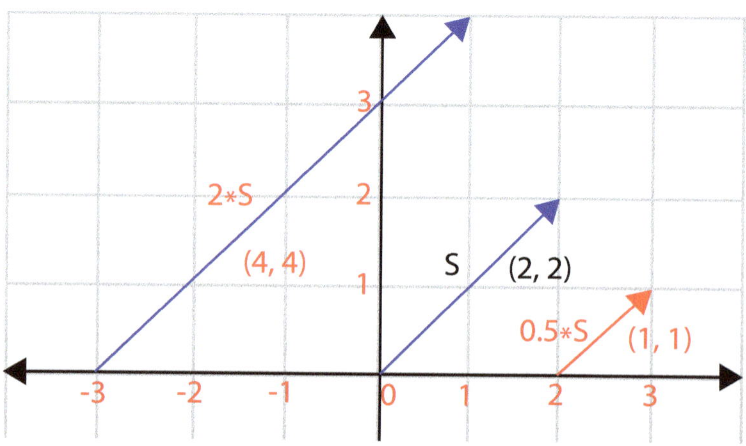

Figure 36.9 Scaling vector S by 0.5 and 2

Cartesian coordinate system

A Cartesian coordinate system is a coordinate system that specifies each point uniquely in a plane by a set of numerical coordinates, which are the signed distances to the point from two fixed perpendicular oriented lines, called axes, measured in the same unit of length, e.g. *Figure 36.9*.

Vector Length

A vector has a length. The length of a vector is the distance from its starting point to its ending point. The length is also known as the **magnitude of a vector**.

Using Pythagoras' theorem the length or magnitude of a vector **S** may be computed as follows:

$$|S| = \sqrt{S_x^{\,2} + S_y^{\,2}}$$

|S| means take the magnitude of **S**.

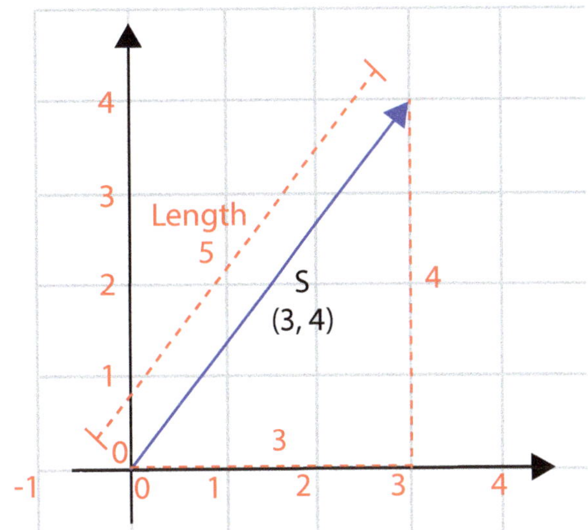

Figure 36.10 Using Pythagoras' theorem to calculate the length or magnitude of a vector S

Vector Normalization

A **normalised vector** is a vector with a magnitude that is always 1.0. A normalised vector is also referred to as a **unit vector**.

To create a normalised vector, each component of the vector is divided by the magnitude of the vector.

The result is a vector pointing in the same direction as the original but with length 1.0.

If the vector to be normalised is **V**, and the normalised result is **N** then

$$\mathbf{N} = \frac{1}{|\mathbf{V}|} * \mathbf{V} = \begin{bmatrix} \dfrac{V_x}{\sqrt{V_x^{\,2} + V_y^{\,2}}} \\ \dfrac{V_y}{\sqrt{V_x^{\,2} + V_y^{\,2}}} \end{bmatrix}$$

Unit vectors *i* and *j*

A vector **r** multiplied by a scalar *n* is equal to *n***r**. Its direction is unchanged and its magnitude is *n* times the original magnitude. The unit vectors **i** and **j** can be used to define the orientation of a vector quantity where **i** points in the X-axis direction and **j** in the Y-axis direction. A vector **r** expressed in terms of its component in X-axis direction, r_x, and its component in the Y-axis direction, r_y, becomes

$$\mathbf{r} = r_x\mathbf{i} + r_y\mathbf{j}$$

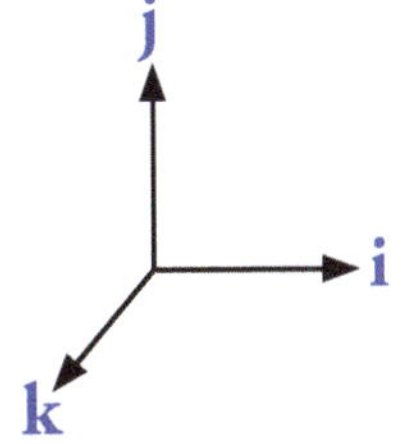

In three dimensions it becomes

$$\mathbf{r} = r_x\mathbf{i} + r_y\mathbf{j} + r_z\mathbf{k}$$

where the component of vector **r** in the Z-axis direction is r_z, and **k** is the unit vector that points in the Z-axis direction. We say that the vector **r** has been resolved into its two or three components, r_x and r_y, or r_x, r_y and r_z.

Practical application of position and direction vectors

In geometry, a position vector (also known as a location vector or radius vector) represents the position of a point P in space in relation to an arbitrary reference origin O. The symbols **r** or **s** are often used to denote a position vector.

The position vector **r** shown in *Figure 36.11* represents the position, at some time *t*, of a particle of mass *m* moving with velocity **v**. At time *t*, the particle is at position P.

Note that the position vector **r**, as with all position vectors, is tied to some origin O, whilst its other end is tied to the body of the particle.

The direction vector **v** possesses both magnitude and direction.

The magnitude |**v**| represents the speed with which the particle is moving at time *t*, and the direction of movement at this time is represented by the vector's pointing direction.

At some later time t_1 the particle will be located at a different position.

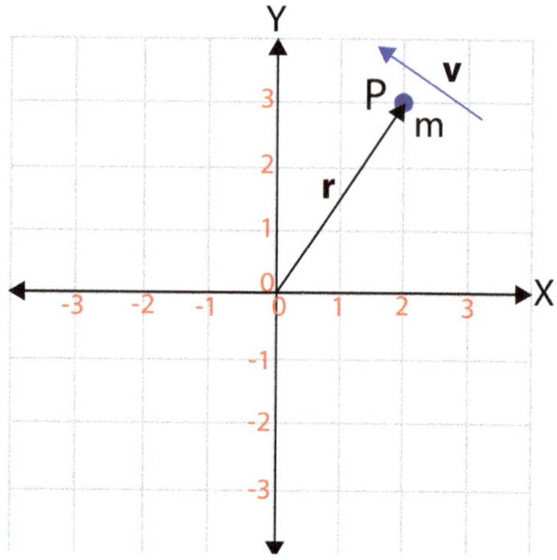

Figure 36.11 Particle of mass m at position P at time t moving with velocity v

We can calculate the new position P_1 at time t_1 by adding the amount of movement in the X direction to the particle's X-coordinate at time *t*, and the amount of movement in the Y direction to the particle's Y-coordinate at time *t* as follows

$$X_{NEW} = X_{OLD} + X_{MOVEMENT}$$

$$Y_{NEW} = Y_{OLD} + Y_{MOVEMENT}$$

X_{NEW} is the new X-coordinate and Y_{NEW} is the new Y-coordinate.

Effectively, the end point of position vector **r** has been moved. This movement is called **translation**.

Figure 36.12 shows the new position vector $\mathbf{r}_{new}$ at time t_1. The velocity has remained unchanged.

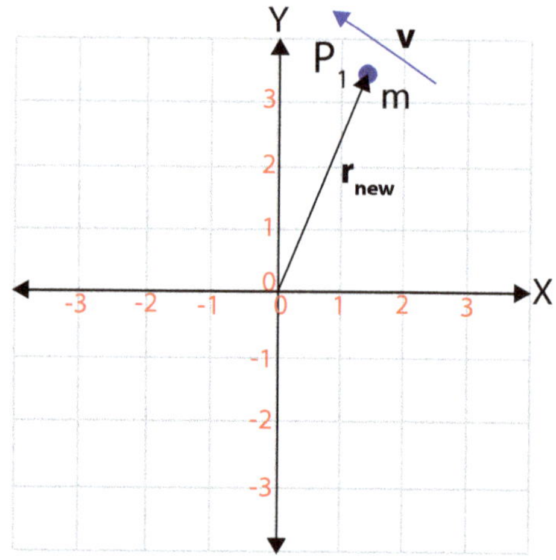

Figure 36.12 Particle of mass m at position P_1 at time t_1 moving with velocity v

The concept of translation does not make sense for a direction or free vector (see *Figure 36.2*). Vector **v** can be moved upwards or downwards, forwards or backwards, and, if its length and direction remain unchanged, it is still vector **v**.

The difference between a position vector and a direction vector is that the former is anchored at one end to an origin whilst the latter does not have to be. This difference has consequences for the way that vector transformations are represented by matrices. Matrices and their role in transforming vectors is the subject of the next few sections.

Matrices

Purpose: To understand the concept of a matrix(plural matrices) and matrix operations

A matrix (plural matrices) is an array of numbers. It can be one-dimensional, two-dimensional, or many dimensional - and in this repect is similar to arrays used in a programming language.

Figure 36.13 shows an example of a two-dimensional matrix, **M**.

It consists of two rows and two columns.

$$M = \begin{bmatrix} 2 & 3 \\ 3 & 4 \end{bmatrix}$$

Figure 36.13 Two-dimensional matrix M

What might this matrix **M** represent?

Consider the following two simultaneous equations in x and y:

$$2x + 3y = 11 \quad \text{——①}$$
$$3x + 4y = 15 \quad \text{——②}$$

To solve for x, we can multiply the first equation ① by 4 and the second equation ② by 3 to create ③ and ④ then subtract the second ④ from the first ③:

4 x ① ⇒ $8x + 12y = 44$ ——③

3 x ② ⇒ $9x + 12y = 45$ ——④

③ - ④ ⇒ $-x = -1 \Rightarrow x = 1$

To solve for y, we can multiply the first equation ① by 3 and the second equation ② by 2 to create ⑤ and ⑥ then subtract the second ⑥ from the first ⑤:

3 x ① ⇒ $6x + 9y = 33$ ——⑤

2 x ② ⇒ $6x + 8y = 30$ ——⑥

⑤ - ⑥ ⇒ $y = 3$

Representing two simultaneous equations by matrices

We start by representing equations ① and ② as shown in *Figure 36.14* where * is the symbol used for multiplication.

$$\begin{bmatrix} 2 & 3 \\ 3 & 4 \end{bmatrix} * \begin{bmatrix} x \\ y \end{bmatrix} = \begin{bmatrix} 11 \\ 15 \end{bmatrix}$$

Figure 36.14 Two simultaneous equations represented by three matrices

Figure 36.14 contains three matrices:

- A 2 x 2 matrix **M** $\begin{bmatrix} 2 & 3 \\ 3 & 4 \end{bmatrix}$
- A 2 x 1 column matrix **V** $\begin{bmatrix} x \\ y \end{bmatrix}$
- A 2 x 1 column matrix **C** $\begin{bmatrix} 11 \\ 15 \end{bmatrix}$

2 x 2 means 2 rows by 2 columns

2 x 1 means 2 rows by 1 column

The column matrices **V** and **C** are identical in representation to a column vector which we introduced earlier in the chapter. Column matrices are often referred to as column vectors.

To reassemble simultaneous equations ① and ② from the three matrices, we multiply the column matrix **V** by the first row of **M**, then by the second row of **M**, to obtain a new column matrix as shown in *Figure 36.15*.
The corresponding components in **M** and **V** were multipled as shown in *Figure 36.15* then added,
e.g. first row and first column: 2 and x, 3 and y ⇒ 2x + 3y.
From this new column matrix, it is possible to reassemble the original simultaneous equations as shown.

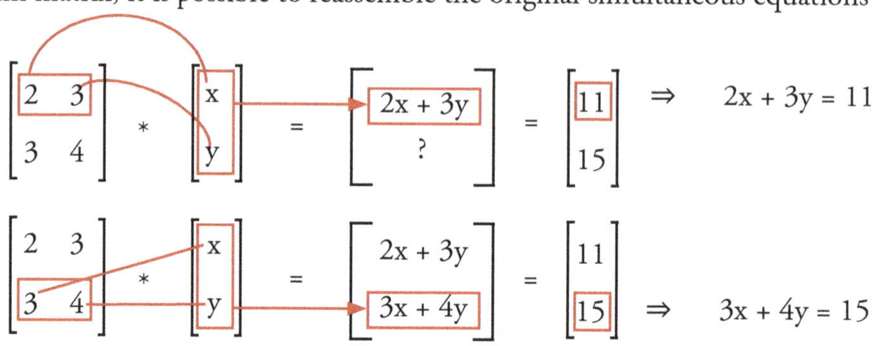

Figure 36.15 Matrix multiplication: 2 x 1 column matrix multiplied by a 2 x 2 matrix to produce a 2 x 1 column matrix

Generalising,

Consider the following two simultaneous equations in x and y:

$$ax + cy = s \quad \text{——①}$$

$$bx + dy = t \quad \text{——②}$$

where a = 2, b = 3, c = 3, d = 4, s = 11, and t = 15.

To solve for *x*, we can multiply the first equation① by *d* and the second equation ② by *c* to create ③ and ④ then subtract the second ④ from the first ③:

d x ① ⇒ $adx + cdy = ds$ ——③

c x ② ⇒ $bcx + cdy = ct$ ——④

③ - ④ ⇒ $(ad - bc)x = ds - ct \Rightarrow x = \dfrac{ds - ct}{ad - bc}$

To solve for *y*, we can multiply the first equation ① by *b* and the second equation ② by *a* to create ⑤ and ⑥ then subtract the second ⑥ from the first ⑤:

b x ① ⇒ $abx + bcy = bs$ ——⑤

a x ② ⇒ $abx + ady = at$ ——⑥

Multiply top and bottom by -1

⑤ - ⑥ ⇒ $(bc - ad)y = bs - at \Rightarrow y = \dfrac{bs - at}{bc - ad} \Rightarrow y = \dfrac{at - bs}{ad - bc}$

The two simultaneous equations ① and ② may be represented in matrix form as shown in *Figure 36.16*.

$$\begin{bmatrix} a & c \\ b & d \end{bmatrix} * \begin{bmatrix} x \\ y \end{bmatrix} = \begin{bmatrix} s \\ t \end{bmatrix}$$

Figure 36.16 Two simultaneous equations represented by three matrices

or $\quad \mathbf{M} * \mathbf{V} = \mathbf{C}$ where $\mathbf{M} = \begin{bmatrix} a & c \\ b & d \end{bmatrix}$ $\quad \mathbf{V} = \begin{bmatrix} x \\ y \end{bmatrix}$ and $\quad \mathbf{C} = \begin{bmatrix} s \\ t \end{bmatrix}$

Solving the two simultaneous equations using determinants

A square array of numbers or variables enclosed between vertical lines is called a **determinant**. A determinant is different from a matrix in that a determinant has a numerical value, whereas a matrix does not. The determinant **D** shown in *Figure 36.17* has two rows and two columns and is evaluated as shown.

$$\mathbf{D} = \begin{vmatrix} a & c \\ b & d \end{vmatrix} = ad - bc$$

Figure 36.17 Determinant evaluation

If matrix **M** = $\begin{bmatrix} a & c \\ b & d \end{bmatrix}$

Then, determinant **M** = determinant $\begin{bmatrix} a & c \\ b & d \end{bmatrix} = \begin{vmatrix} a & c \\ b & d \end{vmatrix} = ad - bc$

But the solutions to simultaneous equations (1) and (2) were expressed as follows

$$x = \frac{ds - ct}{ad - bc} \qquad \text{and} \qquad y = \frac{at - bs}{ad - bc}$$

which is $x = \dfrac{ds - ct}{\det \mathbf{M}}$ $\qquad y = \dfrac{at - bs}{\det \mathbf{M}}$

where det **M** is determinant **M**.

ds - ct and at - bs also look like determinants.

Let det **X** = ds - ct and det **Y** = at - bs then **X** = $\begin{bmatrix} s & c \\ t & d \end{bmatrix}$ and **Y** = $\begin{bmatrix} a & s \\ b & t \end{bmatrix}$

Thus, to solve for *x*, replace the first column of matrix **M** by matrix **C**, then $x = \dfrac{\det \mathbf{X}}{\det \mathbf{M}}$ where **C** = $\begin{bmatrix} s \\ t \end{bmatrix}$

To solve for *y*, replace the second column of **M** by matrix **C**, then $y = \dfrac{\det \mathbf{Y}}{\det \mathbf{M}}$ where **C** = $\begin{bmatrix} s \\ t \end{bmatrix}$

Table 36.1 shows a program that uses matrices and determinants to solve two simultaneous equations in x and y.

Questions

1. What are the dimensions of the following matrices?

   (a) $\begin{bmatrix} 3 & 2 \\ 4 & 5 \end{bmatrix}$ (b) $\begin{bmatrix} 3 \\ 2 \end{bmatrix}$ (c) $\begin{bmatrix} 3 & 2 \end{bmatrix}$ (d) $\begin{bmatrix} 3 & 2 & 6 \\ 4 & 5 & 8 \end{bmatrix}$ (e) $\begin{bmatrix} 3 & 2 \\ 6 & 4 \\ 4 & 5 \end{bmatrix}$

2. Evaluate the following

   (a) $\begin{bmatrix} 3 & 2 \\ 4 & 5 \end{bmatrix} * \begin{bmatrix} 3 \\ 2 \end{bmatrix}$ (b) $\begin{bmatrix} 3 & 2 & 6 \\ 4 & 5 & 8 \\ 2 & 3 & 4 \end{bmatrix} * \begin{bmatrix} 3 \\ 6 \\ 4 \end{bmatrix}$ (c) $\begin{bmatrix} 3 & 2 & 6 \\ 4 & 5 & 8 \\ 2 & 3 & 4 \end{bmatrix} * \begin{bmatrix} 2 & 4 \\ 5 & 1 \\ 4 & 3 \end{bmatrix}$ (d) det $\begin{bmatrix} 3 & 2 \\ 4 & 5 \end{bmatrix}$

Tasks

1. Use the program in *Table 36.1* to solve the following simultaneous equations for x and y. Check your solutions.

(a) $4x + y = 7$, $x + 2y = 9$ (b) $8x + 2y = 46$, $7x + 3y = 47$ (c) $2x + 3y = 31$, $4x + 2y = 34$

Download **SolvingSimultaneousEquations** from www.educational-computing.co.uk/DelphiBookCode/DelphiCode.html

```
Program SolvingSimultaneousEquations;

{$APPTYPE CONSOLE}
Uses
  System.SysUtils;
Type
  TMatrix = Array[0..1] Of Array[0..1] Of Real;
  TVector = Array[0..1] Of Real;

Var
  Matrix : TMatrix;
  VariablesVector, ConstantsVector : TVector;
  Ch : Char;

Function Determinant(Matrix : TMatrix) : Real;
  Begin
    Result := Matrix[0, 0] * Matrix[1, 1] - Matrix[1, 0] * Matrix[0,1];
  End;

Procedure Solve (Matrix : TMatrix; ConstantsVector : TVector;
                 Var VariablesVector : TVector);
  Var
    k : Integer;
    DeterminantM, DeterminantX, DeterminantY : Real;
    DeterminantXMatrix, DeterminantYMatrix : TMatrix;
  Begin
    DeterminantM := Determinant(Matrix);
    DeterminantXMatrix[0, 0] := ConstantsVector[0];
    DeterminantXMatrix[0, 1] := ConstantsVector[1];
    DeterminantXMatrix[1, 0] := Matrix[0,1];
    DeterminantXMatrix[1, 1] := Matrix[1, 1];
    DeterminantYMatrix[0, 0] := Matrix[0, 0];
    DeterminantYMatrix[0, 1] := Matrix[1, 0];
    DeterminantYMatrix[1, 0] := ConstantsVector[0];
    DeterminantYMatrix[1, 1] := ConstantsVector[1];
    DeterminantX := Determinant(DeterminantXMatrix);
    DeterminantY := Determinant(DeterminantYMatrix);
    VariablesVector[0] := DeterminantX/DeterminantM;
    VariablesVector[1] := DeterminantY/DeterminantM;
  End;
Begin
  Repeat
    Repeat
      Write('Matrix[0, 0]: '); Readln(Matrix[0, 0]); // := 2;
      Write('Matrix[0, 1]: '); Readln(Matrix[0, 1]); // := 3;
      Write('Matrix[1, 0]: '); Readln(Matrix[1, 0]); // := 3;
      Write('Matrix[1, 1]: '); Readln(Matrix[1, 1]); // := 4;
      Writeln('Matrix row 0: ', Matrix[0,0] :2:1, ' ', Matrix[0,1] :2:1);
      Writeln('Matrix row 1: ',Matrix[1,0 ] :2:1, ' ', Matrix[1,1] :2:1);
      Write('Correct Y/N? '); Readln(Ch);
    Until Ch In ['y', 'Y'];
    VariablesVector[0] := 0;
    VariablesVector[1] := 0;
    Repeat
      Write('Constants Vector[0]: '); Readln(ConstantsVector[0]); // := 11;
      Write('Constants Vector[1]: '); Readln(ConstantsVector[1]); // := 15;
      Write('Correct Y/N? '); Readln(Ch);
    Until Ch In ['y', 'Y'];
    Solve(Matrix, ConstantsVector, VariablesVector);
    Writeln('x = ', VariablesVector[0] :16:14);
    Writeln('y = ', VariablesVector[1] :16:14);
    Write('Another go Y/N? '); Readln(Ch);
  Until Ch In ['n', 'N'];
End.
```

Table 36.1 Program that uses matrices and determinants to solve two simultaneous equations for x and y

Multiplying a 2 x 2 matrix by a 1 x 2 row matrix

In the previous section, we explored how to multiply a 2 x 1 column matrix by a 2 x 2 matrix.

Figure 36.18 shows how to multiply a 2 x 2 matrix by a 1 x 2 row matrix.

Multiply the corresponding components then add, e.g. first row and first column: 2 and x, 3 and y ⇒ 2x + 3y.

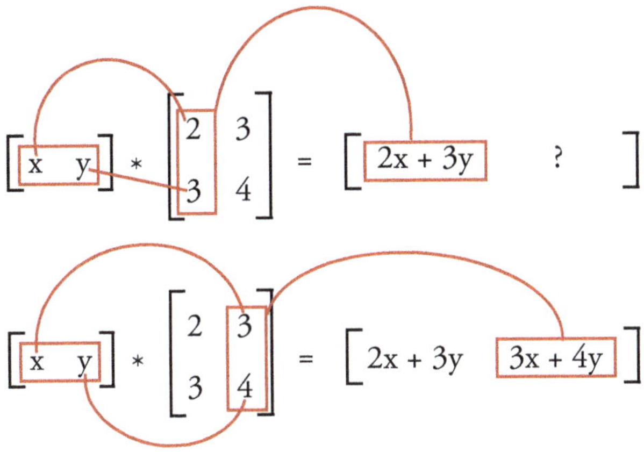

Figure 36.18 Matrix multiplication: multiplying a 2 x 2 matrix by a 1 x 2 row matrix to produce a 1 x 2 matrix

Questions

3 Evaluate the following

(a) $\begin{bmatrix} 3 & 2 \end{bmatrix} * \begin{bmatrix} 3 & 2 \\ 4 & 5 \end{bmatrix}$ (b) $\begin{bmatrix} 3 & 2 & 6 \\ 4 & 5 & 8 \end{bmatrix} * \begin{bmatrix} 3 & 2 \\ 6 & 4 \\ 4 & 5 \end{bmatrix}$ (c) $\begin{bmatrix} 3 & 2 & 6 \\ 4 & 5 & 8 \end{bmatrix} * \begin{bmatrix} 3 & 2 & -1 \\ 6 & 4 & 2 \\ 4 & 5 & 3 \end{bmatrix}$

4 Evaluate the following

(a) $\begin{bmatrix} 3 & 2 \\ 4 & 3 \end{bmatrix} * \begin{bmatrix} 3 & -2 \\ -4 & 3 \end{bmatrix}$ (b) $\begin{bmatrix} 3 & 2 & -1 \\ 6 & 4 & 2 \\ 4 & 5 & 3 \end{bmatrix} * \begin{bmatrix} 1 & 0 & 0 \\ 0 & 1 & 0 \\ 0 & 0 & 1 \end{bmatrix}$ (c) $\begin{bmatrix} 1 & 0 & 0 \\ 0 & 1 & 0 \\ 0 & 0 & 1 \end{bmatrix} * \begin{bmatrix} 3 & 2 & -1 \\ 6 & 4 & 2 \\ 4 & 5 & 3 \end{bmatrix}$

5 Evaluate the following

(a) $\begin{bmatrix} 3 & 2 & -1 \\ 6 & 4 & 2 \\ 4 & 5 & 3 \end{bmatrix} * \begin{bmatrix} 2 & 4 & 6 \\ 3 & 3 & 5 \\ 1 & 4 & 2 \end{bmatrix}$ (b) $\begin{bmatrix} 2 & 4 & 6 \\ 3 & 3 & 5 \\ 1 & 4 & 2 \end{bmatrix} * \begin{bmatrix} 3 & 2 & -1 \\ 6 & 4 & 2 \\ 4 & 5 & 3 \end{bmatrix}$

6 In which of the following can we form the products A*B and/or B*A

(a) $A = \begin{bmatrix} 6 & 3 \\ 5 & 2 \end{bmatrix}$ $B = \begin{bmatrix} 2 & 4 \\ 1 & 7 \end{bmatrix}$ (b) $A = \begin{bmatrix} 3 & 2 \\ 6 & 4 \\ 4 & 5 \end{bmatrix}$ $B = \begin{bmatrix} 3 & 2 & 6 \\ 4 & 5 & 8 \end{bmatrix}$

(c) $A = \begin{bmatrix} 6 & 3 \\ 5 & 2 \end{bmatrix}$ $B = \begin{bmatrix} 3 & 2 \\ 6 & 4 \\ 4 & 5 \end{bmatrix}$

Transformations

It is possible to perform transformations on a point in space using matrix multiplication because

- a point in space may be represented by a row matrix V, e.g. $\begin{bmatrix} 2 & 3 \end{bmatrix}$ or a column matrix $\begin{bmatrix} 2 \\ 3 \end{bmatrix}$ and,
- it is possible to multiply one matrix with another,

Scaling

Earlier in the chapter, we showed how to scale the *x* and *y* coordinates of a point by multiplying each of its *x* and *y* coordinates by an appropriate scaling factor, X_{SC}, for the *x* coordinate and Y_{SC} for the *y* coordinate as follows

$$X_{NEW} = X_{OLD} * X_{SC}$$

$$Y_{NEW} = Y_{OLD} * Y_{SC}$$

In matrix notation, scaling is achieved as shown in *Figures 36.19* and *36.20*.

Row matrix → $\begin{bmatrix} X_{NEW} & Y_{NEW} \end{bmatrix} = \begin{bmatrix} X_{OLD} & Y_{OLD} \end{bmatrix} * \begin{bmatrix} X_{SC} & 0 \\ 0 & Y_{SC} \end{bmatrix}$ ← Transformation matrix

Figure 36.19 Matrix multiplication: multiplying a 2 x 2 matrix by a 1 x 2 row matrix to produce a scaling

$\begin{bmatrix} X_{NEW} \\ Y_{NEW} \end{bmatrix} = \begin{bmatrix} X_{SC} & 0 \\ 0 & Y_{SC} \end{bmatrix} * \begin{bmatrix} X_{OLD} \\ Y_{OLD} \end{bmatrix}$ ← Column matrix

Figure 36.20 Matrix multiplication: multiplying a 2 x 1 column matrix by a 2 x 2 matrix to produce a scaling

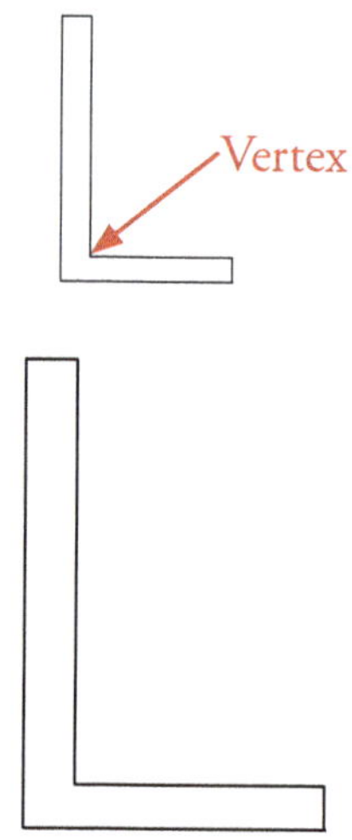

Figure 36.21 Scaling an object - a letter L - by scaling its vertices

Multiplying the transformation matrix and the column matrix from the righthand side of *Figure 36.20*, we obtain the result shown in *Figure 36.22*.

$$\begin{bmatrix} X_{NEW} \\ Y_{NEW} \end{bmatrix} = \begin{bmatrix} X_{SC} * X_{OLD} \\ Y_{SC} * Y_{OLD} \end{bmatrix}$$

Figure 36.22 Result of multiplying the column matrix by the transformation matrix

To scale an object constructed of lines as shown in *Figure 36.21*, we just need to apply an appropriate scaling transformation matrix to each row/column matrix representing a point where two lines meet, i.e. a vertex.

Questions

7 By what factor are the x, y coordinates of position vector $\begin{bmatrix} 2 \\ 3 \end{bmatrix}$ changed by the scaling matrix $\begin{bmatrix} 6 & 0 \\ 0 & 6 \end{bmatrix}$?

8 Write down the 2 x 2 matrix that causes a stretching by 3 in the X-axis direction, and a shrinking by 0.5 in the Y-axis direction.

9 The scaling matrix $\begin{bmatrix} -1 & 0 \\ 0 & 1 \end{bmatrix}$ when applied to the vector $\mathbf{r} = \begin{bmatrix} 2 \\ 3 \end{bmatrix}$ representing point P reflects **r** in the Y-axis. Draw the reflected vector on a copy of the given diagram.

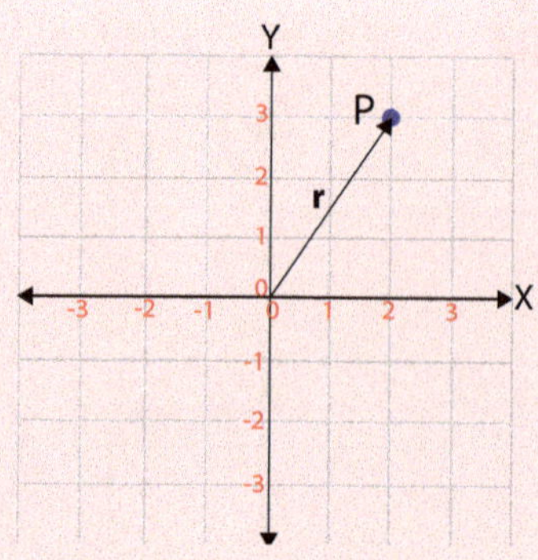

10 Write down the scaling vector that will reflect vector r in the X-axis.

Two-dimensional rotation

If a point (Xold, Yold) in a polygon is rotated about the origin (0, 0) through an angle ε as shown in *Figure 36.23*, the new position (Xnew, Ynew) is given by

Xnew = R * Cos(θ + ε)

Ynew = R * Sin(θ + ε)

But, using trigonometirc identities

Cos(θ + ε) = Cos θ * Cos ε - Sin θ * Sin ε

and

Sin(θ + ε) = Sin θ * Cos ε + Cos θ * Sin ε

Therefore,

Xnew = R * (Cos θ * Cos ε - Sin θ * Sin ε)

Xnew = R * Cos θ * Cos ε - R * Sin θ * Sin ε

Ynew = R * (Sin θ * Cos ε + Cos θ * Sin ε)

Ynew = R * Sin θ * Cos ε + R * Cos θ * Sin ε

Using Xold = R * Cos θ and Yold= R * Sin θ

Therefore

Xnew = Xold * Cos ε - Yold * Sin ε ——(1)

Ynew = Yold * Cos ε + Xold * Sin ε

Rearranging the right hand side

Ynew = Xold * Sin ε + Yold * Cos ε ——(2)

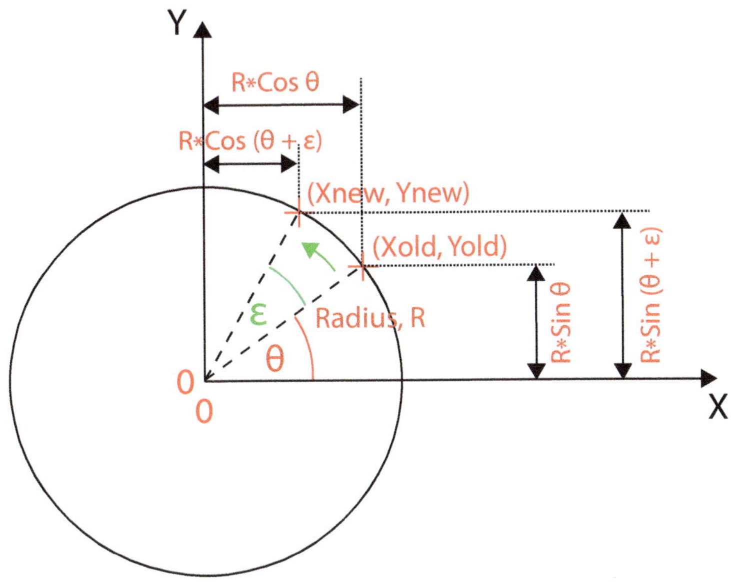

Figure 36.23 Rotating a point through angle ε from (Xold, Yold) to (Xnew, Ynew)

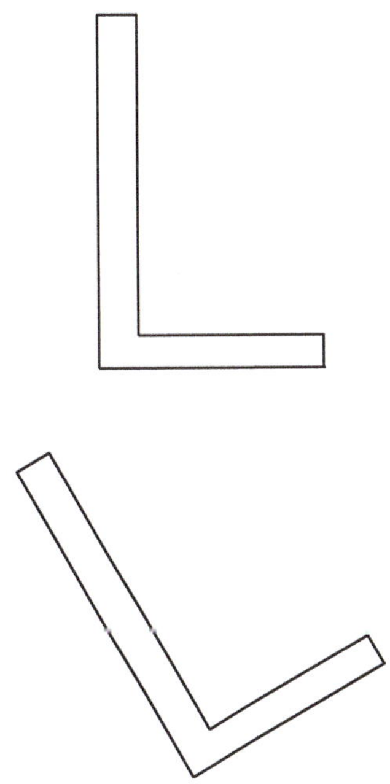

Figure 36.24 Rotating a letter L through 30° counter clockwise

We can write equations (1) and (2) in matrix form for a row matrix as follows

$$[Xnew, Ynew] = [Xold, Yold] * \begin{bmatrix} \text{Cos } \varepsilon & \text{Sin } \varepsilon \\ \text{-Sin } \varepsilon & \text{Cos } \varepsilon \end{bmatrix}$$

and for a column matrix as follows

$$\begin{bmatrix} Xnew \\ Ynew \end{bmatrix} = \begin{bmatrix} \text{Cos } \varepsilon & \text{-Sin } \varepsilon \\ \text{Sin } \varepsilon & \text{Cos } \varepsilon \end{bmatrix} * \begin{bmatrix} Xold \\ Yold \end{bmatrix}$$

Now that we have a transformation matrix for rotating a single point about the origin by an angle ε in the two-dimensional X-Y plane, we can apply this to every point of a two-dimensional object such as the letter L shown in *Figure 36.24*.

Questions

11 The position vector $\begin{bmatrix} 2 \\ 3 \end{bmatrix}$ is rotated through an angle of 30° anticlockwise about the origin.

(a) What is the transformation matrix?

(b) What is the resulting position vector?

12 (a) Using a copy of the given grid, sketch the triangle whose vertices have coordinates (0, 0), (1, 2) and (1, 0).

The triangle is rotated through an angle of 60° anticlockwise about the origin.

(b) What is the transformation matrix?

(c) Calculate the coordinates of the vertices of the transformed triangle.

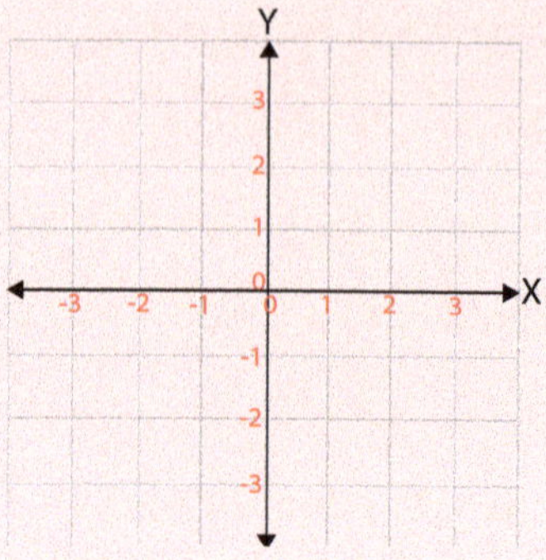

Shear

The shearing transformation has the effect of translating(moving) differents parts of the object by different amounts so that distortion results as shown in *Figures 36.26* and *36.27*.

Shear in the X-direction is given by

Xnew = Xold + Yold * Xsh

Ynew = Yold

Shear in the Y-direction is given by

Xnew = Xold

Ynew = Yold + Xold * Ysh

The matrix equivalents of these formula are shown in *Figure 36.25*.

$$\begin{bmatrix} \text{Xnew, Ynew} \end{bmatrix} = \begin{bmatrix} \text{Xold, Yold} \end{bmatrix} * \begin{bmatrix} 1 & 0 \\ \text{Xsh} & 1 \end{bmatrix}$$

$$\begin{bmatrix} \text{Xnew, Ynew} \end{bmatrix} = \begin{bmatrix} \text{Xold, Yold} \end{bmatrix} * \begin{bmatrix} 1 & \text{Ysh} \\ 0 & 1 \end{bmatrix}$$

$$\begin{bmatrix} \text{Xnew} \\ \text{Ynew} \end{bmatrix} = \begin{bmatrix} 1 & \text{Xsh} \\ 0 & 1 \end{bmatrix} * \begin{bmatrix} \text{Xold} \\ \text{Yold} \end{bmatrix}$$

$$\begin{bmatrix} \text{Xnew} \\ \text{Ynew} \end{bmatrix} = \begin{bmatrix} 1 & 0 \\ \text{Ysh} & 1 \end{bmatrix} * \begin{bmatrix} \text{Xold} \\ \text{Yold} \end{bmatrix}$$

Figure 36.25 Matrix equivalents of the shear formula

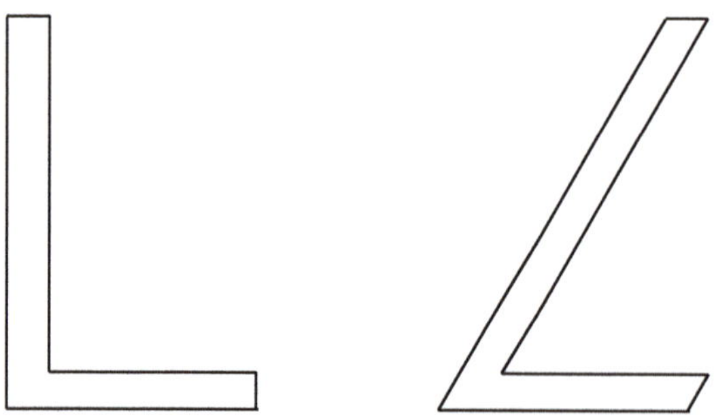

Figure 36.26 Horizontal shear

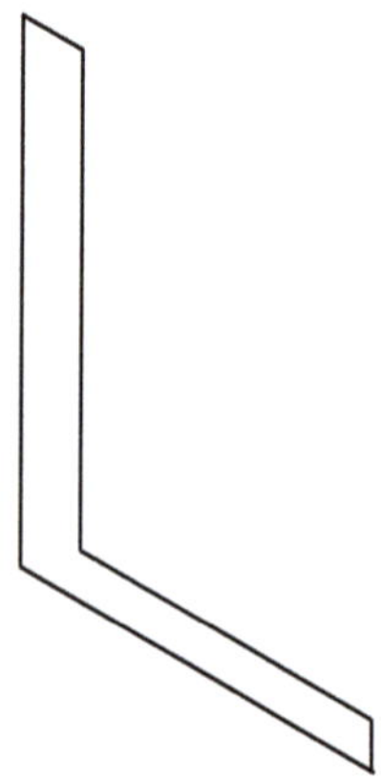

Figure 36.27 Vertical shear

Homogeneous coordinates

Purpose: To understand the role of homogeneous coordinates

In the previous section, matrix methods were given for dealing with all the transformations except translations. There is a reason for this: matrix multiplication cannot deal with translation in the normal coordinate system.

Enter homogeneous coordinates which provide a coordinate system in which matrix multiplication is supported for all the transformations, i.e. translation, scaling and rotation.

Homogeneous coordinates are of a dimension one higher than that of the space they are applied to.

For two dimensional space, homogeneous coordinates take the form (Wx, Wy, W). Therefore, a 3 x 3 transformation matrix is required for translation, scaling and rotation.

For three dimensional space, homogeneous coordinates take the form (Wx, Wy, Wz, W). Therefore, a 4 x 4 transformation matrix is required for translation, scaling and rotation.

After a transformation has been applied to a row or column matrix, the latter are converted back to Cartesian coordinates by first dividing the homogeneous coordinates by the W-coordinate and then omitting the latter.

Any value other than 0 may be used for W, but usually 1 is chosen.

Consider the point (3, 5) in two-dimensional space that uses the Cartesian coordinate system.

In the homogeneous coordinate system, the point is represented by (3, 5, 1) where Wx = 3, Wy = 5 and W = 1.

Figure 36.28 shows a mapping of the Cartesian coordinates of a point in 2-D space to homogeneous coordinates and vice versa.

Cartesian to homogeneous
(3, 5) ⟶ (3, 5, 1)

Homogeneous to Cartesian
(6, 2, 2) ⟶ (3, 1)

Figure 36.28 Mapping from Cartesian coordinates to homogeneous coordinates and vice versa

Translation

The following transformation matrix **M** is used to translate a point (Xold, Yold) by the amounts Xmv and Ymv:

$$\mathbf{M} = \begin{bmatrix} 1 & 0 & Xmv \\ 0 & 1 & Ymv \\ 0 & 0 & 1 \end{bmatrix}$$

The transformation of point P, column matrix $\mathbf{v}_P$, to point T, column matrix $\mathbf{v}_T$, is obtained by performing the matrix-vector multiplication $\mathbf{M}*\mathbf{v}_p$

$$\mathbf{v}_T = \mathbf{M}*\mathbf{v}_p$$

Can also be written as $\mathbf{v}_T = \mathbf{M}.\mathbf{v}_p$ where . means multiply.

where we refer to each column matrix as a vector $\mathbf{v}_T = \begin{bmatrix} Xnew \\ Ynew \\ W \end{bmatrix}$ $\mathbf{v}_p = \begin{bmatrix} Xold \\ Yold \\ 1 \end{bmatrix}$

Expanding, this becomes

$$\begin{bmatrix} Xnew \\ Ynew \\ W \end{bmatrix} = \begin{bmatrix} 1 & 0 & Xmv \\ 0 & 1 & Ymv \\ 0 & 0 & 1 \end{bmatrix} * \begin{bmatrix} Xold \\ Yold \\ 1 \end{bmatrix} = \begin{bmatrix} Xold + Xmv \\ Yold + Ymv \\ 1 \end{bmatrix}$$

We learned earlier in this chapter that translation does not make sense for direction vectors (see *Figure 36.2*) since direction vectors are not anchored at the origin of the Cartesian coordinate system.

The homogeneous coordinate system distinguishes between position vectors (points) and direction vectors.

Points are positions specified by two coordinates (position vectors) with respect to the origin and two orthogonal axes.

Both position vectors and direction vectors can be represented by column vectors (column matrices) in homogeneous coordinates with the difference that position vectors have a 1 in the third position in two-dimensional systems whereas direction vectors have zero in this position, e.g direction vector **V** shown in *Figure 36.29*.

$$\mathbf{V} = \begin{bmatrix} Xold \\ Yold \\ 0 \end{bmatrix}$$

Figure 36.29 Direction vector showing homogeneous coordinates

The consequence is that the translation transformation fails to apply a translation. Try the matrix multiplication shown in *Figure 36.30* for yourself to check that this is indeed the outcome.

$$\begin{bmatrix} Xnew \\ Ynew \\ W \end{bmatrix} = \begin{bmatrix} 1 & 0 & Xmv \\ 0 & 1 & Ymv \\ 0 & 0 & 0 \end{bmatrix} * \begin{bmatrix} Xold \\ Yold \\ 0 \end{bmatrix} = \begin{bmatrix} Xold \\ Yold \\ 0 \end{bmatrix}$$

Figure 36.30 Attempt to apply a translation transformation matrix to a direction vector

Note that the transformation matrix has 0 in the third column where there was a 1 before, although this is not necessary in order to get the given outcome.

For the purposes of this exercise, converting back to Cartesian coordinates skips the division by W operation. All that is required is to drop the W coordinate but then such a transformation would not be used anyway.

Rotation

The following transformation matrix **R** in homogeneous coordinates is used to rotate a point P, (Xold, Yold) in Cartesian coordinates and represented by a column vector, counterclockwise in the X-Y plane by an angle ε measured with respect to the X axis.

$$\mathbf{R} = \begin{bmatrix} Cos\ \varepsilon & -Sin\ \varepsilon & 0 \\ Sin\ \varepsilon & Cos\ \varepsilon & 0 \\ 0 & 0 & 1 \end{bmatrix}$$

The transformation of point P, column matrix $\mathbf{v}_P$, to point T, column matrix $\mathbf{v}_T$, is obtained by performing the matrix-vector multiplication $\mathbf{M}.\mathbf{v}_P$

$$\mathbf{v}_T = \mathbf{M}.\mathbf{v}_P$$

$$\begin{bmatrix} Xnew \\ Ynew \\ W \end{bmatrix} = \begin{bmatrix} Cos\ \varepsilon & -Sin\ \varepsilon & 0 \\ Sin\ \varepsilon & Cos\ \varepsilon & 0 \\ 0 & 0 & 1 \end{bmatrix} * \begin{bmatrix} Xold \\ Yold \\ 1 \end{bmatrix} = \begin{bmatrix} Cos\ \varepsilon * Xold - Sin\ \varepsilon * Yold \\ Sin\ \varepsilon * Xold + Cos\ \varepsilon * Yold \\ 1 \end{bmatrix}$$

where we refer to each column matrix as a vector, i.e. $\mathbf{v}_T = \begin{bmatrix} Xnew \\ Ynew \\ W \end{bmatrix}$ $\mathbf{v}_P = \begin{bmatrix} Xold \\ Yold \\ 1 \end{bmatrix}$

Scaling

The scaling transformation matrix changes the size of an object by expanding or contracting the object's vertices along the two axes in a two-dimensional system.

The following transformation matrix **S** in homogeneous coordinates is used to scale a vertex P, (Xold, Yold) in Cartesian coordinates, by Sx in the X-direction and by Sy in the Y-direction

$$\mathbf{S} = \begin{bmatrix} Sx & 0 & 0 \\ 0 & Sy & 0 \\ 0 & 0 & 1 \end{bmatrix}$$

The transformation of point P, column matrix $\mathbf{v}_P$, to point T, column matrix $\mathbf{v}_T$, is obtained by performing the matrix-vector multiplication $\mathbf{S}.\mathbf{v}_P$

$$\mathbf{v}_T = \mathbf{M}.\mathbf{v}_P$$

$$\begin{bmatrix} Xnew \\ Ynew \\ W \end{bmatrix} = \begin{bmatrix} Sx & 0 & 0 \\ 0 & Sy & 0 \\ 0 & 0 & 1 \end{bmatrix} * \begin{bmatrix} Xold \\ Yold \\ 1 \end{bmatrix} = \begin{bmatrix} Sx * Xold \\ Sy * Yold \\ 1 \end{bmatrix}$$

where we refer to each column matrix as a vector, i.e. $\mathbf{v}_T = \begin{bmatrix} Xnew \\ Ynew \\ W \end{bmatrix}$ $\mathbf{v}_P = \begin{bmatrix} Xold \\ Yold \\ 1 \end{bmatrix}$

Concatenating transformations

The preceding sections have shown that performing translation, rotation and scaling of a point (position vector) can be achieved by a simple matrix-vector multiplication operation. Multiplying a position vector by a sequence of matrices can apply a sequence of transformations. This can be done by first multiplying all the transformation matrices together to produce a single matrix **T** representing the entire transformation sequence. This matrix can then be used to transform points (position vectors) directly from their old positions to their new positions. Combining the transformation matrices in this way produces what is called a concatenation or composition matrix.

For example each of the following achieve a different transformation because the order in which translation, scaling and rotation are applied matters,

$$\mathbf{T} = \begin{bmatrix} 1 & 0 & Xmv \\ 0 & 1 & Ymv \\ 0 & 0 & 1 \end{bmatrix} * \begin{bmatrix} Sx & 0 & 0 \\ 0 & Sy & 0 \\ 0 & 0 & 1 \end{bmatrix} * \begin{bmatrix} \text{Cos } \varepsilon & \text{-Sin } \varepsilon & 0 \\ \text{Sin } \varepsilon & \text{Cos } \varepsilon & 0 \\ 0 & 0 & 1 \end{bmatrix} = \begin{bmatrix} Sx*\text{Cos } \varepsilon & \text{-}Sx*\text{Sin } \varepsilon & Xmv \\ Sy*\text{Sin } \varepsilon & Sy*\text{Cos } \varepsilon & Ymv \\ 0 & 0 & 1 \end{bmatrix}$$

$$\mathbf{T} = \begin{bmatrix} Sx & 0 & 0 \\ 0 & Sy & 0 \\ 0 & 0 & 1 \end{bmatrix} * \begin{bmatrix} 1 & 0 & Xmv \\ 0 & 1 & Ymv \\ 0 & 0 & 1 \end{bmatrix} * \begin{bmatrix} \text{Cos } \varepsilon & \text{-Sin } \varepsilon & 0 \\ \text{Sin } \varepsilon & \text{Cos } \varepsilon & 0 \\ 0 & 0 & 1 \end{bmatrix} = \begin{bmatrix} Sx*\text{Cos } \varepsilon & Sy*\text{Sin } \varepsilon & Sx*Xmv \\ \text{-}Sx*\text{Sin } \varepsilon & Sy*\text{Cos } \varepsilon & Sy*Ymv \\ Sx*Xmv & Sy*Ymv & 1 \end{bmatrix}$$

$$\mathbf{T} = \begin{bmatrix} Sx & 0 & 0 \\ 0 & Sy & 0 \\ 0 & 0 & 1 \end{bmatrix} * \begin{bmatrix} \text{Cos } \varepsilon & \text{-Sin } \varepsilon & 0 \\ \text{Sin } \varepsilon & \text{Cos } \varepsilon & 0 \\ 0 & 0 & 1 \end{bmatrix} * \begin{bmatrix} 1 & 0 & Xmv \\ 0 & 1 & Ymv \\ 0 & 0 & 1 \end{bmatrix} = \begin{bmatrix} Sx*\text{Cos } \varepsilon & Sx*\text{Sin } \varepsilon & (Sx*\text{Cos } \varepsilon)*Xmv - (Sx*\text{Sin } \varepsilon)*Ymv \\ \text{-}Sy*\text{Sin } \varepsilon & Sy*\text{Cos } \varepsilon & (Sy*\text{Sin } \varepsilon)*Xmv + (Sy*\text{Cos } \varepsilon)*Ymv \\ 0 & 0 & 1 \end{bmatrix}$$

Rotation, scaling then translation using a concatenation matrix of a position vector

We may multiply the three transformation matrices, rotation A, scaling B and translation C in stages. We may first calculate A*B or we may first calculate B*C. The same final product ABC is obtained either way.

Figure 36.31 shows the result of multiplying A by B first.

$$\mathbf{T} = \overset{\text{A}}{\begin{bmatrix} \text{Cos } \varepsilon & \text{-Sin } \varepsilon & 0 \\ \text{Sin } \varepsilon & \text{Cos } \varepsilon & 0 \\ 0 & 0 & 1 \end{bmatrix}} * \overset{\text{B}}{\begin{bmatrix} Sx & 0 & 0 \\ 0 & Sy & 0 \\ 0 & 0 & 1 \end{bmatrix}} * \overset{\text{C}}{\begin{bmatrix} 1 & 0 & Xmv \\ 0 & 1 & Ymv \\ 0 & 0 & 1 \end{bmatrix}} = \begin{bmatrix} Sx*\text{Cos } \varepsilon & \text{-}Sy*\text{Sin } \varepsilon & 0 \\ Sx*\text{Sin } \varepsilon & Sy*\text{Cos } \varepsilon & 0 \\ 0 & 0 & 1 \end{bmatrix} * \begin{bmatrix} 1 & 0 & Xmv \\ 0 & 1 & Ymv \\ 0 & 0 & 1 \end{bmatrix}$$

Figure 36.31 Rotation, scaling then translation transformations, first stage multiplication

Figure 36.32 shows the outcome of the final stage multiplication.

$$\mathbf{T} = \begin{bmatrix} Sx*\text{Cos } \varepsilon & \text{-}Sy*\text{Sin } \varepsilon & 0 \\ Sx*\text{Sin } \varepsilon & Sy*\text{Cos } \varepsilon & 0 \\ 0 & 0 & 1 \end{bmatrix} * \begin{bmatrix} 1 & 0 & Xmv \\ 0 & 1 & Ymv \\ 0 & 0 & 1 \end{bmatrix} = \begin{bmatrix} Sx*\text{Cos } \varepsilon & \text{-}Sy*\text{Sin } \varepsilon & (Sx*\text{Cos } \varepsilon)*Xmv - (Sy*\text{Sin } \varepsilon)*Ymv \\ Sx*\text{Sin } \varepsilon & Sy*\text{Cos } \varepsilon & (Sx*\text{Sin } \varepsilon)*Xmv + (Sy*\text{Cos } \varepsilon)*Ymv \\ 0 & 0 & 1 \end{bmatrix}$$

Figure 36.32 Rotation, scaling then translation transformations, final stage multiplication

Figure 36.33 shows a cropped screenshot of the outcome of executing program **RotateScaleMove** which uses the concatenation transformation matrix **T** shown in *Figure 36.32* to rotate a position vector (100, 0) through 90°. The original position vector is shown in blue and the rotated position vector is shown in red.

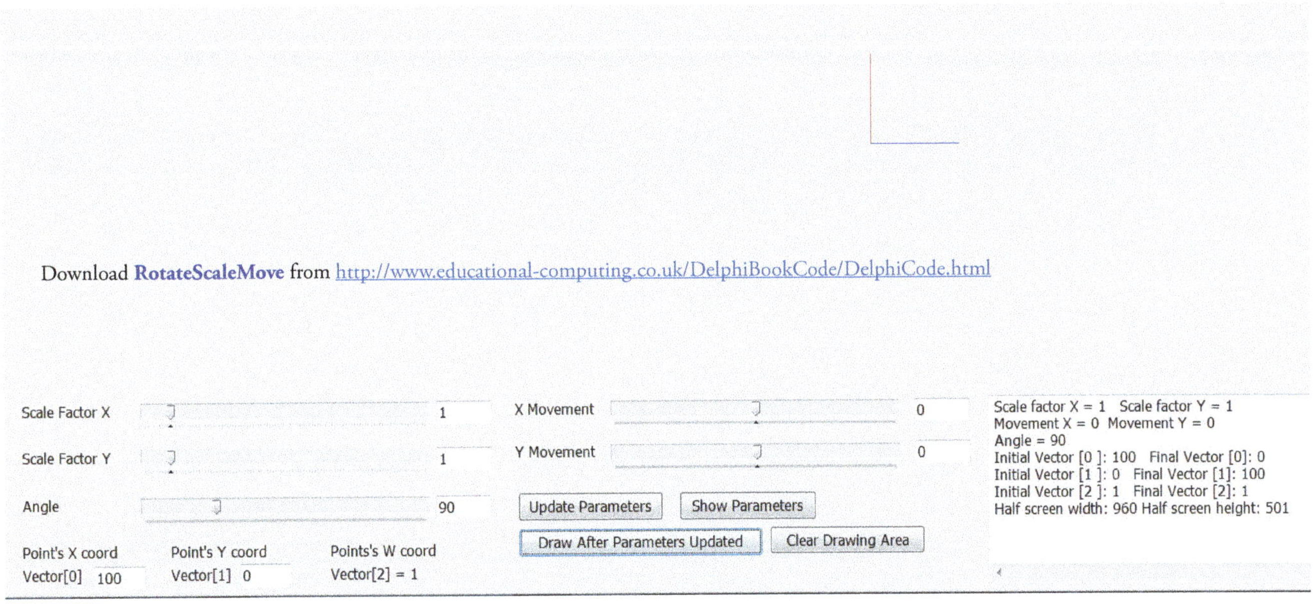

Figure 36.33 Cropped screenshot showing outcome of program RotateScaleMove in execution with rotation angle 90°, original position vector shown in blue, rotated position vector shown in red

Using a concatenation matrix to rotate, scale then move an L-shaped object

Figure 36.34 shows a cropped screenshot of the outcome of executing program **LShapeProject** with rotation angle set at 45°. The original position of the L-shaped object is shown in blue and the rotated object in red. Essentially the program has applied the concatenation matrix **T** to the position vector of each point, i.e. vertex, at which the straight lines defining the L-shaped object meet. The new endpoint position vectors are then used to redraw the L-shaped object.

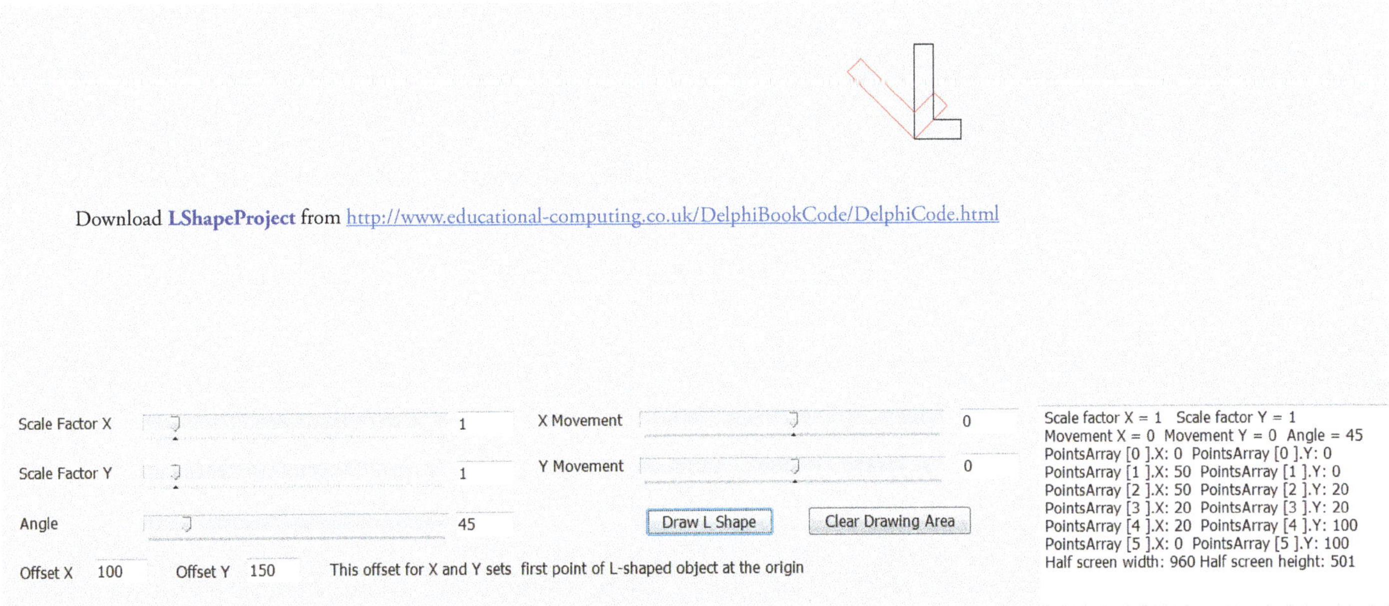

Figure 36.34 Cropped screenshot showing outcome of program LShapeProject in execution with rotation angle 45°, original position of object shown in blue, rotated object shown in red

Figure 36.35 shows a cropped screenshot of the outcome of executing program **LShapeProject** with rotation angle set at 45°, Scale Factor X and Y set to 2. The original position of the L-shaped object is shown in blue and the rotated object in red before and after the scaling.

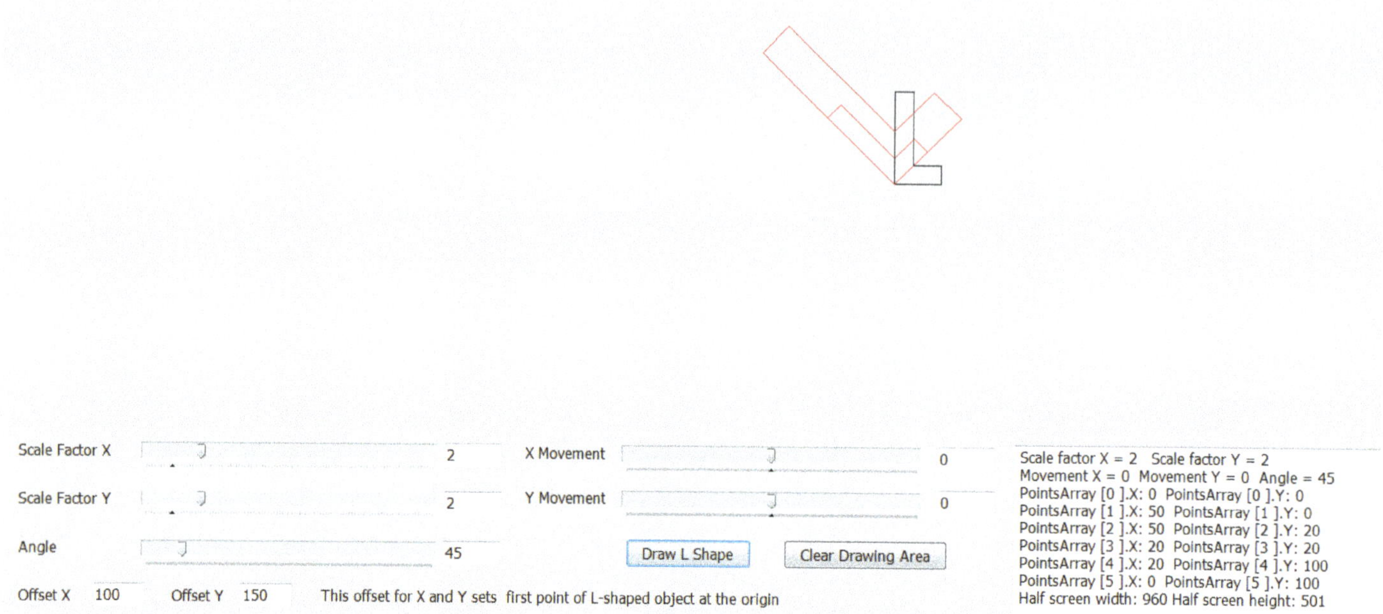

Figure 36.35 Cropped screenshot showing outcome of program LShapeProject in execution with rotation angle 45°, scale factor X and Y = 2, original position of object shown in blue, rotated object shown in red unscaled and scaled

Figure 36.36 shows a cropped screenshot of the outcome of executing program **LShapeProject** with X Movement set to 90, original position of object shown in blue, object in new position shown in red.

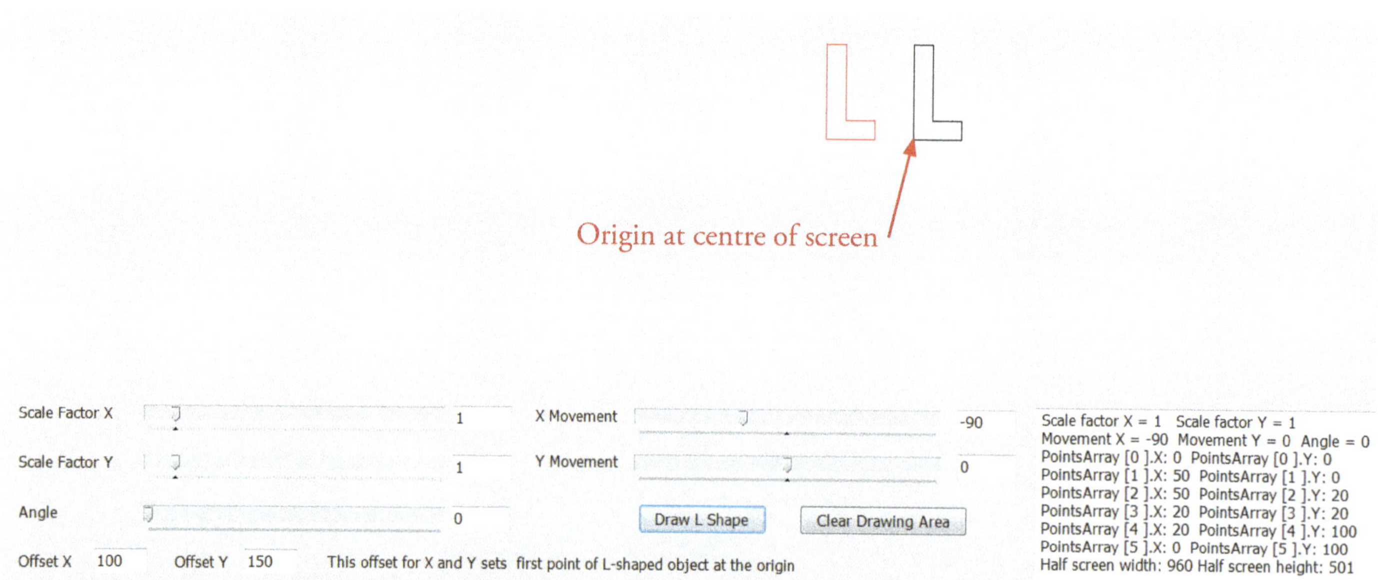

Figure 36.36 Cropped screenshot showing outcome of program LShapeProject in execution with X Movement = 90, original position of object shown in blue, object in new position shown in red

Figure 36.37 shows a cropped screenshot of the outcome of executing program **LShapeProject** with rotation angle 45°, X Movement set to 90, original position of object shown in blue, object in new position shown in red. *Figure 36.37* highlights that using a concatenation matrix raises an issue regarding rotation. Not only has the L-shaped object rotated but so has the coordinate system. The translation along the X-axis has taken place with the X-axis also rotated through 45°. One way that this change of coordinate orientation can be corrected is by adjusting the Y Movement in the opposite direction to the X Movement as show in *Figure 36.38*. This exercise illustrates that care needs to be exercised when applying multiple transformations. The maths behind transformations has been touched upon lightly in this chapter and is a preparation for Open GL graphics which is covered in a later chapter. Matrices and the W coordinate play a big role in **OpenGL** graphics so it is important that you have been introduced to these in this chapter.

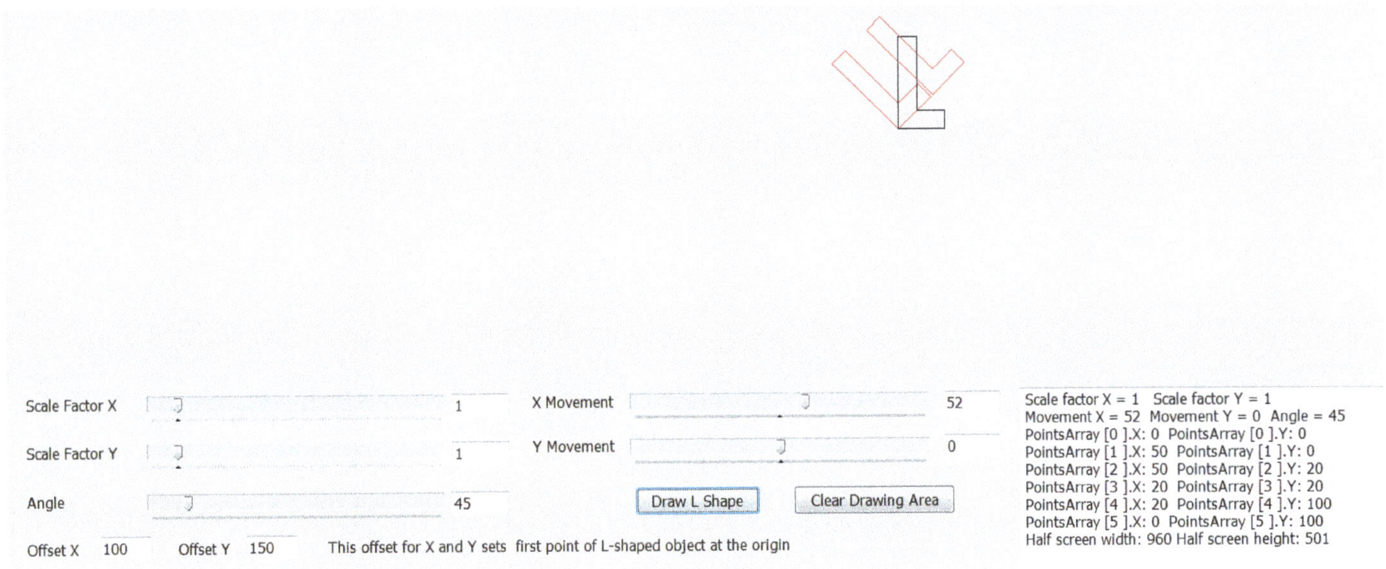

Figure 36.37 Cropped screenshot showing outcome of program LShapeProject in execution with rotation angle 45°, X Movement = 52, original position of object shown in blue, object in new position shown in red

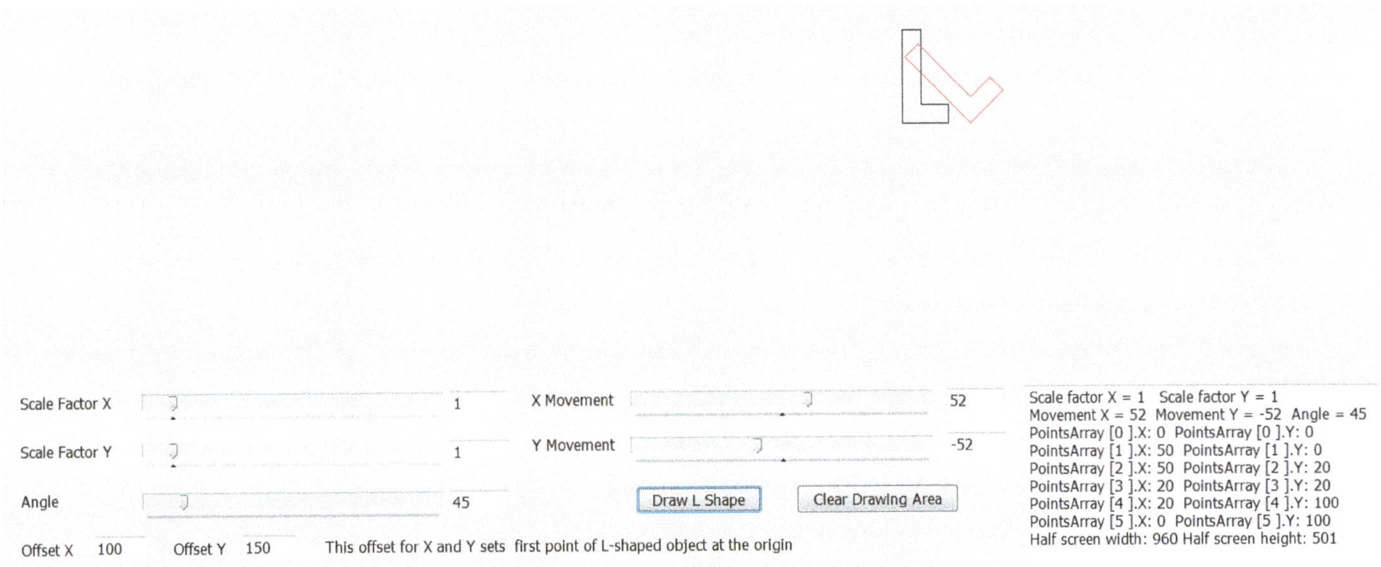

Figure 36.38 Cropped screenshot showing outcome of program LShapeProject in execution with rotation angle 45°, X Movement = 52 and Y Movement = -52, original position of object shown in blue, object in new position shown in red

Offset X and Offset Y

In each of *Figures 36.34* to *36.38* an offset setting has been used in order to locate the L-shaped object at the origin. The origin is situated at the centre of the screen, X, Y coordinates **ScreenWidth Div 2** and **ScreenHeight Div 2,** respectively. *Figure 36.39* shows the effect of rotation of the L-shaped object when these two offset values are zero.

The bottom, left vertex of the L-shaped object is no longer anchored at the origin, instead the object "orbits" about this origin.

Figure 36.39 Cropped screenshot showing outcome of program LShapeProject in execution with rotations of 45°, 90°, 135°, 180°, 235°, 270°, Offset X = 0 and Offset Y = 0, original position of object shown in blue, object in new positions shown in red

Tasks

2 Use the program **RotateScaleMove** from http://www.educational-computing.co.uk/DelphiBookCode/DelphiCode.html to carry out the following exercises

(a) Set Point's Y coordinate to 0, click button **Update Parameters** then button **Draw After Parameters Updated.**

(b) Set **Scale Factor X** slider to 3 (use left and right arrow keys to make fine adjustments). Click button **Update Parameters** then button **Draw After Parameters Updated.**

(c) Click button **Clear Drawing Area**. Set **Angle** slider to 90. Click button **Update Parameters** then button **Draw After Parameters Updated.**

(d) Set **Y Movement** slider to 100. Click button **Update Parameters** then button **Draw After Parameters Updated**. Explain the resulting position vector shown in *Figure 36.40*.

(e) Set **X Movement** slider to -33. Click button **Update Parameters** then button **Draw After Parameters Updated.** Explain the resulting position vector shown in *Figure 36.41*.

(f) Set **X Movement** slider to -66.
Click button **Update Parameters** then button **Draw After Parameters Updated.**
Explain the resulting position vector.

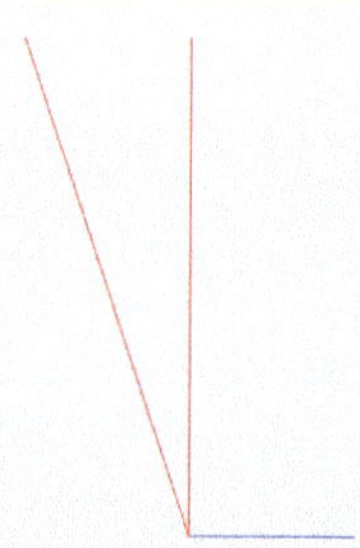

Figure 36.40

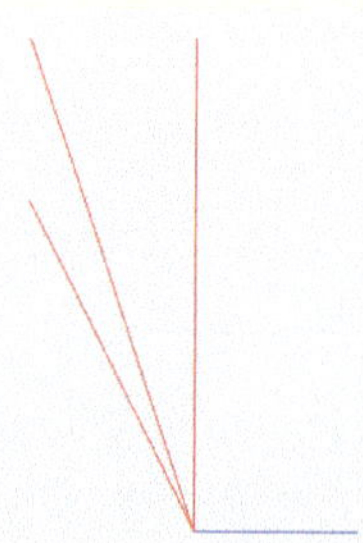

Figure 36.41

(f) Set **X Movement** slider to 100.
Click button **Update Parameters** then button **Draw After Parameters Updated.**
Explain the resulting position vector.

37 Graphics

Introduction to graphics

Purpose: To learn how to use VCL's drawing canvas

The device context

Microsoft's Windows operating system manages multiple applications by limiting each application's use of the full screen to one or more rectangles called windows. For the programmer, this means that their program should not write text and graphics directly to screen locations. Instead, it should draw only into a window's client area, the area inside the window frame of a form, a button or some other control. Such an area for drawing on the screen is called a display context. Microsoft Windows interacts directly with the drawing surface on behalf of the application but consults an area of memory set aside to store attributes such as brush and fill colour, the logical and physical device structures, window size and position, etc. This area of memory is called a Device Context. Each form that Delphi creates is a Window. As such a form has a Device Context.

Device contexts thus represent specific areas on the screen, from the surface of a control (such as a button) to the entire surface of a window or even the screen itself. They can also represent the surface of a printer or plotter.

Direct access to a form's Device Context is made via a pointer (32-bit unsigned integer) called a handle, a variable of type HDC (Handle to a Device Context).

> **Key concept**
> **Device context:**
> A device context represents a specific area on the screen, from the surface of a control (such as a button) to the entire surface of a window or even the screen itself. A device context can also represent the surface of a printer or plotter. It does so by setting aside an area of memory to store attributes for a particular window, e.g. window size and position, brush colour, fill colour, etc.

Drawing on the screen and the role of the handle

A user's application that needs to interact with an output device such as a VDU must first use software in the Windows operating system GDI (Graphics Device Interface) kernel and this in turn calls on software in the VDU's device driver.

To draw on a graphics output device such as the screen or printer, a handle to a Device Context (DC) is required. A handle is simply a number that Windows uses for internal reference to an object, e.g. each form and each control on a form, a button, is a window object. Therefore, every window has a handle, a reference number, that Windows uses when it needs to access the window.

By assigning handles to an application, Windows effectively grants the application permission to use the device associated with each handle.

A specific handle is then included as an argument to the GDI functions e.g. **TextOut**, to identify to Windows the device to draw graphics on. In the case of the screen, the handle references the DC for a particular window and using this handle, Windows is able to paint in the client area of the window, e.g. the client area of a form.

> **Key term**
> **Handle:**
> A handle is a unique number that serves as an index into a table of pointers managed by Windows for the management of resource objects.
> The pointers point to memory locations that govern the appearance and behaviour of these objects, e.g. a window on the screen
> There are handles for different types of resource/object. For example, a window handle (hWND) is a unique identifier that Windows assigns to each created window.

To retrieve a handle to a device context, an application calls the **GetDC** function, passing it the handle of the window whose surface is to be drawn upon. It is very important to call the **ReleaseDC** function when the application has finished drawing its output, as neglecting to release the device context can cause Windows to lock up.

To avoid having to work directly with device contexts, Delphi has provided the **TCanvas** object type.

However, before examining the use of the **TCanvas** object type, we will consider device contexts directly:

1. **Start** a new VCL application.
2. **Place** a button `Button1` on the form.
3. **Create** the **OnClick** event handler for `Button1` (double click `Button1`) and enter the code shown in *Table 37.1*.

```
Procedure TForm1.Button1Click(Sender: TObject);
 Var
    h : HDC;                 Delphi 7: Remove WinApi
  Begin
    h := GetDC(Form1.Handle);
    WinApi.Windows.TextOut(h,0,0,PChar('Hello'),5);
    ReleaseDC(Form1.Handle,h);
  End;
```

Table 37.1 Delphi 10.3 OnClick event handler code for Button1

PChar is a datatype which is a pointer to a character string.

PChar() is a function that returns a pointer of datatype **PChar.**

WinApi.Windows.TextOut writes a string within the window with handle `h`, starting at **x = 0** and **y = 0** relative to top left corner of window. 5 is a count parameter which specifies the number of characters in the string '`Hello`'.

Figure 37.1 DeviceContextProject in execution

4. **Save** Project as **DeviceContextProject.dpr** or **DeviceContextProject.dprog**, depending on the version of Delphi, in new folder **DeviceContextProject.**
5. **Save** unit as **DeviceContextUnit.pas.**
6. **Compile|Build|Run** - press **Ctrl F9**.

Figure 37.1 shows the result when `Button1` is clicked.

7. **Amend** the **OnClick** event handler for `Button1` as shown in *Table 37.2*.
8. **Save** unit.
9. **Compile|Build|Run** - press **Ctrl F9**.

Figure 37.2 shows the result when `Button1` is clicked.

```
Procedure TForm1.Button1Click(Sender: TObject);
  Var
    h : HDC;                 Delphi 7: Remove WinApi
  Begin
    h := GetDC(Form1.Handle);
    WinApi.Windows.SetBkColor(h,222);
    WinApi.Windows.SetTextColor(h,65000);
    WinApi.Windows.TextOut(h,0,0,PChar('Hello'),5);
    ReleaseDC(Form1.Handle,h);
  End;
```

Table 37.2 Amended Delphi 10.3 OnClick event handler for Button1

10. Add a second button, `Button2`, to the form as shown in *Figure 37.3* but without `Hello` text.

11. Add the additional code shown in *Table 37.3* to the **OnClick** event handler for `Button1`.

12. Save unit.

13. Compile|Build|Run - press **Ctrl F9**.

Figure 37.3 shows the result when `Button1` is clicked.

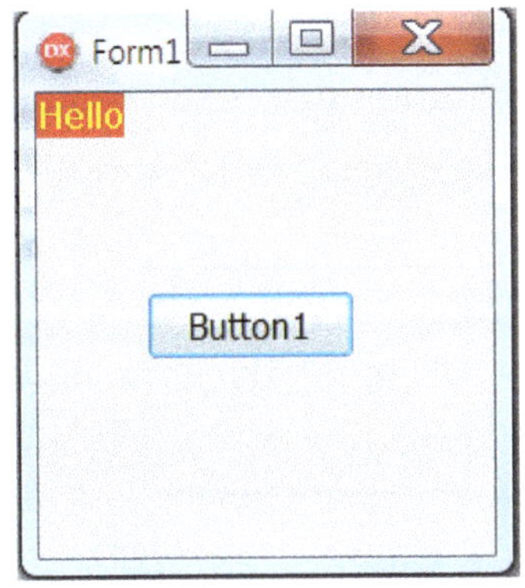

Figure 37.2 Amended DeviceContextProject in execution

```
Procedure TForm1.Button1Click(Sender: TObject);
 Var
   h : HDC;                  Delphi 7: Remove WinApi
 Begin
   h := GetDC(Form1.Handle);
   WinApi.Windows.SetBkColor(h,222);
   WinApi.Windows.SetTextColor(h,65000);
   WinApi.Windows.TextOut(h,0,0,PChar('Hello'),5);
   ReleaseDC(Form1.Handle,h);
   h := GetDC(Button2.Handle);
   WinApi.Windows.TextOut(h,0,0,PChar('Hello'),5);
   ReleaseDC(Button2.Handle,h);
 End;
```

Table 37.3 Amended Delphi 10.3 OnClick event handler code for Button1 that writes text to Form1 and Button2

Figure 37.3 Further amended DeviceContextProject in execution

14. Add the additional code shown in *Table 37.4* to the **OnClick** event handler for `Button1`.

15. Save unit.

16. Compile|Build|Run - press **Ctrl F9**.

Figure 37.4 shows the result when `Button1` is clicked. We have used 0 for the handle number of the whole screen.

```
Procedure TForm1.Button1Click(Sender: TObject);
 Var
   h : HDC;                  Delphi 7: Remove WinApi
 Begin
   h := GetDC(Form1.Handle);
   WinApi.Windows.SetBkColor(h,222);
   WinApi.Windows.SetTextColor(h,65000);
   WinApi.Windows.TextOut(h,0,0,PChar('Hello'),5);
   ReleaseDC(Form1.Handle,h);
   h := GetDC(Button2.Handle);
   WinApi.Windows.TextOut(h,0,0,PChar('Hello'),5);
   ReleaseDC(Button2.Handle,h);
   h := GetDC(0);//Handle number of whole screen is 0
   WinApi.Windows.TextOut(h,0,0,PChar('Hello'),5);
   ReleaseDC(0,h);
 End;
```

Table 37.4 Amended Delphi 10.3 OnClick event handler code for Button1 that writes text to Form1, Button2 and the screen

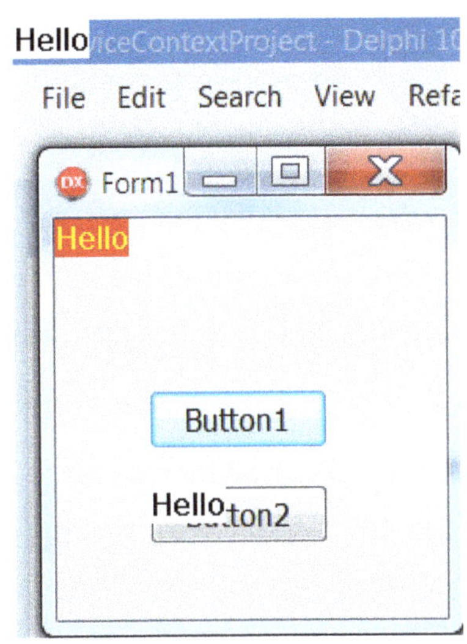

Figure 37.4 The result of another amendment to DeviceContextProject

TCanvas object type

An application that needs to interact with an output device such as a VDU must first use software in the Windows operating system GDI kernel, this in turn calls on software in the VDU's device driver. as shown in *Figure 37.5*.

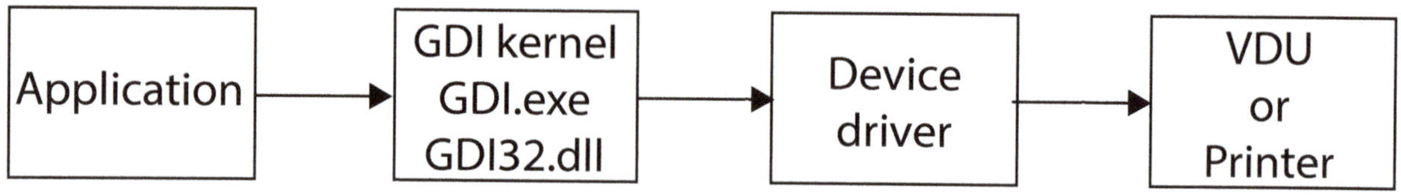

Figure 37.5 Interaction of an application with a VDU or printer

Delphi encapsulates the majority of GDI routines such as **LineTo** and **MoveTo** in a **TCanvas** object.

Examples of these and other drawing routines are shown in *Table 37.5*.

Drawing routines	Drawing routines
Arc	Chord
Create	Destroy
Draw	Ellipse
FillRect	FloodFill
LineTo	MoveTo
Pie	Polygon
PolyLine	Rectangle
RoundRect	TextHeight
TextOut	TextRect
TextWidth	

Table 37.5 Delphi GDI drawing functions

The most commonly used graphical objects in Windows' drawing routines are the pen and the brush.

In Delphi, both the brush and pen objects are encapsulated as the **Brush** and **Pen** properties of a **TCanvas** object.

Brush - defines a colour and a pattern for filling the interiors of closed shapes, such as rectangles.

Pen - determines the characteristics of lines drawn on the **TCanvas** object, such as the line's thickness and colour.

All Delphi forms already contain a **TCanvas** object called **Canvas** which provides access to a graphical area on which shapes can be drawn.

Coordinates

Most GDI drawing routines require a set of coordinates that specify the location where drawing is to occur. These coordinates are based on a unit of measurement, the pixel (the smallest addressable region of a screen).

The GDI co-ordinate system use an X,Y axis system.

It has three co-ordinate systems to plot areas on drawing surfaces called the device, logical and world coordinates. We are only interested for the moment in the first two.

Device Coordinates

Device coordinates refer to the device on which the GDI is running. Its measurements are in pixels, and the orientation has the horizontal and vertical axes increasing from **left to right** and **top to bottom**. For example, if windows is running on a 1024 x 768 pixel display, the coordinates at the top-left corner on the device are (0,0) and the bottom-right coordinates are (1023, 767).

Logical Coordinates

Logical coordinates refer to the coordinates system used by any area in the GDI system that has a device context such as a screen, a form, or a form's client area. *Figure 37.6* shows how these three co-ordinate system apply.

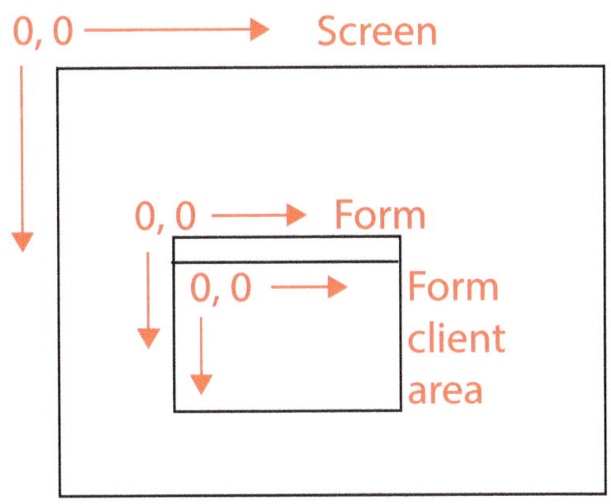

Figure 37.6 Coordinate system for screen, form and form's client area

- **Screen** coordinates refer to the display device and are in pixels (a pixel is the smallest addressable region of a display). On a 1024 x 768 display, **Screen.Width** and **Screen.Height** are also 1024 and 768 pixels, respectively.
  Using **GetDC** with argument value 0 gets a canvas handle to the whole screen using a canvas object of type **TCanvas**:

```
ACanvasObject.Handle := GetDC(0);
```

- **Form** coordinates and window coordinates are the same and refer to an entire form or window, including the caption bar and borders. Delphi doesn't provide a Device Context to a form through a form's property, but it is possible to obtain one by using the Win32 API function **GetWindowDC()** and a canvas object of type **TCanvas**, as follows:

```
ACanvasObject.Handle := GetWindowDC(Form1.Handle);
```

- A form's **client-area** coordinates refer to a form's client area. Every form already has a **TCanvas** object via its **Canvas** property which provides the handle to its client area and whose measurements are obtained from the form's **ClientWidth** and **ClientHeight** properties.

Co-ordinate Mapping

How do device coordinates differ from logical coordinates?

Device coordinates are measured relative to the top left corner of the screen.

Logical coordinates are measured relative to the top left corner of a form or its client area.

As a form can be positioned anywhere on the screen, its top left corner screen coordinates or top left corner client area coordinates change as the form is moved to different positions on the screen.

However, its logical coordinates of the top left corner remain unchanged at (0,0) when the form is repositioned. Only when the form is placed up against the top left corner of the screen are both co-ordinate systems in agreement.

How to draw on the canvas

Drawing lines with MoveTo and LineTo

The **Canvas** property of a form is used to access the various GDI drawing routines, e.g.

> **Canvas.MoveTo(x1,y1)** moves the drawing cursor to position with x-coord, **x1** and y-coord, **y1** measured from the top left corner of the form's client area.
>
> **Canvas.Pen.Color := clRed** sets the drawing pen's colour to red.
>
> **Canvas.LineTo(x2, y2)** draws a line from the current position of the drawing cursor to the point with x-coord, **x2** and y-coord, **y2**. The current x and current y values of the pen are set to the end of the line after the line has been drawn.

1. **Start** a new VCL application.
2. **Place** a button `Button1` on the form.

3. **Create** the **OnClick** event handler for `Button1` (double click `Button1`) and enter the code shown in *Table 37.6*.
4. **Save** Project as **SimpleLineProject.dpr** or **SimpleLineProject.dprog**, depending on the version of Delphi, in new folder **SimpleLineProject**.
5. **Save** unit as **SimpleLineUnit.pas**.
6. **Compile|Build|Run** - press **Ctrl F9**.

Figure 37.7 shows the result when `Button1` is clicked.

```
Procedure TForm1.Button1Click(Sender: TObject);
  Begin
    Canvas.Pen.Color := clRed;
    Canvas.MoveTo(0, 0);
    Canvas.LineTo(ClientWidth, ClientHeight);
  End;
```

Table 37.6 OnClick event handler code for Button1 that draws a diagonal red line form the top left corner to the bottom right corner of the form's client area

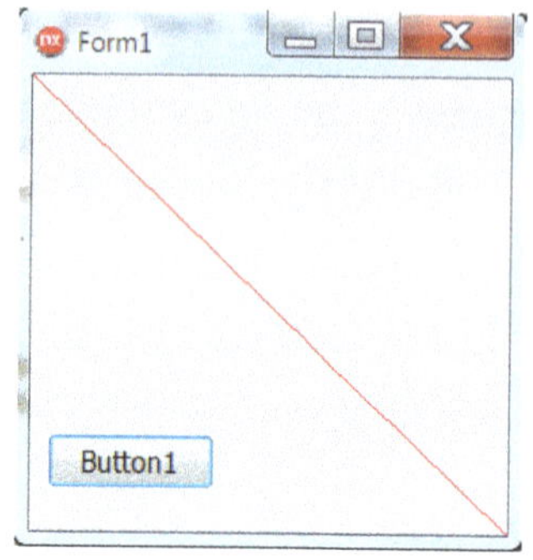

Figure 37.7 Output from SimpleLineProject in execution

Drawing rectangles

1. **Start** a new VCL application.
2. **Place** a button `Button1` on the form.
3. **Create** the **OnClick** event handler for `Button1` (double click `Button1`) and enter the code shown in *Table 37.7*.
4. **Save** Project as **SimpleRectangleProject.dpr** or **SimpleRectangleProject.dprog**, depending on the version of Delphi, in new folder **SimpleRectangleProject**.
5. **Save** unit as **SimpleRectangleUnit.pas**.
6. **Compile|Build|Run** - press **Ctrl F9**.

Figure 37.8 shows the result when `Button1` is clicked.

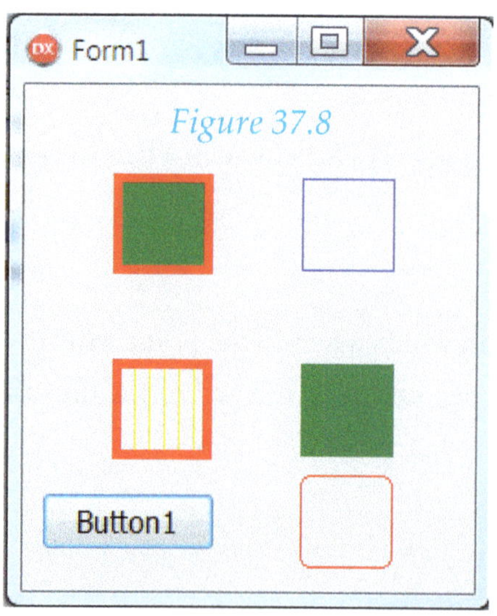

Figure 37.8

```
Procedure TForm1.Button1Click(Sender: TObject);
  Var
    x1, x2,  y1, y2 : Integer;
    Rect : TRect;
 Begin
   x1 := 50;
   y1 := 50;
   x2 := 100;
   y2 := 100;
   Canvas.Pen.Color := clRed;
   Canvas.Pen.Width := 5;
   Canvas.Brush.Style := bsSolid;
   Canvas.Brush.Color := clGreen;
   Canvas.Rectangle(x1, y1, x2, y2);
   Canvas.Brush.Color := clGreen;
   Rect := TRect.Create(150, 150, 200, 200);
   Canvas.FillRect(Rect);
   Canvas.Brush.Color := clBlue;
   Canvas.Brush.Style := bsSolid;
   Rect.Left := 150;
   Rect.Top := 50;
   Rect.Right := 200;
   Rect.Bottom := 100;
   Canvas.FrameRect(Rect);
   Canvas.Brush.Color := clYellow;
   Canvas.Brush.Style := bsVertical;
   Rect.Left := 50;
   Rect.Top := 150;
   Rect.Right := 100;
   Rect.Bottom := 200;
   Canvas.Rectangle(Rect);
   Canvas.Brush.Style := bsClear;
   Canvas.Pen.Width := 1;
   Canvas.RoundRect(150, 210, 200, 260, 10, 10);
 End;
```

Table 37.7 OnClick event handler code for Button1 that draws rectangles, unfilled and filled with border and without

Canvas.Rectangle: Draws a rectangle on the canvas - *Figure 37.9*.

Figure 37.9

Use **Rectangle** to draw a rectangle using **Pen** and fill it with **Brush**. Specify the rectangle's coordinates in one of two ways:

1. Giving four coordinates that define the upper left corner at the point (x1, y1) and the lower right corner at the point (x2, y2) - *Table 37.8*.
2. Using a **TRect** type - *Table 37.9*.

```
x1 := 50;
y1 := 50;
x2 := 100;
y2 := 100;
Canvas.Pen.Color := clRed;
Canvas.Pen.Width := 5;
Canvas.Brush.Style := bsSolid;
Canvas.Brush.Color := clGreen;
Canvas.Rectangle(X1, Y1, X2, Y2);
```

Table 37.8

Canvas.FillRect: Used to fill a rectangular region without drawing the boundary in the current pen - *Figure 37.10*. Fills a rectangular region using the current brush. The region is filled including the top and left sides of the rectangle, but excluding the bottom and right edges - *Table 37.9*.

Figure 37.10

```
Canvas.Brush.Color := clGreen;
Rect := TRect.Create(150, 150, 200, 200);
Canvas.FillRect(Rect);
```

Table 37.9

Canvas.FrameRect: Draws a rectangle using the **Brush** of the canvas to draw the border - *Figure 37.11*. **FrameRect** draws a 1 pixel wide border around a rectangular region. **FrameRect** does not fill the interior of the rectangle with the **Brush** pattern - *Table 37.10*.

Figure 37.11

```
Canvas.Brush.Color := clBlue;
Canvas.Brush.Style := bsSolid;
Rect.Left := 150;
Rect.Top := 50;
Rect.Right := 200;
Rect.Bottom := 100;
Canvas.FrameRect(Rect);
```

Table 37.10

Canvas.RoundRect: Draws a rectangle with rounded corners on the canvas - *Figure 37.12*. **RoundRect** draws a rounded rectangle using **Pen** and fills it with **Brush**. The rectangle has edges defined by the points (x1,y1), (x2,y1), (x2,y2), (x1,y2), with shaved corners to create a rounded appearance. The curve of the rounded corners matches the curvature of an ellipse with width x3 and height y3 - *Table 37.11*.

Figure 37.12

```
Canvas.Brush.Style := bsClear;
Canvas.Pen.Width := 1;
Canvas.RoundRect(150, 210, 200, 260, 10, 10);
                  x1   y1   x2   y2  x3  y3
```

Table 37.11

Pen colour

Windows makes use of 24 bits to store the selected pen colour (actually the colour value is stored in a 32-bit long integer but the high order byte is always zero). For the colour range from black to white the selected pen colour ranges from 0 to 16777215 in decimal and 000000_{16} to $FFFFFF_{16}$ in hexadecimal.

Table 37.12 shows some colour constants and their numeric value.

Colour	Decimal Value	Hexadecimal Value
clBlack	0	000000
clMaroon	128	000080
clRed	255	0000FF
clGreen	32768	008000
clLime	65280	00FF00
clTeal	8421376	808000
clBlue	16711680	FF0000
clWhite	16777215	FFFFFF

Table 37.12 Some colour constants and their numeric value

Using 24 bits makes it possible to allocate one byte (8 bits to each primary colour) i.e. one byte for red, one byte for green and one byte for blue.

31 Blue	Green	Red 0
00-FF	00-FF	00-FF

Table 37.13 Red, Green, Blue division of 24 bits

Drawing pixels

The **Canvas** object has a property **Pixels[x, y: Integer]** of type **TColor** whose type definition is as follows:

Type TColor = -2147483648..2147483647;

The relevant range of **TColor** is 0 to 16777215.

The **Pixels** property has a getter method which is called each time the color of a pixel in the Pixels property is read.

The getter method returns the color on the drawing surface at a specific pixel position, **x**, **y**, within the current clipping region. If the position is outside the clipping rectangle, -1 is returned.

It has a setter method which is called to change the color of individual pixels on the drawing surface.

1. **Start** a new VCL application.
2. **Place** a **TTimer** component, `Timer1`, on the form.
3. **Create** the **OnClick** event handler for `Timer1` (double click `Timer1)` and enter the code shown in *Table 37.14*.
4. **Set** the **Interval** property of `Timer1` to 1 millisecond.
5. **Save** Project as **DrawingPixelsProject.dpr** or **DrawingPixelsProject.dprog**, depending on the version of Delphi, in new folder **DrawingPixelsProject**.
6. **Save** unit as **DrawingPixelsUnit.pas**.
7. **Compile**|**Build**|**Run** - press **Ctrl F9**.

Figure 37.13 shows the result.

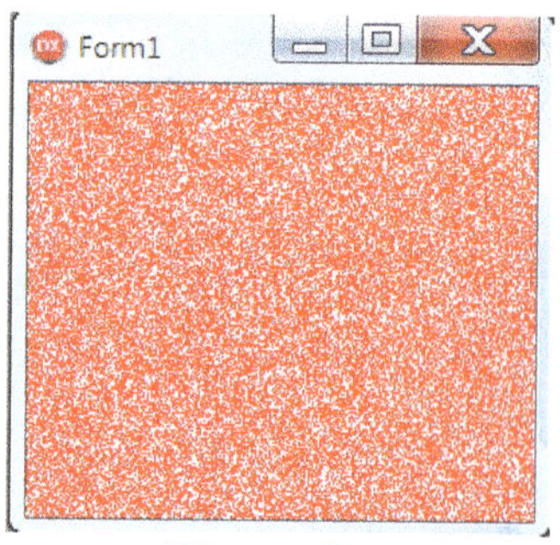

Figure 37.13

The function **rgb** returns a 32-bit integer (highest-order byte 0) which represents a 24 bit colour value. It takes three parameters of type byte, representing the red, green and blue colour components, respectively.

```
Procedure TForm2.Timer1Timer(Sender: TObject);
  Var
    i : Integer;
  Begin
    For i := 0 To 99      Setter method called to write rgb value
      Do Canvas.Pixels[Random(ClientWidth), Random(ClientHeight)]
                          := rgb(255, 0, 0);
  End;                           Red Green Blue
```

Table 37.14

Programming tasks

1. Adapt program DrawingPixelsProject to use:
   - Blue pixels
   - Green pixels
   - Random(256) to generate red, green and blue colour values randomly, each in range 0..255.

Reading Pixels

1. **Start** a new VCL application.
2. **Place** four **TPanel** controls on the form arranged as shown in *Figure 37.14* and aligned as follows:
    - `Panel1` aligned **Top**
    - Next `Panel2` aligned **Top**
    - Then `Panel3` aligned **Top**
    - `Panel4` aligned **Client.**

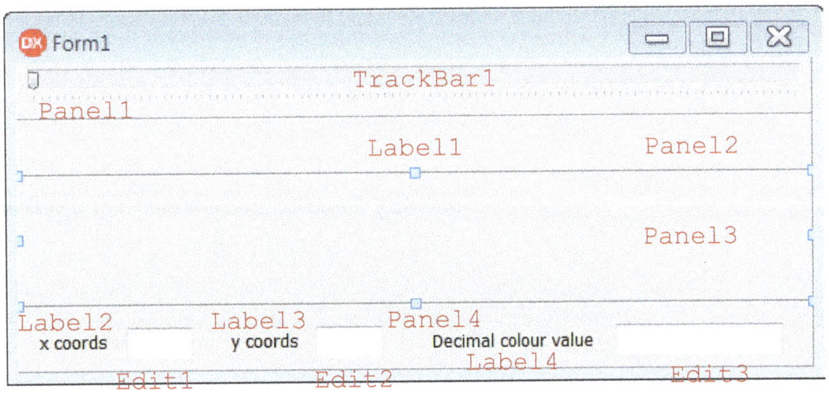

Figure 37.14 UI design for DrawingPixelsProject

3. **Place** four **TLabel** controls, `Label1` on `Panel2`, `Label2`, `Label3` and `Label4` on `Panel4` arranged as shown in *Figure 37.14* and captioned as follows:
    - **Label1**'s caption an empty string
    - **Label2**'s caption the string 'x coords'
    - **Label3**'s caption the string 'y coords'
    - **Label4**'s caption the string 'Decimal colour value'.
4. **Place** three **TEdit** controls on `Panel4` arranged as shown in *Figure 37.14* each with an empty **Text** property.
5. **Place** a TTrackBar component, `TrackBar1`, on Panel 1.
6. **Enter** the **Type** definition for `TMyPanel` as shown in *Table 37.15*.
7. **Create** the **OnChange** event handler for `TrackBar1` and enter the code shown in *Table 37.15*.
8. **Create** the **OnMouseDown** event handler for `Panel3` and enter the code shown in *Table 37.15*.
9. **Create** the **OnMouseMove** event handler for `Panel3` and enter the code shown in *Table 37.15*.
10. **Save Project** as **ReadingPixelsProject.dpr** or **ReadingPixelsProject.dprog**, depending on the version of Delphi, in new folder **ReadingPixelsProject**.
11. **Save** unit as **ReadingPixelsUnit.pas**.
12. **Compile|Build|Run** - press **Ctrl F9**.

Figure 37.15 shows the result when the trackbar is moved and the mouse left button is clicked with the mouse over `Panel3`. The pixel under the mouse pointer at **x** = 371 and **y**= 106 is read and its colour value in decimal is displayed in `Edit3`.

```
Implementation
{$R *.dfm}
Type
  TMyPanel = Class(TPanel);
Procedure TForm1.Panel3MouseDown(Sender: TObject; Button: TMouseButton;
                                 Shift: TShiftState; X, Y: Integer);
  Begin
    Edit3.Text := IntToStr(TMyPanel(Sender).Canvas.Pixels[x, y]);
  End;
Procedure TForm1.Panel3MouseMove(Sender: TObject; Shift: TShiftState;
                                 X, Y: Integer);
  Begin
    Edit1.Text := IntToStr(x);
    Edit2.Text := IntToStr(y);
  End;
Procedure TForm1.TrackBar1Change(Sender: TObject);
  Begin
    Label1.Caption := 'Decimal colour value = ' + IntToStr(Round((TrackBar1.Position * 16777215)/100));
    Panel3.Color := Round((TrackBar1.Position * 16777215)/100);
  End;
End.
```

Table 37.15 OnClick event handlers code Panel3MouseDown, Panel3MouseMove and TrackBar1Change events

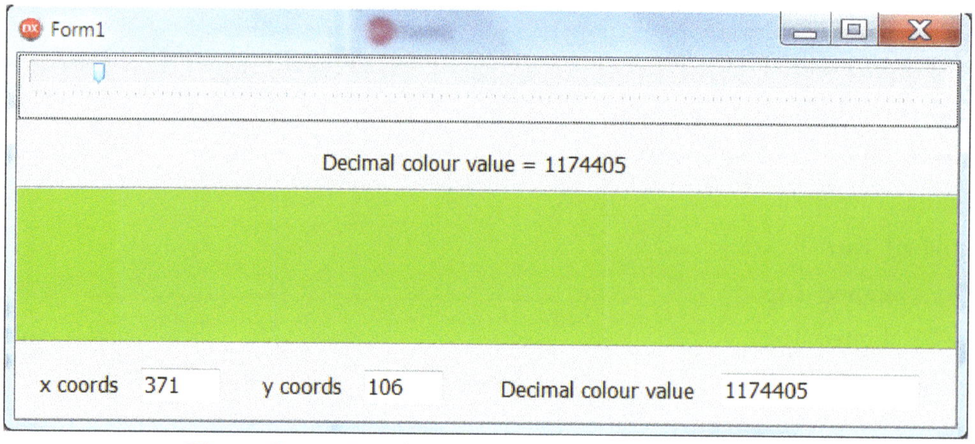

Figure 37.15 ReadingPixelsProject in execution

TPanel has a **Canvas** property but unfortunately it has **Protected**[1] status, therefore, its use is restricted to its class (i.e. the unit in which its class is defined) and its descendent classes. To get around this in **ReadingPixelsProject** we must define a descendent class in the **ReadingPixelsProject**'s unit, **ReadingPixelsUnit**.
For example,

```
Type TMyPanel = Class(TPanel);
Procedure TForm1.Panel3MouseDown(Sender: TObject; Button: TMouseButton;
                                 Shift: TShiftState; X, Y: Integer);
  Begin
    Edit3.Text := IntToStr(TMyPanel(Sender).Canvas.Pixels[x, y]);
  End;
```

gives access to the **Canvas** property of a **TPanel** object, **Panel3**. The coordinates x, y are relative to `Panel3` with the top left corner having x, y coordinates of 0, 0.

Drawing Polygons

A polygon is any closed shape of n sides, e.g. a triangle is a closed shape of three sides. Polygons are drawn using the attributes set by both the **Pen** and **Brush** properties. The **Pen** property determines the outline of the polygon, and the **Brush** property determines how the polygon is filled. Several methods exist that draw polygons of different shapes, from rectangles to circles. The **Polygon** method of **TCanvas** objects can be used to draw polygons of any arbitrary shape simply by passing it an open array of **TPoint** structures.

Table 37.16 shows how the **Polygon** method of the form's canvas can be used to draw a triangle and a rectangle. The result of clicking the **Draw Polygons** button is shown in *Figure 37.16*.

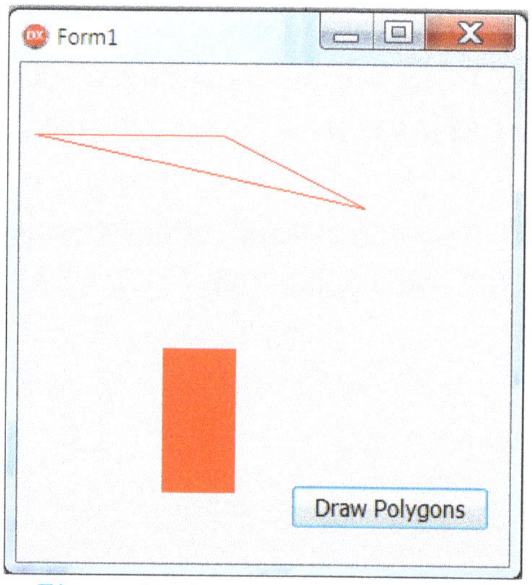

Figure 37.16 Using the Polygon method to draw a triangle and a rectangle

```
Procedure TForm1.DrawPolygonsClick(Sender: TObject);
  Begin
    Canvas.Brush.Color := clBtnFace;//Same colour as form
    Canvas.Pen.Color := clRed;
    Canvas.Polygon([Point(10,50), Point(140,50), Point(240,100)]);
    Canvas.Brush.Color := clRed;
    Canvas.Polygon([Point(100,200), Point(150,200), Point(150,300), Point(100,300)]);
  End;
```

Table 37.16 OnClick event handler to draw an unfilled triangle and a filled rectangle

1 See Chapter 21

The **Polygon** method draws a series of lines on the canvas connecting the points passed in and closing the shape by drawing a line from the last point to the first point, e.g. `Point(240, 100)` to `Point(10, 50)`.

After drawing the complete shape, **Polygon** fills the shape using the value of **Brush**.

The `[Point(10,50), Point(140,50), Point(240,100)]` parameter is an array of points that give the vertices of the polygon.

Canvas.Polygon is defined in **Vcl.Graphics.TCanvas** as

```
Procedure Polygon(const Points: array of TPoint); override;
```

Points is an open array[2].

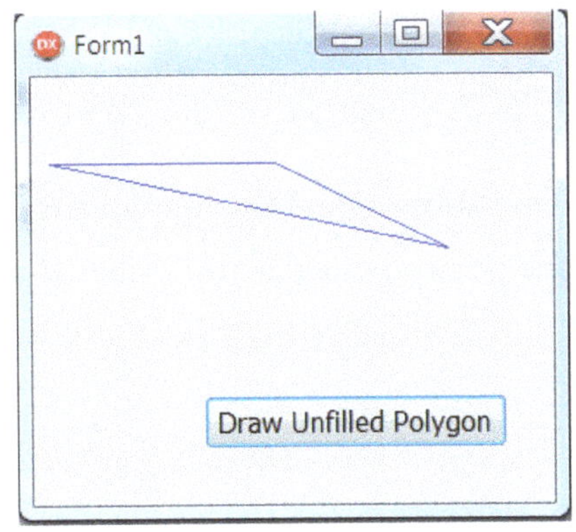

Figure 37.17 Using the PolyLine method to draw a triangle

Typically, **Polygon** is used to draw a filled polygon. The appearance of the triangle in *Figure 37.16* was created without an apparent fill colour by setting **Brush** to the same colour as the background, i.e. **btnface**.

To avoid filling the polygon the method **PolyLine** is used in place of the method **Polygon**.

In order to close the polygon, **PolyLine** requires that an extra **Point** must be added to the open array parameter. This point should have the same value for the x, y coordinates as the first **Point**, i.e. `Point(10, 50)` as shown in *Table 37.17*.

The result of clicking the **Draw Unfilled Polygon** button is shown in *Figure 37.17*.

```
Procedure TForm1.DrawUnfilledPolygonClick(Sender: TObject);
  Begin
    Canvas.Pen.Color := clBlue;
    Canvas.PolyLine([Point(10,50), Point(140,50), Point(240,100), Point(10,50)]);
  End;
```

Table 37.17 OnClick event handler to draw an unfilled triangle

Drawing circles

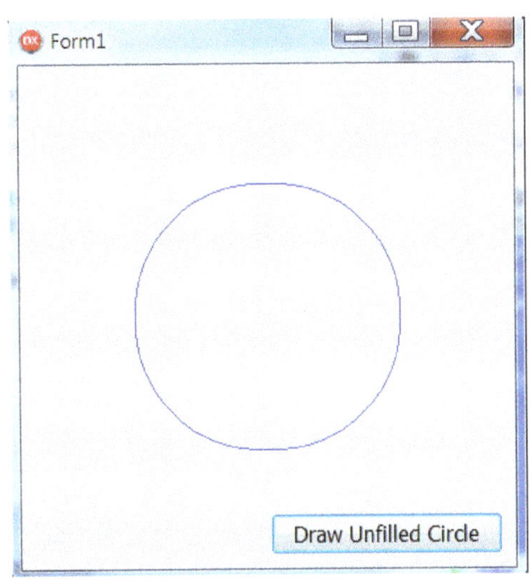

Figure 37.18 Drawing an unfilled circle using connected line segments

A simple way to draw a circle is by connecting a sizeable number of line segments to form a polygon which, although not a true circle, is good enough. At moderately small radii, the polygon will appear sufficiently curved to have the appearance of a circle as shown in *Figure 37.18*.

Before exploring how this is done in code, we need to visit some trigonometry.

The coordinates (X, Y) of all points on a circle with radius R, centred at (XCentre, YCentre), is given by the formulae:

$$X = XCentre + R * \text{Cos } A$$

$$Y = YCentre + R * \text{Sin } A$$

where angle A is as shown in *Figure 37.19*.

(Sin = Opposite/Hypoteneuse; Cos = Adjacent/Hypoteneuse).

www.educational-computing.com/DelphiBook/Code/Chapter37/CirclePolyLineProject.rar

2 See Chapter 14

Angle A goes from 0 to 360° or from 0 to 2π radians.

Angle A varies over this range in infinitessimal steps but for most computer graphics, it is possible to use finite steps, e.g. 5°, and still get good results.

By using trigonometric identities, the computer can be saved from having to calculate sine and cosine for each new angle (A + N times AngleStep) over the 360° range.

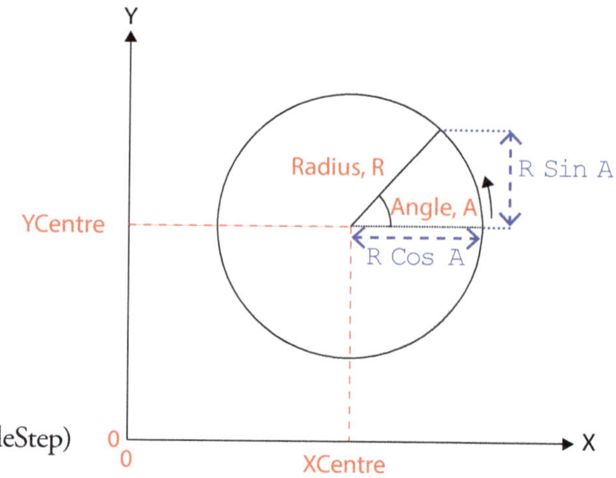

Figure 37.19 Circle centred at (XCentre, YCentre) with radius R

Trigonometric identities:

Cos (A + AngleStep) = Cos (A) * Cos (AngleStep) - Sin (A) * Sin (AngleStep)

Sin (A + AngleStep) = Sin (A) * Cos (AngleStep) + Cos (A) * Sin (AngleStep)

If we abbreviate AngleStep to ΔA, and use the values of X and Y at one point to calculate the values at the adjoining point, then the ith and $(i + 1)^{th}$ coordinates are given by

X(i) = XCentre + R * Cos (A)

Y(i) = YCentre + R * Sin(A)

X(i + 1) = XCentre + R * Cos (A + ΔA)

Y(i + 1) = YCentre + R * Sin(A + ΔA)

Rearranging the equations for X(i) and Y(i) as follows

R * Cos (A) = X(i) - XCentre

R * Sin(A) = Y(i) - YCentre

Then

X(i + 1) = XCentre + R * Cos (A) * Cos(ΔA) - R * Sin(A) * Sin(ΔA)

Y(i + 1) = YCentre + R * Sin(A) * Cos (ΔA) + R * Cos(A) * Sin(ΔA)

Substituting for R * Sin (A) and R * Cos(A) we obtain

X(i + 1) = XCentre + (X(i) - XCentre) * Cos(ΔA) - (Y(i) - YCentre) * Sin(ΔA) —(1)

Y(i + 1) = YCentre + (Y(i) - YCentre) * Cos (ΔA) + (X(i) - XCentre) * Sin(ΔA) —(2)

Equations 1 and 2 describe each point using only angle ΔA, and coordinates XCentre and YCentre. Starting the circle at A = 0 and i = 1, we obtain

X(0) = XCentre + R because Cos(0) = 1

Y(0) = YCentre because Sin(0) = 1

The next coordinate values are

X(1) = XCentre + (X(1) - XCentre) * Cos(ΔA) - (Y(0) - YCentre) * Sin(ΔA)

Y(1) = YCentre + (Y(1) - YCentre) * Cos (ΔA) + (X(0) - XCentre) * Sin(ΔA)

Substituting for X(0) and Y(0)

X(1) = XCentre + R * Cos(ΔA)

Y(1) = YCentre + R* Sin(ΔA)

All subsequent X, Y coordinate values will involve R, Sin(ΔA) and Cos(ΔA), only.

Therefore, we only need to calculate Sin(ΔA) and Cos(ΔA) once for a given ΔA.

Table 37.18 shows a function which starts with X(0) and Y(0) then uses equations 1 and 2 to calculate the remaining points. In order to close the polygon, we need to add another point to the end of the array thereby connecting the last calculated point the first point. This is achieved by adding X(0) and Y(0) to the `CircleOfPoints` array as follows

```
CircleOfPointsArrayDouble[NoOfPoints].x := X(0);
CircleOfPointsArrayDouble[NoOfPoints].y := Y(0);
```

`NoOfPoints` is equal to the number of line segments that need to be drawn. `TotalNoOfPoints` is thus one more than `NoOfPoints`.

```
Function TForm1.CalculateCirclePoints(XCentre, YCentre, Radius, NoOfPoints : Integer) : TCircleOfPoints;
  Var
    AngleStep : Double;
    CosStep, SinStep, XDifference, YDifference : Double;
    i : Integer;
    CircleOfPointsArrayDouble : TCircleOfPointsDouble;
    CircleOfPointsArrayInteger : TCircleOfPoints;
  Begin
    AngleStep := 360/NoOfPoints;
    CosStep := Cos(DegToRad(AngleStep));
    SinStep  := Sin(DegToRad(AngleStep));
    CircleOfPointsArrayDouble[0].x := XCentre + Radius;
    CircleOfPointsArrayDouble[0].y := YCentre;
    For i := 1 To NoOfPoints - 1
      Do
        Begin
          XDifference := CircleOfPointsArrayDouble[i - 1].x - XCentre;
          YDifference := CircleOfPointsArrayDouble[i - 1].y - YCentre;
          CircleOfPointsArrayDouble[i].x := XCentre + XDifference*CosStep - YDifference*SinStep;
          CircleOfPointsArrayDouble[i].y := YCentre + XDifference*SinStep + YDifference*CosStep;
        End;
    CircleOfPointsArrayDouble[NoOfPoints].x := CircleOfPointsArrayDouble[1].x;
    CircleOfPointsArrayDouble[NoOfPoints].y := CircleOfPointsArrayDouble[1].y;
    For i := 1 To TotalNoOfPoints
      Do
        Begin
          CircleOfPointsArrayInteger[i].x := Round(CircleOfPointsArrayDouble[i].x);
          CircleOfPointsArrayInteger[i].y := Round(CircleOfPointsArrayDouble[i].y);
        End;
    Result := CircleOfPointsArrayInteger;
  End;
```

To avoid propagating rounding errors the X, Y points for drawing a circle are calculated as doubles not integers.

PolyLine uses zero-indexed arrays

The X, Y points for drawing a circle are rounded to integers because PolyLine requires integer coordinates.

Table 37.18 Function which calculates points which will be used to draw a circle

Table 37.19 shows the event handler `DrawUnfilledCircleClick` which when called, draws a **PolyLine** circle using integer-valued point coordinates, **X** and **Y**, stored in `CircleOfPointsArrayInteger`.

```
Procedure TForm1.DrawUnfilledCircleClick(Sender: TObject);
  Var
    CircleOfPointsArrayInteger : TCircleOfPoints;
    Radius : Integer;
  Begin
    Radius := StrToInt(edtRadius.Text);
    CircleOfPointsArrayInteger := CalculateCirclePoints(Form1.ClientWidth Div 2, Form1.ClientHeight Div 2,
                                                        Radius, TotalNoOfPoints - 1);
    Canvas.Pen.Color := clBlue;
    Canvas.PolyLine(CircleOfPointsArrayInteger);
  End;
```

Table 37.19 OnClick event handler to draw an unfilled circle

Table 37.20 shows the **Const** and **Type** definitions that the code in *Table 37.18* and *Table 37.19* rely upon.

Figure 37.20 shows the output from **CirclePolyLineProject** for radii, 50, 100, 150 and number of points 65.

```
Const
  TotalNoOfPoints = 65;
Type
  TPointRecordDouble = Record
                          x : Double;
                          y : Double;
                        End;
  TCircleOfPointsDouble =  Array[0..TotalNoOfPoints - 1] Of TPointRecordDouble;
  TCircleOfPoints = Array[0..TotalNoOfPoints - 1] Of TPoint;

  TForm1 = Class(TForm)
             DrawUnfilledCircle: TButton;
             edtRadius: TEdit;
             lblRadius: TLabel;
             Procedure DrawUnfilledCircleClick(Sender: TObject);
             Function CalculateCirclePoints(XCentre, YCentre, Radius, NoOfPoints : Integer) : TCircleOfPoints;
           End;
```

Note

Ctrl Shift C is a shortcut which will generate the skeleton code for function CalculateCirclePoints. Place cursor on same line as this function in the class definition and press Ctrl Shift C key combination at the same time.

Table 37.20 Const and Type definitions for CirclePolyLineProject

Varying the number of points

In order to vary the number of points stored in the array passed to **PolyLine**, we need to use an array type whose size is expressed at run time. This type of array is called a dynamic array[3]. The revised **Type** definition is shown in *Table 37.21*.

```
Type
  TPointRecordDouble = Record
                          x : Double;
                          y : Double;
                        End;
  TCircleOfPointsDouble =  Array Of TPointRecordDouble;
  TCircleOfPoints = Array Of TPoint;
```

Table 37.21 Revised Type definition showing change to dynamic arrays

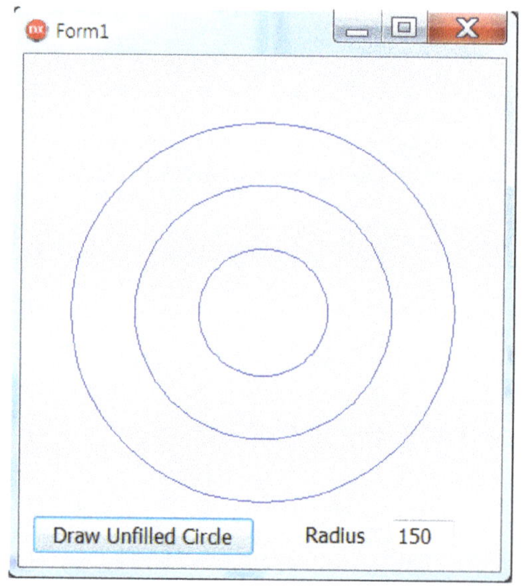

Figure 37.20 Circles centred at (XCentre, YCentre) with various radii

The necessary revisions to `CalculateCircleOfPoints` are shown in red in *Table 37.22*. Dynamic arrays use 0-based indexing.

Figure 37.21 shows the User Interface (UI) design.

Table 37.23 shows the on click event handler which draws the polygon. `TMyPanel` is necessary to overcome the protected status of **TCanvas** property of **TPanel** - *Table 37.24*.

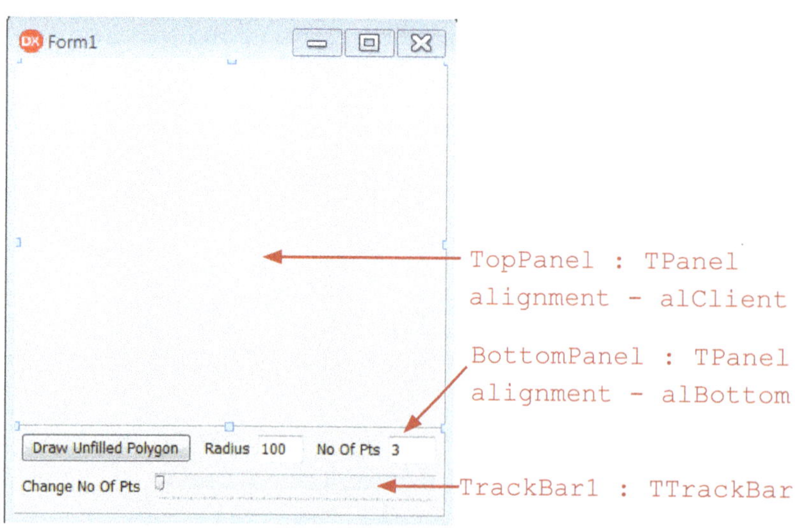

Figure 37.21 UI design

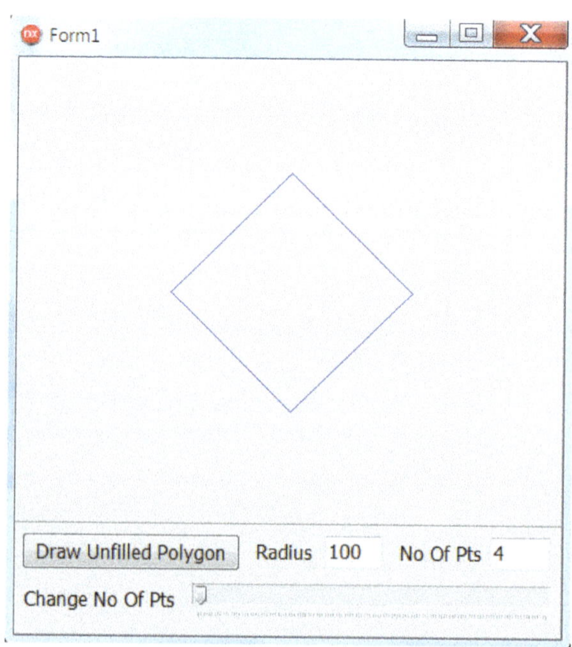

Figure 37.22 Drawing with No Of Pts = 4 generates a rectangle

3 Dynamic arrays: see Chapter 14.

```
Function TForm1.CalculateCirclePoints(XCentre, YCentre, Radius, NoOfPoints : Integer) : TCircleOfPoints;
  Var
    AngleStep : Double;
    CosStep, SinStep, XDifference, YDifference : Double;
    i : Integer;
    CircleOfPointsArrayDouble : TCircleOfPointsDouble;
    CircleOfPointsArrayInteger : TCircleOfPoints;
  Begin
    SetLength(CircleOfPointsArrayDouble, NoOfPoints + 1);
    SetLength(CircleOfPointsArrayInteger, NoOfPoints + 1);
    AngleStep := 360/NoOfPoints;
    CosStep := Cos(DegToRad(AngleStep));
    SinStep  := Sin(DegToRad(AngleStep));
    CircleOfPointsArrayDouble[0].x := XCentre + Radius;
    CircleOfPointsArrayDouble[0].y := YCentre;
    For i := 1 To NoOfPoints - 1
      Do
        Begin
          XDifference := CircleOfPointsArrayDouble[i - 1].x - XCentre;
          YDifference := CircleOfPointsArrayDouble[i - 1].y - YCentre;
          CircleOfPointsArrayDouble[i].x := XCentre + XDifference*CosStep - YDifference*SinStep;
          CircleOfPointsArrayDouble[i].y := YCentre + XDifference*SinStep + YDifference*CosStep;
        End;
    CircleOfPointsArrayDouble[NoOfPoints].x := CircleOfPointsArrayDouble[0].x;
    CircleOfPointsArrayDouble[NoOfPoints].y := CircleOfPointsArrayDouble[0].y;
    For i := 0 To NoOfPoints
      Do
        Begin
          CircleOfPointsArrayInteger[i].x := Round(CircleOfPointsArrayDouble[i].x);
          CircleOfPointsArrayInteger[i].y := Round(CircleOfPointsArrayDouble[i].y);
        End;
    Result := CircleOfPointsArrayInteger;
  End;
```

Table 37.22 Revised CalculateCircleOfPoints showing the use of 0-based indexed dynamic arrays

```
Procedure TForm1.DrawUnfilledPolygonClick(Sender: TObject);
  Var
    CircleOfPointsArrayInteger : TCircleOfPoints;
    Radius, NoOfPoints : Integer;
  Begin
    NoOfPoints := TrackBar1.Position;
    SetLength(CircleOfPointsArrayInteger, NoOfPoints + 1);
    Radius := StrToInt(edtRadius.Text);
    CircleOfPointsArrayInteger := CalculateCirclePoints(TopPanel.ClientWidth Div 2,
                                                        TopPanel.ClientHeight Div 2,
                                                        Radius, NoOfPoints);
    TMyPanel(TopPanel).Canvas.Pen.Color := clBlue;
    TMyPanel(TopPanel).Canvas.PolyLine(CircleOfPointsArrayInteger);
    TrackBar1.SetFocus;
  End;
```

Table 37.23 On click event handler DrawUnFilledPolygonClick

```
TMyPanel = Class(TPanel);
```

Table 37.24 TMyPanel overcomes the protected status of TCanvas property of TPanel

Table 37.25 shows the **On change** event handler `TrackBar1Change`.

Figure 37.23 shows the polygon which is drawn when no of points = 12.

```
Procedure TForm1.TrackBar1Change(Sender: TObject);
  Begin
    edtNoOfPts.Text := IntToStr(TrackBar1.Position);
  End;
```

Table 37.25 On change event handler TrackBar1Change

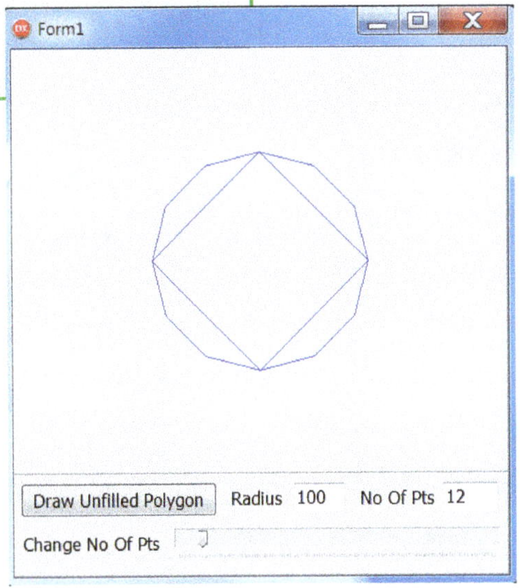

Figure 37.23 Drawing with No Of Pts = 12 generates an approximation to a circle

Programming tasks

2. Download CirclePolyLineExpProject from
www.educational-computing.com/DelphiBook/Code/Chapter37/CirclePolyLineExpProject.rar

Experiment with different no of points and radii.

Rotating a polygon

If a point (Xold, Yold) in a polygon is rotated about the origin (0, 0) through an angle ε, the new position (Xnew, Ynew) is given by

Xnew = R * Cos(θ + ε)

Ynew = R * Sin(θ + ε)

But

Cos(θ + ε) = Cos θ * Cos ε - Sin θ * Sin ε

and

Sin(θ + ε) = Sin θ * Cos ε + Cos θ * Sin ε

Therefore,

Xnew = R * (Cos θ * Cos ε - Sin θ * Sin ε)

Xnew = R * Cos θ * Cos ε - R * Sin θ * Sin ε

Ynew = R * (Sin θ * Cos ε + Cos θ * Sin ε)

Ynew = R * Sin θ * Cos ε + R * Cos θ * Sin ε

Using Xold = R * Cos θ and Yold= R * Sin θ

Therefore

Xnew = Xold * Cos ε - Yold * Sin ε ——(3)

Ynew = Yold * Cos ε + Xold * Sin ε

Rearranging the right hand side

Ynew = Xold * Sin ε + Yold * Cos ε ——(4)

We can write this in matrix form as follows

$$(Xnew, Ynew) = (Xold, Yold) * \begin{pmatrix} \cos \varepsilon & \sin \varepsilon \\ -\sin \varepsilon & \cos \varepsilon \end{pmatrix}$$

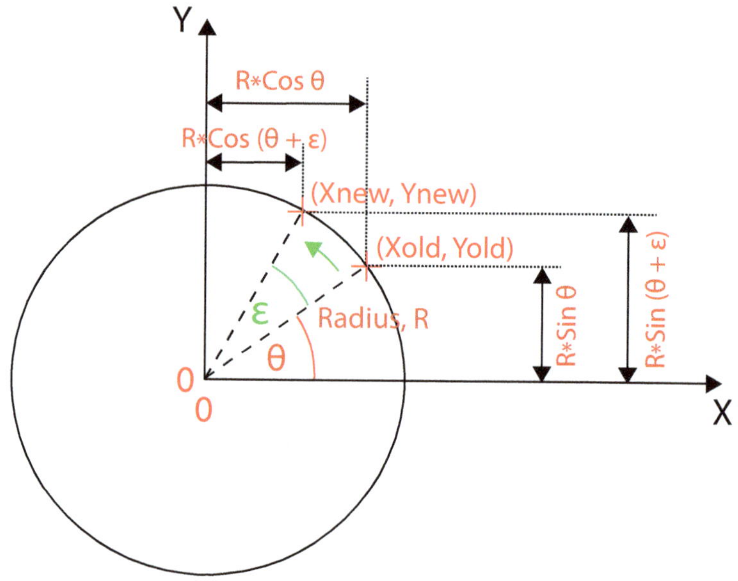

Figure 37.24 Rotating a point through angle ε from (Xold, Yold) to (Xnew, Ynew)

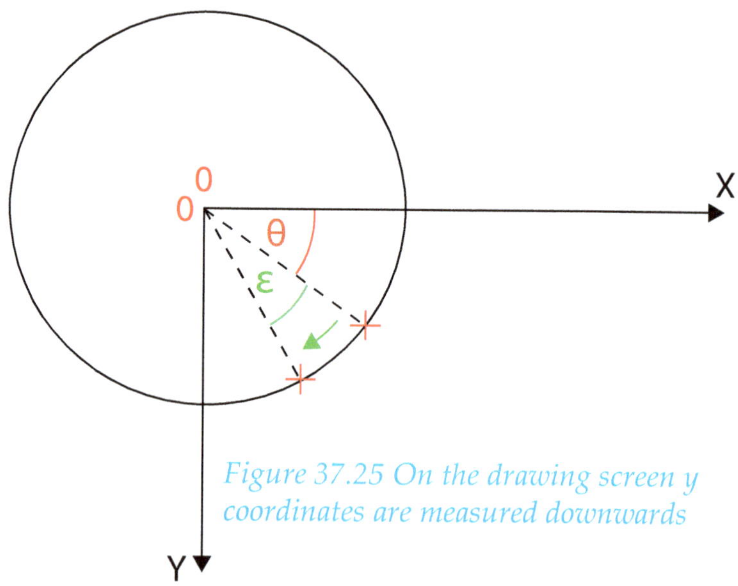

Figure 37.25 On the drawing screen y coordinates are measured downwards

Now that we have a formula for rotating a single point about the origin in the two-dimensional X-Y plane, we can apply this to every point of a two-dimensional object.

For the drawing screen, the origin is located in the topmost left corner, the Y-axis grows downwards.

Therefore to rotate an object clockwise on the screen, angle ε is positive. To rotate an object anticlockwise, angle ε is negative.

Figures 37.26, 37.27 show a square rotated clockwise and anticlockwise 20° using the equations **3** and **4**, above.

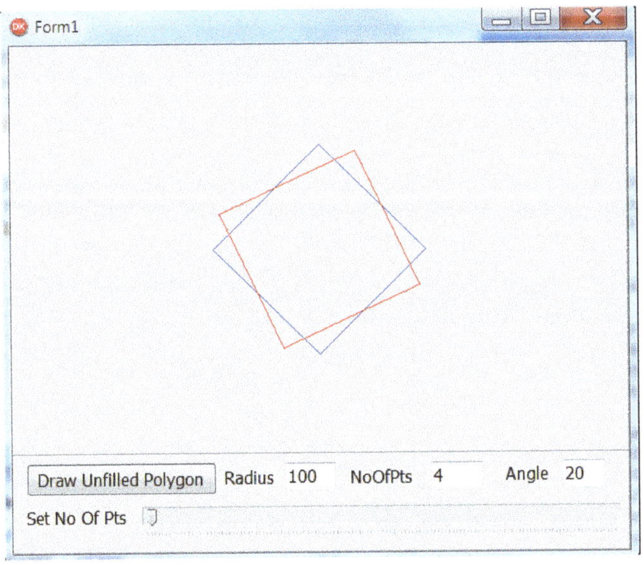

Figure 37.26 A blue square of side 100 rotated clockwise 20°, shown as a red square

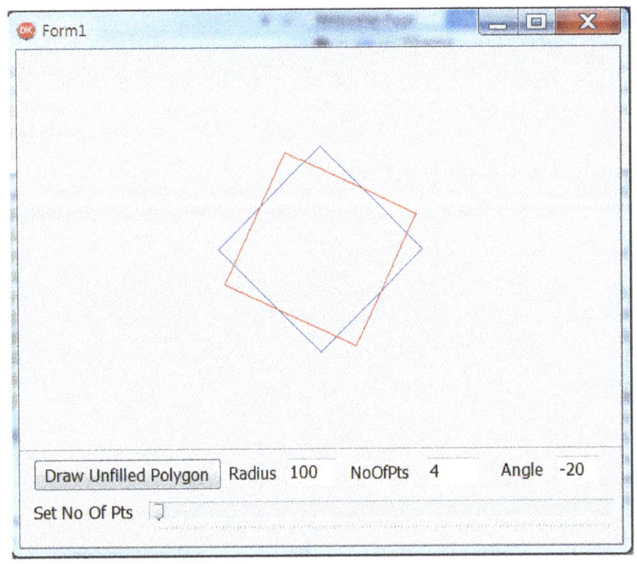

Figure 37.27 A blue square of side 100 rotated anticlockwise 20°, shown as a red square

Table 37.26 shows the code which calculates, using the rotation formulae, the coordinates after rotation of the polygon `CircleOfPointsArrayDouble`. It returns a rounded version, CircleOfPointsArrayInteger, which can be used by **Canvas.PolyLine** method of `TMyPanel(TopPanel.`

```
Function TForm1.RotateCirclePoints(CircleOfPointsArrayDouble : TCircleOfPointsDouble;
                                   Angle : Double; XCentre, YCentre : Integer) : TCircleOfPoints;
  Var
    i : Integer;
    CircleOfPointsArrayInteger : TCircleOfPoints;
    SinAngle, CosAngle, OldX, OldY : Double;
  Begin
    SetLength(CircleOfPointsArrayInteger, Length(CircleOfPointsArrayDouble));
    SinAngle := Sin(DegToRad(Angle));
    CosAngle := Cos(DegToRad(Angle));
    For i := 0 To Length(CircleOfPointsArrayDouble) - 1
      Do
        Begin
          OldX := CircleOfPointsArrayDouble[i].x - XCentre;
          OldY := CircleOfPointsArrayDouble[i].y - YCentre;
          CircleOfPointsArrayDouble[i].x := CosAngle * OldX - SinAngle * OldY + XCentre;
          CircleOfPointsArrayDouble[i].y := SinAngle * OldX + CosAngle * OldY + YCentre;
        End;
    For i := 0 To Length(CircleOfPointsArrayDouble) - 1
      Do
        Begin
          CircleOfPointsArrayInteger[i].x := Round(CircleOfPointsArrayDouble[i].x);
          CircleOfPointsArrayInteger[i].y := Round(CircleOfPointsArrayDouble[i].y);
        End;
    Result := CircleOfPointsArrayInteger;
  End;
```

Table 37.26 Function RotateCircleOfPoints calculates, using the rotation formulae, the coordinates after rotation of the polygon CircleOfPointsArrayDouble

Programming tasks

3. Using as a basis the project CirclePolyLineExpProject, write and test a function which scales any polygon drawn in CirclePolyLineProject by an equal factor in the X and Y directions.
The CirclePolyLineProject may be download from
www.educational-computing.com/DelphiBook/Code/Chapter37/CirclePolyLineExpProject.rar

Drawing Ellipses

Figure 37.28 shows in red, a curve known as an ellipse centered at the origin with width 2*a* and height 2*b* (major axis = 2a and minor axis = 2b).

Every point on the ellipse is given by

$$\frac{x^2}{a^2} + \frac{y^2}{b^2} = 1$$

Figure 37.28 shows a way of constructing an ellipse for a given *a* and *b*. First two concentric circles are drawn, one with radius *a* and another with radius *b*. A rotating arm 0BA, anchored at the origin, moves in an anticlockwise direction from θ = 0 to θ = 2π.

For any point P on the ellipse

$$x = a\cos\theta$$

$$y = b\sin\theta$$

This pair of equations is known as the parametric equations of an ellipse.

The parameter *a* is called the major axis of the ellipse and the parameter *b*, the minor axis.

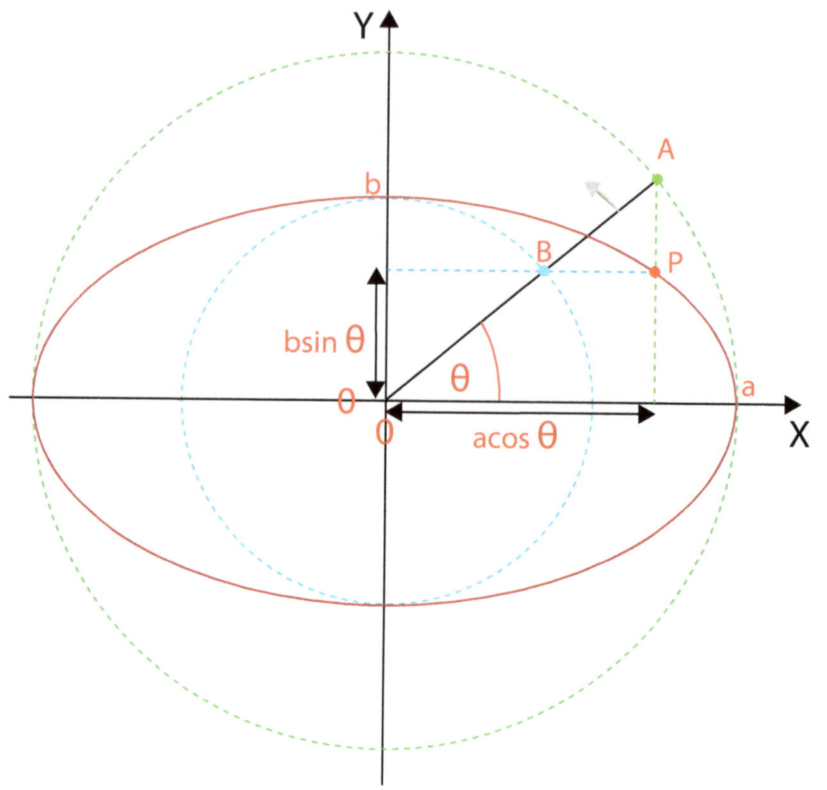

Figure 37.28 Construction of an ellipse from a parametric equation

When θ = 0

$$x = a$$

$$y = 0$$

When θ = $^{\pi}/_{2}$

$$x = 0$$

$$y = b$$

θ is called the eccentric anomaly.

www.educational-computing.com/DelphiBook/Code/Chapter37/EllipsePolyLineProject.rar

Figure 37.29 shows the output of application **EllipsePolyLineProject** for major axis 200 and minor access 100.

The function `CalculateEllipsePoints` which calculates the points that **PolyLine** uses to draw the ellipse in *Figure 37.29* is shown in *Table 37.27*.

If we use the same value for the major and minor axes then the ellipse that is drawn is a circle.

A major saving in computation time may be achieved by expoiting the inherent symmetry of the ellipse

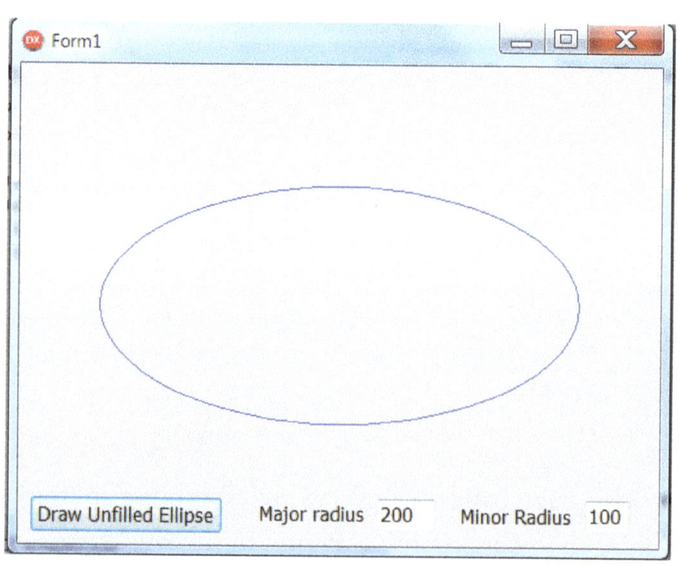

Figure 37.29 Drawing an ellipse using EllipsePolyLineProject

```
Function TForm1.CalculateEllipsePoints(XCentre, YCentre, MajorRadius,
                        MinorRadius, NoOfPoints : Integer) : TCircleOfPoints;
  Var
    AngleStepInDegrees, AngleStepInRadians : Double;
    AngleInRadians, XDifference, YDifference : Double;
    i : Integer;
    CircleOfPointsArrayDouble : TCircleOfPointsDouble;
    CircleOfPointsArrayInteger : TCircleOfPoints;
  Begin
    AngleStepInDegrees := 360/NoOfPoints;
    AngleStepInRadians := DegToRad(AngleStepInDegrees);
    AngleInRadians := 0;
    CircleOfPointsArrayDouble[0].x := XCentre + MajorRadius;
    CircleOfPointsArrayDouble[0].y := YCentre;
    For i := 1 To NoOfPoints - 1
      Do
        Begin
          AngleInRadians := AngleInRadians + AngleStepInRadians;
          CircleOfPointsArrayDouble[i].x := XCentre + MajorRadius*Cos(AngleInRadians);
          CircleOfPointsArrayDouble[i].y := YCentre + MinorRadius*Sin(AngleInRadians);
        End;
    CircleOfPointsArrayDouble[NoOfPoints].x := CircleOfPointsArrayDouble[0].x;
    CircleOfPointsArrayDouble[NoOfPoints].y := CircleOfPointsArrayDouble[0].y;
    For i := 0 To NoOfPoints
      Do
        Begin
          CircleOfPointsArrayInteger[i].x := Round(CircleOfPointsArrayDouble[i].x);
          CircleOfPointsArrayInteger[i].y := Round(CircleOfPointsArrayDouble[i].y);
        End;
    Result := CircleOfPointsArrayInteger;
  End;
```

PolyLine uses 0-indexed arrays

Table 37.27 Function CalculateEllipsePoints which uses the parametric equation for an ellipse to calculate 64 x, y points at approximately 6° intervals between 0 and 360°

Programming tasks

4. Make the necessary changes to function `CalculateEllipsePoints` to allow ellipses to be drawn with an angle φ between the major axis *a* and the x axis. Use the equations

$$x = a \cos \theta \cos \varphi - b \sin \theta \sin \varphi$$

$$y = a \cos \theta \sin \varphi + b \sin \theta \cos \varphi$$

Parametric description of a line

Euclid established some 2300 years ago that it is only possible to draw one straight line between any two separate points. The x and y coordinates of all points through which the line passes are all given by the equation

$$y = mx + c$$

where *m* is the gradient of the line and *c* is the intercept on the y axis.

Suppose the two end point x, y coordinates of the line that we wish to draw are (x_1, y_1) and (x_2, y_2) then the gradient *m* is given by

$$\frac{y_2 - y_1}{x_2 - x_1}$$

If $(x_1, y_1) = (1, 4)$ and $(x_2, y_2) = (2, 6)$ then $m = \dfrac{6 - 4}{2 - 1} = 2$

Therefore,

$$y = 2x + c$$

Using $x_1 = 1$ and $y_1 = 4$ in $y = mx + c$, we can determine *c* as follows

$$y = 2x + c \Rightarrow 4 = 2 \times 1 + c \Rightarrow c = 2$$

Therefore, the line with end points $(x_1, y_1) = (1, 4)$ and $(x_2, y_2) = (2, 6)$ is described by the equation

$$y = 2x + 2$$

Whilst this equation describes any point between the two given end points, it is also describes every point beyond the end points. With this description, a line is infinitely long.

To overcome this difficulty, we resort to a parametric description of the line. With this description, any point on the line joining the two points (x1, y1) and (x2, y2) has the coordinates

$$x = x_1 + t * (x_2 - x_1)$$

$$y = y_1 + t * (y_2 - y_1)$$

where, if the points are to lie within the end points, t must run from 0 to 1 inclusive. Thus all points lying on the line segment from (1, 4) to (2, 6) have the coordinates

$$x = 1 + t * (2 - 1)$$

$$y = 4 + t * (6 - 4)$$

i.e.

$$x = 1 + 2 * t$$

$$y = 4 + 2 * t$$

providing that t lies between 0 and 1.

Figure 37.30 shows the user interface of an application which uses a parametric formula to generate the x, y coordinates of the pixels to illuminate.

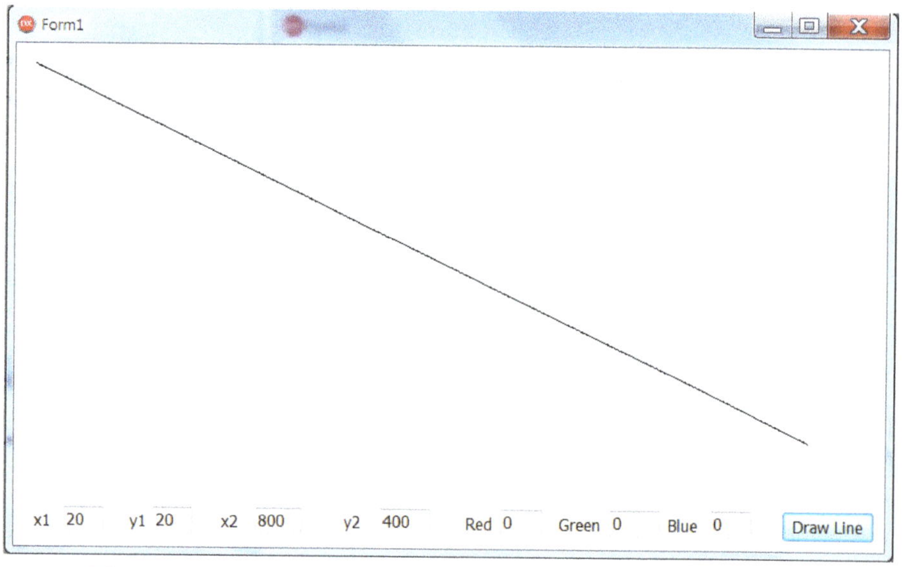

Figure 37.30 Drawing a line using a parametric formula to generate the x, y coordinates of the pixels to illuminate

Table 37.28 shows the on click handler for the **Draw Line** button which generates the x, y coordinates of the pixels which define the line in the colour determined by the red, green and blue settings.

```
Procedure TForm1.DrawLineClick(Sender: TObject);
  Var
    x, y, t : Single;
  Begin
    //X = X1 + (X2 - X1) * t
    //X = Y1 + (Y2 - Y1) * t
    t := 0.0;
    Repeat
      x := StrToInt(edtX1.Text) + (StrToInt(edtX2.Text) - StrToInt(edtX1.Text)) * t;
      y := StrToInt(edtY1.Text) + (StrToInt(edtY2.Text) - StrToInt(edtY1.Text)) * t;
      Canvas.Pixels[Round(x), Round(y)] := rgb(StrToInt(edtRed.Text), StrToInt(edtGreen.Text),
                                          StrToInt(edtBlue.Text));
      t := t + 0.001;
    Until (Abs(t - 1.0)) <= 0.001;
  End;
```

Table 37.28 On click event handler DrawLineClick which draws a line by plotting pixels with pixel position determined by parametric formula

What does parametric mean?

The parametric description of a line is shown in equations 5 and 6

$$x = x_1 + t * (x_2 - x_1) \quad \text{—⑤}$$

$$y = y_1 + t * (y_2 - y_1) \quad \text{—⑥}$$

Equations 5 and 6 are a mathematical description of how to calculate the x, y coordinates of any point on the line joining the two points (x1, y1) and (x2, y2).

We can rewrite equations 5 and 6 as follows

$$f_x(t) = x_1 + t * (x_2 - x_1) \quad \text{—⑦}$$

$$f_y(t)= y_1 + t * (y_2 - y_1) \quad \text{—⑧}$$

The notation *f(t)* is the standard way to show a function (by convention called *f* if we're only listing one). The output of *f* changes based on one variable (in this case, *t*). Change *t*, and the output for *f(t)* changes.

In this example, we have two functions, $f_x(t)$ and $f_y(t)$, but only one variable, *t*. If the value for *t* is changed, the outcome of each of $f_x(t)$ and $f_y(t)$ is changed.

A line is just a special case of a set of geometric shapes which we call curves. Another example of a curve is a circle.

A mathematical description of how to calculate the x, y coordinates of any point on a circle of radius R centred at xCentre, yCentre is

$$x = xCentre + R * \text{Cos } A \quad \text{—⑨}$$

$$y = yCentre + R * \text{Sin } A \quad \text{—⑩}$$

where A varies from 0 to 2π.
Rewriting 9 and 10, we obtain two functions $f_x(A)$ and $f_y(A)$ of a single variable *A*.

$$f_x(A) = xCentre + R * \text{Cos } A \quad \text{—⑪}$$

$$f_y(A)= yCentre + R * \text{Sin } A \quad \text{—⑫}$$

The set of functions defined in 7, 8, 11 and 12 describe a line and a circle, respectively. However, unlike normal functions, e.g. y = mx +c, the equations don't define a y coordinate in terms of an x coordinate, but instead link the values to a "control" variable, *t* or *A*.

We call these parametric "functions" or parametric-described curves or just parametric curves.

If *t* or *A* is varied then with every change two values are obtained, the x, y coordinates of a point on a line or a circle.

Bezier curves

Bézier curves are a form of "parametric" function. They take a set of points, and generate values somewhere "between" those points. (One of the consequences of this is that it is not possible to generate a point that lies outside the outline for the control points, commonly called the "convex hull" for the curve).

A French engineer Pierre Bézier developed Bézier curves for use in the design of Renault automobile bodies. A Bézier curve - *Figure 37.31* - between given start and end points, $\mathbf{P_0}$ and $\mathbf{P_2}$, is an approximating curve formed by adding a sequence of polynomial functions which have been created from the coordinates of a given set of control points $\mathbf{P_1}$.

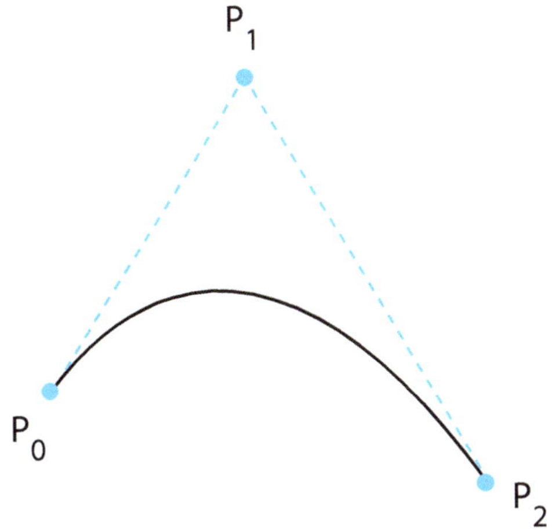

Figure 37.31 Three point Bezier curve

Delphi supports Bézier curves with method **PolyBezier(Const Points : Array Of TPoint)** belonging to the class **TCanvas**. **TPoint** is a record structure consisting of two fields, **X** and **Y**. As a VCL form has a **TCanvas** property, **Canvas**, we can call **Canvas.PolyBezier** to draw a Bézier curve on the client area of the form.

Canvas.PolyBezier requires a minimum of four points for any independent Bézier curve: the point to start the curve on, the point to end the curve on and two control points - *Figure 37.32*. For the four point Bézier curve the **Points** array must be populated as follows:

Points[0] - start point X, Y coordinates

Points[1] - first control point X, Y coordinates

Points[2] - second control point X, Y coordinates

Points[3] - end point X, Y coordinates

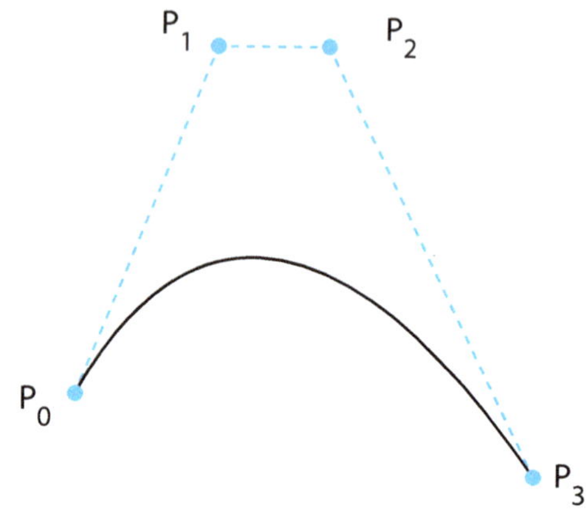

Figure 37.32 Four point Bezier curve

To draw more curves requires adding more points to the array **Points**. However, we must be careful when adding more control points to ensure that the total number of points is always three times the number of curves to be drawn plus one, because each Bézier curve requires two control points and an endpoint but the first requires, in addition, a start point. Each subsequent curve starts from the end point of the previous curve so requires only three points.

An important property of any Bézier curve is that it lies within the **convex hull** (polygon boundary) of the control points. This ensures that the curve smoothly follows the control points without erratic oscillations - *Figure 37.33*.

The polynomials that shape the Bézier curve are called blending finctions because they blend the points to form a composite function describing the curve. This composite is a polynomial of degree one less than the number of points. Three points generate a parabola - *Figure 37.31*. Four points generate a cubic curve - *Figure 37.32* and *Figure 37.33*. The general cubic function has the form

$$y = ax^3 + bx^2 + cx + d$$

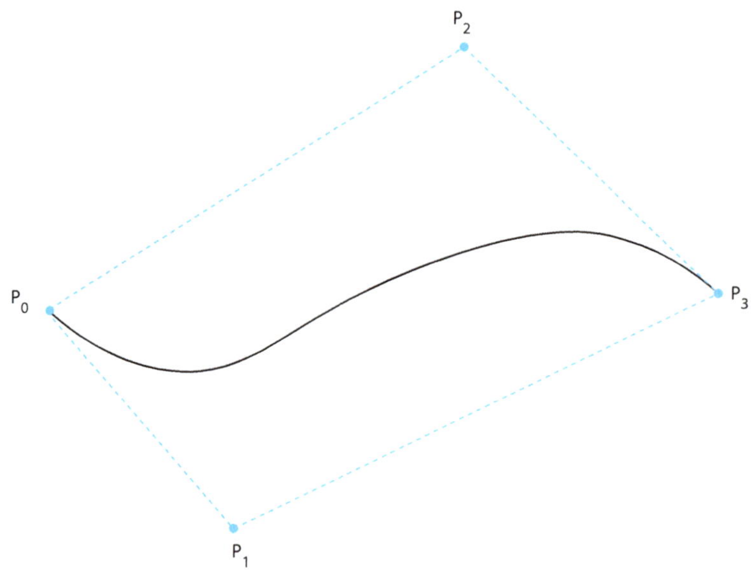

Figure 37.33 Four point Bezier curve illustrating the important property that the curve always lies within the convex hull (polygon boundary) of the control points

Background

See Professor John Kennedy's 'An Introduction to Bezier Curves' paper:
https://drive.google.com/file/d/1jRn_Q-XstNfTru-yg0htZq7ltRtT3IjP/view
and his maths papers and software:
https://sites.google.com/view/johnkennedyghome/home/downloadable-math-software
https://sites.google.com/view/johnkennedyghome/home/downloadable-math-papers

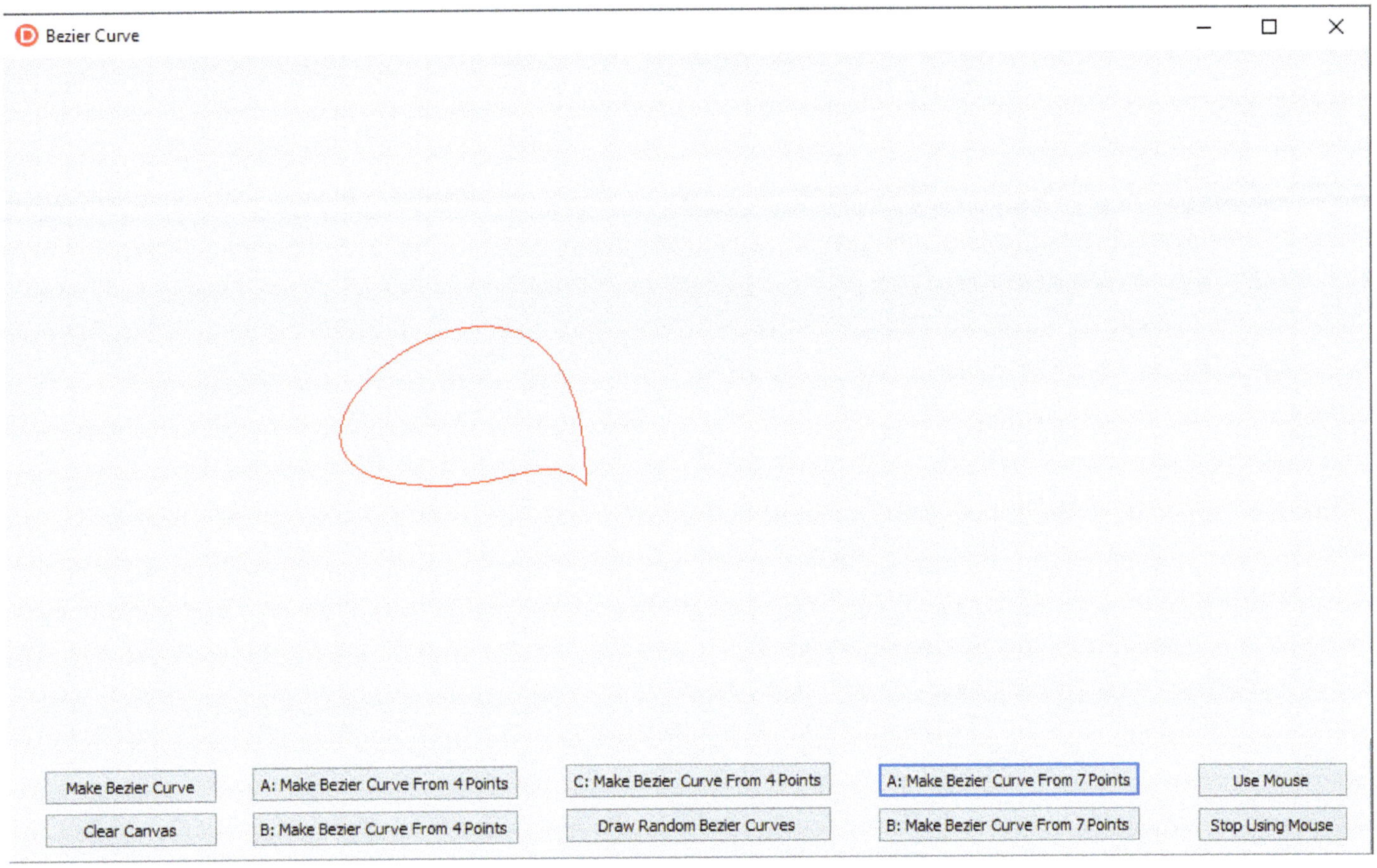

Figure 37.34 BezierCurveProject.dpr in execution

```
Unit BezierCurveUnit;
Interface
Uses
  Winapi.Windows, Winapi.Messages, System.SysUtils, System.Variants,
  System.Classes, Vcl.Graphics, Vcl.Controls, Vcl.Forms, Vcl.Dialogs,
  Vcl.StdCtrls, Vcl.ExtCtrls;
Type
  TfrmBezierCurve = Class(TForm)
                    btnMakeBezierCurve : TButton;
                    btnMakeBezierCurveFrom4Points : TButton;
                    btnMakeBezierCurveFrom7PointsA : TButton;
                    btnMakeBezierCurveFrom4PointsB : TButton;
                    Panel1 : TPanel;
                    btnMakeBezierCurveFrom4PointsC : TButton;
                    btnMakeBezierCurveFrom7PointsB : TButton;
                    btnClearCanvas : TButton;
                    btnDrawRandomBezierCurves : TButton;
                    btnUseMouse : TButton;
                    btnStopUsingMouse : TButton;
                    Procedure btnMakeBezierCurveClick(Sender : TObject);
                    Procedure btnMakeBezierCurveFrom4PointsAClick(Sender : TObject);
                    Procedure btnMakeBezierCurveFrom4PointsBClick(Sender : TObject);
                    Procedure btnMakeBezierCurveFrom4PointsCClick(Sender : TObject);
                    Procedure btnMakeBezierCurveFrom7PointsBClick(Sender : TObject);
                    Procedure btnMakeBezierCurveFrom7PointsAClick(Sender : TObject);
                    Procedure btnClearCanvasClick(Sender : TObject);
                    Procedure btnDrawRandomBezierCurvesClick(Sender : TObject);
                    Procedure FormCreate(Sender : TObject);
                    Procedure FormDestroy(Sender : TObject);
                    Procedure FormMouseUp(Sender : TObject; Button : TMouseButton;
                                          Shift: TShiftState; X, Y : Integer);
                    Procedure btnUseMouseClick(Sender : TObject);
                    Procedure btnStopUsingMouseClick(Sender : TObject);
                  End;
Var
  frmBezierCurve : TfrmBezierCurve;
  BezierCurveArray : Array Of TPoint;
```

Table 37.29 BezierCurveUnit.pas declaration section

```
Implementation
Var
  UseMouseForControlPoint : Boolean = False;
{$R *.dfm}
Procedure WriteBezierArrayToConsole;
  Var
    i : Integer;
  Begin
    For i := Low(BezierCurveArray) To High(BezierCurveArray)
      Do Writeln('BezierCurveArray[',i,'].x = ', BezierCurveArray[i].x,
                 ' BezierCurveArray[',i,'].y = ',BezierCurveArray[i].y);
    Writeln('--------------------------------------------------------------');
  End;
Procedure TfrmBezierCurve.btnMakeBezierCurveFrom7PointsAClick(Sender : TObject);
  Begin
    Canvas.Pen.Color := clRed;
    SetLength(BezierCurveArray, 7);
    BezierCurveArray[0] := TPoint.Create(300,300);
    BezierCurveArray[1] := TPoint.Create(100,300);
    BezierCurveArray[2] := TPoint.Create(400,50);
    BezierCurveArray[3] := TPoint.Create(400,300);
    BezierCurveArray[4] := TPoint.Create(375,275);
    BezierCurveArray[5] := TPoint.Create(350,300);
    BezierCurveArray[6] := TPoint.Create(300,300);
    WriteBezierArrayToConsole;
    Canvas.PolyBezier(BezierCurveArray);
  End;
Procedure TfrmBezierCurve.btnMakeBezierCurveFrom4PointsAClick(Sender : TObject);
  Begin
    Canvas.Pen.Color := clRed;
    SetLength(BezierCurveArray, 4);
    BezierCurveArray[0] := TPoint.Create(50,300);
    BezierCurveArray[1] := TPoint.Create(150,100);
    BezierCurveArray[2] := TPoint.Create(250,100);
    BezierCurveArray[3] := TPoint.Create(300,400);
    WriteBezierArrayToConsole;
    Canvas.PolyBezier(BezierCurveArray);
  End;
Procedure TfrmBezierCurve.btnStopUsingMouseClick(Sender : TObject);
  Begin
    UseMouseForControlPoint := False;
  End;
Procedure TfrmBezierCurve.btnUseMouseClick(Sender : TObject);
  Begin
    UseMouseForControlPoint := True;
  End;
Procedure TfrmBezierCurve.FormCreate(Sender : TObject);
  Begin
    AllocConsole;
    // Change color attributes
   // SetConsoleTextAttribute(GetStdHandle(STD_OUTPUT_HANDLE),
   //                                       FOREGROUND_BLUE);
  End;
Procedure TfrmBezierCurve.FormDestroy(Sender : TObject);
  Begin
    FreeConsole;
  End;
Procedure TfrmBezierCurve.btnMakeBezierCurveFrom4PointsBClick(Sender : TObject);
  Begin
    Canvas.Pen.Color := clRed;
    SetLength(BezierCurveArray, 4);
    BezierCurveArray[0] := TPoint.Create(50,300);
    BezierCurveArray[1] := TPoint.Create(150,100);
    BezierCurveArray[2] := TPoint.Create(200,500);
    BezierCurveArray[3] := TPoint.Create(300,250);
    WriteBezierArrayToConsole;
    Canvas.PolyBezier(BezierCurveArray);
  End;
Procedure TfrmBezierCurve.btnClearCanvasClick(Sender : TObject);
  Begin
    Canvas.FillRect(Rect(0, 0, ClientWidth, ClientHeight - Panel1.Height));
  End;
```

Table 37.30 BezierCurveUnit.pas first implementation section

```
Procedure TfrmBezierCurve.btnMakeBezierCurveFrom4PointsCClick(Sender : TObject);
  Begin
    Canvas.Pen.Color := clRed;
    SetLength(BezierCurveArray, 4);
    BezierCurveArray[0] := TPoint.Create(50,200);
    BezierCurveArray[1] := TPoint.Create(150,100);
    BezierCurveArray[2] := TPoint.Create(300,300);
    BezierCurveArray[3] := TPoint.Create(450,200);
    WriteBezierArrayToConsole;
    Canvas.PolyBezier(BezierCurveArray);
  End;
Procedure TfrmBezierCurve.btnMakeBezierCurveFrom7PointsBClick(Sender : TObject);
  Begin
    Canvas.Pen.Color := clRed;
    SetLength(BezierCurveArray, 7);
    BezierCurveArray[0] := TPoint.Create(50,300);
    BezierCurveArray[1] := TPoint.Create(150,50);
    BezierCurveArray[2] := TPoint.Create(250,400);
    BezierCurveArray[3] := TPoint.Create(350,300);
    BezierCurveArray[4] := TPoint.Create(350,300);
    BezierCurveArray[5] := TPoint.Create(450,100);
    BezierCurveArray[6] := TPoint.Create(600,300);
    WriteBezierArrayToConsole;
    Canvas.PolyBezier(BezierCurveArray);
  End;
Procedure TfrmBezierCurve.FormMouseUp(Sender : TObject; Button : TMouseButton;
                                      Shift : TShiftState; X, Y : Integer);
  Begin
   Canvas.Pen.Color := clRed;
   If UseMouseForControlPoint
     Then
       If (Y > Panel1.Height)
        Then
          Begin
            SetLength(BezierCurveArray, 4);
            BezierCurveArray[0] := TPoint.Create(50,200);
            BezierCurveArray[1] := TPoint.Create(150,100);
            BezierCurveArray[2] := TPoint.Create(X,Y);
            BezierCurveArray[3] := TPoint.Create(450,200);
            WriteBezierArrayToConsole;
            Canvas.PolyBezier(BezierCurveArray);
          End;
  End;
Procedure TfrmBezierCurve.btnDrawRandomBezierCurvesClick(Sender : TObject);
  Var
    i: Integer;
  Begin
    Canvas.Pen.Color := clRed;
    SetLength(BezierCurveArray, 4);
    For i := Low(BezierCurveArray) To High(BezierCurveArray)
      Do
        Begin
          BezierCurveArray[i].x := Random(ClientWidth);
          BezierCurveArray[i].y := Random(ClientHeight);
          Writeln('BezierCurveArray[',i,'].x = ', BezierCurveArray[i].x,
                  ' BezierCurveArray[',i,'].y = ',BezierCurveArray[i].y);
        End;
    Writeln('--------------------------------------------------------------');
    Canvas.PolyBezier(BezierCurveArray);
  End;
Procedure TfrmBezierCurve.btnMakeBezierCurveClick(Sender : TObject);
  Begin
    Canvas.Pen.Color := clRed;
    SetLength(BezierCurveArray, 7);
    BezierCurveArray[0] := TPoint.Create(50,300);
    BezierCurveArray[1] := TPoint.Create(100,50);
    BezierCurveArray[2] := TPoint.Create(250,200);
    BezierCurveArray[3] := TPoint.Create(400,50);
    BezierCurveArray[4] := TPoint.Create(500,300);
    BezierCurveArray[5] := TPoint.Create(600,300);
    BezierCurveArray[6] := TPoint.Create(700,200);
    WriteBezierArrayToConsole;
    Canvas.PolyBezier(BezierCurveArray);
  End;
End.
```

Table 37.31 BezierCurveUnit.pas remainder implementation section

38 Sound applications in Delphi

Playing sounds in Delphi

Purpose: To learn to write Delphi applications which play sound

Using Winapi.MMSystem

The **PlaySound** function in **Winapi.MMSystem** plays a sound specified by a given file name, resource, or system event. For example,

```
PlaySound(PChar(FileName), 0, SND_ASYNC Or SND_LOOP);
```

where the flags mean

SND_SYNC = 0	Start playing, and wait for the sound to finish
SND_ASYNC = 1	Start playing, and don't wait to return
SND_LOOP = 8	Keep looping the sound until another sound is played

To stop a sound which is playing use

```
PlaySound(Nil, 0, 0);
```

Before **PlaySound** came on the scene **sndPlaySound** was used but this is now obsolete although still retained for backward compatibility only.

Table 38.1 shows how both of these may be used to play a **WAV** file.

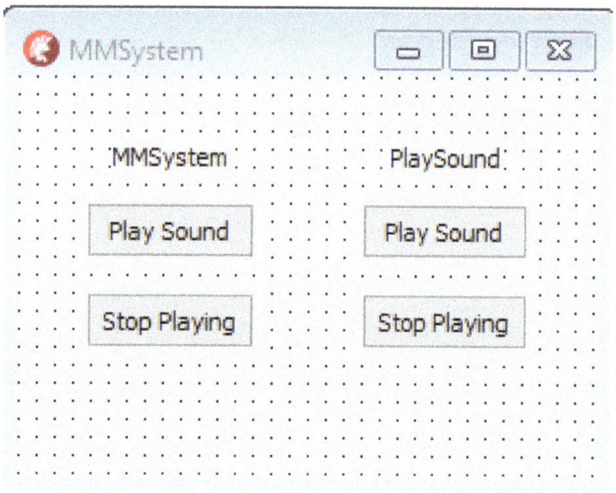

Figure 38.1 User Interface design

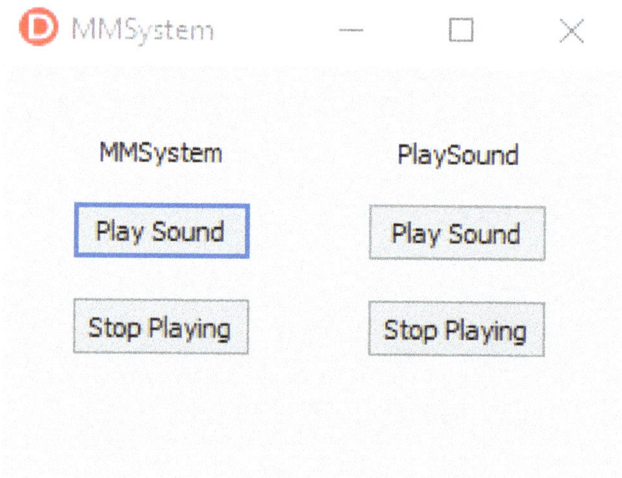

Figure 38.2 MMSystemProject in execution

Create a new VCL project and save it as `MMSystemProject.dproj` in folder `MMSystem`.

Add four buttons and two labels as shown in *Figure 38.1*.

Change their names and captions as shown in *Figure 38.1* and *Table 38.1*.

Create OnClick event handlers for each of the buttons and **insert** the respective code shown in *Table 38.1*.

Save the unit as `MMSystemUnit.pas` in folder `MMSystem`.

Build the project (**SHIFT F9**).

Download the zip file of `142901__fight2flyphoto__two-spitfires-flyby.wav` from www.educational-computing.co.uk/DelphiBookCode/DelphiCode.html. and save in `MMSystem\Win32\Debug` i.e. the same folder as `MMSystemProject.exe.`

Now **run** the project (**F9**) and **click** the **Play Sound** button beneath the label **MMSystem** and then to finish, **click** the **Stop Playing** button beneath **MMSystem**.

Repeat for the buttons beneath label **PlaySound**.

```
Unit MMSystemUnit;
Interface
Uses
  Winapi.Windows, Winapi.Messages, System.SysUtils, System.Variants, System.Classes, Vcl.Graphics,
  Vcl.Controls, Vcl.Forms, Vcl.Dialogs, Vcl.StdCtrls;
Type
  TfrmMMSystem = Class(TForm)
                  btnPlaySound: TButton;
                  btnStopPlaying: TButton;
                  btnPlaySound1: TButton;
                  lblMMSystem: TLabel;
                  btnStopPlaying1: TButton;
                  lblPlaySound: TLabel;
                  Procedure btnPlaySoundClick(Sender : TObject);
                  Procedure btnStopPlayingClick(Sender : TObject);
                  Procedure btnPlaySound1Click(Sender : TObject);
                  Procedure btnStopPlaying1Click(Sender : TObject);
                End;
Var
  frmMMSystem: TfrmMMSystem;
Implementation
  {$R *.dfm}
  Uses Winapi.MMSystem;
  Const
    cnstFileName = '142901__fight2flyphoto__two-spitfires-flyby.wav';
  {Spitfire WAV used under licence: https://creativecommons.org/licenses/by/3.0/}

  Procedure TfrmMMSystem.btnPlaySound1Click(Sender : TObject);
    Begin
      If FileExists(cnstFileName)
        Then PlaySound(PChar(cnstFileName), 0, SND_ASYNC Or SND_LOOP);
    End;

  Procedure TfrmMMSystem.btnPlaySoundClick(Sender : TObject);
    Begin
      sndPlaySound(cnstFileName,
        SND_NODEFAULT Or SND_ASYNC Or SND_LOOP);
    End;

  Procedure TfrmMMSystem.btnStopPlaying1Click(Sender : TObject);
    Begin
      PlaySound(Nil, 0, 0);
    End;

  Procedure TfrmMMSystem.btnStopPlayingClick(Sender : TObject);
    Begin
      sndPlaySound(nil, 0); // Stops the sound
    End;
End.
```

Table 38.1 Using MMSystem library to play the sound of two spitfires in a flypass

Installing Microsoft's speech api

The current version of Microsoft's speech api, at the time of writing **SAPI 5.4**, can only be imported successfully into Delphi 10.4.2 (latest version of Delphi at the time of writing) after the file **tlibimp.sym** located in `C:\Program Files (x86)\Embarcadero\Studio\21.0\bin` is edited. This file is the configuration file for the type library importer used by the IDE (and the command-line utility **TLibImp.exe**). **SAPI 5.4** type library defines its own versions of the already-defined-in-Delphi interfaces **IStream** and **ISequentialStream**.

Open tlibimp.sym in a text editor and insert two semicolons at the beginning of the lines defining **IStream** and **ISequentialStream** as shown in *Figure 38.3*. **Save** the edited file (you may need administrator rights to do this).

The Delphi IDE will then ignore these two lines when it reads **tlibimp.sym**.

```
;;=====================================================================;;
;; Names listed in this section are skipped by the importer
;; Built-in Interfaces, such as IUnknown and IDispatch are listed
;; here
;;=====================================================================;;
[BuiltInInterfaces]
{00020400-0000-0000-C000-000000000046}=IDispatch
{00000000-0000-0000-C000-000000000046}=IUnknown
;; {0000000C-0000-0000-C000-000000000046}=IStream
;; {0C733A30-2A1C-11CE-ADE5-00AA0044773D}=ISequentialStream
```

Figure 38.3 A section of file tlibimp.sym containing IStream and ISequentilaStream

Launch the Delphi IDE and select **Component|Import Component** to bring up the **Type of Component** window - *Figure 38.4*.

With **Import a Type Library** selected **click Next** to bring up the **Registered Type Libraries** window - *Figure 38.5*.

Scroll down to locate the **Microsoft Speech Object Library 5.4** - **sapi.dll** (don't use **sapi_onecore.dll** which was produced by Microsoft for the mobile market, originally).

Click Next to bring up the **Component window** which allows the palette page for this component to be specified - *Figure 38.6.*

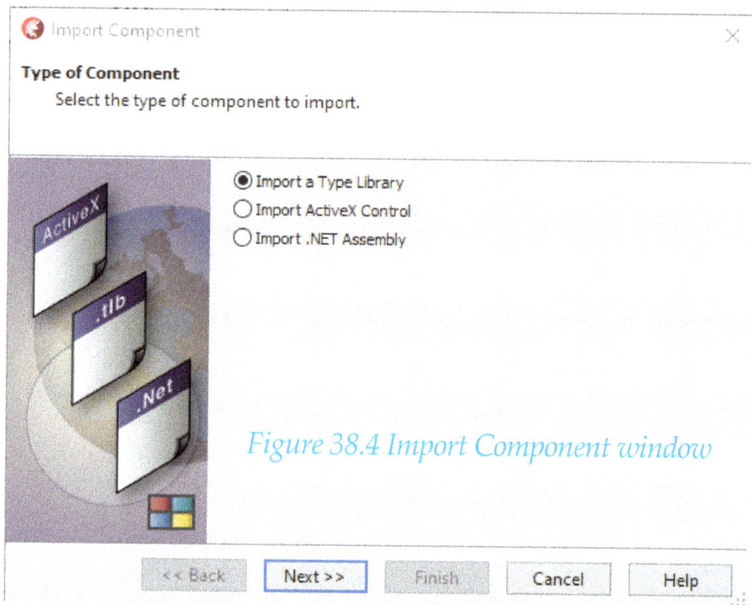

Figure 38.4 Import Component window

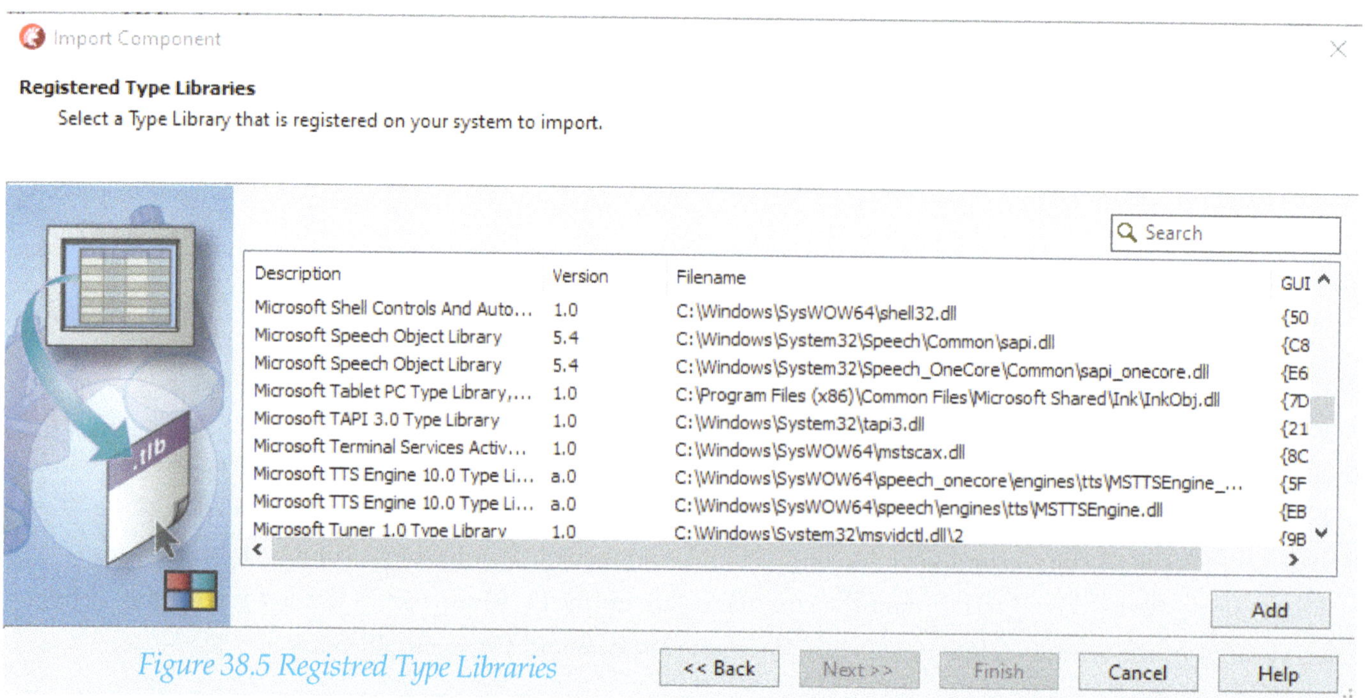

Figure 38.5 Registred Type Libraries

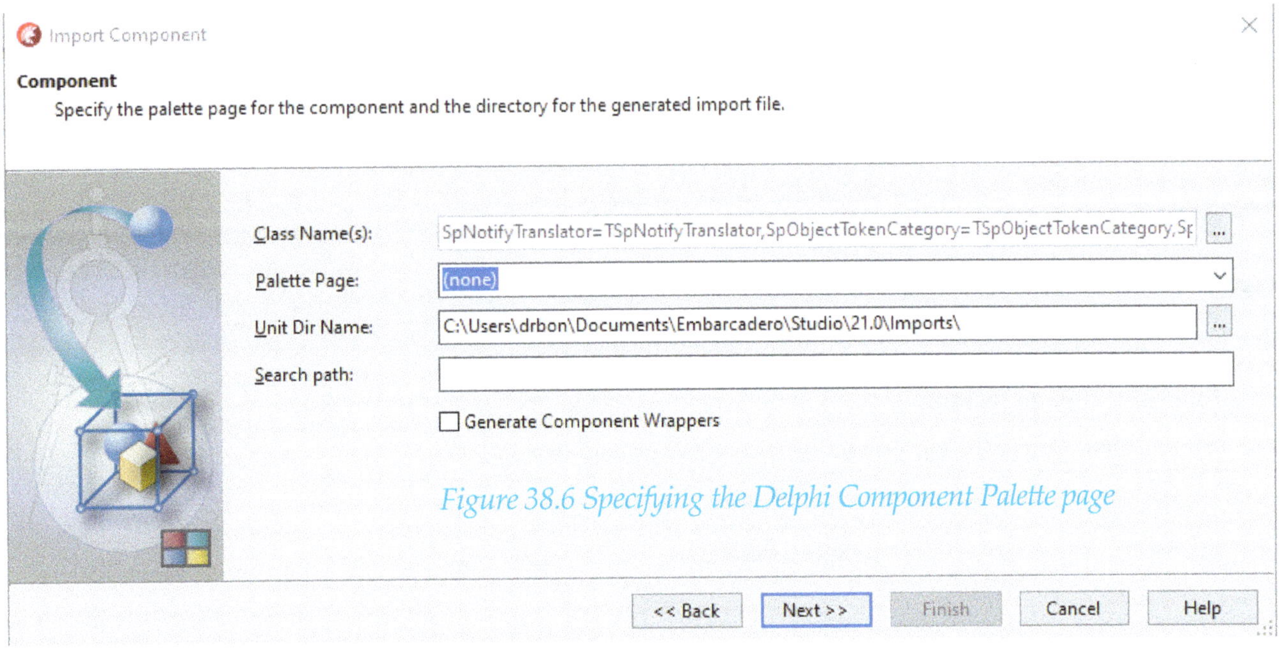

Figure 38.6 Specifying the Delphi Component Palette page

Change the **Palette Page** field from **(none)** to **SAPI54**.

Tick **Generate Component Wrappers**.

Click **Next**, then **select** **Install to New Package** and **click** **Next** again.

Enter `SAPI54` into the **Package name** field and `Speech API 5.4` into the **Description** field.

Click **Finish**.

The new package will now be created with the addition of a type library import unit, and the IDE will build the package. The **Confirm** window shown in *Figure 38.7* may pop up. In which case, **tick** the '**Remember selection and don't prompt again**' box then **click** the **Yes** button.

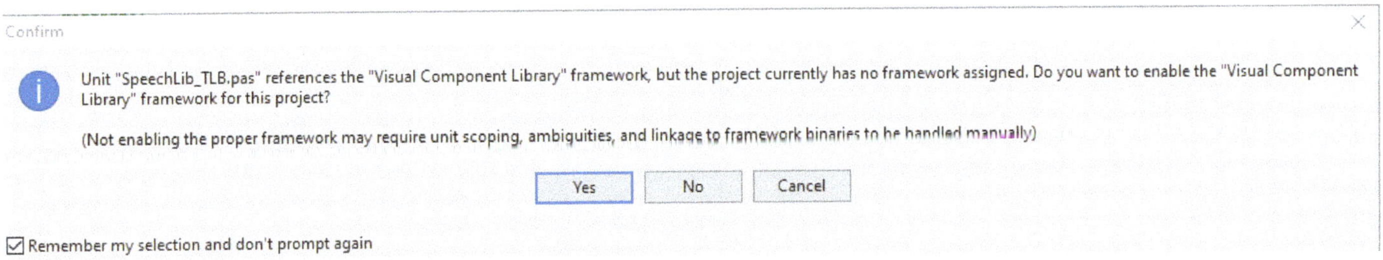

Figure 38.7 Enabling the VCL framework for the project

The component palette will now contain the tab **SAPI54** as shown in *Figure 38.8*.

Select **File|Close All**.

Each component in this tab is named after the primary interface it implements. So for example, the **TSpVoice** component implements the **SpVoice** interface. Documentation on all these interfaces is located in the SAPI 5.4 SDK documentation.

Text to speech simple example

Start a new VCL project.

Add a **TMemo** component and a **TButton** component to the form and arrange as shown in *Figure 38.9*.

Change the name of the **TButton** component to `btnSpeak` and its caption to `Speak`.

Change the name of the form to `frmTextToSpeech` and its caption to `Text To Speech`.

Change the name of the **TMemo** component to `memText`.

Replace the contents of `memText` **Lines** property in the **String List Editor** with the contents of the text file `Sonnet116.txt` (download from www.educational-computing.co.uk/DelphiBookCode/DelphiCode.html) - *Figure 38.9*.

Add a **TSPVoice** component from the **SAPI54** tab to the form.

Arrange the components on the form as shown in *Figure 38.10*.

Double click the Speak button to create an OnClick event handler.

Add the following code to its body

```
SpVoice1.Speak(memText.Text, SVSFlagsAsync);
```

Save the project as `TextToSpeechProject` in folder `TextToSpeech` and **save** the unit as `TextToSpeechUnit` in the same folder.

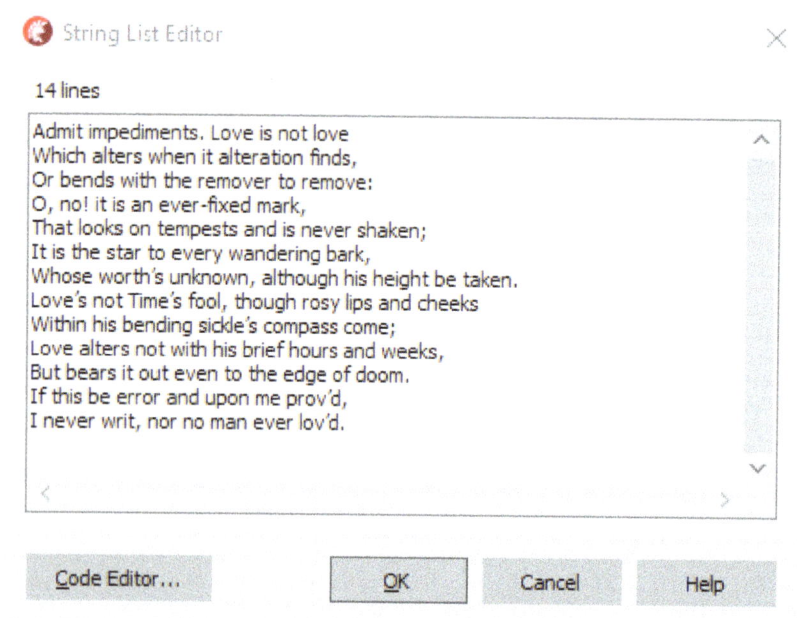

Figure 38.9 String List Editor for memText Lines property

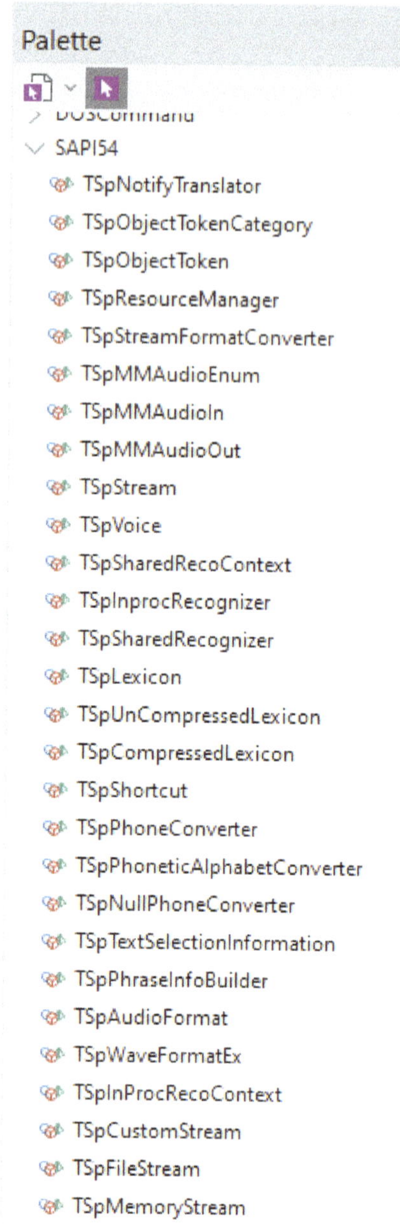

Figure 38.8 SAPI54 tab contents

Now **run** the project (F9) and **click** the `Speak` button. The text in the memo box should now be spoken by the computer.

Click the close icon to close the application.

Add another **TButton**, change its name to btnStopSpeech and its caption to `StopSpeech`.

Double click this button and add the following code to its body

```
SpVoice1.Speak('', SVSFPurgeBeforeSpeak);
```

File|Save All.

Run the project (**F9**) and start and stop the speech.

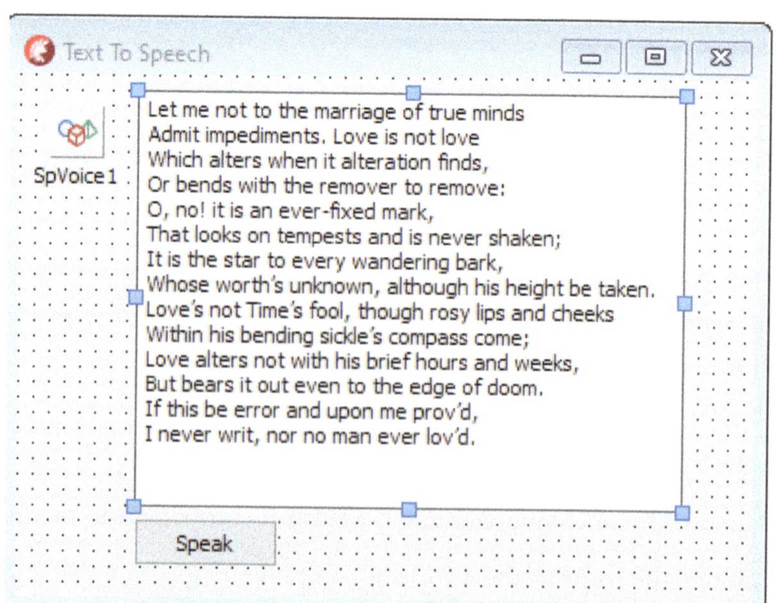

Figure 38.10 Text To Speech user interface

Close the application.

Now select SpVoice1 and in the Object Inspector select the Events tab.

Double click in the field for the **OnWord** event to create the event handler

```
TfrmTextToSpeech.SpVoice1Word(ASender : TObject; StreamNumber : Integer;
  StreamPosition : OleVariant; CharacterPosition, Length : Integer);
```

Add the following code to its body

```
memText.SelStart := CharacterPosition;
memText.SelLength := Length;
```

Set HideSelection to **False** for `memText` in the **Object Inspector** properties tab.

File|Save All.

Run the project (**F9**) and click the `Speak` button.

Each word as it is spoken should now be highlighted in blue - *Figure 38.11*.

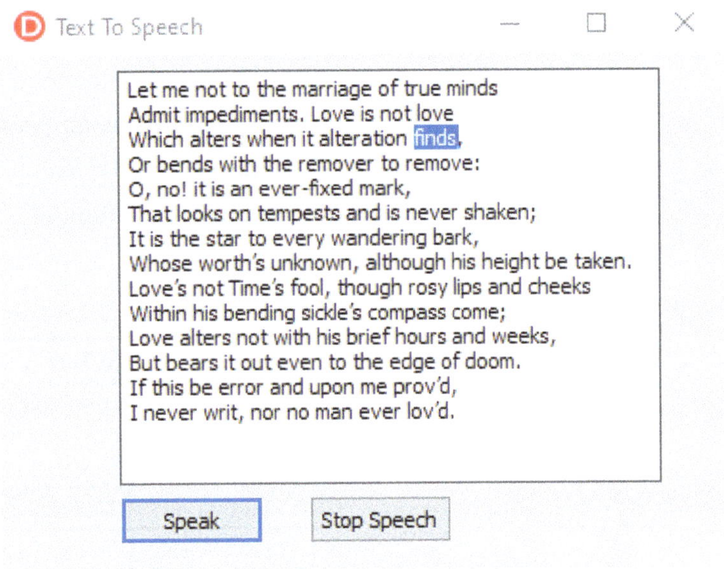

Figure 38.11 TextToSpeechProject in execution showing the spoken word highlighted in blue

39 VCL components 1

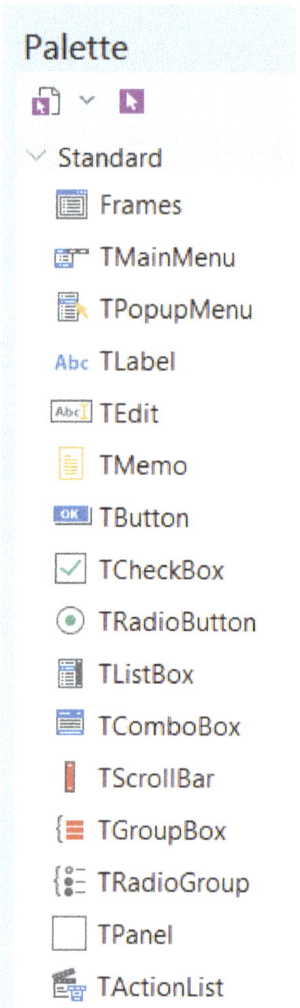

Fig. 39.1 Standard component palette Delphi 10.3

Introduction to VCL components

Purpose: To learn how to use Delphi components

Delphi comes with a large number of ready-to-use components.

These are largely based on Windows predefined controls. Controls are Microsoft® Windows' term for what Delphi calls components.

A control is technically a predefined window that has a specific behaviour and some styles and is capable of responding to specific messages.

The Windows predefined controls that will be considered in this chapter are located in the **Standard** component palette. These are the ones that you will use most often. *Figure 39.1* shows the standard component palette for **Delphi Community Edition 10.3** (the list of components has remained the same since **Delphi 7**). *Table 39.1* summarises what these components are used for.

Name	What it is used for
Frames	A frame (TFrame), like a form, is a container for other components. It can be saved on the Tool palette for easy reuse in different parts of the application.
TMainMenu	To design ordinary menus.
TPopUpMenu	To design pop-up menus.
TLabel	Used to label other components.
TEdit	To create a text box, a rectangular area, in which a user can enter one line of text.
TMemo	To create a text box in which a user can enter multiple lines of text.
TButton	To create buttons on screen that when clicked do something.
TCheckBox	To create options each consisting of two possibilities.
TRadioButton	To create a group of mutually exclusive options.
TListBox	To display a list of choices and also list images.
TComboBox	To enable a list box to be combined with an editable area to allow users to choose an item from a list or to enter their own choice directly.
TScrollBar	To provide a method for scrolling through a range of items.
TGroupBox	To group items so that they behave as a unit.
TRadioGroup	To create a special type of group box that makes it easier to work with radio buttons.
TPanel	To create a container component for other components that are to be treated as a group.
TActionList	To create a list of actions (or commands) that indicate 1. the operation to carry out when a menu item or button is clicked 2. the status updates to apply to all the elements linked to the action.

Table 39.1 What the standard components are used for

Using TMainMenu, TPopUpMenu, TButton and TMemo components

Start a new application in Delphi, **File/New/Application** or **File/New/VCL Forms Application - Delphi**.

This produces a **dpr/dproj** file and a **Unit1** file that the programmer can edit through the IDE.

It also creates a **dfm** file behind the scenes which corresponds to the form, `Form1`, that is visible in the IDE.

Save the project renaming `Project1` with the name `MainMenu` in a folder `MainMenuProject`.

Save the unit as `MainMenuUnit.pas`.

Change the name of the form to `frmMainMenu` and its caption to `Main Menu Example`.

Drop a `TMainMenu`, a `TPopUpMenu`, a `TButton` and a `TMemo` component on the form as shown in *Figure 39.2*.

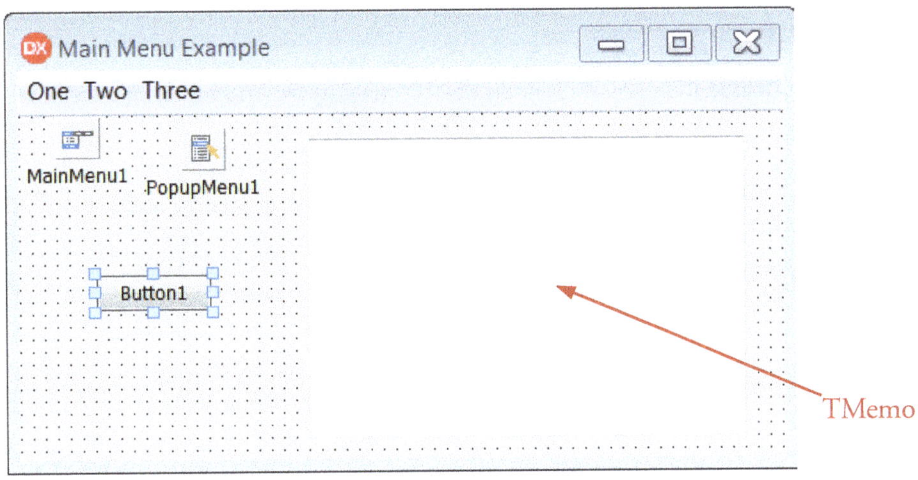

Fig. 39.2 Using TMainMenu, TPopUpMenu, TButton, TMemo from the Standard component palette Delphi 10.3

- Double click (or click on **...**) in the **Items** property **(Menu)** for `MainMenu1` shown in *Figure 39.3*, or
- Double click inside `MainMenu1` on form to bring up the **Menu Designer** window shown in *Figure 39.4*.

On the first occasion, a blank menu item is highlighted in the **Menu Designer**. Change the **Caption** property for the blank menu item to `One` as shown in *Figure 39.4*. Move to the next two columns in turn and enter `Two` and `Three`, respectively, for the blank menu item. Delphi assigns a **Name** property value based on the **Caption** property value, e.g. `One1`.

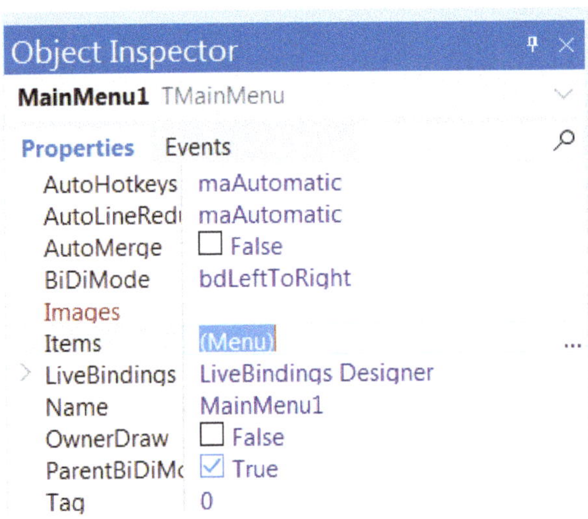

Fig. 39.3 Properties tab for MainMenu1 object

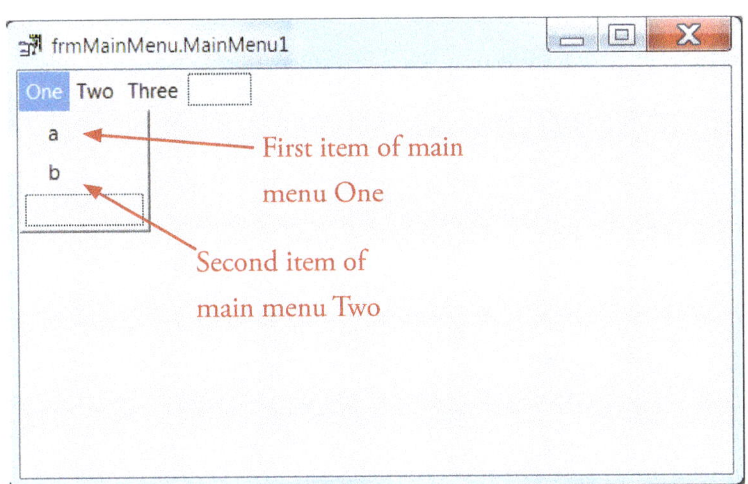

Fig. 39.4 Menu Designer window that appears on clicking on (Menu) ... in Items property

Each time a new menu item is added, e.g. `Five`, a dotted box is added below and to the right as shown in *Figure 39.5*. The box below corresponds to the first item of the main menu item and the one to the right the next main menu item. *Figure 39.4* shows that the first main menu item `One` already has two items belonging it, `a` and `b`, respectively.

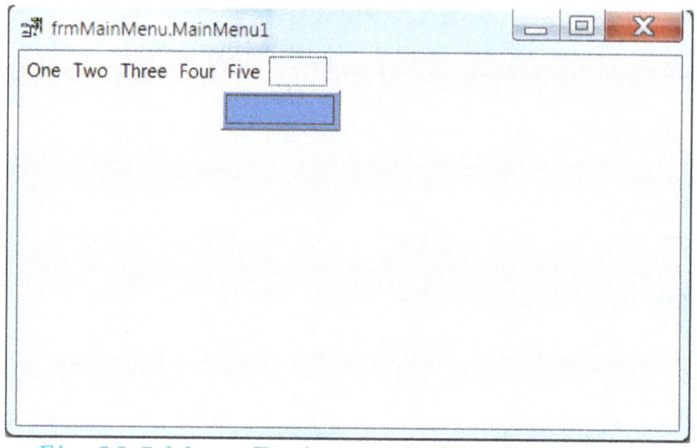

Fig. 39.5 Menu Designer window showing new main menu and new first item options

Deleting main menu items is achieved by selecting the main menu item in the **Menu Designer**, clicking the right mouse button and clicking the **Delete** option in the pop up menu (speedmenu) as shown in *Figure 39.6*.

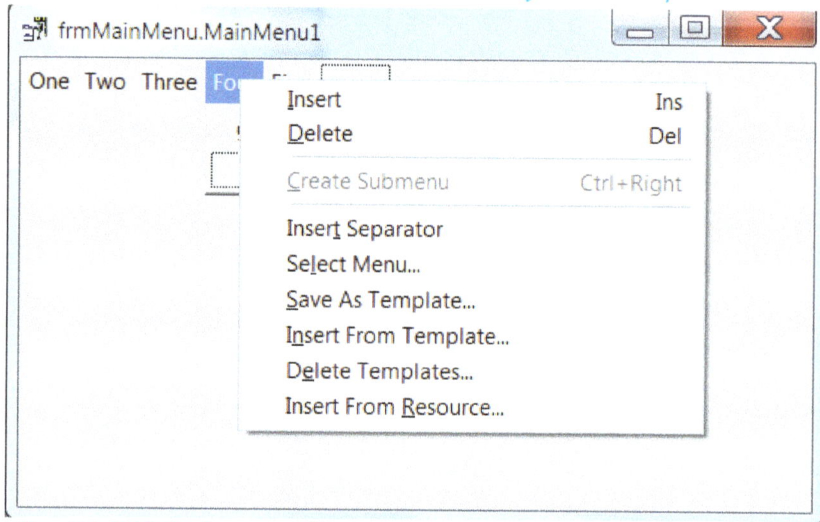

Fig. 39.6 Deleting a main menu item by clicking the right mouse button whilst within Menu Designer and selecting delete

Inserting a separator between items in a main menu option is achieved by selecting the main menu item in the **Menu Designer**, clicking the right mouse button and clicking the **Insert Separator** option in the pop up menu as shown in *Figure 39.7*.

Tables 39.2 and *39.3* show the source code for the **Implementation** and **Interface** sections, respectively, of `MainMenuUnit.pas`.

Each `TfrmMainMenu` **OnClick** event handler has been created by double-clicking the respective main menu item, e.g. `TfrmMainMenu.OneClick`.

`Memo1.Lines.Append('''Two'' on main menu clicked')` adds a line of text immediately after the previous line. (NB the use of two single quotes on each side of `Two` to achieve one single quote on each side when displayed).

Figure 39.8 shows `MainMenuProject` in execution and after main menu items `One`, `Two` and `Three` have been clicked more than once and in the order shown in the **TMemo** window.

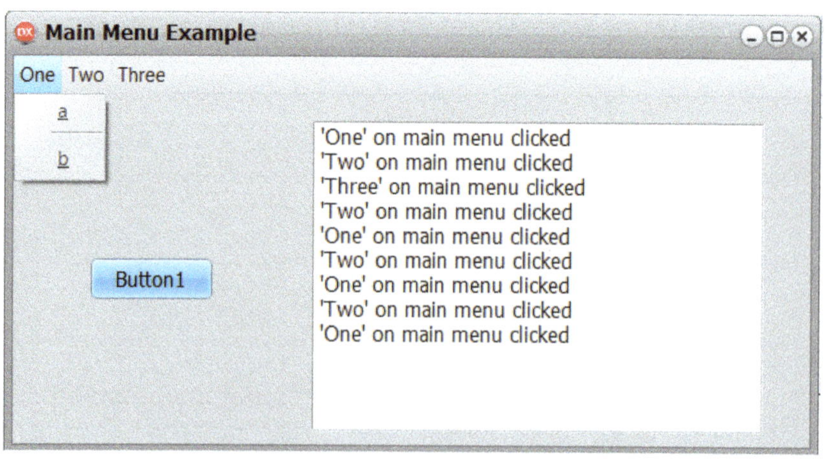

Fig. 39.8 MainMenuProject in execution with default style Aqua Light Slate selected in Project | Options | Appearance

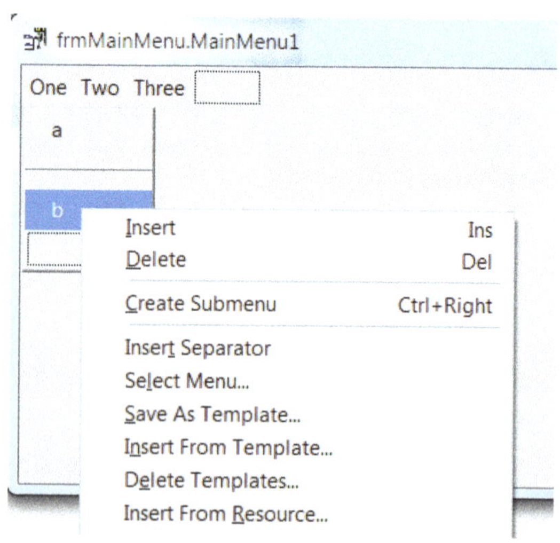

Fig. 39.7 Creating a separator in main menu item by clicking the right mouse button whilst within Menu Designer and selecting Insert Separator

```
Implementation
{$R *.dfm}
Procedure TfrmMainMenu.c1Click(Sender: TObject);
  Begin
    ShowMessage('''c'' clicked on main menu');
  End;
Procedure TfrmMainMenu.d1Click(Sender: TObject);
  Begin
    ShowMessage('''d'' clicked on main menu');
  End;
Procedure TfrmMainMenu.e1Click(Sender: TObject);
  Begin
    ShowMessage('''e'' clicked on main menu');
  End;
Procedure TfrmMainMenu.f1Click(Sender: TObject);
  Begin
    ShowMessage('''f'' clicked on main menu');
  End;
Procedure TfrmMainMenu.OneClick(Sender: TObject);
  Begin
    Memo1.Lines.Append('''One'' on main menu clicked');
  End;
Procedure TfrmMainMenu.ThreeClick(Sender: TObject);
  Begin
    Memo1.Lines.Append('''Three'' on main menu clicked');
  End;
Procedure TfrmMainMenu.TwoClick(Sender: TObject);
  Begin
    Memo1.Lines.Append('''Two'' on main menu clicked');
  End;
Procedure TfrmMainMenu.a1Click(Sender: TObject);
  Begin
    ShowMessage('''a'' clicked on main menu');
  End;
Procedure TfrmMainMenu.a2Click(Sender: TObject);
  Begin
    ShowMessage('You clicked ''a'' on pop up menu');
  End;
Procedure TfrmMainMenu.b1Click(Sender: TObject);
  Begin
    ShowMessage('''b'' clicked on main menu');
  End;
Procedure TfrmMainMenu.b2Click(Sender: TObject);
  Begin
    ShowMessage('You clicked ''b'' on pop up menu');
  End;
Procedure TfrmMainMenu.Button1Click(Sender: TObject);
  Begin
    PopUpMenu1.Popup(Mouse.CursorPos.X, Mouse.
CursorPos.Y);
  End;
End.
```

Table 39.2 MainMenuUnit.pas Implementation section containing event handlers for main menu items and Button1

```
Unit MainMenuUnit;
Interface
Uses
  Winapi.Windows, Winapi.Messages, System.SysUtils,
  System.Variants, System.Classes, Vcl.Graphics,
  Vcl.Controls, Vcl.Forms, Vcl.Dialogs, Vcl.Menus,
  Vcl.StdCtrls;
Type
  TfrmMainMenu = Class(TForm)
                   MainMenu1 : TMainMenu;
                   One : TMenuItem;
                   a1 : TMenuItem;
                   b1 : TMenuItem;
                   Two : TMenuItem;
                   Three : TMenuItem;
                   c1 : TMenuItem;
                   d1 : TMenuItem;
                   e1 : TMenuItem;
                   f1 : TMenuItem;
                   Button1 : TButton;
                   PopupMenu1 : TPopupMenu;
                   a2 : TMenuItem;
                   b2 : TMenuItem;
                   Memo1 : TMemo;
                   N1 : TMenuItem;
                   Procedure b1Click(Sender: TObject);
                   Procedure c1Click(Sender: TObject);
                   Procedure d1Click(Sender: TObject);
                   Procedure e1Click(Sender: TObject);
                   Procedure f1Click(Sender: TObject);
                   Procedure Button1Click(Sender:
                                          TObject);
                   Procedure b2Click(Sender: TObject);
                   Procedure a2Click(Sender: TObject);
                   Procedure a1Click(Sender: TObject);
                   Procedure OneClick(Sender: TObject);
                   Procedure TwoClick(Sender: TObject);
                   Procedure ThreeClick(Sender:
                                          TObject);
                 End;
Var
  frmMainMenu : TfrmMainMenu;
```

Table 39.3 MainMenuUnit.pas Interface section

(Download from www.educational-computing.com/DelphiBook/Code/Chapter39/MainMenuProject.rar)

Programming Task

1. Add main menu item `Four` to the `MainMenuProject`.
   Add to this main menu item, two menu items `g` and `h`.
   Create event handlers for all three new items, `Four`, `g` and `h`, similar in action to those that exist already.
   Run and test your modified program.

Creating a menu from a template

Delphi comes with a few pre-built menu templates. It is also possible to create your own menu templates for reuse.

Start a new application in Delphi, **File/New/Application** or **File/New/VCL Forms Application - Delphi**.

Save the project, renaming `Project1` with the name `MainMenuTemplate` in a folder

`MainMenuFromTemplateProject`.

Save the unit as `MainMenuFromTemplateUnit.pas`.

Change the name of the form to `frmMainMenuFromTemplate` and its caption to `Main Template Menu Example`.

Drop a `TMainMenu` component on the form and double click it to bring up the **Menu Designer.**

1. Click on the right mouse button to open up the speedmenu
2. Select **Insert From Template** from the speedmenu.

This brings up the menu of options shown in *Figure 39.9*.

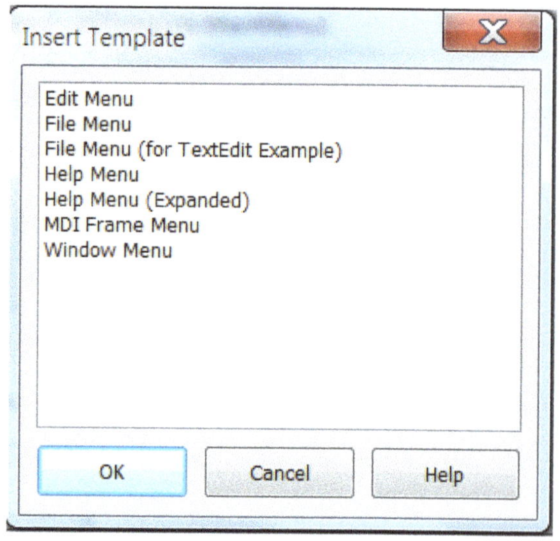

Fig. 39.9 Insert Template options

Select **File Menu**.

Repeat steps 1 and 2 and, in turn, select **Edit Menu** then **Window Menu** then **Help Menu**.

Figure 39.10 shows the result of adding these main menu items and the items in the **File** menu.

The **Object Inspector** view is included in *Figure 39.10* in order to show how accelerator keys are set up by prefacing the caption with &, e.g. `&File`. Accelerator keys are indicated by an underline, e.g. `File`. An accelerator key allows a user to press ALT and the underlined key to produce the same effect as clicking the menu item.

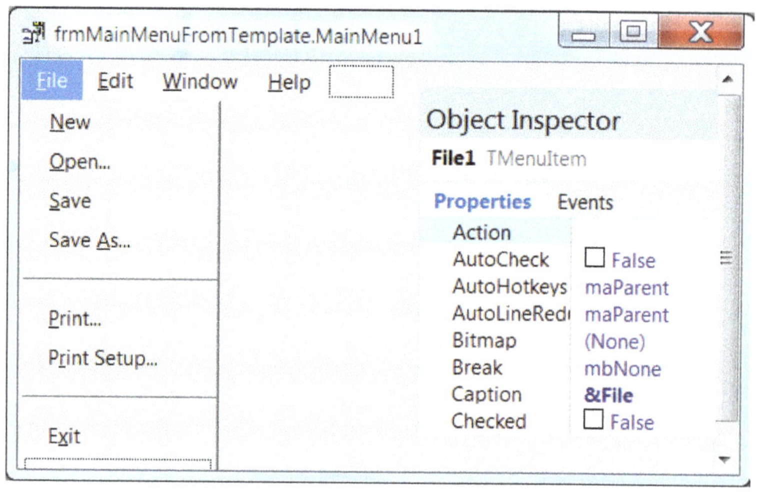

Fig. 39.10 Menu Designer showing menu templates File, Edit, Window and Help added to form

Figure 39.11 shows `MainMenuFromTemplate` project in execution with the **Edit** menu currently selected.

At design time, menu items may be moved by dragging and dropping them. A menu item may be removed by selecting the menu item and pressing the **Del** key or by clicking the right mouse button and selecting Delete from the speedmenu.

Figure 39.12 shows how a keyboard shortcut can be added to a menu item, item 'a' in this instance in `MainMenuProject` application.

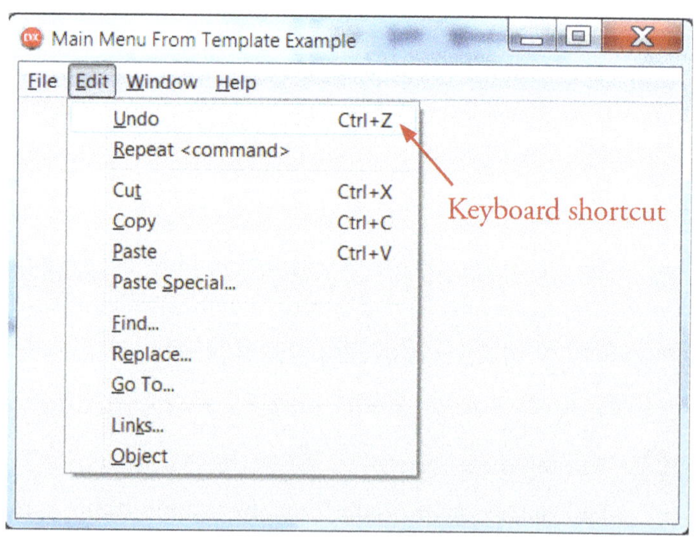

Fig. 39.11 MainMenuFromTemplate in execution showing pre-built Edit menu options

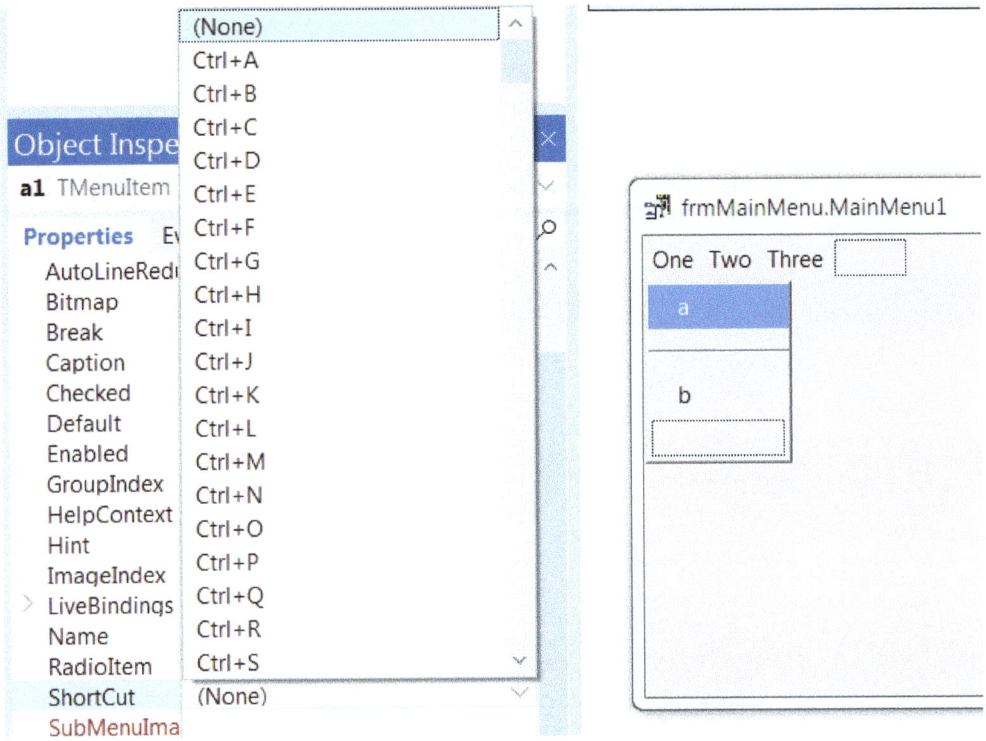

Fig. 39.12 Creating a keyboard shortcut for a menu item

TMemo component

TMemo as we have seen is a text box that handles multiple lines of text.

The text is stored in the **Lines** property as numbered lines, with the numbering starting from 0.

Figure 39.13 shows the Object Inspector for a **TMemo** object, `Memo1`.

The property **MaxLength** sets the maximum number of characters that can be entered except when its value is 0 which denotes no limit.

Clicking the ellipsis (...) in the **(TStrings)** field of the **Lines** property brings up the **String List Editor** as shown in *Figure 39.14*.

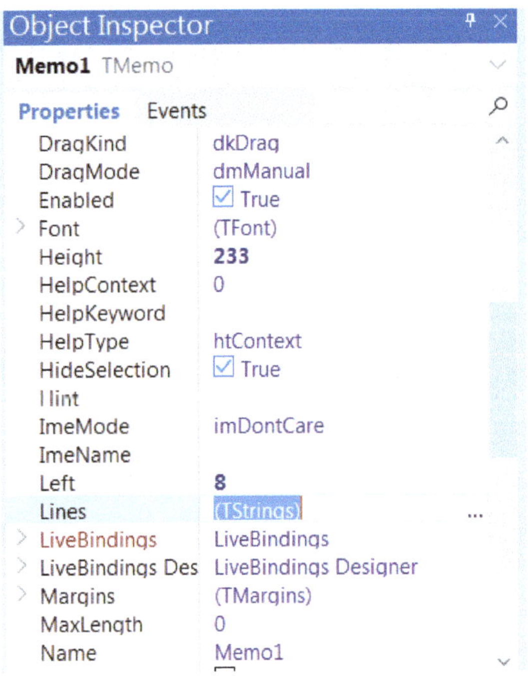

Fig. 39.13 Object Memo1 of type TMemo and some of its properties

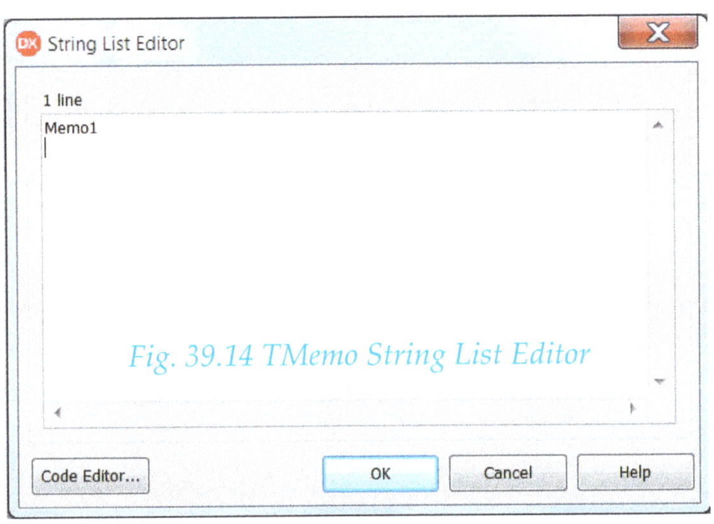

Fig. 39.14 TMemo String List Editor

Lines of text may be directly entered into the editor window, edited or any existing lines deleted.

The total number of lines is recorded in a read only property (not visible in the Object Inspector) but accessible with `Memo1.Lines.Count`.

If the WordWrap property is true, the text in the window is wrapped at the right margin so that it fits in the client area - Figure 39.15.

The ScrollBars property allows scrollbars to be assigned to the TMemo window. Its property options are ssBoth, ssHorizontal, ssNone, ssVertical.

Figure 39.16 demonstrates the use of scrollbars.

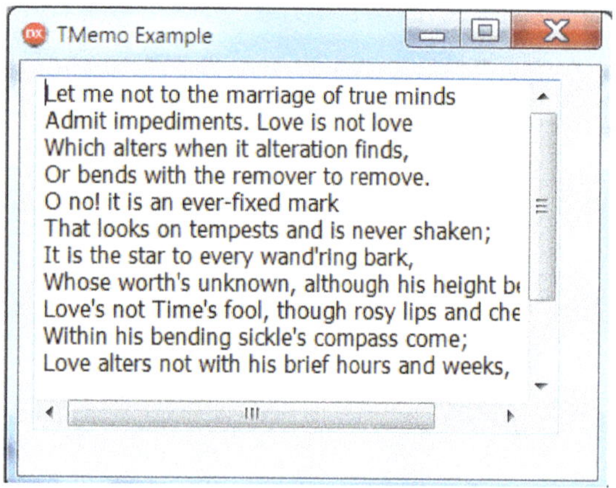

Fig. 39.16 Demonstrating the use of scrollbars

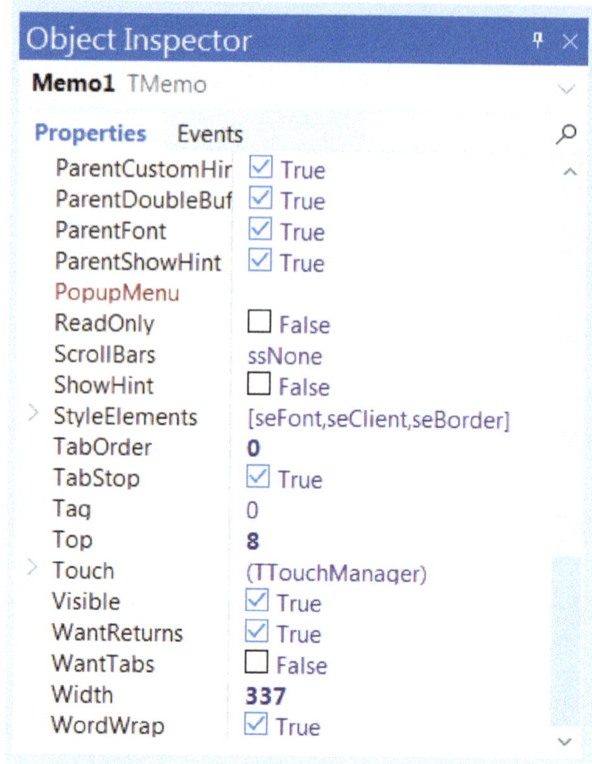

Fig. 39.15 Object Memo1 of type TMemo and some more of its properties

Table 39.4 shows the source code for the FormCreate event handler which first clears the memo box (TMemo window) before loading the text of a text file 'Sonnet116.txt'.

Table 39.5 shows examples of the use of some properties/methods of TMemo and Table 39.6 shows the implementation section of a program TMemoWithButtonsProject that demonstrates the use of some of these.

```
Unit TMemoUnit;
Interface
Uses
  Winapi.Windows, Winapi.Messages, System.SysUtils,
  System.Variants, System.Classes, Vcl.Graphics,
  Vcl.Controls, Vcl.Forms, Vcl.Dialogs, Vcl.StdCtrls;
Type
  TfrmMemoExample = Class(TForm)
                      Memo1 : TMemo;
                      Procedure FormCreate(Sender: TObject);
                    End;
Var
  frmMemoExample : TfrmMemoExample;
Implementation
{$R *.dfm}
Procedure TfrmMemoExample.FormCreate(Sender: TObject);
  Begin
    Memo1.Lines.Clear;
    Memo1.Lines.LoadFromFile('Sonnet116.txt');
  End;
End.
```

Table 39.4 Using FormCreate event handler to load the contents of a text file into Lines

Figure 39.17 shows `TMemoWithButtonsProject.dproj` in execution, button `Load File` clicked.

(Download from www.educational-computing.com/DelphiBook/Code/Chapter39/TMemoComponentWithButtons.rar)

Property/Method	Example
Memo1.Lines.Text	`Memo1.Lines.Text := 'Lots of text'#10'Lots more'#10'and more';`
Memo1.Lines.LoadFromFile(FileName)	`Memo1.Lines.LoadFromFile('Sonnet116.Txt');`
Memo1.Lines[n]	`Memo1.Lines[2] := 'Hello world!';`
Memo1.Lines.Append(AString)	`Memo1.Lines.Append('Appending a line of text');`
Memo1.Lines.Delete(n)	`Memo1.Lines.Delete(0);`
Memo1.Lines.Move(n, m)	`Memo1.Lines.Move(0,3);`
Memo1.Lines.Exchange(n, m)	`Memo1.Lines.Exchange(0,2);`
Memo1.Lines.Insert(0, AString)	`Memo1.Lines.Insert(0,'Hello World!');`
Memo1.Alignment	`Memo1.Alignment := taCenter;`

Table 39.5 Examples of the use of some properties/methods of TMemo

P

```
Implementation
{$R *.dfm}
Procedure TfrmMemoExample.btnAssignTextClick(Sender: TObject);
  Begin
    Memo1.Lines.Text := 'Lots of text'#10'Lots more'#10'and more';
  End;
Procedure TfrmMemoExample.btnLoadFileClick(Sender: TObject);
  Begin
    Memo1.Lines.Clear;
    Memo1.Lines.LoadFromFile('Sonnet116.Txt');
  End;
Procedure TfrmMemoExample.btnIndexIntoLineClick(Sender: TObject);
  Begin
    Memo1.Lines.Clear;
    Memo1.Lines.LoadFromFile('Sonnet116.Txt');
    Memo1.Lines[2] := 'Hello world!';
  End;
Procedure TfrmMemoExample.btnAppendLineClick(Sender: TObject);
  Begin
    Memo1.Lines.Clear;
    Memo1.Lines.Text := 'Lots of text'#10'Lots more'#10'and more';
    Memo1.Lines.Append('Appending a line of text');
  End;
Procedure TfrmMemoExample.btnDeleteLineClick(Sender: TObject);
  Begin
    Memo1.Lines.Clear;
    Memo1.Lines.LoadFromFile('Sonnet116.Txt');
    If MessageDlg('Do you want to delete the first line?',
                  mtCustom, [mbYes, mbNo], 0) = mrYes
      Then Memo1.Lines.Delete(0);
  End;
Procedure TfrmMemoExample.btnMoveLineClick(Sender: TObject);
  Begin
    Memo1.Lines.Clear;
    Memo1.Lines.LoadFromFile('Sonnet116.Txt');
    If MessageDlg('Do you want to move the line with index 0 to become line with index 3?',
                  mtCustom, [mbYes, mbNo], 0) = mrYes
      Then Memo1.Lines.Move(0,3);
  End;
Procedure TfrmMemoExample.btnExchangeLinesClick(Sender: TObject);
  Begin
    Memo1.Lines.Clear;
    Memo1.Lines.LoadFromFile('Sonnet116.Txt');
    If MessageDlg('Do you want to exchange the line with index 0 to line with index 2?',
                  mtCustom, [mbYes, mbNo], 0) = mrYes
      Then Memo1.Lines.Exchange(0,2);
End;
Procedure TfrmMemoExample.btnJustificationClick(Sender: TObject);
  Begin
    Memo1.Lines.Clear;
    Memo1.Lines.Text := 'Lots of text'#10'Lots more'#10'and more';
    If MessageDlg('Do you want to switch to right justify the text?',
                  mtCustom, [mbYes, mbNo], 0) = mrYes
      Then Memo1.Alignment := taRightJustify;
    If MessageDlg('Do you want to switch to centre the text?',
                  mtCustom, [mbYes, mbNo], 0) = mrYes
      Then Memo1.Alignment := taCenter;
    If MessageDlg('Do you want to switch to left justify the text?',
                  mtCustom, [mbYes, mbNo], 0) = mrYes
      Then Memo1.Alignment := taLeftJustify;
  End;
End.
```

Table 39.6 TMemoWithButtonsProject.dproj, unit TMemoWithButtonsUnit implementation section

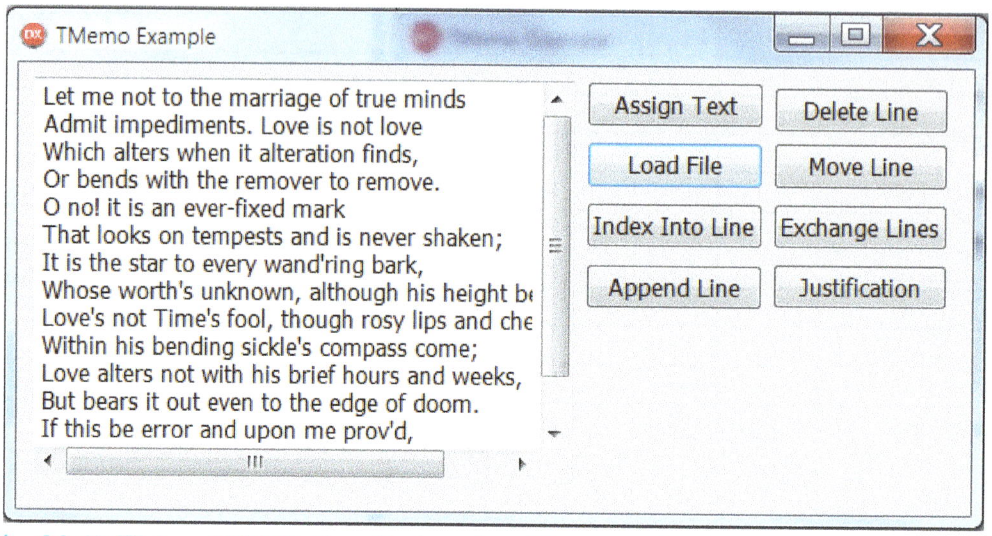

Fig. 39.17 TMemoWithButtonsProject.dproj in execution, button Load File clicked

TMemo also supports a

1. Save to file method, e.g. `Memo1.Lines.SaveToFile(FileName);`
2. Copy to clipboard method, e.g. `Memo1.CopyToClipboard;`
3. Paste from clipboard method, e.g. `Memo1.PasteFromClipboard;`

It is possible to also use *Ctrl C* to copy text highlighted in the TMemo text box to the Windows clipboard and *Ctrl V* to paste text from the Windows clipboard to the selected position within the TMemo text box.

Save to file, copy to clipboard, paste from clipboard and clear functionality have been added to the TMemo project and the modified project saved as `TMemoClipboardProject` and its modified unit as `TMemoClipboardUnit`.

Figure 39.18 shows program `TMemoClipboardProject` in execution.

A TSaveTextFileDialog non-visual component from the Dialogs tab was also added to allow specification of the path and filename of the text file in which the contents of the TMemo text box are to be saved using event handler `btnSaveToFileClick`- *Table 39.7*.

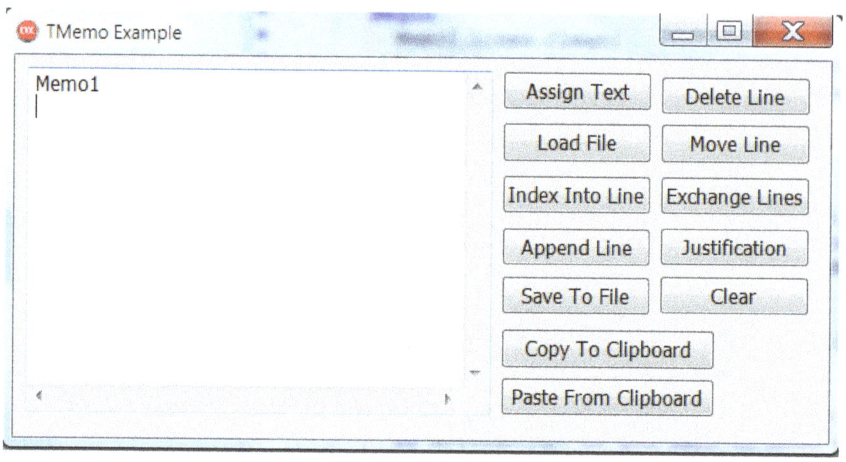

Fig. 39.18 TMemoClipboardProject.dproj in execution

```
Procedure TfrmMemoExample.btnSaveToFileClick(Sender: TObject);
 Begin
   If SaveTextFileDialog1.Execute
     Then
       Begin
         If FileExists(SaveTextFileDialog1.FileName)
           Then Raise Exception.Create('File already exists.')
           Else Memo1.Lines.SaveToFile(SaveTextFileDialog1.FileName);
       End;
 End;
```
P

Table 39.7 TMemoClipboardUnit event handler for the Save To File button

(Download from www.educational-computing.com/DelphiBook/Code/Chapter39/TMemoClipboard.rar)

Programming Task

2. Modify application `TMemoClipboard` so that it
   1. Prompts user for line number of line to be deleted and then uses this number to delete the line
   2. Prompts user for line number of line to be selected and and then its value is displayed by ShowMessage
   3. Prompts user for line numbers of lines to be exchanged and then uses these to exchange these lines
   4. Prompts user for line numbers of lines required by `Move` and then uses these to apply `Move`
   5. Inserts a given string value supplied by user at given line number supplied by user.
3. Modify TfrmMemoExample.btnLoadFileClick to use TOpenTextFileDialog from the Dialogs tab to open a selected text file.

Using TListBox and TComboBox components

The **TListBox** component enables a user to select an item from a scrollable list of string items as shown in *Figure 39.19*.

The list of items can be created in the **Items** property editor box or from executable code - *Table 39.8*. The **Items** property editor box can be brought up by clicking on **...** in the **Items** property shown in *Figure 39.20*.

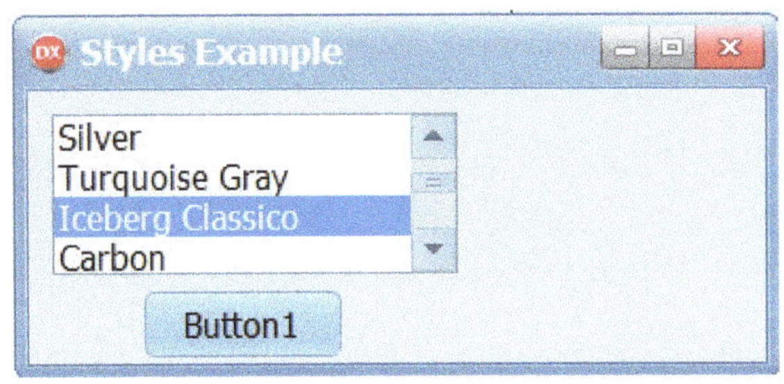

Fig. 39.19 Delphi 10.3 VCL application TListBoxProject in execution

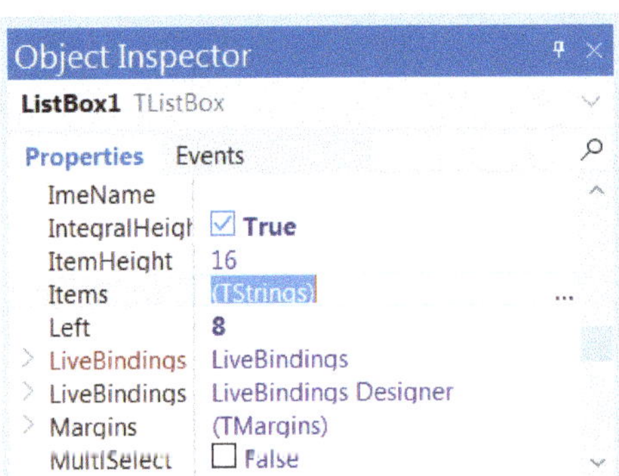

Fig. 39.20 ListBox1 Properties

The application `TListBoxProject` whose unit is shown in *Table 39.8* has been designed to allow the user to select the Graphical User Interface (GUI) style from the style options offered in the list box.

The ability to choose different GUI styles has been available since Delphi XE2.

The default style is chosen on the **Project|Options|Appearance** page as shown in *Figure 39.21*. The default style is selected from the list box

P

```
Unit TListBoxUnit;
Interface
Uses
  Winapi.Windows, Winapi.Messages, System.SysUtils,
  System.Variants, System.Classes, Vcl.Graphics,
  Vcl.Controls, Vcl.Forms, Vcl.Dialogs,
  Vcl.StdCtrls, Vcl.Themes, Vcl.Styles;
Type
  TfrmStylesExample = Class(TForm)
                      btnChangeStyle : TButton;
                      ListBox1 : TListBox;
                      Procedure FormCreate(Sender: TObject);
                      Procedure RefreshStylesList;
                      Procedure ChangeStyleClick(Sender: TObject);
                    End;
Var
  frmStylesExample : TfrmStylesExample;
Implementation
{$R *.dfm}
Procedure TfrmStylesExample.btnChangeStyleClick(Sender: TObject);
  Begin
    If ListBox1.ItemIndex <> -1
      Then TStyleManager.SetStyle(ListBox1.Items[ListBox1.ItemIndex]);
  End;
Procedure TfrmStylesExample.FormCreate(Sender: TObject);
  Begin
    RefreshStylesList;
  End;
Procedure TfrmStylesExample.RefreshStylesList;
  Var
    StyleName : String;
  Begin
    ListBox1.Clear;
    For StyleName In TStyleManager.StyleNames
      Do ListBox1.Items.Add(StyleName);
    ListBox1.ItemIndex := 0;
  End;
End.
```

These two libraries need to be added

Table 39.8 Application TListBoxProject, unit TListBoxUnit

(Download from www.educational-computing.com/DelphiBook/Code/Chapter39/TListBoxProject.rar)

populated with the items that have been ticked in the custom styles window.

Table 39.9 shows the main program, `Program TListBoxProject`, (Project|View Source) and the statement that sets the default style:

```
TStyleManager.TrySetStyle('Iceberg
        Classico');
```

TrySetStyle() is a method of the class **TStyleManager**.

```
Program TListBoxProject;
Uses
  Vcl.Forms,
  TListBoxUnit in 'TListBoxUnit.pas' {StylesExample},
  Vcl.Themes,
  Vcl.Styles;
{$R *.res}
Begin
  Application.Initialize;
  Application.MainFormOnTaskbar := True;
  TStyleManager.TrySetStyle('Iceberg Classico');
  Application.CreateForm(TfrmStylesExample, frmStylesExample);
  Application.Run;
End.
```

Table 39.9 Application TListBoxProject main program

The unit of this application, *Table 39.8*, contains an **OnClick** event handler that changes the style when the `ChangeStyle` button is clicked:

```
Procedure TfrmStylesExample.ChangeStyleClick(Sender: TObject);
  Begin
    If ListBox1.ItemIndex <> -1
      Then TStyleManager.SetStyle(ListBox1.Items[ListBox1.ItemIndex]);
  End;
```

`ListBox1.Items` is a list of strings.

`ListBox1.ItemIndex` is the index of the currently selected string, i.e. style name.

Therefore,

`ListBox1.Items[ListBox1.ItemIndex]`

stores the style name of the currently selected item of `ListBox1`.

Calling `TStyleManager.SetStyle` then sets the GUI style to the currently selected style.

The list box is populated by calling procedure

`TStylesExample.RefreshStylesList`

which is done when the form is created.

Table 39.10 shows how `ListBox1` is populated with style names.

`RefreshStylesList` first clears `ListBox1` before populating `ListBox1.Items` with the names of the custom styles that were ticked in **Project|Options|Appearance**. These styles are bundled with the executable that is created when the project is built.

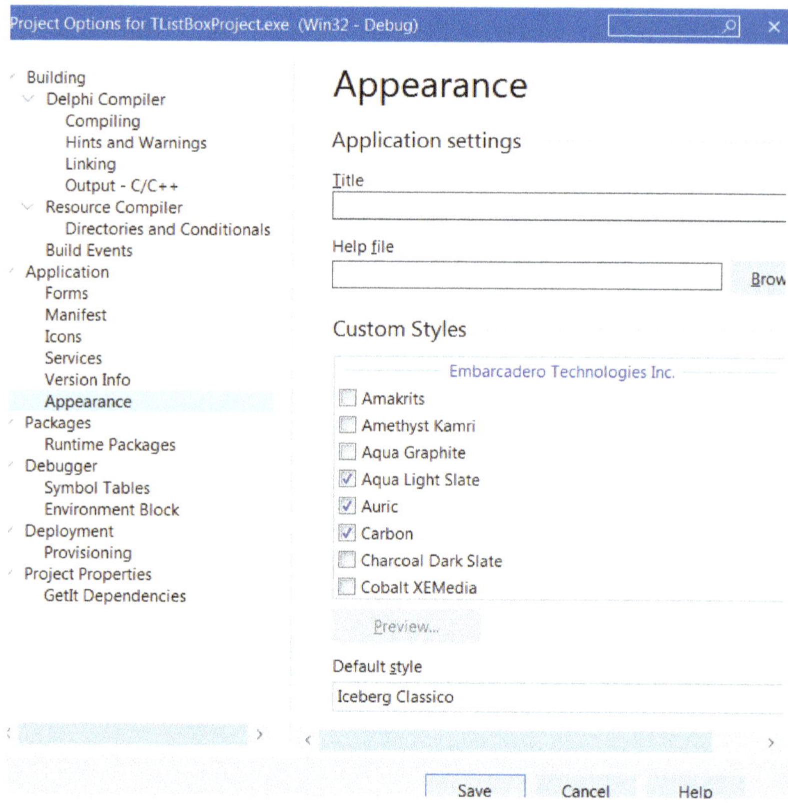

Fig. 39.21 Selecting custom styles via Project|Options|Appearance

A **TListBox** does allow multiple items to be selected together if the property **MultiSelect** is set to **True**. Obviously, this does not make sense for the styles example we have considered but there are situations where this might be usefully employed.

The **IntegralHeight** property of the list box was set to **True** to make sure that the list box cannot be resized in such a way that an item is only partly visible.

```
Procedure TfrmStylesExample.RefreshStylesList;
  Var
    StyleName : String;
  Begin
    ListBox1.Clear;
    For StyleName In TStyleManager.StyleNames
      Do ListBox1.Items.Add(StyleName);
    ListBox1.ItemIndex := 0;
  End;
```

Table 39.10 Shows how ListBox1 is populated

(Download from www.educational-computing.com/DelphiBook/Code/Chapter39/ComboBoxProject.rar)

A **TComboBox** serves a similar purpose to a **TListBox** which is to store a list of strings.

However, it differs from a **TListBox** in three respects

1. The full list of items to select from is hidden, as a result it uses less screen space
2. An item not present in the list can be entered in the combobox by typing its name in the box's edit field
3. It does not support multiple selection of items.

The unit `ComboBoxUnit` for the Delphi 10.3 VCL application `ComboBoxProject` is shown in *Table 39.11*.

Figure 39.22 shows the `ComboBoxProject` immediately after launch. The control's edit field is clearly shown.

The list of items shown in *Figure 39.23* was added via **String List Editor** launched from the **TComboBox** property **Items** by clicking **...** the ellipsis symbol. The edit field was emptied by clearing the `ComboBox1.Text` field.

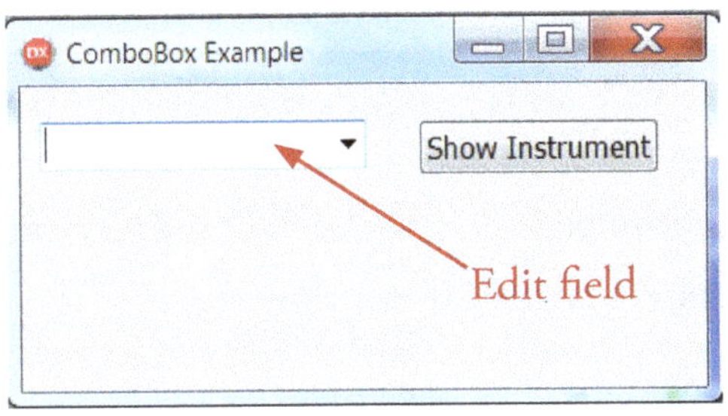

Fig. 39.22 ComboBox project in execution showing the edit field

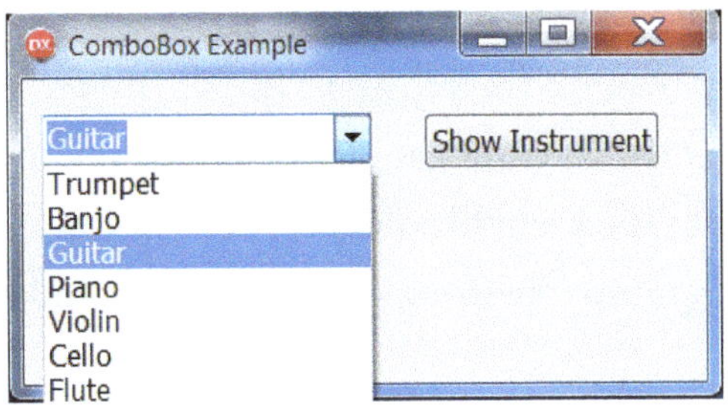

Fig. 39.23 ComboBox project in execution showing the selection of Guitar from the list of items

The event handler for the `Show Instrument` button has to check whether an item from the list of strings has been selected ot a new item has been entered via the edit field. For the latter case,

`ComboBox1.ItemIndex = -1`

and

`Length(ComboBox1.Text)>0`.

For the former,

`ComboBox1.ItemIndex`

contains the index of the selected item, 0 for the first, 1 for the second, and so on.

By changing **Sorted** to **True** in the properties tab of `ComboBox1`, the list of items will appear in ascending alphabetical order.

```
Unit ComboBoxUnit;
Interface
Uses
  Winapi.Windows, Winapi.Messages, System.SysUtils,
   System.Variants, System.Classes, Vcl.Graphics,
  Vcl.Controls, Vcl.Forms, Vcl.Dialogs, Vcl.StdCtrls;
Type
  TfrmComboBoxExample = Class(TForm)
                          ComboBox1 : TComboBox;
                          btnShowInstrument : TButton;
                          Procedure btnShowInstrumentClick(Sender: TObject);
                        End;
Var
  frmComboBoxExample : TfrmComboBoxExample;
Implementation
{$R *.dfm}
Procedure TfrmComboBoxExample.btnShowInstrumentClick(Sender: TObject);
  Begin
    If ComboBox1.ItemIndex <> -1
      Then ShowMessage(ComboBox1.Items[ComboBox1.ItemIndex])
      Else
        If Length(ComboBox1.Text) > 0
          Then ShowMessage(ComboBox1.Text)
          Else ShowMessage('Nothing selected');
  End;
End.
```

P

Table 39.11 Application ComboBoxProject, unit ComboBoxUnit

Programming Task

4. Add two more items, *tuba* and *cornet*, to ComboBox1 in application ComboBoxProject. Set Sorted to True. Run the application again to check that these items now appear and in the correct alphabetical order.
5. Add more styles to ListBox1 in application TListBoxProject. Run the application again and check that you can change the default style to each of the new styles.

(Download from www.educational-computing.com/DelphiBook/Code/Chapter39/CheckBoxRadioButtonProject.rar)

Using TCheckBox and TRadioButton components

The **TCheckBox** component/control presents a single option which may either be ticked or unticked as shown in *Figure 39.24*.

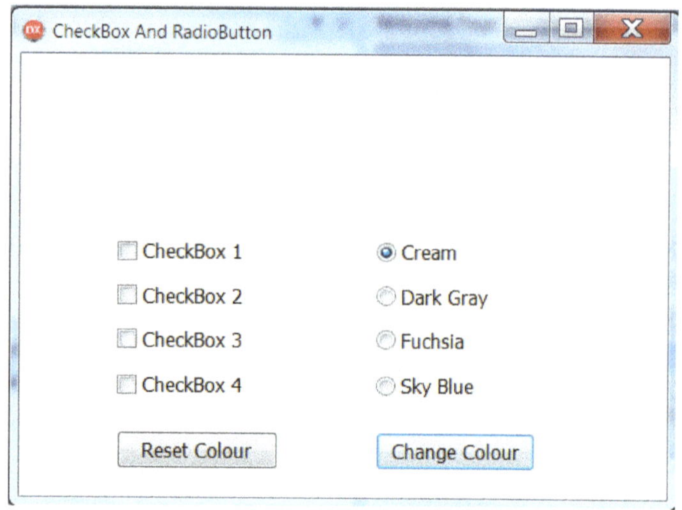

Fig. 39.24 CheckBoxRadioButtonProject in execution

Clicking the control's caption, e.g. `CheckBox 1`, or the tick box generates an **OnClick** event whether checked or unchecked. Checkboxes are used whenever a user needs to enable or disable multiple options.

Table 39.12 shows the **Implementation** section of the `CheckBoxRadioButtonUnit` for Windows VCL application `CheckBoxRadioButtonProject`.

Table 39.13 shows the **Interface** section for this unit.

Each checkbox has an event handler to handle the **OnClick** event. The event handler accesses the **Checked** property of the control, e.g. `CheckBox1`, and responds by assigning the appropriate string to the **TLabel** component using an If statement as shown below

```
If CheckBox1.Checked
     Then Label1.Caption := 'CheckBox 1 Checked'
     Else Label1.Caption := '';
```

```
Var
  frmCheckBoxAndRadioButton : TfrmCheckBoxAndRadioButton;
Implementation
{$R *.dfm}
Procedure TfrmCheckBoxAndRadioButton.btnChangeColourClick(Sender: TObject);
  Begin
    If RadioButton1.Checked
      Then frmCheckBoxAndRadioButton.Color := clCream;
    If RadioButton2.Checked
      Then frmCheckBoxAndRadioButton.Color := clDkGray;
    If RadioButton3.Checked
      Then frmCheckBoxAndRadioButton.Color := clFuchsia;
    If RadioButton4.Checked
      Then frmCheckBoxAndRadioButton.Color := clSkyBlue;
  End;
Procedure TfrmCheckBoxAndRadioButton.btnResetColourClick(Sender: TObject);
  Begin
    frmCheckBoxAndRadioButton.Color := clBtnface;
  End;
Procedure TfrmCheckBoxAndRadioButton.CheckBox1Click(Sender: TObject);
  Begin
    If CheckBox1.Checked
      Then Label1.Caption := 'CheckBox 1 Checked'
      Else Label1.Caption := '';
  End;
Procedure TfrmCheckBoxAndRadioButton.CheckBox2Click(Sender: TObject);
  Begin
    If CheckBox2.Checked
      Then Label2.Caption := 'CheckBox 2 Checked'
      Else Label2.Caption := '';
  End;
Procedure TfrmCheckBoxAndRadioButton.CheckBox3Click(Sender: TObject);
  Begin
    If CheckBox3.Checked
      Then Label3.Caption := 'CheckBox 3 Checked'
      Else Label3.Caption := '';
  End;
Procedure TfrmCheckBoxAndRadioButton.CheckBox4Click(Sender: TObject);
  Begin
    If CheckBox4.Checked
      Then Label4.Caption := 'CheckBox 4 Checked'
      Else Label4.Caption := '';
  End;
End.
```

Table 39.12 Implementation section of application CheckBoxRadioButtonProject, unit CheckBoxRadioButtonUnit

```
Unit CheckBoxRadioButtonUnit;
Interface
Uses
  Winapi.Windows, Winapi.Messages, System.SysUtils,
  System.Variants, System.Classes, Vcl.Graphics,
  Vcl.Controls, Vcl.Forms, Vcl.Dialogs, Vcl.StdCtrls;
Type
  TfrmCheckBoxAndRadioButton = Class(TForm)
                                  CheckBox1 : TCheckBox;
                                  CheckBox2 : TCheckBox;
                                  CheckBox3 : TCheckBox;
                                  CheckBox4 : TCheckBox;
                                  RadioButton1: TRadioButton;
                                  RadioButton2: TRadioButton;
                                  RadioButton3: TRadioButton;
                                  RadioButton4: TRadioButton;
                                  btnChangeColour: TButton;
                                  Label1 : TLabel;
                                  Label2 : TLabel;
                                  Label3 : TLabel;
                                  Label4 : TLabel;
                                  btnResetColour: TButton;
                                  Procedure btnChangeColourClick(Sender: TObject);
                                  Procedure CheckBox1Click(Sender: TObject);
                                  Procedure CheckBox2Click(Sender: TObject);
                                  Procedure CheckBox3Click(Sender: TObject);
                                  Procedure CheckBox4Click(Sender: TObject);
                                  Procedure btnResetColourClick(Sender: TObject);
                                End;
```

Table 39.13 Interface section of application CheckBoxRadioButtonProject, unit CheckBoxRadioButtonUnit

A **TRadioButton** control can be used in two possible ways:

1. When the alternative state in a two-choice option is not evident such as shown in *Figure 39.25*. If a single checkbox was used with caption `Global`, instead, it would not be obvious that the checkbox indicated option `Local` when unticked.
2. When a choice between more than two states needs to be offered as shown in *Figure 39.24*.

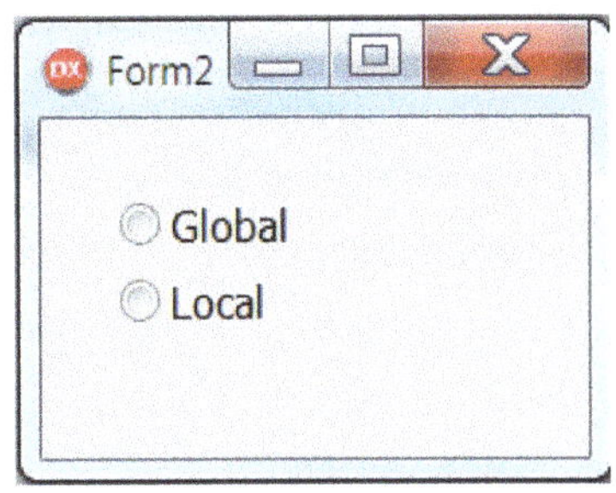

Fig. 39.25 Two RadioButtons

The **OnClick** event for a **TRadioButton** is triggered only when it is checked unlike the **TCheckBox** control.

Hence the application uses a **TButton** control, `btnChangeColour`, and an **OnClick** event handler for this button to read the state of each **TRadioButton** control in turn to decide which colour to change the form to, if at all - *Figure 39.14*.

```
Procedure TfrmCheckBoxAndRadioButton.btnChangeColourClick(Sender: TObject);
  Begin
    If RadioButton1.Checked
      Then frmCheckBoxAndRadioButton.Color := clCream;
    If RadioButton2.Checked
      Then frmCheckBoxAndRadioButton.Color := clDkGray;
    If RadioButton3.Checked
      Then frmCheckBoxAndRadioButton.Color := clFuchsia;
    If RadioButton4.Checked
      Then frmCheckBoxAndRadioButton.Color := clSkyBlue;
  End;
```

Table 39.14 Event handler for Change Colour button

Introduction to VCL components

Purpose: To learn how to use Delphi components

Using TGroupBox, TRadioGroup and TPanel controls

Grouping controls act as containers for other standard controls. Each contained control is a child window of the parent grouping control.

The TGroupBox control is used mainly to visually indicate a group of functionally related controls. For example, a group of TEdit boxes and TLabels that together serve to collect a customer's details as shown in *Figure 40.1*.

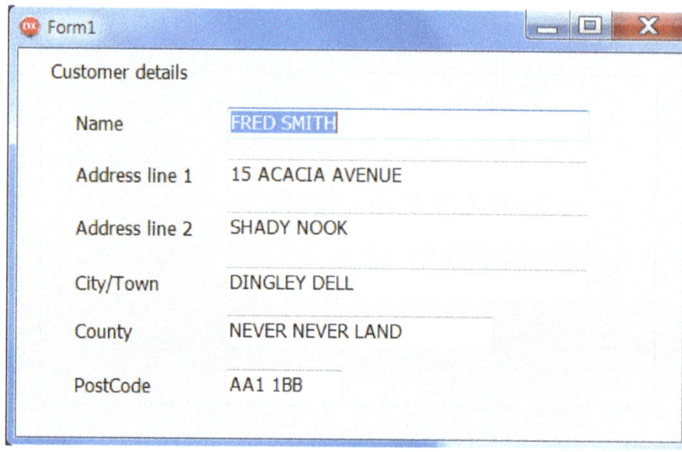

Fig. 40.1 Application GroupBoxProject in execution

Table 40.1 shows the unit `GroupBoxUnit` for the Windows VCL application `GroupBoxProject`. The application accepts customer details in any letter case before converting the details to upper case. The Delphi UpperCase function is used to perform this conversion.

The application shares the event handler `TForm1.Edit1Exit` amongst all the `TEdit` controls.

```
Procedure TForm1.Edit1Exit(Sender: TObject);
  Begin
    TEdit(Sender).Text :=
           UpperCase(TEdit(Sender).Text);
  End;
```

The OnExit event fires when the TEdit control ceases to be active, i.e. the focus moves to another control.

TEdit(Sender) casts the Sender object to TEdit so that its Text property can be accessed. Sender identifies which TEdit control fired the OnExit event,

e.g. `Edit3`.

It is more natural to press enter to finish data entry in one TEdit field and to move to the next field.

The event handler that handles this is

```
Unit GroupBoxUnit;
Interface
Uses
  Winapi.Windows, Winapi.Messages, System.SysUtils,
  System.Variants, System.Classes, Vcl.Graphics,
  Vcl.Controls, Vcl.Forms, Vcl.Dialogs, Vcl.StdCtrls;
Type
  TForm1 = Class(TForm)
            GroupBox1: TGroupBox;
            Edit1 : TEdit;
            Edit2 : TEdit;
            Edit3 : TEdit;
            Label1 : TLabel;
            Label2 : TLabel;
            Label3 : TLabel;
            Label4 : TLabel;
            Label5 : TLabel;
            Label6 : TLabel;
            Edit4 : TEdit;
            Edit5 : TEdit;
            Edit6 : TEdit;
            Procedure Edit1Exit(Sender: TObject);
            Procedure Edit1KeyPress(Sender: TObject;
                                    Var Key: Char);
          End;
Var
  Form1 : TForm1;
Implementation
{$R *.dfm}
Procedure TForm1.Edit1Exit(Sender : TObject);
  Begin
    TEdit(Sender).Text := UpperCase(TEdit(Sender).Text);
  End;
Procedure TForm1.Edit1KeyPress(Sender : TObject;
                               Var Key : Char);
  Begin
    If Key = #13 //can use Chr(vkReturn) in place of #13
      Then
        Begin
          TEdit(Sender).Text := UpperCase(TEdit(Sender).Text);
          SelectNext(Sender as TWinControl,True,True) ;
          Key := #0;
        End;
  End;
End.
```

Table 40.1 Application GroupBoxProject, unit GroupBoxUnit

`TForm1.Edit1KeyPress(Sender : TObject; var Key : Char)` and the event is OnKeyPress.

The key pressed is passed to this handler which checks for the *Enter* key code #13. The Delphi procedure **SelectNext** moves the focus to the next control which happens to be a **TEdit** box whilst there are more customer details to enter.

`Key := #0;` is required because two Windows messages are generated when a key is pressed WM_KEYDOWN and WM_CHAR. Setting `Key`'s value to zero suppresses the effect of WM_CHAR. Lastly, for the application to handle keyboard events. the **KeyPreview** property of the form must be set to **True**. The TAB key can be used in Windows applications to move between controls. Each control on the form has a **TabOrder** property which determines the order in which the control is visited when the TAB key is pressed. For the application `GroupBoxProject` shown in *Figure 40.1*, to support the expected transition between the **TEdit** boxes, the tab order should increase by 1 each time in going from the first **TEdit** box at the top of the form to the last **TEdit** box at the bottom. This is the case as inspection of the **TabOrder** property for each of the six **TEdit** controls shows progression from 0 to 5. As the application has been programmed to treat pressing the *Enter* key as equivalent to pressing the TAB key, the corresponding tab order applies to the movement between the **TEdit** controls.

The **TRadioGroup** control provides an alternative to creating and placing each **TRadioButton** on the form manually. A **TRadioButton** is created for each item in the **Items** property. The created **TRadioButton**s are arranged in the number of columns specified by the **Columns** property. The currently selected **TRadioButton** is returned in **ItemIndex**. *Figure 40.2* shows Windows VCL application `TRadioGroupProject` in execution.

Figure 40.3 shows the second **TRadioGroup** control's **Columns** property set to 2.

Clicking the ellipsis **...** shown in *Figure 40.4* brings up the **String List Editor** which is used to create five **TRadioButtons** and their captions - *Figure 40.5*.

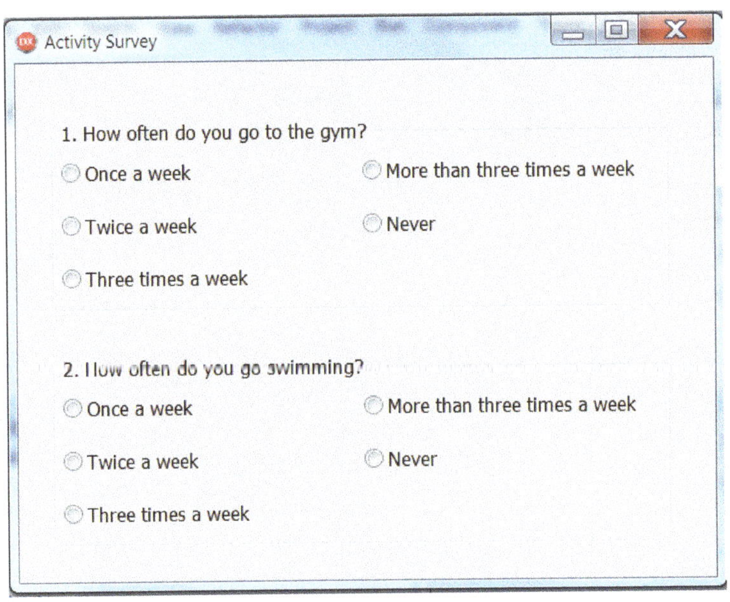

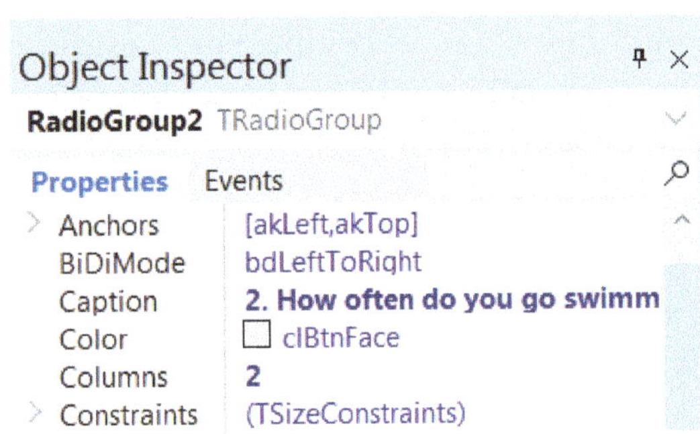

Fig. 40.3 Object Inspector showing second TRadioGroup control's Columns property set to 2

Fig. 40.2 Application TRadioGroupProject in execution

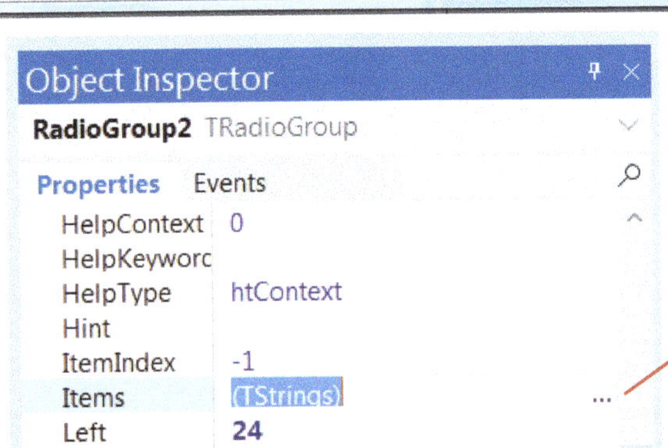

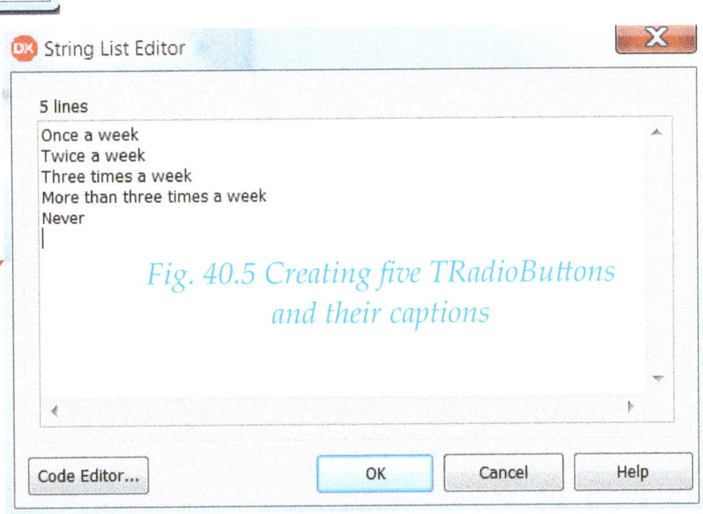

Fig. 40.5 Creating five TRadioButtons and their captions

Fig. 40.4 Object Inspector showing second TRadioGroup control's Items property

The TPanel control/component is used as a container for other controls which may be dropped on it. It is used to group components in order to achieve a particular layout effect. It appears as a rectangular window with bevelled edges as shown in the Windows VCL application in *Figure 40.6*. It is similar to TLabel in that it has a Caption property whose value is displayed in the middle of the TPanel control. However, being a windowed control, it has more extensive capabilities then the non-windowed control TLabel.

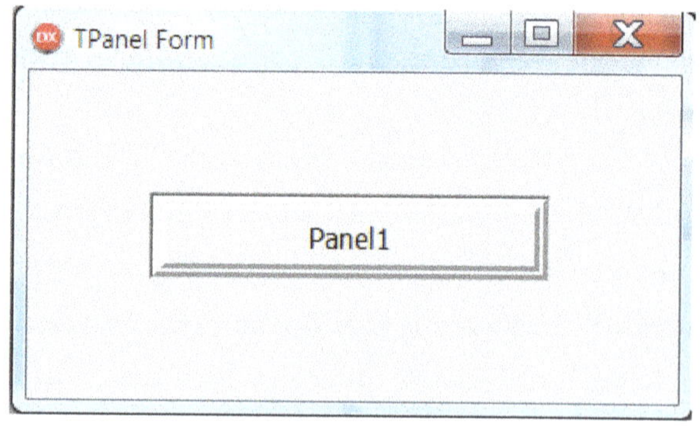

Fig. 40.6 TPanelProject in execution

TPanel has properties that control the two bevels, BevelInner and BevelOuter, that make up the panel's border. BevelInner controls the appearance of the inner bevel. BevelOuter controls the appearance of the outer bevel. BevelWidth controls the width of the bevels. BevelInner and BevelOuter properties can have the values bvNone, bvLowered, bvRaised and bvSpace. *Figure 40.7* shows the Object Inspector view of some of `Panel1`'s properties, in particular the settings for the various bevel properties for the panel shown in *Figure 40.6*.

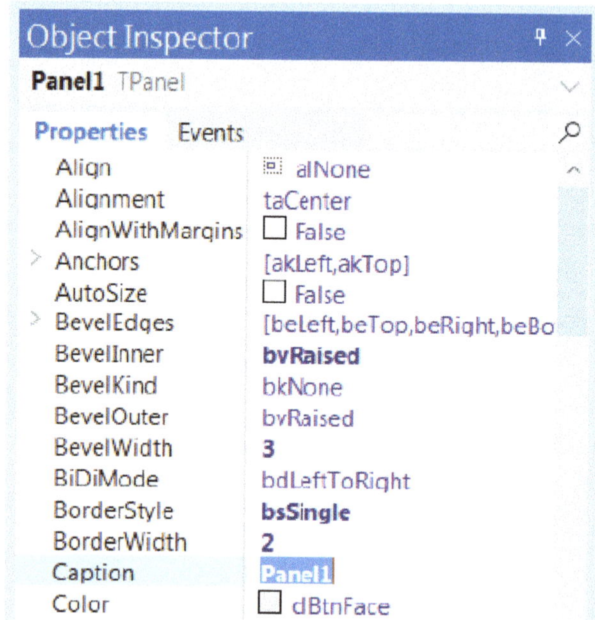

Fig. 40.7 Object Inspector view of some of Panel1's properties

Figure 40.8 shows `TPanelButtonsProject` in execution. This project uses a TPanel component to organise the layout of three buttons dropped onto the panel with the alignment of each set to alLeft.

Table 40.2 shows the unit for application `TPanelButtonsProject`. The OnClick event handlers for buttons `Button2` and `Button3` have been set to `TForm1.Button1Click`.

```
Unit TPanelButtonsUnit;
Interface
Uses
  Winapi.Windows, Winapi.Messages, System.SysUtils,
  System.Variants, System.Classes, Vcl.Graphics,
  Vcl.Controls, Vcl.Forms, Vcl.Dialogs, Vcl.Buttons,
  Vcl.ExtCtrls, Vcl.StdCtrls;
Type
  TForm1 = Class(TForm)
             Panel1 : TPanel;
             Memo1 : TMemo;
             Button1 : TButton;
             Button2 : TButton;
             Button3: TButton;
             Procedure Button1Click(Sender: TObject);
           End;
Var
  Form1 : TForm1;
Implementation
{$R *.dfm}
Procedure TForm1.Button1Click(Sender: TObject);
  Begin
    Memo1.Lines.Append(TButton(Sender).Name + ' clicked');
  End;
End.
```

Table 40.2 Application TPanelButtonsProject, unit TPanelButtonsUnit

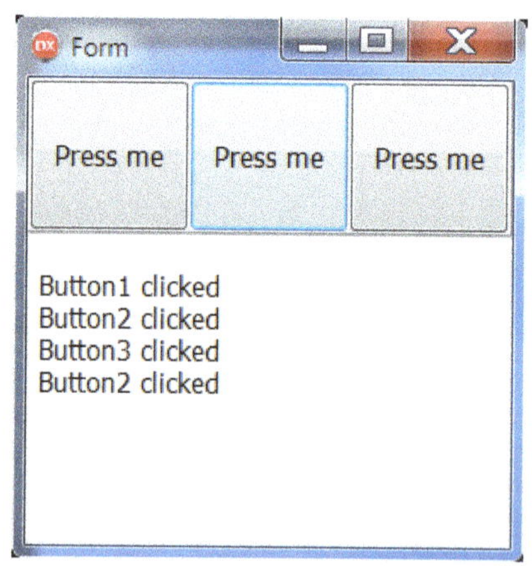

Fig. 40.8 TPanelButtonsProject in execution

Many controls are able to display scrollbars automatically when needed, e.g. TMemo. However, situations may arise when a separate scrollbar is required. *Figure 40.9* shows a simple example of such use.

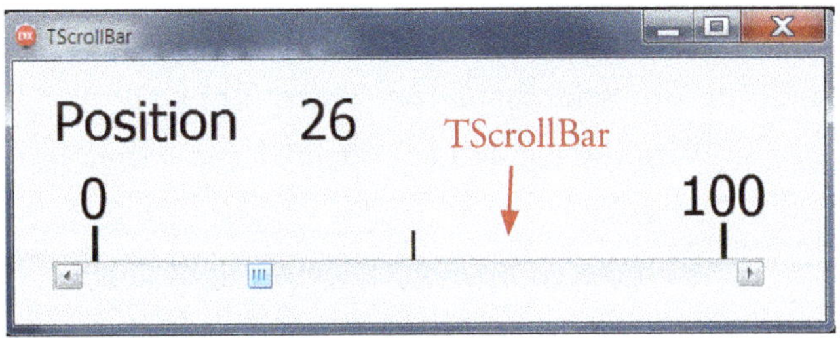

Fig. 40.9 TScrollBarProject in execution

The orientation may be set to **sbHorizontal** or **sbVertical** through the **Kind** property. *Figure 40.9* shows the case when **Kind** has the value **sbHorizontal**.

The range of values is set through the **Min** and **Max** properties.

The **OnChange** event is used to react to any changes to the position of the scrollbar cursor.

Table 40.3 shows the unit for the application `TScrollBarProject`.

```
Unit TScrollBarUnit;
Interface
Uses
  Winapi.Windows, Winapi.Messages, System.SysUtils,
  System.Variants, System.Classes, Vcl.Graphics,
  Vcl.Controls, Vcl.Forms, Vcl.Dialogs, Vcl.StdCtrls;
Type
  TForm1 = Class(TForm)
             ScrollBar1 : TScrollBar;
             lblPosition : TLabel;
             lblPositionValue : TLabel;
             lblZero : TLabel;
             lbl100 : TLabel;
             lblZeroMark : TLabel;
             lbl100Mark : TLabel;
             lbl50Mark : TLabel;
             Procedure ScrollBar1Change(Sender: TObject);
           End;
Var
  Form1 : TForm1;
Implementation
{$R *.dfm}
Procedure TForm1.ScrollBar1Change(Sender: TObject);
  Begin
    lblPositionValue.Caption := IntToStr(ScrollBar1.Position);
  End;
End.
```

Table 40.3 Application TScrollBarProject, unit TScrollBarUnit

Adding components to a form

There are two ways to place a component from the **Component/Tool Palette** on a form:

1. Double click on the component in the **Component Palette** to add it to the form. It is placed with its default size and shape in the middle of the form or to the lower right of any components already located in the middle.
2. Adding a component at a specific position is done as follows
    1. Select the component in the **Component/Tool Palette**.
    2. Click the required position on the form for the upper-left corner of the component. The component will then appear with its default size at this position.
    3. If the component is required to be larger or smaller than the default size then the mouse pointer should be positioned as in 2, but the left mouse button should not be released until the mouse pointer has been dragged to give the required size.

Adding multiple components to a form

Adding more than one component of the same type to a form can be done as follows

1. Hold down SHIFT
2. Click the component in the **Component/Tool Palette** then release the SHIFT key. The selected component will remain selected.
3. Click the position on the form for the upper-left corner of each copy.

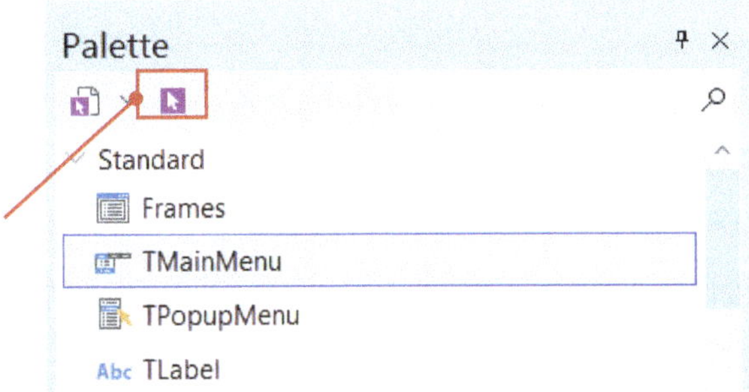

Fig. 40.10 Selecting multiple components

Figure 40.10 shows **TMainMenu** selected with SHIFT. To deselect and return to the usual method of selecting components, click on the pointer icon.

Moving components

There are two ways that a component can be moved to a new location

1. With the component selected, place the mouse inside the control and drag the component to its new location.
2. With the component selected, hold down the CTRL key, move the component in the required direction by pressing the corresponding ARROW key repeatedly until the new position is achieved.

Aligning components

First select the components to align.

There are two ways that this can be done

1. Hold down the SHIFT key whilst clicking on the components to align.
2. Hold down the left mouse button and drag the dotted rectangle until it contains the components to select.

Choose **Edit|Align** to bring up the **Alignment Dialog** window which can be used to precisely align a group of components on a form as shown in *Figure 40.11*.

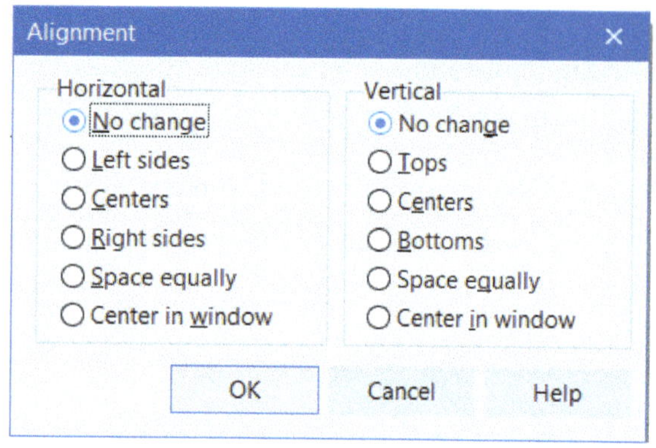

Fig. 40.11 Alignment dialog window

Resizing and reshaping components

The easiest way of resizing/reshaping a component is to select it and then drag the resizing handles in the required direction - *Figure 40.12*.

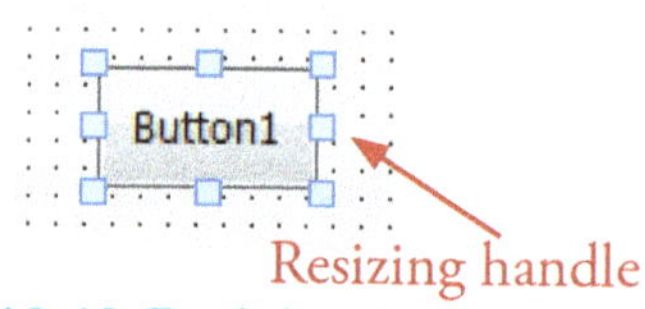

Fig. 40.12 Resizing handles

The alternative is to select the component and then choose **Edit|Size** to bring up the **Size Dialog** window - *Figure 40.13*.

Cutting, copying, pasting and deleting components

Use the following

1. CTRL-X to cut a selected component
2. CTRL-C to copy a selected component
3. CTRL-V to paste a copied/cut component to a form. The pasted component gets a new name but otherwise the same properties as the cut/copied component. The pasted component will acquire any event handlers associated with the cut/copied component.
4. Pressing the DEL key when a component is selected deletes the component. Alternatively, use **Edit|Delete** to delete the selected component. **Edit|Undelete** undeletes the deleted component provided that nothing else has been done subsequently.

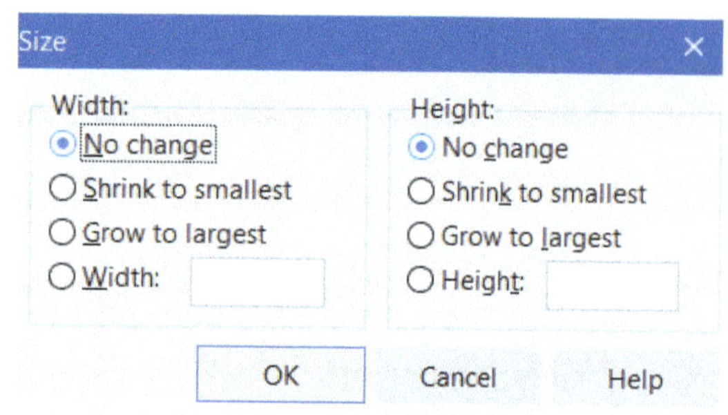

Fig. 40.13 Size dialog window

Using the IDE effectively

See *Chapter 54*.

41 FireMonkey components 1

Introduction to FireMonkey components

Purpose: To understand how FireMonkey differs from VCL

FireMonkey is a set of components for developing cross-platform applications - Windows 32-bit, Windows 64-bit, Android, iOS (iPhone and iPad), macOS and Linux, currently.

Control emulation

With FireMonkey, every visual control is an emulation of controls built into the operating system. This means that visual controls such as **TButton** are constructed from drawing primitives, i.e. drawing commands such as `MoveTo(x1, y2)`, `LineTo(x2, y2)`, etc, which create the required visual shape, appropriately styled for the particular operating system.

On the other hand, visual controls in the VCL framework rely on the controls that already exist in the particular version of the Windows operating system. To achieve this, the VCL simply places a wrapper around Windows' own controls in order to abstract away the complex details of working with these controls. For example, **TButton** is a wrapper around Windows' own button control. This wrapper presents a set of button properties, methods and events for Delphi applications at a level of abstraction that is easier to work with.

Child-parent relationship

In FireMonkey, all controls can act as containers for other controls unlike VCL which is restricted to just a few controls for this purpose, e.g. **TPanel**.

This means it is possible in FireMonkey, for example, to add an image (an icon) to a button to convey the button's purpose eliminating the need to do this in text - *Figure 41.1*.

Fig. 41.1 Child image of button control parent

The relationship between button and image is a parent-child one with the image a child of a button, the parent. Move the button on the form to a new position and the image moves with the button because it is in a parent-child relationship.

This can be exploited, for example, on forms in which labels are associated with other controls. By making the other controls children of these labels, the controls maintain their relative positions to their labels when either are moved to new positions on the form.

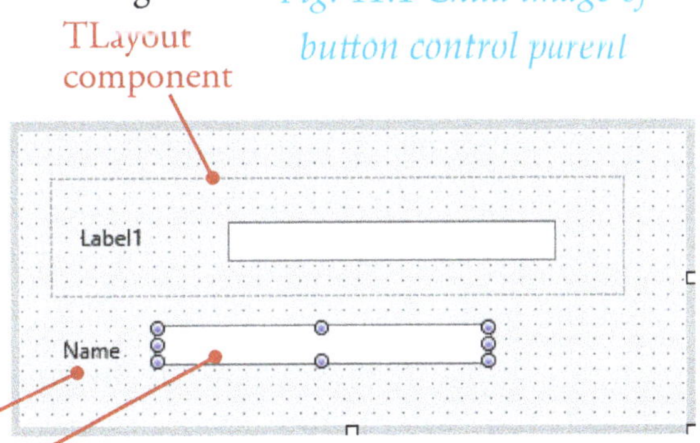

Fig. 41.2 Child TLabel, Name, of edit control parent and an alternative using TLayout

Figure 41.2 shows an example of a label with text `Name` linked by a parent-child relationship to an edit box. The label's property `Position.x` has been set to -50 to position label `Name` to left of edit box. When the edit box is moved, the label `Name` moves with it to maintain its position relative to the edit box. *Figure 41.2* also shows an alternative way that uses a **TLayout** component to keep a label, `Label1`, and an edit box together. *Figure 41.3* shows the structure view of `Form1` and its controls/components shown in *Figure 41.2*.

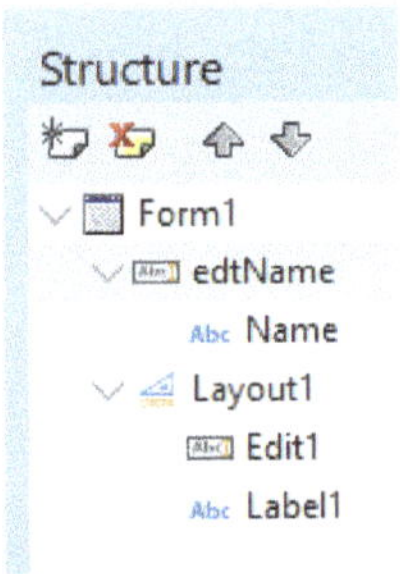

Fig. 41.3 Structure view of child label of edit control parent and an alternative using TLayout

Styles

In the VCL, the appearance of controls is defined by the Windows operating system[1].

In FireMonkey, the application's appearance is completely controlled by FireMonkey with the consequence that its appearance is changed automatically to fit the styling of the current operating system or if required, completely customised.

This ability of FireMonkey to change the appearance of an application automatically without the requirement for the programmer to produce different versions of an application, one per platform, is the key to supporting multi-device development. The look and feel of an application changes automatically to fit the particular target platform. The key is styled controls. *Figure 41.4* shows how the style of a button on a form changes as the operating system is changed in the **Style** window.

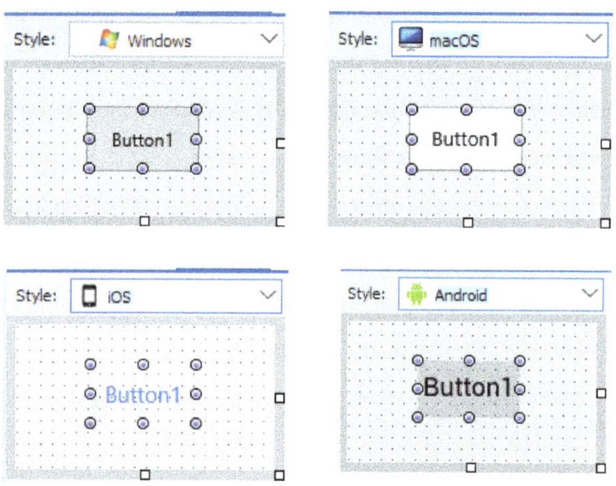

Fig. 41.4 A button's appearance in Winodws, macOS, iOS and Android

Each FireMonkey control has an associated style which determines the control's appearance. A style is built up from drawing primitives and other components, e.g. the style for **TPanel** is simply **TRectangle**. New styles may be created and named. For example, a new style can be created and named based on a button with an image on it.

This new style may then be applied to any button placed on a form to turn the button into a button with an image on it. Delphi has a number of built-in named button styles some of which are shown in *Figure 41.5*.

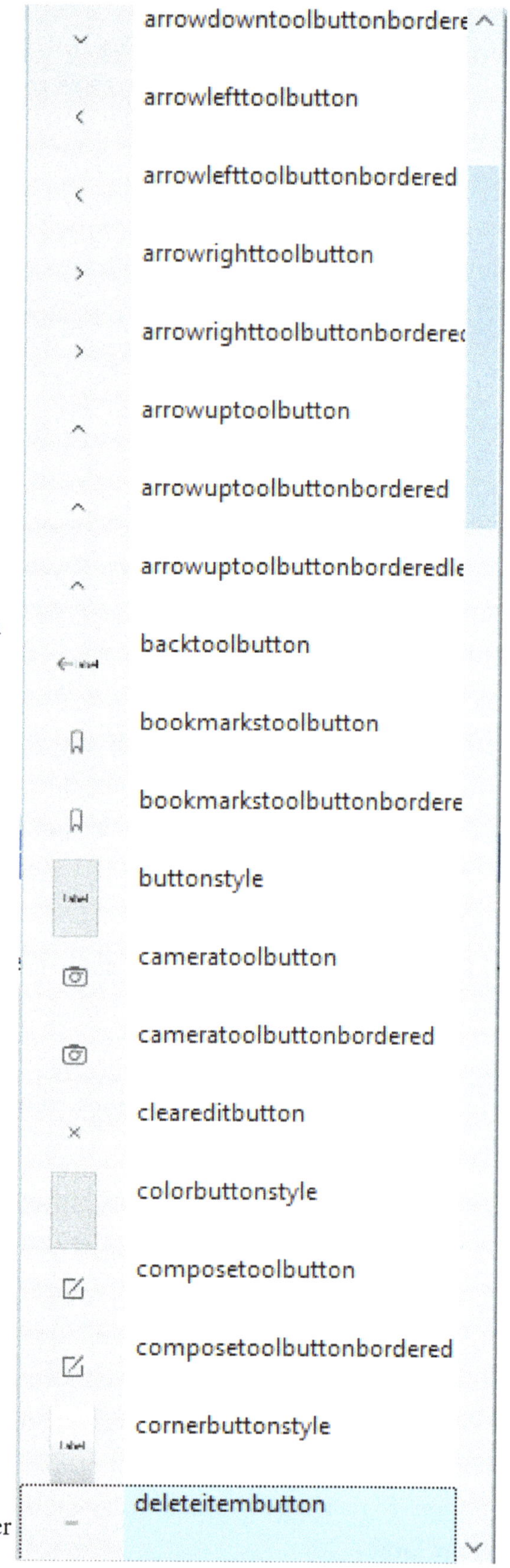

Fig. 41.5 Some button styles already builtin to Delphi

Figure 41.6 shows how a particular button style, **deleteitembutton** is selected from a dropdown list and applied to a button on a form. The appearance of this button style varies to fit the particular platform style for a delete item button.

1 Since XE2 the appearance of a VCL control can be customised with VCL styles.

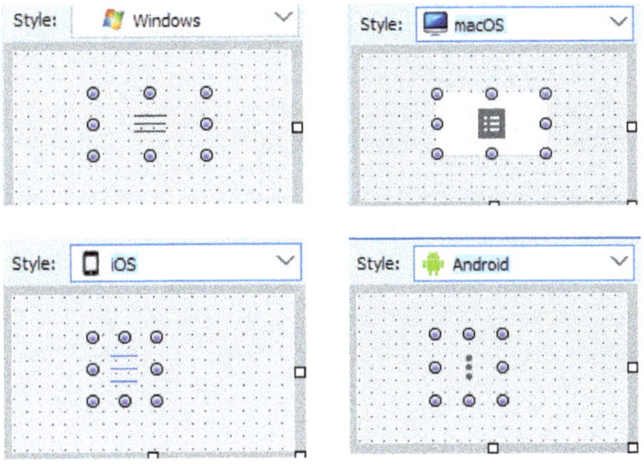

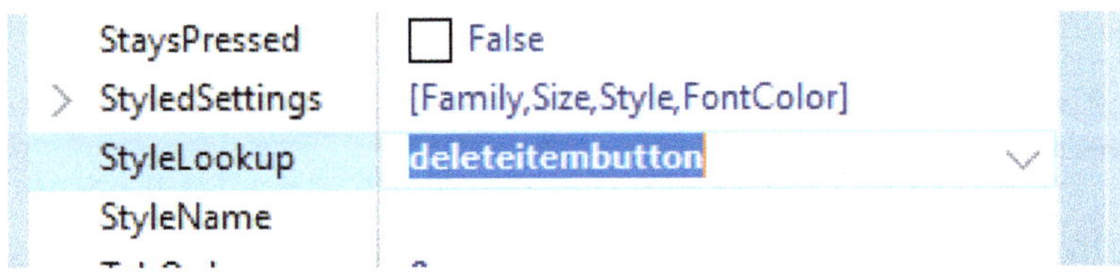

Fig. 41.6 deleteitembutton style applied to button on a form

Purpose: To learn how to install and set up Delphi 10.3 Community edition for multi-device application development (and later versions)

Although it is possible to just focus on Windows desktop initially, it is better to start with an installation of Delphi that will allow Windows desktop, Android, iOS and macOS multi-device application development.

Figure 41.7 shows via the **Tools|Manage Platform Platform** tab window for **RAD Studio 10.3.2** that **Delphi 10.3.2** used the following installation options when being installed:

1. Delphi Windows 64-bit Community
2. Delphi Windows 32-bit Community
3. Delphi macOS Community
4. Delphi iOS Community
5. Delphi Android Community

It is possible to install any of these options after the initial installation if they were not included initially.

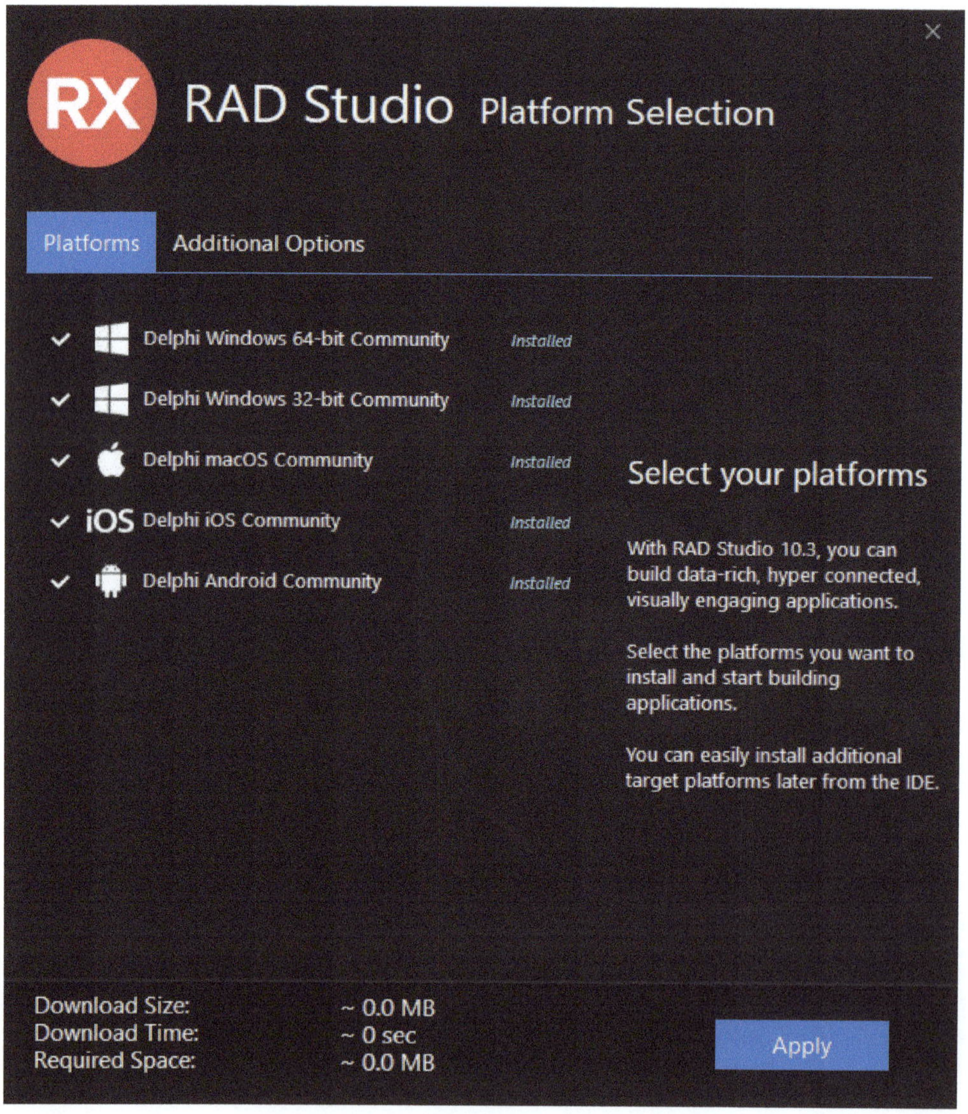

Fig. 41.7 RAD Studio Platform Selection Delphi 10.3

Later versions of Delphi should install in a similar manner. *Figure 41.8* shows the **Tools|Manage Platform Additonal Options** tab window. With the exception of **Additonal Languages** all the options have been installed. Using the installation options shown in *Figures 41.7* and *41.8*, the installation process for **Delphi 10.3.2** should proceed seamlessly with the end result being an environment set up for desktop and mobile/tablet multi-device programming.

The **SDK Manager** can be used to check that the **SDK**, **NDK** and **Java** configuration has been set up correctly for Android development - **Tools | Options | Deployment | SDK Manager**. *Figure 41.9* shows the menu part of the **Tools | Options** window.

Figure 41.10 shows the **SDK** tab window of the **SDK Manager**. *Figure 41.11* shows the **Java** tab window of the **SDK Manager**. *Figure 41.12* shows the **NDK** tab window of the **SDK Manager**.

Thankfully, the installer has set up all the necessary configurations of **SDK**, **NDK** and **Java**.

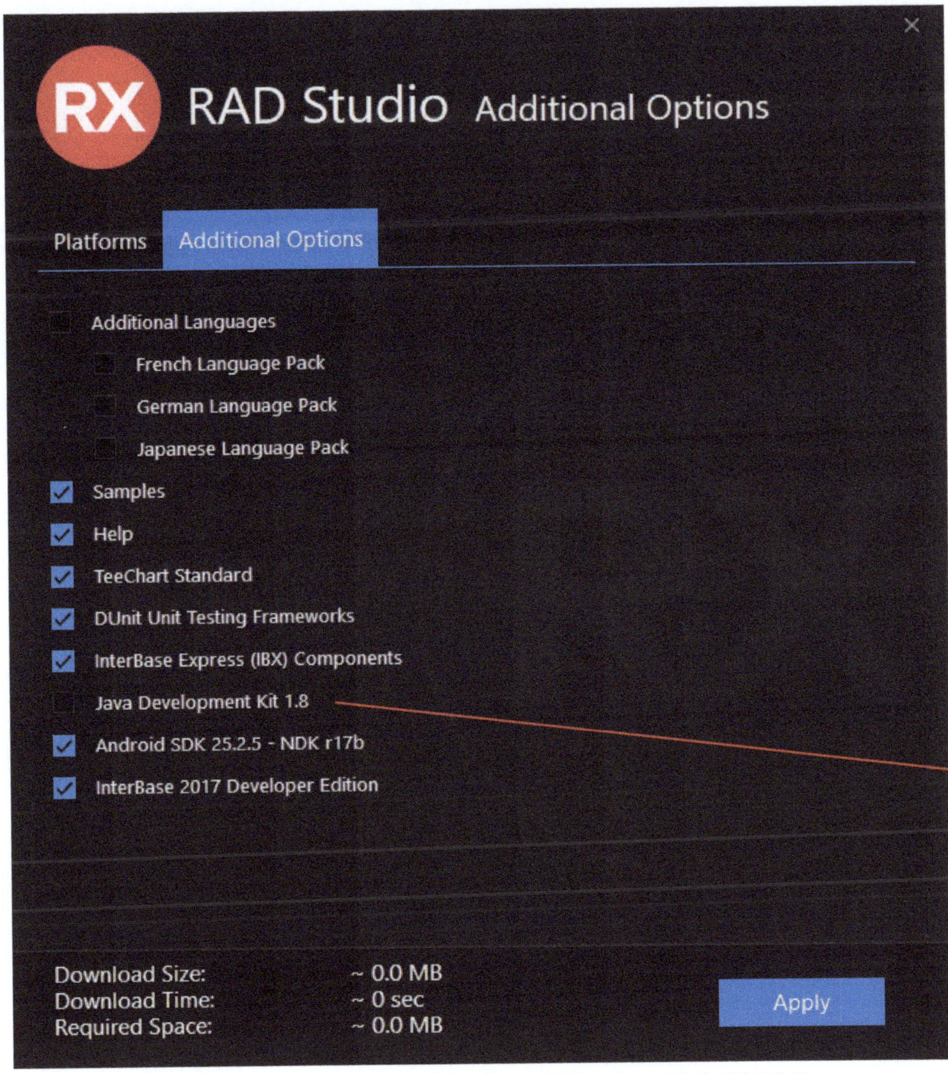

Fig. 41.8 RAD Studio Platform Selection Delphi 10.3

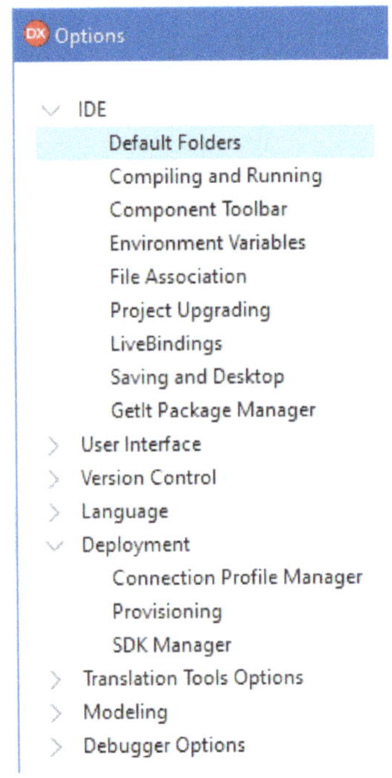

Fig. 41.9 Tools | Options

Java Development Kit 1.8 not ticked because it was already installed on the development computer. This may not be the case for you so tick this box.

Fig. 41.10 SDK Manager Delphi 10.3.2, SDK tab window

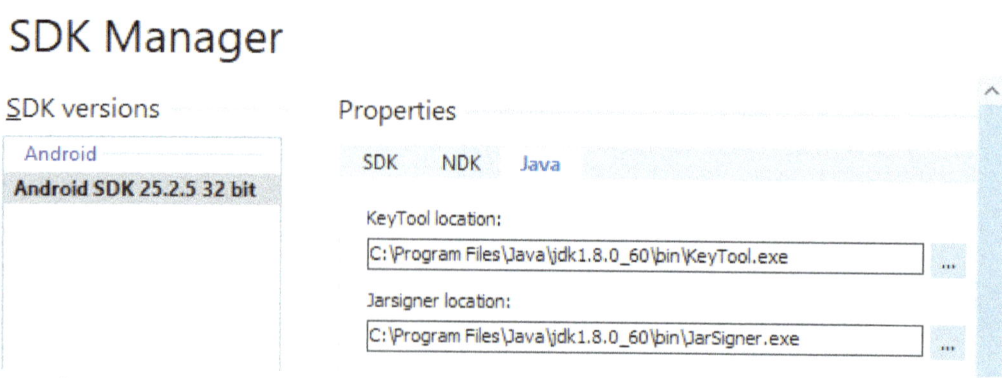

Fig. 41.11 SDK Manager Delphi 10.3.2, Java tab window

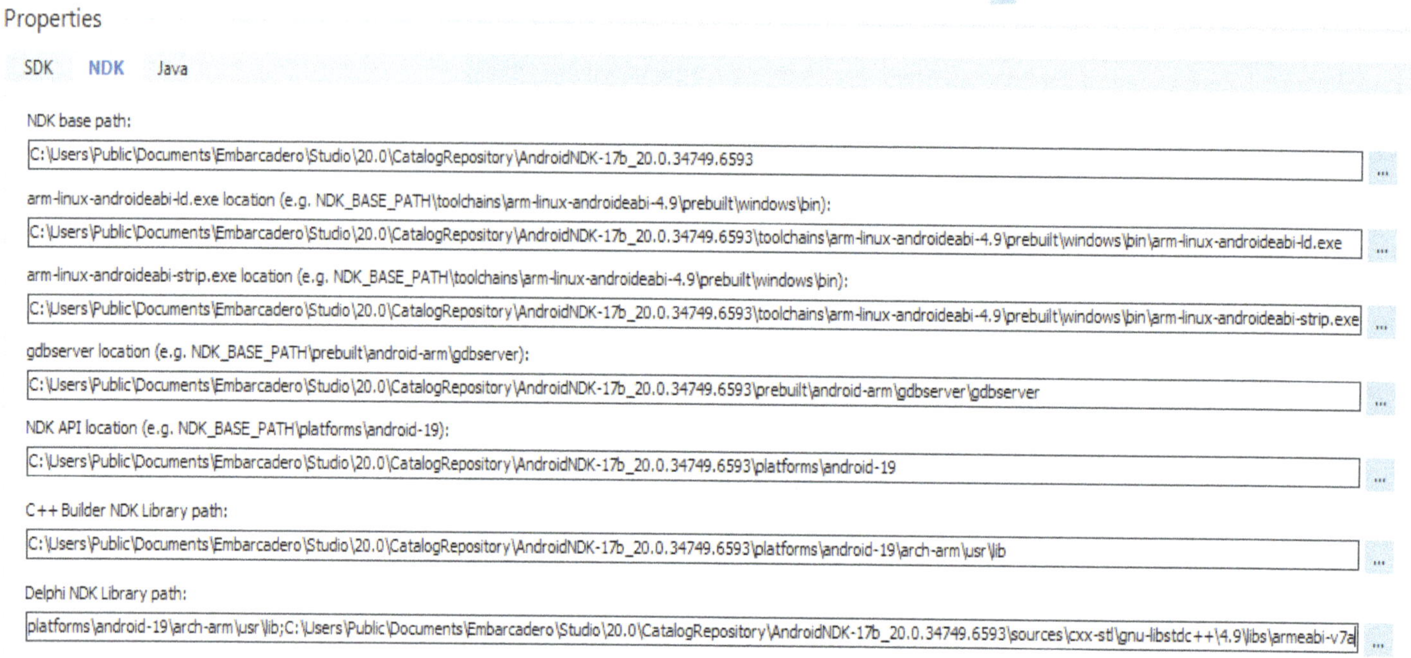

Fig. 41.12 SDK Manager Delphi 10.3, NDK tab window

Working with an Android device requires that an appropriate USB driver is installed since the installed Windows driver is not adequately provisioned to support multi-device applications. Embarcadero recommends installing the Google USB driver and enabling this driver. This should disable the Windows USB driver but if it doesn't then this needs to be done - **Settings|Devices|Devices and printers**.

If a device specific USB driver(s) is available then download and install this. This is the case for the **Samsung Galaxy S8+** used in this chapter to demonstrate some multi-device applications. *Figure 41.13* shows the USB drivers that have been installed for this Android device. The ADB (Android Debugging Bridge) driver is used when debugging an application installed and running on the Android device.

The installation is now ready to support the creation of our first multi-device application for Windows desktop and Android.

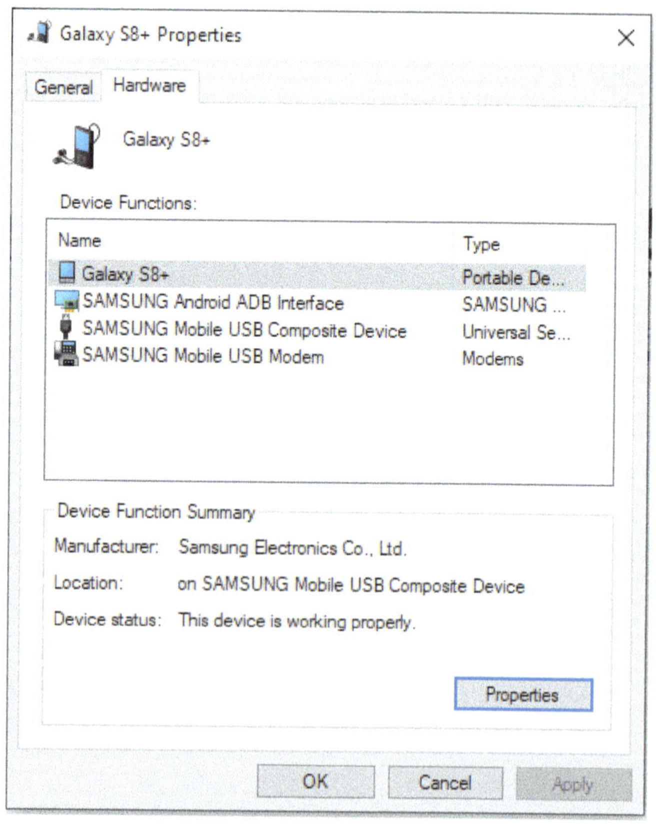

Fig. 41.13 Samsung Galaxy S8+ properties

(Download from www.educational-computing.com/DelphiBook/Code/Chapter41/SpeedButtonDrawnProject.rar)

Illustrating the vector nature of FireMonkey controls

Create a Multi-Device Application - **File|New|Multi-Device Application**. Place a **TToolBar**, `ToolBar1`, on the form and set its alignment to **Top**.

Place a **TSpeedButton** on the **TToolBar** control, `ToolBar1`. Set its alignment to **Left**. Place **TPath** on the **TSpeedButton** control, `SpeedButton1`. The Structure pane should resemble that shown in *Figure 41.14*.

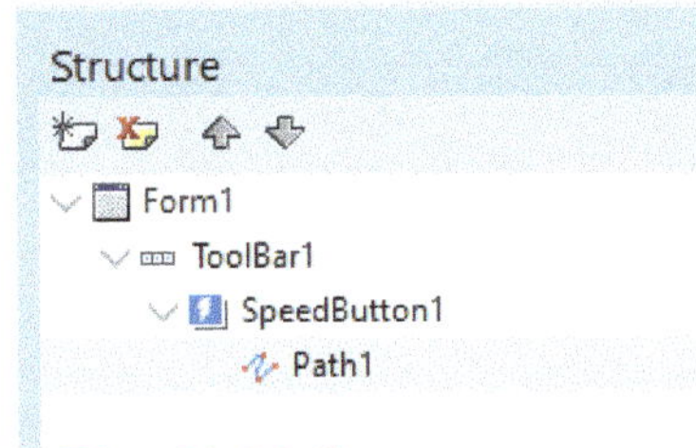

Fig. 41.14 Structure pane

Select the **TPath** component, `Path1`, and click the ellipsis (**...**) shown in *Figure 41.15* for **(PathData)** to bring up the **Path Designer** shown in *Figure 41.16*. Enter the path data shown in *Figure 41.17*. The path data are vector drawing commands to draw three equally spaced vertically aligned horizontal lines. Click on **OK**. *Figure 41.18* shows the speed button with the glyph of three horizontal lines.

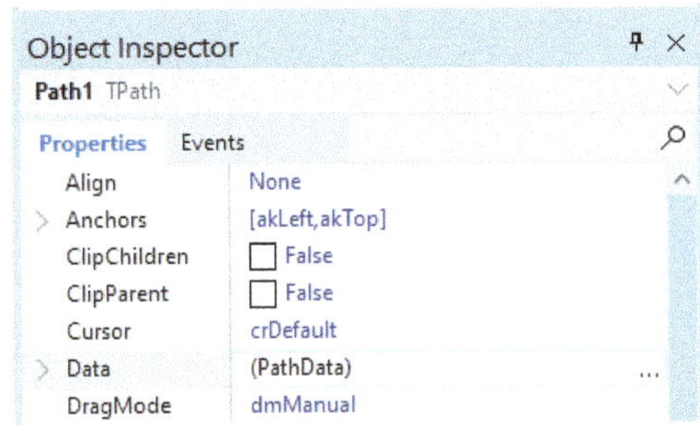

Fig. 41.15 Object Inspector

Figure 41.19 shows the application in execution after some additional styling. An event handler has been added - *Table 41.1*. The **HitTest** property of `Path1` must be set to **False** so that a click on `SpeedButton1` is not intercepted and trapped by `Path1` since it is in front of `SpeedButton1` but is handled by `SpeedButton1`'s **OnClick** event handler.

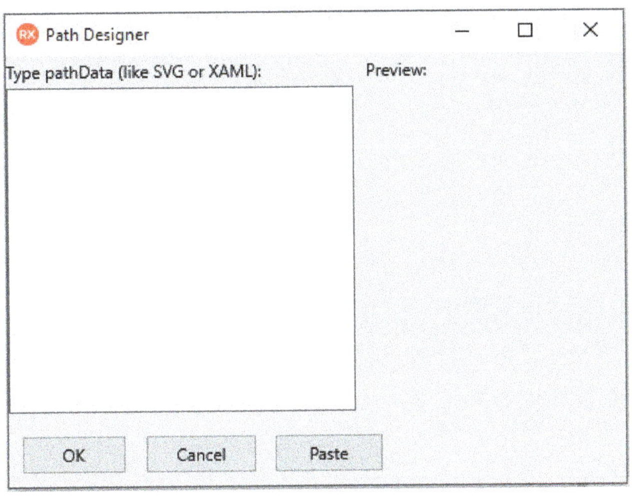

Fig. 41.16 Path Designer

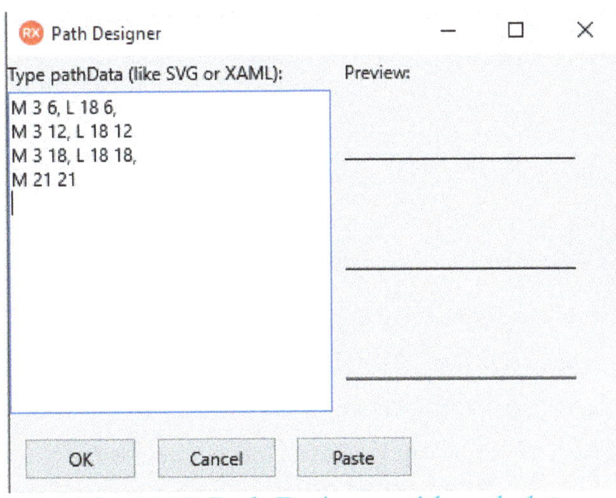

Fig. 41.17 Path Designer with path data

Fig. 41.18 Form with customised speedbutton

Fig. 41.19 Form with additional styling

```
Unit SpeedButtonUnit;
Interface
Uses
  System.SysUtils, System.Types, System.UITypes,
  System.Classes, System.Variants,
  FMX.Types, FMX.Controls, FMX.Forms, FMX.Graphics,
  FMX.Dialogs, FMX.Objects, FMX.StdCtrls,
  FMX.Controls.Presentation, FMX.Layouts;
Type
  TForm1 = Class(TForm)
             ToolBar1: TToolBar;
             SpeedButton1: TSpeedButton;
             Path1: TPath;
             Panel1: TPanel;
             StyleBook1: TStyleBook;
             Procedure SpeedButton1Click(Sender: TObject);
           End;
Var
  Form1: TForm1;
Implementation
{$R *.fmx}

Procedure TForm1.SpeedButton1Click(Sender: TObject);
  Begin
    ShowMessage('SpeedButton clicked!')
  End;
End.
```

Table 41.1 SpeedButtonUnit with OnClick event handler

(Download from www.educational-computing.com/DelphiBook/Code/Chapter41/RotatedControlsProject.rar)

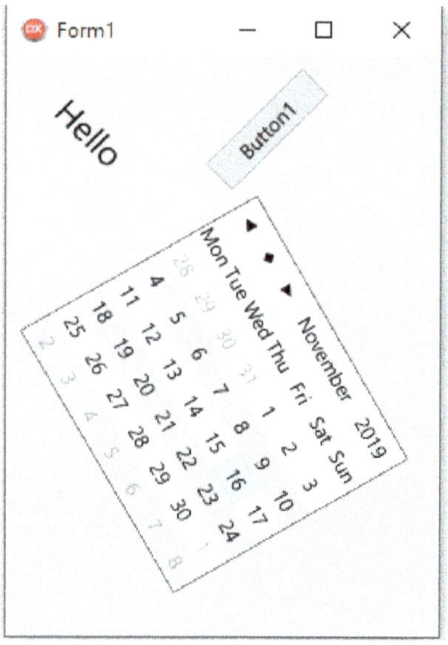

Fig. 41.20 Form containing three controls rotated at various rotation angles

Another feature of the vector nature of FireMonkey controls is the ability to rotate these controls on a form. *Figure 41.20* shows an example application in which three controls/components have been rotated at design time, 45, -45 and 60 degrees. *Figure 41.21* shows the **RotationAngle** property set to 45 degrees for `Label1`. The ability to easily rotate controls will be exploited in making an analogue clock application in *Chapter 42*.

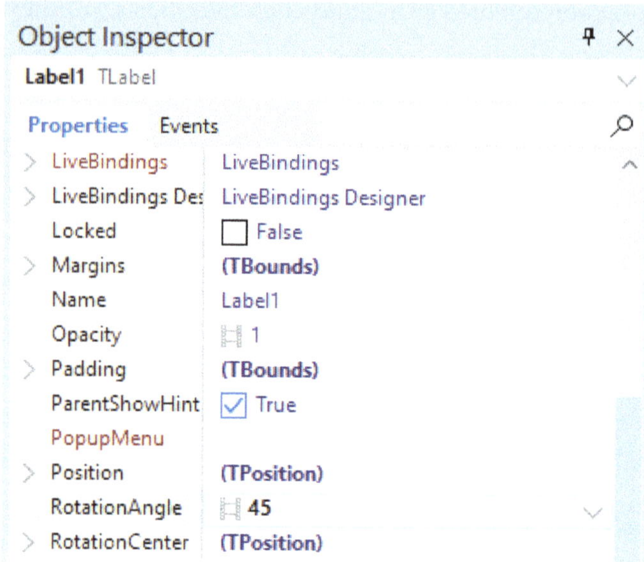

Fig. 41.21 Object Inspector showing rotation angle set to 45 degrees for Label1

Purpose: To learn how to develop applications for Windows Desktop and Android

Create a multi-device application in **Delphi 10.3.2** or later, **File|New|Multi-Device Application**. Select **Blank application**. *Figure 41.22* shows the **Projects window** for this multi-device application, `Project1.dprog`. It also shows a connected Android device under **Target**, SM-G955F. This is a SamSung Galaxy S8+ mobile phone which has been connected by USB cable to the Windows 10 development computer.

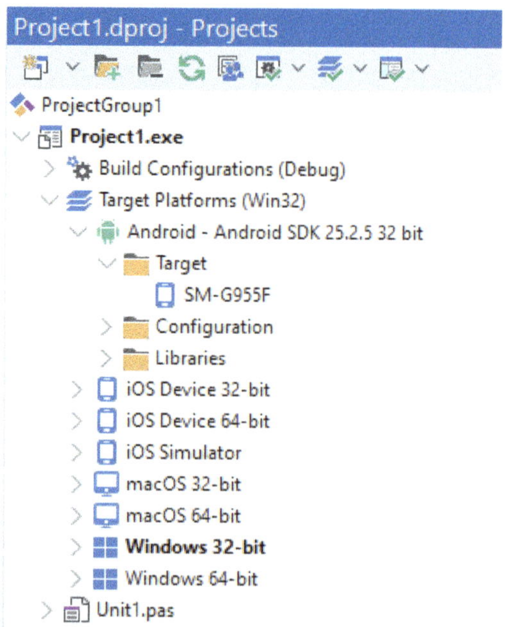

Fig. 41.22 New multi-device project showing connected Android device SM-G955F

Figure 41.23 shows the **Toolbar** default settings Selected **Target Platform**: ***Window 32-bit***, **Style:** ***Windows***, **View:** ***Master***.

Add a **TButton** control to the form and set its **Align** property to **Center**.

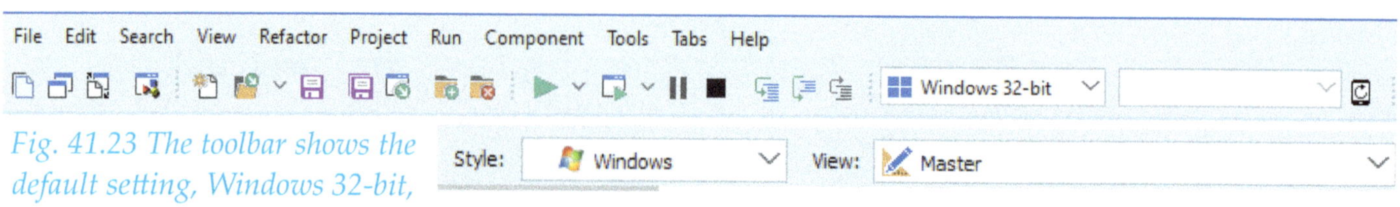

Fig. 41.23 The toolbar shows the default setting, Windows 32-bit, Style: Windows, View: Master

Set the form's **Width** and **Height** properties to `200`. The outcome should be similiar to that shown in *Figure 41.24*. Double click the button to create an **OnClick** event handler.

Add `ShowMessage('Hello World!')` to this handler as shown below

```
Procedure TForm1.Button1Click(Sender : TObject);
  Begin
    ShowMessage('Hello World!');
  End;
```

Run without debugging (Shift Ctrl F9). Click on `Button1` to show message `'Hello World'`.

Kill the running application to return to the IDE.

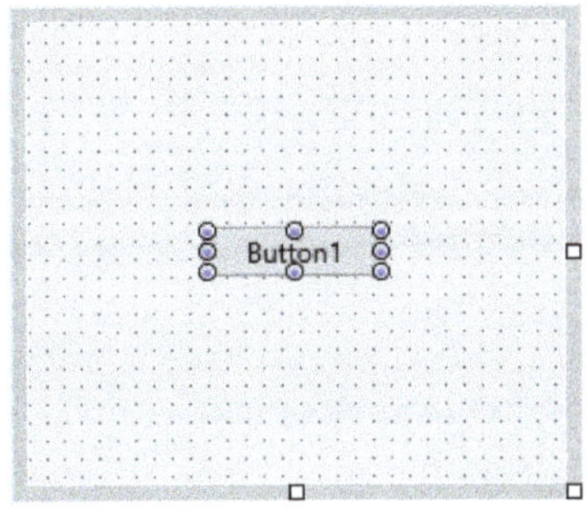

Fig. 41.24 Project1 form with TButton control, Button1

Now change option **Windows 32-bit** in the **Toolbar** to **Android** as shown in *Figure 41.25*. The target **SM-G955F** appears automatically (eventually) if connected by USB and its presence is registered in the **Projects** window. Change the style to **Android**. The appearance of `Button1` changes as shown in *Figure 41.26*.

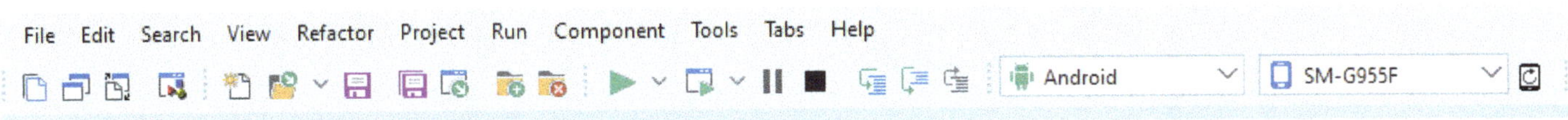

Fig. 41.25 Android operating system option selected

To visualise what the application will look like on the target **SM-G955F** we must change the **View** from **Master** to the Android device nearest in aspect ratio to **SM-G955F**.

Figure 41.27 shows the state just before selecting **Android 5" phone**. It appears as a **Created** option because this option was previously selected on the development computer. *Figure 41.28* shows the state after switching the view.

Figure 41.29 shows the form's appearance after the view has changed to **Android 5" phone**.

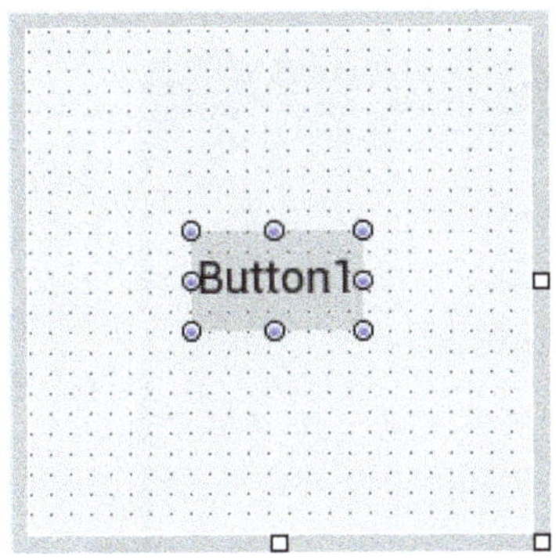

Fig. 41.26 Project1 form with Android style

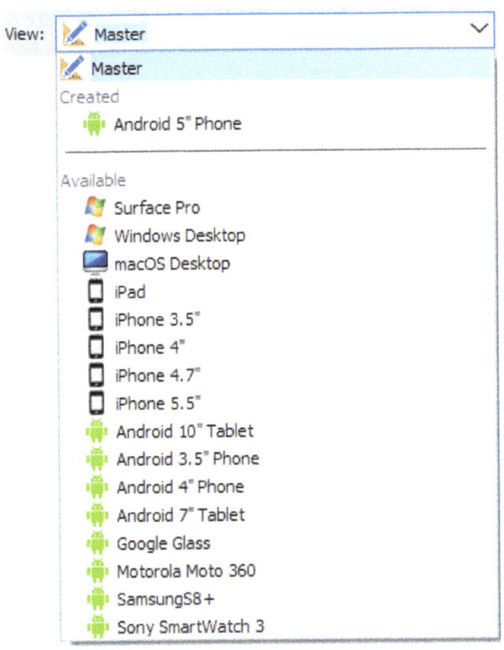

Fig. 41.27 About to switch from Master to Android 5" phone

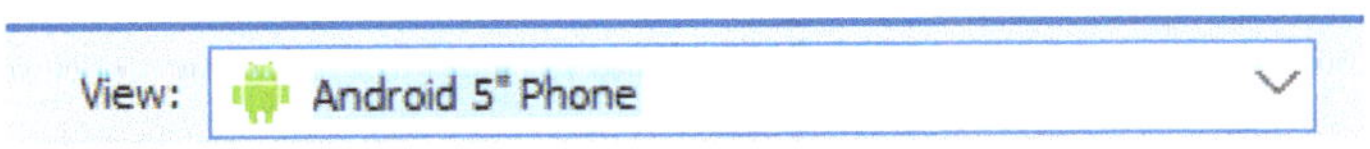

Fig. 41.28 View after switch

> The available views do not cover all the possible mobile phone/tablet form factors. However, Delphi takes account of the actual form factor of the device when building the mobile phone/tablet application. Views and Styles are design-time settings. When building an application only the target setting matters. However, to delete a control on a form the view setting must be Master

Fig. 41.29 Emulation of Android 5" phone

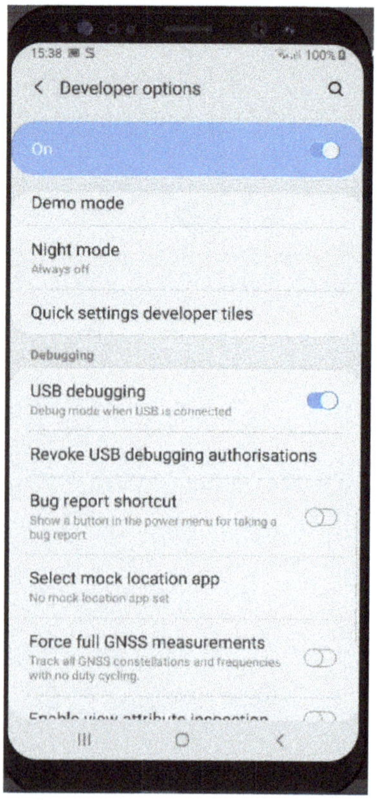

Fig. 41.30 USB debugging

Developer options and USB debugging must be enabled on the target device. On a SamSung S8+, go to Settings then Developer options. Turn on Developer options and USB debugging as shown in *Figure 41.30*. However, Developer Options are normally hidden, so go to Settings|About Phone|Software information, touch Build number seven times and the Developer options menu will appear under Settings. Now enable USB debugging.

Save the project as `TestProject.dprog` and the unit as `TestUnit.pas` in folder `TestProject`.

Now Run without debugging (Shift Ctrl F9). Delphi produces an Android Package Kit (apk for short) file used by the Android operating system for distribution and installation of mobile apps. `TestProject.apk` is the equivalent of `TestProject.exe` which Delphi creates for the Windows operating system. *Figure 41.31* shows `TestProject.apk` installed and executing on SamSung S8+ mobile phone. *Figure 41.32* shows the behaviour of `TestProject.apk` when `Button1` is clicked.

Fig. 41.31 Screencast of TestProject executing on SamSung S8+

Avoid using ShowMessage on an Android device for anything other than simple demonstrations such as the example shown in *Figure 41.32*. The Android operating system is not designed to handle VCL modal dialogs such as MessageDlg, InputBox, InputQuery and ShowMessage.

Use FMX.DialogService.TDialogService.ShowMessage instead for FireMonkey applications. Add FMX.DialogService to the Uses statement.

Fig. 41.32 Screencast of TestProject executing on SamSung S8+

TDialogService.ShowMessage is a class method supplied with FMX.DialogService that can work synchronously or asynchronously depending on the preferred mode set by the programmer for TDialogService:

```
TDialogService.ShowMessage('Hello
                World');
```

The method is prefaced by the class name TDialogService because it is a class method.

When PreferredMode is set to Platform, the called version of ShowMessage is the one that is appropriate for the operating system. The following code sets the preferred mode to Platform.

```
TDialogService.PreferredMode := TDialogService.TPreferredMode.Platform;
```

Table 41.2 show the unit code for an application which calls TDialogService.ShowMessage when `Button1` is clicked.

Figure 41.33 shows the result of clicking `Button1` on the screen of an Android device.

To obtain input whilst ensuring proper working on Android devices, we use FMX.DialogService.TDialogService.InputQuery.

(Download from www.educational-computing.com/DelphiBook/Code/Chapter41/TestProjectFMXDialogService.rar)

```
Unit TestDialogServiceUnit;
Interface
Uses
  System.SysUtils, System.Types, System.UITypes, System.Classes,
  System.Variants,
  FMX.Types, FMX.Controls, FMX.Forms, FMX.Graphics, FMX.Dialogs,
  FMX.Controls.Presentation, FMX.StdCtrls, FMX.DialogService;
Type
  TForm1 = Class(TForm)
             Button1: TButton;
             Procedure Button1Click(Sender: TObject);
           End;
Var
  Form1: TForm1;
Implementation
{$R *.fmx}
Procedure TForm1.Button1Click(Sender: TObject);
  Begin
    TDialogService.PreferredMode := TDialogService.TPreferredMode.Platform;
    TDialogService.ShowMessage('Hello World');
  End;
End.
```

P

Table 41.2 Using FMX.DialogService.TDialogService.ShowMessage

Fig. 41.33 Screencast of TestProjectFMXDialogService executing on SamSung S8+

InputQuery is able to display a dialog box containing multiple fields.

For example, we are able to use the procedure version of **InputQuery** to obtain a username and a password from the user as follows

Caption — Prompts — Default values

```
TDialogService.InputQuery('LogIn', ['Username ', #1'Password '], ['', ''],
      Procedure(Const AResult : TModalresult;
                Const AValues : Array Of String)
                Begin
                  Username := AValues[0];
                  Password := AValues[1]
                End);
```

Anonymous procedure

#1 directive to not show password characters as plain text but instead as asterisks

Figure 41.34 shows the form design for application `TestProjectDialogServiceInputQuery` and *Figure 41.35* its structure. *Figure 41.36* shows `TestProjectDialogServiceInputQuery` in execution, with the **Login** button clicked, and the **InputQuery** dialog box displayed.

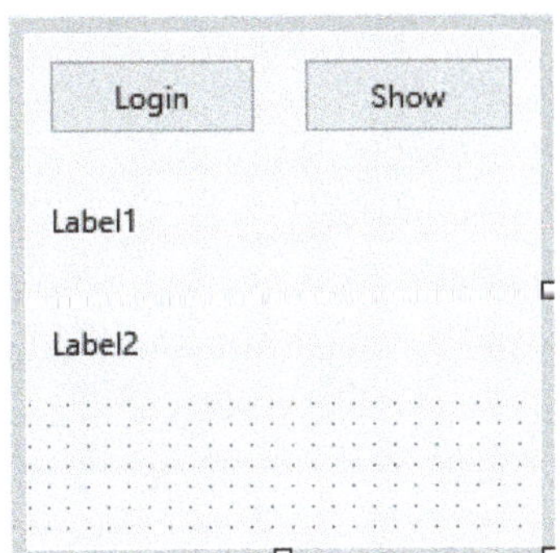

Fig. 41.34 Form design for application TestProjectDialogServiceInputQuery

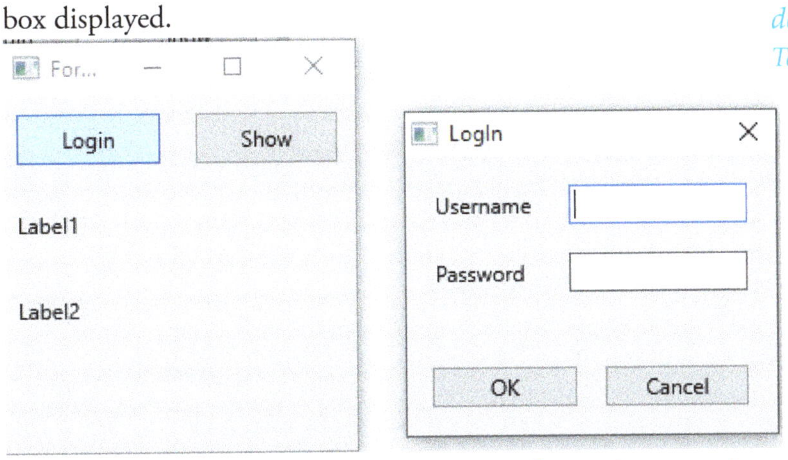

Fig. 41.36 TestProjectDialogServiceInputQuery in execution, Login button clicked, InputQuery dialog box displayed

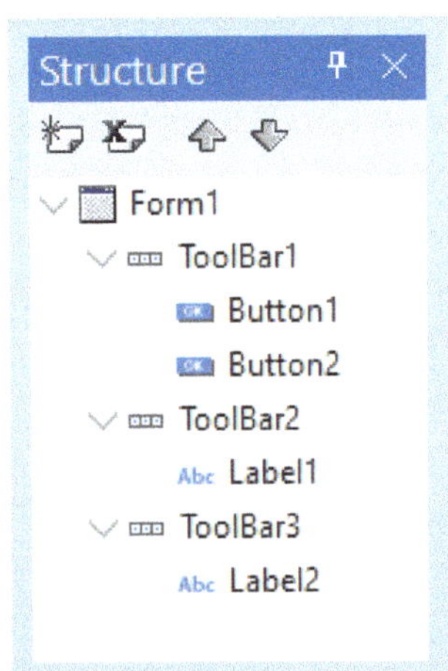

Fig. 41.35 Structure window for the design with code shown in Figure 41.27

(Download from www.educational-computing.com/DelphiBook/Code/Chapter41/TestProjectFMXDialogServiceInputQuery.rar)

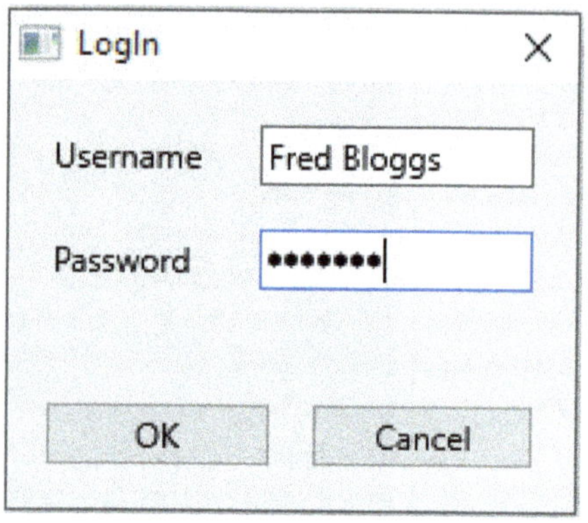

Fig. 41.37 User input into the two TEdit boxes

If the `OK` button is clicked - *Figure 41.37* - the two values for username and password are assigned to the string variables `UserName` and `Password` shown in *Table 41.3* before the dialog window is closed. The action of closing the dialog window calls the anonymous procedure which assigns the values collected in `AValues[0]` and `AValues[1]` from the two edit boxes to `Username` and `Password` as follows

`Username := AValues[0]; Password := AValues[1];`

Anonymous procedures are covered in *Chapter 44*.

Figure 41.38 shows the output after the `Show` button is clicked.

```
Unit TestDialogServiceInputQueryUnit;
Interface
Uses
  System.SysUtils, System.Types, System.UITypes,  System.Classes,
  System.Variants,  FMX.Types, FMX.Controls, FMX.Forms, FMX.Graphics,
  FMX.Dialogs, FMX.Controls.Presentation, FMX.StdCtrls, FMX.DialogService;
Type
  TForm1 = Class(TForm)
           Button1: TButton;
           Button2: TButton;
           Label1: TLabel;
           Label2: TLabel;
           ToolBar1: TToolBar;
           ToolBar2: TToolBar;
           ToolBar3: TToolBar;
           Procedure Button1Click(Sender: TObject);
           Procedure Button2Click(Sender: TObject);
         End;
Var
  Form1: TForm1;
Implementation
{$R *.fmx}
Var
  Username, Password : String;
Procedure TForm1.Button1Click(Sender: TObject);
  Begin
    TDialogService.PreferredMode := TDialogService.TPreferredMode.Platform;
    TDialogService.InputQuery('LogIn', ['Username ', #1'Password '], ['', ''],
      Procedure(Const AResult : TModalresult;
                Const AValues : Array Of String)
                Begin
                  Username := AValues[0];
                  Password := AValues[1]
                End);
  End;

Procedure TForm1.Button2Click(Sender: TObject);
  Begin
    Label1.Text := '   Username: ' + Username;
    Label2.Text := '   Password: ' + Password;
  End;
End.
```

Table 41.3 Using FMX.DialogService.TDialogService.InputQuery

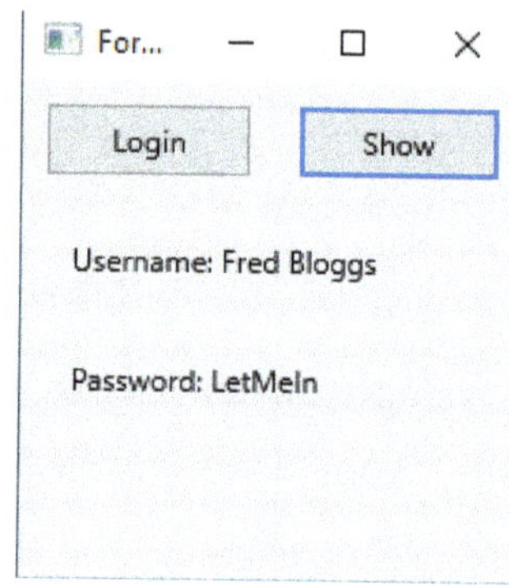

Fig. 41.38 Output after Show button clicked

The text `Label1` and text `Label2` shown in *Figure 41.36* on the form change to

`Username: Fred Bloggs`

`Password: LetMeIn`

Purpose: To learn how to develop applications for OSX and iOS[2]

If the Windows development computer and the destination Apple MacBook or other Apple computer are set up and configured for deployment of a Delphi application then deploying an application from a Windows development machine to an Apple MacBook or other running macOS 64-bit starts with selecting macOS 64-bit in the Delphi toolbar as shown in *Figure 41.39*. The setting of the **Style** and **View** windows (dropdown boxes) shown in *Figure 41.40* are irrelevant as far as deployment is concerned.

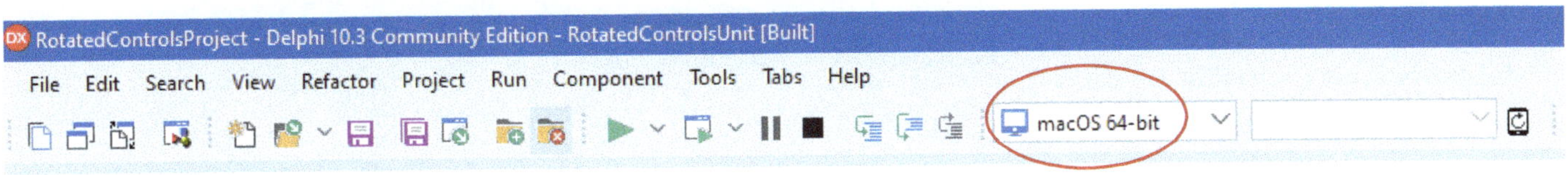

Fig. 41.39 Windows 10 Delphi toolbar with target set to macOS 64-bit

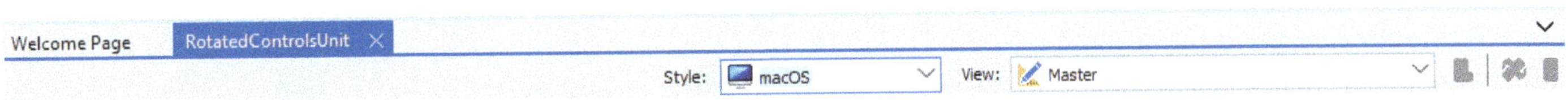

Fig. 41.40 Windows 10 Delphi toolbar with style set to macOS and view Master

The **Style** window setting is used at design time to style the appearance of controls for a specific target, i.e. controls may be customised for specific targets, e.g. macOS (In *Chapter 42*, the noughts and crosses exercise has styling set up separately for each target).

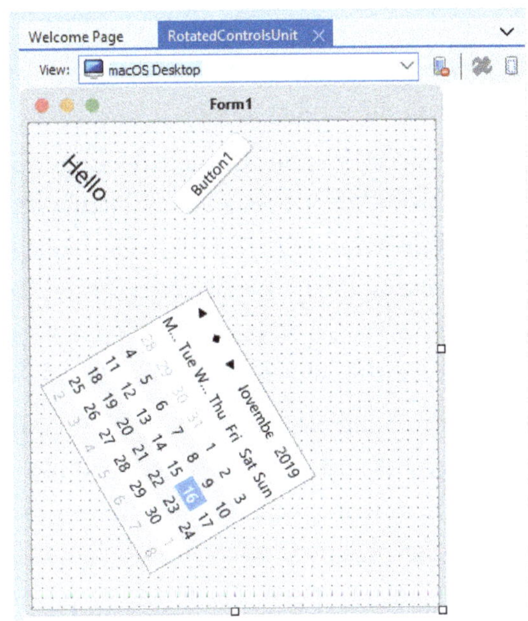

Fig. 41.41 Windows 10 Delphi toolbar with view set to macOS Desktop

The **View** window setting is used to switch from the **Master** view to a specific available target view as shown in *Figure 41.41* for the `RotatedControlsProject` (on deployment Delphi uses the actual device's form factor to configure the executable's actualUI). Incidently, it is worth noting now that to delete a form component/control, Delphi must be in **Master** view mode.

Figure 41.42 shows the `RotatedControlsProject` deployed to executing on Apple MacBook Pro running **macOS Catalina version 10.15.1**.

Setting up MacBook for deployment of Delphi applications

PAServer, the Platform Assistant Server Application, must be installed on the Mac or MacBook and up and running. The macOS installer for the Platform Assistant (**PAServer**) and the **PAServer Manager** are named **PAServer20.0.pkg** (this may change with later versions of Delphi, so check). **PAServer** installer is located in the **PAServer** directory inside the RAD Studio installation directory (hence you should always be able to get the correct **PAServer** for your version of Delphi). The RAD Studio installation directory is, for example for Delphi Rio, `C:\Program Files (x86)\Embarcadero\Studio\20.0\PAServer\PAServer20.0.pkg`.

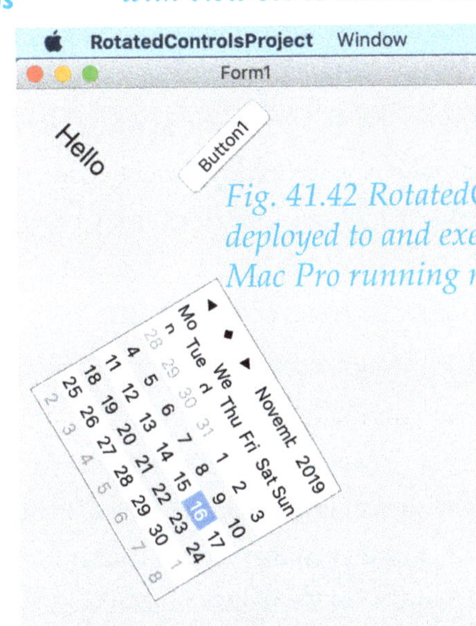

Fig. 41.42 RotatedControlsProject deployed to and executing on Apple Mac Pro running macOS Catalina

---

2 A Mac or MacBook is required for iPhone/iPad development

Alternatively, it can be downloaded from Embarcadero's website but make sure that you choose the version that matches your current Delphi release.

Next the .pkg file should be copied to a local directory on the Mac/MacBook (the Windows development computer and the Mac/MacBook are typically part of the same local area network but an alternative could be Windows running on the Mac/MacBook in a virtual machine created by Parallels Desktop or VMWare Fusion). Double clicking the .pkg file in Finder on the Mac/MacBook launches the installer for Platform Assistant Server. By default Platform Assistant is installed on the primary disk on the Mac/MacBook in the Applications folder.

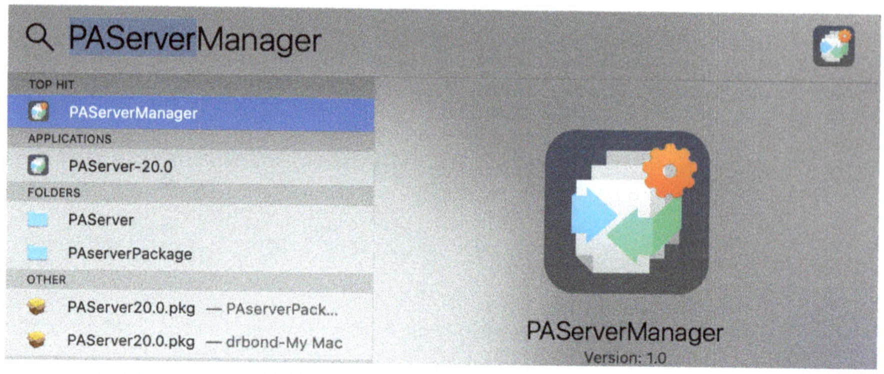

Fig. 41.43 Locating PAServerManager using macOS application search

After the installation is complete, locate PAServerManager using macOS application search (magnifying glass icon top right of the toolbar) as shown in *Figure 41.43*. Double click PAServerManager (`PAServerManager.app`) to launch it, and to attach it to the toolbar as shown in *Figure 41.44*.

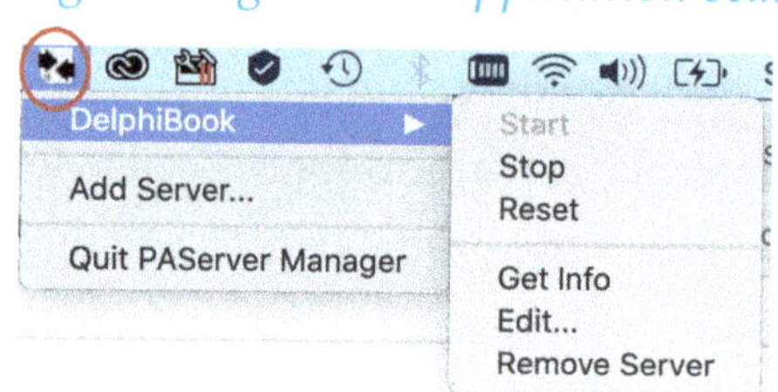

Fig. 41.44 PAServerManager in the toolbar

Clicking on its icon in the toolbar brings down the menu Add Server|Quit PAServer Manager. Clicking on Add Server brings up the window shown in *Figure 41.45*. The name `DelphiBook` was entered in the Name labelled edit box to create a named PAServer, `DelphiBook`. *Figure 41.44* shows the result of creating server `DelphiBook` and starting it.

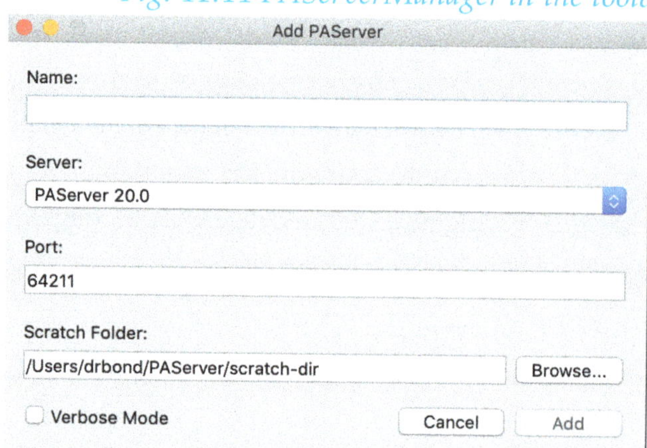

Fig. 41.45 Adding a PAServer using PAServerManager

In order to build OSX projects and iOS projects, Delphi must discover and set paths to required files on the Mac/MacBook as well as pulling some development files (header files) from the Mac/MacBook into the Windows development computer. These files are provided by XCode and accessed via PAServer running on the MacBook. Therefore, the relevant version of XCode and XCode Command Line Tools must be installed on the MacBook (relevant for the OSX version and the iOS device and its operating system version).

The `RotatedControlsProject` shown deployed and executing in *Figure 41.42* used XCode 11.1 installed on a MacBook. This works fine for OSX Catalina development but does not work with iOS 13.2 onwards which require later versions of XCode. XCode and XCode Command Line Tools may be downloaded for free from the App Store or from http://developer.apple.com/downloads. The latter requires that you register as an Apple Developer (free option) - http://developer.apple.com/programs/register.

To check that XCode Command Line Tools are installed on your Mac/MacBook:

1. Start XCode on the Mac/MacBook
2. Choose Preferences from the XCode menu
3. In the general window, click the Locations tab
4. On the Locations window, check the Command Line Tools option shows the XCode version (with which the Command Line Tools were installed) - *Figure 41.46*. This means that the Command Line Tools are already installed and that you do not need to install them.

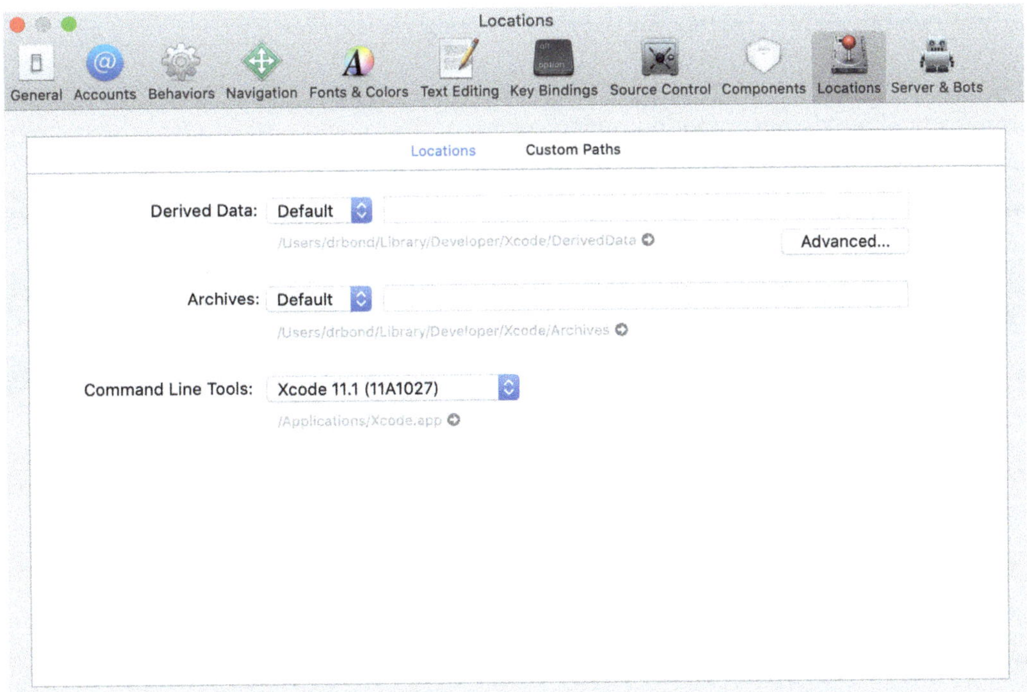

Fig. 41.46 XCode Locations window showing that Command Line Tools XCode 11.1 installed

When **PAServer** `DelphiBook` is started, a terminal window is created as shown in *Figure 41.47*. The no password option has been chosen. Select **Tools|Options|Deployment|Connection Profile Manager** on the Windows development computer to launch the **Connection Profile Manager** window - *Figure 41.48*.

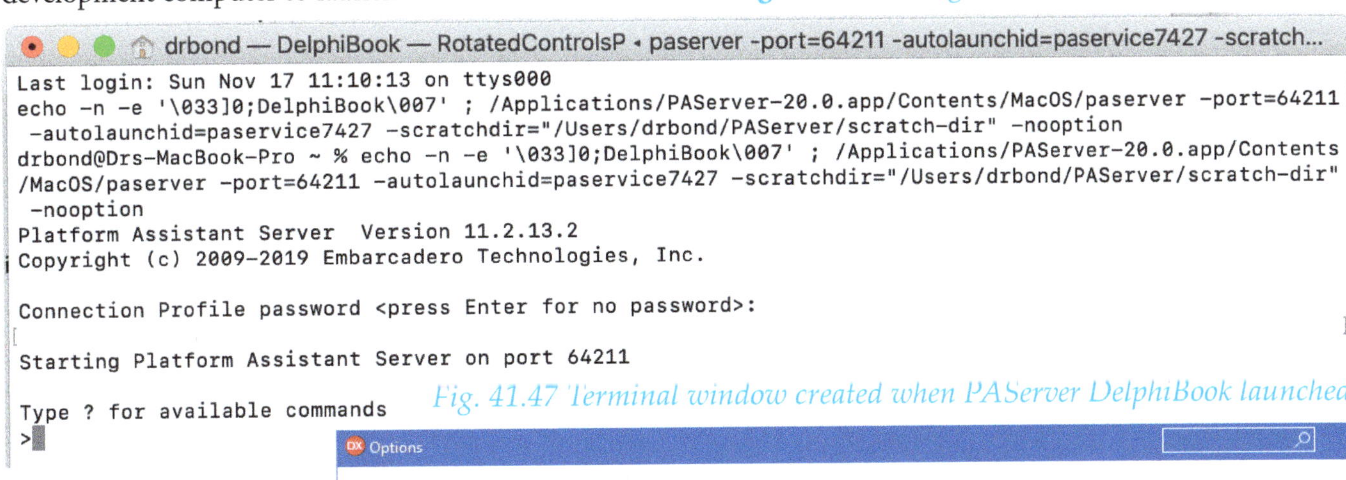

Fig. 41.47 Terminal window created when PAServer DelphiBook launched

Add a profile for **macOS 64-bit** platform. Note its **IP address** and enter it into the **Host name** field. Use the default port `64211` and do not enter a password. Click on **Test Connection**. If the **PAServer** is running in the MacBook and the configuration is correct the `Connection succeeded` message shown in *Figure 41.49* should appear.

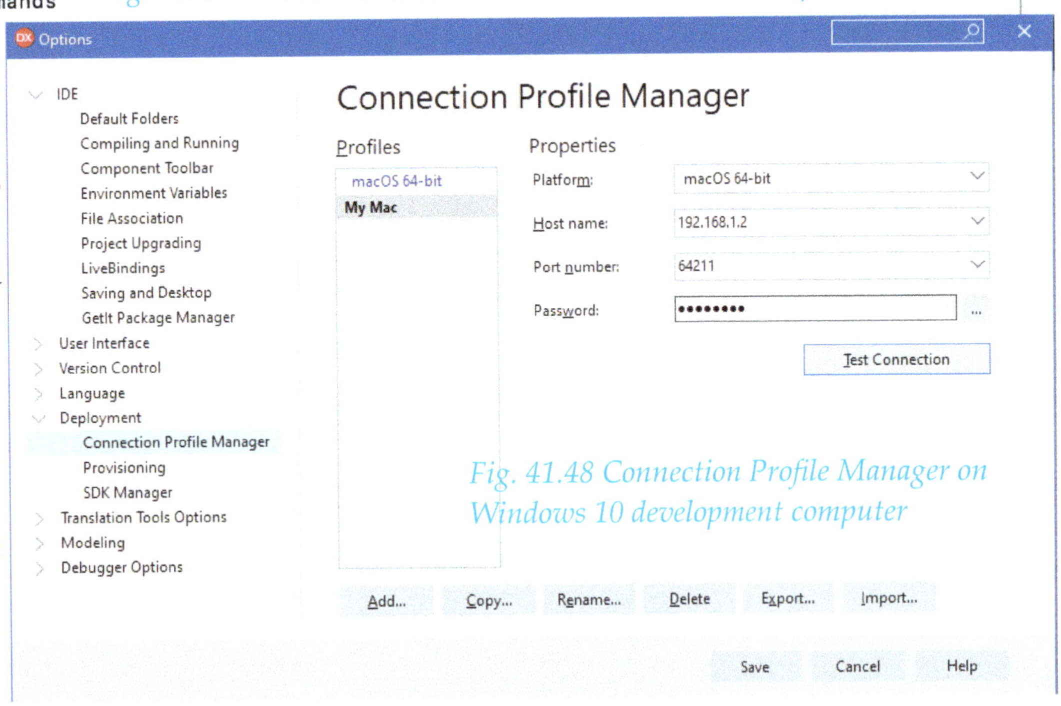

Fig. 41.48 Connection Profile Manager on Windows 10 development computer

Select the build type **macOS 64-bit - Normal** in the **Provisioning** window as shown in *Figure 41.50*.

Figure 41.51 shows the **SDK Manager** window. Selecting **Mac OSX 10.15** reveals that the correct sdk, **MacOSX10.15.sdk** is available from the given path.

This matches the version of the operating system running in the Apple MacBook - *Figure 41.52*.

Both Windows computer and Apple MacBook are now configured for building, deploying, executing and debugging a Delphi application.

Figure 41.42 earlier in this chapter shows one example of a Delphi cross-platform application executing on an Apple MacBook.

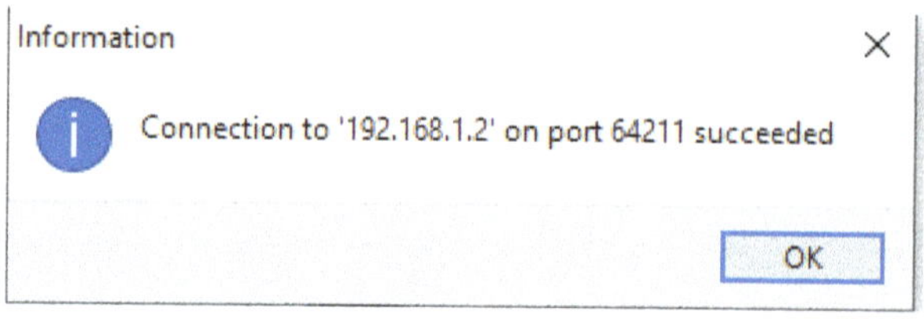

Fig. 41.49 Testing the connection between the Windows development computer and the Apple Mac at 192.168.1.2

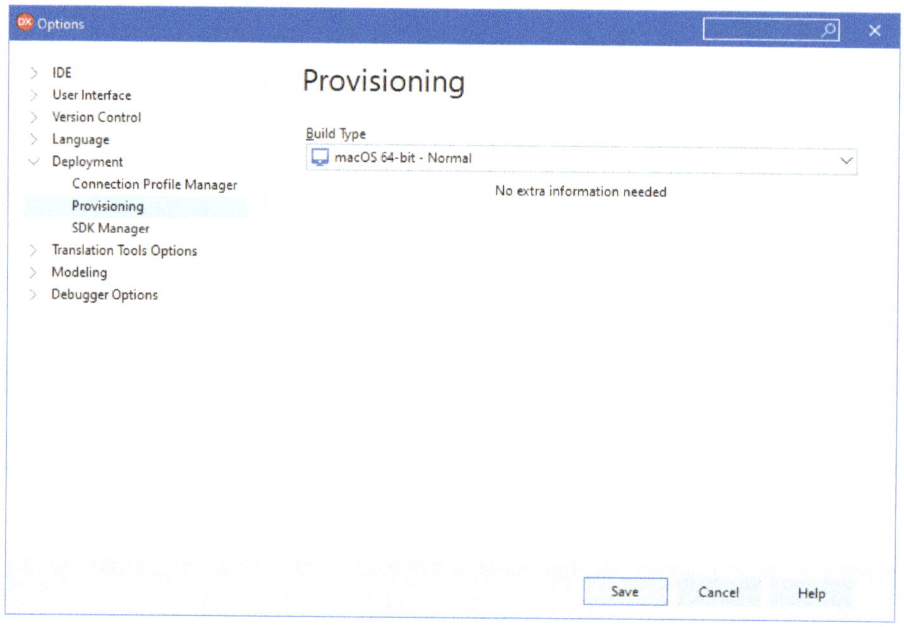

Fig. 41.50 Provisioning window showing that the macOS 64-bit - Normal build type has been selected

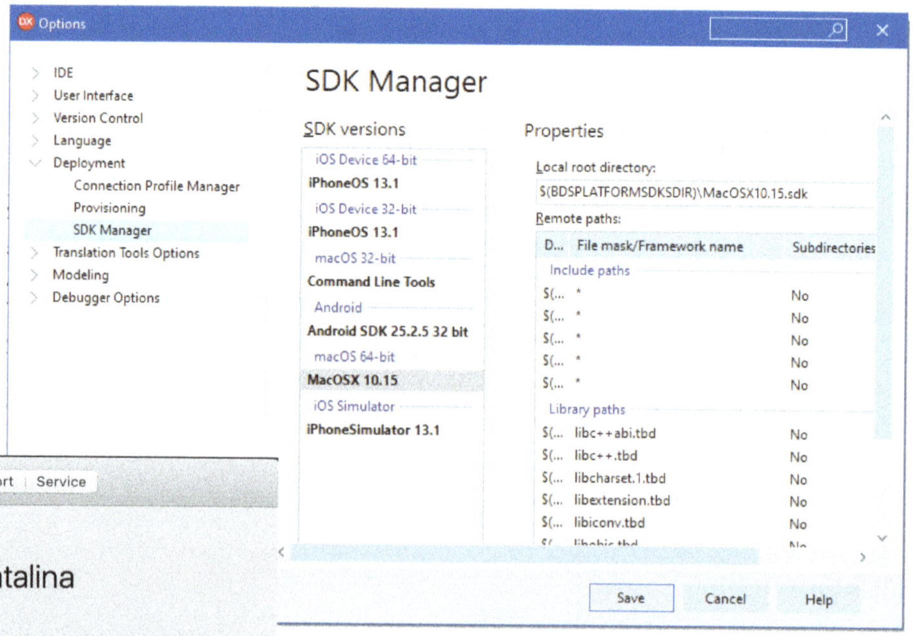

Fig. 41.51 SDK Manager window showing that when the macOS X 10.15 has been selected its SDK MacOSX10.15.sdk is available from the given path

Fig. 41.52 Apple Mac about window showing that its operating system is version 10.15.1

Setting up an Apple MacBook for deployment of Delphi applications to iOS devices

Firstly, the currently installed XCode 11.1 was renamed to avoid conflict, then XCode 11.2.1 was installed from the App Store and launched with an iPhone 11 connected to an Apple MacBook. Window|Devices and Simulators was selected in Xcode and configured to connect to "`Kevin's iPhone`" as shown in *Figure 41.53*.

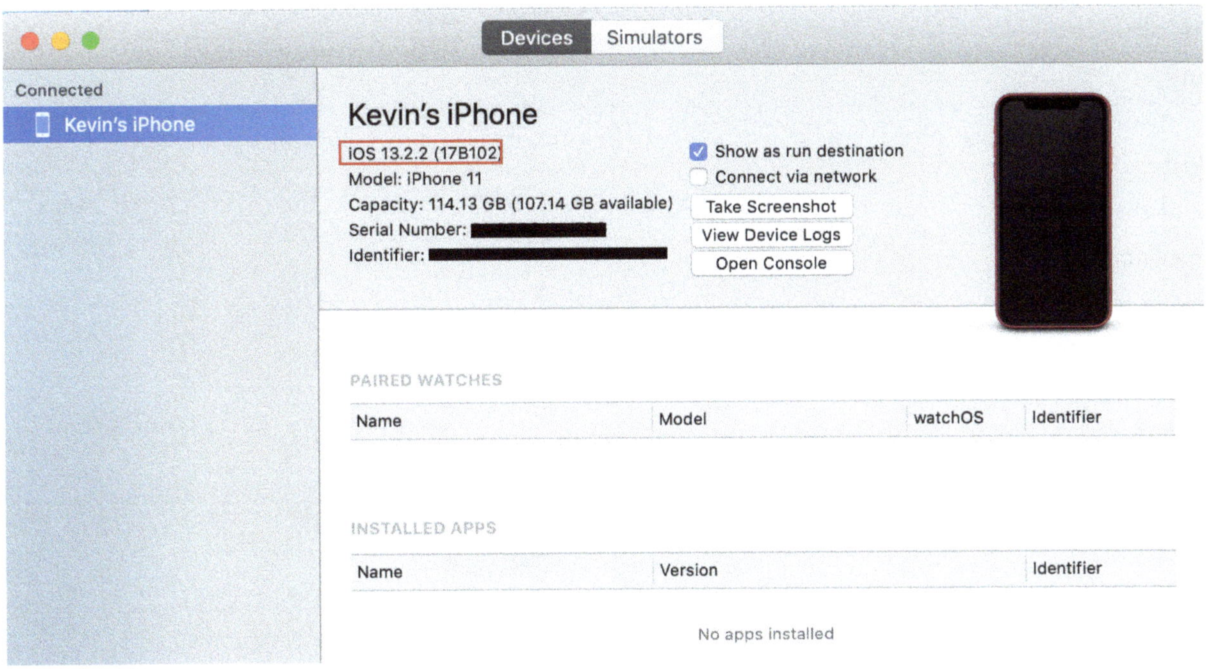

Fig. 41.53 XCode 11.2.1 Window | Devices and Simulators with iPhone 11 running operating system iOS 13.2.2

XCode 11.1 does not support iOS 13.2.2 and so was replaced by XCode 11.2.1. The mobile landscape changes so frequently that this can cause issues for Delphi mobile development, especially Apple iOS.

Also, Delphi 10.3.3 is required for iOS 13.2 development.

Delphi 10.3.2 works with devices running iOS up to iOS 13.1.

Delphi 10.3.3 was released on November 21st 2019. This section uses Delphi 10.3.3 Enterprise version but the Community Edition 10.3.3 ot later is perfectly adequate for this task and many others.

To develop for an iPhone or iPad requires an Apple ID from appleID.apple.com - *Figure 41.54*.

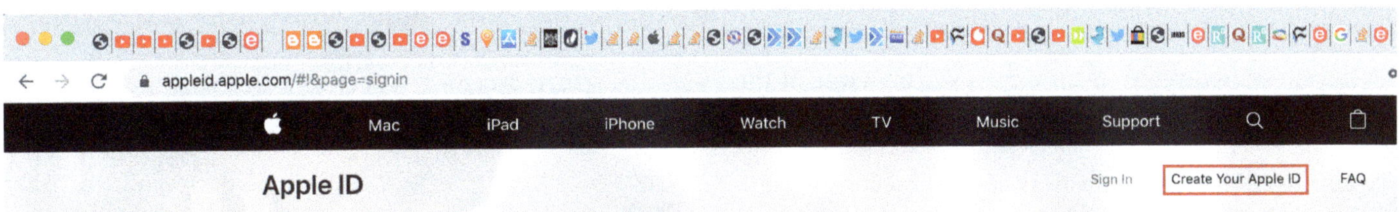

Fig. 41.54 Creating an Apple ID

You will be required to enter your name, date of birth, email address, password and the answers to some security questions, e.g. "your favourite pet's name". Your Apple ID will be the email address that you supply. It is also possible to create an Apple ID from within XCode|Preferences|Accounts.

Click on XCode|Preferences in XCode and select Accounts to bring up a window similar to the one shown in *Figure 41.55*. This window shows that an existing Apple ID has been selected already (partially obscured for security reasons). If no Apple ID shows then click on + sign at the bottom of the Apple IDs' window to add an Apple ID.

Now click on Manage Certificates to generate a development certificate to use to sign generated apps during the development phase. A signing certificate is generated for the given Apple ID and when done the information shown in *Figure 41.56* appears. Click on Done.

(Download from www.educational-computing.com/DelphiBook/Code/Chapter41/NoughtsAndCrossesProjectExp.rar)

To view this certificate in greater detail requires that application **Keychain Access** is run and the corresponding development certificate selected using **Window|Keychain Viewer**. *Figure 41.57* shows some of the information contained in the first section of this certificate. Note that the **Organisational Unit** is `UTU422L452`. This is otherwise known as the **Team ID**.

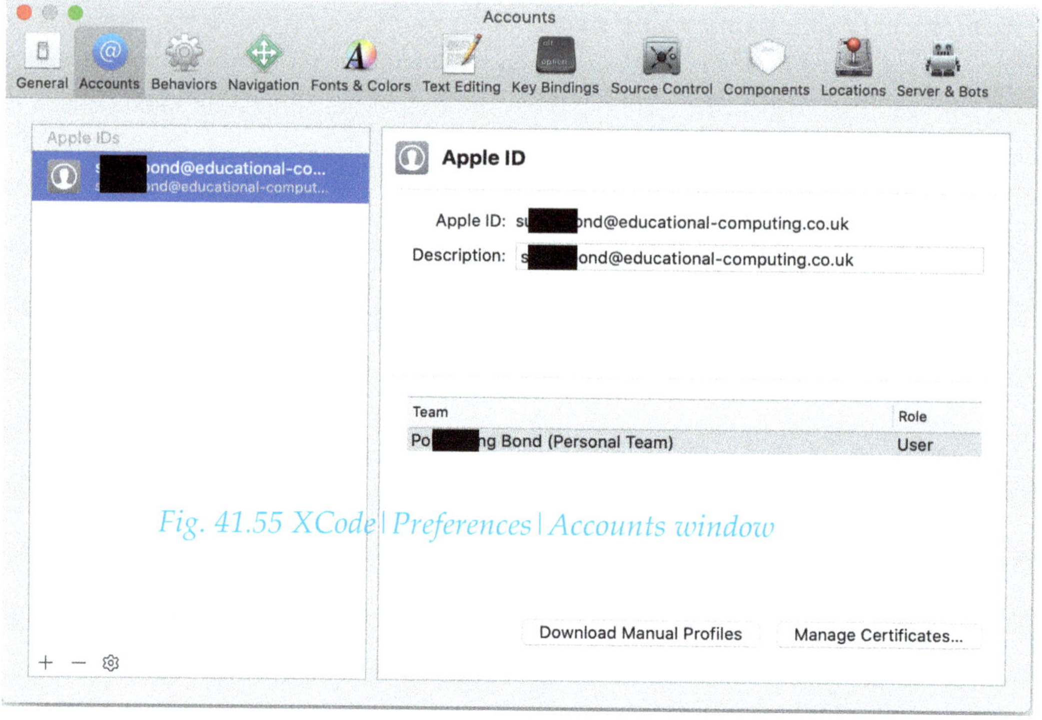

Fig. 41.55 XCode | Preferences | Accounts window

We need to create a **Bundle ID** to uniquely identify an application in Apple's ecosystem. Since this chapter is about local app development we just need to make sure that the **Bundle ID** is unique within the local Apple system. The developer chooses the **Bundle ID**. Typically, the name of the application is appended to a reverse domain, e.g. uk.co.educational-computing. However, in this chapter, ECS will be used in place of the reverse domain. The application is a noughts and crosses game whose development is covered in *Chapter 42*. The name of the application is `NoughtsAndCrossesProjectExp`.

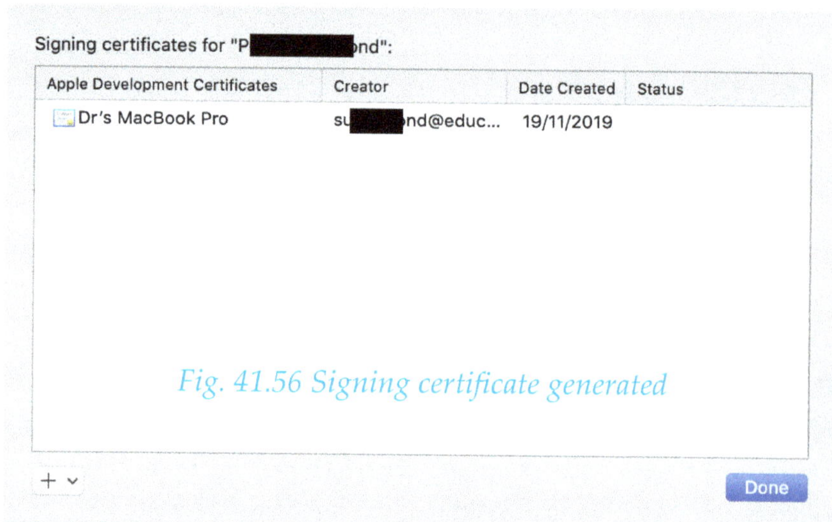

Fig. 41.56 Signing certificate generated

We also need an **App ID**. This is created by combining the **Team ID** with the **Bundle ID**. For the noughts and crosses application, the **App ID** will be

`UTU422L452.ECS.NoughtsAndCrossesProjectExp`

Fig. 41.57 Keychain Access | Window | Keychain Viewer certificate

Unlike Android, it is not possible to install just any app on an iOS device. It has to be signed by Apple first. Both a **Signing Certificate** and a **Provisioning Profile** (**Development** for local development and testing or **Distribution** for uploading to App Store) are therefore required.

An app undergoing development will need testing whether or not the intention is to send it to Apple for approval for sale via the App Store. A provisioning profile links the target device to a developer account. During development, the developer chooses which devices can run the app and what services the app can access. A provisioning profile is downloaded from the developer's account and embedded in the app bundle, and the entire bundle is code-signed. A (**Team**) **Development Provisioning Profile** must be installed on each device on which the app is intended to run. Each (**Team**) **Development Provisioning Profile** contains

1. **App ID** - **Team ID**, **Bundle ID**, e.g. `UTU422L452.ECS.NoughtsAndCrossesProjectExp`
2. **Development Certificate** for developers in the team to use when testing the app on a device while writing code; public key part of the public-private key encryption algorithm sent to device, private part used to sign the app
3. List of devices that the app can run on

When a device such as an iPhone is connected to **XCode** running in a Mac or MacBook and an app is installed on the device by **XCode**, the following takes place

1. the **Provisioning Profile** in the Mac/MacBook examines the **Developer Certificate** in the Mac/MacBook's key chain (*Figure 41.57*)
2. **XCode** uses the certificate to sign the code with the private key associated with the certificate
3. the device's unique identifier (**UUID**) is matched with the device IDs in the **Provisioning Profile**
4. the **Bundle ID** part of the **App ID** in the **Provisioning Profile** is matched with the bundle identifier in the app; the **Team ID** of the **App ID** in the **Provisioning Profile** is matched with the **Team ID** in the app
5. the service entitlements required are associated with the **App ID**
6. the public key of the certificate stored in the device is matched to the private key used to sign the app.

The difference between **Development** and **Distribution Profiles** is that **Distribution Profiles** don't specify any **Device IDs**. A **Distribution Profile** is used to submit an app to the App Store for distribution. After the app is reviewed by Apple, Apple signs it with their own signature that can run on any device. A third kind of profile, an **Ad-Hoc Profile**, is used when the app is to be released to a limited number of registered devices.

Preparing iOS device for development

You may get the error message on attaching your **iOS** mobile device, e.g. iPhone 11, to a Mac or MacBook running **XCode**: "Development cannot be enabled while your computer is locked. Please unlock your device and reattach." One solution is to

1. Disconnect the mobile device/tablet from the Mac or MacBook and close **XCode**
2. On the mobile device/tablet select **Settings|General|Reset**, then tap **Reset Location & Privacy**
3. Plug mobile device/tablet back into the Mac or MacBook whence a prompt should appear on the mobile device/tablet to **Trust** the MacBook, tap **Trust**
4. Reopen **XCode**
5. Test the connection by building a project, `Test1`, in **XCode** (**File|New|Project**, accept the default **Single View App** which just writes "`Hello, World!`" to the mobile/tablet's screen) as shown in *Figure 41.58*.

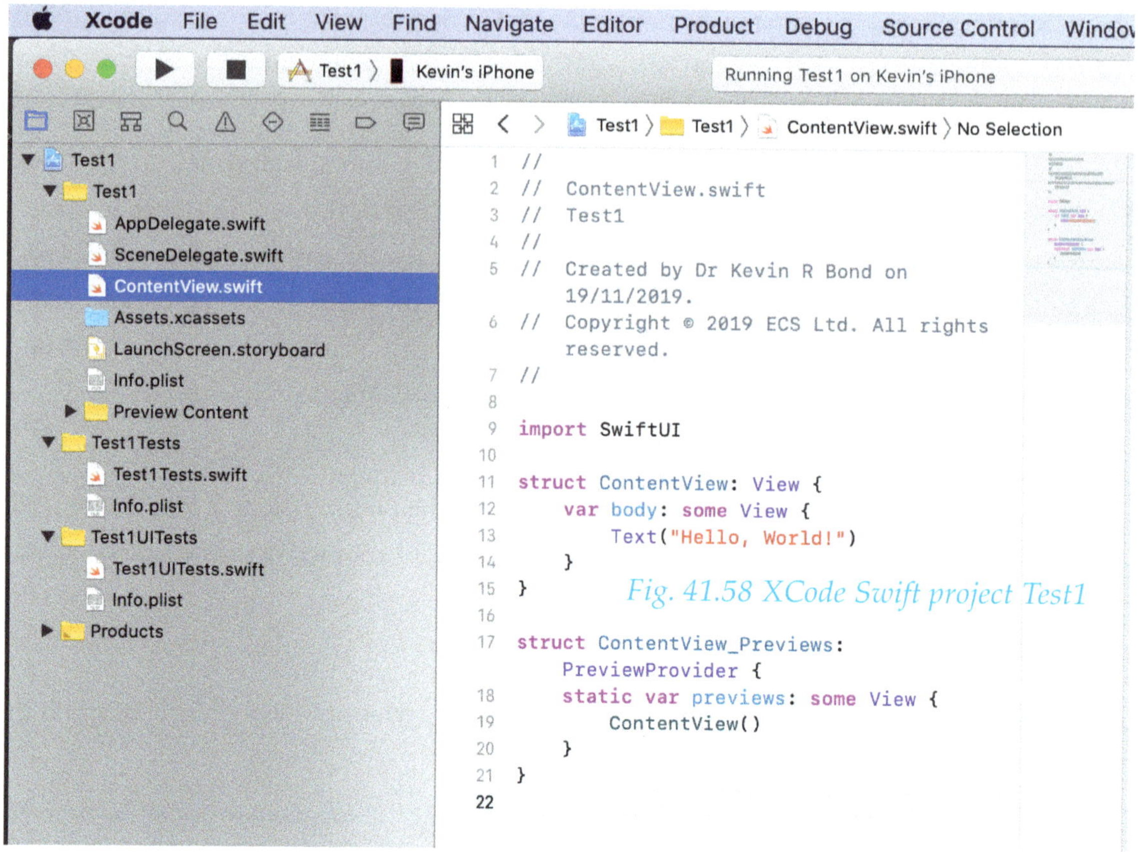

Fig. 41.58 XCode Swift project Test1

Set the **iOS deployment Target** as shown in *Figure 41.59*.
Set the **Signing & Capabilities** for Swift app with **Bundle ID** `ECS.Test1` as shown in *Figure 41.60*.
Now build and deploy this app to iPhone.
Figure 41.61 shows app `Test1` executing on the iPhone 11 connected to the MacBook. The program shown in *Figure 41.58* was modifed by changing "`Hello, World!`" to "`Hello, World 2`" just to show it could be done.

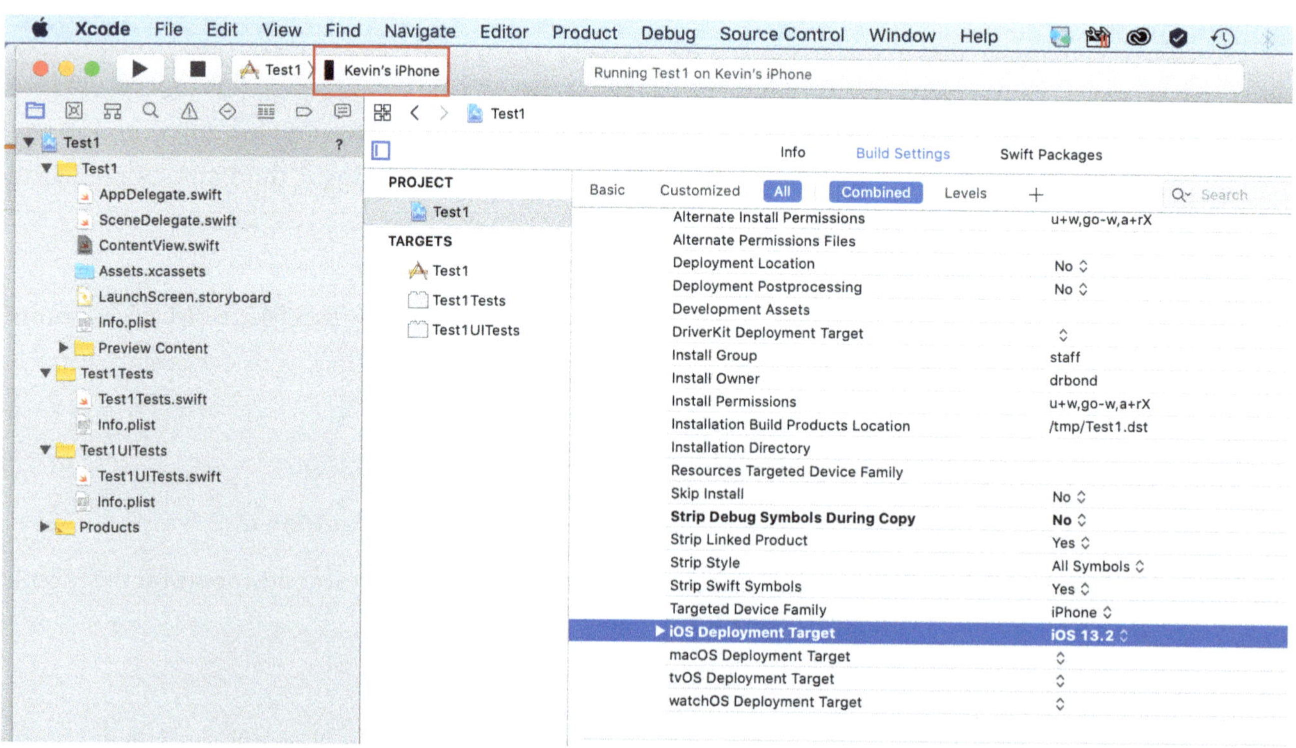

Fig. 41.59 Setting iOS Deployment target

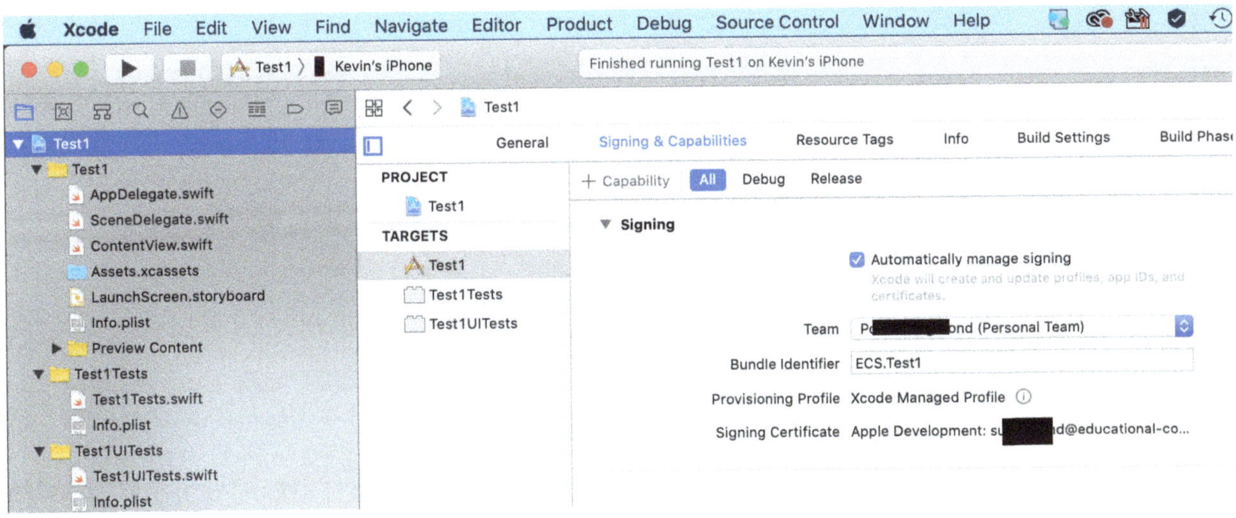

Fig. 41.60 Setting up signing for Swift app ECS.Test1

With the free **Developer** account, Apple allows up to ten **App IDs** to be created every seven days and allows a maximum of three apps at any one time to be installed on an iOS device.

Building, deploying and launching a Delphi app on an iPhone 11

Having tested that the set up for deploying and launching an app to the iPhone 11 is functioning in **XCode**, it is time to test the process with a **Delphi** cross-platform app.

Close **XCode** on the Apple Mac/MacBook.

On the Windows development computer, launch **Delphi 10.3.3**.

Load `NoughtsAndCrossesProjectExp.dproj`.

Select **Project|Options|Version Info** as shown in *Figure 41.62* and change the **CFBundleIdentifier** to `ECS.$(ModuleName)`. Test the connection to the Mac/MacBook is successful as before - *Figures 41.48*, *41.49*.

Fig. 41.61 Test1 app running on an iPhone 11

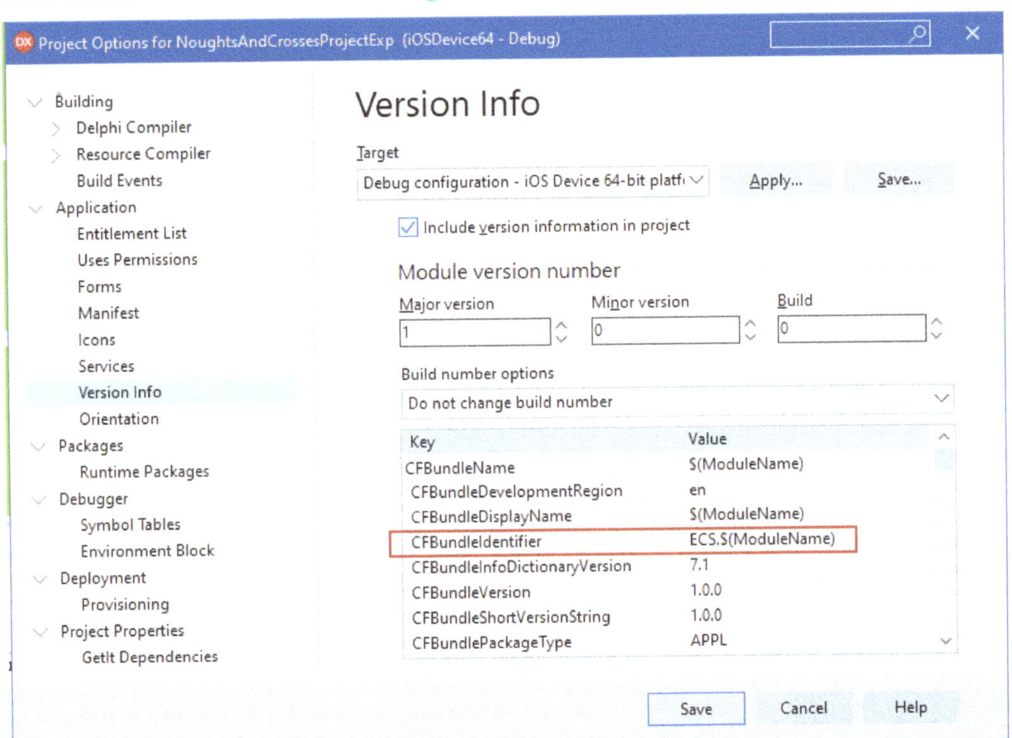

Fig. 41.62 Setting Bundle ID to ECS.NoughtsAndCrossesProjectExp

Select target **iOS Device 64-bit** `Kevin's iPhone` (substitute your iPhone name)- see *Figures 41.63* and *41.64*.

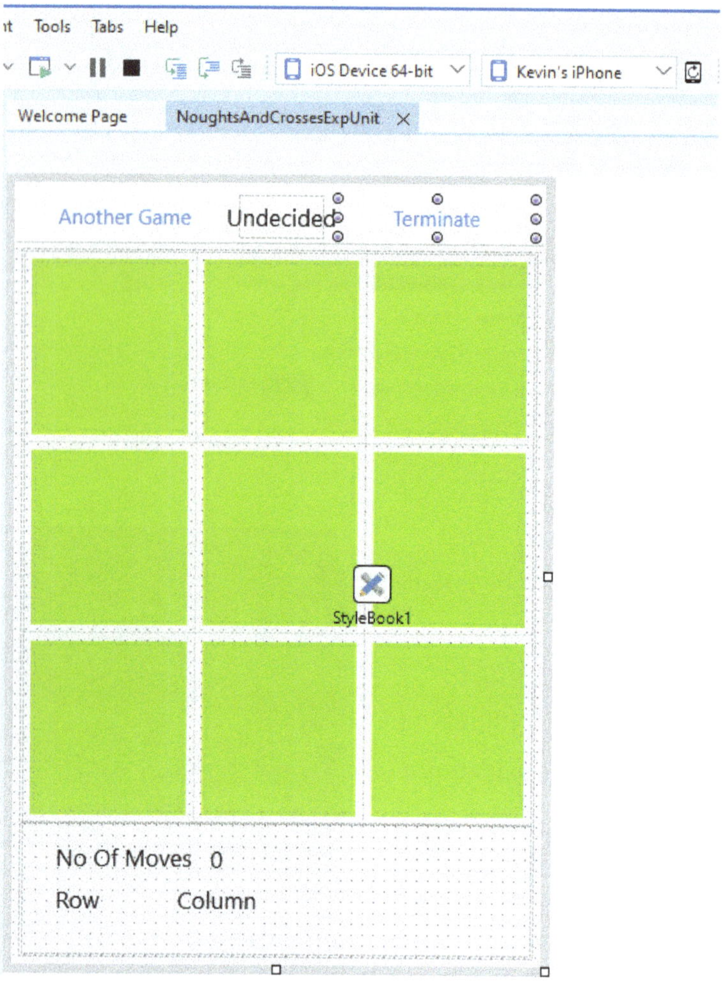

Fig. 41.63 User Interface design for noughts and crosses game, target iOSDevice 64-bit, Kevin's iPhone

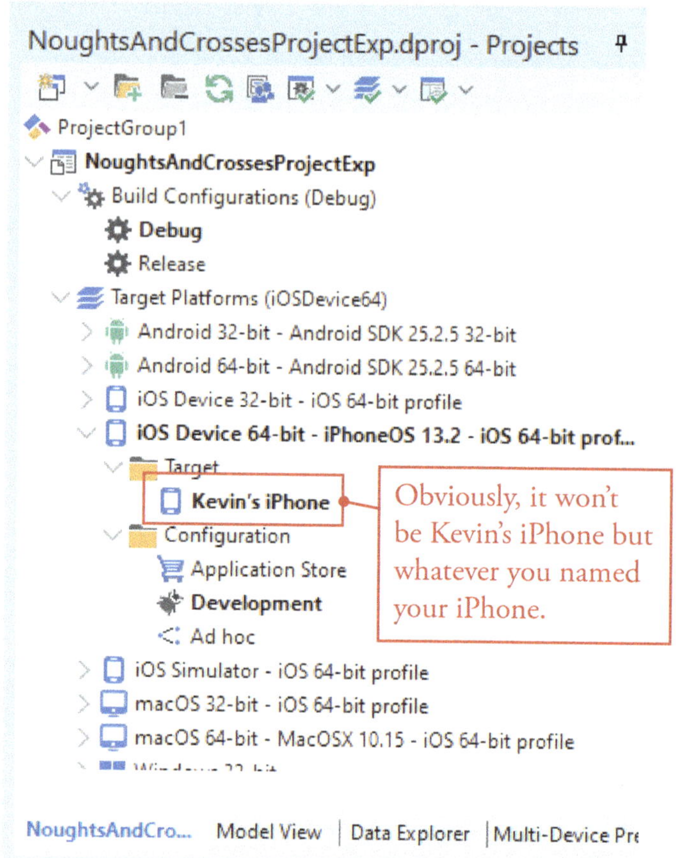

Fig. 41.64 Projects window showing settings for NoughtAndCrossesProjectExp

In **Tools|Options|Deployment|Provisioning** make sure that **Provision Profile** and **Developer Certificate** are set to **<Auto>**. This selection will select the **Developer Certificate** that was used before - *Figure 41.57* - and will create a **Provisioning Profile** for the specified iPhone and the app `NoughtsAndCrossesProjectExp`. (If Delphi is unable to create a provisioning profile then it must be done in **XCode** on the Mac/MacBook by creating a **Swift Project** with the same name and **Building a Profile** for this[3]). Delphi iPhone development is not for the faint-hearted! Check in **Tools|Options|Deployment|SDK Manager** that an SDK has been installed that will support the current iOS operating system - *Figure 41.51*. Use the **Add** button to set up and install the required SDK, if not.

Now **Run without Debugging** (Shift+CTRL+F9).

The initiated process will pass through five stages:

1. Compiling
2. Linking
3. Provisioning
4. Deploying
5. Signing
6. Launching

At the **Signing** stage, a pop-up window will appear on the Mac/MacBook '*codesign wants to access key "Apple Development:* [redacted] *(*[redacted]*)" in your keychain*' prompting the user for their password.

3 See next page for more detail on Provisioning Profiles.

Enter the password that you use for your Mac/MacBook and again when the same pop-up window appears again. The app should appear as an icon on the home screen of the iPhone at the end of this process - *Figure 41.65* - and should launch automatically if the app is trusted - *Figure 41.66*.

Fig. 41.65 NoughtAndCrossesProjectExp icon on home screen

Fig. 41.66 NoughtAndCrossesProjectExp in execution

If the application doesn't launch automatically, click on the icon. If a window then appears on the iPhone that states that apps from the named **Developer** are not trusted, click on **Settings|General|Device Management|Apple Development: ......** and select **Trust**. - *Figure 41.67*.

Note that the `Terminate` button will not work in an iPhone because apps are not allowed to be closed in this way - use the iPhone way.

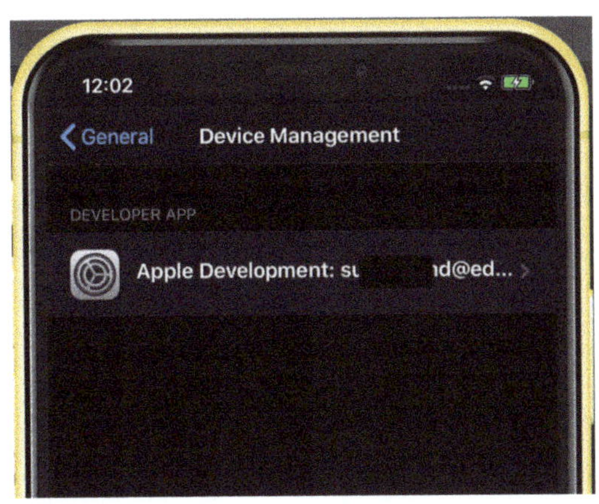

Fig. 41.67 Setting Apple Development for given Apple ID to Trust

Solving problems with Provisioning Profiles and Developer Certificates

From **Tools|Options|Deployment|Provisioning** select a pre-created **Provision Profile** (created from **XCode**) as shown in *Figure 41.68*.

With **<Auto>** selected in the **Developer Certificate** field an **iOS Provisioning Profile** should be loaded, e.g. `ECS.NoughtsAndCrossesProjectExp`.The corresponding **Developer Certificate** will then be loaded.

Two **Organisation Identifiers**, `ECS` and `ECS1` have been used corresponding to two different **Apple IDs**.

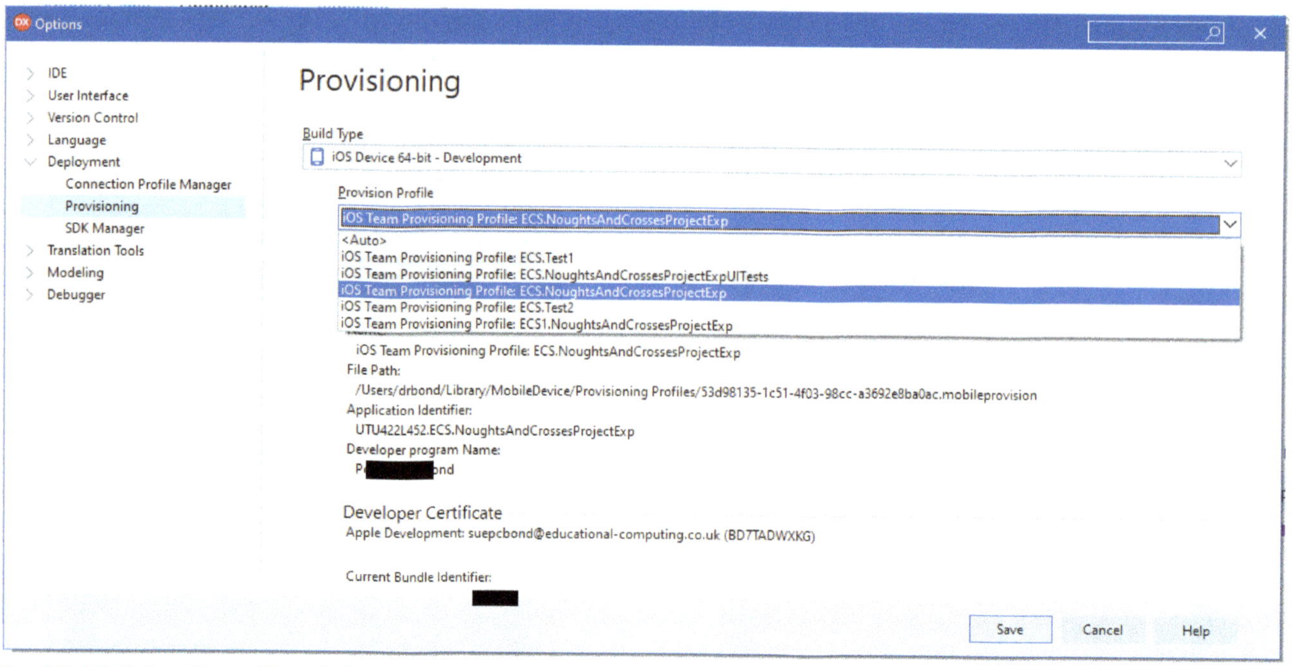

Fig. 41.68 Selecting a Provisioning Profile and automatically loading the corresponding Developer Certificate

The *Provisioning Profiles* are stored on the Mac/MacBook in a folder with path `~Library/MobileDevice/ProvioningProfiles/` (use **Finder|Go|GoTo**). *Figure 41.69* shows the currently stored **Profiles** for the MacBook used in this chapter. *Figures 41.70*, *41.71*, *41.72* show the stages involved in creating a new Provisioning Profile.

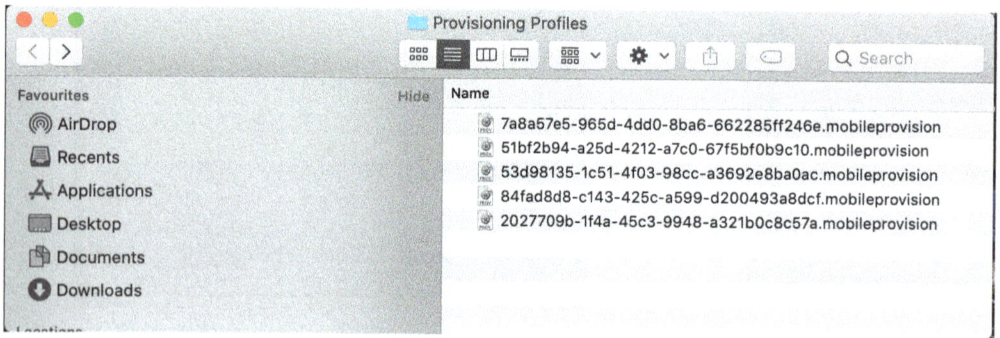

Fig. 41.69 MacBook folder storing Provisioning Profiles created by XCode

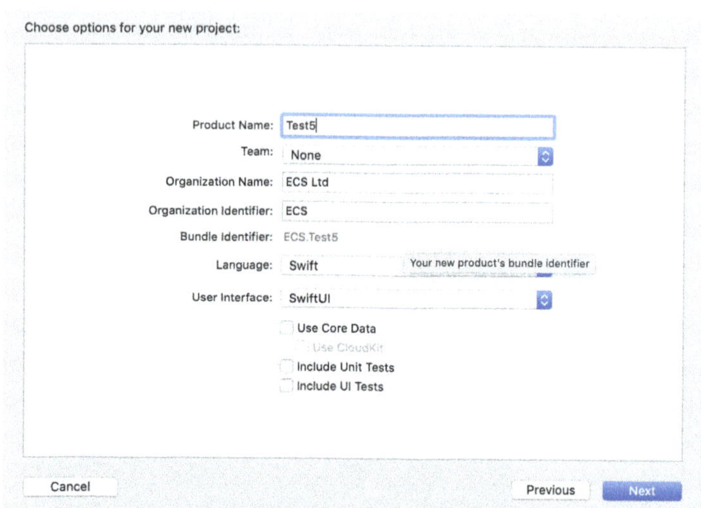

Fig. 41.70 Create a new XCode Project | Single App Test5

Fig. 41.71 Signing & Capabilities

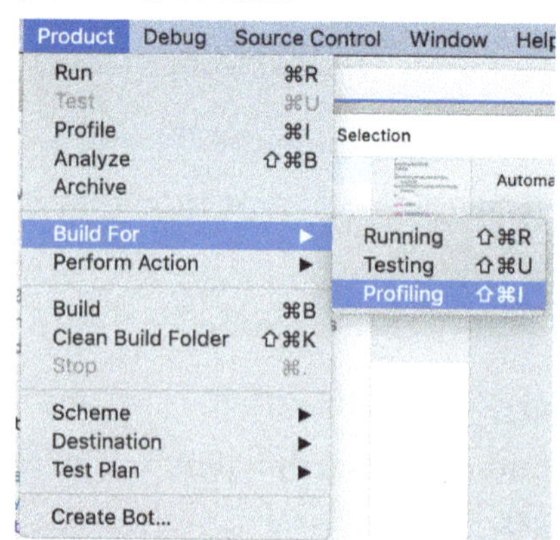

Fig. 41.72 Building a Profile for ECS.Test5

Programming Tasks

1. Create a single form multi-device Windows Firemonkey application which converts centimetres to inches. The centimetre value is entered in an edit box labelled "Input value in centimetres". The edit box should be a container for the TLabel component. The equivalent value in inches is displayed by the Text field of a TLabel component when a button labelled "Convert" is clicked. Build for 32-bit or 64-bit and run.

2. Modify the application in programming task 1 to use two labelled edit boxes, one for centimetres and one for inches. Use the labels, "Centimetres" and "Inches", respectively. Each edit box should be a container for their corresponding label. Use two buttons, one to convert from centimetres to inches and one to convert from inches to centimetres. Build for 32-bit or 64-bit and run.

3. Create a single form multi-device Windows Firemonkey application which converts kilograms to pounds and vice versa. The kilograms value is entered in an edit box labelled "Kilograms" and the output appears in an edit box labelled "Pounds". Each edit box should be a container for their corresponding label. The roles of the edit boxes are reversed when converting in the opposite direction. Use two buttons, one to convert from kilograms to pounds and one to convert from pounds to kilograms. Build for 32-bit or 64-bit and run.

4. Modify the application in task 3 to convert from kilograms to stones and pounds only. Use a labelled edit box for the stones result and a labelled edit box for the pounds result. Build and run.

5. Select and configure a platform other than Windows for the application developed in task 1 or 2. Build and run.

6. Load the RotatedControlsProject. Using Windows as the target, build for 32-bit or 64-bit and run the application. Now experiment with changing the angles at which each control is rotated. Build and run. Select and configure a platform other than Windows for the application. Build and run.

7. Load the TestProjectFMXDialogService project. Select and configure a platform other than Windows for the application. Build and run.

42 FireMonkey components 2

Developing with FireMonkey components

Purpose: To understand how to create custom styles with FireMonkey

Start a new Blank Multi-Device Application.
Save in a separate folder `CustomStyleTest` as

`CustomStyleTestProject.dproj`

and `CustomStyleTestUnit.pas`.

Add a TPanel component, `Panel1`, to the form. Adjust size of form so that it is just greater than `Panel1` as shown in *Figure 42.1*. Select Windows 64-bit and right click `Panel1` on the form and select `Edit Custom Style` to bring up the Style Designer - *Figure 42.4*. As TPanel inherits from TRectangle, the Style Designer shows a TRectangle control. This control has a Fill property. Change the Fill|Color to Chartreuse and change the Name field to `PanelStyleChartreuse`. The Platform field in the Style Designer - *Figure 42.4* - shows Windows 10 Desktop so this custom style will apply to Windows 10 Desktop applications only. Close the Style Designer by clicking the cross in the tab and click Yes when prompted to apply changes.

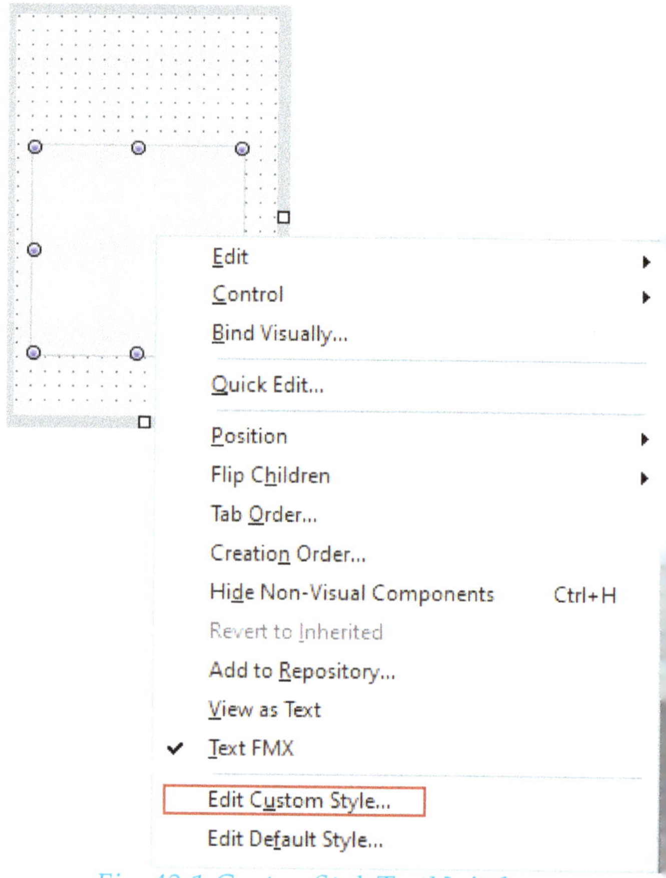

Fig. 42.1 CustomStyleTestUnit form, Panel1 right clicked

If this is the first time that changes are applied, Delphi adds a TStyleBook component, `TStyleBook1`, to the form as shown in *Figure 42.2*. The TPanel control's colour is now `Chartreuse`.

The available styles are revealed by expanding Styles in the Structure window - *Figure 42.3*.

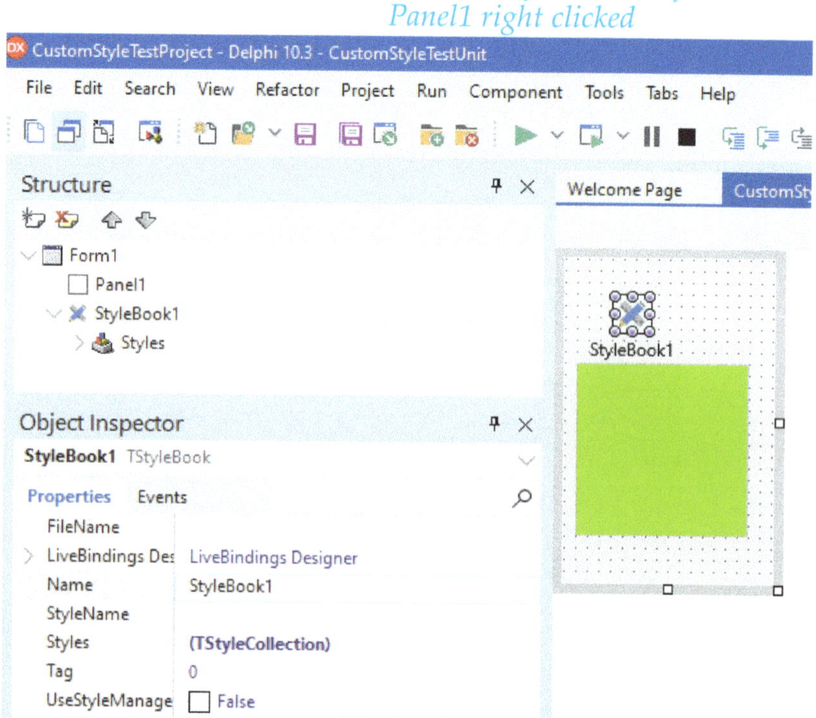

Fig. 42.2 Panel1 now filled with colour Chartreuse and StyleBook1 added

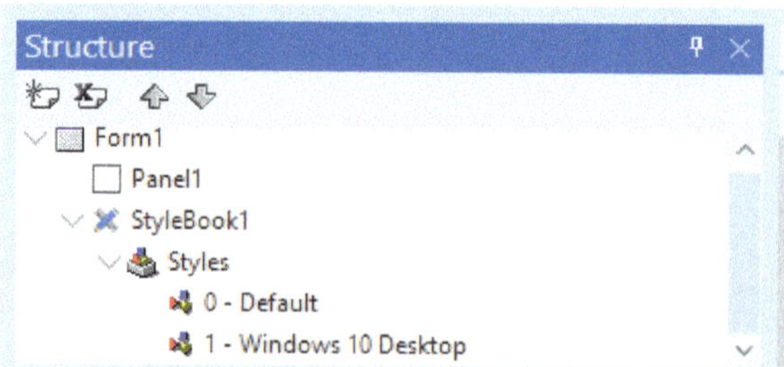

Fig. 42.3 Structure window

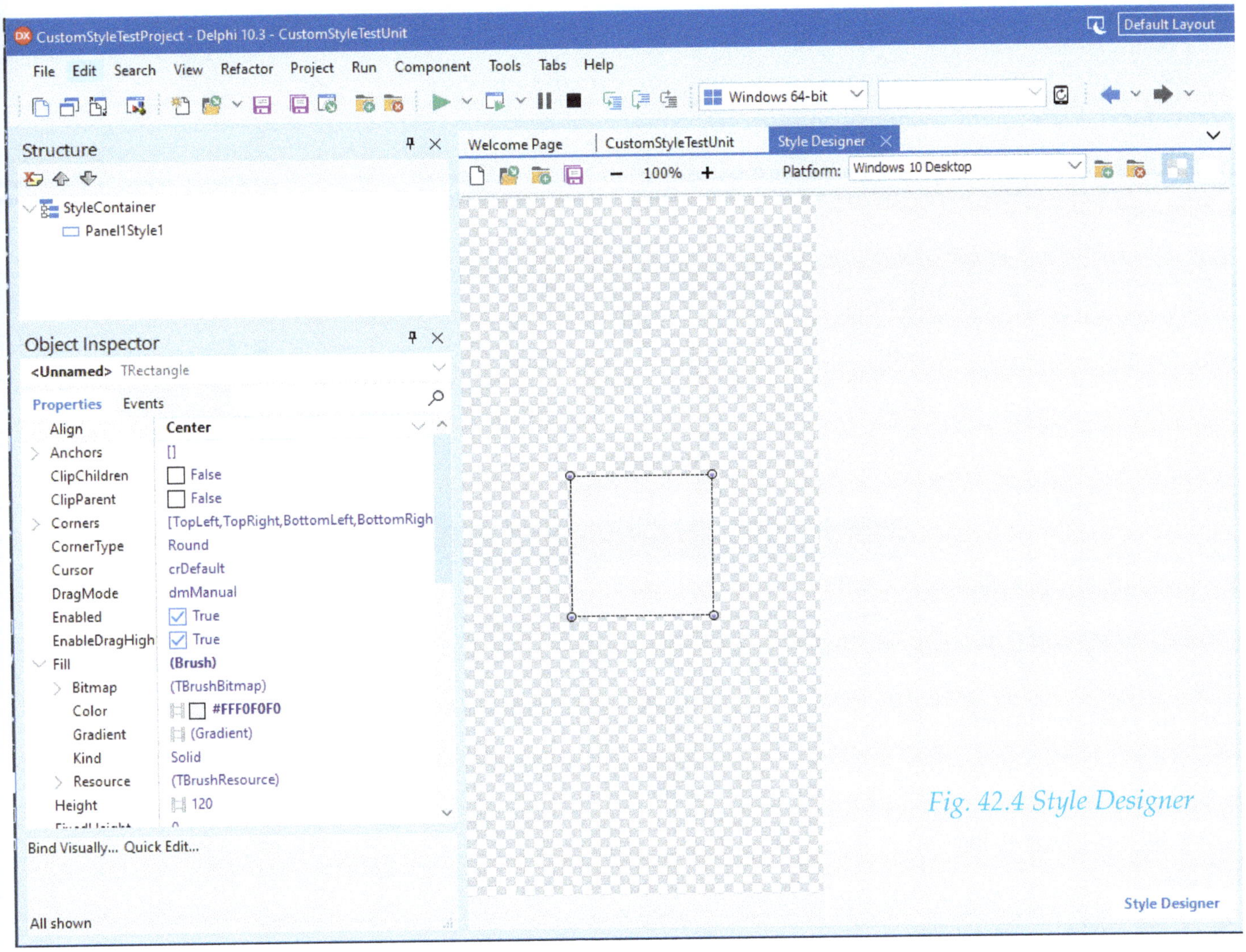

Fig. 42.4 Style Designer

Figure 42.5 shows that the **StyleName** property field has been set to `Panel1Style1` for `PanelStyleChartreuse`.

Figure 42.6 shows that a new custom style named `Panel1Style1` has been created and applied to the **StyleLookUp** field of `Panel1`. The default style is `panelstyle`, the intial style for `Panel1`.

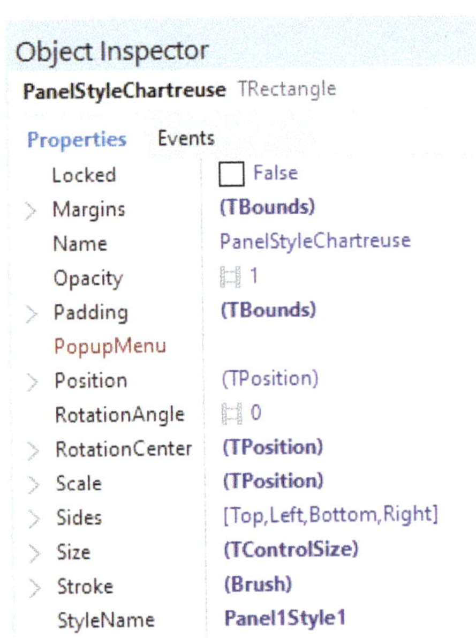

Fig. 42.5 Object Inspector reveals new style as StyleName Panel1Style1

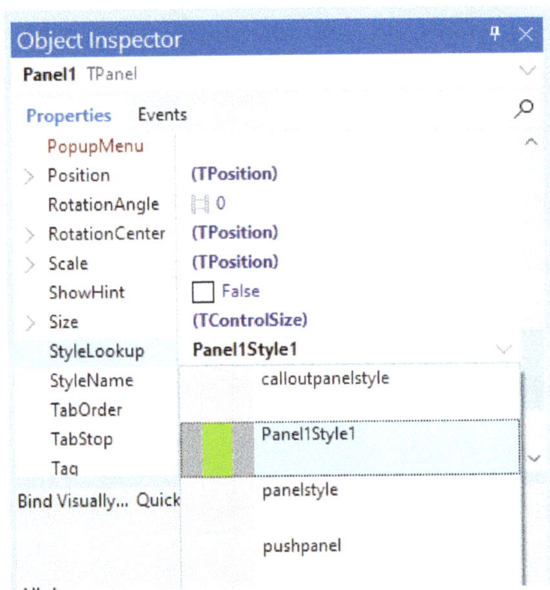

Fig. 42.6 Object Inspector reveals new style added to StyleLookUp

Purpose: To learn how to use anchors

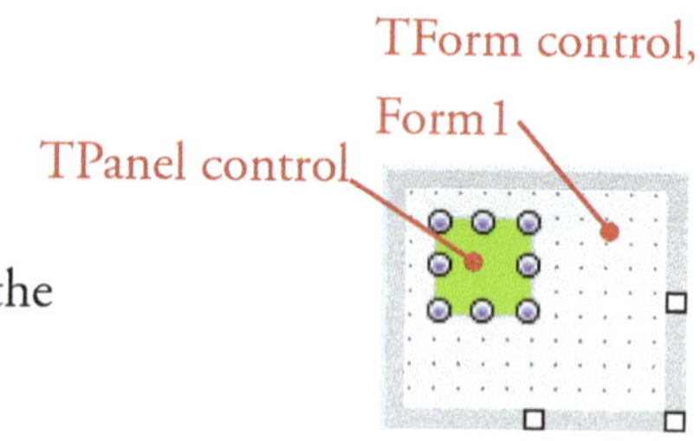

Fig. 42.8 Master view of Form1 containing custom-styled TPanel control, colour Chartreuse

Anchors are used to set the way a control resizes and moves around when the form changes. Each control has 0 to 4 anchors.

The position of the control relative to one or more edge(s) of parent may be set as follows:

- Top
- Bottom
- Left
- Right
- Any combination of the above

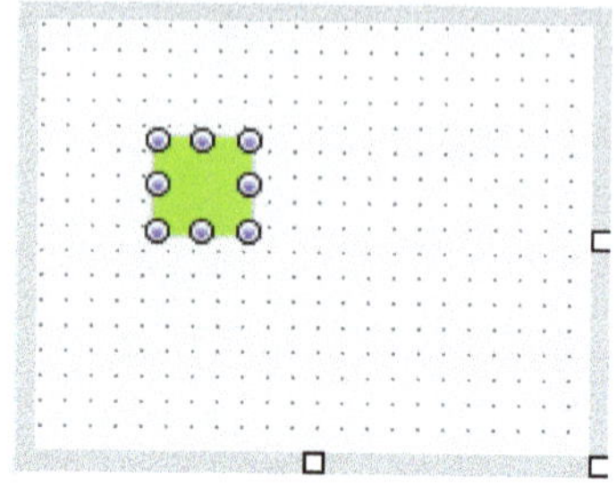

Fig. 42.9 No anchors, form enlarged

The default is **Top**, **Left**.

Typically, the **Object Inspector** is used to set the values of these anchors at design time. *Figure 42.7* shows the **Anchors** property in the **Object Inspector**. The anchors have field names **akLeft**, **akTop**, **akRight** and **akBottom**.

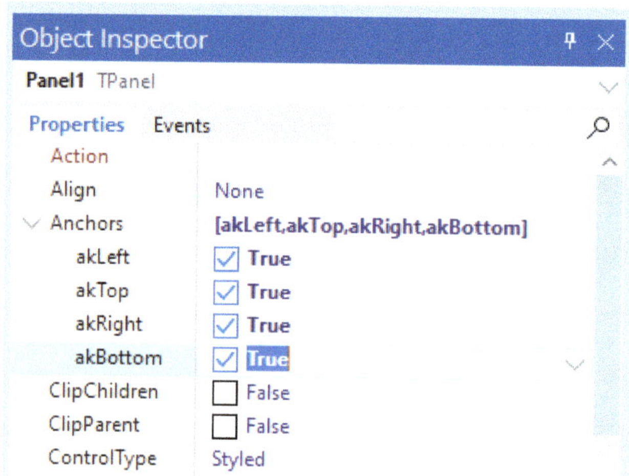

Fig. 42.7 The Anchors property exposed in the Object Inspector

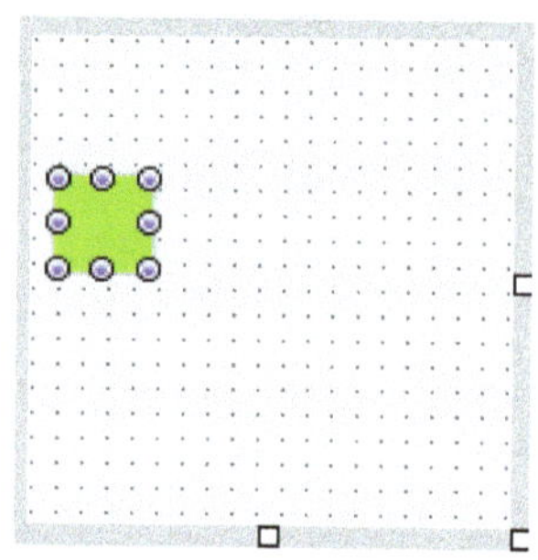

Fig. 42.10 Anchor - Left, form enlarged

The custom-styled **TPanel** control, `Panel1`, shown in *Figure 42.8* is contained within its parent, a **TForm** control, `Form1`.

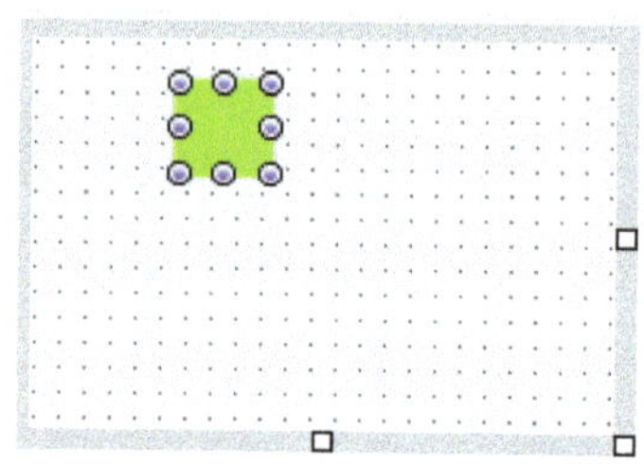

Fig. 42.11 Anchor - Top, form enlarged

Figures 42.9, *42.10*, *42.11*, *42.12* show the effect of the different anchors when applied singly to the **TPanel** control of *Figure 42.8* and the form, `Form1`, is enlarged at design time. Note that the width and height of `Panel1` remain unaltered. *Figure 42.13* shows the result of enlarging the form in *Figure 42.8* when both **Left** and **Top** anchors of the **TPanel** control are selected. Note that the width and height of `Panel1` again remain unaltered.

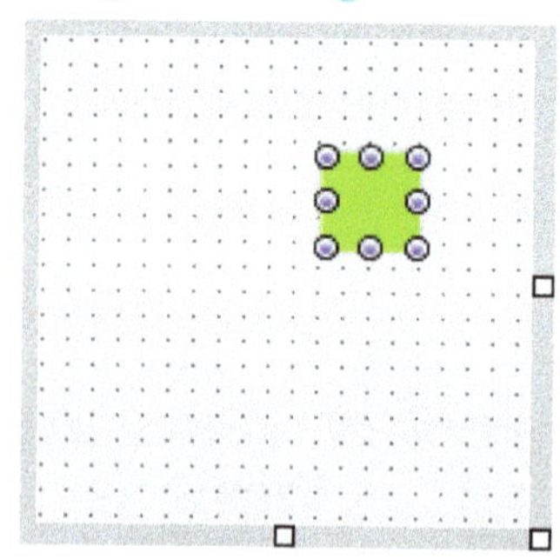

Fig. 42.12 Anchor - Right, form enlarged

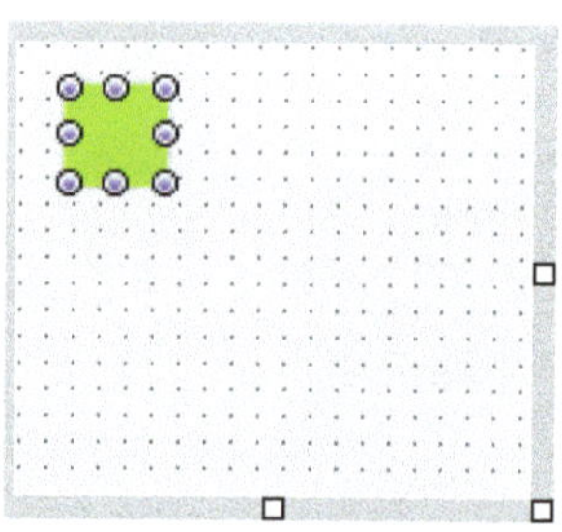

Fig. 42.13 Anchor - Left, Top, form enlarged

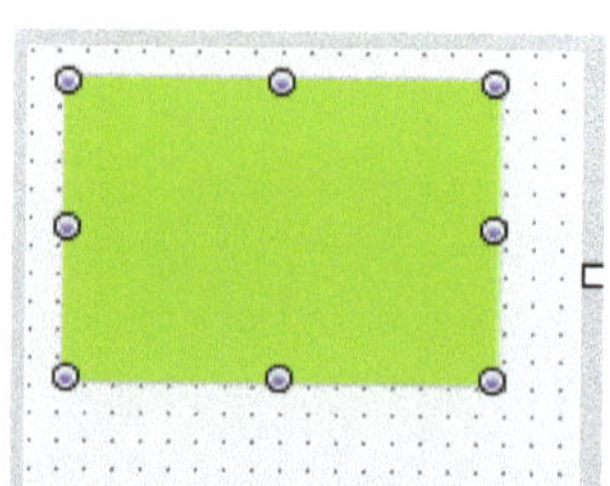

Fig. 42.14 Anchor - Left, Top, Right, Bottom form enlarged

Figure 42.14 shows the result of enlarging the form in *Figure 42.8* at design time when all four anchors are selected. The width and height of `Panel1` change.

Purpose: To learn how to use alignment

The anchors property enables a control to maintain a specified relationship with an edge of a parent as illustrated in the last section. If instead, we want the control to lie along an edge of its parent then we use the **Align** property of the control. The default is **None**.

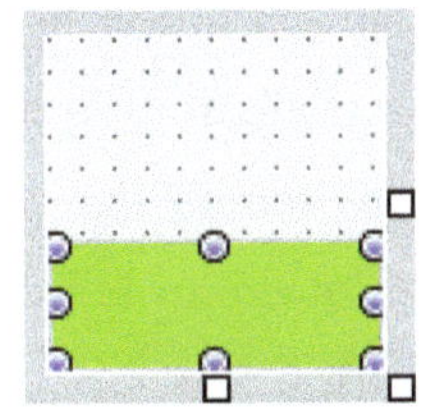

Fig. 42.15 Alignment - Bottom

Figure 42.15 shows the result of using the **Object Inspector** to set the **Align** property to **Bottom**, of the custom-styled **TPanel** control, `Panel1`, shown in *Figure 42.8*. The height value of `Panel1` in *Figure 42.8* is preserved but its width and position are changed so that it lies along the bottom edge. Now, when the form is enlarged, the height of `Panel1` is preserved but its width increases so that it continues to lie along the bottom edge - *Figure 42.16*. The respective effect for the other edges is achieved with alignment settings **Top**, **Left** and **Right**. *Figure 42.17* shows that when **Align** is **Top**, `Panel1`'s position changes and its width increases so that it lies along the top edge, but the height of `Panel1` remains the same.

Fig. 42.16 Alignment - Bottom, form enlarged

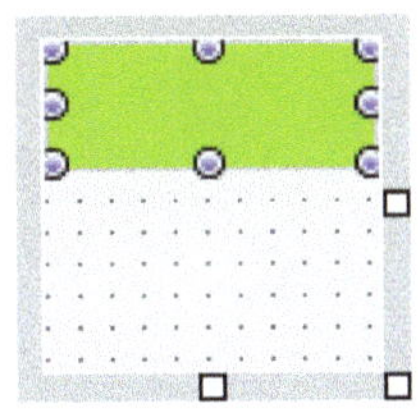

Fig. 42.17 Alignment - Top

Figure 42.18 shows that when **Align** is **Left**, its position changes and its height increases so that it lies along the left edge, but the width of `Panel1` remains the same.

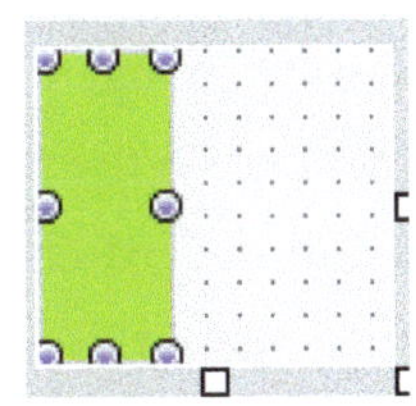

Fig. 42.18 Alignment - Left

Figure 42.19 shows the effect on `Panel1` in *Figure 42.8* when **Align** for `Panel1` is set to **Center** (US spelling). The width and height of `Panel1` are unaltered.

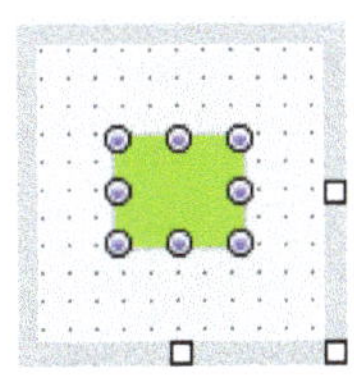

Fig. 42.19 Alignment - Center (US spelling)

Figure 42.20 shows the effect on `Panel1` in *Figure 42.19* when the form is enlarged. Again, the width and height of `Panel1` are unaltered.

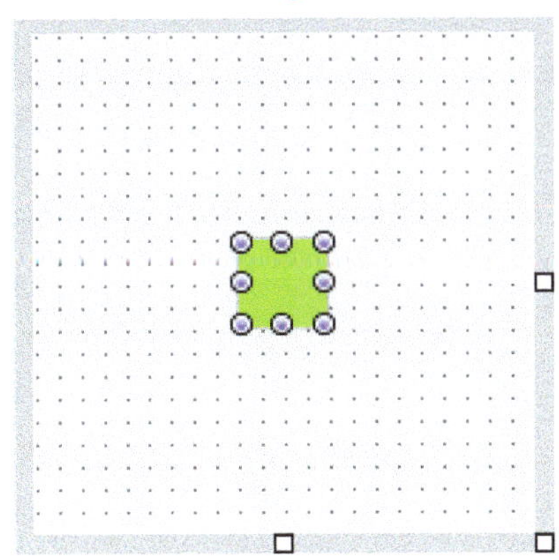

Fig. 42.20 Alignment - Centre, form enlarged

Figure 42.21 shows that if `Panel1`'s **Align** property is set to **Scale**, `Panel1` in *Figure 42.8* resizes and moves to maintain the relative position and size as its parent, `Form1`, is resized.

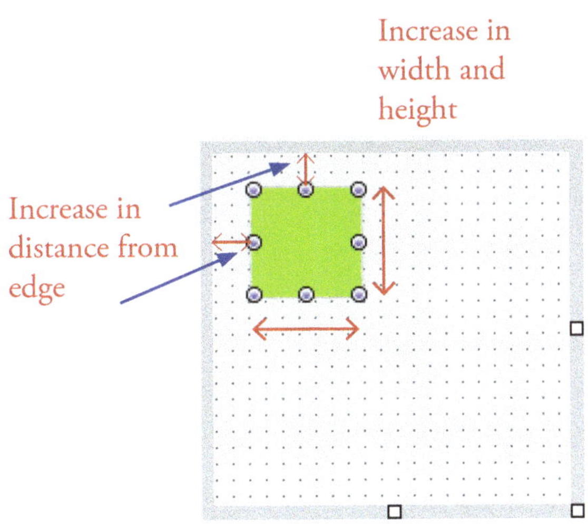

Fig. 42.21 Alignment - Scale, form enlarged

Figure 42.22 shows a form containing two custom-styled **TPanel** components, one with **Align** set to **Bottom** (red **TPanel** control) and one with **Align** set to **None** (chartreuse **TPanel** control)

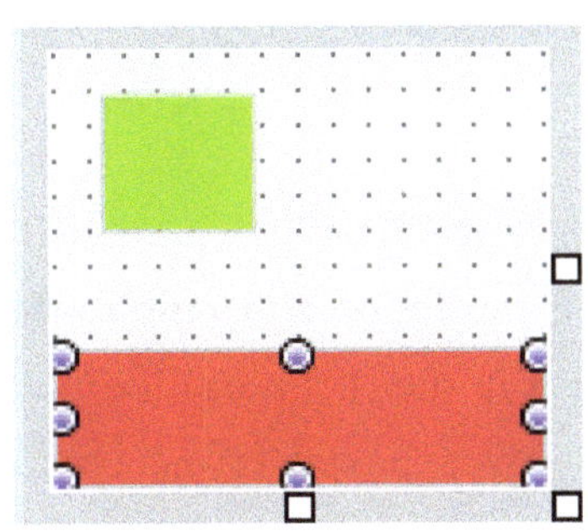

Fig. 42.22 Two custom-styled TPanel controls with align set to None and Bottom, respectively

Figure 42.23 shows the same form but with the chartreuse **TPanel** control's **Align** property set to **Client**. The **Client** setting causes the control to resize to fill the client area of its parent, the form.

As there is another bottom-pinned control already occupying part of the parent area, the chartreuse-coloured control resizes to fit the remaining parent area. *Figure 42.24* shows the client area of an example form, `Form1` for a Windows 64-bit desktop application.

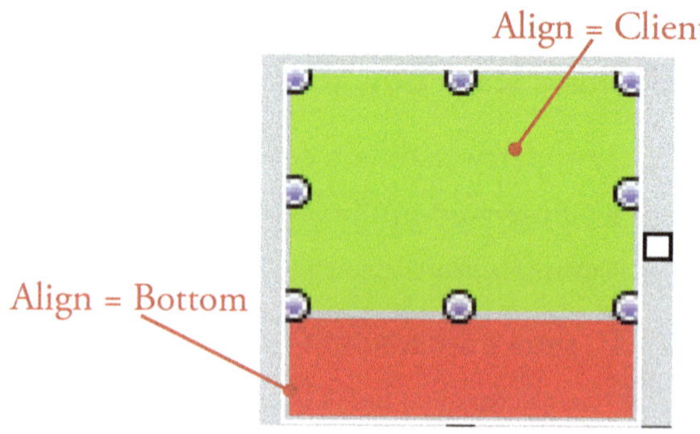

Fig. 42.23 Two custom-styled TPanel controls with align set to Client and Bottom, respectively

Figure 42.25 shows two **TPanel** controls with their **Align** property both set to **Bottom**.

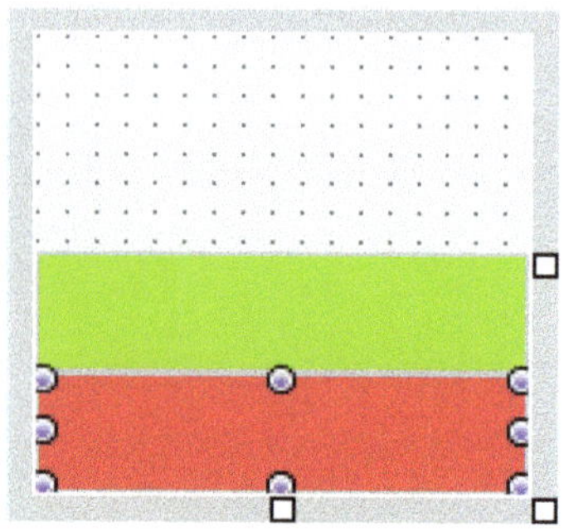
Fig. 42.25 Two custom-styled TPanel controls, Align set to Bottom for both

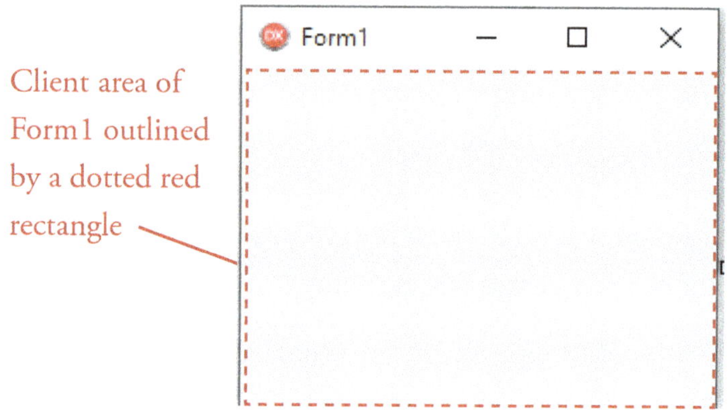

Fig. 42.24 FireMonkey Windows 64-bit desktop application

If the chartreuse-coloured **TPanel** control's **Align** property is now changed to **MostBottom** then this control is pinned to the very bottom of the form's client area and the red-coloured **TPanel** control moves to above it, as shown in *Figure 42.26*.

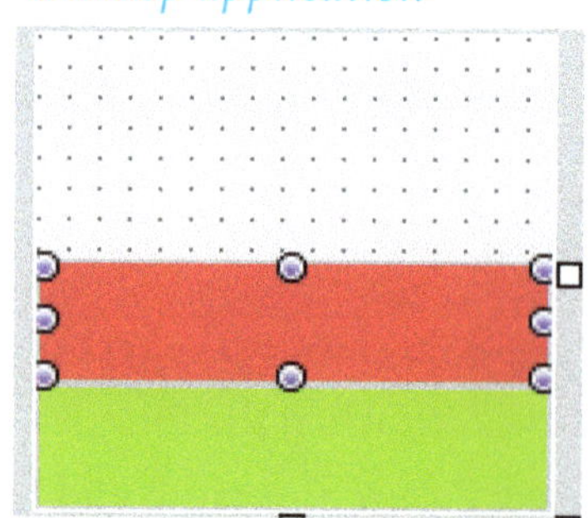
Fig. 42.26 Two custom-styled TPanel controls, red-coloured Align's property set to Bottom as before, chartreuse-coloured Align setting changed to MostBottom

MostTop, **MostLeft** and **MostRight** are also available.

Figures 42.27 and *42.28* illustrate the use of **FitLeft**. The **TPanel** control resizes to partially fit the parent area by preserving the aspect ratio. The control moves to and pins to the left side of the parent.

FitTop, **FitBottom** and **FitRight** are also available.

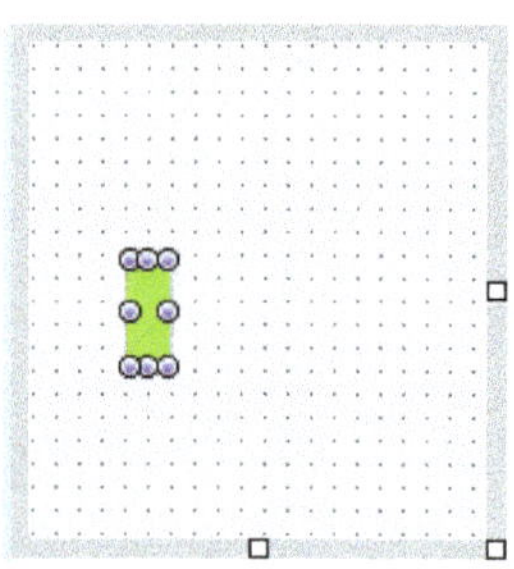
Fig. 42.27 Custom-styled TPanel control, Align set to None

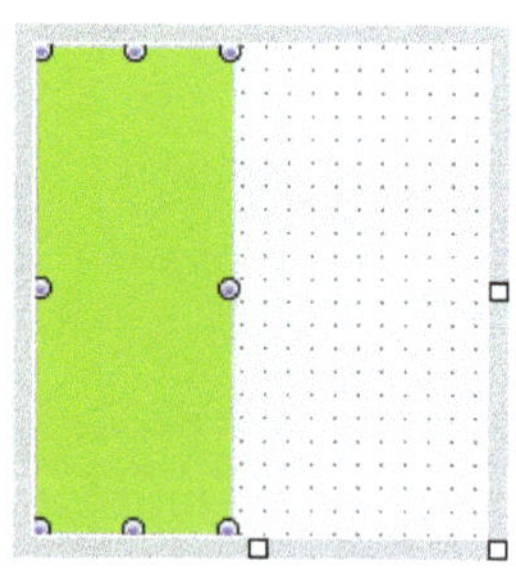
Fig. 42.28 Custom-styled TPanel control, Align set to FitLeft

Align property value **Contents** is similar to **Client** but differs in resizing to fill the entire bounds of its parent, to the extent of overlapping it and any other control present in the client area. *Figure 42.29* shows the result of setting the **Align** property of the red **TPanel** control in *Figure 42.26* to **Contents**.

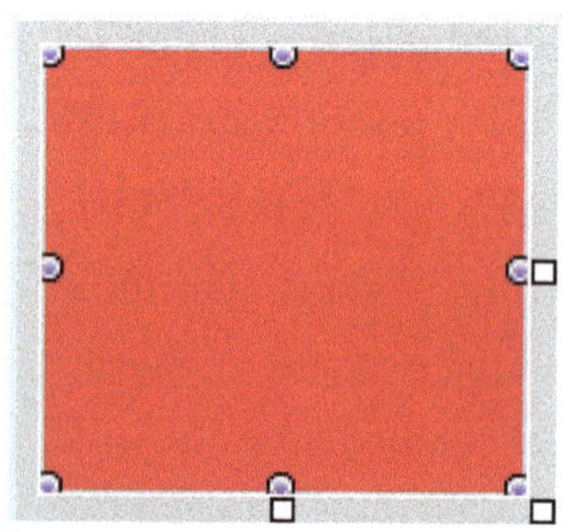
Fig. 42.29 Two custom-styled TPanel controls, chartreuse-coloured Align setting set to MostBottom, as before, and red-coloured Align's property set to Contents

Purpose: To learn how to use layouts

FireMonkey layouts are containers for other graphical objects that can be used to build visually attractive and complex user interfaces. FireMonkey layouts offer the possibility to manipulate a group of controls as a whole as well as enabling the arrangement, sizing, and scaling of their child controls, Complex user interfaces may be constructed, relatively easily, by just using properties such as **Position**, **Align**, **Margins**, and **Padding** with **Anchors** and layouts - see *Figure 42.30*.

Fig. 42.30 User Interface design of a calculator application

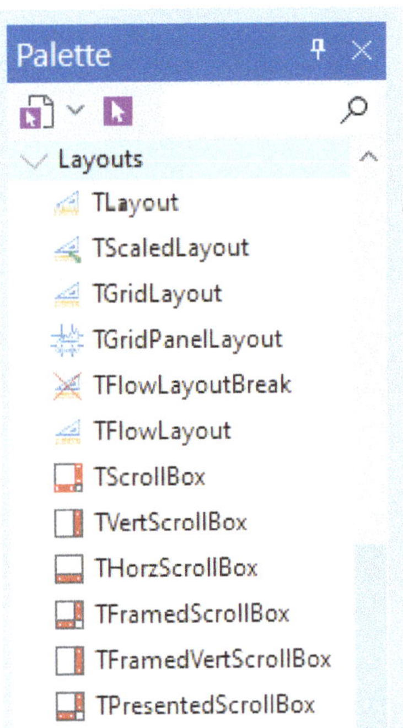

Fig. 42.31 Tool Palette, Layouts

The available layouts are located in the **Tool Palette**, under the **Layouts** category - *Figure 42.31*.

An instance of **TLayout** is a simple container which is a parent to the other controls that it contains and which can be manipulated as a group, e.g. rotated, hidden or made visible by setting the **TLayout** instance's **Visible** property to **True** or **False**.

TLayout is visible at design time but not runtime and does not automatically set any properties of its children.

Figure 42.32 shows a form at design time containing four **TLayout** controls, each containing a custom-styled **TPanel** control, colour chartreuse, and each of these, a **TText** control (**TText** is similar to **TCaption** but is less customisable than **TCaption**).

First, `Layout1` was created containing one **TPanel** and one **TText** control with its **Text** property set to 'X'. This layout was then copied three times and the **x** and **y Position** properties of each copy and the original, `LayOut1`, set to achieve a grid arrangement as shown in *Figure 42.32*. The **TStyleBook** control, `StyleBook1`, was created when the **TPanel** control, `Layout1`, was custom styled. It is only visible at design time. The align property of each **TLayout** control was set to `Scale`. The align property of each **TPanel** control was set to `Client` and each **TText** to `Center`.

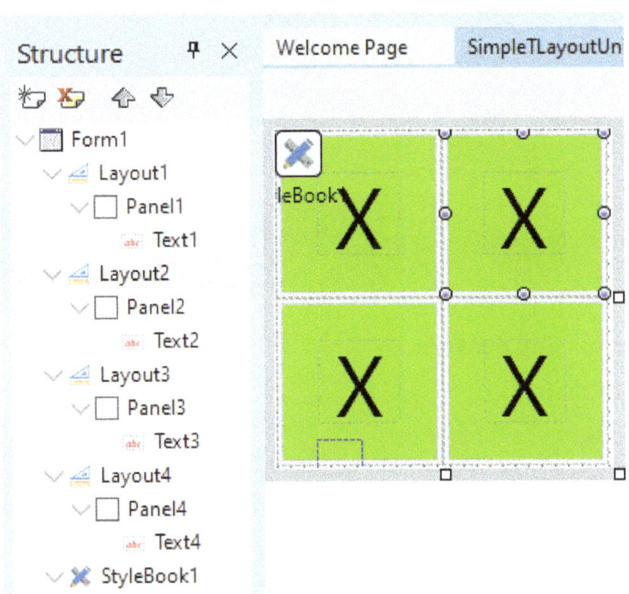

Fig. 42.32 Creating four TLayout containers each containing a TPanel and a TText control

(Download from www.educational-computing.com/DelphiBook/Code/Chapter41/SimpleTLayout.rar)

Add a fifth **TLayout** control, `Layout5`, and arrange for it to be the parent of `Layout1` to `Layout4` inclusive, as shown in the **Structure** pane in *Figure 42.33*. Set the align property of `Layout5` to `Client` so that it fills the client area of the form, `Form1`.

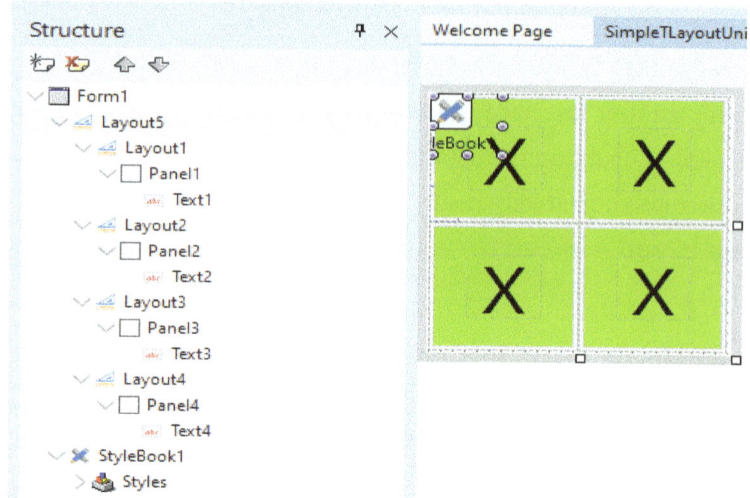

Fig. 42.33 Placing the four TLayout containers inside a fifth TLayout control

Save project as `SimpleTLayoutProject.dprog`.

Figure 42.34 shows this project in execution.

Figure 42.35 shows the same project in execution but after scaling the form.

On scaling the form, the container `Layout5` expands so that it continues to fill the form's client area whilst`Layout1` to `Layout4` scale accordingly because they are contained by `Layout5` and their alignment is set to `Scale`.

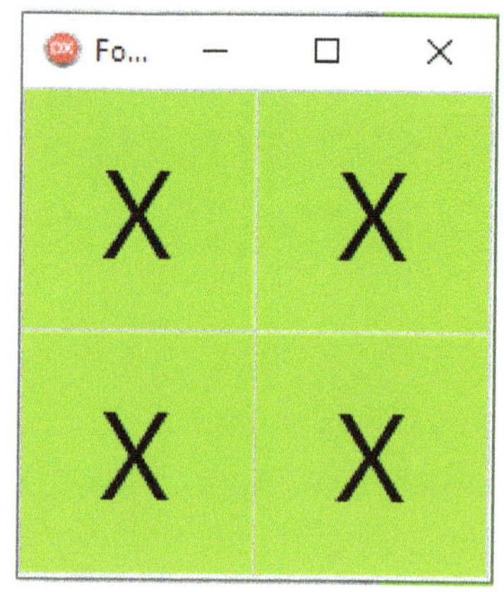

Fig. 42.34 SimpleTLayoutProject in execution

Margins and padding may be used to make clearer the boundaries between each panel and between the form and the panels as shown in *Figure 42.36*.

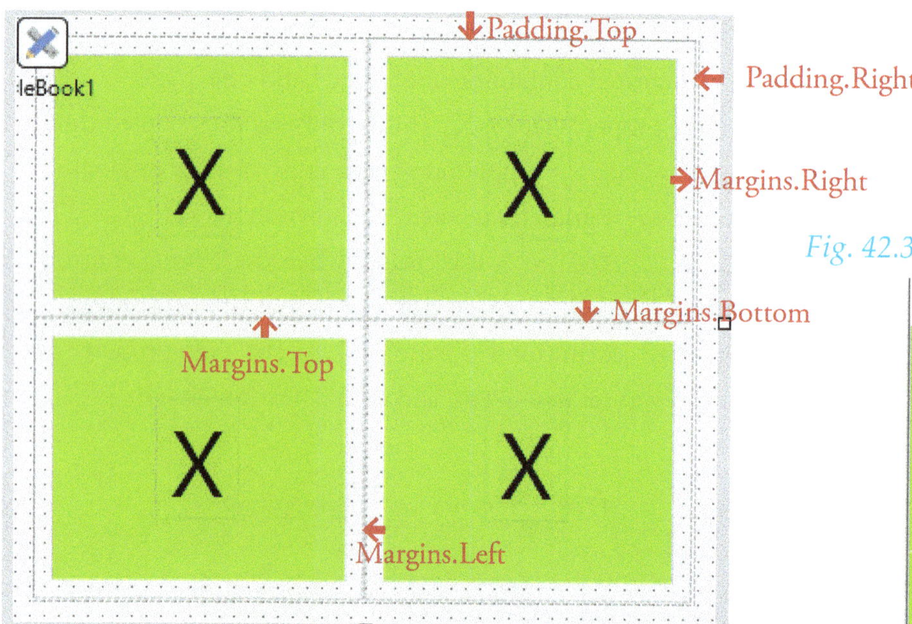

Fig. 42.36 SimpleTLayoutProject using margins and padding

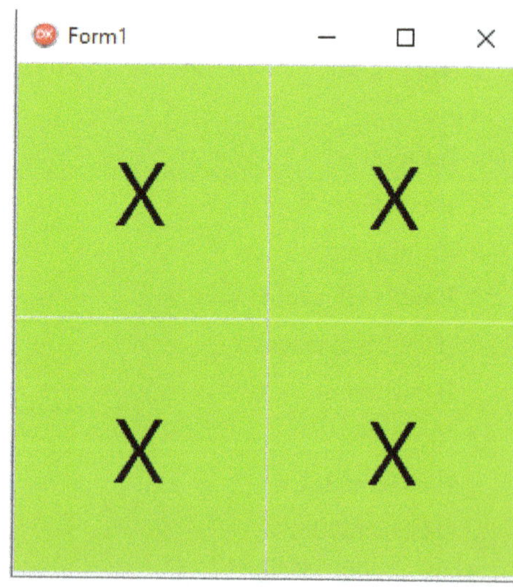

Fig. 42.35 SimpleTLayoutProject in execution with form scaled at runtime

Padding sets the spacing between parent and its children. *Figure 42.37* shows the **Bottom**, **Left**, **Right** and **Top** settings for the **Padding** property of `Form1` which are responsible for the padding shown in *Figure 42.36*.

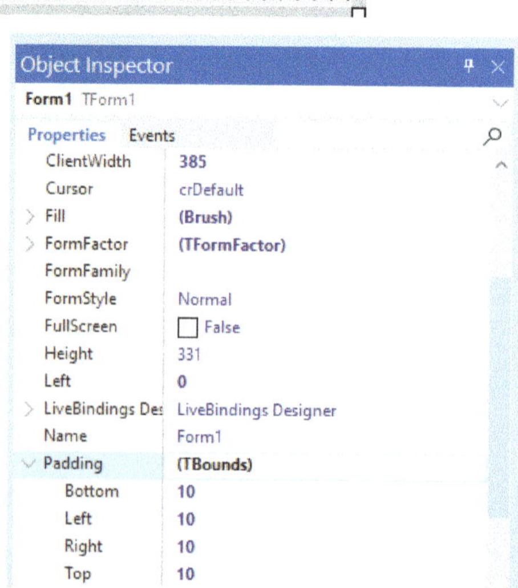

Fig. 42.37 Setting Padding property of Form1 to 10, Left, Right, Top and Bottom

Margins set the spacing between siblings and to the edges of their parent.

Figure 42.38 shows the Object Inspector settings for the **Margins** property of `Panel1`. Similar settings were applied to the **Margins** property of the other panel components.

Figure 42.39 shows the **SimpleTLayoutProject** in execution with margins and padding.

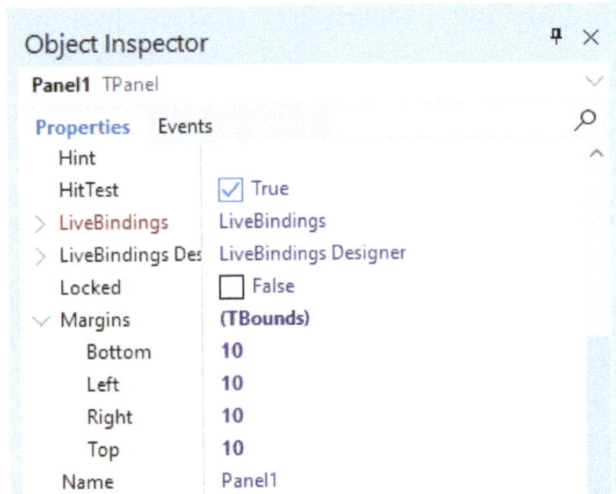

Fig. 42.38 Setting Margins property of Form1 to 10, Left, Right, Top and Bottom

Fig. 42.39 SimpleTLayoutProject in execution showing margins and padding

Fig. 42.40 SimpleTLayoutProject in execution and scaled down to show clipping for Panel2, Panel3 and Panel4

When the **BorderStyle** property of `Form1`is set to **Sizeable** the form is resizable. However, this creates a problem if the **ClipChildren** property of a **TPanel** component is not set to **True**. *Figure 42.40* shows what happens on scaling down `Form1` when the **ClipChildren** property of `Panel1` is **False** and **True** for the other panels. Of course, it is possible to stop a form being scaled. To do this set the **BorderStyle** property of the form to **Single**. It might also be a good idea at the same time to set its **Position** property to **DesktopCenter.**

TLayout is one of several layout containers available from the **Layouts** tab of the component **Palette** - *Figure 42.41*.

In the next section we will use **TGridPanelLayout** to build a noughts and crosses board game.

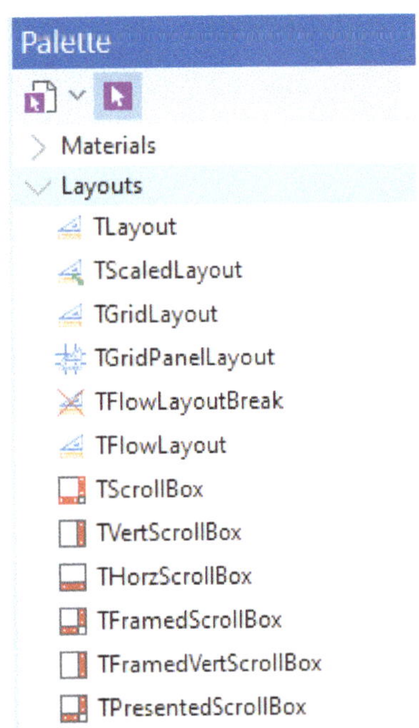

Fig. 42.41 Layouts tab of component Palette

Purpose: To learn how to develop a multi-device board game

We will build a single form application with FireMonkey that can be deployed to all GUI-supported platforms.

Create a Blank Multi-Device Application - **File|New|Multi-Device Application**. Save the project as `NoughtsAndCrossesProject` and its unit as `NoughtsAndCrossesUnit`.

1. Place a **TLayout** container on the form, set its **Align** property to **Client** and its **Name** property to `GameAreaLayout`. Rename `Form1`, `OsAndXsForm`. Set the form's **Width** to 387 and its **Height** to 574. Set its **Caption** to `Noughts and Crosses`.
2. Place a **TToolBar** control on the form and set its **Align** property to **MostTop**, and its **Height** property to 44.
3. Place a **TLayout** container on `GameAreaLayout`, set its **Align** property to **Bottom**, its **Height** property to 113 and its **Name** property to `BottomOfFormLayout`.
4. Place a **TGridPanelLayout** on `GameAreaLayout`, set its **Align** property to **Client** and its **Name** property to `GridPanelLayout`.
5. Click the ellipsis in the value field of property **ColumnCollection** of `GridPanelLayout` (*Figure 42.43*) to bring up the **ColumnCollection** editor - *Figure 42.44*. Click the icon to add a new column. Adjust the **Value** field of each column until each is approximately 33.33% - *Figure 42.45*. You will need several attempts to achieve this.

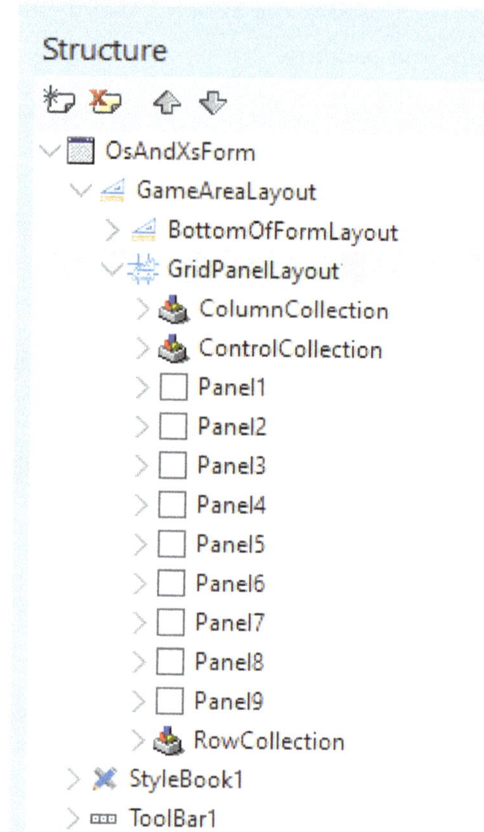

Fig. 42.42 Structure pane for NoughtsAndCrossesProject

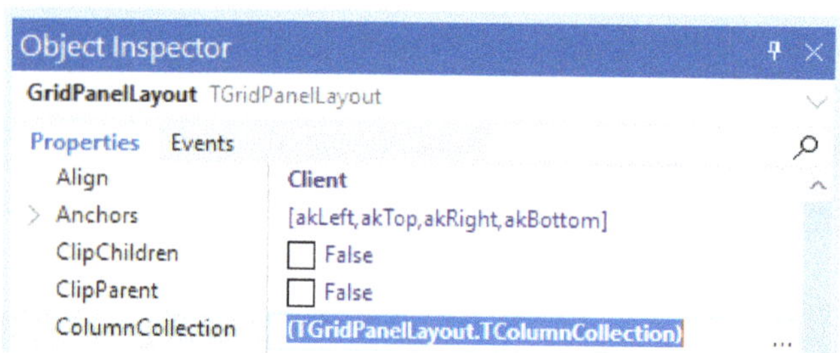

Fig. 42.43 Object Inspector showing GridPanelLayout ColumnCollection property

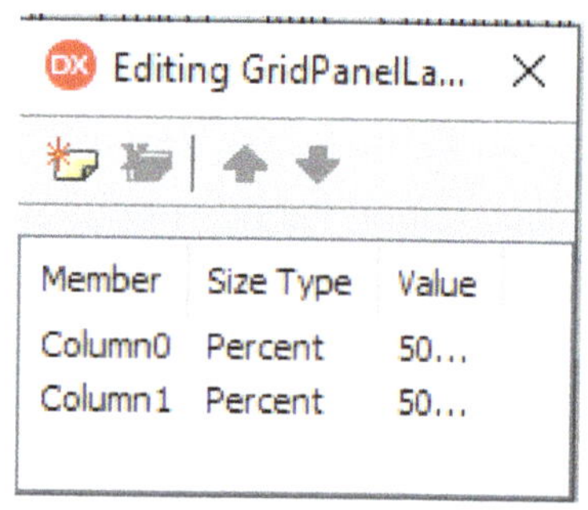

Fig. 42.44 Editing GridPanelLayout. ColumnCollection

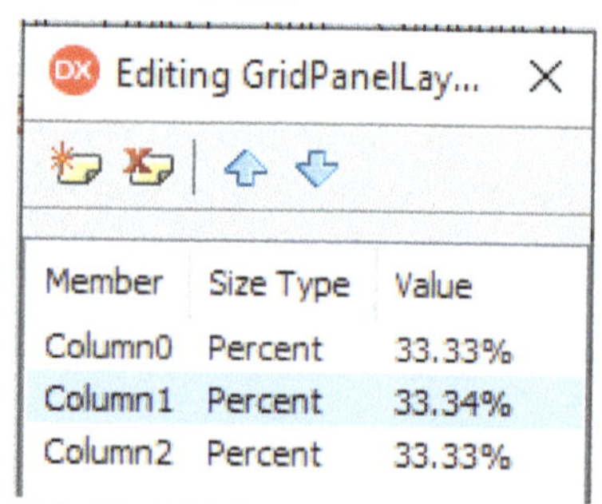

Fig. 42.45 Editing GridPanelLayout. ColumnCollection

6. Click the ellipsis in the value field of property **RowCollection** of `GridPanelLayout` to bring up the **RowCollection** editor. Click the icon to add a new row. Adjust the **Value** field of each row until each is approximately 33.33%. You will need several attempts to achieve this.
7. Select `GridPanelLayout` and add a **TPanel** component to the grid. This panel, `Panel1`, will be assigned automatically to the first grid cell
8. Select **Style: Windows 64-bit**, **View: Master** and right click `Panel1` on the form and select `Edit Custom Style` to bring up the **Style Designer** - *Figure 42.4*. Change the **Fill|Color** to **Chartreuse** as described in the opening section of this chapter, set **Align** to **Client** and **Margins** all to 4. Click **File|Save All**.

9. Copy and paste Panel1 eight times. The eight additional panels, Panel2 to Panel9, will be assigned automatically row by row to the grid as shown in *Figure 42.46*. Property **StyleLookUp** should be Panel1Style1, the custom style created in bullet 8 which sets the panels' fill color to Chartreuse. Click **File|Save All**.
10. Set GameAreaLayout's **Padding** to all 6. OsAndXsForm should now look as shown in *Figure 42.46* and the **Structure** pane as shown in *Figure 42.42*.
11. Add a **TText** component to Panel1, set **Align** to **Client**, set **HitTest** to **True** then copy and paste to the other panels.
12. Change Text1.Tag to 11, Text2.Tag to 12, Text3.Tag to 13, Text4.Tag to 21, Text5.Tag to 22, Text6.Tag to 23, Text7.Tag to 31, Text8.Tag to 32, Text9.Tag to 33. Click **File|Save All**.

Fig. 42.46 OsAndXsForm

13. Place two **TButton** controls on the **TToolBar** control, ToolBar1. Change **Name** property of the first to **btnAnotherGame** and the second to **btnTerminate**. Set **Align** property of first button to **MostLeft** and set **Align** property of second button to **MostRight**. Set the **Width** of each to 150. Set the **Text** property of the first to Another Game and the second to Terminate. Set **Margins.Bottom**, **Left**, **Right** to 4 and **Margins.Top** to 8 for both buttons.
14. Add a **TLayout** container to ToolBar1. Change its Name to StateOfGameLayout. Set its **Align** property to **Client**. Set **Margins.Bottom**, **Left**, **Right** to 4 and **Margins.Top** to 8. Click **File|Save All**.
15. Place a **TLabel** component on StateOfGameLayout. Change its **Name** to lblStateOfGame, its **Align** property to **Center**, its **Text** property to to Undecided, its **Width** to 151, its **TextSettings|HorzAlign** to **Center**.
16. Place four **TLabel** components on BottomOfFormLayout. Change their **Name** property to lblColumn, lblRow, lblNextSymbol, lblNoOfMoves, respectively. Set the **Text** property of lblColumn to Column, lblRow to to Row, lblNoOfMoves1 to No Of Moves. Clear the **Text** property field of lblNextSymbol.
17. Set lblNoOfMoves's **Position.X** to 25 and **Position.Y** to 16.
18. Set lblRow's **Position.X** to 25 and **Position.Y** to 47.
19. Set lblColumn's **Position.X** to 114 and **Position.Y** to 47.
20. Set lblNextSymbol's **Position.X** to 208 and **Position.Y** to 16.
21. Add a **TLabel** component to lblColumn. Change its **Name** to lblColumnNo. Set **Position.X** to 64, **Position.Y** to 0, **Width** to 25. Clear the **Text** property field.
22. Add a **TLabel** component to lblRow. Change its **Name** to lblRowNo. Set **Position.X** to 39, **Position.Y** to 0, **Width** to 25. Clear the **Text** property field.
23. Add a **TLabel** component to lblNoOfMoves. Change its **Name** to lblNumber. Set **Position.X** to 113, **Position.Y** to 0, **Width** to 19. Set **Text** property field to 0. Click **File|Save All**.
24. Now **Run (F9)** the program. The result is shown in *Figure 42.47*.

(Download from www.educational-computing.com/DelphiBook/Code/Chapter42/FormCreate.txt)

A two-dimensional array `GridArray` will used to keep track of the state of the game. Its structure is as follows

```
TGridArray = Array[1..3,1..3] Of TSquareState;
```

`TSquareState` is a user-defined enumerated type defined as follows

```
TSquareState = (Empty, SquareCross,
                SquareNought);
```

Add `TSquareState` and `TGridArray` definitions in that order to the **Type** area of the **Interface** section of the unit code.

Variable `GridArray` is declared as follows

```
GridArray : TGridArray;
```

The following nested for loop will be used to initialise `GridArray` at the beginning of each game:

```
For Row := 1 To 3
  Do
    For Column := 1 To 3
      Do GridArray[Row, Column] := Empty;
```

Two other user-defined enumerated types need to be added to the **Type** area of the **Interface** section.

```
TSymbol = (Nought, Cross);

TGameState = (GameUndecided, Draw,
              NoughtWin, CrossWin);
```

Fig. 42.47 GUI for Noughts and Crosses

Select the `OsAndXsForm` in the Object Inspector and its **Events** tab. Double click in the **OnCreate** empty field to create an event handler `FormCreate` - *Figure 42.48*.

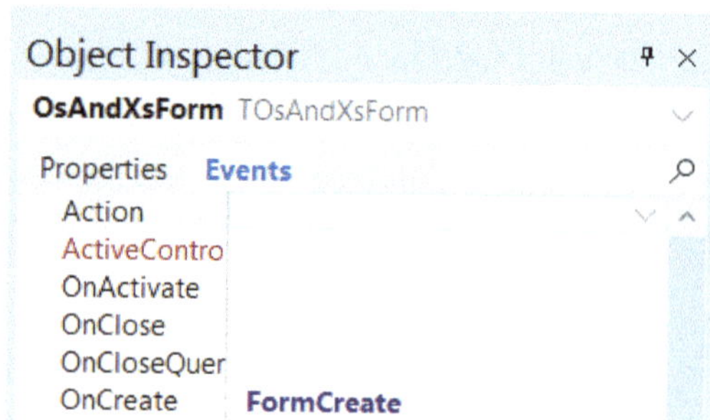

Fig. 42.48 FormCreate event handler

```
Procedure TOsAndXsForm.FormCreate(Sender: TObject);
  Var
    Row, Column : Integer;
  Begin
    NoOfMoves := 0;
    Player1Symbol := Cross;
    Player2Symbol := Nought;
    lblNextSymbol.Text := 'X starts';
    If (NoOfGamesPlayed Mod 2) = 0
      Then InitialiseCurrentSymbol(Cross)
      Else InitialiseCurrentSymbol(Nought);
    For Row := 1 To 3
      Do
        For Column := 1 To 3
          Do GridArray[Row, Column] := Empty;
  End;
```
P

Table 42.1 OnCreate event handler, FormCreate

```
Private
  Player1Symbol : TSymbol;
  Player2Symbol : TSymbol;
  NoOfMoves : Integer;
  CurrentSymbol : TSymbol;
```
P

Table 42.2 Private fields of class TOsAndXsForm

Switch from the **Form** view to the **Unit** view and add code to the skeleton code for `FormCreate` so that it is as shown in *Table 42.1*.

Add the private fields shown in *Table 42.2* to the class `TOsAndXsForm`. Update the global variables section to that shown in *Table 42.43*.

(Download from www.educational-computing.com/DelphiBook/Code/Chapter42/Variables.txt)

Add the method header

```
Procedure InitialiseCurrentSymbol(InitialSymbol : TSymbol);
```

to the class `TOsAndXsForm` in the **Interface** section and the code shown in *Table 42.4* to the **Implementation** section.

```
Var
  OsAndXsForm: TOsAndXsForm;
  WhoGoesFirst : TSymbol;
  GridArray : TGridArray;
  GameOutcome : GameStateType = GameUndecided;
  NoOfGamesPlayed : Integer = 0;
  WinningRow : Integer = 0;
  WinningColumn : Integer = 0;
  WinningDiagonal : Integer = 0;
```

Table 42.3 Global variable declarations and initialisation

```
Procedure TOsAndXsForm.InitialiseCurrentSymbol(InitualSymbol : TSymbol);
  Begin
    CurrentSymbol := InitialSymbol;
  End;
```

Table 42.4 Method TOsAndXsForm.InitialiseCurrentSymbol

Select `Text1` in the Object Inspector and its **Events** tab. Double click in the **OnClick** empty field to create an event handler `Text1Click` - *Figure 42.49*.

Add the code shown in *Table 42.5* to the body of this event handler.

Add `Text1Click` to the **OnClick** field of each of `Text2` to `Text9`.

Click **File|Save All**.

Now **Run (F9)** and test the program.

Figure 42.50 shows the result of clicking on the middle square.

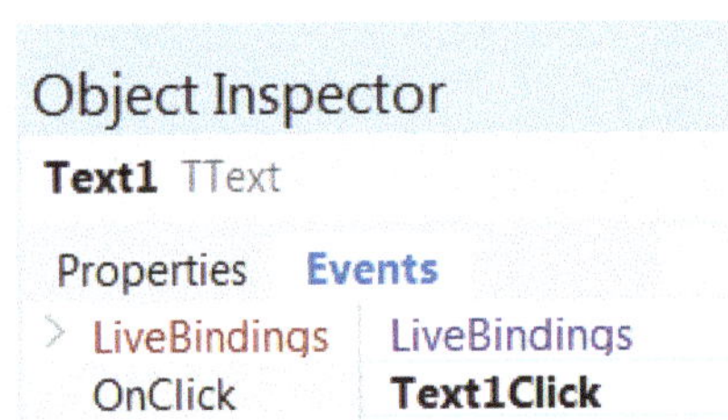

Fig. 42.49 Text1Click event handler

Figure 42.51 shows the result of clicking on the square to the right of the middle square.

Fig. 42.50 Executing Noughts and Crosses and clicking on the middle square

Fig. 42.51 Executing Noughts and Crosses and clicking on the square to the right of the middle square

(Download from www.educational-computing.com/DelphiBook/Code/Chapter42/ProcedureTOsAndXsFormText1Click.txt)

```
Procedure TOsAndXsForm.Text1Click(Sender: TObject);
  Var
    RowNo, ColumnNo : Integer;
  Begin
    If GameOutcome = GameUndecided
      Then
        Begin
          If (Sender is TText)
            Then
              Begin
                (Sender As TText).TextSettings.Font.Size := 60;
                RowNo := (Sender As TText).Tag Div 10;
                ColumnNo := (Sender As TText).Tag Mod 10;
                If GridArray[RowNo, ColumnNo] = Empty
                  Then
                    Begin
                      If CurrentSymbol = Cross
                        Then
                          Begin
                            (Sender As TText).Text := 'X';
                            GridArray[RowNo, ColumnNo] := SquareCross;
                            CurrentSymbol := Nought;
                            lblNextSymbol.Text := 'O plays next';
                          End
                        Else
                          Begin
                            (Sender As TText).Text := 'O';
                            GridArray[RowNo, ColumnNo] := SquareNought;
                            CurrentSymbol := Cross;
                            lblNextSymbol.Text := 'X plays next';
                          End;
                      NoOfMoves := NoOfMoves + 1;
                      lblRowNo.Text := IntToStr(RowNo);
                      lblColumnNo.Text := IntToStr(ColumnNo);
                      lblNumber.Text := IntToStr(NoOfMoves);
                    End;
              End;
        End;
  End;
```

Table 42.5 Initial code of OnClick event handler, Text1Click

The event handler `Text1Click` is called when a mouse click occurs over a square. The component which is clicked is identified in the parameter **Sender**. If it is a **TText** component and the game is not yet decided then the `RowNo` and `ColumnNo` of the clicked square is calculated from its **Tag** property. The `GridArray` cell with this `RowNo` and `ColumnNo` is then checked. If it is empty then the **Text** property of the **TText** component associated with the corresponding square is assigned an 'X' or an 'O' depending on the value of `CurrentSymbol`. The value of `CurrentSymbol` and the **Text** property of label `lblNextSymbol` are then changed as shown in *Table 42.6*.

```
If CurrentSymbol = Cross
  Then
    Begin            <- Casting from TObject to TText
      (Sender As TText).Text := 'X';
      GridArray[RowNo, ColumnNo] := SquareCross;
      CurrentSymbol := Nought;
      lblNextSymbol.Text := 'O plays next'
    End
  Else
    Begin
      Sender As TText).Text := 'O';
      GridArray[RowNo, ColumnNo] := SquareNought;
      CurrentSymbol := Cross;
      lblNextSymbol.Text := 'X plays next'
    End;
```

Table 42.6 Section of code from OnClick event handler, Text1Click, which updates game

(Download from www.educational-computing.com/DelphiBook/Code/Chapter42/TestStateOfBoard.txt)

(Download from www.educational-computing.com/DelphiBook/Code/Chapter42/GameOutcome.txt)

Following the successfully placement on the grid of an 'X' or an 'O', the state of the game must be checked by calling the function `TestStateOfBoard` and recording the result returned in variable `GameOutcome`. as shown in *Table 42.7*. Add this code to the end of the event handler, `Text1Click`.

```
GameOutcome := TestStateOfBoard;
If (GameOutcome = NoughtWin)
  Then lblStateOfGame.Text := 'Nought wins!';
If (GameOutcome = CrossWin)
  Then lblStateOfGame.Text := 'Cross wins!';
If Not (GameOutcome = GameUndecided)
  Then
    Begin
      {Change colour of winning squares to red}
    End;
```

Table 42.7 Section of code fromOnClick event handler, Text1Click, which updates game

The code of function `TestStateOfBoard` is shown in *Table 42.8*. Add `Function TestStateOfBoard : TGameState;` to class `TOsAndXsForm` in the **Interface** section.

Add `Function TOsAndXsForm.TestStateOfBoard : TGameState;` to the **Implementation** section.

Click **File|Save All**.

Now **Run (F9)** and test the program.

```
Function TOsAndXsForm.TestStateOfBoard : TGameState;
  Var
    i, j : Integer;
  Begin
    Result := GameUndecided;
    For i := 1 To 3
      Do
        Begin
          If (GridArray[i, 1] = GridArray[i, 2])
              And (GridArray[i, 2] = GridArray[i, 3])
                And (GridArray[i, 1] <> Empty)
            Then
              If GridArray[i, 1] = SquareCross
                Then
                  Begin
                    Result := CrossWin;
                    WinningRow := i;
                    Exit;    // Exit function
                  End
                Else
                  Begin
                    Result := NoughtWin;
                    WinningRow := i;
                    Exit;
                  End;
        End;
    For j := 1 To 3
      Do
        Begin
          If (GridArray[1, j] = GridArray[2, j])
              And (GridArray[2, j]= GridArray[3, j])
                And (GridArray[1, j] <> Empty)
            Then
              If GridArray[1, j] = SquareCross
                Then
                  Begin
                    Result := CrossWin;
                    WinningColumn := j;
                    Exit;
                  End
                Else
                  Begin
                    Result := NoughtWin;
                    WinningColumn := j;
                    Exit;
                  End;
        End;
    If (GridArray[1, 1] = GridArray[2, 2])
        And (GridArray[2, 2] = GridArray[3, 3])
          And (GridArray[1, 1] <> Empty)
      Then
        Begin
          If GridArray[1, 1] = SquareCross
            Then Result := CrossWin
            Else Result := NoughtWin;
            WinningDiagonal := 1;
            Exit;
        End;
    If (GridArray[1, 3] = GridArray[2, 2])
        And (GridArray[2, 2] = GridArray[3, 1])
          And (GridArray[1, 3] <> Empty)
      Then
        Begin
          If GridArray[1, 3] = SquareCross
            Then Result := CrossWin
            Else Result := NoughtWin;
            WinningDiagonal := 2;
        End;
  End;
```

Table 42.8 Function TOsAndXsForm.TestStateOfBoard

Double click button `Terminate` and add the following code to the event handler `TOsAndXsForm.btnTerminateClick`:

```
Application.Terminate;
```

Double click button `Another Game` and add the code shown in *Table 42.9* to the event handler `TOsAndXsForm.btnAnotherGameClick`.

(Download from www.educational-computing.com/DelphiBook/Code/Chapter42/AnotherGameClick.txt)

```
Procedure TOsAndXsForm.btnAnotherGameClick(Sender: TObject);
  Var
    Row, Column : Integer;
  Begin
    NoOfGamesPlayed := NoOfGamesPlayed + 1;
    NoOfMoves := 0;
    Player1Symbol := Cross;
    Player2Symbol := Nought;
    If (NoOfGamesPlayed Mod 2) = 0
      Then InitialiseCurrentSymbol(Cross)
      Else InitialiseCurrentSymbol(Nought);
    For Row := 1 To 3
      Do
        For Column := 1 To 3
          Do GridArray[Row, Column] := Empty;
    Text1.Text := ''; Text2.Text := ''; Text3.Text := ''; Text4.Text := '';
    Text5.Text := ''; Text6.Text := ''; Text7.Text := ''; Text8.Text := '';
    Text9.Text := '';
    Panel1.StyleLookup := 'Panel1Style1'; Panel2.StyleLookup := 'Panel1Style1';
    Panel3.StyleLookup := 'Panel1Style1'; Panel4.StyleLookup := 'Panel1Style1';
    Panel5.StyleLookup := 'Panel1Style1'; Panel6.StyleLookup := 'Panel1Style1';
    Panel7.StyleLookup := 'Panel1Style1'; Panel8.StyleLookup := 'Panel1Style1';
    Panel9.StyleLookup := 'Panel1Style1';
    WinningRow := 0;
    WinningColumn := 0;
    WinningDiagonal := 0;
    lblStateOfGame.Text := 'Undecided';
    lblRowNo.Text := '';
    lblColumnNo.Text := '';
    GameOutcome := GameUndecided;
    If (NoOfGamesPlayed Mod 2) = 0
      Then lblNextSymbol.Text := 'X starts'
      Else lblNextSymbol.Text := 'O starts'
  End;
```

Table 42.9 Event handler TOsAndXsForm.btnAnotherGameClick

Figure 42.52 shows that it is possible to indicate a win state not only by text message, e.g. "Cross wins!" but also by changing the colour of the squares.

The code to do this is shown in *Table 42.10*. Use this code to replace the corresponding code from *Table 42.7* in the event handler `Text1Click`. The custom style `Panel1Style2` needs to be created. The easiest way to do this is to `copy Panel1Style1`, rename it `Panel1Style2` then select **Fill|Color Red** before saving. Remember that the custom styles are platform specific, e.g. Windows 10 Desktop.

Select **StyleBook1|Styles|Windows 10 Desktop** in the **Structure Pane** as shown in *Figure 42.53* (it will be **Windows 7 Desktop** if your O.S. is Windows 7).

In the **Object Inspector** click on the ellipsis (...) in the **Resource** property field as shown in *Figure 42.54*. This launches the **Style Designer**. Right click `Panel1Style1` select **Edit|Copy**. Select and right click **StyleContainer**, select **Edit|Paste** to create

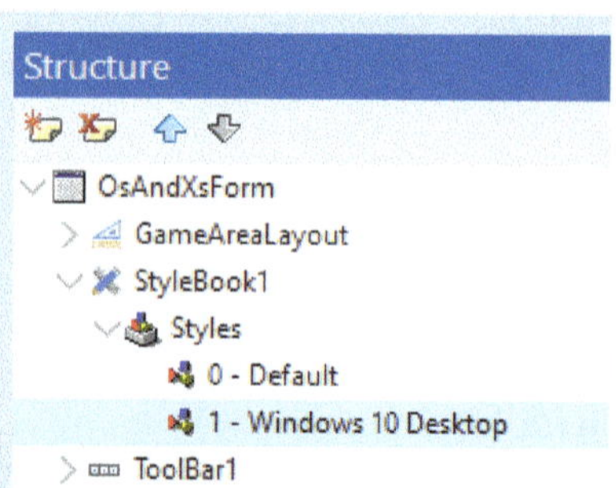

Fig. 42.53 Structure Pane

Fig. 42.52 Winning configuration indicated in red

(Download from www.educational-computing.com/DelphiBook/Code/Chapter42/RedSquares.txt)

a second `Panel1Style1` in the **Structure Pane**.

Select the copy `Panel1Style1` in the **Structure Pane** and change its **StyleName** property value to `Panel1Style2` as shown in *Figure 42.56*.

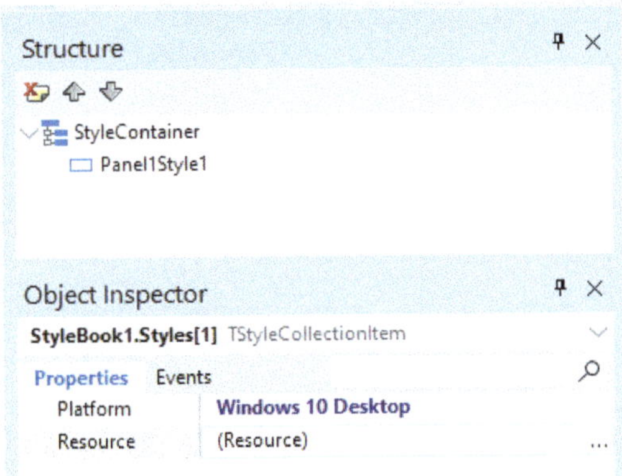

Fig. 42.54 Resource property

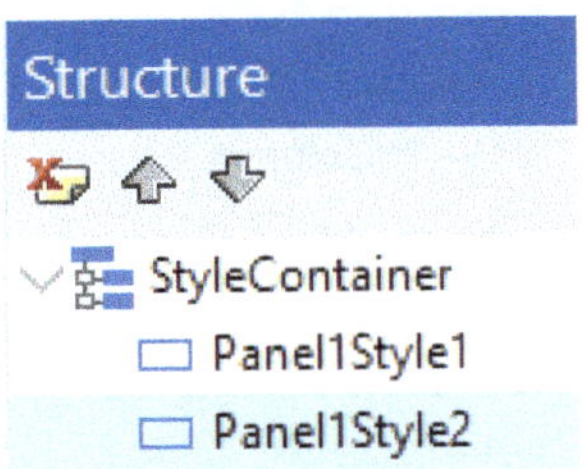

Fig. 42.56 Structure Pane

Select **Fill|Color|Red** for `Panel1Style2`.

Close the **Style Designer**, selecting **Save** to save the new style `Panel1Style2`.

Click **File|Save All**.

Now **Run (F9)** and test the program.

Finally, we need to take account of a draw, when all nine squares are occupied but no winner, by adding the following code to the end of event handler `Text1Click`:

```
If (GameOutcome = GameUndecided)
      And (NoOfMoves = 9)
  Then
    Begin
      lblStateOfGame.Text := 'Draw';
      GameOutcome := Draw;
      lblNextSymbol.Text := '';
    End;
```

Click **File|Save All**.

Now **Run (F9)** and test the program.

```
If Not (GameOutcome = GameUndecided)                                    P
  Then
    Begin
      lblNextSymbol.Text := '';
      If WinningRow <> 0
        Then
          Case WinningRow Of
            1 : Begin
                  Panel1.StyleLookup := 'Panel1Style2';
                  Panel2.StyleLookup := 'Panel1Style2';
                  Panel3.StyleLookup := 'Panel1Style2';
                End;
            2 : Begin
                  Panel4.StyleLookup := 'Panel1Style2';
                  Panel5.StyleLookup := 'Panel1Style2';
                  Panel6.StyleLookup := 'Panel1Style2';
                End;
            3 : Begin
                  Panel7.StyleLookup := 'Panel1Style2';
                  Panel8.StyleLookup := 'Panel1Style2';
                  Panel9.StyleLookup := 'Panel1Style2';
                End;
          End;
      If WinningColumn <> 0
        Then
          Case WinningColumn Of
            1 : Begin
                  Panel1.StyleLookup := 'Panel1Style2';
                  Panel4.StyleLookup := 'Panel1Style2';
                  Panel7.StyleLookup := 'Panel1Style2';
                End;
            2 : Begin
                  Panel2.StyleLookup := 'Panel1Style2';
                  Panel5.StyleLookup := 'Panel1Style2';
                  Panel8.StyleLookup := 'Panel1Style2';
                End;
            3 : Begin
                  Panel3.StyleLookup := 'Panel1Style2';
                  Panel6.StyleLookup := 'Panel1Style2';
                  Panel9.StyleLookup := 'Panel1Style2';
                End;

          End;
      If WinningDiagonal <> 0
        Then
          Case WinningDiagonal Of
            1 : Begin
                  Panel1.StyleLookup := 'Panel1Style2';
                  Panel5.StyleLookup := 'Panel1Style2';
                  Panel9.StyleLookup := 'Panel1Style2';
                End;
            2 : Begin
                  Panel3.StyleLookup := 'Panel1Style2';
                  Panel5.StyleLookup := 'Panel1Style2';
                  Panel7.StyleLookup := 'Panel1Style2';
                End;
          End;
    End;
```

Table 42.10 More code for Event handler TOsAndXsForm.Text1Click

(Download from www.educational-computing.com/DelphiBook/Code/Chapter42/NoughtsAndCrosses.rar)

To deploy `NoughtsAndCrosses` to an Android device successfully, requires that `Panel1Style1` and `Panel1Style2` are created for the Android platform, first. Connect an Android device via USB to the development computer. Select **Android 32-bit** or **Android 64-bit** and then select the corresponding target - *Figure 42.57*.

Fig. 42.57 Selecting Android 32-bit for a SamSung S8+target

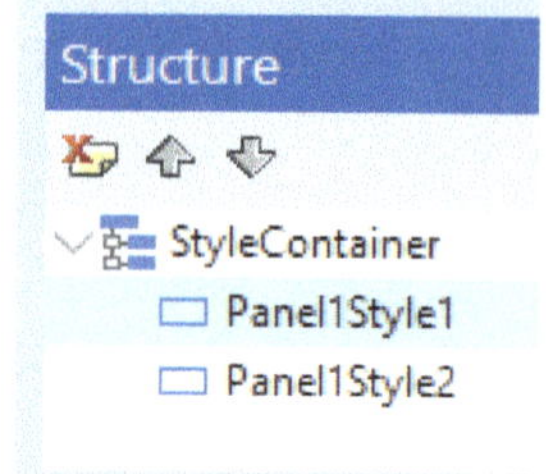

Fig. 42.58 Structure Pane showing the newly created styles in the Style Container

Select **View: Master**.

Adding a **TPanel** component, `Panel10`, temporarily, is the surest way of being able to create the required custom styles. Right click the added panel and select **Edit Custom Style**. Ensure that the **Platform** field shows **AndroidL Light**, before renaming `Panel10Style1`, `Panel1Style1`. Change **Fill|Color** to **Chartreuse**. Copy and paste `Panel1Style1` then rename `Panel1Style2`. Change its **Fill|Color** to **Red**. Finally delete `Panel10`. *Figure 42.58* shows that the **StyleContainer** now contains `Panel1Style1` and `Panel1Style2`. Save the newly created styles. *Figure 42.59* shows the change to the **Structure Pane** which now includes the new style **AndroidL Light**. Click **File|Save All**.

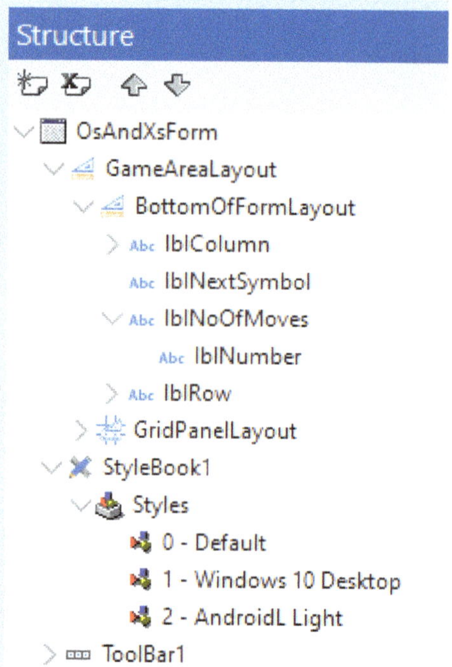

Fig. 42.59 Structure Pane showing the newly created AndroidL Light Style

Now **Run (F9)** and deploy the program to the connected Android device. *Figure 42.60* shows `NoughtsAndCrosses` executing on a SamSung S8+ connected to the development computer via USB. The required custom styles must be created for each type of device to which the `NoughtsAndCrosses` program is to be deployed, e.g. an iPhone.

Fig. 42.60 Samsung S8+ running NoughtsAndCrosses

TGridPanelLayout is one of several possible layout containers. TGridLayout is similar to TGridPanelLayout but unlike a TGridPanelLayout container doesn't allow a child control placed in a cell of the grid to be manually resized, aligned or anchored. With TGridLayout, the Height and Width properties of a child control are automatically set to fit the grid cell.

TFlowLayout arranges the child controls as if they were words in a a paragraph, i.e. they are arranged and displayed in the layout in the order in which they were added. TFlowLayoutBreak is used to change to the next line.

Programming Task

1. Modify the Noughts and Crosses application to make it a computer versus human game.
The computer should always go first and its symbol should always be an X.
Use the **following rules** for the computer's moves:
Computer's moves:
Move 1: The computer must place an X in a corner.
Move 2: The computer must place an X in the opposite corner to move 1, if free, **Otherwise** it should place an X in a corner which is free.
Move 3: If 2 Xs and a space are in a line **Then** the computer should place an X in the space,
Else If 2 Os and a space are in a line **Then** the computer should place an X in the space,
Otherwise the computer should place an X in a free corner.
Move 4: The same as Move 3.
Move 5: The computer should place an X in the free space.

Purpose: To learn how to develop a multi-device application that uses rotation

The animation that we will create is an analogue clock[1] shown in *Figure 42.61*.

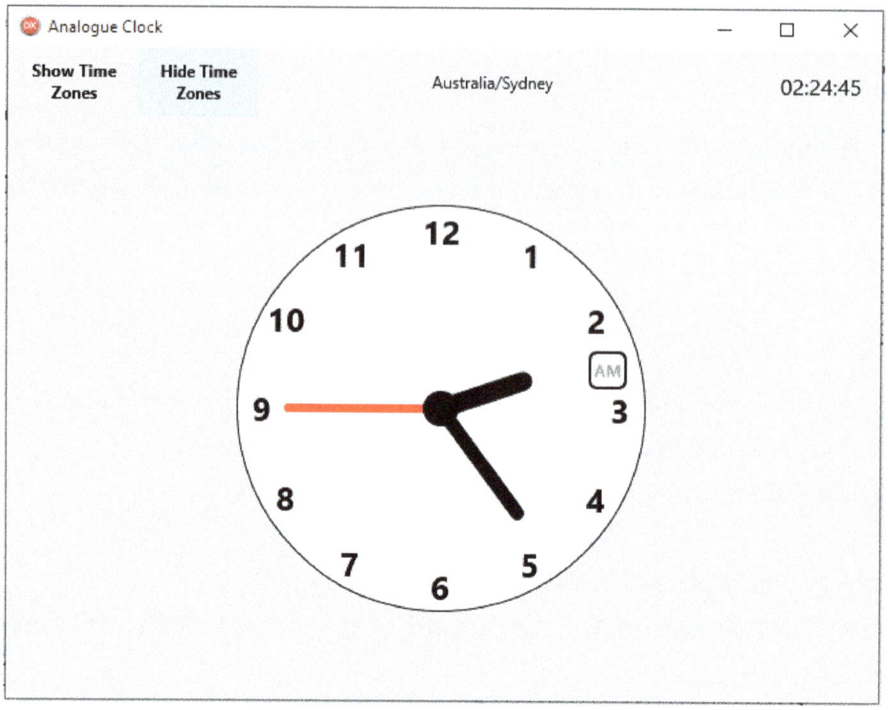

Fig. 42.61 AnalogueClockWithTimeZones in execution, time zone set to Sydney Australia

Create a Blank Multi-Device Application - **File|New|Multi-Device Application**. Save the project as `AnalogueClockWithTimeZones` and its unit as `AnalogueClockWithTimeZonesUnit`.

1. Set **Width** property of the form, `Form1`, to 640 and its **Height** property to 480. Set `Form1`'s **Caption** property to `Analogue Clock`.
2. Place a **TCircle** control, `Circle1`, on the form, `Form1`. Set its **Align** property to **Center**, its **Width** and **Height** properties to 300, its **Fill|Color** to **White**.
3. Place a **TLayout** container, `Layout1`, on the **TCircle** control, set its **Height** property to 300, and its **Width** to 37.5. Set **Position.X** to 131 and its **Position.Y** to 0. *Figure 42.62* shows the result of the first three steps.
4. Place a **TText** control, `Text1`, on the **TLayout** control, `Layout1`, set its **Height** property to 37.5, and its **Width** to 37.5. Set its **Position.X** to 0, and its **Position.Y** to 0. Set its **Text** property to `12`. Set **TextSettings.HorzAlign** and **TextSettings.VertAlign** to **Center**. Set **TextSettings.Font.Size** to 24. Set **TextSettings.Font.Style** to [fsBold]. Set **TextSettings.Font.FontColor** to **Black** - *Figure 42.63*.
5. Place a **TRoundRect** control on the the **TCircle** control, `Layout1`. Set its **Fill.Color** to **Black**. Set its **Width** to 14 and its **Height** to 70. Set **Position.X** to 143 and **Position.Y** to 80. Rename it `rrHour`.

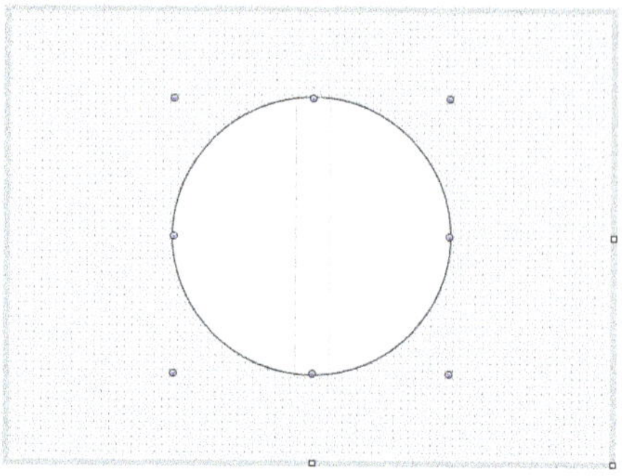

Fig. 42.62 TLayout container on TCircle on TForm

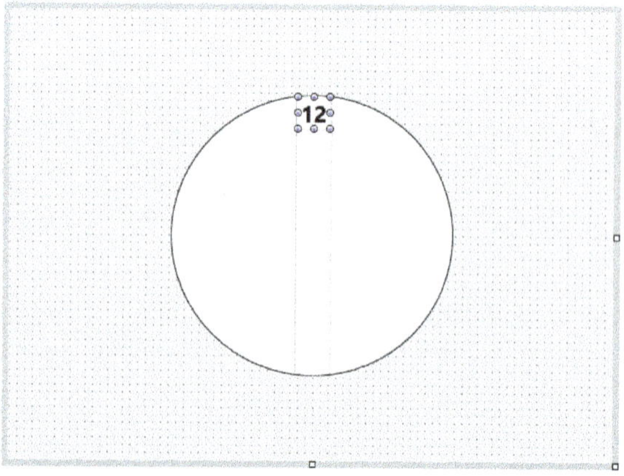

Fig. 42.63 TText on TLayout container on TCircle on TForm

1 Based on an idea from Harry Stahl's book Cross-Platform Development with Delphi 10.2 & FireMonkey

(Download from www.educational-computing.com/DelphiBook/Code/Chapter42/FormCreateBasic.txt)

6. Place another TRoundRect control on the the TCircle control, Layout1. Set its Fill.Color property to Red. Set its Width to 10 and its Height to 100. Set Position.X to 145 and Position.Y to 50. Rename it rrMinute.
7. Place another TRoundRect control on the the TCircle control, Layout1. Set its Fill|Color to Red. Set its Width to 6 and its Height to 115. Set Position.X to 147 and Position.Y to 35. Rename it rrSecond. - *Figure 42.64*.

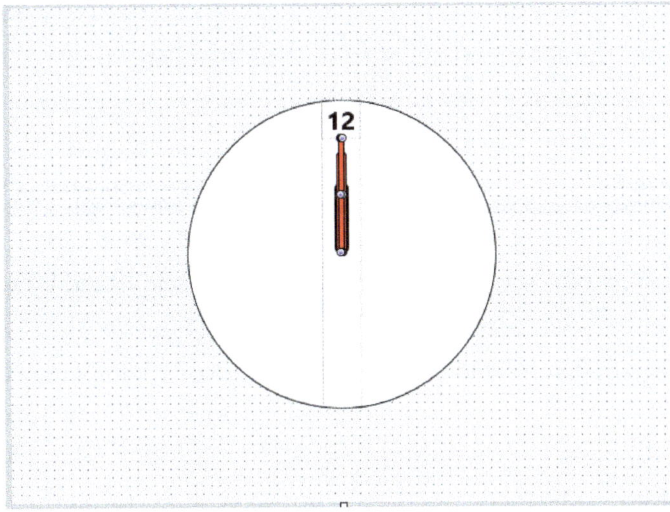

Fig. 42.64 Clockface with hour, minute and second hands

8. Place a TLayout container, Layout2, on Form1, set its Align property to Top, set its Height to 50.
9. Place two TSpeedButton controls on Layout2 and set the Align property of SpeedButton1 to MostLeft, and SpeedButton2 to Left. Change the Text property of SpeedButton1 to Show Time Zones and SpeedButton2 to Hide Time Zones. Set TextSettings.WordWrap to True for both. Set the Width property of the SpeedButton1 to 97 and the SpeedButton2 to 89.
10. Place two TText controls on Layout2. Set the first's Width to 345 and Height to 33. Set the second's Align property to Right and Width to 88. Set Position.X of the first to 184 and Position.Y to 8.
11. Select Layout1 and set its StyleName property to ClockFaceNoStyle.
12. Select Form1 and the Events tab in the Object Inspector. Double click the OnCreate event field to create the event handler, TForm1.FormCreate. Insert code from *Table 42.11* into the event handler. Add variable declaration Var CurrentTimeZone : String; after {$R *.fmx} in the the Implementation section.

```
Procedure TForm1.FormCreate(Sender: TObject);
  Var
    i : Integer;
    ClockFaceLayout : TLayout;
    ClockFaceNo : TText;
  Begin
    For i := 1 To 11
      Do
        Begin
          ClockFaceLayout := TLayout(Circle1.FindStyleResource('ClockFaceNoStyle', True));
          If ClockFaceLayOut <> Nil
            Then
              Begin
                ClockFaceLayOut.Parent := Circle1;
                ClockFaceLayOut.RotationAngle := i * 30;
                ClockFaceNo := TText(ClockFaceLayOut.Children[0]);
                If ClockFaceNo <> Nil
                  Then
                    Begin
                      ClockFaceNo.Text := i.ToString;
                      ClockFaceNo.RotationAngle := (i * 30) * -1;
                    End;
              End;
        End;
     Text2.Text := 'etc/GMT';
     CurrentTimeZone := Text2.Text;
  End;
```

Table 42.11 Event handler TForm1.FormCreate

```
ClockFaceLayout := TLayout(Circle1.FindStyleResource('ClockFaceNoStyle', True));
```

After the above statement from event handler FormCreate is executed, ClockFaceLayout either contains **Nil** or a reference to a copy of a **TLayout** object with **StyleName** property ClockFaceNoStyle, i.e. Layout1. **FindStyleResource** returns the resource object linked directly to the control Circle1 or if none exists then it searches amongst the control's children for a style resource ClockFaceNoStyle. Of course, it matches resource object Layout1 because this object has **StyleName** ClockFaceNoStyle and is a child object of Circle1.
A copy of Layout1 is therefore returned, referenced by variable ClockFaceLayout.
The following code sets the parent of this copy to Circle1 before rotating the copy through a multiple of 30 degrees determined by the current value of i which may be an integer from 1 to 11.

```
ClockFaceLayOut.Parent := Circle1;
ClockFaceLayOut.RotationAngle := i * 30;
```

Next, a reference, ClockFaceNo, is obtained, using the following code, to the **TText** control child of the copy of Layout1

```
ClockFaceNo := TText(ClockFaceLayOut.Children[0]);
```

The following code changes the **Text** property of the **TText** control referenced by ClockFaceNo to the current value of i (i cycles through 1 to 11) before rotation through a multiple of 30 degrees anticlockwise (times -1) from the x-axis of the rotated **TLayout** copy.

```
ClockFaceNo.Text := i.ToString;
ClockFaceNo.RotationAngle := (i * 30) * -1;
```

Figure 42.65 shows the **TLayout** copy rotated clockwise through 90 degrees (i = 3) and its **TText** control changed to showing **Text** property value 3. It is clear from this figure that the **TText** control must be rotated anticlockwise by 90 degrees if it is to display as shown in *Figure 42.66*.
Figure 42.66 shows the result when AnalogueClockWithTimeZones is executed.

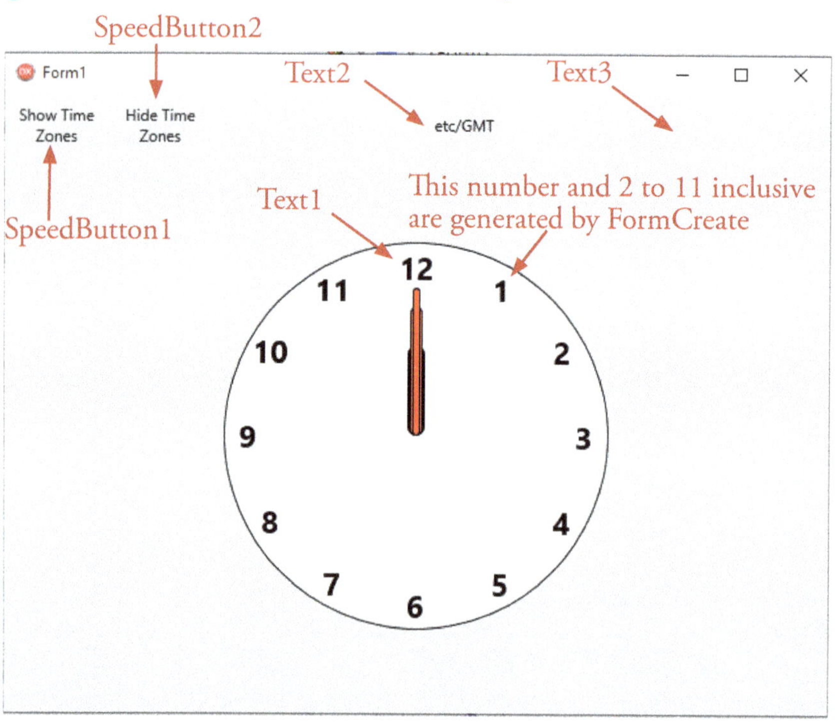

Fig. 42.66 AnalogueClockWithTimeZones in execution, time zone Greenwich Mean Time

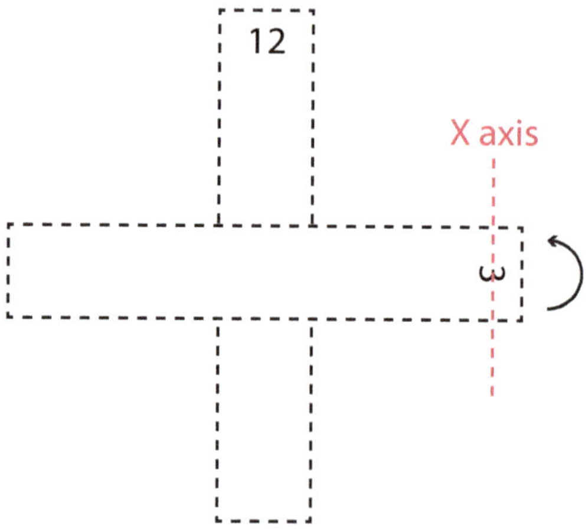

Fig. 42.65 TLayout original and a copy which has been rotated through 90 degrees clockwise

13. Add a **TTimer** control, Timer1, to the form. Set **Enabled** property to **True** and **Interval** to 1000 - *Figure 42.67*. The **Structure** pane in *Figure 42.68* shows the design so far.

(Download from www.educational-computing.com/DelphiBook/Code/Chapter42/TimerVersion1.txt)

```
Procedure TForm1.Timer1Timer(Sender: TObject);
  Var
    Hour, TwelveHour, Minute, Second : Word;
    strHour, strMinute, strSecond : String;
    DateTime : TDateTime;
  Begin
    DateTime := Now;
    Hour := HourOf(DateTime);
    TwelveHour := Hour Mod 12;
    Minute := MinuteOf(DateTime);
    Second := SecondOf(DateTime);
    rrHour.RotationAngle := 30 * TwelveHour + Round(Minute/2.17);
    rrMinute.RotationAngle := 6 * Minute;
    rrSecond.RotationAngle := 6 * Second;
    strHour := Hour.ToString;
    strMinute := Minute.ToString;
    strSecond := Second.ToString;
    If (Length(strMinute) < 2)
      Then strMinute := '0' + strMinute;
    If (Length(strSecond) < 2)
      Then strSecond := '0' + strSecond;
      If (Length(strHour) < 2)
      Then strHour := '0' + strHour;
    Text3.Text := strHour + ':' + strMinute + ':' + strSecond;
  End;
```

Table 42.12 Event handler TForm1.Timer1Timer

14. Select `Timer1` and the **Events** tab in the Object Inspector. Double click the **OnTimer** event field to create the event handler, `TForm1.Timer1Timer`. Insert code from *Table 42.12* into the event handler.
15. Add **System.DateUtils** to the **Uses** clause of the **Interface** section.

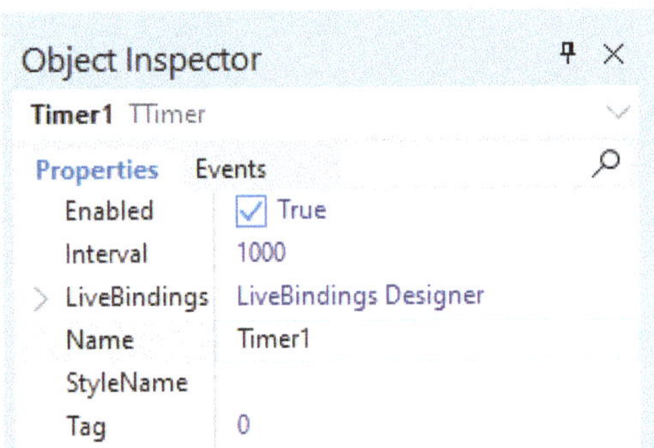

Fig. 42.67 Timer1 property settings

The next stage is to configure the rotation centre of rectangles `rrHour`, `rrMinute`, `rrSecond`. The coordinates of the rotation centre take values in the range 0 through 1. The point with the coordinates (0, 0) corresponds to the upper left corner of the control as shown in *Figure 42.69*.

To rotate the hour, minute and second hands about the midpoint of the bottom edge of each, we need to set their **RotationCenter.X** property to 0.5 and their **RotationCenter.Y** property to 1.

16. Set **RotationCenter.X** property to 0.5 and **RotationCenter.Y** property to 1 for `rrHour, rrMinute` and `rrSecond`.

Click **File|Save All**.

Now **Run (F9)** and test the program.

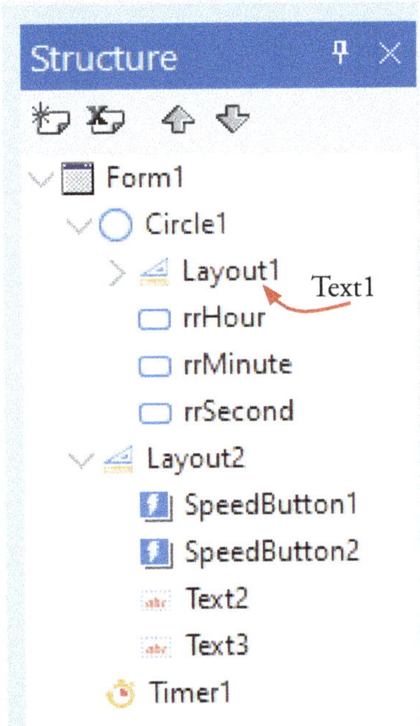

Fig. 42.68 Structure pane showing design so far

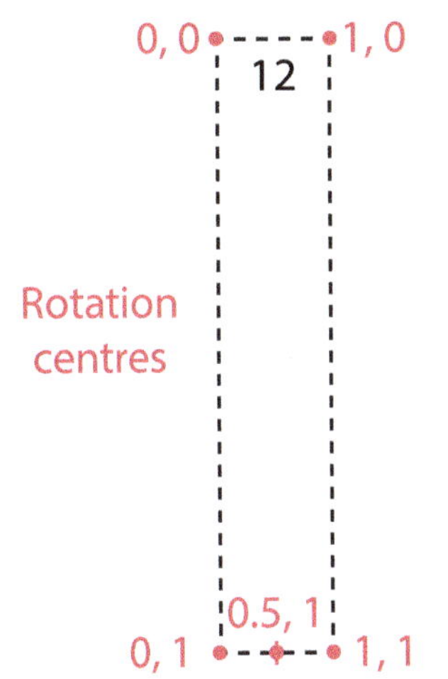

Fig. 42.69 Coordinates of some rotation centres for a rectangular-shaped control

Figure 42.70 shows `AnalogueClockWithTimeZones` in execution with clock hands movement and time displayed digitally. The event handler `Timer1Timer` is called every second because its **Interval** property has been set to 1000. This property's units are milliseconds, 1000 milliseconds = 1 second.

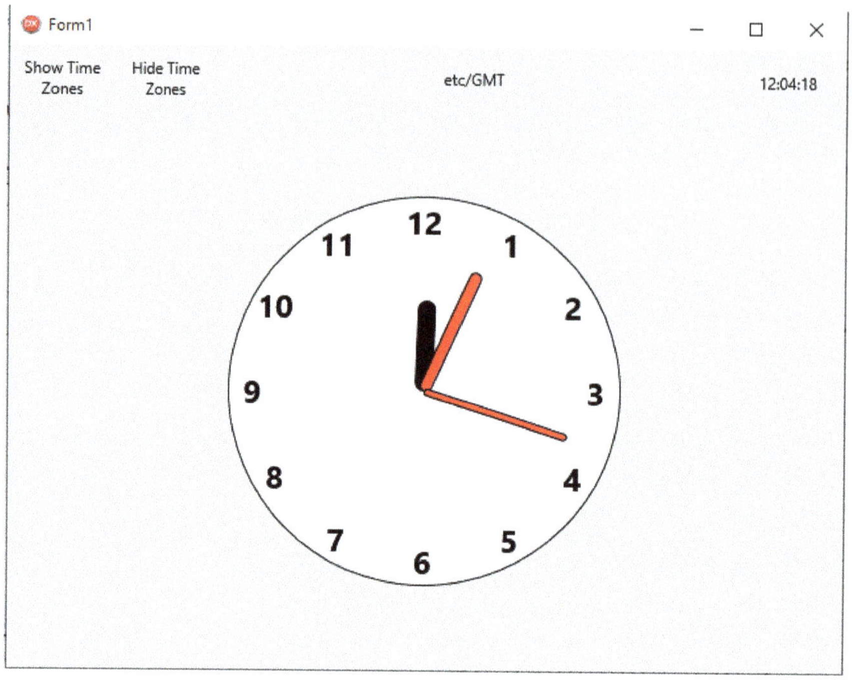

Fig. 42.66 AnalogueClockWithTimeZones in execution with clock hands movement

Questions

1. Explain the following snippets of code extracted from event handler `TForm1.Timer1Timer` shown in *Table 42.12*.

(a)

```
DateTime := Now;
Hour := HourOf(DateTime);
TwelveHour := Hour Mod 12;
Minute := MinuteOf(DateTime);
Second := SecondOf(DateTime);
```

(b)

```
rrHour.RotationAngle := 30 * TwelveHour + Round(Minute/2.17);
rrMinute.RotationAngle := 6 * Minute;
rrSecond.RotationAngle := 6 * Second;
```

(c)

```
strMinute := Minute.ToString;
strSecond := Second.ToString;
If (Length(strMinute) < 2)
  Then strMinute := '0' + strMinute;
If (Length(strSecond) < 2)
  Then strSecond := '0' + strSecond;
  If (Length(strHour) < 2)
  Then strHour := '0' + strHour;
Text3.Text := strHour + ':' + strMinute + ':' + strSecond;
```

It is not possible with the current design to distinguish AM from PM.

17. Add a **TRectangle** control, `Rectangle1`, to `Circle1`. Set its **Position.X** property to 258 and its **Position.Y** property to 107. Set its **Height** to 28 and its **Width** to 28. Set its **XRadius** property to 5 and its **YRadius** property to 5.
    Set **Fill.Color** to **White**.
18. Add a **TText** control, `Text4`, to `Rectangle1`. Set its **Height** to 26 and its **Width** to 26. Set **Align** to **Center**.
19. Add the following code to the end of event handler `Timer1Timer`:

```
If IsPm(DateTime)
  Then Text4.Text :=  'PM'
  Else Text4.Text := 'AM';
```

Click **File|Save All**.

Now **Run (F9)** and test the program.

Figure 42.67 shows the result.

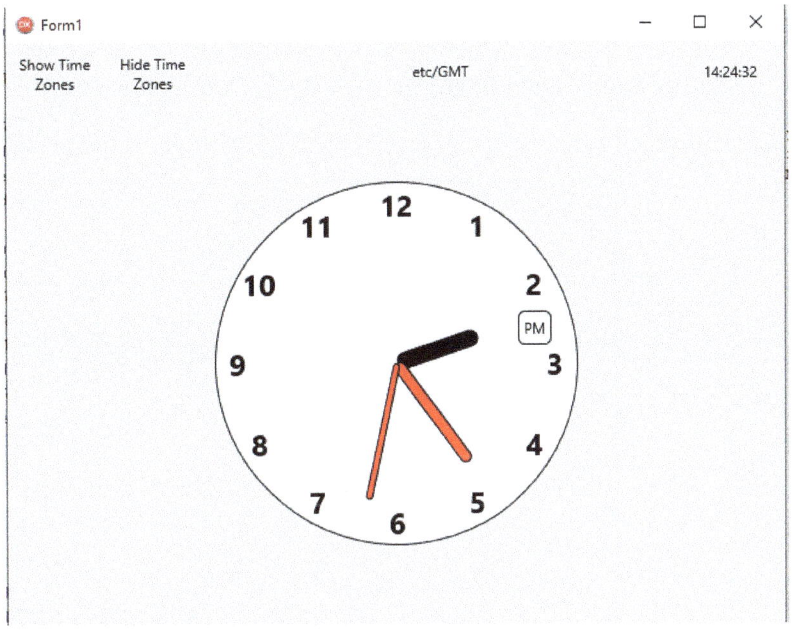

Fig. 42.67 AnalogueClockWithTimeZones in execution with clock hands movement and AM/PM indication

The clock hands need to show that they are anchored.

20. Add a **TCircle** control, `Circle2`, to `Circle1`. Set its **Align** property to **Center**. Set its **Width** and **Height** to 26. Set its **Fill.Color** property to **Black**.

Click **File|Save All**.

Now **Run (F9)** and test the program.

Figure 42.68 shows the result.

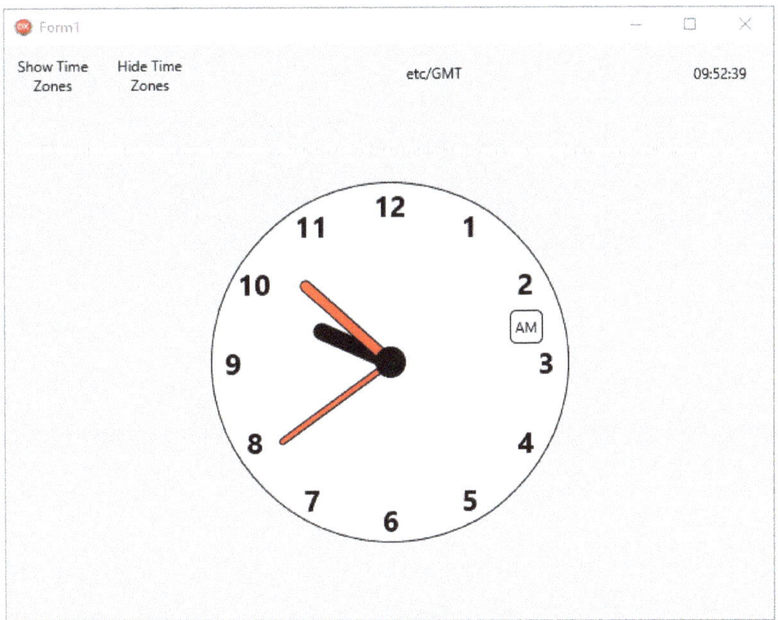

Fig. 42.68 AnalogueClockWithTimeZones in execution with clock hands anchored

The analogue clock application is only capable of showing the time for a single time zone. To change the application to one that supports selection of other time zone requires that a list of possible time zones be added.

We need to add a time zone unit `TZDB` to the **Uses** clause of the **Interface** section and install `TZDB.pas`, `TZDB.ico` and `TZDB.res` into the application's source code folder.

This unit contains the whole pre-compiled **TZ** database and all the code required to interpret it. The **TZ** database is a collaborative compilation of information about the world's time zones, primarily intended for use with computer programs and operating systems. (https://www.iana.org/time-zones).

View `TZDB.pas` at https://github.com/pavkam/tzdb/blob/master/dist/TZDB.pas.

Download the **TZDB** library from https://github.com/pavkam/tzdb by clicking on **Clone or download|Download ZIP**.

Unzip the download and save to a folder.

21. Copy `TZDB.pas`, `TZDB.ico` and `TZDB.res` from `tzdb-master|dist` folder to the folder containing `AnalogueClockWithTimeZones.dproj`.
22. Add `LTimeZone : TBundledTimeZone;` to the **Var** declaration region of the **Implementation** section.
23. Add the time zone unit `TZDB.pas` to the **Uses** clause of the **Interface** section.
24. Add a **TListView** control, `ListView1`, to `Form1`. Set its **CanSwipeDelete** to **False**. Set its **Width** to 1. Set its **StyleLookUp** property to **listviewstyle**. Set its **EditMode** to **True**.
25. Add `LTZID : String; LItem : TListViewItem;` to **Var** declaration of event handler `FormCreate`.
26. Insert the code shown in red in *Table 42.13* into event handler `FormCreate`.
27. Double click `SpeedButton1` (`Show Time Zones` on form) to create event handler `SpeedButton1Click`.

```
Procedure TForm1.FormCreate(Sender: TObject);
  .....
  Begin
    .....
    For i := 1 To 11
      Do
        Begin
          .....
        End;
    ListView1.BeginUpdate;
    Try
      For LTZID in TBundledTimeZone.KnownTimeZones(True)
        Do
          Begin
            LItem := ListView1.Items.Add;
            LItem.Text := LTZID;
          End;
     Finally
       ListView1.EndUpdate;
     End;
     ListView1.SetFocus;
     LTimeZone := TBundledTimeZone.GetTimeZone('etc/GMT');
     Text2.Text := 'etc/GMT';
     CurrentTimeZone := Text2.Text;
  End;
```

P

Table 42.13 Code in red to insert into event handler TForm1.FormCreate

28. Add the statement `ListView1.Width := 250;` to this event handler.
29. Double click `SpeedButton2` (Hide Time Zones on form) to create event handler `SpeedButton1Click`.
30. Add the statement `ListView1.Width := 0;` to this event handler.

Click **File|Save All**.

Now **Run (F9)** and test the program.

Figure 42.69 shows the result when `Show Time Zones` is clicked.

Changing time zone requires an event handler to this when a different time zone is selected from `ListView1`.

31. Change to the **Events** tab of `ListView1` and double click in the field of **OnItemClick** to create event handler `ListView1ItemClick`.

32. Insert the code shown in red in *Table 42.14* into event handler `ListView1ItemClick`.

33. Add `SelectedItem : TListViewItem;` to **Var** declaration of **Implementation** section.

Click **File|Save All**.

Now **Run (F9)** and test the program.

Figure 42.70 shows the result when `Show Time Zones` and then `Africa/Asmara` are clicked.

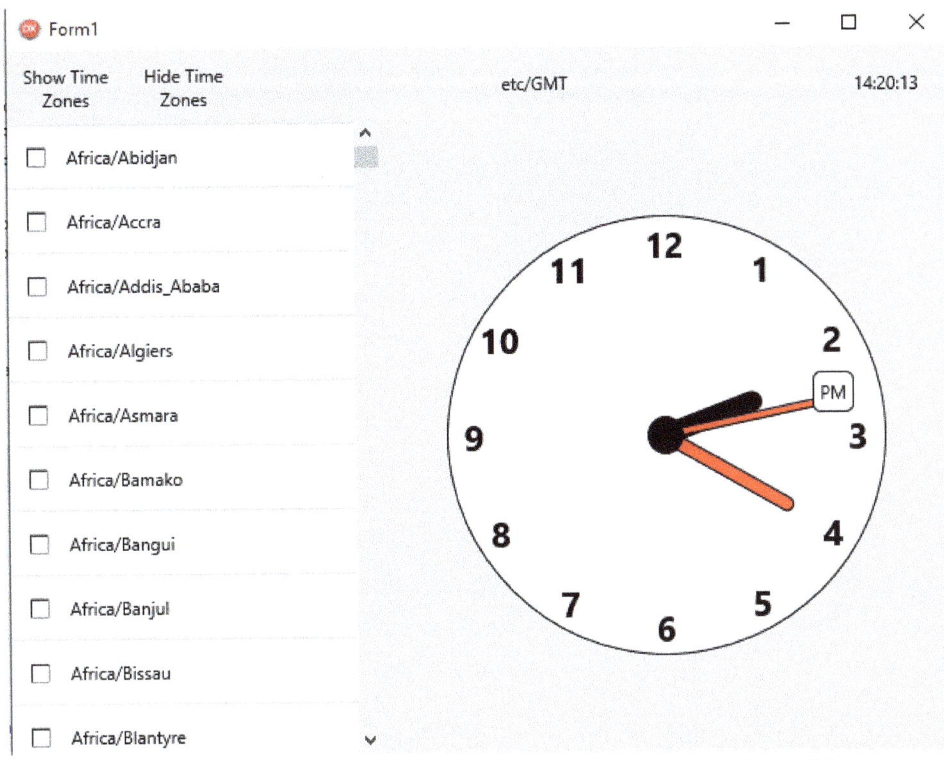

Fig. 42.69 AnalogueClockWithTimeZones in execution with Show Time Zones clicked

To apply the selected time zone to the clock, change

```
DateTime := Now;
```

to

```
DateTime := LTimeZone.ToLocalTime(Now);
```

in event handler `Timer1Timer`.

Click **File|Save All**.

Now **Run (F9)** and test the program.

Figure 42.71 shows the result when `Show Time Zones` and then `Australia/Sydney` are clicked. The time shown by the clock changes to show Sydney time.

```
Procedure TForm1.ListView1ItemClick(Sender: TObject);
  Var
    SelectedItem : TListViewItem;
  Begin
    If SelectedItem <> Nil
      Then SelectedItem.Checked := False;
    If AItem <> Nil
      Then
        Begin
          Text2.Text := AItem.Text;
          CurrentTimeZone := Text2.Text;
          SelectedItem := AItem;
        End
      Else Text2.Text := CurrentTimeZone;
    LTimeZone := TBundledTimeZone.GetTimeZone(Text2.Text);
  End;
```

Table 42.14 Code to insert into event handler TForm1.ListView1ItemClick

34. Finally change the **Caption** property of `Form1` to `Analogue Clock`.

Click **File|Save All**.

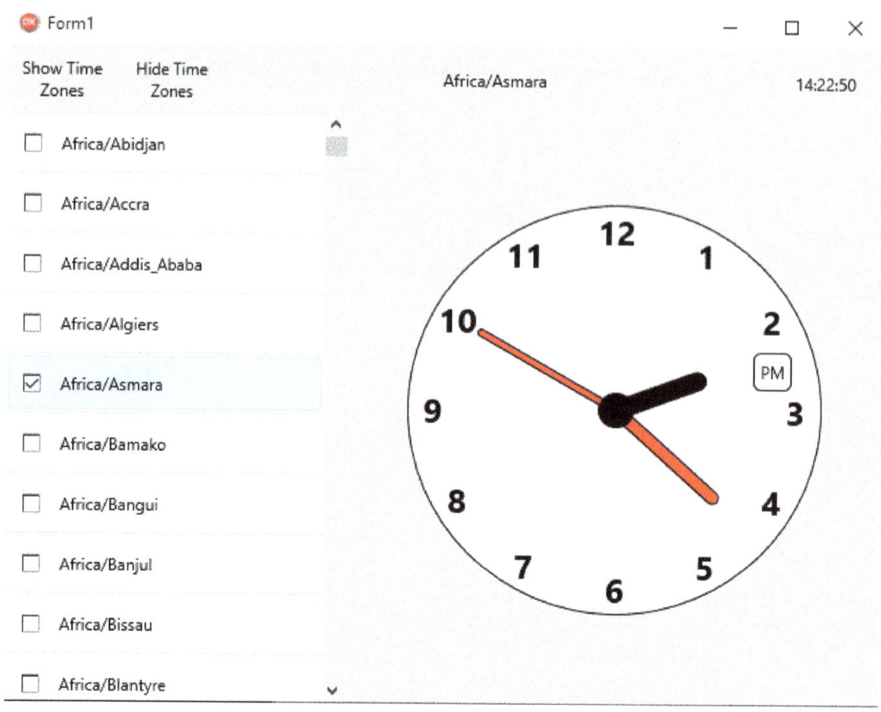

Fig. 42.70 AnalogueClockWithTimeZones in execution with Show Time Zones and then Africa/Asmara clicked

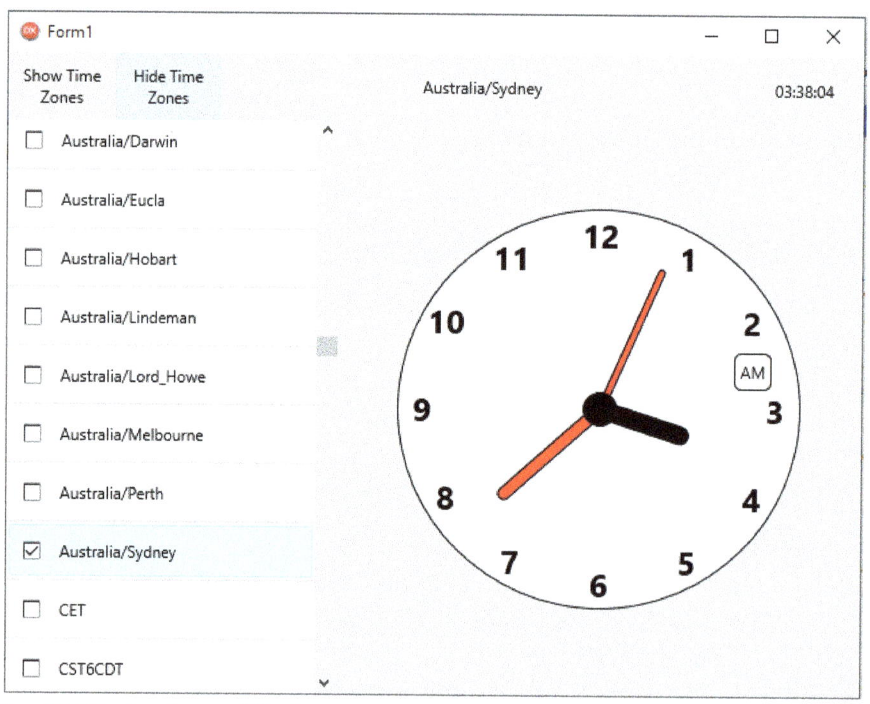

Fig. 42.71 AnalogueClockWithTimeZones in execution fully operational

(Download from www.educational-computing.com/DelphiBook/Code/Chapter42/AnalogueClockWithTimeZones.rar)

Purpose: To learn how to configure a multi-device application for a different target device

The Analogue Clock application was developed on a Windows 10 PC with target operating system set to Windows 64-bit and target device Windows desktop.

Adjustments may be needed to fit the application to a different target device, e.g. a Samsung S8+ mobile phone.

In this section, the target device will be a Samsung S8+ device in developer's mode connected via USB to the Windows 10 development PC.

1. First select the operating system and the target device as shown in *Figure 42.72* and *Figure 42.73*.

Fig. 42.72 Toolbar options windows for target operating system and device

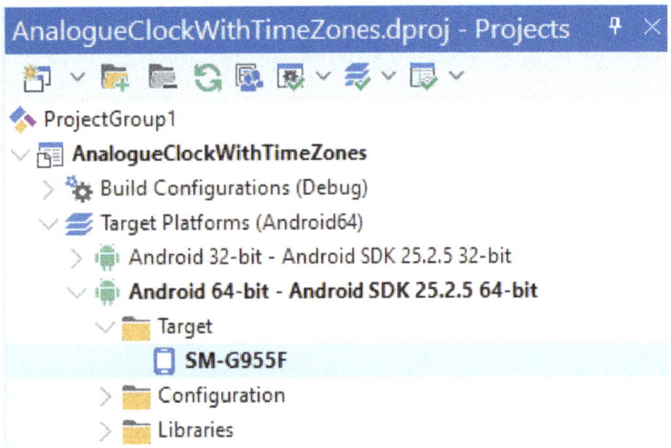

Fig. 42.73 Projects pane for AnalogueClockWithTimeZones

2. Select **Style: Android** and **View: Android 5" Phone**. The UI design changes to that shown in *Figure 42.73*.
3. Set **Align** property for `SpeedButton2` to **Most Left**.
4. Set **Align** property for `Text2` to **Most Left**. Set its **Width** to 169.

Click **File|Save All**.

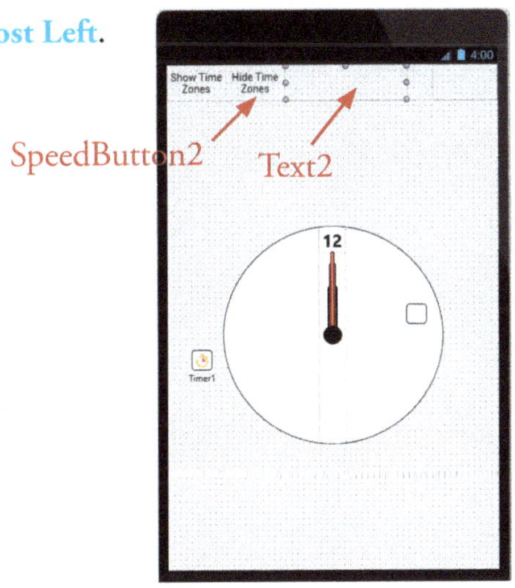

Fig. 42.73 UI design mode for Android 5" Phone

Fig. 42.74 AnalogueClockWithTimeZones executing on Samsung S8+

Now **Run (F9)** and deploy to the target device, a Samsung S8+ mobile phone.

Figure 42.74 shows `AnalogueClockWithTimeZones` executing on the target device with time zone `Africa|Casablanca` selected.

Figure 42.75 shows the application executing on the target device after `Show Time Zones` clicked and `America/Blanc-Sabon` selected.

Fig. 42.75 ShowTimeZones clicked

The original settings are restored on switching back to Windows 64-bit, target Windows desktop. This means that the project maintains one set of settings for the Windows target and a different set for the Android target. Delphi does this using the resource directive **$R** placed at the beginning of the **implementation** section of the unit as shown below for Windows desktop and Android 5" Phone

```
Implementation
{$R *.fmx}
{$R *.LgXhdpiPh.fmx ANDROID}
```

A resource directive is added for each target. *Figure 42.76* shows the resource directive list for three different Android targets, an Apple Mac laptop and Windows desktop., which is placed in the **implementation** section of the unit.

```
{$R *.fmx}
{$R *.NmXhdpiPh.fmx ANDROID}
{$R *.LgXhdpiPh.fmx ANDROID}
{$R *.SmXhdpiPh.fmx ANDROID}
{$R *.Macintosh.fmx MACOS}
```

Fig. 42.76 Resource directives for different targets

Programming Task

2 Build and deploy `AnalogueClockWithTimeZones` to an Android or Apple device.

43 Debugging

Debugging

Purpose: To learn methods for debugging a program

What is debugging?

Debugging is the process of detecting and removing errors (referred to as "bugs") in a program that can cause the program to behave unexpectedly or crash at runtime.

Debugging tools (called debuggers) are used to support the programmer in identifying coding errors. They allow the programmer to examine the program state when the error(s) occurs and to check on the possible cause(s). A debugger allows a programmer to trace the program execution step-by-step and to stop the execution at any point in order to examine the current value of variables, modify their values, view the program output.

Use a console screen

The simplest approach and one that directly avoids using the resident debugger, is to output the state of variables to the running program's output window in the case of a console application or to a separate console window in the case of a GUI application. Using a separate console window offers more screen estate for viewing/reviewing the debugging information for a GUI application.

Table 43.2 shows a highly contrived example program which contains a logic error. It does not always calculate a correct quotient and a correct remainder. For example, some but not all values from *Table 43.1* invoke an exception because the calculated quotient and the calculated remainder do not match the expected results.

Test case	Dividend	Divisor	Result
1	7	2	Quotient = 3, Remainder = 1
2	8	2	Quotient = 3, Remainder = 2 Quotients failed to match... Remainders failed to match...
3	4	1	Quotient = 3, Remainder = 1 Quotients failed to match... Remainders failed to match...
4	9	3	Quotient = 2, Remainder = 3 Quotients failed to match... Remainders failed to match...
5	9	4	Quotient = 2, Remainder = 1

Table 43.1 Some values with which to test the integer division program

Assert is used in the following code snippet to assist debugging the program by evaluating a specified test expressed as a Boolean expression:

```
Try
  Assert(Quotient = (Dividend Div Divisor), 'Quotients Failed to match');
Except
  On E : Exception Do Writeln(E.Message);
End
```

If the Boolean test fails, **Assert** raises an **EAssertionFailed** exception. The exception object is created with the specified string which forms part of **E.Message** together with the complete path, filename, and the line number on which **Assert** failed.

The code in *Table 43.2* also illustrates adding a **Writeln** statement to provide the state of variable `r` inside the **While** loop of the function call `GetQuotient` where the quotient is calculated.

```
//Writeln('Inside while, value of r = ', r);
```

It is shown in *Table 43.2* commented out, uncomment this statement and run the program.

P

```
Program ConsoleModeIntegerDivisionIncorrectProject;
{$APPTYPE CONSOLE}
{$R *.res}
Uses
  System.SysUtils;
Function GetQuotient(x, y : Integer) : Integer;
  Var
    q, r : Integer;
  Begin
    r := x;
    q := 0;
    While r > y
      Do
        Begin
          //Writeln('Inside while, value of r = ', r);
          r := r - y;
          q := q + 1;
        End;
    Result := q;
  End;
Function GetRemainder(x, y : Integer) : Integer;
  Var
    q, r : Integer;
  Begin
    r := x;
    q := 0;
    While r > y
      Do
        Begin
          r := r - y;
          q := q + 1;
        End;
    Result := r;
  End;
Var
  Dividend, Divisor, Quotient, Remainder : Integer;
Begin
  Repeat
    Write('Input dividend: ');
    Readln(Dividend);
    If (Dividend <> -1)
      Then
        Begin
          Write('Input divisor: ');
          Readln(Divisor);
        End;
    If (Dividend >= 0) And (Divisor > 0)
      Then
        Begin
          Quotient := GetQuotient(Dividend, Divisor);
          Writeln('Quotient = ', Quotient);
          Remainder := GetRemainder(Dividend, Divisor);
          Writeln('Remainder = ', Remainder);
          Try
            Assert(Quotient = (Dividend Div Divisor), 'Quotients Failed to match');
          Except
            On E : Exception Do Writeln(E.Message);
          End;
          Try
            Assert(Remainder = (Dividend Mod Divisor), 'Remainders Failed to match');
          Except
            On E : Exception Do Writeln(E.Message);
          End;
        End;
  Until Dividend = -1;
  Write('Press return to exit application');
  Readln;
End.
```

Table 43.2 Integer division program with a logic error

Figure 43.1 shows the console window output for the first three test cases from *Table 43.1*. Inspection of the output should identify the error: the condition in the two **While** statements should be `r >= y` not `r > y`. Satisfy yourself that this is the case by running the program again after making the correction to both functions.

```
D:\IntegerDivisionTest\Win32\Debug\ConsoleModeIntegerDivisionIncorrectProject.exe
Input dividend: 7
Input divisor: 2
Inside while, value of r = 7
Inside while, value of r = 5
Inside while, value of r = 3
Quotient = 3
Remainder = 1
Input dividend: 8
Input divisor: 2
Inside while, value of r = 8
Inside while, value of r = 6
Inside while, value of r = 4
Quotient = 3
Remainder = 2
Quotients failed to match (D:\IntegerDivisionTest\ConsoleModeIntegerDivisionIncorrectProject.dpr, line 60)
Remainders failed to match (D:\IntegerDivisionTest\ConsoleModeIntegerDivisionIncorrectProject.dpr, line 65)
Input dividend: 4
Input divisor: 1
Inside while, value of r = 4
Inside while, value of r = 3
Inside while, value of r = 2
Quotient = 3
Remainder = 1
Quotients failed to match (D:\IntegerDivisionTest\ConsoleModeIntegerDivisionIncorrectProject.dpr, line 60)
Remainders failed to match (D:\IntegerDivisionTest\ConsoleModeIntegerDivisionIncorrectProject.dpr, line 65)
Input dividend:
```

Figure 43.1 Console window output from Integer division program

Table 43.3 and *Table 43.4* show the graphical user interface code equivalent of the console program.

The compiler directive **{$APPTYPE CONSOLE}** was added to the program source (*Table 43.4*) in order to open a console window alongside the GUI window when the program `IntegerDivisionProject` is run.

Figure 43.2 shows the user interface design and the result of calculating the quotient and remainder for dividend 7 and divisor 2 when the program `IntegerDivisionProject` is run.

The presence of a console window enables the following `Writeln` statements within the code to be successfully executed:

```
Writeln('Inside quotient while, value of r = ', r);
Writeln('Inside remainder while, value of r = ', r);
Writeln('Quotient = ', edtQuotient.Text);
Writeln('Remainder = ', edtRemainder.Text);
```

Figure 43.3 shows the console window output for the first and second test cases from *Table 43.1*.

The `Assert` statements were edited to use `ShowMessage` instead of `Writeln` but the program would still have worked if `Writeln` had been used except output would have directed to the console window.

Figure 43.4(a) and *Figure 43.4(b)* show the two `Assert` statements using `ShowMessage` to report an error with the calculation of the quotient and remainder for dividend 8 and divisor 2.

```
Z:\ProductionChapters\DelphiBoo...
Inside quotient while, value of r = 7
Inside quotient while, value of r = 5
Inside quotient while, value of r = 3
Quotient = 3
Inside remainder while, value of r = 7
Inside remainder while, value of r = 5
Inside remainder while, value of r = 3
Remainder = 1
Inside quotient while, value of r = 8
Inside quotient while, value of r = 6
Inside quotient while, value of r = 4
Quotient = 3
Inside remainder while, value of r = 8
Inside remainder while, value of r = 6
Inside remainder while, value of r = 4
Remainder = 2
```

Figure 43.3 Console window output from GUI integer division program

```
Unit IntegerDivisionUnit;
Interface
Uses
  Winapi.Windows, Winapi.Messages, System.SysUtils, System.Variants, System.Classes, Vcl.Graphics,
  Vcl.Controls, Vcl.Forms, Vcl.Dialogs, Vcl.StdCtrls;
Type
  TfrmIntegerDivision = Class(TForm)
                         btnCalculateQuotient: TButton;
                         btnCalculateRemainder: TButton;
                         edtDividend: TEdit;
                         edtDivisor: TEdit;
                         lblDividend: TLabel;
                         lblDivisor: TLabel;
                         edtQuotient: TEdit;
                         lblQuotient: TLabel;
                         lblRemainder: TLabel;
                         edtRemainder: TEdit;
                         Procedure btnCalculateQuotientClick(Sender : TObject);
                         Procedure btnCalculateRemainderClick(Sender : TObject);
                       End;
Var
  frmIntegerDivision: TfrmIntegerDivision;
Implementation
  {$R *.dfm}
  Function GetQuotient(x, y : Integer) : Integer;
  Var
    q, r : Integer;
  Begin
    r := x;
    q := 0;
    While r > y
      Do
        Begin
          Writeln('Inside quotient while, value of r = ', r);
          r := r - y;
          q := q + 1;
        End;
    Result := q;
  End;
  Function GetRemainder(x, y : Integer) : Integer;
  Var
    q, r : Integer;
  Begin
    r := x;
    q := 0;
    While r > y
      Do
        Begin
          Writeln('Inside remainder while, value of r = ', r);
          r := r - y;
          q := q + 1;
        End;
    Result := r;
  End;
  Procedure TfrmIntegerDivision.btnCalculateQuotientClick(Sender : TObject);
    Begin
      If (StrToInt(edtDividend.Text) >= 0) And (StrToInt(edtDivisor.Text) > 0)
      Then
        Begin
          edtQuotient.Text := IntToStr(GetQuotient(StrToInt(edtDividend.Text), StrToInt(edtDivisor.Text)));
          Writeln('Quotient = ', edtQuotient.Text);
          Try
            Assert(StrToInt(edtQuotient.Text) = StrToInt(edtDividend.Text) Div StrToInt(edtDivisor.Text),
                                                'Quotients failed to match');
          Except
            On E : Exception Do ShowMessage(E.Message); // Writeln(E.Message);
          End;
        End;
    End;
  Procedure TfrmIntegerDivision.btnCalculateRemainderClick(Sender : TObject);
    Begin
      If (StrToInt(edtDividend.Text) >= 0) And (StrToInt(edtDivisor.Text) > 0)
      Then
        Begin
          edtRemainder.Text := IntToStr(GetRemainder(StrToInt(edtDividend.Text), StrToInt(edtDivisor.Text)));
          Writeln('Remainder = ', edtRemainder.Text);
          Try
            Assert(StrToInt(edtRemainder.Text) = StrToInt(edtDividend.Text) Mod StrToInt(edtDivisor.Text),
                   'Remainder failed to match');
          Except
            On E : Exception Do ShowMessage(E.Message); // Writeln(E.Message);
          End;
        End;
    End;
End.
```

Table 43.3 GUI integer division unit with a logic error

```
Program IntegerDivisionProject;
{$APPTYPE CONSOLE}
Uses
  Vcl.Forms,IntegerDivisionUnit in 'IntegerDivisionUnit.pas'
{frmIntegerDivision};
{$R *.res}
Begin
  Application.Initialize;
  Application.MainFormOnTaskbar := True;
  Application.CreateForm(TfrmIntegerDivision, frmIntegerDivision);
  Application.Run;
End.
```

Added to source code (Project|View Source).

Table 43.4 GUI integer division program source

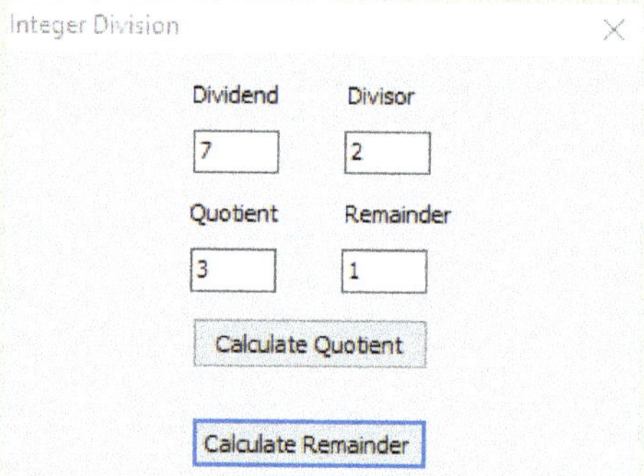

Figure 43.2 GUI integer division program in execution

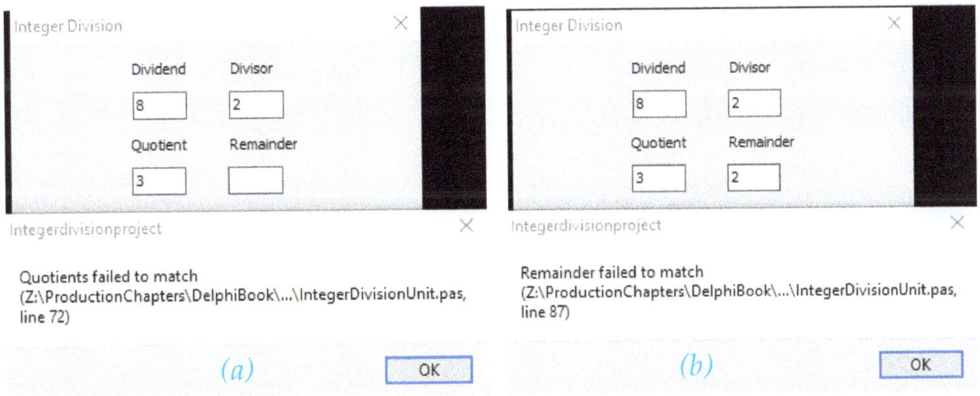

Figure 43.4 Output from GUI integer division program for dividend 8 and divisor 2

OutputDebugString

The **OutputDebugString** function is defined in the **Win32 API**, in the **RTL** unit **Winapi.Windows**. It is used as follows

```
Uses
  Winapi.Windows;
...
Var
  AMessage : String;
Begin
  OutputDebugString('This is one way of outputting a message');
  AMessage := 'This is another way of outputting a message';
  OutputDebugString(PChar(Message));
...
End.
```

To use **OutputDebugString** in the IDE the program must be run in **Debugger** (debug) mode, i.e. **Run** (**F9**). *Figure 43.5* shows the console mode integer division program executing in debug mode. **OutputDebugString** output for dividend value 7 and divisor value 2 appears in the **Events** window shown in *Figure 43.5* and *Figure 43.6*. The console window is shown in *Figure 43.7*.

If the program is run in standalone mode, i.e. outside of the IDE, then output by **OutputDebugString** can be captured by the application **DebugView** (`dbgview.exe`) - *Figure 43.8* -which is available from **SysInternals** (**Microsoft**) - download from https://docs.microsoft.com/en-us/sysinternals/downloads/debugview.

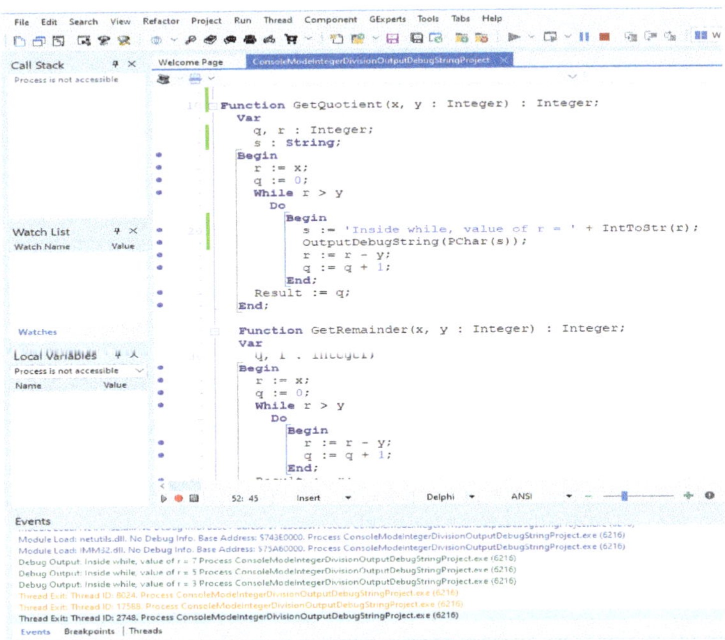

Figure 43.5 IDE showing use of OutputDebugString

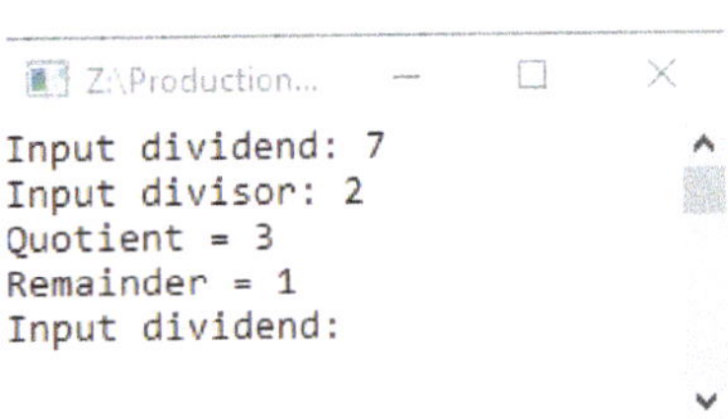

Figure 43.7 Console window

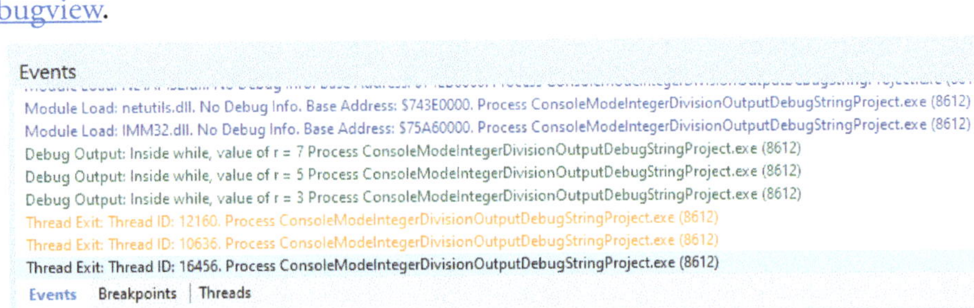

Figure 43.6 ConsoleModeIntegerDivisionOutputDebugStringProject executing within IDE (Run(F9)) with dividend value 7 and divisor value 2

For clarity and ease of use, the author prefers a console mode window and **Writeln** over **OutputDebugString**.

Also, if **OutputDebugString** is called repeatedly or in a loop, it may cause some performance overhead. In the case of graphics applications such as simulations involving a large number of onscreen moving objects a separate console mode window is the better option.

However, **DebugView** does allow debug output to be routed to any computer on a network that is reachable via TCP/IP.

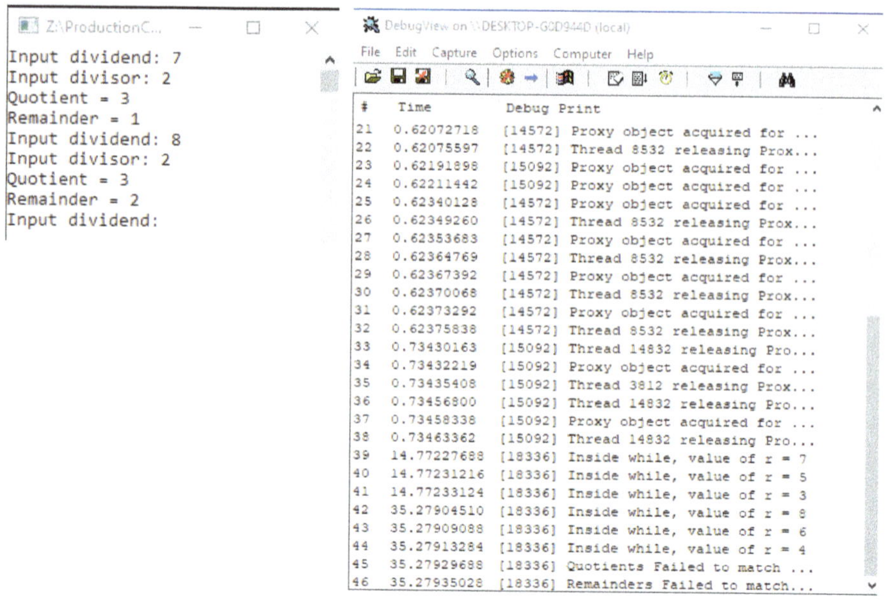

Figure 43.8 Console window together with DebugView for dividend 7 and divisor 2, dividend 8 and divisor 2 respectively

Also, Delphi allows conditional compilation of **OutputDebugString** statements so that they don't need to be removed or commented out in the release version. Instead they just need to be surrounded as follows

```
{$IFDEF ODS}
  OutputDebugString('This is a message');
{$ENDIF}
```

The Debugger

Download and open the `IntegerDivisionProject` in the IDE.

In the project window (*Figure 43.9*) note the following:

- **Project|Compile** compile only those files that have changed since the last build as well as any files that depend on them. Compiling does not execute the application
- **Project|Build** compile all of the source code in the current project, regardless of whether any source code has changed. Building is useful when unsure of which files have changed, or if project or compiler options have changed.

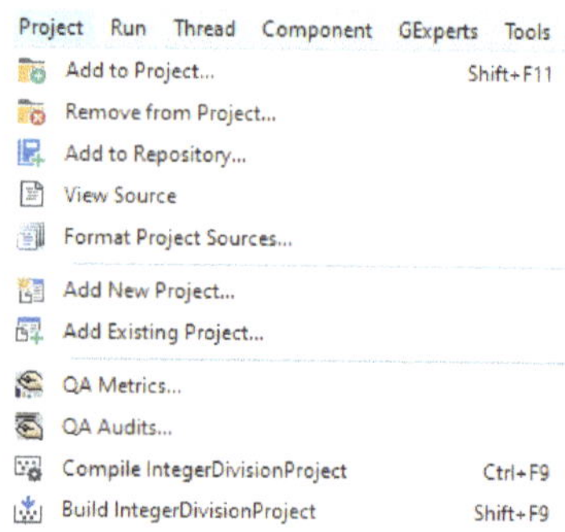

Figure 43.9 Project window

If the selected build configuration is **Debug** then the output of compiling/building is an **exe** in a subfolder `Debug` which itself is contained in a subfolder named after the selected target platform, e.g. `Win32`.

When a program is ready for release the target platform is changed to **Release**.

Executing a program is not the same as compiling/building.

However, **Run|Run (F9)** does compile any changed source code and, if the compile is successful, executes the application in debug mode meaning that the application may be debugged in the IDE. If the program/application has already been successfully compiled then **Run|Run (F9)** simply executes the application in debug mode in the IDE. The debug toolbar icon **Run**(**F9**) button may also be used.

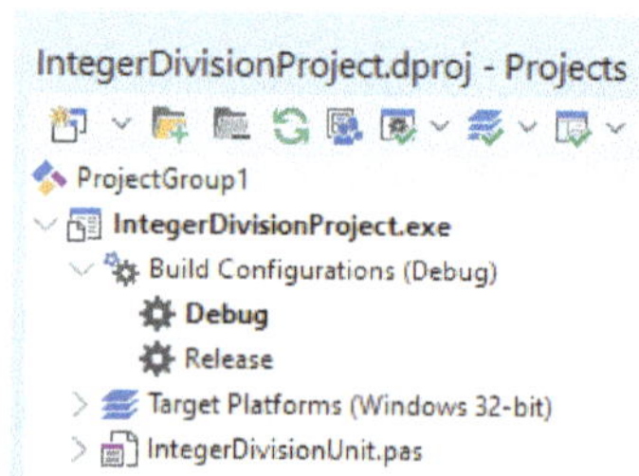

Figure 43.10 Project Manager window showing that the selected build configuration is Debug

Run Without Debugging (**Shift + Ctrl + F9**) compiles any changed source code, and if the compile is successful, executes the application without invoking the debugger built into the IDE. The debug toolbar icon ▶ **Run Without Debugging** (**Shift + Ctrl + F9**) button may also be used.

The above commands are also available from the **context menu** of the project node in the **Project Manager**, opened by right clicking on the project node - `IntegerDivisionProject` - as shown in *Figure 43.11*. The generated files from a previous build may be deleted with the **Clean** command from the same context menu.

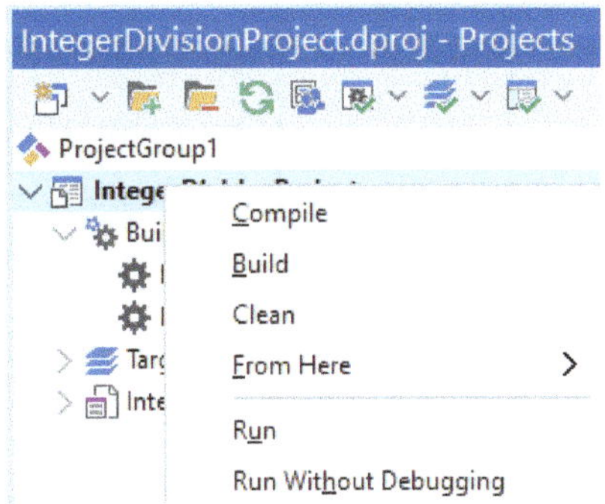

Figure 43.11 Context menu in Project Manager window showing some but not all options

If the debugger support of the IDE is required then the application must be run with the debugging option. Before or when the application is running, breakpoints can be set and variables inspected.

During a debugging session any line of the source code that is eligible for a breakpoint is marked with a blue dot • in the left gutter of the **Code Editor**. Clicking on the blue dot sets a breakpoint. The blue dot is then replaced by a multi-coloured one. Clicking the latter cancels the breakpoint.

Breakpoints are displayed in the **Breakpoint List** window, available by selecting **View|Debug Windows|Breakpoints** - *Figure 43.12*. The breakpoint at line 36 was set by clicking on the blue dot at line 36. Note that the blue dot changes colour to indicate that a breakpoint is enabled on this line and the debugger is active. Clicking on the `Calculate Quotient` button invokes a call to function `GetQuotient`. The function is entered and execution breaks at lines 36 on the statement `r := x`.

The **Local Variables** window (**View|Debug Windows|Local Variables** if not open) is now populated with the current values of the variables belonging to function `GetQuotient` as shown in *Figure 43.12*.

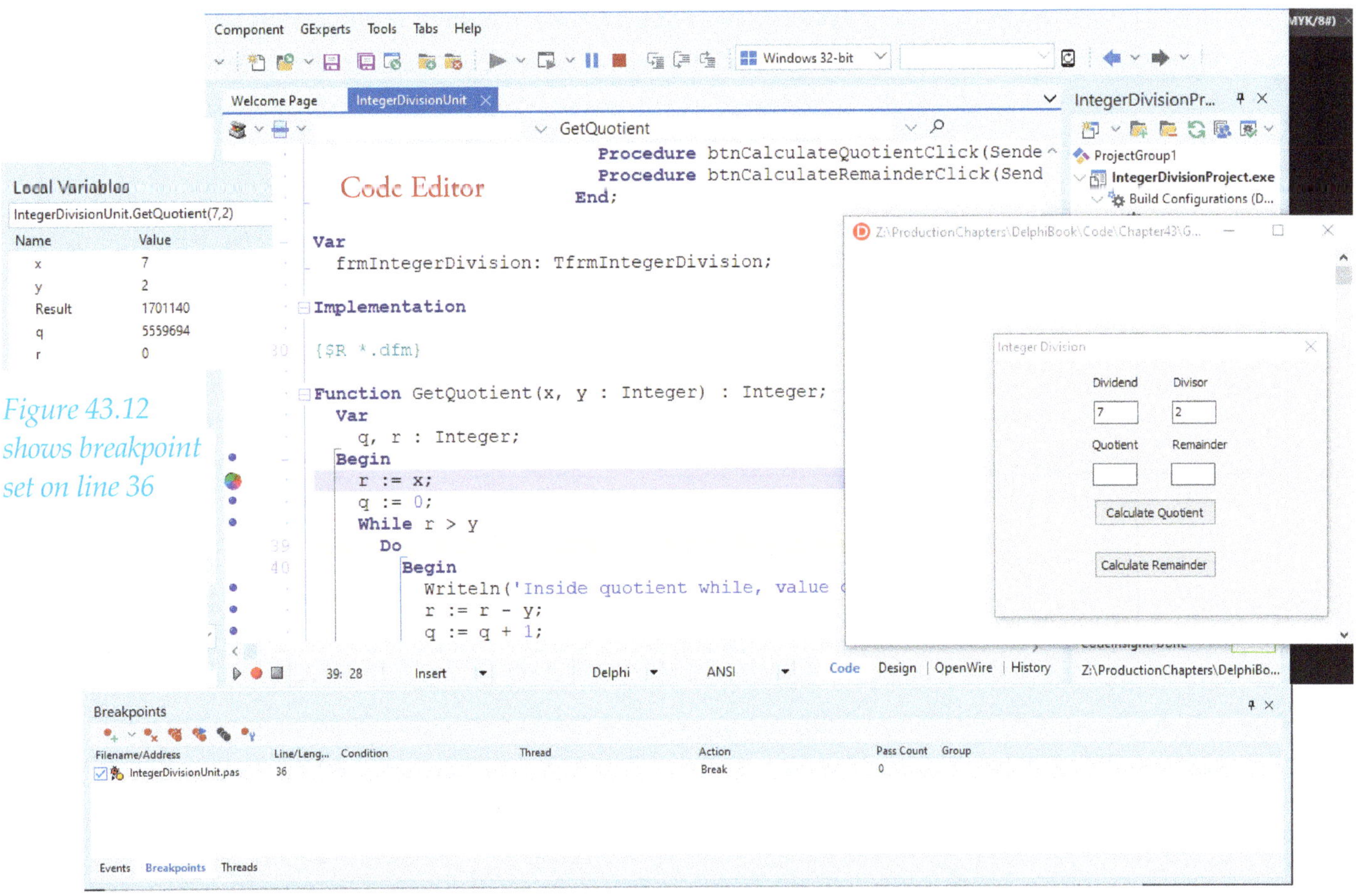

Figure 43.12 shows breakpoint set on line 36

Table 43.4 shows the most useful debugging commands and their shortcuts. *Figure 43.13* shows the debug toolbar.

Keyboard shortcut	IDE command	Description
F8	Run|Step Over (Badly named: doesn't mean this literally)	The program execution has stopped on a breakpoint: pressing **F8** instructs the debugger to execute the line of code at the breakpoint. If the line contains a function, **Step Over** executes the function and then stops at the first line after the function call.
F4	Run|Run to Cursor	The program execution has stopped on a breakpoint: pressing **F4** causes the debugger to resume program execution but then break at the current position of the cursor. This is an example of an implicit breakpoint. Breakpoints placed in the left gutter of the code editor are explicit breakpoints. If the original explicit breakpoint is removed: repositioning the cursor and pressing **F4** causes execution to resume but to break again at the new position of the cursor.
F7	Run|Trace Into	The program execution has stopped on a breakpoint: pressing **F7** instructs the debugger to execute the line of code at the breakpoint. If the line contains a function, the debugger enters the body of the function and then stops at the first line of code. The **Trace Into** command enables tracing into the code of any function or procedure. Instead of executing the function or procedure and returning to the next line after the function/procedure call as **Step Over** does, **Trace Into** places the execution point on the first source code line in the function or procedure being called.
Shift F7	Run|Trace To Next Source Line	If the execution point is on a Windows API function that uses a callback, using **Trace To Next Source Line** will jump the execution point to the first line in the callback function. The effect is similar to **Trace Into.**
Shift F8	Run|Run Until Return	If the current execution is paused inside a function then pressing **Shift F8** executes the function and then stops when execution reurns from the function. This is useful when the debugger ends up pausing execution in a function that you don't want to have to step through. SHIFT-F8 will get you out very quickly. (WARNING: Don't use SHIFT-F8 from inside an assembly-code routine that plays around with the stack. Unpredictable behavior can result. **F4** to the bottom of it instead.).
Ctrl F2	Run|Program Reset	Terminates the execution of a single process that is currently under the debugger's control.
	Run|Detach From Program	Unloads the process from the debugger's control without actually terminating it.
F9	Run with debugging	To make the application's user interface the focus again during debugging just press **F9** again.

Table 43.4 Useful debugging commands and their keyboard shortcuts

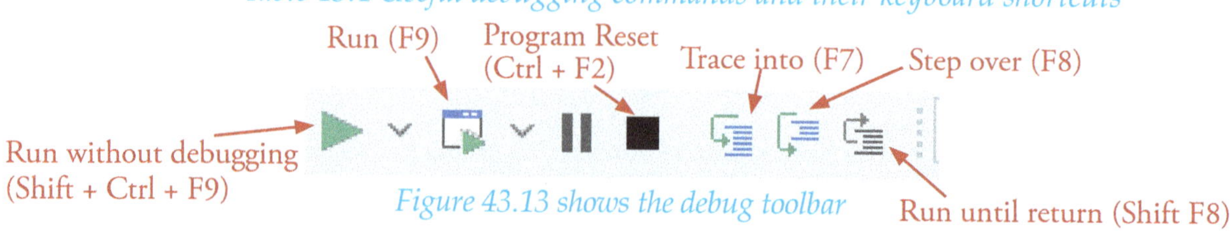

Figure 43.13 shows the debug toolbar

Ctrl + Alt + W or **View|Debug Windows|Watches** brings up the **Watches** window.

To add an instance of a variable to the **Watch List**, e,g, `r`, **run** the program in the debugger.
Set breakpoint on `r := x` in the **GetQuotient** function.
Highlight the variable `r` in the source code then **drag** it to the **Watches** window *Figure 43.14*.
Enter 7 for the dividend and 2 for the divisor. **Click** **Calculate Quotient** button. *Figure 43.15* shows the state recorded in both the **Watches** and the **Local Variables** windows when the breakpoint is encountered.
Press **F8** to execute `r := x`.
Figure 43.16 shows that the **Value** field for `r` has changed to 7 in both the **Watches** and the **Local Variables** windows.
With `r` selected in the **Watches** window, **press** Ctrl + U or right click `r` on the highlight to bring up the **Evaluate/ Modify** window - *Figure 43.17*. The value of `r` may now be altered if necessary which it isn't in this example. Or an expression containing `r`, e.g. `r = 3` may be constructed.

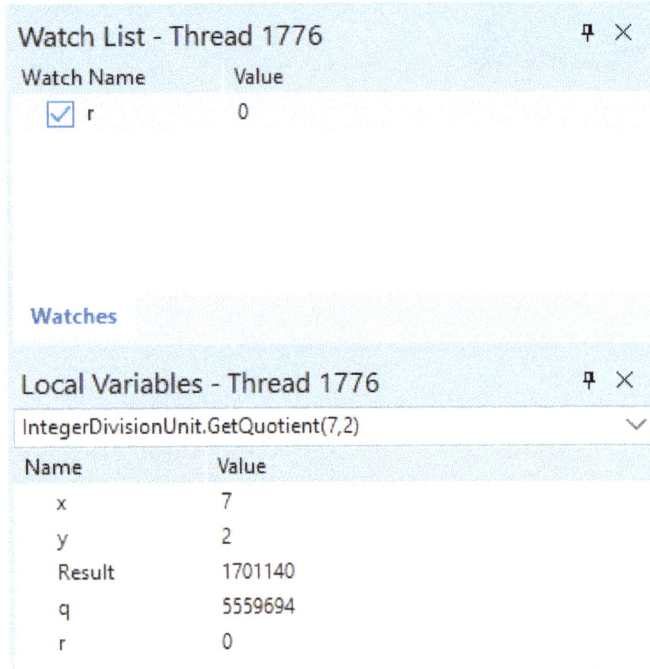

Figure 43.15 shows the state recorded in the Watches and Local Variables windows on hitting the breakpoint

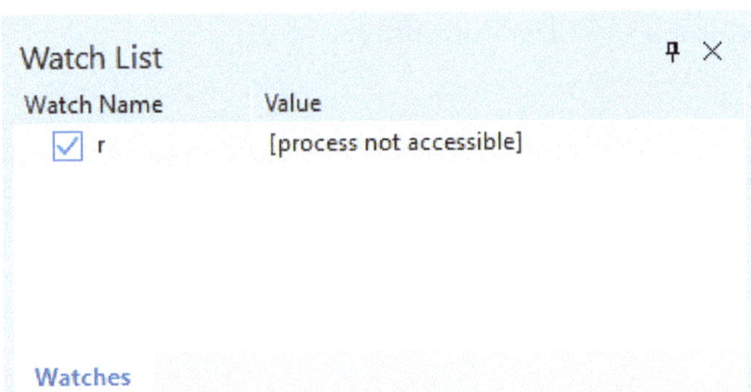

Figure 43.14 shows the Watches window with variable r in the watch list

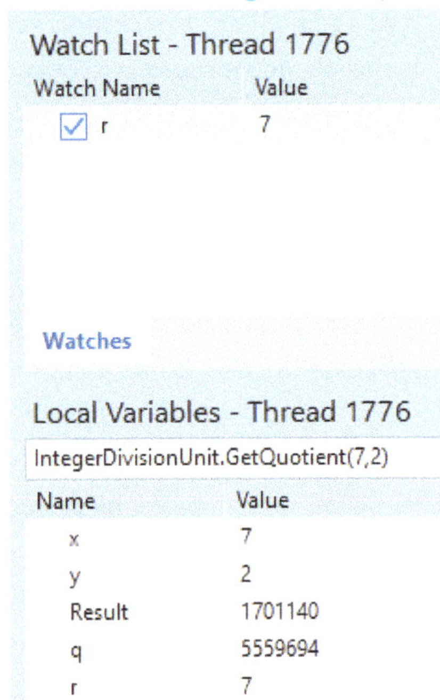

Figure 43.16 shows the Watches and Local Variables windows after F8 pressed

Construct this expression, **click** **Watch** icon and **observe** that the **Watches** window changes to that shown in *Figure 43.=18*.

Single step through the program (**F8**) until the **Watches** window shows that the expression `r = 3` becomes **True**.

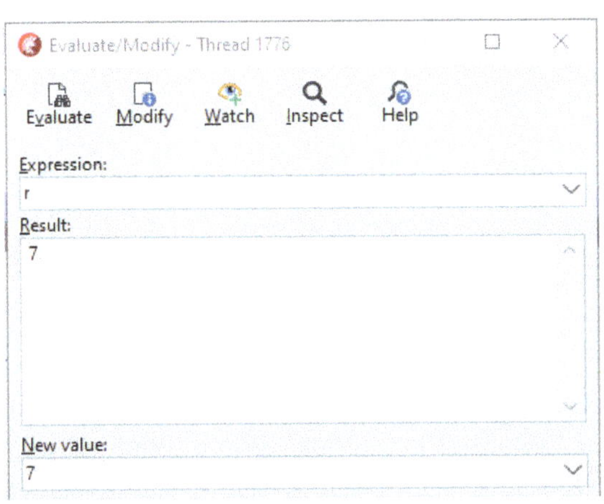

Figure 43.17 shows the Evaluate/Modify window with r = 7

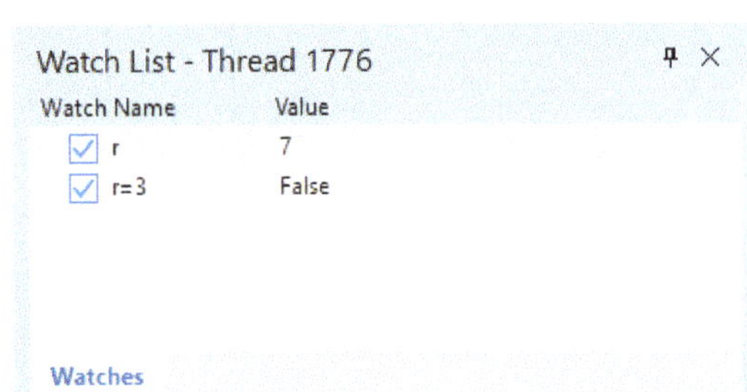

Figure 43.18 Watch List now contains a condition expression r = 3

44 Anonymous methods

First-class objects

Purpose: To learn what is meant by a first-class object

First-class objects (or values)

First-class objects (or values) are objects which may

- appear in expressions (expressions such as $5 + 3 \times y^3$)
- be assigned to a variable
- be assigned as arguments to functions
- be returned by function calls

Typical first-class objects in many programming languages are integers, floating-point values, characters and strings.

For example,

`x := 5;` is an assignment statement in which the first-class value `5` is assigned to the variable `x`.

`MyStringVar := Uppercase('Hello World!');`

is an assignment statement containing a function call `Uppercase` with argument

`'Hello World!'`

which is a first-class value of type `string`. This function returns a first-class value of type `string`

`'HELLO WORLD!'`

Functions as first-class objects

In functional programming languages and in some imperative programming languages a function is a first-class object. This means that it can

- appear in expressions
- be assigned to a variable
- be passed as an argument to another function
- be returned as the result of a function call.

When a function is a first-class object it is called a **first-class function**.

> **Key principle**
>
> **Partial function application:**
> Any function taking two or more arguments can be partially applied to one or more arguments.

Figure 44.1 shows a multiplication function which is assigned in an assignment statement to a variable `f`. This function takes a pair of integers and returns an integer, i.e. in partial function application notation

`Integer -> Integer -> Integer`

If the function is applied to two arguments, the result is a number; so that, for instance, `3*6` equals `18`.

What happens if the function is applied to one argument, e.g. `3`? The result that is returned is a single argument function `MultiplyBy3`. This is a function of a more specialised nature, this time a function `MultiplyBy3` with one argument `j`.

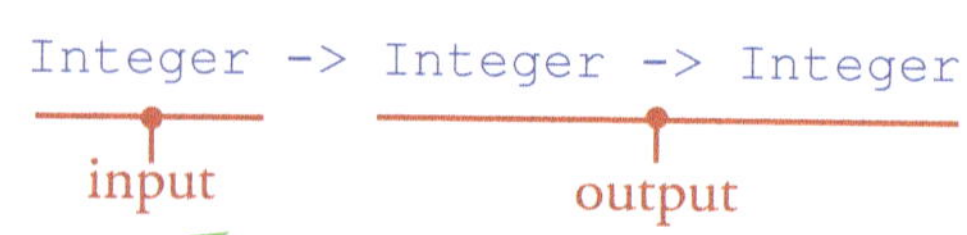

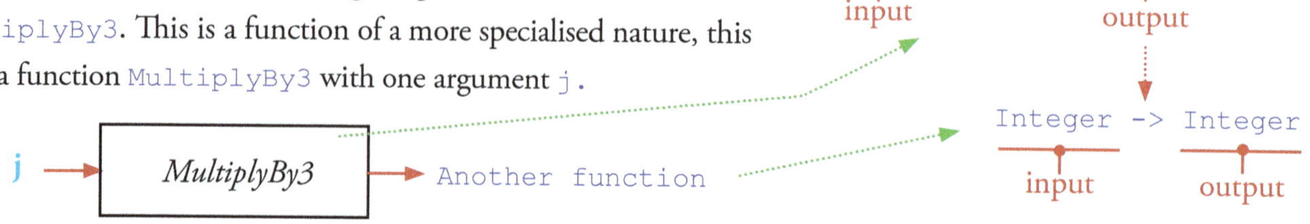

To evaluate `3 * 6` we call `f(3)` and then apply it to argument `6`:

```
f(3)(6)
```

The result is then written to the output window by the statement

```
Writeln(f(3)(6));
```

This is an example of **partial function application**.

Anonymous functions

An **anonymous function** is a special kind of first-class function that is declared inline, without naming it. The program shown in *Table 44.1* shows an example of how an anonymous function is declared:

```
Function(y : Integer) : Integer
  Begin
    Writeln('Inside anonymous method, x: ', x);
    Writeln('Inside anonymous method, y: ', y);
    Result := x * y;
  End;
```

Parameter x comes from the block which surrounds the anonymous function - see Table 44.1.

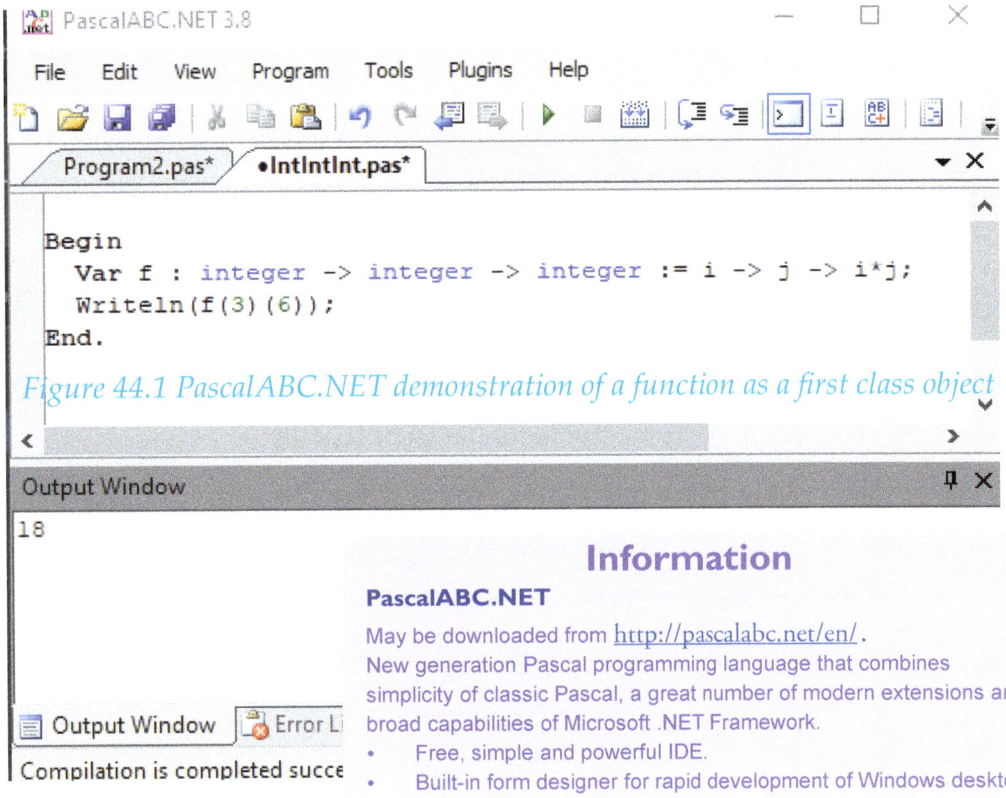

Figure 44.1 PascalABC.NET demonstration of a function as a first class object

Information

PascalABC.NET

May be downloaded from http://pascalabc.net/en/.

New generation Pascal programming language that combines simplicity of classic Pascal, a great number of modern extensions and broad capabilities of Microsoft .NET Framework.

- Free, simple and powerful IDE.
- Built-in form designer for rapid development of Windows desktop applications.
- Free LGPLv3 license.

This function is assigned to variable `Result` which is of type `TFunctionOfInteger`, a function reference. This means that the anonymous function is a **first-class function**.

Function `f` is therefore a single argument function which returns a reference to a function of a single argument. We therefore have what we need to create a partial function, e.g. `f(3)` and apply this to a single integer argument, e.g. `f(3)(4)` just as we did in the **PascalABC.NET** example shown in *Figure 44.1*.

The Delphi program shown in *Table 44.1* demonstrates writing the result of partial function application with the statement `Writeln(f(3)(4));`

It is also possible to assign the partial function `f(3)` to a variable `g` of type `TFunctionOfInteger` and then apply `g` to the single argument 4 as shown in *Table 44.1* writing the result returned as follows `Writeln(g(4));`

```
Program PartialFunctionApplicationProject;
{$APPTYPE CONSOLE}
{$R *.res}
Uses
  System.SysUtils;
Type
  TFunctionOfInteger = Reference to Function(x : Integer) : Integer;
Function f(x : Integer) : TFunctionOfInteger;
  Begin
    Result := Function(y : Integer) : Integer
              Begin
                Writeln('Inside anonymous method, x: ', x);
                Writeln('Inside anonymous method, y: ', y);
                Result := x * y;
              End;
  End;
Var
  g : TFunctionOfInteger;
Begin
  g := f(3); {Assign a partial function f(3) to variable g}
  Writeln(g(4)); {Apply the partial function to argument 4}
  Writeln(f(3)(4)); {Apply partial function f(3) to argument4}
  Readln;
End.
```

Table 44.1 Partial function application using an anonymous function

Figure 44.2 shows the console output window for `PartialFunctionApplicationProject` in execution.

```
Z:\ProductionChapters\DelphiBook\Code\Chapter44\PartialFunctionApplication\...
Inside anonymous method, x: 3
Inside anonymous method, y: 4
12
Inside anonymous method, x: 3
Inside anonymous method, y: 4
12
```

Figure 44.2 Console window output from PartialFunctionApplicationProject

Closure

A **closure** is a technique for implementing name binding in a language with first-class functions in the situation where the name would otherwise not be within scope lexically.

Operationally, a closure is a record storing a function together with an environment.

For example, in *Table 44.1* the anonymous function references a variable `x` which is not directly associated with the function either as an argument passed to the function or as a locally-defined variable:

```
Result := Function(y : Integer) : Integer
            Begin
              Writeln('Inside anonymous method, x: ', x);
              Writeln('Inside anonymous method, y: ', y);
              Result := x * y;
            End;
```

This function gets the value to use for `x` from the surrounding environment, i.e. the argument passed to function `f`.

For example, at the time of the function call f(3)(4), the anonymous function gets the value 3 from the environment which has bound x to this value.

Simple example of the use of partial function application

The program shown in *Table 44.2* extends the `PartialFunctionApplicationProject` application so that when run it generates a times table output shown in *Figure 44.3*.

```
Program TimesTable;
{$APPTYPE CONSOLE}
{$R *.res}
Uses
  System.SysUtils;
Type
  TFunctionOfInteger = Reference to Function(x : Integer) : Integer;
Function f(x : Integer) : TFunctionOfInteger;
  Begin
    Result := Function(y : Integer) : Integer
                Begin
                  Result := x * y;
                End;
  End;
Begin
  For Var i := 1 To 12
    Do
      Begin
        For Var j := 1 To 12
          Do Write(f(i)(j), ' ');
        Writeln;
      End;
  Readln;
End.
```

Table 44.2 Partial function application using an anonymous function

Whilst this is a highly contrived example - `Write(i * j, ' ');` produces the same output - it illustrates the application of the concept of an anonymous function and the concept of partial function application, both very powerful concepts.

```
Z:\ProductionChapters\DelphiBook\Code\Chapter44\TimesTa...
1   2   3   4   5   6   7   8   9   10  11  12
2   4   6   8   10  12  14  16  18  20  22  24
3   6   9   12  15  18  21  24  27  30  33  36
4   8   12  16  20  24  28  32  36  40  44  48
5   10  15  20  25  30  35  40  45  50  55  60
6   12  18  24  30  36  42  48  54  60  66  72
7   14  21  28  35  42  49  56  63  70  77  84
8   16  24  32  40  48  56  64  72  80  88  96
9   18  27  36  45  54  63  72  81  90  99  108
10  20  30  40  50  60  70  80  90  100 110 120
11  22  33  44  55  66  77  88  99  110 121 132
12  24  36  48  60  72  84  96  108 120 132 144
```

Figure 44.3 Console window output from TimesTable.exe

Higher order functions

We have learned that a first class function is a function that may be passed as an argument to another funtion. The functions that accept a first class function as an argument are called **higher order functions**. Higher order functions are a powerful means of abstraction.

Table 44.3 shows the use of a higher order function `Map` which takes a function `f` as its first argument and then applies this function to every element of its second argument, an `array of integer`. The result is returned in another array. The main block of this program then iterates over the elements of the returned array - *Figure 44.4*.

We may define another function, say, `Cube`, which cubes its integer argument `x`. and then call `Map(Cube, AnArrayOfIntegers)` to cube every integer in `AnArrayOfIntegers`.

```
Program SimpleMapProject;
{$APPTYPE CONSOLE}
{$R *.res}
Uses
  System.SysUtils;
Type
  TFunctionOfInteger = Reference to Function(x : Integer): Integer;
  TArrayOfIntegers = Array Of Integer;
Function Sqr(x : Integer) : Integer;
  Begin
    Result := x * x;
  End;
Function Map(f : TFunctionOfInteger; ArrayOfIntegers : TArrayOfIntegers) : TArrayOfIntegers;
  Var
    ArrayOfMappedIntegers : TArrayOfIntegers;
  Begin
    SetLength(ArrayOfMappedIntegers, Length(ArrayOfIntegers));
    For Var i In ArrayOfIntegers
      Do ArrayOfMappedIntegers[i - 1] := f(ArrayOfIntegers[i - 1]);
      Result := ArrayOfMappedIntegers;
  End;
Var
  AnArrayOfIntegers : TArrayOfIntegers = [1, 2, 3, 4, 5, 6, 7, 8, 9, 10];
  AnotherArrayOfIntegers : TArrayOfIntegers;
Begin
  Writeln('Length of array: ', Length(AnArrayOfIntegers));
  Writeln('First element of this array: ', AnArrayOfIntegers[0]);
  AnotherArrayOfIntegers := Map(Sqr, AnArrayOfIntegers);
  Var  i : Integer;
  Writeln('Contents of returned array');
  For i := 1 To Length(AnotherArrayOfIntegers)
    Do Writeln(i : 4, ' : ', AnotherArrayOfIntegers[i - 1]);
  Readln;
End.
```

Table 44.3 Higher order function example

```
Z:\ProductionChapters\DelphiBook\Code\Chapter44\SimpleMap\Win32\Debug\SimpleMapProject.exe

Length of array: 10
First element of this array: 1
Contents of returned array
   1 : 1
   2 : 4
   3 : 9
   4 : 16
   5 : 25
   6 : 36
   7 : 49
   8 : 64
   9 : 81
  10 : 100
```

Figure 44.4 Console window output from SimpleMapProject.exe

Doing calculus with higher order functions

In calculus the derivative of a function is another function.

Using Newton's notation, the derivative of a function f(x) is a function f'(x) defined as follows

$$f'(x) = \lim_{h \to 0} \frac{f(x + h) - f(x)}{h}$$

The derivative is defined as "the limit as h goes to zero".
For example, the derivative of $f(x) = x^3$ is a new function $f'(x) = 3x^2$.
A good approximation of the limit may be achieved by using small, positive values of h, such as h = 0.00001.
Even greater precision is possible by making h smaller.
Table 44.4 shows how we may use a higher-order function `Derivative` that takes a function and a value `h` as an argument, and returns another function that is the approximate derivative for that value of `h`. The returned function takes an argument `x` and via closure returns the approximate value of the derivative at that value `x` for the given `h`.

For example,

```
g := Derivative(Square, DoubleDouble(0.000000000000000000000000000000000000000000000001));
Writeln(FloatToStr(g(DoubleDouble(10))));
```

computes the approximate value of the derivative of $f(x) = x^2$ at the value `x = 10` for `h = 0.000000000000000000000000000000000000000000000001`.

The program `DerivativeHighPrecisionProject` uses the multi-precision floating point library `Neslib.MultiPrecision` which may be downloaded from https://github.com/neslib/Neslib.MultiPrecision.

Of course, the built-in data type `Double` may be used instead but with the consequence that the computed derivatives will be of lower precision. *Figure 44.5* shows the console output when this program is run.

```
Program DerivativeHighPrecisionProject;
{$APPTYPE CONSOLE}
{$R *.res}
Uses
  System.SysUtils,
  Neslib.MultiPrecision;
Type
    TFuncOfDouble = Reference to Function(x : DoubleDouble) : DoubleDouble;
Function Square(x : DoubleDouble) : DoubleDouble;
  Begin
    Result := x * x;
  End;
Function Cube(x : DoubleDouble) : DoubleDouble;
  Begin
    Result := x * x * x;
  End;

Function Derivative (f : TFuncOfDouble; h : DoubleDouble) : TFuncOfDouble;
  Begin
    Result := Function(x : DoubleDouble) :  DoubleDouble
                Begin
                  Result := (f(x + h) - f(x))/h;
                End;
  End;
Var
  g : TFuncOfDouble;
Begin
  g := Derivative(Square, DoubleDouble(0.000000000000000000000000000000000000000000000001));
  Writeln(FloatToStr(g(DoubleDouble(10))));
  g := Derivative(Cube, DoubleDouble(0.0000000000000000000000000000000000000000000000000000000001));
  Writeln(FloatToStr(g(DoubleDouble(5))));
  Readln;
End.
```

P

Table 44.4 Higher order function example

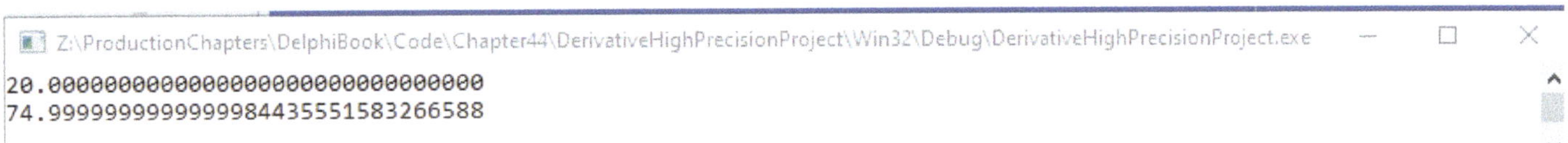

Figure 44.5 Console window output from DerivativeHighPrecisionProject.exe

MapReduce

A class may have a generic method, i.e. a method that acts on a generic or generalised type `T`. For example, a generic method of a class may be defined with the following method signature

```
Procedure SomeName<T>(SomeParameter : T);
```

It may also have class methods as well as object methods. An object method acts on an object whilst a class method acts on a class. An object method requires an object to be instantiated and uses the reference to the object when calling the object method. A class method uses a class reference, e.g. `TList` in `TList.Create` when calling the class method `Create`, a special class method called a constructor.

Table 44.5 shows a class with three generic methods

```
Class Function Map<T> (InputArray : TArray<T>;
                       MapFunction : TFunc<T, T>) : TArray<T>;
Class Function Reduce<T : Record> (InputArray : TArray<T>;
                                   ReduceFunction : TFunc<T, T, T>; InitValue : T) : T;
Class Function Filter<T> (InputArray : TArray<T>;
                          FilterFunction: TFunc<T, Boolean>) : TArray<T>;
```

`Class Function Map<T>` has two input arguments, `InputArray` and `MapFunction` and it returns an array of element type `T`. `InputArray`'s type is an array type with a generic element type `T`.

`MapFunction : TFunct<T, T>` means that this function returns a reference to a function with a single input argument of type `T` and a result type `T`.

`Class Function Reduce<T : Record>` has three input arguments, `InputArray`, `ReduceFunction` and `InitValue` and it returns a value of type `T`.

`InputArray`'s type is an array type with a generic element type `T : Record`, i.e. a record type with generic field type.

`ReduceFunction : TFunct<T, T, T>` means that this function returns a reference to a function with two input arguments of type `T` and a result type `T`. `InitValue` is of type `T`.

`Class Function Filter<T>` has two input arguments, `InputArray` and `FilterFunction` and it returns an array of element type `T`.

`InputArray`'s type is an array type with a generic element type `T`.

`FilterFunction : TFunct<T, Boolean>` means that this function returns a reference to a function with a single input argument of type `T` and a result type `Boolean`.

Figure 44.6 shows the output when the program shown in *Table 44.5* is run.

In *Table 44.6* the `MapFunction` is implemented as an anonymous function as follows

```
Function(Item : Integer) : Integer
  Begin
    Result := Item * Item;
  End
```

The `ReduceFunction` is implemented as an anonymous function as follows

```
Function(Term1, Term2 : Integer) : Integer
  Begin
    Result := Term1 + Term2;
  End
```

The `FilterFunction` is implemented as an anonymous function as follows

```
Function (Item : Integer) : Boolean
  Begin
    Result := Item Mod 2 = 0;
  End
```

Figure 44.6 shows the output when the program shown in *Table 44.6* is run.

```
Unit Unit1HigherOrderFunctionsUnit;
Interface
  Uses System.Generics.Collections, System.SysUtils, System.Classes;
  Type
    THigherOrder = Class Sealed
                     Class Function Map<T> (InputArray : TArray<T>;
                                            MapFunction : TFunc<T, T>) : TArray<T>;
                     Class Function Reduce<T : Record> (InputArray : TArray<T>;
                                          ReduceFunction : TFunc<T, T, T>; InitValue : T) : T;
                     Class Function Filter<T> (InputArray : TArray<T>;
                                               FilterFunction: TFunc<T, Boolean>) : TArray<T>;
                   End;
Implementation
  Class Function THigherOrder.Filter<T>(InputArray : TArray<T>;
                                        FilterFunction : TFunc<T, Boolean>) : TArray<T>;
    Var
      List : TList<T>;
    Begin
      List := TList<T>.Create;
      Try
        For Var i := 0 To Length(InputArray) - 1
          Do
            If FilterFunction(InputArray[i])
              Then List.Add(InputArray[i]);
        Result := List.ToArray;
      Finally
        List.Free;
      End;
    End;
  Class Function THigherOrder.Map<T>(InputArray : TArray<T>;
                                     MapFunction : TFunc<T, T>) : TArray<T>;
    Begin
      SetLength(Result, Length(InputArray));
      For Var i := 0 To Length(InputArray) -1
        Do Result[i] := MapFunction(InputArray[i]);
    End;
  Class function THigherOrder.Reduce<T>(InputArray : TArray<T>;
                                        ReduceFunction: TFunc<T, T, T>; InitValue: T) : T;
    Begin
      Result := InitValue;
      For Var n In InputArray
        Do Result := ReduceFunction(Result, n);
    End;
End.
```

Table 44.5 Class methods for Map, Reduce and Filter

```
Z:\ProductionChapters\DelphiBook\Code\Chapt...
 94 squared = 8836
 95 squared = 9025
 96 squared = 9216
 97 squared = 9409
 98 squared = 9604
 99 squared = 9801
100 squared = 10000
Press return to continue...
Sum of first 100 positive integers squared = 338350
Press return to continue...
```

```
Z:\ProductionChapters\DelphiBook\Code\Chapt...
Next even positive integer between 1 and 100 = 86
Next even positive integer between 1 and 100 = 88
Next even positive integer between 1 and 100 = 90
Next even positive integer between 1 and 100 = 92
Next even positive integer between 1 and 100 = 94
Next even positive integer between 1 and 100 = 96
Next even positive integer between 1 and 100 = 98
Next even positive integer between 1 and 100 = 100
Press return to continue...
Sum of first 100 positive even integers = 2550
Press return to end...
```

Figure 44.6 Console window output from HigherOrderFunctionsProject.exe

P

```
Program HigherOrderFunctionsProject;
{$APPTYPE CONSOLE}
{$R *.res}
Uses
  System.SysUtils,
  Unit1HigherOrderFunctionsUnit in 'Unit1HigherOrderFunctionsUnit.pas';

Var
  InputData : TArray<Integer>;
  OutputData : TArray<Integer>;
Begin
  Try
    Setlength(InputData, 100);
    For Var i := 0 To Length(InputData) - 1 Do InputData[i] := i + 1;
    OutputData := THigherOrder.Map<Integer>(InputData,
                                       Function(Item : Integer) : Integer
                                         Begin
                                           Result := Item * Item;
                                         End);
    For Var i := 0 To Length(OutputData) - 1
      Do Writeln(i + 1 : 4, ' squared = ', OutputData[i]);
    Write('Press return to continue...');
    Readln;
    Var ReduceResult := THigherOrder.Reduce<Integer>(OutputData,
                                                Function(Term1, Term2 : Integer) : Integer
                                                  Begin
                                                    Result := Term1 + Term2;
                                                  End, 0);
    Writeln('Sum of first 100 positive integers squared = ', ReduceResult);
    Write('Press return to continue...');
    Readln;
    OutputData := THigherOrder.Filter<Integer>(InputData,
                                           Function (Item : Integer) : Boolean
                                             Begin
                                               Result := Item Mod 2 = 0;
                                             End);
    For Var i := 0 To Length(OutputData) - 1
      Do Writeln('Next even positive integer between 1 and 100 = ', OutputData[i]);
    ReduceResult := THigherOrder.Reduce<Integer>(OutputData, Function(Term1, Term2 : Integer) : Integer
                                                          Begin
                                                            Result := Term1 + Term2;
                                                          End, 0);
    Write('Press return to continue...');
    Readln;
    Writeln('Sum of first 100 positive even integers = ', ReduceResult);
  Except
    On E: Exception
      Do Writeln(E.ClassName, ' : ', E.Message);
  End;
  Write('Press return to end...');
  Readln;
End.
```

Table 44.6 Using higher order functions Map, Reduce and Filter

45 Measuring time

Measuring time

Purpose: To learn how to use time measurement in Delphi

Using GetTickCount

Function **GetTickCount** and function **GetTickCount64** return the number of milliseconds since the operating system started. **GetTickCount** returns a 32 bit **DWord** which wraps every 49.7 days. Therefore it is better to use **GetTickCount64** (available since Windows Vista) which uses 64 bits.

Unfortunately, the resolution of the system timer which **GetTickCount** and **GetTickCount64** rely upon is typically in the range of 10 milliseconds to 16 milliseconds.

Figure 45.1 shows a simple use of **GetTickCount64**. The procedure **Sleep** pauses program execution for 1000 milliseconds.

Figure 45.2 shows the output from `GetTickCountProject` when executed.

```
Program GetTickCountProject;
{$APPTYPE CONSOLE}
{$R *.res}
Uses
  System.SysUtils,
  WinAPI.Windows;
Var
  Ticks : UInt64;
Begin
  Ticks := GetTickCount64;
  Sleep(1000); {Program execution paused for 1000 milliseconds}
  Writeln('ProcessingTime: ', (GetTickCount64 - Ticks).ToString, ' milliseconds');
  Readln;
End.
```

P

Figure 45.1 Using GetTickCount64

```
Z:\ProductionChapters\DelphiBook\Code\Chapter45\GetTickCountProject\Win32\Debug\GetTickCountProject.exe
ProcessingTime: 1015 milliseconds
```

Figure 45.2 GetTickCountProject in execution

Using TStopwatch

To solve the limited resolution and obtain sub-millisecond accuracy we turn to the type **TStopwatch** in the **System.Diagnostics** unit. A **TStopwatch** instance measures elapsed time by counting timer ticks in the underlying timer mechanism. If the installed hardware and operating system support a high-resolution performance counter, then the **TStopwatch** class uses that counter to measure elapsed time. Otherwise, the Stopwatch class uses the system timer to measure elapsed time.

Function **StartNew** is used to initialize and return a new **TStopwatch** value. **StartNew** sets the newly created stopwatch to "started". If a stopped stopwatch is required then use the **Create** method.

Figure 45.3 shows a program that uses a stopwatch of type **TStopwatch**.

Figure 45.4 shows it in execution timing the execution of `Sleep(1000)`.

```
Program StopwatchProject;
{$APPTYPE CONSOLE}
{$R *.res}
Uses
  System.SysUtils, System.Diagnostics;
Var
  Stopwatch : TStopwatch;
Begin
  StopWatch := TStopwatch.StartNew;{Gets an instance of a TStopwatch and starts it ticking}
  Sleep(1000); {Program execution paused for 1000 milliseconds}
  StopWatch.Stop;
  Writeln('ProcessingTime: ', Stopwatch.Elapsed.TotalMilliseconds.ToString, ' milliseconds');
  Readln;
End.
```

Figure 45.3 StopwatchProject which relies on TStopwatch

```
Z:\ProductionChapters\DelphiBook\Code\Chapter45\TStopWatchProject\Win32\Debug\StopwatchProject.exe
ProcessingTime: 1002.4814 milliseconds
```

Figure 45.4 StopwatchProject in execution

The frequency of the timer that the stopwatch relies upon is measured in ticks per second. The program shown in *Figure 45.5* obtains this frequency using the **Frequency** property. The reciprocal of the value returned gives the time interval between ticks in seconds, i.e. the resolution of the timer. If this value is multiplied by 1000000, the time interval will be converted to microseconds. For the computer this program executes on, the timer used is a high resolution one. The program confirms this by obtaining the value of property **IsHighResolution**.

```
Program StopwatchPrecisionProject;
{$APPTYPE CONSOLE}
{$R *.res}
Uses
  System.SysUtils, System.Diagnostics;
Var
  Stopwatch : TStopwatch;
Begin
  Stopwatch := TStopwatch.Create;
  Writeln('Maximum precision is ', Stopwatch.IsHighResolution);
  Writeln('Stopwatch frequency: ', Stopwatch.Frequency, 'ticks per second');
  Writeln('Maximum precision: ' + (1000000/Stopwatch.Frequency).ToString
                                + ' microseconds');

  Readln;
End.
```

Figure 45.5 StopwatchPrecisionProject

```
Z:\ProductionChapters\DelphiBook\Code\Chapter45\StopwatchFrequencyProject\Win32\Debug\StopwatchPrecisionProject.exe
Maximum precision is TRUE
Stopwatch frequency: 10000000 ticks per second
Maximum precision: 0.1 microseconds
```

Figure 45.6 StopwatchPrecisionProject in execution

46 Sensors

Sensors

Purpose: Introduction to using Delphi to interact with Bluetooth Low Energy sensors

The Bluetooth framework was introduced in XE7 with support for both VCL and FireMonkey applications. This framework makes it possible to connect to a large number of devices including desktop computers, phones, smart watches, heart rate monitors, weighing scales and many more devices.

Bluetooth Low Energy (BLE)

What is it?

Bluetooth Low Energy is a short range wireless technology for applications that operate with low-power and low-bandwidth requirements, i.e. battery powered applications which need the battery to last for a few years and which transmit a small amount of data at a time.

Table 46.1 shows how Bluetooth compares with other communication technologies. Bluetooth **v1.1** to **v2.0** is known as Classic Bluetooth. Bluetooth **v.4.0** and **v.5.0** are known as Bluetooth Low Energy or BLE.

Bluetooth	Ethernet	Wi-Fi	Modems
version 1.1 : 1 Mbps	802.3i : 10 Mbps	802.11 : 2 Mbps	V.21 : 0.3 kbps
version 2.0 : 3 Mbps	802.3u : 100 Mbps	802.11b : 11 Mbps	V.22 : 1.2 kbps
version 2.0 : 54 Mbps	802.3ab : 1000 Mbps	802.11g : 54 Mbps	V.32 : 9.6 kbps
version 4.0 : 0.3 Mbps	802.3an : 10000 Mbps	802.11n : 135 Mbps	V.34 : 28.6 kbps
version 5.0 : 2 Mbps			

Table 46.1 Communication technologies and their data bit rates

Bluetooth Classic is designed for transmitting continuous streams of data such as music playback whereas BLE is optimized for power efficiency. BLE has a peak current consumption during radio transmission of under 15mA, typically, and a chip operating voltage of 1.1V. This gives a peak power consumption value of 1.1V x 15mA = 16.5mW (Power = Voltage x Current). This makes it perfect for sensor-based or Internet of Things (IoT) use cases.

BLE operates in the 2.4 GHz ISM (Industrial, Scientific and Medical) wireless band with a range of 10-30 metres (v4.0), typically. The current version, Bluetooth version 5, was introduced in December 2016. It has a range of up to 50 metres.

> **Information**
>
> There are three Bluetooth device types:
> Bluetooth Smart which operates in single mode and offers only BLE;
> Bluetooth Smart Ready which operates in dual mode and offers both BLE and Bluetooth Classic;
> Bluetooth which offers Bluetooth Classic only.

The central-peripheral relationship in BLE

Devices such as laptop/desktop computers e.g. Apple Mac Pro/Apple iMac, or tablet or mobile phone are able to connect to multiple peripherals (external BLE devices) simultaneously, but each BLE device, e.g. heart rate monitor, acting as a peripheral can typically only interact with one central (device) at a time. BLE peripherals advertise their presence - see *Figure 46.2* - so that central devices may discover them. If a discovered BLE device is subsequently connected to a central, it stops advertising as a peripheral since it can no longer form a connection with other devices. The relationship between a BLE central and peripheral can be viewed as a client-server relationship - *Figure 46.1*. The server (peripheral) hosts a GATT (Generic **ATT**ribute profile) database that provides information which the client (central) accesses via BLE. In Bluetooth, all objects are identified by UUIDs. A UUID is a universally unique identifier used to label information. Bluetooth maintains a database of assigned numbers for standard objects, and assigns sub-ranges for vendors (that have paid enough for a reservation). The official Bluetooth website lists the **UUID**s of GATT services and characteristics as 16-bit (2-byte) values, e.g. `0x180F` for the **Battery Service** - https://www.bluetooth.com/specifications/assigned-numbers/

When dealing with UUIDs on Android, the 16-bit values are required to be used together with a base UUID of `00000000-0000-1000-8000-00805F9B34FB`, so the fully-qualified UUID for the Battery Service is:

`0000180F-0000-1000-8000-00805F9B34FB`

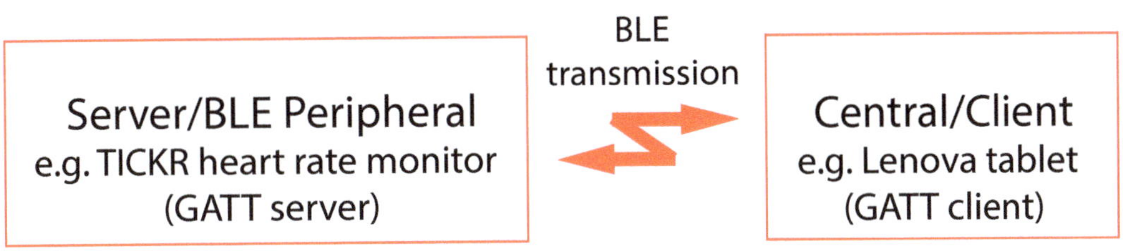

Figure 46.1 BLE peripheral communicating in a client-server relationship with BLE central executing a BLE app

GATT service

A **GATT service** is a collection of characteristics (data fields) that describes a feature of a device, e.g the state of the battery.

GATT characteristic

A **GATT characteristic** is an entity (e.g. data field) containing meaningful data that can typically be read from or written to, e.g. the battery level - see *Figure 46.2*.

Figure 46.3 shows other services available from the TICKR device, in particular the HEART RATE service. It has two characteristics: HEART RATE MEASUREMENT and BODY SENSOR LOCATION. This app has been designed to read and display the data associated with the HEART RATE MEASUREMENT characteristic when the **Read Characteristic** button is clicked - *Figure 46.4*.

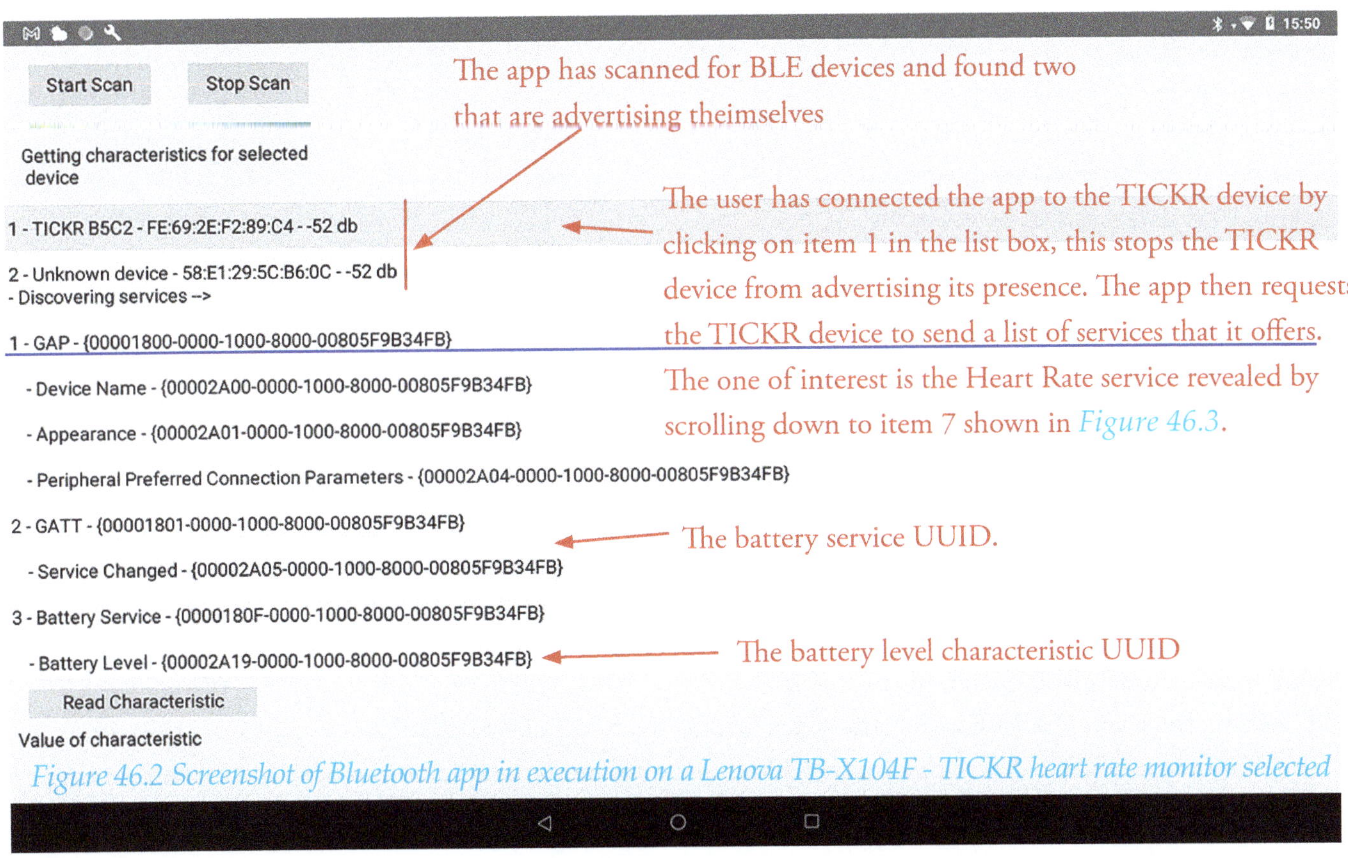

Figure 46.2 Screenshot of Bluetooth app in execution on a Lenova TB-X104F - TICKR heart rate monitor selected

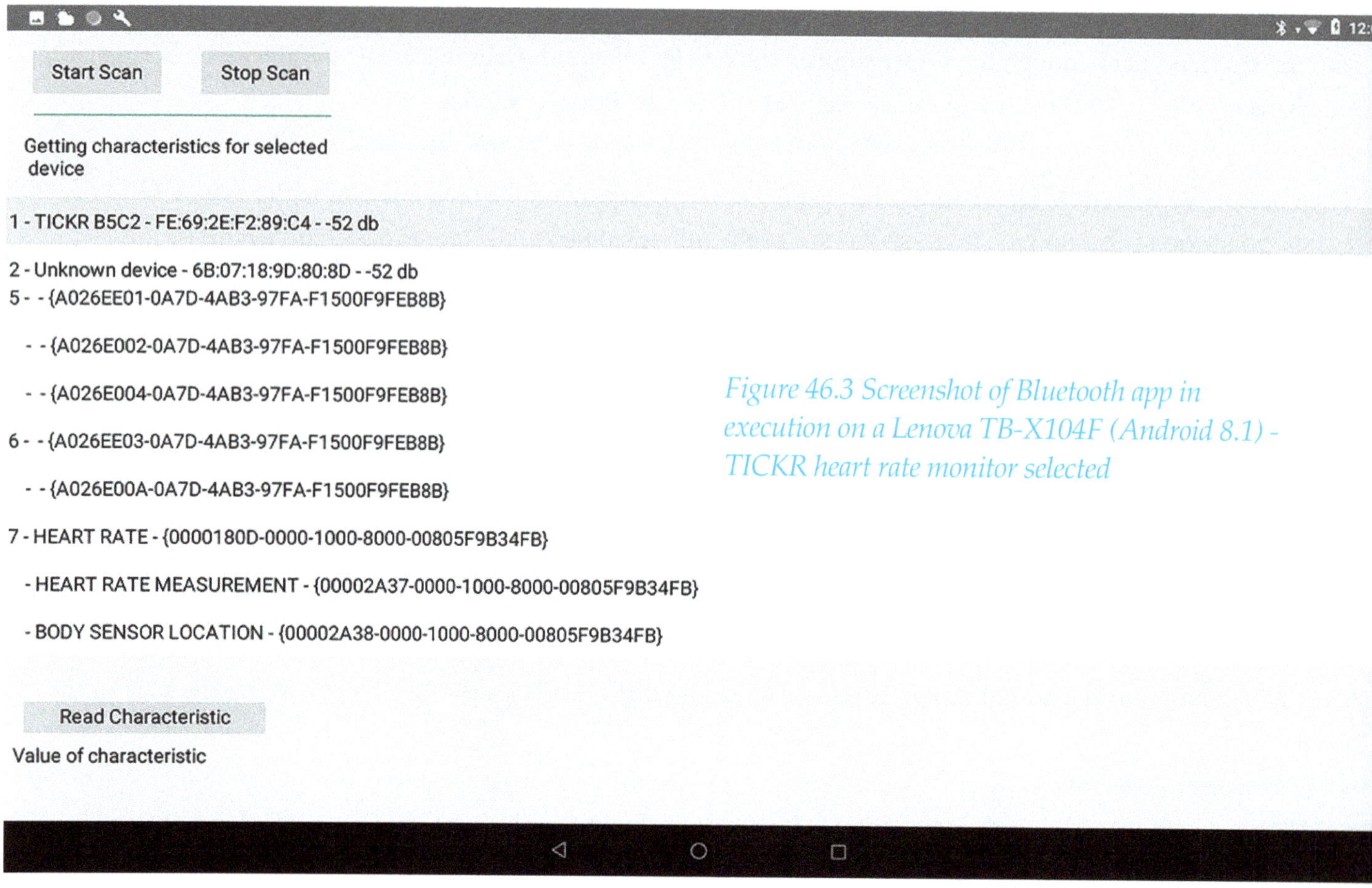

Figure 46.3 Screenshot of Bluetooth app in execution on a Lenova TB-X104F (Android 8.1) - TICKR heart rate monitor selected

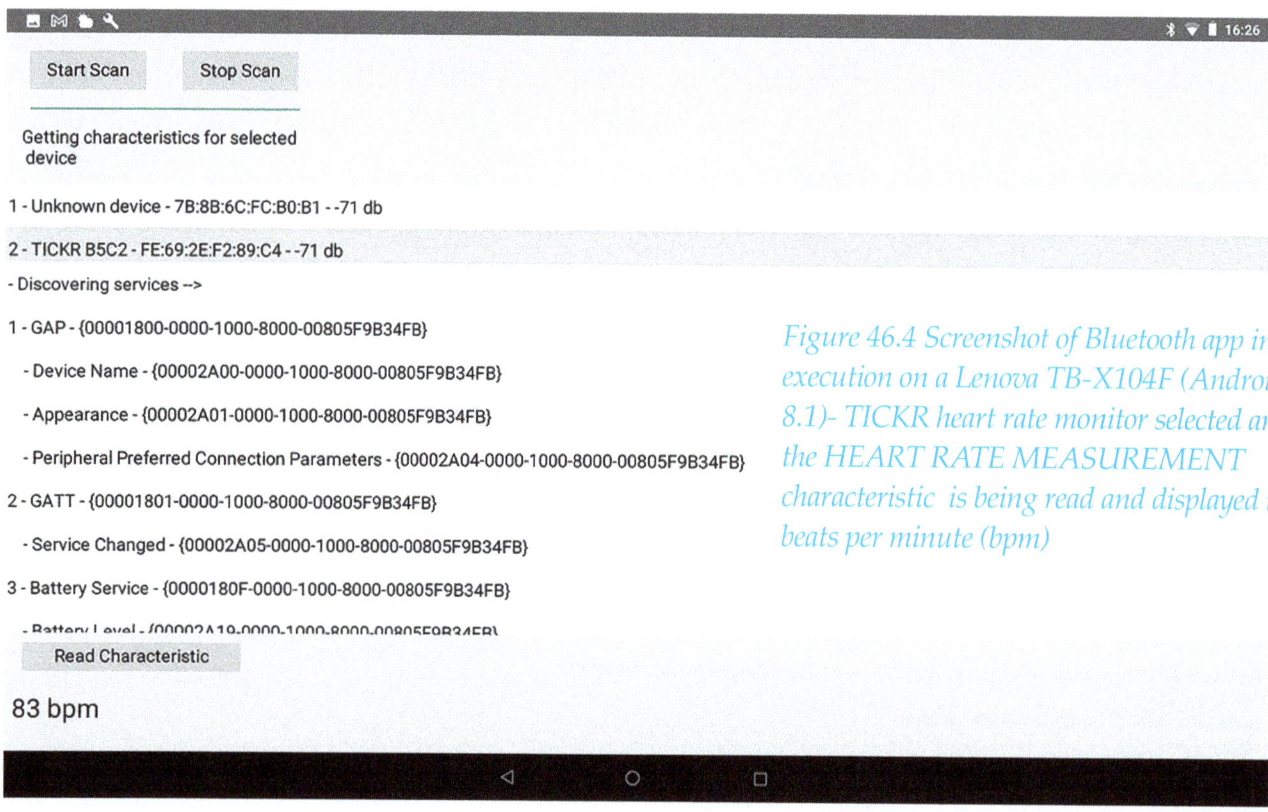

Figure 46.4 Screenshot of Bluetooth app in execution on a Lenova TB-X104F (Android 8.1)- TICKR heart rate monitor selected and the HEART RATE MEASUREMENT characteristic is being read and displayed in beats per minute (bpm)

BLE operations

There are three common BLE operations:

1. Write: The client (the BLE application) writes some bytes to a characteristic or descriptor on the server (BLE device). GATT descriptors contain additional information and attributes of a GATT characteristic. They can be used to describe the characteristic's features or to control certain behaviours of the

characteristic, e.g. enable reading/disable reading.
The server's firmware processes the write and performs some server-side (BLE device) operation in response to it. E.g, a smart thermostat may have a characteristic that changes the target temperature when written to.

2. Read: The client (the BLE application) reads the value of a characteristic or descriptor on the server (BLE device) and transforms it to a user-meaningful representation as prescribed by the BLE device's manufacturer. E.g., a heart rate monitor will have a characteristic whose value represents the current heart rate.
3. Notify/Indicate: The client (app) subscribes to a characteristic for notifications or indications, and is notified by the server (BLE device) when the value of the characteristic changes. A light sensor may have a notifiable characteristic that will report changes in light level when it's subscribed to.

Declaring required permissions in the Android Manifest

This section covers setting up a client application for an Android client - probably the easiest to demonstrate or work with. Working with iOS devices (smart phone/iPad) requires an Apple laptop/desktop and ideally, an app developer account. Windows BLE operation can be difficult to set up and not all Windows machines support BLE.

Start a new multi-device application (File|New|Multi-Device Application - Delphi then **select** Blank Application). In the menu bar of the IDE, **select** **Android 32-bit** (or **Android 64-bit** if your Android device is 64 bits) and the Android device on which the application will be installed, e.g. see *Figure 46.6*. **Set** the Style to **Android** and the View to **Master**. **Select** Project|Options|Uses Permissions and **tick** Bluetooth, Bluetooth admin and Access fine location as shown in part in *Figure 46.5*. **Click** Save.

These permissions are required for the following reasons:

- BLUETOOTH: Allows the app to connect to Bluetooth devices.
- BLUETOOTH_ADMIN: Allows the app to scan for and bond (used when an encrypted link is required) with Bluetooth devices.
- ACCESS_FINE_LOCATION: As of **Android MarshMallow (6.0)** and above, location permission is required for the app to get BLE scan results. The main motivation for this requirement is users' privacy. A BLE scan can often unintentionally reveal the user's location to unscrupulous app developers. Prior to **Android 10**, ACCESS_COARSE_LOCATION can be used to gain access to BLE scan results, however, it is best to use ACCESS_FINE_LOCATION, instead, since it works for all versions of Android.

Of the three declared permissions, only location is considered, in Android terms, a dangerous permission. This means that the user needs to explicitly grant location access to the app at install time. The app should therefore inform the user that their location will not be used for anything other than ensuring that BLE scanning works.

Add three panels (`TPanel`), `Panel1`, `Panel2` and `Panel3`, to the form. **Set** the **Align** property of `Panel1` to **Client**. **Set** the **Align** property of `Panel3` to **Bottom**. **Set** the **Align** property of `Panel2` to **Top**. **Add** two buttons, `Button1`, `Button2`, a label, `Label1`, and a progress bar (**TProgressBar**) to `Panel2`. **Add** a button, `Button3`, and a label, `Label2`, to `Panel3`. **Arrange** as shown in *Figure 46.7*. **Add** a **TBluetoothLE** and a **TTimer** component from the System Tool/ Component Palette to the form. **Change** the form's **Name** property to `frmBluetoothLEScanner` and its **Caption** property to `BluetoothLE Scanner`. **Change** the **Name** property of `Button1` to `btnStartScan` and the **Name** property of `Button2` to `btnStopScan`. **Change** their **Caption** properties to `Start Scan` and `Stop Scan`, respectively. **Change** the **Name** property of `Label1` to `lblTopPanel` and its **Text** property to `BLE Peripherals`. **Change** the **Name** property of `Button3` to `btnReadCharacteristic` and its **Text** property to `Read Characteristic`. **Change** the **Name** property of `Label2` to `lblBottomPanel` and its **Text** property to `Value of characteristic`.

Double click button `Start Scan` to create an **OnClick** event handler,

```
Procedure TfrmBluetoothLEScanner.btnStartScanClick(Sender : TObject).
```

Add to its body

```
lblTopPanel.Text := 'BLE Peripherals';
PermissionsService.RequestPermissions(
        [FLocationPermission], RequestPermissionsResult, DisplayRationale);
```

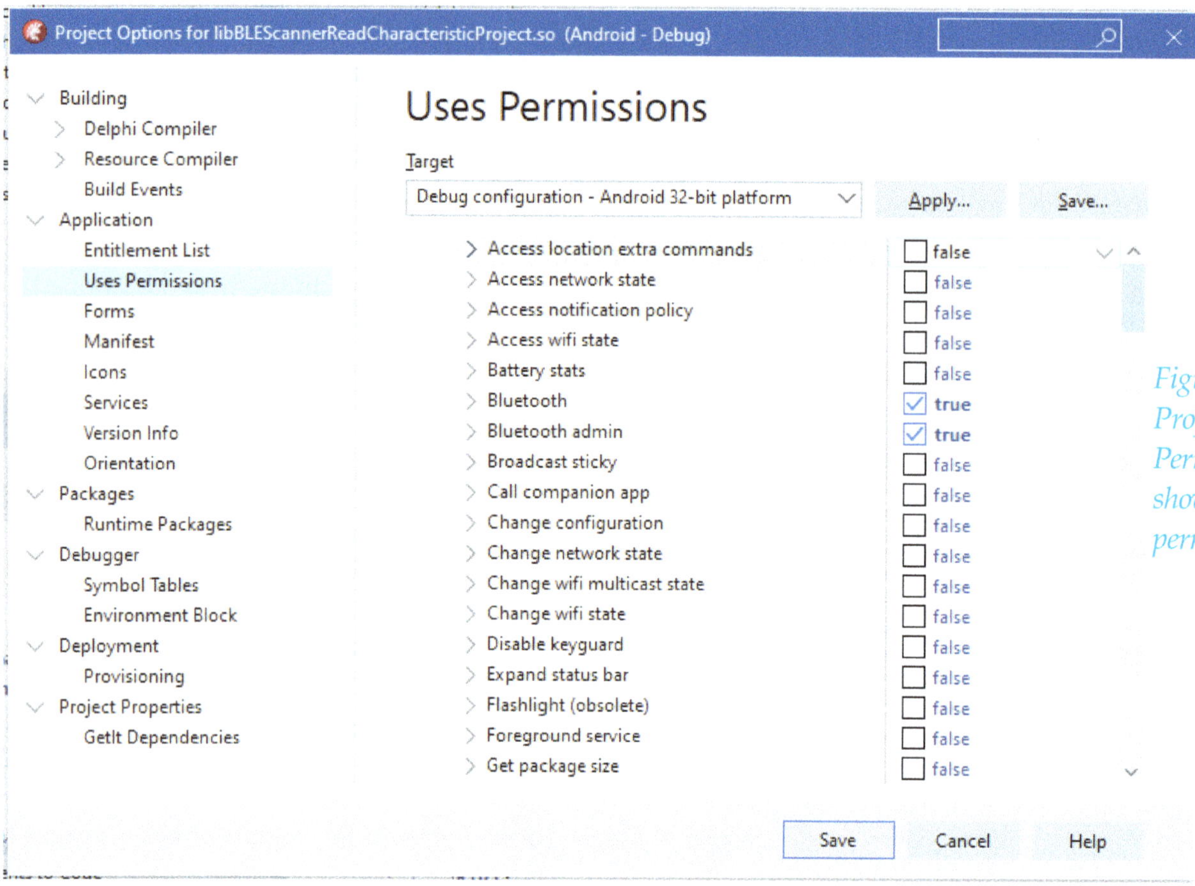

Figure 46.5 Project | Options | Uses Permissions window showing the first few permissions options

Add `System.Permissions` to the **Uses** clause in the **Interface** section. **Add** `FLocationPermission : String;` to the **Private** section of the **Class** definition.

Select the form in the **Object Inspector**, and then the **Events** tab. **Double click** the **OnCreate** field to create an **OnCreate** event handler for the form and **add** the following to its body

```
{$IFDEF ANDROID}
  FLocationPermission := JStringToString(
    TJManifest_permission.JavaClass.ACCESS_FINE_LOCATION);
{$ENDIF}
```

Add the following to the beginning of the **Implementation** section

```
Uses
  {$IFDEF ANDROID}
    Androidapi.Helpers,
    Androidapi.JNI.JavaTypes,
    Androidapi.JNI.Os,
  {$ENDIF}
  FMX.DialogService;
```

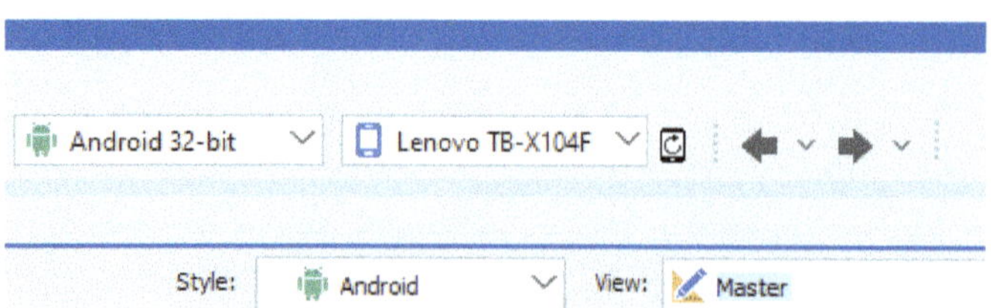

Figure 46.6 UI design for Android device

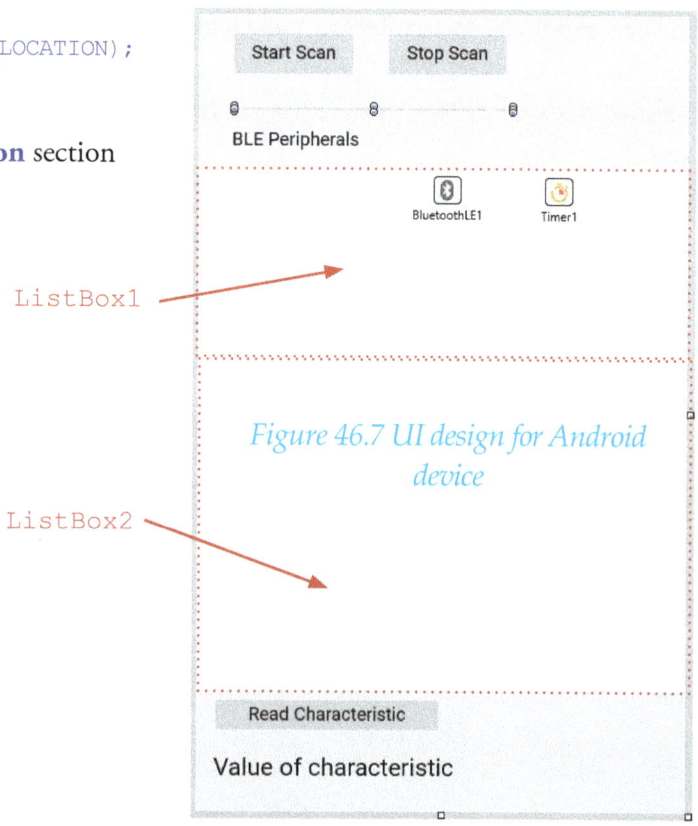

Figure 46.7 UI design for Android device

The RequestPermissions procedure's signature is defined in unit System.Permissions as follows

```
Procedure RequestPermissions(Const APermissions : TArray<String>;
  Const AOnRequestPermissionsResult : TRequestPermissionsResultProc;
  AOnDisplayRationale : TDisplayRationaleProc = nil); Overload; Virtual;
```

It is called as follows

```
PermissionsService.RequestPermissions([FLocationPermission],
                                      RequestPermissionsResult, DisplayRationale);
```

FLocationPermission has already been initialised to ACCESS_FINE_LOCATION.

The second and third parameters must each reference a procedure - RequestPermissionsResult and DisplayRationale, respectively. The first procedure if successful starts the BLE discovery process. The second informs the user why his/her permission is required and attempts to obtain this permission.

Add the following object method declaration to the **Private** section of the class definition

```
Procedure RequestPermissionsResult(Sender : TObject;
                                   Const APermissions : TArray<String>;
                                   Const AGrantResults : TArray<TPermissionStatus>);
```

Place the cursor in this declaration and **press** the key combination **CTRL+SHIFT+C** to create the skeleton code for this method in the **Implementation** section. **Add** the code shown in *Table 46.2* to the body of this object method.

In a similar way create another object method declaration and implementation as shown below and in *Table 46.3*.

```
Procedure DisplayRationale(Sender : TObject;
           Const APermissions : TArray<String>; Const APostRationaleProc : TProc);
```

Add a **TListBox** component, ListBox1, to Panel1 and **set** its **Align** property to **Top**. **Add** another **TListBox** component, ListBox2, to Panel1 and **set** its **Align** property to **Client**. **Adjust** their heights so that they are roughly in the proportions shown by the dotted red rectangles in *Figure 46.7*.

Add the following object method declaration to the **Private** section of the class definition

```
Procedure StartBLEDiscovery;
```

```
Procedure TfrmBluetoothLEScanner.RequestPermissionsResult(Sender : TObject;
                                      Const APermissions : TArray<String>;
                                      Const AGrantResults : TArray<TPermissionStatus>);
  Begin
    // 1 permission involved: ACCESS_FINE_LOCATION
    If (Length(AGrantResults) = 1) And (AGrantResults[0] = TPermissionStatus.Granted)
      Then StartBLEDiscovery
      Else TDialogService.ShowMessage('Cannot start BLE scan as the permission has not been granted');
  End;
```

Table 46.2 Object method TfrmBluetoothLEScanner.RequestPermissions

```
Procedure TfrmBluetoothLEScanner.DisplayRationale(Sender : TObject;
          Const APermissions : TArray<String>; Const APostRationaleProc : TProc);
  Begin
    TDialogService.ShowMessage('We need to be given permission to discover BLE devices',
      Procedure(Const AResult : TModalResult)
        Begin
          APostRationaleProc;
        End);
  End;
```

Table 46.3 Object method TfrmBluetoothLEScanner.DisplayRationale

Create the object method implementation as shown in *Table 46.4*. **Add** the following field definitions to the **Private** section of the class

```
Scanning : Boolean;
ScanningStart : Cardinal;
```

Set the **Interval** property of `Timer1` to 1000 (1 second in milliseconds) and **Enabled** property to **False**.
Define a constant, `ScanningTime`, in the **Interface** section as follows

```
Const
  ScanningTime = 10000; // 10s in milliseconds
```

`BluetoothLE1.DiscoverDevices(ScanningTime)` starts a discovery operation to find BLE devices using Bluetooth Low Energy. `ScanningTime` is a timeout argument which is how much time the application has allocated to it for discovering BLE devices using Bluetooth Low Energy. There are overloaded versions of `DiscoverDevices` that allow the application to specify an array or a list of service UUIDs to look for in BLE devices. The discovery operation will then ignore any BLE device that does not provide at least one service with an UUID specified in the array/list. When the discovery operation is finished, the `OnEndDiscoverDevices` event fires. `OnEndDiscoverDevices` provides a list of discovered BLE devices.

```
Procedure TfrmBluetoothLEScanner.StartBLEDiscovery;
  Begin
    If Not Scanning
      Then
        Begin
          Listbox1.Clear;
          {TThread.GetTickCount returns the number of milliseconds that
          have elapsed since the system was started.}
          ScanningStart := TThread.GetTickCount;
          BluetoothLE1.DiscoverDevices(ScanningTime);
          ProgressBar1.Value := 0;
          Timer1.Enabled := True;
          Scanning := True;
        End;
  End;
```

Table 46.4 Object method TfrmBluetoothLEScanner.StartBLEDiscovery

Select the **Events** tab for `BluetoothLE1` in the **Object Inspector** and **double click** the field for **OnEndDiscoverDevices** to create the event handler

```
Procedure TfrmBluetoothLEScanner.BluetoothLE1EndDiscoverDevices(
  Const Sender : TObject; Const ADeviceList : TBluetoothLEDeviceList);
```

Expand the skeleton event handler in the **Implementation** section with the code shown in *Table 46.5*.
Check that the **Max** and **Min** properties of `ProgressBar1` are 100 and 0, **correct** these properties if not.
Select the **Events** tab for `Timer1` in the **Object Inspector** and **double click** the field for **OnTimer** to create the event handler `Procedure TfrmBluetoothLEScanner.Timer1Timer(Sender : TObject)`.

Expand the skeleton event handler in the **Implementation** section with the code shown in *Table 46.6*.

Save All (**SHIFT+CTRL+S**) in folder `BLEScanner`- use project name `BLEReadCharacteristicProject.dproj` and unit name `BLEReadCharacteristicUnit.pas`.
Run without debugging[1] (**SHIFT+CTRL+F9**) and **click** **Start Scan**. *Figure 46.7* shows the result after the scan is finished for the author's BLE devices. The scan has identified two named BLE devices:

---

1 Debugging must be enabled on the client, e.g. tablet, on which the app is to run.

1. TICKR B5C2 - chest worn heart rate monitor.
2. CC2650 Sensor Tag - Texas Instrument BLE device.

and three unnamed devices.

Double click button `Stop Scan` to create an **OnClick** event handler,

```
Procedure TfrmBluetoothLEScanner.btnStopScanClick(Sender : TObject).
```

Add to its body

```
Timer1.Enabled := False;
Scanning := False;
BluetoothLE1.CancelDiscovery;
```

```
Procedure TfrmBluetoothLEScanner.BluetoothLE1EndDiscoverDevices(
                Const Sender : TObject; Const ADeviceList : TBluetoothLEDeviceList);
  Var
    DiscoveredDevicesCount : Integer;
    DiscoveredDeviceIndex : Integer;
    DiscoveredDevice : TBluetoothLEDevice;
    DiscoveredDeviceName : String;
  Begin
    If Scanning
      Then ProgressBar1.Value := ProgressBar1.Max;
    Timer1.Enabled := False;
    Scanning := False;
    DiscoveredDevicesCount := BluetoothLE1.DiscoveredDevices.Count;
    lblTopPanel.Text := 'No of discovered devices = ' + DiscoveredDevicesCount.ToString;
    For DiscoveredDeviceIndex := 0 To DiscoveredDevicesCount - 1
      Do
        Begin
          DiscoveredDevice := BluetoothLE1.DiscoveredDevices[DiscoveredDeviceIndex];
          DiscoveredDeviceName := DiscoveredDevice.DeviceName;
          If DiscoveredDeviceName = ''
            Then DiscoveredDeviceName := 'Unknown device';
          DiscoveredDeviceName := (DiscoveredDeviceIndex + 1).ToString
                                  + ' - ' + DiscoveredDeviceName
                                  + ' - ' + DiscoveredDevice.Identifier;
          Listbox1.Items.Add(DiscoveredDeviceName)
        End;
End;
```

Table 46.5 Event handler TfrmBluetoothLEScanner.BluetoothLE1EndDiscoverDevices

```
Procedure TfrmBluetoothLEScanner.Timer1Timer(Sender : TObject);
  Var
    TimeElapsed : Cardinal;//Represents an unsigned 32-bit integer type = 0..4294967295
  Begin
    TimeElapsed := TThread.GetTickCount - ScanningStart;
    ProgressBar1.Value := ProgressBar1.Max * (TimeElapsed.ToSingle / ScanningTime);
  End;
```

Table 46.6 Event handler TfrmBluetoothLEScanner. Timer1Timer

Select the Events tab for `ListBox1` in the Object Inspector and **double click** the field for OnClick to create the event handler

```
Procedure TfrmBluetoothLEScanner.ListBox1Click (Sender : TObject).
```

Expand the skeleton event handler in the Implementation section with the code shown in *Table 46.7*.

This event handler calls the class method `CreateAnonymousThread` that creates an instance of an internally derived TThread thread that calls the anonymous method

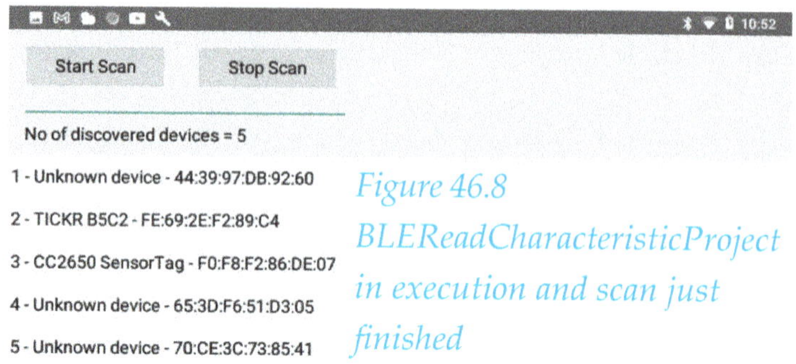

Figure 46.8 BLEReadCharacteristicProject in execution and scan just finished

```
Procedure
  Begin
    lblTopPanel.Text := 'Getting ...';
    If Not BluetoothLE1.DiscoveredDevices[ListBox1.ItemIndex].DiscoverServices
      Then TThread.Synchronize(Nil,
                Procedure
                  Begin
                    Listbox2.Items.Add('- Service discovery not allowed');
                    Listbox1.Enabled := True;
                  End);
  End);
```

The Start method must be called on this thread as shown in *Table 46.7* because it is placed in a suspended state on creation.

If services cannot be discovered then the anonymous procedure

```
Procedure
  Begin
    Listbox2.Items.Add('- Service discovery not allowed');
    ListBox1.Enabled := True;
  End);
```

is called.

```
Procedure TfrmBluetoothLEScanner.ListBox1Click(Sender : TObject);
  Begin
    btnStopScanClick(Sender);
    ListBox2.Clear;
    ListBox2.Items.Add('<-- Discovering services -->');
    TThread.CreateAnonymousThread(
      Procedure
        Begin
          lblTopPanel.Text := 'Getting characteristics for selected device';
          If Not BluetoothLE1.DiscoveredDevices[ListBox1.ItemIndex].DiscoverServices
            Then TThread.Synchronize(Nil,
                      Procedure
                        Begin
                          ListBox2.Items.Add('- Service discovery not allowed');
                          ListBox1.Enabled := True;
                        End);
        End).Start;
    ListBox1.Enabled := False;
  End;
```

Table 46.7 Event handler TfrmBluetoothLEScanner.ListBox1Click

To avoid multithread conflicts accessing `ListBox1` and `ListBox2`, this anonymous procedure is executed in the main thread which is achieved by calling it from within `TThread.Synchronize`. Execution of the current thread is suspended while this anonymous procedure executes in the main thread. The parameter occupied by **Nil** can used to pass information to the main thread, as none is required **Nil** is used.

The **DiscoverServices** method is called to search for the available services on the selected BLE device.

The **OnServicesDiscovered** event fires when the discovery operation finishes unless the service discovery operation fails. **OnServicesDiscovered** occurs once per BLE device. The handler of **OnServicesDiscovered** receives the following parameters:

- **Sender** is the discovered device.
- **AServiceList** is a list of services that the discovered device provides.

Select the **Events** tab for `BluetoothLE1` in the **Object Inspector** and **double click** the field for **OnServicesDiscovered** to create the event handler

```
Procedure TfrmBluetoothLEScanner.BluetoothLE1ServicesDiscovered(
      Const Sender : TObject; Const AServiceList : TBluetoothGattServiceList);
```

Expand the skeleton event handler in the **Implementation** section with the code shown in *Table 46.8*.

Save All (SHIFT+CTRL+S).

Run without debugging (SHIFT+CTRL+F9) and **click** **Start Scan** then **click** on a discovered device to get its services and characteristics.

```
Procedure TfrmBluetoothLEScanner.BluetoothLE1ServicesDiscovered(
  Const Sender : TObject; Const AServiceList : TBluetoothGattServiceList);
  Var
    ServiceIndex: Integer;
    CharacteristicIndex: Integer;
  Begin
    If AServiceList.Count > 0
      Then
        Begin
          For ServiceIndex := 0 To AServiceList.Count - 1
            Do
              Begin
                Service := AServiceList[ServiceIndex];
                ListBox2.Items.Add((ServiceIndex + 1).ToString
                                    + ' - ' + Service.UUIDName
                                    + ' - ' + Service.UUID.ToString);
                For CharacteristicIndex := 0 To Service.Characteristics.Count - 1
                  Do
                    Begin
                      Characteristic := Service.Characteristics[CharacteristicIndex];
                      ListBox2.Items.Add('     - ' + Characteristic.UUIDName
                                          + ' - ' + Characteristic.UUID.ToString);
                    End;
              End;
        End
      Else ListBox2.Items.Add('- Access not allowed or no service available');
    ListBox1.Enabled := True;
  End;
```

Table 46.8 Event handler TfrmBluetoothLEScanner.BluetoothLE1ServicesDiscovered

Figure 46.9 shows some of the services and characteristics for the selected BLE device, a **Texas Instruments CC2650 Sensor Tag**, the server, connected to the client (app running on a Lenova tablet). By scrolling down, the more interesting services[2], items labelled 5 to 7, are brought into view.

Service 5 is a temperature service which hasn't worked since 2017 when Texas Instruments withdrew the Infra Red thermopile temperature chip, TMP007[3].

Service 6 is a humidity service which is functioning and which also senses temeperature.

Service 7 is a barometric pressure sensor which also senses temperature.

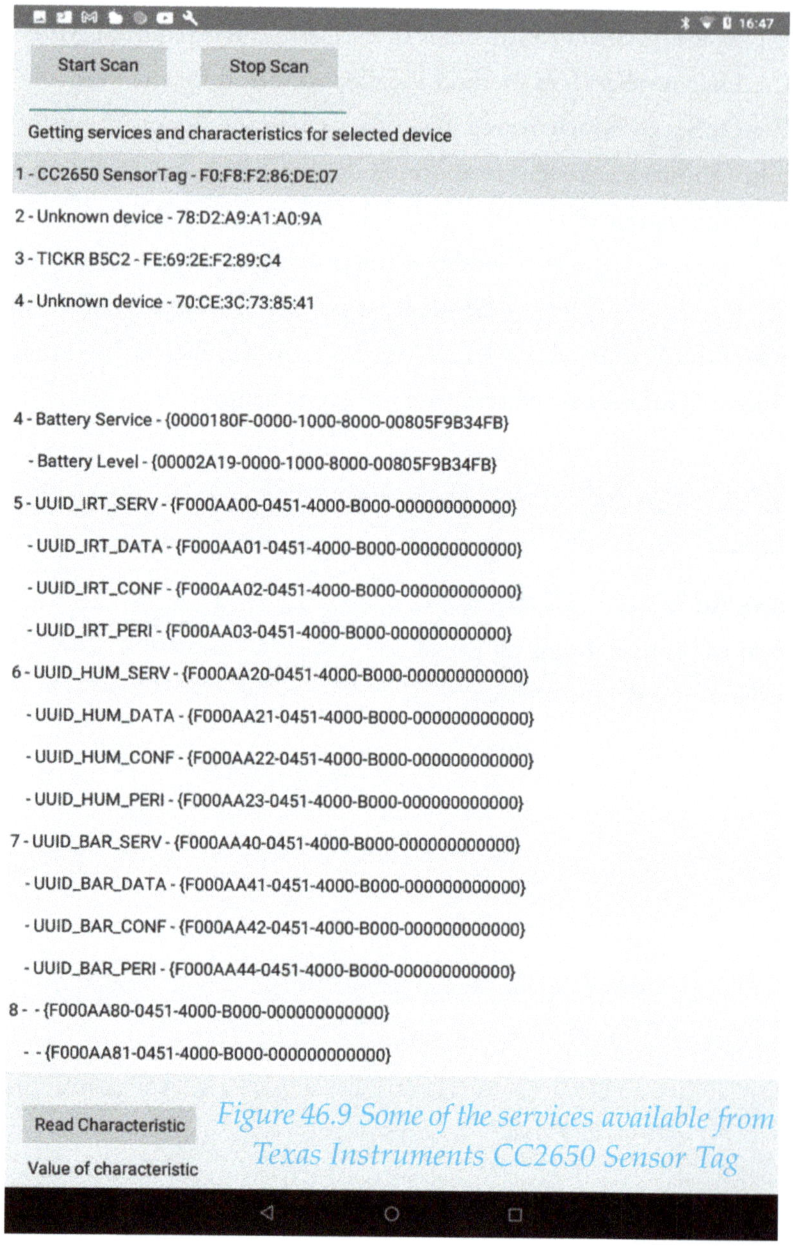

Figure 46.9 Some of the services available from Texas Instruments CC2650 Sensor Tag

Heart rate measurement

Heart rate measurement is fairly straightforward to implement. A quick look at the bluetooth specifications document

https://btprodspecificationrefs.blob.core.windows.net/assigned-values/16-bit%20UUID%20Numbers%20Document.pdf

reveals that UUID 2A37 (*Figure 46.10*) has been allocated to heart rate measurement.

When dealing with UUIDs on Android, the 16-bit values are required to be used together with a base UUID of `00000000-0000-1000-8000-00805F9B34FB`, so the fully-qualified UUID for the Heart Rate Measurement characteristic is: `00002A37-0000-1000-8000-00805F9B34FB`.

The same document reveals that the Heart Rate service has UUID `180D` (*Figure 46.11*), so its fully-qualified UUID is `0000180D-0000-1000-8000-00805F9B34FB`.

Add the following constant definitions to the existing **Const** section of the application.

```
HRSERVICE : TBluetoothUUID = '{0000180D-0000-1000-8000-00805F9B34FB}';
HRMEASUREMENT_CHARACTERISTIC : TBluetoothUUID = '{00002A37-0000-1000-8000-00805F9B34FB}';
```

GATT Characteristic and Object Type	0x2A34	Glucose Measurement Context
GATT Characteristic and Object Type	0x2A35	Blood Pressure Measurement
GATT Characteristic and Object Type	0x2A36	Intermediate Cuff Pressure
GATT Characteristic and Object Type	0x2A37	Heart Rate Measurement
GATT Characteristic and Object Type	0x2A38	Body Sensor Location

Figure 46.10 Some GATT Characteristic allocated UUIDs

2 https://usermanual.wiki/Document/CC265020SensorTag20Users20Guide2020Texas20Instruments20Wiki.2070227354.pdf
3 https://www.mouser.com/PCN/Texas_Instruments_PCN20171205004_20171206152122163.pdf

GATT Service	0x1809	Health Thermometer
GATT Service	0x180A	Device Information
GATT Service	0x180D	Heart Rate
GATT Service	0x180E	Phone Alert Status
GATT Service	0x180F	Battery
GATT Service	0x1810	Blood Pressure

Figure 46.11 Some GATT Services allocated UUIDs

The **Heart Rate Service 1.0** specification document may be downloaded from https://www.bluetooth.com/specifications/specs/. In typical applications, the **Heart Rate Measurement** characteristic is notified approximately once per second and includes the **Heart Rate Measurement Value** field which contains the measurement in beats per minute. Heart rate measurement is a notification service so must be subscribed to according to this specification.

Double click the `Read Characteristic` button to create an **OnClick** event handler. **Add** the code shown in *Table 46.9* to its body. The call

```
BluetoothLE1.SubscribeToCharacteristic(ADevice, Characteristic);
```

sets up the heart rate monitor BLE device to notify the client (app) when the heart rate measurement changes. **Select** the **Events** tab for `BluetoothLE1` in the **Object Inspector** and **double click** the field for **OnCharacteristicRead** to create the event handler

```
Procedure TfrmBluetoothLEScanner.BluetoothLE1CharacteristicRead(
          Const Sender : TObject;
          Const ACharacteristic : TBluetoothGattCharacteristic;
          AGattStatus : TBluetoothGattStatus);
```

```
Procedure TfrmBluetoothLEScanner.btnReadCharacteristicClick(Sender : TObject);
  Var
    ADevice : TBluetoothLEDevice;
  Begin
    Service := Nil;
    Characteristic := Nil;
    ADevice := BluetoothLE1.DiscoveredDevices[ListBox1.ItemIndex];
    lblBottomPanel.Text := ADevice.Identifier;
    Service := BluetoothLE1.GetService(ADevice, HRSERVICE);
    If Service <> Nil
      Then
        Begin
          Characteristic := BluetoothLE1.GetCharacteristic(Service, HRMEASUREMENT_CHARACTERISTIC);
          If Characteristic <> Nil
            Then
              Begin
                lblBottomPanel.Text := Characteristic.UUIDName;
                BluetoothLE1.SubscribeToCharacteristic(ADevice, Characteristic);
              End
            Else lblBottomPanel.Text := 'No Characteristic.UUIDName';
        End
      Else
        Begin
          lblTopPanel.Font.Size := 26;
          lblTopPanel.Text := 'Service not found';
        End;
  End;
```

Table 46.9 Event handler TfrmBluetoothLEScanner.btnReadCharacteristicClick

Expand the skeleton event handler in the **Implementation** section with the code shown in *Table 46.10*.
The **OnCharacteristicRead** event fires whenever the app is notified by the BLE device of a change in heart rate. According to the HRS_SPEC_V10.pdf document, the **Heart Rate Value Format** bit (bit 0 of the **Flags** field, `Bytes[0]`) indicates if the data format of the **Heart Rate Measurement Value** field is in a format of `UINT8` or `UINT16`. When the **Heart Rate Value** is sent in `UINT8` format, the **Heart Rate Value Format** bit is set to 0. When the **Heart Rate Value** is sent in `UINT16` format, the **Heart Rate Value Format** bit is set to 1. Hence the

```
Procedure TfrmBluetoothLEScanner.BluetoothLE1CharacteristicRead(
            Const Sender : TObject; Const ACharacteristic : TBluetoothGattCharacteristic;
            AGattStatus : TBluetoothGattStatus);
  Var
    Bytes : TBytes;
    HeartRate : Integer;
  Begin
    If aGattStatus = TBluetoothGattStatus.Success
      Then
        Begin
          Bytes := ACharacteristic.Value;
          If (Bytes[0] And $1) = 0
            Then HeartRate := Bytes[1]
            Else HeartRate := Bytes[1] + (Bytes[2] * 16);
          lblBottomPanel.Text := 'Heart Rate: ' + HeartRate.ToString + ' bpm';
        End
      Else lblBottomPanel.Text := 'Gatt status is not SUCCESS. Cannot read characteristic.';
  End;
```

Table 46.10 Event handler TfrmBluetoothLEScanner.BluetoothLE1CharacteristicRead

test `(Bytes[0] And $1) = 0` in the event handler shown in *Table 46.10*. The **Heart Rate Value** occupies `Bytes[1]` if `UINT8` and `Bytes[1]` and `Bytes[2]` if `UINT16`. The value of the **Heart Rate Value Format** bit may change during a connection but this will only occur if the heart rate exceeds 255 bpm.
The heart rate monitor used to test the application is a Wahoo TICKR which may be purchased for about £40.
Save All (SHIFT+CTRL+S).
Run without debugging (SHIFT+CTRL+F9) and **click** Start Scan then **click** on a discovered device to get its services and characteristics.
Click the `Read Characteristic` button to start the heart rate reading process. *Figure 46.12* shows the app executing on a Lenova tablet.

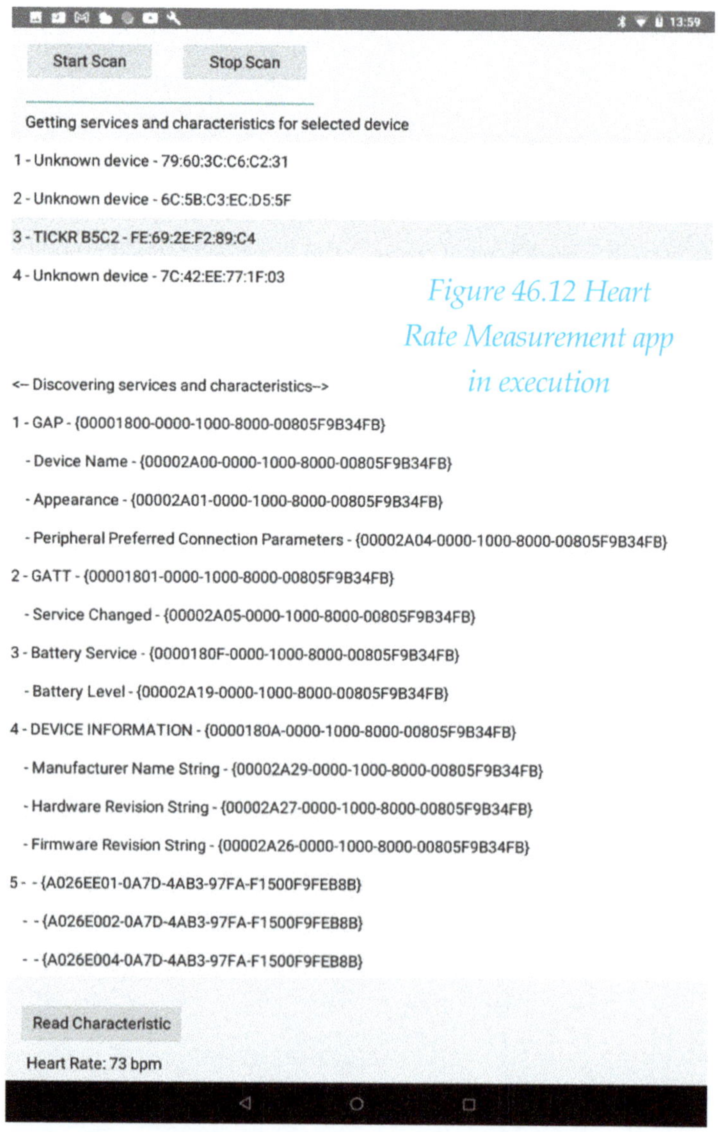

Figure 46.12 Heart Rate Measurement app in execution

LightBlue®

When debugging Delphi BLE apps it is useful to have an independent and reliable means of discovering and scanning BLE devices. LightBlue® is an application that connects to devices that use Bluetooth Low Energy. With LightBlue®, it is possible to scan, connect to and browse any nearby BLE device. The app is free and may be downloaded from Google Play Store or from Apple's App Store.

47 Introduction to OpenGL

Introduction to OpenGL

Purpose: To become familiar with graphics based on OpenGL

OpenGL

OpenGL is a worldwide standard for 3D computer graphics programming. It has its origins in the earlier GL ("Graphics Library") system which was invented by Silicon Graphics Inc. as the means for programming their high-performance specialised graphics workstations. GL was subsequently adapted by various people to run on other types of machine. In 1992, a variation of GL called OpenGL was announced. OpenGL differs from GL in that OpenGL was intentionally designed to be platform-independent, so that it would work across a whole range of computer hardware, not just Silicon Graphics machines.

OpenGL itself is not a programming language, or a software library. It is a specification of an Application Programming Interface (API) for computer graphics programming. As such, OpenGL defines a set of functions for doing computer graphics, e.g. **glVertex3f**, **glColor3f**. These functions must be implemented before they can be used to perform graphics on a particular machine, i.e. an implementation of OpenGL is required for the particular machine and its operating system.

Drawing two-dimensional objects

Table 47.1 shows a procedure that makes a rectangle by specifying its four corners (vertices) using X-axis coordinates `Left`, `Right`, and Y-coordinates `Top`, `Bottom`, and the line drawing and fill colour using three parameters `r`, `g` and `b` corresponding to red, green and blue. The type `GLfloat` is a synonym for `Single`. *Figure 47.1* shows the coordinate system.

```
Procedure TfrmOpenGL.MakeRectangle(Left, Right,
                                   Top, Bottom,
                                   r, g, b : GLfloat);
  Begin
    glBegin(GL_POLYGON);
      glColor3f(r, g, b);//r,g,b values 0.0 to 1.0
      glVertex2f(Left, Bottom);
      glVertex2f(Right, Bottom);
      glVertex2f(Right, Top);
      glVertex2f(Left, Top);
    glEnd;
  End;
```

P

Table 47.1 OpenGL commands to make a rectangle

In OpenGL, an object is usually constructed first in local space and then scaled and moved to world space.

In local space, the origin of the coordinate system is placed at the centre of the object.

For example, to make a red rectangle with sides of equal length, `MakeRectangle` would be called as follows

```
MakeRectangle(-1.0,+1.0,-1.0,+1.0,1,0,0);
```

Figure 47.2 shows the local space coordinate system used to make this rectangle.

To place this rectangle in the world system, the rectangle is moved to the right 1 unit from the origin along the X-axis and 5 units backwards from the origin along the Z-axis in the negative direction using

```
glTranslate(1.0, 0.0, -5.0);
```

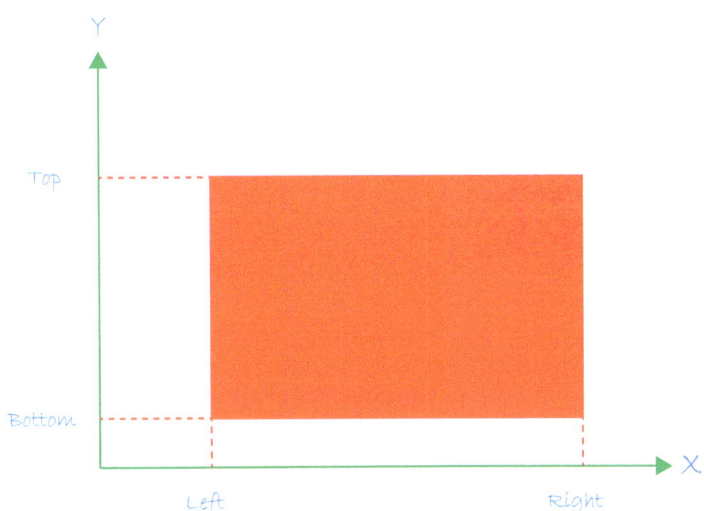

Figure 47.1 Coordinate system

The result is shown in *Figure 47.3* which shows the rectangle's location after translation to world space coordinates.

The coordinates of top left vertex of the rectangle are labelled $(x_{eye}, y_{eye}, z_{eye})$ in *Figure 47.4*. These are the X, Y and Z distances with reference to the eye located at the origin of the world coordinate system shown in *Figure 47.4*. This vertex and the other three vertices of the square are mapped onto the two-dimensional surface located at **P** in *Figure 47.4*, a distance `-n` along the Z-axis, using a projection matrix set up as follows

```
glMatrixMode(GL_PROJECTION); //Create Projection Matrix
glLoadIdentity; // Clear Projection matrix
glFrustum(l, r, b, t, n, cFarZ);
```

In the **Cartesian** world or **Euclidean** world two parallel lines can never intersect unlike in the perspective world, where parallel lines converge in the distance.

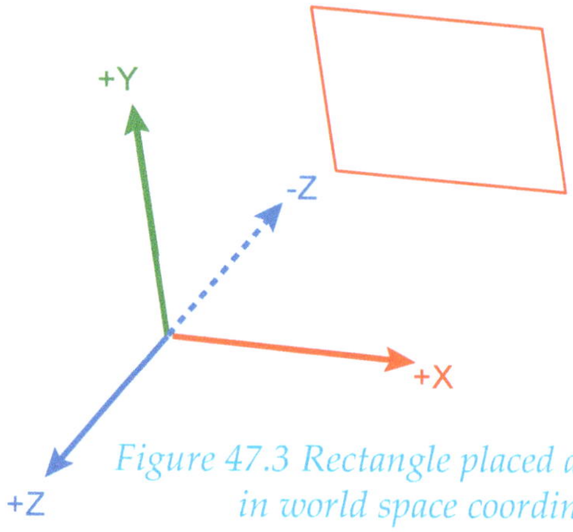

Figure 47.3 Rectangle placed at (1, 0.0, -5) in world space coordinates

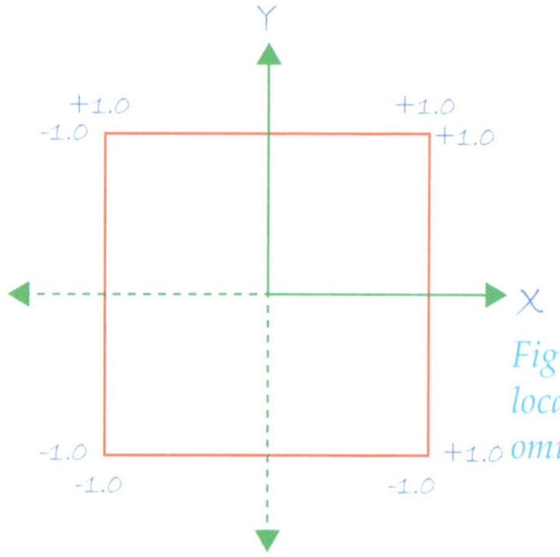

Figure 47.2 A rectangle drawn in local space coordinates (fill colour omitted for clarity)

The projection modelled in *Figure 47.4* is a perspective one in which lines headed in the Z-axis direction converge at infinity. To model this convergence, a fourth coordinate, w, is added to the world space coordinates as follows

$$(x_{eye}, y_{eye}, z_{eye}, w_{eye})$$

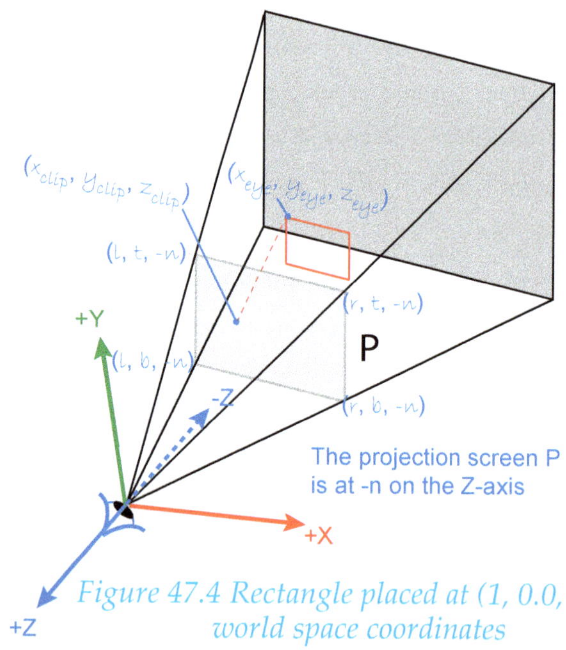

Figure 47.4 Rectangle placed at (1, 0.0, -5) in world space coordinates

These are known as **homogeneous coordinates** to distinguish them from **Cartesian space** or **Euclidean space coordinates**. The coordinate w is needed in order to handle perspective. We map between the two coordinate systems as follows

$$(x_{eye})_{cartesian} = \frac{(x_{eye})_{homogeneous}}{w}$$

$$\begin{pmatrix} x_{clip} \\ y_{clip} \\ z_{clip} \\ w_{clip} \end{pmatrix} = M_{projection} \cdot \begin{pmatrix} x_{eye} \\ y_{eye} \\ z_{eye} \\ w_{eye} \end{pmatrix}$$

Figure 47.5 Perspective projection

Before applying the perspective projection operation, the values of $(x_{eye})_{cartesian}$ and $(x_{eye})_{homogeneous}$ are identical which requires that $w = 1$. This is no longer the case after applying the perspective projection shown in *Figure 47.5*, i.e. $w_{clip} \neq 1$.

Also, projecting onto **P** means $z_{clip} = -n$ and

$$x_{clip} = \frac{-n \cdot x_{eye}}{z_{eye}} \qquad y_{clip} = \frac{-n \cdot y_{eye}}{z_{eye}}$$

The projection matrix $M_{projection}$ maps eye coordinates to clip coordinates.

In *Figure 47.4* the second grey panel is located at -cFarZ along the Z-axis.

The descriptive name for the truncated pyramid shape defined by the two greyed panels in *Figure 47.4* is a **frustum**.

After the eye coordinates have been transformed by multiplying by matrix $M_{projection}$, the clip coordinates are still **homogeneous coordinates**. These are now transformed back into Cartesian coordinates by dividing by w_{clip} to produce **normalised device coordinates** (NDC) - *Figure 47.6*.

Normalised Device Coordinates (NDC)

$$\begin{pmatrix} x_{ndc} \\ y_{ndc} \\ z_{ndc} \end{pmatrix} = \begin{pmatrix} x_{eye}/w_{clip} \\ y_{eye}/w_{clip} \\ z_{eye}/w_{clip} \end{pmatrix}$$

Figure 47.6 Normalised device coordinates

Information

See Professor John Kennedy's '3-Dimensional Graphing Transformations' paper:
https://drive.google.com/file/d/1se-RQQeeESp6mm3A_xoBJg-8zRiGaDIO/view

Frustum culling (clipping) is performed on the clip coordinates, just before dividing by w_{clip}. The clip coordinates x_{clip}, y_{clip}, z_{clip} are tested by comparing with w_{clip}. If any clip coordinate is less than $-w_{clip}$ or greater than $+w_{clip}$, then the vertex is discarded. The edges of any affected polygons are then reconstructed where partial clipping has occurred.

In perspective projection, a 3D point in a truncated pyramid frustum (eye coordinates) is mapped to a cube (NDC) as shown in *Figure 47.7*.

The X coordinate range [l, r] is mapped to [-1, 1].

The Y coordinate range [b, t] is mapped to [-1, 1].

The Z coordinate range [-n, -cFarZ] is mapped to [-1, 1].

The normalised device coordinates are now mapped to the window coordinates of the display device.

Given a window of width, width, and height, height, located at x_{window}, y_{window}, the relationship between NDC and the window coordinates is linear and is as follows

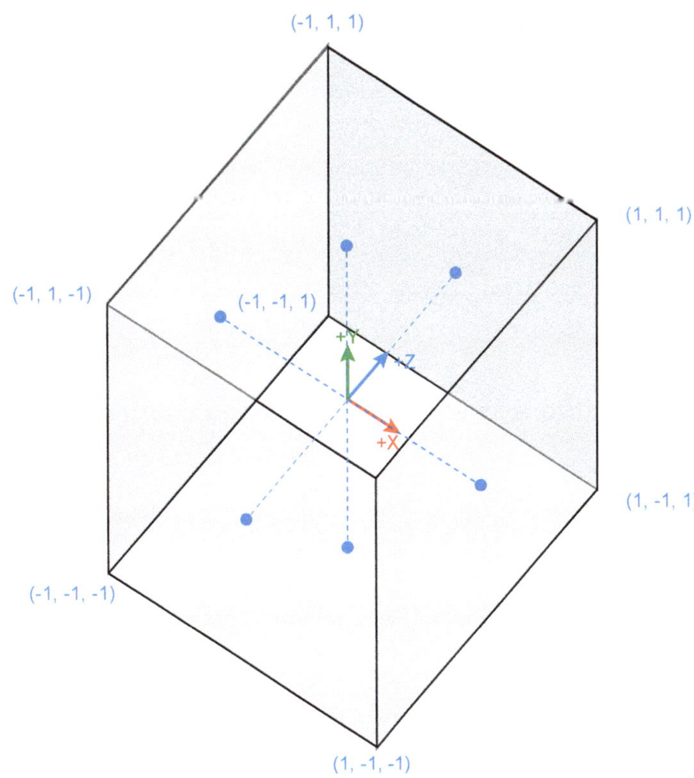

Figure 47.7 Normalised device coordinates

X-axis: -1 → x_{window} **Y-axis:** -1 → y_{window} **Z-axis:** -1 → n

X-axis: +1 → width + x_{window} **Y-axis:** +1 → height + y_{window} **Z-axis:** +1 → cFarZ

A depth test is performed on the z_{window} values to determine when an object is front of another. The outcome of the depth test determines whether one object should fully or partially cover another object when both are rendered (drawn) on the screen. The x_{window} and y_{window} values encode the perpective.

$$\begin{pmatrix} x_{window} \\ y_{window} \\ z_{window} \end{pmatrix} = \begin{pmatrix} \frac{width}{2} x_{ndc} + \left(x + \frac{width}{2}\right) \\ \frac{height}{2} y_{ndc} + \left(y + \frac{height}{2}\right) \\ \left(\frac{cFarZ - n}{2}\right) z_{ndc} + \left(\frac{cFarZ + n}{2}\right) \end{pmatrix}$$

Figure 47.8 Mapping from NDC coordinates to window coordinates

As the transformed depth coordinate moves further away from the near clipping plane P, its location becomes increasingly less precise.

Table 47.2 shows `MakeRectangle` being used to create two rectangles, one red (rgb value: `1, 0, 0`), and one green (rgb value: `0, 1, 0`). Each rectangle is magnified 3x in the X, Y and Z directions by applying the OpenGL command `glScale(3, 3, 3)` to it.

P

```
Procedure TfrmOpenGL.Draw;
  Begin
    glClearColor(1.0, 1.0, 1.0, 1.0);
    glClear(GL_COLOR_BUFFER_BIT or GL_DEPTH_BUFFER_BIT);
    glMatrixMode(GL_MODELVIEW); //Creates 4 x 4 ModelView matrix
    glLoadIdentity; //Sets ModelView matrix to Identity matrix
    glTranslate(1, 0.0, -5); //Add translation after scaling added to ModelView matrix
    glScale(3,3,3); //Add scaling first to ModelView matrix
    MakeRectangle(-1.0, +1.0, -1.0, +1.0, 1.0, 0.0, 0.0); //Local coordinates view
    glLoadIdentity; //Sets ModelView matrix to Identity matrix, i.e. default state
    glTranslate(2, 1, -5); //Add translation after scaling added to ModelView matrix
    glScale(3,3,3); //Add scaling first to ModelView matrix
    MakeRectangle(-1.0, +1.0, -1.0, +1.0, 0.0, 1.0, 0.0);  //Local coordinates view
    //Force OpenGL commands to execute
    SwapBuffers(wglGetCurrentDC); //Uses double buffering to avoid flicker
  End;
```

Table 47.2 OpenGL commands to make a rectangle

Each magnified rectangle is then moved to a position in world coordinate space, using the OpenGL command `glTranslate (1, 0.0, -5)` for the red rectangle, and `glTranslate (2, 1, -5)` for the green rectangle.

The **ModelView** matrix is a 4 x 4 matrix that is cleared by loading it with the **Identity matrix** - *Figure 47.9*.

$$\begin{bmatrix} 1 & 0 & 0 & 0 \\ 0 & 1 & 0 & 0 \\ 0 & 0 & 1 & 0 \\ 0 & 0 & 0 & 1 \end{bmatrix}$$

Figure 47.9 Identity matrix

`glScale(3, 3, 3)` modifies the **ModelView** matrix as shown in *Figure 47.10*. The general form of the **ModelView** scaling matrix is shown in *Figure 47.11*.

The general form of the **ModelView** translation matrix is shown in *Figure 47.12*. The centre of the object in local coordinate space is moved X units in the X direction, Y units in the Y direction and Z units in the Z direction. The **ModelView** matrix for `glTranslate(1, 0.0, -5)` alone is shown in *Figure 47.13*. Combining both scaling and translation, the **ModelView** matrix for `glScale(3, 3, 3)` followed by `glTranslate(1, 0.0, -5)` becomes the matrix shown in *Figure 47.15*.

Note that multiplying the translation matrix by the scaling matrix results in a different ModelView matrix.

Order is important.

The position vector for the upper left vertex of the red rectangle in local space is shown in *Figure 47.14*. After matrix multiplication by the ModelView matrix shown in *Figure 47.15*, the position vector in world space is as shown in *Figure 47.16*.

$$\begin{bmatrix} 3 & 0 & 0 & 0 \\ 0 & 3 & 0 & 0 \\ 0 & 0 & 3 & 0 \\ 0 & 0 & 0 & 1 \end{bmatrix}$$

Figure 47.10 Scaling by 3 matrix

$$\begin{bmatrix} S_x & 0 & 0 & 0 \\ 0 & S_y & 0 & 0 \\ 0 & 0 & S_z & 0 \\ 0 & 0 & 0 & 1 \end{bmatrix}$$

Figure 47.11 Scaling by S_x, S_y, S_z matrix

$$\begin{bmatrix} 1 & 0 & 0 & X \\ 0 & 1 & 0 & Y \\ 0 & 0 & 1 & Z \\ 0 & 0 & 0 & 1 \end{bmatrix}$$

Figure 47.12 Translation matrix - movement by X, Y, Z

$$\begin{bmatrix} 1 & 0 & 0 & 1 \\ 0 & 1 & 0 & 0 \\ 0 & 0 & 1 & -5 \\ 0 & 0 & 0 & 1 \end{bmatrix}$$

Figure 47.13 Translation by 1 unit in X direction, 0 units in Y direction, and 5 units in the -Z direction

$$\begin{bmatrix} -1 \\ 1 \\ 0 \\ 1 \end{bmatrix}$$

Figure 47.14 Position vector of upper left vertex of red rectangle in local view coordinates

$$\begin{bmatrix} 1 & 0 & 0 & 1 \\ 0 & 1 & 0 & 0 \\ 0 & 0 & 1 & -5 \\ 0 & 0 & 0 & 1 \end{bmatrix} * \begin{bmatrix} 3 & 0 & 0 & 0 \\ 0 & 3 & 0 & 0 \\ 0 & 0 & 3 & 0 \\ 0 & 0 & 0 & 1 \end{bmatrix} = \begin{bmatrix} 3 & 0 & 0 & 1 \\ 0 & 3 & 0 & 0 \\ 0 & 0 & 3 & -5 \\ 0 & 0 & 0 & 1 \end{bmatrix}$$

Figure 47.15 ModelView matrix created by multiplying the scaling matrix by the translation matrix

Note

If the ModelView matrix in Figure 47.16 is replaced by the Identity matrix, the position vector after the multiplication will be the same as the position vector before.

$$\begin{bmatrix} 3 & 0 & 0 & 1 \\ 0 & 3 & 0 & 0 \\ 0 & 0 & 3 & -5 \\ 0 & 0 & 0 & 1 \end{bmatrix} * \begin{bmatrix} -1 \\ 1 \\ 0 \\ 1 \end{bmatrix} = \begin{bmatrix} -2 \\ 3 \\ -5 \\ 1 \end{bmatrix}$$

Figure 47.16 Position vector of upper left vertex of red rectangle multiplied by ModelView matrix

The OpenGL command combination

```
glClearColor(1.0,1.0,1.0, 1.0);
glClear(GL_COLOR_BUFFER_BIT);
```

sets the colour of the window which renders the OpenGL scene. The OpenGL command `glClearColor(1.0,1.0,1.0, 1.0)` sets the clearing colour to white(rgb colour: `1.0,1.0,1.0`). The fourth parameter, the alpha value, sets the transparency. to none.The next line `glClear(GL_COLOR_BUFFER_BIT)` clears the entire window to the current clearing colour.

GL_COLOR_BUFFER_BIT indicates which buffer is to be cleared, i.e. the colour buffer where the image to be displayed on the screen is stored The colours of the pixels that are displayed in the window are stored in a buffer (area of memory), called the colour buffer, in the graphics hardware in bitplanes as shown in *Figure 47.17*. The red, green, blue and alpha (RGBA) values of a pixel are stored directly in these bitplanes.

Depth information is stored in another buffer called the depth buffer. The depth buffer is indicated by GL_DEPTH_BUFFER_BIT. The OpenGL command glClear(GL_DEPTH_BUFFER_BIT) clears the depth buffer.

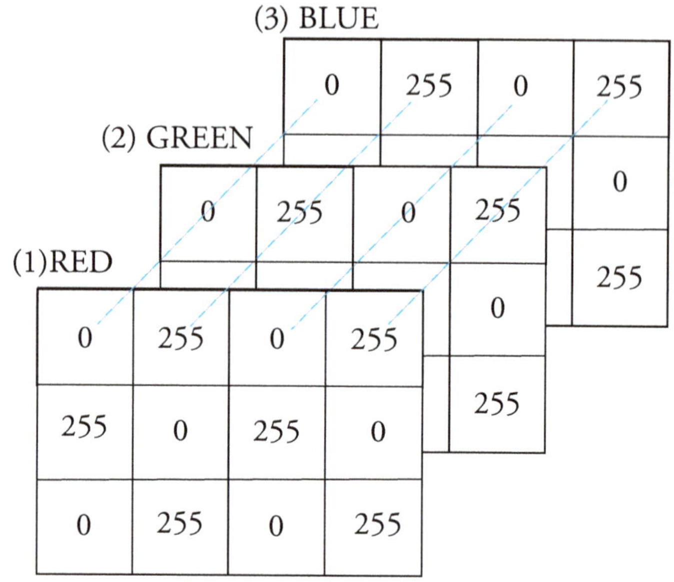

Figure 47.17 The red, green and blue bitplanes (the alpha bitplane is not shown) for 4 x 3 pixel window, r value 1.0 translates to 255, etc.

To clear both we use

```
glClear(GL_COLOR_BUFFER_BIT or GL_DEPTH_BUFFER_BIT);
```

The clearing colour only needs to be set once. Thereafter, the application will remember its value in a state variable. With the colour buffer now describing the scene set up, procedure Draw calls SwapBuffers(wglGetCurrentDC) to cause the screen to use this buffer.

Before any drawing operation can be carried out the OpenGL environment must be initialised. *Table 47.3* shows a procedure that does this. The viewing area or region of the screen that the image occupies is set to be the entire client area of the form frmOpenGL using

```
glViewPort(0, 0, frmOpenGL.ClientWidth, frmOpenGL.ClientHeight);
```

Next a 4 x 4 matrix called the projection matrix is created. It is then initialised with the Identity matrix (see *Figure 47.9*). The projection matrix will be used to define a viewing volume. The viewing volume is used in two ways:

1. It determines how an object is projected onto the screen, i.e. by perspective or by orthographic projection.
2. It defines which objects or which portions of objects are clipped out of the final image.

If the projection is to match how objects appear to us in daily life then the projection matrix must be set to perspective mode. Perspective mode makes objects farther away appear smaller and makes straight lines appear to converge in the distance. Perspective projection is set up by calling glFrustum as shown in *Table 47.3*.
Depth testing is enabled with glEnable(GL_DEPTH_TEST).
Finally, we switch the mode to GL_MODELVIEW so that modelling and viewing transformations may occur.

```
Procedure GLInit;
  Const
    cLeft = -1; cRight = +1; cBottom = -1; cTop = +1; cNearZ = 0.3; cFarZ = 25;
  Begin
    glViewPort(0, 0, frmOpenGL.ClientWidth, frmOpenGL.ClientHeight);
    glMatrixMode(GL_PROJECTION); //Create Projection Matrix
    glLoadIdentity; // Set Projection matrix to Identity matrix
    glFrustum(cLeft, cRight, cBottom, cTop, cNearZ, cFarZ); //Set perspective view
    glEnable(GL_DEPTH_TEST); //Enable depth testing in Normalised Device Coordinates View
    glMatrixMode(GL_MODELVIEW);
  End;
```

Table 47.3 Initialisation of the OpenGL evironment, perspective projection

The `OnCreate` event handler shown in *Table 47.4* obtains a handle to the form `frmOpenGL`'s device context (see *Chapter 37*). The pixel format is then set by calling `SetupPixelFormat(HandleOfDeviceContext)`. Next an OpenGL window, `RenderingContext`, is created by calling `wglCreateContext(HandleOfDeviceContext)`. This window is then made active by calling `wglMakeCurrent(HandleOfDeviceContext, RenderingContext)`. Finally, the OpenGL environment is initialised by calling `GLInit`.

```
Procedure TfrmOpenGL.FormCreate(Sender : TObject);
  Var
    HandleOfDeviceContext : HDC;
    RenderingContext : HGLRC;    //THandle
  Begin
    HandleOfDeviceContext := GetDC(frmOpenGL.Handle);
    SetupPixelFormat(HandleOfDeviceContext);
    RenderingContext := wglCreateContext(HandleOfDeviceContext); //makes OpenGL window
    wglMakeCurrent(HandleOfDeviceContext, RenderingContext); //makes OpenGL window active
    GLInit; //initialize OpenGL
  End;
```

Table 47.4 Creating a rendering window for the OpenGL commands

Table 47.5 shows the `OnPaint` event handler that is called whenever the form is repainted, e.g. when created, moved or uncovered. The OpenGL scene is therefore drawn every time this event is triggered.

Reducing the form in size may not trigger the `OnPaint` event handler so the second event handler in *Table 47.5* is necessary in order to force a repaint.

```
Procedure TfrmOpenGL.FormPaint(Sender : TObject);
  Begin
    Draw;
  End;

Procedure TfrmOpenGL.FormResize(Sender: TObject);
  Begin
    Repaint;
  End;
```

Table 47.5 OnPaint and OnResize event handlers

Table 47.6 and *Table 47.7* show the full source code for unit `TwoDRectangle.pas` described procedure by procedure in *Tables 47.1* to *47.5*.

Figure 47.18 shows the compiled project `TwoDRectangleProject.dpr` in execution.

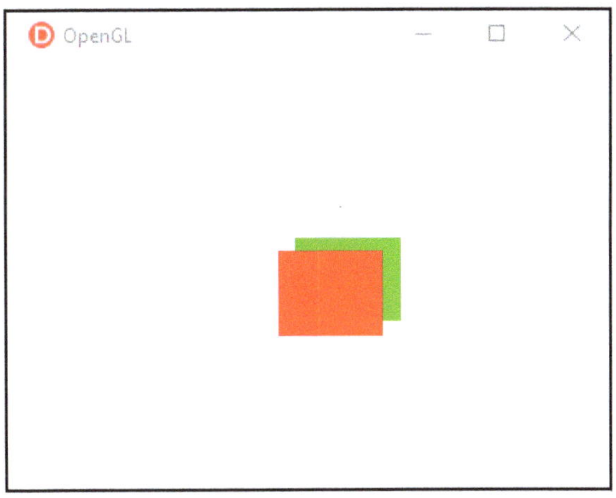

Figure 47.18 TwoDRectangleProject

Now let's suppose that we want to rotate the red rectangle about the Z-axis in its local space (centred on the red rectangle).

There are two ways that this can be done:

1. Rotate the red rectangle before it is translated to world space.
2. Translate the red rectangle in world space to the origin, rotate the red rectangle then translate back to its original position in world space.

Note

`glRotate(Angle, X-axis, Y-axis, Z-axis`

In the first method, procedure `Draw` needs to be modified as follows

```
glTranslate(1, 0.0, -5);
glScale(3, 3, 3);
glRotate(45, 0, 0, 1); //Rotation is applied first then scaling then translation
MakeRectangle(-1.0, +1.0, -1.0, +1.0, 1.0, 0.0, 0.0);
```

Figure 47.19 shows the result for rotation by 45° about the Z-axis in local space before translation to world space.

```
Unit TwoDRectangleUnit;
Interface
Uses
  Winapi.Windows, Winapi.Messages, System.SysUtils, System.Variants, System.Classes,
  Vcl.Graphics,  Vcl.Controls, Vcl.Forms, Vcl.Dialogs, OpenGL, Vcl.StdCtrls, Vcl.ExtCtrls;
Type
  TfrmOpenGL = Class(TForm)
                 Procedure FormCreate(Sender: TObject);
                 Procedure FormPaint(Sender: TObject);
                 Procedure MakeRectangle(Left, Right, Top, Bottom, r, g, b : GLfloat);
                 Procedure Draw;
                 Procedure FormResize(Sender: TObject);
                 Procedure FormDestroy(Sender : TObject);
               End;
Var
  frmOpenGL: TfrmOpenGL;
  RenderingContext : HGLRC;   //THandle
Implementation
{$R *.dfm}
  Procedure SetUpPixelFormat(DeviceContext : HDC);
    Const
      pfd : TPIXELFORMATDESCRIPTOR =
        (
          nSize : sizeof(TPIXELFORMATDESCRIPTOR);// size
          nVersion : 1;// version
          dwFlags : PFD_SUPPORT_OPENGL or PFD_DRAW_TO_WINDOW or PFD_DOUBLEBUFFER;
          iPixelType : PFD_TYPE_RGBA; // color type
          cColorBits : 24;                   // preferred color depth
          cRedBits : 0; cRedShift : 0;       // color bits (ignored)
          cGreenBits : 0;  cGreenShift : 0;
          cBlueBits : 0; cBlueShift : 0;
          cAlphaBits : 0;  cAlphaShift : 0;    // no alpha buffer
          cAccumBits : 0;
          cAccumRedBits : 0;                 // no accumulation buffer,
          cAccumGreenBits : 0;       // accum bits (ignored)
          cAccumBlueBits : 0;
          cAccumAlphaBits : 0;
          cDepthBits : 16;                   // depth buffer
          cStencilBits : 0;          // no stencil buffer
          cAuxBuffers : 0;                   // no auxiliary buffers
          iLayerType : FD_MAIN_PLANE;        // main layer
          bReserved : 0;
          dwLayerMask : 0;
          dwVisibleMask : 0;
          dwDamageMask : 0; // no layer, visible, damage masks
        );
    Var
      PixelFormat : Integer;
    Begin
      PixelFormat := ChoosePixelFormat(DeviceContext, @pfd);
      If (PixelFormat = 0)
        Then Exit;
      If (SetPixelFormat(DeviceContext, PixelFormat, @pfd) <> TRUE)
        Then Exit;
    End;
```

Table 47.6 First section of unit TwoDRectangleUnit.pas

P

```
Procedure GLInit;
  Const
    cLeft = -1; cRight = +1; cBottom = -1; cTop = +1; cNearZ = 0.3; cFarZ = 25;
  Begin
    glViewPort(0, 0, frmOpenGL.ClientWidth, frmOpenGL.ClientHeight);
    glMatrixMode(GL_PROJECTION); //Create Projection Matrix
    glLoadIdentity; // Set Projection matrix to Identity matrix
    glFrustum(cLeft, cRight, cBottom, cTop, cNearZ, cFarZ); //Set perspective view
    //glOrtho(-10, 10, -10.0, 10, 0, 25.0);
  //  glMatrixMode(GL_MODELVIEW);  //Create ModelViewMatrix
    glEnable(GL_DEPTH_TEST); //Enable depth testing in Normalised Device Coordinates View
    glMatrixMode(GL_MODELVIEW);
  End;
Procedure TfrmOpenGL.FormCreate(Sender: TObject);
  Var
    HandleOfDeviceContext : HDC;
  Begin
    HandleOfDeviceContext := GetDC(frmOpenGL.Handle); //Any windowed control may be used here
    SetupPixelFormat(HandleOfDeviceContext);
    RenderingContext := wglCreateContext(HandleOfDeviceContext); //makes OpenGL window
    glMakeCurrent(HandleOfDeviceContext, RenderingContext);   //makes OpenGL window active
    GLInit; //initialize OpenGL
  End;
Procedure TfrmOpenGL.FormPaint(Sender: TObject);
  Begin
   Draw;
  End;
Procedure TfrmOpenGL.FormResize(Sender: TObject);
  Begin
    Repaint;
  End;
Procedure TfrmOpenGL.MakeRectangle(Left, Right, Top, Bottom, r, g, b : GLfloat);
  Begin
    glBegin(GL_POLYGON);
      glColor3f(r, g, b);
      glVertex2f(Left, Bottom);
      glVertex2f(Right, Bottom);
      glVertex2f(Right, Top);
      glVertex2f(Left, Top);
    glEnd;
  End;
```

```
Procedure TfrmOpenGL.FormDestroy(Sender : TObject);
  Begin
    wglMakeCurrent(0,0);
    wglDeleteContext(RenderingContext);
  End;
```

```
Procedure TfrmOpenGL.Draw;
  Begin
    glClearColor(1.0, 1.0, 1.0, 1.0);
    glClear(GL_COLOR_BUFFER_BIT or GL_DEPTH_BUFFER_BIT);
    glMatrixMode(GL_MODELVIEW);
    glLoadIdentity; //Sets ModelView matrix to Identity matrix
    glTranslate(1, 0.0, -5);  //Change ModelViewMatrix (World coordinates view)
    glScale(3,3,3); //Change ModelViewMatrix
    MakeRectangle(-1.0, +1.0, -1.0, +1.0, 1.0, 0.0, 0.0);   //Make object in Local coordinates view
    glLoadIdentity; //Sets ModelView matrix to Identity matrix, i.e. default state
    glTranslate(2, 1, -5);  //World coordinates view
    glScale(3,3,3);
    MakeRectangle(-1.0, +1.0, -1.0, +1.0, 0.0, 1.0, 0.0);  //Local coordinates view
    //Force OpenGL commands to execute
    SwapBuffers(wglGetCurrentDC); //Uses double buffering to avoid flicker
  End;
End.
```

Table 47.7 Second section of unit TwoDRectangleUnit.pas

(www.educational-computing.co.uk/DelphiBookCode/DelphiCode.html)

To enable comparison, the green rectangle is drawn with zero Y translation, i.e.

```
glTranslate(2, 0, -5);
glScale(3,3,3);
MakeRectangle(-1.0, +1.0, -1.0, +1.0, 0.0, 1.0, 0.0);
```

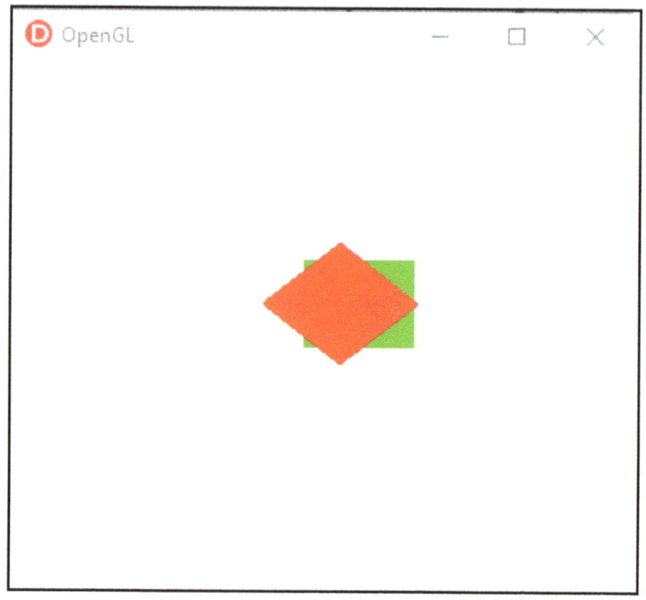

Figure 47.19 TwoDRectangleWithRotationProject rotation about Z-axis

The ModelView matrix that rotates a position vector by angle A about the Z-axis in an anticlockwise direction is shown in *Figure 47.20*.

$$\begin{bmatrix} \cos A & -\sin A & 0 & 0 \\ \sin A & \cos A & 0 & 0 \\ 0 & 0 & 1 & 0 \\ 0 & 0 & 0 & 1 \end{bmatrix}$$

Figure 47.20 ModelView matrix that rotates a position vector by angle A about the Z-axis

The ModelView matrix that rotates a position vector by angle A about the Z-axis in an anticlockwise direction, scaling in each direction by 3 and then translation to X = 1 and Z = -5 is shown in *Figure 47.21.*

$$\begin{bmatrix} 3\cdot\cos A & -3\cdot\sin A & 0 & 1 \\ 3\cdot\sin A & 3\cdot\cos A & 0 & 0 \\ 0 & 0 & 3 & -5 \\ 0 & 0 & 0 & 1 \end{bmatrix}$$

Figure 47.21 ModelView matrix that rotates a position vector by angle A about the Z-axis, scales in each direction by 3 and then translates to X = 1 and Z = -5

The position vector of the upper left vertex of the red rectangle after multiplication by the ModelView matrix for rotation by angle 45° about the Z-axis in an anticlockwise direction, scaling in each direction by 3 and then translation to X = 1 and Z = -5 is shown in *Figure 47.22.*

$$\begin{bmatrix} 3\cdot\cos 45 & -3\cdot\sin 45 & 0 & 1 \\ 3\cdot\sin 45 & 3\cdot\cos 45 & 0 & 0 \\ 0 & 0 & 3 & -5 \\ 0 & 0 & 0 & 1 \end{bmatrix} * \begin{bmatrix} -1 \\ 1 \\ 0 \\ 1 \end{bmatrix} = \begin{bmatrix} 1 - 3\cdot(\cos 45 - \sin 45) \\ 3\cdot(\cos 45 - \sin 45) \\ -5 \\ 1 \end{bmatrix} = \begin{bmatrix} 1 \\ 0 \\ -5 \\ 1 \end{bmatrix}$$

Figure 47.22 Position vector of upper left vertex of red rectangle multiplied by ModelView matrix

(www.educational-computing.co.uk/DelphiBookCode/DelphiCode.html)

Changing the view

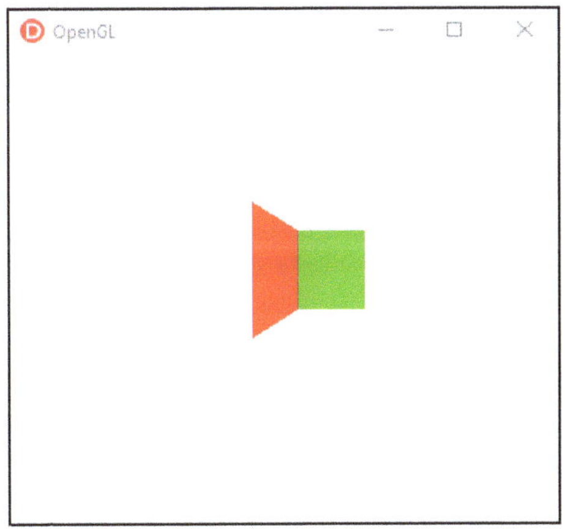

Figure 47.23 TwoDRectangleWithRotationProject rotation about Y-axis

Figure 47.23 shows the result for rotation by 45° about the Y-axis in local space before translation to world space.

Figure 47.4 shows an eye view of the rectangle in world space view. We can replace the eye by a camera and achieve the same projection onto the two-dimensional window shown in *Figure 47.23*. What view would result if the eye/camera could be shifted away from the origin or if the eye/camera could be rotated to point in a different direction?

Unfortunately, OpenGL doesn't explicitly support a specific matrix for camera transformation or for that matter, a camera object. Instead, the entire world space scene must be transformed, with the camera remaining fixed at the origin (0,0,0), looking along -Z axis, to produce a result that the camera would have produced if moveable.

Rotating the eye/camera clockwise 45° about the Y-axis is equivalent to rotating the scene anticlockwise 45°. So in the example shown in *Figure 47.24*, the scene is rotated by constructing the `GL_MODELVIEW` matrix for each rectangle as follows

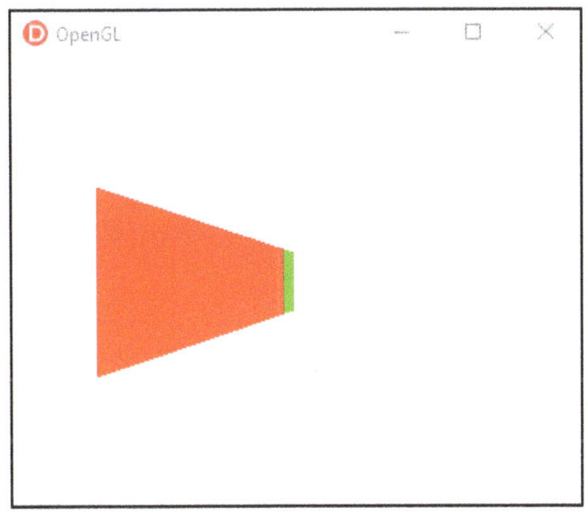

Figure 47.24 TwoDRectangleWithViewRotationProject rotation about Y-axis, +45°

```
glMatrixMode(GL_MODELVIEW);
glLoadIdentity;
glRotate(45, 0, 1, 0);// scene rotation
glTranslate(1, 0.0, -5);
glScale(3,3,3);
MakeRectangle(-1.0, +1.0, -1.0, +1.0, 1.0, 0.0,
0.0);
glLoadIdentity;
glRotate(45, 0, 1, 0);//scene rotation
glTranslate(2, 0, -5);
glScale(3,3,3);
MakeRectangle(-1.0, +1.0, -1.0, +1.0, 0.0, 1.0, 0.0);
```

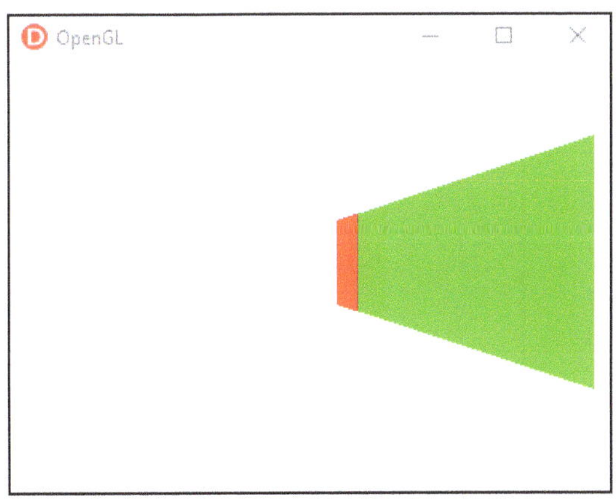

Figure 47.24 TwoDRectangleWithViewRotationProject rotation about Y-axis, -45°

The *GL_MODELVIEW* matrix in fact combines the viewing matrix and modelling matrix into one matrix.

Figure 47.25 shows the transformation of a cube from local space to screen space through world space, view space and clip space.

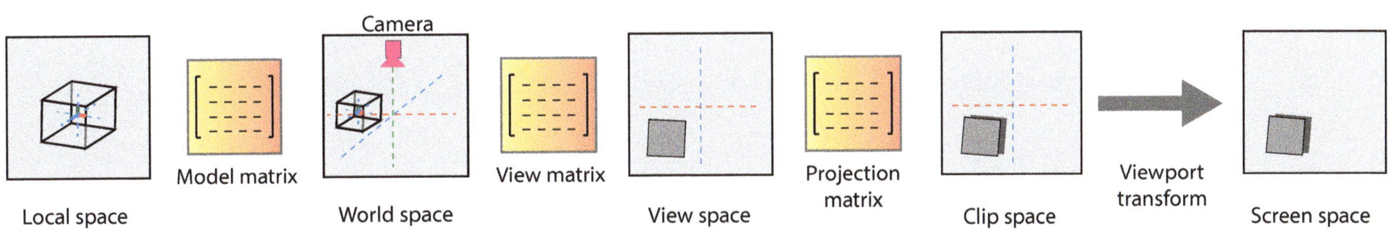

Figure 47.25 The transformations from local space to screen space

(www.educational-computing.co.uk/DelphiBookCode/DelphiCode.html)

Orthographic projection

In this projection, objects are mapped directly onto the screen without affecting their relatve sizes. Parallel lines remain parallel lines. This type of projection is used in applications where the final image needs to reflect the measurements of objects, rather than how they might look, e.g. in architectural plans.

```
Procedure GLInit;
  Const
    cLeft = -10; cRight = +10; cBottom = -10; cTop = +10; cNearZ = 0.0; cFarZ =
25;
  Begin
    glViewPort(0, 0, frmOpenGL.ClientWidth, frmOpenGL.ClientHeight);
    glMatrixMode(GL_PROJECTION); //Create Projection Matrix
    glLoadIdentity; // Set Projection matrix to Identity matrix
    glOrtho(cLeft, cRight, cBottom, cTop, cNearZ, cFarZ); //Set orthographic view
    glEnable(GL_DEPTH_TEST); //Enable depth testing in Normalised Device Coordinates View
    glMatrixMode(GL_MODELVIEW);
  End;
```

Table 47.8 Initialisation of the OpenGL evironment orthographic projection

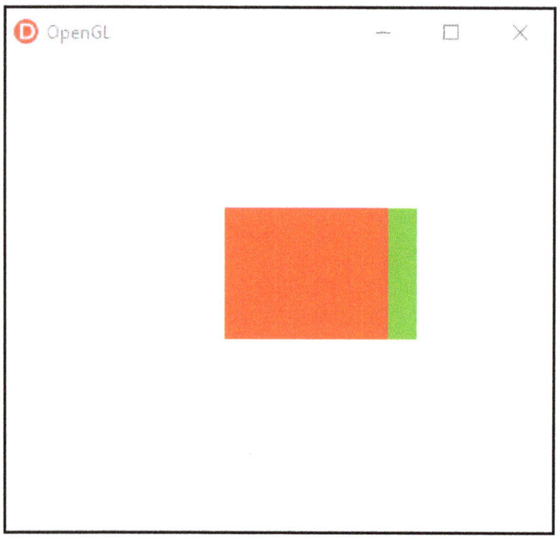

Figure 47.26 TwoDRectangleWithViewRotationProject zero rotation about Y-axis

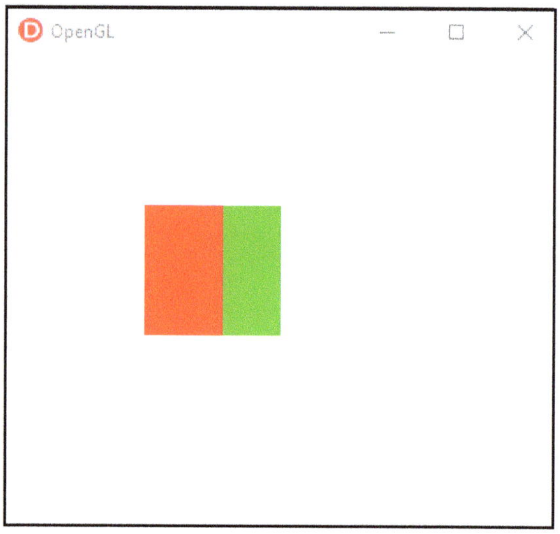

Figure 47.27 TwoDRectangleWithViewRotationProject rotation about Y-axis, 45°

(www.educational-computing.co.uk/DelphiBookCode/DelphiCode.html)

48 More OpenGL

Introduction to OpenGL

Purpose: To become familiar with graphics based on OpenGL

OpenGL

Delphi versions since XE2 have provided support for OpenGL graphics via FireMonkey. However, its OpenGL implementation is limited to a few high level design time components and objects - see **Palette** of a multi-device 3D application. It is possible to leverage more OpenGL functions by writing code directly in a FireMonkey application but this is best avoided until you have gained more experience with OpenGL.

Instead, we will start with an OpenGL implementation called **GLScene** that offers a fuller range of options and a better introduction for exploring OpenGL whilst masking most of the intricacies of OpenGL.

GLScene

GLScene is a free OpenGL-based library for the Delphi programming language, C++ and Free Pascal. It provides visual components and objects which allow 3D scenes to be described and rendered in code.

Figure 48.1 shows a fractal generated scene produced with **GLScene v2.0** (released August 2020) in **Delphi 10.4** running on **Windows 10**.

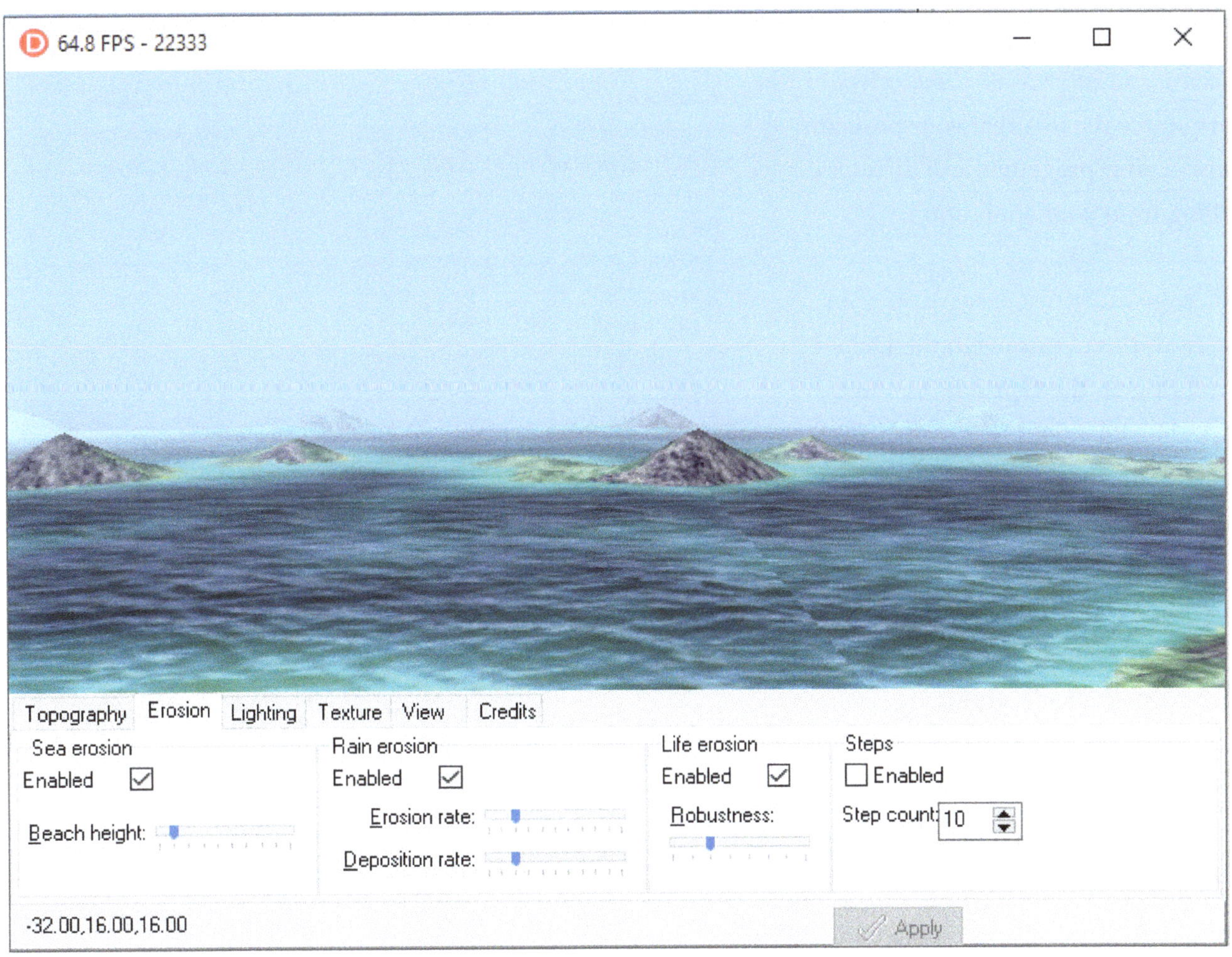

Figure 48.1 Fractal generated scene produced with GLScene v2.0 (released August 2020) in Delphi 10.4 runing on Windows 10.

Setting up GLScene

After downloading the latest version of GLScene, extract to a directory that you have access to. *Figure 48.2* shows the extracted contents of **GLScene v2.0**.

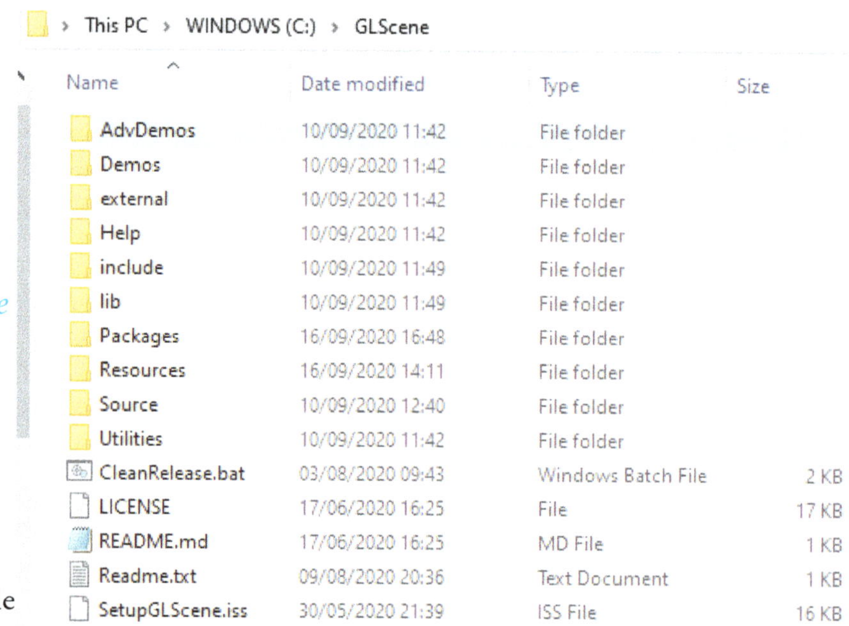

Figure 48.2 Extracted contents of GLScene v2.0.

The first thing that must be done is to copy the **GLScene dlls** from the `external` directory to `Windows System32` and `SysWOW64` directories. You will need to **Runas administrator** to do this.

Change to directory `external` - see *Figure 48.2*.

A batch file, `SetupDLLs.bat`, is provided to make the task of copying the dlls to their respective destination directories more manageable.

Right click with the mouse on this batch file and select **Runas administrator**. **Provide** the administrator's password when prompted, if required.

If you cannot place these **dlls** in the `System32` and `SysWOW64` directories, you may place the **dlls** that your program requires in your program's **.exe** directory for calling from your application.

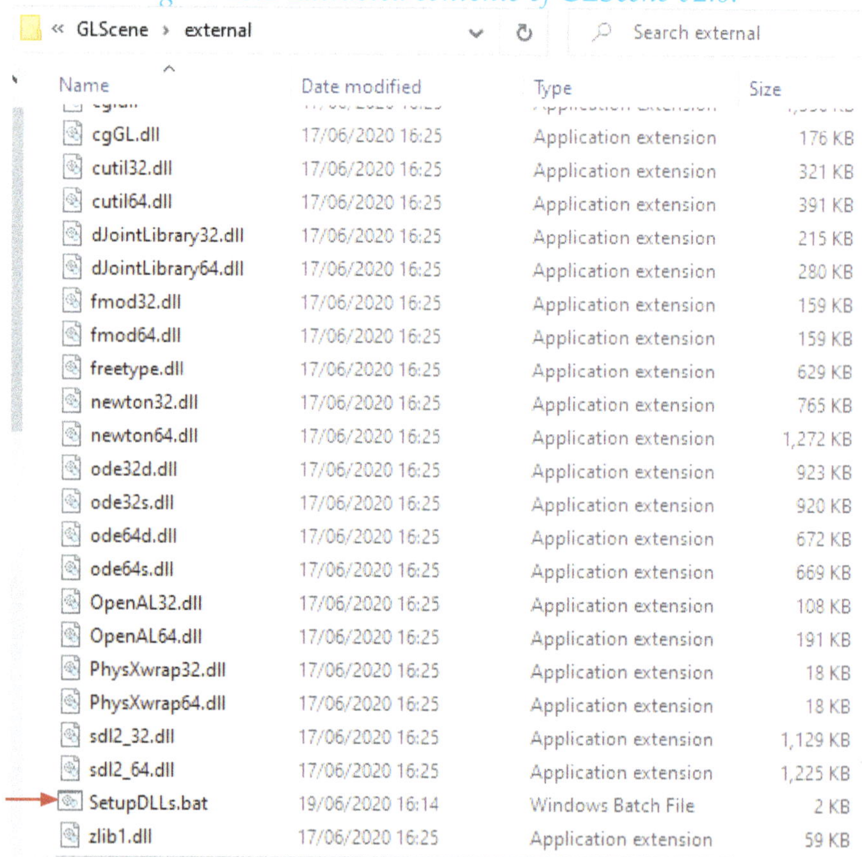

Figure 48.3 Contents of External directory

Installing GLScene components

Click Tools then **Options** in the Delphi IDE to bring up the **Options** window. **Click Language** then **Delphi** and **select Library** as shown in *Figure 48.4*. **Click** the ellipsis (**...**) button for the **Library Path** to bring up the window shown in *Figure 48.5*. **Overwrite** the field labelled **Greyed items denote invalid path** contents with the path to `GLScene\Lib\Win32` directory. **Click** the **Add** button to add this path to the list of paths. *Figure 48.5* shows that this path has already been added.

Open `GLScene.groupproj` located in directory `\GLScene\Packages\` using menu item **File|Open Project...(Ctrl+F11)** in the Delphi IDE - see *Figure 48.6*.

Information

Obtaining GLScene:
Download the latest version of GLScene from https://sourceforge.net/projects/glscene/files/GLScene.

The **Project Manager** window of the IDE should now show a list of projects with **.bpl** extensions.

A package, e.g. `GLScene_DT.bpl`, is a specially compiled library used by applications, the IDE, or both.

On **Win32**, package files end with the **.bpl** (Borland package library) extension.

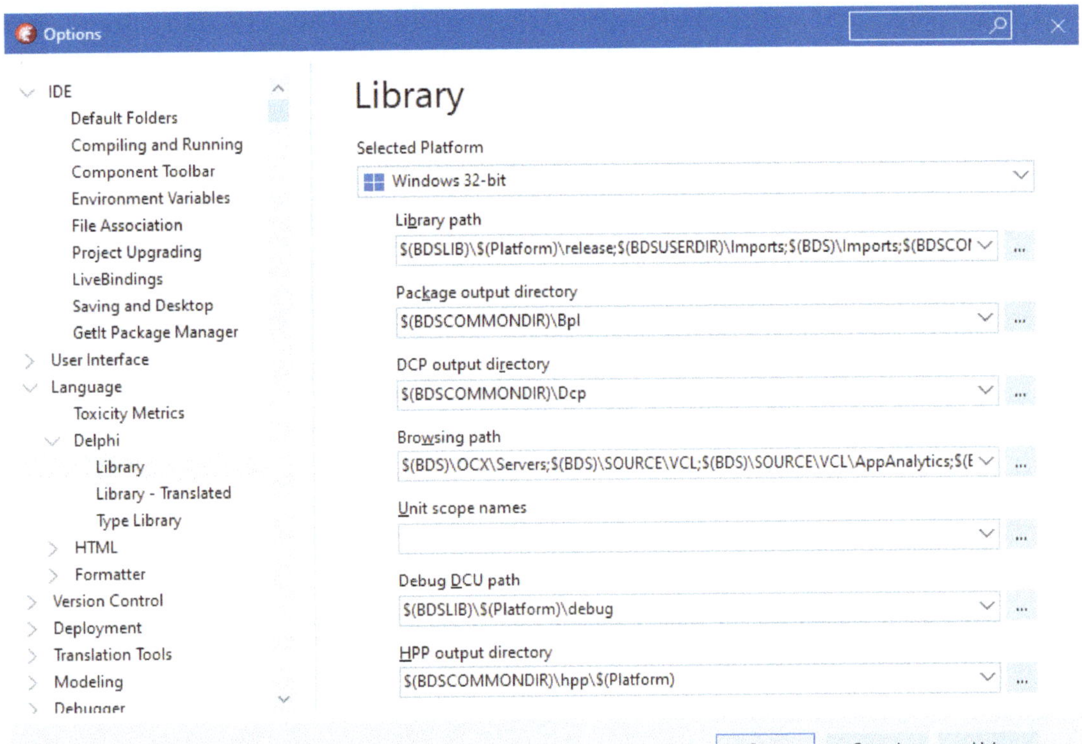

Figure 48.4 Options window

Packages allow the location of object code to be rearranged without affecting the source code.

Design-time packages, e.g. `GLScene_DT.bpl`, are used to install components in the IDE and to create special property editors for custom components.

Runtime packages, e.g. `GLScene_RT.bpl`, provide functionality when a user runs an application.
A single package can function at both design time and runtime, and design-time packages frequently work by referencing runtime packages in their requires clauses.

Ordinarily, packages are loaded statically when an applications starts.

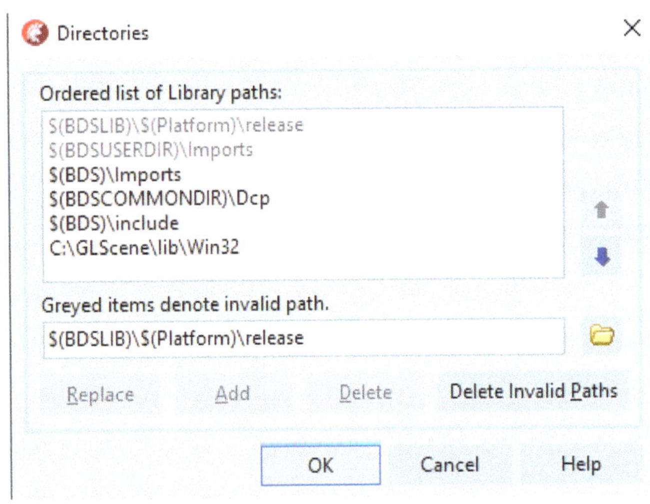

Figure 48.5 Library path pop-up window

Each package is declared in a separate source file, which should be saved with the **.dpk** extension to avoid confusion with other files containing Delphi code.

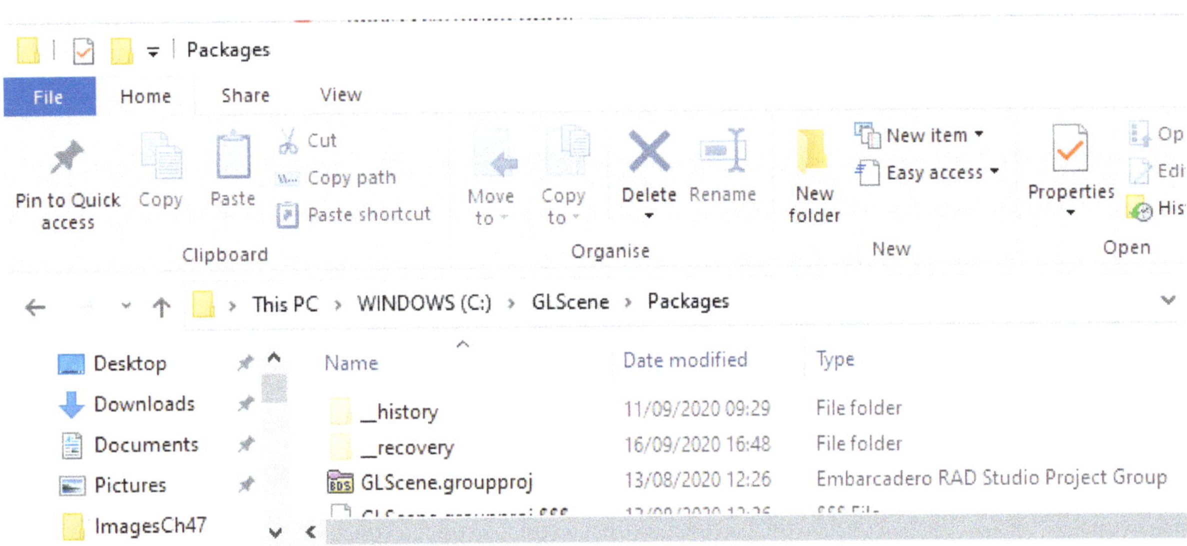

Figure 48.6 Packages directory

A package source file does not contain type, data, procedure, or function declarations. Instead, it contains:

- a name for the package.
- a list of other packages required by the new package. These are packages to which the new package is linked.
- a list of unit files contained by, or bound into, the package when it is compiled.

The package is essentially a wrapper for these source-code units, which provide the functionality of the compiled package.

An example of a package source file is shown in *Table 48.1*.

A compiled package involves several generated files.

For example, the source file for the package called **GLScene_RT** is `GLScene_RT.dpk`, from which the compiler generates an executable and a binary image called `GLScene_RT.bpl` and `GLScene_RT.dcp`, respectively.

GLScene_RT is used to refer to the package in the requires clauses of other packages, or when using the package in an application. Package names must be unique within a project.

```
Package GLScene_Physics_DT;
  {$R *.res}
  {$R 'GLScenePhysics.res'}
  ...
  {$IOCHECKS ON}
  {$LOCALSYMBOLS ON}
  {$LONGSTRINGS ON}
  {$OPENSTRINGS ON}
  {$OPTIMIZATION OFF}
  {$OVERFLOWCHECKS OFF}
  {$RANGECHECKS OFF}
  {$REFERENCEINFO ON}
  ...
  {$DESCRIPTION 'GLScene Physics Managers'}
  {$DESIGNONLY}
  {$IMPLICITBUILD ON}
  Requires
    rtl,
    vcl,
    GLScene_Physics_RT,
    GLScene_RT;
  Contains Physics.Register in '..\Source\Physics.Register.pas';
End.
```

Table 48.1 Contents of package source file GLScene_Physics_DT.dpk

Figure 48.7 shows the **Project manager** window with `GLScene_GPU_RT.bpl` expanded to reveal the binary images that it requires.

Figure 48.8 shows the **Project manager** window with `GLScene_GPU_RT.bpl` expanded to reveal the unit files that it contains.

Click on **Project** in Delphi IDE, select **Options** to bring up the **Project Option** window for **GLScene** then click **Delphi Compiler**. *Figure 48.9* shows the window that appears. Note that the **Unit output directory** field contains the path `..\lib\$(Platform)`.

As the target is the **Windows 32-bit platform**, the **Unit output directory** is set to `..\lib\Win32`.

Right click the highest **.bpl** in the **Project manager** then compile **GLScene**'s packages for **Win32** using **From Here|Compile All From Here** - *Figure 48.10*. This will create Delphi compiled units, extension **.dcu**, in the `\lib\Win32` directory for all the packages - *Figure 48.11*.

Click **Component** in the Delphi IDE then **Install Packages**. This brings up the window shown in *Figure 48.12*.

Click the **Add** button to bring up the window shown in *Figure 48.13*.

Hold down the **Ctrl** key and **click** every **DT** (Design Time) **bpl** file. **Click** the **Open** button to start the install process.

When the install operation is complete, close `GLScene.groupproj`.

If the installation is successful then the following component groups will have been added to the component palette window:

- **GLScene**
- **GLScene PFX**
- **GLScene Utils**
- **GLScene Terrain**
- **GLScene Shaders**
- **GLScene GPU Computing**
- **GLScene Physics**

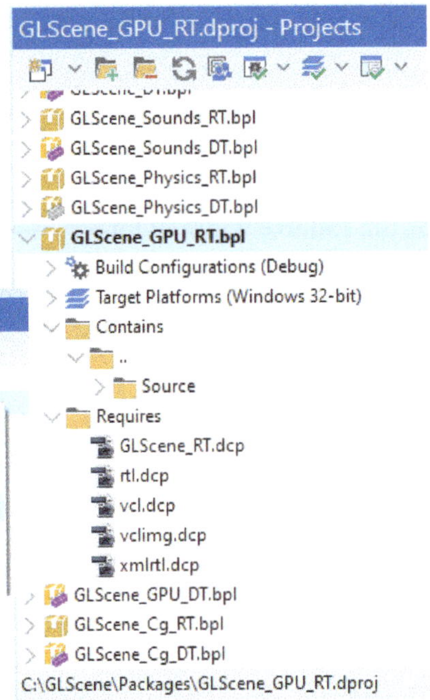

Figure 48.7 Project manager window with GLScene_GPU_RT.bpl expanded to show the binary images that it requires

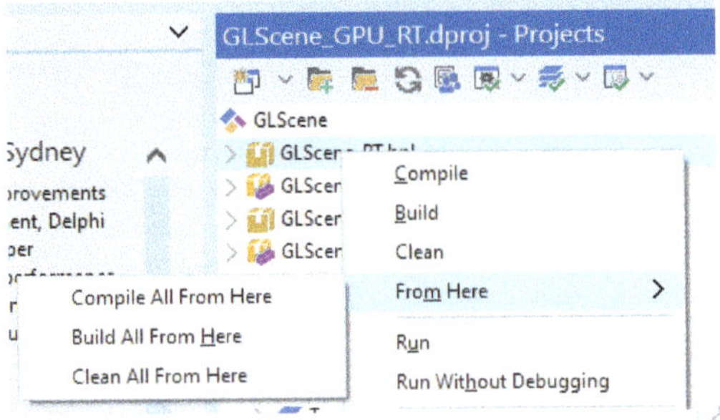

Figure 48.10 Compile All From Here

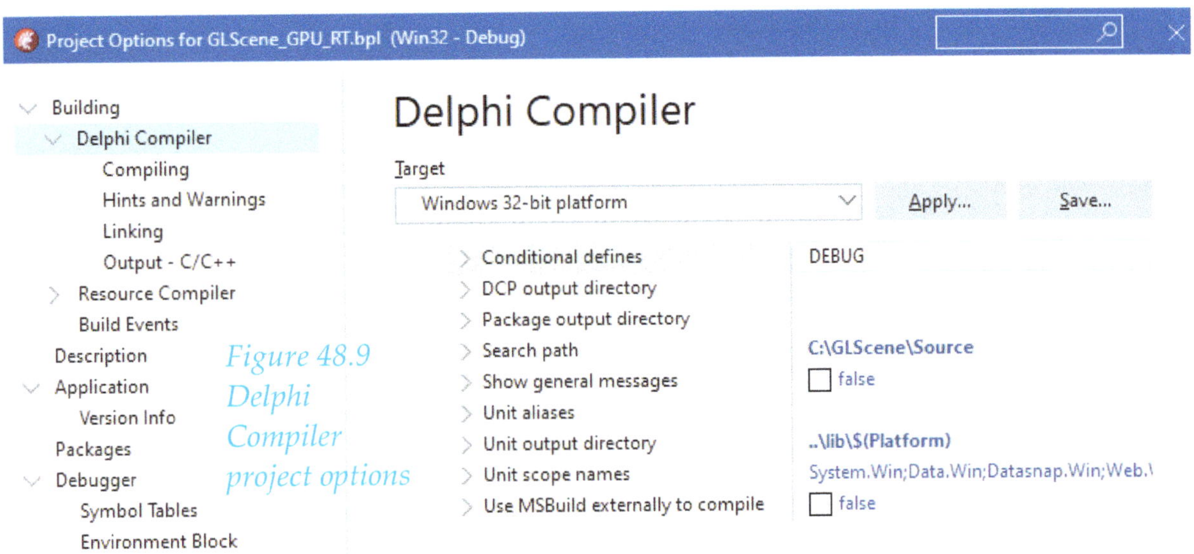

Figure 48.9 Delphi Compiler project options

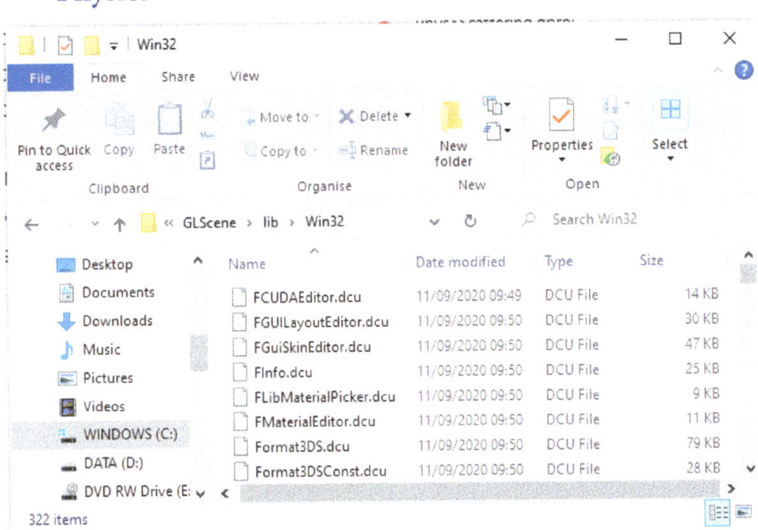

Figure 47.11 Shows some Delphi compiled units in \lib\Win32 directory

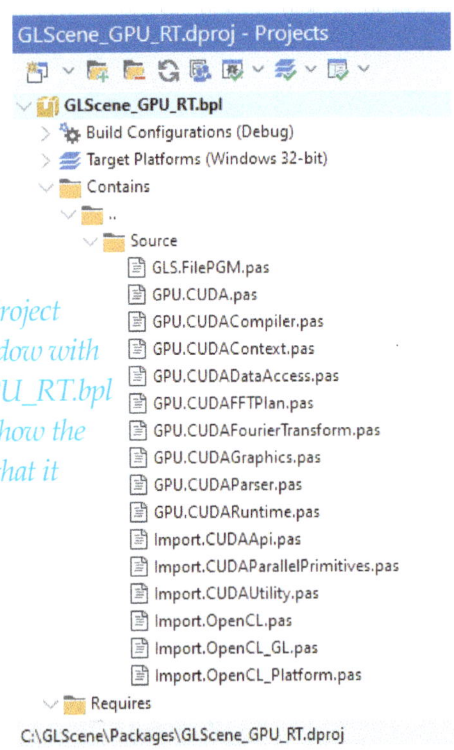

Figure 48.8 Project manager window with GLScene_GPU_RT.bpl expanded to show the the unit files that it contains

The **Palette** window will not be visible until a new or existing Delphi project is opened.

Figure 48.14 shows a section of the **Palette** window for a new **Windows VCL Delphi Application**.

The **Palette** window for a **Multi-Device Delphi Application** is similar.

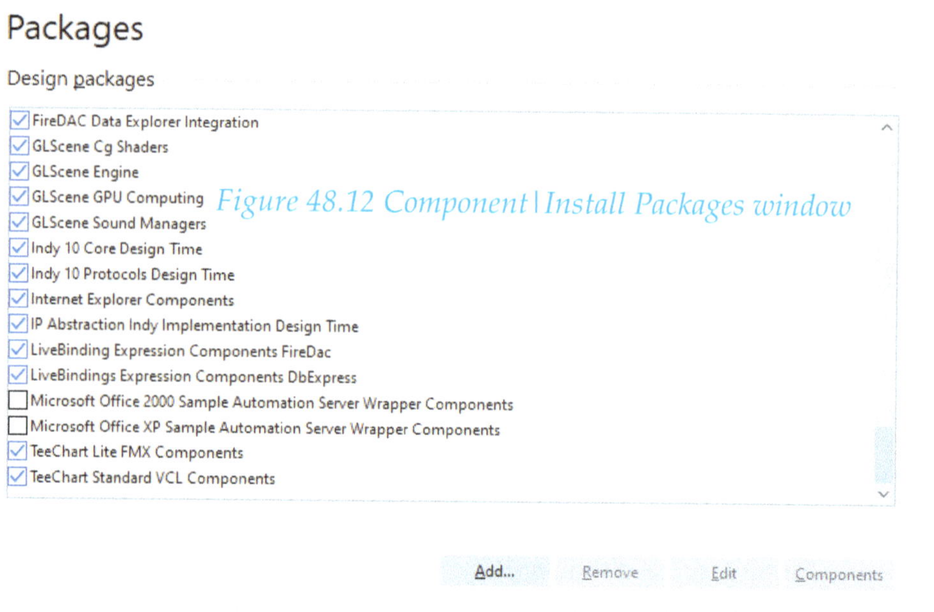

Figure 48.12 Component|Install Packages window

First GLScene project

Create a new Windows VCL application (**File|New**).

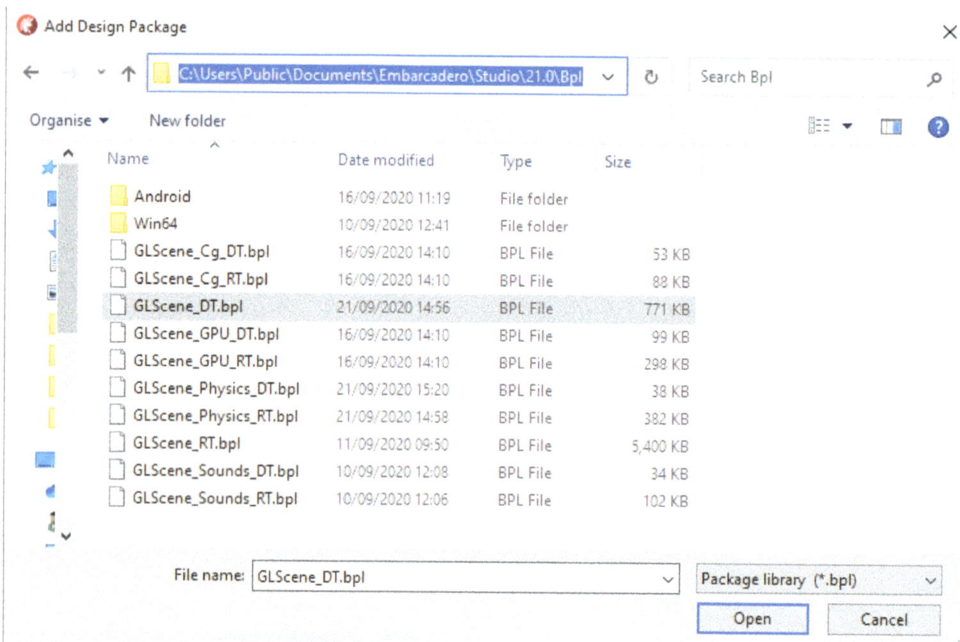

Figure 48.13 Add Design Package window

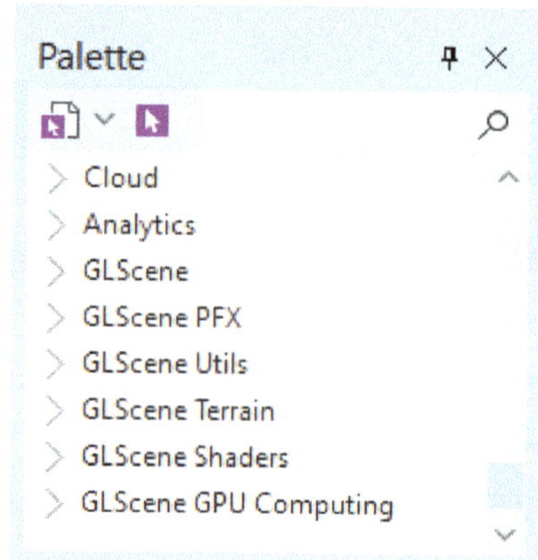

Figure 48.14 Component Palette

Save the project as `EarthMapSphereProject` and the unit as `EarthMapSphereUnit` (**File|Save Project As...**).

1. **Add** a **TGLScene** object from the **GLScene** palette.
2. **Add** a **TGLSceneViewer** from the **GLScene** palette.
3. In the **Structure** pane, **right click** `GLScene1` to bring up the window shown in *Figure 48.15* then **click** left mouse button on **Show Scene Editor** to bring up **GLScene Editor** shown in *Figure 48.16*.
4. **Click** **Scene objects** to bring up the window shown in *Figure 48.17*.
5. **Click** **Add object** to bring up the objects window shown in *Figure 48.18*.
6. **Click** **Camera**, **LightSource** and from **Basic geometry**, **click** **Sphere**. The **Structure** pane should now resemble *Figure 48.19*.

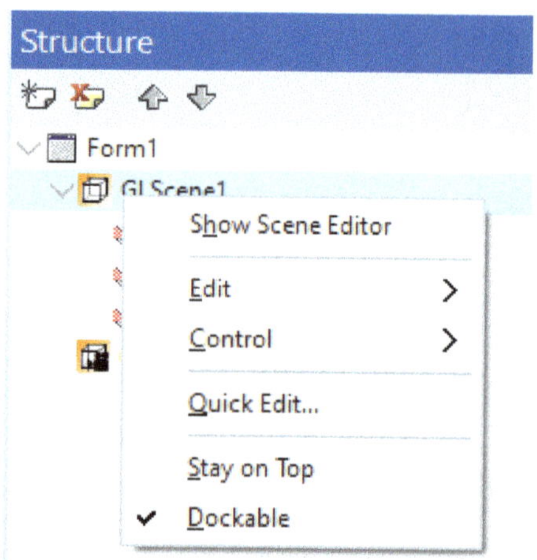

Figure 48.15 Window that pops up when right mouse button clicked over GLScene1

Figure 48.20 shows a viewing window on a scene comprising two spheres, a camera and a light source. First we need to understand how to position the camera and the light source. Camera and light source will not be visible in our scene but we can position each by setting their properties in the **Object Inspector**.

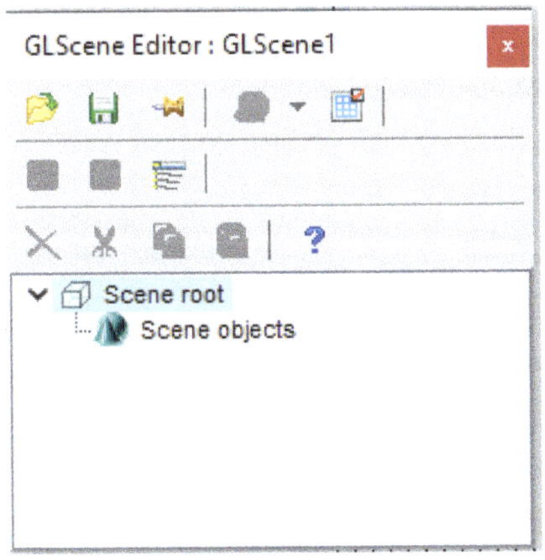

Figure 48.16 GLScene Editor

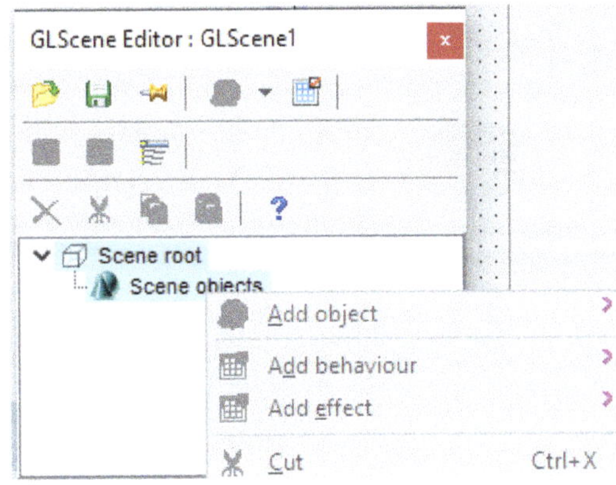

Figure 48.17 Scene objects menu

Figure 48.21 shows the appearance at design time of `Form1` for one configuration of property settings for `GLSphere1`, `GLCamera1`, `GLLightSource1`, `GLSceneViewer1` and `Form1`. Before listing these property settings, we will take a look at how this graphical output has been achieved.

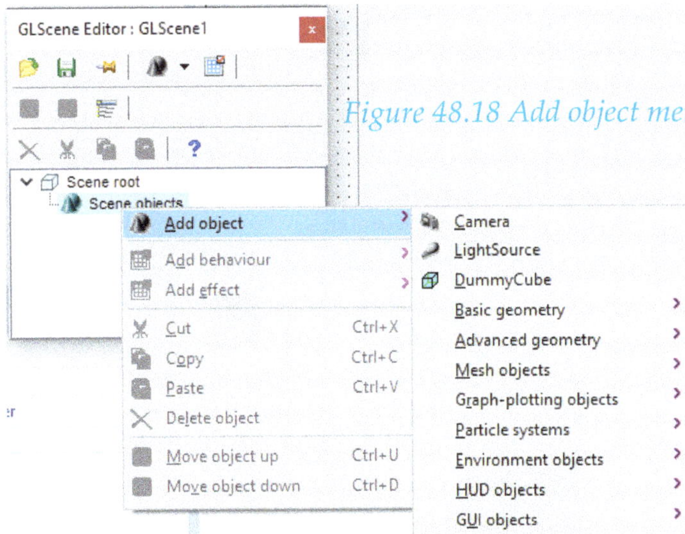

Figure 48.18 Add object menu

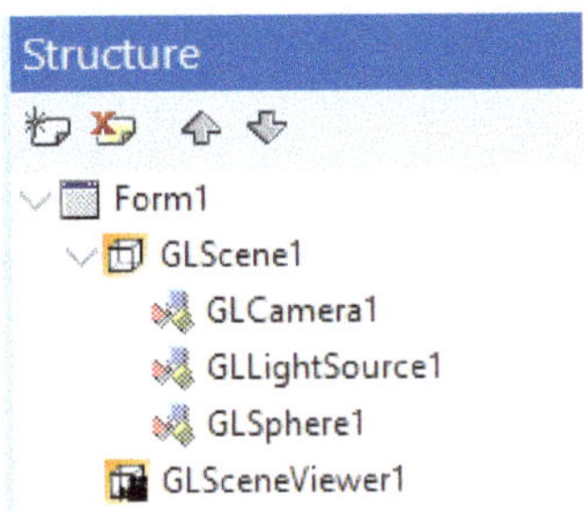

Figure 48.19 Structure pane for EarthMapSphereProject

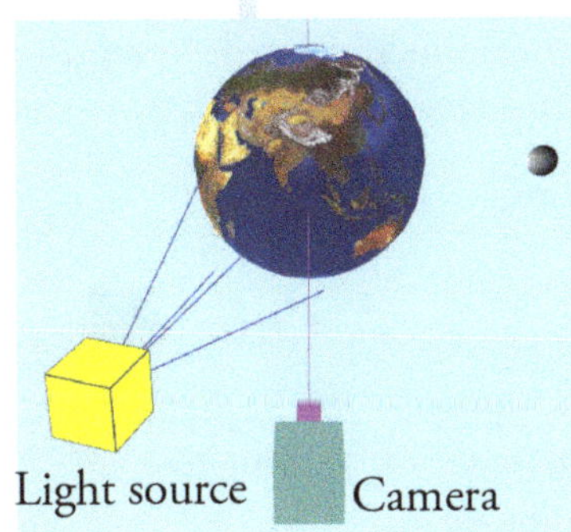

Figure 48.20 Light source, camera and two spheres

GLScene provides wrappers for **OpenGL** to make the task of working with 3D objects much easier.

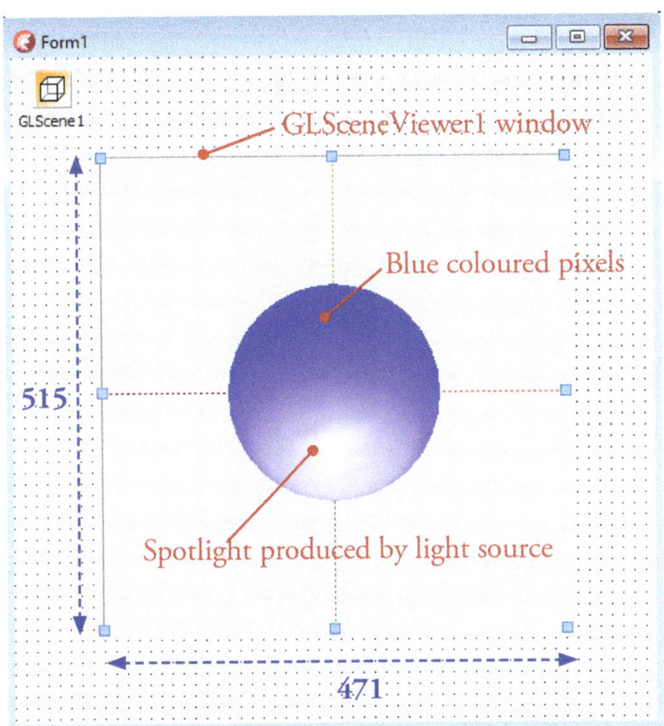

Figure 48.21 Design-time view of EarthMapSphereProject Form1

In **OpenGL** everything is in 3D space, but the screen or a window of the screen is a 2D array of pixels (e.g. `GLSceneViewer1` window in *Figure 48.21*). Therefore, a significant part of **OpenGL**'s work is about transforming 3D coordinates to 2D pixels. This task is managed by the graphics pipeline of **OpenGL**. The process is

3D coordinates → 2D coordinates → actual coloured pixels.

The graphics pipeline is divided into several steps where each step requires the output of the previous step as its input - *Figure 48.22*.

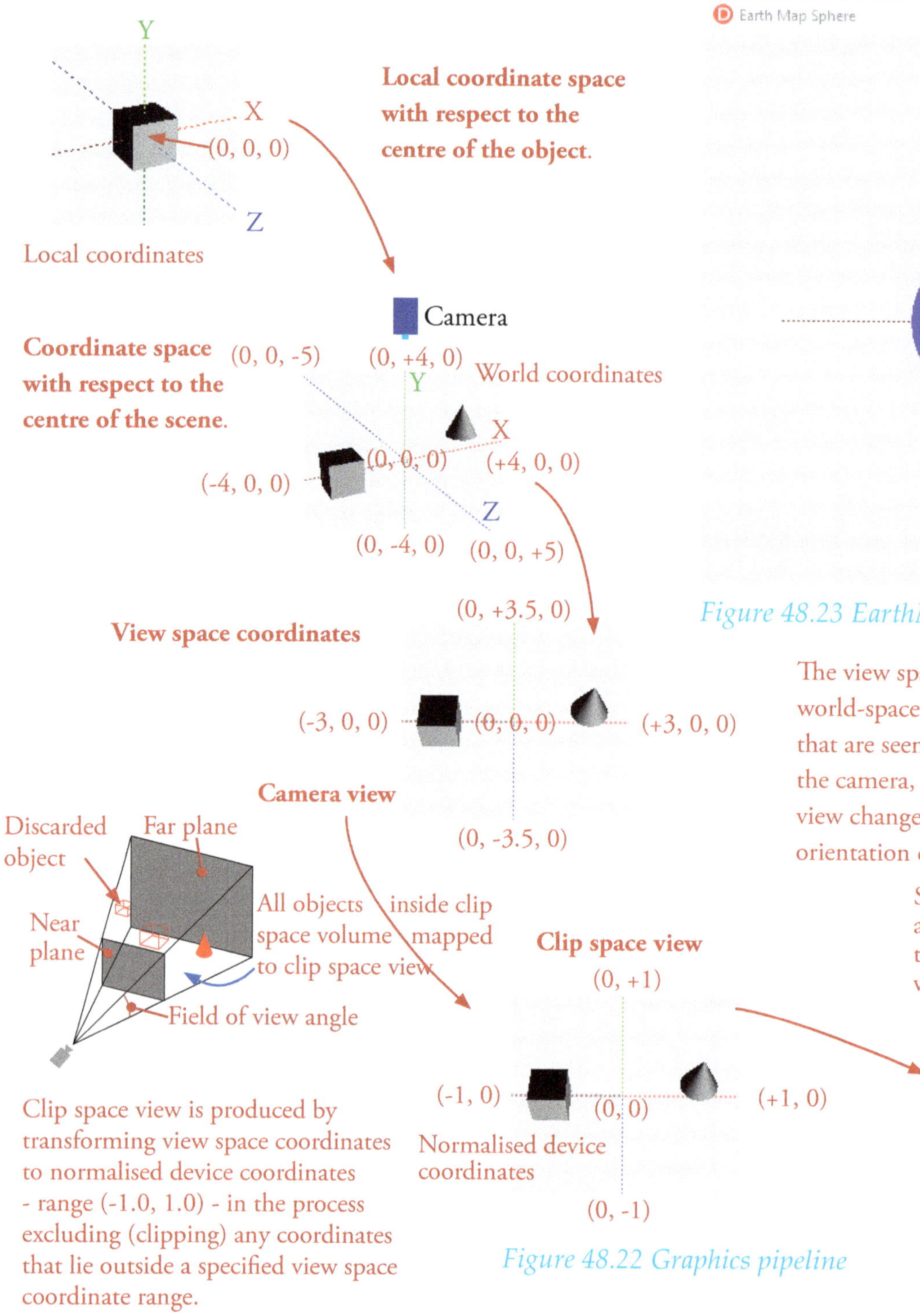

Figure 48.22 Graphics pipeline

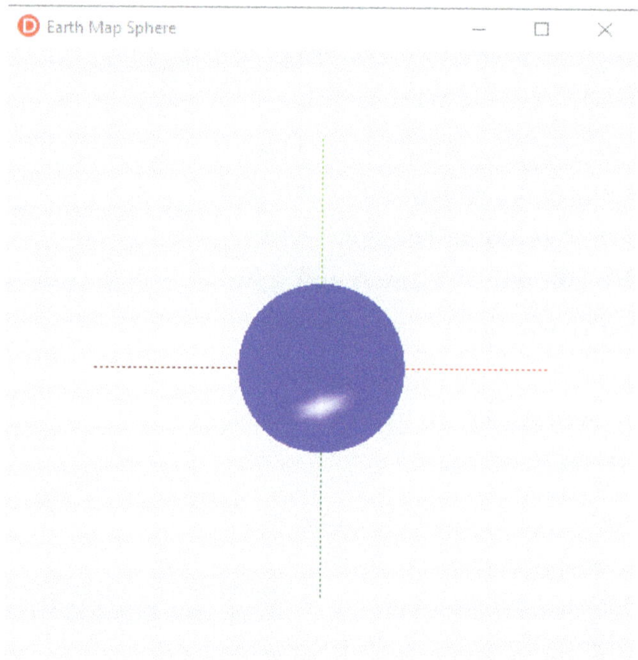

Figure 48.23 EarthMapSphereProject in execution

Let's now return to the `EarthMapSphereProject` so that we may explore how **GLScene** supports **OpenGL**.

Change the form's name to `frmEarthMapSphere` and its caption to `Earth Map Sphere`.

Select the components shown in *Table 48.2* in turn and **set** their properties in the **Object Inspector** as shown in *Table 48.2*.

Press **Shift+Ctrl+S** to save the project and unit file to folder `FirstExerciseSphereWithEarthMap`.

Press **F9** to compile and run the project.

Figure 48.23 shows the result.

Press **Ctrl + F2** to stop the execution. **Change** the **Slices** and **Stacks** properties of `GLSphere1` to 32 to make the profile of the sphere sharper. **Press** **Shift+Ctrl+S** to save the project and unit file.

GLSceneViewer1	**GLSphere1**	**GLCamera1**
Camera : **GLCamera1**	Direction.X : 0	CameraStyle : csPerspective
FieldOfView : 150	Direction.Y : 0	Direction.X : 0
Height : 337	Direction.Z : 1	Direction.Y : 0
Left : 64	Material.FrontProperties.Diffuse : clrBlue	Direction.Z : -1
Top : 72	Material.FrontProperties.Ambient : clrBlue	DepthOfView : 100
Width : 329	Material.FrontProperties.Emission : clrGray20	FocalLength : 50
	Material.FrontProperties.Shininess : 128	NearPlaneBias : 1
GLLightSource1	Material.FrontProperties.Specular : clrWhite	Position.X : 0
Ambient : clrBlue	Material.BlendingMode : bmOpaque	Position.Y : 0
Diffuse : clrWhite	Position.X : 0	Position.Z : 5
LightStyle : IsSpot	Position.Y : 0	SceneScale : 1
Position.X : 0	Position.Z : 0	TargetObject : GLSphere1
Position.Y : -5	Radius : 1	
Position.Z : 5	RollAngle : 0	
Shining : True	Scale.X : 1	
Specular : clrWhite	Scale.Y : 1	
SpotCutOff : 180	Scale.Z : 1	
SpotDirect.X : 0	ShowAxes : True	
SpotDirection.Y :	Up.X : 0	
SpotDirection.Z : -1	Up.Y : 1	
	Up.Z : 0	

Table 48.2 Property settings for GLSceneViewer1, GLLightSource1, GLSphere1 and GLCamera1

First GLScene project extended

Copy the contents of folder `FirstExerciseSphereWithEarthMap` to a new folder `SecondExerciseSphereWithEarthMap` and open this project in the Delphi IDE.

Copy image file `Earth.jpg` to folder `SecondExerciseSphereWithEarthMap`.

www.educational-computing.com/DelphiBook/Code/Chapter48/Earth.jpg

Select `GLSphere1` in the **Object Inspector**.

Click the ellipsis (**...**) in the property field of **Material**|**Texture**|**Image** to open the folder shown in *Figure 48.24*. **Select** `Earth.jpg` and **click** **Open**.

Click the ellipsis (**...**) in `GLSphere1`'s **Material** property field to bring up the **Material Editor** shown in *Figure 48.25*. **Deselect** the **Disabled** checkbox then **click** **OK**.

The map of the earth should now be visible and wrapped around `GLSphere1`.

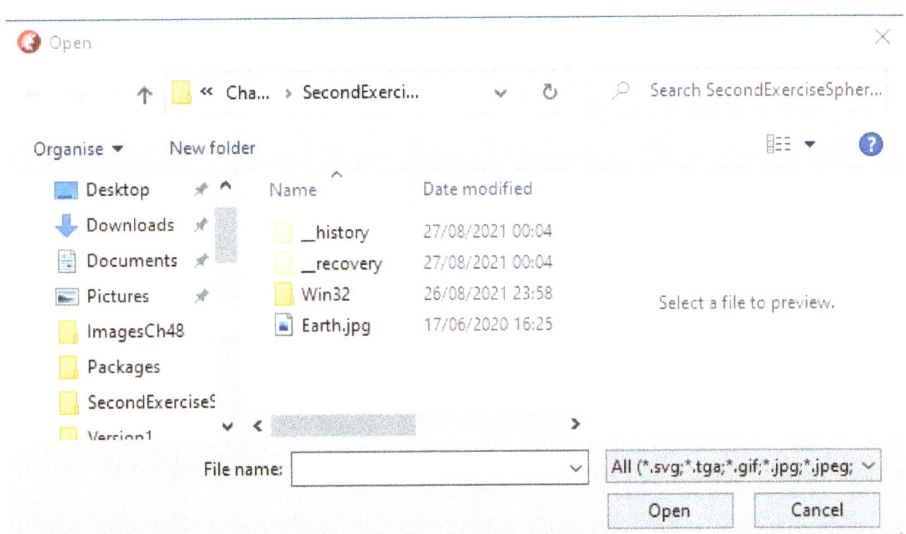

Figure 48.24 Folder SecondExerciseSphereWithEarthMap

(www.educational-computing.co.uk/DelphiBookCode/DelphiCode.html)

Add a **TGLCadencer** component from the **GLScene** palette to the form.

This component was chosen in order to illustrate the difference between a timer and a cadencer. The cadencer component triggers "progression events". Unlike a timer component, progression events do not happen at a fixed interval. Instead, they usually happen once the previous frame is complete.

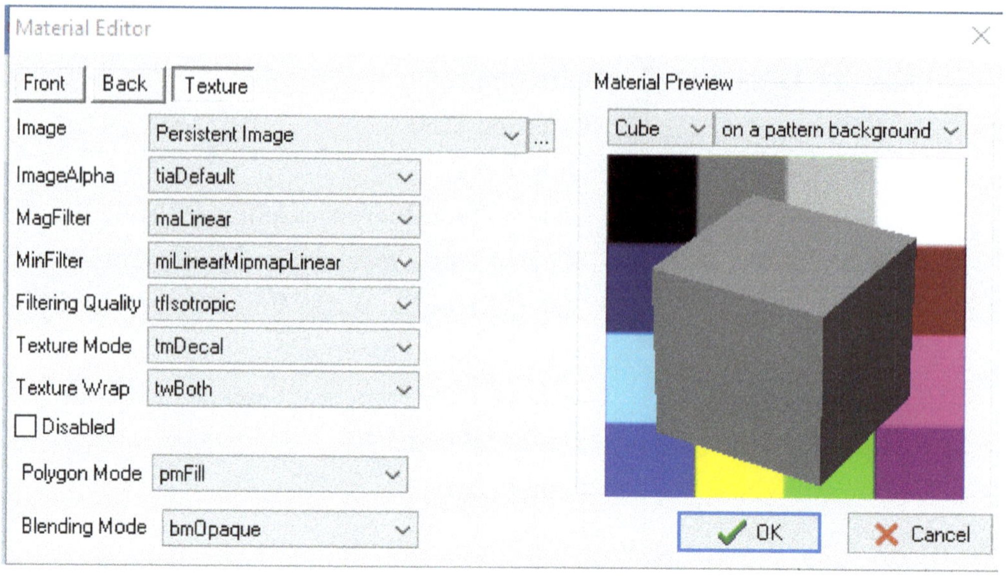

Figure 48.25 Material Editor

A **TGLCadencer** component takes account of the fact that scene rendering may take a variable amount of time depending on factors such as the scene's complexity and the rendering hardware. In contrast, a **TTimer** component operates at a pre-configured rate and therefore ignores whether frame rendering is complete or not. Using a **TTimer** component can thus result in noticeable flickering of the rendered scene. On the other hand, much smoother scene rendering is achieved with a **TGLCadencer** component because it supports frame by frame synchronisation and therefore synchronised updation of objects.

The process of rendering a frame results in the occurrence of an **OnProgress** event when the rendering is complete. Every **GLScene** object has an **OnProgress** event where all extra actions that are required to be executed every time the scene is rendered may be coded. Double clicking an object in the **Object Inspector** adds an **OnProgress** event to the form.

The **onProgress** event handler has two parameters:

1. **deltaTime** - the time period in seconds between when the rendering of last frame is completed and when rendering of the current frame is completed. This depends on the frame rate. The ideal frame rate is 30 frames per second - **deltaTime** 0.033333 seconds. Slower frame rates can result in jerkier motion. It is important to do any calculations related to time using **deltaTime**, e.g.

   ```
   GLSphere1.TurnAngle := GLSphere1.TurnAngle + 100*deltaTime;
   ```

   rotates a sphere, `GLSphere1`, with speed of 100 angular units per second about the turn axis where the angular unit is **deltaTime** degrees. This ensures that the rotation speed is independent of the frame rate (faster hardware results in a smaller rotation unit but more scene renders per second; slower hardware results in a larger rotation unit but fewer scene renders per second).

2. **newTime** - is the current time. Subtracting the current and previous **newTime** (time between consecutive progression events) computes **deltaTime** since **deltaTime** is the time interval between progression events.

TGLCadencer has an **Enabled** property which can be set to turn on the **TGLCadencer** component and reset to turn it off. When it is turned off the scene is frozen. **TGLCadencer** supports several modes of operation, **cmASAP** is the default mode. This mode progresses the scene whenever it can, giving it the highest priority.

We need to add more components to produce a rotating earth with a background of stars:

1. In the **Structure** pane, **right click** `GLScene1` to bring up the window shown in *Figure 48.15* then **click** left mouse button on **Show Scene Editor** to bring up **GLScene Editor** shown in *Figure 48.16*.
2. **Click Scene objects** to bring up the window shown in *Figure 48.17*.
3. **Click Add object** to bring up the objects window shown in *Figure 48.18*.
4. **Click DummyCube** to add a **TGLDummyCube**, `GLDummyCube1`. **Repeat** to add another, `GLDummyCube2`.
5. **Select** `GLDummyCube2` then **right click** it to bring up the **Add Object** menu. **Select Add Object** then **select Environment objects** and from these objects **select SkyDome**. to add `GLSkyDome1` object to `GLDummyCube2`.
6. **Make** `GLDummyCube1` the parent of `GLSphere1` by moving the latter in the **GLScene Editor** window to beneath `GLDummyCube1` - *Figure 48.26* shows the result.

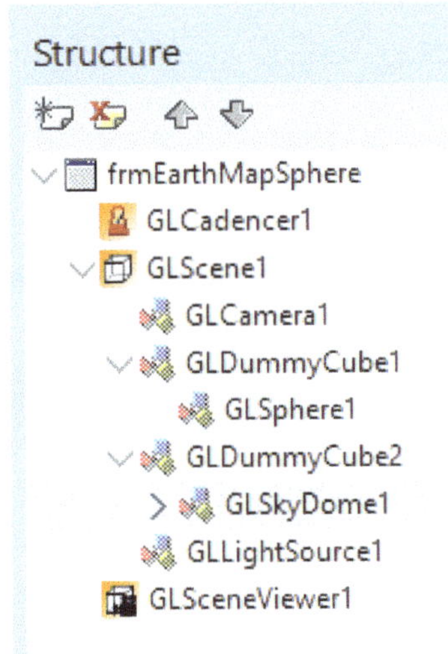

Figure 48.26 Structure pane

Make sure that the **Scene** property of `GLCadencer1` is set to `GLScene1`.
Make sure that the property **Direction.Z** of `GLSkyDome1` is set to `1`.
Select the form `frmEarthMapSphere`. In the **Events** tab **double click** the **OnCreate** event to create event handler `FormCreate`.

Add the code shown in *Table 48.3* to its body. This code will load the star map[1] `'Yale_BSC.stars'` into `GLSkyDome1`'s **Stars** property. **Place** the star map file where the executable of the Delphi program can find it. To locate the executable's path programmatically use

```
Path := ExtractFilePath(Paramstr(0));
```

`Path` is a user-defined variable of type **String**.

Select `GLSphere1` then in the **Events** tab **double click** the **OnProgress** event to create event handler `GLSphere1Progress`.

Add the code shown in *Table 48.3* to its body.

Set the **Align** property of `GLSceneViewer1` to **alClient** so that it fills the client area of the form.

Press Shift+Ctrl+S to save the project and unit file to folder `FirstExerciseSphereWithEarthMap`.
Press F9 to compile and run the project.
Figure 48.27 shows the result.

The earth rotates at a steady rate against a backdrop of stars.

Figure 48.27 Rotating earth against a backdrop of stars

Second GLScene project extended

Copy the contents of folder `SecondExerciseSphereWithEarthMap` to a new folder `Sputnik` and open this project in the Delphi IDE.

1 http://tdc-www.harvard.edu/catalogs/bsc5.html

(www.educational-computing.co.uk/DelphiBookCode/DelphiCode.html)

P

```
Unit EarthMapSphereUnit;
Interface
Uses
  Winapi.Windows, Winapi.Messages, System.SysUtils, System.Variants, System.Classes,
  Vcl.Graphics, Vcl.Controls, Vcl.Forms, Vcl.Dialogs, GLS.SceneViewer, GLS.BaseClasses,
  GLS.Scene, GLS.Objects, GLS.Coordinates, GLS.Cadencer, GLS.SkyDome;
Type
  TfrmEarthMapSphere = Class(TForm)
                        GLScene1: TGLScene;
                        GLSceneViewer1: TGLSceneViewer;
                        GLCamera1: TGLCamera;
                        GLLightSource1: TGLLightSource;
                        GLSphere1: TGLSphere;
                        GLCadencer1: TGLCadencer;
                        GLSkyDome1: TGLSkyDome;
                        GLDummyCube1: TGLDummyCube;
                        GLDummyCube2: TGLDummyCube;
                        Procedure GLSphere1Progress(Sender : TObject;
                                    Const deltaTime, newTime : Double);
                        Procedure FormCreate(Sender : TObject);
                      End;
Var
  frmEarthMapSphere: TfrmEarthMapSphere;
Implementation
Uses System.UITypes;
{$R *.dfm}
Procedure TfrmEarthMapSphere.FormCreate(Sender : TObject);
  Begin
    GLSkydome1.Bands.Clear;
    If FileExists('Yale_BSC.stars')
      Then GLSkydome1.Stars.LoadStarsFile('Yale_BSC.stars');
  End;
Procedure TfrmEarthMapSphere.GLSphere1Progress(Sender : TObject; Const deltaTime, newTime : Double);
  Begin
    GLSphere1.TurnAngle := GLSphere1.TurnAngle + 100*deltaTime;
  End;
End.
```

www.educational-computing.com/DelphiBook/Code/Chapter48/Yale_BSC.stars

Table 48.3 EarthMapSphereUnit.Pas in SecondExerciseSphereWithEarthMap folder

1. In the **Structure** pane, **right click** GLScene1 to bring up the **Show Scene Editor** window then **click** left mouse button on **Show Scene Editor** to bring up **GLScene Editor**.
2. **Right Click GLDummyCube1** to bring up **Add Object** window. and from the **Basic Geometry select Sphere** to add a sphere, GLSphere2, to GLDummyCube1.
3. **Set** its **Radius** property to 0.05, its **Slices** and **Stacks** properties to 32. **Set Position.Y** property to 2. **Set ShowAxes** property to **False**. **Set** the **FrontProperties** and **BackProperties** property fields for **Diffuse**, **Emission** and **Specular** to **clrBrown**.
4. **Add GLS.Keyboard** to the **Uses** clause of the **Interface**.

(www.educational-computing.co.uk/DelphiBookCode/DelphiCode.html)

5. **Create** an **OnProgress** event handler for `GLSphere2` and **add** the code shown in *Table 48.4* to its body. **Add** the variable declaration shown in *Table 48.4* to the **Implementation** section.

6. **Add** a **TGLSoundLibrary** and a **TGLSMFMOD** component from the **GLScene** palette to the form.

7. **Add** **GLS.FileMP3** to the **Uses** clause in the Interface.

8. **Add** `GLSoundLibrary1.Samples.AddFile('Sputnik.mp3', 'Sputnik.mp3');` to the event handler `FormCreate`.

9. **Select** `GLSMFMOD1` and **set** the **Cadencer** property to `GLCadencer1`, **set** the **Listener** property to `GLSphere1`, **set** its **Active** property to **True**.

10. **Select** `GLSMFMOD1` and **open** its tree. **Right click** on **Sources** and then **select** **Add item**. In the **Object Inspector** **set** the **SoundLibrary** property to `GLSoundLibrary1`, the **SoundName** property to `Sputnik.mp3`, the **NbLoops** property to 10000.

P

```
Var
  Theta : Double;
  Speed : Double = 0.0005;

Procedure TSimpleSphereAnimation.GLSphere2Progress(Sender: TObject; Const deltaTime,newTime: Double);
  Begin
    // handle keypresses
    If IsKeyDown(VK_UP)
      Then Speed := 2 * deltaTime;
    If IsKeyDown(VK_RIGHT)
      Then Speed := 4 * deltaTime;
    If IsKeyDown(VK_LEFT)
      Then Speed := 0.5 * deltaTime;
    If IsKeyDown(VK_DOWN) Then Speed := deltaTime;
    If IsKeyDown(VK_ESCAPE)
      Then Close;
    Theta := (Theta + Speed);
    If (Abs(Theta - (2 * 3.142)) < 0.001)
      Then Theta := 0.0;
    GLSphere2.Position.Z := 2 * cos(Theta);
    GLSphere2.Position.Y := 2 * sin(Theta);
  End;
```

Table 48.4 Event handler for OnProgress event for GLSphere2

Place the star map file, `'Yale_BSC.stars'`, and the sound file, `'Sputnik.mp3'`, where the executable of the Delphi program can find it.

Press Shift+Ctrl+S to save the project and unit file to folder `Sputnik`.

Press F9 to compile and run the project.

Figure 48.28 shows the result. When the program is executing the sound made by Sputnik is played.

(`'Sputnik.mp3'` downloaded from http://www.ddlus.de/spacesounds%201.html was digitized and kindly provided by Federico Manzini)

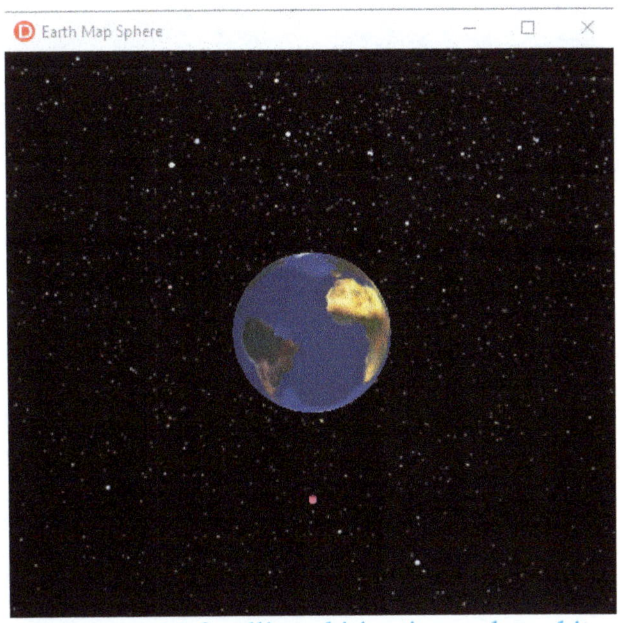

Figure 48.28 Satellite orbiting in a polar orbit about a rotating earth

Heightmaps

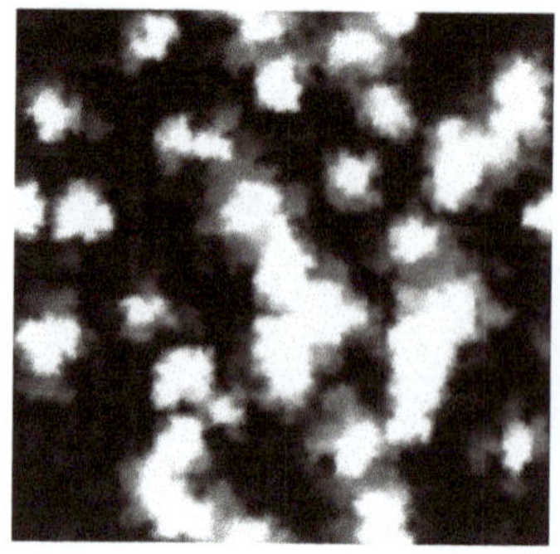

Figure 48.29 Bitmap image of file Heightmap.bmp which is used in the program HeightMapDemoProject.dpr

In computer graphics, a heightmap is a two dimensional raster/bitmap representation of a three dimensional terrain map as viewed from above - *Figure 48.29* - in which each pixel stores a value/values that represent surface elevation data. The heightmap is used to elevate a 3D mesh so that it can represent the contouring of a terrain. The brighter areas in *Figure 48.29* represent higher terrain, e.g. mountains, while the darker areas represent lower regions , e.g. valleys.

The data stored in the heightmap, `Heightmap.bmp`, shown as a bitmap image in *Figure 48.29* is interpreted as height above a base level of the terrain being modelled. This information is coded as a greyscale image, with black representing minimum height and white representing maximum height. The amount of displacement for each unit of the height data is specified by the program that renders the heightmap - *Figure 48.30*. Heightmaps may be created using propriety software such as World Machine - www.world-machine.com - or 3D-Mapper - 3d-map-generator.com or using free software such as terrain.party. One or more textures are then applied to the mesh to generate the terrain as shown in *Figure 48.31* and *Figure 48.32*.

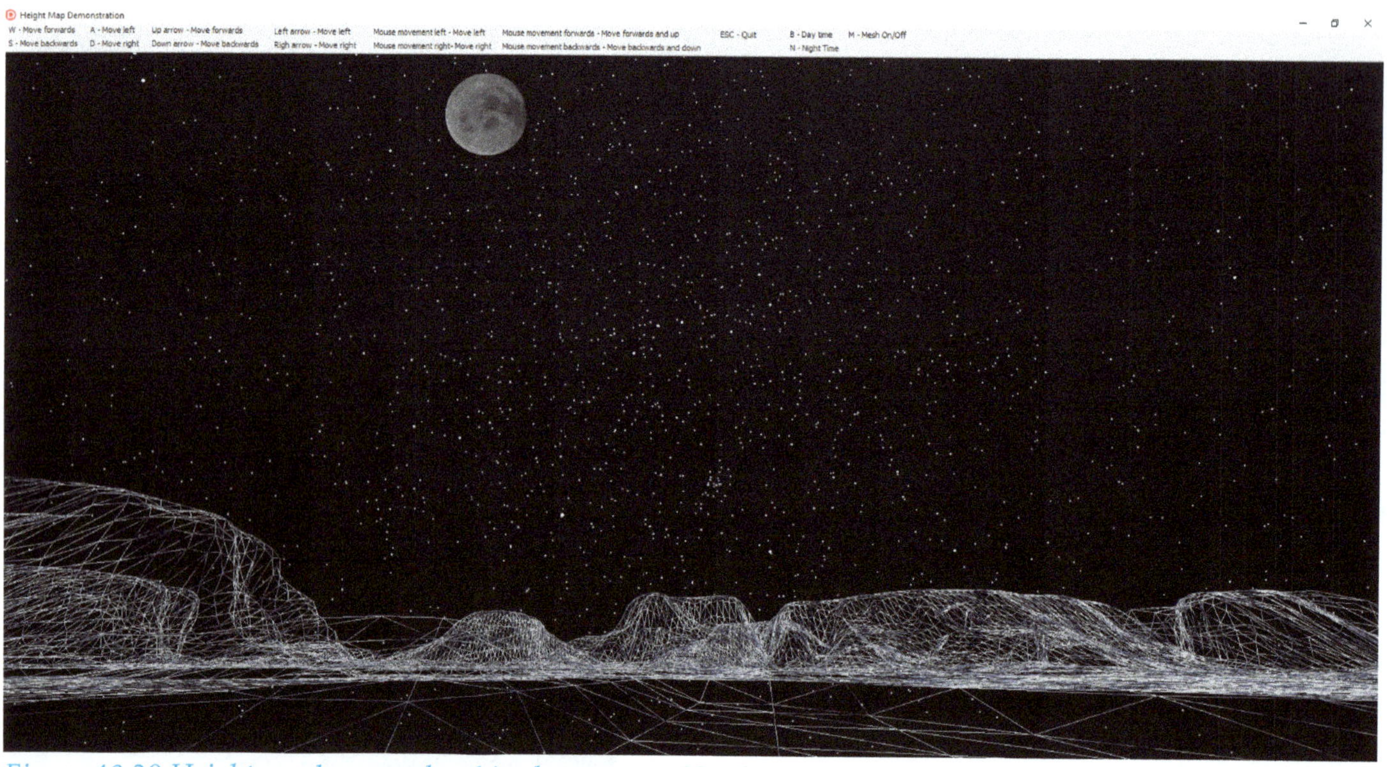

Figure 48.30 Heightmap.bmp rendered in the program HeightMapDemoProject.dpr to raise the mesh as shown

HeightMapDemoProject (Based on Terrain demo source code including images and sound files from GLScene released under Mozilla Public License Version 2.0 **http://mozilla.org/MPL/2.0/**

Create a new Windows VCL application (**File|New**).

Save the project as `HeightMapDemoProject` and the unit as `HeightMapDemoUnit` (**File|Save Project As...**) in folder `HeightMapDemo`.

1. **Add** a **TGLScene** object from the **GLScene** palette to the form.
2. **Add** a **TPanel** component, `Panel1`, from the **Standard** component palette and **place** on the form.
3. **Select** its **Align** property and set to **alTop**.

Figure 48.31 Heightmap.bmp rendered textured with Snow512.jpg and Detailmap.jpg in the program HeightMapDemoProject.dpr to cover the mesh the mesh as shown in night time view

Figure 48.32 Heightmap.bmp rendered textured with Snow512.jpg and Detailmap.jpg in the program HeightMapDemoProject.dpr to cover the mesh the mesh as shown in day time view

4. **Add** a **TGLSceneViewer** from the **GLScene** palette to the form.
5. **Select** its **Align** property and **set** to **alClient**.
6. In the **Structure** pane, **select** and then **right click** `GLScene1` and **select** the **Show Scene Editor** to bring up the **GLScene Editor** window.
7. **Select** and **right click** **Scene objects** then **click** **Add object** to bring up the objects window.

8. **Click DummyCube** to add a dummy cube, GLDummyCube1 to the scene and then **select Scene objects** and **repeat** to create another, GLDummyCube2. The background needs to be in its own dummy cube, GLDummyCube2 for it to render correctly..
9. In the Structure pane, **select** and then **right click** GLScene1 then **click** left mouse button on Show Scene Editor to bring up GLScene Editor. **Select** and then **right click** GLDummyCube2 then **Add object** from the popup window. **Select** Environment objects palette and **select SkyDome**.
10. In the Scene Editor, **select** GLDummyCube2 then in the Object Inspector **click** the ellipsis (**...**) for **(TGLSkyDomeBands)** property. **Select** the **0-0:** option in the Editing GLSkyDome1Bands popup window and **set** the **StartAngle** property to -5 and the **StopAngle** property to 25. **Select** the **0-1:** option in the Editing GLSkyDome1Bands popup window and **set** the **StartAngle** property to 25 and the **StopAngle** property to 90. **Set Direction.Y** to 1, **Position.Y** to 1 and **Up.Z** to -1. All other **Direction**, **Position** and **Up** settings should be 0.
11. In the Structure pane, **select** and then **right click** GLScene1 then **click** left mouse button on Show Scene Editor to bring up GLScene Editor. **Select** and then **right click** GLDummyCube2 then **select Add object** from the popup window. **Select** Mesh objects palette and **select Terrain renderer** to add GLTerrainRenderer1 to the GLDummyCube2.
12. **Add** a **TGLBitmapHDS** component, GLBitmapHDS1, from the GLScene Terrain component palette to the form. **Use** the Object Inspector to set its **InfiniteWrap** property to **True**. This is done so that as the user moves about the scene the user will always see terrain.
13. **Set** the following properties for GLTerrainRenderer1 as shown
    a. **ClodPrecision** to 1000
    b. **Direction.Y** to 1, other directions to 0
    c. **HeightDataSource** to **GLBitmapHDS1**
    d. **Position.X** to 0, **Position.Y** to 0, **Position.Z** to 0.
    e. **Scale.X** to 10, **Scale.Y** to 10 and **Scale.Z** to 0.4
    f. **Up.Z** to 1, **Up.X** to 0, **Up.Y** to 0
    g. **QualityDistance** to 1000
    h. **QualityStyle** to **hrsFullGeometry**
    i. **Set Material.Texture.ImageAlpha** to **tiaImageFromIntensity** and **Material.PolygonMode** to **pmLines**.
    j **Accept** the default values for all the other properties.
14. **Select** GLScene1 and bring up the GL Scene Editor as before. **Select** GLDummyCube1 then **right click** and **select Add object** then **Camera** to add GLCamera1 to GLDummyCube1.
15. **Set** the following properties for GLCamera1 as shown
    a. **DepthOfView** to 1000
    b. **Direction.Z** to -1, **Direction.X** to 0, **Direction.Z** to 0.
    c. **FocalLength** to 1000
    d. **Position.Y** to 4, **Position.X** to 0, **Position.Y** to 0.
    e. **Leave TargetObject** blank
    f. **Up.Y** to 1, **Up.X** to 0, **Up.Z** to 0.

16. **Set** GLSceneViewer1 **Camera** property to GLCamera1.
17. The user interface should show two regions, one skylike and the other black as shown in *Figure 48.33*.
18. In the **Object Inspector**, **select** the form and **change** its **Name** property to HeightMapDemo and its **Caption** property to Height Map Demonstration. In the **Events** tab **double click** **OnCreate** to create an event handler THeightMapDemo.FormCreate. **Add** the code shown in *Table 48.5*. **Set** **WindowState** to **wsMaximized**.

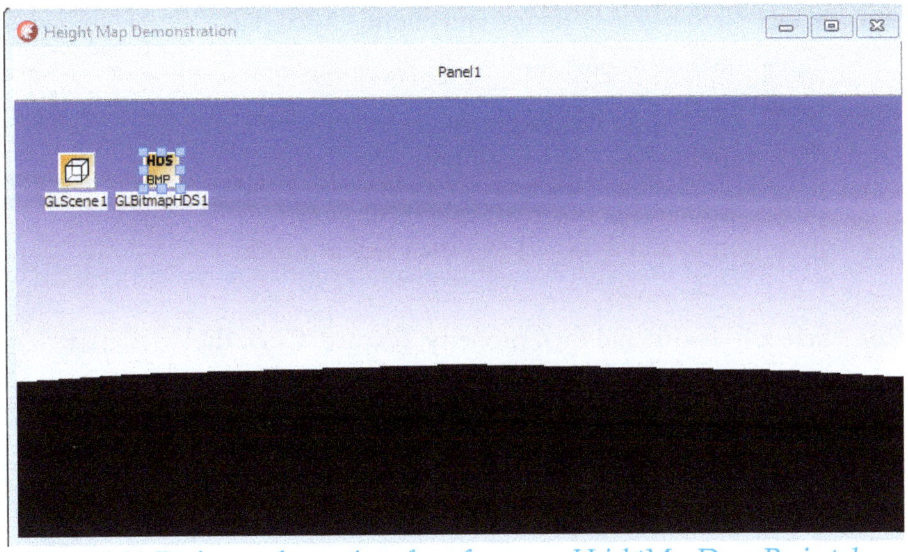

Figure 48.33 Design mode user interface of program HeightMapDemoProject.dpr

```
Procedure THeightMapDemo.FormCreate(Sender : TObject);
  Begin
    GLBitmapHDS1.Picture.LoadFromFile('HeightMap.bmp');
    SetCursorPos(Width Div 2, Height div 2);
  End;
```

Table 48.5 FormCreate event handler which loads heigthmap

19. In the **Structure** pane, **select** and then **right click** GLScene1 then **click** left mouse button on **Show Scene Editor** to bring up **GLScene Editor**. **Select** and then **right click** GLDummyCube1 then **Add object** from the popup window. **Select** **LightSource** palette to add a camera GLLightSource1. **Set** **LightStyle** to **IsSpot**, **Ambient**, **Diffuse** and **Specular** to **clrWhite**, **Shining** to **True** and **CutOff** to 180. **Set** **SpotDirection.Z** to -1, the other fields to 0. **Position.Y** to 4, the other fields to 0.
20. **Press** **Shift+Ctrl+S** to save the project and unit file to folder HeightMapDemo.
21. **Press** **Shift + F9** to build the project.
22. **Place** the bitmap file HeightMap.bmp where the executable can find it.
23. **Press** **F9** to run the project. *Figure 48.34* shows the result.

Figure 48.34 HeightMapDemoProject.dpr in execution in mesh mode (pmLines)

24. **Select** `GLTerrainRender1` and **change** **Material.PolygonMode** to **pmLines**.
25. **Select** **TerrainEx** property of `GLTerrainRender1`, **click** the ellipsis (**...**) to bring up the **Editing GLRender1.TerrainEx** window. **Click** the **Add New (Ins)** icon to add **0-Tex[0]** and then **repeat** to add **1-Tex[1]** as shown in *Figure 48.35*.

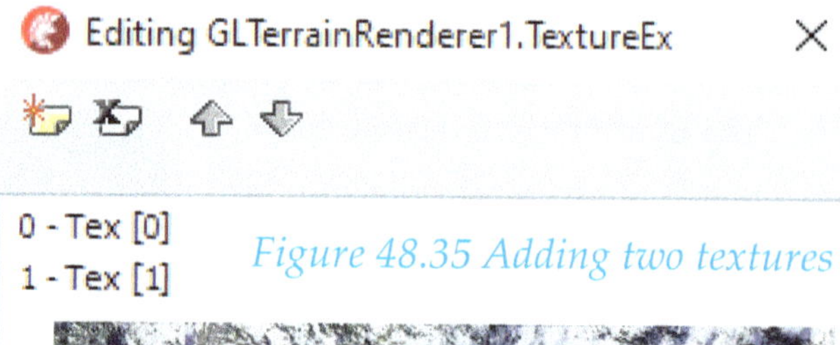

Figure 48.35 Adding two textures

26. **Select** **0-Tex[0]** and then property **Texture**. **Click** the ellipsis (**...**) to open a file explorer window. **Find** and **load** `Snow512.jpg`. **Set** **Texture.Disabled** to **False**. **Set** **DepthTextureMode** to **dtmLuminance**. **Set** **Texture.TextureMode** to **tmReplace**. *Figure 48.36* shows the image stored in file `Snow512.jpg`.

Figure 48.36 Snow512.jpg

27. **Select** **0-Tex[1]** and then property **Texture**. **Click** the ellipsis (**...**) to open a file explorer window. **Find** and **load** `DetailMap.jpg`. **Set** **Texture.Disabled** to **False**. **Set** **DepthTextureMode** to **dtmLuminance**. **Set** **Texture.TextureMode** to **tmModulate**. *Figure 48.37* shows the image stored in file `DetailMap.jpg`.
28. **Press** **Shift+Ctrl+S** to save the project and unit file to folder `HeightMapDemo`.
29. **Press** **Shift + F9** to build the project.
30. **Press** **F9** to run the project.*Figure 48.38* shows the result.
31. **Experiment** with the other **TextureMode** properties for **0-Tex[0]**.
32. **Add** the following units to the **Uses** clause: `GLS.Keyboard`, `Vcl.Imaging.GIFImg`, `GLS.Color`, `GLS.State`, `GLS.VectorGeometry`.
33. **Add** a **TGLCadencer** component `GLCadencer1` to the form.

Figure 48.37 DetailMap.jpg

Figure 48.38 HeightMapDemoProject.dpr in execution in fill mode (pmFill) with two textures

34. In the **Events** tab of `GLCadencer1`, **double click** the **OnProgress** property field to create an event handler `GLCadencer1Progress`. **Add** the code shown in *Table 48.6*. **IsKeyDown** is supplied by unit `GLS.Keyboard`. **ClampValue** by unit `GLS.VectorGeometry`, **pmLines** and **pmFill** by `GLS.State`, **TGIFColorMap** by `Vcl.Imaging.GIFImg`, **clrNavy**, etc by **GLS.Color**.

```
Procedure THeightMapDemo.GLCadencer1Progress(Sender : TObject; Const deltaTime, newTime : Double);
  Var
    MovementStep : single;
    Color : TGifColor;
  Begin
    With Mouse.CursorPos, GLCamera1, Screen
      Do
        Begin
          GLDummyCube1.Turn((X - (Width Div 2)) * 0.2);
          PitchAngle := ClampValue(PitchAngle + ((Height Div 2) - Y) * 0.2, -90, 90);
          SetCursorPos(Width Div 2, Height Div 2);
        End;
    If IsKeyDown(vk_lshift)
      Then MovementStep := 200 * deltaTime
      Else MovementStep := 50 * deltaTime;
    If IsKeyDown(Ord('W')) Or IsKeyDown(vk_up)
      Then GLDummyCube1.Move(-1 * MovementStep);
    If IsKeyDown(Ord('S')) Or IsKeyDown(vk_down)
      Then GLDummyCube1.Move(0.85 * MovementStep);
    If IsKeyDown(Ord('A')) Or IsKeyDown(vk_left)
      Then GLDummyCube1.Slide(0.7 * MovementStep);
    If IsKeyDown(Ord('D')) Or IsKeyDown(vk_right)
      Then GLDummyCube1.Slide(-0.7 * MovementStep);
    If IsKeyDown(Ord('M'))
      Then
        With GLTerrainRenderer1.Material
          Do
            If PolygonMode = pmLines
              Then  PolygonMode := pmFill
              Else PolygonMode := pmLines;
    If IsKeyDown(Ord('N'))
      Then
        Begin
          If FileExists('Yale_BSC.stars')
            Then GLSkydome1.Stars.LoadStarsFile('Yale_BSC.stars');
          GLSceneViewer1.Buffer.BackgroundColor := clBlack;
          Color.Red := 0; Color.Green := 0; Color.Blue := 8;
          GLSkyDome1.Bands[0].StopColor.AsWinColor := TGIFColorMap.RGB2Color(Color);
          Color.Red := 0; Color.Green := 0; Color.Blue := 0;
          GLSkyDome1.Bands[0].StartColor.AsWinColor := TGIFColorMap.RGB2Color(Color);
          Color.Red := 0; Color.Green := 0; Color.Blue := 16;
          GLSkyDome1.Bands[1].StopColor.AsWinColor := TGIFColorMap.RGB2Color(Color);
          Color.Red := 0; Color.Green := 0; Color.Blue := 8;
          GLSkyDome1.Bands[1].StartColor.AsWinColor := TGIFColorMap.RGB2Color(Color);
          GLSprite1.Visible := True;
          GlSprite2.Visible := False;
        End;
    If IsKeyDown(Ord('B'))
      Then
        Begin
          GLSkyDome1.Bands[1].StopColor.Color := clrNavy;
          GLSkyDome1.Bands[1].StartColor.Color := clrBlue;
          GLSkyDome1.Bands[0].StopColor.Color := clrBlue;
          GLSkyDome1.Bands[0].StartColor.Color := clrWhite;
          GLSceneViewer1.Buffer.BackgroundColor := clBlack;
          GLSkydome1.Stars.Clear;
          GLSprite1.Visible := False;
          GlSprite2.Visible := True;
        End;
    GLDummyCube1.Position.Y := GLTerrainRenderer1.InterpolatedHeight(GLDummyCube1.AbsolutePosition);
    If IsKeyDown(vk_escape)
      Then Close;
  End;
```

Table 48.6 GLCadencer1Progress event handler

35. **Place** the file `Yale_BSC.stars` where the executable can find it.
36. In the **Events** tab of the form `HeightMapDemo`, **double click** the **OnShow** property field to create an event handler `FormShow`. **Add** the code shown in *Table 48.7*.

```
Procedure THeightMapDemo.FormShow(Sender : TObject);
  Begin
    GLCadencer1.Enabled := True;
  End;
```

Table 48.7 FormShow event handler

37. **Press** Shift+Ctrl+S to save the project and unit file to folder `HeightMapDemo`.
38. **Press** Shift + F9 to build the project.
39. **Press** F9 to run the project.
40. The scene may now be navigated as follows
    a. W - Move forwards, A - Move left, S - Move backwards, D - Move right
    b. Up arrow key - Move forwards, Left arrow key - Move left, Down arrow key - Move backwards, Right arrow key - Move right
    c. Mouse movement left - Move left, Mouse movement right - Move right, Mouse movement forwards - Move forwards, Mouse movement backward - Move backwards
    d. B- Day time, N- Night time, M - Mesh On/Off, Escape key - Quit
41. *Figure 48.39* shows the result.
42. **Select** `GLScene1` and bring up the **GL Scene Editor** as before. **Select** `GLSkyDome1` under `GLDummyCube2` then **right click** and **select** **Add object** then **Basic Geometry**, **add** a **GLSprite**, `GLSprite1` to `GLSkyDome1`.

Figure 48.39 HeightMapDemoProject.dpr in execution with some forwards movement with night time mode selected. Note the star sky.

43. **Select** `GLSprite1` and **set** its properties as follows
    a. **Material.BlendingMode** to **bmTransparency**, **Material.DepthProperties.DepthCompareFunction** to **Always**
    b. **Material.Texture.ImageAlpha** to **tiaAlphaFromIntensity**
    c. **Material.Texture.TextureMode** to **tmAdd**, **Material.DepthProperties.DepthWrite** to **False**

d. **Material.Texture.TextureFormat**to **tfRGBA16** (image was saved as RGB 16 bits per channel in png format), **Material.DepthProperties.DepthTest** to **True**

e. **Material.Texture.ImageAlpha** to **tiaBottomRightPointColorTransparent** (picking a black area in the bottom right corner as the colour to make transparent)

f. **Material.Texture.Disabled** to **False**

g. **Direction.Z** to 1, the rest to 0

h. **Position.X** to -1.5, **Position.Y** to 1, **Position.Z** to 0

i. **Scale.X**, **Scale.Y** and **Scale.Z** to 0.2

j. **Up.Y** to 1, **Up.X** to 0, **Up.Z** to 0

k. **Visible** to **False**

44. **Select Material.Texture.Image** and **load** image `MoonRGBA16BitsPerChannel.png` (*Figure 48.40*).

Figure 48.40 MoonRGBA16BitsPerChannel.png

45. **Uncomment** the statements shown in *Table 48.6* that reference `GLSprite1`

46. **Press Shift+Ctrl+S** to save the project and unit file to folder `HeightMapDemo`.

47. **Press Shift + F9** to build the project.

48. **Press F9** to run the project. *Figure 48.41* shows the result when the night mode is selected.

Figure 48.41 HeightMapDemoProject.dpr in execution, night time mode selected

49. **Select** `GLScene1` and bring up the **GL Scene Editor** as before. **Select** `GLSkyDome1` under `GLDummyCube2` then **right click** and **select Add object** then **Basic Geometry**, **add** a **GLSprite**, `GLSprite2` to `GLSkyDome1`.

50. **Select** `GLSprite2` and **set** its properties as follows

a. **Material.BlendingMode** to **bmAdditive**, **Material.DepthProperties.DepthCompareFunction** to **Always**

b. **Material.MaterialOptions** to **[moIgnoreFog]**, **Material.DepthProperties.DepthWrite** to **False**
c. **Material.Texture.TextureMode** to **tmReplace**, **Material.DepthProperties.DepthTest** to **True**
d. **Material.Texture.TextureFormat** to **tfRGBA**,
e. **Material.Texture.ImageAlpha** to **tiaBottomRightCornerPointTransparent**
f. **Material.Texture.Disabled** to **False**
g. **Direction.Z** to 1, the rest to 0
h. **Position.X** to -1, **Position.Y** to 1, **Position.Z** to 0;
i. **Up.Y** to 1, the rest to 0.

51. **Select** **Material.Texture.Image** and **load** image `Flare.bmp` (*Figure 48.42*).

52. **Uncomment** the statements shown in *Table 48.6* that reference `GLSprite2`.

53. **Press** **Shift+Ctrl+S** to save the project and unit file to folder `HeightMapDemo`.

54. **Press** **Shift + F9** to build the project.

Figure 48.42 Flare.bmp

Figure 48.43 HeightMapDemoProject.dpr in execution

55. **Press** **F9** to run the project. *Figure 48.43* shows the result when the night mode is selected.

56. Now **add** a **TGLSoundLibrary** component, `GLSoundLibrary1`, and a **TGLSMBass** component, `GLSMBass1`, to the form.

57. **Select** the **Samples** property of `GLSoundLibrary1` and **click** the ellipsis (**...**) to bring up the **Editing GLSoundLibrary1.Samples** window. **Click** **Add New (Ins)** icon to add a new item. **Select** the **Data** property and **click** the ellipsis (**...**) to bring up the open file window. **Select** and **open** `ChillyWind.mp3`. The **Name** property value will be assigned the filename automatically. **Add** another item, this time open `Howl.mp3`.

58. **Select** `GLSMBass1` and **set** its properties as follows

a. **Active** to **True**
b. **Algorithm3D** to **algFull**

c. **Cadencer** to **GLCadencer1**

d. **Listener** to **GLCamera1**

59. **Add** two **TTimer** components, `Timer1` and `Timer2` to the form. **Set** their **Enabled** property to **True**.

60. **Select** the **Event** tab of `Timer1` in the **Object Inspector** and **double click** the **OnTimer** event field ito create an event handler `Timer1Timer`. **Add** the code shown in *Table 48.8* to its body.

61. **Select** the **Event** tab of `Timer2` in the **Object Inspector** and **double click** the **OnTimer** event field ito create an event handler `Timer2Timer`. **Add** the code shown in *Table 48.9* to its body.

The component `GLSMBass1` is associated with `GLCamera1` by assignment - see bullet 58.d. `GetOrCreateSoundEmitter(GLCamera1)` creates an object with a **Source.SoundLibrary** property. By assigning `GLSoundLibrary1` to this property and then assigning `GLSoundLibrary1.Samples[0].Name` to `Source.SoundName`, the mp3 sound file `ChillyWind.mp3` may be played when the event handler `Timer1Timer` is called. In a similar manner the mp3 sound file `Howl.mp3` may be played when the event handler `Timer2Timer` is called.

62. **Press** **Shift+Ctrl+S** to save the project and unit file to folder `HeightMapDemo`.

```
Procedure THeightMapDemo.Timer1Timer(Sender : TObject);
  Begin
    With GetOrCreateSoundEmitter(GLCamera1)
      Do
        Begin
          Source.SoundLibrary := GLSoundLibrary1;
          Source.SoundName := GLSoundLibrary1.Samples[0].Name;
          Source.Volume := Random * 0.5 + 0.5;
          Playing := True;
        End;
    Timer1.Enabled := False;
    Timer1.Interval := 1500 + Random(1500);
    Timer1.Enabled := True;
  End;
```

Table 48.8 Timer1Timer event handler

```
Procedure THeightMapDemo.Timer2Timer(Sender : TObject);
  Begin
    With GetOrCreateSoundEmitter(GLCamera1)
      Do
        Begin
          Source.SoundLibrary := GLSoundLibrary1;
          Source.SoundName := GLSoundLibrary1.Samples[1].Name;
          Source.Volume := Random * 0.5 + 0.5;
          Playing := True;
        End;
    Timer2.Enabled := False;
    Timer2.Interval := 2000 + Random(5000);
    Timer2.Enabled := True;
  End;
```

Table 48.9 Timer2Timer event handler

63. **Press** **Shift + F9** to build the project.

64. **Press** **F9** to run the project. The executing program now has sound to accompany the bleak environment.

65. **Stop** the program running - **Ctrl + F2**.

66. **Clear** `Panel1`'s caption.

67. **Add** 17 **TLabel** components to `Panel1` and position as shown in *Figure 48.44*.
68. **Rename** them as shown in *Table 48.10*.
69. **Set** the **Caption** property in the **Object Inspector** for each label to the value indicated in *Table 48.11*.
70. **Press** Shift+Ctrl+S to save the project and unit file.
71. **Press** Shift + F9 to build the project.
72. **Press** F9 to run the project.
73. **Use** the keys **WSAD** to move around the scene.
74. **Toggle** the mesh on and off using the **M** key.
75. **Switch** to the night time view by pressing the **N** key.
76. **Return** to day time view by pressing the **B** key.
77. **Test** the arrow keys on the keyboard.
78. **Move** the mouse to navigate left/right and up/down.
79. **Press** and hold down the Shift key and **repeat** 73 to 77.
80. **Press** the escape key to exit the program.

```
lblWMoveForwards : TLabel;
lblSMoveBackwards : TLabel;
lblAMoveLeft : TLabel;
lblDMoveRight : TLabel;
lblMMeshOnOff : TLabel;
lblNightTime : TLabel;
lblBDayTime : TLabel;
lblUpArrowMoveForwards : TLabel;
lblDownArrowMoveBackwards : TLabel;
lblLeftArrowMoveLeft : TLabel;
lblRighArrowMoveRight : TLabel;
lblMouseMovementLeft : TLabel;
lblMouseMovementRight : TLabel;
lblMouseMovementForwards : TLabel;
lblMouseMovementBackwards : TLabel;
lblESCQuit : TLabel;
```

Table 48.10 Labels added to Panel1

```
lblWMoveForwards.Caption = 'W - Move forwards'
lblSMoveBackwards.Caption = 'S - Move backwards'
lblAMoveLeft.Caption = 'A - Move left'
lblDMoveRight.Caption = 'D - Move right'
lblMMeshOnOff.Caption = 'M - Mesh On/Off'
lblNightTime.Caption = 'N - Night Time'
lblBDayTime.Caption = 'B - Day time'
lblUpArrowMoveForwards.Caption = 'Up arrow - Move forwards'
lblDownArrowMoveBackwards.Caption = 'Down arrow - Move backwards'
lblLeftArrowMoveLeft.Caption = 'Left arrow - Move left'
lblRightArrowMoveRight.Caption = 'Right arrow - Move right'
lblMouseMovementLeft.Caption = 'Mouse movement left - Move left'
lblMouseMovementRight.Caption = 'Mouse movement right- Move right'
lblMouseMovementForwards.Caption = 'Mouse movement forwards - Move forwards and up'
lblMouseMovementBackwards.Caption = 'Mouse movement backwards - Move backwards and down'
lblESCQuit.Caption = 'ESC - Quit'
lblShiftCaption = 'Press Shift to speed up movement'
```

Table 48.11 Label captions

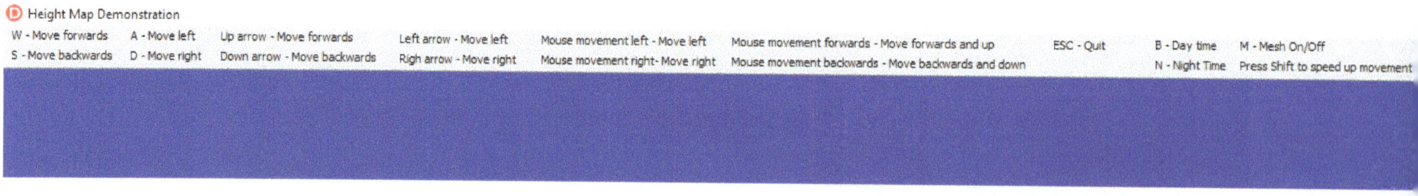

Figure 48.44 Shows the positions of the various labels added to Panel1

Particles in a box in two dimensions

Create a new Windows VCL application (**File|New**).

Save the project as `ParticlesInBoxProject` and the unit as `ParticlesInBoxUnit` (**File|Save Project As...**) in folder `ParticlesInABoxInTwoDimensions`.

1. **Add** a **TGLScene** object from the **GLScene** palette to the form.

2. **Add** a **TGLSceneViewer** from the **GLScene** palette to the form.
3. **Select** its **Align** property and **set** to **alClient**.
4. In the **Structure** pane, **select** and then **right click** `GLScene1` and **select** the **Show Scene Editor** to bring up the **GLScene Editor** window.
5. **Select** and **right click** **Scene objects** then **click** **Add object** to bring up the objects window.
6. **Click** **DummyCube** to add a dummy cube, `GLDummyCube1` to the scene.
7. **Select** and **right click** **Scene objects** then **click** **Add object** to bring up the objects window. **Select** `GLDummyCube1` in the **GLScene Editor** window. **Right click** `GLDummyCube1` and **select** **Add Object** then **Camera**. **Make** `GLDummyCube1` the **TargetObject** property value of `GLCamera1`. **Accept the default settings for** `GLCamera1`. **Set** `GLSceneViewer1`'s **Camera** property to `GLCamera1`.
8. **Add** a **TGLMaterialLibrary** component from the **GLScene** palette, `GLMaterialLibrary1`, to the form.
9. **Click** the ellipsis (...) in the **Materials** property of `GLMaterialLibrary1` to bring up the **Editing GLMaterialLibrary1.Materials** window. **Add** an item by clicking on the **Add New(Ins)** icon. **Name** the new item `LibMaterial`.
10. **Select** `0-LibMaterial` in the **Structure** window.
11. **Click** on **(TGLTextureImage)** in the property **Image** to bring up the open file window.
12. **Select** `RedCircle3.png` and open.
13. **Set** the properties as shown in *Figure 48.45*.

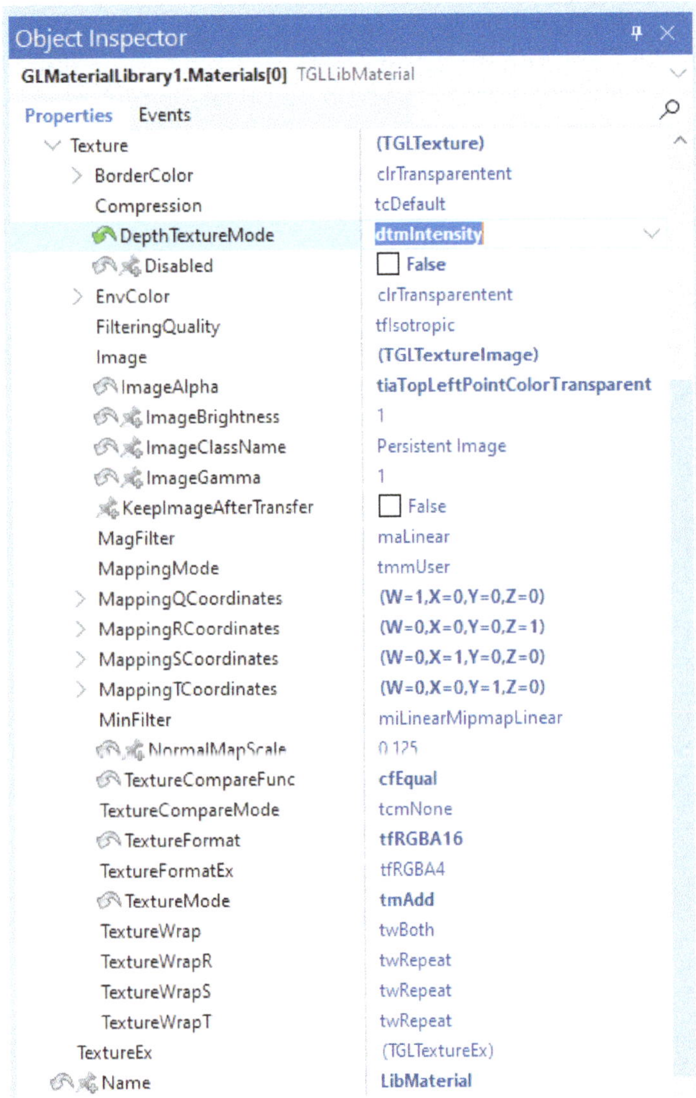

Figure 48.45 Object Inspector

`RedCircle3.png` is a 148 x 148 pixels image with a transparent black background - *Figure 48.46*. By setting **ImageAlpha** to **tiaTopLeftPointColourTransparent** the program will treat the black area surrounding the circle as transparent. This enables the underlying background colour to substitute for the black colour of this area. The image is saved in RGBA 16-bit format so **TextureFormat** is set to **tfRGBA16**. Using an 8-bit image would place less processing demand on the program.

14. **Add** a **TGLCadencer** component from **GLScene** palette, `GLCadencer1`, to the form.
15. **Set** its **Scene** property to `GLScene1`.
16. **Set** `Form1`'s **BorderWidth** to 10 and border **Color** to **clBlack**. **Set** its **Height** property to 546 and its **Width** to 724.
17. **Press** **Shift+Ctrl+S** to save the project and unit file to folder `ParticlesInABoxInTwoDimensions`.

Figure 48.46 RedCircle3.png

18. **Create** constant definitions, record type and variables in addition to `Form1` as shown in *Table 48.12*.

19. **Make** sure that the **Uses** statement includes all the libraries shown in *Table 48.12*. (Pressing **Ctrl + Shift + A** when the mouse cursor is in a type name brings up a window from which it is usually possible to select the unit to add it automatically). **GLScene** has its own **TVector** type. But the program could need more than offered by **GLScene**'s **TVector** so it was decided to use `System.Math.Vectors.TVector`. We could have used the more powerful **GLS.Vector.Geometry** vector support but not on this occasion.

```
Unit ParticlesInBoxUnit;
Interface
Uses
  Winapi.Windows, Winapi.Messages, System.SysUtils, System.Variants,
  System.Classes, Vcl.Graphics, Vcl.Controls, Vcl.Forms, Vcl.Dialogs,
  GLS.Scene, GLS.Objects, GLS.HUDObjects, GLS.Coordinates, GLS.BaseClasses,
  GLS.SceneViewer, GLS.Material, GLS.Cadencer,GLS.FullScreenViewer,
  GLS.Collision, GLS.DCE, GLS.XCollection, Math, System.Math.Vectors;
Type
  TForm1 = Class(TForm)
           GLSceneViewer1 : TGLSceneViewer;
           GLScene1 : TGLScene;
           GLCamera1 : TGLCamera;
           GLDummyCube1 : TGLDummyCube;
           GLMaterialLibrary1 : TGLMaterialLibrary;
           GLCadencer1 : TGLCadencer;
           Procedure GLCadencer1Progress(Sender : TObject;
                                         Const deltaTime,
                                         newTime: Double);
           Procedure FormCreate(Sender : TObject);
           Procedure FormDestroy(Sender : TObject);
           Procedure FormActivate(Sender : TObject);
         End;
Const
  cnstNoOfSprites = 10;//Maybe up to 1000
  cnstSpriteSize = 20;//May be 10
  cnstTemperature = 300;
  cnstTemperatureDeviation = 150;
Type
  TSprite = Record
            GLHudSprite : TGLHudSprite;
            WallCollisionX : Boolean;
            WallCollisionY : Boolean;
            VelocityVector : System.Math.Vectors.TVector;
            PositionVector : System.Math.Vectors.TVector;
          End;
  TSpriteArray = Array[0..cnstNoOfSprites - 1] Of TSprite;
Var
  Form1 : TForm1;
  SpriteArray : TSpriteArray;
  CollisionDetected : Boolean = False;
```

Table 48.12 Declarations for ParticlesInBoxUnit

20. **Create** event handlers for `Form1` for events, **OnCreate**, **OnActivate**, **OnDestroy**. **Add** the code shown in *Table 48.13* to the corresponding body.

21. **Select** the **Events** page of `GLCadencer1` and **double click** the **OnProgress** event to produce an event handler `GLCadencer1Progress`. **Add** the code shown in *Table 48.14*.

22. **Press** **Shift+Ctrl+S** to save the project and unit file to folder `ParticlesInABoxInTwoDimensions`.

23. **Press** **Shift + F9** to build the project.

24. **Press** **F9** to run the project.

25. *Figure 48.47* shows the result.

26. **Stop** the program running - **Ctrl + F2**.

27. **Change** `cnstNoOfSprites` to 100.

28. **Press** **Shift+Ctrl+S** to save the project and unit file.

29. **Press** **F9** to run the project (it will be rebuilt).

30. *Figure 48.47* shows the result.

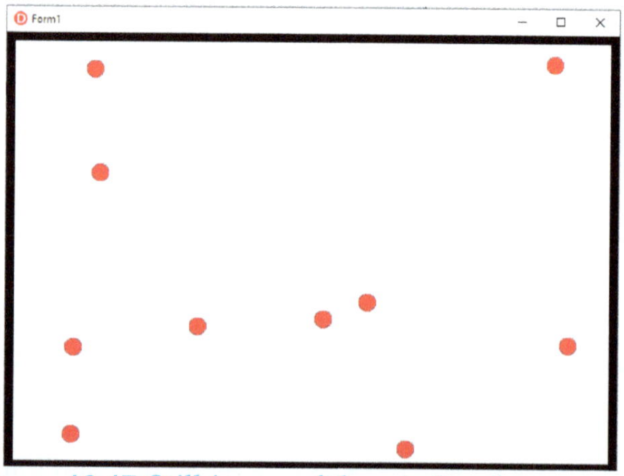

Figure 48.47 Still image of the window for ParticlesInBoxProject in execution with 10 particles

31. *Figure 48.48* shows the result.
32. **Stop** the program running - **Ctrl + F2**.
33. **Change** `cnstNoOfSprites` to 100.
34. **Press Shift+Ctrl+S** to save the project and unit file.
35. **Press F9** to run the project (it will be rebuilt).
36. *Figure 48.49* shows the result.

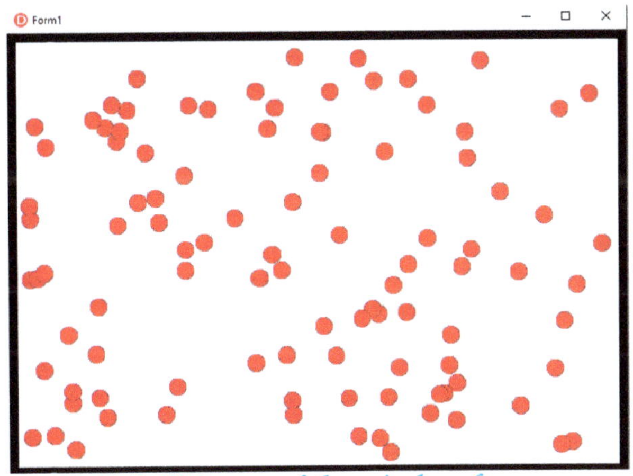

Figure 48.48 Still image of the window for ParticlesInBoxProject in execution with 100 particles

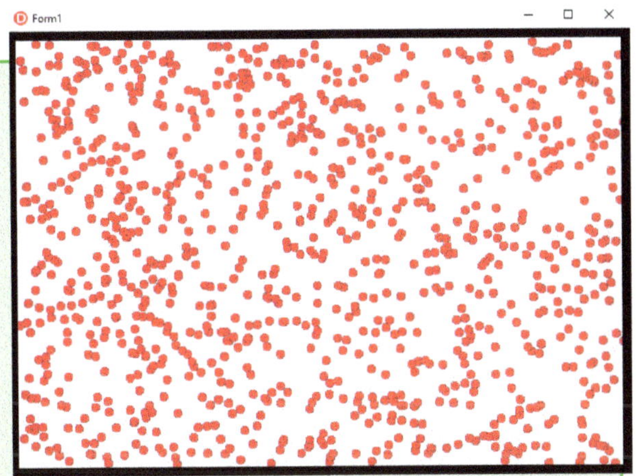

Figure 48.49 1000 particles, particles size 10

```
Implementation
{$R *.dfm}
Procedure TForm1.FormActivate(Sender : TObject);
  Begin
    GLCadencer1.Enabled := True;
  End;
Procedure TForm1.FormCreate(Sender : TObject);
  Var
    i : Integer;
    RandomXValue, RandomYValue : Single;
  Begin
    Randomize;
    For i := 0 To cnstNoOfSprites - 1
      Do
        Begin
          SpriteArray[i].GLHudSprite := TGLHudSprite.Create(Form1);
          SpriteArray[i].GLHudSprite.Width := cnstSpriteSize;
          SpriteArray[i].GLHudSprite.Height := cnstSpriteSize;
          SpriteArray[i].WallCollisionX := False;
          SpriteArray[i].WallCollisionY := False;
          SpriteArray[i].GLHudSprite.Material.MaterialLibrary := GLMaterialLibrary1;
          SpriteArray[i].GLHudSprite.Material.LibMaterialName := 'LibMaterial';
          SpriteArray[i].GLHudSprite.Material.Texture.Disabled := False;
          {--------------------------------------------------------------------------------}
          Repeat
            RandomXValue := Random(Form1.ClientWidth - 3*cnstSpriteSize);
          Until (RandomXValue > 0);
          Repeat
            RandomYValue := Random(Form1.ClientHeight  - 3*cnstSpriteSize);
          Until (RandomYValue > 0);
          SpriteArray[i].PositionVector := System.Math.Vectors.TVector.Create(RandomXValue, RandomYValue);
          Repeat
            RandomXValue := RandG(cnstTemperature, cnstTemperatureDeviation);
          Until (RandomXValue > 0);
          Repeat
            RandomYValue := RandG(cnstTemperature, cnstTemperatureDeviation);
          Until (RandomYValue > 0);
          SpriteArray[i].VelocityVector := System.Math.Vectors.TVector.Create(RandomXValue, RandomYValue);
          {--------------------------------------------------------------------------------}
          SpriteArray[i].GLHudSprite.Position.X := SpriteArray[i].PositionVector.X;
          SpriteArray[i].GLHudSprite.Position.Y := SpriteArray[i].PositionVector.Y;
          SpriteArray[i].GLHudSprite.Tag := i;
          If (i Mod 2 = 0)
            Then SpriteArray[i].VelocityVector.X := - SpriteArray[i].VelocityVector.X
            Else SpriteArray[i].VelocityVector.Y := - SpriteArray[i].VelocityVector.Y;
          SpriteArray[i].GLHudSprite.Parent := GLDummyCube1;
        End;
  End;
Procedure TForm1.FormDestroy(Sender : TObject);
  Var i : Integer;
  Begin
    For i := 0 To cnstNoOfSprites - 1
      Do SpriteArray[i].GLHudSprite.Free;
  End;
```

Table 48.13 Form event handlers

```
Procedure TForm1.GLCadencer1Progress(Sender : TObject; Const deltaTime,
                                     newTime : Double);
  Var
    i : Integer;
  Begin
    For i := 0 To cnstNoOfSprites - 1
      Do
        Begin
          If ((SpriteArray[i].PositionVector.X < (cnstSpriteSize/2))
            Or (SpriteArray[i].PositionVector.X > (Form1.ClientWidth)))
              And Not SpriteArray[i].WallCollisionX
                Then
                  Begin
                    SpriteArray[i].VelocityVector.X := -SpriteArray[i].VelocityVector.X;
                    SpriteArray[i].WallCollisionX := True;
                  End;
          If ((SpriteArray[i].PositionVector.Y < cnstSpriteSize/2)
              Or (SpriteArray[i].PositionVector.Y > (Form1.ClientHeight - cnstSpriteSize/2)))
                And Not SpriteArray[i].WallCollisionY
                Then
                  Begin
                    SpriteArray[i].VelocityVector.Y := -SpriteArray[i].VelocityVector.Y;
                    SpriteArray[i].WallCollisionY := True;
                  End;
          SpriteArray[i].PositionVector.X := SpriteArray[i].PositionVector.X
                                    + SpriteArray[i].VelocityVector.X*deltaTime;
          If SpriteArray[i].WallCollisionX
            Then
              Begin
                If SpriteArray[i].PositionVector.X <= cnstSpriteSize/2
                  Then SpriteArray[i].PositionVector.X := Round(cnstSpriteSize);
                If SpriteArray[i].PositionVector.X >= (Form1.ClientWidth - Round(cnstSpriteSize/2))
                 Then SpriteArray[i].PositionVector.X := Form1.ClientWidth - Round(cnstSpriteSize);
              End;
          SpriteArray[i].PositionVector.Y := SpriteArray[i].PositionVector.Y
                                    + SpriteArray[i].VelocityVector.Y*deltaTime;
          If SpriteArray[i].WallCollisionY
            Then
              Begin
                If SpriteArray[i].PositionVector.Y <= cnstSpriteSize/2
                  Then SpriteArray[i].PositionVector.Y := Round(cnstSpriteSize);
                If SpriteArray[i].PositionVector.Y >= (Form1.ClientHeight -cnstSpriteSize/2)
                 Then SpriteArray[i].PositionVector.Y := Form1.ClientHeight - Round(cnstSpriteSize);
              End;
          SpriteArray[i].GLHudSprite.Position.X := SpriteArray[i].PositionVector.X;
          SpriteArray[i].GLHudSprite.Position.Y := Form1.ClientHeight - SpriteArray[i].PositionVector.Y;
          If SpriteArray[i].WallCollisionX Then SpriteArray[i].WallCollisionX := False;
          If SpriteArray[i].WallCollisionY Then SpriteArray[i].WallCollisionY := False;
        End;
  End;
```

Table 48.14 Event handler GLCadencer1Progress

Two spheres colliding in a box

Create a new Windows VCL application (**File|New**).

Save the project as `TwoSpheresCollidingProject` and the unit as `TwoSpheresCollidingUnit` (**File|Save Project As...**) in folder `TwoSpheresColliding`.

1. **Add** a **TGLScene** object, a **TGLSceneViewer object**, a **TGLCollisionManager** object and a **TGLCadencer** object to the form.
2. **Rename** the form `frmTwoSpheresColliding` and **change** its caption to `Two Spheres Colliding`.
3. **Add** the objects shown in *Figure 48.51* to `GLScene1`.

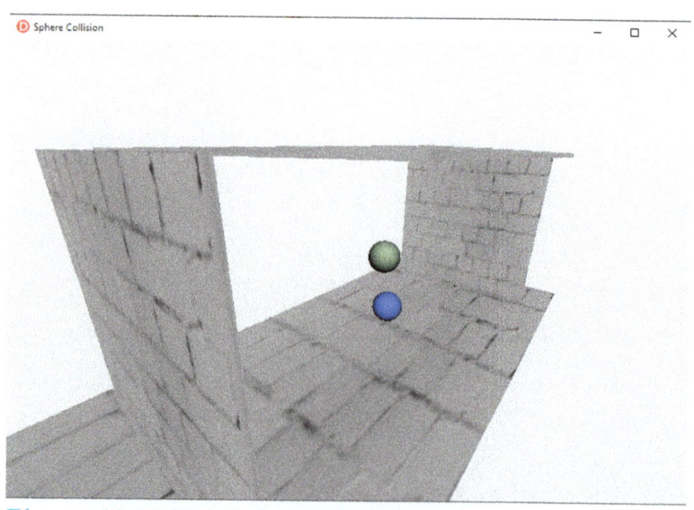

Figure 48.50 TwoSpheresCollidingProject in execution

```
Unit TwoSpheresCollidingUnit;
Interface
Uses
  Winapi.OpenGL, System.SysUtils, System.Classes, Vcl.Graphics, Vcl.Controls,
  Vcl.Forms, Vcl.Dialogs, Vcl.ComCtrls, Vcl.StdCtrls, GLS.Scene,  GLS.VectorTypes,
  GLS.Objects, GLS.Collision, GLS.SceneViewer, GLS.Coordinates,
  GLS.BaseClasses, GLS.Cadencer, GLS.Mesh, GLS.Trail;
Type
  TfrmTwoSpheresColliding = Class(TForm)
                               GLScene1 : TGLScene;
                               GLSceneViewer1 : TGLSceneViewer;
                               CollisionManager1 : TGLCollisionManager;
                               GLCamera1 : TGLCamera;
                               GLLightSource1 : TGLLightSource;
                               Sphere1 : TGLSphere;
                               Sphere2 : TGLSphere;
                               GLCadencer1 : TGLCadencer;
                               GLCube1 : TGLCube;
                               GLCube2 : TGLCube;
                               GLDummyCube1 : TGLDummyCube;
                               GLCube3 : TGLCube;
                               GLCube4 : TGLCube;
                               Procedure CollisionManager1Collision(Sender : TObject; Object1,
                                 Object2 : TGLBaseSceneObject);
                               Procedure GLCadencer1Progress(Sender : TObject; Const deltaTime,
                                 newTime : Double);
                             End;
Var
  frmTwoSpheresColliding : TfrmTwoSpheresColliding;
Implementation
{$R *.DFM}
Var
  Direction1 : Integer = 1;
  Direction2 :  Integer = 1;
Procedure TfrmTwoSpheresColliding.CollisionManager1Collision(Sender : TObject; Object1,
  Object2 : TGLBaseSceneObject);
  Begin
    If (((Object1.Name = 'GLCube1') And (Object2.Name = 'Sphere1'))
      Or ((Object1.Name = 'Sphere1') And (Object2.Name = 'GLCube1')) )
      Then Direction1 := -Direction1;
    If (((Object1.Name = 'GLCube2') And (Object2.Name = 'Sphere1'))
      Or ((Object1.Name = 'Sphere1') And (Object2.Name = 'GLCube2')) )
      Then Direction1 := -Direction1;
    If ((Object1.Name = 'Sphere1') And (Object2.Name = 'Sphere2'))
      Or ((Object1.Name = 'Sphere2') And (Object2.Name = 'Sphere1'))
      Then
        Begin
          Direction1 := -Direction1;
          Direction2 := -Direction2;
        End;
      If (((Object1.Name = 'Sphere2') And (Object2.Name = 'GLCube3'))
        Or ((Object1.Name = 'GLCube3') And (Object2.Name = 'Sphere2')) )
        Then Direction2 := -Direction2;
      If (((Object1.Name = 'Sphere2') And (Object2.Name = 'GLCube4'))
        Or ((Object1.Name = 'GLCube4') And (Object2.Name = 'Sphere2')) )
        Then Direction2 := -Direction2;
  End;
Procedure TfrmTwoSpheresColliding.GLCadencer1Progress(Sender : TObject; Const deltaTime,
  newTime : Double);
  Begin
    Sphere1.Position.Z :=  Sphere1.Position.Z - Direction1 * 10*deltaTime;
    Sphere2.Position.Y := Sphere2.Position.Y - Direction2 * 10*deltaTime;
    CollisionManager1.CheckCollisions;
  End;
End.
```

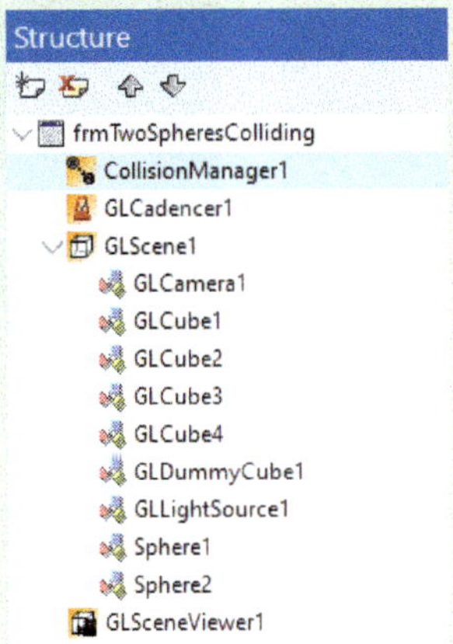

Figure 48.51 Structure window for TwoSpheresCollidingUnit

Table 48.15 TwoSpheresCollidingUnit.pas

Where is GLScene used?

Eurofins EAG Laboratories, the global leader in materials testing services and part of Eurofins Scientific, uses Delphi and GLScene for visualising 2D and 3D surfaces from data produced by atomic force microscopes and optical profilometers. *Figure 48.52* shows the 3D rendered surface of a grasshoppers eye which has been scanned at very high resolution. The software, EAG's Atomic Force Microscope (AFM) and Optical Profilometry Viewer, was written in Delphi and GLScene. The software enables the 3D image to be tilted and rotated. The partial image to the left is the 2D view of the same image. *Figure 48.53* shows a 2D rendered image of a rose petal, the partial image to the right is the 3D view of the same image.

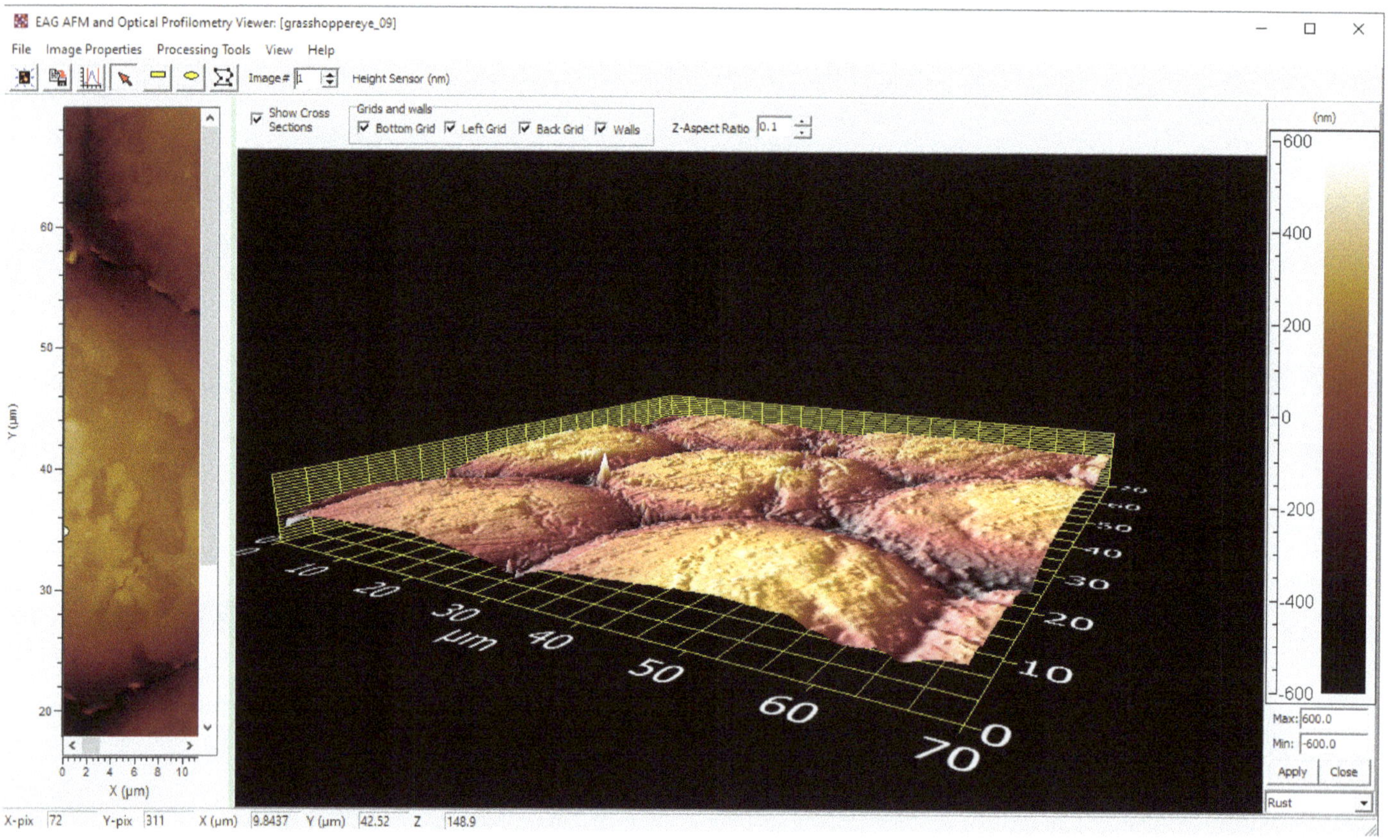

Figure 48.52 3D image of a grasshoppers eye displayed by EAG AFM and Optical Profilometry Viewer written in Delphi with GLScene - software and image Copyright © Eurofins Scientific www.eurofinsEAG.com.

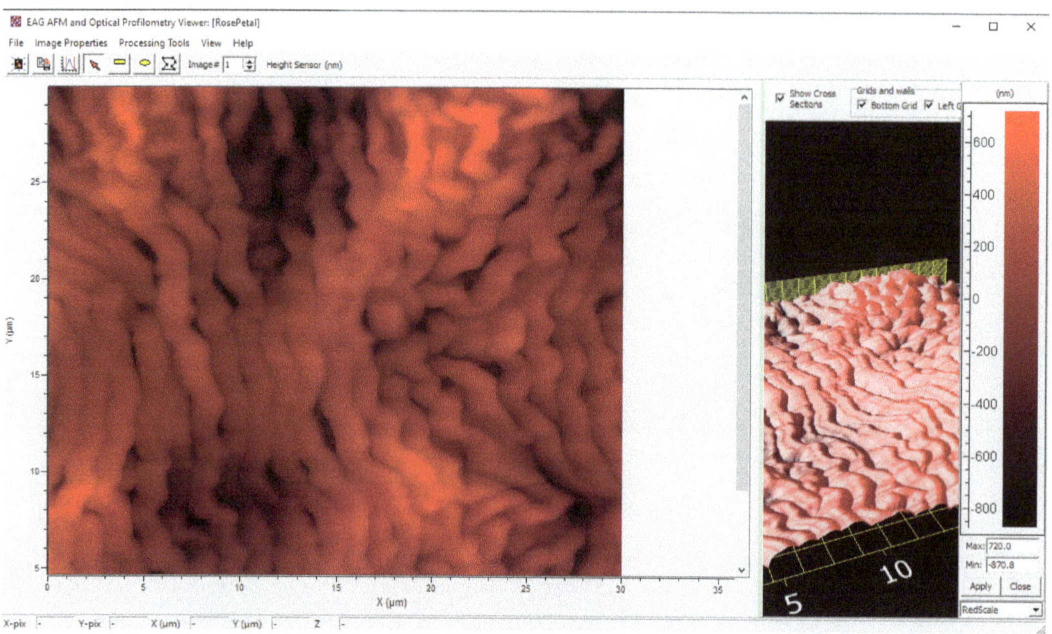

Figure 48.53 3D image of a rose petal displayed by EAG AFM and Optical Profilometry Viewer written in Delphi with GLScene - software and image Copyright © Eurofins Scientific www.eurofinsEAG.com.

49 Game engines

Introduction to game engines

Purpose: To become familiar with Gorilla 3D

Gorilla 3D

Download the installation packages for your version of Delphi from https://gorilla3d.de/files/?dir=packages/

e.g. https://gorilla3d.de/files/?dir=packages/10.4.2

Install these packages in your version of Delphi by following the instructions in `Installation.txt`.

After restarting the IDE and creating a new Multi-device application the Gorilla 3D component palette tabs should be visisble in the component palette as shown in *Figure 49.1*.

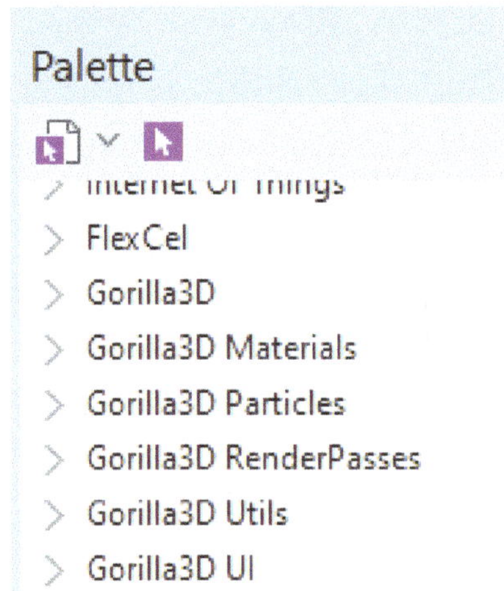

Figure 49.1 Component palette showing Goriall3D installed component palettes

Download demos from https://gorilla3d.de/files/?dir=demos/.

Figure 49.2 shows a screenshot of the executing Physics Particle demo.

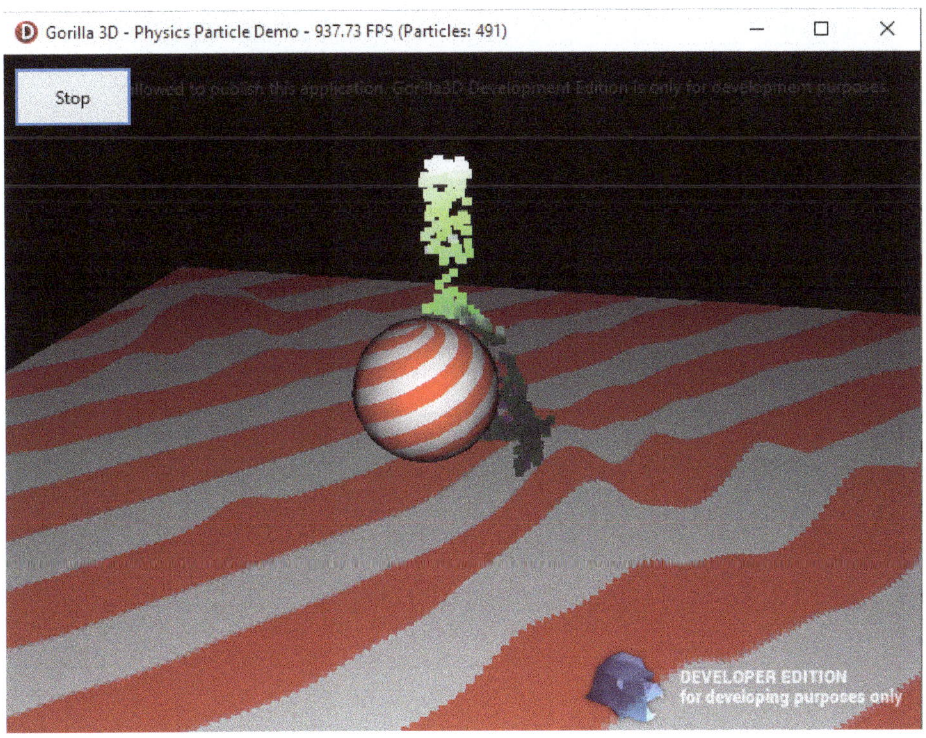

Figure 49.2 Gorilla 3D Physcis Particle Demo

Castle game engine

The Castle game engine has been available for several years but only for Free Pascal. However, there is an ongoing initiative to port this engine to Delphi - see

https://castle-engine.io/wp/2021/09/17/delphi-porting-progress-basic-cge-window-with-images-and-text-works/.

50 COM and OLE - Microsoft Excel, Word

Component Object Model (COM)

Purpose: To learn how to connect a Delphi application to Microsoft® Excel and Word

What s COM?

The Component Object Model (COM) is a technology that dates from the early 1990s but which is still present today as a core part of Microsoft Office, APIs such as Direct3D and WinRT.

By provide OOP functionality in a language neutral manner through object interfaces based on the base COM interface, **IUnknown**. By good fortune or design, Delphi's **IInterface** type matches **IUnknown** exactly.

OLE Automation

COM is used by OLE Automation, in which one application exposes special COM interfaces in order to be programmatically controlled by another. Delphi may be used to to control the constituent programs of Microsft Office, Excel and Word. The latter are called Automation servers when controlled in this way. The Automation objects of Automation servers expose two types of interface:

1. Early binding
2. Late binding

Early binding

Early binding uses interface references in exactly the same way that objects in Delphi are accessed through interfaces (see *Chapter 26*). In Early binding, the Delphi application has access to all the types of the Automation server via imported units. The units for Office are Word2000, Excel2000. These imported units contain a series of interfaces and constants, together with factory classes (refer to *Chapter 26* for an explanation) for the **CoClasses**.

For example, if we wanted to control Microsoft Word and use it to create a new Word document then we need to declare a variable of type **Word2000.WordApplication** and a variable of type WordDocument as follows

```
Var
  WordApplication : Word2000.WordApplication;
  NewDocument : WordDocument;
```

We also need to add to the implementation section

```
Uses Word2000;
```

Create a new Windows VCL application and **save** the project as `OLEEarlyBindingProject.dproj` and the unit as `OLEEarlyBindingUnit.pas` in folder `OLEEarlyBindingSimple`.

Add a button to the form, rename `btnCreateWordDocument` and set its caption to `Create Word Document` *Figure 50.1*.

Change the form's name to `frmEarlyBinding` and its caption to `Early Binding`.

Add `System.IOUtils` to the **Interface Uses** clause so that **TPath** may be used.

Create a procedure `CreateWordDocument(Const Filename : String)` in the implementation section and **add** the code shown in *Table 50.1* to its body. **Const** (constant) parameters are similar to value parameters, except that you cannot assign a value to a constant parameter within the body of a procedure or function, nor can you pass one as a var parameter to another routine. Using **const** allows the compiler to optimize code for structured and string-type parameters.

Create an **OnClick** event handler on the button and **add** the code shown in *Table 50.1* to its body.

Save All (**Shift + Ctrl + S**).

Now **run** the project and **click** on the button to create `Testkrb2.doc` in the user's documents folder.

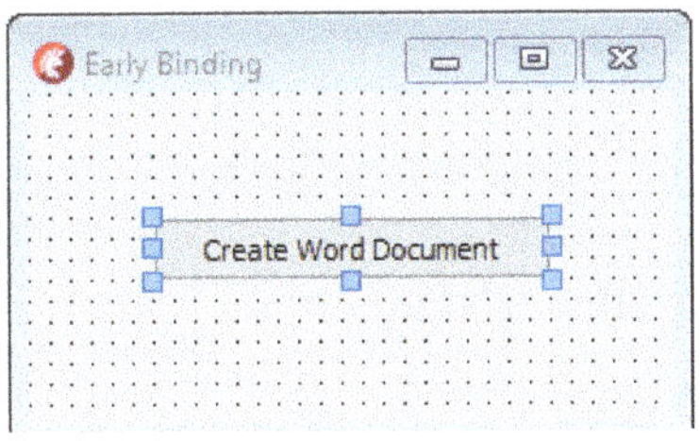

Figure 50.1 OLEWordEarlyBindingProject

```
Unit OLEEarlyBindingUnit;

Interface

Uses
  Winapi.Windows, Winapi.Messages, System.SysUtils, System.Variants,
  System.Classes, Vcl.Graphics, Vcl.Controls, Vcl.Forms, Vcl.Dialogs,
  Vcl.StdCtrls, System.IOUtils;

Type
  TfrmEarlyBinding = Class(TForm)
                       btnCreateWordDocument : TButton;
                       Procedure btnCreateWordDocumentClick(Sender : TObject);
                     End;

Var
  frmEarlyBinding: TfrmEarlyBinding;

Implementation

{$R *.dfm}
  Uses Word2000;
  Procedure CreateWordDocument(Const Filename : String);
    Var
      WordApplication : Word2000.WordApplication;
      NewDocument : WordDocument;
    Begin
      WordApplication := CoWordApplication.Create;
      NewDocument := WordApplication.Documents.Add(EmptyParam, EmptyParam,
                       EmptyParam, EmptyParam);
      NewDocument.Content.text := 'Hello World!';
      NewDocument.SaveAs(TPath.Combine(TPath.GetDocumentsPath, FileName),
                         EmptyParam, EmptyParam, EmptyParam, EmptyParam,
                         EmptyParam, EmptyParam, EmptyParam, EmptyParam,
                         EmptyParam, EmptyParam);
      WordApplication.Quit(False, False, False);
    End;

  Procedure TfrmEarlyBinding.btnCreateWordDocumentClick(Sender : TObject);
    Begin
      CreateWordDocument('TestKrb2.doc');
    End;
End.
```

Table 50.1 Early binding Delphi application which connects to Microsoft Word

Early binding frequently requires **EmptyParam** to be passed as a parameter when a method is called. **EmptyParam** is a function from `System.Variants` that returns a **Variant** containing a special value which OLE Automation interprets as whatever default value is appropriate. Other idiosyncracies make early binding awkward to use.

Late binding

This uses a scripting approach in which method and property names are looked up dynamically at runtime.

For example, if we wanted to control Microsoft Word and use it to create a new Word document then a variable of type **OleVariant** or **Variant** needs to be declared for the Word application and for the new document as follows

```
Var
  WordApplication, NewDocument : OleVariant;
```

An Ole object would then be created and referenced by `WordApplication` as follows

```
WordApplication := CreateOleObject('Word.Application');
```

The Delphi function `CreateOleObject` is the direct equivalent of `CreateObject` in VBScript or Visual Basic for Applications (VBA). This has implications for the speed of execution of the automation since under the hood it is a script that is executed on the Automation server.

Using the type **OleVariant** instead of the type **Variant** ensures that the mapping form Delphi to scripting language does not use any data structures that the script engine cannot understand. If the type **Variant** is used, Delphi will do its best to convert Delphi data structures to scripting language structures but there is no gurantee that it will always be successful.

Create a new **Windows VCL application** and **save** the project as `OLEWordLateBindingProject.dproj` and the unit as `OLEWordLateBindingUnit.pas` in folder `OLEWordLateBindingSimple`.

Add a button to the form, rename `btnCreateWordDocument` and set is caption to `Create Word Document`.

Change the form's name to `frmLateBinding` and its caption to `Late Binding`.

Add `System.IOUtils` to the **Interface Uses** clause so that **TPath** may be used.

Add `System.Win.ComObj`, `System.Variants` to the **Interface Uses** clause so that **OleVariant** and **CreateOleObject** may be used.

Create a procedure `CreateWordDocument(Const Filename : String)` in the implementation section and **add** the code shown in *Table 50.2* to its body.

Create an **OnClick** event handler on the button and **add** the code shown in *Table 50.2* to its body.

Save All (**Shift + Ctrl + S**).

Now **run** the project (*Figure 50.2*) and **click** on the button to create `Testkrb1.doc` in the user's documents folder.

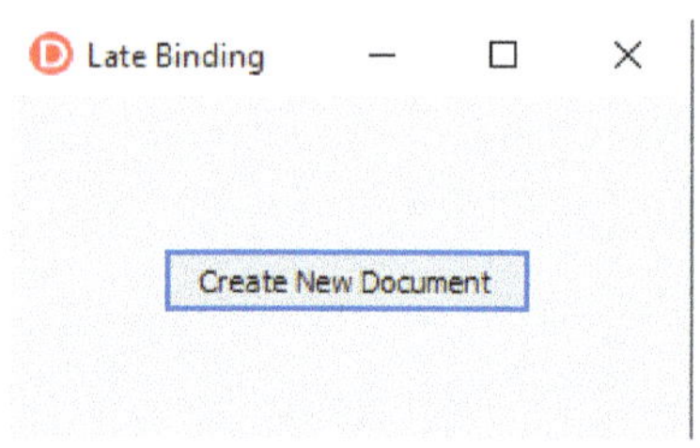

Figure 50.2 OLEWordLateBindingProject

```
Unit OLEWordLateBindingUnit;

Interface

Uses
  Winapi.Windows, Winapi.Messages, System.SysUtils, System.Variants,
  System.Classes, Vcl.Graphics, Vcl.Controls, Vcl.Forms, Vcl.Dialogs,
  System.Win.ComObj, System.IOUtils, Vcl.StdCtrls;

Type
  TfrmLateBinding = Class(TForm)
                      btnCreateNewDocument : TButton;
                      Procedure btnCreateNewDocumentClick(Sender : TObject);
                    End;

Var
  frmLateBinding : TfrmLateBinding;

Implementation
{$R *.dfm}

Procedure CreateWordDocument(Const Filename : String);
  Var
    WordApplication , NewDocument : OleVariant;
  Begin
    WordApplication := CreateOleObject('Word.Application');
    NewDocument := WordApplication.Documents.Add;
    NewDocument.Content := 'Hello World';
    NewDocument.SaveAs(TPath.Combine(TPath.GetDocumentsPath, FileName));
    WordApplication.Quit;
  End;

Procedure TfrmLateBinding.btnCreateNewDocumentClick(Sender : TObject);
  Begin
    CreateWordDocument('Testkrb1.doc');
  End;

End.
```

Table 50.2 Late binding Delphi application which connects to Microsoft Word

Running an Excel spreadsheet macro from Delphi

As **Late binding** relies on running a script under the hood, we may prepare a script and run the script explicitly. from Delphi.

Open a blank workbook in **Excel**.

Select `Sheet1` then the **View** tab.

Select Macros then **Record Macro...**

Enter the name `Macro1` for this macro and **accept** store in the current workbook.

Enter the sequence 1, 2, 3, 4, 5, 6, one number per cell, in column `A`.

Enter `=$A1*2` in cell `B1`, then **copy** the formula to the next five cells in this column.

With column `B` items selected as shown in *Figure 50.3*, **click** the **Insert** tab, **select** the **Insert Line Chart** option and then **Line Chart with Markers**.

Reposition the chart as shown in *Figure 50.3*.

Select View|Macros|Stop Recording.

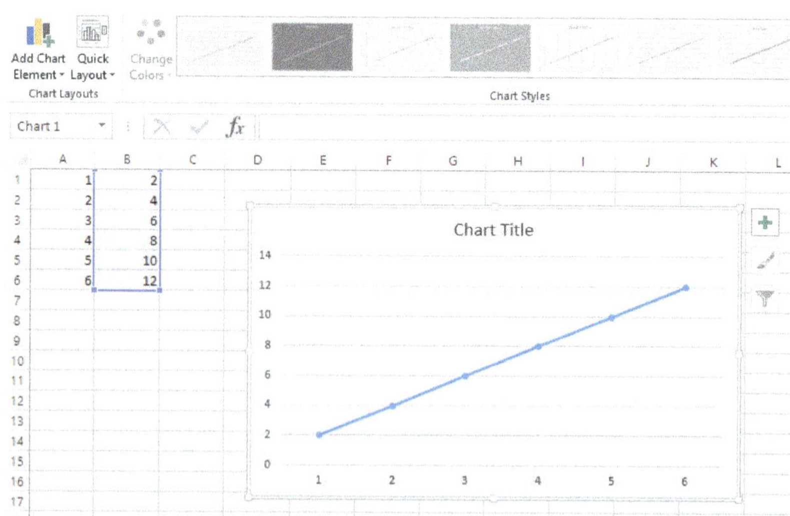

Figure 50.3 Spreadsheet produced by instructions shown in the text

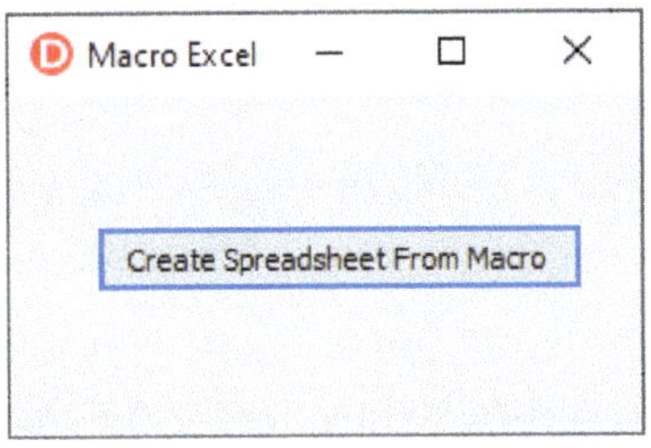

Figure 50.4 LateBindingMacroExcelProject

Save the spreadsheet as `Macro1Book1.xls`.

Delete the chart and the two columns of data.

Save the altered spreadsheet as `Macro1Book1Empty.xls`.

This spreadsheet will still contain macro `Macro1`.

Create a new **Windows VCL application** and **save** the project as `LateBindingMacroExcelProject.dproj` and the unit as `LateBindingMacroExcelUnit.pas` in folder `LateBindingMacroExcel`.

Add a button to the form, **rename** it `btnCreateSpreadsheetFromMacro` and **set** is caption to `Create Spreadsheet From Macro` *Figure 50.4*.

Add `ComObj`, `System.Variants` and `System.SysUtils` to the `Uses` section.

Create an **OnClick** event handler on the button and **add** the code shown in *Table 50.3* to its body.

Save All (**Shift + Ctrl + S**).

Make sure that `Macro1Book1Empty.xls` is stored in the same directory as `LateBindingMacroExcelProject.exe`.

Now **run** the project (*Figure 50.4*) and **click** on the button. The updated spreadsheet is saved as `Macro1Book1Updated.xls`. The path to the executable is returned by `ExtractFileDir(ParamStr(0))`.

```
Unit LateBindingMacroExcelUnit;

Interface

Uses
  Winapi.Windows, Winapi.Messages, System.Variants,
  System.Classes, Vcl.Graphics, Vcl.Controls, Vcl.Forms, Vcl.Dialogs,
  Vcl.StdCtrls, ComObj, System.SysUtils;

Type
  TfrmMacroExcel = Class(TForm)
                     btnCreateSpreadsheetFromMacro: TButton;
                     Procedure btnCreateSpreadsheetFromMacroClick(Sender : TObject);
                   End;

Var
  frmMacroExcel : TfrmMacroExcel;

Implementation

{$R *.dfm}

Procedure TfrmMacroExcel.btnCreateSpreadsheetFromMacroClick(Sender : TObject);
  Var
    Excel : OleVariant;
  Begin
    Try
      Try
        Excel := CreateOleObject('Excel.Application');
        Excel.Workbooks.Open(ExtractFileDir(ParamStr(0)) + '\' + 'Macro1Book1Empty.xls');
        Excel.Run('Macro1');
        Excel.Workbooks[1].SaveAs(ExtractFileDir(ParamStr(0)) + '\' + 'Macro1Book1Updated.xls');
        Excel.WorkBooks[1].Close;
      Except
        On E : Exception
          Do ShowMessage(E.ClassName + ': ' + E.Message);
      End;
    Finally
      Excel.Quit;
    End;
  End;
End.
```

Table 50.3 Late binding Delphi application which connects to Microsoft Excel then runs a macro, Macro1, to create the contents of the spreadsheet

Basing Delphi code on an Excel spreadsheet macro

Create a macro recording for a spreadsheet with chart as described in the previous section and shown in *Figure 50.3*. **View** the macro in Excel before closing the spreadsheet. **Click** the **Edit** button to bring up the Microsoft Visual Basic for Applications window. **Copy** the macro code from the edit window and save it in a text editor. *Table 50.4* shows the contents of this macro.

Create a new **Windows VCL application** and **save** the project as `CreatingExcelProject.dproj` and the unit as `CreatingExcelUnit.pas` in folder `CreatingExcel`.

Add a button to the form, rename `btnCreateSpreadsheet` and **set** its caption to `Create Spreadsheet`.

Change the form's name to `frmLateBindingExcel` and its caption to `Late Binding Excel`.

Add `ComObj`, `ExcelXP`, `OfficeXP`, `System.Variants` to the **Interface Uses** clause.

Add a **TFileSaveDialog** component to the form so that the user can specify the name of the Excel spreadsheet file when it is saved.

Create an **OnClick** event handler on the button and **add** the code shown in *Table 50.5* to its body.

This code is a mapping of the macro shown in *Table 50.4* into the corresponding Delphi code.

Save All (**Shift + Ctrl + S**).

Now **run** the project (*Figure 50.5*) and **click** on the button to create a spreadsheet containing two columns of data and a chart.

```
Range("A1").Select
ActiveCell.FormulaR1C1 = "1"
Range("A2").Select
ActiveCell.FormulaR1C1 = "2"
Range("A3").Select
ActiveCell.FormulaR1C1 = "3"
Range("A4").Select
ActiveCell.FormulaR1C1 = "4"
Range("A5").Select
ActiveCell.FormulaR1C1 = "5"
Range("A6").Select
ActiveCell.FormulaR1C1 = "6"
Range("B1").Select
ActiveCell.FormulaR1C1 = "=RC1*2"
Range("B1").Select
Selection.AutoFill Destination:=Range("B1:B6"), Type:=xlFillDefault
Range("B1:B6").Select
ActiveSheet.Shapes.AddChart2(332, xlLineMarkers).Select
ActiveChart.SetSourceData Source:=Range("Sheet1!$B$1:$B$6")
```

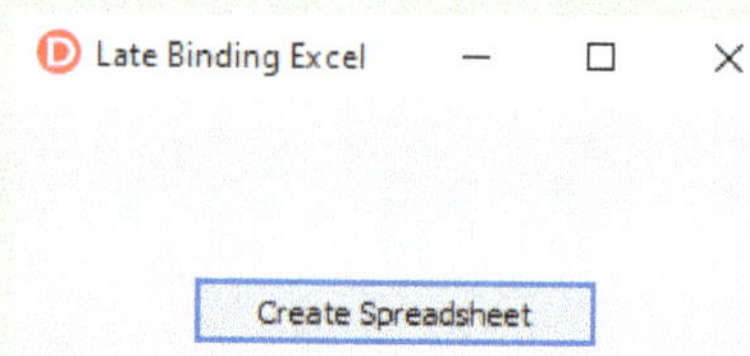

Figure 50.5 LateBindingCreateExcelProject

Table 50.4 Recorded macro for spreadsheet shown in Figure 50.3

Save as `Test1.xlsx` (default extension is `xlsx`).

Open in Excel and confirm that the spreadsheet is as expected.

Now **change** the `AddChart2` statement to

```
Excel.Application.ActiveSheet.Shapes.AddChart2(332,
xlXYScatterLinesNoMarkers, 10, 100).Select;
```

and **run** the program again. The third and fourth parameters set the **Left** and **Top** positions, in points, of the left and top edges of the chart respectively, relative to the anchor (see https://docs.microsoft.com/en-us/office/vba/api/excel.shapes.addchart2).

Figure 50.6 shows the result.

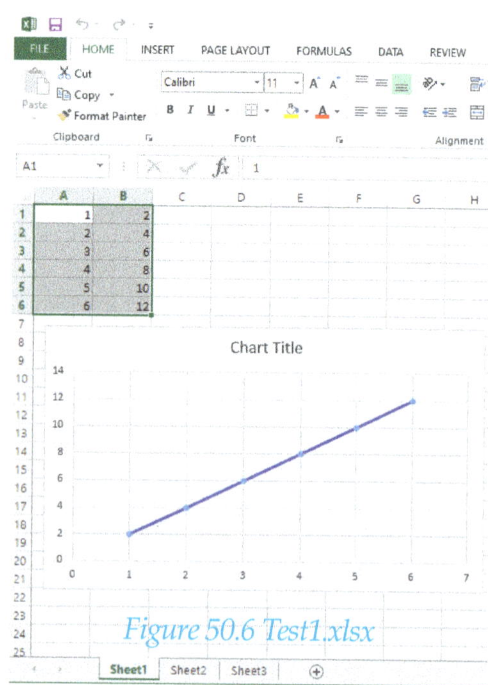

Figure 50.6 Test1.xlsx

```
Unit CreatingExcelUnit;
Interface
Uses
  Winapi.Windows, Winapi.Messages, System.SysUtils, System.Variants, System.Classes, Vcl.Graphics,
  Vcl.Controls, Vcl.Forms, Vcl.Dialogs, Vcl.StdCtrls, ComObj, ExcelXP, OfficeXP;
Type
  TfrmLateBindingExcel = Class(TForm)
                           btnCreateSpreadsheet: TButton;
                           FileSaveDialog1 : TFileSaveDialog;
                           Procedure btnCreateSpreadsheetClick(Sender : TObject);
                         End;
Var
  frmLateBindingExcel : TfrmLateBindingExcel;

Implementation

{$R *.dfm}

Procedure TfrmLateBindingExcel.btnCreateSpreadsheetClick(Sender : TObject);
Var
  Workbook, Worksheet : OleVariant;
  Excel : OleVariant;
  Begin
    Try
      Try
        Excel := CreateOleObject('Excel.Application');
        Excel.Workbooks.Add;
        WorkBook := Excel.Workbooks[1];
        WorkSheet := WorkBook.Worksheets[1];
        WorkSheet.Range['A1'].Select;
        Excel.Application.ActiveCell.FormulaR1C1:= '1';
        WorkSheet.Range['A2'].Select;
        Excel.Application.ActiveCell.FormulaR1C1:= '2';
        WorkSheet.Range['A3'].Select;
        Excel.Application.ActiveCell.FormulaR1C1:= '3';
        WorkSheet.Range['A4'].Select;
        Excel.Application.ActiveCell.FormulaR1C1:= '4';
        WorkSheet.Range['A5'].Select;
        Excel.Application.ActiveCell.FormulaR1C1:= '5';
        WorkSheet.Range['A6'].Select;
        Excel.Application.ActiveCell.FormulaR1C1:= '6';
        WorkSheet.Range['B1'].Select;
        Excel.Application.ActiveCell.FormulaR1C1:= '=RC1*2';//row relative addressing, column absolute
        Excel.Application.Selection.Copy;
        WorkSheet.Range['B1','B6'].Select;
        Excel.Application.ActiveSheet.Paste;
        Excel.Application.CutCopyMode:= False;
        {-----------------------------------------------------------------------------------------}
        Worksheet.Range['A1:B6'].Select;
        Excel.Application.ActiveSheet.Shapes.AddChart2(332, xlXYScatterLinesNoMarkers).Select;
        Excel.Application.ActiveChart.SetSourceData(Source:= Worksheet.Range['Sheet1!$A$1:$B$6']);
        Excel.Application.ActiveChart.FullSeriesCollection[1].Select;
        Excel.Application.Selection.Format.Line.Visible:= msoTrue;
        Excel.Application.Selection.Format.Line.ForeColor.RGB:= clBlue;
        Excel.Application.Selection.Format.Line.Transparency:= 0;
        Excel.Application.Selection.MarkerStyle:= -4105;
        {-----------------------------------------------------------------------------------------}
        FileSaveDialog1.DefaultFolder := ExtractFileDir(ParamStr(0)) + '\';
        FileSaveDialog1.DefaultExtension := 'xlsx';
        FileSaveDialog1.Execute;
        Excel.Workbooks[1].SaveAs(FileSaveDialog1.FileName);
        Excel.WorkBooks[1].Close;
      Except
        On E : Exception
          Do ShowMessage(E.ClassName + ': ' + E.Message);
      End;
    Finally
      Excel.Quit;
    End;
  End;
End.
```

Table 50.5 Late binding Delphi application which connects to Microsoft Excel to create the contents of the spreadsheet

WINSOFT® Direct Office

WINSOFT supplies a set of components that support the processing of .docx, .pptx and .xlsx documents. Microsoft Office installation is not required. **Download** and **install** Direct Office from https://winsoft.sk/officecs.htm. Direct Office comes with a large number of demo programs which are sufficient to use for learning how to use Direct Office components with Delphi. The trial version is free and fully featured. It works with Delphi versions from Delphi 7 onwards.

TMS FlexCel for VCL & FMX

FlexCel for VCL / FireMonkey from TMS Components is a suite of Delphi components that support the manipulation of Excel files. It can read or create complex spreadsheets, on Windows or macOS (it is cross platform so can also work with iOS, Android and Linux) and on machines without Excel installed. Extensive documentation is available from https://doc.tmssoftware.com/flexcel/vcl/index.html.

FlexCel may be downloaded from https://www.tmssoftware.com/site/flexcel.asp#product-downloads. It supports Delphi versions from XE onwards.

It is free for non-commercial use. A free academic licence is also available for schools and colleges.

When FlexCel is installed, it also installs a tool called APIMate. It is accessible from the **Start Menu** by searching for APIMate.

It is also possible to download APIMate for Windows or macOS from https://download.tmssoftware.com/flexcel/tools/net/ApiMate.zip

and https://download.tmssoftware.com/flexcel/tools/net/ApiMate.dmg respectively.

Launch APIMate and **select Open File**. then **locate** `Test1.xlsx` used in the earlier exercise. **Click** the **Open** button. **APIMate** will now parse `Test1.xlsx` and generate the Delphi code that when run will recreate `Test1.xlsx` - *Figure 50.7*. **Download** `FlexCelAPIMateExampleProject` from www.educational-computing.co.uk/DelphiBookCode/DelphiCode.html. This project was created by copying the Delphi code from **APIMate** (*Figure 50.7*). The **FileSaveDialog** component was added to the form and used in place of `OpenDialog1` in the **APIMate** code - *Figure 50.8*.

When the Delphi project is run, `Test1.xlsx` contents are regenerated.

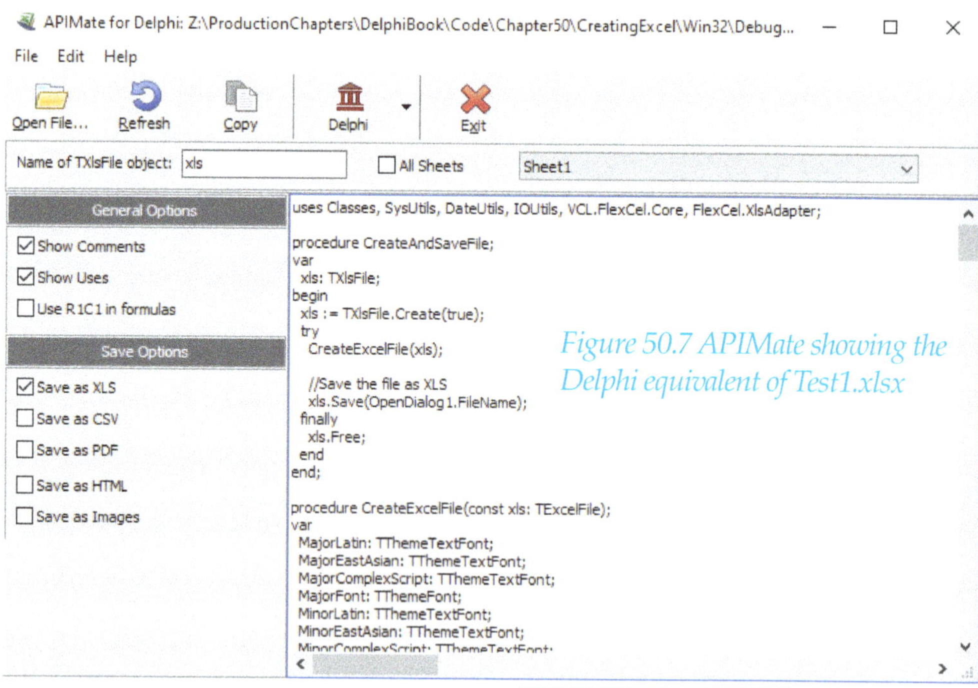

Figure 50.7 APIMate showing the Delphi equivalent of Test1.xlsx

Exporting a spreadsheet to pdf

Create a new Windows VCL application and **save** the project as `FlexCelToPDFProject.dproj` and the unit as `FlexCelToPDFProjectUnit.pas` in folder `FlexCelToPDF`.

Add a button to the form, rename `btnFlexCelToPDF` and **set** its caption to `FlexCel To PDF`.

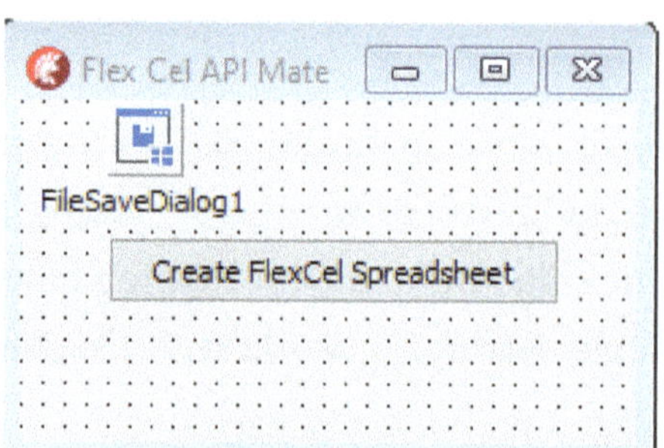

Figure 50.8 FlexCelAPIMateExampleProject user interface design

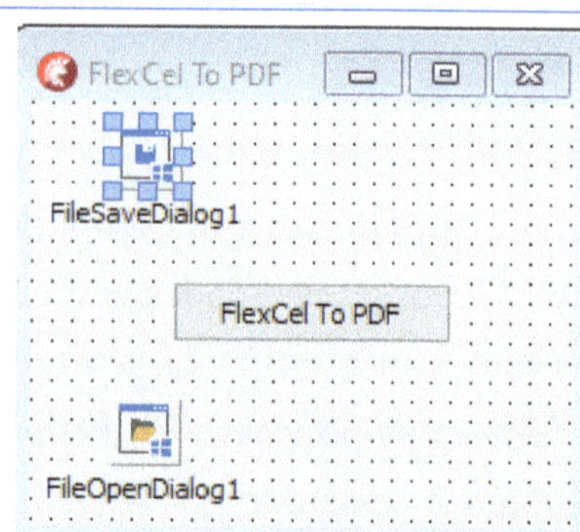

Figure 50.9 FlexCelToPDFProject UI design

Change the form's name to `frmFlexCelToPDF` and its caption to `FlexCel To PDF`.

Add `VCL.FlexCel.Core`, `FlexCel.XlsAdapter`, `FlexCel.Render` to the **Interface Uses** clause.

Add a **TFileSaveDialog** component to the form as shown in *Figure 50.9* so that the user can specify the name of the Excel spreadsheet file when it is saved.

Create an **OnClick** event handler on the button and **add** the code shown in *Table 50.5* to its body.

Save All (**Shift + Ctrl + S**).

Now **run** the project and **click** on the button. **Open** `Test1.xlsx` by supplying the filename `Test1` (the open file dialog will automatically append the extension `xlsx`). When prompted to save use `Test1` (the file save dialog will automatically append the extension `xlsx`). *Figure 50.10* shows the resulting contents of the pdf file that is produced.

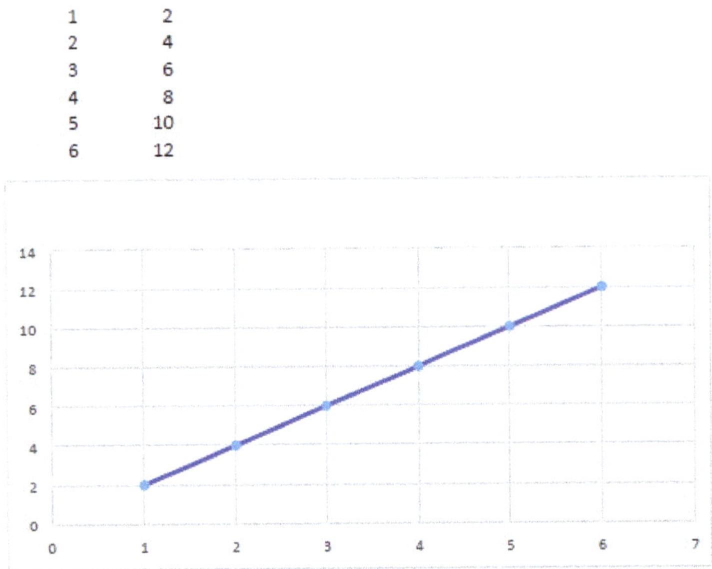

Figure 50.10 shows the contents of Test1.pdf

```
Interface

Uses
  Winapi.Windows, Winapi.Messages, System.SysUtils, System.Variants,
  System.Classes, Vcl.Graphics, Vcl.Controls, Vcl.Forms, Vcl.Dialogs,
  Vcl.StdCtrls, VCL.FlexCel.Core, FlexCel.XlsAdapter, FlexCel.Render;

Type
  TfrmFlexCelToPDF = Class(TForm)
                       btnFlexCelToPDF : TButton;
                       FileSaveDialog1 : TFileSaveDialog;
                       FileOpenDialog1 : TFileOpenDialog;
                       Procedure btnFlexCelToPDFClick(Sender : TObject);
                     End;

Var
  frmFlexCelToPDF : TfrmFlexCelToPDF;

Implementation

{$R *.dfm}
Procedure ExportToPdf(Const InFile, OutFile : String);
  Var
    xls: TXlsFile;
    pdf: TFlexCelPdfExport;
  Begin
    xls := TXlsFile.Create(InFile);
    Try
      pdf := TFlexCelPdfExport.Create(xls, true);
      Try
        pdf.Export(OutFile);
      Finally
        pdf.Free;
      End;
    finally
      xls.Free;
    End;
  End;
Procedure TfrmFlexCelToPDF.btnFlexCelToPDFClick(Sender : TObject);
  Begin
    FileOpenDialog1.DefaultFolder := ExtractFileDir(ParamStr(0)) + '\';
    FileOpenDialog1.DefaultExtension := 'xlsx';
    FileOpenDialog1.Execute;
    FileSaveDialog1.DefaultFolder := ExtractFileDir(ParamStr(0)) + '\';
    FileSaveDialog1.DefaultExtension := 'pdf'
    FileSaveDialog1.Execute;
    ExportToPdf(FileOpenDialog1.Filename, FileSaveDialog1.Filename);
  End;
End.
```

Table 50.6 FlexCelToPDFUnit.pas

51 Git and GitHub

Git

Purpose: To learn how to use Git and GitHub

Git

Git is a version control system (VCS) that makes it possible to manage and keep track of the source code history of projects.

Version control is a system that records changes to a file or set of files over time so that specific versions may be recalled at anytime in the future. In this chapter the file or files of interest are software source code files but it is possible to use a version control system for any type of computer file. Using a version control system is particularly useful when there is a need to revert files or an entire project back to a previous state perhaps because something has gone wrong.

Git is unlike other VCSs in that it stores its data as a set of snapshots. Everytime the state of the project or a file is committed, Git basically takes a picture of what all the files look like at that moment and stores a reference to this snapshot. If a file has not changed, Git just stores a link to the previous identical file that it has already stored.

A programmer usually configures Git to work with local storage, only committing to a remote server at the end of the day for additional security. This means that Git can operate even when the computer is offline.

Installing Git

Download the installer exe file from https://gitforwindows.org/ and run it.

At the time of writing, this is `Git-2.31.1-64-bit.exe` for a 64-bit machine.

Figure 51.1 shows part of the **Start menu** of a 64-bit machine on which Git has been installed. Selecting **Git GUI** brings up the window shown in Figure 51.2.

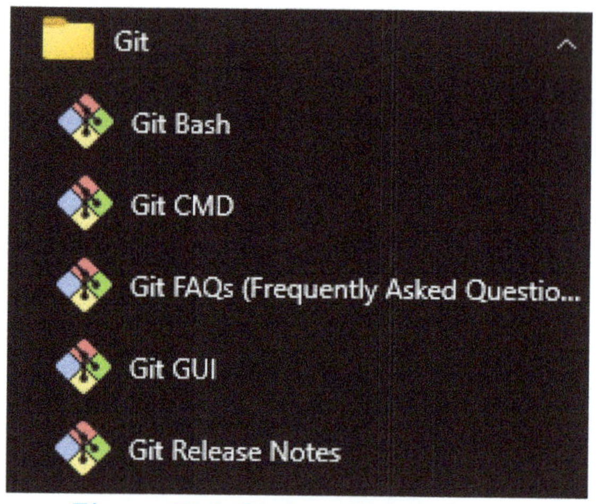

Figure 51.1 Git installed and accessible from the Start menu

Figure 51.2 Git GUI window

A folder for a repository has already been created on drive D:

`D:/GitRepository/Repo1`

Double clicking `D:/GitRepository/Repo1` opens this empty repository in the window shown in Figure 51.3.

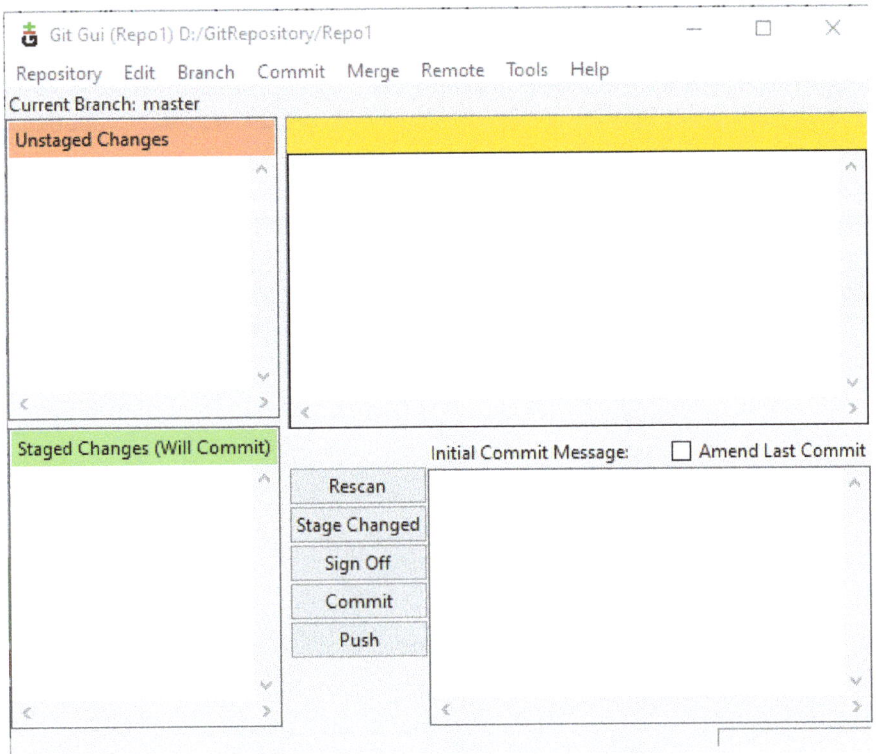

Figure 51.3 Window on Git repository D:/GitRepository/Repo1

GitHub

GitHub is a cloud-based hosting service that is often used to manage Git repositories. Sign up to a free account on GitHub in the cloud - https://github.com/.

Git is the tool and GitHub is the service for projects that use Git.

GitHub Desktop installs on a local machine and connects to both Git locally and to GitHub in the cloud when this option is selected. GitHub simplifies working with Git.

Download the installer exe file, `GitHubDesktopSetup-x64.exe`, for a 64-bit machine from

https://desktop.github.com/

and run it. **Launch** GitHub Desktop from the Start menu to bring up the window shown in *Figure 51.5* on the next page.

Delphi and Git

Git is integrated with later versions of Delphi. First Delphi must be configured to work with Git.

Select Tools|Options|Version Control|Git as shown in *Figure 51.4*.

Make sure that the path to Git's executable is present, if not add it. **Add** the user name and email address that was used when setting up using GitHub with Git. **Save** this configuration.

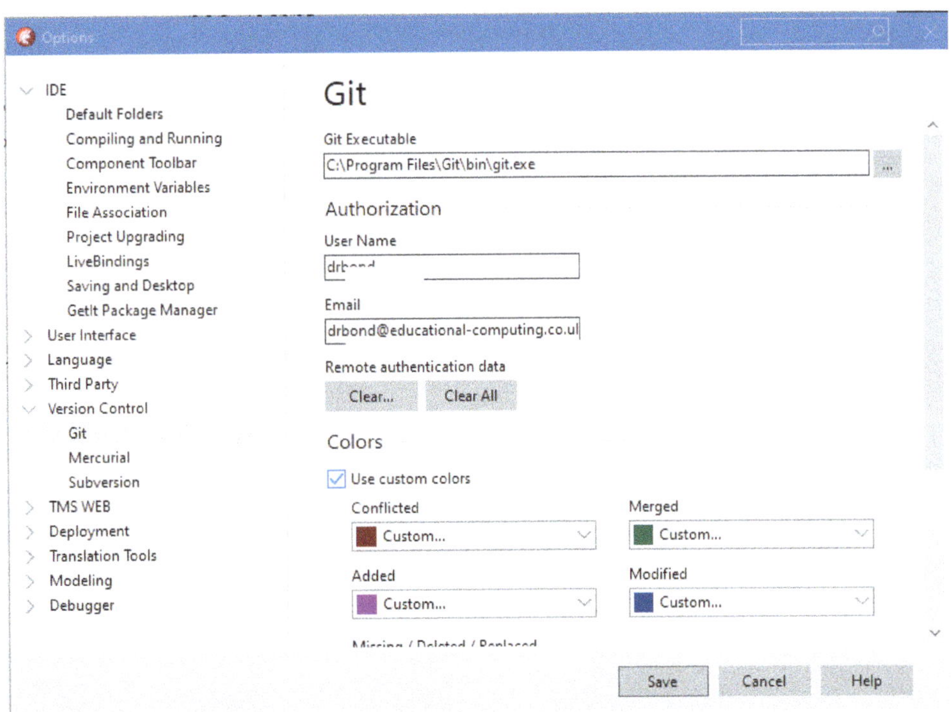

Figure 51.4 Configuring Delphi to work with Git

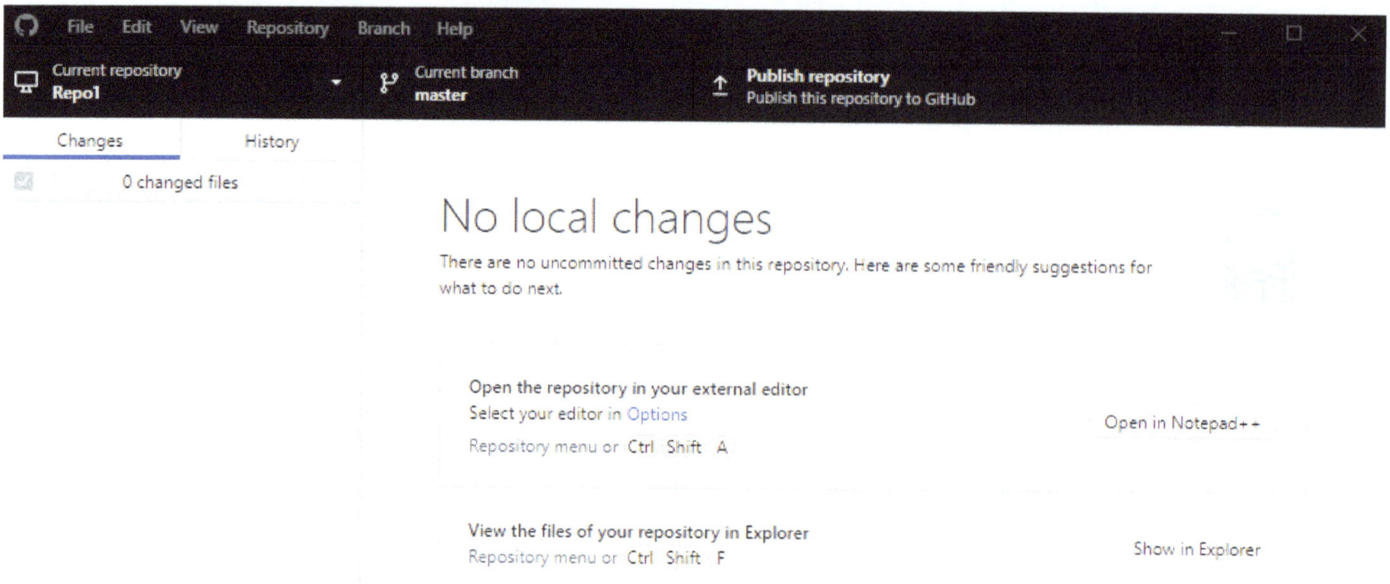

Figure 51.5 GitHub Desktop connected to Git local repository D:/GitRepository/Repo1

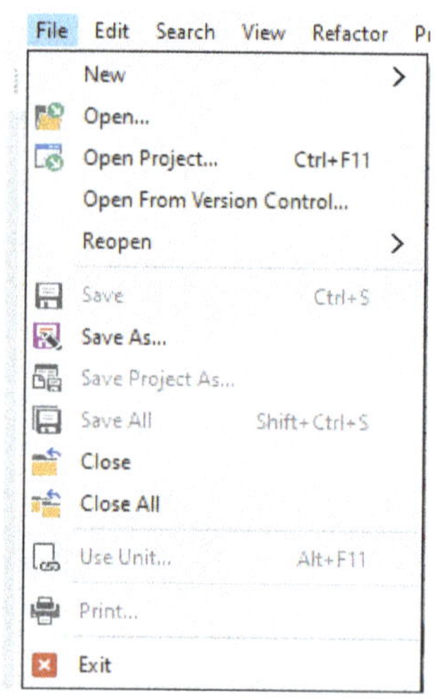

Figure 51.6 Opening a project from a Git repository

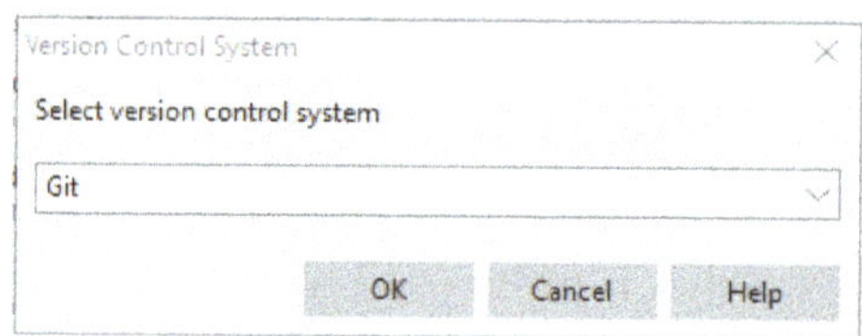

Figure 51.7 Selecting a VCS

Cloning a Delphi project on a Git public repository

Select File|Open From Version Control... - *Figure 51.6* - to bring up the Version Control System window shown in *Figure 51.7*. **Accept** the default selection **Git**. The Clone window should now appear - *Figure 51.8*. **Paste** https://github.com/HeidiSQL into the **Source** field and a path for the **Destination**. **Click** **OK**. Cloning should now begin - *Figure 51.9* - and when finished the cloned files should appear in the **Project Manager** window.

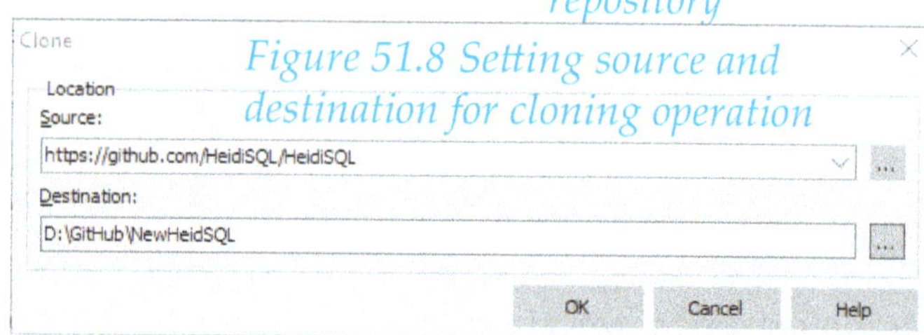

Figure 51.8 Setting source and destination for cloning operation

Creating a local repository

Close **HeidSQL**. **Switch** focus to **GitHub Desktop**. **Select** **File|New repository** - *Figure 51.10* - to create a new repository. In the window that now appears - *Figure 51.11* - **enter** a name, a description, and a local path for the repository. **Tick** the "**Initialize this repository with a README**" file. **Select** **Delphi** for **GitIgnore** so that files that do not need to be backed up are ignored. The option to include a license may be ignored if one is not required. **Click** **Create repository**. GitHub Desktop is used to show the new respository - *Figure 51.12*. **Click** Publish repository to copy it to a GitHub in the cloud account (this needs

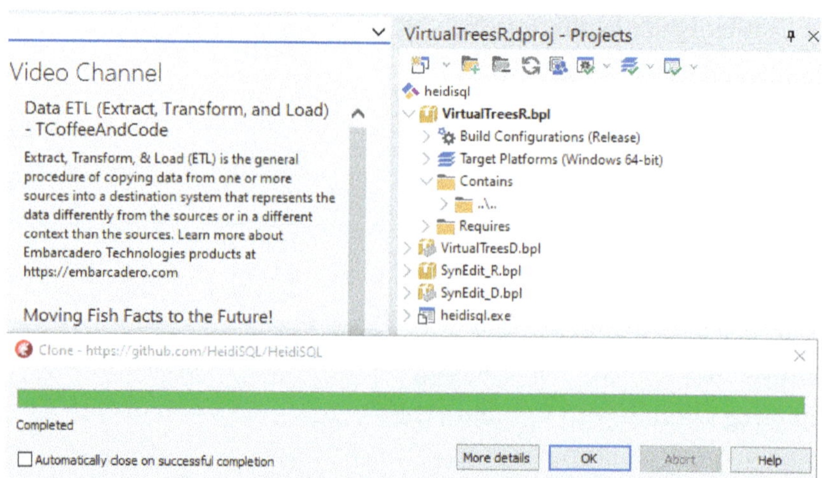

Figure 51.9 HeidiSQL cloned and opened in Delphi

to be set up in advance). **Complete** the fields of the next window - *Figure 51.13* - and **click Publish repository**. The current branch (main) should now be published to the cloud - *Figure 51.14*.

Figure 51.15 shows the contents of the local folder that is created by GitHub Desktop. Note that it is unnecessary to include `Chapter51` in the path as a folder is automatically created from the name for the repository. **Select File|New|Windows VCL Application - Delphi** to create a new Delphi application. **Add** a TButton control to the form. **Save** this project and its unit to the `Chapter51` repository using `GitProject` and `GitUnit` as project and unit names, respectively. *Figure 51.17* shows the new contents of folder `Chapter51`. These changes to the Git repository may be viewed in GitHub Desktop - *Figure 51.18*. **Add** a description name - the author has added "**Initial VCL design**" - and a description then **click Commit to main** to commit the changes. Now **push** this commit to the cloud - *Figure 51.16*. **Add** another button, **reposition** the first then **save**. *Figure 51.19* shows that the changes have been logged by Git. **Commit to main** after adding a description name, e.g. "**Added another button**". **Push** to the cloud. Now suppose that you want to revert to the previous version which had only one button. **Close** the application then **switch** focus to GitHub Desktop and **right click** "**Added another button**" in the **History** window. In the popup window, **click Revert changes in commit**. Now **reload** the application in Delphi to get the previous version.

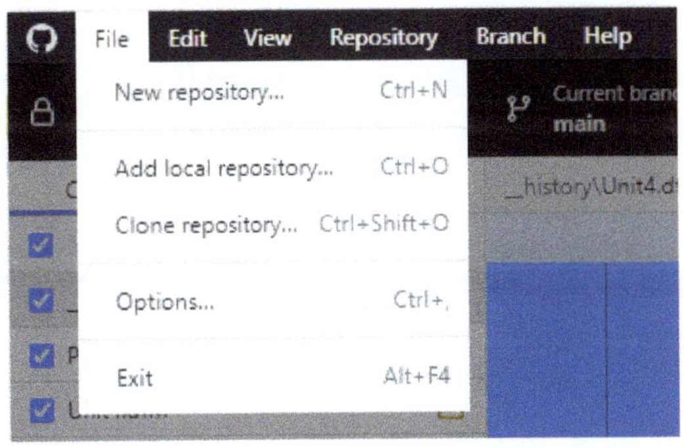

Figure 51.10 Creating a new repository form GitHub

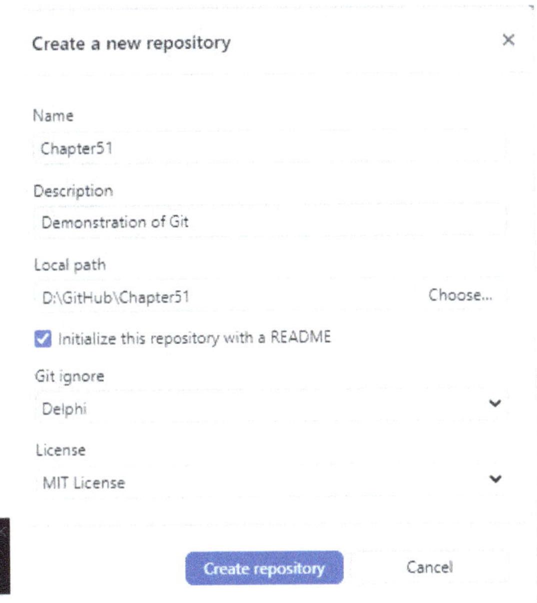

Figure 51.11 Setting up the new repository

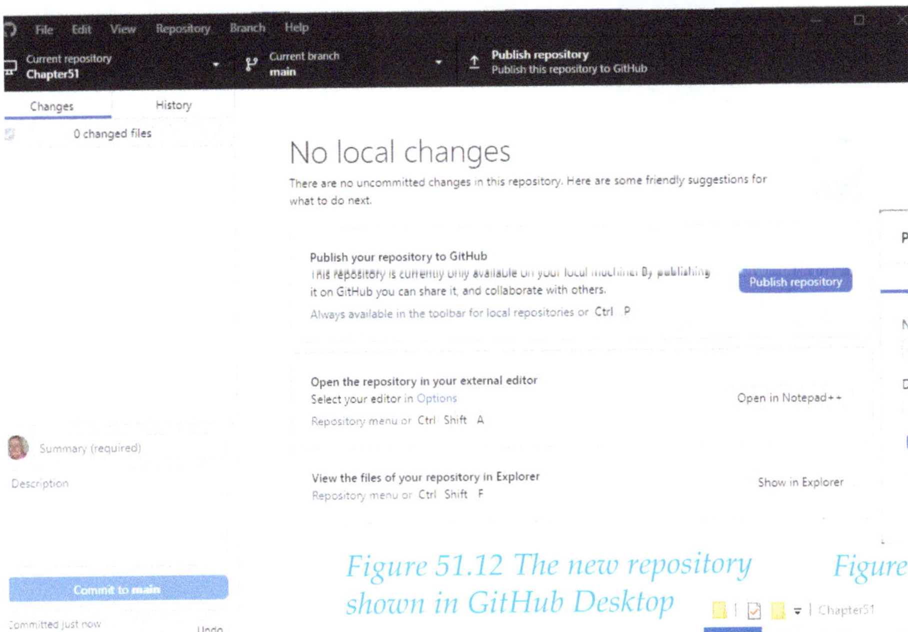

Figure 51.12 The new repository shown in GitHub Desktop

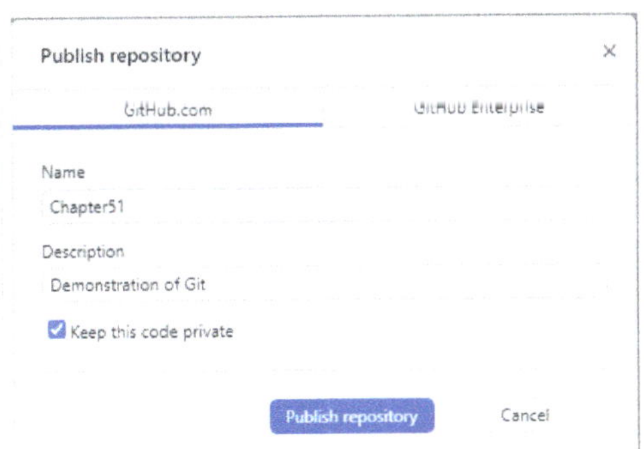

Figure 51.13 Publishing the repository to the cloud

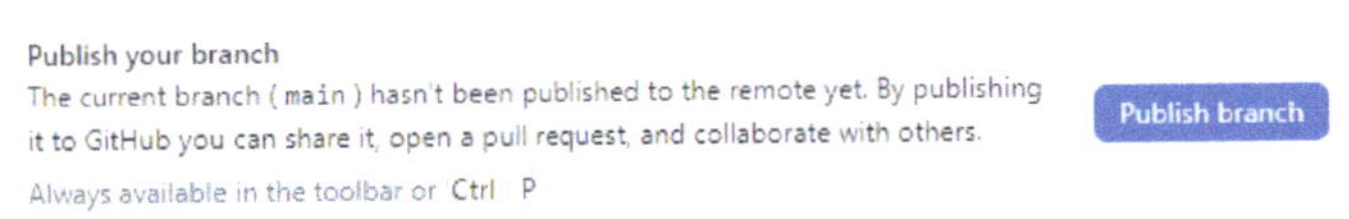

Figure 51.14 Publishing the current branch (main) to the repository in the cloud

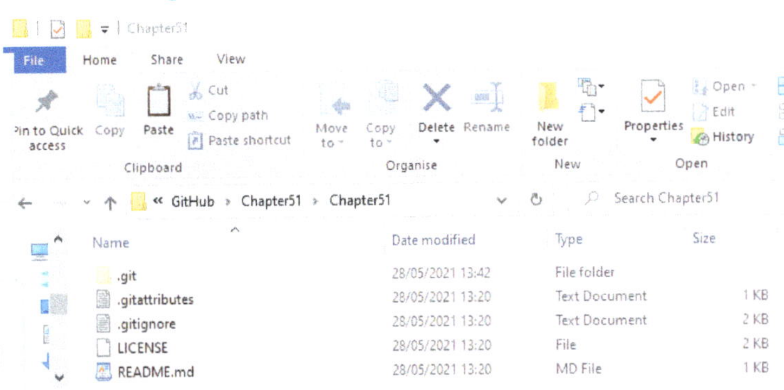

Figure 51.15 Chapter51 folder with contents created by Git

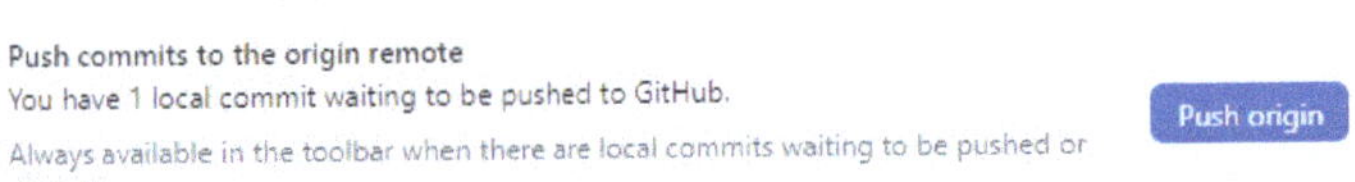

Figure 51.16 Pushing the commit to the cloud

After some practice with GitHub and Git, your confidence in using these will grow. For more guidance and support the following videos (recommended by Ian Barker - https://www.youtube.com/watch?v=JSswgwPbjNs) are worth looking at

Git' Delphi - https://fixedbycode.blogspot.com/2015/02/git-delphi.html

The beginners' guide to contributing to a GitHub project - https://akrabat.com/the-beginners-guide-to-contributing-to-a-github-project

Ian Barker's blog on his Git and GitHub webinair - https://tinyurl.com/delphigit

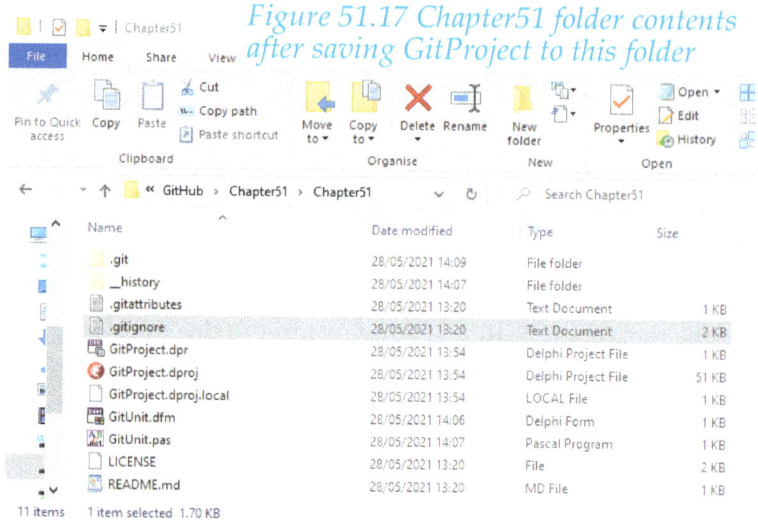

Figure 51.17 Chapter51 folder contents after saving GitProject to this folder

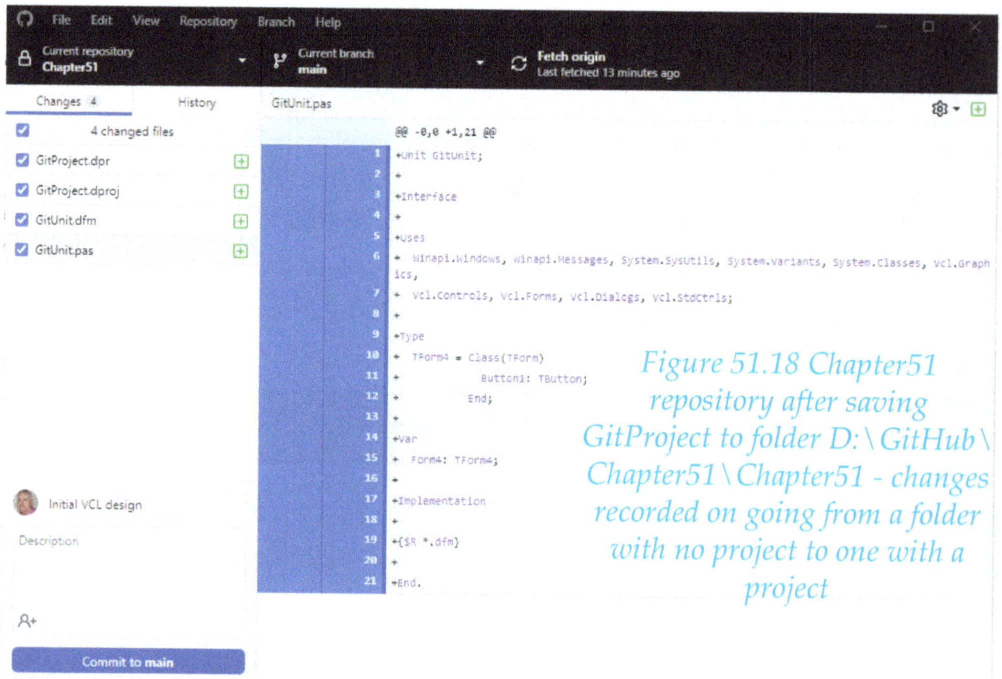

Figure 51.18 Chapter51 repository after saving GitProject to folder D:\GitHub\Chapter51\Chapter51 - changes recorded on going from a folder with no project to one with a project

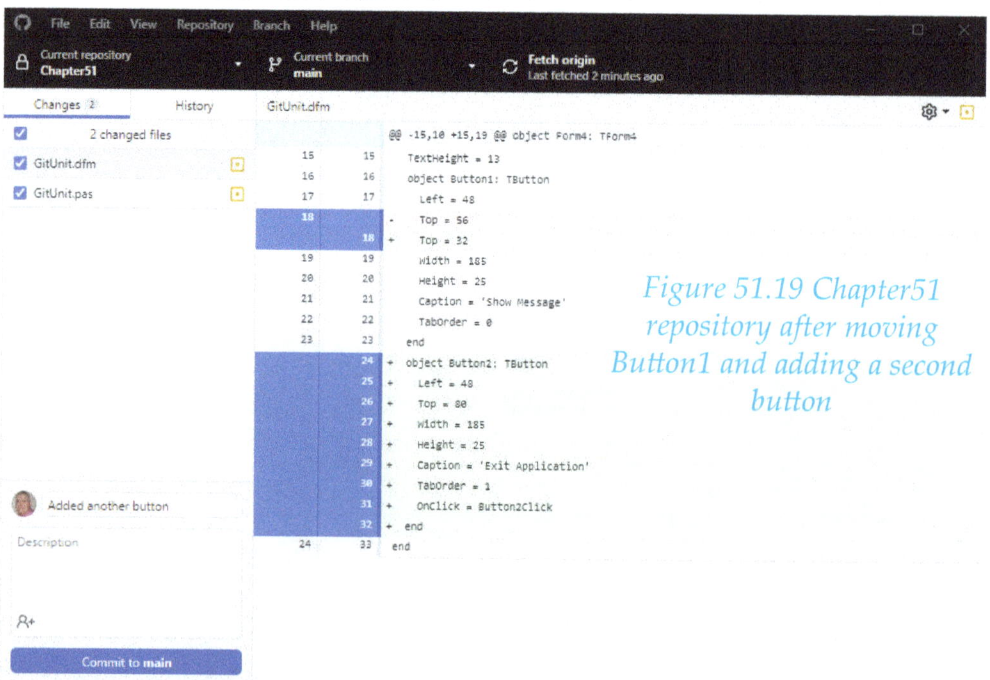

Figure 51.19 Chapter51 repository after moving Button1 and adding a second button

52 Unit testing

Unit testing

Purpose: To learn how to use unit tests

A **unit test** is an automated piece of code that invokes the unit of work being tested, and then checks some assumptions about a single end result of that unit.

Table 52.1 shows the unit of work that is to be tested.

```
Unit UnitUnderTest;
Interface
  Function Add(Value1, Value2 : Integer) : Integer;
Implementation
  Function Add(Value1, Value2 : Integer) : Integer;
    Begin
      Result := Value1 + Value2;
    End;
End.
```

Table 52.1 Unit under test

Table 52.2 shows an example of an automated piece of code `TestUnit.Pas` which tests/invokes the unit `UnitUnderTest.Pas` in order to check the assumption that the function `Add` in `UnitUnderTest` does add two values, `Value1` and `Value2`, as expected.

Table 52.3 shows the program that runs the unit test.

The program uses a unit testing IDE plugin for Delphi called **TestInsight** which supports all versions from XE and higher.

TestInsight integrates unit testing into the Delphi IDE so that when the program shown in *Table 52.3* is compiled and run the test cases are applied to the unit under test and the outcome is reported as shown in *Figure 52.2* provided **TestInsight** has been enabled.

```
Unit TestUnit;
Interface
  Uses DUnitX.TestFramework;
  Type
    [TestFixture]
    TMyTestObject = Class(TObject)
      Public
        [TestCase('1 and 1', '1,1,2')]
        [TestCase('1 and 2', '1,2,3')]
        [TestCase('1 and 3', '1,2,4')]
        Procedure TestAdd(Value1, Value2, Expected : Integer);
        [TestCase]
        Procedure TestPass;
        [TestCase]
        Procedure TestFail;
      End;
Implementation
{TMyTestObject}
  Uses UnitUnderTest;
  Procedure TMyTestObject.TestAdd(Value1, Value2, Expected: Integer);
    Var
      Actual : Integer;
    Begin
      Actual := Add(Value1,Value2);
      Assert.AreEqual(Expected, Actual);
    End;
  Procedure TMyTestObject.TestFail;
    Begin
      Assert.Fail('Ooops!');
    End;
  Procedure TMyTestObject.TestPass;
    Begin
      Assert.Pass('OK');
    End;
Initialization
  TDUnitX.RegisterTestFixture(TMyTestObject);
End.
```

Table 52.2 TestUnit with three test cases for tesing Add function

First **TestInsight** must be downloaded and installed:

https://files.spring4d.com/TestInsight/1.2.0.0/TestInsightSetup.zip.

In order to make **TestInsight** work with your project, it needs to have the **TESTINSIGHT** compiler directive defined in the project - *Figure 52.1*.

```
Program IntroToUnitTestingProject;
Uses
  TestInsight.DUnitX,
  TestCasesUnit in 'TestCasesUnit.pas',
  UnitUnderTest in 'UnitUnderTest.pas';
Begin
  TestInsight.DUnitX.RunRegisteredTests;
End.
```

Table 52.3 Program that runs the tests

This can be done quickly with the context menu in the project manager - *Figure 52.1* - **right click** `IntroToUnitTestingProject.exe` to bring up the context menu. **Click** **Options** then add **TESTINSIGHT** to Conditional defines as shown. At the same time enable **TestInsight Project**.

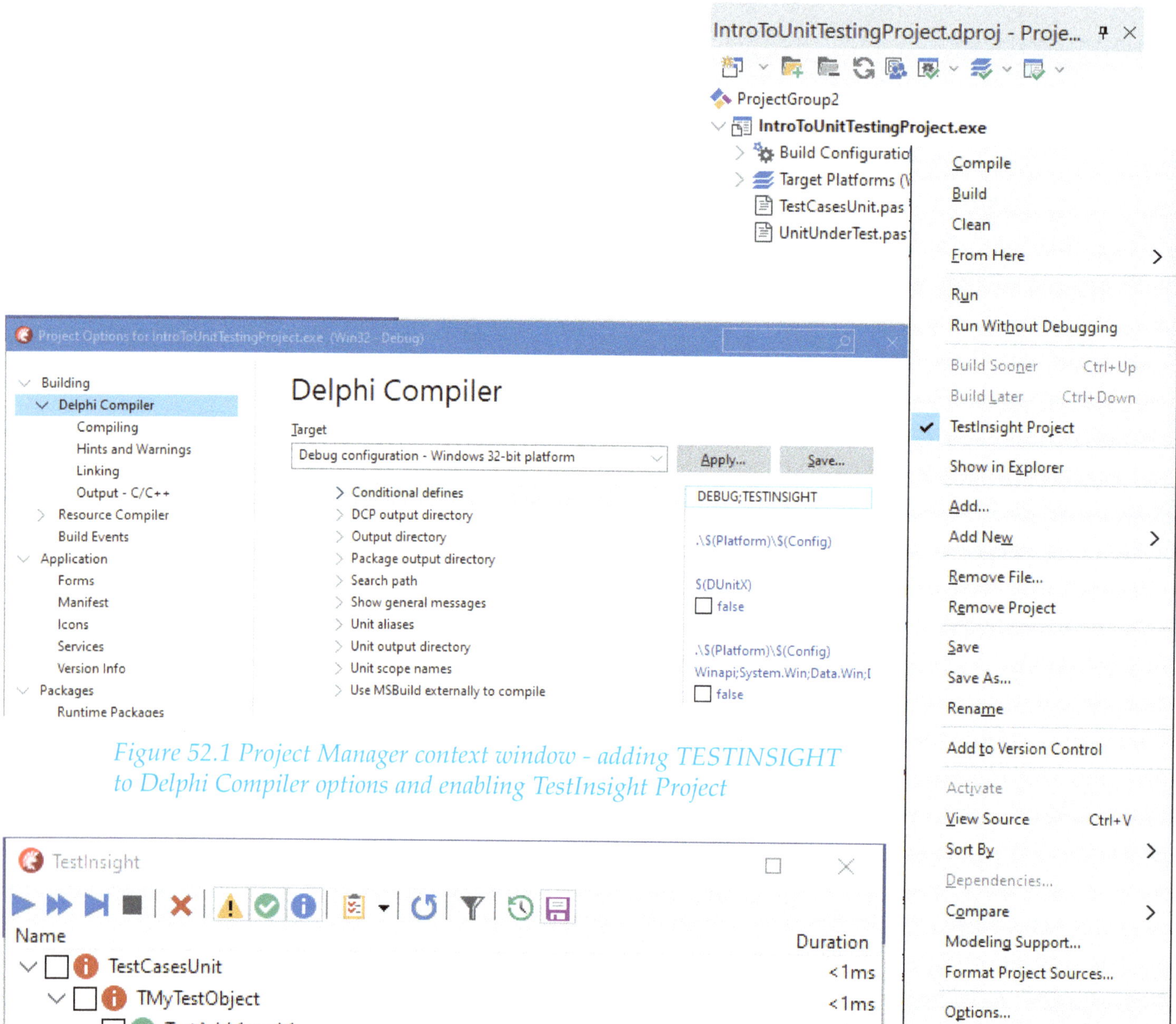

Figure 52.1 Project Manager context window - adding TESTINSIGHT to Delphi Compiler options and enabling TestInsight Project

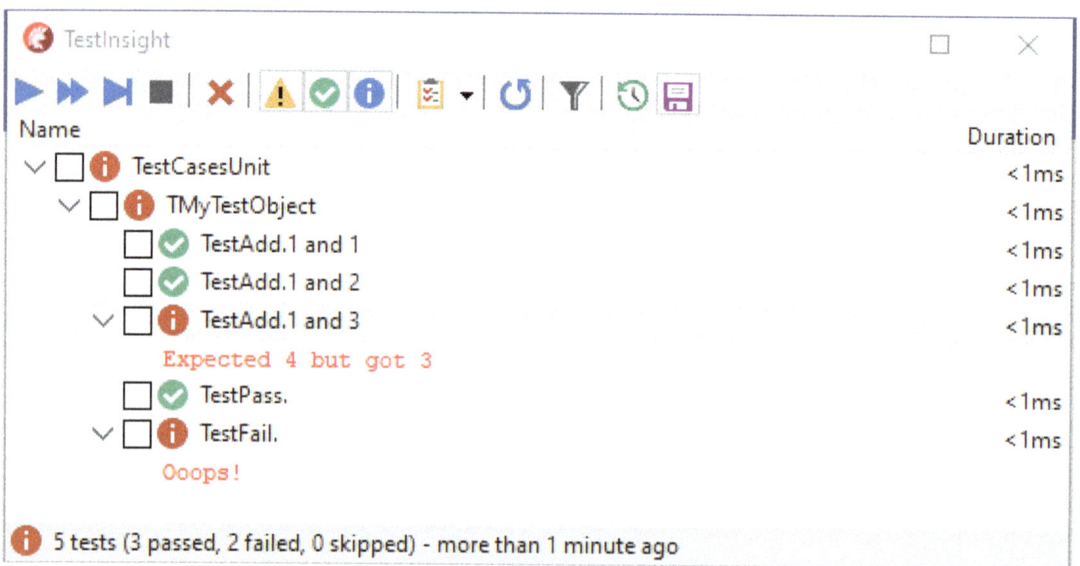

Figure 52.2 TestInsight window showing the results of testing

This project was created by selecting **File|New|Other|DUnitX|DUnitX Project** - *Figure 52.3* - and accepting the options shown in *Figure 52.4*. The `IFDEF/IFNDEF` statements were removed from the source shown in *Table 52.3* in order to focus on the essentials but leaving these statements alone will produc the same behaviour shown in

Figure 52.2. Alternatively, selecting **File|New|Other|Other|Unit Test|Test Project** will create a template that may be modified as shown in *Tables 52.1*, *52.2*, *52.3* in order to use **TestInsight**.

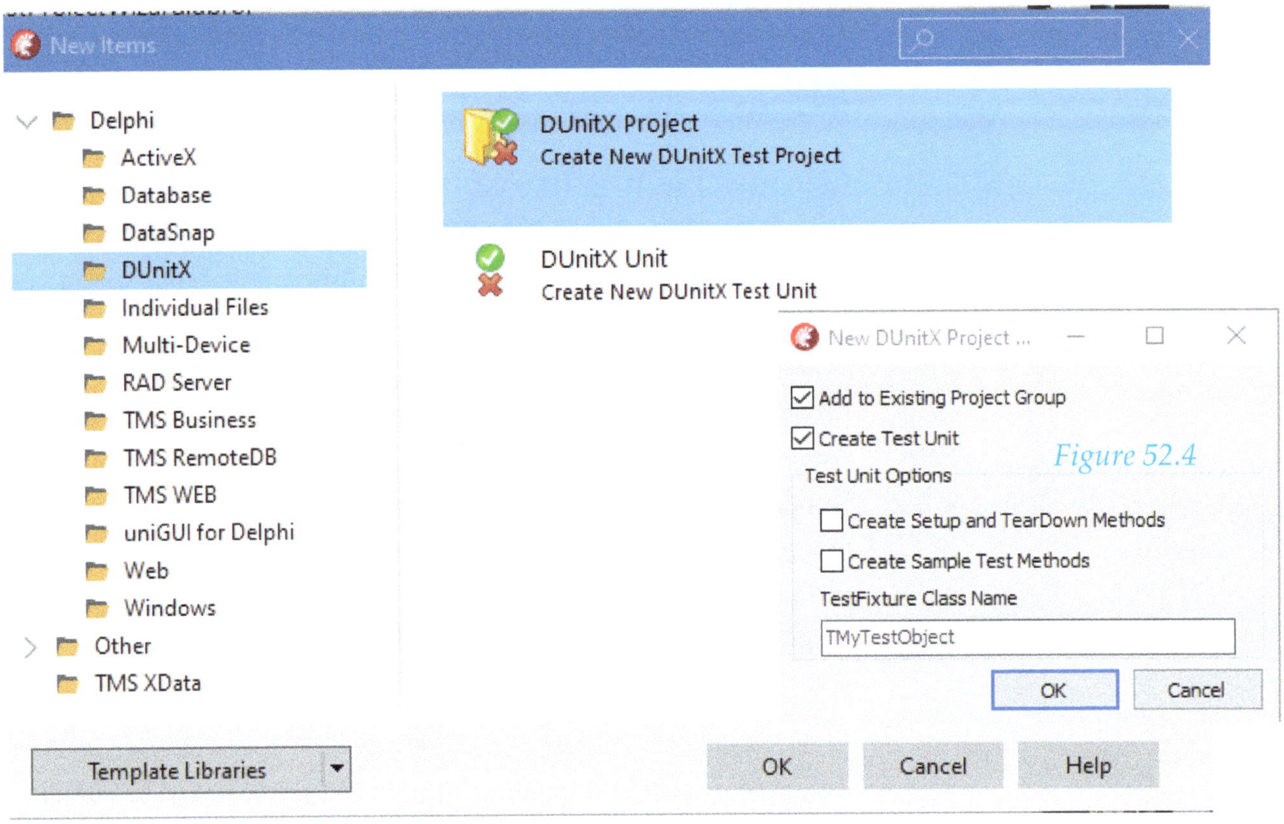

Figure 52.3 Creating a DUnitX Project

Add the unit to be tested if it exists to the project - **Project|Add to Project...** -or create a new unit - **File|New|Unit - Delphi**.

Using the syntax required by **TestInsight**, **add** test cases to be applied to function `Add`, e.g.

```
[TestCase('1 and 1', '1,1,2')]
[TestCase('1 and 2', '1,2,3')]
[TestCase('1 and 3', '1,2,4')]
Procedure TestAdd(Value1, Value2, Expected : Integer);
[TestCase]
Procedure TestPass;
[TestCase]
Procedure TestFail;
```

In `[TestCase('1 and 1', '1,1,2')]`, the string value `'1,1,2'` means when `Value1 = 1` and `Value2 = 1` the expected output is `2`. The string value `'1 and 1'` identifies the test when its outcome is reported.

The following test cases call the procedures `TestPass` and `TestFail`

```
[TestCase]
Procedure TestPass;
[TestCase]
Procedure TestFail;
```

Their implementations illustrate how to report a pass and a fail using `Assert.Pass` and `Assert.Fail`, respectively. This example is a trivial use for illustration purposes only. In a real world example, `Assert.Pass` and `Assert.Fail` would be used in a single procedure with multiple paths of execution so that more sophisticated testing may be carried out.

53 Installing packages

Introduction to installing packages

Purpose: To become familiar with packages

Dynamic-link libraries

What is a dynamic-link library?

A dynamic-link library (DLL) is a library of compiled code with a separate existence but which links[1] to an application's exe when the exe is loaded into memory or later when the exe is in execution. The DLL contains subroutines that may be called from the exe[1] to which it is linked. On Windows, DLLs are a way of sharing compiled code between executables of different programs. The Windows operating system APIs, for example, are DLLs that are available to user programs compiled for the Windows operating system. Also, subroutines of a DLL created in Delphi may be used by programs written in other programming languages, e.g. C#.

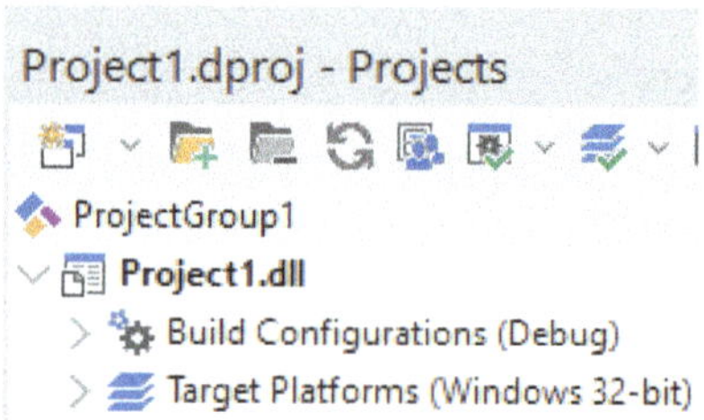

Figure 53.1 Project1 in Project Manager window

Programs that use code compiled into a shared dll produce smaller executables when compiled and therefore have a smaller memory footprint when loaded.

A single copy of a DLL residing in memory may be linked to multiple executables thus saving memory space.

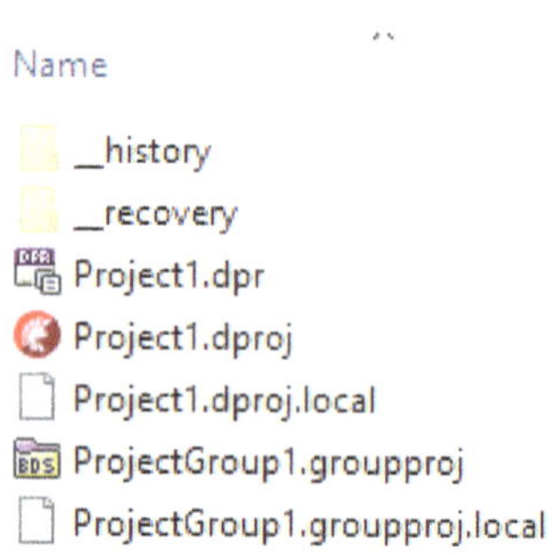

Figure 53.2 Folder LibraryDLLProject

Writing a dynamic-link library

Select File|New|Other|Delphi|Dynamic library to create `Project1.dpr` as shown in *Table 53.1*.

Select File|Save All in folder `LibraryDLLProject` - *Figure 53.2*. The source is saved in `Project1.dpr` but compiles to `Project1.dll` - *Figure 53.1*.

```
Library Project1;
{ Important note about DLL memory management: ShareMem must be the
  first unit in your library's USES clause AND your project's (select
  Project-View Source) USES clause if your DLL exports any procedures or
  functions that pass strings as parameters or function results. This
  applies to all strings passed to and from your DLL--even those that
  are nested in records and classes. ShareMem is the interface unit to
  the BORLNDMM.DLL shared memory manager, which must be deployed along
  with your DLL. To avoid using BORLNDMM.DLL, pass string information
  using PChar or ShortString parameters. }
Uses
  System.SysUtils, System.Classes;
{$R *.res}
Begin
End.
```

This may be ignored - it was relevant in the 1990s but not now.

Table 53.1 Project1.dpr

1 Or executable code in another DLL.

Right click ProjectGroup1 in the Project Manager and **save** the project group - *Figure 53.1*.

Delete the comment then **add** a function AddTwoIntegers followed by the statement Exports AddTwoIntegers; as shown in *Table 53.2*.

```
Library Project1;
Uses
  System.SysUtils, System.Classes;
{$R *.res}
Function AddTwoIntegers(First, Second : Integer) : Integer;
  Begin
    Result := First + Second;
  End;
Exports AddTwoIntegers;
Begin
End.
```

Table 53.2 Project1.dpr

The export statement specifies the names of procedures or functions that are callable from code that exists independently elsewhere and is not part of the library.

File|Save All.

Open Build Configurations in the Project Manager window and **select** Release.

Right click Project1.dll in the Project Manager window and **select** Build to create Project1.dll in the Win32\Release folder (Target Platforms (Windows 32-bit) setting).

File|Close All.

Select File|New|Console Application - Delphi to create a console application.

File|Save Project As UsingADLLProject.dproj in folder UsingADLLProject.

Add the code shown in *Table 53.3*. The following shows the import declaration which enables the function AddTwoIntegers located in Project1.dll to be called from UsingADLLProject.exe:

```
Function AddTwoIntegers(First, Second : Integer) : Integer;
         External 'Project1.dll';
```

Open Build Configurations in the Project Manager window and **select** Release.

Right click UsingADLLProject.exe in the Project Manager window and **select** Build to create UsingADLLProject.exe in the Win32\Release folder (Target Platforms (Windows 32-bit) setting).

Copy Project1.dll to this folder. **Select** Run Without Debugging (Shift Ctrl F9) to run UsingADLLProject.exe.

Figure 53.3 shows the console window output. Note that the result displayed by UsingADLLProject.exe has been calculated by using code located in Project1.dll.

```
Program UsingADLLProject;
{$APPTYPE CONSOLE}
{$R *.res}
Uses
  System.SysUtils;
Function AddTwoIntegers(First, Second : Integer) : Integer;
  External 'Project1.dll';
Begin
  Writeln('4 + 8 = ', AddTwoIntegers(4, 8));
  Readln;
End.
```

Table 53.3 UsingADLLProject.dpr

Figure 53.3 UsingADLLProject in execution

Download and **unzip** Dependencies an open source version of Dependency Walker from https://github.com/lucasg/Dependencies. (Dependency Walker doesn't work on the latest version of Windows 10).

Run `DependenciesGUI.exe` and **select** `File|Open UsingADLLProject.exe`. *Figure 53.4* shows the DLLs that `UsingADLLProject` depends upon including `Project1.dll`. (The exe and DLL were moved to the D:\drive).

Right click `D:\UsingADLLProject\Project1.dll` to bring up the window shown in *Figure 53.5*. The upper right pane shows that this DLL exports a function `AddTwoIntegers`.

Figure 53.5 shows the **delayed** field setting is **False**. The value of this field determines whether `Project1.dll` is loaded at the time that `UsingADLLProject` is loaded (value is **False**), i.e. at load time, or at runtime (value is **True**) when loading is delayed until the time `AddTwoIntegers` is called.

This field value is set to **True** when the **delayed** keyword is used in `UsingADLLProject` as follows

```
Function AddTwoIntegers(First, Second : Integer) : Integer;
    External 'Project1.dll' Delayed;
```

`UsingADLLProject` is a trivial example chosen to illustrate the basics. For larger projects, especially those that make use of shared DLLs, deciding whether to link at load time or at runtime becomes more important.

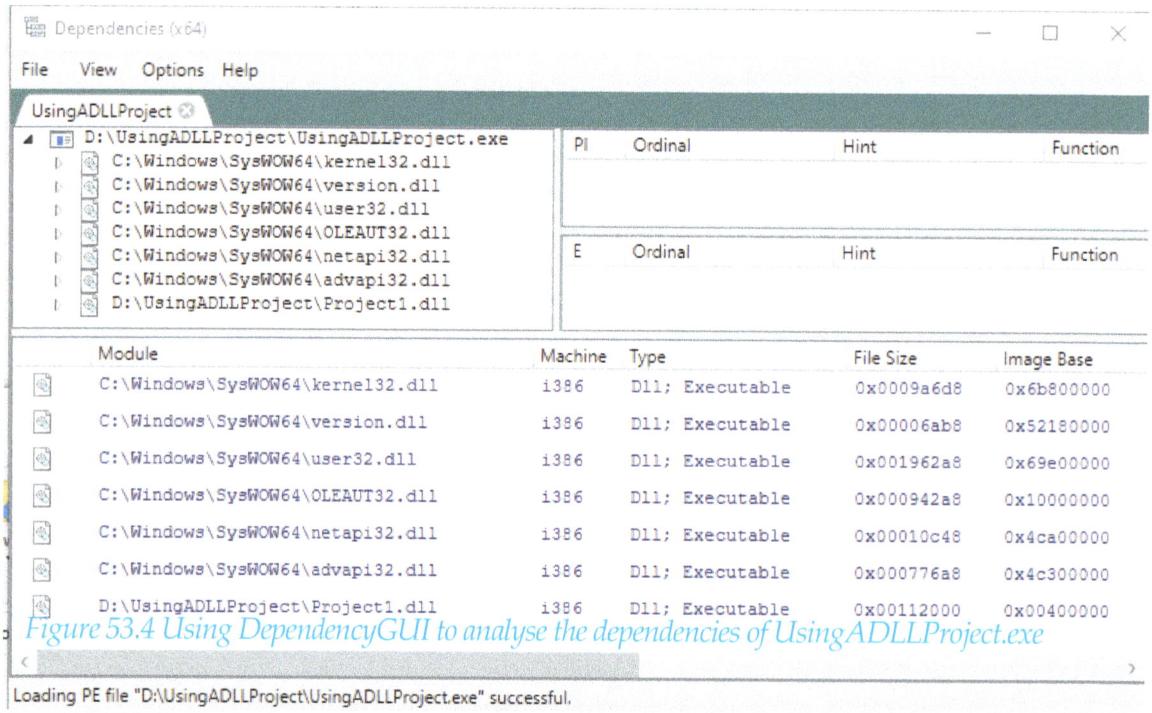

Figure 53.4 Using DependencyGUI to analyse the dependencies of UsingADLLProject.exe

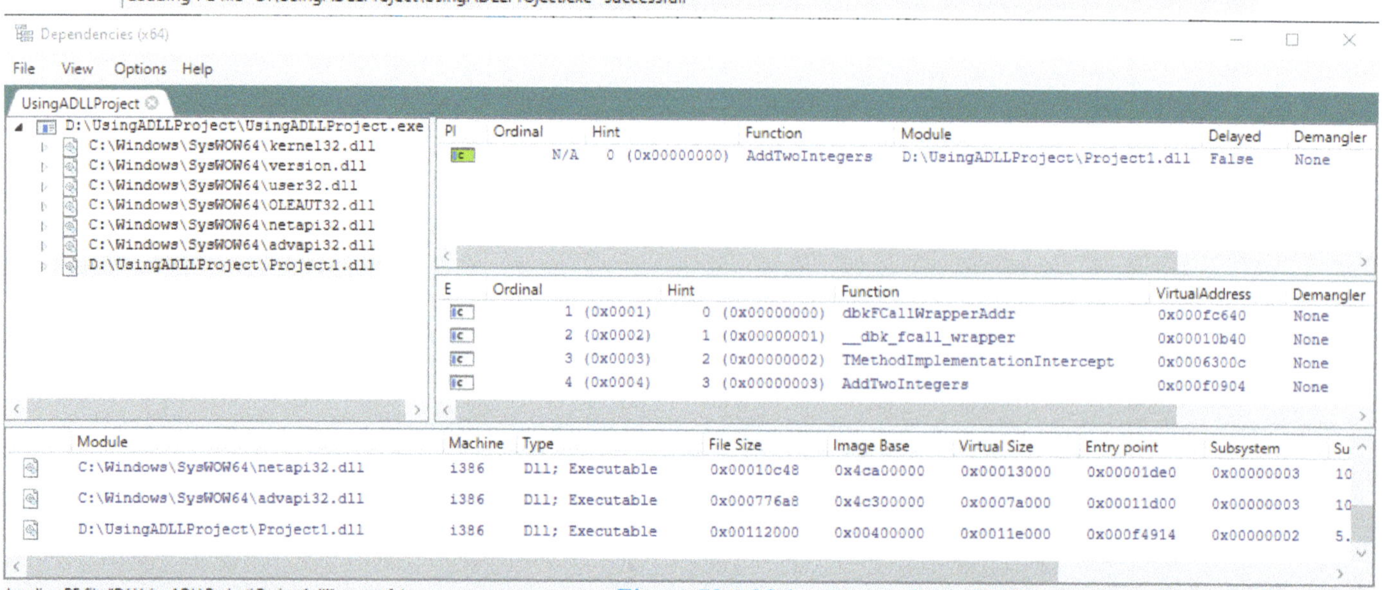

Figure 53.5 Using DependencyGUI to analyse Project1.dll

Delphi packages

Delphi packages are Embarcadero's way of using dynamic-link libraries to reduce the size of executables. Code that would have been compiled into an executable is instead independently compiled into a package. An example of a Delphi program written in this way is the Delphi IDE. Different functionalities are implemented in separate packages. Ths enables Embarcadero to maintain different editions of the product: the **Community edition**; the **Professional edition**; the **Enterprise edition** and the **Architect edition**, each created with a different set of packages. The technology of packages also allows third party components to be installed (or uninstalled) in the IDE without having to rebuild the IDE.

The original thinking behind the use of packages was to reduce the size of executables, especially in the case of a suite of Delphi applications each of which, without the technology of packages, could contain the same standard library code. This duplication is avoided when applications are built to link to pre-built packages for the RTL (Runtime library), VCL and FireMonkey instead of having these libraries compiled into every executable.

Create a VCL application with a few buttons and save as `EXESizeProject.dproj` in folder `EXESizeProject`.
Select **Project|Options|Packages|Runtime Packages** and **set** **Link with runtime packages** to **false**. - *Figure 53.6.*

Now **build** the project and **check** the size of the executable - *Figure 53.7*.
Revisit the project options and **set** **Link with runtime packages** to **true**.
Now **build** the project and **check** the size of the executable - *Figure 53.8*. Note the considerable reduction in the size of the exe.
A package source file does not contain type, data, procedure, or function declarations.
Instead, it contains:

- a name for the package,
- a list of other packages required by the new package. These are packages to which the new package is linked,
- a list of unit files contained by, or bound into, the package when it is compiled. The package is essentially a wrapper for these source-code units, which provide the functionality of the compiled package.

The packages that `EXESizeProject` links to have been previously compiled. This highlights an issue with Delphi packages: packages can only be installed and used in the same version of Delphi used to compile them because their DCU (Delphi Compiled Units) files are version dependent.

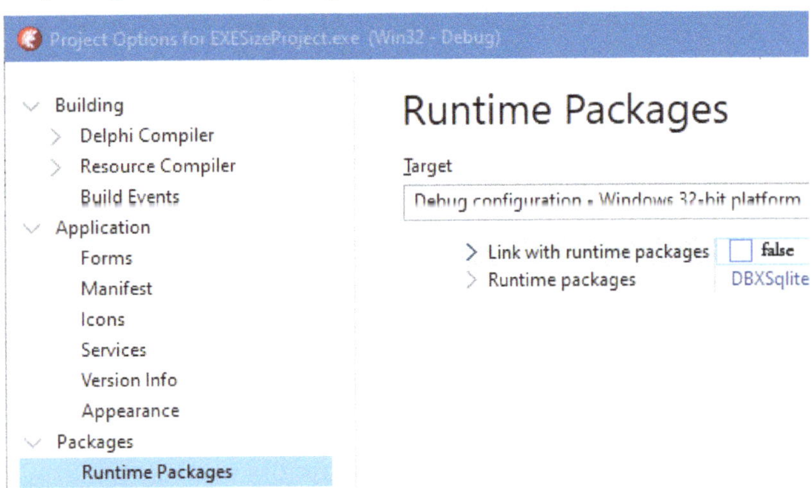

Figure 53.6 Configuring Project Options for Runtime Packages

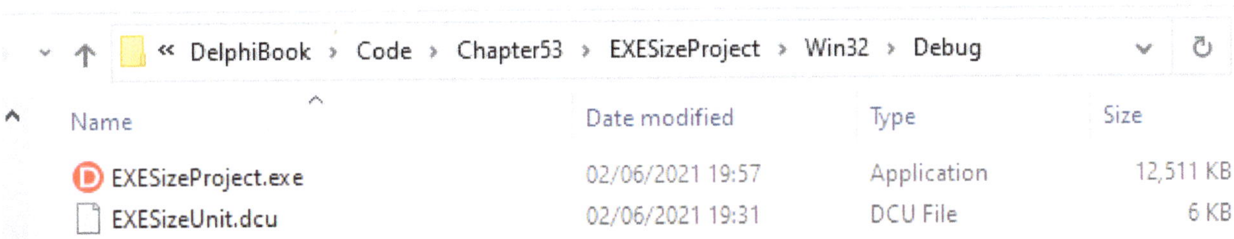

Figure 53.7 EXESizeProject built without runtime standard libraries (packages)

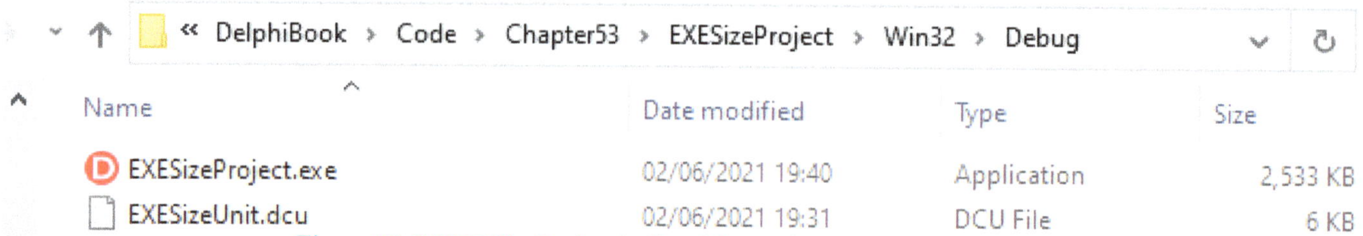

Figure 53.8 EXESizeProject built with runtime standard libraries (packages)

This means that to install a new component(s) in the IDE

- the source code is required (so it can be installed in any version)
- the package containing the component(s) must be compiled for every Delphi version in which it is to be installed.

Creating your own package

Select File|New|Package - Delphi to create a new package, `Package1`.

The project group for this package is shown in *Figure 53.9* in the Project Manager.

Right click `Package1.bpl` in the Project Manager and **select** View Source from the pop-up menu.

Figure 53.10 shows the source code for `Package1` that is now displayed in the editor window of the IDE.

Select File|Save All. and **save** in folder `PackageProject1`.

Figure 53.11 shows the contents of the folder `PackageProject1`.

The source code is saved in `Package1.dpk`. **Open** this file in another editor such as WordPad or NotePad++ to verify this.

Right click `Package1.bpl` in the Project Manager and **select** Build from the pop-up menu. The Delphi compiler automatically saves compiled packages in `C:\Users\Public\Documents\Embarcadero\Studio\21.0\Bpl` and `C:\Users\Public\Documents\Embarcadero\Studio\21.0\DCP`.

Delphi uses these folders so that compiled packages that applications and the IDE rely on may be easily located. It is more convenient for this simple exercise, however, to use the project folder for the compiler's output.

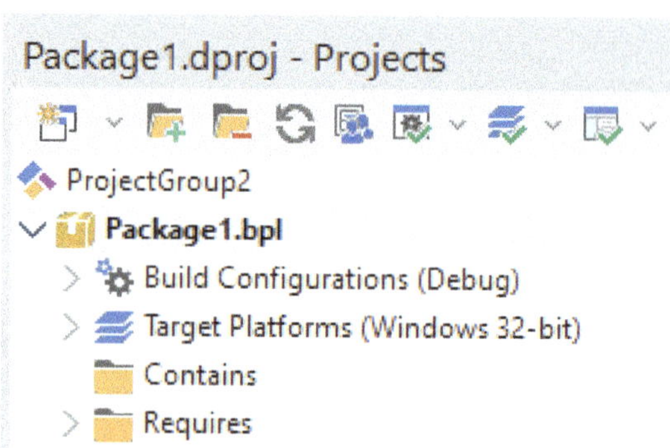

Figure 53.9 Project Manager Package1

To make the change from using the default folders, **select** Project|Options|Delphi Compiler and **make** the **DCP output directory** and the **Package output directory** the same as the **Unit output directory** as shown in *Figure 53.12*.

.\$(Platform)\$(Config) means: starting from the current directory, **change** to the subdirectory named by environment variable **$(Platform)** and then **change** to the subdirectory named by environment variable **$(Config)**.

This creates the path `PackageProject1\Win32\Debug` for the compiler's output. for the current configuration.

Now **right click** `Package1.bpl` in the Project Manager and **select** Build from the pop-up menu.

Figure 53.13 shows the contents of the folder `PackageProject1\Win32\Debug` after compilation. Note that two files have been created[2]:

- `Package1.bpl`
- `Package1.dcp`

---

2 Suppress the output of .bpi files by selecting Output DCUs only for Project|Options|Delphi Compiler|C/C++ Output File generation

`Package1.bpl` (Borland package library) is an executable file in the form of dynamic-link library with special Borland-specific features.

`Package1.dcp` or Delphi compiled package (DCP) file is a binary image containing a package header and a concatenation of all Delphi compiled unit files in the package, including all symbol information required by the compiler and linker. We haven't added any units yet. This is the next task.

Right click `Package1.bpl` in the **Project Manager** and **select** **Add New|VCL Form** from the pop-up menu.

Figure 53.14 shows the **Project Manager** window. The file `rtl.dcp` was automatically added to the **Requires** section at the time the package was created. The **Contains** section was empty initially but it now shows the newly created unit, `Unit1.pas`. Selecting the chevron associated with `Unit1.pas` reveals `Unit1.dfm`.

Now **right click** `Package1.bpl` and **select** **Build** from the pop-up menu.

```
package Package1;

{$R *.res}
{$IFDEF IMPLICITBUILDING This IFDEF should not be used by users}
{$ALIGN 8}
{$ASSERTIONS ON}
{$BOOLEVAL OFF}
{$DEBUGINFO OFF}
{$EXTENDEDSYNTAX ON}
{$IMPORTEDDATA ON}
{$IOCHECKS ON}
{$LOCALSYMBOLS ON}
{$LONGSTRINGS ON}
{$OPENSTRINGS ON}
{$OPTIMIZATION OFF}
{$OVERFLOWCHECKS OFF}
{$RANGECHECKS OFF}
{$REFERENCEINFO ON}
{$SAFEDIVIDE OFF}
{$STACKFRAMES ON}
{$TYPEDADDRESS OFF}
{$VARSTRINGCHECKS ON}
{$WRITEABLECONST OFF}
{$MINENUMSIZE 1}
{$IMAGEBASE $400000}
{$DEFINE DEBUG}
{$ENDIF IMPLICITBUILDING}
{$IMPLICITBUILD ON}

requires
  rtl;

end.
```

Figure 53.10 Source code for Package1

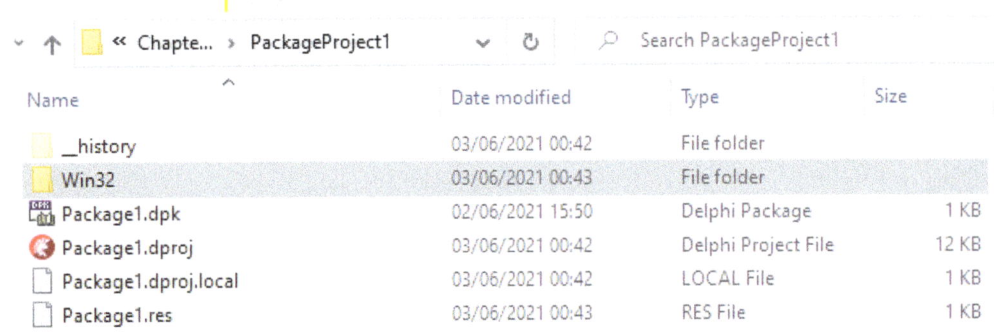

Figure 53.11 Project folder contents

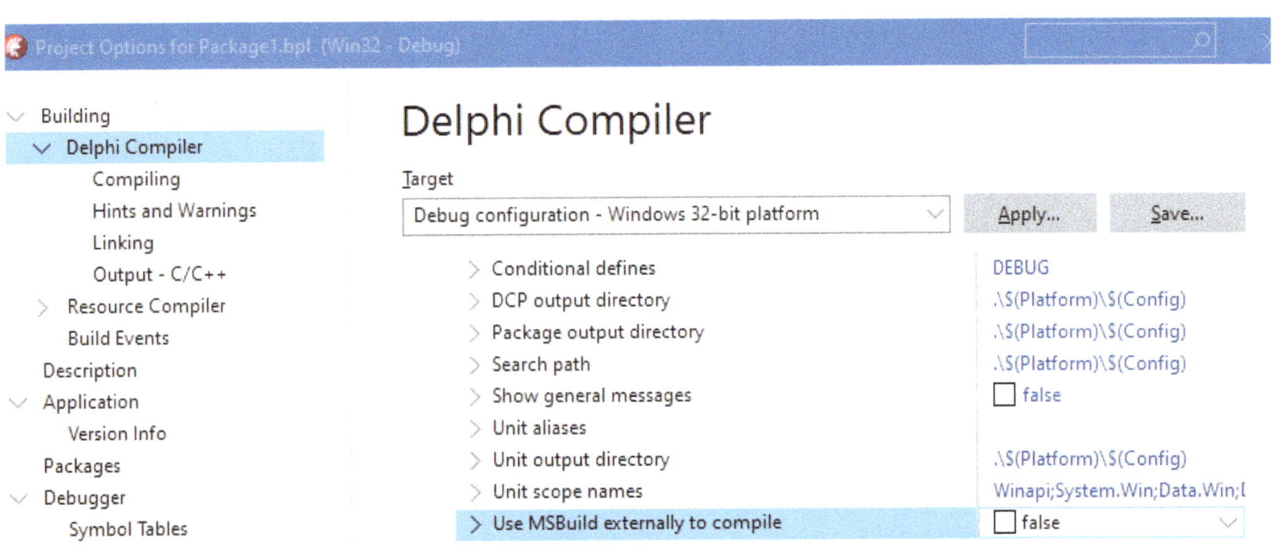

Figure 53.12 Project compiler options

Confirm when prompted by the compiler that the VCL library should be included (`vcl.dcp` added to the **Requires** section). The VCL library is required by `Unit1.pas`. The file `vcl.dcp` contains a list of all the DCUs (Delphi compiled units) belonging to the VCL library.

Figure 53.13 Folder PackageProject1\Win32\Debug

When the build (compilation) is finished folder `PackageProject1\Win32\Debug` contains in addition to a modified `Package1.bpl` and modified `Package1.dcp`, the compiled `Unit1` - `Unit1.dcu` - as shown in *Figure 53.15*.

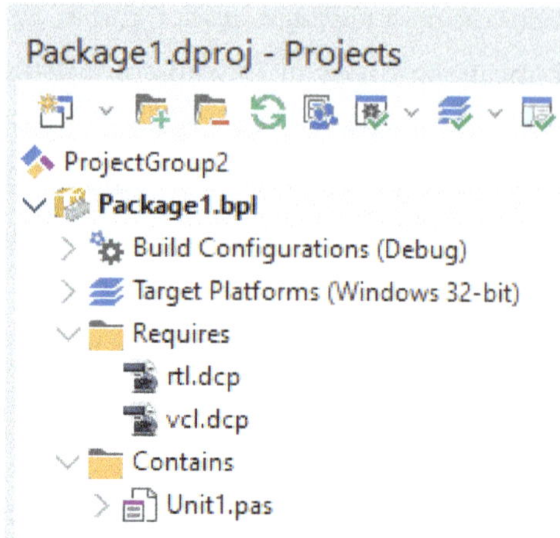

Figure 53.14 Project Manager window after compilation

When is the DCP used and when is the BPL used?

If we build an application to load a package, say `Package1`, at runtime when the application's executable is loaded into memory, the package's **BPL** (executable Borland Package Library) is loaded, e.g. `Package1.bpl`.

Select **File|New|Package - Delphi** to create a new package, `Package1`.
Select **Project|Options|Description** and **set** **Usage options** to **Runtime only** as shown in *Figure 53.16*.
Save this package in folder `Experimental`.
Right click `Package1.bpl` in the **Project Manager** and **select** **Add New|Unit** from the pop-up menu.
Add the code shown in *Table 53.4* to thus unit and **save**.
Set the compiler options as shown in *Figure 53.12*.

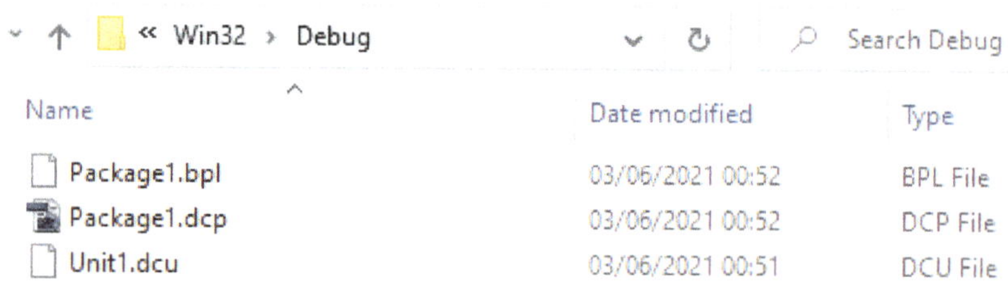

Figure 53.15 Folder PackageProject1\Win32\Debug

Now **right click** `Package1.bpl` and **select** **Build** from the pop-up menu.
Copy `Package1.bpl` to `C:\Users\Public\Documents\Embarcadero\Studio\21.0\Bpl` and `Package1.dcp` to `C:\Users\Public\Documents\Embarcadero\Studio\21.0\DCP`.
These two folders are on the compiler's search path by default.
File|Close All.
Select **File|New|Console Application - Delphi**.
Select **File|Save Project As** `Project1.dproj` in folder `ConsoleAppLoadPackageWithApp`.
Select **Project|Options|Packages|Runtime Packages** and **set** **Link with runtime packages** to **True**.
Select the next option **Runtime Packages** and click the ellipsis **...** to bring up the window shown in *Figure 53.17*.

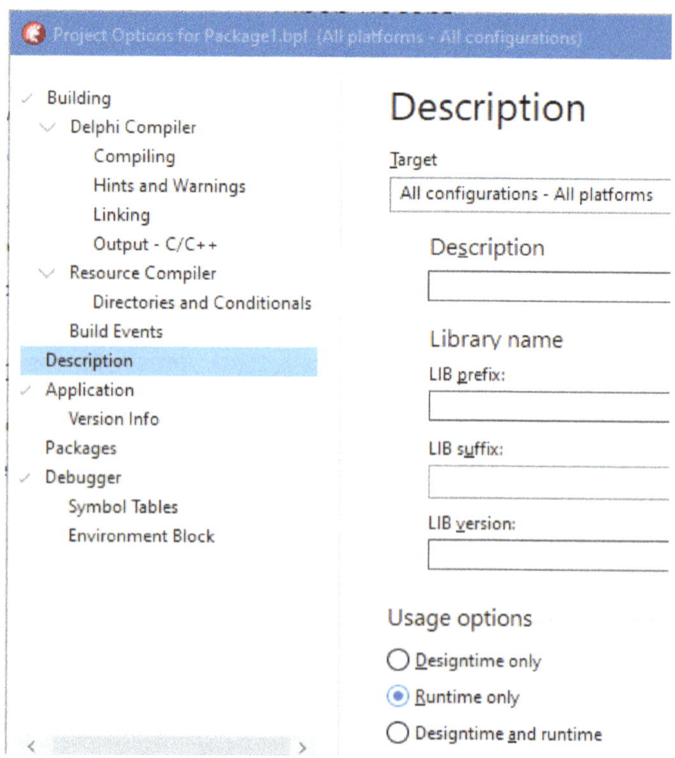

Figure 53.16 Project|Options|Description

```
Unit Unit1;
Interface
  Function AddTwoIntegers(First, Second : Integer) : Integer;
  Exports AddTwoIntegers;
Implementation
  Function AddTwoIntegers(First, Second : Integer) : Integer;
    Begin
      Result := First + Second;
    End;
End.
```

Table 53.4 Unit1.pas

`Package1` needs to be added as shown in *Figure 53.17*.

This can be done in one of two ways:

- If the name cannot be recalled then **select** the folder icon shown in *Figure 53.17* to bring up the **Add Runtime Package** window shown in *Figure 53.18*. **Browse** for the package using the **Browse** button.
- Alternatively, **add** the name directly.

With the **Add Runtime Package** window open, it is also possible to add the folder containing `Package1` to the **Search Path**. Instead, we chose to place `Package1.bpl` and `Package1.dcp` in the default folders which are already in the compiler's search path.

Add the code shown in *Table 53.5* to the project.

Interestingly, `Unit1.dcu` is not required in order to successfully compile and build `Project1`. The compiler instead searches for `Package1.dcp` and uses the information it contains to resolve both the unit name and the external function `AddTwoIntegers` reference.

Now **right click** `Project1.bpl` in the **Project Manager** and **select** **Build** from the pop-up menu.

Instead of running `Project1.exe` from the folder where the compiler placed it, **copy** it to a new folder `Project1ExeLoadtime` as shown in *Figure 53.19*. **Run** it from this folder.

Figure 53.20 shows the result of adding 4 and 5.

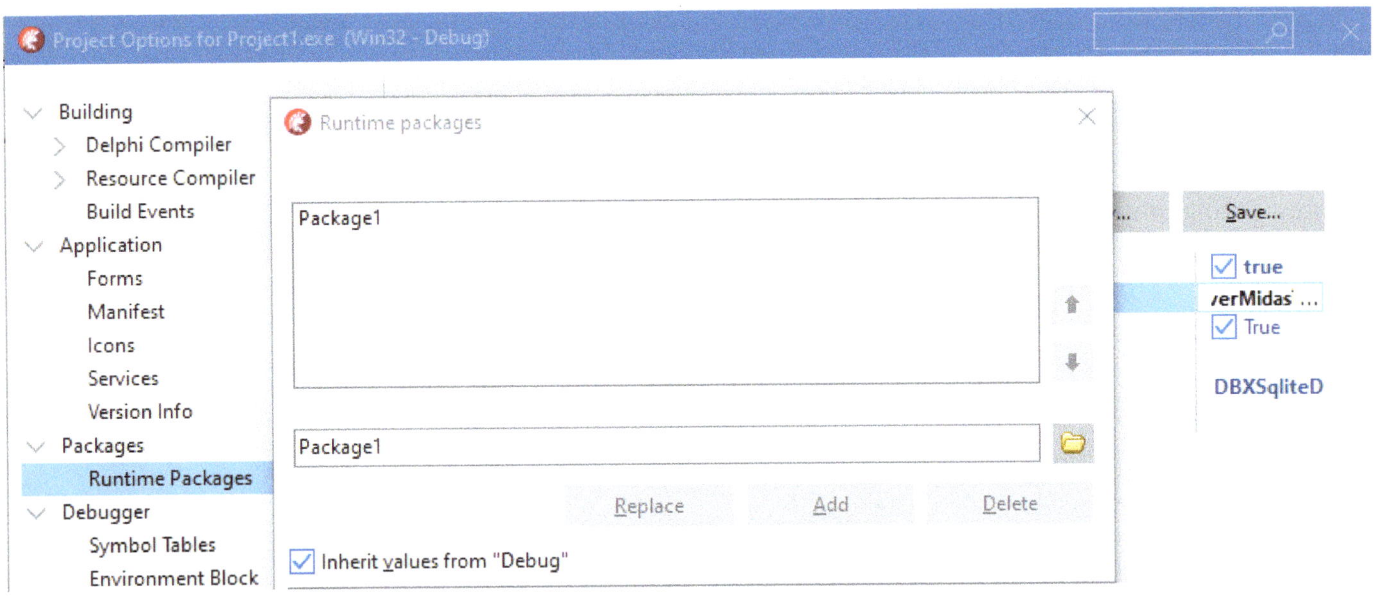

Figure 53.17 Project | Options | Packages | Runtime Packages

What gets loaded[3] along with `Project1.exe` to enable two integers to be added? It is the dynamic-link library `Package1.bpl`.

If the `Project1.exe` is run on a different machine from the one it was compiled on then `Package1.bpl` must be placed in the same directory as `Project1.exe` otherwise it won't be able to load the package it needs..

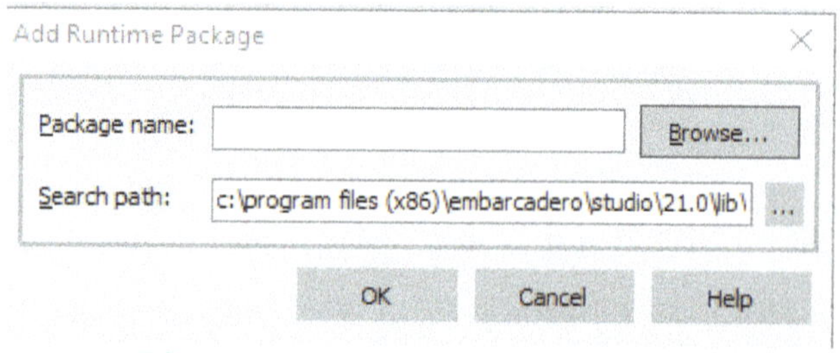

Figure 53.18 Add Runtime Package

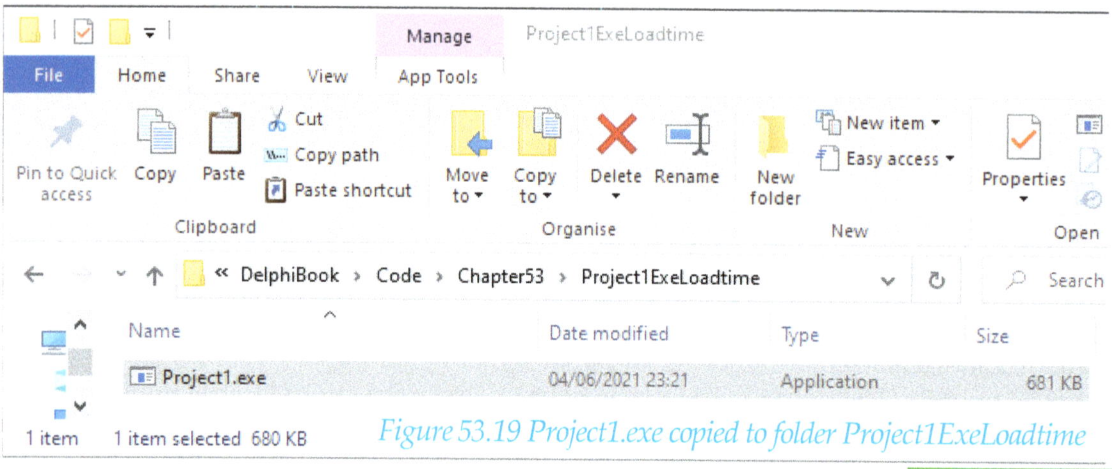

Figure 53.19 Project1.exe copied to folder Project1ExeLoadtime

Figure 53.20 Project1.exe launched into execution from folder Project1ExeLoadtime

```
Program Project1;
{$APPTYPE CONSOLE}
{$R *.res}
Uses
  System.SysUtils, Unit1;
Begin
  Writeln(AddTwoIntegers(4,5));
  Readln;
End.
```

Table 53.5 Project1.dpr

Loading a package dynamically when the program requires it

Table 53.6 shows how a program can be written to dynamically load a package, `Package1.bpl` at runtime when it is needed - the same `package.bpl` as used for the program in *Table 53.5.* The **Project Options** need to be set as before.

The compiler uses `Package1.dcp` to enable `Project1` to be successfully compiled as long as it is in the compiler's search path.

```
Program Project1;
{$APPTYPE CONSOLE}
{$R *.res}
Uses
  System.SysUtils, WinAPI.Windows, Unit1;
Type
  TGetAddTwoIntegers = Function(First, Second : Integer) : Integer;
Var
  Handle: HMODULE;
  GetAddTwoIntegers : TGetAddTwoIntegers;
Begin
  Handle := LoadPackage('Package1.bpl');
  If Handle <> 0
    Then
      Begin
        Writeln('Package1 is Loaded');
        @GetAddTwoIntegers := GetProcAddress(Handle, 'AddTwoIntegers');
        If @GetAddTwoIntegers <> Nil
          Then Writeln(AddTwoIntegers(4, 5));
      End
    Else Writeln('Not Loaded');
  UnloadPackage(Handle);
  Readln;
End.
```

Table 53.6 Project1.dpr loads Package1.bpl after Project1 has started execution

3 This can be see with Process Monitor from www.sysinternals.com by setting the filter to **Process Name** ends with `Project1.exe`.

(www.educational-computing.co.uk/DelphiBookCode/DelphiCode.html)

When are DCUs needed?

Packages are of two main types:

- Design-time
- Runtime

Only design-time packages are allowed to link against IDE internals.

DCUs are need if an application uses components provided by a design-time package. The application will link to the DCUs at compile/build-time (i.e. application is not built with runtime packages). In this instance, the package's DCUs must be in a directory located on the IDE's library path.

Installing GLScene using both design-time and runtime packages

Download `GLScene_v2.0_VCL_Win32_Win64.zip` from www.glscene.org (redirects to http://glscene.sourceforge.net/wikka/) and **unzip** to folder `GLScene` - *Figure 53.21*.

GLScene is an OpenGL based 3D library of visual components and objects for Delphi, C++Builder and FreePascal. By providing visual components and objects that encapsulate OpenGL, GLScene elevates OpenGL to a level of abstraction that makes it easier to create and render 3D scenes.

Open the `Packages` folder - *Figure 53.22* - to reveal the design-time and runtime packages, e.g. `GLScene_Cg_DT.dpk` and `GLScene_Cg_RT.dpk`.

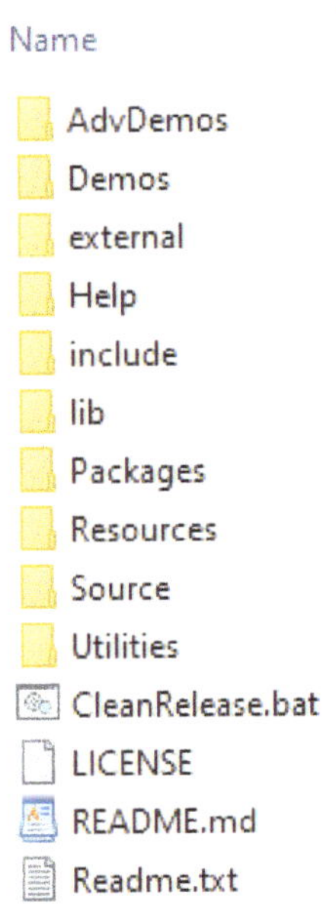

Figure 53.21 Contents of folder GLScene

Launch Delphi and **open** (File|OpenProject...) `GLScene.groupproj`. *Figure 53.23* shows the resulting contents of the Project Manager window.

Before compiling the packages we need to install some DLLs. An installation guide, `InstallationGLS.pdf,` is provided in folder `..\GLScene\Help`. The essential installation instructions are as follows:

- **Run** `SetupDLLs.bat` located in folder `..\GLScene\external` as administrator to copy third party dynamic libraries into `C:\Windows\System32` and `C:\Windows\SysWOW64` folders. The latter folder is where 32-bit DLLs go on a 64-bit Windows machine. This version of GLScene links to a DLL named `newton.dll` not `newton32.dll` and newton64.dll which the batch file copies. Rename these `newton.dll` where they are stored.
- **Setup** Delphi Library Path in **Tools|Options|Language|Delphi|Library** dialogue: **add** path to GLScene source - `..\GLScene\Source`.
- **Right click** each BPL file in the Project Manager window and compile GLScene's packages for Win32 using "**Compile All From Here**".
- **Right click** each design-time package in the Project Manager window and click **Install** - *Figure 53.23* - to install GLScene components to the Component Palette - *Figure 53.24*.

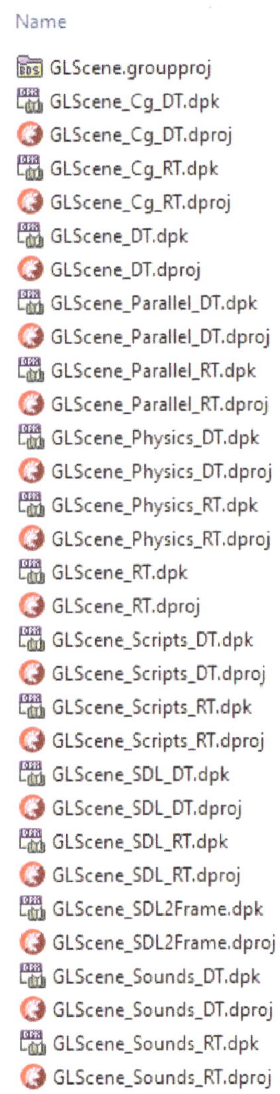

Figure 53.22 Contents of folder GLScene/Packages

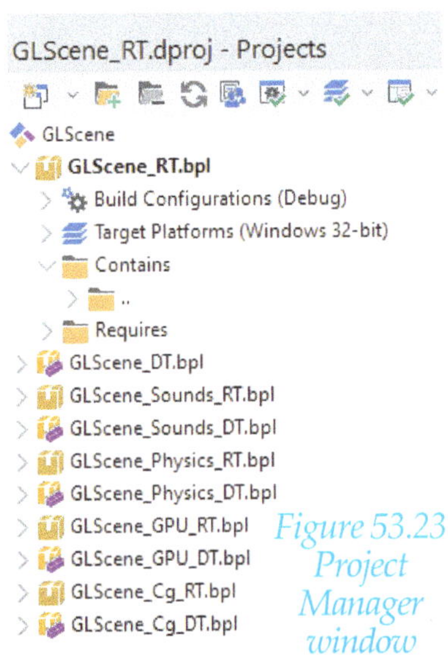

Figure 53.23 Project Manager window

GLScene comes with a large number of demo projects.

(www.educational-computing.co.uk/DelphiBookCode/DelphiCode.html)

Open `Meshes.groupproj` in the `...\GLScene\Demos\Delphi\meshes` folder.
Right click `Ducky.exe` in the **Project Manager** window and select **Run Without Debugging**.
Figure 53.25 shows two examples of the output produced by the running program when the wireframe option is selected and one example when it isn't. *Table 53.7* shows the source code (`Unit1.pas`) responsible for calling the GLScene library routines that create these examples. *Figure 53.26* shows the form, `Ducky (Unit1.dfm),` that corresponds to `Unit1.pas`. *Figure 53.27* shows the **Structure window** with three main design-time components: `GLScene1`, `GLSceneViewer1` and `Panel1`. These are selected from the **Component Palette**. `GLActor1`, `GLDummyCube1`, `GLCamera1` and `GLLightSource1` are components added to `GLScene1` using the **Scene Editor** - *Figure 53.28*.

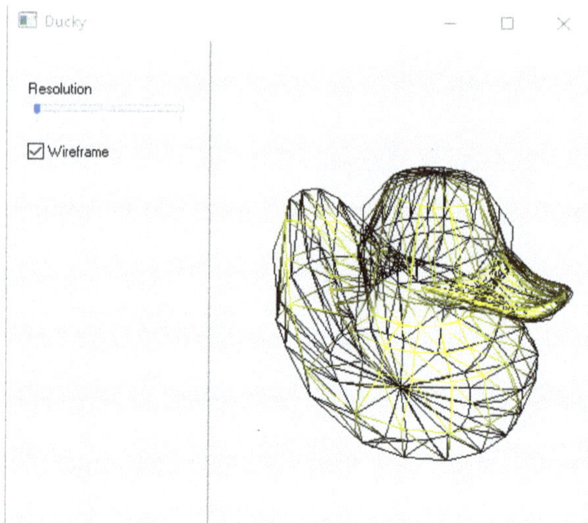

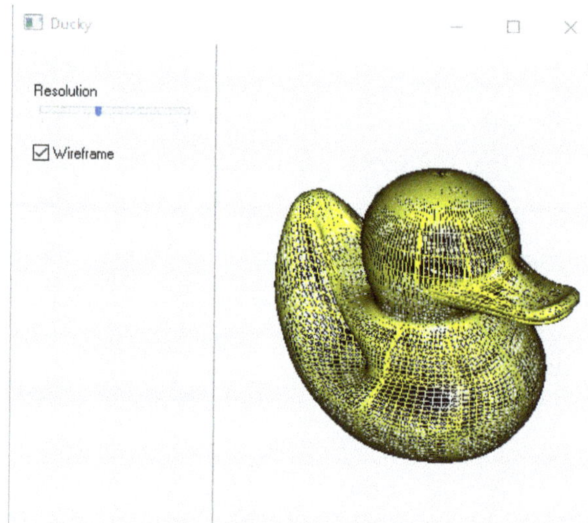

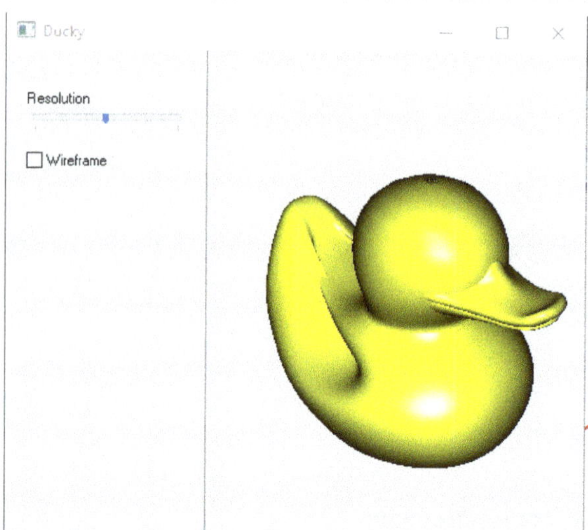

Figure 53.25 Ducky examples from GLScene Meshes demos folder: low resolution wireframe; medium resolution wireframe; medium resolution no wireframe

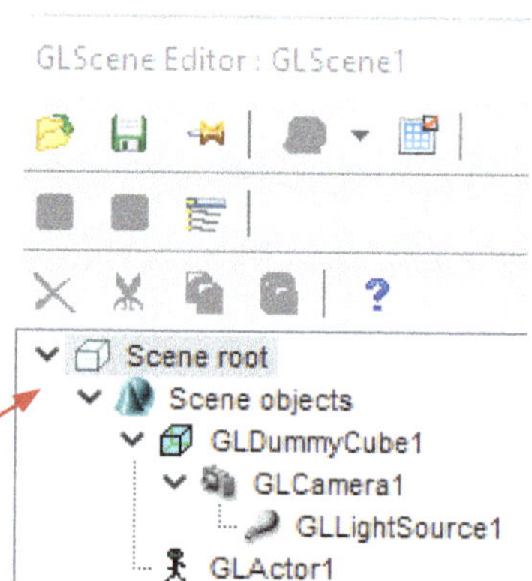

Figure 53.28 Ducky GLScene Editor

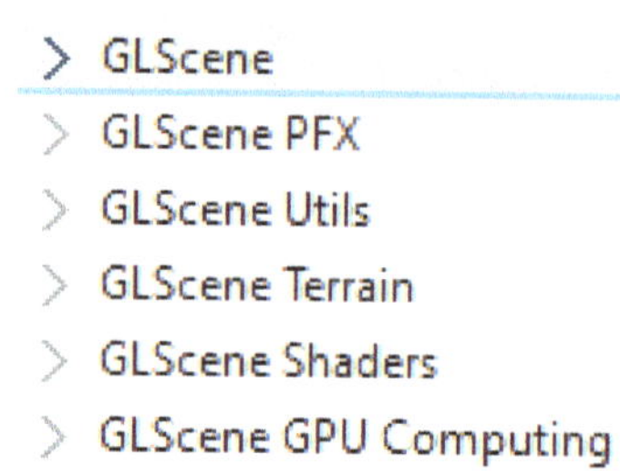

Figure 53.24 Part of the component palette

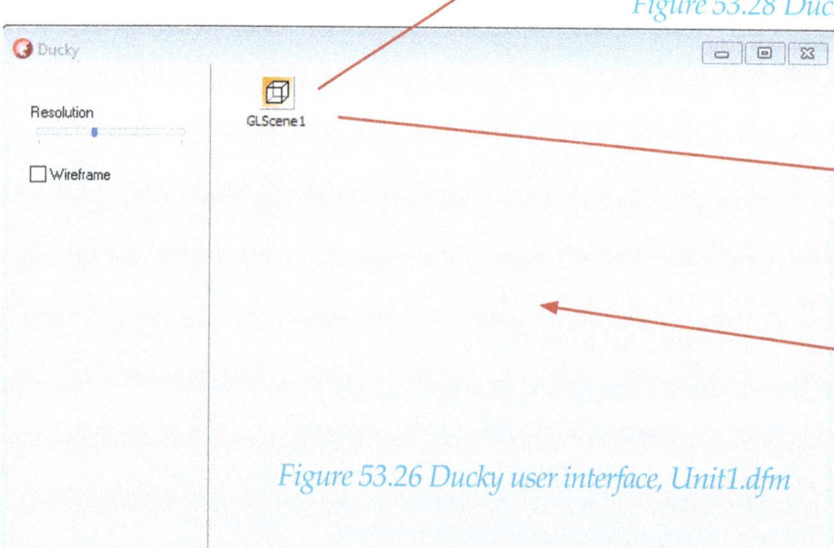

Figure 53.26 Ducky user interface, Unit1.dfm

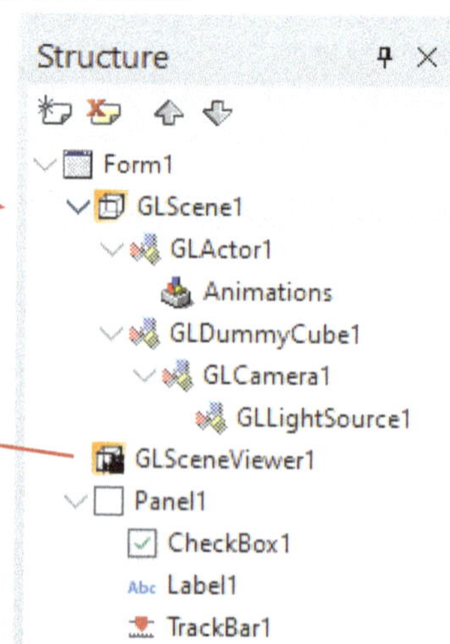

Figure 53.27 Ducky Structure window

(www.educational-computing.co.uk/DelphiBookCode/DelphiCode.html)

P

```
Unit Unit1;
Interface
Uses
  Winapi.OpenGL, System.SysUtils,System.Classes, Vcl.Graphics, Vcl.Controls,
  Vcl.Forms, Vcl.Dialogs, Vcl.ExtCtrls, Vcl.ComCtrls, Vcl.StdCtrls, GLS.Scene,
  GLS.VectorTypes, GLS.PersistentClasses, GLS.VectorFileObjects, GLS.Objects,
  GLS.SceneViewer, GLS.ParametricSurfaces, GLS.VectorGeometry, GLS.VectorLists,
  GLS.Texture, GLS.Coordinates, GLS.Material, GLS.State, GLS.BaseClasses, GLS.FileNurbs,
  GLS.Utils;
Type
  TForm1 = Class(TForm)
             GLScene1: TGLScene; GLCamera1: TGLCamera; GLDummyCube1: TGLDummyCube;
             GLLightSource1: TGLLightSource; Panel1: TPanel; GLSceneViewer1: TGLSceneViewer;
             TrackBar1: TTrackBar; Label1: TLabel; CheckBox1: TCheckBox; GLActor1: TGLActor;
             Procedure GLSceneViewer1MouseDown(Sender: TObject; Button: TMouseButton;
                    Shift: TShiftState; X, Y: Integer);
             Procedure GLSceneViewer1MouseMove(Sender: TObject; Shift: TShiftState; X, Y: Integer);
             Procedure FormCreate(Sender: TObject);
             Procedure TrackBar1Change(Sender: TObject);
             Procedure CheckBox1Click(Sender: TObject);
             Public
              mx, my: Integer;
            End;
Var
  Form1: TForm1;
Implementation
{$R *.dfm}
Procedure TForm1.FormCreate(Sender: TObject);
  Var
    cp: TAffineVectorList;
  Begin
    SetGLSceneMediaDir();
    // Load the nurbs data
    GLActor1.LoadFromFile('duck1.nurbs');
    GLActor1.AddDataFromFile('duck2.nurbs');
    GLActor1.AddDataFromFile('duck3.nurbs');
    { Translate Actor based on the first mesh object's average
      control point. Quick and dirty ... or maybe just dirty :P }
    cp := TMOParametricSurface(GLActor1.MeshObjects[0]).ControlPoints;
    GLActor1.Position.Translate(VectorNegate(VectorScale(cp.Sum, 1 / cp.Count)));
  End;
Procedure TForm1.GLSceneViewer1MouseDown(Sender: TObject; Button: TMouseButton;
  Shift: TShiftState; X, Y: Integer);
  Begin
    mx := X;
    my := Y;
  End;
Procedure TForm1.GLSceneViewer1MouseMove(Sender: TObject; Shift: TShiftState; X, Y: Integer);
  Begin
    If ssLeft In Shift
      Then GLCamera1.MoveAroundTarget(my - Y, mx - X);
    mx := X;
    my := Y;
  End;
Procedure TForm1.TrackBar1Change(Sender: TObject);
  Var
    i: Integer;
  Begin
    For i := 0 to 2
      Do TMOParametricSurface(GLActor1.MeshObjects[i]).Resolution := TrackBar1.Position;
    GLActor1.StructureChanged;
  End;
Procedure TForm1.CheckBox1Click(Sender: TObject);
  Begin
    With GLActor1.Material
      Do
        Begin
          If CheckBox1.Checked
            Then
              Begin
                PolygonMode := pmLines;
                FaceCulling := fcNoCull;
              End
            Else
              Begin
                PolygonMode := pmFill;
                FaceCulling := fcBufferDefault;
              End;
        End;
  End;
End.
```


Table 53.7 Ducky demo Unit1.pas

54 Using the IDE more effectively

Using keyboard shortcuts

Purpose: To learn how to speed up development

Why use keyboard shortcuts?

Using keyboard shortcuts can save you time when typing code, deleting code, navigating code, and it is almost always faster than using a mouse.

Useful keyboard shortcuts

Start a new console application (**File|New|Console Application - Delphi**).

Add a unit (**File|New|Unit -Delphi**) to this application.

Now **save** the application's project source as `ConsoleClassProject.dproj` (*Table 54.1*) and its unit as `ConsoleClassUnit.pas` (*Table 54.2*) in folder `ConsoleClassApplication`.

Add the keyword **Type** to the **Interface** section of `ConsoleClassUnit.pas` followed by a blank line.

With the cursor on the blank line type **classf** (short for class declaration full) and then press the key combination **Ctrl + J** to insert the class template **TMyClass** shown in *Table 54.3*.

Remove (TComponent).

Now **move** the cursor to the blank line below the **Public** keyword then type **propgs** (short for property with getter and setter). Next **press** the key combination **Ctrl + J** to insert the property template shown in *Figure 54.1*.

Now while `name` is highlighted and `type` is outlined by a blue rectangle (otherwise this step won't work), **change** it to `Name` then **tab** to highlight `type` and change this to `String`. Next **press** the **Enter** key to create the getter and setter code. The result is shown in *Table 54.4*.

Note that by using just a few keystrokes a compilable class, `TMyClass`, has been produced.

```
Program ConsoleClassProject;

{$APPTYPE CONSOLE}
{$R *.res}

Uses
  System.SysUtils,
  ConsoleClassUnit In 'ConsoleClassUnit.pas';

Begin
  Try
    { TODO -oUser -cConsole Main : Insert code here }
  Except
    On E : Exception Do
      Writeln(E.ClassName, ': ', E.Message);
  End;
End.
```

Table 54.1 ConsoleClassProject source

```
Unit ConsoleClassUnit;

Interface

Implementation

End.
```

Table 54.2 ConsoleClassUnit source

```
Unit ConsoleClassUnit;

Interface
  Type
    TMyClass = Class(TComponent)
      Private

      Protected

      Public

      Published

    End;
Implementation

End.
```

Table 54.3 ConsoleClassUnit source with keyboard shortcut created property template

```
Property name : type Read Getname Write Setname;
```

Figure 54.1 Property template in SynEdit mode showing four jump points

Check that this is the case by pressing **Ctrl + F9** (**Compile ConsoleClassProject**).

The template names **classf** and **propgs** are examples of **Live Templates**. **Live Templates** are reusable skeleton code statements.

Pressing the key combination **Ctrl + J** anywhere in the code editor brings up the **Live Template** menu window shown in *Figure 54.2*. The template names **classf** and **propgs** could have been selected from this menu window.

Templates have **jump points** which are placeholders for key entry fields. **Jump points** allow navigation between elements in a template using **Tab** for forward navigation and **Shift + Tab** for backward navigation. Some **jump points** are editable, e.g. those belonging to **propgs** - *Figure 54.1* - indicated by highlighting and outlining (the template is in **SynEdit** mode when this occurs). Pressing **Esc**, **Enter**, or pressing the **Tab** key from the last **jump point** exits **SyncEdit** mode and returns the **Code Editor** to its regular edit mode.

Place the cursor on `Procedure TMyClass.SetName(Const Value : String)` in the **Implementation** section of `ConsoleClassUnit.pas`.

Pressing the key combination **Ctrl + Shift + Up Arrow** moves the cursor to the location of `TMyClass.SetName` in the **Interface** section.

Pressing the key combination **Ctrl + Shift + Down Arrow** moves the cursor to the location of `TMyClass.SetName` in the **Implementation** section.

```
Unit ConsoleClassUnit;

Interface

Type
  TMyClass = Class
  Private
    Function GetName : String;
    Procedure SetName(Const Value : String);

  Protected

  Public
    Property Name : String Read GetName Write SetName;
  Published

  End;

Implementation

{ TMyClass }

Function TMyClass.GetName : String;
  Begin

  End;

Procedure TMyClass.SetName(Const Value : String);
  Begin

  End;

End.
```

Table 54.4 ConsoleClassUnit source

```
template arrayd   array declaration (variable)
template begin   begin...end;
template case   case statement
template class   class declaration (full with section comments)
template classc   class declaration (with Create/Destroy overrides)
template classd   class declaration (no parts)
template classf   class declaration (full)
template CreateC   TComponent descendant constructor
template else   else begin...end;
template enum   enumeration declaration
template for   for (no begin/end)
template forb   for loop
template forin   for in loop
template forr   for loop (reverse)
template function   function declaration
template if   if (no begin/end)
template ifb   if statement
template ife   if then (no begin/end) else (no begin/end)
template ifeb   if then else
template ifnass   Creates code that checks for nil and then creates an instance if needed
template ifnil   Creates code that checks for nil and then creates an instance if needed
template para   Creates an XMLDoc <para> tag
template param   Creates an XMLDoc <param> tag
template procedure   procedure declaration
template prop   Creates a property declaration with any getter and setter
template propf   Creates a property declaration with a simple field name for the getter and setter
template propgs   Creates a property declaration with getter and setter methods
template propro   Creates a read only property declaration
template proprof   Creates a read only property declaration
template raise   Create and raise an instance of an Exception class
template region   create or surround code with a region
template remarks   Creates an XMLDoc <remarks> tag
template repeat   repeat ... until loop
```

Figure 54.2 Section of Live Template menu window (Ctrl + J)

Add `NameValue : String;` before `Function GetName` in the class definition.

Add `NameValue := Value;` to the body of `SetName` in the **Implementation** section.

Add `Result := NameValue;` to the body of `GetName` in the **Implementation** section.

Shift + Ctrl + S to save all.

Switch the focus to `ConsoleClassProject source`.

Delete the **Try Except End** statement.

Add before the **Begin End** block `Var Object1 :` then **press** the key combination Ctrl + Space to bring up the CodeInsight window. **Select** `TMyClass` from the window. **Close** the statement with a semicolon.

In the **Begin End** block type Object1 := then **press** the key combination Ctrl + Space to bring up the CodeInsight window. again - *Figure 54.3*. **Select** `TMyClass`. Now **type** a fullstop (`TMyClass.`) to invoke the `CodeInsight` window again and **select** `Create`.

On the next line **type** `Object1.` to invoke the CodeInsight window and **select** property `Name`. If the CodeInsight window should disappear before you can do this, just type Ctrl + Space to bring it up again.

Figure 54.4 shows a section of this window.

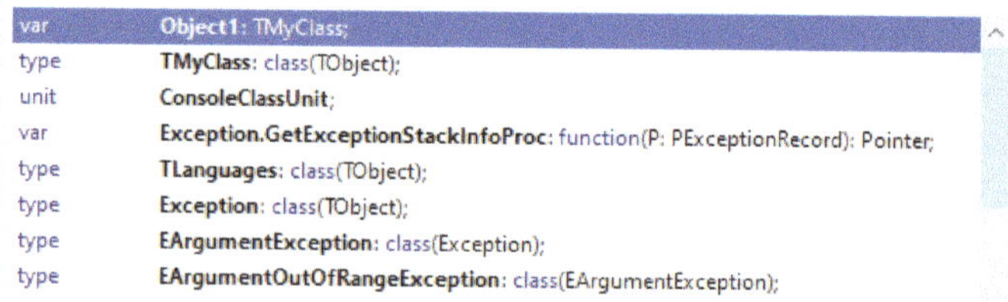

Figure 54.3 Section of CodeInsight window (Ctrl + Space)

Complete the statement as follows:

```
Object1.Name := 'Harry';
```

then **add** the following two statements on the next two lines:

```
Writeln(Object1.Name);
Readln;
```

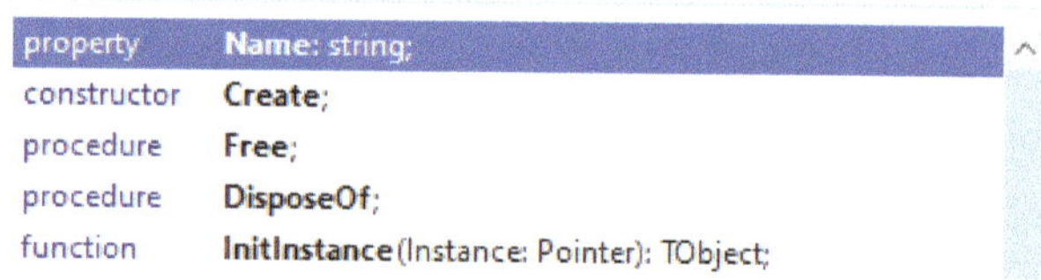

Figure 54.4 Section of CodeInsight window (Ctrl + Space)

Shift + Ctrl + S to save all.

Press F9 to compile, link and run.

Figure 54.5 shows the output from the executing `ConsoleClassProject`.

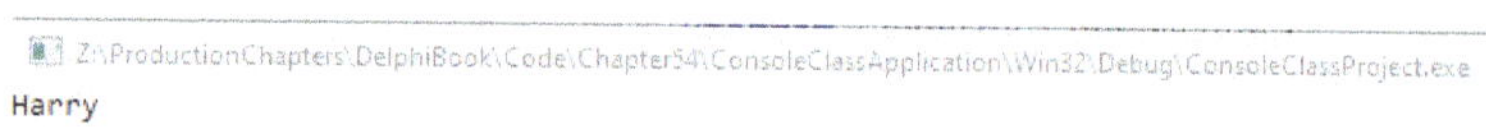

Figure 54.5 ConsoleClassProject in execution

Return to the Code Editor and **delete** `{ TMyClass }` from the **Implementation** section of `ConsoleClassUnit` as follows:

- **Move** the cursor to this line
- **Press** the key combination Ctrl + Y.

We don't need keywords **Protected** or **Published** in `TMyClass`. **Use** Ctrl + Y to delete these and all blank lines.

The author prefers a layout style for class definitions which differs from that of the house style used by Embarcadero. Embarcadero treat `TMyClass End` as block delimiters whereas the author prefers `Class End` - *Figure 54.6*. A dotted line has been added to *Figure 54.6* to show the important alignment.

Keyboard shortcuts may be used to indent not just a single line but a whole block. In the current layout shown in *Figure 54.7* **move** the cursor to the line containing the keyword **Private**, positioning it before this keyword. **Press** the key combination Shift + End key to select the text from the cursor position to the end of line. **Repeatedly press** Shift + Down Arrow to select all the lines below the current one down to and including the line containing `End;`. To indent the highlighted block **press** Ctrl + Shift + I. (Ctrl + Shift + U unindents). Unfortunately, if the indent is set to two columns, the alignment will be one column off. Final adjustment must now take place a line at a time using the space key to achieve the layout shown in *Figure 54.6*.

Blocks of selected code may be commented out using Ctrl + / and the effect reversed by applying Ctrl + / again.

To comment out a single line just **place** the cursor on the line and **press** Ctrl + /. The effect is reversed by applying Ctrl + / again.

```
TMyClass = Class
           Private
             NameValue : String;
             Function GetName : String;
             Procedure SetName(Const Value : String);
           Public
             Property Name : String Read GetName Write SetName;
           End;
```

Figure 54.6 Layout style preferred by author

```
TMyClass = Class
Private
  NameValue : String;
  Function GetName : String;
  Procedure SetName(Const Value : String);
Public
  Property Name : String Read GetName Write SetName;
End;
```

Figure 54.7 Current layout

Add the block of text shown below the keyword **Implementation** in *Figure 54.8*. **Highlight** this block of text then press Ctrl + / once to comment each line in one go - *Figure 54.9*.

```
Implementation
  This is
  an example
  of the
  use of keyboard shortcuts
```

Figure 54.8 Preparation for setting comments with Ctrl + /

```
Implementation
  //This is
  //an example
  //of the
  //use of keyboard shortcuts
```

Figure 54.9 Comments created

Unlike other object-oriented languages, Delphi separates a class definition from its implementation. Some programmers see this as a disadvantage but Delphi programmers don't because they know that they can move between the two using Ctrl + Shift + Up Arrow and Ctrl + Shift + Down Arrow. They also know that templates are available that generate a skeleton class definition. But how can the amount of typing be reduced when a class definition is extended with a new method? Fortunately, Ctrl + Shift + C will populate the **Implementation** section with the necessary skeleton code for the new method.

Add the following to the **Public** section of `TMyClass`, placed after the **Property** statement:

```
Function GetLengthOfName : Integer;
```

Press Ctrl + Shift + C to generate the skeleton implementation of the method `TMyClass.GetLengthOfName` in the **Implementation** section - *Figure 54.10*.

```
Implementation

 // This is
 // an example
 // of the
 // use of keyboard shortcuts

Function TMyClass.GetLengthOfName : Integer;
  Begin

  End;

Function TMyClass.GetName : String;
  Begin
    Result := NameValue;
  End;
```

Figure 54.10 New method TMyClass.GetLengthOfName generated by Ctrl+Shift+C

Place the cursor anywhere in an identifier, e.g. `NameValue` in *Figure 54.7*, and **double click** with the mouse to select the word. Ctrl + Click on a variable to go to its declaration.

A variable may be declared given an undeclared identifier, e.g. `myvar`, that exists within a **procedure block scope**, if the cursor is placed on the identifier and Ctrl + Shift + V pressed. *Figure 54.11* shows the popup window that results for identifier myvar. Using this shortcut creates a local variable `myvar` of the type selected from the **Type** listbox.

In a similar manner, an identifier referenced by an object reference, e.g. `Form1.testvar` may be declared as a field of the class of `Form1` by pressing Ctrl + Shift + D.

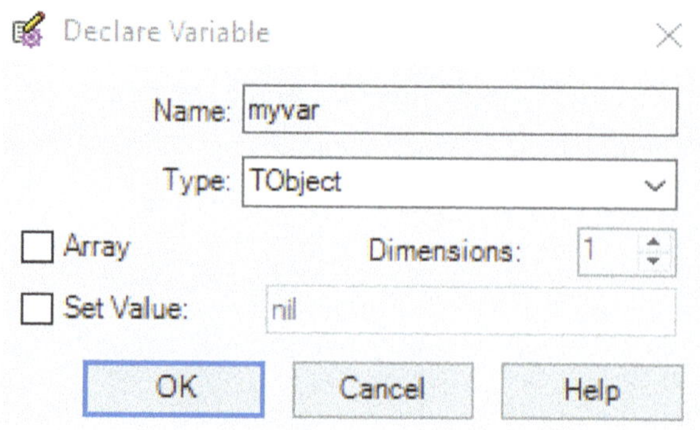

Figure 54.11 Popup window for declaring local variable myvar

Let's say you want to use **ShowMessage** in a Vcl application but you have forgotten which unit it is defined in then **Ctrl + Shift + A** will bring up a **Find Unit** window with the unit that you require specified in the window - *Figure 54.12*.

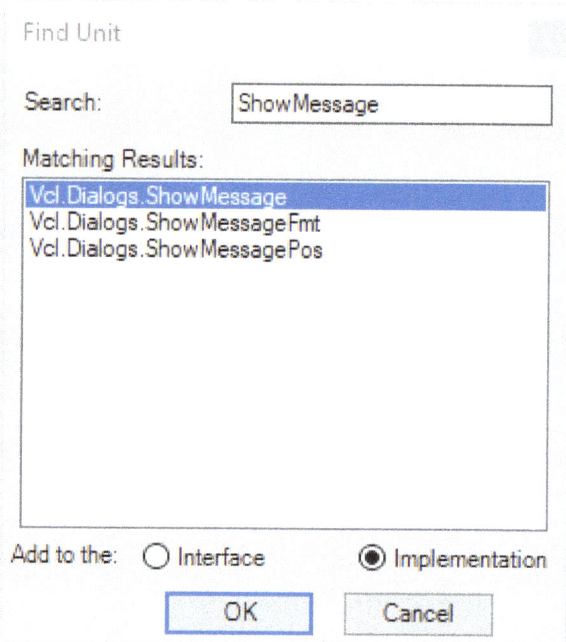

Figure 54.12 Find Unit invoked by Ctrl + Shift + A

Ctrl + F launches the search box and locates it at the bottom of the **Code Editor** window.

Placing the cursor on a unit identifier, e.g. **Vcl.Forms**, and pressing **Ctrl + Enter** will open up the unit in the IDE so that it may be inspected.

Ctrl + Click on an identifier, e.g. **ShowMessage**, will open up the unit containing this identifier in the IDE, in this case **Vcl.Dialogs**. Try the identifier **Application** in the source of a Vcl application (**Project|View Source**).

GExperts software

GExperts is a free set of tools built to increase the productivity of Delphi and C++Builder programmers by adding several features to the IDE. It is available from http://www.gexperts.org/download/. and installs into the **Delphi IDE Toolbar** - *Figure 54.13*.

Figure 54.13 GExperts in toolbar

Setting up favourites

GExperts makes it possible to have your favourite applications to hand from within the IDE. It is often useful to be able to step out of the IDE and into another application or application + file, e.g. Acrobat reader + pdf. If **GExperts** is installed in the IDE then the IDE has an option to set up a list of favourite files as shown in *Figure 54.14* and *Figure 54.15*.

Selecting **File|Favourites** allows a specific favourite to be opened by selecting it from the popup menu, e.g. **notepad++.exe** shown in *Figure 54.14*.

The option **X Configure...** when selected brings up the window shown in *Figure 54.15*.

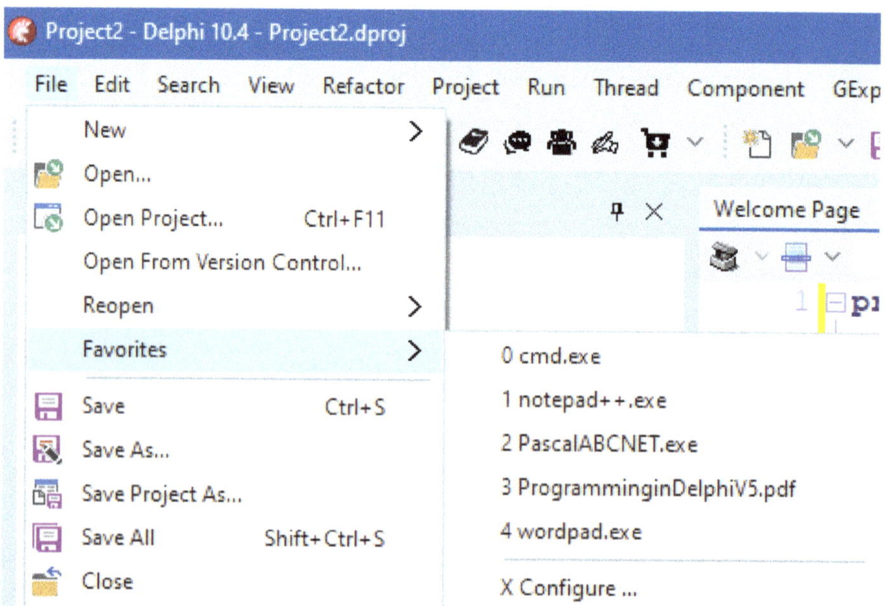

Figure 54.14 Using File|Favourites to set up shortcut links to other applications

Selecting File|New File in this window brings up a window which allows a new favourite to be added to the collection.

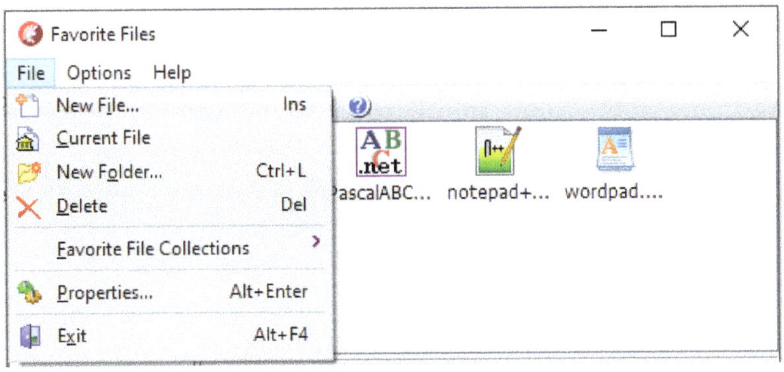

Figure 54.15 Setting up shortcut link to another application

Using the clipboard history

GExperts provides a Clipboard History window that can be quite useful to have when you want to copy snippets of code in advance from elsewhere, say Notepad++, which you may have opened from File|Favourites. Just highlight the snippet in Notepad++ then copy it (CTRL + C) to the clipboard. It will automatically appear in the GExperts Clipboard History window - see *Figure 54.16*. **Double click** the item reference in the upper window of the Clipboard History window of the snippet that you want, then **position** the cursor in the Delphi code at the place you want to insert the snippet, then **press** Ctrl + V. Of course, you can copy and paste from one application to another without relying on GExperts but there are circumstances where you may want to avoid switching between Delphi and another application. This is where GExperts can be useful. Or you may have copied or cut (Ctrl + X) several parts of a Delphi program you are working on and want to place one or more of these snippets back in the program. These snippets will be available in the GExperts Clipboard History window.

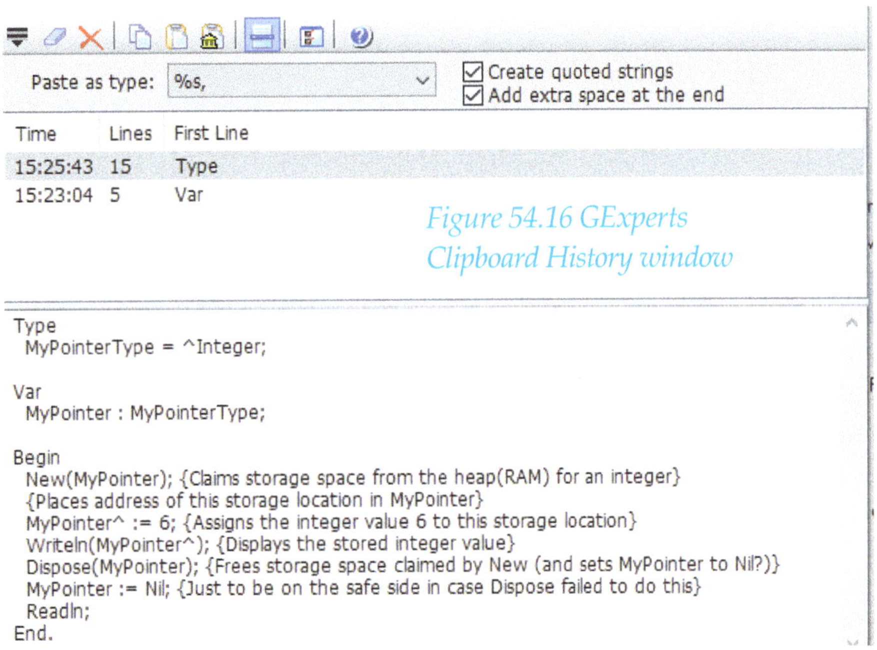

Figure 54.16 GExperts Clipboard History window

55 Introduction to databases

First database project

Purpose: To learn how to create a database application

Setting up an ADO connection

Launch Delphi

Select File|New|VCL Forms Application.

Delphi presents a new project and a blank form for you to use.

You are now going to place on the blank form non-visual components from the Tool Palette that will work with a Microsoft Access database, DBDemos.mdb:

- TADOConnection component from the ADO page in Delphi 7 and dbGo page in Delphi 2009 onwards
- TADOTable component from the ADO page in Delphi 7 and dbGo page in Delphi 2009 onwards
- TDataSource component from the Data Access page
- TDBGrid component from the Data Controls page

Information

DBDemos.mdb is supplied with your version of Delphi. It may be located in folder C:\Program Files\Common Files\Embarcadero Shared\Data in later versions of Delphi. COPY to your work area. Alternatively, download from www.educational-computing.com/DelphiBook/Code/dbdemos.rar

Resource

Download IntroductionToADO project from www.educational-computing.co.uk/DelphiBookCode/DelphiCode.html

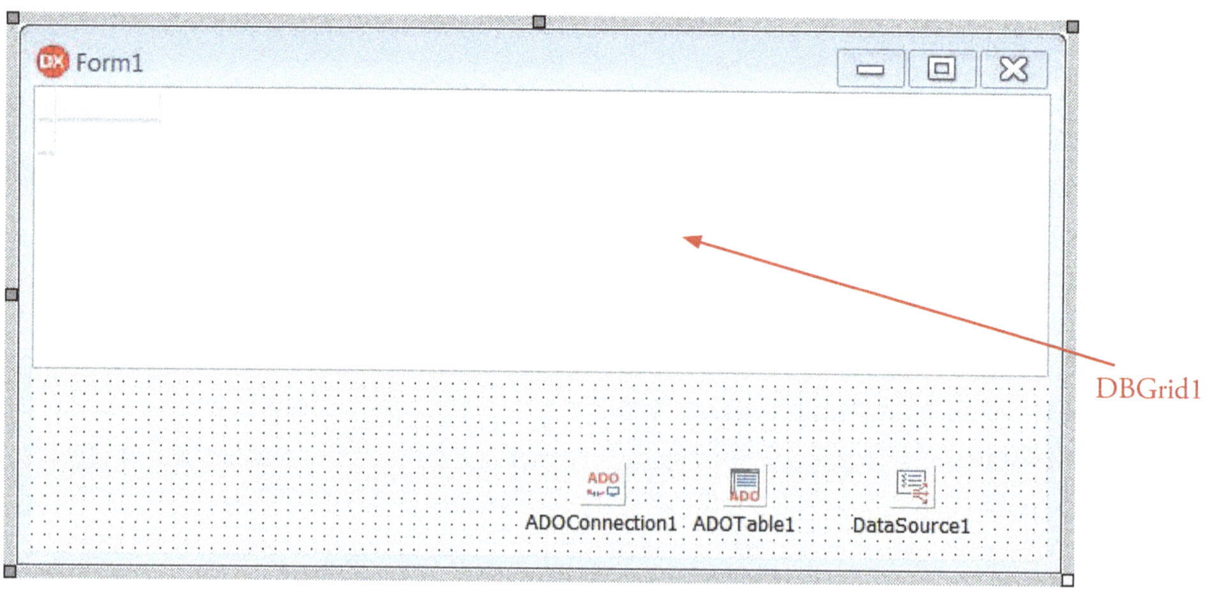

Fig. 55.1 Community Edition Form1 layout

Adjust **DBGrid1** as shown in *Figure 55.1*.

Next, **set** the **ConnectionString** property of the ADOConnection component as follows:

1. With the ADOConnection selected, **find** the **ConnectionString** property in the Object Inspector.
2. **Double click** the white space or click the ellipsis (...) of **ConnectionString** to bring up the **ConnectionString dialogue window** - *Figure 55.2*.
3. **Click** Build to bring up the **Data Link Properties** window - *Figure 55.3*.

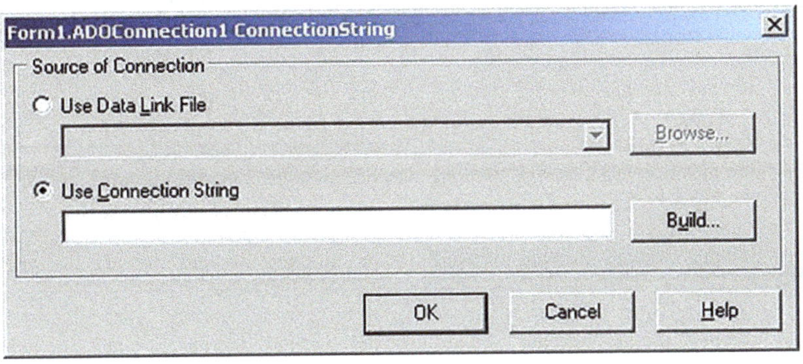

Fig. 55.2 Delphi 7 Connection string dialogue window

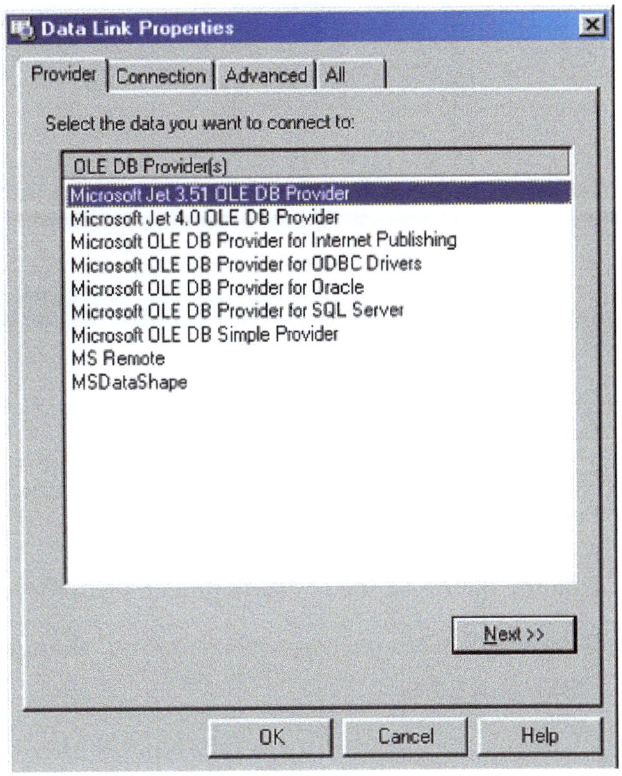

Fig. 55.3 Delphi 7 Data Link Properties window

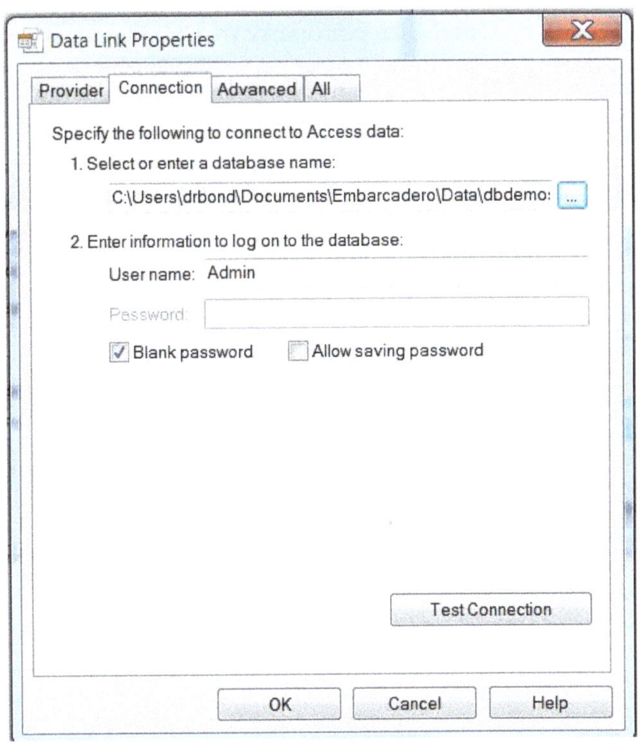

Fig. 55.4 Community Edition Connection tab of Data Link Properties window

Highlight **Microsoft Jet 4.0 OLE DB Provider** then click **Next** to tab to the **Connection** window. - *Figure 55.4*.

Click on **Select** or **enter** a database name.

Select **DBDemos.mdb**.

Check **Blank password box**.

Click **Test Connection**.

If the connection works then the **Microsoft Data Link** pop-up window shown in *Figure 55.5* should appear.

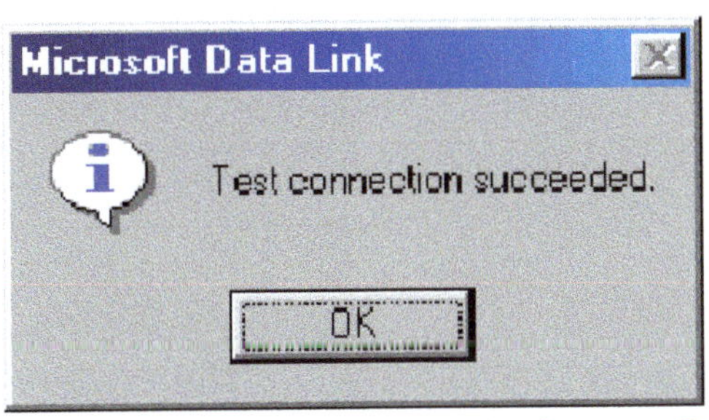

Fig. 55.5 Delphi 7 Pop-up window confirming connection succeeded

Click **OK**.

The window shown in *Figure 55.6* should appear showing that a value for the connection string has been assigned.

Click **OK** again to close this window.

Set the **Login Prompt** of the **ADOConnection** component to **False**.

Make sure that the **Connected** property is **True** (double click **False** if it isn't).

With the **ADOTable** component selected, **set** its **Connection** property to **ADOConnection1**.

With the **ADOTable** component selected, **change** its **TableName** property to **Country** by selecting this table from the **ListBox**.

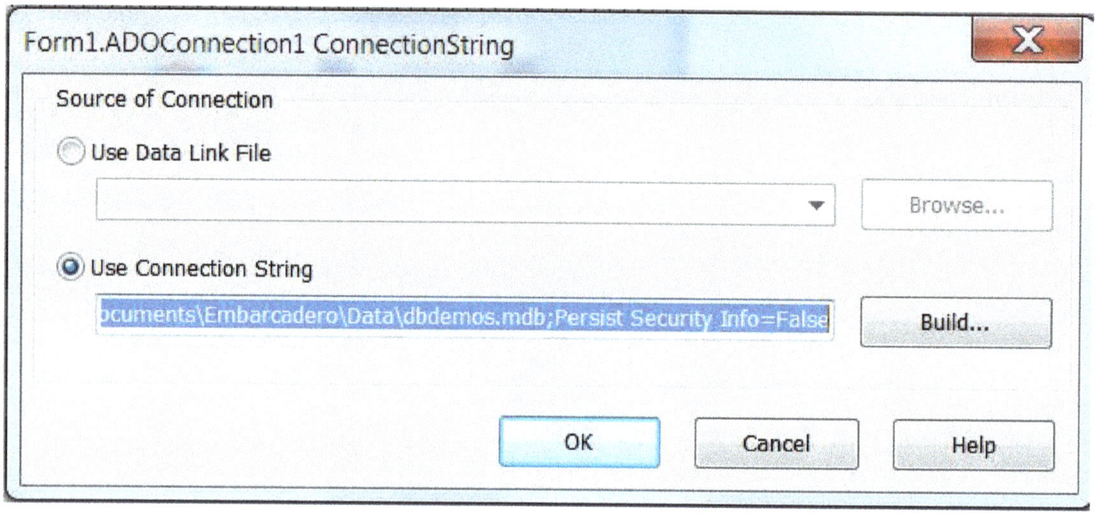

Fig. 55.6 Community Edition Connection String created

Change the ADOTable's **Name** property to **DBDemosTable**.

With the DataSource component selected, **change** the **DataSet** property of the DataSource component to **DBDemosTable**.

Change its **Name** property to **DBDemosSource**.

With the DBGrid component selected, **change** its **Name** property to **DBDemosGrid**.

Change its **DataSource** property to **DBDemosSource**.

Make the **DBDemosTable** active by selecting the **Active** property and double clicking on **False**. The DBGrid component should fill with data as shown in *Figure 55.7*.

Save your project in a folder named Introduction. Use the Project name IntroductionToADO.

Accept the default name for the unit.

Now **Build (Shift F9)** and **Run (F9)** your project. *Figure 55.8* shows the result of executing the project. Use the scroll bars to scroll through the data.

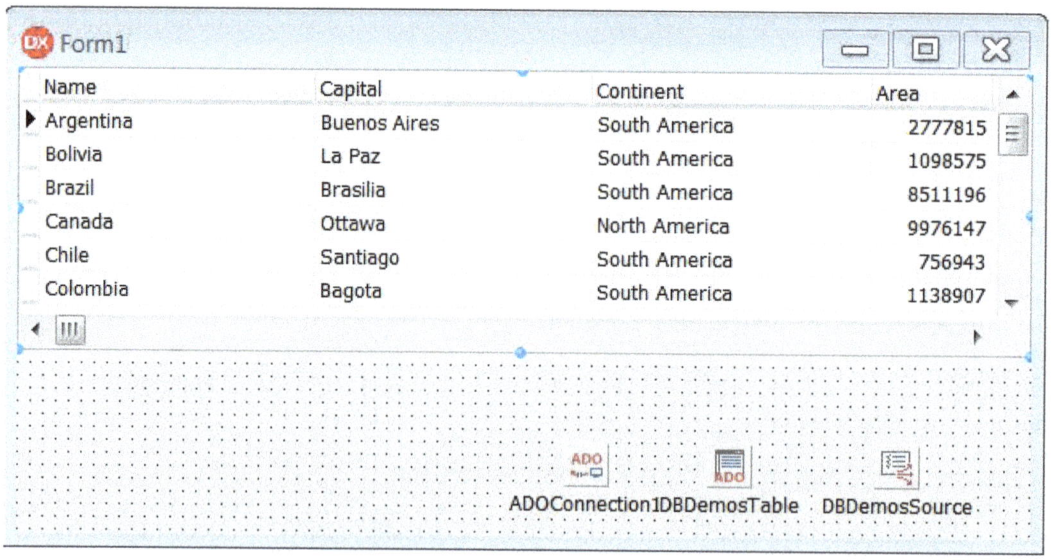

Fig. 55.7 Community Edition Form1 showing the design mode view of Country table data

Setting up a FireDac connection

FireDac was introduced in Delphi XE3 as a full replacement for everything that has been used previously for database connectivity.

FireDac is a fully robust bidirectional, high performance database system which works with many different database systems.

It is a native Delphi implementation and therefore works wherever it is possible to do Delphi development, i.e.

- On mobile devices to access mobile databases such as SQLLite, Interbase ToGo or IBLite
- On a server or desktop to access any available databases
- With DataSnap to provide DataSnap services that expose backend enterprise databases.

On mobile devices databases it is restricted to SQLLite, Interbase ToGo and IBLite.

To access other databases from a mobile device requires tha use of DataSnap.

FireDAC works with both FireMonkey and VCL.

Launch Delphi Community Edition 10.2.3 (or earlier version back to Delphi XE3).

Select File|New VCL Forms Application - Delphi.

Delphi presents a new project and a blank form for you to use.

You are now going to place on the blank form non-visual components from the Tool Palette that will work with a Microsoft Access database, DBDemos.mdb:

- TFDConnection component from the FireDac page of the Tool Palette
- TFDTable component from the FireDAC page - change **Name** to **FDDBDemosTable**
- TDataSource component from the Data Access page - change **Name** to **DBDemosSource**
- TDBGrid component from the Data Controls page - change **Name** to **DBDemosGrid**

Adjust **DBDemosGrid** as shown in *Figure 55.8*.

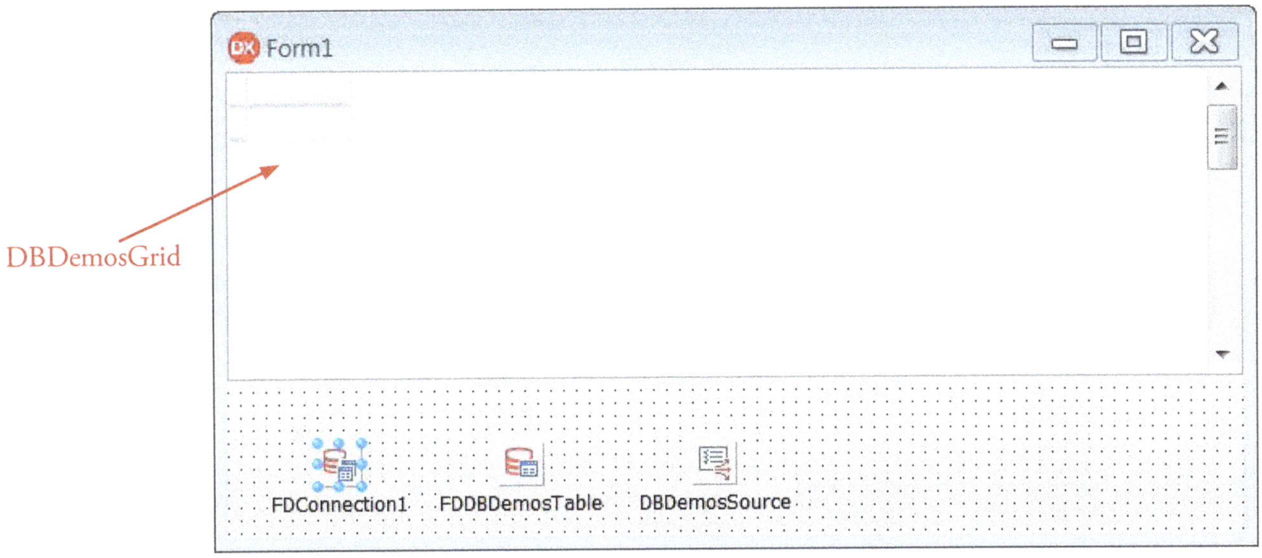

Fig. 55.8 Community Edition Form1 showing the design mode view positioning of DBGrid component

Next, **set** the FDConnection component as follows:

1. **Double click** the FDConnection to bring up the **FireDAC Connection Editor window** - *Figure 55.9*.
2. **Select** **MsAcc** from the **DriverID** listbox to select the Microsoft Access driver identifier- *Figure 55.10*.
3. **Select** the path to **DBDemos.mdb** for the database - *Figure 55.10*.
4. **Use** **Admin** for **User_Name** - *Figure 55.10*.
5. **Leave** the **Password** box blank - *Figure 55.10*.
6. **Click** **Test**. FireDAC responds by displaying the **Login dialogue** window shown in *Figure 55.11*. **Click** **OK** as a password is not required. If a connection is established the pop-up window shown in *Figure 55.12* should appear.
7. **Click** OK to close the **Connection established successfully** window.
8. **Set** the **LogIn Prompt** of the FDConnection component to **False**.
9. **Make** sure that the **Connected** property of the FDConnection component is **True** (double click **False** if it isn't).

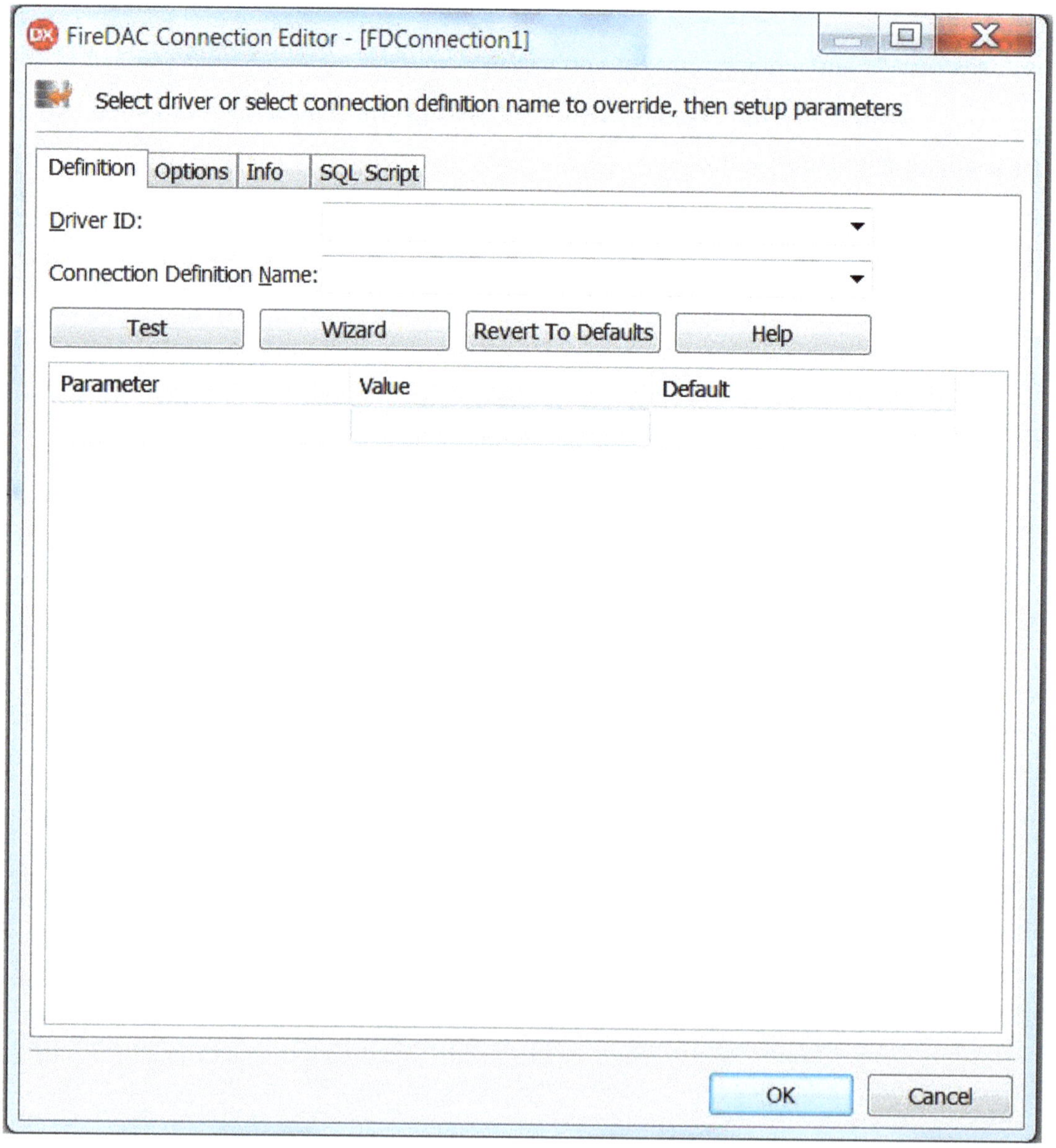

Fig. 55.9 Community Edition Form1 showing FireDACConnection Editor

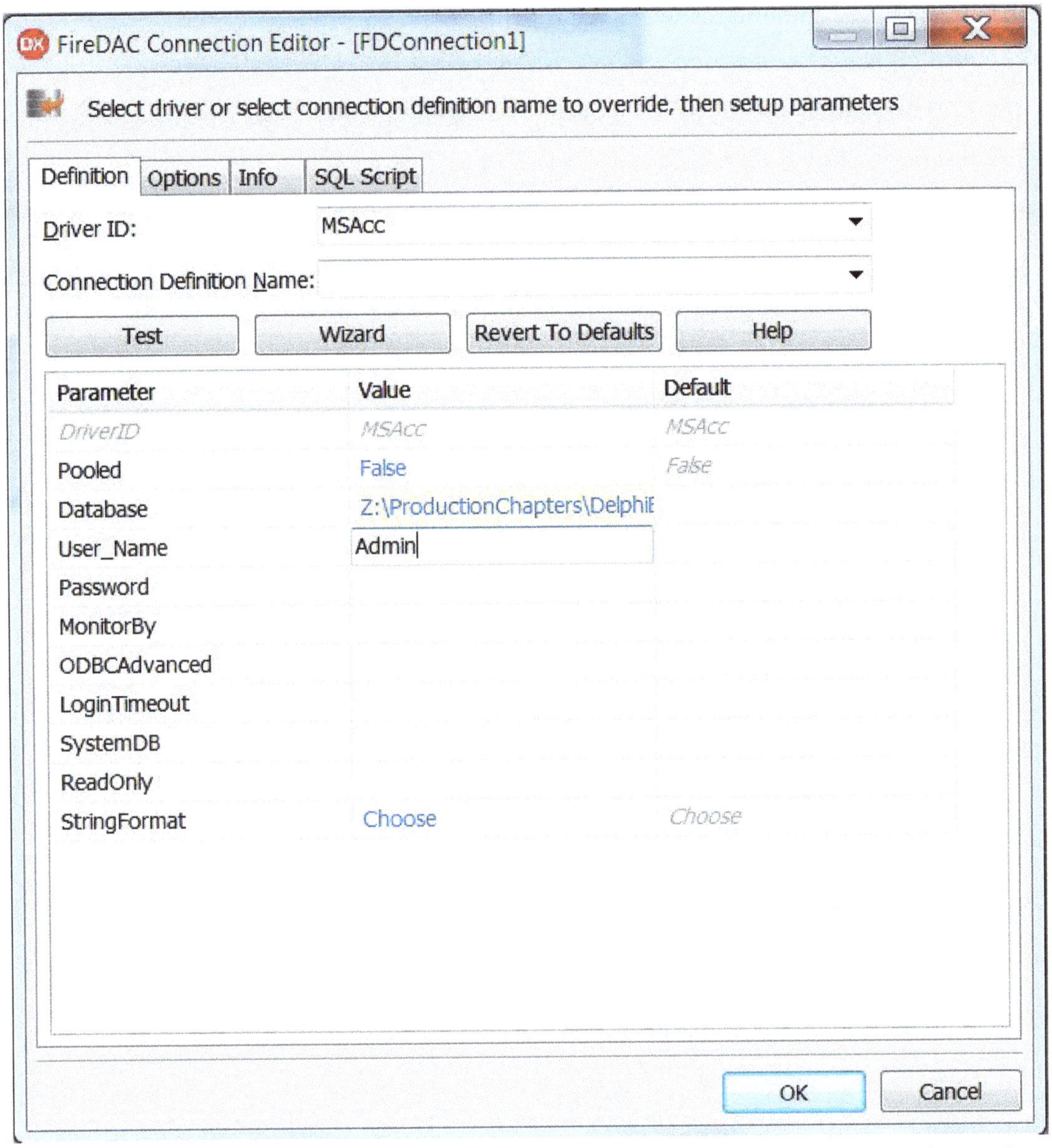

Fig. 55.10 Community Edition showing FireDAC Connection Editor with configuration data

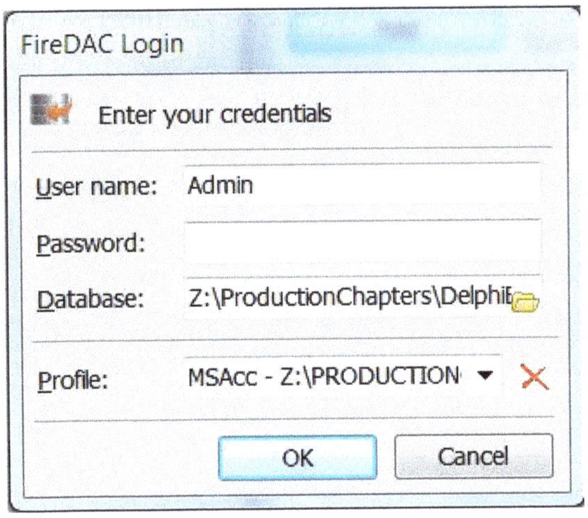

Fig. 55.11 Login dialogue window

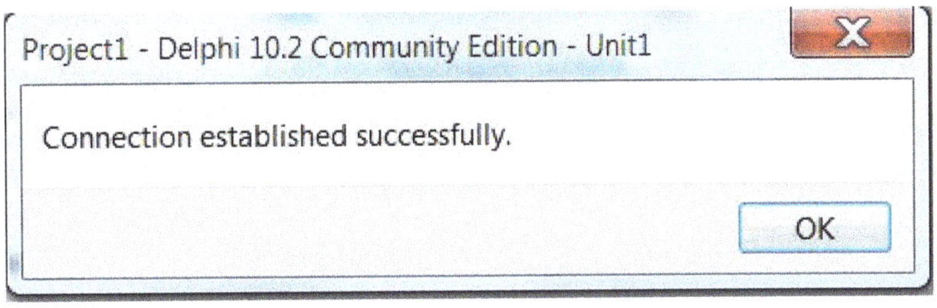

Fig. 55.12 Community Edition Connection established window

10. With the **FDTable** component selected, **set** its **Connection** property to **FDConnection1** (it should be set automatically).
11. With the **FDTable** component selected, **change** its **TableName** property to **Country** by selecting this table from the **ListBox**.

12. With the DataSource component selected, **change** the **DataSet** property of the DataSource component to **FDDBDemosTable**.

13. **Make** the FDDBDemosTable active by selecting the **Active** property and double clicking on **False**. The DBGrid component should fill with data as shown in *Figure 55.13*.

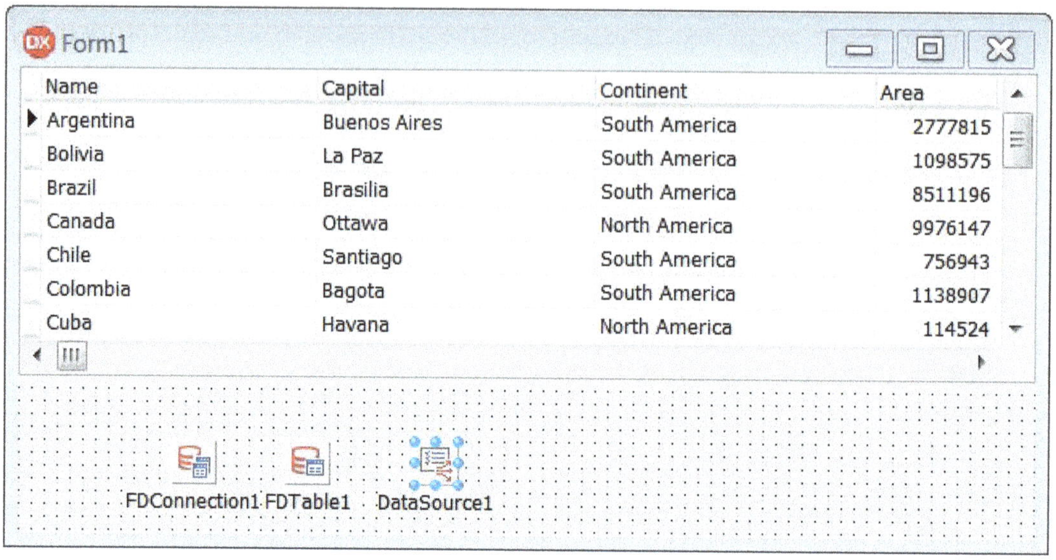

Fig. 55.13 Community Edition Design view of Country table dataset

Save your project in a folder named FDIntroduction. Use the Project name IntroductionToFD.

Accept the default name for the unit.

Now **Build (Shift F9)** and **Run (F9)** your project. *Figure 55.14* shows the result of executing the project.

Use the scroll bars to scroll through the data.

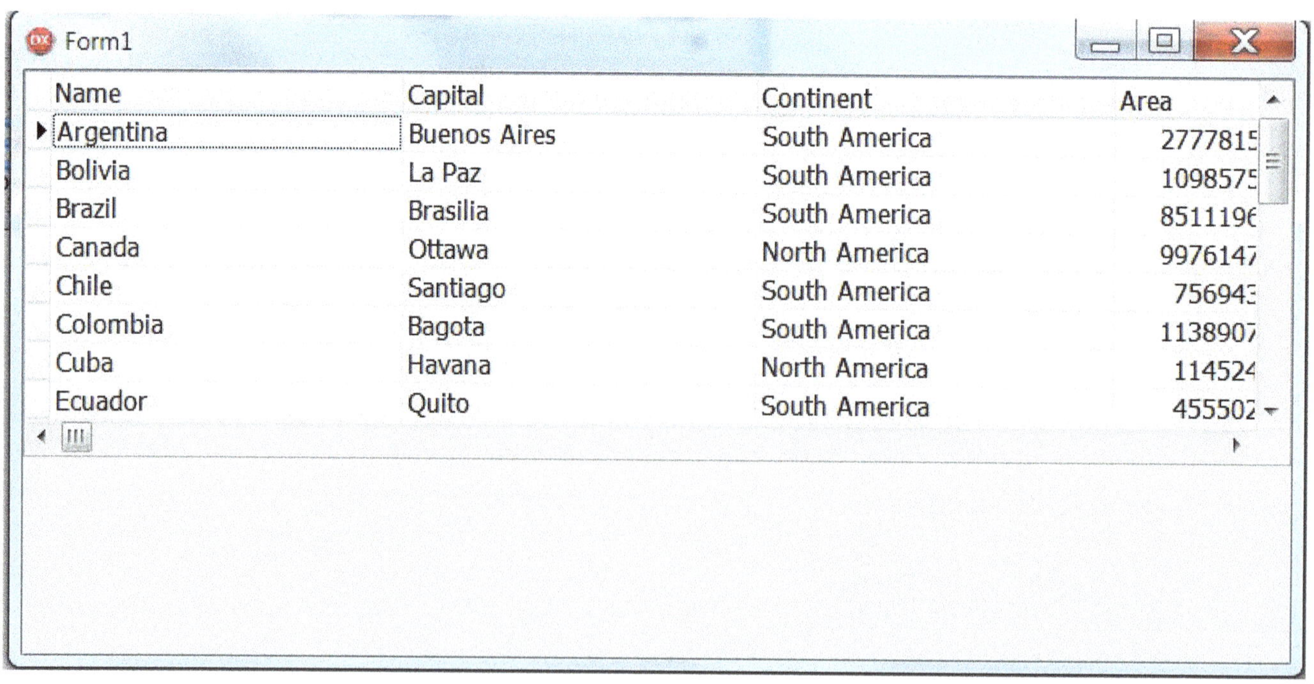

Fig. 55.14 Community Edition runtime view of Country table dataset

Note that if you are using a version of Delphi earlier than XE8, you might get a runtime error which is caused by missing units. This is easily remedied by dropping two components. The first is the physical driver link component associated with the database driver that you are using, e.g. **FDPhysMSAccessDriverLink** from the **FireDac Links** page of the **Tool Palette**. The second component is the **FDGUIxWaitCursor** component from the **FireDAC UI** page of the **Tool Palette**.

FireDAC doesn't use these components as such and therefore it is not required that you set any of their properties. Instead what the **FireDAC** application requires is the presence of the units associated with these components in the application's **Uses** clause. After saving or compiling your application these components may be removed. However, leaving these on the form does no harm.

The **Info** page of **FireDAC**'s **Connection Editor** contains details about the connection that has been established when you have tested the connection - *Figure 55.15*. This page can provide useful information with which to debug any errors such as the wrong version of the client driver that may occur when connecting to a database.

Fig. 55.15 Community Edition Connection Editor Info page

56 Creating and executing SQL statements at runtime

First database project (continued)

Purpose: To learn how to create and execute SQL statements at runtime

Querying a Database

Using a Memo Box to Create and Execute SQL Statements at Runtime

Create a new VCL Forms application and **save** in a folder named ADOQuerywithMemoBox. **Name** the project ADOQuery, accept the default name for the unit.

Add an ADOConnection component and an ADOQuery component to the form (ADO or dbGo).

From the Standard tab **select** a Panel component and place on the form.

Set the Panel component's Align property to **alTop**. ← Use visual wizard if it presents and click on top bar.

Place a DBGrid component from the Data Controls tab on the panel.

Set its **Align** property to **alClient**. ← Use visual wizard if it presents and click on middle bar.

Select the ADOConnection component and in the Object Inspector **select** the **ConnectionString** property.

Double click the **value field** to bring up the Connection String editor.

Click Build to bring up the **Data Link** properties window. Select **Microsoft jet 4.0 OLE DB** provider.

Click Next to switch to the Connection tab.

Select the path to **DBDemos.mdb. Click** Test Connection. Assuming that the test is successfully, **click OK** and then **OK** again to finish setting up the connection.

> **Resource**
>
> Download ADOQuerywithMemoBox project from www.educational-computing.co.uk/DelphiBookCode/DelphiCode.html

Change the **LoginPrompt** property of **ADOConnection1** to **False**.

Click on **ADOQuery1** component. **Select** its **Connection** property to **ADOConnection1**.

Add a **DataSource** component from the Data Access tab.

Select DataSource1 and **set** its **DataSet** property to **ADOQuery1**.

Select the **DBGrid1** component and **set** its **DataSource** property to **DataSource1**.

From the Standard tab **add** three **Buttons** and a **Memo box.**

Change the **Name** property of the first button to **Select** and its **Caption** property to **Select**.

Change the **Name** property of the second button to **ExecSql** and its **Caption** property to **Exec SQL**.

Change the **Name** property of the third button to **Terminate** and its **Caption** property to **Terminate**.

Change the **Name** property of the memo box to **SQLMemo**.

Select the **Lines** property of SQLMemo. **Double click** its **value field** to bring up the **Strings List editor.**

Clear the contents.

When the design of the program has been finished, the form at design time should now resemble *Figure 56.1*.

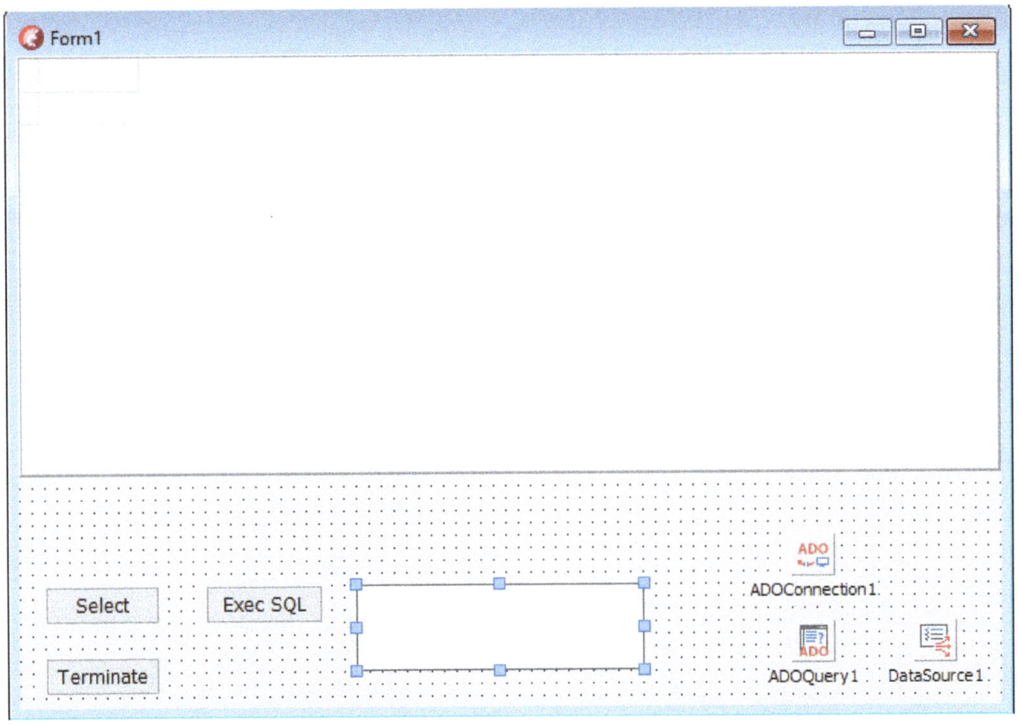

Fig. 56.1 Delphi Community Edition querying a database form

Double click the **Select button** on the form to create an event handler.

Add the following code:

```
ADOQuery1.DisableControls;
Try
  ADOQuery1.Close;
  ADOQuery1.SQL.Clear;
  ADOQuery1.SQL.Add(SQLMemo.Lines.Text);
  ADOQuery1.Open;
Finally
  ADOQuery1.EnableControls;
End;
```

Click File|Save to ensure units for the added components are added to the Uses statement.

Double click the **Exec SQL** button on the form to create an event handler.

Add the following code:

```
ADOQuery1.DisableControls;
Try
  ADOQuery1.Close;
  ADOQuery1.SQL.Clear;
  ADOQuery1.SQL.Add(SQLMemo.Lines.Text);
  ADOQuery1.ExecSql;
Finally
  ADOQuery1.EnableControls;
End;
```

Double click the **Terminate button** and **add** the following code to the event handler:

```
Application.Terminate;
```

Make the form the focus so that **Form1's OnActivate** event handler can be selected from the **Events** tab.

Double click its **Value** field to create an event handler.

Add the following code to this event handler:

```
Form1.WindowState := wsMaximized;
```

Save the program and then **run it.**

Try the following SQL in the **Memo box**:

1. `Select * From Country` (then click the Select button.)
2. `Select * From Customer` (then click the Select button.)
3. `Select * From Employee` (then click the Select button.)
4. `Select * From Items` (then click the Select button.)
5. `Select Name, Continent, Population From Country`
6. `Select Name, Continent From Country Order By Continent Asc`
7. `Select Name, Continent From Country Order By Continent Desc`
8. `Select Continent, Sum(Population) From Country Group By Continent`
9. `Insert Into Country (Name, Continent) Values('DG', 'XY')` (Click Exec SQL button)
10. `Update Country Set Continent = 'KL' Where Country.Name = 'DG'` (Click Exec SQL button)
11. `Delete From Country Where Name = 'DG'` (Click Exec SQL button)

The **ExecSQL** method is used to execute queries that do not return a cursor to data, e.g. Insert, Update, Delete.

A cursor is used in conjunction with a dataset. A cursor is a pointer to the current row in the dataset.

57 Using DBEdit boxes

Resource

Download ADODBEdit project from www.educational-computing.co.uk/DelphiBookCode/DelphiCode.html

First database project (continued)

Purpose: To learn how to use DBEdit boxes

Using DBEdit Boxes

Start a new VCL application. **Save** the project in folder `ADODBEdit` with project name `ADODBEdit`. **Save** unit using default name in the same folder.

Place on form

- ADOConnection component from the ADO tab in Delphi 7 and dbGo page in Delphi 2009 onwards
- ADOTable component from the ADO tab in Delphi 7 and dbGo page in Delphi 2009 onwards
- DataSource component from the Data Access tab
- Five DBEdit components from the Data Controls tab.

Set up the ADOConnection as in *Chapter 56* but don't change its name.

Set up the ADOTable as in *Chapter 56* but don't change its name. **Select** **Country** as **TableName**. **Make** this table **active**.

Set up the DataSource as in *Chapter 56* but don't change its name.

For each of the DBEdit components **make** the **DataSource** property **DataSource1**.

For **DBEdit1 DataField** property **select** the **Name** field of **Country** table from the **ListBox**.

For **DBEdit2 DataField** property **select** the **Capital** field of **Country** table from the **ListBox**.

For **DBEdit3 DataField** property **select** the **Continent** field of **Country** table from the **ListBox**.

For **DBEdit4 DataField** property **select** the **Population** field of **Country** table from the **ListBox**.

For **DBEdit5 DataField** property **select** the **Area** field of **Country** table from the **ListBox**.

Add three buttons:

- **Rename** first button **Next** and its **caption** similarly
- **Rename** second button **Previous** and its **caption** similarly
- **Rename** the third **Terminate** and its **caption** similarly

Double click the **Name** button on the form to create an event handler.

Add the following code to the event handler:

```
ADOTable1.Next;
```

Double click the **Previous** button on the form to create an event handler.

Add the following code to the event handler:

```
ADOTable1.Prior;
```

Double click Terminate button and **add** the following code to the event handler:

```
Application.Terminate;
```

Save all.

Run the program. The result should be as shown in *Figure 57.1*.

Click on button **Next** to advance one record (unless already at the end of the dataset).

Click on button **Previous** to go back one record (unless already at the beginning of the dataset)

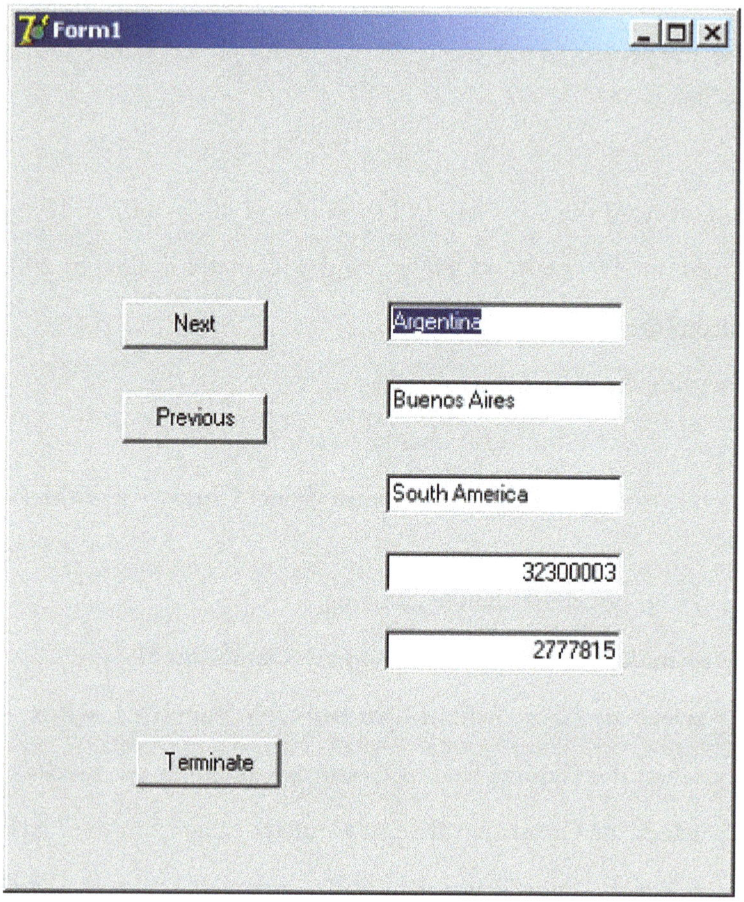

Fig. 57.1 DBEdit form for Delphi 7

Click on button **Terminate** to close the program.

58 Using tables

First database project (continued)

Purpose: To learn how to use tables

> **Resource**
>
> Download ADOTables project from www.educational-computing.co.uk/DelphiBookCode/DelphiCode.html

Using Tables

Launch Delphi

Select File|New|VCL Application.

Delphi presents a new project and a blank form for you to use. **Save** the project in folder `ADODBTables` with project name `ADODBTables.` **Save** unit using default name in the same folder.

You are now going to place non-visual components on the blank form that will work with a Microsoft® Access database, **DBDemos.mdb**:

- ADOConnection component from the ADO tab in Delphi 7 and dbGo page in Delphi 2009 onwards
- ADOTable component from the ADO tab in Delphi 7 and dbGo page in Delphi 2009 onwards
- DataSource component from the Data Access tab
- DBGrid component from the Data Controls tab.

In design view, the view that you are currently working in, components are displayed in a form along with their names.

Delphi assigns each component placed on a form a generic name that identifies what kind of component it is, e.g., **DataSource1** and **ADOTable1**, **DBGrid1.**

Change these names to more descriptive names (for example, if the database name is **Country** then change **DataSource1** to **CountrySource, ADOTable1** to **CountryTable**, **DBGrid1** to **CountryDBGrid**, **DataSource1** to **CountryDataSource**) but don't do it just yet.

To change the name of a component,

1. **Select** the component by clicking its icon on the form.
2. **Edit** the component's **Name** property in the Object Inspector (**Press** F11 if the Object Inspector is not visible).

Next, set the **ConnectionString** property of the **ADOConnection** component.

With the **ADOConnection** selected **find** the **ConnectionString** property in the Object Inspector.

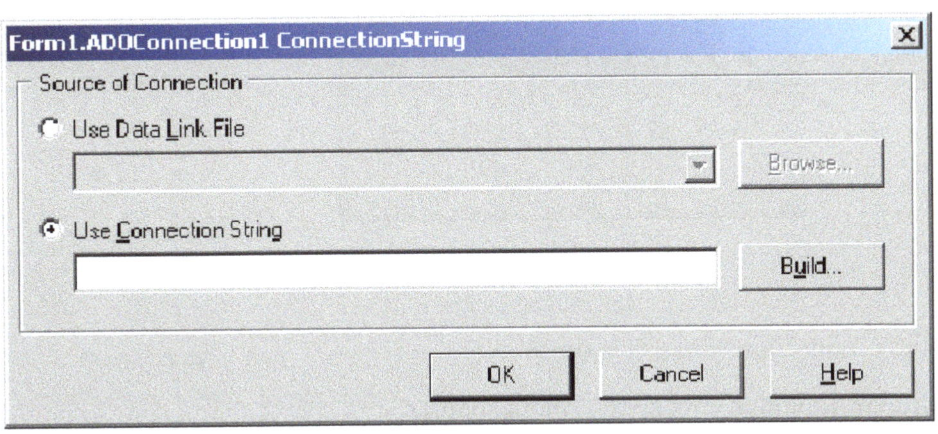

Fig. 58.1 Connection string dialogue window

Double click the white space or click the ellipsis (...) of **ConnectionString** to bring up the **ConnectionString** dialogue.

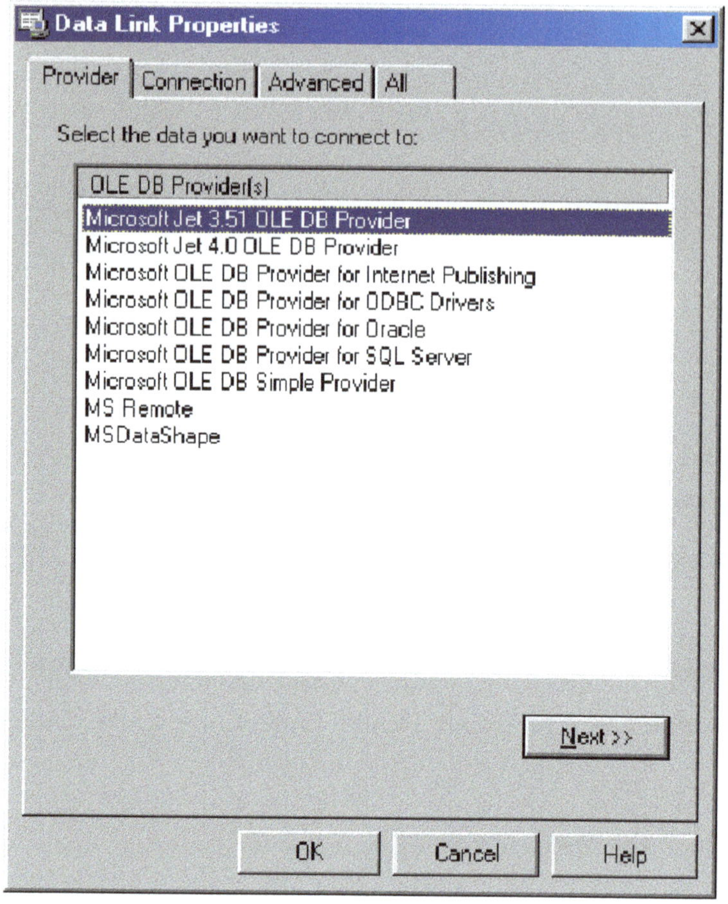

Fig. 58.2 Data Link Properties window Provider tab

Click Build to bring up the **Data Link** properties window - *Figure 58.2*.

Highlight Microsoft Jet 4.0 OLE DB Provider then **click Next** to tab to the **Connection** page - *Figure 58.3*.

Click on **Select** or enter a database name. **Select DBDemos.mdb**.

Check Blank password box.

Click Test Connection.

Fig. 58.4 Confirmation that connection successful pop-up window

If the connection works then the pop-up window should in *Figure 58.4* should appear.

Click OK.

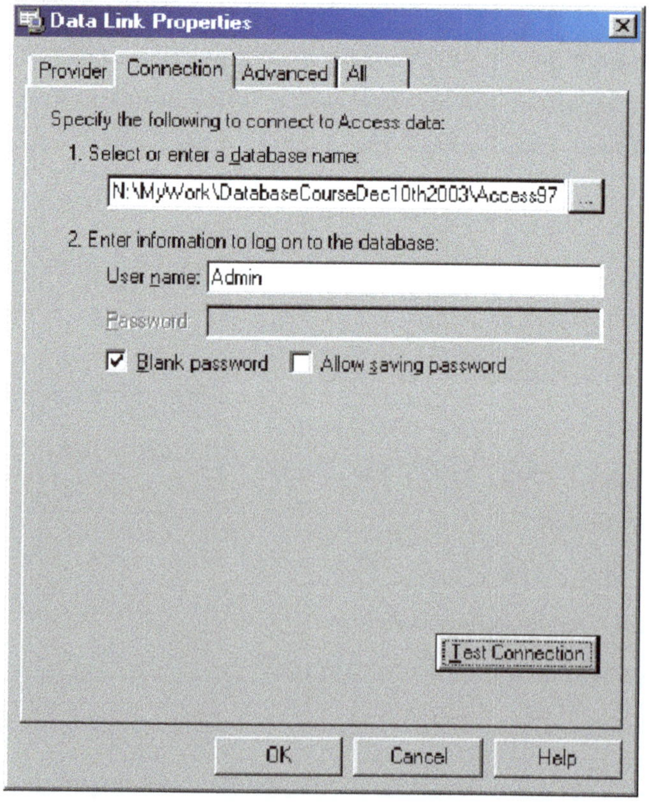

Fig. 58.3 Data Link Properties window Connection tab

Click **OK** again to return to the Connection string dialogue window - *Figure 58.5*.

Click **OK** to close this window.

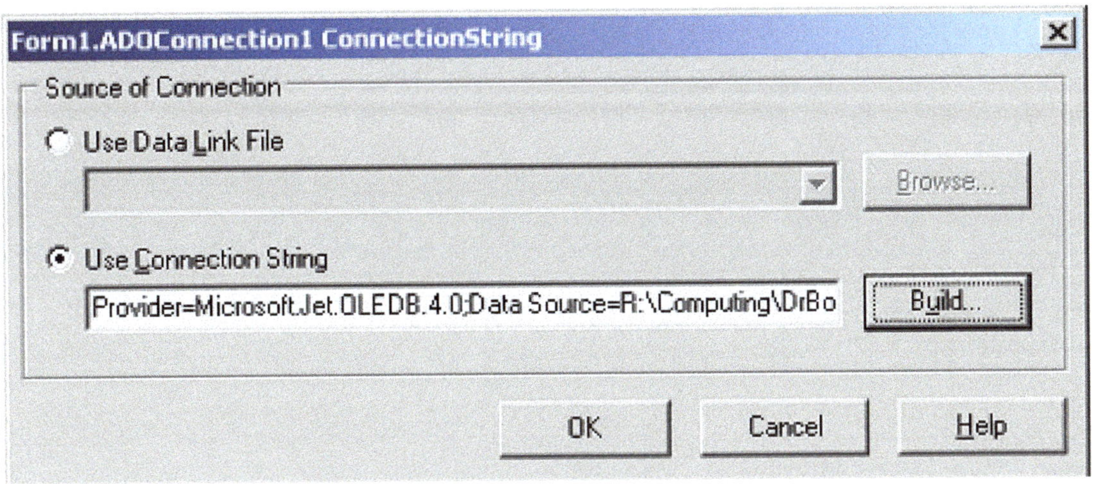

Fig. 58.5 Connection string dialogue window with completed Connection String field

Set the **Login Prompt** of the **ADOConnection** component to **False**.

With the **ADOTable** component selected, **make** the **connection** property **ADOConnection1**, **change** its **TableName** property to **Country**.

Change its **Name** property to **DBDemosTable**.

With the **Data Source** component selected, **change** the **DataSet** property of the **Data Source** component to **DBDemosTable**.

Change its **Name** property to **DBDemosSource**.

With the **DBGrid** component selected, **change** its **Name** property to **DBDemosGrid**.

Change its **DataSource** property to **DBDemosSource**.

Place two **buttons** and a **combo box** component from the **Standard** tab on the form. **Change** the **Name** property of the buttons to **OpenTable** and **CloseTable** respectively.

Change the **Name** property of the combo box to **TablesComboBox**.

Change the **Caption** property of the two buttons to **Open Table** and **Close Table** respectively.

Add the following strings, which are the names of the tables in **DBDemos.mdb** database, to the **Item** property of the **TableComboBox**:

```
Country
Customer
Employee
Items
NextCust
NextItem
NextOrd
Orders
Parts
Vendors
```

Delete from the **Text** property of **TableComboBox** the string **TablesComboBox** to leave a blank field.

The form should now look like that shown in *Figure 58.6*, if using Delphi Community Edition 10.2.

Save all.

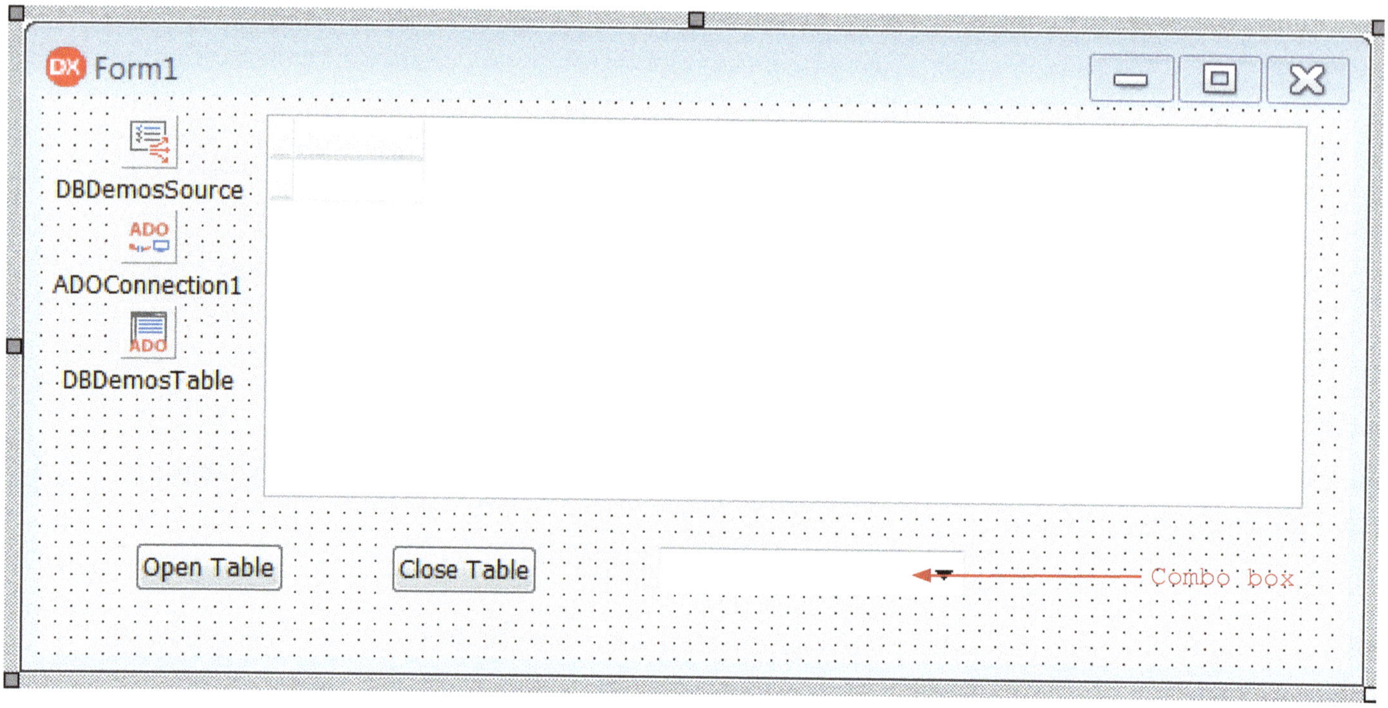

Fig. 58.6 Form design in Delphi Community Edition 10.2

Opening and Closing Datasets

To read from or write data to a table or through a query, an application must first open a dataset.

There are two ways to **open** a dataset:

- **Set** the **Active** property of the dataset to **True**, either at design time in the Object Inspector, or in code at runtime:

```
DBDemosTable.Active := True;
```

- **Call** the **Open** method for the dataset at runtime:

```
DBDemosTable.Open;
```

There are also two ways to **close** a dataset:

- **Set** the **Active** property of the dataset to **False**, either at design time in the Object Inspector, or in code at runtime:

```
DBDemosTable.Active := False;
```

- **Call** the **Close** method for the dataset at runtime:

```
DBDemosTable.Close;
```

It is possible to write a program, which can open and display any table in a database.

This is the purpose of the form shown in *Figure 58.6* and the program that supports it.

Double click the **Open Table** button and create the following procedure:

```
Procedure TForm1.OpenTableClick(Sender : TObject);
  Begin
    DBDemosTable.TableName := TablesComboBox.Text;
    DBDemosTable.Open;
  End;
```

Now **double click Close Table** button and create the following procedure:

```
Procedure TForm1.CloseTableClick(Sender : TObject);
  Begin
    DBDemosTable.Close;
  End;
```

Run the program. **Select Country** in the **Combo Box. Click Open Table** button. You will see data from this table in the grid similar to that shown in *Figure 58.7*. **Close** this table and **open** another.

Fig. 58.7 Delphi Community Edition 10.2 running program showing Country table

59 Navigating a dataset

First database project (continued)

Purpose: To learn how to navigate a dataset

Navigating Datasets

Each active dataset has a cursor, or pointer, to the current row in the dataset. The current row in a dataset is the one whose values can be manipulated with edit, insert, and delete methods. Don't type in the following procedures. Page 840 instructs you to **add** seven buttons and an edit box. The event handlers for each of these buttons are described below. Event handlers are created by double clicking on the corresponding form component.

The **First** method moves the cursor to the first row in a dataset and sets the **BOF** property to **True**.

Example 1:

```
Procedure TForm1.FirstClick(Sender : TObject);
  Begin
    DBDemosTable.First;
  End;
```

Resource

Download ADONavigatingDataSets project from www.educational-computing.co.uk/DelphiBookCode/DelphiCode.html

The **Last** method moves the cursor to the last row in a dataset and sets the **EOF** property to **True**.

Example 2:

```
Procedure TForm1.LastClick(Sender : TObject);
 Begin
   DBDemosTable.Last;
 End;
```

The **Next** method moves the cursor forward one row in the dataset and sets the **BOF** property to **False** if the dataset is not empty.

Example 3:

```
Procedure TForm1.NextClick(Sender : TObject);
  Begin
    DBDemosTable.Next;
  End;
```

The **Prior** method moves the cursor back one row in the dataset, and sets **EOF** to **False** if the dataset is not empty.

Example 4:

```
Procedure TForm1.PriorClick(Sender : TObject);
  Begin
    DBDemosTable.Prior;
  End;
```

MoveBy enables you to specify how many rows forward or back to move the cursor in a dataset. Movement is relative to the current record at the time that **MoveBy** is called. This function takes an integer parameter, the number of records to move. Positive integers indicate a forward move and negative integers indicate a backward move.

Example 5:

```
Procedure TForm1.MoveByClick(Sender : TObject);
  Begin
    DBDemosTable.MoveBy(StrToInt(MoveByEdit.Text));
  End;
```

Marking and Returning to Records

In addition to moving from record to record in a dataset, it is possible to mark a particular location in a dataset so that it can be returned to quickly.

The **Bookmark** property indicates which bookmark among any number of bookmarks in the application is current. **Bookmark** is a string that identifies the current bookmark.

To create a bookmark, declare a variable of type **TBookmark** in the application, then call **GetBookmark** to allocate storage for the variable and set its value to a particular location in a dataset.

Example 6:

```
Var
  Bookmark : TBookmark;
Procedure TForm1.SetBookmarkClick(Sender : TObject);
  Begin
    DBDemosTable.FreeBookmark(Bookmark);
    Bookmark := DBDemosTable.GetBookmark;
  End;
```

When passed a bookmark, **GoToBookmark** moves the cursor for the dataset to the location specified in the bookmark.

Example 7:

```
Procedure TForm1.GoToBookmarkClick(Sender : TObject);
  Begin
    DBDemosTable.GoToBookmark(Bookmark);
  End;
```

To give a user of the form shown in *Figure 58.6*, *Chapter 58*, the ability to navigate through the displayed table, **add** seven **buttons** and one **edit box** from the **Standard** tab. **Change** the **Name** property of the buttons to **First**, **Last**, **Next**, **Prior**, **MoveBy**, **SetBookmark** and **GoToBookmark**, respectively. **Change** the **Caption** property of these buttons to **First**, **Last**, **Next**, **Prior**, **Move By**, **Set Bookmark** and **Go To Bookmark** respectively. Finally, **change** the **Name** of the **edit box** to **MoveByEdit** and **set** its **Text** property to **blank**.

Figure 59.1 shows the form after the addition of these components.

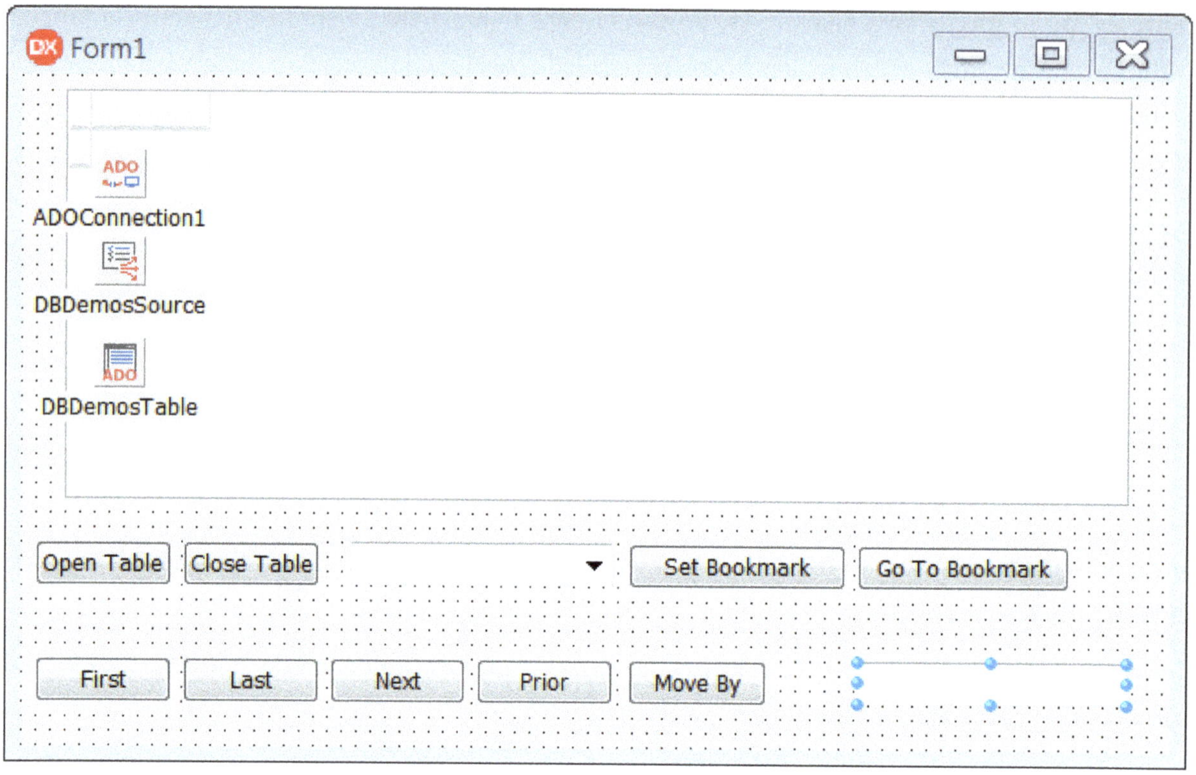

Fig. 59.1 Navigating a dataset form in Delphi Community Edition 10.2

Double click each button and add its corresponding code from examples 1 to 7.

Save in a folder named ADONavigatingDatasets. **Name** the project ADONavigatingDatasets, accept the default name for the unit.

Now **run** and **test** that each button works as described.

Searching Datasets

Locate moves the cursor to the first row matching a specified set of search criteria. In its simplest form, you pass **Locate** the name of a column to search, a field value to match, and an options flag specifying whether the search is case-sensitive or if it can use partial-key matching. However, it is better to use SQL. SQL queries in Delphi are covered later in *Chapter 61*.

Add another Button to the form and change its **Name** and **Caption** properties to **Locate.**

Add another Edit **box** component to the form and change its **Name** property to **LocateEdit**. **Change** its **Text** property to **blank**.

Resource

Download project ADONavigatingDataSetsFilter from www.educational-computing.co.uk/DelphiBookCode/DelphiCode.html

Example 8:

Double click the **Locate** button and **add** the following code:

```
Procedure TForm1.LocateClick(Sender : TObject);
  Var
    LocateSuccess : Boolean;
  Begin
    LocateSuccess := DBDemosTable.Locate('Name', LocateEdit.Text,
                                          [LoPartialKey, LoCaseInsensitive]);
  End;
```

Save all then **run** this program. **Open** the **Country** table and enter the country name **Guyana** into the **LocateEdit** box. Click the **Locate** button.

The cursor should move to the row with **Name** field value **Guyana**. as shown in *Figure 59.2*.

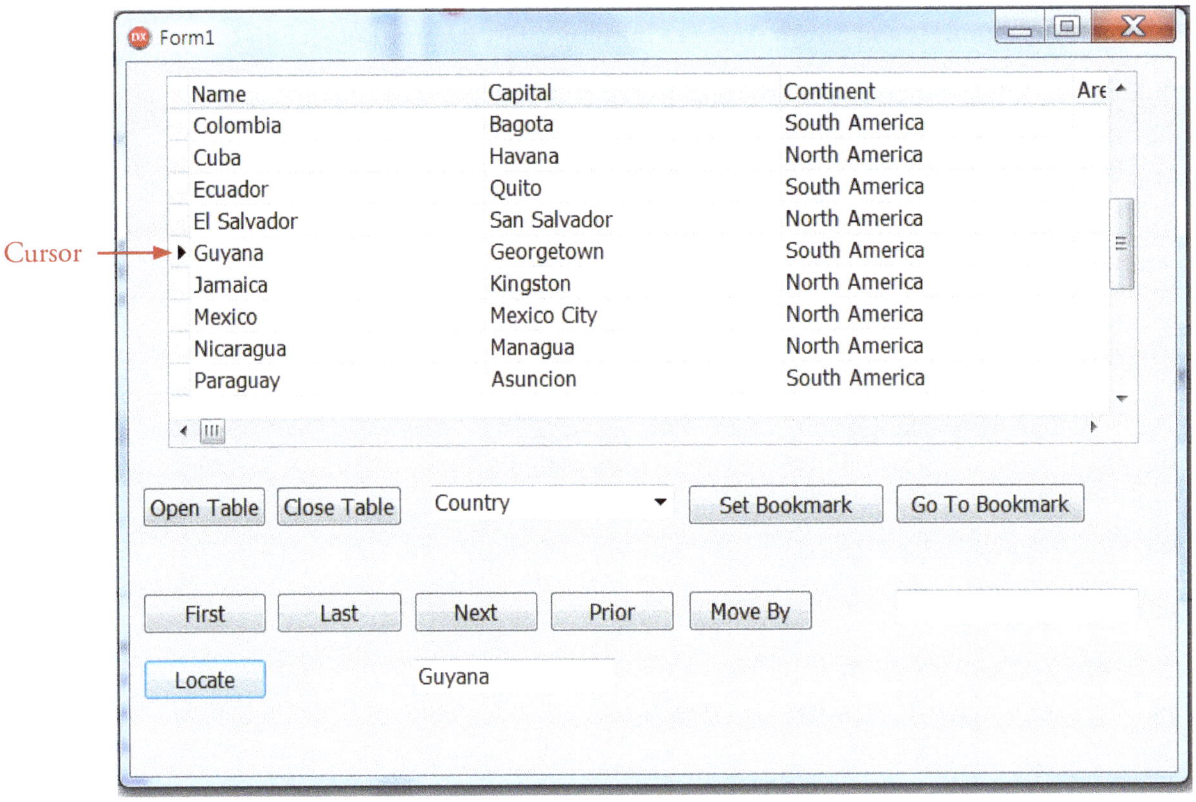

Fig. 59.2 Using Locate in Delphi Community Edition 10.2 to locate record for Guyana

The first parameter in the **DBDemosTable.Locate** function corresponds to a column name in the table. The second parameter is the search value on which this column is searched for a match. The third parameter sets the type of match that is applied.

It is possible to search for a match on more than one column. **Change** the name of **LocateEdit** to **LocateEdit1**. **Add** another **Edit box** to the form. Name this **Edit box** **LocateEdit2**. **Change** the procedure as follows:

Example 9:

Double click the **Locate** button and **change** the code as follows:

```
Procedure TForm1.LocateClick(Sender: TObject);
  Var
    LocateSuccess : Boolean;
  Begin
    LocateSuccess :=
    DBDemosTable.Locate('Name; Continent',
    VarArrayOf([LocateEdit1.Text,
    LocateEdit2.Text]),  [LoPartialKey,
    LoCaseInsensitive]);
  End;
```

VarArrayOf is a variant array that is assigned two values. One from the **Text** property of **Edit box** **LocateEdit1** and one from **LocateEdit2**.

The two column names are **Name** and **Continent.** A semicolon separates these.

Add a Label component to **LocateEdit1** and another one to **LocateEdit2**. **Change** the **Name** property of the first Label to **NameLabel** and the second to **ContinentLabel**. **Change** the caption property to **Name** and **Continent**, respectively.

Run this program and enter **Bolivia** and **South America** into **LocateEdit1** and **LocateEdit2** respectively.

The cursor should move to the row containing **Bolivia** as shown in *Figure 59.3*.

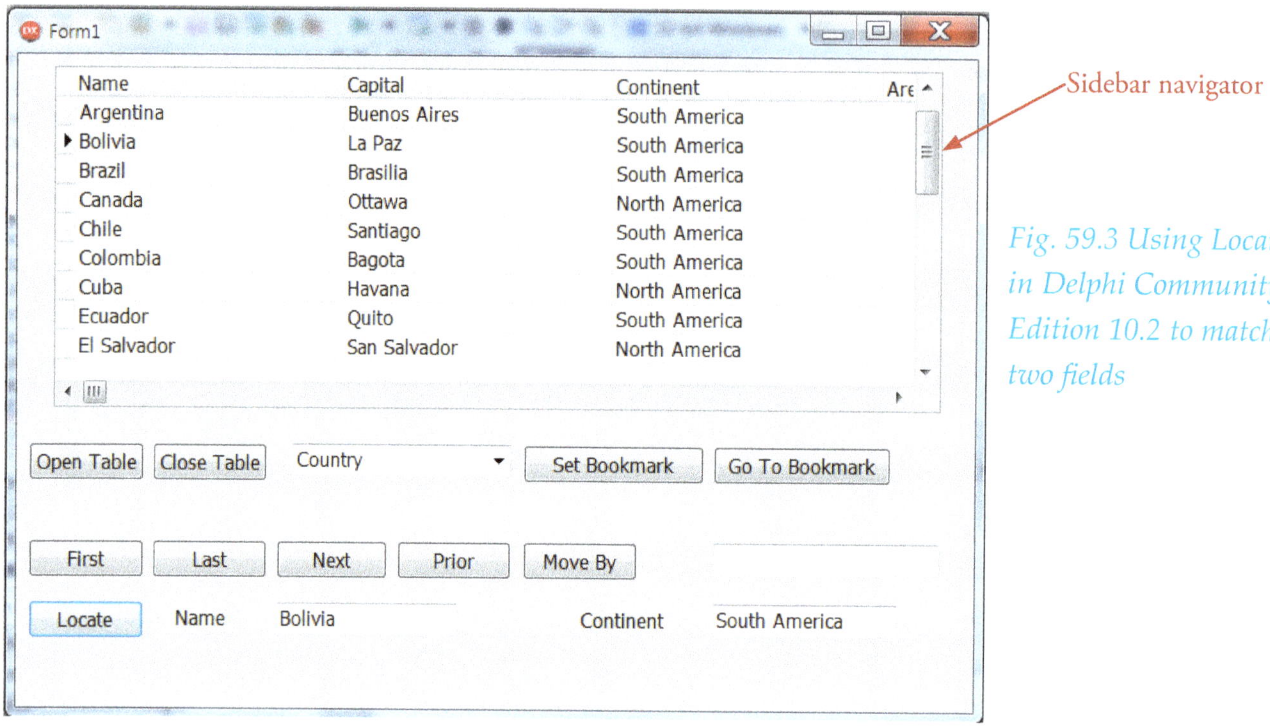

Fig. 59.3 Using Locate in Delphi Community Edition 10.2 to match two fields

Use sidebar navigator to navigate away for **Bolivia**'s record. Now **change** the **Continent** value to **North America** and **click Locate** button. This time the cursor remains where it is because the **locate** action fails to match the **Continent** field value.

Enabling and Disabling Filtering

Enabling filters on a dataset is a three-step process:

- **Create** a filter.
- **Set** filter options for string-based filter tests, if necessary.
- **Set** the Filtered property to True.

Resource

Download project ADONavigatingDataSetsFilterFind from www.educational-computing.co.uk/DelphiBookCode/DelphiCode.html

When filtering is enabled, only those records that meet the filter criteria are available to an application.

Add another Button to the form and change its **Name** and **Caption** properties to **Filter.**

Add another Edit **box** component to the form and change its **Name** property to **FilterEdit**. **Change** its **Text** property to **blank**.

Example 10:

Figure 59.4 shows a form for using a filter. **Double click** the **Filter** button and add the following code to the event handler:

```
Procedure TForm1.FilterClick(Sender : TObject);
  Begin
    {DBDemosTable.FilterOptions := [foCaseInsensitive];}
    DBDemosTable.Filter := FilterEdit.Text;
    DBDemosTable.Filtered := True;
  End;
```

The first line is commented out because **FilterOptions** do not work with ADO tables.

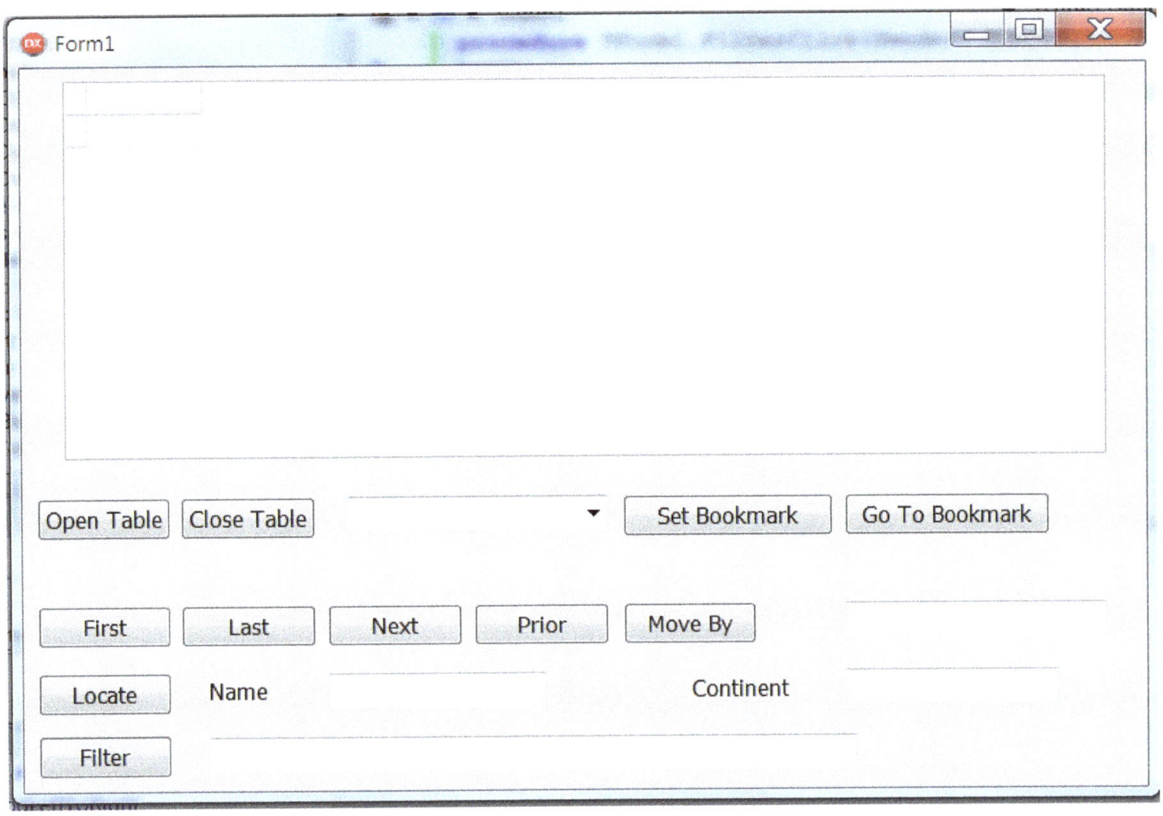

Fig. 59.4 Adding a filter on a dataset to the form, Delphi Community Edition 10.2

Figure 59.5 shows a filter in action on the **Country** table.

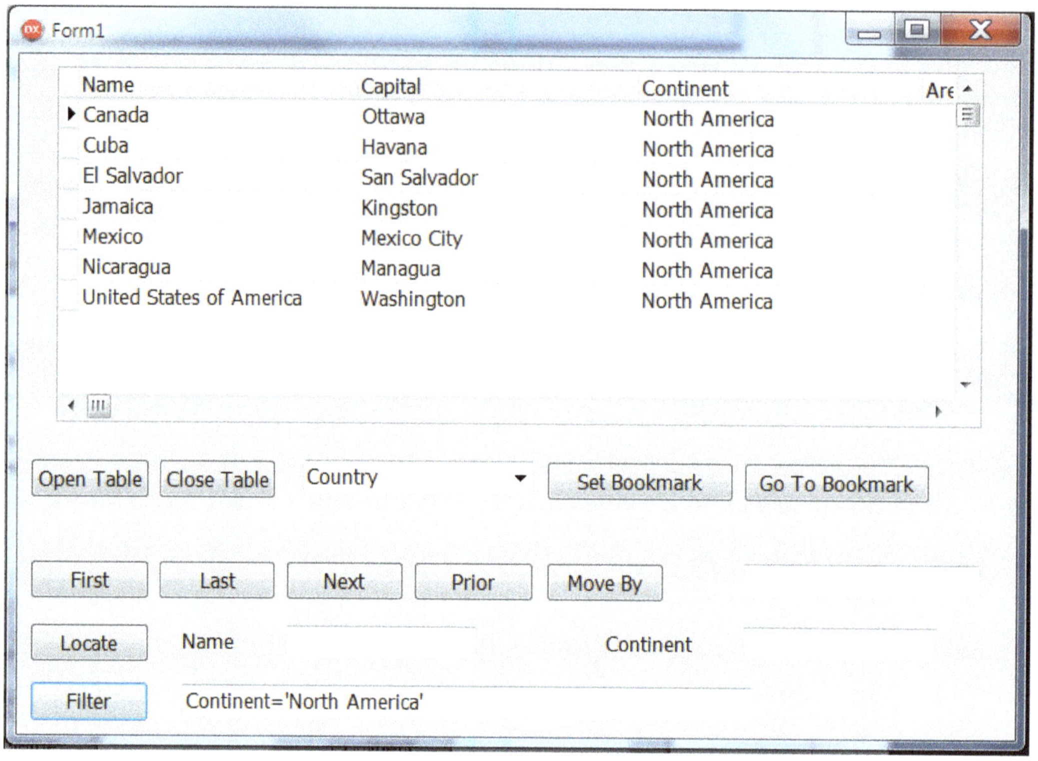

Fig. 59.5 Filter in action on table Country, Delphi Community Edition 10.2

There are four dataset methods that enable navigation among records in a filtered dataset.

1. **FindFirst** Moves to the first record in the dataset that matches the current filter criteria.

   Example 11:

```
Procedure TForm1.FindFirstClick(Sender : TObject);
  Begin
    {DBDemosTable.FilterOptions :=
                        [foCaseInsensitive];}
    DBDemosTable.Filter := FilterEdit.Text;
    DBDemosTable.FindFirst;
  End;
```

2. **FindLast** Moves to the last record in the dataset that matches the current filter criteria.

   Example 12:

```
Procedure TForm1.FindLastClick(Sender : TObject);
  Begin
    {DBDemosTable.FilterOptions := [foCaseInsensitive];}
    DBDemosTable.Filter := FilterEdit.Text;
    DBDemosTable.FindLast;
  End;
```

3. **FindNext** Moves from the current record in the filtered dataset to the next one.

Example 13:

```
Procedure TForm1.FilterClick(Sender : TObject);
  Begin
    {DBDemosTable.FindNextOptions := [foCaseInsensitive];}
    DBDemosTable.Filter := FilterEdit.Text;
    DBDemosTable.FindNext;
  End;
```

4. **FindPrior** Moves from the current record in the filtered dataset to the previous one.

Example: 14

```
Procedure TForm1.FindPriorClick(Sender : TObject);
  Begin
    {DBDemosTable.FilterOptions := [foCaseinSensitive];}
    DBDemosTable.Filter := FilterEdit.Text;
    DBDemosTable.FindPrior;
  End;
```

Figure 59.6 shows an example of the use of the navigation buttons on a filtered dataset where the filter is the continent of North America.

Add four more **Buttons** to the form and change their **Name** and **Caption** properties to match *Figure 59.6*.
Create event handlers as shown in **Examples 11** to **14**.
Save in a folder named ADONavigatingDatasetsFilter. **Name** the project ADONavigatingDatasetsFilter, accept the default name for the unit.
Now **run** and **test** that each button works as described.

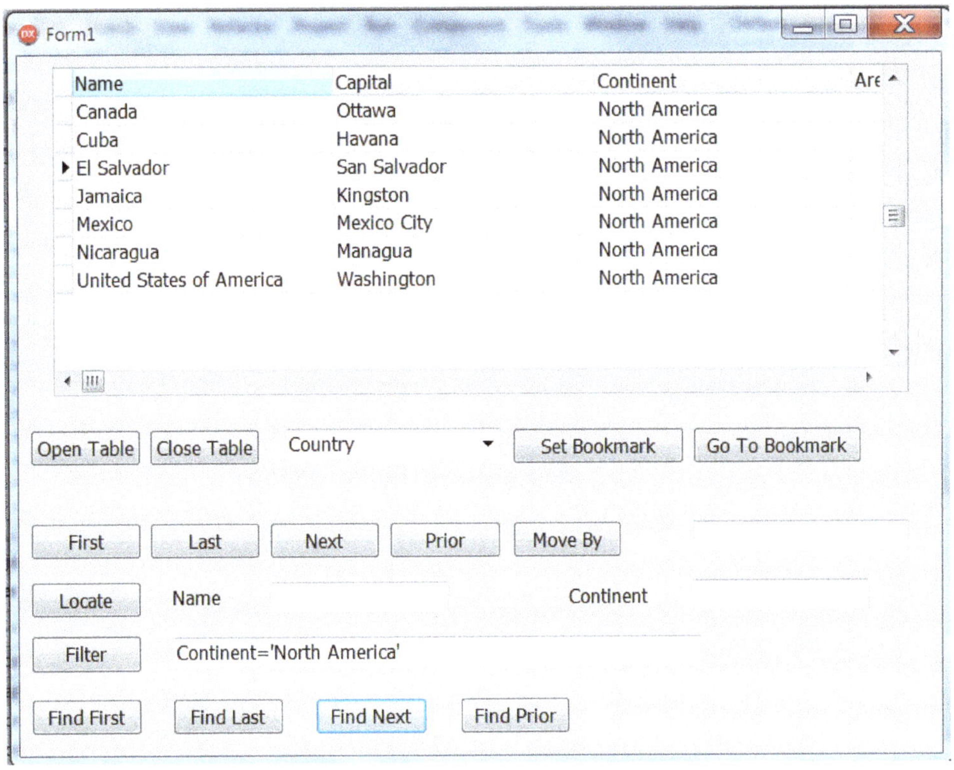

Fig. 59.6 Filter in action with navigation on table Country , Delphi Community Edition 10.2

Disabling filtering is achieved by

```
DBDemosTable.Filtered := False;
```

It is possible to add another button, say, with its **Caption** set to **Disable Filtering**, and a button click event handler containing this statement for this button, but we won't. Instead we can just clear the filter edit box and click on the **Filter** button to display the entire contents of the table.

60 Editing a dataset

First database project (continued)

Purpose: To learn how to edit a dataset

Editing Datasets

A dataset must be in **dsEdit** mode before an application can modify records. Once a dataset is in **dsEdit** mode a user can modify the field values for the current record that appears in any data-aware controls on a form.

Figure 60.1 shows the form after adding a button for each operation in this section, creating button click event handlers for each, running the program and clicking on the **Edit** button. Note that the cursor changes to I.

These operations are: **Edit**, **Append**, **Insert**, **Post**, **Delete** and **Cancel**.

Example 1:

```
Procedure TForm1.EditClick(Sender: TObject);
  Begin
    DBdemosTable.Edit;
  End;
```

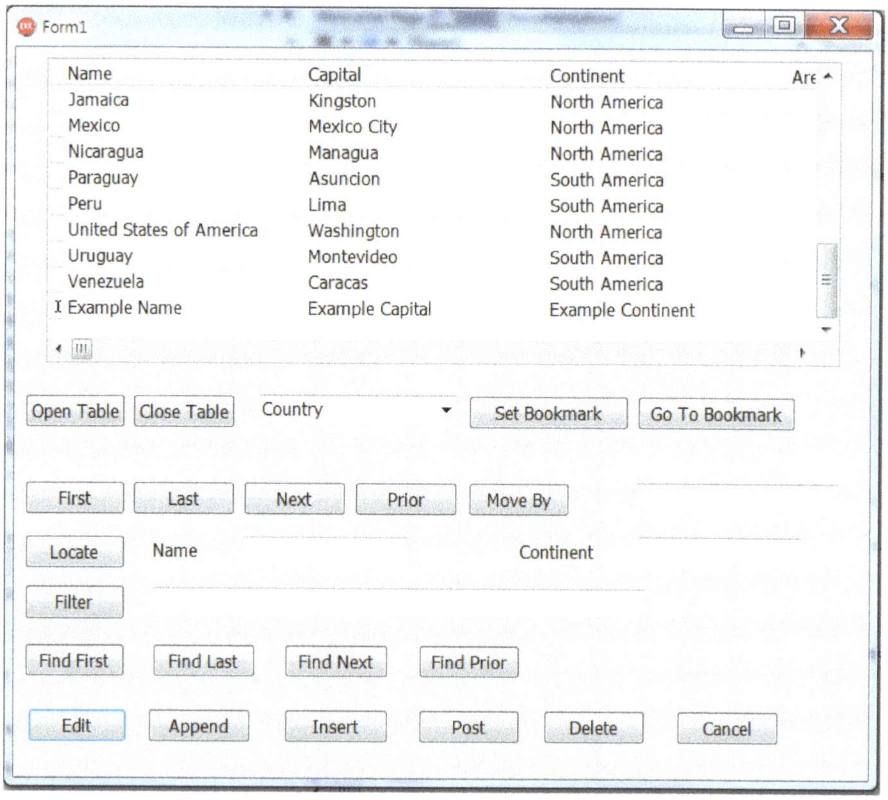

Fig. 60.1 Editing a dataset in Delphi Community Edition 10.2

Adding New Records

A dataset must be in **dsInsert** mode before an application can add new records. In code, it is possible to use the **Insert** or **Append** methods to put a dataset into **dsInsert** mode. Once a dataset is in **dsInsert** mode, a user or application can enter values into fields associated with the new record.

Inserting Records

Insert opens a new, empty record before the current record, and makes the empty record the current record so that field values for the record can be entered either by a user or by application code.

Example 2:

```
Procedure TForm1.InsertClick(Sender : TObject);
  Begin
    DBDemosTable.Insert;
  End;
```

When an application calls **Post,** a newly inserted record is written to the dataset.

Resource

Download ADOEditingDatasets project from www.educational-computing.co.uk/DelphiBookCode/DelphiCode.html

Appending records

Append opens a new, empty record at the end of the dataset, and makes the empty record the current one so that field values for the record can be entered either by a user or by application code.

Example 3:

```
Procedure TForm1.AppendClick(Sender: TObject);
  Begin
    DBDemosTable.Append;
  End;
```

When an application calls **Post**, a newly appended record is written to the dataset.

Deleting Records

Delete deletes the current record from a dataset and puts the dataset in **dsBrowse** mode. The record that followed the deleted record becomes the current record.

Example 4:

```
Procedure TForm1.DeleteClick(Sender: TObject);
  Begin
    DBDemosTable.Delete;
  End;
```

Posting Data to the Database

Post writes changes made to the current record to the database.

Example 5:

```
Procedure TForm1.PostClick(Sender: TObject);
  Begin
    DBDemosTable.Post;
  End;
```

Cancelling Changes

An application can undo changes made to the current record at any time, if it has not yet directly or indirectly called **Post**. A call to **Cancel** can return the record back to its original values.

Example 6:

```
Procedure TForm1.CancelClick(Sender: TObject);
  Begin
    DBDemosTable.Cancel;
  End;
```

Add six buttons from the Standard tab to your program from *Chapter 59*. **Change** the **Name** property of the buttons to **Edit, Append, Insert, Post, Delete, Cancel**. **Change** the **Caption** property of these buttons to **Edit, Append, Insert, Post, Delete, Cancel** respectively. **Double click** each in turn and **add** the corresponding code from Examples 1 to 6 to the body of each event handler.

Save the project in folder `ADODBEditingDataSets` with project name `ADODBEditingDataSets`. **Save** unit using default name in the same folder.

Run the project and **test** that each button works as expected.

61 SQL and the ADOQuery component

Using SQL queries

Purpose: To learn how to perform SQL queries with the ADOQuery component

SQL is a standard language for storing, manipulating and retrieving data in databases.

Launch Delphi

Select File|New|VCL Forms Application.

Delphi presents a new project and a blank form for you to use.

In order to work with the Microsoft Access database, **DBDemos.mdb**, you will need to place the following non-visual components on the blank form:

- ADOConnection component from the ADO tab in Delphi 7 and dbGo page in Delphi 2009 onwards
- ADOQuery component from the ADO tab in Delphi 7 and dbGo page in Delphi 2009 onwards
- DataSource component from the Data Access tab
- DBGrid component from the Data Controls tab.

Select the **ConnectionString** property of the ADOConnection component and **double click** the blank space or click the ellipsis. The window shown in *Figure 61.1* should appear.

Click the **Build** button to bring up the Data Link Properties window shown in *Figure 61.2*.

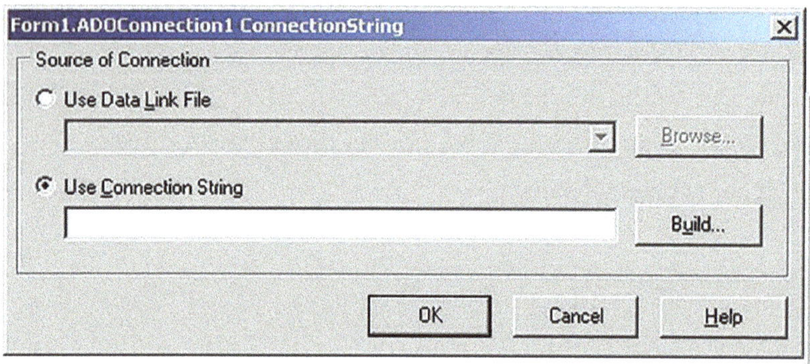

Fig. 61.1 Delphi 7 ConnectionString window

Resource

Download BasicSelectFromCountry project from www.educational-computing.co.uk/DelphiBookCode/DelphiCode.html

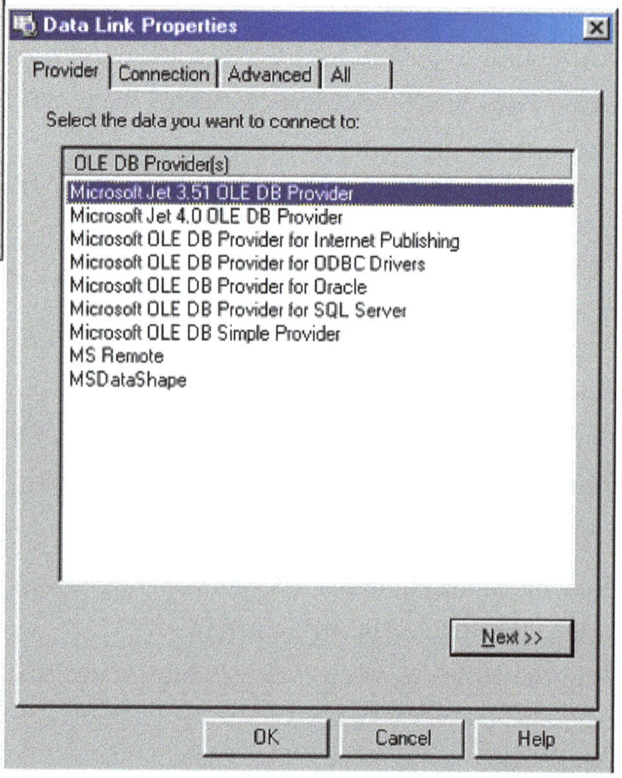

Fig. 61.2 Delphi 7 Data Link Properties window

Highlight the **Microsoft Jet 4.0 OLE DB Provider** or later version then press the next button to go to the **Connection** tab.

Select the **DBDemos.mdb** database stored in your work area - *Figure 61.3*.

Information

DBDemos.mdb is supplied with your version of Delphi. It may be located in folder C:\Program Files\Common Files\Embarcadero Shared\Data in later versions of Delphi.
Microsoft Jet 4.0 OLE DB driver may or may not be installed on your machine. Furthermore, it needs a 32 bit operating system to function. However the driver can be forced to work in a 64 bit environment - see https://www.codicode.com/art/64_bit_version_of_jet.aspx.
There is a 64 bit version, Microsoft.ACE.OLEDB.12.0, which can be obtained from https://www.microsoft.com/en-us/download/details.aspx?id=13255.
Microsoft Jet 4.0 OLE DB driver can be obtained from the same link if it isn't present already on your machine.

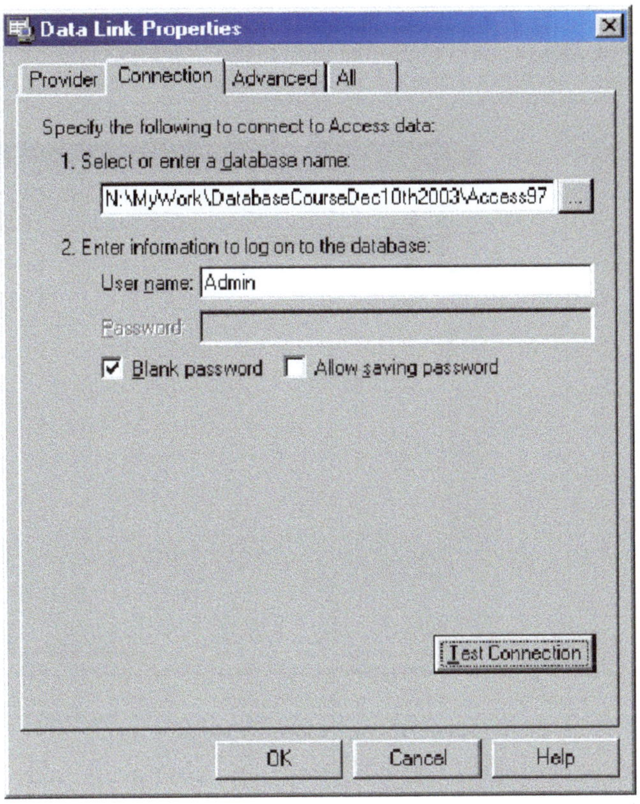

Fig. 61.3 Delphi 7 Data Link Properties Connection window

Test the connection - *Figure 61.4*.

Click OK if the test is satisfactory.

Fig. 61.4 Delphi 7 Data Link window

Click OK to exit the **ConnectionString** window.

Select the **ADOConnection1** component.

In the Object Inspector **change** the **LoginPrompt** property to **False**.

Select the **Connected** property and **double click** its **value** to change it to **True**. **ADOConnection1** should now connect to **DBDemos** database. The **connected** property will show **True** if this is the case.

Select ADOQuery1 component on the form. In the Object Inspector, **select** the **Connection** property and **change** it to **ADOConnection1**.

Select the DataSource component and in the Object Inspector **change** its DataSet property to ADOQuery1.

Select the DBGrid component and in the Object Inspector **change** its DataSource property to DataSource1.

Select the ADOQuery component and in the Object Inspector **select** the SQL property.

Double click TStrings or **click** the ellipsis to open an SQL String List editor.

Enter the SQL statement **Select * From Country** shown in *Figure 61.5* and **click** **OK**.

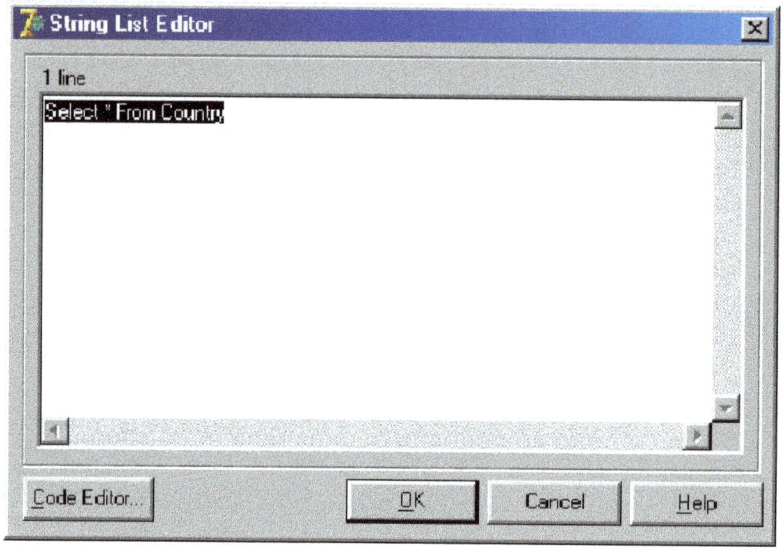

Fig. 61.5 Delphi 7 String List Editor window

Select the **Active** property of **ADOQuery1** and **change** its value to **True** to display all the records from the **Country** table. Notice that the records appear whilst the form is in design mode.

Figure 61.6 shows the results set from **ADOQuery1** when **Delphi 10.2.3 Community edition** is used instead of **Delphi 7**.

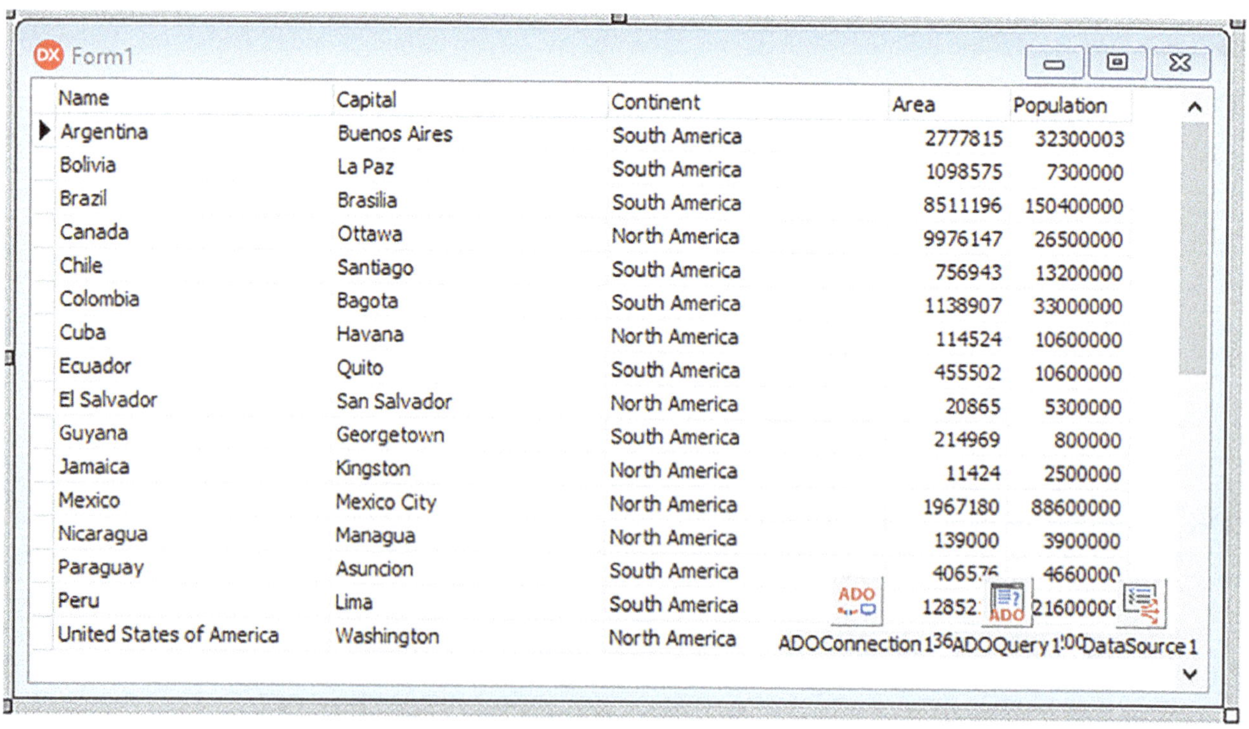

Name	Capital	Continent	Area	Population
Argentina	Buenos Aires	South America	2777815	32300003
Bolivia	La Paz	South America	1098575	7300000
Brazil	Brasilia	South America	8511196	150400000
Canada	Ottawa	North America	9976147	26500000
Chile	Santiago	South America	756943	13200000
Colombia	Bagota	South America	1138907	33000000
Cuba	Havana	North America	114524	10600000
Ecuador	Quito	South America	455502	10600000
El Salvador	San Salvador	North America	20865	5300000
Guyana	Georgetown	South America	214969	800000
Jamaica	Kingston	North America	11424	2500000
Mexico	Mexico City	North America	1967180	88600000
Nicaragua	Managua	North America	139000	3900000
Paraguay	Asuncion	South America	4065[illegible]	4660000
Peru	Lima	South America	12852[illegible]	2160000[illegible]
United States of America	Washington	North America		

Fig. 61.6 Delphi 10.2.3 Community edition design mode results set window for the application

Now **edit** the **SQL** property of **ADOQuery1** so that the SQL query is

as follows: `Select * From Country`

```
Where Continent = :ContinentValue
```

Note that the ':' denotes that **ContinentValue** is a parameter.

The value for this parameter will be supplied at run time.

> **Resource**
>
> Download project ParameterisedSelectFromCountryWhereContinent from www.educational-computing.co.uk/DelphiBookCode/DelphiCode.html

First **select** the **Parameters** property of **ADOQuery1** in the Object Inspector.

Double click its **Value** field or **click** the ellipsis.

Select ContinentValue in the pop-up window.

Accept DataType value **ftWideString**, Direction value **pdInput** shown in the Object Inspector.

Close the pop-up window by clicking on the cross.

Add one **Button** from the **Standard** tab. **Change** its name to **ExecuteQuery** and its **caption** to **Execute Query**.

Add an **Edit box** from the **Standard** tab and **rename** it **ContinentValueEdit**. **Clear** its **Text** property.

Now **double click** the **Execute Query** button to create an event handler template.

Add the body of the following code to this event handler, **TForm1.ExecuteQueryClick**:

```
Procedure TForm1.ExecuteQueryClick(Sender: TObject);
  Begin
    ADOQuery1.DisableControls;
    Try
      ADOQuery1.Close;
      ADOQuery1.Parameters.ParamValues['ContinentValue'] := ContinentValueEdit.Text;
      ADOQuery1.Open;
    Finally
      ADOQuery1.EnableControls;
    End;
  End;
```

Run this program and enter the value **North America** into the **Edit box**.

Click the **Execute Query** button. A result similar to that shown in *Figure 61.7* should appear.

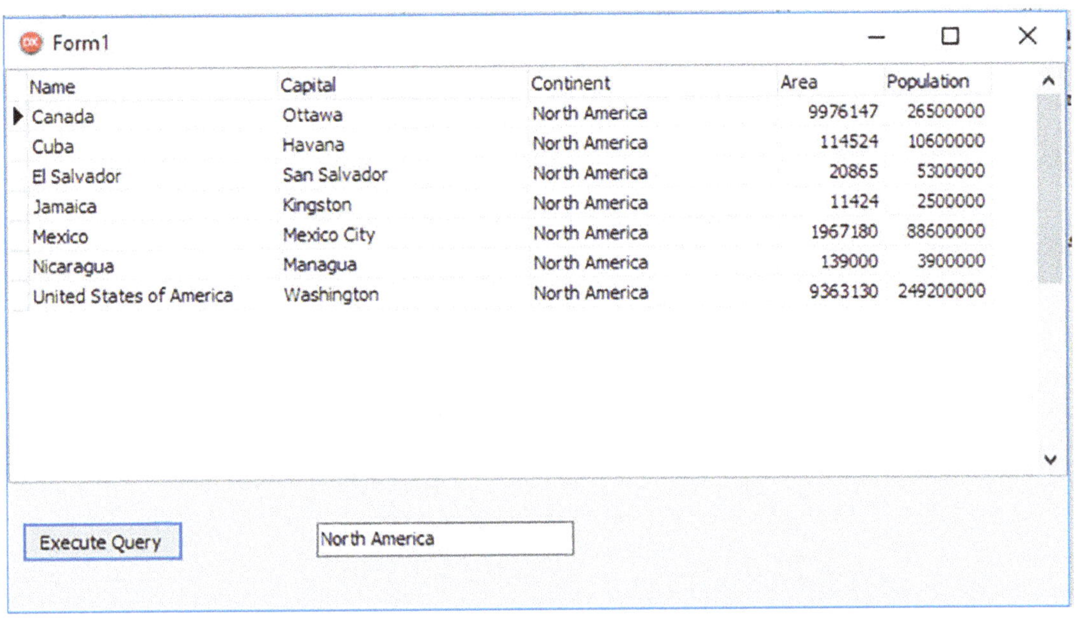

Fig. 61.7 Results set window for the application in Delphi 10.2.3 Community edition

Using Insert, Update and Delete Queries

Now **add** three more buttons to the form and **change** the **Name** property of each, in turn, to the following:

Insert

Update

Delete

and their captions respectively to

Insert

Update

Delete

> **Resource**
>
> Download InsertUpdateDeleteQuery project from
> www.educational-computing.co.uk/DelphiBookCode/DelphiCode.html

Add three more ADOQuery components to the form and change the **Name** property of each, in turn, to the following:

ADOQueryInsert

ADOQueryUpdate

ADOQueryDelete

For each new query the **Connection** property must be **set** to **ADOConnection1**.

Change the **Execute Query** button's **Caption** property to **Parameter Select** and its **Name** property to **ParameterSelect**.

Add another button and **change** its **Name** property to **Select** and its **Caption** property to **Select.**

Add another **ADOQuery** component and change its **Name** property to **ADOQuerySelect** and its **Connection** property to **ADOConnection1**.

Add a Label component and change its **Caption** property to **Continent**. **Change** its **AutoSize** property to **false** and its **Alignment** property to **taCenter.** **Change** its **Font** property to size **12** and its **Layout** property to **tlCenter**. Position this label over the Edit box **ContinentValueEdit.**

Double click the **Select** button to create an event handler **Procedure SelectClick**.

Add the following code to the body of this event handler:

```
DataSource1.DataSet := ADOQuerySelect;
ADOQuerySelect.DisableControls;
Try
  ADOQuerySelect.Close;
  ADOQuerySelect.Open;
Finally
  ADOQuerySelect.EnableControls;
End;
```

Select the ADOQuerySelect query component on the form and **select** its **SQL** property in the Object Inspector. **Double click** its **value** field to open the **Strings List editor**. **Add** the following SQL statement:

```
Select * From Country
```

Double click the **Insert** button and add the following code to the created event handler template.

```
ADOQueryInsert.DisableControls;
Try
  ADOQueryInsert.Close;
  ADOQueryInsert.ExecSQL;
Finally
    ADOQueryInsert.EnableControls;
End;
```

Select the ADOQueryInsert query component on the form and **select** its **SQL** property in the Object Inspector. **Double click** the value field to run the String List editor. **Add** the following SQL statement:

Insert Into Country (Name, Continent)

Values ('Never Never Land', 'The Moon')

Add another Edit box component from the Standard component tab to the form. **Change** its **Name** property to **NameValueEdit**.

Add a Label component from the Standard tab to the form positioned just to the left of the newly added Edit box. **Change** its **Caption** to **Use for Delete** and **Update**. **Change** its font size to 12.

Double click the **Update** button and **add** the following code to the created event handler template.

```
ADOQueryUpdate.DisableControls;
Try
  ADOQueryUpdate.Close;
  ADOQueryUpdate.Parameters.ParamValues['NameValueToUpdate'] := NameValueEdit.Text;
  ADOQueryUpdate.ExecSQL;
Finally
  ADOQueryUpdate.EnableControls;
End;
```

Select the ADOQueryUpdate query component on the form and **select** its **SQL** property in the Object Inspector. **Double click** the **value** field to run the String List editor. Add the following SQL statement:

```
Update Country
  Set Name = 'Never Never Never Land'
  Where Country.Name = :NameValueToUpdate
```

Click on the **Parameters** property of **ADOQueryUpdate** and **check** that a parameter **NameValueToUpdate** has been created with data type **WideString**.

Double click the **Delete** button and **add** the following code to the created event handler template.

```
ADOQueryDelete.DisableControls;
Try
  ADOQueryDelete.Close;
  ADOQueryDelete.Parameters.ParamValues['NameValueToDelete'] := NameValueEdit.Text;
  ADOQueryDelete.ExecSQL;
Finally
    ADOQueryDelete.EnableControls;
End;
```

Select the ADOQueryDelete query component on the form and **select** its **SQL** property in the Object Inspector. **Double click** the **value** field to run the **String List editor**. **Add** the following SQL statement:

```
Delete
   From Country
      Where Name = :NameValueToDelete
```

Click on the **Parameters** property of **ADOQueryDelete** and **check** that a parameter **NameValueToDelete** has been created with data type **WideString**.

The form should now appear in design view as shown in *Figure 61.8*.

Run the program and **try** each SQL command in turn as instructed below.

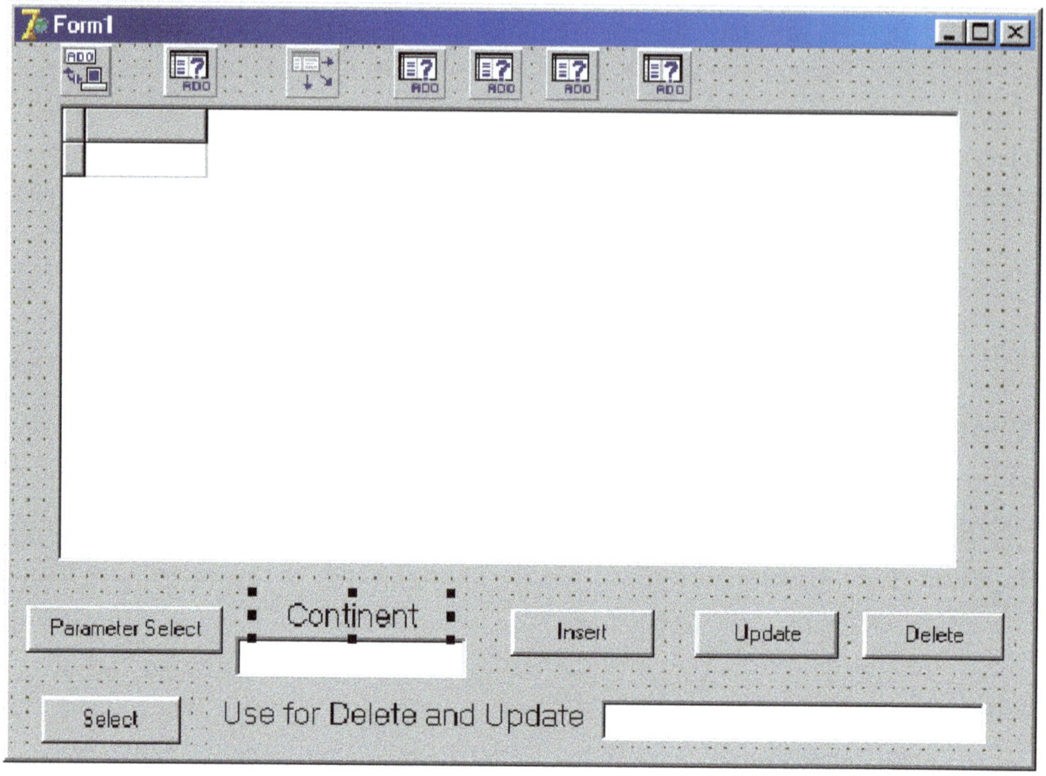

Fig. 61.8 Delphi 7 form design for select, insert, update, delete

1. **Click** the **Select** button to see all records in the **Country** table - *Figure 61.9*.

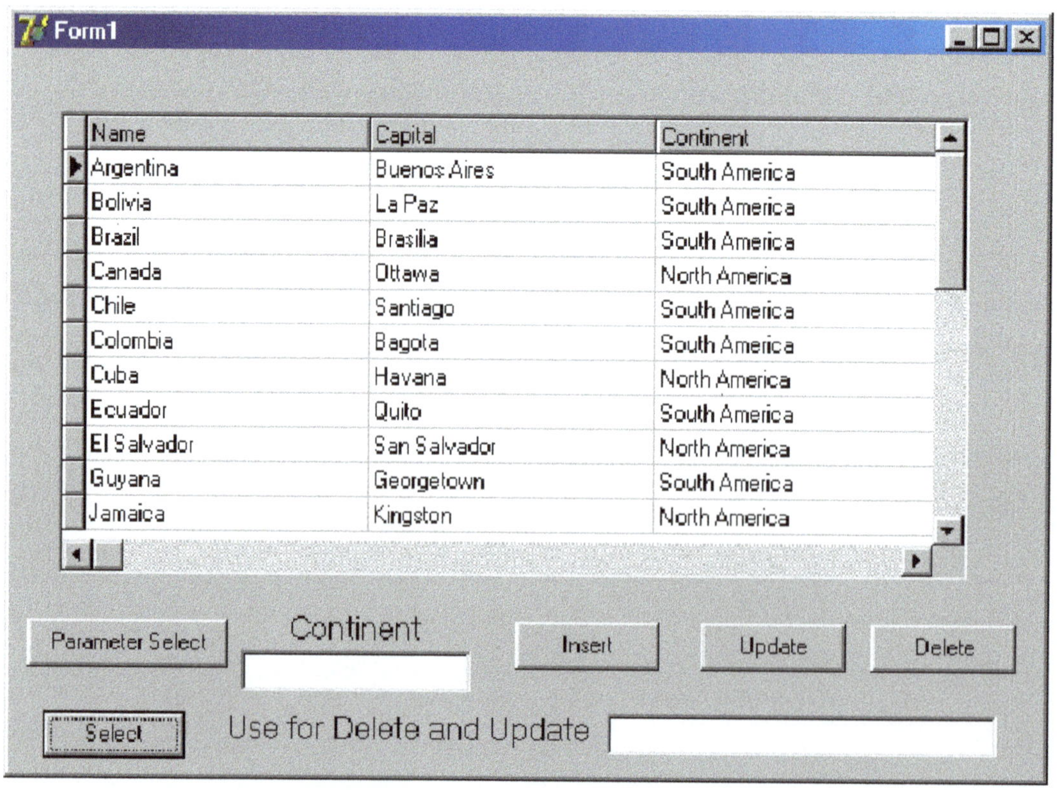

Fig. 61.9 Delphi 7 results set for Select operation

2. Now **enter** **North America** in the **Continent** parameter **edit box.**

Click the **Parameter Select** button to see only records in the North American continent - *Figure 61.10*.

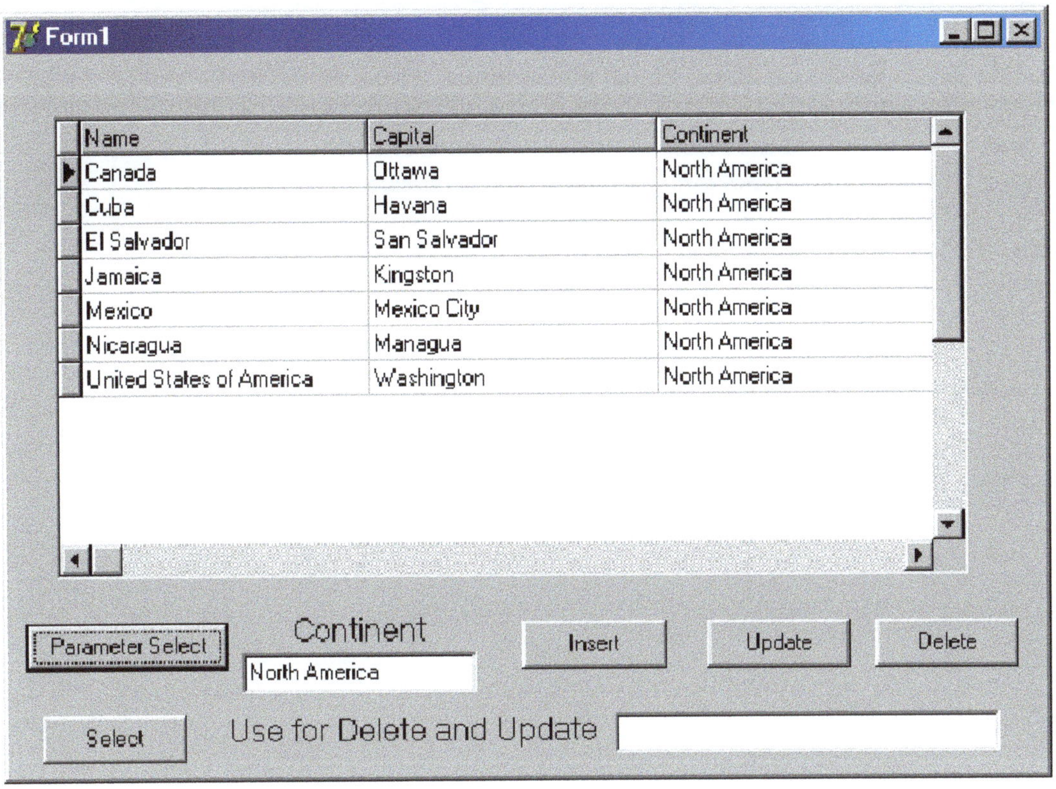

Fig. 61.10 Delphi 7 results set for Parameter Select operation

3. **Click** the **Insert** button to insert the **Never Never Land** record.

Click the **Select** button to see the result - *Figure 61.11*.

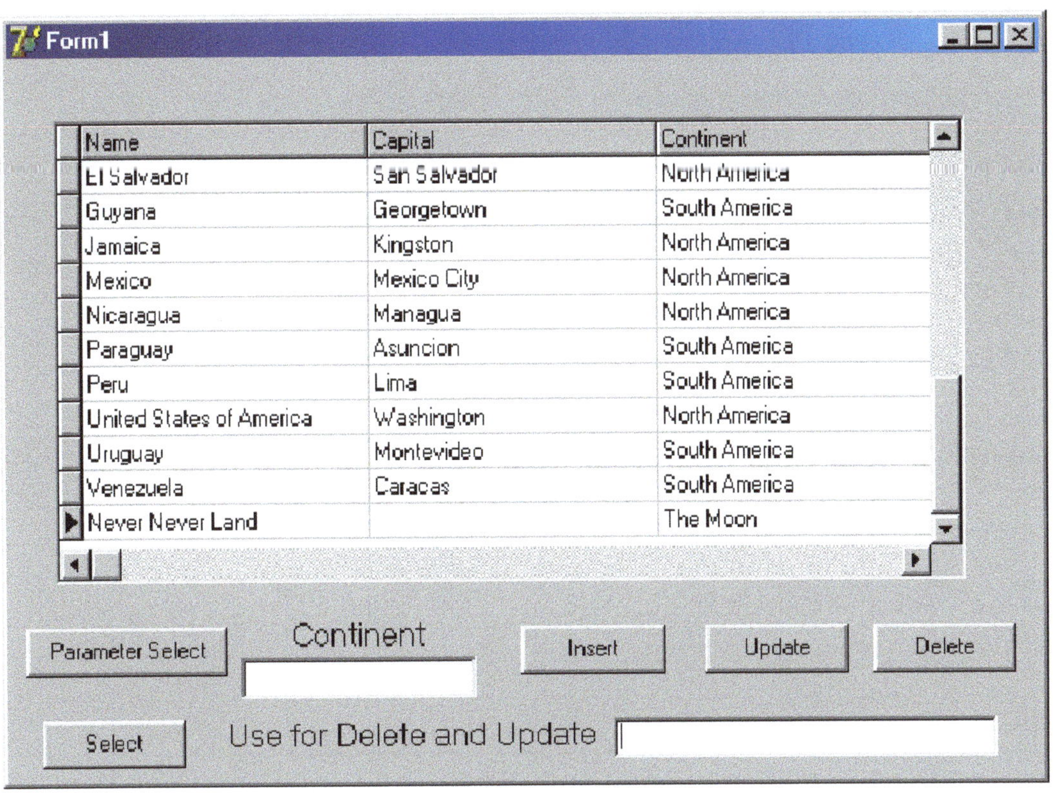

Fig. 61.11 Delphi 7 results set for Insert operation followed by Select operation operation

4. Enter the value **Never Never Land** into the **Use for Delete and Update edit box**.

Click the **Update** button. To see the change, **click** the **Select** button - *Figure 61.12*.

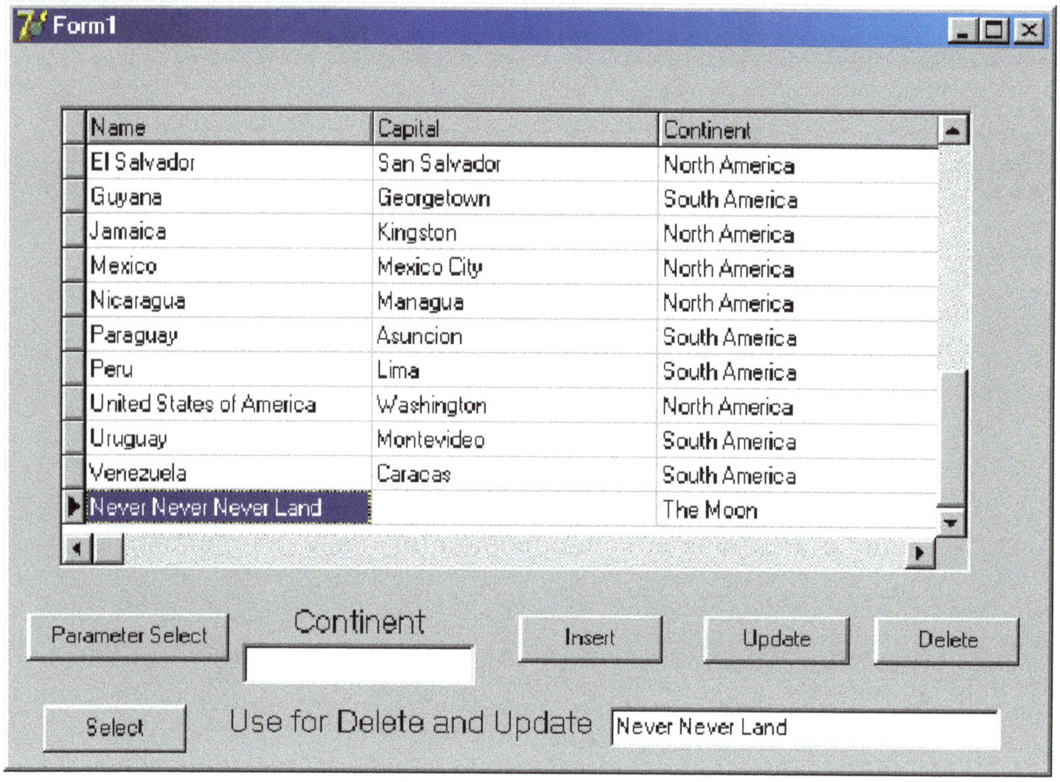

Fig. 61.12 Delphi 7 results set for Update operation followed by Select operation operation

The **Update** operation applied the SQL shown below to update '**Never Never Land**' to '**Never Never Never Land**'

```
Update Country
  Set Name = 'Never Never Never Land'
  Where Country.Name = :NameValueToUpdate
```

5. Enter the value **Never Never Never Land** into the **Use for Delete and Update edit box**.

Click the **Delete** button. To see the change, **click** the **Select** button.

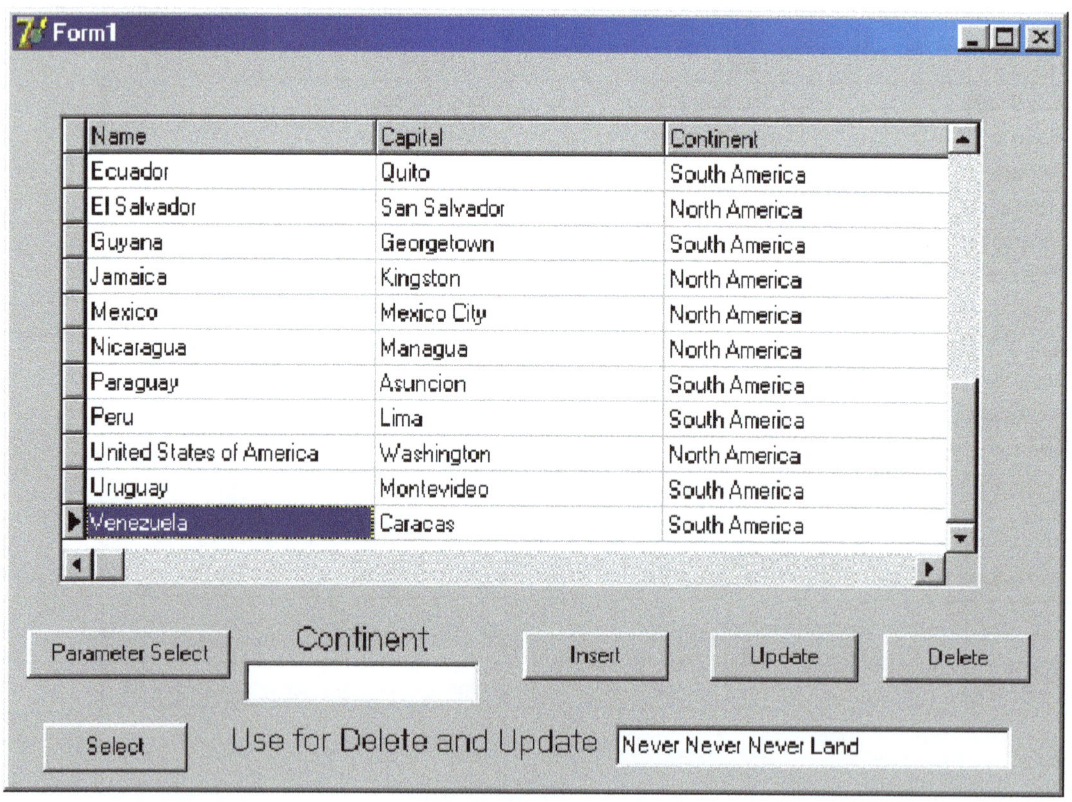

Fig. 61.13 Delphi 7 results set for Delete operation followed by Select operation operation

The last record in the results set is now **Venezuela**'s record - see *Figure 61.13* - whereas previously it was **Never Never Never Land**'s record - see *Figure 61.12*.

Programming Task

1. Amend ADOQueryInsert's SQL property from

```
Insert Into Country (Name, Continent)
Values ('Never Never Land', 'The Moon')
```

to

```
Insert Into Country (Name)
Values (:NameValueToInsert)
```

Check that a parameter NameValueToInsert has been created with data type WideString.
Amend Procedure TForm1.InsertClick to assign the value in the NameValueEdit box to this parameter before ExecSQL is called.
Test that your amendment allows a country name Never Never Land to be inserted.

62 Exploring SQL

Exploring Structured Query Language (SQL)

Purpose: To learn how to use SQL queries against any database

Using CuteSQL to execute SQL queries

To apply SQL statements and commands against **DBDemos.mdb** directly, we need a tool that can connect via ADO and execute any valid SQL statement or command that we submit. CuteSQL is just such a tool, but there are others that can be used. Further SQL tutorials are available at https://www.w3schools.com/sql/default.asp.
CuteSQL is freeware produced originally by the now defunct CharonWare®.
A copy may be downloaded from www.educational-computing.co.uk/DelphiBook/CuteSQL.zip.

Extract the contents and **run** the installer.

Launch CuteSQL and ignore the registration code field, just **click** **Start working** - *Figure 62.1*.

The split window view - *Figure 62.2* - shows an upper pane for entering SQL queries and commands, and a lower pane with two tabs, one with a grid to show the result set returned and one to show the success or failure with reason(s) of the operation .

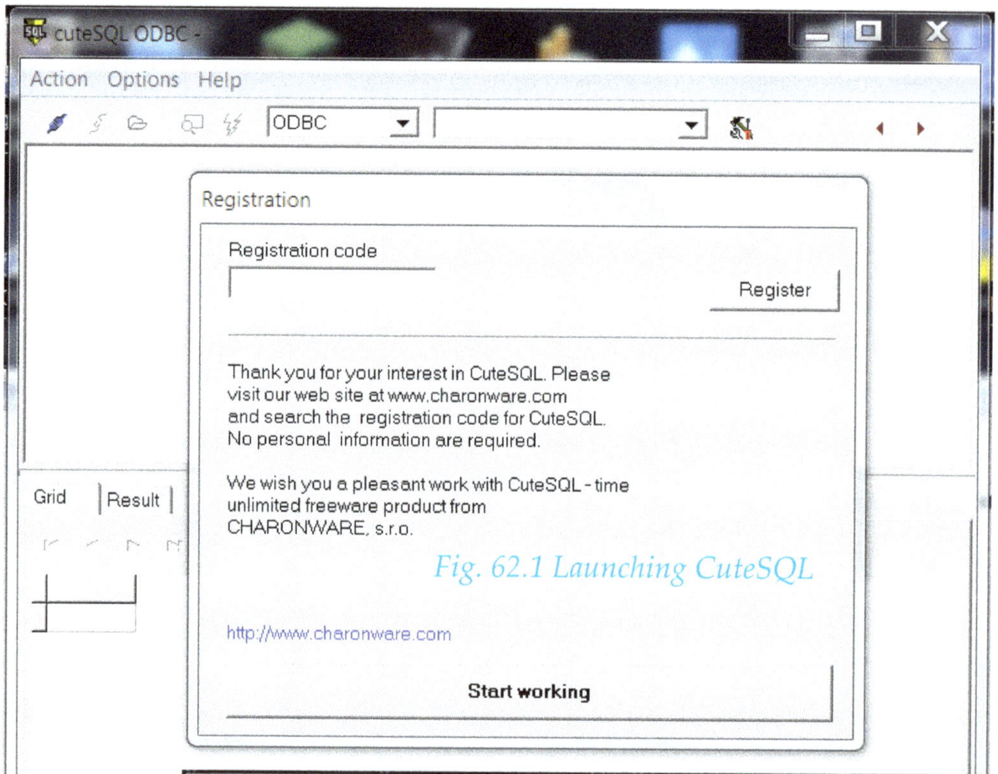

Fig. 62.1 Launching CuteSQL

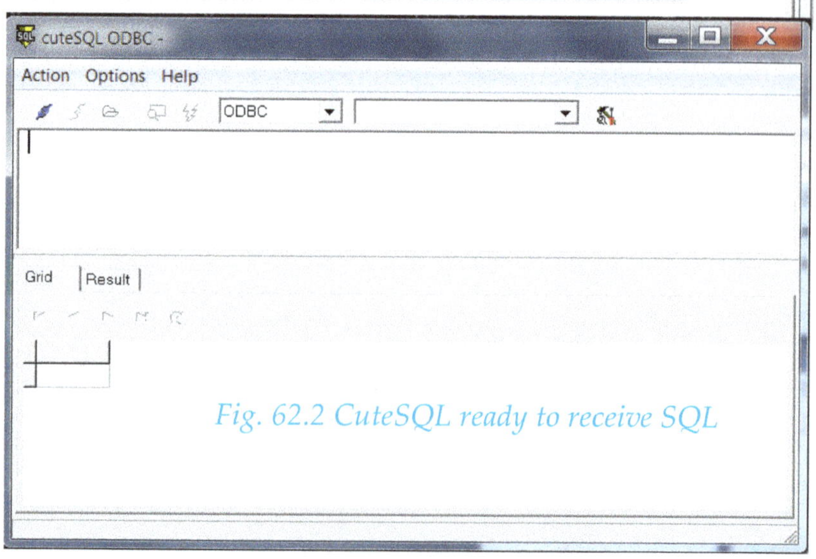

Fig. 62.2 CuteSQL ready to receive SQL

Resource

Download from www.educational-computing.co.uk/DelphiBook/CuteSQL.zip

Using CuteSQL, establish an ADO connection to DBDemos.mdb as follows:

Copy DBDemos.mdb from its location, e.g. **C:\Program Files (x86)\Common Files\Borland Shared\Data** to your work folder.

Launch CuteSQL and **select** ADO from the drop-down list or list box - *Figure 62.3*.

Click on icon next to edit box.

Select **Provider** tab from the **Data Link Properties** and highlight **Microsoft Jet 4.0 OLE DB Provider** then **click** **Next** to tab to the **Connection** page.

Click on **Select or enter a database name**. **Select** **DBDemos.mdb**.

User name should be **Admin**.

Check **Blank** password box.

Click **Test Connection**.

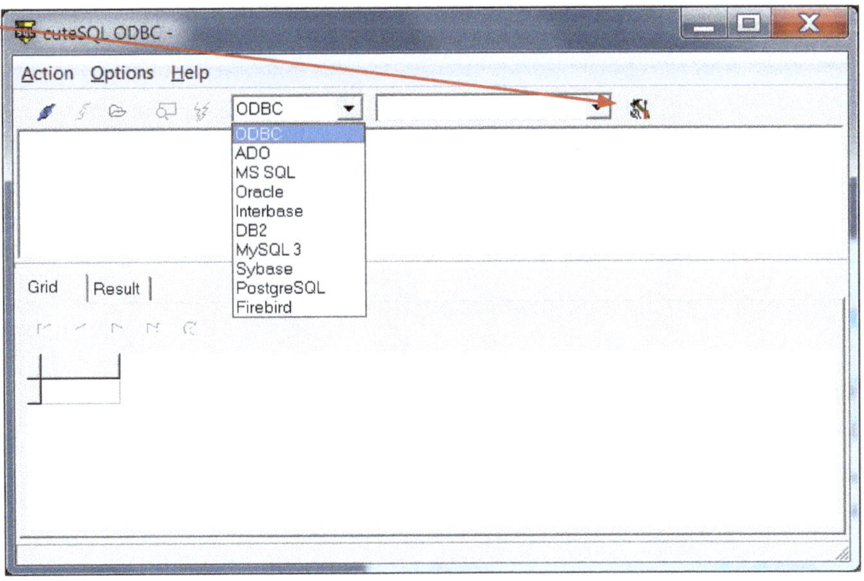

Fig. 62.3 Setting up an ADO connection

If the connection is working then the pop-up window shown in *Figure 62.4* should appear.

Click **OK**.

Now **click** **Action/connect.**

Click **OK** if asked to login to database, you don't need to supply a **User name** or **password**. You should now be connected to DBDemos.mdb.

You are ready to write and execute SQL queries.

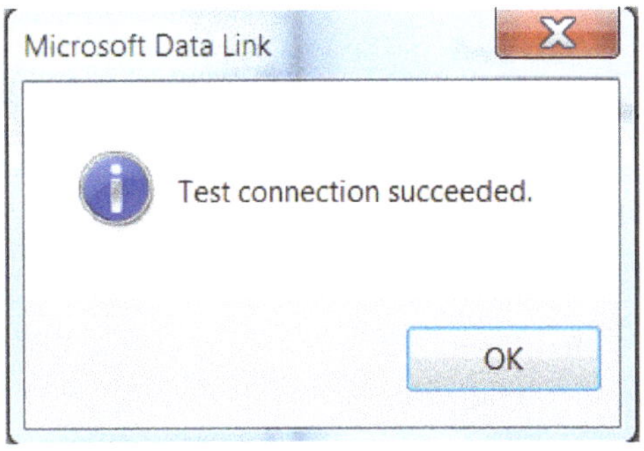

Fig. 62.4 ADO connection test

From the **Action** drop-down menu or by using the icons shown in *Figure 62.5*:

Use **Execute SQL query** for all **Select** queries

Use **Execute SQL Command** for all commands (**Insert**, **Update**, **Delete**)

Fig. 62.5 Execute SQL query, execute SQL command

Using **Select * From** .... familiarise yourself with the attributes (fields) and contents of the following tables:

Country
Customer
Employee
Items
NextCust
NextItem
NextOrd
Orders
Parts
Vendors

Exercises to try

Exercise 1 - Figure 62.6

```
Select * From Country
  Order By Capital ASC
```

Returns result set showing all fields of **Country** table arranged in ascending alphabetical order on **Capital** field.

ASC means ascending order. '*' means all fields.

Order By means order the result set on the given field. If **ASC** is omitted then ordering is ascending by default.

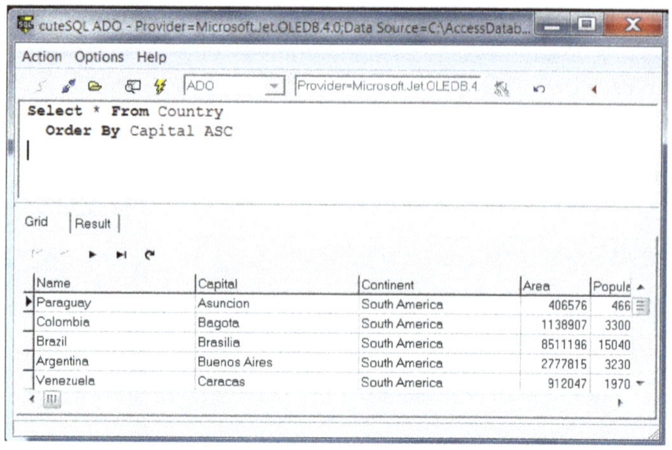

Fig. 62.6 Exercise 1 result set

Exercise 2 - Figure 62.7

```
Select * From Country
  Order By Capital DESC
```

Returns result set showing all fields of **Country** table arranged in descending alphabetical order on **Capital** field.

DESC means descending order.

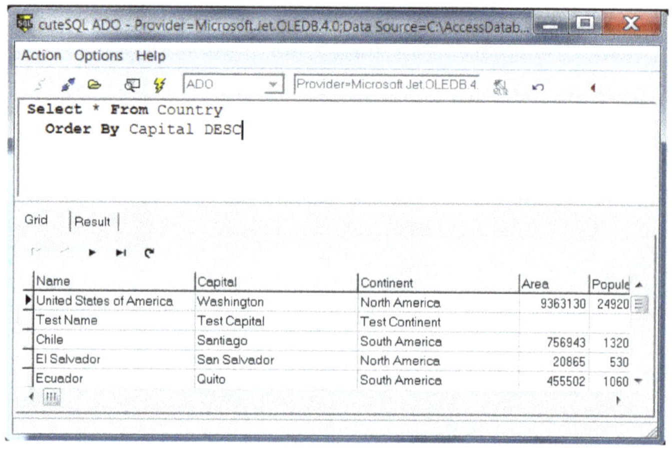

Fig. 62.7 Exercise 2 result set

Exercise 3 - Figure 62.8

```
Select Name, Capital, Continent, Population
  From Country
    Where Population > 100000
```

Returns result set showing the specified fields of **Country** table for rows where the **Population** field value exceeds **100000**.

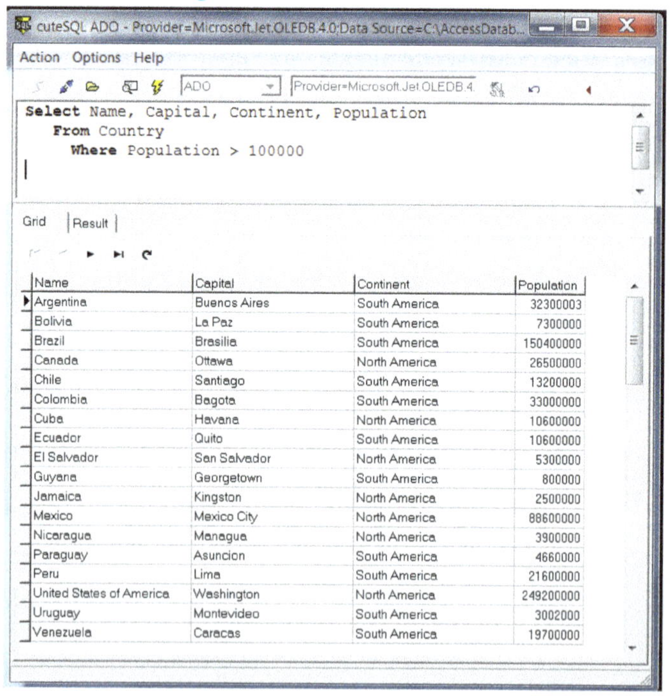

Fig. 62.8 Exercise 3 result set

Exercise 4 - Figure 62.9

```
Select Name, Capital, Continent, Population
  From Country
    Where (Population > 100000)
      And (Continent = 'South America')
```

Returns result set showing the specified fields of **Country** table for rows where the **Population** field value exceeds **100000** and the **Continent** field value matches **South America**.

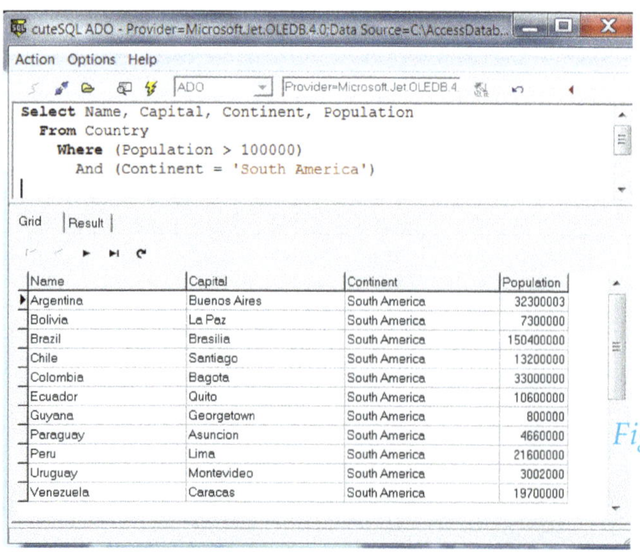

Fig. 62.9 Exercise 4 result set

Resource

Download from www.educational-computing.co.uk/DelphiBookCode/DelphiCode.html
Chapter 62/SQL.rar

Exercise 5 - *Figure 62.10*

```
Select Name, Capital, Continent, Area, Population
  From Country
    Where (Population > 100000000) Or (Population < 1000000)
```

Returns result set showing the specified fields of **Country** table for rows where the **Population** field value exceeds `100000000` or **Population** field value falls below `1000000`.

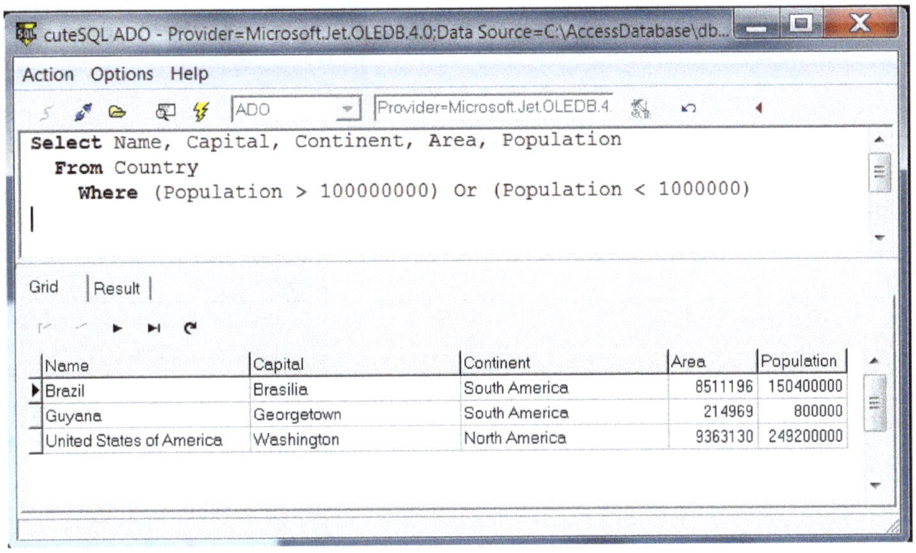

Fig. 62.10 Exercise 5 result set

Exercise 6 - *Figure 62.11*

```
Select Count(*) As NoOfCountries
  From Country
```

Returns count of number of rows in **Country** table, the count is referenced by a virtual field called **NoOfCountries**.

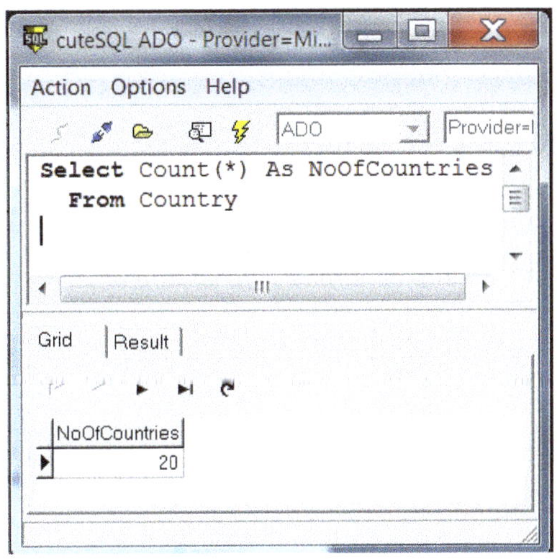

Fig. 62.11 Exercise 6 result

Exercise 7 - *Figure 62.12*

```
Select Count(*) As NoOfContinent
  From Country
    Where Continent = 'North America'
```

Returns count of number of rows in **Country** table where the **Continent** field matches **North America,** the count is referenced by a virtual field called **NoOfCountries.**

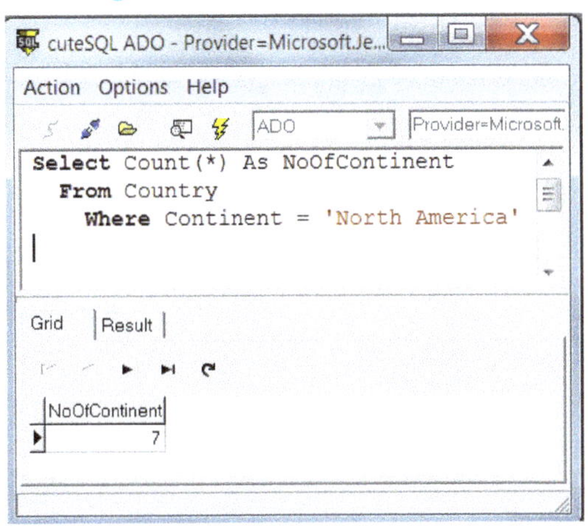

Fig. 62.12 Exercise 7 result

Exercise 8 - *Figure 62.13*

```
Select Avg(Population) As AveragePop
  From Country
```

Returns the average population of countries in the **Country** table, the average population is referenced by a virtual field called **AveragePop**.

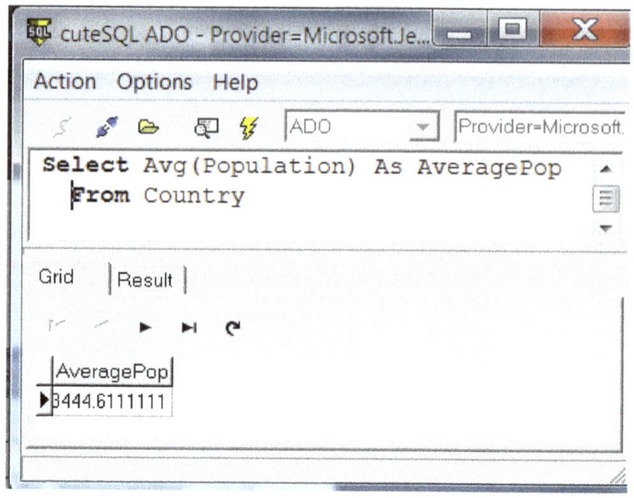

Fig. 62.13 Exercise 8 result

Exercise 9 - *Figure 62.14*

```
Select Max(Population)
  From Country
```

Returns the largest population amongst the countries in the **Country** table.

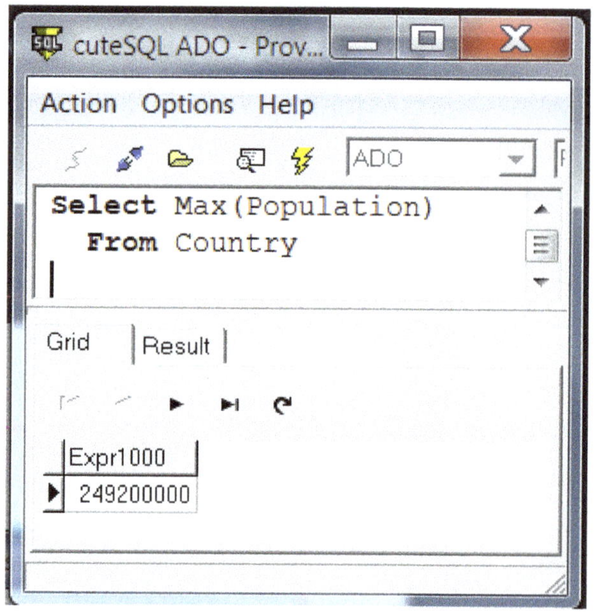

Fig. 62.14 Exercise 9 result

Question

1. What necessary change must be made to the SQL in Exercise 9 for the column heading Expr1000 to be replaced by MaxPop?

Exercise 10 - *Figure 62.15*

```
Select Min(Population)
  From Country
```

Returns the smallest population amongst the countries in the **Country** table.

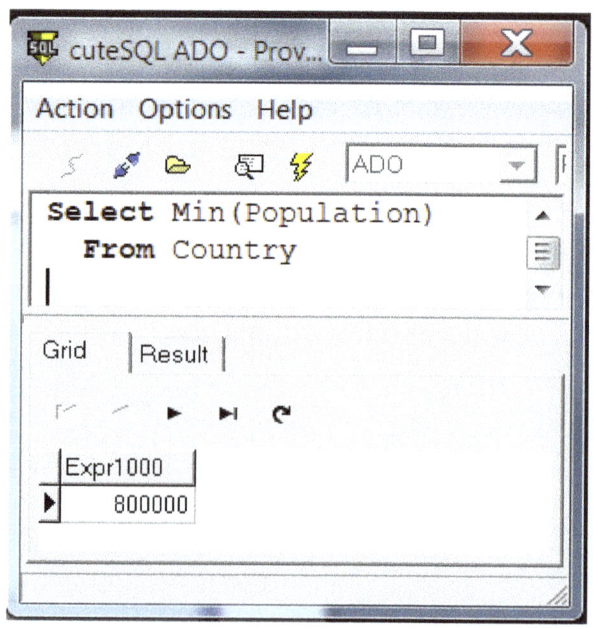

Fig. 62.15 Exercise 10 result

Exercise 11 - *Figure 62.16*

```
Select Sum(Population)
  From Country
```

Returns the result of adding together the population of all the countries in the **Country** table.

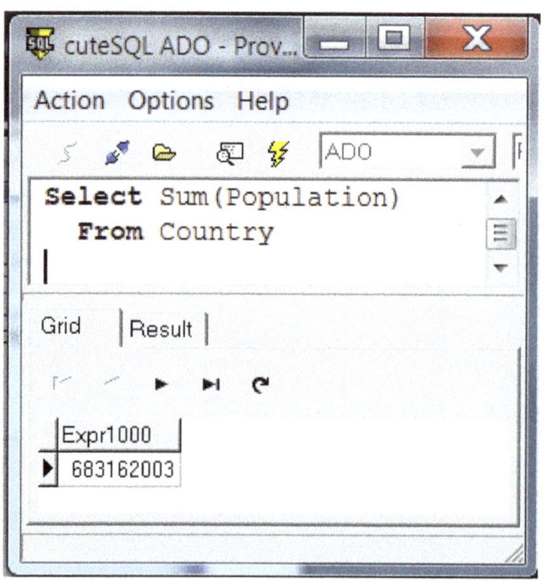

Fig. 62.16 Exercise 11 result

Exercise 12 - *Figure 62.17*

```
Select * From Customer
  Order by Customer.CustNo
```

Figure 62.17 shows a cropped image of the result set for this SQL query. Note that the field reference for the **Order By** clause is **Customer.CustNo**. It is written this way to indicate that field **CustNo** to use is the one belonging to the **Country** table. It is unnecessary to qualify **CustNo** in this way when the query refers to only one table as there is no ambiguity. But we are anticipating the case where more than one table is involved and where **CustNo** appears in each. In this scenario, we must be clear which **CustNo** we are referring to.

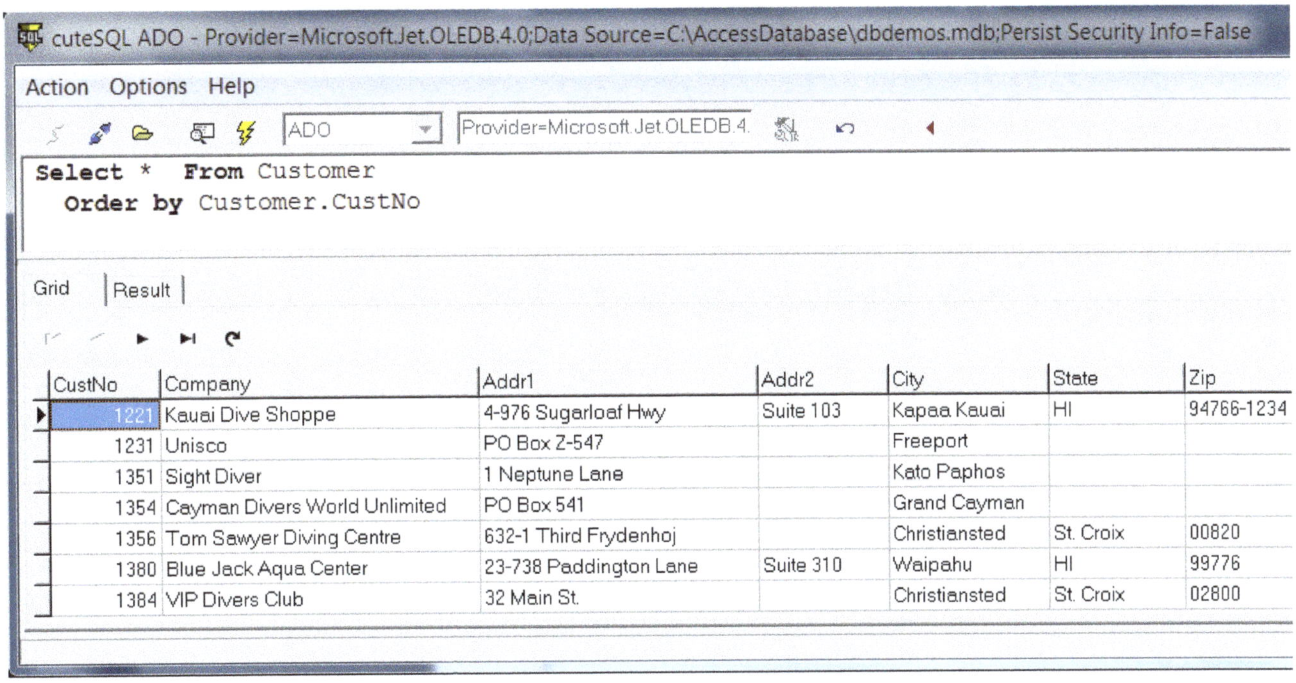

Fig. 62.17 Exercise 12 result set

Exercise 13 - *Figure 62.18*

```
Select * From Orders
  Order by Orders.OrderNo
```

Figure 62.18 shows a cropped image of the result set of this SQL query. The fields of **Orders** table are arranged in ascending numerical order on **OrderNo** field of the **Orders** table.

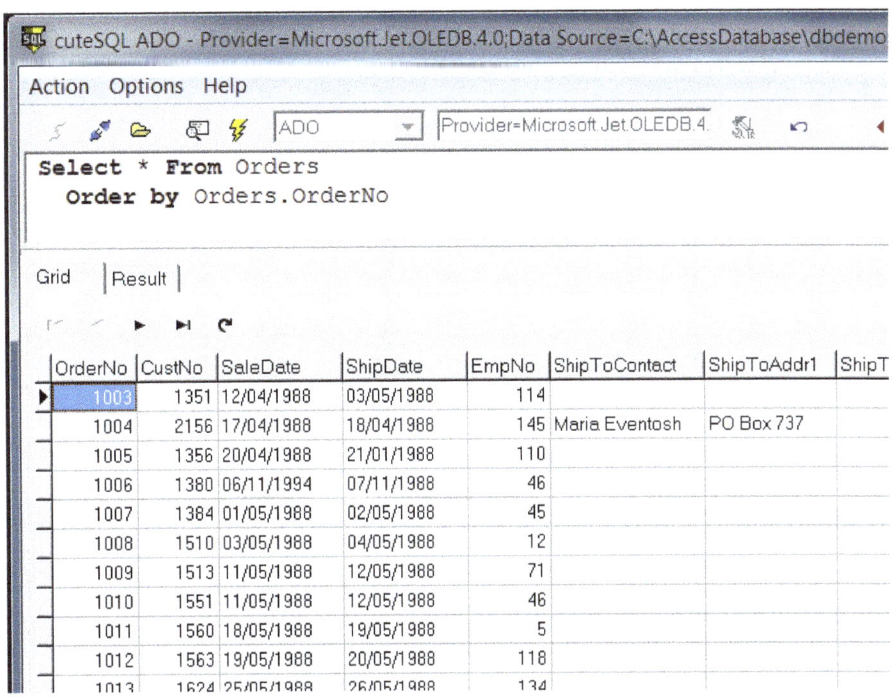

Fig. 62.18 Exercise 13 result set

Exercise 14 - *Figure 62.19*

```
Select Customer.Company, Orders.OrderNo, Customer.OrderNo
  From Customer, Orders
    Where (Orders.CustNo = Customer.CustNo)
      Order By Customer.Company, Orders.OrderNo
```

In this query, the **From Customer, Orders** clause is responsible for joining the rows of **Customer** and **Orders** tables together with **Where (Orders.CustNo = Customer.CustNo)**, i.e. where the **CustNo** in each matches. *Figure 62.19* shows that this is the case. The result set is first ordered in ascending order by **Company** and then for each **Company** value, ordered by **OrderNo**.

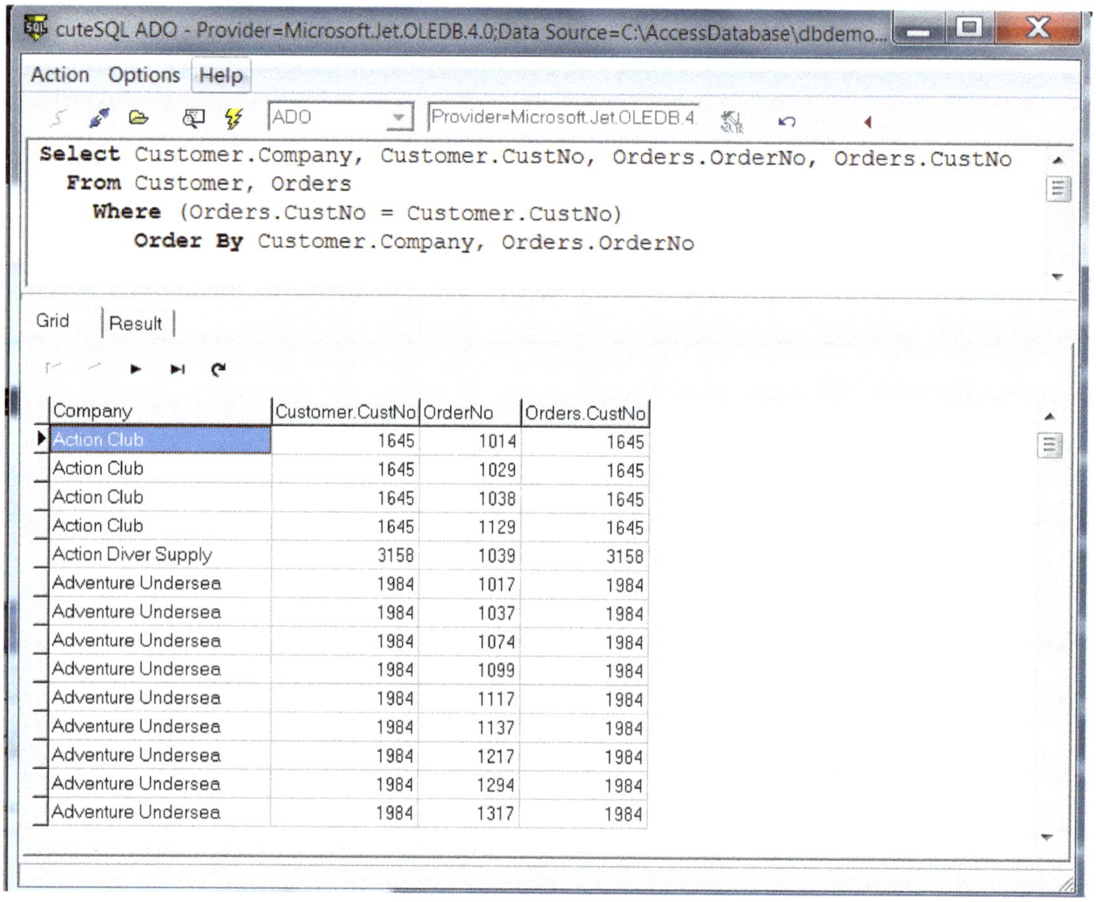

Fig. 62.19 Exercise 14 result set

Exercise 15 - *Figure 62.20*

```
Select Customer.Company
  From Customer, Orders
    Where (Orders.CustNo = Customer.CustNo) And (Orders.OrderNo = 1039)
```

In this query, the **From Customer, Orders** clause is responsible for joining the rows of **Customer** and **Orders** tables together with the Where clause, i.e. where the **CustNo** in each matches and **OrderNo** is the specific value **1039**. *Figure 62.20* shows that this condition is only true for one row with the company name **Action Diver Supply.** This particular field is selected from the matched row by the **Select Customer.Company** clause.

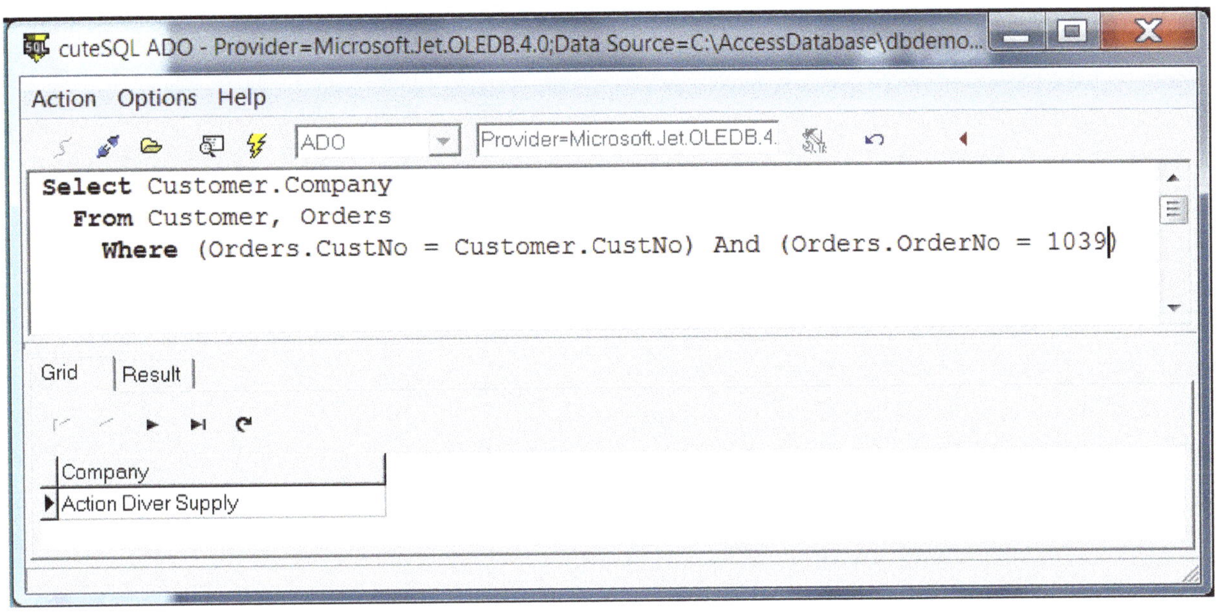

Fig. 62.20 Exercise 15 result set

Exercise 16 - *Figure 62.21*

```
Select Items.OrderNo, Parts.Description
  From Items, Parts
    Where Items.PartNo = Parts.PartNo
      Order By Items.OrderNo
```

Items such as a regulator system, a chisel point knife, etc can appear on a particular order, i.e. an order can be made up of more than one item. The items on a particular order are stored in a separate table **Items** and linked to the **Order** table by the common field **OrderNo**. This SQL query joins the rows of the tables **Items** and **Parts** with matching **PartNo** values and then selects a result set consisting of **OrderNo** and a description of each item on the order. The result set is ordered in ascending order on **OrderNo**.

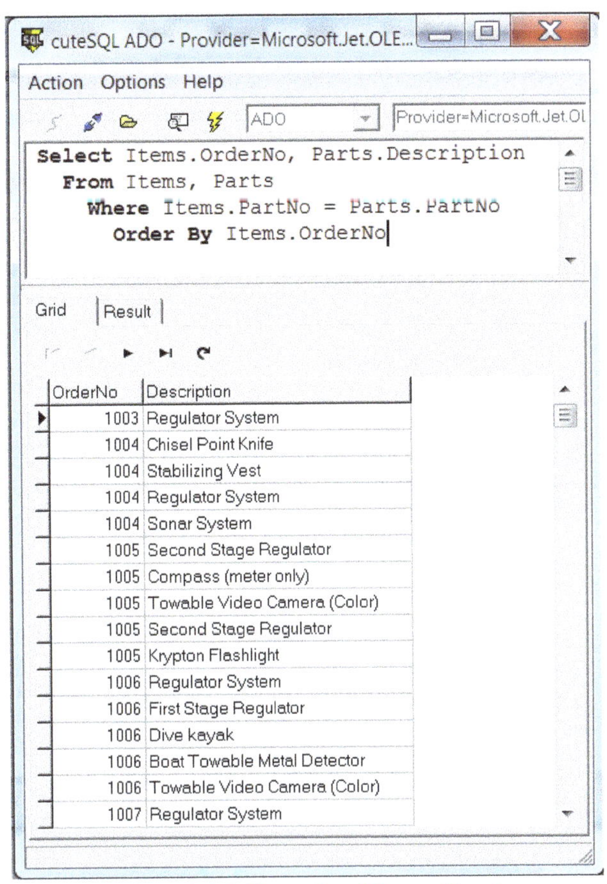

Fig. 62.21 Exercise 16 result set

Exercise 17 - Figure 62.22

```
Select CustNo
  From Orders
    Where Orders.PaymentMethod = 'Visa'
```

In this query, **CustNos** are selected from the table **Orders** where the method of payment is **Visa**. There are **33** rows in the result set shown in *Figure 62.22* but this number includes duplicate **CustNos**. There are actually only **19** unique **CustNos**.

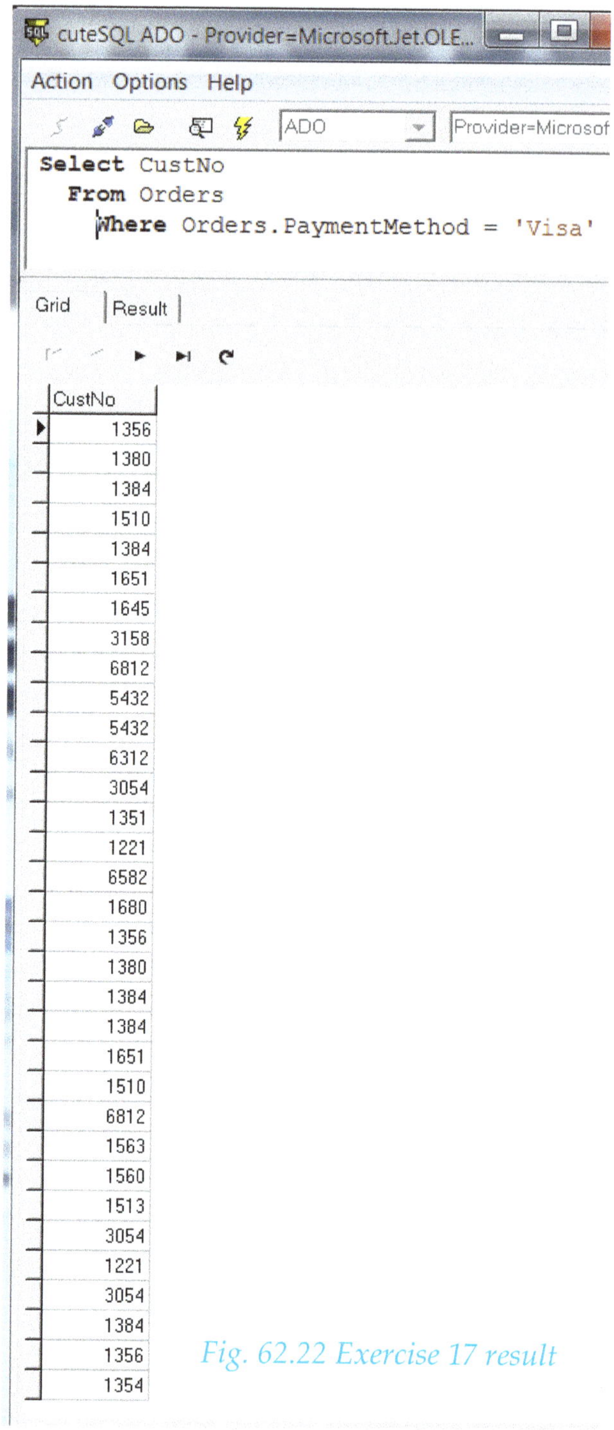

Fig. 62.22 Exercise 17 result

Exercise 18 - Figure 62.23

```
Select Count(*)From Customer
  Where Customer.CustNo
    In (Select CustNo From Orders
          Where Orders.PaymentMethod = 'Visa')
```

The **In** operator tests for membership of the **Select** subquery (Exercise 17) result set, in this query the test is **Customer.CustNo** membership of the subquery result set. Nineteen **CustNos** in the Customer table are present in the subquery result set. These **19** are counted by the **Count(*)** operation with the outcome shown in *Figure 62.23*.

The **In** operator allows allows multiple values to be specified in a **Where** clause. The **In** operator is shorthand for multiple **Or** conditions.

Programming Tasks

1. Change **Orders.PaymentMethod** to '**Credit**'. Compare result with original query. How many rows are there in the subquery result set?
2. Change **Select Count(*)** to **Select Customer.Company** and run queries with '**Credit**' and then'**Visa**' for **PaymentMethod**.

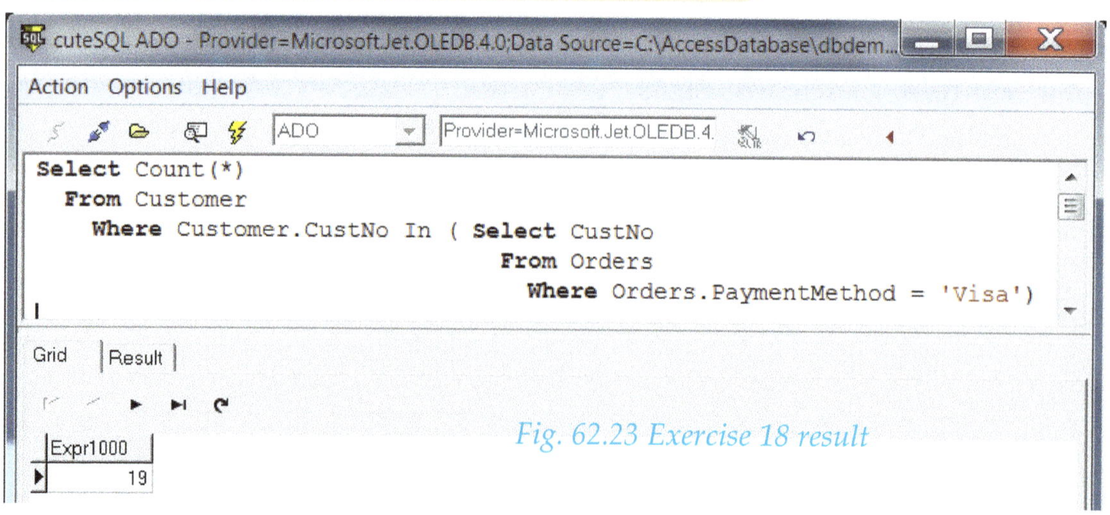

Fig. 62.23 Exercise 18 result

Programming Tasks

3. Write a query which returns OrderNo, CustNo and Company where OrderNo = 1003.

4. Write a query which returns OrderNo, Company, PartNo and Description where OrderNo = 1004.

Exercise 19 - *Figure 62.24*

```
Select Country.Name From Country Where Country.Population
  In (Select Max(Country.Population)
            From Country)
```

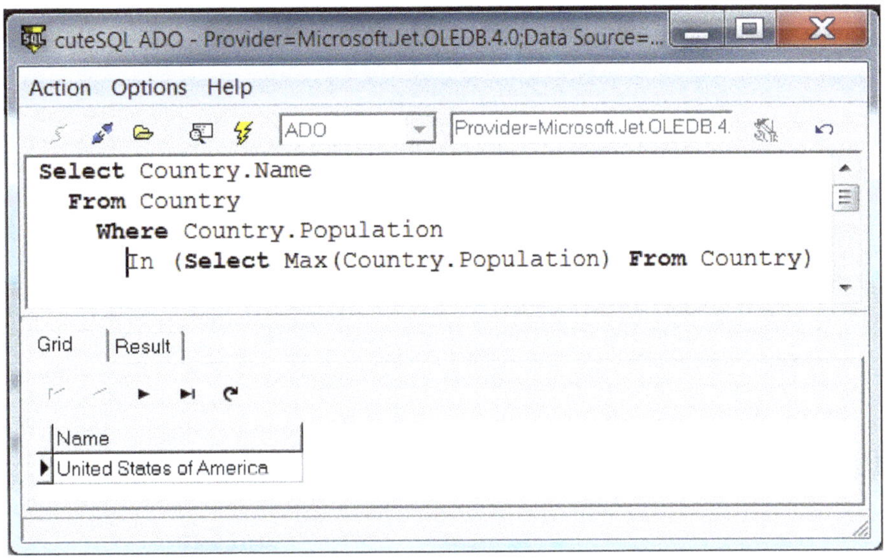

Fig. 62.24 Exercise 19 result

The subquery **Select Max...** returns a single result which is the largest population value amongst countries in the **Country** table. The query then selects the country name whose population value is equal to the subquery's returned result, i.e. **United States of America**.

Since a single result is returned the **In** operator can be replaced by the **=** operator as follows

```
Select Country.Name
  From Country
    Where Country.Population = (Select Max(Country.Population) From Country)
```

Exercise 20 - *Figure 62.25*

```
Select Orders.OrderNo
  From Orders
    Where Orders.SaleDate < #20/04/1988#
```

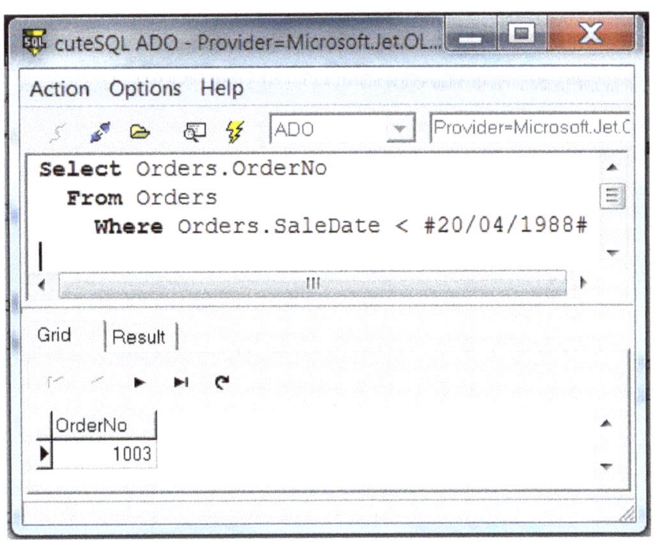

Fig. 62.25 Exercise 20 result

This query selects order numbers form the **Orders** table where the date of sale occurs before **20/4/1988**.
The date literal value **20/4/1988** has to be delimited and in this example the special character **#** is used.

Exercise 21 - *Figure 62.26*

```
Select Orders.OrderNo, Items.ItemNo
  From Orders INNER JOIN Items
    On Orders.OrderNo = Items.OrderNo
```

This query uses a different way of joining two tables together using matching values of a common field. This is called an inner join.

Exercise 22 - *Figure 62.27*

```
Select Items.OrderNo, Items.ItemNo,
         Items.PartNo
  From Items Where Items.PartNo
    In (Select Parts.PartNo From Parts
         Where Parts.Description =
           'Dive kayak')
```

In this query, the subquery returns a single result which is the **PartNo** for a part with description **Dive Kayak**. This has value **900**. The query then returns a result set of all orders that feature this part number. The = sign could have been used instead of the **In** operator but the latter was chosen so that Not could be demonstrated in the next exercise.

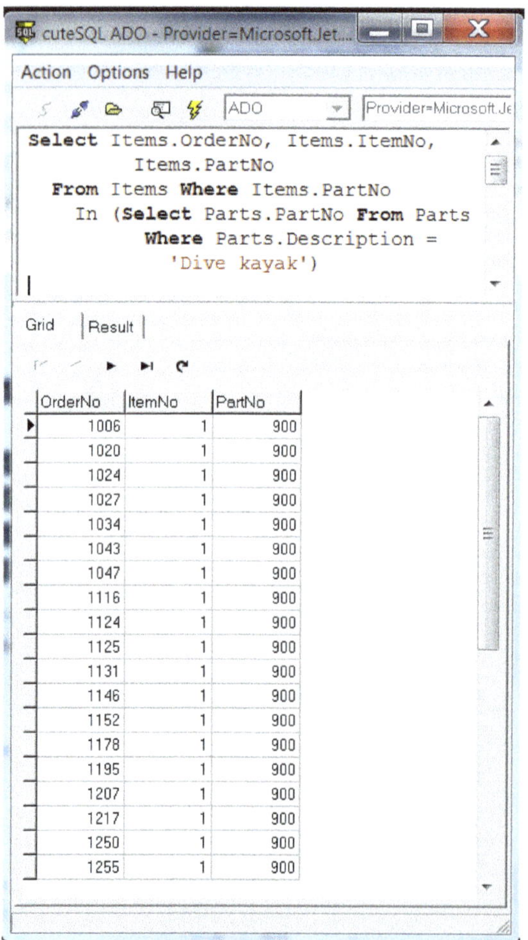

OrderNo	ItemNo	PartNo
1006	1	900
1020	1	900
1024	1	900
1027	1	900
1034	1	900
1043	1	900
1047	1	900
1116	1	900
1124	1	900
1125	1	900
1131	1	900
1146	1	900
1152	1	900
1178	1	900
1195	1	900
1207	1	900
1217	1	900
1250	1	900
1255	1	900

Fig. 62.27 Exercise 22 result set

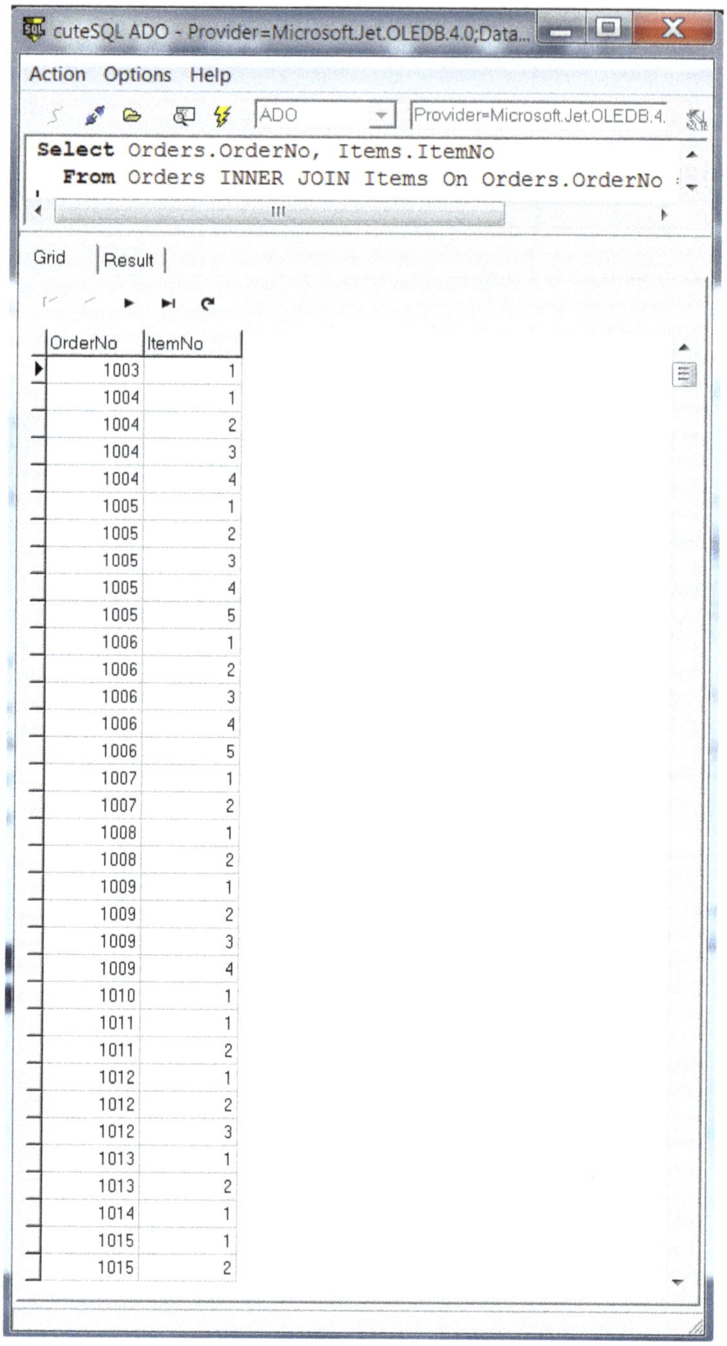

OrderNo	ItemNo
1003	1
1004	1
1004	2
1004	3
1004	4
1005	1
1005	2
1005	3
1005	4
1005	5
1006	1
1006	2
1006	3
1006	4
1006	5
1007	1
1007	2
1008	1
1008	2
1009	1
1009	2
1009	3
1009	4
1010	1
1011	1
1011	2
1012	1
1012	2
1012	3
1013	1
1013	2
1014	1
1015	1
1015	2

Fig. 62.26 Exercise 21 result set

Exercise 23

```
Select Items.OrderNo, Items.ItemNo, Items.PartNo
   From Items
    Where Items.PartNo
      Not In (
        Select Parts.PartNo From Parts
          Where Parts.Description = 'Dive Kayak')
```

This query selects every item whose **PartNo** value is not 900.

Exercise 24

```
Select * From Orders Where SaleDate > Date()
```

This query selects all rows of the **Orders** table where the **SaleDate** field value is after the current date returned by **Date()**.

Exercise 25

```
Select * From Orders Where SaleDate < Date()
```

This query selects all rows of the **Orders** table where the **SaleDate** field value is before the current date returned by **Date()**.

Exercise 26 - *Figure 62.28*

```
Select * From Employee Where EmpNo Between 6 And 10
```

This query selects all rows of the **Employee** table with **EmpNo** in the range **6** to **10** inclusive, i.e. 6 or 7 or 8 or 9 or 10.

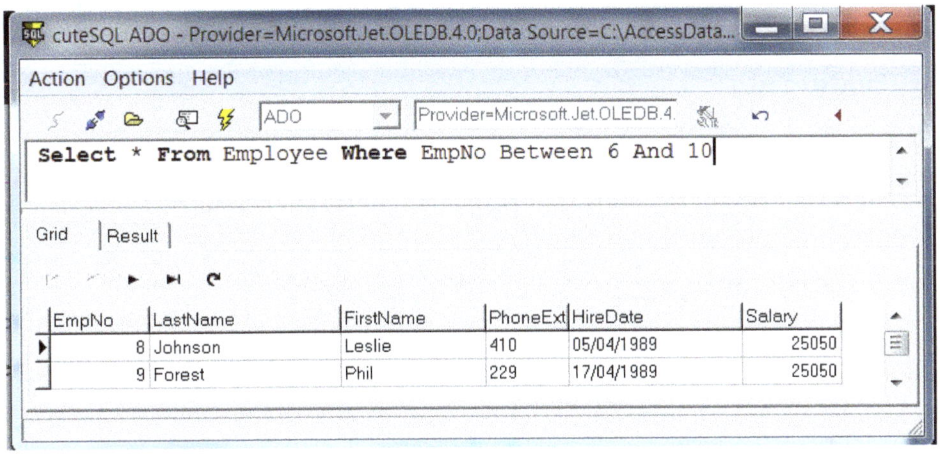

Fig. 62.28 Exercise 26 result set

Fig. 62.29 Exercise 27 result set

Exercise 27 - *Figure 62.29*

```
Select EmpNo From Orders Order By EmpNo
```

This query selects the value of the **EmpNo** field from each row of the **Orders** table, ordering the results set in ascending order on **EmpNo**. *Figure 62.29* shows the first part of the result set which contains **208** rows.

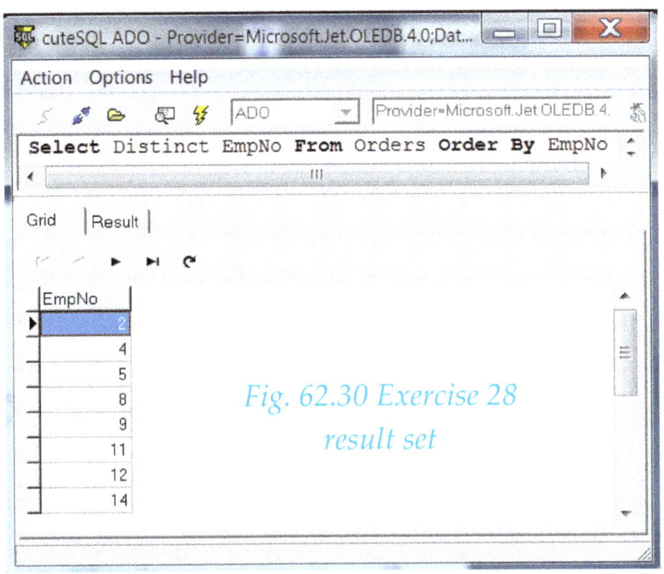

Fig. 62.30 Exercise 28 result set

Exercise 28 - *Figure 62.30*

```
Select Distinct EmpNo From Orders
  Order By EmpNo
```

This query selects the value of the **EmpNo** field from each row of the **Orders** table, eliminating duplicate values before ordering the results set in ascending order on **EmpNo**.

Exercise 29 - *Figure 62.31*

```
Select Distinct EmpNo
  From Orders
    Where EmpNo In (1,2,3,4)
      Order By EmpNo
```

This query subsets the returned result set by restricting **EmpNo** to the values in the set consisting of members 1, 2, 3 and 4.

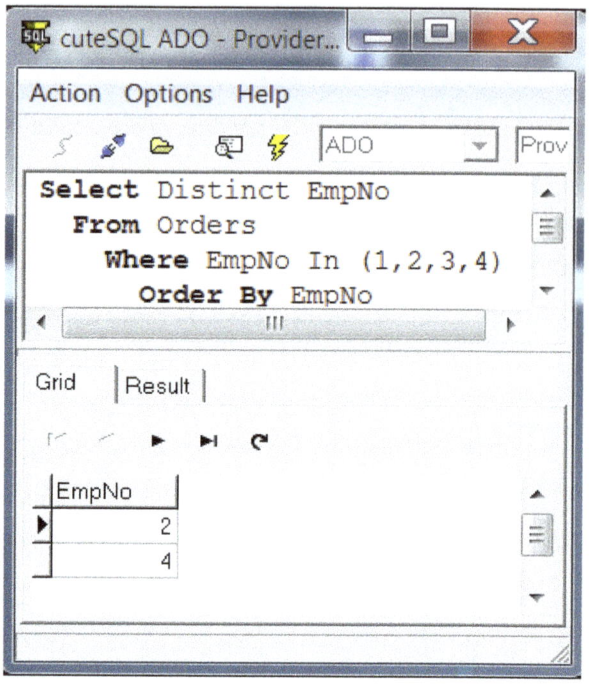

Fig. 62.31 Exercise 29 result set

Exercise 30 - *Figure 62.32*

```
Select EmpNo, OrderNo, SaleDate
  From Orders
    Where SaleDate < #3/1/1989#
      Group By EmpNo, OrderNo, SaleDate
```

This query groups the results together by **EmpNo** and the corresponding **OrderNo** and **SaleDate** where **SaleDate** is before **3/1/1989** as shown in *Figure 62.32*. *Figure 62.32* shows only the first part of the result set.

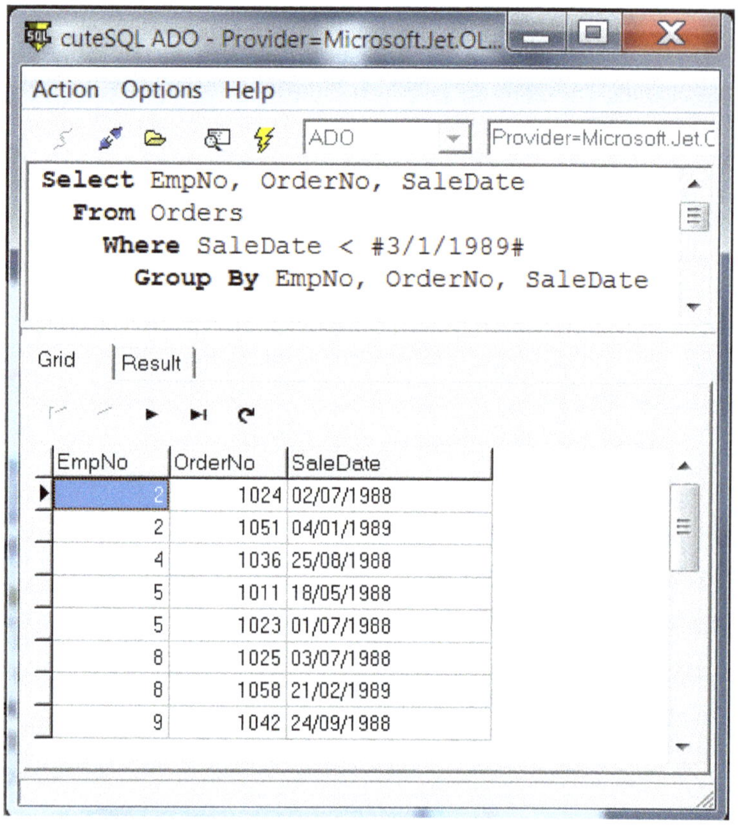

Fig. 62.32 Exercise 30 result set

63 Introduction to Interbase

Using Interbase 2017

Purpose: To learn how to create an Interbase 2017 database

Using Interbase Server Manager

Launch Interbase Server Manager from the Start Menu Embarcadero Interbase 2017 program group- *Figure 63.1*.

Make sure that the *Run the Interbase server as a Windows service* option is selected as shown in *Figure 63.2*.

Make sure that Interbase Server 2017 is shown running - *Figure 63.2* - click on the Start button if not. This is a local server running on the computer from which it was launched.

Figure 63.3 shows that Interbase 2017 Guardian and Interbase Server are started as expected. These two services run together on the local machine. The Guardian process monitors the uptime of the Interbase server.

Fig. 63.1 Start Menu Embarcadero Interbase 2017

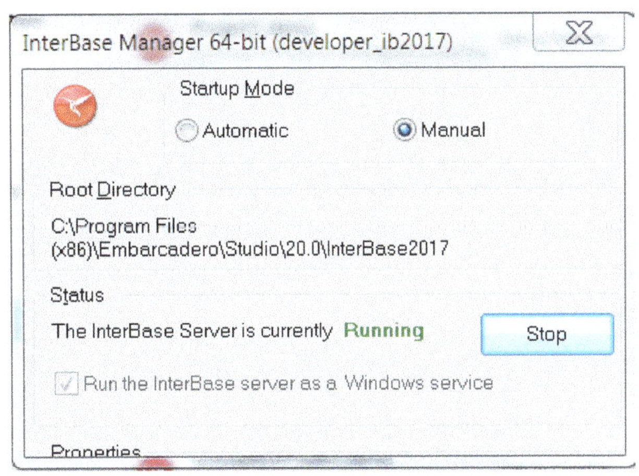

Fig. 63.2 Embarcadero Server Manager 64-bit 2017

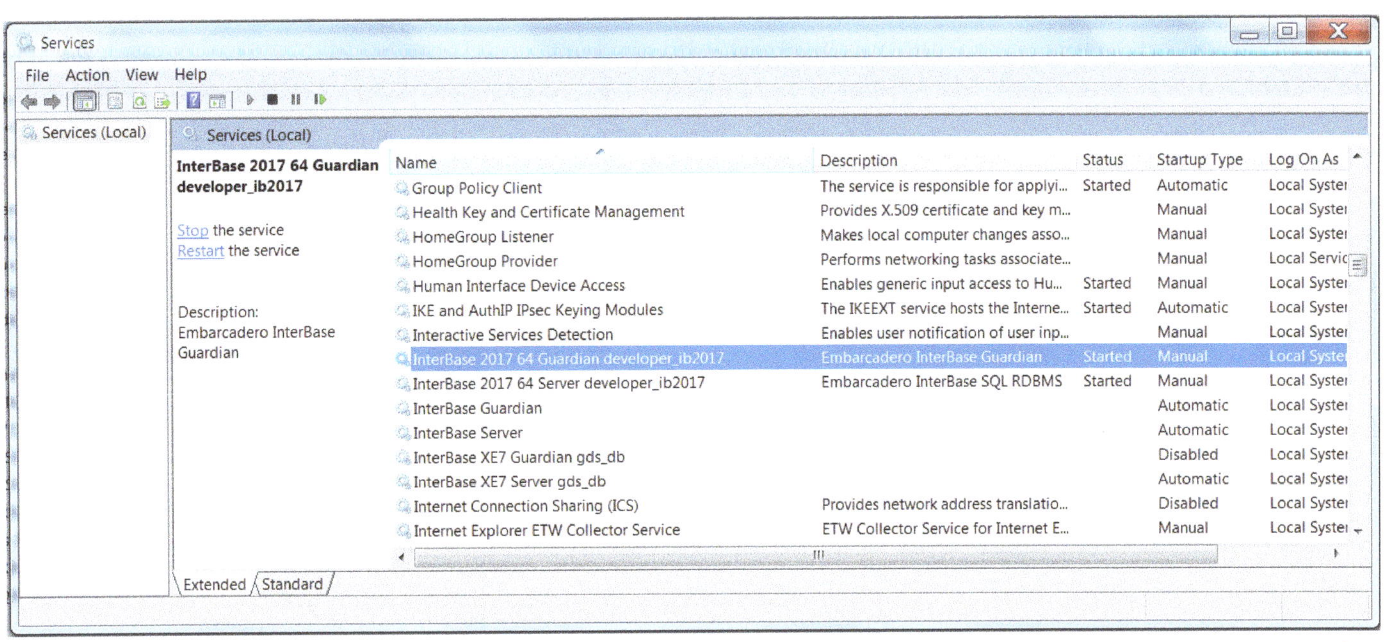

Fig. 63.3 Windows Services showing that Interbase 2017 Guardian and Interbase 2017 server are started

Creating and registering a database on the server

Interbase databases are accessed through an Interbase server. Before this can happen, a database must exist and be registered with the server.

Launch IBConsole from the Start Menu - *Figure 63.1*.

Select LocalServer - developer_ib2017 (or if not available, LocalServer - gds_db) shown in *Figure 63.4* then **click** Server in the toolbar to bring down the menu shown in *Figure 63.5*. It is also possible to to do this by right clicking LocalServer - developer_ib2017 (or LocalServer - gds_db)in the upper left pane.

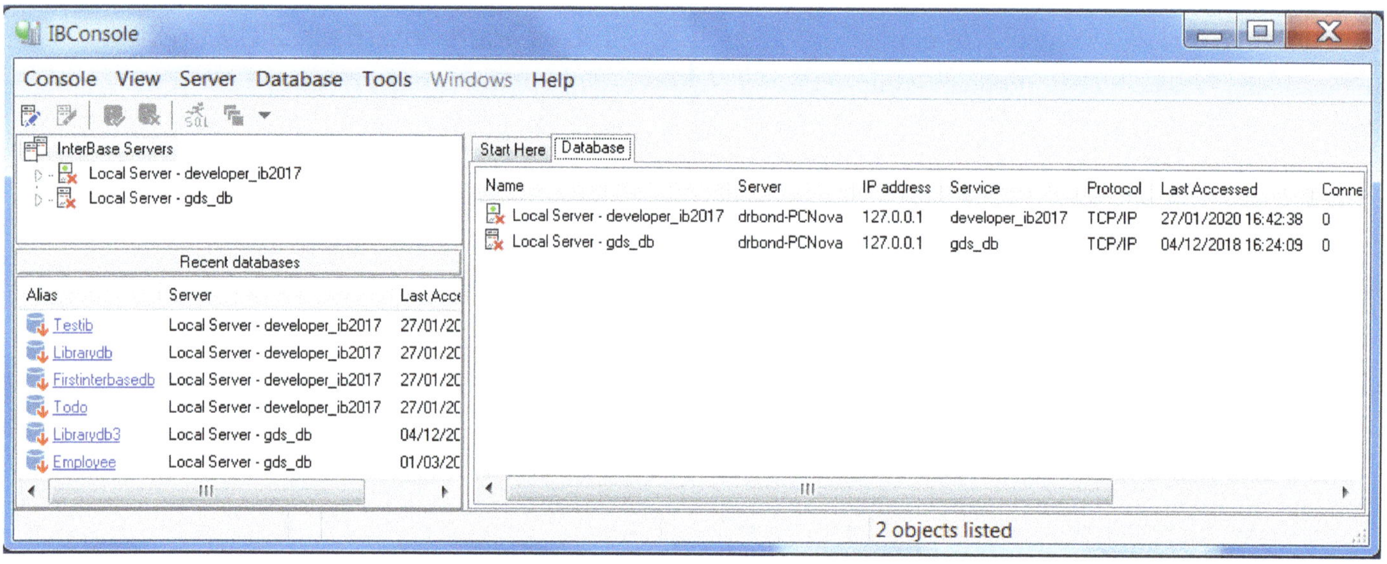

Fig. 63.4 IBConsole showing two available servers, developer_ib2017 and gds_db

Click Login to launch the Server Login window - *Figure 61.6*.

Enter the Database Administrator's User Name, `SYSDBA`, and the administator's Password, `masterkey`, then **click** the Login button.

Figure 63.7 shows that the developer_ib2017 local server is now active.

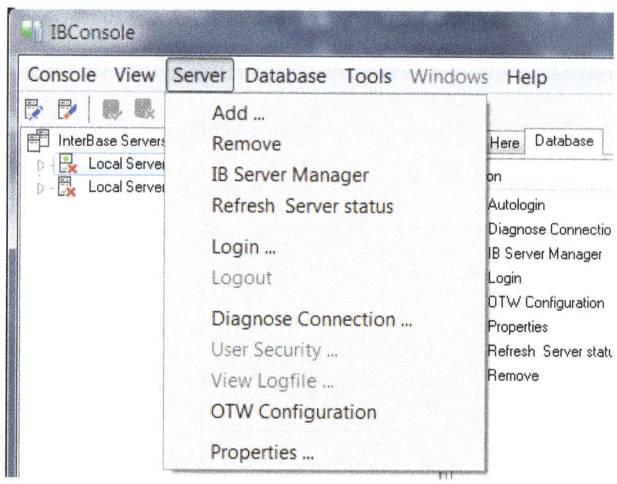

Fig. 63.5 Server dropdown menu

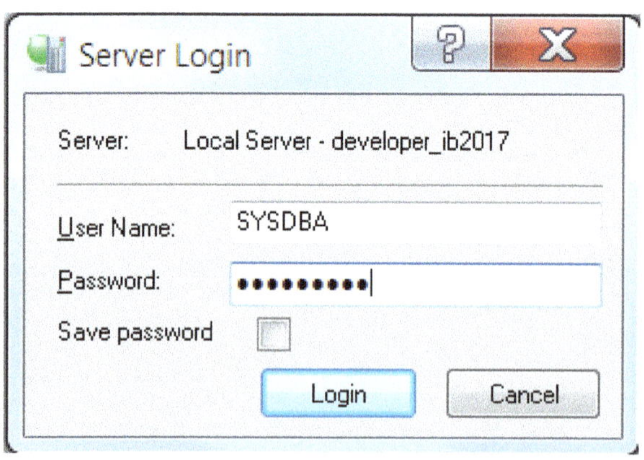

Fig. 63.6 Server login

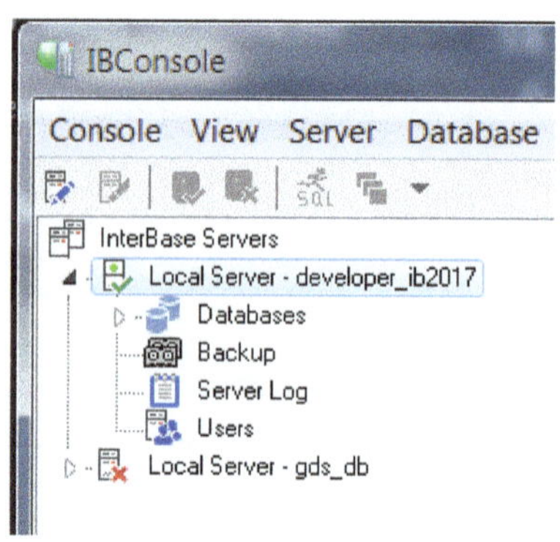

Fig. 63.7 Logged in to local server

Click Database in the toolbar to bring down the menu shown in *Figure 63.8*.

Click Create Database to bring up the Create Database window shown in *Figure 63.9*. Alternatively, if the required database exists already then **click** Add instead.

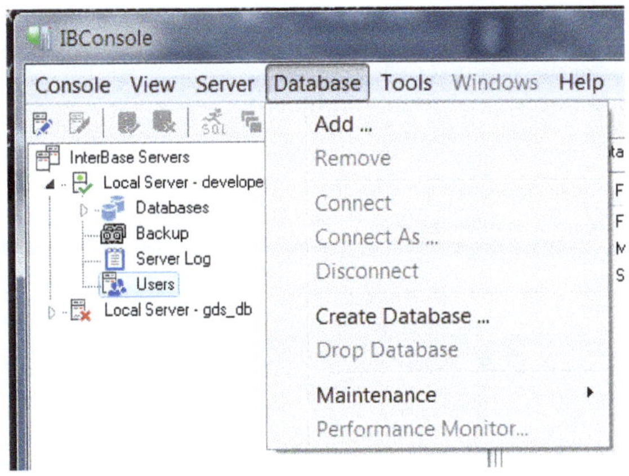

Fig. 63.8 Database dropdown menu

Databases must be created on the same drive as Interbase server e.g. the C: drive.

Click on the ellipsis (...) button in the Create Database window to bring up the Specify Database window shown in *Figure 63.10*.

Navigate to the folder/subfolder on the local drive in which to create the database. **Type** a suitable filename for this database.

For this exercise the folder path is `C:\Users\drbond` and the chosen filename is `TestDB` - *Figure 63.11*.

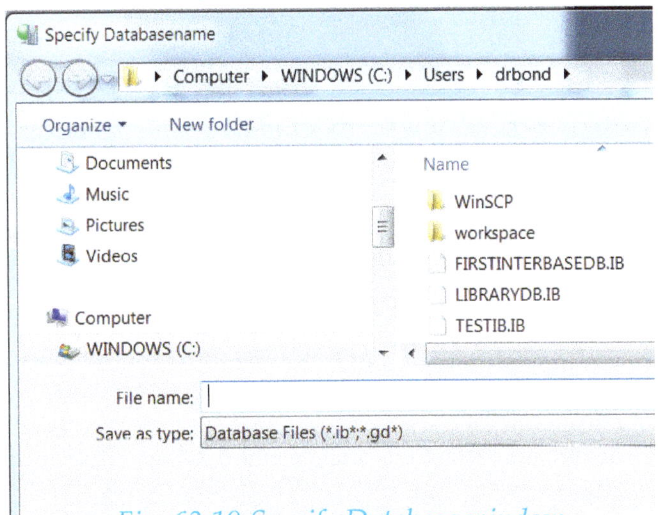

Fig. 63.10 Specify Database window

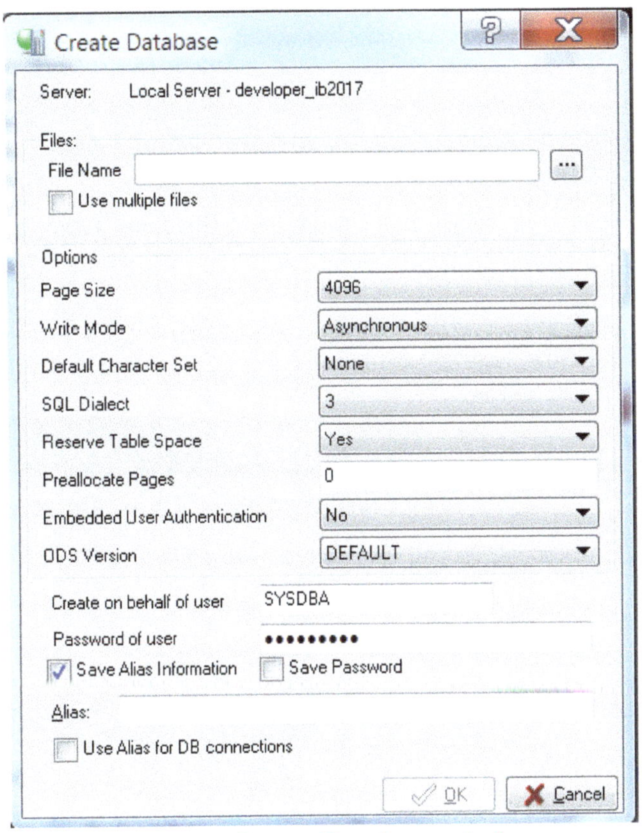

Fig. 63.9 Create Database window

Set the Alias field to `MyFirstDatabase` and ensure that the Save Alias information and the Use Alias for DB Connections boxes are ticked. In the next chapter we will use this alias to make a connection to the TestDB database from a Delphi program.

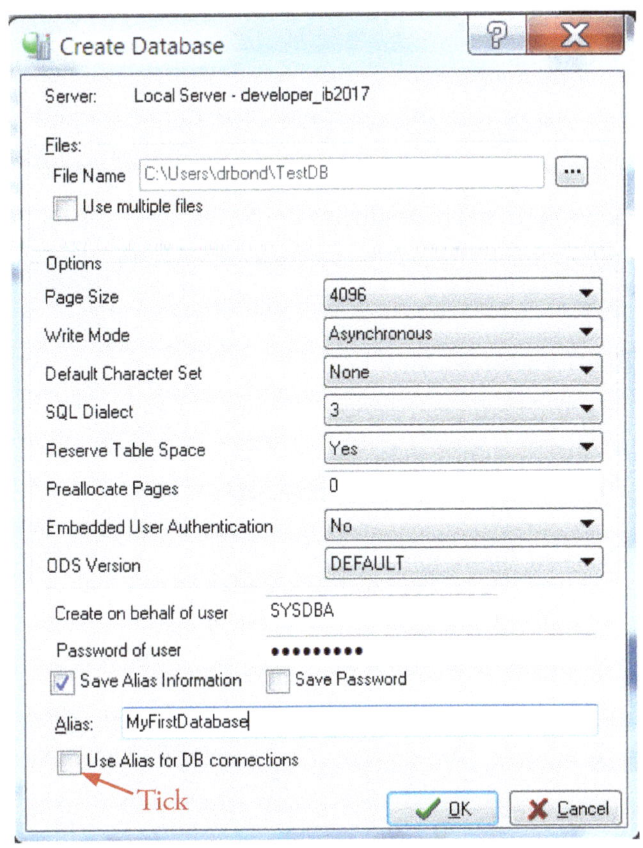

Fig. 63.11 Specify Database window with set up data

Click OK to bring up the Database Connect Window shown in *Figure 63.12*. Make sure that Use DBAliasname box is ticked.

Enter the password `masterkey` and click Connect.

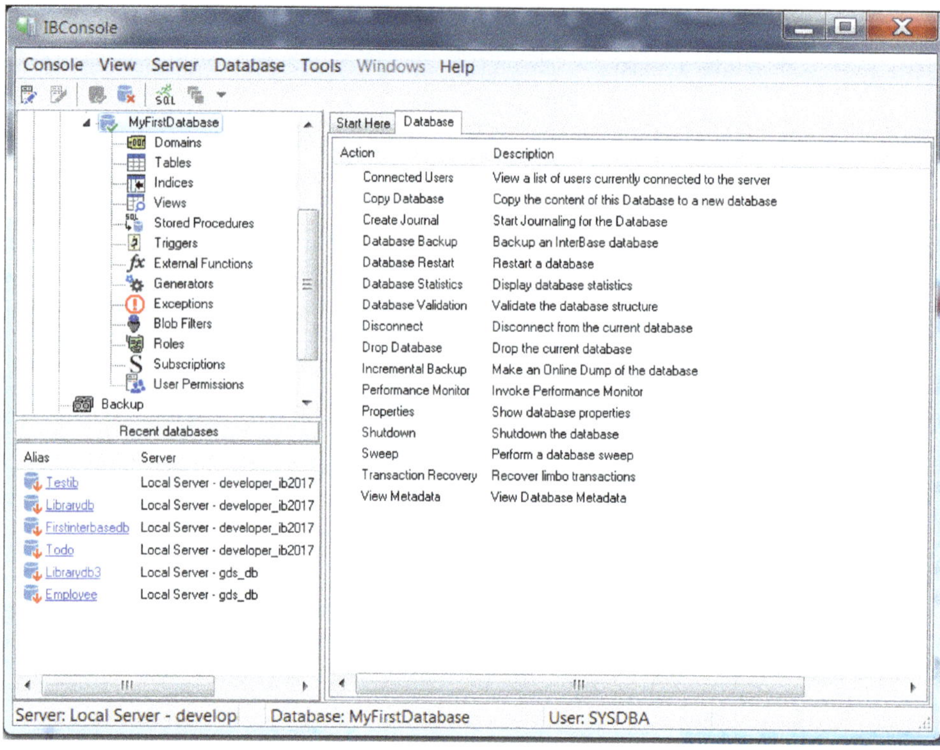

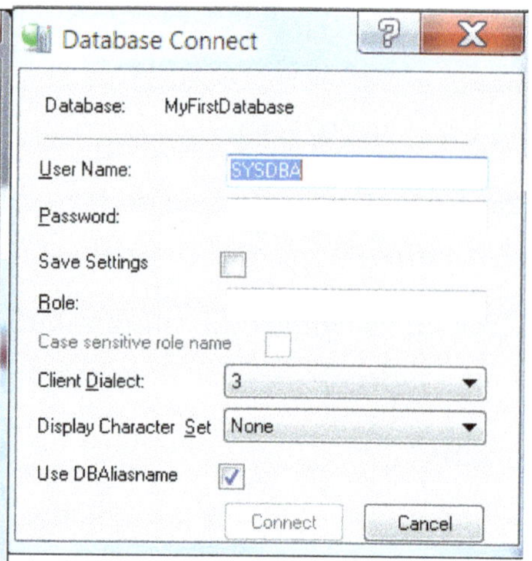

Fig. 63.12 Database Connect window for MyFirstDatabase

Fig. 63.13 MyFirstDatabase registered and connected to the local Interbase server

This action creates the database `TestDB` with alias `MyFirstDatabase`, registers it on the local Interbase server as shown in *Figure 63.13* and connects to it.

Creating a table

An Interbase database is a relational database. Relational databases are based on tables which `TestDB` does not yet possess. The next task, therefore, is to create at least one table.

Make sure that `TestDB`/`MyFirstDatabase` is connected and highlighted as shown in *Figure 63.13*.

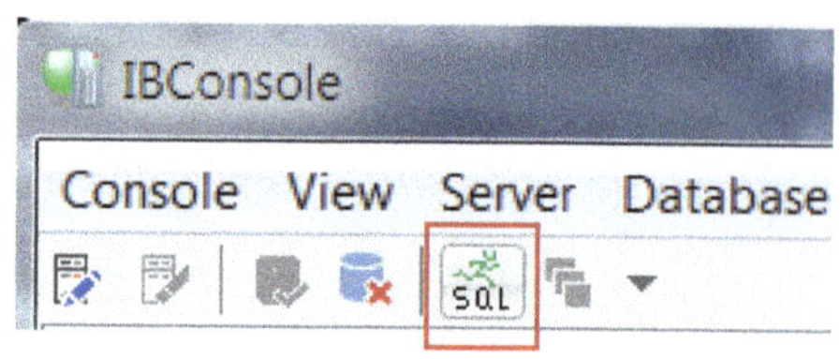

Fig. 63.14 SQL option

Click on the icon SQL in the toolbar ribbon - *Figure 63.14* - to bring up the InteractiveSQL(ISQL) window as shown in *Figure 63.15*.

Click Query in the toolbar to bring down the menu shown *Figure 63.16*.

Click Load Script and locate and load DDL script `TestDB.sql` into ISQL as shown in *Figure 63.17*.

DDL is an acronym for Data Definition Language.

To create the table **Student** we must execute this script.

Click the Execute Query icon shown in *Figure 63.18*.

This creates the **Student** table.

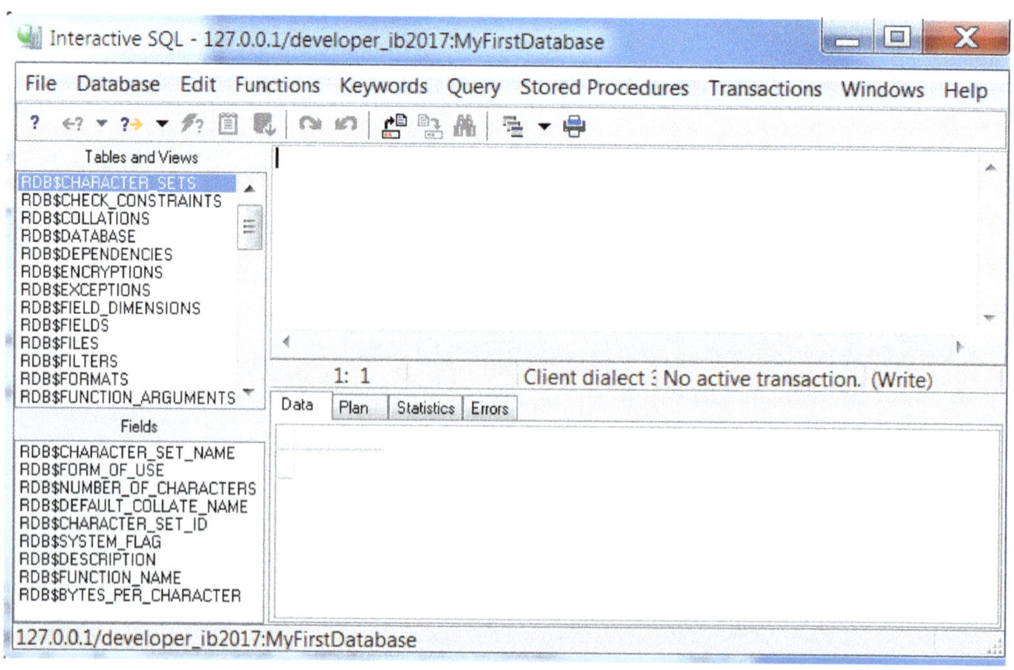

Fig. 63.15 Interactive SQL Window

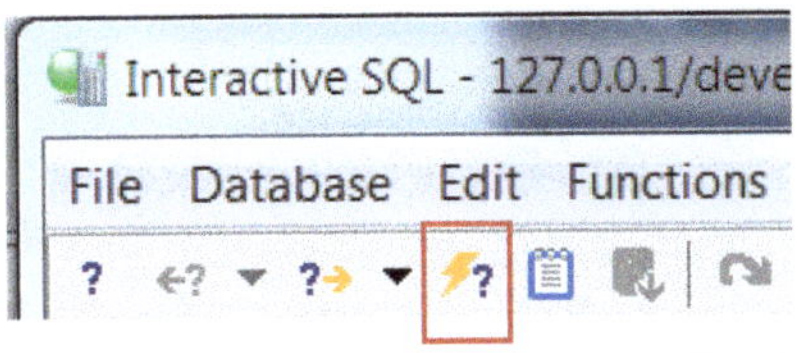

Fig. 63.18 Execute Query (F5)

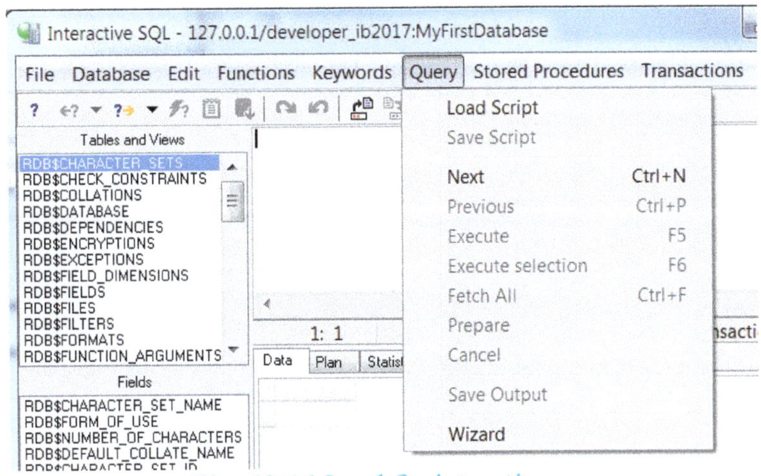

Fig. 63.16 Load Script option

Scroll down to locate the **Student** table row as shown in *Figure 63.19*.

Double click on `Student` in this row to bring up a second window and its **Properties** page as shown in *Figure 63.19*.

Click on the **Data tab** to bring up the page shown in *Figure 63.20*.

We can use this page to populate the database `TestDB`/`MyFirstDatabase` with data.

Replace the **<null>** fields with `1`, `Bond`, `Kevin`, respectively as shown in *Figure 63.21*, then **click** the insert record icon **+**. to insert the record into table `Student` - *Figure 63.22*.

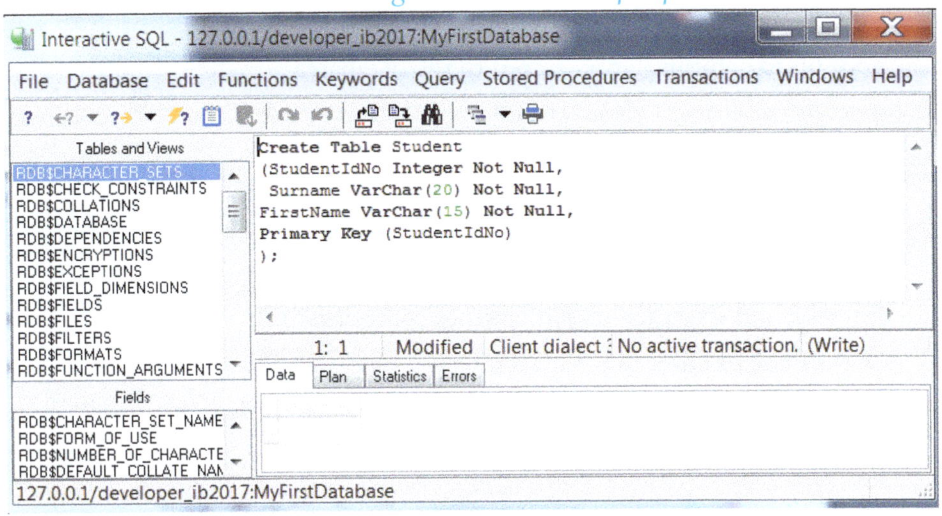

Fig. 63.17 DDL Script TestDB.sql loaded into Interactive SQL

More records can be inserted using this method or we can use the **Interactive SQL** window and a method based on the SQL **Insert** statement.

Before we do we must commit the changes made to the database, in particular the changes to table `Student`.

Close the **Properties** page.

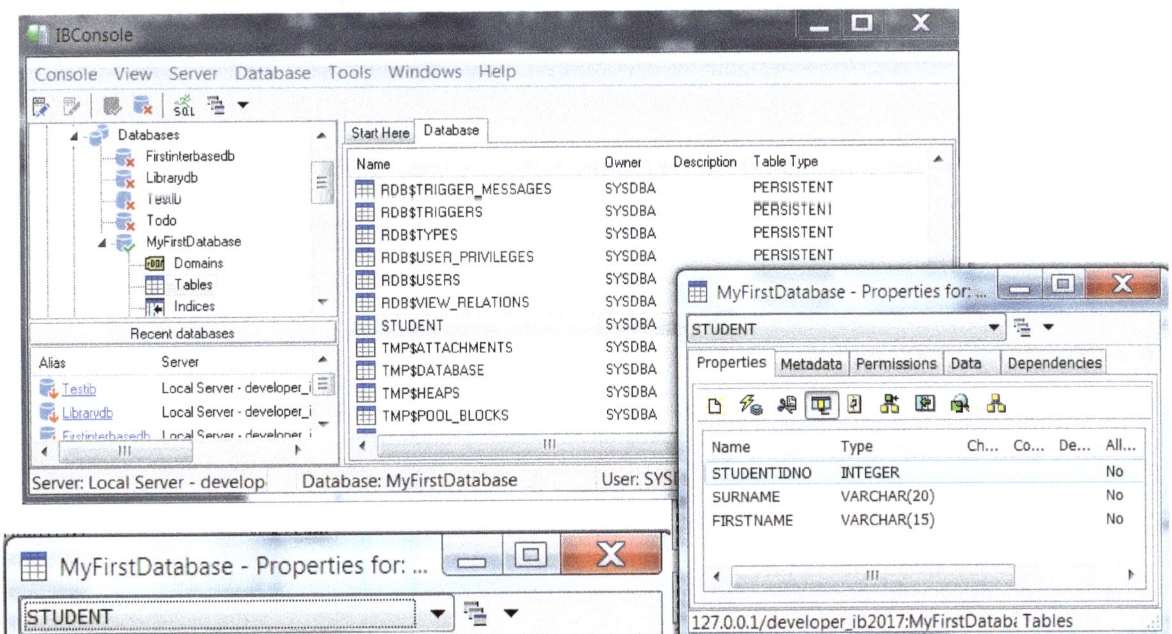

Fig. 63.19 Table Student

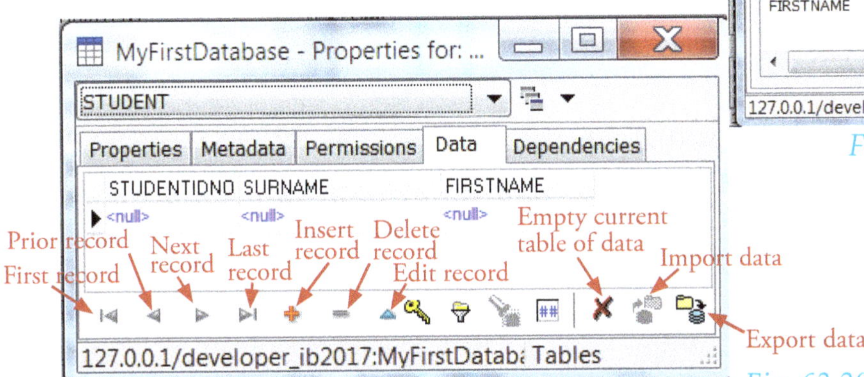

Fig. 63.20 Data page for table Student

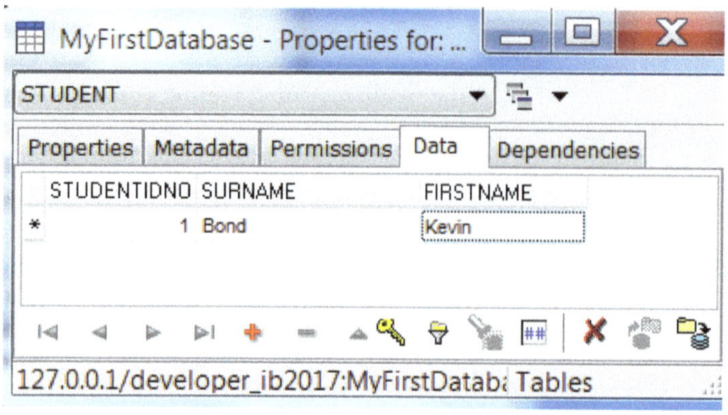

Fig. 63.21 Preparing a student record for insertion into table Student

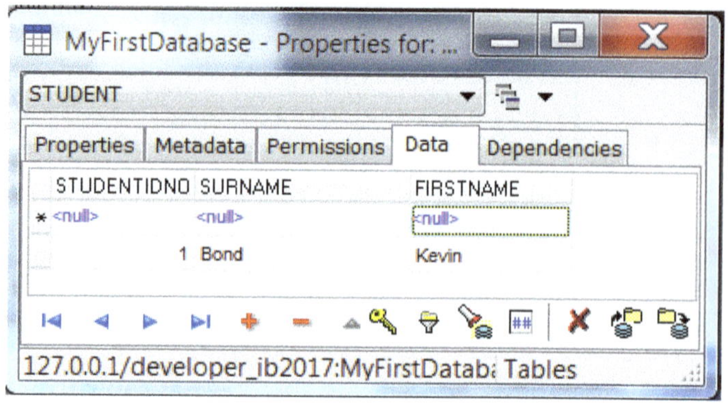

Fig. 63.22 Student record for Bond inserted into table Student

Click the **Yes** button on the **Commit/Rollback** window that pops up to commit `Bond`'s record to the database, permanently. Inserting a record into the database is a two stage process:

1. The first stage inserts the record into the database temporarily;
2. In the second stage, the record is either committed to the database in order to make its insertion permanent or it is removed from the database by rolling back the transaction.

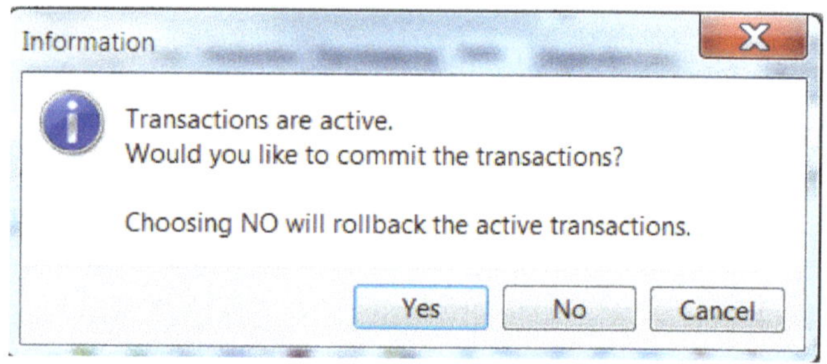

Fig. 63.23 Commit/Rollback window

A transaction is an indivisible unit of work which in this case consists of the two stages just described, an action such as **Insert** record followed by **Commit** or **Rollback**.

The second stage is important because errors can arise when making changes to a database which if ignored can leave a database in an inconsistent state.

Figure 63.20 shows only a part of the data page's toolbar. The expanded window of this page - *Figure 63.24* - shows a button, `Commit & Refresh`, that can be used to commit transactions and refresh the data displayed.

Fig. 63.24 Data page's toolbar options

Using SQL to insert records

Data can also be added to a table of a database using SQL. *Figure 63.25* shows an **Insert** statement that when executed inserts a record with the values `2`, '`Bloggs`', '`Fred`' for fields `StudentIDNo`, `Surname` and `Firstname`, respectively, into table `Student`.

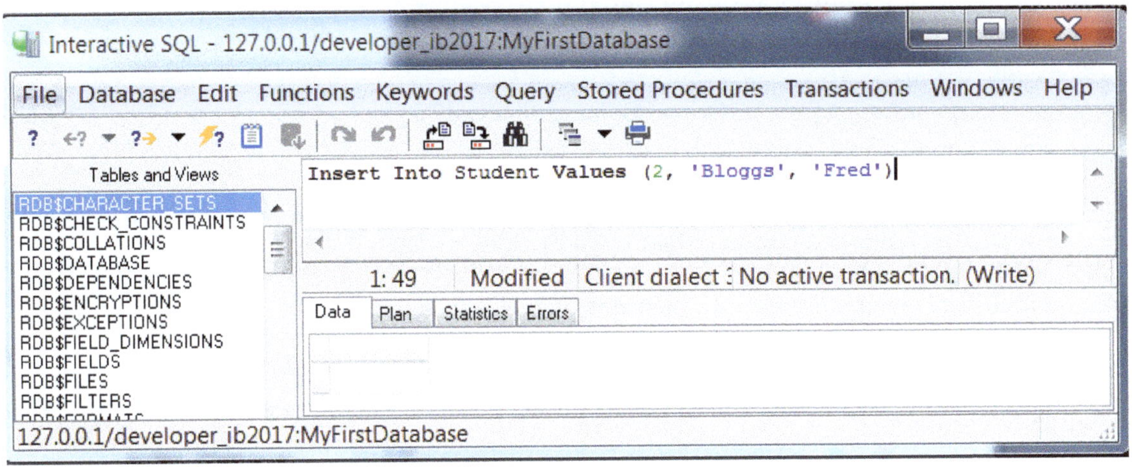

Fig. 63.25 Insert operation

Launch Interactive SQL within IBConsole.

Enter the **Insert** statement as shown in *Figure 63.25* into Interactive SQL.

Click the **Execute Query** icon to execute the **Insert** statement.

Click the **Commit Work** icon to commit the new record to the database.

We can use an SQL Select statement to check that the record has indeed been added to the database.

Enter `Select * From Student` into **Interactive SQL**:

Click the **Execute Query** icon to execute the query.

The Select statement in the upper pane disappears and the result set returned is displayed in the lower pane of the **ISQL** window as shown in *Figure 63.26*.

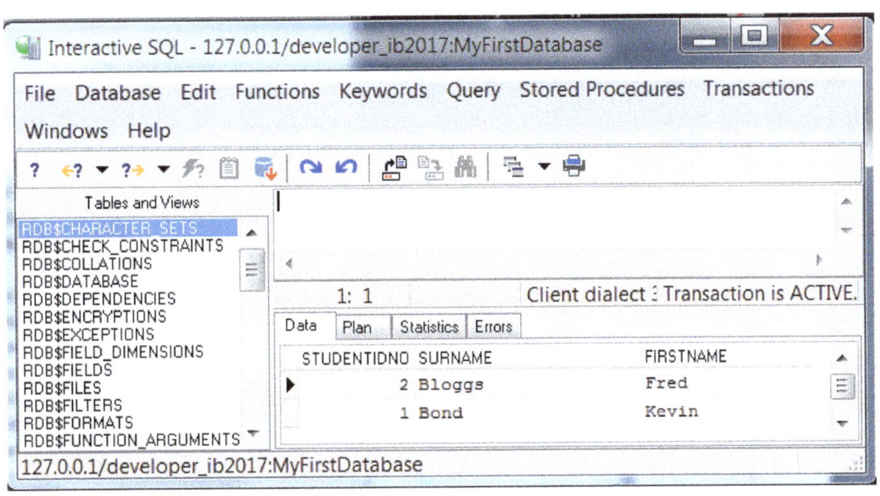

*Fig. 63.26 Result set from Select * From Student operation*

Generators

In Interbase, if we want a numeric field to automatically increment its value by a fixed amount each time a record is inserted we have to rely on a generator. A generator is a mechanism that creates a unique, sequential number each time it is called upon. A generator applies to the whole database.

A generator is typically used for a primary key field, e.g. `StudentIDNo`.

In Interbase, a generator is created with the statement

Create Generator *name*;

e.g. **Create Generator** `StudentIDNo_Gen`;

When using Interactive SQL we haven't needed to use a semicolon at the end of an SQL/DDL statement on the occasions where only a single statement has been executed. However, it is good practice to use a semicolon. Semicolons are essential if we are executing more than one SQL/DDL statement.

Create Generator declares a generator with the specified name to the database and sets its starting value to zero (the default). If a starting value other than 0 is required then another DDL statement, **Set Generator**, must be used, e.g.

Set Generator `StudentIDNo_Gen` **To** 1000;

Set Generator sets a starting value for a newly created generator, or resets the value of an existing generator. The new value for the generator can be an integer from 2^{63} to 2^{63} -1.

Once a generator has been created, it exists within the database waiting to generate numbers.

It relies on a function call, **Gen_ID**(), to generate a new sequential number, e.g.

Gen_ID(`StudentIDNo_Gen`, 1)

The syntax of this call is

Gen_ID(*NameOfGenerator*, *Step*)

Step defines the amount by which the current value should be incremented (or decremented)

Figure 63.27 shows the DDL statements which create a generator and set its starting value to 2.

The value 2 has been chosen as the starting value because this generator will be used to insert new records into table `Student` and this table already has a record with primary key 2.

Figure 63.28 shows the use of the **Gen_ID**() function in an **Insert** statement. The function call to **Gen_ID** returns the current value of the generator `StudentIDNo_Gen` + the step value 1, i.e. 2 + 1 = 3. The **Insert** statement uses this value for its first field whilst the generator updates its current value to 3.

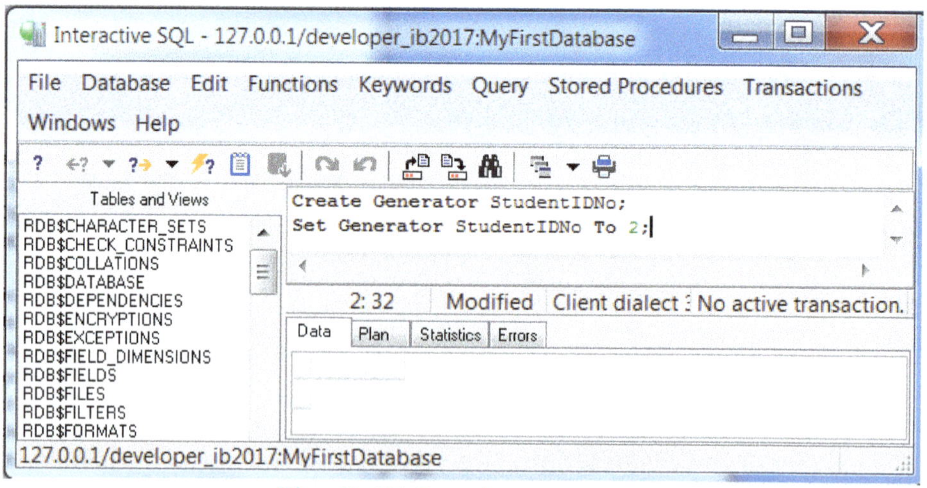

Fig. 63.27 Creating a generator

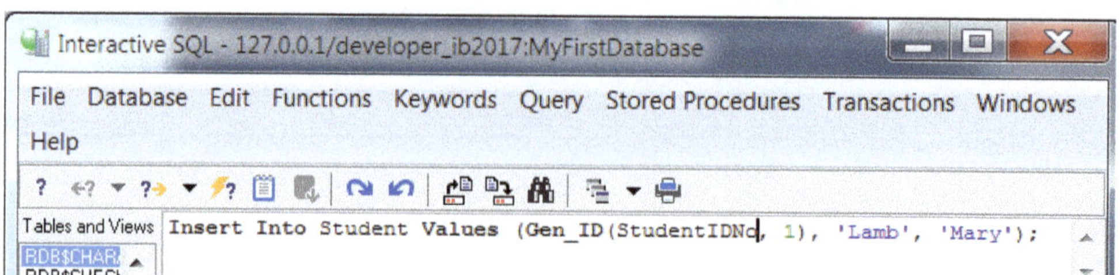

Fig. 63.28 Using Gen_ID in an insert statement

Figure 63.29 shows that `StudentIDNo` has been added to the list of generators and its current value before `Mary Lamb`'s record is inserted is 2.

After `Mary Lamb`'s record is inserted its current value is 3 - *Figure 63.30*.

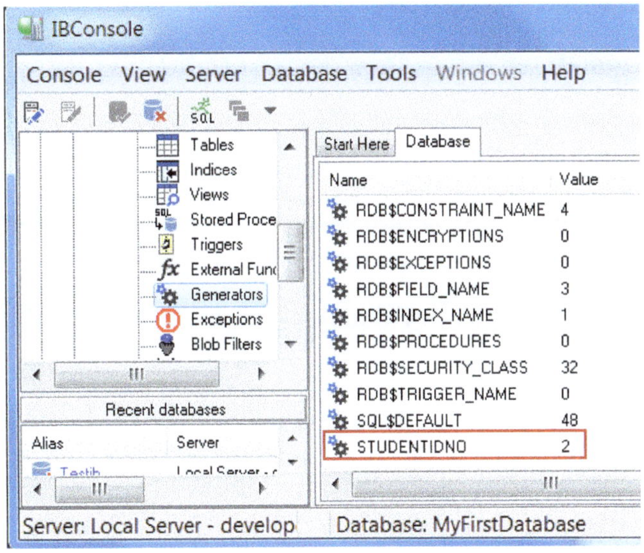

Fig. 63.29 List of generators including StudentIDNo in IBConsole and its value before Mary Lamb's record inserted

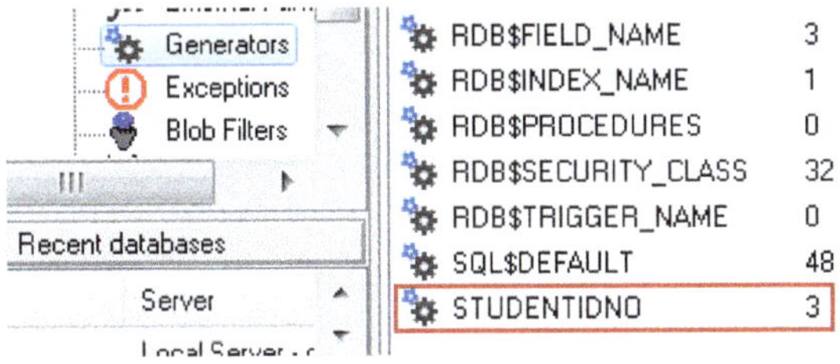

Fig. 63.30 StudentIDNo generator in IBConsole and its value after Mary Lamb's record inserted

Creating a multiple table database

Launch IBConsole from the Start Menu - *Figure 63.1*.

Select LocalServer - developer_ib2017 shown in *Figure 63.4* then **click** Server in the toolbar to bring down the menu shown in *Figure 63.5*. It is also possible to to do this by right clicking LocalServer - developer_ib2017 in the upper left pane.

Click Login to launch the Server Login window - *Figure 63.6*.

Enter the Database Administrator's User Name, `SYSDBA`, and the administator's Password, `masterkey`, then **click** the Login button.

Figure 63.7 shows that the developer_ib2017 local server is now active.

Click Database in the toolbar to bring down the menu shown in *Figure 63.8*.

Click Create Database to bring up the Create Database window shown in *Figure 63.9*. Alternatively, if the required database exists already then **click** Add instead.

Databases must be created on the same drive as Interbase server e.g. the C: drive.

Click on the ellipsis (...) button in the Create Database window to bring up the Specify Database window shown in *Figure 63.10*.

Navigate to the folder/subfolder on the local drive in which to create the database. **Type** a suitable filename for this database.

For this exercise the folder path is `C:\Users\drbond` and the chosen filename is `LibDB.ib`. **Add** alias `Library`.

Click OK to bring up the Database Connect Window.

Enter the password `masterkey` and click Connect.

Database `LibDB.ib` alias `Library` should now be registered and a connection to it open on the Interbase server as shown in *Figure 63.31*.

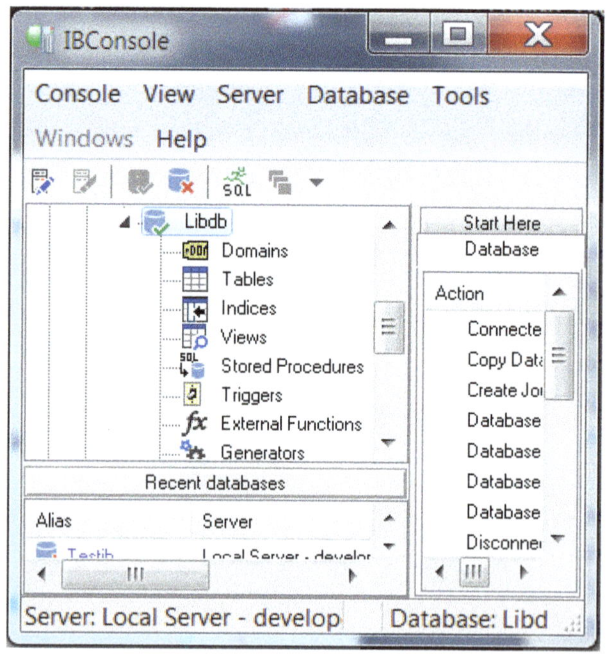

Fig. 63.31 LibDB.ib registered and connected, alias Libdb

Click on the icon SQL in the toolbar ribbon to bring up the InteractiveSQL(ISQL) window.

Click Query in the toolbar to bring down the menu shown *Figure 63.16*.

Click Load Script and locate and load DDL script `CreateLibDatabase.sql` - *Table 63.1* - into ISQL.

Click the Execute Query icon to create tables `Student`, `Book` and `Loan`.

Double click Tables icon - *Figure 63.32* - in IBConsole and check that tables `Student`, `Book` and `Loan` have been created.

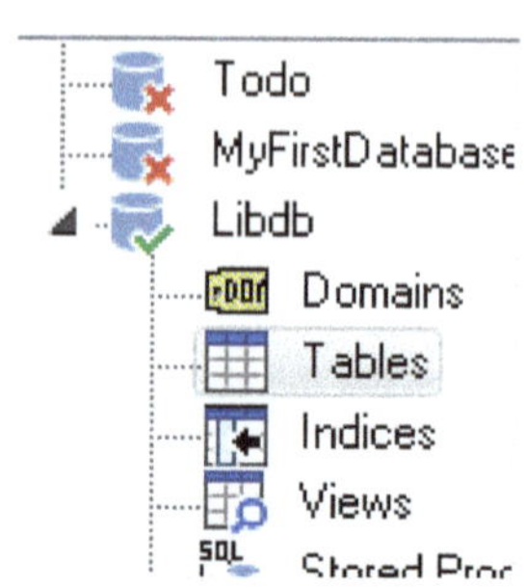

Fig. 63.32 IBConsole Libdb database

Click Load Script and locate and load DDL script `InsertIntoStudent.sql` - *Table 63.2* - into ISQL.

Click the Execute Query icon to insert student data into table `Student`.

Download from www.educational-computing.co.uk/DelphiBookCode/DelphiCode.html
Chapter 63: CreateLibDatabase.sql, InsertIntoStudent.sql, InsertIntoBook.sql, InsertIntoLoan.sql

Click Load Script and locate and load DDL script `InsertIntoBook.sql` - *Table 63.3* - into ISQL.

Click the Execute Query icon to insert book data into table `Book`.

Click Load Script and locate and load DDL script `InsertIntoLoan.sql` - *Table 63.4* - into ISQL.

Click the Execute Query icon to insert loan data into table `Loan`.

Enter the following into ISQL:

```
Select * From Student
```

Click the Execute Query icon.

Check that result set is as expected.

Enter the following into ISQL:

```
Select * From Book
```

Click the Execute Query icon.

Check that the result set is as expected.

Enter the following into ISQL:

```
Select * From Loan
```

Click the Execute Query icon.

Check that the result set is as expected.

Figure 63.33 shows the results set for the query `Select * From Loan`.

```
Create Table Student
(StudentIdNo Integer Not Null,
 Surname VarChar(20) Not Null,
 FirstName VarChar(15) Not Null,
Primary Key (StudentIdNo)
);

Create Table Book
(BookIdNo Integer Not Null,
 Title VarChar(80) Not Null,
 ISBN VarChar(13) Not Null,
 Primary Key (BookIdNo)
);

Create Table Loan
(BookIdNo Integer Not Null,
 StudentIdNo Integer Not Null,
 LoanDate Date Not Null,
 Primary Key (BookIdNo),
 Foreign Key (StudentIdNo) References Student(StudentIdNo),
 Foreign Key (BookIdNo) References Book(BookIdNo)
);

Create Unique Index BookIDIndex On Book(BookIdNo);
Create Unique Index StudentIdNo On Student(StudentIdNo);
Create Unique Index LoanBookIdNoIndex On Loan(BookIdNo);
Create Index LoanStudentIdNoIndex On Loan(StudentIdNo);
```

The Create Unique Index and Create Index statements are unnecessary for fields defined with a primary key or a foreign key in a table as Interbase automatically generates a corresponding ascending index and enforces the uniqueness constraint required by the relational model.

Table 63.1 CreateLibDatabase.sql script

```
Insert Into Student(StudentIdNo, Firstname, Surname) Values(1, 'James', 'Bond');
Insert Into Student(StudentIdNo, Firstname, Surname) Values(2, 'Fred', 'Bloggs');
Insert Into Student(StudentIdNo, Firstname, Surname) Values(3, 'Mary', 'Moffet');
Insert Into Student(StudentIdNo, Firstname, Surname) Values(4, 'Joe', 'Smith');
Insert Into Student(StudentIdNo, Firstname, Surname) Values(5, 'Jane', 'Brown');
Insert Into Student(StudentIdNo, Firstname, Surname) Values(6, 'Mo', 'Ali');
Insert Into Student(StudentIdNo, Firstname, Surname) Values(7, 'Faiza', 'Shah');
Insert Into Student(StudentIdNo, Firstname, Surname) Values(8, 'Mick', 'Hancock');
Insert Into Student(StudentIdNo, Firstname, Surname) Values(9, 'Sarah', 'Choo');
Insert Into Student(StudentIdNo, Firstname, Surname) Values(10, 'Nancy', 'Bowden');
Insert Into Student(StudentIdNo, Firstname, Surname) Values(11, 'Choy', 'Pen');
Insert Into Student(StudentIdNo, Firstname, Surname) Values(12, 'Dan', 'Switzer');
Insert Into Student(StudentIdNo, Firstname, Surname) Values(13, 'Alan', 'Chomsky');
Insert Into Student(StudentIdNo, Firstname, Surname) Values(14, 'Alice', 'Springs');
Insert Into Student(StudentIdNo, Firstname, Surname) Values(15, 'Dipak', 'Patel');
Insert Into Student(StudentIdNo, Firstname, Surname) Values(16, 'Aisha', 'Singh');
```

Table 63.2 InsertIntoStudent.sql script

```
Insert Into Book (BookIdNo, Title,ISBN) Values(1, 'A Level Computer Science for AQA Unit 1',
'9780992753610');
Insert Into Book (BookIdNo, Title,ISBN) Values(2, 'A Level Computer Science for AQA Unit 1',
'9780992753610');
Insert Into Book (BookIdNo, Title,ISBN) Values(3, 'A Level Computer Science for AQA Unit 1',
'9780992753610');
Insert Into Book (BookIdNo, Title,ISBN) Values(4, 'A Level Computer Science for AQA Unit 1',
'9780992753610');
Insert Into Book (BookIdNo, Title,ISBN) Values(5, 'A Level Computer Science for AQA Unit 2',
'9780992753627');
Insert Into Book (BookIdNo, Title,ISBN) Values(6, 'A Level Computer Science for AQA Unit 2',
'9780992753627');
Insert Into Book (BookIdNo, Title,ISBN) Values(7, 'A Level Computer Science for AQA Unit 2',
'9780992753627');
Insert Into Book (BookIdNo, Title,ISBN) Values(8, 'A Level Computer Science for AQA Unit 2',
'9780992753627');
Insert Into Book (BookIdNo, Title,ISBN) Values(9, 'AS Level Computer Science for AQA Units 1 & 2',
'9780992753634);
Insert Into Book (BookIdNo, Title,ISBN) Values(10, 'AS Level Computer Science for AQA Units 1 & 2',
'9780992753634');
Insert Into Book (BookIdNo, Title,ISBN) Values(11, 'AS Level Computer Science for AQA Units 1 & 2',
'9780992753634');
Insert Into Book (BookIdNo, Title,ISBN) Values(12, 'AS Level Computer Science for AQA Units 1 & 2',
'9780992753634');
Insert Into Book (BookIdNo, Title,ISBN) Values(13,
'How to Program Effectively in Delphi for AS/A Level Computer Science', '9780992753696');
Insert Into Book (BookIdNo, Title,ISBN) Values(14,
'How to Program Effectively in Delphi for AS/A Level Computer Science', '9780992753696');
Insert Into Book (BookIdNo, Title,ISBN) Values(15,
'How to Program Effectively in Delphi for AS/A Level Computer Science', '9780992753696');
Insert Into Book (BookIdNo, Title,ISBN) Values(16,
'How to Program Effectively in Delphi for AS/A Level Computer Science', '9780992753696');
Insert Into Book (BookIdNo, Title,ISBN) Values(17, 'GCSE Computer Science for AQA', '9780992753641');
Insert Into Book (BookIdNo, Title,ISBN) Values(18, 'GCSE Computer Science for AQA', '9780992753641');
Insert Into Book (BookIdNo, Title,ISBN) Values(19, 'GCSE Computer Science for AQA', '9780992753641');
Insert Into Book (BookIdNo, Title,ISBN) Values(20, 'GCSE Computer Science for AQA', '9780992753641');
```

Table 63.3 InsertIntoBook.sql script

```
Insert Into Loan(BookIdNo, StudentIdNo,LoanDate)
Values(1,2, '11.6.2020');
Insert Into Loan(BookIdNo, StudentIdNo,LoanDate)
Values(2,4, '12.6.2020');
Insert Into Loan(BookIdNo, StudentIdNo,LoanDate)
Values(5,4, '15.6.2020');
Insert Into Loan(BookIdNo, StudentIdNo,LoanDate)
Values(4,5, '8.7.2020');
Insert Into Loan(BookIdNo, StudentIdNo,LoanDate)
Values(10,5, '8.7.2020');
Insert Into Loan(BookIdNo, StudentIdNo,LoanDate)
Values(13,5, '12.7.2020');
Insert Into Loan(BookIdNo, StudentIdNo,LoanDate)
Values(14,8, '15.7.2020');
```

Table 63.4 InsertIntoLoan.sql script

Finally **commit** the transactions to the database.

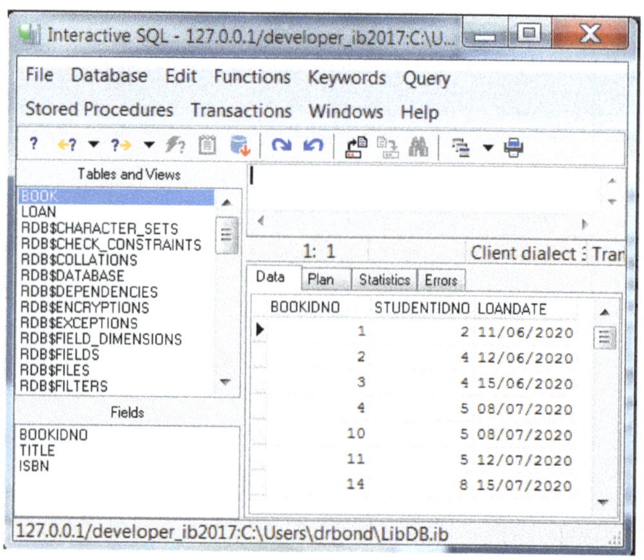

*Fig. 63.33 Select * From Loan query result set*

Download from www.educational-computing.co.uk/DelphiBookCode/DelphiCode.html
Chapter 63: CreateViewBooksOverdue.sql

Working with dates in Interbase

If a fullstop is used as a separator of an all-numeric date in which the year (a four digit value) comes last then Interbase assumes the format is Day-Month-Year, e.g. `12.6.2020` is 12th June 2020 - see *Table 63.4*.

For more information see docwiki.embarcadero.com/Interbase/2020/en/Working_with_Dates_and_Times.

Views

In SQL, a view is a virtual table based on the result set of an SQL statement.

A view contains rows and columns, just like a real table. The fields in a view are fields from one or more real tables in the database. A view appears as a single table even though its data may come from more than one table.

Enter the SQL statement into **ISQL**

```
Create View BooksOverdue(BorrowerID, Name, TitleOfBook, BorrowedOn)
  As
    Select Loan.StudentIdNo, Student.Surname, Book.Title, Loan.LoanDate
      From Loan, Student, Book
        Where (Loan.StudentIdNo = Student.StudentIdNo) And (Loan.BookIdNo = Book.BookIDNo)
               And LoanDate + 21 < 'Today';
```

Execute this statement.

Depending on when you are reading this chapter, there may or may not be books that are overdue.

Interbase evaluates the expression `LoanDate + 21` and returns a date value 21 days onwards from the given loan date. '**Today**' returns today's date as a string which is then cast by Interbase to data type **Date** in order to evaluate the comparison. Therefore, inorder to test the view `BooksOverdue` we need to insert a record with a loan date which is more than 21 days before today's date.

Enter the SQL statement into **ISQL**

```
Insert Into Loan(BookIdNo, StudentIdNo,LoanDate) Values(11,6, Cast('Today' As Date) - 31);
```

Execute this statement.

A **Cast** operation is necessary to cast the string returned by '**Today**' into a **Date** data type in order to subtract 31 days from this date. Subtraction is defined for a **Date** data type but not for **String** data type.

Next using **ISQL**, **enter** and **execute** the SQL statement

```
Select * From BooksOverdue;
```

Given that only one book is overdue, the result set for this operation is shown in *Figure 63.34*.

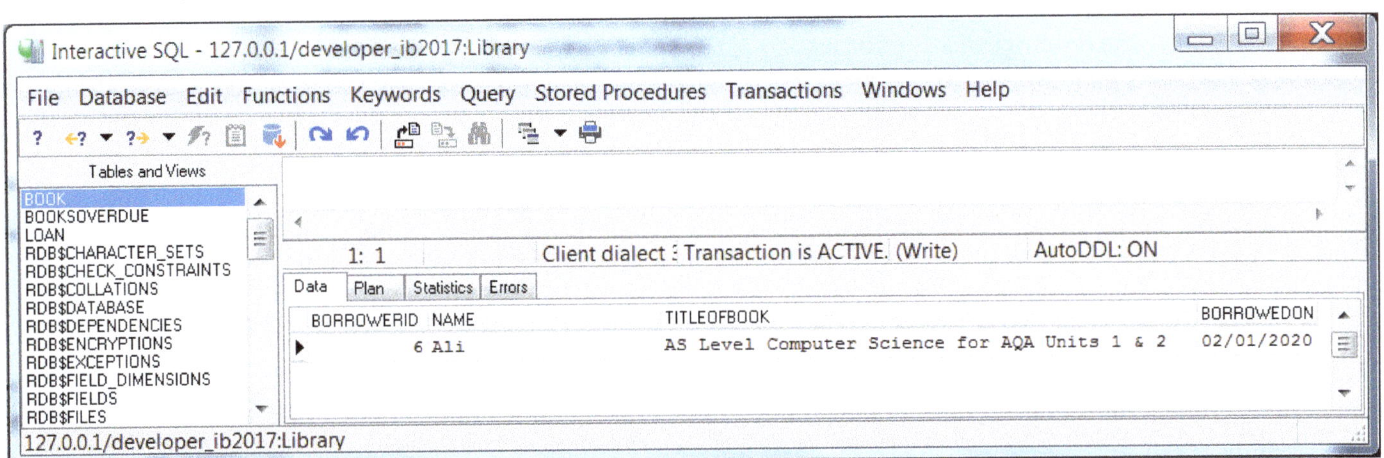

Fig. 63.34 Borrowers with overdue books

Using **ISQL**, **enter** and **execute** the SQL statement

```
Select * From Loan;
```

The result set for this operation is shown in *Figure 63.35*.

BOOKIDNO	STUDENTIDNO	LOANDATE
1	2	11/06/2020
2	4	12/06/2020
5	4	15/06/2020
4	5	08/07/2020
10	5	08/07/2020
13	5	12/07/2020
14	8	15/07/2020
11	6	02/01/2020

Fig. 63.35 Result set showing all loans

It would helpful if the result set returned by `Select * From BooksOverdue;` included a calculation of the number of days overdue. The simplest way of achieving this is to replace the current view `BooksOverdue` as follows:

1. **Commit** the current work by clicking the **Commit Work** icon in the ISQL ribbon (*Figure 63.36*) or pressing **F9** or entering and executing **Commit;** in the ISQL window.

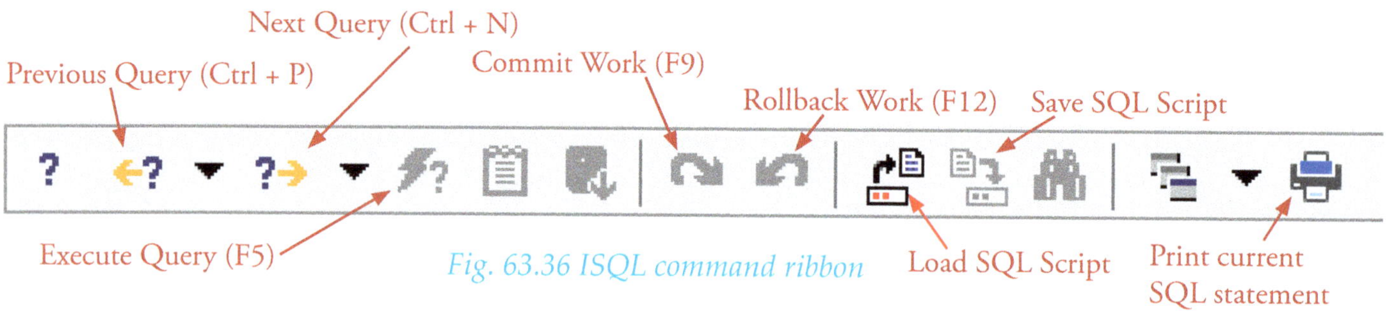

Fig. 63.36 ISQL command ribbon

2. **Enter** the SQL statement.

```
Drop View BooksOverdue;
```

3. **Execute** the SQL statement.

www.educational-computing.co.uk/DelphiBookCode/DelphiCode.html
Chapter 63: CreateViewBooksOverdueM.sql

4. **Enter** the SQL statement

```
Create View BooksOverdue(BorrowerID, Name, TitleOfBook, BorrowedOn, NoOfDaysOverdue)
  As
    Select Loan.StudentIdNo, Student.Surname, Book.Title,
           Loan.LoanDate, current_date - LoanDate
      From Loan, Student, Book
        Where (Loan.StudentIdNo = Student.StudentIdNo) And (Loan.BookIdNo = Book.BookIDNo)
              And LoanDate + 21 < 'Today';
```

5. **Execute** the SQL statement.

To check that the altered view performs as expected **enter** and **execute** the following SQL ststement

```
Select * From BooksOverdue;
```

Figure 63.37 shows the result set that is returned.

BORROWERID	NAME	TITLEOFBOOK	BORROWEDON	NOOFDAYSOVERDUE
6	Ali	AS Level Computer Science for AQA Units 1 & 2	02/01/2020	31

Fig. 63.37 Result set Select statement using new view

The field `NoOfDaysOverdue` is included in the new view and its value is obtained by evaluating

```
current_date - LoanDate
```

Interbase performs a subtraction operation on the date value returned by **current_date**, an Interbase function, and the date value stored in `LoanDate`.

Users and the view mechanism and permissions

The Database Administrator

When Interbase is installed it has a default user SYSDBA. SYSDBA is known as the Database Administrator or DBA because user SYSDBA has full control over the server, databases registered on the server and the setting up of other users of the server and what operations they are allowed to perform.

Users of the database

One of the first tasks for SYSDBA is to create and register other users of the server.

Table 63.5 shows some other users in addition to *SYSDBA* of a library system.

User	Name of person	Role	Password
SYSDBA	Kevin Bond	Database Administrator	masterkey
MSmith	Mary Smith	Chief librarian	password1
JBloggs	Joe Bloggs	Library assistant	password2
PTeng	Poh-Cheng Teng	Library assistant	password3

Table 63.5 Users and their roles

Click on Server in IBConsole and then User Security. This brings up the window shown in *Figure 63.38*.

Click on the New button to create the first of three new users (*Table 63.5*), `Mary Smith`.

Click the Apply button after entering the relevant details for the new user.

After setting up the third new user click the Close button.

Now **click** the Users icon in IBConsole to reveal the registered Users on the Local Server as shown in *Figure 63.39*.

Right click the `Library` alias in IBConsole and select Disconnect to disconnect the `Library` database from the server.

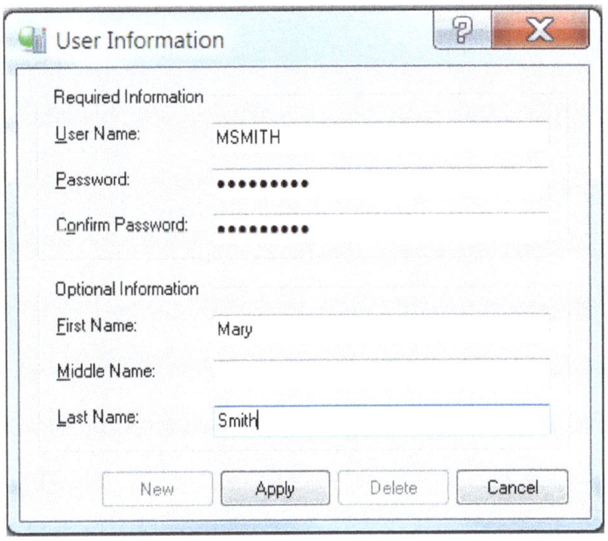

Fig. 63.38 Setting up a new user

Click Database in the toolbar to bring down the menu shown in *Figure 63.8*.

Click Create Database to bring up the Create Database window shown in *Figure 63.9*. Alternatively, if the required database exists already then **click** Add instead.

Databases must be created on the same drive as Interbase server e.g. the C: drive.

Click on the ellipsis (...) button in the Create Database window to bring up the Specify Database window shown in *Figure 63.10*.

Navigate to the folder/subfolder on the local drive in which to create the database. **Type** a suitable filename for this database.

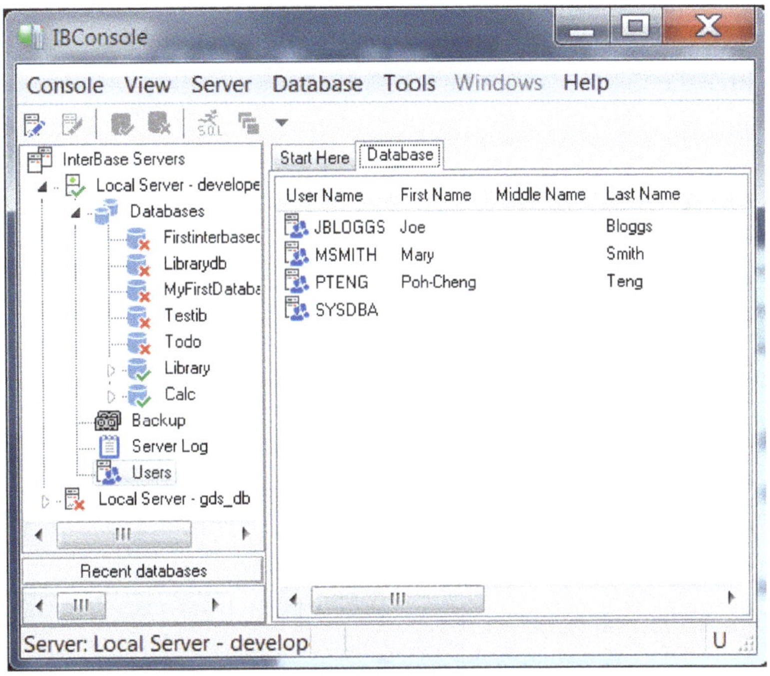

Fig. 63.39 Registered users

For this exercise the folder path is

`C:\Users\drbond\NewLibrary`

and the chosen filename is `NewLibDB.ib`.

Add alias `NewLibDB`.

Click OK to bring up the Database Connect Window.

Enter the password `password1` and click Connect.

Database `NewLibDB.ib` alias `NewLibDB` should now be registered and a connection to it open on the Interbase server.

Click on the icon SQL  in the toolbar ribbon to bring up the InteractiveSQL(ISQL) window.

Click Query then Load Script and **locate** and **load** DDL script `CreateLibraryWithDomains.sql` - *Table 63.6* - into ISQL.

Click the Execute Query icon to create tables `Student`, `Book`, `BookCopy` and `Loan`.

Double click Tables icon in IBConsole and check that tables `Student`, `Book`, `BookCopy` and `Loan` have been created.

Click Load Script and **locate** and **load** DDL script `InsertIntoNewStudent.sql` into ISQL.

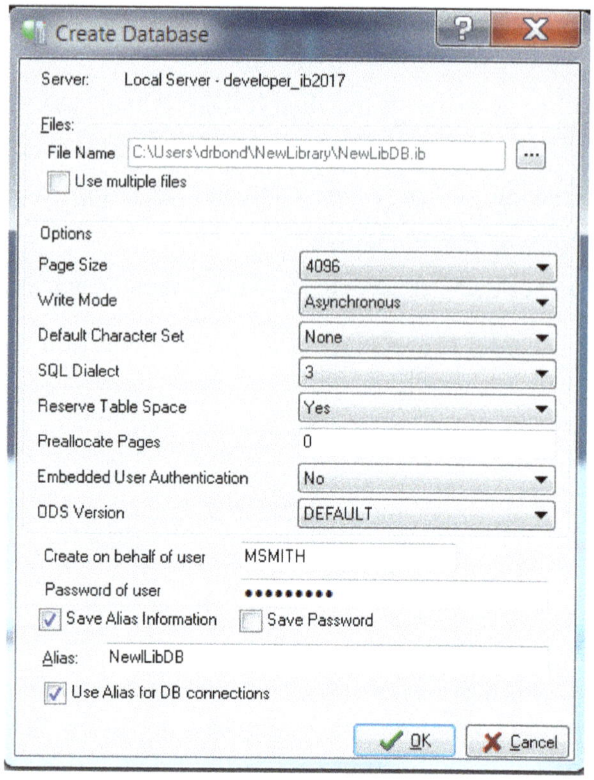

Fig. 63.40 Creating a new database with owner MSmith

Click the Execute Query icon to insert student data into table `Student`.

Click Load Script and locate and load DDL script `InsertIntoNewBook.sql` into ISQL.

Click the Execute Query icon to insert book data into table `Book`.

Click Load Script and locate and load DDL script `InsertIntoNewBookCopy.sql` into ISQL.

Click the Execute Query icon to insert book data into table `BookCopy`.

Click Load Script and locate and load DDL script `InsertIntoNewLoan.sql` - *Table 63.4* - into ISQL.

Click the Execute Query icon to insert loan data into table `Loan`.

Enter the following into ISQL: `Select * From Student`

Click the Execute Query icon.

Check that result set is as expected.

Enter the following into ISQL: `Select * From Book`

Click the Execute Query icon.

Check that the result set is as expected.

Enter the following into ISQL: `Select * From BookCopy`

Click the Execute Query icon.

Check that the result set is as expected.

Enter the following into ISQL: `Select * From Loan`

Click the Execute Query icon.

Check that the result set is as expected.

Download from www.educational-computing.co.uk/DelphiBookCode/DelphiCode.html
Chapter 63: InsertIntoNewStudent.sql, InsertIntoNewBook.sql, InsertIntoNewLoan.sql, InsertIntoNewBookCopy.sql

Download from www.educational-computing.co.uk/DelphiBookCode/DelphiCode.html
Chapter 63: CreateLibraryWithDomains.sql, ViewBooksViewLoans.sql

A multi-user database

The owner of the database `NewLibDB` is user `MSmith`. Currently this database is only accessible by `MSmith` and the database administrator, `SysDBA`.

To make the database accessible to other users we need to use the **Grant** command. However, care should be taken to grant only specific necessary actions from the set **Select**, **Insert**, **Update**, **Delete**. Also, the particular views granted to each user should be a carefully chosen subset of data that matches the privilege level of the respective users. *Table 63.7* shows two **Create View** statements which create views that could be used for library assistants.

```
Create View ViewBooks(ISBN,BookTitle, Author)
  As
    Select ISBN, Title,
      AuthorSurname || ', ' || AuthorInitials
    From Book;

Create View ViewLoans(BorrowerID, Name,
         BookTitle, BorrowedOn, NoOfDaysOnLoan)
  As
    Select Loan.StudentIdNo,
      Student.Surname, Book.Title,
        Loan.LoanDate,
          current_date - LoanDate
    From Loan, Student, Book, BookCopy
      Where
       (Loan.StudentIdNo = Student.StudentIdNo)
      And (Loan.BookCopyIdNo = BookCopy.BookCopyIDNo)
      And (BookCopy.BookIDNo = Book.BookIDNo);
```

Table 63.7 ViewBooksViewLoans.sql

With `MSmith` connected to `NewLibDB`, **click** on the icon **SQL** in the toolbar ribbon to bring up the **IntcractiveSQL**(**ISQL**) window.

Click **Query** then **Load Script** and **locate** and **load** DDL script `ViewBooksViewLoans.sql` - *Table 63.7* - into **ISQL**.

Click the **Execute Query** icon to create views `ViewBooks`, and `ViewLoans`.

Double click **Views** icon in IBConsole and check that views `ViewBooks`, and `ViewLoans` have been created as shown in *Figure 63.41*.

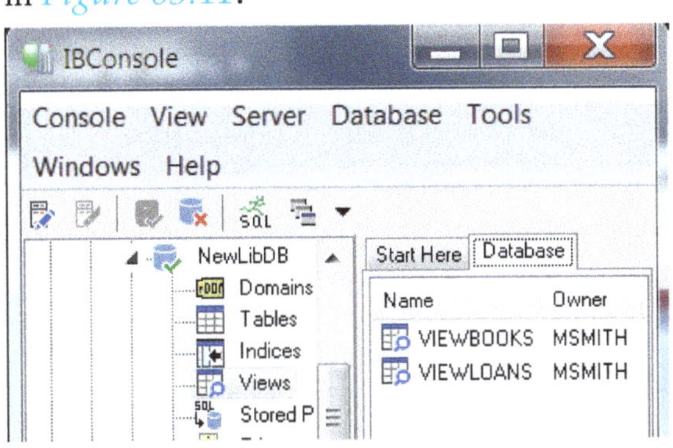

Fig. 63.41 Views

```
Create Domain SurnameType As VarChar(20);

Create Domain StudentIdNoType As Integer
  Check (Value Between 1 And 2000);

Create Domain BookIdNoType As Integer
  Check (Value Between 1 And 1000);

Create Domain BookCopyIdNoType As Integer
  Check (Value Between 1 And 6000);

Create Table Student
  ( StudentIdNo StudentIdNoType Not Null,
    Surname SurnameType Not Null,
    FirstName VarChar(10) Not Null,
    Primary Key (StudentIdNo)
  );

Create Table Book
  ( BookIdNo BookIdNoType Not Null,
    Title VarChar(80) Not Null,
    ISBN Char(13) Not Null,
    DeweyNo Char(3) Not Null,
    PublisherName VarChar(40),
    AuthorSurname SurnameType Not Null,
    AuthorInitials VarChar(2),
    Primary Key (BookIdNo)
  );

Create Table BookCopy
  ( BookCopyIdNo BookCopyIdNoType Not Null,
    BookIdNo BookIdNoType Not Null,
    Primary Key (BookCopyIdNo),
    Foreign Key (BookIdNo) References
                   Book (BookIdNo)
  );

Create Table Loan
  ( BookCopyIdNo BookCopyIdNoType Not Null,
    StudentIdNo StudentIdNoType Not Null,
    LoanDate Date Not Null,
    Primary Key (BookCopyIdNo),
    Foreign Key (StudentIdNo) References
                 Student (StudentIdNo),
    Foreign Key (BookCopyIdNo) References
                 BookCopy(BookCopyIdNo)
  );

Create Unique Index BookIdNoIndex On
                   Book (BookIdNo);
Create Unique Index StudentIdNoIndex On
                   Student (StudentIdNo);
Create Unique Index BookCopyIdNoIndex On
                   BookCopy (BookCopyIdNo);
Create Unique Index LoanBookIdNoIndex On
                   Loan(BookCopyIdNo);
Create Index LoanStudentIdNoIndex On Loan
              (StudentIdNo);

Commit;
```

Table 63.6 CreateLibraryWithDomains.sql script

The next stage grants permissions to users `JBloggs` and `PTeng`.

Click **Query** then **Load Script** and **locate** and **load** DDL script `GrantViewBooksViewLoans.sql` - *Table 63.8* - into **ISQL**.

Click the **Execute Query** icon to grant **Select** only permissions to these users.

```
Grant Select On ViewBooks To JBloggs;
Grant Select On ViewBooks To PTeng;
Grant Select On ViewLoans To JBloggs;
Grant Select On ViewLoans To PTeng;
```

Table 63.8 GrantViewBookViewLoans.sql script

Double click Views icon in IBConsole and right click `ViewBooks`, select **Properties** from the submenu.
In the window that pops up select the **Permissions** tab to reveal permissions for `NewLibDB` owner `MSmith`, user `JBloggs` and user `PTeng` on the view `ViewBooks` - *Figure 63.42*.
Right click `NewLibDB` in IBConsole and **select** **Disconnect** from the database `NewLibDB` and then **select** **Connect As** then enter for **User Name:**, `JBloggs` and for **Password:** `password2`.
With `JBloggs` connected to `NewLibDB`, **click** on the icon **SQL** in the toolbar ribbon to bring up the **InteractiveSQL**(**ISQL**) window.
Enter `Select * From ViewBooks` into **ISQL**.

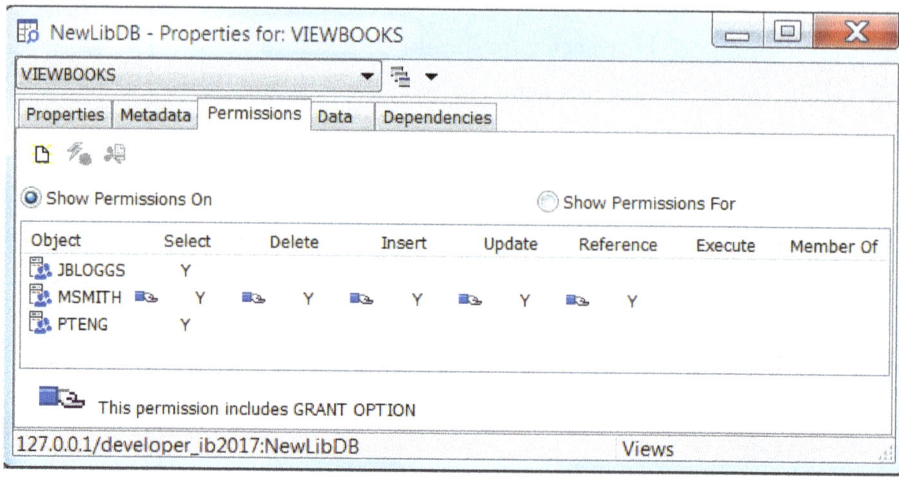

Fig. 63.42 Permissions for ViewBooks view

Click the **Execute Query** icon to obtain the result set shown in *Figure 63.43*.

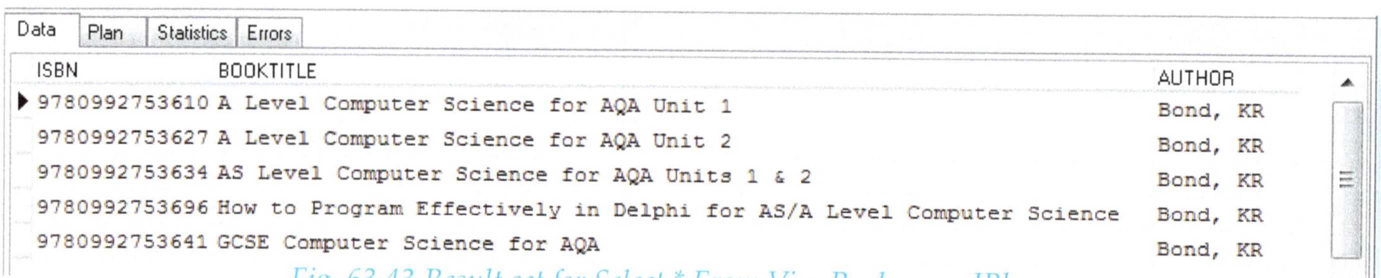

ISBN	BOOKTITLE	AUTHOR
9780992753610	A Level Computer Science for AQA Unit 1	Bond, KR
9780992753627	A Level Computer Science for AQA Unit 2	Bond, KR
9780992753634	AS Level Computer Science for AQA Units 1 & 2	Bond, KR
9780992753696	How to Program Effectively in Delphi for AS/A Level Computer Science	Bond, KR
9780992753641	GCSE Computer Science for AQA	Bond, KR

*Fig. 63.43 Result set for Select * From ViewBooks user JBloggs*

The insert operation `Insert Into ViewBooks Values('9780992753656', 'Teaching Database Theory', 'Bond, KR')` doesn't make logical sense, whichever user is connected, because the view `ViewBooks` is a virtual table. Views tend to be used to hide information about the underlying real tables as well as to create a useful and convenient tailored view of the database.

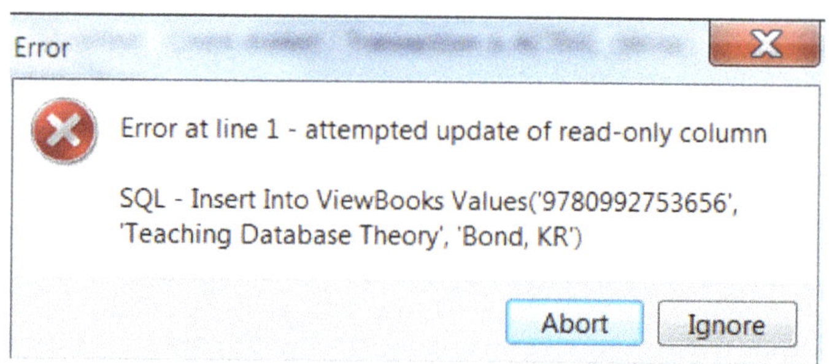

Fig. 63.44 Error message caused when an insert operation is attempted on a virtual table

Permissions are used to restrict what operations a user may execute. User `JBloggs` has not been granted any permissions on table `Book`, therefore, the attempted operations shown in *Figure 63.45* and *Figure 63.46* result in the given error messages.

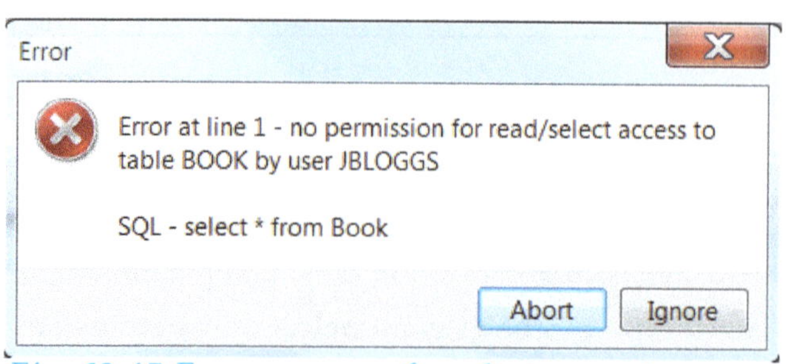

Fig. 63.45 Error message for select operation on table Book by user JBloggs

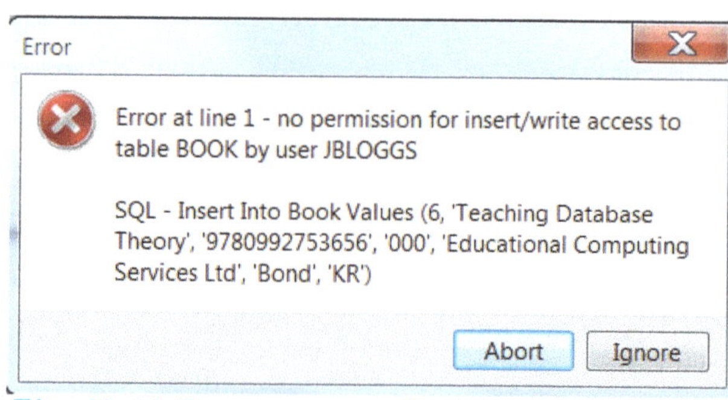

Fig. 63.46 Error message for insert operation on table Book by user JBloggs

Domains

Domains are similar to data type definitions in Pascal but differ by offering more than data typing.

A domain created in an Interbase database specifies a unique name for the domain, and defines various attributes and constraints that may be applied to one or more columns (fields) of the database.

These attributes include:

- Datatype
- Default values and NULL status
- CHECK constraints

For example,

```
                                   Default value
 Unique name   Datatype
Create Domain YesNo As Char(1) Default 'N'
  Check (Value In ('Y', 'N'));

    Check constraint
```

The datatype is the only required attribute that must be set for the domain—all other attributes are optional.

When creating a new column in an Interbase table you must always define its datatype. This establishes the set of valid data that the column can contain.
Only values that can be represented by that datatype are allowed.
Besides establishing the set of valid data that a column can contain, the datatype defines the kinds of operations that may be performed on the data. For example, numbers in INTEGER columns can be manipulated with arithmetic operations, while CHARACTER columns cannot.
The datatype also defines how much space each data item occupies on the disk. Choosing an optimum size for the data value is an important consideration when disk space is limited, especially if a table is very large.

InterBase supports the following datatypes:

- INTEGER and SMALLINT
- FLOAT and DOUBLE PRECISION
- NUMERIC and DECIMAL
- DATE, TIME, and TIMESTAMP
- CHARACTER and VARYING CHARACTER
- BLOB

InterBase provides the binary large object (BLOB) datatype to store data that cannot easily be stored in one of the standard SQL datatypes. A BLOB is used to store very large data objects of indeterminate and variable size, such as bitmapped graphics images, vector drawings, sound files, video segments, chapter or book-length documents, or any other kind of multimedia information.

InterBase also supports arrays of most datatypes. An array is a matrix of individual items composed of any single InterBase datatype (except BLOB). An array can have from 1 to 16 dimensions. An array can be handled as a single entity, or manipulated item-by-item.

A TIMESTAMP datatype is supported that includes information about year, month, day of the month, and time. The TIMESTAMP datatype is stored as two long integers, and requires conversion to and from InterBase when entered or manipulated in a host-language program. The DATE datatype includes information on the year, month, and day of the month. The TIME datatype includes information about time in hours, minutes, seconds, and tenths, hundredths, and thousandths of seconds.

Interbase data types conform to SQL datatypes.

Interbase datatypes:

```
< datatype> = SMALLINT| INTEGER| FLOAT| DOUBLE PRECISION
              | {DECIMAL | NUMERIC} [( precision [, scale])]
              | {DATE | TIME | TIMESTAMP}
              | {CHAR | CHARACTER | CHARACTER VARYING | VARCHAR}
              [( int)] [CHARACTER SET charname]
              | {NCHAR | NATIONAL CHARACTER | NATIONAL CHAR} [VARYING] [( int)]
              |BOOLEAN
<array_dim> = [x:y [, x1:y1 ...]]
```

Symbol | means OR. Symbols [] mean optional. Symbols {} mean the enclosed datatypes draw their values from a particular set.

Note The outermost (in **blue bold** typeface) brackets must be included when declaring arrays.

Examples

Datatype definition:

```
Create Domain SurnameType As VarChar(20);
```

Datatype and constraint definition:

```
Create Domain StudentIdNoType As Integer
   Check (Value Between 1 And 2000);
```

An optional default value may be defined that is automatically entered into a column if an explicit value is not specified.

```
Create Domain YesNo As As Char(1)
  Default 'N' Check (Value In ('Y', 'N'));
```

For more information on domains and how to use them see:

http://docwiki.embarcadero.com/InterBase/2020/en/Using_the_VALUE_Keyword
http://docwiki.embarcadero.com/InterBase/2020/en/Specifying_Domain_CHECK_Constraints

For more information on Interbase datatypes and how to use them see:

http://docwiki.embarcadero.com/InterBase/2020/en/Integer_Data_Types
http://docwiki.embarcadero.com/InterBase/2020/en/Fixed-decimal_Data_Types
http://docwiki.embarcadero.com/InterBase/2020/en/Floating-point_Data_Types
http://docwiki.embarcadero.com/InterBase/2020/en/Date_and_Time_Data_Types
http://docwiki.embarcadero.com/InterBase/2020/en/Specifying_a_Character_Set
http://docwiki.embarcadero.com/InterBase/2020/en/Fixed-length_Character_Data
http://docwiki.embarcadero.com/InterBase/2020/en/Variable-length_Character_Data
http://docwiki.embarcadero.com/InterBase/2020/en/The_BOOLEAN[1]_Data_Type
http://docwiki.embarcadero.com/InterBase/2020/en/Defining_BLOB_Data_Types
http://docwiki.embarcadero.com/InterBase/2020/en/BLOB_Columns

1 BOOLEAN type added to later versions of Interbase

Download from www.educational-computing.co.uk/DelphiBookCode/DelphiCode.html

Chapter 63: CreateLibraryWithDomainsM.sql, InsertIntoNewStudent.sql, InsertIntoNewBook.sql, InsertIntoNewLoan.sql, InsertIntoNewBookCopy.sql

Modified library exercise

The DDL script shown in *Table 63.8* shows a modified `BookCopy` table containing a new field `OnLoan` of datatype `YesNo`.

`YesNo` is a user-defined datatype with a default value 'N' and a constraint which permits only the characters 'Y' and 'N' to be stored.

Its definition is as follows

```
Create Domain YesNo As Char(1) Default 'N'
  Check (Value In ('Y', 'N'));
```

Create a new database with owner `MSmith`, alias `NewLibDBModified`, save as `NewLibDBModified.ib` on a local drive. Connect the server to this database and launch interactive SQL.

Load and execute the script

`CreateLibraryWithDomainsM.sql`

Now load and execute the following scripts in sequence:

`InsertIntoNewStudent.sql`

`InsertIntoNewBook.sql`

`InsertIntoNewBookCopy.sql`

`InsertIntoNewLoan.sql`

Enter the following into **ISQL**:

```
Select * From BookCopy
```

Click the **Execute Query** icon.

The result set is shown in *Figure 63.47*.

Data | Plan | Statistics | Errors

BOOKCOPYIDNO	BOOKIDNO	ONLOAN
1	1	N
2	1	N
3	1	N
4	1	N
5	2	N
6	2	N
7	2	N
8	2	N
9	3	N
10	3	N
11	3	N
12	3	N
13	4	N
14	4	N
15	4	N
16	4	N
17	5	N
18	5	N
19	5	N
20	5	N

*Fig. 63.47 Select * From BookCopy result set*

```
Create Domain SurnameType As Varchar(20);
Create Domain BookIdNoType As Integer
  Check (Value Between 1 and 1000);
Create Domain BookCopyIdNoType As Integer
  Check (Value Between 1 and 6000);
Create Domain StudentIdNoType As Integer
  Check (Value Between 1 And 2000);
Create Domain YesNo As Char(1) Default 'N'
  Check (Value In ('Y', 'N'));

Create Table Student  (
  StudentIdNo StudentIdNoType NOT NULL,
  Surname SurnameType NOT NULL,
  FirstName Varchar(10) NOT NULL,
  Primary Key (StudentIdNo)
);

Create Table Book  (
  BookIdNo BookIdNoType NOT NULL,
  Title Varchar(80) NOT NULL,
  ISBN Char(13) NOT NULL,
  DeweyNo Char(3) NOT NULL,
  PublisherName Varchar(40),
  AuthorSurname SurnameType NOT NULL,
  AuthorInitials Char(2),
  Primary Key (BookIdNo)
);

Create Table BookCopy  (
  BookCopyIdNo BookCopyIdNoType NOT NULL,
  BookIdNo BookIdNoType NOT NULL,
  OnLoan YesNo NOT NULL,
  Primary Key (BookCopyIdNo),
  Foreign Key (BookIdNo) references
   Book (BookIdNo)
);

Create Table Loan  (
  BookCopyIdNo BookCopyIdNoType NOT NULL,
  StudentIdNo StudentIdNoType NOT NULL,
  LoanDate Date NOT NULL,
  Primary Key (BookCopyIdNo),
  Foreign Key (StudentIdNo) references
    Student (StudentIdNo),
  Foreign Key (BookCopyIdNo) references
    BookCopy (BookCopyIdNo)
);

Create Unique Index BookIdNoIndex
  On Book (BookIdNo);
Create Unique Index StudentIdNoIndex
  On Student (StudentIdNo);
Create Unique Index BookCopyIdNoIndex
  On BookCopy (BookCopyIdNo);
Create Unique Index LoanBookIdNoIndex
  On Loan(BookCopyIdNo);
Create Index LoanStudentIdNoIndex
  On Loan (StudentIdNo);
Create Index BookCopyBookIdNoIndex
  On BookCopy (BookIdNo);
```

Table 63.8 CreateLibraryWithDomainsM.sql script

The script

`InsertIntoNewBookCopy.sql`

contains the insert statements that created table `BookCopy` e.g.

```
Insert Into BookCopy(BookCopyIdNo, BookIDNo)
                    Values(1,1);
```

The value 'N' for column `ONLOAN` has been inserted automatically because this column draws its values from a domain with default value 'N'.

The insert statements in script `InsertIntoNewBookCopy.sql` must specify the fieldnames of the two fields for which values have been supplied because there are more than these fields in the table `BookCopy`. In fact there are three fields:

1. `BookCopyIdNo`
2. `BookIDNo`
3. `OnLoan`

Contrast this with the insert statements in script `InsertIntoNewBook.sql` which don't because each SQL statement supplies a value for every field.

The book copies with `BookCopyIdNo` values of 1, 2, 4, 5, 10, 13, 14 are on loan - see `InsertIntoNewLoan.sql` - yet their `OnLoan` field in the `BookCopy` table indicates with value '`N`' that they are not - *Figure 63.47*.

The database is therefore inconsistent.

This is fixed with the following SQL data manipulation language (DML) statement:

```
Update BookCopy Set OnLoan = 'Y'
  Where BookCopyIdNo In (Select BookCopyIdNo From Loan);
```

Followed by the commit statement

```
Commit;
```

Enter and **execute** these two statements in **ISQL**.

Enter the following into **ISQL**:

```
Select * From BookCopy
```

Click the **Execute Query** icon.

The result set is shown in *Figure 63.48*.

Clearly, the database will be temporarily in an inconsistent state in between the two operations:

Operation 1: insert a new loan into the `Loan` table

Operation 2: update the corresponding `BookCopy` table row to reflect that a specific copy of a book is now on loan.

One solution that overcomes this problem uses a trigger to combine the two operations.

Data | Plan | Statistics | Errors

BOOKCOPYIDNO	BOOKIDNO	ONLOAN
1	1	Y
2	1	Y
3	1	N
4	1	Y
5	2	Y
6	2	N
7	2	N
8	2	N
9	3	N
10	3	Y
11	3	N
12	3	N
13	4	Y
14	4	Y
15	4	N
16	4	N
17	5	N
18	5	N
19	5	N
20	5	N

*Fig. 63.48 Select * From BookCopy result set*

Triggers

A trigger is a self-contained program associated with a table or view that automatically performs an action when a row in the table or view is inserted, updated, or deleted.

A trigger is never called directly.

Instead, when an application or user attempts to **Insert, Update**, or **Delete** a row in a table, any triggers associated with that table and operation automatically execute, or fire.

A trigger is composed of a header and a body.

Create Trigger defines a new trigger to a database.

Table 63.9 Trigger SetOnLoanToY when loan record updated

For example,

```
Create Trigger SetOnLoanToY For Loan
  After Insert
  As
    Begin
      Update BookCopy Set OnLoan = 'Y'
        Where BookCopyIdNo = NEW.BookCopyIdNo;
    End;
```

Annotations: Table name; Trigger name; Header; Operation that fires trigger; Action carried out by trigger; Body

With `LibDBModified` database connected and selected in IBConsole.

Launch ISQL from IBConsole.

Click Query|Load Script and **select** script `SetOnLoanToY.sql`

Figure 63.49 shows **ISQL** window with script `SetOnLoanToY` loaded.

Execute this script to create trigger `SetOnLoanToY`. **Close ISQL**.

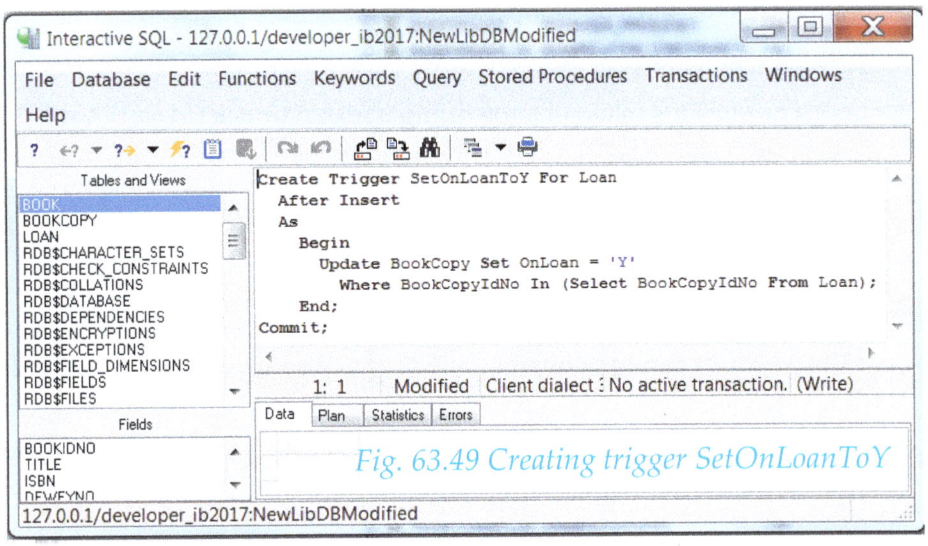

Fig. 63.49 Creating trigger SetOnLoanToY

Select **Triggers** under `NewLibDBModified` in IBConsole:

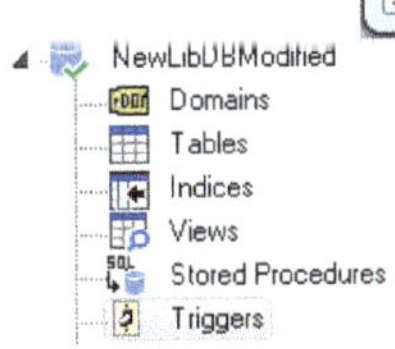

Double click `SETONLOANTOY` in right pane of IBConsole:

to bring up the Trigger window for `SETONLOANTOY`.

Select the **MetaData** tab to reveal the metadata for this trigger - *Figure 63.50*.

Note that IBConsole has

- added **SET TERM ^ ;** to switch the terminator symbol from ';' to '^' temporarily.
- replaced ';' by '^' in script.

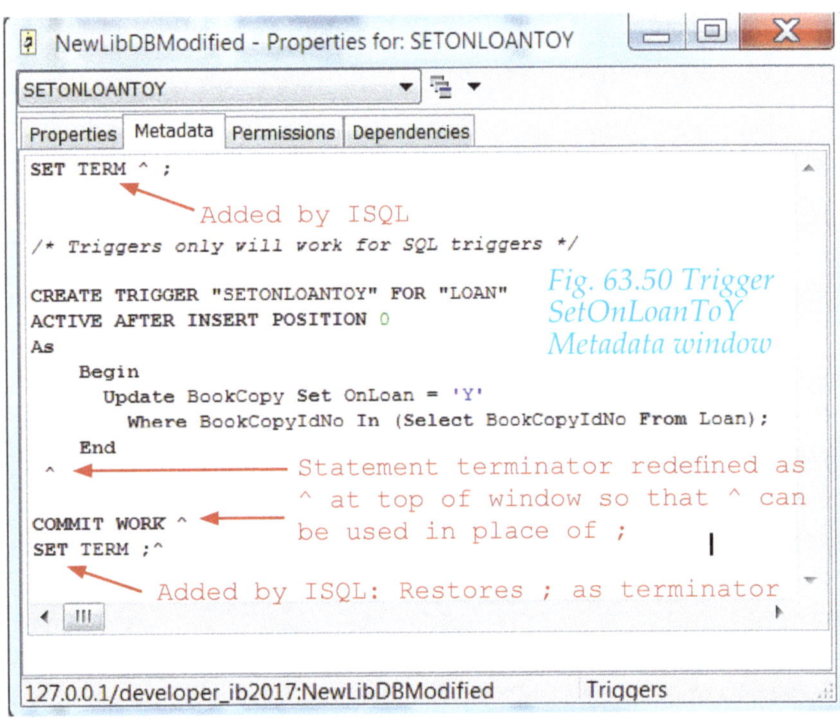

Fig. 63.50 Trigger SetOnLoanToY Metadata window

Download from www.educational-computing.co.uk/DelphiBookCode/DelphiCode.html
Chapter 63: SetOnLoanToN.sql

Enter the following statements

```
Insert Into Loan Values (3, 7, 'today');
Commit;
```

Click [SQL] to execute these statements.

Figure 63.51 shows a new loan record in table `Loan` with `BookCopyIdNo` 3 as expected.

Figure 63.52 shows that the `OnLoan` field of the record in table `BookCopy` with `BookCopyIdNo` 3 has changed as expected to 'Y'.

Data | Plan | Statistics | Errors

BOOKCOPYIDNO	STUDENTIDNO	LOANDATE
1	2	11/06/2020
2	4	12/06/2020
5	4	15/06/2020
4	5	08/07/2020
10	5	08/07/2020
13	5	12/07/2020
14	8	15/07/2020
3	7	06/02/2020

Fig. 63.51 New loan record added to Loan table by insert statement

With triggers, Interbase provides two context variables that maintain information about the row being inserted, updated or deleted.

- **OLD**.fieldname refers to the current or previous values in a row being updated or deleted. It is not relevant for **Insert** triggers.
- **NEW**.fieldname refers to the new values in a row being inserted or updated. It is not relevant for **Delete** triggers.

The reverse of adding a loan record is deleting a loan record. When a loan record is deleted, its corresponding `BookCopy` `OnLoan` field must be changed from 'Y' to 'N'.

The trigger that does this is shown in *Table 63.10*.

```
Create Trigger SetOnLoanToN For Loan
  Before Delete
  As
  Begin
    Update BookCopy Set OnLoan = 'N'
      Where BookCopyIdNo = OLD.BookCopyIdNo;
  End;
```

Table name
Header
Trigger name
Operation that fires trigger
Body
Action carried out by trigger

Table 63.10 Trigger SetOnLoanToN when loan record deleted

Information

The CREATE TRIGGER statement includes DML statements that are nested inside the DDL CREATE TRIGGER statement, i.e. Update. In order for InterBase to correctly parse and interpret a trigger, Interbase needs a way to terminate the CREATE TRIGGER which is different from how the individual DML statements inside the CREATE TRIGGER are terminated, otherwise the trigger would terminate on encountering the first ';'. This is accomplished with the SET TERM statement.

Data | Plan | Statistics | Errors

BOOKCOPYIDNO	BOOKIDNO	ONLOAN
1	1	Y
2	1	Y
3	1	Y
4	1	Y
5	2	Y
6	2	N
7	2	N
8	2	N
9	3	N
10	3	Y
11	3	N
12	3	N
13	4	Y
14	4	Y
15	4	N
16	4	N
17	5	N
18	5	N
19	5	N
20	5	N

Fig. 63.52 OnLoan field of record with BookCopyIdNo changed to 'Y'

Launch **ISQL** from IBConsole.
Enter and **execute** the **DDL** shown in *Table 63.10*.
Enter and **execute** the following statements

```
Delete From Loan Where BookCopyIdNo = 3;
Commit;
```

Check that both tables, `Loan` and `BookCopy`, have been changed as expected: record with `BookCopyIdNo` 3 removed from `Loan` and `OnLoan` field in `BookCopy` table changed to 'N' for record with `BookCopyIdNo` 3.

Download from www.educational-computing.co.uk/DelphiBookCode/DelphiCode.html
Chapter 63: CreateGeneratorsNewLibDBModified.sql

Creating a trigger for a generator

A trigger can be used to call a generator when a new sequential number is needed, e.g. a new primary key value.

We can use triggers to automate the process of generating primary key values for primary keys `StudentIdNo`, `BookIdNo` and `BookCopyIdNo`. First we need to create the necessary generators and then we need to create triggers which fire when a new record is about to be inserted into tables `Student`, `Book` or `BookCopy`.

Launch ISQL from IBConsole.
Enter and **execute,** in turn, the DDL statements shown in *Table 63.11, Table 63.12, Table 63.13* and *Table 63.14*.

```
Create Generator StudentIdNo_Gen;
Set Generator StudentIdNo_Gen To 1;
Create Generator BookIdNo_Gen;
Set Generator BookIdNo_Gen To 1;
Create Generator BookCopyIdNo_Gen;
Set Generator BookCopyIdNo_Gen To 1;
```

Table 63.11 DDL statements to create generators for NewLibDBModified

```
Create Trigger Insert_StudentIDNo
  For Student
    Before Insert
  As
Begin
  /* increment generator, grab next ID
     and assign to the primary key column */
  NEW.StudentIdNo = GEN_ID (StudentIdNo_Gen, 1);
End;
```

Table 63.12 Creating a trigger which generates a new StudentIdNo

```
Create Trigger Insert_BookIDNo
  For Book
    Before Insert
  As
Begin
  /* grab next ID, increment generator,
     and assign to the primary key column */
  NEW.BookIdNo = GEN_ID (BookIdNo_Gen, 1);
End;
```

Table 63.13 Creating a trigger which generates a new BookIdNo

```
Create Trigger Insert_BookCopyIDNo
  For BookCopy
    Before Insert
  As
Begin
  /* grab next ID, increment generator,
     and assign to the primary key column */
  NEW.BookCopyIdNo = GEN_ID (BookCopyIdNo_Gen, 1);
End;
```

Table 63.14 Creating a trigger which generates a new BookCopyIdNo

SQL consists of DML and DDL commands.

DML or Data Manipulation Language consists of the SQL commands Select, Insert, Update and Delete.

In order to test the triggers and generators, we need to delete all data from the database `NewLibDBModified` first.

Table 63.15 shows the delete statements and the order in which they should be executed to carry out this task.

The order of execution matters becasue we cannot delete all the data in table `BookCopy` whilst corresponding `BookCopyIdNo` and `StudentIdNo` values exist in table `Loan`.

Similarly we cannot delete all the data in table `Book` whilst corresponding `BookIdNo` values exist in table `BookCopy`.

```
Delete From Loan;
Delete From BookCopy;
Delete From Book;
Delete From Student;
Commit;
```

Table 63.15 DML statements to delete all the data from the database NewLibDBModified

Executing the delete statements in this order preserves **referential integrity**, i.e. a `BookIdNo` in table `BookCopy` references a record that exists with this `BookIdNo` in table `Book`.

We now need to recreate data for database `NewLibDBModified`. We use new scripts shown in Table 63.16, Table 63.17 and Table 63.18 to regenerate data for tables `Book`, `Student` and `BookCopy` and previously used script `InsertIntoNewLoan.sql` for table `Loan`.

```
Insert Into Book(Title, ISBN, DeweyNo, PublisherName, AuthorSurName, AuthorInitials)
  Values('A Level Computer Science for AQA Unit 1', '9780992753610', '000',
         'Educational Computing Services Ltd', 'Bond', 'KR');
Insert Into Book(Title, ISBN, DeweyNo, PublisherName, AuthorSurName, AuthorInitials)
  Values('A Level Computer Science for AQA Unit 2', '9780992753627', '000',
         'Educational Computing Services Ltd', 'Bond', 'KR');
Insert Into Book(Title, ISBN, DeweyNo, PublisherName, AuthorSurName, AuthorInitials)
  Values('AS Level Computer Science for AQA Units 1 & 2', '9780992753634', '000',
         'Educational Computing Services Ltd', 'Bond', 'KR');
Insert Into Book(Title, ISBN, DeweyNo, PublisherName, AuthorSurName, AuthorInitials)
  Values('How to Program Effectively in Delphi for AS/A Level Computer Science', '9780992753696',
         '005', 'Educational Computing Services Ltd', 'Bond', 'KR');
Insert Into Book(Title, ISBN, DeweyNo, PublisherName, AuthorSurName, AuthorInitials)
  Values('GCSE Computer Science for AQA', '9780992753641', '000', 'Educational Computing Services Ltd',
         'Bond', 'KR');
Commit;
```

P

Table 63.16 InsertIntoNewBookWithGen.sql script

```
Insert Into Student(Firstname, Surname) Values('James', 'Bond');
Insert Into Student(Firstname, Surname) Values('Fred', 'Bloggs');
Insert Into Student(Firstname, Surname) Values('Mary', 'Moffet');
Insert Into Student(Firstname, Surname) Values('Joe', 'Smith');
Insert Into Student(Firstname, Surname) Values('Jane', 'Brown');
Insert Into Student(Firstname, Surname) Values('Mo', 'Ali');
Insert Into Student(Firstname, Surname) Values('Faiza', 'Shah');
Insert Into Student(Firstname, Surname) Values('Mick', 'Hancock');
Insert Into Student(Firstname, Surname) Values('Sarah', 'Choo');
Insert Into Student(Firstname, Surname) Values('Nancy', 'Bowden');
Insert Into Student(Firstname, Surname) Values('Choy', 'Pen');
Insert Into Student(Firstname, Surname) Values('Dan', 'Switzer');
Insert Into Student(Firstname, Surname) Values('Alan', 'Chomsky');
Insert Into Student(Firstname, Surname) Values('Alice', 'Springs');
Insert Into Student(Firstname, Surname) Values('Dipak', 'Patel');
Insert Into Student(Firstname, Surname) Values('Aisha', 'Singh');
Commit;
```

Table 63.17 InsertIntoNewStudentWithGen.sql script

```
Insert Into BookCopy(BookIDNo) Values(1);
Insert Into BookCopy(BookIDNo) Values(1);
Insert Into BookCopy(BookIDNo) Values(1);
Insert Into BookCopy(BookIDNo) Values(1);
Insert Into BookCopy(BookIDNo) Values(2);
Insert Into BookCopy(BookIDNo) Values(2);
Insert Into BookCopy(BookIDNo) Values(2);
Insert Into BookCopy(BookIDNo) Values(2);
Insert Into BookCopy(BookIDNo) Values(3);
Insert Into BookCopy(BookIDNo) Values(3);
Insert Into BookCopy(BookIDNo) Values(3);
Insert Into BookCopy(BookIDNo) Values(3);
Insert Into BookCopy(BookIDNo) Values(4);
Insert Into BookCopy(BookIDNo) Values(4);
Insert Into BookCopy(BookIDNo) Values(4);
Insert Into BookCopy(BookIDNo) Values(4);
Insert Into BookCopy(BookIDNo) Values(5);
Insert Into BookCopy(BookIDNo) Values(5);
Insert Into BookCopy(BookIDNo) Values(5);
Insert Into BookCopy(BookIDNo) Values(5);
Commit;
```

Table 63.18 InsertIntoNewBookCopyWithGen.sql script

Launch ISQL.

Select Query|Load Script and load and execute the following scripts, in turn:

1. `InsertIntoNewBookWithGen.sql`
2. `InsertIntoNewStudentWithGen.sql`
3. `InsertIntoNewBookCopyWithGen.sql`
4. `InsertIntoNewLoan.sql`

Figure 63.53 shows the result set from executing `Select * From Book`.

Note `BookIdNo`s generated and inserted in sequence row by row. **Check** that the other tables have data as expected.

Data | Plan | Statistics | Errors

BOOKIDNO	TITLE	ISBN	DEWEYNO	PUBLISHERNAME	AUTHORSURNAME	AUTHORINITIALS
1	A Level Computer Science for AQA Unit 1	9780992753610	000	Educational Computing Services Ltd	Bond	KR
2	A Level Computer Science for AQA Unit 2	9780992753627	000	Educational Computing Services Ltd	Bond	KR
3	AS Level Computer Science for AQA Units 1 & 2	9780992753634	000	Educational Computing Services Ltd	Bond	KR
4	How to Program Effectively in Delphi for AS/A Level Computer Science	9780992753696	005	Educational Computing Services Ltd	Bond	KR
5	GCSE Computer Science for AQA	9780992753641	000	Educational Computing Services Ltd	Bond	KR

*Fig. 63.53 Result set from Select * From Book*

Stored Procedures

A stored procedure is a series of SQL commands stored as a self-contained program in the database.

They may be executed by the **Execute Procedure** command followed by the procedure name and any parameters or be used in place of a table name in a **Select** statement.

For example, the task of calculating fines on overdue books is one that will need to be carried out on the library database from time to time. This task can be assigned to a stored procedure attached to the database.

Table 63.19 shows an SQL script, `CalculateFinesProc.sql`, for creating a stored procedure `CalculateFines` which selects records from table `Loan` for which the current date is greater than or equal to the loan date + 21 days and which then inserts these records into table `Fines` using local variables `:BookCopyIdNoVar`, `:StudentIdNoVar`, `:LoanDateVar` which temporarily store the data extracted by the select operation. Before selecting records, the stored procedure deletes all existing records in table `Fines` by executing the SQL statement `Delete From Fines;`. Table `Fines` must exist before `CalculateFines` is created.

The form of a stored procedure which does not return any results to the calling agent is as follows

```
Create Procedure <procedure name>
  As
     Declare Variable <variable name> <datatype>;
     Declare ....;
     Begin
       Command 1;
       Command 2;
       ....
     End
```

When a variable is referenced in the body of the stored procedure, the symbol ':' is used in front of it to mean that the variable's value is to be set or to be read.

```
Set Term ^ ;
CREATE PROCEDURE CalculateFines
  As
    Declare Variable BookCopyIdNoVar Integer;
    Declare Variable StudentIdNoVar Integer;
    Declare Variable LoanDateVar Date;
    Begin
      Delete From Fines;
      For Select BookCopyIdNo, StudentIdNo, LoanDate From Loan
        Where (Current_date - LoanDate - 21 ) >= 0
              Into :BookCopyIdNoVar, :StudentIdNoVar, :LoanDateVar
          Do Insert Into Fines(BookCopyIdNo, StudentIdNo, Loan_Date, Date_Fine_Calculated)
               Values (:BookCopyIdNoVar, :StudentIdNoVar, :LoanDateVar, current_date);
    End ^
Set Term ; ^
```

P

Table 63.19 CalculateFinesProc.sql script

The stored procedure `CalculateFines` uses a **For Select Where Into Do** command

```
For Select BookCopyIdNo, StudentIdNo, LoanDate From Loan
        Where (Current_date - LoanDate - 21 ) >= 0
          Into :BookCopyIdNoVar, :StudentIdNoVar, :LoanDateVar
  Do
```

There are two constructs at work here:
1. Select From Where Into
2. For Do

The script which creates table `Fines` is shown in *Table 63.20*.

The field `Fine_In_Pounds` is a calculated field which adds the product of number of days overdue and £0.05 to £1.00. Fines are calculated at £0.05 per day with an automatic surcharge of £1.00 for exceeding the loan period of 21 days.

```
Create Table Fines
(BookCopyIdNo BookCopyIdNoType Not Null,
 StudentIdNo StudentIdNoType Not Null,
 Loan_Date Date Not Null,
 Date_Fine_Calculated date Not Null,
 Fine_In_Pounds Computed By
                  (1.00 + (current_date - Loan_Date - 21)*0.05),
 Primary Key (BookCopyIdNo),
 Foreign Key (StudentIdNo) references Student (StudentIdNo),
 Foreign Key (BookCopyIdNo) references BookCopy (BookCopyIdNo)
);
Create Unique Index FinesBookCopyIdNoIndex On Fines (BookCopyIdNo);
Commit;
```

P

Table 63.20 CreateTableFines.sql script

Launch ISQL.

Select Query|Load Script and load and execute the script, `CreateTableFines.sql`, to create the empty table `Fines`.

Select Query|Load Script and load and execute the script, `CalculateFinesProc.sql`, to create the stored procedure `CalculateFines`. - *Figure 63.54*.

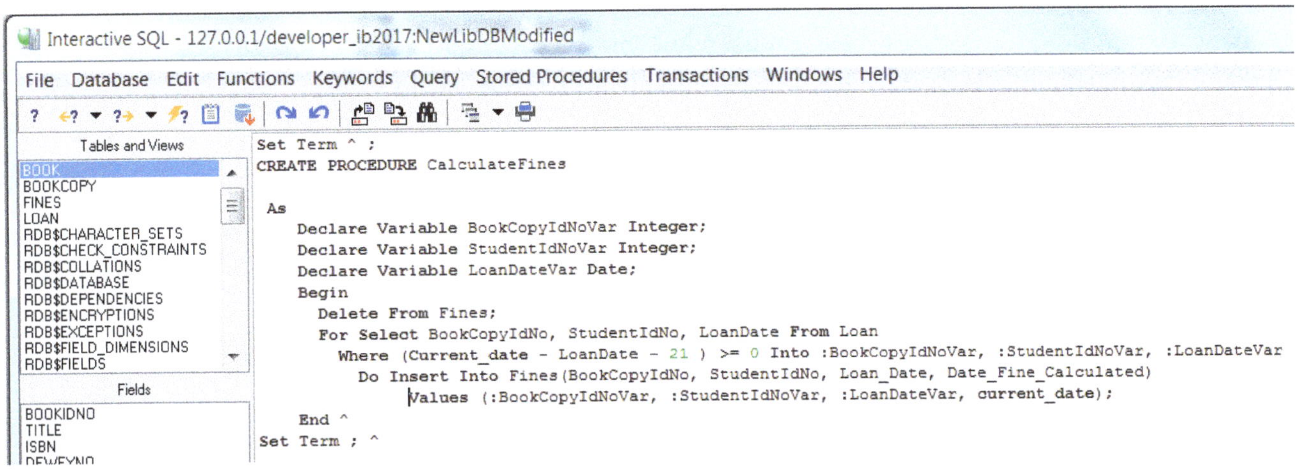

Fig. 63.54 Script CalculateFinesProc.sql loaded into ISQL

Close ISQL.

Click on the Stored Procedures node in IBConsole as shown in *Figure 63.55*. You should see stored procedure `CalculateFines` in the database tab.

Launch ISQL.

Enter and **execute** `CalculateFines` as shown in *Figure 63.56*. **Commit** the transaction.

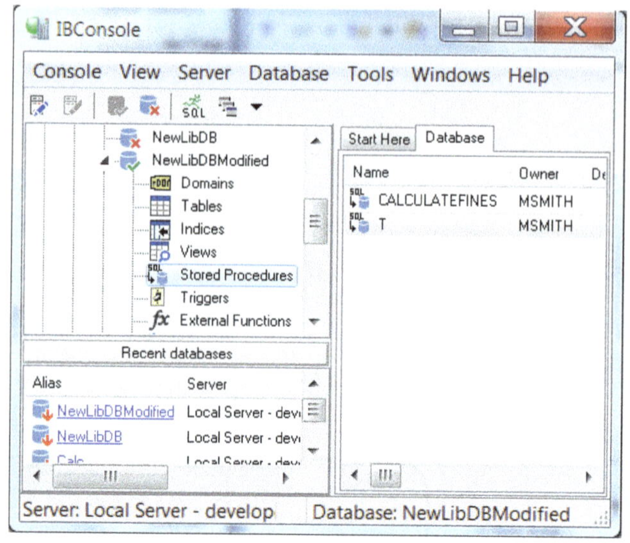

Fig. 63.55 StoredProcedures node in IBConsole

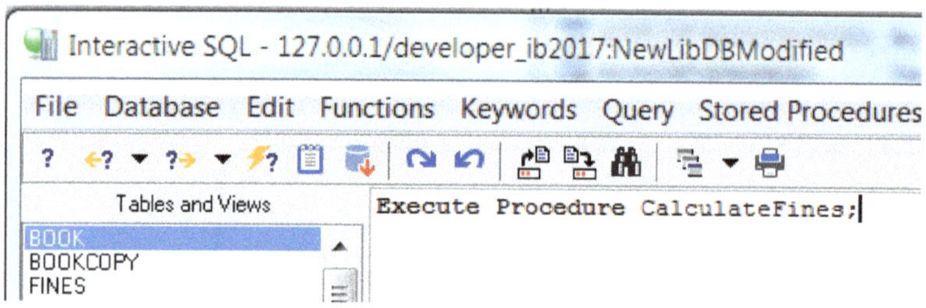

Fig. 63.56 Execute Procedure CalculateFines

Enter and **execute** `Select * From Fines;`

The result set is shown in *Figure 63.57*.

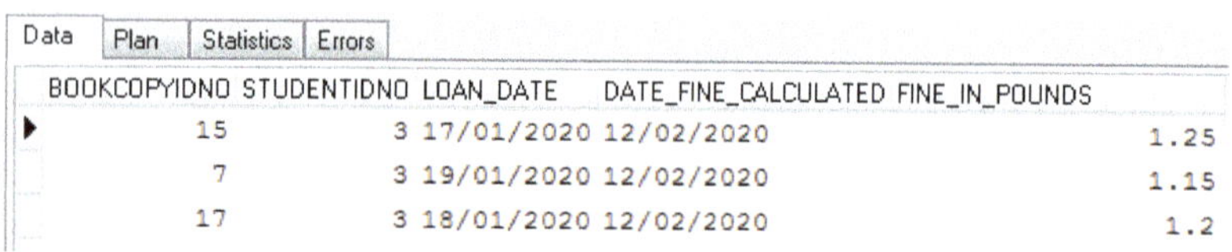

BOOKCOPYIDNO	STUDENTIDNO	LOAN_DATE	DATE_FINE_CALCULATED	FINE_IN_POUNDS
15	3	17/01/2020	12/02/2020	1.25
7	3	19/01/2020	12/02/2020	1.15
17	3	18/01/2020	12/02/2020	1.2

*Fig. 63.57 Result set for Select * From Fines*

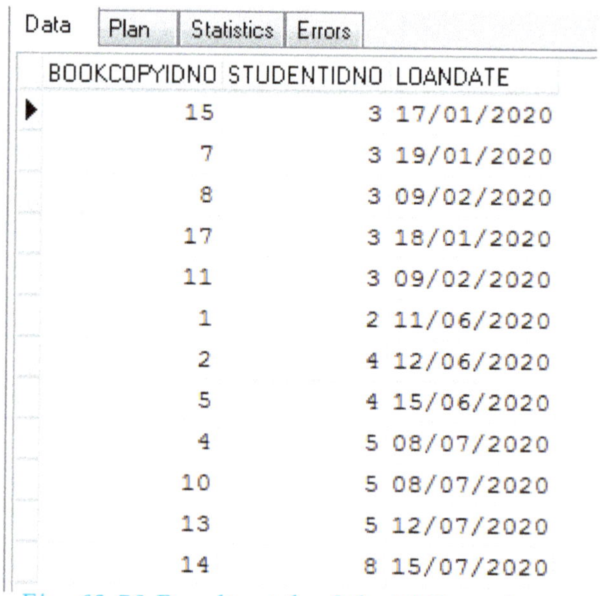

BOOKCOPYIDNO	STUDENTIDNO	LOANDATE
15	3	17/01/2020
7	3	19/01/2020
8	3	09/02/2020
17	3	18/01/2020
11	3	09/02/2020
1	2	11/06/2020
2	4	12/06/2020
5	4	15/06/2020
4	5	08/07/2020
10	5	08/07/2020
13	5	12/07/2020
14	8	15/07/2020

*Fig. 63.58 Result set for Select * From Loan*

`CalculateFines` was executed on February 12th 2020 on the `Loan` table data shown in *Figure 63.58*.

The data in this table are not very realistic since loan dates exist well in advance of the current date. As well as data inserted by script, additional data has been added to this table using Insert Into statements executed within ISQL in order that the `Fines` table would have some overdue records to demonstrate calculating fines.

The current practice applied to relational databases is to use singular names for tables which reflect the purpose of the tables, e.g. `Book`. The name of table `Fines` needs to change because it is neither plural nor truly reflective of the purpose of the table, i.e. to record books which are overdue along with an identifier that identifies the borrower. A better name is `OverdueLoan` because *Loan* implies a borrowed book and its associated borrower; and *Overdue* implies that its loan period has been exceeded with a consequent financial penalty.

Launch ISQL.

Enter and **execute**

```
Delete From Fines;
Commit;
```

Enter and **execute**

```
Drop Procedure CalculateFines;
Commit;
```

Enter and **execute**

```
Drop Table Fines;
Commit;
```

Information

If ISQL won't allow table Fines to be deleted it could be because it still contains data or because it is still part of a transaction.

Disconnect the database and reset the Interbase server. Restart the server. This should fix the issue. Waiting a short period of time should also clear a pending transaction.

Select Query|Load Script and load and execute the script, `CreateTableOverdueLoan.sql`. to create the empty table `OverdueLoan`.

Select Query|Load Script and load and execute the script, `CalculateOverdueLoanProc.sql` to create the stored procedure `CalculateOverdueLoan`.

Test the changes by executing stored procedure `CalculateOverdueLoan`.

We may also create stored procedures which receive one or more inputs from the calling agent and which may return one or more values to the calling agent.

Table 63.21 shows a script to create a stored procedure, `StudentWithOverdueLoan`, which returns a single value `Student_With_Id` of data type `Integer`. each time it is called.

```
Set Term ^ ;
Create Procedure StudentWithOverdueLoan
  Returns (Student_With_Id Integer)
  As
    Begin
      For Select Distinct StudentIdNo From OverdueLoan
            Into :Student_With_Id
        Do Suspend;
    End ^
Set Term ; ^
Commit;
```

Table 63.21 StudentWithOverdueLoanProc.sql script

Launch ISQL.

Select Query|Load Script and load and execute the script `StudentWithOverdueLoanProc.sql` to create the stored procedure `StudentWithOverdueLoan`.

Enter and **execute** `Select * From StudentWithOverdueLoan;`

The stored procedure selects the next `StudentIdNo` value from the table `OverdueLoan`. The Suspend command then suspends execution of the stored procedure and returns this value to the `Select` statement that called the stored procedure. Since `Select` searches for all matches, the stored procedure is called again and so on until there are no more values to return.

The result set is shown in *Figure 63.59*.

The `Loan` table contained records for two students with overdue loans, `StudentIdNo` 2 and 3.

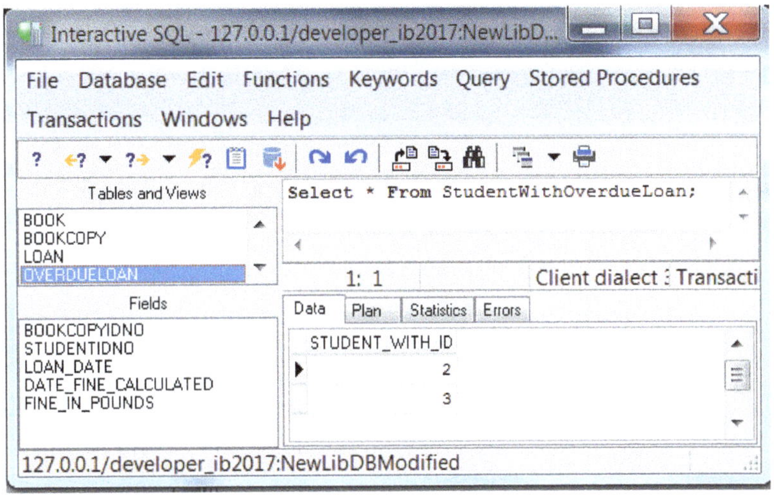

*Fig. 63.59 Result set for Select * From StudentWithOverdueLoan*

In fact, the `Loan` table contained three overdue loans for student 3 but the `Distinct` keyword forced `Select` to use only one instance of student 3.

When a stored procedure relies on **Suspend** to achieve its goal, we use **Select * From** *<stored procedure name>;* instead of **Execute Procedure** *<stored procedure name>;*

Table 63.22 shows a script to create a stored procedure, `SumFineOfStudentInOverdueLoan`, which takes a single input, `StudentIdNoVar` of data type `Integer`, and which returns a single value `Unpaid_Fines`, of data type `Decimal(5, 2)`.

The result set is shone in *Figure 63.60*.

Stored procedure `SumFineOfStudentInOverdueLoan` uses an aggregate function **Sum** to accumulate the fines due for the three instances of student 3 in the table `OverdueLoan`.

```
Set Term ^ ;
Create Procedure SumFineOfStudentInOverdueLoan(StudentIdNoVar Integer)
  Returns (Student_With_Id Int, Unpaid_Fines Decimal(5, 2))
  As
    Begin
      For Select Sum(Fine_In_Pounds) From OverdueLoan
           Where StudentIdNo = :StudentIdNoVar Into :Unpaid_Fines
        Do Student_With_Id = :StudentIdNoVar;
    End ^
Set Term ; ^
Commit;
```

Table 63.22 SumFineOfStudentInOverdueLoanProc.sql script

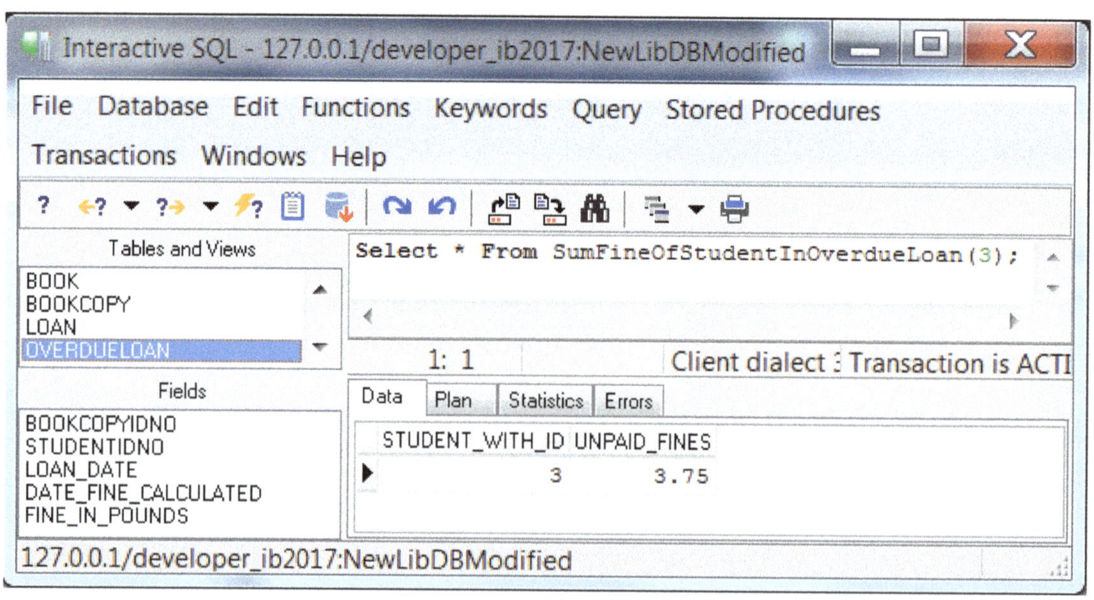

Fig. 63.60 Result set for Execute Procedure SumFineOfStudentInOverdueLoan

Why use stored procedures?

1. Stored procedures supplement SQL with variables, comments, assignment statements, declarative statements, conditional testing and looping programming elements as shown in *Table 63.23*. These enhancements enable much more to be done than is possible with SQL alone.

Construct	Example
Comments	`/* This is a comment*/`
Begin End compound statement	See While Do below
Assignment statements	`i = i + 1;`
If <condition> Then Else	If Exists(Select UserId From LogInDetails Where UserId = :UserIdVar) Then LogInDetails.Password = :NewPasswordVar Else Insert Into LogInDetails (UserId, Password) Values :UserIdVar, :NewPasswordVar;

While <condition> Do	Set Term ^ ;
	Create Procedure FirstFourStudentRecords
	Returns (SurnameVar VarChar(30), FirstNameVar VarChar(30))
	As
	  Declare Variable i Integer;/*Declarative statement*/
	Begin
	  i = 1;
	  While (i < 5) Do
	    Begin
	      Select Surname, Firstname From Student
	         Where StudentIdNo = :i Into :SurnameVar, :FirstNameVar;
	      i = i + 1;
	      Suspend;
	    End ← Note: no terminator symbol
	End ^
	Set Term ; ^
	Commit;

Table 63.23 Available enhancements to SQL

2. Complex tasks may be split into smaller more logical modules. These can then use the fact that stored procedures can be invoked by each other.

3. Stored procedures give full access to SQL and the database's metadata, e.g. see script shown in *Table 63.24* which excludes system tables by exploiting the fact that all contain a '$' in their name.

```
Set Term ^ ;                                                    P
Create Procedure SelectMetadata
Returns (RelationVar VarChar(50))
As
Begin
   For Select rdb$relation_name From rdb$relations
         Where Not (rdb$relation_name containing '$')
           Into :RelationVar
      Do Suspend;
End ^
Set Term  ; ^
Commit;
```

Table 63.24 SelectMetadatataProc.sql script

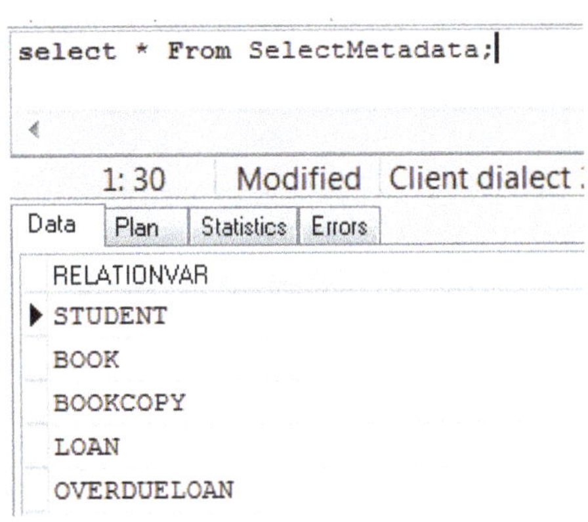

*Fig. 63.61 Result set for Select * From Metadata*

4. Stored procedures offer enhanced security. If database operations such as **Insert**, **Alter**, **Drop** or **Select** can only be performed on a table by stored procedures, then a user's access to the table can be carefully controlled so that only that which is permitted via stored procedures is possible. The user's access rights are restricted to executing the stored procedure (execute access only), all other type of access are denied.
5. Stored procedures make the front end to the database irrelevant, whether it be Delphi, PHP, C# or some other programming language.
6. Interbase is a client/server database management system. As such an Interbase server may very well be accessed across a network. Using stored procedures makes it possible to offload application processes from the client to the server, thus reducing network traffic.

Interbase UDF library

Interbase provides a number of frequently needed functions in the form of a UDF library, named `ib_udf.dll` on Windows platforms and `ib_udf` on UNIX platforms.

On the Windows 7 machine on which this book is being written `ib_udf.dll` is located in the folder whose path is

```
C:\Program Files (x86)\Embarcadero\Studio\20.0\InterBase2017\UDF
```

Locate a copy of the script `ib_udf.sql` and **load** it into IBConsole's **ISQL**.

Information

```
e.g. C:\ProgramData\Embarcadero\Interbase\developer_ib2020\examples\ib_udf.sql
```

Execute this script to make the UDF functions available.

A list of these functions can be obtained from

http://docwiki.embarcadero.com/InterBase/2020/en/The_InterBase_UDF_Library

and from the **External Functions** tab as shown in *Figure 63.62*. after they have been installed.

Launch **ISQL**.

Enter and **execute**

UDF function StrLen returns length of string

```
Select StrLen(Surname) From Student;
```

Figure 63.63 shows the result set returned from this query.

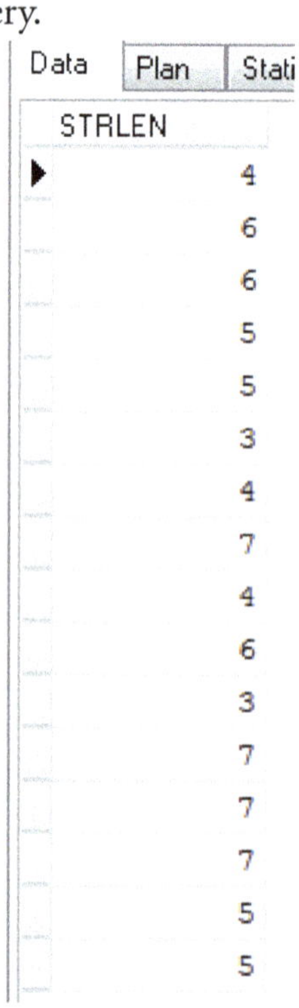

Fig. 63.63 Result set

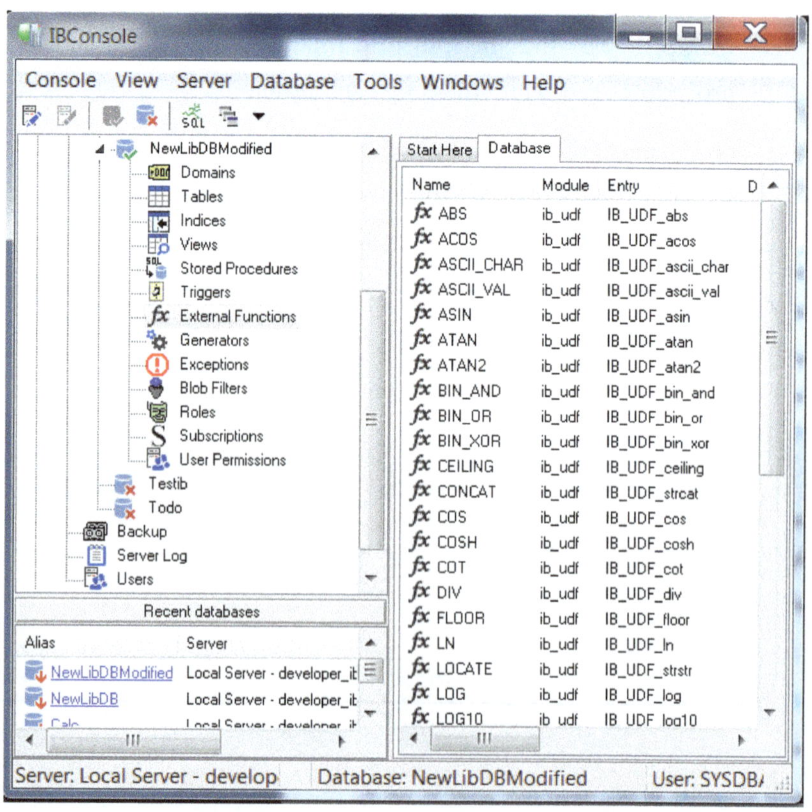

Fig. 63.62 External Functions tab - NewLibDBModified

Roles

A role is a named group of privileges such as permission to use **Select**, **Insert**,etc. It simplifies granting user rights as multiple users can be granted the same role. Should it become necessary to alter the rights of these users, only the role has to be changed.

For example, suppose that we wish to grant certain library staff **Select**, **Insert**, **Update** and **Delete** rights to the tables `Book`, `Student`, `BookCopy` and `Loan` in database `NewLibDBModified` and then later remove these rights.

For convenience, we create a role with the name `Librarian` using the following DDL statement

```
Create Role Librarian;
```

We then grant the required access permissions as follows

```
Grant Select, Insert, Delete, Update On Book To Librarian;
Grant Select, Insert, Delete, Update On Student To Librarian;
Grant Select, Insert, Delete, Update On BookCopy To Librarian;
Grant Select, Insert, Delete, Update On Loan To Librarian;
```

Finally we assign users `MSmith` and `JBloggs` to role `Librarian` using the following

```
Grant Librarian To MSmith, JBloggs;
```

Of course, user `MSmith` already has full access as owner of the database but we have included `MSmith` for consistency.

```
Create Role Librarian;
Grant Select, Insert, Delete, Update On Book To Librarian;
Grant Select, Insert, Delete, Update On Student To Librarian;
Grant Select, Insert, Delete, Update On BookCopy To Librarian;
Grant Select, Insert, Delete, Update On Loan To Librarian;
Commit;
```

P

Table 63.25 CreateRoleLibrarian.sql script

Connect to database `NewLibDBModified` as user `SYSDBA` (password `masterkey`) or `MSmith` (password `password1`).

Launch ISQL.

Select Query|Load Script and load and execute the script `CreateRoleLibrarian.sql` to create role `Librarian`.

Enter and **execute**

```
Grant Librarian To MSmith, JBloggs;
Commit;
```

Disconnect from the database and connect as `JBloggs`.as shown in *Figure 63.63*.

Launch ISQL.

Enter and **execute** `Select * From Book;`

The error message window shown in *Figure 63.64* should pop up because `JBloggs` connected without selecting `Librarian` role.

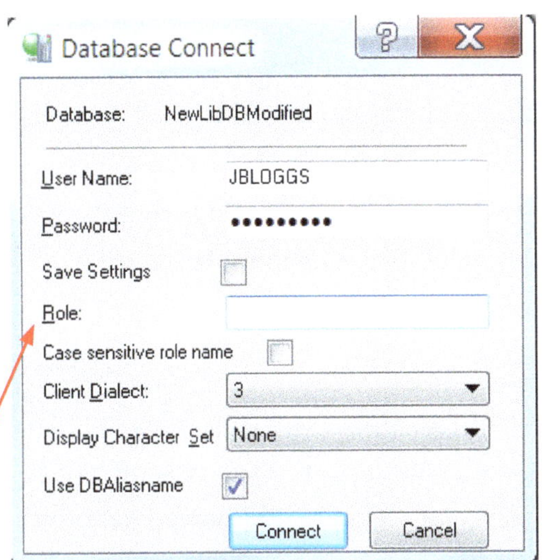

Fig. 63.63 Connect As JBloggs

Disconnect and reconnect as `JBloggs` but this time enter `Librarian` in `Role` field as shown in *Figure 63.65*.

Launch ISQL.

Enter and **execute** `Select * From Book;`

This time the select statement should be successful.

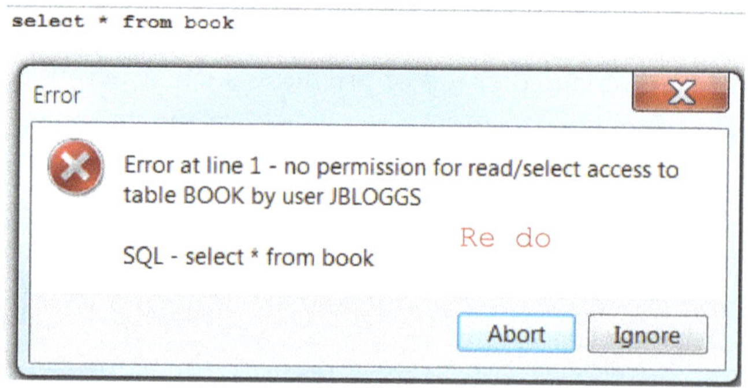

Fig. 63.64 JBloggs does not have permisiion to perform select operation on book table

To remove a role from user, make sure that you are connected to `NewLibDBModified` as the administrator `SYSDBA` or the owner `MSmith`.

Launch ISQL.

Enter and **execute**

```
Revoke Librarian From JBloggs;
Commit;
```

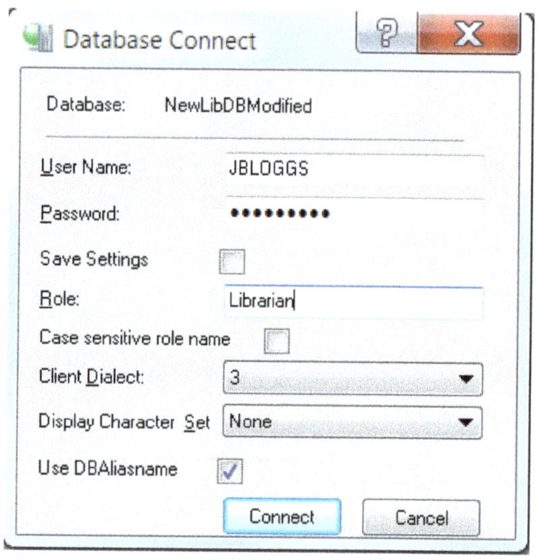

Fig. 63.65 Connect As JBloggs

Indexes

The DDL following statement creates an index on the book table

```
Create Unique Index BookIdNoIndex
  On Book (BookIdNo);
```

The purpose of this index with name `BookIdNoIndex` is similar to that of the index found at the back of a physical book, i.e. to facilitate rapid searching, in this case on the unique field `BookIdNo` of `Book`.

An index is an ordered list of pointers into a table which is used to provide speedier data access.

If the indexed field, e.g. `BookIdNo`, is unique there is only one pointer per field value.

An index is part of a table's physical on-disk structure. It is used to improve the performance of queries on the indexed table.

For fields defined with a primary key or a foreign key in a table, Interbase should automatically generate a corresponding ascending index and apply the uniqueness constraint required by the relational model.

If the field that is indexed is not unique then the DDL drops the **Unique** keyword, e.g.

```
Create Index BookCopyBookIdNoIndex
  On BookCopy (BookIdNo);
```

Alter

Alter is the SQL command used to modify database objects, e.g. databases, tables, procedures, views, domains, triggers, generators, etc can all be changed using the **Alter** command.

The Case tool, **Case Studio 2.23**, which was used to generate the script shown in *Table 63.26* from the E-R diagram shown in *Figure 63.66*, uses **Alter** to add foreign keys to the `Loan` and `BookCopy` tables.

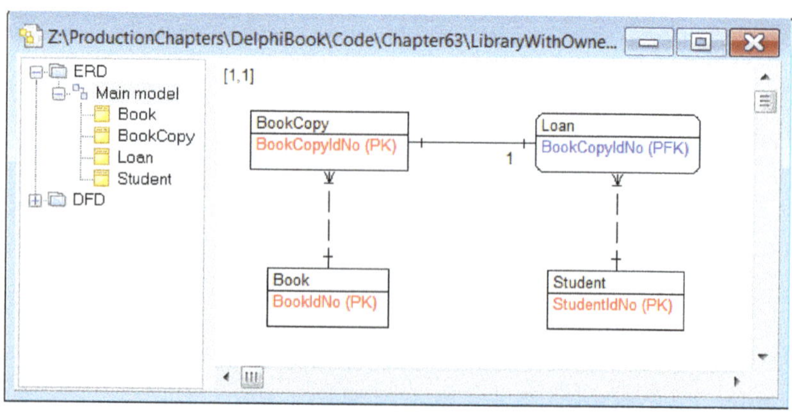

Fig. 63.66 Library Entity Relationship (E-R) diagram drawn in Case Studio 2.23

```
Create Domain SurnameType As Varchar(20);
Create Domain ....;
Create Table Student   (
        StudentIdNo Integer NOT NULL Check (Value Between 1 And 2000),
        Surname Varchar(20) NOT NULL,
        FirstName Varchar(10) NOT NULL,
 Primary Key (StudentIdNo)
);
Create Table Book   (
        BookIdNo Integer NOT NULL Check (Value Between 1 and 1000),
        ....,
 Primary Key (BookIdNo)
);
Create Table BookCopy   (
        BookCopyIdNo Integer NOT NULL Check (Value Between 1 and 6000),
        ....,
 Primary Key (BookCopyIdNo)
);
Create Table Loan   (
        BookCopyIdNo Integer NOT NULL Check (Value Between 1 and 6000),
        ....,
 Primary Key (BookCopyIdNo)
);
Alter Table Loan add Foreign Key (StudentIdNo)
  references Student (StudentIdNo) on update no action on delete no action;
Alter Table BookCopy add Foreign Key (BookIdNo)
  references Book (BookIdNo) on update no action on delete no action;
Alter Table Loan add Foreign Key (BookCopyIdNo)
  references BookCopy (BookCopyIdNo) on update no action on delete no action;
```

Table 63.26 LibraryCaseTool.sql script

Lettercase of SQL Keywords

We have already covered several SQL keywords such as **Select**, **Insert**, **Create** which have been written in a mix of uppercase and lowercase letters with the first letter of each capitalised. This isn't the only way that the SQL keywords can be written. Some developers prefer to make all keywords uppercase, others prefer all lowercase, and some mix and match. It is a matter of preference.

Which version of Interbase?

Delphi 7 shipped with version 6.0 of Interbase whilst the latest version Delphi 10.3.3 ships with version 2020 of Interbase.

In early 2000, Borland/Inprise announced that Interbase would be released under open-source and a variant of Mozilla Public Licence. Borland/Inprise continued to support the open source version correcting a backdoor used id/password present in all versions since 1994 . However, in 2001 Borland/Inprise discontinued support for the open source variant which then became a separate fork supported by the Firebird project which is still active with the release in January 2020 of Firebird version 3.0. *Figure 63.67* shows the About window for Interbase 6.1, the last open-source version supported by Borland/Inprise. The backdoor userid/password issue was fixed in this version.

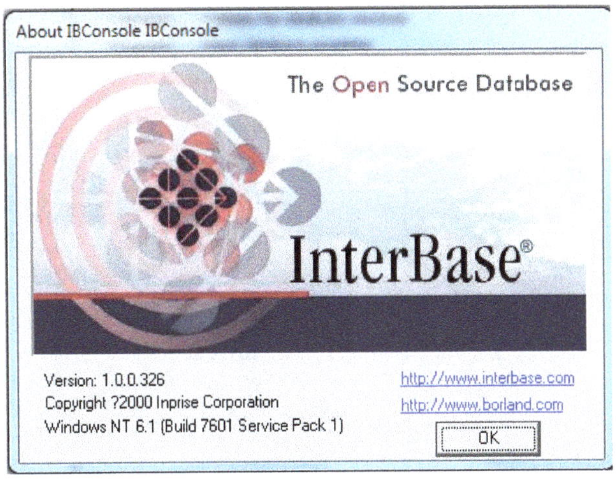

Fig. 63.67 Interbase 6.1 open source version

Migrating a database from an earlier version of Interbase

The example task described below converts an Interbase XE3 database to an Interbase 2017 database by making a back up copy of the XE3 database on a local Interbase XE3 server first, before restoring this back up from a local Interbase 2017 server. The latter converts the XE3 database into the format required for the 2017 server. A similar process can be used to migrate an Interbase 2017 database to an Interbase 2020 database or an Interbase 6 database to any later version of Interbase.

Figure 63.68 shows local server Interbase XE3 running as a service on a Windows 7 computer.
Figure 63.69 shows the system administrator SYSDBA logged in to local server Interbase XE3 in IBConsole and connected to an Interbase XE3 database `CSBookDatabase.gdb`, alias `Csbookdatabase`.
In order to migrate this database to Interbase 2017 we must first back up the database.
To do this, we must select **Backup** from the menu option **Database|Maintenance|Backup/Restore** shown in *Figure 63.70*. The **Database Backup** window will then be displayed - *Figure 63.71*. An alias and a filepath must be entered in the the **Backup File(s)** section.

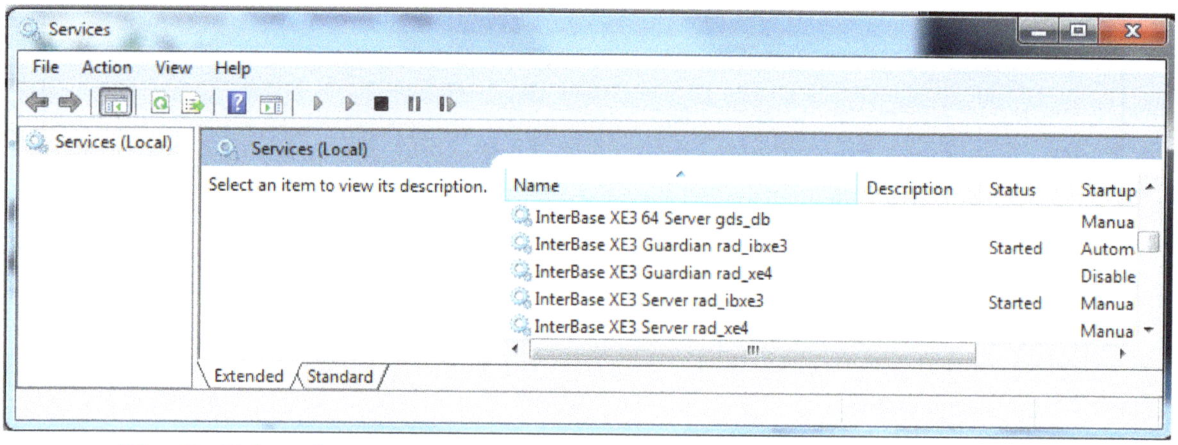

Fig. 63.68 Interbase XE3 shown running as a service on a Windows 7 computer

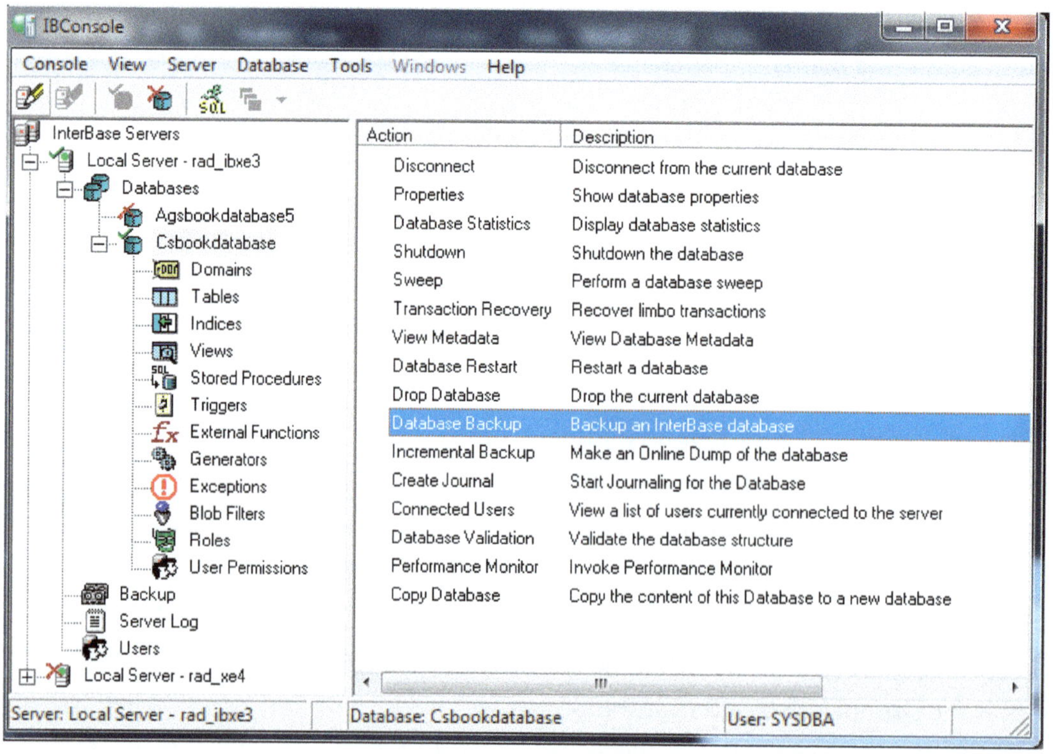

Fig. 63.69 Local server Interbase XE3 and a connected Interbase XE3 database CsBookDatabase.gdb

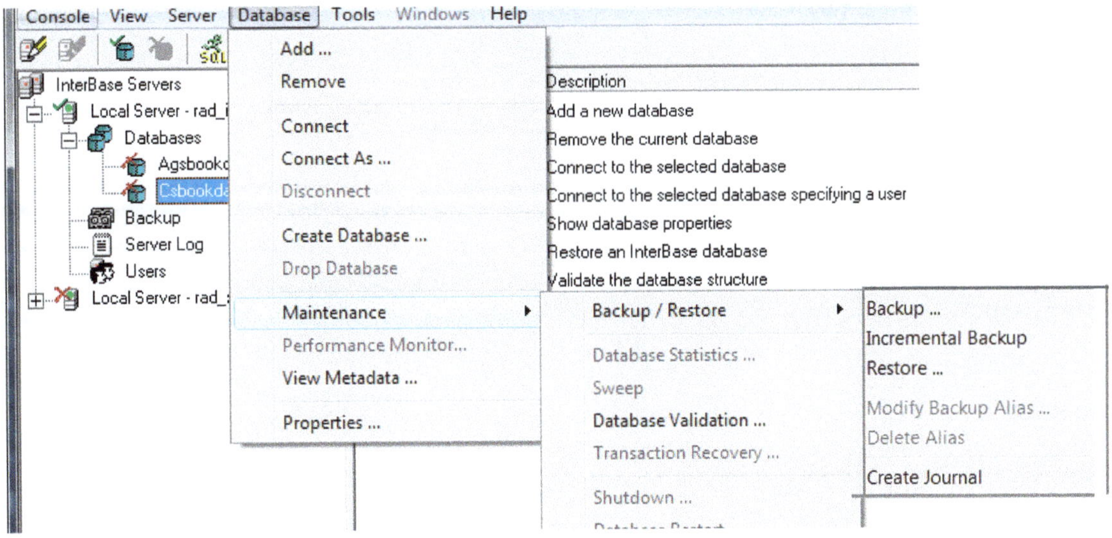

Fig. 63.70 Using the Database|Maintenance|Backup/Restore|Backup menu option to backup CSBookDatabase.gdb

This example, uses the alias and file path `CSBookDatabase` and `C:\CSBookDatabase.ibk`, respectively.

Under the **Options** section, the **Verbose Output** is set to **To Screen**.

Next the **OK** button is clicked to start the backup.

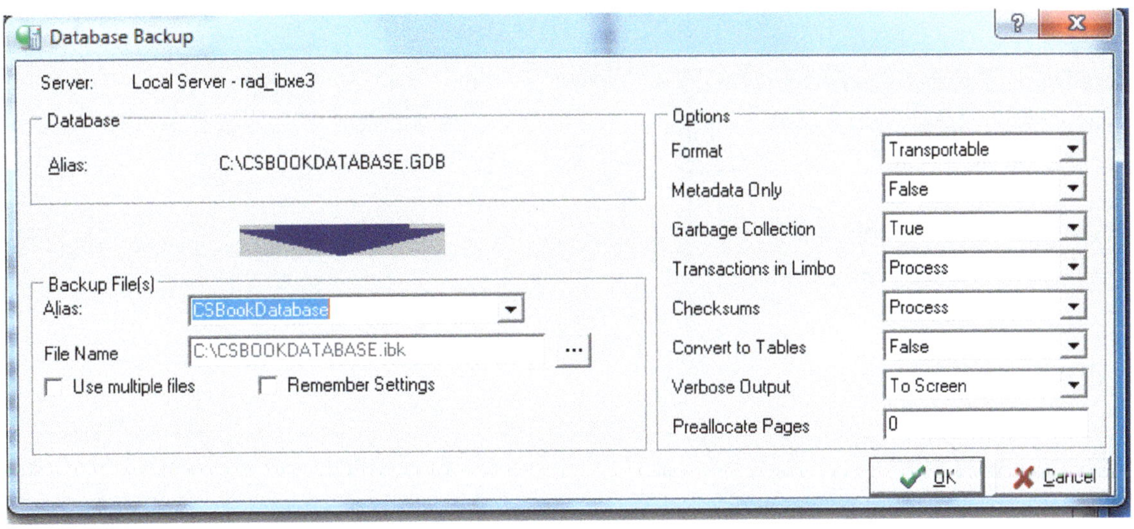

Fig. 63.71 Using the Database|Maintenance|Backup/Restore|backup menu option to backup CSBookDatabase.gdb

The backup details are displayed in the **Database Backup** screen.

When the back up has completed successfully, an **Information** screen is displayed.

Clicking the **OK** button closes this window. Clicking on  closes the **Database Backup** window.

Interbase server XE3 must now be stopped.

This is done by launching **Control Panel** then selecting **System and Security** followed by **Administrative Tools**. **Services** is clicked and then **Interbase XE3** is right-clicked and **Stop** clicked in the drop-down menu.

Next Interbase 2017 is started (there are two ways this can be done: from the Start Menu by selecting **Interbase Server Manager** and then **Start** or from **Control Panel|System and Security| Administrative Tools| Services**) then **Start**).

IBConsole must be launched and **Server|Add** clicked to add `Local Server developer_ib2017`, if not already present.

Next the administrator must be logged in as shown in *Figure 63.72*.

The administrator must then select **Database|Backup/Restore|Restore** as shown in *Figure 63.73*.

Clicking **Restore** launches the window shown in *Figure 63.74*.

Under the **Options** section, **Overwrite** must be set to **True**.

The **Alias** and **File Name** fields are set to `CSBookDatabase` and `C:\Users\drbond\CSBookDatabase.ib`, respectively.

Under the **Options** section, the **Verbose Output** is set to **To Screen**.

Next the **OK** button is clicked to start the restore.

The restore details are displayed in the **Database Restore** screen shown in *Figure 63.75*.

When the restore operation has completed successfully, an **Information** screen is displayed as shown in *Figure 63.75*.

Figure 63.76 demonstrates a successful migration of `CSBookDatabase.gdb` from Interbase XE3 to Interbase 2017 as `CSBookDatabase.ib`.

Figure 63.77 shows a restore operation on an Interbase 2020 local server which converts an Interbase 2017 database backup copy `CSBookDatabase.ibk` to an Interbase 2020 database `CSBookDatabase2020.ib`.

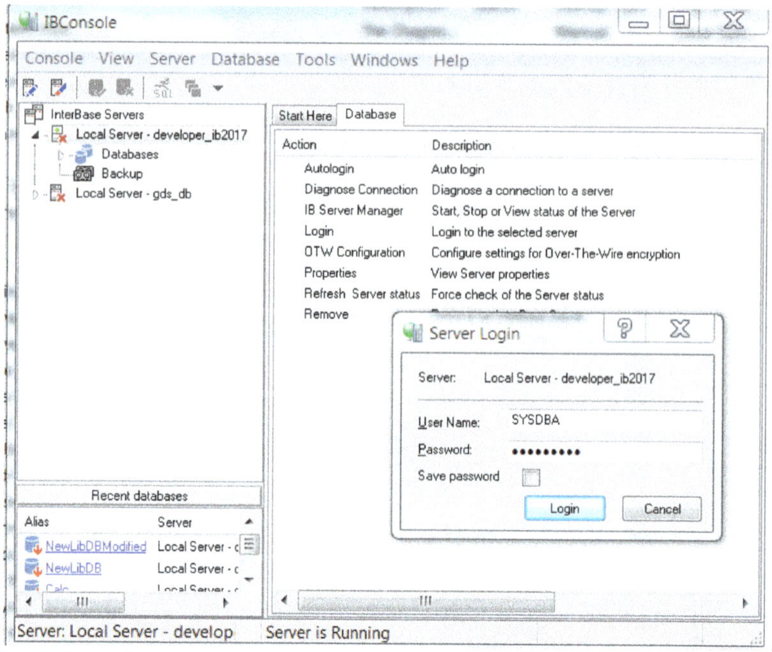

Fig. 63.72 Logging in as Administrator to Local Server developer_ib2017

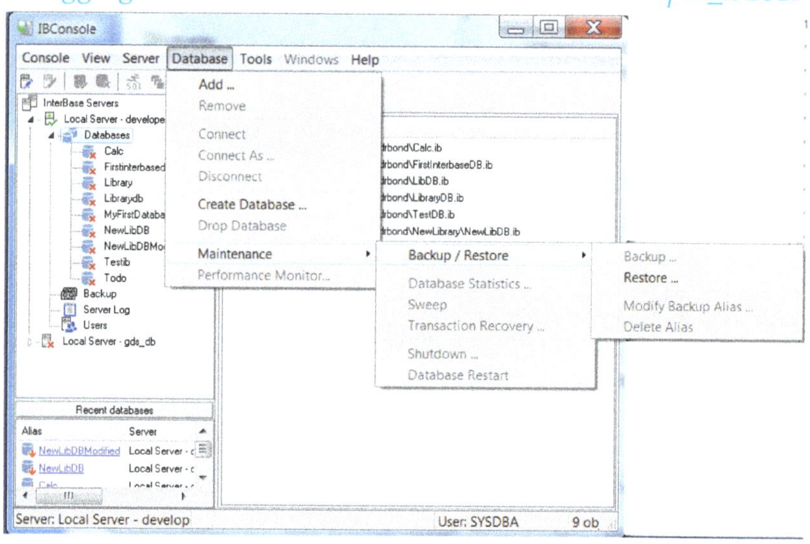

Fig. 63.73 Selecting Restore from back up CSBookDatabase.ibk

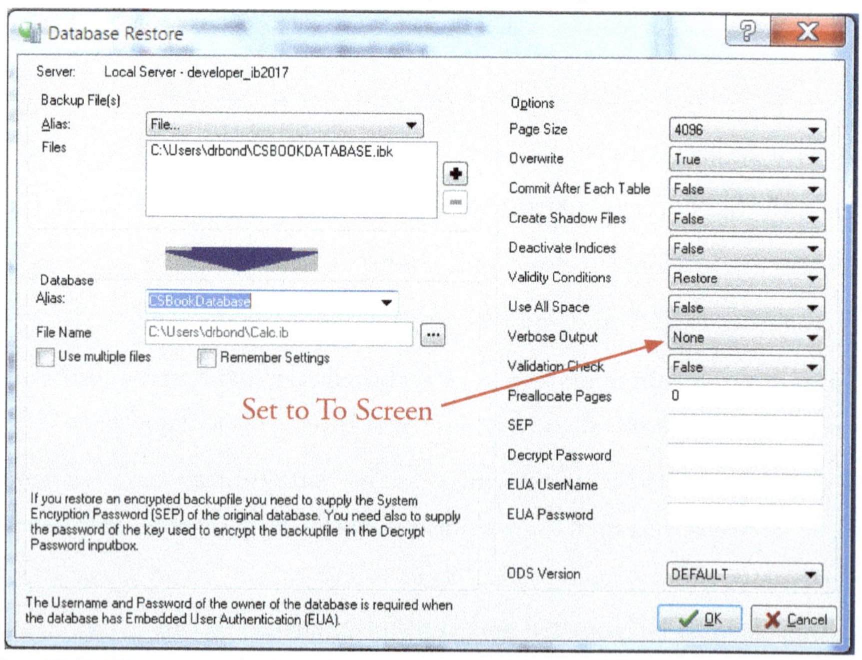

Fig. 63.74 Restore window for creating CSBookDatabase.ib from backup

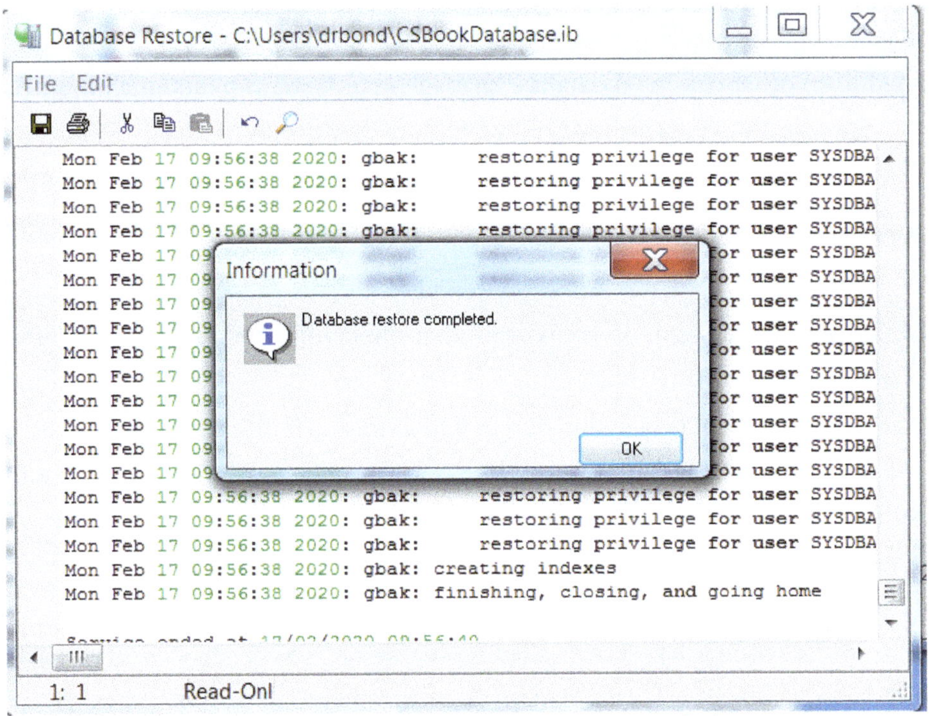

Fig. 63.75 Database Restore progress window

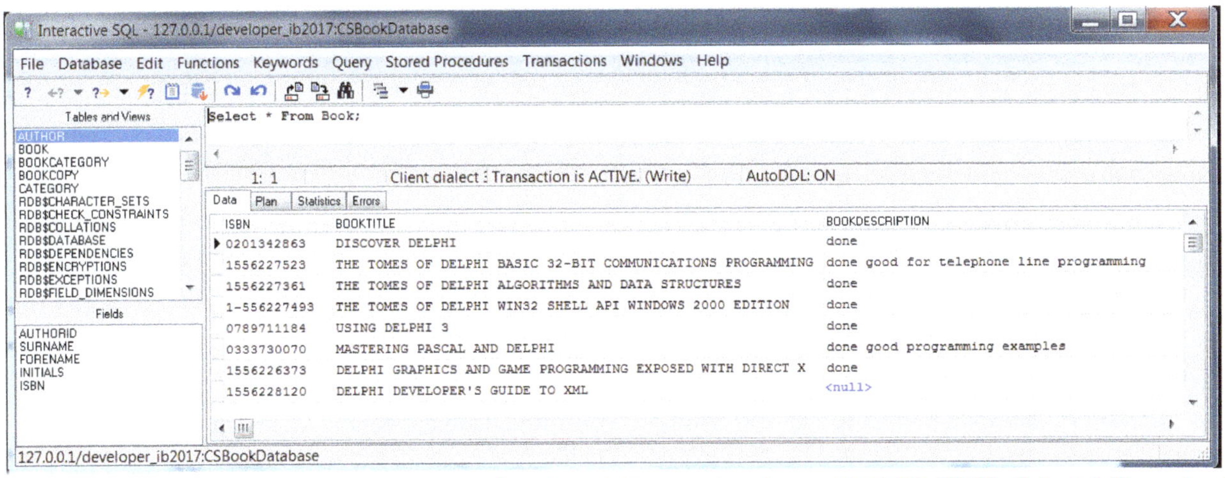

*Fig. 63.76 CSBookDatabase.ib connected to Local Server developer_ib2017, ISQL Select * From book*

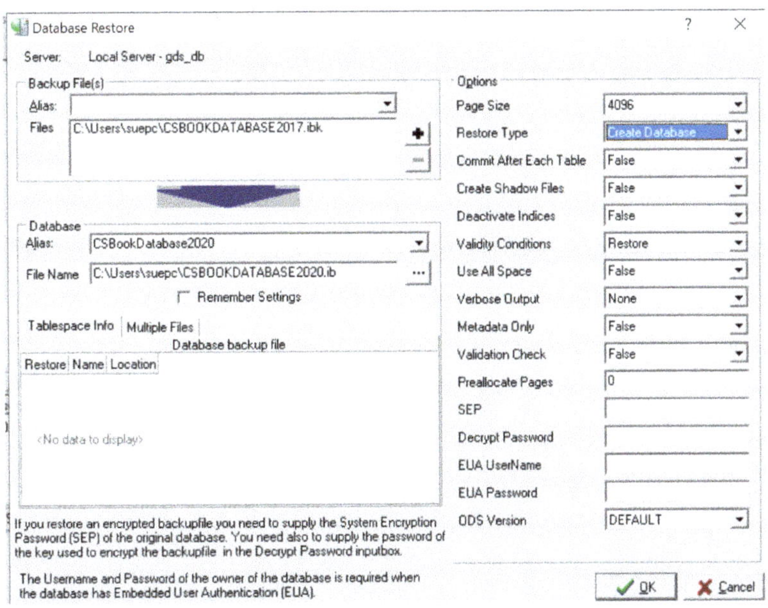

Fig. 63.77 Database restore operation on an Interbase 2020 server which converts an Interbase 2017 database backup to an Interbase 2020 database CSBookDatabase2020.ib

Why use Interbase?

Interbase is distiguished from other relational database management systems by its small footprint, close to zero administration requirements and multi-generational architecture. It runs on Microsoft Windows, macOS, Linux, Solaris as well as iOS and Android. Interbase can be run as an embedded database or a regular server.

A full Interbase server installation requires around 40 MB on disk. A minimum Interbase client install requires about 400 KB of disk space.

Since Interbase XE, Interbase includes 256 bit encryption that offers full database, table or column data encryption.

Multi-generational architecture

Interbase is a client-server database manangement system which means multiple clients may access the server simultaneously. Access to a common database, by mutiple users simultaneously, must be carefully controlled so that updates from multiple clients do not overwrite each other. One such technique that overcomes this potential problem is **blocking** which esssentially blocks access to a particular record to all clients attempting access except one by placing a lock on the record. This can slow access and is inconvenient to interactive clients. Interbase instead uses a different technique to control concurrent access called multiversion concurrency control. Each transaction creates a version of the record. Upon the write step, the update will fail rather than be blocked initially.

Interbase also uses multi-generational records to implement rollbacks, i.e. recovery from an error or potential inconsistency, rather than transaction logs.

This approach works well except under certain circumstances when certain operations perform slowly compared to a more traditional implementation such as locks. One example is SQL Count.

How is SQL pronounced?

The author pronounces SQL as "es-queue-el" and not "sequel". The consequence is that when writing about SQL, "an" and not "a" is used, e.g. "an SQL statement" and not "a SQL statement".

The original SQL standard declared the offical pronunciation for SQL as "es-queue-el". However, many English-speaking database professionals still use the non-standard pronunciation "sequel".

The first draft of SQL was in fact Structured English Query Language and its acronym was SEQUEL. However, because the acronym was a violation of a trademark, the name was changed to Structured Query Language and abbreviated as SQL. So it was intended originally to be pronounced as SEQUEL.

Data Security in Interbase

See MT Kelly article

https://community.idera.com/developer-tools/b/blog/posts/data-security-in-interbase?utm_source=Eloqua&utm_medium=email&utm_content=Promotion-200219-InterBaseDisasterRecovery

Recovery from a crash

Rollback - see Bill Todd's article *Interbase: What sets it apart.*

edn.embarcadero.com/kr/print/27007

Also see online slide presentation:

pdfslide.net/documents/1096-understanding-interbase-transactions-bill-todd-the-database-group-inc.html

On-Disk Structure (ODS)

Each release of Interbase has a specific internal file format. Interbase distinguishes one internal file format from another by recording an on-disk structure (ODS) number in the database file, e.g. 17.1. The number before the decimal point refers to the major ODS version. For example, Interbase 2017 has major ODS version number 17, Interbase 2020 has major ODS version number 18. Interbase 2020 still supports older ODS versions ODS 13 through to ODS 17. Therefore, Interbase server 2020 can successfully connect to an Interbase 2017 database, for example. Interbase databases older than ODS 13 should be backed up from an Interbase server that they can connect to and then restored by an Interbase server with ODS version number later than or equal to ODS 13 in order to connect to Interbase 2017 or 2020. *Table 63.27* shows Interbase servers and their corresponding ODS numbers.

Server Version	ODS number
Interbase 6.0	10.0 can support 9.0/9.1
Interbase 7.0	11.0 can support 10.0
Interbase 7.1	11.1, can support 10.0
Interbase 7.5	11.2, can support 10.0
Interbase 2007	12.0, can support 11.x
Interbase 2009	13.1, can support 12.0
Interbase XE, XE3	15.0, can support 13.1
Interbase XE 7	16.0, can support 13, 15
Interbase 2017	17, can support 13, 15
Interbase 2020	18, can support 13, 15, 17

Table 63.27 Interbase server versions and their On-Disk Structure (ODS) number

Exporting data from an Interbase database

Data may be exported from an Interbase database table such as table `Student` shown in *Figure 63.78*

Double click the table in the **Database** pane to bring up the **Properties** window.

Select the **Data** tab in the **Properties** pane - *Figure 63.79* - then **click** the **Export data** button.

Specify the path and filename of the file that will store the exported data - `Student.txt`.

Table 63.28 shows the contents and format of this text file, `Student.txt`, after a successful export.

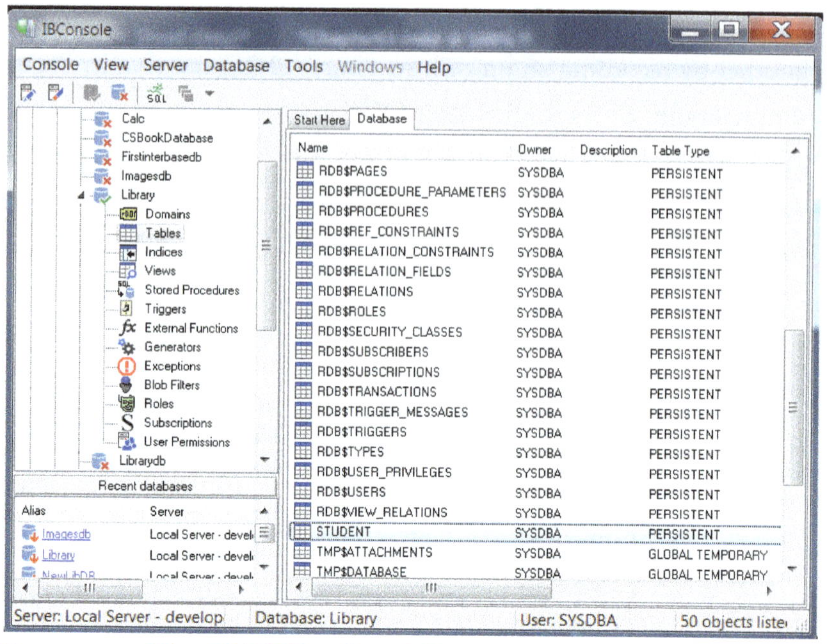

Fig. 63.78 Database LibDB.ib (alias Library)

```
STUDENTIDNO   SURNAME                FIRSTNAME
===========   ====================   ===============
1             Briggs                 James
2             Bloggs                 Fred
3             Moffet                 Mary
4             Smith                  Joe
5             Brown                  Jane
6             Ali                    Mo
7             Shah                   Faiza
8             Hancock                Mick
9             Choo                   Sarah
10            Bowden                 Nancy
11            Pen                    Choy
12            Switzer                Dan
13            Chomsky                Alan
14            Springs                Alice
15            Patel                  Dipak
16            Singh                  Aisha
17            Zaks                   Matt
```

Table 63.28 Contents of Student.txt produced by clicking Export data icon in IBConsole with Data tab selected for table Student

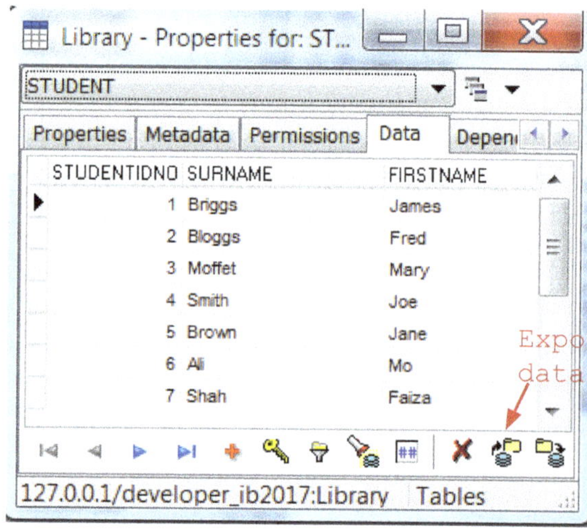

Fig. 63.79 Data tab for table Student

Importing data into an Interbase database

Create a database `ImportData.ib` with alias `ImportData`.

Use the script `CreateLibDatabase.sql` to create tables for this database including table `Student`.

Double click table `Student` - *Figure 63.80*.

Select the **Data** tab in the **Properties** pane - *Figure 63.81* - then **click** the **Import data** button to bring up the **Import to data to table** window - *Figure 63.82* - which will be blank initially. *Figure 63.82* shows the stage after the

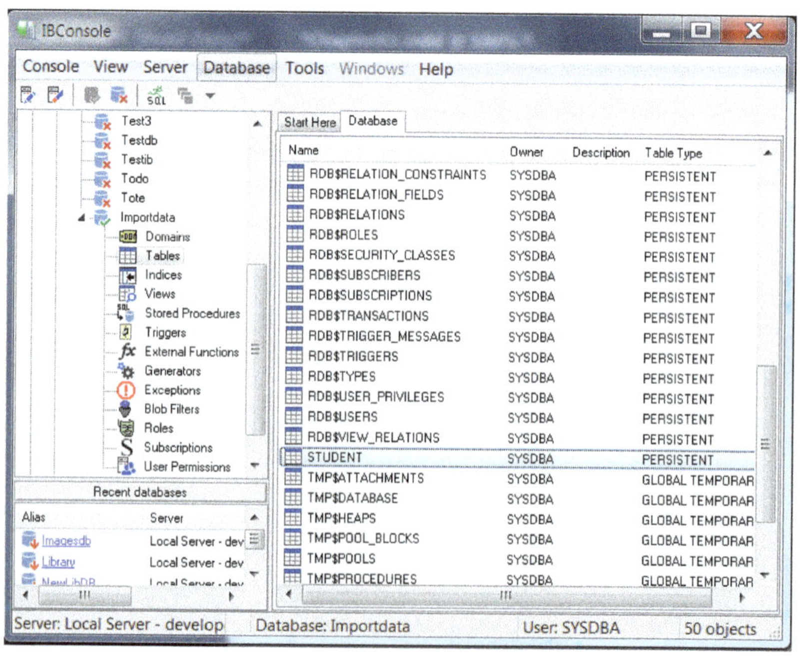

Fig. 63.80 Database ImportData.ib (alias Importdata)

text file `Student.txt` has been opened in the **Open file dialogue** window - *Figure 63.83*.

Set Skip Headerlines to 2 - *Figure 63.84*.

Select `StudentIDNo` in the lower left pane.

Starting from the left, highlight `StudentIDNo` in the upper pane as shown in *Figure 63.84*. Highlighting in this way ensures that the **Position** column will be 1 as it needs to be.

Click the Assign to Column button.

The **Position** and **Size** columns will now show 1 and 11, as shown in *Figure 63.84*.

Select `Surname` in the lower left pane and repeat the process. *Figure 63.85* shows the stage when in the lower left pane, all three fields of table `Student` have been have been processed and linked to the columns of the text file data.

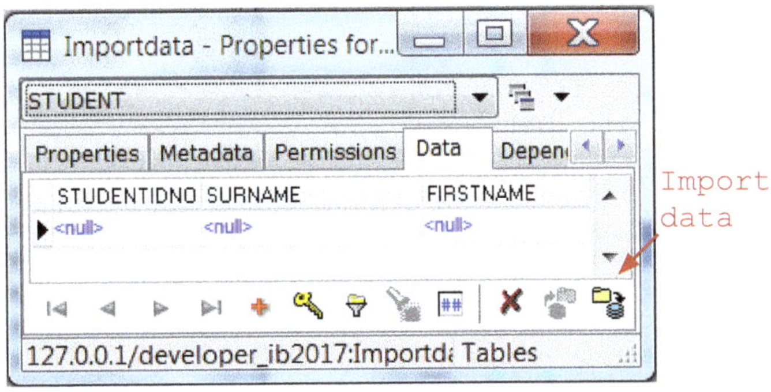

Fig. 63.81 Data tab for table Student

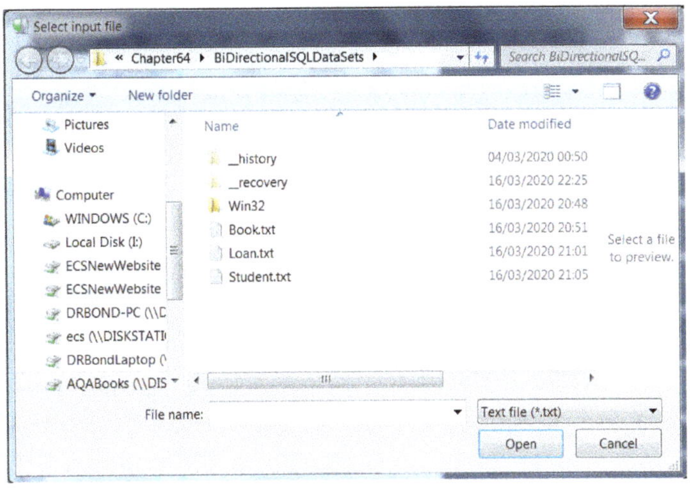

Fig. 63.83 Open file dialogue to select file containing data to import

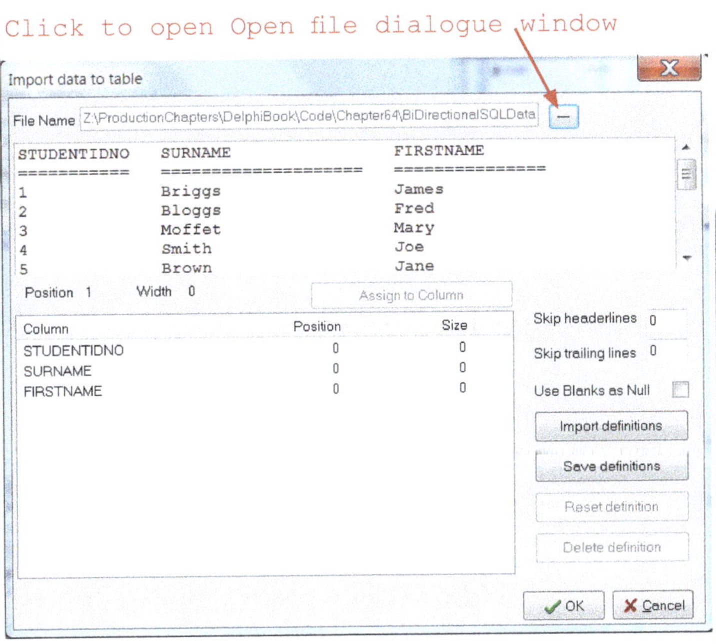

Fig. 63.82 Import data to table window

Click the **OK** button to start the import process.

The message window shown in *Figure 63.86* pops up when the data has been imported.

Figure 63.87 shows that table `Student` is now populated with the imported data.

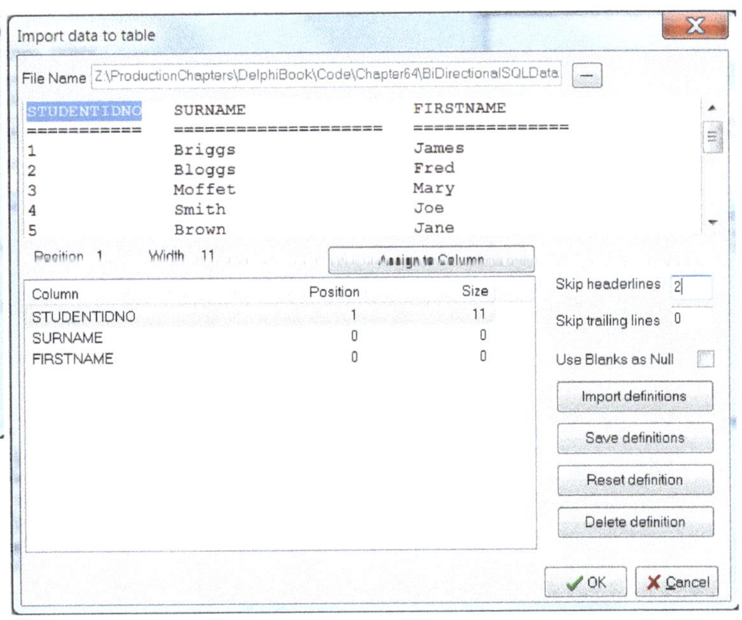

Fig. 63.84 Mapping table fields to text file fields - first field

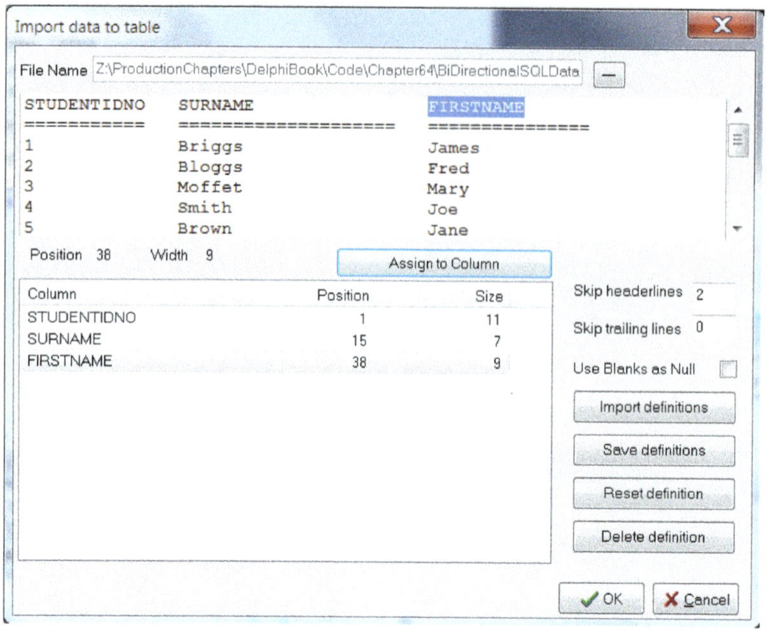

Fig. 63.85 Mapping table fields to text file fields - all done

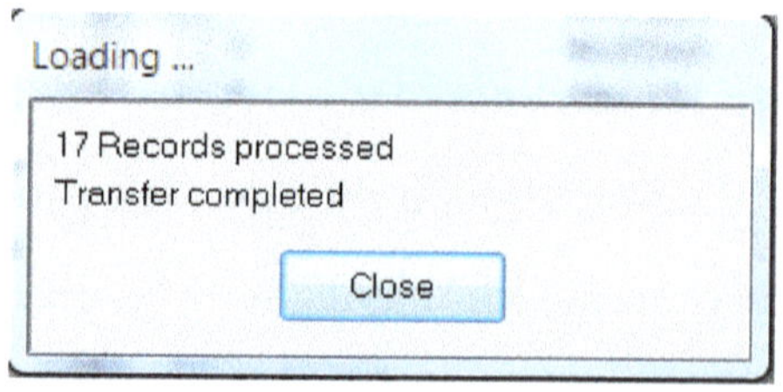

Fig. 63.86 Transfer completed message window

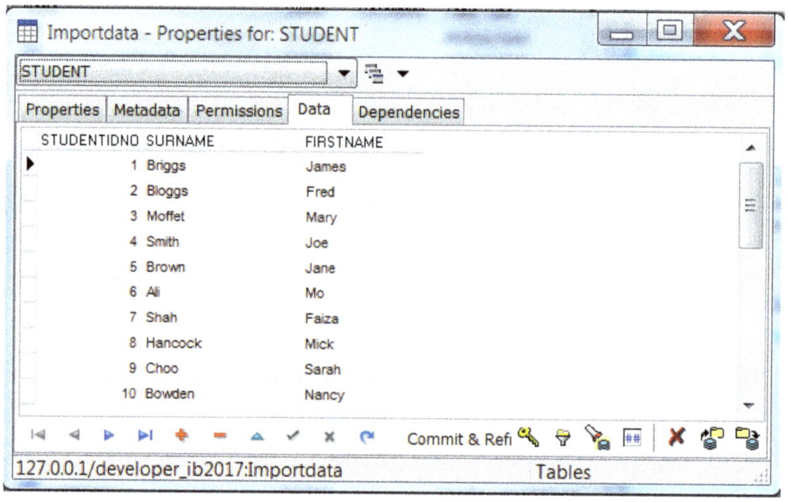

Fig. 63.87 Table Student populated with data form text file Student.txt

64 Using Delphi with Interbase

First database project

Purpose: To learn how to use tables

Delphi Community Edition 10.3.2 or later

Delphi 10.3.2 and 10.3.3 will both work with Interbase 2017 and Interbase 2020. These database tools may be downloaded from https://www.embarcadero.com/products/interbase/developer/free-download. The contents of this chapter are still relevant even if you are using a later version of Delphi. Just use the shipped version of Interbase that is compatible with your version of Delphi - see *Chapter 63* for an explanation of the on-disk structure (ODS) version numbering and compatibility issues with Interbase databases created with earlier versions of Interbase.

After installing, you should start the Interbase server preferably as a service. **Launch** Control Panel then **select** System and Security followed by Administrative Tools. **Double click** Services - *Figure 64.1* - to launch the Services window - *Figure 64.2*. **Right click** on InterBase 2017 64 Server developer_ib2017 or the relevant Interbase server and **click** Start in the drop-down menu if the server is not already started. If InterBase 2017 64 Guardian developer_ib2017 is also installed then you can **Right click** on this and **click** Start in the drop-down menu instead.

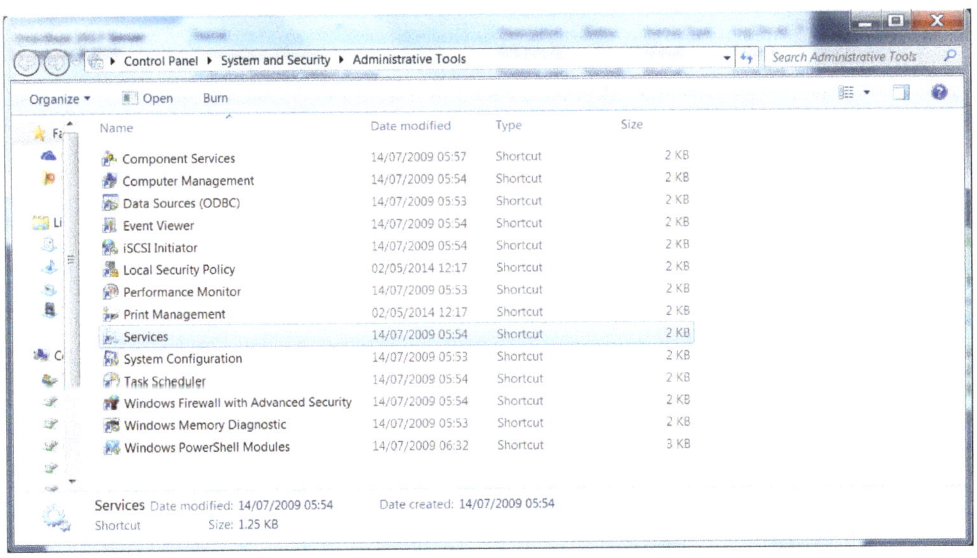

Fig. 64.1 Microsoft Windows 7 Administrative Tools

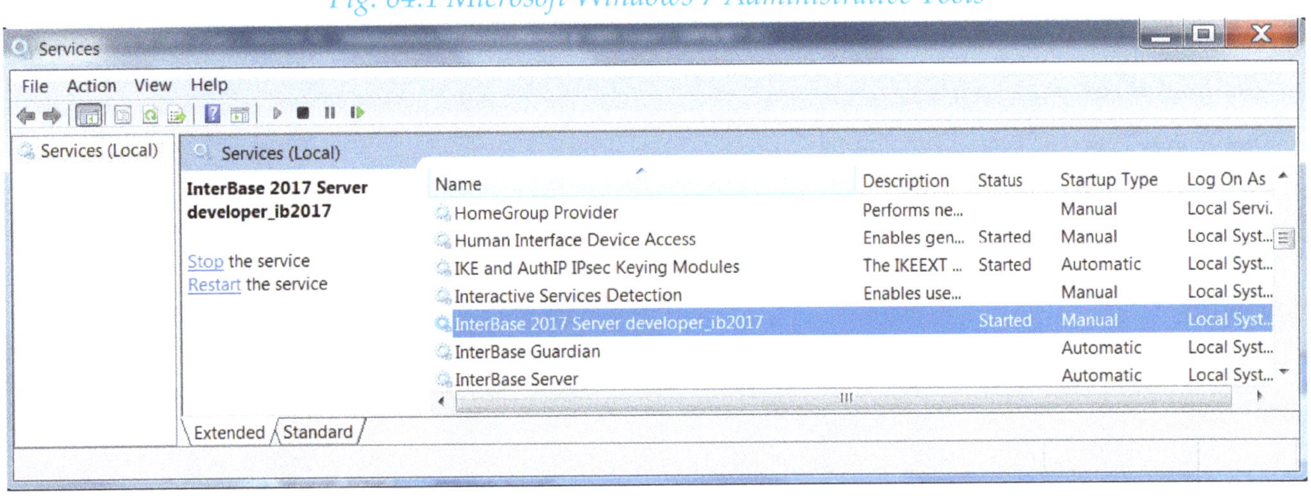

Fig. 64.2 Microsoft Windows 7 Services window showing that Interbase Server 2017 is started

www.educational-computing.com/DelphiBook/Code/Chapter64/LibraryLoansTableExercise.rar

Launch Delphi

Select File|New|VCL Application.

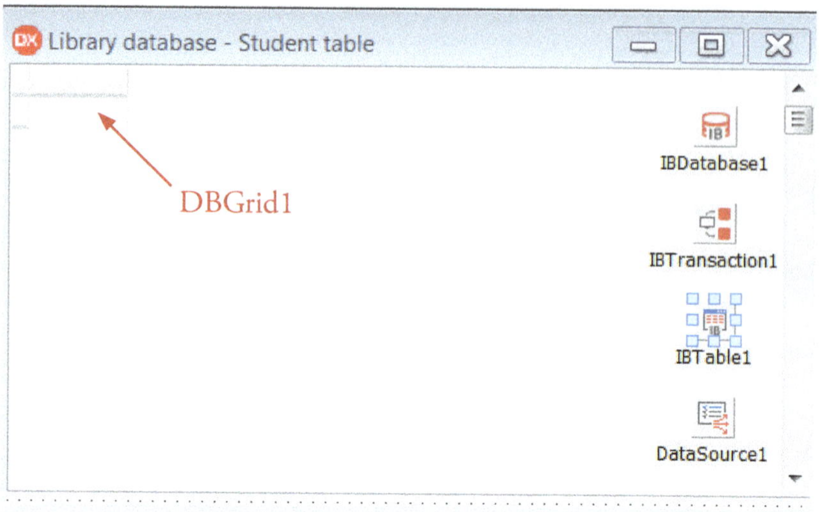

Fig. 64.3 Form1 for LibraryLoansTable project

- **Select** the form, `Form1`, and change its caption to `Library database - Student table` - see *Figure 64.3*.
- **Place** an TIBDatabase component, `IBDatabase1`, an TIBTransaction component, `IBTransaction1`, and an TIBTable component, `IBTable1`, from the Interbase palette on this form as shown in *Figure 64.3*.
- **Place** a TDBGrid from the Data Controls palette on the form - `DBGrid1` - as shown in *Figure 64.3*.
- **Place** a TDataSource component from the Data Access palette on the form - `DataSource1`.

Save the project (**Save All**) in a folder `LibraryLoansTableExercise`.

- **Save** the unit as `LibraryLoansTableUnit.pas`
- **Save** the project as `LibraryLoansTable.dproj.`

Download LibDB.ib from

www.educational-computing.com/DelphiBook/Code/Chapter64/LibDB.ib.

(This is an Interbase 2017 created database, other versions are available - see www.educational-computing.co.uk/DelphiBookCode/DelphiCode.html).

Databases must be created on the same drive as Interbase server e.g. the C: drive.

Copy LibDB.ib to a folder on the C: drive.

In this example, **LibDB.ib** has been copied to `C:\Users\drbond\`.

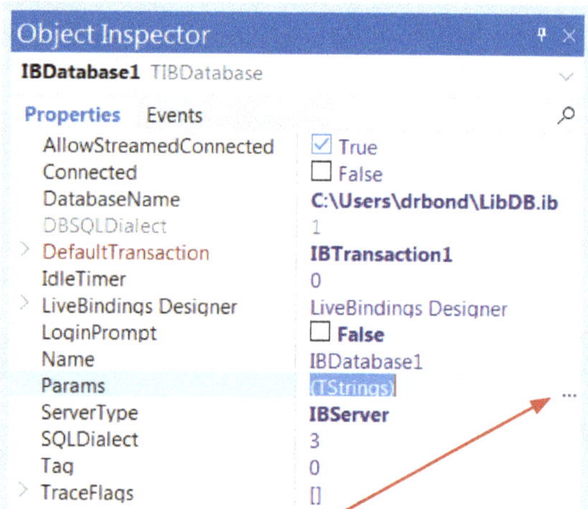

Fig. 64.4 Object Inspector settings for IBDatabase1

Select `IBDatabase1` and from the **Object Inspector** view shown in *Figure 64.4*

- **Set DatabaseName** to `C:\Users\drbond\`
- **Set DefaultTransaction** to `IBTransaction1`
- **Set LoginPrompt** to `False`
- **Set ServerType** to `IBServer`.

Click ellipsis (...) in property **Params** to bring up the **String List Editor** shown in *Figure 64.5*.

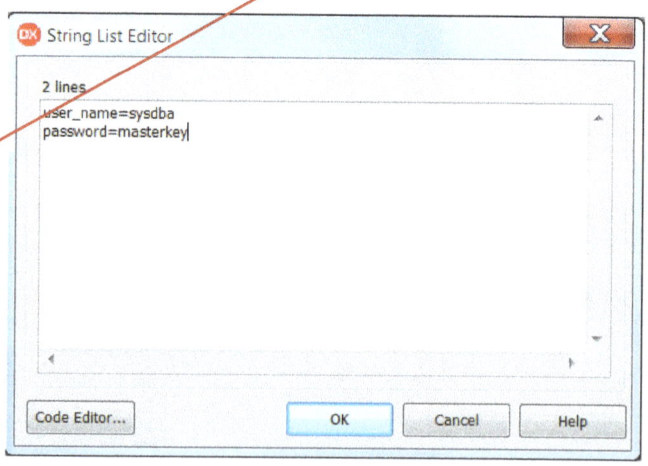

Fig. 64.5 String List Editor for IBDatabase1

Add the strings

- `user_name=sysdba`
- `password=masterkey` as shown in *Figure 64.5*.

Click OK.

Select `IBTransaction1` and from the **Object Inspector** shown in *Figure 64.6*

- **Set DefaultDatabase** to `IBDatabase1`.

Select `IBDatabase1` and from the **Object Inspector**

- **Change** the **Connected** field of `IBDatabase1` - *Figure 64.4* - to `True` to connect the database `LibDB.ib`.

  If you are unable to connect, try resetting the server first[1].

Select `IBTable1` and from the **Object Inspector** shown in *Figure 64.7*

- **Set Database** to `IBDatabase1`
- **Set TableName** to `Student`
- **Set Active** to `True`.

Select `DataSource1` and from the **Object Inspector** shown in *Figure 64.8*

- **Set DataSet** to `IBTable1`.

Select `IBDBGrid1` and from the **Object Inspector** shown in *Figure 64.9*

- **Set DataSet** to `IBTable1`.

Data from table `Student` should now appear at design time in `DBGrid1` as shown in *Figure 64.10*.

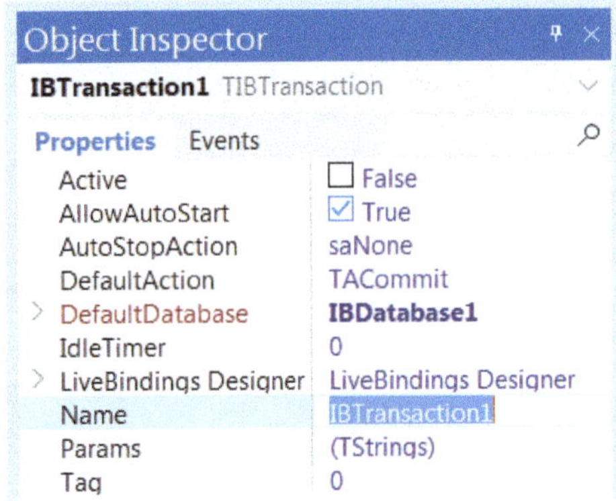

Fig. 64.6 Object inspector for IBTransaction1

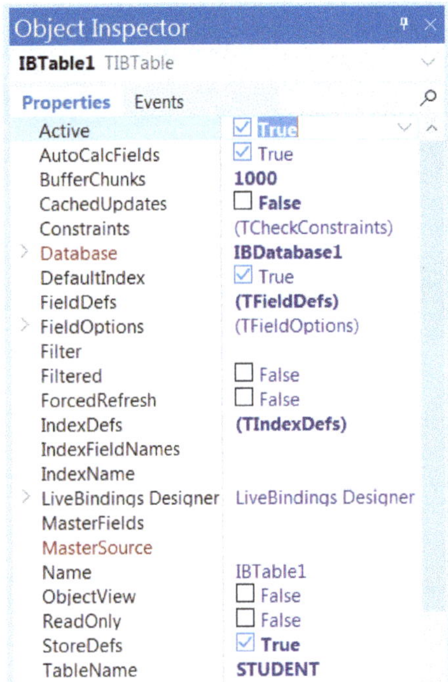

Fig. 64.7 Object inspector for IBTable1

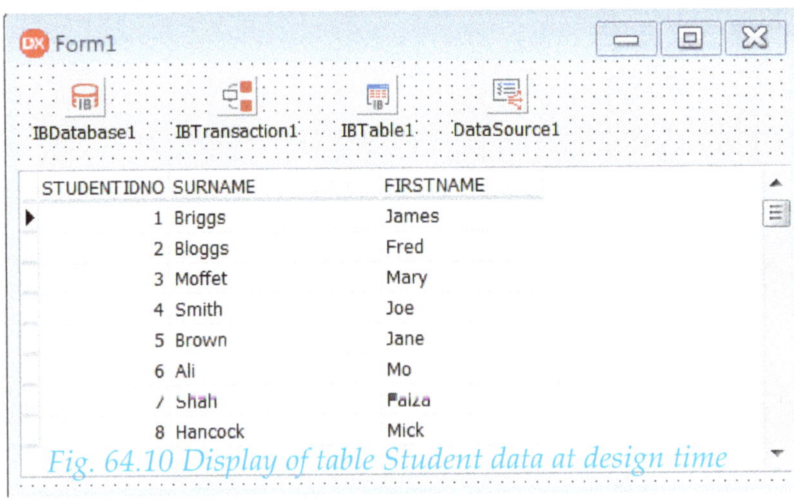

Fig. 64.10 Display of table Student data at design time

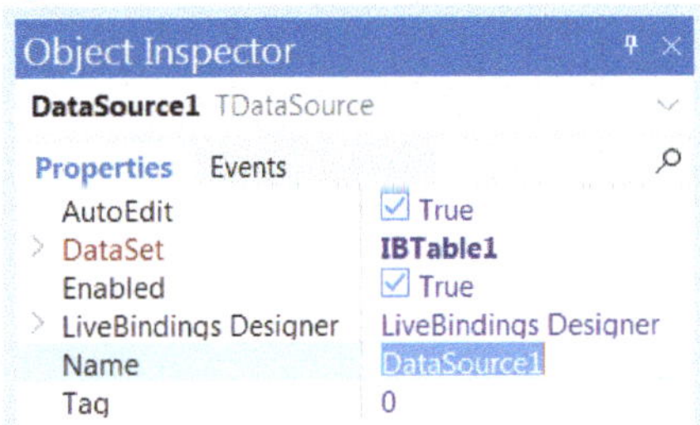

Fig. 64.8 Object inspector for DataSource1

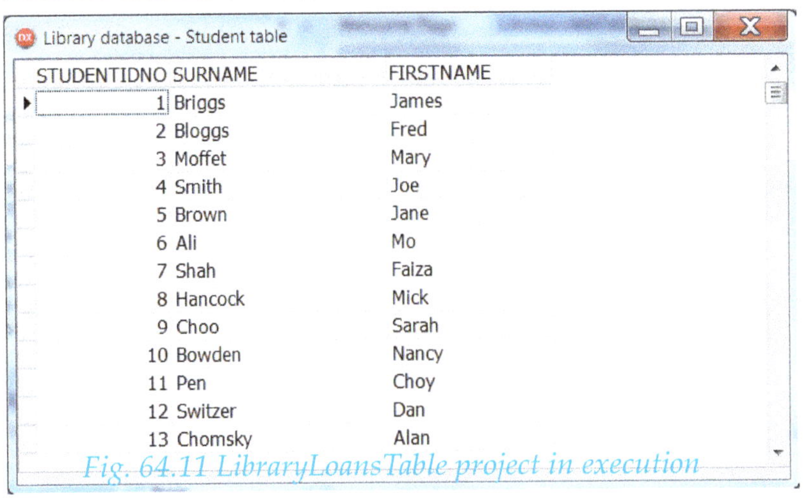

Fig. 64.11 LibraryLoansTable project in execution

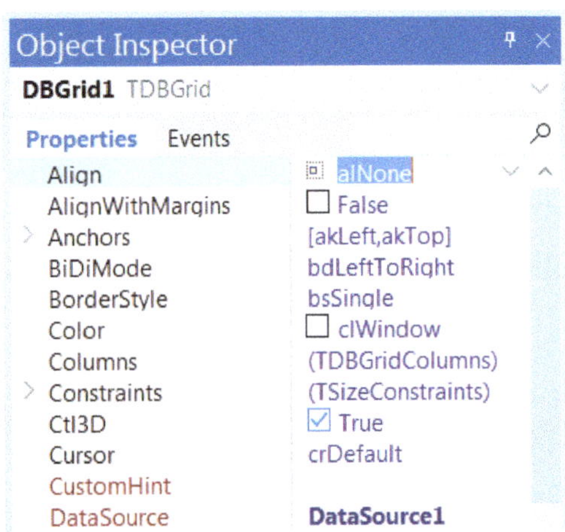

Fig. 64.9 Object inspector for DBGrid1

1 Limited to work only for 48 hours, after that time new connections are disallowed, it will then be necessary to reset the server.

```
Developer edition of Interbase: Limited
to a maximum of 20 users and 80 logical
connections to the server. It also needs
restarting every 48 hours.
```

Click File|Save All.

Click ▶ to compile and execute `LibraryLoansTable` project.

Figure 64.11 shows the executing project window.

Close the application by clicking ✕.

Place a **TDBNavigator** from the **Data Controls** palette on the form - `DBNavigator1` - as shown in *Figure 64.12*.

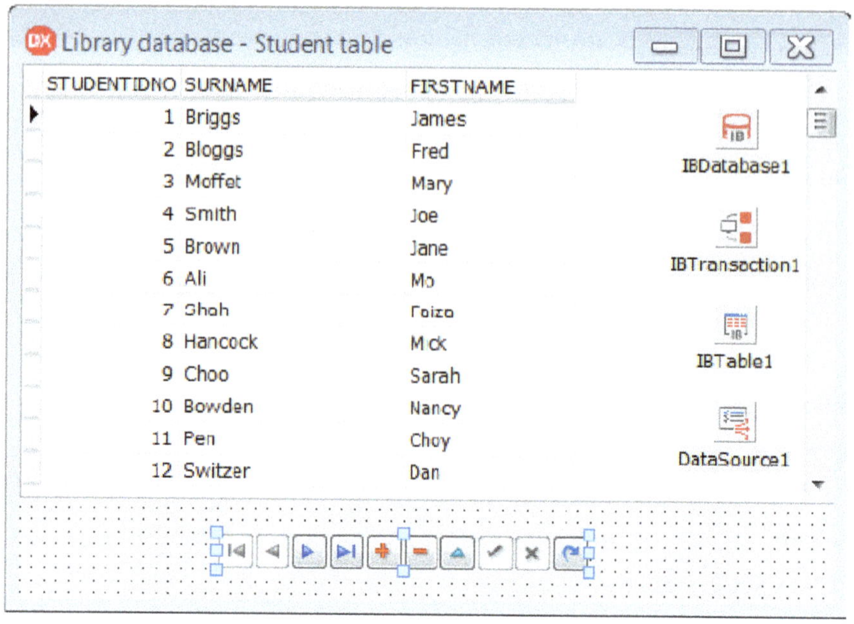

Fig. 64.12 DBNavigator1 placed on form, Form1

Select `DBNavigator1` and from the **Object Inspector set DataSource** to `DataSource1` as shown in *Figure 64.13*.

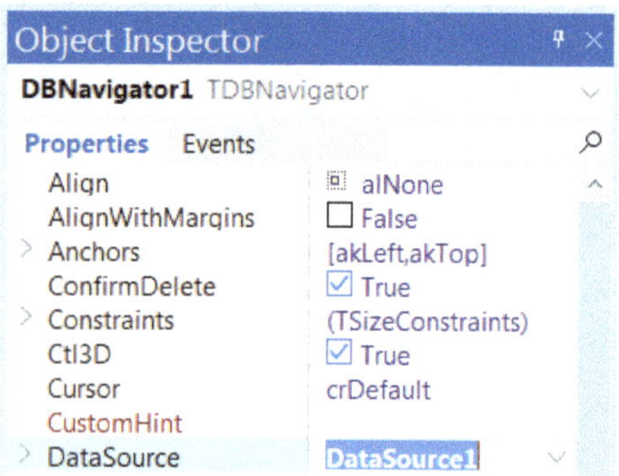

Fig. 64.13 Object inspector, DBNavigator1

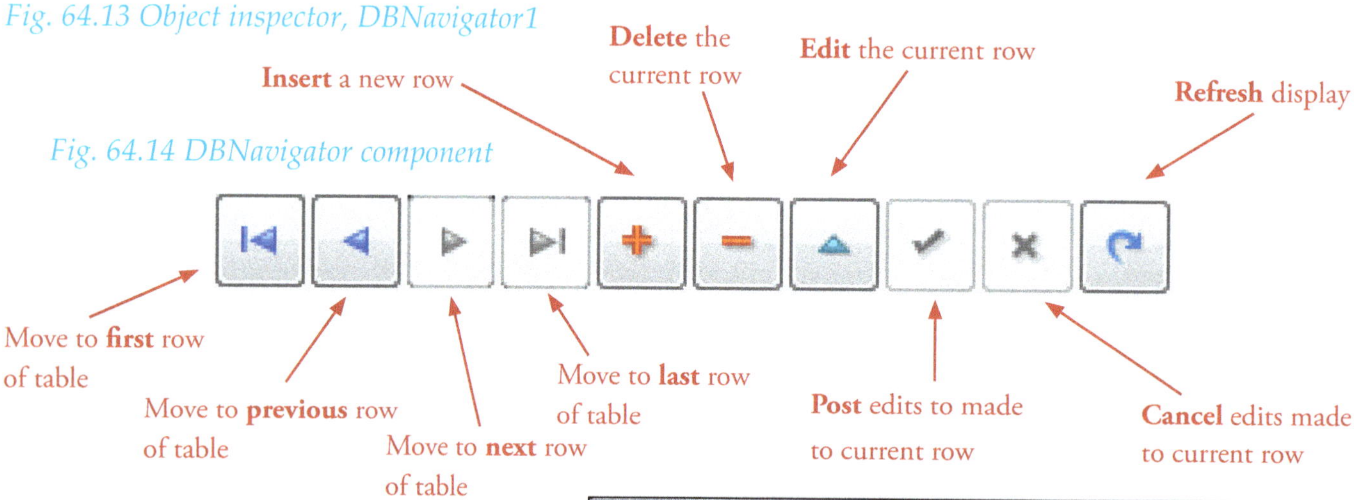

Fig. 64.14 DBNavigator component

Figure 64.14 shows how the buttons of the **DBNavigator** component `DBNavigator1` may be used to access and control the data in table `Student`.

Click File|Save All.

Click ▶ to compile and execute `LibraryLoansTable` project.

Figure 64.15 shows the executing project window.

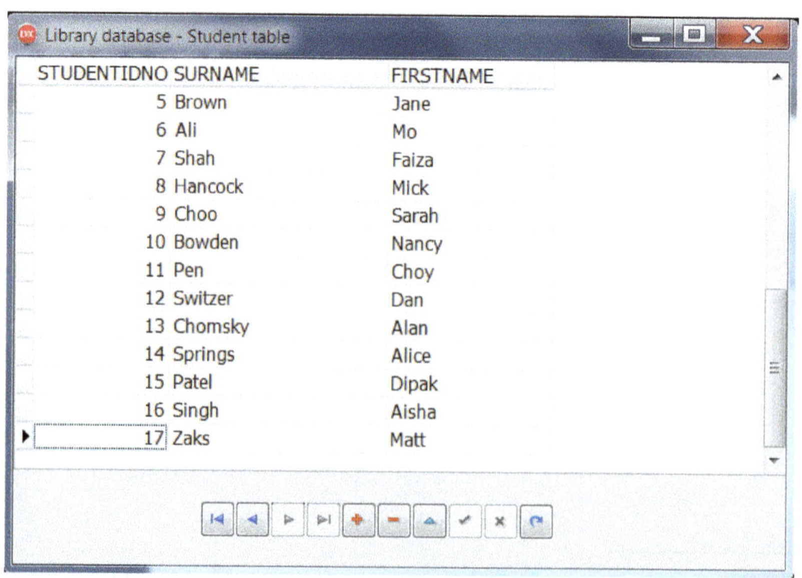

Fig. 64.15 LibraryLoansTable project in execution

Using the **DBNavigator** component it is possible to

- **Navigate** back and forth through the data in table `Student`
- **Edit** and **post** the edits to the database
- **Insert** a new row and **delete** a row
- **Cancel** edits to the current row.

The purpose of each button on the **DBNavigator** bar is described in *Table 64.1*.

Button	Purpose
First	Calls the table's First method to set the current row to be the first row.
Previous	Calls the table's Prior method to set the current row to be the previous row.
Next	Calls the table's Next method to set the current row to be the next row.
Last	Calls the table's Last method to set the current row to be the last row.
Insert	Calls the table's Insert method to insert a new row before the current row, and set the table in Insert state.
Delete	Deletes the current row. If the ConfirmDelete property is True it prompts for confirmation before deleting.
Edit	Puts the table in Edit state so that the current row can be modified.
Post	Writes changes in the current row to the database.
Cancel	Cancels edits to the current row, and returns the table to Browse state.
Refresh	Clears data control display buffers, then refreshes its buffers from the physical table or query. Useful if the underlying data may have been changed by another application.

Table 64.1 DBNavigator component explained

Querying a Database

Letting a user browse through an entire table of data and view the contents of any row of the table is one way that data in a database may be accessed. Sometimes, however, the requirement is for a user to be able to view or edit only rows containing a certain attribute value. This is called **querying a database**.

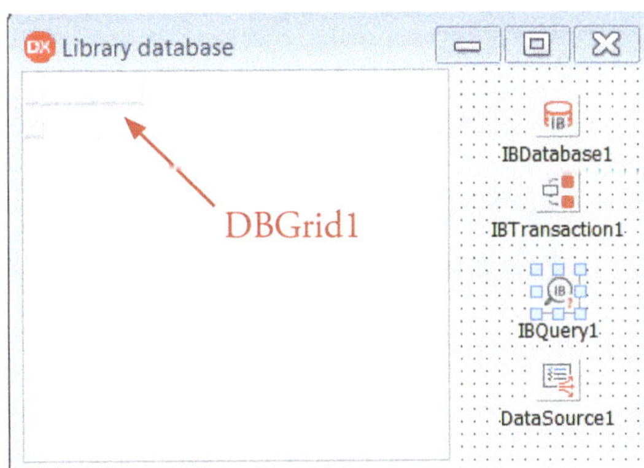

Fig. 64.16 LibraryLoansQuery project form, Form1

In Delphi this can be done using a **TQuery** object.

Launch Delphi

Select **File|New|VCL Application**.

- **Select** the form, `Form1`, and change its caption to `Library database` as shown in *Figure 64.16*.
- **Place** an **TIBDatabase** component, `IBDatabase1`, an **TIBTransaction** component, `IBTransaction1`, and an **TIBQuery** component, `IBQuery1`, from the **Interbase** palette on this form as shown in *Figure 64.16*.
- **Place** a **TDBGrid** from the **Data Controls** palette on the form - `DBGrid1` - as shown in *Figure 64.16*.
- **Place** a **TDataSource** component from the **Data Access** palette on the form - `DataSource1`.

Save the project (**Save All**) in a folder `LibraryLoansQueryExercise`:

- **Save** the unit as `LibraryLoansQueryUnit.pas`
- **Save** the project as `LibraryLoansQuery.dproj`.

www.educational-computing.com/DelphiBook/Code/Chapter64/LibraryLoansQueryExercise.rar

Download LibDB.ib from

www.educational-computing.com/DelphiBook/Code/Chapter64/LibDB.ib

This is an Interbase 2017 created database, other versions are available:

www.educational-computing.co.uk/DelphiBookCode/DelphiCode.html

Databases must be created on the same drive as Interbase server, e.g. the C: drive.
Copy LibDB.ib to a folder on the C: drive.
In this example, **LibDB.ib** has been copied to `C:\Users\drbond\`.
Select `IBDatabase1` and from the **Object Inspector** view shown in *Figure 64.4*

- **Set DatabaseName** to `C:\Users\drbond\`
- **Set DefaultTransaction** to `IBTransaction1`
- **Set LoginPrompt** to `False`
- **Set ServerType** to `IBServer`.

Click ellipsis (...) in property **Params** to bring up the **String List Editor** shown in *Figure 64.5*.
Add the strings `user_name=sysdba`, `password=masterkey` as shown in *Figure 64.5*.
Click `OK`.

Select `IBTransaction1` and from the **Object Inspector** shown in *Figure 64.6*

- **Set** Default**Database** to `IBDatabase1`.
  Make **Active** property `True`.

Select `IBDatabase1` and from the **Object Inspector**

- **Change** the **Connected** field of `IBDatabase1` - *Figure 64.4* - to `True` to connect the database `LibDB.ib`.
  If you are unable to connect, try resetting the server first.

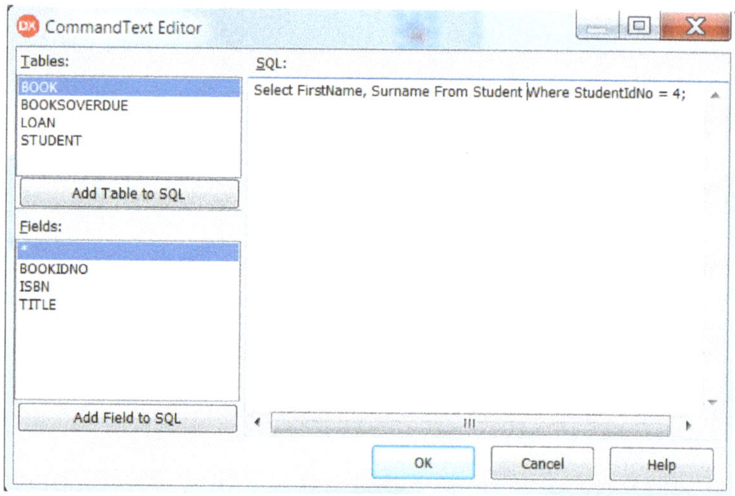

Fig. 64.17 SQL string for IBQuery1

Select `IBQuery1` and from the **Object Inspector**

- **Set Database** to `IBDatabase1`
- **Select SQL** in Object Inspector and click the ellipsis (...)
- **Add** the SQL statement:

```
Select FirstName, Surname
  From Student Where StudentIdNo = 4;
```

  as shown in *Figure 64.17*.
- **Close** the **CommandText Editor** window.
- **Set Transaction** to `IBTransaction1`

Select `DataSource1` and from the **Object Inspector**

- **Set DataSet** to `IBQuery1`.

Select `IBDBGrid1` and from the **Object Inspector**

- **Set DataSource** to `DataSource1`.

Select `IBQuery1` and from the **Object Inspector** set **Active** to `True`.
Data returned by the query should now appear at design time in `DBGrid1` as shown in *Figure 64.18*.

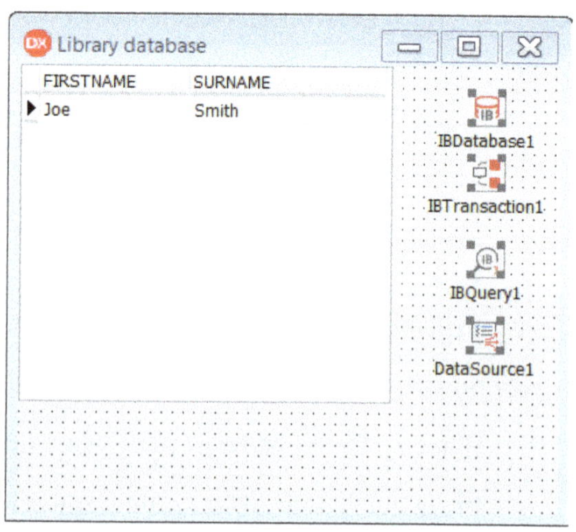

Fig. 64.18 LibraryLoansQuery project at design time showing the result of making IBQuery1 active

www.educational-computing.com/DelphiBook/Code/Chapter64/LibraryLoansDynamicQueryExercise.rar

Click File|Save All.

Click ▶ to compile and execute `LibraryLoansQuery` project.

Figure 64.19 shows the executing project window.

Close the application by clicking ✕.

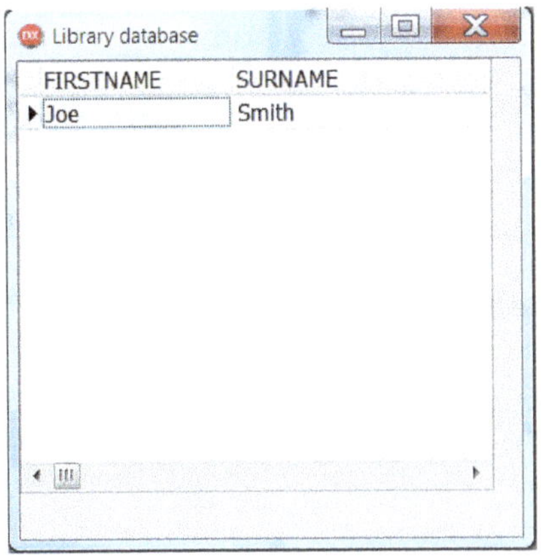

Fig. 64.19 LibraryLoansQuery in execution

Dynamic query

The previous example made use of a **static query**. That is, a query that is set at design time. The results of this query may be displayed at design time if the query is made active at design time. The word static means that the query cannot be modified at runtime.

A query can be made inactive at runtime by setting its **Active** property to `False`, as follows:

```
IBQuery1.Active := False;
```

A **dynamic query** is a query that may be modified during program execution.

To illustrate the use of a dynamic query

- **Add** a **TButton** control, `Button1`, from the **Standard** palette to the form as shown in *Figure 64.20*.
- **Change** its caption and its name to `SetQuery`.

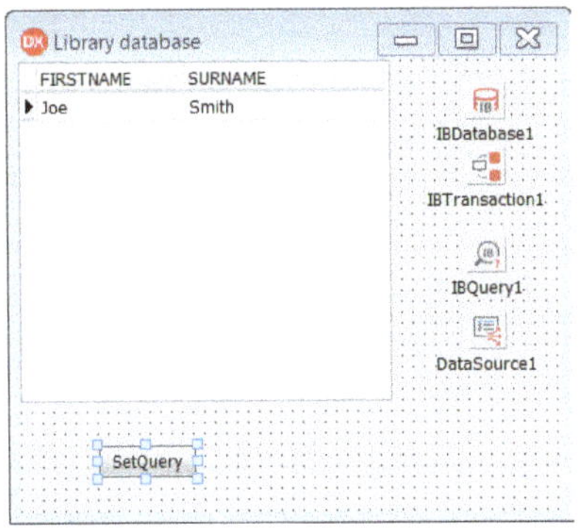

Fig. 64.20 SetQuery button added to form

Select `IBQuery1` on the form.

Select its **SQL** property in the Object Inspector and click the ellipsis (...) to bring up the **CommandText Editor**.

Delete any existing SQL statements.

Enter `Select FirstName, Surname From Student Where StudentIdNo = :QueryStudentIdNo`

Close the **CommandText Editor** window by clicking on **OK**.

With `IBQuery1` select **Params** property in the Object Inspector and click the ellipsis (...) to bring up the **Editing IBQuery1.Params** window as shown in *Figure 64.21*.

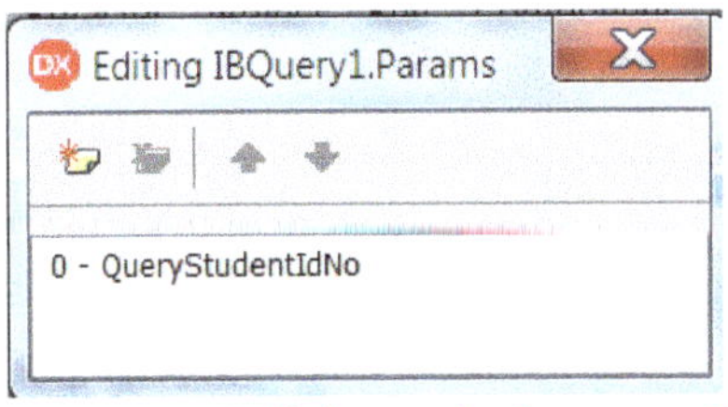

Fig. 64.21 Editing window to edit QueryStudentIdNo parameter

Click 0 - QueryStudentIdNo to highlight it. The Object Inspector will now show the properties of this parameter - *Figure 64.22*.

Change the **DataType** field to **ftInteger**.

Click ✕ in the Editing **IBQuery1.Params** window to close it.

Double click the `SetQuery` button to create an event handler `SetQueryClick`.

Add the code shown in *Table 64.2* to this event handler

```
TForm1.SetQueryClick(Sender: TObject)
```

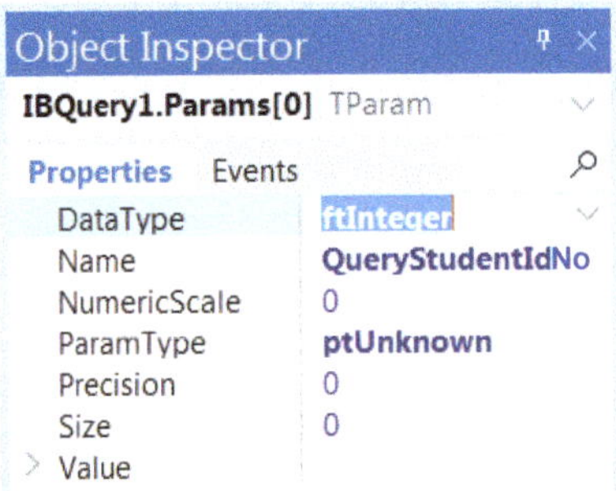

Fig. 64.22 Object Inspector for IBQuery1.Params[0]

Save the project (**Save Project As**) in folder

`LibraryLoansDynamicQueryExercise`

- **Save** the project as `LibraryLoansQuery.dproj`.

Save the unit (**Save As**) in folder `LibraryLoansDynamicQueryExercise`.

- **Save** the unit as `LibraryLoansDynamicQueryUnit.pas`

Click ▶ to compile and execute `LibraryLoansDynamicQuery` project.

Figure 64.23 shows the executing project window.

Close the application by clicking ✕.

```
Procedure TForm1.SetQueryClick(Sender: TObject);
Var
  InputStudentIDNo : String;
Begin
  InputStudentIDNo :=
    InputBox ('Set the StudentIDNo attribute',
              'Enter StudentID:',
              '');
  Query1.DisableControls;
  Try
    IBQuery1.Active := False;
    IBQuery1.Params[0].AsInteger := StrToInt(InputStudentIDNo);
    IBQuery1.Active := True;
  Finally IBQuery1.EnableControls;
  End;
End;
```

P

```
IBQuery1.ParamByName('QueryStudentIdNo').AsInteger
        := StrToInt(InputStudentID);
```

is an alternative way of using the parameter.

Table 64.2 SetQueryClick event handler

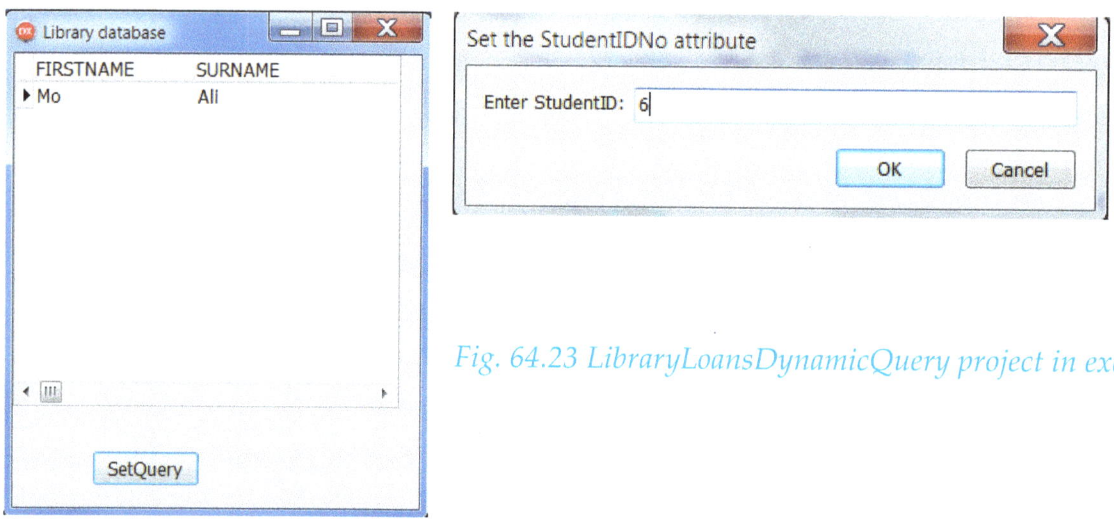

Fig. 64.23 LibraryLoansDynamicQuery project in execution

InputBox is a Delphi function that displays a dialogue box.

The variable `InputStudentIDNo` collects the value typed by the user.

`IBQuery1.DisableControls` disables all data control components connected to `IBQuery1`, e.g. `DBGrid1`.

A **Try…Finally** block is then executed as follows:

```
Try
  IBQuery1.Active := False;
  IBQuery1.Params[0].AsInteger := StrToInt(InputStudentIDNo);
  IBQuery1.Active := True;
Finally IBQuery1.EnableControls;
End;
```

The code between **Finally** and **End** is always executed, and so no matter what happens during the execution of the statements between the **Try** and the **Finally**, the **Query** component is always enabled using

```
IBQuery1.EnableControls
```

The code between **Try** and **Finally** sets the **Active** property of `IBQuery1` to `False` because the value of a SQL query parameter cannot be changed while the Query component is active.

The collected `InputStudentIDNo` value is converted into an integer value and then assigned to the parameter `QueryStudentIDNo`. Internally this is referenced as `IBQuery1.Params[0]`. The **AsInteger** method ensures an integer value is assigned to the parameter.

The `QueryStudentIDNo` parameter is the only parameter the SQL has; it's considered parameter 0. If a second SQL parameter existed, it would be parameter 1, and so on.

A **Try** block is a way of protecting against an error. If any error occurs during the execution of the statements between **Try** and **Finally**, the procedure will abort, and later an error message will be displayed to the user. Any statements associated with the **Finally** part will execute as any exception aborts the procedure.

Datasets

In Delphi the fundamental unit for accessing data is the dataset family of objects. A database application uses datasets for all database access. Generally, a dataset object represents a specific table belonging to a database, or it represents a query or stored procedure that accesses a database.

To read or write data in a table or through a query, an application must first open a dataset (table). One of two ways may be used to do this:

1. **Set** the **Active** property of the dataset to `True`, either at design time in the Object Inspector, or in code at runtime:
   ```
   IBTable1.Active := True;
   ```
2. **Call** the **Open** method for the dataset at runtime:
   ```
   IBTable1.Open;
   ```

There are two ways to close a dataset:

1. **Set** the **Active** property of the dataset to `False`, either at design time in the Object Inspector, or in code at runtime:
   ```
   IBQuery1.Active := False;
   ```
2. **Call** the **Close** method for the dataset at runtime:
   ```
   IBQuery1.Close;
   ```

Creating SQL Statements at RunTime

An entire SQL statement may be constructed at runtime as follows:

1. **Select** **File|New|VCL Application**.
2. **Add** a **TIBDatabase**, **TIBTransaction**, **TIBQuery**, **TDataSource** and **TDBGrid** component to the form.
3. **Select** **DatabaseName** property for `IBDatabase1` and **set** its path to `LibDB.ib`, e.g. in my case `C:\Users\drbond\LibDB.ib`.
4. **Select** **Transaction** property and **set** it to `IBTransaction1`.
5. **Set** **LoginPrompt** to `False`
6. **Set** **ServerType** to `IBServer`.

www.educational-computing.com/DelphiBook/Code/Chapter64/RuntimeSQL.rar

7. **Click** ellipsis (**...**) in property **Params** to bring up the **String List Editor**. **Add** the strings `user_name=sysdba` and `password=masterkey`. **Click OK**.
8. **Select Connected** and set to `True` (if this fails reset Interbase server if necessary to enable the connection).
9. **Select** `IBTransaction1` and set its **Transaction** property to `IBDatabase1`. Set its **Active** property to `True`.
10. **Add** a button to the form and **rename** its **Caption** and **Name** properties `ExecuteQuery`.
11. **Select** `IBQuery1` and **set** its **Database** property to `IBDatabase1`.
12. **Select** `DataSource1` and **set** its **DataSet** property to `IBQuery1`.
13. **Select** `DBGrid1` and **set** its **DataSource** property to `DataSource1`.
14. **Double click** this button and **add** the block of code shown in *Table 64.3* to event handler `Procedure TForm1.ExecuteQueryClick(Sender: TObject)`.
15. **Save** the project using **Save Project As** from the **File** menu in folder `RuntimeSQL`. **Choose** `RuntimeSQL.Pas` for the unit file and `RuntimeSQLProject.dproj` for the project file.

Click ▶ to compile and execute `RuntimeSQLProject` project.

Figure 64.24 shows the executing project window.

Close the application by clicking ✖.

```
Procedure TForm1.ExecuteQueryClick(Sender: TObject);
Var
  AttributeString,
  RelationalOperatorString,
  AttributeValueString : String;
Begin
  AttributeString :=
        InputBox('Set the Attribute',  'Enter an Attribute','');
  RelationalOperatorString :=
         InputBox('Set the Relational Operator',
         'Enter a relational operator, one of <,>,<=,>=,<>,=','');
  AttributeValueString := InputBox('Set the Attribute Value',
                                   'Enter an attribute value','');
  IBQuery1.DisableControls;
  Try
    IBQuery1.Active := False;
    IBQuery1.SQL.Clear;
    IBQuery1.Filtered := True;
    IBQuery1.FilterOptions := [foCaseInsensitive];
    IBQuery1.SQL.Add(Concat('Select * From Student Where ',
                       AttributeString,
                       RelationalOperatorString,
                       AttributeValueString));
    IBQuery1.Active := True;
  Finally IBQuery1.EnableControls;
  End;
End;
```

Table 64.3 ExecuteQueryClick event handler

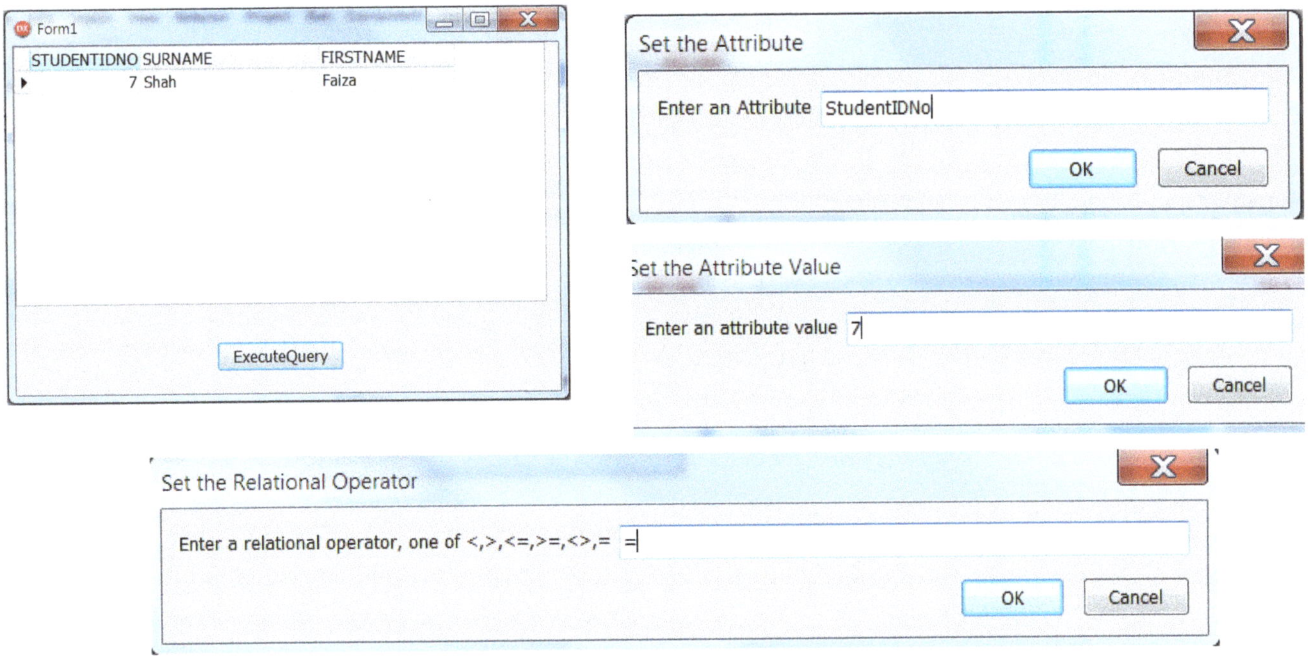

Fig. 64.24 RuntimeSQLProject project in execution

Using the Link in a Master/Detail Form

Launch Delphi. www.educational-computing.com/DelphiBook/Code/Chapter64/MasterDetailExercise.rar

Select File|New|VCL Application.

Add a TIBDatabase and a TIBTransaction to the form.

Place on the form: two TBTable components from the Interbase palette, two TDataSource components from the Data Access palette, a TDBEdit box, a TDBGrid and one TDBNavigator bar from the Data Controls palette.

Select **DatabaseName** property for `IBDatabase1` and **set** its path to `LibDB.ib`, e.g. in my case `C:\Users\drbond\LibDB.ib`.

Select **Transaction** property and **set** it to `IBTransaction1`.

Set **LoginPrompt** to `False`

Set **ServerType** to `IBServer`.

Click ellipsis (...) in property **Params** to bring up the **String List Editor**. **Add** the strings `user_name=sysdba` and `password=masterkey`. **Click** **OK**.

Select **Connected** and set to `True` (if this fails reset Interbase server if necessary to enable the connection).

Select `IBTransaction1` and set its **Transaction** property to `IBDatabase1`. Set its **Active** property to `True`.

Click `IBTable1` and **set** its **DatabaseName** to `Database1`, its **TableName** to `Student`.

Click `IBTable2` and **set** its **DatabaseName** to `Database1`, its **TableName** to `Loan`.

Select `DataSource1` and **connect** it to `IBTable1`.

Select `DataSource2` and **connect** it to `IBTable2`.

Select `IBTable2` and **set** its **MasterSource** property to `DataSource1`.

Click the **MasterFields** property and then the ellipsis (...) to bring up the **Field Link Designer** window shown in *Figure 64.25*.

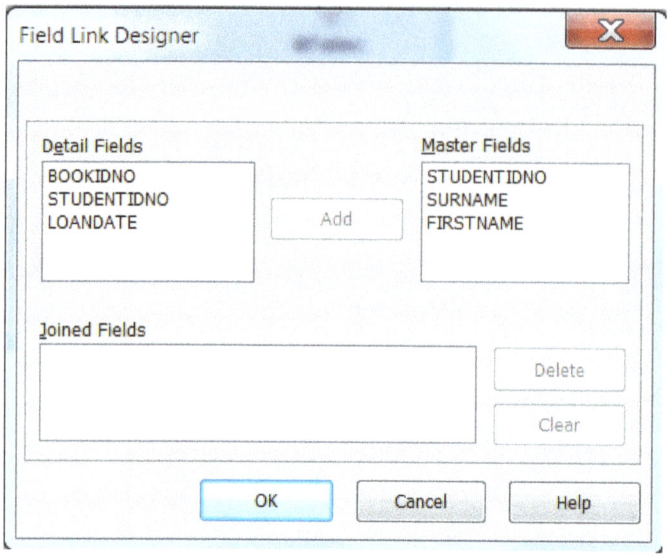

Fig. 64.25 Field Link Designer launched from IBTable2 MasterDetails property

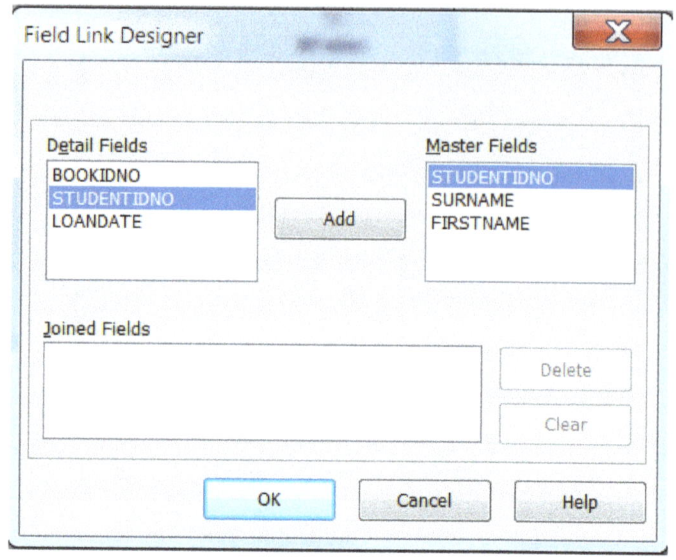

Fig. 64.26 Selecting StudentIDNo in Detail Fields and Master Fields

Select `StudentIDNo` in the **Detail Fields** box and `StudentIDNo` in the **Master Fields** box, as shown in *Figure 64.26*.

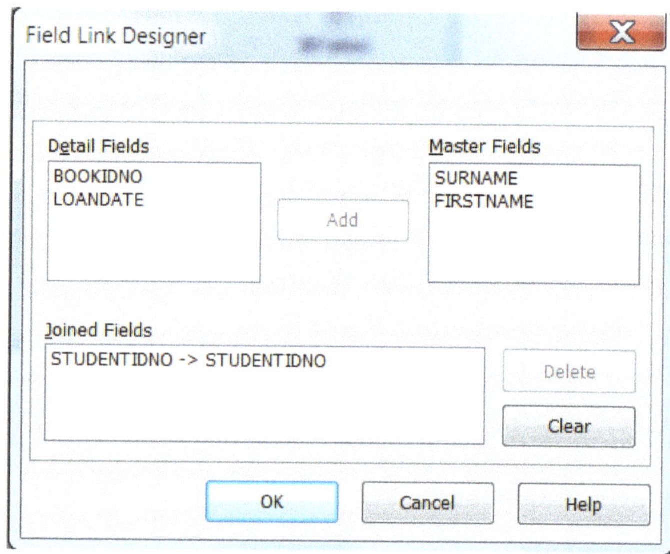

Fig. 64.27 StudentIDNo field in IBTable2 (the detail) now linked to StudentIDNo field in IBTable1 (the master)

Click Add to join the two attributes (fields) as shown in *Figure 64.27*.

Click OK.

Click on `DBEdit1` and **connect** its **DataSource** property to `DataSource1`.

Set its **DataField** property to `StudentIDNo`.

Click on `DBGrid1` and **connect** its **DataSource** property to `DataSource2`.

Select `DBNavigator1` and **connect** its **DataSource** property to `DataSource1`.

Set the **Active** property of `IBTable1` and `IBTable2` to `True`.

Add a **TLabel** component from the **Standard** palette to the form to label the **DBEdit** box. **Change** its **Caption** property to `StudentIDNo`.

Save the project using **Save Project As** from the **File** menu in folder `MasterDetailExercise`.

Choose `MasterDetailUnit.Pas` for the unit file and `MasterDetailProject.dproj` for the project file.

Click ▶ to compile and execute `MasterDetailProject` project.

Figure 64.28 shows the executing project window with a second grid which has not yet been added to the project. **Click** the relevant buttons on the navigator bar to see loans for different students.

Close the application by clicking ✕.

It would be useful to see the title of a book (e.g. `BookIDNo` 13) which is shown on loan to a particular student with `StudentIDNo` 5. This information is linked to `BookIDNo` in the `Book` table.

Add another **TIBTable** component, `IBTable3`, from the **Interbase** palette to the form.

Add another TDataSource component, `DataSource3`, from the Data Access palette.

Add another TDBGrid, `DBGrid2`, from the Data Controls palette. Arrange as shown in *Figure 64.29*.

Connect `DBGrid2`'s **DataSource** field to `DataSource3`.

Select `DataSource3` and **set** its **DataSet** property to `IBTable3`.

Select `IBTable3` and **set** its **MasterSource** property to `DataSource2`. **Set** its **Active** property to `True`.

Click the **MasterFields** property and then the ellipsis (...) to bring up the **Field Link Designer** window.

Select `BookIDNo` in the **Detail Fields** box and `BookIDNo` in the **Master Fields** box, as shown.

Click Add to join the two attributes (fields).

Click OK.

Click Save All.

Click ▶ to compile and execute `MasterDetailProject` project.

Figure 64.28 shows the executing project window with the second grid showing the information on the title of the book with `BookIDNo` 13 on loan to student `StudentIDNo` 5.

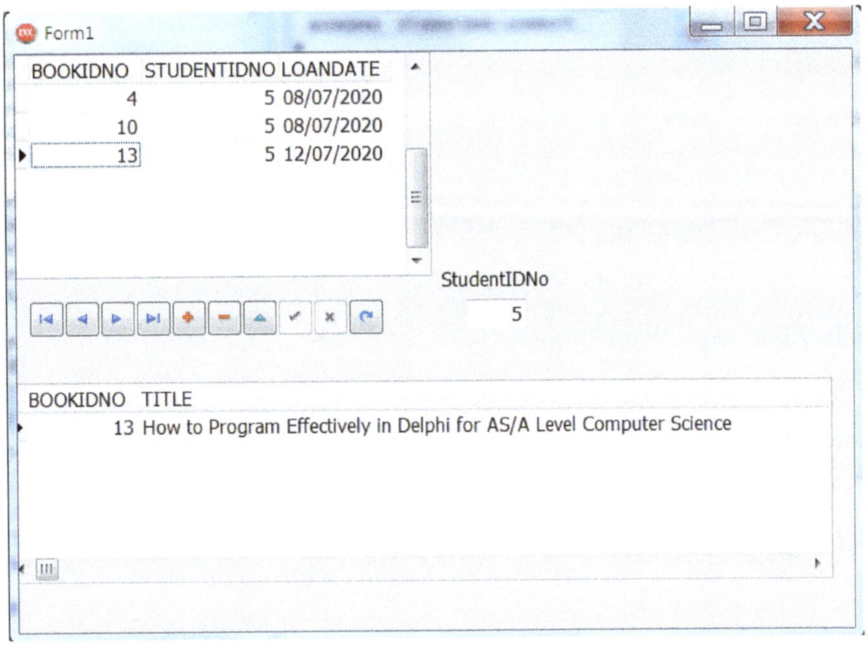

Fig. 64.28 MasterDetailProject in execution

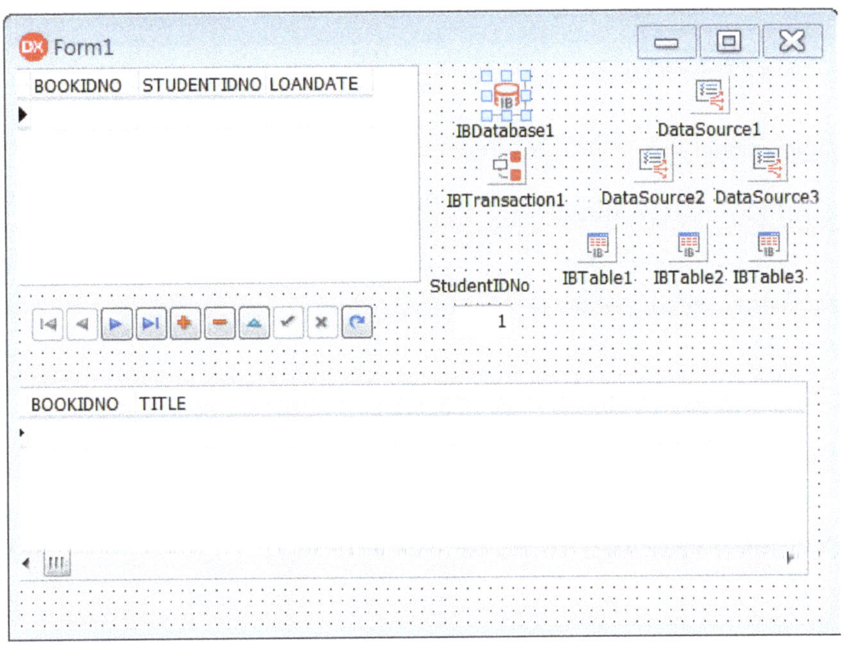

Fig. 64.29 MasterDetailProject with additional table and grid

Click the relevant buttons on the navigator bar to see book loans and the corresponding book titles for different students.

Close the application by clicking ✕.

www.educational-computing.com/DelphiBook/Code/Chapter64/LibraryBooksOverdue.rar

Accessing a view created for an Interbase database

To reset the Interbase server, in Services right click Interbase Guardian (whichever version you are using) then select Stop. Once stopped restart by right clicking Interbase Guardian then select Start.

Launch Delphi.

Select File|New|VCL Application.

Add a TIBDatabase and a TIBTransaction to the form.

Place on the form: one IBQuery component, `IBQuery1`, from the Interbase palette, one TDataSource component, `DataSource1`, from the Data Access palette, a TDBGrid component, `DBGrid1` from the Data Controls palette.

Select DatabaseName property for `IBDatabase1` and **set** its path to `LibDB.ib`, e.g. in my case `C:\Users\drbond\LibDB.ib`.

Select DefaultTransaction property and **set** it to `IBTransaction1`.

Set LoginPrompt to `False`

Set ServerType to `IBServer`.

Click ellipsis (...) in property Params to bring up the String List Editor.

Add the strings `user_name=sysdba` and `password=masterkey`.

Click OK.

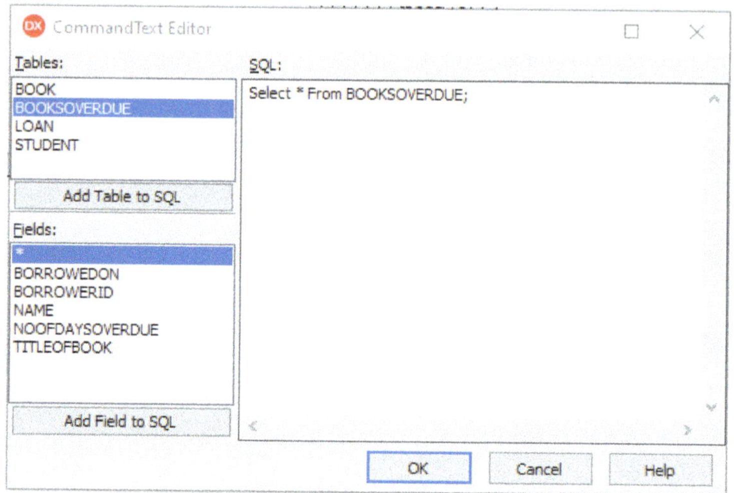

Fig. 64.30 CommandText Editor SQL for View BooksOverdue

Select Connected and set to `True` (if this fails reset Interbase server if necessary to enable the connection).

Select `IBTransaction1` and set its DefaultDatabase property to `IBDatabase1`. Set its Active property to `True`.

Select `DBGrid1`, set its Constraints|MinWidth property to 1000.

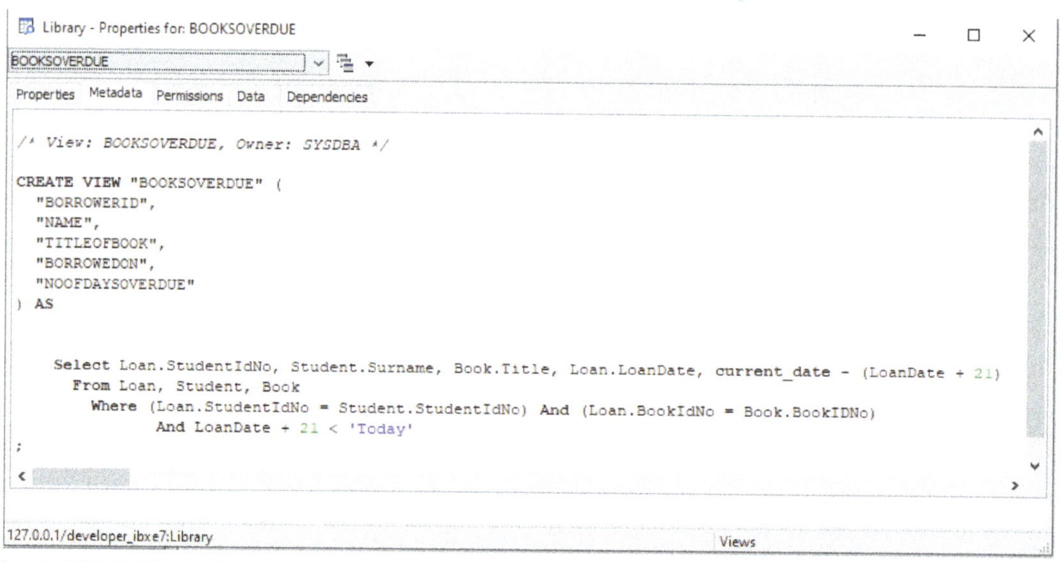

Fig. 64.31 IBConsole showing view BooksOverdue for database alias Library (LibDB.ib)

Select `IBQuery1` and from the Object Inspector

- **Set** Database to `IBDatabase1`
- **Select** SQL in Object Inspector and click the ellipsis (...)
- **Add** the SQL statement:

```
Select * From BooksOverdue;
```

  as shown in *Figure 64.30*.

- **Close** the CommandText Editor window.
- **Set** Transaction to `IBTransaction1`

Select DataSource1 and from the **Object Inspector**

- **Set DataSet** to IBQuery1.

Select IBDBGrid1 and from the **Object Inspector**

- **Set DataSource** to DataSource1.

Select IBQuery1 and from the **Object Inspector** set **Active** to True.

Data returned by the query should now appear at design time in DBGrid1.

Save the project using **Save Project As** from the **File** menu in folder LibraryBooksOverdue

Choose LibraryBooksOverdueUnit.Pas for the unit file and LibraryBooksOverdueProject.dproj for the project file.

Click ▶ to compile and execute LibraryBooksOverdueProject project.

Figure 64.32 shows the executing project with the data returned by the query appearing in the grid.

The date on which the query is executed determines which records are returned.

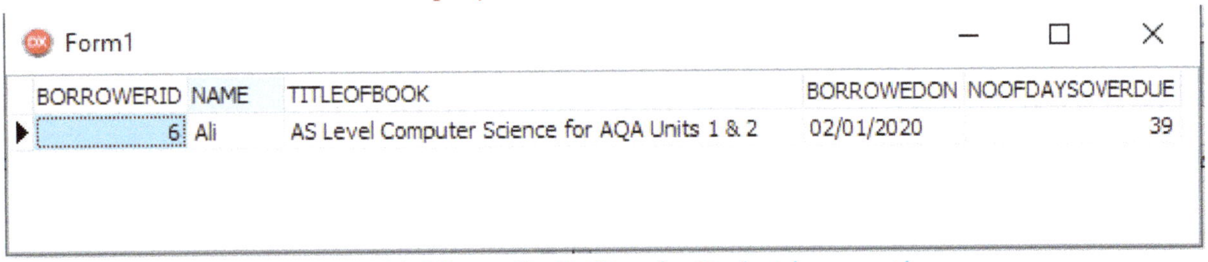

Fig. 64.32 LibraryBooksOverdueProject in execution

Bi-directional SQL datasets

Launch Delphi www.educational-computing.com/DelphiBook/Code/Chapter64/LibraryLoans.rar

Select File|New|VCL Application.

- **Place** a TIBDatabase component from the Interbase palette on the form.
- **Place** a TIBTransaction component from the Interbase palette on the form.
- **Place** TIBDataSet from Interbase palette on the form
- **Place** a TDBGrid from the Data Controls palette on the form.
- **Place** a TDataSource component from the Data Access palette on the form.

Information

Bi-directional:

Bi-directional means that data may be transferred from the application to the database (insert, update operations) and vice versa (select operations).

Place four buttons from the Standard palette on the form and change name of each as follows:

Select

Insert

Post

Commit

Place a single TEdit box from the Standard palette on the form.

Delete Edit1 from its **text property** field.

Change its name to **StudentIDNo**.

Place a single TLabel component from the Standard palette on the form.

Change its **Caption** property to Student ID No.

The form should now look as shown in *Figure 64.33*.

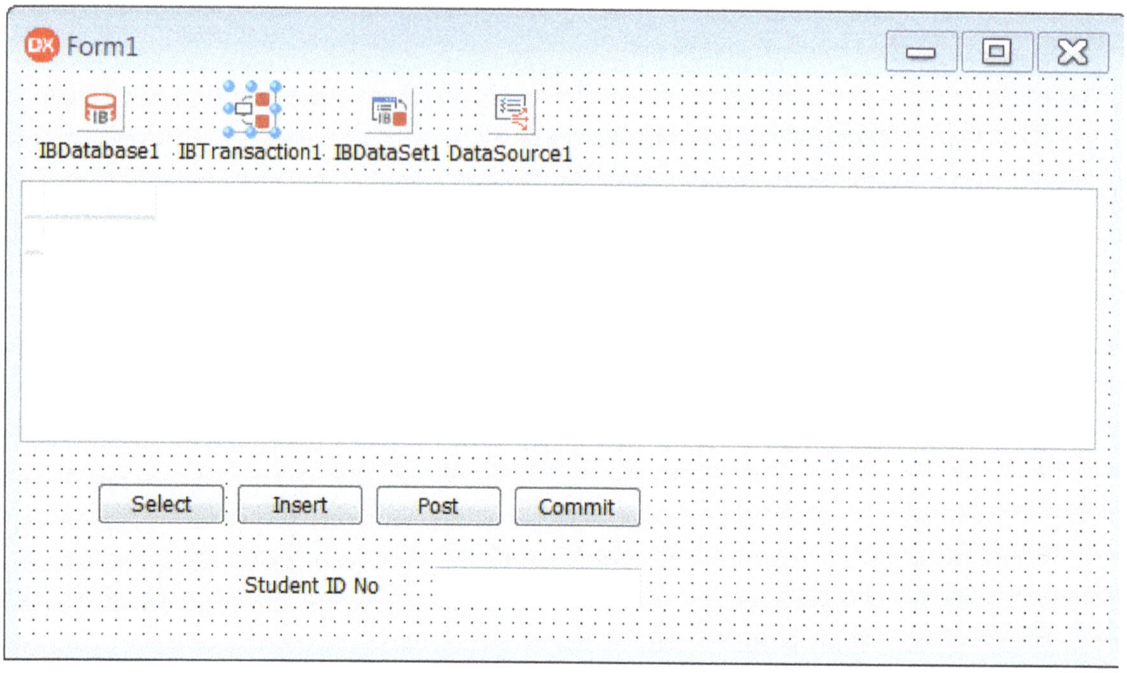

Fig. 64.33 Form1 design

We now require a database to connect to.

We will use IBConsole for Interbase 2017 to create a library loans database.

Launch IBConsole for Interbase 2017.

Right click **Local Server - developer_ib2017** to bring up the **Login** window - *Figure 64.34*.

Enter the password **masterkey**.

If successful, `Local Server - developer_ib2017` icon will lose its little red cross and the icon will show a green tick to indicate that it is now connected - *Figure 64.35*.

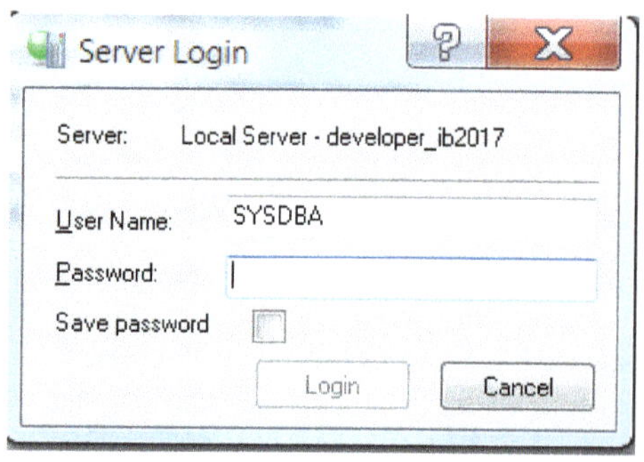

Fig. 64.34 IBConsole Local Server developer_ib2017 pop up login window

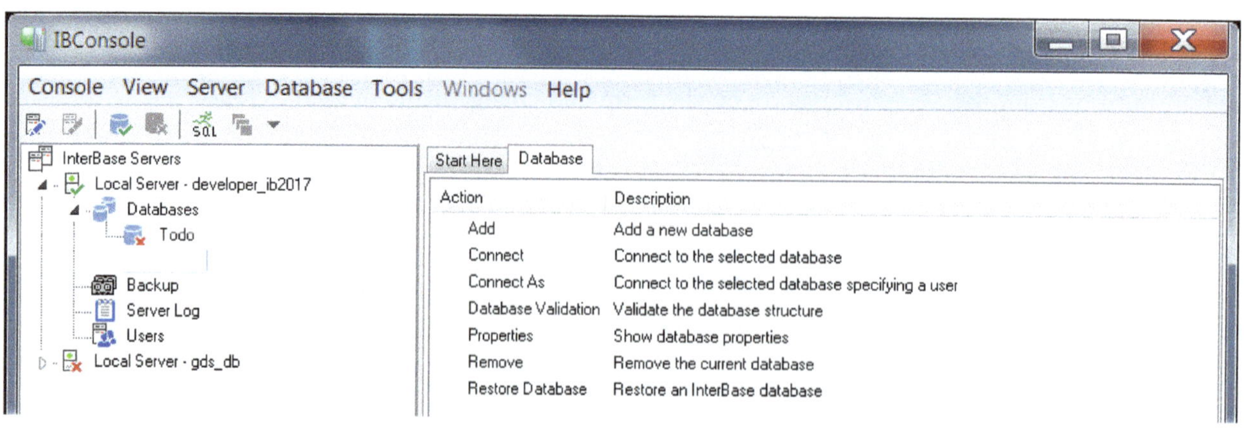

Fig. 64.35 IBConsole connected to Local Server developer_ib2017

If the **Library** database, **LibDB.ib**, does not already exist it needs to be created.

LibDB.ib may be downloaded from www.educational-computing.com/DelphiBook/Code/Chapter64/LibDB.ib. Alternatively it may be created from a script(s) (see *Table 64.4*) obtainable from www.educational-computing.co.uk/DelphiBookCode/DelphiCode.html.

For **Delphi** and **IBConsole** to work successfully with this database or any database, for that matter, **the database must be stored on a local drive and not a network drive**.

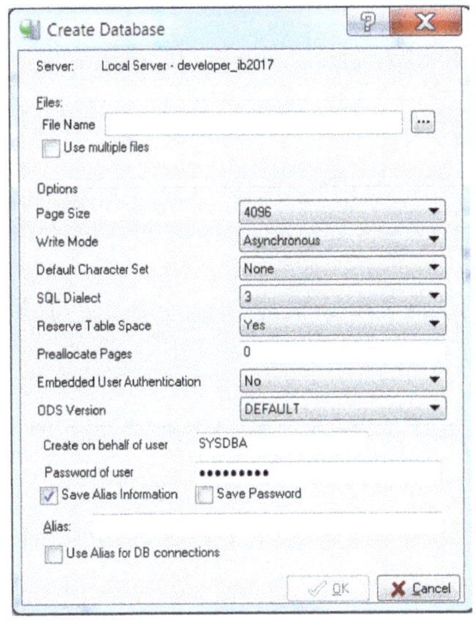

Fig. 64.36 Create Database window

If creating from a script, **IBConsole** is needed in order to execute the DDL script to create the tables of the database **LibDB.ib**. A skeletal database **LibDB.ib** without its tables must be created first in this case.

Click **Database|Create Database** to bring up the **Create Database** window. Alternatively, if the required database exists already then **click** **Database|Add** instead.

Databases must be created on the same drive as Interbase server e.g. the C: drive.

Click on the ellipsis (**...**) button in the **Create Database** window to bring up the **Specify Database** window - *Figure 64.36.*

Navigate to the folder/subfolder on the local drive in which to create the database.

Type a suitable filename for this database.

For this exercise, the folder path is `C:\Users\drbond` (it will be different for you) and the chosen filename is `LibDB.ib`. **Add** alias `Library`.

Enter user SYSDBA and password masterkey.

Click **OK**. Database `LibDB.ib` alias `Library` should now be registered and a connection to it open on the Interbase server.

Click **SQL** in the toolbar to bring up the **ISQL** window as shown in *Figure 64.37*.

Click **SQL|Query** in the toolbar to bring down the menu shown *Figure 64.37*.

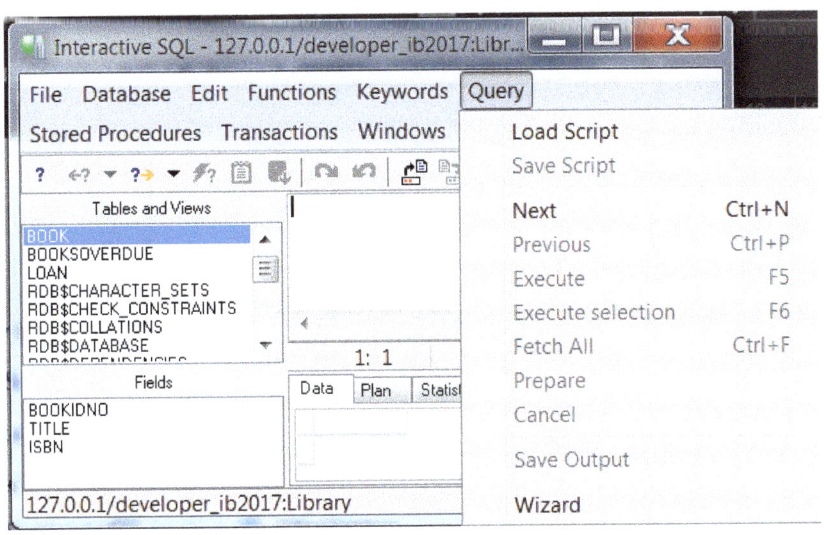

Fig. 64.37 ISQL showing Query dropdown menu

Click **Load Script** and **locate** and **load** DDL script `Library.sql` into **ISQL**. - *Table 64.4*.

```
Create Table Student
(StudentIdNo Integer Not Null,
 Surname VarChar(20) Not Null,
 FirstName VarChar(15) Not Null,
 Primary Key (StudentIdNo)
);
Create Table Book
(BookIdNo Integer Not Null,
 Title VarChar(80) Not Null,
 ISBN VarChar(13) Not Null,
 Primary Key (BookIdNo)
);
Create Table Loan
(BookIdNo Integer Not Null,
 StudentIdNo Integer Not Null,
 LoanDate Date Not Null,
 Primary Key (BookIdNo),
 Foreign Key (StudentIdNo)
   References Student(StudentIdNo),
 Foreign Key (BookIdNo)
  References Book(BookIdNo)
);
```

Table 64.4 Library.sql script

Click the **Execute Query** icon to create tables `Student`, `Book` and `Loan`.

Double click **Tables** icon in IBConsole and check that tables `Student`, `Book` and `Loan` have been created.

Click **Load Script** and locate and load DDL script `InsertIntoStudent.sql` into **ISQL**.

Click the **Execute Query** icon to insert student data into table `Student`.

Click **Load Script** and locate and load DDL script `InsertIntoBook.sql` into **ISQL**.

Click the **Execute Query** icon to insert book data into table `Book`.

Click **Load Script** and locate and load DDL script `InsertIntoLoan.sql` into **ISQL**.

Click the **Execute Query** icon to insert loan data into table `Loan`.

Enter the following into **ISQL**:

```
Select * From Student
```

Click the **Execute Query** icon.

The result set is shown in *Figure 64.38*.

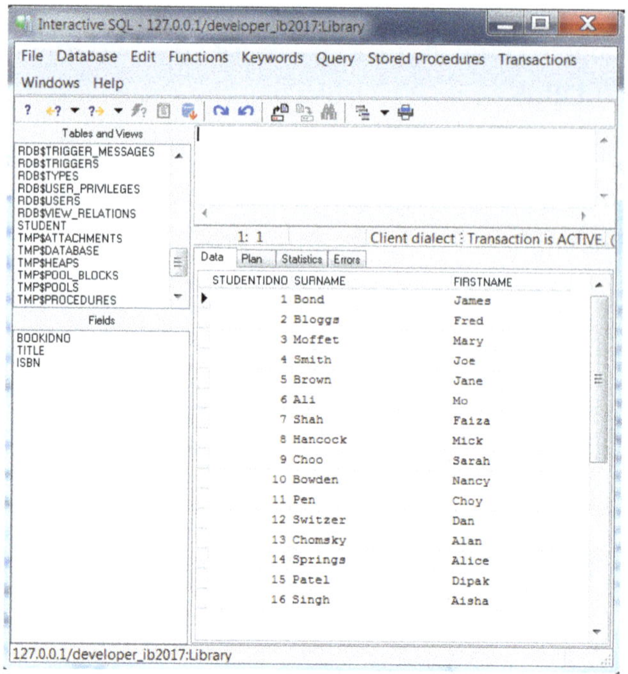

*Fig. 64.38 ISQL showing result set for Select * From Student*

Enter the following into **ISQL**:

```
Select * From Book
```

Click the **Execute Query** icon.

The result set is shown in *Figure 64.39*.

Enter the following into **ISQL**:

```
Select * From Loan
```

Click the **Execute Query** icon.

The result set is shown in *Figure 64.40*.

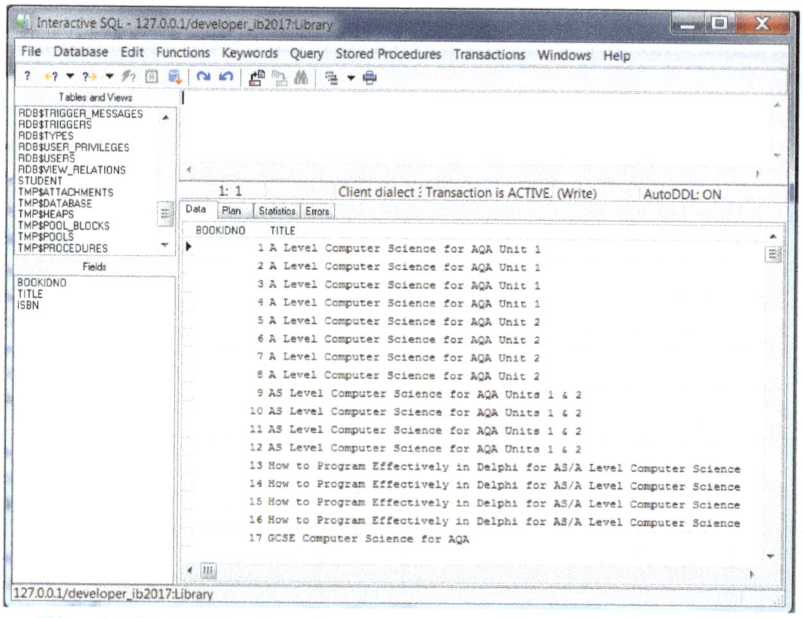

*Fig. 64.39 ISQL showing result set for Select * From Book*

Switch to Delphi and set **IBDatabase1.DatabaseName** to the correct path to its location, e.g. `C:\Users\drbond\LibDB.ib`.

Set **IBDatabase1.DefaultTransaction** to **IBTransaction1**.

Set **IBTransaction1.DefaultDatabase** to **IBDatabase1**.

Set **DBGrid1.DataSource** to **DataSource1**.

Set **DataSource1.DataSet** to **IBDataSet1**.

Set **DataSource1.AutoEdit** to **True**.

Set **IBDataSet1.Database** to **IBDatabase1**.

Select **IBDatabase1**.

Set **LoginPrompt** to `False`

Set **ServerType** to `IBServer`.

Click ellipsis (...) in property **Params** to bring up the **String List Editor**.

Add the strings `user_name=sysdba` and `password=masterkey`.

Click **OK**.

In the Object Inspector **click** on **Connected** property and **select** **True** to connect to database.

`C:\Users\drbond\LibDB.ib`.

Select the **IBDataSet** component.

In the object inspector **double click** the ellipsis (...) for **ModifySQL** and add the **Update** statement shown in *Figure 64.41*.

In the object inspector **double click** the ellipsis (...) for **InsertSQL**, **RefreshSQL**, **SelectSQL** and add the corresponding statements referenced in *Figure 64.41*.

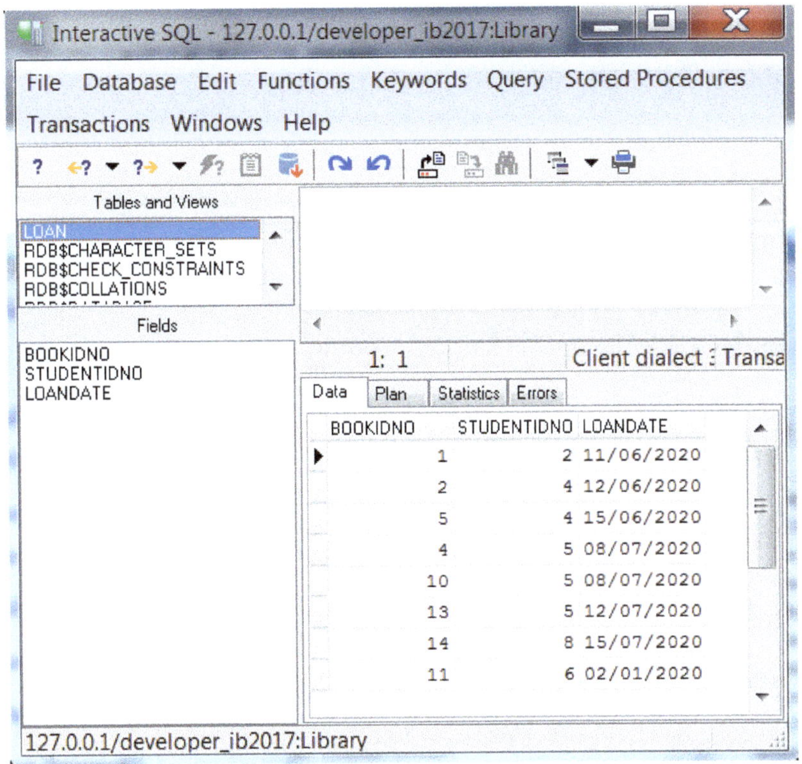

*Fig. 64.40 ISQL showing result set for Select * From Loan*

Open InsertSQL

Add

```
Insert Into Student
  (StudentIDNo, Surname, Firstname)
Values
  (:StudentIDNo,:Surname, :Firstname)
```

Open ModifySQL

Add

```
Update Student Set Surname=:Surname
Where StudentIDNo = :Old_StudentIDNo
```

Open RefreshSQL

Add

```
Select * From Student Where
StudentIDNo = :Old_StudentIDNo
```

Open SelectSQL

Add

```
Select * From Student Where
StudentIDNo = :StudentIDNo
```

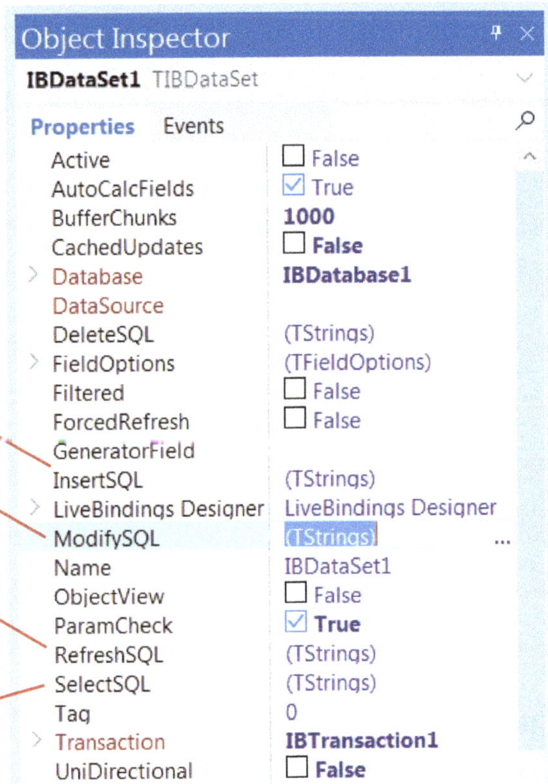

Fig. 64.41 Object inspector for IBDataSet1

Double click the button labelled **Select.**

Add the following code to the event handler:

```
IBDataSet1.Close;
IBDataSet1.ParamByName('StudentIDNo').AsInteger := StrToInt(StudentIDNo.Text);
IBDataSet1.Open;
```

Double click the button labelled **Insert**.

Add the following code to the event handler:

```
IBDataSet1.Open;
IBDataSet1.Insert;
```

Double click the button labelled **Post**. **Add** the following code to the event handler:

```
IBDataSet1.Post;
```

Double click the button labelled **Commit**. Add the following code to the event handler:

```
IBTransaction1.Commit;
```

Save the project (**Save All**) in a folder `LibraryLoans`:

- Save the unit as `LibraryLoansUnit.pas`
- Save the project as `LibraryLoans.dproj`.

Compile and then **run** the project. *Figure 64.42* shows the `LibraryLoans` project in execution.

Enter the value 1 into the `Student ID No` edit box - a student record with this ID should already exist.

Click the **Select** button.

You should see only one record, the one with

`StudentIDNo` = 1.

as shown in *Figure 64.43.*

Next, **change** the `Surname` field to a new surname, 'Briggs', press return when you have finished making the change.

Click the **Post** button.

View the change in **IBConsole** to check that it has occurred.

Click Select with the **Edit** box showing value 1.

You should now see the Delphi program display the new value of the `Surname` field.

Click the **Insert** button.

A blank record line should now appear as shown in *Figure 64.44.*

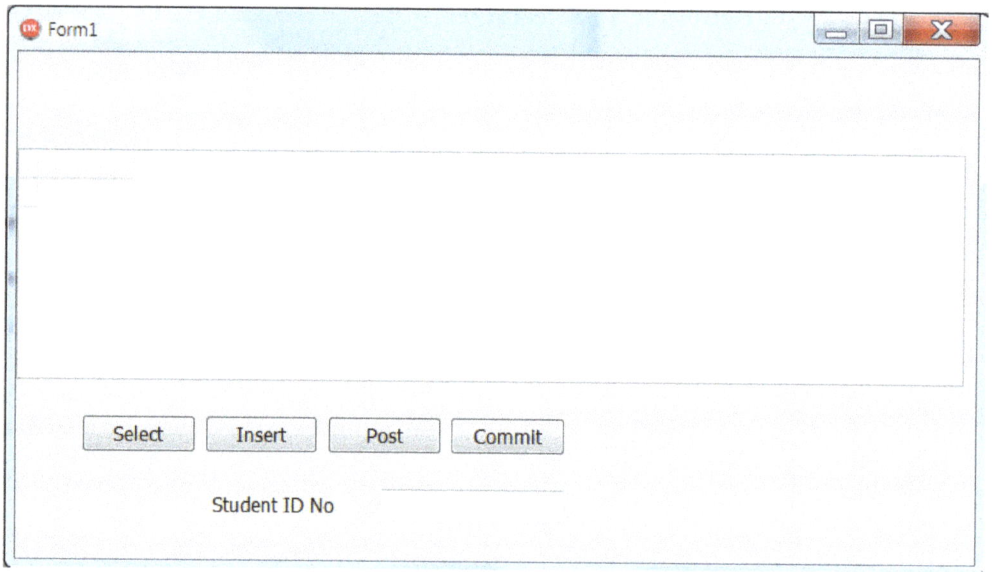

Fig. 64.42 LibraryLoans project in execution

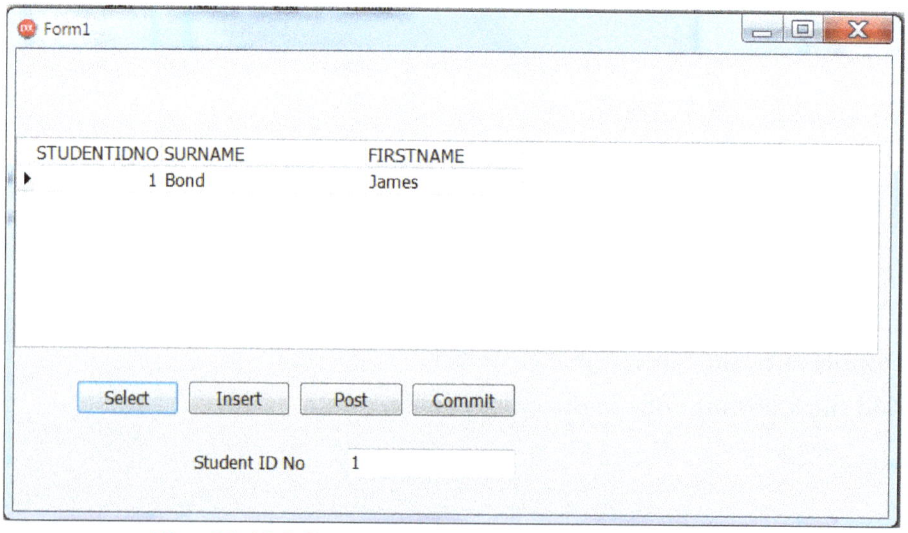

Fig. 64.43 LibraryLoans project in execution after Select clicked, Student ID No = 1

Enter a unique value for `StudentIDNo` e.g.`17` and something sensible for the other two fields, e.g. `Zaks` and `Matt`.

Click on **Post**.

To view new record enter its primary key value into the **Edit** box and **click** the **Select** button - *Figure 64.45*.

The **Select** statement could have been written to just return all records. **Modify** the **Select** statement so that it reads as follows:

```
Select * From Student
```

Update and **Insert** will still work. For **Update** simply position the mouse, for example, in the surname field that needs modifying, make the required changes then click the `Post` button.

To have both a **Select** and a **Select All** requires a different method of assigning the corresponding SQL **Select** statement. **Modify** the **Select** button event handler so that it reads as shown in *Table 64.5*.

Add another button from the Standard Palette, name it `SelectAll` and **change** its caption to `Select All`.

Double click this button to create an event handler.

Modify the `Select All` event handler so that it reads as shown in *Table 64.6*.

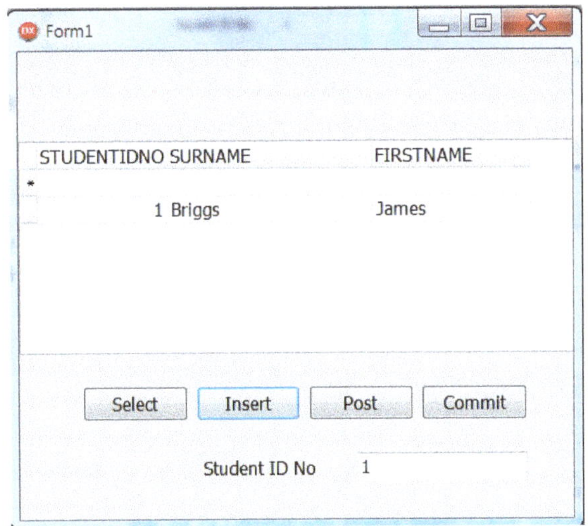

Fig. 64.44 LibraryLoans project Insert button clicked

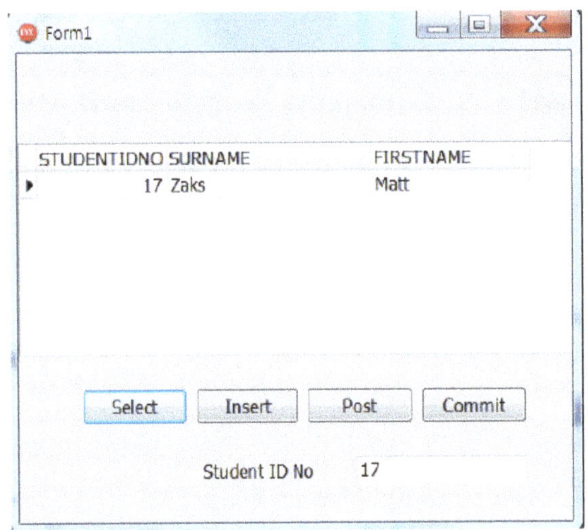

Fig. 64.45 LibraryLoans project Select button clicked

```
IBDataSet1.Close;
IBDataSet1.SelectSQL.Clear;
IBDataSet1.SelectSQL.Add('Select * From Student Where StudentIDNo = :StudentIDNo');
IBDataSet1.ParamByName('StudentIDNo').AsInteger := StrToInt(StudentIDNo.Text);
IBDataSet1.Open;
```

*Table 64.5 Select * From Student using ParamByName*

Save the project using **Save Project As** from the **File** menu in folder `LibraryLoansExtended`

Save As `LibraryLoansUnit.Pas` in folder `LibraryLoansExtended`

```
IBDataSet1.Close;
IBDataSet1.SelectSQL.Clear;
IBDataSet1.SelectSQL.Add('Select * From Student');
IBDataSet1.Open;
```

*Table 64.6 Select * From Student*

Click to compile and execute `LibraryLoans` project.

Click the `Select All` button.

Figure 64.46 shows the result.

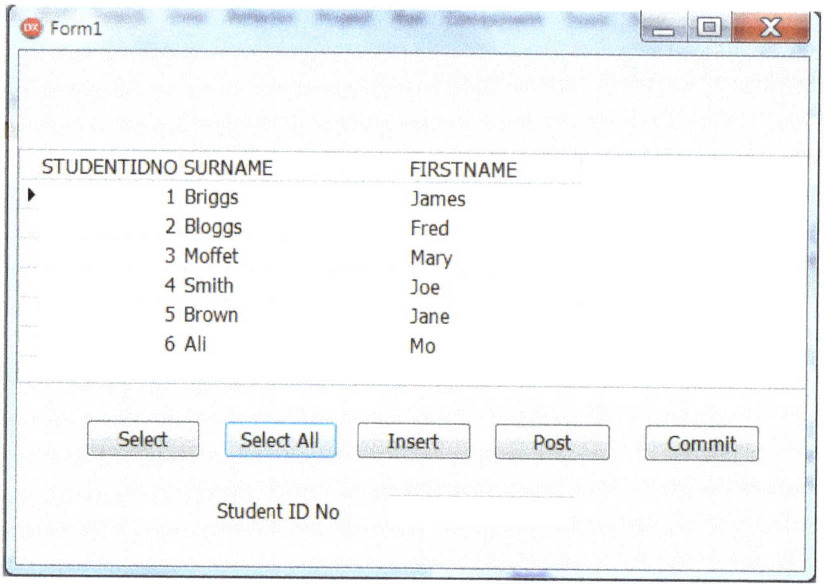

Fig. 64.46 LibraryLoans project Select All button clicked

Now **add** a button from the **Standard** palette. **Change** the name of this button to `Delete`.

Select `IBDataSet1` so that its properties are visible in the Object Inspector. **Open** the **DeleteSQL** property and **add** the following:

```
Delete From Student Where StudentIDNo = :Old_StudentIDNo
```

Double click the `Delete` button and add the following code:

```
IBDataSet1.Delete;
```

Click Save All to save both the unit and the project.

Click ▶ to compile and execute `LibraryLoans` project.

Click `Select All`.

Move the cursor onto the last but one row of the grid.

Click the `Delete` button. This row should disappear.

Click the `Commit` button.

Click the `Select All` button and **confirm** that the last but one record has disappeared.

Add a button from the **Standard** palette. **Change** its **name** property to `SelectAllOrdered` and its **caption** to `Select All Ordered`.

Double click this new button and **add** the code shown in *Table 64.7*.

```
IBDataSet1.Close;
IBDataSet1.SelectSQL.Clear;
IBDataSet1.SelectSQL.Add('Select * From Student Order By StudentIdNo');
IBDataSet1.Open;
```

*Table 64.7 Select * From Student Order By StudentIDNo*

Click Save All to save both the unit and the project.

Click ▶ to compile and execute `LibraryLoans` project.

Figure 64.47 shows the result.

Add a button from the **Standard** palette. **Change** its **name** property to `Refresh`.

Double click this new button and **add** the code

```
IBDataSet1.Refresh;
```

Click Save All to save both the unit and the project.

Click ▶ to compile and execute `LibraryLoans` project.

Data is re-fetched from the database when the **Refresh** method of `DataSet1` is called. This ensures that the application has the latest data from the database.

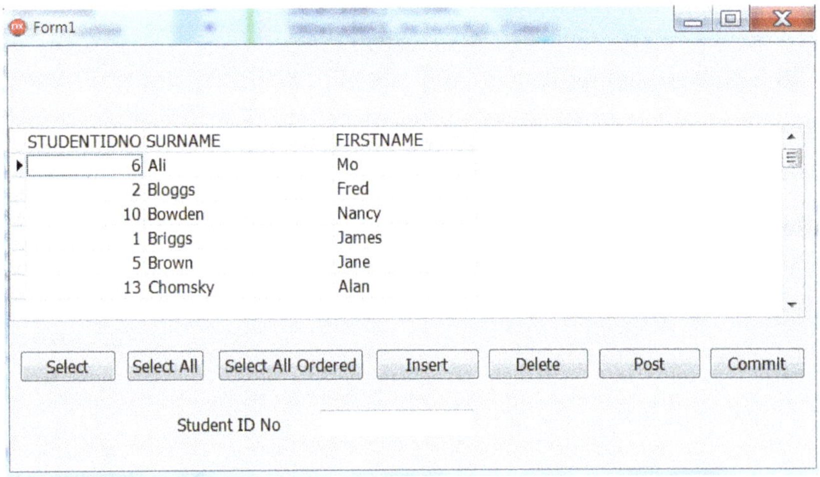

Fig. 64.47 LibraryLoans project Select All Ordered button clicked

Using a Generator

The operation of inserting a new record into the database requires that a blank row is first created in `DBGrid1`. This is done by clicking the `Insert` button. Values for the the fields `StudentIDNo`, `Surname` and `FirstName` must then be inserted in the correct place in the blank row. Finally the `Post` button must be clicked to post the new record to the database. However, the requirement for a unique `StudentIDNo` value to be entered creates a potential problem: the value chosen must not exist already in the database in table `Student`.

It would be much better if the database itself supplied the `StudentIDNo` value.

Fortunately, Interbase can do this via its **generator** mechanism.

Open IBConsole, and connect to `LibDB.ib`, if not already connected.

Click on **SQL** to open the **Interactive SQL** window.

Type the following into the window:

```
Create Generator Gen_StudentIDNo
```

Execute this query. **Check** in **IBConsole** that this generator has been created - see *Figure 64.48*.

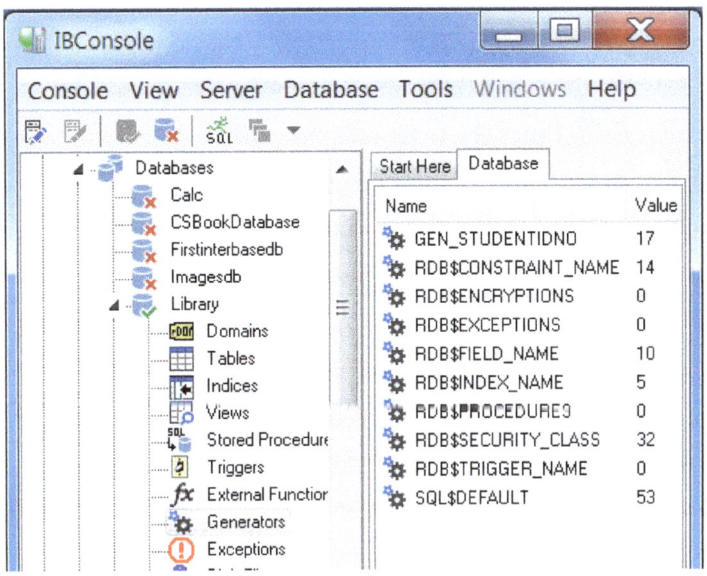

Fig. 64.48 Generators for Library database

Return to Delphi, select `IBDataSet1` and make its properties visible in the Object Inspector.

Select its **Generator** property and **click** on the ellipsis (...) to open the generator window.

Select `GEN_STUDENTIDNO` for the **Generator** value, `STUDENTIDNO` for the **Field** value associated with this particular generator, **Increment By** value 1, and `On Post` for the **Apply Event** option as shown in *Figure 64.49*.

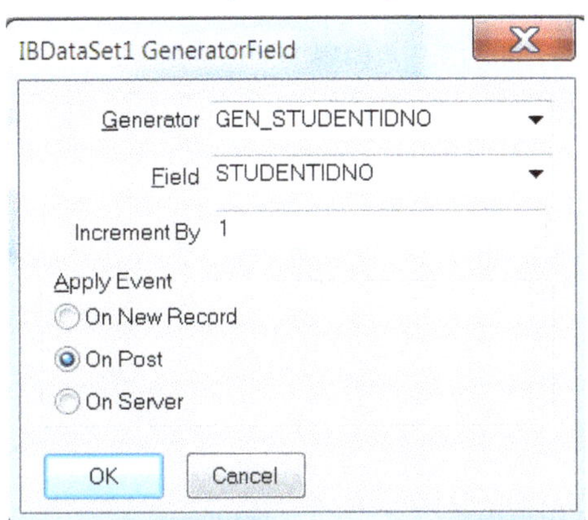

Fig. 64.49 Selecting Gen_StudentIDNo for field StudentIDNo

Click OK.

Switch to IBConsole.

Click Generators under `Library` then **double click** `GEN_STUDENTIDNO` in the **Database** tab located in the right window.

The pop-up window shown in *Figure 64.50* should appear showing the current value of the generator `GEN_STUDENTIDNO`.

Figure 64.50 shows the current value to be 18 corresponding to the last record posted, "`18, Choy, Ping Cheng`" shown in *Figure 64.51*.

The next record posted will use the next generated value 19 and this value will subsequently appear as the generator `GEN_STUDENTIDNO`'s current value.

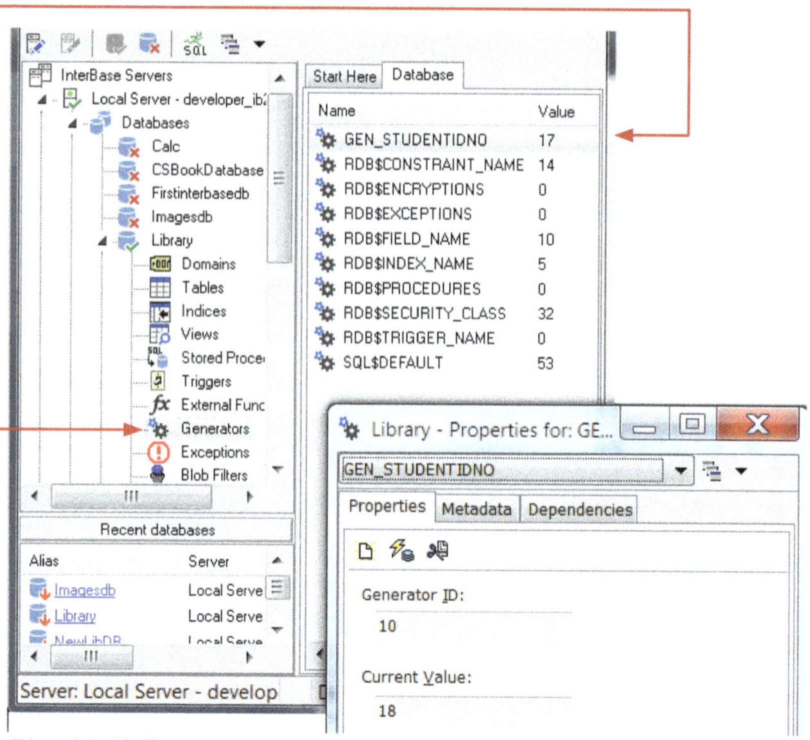

Fig. 64.50 Pop-up window which appears after clicking Generators then double-clicking GEN_STUDENTIDNO

It is possible to set the **Current Value** to a different value by clicking on the icon in the properties tab shown in *Figure 64.50* to bring up the window shown in *Figure 64.52*. The current value is shown in the **Value** field. Enter the new value into this field and click **OK** when done. Take care not to set a value which will clash with an existing value in the database table `Student`.

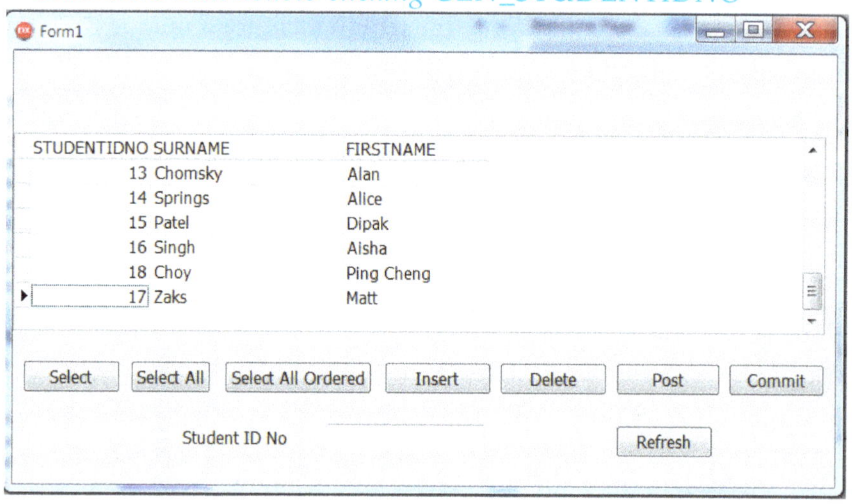

Fig. 64.51 Select All clicked then cursor moved to last row

Figure 64.51 shows three columns of data but when inserting a new record only two are required, `Surname` and `FirstName`, as `StudentIdNo` is generated automatically on posting the new record to the database.

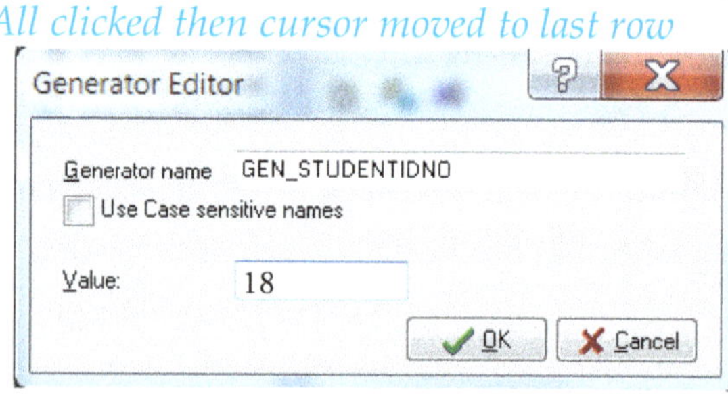

Fig. 64.52 Changing the generator's value

The solution is to hide the `StudentIdNo` column in `DBGrid1` by setting its **Visible** property to `False`.

Double click the `Insert` button in **Design mode** in the **Delphi IDE**.

Change the body of the event handler `TForm1.InsertClick(Sender: TObject)` so that it reads as follows

```
IBDataSet1.Open;
IBDataSet1.Insert;
DBGrid1.Columns[0].Visible := False;
```

The columns have index values 0, 1 and 2, respectively. Therefore, column `StudentIDNo` corresponds to index 0.

Figure 64.53 shows `DBGrid1` after the `Insert` button is clicked with `DataSet1` yet to be opened (application just launched). Note that there is no `StudentIDNo` column.

Click the `Select All` button to open `DataSet1` and to show all records in table `Student`.

Move the cursor to the last record using the scroll bars.

Now **click** the `Insert` button.

A blank row will appear below the last record.

Enter a value for the `Surname` field and for the `FirstName` field then click the `Post` button to write the record to the database table `Student`. *Figure 64.54* shows the new record "`Cleland`, `Sam`" before posting.

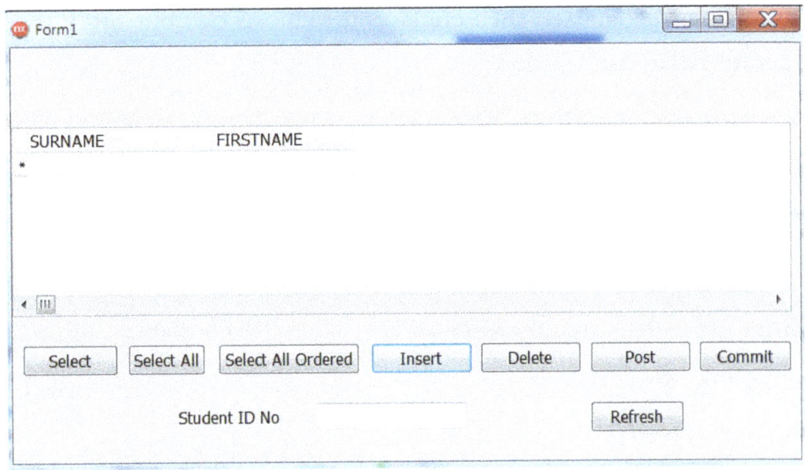

Fig. 64.53 DBGrid1 after clicking the Insert button with DataSet1 closed

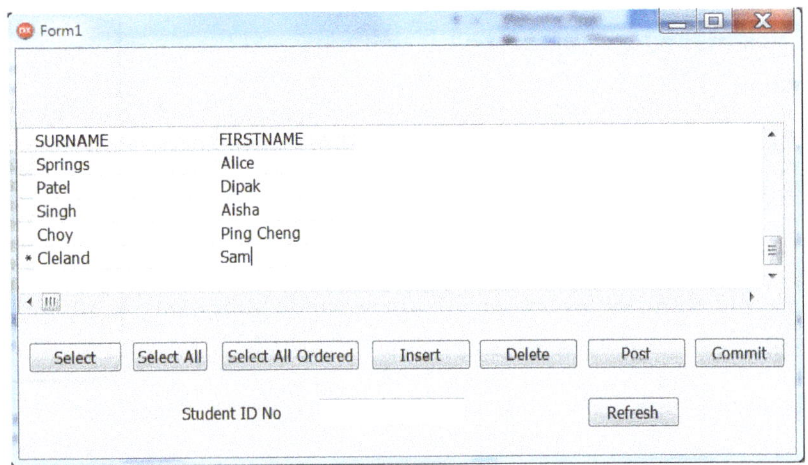

Fig. 64.54 DBGrid1 after clicking the Insert button with DataSet1 open

Storing and accessing images in an Interbase database

www.educational-computing.com/DelphiBook/Code/Chapter64/ImagesDatabase.rar

Use the data type **Blob** (Binary large object) to store images in an Interbase database.

This data type may be subtyped in order to accommodate the many native data types that can be defined as **Blob** data. Interbase provides two predefined types:

1. An unstructured subtype generally applied to binary data - **sub_type 0**
2. A structured subtype for plain text - **sub_type 1**.

Rather than storing **Blob** data directly in the **Blob** field of a table record, Interbase stores a **Blob ID**. A **Blob ID** is a unique numeric value that references **Blob** data. The **Blob** data is stored elsewhere in the database, in a series of **Blob** segments. A segment is a unit of storage used by Interbase for **Blob** data. It is the amount of data that is transferred in one read or write operation. Therefore, when an application creates a **Blob**, it must write data to it a segment at a time. When an application reads a **Blob**, it reads a segment at a time.

Launch **IBConsole**.

Click **Database|Create Database** to bring up the **Create Database** window. Alternatively, if the required database exists already then **click** **Database|Add** instead.

Databases must be created on the same drive as Interbase server e.g. the C: drive.

If creating the database then **click** on the ellipsis (...) button in the **Create Database** window to bring up the **Specify Database** window.

Navigate to the folder/subfolder on the local drive in which to create the database.
Type a suitable filename for this database.

For this exercise, the folder path is `C:\Users\drbond` (it will be different for you) and the chosen filename is `ImagesDB.ib`. **Add** alias `ImagesDB`. www.educational-computing.com/DelphiBook/Code/Chapter64/ImagesDB.ib

Enter user `SYSDBA` and password `masterkey` (this step is required if adding an existing database)

Click OK. Database `ImagesDB.ib` alias `ImagesDB` should now be registered and a connection to it open on the Interbase server.

www.educational-computing.com/DelphiBook/Code/Chapter64/Image.sql

```
Create Table Image
(
  PictureID Integer Not Null,
  CopyrightOwner VarChar(60),
  Country VarChar(30),
  Location VarChar(30),
  Picture BLOB Sub_Type 0 Segment Size 32000,
  Description VarChar(60),
 PRIMARY KEY (PictureID)
);
CREATE GENERATOR GenPictureID;
COMMIT;
```

Table 64.8 Image.sql script

Click SQL in the toolbar to bring up the **ISQL** window.

Click SQL|Query in the toolbar to bring down the menu.

Click Load Script and **locate** and **load** DDL script `Images.sql` into **ISQL**.

Click the **Execute Query** icon to create table `Image`.

Double click Tables icon in IBConsole and check that table `Image` has been created.

Launch Delphi. Make sure that Interbase server is running. You may need to reset the server if you are using the developer version which sets a time limit on continuous running.

Select File|New|VCL Application.

Set `Form1`'s **Height** property to 777 and its **Width** property to 1198.

Place a **TIBDatabase** component from the **Interbase** palette on the form.

Place a **TIBTransaction** component from the **Interbase** palette on the form.

Place a **TIBDataSet** component from **Interbase** palette on the form

Place a **TDataSource** component from the **Data Access** palette on the form.

Place an **TOpenDialog** component from the **Dialogs** palette on the form.

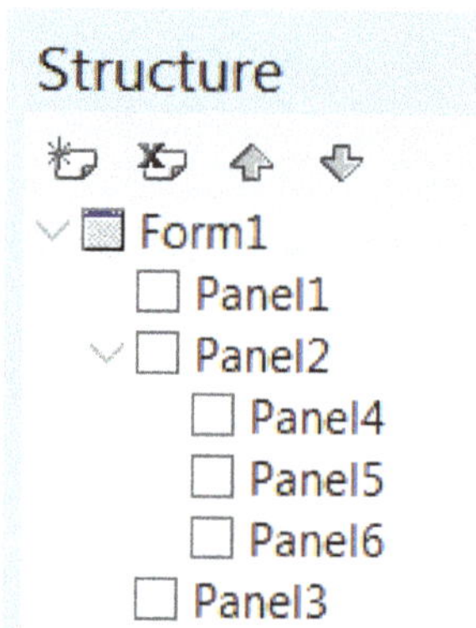

Fig. 64.55 Structure window showing arrangement of panels

Place six panels from the **Standard** palette on the form and arrange as shown in *Figures 64.55* and *64.56*.

Set `Panel1`'s **Align** property to **alBottom** and its **Height** property to 54.

Move `Panel2` above `Panel1`.

Set `Panel2`'s **Align** property to **alBottom** and its **Height** property to 568.

Move `Panel3` above `Panel2`.

Set `Panel3`'s **Align** property to **alClient**.

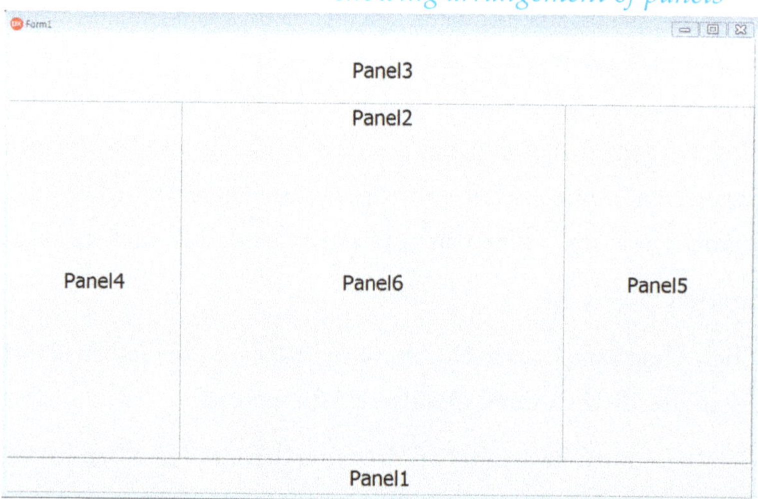

Fig. 64.56 Panel layout for Images database user interface

Set `Panel4`'s **Align** property to **alLeft** and its **Width** to 274.

Set `Panel5`'s **Align** property to **alRight** and its **Width** to 299.

Set `Panel6`'s **Align** property to **alClient**.

Place a **TDBGrid** component, `DBGrid1`, from the **Data Controls** palette on `Panel3`.

Set `DBGrid1`'s **Align** property to **alClient**.

Place a **TDBImage** component, `DBImage1`, from the **Data Controls** palette on `Panel6`.

Set `DBImage1`'s **Align** property to **alClient**.

Place twelve buttons from the **Standard** palette on `Panel5` as shown in *Figure 64.57* and change **Name** and **Caption** properties of each as follows:

- `btnSelect` and `Select`
- `btnSelectAll` and `Select All`
- `btnInsert` and `Insert`
- `btnInsertPicture` and`InsertPicture`
- `btnDelete` and `Delete`
- `btnPost` and `Post`
- `btnCommit` and `Commit`
- `btnTerminate` and `Terminate`
- `btnFirst` and `First`
- `btnNext` and `Next`
- `btnPrevious` and `Previous`
- `btnLast` and `Last`

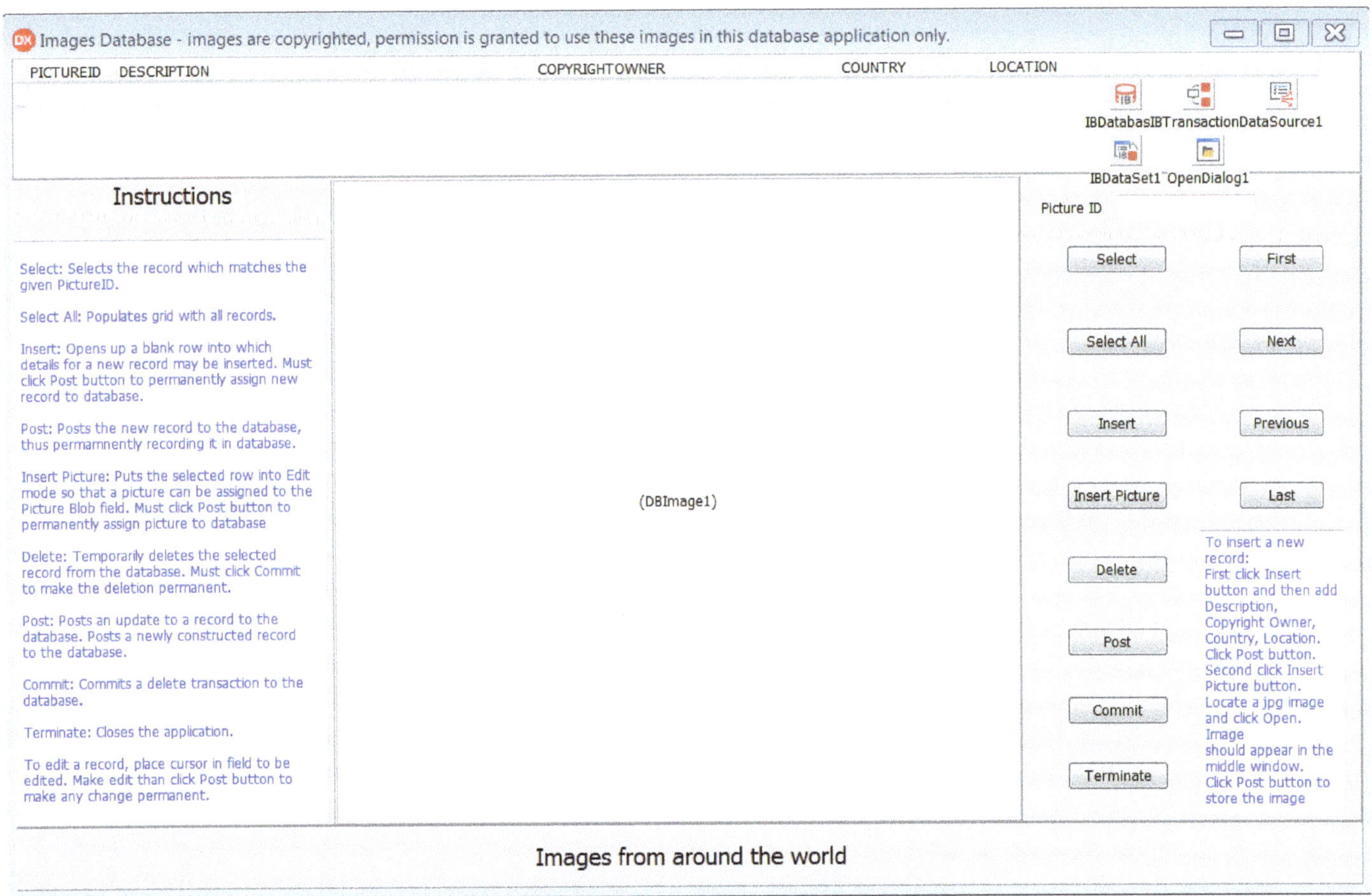

Fig. 64.57 User interface for images database project

To align the buttons, hold down the shift key whilst clicking on buttons to create a group as shown in *Figure 64.58*.

Right click with the mouse pointer to bring up the menu shown in *Figure 64.58*.

Click on **Position** option, then **Align** to bring up the **Alignment** submenu shown in *Figure 64.59*.

Select Left then click **OK** to align the left side of each button in the group.

Repeat the exercise but this time select **Space Equally**.

Use this alignment method to align the second column of buttons.

Place a single **TEdit** box from the **Standard** palette on `Panel5`.

Delete `Edit1` from its **Text** property field. **Change** its name to `edtPictureID`.

Place a single **TLabel** component from the **Standard** palette on `Panel5`.

Change its **Caption** property to `PictureID` and its **Name** to `lblPictureID`.

Arrange both as shown in *Figure 64.57*.

Select `Panel4` and change its **VerticalAlignment** property to **taAlignTop**.

Change its **Caption** to `Instructions`.

The form should now look as follows:

Change `Form1`'s **Caption** to `Images Database - images are copyrighted, permission is granted to use these images in this database application only`. Change its `Name` property to `frmImagesDatabase`.

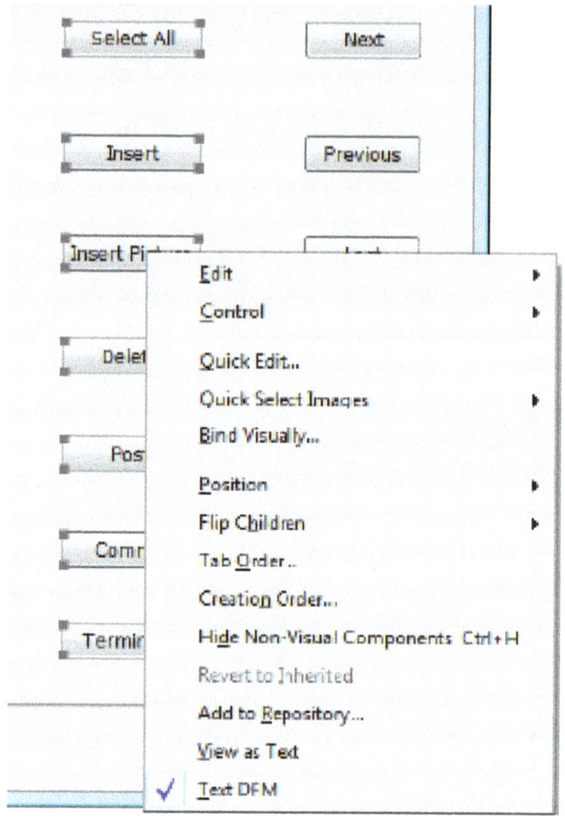

Fig. 64.58 Aligning buttons

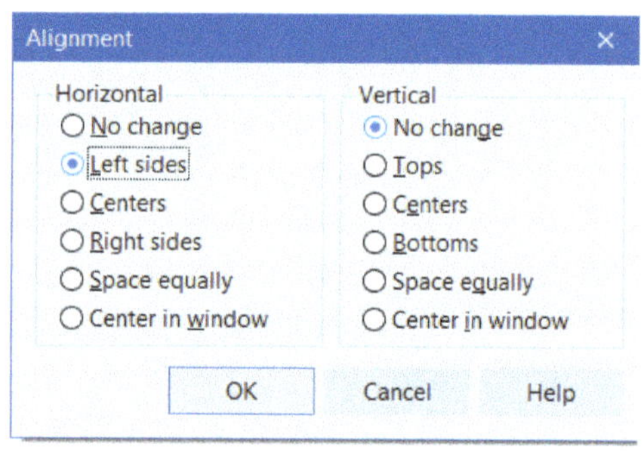

Fig. 64.59 Alignment submenu

Place a **TMemo** component, `Memo1`, from the **Standard** palette on `Panel4` and position as shown in *Figure 64.57*.

Place a **TMemo** component, `Memo2`, from the **Standard** palette on `Panel5` and position as shown in *Figure 64.57*.

`Memo1`: **Height** = 513; **Width** = 275.

`Memo2`: **Height** = 262; **Width** = 129.

Select the **Lines** property of each in turn and click the ellipsis (...) in the **TStrings** field to bring up the **String List Editor. Download** the text for each from

www.educational-computing.co.uk/DelphiBookCode/Memo1Lines.txt

and www.educational-computing.co.uk/DelphiBookCode/Memo2Lines.txt

Select Panel1 and **change** its **Caption** property to `Images from around the world`.

Set DatabaseName property of `IBDatabase1` to `C:\Users\drbond\ImagesDB.ib` (your path will be different).

Set DefaultTransaction property of `IBDatabase1` to `IBTransaction1`.

Set **DefaultDatabase** property of `IBTransaction1` to `IBDatabase1`.

Set **DataSource** property of `DBGrid1` to `DataSource1`.

Set **DataSet** property of `DataSource1` to `IBDataSet1`. **Set** `DataSource1.AutoEdit` to **True**.

Select `DBImage1`. **Set** its **DataSource** property to `DataSource1`, its **DataField** to `Picture`, its **Stretch** property and its **Proportional** property to **True**.

Select `IBDatabase1` so it is available in the Object Inspector. **Click** on its **Connected** property and **select** **True** to connect to the database `C:\Users\drbond\ImagesDB.ib`.

Select `IBDataSet1` component. **View** in object inspector.

Click the ellipsis (...) in the **GeneratorField** property to set the generator as shown in *Figure 64.60*.

Add the SQL statements shown in *Figure 64.60* to the corresponding fields of `IBDataSet1`.

Save the project (**Save All**) in a folder `ImagesDatabase`:

- Save the unit as `ImagesDatabaseUnit.pas`
- Save the project as `ImagesDatabaseProject.dproj`.

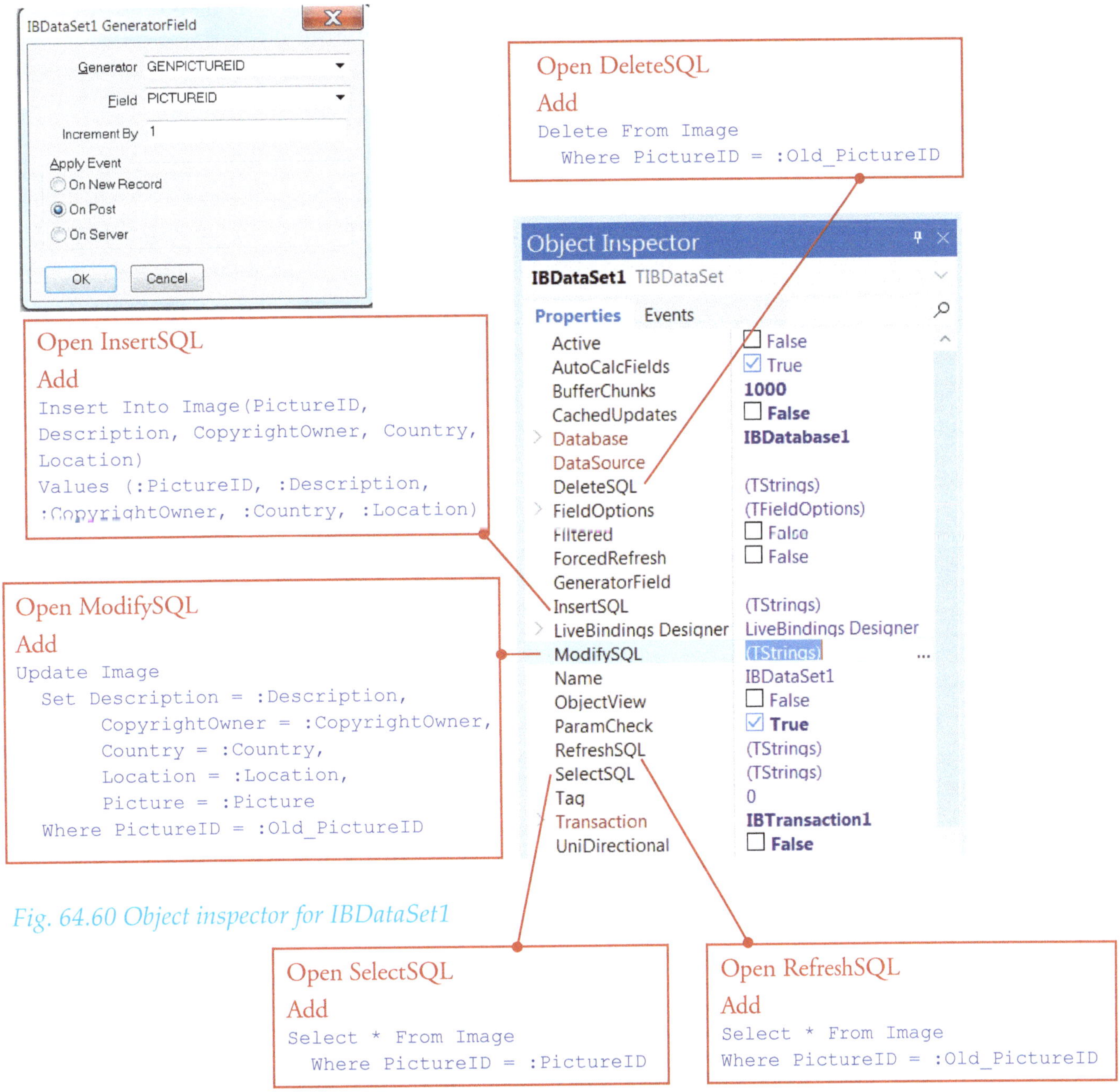

Fig. 64.60 Object inspector for IBDataSet1

Double click the button labelled `Select` to create the event handler `TfrmImagesDatabase.SelectClick`. **Add** the code shown in *Table 64.9* to the body of this event handler.

```
Procedure TfrmImagesDatabase.btnSelectClick(Sender: TObject);
Begin
  DisableMoveButtons;
  DBGrid1.Columns[0].ReadOnly := True; DBGrid1.Columns[0].Visible := True;
  IBDataSet1.Close;
  If Length(PictureID.Text) <> 0
    Then
      Begin
        IBDataSet1.SelectSQL.Clear;
        IBDataSet1.SelectSQL.Add('Select * From Image Where PictureID = :PictureID');
        IBDataSet1.ParamByName('PictureID').AsInteger := StrToInt(PictureID.Text);
        IBDataSet1.Open;
        If Not IBDataSet1.IsEmpty
          Then
            If (Length(DBGrid1.Fields[3].Text) <> 0) And (Length(DBGrid1.Fields[4].Text) <> 0)
                  And (Not DBImage1.Picture.Graphic.Empty)
              Then Panel1.Caption := 'Image from ' + DBGrid1.Fields[4].Text
                                          + ', ' + DBGrid1.Fields[3].Text
              Else Panel1.Caption := 'Images from around the world';
      End
    Else ShowMessage('You have''t entered a Picture ID');
End;
```

Annotations: Ensures that PictureID column cannot be edited (ReadOnly); Ensures that PictureID column visible (Visible); IBDataSet1 must be closed in order to edit its SQL (IBDataSet1.Close); Checks that TEdit box not empty (If Length(PictureID.Text) <> 0); TEdit box (PictureID.Text); Checks that a record is returned (If Not IBDataSet1.IsEmpty); Constructs a string from location and country information and assigns this to Caption for Panel1.

P

Table 64.9 Event handler which is invoked when the Select button clicked

Two utility procedures that enable and disable the navigation buttons, `First`, `Next`, `Previous` and `Last` are needed. These buttons are only required to be active when the `Select All` button is clicked.

Create these two procedures as private methods of objects of class `TfrmImagesDatabase` as shown in *Table 64.10*.

```
Procedure TfrmImagesDatabase.DisableMoveButtons;
Begin
  btnFirst.Enabled := False;
  btnNext.Enabled := False;
  btnPrevious.Enabled := False;
  btnLast.Enabled := False;
End;

Procedure TImagesDatabase.EnableMoveButtons;
Begin
  btnFirst.Enabled := True;
  btnNext.Enabled := True;
  btnPrevious.Enabled := True;
  btnLast.Enabled := True;
End;
```

```
TImagesDatabase = Class(TForm)
    IBDatabase1: TIBDatabase;
    IBTransaction1: TIBTransaction;
    ...
  Private
    Procedure DisableMoveButtons;
    Procedure EnableMoveButtons;
  Public
    { Public declarations }
  End;
```

P

Table 64.10 Two utility procedures to disable and enable buttons First, Next, Previous and Last

Place their code in the **Implementation** section.

Double click the button labelled `Select All` to create `TfrmImagesDatabase.SelectAllClick` event handler.

```
Procedure TfrmImagesDatabase.btnSelectAllClick(Sender: TObject);
Begin                                          Enables First, Next, Previous, Last buttons
  EnableMoveButtons;
  DBGrid1.Columns[0].ReadOnly := True; DBGrid1.Columns[0].Visible := True;
  IBDataSet1.Close;
  IBDataSet1.SelectSQL.Clear;                  Ensures that PictureID column visible
  IBDataSet1.SelectSQL.Add('Select * From Image Order By PictureID');
  IBDataSet1.Open;
  btnFirstClick(Self);                         Set cursor to point to first record
End;
```

Table 64.11 Event handler which is invoked when the Select All button clicked

Add the code shown in Table 64.11 to the body of this event handler.

Double click the button labelled `Insert` to create `TfrmImagesDatabase.InsertClick` event handler.

Add the code shown in Table 64.12 to the body of this event handler.

```
Procedure TfrmImagesDatabase.btnInsertClick(Sender: TObject);
Begin                        Insert opens a blank row so need to revert to general caption
  Panel1.Caption := 'Images from around the world';
  DisableMoveButtons;        Disables First, Next, Previous, Last buttons
  IBDataSet1.Close;
  IBDataSet1.SelectSQL.Clear;        This SQL clears DBGrid1when IBDataSet1 opened
  IBDataSet1.SelectSQL.Add('Select * From Image Where PictureID = :Old_PictureID');
  DBgrid1.Columns[0].Visible := False;  Hides PictureID column, PictureID generated by generator not user
  IBDataSet1.Open;           DBGrid1 cleared at this point leaving a single blank row visible
  IBDataSet1.Insert;         Operation which places IBDataSet1 into insert mode (State = dsInsert) and
End;                         marks blank row with an asterisk
```

Table 64.12 Event handler which is invoked when the Insert button clicked

Double click the button labelled `Select All` to create `TfrmImagesDatabase.InsertPictureClick` event handler.

Add the code shown in Table 64.13 to the body of this event handler.

Double click the button labelled `Post` to create `TfrmImagesDatabase.PostClick` event handler.

Add the code shown in Table 64.14 to the body of this event handler.

The state of `IBDataSet1` is switched to edit mode (**State = dsEdit**) when the cursor is placed in cell of `DBGrid1`. Changes may then be made to the data in that cell and any other cell in the containing row with the exception of the `PictureID` cell which is read only (the `PictureID` column is made read only in the event handlers that are called when either the `Select` button or the `Select All` button is clicked). To make any edits permanent, the `Post` button must be clicked.

```
Procedure TfrmImagesDatabase.btnInsertPictureClick(Sender: TObject);     Need to add unit JPEG
Var                                                                       to Uses clause
    B: TJPEGImage;
  Begin
    DisableMoveButtons;  <-- Disables First, Next, Previous, Last buttons
    If IBDataSet1.Active  <-- Need to have a record to insert picture into
      Then
        Begin  <-- Opens a window on the file system so a JPEG image file can be selected
         If OpenDialog1.Execute
           Then
             Begin  <-- Creates a JPEG object and assigns its address in memory to variable B
               B := TJPEGImage.Create;
               Try  <-- TJPEGImage object method called to load image file into memory
                 B.LoadFromFile(OpenDialog1.Filename);
                 IBDataSet1.Edit;  <-- Put IBDataSet1 into edit mode (state = dsEdit)
                 DBImage1.Picture.Assign(B);  <-- JPEG data copied to Picture field of DBImage1
                 If (Length(DBGrid1.Fields[3].Text) <> 0) And (Length(DBGrid1.Fields[4].Text) <> 0)
                       And (Not DBImage1.Picture.Graphic.Empty)
                   Then Panel1.Caption := 'Image from ' + DBGrid1.Fields[4].Text
                                                 + ', ' + DBGrid1.Fields[3].Text
                   Else Panel1.Caption := 'Images from around the world';
               Finally
                 B.Free;
               End;
             End;
        End
      Else ShowMessage('DataSet closed - use Insert first to create a new record or select a specific record');
  End;
```

Annotations: "Check there is data in Country and Location fields" (points to the If (Length(...)) line); "Constructs a string from location and country information and assigns this to Caption for Panel1" (points to the Panel1.Caption assignment).

Table 64.13 Event handler which is invoked when the Insert Picture button clicked

```
Procedure TfrmImagesDatabase.btnPostClick(Sender: TObject);
Begin
  DisableMoveButtons;  <-- Disables First, Next, Previous, Last buttons
  DBGrid1.Columns[0].Visible := True;  <-- Makes PictureID column visible so that on posting
                                           an insert the newly allocated PictureID can be seen.
                                           Unhides the PictureID column if an edit is posted.
  If (IBDataSet1.State = dsEdit) Or (IBDataSet1.State = dsInsert)  <-- Checks that IBDataSet1 in an edit or insert state
    Then IBDataSet1.Post;
  If (Length(IBDataSet1.SelectSQL.Text) = 40) Then EnableMoveButtons;  <-- Checks if SQL is Select All which
                                                                           is the only SQL with length 40
  If IBDataSet1.Active And (DBImage1.Picture.Graphic.Empty = False)
    Then  <-- If IBDataSet1 open and the display shows a picture and location and country information is available
      If (Length(DBGrid1.Fields[3].Text) <> 0) And (Length(DBGrid1.Fields[4].Text) <> 0)    show this
           And (Not DBImage1.Picture.Graphic.Empty)                                           information
        Then Panel1.Caption := 'Image from ' + DBGrid1.Fields[4].Text + ', ' + DBGrid1.Fields[3].Text
        Else Panel1.Caption := 'Images from around the world';
End;
```

Table 64.14 Event handler which is invoked when the Post button clicked

The rows returned by `Select All` may be scrolled through by clicking the `First`, `Next`, `Previous` and `Last` buttons or by using the scroll bars on the right side of the grid - *Figure 64.61*. The event handler shown in *Table 64.15* is invoked whenever the rows of `DBGrid1` are scrolled through whether by the scroll bars or by the buttons `First`, `Next`, `Previous` and `Last` or when the cursor is placed in the grid, e.g. when data from *IBDataSet1* is sent to the grid by a `Select` or `Select All`.

To create event handler `IBDataSet1AfterScroll`, **select** IBDataBase1 and then in the **Object Inspector**, **select** the **Events** tab and double click the empty field for the event **AfterScroll**.

Add the code shown in *Table 64.15* to this event handler.

```
Procedure TfrmImagesDatabase.IBDataSet1AfterScroll(DataSet: TDataSet);
Begin
  If (Length(DBGrid1.Fields[3].Text) <> 0) And (Length(DBGrid1.Fields[4].Text) <> 0)
        And (Not DBImage1.Picture.Graphic.Empty)
    Then Panel1.Caption := 'Image from ' + DBGrid1.Fields[4].Text + ', '
                             + DBGrid1.Fields[3].Text
    Else Panel1.Caption := 'Images from around the world';
End;
```

Table 64.15 Event handler which is invoked when the scroll buttons are used

By clicking a cell in the grid, `DBGrid1`, and making a change to its data, `IBDataSet1` is placed in edit mode (**State = dsEdit**). The cursor on the left-hand side of the grid changes from ▶ to I and back to ▶ on clicking button `Post` - *Figures 64.61* and *64.62*.

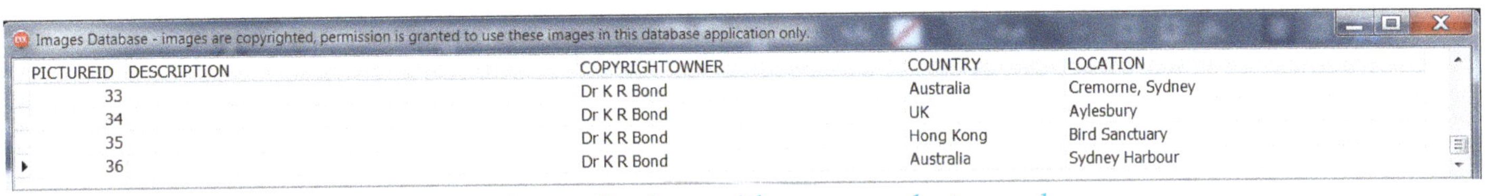

Fig. 64.61 Image database with cursor on last record

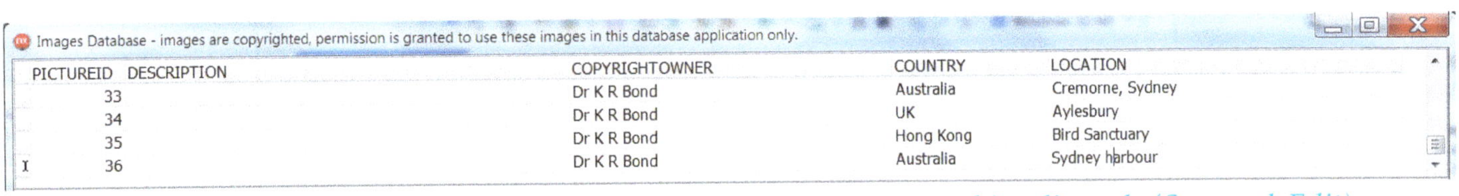

Fig. 64.62 Image database with cursor on last record and last record in edit mode (State = dsEdit)

It is important that the user cannot edit the `PictureID` column as the values in this column are primary key values. To prevent editing of the values in the `PictureID` column, we make it read only.

There are two ways that this can be done:

1. When the form is activated
2. When a cell in `DBGrid1` is clicked.

Table 64.16 and *Table 64.17* show two event handlers which implement these two ways.

Using the **Events** tab of form `ImagesDatabase` in the **Object Inspector**, double click the empty field for the event **OnActivate** to create the event handler `TfrmImagesDatabase.FormActivate`.

Add the code shown in *Table 64.16*.

```
Procedure TfrmImagesDatabase.FormActivate(Sender: TObject);
Begin
  DisableMoveButtons;
  DBGrid1.Columns[0].ReadOnly := True;
End;
```

Table 64.16 Event handler which is invoked when the application's form is activated

Using the **Events** tab of `DBGrid1` in the **Object Inspector**, **double click** the empty field for the event **OnCellClick** to create the event handler `TfrmImagesDatabase.DBGrid1CellClick`.
Add the code shown in *Table 64.17*.

```
Procedure TfrmImagesDatabase.DBGrid1CellClick(Column: TColumn);
Begin
  DBGrid1.Columns[0].ReadOnly := True;
End;
```

P

Table 64.17 Event handler which is invoked when a cell of DBGrid1 is clicked

Event handlers for the navigation buttons, `First`, `Next`, `Previous` and `Last` are created by **double clicking** the corresponding button and then adding the code shown in *Tables 64.18*, *64.19*, *64.20* and *64.21*, respectuvely.

```
Procedure TfrmImagesDatabase.FirstClick(Sender: TObject);
Begin
  IBDataSet1.First;
End;
```

P

Table 64.18 Event handler which is invoked when button First is clicked

```
Procedure TfrmImagesDatabase.NextClick(Sender: TObject);
Begin
  IBDataSet1.Next;
End;
```

P

Table 64.19 Event handler which is invoked when button Next is clicked

```
Procedure TfrmImagesDatabase.PreviousClick(Sender: TObject);
Begin
  IBDataSet1.Prior;
End;
```

P

Table 64.20 Event handler which is invoked when button Previous is clicked

```
Procedure TfrmImagesDatabase.LastClick(Sender: TObject);
Begin
  IBDataSet1.Last;
End;
```

P

Table 64.21 Event handler which is invoked when button Last is clicked

Double click the `Commit` button to create the event handler `TfrmImagesDatabase.CommitClick` and **add** the code shown in *Table 64.22*.

```
Procedure TfrmImagesDatabase.CommitClick(Sender: TObject);
Begin
  IBTransaction1.Commit;
  Panel1.Caption := 'Images from around the world';
End;
```

Table 64.22 Event handler which is invoked when button Commit is clicked

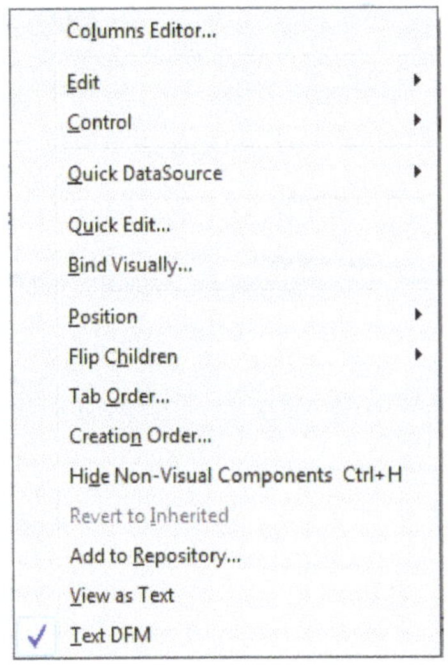

Fig. 64.63 Pop up window when DBGrid1 right clicked

Double click the `Terminate` button to create the event handler `TImagesDatabase.TerminateClick` and **add** the code shown in *Table 64.23*.

```
Procedure TfrmImagesDatabase.TerminateClick(Sender: TObject);
Begin
  Application.Terminate;
End;
```

Table 64.23 Event handler which is invoked when button Terminate is clicked

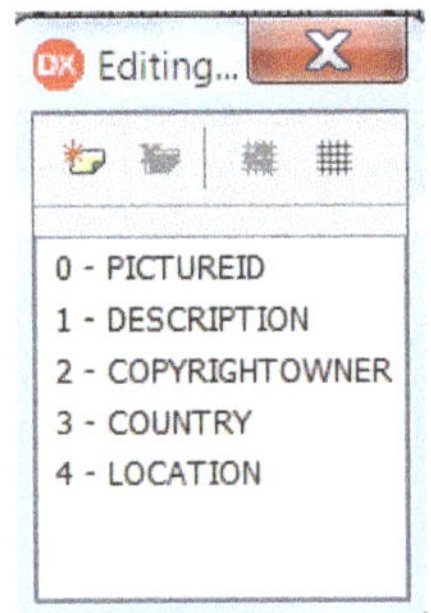

Fig. 64.64 Edit window

Click Save All to save both the unit and the project.

Images will not display in the **Blob** column in `DBGrid1` so this column needs to be removed from `DBGrid1`.

Right click `DBGrid1` to bring up the window shown in *Figure 64.63*.

Click **Columns Editor...** to bring up the window shown in *Figure 64.64*.

Figure 64.64 shows the fields that remain after the **Blob** field has been removed by selecting it and then clicking (greyed out in *Figure 64.64*).

Click to compile and execute `ImagesDatabase` project.

Fig. 64.65 ImagesDatabase application in execution showing data with added

Parameters used in IBDataSet1

The SQL statements specified in the Object Inspector for `IBDataSet1` are known as base statements. These base statements are required for Delphi to be able to compile the application.

The current field value may be accessed in the SQL statement using **:FieldName**, and the old field value using **OLD_FieldName**. The old field value mechanism is used when the search term in the **Where** clause relies on a field whose value will be changed.

For example in the following SQL `ItemNo` could originally have been 56 but is changed by the SQL statement to 65, say:

```
Update StockInventory
  Set StockInventory.ItemNo = :ItemNo
    Where (StockInventory.ItemNo = OLD_ StockInventory.ItemNo)
```

Insert

The following **Insert** SQL assigns the corresponding column values in the current row of `DBGrid1` to parameters `:PictureID, :Description, :CopyrightOwner, :Country, :Location`.

```
Insert Into Image(PictureID, Description, CopyrightOwner, Country, Location)
  Values (:PictureID, :Description, :CopyrightOwner, :Country, :Location)
```

Select

The following **Select** SQL assigns the corresponding column value for `PictureID` in the current row of `DBGrid1` to parameter `:PictureID`

```
Select * From Image
  Where PictureID = :PictureID
```

Update (Modify)

The following **Update** SQL assigns the corresponding column values in the current row of `DBGrid1` to parameters `:Description, :CopyrightOwner, :Country, :Location, :Picture` and uses the original value of `PictureID` which in this case does not change because the application has been designed to prevent the user from changing it. The latter means that `:PictureID` could have been used instead of `OLD_PictureID`.

```
Update Image
  Set Description = :Description,
      CopyrightOwner = :CopyrightOwner,
      Country = :Country,
      Location = :Location,
      Picture = :Picture
  Where PictureID = :Old_PictureID
```

Delete

The value of `:Old_PictureID` that is used is the corresponding column value in `DBGrid1` for the currently selected row. `Old_PictureID` is typically used but depending on context `:PictureID` works successfully.

```
Delete From Image
  Where PictureID = :Old_PictureID
```

Refresh

This is typically relevant where a change in one table requires that another table be refreshed to reflect the change.

```
Select * From Image
  Where PictureID = :Old_PictureID
```

Refreshes a single row.

www.educational-computing.com/DelphiBook/Code/Chapter64/ImagesDatabaseWithDataModule.rar

Data module

A data module (**TDataModule**) is a form that contains non-visual components used by the application as shown in *Figure 64.66*.

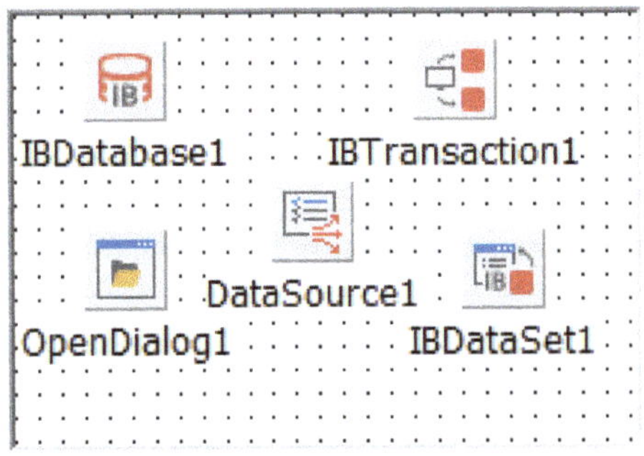

Fig. 64.66 Data module form, DataModule1 containing non-visual components for application ImagesDataBaseWithDataModuleProject

Save the `ImagesDatabaseProject` and its unit `ImagesDatabaseUnit.pas` in folder `ImagesDatabaseWithDataModule` as

- `ImagesDatabaseWithDataModuleProject`
- `ImagesDataBaseWithBackUpUnit.pas`

To add a data module unit to the project, click **File|New|Other|Database** in the Delphi IDE to bring up the **Data Module** window as shown in *Figure 64.67*.

Click the **OK** button to add a data module unit, `DataModule1`, to the project.

Save As `DataModuleUnit.pas`.

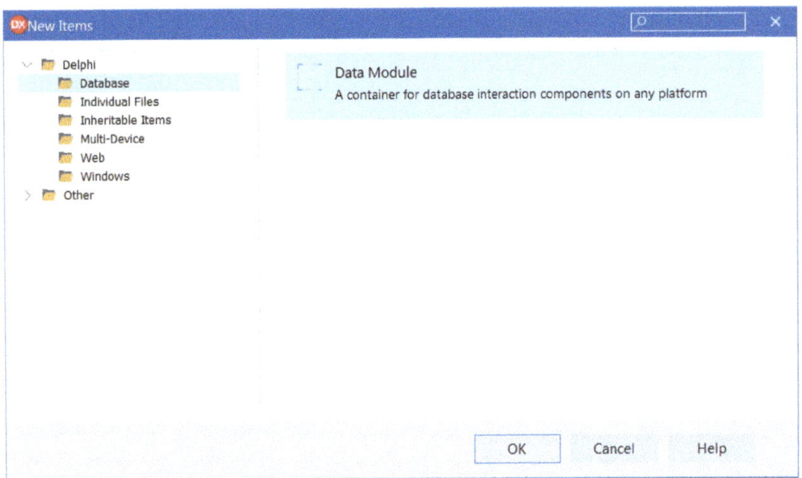

Fig. 64.67 File|New|Other|Database window

Place the following on the **Data Module** unit's form, `DataModule1` as shown in *Figure 64.66*:

- a **TIBDatabase** component (`IBDatabase1`)
- a **TIBTransaction** component (`IBTransaction1`)
- a **TIBDataSet** component (`IBDataSet1`)
- A **TDataSource** component (`DataSource1`)
- A **TOpenDialog** component (`OpenDialog1`).

Remove the corresponding components from `frmImagesDatabase`.

Make sure that the `ImagesDataBaseWithBackUpUnit.pas` uses clause in the **Interface** section includes the `DataModuleUnit` as shown below

```
Uses
  Winapi.Windows, Winapi.Messages, System.SysUtils, System.Variants, System.Classes,
  Vcl.Graphics, Vcl.Controls, Vcl.Forms, Vcl.Dialogs, Data.DB, Vcl.StdCtrls, Vcl.DBCtrls,
  Vcl.Grids, Vcl.DBGrids, IBX.IBCustomDataSet, IBX.IBDatabase, JPEG,  Vcl.ExtCtrls,
  DataModuleUnit;
```

Make sure that the **Implementation** section of `DataModuleUnit.pas` includes `ImagesDataBaseWithBackupUnit;` as shown below

```
Implementation
{%CLASSGROUP 'Vcl.Controls.TControl'}
{$R *.dfm}
Uses ImagesDataBaseWithBackupUnit;
```

Information

Data module:

A data module provides a convenient organisational tool that can be used to isolate the parts of an application that handle database connectivity and business rules.

Placing `Uses ImagesDatabaseWithBackUpUnit` in the **Implementation** section avoids a circular reference error which would occur if placed in the **Interface** section.

Select `IBDataSet1` and in its **Events** tab in the **Object Inspector** double click the **AfterScroll** field to create the event handler `IBDataSet1AfterScroll`.

Add the code shown in *Table 64.24*.

```
Procedure TDataModule1.IBDataSet1AfterScroll(DataSet: TDataSet);
Begin
  If (Length(frmImagesDatabase.DBGrid1.Fields[3].Text) <> 0)
        And (Length(frmImagesDatabase.DBGrid1.Fields[4].Text) <> 0)
        And (Not frmImagesDatabase.DBImage1.Picture.Graphic.Empty)
    Then frmImagesDatabase.Panel1.Caption := 'Image from ' + frmImagesDatabase.DBGrid1.Fields[4].Text
                                             + ', ' + frmImagesDatabase.DBGrid1.Fields[3].Text
    Else frmImagesDatabase.Panel1.Caption := 'Images from around the world';
End;
```

Table 64.24 Event handler TDataModule1.IBDataSet1AfterScroll

Remove `IBDataSet1AfterScroll` from both the **Implementation** section and the class definition in `ImagesDataBaseWithBackUpUnit.pas`. Later when the application is compiled you will be asked to confirm the removal of the remaining internal reference to `ImagesDataBaseWithBackUpUnit.pas`.

Set up `IBDatabase1`, `IBDatabase1`, `IBTransaction1`, `IBDataSet1`, `DataSource1` as before.

We now need to use the refactoring tool in the IDE to make necessary changes to the instances in the source code in `ImagesDataBaseWithBackUpUnit.pas` which reference the components that were moved to `DataModuleUnit.pas`.

Position the cursor immediately before the first instance of `IBDataSet1` in procedure `TfrmImagesDatabase.btnDeleteClick`.

Click **Refactor|Rename** in the IDE

Add `DataModule1.` to the identifier as shown in *Figure 64.68*.

Untick "**View references before refactoring**" then **click** the **OK** button (greyed out in *Figure 64.68* because the refacoring has been done already).

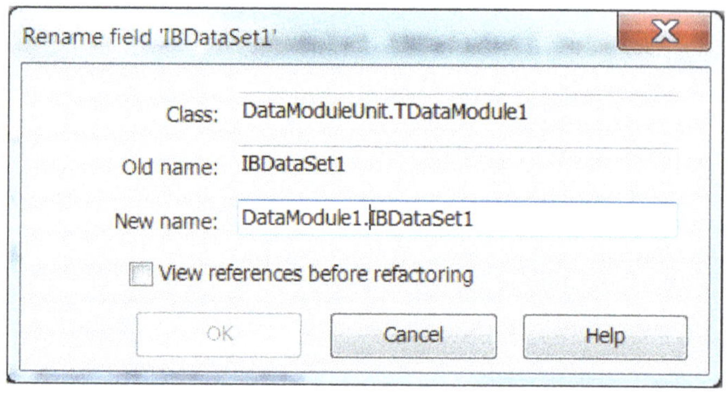

Fig. 64.68 Refactoring identifiers in ImagesDataBaseWithBackUpUnit.pas

Repeat the exercise until changes have been made as necessary to all identifiers in `ImagesDataBaseWithBackUpUnit.pas` of components that have been relocated to `DataModuleUnit.pas`.

Click **Save All** to save both the unit and the project.

Click ▶ to compile and execute `ImagesDatabaseWithDataModuleProject`.

Check that the application works as before.

www.educational-computing.com/DelphiBook/Code/Chapter64/ImagesDatabaseWithDataModule.rar

Backing up and restoring from backup the images database

With `ImagesDatabaseWithDataModuleProject` loaded in the IDE, **click File|New|VCL Form - Delphi** to create a new form and corresponding unit.

Save this unit as `PasswordUnit.pas`.

Change the **Name** property of the form to `PasswordForm` and its **Caption** to `Password Form`.

Add the following from the **Standard** palette to the form

- two **TEdit** components, `Edit1` and `Edit2`
- two **TLabel** components, `Label1` and `Label2`
- two **TButton** components, `Button1` and `Button2`

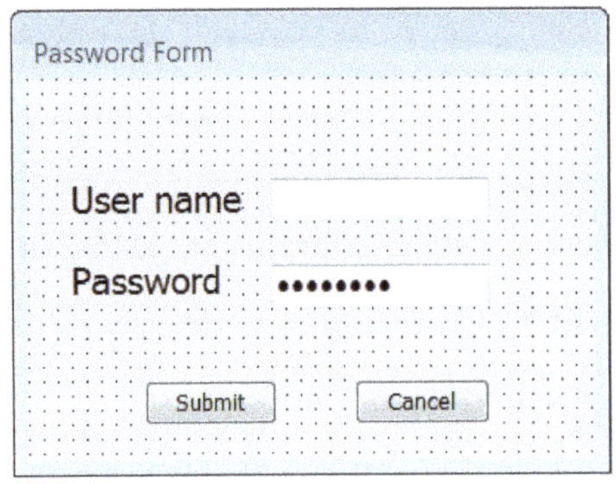

Fig. 64.69 Password form

Change the **Name** property of the two **TEdit** components to `edtUserName` and `edtPassword`, respectively.

Delete the text in the **Text** property of `edtUserName` so the field is now blank.

Change the **PasswordChar** field of `edtPassword` to the asterisk character * and **type** any 8 characters in the **Text** property field in order to populate it with eight asterisks as shown in *Figure 64.69*.

Change the **Caption** property of `Label1` to `User name` and that of `Label2` to `Password`.

Change the **Name** property of the two **TButton** components to `btnSubmit` and `btnCancel`, respectively.

Change the **Caption** property of `btnSubmit` to `Submit` and that of `btnCancel` to `Cancel`.

Set the **Position** property of `PasswordForm` to **poMainFormCenter**.

Set the **BorderIcons** property of `PasswordForm` to all **False**.

Set the **Height** property of `PasswordForm` to 259.

Set the **Width** property of `PasswordForm` to 332.

Arrange these components on the form as shown in *Figure 64.69*.

Click Save All to save both the unit and the project.

Click File|New|VCL Form - Delphi to create another new form and corresponding unit.

Save this unit as `AdminUnit.pas`.

Change the **Name** property of the form to `AdminForm` and its **Caption** to `Admin Form`.

Add three **TButton** components, `Button1`, `Button2`, and `Button3`, from the **Standard** palette to the form.

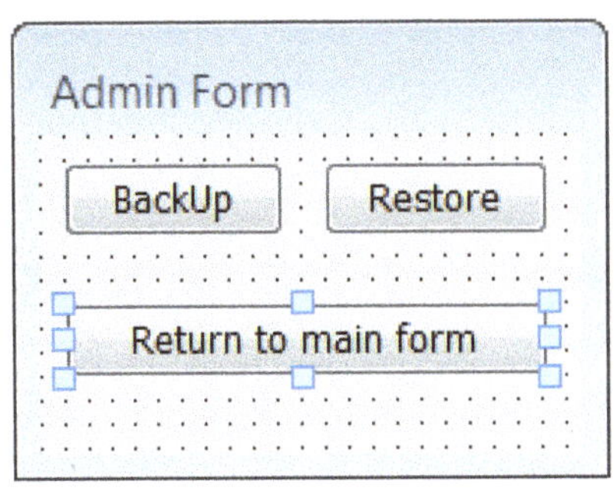

Fig. 64.70 Admin form

Change the **Name** property of the three **TButton** components to `btnBackUp`, `btnRestore` and `btnImagesDatabase`, respectively.

Change the **Caption** property of `btnBackUp` to `BackUp`, `btnRestore` to `Restore`, and `btnImagesDatabase` to `Return To main form`.

Set the **Position** property of `AdminForm` to **poMainFormCenter**.

Set the **BorderIcons** property of `AdminForm` to all **False**.

Set the **Height** property of AdminForm to 153.

Set the **Width** property of AdminForm to 200.

Arrange these components on the form as shown in *Figure 64.70*.

Click Save All to save both the unit and the project.

Add ImagesDatabaseWithBackUpUnit and DataModuleUnit to the uses clause in the **Interface** section of AdminUnit.pas.

Add AdminUnit to the uses clause in the **Implementation** section of PasswordUnit.pas.

Add PasswordUnit to the uses clause in the **Interface** section of ImagesDataBaseWithBackUpUnit.pas.

Switch to the DataModuleUnit.

Add a **TOpenDialog** component, OpenDialog2, from the **Dialogs** palette to DataModule1 form.

Add a **TIBBackupService** component, IBBackupService1, and a **TIBRestoreService** component, IBRestoreService1, from the **Interbase Admin** palette to DataModule1 form.

Double click the BackUp button shown in *Figure 64.70* to create the event handler

TAdminForm.btnBackUpClick

Add the code shown in *Table 64.25* to this event handler.

```
Procedure TAdminForm.btnBackUpClick(Sender: TObject);
Begin
  DataModule1.IBBackupService1.Attach;
  ShowMessage('Get file name of database to be backed up');
  If DataModule1.OpenDialog1.Execute
    Then
      Begin
        Try
          DataModule1.IBBackupService1.DatabaseName := DataModule1.OpenDialog1.Filename;
          ShowMessage(DataModule1.IBBackupService1.DatabaseName);
          ShowMessage('Get file name of backup file - must be on local drive');
          If DataModule1.OpenDialog2.Execute
            Then DataModule1.IBBackupService1.BackupFile.Text := DataModule1.OpenDialog2.FileName;
          ShowMessage(DataModule1.IBBackupService1.BackupFile.Text);
          If (DataModule1.IBBackupService1.DatabaseName <> '')
              And (DataModule1.IBBackupService1.BackupFile.Text <> '')
            Then
              Begin
                ShowMessage('Backing up');
                DataModule1.IBBackupService1.ServiceStart;
                ShowMessage('Database backed up');
              End;
        Except
          ShowMessage('Something has gone wrong');
        End;
      End;
  DataModule1.IBBackupService1.Detach;
End;
```

P

Table 64.25 Event handler TAdminForm.btnBackUpClick

Double click the Restore button shown in *Figure 64.70* to create the event handler

TAdminForm.btnRestoreClick

Add the code shown in *Table 64.26* to this event handler.

Double click the `Return to main form` button shown in *Figure 64.70* to create the event handler

`TAdminForm.btnImagesDatabaseClick`

Add the code shown in *Table 64.27* to this event handler.

```
Procedure TAdminForm.btnRestoreClick(Sender: TObject);
Begin
  DataModule1.IBDatabase1.Connected := False;
  DataModule1.IBRestoreService1.Attach;
  DataModule1.IBRestoreService1.DatabaseName.Text := 'C:\Users\drbond\ImagesDB.ib';
  DataModule1.IBRestoreService1.BackupFile.Text := 'C:\Users\drbond\ImagesDB.ibk';
  DataModule1.IBRestoreService1.Options := [Replace];
  DataModule1.IBRestoreService1.ServiceStart;
  ShowMessage('Database restored');
  DataModule1.IBDatabase1.Connected := True;
End;
```

P

Table 64.26 Event handler TAdminForm.btnRestoreClick

```
Procedure TAdminForm.btnImagesDatabaseClick(Sender: TObject);
Begin
  frmImagesDatabase.Visible := True;
  DataModule1.IBDataSet1.Close;
  frmImagesDatabase.Panel1.Caption := 'Images from around the world';
  AdminForm.Hide;
End;
```

P

Table 64.27 Event handler TAdminForm.btnImagesDatabaseClick

Switch to the `Password Form` (`PasswordUnit.pas`) shown in *Figure 64.69*.

Double click the `Submit` button shown in *Figure 64.69* to create the event handler

`TPasswordForm.btnSubmitClick`

Add the code shown in *Table 64.28* to this event handler.

From a security point of view it is not a good idea to store user names and passwords in the source code. Even when the source code is compiled, usernames and passwords are embedded in the compiled code and can still be read using a hex reader and a knowledge of ASCII or Unicode codes.

```
Procedure TPasswordForm.btnSubmitClick(Sender: TObject);
Begin
  If (edtUserName.Text = 'Admin') And (edtPassword.Text = 'LetMeIn')
    Then
      Begin
        edtUserName.Text := '';
        edtPassword.Text := 'password';
        AdminForm.Show;
        PasswordForm.Hide;
      End
    Else ShowMessage('Incorrect details');
End;
```

P

Table 64.28 Event handler TPasswordForm.btnSubmitClick

As we are not building a production system we will live with this issue.

Double click the `Cancel` button shown in *Figure 64.69* to create the event handler

`TPasswordForm.btnCancelClick`

Add the code shown in *Table 64.29* to this event handler.

```
Procedure TPasswordForm.btnCancelClick(Sender: TObject);
Begin
  PasswordForm.Hide;
End;
```

P

Table 64.29 Event handler TPasswordForm.btnCancelClick

Add a **TButton** component to `Panel1` of the `frmImagesDatabase` form, positioned as shown in *Figure 64.71*. **Change** its **Name** and **Caption** properties to `Maintenance`. **Double click** this button to create an **OnClick** event handler. **Add** `PasswordForm.Show;` to its body.

Click Save All to save both the unit and the project.

Click ▶ to compile and execute `ImagesDatabaseWithDataModuleProject` project.

Click the `Maintenance` button shown in *Figure 64.71* to launch the `Password Form`.

Enter user name `Admin` and password `LetMeIn`.

Click the `Submit` button to launch the `Admin Form`.

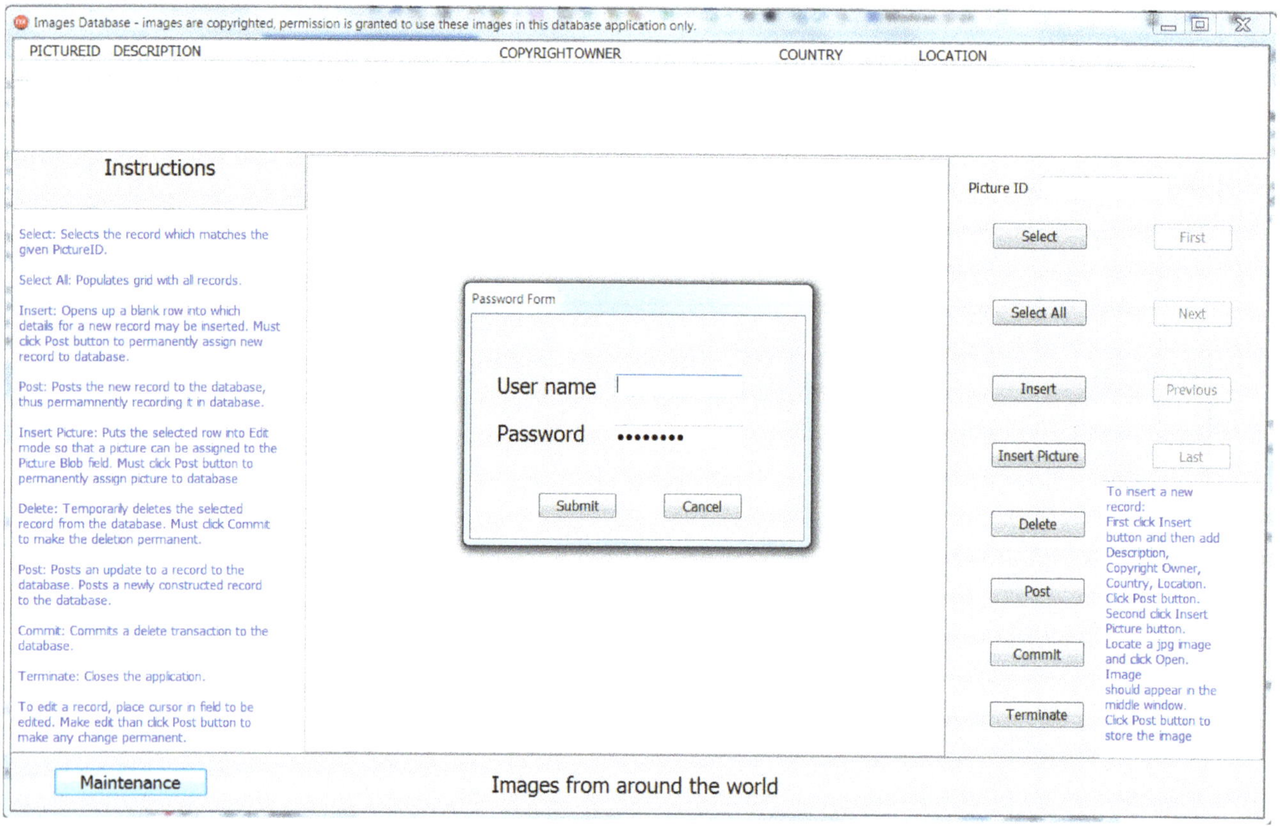

Fig. 64.71 Shows Password form in centre of the application's main form when Maintenance button clicked

Figure 64.72 shows the `Admin Form` which appears in the centre of the application's main form when the `Submit` button is clicked and the user name and password are correct.

Click the `BackUp` button on the `Admin Form` to start preparations to backup the images database.

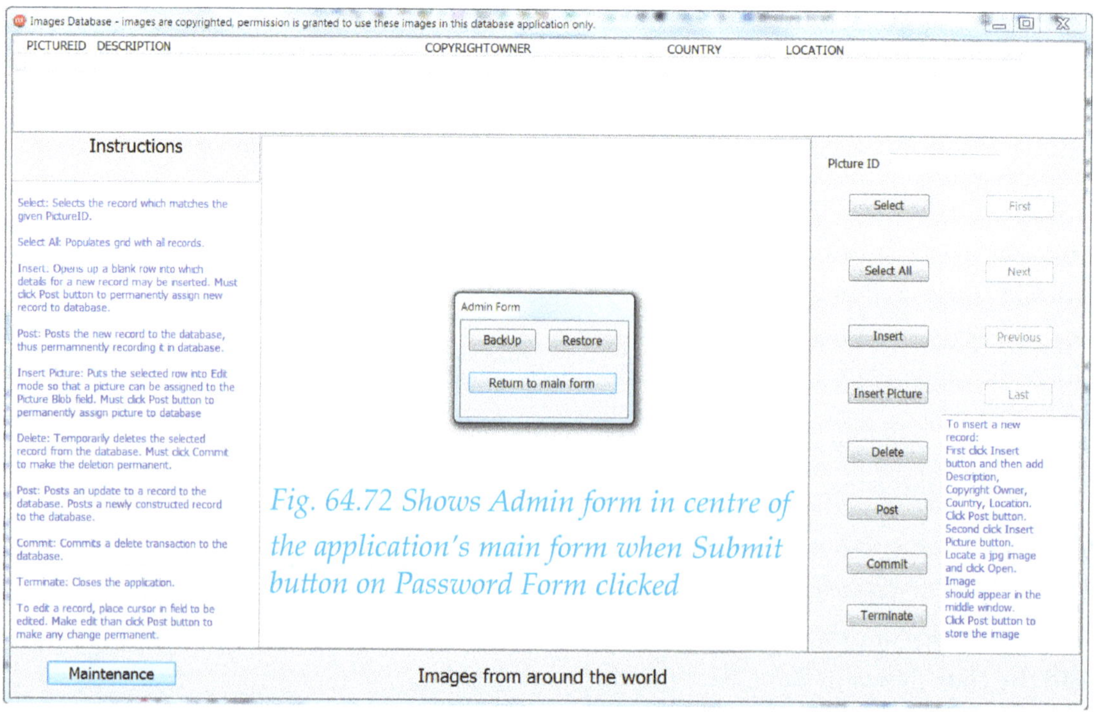

Fig. 64.72 Shows Admin form in centre of the application's main form when Submit button on Password Form clicked

The **Database Login** form - *Figure 64.73* - pops up.

Enter `sysdba` for user name and `masterkey` for password then click `OK`.

A production system should not rely on the default administrator's password `masterkey`, so this password should be changed.

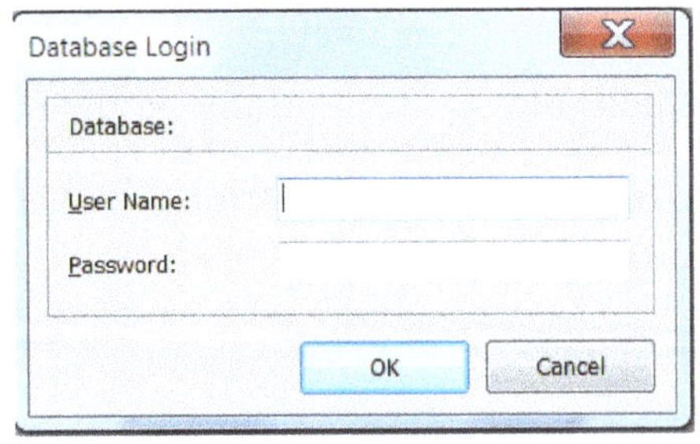

Fig. 64.73 Shows Database Login form which pops up when BackUp button on Admin Form clicked

If the database login succeeds then the message window shown in *Figure 64.74* should appear. **Click** `OK`.

The open file dialog window shown in *Figure 64.75* should now appear, of course with a path that is specific to your set up.

Select database `IMAGESDB.IB` and click `Open`.

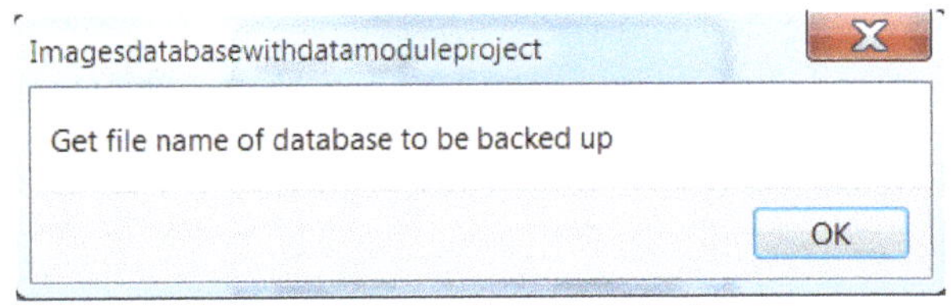

Fig. 64.74 First message window

The message window shown in *Figure 64.76* should appear. showing the path and filename of the database to be backed up. **Click** `OK`.

The open file dialog window shown in *Figure 64.77* should now appear.

The filename, `IMAGESDB.IBK`, for the backup file has already been entered. **Click** `Open`.

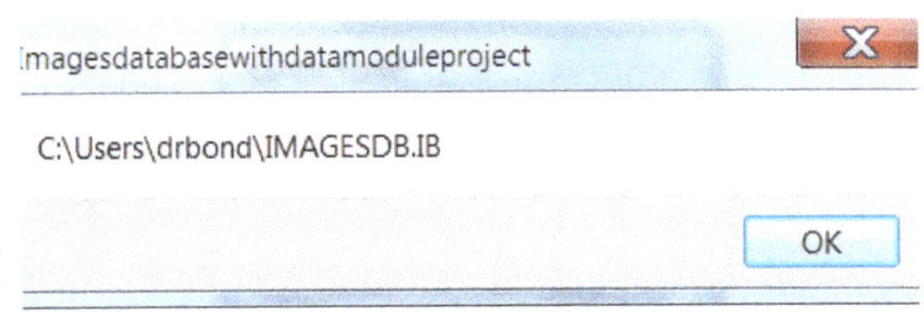

Fig. 64.76 Second message window

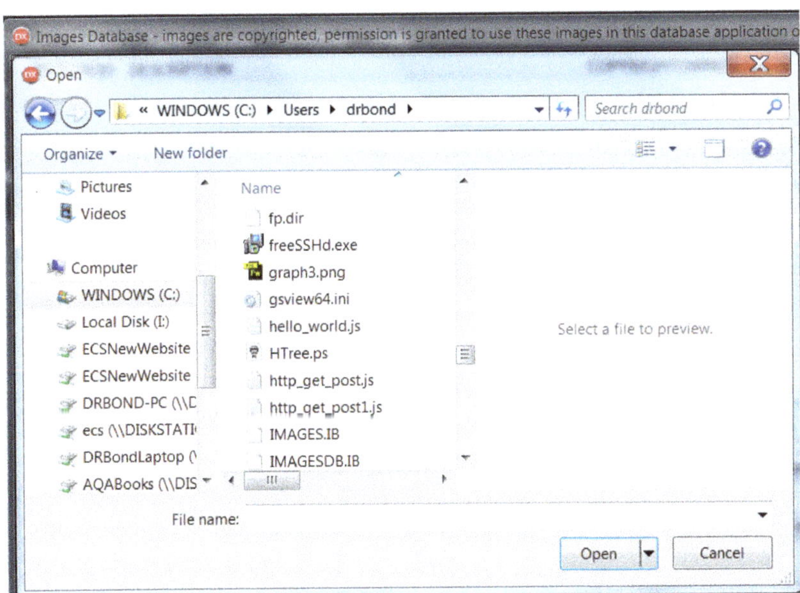

Fig. 64.75 Selecting database to be backed up

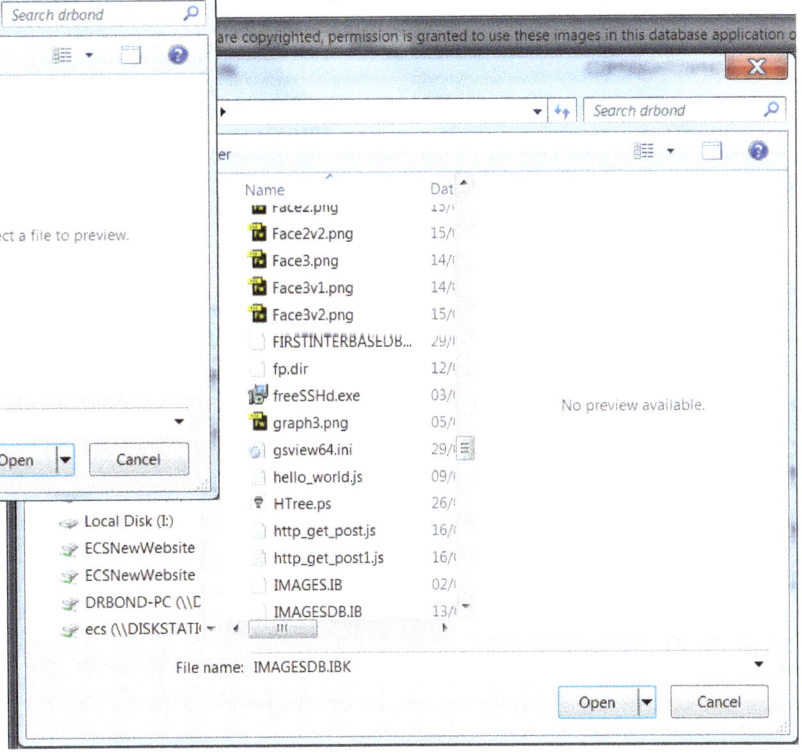

Fig. 64.77 Selecting backup path and filename

The message window shown in *Figure 64.78* should appear showing the path and filename of the backup file. **Click** `OK`.

The backup process should now begin. Two more message windows appear during this process, one stating `Backing up` and the second `Database backed up`. **Click** `OK` each time.

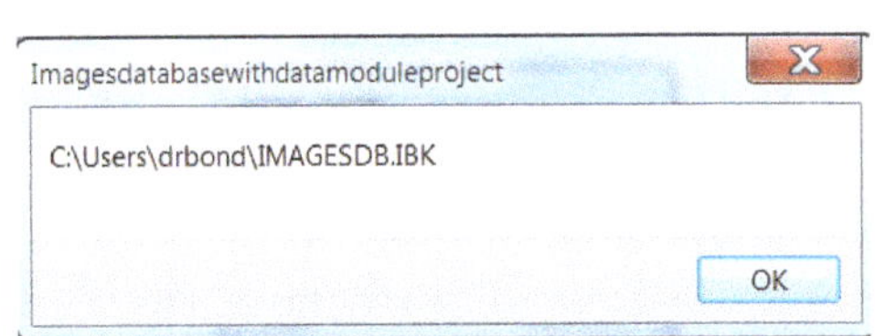

Fig. 64.78 Third message window

www.educational-computing.com/DelphiBook/Code/Chapter64/NewLibDBModified5.ib

Restoring from backup

Click the `Restore` button on the `Admin Form` to start preparations to backup the images database.

The **Database Login** form - *Figure 64.73* - pops up.

Enter `sysdba` for user name and `masterkey` for password then click `OK`.

If the database login succeeds then the restoration process should begin. If successful, the message window shown in *Figure 64.79* confirming that the database has been restored should appear. **Click** `OK`.

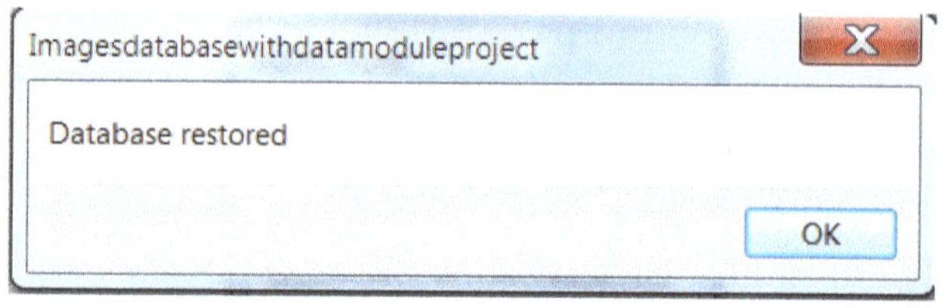

Fig. 64.79 Database restored message window

Click the `Return to main form` button to return to the main form.

Click the `Terminate` button to exit the application.

Using Delphi to call stored procedures

Chapter 63 covered setting up a stored procedure for an Interbase database, `NewLibDBModified5.ib` (alias `NewLibDBModified`). Stored procedures are stored with the server and are called from a client application.

Figure 64.80 shows stored procedures attached to database `NewLibDBModified5.ib`, alias `NewLibDBModified`.

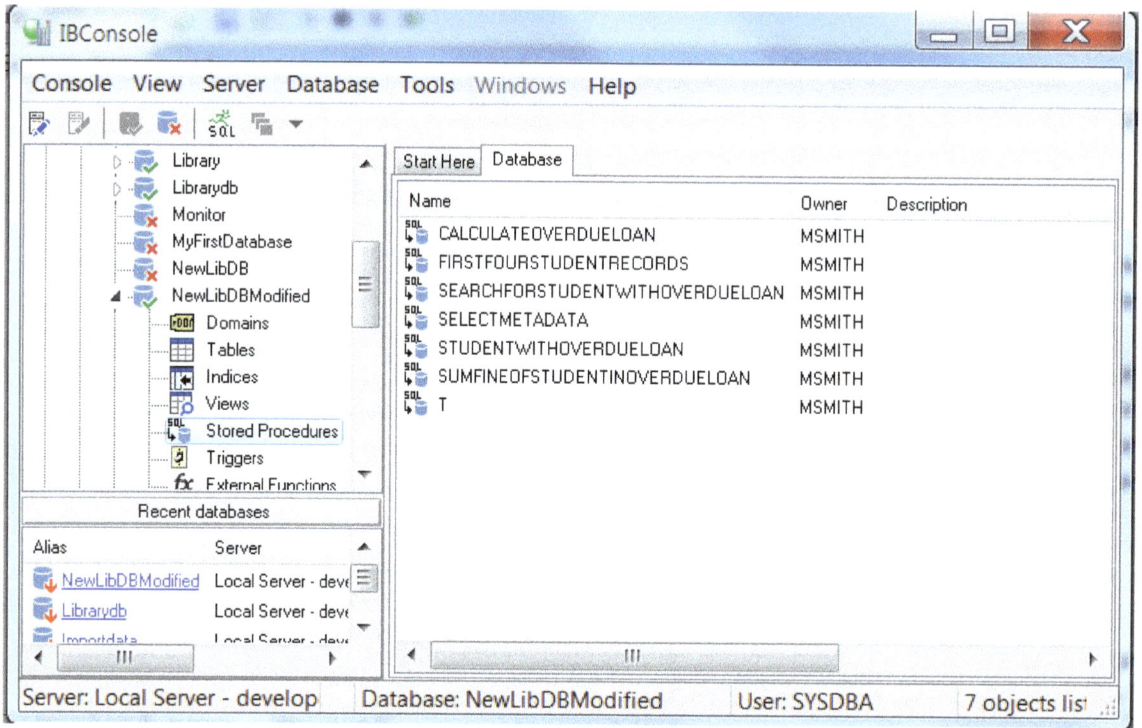

Fig. 64.80 List of stored procedures attached to database NewLibDBModified5.ib (alias NewLibDBModified

Launch Delphi.

Select **File|New|VCL Application**.

Set `Form1`'s **Height** property to 377 and its **Width** property to 660.

Place a **TIBDatabase** component, `IBDatabase1`, from the **Interbase** palette on the form.

Place a **TIBTransaction** component, `IBTransaction1`, from the **Interbase** palette on the form.

Place a **TIBStoredProc** component, `IBStoredProc1`, from **Interbase** palette on the form.

Place a **TIBTable** component, `IBTable1`, from **Interbase** palette on the form.

www.educational-computing.com/DelphiBook/Code/Chapter64/StoredProcedureExercise.rar

Place a **TDataSource** component, `DataSource1`, from the **Data Access** palette on the form.

Place a **TDBGrid** component, `DBGrid1`, from the **Data Controls** palette on the form.

Place three **TButton** components, `Button1`, `Button2`, `Button3`, from the **Standard** palette on the form.

Place a **TLabel** component, `Label1`, from the **Standard** palette on the form.

Arrange the components/controls as shown in *Figure 64.81*.

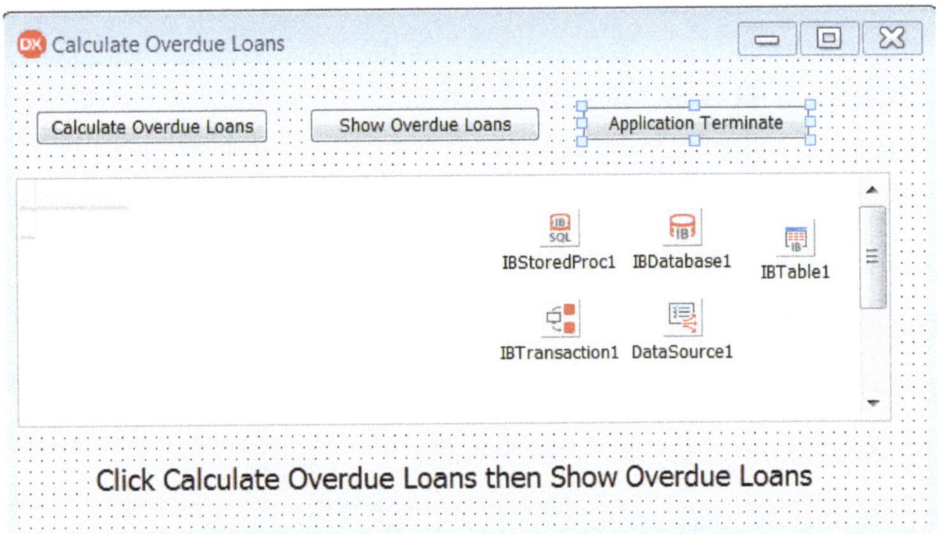

Fig. 64.81 User interface design for CalculateOverdueLoansProject

Change the **Name** property of `Form1` to `CalculateOverdueLoansForm`.

Change its `Caption` property to `Calculate Overdue Loans`.

Change the **Name** property of `Button1` to `ExecuteStoredProcedure`.

Change its `Caption` property to `Calculate Overdue Loans`.

Change the **Name** property of `Button2` to `ShowOverdueLoans`.

Change its `Caption` property to `Show Overdue Loans`.

Change the **Name** property of `Button3` to `ApplicationTerminate`.

Change its `Caption` property to `Application Terminate`.

Change the **Name** property of `Label1` to `lblInstructions`.

Change its `Caption` property to `Click Calculate Overdue Loans then Show Overdue Loans`.

Select `IBDatabase1` and in Object Inspector

- **Set DatabaseName** property path e.g. `C:\Users\drbond\NewLibrary\NewLibDBModified5.ib`
- **Set** its **Transaction** property to `IBTransaction1`
- **Set LogInPrompt** to **False**
- **Set Params** property to

  username=MSmith

  password=password1
- **Set Connected** property to **True**.

Select `IBTransaction1` and in Object Inspector **set DefaultDatabase** to `IBDatabase1`.

Select `IBTable1` and in Object Inspector **set Database** property to `IBDatabase1` and **TableName** to `OVERDUELOAN`.

Select `DataSource1` and in Object Inspector **set DataSet** property to `IBTable1`.

Select `DBGrid1` and in Object Inspector **set DataSource** property to `DataSource1`.

Select `IBStoredProc1` and in Object Inspector **set** its properties as shown in *Figure 64.82*.

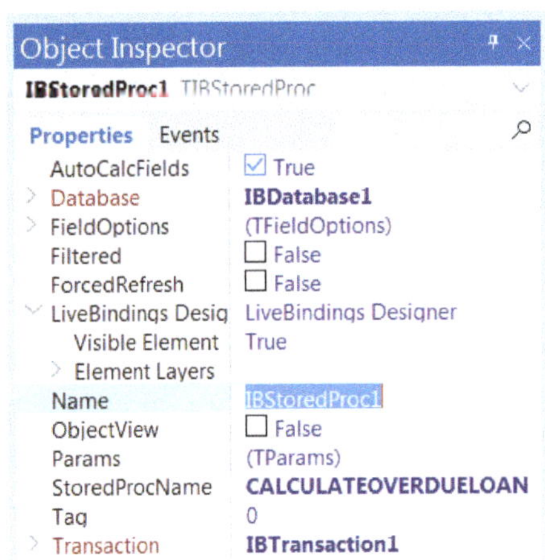

Fig. 64.82 Object Inspector for IBStoredProc1 showing setup for Database and StoredProcName properties

Double click the button with caption `Calculate Overdue Loans` to create an **OnClick** event handler.

Add the code `IBStoredProc1.ExecProc;` to its body.

Double click the button with caption `Show Overdue Loans` to create an **OnClick** event handler.
Add the code `IBTable1.Open;` to its body.

Double click the button with caption `Application Terminate` to create an **OnClick** event handler.
Add the code `Application.Terminate;` to its body.

Save the project using **Save Project As** from the **File** menu in folder `StoredProcedureExercise`.

Choose `StoredProcedureUnit.Pas` for the name of the unit file and `StoredProcedureProject.dproj` for the name of the project file.

Click ▶ to compile and execute `StoredProcedureProject`.

Figure 64.83 shows the executing project following the two steps

1. `Calculate Overdue Loans`
2. `Show Overdue Loans`

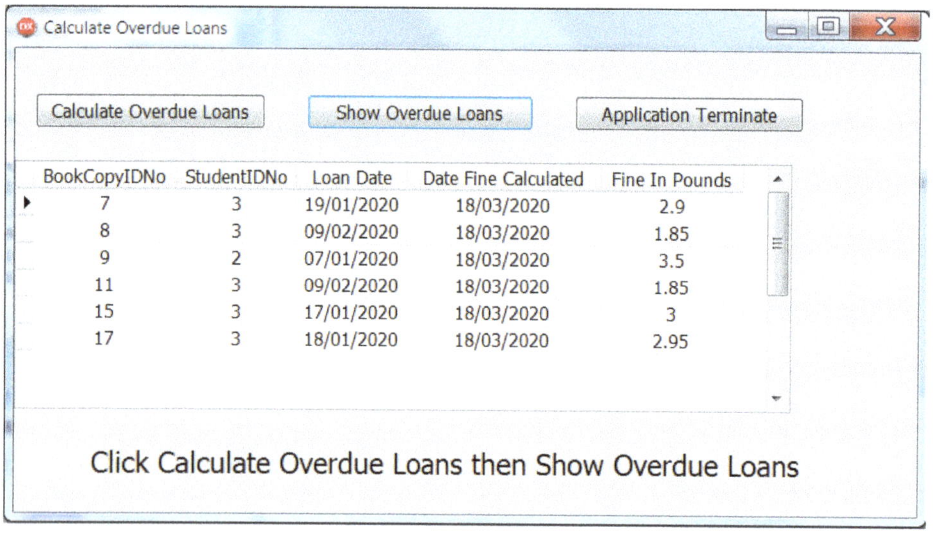

Fig. 64.82 CalculateOverdueLoansProject in execution

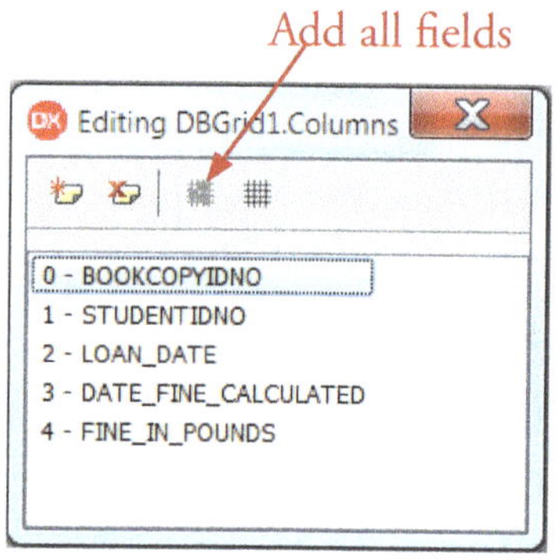

Fig. 64.83 Editing DBGrid1 columns

Formatting DBGrid1

A further stage was applied to `DBGrid1` to format each column heading and its alignment and the alignment of the content in each.

The stage consists of the following steps (steps 4 to 7 use a specific example)

1. **Right click** anywhere in `DBGrid1` to bring up a menu
2. **Select** the **Columns editor** from this menu to bring up the editor shown in *Figure 64.83*
3. **Click** the **Add all fields** icon to add the five fields shown in *Figure 64.83*
4. **Click** on `4 - FINE_IN_POUNDS` to show the properties of column 4 in the Object Inspector (`DBGrid1.Columns[4]`) - *Figure 64.84*
5. **Set** the **Alignment** property to **taCentre**
6. **Set** the **Title|Alignment** to **taCenter**
7. **Set** the **Title|Caption** to `FineInPounds`

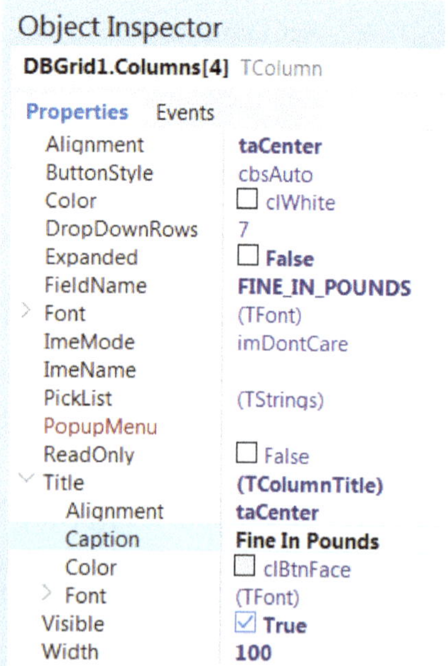

Fig. 64.84 Object Inspector showing properties of DBGrid1.Columns[4]

The **FieldName** property `FINE_IN_POUNDS` refers to the field with the same name in the table `OVERDUELOANS`.
The **Title|Caption** property refers to the column heading.

65 Data modelling tools for database design

Data modelling tools

Purpose: To learn how to use a data modelling tool for database design

Download ERD Concepts 8[1] from https://www.erdconcepts.com/ or www.educational-computing.com/DelphiBook/Code/Chapter65/erdconcepts804_x86_reg.exe, www.educational-computing.com/DelphiBook/Code/Chapter65/erdconcepts804_x64_reg.exe and install.

Launch ERD Concepts 8 and **load** `GradingExample.ecm` from the `Model\Examples folder` (`..\Documents\ERD Concepts 8\Model\Examples`. *Figure 65.1* shows the E-R diagram for this example as displayed in the main window of ERD Concepts 8.

Select **Database|Generate Database...** to launch the **Generate Database** window - *Figure 65.2*. **Click** **Execute** to generate a DDL (Data Definition Language) script, `GradingExample_script.ddl`, shown in abbreviated form in *Table 65.1*. This script appears in the **DDL Viewer** window part of which is shown in *Figure 65.3*. By clicking the **Execute SQL** button and then from the **Database Connections using ADO** window (*Figure 65.4*), making a connection to the PostgreSQL database `StudentGradingSystem` (previously created with **pgAdmin4** but without tables, etc), it is possible to populate this database with the tables designed in ERD Concepts 8 - *Figure 65.1*. However, the usual way is to paste and execute the script in the SQL window of **pgAdmin 4** (current version of the PostgreSQL administration tool) to produce the tables, etc.

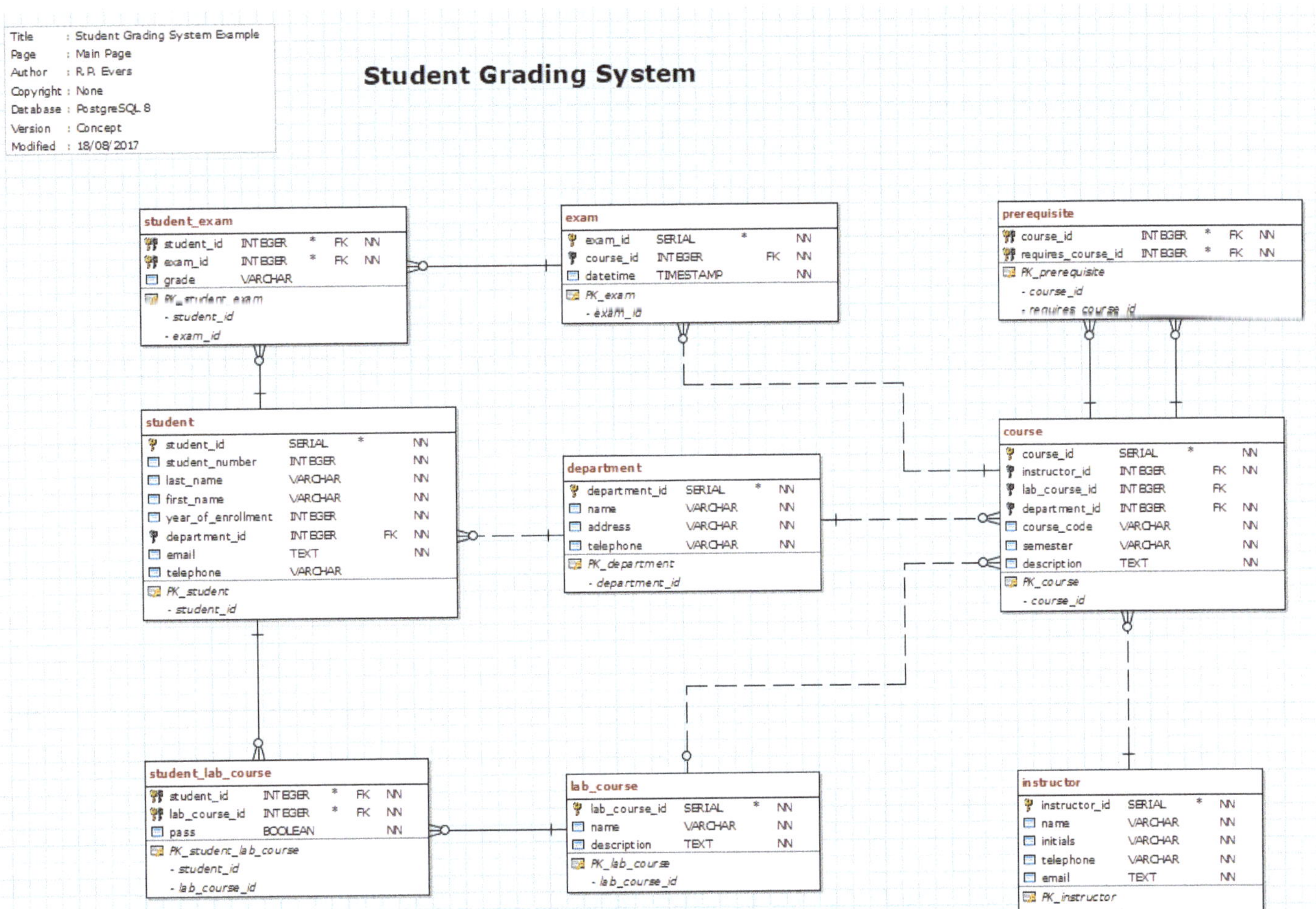

Figure 65.1 E-R diagram for a Student Grading System

1 ERD Concepts 8 was made available in 2018 with a MIT license. It is completely free.

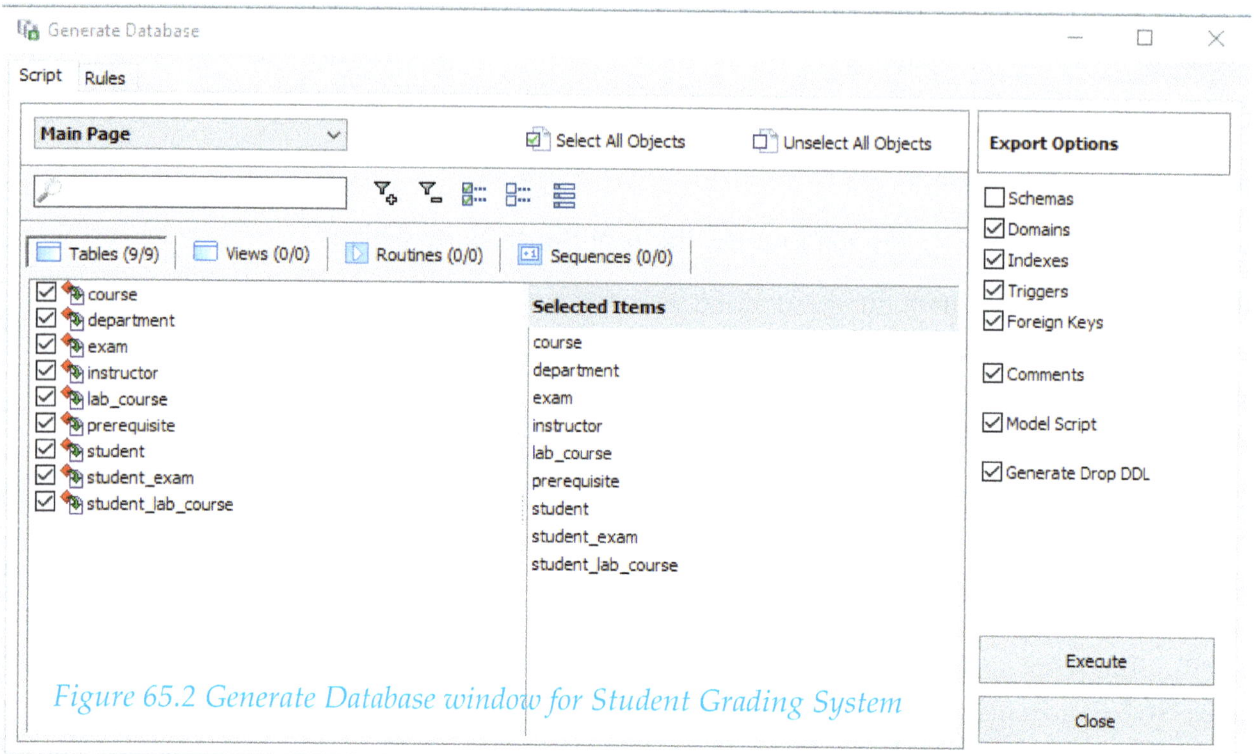

Figure 65.2 Generate Database window for Student Grading System

```
/*==========================================================================*/
/* DDL SCRIPT                                                               */
/*==========================================================================*/
/*  Title    : Student Grading System Example                               */
/*  FileName : GradingExample.ecm                                           */
/*  Platform : PostgreSQL 8                                                 */
/*  Version  : Concept                                                      */
/*  Date     : 21 June 2021                                                 */
/*==========================================================================*/
/*==========================================================================*/
/* CREATE TABLES                                                            */
/*==========================================================================*/

CREATE TABLE instructor (
  instructor_id SERIAL,
  name VARCHAR(40) NOT NULL,
  initials VARCHAR(40) NOT NULL,
  telephone VARCHAR(10) NOT NULL,
  email TEXT NOT NULL,
  CONSTRAINT PK_instructor PRIMARY KEY (instructor_id)
);

CREATE TABLE lab_course (
  lab_course_id SERIAL,
  name VARCHAR(40) NOT NULL,
  description TEXT NOT NULL,
  CONSTRAINT PK_lab_course PRIMARY KEY (lab_course_id)
);

...
CREATE TABLE student (
  student_id SERIAL,
  student_number INTEGER NOT NULL,
  last_name VARCHAR(40) NOT NULL,
  first_name VARCHAR(40) NOT NULL,
  year_of_enrollment INTEGER NOT NULL,
  department_id INTEGER NOT NULL,
  email TEXT NOT NULL,
  telephone VARCHAR(10),
  CONSTRAINT PK_student PRIMARY KEY (student_id)
);
...
```

Table 65.1 Abbreviated DDL script GradingExample_create.ddl for a PostgreSQL 8 database

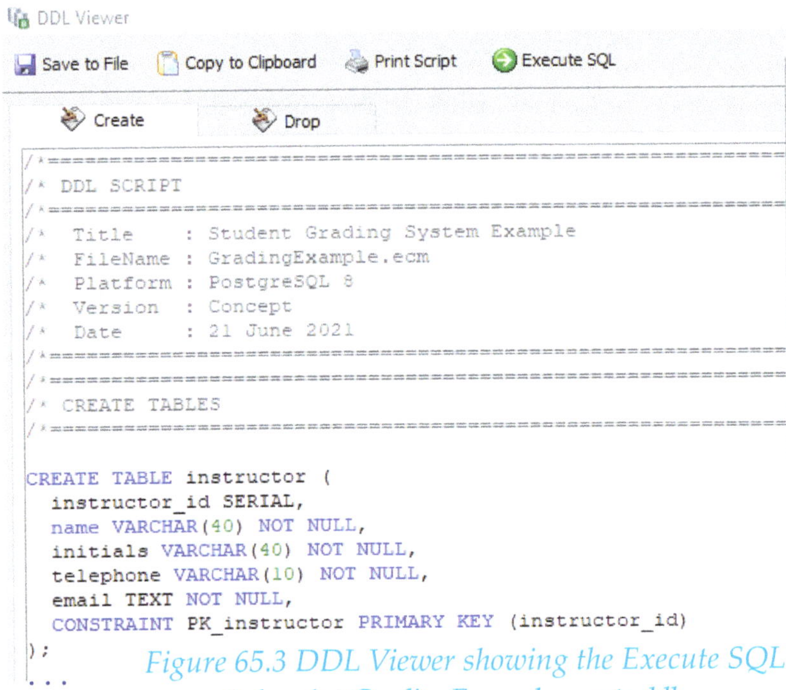

Figure 65.3 DDL Viewer showing the Execute SQL button and part of generated script GradingExample_create.ddl

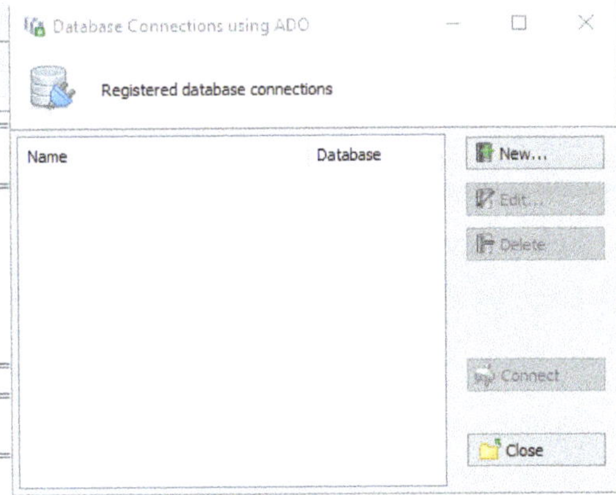

Figure 65.4 Database Connections using ADO window

Simpler example to try

Select File|New and Interbase 2017 to create a new model. **Save As** `Library.ecm`.

Using the drawing palette (*Figure 65.5*) pinned to the left edge of the modelling window:

- **Select** the New Table icon and **paste** in the window three times
- **Right click** the first table in the window and **select** Edit from the popup window and **rename** it `Student` as shown in *Figure 65.6*
- **Right click** in the window and **select** New to create a new field `NEW_COLUMN`
- **Highlight** `NEW_COLUMN` and **change** its name to `StudentIdNo`
- **Left click** the **Data type** field and **select** **Integer** from the dropdown list
- **Left click** the **PK** checkbox to make this field the primary key

Figure 65.5

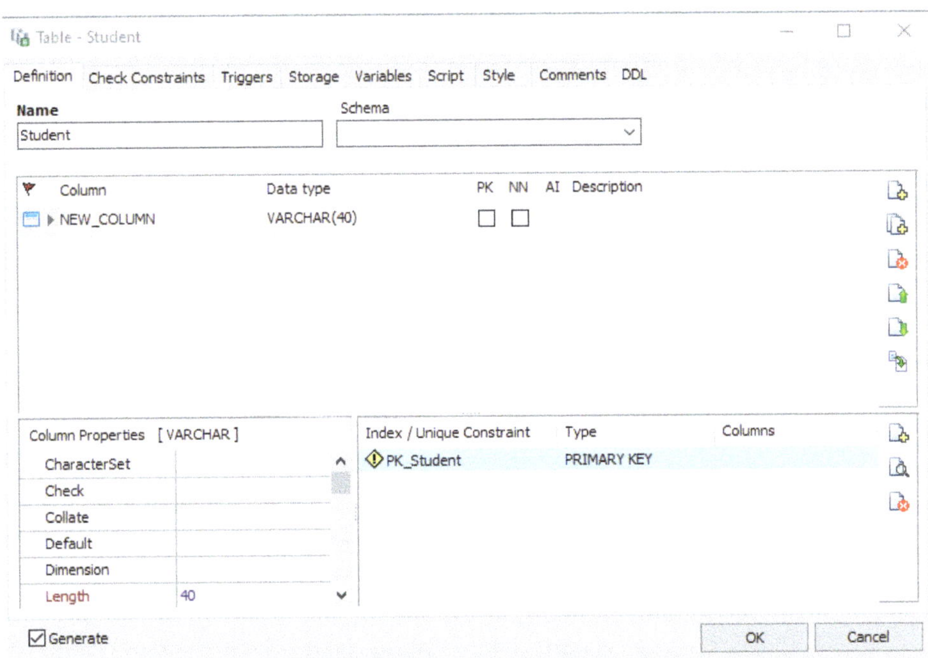

Figure 65.6 Table Student in edit mode

- **Add** the fields `Surname` and `FirstName` as shown in *Figure 65.7* specifying **VarChar** length via the **Column Properties** Length field, **click** the **NN** (Not Null) checkbox in each case
- **Repeat** the exercise for the `Book` table as shown in *Figure 65.7*, **click** the **NN** (Not Null) checkbox for the `Title` and `ISBN` fields
- **Add** the field `LoanDate` to the `Loan` table, **click** the **NN** (Not Null) checkbox
- **Select** the relationship icon from the drawing palette, **click** on the `Student` table and then the `Loan` table to create a one-to-many relationship as shown in *Figure 65.7*; `StudentIdNo` is automatically added to the `Loan` table as a foreign key
- **Select** the relationship icon from the drawing palette, **click** on the `Book` table and then the `Loan` table to create a one-to-many relationship as shown in *Figure 65.7*; `BookIdNo` is automatically added to the `Loan` table as a foreign key
- **Put** the `Loan` table into edit mode and **click** the **PK** checkbox for fields `StudentIdNo` and `BookIdNo` to make both primary key fields; the `Loan` table now has a composite primary key (primary key consists of more than one field).
- **Save All.**
- **Select** **Database|Generate Database...|Select All Objects|Execute** to generate DDL script shown in *Figure 65.8*
- **Select** **Save to File** and save this script as `Library_create.ddl`
- **Launch** **IBConsole** (Interbase 2020[2] is running as a service) - *Figure 65.9*
- **Use** **Interbase Server Manager** to check that the Interbase server is running
- **Open** **Local Server - gds_db** (**Double click** the icon) in **IBConsole**

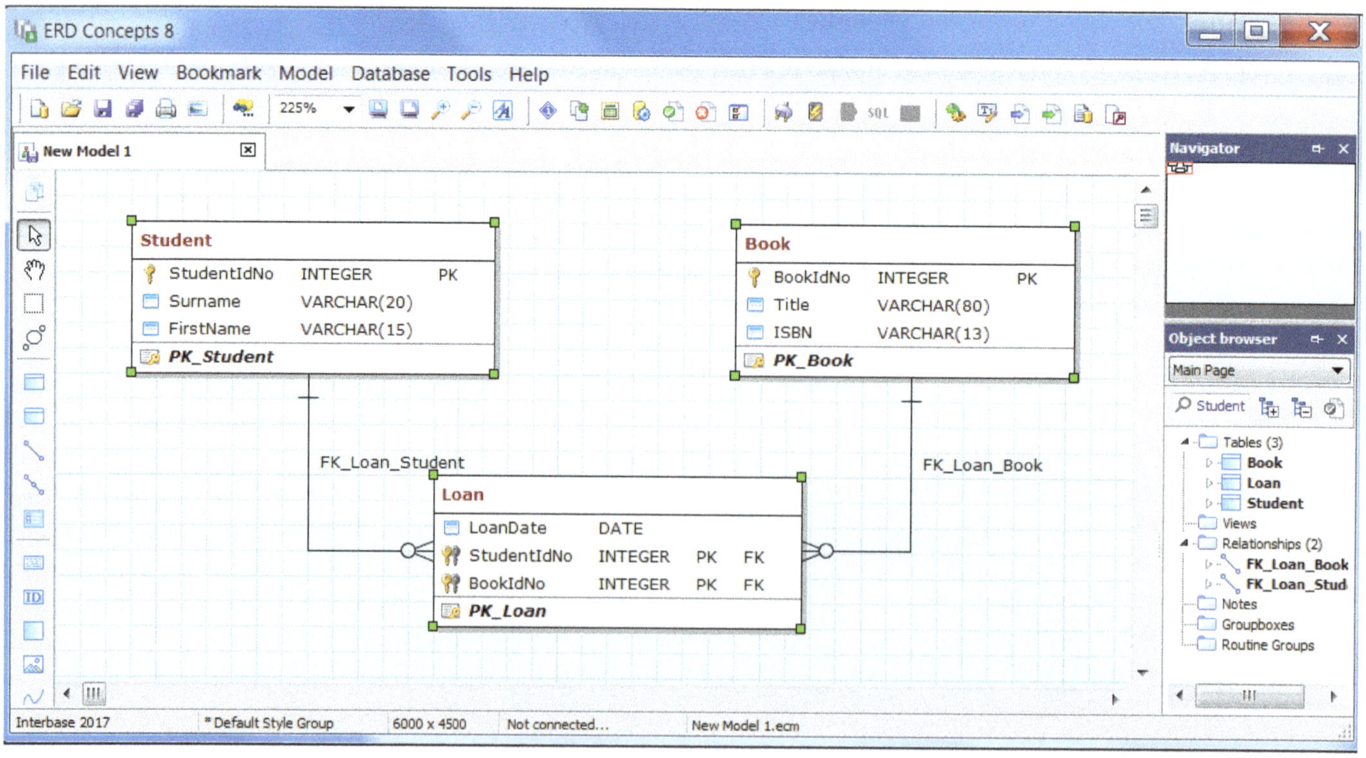

Figure 65.7 E-R diagram showing attributes and relationships for the three tables

2 Although the script generated is for Interbase 2017, it will generate an Interbase 2020 database

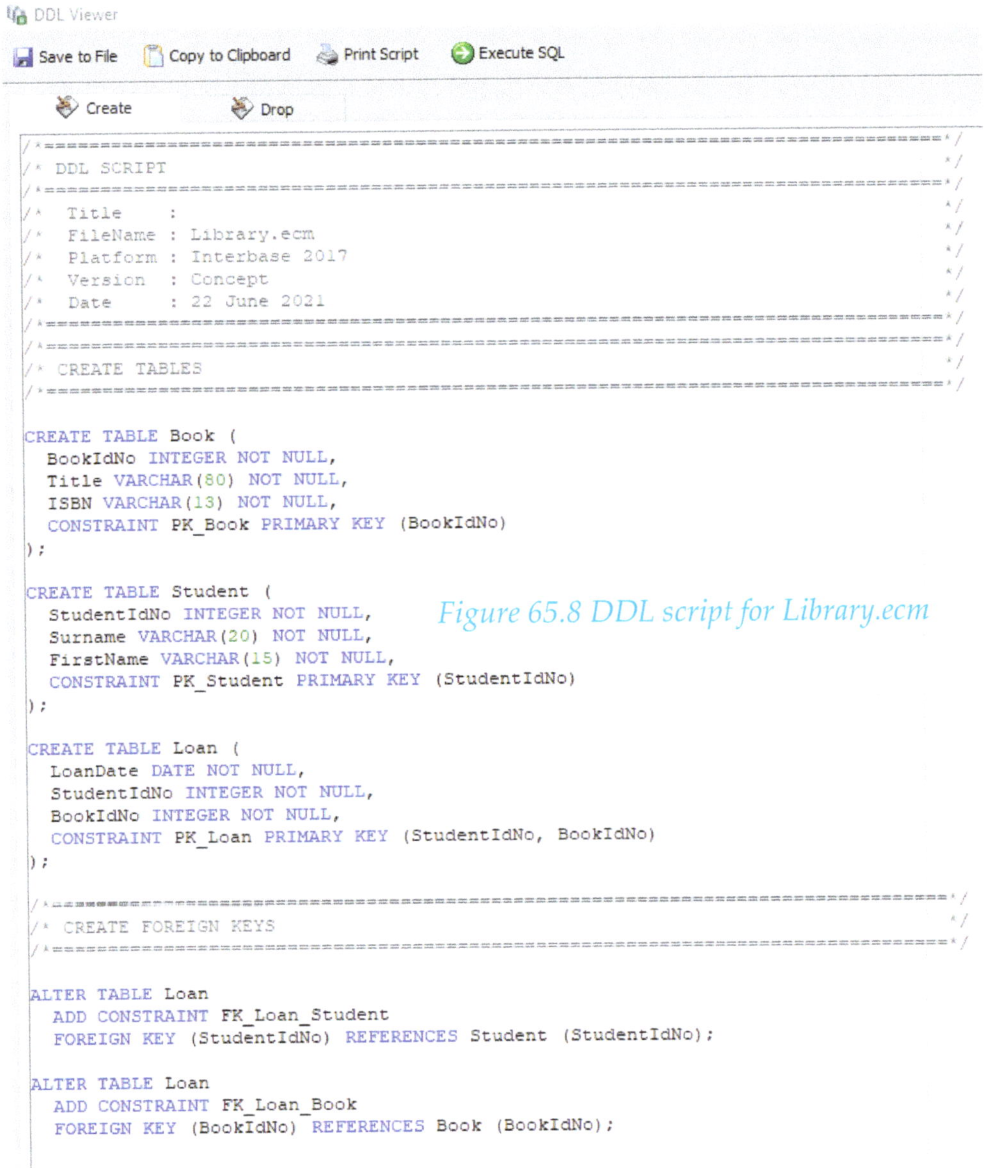


```
/*===========================================================================*/
/* DDL SCRIPT                                                                */
/*===========================================================================*/
/*  Title     :                                                              */
/*  FileName : Library.ecm                                                   */
/*  Platform : Interbase 2017                                                */
/*  Version  : Concept                                                       */
/*  Date     : 22 June 2021                                                  */
/*===========================================================================*/
/*===========================================================================*/
/* CREATE TABLES                                                             */
/*===========================================================================*/

CREATE TABLE Book (
  BookIdNo INTEGER NOT NULL,
  Title VARCHAR(80) NOT NULL,
  ISBN VARCHAR(13) NOT NULL,
  CONSTRAINT PK_Book PRIMARY KEY (BookIdNo)
);

CREATE TABLE Student (
  StudentIdNo INTEGER NOT NULL,
  Surname VARCHAR(20) NOT NULL,
  FirstName VARCHAR(15) NOT NULL,
  CONSTRAINT PK_Student PRIMARY KEY (StudentIdNo)
);

CREATE TABLE Loan (
  LoanDate DATE NOT NULL,
  StudentIdNo INTEGER NOT NULL,
  BookIdNo INTEGER NOT NULL,
  CONSTRAINT PK_Loan PRIMARY KEY (StudentIdNo, BookIdNo)
);

/*===========================================================================*/
/* CREATE FOREIGN KEYS                                                       */
/*===========================================================================*/

ALTER TABLE Loan
  ADD CONSTRAINT FK_Loan_Student
  FOREIGN KEY (StudentIdNo) REFERENCES Student (StudentIdNo);

ALTER TABLE Loan
  ADD CONSTRAINT FK_Loan_Book
  FOREIGN KEY (BookIdNo) REFERENCES Book (BookIdNo);
```

Figure 65.8 DDL script for Library.ecm

- **Select** Database|Create Database in IBConsole and **use** file name `Library` on a local drive (must be a local drive - **click** ellipsis **...** and **save** to local drive) **enter** `SYSDBA` for the user and `masterkey` for the password; **check** **Save Alias Information** and **Save Password**; **accept** `Library` as the alias; **click** **OK** - *Figure 65.10*
- **Select** the SQL icon to open the Interactive SQL window
- **Select** Query|Load Script and **locate** `Library_create.ddl`, **open.**
- **Click** **F5** to run the script - *Figure 65.11* shows that the tables have been created

The tables may now be populated with data.

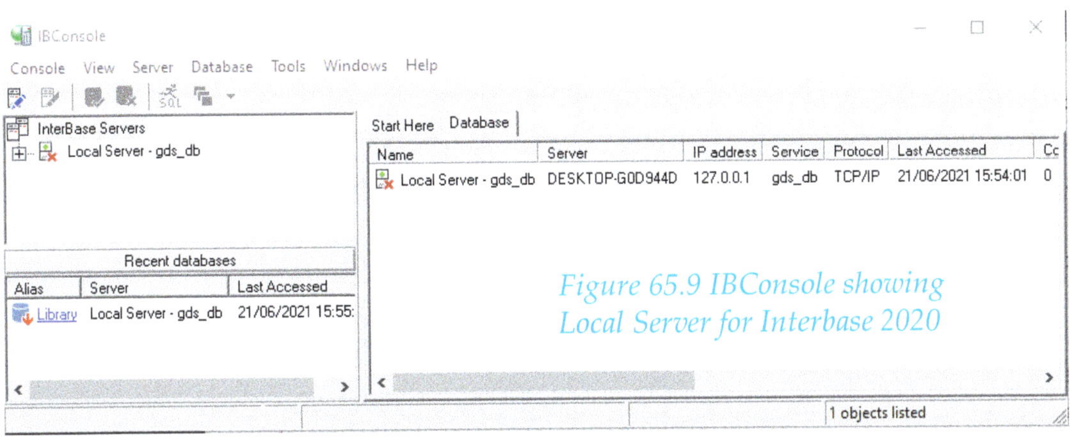

Figure 65.9 IBConsole showing Local Server for Interbase 2020

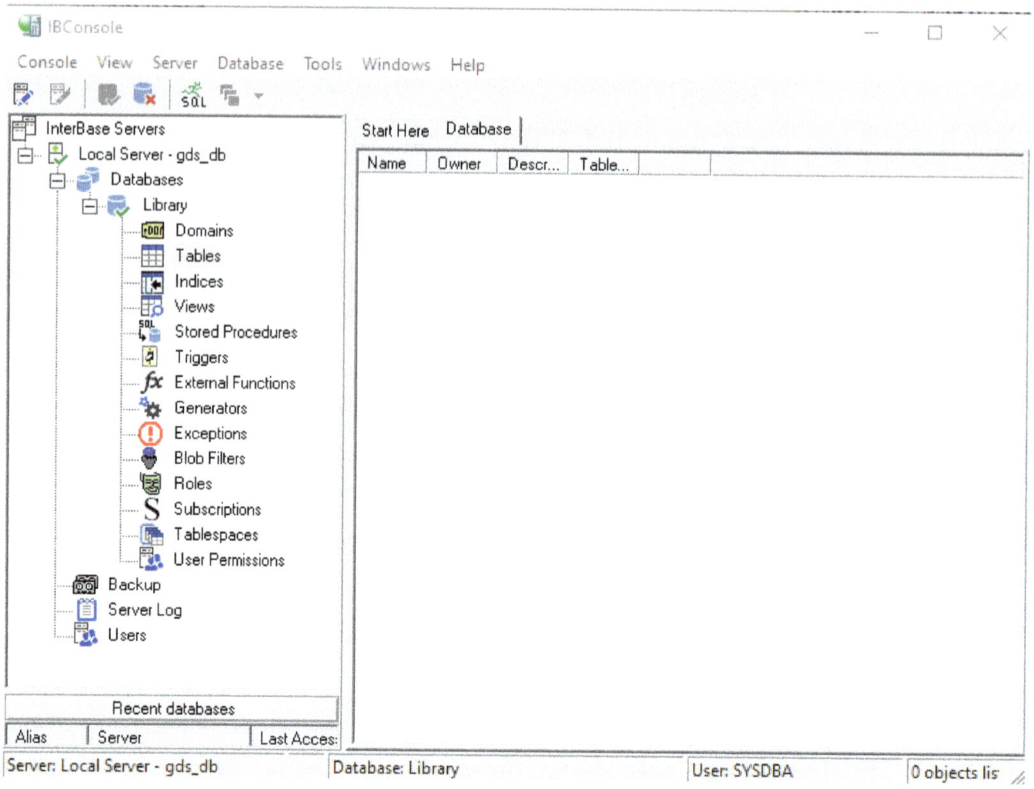

Figure 65.10 Library database created but no tables yet

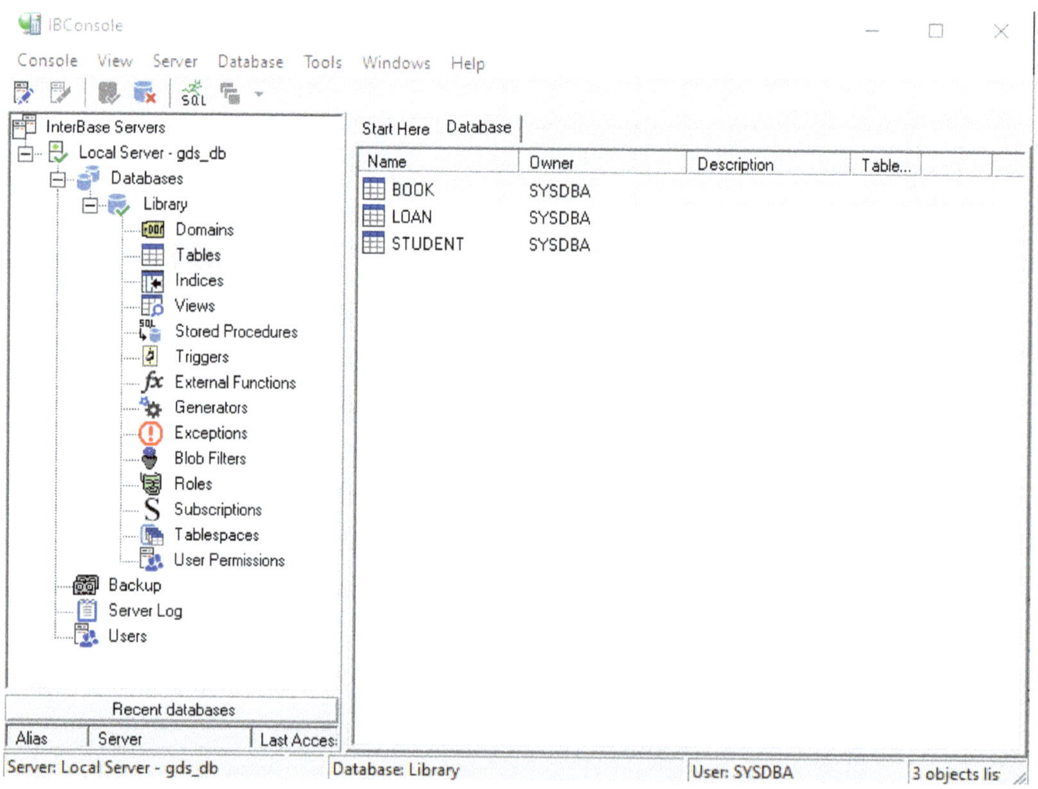

Figure 65.11 Library database tables created from DDL script

TMS Data Modeller

TMS offer an academic license for its products - visit www.tmssoftware.com for its offers. The academic versions are fully functional and fully free for students and teachers for non-commercial use.

The version of TMS Data Modeller used in this section is the trial version (found in the Business category).

Launch TMS Data Modeller and **select File|New|New Project**. **Select Interbase 2017** as the target database as shown in *Figure 65.12*. **Create** the E-R diagram shown in *Figure 65.13* for the same Library database as the previous example then select **Home|Generate script** to generate the DDL script shown in *Figure 65.14*. **Save** the DDL script as `TMSLibraryScript.sql`.

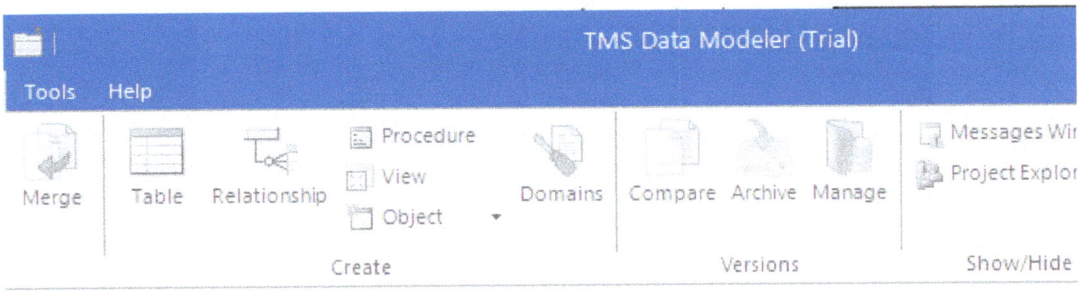

Figure 65.12 Creating a new project in TMS Data Modeller

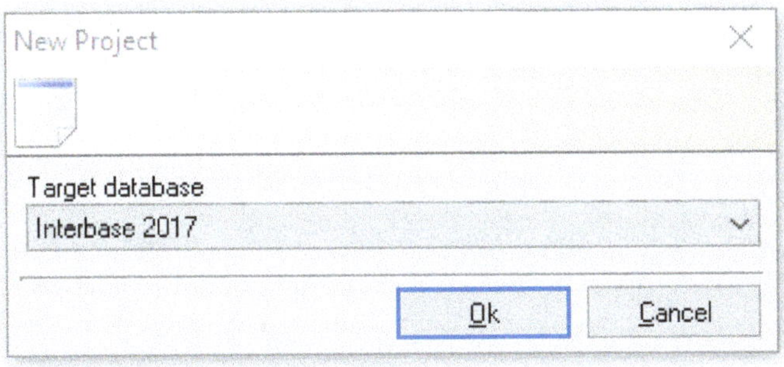

No version

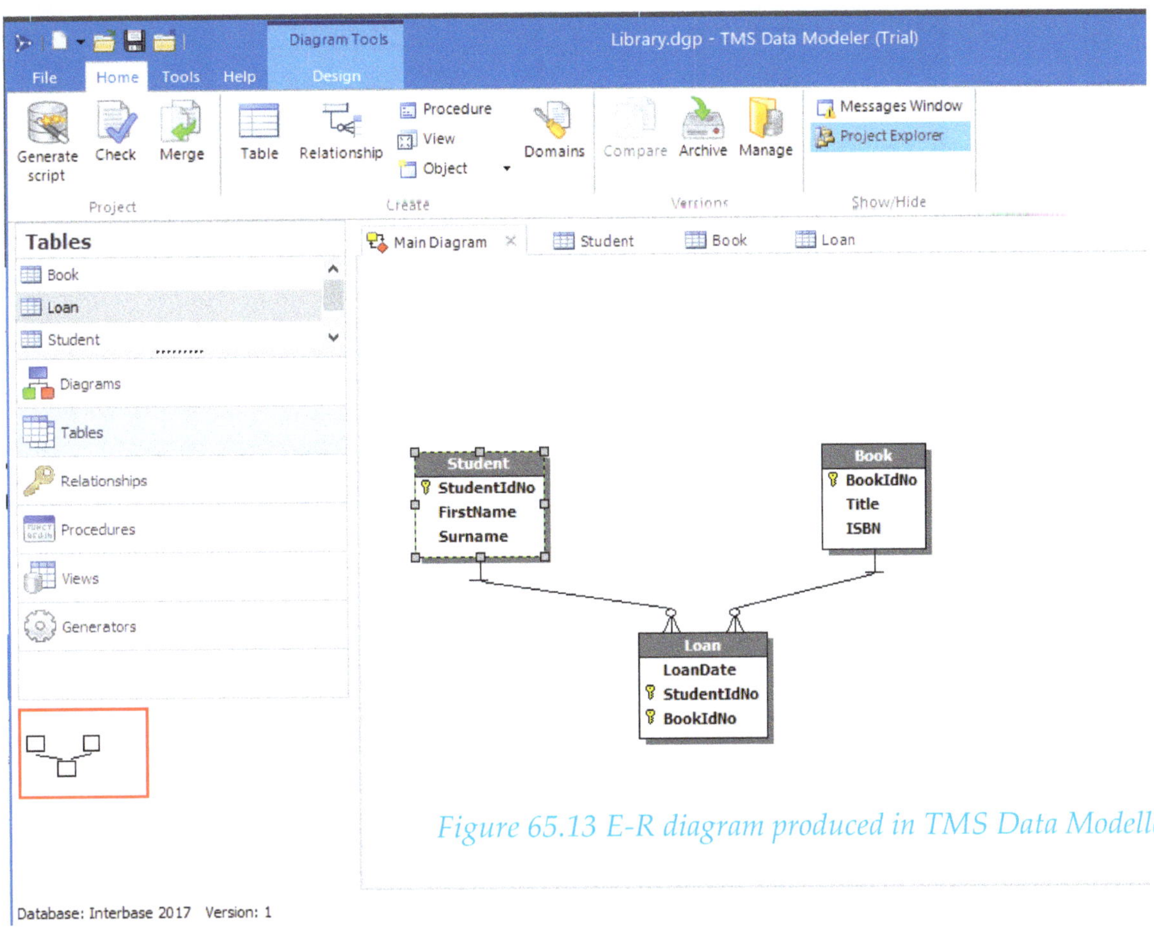

Figure 65.13 E-R diagram produced in TMS Data Modeller

Launch IBConsole and **create** database `TMSLIBRARY.IB` on a local drive.

Load the script `TMSLIbraryScript.sql` in the SQL Interactive window and **execute** the script to create the three linked tables, `Student`, `Loan` and `Book`.

```
CREATE TABLE Loan (
  LoanDate DATE NOT NULL,
  StudentIdNo INTEGER NOT NULL,
  BookIdNo INTEGER NOT NULL,
  CONSTRAINT PrimaryKey3 PRIMARY KEY (StudentIdNo,BookIdNo)
);

CREATE TABLE Book (
  BookIdNo INTEGER NOT NULL,
  Title VARCHAR(80) NOT NULL,
  ISBN VARCHAR(13) NOT NULL,
  CONSTRAINT PrimaryKey2 PRIMARY KEY (BookIdNo)
);

CREATE TABLE Student (
  StudentIdNo INTEGER NOT NULL,
  FirstName VARCHAR(15) NOT NULL,
  Surname VARCHAR(20) NOT NULL,
  CONSTRAINT PrimaryKey1 PRIMARY KEY (StudentIdNo)
);

ALTER TABLE Loan ADD CONSTRAINT Book_Loan_1
  FOREIGN KEY (BookIdNo)
  REFERENCES Book (BookIdNo);

ALTER TABLE Loan ADD CONSTRAINT Book_Loan
  FOREIGN KEY (StudentIdNo)
  REFERENCES Student (StudentIdNo);
```

Figure 65.14 DDL script produced in TMS Data Modeller

Why use a data modelling tool

The database structure may be need to change several times during development. Using a higher level tool such as ERD Concepts 8 or TMS Data Modeller makes it easy to incorporate these changes by simply modifying the E-R model before recreating the modified database structure from a new script.

TMS Data Modeller is likely to be supported for many years whilst ERD Concepts 8 is the last version that will be created as development has ceased. The choice is yours.

66 Project preparation

Choosing a project

Purpose: To learn how to structure choosing a project

Why is a project a part of your course?

A major focus of computer science is algorithms and their application to processing of information. Therefore, it is important that you demonstrate that you can solve an information-processing problem using the most appropriate means available. A project is an excellent means by which you can demonstrate this capability.

What am I expected to produce?

To satisfy the examiners you are expected to produce a working computer-based system to a specification that you have drawn up in consultation with a contracting customer (end user), e.g. a physics teacher who wishes to demonstrate Maxwell's Demon to his classes. The specification is a detailed statement of what it is you are being asked by the contracting customer/end user to produce. The contracting customer is the person you ship the finished product to and who evaluates whetehr you have met their requirements. This contracting customer or end user may then use the product with his/her users/customers.

You are also expected to document the system that you have produced.

How do I choose a suitable project?

You are more likely to develop a successful project if you aim to solve a genuine problem experienced by a real person. This person who is called the contrating customer/end-user should not be you. The person can be a relative, a friend, a teacher at your school or college or someone that you have been introduced to for the purpose of choosing a project. Projects based upon invented problems and in which a student acts as his/her own end-user result in artificial and unrealistic solutions. Firstly, such projects are usually associated with a specification that changes during the design and implementation stages of the project. When a student experiences a little difficulty with an aspect of the design and/or implementation there is a temptation to decide it is easier to change the specification than overcome the difficulty. This has been described as the "shifting the goal posts" syndrome. Secondly, the evaluation process is weakened because there is no independent and reliable yardstick by which the effectiveness of the solution can be measured. The evaluation process checks the solution against the original specifications in order to establish that a solution has been produced as required. When you act as your own contracting customer/end-user you cannot by definition be independent.

Sources of ideas for a project

You will be spending a lot of time working on your project, so it is important that you choose something that interests you and that you will enjoy tackling. Often this can be achieved by looking for a problem to solve in an area in which you have some experience or interest. This might be a hobby, a sport that you play or watch; a club or society you belong to or perhaps something you are currently studying. Secondly, you will need to interact with the person acting as your real end-user/customer at the specification stage and later at the evaluation phase. Therefore, you need to ensure that the person for whom you are solving a problem can spare the necessary time to communicate his/her requirements and that they will be available to pass comment at the stage when a working system is produced. The amount of contracting customer/end-user's time that is required varies from project to project but can be as much as eight hours.

Scope of project

The project that you choose needs to be sufficiently meaty to enable you to gain the maximum possible marks but not so ambitious that you cannot get it finished in the time available. A natural tendency is to choose a project for which a solution can be visualised almost immediately. Such a project is unlikely to be of sufficient scope to satisfy the examiners. One test that can be used to decide whether a project is of adequate scope asks the student to specify an outline of the problem to be solved. When this is examined the outline often includes the solution to the problem. At the other extreme are projects that purport to be for large commercial organisations, for example, a stock control system for a large supermarket retailer. A good guideline here is to answer the question: "Will the solution that you can provide have a realistic chance of being used?" The same question can be used to reject a project that might initially seem to be of adequate scope but for which the volume of data is so small as to make a non-computer-based solution more attractive. For example, keeping records of ten people in the table-tennis club who each pay an annual subscription of £10.00 would be easier to manage manually using a paper-based system.

Technically how good do I have to be?

A major objective of the project is to produce a working system. You must be technically competent to tackle your chosen project. This has implications for the hardware and software that you will use. Coding your solution in an unfamiliar programming language that you will have to learn after starting your project is not a sensible course to follow. Learning a new programming language is not an objective of the project. You should also ensure that you are able to call on expert help when you do have a problem with the software that you have chosen to use.

Defining the problem

You should not begin to solve a problem until you have defined the problem that you are going to solve. This may seem a rather obvious statement but a surprising number of unsuccessful projects have begun without a student having a clear idea of what it is that he/she is tackling. Therefore, every project should begin with a clear statement that specifies the problem that is to be solved.

E.g. *Problem definition for Princes Risborough Tennis Club's Membership Database*

> The current system identifies members of the tennis club for whom a subscription renewal is due in the following month. It generates and sends renewal notices specifying the correct category of renewal fee followed by overdue subscription reminders if necessary. The current system is entirely paper-based and operated manually by the club's secretary. This was a manageable task when the membership was low (20 members) and there was only one fee category but now that the membership has grown to over 200 with four different categories of membership subscription, it has become an excessive time-burden for the secretary maintaining the paperwork. Furthermore, complaints have been received from some members that they have received a demand for payment which has not been applicable.

This definition is sufficiently clear for your project supervisor (your computer science teacher) to understand the problem that you intend to solve and to assess firstly, whether it will satisfy the criteria of the examiners and secondly, whether you are likely to be successful in tackling it.

The problem is not how to produce a computer-based subscription system. That is just one possible solution to the problem. The real problem is that *the secretary is finding it difficult to keep track of membership subscriptions payments with the current manual system.*

Your supervisor will want to know who will be the proposed contracting customer/end-user. In the above example, it should be the club secretary. The problem definition should be shown to the end-user in order to check that the end-user agrees with your understanding of the problem to be solved.

What are you expected to do after you have defined a problem?

In the commercial world, the next stage would be a low-cost brief mini-investigation to consider how best to solve the problem before a significant commitment of a company's or an organisation's funds are committed to the project. This is known as a feasibility study. Its objective is to investigate the potential for a new system. The outcome of this study might be

- to reject a computer-based solution perhaps on cost grounds or because no significant benefit would be gained or simply that such a solution is not possible
- to recommend that no software development takes place but instead a special-purpose application package be purchased which has already been designed to solve a similar problem
- to recommend committing funds to developing a software and hardware solution to the problem

In your case, your supervisor will have assessed the feasibility of your project and given you feedback. Assuming approval has been given for you to develop the project you may now begin the next stage of a project: ANALYSIS.

Analysis

The objective of analysis is to answer the question: *Exactly what must the system do?*

What must be done must be decided before considering how it should be done.

A significant percentage of the marks for the project are awarded for an 'analysis of the end-user's requirements'. This will include finding out how the current system (if there is one) works and what the inputs and outputs are. Most importantly, it will include finding out what the end-user would like the new system to do. Analysis or systems analysis to give it its full name must establish the requirements for the new system.

The analyst will use their understanding of the proposed new system to build models that represent this understanding. These models may then be shown to the end-user who can check that the analyst has indeed understood the requirements of the end-user. The different modelling techniques that an analyst may use are

- Data Flow Diagrams
- E-R diagrams
- Data dictionary
- Object analysis diagrams

Summarising the objectives

The objectives of the proposed new system need to be formally identified and stated.

Objectives are usually at two levels of detail. At the highest level there are those that state the purpose or overall objective of the system. Naturally, these are in broad general terms and are usually qualitative. At the second level somewhat more detailed objectives are set. These are both qualitative and quantitative. The quantitative ones are measurable and can therefore be used to evaluate the effectiveness of your solution. Where possible you should include both qualitative and quantitative objectives but the latter should predominate because they give the clearest guidance for the design stage.

An example of a qualitative objective is:

"It should be easy to locate details of a particular member of the tennis club"

An example of a quantitative objective is:

"It should be possible to locate any member's details in under 5 seconds"

The more clearly your objectives are stated, the easier it will be for your end-user to check that your understanding of his/her requirements has been achieved. It will also be easier to evaluate how closely your final solution satisfies the objectives.

The objectives of a proposed new membership subscription system for Princes Risborough tennis club might be as follows:

Overall objectives:

To create a system that will automate the process of identifying, notifying and reminding members whose subscriptions are due.

Specific objectives of the system

These may be classified into the input requirements, output requirements, processing requirements, performance requirements, and data storage requirements.

The input, output and processing requirements are often lumped together as shown below.

Input, processing and output requirements

The system to be created must

1. Automatically produce a list of members whose subscriptions are due.
2. Automatically print a standard letter (contents specified by club secretary) with forename, surname, address, membership number, category of membership, subscription and date due inserted into the letter for each member one month in advance of the date when the subscription falls due unless the subscription has been paid (mail-merge application). The member's record must record that a letter has been generated and the date it was generated.
3. Allow a subscription payment to be recorded. The club secretary is to enter the member's membership number, the date of payment and the amount paid. The system should locate the correct member's record and check the subscription fee due against amount paid then if correct record the date of payment and increment the number of years of membership. If incorrect the system should display an appropriate error message.
4. Automatically print one standard letter (contents specified by club secretary) with the name, address, subscription, date when it fell due and the date of the previous notification for each member whose subscription is overdue by two weeks. The member's record must record that a letter has been generated and the date it was generated.
5. Automatically generate one more reminder letter (contents specified by club secretary) for each member whose subscription is four weeks overdue. The member's record must record that a letter has been generated and the date it was generated.
6. Automatically cancel membership for each member whose subscription is eight weeks overdue and print a standard letter (contents specified by club secretary) of notification of termination of club membership with name, address and dates of previous three letters inserted. The cancelled member's record should not be deleted, however.
7. Allow the club secretary to search for a members' details by surname and membership number in order to view a member's full details.
8. Allow the club secretary to add details of a new member. System should allocate a unique four-digit membership number automatically.
9. Allow the club secretary to amend details of a member with the exception of the member's membership number.
10. Allow club secretary to delete a member from the system.
11. Allow the club secretary to print an alphabetically ordered list of selected members from a single individual to all members together with specified fields of their details.

12. Allow the club secretary to create a new standard letter and to print this letter for selected members (new mail-merge application).
13. Allow the club secretary to print one or more blank membership forms on demand using a supplied design.
14. Allow the club secretary to print an alphabetically ordered list of members and specified fields of their details whose membership renewal is due within four weeks of a specified date.
15. Allow the club secretary to print an alphabetically ordered list of members whose membership renewal is now overdue together with specified fields of their details.
16. Allow the club secretary to view and print details of members whose membership has been cancelled since a specified date. The printed output should be alphabetically sorted if more than one member is specified.
17. Allow the club secretary to interrogate the system for the following information and to print this information on demand:
    1. total number of members in each category
    2. total number of members
    3. total subscription receipts between two specified dates
    4. total of subscriptions due in the next four weeks
    5. total of subscriptions overdue
    6. total number of memberships cancelled between two specified dates
    7. total number of new memberships between two specified dates
    8. total number of membership renewals that are overdue by specified period.
18. Allow the club secretary to set a password on the system.
19. Allow the club secretary to command the system to back up the members' data.
20. Allow the club secretary to command the system to be restored from a backup copy.

The use of a number scheme rather than a bullet point scheme is very important for later when you need to refer to a specific objective.

Performance requirements

1. It should take less than 5 seconds to look up a given member's details.
2. It should take less than 30 seconds for the system to extract and display on a visual display unit any of the totals specified in input process-output requirement 17.
3. It should be made as easy as possible for the club secretary to create a new mail-merge application.
4. It should be made as easy as possible for the club secretary to select a particular activity and to switch between activities.

Data requirements

1. The system should record the following information about a member:
    1. Membership number
    2. Surname
    3. Forename
    4. Address
    5. Home telephone number
    6. Mobile telephone number
    7. Membership category code
    8. Number of years of membership
    9. Date of payment of subscription
    10. Date next subscription falls due
    11. Subscription renewal notice sent
    12. Date subscription renewal notice sent
    13. First overdue reminder sent
    14. Date first overdue reminder sent
    15. Second overdue reminder sent
    16. Date second reminder sent
    17. Membership cancelled
    18. Date membership cancelled

2. The system should record the following information about membership categories
    1. Membership category code
    2. Category description
    3. Subscription fee
3. The system will need to be able to store some 200 member records, initially, but cater for an expansion of up to 1000 members
4. The system should cater for 10 categories of membership, initially, but allow expansion up to 20 categories. The ten categories to be recorded together with their current subscription fees are as follows:

	Membership Category Code	**Subscription Fee**
(i)	full adult	£200
(ii)	weekend adult	£100
(iii)	evening only adult	£100
(iv)	morning adult	£50
(v)	afternoon adult	£50
(vi)	full junior	£100
(vii)	weekend junior	£50
(viii)	evening junior	£50
(ix)	novice	£30
(x)	trial	£10

Context Diagram

The analyst should start with a context diagram before drawing a full-blown data flow diagram. This diagram will only use the source/destination and data flow symbols from the set of symbols used to draw data flow diagrams. A blank circle will be drawn where the rest of the data flow diagram should appear. This blank circle will enclose the system. The sources and destinations and the data flows to and from the system will appear in the rest of the diagram - *Figure 66.1*.

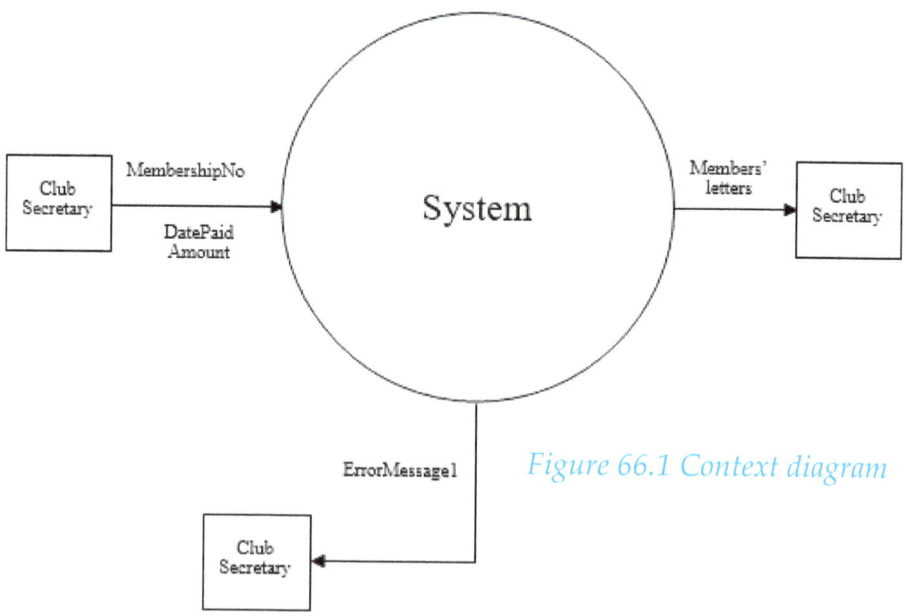

Figure 66.1 Context diagram

Why draw this very high level diagram?

The answer is that it will focus on the inputs and outputs of the system. This diagram can be used to design the user interface. The simplified context diagram shows one input and two outputs. The diagram has one source and two destinations - all three are Club Secretary. The data flows are labelled. In order for this context diagram to be useful to a designer, the data flows must be defined. For this purpose the diagram must be accompanied by a data dictionary. For example, the data flow labelled `ErrorMessage1` should have the following entry in a data dictionary - *Table 66.1*.

Name	Alias	Description	Data type	Size/Range
ErrorMessage1	An error message	No such Member	String	14 characters

Table 66.1 Data dictionary

The context diagram plus its associated data dictionary should contain enough information for a user interface designer to work with this information to produce a user-interface that could be shown to the end-user.

Level One DFD (Data Flow Diagram)

The next stage is to add the high level processes, data stores and data flows inside the system. The blank circle is replaced by a high level representation of the proposed system. - *Figure 66.2*.

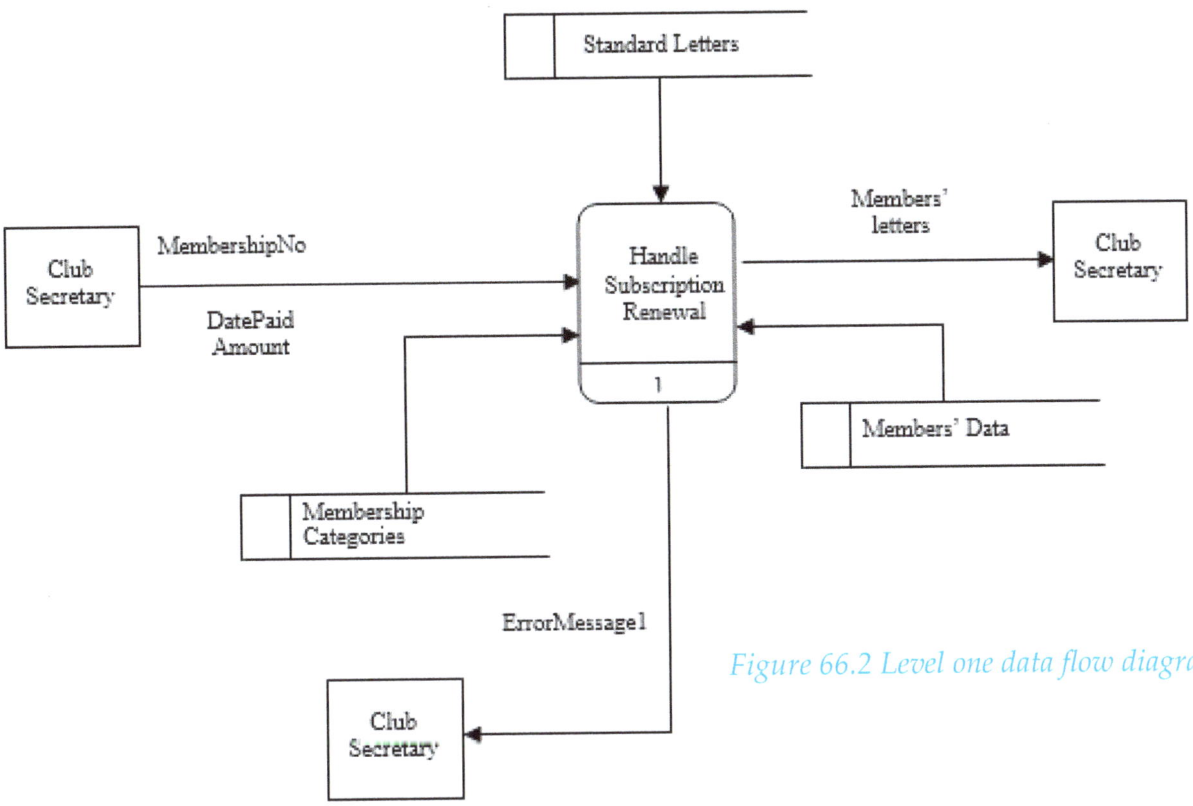

Figure 66.2 Level one data flow diagram

Finally, you may wish to draw the Level Two data flow diagrams for this project. The first one has been done for you in *Figure 66.3*.

Exercise

Download[1] the Level Two data flow diagrams (`DFDsForPrincesRisboroTennisClub.doc`). Use these to extract the user interface parts and create a full context diagram for the Princes Risborough Tennis Club project. To avoid the context diagram becoming too cluttered you may wish to draw more than one context diagram, with each representing a part of the user interface.

Business Algorithms

Sometimes a project will need to use algorithms supplied by the end-user. These are algorithms used by the existing system or that would be used if a system existed. An example from another scenario is an algorithm for calculating interest on an investment (*Table 66.2*), e.g. if a customer invests £100 how much interest would be earned in the first year of the investment and in subsequent years?

1 See www.educational-computing.com/DelphiBook/DelphiCode.html

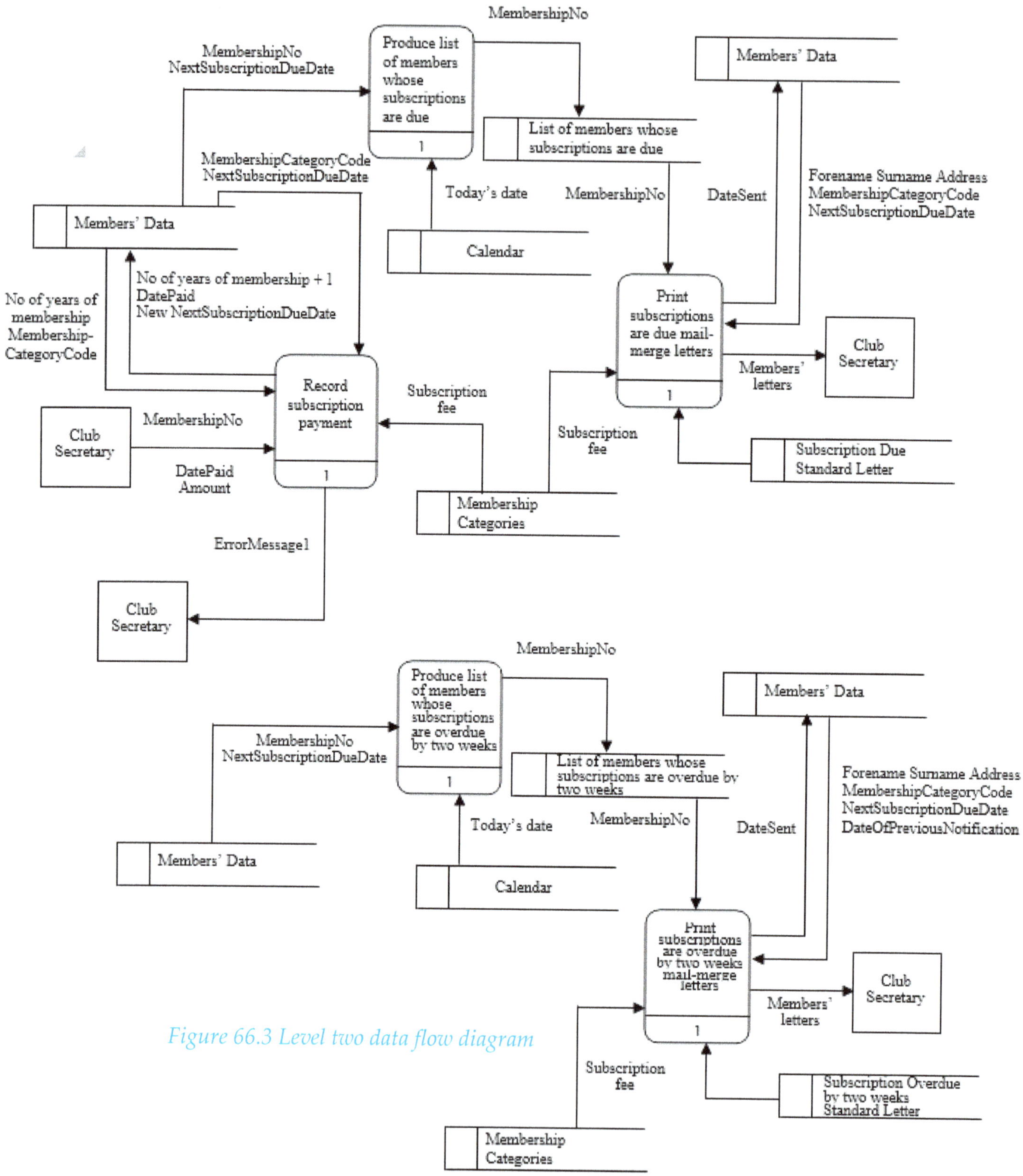

Figure 66.3 Level two data flow diagram

Business algorithm:

Table 66.2 Algorithm for calculating interest

```
APR := 0.05;
Year := 0;
Repeat
  Year := Year + 1;
  Interest := SumInvested * APR;
  SumInvested := SumInvested + Interest;
Until Year = NoOfYearsRequested;
```

Entity Relationship Diagram

Before drawing the data flow diagrams you may wish to identify the entities in the system – the things for which your project will store data. Next, you need to identify(spot) the relationships between the entities – one-to-one, one-to-many, many-to-many. Finally, a diagram needs to be drawn which shows the entities and the relationships between these – the Entity-Relationship or E-R diagram - *Figure 66.4*.

Figure 66.4 E-R diagram

Entity Description

Finally, each entity must be "described". "Described" has a specific meaning in this context. Essentially this means writing the entity name followed by its attributes enclosed in brackets. The entity identifier must be clearly indicated by an underline. The description for the entities in this project are as follows:

```
Member(MembershipNumber, Surname, Forename, Address, HomeTelephoneNumber,
       WorkTelephoneNumber, MembershipCategoryCode, NumberOfYearsOfMembership,
       DateOfPaymentOfSubscription, DateNextSubscriptionFallsDue,
       SubscriptionRenewalNoticeSent, DateSubscriptionRenewalNoticeSent,
       FirstOverdueReminderSent, DateFirstOverdueReminderSent,
       SecondOverdueReminderSent, DateSecondReminderSent, MembershipCancelled,
       DateMembershipCancelled)
MembershipCategory(MembershipCategoryCode, CategoryDescription, SubscriptionFee)
```

The data requirements section of this document was used to construct the entity descriptions.

Constraints

Hardware

In order to run Microsoft® Access 2016 and to be able to perform a mail merge using Word:

Operating system: Windows 10 for PC

Processor: 1.6 GHz, Dual-Core Processor

RAM: 4 GB for 64-bit Systems and 2 GB for 32-bit Systems

Hard Disk Space: 4 GB

Graphics Card: DirectX 10 Graphics Card

Display Resolution: 1024×468 A

The user has a HP 24-dp0002na 23.8" AMD Ryzen 5, 256 GB SSD running Windows 10, which will be perfectly suitable, and similar machines are available for development work at the School.

Software

The club secretary already has MS Access 2016 and is keen to see it used for this project because he has some experience using it already. However, he is prepared to accept a well-reasoned case for an alternative approach that requires no additional expenditure.

Users

Access to the system is to be restricted to the club secretary.

Time

The project should be completed and fully documented by ....

User's level of information technology skills

Mr Smith is familiar with Word and has good keyboard skills, so he should have no problem entering data and learning how to use the system. Mr Smith is keen to use his Microsoft Access 2016 skills.

Limitations

System boundaries (scope of proposed system)

The system to be developed is to focus solely on dealing with subscription renewals. It will not include keeping the accounts of the tennis club or any other aspect of running the club.

67 Using the Low Code App Wizard

Using the Low Code App Wizard for FireMonkey

Purpose: To understand what is meant by Low Code and how to use this approach

Embarcadero's **Low Code App Wizard for FireMonkey** for Delphi makes it possible to quickly create a cross-platform application from existing templates containing the basic functionality required of every mobile app. It comes with a set of tests that may be applied to check that as the application is extended/customised, its quality is maintained. **Low Code** means *minimal coding* by configuring a template and adjusting its settings using the RAD approach of Delphi. **Low code** supports extensibility. Given the supplied **Low Code** design, it is possible to extend it by copying, adapting and configuring its existing templates whilst writing a minimal amount of code.

The **Low Code App** wizard may be downloaded and installed by selecting **Tools|GetIt Package Manager** - *Figure 67.1* and then **FireMonkey App Wizard** - *Figure 67.2*.

Once the wizard is installed, **select** **File|New|Multi-Device|FireMonkey Template App** - *Figure 67.3* - to create a Delphi FireMonkey application. The window shown in *Figure 67.4* appears next. **Enter** a name for the project and **select** a folder for the project. **Untick** the **Data Layer** box to avoid working with a database at this stage. **Click** the **Next** button to bring up the **Application Screens** window - *Figure 67.5*. **Accept** the given selections by clicking **Next**. *Figure 67.6* shows the design view for unit `view.pas` with a **Samsung G955F** mobile phone connected via usb to a computer running **Delphi 10.4.2** on **Windows 10**.

Figure 67.2 FireMonkey App Wizard

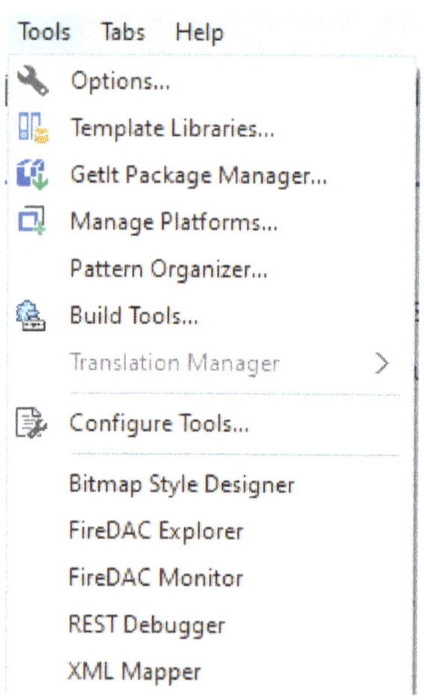

Figure 67.1 Tools menu

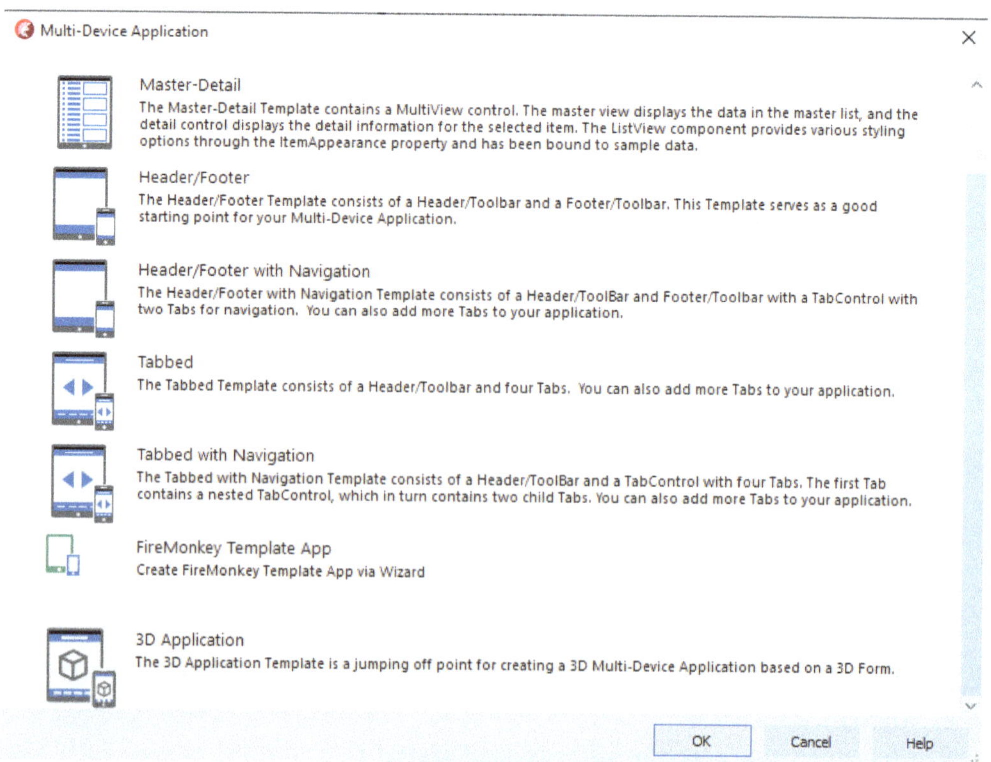

Figure 67.3 FireMonkey Template App

If when you run the application a syntax error occurs, edit `view.pas` which at the time of writing contains a superfluous and orphaned `{$IFDEF}` statement. It is easy to spot.

Or in **Project|Options|Compiling|Require** set flag for option `$IF to be terminated by $IFEnd.`

Figure 67.7 shows the launch screen when the application is installed and run on the **Samsung G955F**. The application is not set up to accept an email address and a password so don't enter anything into the edit boxes. Instead, just click **sign in** to gain access to the home screen - *Figure 67.8* - showing a hamburger menu ☰ . *Figure 67.9* shows the window that appears when the hamburger menu is clicked. *Figure 67.10* shows the window that appears if the **Settings** option is selected. The **Low Code App Wizard** supplies enough functionality for the basis from which mobile phone or tablet apps may be developed.

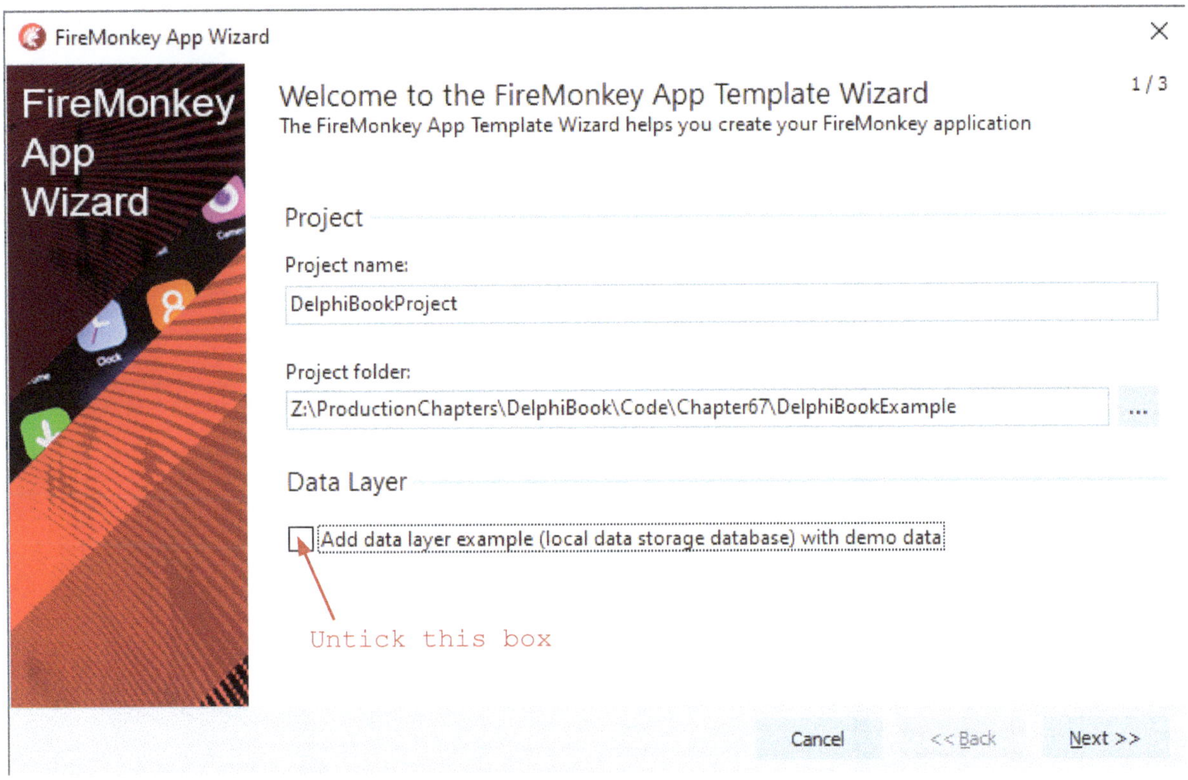

Figure 67.4 Setting up the project

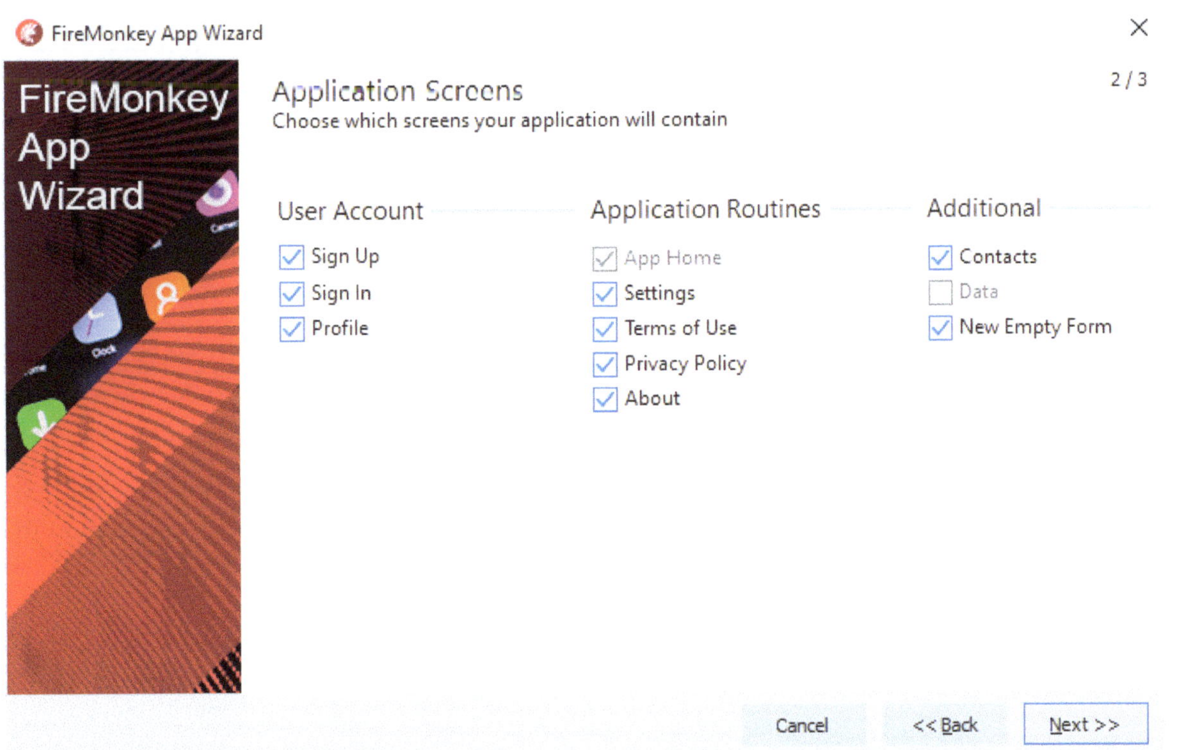

Figure 67.5 Selecting the screens to include in the application - App Home will always be provided hence it is greyed out

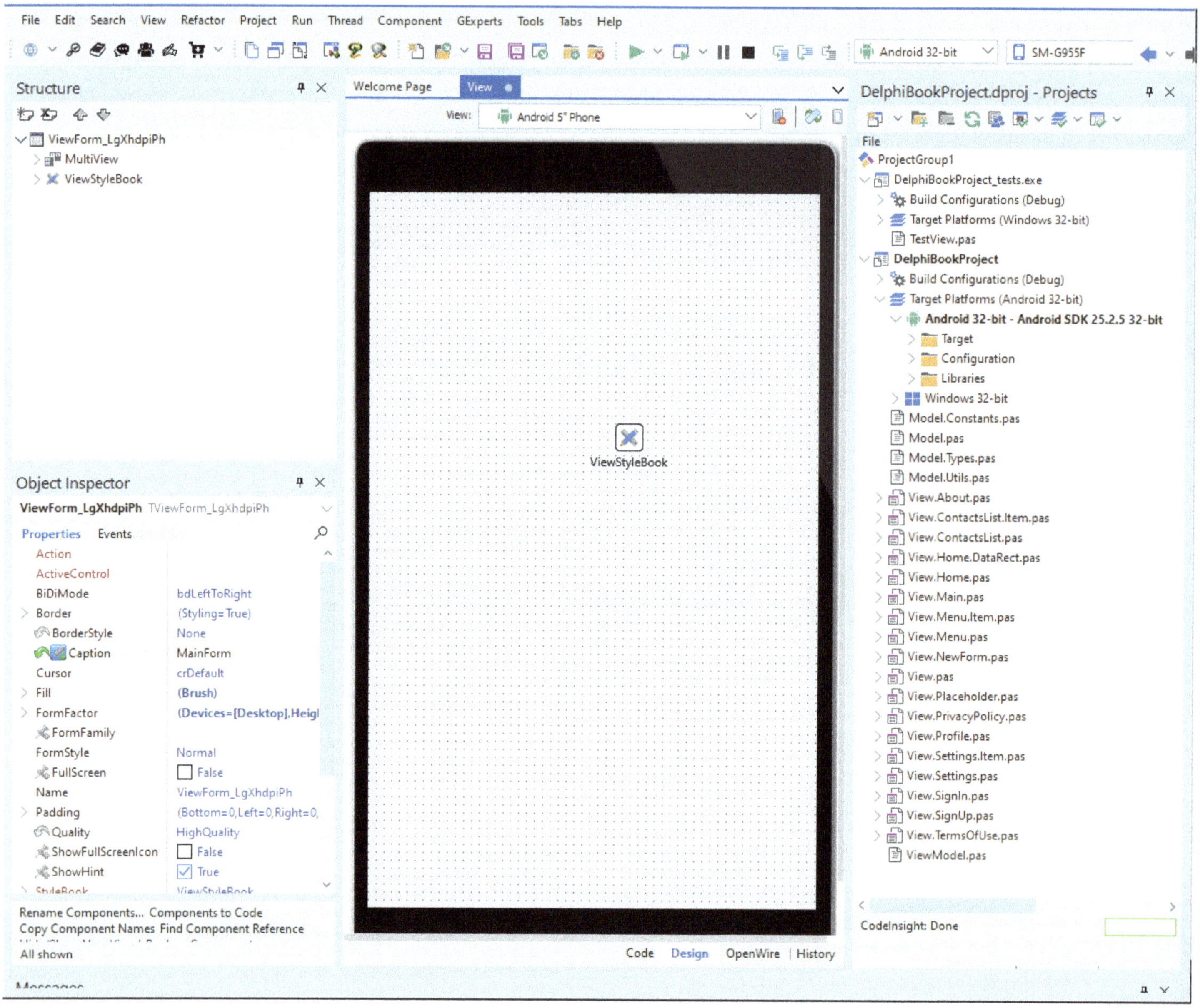

Figure 67.6 The design view for Samsung G955F mobile phone showing the list of units that are created automatically

Low Code App Wizard Database example

In this example, the **Low Code App Wizard** will work with a database, `employee.gdb`, that comes with the wizard. This may be replaced with an alternative if desired and the screen that displays data edited to work with the alternative database.

Select **File|New|Multi-Device|FireMonkey Template App** to create a Delphi FireMonkey application. **Enter** a name for the project and **select** a folder for the project. This time the **Data Layer** box needs to be ticked and when the application is installed and run in the target device (a Lenova tablet in this example), the `DB Access` fields shown on the home screen are populated with data from a database record. An extra field labelled `Data` appears on the **Hamburger menu** screen which when selected on the Lenova tablet brings up a list view of data from the employee database - *Figure 67.11*.

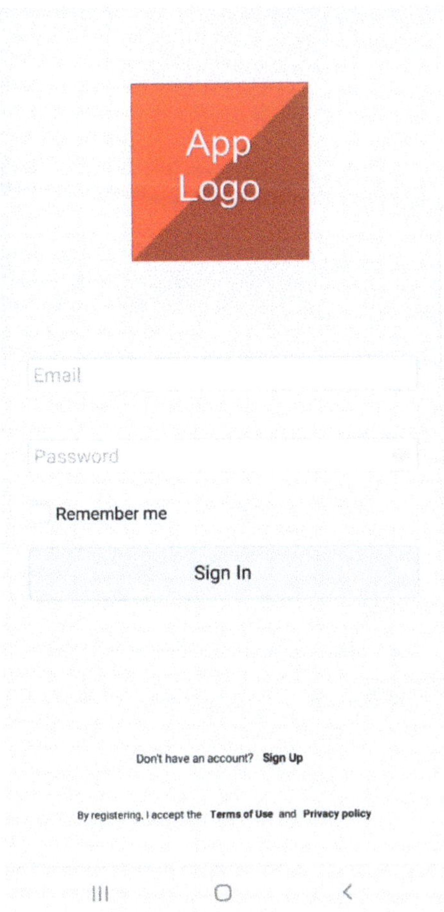

Figure 67.7 Launch screen

Figure 67.8 Home screen showing hamburger menu

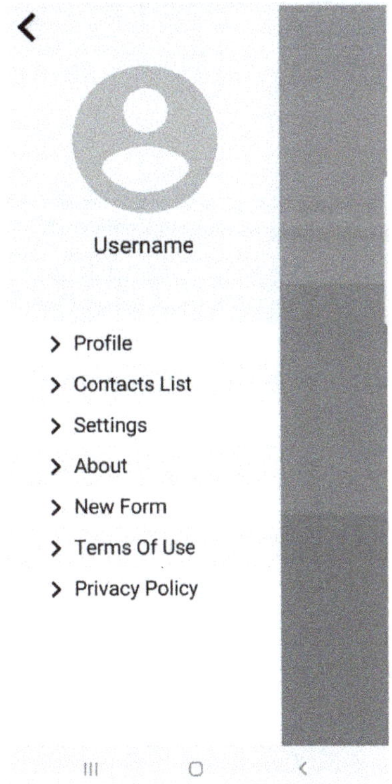

Figure 67.9 Hamburger menu

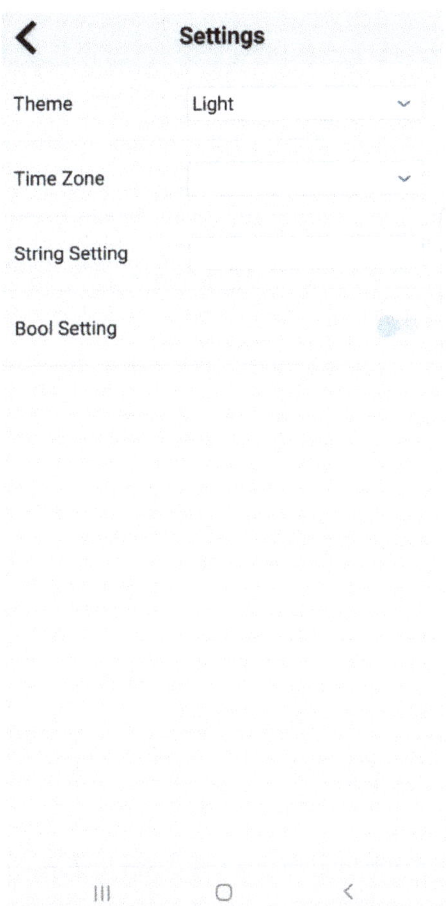

Figure 67.10 Settings screen

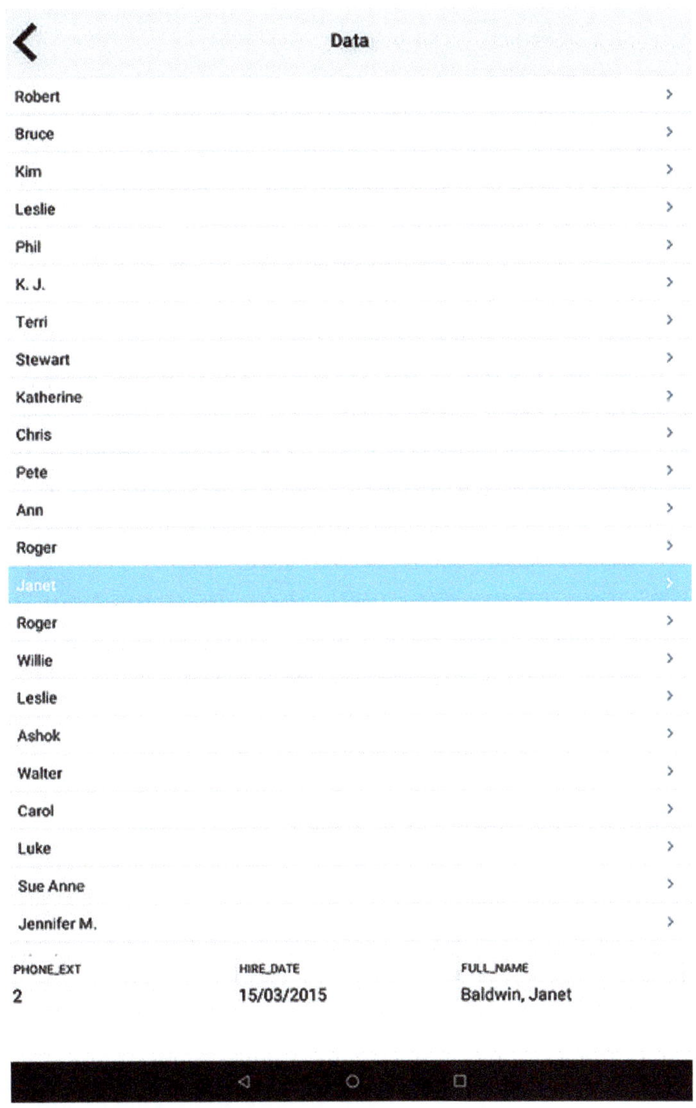

Figure 67.11 Database example

68 Using low code wizards with REST

Embarcadero's REST Debugger

Purpose: To understand how to use Embarcadero's REST Debugger

Embarcadero's **REST Debugger** is a tool that can be used to test and debug **REST** queries.

It is available in the IDE from **Tools | REST Debugger** or as an independent download from https://www.embarcadero.com/free-tools/rest-debugger.

To install in the IDE, if not already present, visit https://docwiki.embarcadero.com/RADStudio/Sydney/en/Installing_the_REST_Debugger.

Songsterr has an open **Application Programming Interface (API)** which makes it possible to write programs to obtain publicly available **Songsterr** data using REST (See https://www.songsterr.com/a/wa/api).

Launch the **REST Debugger**. **Enter** the base **URL**, http://www.songsterr.com/a/ra in the **URL** field of the **Request** tab of the **REST Debugger** and **select** method **GET**. **Open** the **Parameters** tab and **enter** the **Resource** identifier, `songs.json`. **Click** the **Add** button and in the pop-up window, **select GET/POST**, enter `pattern` in the **Name** field and `Beatles` in the **Value** field. **Click** the **Apply** button. **Click** the **Send Request** button. *Figure 68.1* reveals in the Tabular Data tab of the **REST Debugger**, the song data response for this request.

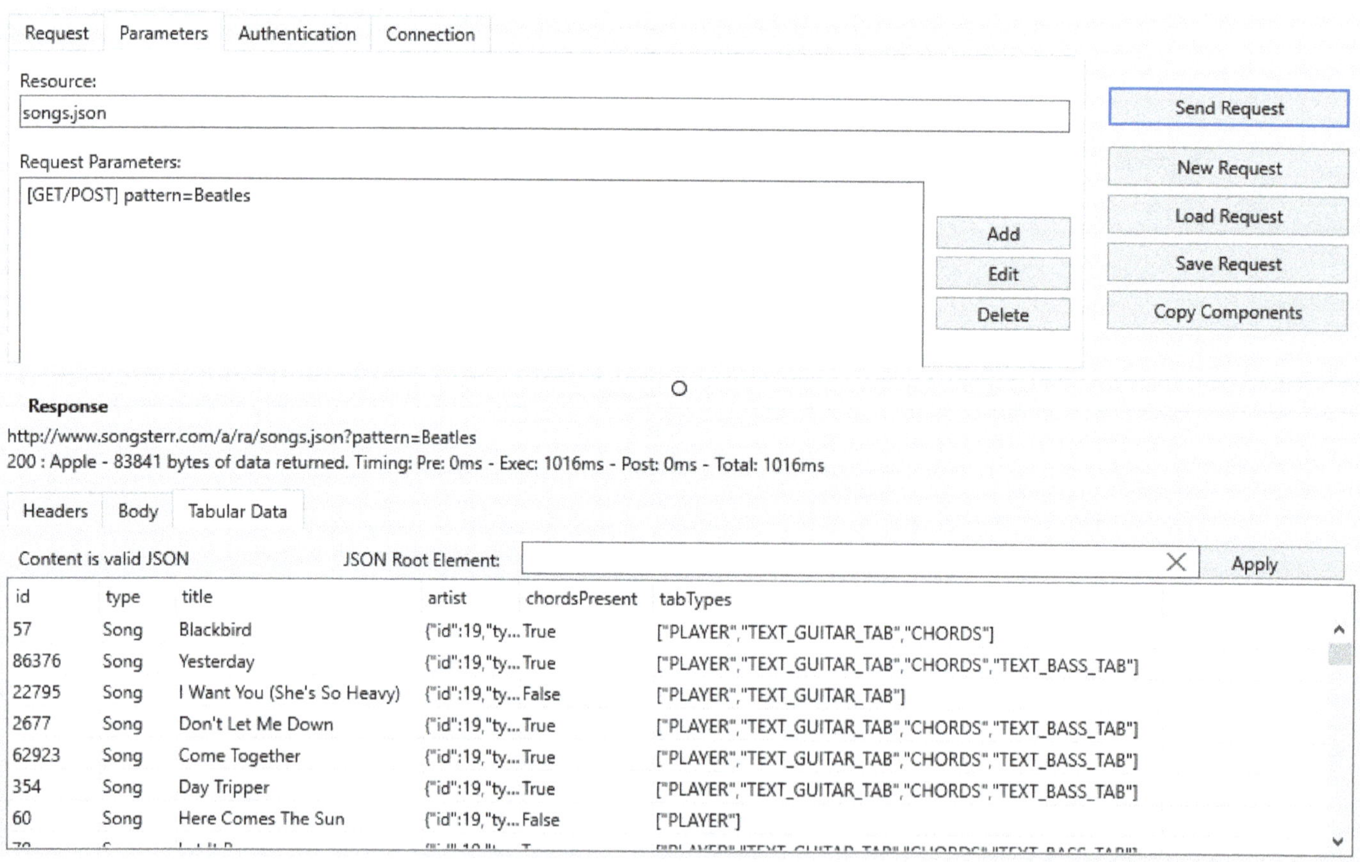

Fig. 68.1 Beatles song data returned in response to REST request sent by REST Debugger

Twitter application

Watch Alister Christie of Learn Delphi TV explain how to access a Twitter account using low code and the REST Debugger -
https://learndelphi.org/discover-how-to-use-the-rest-debugger-in-delphi-to-connect-to-twitter-in-this-new-learn-delphi-video-tutorial/

69 Introduction to FireDAC database programming

Using FireDAC to connect to a database

Purpose: To be familiar with using FireDAC to connect to a database

Introduction

FireDAC was introduced in Delphi XE3 in 2013. It has become the technology to use in Delphi for working with databases. It is supported on all Delphi's platforms: Windows, Mac OS, iOS, Android and Linux.

FireDAC provides drivers for almost every relational database and a non-relational database, MongoDB (MongoDB is a document database, which means it stores data in JSON-like documents).

It has native support for Oracle, IBM DB2, MS SQL Server, Interbase, SAP SQL Anywhere, SAP Advantage Database Server and Teradata, Firebird, MongoDB, MySQL, PostgresSQL and SQLite.

FireDAC also supports two bridging drivers, one for ODBC and another for dbExpress. Using the FireDAC ODBC driver makes it possible to work with virtually any relational database that exists.

Using TFDConnection and TFDTable in a VCL application

P

Launch Delphi, **select** File|New|Windows VCL Application-Delphi.

Select File|New|Other|Database|Data Module to create a new unit, `Unit2`, and a **TDataModule** form, `DataModule1`. **Save** the project as `FireDACProject1.proj` in folder `FireDACProject1`.

Save `Unit1` as `MainFormUnit.pas` and `Unit2` as `DataModuleUnit.pas` in folder `FireDACProject1`.

Add a TFDConnection component, `FDConnection1`, from the FireDAC page of the component palette to the TDataModule form, `DataModule1`.

Double click this component to open the FireDAC Connection editor for `FDConnection1` - *Figure 69.1*.

Select IB from the dropdown listbox for the **Driver ID**.

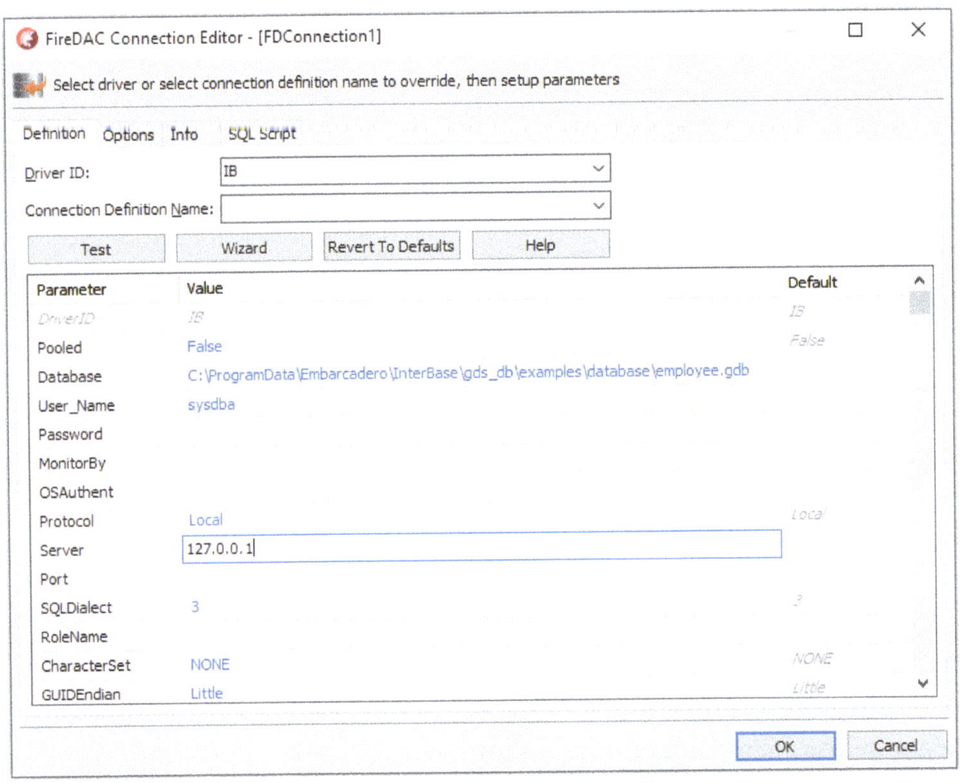

Fig. 69.1 FireDAC Connection Editor

Select database, `employee.gdb`, supplied with Interbase (this should ensure a match between database version and Interbase server version, i.e. same on-disk-structure) by providing its full path

`C:\ProgramData\Embarcadero\InterBase\gds_db\examples\database\employee.gdb`

Enter User_Name, `sysdba`, the user name for the database administrator.

Enter `127.0.0.1` or `localhost` in the **Server** field.

Click the `Test` button to bring up the **Login** window shown in *Figure 69.2*.

Enter `masterkey` for the password and click **OK**.

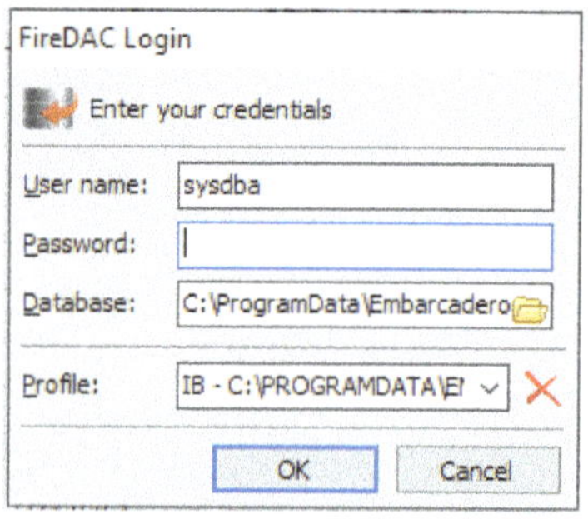

Fig. 69.2 FireDac Login window

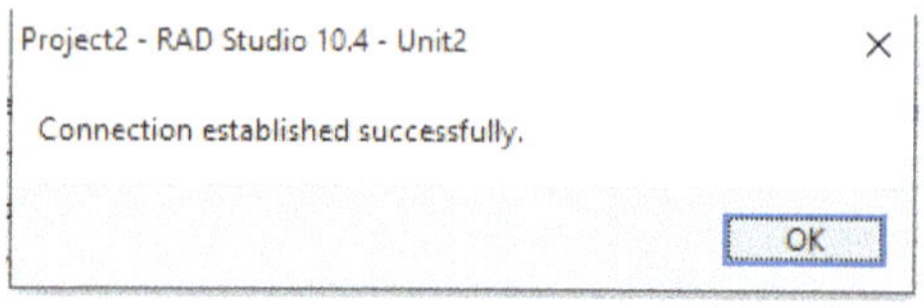

Fig. 69.3 Connection established successfully window

Fig. 69.4 Interbase 2020 in Start Menu

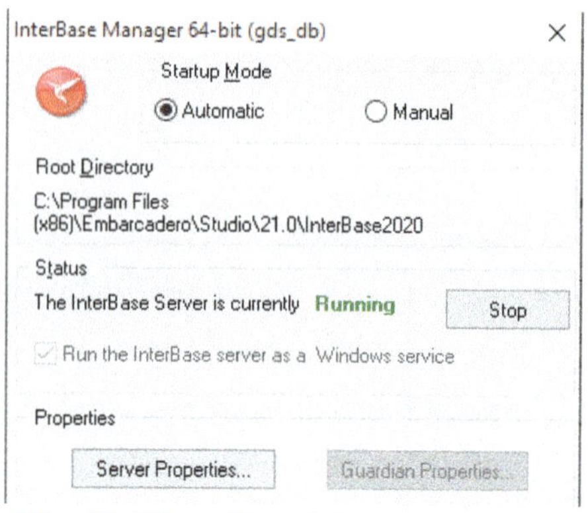

Fig. 69.5 Interbase Manager window

If successful then the window shown in *Figure 69.3* should pop up. If not, it may be because the **Interbase server** is not running or the maximum allowed number of connections for the **Developer version** of Interbase has been reached already. To fix this, **run** the **Interbase Server Manager** and start or stop/start the server - *Figure 69.4* and *Figure 69.5* and try connecting again. The server can also be started or restarted using the **Services** applet from **Administrative tools** of **Windows**.

Click the **OK** button in the popup window shown in *Figure 69.3*.

Select the **SQL Script** tab and enter the following SQL statement in the upper window

```
Select * From Customer
```

Click the green run button to execute the query. The dataset returned appears in the lower window as shown in *Figure 69.6*.

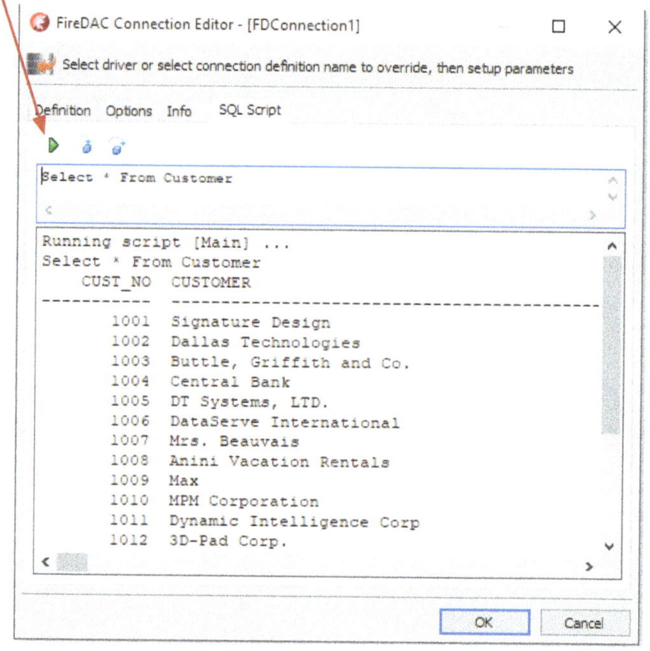

Fig. 69.6 Result set which is returned when the given SQL is executed

Add a **TFDTable** from the **FireDAC** page of the component palette to the **TDataModule** form. Its name should be `FDTable1`.

Set its **Connection** property to `FDConnection1`.

Click the left mouse button on the down arrow in the `FDTable1`'s **TableName** field. If `FDConnection1`'s **Connected** field is `False` then the login dialogue box shown in *Figure 69.2* should appear otherwise a list of table names should be displayed in a drop down menu. **Log in** if necessary, but either way **select** the `Employee` table name. Set `FDTable1`'s **Active** field to `True`.

Switch attention to `Form1` of `Unit1`. **Add** `DataModuleUnit` to the **Uses** statement.

Add a **TPanel** component from the **Standard** page of the **Palette** to `Form1`. Remove its caption, `Panel1`.

Set its **Align** property to **alTop** and its **Height** property to 41.

Add a **TDBNavigator**, `DBNavigator1`, from the **Data Controls** page of the **Palette** and two buttons from the **Standard** page.

Set the **ShowHint** property of `DBNavigator1` to `True`.

Right click the first button and select the **Quick Edit** option from the pop-up menu window - *Figure 69.7*.

Use the **Quick Edit** window to change the button's name and caption as shown in *Figure 69.8*.

Click the button with the tick symbol to set name and caption.

Repeat for the other button and set its name and caption as shown in *Figure 69.9*.

Add a **TDBGrid** component, `DBGrid1`, from the **Data Controls** page of the **Palette** to the form placing it on the region below the **TPanel** component.

Set its **Align** property to **alClient**.

Add a **TDataSource** component, `DataSource1`, from the **Data Controls** page of the **Palette** to the form.

Set its **DataSet** property to `DataModule1.FDTable1`.

Set the **DataSource** property of `DBGrid1` to `DataSource1`.

Add a **TFDGUIxLoginDialog** component from the **FireDAC UI** page of the **Palette**.

Set `FDTable1`'s **Active** property to `True`, if it isn't already.

The grid should now fill with data from table `Employee` as shown in *Figure 69.10* but with a different column layout. More work must be done to achieve the column layout shown in *Figure 69.10*.

Save All.

Compile and **run** the program (**Shift + Ctrl + F9**)[1].

The **FireDAC Login** window should appear as shown in *Figure 69.11* because `FDConnection1`'s **LoginPrompt** property was left set as `True`, the default. **Enter** `masterkey` for the password and click **OK**.

Figure 69.12 shows the program in execution.

Starting at the left end of the navigator bar (`DBNavigator1`), **move** the mouse cursor over each navigator button in turn to reveal a pop-up hint window describing what each does.

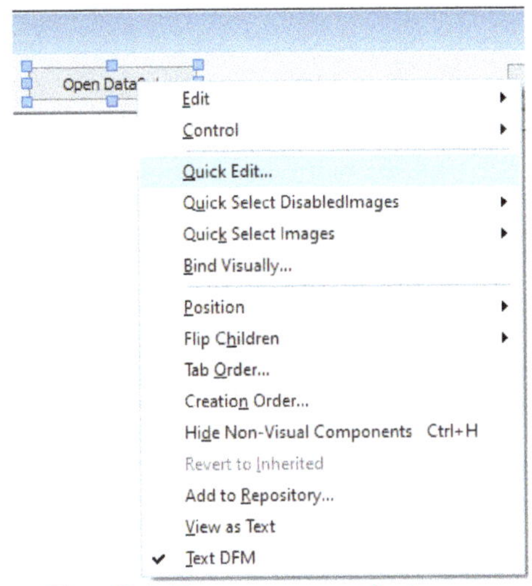

Fig. 69.7 Pop-up menu that appears after right mouse button is clicked

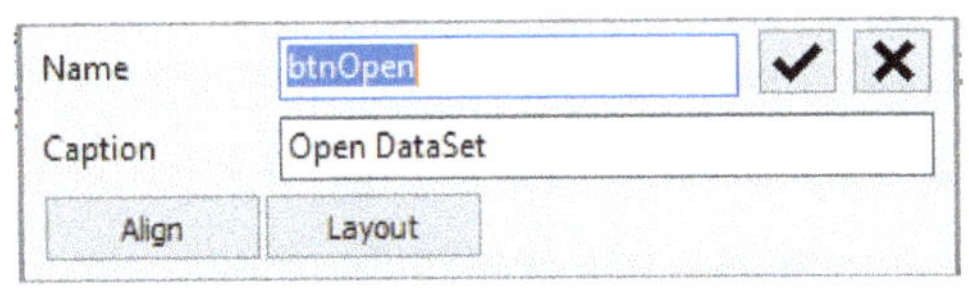

Fig. 69.8 Quick Edit pop-up window

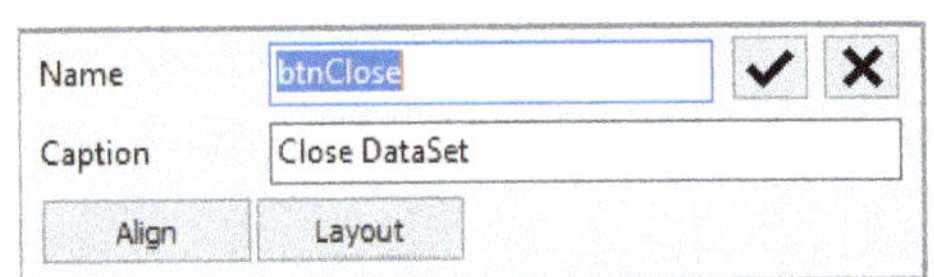

Fig. 69.9 Quick Edit pop-up window

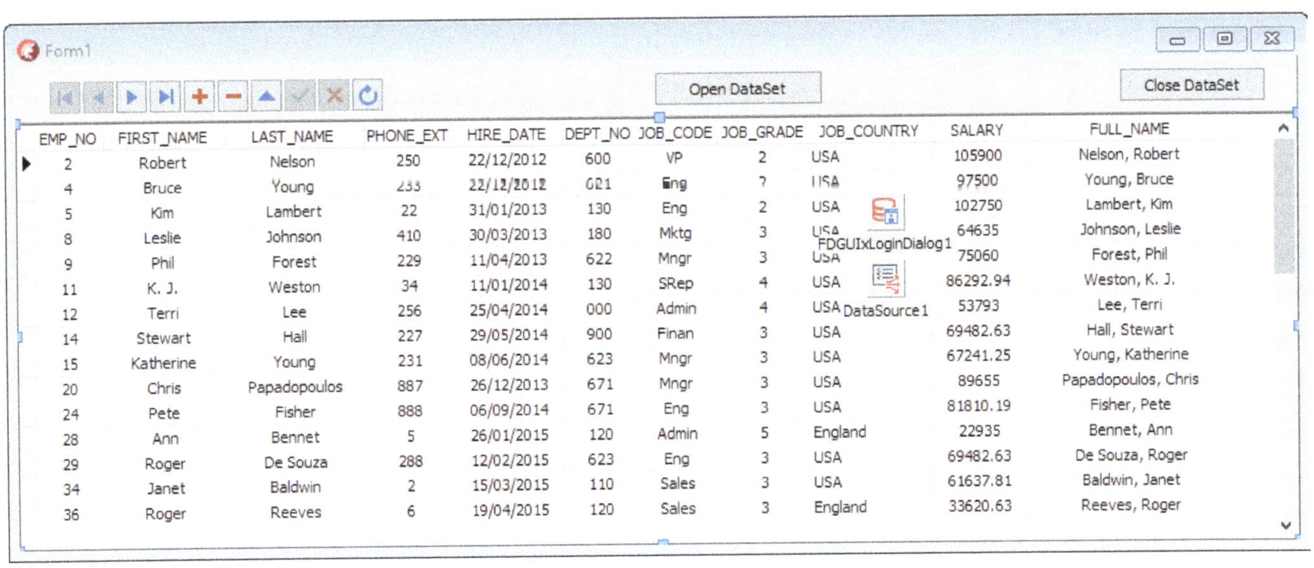

EMP_NO	FIRST_NAME	LAST_NAME	PHONE_EXT	HIRE_DATE	DEPT_NO	JOB_CODE	JOB_GRADE	JOB_COUNTRY	SALARY	FULL_NAME
2	Robert	Nelson	250	22/12/2012	600	VP	2	USA	105900	Nelson, Robert
4	Bruce	Young	233	22/12/2012	621	Eng	2	USA	97500	Young, Bruce
5	Kim	Lambert	22	31/01/2013	130	Eng	2	USA	102750	Lambert, Kim
8	Leslie	Johnson	410	30/03/2013	180	Mktg	3	USA	64635	Johnson, Leslie
9	Phil	Forest	229	11/04/2013	622	Mngr	3	USA	75060	Forest, Phil
11	K. J.	Weston	34	11/01/2014	130	SRep	4	USA	86292.94	Weston, K. J.
12	Terri	Lee	256	25/04/2014	000	Admin	4	USA	53793	Lee, Terri
14	Stewart	Hall	227	29/05/2014	900	Finan	3	USA	69482.63	Hall, Stewart
15	Katherine	Young	231	08/06/2014	623	Mngr	3	USA	67241.25	Young, Katherine
20	Chris	Papadopoulos	887	26/12/2013	671	Mngr	3	USA	89655	Papadopoulos, Chris
24	Pete	Fisher	888	06/09/2014	671	Eng	3	USA	81810.19	Fisher, Pete
28	Ann	Bennet	5	26/01/2015	120	Admin	5	England	22935	Bennet, Ann
29	Roger	De Souza	288	12/02/2015	623	Eng	3	USA	69482.63	De Souza, Roger
34	Janet	Baldwin	2	15/03/2015	110	Sales	3	USA	61637.81	Baldwin, Janet
36	Roger	Reeves	6	19/04/2015	120	Sales	3	England	33620.63	Reeves, Roger

Fig. 69.10 Design view of Form1 showing grid populated with data from the Employee table

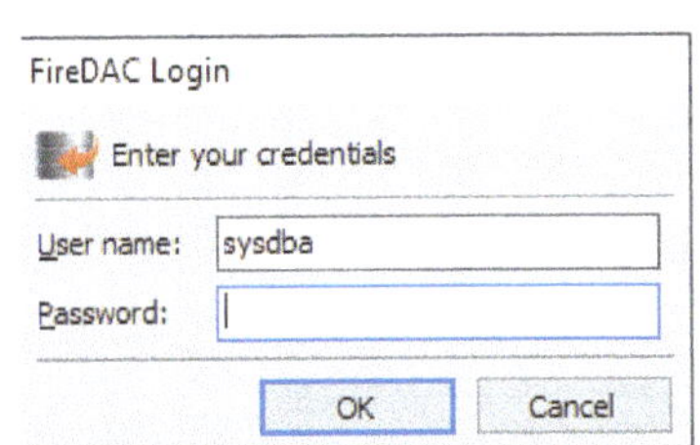

Fig. 69.11 FireDAC Login window

1 In versions prior to Delphi XE8, all required **FireDAC** units were not automatically added to the **uses** clause. The trick that fixes this issue requires that two components, **TFDPhysIBDriverLink** and **TFDGUIxWaitCursor** are added temporarily to the form. Remove these after building the project although no harm is done if left on the form.

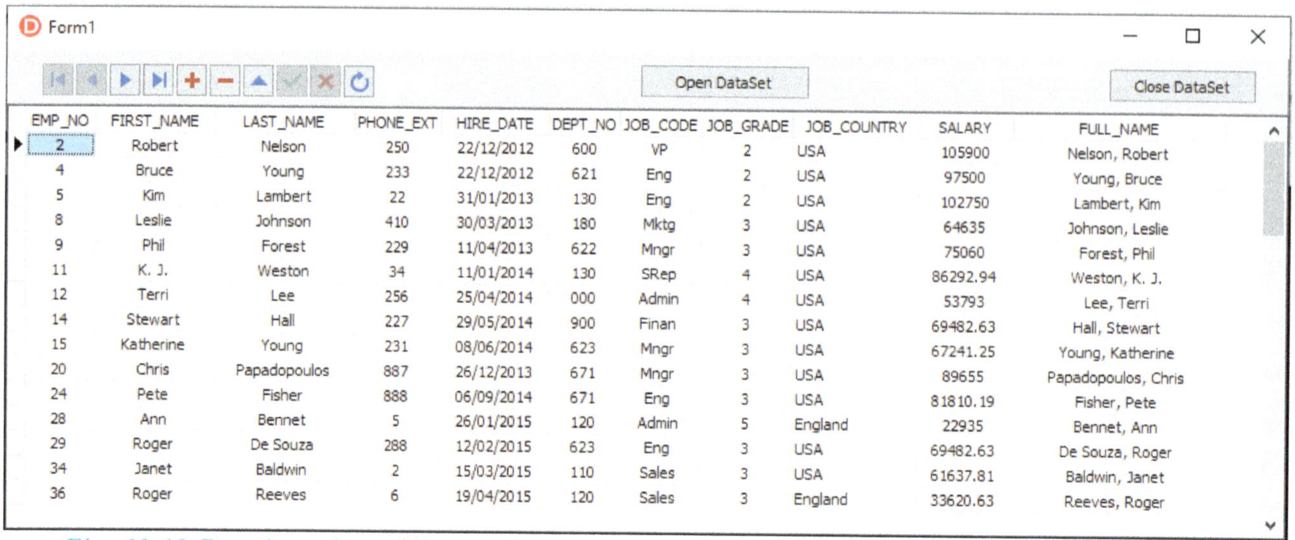

Fig. 69.12 Runtime view of Form1 showing grid populated with data from the Employee table

Scroll down to the row with `EMP_No` 72. **Select** the empty `Phone_Ext` field.

Enter the value 567 and **press** return then **click** the **Post edit** button (✓) in the navigator bar to post the edited record to the database table, `Employee`[2].

Stop the execution of the program and then **run** it again to demonstrate that the record with `EMP_NO` 72 has indeed been changed.

Stop the execution of the program and return to the IDE.

With the mouse cursor over the grid, **click** the right mouse button to bring up the options menu window shown in *Figure 69.13*. **Click** the **Columns Editor** option to bring up the **Columns Editor** window.

This window will be empty initially.

Click the **Add All Fields** icon to add all the fields of table `Employee`.

Select each field in the **Columns Editor** in turn and then in the **Object Inspector** change the **Alignment** and **Title|Alignment** property values to **taCenter**.

The `EMP_NO` column has the identifier `DBGrid1.Columns[0]` in the **Object Inspector**, the `FIRST_NAME` column has the identifier `DBGrid1.Columns[1]`, and so on.

Save All.

Double click the `Open DataSet` button to create an **OnClick** event handler.

Add the following code to the body of this event handler

```
If DataModule1.FDTable1.Active = False
  Then DataModule1.FDTable1.Open;
```

Double click the `Close DataSet` button to create an **OnClick** event handler.

Add the following code to the body of this event handler

```
If DataModule1.FDTable1.Active = True
  Then DataModule1.FDTable1.Close;
```

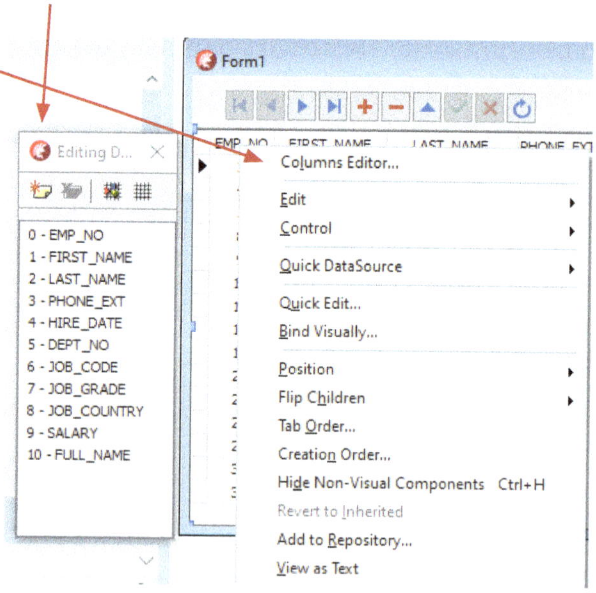

Fig. 69.13 Options menu window for TDBGrid component and Columns Editor window

An alternative way of formatting the grid columns is to select DBGrid1 in the Structure pane and then to select each field in turn in this pane

2 The **Options** property of `DBGrid1` must have **dgEditing** set to `True` for in-grid editing to work. It is by default.

Set `FDTable1`'s **Active** property to `False`.
Save All.
Compile and **run** the program (**Shift + Ctrl + F9**).
The grid will now display with column headings only.
Click the `Open DataSet` button to fill the grid with data.
Click the `Close DataSet` button to return to an empty grid.
Close the application.

Programming tasks

1. Select `DBGrid1` in the Object Inspector. Open up the **Options** property. Change **dgColLines**, **dgRowLines** to `False` and change **dgRowSelect** to `True`. Compile and run the program (**Shift + Ctrl + F9**). Note that the grid lines disappear at both design time and run time. Also, note that selecting a row at runtime highlights the whole row because **dgRowSelect** is `True`. Stop the application and restore the row and column lines and set **dgRowSelect** to `False`. Compile and run the program (**Shift + Ctrl + F9**). This time selecting a row does not highlight the whole row but only an individual cell.

2. Select `DBGrid1` in the Object Inspector. Change the **DrawingStyle** property from **gdsThemed** to **gdsClassic**. Note the effect on the grid. Now change the **DrawingStyle** property from **gdsClassic** to **gdsGradient**. Note the effect on the grid.

3. Replace the `Employee` table with the `Customer` table.
Set the column formatting as before.

MySQL

FireDAC is able to work with many other database systems. One such system, **MySQL**®, started life as an open-source relational database management system. It is now developed, distributed, and supported by Oracle Corporation® but a free community edition is available which is used extensively by many websites. Installing MySQL is made easy with **MySQL Installer** which may be downloaded from dev.mysql.com/downloads - *Figure 69.14*. Download **MySQL Installer 8.0.23** or later - **Windows (x86, 32-bit), MSI Installer** (**mysql-installer-web-community-8.0.23.0.msi**).

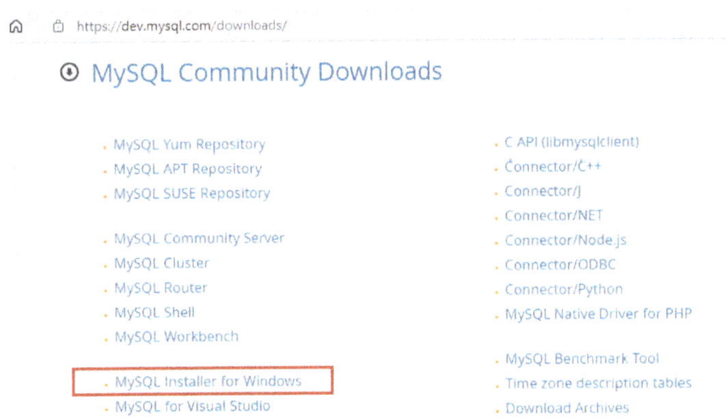

Fig. 69.14 Downloads page for MySQL

Install **MySQL Installer** and then launch it. *Figure 69.15* shows the launched **MySQL Installer** after installing **MySQL Server 5.7.33 x86**, **MySQL Workbench 8.0.23 x64** and the

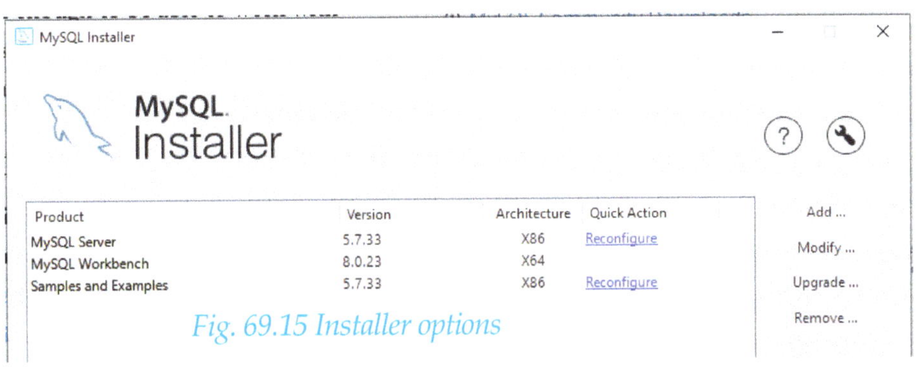

Fig. 69.15 Installer options

folder of **Samples and Examples 5.7.33 x86** for MySQL.

MYSQL Server 5.7.33 is not the most recent MySQL server but it is the most recent 32-bit (x86) server. Later servers are 64-bit. The Delphi IDE is 32-bit, so can only connect to and show data at design time from a MySQL database that is hosted by a local 32-bit MySQL server. However, it is possible to connect to a 64-bit remote MySQL server over TCP/IP and display data at design time.

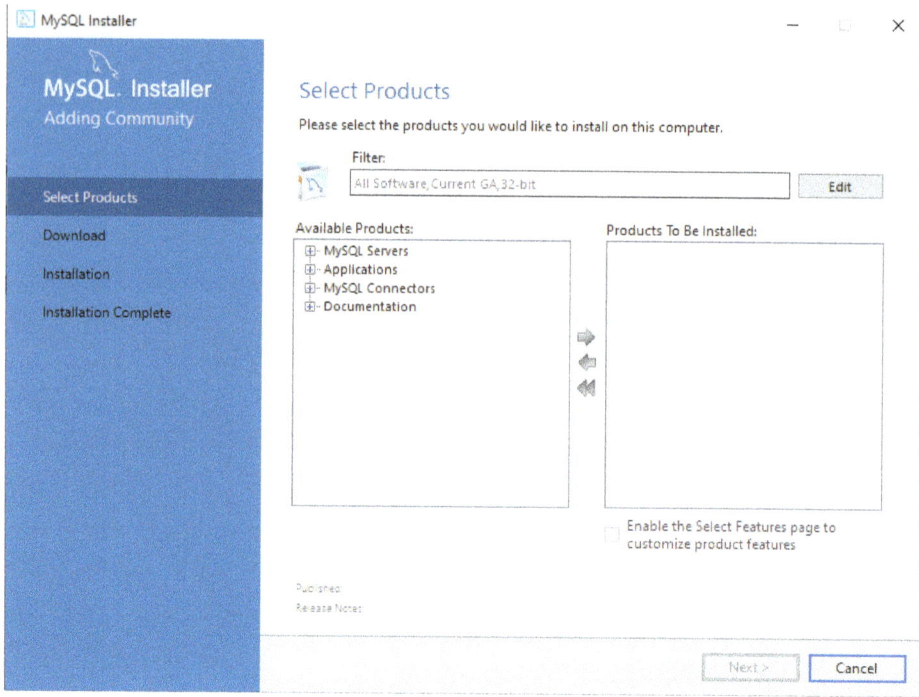

Fig. 69.16 Selecting MySQL products to install - filter set to 32-bit software

Clicking the **Add** button shown in *Figure 69.15* brings up the window shown in *Figure 69.16* from which MySQL servers may be selected for installation. The **Samples and Examples** resource is available from the **Documentation** option. **Install MySQL WorkBench 8.0.23 x64** or later by changing the filter to **Any** as shown in *Figure 69.17*, then open **Applications** and **select**.

When installing or reconfiguring MySQL Server, **install** as a Windows service (*Figure 69.18*) and accept connection via TCP/IP to port 3306, the default port. Set the root user's password.

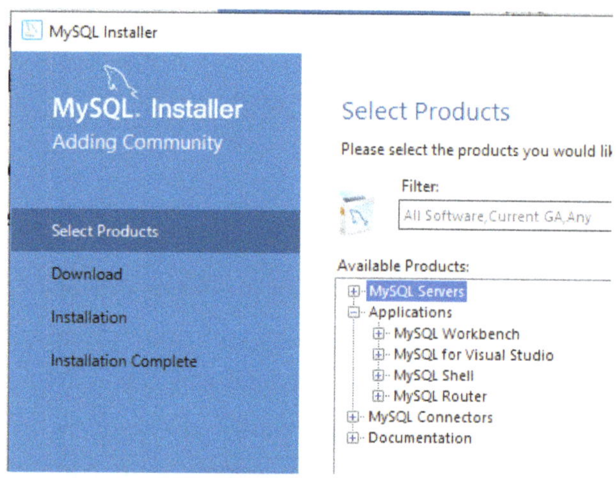

Fig. 69.17 Selecting MySQL products to install - filter set to any software

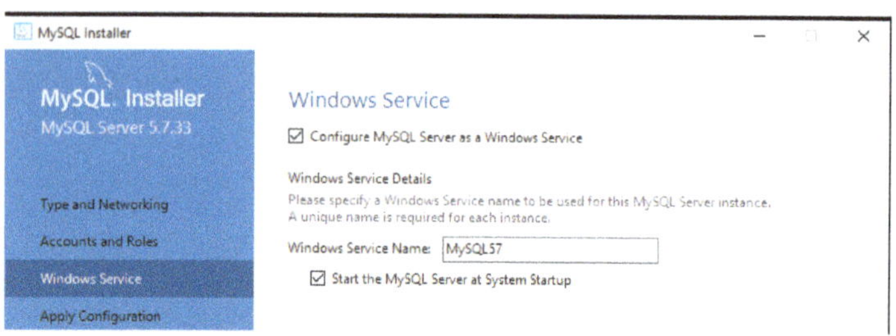

Fig. 69.18 Configuring MySQL server as a Windows service

Open MySQL Workbench. If MySQL Server is up and running on the localhost then the main window of **Workbench** should show a local instance under **MySQL connections** - *Figure 69.19*.

Double click this local instance to connect to the local MySQL server using the login window shown in *Figure 69.20*.

Enter the password that you set for the root user and click **OK**.

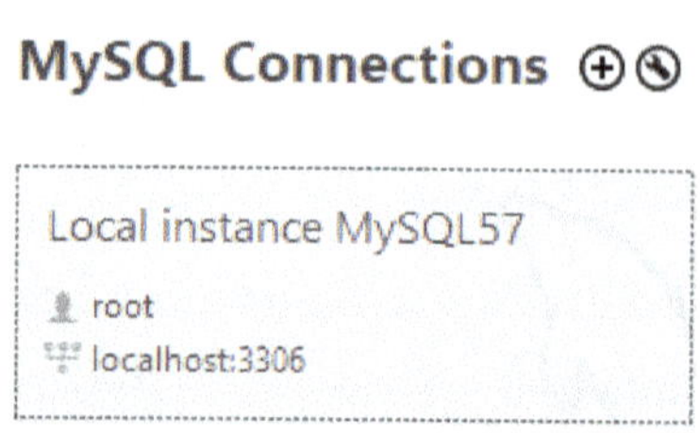

Fig. 69.19 MySQL server running on localhost and listening on port 3306

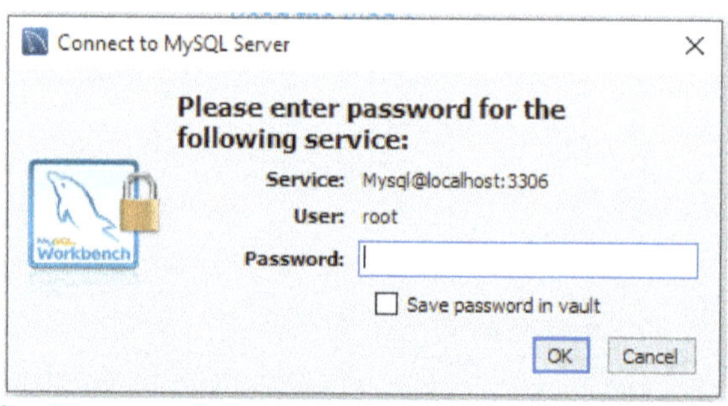

Fig. 69.20 MySQLServer connection login window

Now **select** **Server|Users and Privileges** option from the **Local Instance MySQL57** window to bring up the **Administration** tab - *Figure 69.21*.

Set up a new user, `User1`, by clicking **Add Account** button at bottom of window (not shown in *Figure 69.21*).

Enter the details shown in *Figure 69.22*. It is very important to use the wildcard symbol **%** for the **Limit to Host Matching** field so that the new user may connect to a remote MySQL server. Contrast this with the root user which is restricted to logging in to the localhost only for security reasons - *Figure 69.23*.

Select the **Administrative Roles** and make sure that all checkboxes are deselected. **Select** the **Schema Privileges** tab and tick the **Select** box. **Click** **Add Entry...** button to bring up the **New Schema Privilege Definition** window.

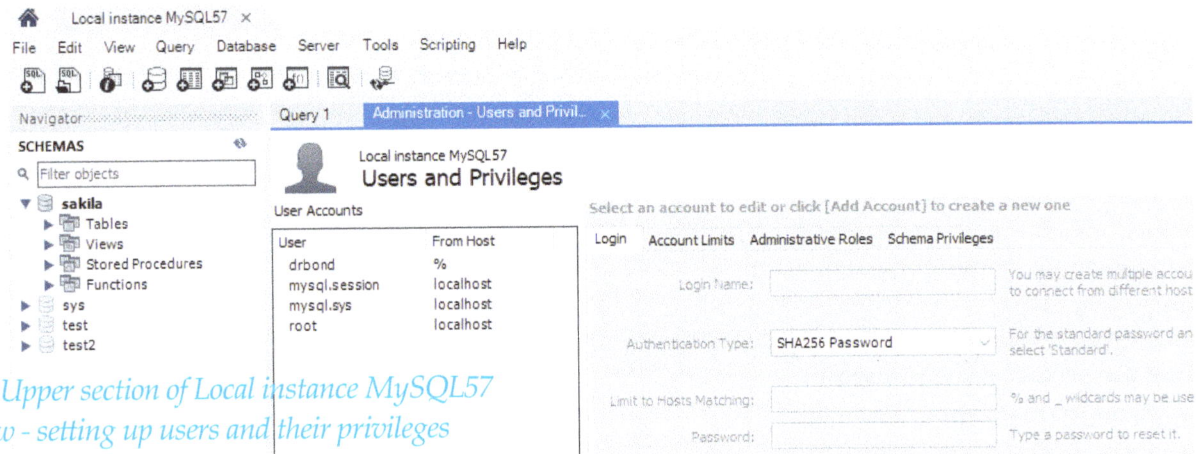

Fig. 69.21 Upper section of Local instance MySQL57 window - setting up users and their privileges

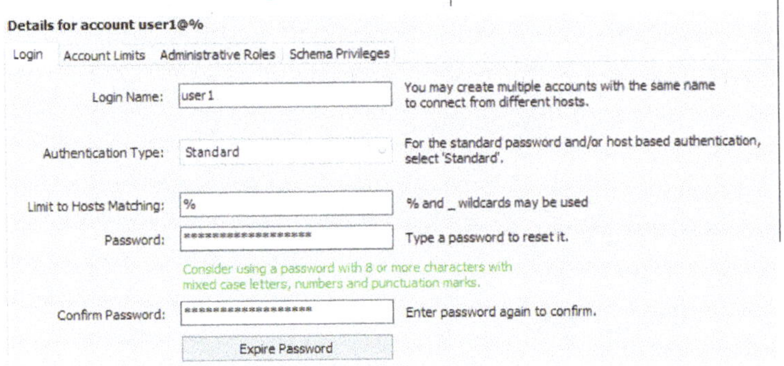

Fig. 69.22 Entering details for new user

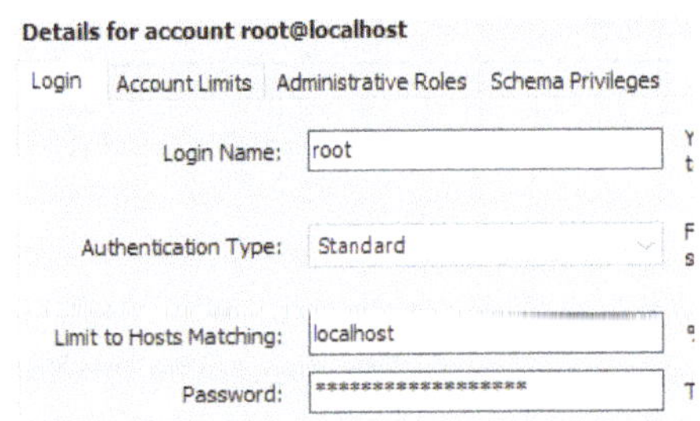

Fig. 69.23 User root restricted to localhost

Click the **Schemas matching pattern** radio button and **add** `sakila%` to the empty field.

Click the **OK** button.

Click the **Select** checkbox in the **Object Rights** panel. **Click** the **Apply** button - *Figure 64.24*.

The next task is to create the `sakila` database from two scripts:

- `sakila-schema.sql`
- `sakila-data.sql`

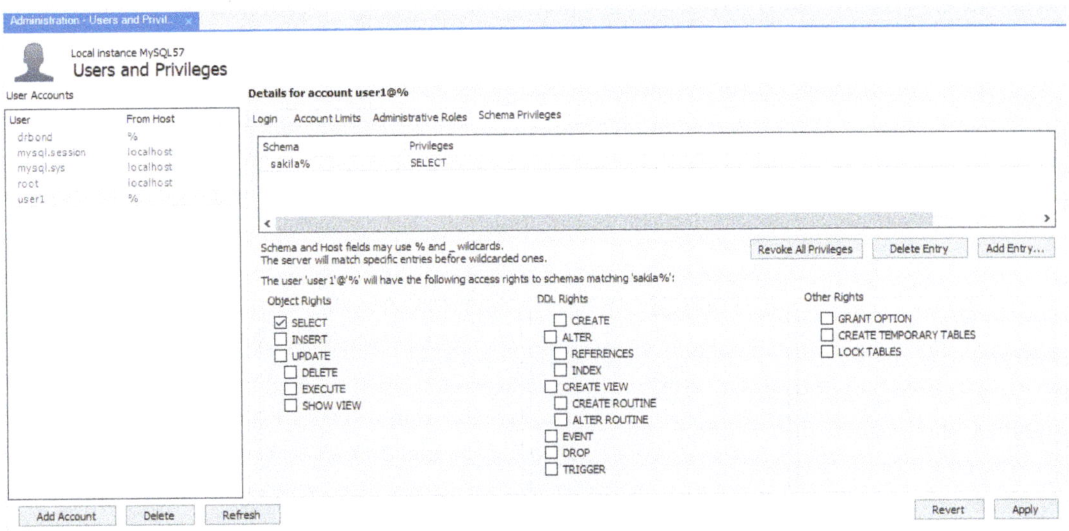

Fig. 69.24 Setting Schema(database) privileges for user1 on any database that begins with name sakila

Launch MySQL Worbench. **Login** to the local instance as `root`.

Click File|Open SQL Script...

Open `sakila-scheme.sql` from its location (`C:\Program Files (x86)\MySQL\Samples and Examples 5.7\Sample Databases\Sakila`)

Execute this script (**Click** ⚡ or **Query|Execute (All or Selection)** or **Ctrl+Shift+Enter**) to create the database structure.

Open `sakila-data.sql` from its location (`C:\Program Files (x86)\MySQL\Samples and Examples 5.7\Sample Databases\Sakila`)

Execute this script (**Click** ⚡ or **Query|Execute (All or Selection)** or **Ctrl+Shift+Enter**) to insert data into the `sakila` database.

The `sakila` database now exists and is shown in the Navigator window by selecting the **Schemas** tab - see *Figure 69.21* and *Figure 69.25*.

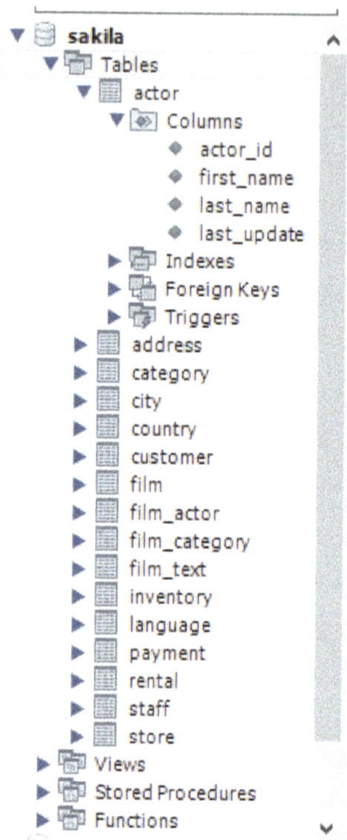

Fig. 69.25 Sakila database structure

Move the mouse pointer over actor to reveal the options menu as shown in *Figure 69.26*.

Click the Table/Result Grid symbol to reveal table data for the `actor` table - *Figure 69.27*.

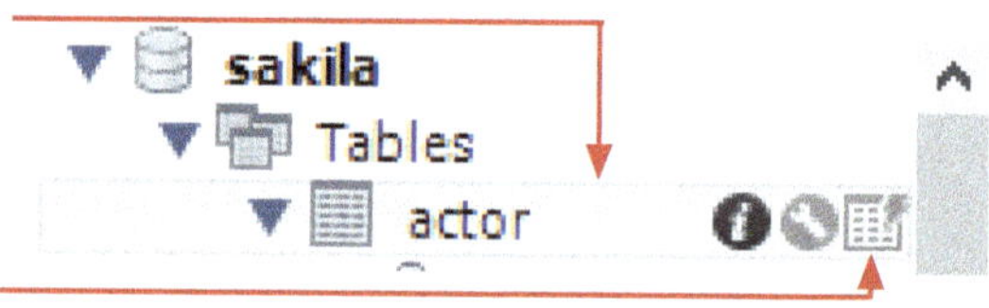

Fig. 69.26 Show data option

Delphi and MySQL

P

Launch Delphi, **select** File|New|Windows VCL Application-Delphi. **Change** the **Name** of `Form1` to `MainForm` and its **Caption** to `Main Form`.

Select File|New|Other|Database|Data Module to create a new unit, `Unit2`, and a TDataModule form, `DataModule1`.

Save `Unit2` as `DataModule.pas` in folder `FireDACSakilaProject`. **Save Project As** `FireDACSakilaProject` in folder `FireDACSakilaProject` and **save** `Unit1`, the main VCL form unit, as `FireDACSakilaUnit` in the same folder.

Click the Data Explorer tab located between the Projects and Palette windows as shown in *Figure 69.28*.

Open the FireDAC option as shown in *Figure 69.29*.

Right click the MySQL Server option to bring up the Add New Connection option as shown in *Figure 69.30*.

This will be used to add a new named connection, `sakila`.

Click the left mouse button with the mouse pointer over **Add New Connection** to bring up the window shown in *Figure 69.31*.

Enter the name `sakila` and click **OK** to bring up the FireDAC Connection Editor window shown in *Figure 69.32*.

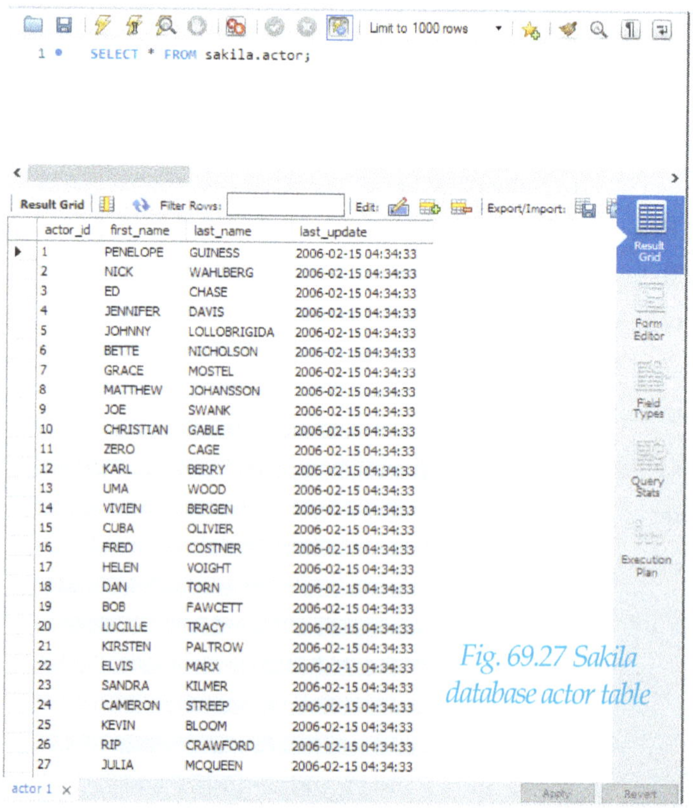

actor_id	first_name	last_name	last_update
1	PENELOPE	GUINESS	2006-02-15 04:34:33
2	NICK	WAHLBERG	2006-02-15 04:34:33
3	ED	CHASE	2006-02-15 04:34:33
4	JENNIFER	DAVIS	2006-02-15 04:34:33
5	JOHNNY	LOLLOBRIGIDA	2006-02-15 04:34:33
6	BETTE	NICHOLSON	2006-02-15 04:34:33
7	GRACE	MOSTEL	2006-02-15 04:34:33
8	MATTHEW	JOHANSSON	2006-02-15 04:34:33
9	JOE	SWANK	2006-02-15 04:34:33
10	CHRISTIAN	GABLE	2006-02-15 04:34:33
11	ZERO	CAGE	2006-02-15 04:34:33
12	KARL	BERRY	2006-02-15 04:34:33
13	UMA	WOOD	2006-02-15 04:34:33
14	VIVIEN	BERGEN	2006-02-15 04:34:33
15	CUBA	OLIVIER	2006-02-15 04:34:33
16	FRED	COSTNER	2006-02-15 04:34:33
17	HELEN	VOIGHT	2006-02-15 04:34:33
18	DAN	TORN	2006-02-15 04:34:33
19	BOB	FAWCETT	2006-02-15 04:34:33
20	LUCILLE	TRACY	2006-02-15 04:34:33
21	KIRSTEN	PALTROW	2006-02-15 04:34:33
22	ELVIS	MARX	2006-02-15 04:34:33
23	SANDRA	KILMER	2006-02-15 04:34:33
24	CAMERON	STREEP	2006-02-15 04:34:33
25	KEVIN	BLOOM	2006-02-15 04:34:33
26	RIP	CRAWFORD	2006-02-15 04:34:33
27	JULIA	MCQUEEN	2006-02-15 04:34:33

Fig. 69.27 Sakila database actor table

Enter the data shown in red in *Figure 69.33* (replace **<LOCAL>** with `127.0.0.1`). **Click OK** to save the settings.

MySQL saves each database table in a separate file unlike many other database systems which use a single file for storing tables. Therefore the **database** field in *Figure 69.33* references a folder. **FireDAC** named connections are stored in a file `FDConnectionDefs.ini` usually located in

`C:\Users\Public\Documents\Embarcadero\Studio\FireDAC`

Figure 69.34 shows a section of the contents of `FDConnectionDefs.ini` and the definition for the named connection `sakila.`

Delphi reads `FDConnectionDefs.ini` at startup and uses what it reads to populate the **Data Explorer** tree for **FireDAC** - *Figure 69.32*.

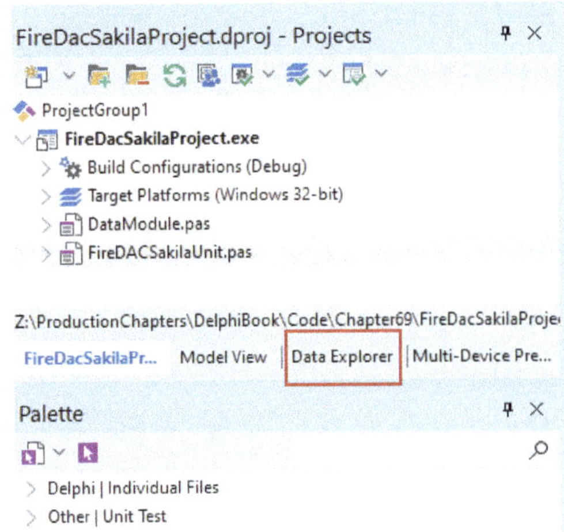

Fig. 69.28 Projects window and the tabs

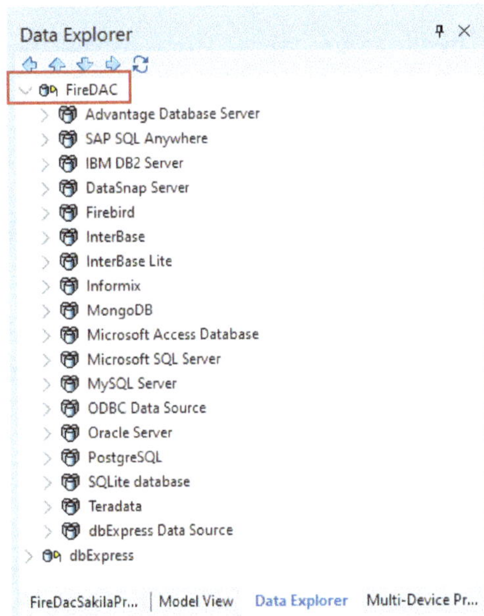

Fig. 69.29 Data Explorer window with FireDAC submenu of connectable database systems

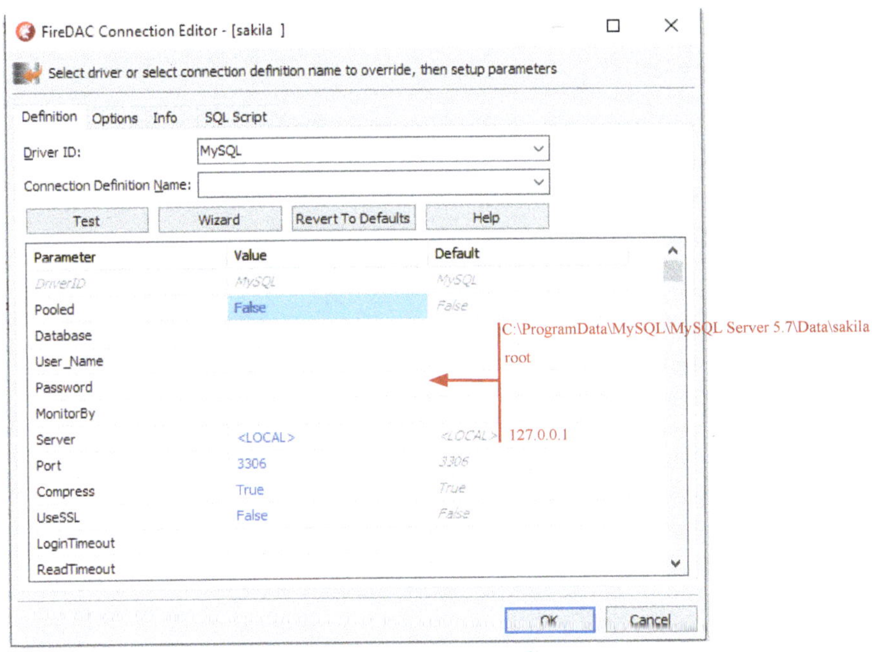

Fig. 69.33 FireDAC Connection Editor

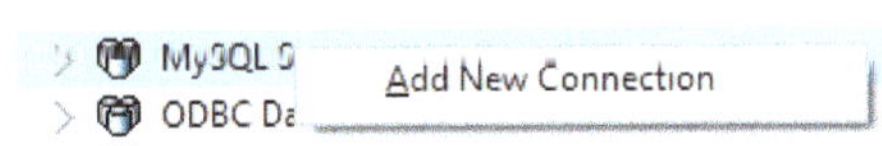

Fig. 69.30 Add New (named) Connection to the MySQL server

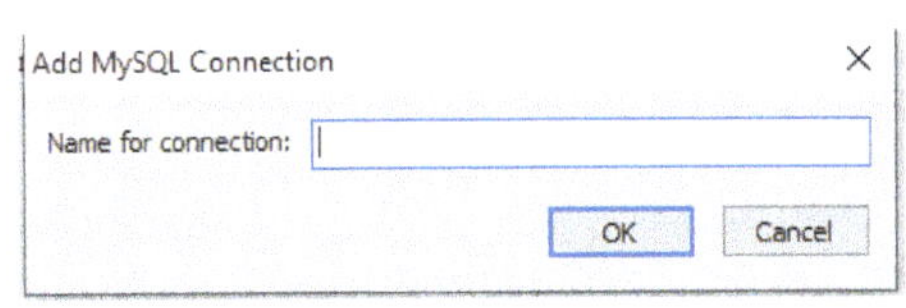

Fig. 69.31 Add MySQL Connection name

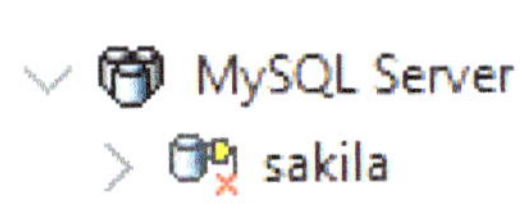

Fig. 69.32 Data Explorer showing MySQL Server and its named connection sakila

```
[IMAGEDB]
DriverID=IB
Protocol=TCPIP
Database=localhost:C:\Users\drbond\imagesdb.ib
User_Name=sysdba
Password=masterkey
CharacterSet=
ExtendedMetadata=True

[LibDB2020]
DriverID=IB
Protocol=TCPIP
Database=localhost:C:\Users\drbond\libdb2020.ib
User_Name=sysdba
Password=masterkey
CharacterSet=
ExtendedMetadata=True

[test]
Database=C:\ProgramData\MySQL\MySQL Server 5.7\Data\test
User_Name=root
Server=127.0.0.1
DriverID=MySQL

[sakila]
Database=C:\ProgramData\MySQL\MySQL Server 5.7\Data\sakila
User_Name=root
Server=127.0.0.1
DriverID=MySQL
```

Fig. 69.34 Section of FDConnectionDefs.ini file where named connections are stored

Add a **TFDConnection** component, `FDConnection1`, from the **FireDAC** page of the component palette to the **TDataModule** form, `DataModule1`. **Rename** this component `SakilaConnection`.

Double click this component to open the **FireDAC Connection editor** for `SakilaConnection` - *Figure 69.35*.

Use `sakila` for the **Database** field (very important that you don't use the actual path to the folder containing this database's table files - Delphi will not recognise the database if you do). Use `root` for the **User_Name** field, `127.0.0.1` for the **Server** field and `3306` for the **Port** field. **Click OK**.

The **MySQL driver** code resides in a **dll** that the program needs to use to gain access to the referenced MySQL database, `sakila`.

The easiest way is to open the file `FDDrivers.ini` in a text editor such as **Notepad++** and add the following before saving the file

```
[MySQL]
VendorLib=C:\Program Files (x86)\MySQL\MySQL Server 5.7\lib\libmysql.dll
```

The file `FDDrivers.ini` is usually located in

```
C:\Users\Public\Documents\Embarcadero\Studio\FireDAC
```

`FDDrivers.ini` is read when Delphi is started so it must be restarted to register any changes made whilst it is running.

Alternatively, **add** a **TFDPhysMySQLDriverLink** component from the **FireDAC Links** tab of the component palette to the data module form. This component's **VendorLib** property must then be assigned the path shown above.

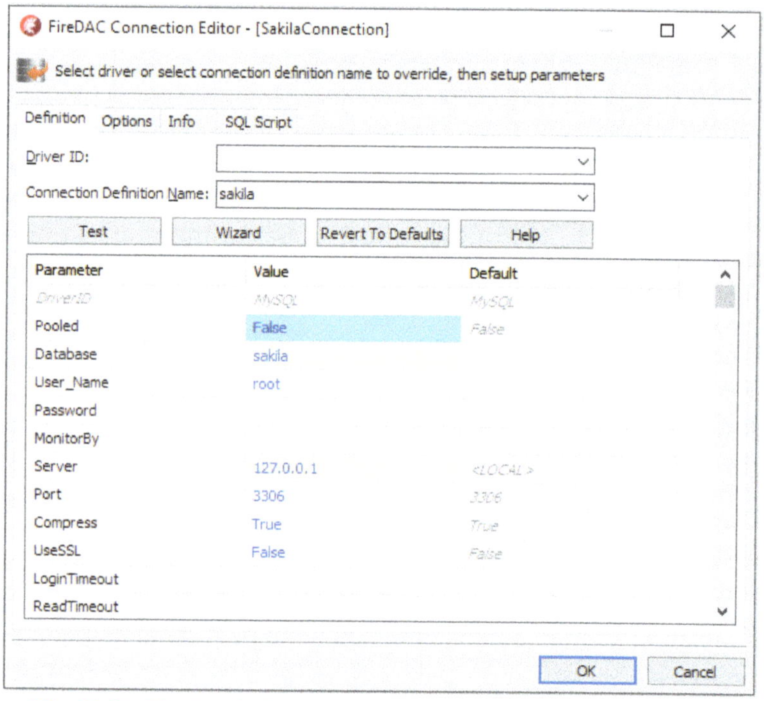

Fig. 69.35 FireDAC Connection Editor window that appears after SakilaConnection double-clicked

Add a **TFDGUIxLoginDialog** component, `FDGUIxLoginDialog1`, to the data module form.

Set LoginDialog property in the **Object Inspector** of `SakilaConnection` to `FDGUIxLoginDialog1` and its **LoginPrompt** property to `True`.

Double click the **Connection** field in the **Object Inspector** of `SakilaConnection` to bring up the **FireDAC Login** window shown in *Figure 69.36*.

Enter the password that you chose when setting up **MySQL** server. If all has worked, the **Connected** property should change from `False` to `True`.

Assuming success, **add** a **TFDTable** component from the **FireDAC** tab of the component palette to the data module form. **Change** its name to `ActorTable`.

Change its **Connection** property in the **Object Inspector** to `SakilaConnection` and its **TableName** property to `sakila.actor`.

Click its **Active** property field to set it to `True`.

Switch to form `MainForm`, unit `FireDACSakilaUnit`. **Add** `DataModule` to the unit's **Uses** statement.

Add four **TPanel** components to the form and **rename** them as follows

```
PanelForTitle
PanelDBNavigator
PanelActorDBGrid
PanelQueryDBGrid
```

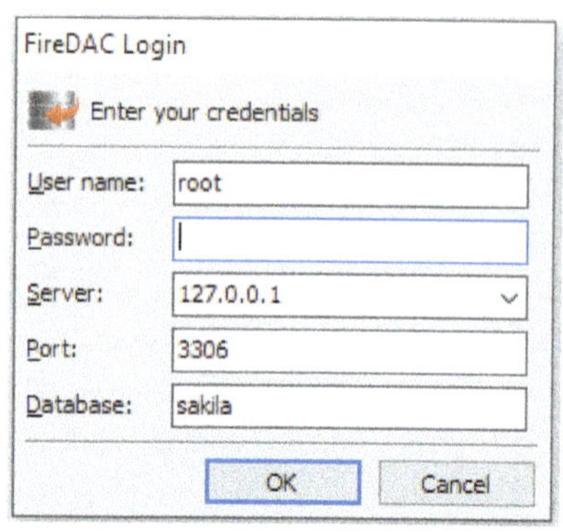

Fig. 69.36 FireDAC Login window for SakilaConnection

Set the **Align** property of `PanelDBNavigator` to **alTop** and its **Height** property to 41.
Set the **Align** property of `PanelForTitle` to **alTop** and its **Height** property to 41.
Set the **Align** property of `PanelActorDBGrid` to **alTop** and its **Height** property to 303.
Set the **Align** property of `PanelQueryDBGrid` to **alClient**.
Place a **TDBGrid** component from the **Data Controls** tab of the component palette on the `PanelActorDBGrid`. **Rename** it `DBGridActorDataSet`.
Set its **Align** property to **alClient**.
Place a **TDBGrid** component from the **Data Controls** tab of the component palette on the `PanelQueryDBGrid`. **Rename** it `DBGridQueryDataSet`. **Set** its **Align** property to **alClient**.
Place a **TDBNavigator** component, `DBNavigator1`, from the **Data Controls** tab of the component palette on the `PanelDBNavigator`. **Set** its **Align** property to **alClient**. and deselect all but **nbFirst**, **nbNext**, **nbPrior** and **nbLast** buttons of **VisibleButtons** property.

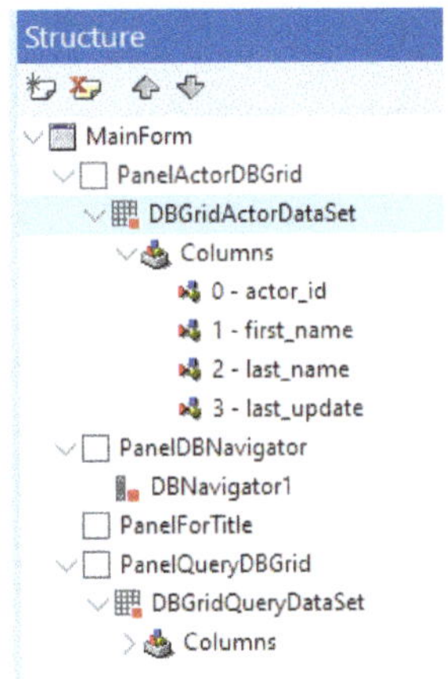

Fig. 69.37 Structure pane

Change the **Caption** property of `PanelForTitle` to `MySQL Database Sakila`. Set its **Alignment** property to **taCenter**.
Open the **Columns** property for `DBGridActorDataSet` in the **Structure** pane as shown in Figure *69.37*. **Select** each column in the **Structure** pane in turn and **change** the two properties **Alignment** and **Title.Alignment** to **taCenter**.
Set `DBGridActorDataSet.Options.dgIndicator` to False and `DBGridActorDataSet.Options.dgRowSelect` to `True`.
Switch to the `DataModule1` form, unit `DataModule`.
Add a **TFDQuery** component form the **FireDAC** tab of the component palette and name it `ActorFilmQuery`.
Add two **TDataSource** components from the **Data Access** tab of the component palette.
Rename them `ActorDataSource` and `FilmDataSource` respectively.
Connect their **DataSet** property to `ActorTable` and `ActorFilmQuery`, respectively.
Switch to form `MainForm`, unit `FireDACSakilaUnit`.
Set the **DataSource** property of `DBGridActorDataSet` to `DataModule1.ActorDataSource`.
Set the **DataSource** property of `DBGridQueryDataSet` to `DataModule1.FilmDataSource`.
Set the **DataSource** property of `DBNavigator1` to `DataModule1.ActorDataSource`.
The `Main Form` should now look very similar to that shown in *Figure 69.38* with the exception of the column headings and widths. To change the column headings to match those of *Figure 69.38*, **edit** the **Title.Caption** property of each column of `DBGridActorDataSet` and `DBGridQueryDataSet`, when the latter becomes available. **Adjust** the column widths by selecting each column in the **Structure** pane.

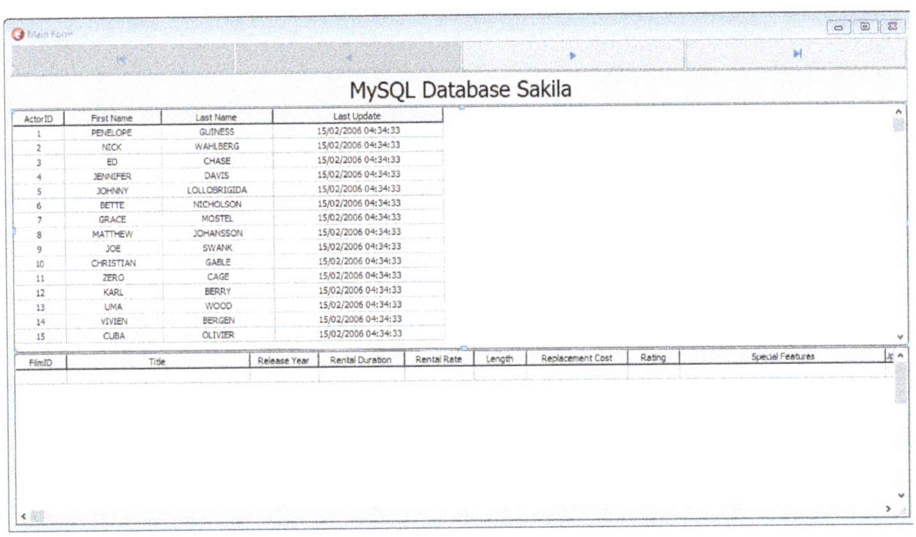

Fig. 69.38 Design stage showing data from the Actor table of sakila database

Select the `ActorFilmQuery` component on the data module form. **Open** the **String List Editor** for the **SQL** property in the **Object Inspector** and add the following select SQL query

```
Select DISTINCT * From film, film_actor, actor
  Where (film.film_id = film_actor.film_id) And (actor.actor_id = film_actor.actor_id)
           And (film_actor.actor_id = :SelectedActor)
```

Click OK.

This SQL Select statement creates a query parameter `SelectedActor` shown in *Figure 69.39*. **Select** this parameter in the **Structure** pane and then set its properties as shown in *Figure 69.39*. The default value for `SelectedActor` is now 1.

Set the **Active** property of `ActorFilmQuery` to `True`.

The `Main Form` should now look similar to that shown in *Figure 69.40*.

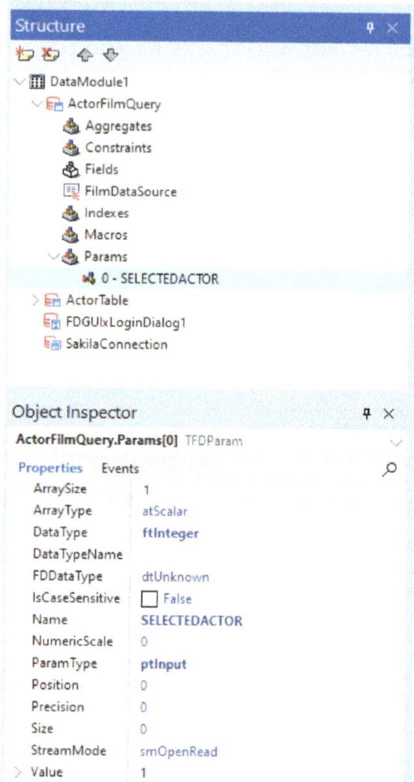

Fig. 69.39 Setting up query parameter SelectedActor

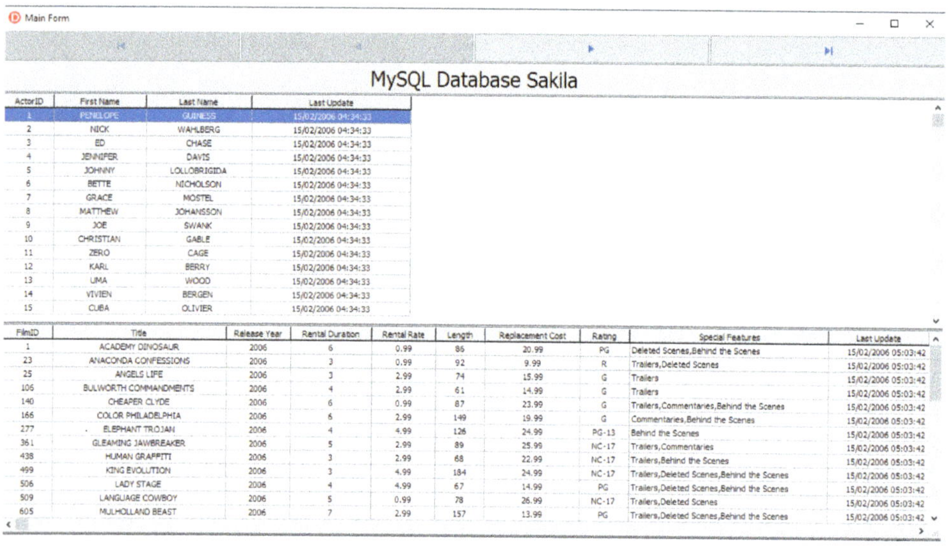

Fig. 69.40 Design stage showing data from the Actor table and using a query, the films that the currently selected actor has acted in

Select `DBNavigator1` and create an **OnClick** event handler adding the code shown in *Table 69.1* to its body.

```
Procedure TMainForm.DBNavigator1Click(Sender : TObject; Button : TNavigateBtn);
  Begin
    With DataModule1
      Do
        Begin
          ActorFilmQuery.DisableControls;
          Try
            ActorFilmQuery.Close;
            ActorFilmQuery.ParamByName('SelectedActor').AsInteger
              := ActorTable.FieldByName('actor_id').AsInteger;
            ActorFilmQuery.Open;
          Finally
            ActorFilmQuery.EnableControls;
          End;
        End;
  End;
```

Table 69.1 Event handler that is called when the navigator buttons of DBNavigator are clicked

Select `DBGridActorDataSet` and create an **OnCellClick** event handler adding the code shown in *Table 69.2* to its body.

```
Procedure TMainForm.DBGridActorDataSetCellClick(Column : TColumn);
  Begin
    With DataModule1
      Do
        Begin
          ActorFilmQuery.DisableControls;
          Try
            ActorFilmQuery.Close;
            ActorFilmQuery.ParamByName('SelectedActor').AsInteger
              := ActorTable.FieldByName('actor_id').AsInteger;
            ActorFilmQuery.Open;
          Finally
            ActorFilmQuery.EnableControls;
          End;
        End;
  End;
```

Table 69.2 Event handler that is called when a cell of grid DBGridActorDataSet is clicked

Save the project and its units by selecting **File|Save All**.
Run the project (**Shift+Ctrl+F9**).
Figure 69.38 shows the application `FireDACSakilaProject` in execution.

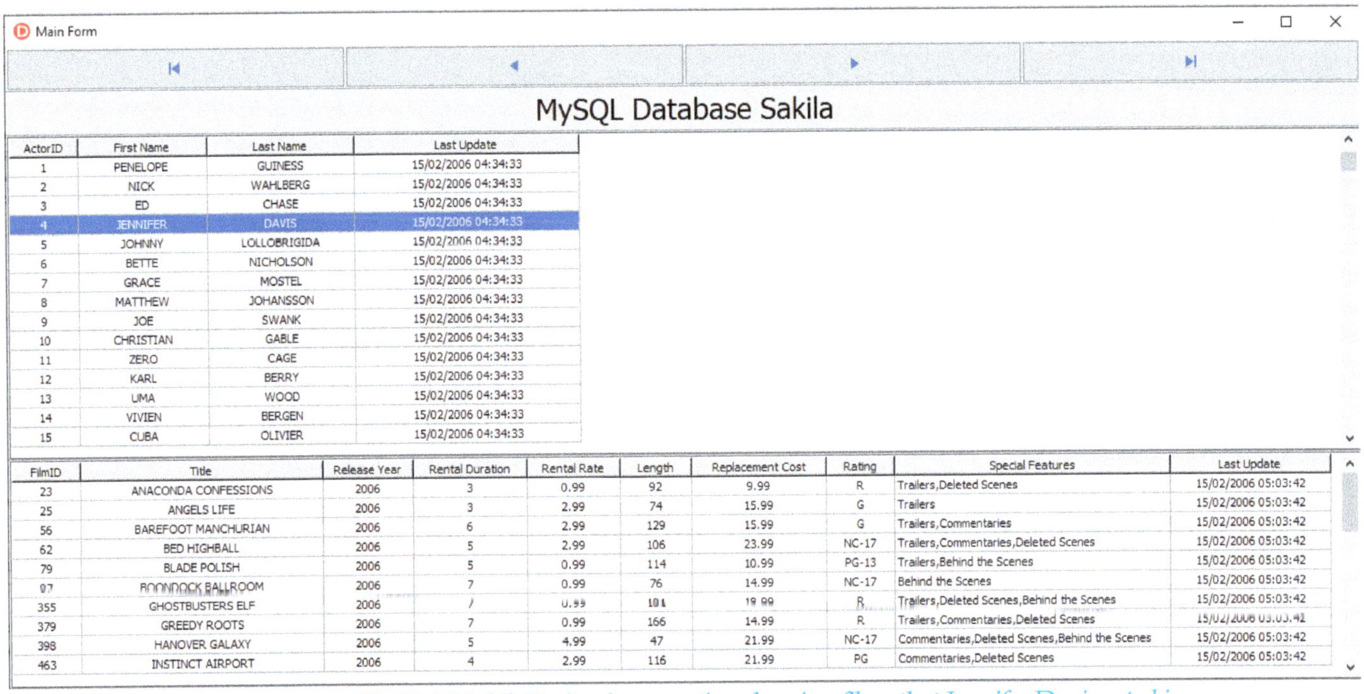

Fig. 69.41 FireDACSakilaProject in execution showing films that Jennifer Davis acted in

Now **set** `DBGridActorDataSet.Options.dgIndicator` to `False` and create the event handler shown in *Table 69.3* for the **AfterScroll** event of the `ActorTable`. **Build** and **run** `FireDACSakilaProject` again. **Change** rows by clicking the far left side of the required row. *Figure 69.42* shows the result.

```
Procedure TDataModule1.ActorTableAfterScroll(DataSet : TDataSet);
  Begin
    With DataModule1
      Do
        Begin
          ActorFilmQuery.DisableControls;
          Try
            ActorFilmQuery.Close;
            ActorFilmQuery.ParamByName('SelectedActor').AsInteger
              := ActorTable.FieldByName('actor_id').AsInteger;
            ActorFilmQuery.Open;
          Finally
            ActorFilmQuery.EnableControls;
          End;
        End;
  End;
```

Table 69.3 Event handler that is called when the grid DBGridActorDataSet is scrolled by selecting a row using the indicator bar on the far left side of the grid

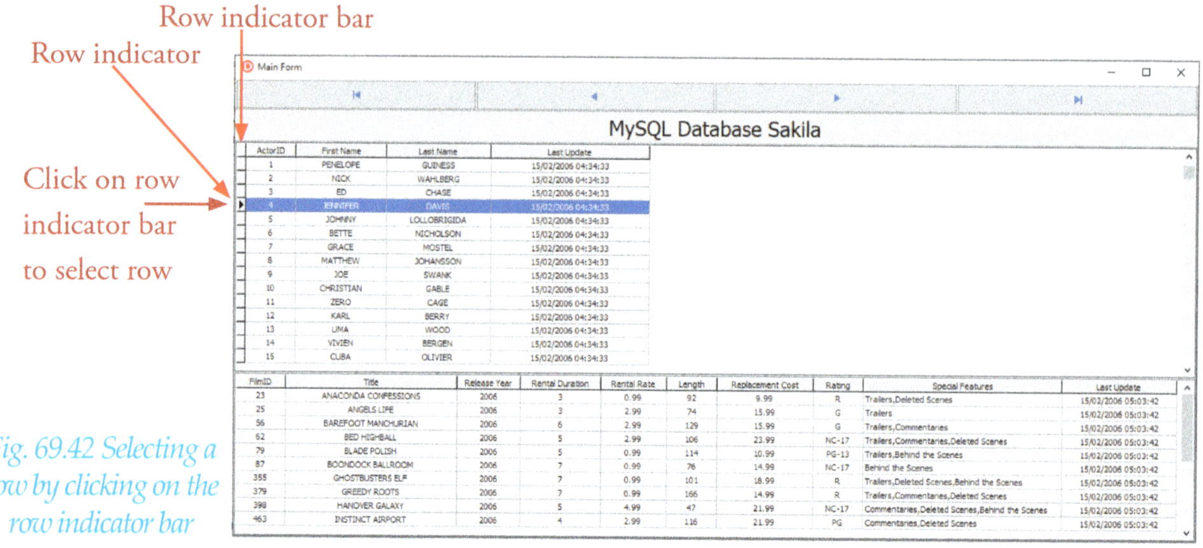

Fig. 69.42 Selecting a row by clicking on the row indicator bar

Setting up other users

It is not a good idea to use the `root` user for connecting to MySQL databases from Delphi programs, generally. It is better to set up users and grant these users access rights that they need to do their job. For example, a user permitted to view data but not change it, or add to it or delete it should be restricted to **Select** only operations. Access rights may be configured in **MySQL Workbench**.

Launch **MySQL Workbench** and **select** `Local Instance MySQL57` (or whatever you called your local instance) then **select** **Server|Users and Privileges**. **Click** the **Add Account** button shown in *Figure 69.43* to add another user. **Choose** a username, e.g. `user1`, set a password and use the wildcard, %, in the **Limit to Host Matching** field. **Switch** to the **Schema Privileges** tab and click **Add Entry** button. **Select** the radio button for **Selected schema** in the **New Schema Privilege Definition** window which pops up. **Select** `sakila` from the dropdown list. **Click** **OK**. In the **Schema Privileges** tab now choose **Select** in the **Object Rights** panel by checking the checkbox. **Click** **Apply**.

Now **run** `FireDACSakilaProject` using user `user1` and check that the data is still viewable.

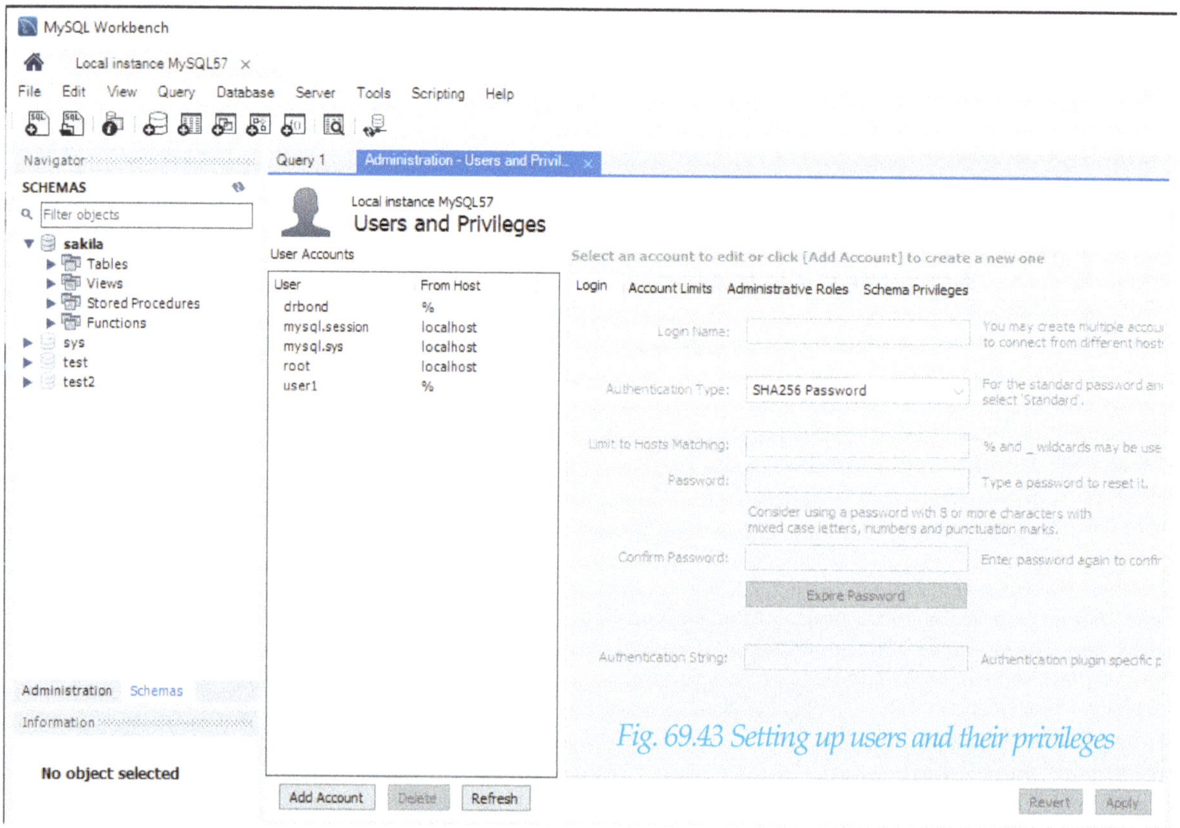

Fig. 69.43 Setting up users and their privileges

Now create another user, `user2`, but this time assign the new user the following object rights

P

Select, **Insert**, **Update** and **Delete**

Create a new Delphi VCL project. **Save** `Unit1`, the main VCL form unit, as `FireDACSakilaStaffUnit` in folder `FireDACSakilaStaffProject` together with the project source, `FireDACSakilaStaffProject.dproj`.

Change the **Name** of `Form1` to `MainForm` and its **Caption** to `Main Form`.

Select **File|New|Other|Database|Data Module** to create a new unit, `Unit2`, and a **TDataModule** form, `DataModule1`.

Save `Unit2` as `DataModule.pas` in folder `FireDACSakilaStaffProject`. **Add** a **TFDConnection** component, `FDConnection1`, from the **FireDAC** page of the component palette to the **TDataModule** form, `DataModule1`.

Rename this component `SakilaConnection`.

Double click this component to open the **FireDAC Connection editor** for `SakilaConnection` - *Figure 69.35*.

Use `sakila` for the **Database** field (very important that you don't use the actual path to the folder containing this database's table files - Delphi will not recognise the database if you do). Set the **Driver ID** to **MySQL**. Use `user2` for the **User_Name** field, `127.0.0.1` for the **Server** field and `3306` for the **Port** field. **Click** **OK**.

Refer to the previous section and use the same approach as before for setting up access to the **MySQL driver** dll.

Add a **TFDGUIxLoginDialog** component, `FDGUIxLoginDialog1`, to the data module form.

Set **LoginDialog** property in the **Object Inspector** of `SakilaConnection` to `FDGUIxLoginDialog1` and its **LoginPrompt** property to `True`.

Double click the **Connection** field in the **Object Inspector** of `SakilaConnection` to bring up the **FireDAC Login** window shown in *Figure 69.33*. **Set** user name to `user2`. **Enter** the password for `user2`. If all has worked, the **Connected** property should change from `False` to `True`.

Add a **TFDTable** component from the **FireDAC** tab of the component palette to the data module form. **Change** its name to `StaffTable`.

Change its **Connection** property in the **Object Inspector** to `SakilaConnection` and its **TableName** property to `sakila.staff` (select from the dropdown list).

Click its **Active** property field to set it to `True`.

Switch to form `MainForm`, unit `FireDACSakilaStaffUnit`.

Set `MainForm` **Height** property to 340.

Add four **TPanel** components to the form and rename them as follows

```
PanelForTitle
PanelForDBNavigator
PanelForStaffDBGrid
PanelForButtons
```

Set the **Align** property of `PanelForDBNavigator` to **alTop** and its **Height** property to 41.

Set the **Align** property of `PanelForTitle` to **alTop** and its **Height** property to 41. **Set** its **Caption** property to `Sakila Database Staff Table` and its **Font|Size** property to 21.

Set the **Align** property of `PanelForStaffDBGrid` to **alTop** and its **Height** property to 183.

Set the **Align** property of `PanelForButtons` to **alClient**.

Place a **TDBGrid** component from the **Data Controls** tab of the component palette on `PanelStaffDBGrid`.

Rename it `DBGridStaffDataSet`.

Set its **Align** property to **alClient**.

Add `DataModule` to the list of units in the **Uses** section of the `FireDACSakilaStaffUnit`.

Set `DBGridStaffDataSet`'s **DataSource** property to `DataModule.DataSource1`.

Data from the `Staff` table should appear in the grid. Grid column widths may be adjusted directly by dragging the column vertical grid lines left or right.

Set DBNavigator1's **DataSource** property to DataModule.DataSource1.

Add three **TButton** components to the PanelForButtons, rename them btnInsert, btnUpdate and btnDelete, respectively. **Change** their captions to Insert, Update and Delete.

The Main Form should now resemble that shown in *Figure 69.44*.

Save All.

Now **build** and **run** the application.

Enter the FireDAC login credentials user2 and the password for user2.

It should now be possible to use the DBNavigator component to

- navigate between the two rows
- edit a row
- insert a new row
- delete a row
- cancel any changes
- commit any changes to the database
- refresh the grid.

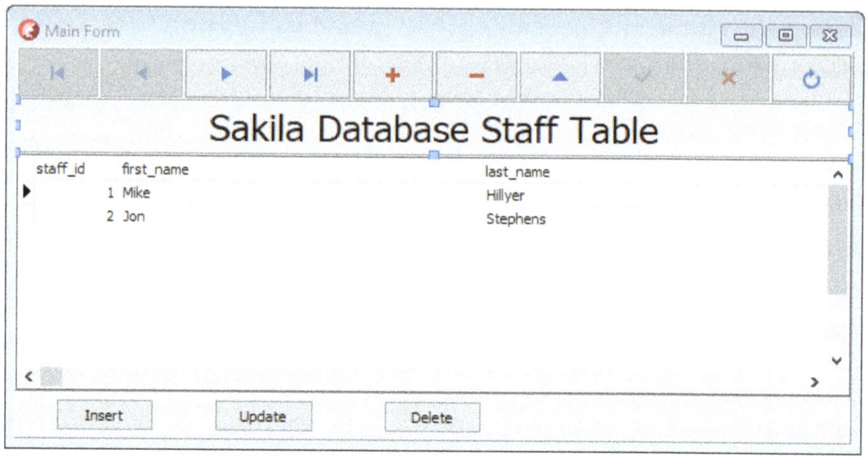

Fig. 69.44 Design of user interface for FireDACSakilaStaffProject

Close the application.

Create a new form (**File|New|VCL Form - Delphi**). **Change** the following properties of this form in the **Object Inspector** as follows

- **BorderStyle** to **bsDialog**
- **Name** to frmStaffData
- **Caption** to Staff Data
- **Width** to 296
- **Height** to 426

Add eight **TEdit** boxes and eight **TLabel** components to the form and rename them as follows

edtFirstName	lblFirstName
edtLastName	lblLastName
edtAddressID	lblAddressID
edtEmail	lblEmail
edtStoreID	lblStoreID
edtActive	lblActive
edtUserName	lblUserName
edtPassword	lblPassword

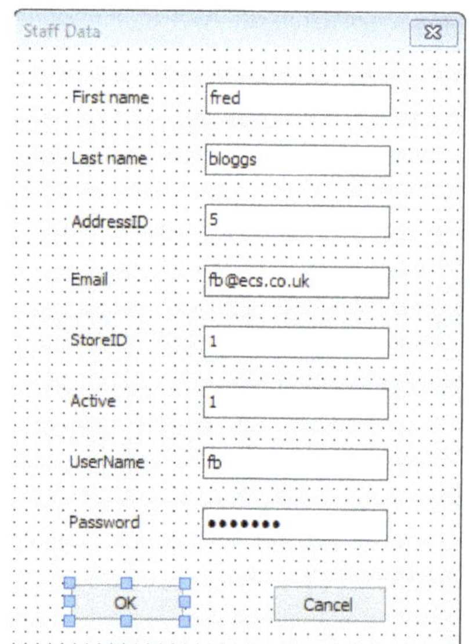

Fig. 69.45 Design of user interface for frmStaffData

Add two **TButton** components to the form, **rename** them btnOK and btnCancel and **change** their captions to OK and Cancel respectively.

Arrange these as shown in *Figure 69.45*. **Set** the **PasswordChar** property of edtPassword to the character '*'.

For convenience, **enter** the data shown in *Figure 69.45*, so that the design can be tested with minimum effort.

Add a reference to the DataModule unit to the list of units in the **Uses** clause of the Interface section. **Add** the statement Uses FireDACSakilaStaffUnit; to the Implementation section just below {$R *.dfm}. **Save** the unit as DataCollection.pas.

Add an **FDQuery** component to form DataModule1 and change its name to FDInsertQuery. **Open** the **SQL String List Editor** by clicking the ellipsis (...) in the **SQL** property field of FDInsertQuery in the **Object Inspector**. **Add** the **SQL Insert** statement shown in *Table 69.4*.

This creates the named parameters shown in *Figure 69.46*.

```
Insert into Staff(staff_id, first_name, last_name, address_id, email,
store_id, active, username, password, last_update) Values(:NextStaffId,
:FirstName, :LastName, :AddressID, :Email, :StoreID, :Active, :UserName,
:Password, :Today);
```

Table 69.4 SQL Insert

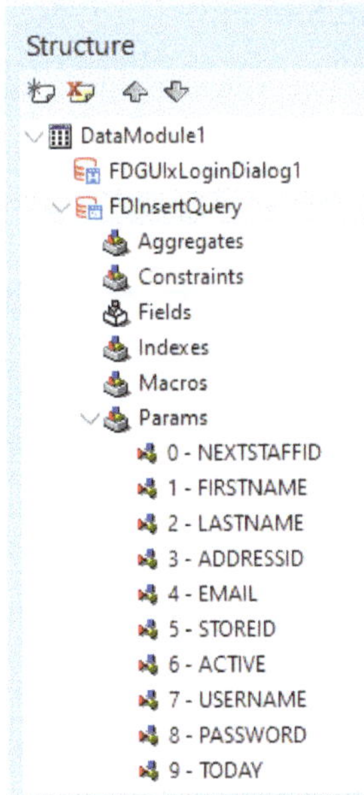

Fig. 69.46 Named parameters for Insert statement

Set the data type in the **Object Inspector** of each named parameter as follows

- `NextStaffID` `ftInteger`
- `FirstName` `ftString`
- `LastName` `ftString`
- `AddressID` `ftInteger`
- `Email` `ftString`
- `StoreID` `ftInteger`
- `Active` `ftInteger`
- `UserName` `ftString`
- `Password` `ftString`
- `Today` `ftDateTime`

Switch to the staff data form, `frmStaffData`.

Double click the `OK` button to create an **OnClick** event handler.

Enter the code shown in *Table 69.5*.

ExecSQLScalar returns the value of the first column in the first row of the first result set, but there is only one value in the result set, the highest value of `staff_id`. Adding one generates the next value.

Double click the `Cancel` button to create an **OnClick** event handler.

Enter the code shown in *Table 69.6*.

```
Procedure TfrmStaffData.btnOKClick(Sender : TObject);
  Var
    NextStaffId : Integer;
  Begin
    frmStaffData.Hide;
    If Not DataModule1.SakilaConnection.Connected
      Then Exit;
    NextStaffId := DataModule1.SakilaConnection.ExecSQLScalar('Select MAX(staff_id) From Staff') + 1;
    DataModule1.FDInsertQuery.ParamByName('NextStaffID').AsInteger := NextStaffId;
    DataModule1.FDInsertQuery.ParamByName('FirstName').AsString := edtFirstName.Text;
    DataModule1.FDInsertQuery.ParamByName('LastName').AsString := edtLastName.Text;
    DataModule1.FDInsertQuery.ParamByName('AddressID').AsInteger := StrToInt(edtAddressID.Text);
    DataModule1.FDInsertQuery.ParamByName('Email').AsString := edtEmail.Text;
    DataModule1.FDInsertQuery.ParamByName('StoreID').AsInteger := StrToInt(edtStoreID.Text);
    DataModule1.FDInsertQuery.ParamByName('Active').AsInteger := StrToInt(edtActive.Text);
    DataModule1.FDInsertQuery.ParamByName('UserName').AsString := edtUserName.Text;
    DataModule1.FDInsertQuery.ParamByName('Password').AsString := edtPassword.Text;
    DataModule1.FDInsertQuery.ParamByName('Today').AsDateTime := Now();
    DataModule1.FDInsertQuery.ExecSQL;
    DataModule1.StaffTable.Refresh;
    MainForm.Visible := True;
  End;
```

Table 69.5 OnClick event handler for the OK button

Select the form and in the **Events** page of the **Object Inspector**, **double click** the empty event handler field of the **OnClose** event to create one. **Fill** the body of this event handler as shown in *Table 69.7*.

```
Procedure TfrmStaffData.btnCancelClick(Sender : TObject);
  Begin
    frmStaffData.Hide;
    MainForm.Visible := True;
  End;
```

Table 69.6 OnClick event handler for the Cancel button

```
Procedure TfrmStaffData.FormClose(Sender : TObject; Var Action : TCloseAction);
  Begin
    frmStaffData.Hide;
    MainForm.Visible := True;
  End;
```

Table 69.7 OnForm event handler

Switch to unit `FireDACSakilaStaffUnit`.

Add the following unit references to the **Uses** clause: `DataModule`, `DataCollection`, `FireDAC.Stan.Param`.

Double click the `Insert` button to create an **OnClick** event handler.

Enter the code shown in *Table 69.8*.

```
Procedure TMainForm.btnInsertClick(Sender: TObject);
  Begin
    DataCollection.frmStaffData.Visible := True;
  End;
```

Table 69.8 OnClick event handler for the Insert button

Double click the `Update` button to create an **OnClick** event handler.

Enter the code shown in *Table 69.9*.

```
Procedure TMainForm.btnUpdateClick(Sender : TObject);
  Var
    intStaffID : Integer;
    strNewPassword : String;
  Begin
    If Not DataModule1.SakilaConnection.Connected
      Then Exit;
    intStaffID := StrToInt(InputBox('Update password', 'Input StaffID of person requesting a password change', '0'));
    strNewPassword := InputBox('Update password', 'Input new password', '');
    DataModule1.SakilaConnection.ExecSQL('Update Staff Set password = :NewPassword, last_update = :LastUpdate'
       + ' where staff_id = :StaffID', [strNewPassword, Now(), intStaffID]);
    DataModule1.StaffTable.Refresh;
  End;
```

Table 69.9 OnClick event handler for the Update button

Double click the `Delete` button to create an **OnClick** event handler.

Enter the code shown in *Table 69.10*.

```
Procedure TMainForm.btnDeleteClick(Sender : TObject);
  Var
    intStaffID : Integer;
  Begin
    If Not DataModule1.SakilaConnection.Connected
      Then Exit;
    intStaffID := StrToInt(InputBox('Delete record', 'Input StaffID of the record you wish to delete', '0'));
    DataModule1.SakilaConnection.ExecSQL('Delete From Staff Where staff_id = :StaffID', [intStaffID]);
    DataModule1.StaffTable.Refresh;
  End;
```

Table 69.10 OnClick event handler for the Delete button

Both `btnUpdateClick` and `btnDeleteClick` rely on the overloaded function `ExecSQL`, in particular, the one with signature

```
Function ExecSQL(Const ASQL: String; AParams: TFDParams): LongInt; Overload;
```

In *Table 69.9*, the formal parameter `ASQL` corresponds to the actual parameter

`'Update Staff Set password = :NewPassword, last_update = :LastUpdate' + ' where staff_id = :StaffID'`

This string defines three SQL params, `NewPassword`, `LastUpdate` and `StaffID`.

In *Table 69.9*, the formal parameter `AParams` corresponds to the actual parameter `[strNewPassword, Now(), intStaffID]`, a list made up of a new password string, a **TDateTime** value returned by `Now()`, and an integer value which should be that of an existing `staff_id`.

Save All.

Build and **run** the application.

Figure 69.47 shows the running application after the `Insert` button has been clicked to insert a new record.

Note that the use of the value 1 for the `Active` field datum results in the stored value `True`. If the value 0 had been used then the stored value would have been `False`.

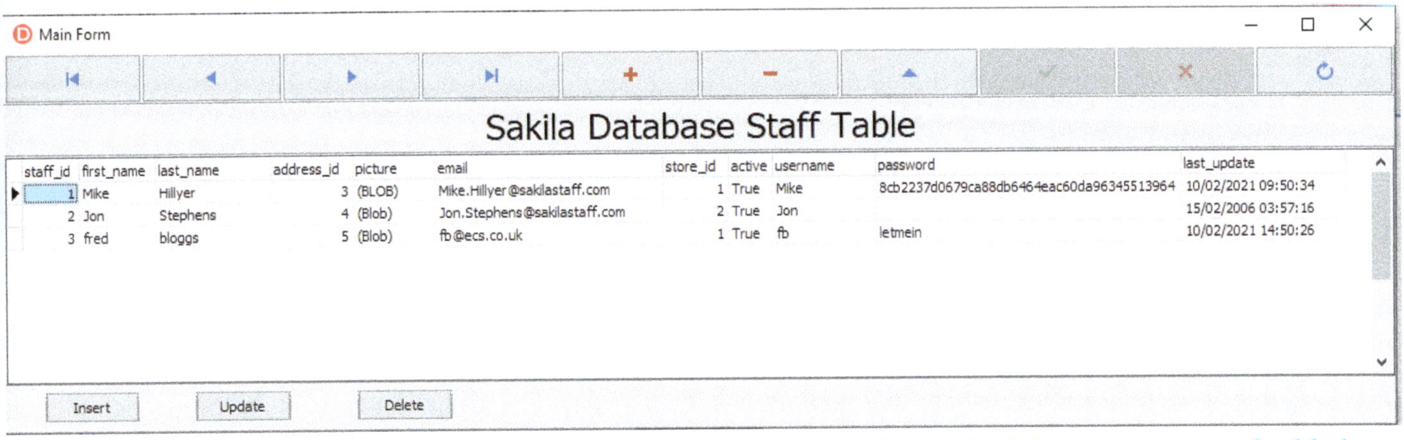

Fig. 69.47 Application FireDACSakilaStaffProject in execution and with one new record added

The application `FireDACSakilaStaffProject` oversimplifies a lot of things in order to introduce the concepts in a simple way. For example, an `address_id` of 5 has been used but where is the corresponding address?

The sakila database structure was developed from a data model that may be viewed in **MySQL Workbench** - **File|Open Model** then select `sakila.mwb`. *Figure 69.48* shows the model in the form of an **E-R diagram**.

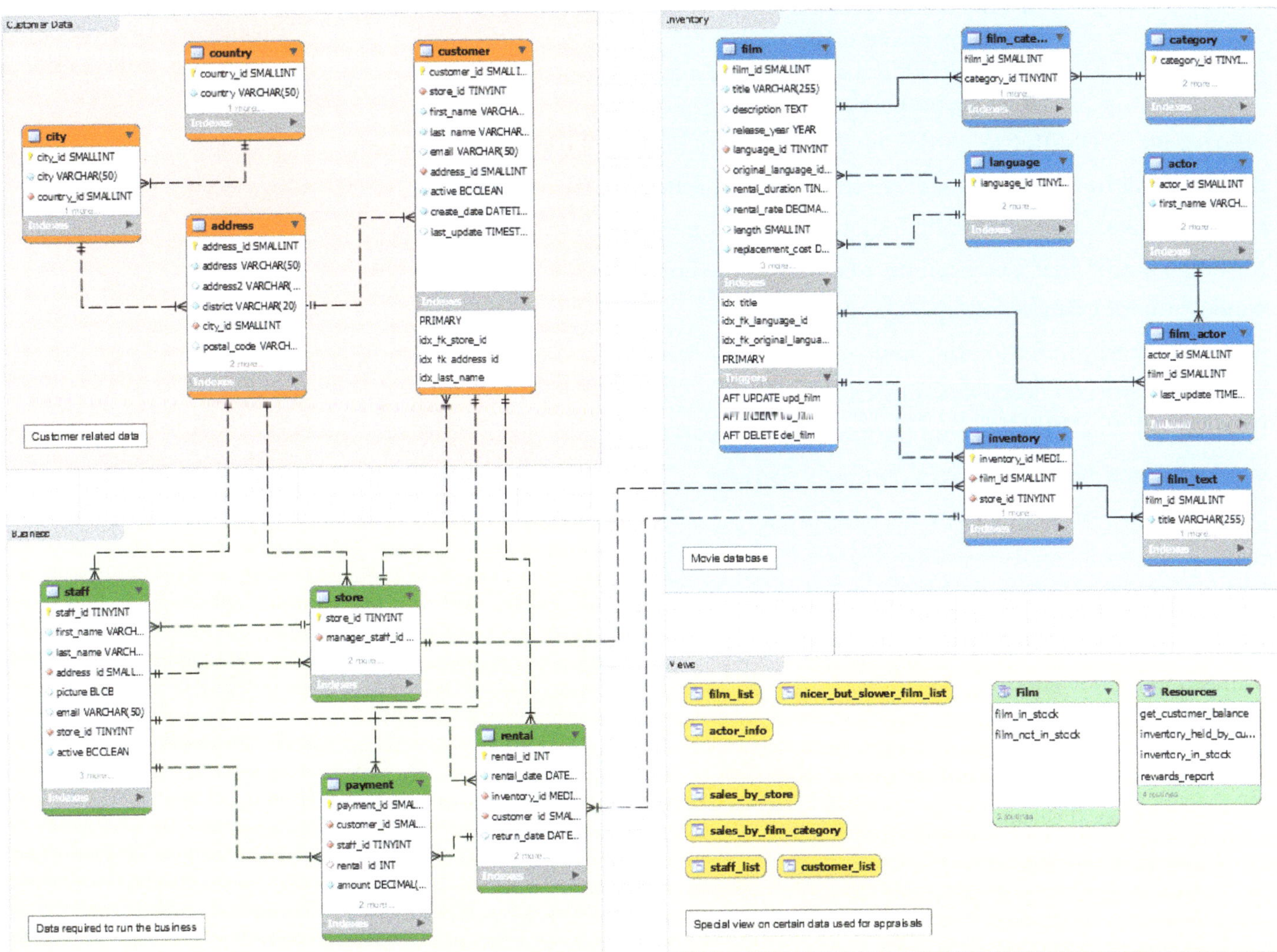

Fig. 69.48 Sakila database data model: Entity-Relationship diagram (released by Oracle® under version 2 of the GNU General Public License (GPLv2))

Programming tasks

4. The column headings of the grid shown in *Figure 69.44* would benefit from being centred. Fields such as `staff_id` would look neater if their data were centred. Apply these changes to `DBGridStaffDataSet`.

5. Use the `Update` button to add a password for staff member with `staff_id` 2.

6. Use the `Delete` button to delete the record for staff member with `staff_id` 3.

7. Create a FireDACSakilaCountryProject similar to FireDACSakilaStaffProject but based on the Country table. The application should be able to show the country data in a grid and insert, update and delete records.

Connecting to a remote MySQL database

Assuming that MySQL Server is running on another machine at ip address 192.168.1.12 and is listening on port 3306, the following information is required in order to connect to a MySQL database on the remote machine

- the username to use for the connection to the remote database
- the password to use
- the ip address of the remote machine
- the port number to use.

The procedure shown in the section ***Setting up other users*** should be followed for setting up user1 on the remote machine with Select access only to the sakila database.

Next set up a MySQL Connection to the remote machine on the local machine using the above information. *Figure 69.49* shows a part of the home window for **MySQL Workbench** before a new connection is set up. *Figure 69.50* shows the location of the home button that a user can use to return to the home window to, for example, set up a new connection.

To create a new connection the home window must be visible, in particular, **MySQL Connections**.

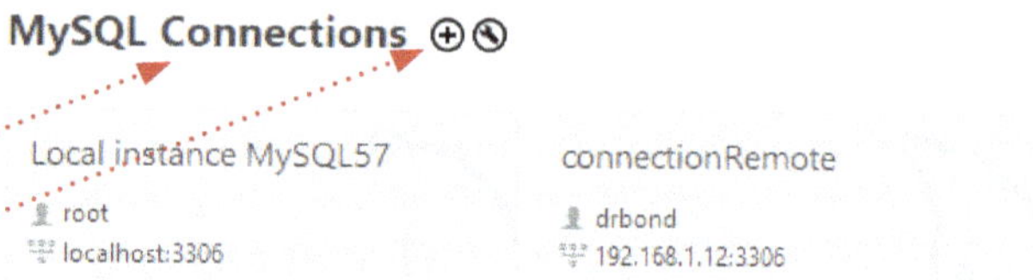

Fig. 69.49 The part of the home window for MySQL Workbench before a new remote connection is set up

Click on the ⊕ icon to bring up the **Setup New Connection** window. **Enter** the data shown in *Figure 69.53* (next page). **Test** the connection using the password for `user1` (set up on remote machine). *Figure 69.51* shows the pop up window that reports a successful test. *Figure 69.52* shows that the new remote connection has been added.

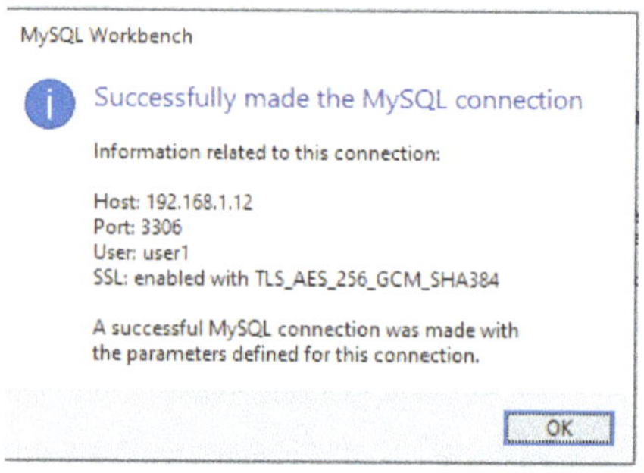

Fig. 69.51 Pop up window reporting that connection test successful

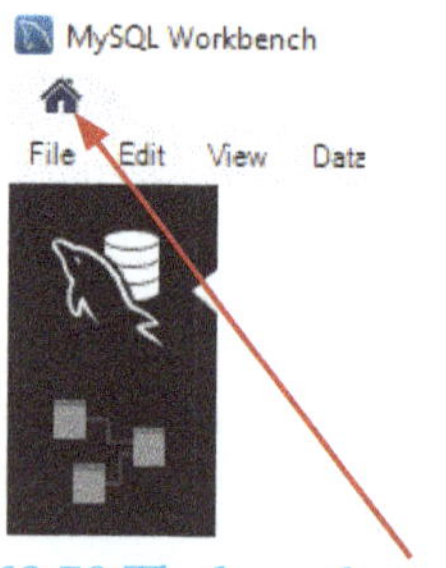

Fig. 69.50 The home button that returns the user to the home window

Failure to connect can result, even if everything else is as it should be, by the settings of the firewall on the remote machine. If this is the case, then the firewall settings need to be changed to accept the ip address of the connecting machine and to allow non-local connections on port 3306.

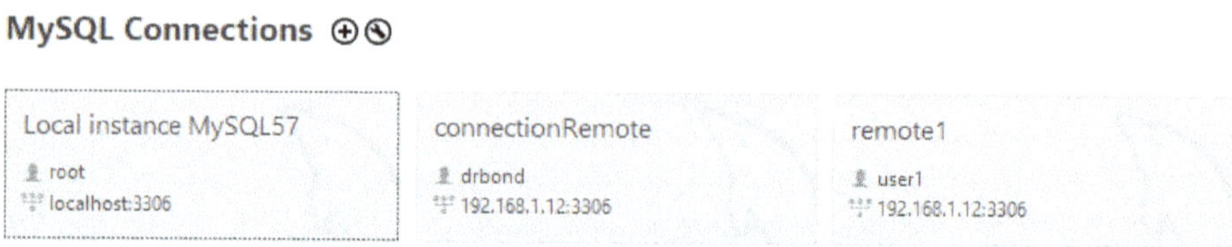

Fig. 69.52 MySQL Connections

Another reason for failure to connect could be that the wild card character % was not used when `user1` was set up on the remote machine. Note `root` cannot be as the username for connecting to a remote machine. It is not allowed.

Save the settings by clicking the **OK** button.

Now **launch** Delphi and and the project `FireDACSakilaStaffProject`.

Save this project and all its units in a new folder `FireDACSakilaStaffRemoteProject` using the filename for the project source file `FireDACSakilaStaffRemoteProject.dprog`

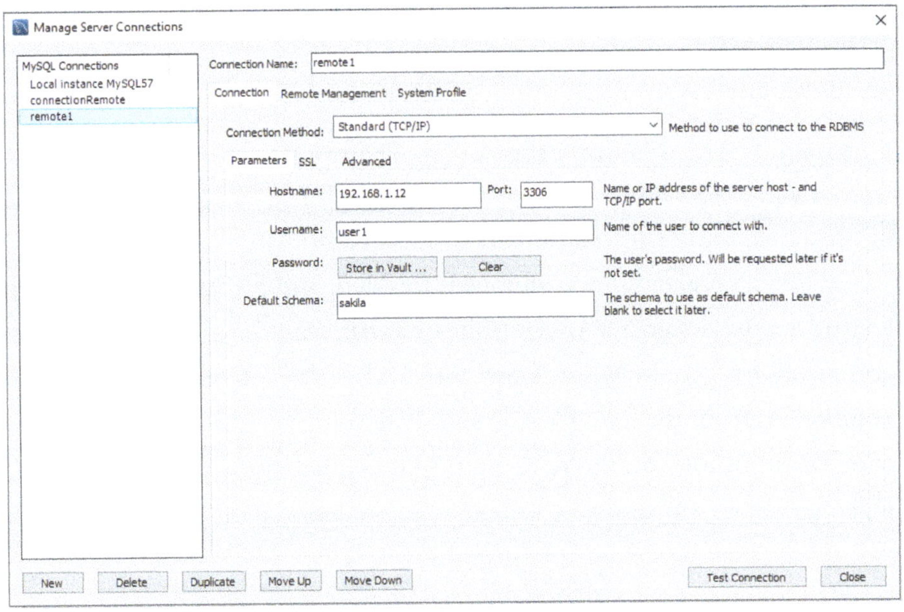

Fig. 69.53 Setting up a new remote connection

Double click `SakilaConnection` on the form `DataModule1` to bring up the **FireDAC Connection** editor. Change **User_Name** to `user1` and **Server** to 192.168.1.12. **Click OK.**

Set SakilaConnection.Connected to `True`. **Set** `StaffTable.Active` to `True`.

Switch to the `FireDACSakilaStaffUnit` form. The grid should now be populated with `Staff` table data from the remotely connected database similar to *Figure 69.47*.

Save All.

Build and **run** the project to get a result similar to *Figure 69.47* before the `Insert` button is clicked.

Defining you own ini file for your Delphi project

If you distribute your Delphi application, you need to supply a copy of the relevant part of `FDConnectionDefs.ini`.

The easiest way to do this is to add a **TFDManager** component, `FDManager1`, to the datamodule form.

Copy the part of `FDConnectionDefs.ini` that references the named connection to be used in your application to a new file, say `connection.ini`. Save this file in the application's current directory.

Add the name `connection.ini` to the **ConnectionDefFileName** property of `FDManager1` in the **Object Inspector**.

With **ConnectionDefFileAutoLoad** set to `True`, `FDManager1` will attempt to open the appropriate definition file before permitting any **FDConnections** to connect.

At design time, the default connection definition file will be used (`FDConnectionDefs.ini`) and at runtime the specified connection definition file, `connection.ini`, will be used.

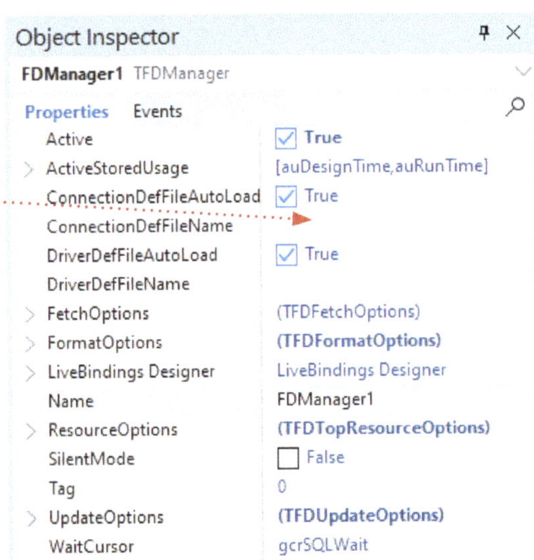

Fig. 69.54 FDManager1 manages loading of the Connection definition file

Using Fast Reports

Purpose: Brief introduction to Fast Reports

FastReport® - is an add-on component for VCL and FMX that allows applications to generate reports designed with a visual report designer at design time or at runtime. **Use Tools|GetIt Package Manager** in the IDE to download and install VCL and FMX versions - see *Figure 70.1*. **Create** a Windows VCL application and **place** a **TfrxReport** component from the **Tool/Component Palette** - *Figure 70.2* - on the form - *Figure 70.3*. **Double click** this component on the form to open up the embedded visual report designer - *Figure 70.4*.

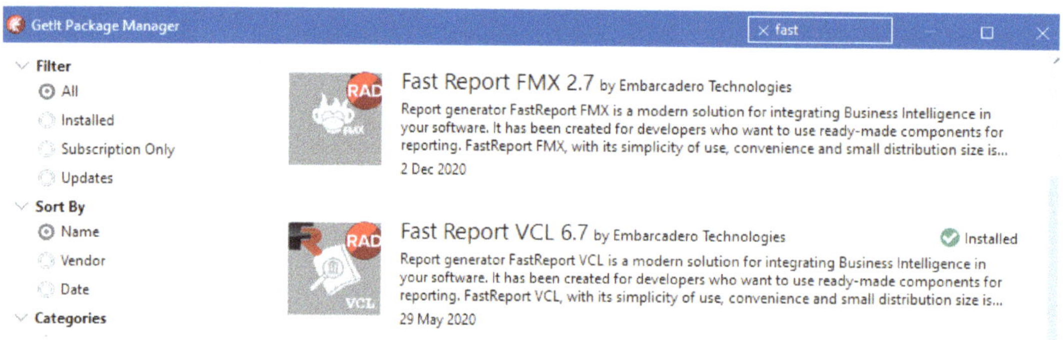

Fig. 70.1 GetIt Package Manager

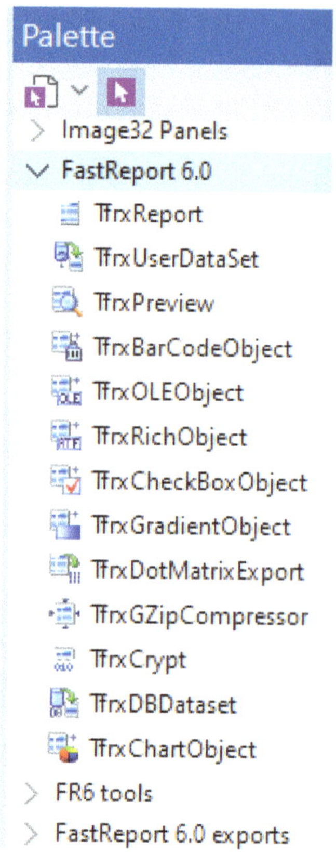

Fig. 70.2 Tool Palette

A report may now be designed by following the guidance provided in the user manual which may be accessed at https://www.fast-report.com/public_download/UserManual-en.pdf.

Fig. 70.3 VCL form

The **TfrxDBDataSet** connector component from the component palette - *Figure 70.2* - may be used to connect a database table (or any other data source, e.g. an array or a file) to a **FastReport** report, e.g. in a mail merge application.

Quick Reports is installed in older versions of Delphi, e.g. Delphi 7. A guide to using **Quick Reports** may be downloaded from www.educational-computing.co.uk/DelphiBookCode/DelphiCode.html.

Fig. 70.4 Embedded visual report designer

71 Database programming for mobile/tablet applications

Database programming for mobile/tablet applications

Purpose: To learn how to create a mobile/tablet application that uses an embedded database

There are two ways that a database may be accessed from a mobile/tablet application:

1. By embedding the database in the device
2. By accessing the database over a network connection.

In this chapter, only the first way will be explored. Delphi supports several different database engines that may be embedded with the database. The chosen database engine for the example in this chapter is IBLite which is more than adequate.

Select File|New|Multi-Device Application - Delphi to create a new multi-device application.

Select Blank Application. **Place** three **TLayout** components from the Layouts components tab on the form. **Set** the **Align** property of the first to **Top** and its name to `TopLayout`, the second, **Bottom** and its name to `BottomLayout`, and the third to **Client** and its name to `ClientLayout`. **Place** a **TListView** component from the Standard components tab on the `ClientLayout` component, **change** its **Name** property to `ListViewOfBookTitles` and its **Align** property to **Client**.

Add a **TLabel** component to `BottomLayout`, **change** its **Name** property to `lblISBN` and its **Align** property to **Top**. **Set** its **Text** property to `ISBN`. **Add** another **TLabel** component to `BottomLayout`, **change** its **Name** prorperty to `lblISBNValue` and its **Align** property to **Client**. **Clear** its **Text** property.

Add a **TLabel** component to `TopLayout`, **change** its **Name** property to `lblBookTitle` and its **Align** property to **Centre**. **Set** its **Text** property to `Book Title` and its **AutoSize** property to **True**. **Adjust** its **Width** property so that its containing box is just large enough in Style **Android** View **Master** (ribbon menu near top of IDE).

Change the **Name** property of the form to `MainForm` and its **Caption** property to `Book Table`.

Save the project as `CSBookDB.dproj` and its unit as `MainFormUnit.pas` in folder `CSBookDatabase`.

Add a **TFDPhysIBDriverLink** component from the FireDAC Links components tab to the form.

Add a **TFDGUIxWaitCursor** component from the FireDAC UI components tab to the form. **Add** a **TFDConnection** component from the FireDAC components tab to the form. **Change** its **Name** property to `FDCSBookDatabaseConnection`. **Change** its **LoginPrompt** property to **False** and **set** its **Params|DriverID** property to **IBLite**.

Add a **TBindSourceDB** components from the LiveBindings components tab to the form. **Add** a **TBindingsList** component, `BindingsList1`, from the LiveBindings Misc components tab to the form. **Double click** `BindingsList1` to bring up the **BindingsList editor** shown in *Figure 71.1*.

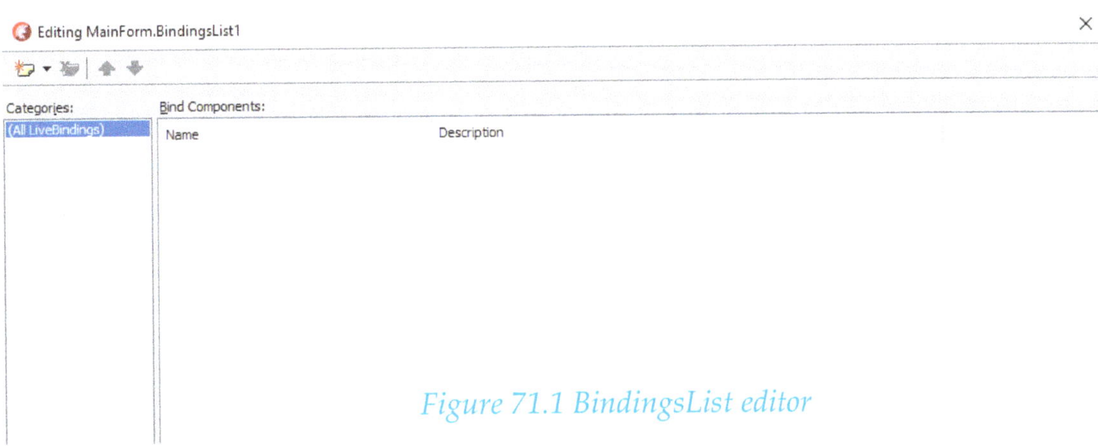

Figure 71.1 BindingsList editor

Click the **New Bindings (Ins)** icon to bring up the **New LiveBinding** window - *Figure 71.2*. **Select TLinkFillControlToField** and click **OK**. The control (another name for a component) `LinkFillControlToField1` should now appear in the **Object Inspector**. **Select** `ListViewOfBookTitles` in the **Control** property field in the **Object Inspector** (click on down arrow to show that this control is available for selection). **Select** `BindSourceDB1` in the **FillDataSource** property field in the **Object Inspector** (click on down arrow to show that this control is available for selection). **Set** the **FillDisplayFieldName** property to the value `BookTitle` (this is a field of the `Book` table in database `CSBookDatabase` that will be used in this application). **Set** the `Track` property to `True`. Close the **BindingsList editor** window.

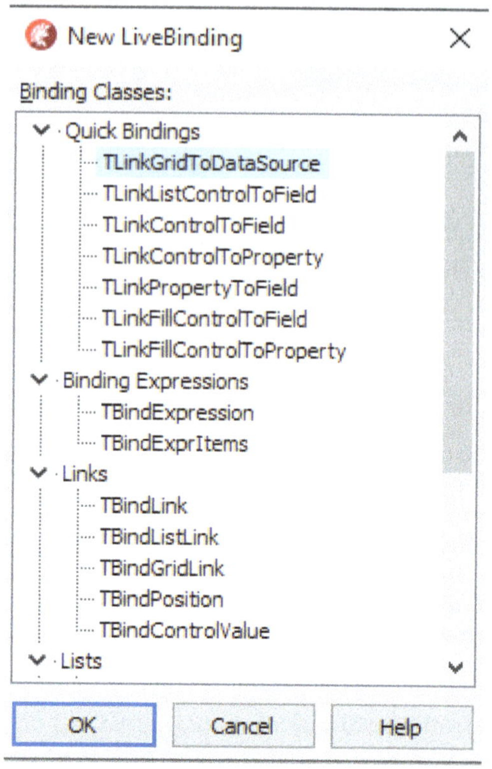

Figure 71.2 New LiveBinding window

Download `CSBOOKDATABASE.IB` from www.educational-computing.co.uk/DelphiBookCode/DelphiCode.html *Chapter 71* and **place** a copy in the folder containing this project[1] - `CSBookDatabase`. **Right click** on `CSBookDB.exe` in the **Projects** window - *Figure 71.3* - to bring up the window shown in *Figure 71.4*. **Select Add...** to bring up the **Add to** project window. **Select** the **Embedded Database Files** filter then **navigate** to the project folder and **select** `CSBOOKDATABASE.IB`.

Click the **Open** button to
(a) add this database to the project and
(b) to open the **Featured Files** window shown in *Figure 71.5*. **Check Interbase ToGo** as shown so that the required instructions for the **Deployment** manifest will be created.

Click the **OK** button. This database will be embedded in the target device together with the application. The **Deployment** manifest may be viewed by selecting **Project|Deployment**. *Figure 71.6* shows part of the deployment manifest for **Android 32-bit** devices employed when debugging the application.

The last line in *Figure 71.6* shows where the database will be placed in the target device.

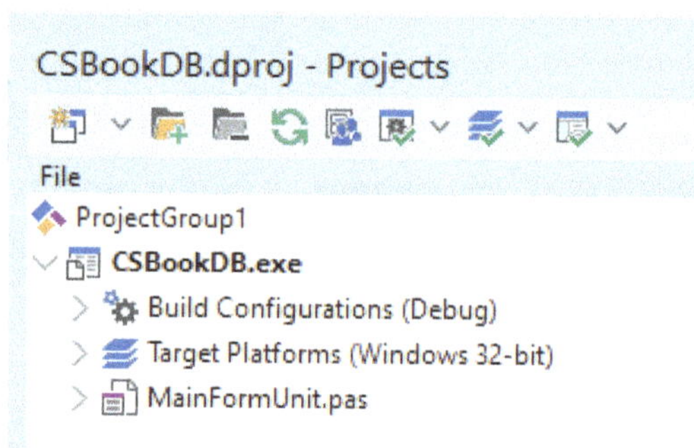

Figure 71.3 Projects window

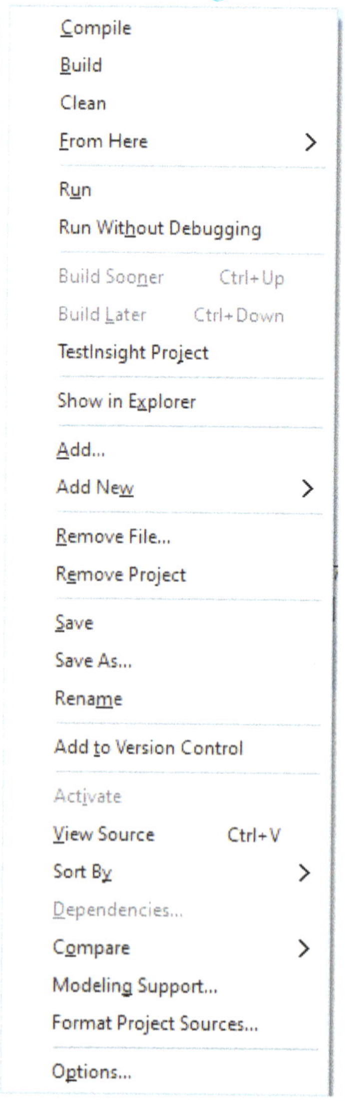

Figure 71.4 Options window

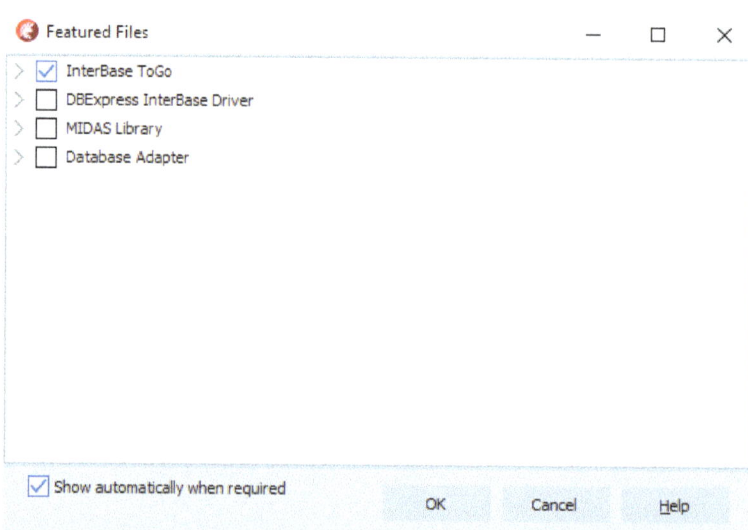

Figure 71.5 Featured Files window showing option Interbase ToGo selected

1 You may have to put this database where it can be found by the exe, i.e. in Debug folder.

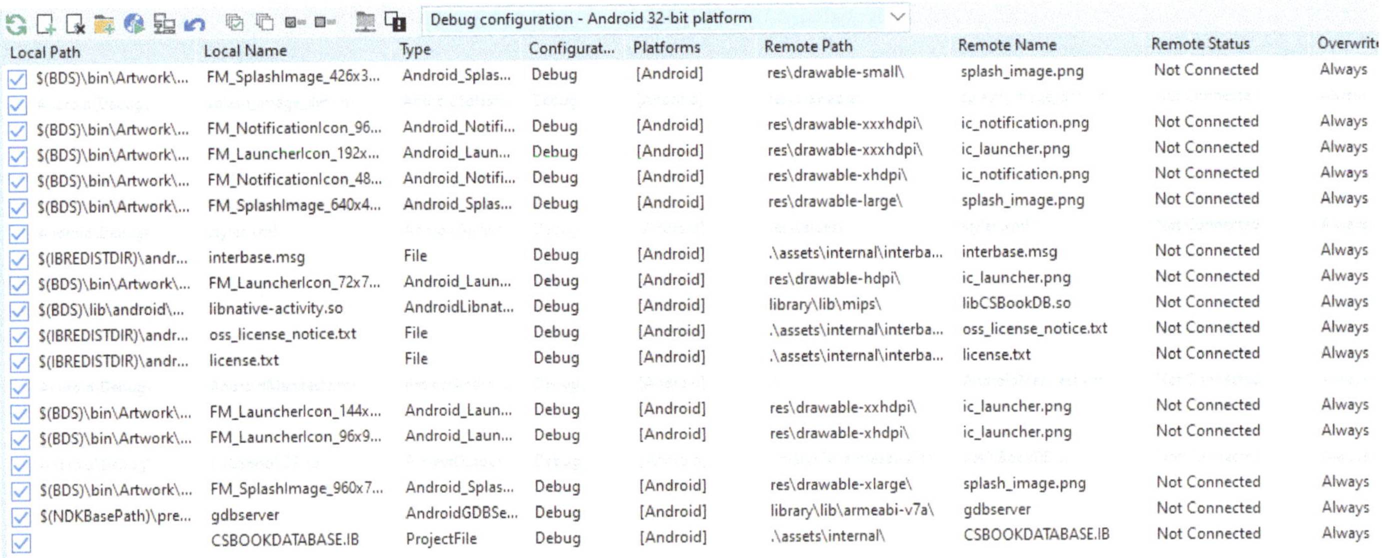

Debug configuration - Android 32-bit platform

Local Path	Local Name	Type	Configurat...	Platforms	Remote Path	Remote Name	Remote Status	Overwrit
$(BDS)\bin\Artwork\...	FM_SplashImage_426x3...	Android_Splas...	Debug	[Android]	res\drawable-small\	splash_image.png	Not Connected	Always
$(BDS)\bin\Artwork\...	FM_NotificationIcon_96...	Android_Notifi...	Debug	[Android]	res\drawable-xxxhdpi\	ic_notification.png	Not Connected	Always
$(BDS)\bin\Artwork\...	FM_LauncherIcon_192x...	Android_Laun...	Debug	[Android]	res\drawable-xxxhdpi\	ic_launcher.png	Not Connected	Always
$(BDS)\bin\Artwork\...	FM_NotificationIcon_48...	Android_Notifi...	Debug	[Android]	res\drawable-xhdpi\	ic_notification.png	Not Connected	Always
$(BDS)\bin\Artwork\...	FM_SplashImage_640x4...	Android_Splas...	Debug	[Android]	res\drawable-large\	splash_image.png	Not Connected	Always
$(IBREDISTDIR)\andr...	interbase.msg	File	Debug	[Android]	.\assets\internal\interba...	interbase.msg	Not Connected	Always
$(BDS)\bin\Artwork\...	FM_LauncherIcon_72x7...	Android_Laun...	Debug	[Android]	res\drawable-hdpi\	ic_launcher.png	Not Connected	Always
$(BDS)\lib\android\...	libnative-activity.so	AndroidLibnat...	Debug	[Android]	library\lib\mips\	libCSBookDB.so	Not Connected	Always
$(IBREDISTDIR)\andr...	oss_license_notice.txt	File	Debug	[Android]	.\assets\internal\interba...	oss_license_notice.txt	Not Connected	Always
$(IBREDISTDIR)\andr...	license.txt	File	Debug	[Android]	.\assets\internal\interba...	license.txt	Not Connected	Always
$(BDS)\bin\Artwork\...	FM_LauncherIcon_144x...	Android_Laun...	Debug	[Android]	res\drawable-xxhdpi\	ic_launcher.png	Not Connected	Always
$(BDS)\bin\Artwork\...	FM_LauncherIcon_96x9...	Android_Laun...	Debug	[Android]	res\drawable-xhdpi\	ic_launcher.png	Not Connected	Always
$(BDS)\bin\Artwork\...	FM_SplashImage_960x7...	Android_Splas...	Debug	[Android]	res\drawable-xlarge\	splash_image.png	Not Connected	Always
$(NDKBasePath)\pre...	gdbserver	AndroidGDBSe...	Debug	[Android]	library\lib\armeabi-v7a\	gdbserver	Not Connected	Always
	CSBOOKDATABASE.IB	ProjectFile	Debug	[Android]	.\assets\internal\	CSBOOKDATABASE.IB	Not Connected	Always

Figure 71.6 Part of the Deployment manifest for the Android 32-bit platform - debug configuration

Right click on **BindSourceDB1** on the form and **select** the option **Bind Visually...** from the popup menu to bring up the **LiveBindings Designer** shown in *Figure 71.7*. This figure confirms that the task of linking `ListViewOfBookTitles` **Item.Text** field to the `BookTitle` field of the `Book` table has been achieved successfully via the `BindingsList1` component. This is the important because the database `CSBOOKDATABASE.IB` will not be opened until the embedded applications runs. Hence, at this stage `BookTitle` in `BindSourceDB1` is shown labelled Invalid).

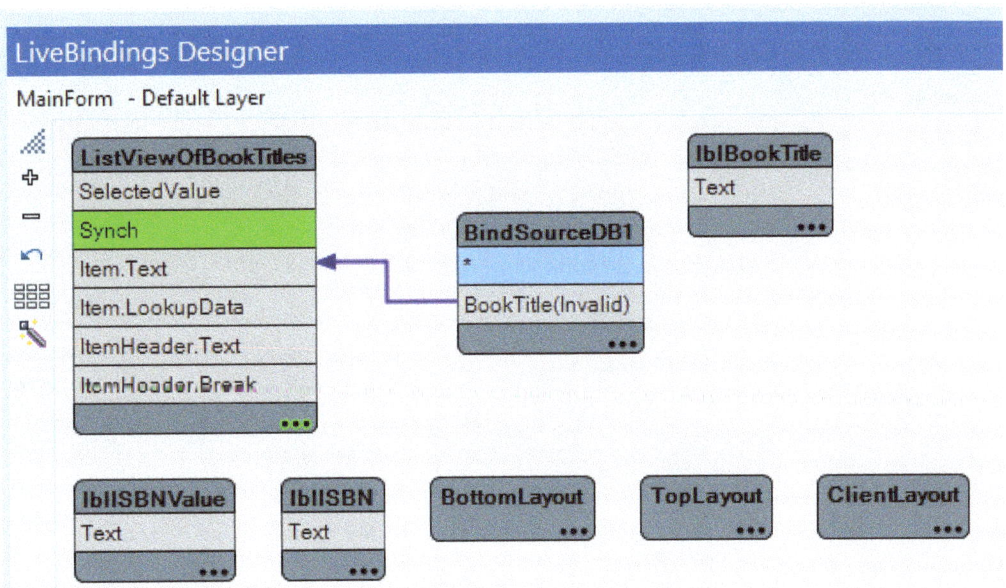

Figure 71.7 LiveBindings Designer

Add a **TFDTable** component from the **FireDAC** components tab. **Change** its name to **FDBookTable**. **Set** the **TableName** property to `Book` and the **IndexFieldNames** property to `ISBN`. The **Connection** property should have set itself to `FDCSBookDatabaseConnection`.

Set the **DataSet** property of `BindSourceDB1` to `FDBookTable`.

We need to create an event handler that will handle setting up the right connection path parameters for the given target. **Close** the **LiveBindings Designer** window. **Select** `FDCSBookDatabaseConnection` and in the **Events** tab page in the **Object Inspector**, **double click** the blank field for **BeforeConnect** to create the event handler `FDCSBookDatabaseConnectionBeforeConnect`. **Add** the code shown in *Table 71.1* to its body.

Add System.iOUTils to the **Uses** section (this is so **TPath** will be recognised).

A connection to the database must be made and the `Book` table opened once the application is finished setting up, i.e. once it transitions into an idle state. The application has an event property called **OnIdle** which is triggered as the application transitions into an idle state. e.g. when it is waiting for input from the user. It is not called continuously unless the **Done** parameter is set to **False**.

Creating an event handler for this event is best done by adding an object method with the signature expected by the **OnIdle** event property, i.e. `OnIdle(Sender : TObject; Var Done : Boolean)` to the class as shown in *Table 71.2*. Opening a connection to the database and the `Book` table needs to happen just once so we need a **Boolean** flag, `FDatabaseOpened`, to record when this has been done - *Table 71.2*. The application sets this to **False** automatically when it launches, initialising this field variable using initialisation code inserted by the compiler. **Place** the cursor in the line of the class definition containing `Procedure OnIdle(Sender : TObject; Var Done : Boolean)` and whilst holding down the key combination **Ctrl+Shift**, **press** the return key to create a template for this procedure in the **Implementation** section. **Add** the code shown in *Table 71.3* to the body of this procedure. This procedure (object method) needs to be associated with the `Application.OnIdle` event property. **Select** the form and **create** an **OnCreate** event handler, `FormCreate`. **Add** the code shown in *Table 71.4* to its body. **Click** **File|Save All** (**Shift+Ctrl+S**).

```
Procedure TMainForm.FDCSBookDatabaseConnectionBeforeConnect(Sender : TObject);
  Begin
    {$IF DEFINED(IOS) or DEFINED(ANDROID)}
    FDBookDatabaseConnection.Params.Values['Database'] := TPath.GetDocumentsPath + PathDelim + 'CSBOOKDATABASE.IB';
    {$ELSEIF DEFINED (MACOS)}
    FDBookDatabaseConnection.Params.Values['Database'] := TPath.GetHomePath + PathDelim + 'CSBOOKDATABASE.IB';
    {$ELSEIF DEFINED(MSWINDOWS)}
    FDBookDatabaseConnection.Params.Values['Database'] := GetCurrentDir + PathDelim + 'CSBOOKDATABASE.IB';
    {$ENDIF}
    FDBookDatabaseConnection.Params.Values['User_name'] := 'sysdba';
    FDBookDatabaseConnection.Params.Values['Password'] := 'masterkey';
  End;
```

Table 71.1 Event handler FDCSBookDatabaseConnectionBeforeConnect

Security-wise, it is not a good idea to embed the username and the password in the code. Strings can be read even when embedded in an exe!

Change this event handler so that it collects both username and password from the user when the program launches - this is tricky but possible on Android which treats input in an asynchronous way.

```
Type
  TMainForm = Class(TForm)
              TopLayout : TLayout;
              BottomLayout : TLayout;
              ClientLayout : TLayout;
              ListViewOfBookTitles : TListView;
              lblISBN : TLabel;
              lblISBNValue : TLabel;
              lblBookTitle : TLabel;
              FDPhysIBDriverLink1 : TFDPhysIBDriverLink;
              FDGUIxWaitCursor1 : TFDGUIxWaitCursor;
              FDCSBookDatabaseConnection : TFDConnection;
              BindingsList1 : TBindingsList;
              BindSourceDB1 : TBindSourceDB;
              LinkFillControlToField1 : TLinkFillControlToField;
              Procedure FDCSBookDatabaseConnectionBeforeConnect(Sender : TObject);
            Private
              FDatabaseOpened : Boolean;
              Procedure OnIdle(Sender : TObject; Var ADone : Boolean);
            End;
```

Table 71.2 TMainForm class definition

```
Procedure TMainForm.OnIdle(Sender : TObject; Var Done : Boolean);
  Begin
    If Not FDatabaseOpened
      Then
        Begin
          Try
            LinkFillControlToField1.AutoActivate := False;
            LinkFillControlToField1.AutoFill := False;
            FDBookDatabaseConnection.Connected := True;
            FDBookTable.Active := True;
            LinkFillControlToField1.BindList.FillList;
          Except
            On E : Exception
              Do ShowMessage(e.Message);
          End;
          FDatabaseOpened := True;
        End;
  End;
```

Table 71.3 Object method OnIdle

```
Procedure TMainForm.FormCreate(Sender : TObject);
  Begin
    Application.OnIdle := OnIdle;
  End;
```

Table 71.4 Event handler FormCreate

Connect an Android device via USB to your Windows computer. **Developer options** and **USB debugging** must be enabled on the target device - see *Chapter 41*.

Chapter 41 also covers potential issues with USB drivers and how to resolve them.

Figure 71.8 Projects window

Sometimes Delphi loads without the required target platform(s). This is easy to fix. Simply **right click** on **Target Platforms (Windows 32-bit)** node or similar node in the **Projects** window then **click Add Platform** - *Figure 71.8* - to bring up the platforms window.

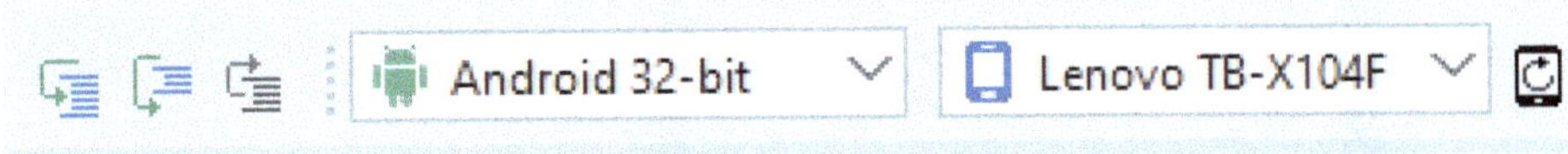

Figure 71.9 IDE Ribbon showing the selected target

The Android device selected for this example is a moderately priced **Lenova TB-X104F** tablet running an Android 32-bit operating system - *Figure 71.9*. The version of Delphi is **10.4.2** and the computer is running **Windows 10** operating system for which the native **Windows USB** driver works perfectly. **Select Style Android** as shown in *Figure 71.11* and adjust field width for the text `Book Title` then **Save All**.

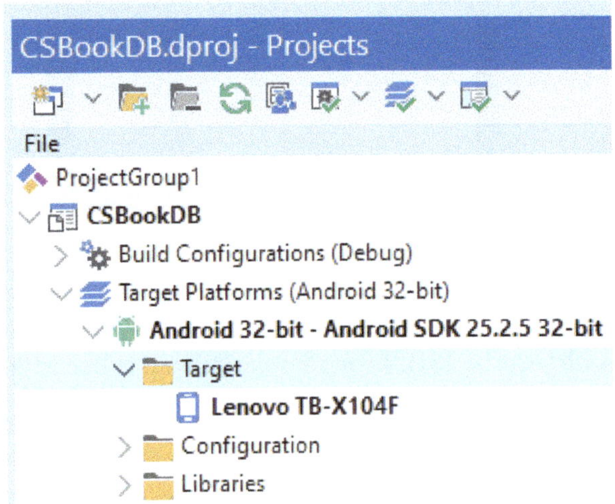

Figure 71.10 Projects window showing Lenova TB-X104F target and debug configuration selected

You should always change style to test that the field width of any strings displayed on the user interface are sufficient to avoid text wrap for the selected style. Also to delete a control/ component from the form, the **Master** view must be selected. *Figure 71.12* shows the design view of the user interface when **Android 7" Tablet** is selected instead of **Master. Select Run|Parameters...** to open the **Project Options LibCSBookDB.so (Android Debug)** window. **Add** the directive **-cleaninstall** to the **Parameters** field. **Click** the **Save** button. **Run with debugging** (F9). *Figure 71.13* shows a screen capture of the application running on the Lenova tablet. **Select Run|Program Reset** to stop the application.

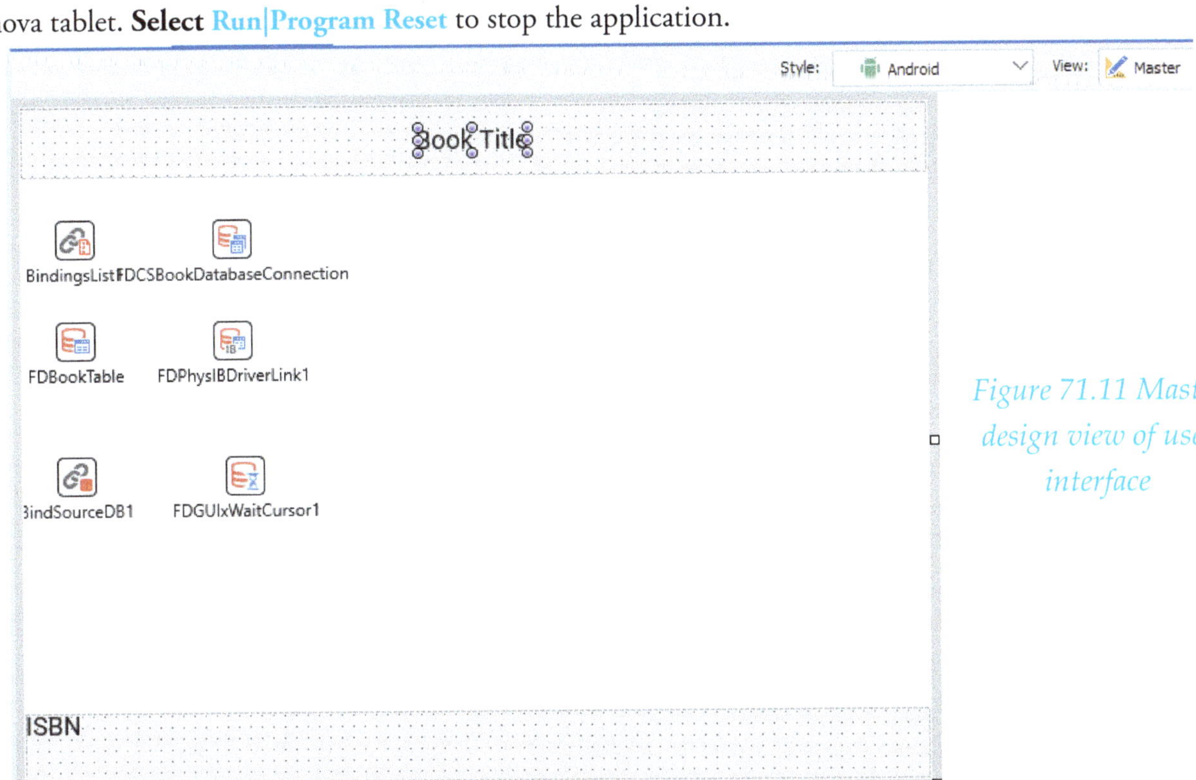

Figure 71.11 Master design view of user interface

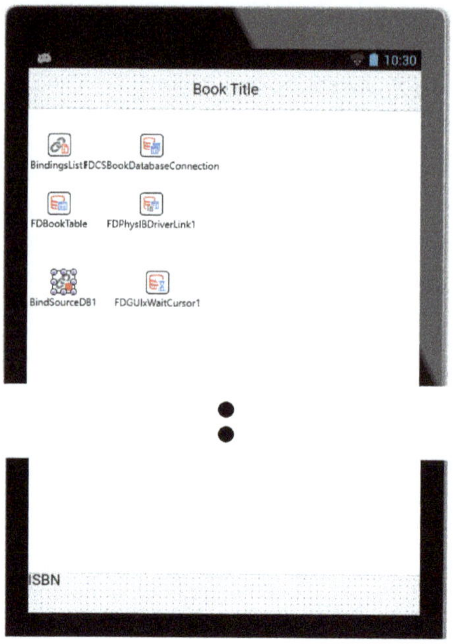

Figure 71.12 Android 7" tablet design view of user interfaces showing a section of the upper part and a section of the lower part

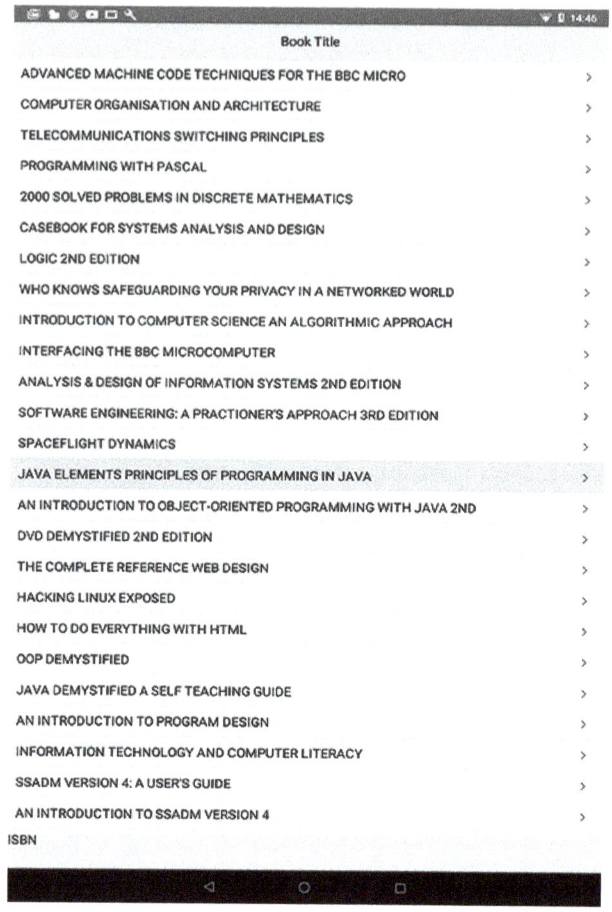

Figure 71.13 Screen capture of application CSBookDB in execution on Lenova tablet

To obtain the ISBN for a book which has been highlighted in the `Book Titles` list shown in *Figure 71.13*, we need to add an **OnItemClick** event handler for `ListViewForBookTitles` and we need to **add** a **TFDQuery** component from the **FireDAC** components tab to the form. **Select** **Master** view and **rename** the **TFDQuery** component `FDQueryForISBN`. **Select** `ListViewForBookTitles` in the **Object Inspector** and **double click** the empty field for property **OnItemClick**. **Add** the code shown in *Table 71.5* to the body of the event handler template. Select `FDQueryForISBN`. **Click** the ellipsis (**...**) for the **SQL** property to bring up the **String List Editor** window. **Add** `Select ISBN From Book where BookTitle = :BookTitle;` and **click** the **OK** button. **Click** the ellipsis (**...**) for the **Params** property to open up the **Editing FDQueryForISBN.Params** window and **check** an entry `0 - BOOKTITLE` has been added. The **Connection** property should have been set automatically to `FDCSBookDatabaseConnection`.

Select **File|Save All** (**Shift+Ctrl+S**). **Run|Run** (**F9**) to run with debugging option. *Figure 71.14* is a screen capture of the running application on the Lenova tablet showing the ISBN for the highlighted book title. **Select** **Run|Program Reset** to stop the application. Now **change** the build configuration to **Release**. **Select** **Run|Parameters...** to open the **Project Options LibCSBookDB.so (Android Release)** window. **Add** the directive **-cleaninstall** to the **Parameters** field. **Click** the **Save** button. **Run|Run without Debugging** (**Shift+Ctrl+F9**) to install and run the application. **Check** that the application behaves as expected. *Figure 71.15* shows the Lenova tablet's apps window and the app icon `CSBookDB`.

```
Procedure TMainForm.ListViewForBookTitlesItemClick(Const Sender : TObject; Const AItem : TListViewItem);
  Begin
    FDQueryForISBN.DisableControls;
    Try
      FDQueryForISBN.Close;
      FDQueryForISBN.Params.ParamValues['BookTitle'] := AItem.Text;
      FDQueryForISBN.Open;
      lblISBNValue.Text := FDQueryForISBN.Fields[0].AsString;
    Finally
      FDQueryForISBN.EnableControls;
    End;
  End;
```

Table 71.5 Event handler ListViewForBookTitlesItemClick

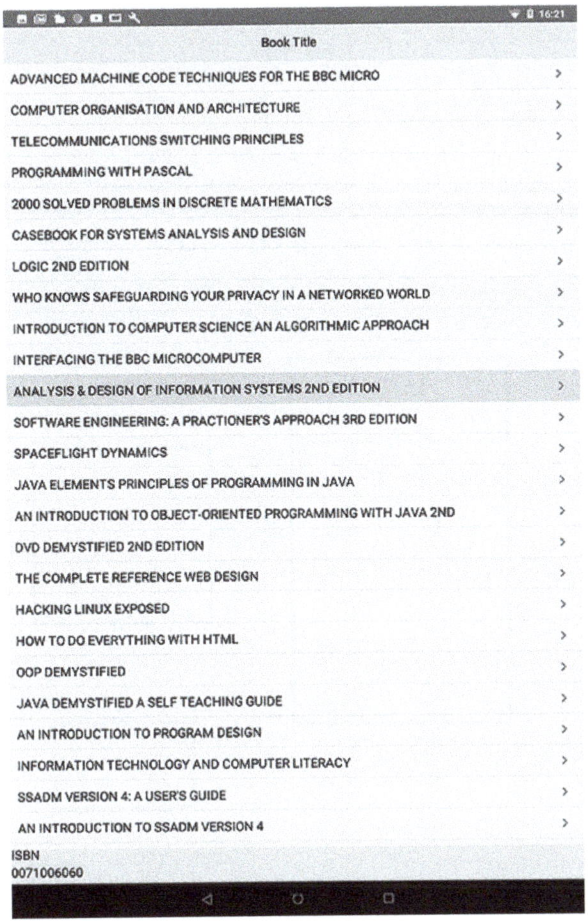

Figure 71.14 Screen capture of application CSBookDB in execution on Lenova tablet

By launching a DOS command shell (cmd) and locating and running **adb shell**, it is possible to access the internal storage of the Lenova tablet as shown in *Figure 71.16*.

The **adb** application enables the Delphi IDE to communicate with the Lenova and debug applications over the USB link. This application is placed in `C:\Users\Public\Documents\Embarcadero\Studio\21.0\CatalogRepository\AndroidSDK-2525-21.0.40680.4203\platform-tools` when **Delphi 10.4.2** is installed. This application, `adb.exe`, was copied to folder `D:\platform-tools` so that a shorter path name could be used in the DOS window. The Android operating system is case sensitive so caremust be be taken when referencing file names/ command names, etc. The command **ls** lists the contents of a folder.

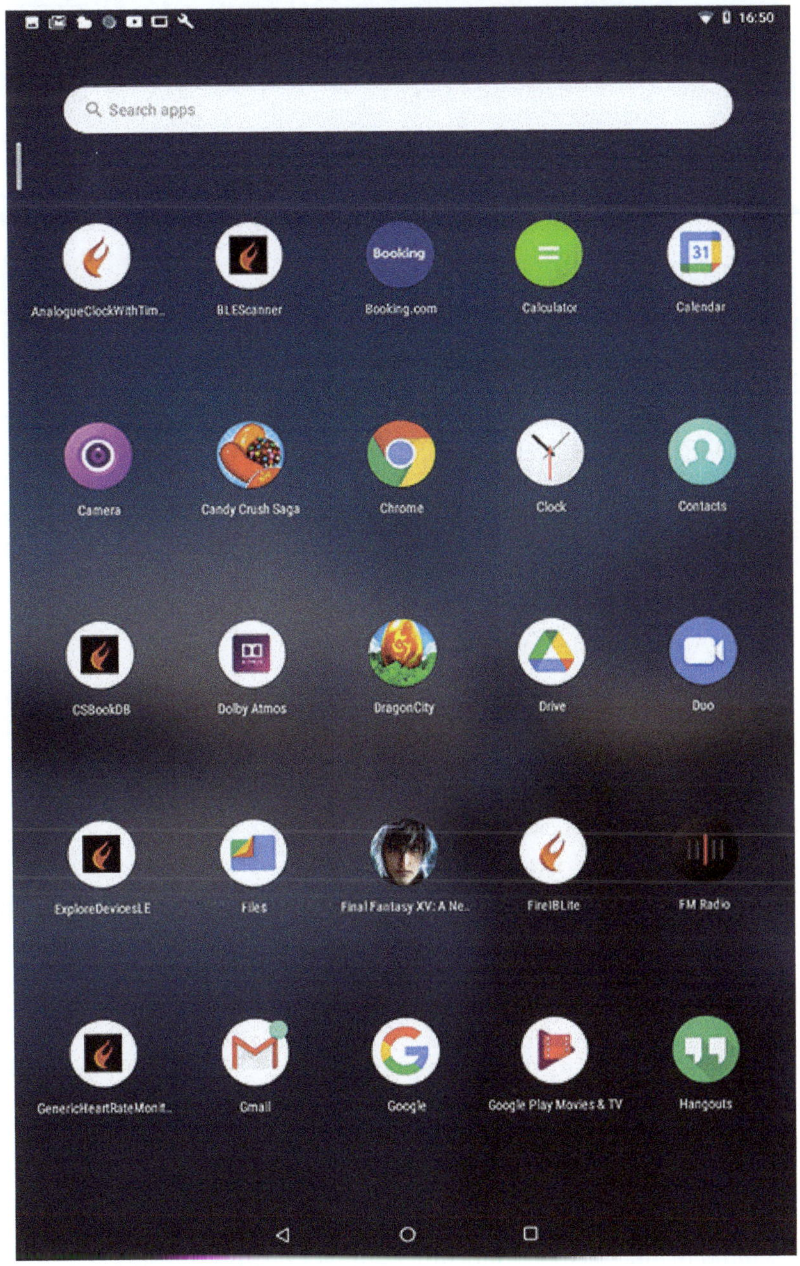

Figure 71.15 Screen capture of Lenova tablet apps window showing the application CSBookDB has been installed

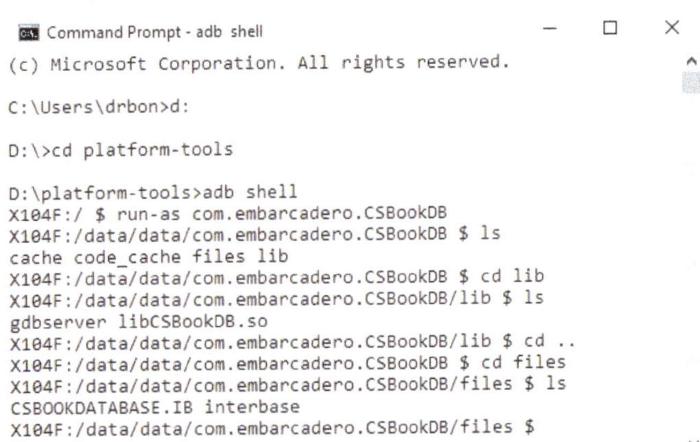

Figure 71.16 Contents of the lib folder on the Lenova showing (a) the executable file libCSBookDB.so and the Interbase\IBLite server - gdbserver - and (b) the files folder contents CSBOOKDATABASE.IB and another folder interbase. The latter contains licence and configuration files

72 REST programming with Delphi

Representational State Transfer (REST)

Purpose: To be familiar with the use of REST

What is REST?

The idea of REST is that application data can be queried and changed using verbs and nouns, represented by HTTP methods and URLs, respectively. A REST request will typically return data in a machine-readable form, such as JSON or XML.

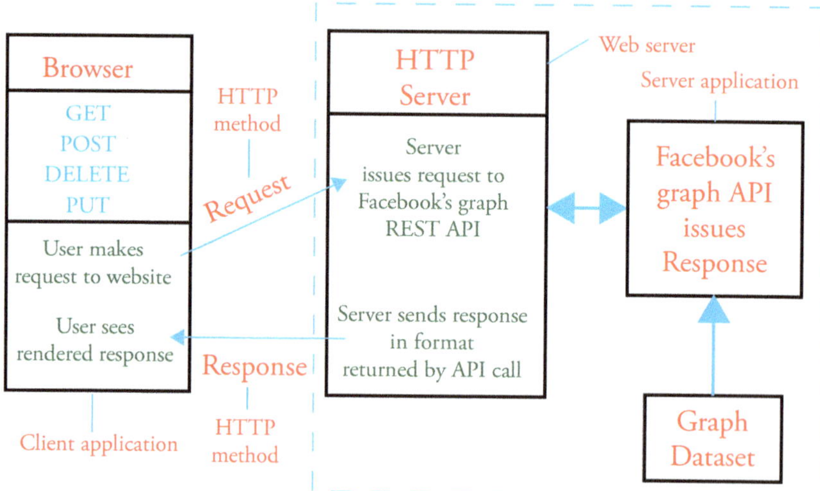

Figure 72.1 Interaction via an HTTP server between a browser and a server application acessing Facebook's social network graph

Suppose that you wanted to order a book from Amazon, the online bookseller. Do you have to download a special app to do this or can you use software that you have on your computer already? Of course, the answer is that you can use browser software you have on your computer already.

Typing the following URL (uniform resource locator) into the address bar of your browser returns a web page that contains information about a resource that Amazon uniquely identifies with the ID 0241003008, i.e. the book *Very Hungry Caterpillar Board Book*:

http://www.amazon.co.uk/Very-Hungry-Caterpillar-Board-Book/dp/0241003008/

Amazon's web site is a web service based on a design pattern called REST which stands for **REpresentational State Transfer**. Central to the concept of REST is the notion of resources. Resources are represented by URIs or Uniform Resource Identifiers, the Amazon example is one such URI. There are two types of URI: URLs and URNs. We will focus on URLs (Uniform Resource Locators). Another key aspect of the design of REST web services is that resources should be linked together and representations of these resources should enable a user to move from one resource to another by following these links.

Figure 72.1 show an interaction via an HTTP server between a client application, a browser, and a server application, that provides a Facebook RESTful web service that accesses Facebook's social network graph dataset of Facebook users. Facebook's graph API is an application programming interface (API) that is run on Facebook servers. If the following URL is typed into the browser's address bar for the scenario in *Figure 72.1* then what is returned is a representation that the browser renders as shown in *Figure 72.2*:

https://graph.facebook.com/4?oauth_token= CAACE......

Figure 72.2 Mark Zuckerberg's user node in Facebook's social network graph, node id is 4. Mark's homepage is www.facebook.com/Zuck. Access to user node 4 has been shut down since version 2.2.

See Task 1 below for how to get an access token (CAACE....) to use with oauth_token.

In the Facebook social network graph, Mark Zuckerberg's user node has the identifier "4", not surprisingly his identifier was one of the very first to be allocated. The representation returned is expressed in JSON (JavaScript Object Notation)

By following the link (https://www.facebook.com/zuck) in the representation shown in *Figure 72.2*, a client application, i.e. a browser, can obtain the next resource representation, Mark Zuckerberg's Facebook home page, from the server application. Facebook's social network graph is, in 2021, the largest social network dataset in the world.

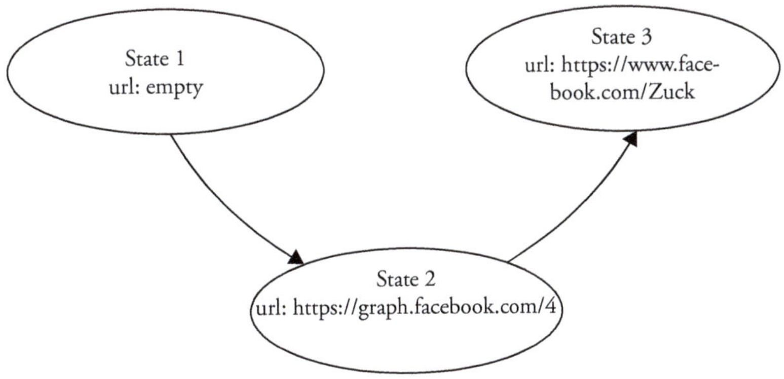

Figure 72.3 The client application's changes of state: each transition to a new state causes the server application to transfer a representation to the client application

Figure 72.3 shows how the client application's state changes as it interacts with the server application which in turn accesses Facebook's social network graph dataset. Thus, the client application changes (transfers) to a new state when it obtains a new resource REpresentation from the server application, this is why REST stands for REpresentational State Transfer!

Background

API:
An API is an application programming interface. An application programming interface separates the data from the operations that may be performed on the data. Applications that use a particular API do not know how the data is stored only how to access it via API calls.

The **REST** architecture is characterised by

- Client-server: separation between server application that offers a service, and the client application that consumes it
- Stateless: each request from a client application must contain all the information required by the server application to carry out the request. Session state is kept entirely on the client not at the server
- Uniform interface: the method of communication between a client application and a server application must be uniform, e.g. via HTTP requests and responses
- Code-on-demand: server applications can provide executable code or scripts for client applications to execute in their context
- Cacheable: the server application must indicate to the client application requests that can be cached
- Every resource has a unique ID, e.g. https://graph.facebook.com/4
- Multiple representations of resources provided for different needs, e.g. html, JSON, XML, jpeg, png, gif, csv
- Resources are linked together, e.g. Facebook's social network graph.

Tasks

1. For this exercise you will need to be on Facebook. Launch Facebook's social network graph explorer tool, https://developers.facebook.com/tools/explorer and select the GET method. Enter `/me` into the field next to GET. Click on Get Access Token and in the pop-up screen select the items that you wish to view. Click on submit.

Questions

1. Explain with an example what is meant by REST.

Uniform interface

Communication between the client application and the server application typically uses HTTP as the **uniform interface**. HTTP provides four principle methods for Creating, Retrieving, Updating and Deleting a resource. The methods are sometimes referred to as **CRUD** operations:

- C – Create
- R – Retrieve
- U – Update
- D - Delete

The HTTP methods that map onto these operations are shown in *Table 72.1*.

HTTP method	Action	Examples
GET	**Retrieve** a resource or a collection of resources	Retrieve Mark Zuckerberg's social network graph entry – `GET /4 HTTP/1.1` `Host: graph.facebook.com` Replace `4` in the `GET` with your id.
POST	**Create** a new resource	Creates a new resource
PUT	**Update** or replace an existing resource	Updates a resource
DELETE	**Delete** a resource	Deletes a resource

Table 72.1 The four HTTP methods for CRUD

The **REST API** created and run at the server may be connected to a relational database such as MySQL. In which case the HTTP verbs will be converted into SQL equivalent database commands as follows :

- GET → SELECT
- POST → INSERT
- DELETE → DELETE
- PUT → UPDATE

in order to carry out operations on the database (see *Chapter 62* for SQL commands).

The REST API may also be connected to a NOSQL database such as MongoDB.

Multiple representations of resources

What is returned to the client application is not the resource but a representation of the resource. The REST service provided by the server application is usually designed to provide at least JSON and XML representations. *Figure 72.4* shows the JSON response. The client application has no knowledge of how the resource is actually stored on the server. The resource sits behind an interface which hides this information. This means that the resource can be restructured without affecting any client application which simply continues to use the uniform interface of **HTTP CRUD** operations.

```
GET /v1/csunit2s/6 HTTP/1.1
Host: cs.apispark.net
Content-Type: application/json
Authorization: Basic
NjY1ZjkyNDUtZTUzNy00MjViLWJhZGI·····
Accept: application/json
Cache-Control: no-cache
```

```
{
  "id": "6",
  "link": [
      "https://cs.apispark.net/v1/csunit2s/subsections/6.1",
      "https://cs.apispark.net/v1/csunit2s/subsections/6.2",
      "https://cs.apispark.net/v1/csunit2s/subsections/6.3"
  ],
  "title": "Fundamentals of computer systems"
}
```

Figure 72.4 JSON representation returned to client application

Delphi and REST

The website apilayer.com offers a suite of Web apis and cloud-based microservice applications that may be used to explore REST and Delphi. Sign up to a free account to obtain an access key. Launch a browser window and use this access key in the following url
http://api.currencylayer.com/api/live?access_key=52f52f[redacted]767a9&currencies=GBP&source=USD

to obtain the current conversion rate from US dollars to pounds sterling. The free account restricts the source currency to US dollars. *Figure 72.5* shows the formatted response to this request that is rendered in the browser window. The resource is located at `api.currencylayer.com` and the path to the resource at this ocation is `/api/live`. An access key is required which is obtained when signing up. The query part is everything after the question mark (access key value partially obscured for privacy reasons), i.e.
The query searches for a match where the currency conversion rate is from 1 US dollar (**source**) to British pounds (**GBP**).

access_key=52f52[redacted]c767a9&currencies=GBP&source=USD

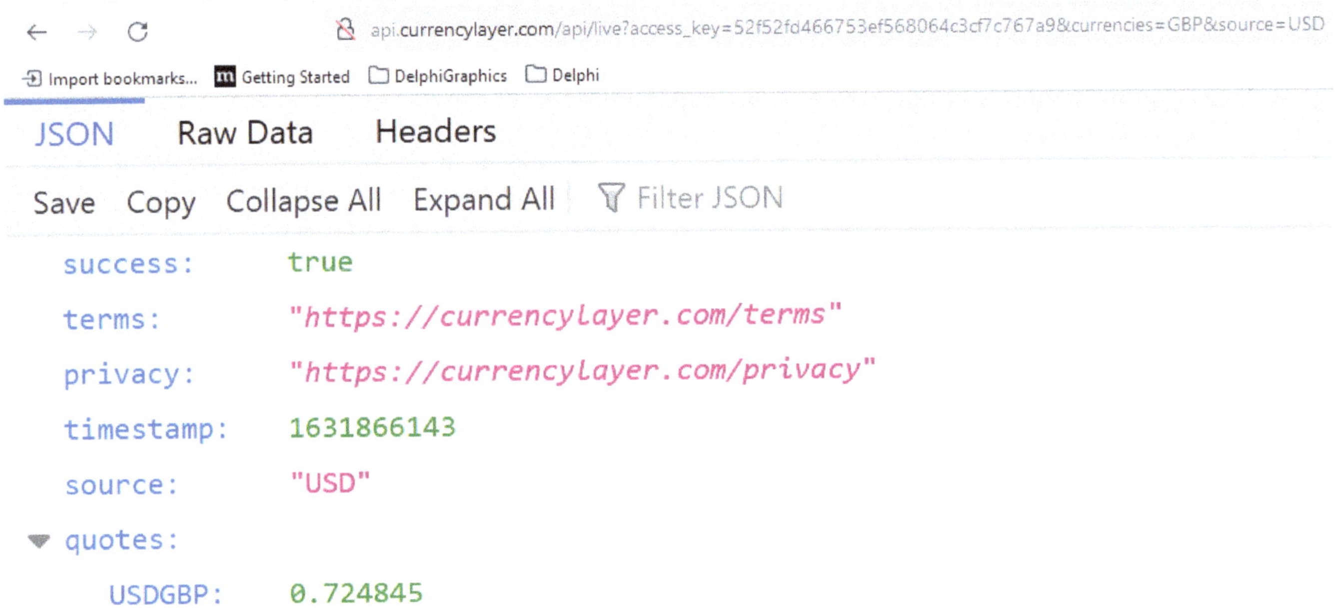

Figure 72.5 Using a free apilayer account and a browser to access the currency converter api of apilayer

Using a Delphi application to obtain currency conversion rates

Create a new Windows VCL application (**File|New**).

Save the project as `RESTCurrencyConverterProject` and the unit as `CurrencyConverterUnit` (**File|Save Project As...**).

1. **Add** a data module to the project - **File|New|Other|Database|Data Module**.
2. **Change** its **Name** property to `DataModuleUnit`.
3. **Add** a **TRESTClient**, a **TRESTRequest**, a **TRESTResponse** and a **TRESTResponseDataSetAdapter** component from the **Rest Client** component palette to the data module form.
4. **Add** a **TMemTable** component from the **FireDAC** component palette to the data module form.

Figure 72.6 shows the **DataModule** form with the added components.

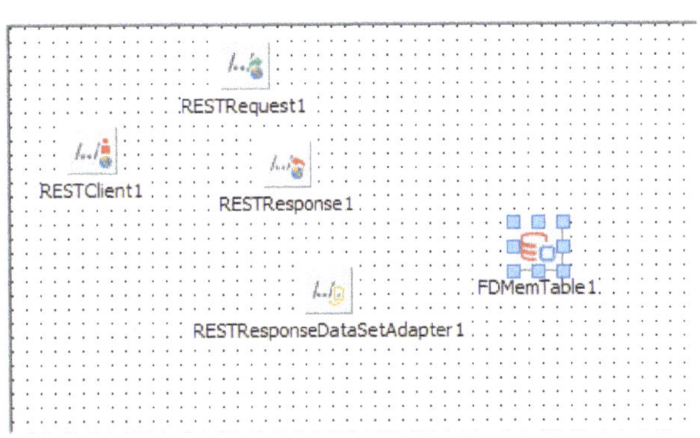

Figure 72.6 DataModule form

The **TRESTClient** component, `RESTClient1`, handles the connection between client and the server (that provides the web service i.e. the currency conversion service. The **TRESTRequest** component, `RESTRequest1`, handles the request i.e. access_key=52f52[redacted]c767a9&currencies=GBP&source=USD.

The **TRESTResponse** component, `RESTResponse1`, collects the JSON formatted response that the server returns. This response is stored in a FireDAC in-memory table, `FDMemTable1`, for convenience. `RESTResponseDataSetAdapter1` provides the connection to this in-memory table (https://www.youtube.com/watch?v=TEP4WcXNpAg). Using a **TFDMemTable** component saves a lot of effort which otherwise would be expended on extracting the currency code-value pairs (https://www.xe.com/iso4217.php). However, both ways will be demonstrated.

5. **Set** the **BaseURL** property of `RESTClient1` to `http://api.currencylayer.com/api`.
6. **Set** the **Client** property of `RESTRequest1` to `RESTClient1`.
7. **Set** the **Method** property of `RESTRequest1` to **rmGET**.
8. **Set** the **Response** property of `RESTRequest1` to `RESTResponse1`.
9. **Click** the value field of the **Params** property for `RESTRequest1` and then **click** on the ellipsis (**...**) of the **Params** property for `RESTRequest1` to bring up the **Editing RESTRequest1.Params** window. **Click** on the **Add New (Ins)** icon to create a new parameter. **Change** the parameter's **Name** property to `access_key` and its **Kind** property to **pkGETorPOST**. **Place** the key that you obtained when you registered with apilayer.com in the **Value** property field.
10. **Create** a second parameter and **set** its **Name** property to `quotes`, its **Kind** property to **pkGETorPOST**, leave its **Value** property blank.
11. **Create** a third parameter and **set** its **Name** property to `source`, its **Kind** property to **pkGETorPOST**, and its **Value** property to **USD**.
12. **Create** a fourth parameter and **set** its **Name** property to `currencies`, its **Kind** property to **pkGETorPOST**, leave its **Value** property blank.
13. **Close** the editing window.
14. **Set** the **Resource** property of `RESTRequest1` to **live**. This selects the resource/path to the live currency rates.
15. **Select** `RESTResponse1` and set its **ContentType** property to **application/json**.
16. **Check** that a valid connection is possible by right clicking on `RESTRequest1`, then selecting **Execute** from the popup window. *Figure 76.7* shows the response for a successful connection attempt.

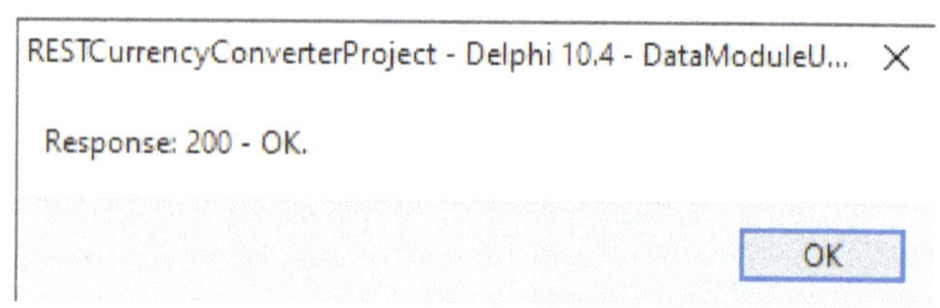

Figure 72.7 Popup window showing response code 200 which is the HTTP code indicating that the connection request was successful

Now to populate `FDMemTable1` with the response:

17. **Set** the **DataSet** property of `RestResponseDataSetAdapter1` to `FDMemTable1`.
18. **Set** the **ResponseJSON** property of `RestResponseDataSetAdapter1` to `RESTResponse1`.
19. **Set** the **StringFieldSize** property of `RestResponseDataSetAdapter1` to `2048`, the **TypesMode** to **Rich**.

20. **Set** the **ContentType** property of `RestResponse1` to `application/json`.
21. **Set** the **RootElement** property of `RestResponseDataSetAdapter1` to `quotes`. This is the key step that sets up a table with name quotes and columns (fields) that correspond to the JSON children of quotes, e.g. `USDGBP`.
22. **Set** the **Active** property of `RestResponseDataSetAdapter1` to **True**. This should create the table quotes with fields and values. To check: **right click** `FDMemTable1` then **select** **Edit DataSet...** in the popup window - *Figure 72.8*.
23. **Select** the `CurrencyConverterUnit` tab then **add** the components arranged as shown in *Figure 72.9*. Change their Name property as shown.

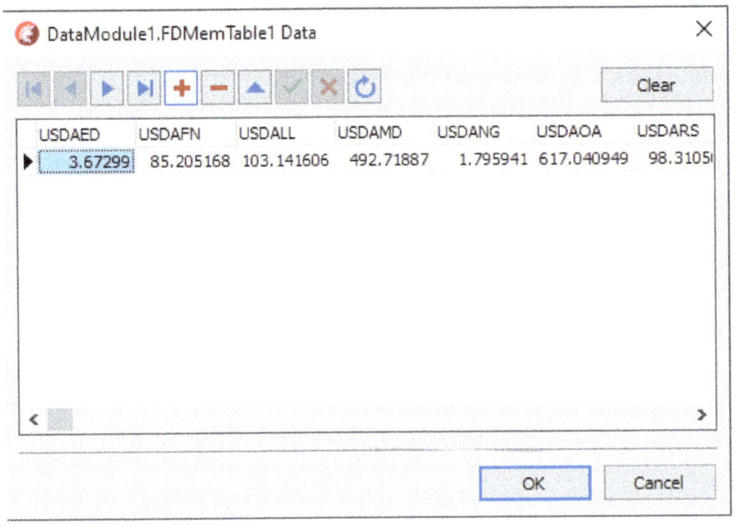

Figure 72.8 Edit DataSet window showing that table with a column for each ISO 4217 Currency Code and its current conversion value for the US dollar

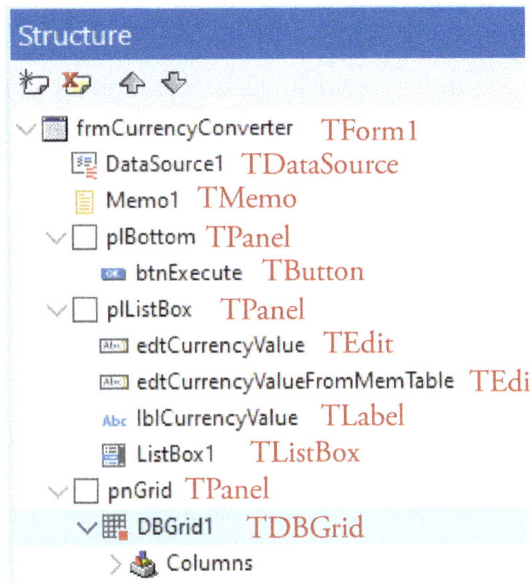

Figure 72.9 Structure window for CurrencyConverterUnit

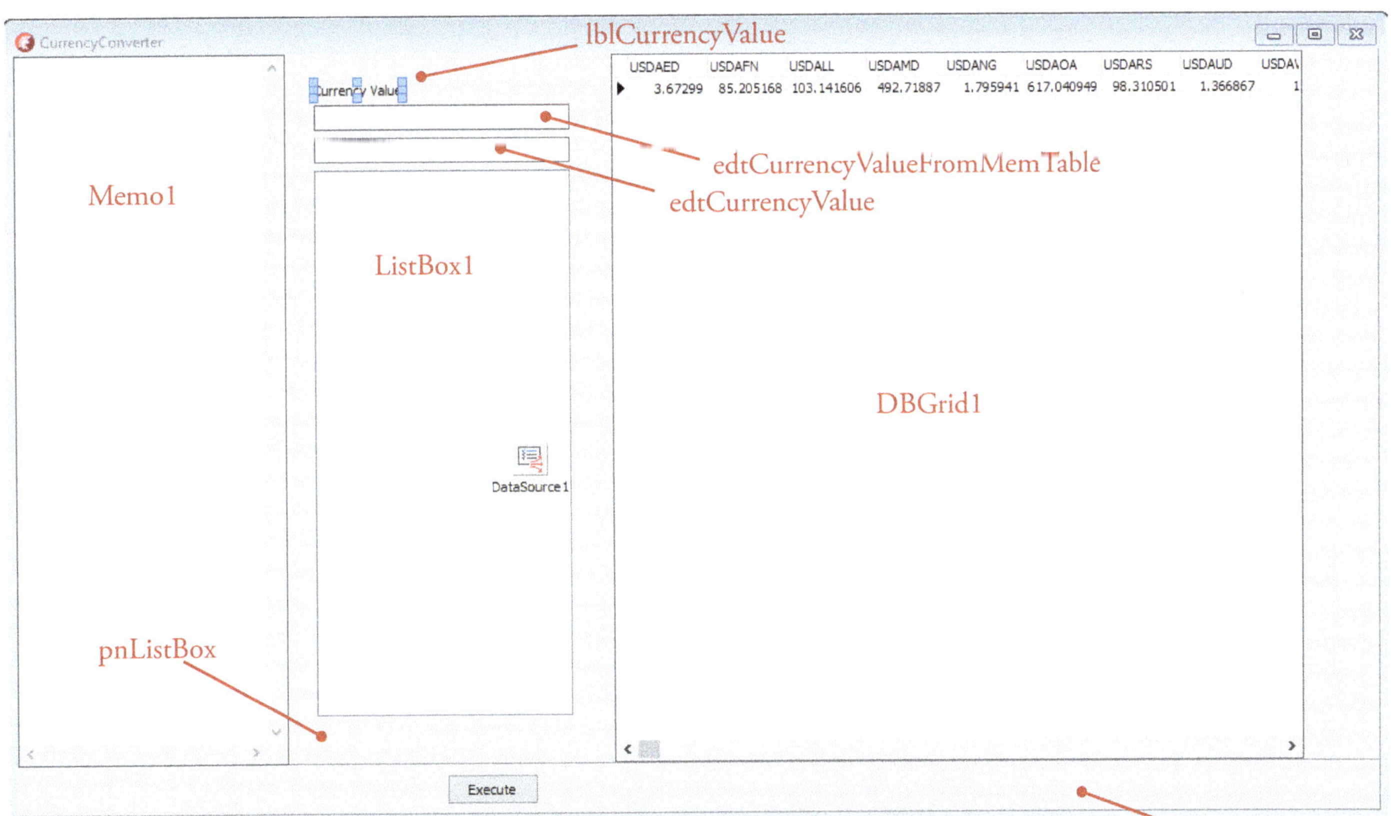

Figure 72.9 CurrencyConverterUnit user interface design

24. **Set** the **Align** property of `pnBottom` to **alBottom**.
25. **Set** the **Align** property of `pnGrid` to **alRight**.
26. **Set** the **Align** property of `Memo1` to **alLeft**.
27. **Set** the **Align** property of `pnListBox` to **alLeft**.
28. **Set** the **DataSet** property of `DataSource1` to `DataModule1.FDMemTable1`.
29. **Set** the **DataSource** property of `DBGrid1` to `DataSource1`. If `DataSource1` is enabled data will appear in `DBGrid1` as shown in *Figure 72.9*.
30. **Double click** the `Execute` button to create an **OnClick** event handler `Procedure TfrmCurrencyConverter.btnExecuteClick`. **Add** the code shown in *Table 72.2* to its body after creating variable `Memo2` as shown. This event handler executes a REST request. The JSON formatted text that is returned is transferred by `RESTClient1` into `RESTResponse1`. This is formatted as JSONText rendering the hierachical nature of the returned JSON as an actual hierachical structure as shown in *Figure 72.10*) and then added to `Memo1`. The remainder of the event handler extracts the ISO standard currency code (although ZWD, Zimbabwe's currency code appears as ZWL. There are other deviations as well) and pastes these to `ListBox1`. `Memo2` retains the currency code- value pairs separated by comma.
31. **Select** `ListBox1` in the **Object Inspector** and **create** an event handler `Procedure TfrmCurrencyConverter.ListBox1Click` for the **OnClick** event. **Populate** its body as shown in *Table 72.2*. When a user clicks on a currency code in `ListBox1`, this event handler puts the currency code and its corresponding value in `edtCurrencyValue` text box, stripping the trailing comma first. The event handler also executes the alternative and easier way of obtaining the data: `edtCurrencyValueFromMemTable.Text := DataModule1.FDMemTable1.FieldByName(s).AsString;` placing the currency value in edit box `edtCurrencyValueFromMemTable` and the code in label `lblCurrencyValue` **Caption** property.
32. **Note** the use utility function `ParseJSON` which is used to remove some unwanted substrings.

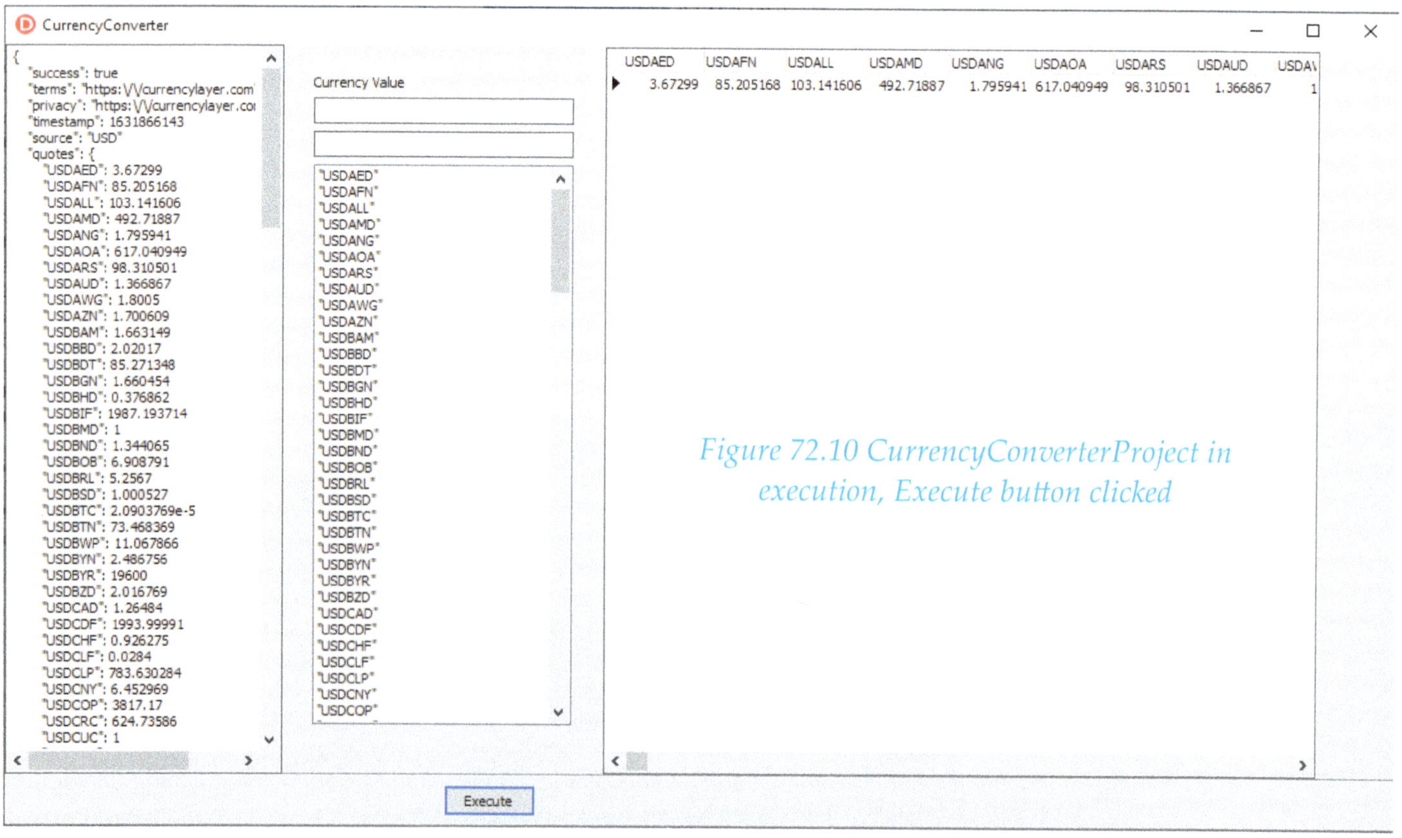

Figure 72.10 CurrencyConverterProject in execution, Execute button clicked

```
Unit CurrencyConvertUnit;

Interface

Uses
  Winapi.Windows, Winapi.Messages, System.SysUtils, System.Variants, System.Classes, Vcl.Graphics,
  Vcl.Controls, Vcl.Forms, Vcl.Dialogs, Vcl.StdCtrls, Vcl.ExtCtrls, Data.DB,
  System.Rtti, System.Bindings.Outputs, Vcl.Bind.Editors, Data.Bind.EngExt,
  Vcl.Bind.DBEngExt, Data.Bind.Components, Data.Bind.DBScope, Vcl.DBCtrls,
  Vcl.Mask, Vcl.Grids, Vcl.DBGrids, FireDAC.Stan.Intf, FireDAC.Stan.Option,
  FireDAC.Stan.Param, FireDAC.Stan.Error, FireDAC.DatS, FireDAC.Phys.Intf,
  FireDAC.DApt.Intf, FireDAC.Stan.Async, FireDAC.DApt, FireDAC.Comp.DataSet,
  FireDAC.Comp.Client;
Type
  TfrmCurrencyConverter = Class(TForm)
                            plBottom : TPanel;
                            btnExecute : TButton;
                            plListBox : TPanel;
                            Memo1 : TMemo;
                            edtCurrencyValue : TEdit;
                            ListBox1 : TListBox;
                            pnGrid : TPanel;
                            DBGrid1 : TDBGrid;
                            DataSource1 : TDataSource;
                            edtCurrencyValueFromMemTable : TEdit;
                            lblCurrencyValue : TLabel;
                            Procedure btnExecuteClick(Sender : TObject);
                            Procedure ListBox1Click(Sender : TObject);
                          End;

Var
  frmCurrencyConverter: TfrmCurrencyConverter;

Implementation

Uses
  DataModuleUnit, System.JSON;

{$R *.dfm}

Var
  Memo2 : TMemo;

Function ParseJSON(strJSON : String) : String;
  Begin
    StrJSON := strJSON.Remove( 0, 11 + AnsiPos('"quotes": {', strJSON)-1 );
    strJSON :- strJSON.Remove(AnsiPos('    }', strJSON), 10);
    Result := strJSON;
  End;

Procedure TfrmCurrencyConverter.btnExecuteClick(Sender : TObject);
  Var
    i : Integer;
    s : String;
  Begin
    DataModule1.RESTRequest1.Execute;
    Memo1.Lines.Add(DataModule1.RESTRequest1.Response.JSONText);
    For i := 0 To Memo1.Lines.Count - 1
      Do Memo1.Lines[i] := Memo1.Lines[i].Remove(Memo1.Lines[i].LastIndexOf(','), 1);
    Memo2 := TMemo.Create(frmCurrencyConverter);
    Memo2.Hide;
    Memo2.Parent :=  frmCurrencyConverter;
    Memo2.Lines.Add(ParseJSON(DataModule1.RESTRequest1.Response.JSONText));

    For i := Memo2.Lines.Count - 1 DownTo 0
      Do
        If Memo2.Lines[i] = ''
          Then Memo2.Lines.Delete(i);
    For i := 0 To Memo2.Lines.Count - 1
      Do
        Begin
          Memo2.Lines[i] := Memo2.Lines[i].TrimLeft;
          ListBox1.Items.Add(Memo2.Lines[i].Remove(AnsiPos(':', Memo2.Lines[i]) - 1, 15));
        End;
    For i := ListBox1.Count - 1 DownTo 0
      Do
        If ListBox1.Items[i] = ''
          Then ListBox1.Items.Delete(i);
    Memo2.Hide;
  End;

Procedure TfrmCurrencyConverter.ListBox1Click(Sender : TObject);
  Var
    s : String;
    i : Integer;
  Begin
    For i := Memo2.Lines.Count - 1 DownTo 0
      Do
        If Memo2.Lines[i].Contains(ListBox1.Items[ListBox1.ItemIndex])
          Then s := Memo2.Lines[i];
    edtCurrencyValue.Text := s.Remove(s.LastIndexOf(','), 1);
    s := '';
    s := ListBox1.Items[ListBox1.ItemIndex];
    s := StringReplace(s,'"','',[rfReplaceAll]);
    edtCurrencyValueFromMemTable.Text := DataModule1.FDMemTable1.FieldByName(s).AsString;
    lblCurrencyValue.Caption := 'Currency ' + s;
  End;
End.
```

Table 72.2 Unit CurrencyConvertUnit.pas

73 TMS Software components

Web application development with Delphi

Purpose: To become familiar with TMS WEB Core

TMS WEB Core makes it possible to develop web(client) applications with Delphi. A Delphi application uses **TMS WEB Core** components to build form-based projects which are then converted into JavaScript when the project is compiled and linked. Applications created in this way must be executed in a web browser.

A knowledge of Object Pascal/Delphi is sufficient to be able to use **TMS WEB Core** to create Single-Page-Applications (SPAs). SPAs rely on a single HTML document for which all application content is dynamically loaded. All that users need to do is open an HTML document in their browser or launch the application.

TMS Software has made it easy to use JavaScript frameworks such as Bootstrap, or to use HTML and CSS directly, to visually enhance TMS WEB Core applications.

Download and **install** **TMS WEB Core** for your version of Delphi from

https://www.tmssoftware.com/site/tmswebcore.asp#product-downloads

TMS Software offers fully functional and fully free versions of TMS products for students and teachers for non-commercial use (academic licence). It is also possible to use the trial version to explore TMS.

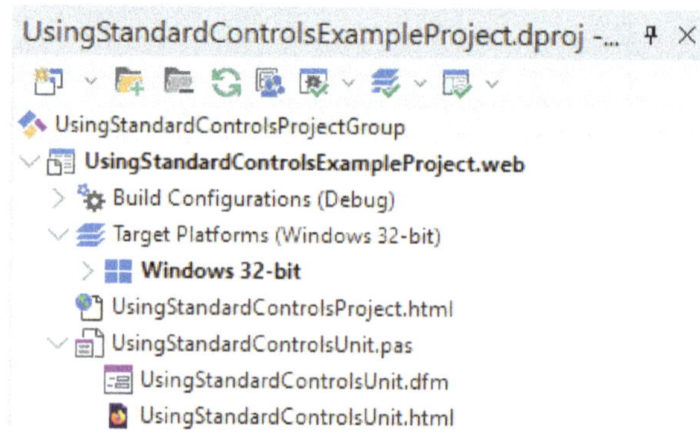

Figure 73.1 Project manager window in Delphi 10.4.2

Using standard controls example

Launch Delphi and then select **File|New|Other|TMS Web Application** to create a new web application. P

Select **File|SaveProject As...** and save the following in folder `UsingStandardControlsExample`

- `UsingStandardControlsUnit.pas`
- `UsingStandardControlsProject.html`
- `UsingStandardControlsExampleProject.dproj`

Right click the project group node in the **Project Manager** (*Figure 73.1*) and **save** project group as `UsingStandardControlsProjectGroup.groupproj`.

Open the **TMS WEB** tab in the **component palette** - *Figure 73.2*.

Add a **TWebLabel**, two **TWebButtons**, a **TWebEdit**, a **TWebMemo**, and a **TWebListBox** to the form as shown in *Figure 73.3*. **Configure** these as shown in *Figure 73.3*.

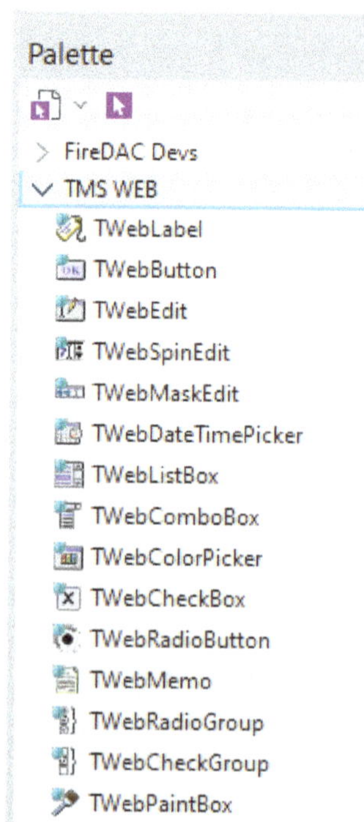

Figure 73.2 Component Palette TMS WEB tab

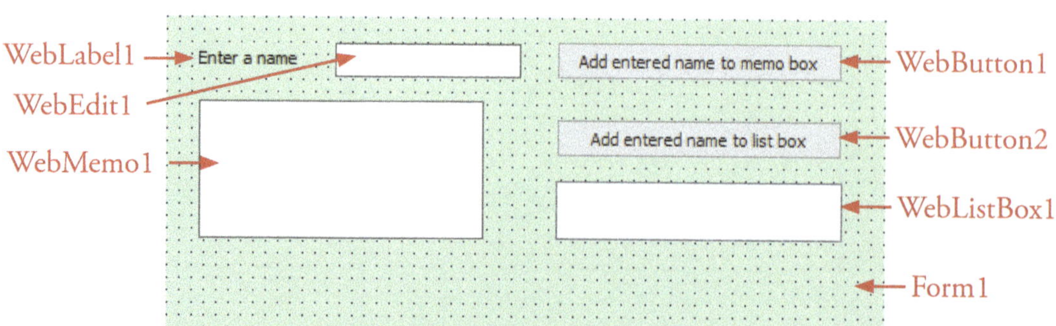

Figure 73.3 Form design

Double click each **TWebButton** component to create **OnClick** event handlers. **Add** the code shown in *Table 73.1*.

Select File|Save All.

Now **select Run Without Debugging**.

The project is compiled and linked then run. The output of the compiling and linking processes is stored in two folders:

1. `Win32\Debug` and
2. `TMSWeb\Debug`

```
Procedure TForm1.WebButton1Click(Sender : TObject);
  Begin
    WebMemo1.Lines.Append(WebEdit1.Text);
  End;

Procedure TForm1.WebButton2Click(Sender : TObject);
  Begin
    WebListBox1.Items.Append(WebEdit1.Text);
  End;
```

Table 73.1 Event handlers for the two TWebButtons

Figure 73.4 and *Figure 73.5* show the contents of each folder.

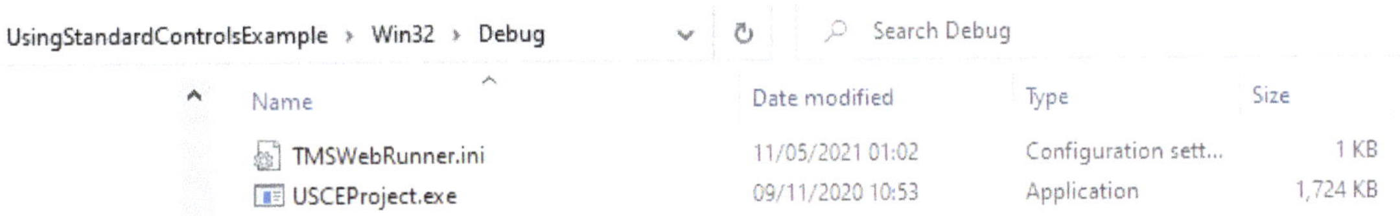

Figure 73.4 Output of Delphi compiler and linker is stored in folder Win32\Debug folder if the Build configuration is Debug.

If the Build configuration is Release then USCEProject.js.map is not generated. This file is needed when debugging the application

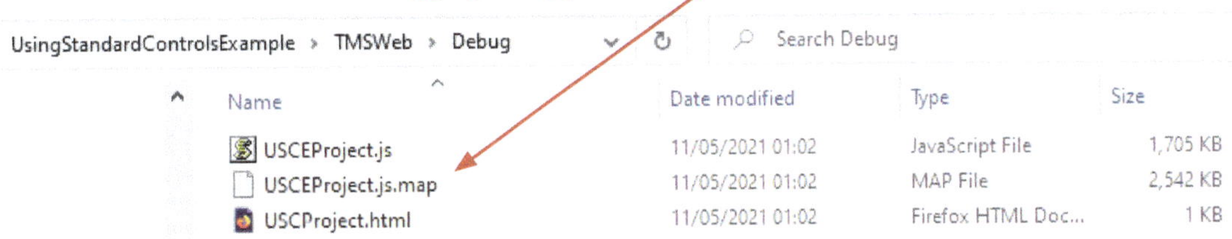

Figure 73.5 Output of transpiler (Object Pascal to JavaScript compiler) is stored in folder TMSWEB\Debug

Using abbreviated file names for presentation purposes,

Table 73.2 shows the contents of `USCProject.html`. This HTML document runs the script `USCEProject.js`.

The outcome of the execution is shown in *Figure 73.7*.

```
<!DOCTYPE html>
<html lang="en">
  <head>
    <meta http-equiv="Content-type" content="text/html; charset=utf-8" />
    <meta name="viewport" content="width=device-width, initial-scale=1">
    <meta >
    <noscript>Your browser does not support JavaScript!</noscript>
    <link rel="icon" href="data:;base64,=">

    <title>TMS Web Project</title>
    <script type="text/javascript" src="USCEProject.js"></script>
    <style>
    </style>
  </head>
  <body>

  </body>
  <script type="text/javascript">
    rtl.run();
  </script>
</html>
```

Table 73.2 USCProject.html

Return to the IDE and **right click** `USCEProject.web` in the **Project Manager** window to bring up the menu shown in *Figure 73.6*.

Click Manage JavaScript Libraries to bring up the **JavaScript Manager** window shown in *Figure 73.8*.

Click the tick box for **Bootstrap 4.3.1** then **click OK**.

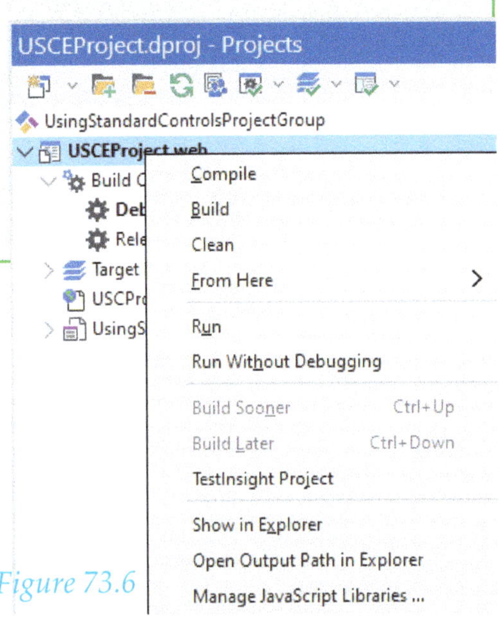

Figure 73.6

Firstly, **ensure** that the **Build Configuration** setting is **Debug** (**Project Manager** panel) and not **Release** then **select** `WebEdit1` on the form. In the Object Inspector, **click** the property **ElementClassName** field to **select** it, then **click** the listbox arrow and **hold** the mouse button down to bring up the **Bootstrap** options shown in *Figure 73.9*.

Select **form-control**. **Repeat** for `WebMemo1` and `WebListBox1`.

Select `WebButton1` and **set** its **ElementClassName** to **btn-primary**. **Select** `WebButton2` and **set** its **ElementClassName** to **btn-success**. Details of these **Bootstrap** classes may be obtained from

https://www.w3schools.com/bootstrap/bootstrap_buttons.asp

Save All then **Run Without Debugging**. The outcome is shown in *Figure 73.10*.

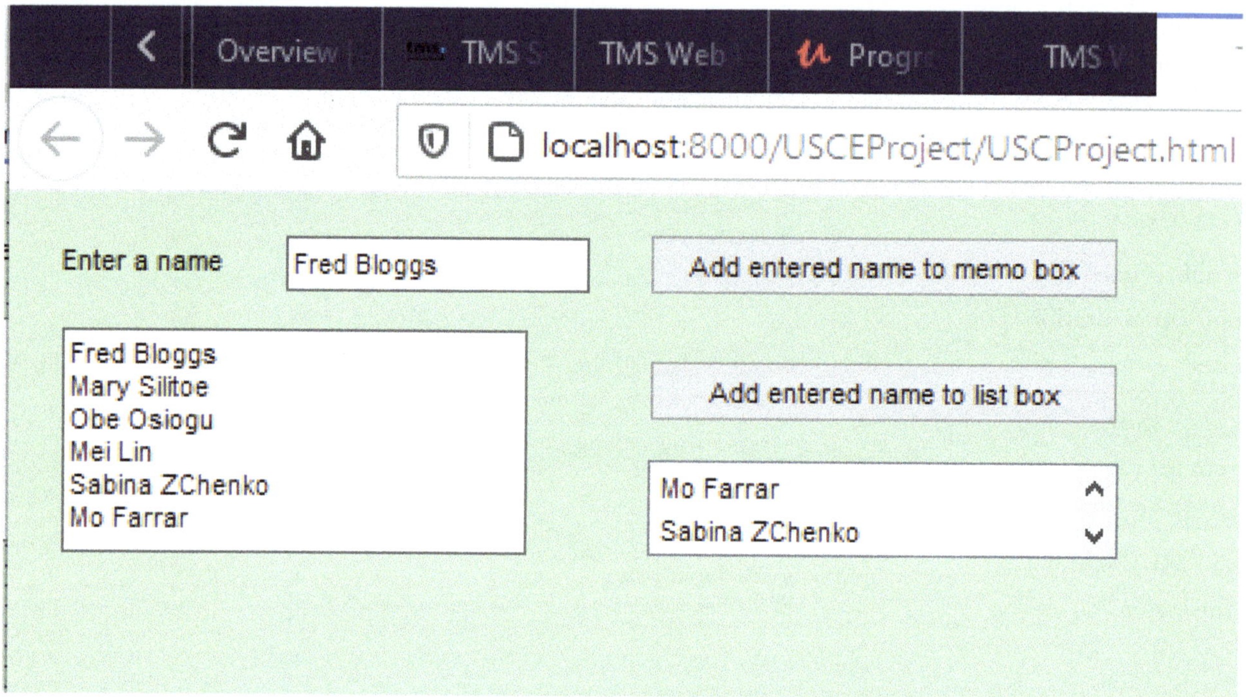

Figure 73.7 UsingStandardControlsExampleProject in execution with some data in a FireFox web browser - Project was resaved as USCEProject.dproj and HTML document as USCProject.html to shorten the url in the address bar for presentation purposes.

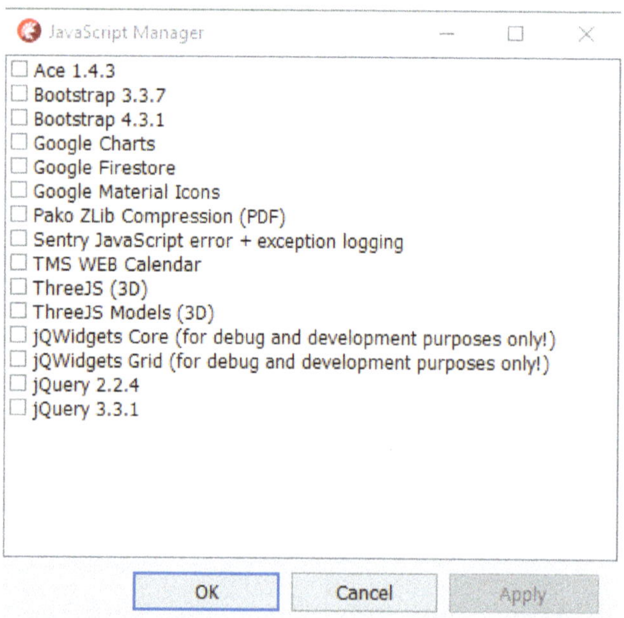

Figure 73.8 JavaScript Manager window

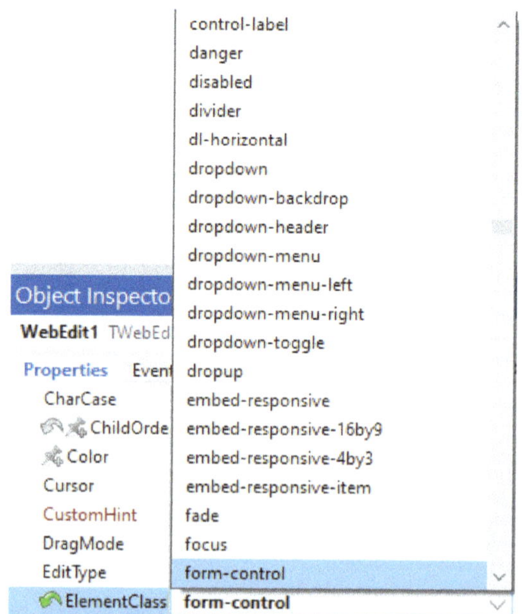

Figure 73.9 Setting ElementClassName to form-control for control WebEdit1

Compiling and linking from the IDE produces an executable `USCEProject.exe` - *Figure 73.4* - that runs on the local machine when **Run Without Debugging** is selected. This executable is actually a web server that listens on port 8000 of the local machine (localhost) and which responds to requests form the web browser - *Figure 73.10*.

If the files from `TMSWeb\Debug`

- `USCEProject.js`
- `USCEProject.js.map`
- `UsingStandardControlsProject.html`
- `UsingStandardControlsUnit.html`

are copied to a public web server, `USCEProject.exe` is not required.

Figure 73.11 shows a FireFox web browser rendering of `USCProject.html` hosted at https://www.educational-computing.com, data has already been added via the web edit box and the two buttons.

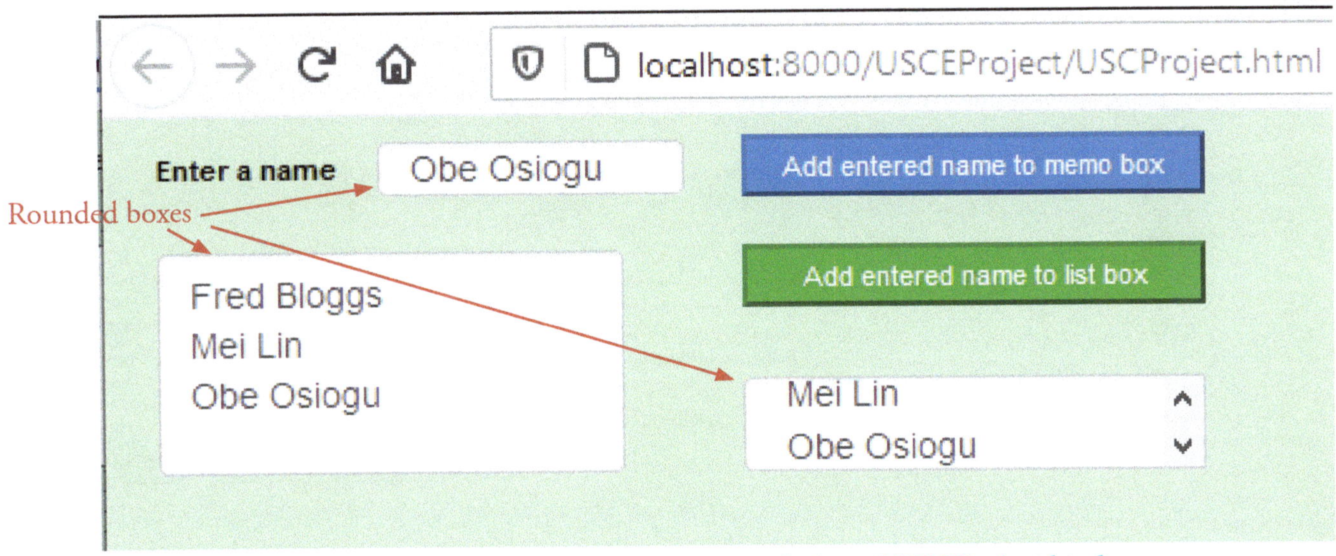

Figure 73.10 FireFox web browser rendering of USCProject.html, data added via the web edit box and the two buttons

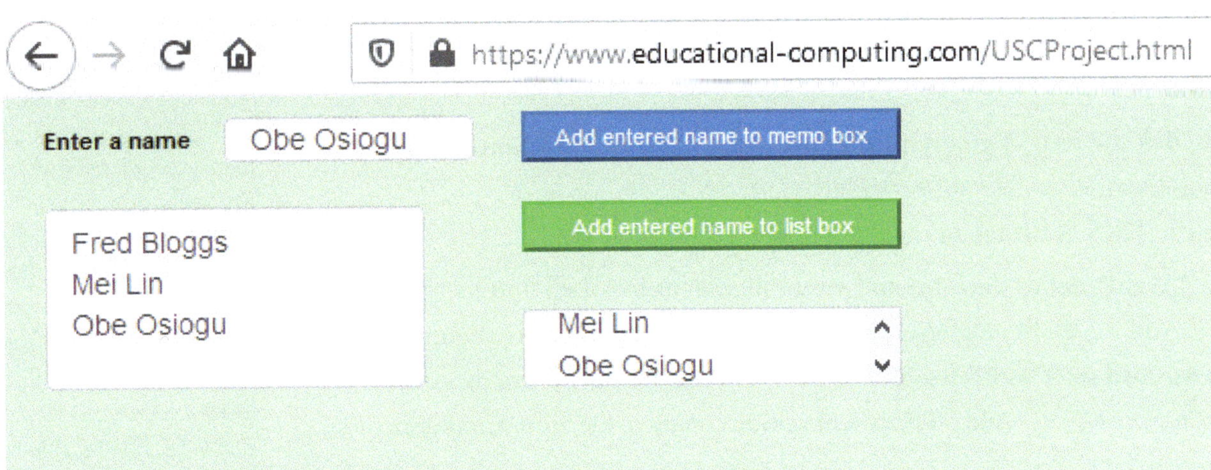

Figure 73.11 FireFox web browser rendering of USCProject.html hosted at www.educational-computing.com, data added via the web edit box and the two buttons

Using Google maps

Figure 73.12 demonstrates that it is possible to make a fully interactive JavaScript/HTML application with Delphi using the **TWebGoogleMaps** component from **TMS Software** (https://www.tmssoftware.com).

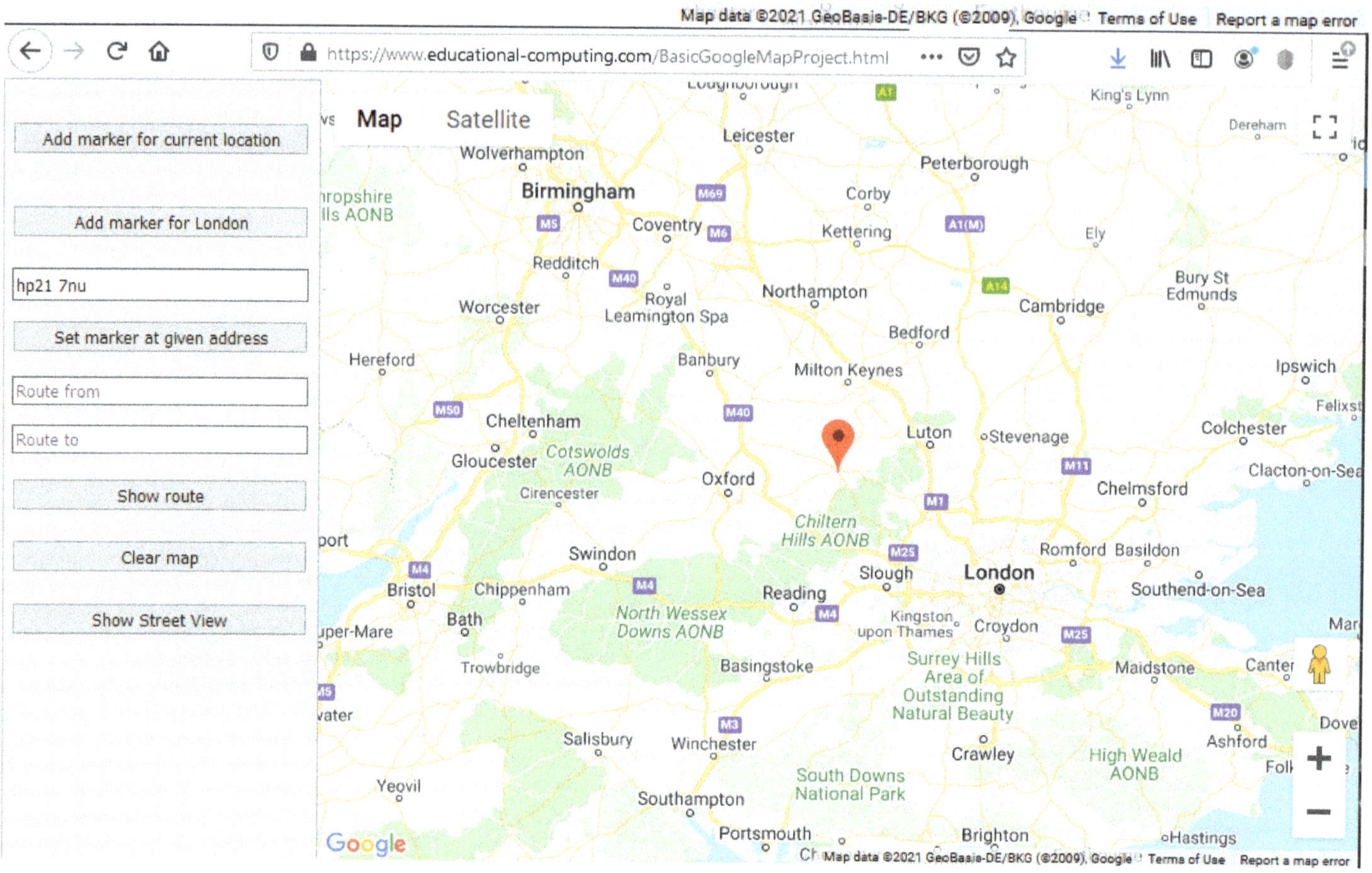

Figure 73.12 FireFox web browser rendering of BasicGoogleMapProject.html hosted at www.educational-computing.com,

Launch Delphi and then select **File|New|Other|TMS Web Application** to create a new web application.

Select **File|SaveProject As...** and save the following in folder `BasicGoogleMapProject`

- `BasicGoogleMapUnit.pas`
- `BasicGoogleMapProject.html`
- `BasicGoogleMapProject.dproj`

Right click the project group node in the **Project Manager** and **save** project group as `BasicGoogleMapProjectGroup.groupproj`.

Open the **TMS WEB** tab in the **component palette** - *Figure 73.2*.

Add a **TWebPanel** to the form and set its alignment to **alLeft** and its **width** to 241. **Add** a **TWebGoogleMaps** control to the form and set its alignment to **alClient. Add** six **TWebButtons** and three **TWebEdit** controls to the panel as shown in *Figure 73.13*. **Add** a **TWebGeolocation** control to the form. **Configure** these as shown in *Figure 73.13*.

Change the names of the buttons respectively to

```
webbtnAddMarkerCurrentLocation
webbtnAddMarkerLondon
webbtnSetMarkerAtAddress
webbtnShowStreetView
webbtnShowRoute
webbtnClearMap
```

Information

Google maps API key:

A Google maps API is needed which may be obtained from https://developers.google.com/maps/documentation/javascript/get-api-key or https://developers.google.com/maps/documentation/embed/get-api-key

YouTube video on how to obtain a free API key: https://www.youtube.com/watch?v=1JNwpp5L4vM

Note that Google no longer provides an API key without requiring you to register a billing account. Instead, it gives $200 of credit which is more than enough to test out projects using Google maps. Check first because Google's policy can change at any time.

Change the **name** property of the form to `frmBasicMaps`. **Set** the anchors for all the controls placed on the panel to

[akLeft,akTop,akRight]

A **Google maps API** is needed which may be obtained by following either link shown in the information panel on the previous page. **Select** the form and in the Object Inspector, **double click** the event **OnCreate** in the **Events** tab to create the event handler `WebFormCreate`. **Add** the API key assignment to the body of this event handler shown in *Table 73.6*.

Double click the button with caption `Add marker for London` to create an **OnClick** event handler. **Add** the variable declaration to `BasicGoogleMapUnit` and the code as shown in *Table 73.3* to the body of this event handler.

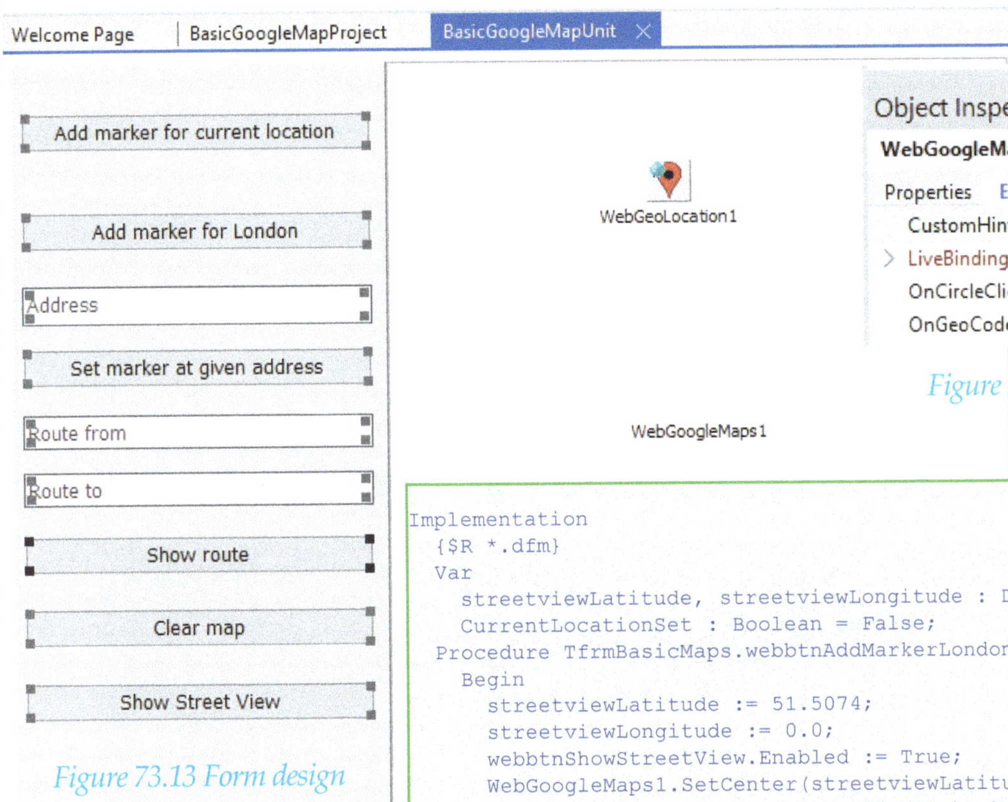

Figure 73.13 Form design

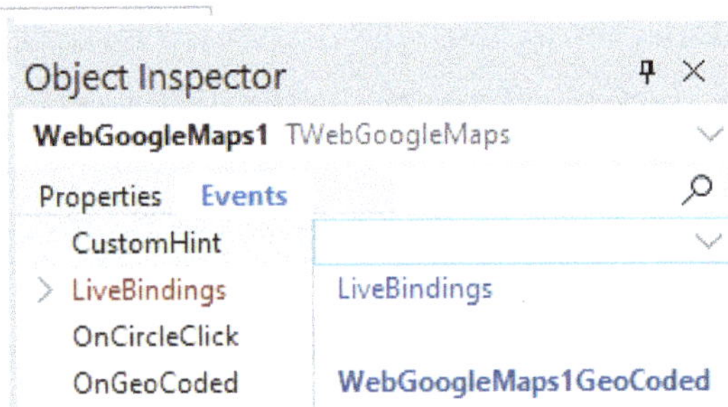

Figure 73.14 Creating event handler

```
Implementation
  {$R *.dfm}
  Var
    streetviewLatitude, streetviewLongitude : Double;
    CurrentLocationSet : Boolean = False;
  Procedure TfrmBasicMaps.webbtnAddMarkerLondonClick(Sender : TObject);
    Begin
      streetviewLatitude := 51.5074;
      streetviewLongitude := 0.0;
      webbtnShowStreetView.Enabled := True;
      WebGoogleMaps1.SetCenter(streetviewLatitude, streetviewLongitude);
      WebGoogleMaps1.AddMarker(streetviewLatitude, streetviewLongitude, 'London');
    End;
```

Table 73.3 OnClick event handler for button with caption Add marker for London

```
Procedure TfrmBasicMaps.webbtnSetMarkerAtAddressClick(Sender : TObject);
  Begin
    If WebEdit1.Text <> ''
      Then
        Begin
          WebGoogleMaps1.GeoCode(WebEdit1.Text);
          webbtnShowStreetView.Enabled := True;
        End
      Else ShowMessage('Please enter an address');
  End;
```

Table 73.4 OnClick event handler for button with caption Set marker at given address

```
Procedure TfrmBasicMaps.WebGoogleMaps1GeoCoded(Sender : TObject;
                                               Lon, Lat : Double);

  Begin
    streetviewLatitude := Lat;
    streetviewLongitude := Lon;
    WebGoogleMaps1.AddMarker(Lat, Lon);
    WebGoogleMaps1.SetCenter(Lat, Lon);
  End;
```

Table 73.5 Event handler for OnGeoCoded event

```
Procedure TfrmBasicMaps.WebFormCreate(Sender : TObject);
  Begin
    WebGoogleMaps1.APIKey := 'AI
  End;
```

Table 73.6 OnCreate event handler for form frmBasicMaps

Double click the button with caption `Set marker for given address` to create an **OnClick** event handler `webbtnSetMarkerAtAddressClick`. **Add** the code shown in *Table 73.4* to the body of this event handler. The procedure call `WebGoogleMaps1.GeoCode(WebEdit1.Text)` converts the address entered in edit box `WebEdit1` to latitude and longitude coordinates. A successful conversion triggers the event **OnGeoCoded**. This event is handled by event handler `WebGoogleMaps1GeoCoded` coded as shown in *Table 73.5*. To create this event handler, **double click** the **OnGeoCode** event property of `WebGoogleMaps1` in the **Object Inspector** as shown in *Figure 73.14* and **add** the code shown in *Table 73.5*.

Double click the button with caption `Show Street View` to create an **OnClick** event handler. **Add** the code shown in *Table 73.7* to the body of this event handler.

Save All then **Run Without Debugging** to launch the application in a local browser.

Click `Set marker at a given address` after entering 'Chilterns' as shown in *Figure 73.15*. **Click** `Show Street View` to open up the street view for this location. *Figure 73.15* shows the street view rotated to look along the road.

```
Procedure TfrmBasicMaps.webbtnShowStreetViewClick(Sender: TObject);
  Begin
    If Not CurrentLocationSet
      Then
        If WebGoogleMaps1.GetCenter(streetviewLatitude, streetviewLongitude)
          Then WebGoogleMaps1.ShowStreetView(streetviewLatitude, streetviewLongitude);
  End;
```

Table 73.7 OnClick event handler for button with caption Show Street View

Figure 73.15 Show Street View rendered in FireFox - Google Street Maps image replaced by an actual image of Peters Lane (Google does not permit the printing of street view images)

The visible width of the location address edit box, `WebEdit1`, is constrained by the panel `WebPanel1`'s width. If an address of even a modest length is entered it will be partially obscured. To remedy this, `WebPanel1` needs to expand when the edit box `WebEdit1` becomes the focus (event **OnEnter**) and contract when the focus moves elsewhere (event **OnExit**). **Create** event handlers for these two events - **double click** these event properties of `WebEdit1` in the **Object Inspector**. **Add** the code shown in *Table 73.8* to these event handlers.

```
Procedure TfrmBasicMaps.WebEdit1Enter(Sender : TObject);
  Begin
    WebPanel1.Width := 400;
  End;
Procedure TfrmBasicMaps.WebEdit1Exit(Sender : TObject);
  Begin
    WebPanel1.Width := 241;
  End;
```

Table 73.8 Event handlers that adjust the width of WebPanel1

Clear the **Text** property of all three edit boxes and **set** the **TextHint** property for each in the **Object Inspector** as follows

```
WebEdit1: Address
WebEdit2: Route from
WebEdit3: Route to
```

Double click the button with caption `Clear map` to create an **OnClick** event handler. **Add** the code shown in *Table 73.9* to the body of this event handler.

```
Procedure TfrmBasicMaps.webbtnClearMapClick(Sender : TObject);
  Begin
    WebGoogleMaps1.HideStreetView;
    WebGoogleMaps1.ClearMarkers;
    WebGoogleMaps1.RemoveDirections;
    CurrentLocationSet := False;
    webbtnShowStreetView.Enabled := False;
  End;
```

Table 73.9 OnClick event handler for button with caption Clear map

Double click the button with caption `Show route` to create an **OnClick** event handler. **Add** the code shown in *Table 73.10* to the body of this event handler.

```
Procedure TfrmBasicMaps.webbtnShowRouteClick(Sender : TObject);
  Begin
    If (WebEdit2.Text <> '') And (WebEdit3.Text <> '')
      Then
        Begin
          WebGoogleMaps1.RemoveDirections;
          WebGoogleMaps1.ShowDirections(WebEdit2.Text, WebEdit3.Text);
        End
      Else ShowMessage('Please enter a from and to address');
  End;
```

Table 73.10 OnClick event handler for button with caption Show route

Save All then **Run Without Debugging** to launch the application in a local browser.

Click `Show route` after entering 'Aylesbury' and 'Portsmouth' for *Route from* and *Route to*, respectively, as shown in *Figure 73.16* to obtain a graphical display of one possible route.

The button with caption `Add marker for current location` is treated differently because it needs to obtain the current location from the computer itself.

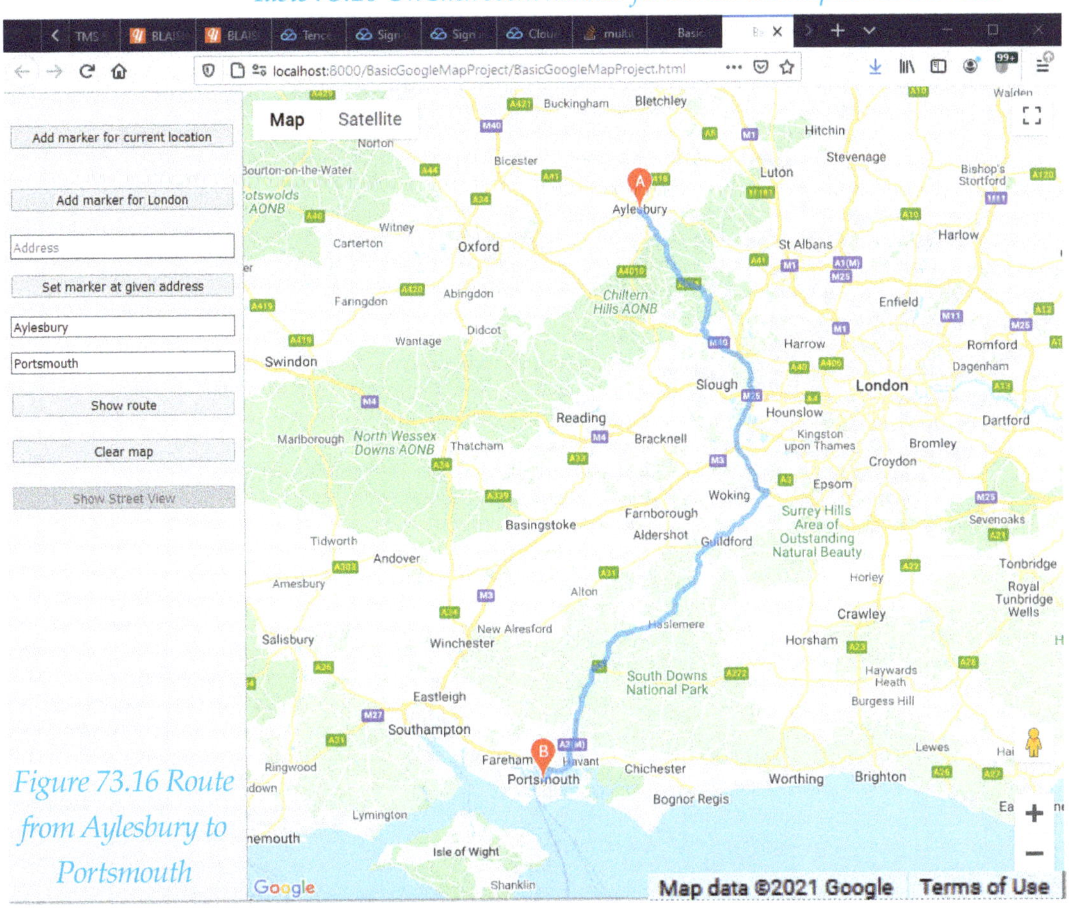

Figure 73.16 Route from Aylesbury to Portsmouth

The event handler for the **OnClick** event is shown in *Table 73.11*.

```
Procedure TfrmBasicMaps.webbtnAddMarkerCurrentLocationClick(Sender : TObject);
  Begin
    If WebGeoLocation1.HasGeolocation
      Then
        Begin
          WebGeoLocation1.GetGeolocation;
          CurrentLocationSet := True;
          webbtnShowStreetView.Enabled := False;
        End;
  End;
```

Table 73.11 OnClick event handler for button with caption Add marker for current location

Set button `Show Street View`'s **Enable** property to false so that this button will be greyed out when the application is launched. This prevents this button from being used after the `Add marker for current location` button is clicked. For some reason, the street view is overriden by the map view. With the application running in a browser, resetting the system by clicking `Clear map` and entering an address instead or clicking the `Add marker for London` button before clicking `Show Street View` enables the correct functioning of street view.

Select `WebGoogleMaps1` and in the **Object Inspector** set the **Options DefaultLatitude** to 51.5074, the **DefaultLongitude** to 0.1272 and the **DefaultZoom** to 8. This ensures that the map is centred on London when the application runs in the browser not Sydney, New South Wales, Australia.

Save All. If the intention is to run the application from a web site, change the **Build configuration** in the **Project Manager** to release. This ensures that the JavaScript file is the smallest possible and the map file is not created.

Click Project|Options|TMS WEB|Compile and check that obfuscation and optimization are enabled - *Figure 73.17*. Obfuscation set to true means that the JavaScript file will be created in a way that makes it difficult to read it in the **Developer Tools** window of the browser running the Javascript file.

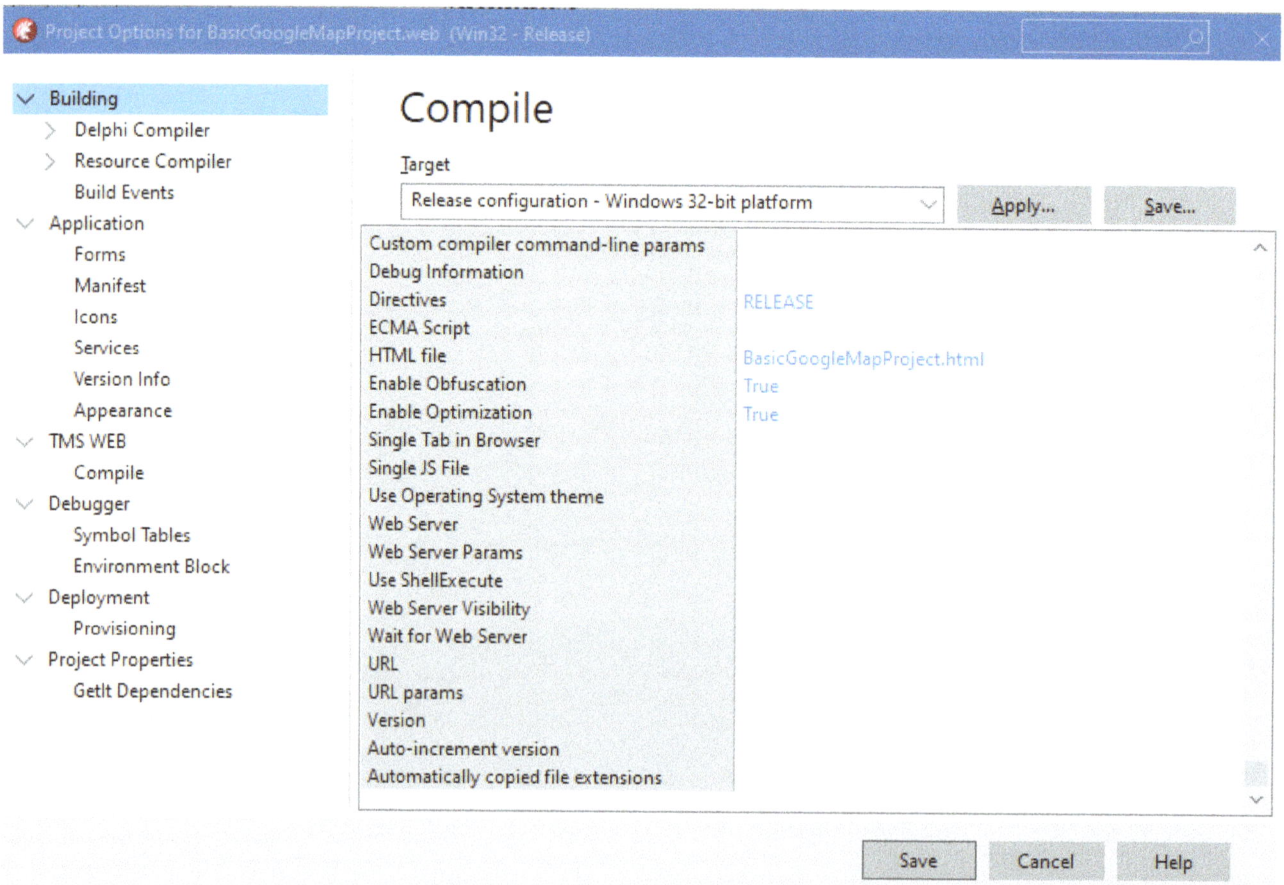

Figure 73.17 Project|Options|TMS WEB|Compile Enable Obfuscation and Enable Optimization set to true

XData server New South Wales public schools map project

The goal of this Delphi project is to generate html and JavaScript code that when run in a web browser displays the locations of public schools of New South Wales, Australia by marker ( ) on a Google map, as shown in *Figure 73.18*.

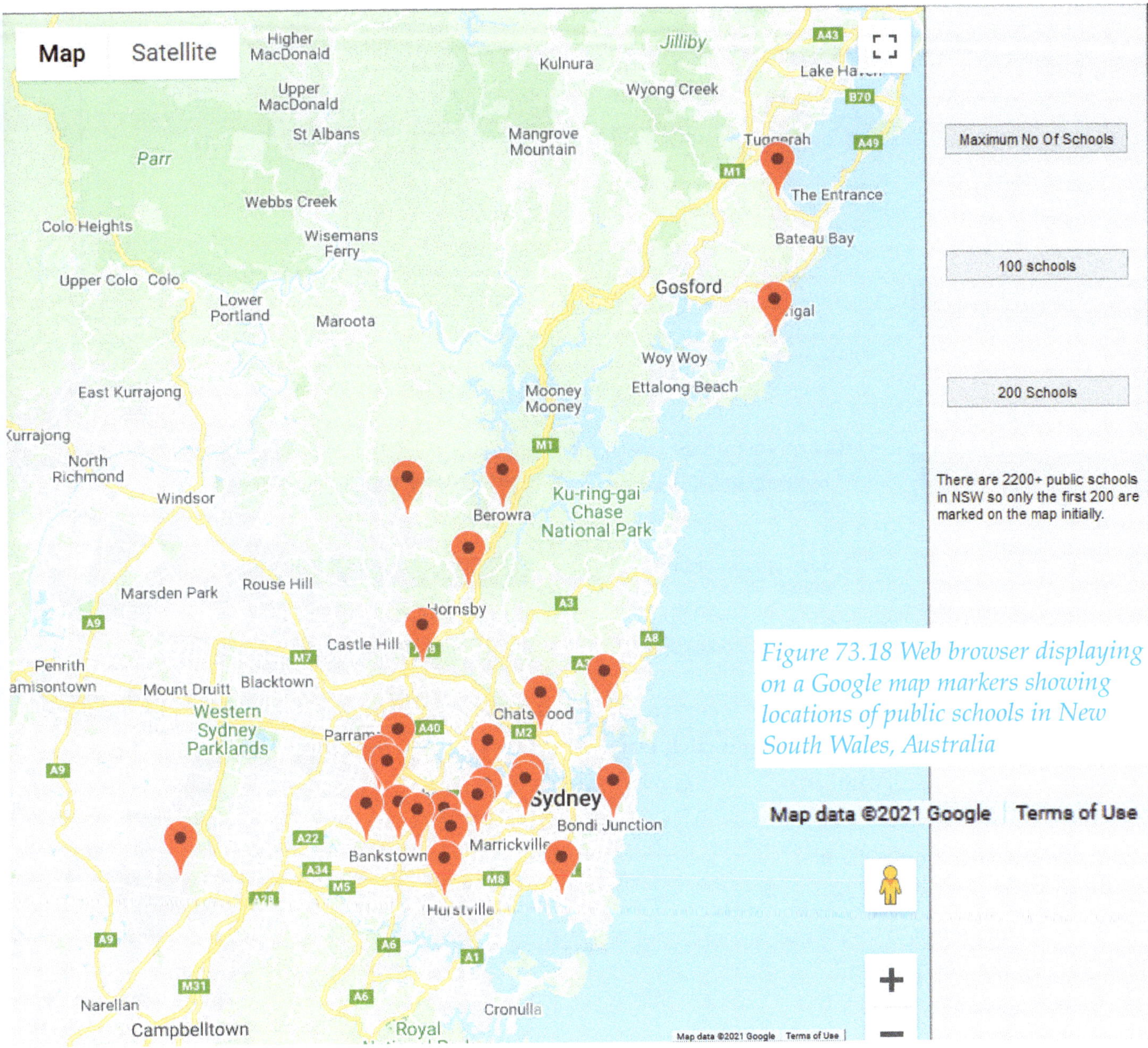

Figure 73.18 Web browser displaying on a Google map markers showing locations of public schools in New South Wales, Australia

The data for this application was stored using **Microsoft® SQL Server Express**[1] in a single-table database. The data for the application was downloaded in csv file format from https://data.cese.nsw.gov.au/data/dataset/nsw-public-schools-master-dataset and used under a Creative Commons Open Data licence (http://www.opendefinition.org/licenses/cc-by) - *Figure 73.21*. The downloaded data was first extracted from the compressed csv file[2] then saved in uncompressed format in `NSW.csv` before being imported into the database.

Launch Microsoft SQL Server Server Management Studio 18 (or the version available to you). Connect to the server using Windows authentication (i.e. Windows domain login) as shown in *Figure 73.20*.

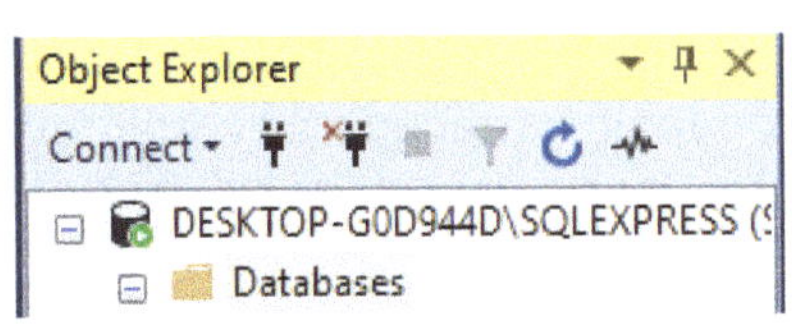

Figure 73.19

1 SQL Server 2019 Express is a free edition of SQL Server, https://www.microsoft.com/en-gb/sql-server/sql-server-downloads

2 The application doesn't need to use a database as it can extract the required data directly from the flat file but a different application might which is why the database approach is illustrated here.

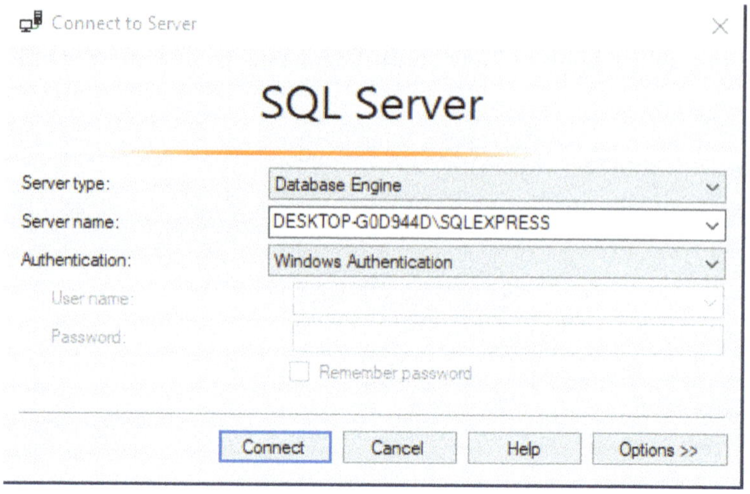

Figure 73.20 Connecting to SQL Server using Windows Authentication

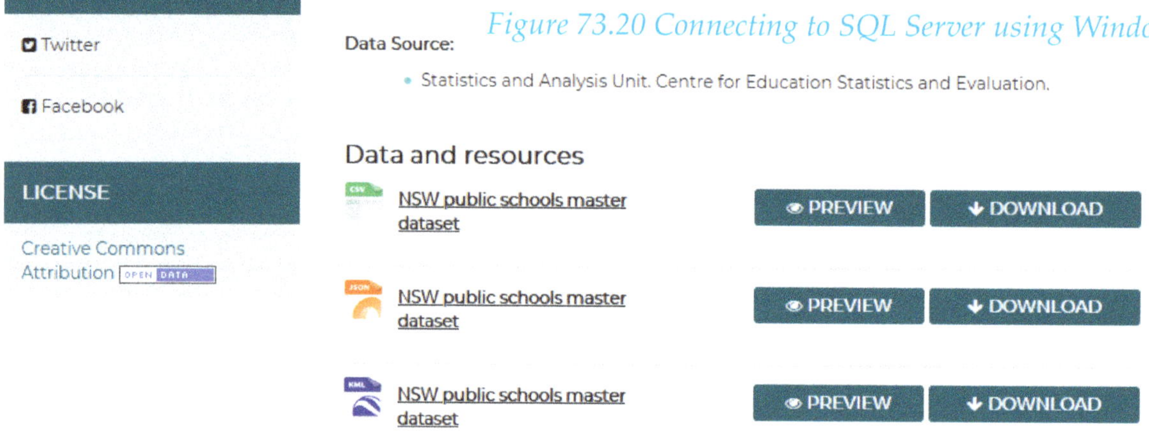

Figure 73.21 Source of csv data: https://data.cese.nsw.gov.au/data/dataset/nsw-public-schools-master-dataset

Create a new database in SQL Server - **right click Databases** (*Figure 73.19*) then **click** the submenu option New Database... (*Figure 73.22*), name it `NSW`. This database will consist of a single table generated from a flat file. **Click** Tasks|Import Flat File... (see *Figure 73.22*) and **select** `NSW.csv`. **Click** through the windows until the **Modify Columns** window is reached. **Modify** the **nvarchar** setting, in most cases to `nvarchar(200)` - *Figure 74.23*. SQL Server estimates the required setting but is unable to anticipate the requirement for every string field. If a string field value is too long for the given setting then the table generation process fails. The setting `nvarchar(200)` is generous enough for success. You may experiment and find that a lower setting works.

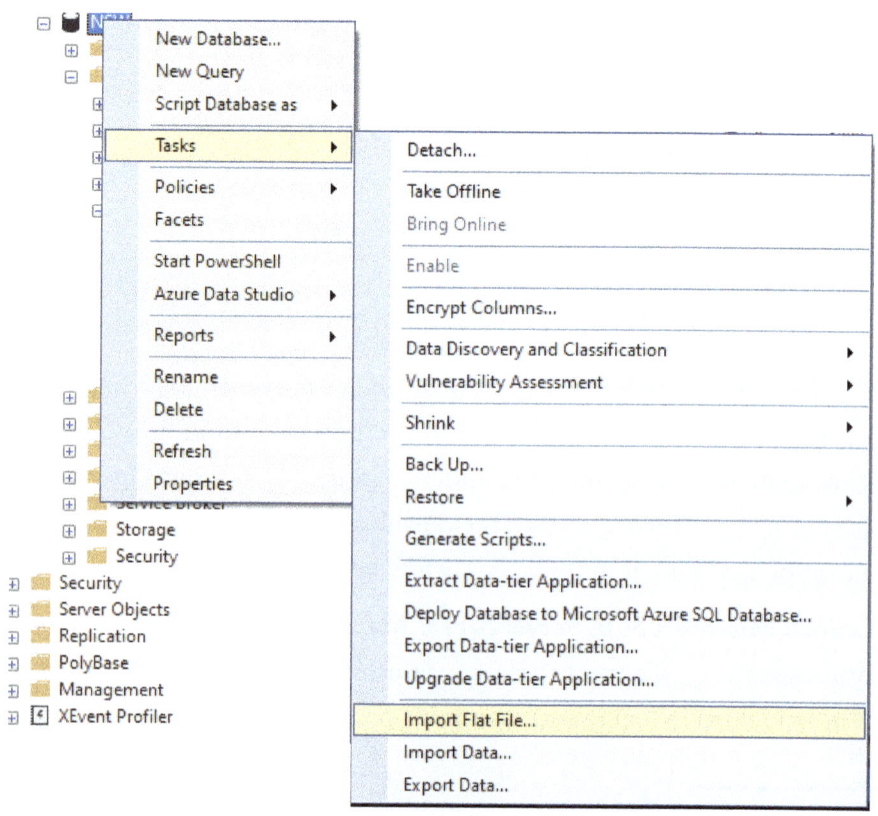

Figure 73.22 Submenus in Microsoft SQL Server Server Management Studio for creating a new database and importing data from a flat file

Select `School_code` for the table's primary key and **select** `Allow Nulls` for every other field. Again, this is done to ensure that table generation is successful. **Complete** the import process.

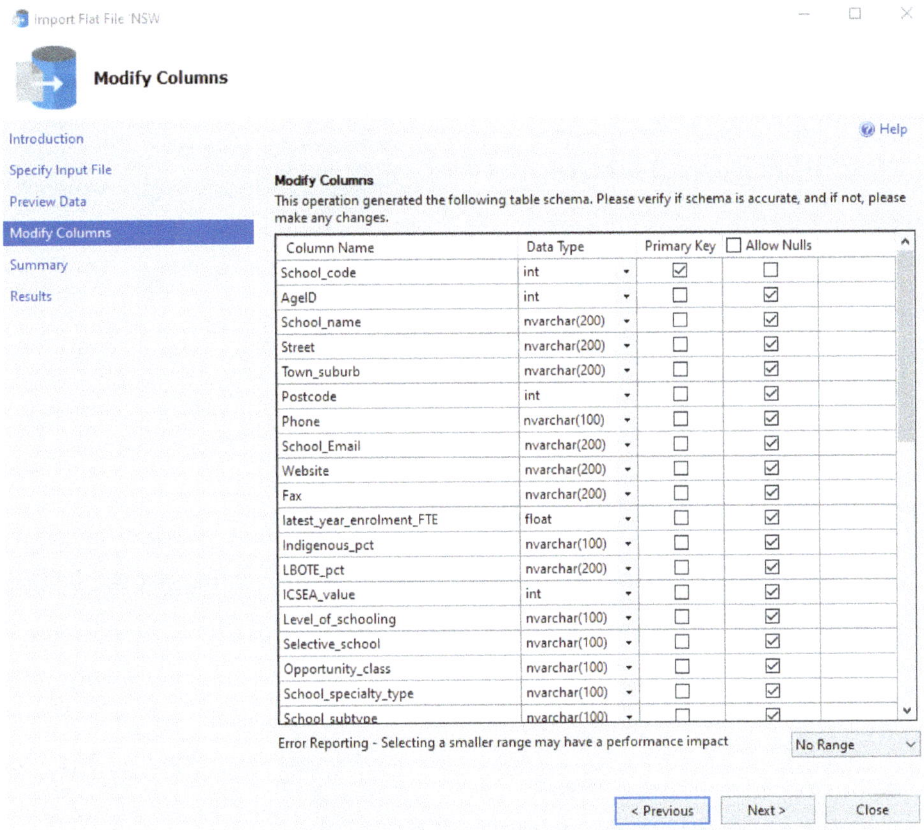

Figure 73.23 Showing changes made to nvarchar settings, selection of primary key and null setting

Figure 73.24 shows some row and column data from the created `NSW` single-table database.

Install TMS WEB Core (free academic licence available or use trial version) if you haven't done so already - https://www.tmssoftware.com.

Install TMS Business Core Library and TMS XData (free academic licence available or use trial version).

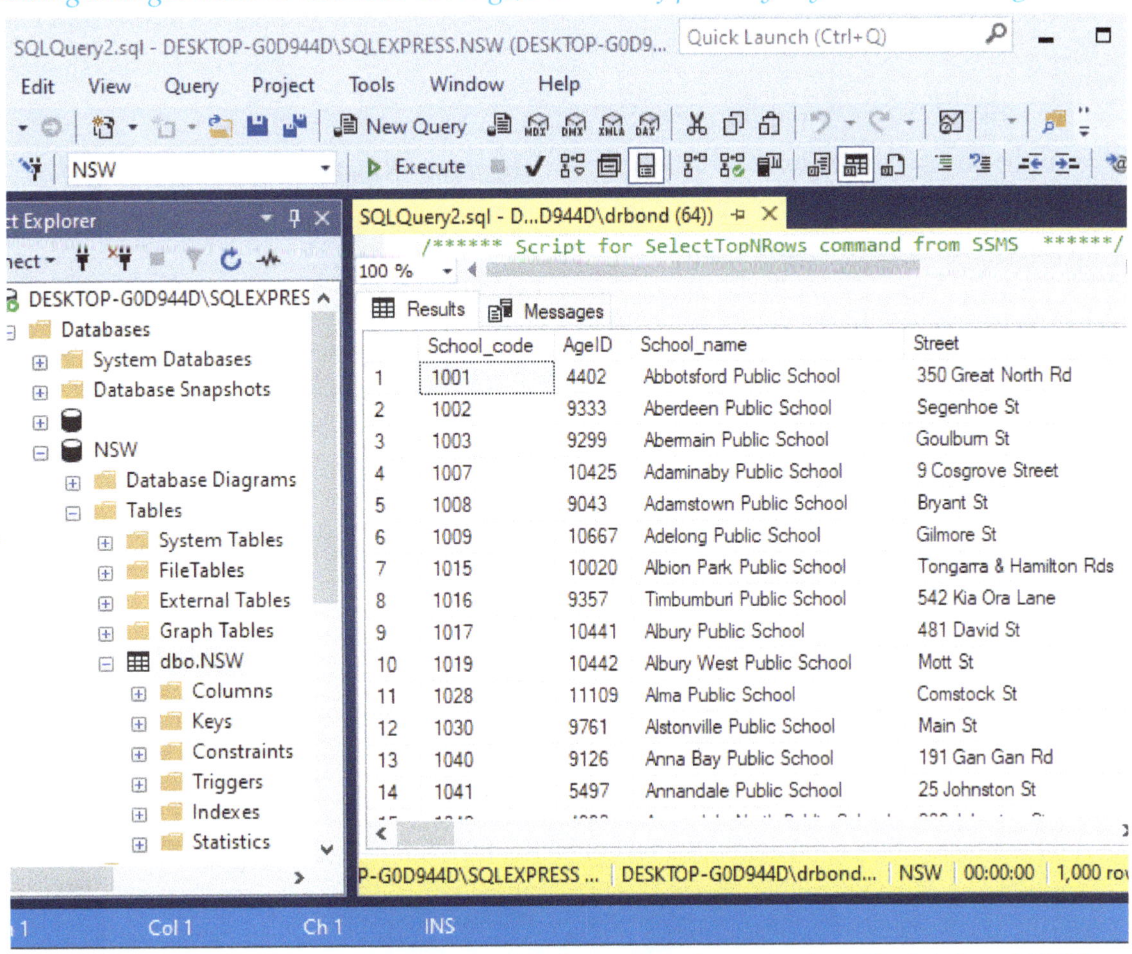

Figure 73.24 Shows some row and column data from single table database NSW

Select

File|New|Other|TMS WEB

to bring up the window shown in *Figure 73.25*.

Select *TMS WEB App + XData Server Group* and **click** `OK` to bring up the window shown in *Figure 73.26a*. **Accept** the default option **VCL Forms Application**, then **click Next** to bring up the window shown in *Figure 73.26b*.

Set the new **XData Server** to use **base url**

http://+:80/DelphiBook

by setting the port to `80` and the path to `DelphiBook` as shown in *Figure 73.26b*.

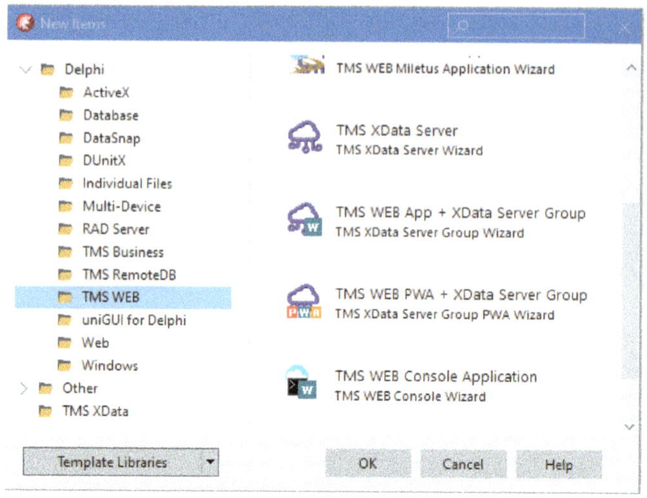

Figure 73.25 Launch window to create a TMS WEB App + XData Server Group

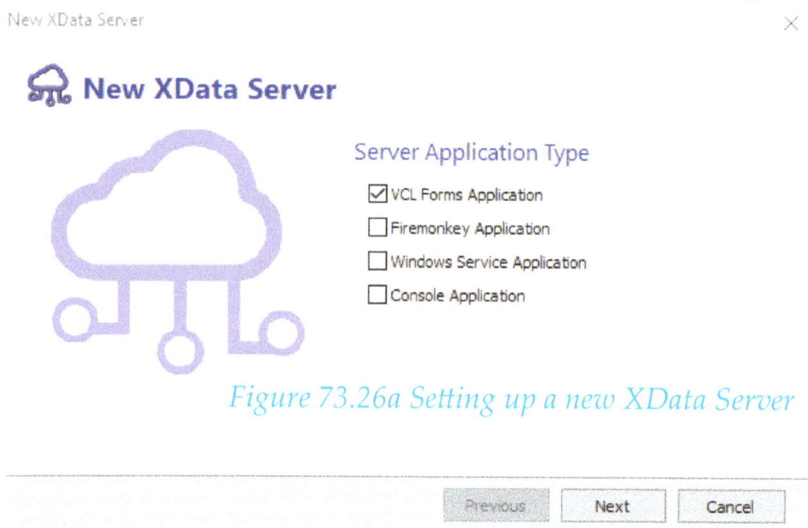

Figure 73.26a Setting up a new XData Server

Click Next to bring up the window shown in *Figure 73.26c*. **Set** the fields as shown.

Click Finish to generate the Project Group `ProjectGroup1` shown in *Figure 73.28*. **Double click** `ConnectionModule.pas` (*Figure 73.27*) to open this unit in the IDE. **Switch** to the form and right click `Connection` (*Figure 73.27*) then **select** option **Connection editor...** to bring up the **FireDac Connection Editor**.

Select Driver ID `MSSQL` and complete the rest of the form as shown in *Figure 73.29*. **Click** the **Wizard** button (*Figure 73.29*) and **select Use Trusted Connection** - *Figure 73.30*. **Click OK** to return to the **FireDac Connection Editor**. **Click** the **Test** button and **enter** your Windows login username and password. **Click OK**. If successful the

Figure 73.26b Setting up a new XData Server to use base url http://+:80/DelphiBook

Figure 73.26c Setting up a new XData Server to connect to a SQL Server database through FireDac

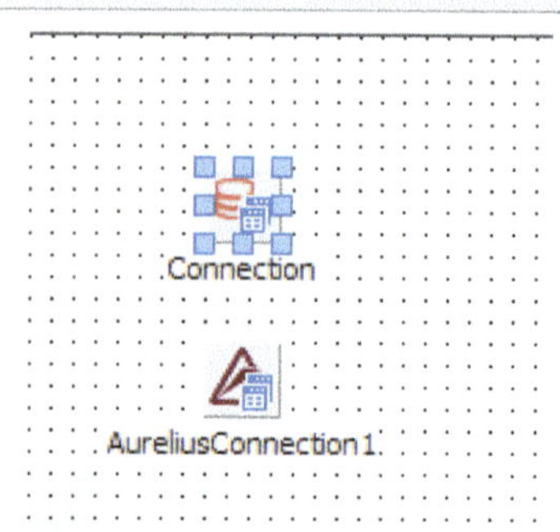

Figure 73.27 ConnectionModule.dfm

window shown in *Figure 73.31* should appear.

Untick LoginPrompt property of the `Connection` component in the Object Inspector.

Now **right click** `AureliusConnection1` (*Figure 73.27*) and **select** the **Connection settings** option to bring up the **Aurelius Connection Editor. Complete** as shown in *Figure 73.32*.

Click Test Connection button. If successful, the window shown in *Figure 73.31* should appear.

Now **right click** `AureliusConnection1` (*Figure 73.27*) again and **select** the **Generate entities from database...** option to bring up the **Aurelius TMS Generate Entities** window as shown in *Figure 73.33*. **Click OK** to generate the entities. The process that now takes place is called **Object Relational Mapping** or **ORM**. The attributes/fields of the table in database `NSW` are mapped to corresponding objects so that data for each attribute may be accessed via their equivalent object (TMS Aurelius calls these entities). A new unit is created (`Unit1.pas`), populated with the necessary class definitions, etc, and assigned to the `VCL_XData_Server` project.

Select `MainForm.pas` and change the caption of the form to `NSW Public Schools server`. **Right**

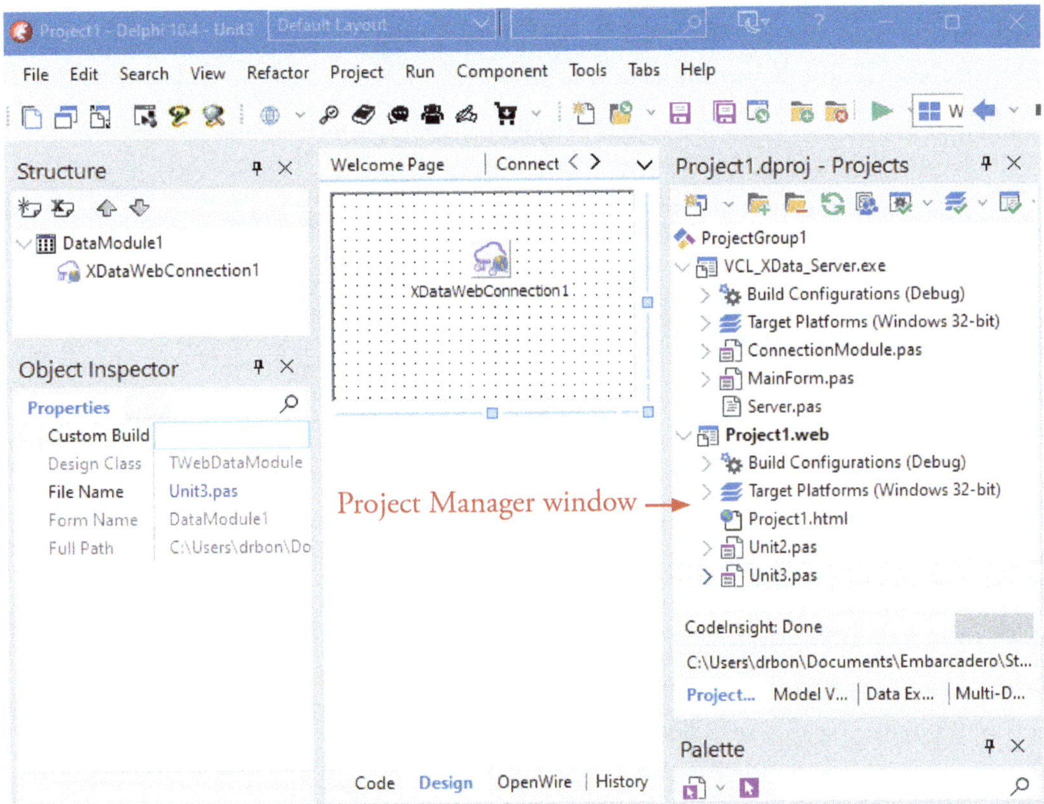

Figure 73.28 ProjectGroup1 set up by TMS WEB App + XData Server Group wizard consisting of a server VCL_XData_Server and a web application, Project1.web

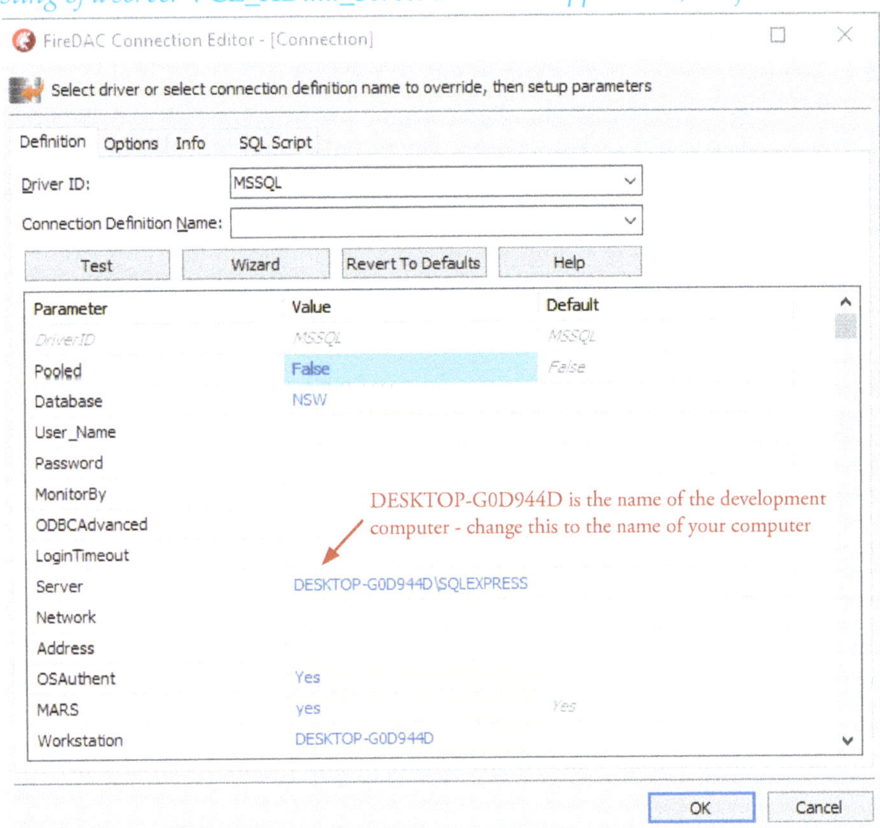

Figure 73.29 FireDac Connection Editor configured for MSSQL database NSW

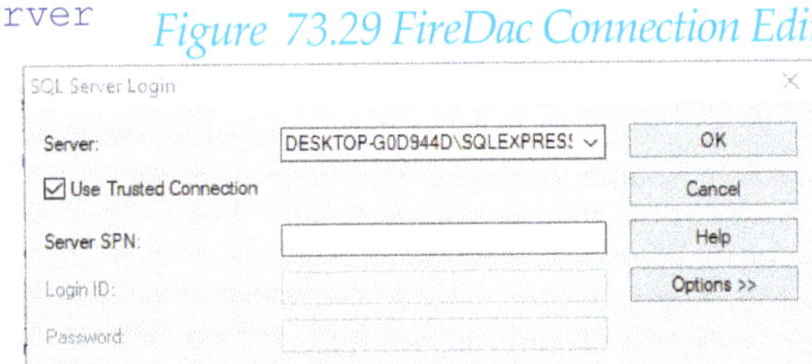

Figure 73.30

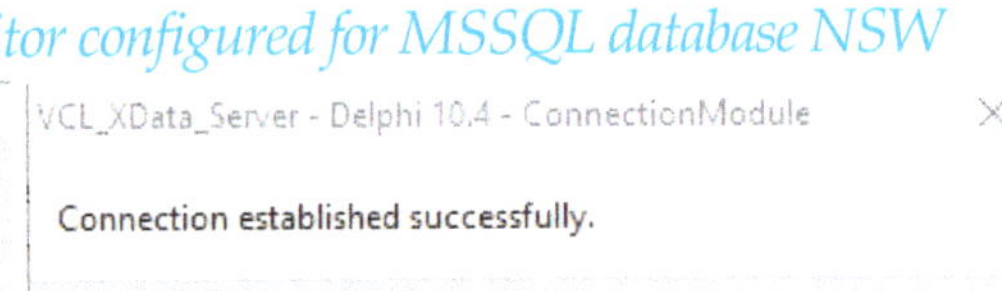

Figure 73.31

click `ProjectGroup1` in the **Project Manager** and **select Save Project Group**. **Save** in folder `XDataBaseMapping`.

Right click `VCL_XData_Server.exe` in the **Project Manager** window and **select Run Without Debugging**. The server should now launch in a window as shown in *Figure 73.34*.

Click the `Project1.web` node in **Project Manager** window (*Figure 73.28*) and **save as** `XDataMapProject.dproj`.

Double click `Unit3.pas` (the unit may be differently numbered, it is the data module unit with component `XDataWebConnection1` - *Figure 73.28*) in the **Project Manager** window to open it in the IDE. **Switch** to its form.

Rename `XDataWebConnection1`, `XDataWebConnection`. Its **URL** property should already be populated with `http://127.0.0.1:80/DelphiBook`.

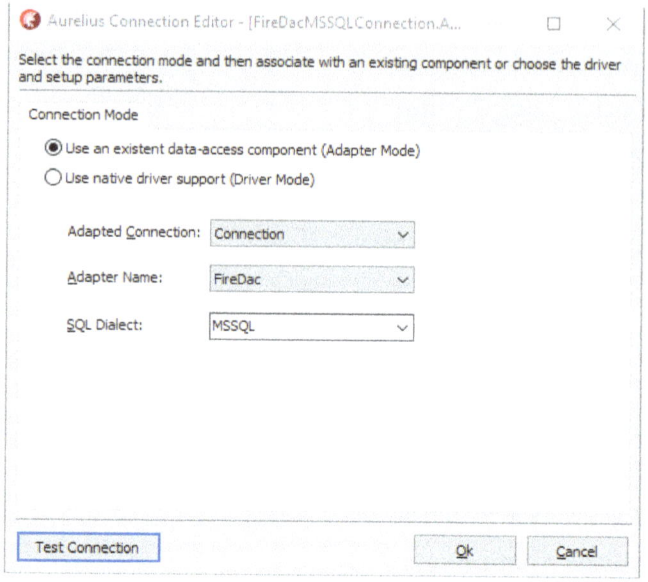

Figure 73.32 Required settings for the Aurelius Connection

Add a `TXDataWebDataSet` component to the form and **rename** it `NSWDataSet`. **Set** its **EntitySetName** to `NSW` and its **Connection** property, if not already set, to `XDataWebConnection`.

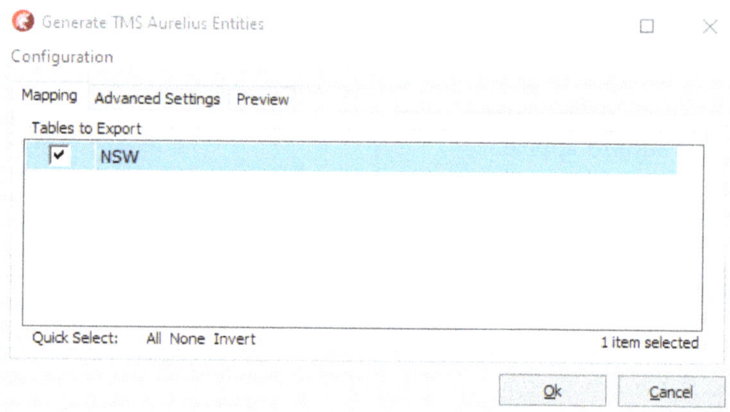

Figure 73.33 Generate entities from database NSW window

With the XData server running, set the **Connected** property of `XDataWebConnection` to `True`.

Right click on `NSWDataSet` component and select the **Fields Editor...** option. **Right click** in the **Fields Editor** window that pops up and **select** the option **Add fields** The window shown in *Figure 73.35* should now appear.

Figure 73.34 XData server now running

Select `School_name`, then whilst holding down the **CTRL** key select `Latitude` and `Longitude`. **Click OK**.

Close the **Fields Editor**.

Double click `Unit2.pas` (the unit may be differently numbered) in the **Project Manager** window to open it in the IDE. **Switch** to its form.

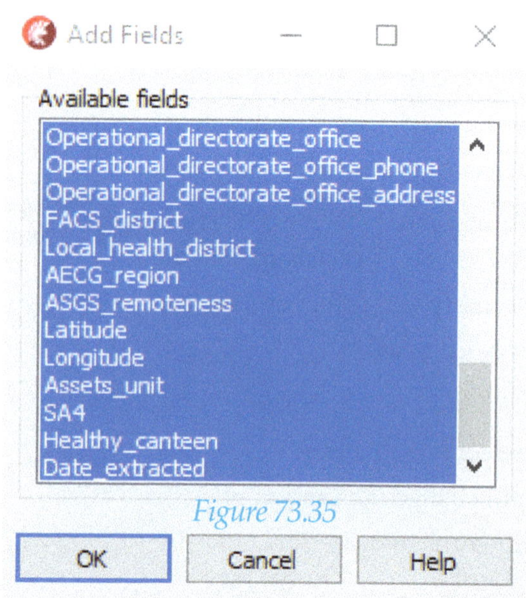

Figure 73.35

Add a `TWebPanel` component to the form and rename it `WebPanel`.

Set its **align** property to **alRight**. **Clear** its **Caption** property.

Select the form and **add** a **TWebGoogleMaps** component to the form. **Rename** it `GoogleMap`. **Set** its **align** property to **alClient**. **Add** an API key to its **APIKey** property. This can be obtained from

https://developers.google.com/maps/documentation/javascript/get-api-key

Select `WebPanel` and **add** three **TWebButton** and one **TWebLabel** components to `WebPanel`. **Set** the button captions to

1. Maximum No Of Schools
2. 100 Schools
3. 200 Schools

Set the **caption** property of the **TWebLabel** component to

`There are 2200+ public schools in NSW so only the first 100 are marked on the map initially.`

Set WordWrap of the **TWebLabel** component property to **True**.

Change the form's **name** and **caption** properties to `frmNSW`. **Size** and **align** the buttons and label as shown in *Figure 73.36* adjusting the panel width accordingly.

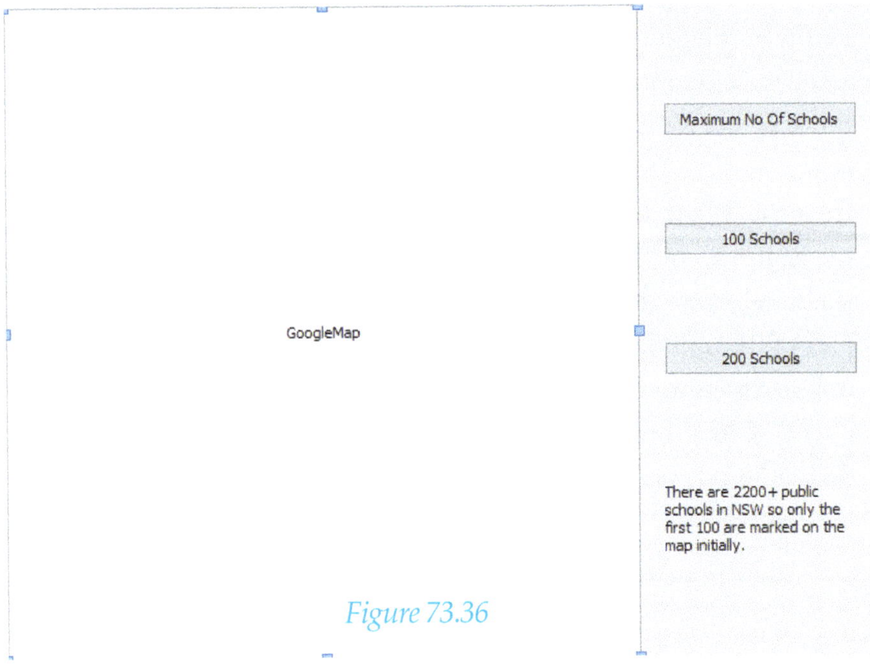

Figure 73.36

Switch to the unit's code and **add** `Unit3` to the **Uses** clause, and procedure `AddMarks` to the form's class definition. With the cursor on the procedure name **press CTRL Shift C** to create the procedure template in the implementation section. **Add** the code shown in *Table 73.12* to the body of this procedure but first create the variable declarations shown in *Table 73.12*.

The statement

```
GoogleMap.AddMarker(DataModule1.NSWDataSetLatitude.AsFloat, DataModule1.NSWDataSetLongitude.AsFloat,
                    DataModule1.NSWDataSetSchool_Name.AsString);
```

adds the default marker, a balloon ( ), at the given latitude and longitude and attaches a string to each which is displayed when the mouse cursor hovers over the corresponding marker - *Figure 73.37*.

Figure 73.37

```
Implementation
  {$R *.dfm}
  Var
    NoOfSchoolsToDisplay : Integer = 100;
    CountingNoOfSchools : Boolean = True;
    NoOfSchools : Integer = 0;
  Procedure TfrmNSW.AddMarkers;
    Var
      i : Integer;
    Begin
      i := 0;
      GoogleMap.ClearMarkers;
      GoogleMap.SetCenter(-33.852728, 151.131206);
      GoogleMap.SetZoom(6);
      DataModule1.NSWDataSet.First;
      While Not DataModule1.NSWDataSet.Eof
        Do
          Begin
            If CountingNoOfSchools
              Then NoOfSchools := NoOfSchools + 1;
            i := i + 1;
            If (i <= NoOfSchoolsToDisplay) And Not DataModule1.NSWDataSet.Eof
              Then
                If Not (DataModule1.NSWDataSetLongitude.AsString = '')
                  Then GoogleMap.AddMarker(DataModule1.NSWDataSetLatitude.AsFloat,
                                           DataModule1.NSWDataSetLongitude.AsFloat,
                                           DataModule1.NSWDataSetSchool_Name.AsString);
            DataModule1.NSWDataSet.Next;
          End;
      If CountingNoOfSchools
        Then CountingNoOfSchools := False;
    End;
```

Table 73.12 Procedure to add balloon markers to a Google map

Latitude, longitude and marker label `NSWDataSetSchool_Name` are read from the **TXDataWebDataSet** component `NSWDataSet`. This dataset obtains its data from the XData server in object form (recall the generate-entities operation performed by the Aurelius component at the server end - part of the unit on the server containing the object-structure of the data is shown in *Table 73.13*). **Close down** the server if it is running. **Switch** to `Server.pas` and enable CORS - see *Table 73.14*.

```
Type
  TNSW = Class;
  TNSWTableDictionary = Class;

  [Entity]
  [Table('NSW')]
  [Id('FSchool_code', TIdGenerator.None)]
  TNSW = Class
           Private
             [Column('School_code', [TColumnProp.Required])]
              FSchool_code: Integer;
             [Column('AgeID', [])]
               FAgeID: Nullable<Integer>;
             [Column('School_name', [], 200)]
               FSchool_name: Nullable<string>;
             [Column('Street', [], 200)]
               FStreet: Nullable<string>;
```

Table 73.13 Part of the unit containing the class definitions for the ORM structure

```
Procedure StartServer;
  Var
    Module : TXDataServerModule;
  Begin
    If Assigned(SparkleServer)
      Then Exit;
    SparkleServer := THttpSysServer.Create;
    Module := TXDataServerModule.Create('http://+:80/DelphiBook',
                                    TFireDacMSSQLConnection.CreatePool(20));
    // Uncomment line below to enable CORS in the server
    Module.AddMiddleware(TCorsMiddleware.Create);
    // Uncomment line below to allow compressed responses from server
    //Module.AddMiddleware(TCompressMiddleware.Create);
    SparkleServer.AddModule(Module);
    SparkleServer.Start;
  End;
```

Table 73.14 StartServer procedure showing the enabling of CORS

Right click `VCL_XData_Server.exe` in the **Project Manager** window and **select Run Without Debugging**.
Switch to the form for unit 2. **Select** `GoogleMap` and then in the **Object Inspector**, **select** the **Events** tab.

Double click OnMapLoaded to create event handler `TfrmNSW.GoogleMapMapLoaded`.
Add the following code to its body

```
Procedure TfrmNSW.GoogleMapMapLoaded(Sender: TObject);
  Begin
    DataModule1.XDataWebConnection.Connected := True;
  End;
```

Switch to the form for unit 3. **Select** `XDataWebConnect` and then in the **Object Inspector**, **select** the **Events** tab.

Double click OnConnect to create event handler `TDataModule1.XDataWebConnectionConnect`.
Add the following code to its body

```
Procedure TDataModule1.XDataWebConnectionConnect(Sender: TObject);
  Begin
    NSWDataSet.Load;
  End;
```

Add `Uses Unit2` to the implementation section of `Unit3`.

Select `XDataWebDataSet` and then in the **Object Inspector**, **select** the **Events** tab.

Double click AfterOpen to create event handler `TDataModule1.XDataWebDataSetAfterOpen`.

Add the code shown in *Table 73.15* to its body.

```
Procedure TfrmNSW.NSWAfterOpen(DataSet: TDataSet);
  Begin
    frmNSW.AddMarkers;
  End;
```

Table 73.15

Switch to `Unit2`'s form.

Double click `WebButton1` (caption: `Maximum No Of Schools`) to create event handler `TfrmNSW.WebButton1Click`.

Add the code shown in *Table 73.16* to its body

```
Procedure TfrmNSW.WebButton1Click(Sender: TObject);
  Begin
    NoOfSchoolsToDisplay := NoOfSchools;
    AddMarkers;
  End;
```

Table 73.16

Double click `WebButton2` (caption: `100 Schools`) to create event handler `TfrmNSW.WebButton2Click`.

Add the code shown in *Table 73.17* to its body

```
Procedure TfrmNSW.WebButton2Click(Sender: TObject);
  Begin
    NoOfSchoolsToDisplay := 100;
    AddMarkers;
  End;
```

Table 73.17

Double click `WebButton3` (caption: `200 Schools`) to create event handler `TfrmNSW.WebButton3Click`.

Add the code shown in *Table 73.18* to its body

```
Procedure TfrmNSW.WebButton3Click(Sender: TObject);
  Begin
    NoOfSchoolsToDisplay := 200;
    AddMarkers;
  End;
```

Table 73.18

Right click `ProjectGroup1` in the **Project Manager** and **select Save Project Group**. **Save** in folder `XDataBaseMapping`.

Right click `XDataMapProject.web` in the **Project Manager** window and **select Run Without Debugging**. *Figure 73.38* shows the result rendered in a browser: **localhost:8000/XDataMapProject/Project1.html**. The default number of schools location-marked is 100.

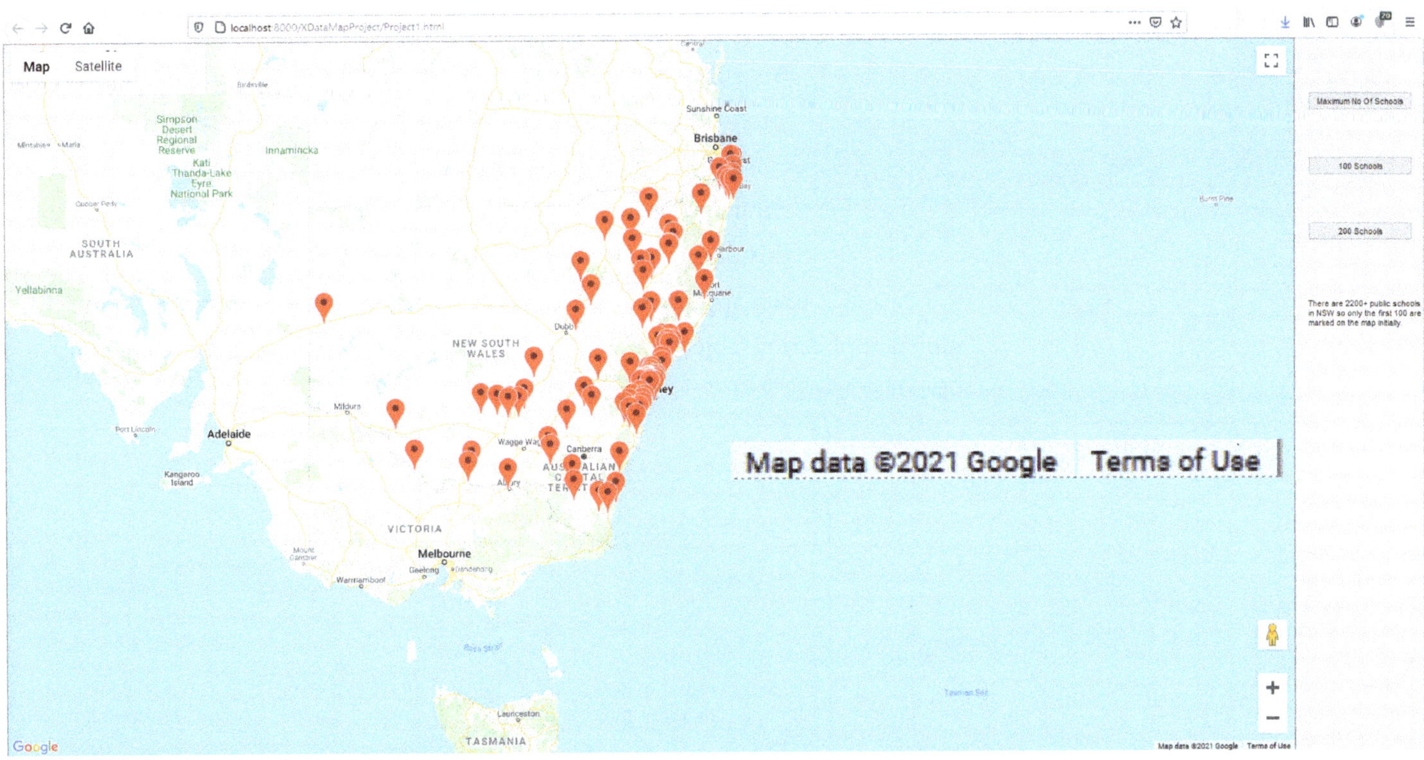

Figure 73.38 Google map showing the locations of 100 public schools in New South Wales Australia

74 Web server applications and databases

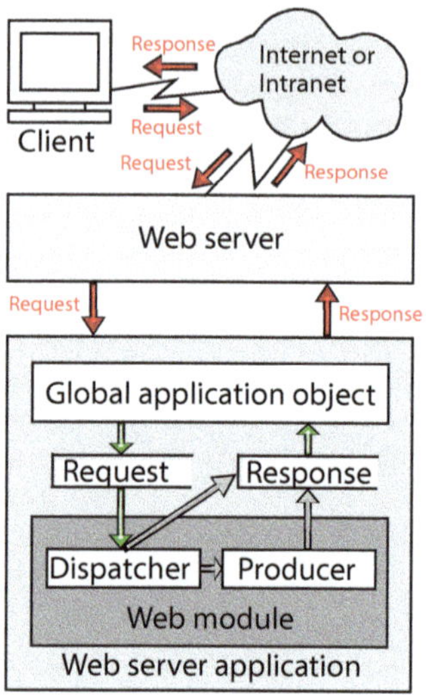

Fig. 74.1 WebBroker technology

Structure of a web server application

Purpose: To be familiar with the structure of a web server application

We learned in *Chapter 32* that a web server works with the HTTP protocol, receiving requests from client browsers and returning a response in the form of one or more web pages. When pages need to be generated dynamically because, for example, they require data from a database then a web server application is required in addition to a web server. It is the job of the web server application to process the request then extract the necessary data from the database before incorporating this data into an HTML document. The web server application then passes this document to the web server which, in turn, sends it to the client.

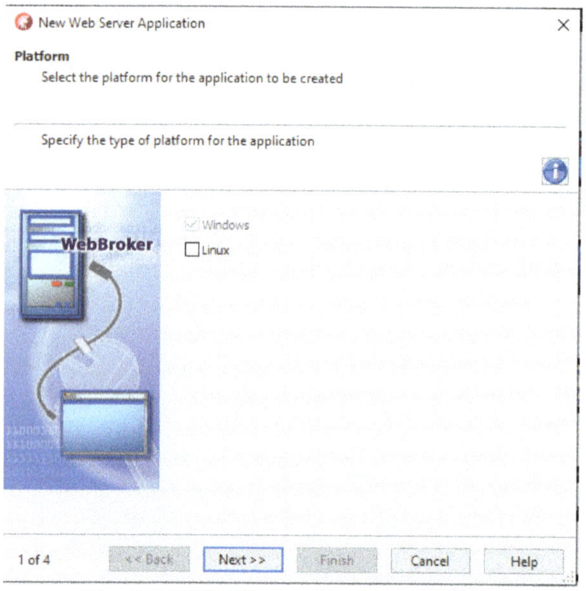

Fig. 74.2 Platform selection window

Chapter 32 introduced Delphi's **WebBroker** technology - *Figure 74.1* - for Web server applications. This chapter explores it in greater depth.

Launch **Delphi**, select **File|New|Other|Web** and then **Web Server Application**. With just the platform type **Windows** selected as shown in *Figure 74.2*, click the **Next >>** button in the **Platform** window. Choose **CGI standalone executable** from the radio button options in the next window. Click **Finish**.

Save the project as `WebCGIProject.dproj` and its unit file `WebModuleUnit1.pas` in folder `WebCGIProject`.

Fig. 74.3 WebModule1 form

A visual object `WebModule1` and associated `dfm` file are also generated - *Figure 74.3* and *Table 74.1* - onto which components are placed that make it possible to connect to a database, retrieve data and create a dynamic web page containing this data. The project source is stored in file `WebCGIProject.dpr` - *Table 74.2*. Each application created with **WebBroker** technology contains a global application object - *Figure 74.1* - which is accessable from the global variable, `Application`.

```
Object WebModule1 : TWebModule1
  OldCreateOrder = False
  Actions = <
    item
      Default = True
      Name = 'DefaultHandler'
      PathInfo = '/'
      OnAction = WebModule1DefaultHandlerAction
    end>
  Height = 230
  Width = 415
End
```

Table 74.1 WebModuleUnit1.dfm

```
Program WebCGIProject;
{$APPTYPE CONSOLE}
Uses
  Web.WebBroker,
  CGIApp,
  WebModuleUnit1 in 'WebModuleUnit1.pas' {WebModule1 : TWebModule};
{$R *.res}
Begin
  Application.Initialize;
  Application.WebModuleClass := WebModuleClass;
  Application.Run;
End.
```

Table 74.2 WebCGIProject.dpr

The global application object encapsulates the operations that handle the application's interaction with the web server. It manages the receipt of requests and the sending out of prepared responses - *Figure 74.1*. After a request is received, the application object sends the request to the dispatcher of the web module for processing - *Figure 74.1*.

The global application object creates and destroys request and response objects shown in *Figure 74.1* as well as specifying their properties.

For CGI applications, the global application object is responsible for creating and destroying application instances, one per request.

The web module (`WebModule1`) in the project is responsible for implementing the business logic of the web server application. It does this via special objects called **actions**. The handler methods of these **action** objects are called to process HTTP requests. In this way, the operations of these **action** objects enable the application to achieve its purpose. Each web module when created contains one **action** object called the `DefaultHandler` - *Figure 74.4* - and an associated handler method called `WebModule1DefaultHandlerAction` - *Table 74.3*. The web server application calls this handler when it cannot process the request in any other way.

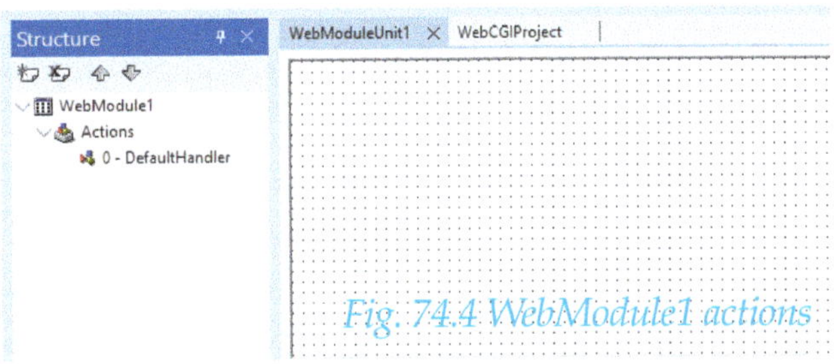

Fig. 74.4 WebModule1 actions

```
Unit WebModuleUnit1;
Interface
Uses
  System.SysUtils, System.Classes, Web.HTTPApp;
Type
  TWebModule1 = Class(TWebModule)
                  Procedure WebModule1DefaultHandlerAction(Sender : TObject;
                               Request : TWebRequest; Response :
                               TWebResponse; Var Handled : Boolean);
                End;
Var
  WebModuleClass : TComponentClass = TWebModule1;
Implementation
{%CLASSGROUP 'System.Classes.TPersistent'}
{$R *.dfm}
  Procedure TWebModule1.WebModule1DefaultHandlerAction(Sender : TObject;
              Request: TWebRequest;
              Response: TWebResponse; Var Handled : Boolean);
    Begin
      Response.Content :=
        '<html>' +
          '<head><title>Web Server Application</title></head>' +
          '<body>Web Server Application</body>' +
        '</html>';
    End;
  End.
```

Table 74.3 WebModuleUnit1.pas

Each new **action** that is created, creates an **action** object which is encapsulated in the web module - *Table 74.4* shows new action object, `WebAction1`, with handler `WebModule1WebAction1Item1Action`. This action object is selected by the web application server by specifying the path `/test`.

The **producer** object in *Figure 74.1* covers a range of possible components that deal with the dynamic generation of web pages and other documents/files.

```
Object WebModule1 : TWebModule1
  OldCreateOrder = False
  Actions = <
    item
      Default = True
      Name = 'DefaultHandler'
      PathInfo = '/'
      OnAction = WebModule1DefaultHandlerAction
    end
    item
      Name = 'WebActionItem1'
      PathInfo = '/test'
      OnAction = WebModule1WebActionItem1Action
    end>
  Height = 230
  Width = 415
End
```

Table 74.4 WebModule1 object

These are located in the **Internet** tab of the component/tool palette and consist of

- **TDataSetPageProducer**
- **TDataSetTableProducer**
- **TSQLQueryTableProducer**
- **TPageProducer**
- **TXMLDocument**
- **TWebFileDispatcher**
- **TWebDispatcher**

A web module also acts as a storage area for non-visual components such as database components and their program code.

Every web module consists of one **TWebDispatcher**. It is possible to add a **TWebDispatcher** component to an existing data module (File|New|Other|Database|Data Module) as long as the automatically generated web module in the web application server is deleted - only one **TWebDispatcher** is allowed per web application server.

CGI web server database application

P

Launch Delphi, select File|New|Other|Web and then Web Server Application. Accept Windows target in the Platform selection window. Choose CGI standalone executable from the radio button options.
Drop a **TDataSetTableProducer** from the Internet tab of the component/tool palette onto the web module form.
From the Interbase tab of the component palette, drop the following onto the web module form:

- a **TIBDatabase** component
- a **TIBTransaction** component.
- a **TIBTable** component.

Set `IBDatabase1.DatabaseName` to `LIBDB2020.IB` for **Interbase 2020** wherever this is stored on a local drive (if you have to work with an older version of Interbase then use the version of the library database that was created for this version - see *Chapter 64*). It is important that you use the version of Interbase that was installed from the installer window of your version of Delphi (**Tools|Manage Platforms|Additonal Options**). Make sure that Interbase server is running. `LIBDB2020.IB` contains three fields, `BookIdNo`, `Title` and `ISBN`.
Set `IBDatabase1.DefaultTransaction` to `IBTransaction1`.
Set `IBDatabase1.LogInPrompt` to `False` and **add** the required login details, `user_name=sysdba`, `passsword=masterkey`, to `IBDatabase1.Params`. **Click** `IBDatabase1.Connected` to connect to the database. `IBDatabase1.Connected` should now be `True` if everything has worked.
Set `IBTransaction1.DefaultDatabase` to `IBDatabase1` and its `Active` property to `True`.
Set `IBTable1.Database` to `IBDatabase1`.
Set `IBTable1.TableName` to `Book`. **Set** `IBTable1.Active` to `True` to check connectivity.
Set `DatSetTableProducer1.DataSet` to `IBTable1`.
Set `DataSetTableProducer1.MaxRows` to 200.
The `TDataSetTableProducer` object produces the result set obtained from data stored in `IBTable1`.
Setting **MaxRows** to 200 limits the result set to 200 rows.
Next **select** the fields from `IBTable1` whose data are to be copied to `DataSetTableProducer1`.
Right click `IBTable1` component on the form and choose Fields Editor.
Right click within the Fields Editor and choose **Add Fields**.
Select only the `BookIDNo` and `Title` fields.
Remove `2- ISBN` from `DatasetTableProducer1|Columns` - **select** then **right click** and from the pop-up menu **choose** `Edit|Delete`.
To add header and footer details to the returned data set which the browser will handle use the **Header** and **Footer** property fields of `DataSetTableProducer1`.
Select the **Header** property field of `DataSetTableProducer1` in the Object Inspector. **Click** the **...** symbol to open the editor.
The **Header** property will contain the first part of an HTML page.
The **Footer** property will contain the last part of this HTML page.
The data set returned will appear between this HTML header and the HTML footer.
Insert the following into the **Header** property:

```
<html>
  <head>
    <title>THIS IS A TEST</title>
  </head>
  <body>
     <center>
       <h1><font color="#FF0000">This is a Test</font></h1>
     </center>
```

Insert the following into **Footer** property:

```
        <hr>
        <p>Report any problems to</p>
        <a href=mailto:drbond@educational-computing.co.uk>Dr Bond</a>
      </body>
    </html>
```

Double click the web module form. The **Action Editor** should pop up. **Click** the **Add** icon to add an **ActionItem**.

Click the **ActionItem** – `WebActionItem1` – in the **Action Editor** to highlight it. Its properties now become available to edit in the **Object Inspector**.

Change the name of the **ActionItem** from `WebActionItem1` to `FirstDataSet`.

Set **PathInfo** to `/First`.

With `FirstDataSet` action selected in the **Structure** window, **click** the **Events** tab in the **Object Inspector**.

Double click the **OnAction** field to produce the event handler template

```
Procedure TWebModule1.WebModule1FirstDataSetAction(Sender : TObject;
          Request : TWebRequest; Response : TWebResponse; var Handled : Boolean);
  Begin

  End;
```

Add the following code to the body of this procedure template:

```
With DataSetTableProducer1
  Do
    Begin
      DataSet.Open;
      Response.Content := DataSetTableProducer1.Content;
      DataSet.Close;
    End;
```

DataSetTableProducer1.Content may be replaced by Content. It has been written this way for clarity.

Save the project as `WebDatabaseProject.dproj` and the unit as `WebModuleUnit.pas` in a folder named `WebDatabaseProject`.

Build (**Shift F9**) the project.

Copy **WebDatabaseProject.exe** to the `cgi-bin` folder of Apache server.

With Apache server[1] configured and running, launch a web browser and enter the url

`http://localhost/cgi-bin/WebDatabaseProject.exe/First`

or if you have set `httpd.conf` to listen on a specific IP address, e.g. 192.168.1.7

`http://192.168.1.7/cgi-bin/WebDatabaseProject.exe/First`

(Use ipconfig from the command line to discover the ip address of your server)

Figure 74.5 shows the web page that is returned and displayed in a web browser.

Your result may look slightly different because your column format settings will be different from those set for this project. How to format columns is described later in this chapter.

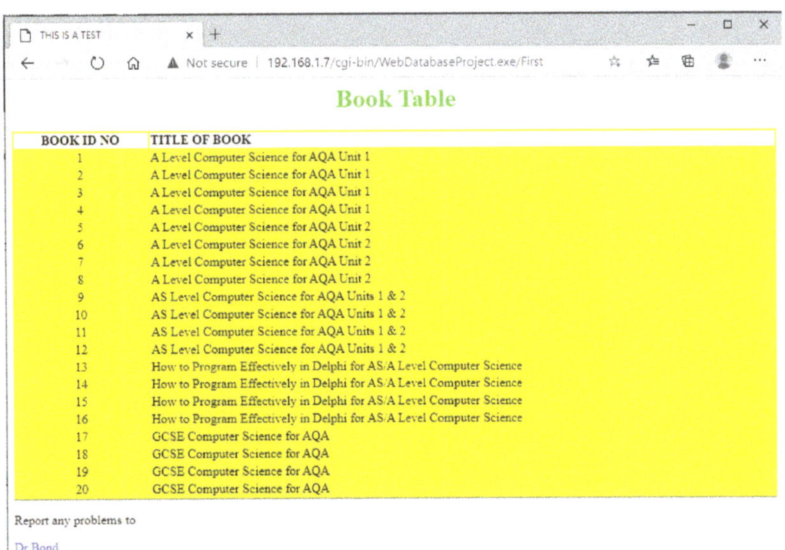

THIS IS A TEST

Not secure | 192.168.1.7/cgi-bin/WebDatabaseProject.exe/First

Book Table

BOOK ID NO	TITLE OF BOOK
1	A Level Computer Science for AQA Unit 1
2	A Level Computer Science for AQA Unit 1
3	A Level Computer Science for AQA Unit 1
4	A Level Computer Science for AQA Unit 1
5	A Level Computer Science for AQA Unit 2
6	A Level Computer Science for AQA Unit 2
7	A Level Computer Science for AQA Unit 2
8	A Level Computer Science for AQA Unit 2
9	AS Level Computer Science for AQA Units 1 & 2
10	AS Level Computer Science for AQA Units 1 & 2
11	AS Level Computer Science for AQA Units 1 & 2
12	AS Level Computer Science for AQA Units 1 & 2
13	How to Program Effectively in Delphi for AS/A Level Computer Science
14	How to Program Effectively in Delphi for AS/A Level Computer Science
15	How to Program Effectively in Delphi for AS/A Level Computer Science
16	How to Program Effectively in Delphi for AS/A Level Computer Science
17	GCSE Computer Science for AQA
18	GCSE Computer Science for AQA
19	GCSE Computer Science for AQA
20	GCSE Computer Science for AQA

Report any problems to

Dr Bond

Fig. 74.5 Web browser window displaying the web page returned by WebDatabaseProject.exe/First

1 See Appendix C at www.educational-computing.com/DelphiBook/DelphiCode.html for how to install and configure Apache 24.

With WebModule1|Actions|0 - DefaultHandler selected in the Structure window, **change** its **Enabled** property to **False** in Object Inspector.

Now **select** action `FirstDataSet` in the Structure window and **change** its **Default** property to **True**.

Save all and then **build** (Shift F9) the project.

Copy WebDatabaseProject.exe to the `cgi-bin` folder of Apache server.
With Apache server running, launch a web browser and enter the url

`http://localhost/cgi-bin/WebDatabaseProject.exe`

or if you have set `httpd.conf` to listen on a specific IP address, e.g. 192.168.1.7

`http://192.168.1.7/cgi-bin/WebDatabaseProject.exe`

The web page shown in *Figure 74.5* is returned as before because the desired action is now the default action.

Now go to another computer connected to the same local area network and on the same subnet.

Launch a browser and enter the url

`http://192.168.1.7/cgi-bin/WebDatabaseProject.exe`

(Replace 192.168.1.7 with the IP address of the Apache web server for your local area network. You will need to have configured Apache web server to listen on this IP address, localhost won't work).

The web page shown in *Figure 74.5* should be returned as before.

Now **create** another action, **name** it `SecondDataSet` and **set** its **PathInfo** property to `/Second`.

Create an **OnAction** event handler for this new action as follows

```
Procedure TWebModule1.WebModule1SecondDataSetAction(Sender : TObject;
          Request : TWebRequest; Response : TWebResponse; var Handled : Boolean);
  Begin
    With DataSetTableProducer1
      Do
        Begin
          DataSet.Open;
          Columns.State := csDefault;
          Response.Content := Content;
          DataSet.Close;
        End;
  End;
```

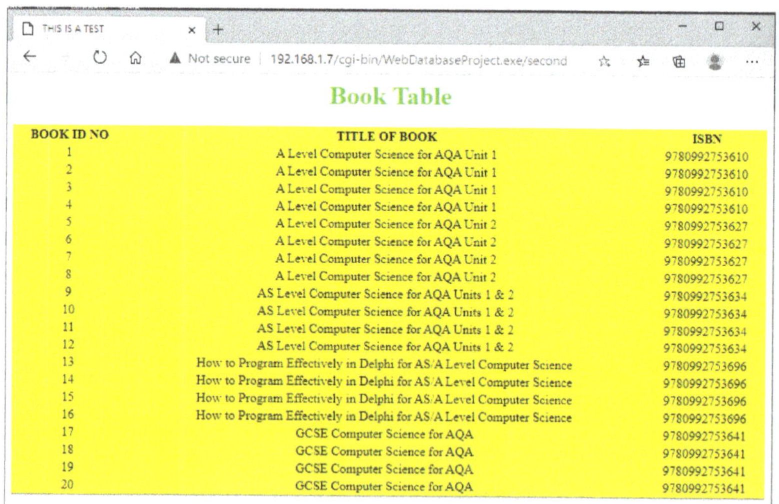

BOOK ID NO	TITLE OF BOOK	ISBN
1	A Level Computer Science for AQA Unit 1	9780992753610
2	A Level Computer Science for AQA Unit 1	9780992753610
3	A Level Computer Science for AQA Unit 1	9780992753610
4	A Level Computer Science for AQA Unit 1	9780992753610
5	A Level Computer Science for AQA Unit 2	9780992753627
6	A Level Computer Science for AQA Unit 2	9780992753627
7	A Level Computer Science for AQA Unit 2	9780992753627
8	A Level Computer Science for AQA Unit 2	9780992753627
9	AS Level Computer Science for AQA Units 1 & 2	9780992753634
10	AS Level Computer Science for AQA Units 1 & 2	9780992753634
11	AS Level Computer Science for AQA Units 1 & 2	9780992753634
12	AS Level Computer Science for AQA Units 1 & 2	9780992753634
13	How to Program Effectively in Delphi for AS/A Level Computer Science	9780992753696
14	How to Program Effectively in Delphi for AS/A Level Computer Science	9780992753696
15	How to Program Effectively in Delphi for AS/A Level Computer Science	9780992753696
16	How to Program Effectively in Delphi for AS/A Level Computer Science	9780992753696
17	GCSE Computer Science for AQA	9780992753641
18	GCSE Computer Science for AQA	9780992753641
19	GCSE Computer Science for AQA	9780992753641
20	GCSE Computer Science for AQA	9780992753641

Report any problems to
Dr Bond

Fig. 74.6 Web browser window displaying the web page returned by WebDatabaseProject.exe/Second

Setting `DataSetTableProducer1.Columns.State` to **csDefault** causes the columns to be generated dynamically, i.e. at runtime. Dynamically generated columns correspond exactly in order and number to the fields of the dataset. In addition, column formatting returns to the default settings.

Save all and then **build** (Shift F9) the project.

Copy `WebDatabaseProject.exe` to the `cgi-bin` folder of Apache server.
With Apache server running, **launch** a web browser and **enter** the url

`http://ip address of your server/cgi-bin/WebDatabaseProject.exe/Second`

Figure 74.6 shows the browser window for url `http://192.168.1.7/cgi-bin/WebDatabaseProject.exe/Second`.
The action that is performed (`Second`) by the web server application generates and delivers a web page containing data for all three fields, `BookIDNo`, `Title`, `ISBN`, of the database `LIBDB2020.IB` to the Apache web server for despatch to the web browser.

Formatting output

Select `DataSetTableProducer1`.

In the **Object Inspector** window, **open** the **Header** field (**double click** ellipsis **...**) in the **String List Editor**. **Click** on **Code Editor** to get a code-layout view of the HTML.

Add the style definition for a **CSS** class `fontcolour` to the `head` section as shown in *Table 74.5*.

Close the **Code Editor** window and when invited **save** its contents.

Select `DataSetTableProducer1|Columns|0 - BookIdNo` in the **Structure** | **Object Inspector** windows.

Change the `DataSetTableProducer1.Columns[0]` properties as shown in *Figure 74.7*.

Table 74.5

```
<head>
  <title>THIS IS A TEST</title>
  <style>
    .fontcolour {color : red;}
  </style>
</head>
```

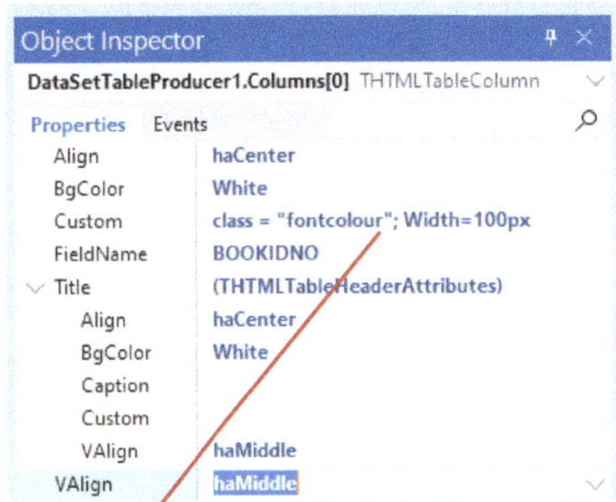

Fig. 74.7 Customising the BookIdNo column

The **Custom** field setting applies the class `fontcolour` to `BookIdNo` values displayed in the returned web page and sets the width of the table column in which these are displayed to 100px.

Figure 74.8 shows the result when this custom formatting is applied.

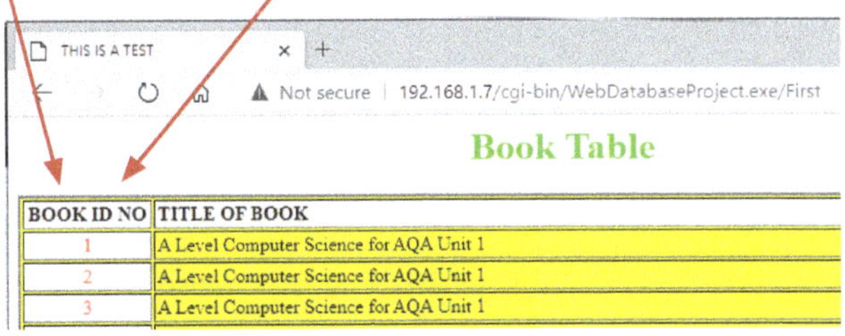

Fig. 74.8 Customising the BookIdNo column

Figure 74.9 encapsulates the web server database application consisting of web browser, intranet/local area network, web server, web server application, Interbase server, Interbase database.

Adding another column at runtime

Now **create** another action, **name** it `ThirdDataSet` and **set** its **PathInfo** property to `/Third`.

Create an **OnAction** event handler for this new action as follows

```
Procedure TWebModule1.WebModule1ThirdDataSetAction(Sender : TObject;
          Request : TWebRequest; Response : TWebResponse; var Handled : Boolean);
 Begin
   With DataSetTableProducer1
     Do
       Begin
         DataSet.Open;
         Columns.Add;
         Columns.Items[2].Field := DataSet.FieldByName('ISBN');
         Columns.Items[2].Custom := 'Width = 100px';
         Response.Content := Content;
         DataSet.Close;
       End;
 End;
```

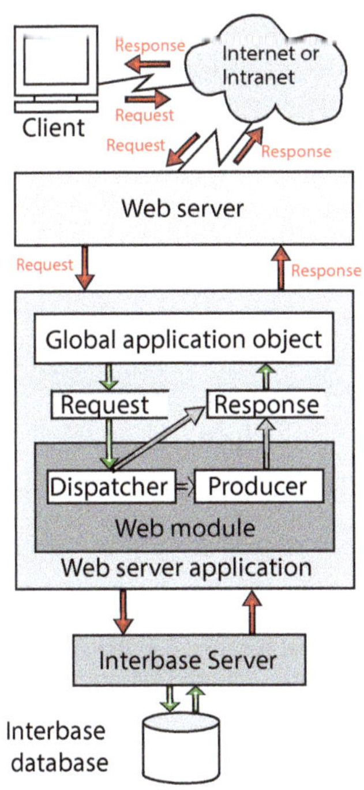

Fig. 74.9 WebBroker technology

A new column is created by `Columns.Add` making three in total.

A field of the dataset is assigned to this third column by

```
Columns.Items[2].Field := DataSet.FieldByName('ISBN');
```

and customised with

```
Columns.Items[2].Custom := 'Width = 100px';
```

Save all and then **build** (Shift F9) the project.

Copy WebDatabaseProject.exe to the `cgi-bin` folder of Apache server.

With Apache server running, **launch** a web browser and **enter** the url

`http://ip address of your server/cgi-bin/WebDatabaseProject.exe/Third`

Figure 74.10 shows the browser window for url `http://192.168.1.7/cgi-bin/WebDatabaseProject.exe/Third`. The action that is performed (`Third`) by the web server application generates and delivers a web page containing data for all three fields, `BookIDNo`, `Title`, `ISBN`, of the database `LIBDB2020.IB` to the Apache web server for despatch to the web browser.

The customisation applied to the first and last columns means that when the browser window is resized horizontally, `Book Id No` and `ISBN` columns remain fixed in width whilst that of the `Title Of Book` column changes.

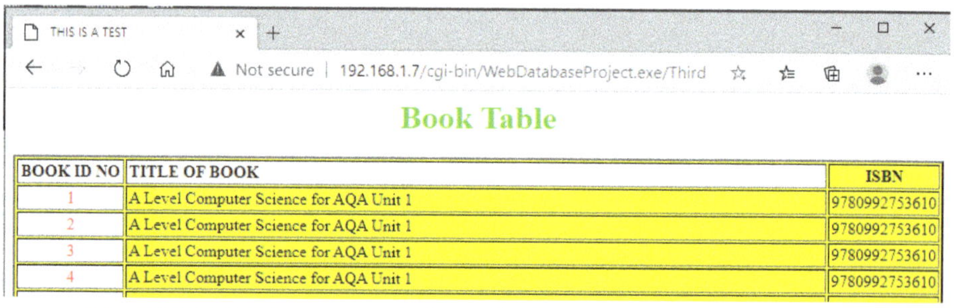

Fig. 74.10 Web browser window displaying part of the web page returned by WebDatabaseProject.exe/Third

Apache dynamic link module

The previous section relied on the CGI (Common Gateway Interface) protocol for communication between the client browser and the Apache web server. On detecting a web page request referencing a CGI application (i.e. one located in the cgi-bin folder), the Apache server launches the application, e.g. `WebDatabaseProject.exe`. Any data sent with the page request is passed by the web server to the CGI application; any output generated by the CGI application is sent by the web server to the client computer. However, CGI is not good at handling multiple requests that arrive together, e.g. from different computers, as the protocol requires a new copy of the CGI application to be launched for each request. Loading multiple copies of the CGI application into memory takes time which reduces the responsiveness of the web server.

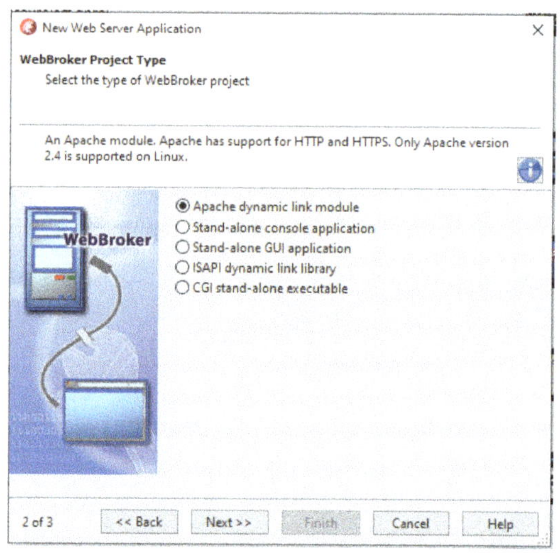

Fig. 74.11 WebBroker Project Type window

It is better to load a copy of the web server application code once and then to access this code from threads of execution running in the Apache server, one thread per request. An Apache web server can do this if the web server application is a library module as Apache has a mechanism for loading library modules and linking to them at the time it is launched.

Creating a Delphi WebBroker Apache dynamic link module

Launch Delphi, select File|New|Other|Web and then Web Server Application. Accept Windows target in the Platform selection window. Choose Apache dynamic link library from the radio button options as shown in *Figure 74.11*. Accept the options shown in *Figure 74.12* and click finish. (Note Apache version 2.0.39 is the highest version supported by Delphi 7). *Table 74.7* shows the source code of the library module that is created - `mod_webbroker.dpr`. *Table 74.8* shows `WebModuleUnit1.pas` and its form window.

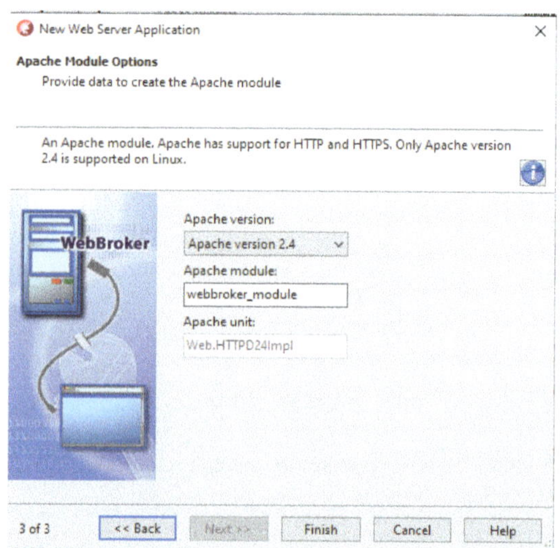

Fig. 74.12 Apache Module Options window

The library module contains the information (shown in red in *Table 74.7*) that is required to configure Apache to load the compiled and linked (build) version of this module - `mod_webbroker.dll`. The produced build (**Shift F9**) version is a dynamic linked library, `mod_webbroker.dll`, hence the `dll` extension. The **Target Platforms** setting in the **Projects** window of the **Delphi IDE** should match the **Apache** target, e.g. 64-bit if the installed **Apache** is the 64-bit version. *Table 74.6* shows the section of `http.conf` containing the script instructions that Apache will use to load `mod_webbroker.dll`. **Add** the lines in red, **save** and **close** `httpd.conf`. Apache is also configured to recognise the virtual directory `xyz` which will be used by web browsers to request execution of `mod_webbroker.dll`.

```
                          :
#LoadModule vhost_alias_module modules/mod_vhost_alias.so
#LoadModule watchdog_module modules/mod_watchdog.so
#LoadModule xml2enc_module modules/mod_xml2enc.so
LoadModule webbroker_module modules/mod_webbroker.dll
  <Location /xyz>
    SetHandler mod_webbroker-handler
  </Location>
                          :
```

Table 74.6 Section of Apache httpd.conf showing reference to mod_webbroker.dll

```
Library mod_webbroker;
Uses
  {$IFDEF MSWINDOWS}
     Winapi.ActiveX,
     System.Win.ComObj,
  {$ENDIF }
  Web.WebBroker,
  Web.ApacheApp,
  Web.HTTPD24Impl,
  WebModuleUnit1 In 'WebModuleUnit1.pas' {WebModule1 : TWebModule};
{$R *.res}
// httpd.conf entries:
//
(*
 LoadModule webbroker_module modules/mod_webbroker.dll
 <Location /xyz>
    SetHandler mod_webbroker-handler
 </Location>
*)
//
// These entries assume that the output directory for this project is the apache/modules directory.
//
// httpd.conf entries should be different if the project is changed in these ways:
//   1. The TApacheModuleData variable name is changed.
//   2. The project is renamed.
//   3. The output directory is not the apache/modules directory.
//   4. The dynamic library extension depends on a platform. Use .dll on Windows and .so on Linux.
//
// Declare exported variable so that Apache can access this module.
Var
  GModuleData : TApacheModuleData;
Exports
  GModuleData name 'webbroker_module';
Begin
  {$IFDEF MSWINDOWS}
    CoInitFlags := COINIT_MULTITHREADED;
  {$ENDIF}
  Web.ApacheApp.InitApplication(@GModuleData);
  Application.Initialize;
  Application.WebModuleClass := WebModuleClass;
  Application.Run;
End.
```

Table 74.7 Delphi WebBroker library module for loading into Apache 2.4

```
Unit WebModuleUnit1;
Interface
Uses
  System.SysUtils, System.Classes, Web.HTTPApp;
Type
  TWebModule1 = Class(TWebModule)
                  Procedure WebModule1DefaultHandlerAction(Sender : TObject;
                    Request : TWebRequest; Response : TWebResponse; var Handled : Boolean);
                End;
Var
  WebModuleClass : TComponentClass = TWebModule1;
Implementation
{%CLASSGROUP 'System.Classes.TPersistent'}
{$R *.dfm}
  Procedure TWebModule1.WebModule1DefaultHandlerAction(Sender: TObject;
              Request: TWebRequest; Response: TWebResponse;
              Var Handled: Boolean);
    Begin
      Response.Content :=
        '<html>' +
        '<head><title>Web Server Application</title></head>' +
        '<body>Web Server Application</body>' +
        '</html>';
    End;
End.
```

Table 74.8 Delphi WebBroker WebModuleUnit1.pas and its form window

Place `mod_webbroker.dll` in the `modules` folder of Apache24.
Launch Apache by double-clicking `httpd.exe` in the `bin` folder of Apache24.

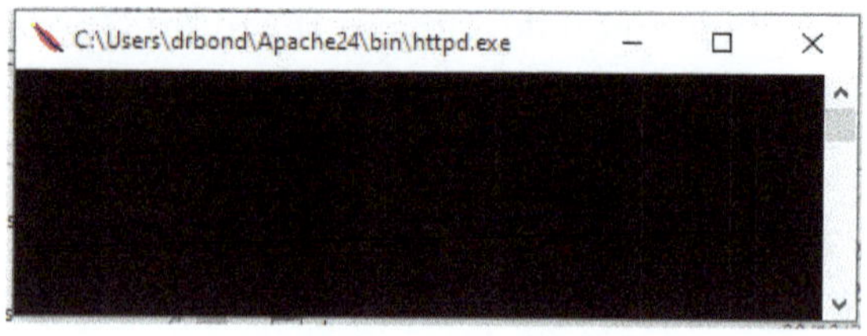

Fig. 74.13 Web server Apache httpd.exe in execution

A command line window should open - *Figure 74.13* - and stay open unless an error has occurred in reading `httpd.conf` or in locating any of the modules marked in httpd.conf `for loading` - look first at `Apache24/logs/error.txt` to discover what might have gone wrong. (For `httpd.exe` to run and the error log file to be opened and written to, Apache24 must be installed in a folder of a local drive which has read/write and executable rights).

Launch a web browser and enter the url

`http://192.168.1.7/xyz`

Replace `192.168.1.7` with the ip address of the machine hosting Apache web server.

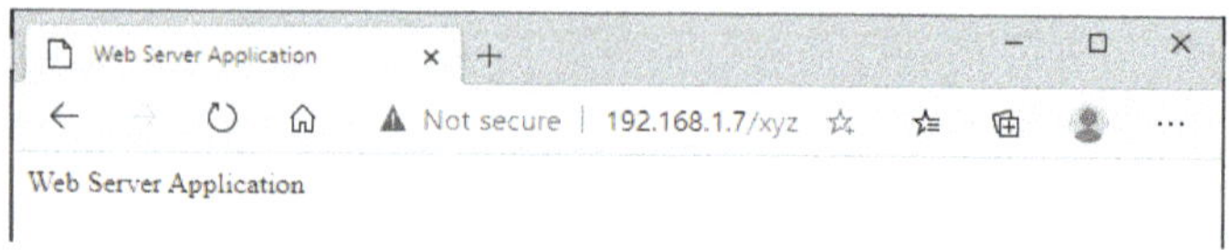

Fig. 74.14 Web page returned for http://192.168.1.7/xyz

Figure 74.14 shows the web page that is returned and rendered in the web browser.

This is the response of the default action since we have no other action than this one currently - see the code in red in *Table 74.8*.

We can edit `httpd.conf` and change the virtual folder `xyz` to anything we like that is a valid folder name. But first Apache web server must be stopped. After the config file has been changed, saved and closed, relaunch Apache so that it reads the new value for the virtual folder.

Save the project in folder `mod_webbrokerprojectfordescription` as `mod_webbroker.dproj` and its unit as `WebModuleUnit1.pas`.

Adding a database

Create a new folder `mod_webbrokerLIBDB2020Project`.

Save the project `mod_webbroker.dproj` from folder `mod_webbrokerprojectfordescription` as `mod_webbroker.dproj` and its unit as `WebModuleUnit1.pas`.

Drop a **TDataSetTableProducer** from the **Internet** tab of the component/tool palette onto the web module form. From the **Interbase** tab of the component/tool palette, **drop** the following onto the web module form:

- a **TIBDatabase** component
- a **TIBTransaction** component.
- a **TIBTable** component.

Use the instructions from section **CGI web server database application** to set up access to `LIBDB2020.ib` and the action `/First` as before together with its **OnAction** event handler `WebModule1WebActionItem1Action`. Omit setting up the **Header** and **Footer** properties.
Set `DataSetTableProducer1.Caption` property to `Dynamic Link Library Example`.
Set `DataSetTableProducer1.CaptionAlignment` to `caTop`.
Right click `DataSetTableProducer1` on the form and **select** **Response Editor** from the pop-up window.
Set **Table Properties**:

- **Align** to **haCenter**
- **Border** to 2
- **Cellpadding** to 3
- **Cellspacing** to 3.

Select DataSetTableProducer1|Columns|0 - BOOKIDNO and **change**

- **Align** to **haCenter**
- **Title|Align** to **haCenter** and **Title|Caption** to Book Id No.

Select DataSetTableProducer1|Columns|1 - TITLE

- **Align** to **haLeft**
- **Title|Align** to **haLeft** and **Title|Caption** to Book Title.

Save All (**CTRL Shift S**).

Build (**Shift F9**) the project.

Place mod_webbroker.dll in the modules folder of Apache24.

Re-launch Apache by double-clicking httpd.exe in the bin folder of Apache24.

Launch a web browser and enter the url

http://192.168.1.7/xyz/First

Replace 192.168.1.7 with the ip address of the machine hosting Apache web server.

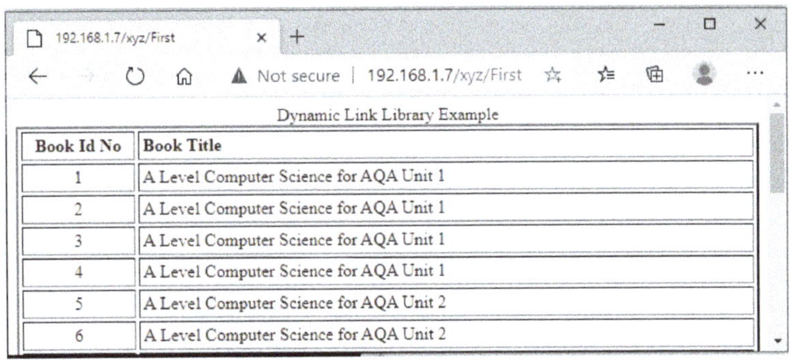

Book Id No	Book Title
1	A Level Computer Science for AQA Unit 1
2	A Level Computer Science for AQA Unit 1
3	A Level Computer Science for AQA Unit 1
4	A Level Computer Science for AQA Unit 1
5	A Level Computer Science for AQA Unit 2
6	A Level Computer Science for AQA Unit 2

Fig. 74.15 Part of the web page returned for http://192.168.1.7/xyz/First

Figure 74.15 shows part of the web page that is returned from the action First and its rendering in the web browser.

Programming tasks

1. Adapt the CGI web server database application WebDatabaseProject.dproj to work with the Student table of LIBDB2020.ib instead of the Book table. The browser should display the values of fields StudentIdNo, Surname and FirstName. StudentIdNo field values should be centered whilst Surname and FirstName field values should be left justified. The column headings should be similarly formatted. Use borders, cell spacing and cell padding similar to that shown in *Figure 74.15*. The table heading centred above the table should be Student Table.

2. Adapt the Delphi WebBroker Apache dynamic link module project mod_webbroker.dproj from the last section to work with the Loan table of LIBDB2020.ib instead of the Book table. The browser should display the values of fields BookIdNo, StudentIdNo and LoanDate. All field values and their column headings should be centered. Use borders, cell spacing and cell padding similar to that shown in *Figure 74.15*. The table heading centred above the tableshould be Loan Table.

Creating web pages with images extracted from a database

P

Create a Delphi WebBroker Apache dynamic link module application as before.

Drop a **TDataSetTableProducer** from the **Internet** tab of the component/tool palette onto the web module form.

From the **Interbase** tab of the component palette, **drop** the following onto the web module form:

- a **TIBDatabase** component
- a **TIBTransaction** component
- a **TIBTable** component.

Use the instructions from section **CGI web server database application** to set up access to the `IMAGE` table of Interbase database `IMAGESDB.IB` and the action `/im` with its **OnAction** event handler `WebModule1WebActionItem1Action`. The body of `WebModule1WebActionItem1Action` should be the same as before.

Select `DataSetTableProducer1` and in the **Object Inspector double click OnFormatCell** in the **Events** tab to create the event handler `DataSetTableProducer1FormatCell`. **Add** the code shown in *Table 74.9*.

```
Procedure TWebModule1.DataSetTableProducer1FormatCell(Sender : TObject; CellRow,
            CellColumn : Integer; Var BgColor : THTMLBgColor; Var Align : THTMLAlign;
            Var VAlign : THTMLVAlign; Var CustomAttrs, CellData : String);
   Begin
     If (CellColumn=4) And (CellRow>0)
      Then CellData := '<img class="contain" src=http://192.168.1.7/imagestream/stream?CellRow='
                    + IntToStr(CellRow) + ' alt="test" >';
   End;
```

See Table 74.12 for definition of CSS class "contain".

Table 74.9 OnFormatCell event handler that handles images

Figure 74.16 shows the contents of the `IMAGE` table displayed in **IBConsole**. The fifth column, (`ColumnNo = 4`), `Picture`, is a `BLOB` field (Binary Large OBject) of `jpeg` images except for the first row (`CellRow = 0`). In order to populate the response object with the correct encoding for `jpeg` images in the fifth column and not the string '(BLOB)', an `img` HTML tag must be used which references an image source as follows `src=http://192.168.1.7/imagestream/stream`.

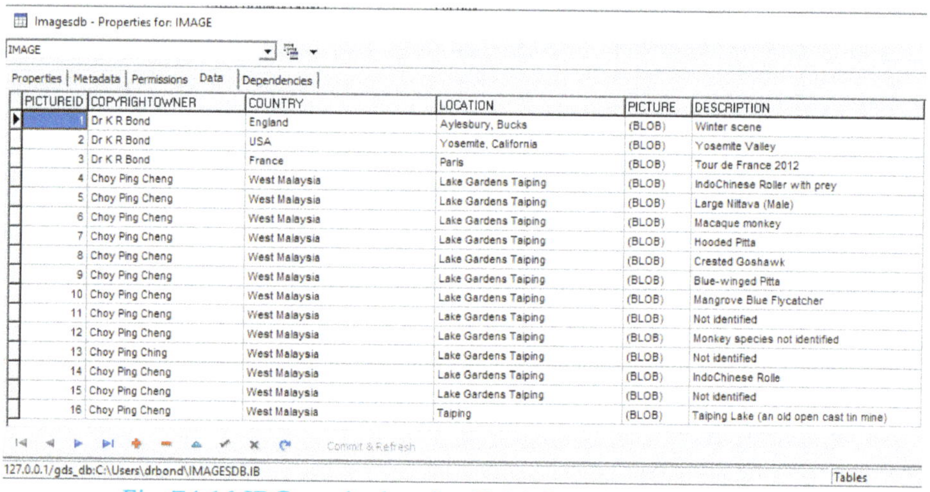

Imagesdb - Properties for: IMAGE

PICTUREID	COPYRIGHTOWNER	COUNTRY	LOCATION	PICTURE	DESCRIPTION
1	Dr K R Bond	England	Aylesbury, Bucks	(BLOB)	Winter scene
2	Dr K R Bond	USA	Yosemite, California	(BLOB)	Yosemite Valley
3	Dr K R Bond	France	Paris	(BLOB)	Tour de France 2012
4	Choy Ping Cheng	West Malaysia	Lake Gardens Taiping	(BLOB)	IndoChinese Roller with prey
5	Choy Ping Cheng	West Malaysia	Lake Gardens Taiping	(BLOB)	Large Niltava (Male)
6	Choy Ping Cheng	West Malaysia	Lake Gardens Taiping	(BLOB)	Macaque monkey
7	Choy Ping Cheng	West Malaysia	Lake Gardens Taiping	(BLOB)	Hooded Pitta
8	Choy Ping Cheng	West Malaysia	Lake Gardens Taiping	(BLOB)	Crested Goshawk
9	Choy Ping Cheng	West Malaysia	Lake Gardens Taiping	(BLOB)	Blue-winged Pitta
10	Choy Ping Cheng	West Malaysia	Lake Gardens Taiping	(BLOB)	Mangrove Blue Flycatcher
11	Choy Ping Cheng	West Malaysia	Lake Gardens Taiping	(BLOB)	Not identified
12	Choy Ping Cheng	West Malaysia	Lake Gardens Taiping	(BLOB)	Monkey species not identified
13	Choy Ping Ching	West Malaysia	Lake Gardens Taiping	(BLOB)	Not identified
14	Choy Ping Cheng	West Malaysia	Lake Gardens Taiping	(BLOB)	IndoChinese Rolle
15	Choy Ping Cheng	West Malaysia	Lake Gardens Taiping	(BLOB)	Not identified
16	Choy Ping Cheng	West Malaysia	Taiping	(BLOB)	Taiping Lake (an old open cast tin mine)

127.0.0.1/gds_db:C:\Users\drbond\IMAGESDB.IB

Fig. 74.16 IBConsole showing IMAGE table of Imagesdb.ib

The action name is `stream` served from an Apache virtual folder `imagestream`. The current row (`IntToStr(CellRow)`) is supplied to action `stream` in in the url parameter `CellRow`. This is needed so that the action can retrieve the corresponding image.

Save the project in folder `mod_webbrokerproject` as `mod_webbroker.dproj` and its unit as `WebModuleUnit1.pas`.

Create a new Delphi WebBroker Apache dynamic link module application and **add** the same components to the webbroker form as before. **Connect** to table `IMAGE` in database `IMAGESDB.IB`.

Create action `WebActionItem1` with `PathInfo /stream`.

Add to the **Implementation** section

```
Var
  Stream : TStream;
```

Create `OnCreate` and `OnDestroy` event handlers for `WebModule1` - *Table 74.10*.

Create OnAction event handler `WebModule1WebActionItem1Action` for `WebActionItem1`.

```
Procedure TWebModule1.WebModuleCreate(Sender : TObject);
  Begin
    Stream := TStream.Create;
  End;
Procedure TWebModule1.WebModuleDestroy(Sender : TObject);
  Begin
    Stream.Free;
  End;
```

Table 74.10 Event handlers for creating and destroying a stream

Add the code to its body as shown in *Table 74.11*. **Save** the project `mod_webstream.dproj` and its unit `WebModuleUnit1.pas` in folder `mod_webstreamproject`.

Build (**Shift F9**) the project.

```
Procedure TWebModule1.WebModule1WebActionItem1Action(Sender : TObject;
            Request : TWebRequest; Response : TWebResponse;
            Var Handled : Boolean);
  Var
    RowNo : Integer;
    Begin
      With DataSetTableProducer1
        Do
          Begin
            DataSet.Open;
            RowNo := Request.QueryFields.Values['CellRow'].ToInteger;
            DataSet.First;
            DataSet.MoveBy(RowNo-1);
            Stream := DataSet.CreateBlobStream(DataSet.FieldByName('Picture'), bmRead);
            Stream.Position := 0;
            Response.ContentStream := Stream;
            Response.ContentType := 'image/jpeg';
            Response.SendResponse;
            DataSet.Close;
          End;
    End;
```

Table 74.11 Streaming the jpeg image data of the Picture field for the specified row via the Response object

Now return to `mod_webbroker.dproj`.

Select `DataSetTableProducer1|Header` property and **make** the contents match that shown in *Table 74.12*.

Select `DataSetTableProducer1|Footer` property and **make** the contents

```
</body>
</html>
```

Right click `DataSetTableProducer1` on form and select **Response Editor**.

Select `Picture` in **Field Name|Field Type** window.

In **Object Inspector**, **set** the **Custom** field to `width=250px`.

Select `PictureId`, `CopyrightOwner`, `Country`, `Location`, `Description`, in turn and **set** their **Custom** field to `width=100px` except `Description` which should be set to `width=150px`.

Save All (**Ctrl Shift S**).

Build (**Shift F9**) the project.

Stop Apache running if it is running.

Edit `httpd.conf` and **add** the lines shown in red in *Table 74.13*.

Save and **close**.

Place `mod_webbroker.dll` and `mod_webstream.dll` in the `modules` folder of Apache24.

Re-launch Apache by double-clicking `httpd.exe` in the `bin` folder of Apache24.

Launch a web browser and enter the url

`http://192.168.1.7/xyz/im`

Replace `192.168.1.7` with the ip address of the machine hosting Apache web server.

```
<html>
  <head>
    <title>Images database</title>
    <style>
      .contain     CSS class definition
        {object-fit: contain;
            width: 100%;
            height: 250px;
        }
    </style>
  </head>
  <body>
    <center>
      <h1>Images database</h1>
    </center>
```

Table 74.12 HTML contents of Header property of DataSetTableProducer1

The object-fit property defines how an element responds to the height and width of its content box.

contain: increases or decreases the size of the image to fill the box whilst preserving its aspect-ratio.

```
                              :
#LoadModule vhost_alias_module modules/mod_vhost_alias.so
#LoadModule watchdog_module modules/mod_watchdog.so
#LoadModule xml2enc_module modules/mod_xml2enc.so
LoadModule webbroker_module modules/mod_webbroker.dll
  <Location /xyz>
    SetHandler mod_webbroker-handler
  </Location>
LoadModule webstream_module modules/mod_webstream.dll
 <Location /imagestream>
    SetHandler mod_webstream-handler
 </Location>
                              :
```

Table 74.13 Section of Apache httpd.conf referencing mod_webbroker.dll and mod_webstream.dll

Figure 74.17 shows part of the web page that is returned from the action `im` and its rendering in Microsoft's Edge web browser running on a Windows 10 machine.

Figure 74.18 shows part of the web page that is returned from the action `im` and its rendering in Apple's Safari web browser running on an iPhone 11 (IP address 192.168.1.14) connected to the same local area network as the web server. *Figure 74.19* shows part of the web page that is returned from the action `im` and its rendering in Google Chrome web browser running on a Samsung S8+ (IP address 192.168.1.4) also connected to the same local area network.

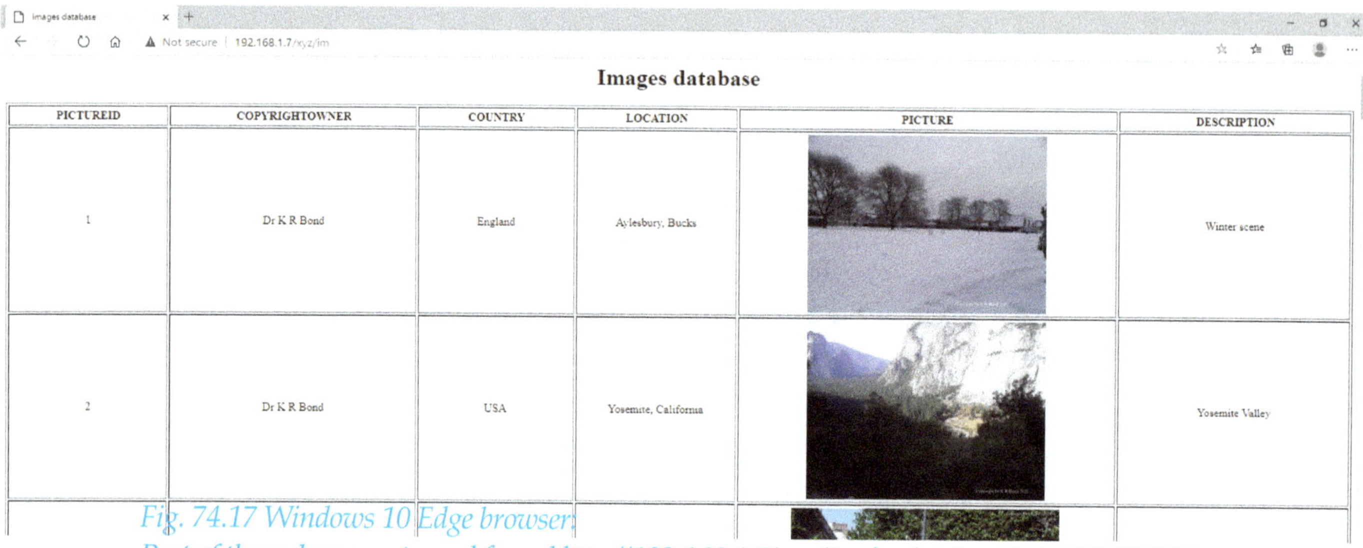

Fig. 74.17 Windows 10 Edge browser: Part of the web page returned for url http://192.168.1.7/xyz/im for database IMAGESDB.IB

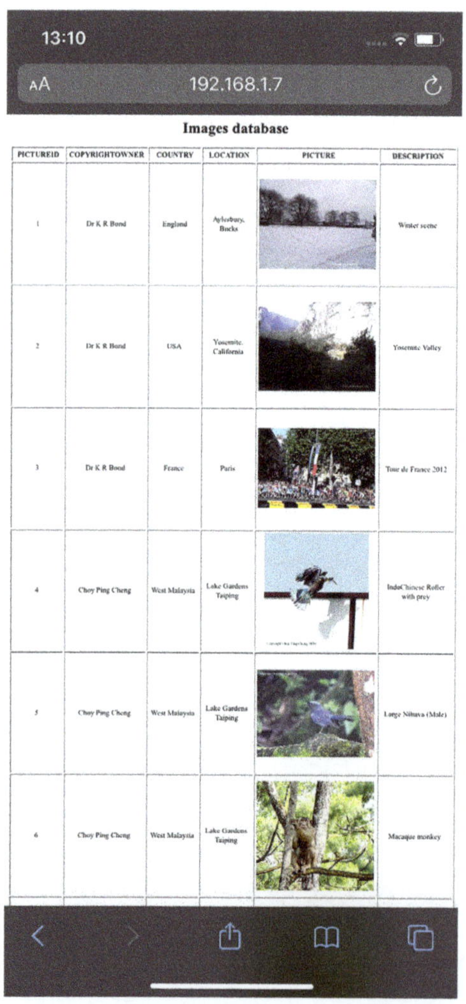

Fig. 74.18 IPhone 11 Safari browser: Part of the web page returned for url http://192.168.1.7/xyz/im for database IMAGESDB.IB

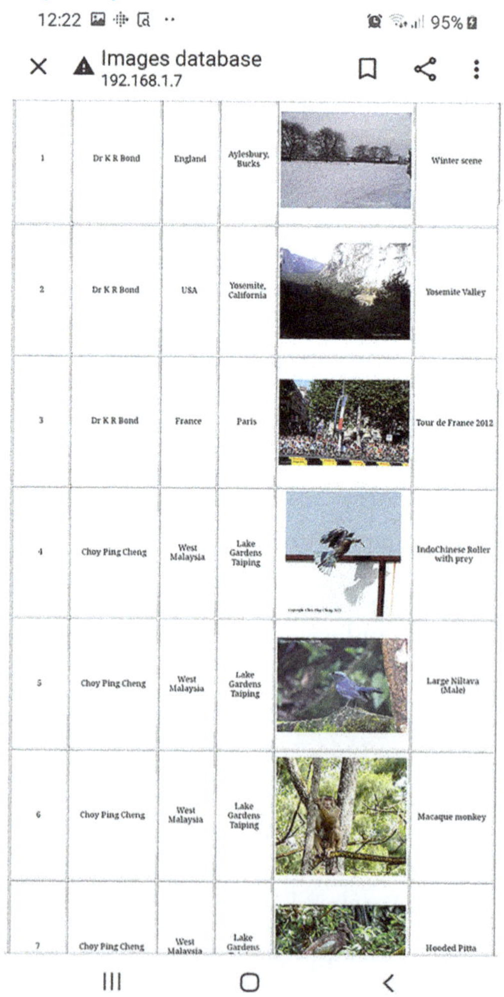

Fig. 74.19 Samsung S8+ Google Chrome browser: Part of the web page returned for url http://192.168.1.7/xyz/im for database IMAGESDB.IB

Querying a database and returning the results as a web page

P

The data returned in a web page might consist of a few rows or a large number of rows depending on the size of the database table. Scrolling through more than a few rows to locate a specific record is not ideal. It would be much better if the number of rows returned could be limited to those of interest. This can be done using **TSQLQueryTableProducer** from the Internet tab of the component palette, and a **TSQLQuery** and a **TSQLConnection** component from the dbExpress tab. Embarcadero deprecates the use of dbExpress components as these are superseded now by the more powerful FireDAC components. However, for backwards compatibility with Delphi versions prior to XE3 and also because **TSQLQueryTableProducer** requires a query component of type **TSQLQuery**, this section will describe the use of these dbExpress components. Generating web pages using a web application that relies upon **FireDAC** components is left as an exercise for the reader.

Launch Delphi, **select** File|New|Other|Web and then Web Server Application. **Accept** Windows target in the Platform selection window. **Choose** Apache dynamic link library from the radio button options.

Save the project as `mod_webbrokerSQL.dproj` in folder `mod_webbrokerSQLProject`. **Save** its unit `WebModuleUnit1.pas` in the same folder.

Make sure that the export statement in `mod_webbrokerSQL.dpr` is as follows

```
Exports
  GModuleData name 'webbrokerSQL_module';
```

From the Internet tab of the component palette, drop a **TSQLQueryTableProducer** on the web module form.

From the dbExpress tab of the component palette, drop the following on the web module form:

- a **TSQLQuery** component
- a **TSQLConnection** component.

Select `SQLConnection1` and double click the **Params** property in the Object Inspector to bring up the Value List Editor. **Set** the **Database** field to the path to `imagesdb.ib` - *Figure 74.20* shows an example - and **set** **User_Name** and **Password**. **Set** `SQLConnection1|LoginPrompt` to `False`.

Set `SQLConnection1`'s **Driver** property to `Interbase Server`.

Attempt to set Connected to `True` (if everything works, it will be successful).

Set `SQLQuery1`'s **SQLConnection** property to `SQLConnection1`.

Set `SQLQuery1`'s **SQL** property via the String List Editor to

```
Select * From image
  Where PictureId = :PictureId
```

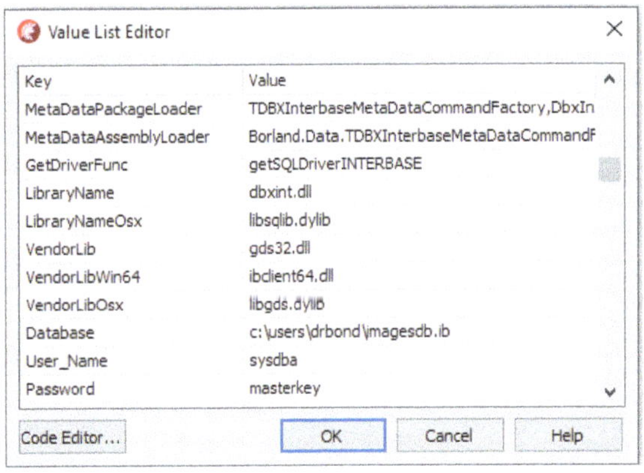

Fig. 74.20 Value List Editor for SQLConnection1 Params field - setting path to imagesdb.ib database

Set `SQLQueryTableProducer1`'s **Query** property to `SQLQuery1`.

Set `SQLQueryTableProducer1`'s **Header** property to that shown in *Table 74.12* but change the `height` property to 400px.

Set `SQLQueryTableProducer1`'s **Footer** property to that shown in *Table 74.14*.

Select `SQLQueryTableProducer1`'s **Columns** property.

Double click **(THTMLTableColumns)** to bring up the Editing SQLQueryTableProducer1.Columns window. **Add** all the fields from `imagesdb.ib` and set the **Table Properties** as shown in *Figure 74.21*.

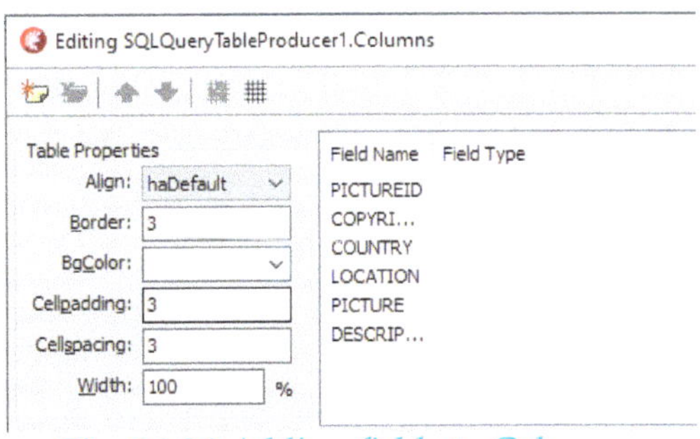

Fig. 74.21 Adding fields to Columns and setting table properties

```
      <br />
      <p></p>
      <hr />
      <form action="http://192.168.1.7/imagedb/query" method = "post">
        <table>
          <tr>
            <td> Picture No <input type="text" name="PictureId" value = "1" size="5" maxlength="5"/></td>
          </tr>
            <tr>
              <td><input type="submit" /></td>
            </tr>
            <tr>
              <td><input type="reset" /></td>
            </tr>
        </table>
      </form>
    </body>
</html>
```

Table 74.14 HTML contents of Footer property of SQLQueryTableProducer1

Select `WebModule1` and create a new **Action** with the **Name** `Query` and **PathInfo** `/query`.

Select this action in the **Structure** pane as shown in *Figure 74.22* and then **double click** the **OnAction** field in the **Events** tab for `WebModule1.Actions[1]` to create the event handler `WebModule1QueryAction`.

Add the code shown in *Table 74.15* to this event handler.

Add the variable declaration to the **Implementation** section

```
Var
     PictureId : Integer = 1;
```

Select `Query|Params|0-PictureId` as shown in *Figure 74.23* and then set **DataType** to **ftInteger** in the Object Inspector.

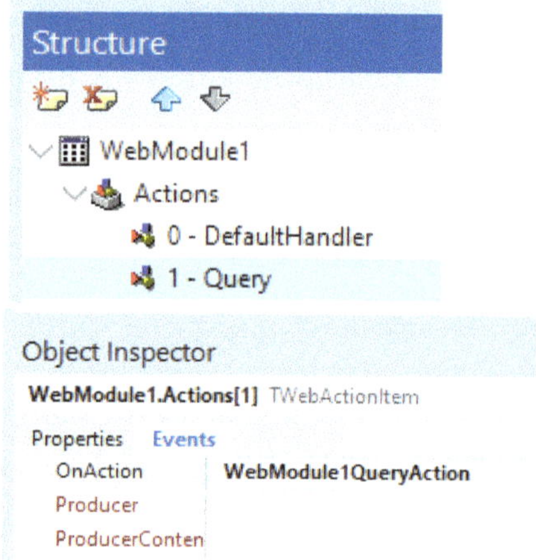

Fig. 74.22 OnAction event handler for Query action

```
Procedure TWebModule1.WebModule1QueryAction(Sender : TObject;
        Request : TWebRequest; Response : TWebResponse; Var Handled : Boolean);
  Begin
    If Request.ContentFields.Values['PictureId'] = ''
      Then PictureId := 1
      Else PictureId := StrToInt(Request.ContentFields.Values['PictureId']);
    SQLQueryTableProducer1.Query.ParamByName('PictureId').AsInteger := PictureId;
    With SQLQueryTableProducer1
      Do
        Begin
          Query.Open;
          Response.Content := SQLQueryTableProducer1.Content;
          Query.Close;
        End;
  End;
```

Request object contains the parameter PictureId's value posted in form element of web page

Assigning the form's submitted PictureId value to the query's parameter value

Table 74.15 Event handler for OnAction event for Query action

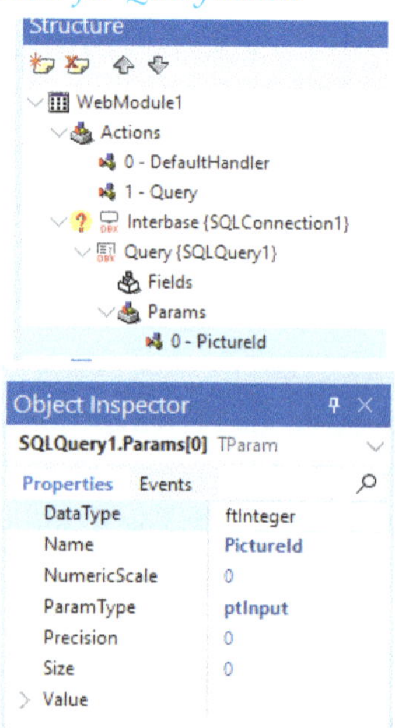

Fig. 74.23 Setting data type of query parameter, PictureId

Select `SQLQueryTableProducer1` and in the **Object Inspector select** the **Events** tab then **double click** the **OnFormatCell** event field to create the `SQLQueryTableProducer1FormatCell` event handler.

Add the code shown in *Table 74.16* to this event handler.

```
Procedure TWebModule1.SQLQueryTableProducer1FormatCell(Sender : TObject; CellRow,
              CellColumn : Integer; Var BgColor : THTMLBgColor; Var Align : THTMLAlign;
              Var VAlign : THTMLVAlign; Var CustomAttrs, CellData : string);
    Begin
      If (CellColumn=4) and (CellRow>0)
        Then CellData := '<img class="contain" src=http://192.168.1.7/imagestream/stream?CellRow='
                          + IntToStr(PictureId) + ' alt="test" >';
    End;
```

Table 74.16 Event handler for OnFormatCell event for SQLQueryTableProducer1

In order for dbExpress components to connect to a database, a `dbxconnections.ini` file must be present in `C:\Users\Public\Documents\Embarcadero\Studio\dbExpress\21.0`. This file is missing in the Delphi 10.4.1 Sydney installation[2]. However, this is easily fixed by creating an empty text file `dbxconnections.ini` and saving it to `C:\Users\Public\Documents\Embarcadero\Studio\dbExpress\21.0`. Delphi will need to be restarted so that it reads the contents of `dbxconnections.ini` on loading the `dbExpress` components. In fact, at the same time the ini file is created, it is possible to add a connection name `[IMAGEDB]` and its specification as shown in *Table 74.17*.

```
[IMAGEDB]
DriverID=IB
Protocol=TCPIP
Database=localhost:C:\Users\drbond\imagesdb.ib
User_Name=sysdba
Password=masterkey
CharacterSet=
ExtendedMetadata=True
```

Table 74.17 File dbxconnection.ini

However, the ini file will be populated with this information when the project `mod_webbrokerSQL.dproj` is saved, including the connection name if one has been assigned in the Object Inspector - *Figure 74.24*.

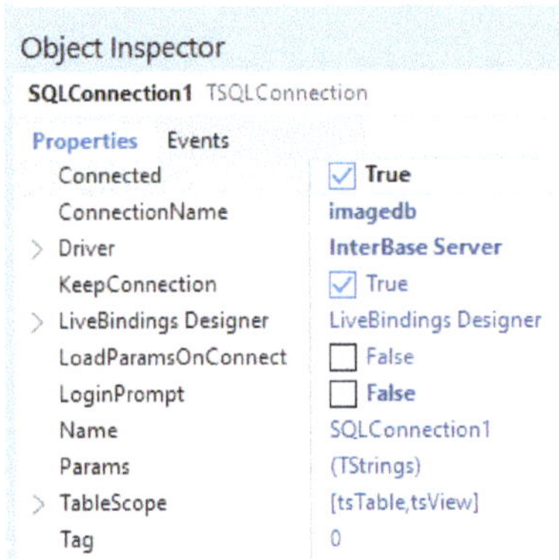

Fig. 74.24 Setting ConnectionName

Save All (Ctrl Shift S).

Build (Shift F9) the project.

Stop Apache running if it is running.

Edit `httpd.conf` and **add** the lines shown in red in *Table 74.18.*

Save and **close**.

Place `mod_webbrokerSQL.dll` and `mod_ webstream.dll` in the `modules` folder of Apache24.

Re-launch Apache by double-clicking `httpd.exe` in the `bin` folder of Apache24.

```
                              :
LoadModule webbroker_module modules/mod_webbroker.dll
 <Location /xyz>
    SetHandler mod_webbroker-handler
 </Location>
LoadModule webstream_module modules/mod_webstream.dll
 <Location /imagestream>
    SetHandler mod_webstream-handler
 </Location>
LoadModule webbrokerSQL_module modules/mod_webbrokerSQL.dll
  <Location /imagedb>
    SetHandler mod_webbrokerSQL-handler
  </Location>
                              :
```

Table 74.18 Section of Apache httpd.conf referencing mod_webbrokerSQL.dll and mod_webstream.dll

Launch a web browser and enter the url

`http://192.168.1.7/imagedb/query`

Replace `192.168.1.7` with the ip address of the machine hosting Apache web server.

Figure 74.25 shows the web page that is returned from the `query` action when 16 is entered in the `Picture No` box and the `Submit` button is clicked or the return/enter key is pressed. The web page returned resets the `Picture No` box to the default value 1.

Different rows of the database table `Image` may be selected by entering a different `Picture No` value.

Figure 74.26 shows the web page that is returned for `Picture No` 23.

2 Embarcadero omitted to include this file

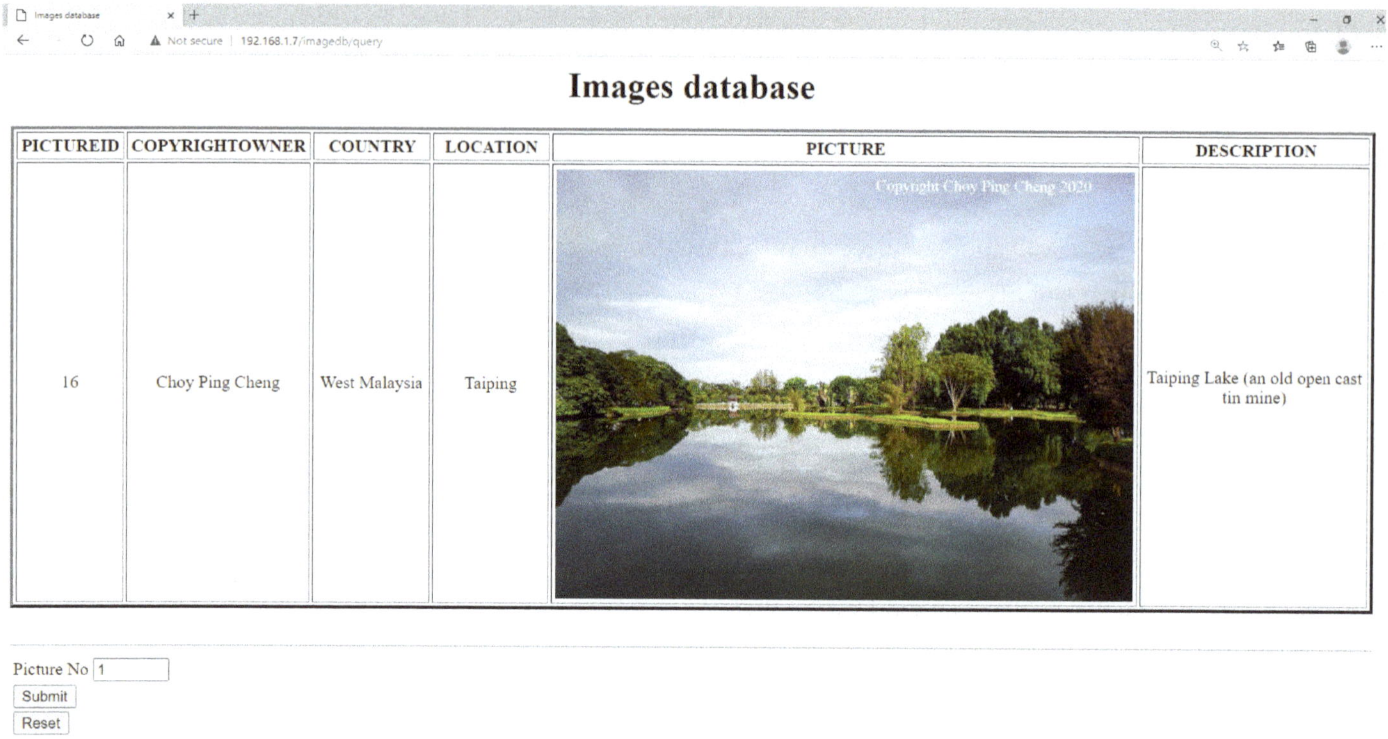

Fig. 74.25 WebBrokerSQLProject returning a web page for url http://192.168.1.7/imagedb/query

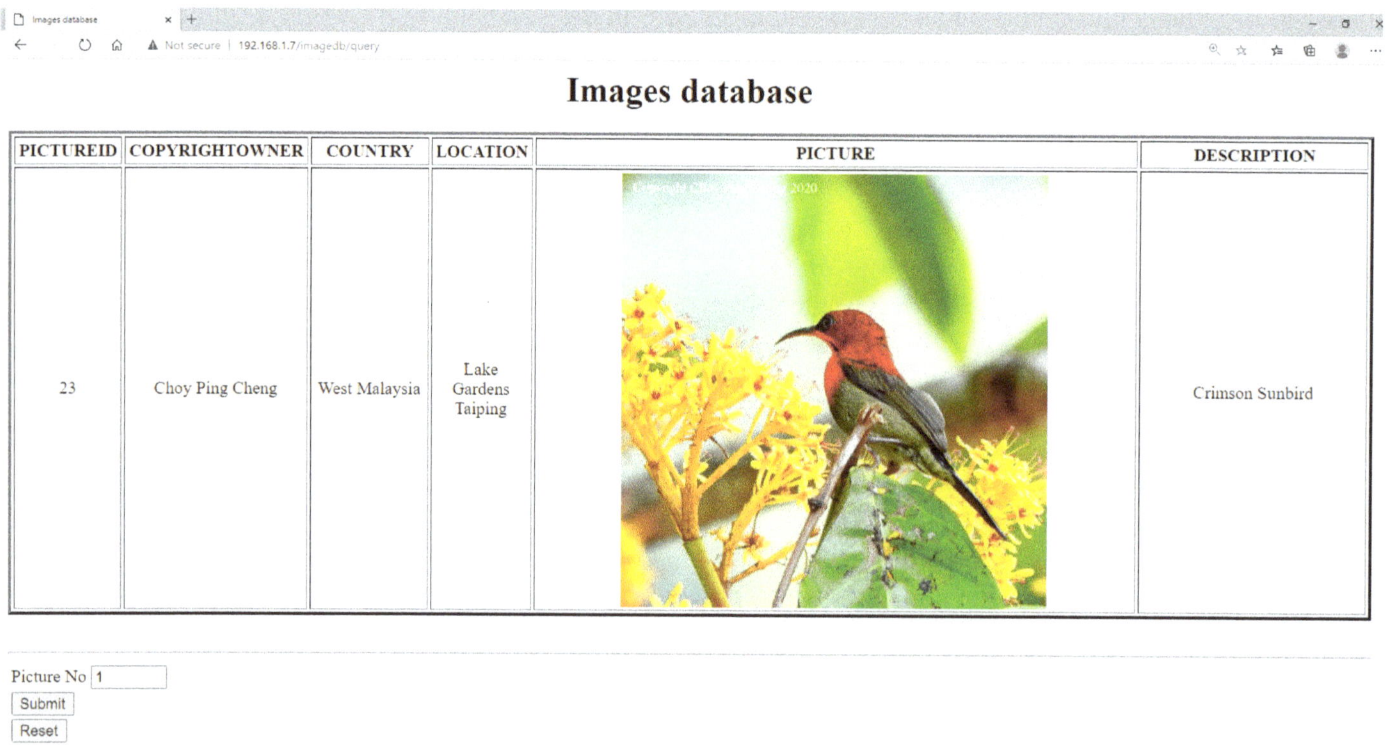

Fig. 74.26 WebBrokerSQLProject returning another web page for url http://192.168.1.7/imagedb/query

75 Machine learning

Machine Learning

Purpose: An introduction to Machine Learning in Delphi

Introduction

There is no unique definition of Machine Learning. Here are two definitions:

> "Machine learning(ML) is the field of study that gives computers the ability to learn without being explicitly programmed" - attributed to Arthur Samuel (1959) but is probably a paraphrase of Samuel's work that appeared later in other works. For example, suppose an email program that you use "looks at" which emails you mark as spam and which you do not, based on this it learns how to better filter spam.

> "Machine learning (ML) is the study of computer algorithms that can improve automatically through experience and by the use of data. It is seen as part of artificial intelligence. Machine learning algorithms build a model based on sample data, known as training data, in order to make predictions or decisions without being explicitly programmed to do so." - attributed to Mitchell, Tom (1997).[1]

There are three concepts at the core of machine learning: data, a model, and learning. Through a learning process, the goal is to find good models that generalise well to yet unseen data given an initial dataset to train on. Using the initial dataset (training data), the parameters of the model are adjusted automatically to arrive at a good correspondence between the output generated by the model and the training data. *Figure 75.1* shows a schematic diagram of the process.

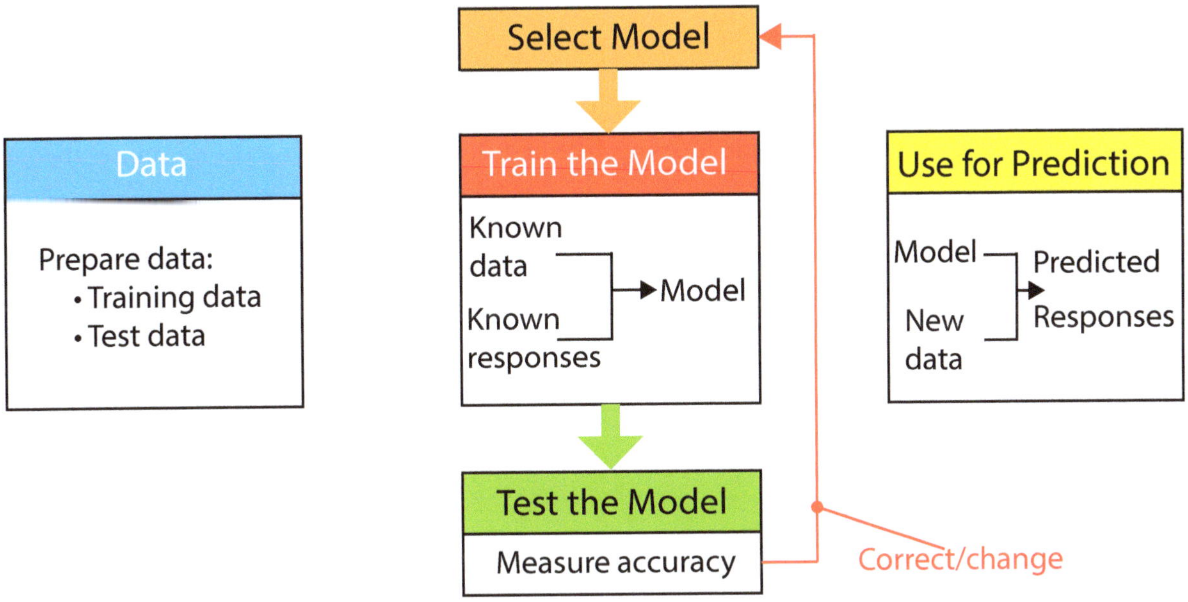

Fig. 75.1 Supervised learning workflow

Consider the simple example of predicting a house price given the land area it occupies. Suppose that some data has already been collected and plotted on a graph of house price against land area as shown in *Figure 75.2*.

1 Machine Learning. New York: McGraw Hill. ISBN 0-07-042807-7. OCLC 36417892. http://www.cs.cmu.edu/~tom/mlbook.html

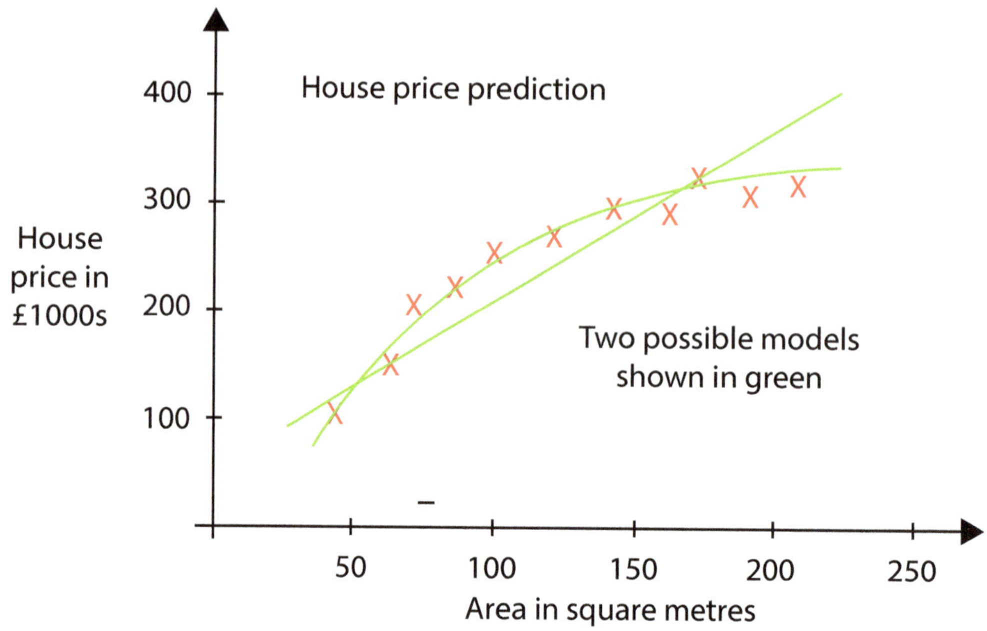

Fig. 75.2 Modelling house prices as a function of land area occupied by house

A linear model might be chosen as a first attempt at modelling house prices as a function of land area occupied by the house. For this linear model, the following hypothesis can be established given that the equation of a straight line is y = mx + c

Hypothesis: PredictedPrice = m x Area + c

Hypothesis: PredictedPrice = f(Area, m, c) = m x Area + c

Parameters/coefficients: m, c

The parameters m and c may be varied to adjust the fit of the model to the given data - see the straight green line in *Figure 75.2*. Our model that predicts the price of a house given its land area is thus a function of Area, m and c until the latter are fixed by the process of machine learning. The best fit for this linear model minimises the mean of the square of the error between the predicted price and the actual price as shown in *Table 75.1*.

$$\text{Cost function} = \frac{\sum_{i=1}^{n}(f(\text{Area}_i, m, c) - \text{ActualPrice})^2}{n}$$

Table 75.1 Mean Squared Error calculation

The mean squared error (MSE) calculated by the formula in *Table 75.1* is called the **Cost Function** in machine learning. Thus to find the optimum values for m and c which minimises the error between prediction and actual, the cost function must be minimised.

There are different forms of MSE formula. Adding a 2 to the denominator makes the calculus of deriving the MSE cleaner.

What has been described is known as **linear regression with one variable**, in this case Area.

The second green line in *Figure 75.2* is another possible model, this time a non-linear one. It actually looks a better fit. For this we use **non-linear regression**.

Classification

The email spam filter machine learning example mentioned in the introduction is an example of a classification problem. For this particular problem two classes exist: spam and not spam which we might express as 0 or 1.

A classification algorithm called **logistic regression** is often used for this type of problem. It is a classification algorithm that assigns observations to a discrete set of classes, two in the case of the spam example. The **logistic regression model** is a linear regression model which uses a more complex cost function. The cost function which is used is the **sigmoid** or **logistic function**. This function replaces the linear function covered in the last section.

The sigmoid or logistic function limits the cost function to between 0 and 1 - see *Figure 75.3*.

In machine learning, the sigmoid function is used to map predictions to probabilities, e.g. the probablity that an email is spam.

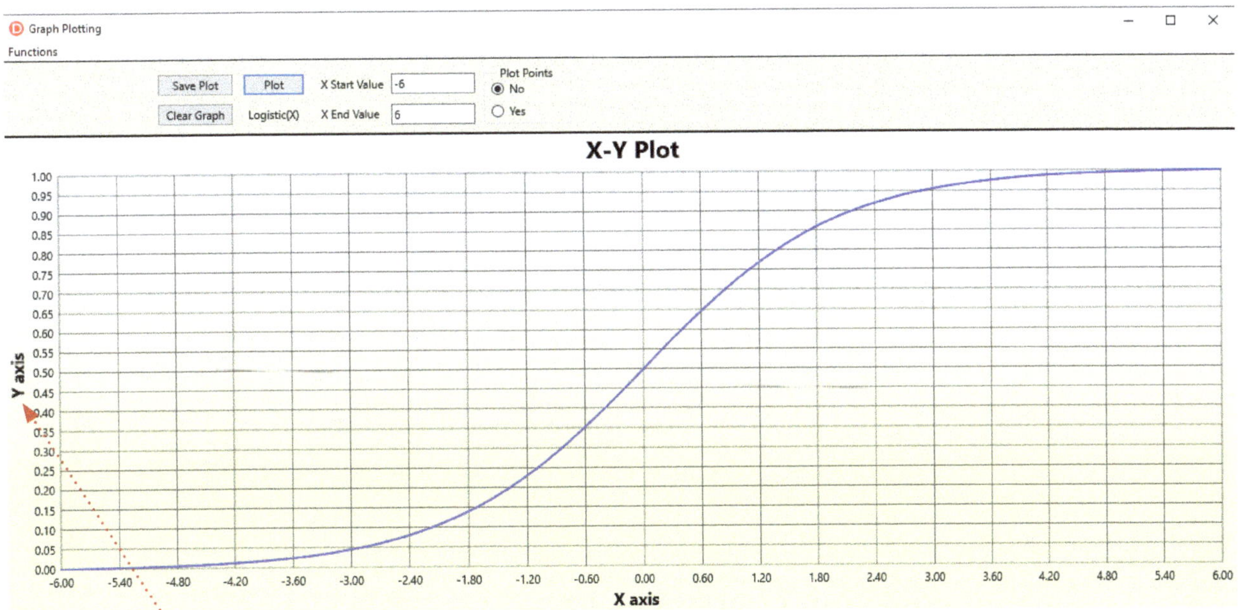

Fig. 75.3 Logistic function plotted using GraphPlotWithFunctionPointers program from Chapter 77

The formula for the sigmoid function is shown in *Table 75.2*.

$$y = f(x) = \frac{1}{1 + e^{-x}} = \frac{e^{+x}}{e^{+x} + 1}$$

Table 75.2 Formula of sigmoid function

When using linear regression we used a formula of the hypothesis i.e. $f(\text{Area}, m, c) = m \times \text{Area} + c$

Generalising and using '.' to indicate multiplication,

$$f(x, m, c) = m.x + c$$

For logistic regression we modify this formula as follows

Let $Z = m.x + c$ then

$$h(x, m, c) = \frac{1}{1 + e^{-Z}} = \frac{1}{1 + e^{-(m.x + c)}}$$

h(x) replaces h(x, m , c) once m and c are determined

Table 75.3 Hypothesis formula for logistic regression

h(x) is our prediction function. If we are deciding on whether an email is spam or not then we rename h(x)

$$\text{Spam}(x)$$

After training on a dataset containing a mix of emails that have already been marked as spam or not spam, the parameters m and c are determined. Given a new email, the value of x is calculated in some pre-determined way. The value of Z may then be calculated from $Z = m.x + c$ and this is fed to Spam(x) to obtain a probability that the email is spam. In *Figure 75.4* the threshold has been set at 0.5. If the calculated probability is above 0.5 the email is classified as spam. If below, it is classified as not spam. Essentially, Spam(x) returns a real value between 0 and 1 that is rounded to an integer value, 0 or 1.

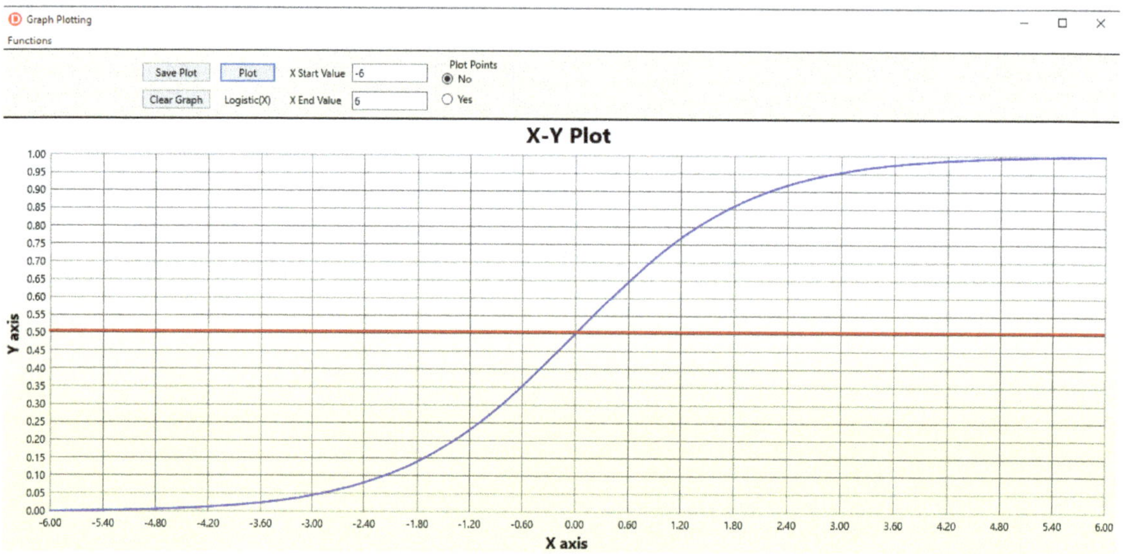

Fig. 75.4 Logistic function with threshold set at 0.5

For logistic regression, the cost function is defined as follows

$$-\log(h(x)) \text{ if } y = 1$$

$$-\log(1 - h(x)) \text{ if } y = 0$$

$$\text{Cost function}(h(x), y) = \begin{cases} -\log(h(x)) & \text{if } y = 1 \\ -\log(1 - h(x)) & \text{if } y = 0 \end{cases}$$

where $y = \text{RoundToInteger}(\text{Spam}(x))$

Table 75.4 Cost function for logistic regression

These two functions (cost function for $y = 0$ and $y = 1$) are compressed into one and the new function is minimised using a technique called **gradient descent**. This technique is too advanced to consider here.

Use **Python4Delphi** to explore logistic regression modelling using a python script[2] for the logistic regression.

Artificial neural networks

Artificial neural networks (ANNs) mimic the neurons in the human brain through a set of algorithms. A typical neuron consists of a cell body (soma), dendrites, and a single axon - *Figure 75.5*. The axon and dendrites are filaments that extrude from the soma. Every neuron has a single axon and many dendrites. The axon extends up to a metre in length in humans, branching as it advances. At the farthest tip of the axon's branches are axon terminals, where the neuron can transmit a signal across the synapse - a joining of an axon terminal and a dendrite branch of another cell.

2 See www.educational-computing.co.uk/DelphiBookCode/DelphiCode.html for a suitable Python script.

Most neurons receive signals via the dendrites and soma and send out signals down the axon. At the majority of synapses, signals cross from the axon of one neuron to a dendrite of another.

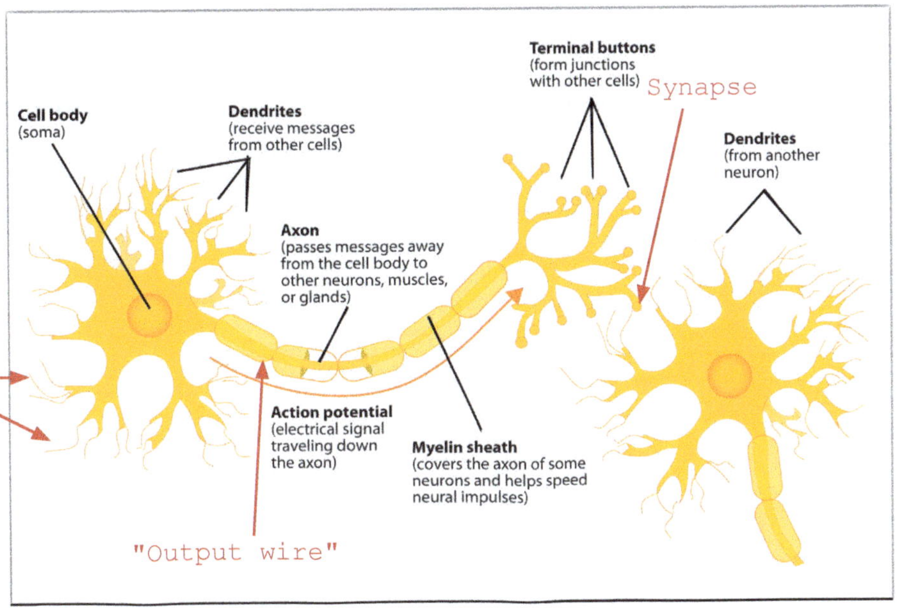

Fig. 75.5 Two connected brain neurons

The signaling process is partly electrical and partly chemical. The neuron generates an all-or-nothing electrochemical pulse called an action potential. This potential travels rapidly along the axon, and activates synaptic connections as it reaches them.

Figure 75.6 shows an artificial neural network consisting of three layers: an input layer, a hidden layer and an output layer.

At a basic level, a neural network consists of four main components:

1. inputs, e.g. x_1 and x_2
2. a bias, e.g. $x_0 = +1$
3. weights, e.g. w_0, w_1, w_2, or
4. threshold e.g. 0.5 in sigmoid function and
5. an output, e.g. Ψ_0 , Ψ_1.

The highly contrived example shown in *Figure 75.6* is a very simplified presentation of an artificial network for distinguishing between images of cats and dogs. The pixels of the image are converted by some algorithm to two real number values, x_1 and x_2. These are fed to the input stage of the neural network along with a bias value, x_0. The input stage consists of three artificial neurons, nodes A, B and C respectively. The weights w_0, w_1, w_2 are applied to these values before summing the products as follows

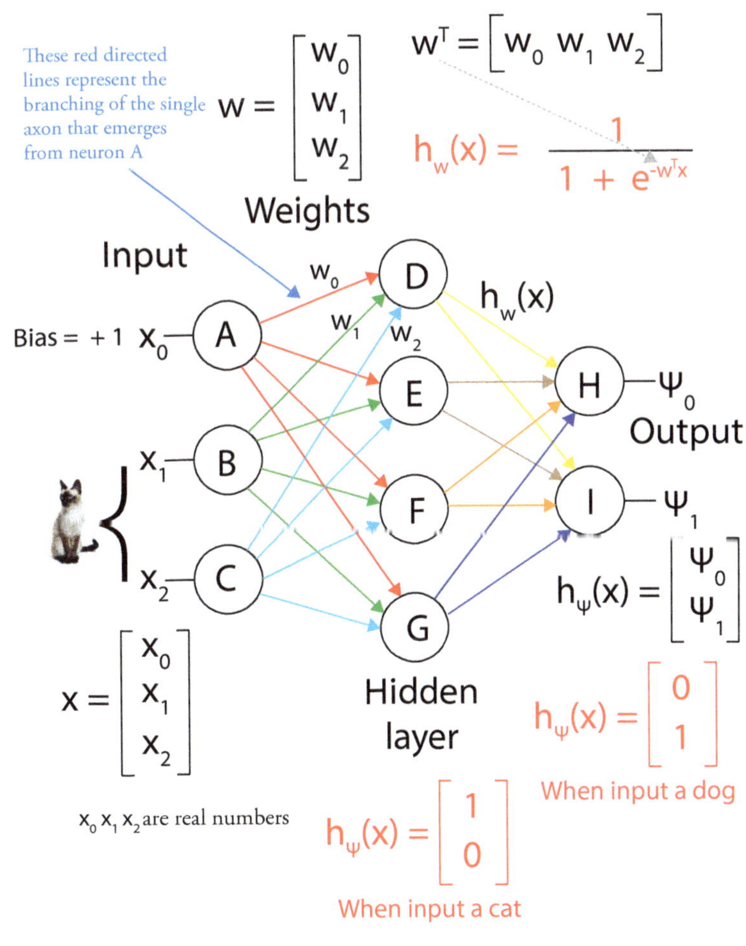

Fig. 75.6 Three layer neural network trained to recognise cats and dogs

$$S = w_0 . x_0 + w_1 . x_1 + w_2 . x_2$$

The result is then fed to neuron D in the hidden layer. Neuron D then applies function $h_w(x)$ to S, i.e. $h_w(S)$ and sends the result to neuron H. Neuron H receives similarly transformed input from neurons E, F and G. Neuron H then applies a threshold, e.g. 0.5, resulting in an output which is either 0 or 1. In a similar fashion, neuron I receives inputs from neurons D, E, F and G and applies the 0.5 threshold resulting in an output which is 0 or 1. The weights, w_0, w_1, w_2 and the weights on the other "axons" emanating from neurons A, B and C are adjusted on training data so that the neural network can be used on new images of cats and dogs, successfully. *Figure 75.7* shows a demonstration of a neural network which uses machine learning components from Mitov software to successfully train a neural network model to recognise two classes.

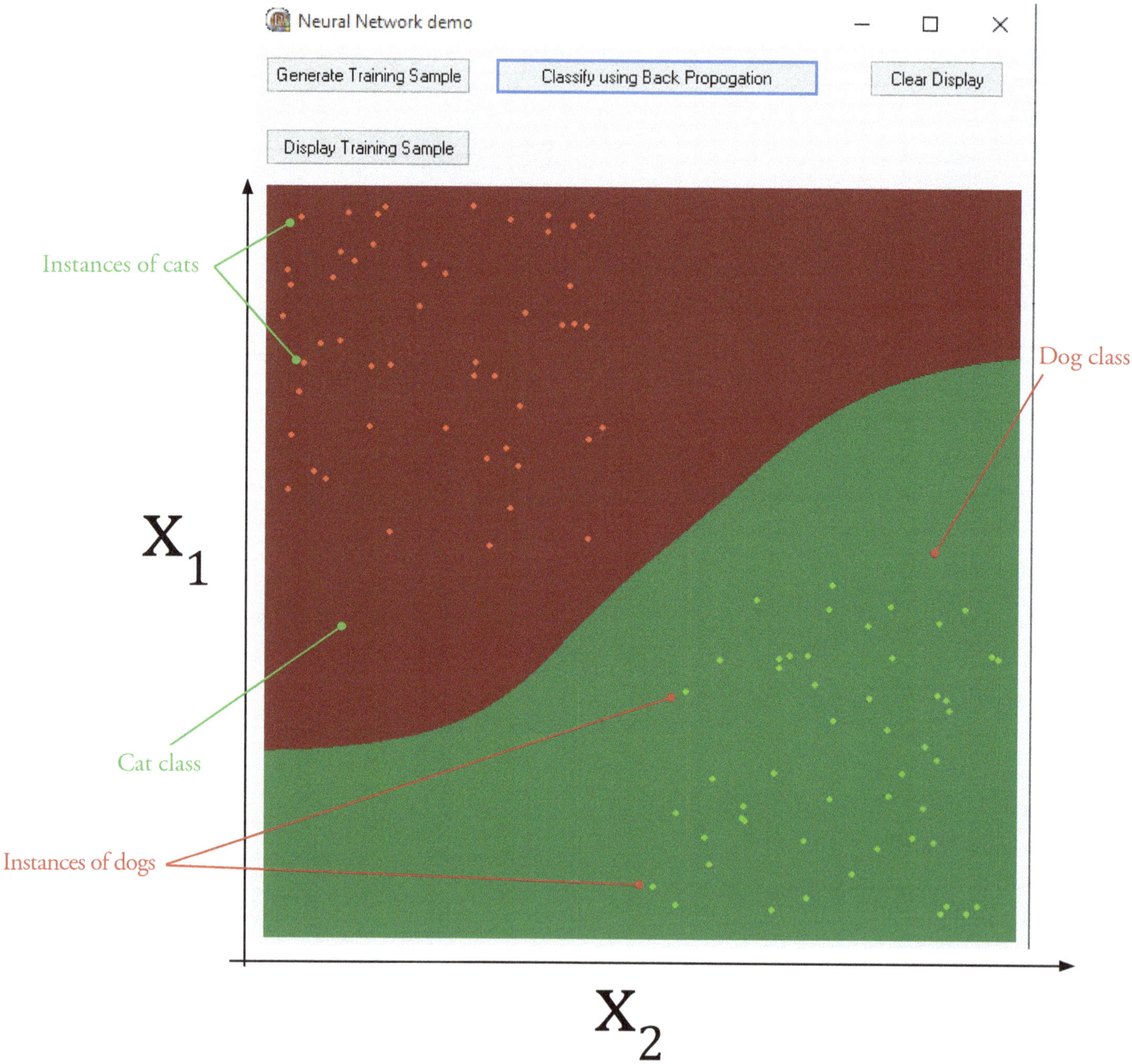

Fig. 75.7 Neural network demo identifying two classes

Neural network demo program

Download and **install** IntelligenceLab for your version of Delphi from

https://www.mitov.com/products/intelligencelab#downloads.

Create a new VCL Delphi application and save as `ILNeuralNetworkDemo.dproj` and `ILNeuralNetworkDemoUnit.pas` in folder `NeuralNetworkDemo`. **Add** and **arrange** the components as shown in *Figure 75.8*.

Change the name of the form to `frmNeuralNetworkDemo` and its caption to `Neural Network demo`.

Change the button names and captions to `btnGenerateTrainingSample`/`Generate Training Sample`, `btnDisplayTrainingSample`/`Display Training Sample`, `btnBackPropagation`/`Classify using Back Propagation`, `btnClearDisplay`/`Clear Display`, respectively.

Create OnClick event handlers for each button and **add** the corresponding code shown in *Table 75.5* to each.

Create object methods `Procedure PlotTheOriginalTrainingSample` and `Procedure GenerateTrainingSample` as shown in *Table 75.5*. **Add** the corresponding code shown in *Table 75.5* and *Table 75.6*.

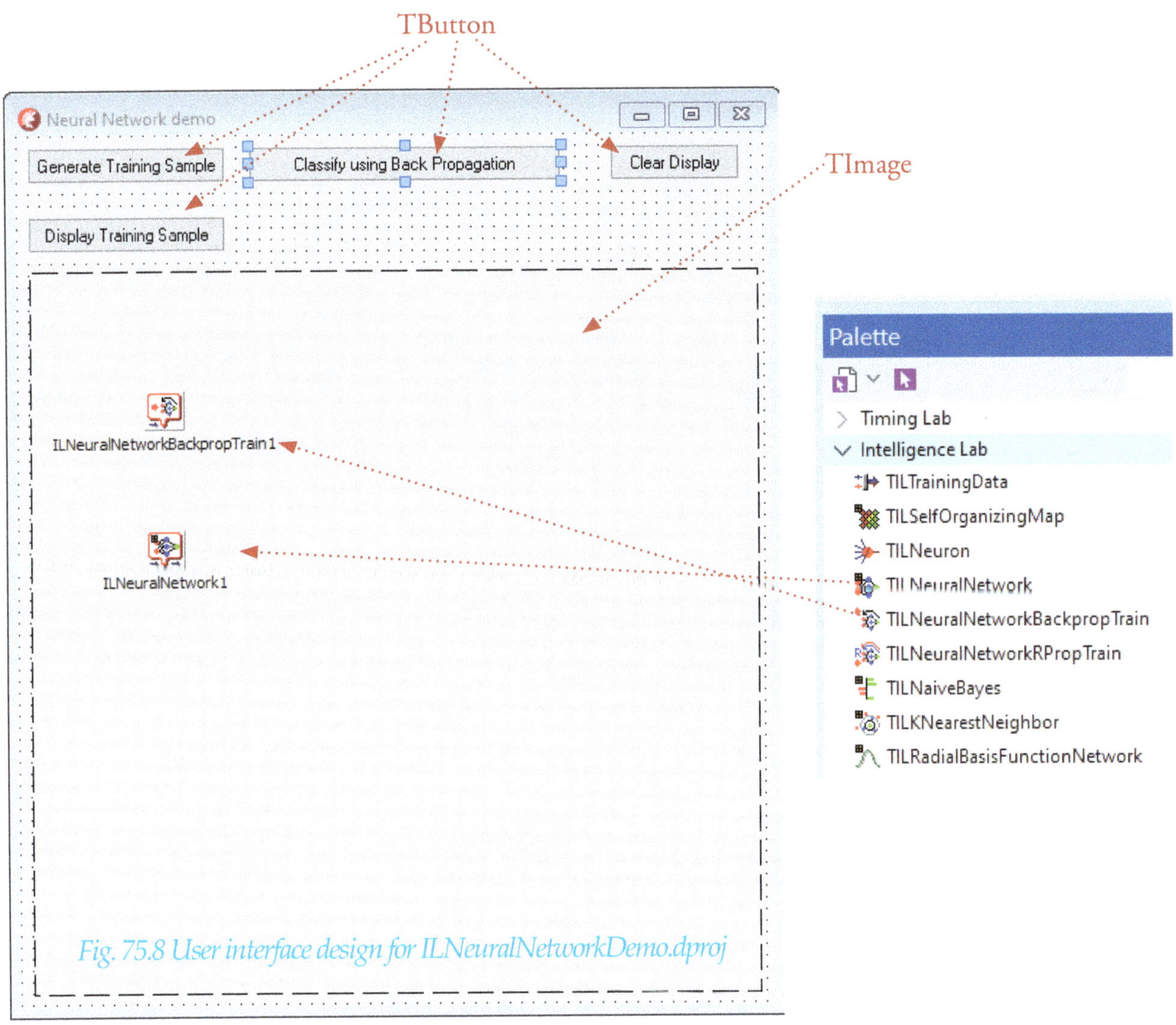

Fig. 75.8 User interface design for ILNeuralNetworkDemo.dproj

Set the **NeuralNetwork** property of `ILNeuralNetworkBackpropTrain1` to `ILNeuralNetwork1`.

Create OnResult event handler - **Events** page of `ILNeuralNetwork1`. **Add** the code shown in *Table 75.6* for event handler `ILNeuralNetwork1Result`.

Save All (Ctrl+Shift+S). **Run without debugging** (Shift+Ctrl+F9).

P

```
Unit ILNeuralNetworkDemoUnit;//Based on Mitov Neural Network demo application
Interface
Uses
  Windows, Classes, Graphics, Controls, Forms,Dialogs, StdCtrls, ExtCtrls, ILNeuralNetwork, LPComponent,
  ILBasicClassifier, Mitov.Types;
Type
  TfrmNeuralNetworkDemo = Class(TForm)
                            Image1 : TImage;
                            btnBackPropagation : TButton;
                            ILNeuralNetwork1 : TILNeuralNetwork;
                            ILNeuralNetworkBackpropTrain1 : TILNeuralNetworkBackpropTrain;
                            btnDisplayTrainingSample : TButton;
                            btnGenerateTrainingSample : TButton;
                            btnClearDisplay : TButton;
                            Procedure btnBackPropogationClick(Sender : TObject);
                            Procedure ILNeuralNetwork1Result(ASender : TObject;
                                   AFeatures : ISLRealBuffer; AResult : TILClassifierResult);
                            Procedure btnDisplayTrainingSampleClick(Sender : TObject);
                            Procedure btnGenerateTrainingSampleClick(Sender : TObject);
                            Procedure btnClearDisplayClick(Sender : TObject);
                            Procedure PlotTheOriginalTrainingSample;
                            Procedure GenerateTrainingSample;
                          End;
Var
  frmNeuralNetworkDemo : TfrmNeuralNetworkDemo;
Implementation
Uses Math;
{$R *.dfm}
Var
  ATrainingData : ISLRealMatrixBuffer = Nil;
  AResponses : ISLRealMatrixBuffer = Nil;
  ATestData : ISLRealBuffer = Nil;
Procedure TfrmNeuralNetworkDemo.btnBackPropagationClick(Sender : TObject);
  Var
    i, j : Integer; aPoint : TPoint;
  Begin
    ILNeuralNetworkBackpropTrain1.Train(ATrainingData, AResponses);
    If ATestData = Nil Then ATestData := TSLRealBuffer.CreateSize(2);
    For i := 0 to 500 - 1
      Do
        For j := 0 to 500 - 1
          Do
            Begin
              ATestData[1] := i;
              ATestData[0] := j;
              ILNeuralNetwork1.Predict(ATestData);
            End;
    PlotTheOriginalTrainingSample;
  End;
Procedure TfrmNeuralNetworkDemo.btnClearDisplayClick(Sender : TObject);
  Var
    i, j : Integer;
  Begin
    For i := 0 To 499
      Do For j := 0 To 499 Do Image1.Picture.Bitmap.Canvas.Pixels[i, j] := RGB(255, 255, 255);
  End;
Procedure TfrmNeuralNetworkDemo.btnDisplayTrainingSampleClick(Sender : TObject);
  Var
    i : Integer; aPoint : TPoint;
  Begin
    Image1.Picture.Bitmap.Width := 500; Image1.Picture.Bitmap.Height := 500;
    PlotTheOriginalTrainingSample;    btnBackPropagation.Enabled := True;
  End;
Procedure TfrmNeuralNetworkDemo.btnGenerateTrainingSampleClick(Sender: TObject);
  Begin
    GenerateTrainingSample; btnDisplayTrainingSample.Enabled := True;
  End;
Procedure TfrmNeuralNetworkDemo.GenerateTrainingSample;
  Var
    i : Integer;
  Begin
    If (ATrainingData = Nil) And (AResponses = Nil)
      Then
        Begin
          ATrainingData  := TSLRealMatrixBuffer.CreateSize(100, 2);
          AResponses   := TSLRealMatrixBuffer.CreateSize(100, 1);
        End;
    For i := 0 to 50 - 1
      Do
        Begin
          AResponses[i, 0] := 1;
          ATrainingData[i, 0] := 10 + Random(230);
          ATrainingData[i, 1] := 10 + Random(230);
        End;
    For i := 50 to 100 - 1
      Do
        Begin
          AResponses[i, 0] := 2;
          ATrainingData[i, 0] := 260 + Random(230);
          ATrainingData[i, 1] := 260 + Random(230);
        End;
  End;
```

Table 75.5 First part of ILNeuralNetworkDemoUnit.pas

```
Procedure TfrmNeuralNetworkDemo.ILNeuralNetwork1Result(ASender : TObject; AFeatures : ISLRealBuffer;
                                                       AResult : TILClassifierResult);
  Begin
    //Result: classifies the x, y pair tested in the first or second category
    If (AResult.Results[0] > 1.5)
      Then Image1.Picture.Bitmap.Canvas.Pixels[Round(AFeatures[0]),
                                          Round(AFeatures[1])] := RGB(0, 127, 0) //Colour green
      Else Image1.Picture.Bitmap.Canvas.Pixels[Round(AFeatures[0]),
                                          Round(AFeatures[1])] := RGB(127, 0, 0); //Colour red
  End;
Procedure TfrmNeuralNetworkDemo.PlotTheOriginalTrainingSample;
  Var
    i : Integer;
    aPoint : TPoint;
  Begin
    For i := 0 to 100 Div 2 - 1
      Do
        Begin
          APoint.x := Round(ATrainingData[i, 0]);
          APoint.y := Round(ATrainingData[i, 1]);
          Image1.Picture.Bitmap.Canvas.Pen.Color := clRed;
          Image1.Picture.Bitmap.Canvas.Brush.Color := clRed;
          Image1.Picture.Bitmap.Canvas.Ellipse(APoint.x - 2, APoint.y - 2,
                                               APoint.x + 2, APoint.y + 2);
          APoint.x := Round( ATrainingData[i + 50, 0]);
          APoint.y := Round( ATrainingData[i + 50, 1]);
          Image1.Picture.Bitmap.Canvas.Pen.Color := clLime;
          Image1.Picture.Bitmap.Canvas.Brush.Color := clLime;
          Image1.Picture.Bitmap.Canvas.Ellipse(APoint.x - 2, APoint.y - 2, APoint.x + 2, APoint.y + 2);
        End;
  End;
End.
```

Table 75.6 Second part of ILNeuralNetworkDemoUnit.pas

Click the `Generate Training Sample` button to initiate a call to `GenerateTrainingSample`. This creates two sets each containing 50 pairs, a pair repesenting a pixel coordinate of `Image1`. A response of 1 is recorded for each pair in the first set, and a response of 2 is recorded for each pair in the second set.

Click the button `Display Training Sample` button to plot each pair on the canvas of the image component, `Image1` - *Figure 75.9*.

Click the `Classify using Back Propagation` button to classify each pair of each set. This calls `ILNeuralNetworkBackpropTrain1.Train(ATrainingData, AResponses)`. `ATrainingData` contains the 100 pairs (first set and second set). `AResponses` contains the corresponding actual outcome which is either 1 or 2. Training the model may take a little while. Once complete, this event handler then sets up test data for each image canvas pixel coordinate, one at a time, and calls for each `ILNeuralNetwork1.Predict(ATestData)` where `ATestData` contains a single coordinate. On generating a prediction result, i.e. 1 or 2, the event handler `ILNeuralNetwork1Result` is called which plots, for the given coordinates, a green pixel if the result is greater than 1.5 or a red pixel if less than or equal to 1.5. The threshold is set at 1.5 because the outcome is 1 or 2 not 0 or 1. The neural network components have been designed to work this way. Finally, the original training sample is replotted to generate the result already shown in *Figure 75.7*.

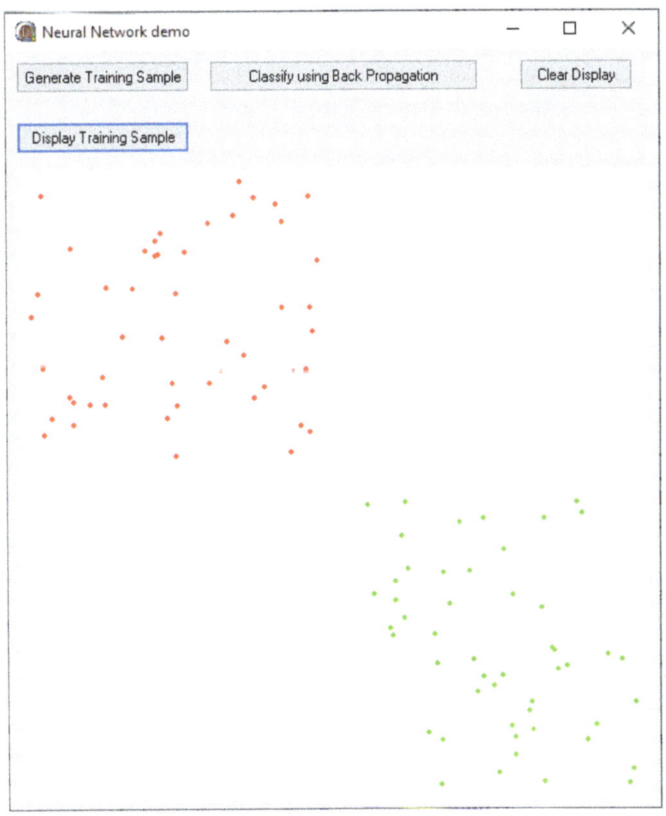

Fig. 75.9 The two sets displayed on the image component

Automatic licence plate recognition

TOpenALPR is a Delphi binding for **OpenALPR** - an open source Automatic License Plate Recognition library. The library analyzes images and identifies licence plates. The output is the text representation of any licence plate characters found in the image.

Create a folder `CarNumberPlateRecognition` on your working drive.

Download and **unpack** `TOpenALPR` from https://github.com/r1me/TOpenALPR.

This creates folder `TOpenALPR-master` - *Figure 75.10*.

Name	Date modified	Type	Size
bin	09/11/2021 23:42	File folder	
examples	06/11/2021 03:00	File folder	
lib	06/11/2021 03:00	File folder	
LICENSE.md	11/04/2018 21:14	MD File	2 KB
openalpr.pas	11/04/2018 21:14	Delphi Source File	21 KB
README.md	11/04/2018 21:14	MD File	3 KB

Fig. 75.10 Contents of folder TOpenALPR-master created by unpacking TOpenALPR.zip

Change to folder `lib`.

Unpack `lib\openalpr-master.zip` in this folder - *Figure 75.11*. **Copy** `openalpr.dll` to `bin\openalpr.dll`

Name	Date modified	Type	Size
LICENSE.txt	16/07/2016 23:16	Text Document	35 KB
note.txt	20/06/2017 20:36	Text Document	1 KB
openalpr.dll	12/06/2017 12:48	Application exten...	2,205 KB
openalpr-master.zip	11/04/2018 21:14	WinRAR ZIP archive	1,043 KB

Fig. 75.11 Contents of folder TOpenALPR-master/bin after unpacking lib\openalpr-master.zip

Download and **unpack** `OpenALPR 2.3.0` from https://github.com/openalpr/openalpr/releases to folder `CarNumberPlateRecognition`.

This creates an `openalpr_32` folder in folder `CarNumberPlateRecognition` containing the files shown in *Figure 75.12*.

Name	Date modified	Type	Size
include	16/07/2016 23:16	File folder	
java	16/07/2016 23:16	File folder	
python	16/07/2016 23:16	File folder	
runtime_data	17/07/2016 20:58	File folder	
samples	16/07/2016 23:16	File folder	
alpr.exe	17/07/2016 20:02	Application	2,287 KB
java_test.bat	16/07/2016 23:16	Windows Batch File	1 KB
liblept170.dll	17/07/2016 15:09	Application exten...	2,288 KB
LICENSE.txt	16/07/2016 23:16	Text Document	35 KB
openalpr.conf	17/07/2016 20:04	CONF File	5 KB
openalpr.dll	17/07/2016 20:04	Application exten...	2,205 KB
openalpr.lib	17/07/2016 20:04	LIB File	11 KB
openalprjni.dll	17/07/2016 20:04	Application exten...	22 KB
openalpr-net.dll	17/07/2016 21:02	Application exten...	2,915 KB
openalprnet-windemo.exe	17/07/2016 21:05	Application	16 KB
openalprpy.dll	17/07/2016 20:04	Application exten...	22 KB
openalpr-static.lib	17/07/2016 20:01	LIB File	3,247 KB
openalpr-utils-calibrate.exe	16/07/2016 23:16	Application	137 KB
openalpr-utils-classifychars.exe	17/07/2016 20:04	Application	2,022 KB
openalpr-utils-tagplates.exe	17/07/2016 20:04	Application	94 KB
opencv_ffmpeg300.dll	17/07/2016 15:20	Application exten...	12,159 KB
opencv_world300.dll	17/07/2016 15:19	Application exten...	11,185 KB
python_test.bat	16/07/2016 23:16	Windows Batch File	1 KB
README.txt	16/07/2016 23:16	Text Document	3 KB
vc_redist.x86.exe	17/07/2016 21:06	Application	13,446 KB

Fig. 75.12 After unpacking openalpr_32.zip

Copy the following files from this folder as instructed:

- all files and sub-directories `openalpr_32\runtime_data` to `bin\runtime_data`
- all files and sub-directories `openalpr_32\samples` to `bin\samples`
- `openalpr_32\openalpr.conf` to `bin\openalpr.conf`
- `openalpr_32\liblept170.dll` to `bin\liblept170.dll`
- `openalpr_32\opencv_ffmpeg300.dll` to `bin\opencv_ffmpeg300.dll`
- `openalpr_32\opencv_world300.dll` to `bin\opencv_world300.dll`

Change to folder `Examples` in folder `TOpenALPR-master`. **Change** to `delphi-vcl-image folder`.

Open `delphi_vcl_image.dproj`, **compile** and **run**.

Click button `Open Image` and **select** `eu-3.jpg` from the `samples` folder.

Click button `Detect plates`. *Figure 75.18* shows the result.

The application has been constructed to perform

1. Text detection - the area where text appears in image eu-3.jpg (*Figure 75.18*) is identified and marked with a yellow rectangle - *Figure 75.13*.
2. Character segmentation - *Figure 75.14*.
3. Character classification - *Figure 75.15*.

Fig. 75.13 Identification of text

Fig. 75.14 Character Segmentation

Fig. 75.15 Character Classification

Text detection may be done by using a sliding window approach with edge detection and then binarisation in which text areas are marked with white pixels and non-text areas are marked with black pixels - *Figure 75.16*. The coordinates of the area in white may then be used to isolate the text area in `eu-3.jpg` ready for character segmentation. A sliding window approach may then be used to segment the character run - *Figure 75.17*.

Character classification using an artificial neural network is a classic machine learning application. The number of artificial neurons required in the output stage of the artificial neural network which recognises all the characters and digits of a car licence plate is the same as the number of characters and digits which need to be recognised.

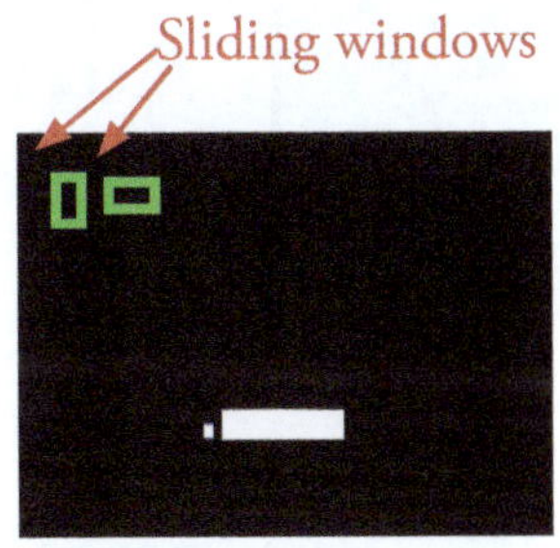

Fig. 75.16 Binarisation of image eu-3.jpg to identify text areas

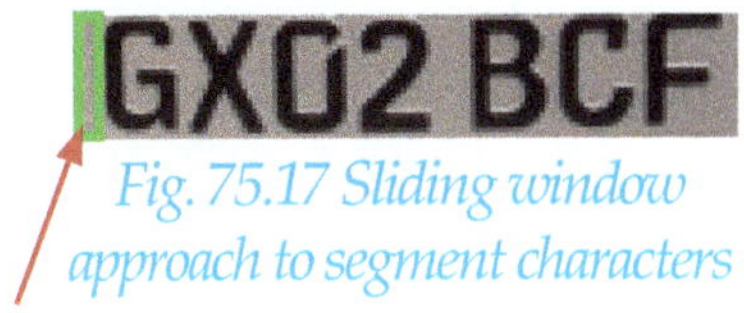

Fig. 75.17 Sliding window approach to segment characters

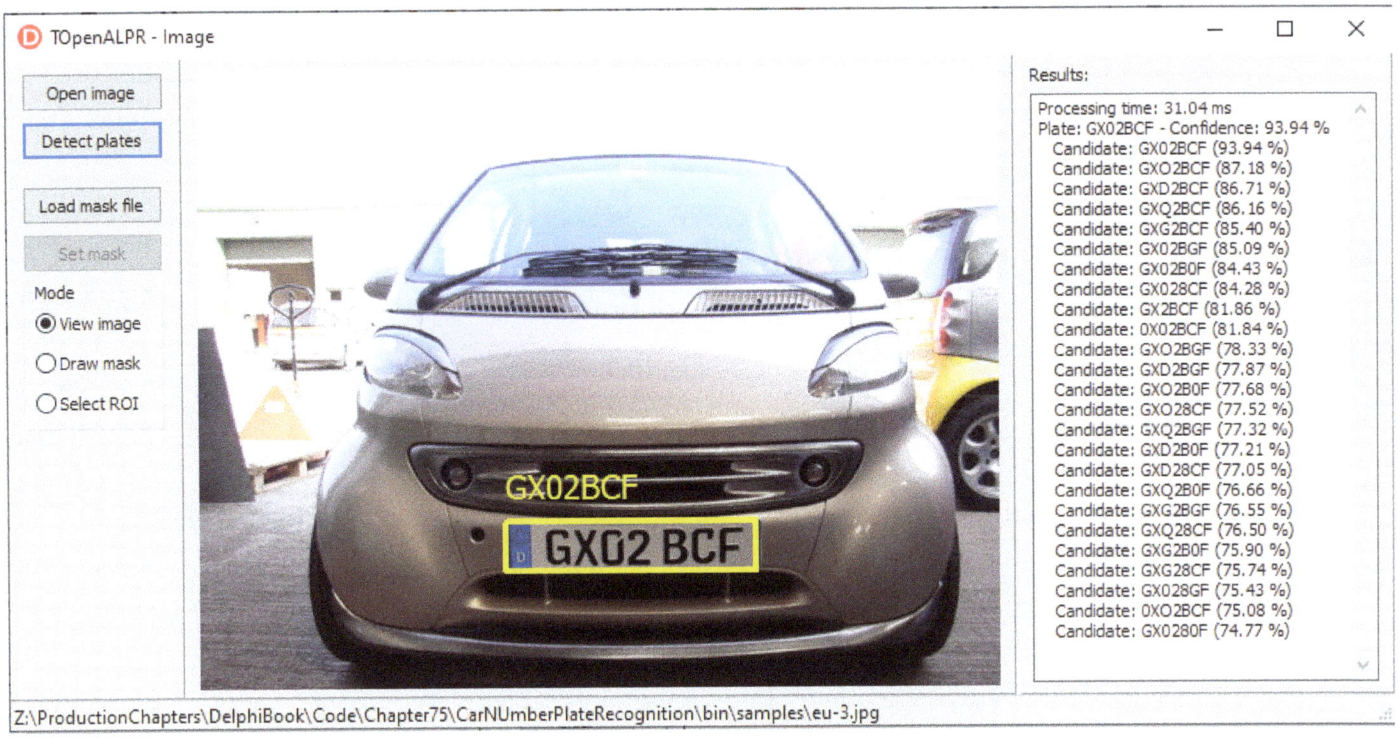

Fig. 75.18 delphi_vcl_Image.dproj in execution, image eu-3.jpg loaded and its number plate identified as GX02BCF with 93.94% confidence

Summary

The field of machine learning is an immense field. We have only touched its surface in this chapter. However, it should now be possible to understand where machine learning sits in relation to the field of Artificial Intelligence (AI). *Figure 75.19* attempts by analogy to show this relationship. Machine learning is a subfield of artificial intelligence. Neural networks are used in machine learning and neural networks make up the backbone of deep learning algorithms. Deep learning algorithms tackle the AI problem of recognising speech or objects in images.To qualify as a deep learning algorithm, the neural network must have more than three node layers (its depth). The car number plate recognition example uses a deep learning convolutional neural network (more than three node layers) to perform edge detection and optical character recognition.

Fig. 75.19 Russina dolls analogy of the relationship between artificial intelligence, machine learning, neural networks, and deep learning

76 Advanced graphics I

Firemonkey 3D

Purpose: To introduce Firemonkey three dimensional graphics

Firemonkey coordinate system

Firemonkey uses the three dimensional coordinate system is shown in *Figure 76.1*. The positive X axis points to the right, the positive Y axis points downwards and the positive Z axis points into the screen.

Wire frame cube

Figure 76.1 also shows a wire frame cube centred on (0, 0, 0), the origin of the three dimensional coordinate system.

The front face of the cube is defined by four vertices numbered 0, 1, 2, 3 using an anti-clockwise winding order (↺), whilst the back face four vertices are numbered 4, 5, 6, 7 in clockwise winding order (↻). The cube is completed by connecting these eight vertices with edges as shown - four edges connecting the four vertices of the front face, four edges connecting the four vertices of the back face and finally four edges connecting the front and back faces.

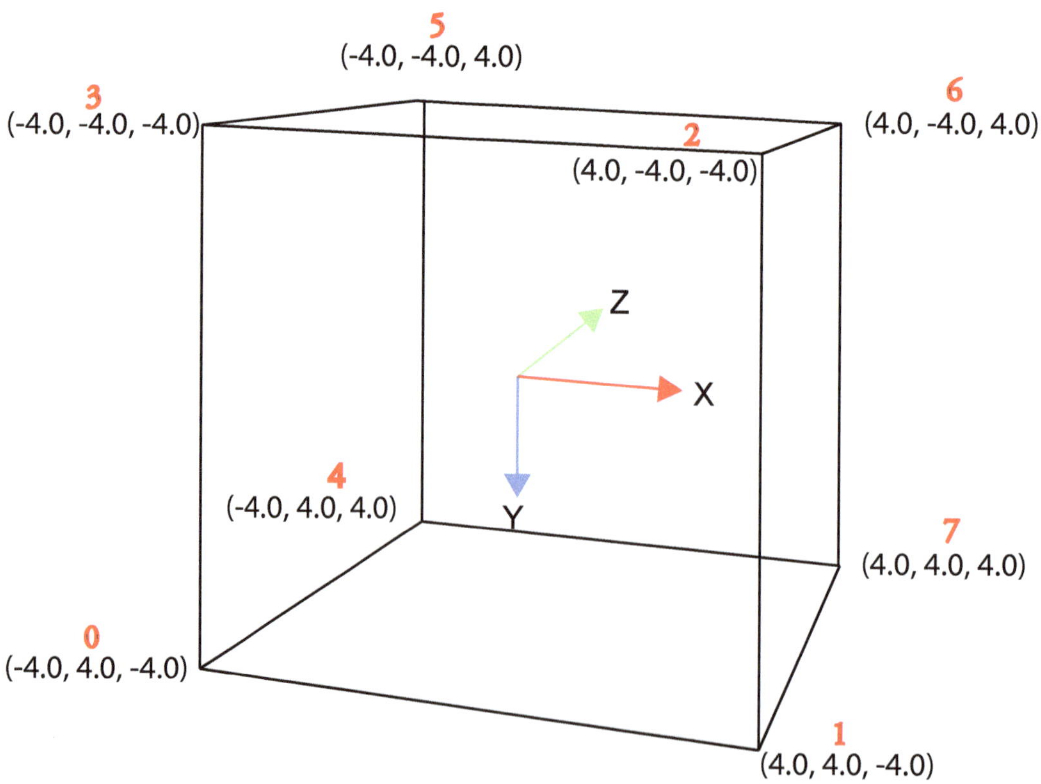

Figure 76.1 Wire frame cube centred on origin of coordinate system

Creating a wireframe cube from scratch in Delphi

Select File|New|Multi-device Application - Delphi then **select** 3D Application from the Multi-device Application window (scroll down to find it) to create a 3D application.

Save the project as `WireFrameCubeProject.dproj` and its form unit as `WireFrameCubeFormUnit.pas`.

Change the **Name** property of the form to `frmWireFrameCube` and its **Caption** property to `Wire Frame Cube`.

Set its **Color** property to **White**. *Table 76.1* shows the source code for this unit.

Now **select** File|New|Unit to create a new unit. **Save** the unit as `WireFrameUnit.pas`.

Add the **Type** definition shown in *Table 76.2* to the **Interface** section of this unit.

Create a **Uses** clause between the keywords **Interface** and **Type** and **add** the following to the clause

System.Classes, System.Generics.Collections, FMX.Types3D, FMX.Controls3D, System.Math.Vectors, System.UITypes;

In theory, placing the cursor over a Delphi type identifier, e.g. **TAlphaColor,** and pressing Shift+Ctrl+A should bring up a window from which **TAlphaColor** 's unit may be chosen, but in practice it doesn't always work as expected.

Place the cursor over `AddEdge` and **press** Shift+Ctrl+C to create a code template for `AddEdge` in the **Implementation** section.

```
Unit WireFrameCubeFormUnit;
Interface
Uses
  System.SysUtils, System.Types, System.UITypes, System.Classes, System.Variants,
  FMX.Types, FMX.Controls, FMX.Forms3D, FMX.Types3D, FMX.Forms, FMX.Graphics,
  FMX.Dialogs;

Type
  TfrmWireFrameCube = Class(TForm3D)
                        Private
                          { Private declarations }
                        Public
                          { Public declarations }
                      End;
Var
  frmWireFrameCube : TfrmWireFrameCube;
Implementation
{$R *.fmx}
End.
```

P

Table 76.1

```
Type
  TPoints3D = Class(TList<TPoint3D>)
              End;
  TEdge = Record
            FromVertex, ToVertex : Integer;
          End;
  TEdges = Class(TList<TEdge>)
             Procedure AddEdge(ptStart, ptEnd : Integer);
           End;
  TWireFrame = Class(TControl3D)
                 Private
                   FDrawColor : TAlphaColor;
                   FEdges : TEdges;
                   FPoints3D : TPoints3D;
                 Public
                   Constructor Create(AOwner : TComponent); Override;
                   Destructor Destroy; Override;
                   Procedure Render; Override;
                   Procedure DrawAxes;
                   Property DrawColor : TAlphaColor read FDrawColor Write FDrawColor;
                   Property Points3D : TPoints3D read FPoints3D;
                   Property Edges : TEdges Read FEdges;
               End;
Implementation
End.
```

P

Table 76.2

Place a cursor over `Create` and **press** **Shift+Ctrl+C** to create code templates in the **Implementation** section for all the methods of the class. *Table 76.3* shows the result. Notice the automatic placement of the **Inherited** keyword. For constructor `Create`, the inherited `Create` method of **TControl3D** needs to be called first.
In the case of the destructor `Destroy`, the inherited Destroy method of **TControl3D** needs to be called but at the end.
In the case of the `Render` method, the inherited `Render` method (from **TControl3D**) needs to be called first.

Add the code shown in *Table 76.4* to the skeleton methods. **Note** that `Create` needs to be explicitly referenced following the inherited keyword because inherited `Create` has a parameter.

```
Implementation
{ TEdges }
Procedure TEdges.AddEdge(ptStart, ptEnd : Integer);
  Begin

  End;
{ TWireFrame }
Constructor TWireFrame.Create(AOwner : TComponent);
  Begin
    Inherited;

  End;
Destructor TWireFrame.Destroy;
  Begin

    Inherited;
  End;
Procedure TWireFrame.DrawAxes;
  Begin

  End;
Procedure TWireFrame.Render;
  Begin
    Inherited;

  End;
End.
```

P

Table 76.3

AddEdge:

```
Var
    Edge : TEdge;
  Begin
    Edge.FromVertex := ptStart;
    Edge.ToVertex := ptEnd;
    Self.Add(edge);
  End;
```

Create:

```
Begin
  Inherited Create(AOwner);
  FPoints3D := TPoints3D.Create;
  FEdges := TEdges.Create;
  FDrawColor := TAlphaColorRec.Black;
End;
```

DrawAxes:

```
Procedure TWireFrame.DrawAxes;
  Var
    ptStart, ptEnd : TPoint3D;
  Begin
    ptStart.X := 0; ptStart.Y := 0; ptStart.Z := 0;
    ptEnd.X := 2; ptEnd.Y := 0; ptEnd.Z := 0;
    Context.DrawLine(ptStart, ptEnd, 1, TAlphaColorRec.Red);
    ptStart.X := 0; ptStart.Y := 0; ptStart.Z := 0;
    ptEnd.X := 0; ptEnd.Y := 1.5; ptEnd.Z := 0;
    Context.DrawLine(ptStart, ptEnd, 1, TAlphaColorRec.Blue);
    ptStart.X := 0; ptStart.Y := 0; ptStart.Z := 0;
    ptEnd.X := 0; ptEnd.Y := 0; ptEnd.Z := 4;
    Context.DrawLine(ptStart, ptEnd, 1, TAlphaColorRec.Green);
  End;
```

Destructor:

```
Begin
  FEdges.Free;
  FPoints3D.Free;
  Inherited;
End;
```

Render:

```
Var
  Edge: TEdge;
Begin
  Inherited;
  For Edge In Edges
    Do Context.DrawLine(Points3D[Edge.FromVertex], Points3D[Edge.ToVertex], 1, DrawColor);
End;
```

Table 76.4

Switch to unit `WireFrameCubeFormUnit`.

Add a **TCamera** component from the **3D Scene** component palette to the form `frmWireFrameCube`.

Set **Position.X** = 0; **Position.Y** = -7; **Position.Z** = -20.

Set **RotationAngle.X** = -20; **RotationAngle.Y** = 0, **RotationAngle.Z** = 0. **Accept** the default settings for its other properties.

Create event handlers for the **OnCreate**, **OnDestroy** and **OnKeyDown** events for the form `frmWireFrameCube`.

Add a field `FWireframe` of type `TWireframe` and a procedure `CreateCube` to the form's type definition as shown in *Table 76.5*.

Add the unit name `WireframeUnit` to the **Uses** clause of the **Interface** (**place** cursor on `TWireframe` and press **Ctrl+Shift+A** to add this unit).

Place cursor over `CreateCube` and **press** **Ctrl+Shift+C** to create a code template in the **Implementation** section.

```
Type
  TfrmWireFrameCube = Class(TForm3D)
                        Camera1 : TCamera;
                        Procedure Form3DCreate(Sender : TObject);
                        Procedure Form3DDestroy(Sender:  TObject);
                        Procedure Form3DKeyDown(Sender : TObject;
                                                Var Key : Word;
                                                Var KeyChar : Char;
                                                Shift : TShiftState);
                        Private
                          FWireframe : TWireframe;
                          Procedure CreateCube;
                      End;
```

P

Table 76.5

Create a variable `pt3D` of type `TPoint3D` in the **Implementation** section.

Add the source code shown in *Table 76.6* to the corresponding methods in the **Implementation** section.

Press **Shift+Ctrl+S** to save the project and unit files.

Press **Shift+Ctrl+F9** to compile and run the project - *Figure 76.2*.

Press the A key on the keyboard to rotate the cube about the Z axis in a clockwise direction.

Press the Z key on the keyboard to rotate the cube about the Z axis in an anti-clockwise direction - *Figure 76.3*.

Press the right arrow key on the keyboard to rotate the cube about the Y axis in a clockwise direction.

Press the left arrow key on the keyboard to rotate the cube about the Y axis in a anti-clockwise direction.

Press the up arrow key on the keyboard to rotate the cube about the X axis in a clockwise direction.

Press the down arrow key on the keyboard to rotate the cube about the X axis in a clockwise direction.

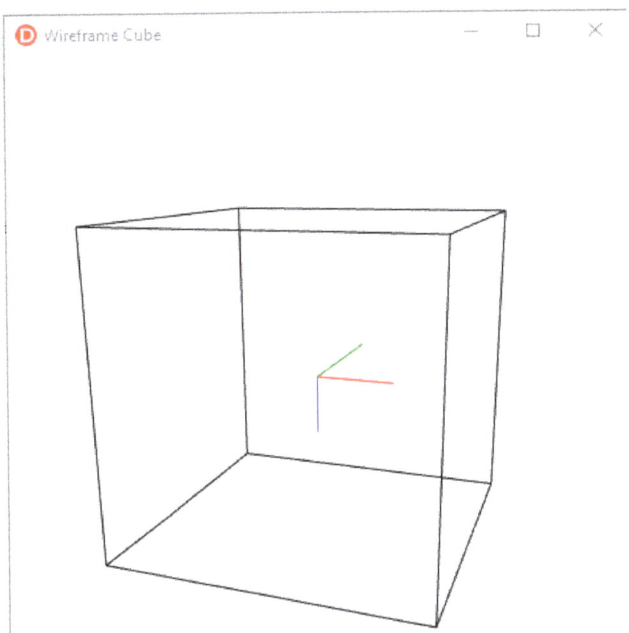

Figure 76.2 WireFrameCubeProject in execution

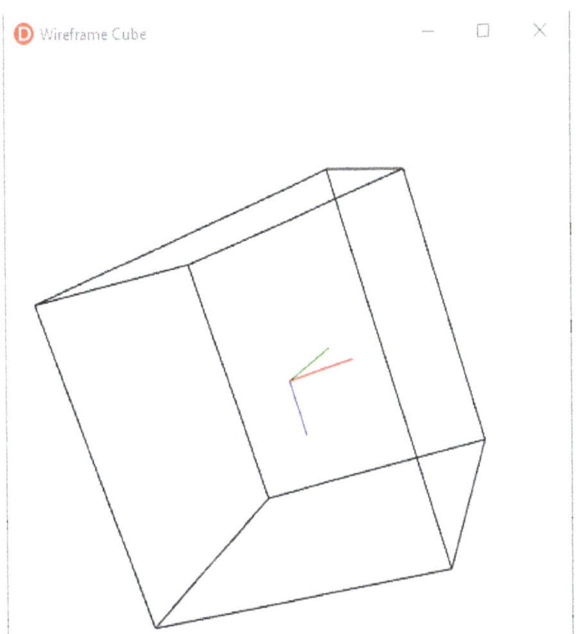

Figure 76.3 Wire frame rotated

```
Implementation
{$R *.fmx}
Var
  pt3D : TPoint3D;
Procedure TfrmWireFrameCube.CreateCube;
  Begin
    With FWireframe
      Do
        Begin
          Points3D.Add(Point3D(-4.0, -4.0,  4.0)); //0
          Points3D.Add(Point3D(4.0, -4.0,  4.0));  //1
          Points3D.Add(Point3D(4.0,  4.0,  4.0));  //2
          Points3D.Add(Point3D(-4.0,  4.0,  4.0)); //3
    // back
          Points3D.Add(Point3D(-4.0, -4.0, -4.0)); //4
          Points3D.Add(Point3D(-4.0,  4.0, -4.0)); //5
          Points3D.Add(Point3D(4.0,  4.0, -4.0));  //6
          Points3D.Add(Point3D(4.0, -4.0, -4.0));  //7
          Edges.AddEdge(0,1); Edges.AddEdge(1,2); Edges.AddEdge(2,3); Edges.AddEdge(3,0);
          Edges.AddEdge(0,4); Edges.AddEdge(1,7); Edges.AddEdge(2,6); Edges.AddEdge(3,5);
          Edges.AddEdge(4,5); Edges.AddEdge(5,6); Edges.AddEdge(6,7); Edges.AddEdge(7,4);
        End;
  End;
Procedure TfrmWireFrameCube.Form3DCreate(Sender: TObject);
  Begin
    FWireframe := TWireframe.Create(Self);
    FWireframe.Parent := Self;
    FWireframe.RotationAngle.Point := Point3D(-5, 20, 0);
    frmWireFrameCube.UsingDesignCamera := True;
    CreateCube;
    pt3D.X := -5; pt3D.Y := 20; pt3D.Z := 0;
  End;
Procedure TfrmWireFrameCube.Form3DDestroy(Sender: TObject);
  Begin
    FWireframe.Free;
  End;
Procedure TfrmWireFrameCube.Form3DKeyDown(Sender: TObject; Var Key: Word; Var KeyChar: Char; Shift: TShiftState);
  Begin
    Case KeyChar Of
      'A', 'a' : Begin
                   pt3D.Z := pt3D.Z + 1;
                   FWireframe.RotationAngle.Point := Point3D(pt3D.X, pt3D.Y, pt3D.Z);
                 End;
      'Z', 'z' : Begin
                   pt3D.Z := pt3D.Z - 1;
                   FWireframe.RotationAngle.Point := Point3D(pt3D.X, pt3D.Y, pt3D.Z);
                 End;
      Else;
    End;
    Case Key Of
      vkLeft :  Begin
                  pt3D.Y := pt3D.Y + 1;
                  FWireframe.RotationAngle.Point := Point3D(pt3D.X, pt3D.Y, pt3D.Z);//Left Arrow key
                End;
      vkRight : Begin
                  pt3D.Y := pt3D.Y - 1;
                  FWireframe.RotationAngle.Point := Point3D(pt3D.X, pt3D.Y, pt3D.Z);//Right Arrow key
                End;
      vkUp :  Begin
                pt3D.X := pt3D.X - 1;
                FWireframe.RotationAngle.Point := Point3D(pt3D.X, pt3D.Y, pt3D.Z);//Left Arrow key
              End;
      vkDown : Begin
                pt3D.X := pt3D.X + 1;
                FWireframe.RotationAngle.Point := Point3D(pt3D.X, pt3D.Y, pt3D.Z);//Right Arrow key
              End;
      Else;
    End;
End.
```

Table 76.6

Creating a wireframe cube using TStrokeCube

Select File|New|Multi-device Application - Delphi then **select** 3D Application from the Multi-device Application window (scroll down to find it) to create a 3D application.

Save the project as `Wireframe3DStrokeCubeProject.dproj` and its form unit as `WireFrameStrokeCubeUnit.pas`.

Change the **Name** property of the form to `frmWireframe3DStrokeCube` and its **Caption** property to `Wireframe 3D StrokeCube`. **Set** its **Color** property to **White**. **Set** its **UsingDesignCamera** property to false so that the scene can be captured and rendered by **Camera1**, instead. The design camera is the default camera. It is fixed in position at -20 units along the Z axis and with **RotationAngle.X** set to -20. If it is not disabled, it will be used at runtime as well as design time.

Add a **TStrokeCube** component, `StrokeCube1`, from the 3D Shapes palette. **Set** its **Depth**, **Height** and **Width** properties to 4 and its **Color** property to **Black**. **Set** its **RotationAngle.X** to -5 and **RotationAngle.Y** to 20.

Add a **TCamera** component, `Camera1`, from the 3D Scenes palette. **Set** its **RotationAngle.X** to -20, **Position.Y** to -3.5 and its **Position.Z** to -3.5.

Select the form and **create** an event handler for the event **OnKeyDown**.

Table 76.7 shows the source code for this unit with the code added for these event handlers.

Press Shift+Ctrl+S to save the project and unit files.

Press Shift+Ctrl+F9 to compile and run the project - *Figure 76.4*.

```
Unit Wireframe3DStrokeCubeUnit;

Interface

Uses
  System.SysUtils, System.Types, System.UITypes, System.Classes, System.Variants,
  FMX.Types, FMX.Controls, FMX.Forms3D, FMX.Types3D, FMX.Forms, FMX.Graphics,
  FMX.Dialogs, System.Math.Vectors, FMX.Controls3D, FMX.Objects3D;

Type
  TfrmWireframe3DStrokeCube = Class(TForm3D)
                              StrokeCube1 : TStrokeCube;
                              Camera1 : TCamera;
                              Procedure Form3DKeyDown(Sender : TObject;
                                                      Var Key: Word;
                                                      Var KeyChar : Char;
                                                      Shift : TShiftState);
                            End;

Var
  frmWireframe3DStrokeCube: TfrmWireframe3DStrokeCube;

Implementation

{$R *.fmx}

Procedure TfrmWireframe3DStrokeCube.Form3DKeyDown(
  Sender : TObject; Var Key : Word; Var KeyChar : Char; Shift : TShiftState);
  Begin
    Case KeyChar Of
      'A', 'a' : StrokeCube1.RotationAngle.Z := StrokeCube1.RotationAngle.Z + 1;
      'Z', 'z' : StrokeCube1.RotationAngle.Z := StrokeCube1.RotationAngle.Z - 1;
      Else;
    End;
    Case Key Of
      vkLeft :  StrokeCube1.RotationAngle.Y := StrokeCube1.RotationAngle.Y + 1;
      vkRight : StrokeCube1.RotationAngle.Y := StrokeCube1.RotationAngle.Y - 1;
      vkUp :  StrokeCube1.RotationAngle.X := StrokeCube1.RotationAngle.X - 1;
      vkDown : StrokeCube1.RotationAngle.X := StrokeCube1.RotationAngle.X + 1;
      Else;
    End;
  End;
End.
```

Table 76.7

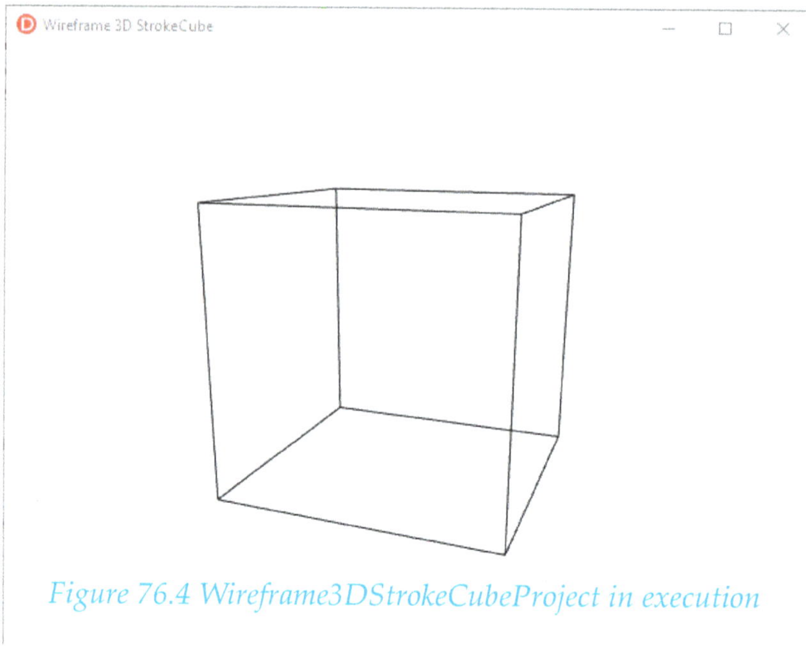

Figure 76.4 Wireframe3DStrokeCubeProject in execution

Creating a filled wireframe cube

Save the project `Wireframe3DStrokeCubeProject.dproj` as `Wireframe3DStrokeCubeFilledProject.dproj` and its form unit `WireFrameStrokeCubeUnit.pas` as `Wireframe3DStrokeCubeFilledUnit.pas`.

Select `StrokeCube1` and **create** an event handler for the event **OnRender**.

Add the code shown in *Table 76.8* to the body of this event handler.

```
Procedure TfrmWireframe3DStrokeCube.StrokeCube1Render(Sender : TObject;
  Context: TContext3D);
  Begin
    Inherited;
    Context.FillCube(TPoint3D.Zero, TPoint3D.Create(4,4,4), 1, TAlphaColorRec.Red);
  End;
```

Table 76.8 Event handler that fills the wireframe cube in red

Change `StrokeCube1`'s **Color** property to red.

Press Shift+Ctrl+S to save the project and unit files.

Press Shift+Ctrl+F9 to compile and run the project - *Figure 76.5*.

Figure 76.5 Wireframe3DStrokeFilledCubeProject in execution

Using TLightMaterialSource to colour a cube

Save the project `Wireframe3DStrokeCubeFilledProject.dproj` as `CubeProject.dproj` and its form unit `Wireframe3DStrokeCubeFilledUnit.pas` as `CubeUnit.pas`.

Delete `StrokeCube1`.

Add a **TCube** component, `Cube1`, from **3D Shapes** to the form. **Set** its **Depth**, **Height** and **Width** properties to 4. **Add** a **TLightMaterialSource** component, `LightMaterialSource1`, from the **Materials** palette to the form.

Set its **Ambient** proprty to red.

Change the **Name** property of the form to `frmCube` and its **Caption** property to `Cube`.

Remove the event handler `TfrmWireframe3DStrokeCube.StrokeCube1Render` and all references to it.
Place the cursor in the first instance of `StrokeCube1` in `Procedure TfrmWireframe3DStrokeCube.Form3DKeyDown` and **press** **Ctrl+Shift+E** to bring up the **Refactor** window. **Change** the **New Name** field to `Cube1`. **Click** the **OK** button. *Table 76.9* shows the revised code for `CubeUnit.pas`.
Toggle to the form view and **select** `Cube1` in the **Structure** window. **Click** the **Material** property of `Cube1` and **select** `LightMaterialSource1`.
Press **Shift+Ctrl+S** to save the project and unit files.

Press **Shift+Ctrl+F9** to compile and run the project - *Figure 76.6*.

```
Unit CubeUnit;
Interface
Uses
  System.SysUtils, System.Types, System.UITypes, System.Classes,
  System.Variants, FMX.Types, FMX.Controls, FMX.Forms3D, FMX.Types3D,
  FMX.Forms, FMX.Graphics, FMX.Dialogs, System.Math.Vectors, FMX.Controls3D,
  FMX.Objects3D,FMX.MaterialSources;
Type
  TfrmCube = Class(TForm3D)
                              Camera1 : TCamera;
                              Cube1 : TCube;
                              LightMaterialSource1 : TLightMaterialSource;
                              Procedure Form3DKeyDown(Sender : TObject;
                                                      Var Key: Word;
                                                      Var KeyChar : Char;
                                                      Shift : TShiftState);
                            End;
Var
  frmCube: TfrmCube;
Implementation
{$R *.fmx}
Procedure TfrmCube.Form3DKeyDown(Sender : TObject;
                                Var Key : Word; Var KeyChar : Char;
                                Shift : TShiftState);
  Begin
    Case KeyChar Of
      'A', 'a' : Cube1.RotationAngle.Z := Cube1.RotationAngle.Z + 1;
      'Z', 'z' : Cube1.RotationAngle.Z := Cube1.RotationAngle.Z - 1;
      Else;
    End;
    Case Key Of
      vkLeft :  Cube1.RotationAngle.Y := Cube1.RotationAngle.Y + 1;
      vkRight : Cube1.RotationAngle.Y := Cube1.RotationAngle.Y - 1;
      vkUp :  Cube1.RotationAngle.X := Cube1.RotationAngle.X - 1;
      vkDown : Cube1.RotationAngle.X := Cube1.RotationAngle.X + 1;
      Else;
    End;
  End;
End.
```

Table 76.9

Using a texture to cover the faces of a cube

Save the project `CubeProject.dproj` as `CubeWithTextureProject.dproj` and its form unit `CubeUnit.pas` as `CubeWithTextureUnit.pas`.

Delete `LightMaterialSource1` then **add** a **TTextureMaterialSource** component, `TextureMaterialSource1`, from the **Materials** palette to the form. In the **Object Inspector**, **click** the **Texture** property ellipsis (**...**) of `TextureMaterialSource1` component then the **Edit...** option to bring up the **Bitmap Editor**. **Click** the **Load** button and **select** `roomwall.jpg` then **click** **OK**. **Select** `Cube1` in the **Structure** window.

Figure 76.6 CubeProject in execution

Change its **Material** property to `TextMaterialSource1`. The result is shown in *Figure 76.7*.

Press Shift+Ctrl+S to save the project and unit files.
Press Shift+Ctrl+F9 to compile and run the project - *Figure 76.8*.

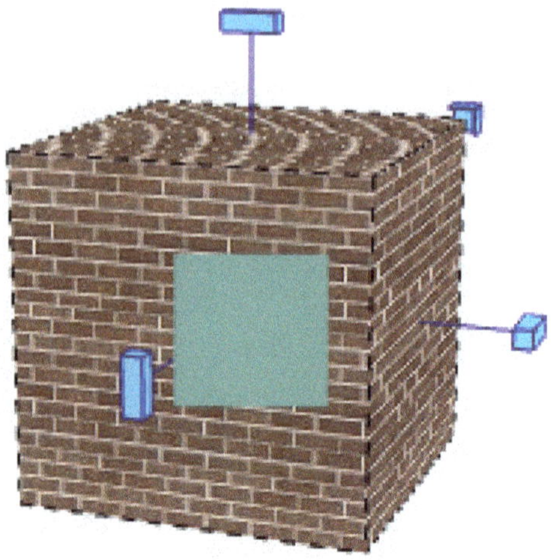

Figure 76.7 CubeWithTextureProject design view

Figure 76.8 CubeWithTextureProject in execution

Information
A material controls how a 3D object appears on the screen. Materials control the colour of the object and how reflective or dull the surface appears.
In addition, most materials take a texture or multiple textures as a parameter(s).
Materials combine textures using different shaders to achieve the final effects.

Textures
Textures are images on the surfaces of objects - see *Figure 76.8*. In the example shown in *Figure 76.6*, a single flat specific colour was applied to the surfaces of the cube - the polygons (rectangles) making up its surfaces were in-filled with red. An object containing several thousand features such as a brick wall, however, could not be rendered in real time quickly enough if treated as several thousand individual objects, one per feature. The solution is to treat the object as one and map a two-dimensional image of a brick wall (maybe captured as a photograph of a real wall) onto the object. *Figure 76.9* shows the process. The pixels in the final image are derived from a set of texels in the original image which are combined to produce the resultant colour used for the framestore pixel. The image rendered to the screen is produced by scanning the framestore (area of memory that stores the current frame) row by row.

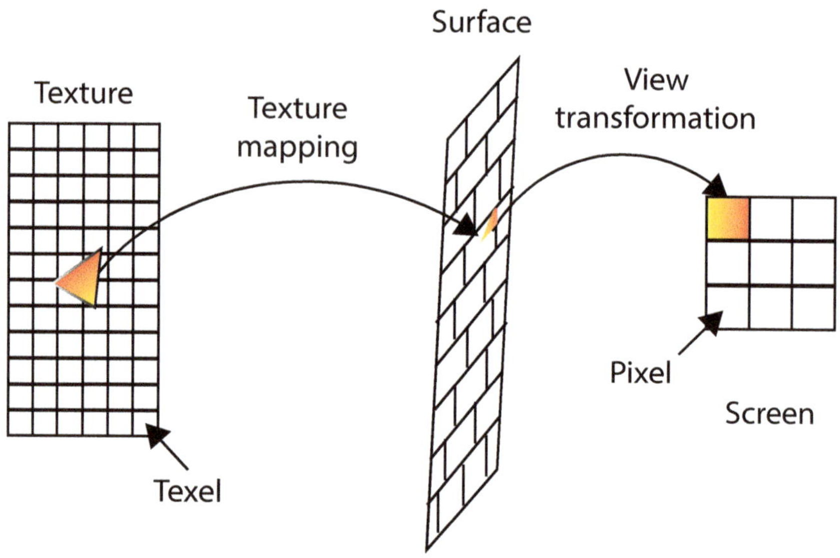

Figure 76.9 Using a texture

The process
A two-dimensional image file is applied to the surface of a 3D model to add color, texture, or other surface detail like glossiness, reflectivity, or transparency. The image file - *Figure 76.10(e)* - is mapped to a **texture map** - *Figure 76.10(d)*. A texture map can be derived from a real-life photo as shown or hand-painted in a graphics application like **Photoshop** or **GIMP** or by computation - see *Figure 76.10*[1].

1 Tschmits, CC BY-SA 3.0 <https://creativecommons.org/licenses/by-sa/3.0>, via Wikimedia Commons

The texture map is created to directly correspond to the UV coordinates of an unwrapped 3D model as shown in *Figure 76.10(b)* (U and V are also the axes of the 2-D texture map). Texture artists when hand painting a texture map usually work in layered files, with the UV coordinates on a semi-transparent layer that the artist uses as a guide for where to place specific details.

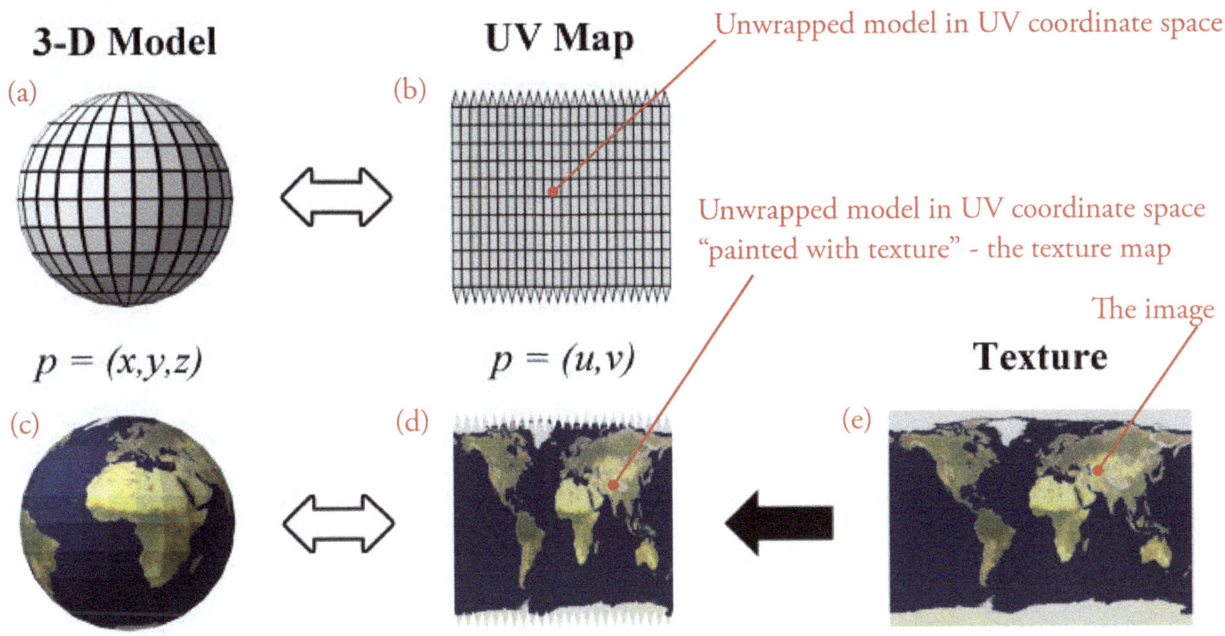

Figure 76.10 Unwrapping a 3-D model to produce a 2-D UV map which is then "painted" with a texture image, https://commons.wikimedia.org/wiki/File:UVMapping.png

Sometimes a texture atlas is used. A **texture atlas** is an image containing multiple smaller images, usually packed together to reduce overall dimensions - *Figure 76.12*. An animated demonstration of the mapping of such an atlas onto the model of a house - *Figure 76.11* - may be run from https://en.wikipedia.org/wiki/Texture_mapping#/media/File:Texture_mapping_demonstration_animation.gif[2]
The model was made with **Blender** and the texture with **GIMP**.

Figure 76.11 House textured from a texture atlas

Figure 76.13 shows a wireframe model of a face[3]. *Figure 76.15* shows the same face with a texture map applied. The texture map is derived from the 2-D image (`Chrome.bmp`) shown in *Figure 76.14*. The unwrapped model in UV coordinate space is shown as a two-dimensional array[3] in *Table 76.10*. In addition to storing the three vertices of each triangle in the mesh, this array also stores the normals assigned to each vertex.

```
unit face_data;
interface
const numVertices   = 473;
      numNormals    = 537; {Some normals are collinear}
      numTriangles = 806;
              { vert1, vert2, vert3, norm1, norm2, norm3 }
const Face : Array[0..805, 0..5] of Integer = (
        (2,1,0 ,0,1,2 ), (3,1,2 ,3,1,0 ), (6,5,4 ,4,5,6 ),
        (4,7,6 ,6,7,4 ),(8,6,7 ,8,4,7 ), (7,9,8 ,7,9,8 ),
        (8,9,10 ,8,9,10 ), (11,8,10 ,11,8,10 ),
        (12,11,10 ,12,11,10 ), (1,12,10 ,1,12,10 ),
        (13,1,10 ,13,1,10 ),(9,13,10 ,14,13,10 ), (0,1,13 ,2,1,13 ), (
        14,0,13 ,15,16,17 ),   (15,14,13 ,18,15,17 ), (9,16,15 ,14,19,18 ),
        ........
```

Table 76.10 Part of face_data.pas which encodes the wireframe model

Figure 76.12 Texture atlas

2 Drummyfish, CC0, via Wikimedia Commons
3 Jan Horn - http://www.sulaco.co.za/opengl_project_chrome_face.htm

The normal assigned to a vertex is computed from the average of the normals of the triangles that meet at that vertex - *Figure 76.16*.

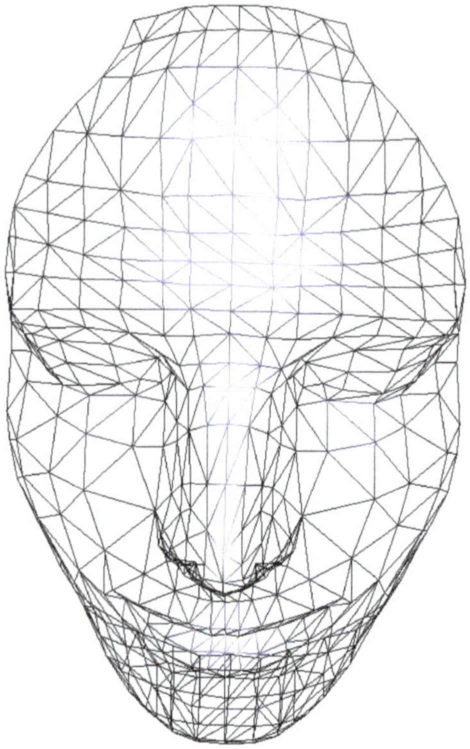

Figure 76.13 Wireframe model of a face

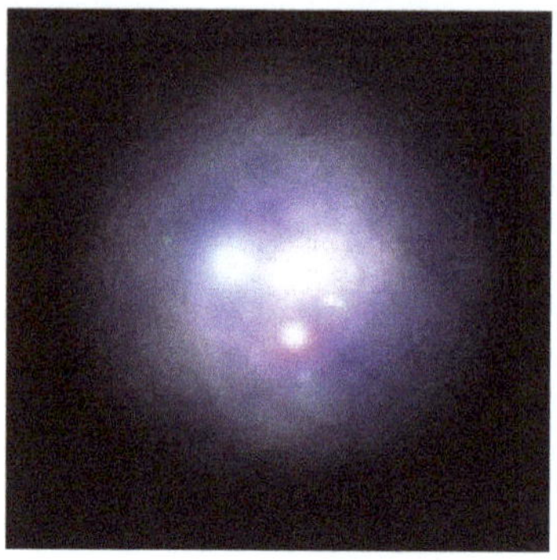

Figure 76.14 2-D texture image

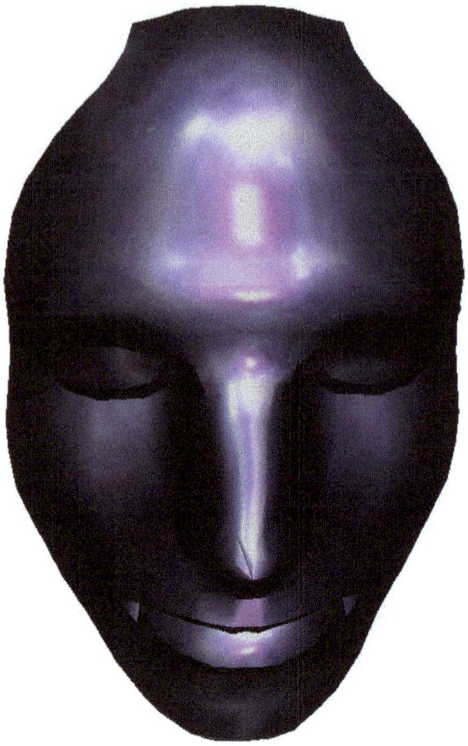

Figure 76.15 Wireframe covered using a two-dimensional texture image mapped onto wireframe model of face

The normals assigned to the vertices (illustrated by an example in *Figure 76.16*) are used to determine how the surface should appear when illuminated by a light source or if at all.

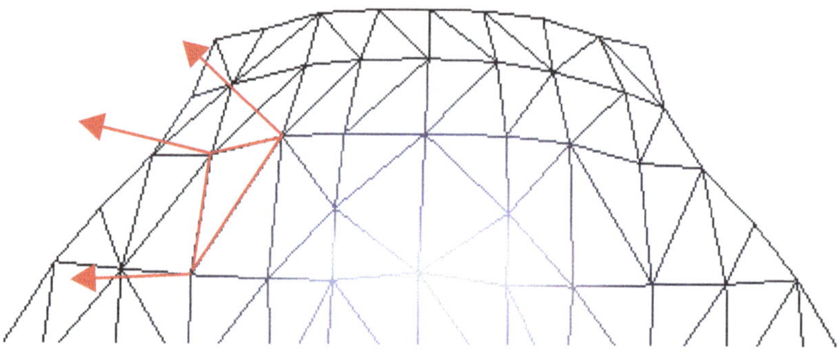

Figure 76.16 Section of the face wireframe showing the normals in red which have been calculated for the three vertices of the given triangle also marked in red

Rotating globe application

So far we have selected a multi-device 3D Delphi application to create a 3D application based on a 3D form.

For this exercise we are going to create a multi-device Delphi application based on a 2D form to which we add a **TViewport3D** as container for 3D objects.

Select **File|New|Multi-device Application - Delphi** then **select** **Blank Application**.

Change the form name to `frmSatelliteOrbitingEarth` and its caption to `Satellite Orbiting Earth`.
Add a **TViewport** component, `Viewport1`, from the **Viewports** palette to the form.
Add a **TDummy** component, `Dummy1`, from the **3D Scene** palette to `Viewport1`.
Add two **TSphere** components from the **3D Shapes** pallete to `Viewport1`.
Add a **TLight** component from the **3D Scene** palette to `Viewport1`. **Set** its **Color** property to **White**, its **Position.Z** property to -5, and its **LightType** to **Spot**.
Change the name of `Sphere1` to `Earth`. **Set** its **Depth**, **Height** and **Width** properties to 5.
Change the name of `Sphere2` to `Satellite`.

Add two **TTextureMaterialSource** components, TextureMaterialSource1 and TextureMaterialSource2 to the form.
Add a **TFloatAnimation**, FloatAnimation1, to the **TSphere** component, Earth.
Set its **Duration** to 10, its **PropertyName** to **RotationAngle.Y**, its **Loop** and **Enabled** properties to **True**.
Set its **StartValue** to 360 and its **StopValue** to 1. This ensures that the Earth sphere rotates anti-clockwise (to make the sun rise in the East).
Add a **TTimer** component, Timer1, to the form. **Set** its **Interval** property to 100 (milliseconds) and its **Enabled** property to **True**. **Create** an **OnTimer** event handler Procedure Timer1Timer. **Add** the code shown in *Table 76.11*.
Download the night sky image by Paul Volkmer[4] from https://unsplash.com/s/photos/night-sky:

paul-volkmer-qVotvbsuM_c-unsplash.jpg

Select frmSatelliteOrbitingEarth in the **Object Inspector**. **Select** **Fill|Bitmap|Bitmap** and **click** the ellipsis (...) then the **Edit...** option to bring up the **Bitmap Editor**. **Load** paul-volkmer-qVotvbsuM_c-unsplash.jpg. **Click** **OK** to return to the **Object Inspector.**
Download and extract **GLScene** from https://sourceforge.net/projects/glscene/. There are two images from the Demos/media folder - moon.bmp and earth.jpg - which we will use as texture images.
Save the project as SatelliteOrbitingEarthProject.dproj and its form unit as SatelliteOrbitingEarthUnit.pas. **Select** TextMaterialSource1. **Click** on the ellipsis (...) of **Texture** property field in the **Object Inspector** then the **Edit...** option to bring up the **Bitmap Editor**. **Load** Earth.jpg. **Click** **OK** to return to the **Object Inspector.**
Repeat for TextMaterialSource2 but this time **load** the image moon.bmp.
Now **select** sphere Earth in the **Object Inspector** and **assign** TextMaterialSource1 to its **Material** property.
Repeat for sphere Satellite but **assign** TextMaterialSource2 to its **Material** property.
Press **Shift+Ctrl+S** to save the project and unit files.
Press **Shift+Ctrl+F9** to compile and run the project - *Figure 76.17*.

```
Unit SatelliteOrbitingEarthUnit;
Interface
Uses
  System.SysUtils, System.Types, System.UITypes, System.Classes, System.Variants,
  FMX.Types, FMX.Controls, FMX.Forms, FMX.Graphics, FMX.Dialogs,
  System.Math.Vectors, FMX.Types3D, FMX.Controls3D, FMX.MaterialSources,
  FMX.Objects3D, FMX.Viewport3D, FMX.Ani;
Type
  TfrmSatelliteOrbitingEarth = Class(TForm)
                                 Viewport3D1 : TViewport3D;
                                 Dummy1 : TDummy;
                                 Earth : TSphere;
                                 Satellite : TSphere;
                                 TextureMaterialSource1 : TTextureMaterialSource;
                                 LightMaterialSource1: TLightMaterialSource;
                                 Light1 : TLight;
                                 Timer1 : TTimer;
                                 FloatAnimation1 : TFloatAnimation;
                                 Procedure Timer1Timer(Sender : TObject);
                               End;
Var
  frmSatelliteOrbitingEarth: TfrmSatelliteOrbitingEarth;
Implementation
{$R *.fmx}
Var
  Angle : Single = 0;
  Counter : Integer = 0;
Procedure TfrmSatelliteOrbitingEarth.Timer1Timer(Sender : TObject);
  Begin
    Counter := (Counter + 1) Mod 360;
    Angle := Angle + 1/(2*cPi);
    Satellite.Position.Y := 5*Cos(Angle);
    Satellite.Position.Z := 5*Sin(Angle);
  End;
End.
```

P

Table 76.11 SatelliteOrbitingEarthUnit.pas

4 https://unsplash.com/license

Figure 76.17 Shows a single frame of Satellite Orbiting Earth Project in execution in which the earth rotates about its axis and the satellite rotates about the earth in a polar orbit

Select the form and **create** an event handler for the event **OnKeyDown**.

Add the code whown in *Table 76.12* to the body of this event handler.

Press Shift+Ctrl+S to save the project and unit files.

Press Shift+Ctrl+F9 to compile and run the project .

```
Procedure TfrmSatelliteOrbitingEarth.FormKeyDown(Sender : TObject;
                                                  Var Key : Word;
                                                  Var KeyChar : Char;
                                                  Shift : TShiftState);
 Begin
   Case Key Of
     vkUp :  Dummy1.Position.Z := Dummy1.Position.Z + 1;
     vkDown : Dummy1.Position.Z := Dummy1.Position.Z - 1;
     vkLeft :  Dummy1.Position.X := Dummy1.Position.X - 1;
     vkRight : Dummy1.Position.X := Dummy1.Position.X + 1;
     Else;
   End;
 End;
```

Table 76.12 Event handler for OnKeyDown event

Use the arrow keys to reposition the combination of earth and satellite in the viewport.

Note that the event handler moves the **TDummy** object, `Dummy1`, but because both earth and satellite objects are children of `Dummy1`, they also move with `Dummy1`.

Mars Perserverance Rover 3D application

Select File|New|Multi-device Application - Delphi then **select** Blank Application to create a 3D application.

Save the project as `ThreeDObjectProject.dproj` and its form unit as `ThreeDObjectUnit.pas` in folder `ThreeDObjectWithPanel`.

Change the **Name** property of the form to `frmThreeDObject` and its **Caption** property to `Three Dimensional Object`. **Set** its **Width** to 1046 and its **Height** to 480.

Add a **TPanel** component to the form and **set** its **Align** property to **Top**, its **Height** property to 200 and its **Name** to `TopPanel`.

Add a **TViewport** component from the **Viewports** components palette. **Set** it **Align** property to **Client**.

Add thirteen **TTrackbar** controls from the **Standard** component palette to the **TopPanel**, arrange as shown in *Figure 76.18*. **Change** their **Name** property as shown in *Table 76.5* (**find** the correponding **Caption** in the table and match to *Figure 76.18*). **Use** copy and paste.

Add and **arrange** twenty six **TLabel** components as shown in *Figure 76.18* (the numeric values are **TLabel** components). **Use** copy and paste. **Change** their **Name** and **Text** properties as shown in *Table 76.14*.

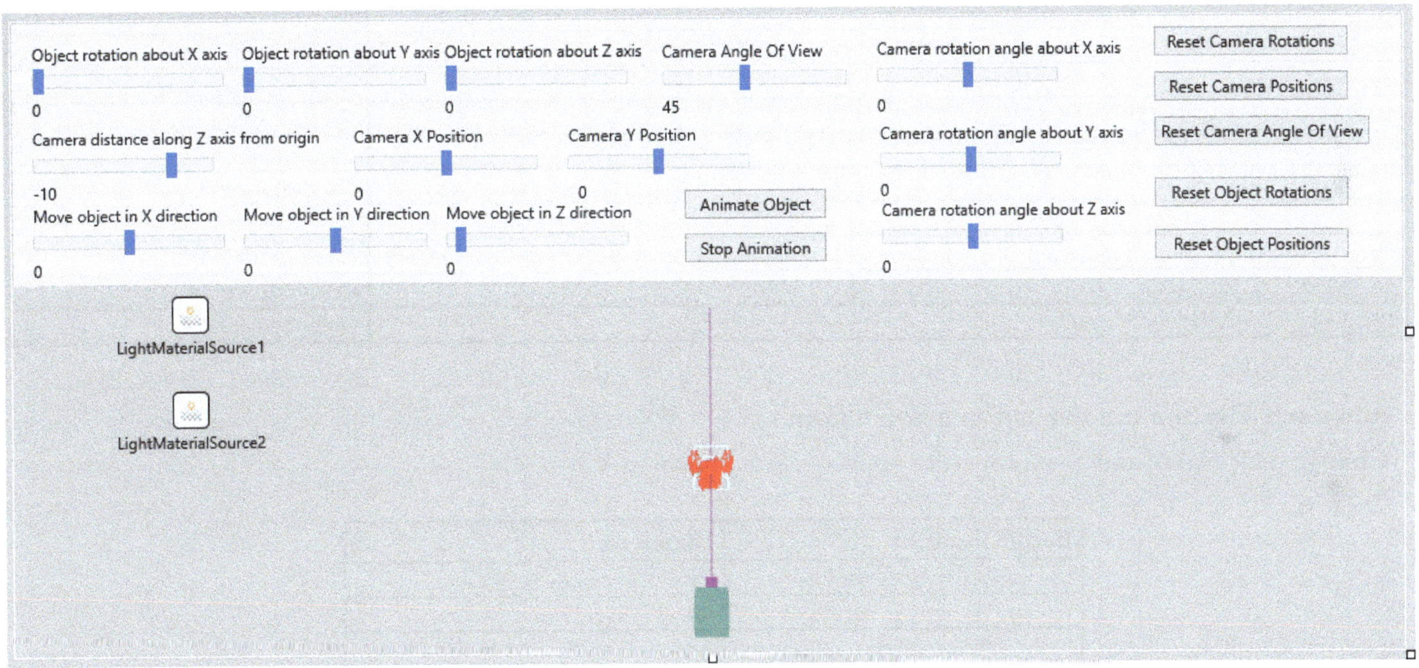

Figure 76.18 User interface form for ThreeDObjectUnit.pas

TrackBar control	Min	Max	Value
`tbXRotation`	0	360	0
`tbYRotation`	0	360	0
`tbZRotation`	0	360	0
`tbCameraViewAngle`	0	100	45
`tbCameraRotationAboutXAxis`	-22	+22	0
`tbCameraRotationAboutYAxis`	-22	+22	0
`tbCameraRotationAboutZAxis`	-180	+180	0
`tbCameraXPosition`	-15	+15	0
`tbCameraYPosition`	-5	5	0
`tbCameraZPosition`	-20	-2	-10
`tbMoveObjectX`	-10	10	0
`tbMoveObjectY`	-5	5	0
`tbMoveObjectZ`	-10	200	0

Table 76.13 TTrackBar controls settings

Name property of component	Text property	Corresponding trackbar
lblModelRotationAboutXAxisCaption	Object rotation about X axis	tbXRotation
lblModelRotationAboutYAxisCaption	Object rotation about Y axis	tbYRotation
lblModelRotationAboutZAxisCaption	Object rotation about Z axis	tbZRotation
lblCameraAngleOfViewCaption	Camera Angle Of View	tbCameraViewAngle
lblCameraRotationAngleAboutXAxisCaption	Camera rotation angle about X axis	tbCameraRotationAboutXAxis
lblCameraRotationAngleAboutZAxisCaption	Camera rotation angle about Z axis	tbCameraRotationAboutZAxis
lblRotationAngleX	0	tbXRotation
lblRotationAngleY	0	tbYRotation
lblRotationAngleZ	0	tbZRotation
lblCameraAngleOfView	45	tbCameraViewAngle
lblCameraRotationAngleAboutXAxis	0	tbCameraRotationAboutXAxis
lblCameraRotationAngleAboutZAxis	0	tbCameraRotationAboutZAxis
lblCameraDistanceAlongZAxisFromOriginCaption	Camera distance along Z axis from origin	tbCameraZPosition
lblCameraZPosition	-10	tbCameraZPosition
lblCameraXPositionCaption	Camera X Position	tbCameraXPosition
lblCameraYPositionCaption	Camera Y Position	tbCameraYPosition
lblCameraRotationAngleAboutYAxisCaption	Camera rotation angle about Y axis	tbCameraRotationAboutYAxis
lblCameraXPosition	0	tbCameraXPosition
lblCameraYPosition	0	tbCameraYPosition
lblCameraRotationAngleAboutYAxis	0	tbCameraRotationAboutYAxis
lblMoveObjectInXDirectionCaption	Move object in X direction	tbMoveObjectX
lblMoveObjectInYDirectionCaption	Move object in Y direction	tbMoveObjectY
lblMoveObjectInZDirectionCaption	Move object in Z direction	tbMoveObjectZ
lblPositionOfObjectAlongXAxis	0	tbMoveObjectX
lblPositionOfObjectAlongYAxis	0	tbMoveObjectY
lblPositionOfObjectAlongZAxis	0	tbMoveObjectZ

Table 76.14 List of TLabel components added to TopPanel and their corresponding trackbars

Add seven **TButton** controls and arrange as shown in *Figure 76.18*.

Change their **Name** and **Text** properties respectively as shown in *Table 76.15*.

Button identifier	Button text
btnResetCameraRotations	Reset Camera Rotations
btnResetCameraPositions	Reset Camera Positions
btnResetCameraAngleOfView	Reset Camera Angle Of View
btnResetObjectRotations	Reset Object Rotations
btnResetObjectPositions	Reset Object Positions
btnAnimate	Animate Object
btnStopAnimation	Stop Animation

Table 76.15 List of TButton components added to TopPanel and their corresponding trackbars

Set the **Min**, **Max** and **Value** properties of the **TTrackBar** controls to the settings shown in *Table 76.13*.

Add a **TModel3D** component from the **3D Shapes** component palette to the **TViewport** component, `ViewPort3D1`.

Add a **TCamera** component from the **3D Scene** component palette to `ViewPort3D1`.

Add a **TLight** component from the **3D Scene** component palette to the **TCamera** component, `Camera1`.

Set the camera **Camera1**'s **Position.Z** property to -10, **leave** its **Position.X** and **Position.Y** properties at 0.

Set its **AngleOfView** property to 45 and its **Projection** property to **Camera**.

Set the **TLight** component's **LightType** property to **Spot** and its **Position** and **Projection** properties as for `Camera1`.

Set **Viewport3D1**'s **UsingDesignCamera** to **False**, its **Color** property to **Lightgray**.

Add a **TSphere** component from **3D Shapes** component palette to `Viewport3D1`.

Set its **Depth**, **Height** and **Width** properties to 5.

Change its **Projection** property to **Screen** and its **WrapMode** to **Fit**.

Set it to the centre of the viewport:

Position.X = 523

Position.Y = 140

(`Viewport3D1`'s **Width** - 1046, and **Height** = 280)

Add a **TLightSourceMaterial** from the **Materials** component palette to the form.

Set its **Diffuse** property to **Slategray**.

Now we need to load `Model3D1` with a 3D model. The one that we will use initially is located in file `Perserverance.dae`. This is a 3D model of the Mars Perseverance Rover[5] vehicle which is obtainable from https://mars.nasa.gov/resources/25042/mars-perseverance-rover-3d-model/ in **glTF** file format.

To obtain this model for yourself, download the **glTF** file, `Perserverence.glb` and then convert to **dae** format using the free **Aspose** converter https://products.aspose.app/3d/conversion/fbx-to-glb - *Figure 76.19*.

Place the converted file `Perserverance.dae` in the project folder `ThreeDObjectWithPanel`.

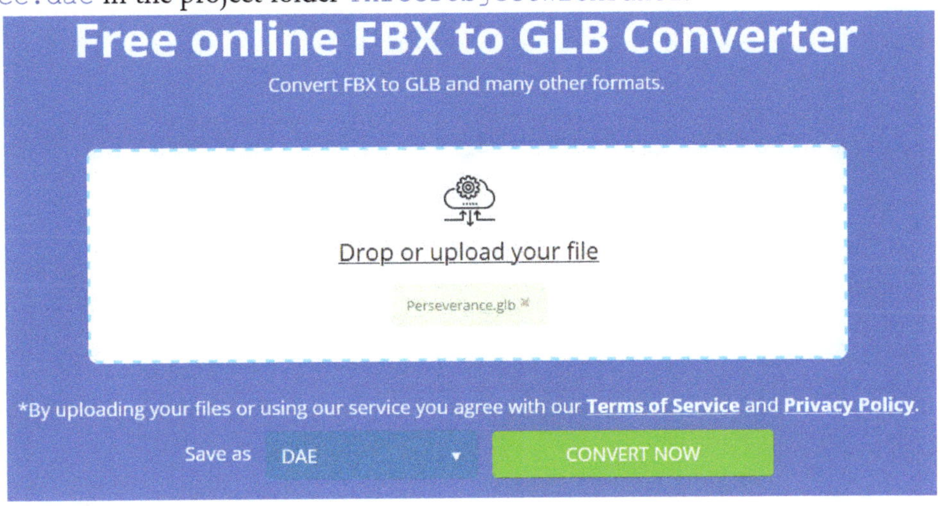

Figure 76.19 Converting Perserverance.glb to Perserverance.dae

Select `Model3D1` and then in the **Object Inspector** click the ellipsis (...) in the property value field for **MeshCollection** to bring up the **Mesh Collection Editor** window.

Click the **Load** button and **load** `Perserverance.dae`. Once loaded (it may take several seconds) **click** the **OK** button (it may take a few more seconds to complete the process).

`Perserverance.dae` may be opened in a text editor such as **NotePad++** as it is in XML format. The editor view reveals that the 3D object is a collection of vertices and triangles in several meshes.

Press **Shift+Ctrl+S** to save the project and unit files.

Select `frmThreeDObject`. In the **Object Inspector**, **select** the events page and **create** two event handlers: one for the **OnCreate** event and one for the **OnResize** event of the form.

Add the code shown in *Table 76.16* to the bodies of these.

Create event handlers for the **OnChange** event for each of the trackbars and **add** the code shown in *Table 76.17*.

Press **Shift+Ctrl+S** to save the project and unit files.

```
Procedure TfrmThreeDObject.FormCreate(Sender : TObject);
  Var
    Mesh : TMesh;
  Begin
    For Mesh In Model3D1.MeshCollection
      Do Mesh.MaterialSource := LightMaterialSource1;
    lblRotationAngleX.Text := FloatToStr(Model3D1.RotationAngle.X);
    lblRotationAngleY.Text := FloatToStr(Model3D1.RotationAngle.Y);
    lblRotationAngleZ.Text := FloatToStr(Model3D1.RotationAngle.Z);
    lblCameraZPosition.Text := FloatToStr(Camera1.Position.Z);
    lblCameraRotationAngleAboutXAxis.Text := FloatToStr(Camera1.RotationAngle.X);
    lblCameraAngleOfView.Text := FloatToStr(Camera1.AngleOfView);
    Sphere1.Position.X := ViewPort3D1.Width / 2;
    Sphere1.Position.Y := ViewPort3D1.Height / 2;
  End;
Procedure TfrmThreeDObject.FormResize(Sender : TObject);
  Begin
    Sphere1.Position.X := ViewPort3D1.Width / 2;
    Sphere1.Position.Y := ViewPort3D1.Height / 2;
  End;
```

Table 76.16 FormCreate and FormResize event handlers

5 NASA/JPL-Caltech

Create event handlers for the **OnClick** event for the first five buttons of *Table 76.15* and **add** the code shown in *Table 76.18*.

```
Procedure TfrmThreeDObject.tbCameraViewAngleChange(Sender : TObject);
  Begin
    Camera1.AngleOfView := tbCameraViewAngle.Value;
    lblCameraAngleOfView.Text := FloatToStr(Camera1.AngleOfView);
  End;
Procedure TfrmThreeDObject.tbCameraXPositionChange(Sender : TObject);
  Begin
    Camera1.Position.X := tbCameraXPosition.Value;
    lblCameraXPosition.Text := FloatToStr(Camera1.Position.X);
  End;
Procedure TfrmThreeDObject.tbCameraYPositionChange(Sender : TObject);
  Begin
    Camera1.Position.Y := tbCameraYPosition.Value;
    lblCameraYPosition.Text := FloatToStr(Camera1.Position.Y);
  End;
Procedure TfrmThreeDObject.tbCameraZPositionChange(Sender : TObject);
  Begin
    Camera1.Position.Z := tbCameraZPosition.Value;
    lblCameraZPosition.Text := FloatToStr(Camera1.Position.Z);
  End;
Procedure TfrmThreeDObject.tbMoveObjectXChange(Sender: TObject);
  Begin
    Model3D1.Position.X := tbMoveObjectX.Value;
   lblPositionOfObjectAlongXAxis.Text := FloatToStr(Model3D1.Position.X);
  End;
Procedure TfrmThreeDObject.tbMoveObjectYChange(Sender: TObject);
  Begin
    Model3D1.Position.Y := tbMoveObjectY.Value;
    lblPositionOfObjectAlongYAxis.Text := FloatToStr(Model3D1.Position.Y);
  End;
Procedure TfrmThreeDObject.tbMoveObjectZChange(Sender: TObject);
  Begin
    Model3D1.Position.Z := tbMoveObjectZ.Value;
   lblPositionOfObjectAlongZAxis.Text := FloatToStr(Model3D1.Position.Z);
  End;
Procedure TfrmThreeDObject.tbCameraRotationAboutXAxisChange(Sender : TObject);
  Begin
    Camera1.RotationAngle.X := tbCameraRotationAboutXAxis.Value;
    If (Camera1.RotationAngle.X < 22.5) And (Camera1.RotationAngle.X > 0)
      Then lblCameraRotationAngleAboutXAxis.Text := FloatToStr(Camera1.RotationAngle.X)
      Else lblCameraRotationAngleAboutXAxis.Text := FloatToStr(Camera1.RotationAngle.X - 360);
  End;
Procedure TfrmThreeDObject.tbCameraRotationAboutYAxisChange(Sender : TObject);
  Begin
    Camera1.RotationAngle.Y := tbCameraRotationAboutYAxis.Value;
    If (Camera1.RotationAngle.Y < 22.5) And (Camera1.RotationAngle.Y > 0)
      Then lblCameraRotationAngleAboutYAxis.Text := FloatToStr(Camera1.RotationAngle.Y)
      Else lblCameraRotationAngleAboutYAxis.Text := FloatToStr(Camera1.RotationAngle.Y - 360);
  End;
Procedure TfrmThreeDObject.tbCameraRotationAboutZAxisChange(Sender : TObject);
  Begin
    Camera1.RotationAngle.Z := tbCameraRotationAboutZAxis.Value;
    lblCameraRotationAngleAboutZAxis.Text := FloatToStr(tbCameraRotationAboutZAxis.Value);
  End;
Procedure TfrmThreeDObject.tbXRotationChange(Sender : TObject);
  Begin
    Model3D1.RotationAngle.X := tbXRotation.Value;
    lblRotationAngleX.Text := FloatToStr(Model3D1.RotationAngle.X);
  End;
Procedure TfrmThreeDObject.tbYRotationChange(Sender : TObject);
  Begin
    Model3D1.RotationAngle.Y := tbYRotation.Value;
    lblRotationAngleY.Text := FloatToStr(Model3D1.RotationAngle.Y);
  End;
Procedure TfrmThreeDObject.tbZRotationChange(Sender : TObject);
  Begin
    Model3D1.RotationAngle.Z := tbZRotation.Value;
    lblRotationAngleZ.Text := FloatToStr(Model3D1.RotationAngle.Z);
  End;
```

P

Table 76.17 OnChange event handlers for the trackbars

P

```
Procedure TfrmThreeDObject.btnResetCameraAngleOfViewClick(Sender : TObject);
  Begin
    tbCameraViewAngle.Value := 45;
    Camera1.AngleOfView := 45;
    lblCameraAngleOfView.Text := FloatToStr(Camera1.AngleOfView);
  End;
Procedure TfrmThreeDObject.btnResetCameraPositionsClick(Sender : TObject);
  Begin
    Camera1.Position.X := 0;
    Camera1.Position.Y := 0;
    Camera1.Position.Z := -10;
    tbCameraXPosition.Value := 0;
    tbCameraYPosition.Value := 0;
    tbCameraZPosition.Value := -10;
    lblCameraXPosition.Text := FloatToStr(Camera1.Position.X);
    lblCameraYPosition.Text := FloatToStr(Camera1.Position.Y);
    lblCameraZPosition.Text := FloatToStr(Camera1.Position.Z);
  End;
Procedure TfrmThreeDObject.btnResetCameraRotationsClick(Sender : TObject);
  Begin
    Camera1.RotationAngle.X := 0;
    Camera1.RotationAngle.Y := 0;
    Camera1.RotationAngle.Z := 0;
    tbCameraRotationAboutXAxis.Value := 0;
    tbCameraRotationAboutYAxis.Value := 0;
    tbCameraRotationAboutZAxis.Value := 0;
    lblCameraRotationAngleAboutXAxis.Text := FloatToStr(Camera1.RotationAngle.X);
    lblCameraRotationAngleAboutYAxis.Text := FloatToStr(Camera1.RotationAngle.Y);
    lblCameraRotationAngleAboutZAxis.Text := FloatToStr(Camera1.RotationAngle.Z);
  End;
Procedure TfrmThreeDObject.btnResetObjectPositionsClick(Sender : TObject);
  Begin
    Model3D1.Position.X := 0;
    Model3D1.Position.Y := 0;
    Model3D1.Position.Z := 0;
    lblPositionOfObjectAlongXAxis.Text := FloatToStr(Model3D1.Position.X);
    lblPositionOfObjectAlongYAxis.Text := FloatToStr(Model3D1.Position.Y);
    lblPositionOfObjectAlongZAxis.Text := FloatToStr(Model3D1.Position.Z);
    tbMoveObjectX.Value := 0;
    tbMoveObjectY.Value := 0;
    tbMoveObjectZ.Value := 0;
  End;
Procedure TfrmThreeDObject.btnResetObjectRotationsClick(Sender : TObject);
  Begin
    Model3D1.RotationAngle.X := 0;
    Model3D1.RotationAngle.Y := 0;
    Model3D1.RotationAngle.Z := 0;
    lblRotationAngleX.Text := FloatToStr(Model3D1.RotationAngle.X);
    lblRotationAngleY.Text := FloatToStr(Model3D1.RotationAngle.Y);
    lblRotationAngleZ.Text := FloatToStr(Model3D1.RotationAngle.Z);
    tbXRotation.Value := 0;
    tbYRotation.Value := 0;
    tbZRotation.Value := 0;
  End;
```

Table 76.18 OnChange event handlers for five of the buttons

Press Shift+Ctrl+S to save the project and unit files.

Press Shift+Ctrl+F9 to compile and run the project.

Figure 76.20 shows the project in execution with the Mars Perseverance Rover vehicle displayed on the screen. The vehicle appears in monochrome (shaded) because just one **TLightMaterialSource** component is used to "colour" the vehicle. To bring a different colour to a specific part of the vehicle, we would need to identify the corresponding mesh and use a second **TLightMaterialSource** with the desired colour setting for its **Diffuse** property. Studying the XML of `Perserverence.dae` in **NotePad++** reveals that the wheels are defined by meshes 27, 28 and 29 (mesh 27 = 6 wheel rims, mesh 28 = 6 sets of wheel spokes, mesh 29 = 6 wheel hubs).

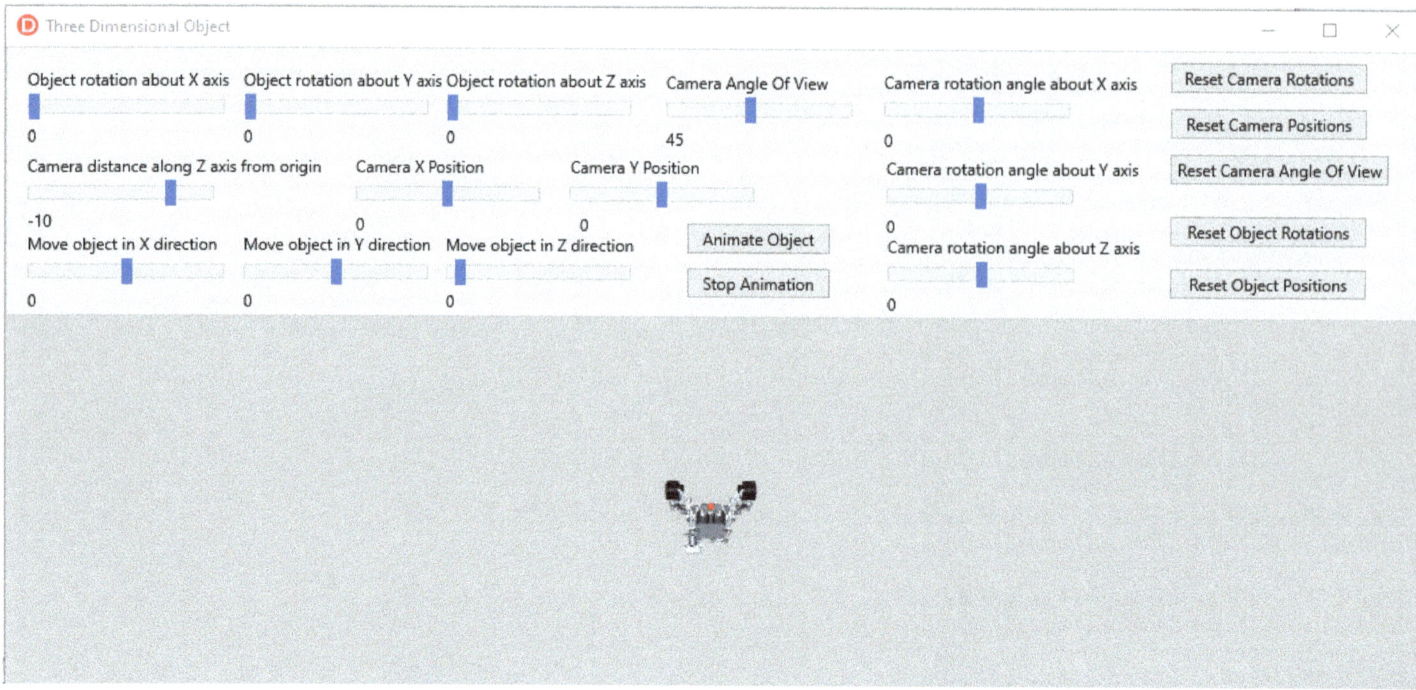

Figure 76.20 ThreeDObjectProject in execution

Add a second **TLightMaterialSource**, `LightMaterialSource2`, to the form and set its **Diffuse** property to **Black**.

Insert the following in the `FormCreate` event handler

```
For i := 27 To 29
  Do Model3D1.MeshCollection[i].MaterialSource := LightMaterialSource2;
```

immediately following

```
For Mesh In Model3D1.MeshCollection
  Do Mesh.MaterialSource := LightMaterialSource1;
```

Press Shift+Ctrl+S to save the project and unit files.

Press Shift+Ctrl+F9 to compile and run the project.

Figure 76.21 shows the Mars Perseverance Rover vehicle displayed with black wheels. The vehicle has been rotated about both Z and Y axes.

Note the red circle (it is located centrally in the viewport). This is the sphere which has been mapped to the screen as a circle because its **Projection** property was set to **Screen**. This setting ensures that the sphere remains fixed in position and immune to any camera movements or changes to the camera's angle of view.

Figure 76.21 Mars Perseverance Rover vehicle, rotated about the Z axis and the Y axis, so that all six black wheels may be shown clearly

Exercises to try

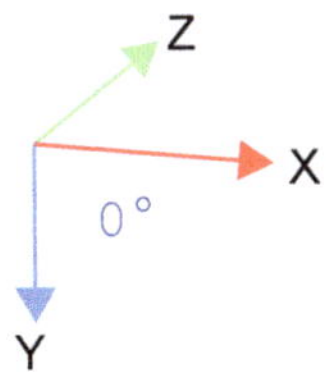

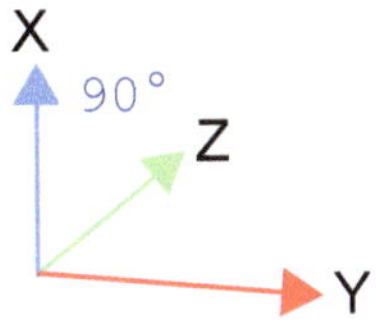

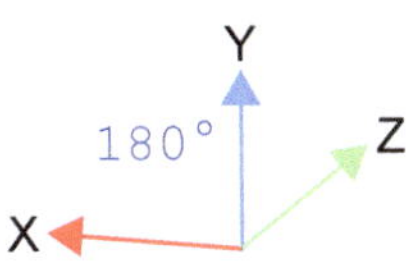

1. **Object rotation about Z-axis**
   Use this slider to rotate the vehicle 180° about the Z-axis (with this trackbar selected - **click** left mouse button - fine adjustment to 180° is achieved by using the arrow keys on the keyboard). *Figure 76.22* shows the result. The red spot is the centrally located sphere, `Sphere1`, which remains in the same position whatever the position of the camera. This sphere is used as a fixed reference against which the movement of the vehicle may be assessed.

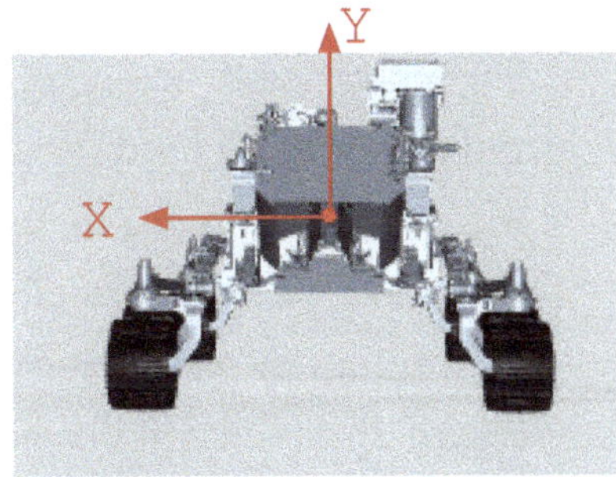

Figure 76.22 Vehicle rotated through 180° about the Z-axis - Z-axis points into page. The coordinate axes on the left of this page show the stages of rotation of the axes.

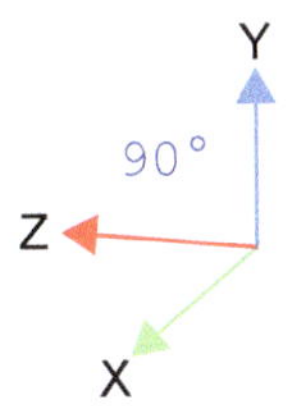

2. **Object rotation about Y-axis**
   Use this slider to rotate the vehicle 90° about the Y-axis after rotation about the Z-axis by 180°. *Figure 76.23* shows the result.

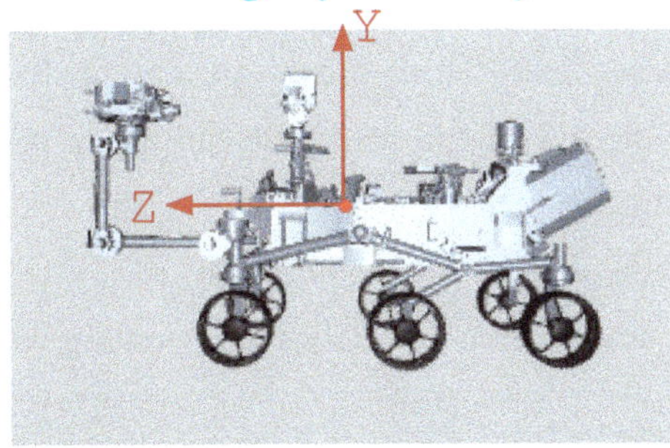

Figure 76.23 Vehicle rotated through 90° about the Y-axis - Z-axis points into page. The coordinate axes on the left of this page shows the rotation of the axes.

3. **Object rotation about X-axis**
   Use this slider to rotate the vehicle 90° about the X-axis after rotation about the Z-axis by 180° and after rotation about the the Y-axis by 90°. *Figure 76.24* shows the result. We conclude from the result that for rotations of the object, the 3D axis system is fixed to the vehicle object, i.e. describes a local space coordinate system for object rotations. Therefore, when the object is rotated, its coordinate system rotates with it.
   Following the three rotations,The X-axis now points out of the paper, the Z-axis downwards and the Y-axis to the left.

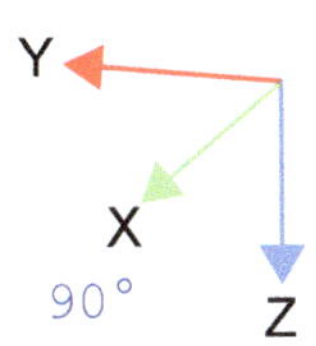

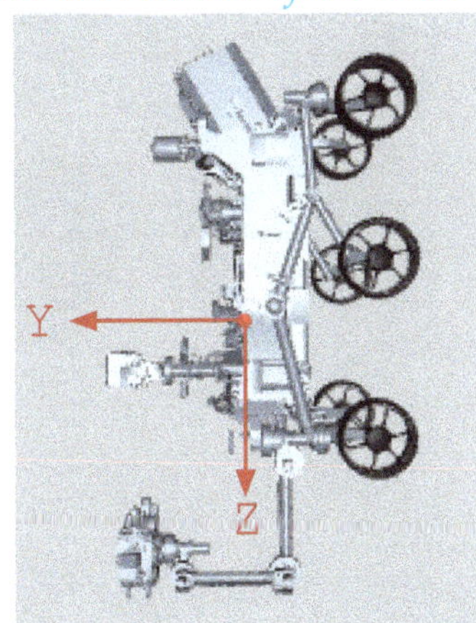

Figure 76.24 Vehicle rotated through 90° about the X-Axis - X-axis points out of page

- The viewport determines where the geometry inside the frustum is going to be rendered on the 2D screen - *Figure 76.25*. The distance along the Z axis between the near plane and the far plane is **n + f** units.
- The line of sight vector originates at the eye point (camera) and points along the positive Z axis. The positive Z axis coincides with the line of sight vector and traverses the centre altitude line of the view pyramid. This altitude line of the pyramid extends along the local positive Z axis from the pyramid's apex until the centre of the pyramid base is reached.
- The figure that is eventually rendered to the user's screen is clipped by a **frustrum** of the view pyramid - the pyramid with its top cut off at the near plane position. Only objects or parts of objects inside this frustum are visible on the user's screen.

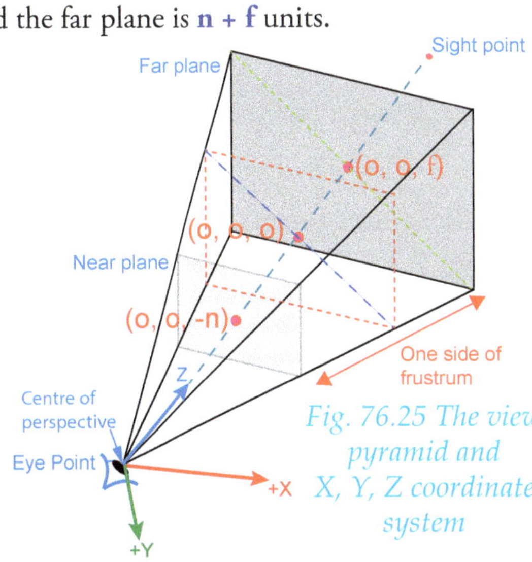

Fig. 76.25 The view pyramid and X, Y, Z coordinate system

- The separation between eye point (camera) and near plane is fixed for a given camera angle of view. Moving the eye point (camera) closer to the origin therefore must brings the near plane closer to the origin. This results in the far plane moving further away from the origin as shown in *Figure 76.26* in order to keep **n + f** the same.

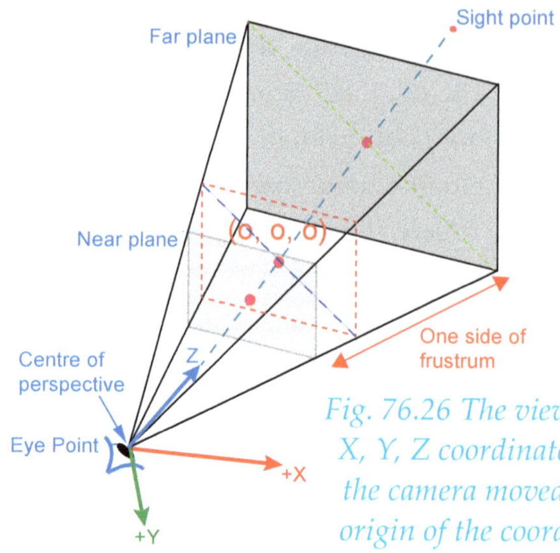

Fig. 76.26 The view pyramid and X, Y, Z coordinate system with the camera moved closer to the origin of the coordinate system

4. **Changing camera distance along Z-axis**

   Use this slider to move the camera closer to the object whilst keeping the camera's angle of view the same at 45°. *Figure 76.27* shows the result. The object is larger and parts of it are clipped because they lie outside the viewing volume defined by view pyramid's frustrum.

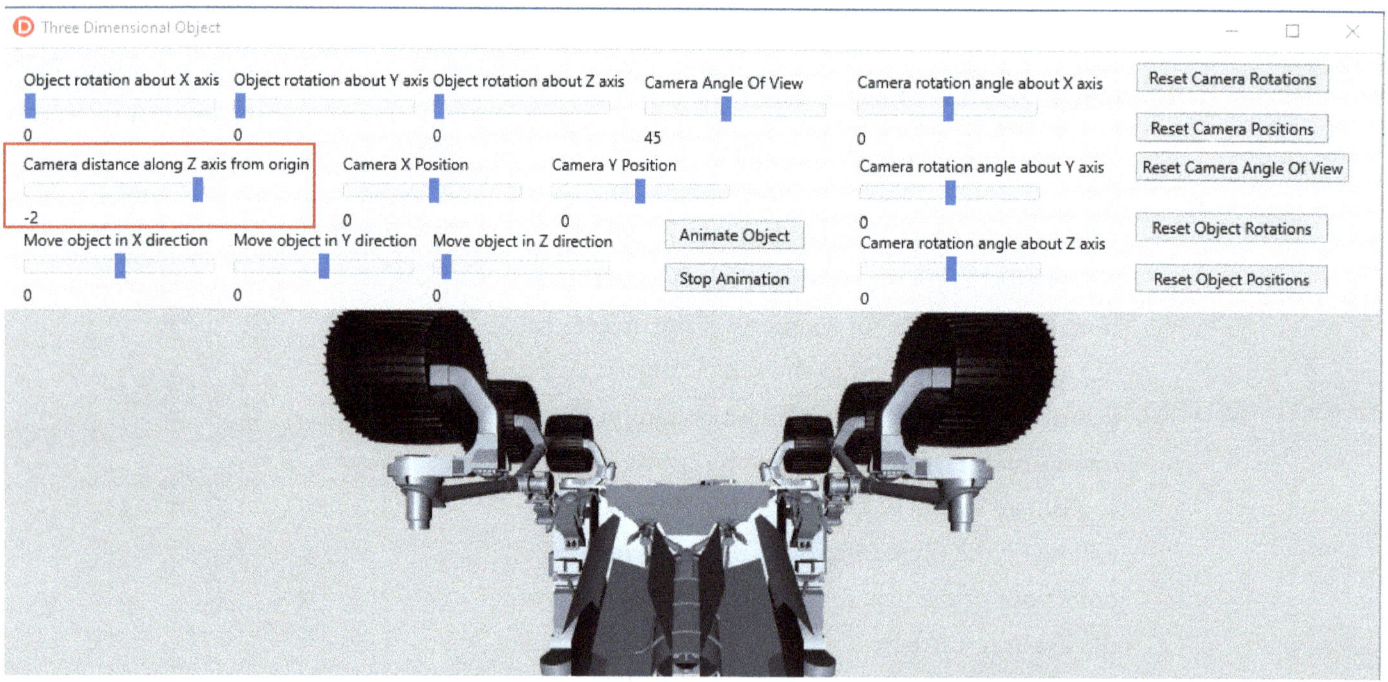

Figure 76.27 The user's screen when camera is moved to Z = -2

Figure 76.28 shows that for the given viewing angle, more and more of the object moves outside the view pyramid as the camera gets closer to the object. It also shows that the object occupies more and more of the field of view, i.e. it grows in size in the viewport - see red dotted light rays.

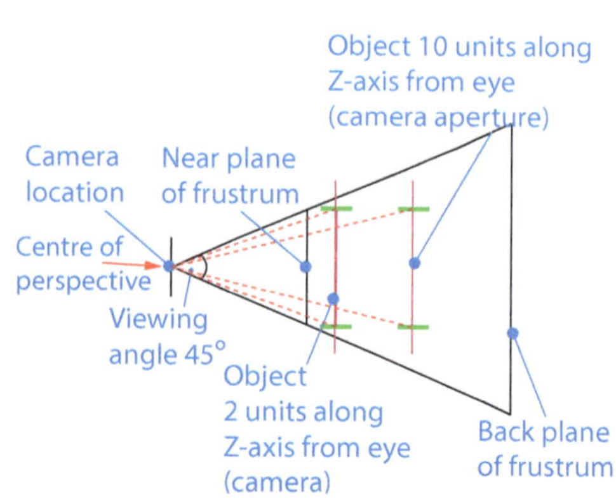

Figure 76.28 Moving camera along Z-axis is equivalent to moving object in opposite direction

5. **Changing camera's view angle**

   With the camera's distance along the Z-axis at -2, **use** this slider to change the camera angle of view to 100°. *Figure 76.29* shows the result. The object has been restored to close to its original size.

   Figure 76.30 shows the new frustrum plan view.

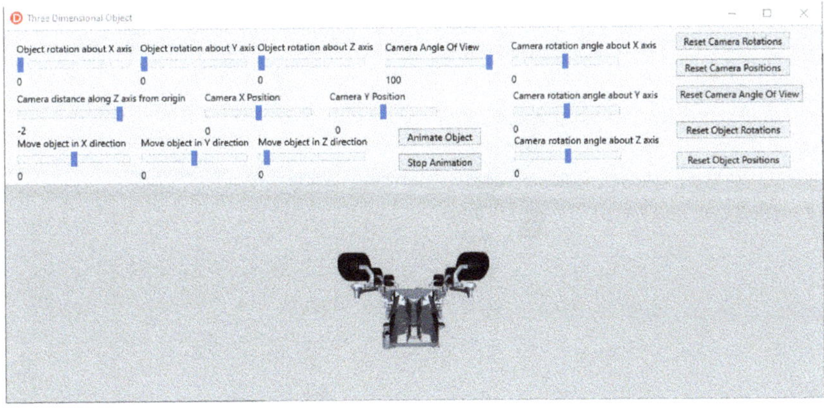

Figure 76.29 Camera at -2 along Z-axis, camera angle of view 100°

6. **Changing the object's position in the X direction**

   Rotate the object 180° about the Z axis. **Move** the object in the X direction -10 units (*Figure 76.31*).

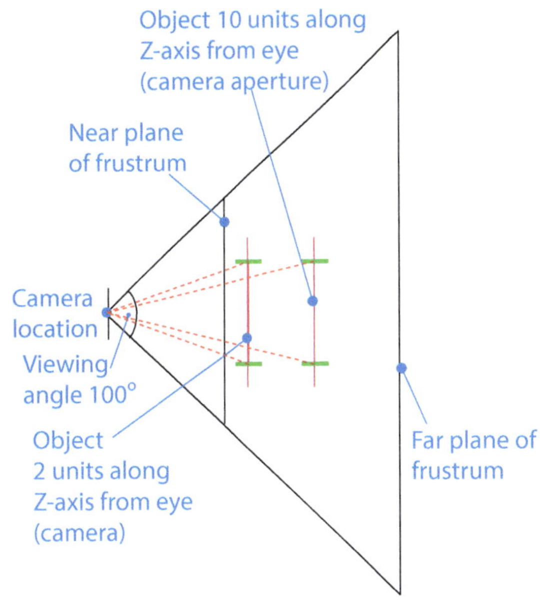

Figure 76.30 Camera's angle of view changed to 100°, camera at -2 along Z axis

7. **Changing the object's position in the Y direction**

   Rotate the object 180° about the Z-axis. **Move** the object in the Y direction -1.5 units (*Figure 76.32*).

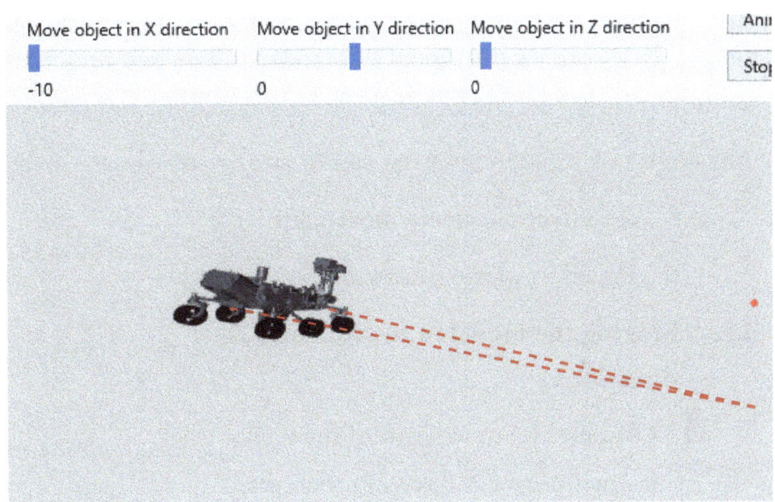

Figure 76.31 Object movement in X direction (perspective point brings side into view)

8. **Changing the object's position in the Z direction**

   Rotate the object 180° about the Z-axis. **Move** the object in the Z direction - 6.8 units (*Figure 76.33*). Fine adjustment of position is possible using the arrow keys on the keyboard.

9. **Changing the object's position in the X direction then rotate camera about Z-axis**

   Move the object 2.5 units in the X direction. **Rotate** the camera about the Z axis 90° aproximately - *Figure 76.34*.

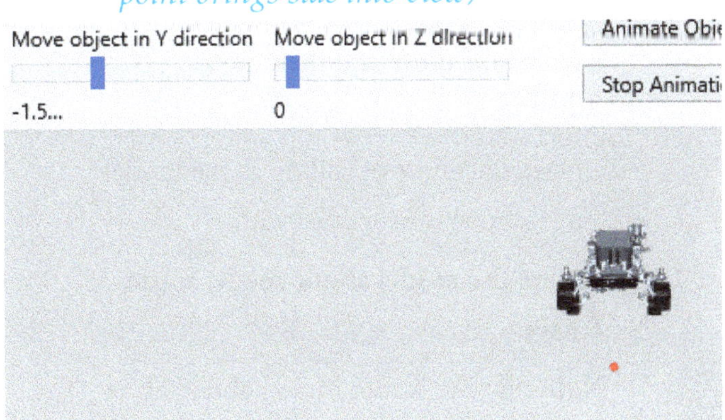

Figure 76.32 Object movement in Y direction

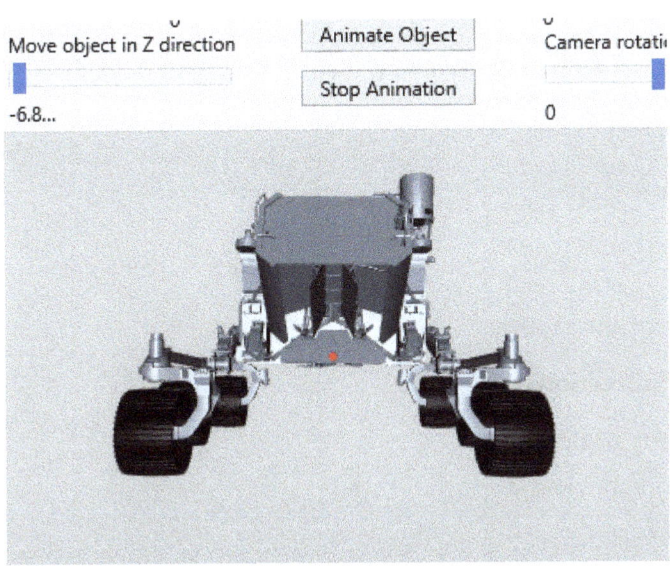

Figure 76.33 Object movement in Z direction

Fine adjustment of position and rotation is possible using the arrow keys on the keyboard.

The object moves along an arc in the opposite direction making its local coordinate system rotate through -90°.

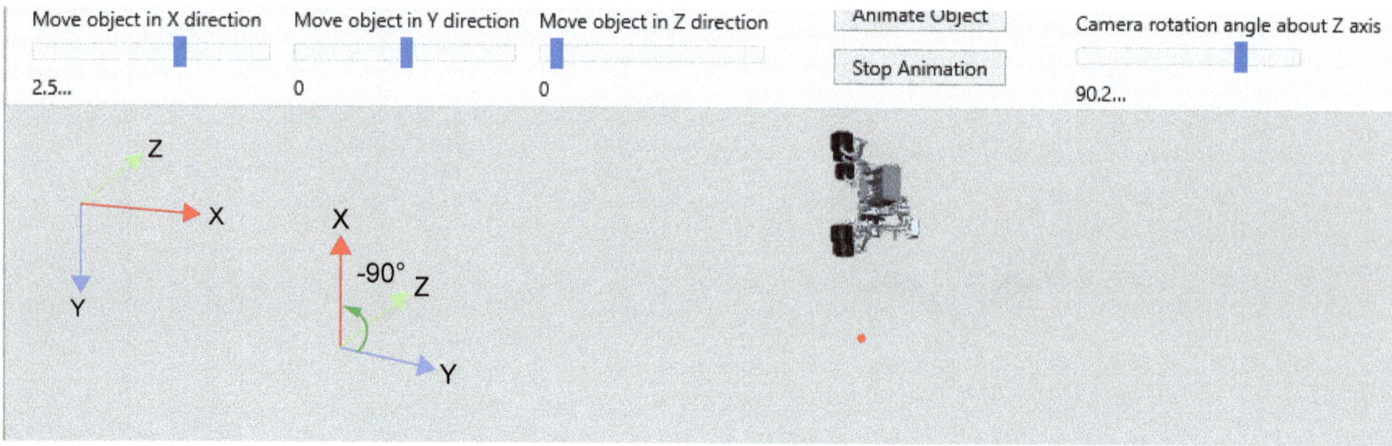

Figure 76.34 Camera rotated 90.2° about the Z axis with object positioned 2.5 units along X axis

10. Rotating the camera about Y-axis

Rotate the camera about the Y axis 11° aproximately with the object at (0, 0, 0) - *Figure 76.35*. Fine adjustment of rotation is possible using the arrow keys on the keyboard.

The object moves in the negative X direction.

Figure 76.37 shows the OpenGL **matrixModelView** program from **Chapter 47**. This program may be downloaded from http://www.songho.ca/opengl/gl_transform.html as **matrixModelView.zip**.

Although this program uses the coordinate system shown in *Figure 76.36*, it nevertheless is useful for showing

- the effect of camera movement
- the effect of the frustrum.

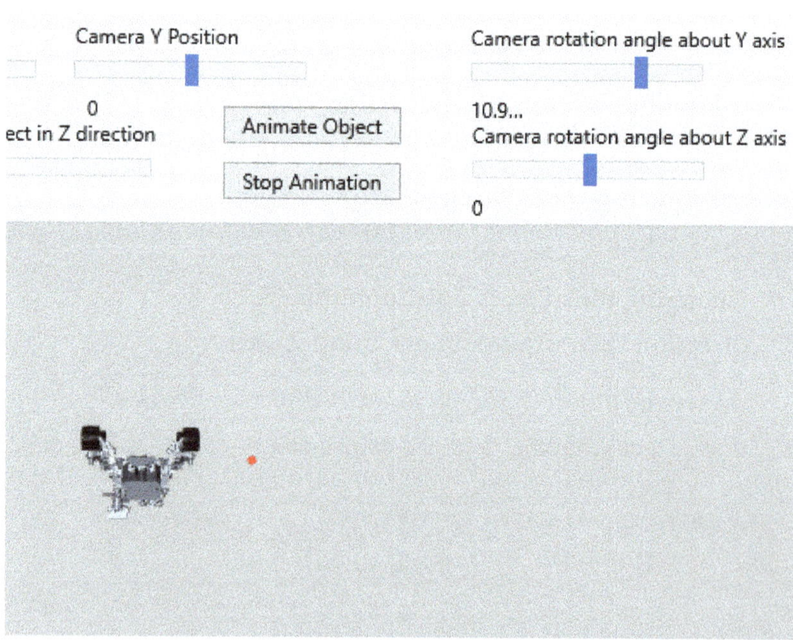

Figure 76.35 Camera rotated 10.9° about the Y axis with object at (0, 0, 0)

11. Moving the model in the X, Y and Z directions

1. **Observe** the movement of the teapot in the positive X direction then the negative X direction and its rendering in the viewport. **Reset** the model. repeat for the Y and then the Z directions. Finally, **reset** the model.
2. **Note** the effect of culling as the model moves outside the frustrum.

12. Rotate the model about the X, Y and Z axes

Note that the teapot rotates about its local coordinate system. **Reset** the model between rotations about each axis. Finally, **reset** the model.

13. Alter the position of the camera in the X, Y and Z directions

Note the movement of the frustrum and the rendering or non-rendering of the teapot in the viewport. **Reset** the camera view between each direction. Finally, **reset** the camera view.

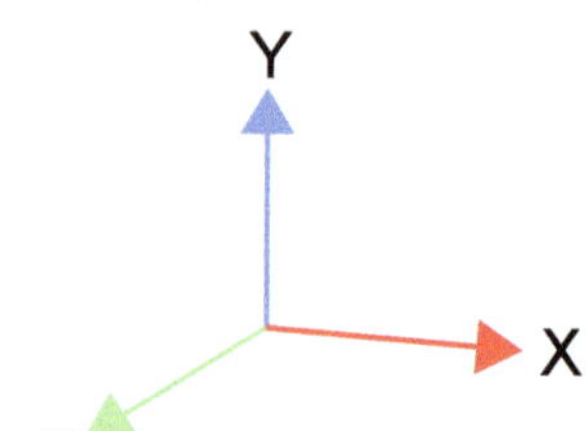

Figure 76.36 Coordinate system for the OpenGL program matrixModelView

14. Alter the pitch, heading and roll angles of the camera

Note the movement of the frustrum and the rendering or non-rendering of the teapot in the viewport. **Reset** the camera view between each angle. Finally, **reset** the camera view.

Hopefully, you will now understand, a little better, the affect of model/object movement/rotation, camera movement/rotation, and finally the movement/rotation of the frustrum and its consequent affect on the rendering of the model/object in the screen space - *Figure 76.38*.

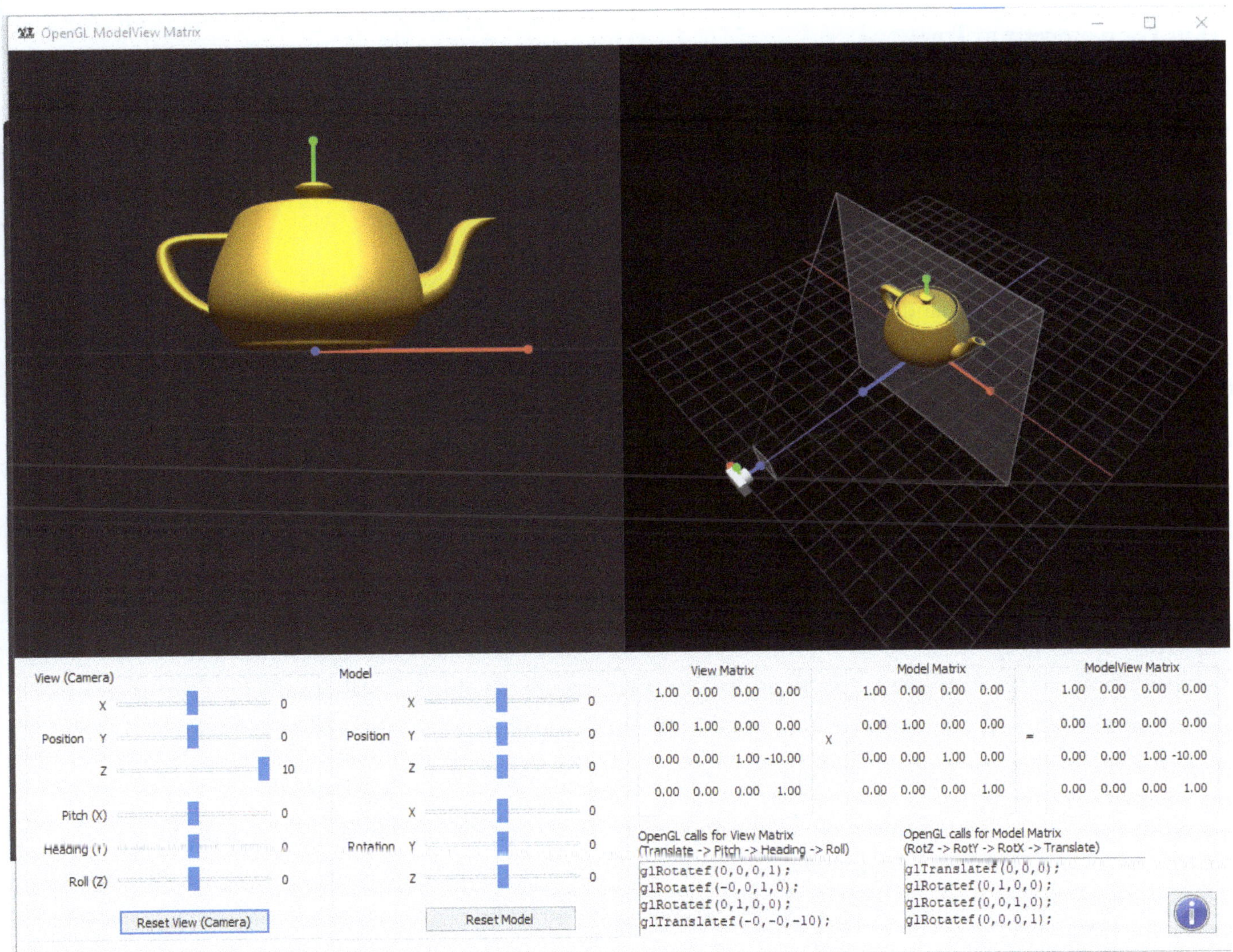

Figure 76.37 OpenGL example to explore a frustrum system - author Song Ho Ahn http://www.songho.ca/

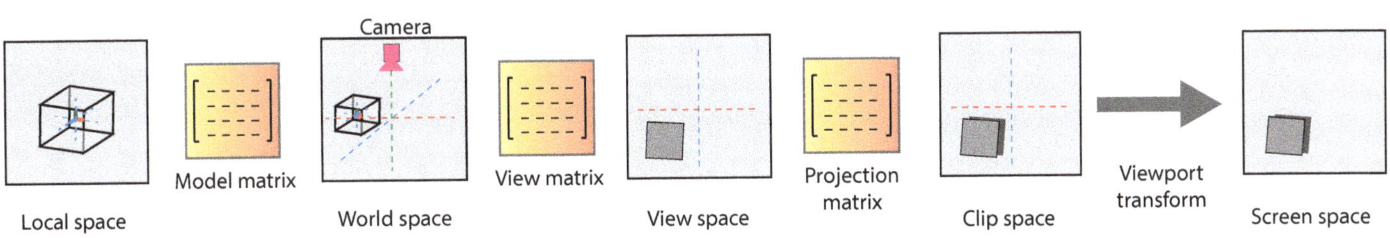

Figure 76.38 The transformations from local space to screen space (The projection matrix transforms the scene so that the frustum becomes a 1x1x1 box. This is done to easily (read: faster) clip the coordinates. Then this box is squished to a 1x1 rectangle, so all coordinates are between 0 and 1. Then the position and size of the viewport are used to transform these coordinates from the 1x1 rectangle to the viewport rectangle.)

Animation

Add a **TFloatAnimation** from the **Animations** component palette to `Model3d1` as shown in *Figure 76.39*.

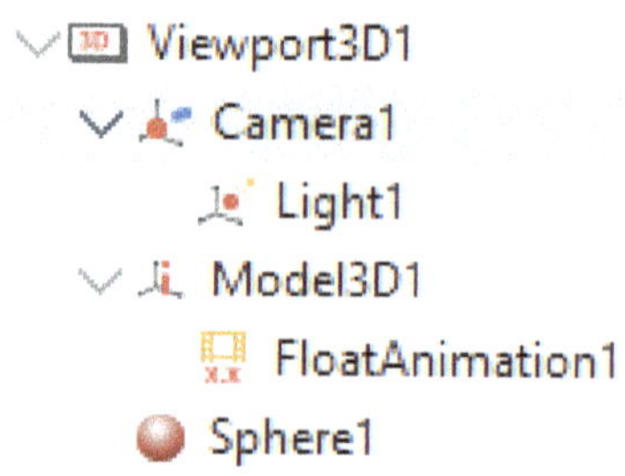

Figure 76.39 Structure window showing Viewport3D1 and its children

Set its **StopValue** property values to +10.

Set its **StartFromCurrent** property to **True**.

Set its property **PropertyName** to **Position.X**.

Set its **Loop** property to **True**.

Set its **Duration** property to **10**. This property value controls the speed of the animation.

Set its **AutoReverse** property to **True**.

Double click `btnAnimate` and `btnStopAnimation` buttons to create two **OnClick** event handlers. **Add** the code shown in *Table 76.19* to these event handlers.

```
Procedure TfrmThreeDObject.btnAnimateClick(Sender : TObject);
  Begin
    FloatAnimation1.Enabled := True;
  End;

Procedure TfrmThreeDObject.btnStopAnimationClick(Sender : TObject);
  Begin
    FloatAnimation1.Enabled := False;
    btnResetObjectPositionsClick(Sender);
    btnResetObjectRotationsClick(Sender);
  End;
```

Table 76.19 OnChange event handlers for five of the buttons

Press **Shift+Ctrl+S** to save the project and unit files.

Press **Shift+Ctrl+F9** to compile and run the project.

Maximise the form.

Rotate the object 180° about the Z axis.

Rotate the object 270° about the Y axis. Remeber that rotations use the object's local coordinates. The orientation of the world coordinates is not changed (only camera rotations can change the relationship with these).

Move the object in the X direction -6.7 units, i.e. 6.7 units to the left.

Click the `Animate Object` button to start the animation. The object should now move across the form to the right in the positive X direction. When it reaches the righthand edge of the form, it should stop and then start off moving in reverse to the left across the form until it reaches its start position whereupon it stops before repeating the movement cycle. To stop the animation at any time press the `Stop Animation` button.

To make the movement more realistic, each wheel should be animated to rotate. This can be attempted in code as follows

```
For Var i := 27 To 28
  Do TAnimator.AnimateFloat(Model3D1.MeshCollection[i],'RotationAngle.Z', 360, 10);
```

Unfortunately, this doesn't work because all six wheels are created together as follows

Mesh 27 = 6 wheel rims, Mesh 28 = 6 sets of wheel spokes, Mesh 29 = 6 wheel hubs

To experiment with rotations of parts of a model (object), you must search for a model which will support this, e.g. a helicopter where there are separate meshes for its rotors. You could try the Mars Ingenuity helicopter 3D model which does support rotor animation (https://mars.nasa.gov/resources/25043/mars-ingenuity-helicopter-3d-model) or alternatively search a specialist site such as https://www.turbosquid.com.

Different platforms

The FireMonkey library supports different 3D APIs:

- DirectX on Windows
- Full OpenGL on Mac
- OpenGL ES on mobiles - a cut down version of the OpenGL library.

Fortunately, Delphi takes care of which API to use, all that a programmer has to do is to select the target platform.

FireMonkey 3D graphics provides the abstract class **TContext3D** that declares virtual drawing methods (see *Table 76.4*) that are implemented differently on different targets.

3D application versus blank multi-device application

We have now covered both types of multi-device application. For a blank application, the programmer has to manually add a viewport whereas in a 3D application, the viewport is provided automatically.

With a blank application, we were able to use 2D controls because essentially our form was derived from **TForm**. In a 3D application, the form is derived from **TForm3D** with the consequence that 2D controls are not directly supported. Instead, we need to use a **T3DLayout** component with its **Projection** property set to **Screen**. The area of the 3D form covered by the **TLayer3D** component now becomes two-dimensional allowing us to place 2D controls on it.

Methane molecule project

Select File|New|Multi-device Application - Delphi then **select** 3D Application from the Multi-device Application window (scroll down to find it) to create a 3D application.

Save the project as `MethaneProject.dproj` and its form unit as `MethaneUnit.pas`.

Change the **Name** property of the form to `frmMethane` and its **Caption** property to `Methane Project`.

Set its **Color** property to **White**.

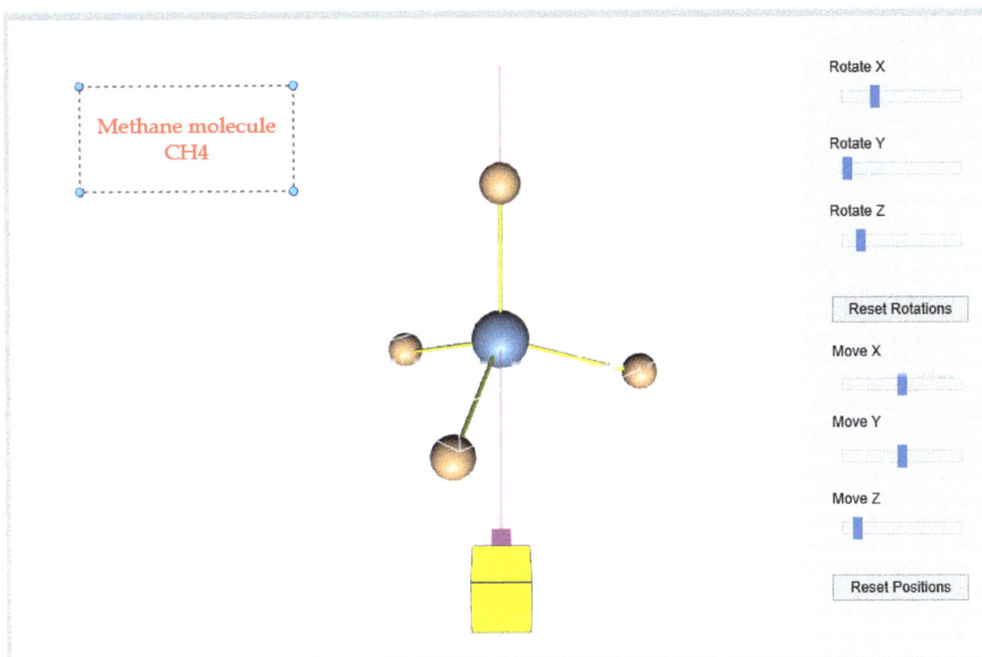

Figure 76.40 User interface for Methane project

Add a **TLayer3D** component from the 3D Layers palette to the form. **Set** its **Projection** property to **Screen**, its **Align** property to **Right** and its **Width** to 150.

Add six **TTrackBar** controls, six **TLabel** components, and two **TButton** controls from the Standard palette to this layer. **Arrange** then as shown in *Figure 76.40*. **Rename** the first three `tbRotateX`, `tbRotateY`, `tbRotateZ`, and the next three `tbMoveX`, `tbMoveY`, `tbMoveZ`, respectively. **Name** the labels `lblRotateX`, `lblRotateY`, `lblRotateZ`, `lblMoveX`, `lblMoveY`, `lblMoveZ`, respectively.

Set their Text property to Rotate X, Rotate Y, Rotate Z, Move X, Move Y, Move Z, respectively. **Rename** the two buttons, btnResetRotations and btnResetPositions, respectively. **Change** their **Text** property to Reset Rotations and Reset Positions, respectively.

Add a **TCamera** component to the form and set its **Position.X** and **Position.Y** properties to 0, and its **Position.Z** property to -10.

Select the form and set its **UsingDesignCamera** property to **False**.

Add a **TDummy** component, Dummy1, from the **3D Scene** palette to the form.

Add a **TCylinder** component, Cylinder1, from the **3D Shapes** palette to the **TDummy** component, **set Depth** and **Width** to 0.1 and **Height** to 4. - *Figure 76.41*.

Do the same for two more **TCylinder** components, Cylinder2 and Cylinder3.

Set the **RotationAngle.Z** to 120 and 240, respectively, for these two cylinders - *Figure 76.42* and *Figure 76.43*.

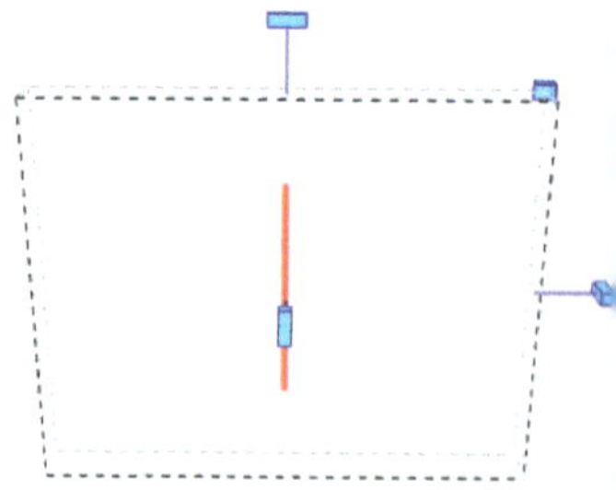

Figure 76.41 TDummy containing one cylinder

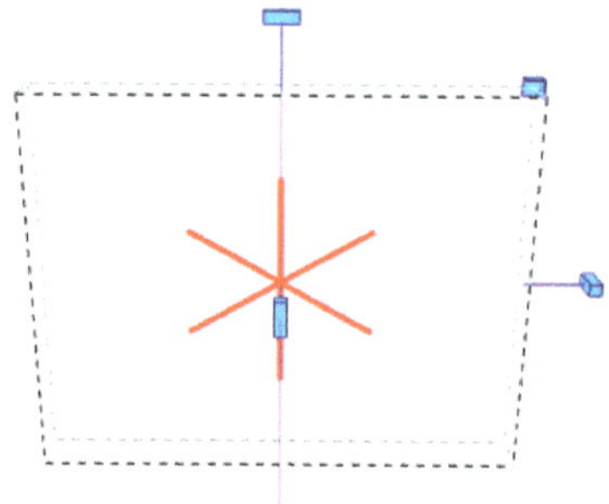

Figure 76.42 TDummy containing three cylinders at 120° to each other

Rotate Cylinder1 anticlockwise about X axis 19.5° - **RotationAngle.X** = -19.5.

Rotate Cylinder2 anticlockwise about X axis 19.5° - **RotationAngle.X** = -19.5.

Rotate Cylinder3 anticlockwise about X axis 19.5° - **RotationAngle.X** = -19.5.

Move Cylinder1 down (+ve) Y axis 1.885 units - elevation of Cylinder3 is shown in *Figure 76.44*, but the same elevation applies to Cylinder1. Cylinder1 is aligned with the Y axis. This means that its lower end is 0.668 units along the Z axis in the positive direction (**Rotate** the red line anticlockwise to align with the Y axis to see this). Therefore, **set Position.Z** to -0.668 to bring its lower end to (0, 0, 0).

Move Cylinder2 leftwards (-ve) along X axis 1.663 units - projection onto X axis is shown for Cylinder3 in *Figure 76.45* but it is the same magnitude for Cylinder2 except it applies to the negative X axis. **Move** Cylinder2 upwards (-ve) along Y axis 0.943 units - projection onto Y axis is shown for Cylinder3 in *Figure 76.45* but it is the same for Cylinder2. **Set Position.Z** to -0.668 to bring its lower end to (0, 0, 0).

Move Cylinder3 rightwards (+ve) along X axis 1.633 units.

Move Cylinder3 upwards (-ve) along Y axis 0.943 units. **Set Position.Z** to -0.668 to bring its lower end to (0, 0, 0).

Figure 76.46 shows the outcome.

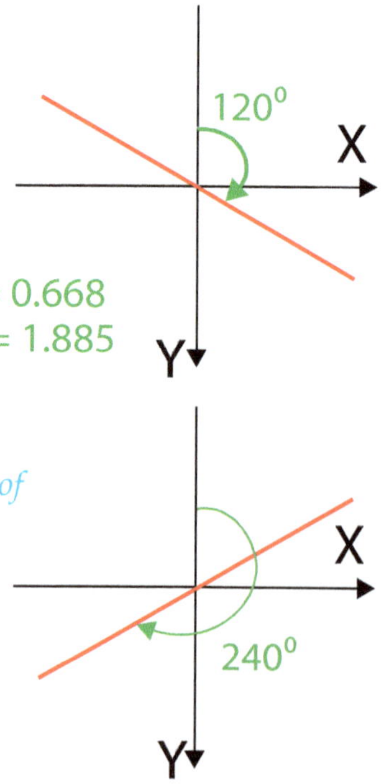

Figure 76.43 Cylinder 2 and Cylinder3 after their respective rotations about the Z axis

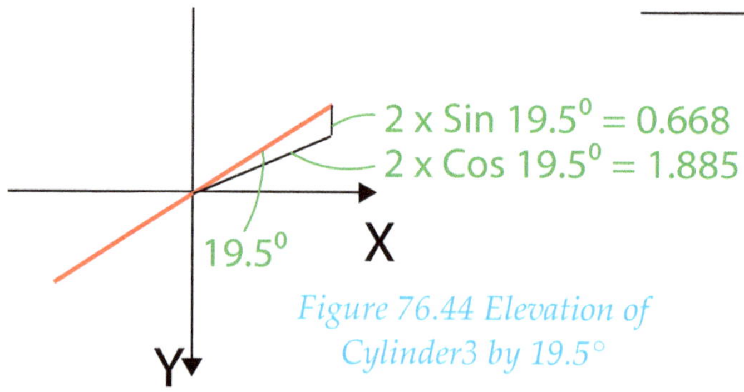

Figure 76.44 Elevation of Cylinder3 by 19.5°

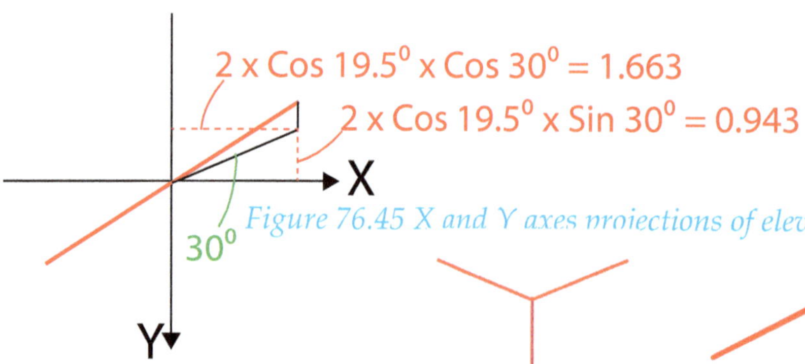

Figure 76.45 X and Y axes projections of elevated Cylinder3

Figure 76.46 Three cylinders elevated and joined at their upper ends shown in plan and side views

Add another **TCylinder**, `Cylinder4`, to `Dummy1`.

Set its **Depth** and **Width** to 0.1 and **Height** to 4. **Set** its **Position.Z** to 2.

Rotate `Dummy1` clockwise about the Y axis by 90° so the Z axis now points to the right as shown in *Figure 76.47* and the X axis now points out of the screen.

Now **rotate** `Cylinder4` about the X axis 90° - **RotationAngle.X = 90**.

The result is shown in *Figure 76.48*.

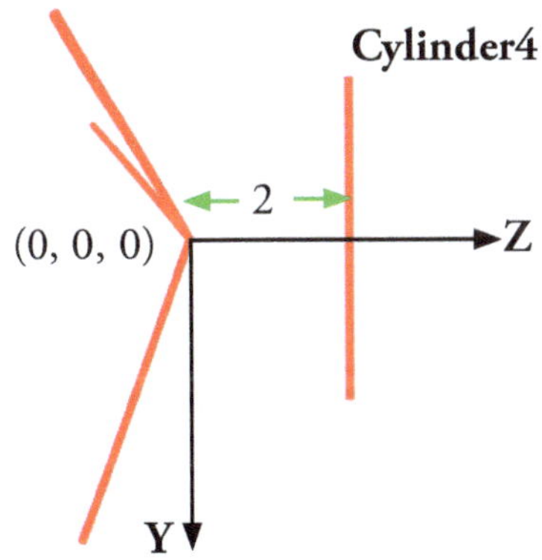

Figure 76.47 Dummy1 rotated about

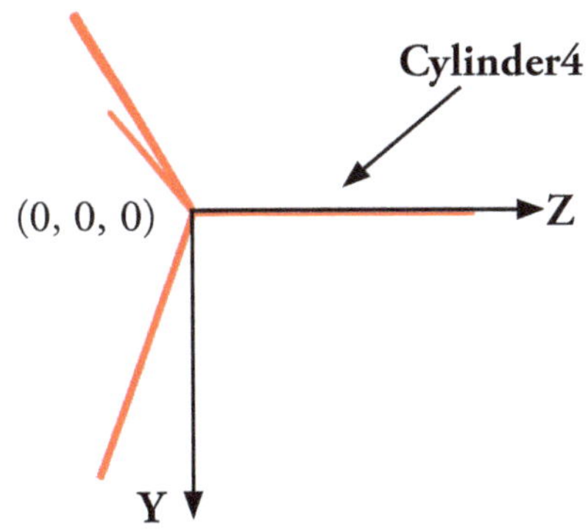

Figure 76.48 Dummy1 rotated about the Y axis by 90° and Cylinder4 rotated about X axis 90°

Add a **TSphere**, `Sphere1`, to `Dummy1`. **Set** its **Depth**, **Height** and **Width** to 1.5.

Its **Position.X**, **Position.Y** and **Position.Z** should be 0, by default.

Set its **SubDivisionsAxes** property to 32 and **SubDivisionsHeight** property to 24 to smooth its surface when rendered.

Figure 76.49 shows the result.

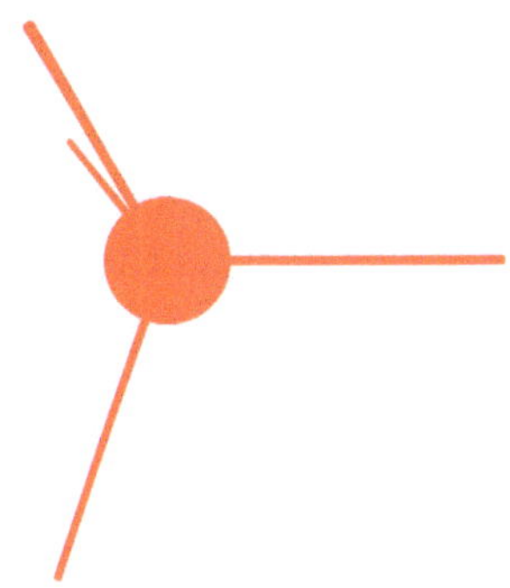

Figure 76.49 TSphere, Sphere1, added

Add four more **TSpheres** to `Dummy1`.

Set their coordinates as follows

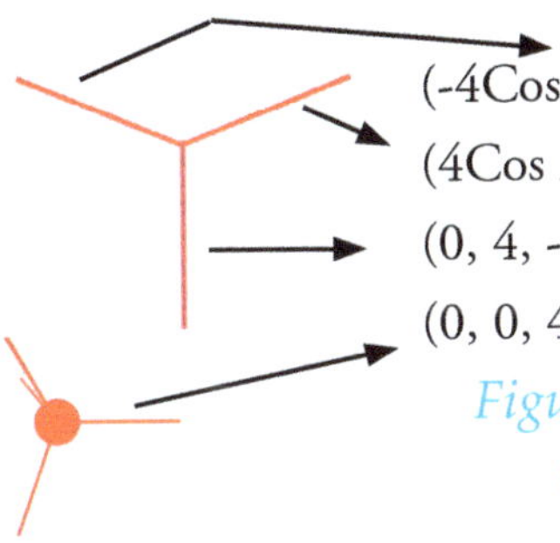

(-4Cos 30, -4Sin 30, -1.336) = (-3.464, -2, -1.336)

(4Cos 30, -4Sin 30, -1.336) = (3.464, -2, -1.336)

(0, 4, -1.336)

(0, 0, 4)

Figure 76.50 Coordinates for the four spheres, Sphere2, ..., Sphere5

Set their **SubDivisionsAxes** to 32 and **SubDivisionsHeight** to 24.

Figure 76.51 shows the result when the program is executed and `Dummy1` is rotated to give a clear view of all five spheres.

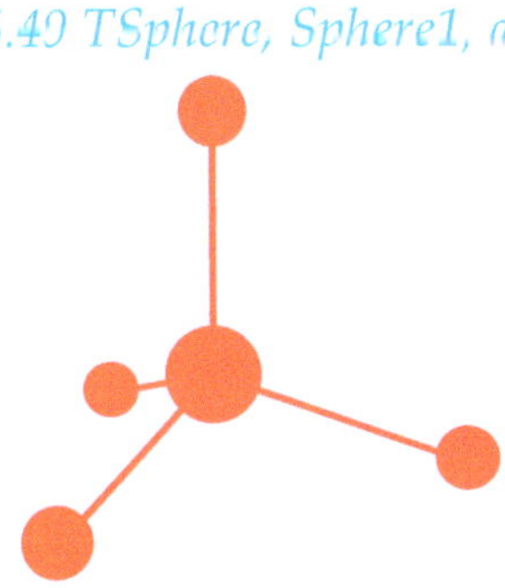

Figure 76.51 The 3D model so far

Add three **TLightMaterialSource** components, `LightMaterialSource1`, `LightMaterialSource2`, `LightMaterialSource3`, from the **Materials** palette to the form. These are needed so that the spheres may reflect light when illuminated.

Assign `LightMaterialSource1` to the **MaterialSource** property of `Sphere2` to `Sphere5`.

Assign `LightMaterialSource2` to the **MaterialSource** property of `Sphere1`.

Assign `LightMaterialSource3` to the **MaterialSource** property of `Cylinder1` to `Cylinder4`.

Set the **Diffuse** property of `LightMaterialSource1` to **SandyBrown**.

Set the **Diffuse** property of `LightMaterialSource2` to **SteelBlue**.

Set the **Diffuse** property of `LightMaterialSource3` to **Yellow**.

Add a **TLight** component, `Light1`, from the **3D Scene** palette to the camera.

LightType property should be **Directional** and **Color White**.

Figure 76.52 shows the result when the program is executed and `Dummy1` is rotated to give a clear view of all five spheres.

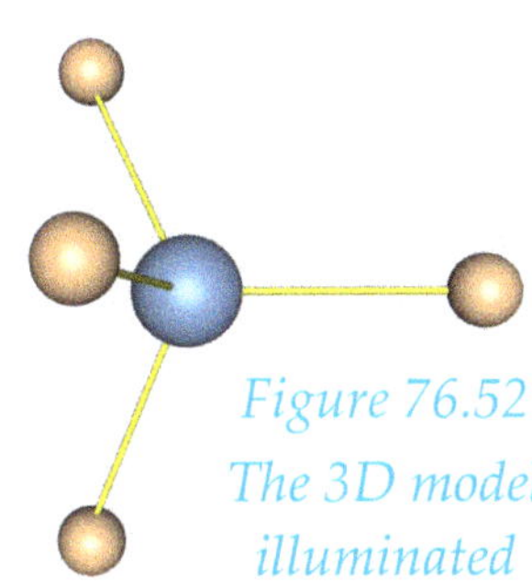

Figure 76.52 The 3D model illuminated

Reset RotationAngle.Y of `Dummy1` to 0.

Set RotationAngle.X of `Dummy1` to 90 and then **set RotationAngle.Z** to 45.

When rotating `Dummy1` about two axes, the order of the rotation operations is important because rotations are not commutative.

Refactor (Ctrl Shift E) the following as shown

- Sphere1 → sphCarbon
- Sphere2 → sphHydrogen4
- Sphere3 → sphHydrogen2
- Sphere4 → sphHydrogen3
- Sphere5 → sphHydrogen1
- Cylinder1 → cylBond1
- Cylinder2 → cylBond2
- Cylinder3 → cylBond3
- Cylinder4 → cylBond4

Add a **TTextLayer3D** component, `TextLayer3D1`, to the form and **set** its **Text** property to `Methane molecule CH4`, its **Color** property to **Red**, its **Font Family** to **Book Antiqua**, its **Font Size** to 18, and its **Font Style** property **fsBold** to True. **Set** its **Position.X** property to 145 and its **Position.Y** property to 98.

Create event handlers for events **OnCreate**, **OnClick** and **OnChange** as shown in *Table 76.20*.

Save All then compile and run.

Figure 76.52 shows the result.

Try rotating and moving the model.

Note that rotating and moving `Dummy1` moves its children i.e the components which collectively make up the methane molecule.

Change the target platform to Android 32-bit if you have an Android device connected to a USB port and build and deploy the Methane project. You may need to set the **Font Size** for the labels and buttons to 10 in the Object Inspector then back to 12 to get the system `Form3DCreate` event handler to correctly resize these for Android (I think it is a bug in Delphi 10.4).

```
Procedure TfrmMethane.btnResetPositionsClick(Sender : TObject);
  Begin
    Dummy1.Position.X := 0;
    Dummy1.Position.Y := 0;
    Dummy1.Position.Z := 0;
    tbMoveX.Value := 0;
    tbMoveY.Value := 0;
    tbMoveZ.Value := 0;
  End;
Procedure TfrmMethane.btnResetRotationsClick(Sender : TObject);
  Begin
    Dummy1.RotationAngle.X := 90;
    Dummy1.RotationAngle.Y := 0;
    Dummy1.RotationAngle.Z := 45;
    tbRotateX.Value := 90;
    tbRotateY.Value := 0;
    tbRotateZ.Value := 45;
  End;
Procedure TfrmMethane.Form3DCreate(Sender : TObject);
  Begin
    {$IFDEF ANDROID}
      btnResetRotations.TextSettings.Font.Size := 10;
      btnResetRotations.Height := 30;
      btnResetPositions.TextSettings.Font.Size := 10;
      btnResetPositions.Height := 30;
      lblRotateX.TextSettings.Font.Size := 10;
      lblRotateY.TextSettings.Font.Size := 10;
      lblRotateZ.TextSettings.Font.Size := 10;
      lblMoveX.TextSettings.Font.Size := 10;
      lblMoveY.TextSettings.Font.Size := 10;
      lblMoveZ.TextSettings.Font.Size := 10;
    {$ENDIF}
  End;
Procedure TfrmMethane.tbMoveXChange(Sender : TObject);
  Begin
    Dummy1.Position.X := tbMoveX.Value;
  End;
Procedure TfrmMethane.tbMoveYChange(Sender : TObject);
  Begin
    Dummy1.Position.Y := tbMoveY.Value;
  End;
Procedure TfrmMethane.tbMoveZChange(Sender : TObject);
  Begin
    Dummy1.Position.Z := tbMoveZ.Value;
  End;
Procedure TfrmMethane.tbRotateXChange(Sender : TObject);
  Begin
    Dummy1.RotationAngle.X := tbRotateX.Value;
  End;
Procedure TfrmMethane.tbRotateYChange(Sender : TObject);
  Begin
    Dummy1.RotationAngle.Y := tbRotateY.Value;
  End;
Procedure TfrmMethane.tbRotateZChange(Sender : TObject);
  Begin
    Dummy1.RotationAngle.Z := tbRotateZ.Value;
  End;
End.
```

Table 76.20 Implementation section of MethaneUnit.pas

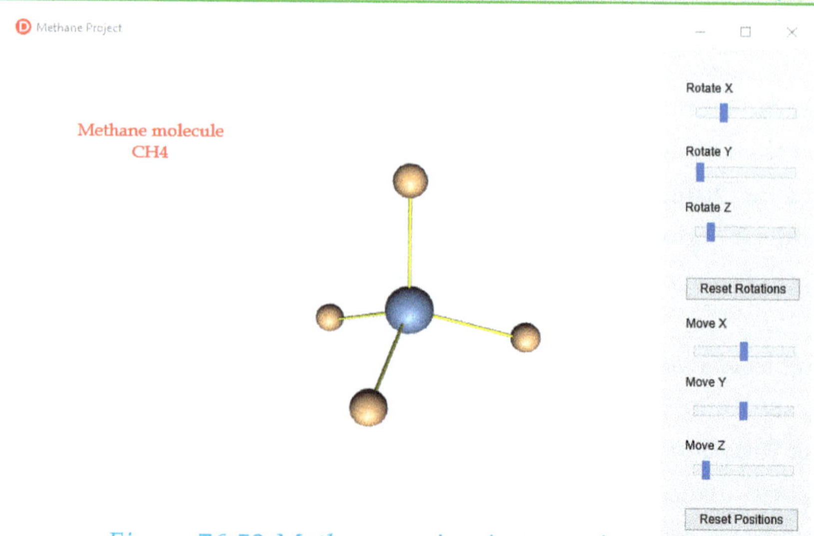

Figure 76.52 Methane project in execution

MoleculeHero[6]

Pawel Glowacki created a more sophisticated molecular modelling application which he called **Molecule Hero**. Sadly Pawel died in 2017 but his application is still available from https://github.com/pglowack/MoleculeHero.

The application reads data from the **Protein Data Bank** - http://www.wwpdb.org/.

Figure 76.53 shows **Molecule Hero** in execution.

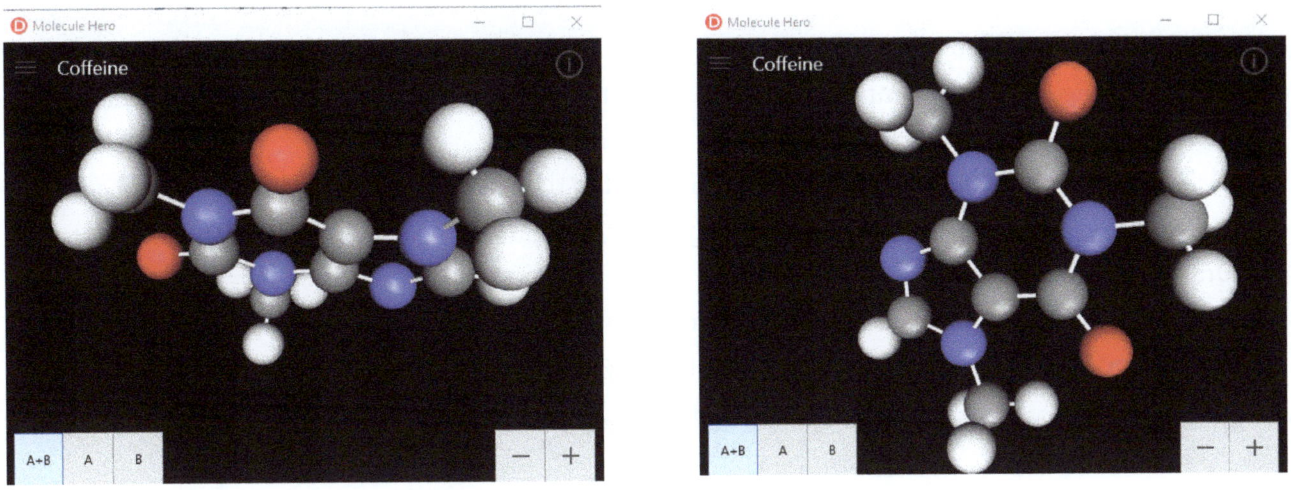

Figure 76.53 Molecule Hero in execution showing two views of the caffeine molecule

6 The MIT License (MIT) Copyright (c) 2015 SUPERLOLO

77 Advanced graphics 2

Graph plotting

Purpose: To learn how to create a Delphi program to graph functions

The options available in Delphi for plotting graphs are

1. TeeChart which provides complete, quick, and easy-to-use charting for business, real-time, financial, and scientific applications.
2. FMX applications (Multi-Device) can use **TPlotGrid** to draw graphs of functions, e.g. sin and cosine - see https://docwiki.embarcadero.com/CodeExamples/Sydney/en/FMXTPlotGrid_(Delphi)
3. Drawing primitives such as **Canvas.DrawLine** - see *Figure 77.1* and *Figure 77.2*.

This chapter uses option 3. It will not be described in detail for space reasons and because much can be learned by examining the source code which is spread over seven sections.

Essentially, the process may be broken down into the following steps:

1. Provide data values in array/list
2. Find minimal and maximal values for X and Y components
3. Calculate linear formulas for mapping data values to screen coordinates
4. Draw line segments applying formulas to get coordinates
5. If needed, draw axes

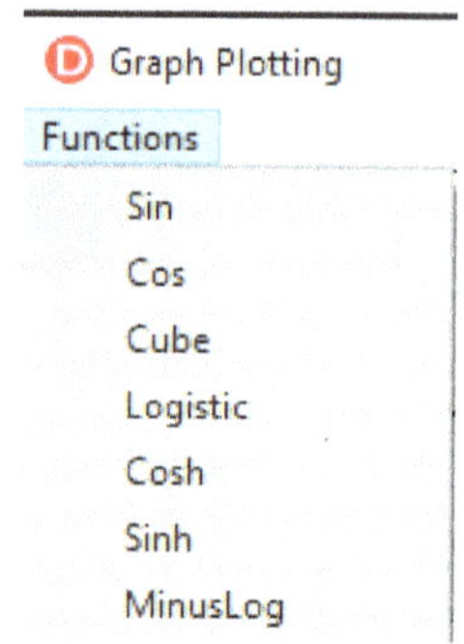

Figure 77.1 Functions menu options

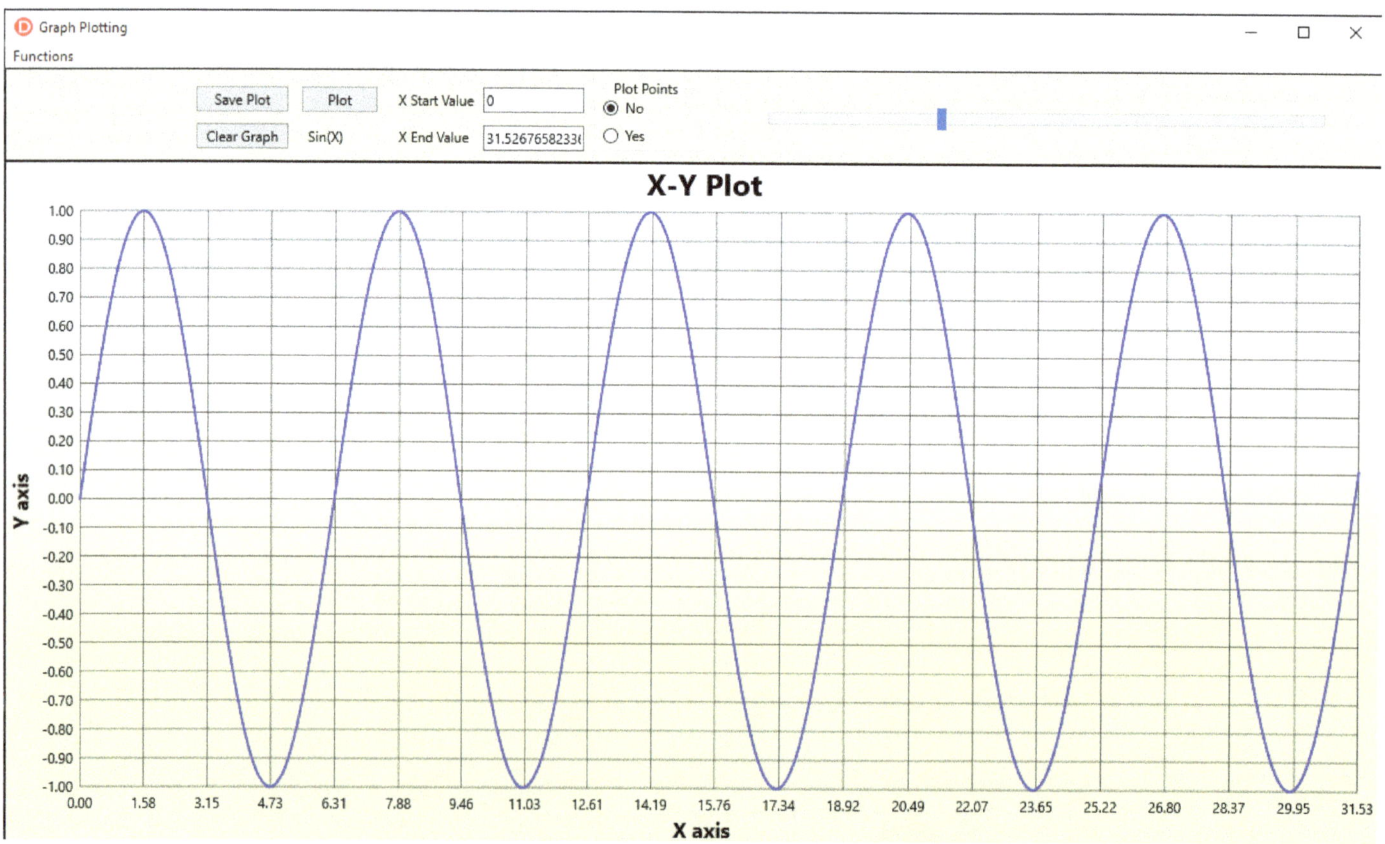

Figure 77.2 GraphPlotWithFunctionPointersProject in execution

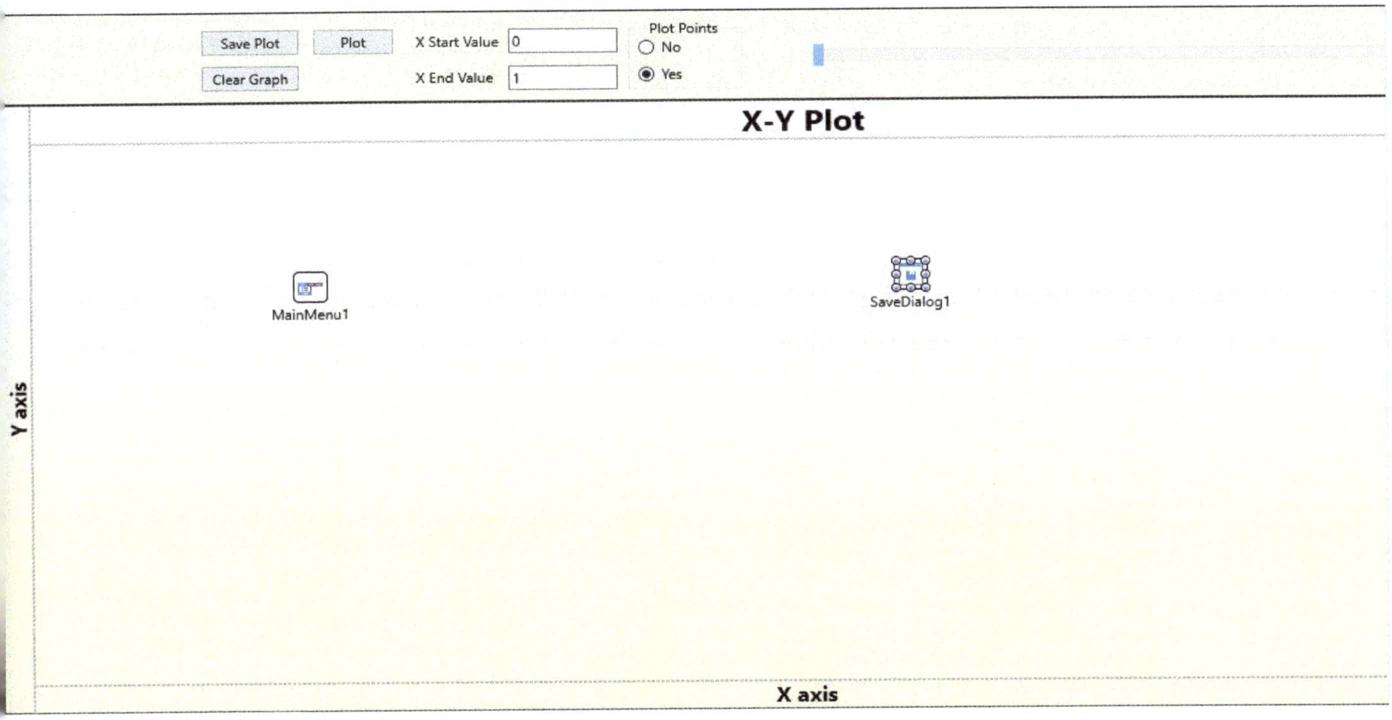

Figure 77.3 GraphPlotWithFunctionPointersProject User Interface design

Create a multi-device application in Delphi with the user interface shown in *Figure 77.3* and *Figure 77.4*. - see *Table 77.2* for the data types and procedures/ functions used. **Create** the event handlers shown in *Table 77.2* to *Table 77.7*.

Create the remaining procedures/functions. **Save**, **Compile** and **run**.

This exercise was inspired by Quark Cube's Creating a Plot (Delphi XE10, FireMonkey) YouTube® exercise.

```
Unit GraphPlotWithFunctionPointers;

Interface

Uses
  System.SysUtils, System.Types, System.UITypes,
  System.Classes, System.Variants, FMX.Types,
  FMX.Controls, FMX.Forms, FMX.Graphics,
  FMX.Dialogs, FMX.Controls.Presentation,
  FMX.StdCtrls, FMX.Layouts,
  FMX.Objects, Math, FMX.ListBox, FMX.Menus, FMX.Edit,
  System.ImageList, FMX.ImgList, Vcl.BaseImageCollection,
  FMX.Printer;

  Const cEulersNumber = 2.71828182845904523536O;
```

Table 77.1 GraphPlotWithFunctionPointers.pas - first section

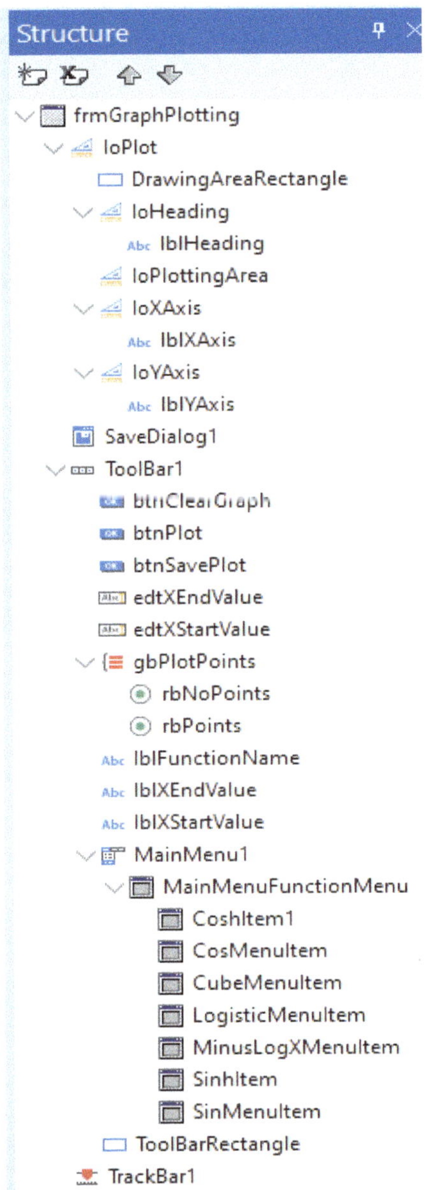

Figure 77.4 Structure window for GraphPlotWithFunctionPointersProject User Interface design

```
TfrmGraphPlotting = Class(TForm)
                    loPlot: TLayout; loXAxis: TLayout;
                    loYAxis: TLayout;loHeading: TLayout;
                    loPlottingArea: TLayout;
                    lblXAxis: TLabel; lblYAxis: TLabel;
                    lblHeading: TLabel;
                    DrawingAreaRectangle: TRectangle;
                    ToolBar1: TToolBar;
                    btnSavePlot: TButton;
                    MainMenu1: TMainMenu;
                    MainMenuFunctionMenu: TMenuItem;
                    SinMenuItem: TMenuItem;
                    CosMenuItem: TMenuItem;
                    CubeMenuItem: TMenuItem;
                    btnPlot: TButton;
                    LogisticMenuItem: TMenuItem;
                    edtXStartValue: TEdit;
                    lblXStartValue: TLabel;
                    edtXEndValue: TEdit;
                    lblXEndValue: TLabel;
                    btnClearGraph: TButton;
                    CoshItem1: TMenuItem; SinhItem: TMenuItem; MinusLogXMenuItem: TMenuItem;
                    lblFunctionName: TLabel;
                    gbPlotPoints: TGroupBox;
                    rbNoPoints: TRadioButton;
                    rbPoints: TRadioButton;
                    ToolBarRectangle: TRectangle;
                    SaveDialog1 : TSaveDialog;
                    TrackBar1: TTrackBar;
                    Procedure FormCreate(Sender : TObject);
                    Procedure btnSavePlotClick(Sender : TObject);
                    Procedure btnPlotClick(Sender : TObject);
                    Procedure SinMenuItemClick(Sender : TObject);
                    Procedure CosMenuItemClick(Sender : TObject);
                    Procedure CubeMenuItemClick(Sender : TObject);
                    Procedure LogisticMenuItemClick(Sender : TObject);
                    Procedure btnClearGraphClick(Sender : TObject);
                    Procedure CoshItem1Click(Sender : TObject);
                    Procedure SinhItemClick(Sender : TObject);
                    Procedure loPlottingAreaPaint(Sender : TObject; Canvas : TCanvas;
                                                  Const ARect : TRectF);
                    Procedure MinusLogXMenuItemClick(Sender : TObject);
                    Procedure TrackBar1Change(Sender: TObject);
                    Private
                      UnitsDisplaySpace : Single;
                      NoOfDecimalPlaces : Integer;
                      GridScale : Integer;
                      StartValue, EndValue : Single;
                      XMax, YMax, XMin, YMin, XRange, YRange : Single;
                      Procedure DrawScales(Canvas : TCanvas; PlottingAreaRectangle : TRectF;
                        NoOfDecimalPlaces, GridScale : Integer; UnitsDisplaySpace : Single);
                      Procedure PlottingArea(Var PlottingAreaRectangle : TRectF;
                         NoOfDecimalPlaces : Integer);
                      Public
                        PlottingData : Array Of TPointF;
                        Procedure GeneratePlotData(FromValue, ToValue : Single);
                        Procedure CheckPlotData;
                        Function CalculateXCoord(XCoord : Single;
                          PlottingAreaRectangle : TRectF) : Single;
                        Function CalculateYCoord(YCoord : Single;
                          PlottingAreaRectangle : TRectF) : Single;
                        Function CalculatePosition(Position : Integer;
                          PlottingAreaRectangle : TRectF) : TPointF;
                        Procedure DrawGraph(PlottingData : Array Of TPointF; aRect : TRectF;
                          Canvas : TCanvas);
                    End;
```

P

Table 77.2 GraphPlotWithFunctionPointers.pas - second section

Table 77.3 GraphPlotWithFunctionPointers.pas - Third section

P

```
  TFunctionVar = Function (Const Argument : Extended) : Extended;

Var
  frmGraphPlotting : TfrmGraphPlotting;
  FunctionVar : TFunctionVar = Nil;
  AnArgument : Integer;
  StateOfCanvas : TCanvasSaveState;
  Cleared : Boolean = True;
  ScalesDrawn : Boolean = False;
Implementation
{$R *.fmx}
  Procedure TfrmGraphPlotting.FormCreate(Sender : TObject);
    Begin
      SinMenuItemClick(Sender);
      edtXEndValue.Text := FloatToStr(2*cPi);
      TrackBar1.Value := 2*cPi;
      TrackBar1.Enabled := True;
    End;
  Procedure TfrmGraphPlotting.btnClearGraphClick(Sender: TObject);
    Var
      aBrush : TBrush;
    Begin
      aBrush := TBrush.Create(TBrushKind.Gradient, $FFF7FDD2);
      loPlottingArea.Canvas.BeginScene;
      loPlottingArea.Canvas.FillRect(loPlottingArea.AbsoluteRect, 1, aBrush);
      loPlottingArea.Canvas.EndScene;
      frmGraphPlotting.Invalidate;
      aBrush.Destroy;
      Cleared := True;
      ScalesDrawn := False;
    End;
  Procedure TfrmGraphPlotting.btnSavePlotClick(Sender : TObject);
    Var
      BitMap : TBitMap;
      PlotAreaRect : TRectF;
    Begin
      PlotAreaRect := RectF(0, 0, loPlot.Width*2, loPlot.Height*2);
      BitMap := TBitMap.Create(Round(PlotAreaRect.Width), Round(PlotAreaRect.Height));
      If SaveDialog1.Execute
        Then
          Begin
            If BitMap.Canvas.BeginScene
              Then
                Begin
                  Try
                    loPlot.PaintTo(BitMap.Canvas, PlotAreaRect);
                  Finally
                    BitMap.Canvas.EndScene;
                  End;
                  BitMap.SaveToFile(SaveDialog1.Filename);
                End;
          End;
    End;
  Procedure TfrmGraphPlotting.btnPlotClick(Sender : TObject);
    Var
      aRect : TRectF;
      StartValue, Endvalue : TPointF;
    Begin
      Cleared := False;
      GeneratePlotData(StrToFloat(edtXStartValue.Text), StrToFloat(edtXEndValue.Text));
      CheckPlotData;
      aRect := loPlottingArea.AbsoluteRect;
      StateOfCanvas := loPlottingArea.Canvas.SaveState;
      DrawGraph(PlottingData, loPlottingArea.AbsoluteRect, loPlottingArea.Canvas);
    End;
```

```
Function TfrmGraphPlotting.CalculatePosition(Position : Integer; PlottingAreaRectangle : TRectF): TPointF;
  Begin
    Result := PointF(CalculateXCoord(PlottingData[Position].X, PlottingAreaRectangle),
                     CalculateYCoord(PlottingData[Position].Y, PlottingAreaRectangle));
  End;
Function TfrmGraphPlotting.CalculateXCoord(XCoord : Single; PlottingAreaRectangle : TRectF): Single;
  Begin
    Result := PlottingAreaRectangle.Left + (((XCoord - XMin)/XRange) * (PlottingAreaRectangle.Width - 5));
  End;
Function TfrmGraphPlotting.CalculateYCoord(YCoord : Single; PlottingAreaRectangle : TRectF): Single;
  Begin
    Result := PlottingAreaRectangle.Bottom - (((YCoord - YMin)/YRange) * PlottingAreaRectangle.Height);
  End;
Procedure TfrmGraphPlotting.CheckPlotData;
  Var
    i, L : Integer;
    Point : TPointF;
  Begin
    XMin := 0; XMax := 1; YMin := 0; YMax := 1;
    If High(PlottingData) >= 0
      Then
        Begin
          Point := PlottingData[0];
          XMin := Point.X;
          YMin := Point.Y;
          YMax := Point.Y;
          L := Length(PlottingData);
          For i := 1 To L - 1
            Do
              Begin
                Point := PlottingData[i];
                If Point.X > XMax
                  Then XMax := Point.X;
                If Point.X < XMin
                  Then XMin := Point.X;
                If Point.Y > YMax
                  Then YMax := Point.Y;
                If Point.Y < YMin
                  Then YMin := Point.Y;
              End;
        End;
    XRange := XMax - XMin;
    YRange := YMax - YMin;
  End;
Procedure TfrmGraphPlotting.GeneratePlotData(FromValue, ToValue : Single);
  Var
    Step, X, Y : Single;
    SizeOfArray, i : Integer;
  Begin
    StartValue := FromValue;
    EndValue := ToValue;
    Step := 0.06125;
    SizeOfArray := Trunc((EndValue - StartValue)/Step) + 1;   //StartValue is not represented accurately
    SetLength(PlottingData, SizeOfArray);
    X := StartValue;
    For i := 0 To Length(PlottingData) - 2
      Do
        Begin
          Y := FunctionVar(X);
          PlottingData[i] := PointF(X, Y);
          X := X + Step;
        End;
     X := EndValue;
     Y := FunctionVar(X);
     PlottingData[Length(PlottingData) - 1] := PointF(X, Y);
  End;
```

P

Table 77.4 GraphPlotWithFunctionPointers.pas - fourth section

```
Procedure TfrmGraphPlotting.loPlottingAreaPaint(Sender : TObject;
                                                 Canvas : TCanvas;
                                                 Const ARect : TRectF);
  Begin
    If Not Cleared Then DrawGraph(PlottingData, aRect, Canvas);
  End;

Procedure TfrmGraphPlotting.PlottingArea(Var PlottingAreaRectangle : TRectF;
                                         NoOfDecimalPlaces : Integer);
  Var
    CurrentPoint : TPointF;
    NextPoint : TPointF;
    S : String;
  Begin
    S := FloatToStrF(YMax, TFloatFormat.ffFixed, 7, NoOfDecimalPlaces);
    CurrentPoint.X := Canvas.TextWidth(S);
    CurrentPoint.Y := Canvas.TextHeight(S);
    S := FloatToStrF(YMin, TFloatFormat.ffFixed, 7, NoOfDecimalPlaces);
    NextPoint.X := Canvas.TextWidth(S);
    NextPoint.Y := Canvas.TextHeight(S);
    If CurrentPoint.X > NextPoint.X
      Then NextPoint.X := CurrentPoint.X;
    If CurrentPoint.Y > NextPoint.Y
      Then NextPoint.Y := CurrentPoint.Y;
    PlottingAreaRectangle.Inflate(-NextPoint.X, -NextPoint.Y);
    NextPoint.X := NextPoint.X * 0.5;
    NextPoint.Y := NextPoint.Y * 0.5;
    PlottingAreaRectangle.Offset(NextPoint.X, -NextPoint.Y);
  End;

Procedure TfrmGraphPlotting.DrawGraph(PlottingData : Array Of TPointF; aRect : TRectF;
                                                              Canvas : TCanvas);
  Var
    i : Integer;
    CurrentPoint : TPointF;
    NextPoint : TPointF;
    PlottingAreaRectangle : TRectF;
    Begin
      PlottingAreaRectangle := aRect;
      NoOfDecimalPlaces := 2;
      UnitsDisplaySpace := 6;
      GridScale := 20;
      Try
        Canvas.BeginScene;
          PlottingArea(PlottingAreaRectangle, NoOfDecimalPlaces);
          DrawScales(Canvas, PlottingAreaRectangle, NoOfDecimalPlaces,
                     GridScale,UnitsDisplaySpace);
          ScalesDrawn := True;
          Canvas.Stroke.Color := TAlphaColors.Blue;
          Canvas.Stroke.Thickness := 2;
          For i := 0 To Length(PlottingData) - 2
            Do
              Begin
                CurrentPoint := CalculatePosition(i, PlottingAreaRectangle);
                NextPoint := CalculatePosition(i + 1, PlottingAreaRectangle);
                Canvas.DrawLine(CurrentPoint, NextPoint, 1);
                If rbPoints.IsChecked
                  Then Canvas.DrawEllipse(RectF(CurrentPoint.X - 1, CurrentPoint.Y - 1,
                                          CurrentPoint.X + 1, CurrentPoint.Y + 1), 1);
              End;
        Finally Canvas.EndScene;
      End;
      If rbPoints.IsChecked
        Then Canvas.DrawEllipse(RectF(NextPoint.X - 1, NextPoint.Y - 1, NextPoint.X + 1,
                                NextPoint.Y + 1), 1);
  End;
```

Table 77.5 GraphPlotWithFunctionPointers.pas - fifth section

```
Procedure TfrmGraphPlotting.DrawScales(Canvas : TCanvas; PlottingAreaRectangle : TRectF;
                                       NoOfDecimalPlaces, GridScale : Integer;
                                       UnitsDisplaySpace : Single);
  Var
    i : Integer;
    CurrentPoint : TPointF; NextPoint : TPointF; Xt : TRectF;
    Step, Position, P : Single;
    S : String;
  Begin
    Canvas.Stroke.Color := TAlphaColors.Black;
    Canvas.Stroke.Thickness := 0.5;
    Step := YRange/GridScale;
    Position := YMin;
    For i := 0 To GridScale
      Do
        Begin
          P := CalculateYCoord(Position, PlottingAreaRectangle);
          S := FloatToStrF(Position, TFloatFormat.ffFixed, 7, NoOfDecimalPlaces);
          CurrentPoint.X := Canvas.TextWidth(S);
          CurrentPoint.Y := Canvas.TextHeight(S) * 0.5;
          Xt := RectF(PlottingAreaRectangle.Left - CurrentPoint.X - UnitsDisplaySpace,
              P - CurrentPoint.Y, PlottingAreaRectangle.Left - UnitsDisplaySpace, P + CurrentPoint.Y);
          Canvas.Fill.Color := TAlphaColors.Black;
          Canvas.FillText(Xt, S, False, 1, [], TTextAlign.Leading);
          Canvas.DrawLine(PointF(PlottingAreaRectangle.Left, P),
                          PointF(PlottingAreaRectangle.Right - 5, P), 1);
          Position := Position + Step;
          If Position > YMax
            Then Position := YMax;
        End;
    Step := XRange/GridScale;
    Position := XMin;
    For i := 0 To GridScale
      Do
        Begin
          P := CalculateXCoord(Position, PlottingAreaRectangle);
          S := FloatToStrF(Position, TFloatFormat.ffFixed, 7, NoOfDecimalPlaces);
          CurrentPoint.X := Canvas.TextWidth(S) * 0.5;
          CurrentPoint.Y := Canvas.TextHeight(S);
          Xt := RectF(P - CurrentPoint.X, PlottingAreaRectangle.Bottom + UnitsDisplaySpace,
             P + CurrentPoint.X, PlottingAreaRectangle.Bottom + UnitsDisplaySpace + CurrentPoint.Y);
          Canvas.Fill.Color := TAlphaColors.Black;
          Canvas.FillText(Xt, S, False, 1, [], TTextAlign.Leading);
          Canvas.DrawLine(PointF(P, PlottingAreaRectangle.Bottom), PointF(P, PlottingAreaRectangle.Top), 1);
          Position := Position + Step;
          If Position > XMax
            Then Position := XMax;
        End;
  End;
Function TestMinusLog2(Const x : Extended) : Extended;
  Begin
    Result := -Log2(x);
  End;
Function LogisticFunction(Const x : Extended) : Extended;
  Var eToTheX : Extended;
  Begin
    eToTheX := Power(cEulersNumber, x);
    Result := eToTheX/(1 + eToTheX);
  End;
Procedure TfrmGraphPlotting.LogisticMenuItemClick(Sender : TObject);
  Begin
    lblFunctionName.Text := 'Logistic(X)';
    FunctionVar := LogisticFunction;
    edtXStartValue.Text := FloatToStr(-6);
    edtXEndValue.Text := FloatToStr(+6);
  End;
Procedure TfrmGraphPlotting.MinusLogXMenuItemClick(Sender : TObject);
  Begin
    lblFunctionName.Text := '- Log2(X)';
    FunctionVar := TestMinusLog2;
    edtXStartValue.Text := FloatToStr(0.1);
    edtXEndValue.Text := FloatToStr(1.0);
  End;
```

Table 77.6 GraphPlotWithFunctionPointers.pas - sixth section

P

```
 Procedure TfrmGraphPlotting.SinhItemClick(Sender : TObject);
   Begin
     lblFunctionName.Text := 'Sinh(X)';
     FunctionVar := Sinh;
     edtXStartValue.Text := FloatToStr(0);
//     edtXEndValue.Text := FloatToStr(2*cPI);
   End;

 Procedure TfrmGraphPlotting.SinMenuItemClick(Sender : TObject);
   Begin
     lblFunctionName.Text := 'Sin(X)';
     FunctionVar := Sin;
     edtXStartValue.Text := FloatToStr(0);
//     edtXEndValue.Text := FloatToStr(2*cPI);
   End;

 Function MyCube(Const x : Extended) : Extended;
   Begin
     Result := x * x * x;
   End;

 Procedure TfrmGraphPlotting.CoshItem1Click(Sender : TObject);
   Begin
     lblFunctionName.Text := 'Cosh(X)';
     FunctionVar := Cosh;
     edtXStartValue.Text := FloatToStr(0);
//     edtXEndValue.Text := FloatToStr(2*cPI);
   End;

 Procedure TfrmGraphPlotting.CosMenuItemClick(Sender : TObject);
   Begin
     lblFunctionName.Text := 'Cos(X)';
     FunctionVar := Cos;
     edtXStartValue.Text := FloatToStr(0);
  //   edtXEndValue.Text := FloatToStr(2*cPI);
   End;

 Procedure TfrmGraphPlotting.CubeMenuItemClick(Sender : TObject);
   Begin
     lblFunctionName.Text := 'Cube(X))';
     FunctionVar := MyCube;
     edtXStartValue.Text := FloatToStr(0);
//     edtXEndValue.Text := FloatToStr(100);
   End;

 Procedure TfrmGraphPlotting.TrackBar1Change(Sender: TObject);
   Begin
     edtXEndValue.Text := FloatToStr(TrackBar1.Value);
     btnClearGraphClick(Sender);
     Application.ProcessMessages;
     If TrackBar1.Enabled
       Then btnPlotClick(Sender)
       Else TrackBar1.Enabled := True;
   End;
End.
```

Table 77.7 GraphPlotWithFunctionPointers.pas - seventh section

Programming Task

1. Change the program so that plotting another function on the grid when the X-axis scale has changed does not overwrite the X-axis scale in all cases.

78 Creating your own components

Creating new components

Purpose: To learn how to create new components

Have you ever wondered how the components available in the component palette of the IDE got to be there? Well, they are installed in the IDE as packages which have been explained already in *Chapter 53*. The process can be illustrated by creating our own components and installing them in the IDE. This is a strength of Delphi: if there is something that you want and which isn't provided in Delphi already then you can implement it in Delphi.
Click the **Component** option in the IDE's menu bar - *Figure 78.1* - to bring up the window shown in *Figure 78.2*.
(In Delphi 7, the equivalent operation is **File|New** and then **select** the **Component** icon in the **New Items** window.)
Click the **New Component** option - *Figure 78.2* - to bring up the window shown in *Figure 78.3*.

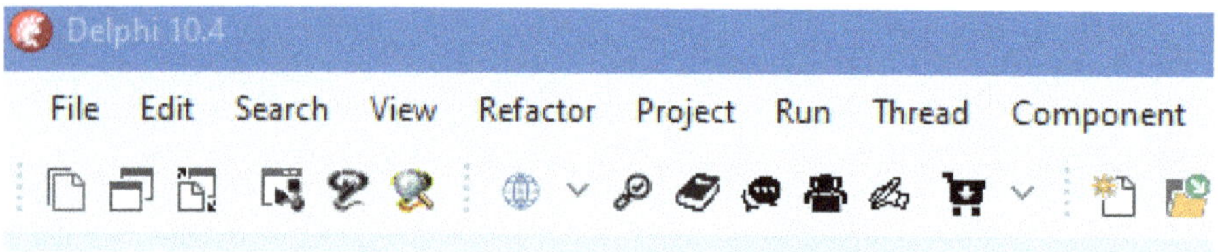

Figure 78.1 Part of the IDE's menu bar showing the Component option

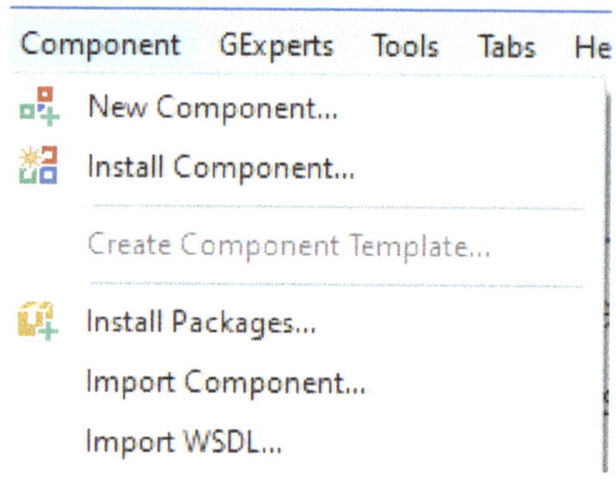

Figure 78.2 Component submenu showing the New Component option

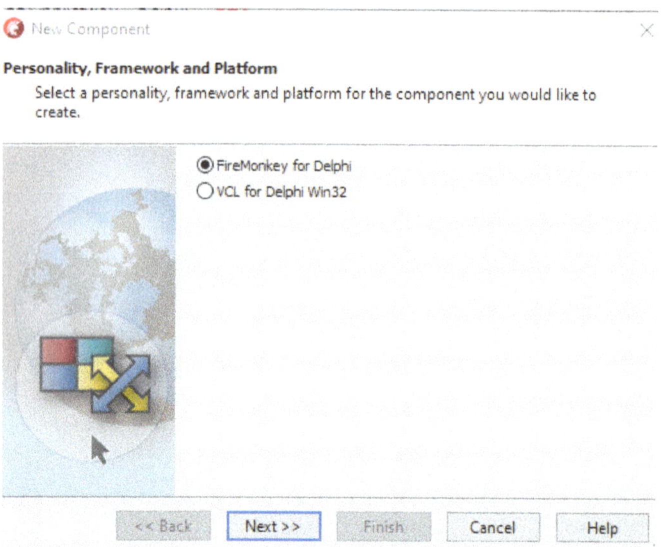

Figure 78.3 New Component window showing Personality, Framework and Platform options

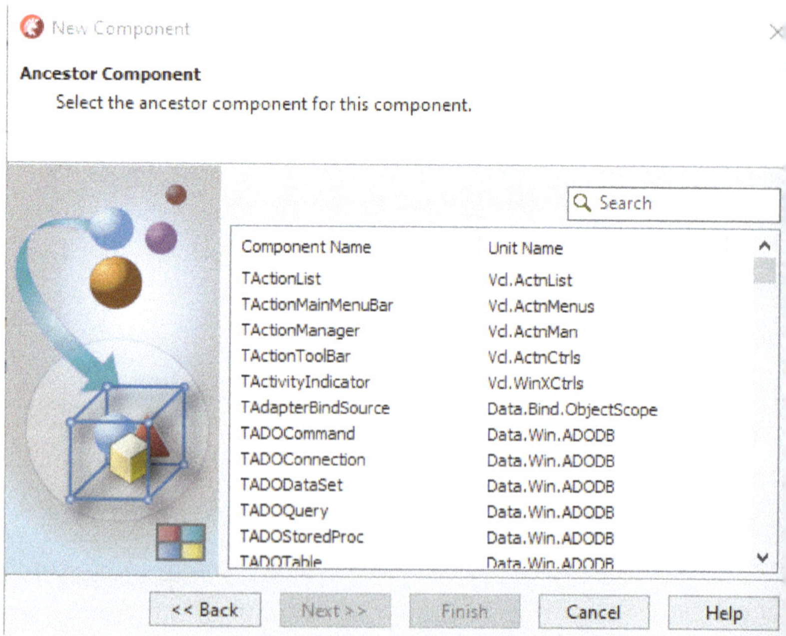

Figure 78.4 New Component window showing Ancestor Component list

Select **VCL for Delphi Win32** then **click** **Next** to bring up the **Ancestor Component** window shown in *Figure 78.4*. **Select** **TButton** from this list then **click** **Next** to bring up the window shown in *Figure 78.5*. The component generating wizard automatically supplies the **Class Name** by appending the next sequence number to **TButton**, the **Ancestor** type. In the example, the sequence number is 1 because there are no previous new button classes. The **Class Name** is therefore **TButton1**. **Change** the **Class Name** to **TNewButton**.

Change the **Unit name** to `NewButton.pas` and **save** to a folder that you have read/write access to - see *Figure 78.6* for an example.
Set the **Search** path to use the path to this folder then **click Next** to bring up the **Create Unit** window - *Figure 78.7*.
Click Finish to create the unit.
Table 78.1 shows `NewButton.pas` formatted according to the author's house style.
Click the **Component** option in the IDE's menu bar - *Figure 78.1* - to bring up the window shown in *Figure 78.2*. **Click** the **Install Component** option - *Figure 78.2* - to bring up the **Install Component** window shown in *Figure 78.8*.
Select `NewButton.pas` for the unit file name.

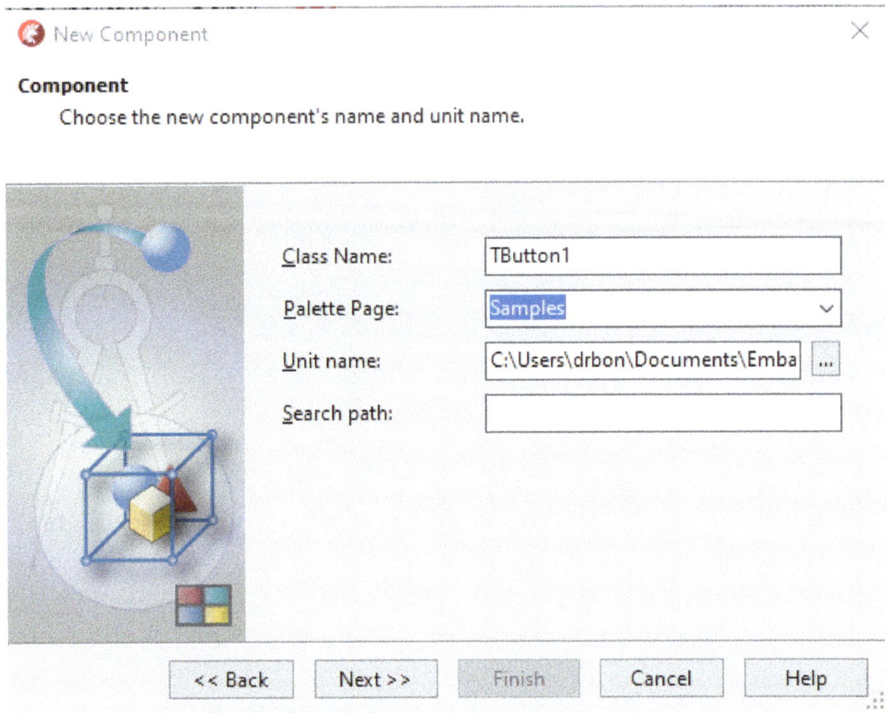

Figure 78.5 New Component window showing Class Name, Palette Page and Unit name default assignments

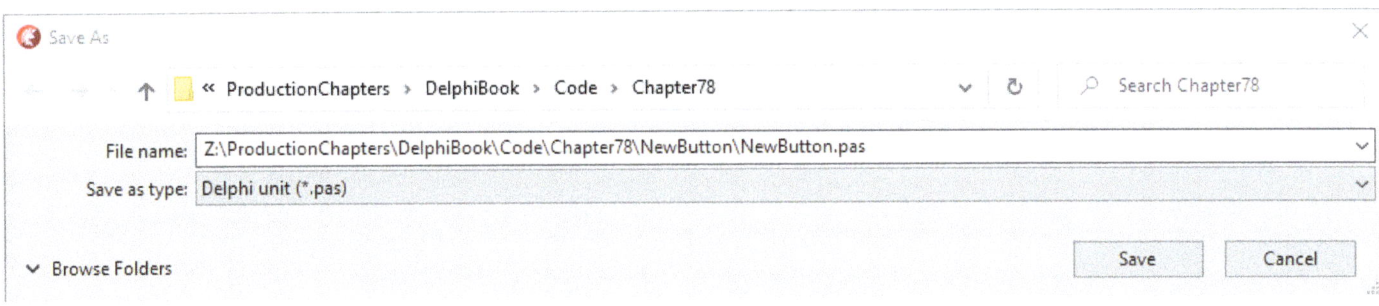

Figure 78.6 Selecting the path for the unit and saving the unit using this path

Select Install into a new package and then **click Next** to bring up the window shown in *Figure 78.9*.
Enter a path + file name for the package. The author has used:
`Z:\ProductionChapters\DelphiBook\Code\Chapter78\NewButton\dclusr.dpk`
Append a path to the end of the **Search path** which corresponds to the path to the package file. **Separate** this new path with a semicolon from the last path in the **Search path** as shown in *Figure 78.9*.
Enter `New Button` for the **Package description** field.
Click Finish.

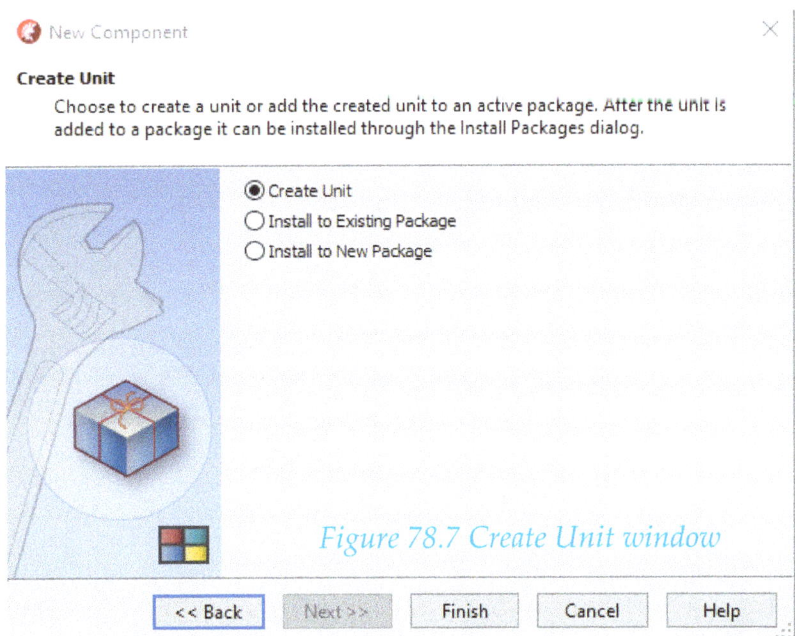

Figure 78.7 Create Unit window

The package `dclusr.dpk` is now compiled to `dclusr.bpl`, a dynamic linked library (*Figure 78.10*) and `dclusr.dcp`.The new component **TNewButton** is registered and installed in the **Samples** component palette.

For an explanation of packages and dynamic linked libraries see *Chapter 53*.

The dynamic linked library `dclusr.bpl` is written to `C:\Users\Public\Documents\Embarcadero\Studio\21.0\Bpl` for Delphi 10.4 - *Figure 78.11*. This is the default folder for this version of Delphi. This bpl is registered in the Windows registry in **Known Packages** - *Figure 78.12*. The class `TNewButton` is registered in the Windows registry in **Palette\Cache** - *Figure 78.13*. An earlier attempt registered a class `TButton1`. *Figure 78.14* shows that `TNewButton` has been installed in the **Samples** component palette.

```
Unit NewButton;
Interface
Uses
  System.SysUtils, System.Classes,
  Vcl.Controls, Vcl.StdCtrls;
Type
  TNewButton = Class(TButton)
               Private
                 { Private declarations }
               Protected
                 { Protected declarations }
               Public
                 { Public declarations }
               Published
                 { Published declarations }
             End;
Procedure Register;
Implementation
  Procedure Register;
    Begin
      RegisterComponents('Samples', [TNewButton]);
    End;
End,
```

Table 78.1 NewButton.pas containing class definition for TNewButton

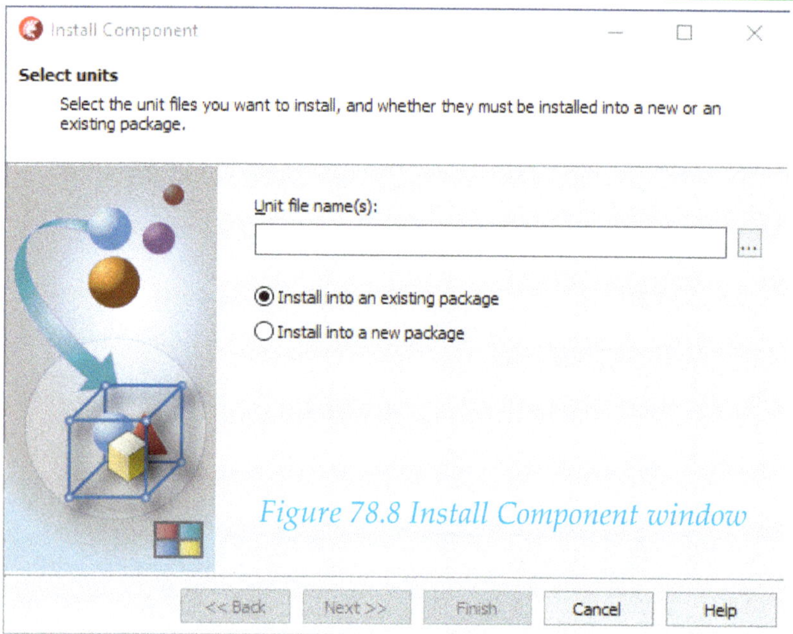

Figure 78.8 Install Component window

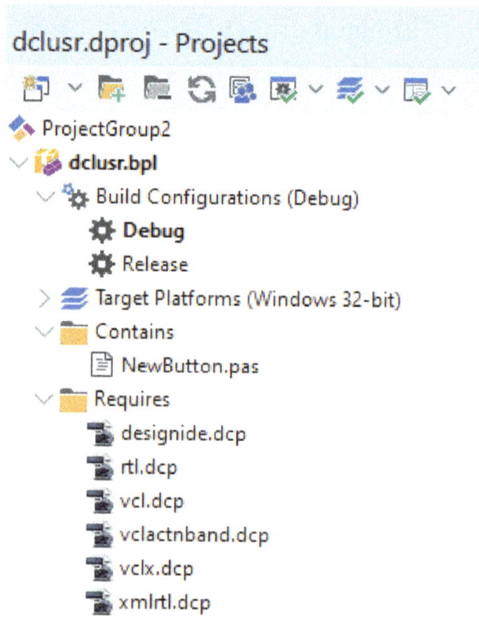

Figure 78.10 Project window showing dclusr.bpl and its dependencies on dcps (Delphi compiled packages)

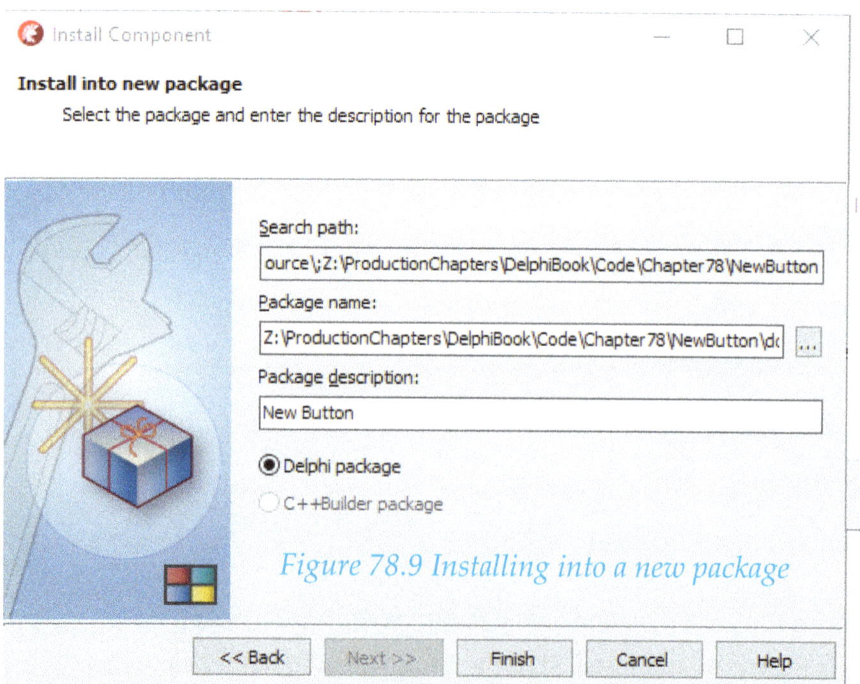

Figure 78.9 Installing into a new package

Figure 78.11 Component successfully registered and installed

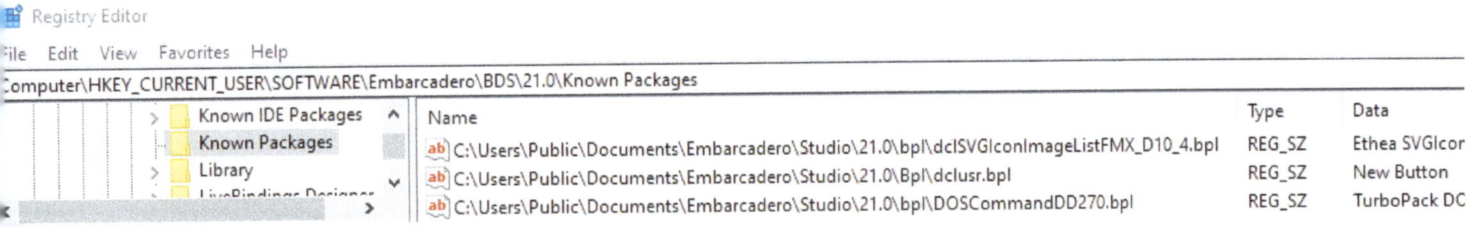

Figure 78.12 Building package dclusr.dpk registers its bpl in Known Packages

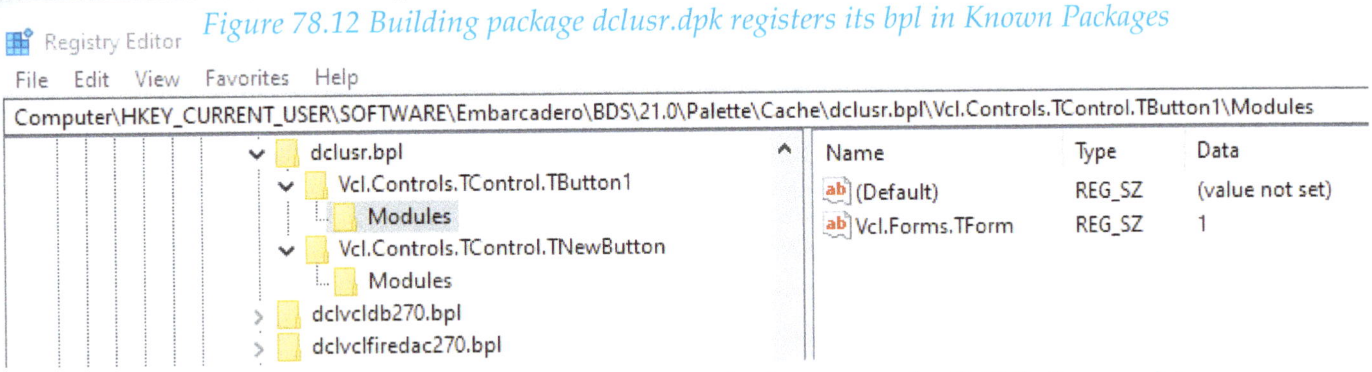

Figure 78.13 Registering TNewButton results in an entry in the Windows registry

The path to `NewButton.pas` needs to be added to the user **Path** environment variable so that the compiler can locate the `NewButton` unit when it is being used in a new project. **Select** **Tools|Options|Environment Variables** then **Path** in the **User System Overrides** window - *Figure 78.15*. **Select** the **Edit** option and then append to the **Variable value** the path to the folder containing `NewButton.pas` - *Figure 78.16*. **Select** **Project|Options|Building|Delphi Compiler** and **add** `.\$(Path)` to the **Search Path** then **Save** - *Figure 78.17*. If this doesn't work when compiling a project **add** the explicit path to **Search Path**.

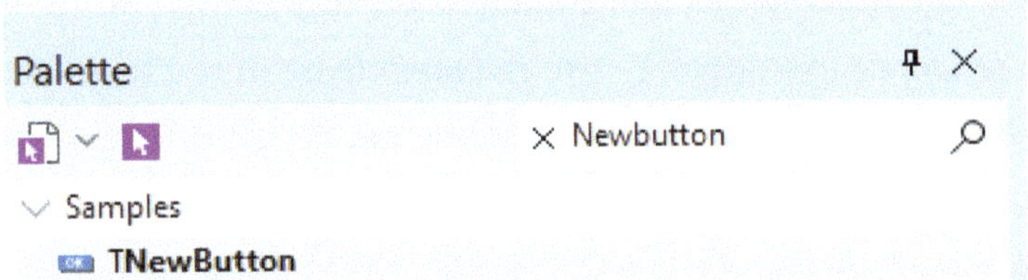

Figure 78.14 Component Palette showing TNewButton control

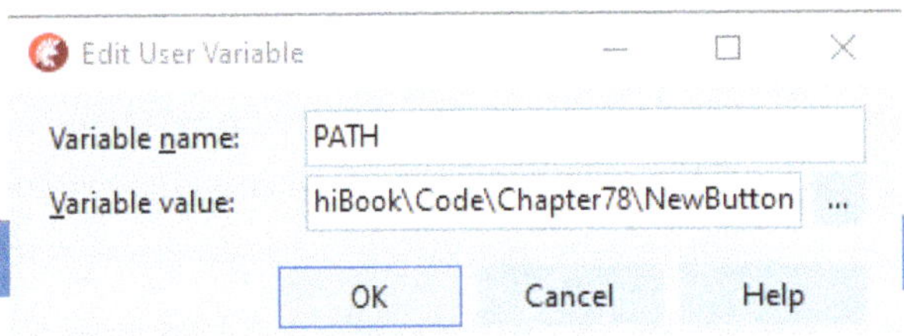

Figure 78.16 Edit User Variable window

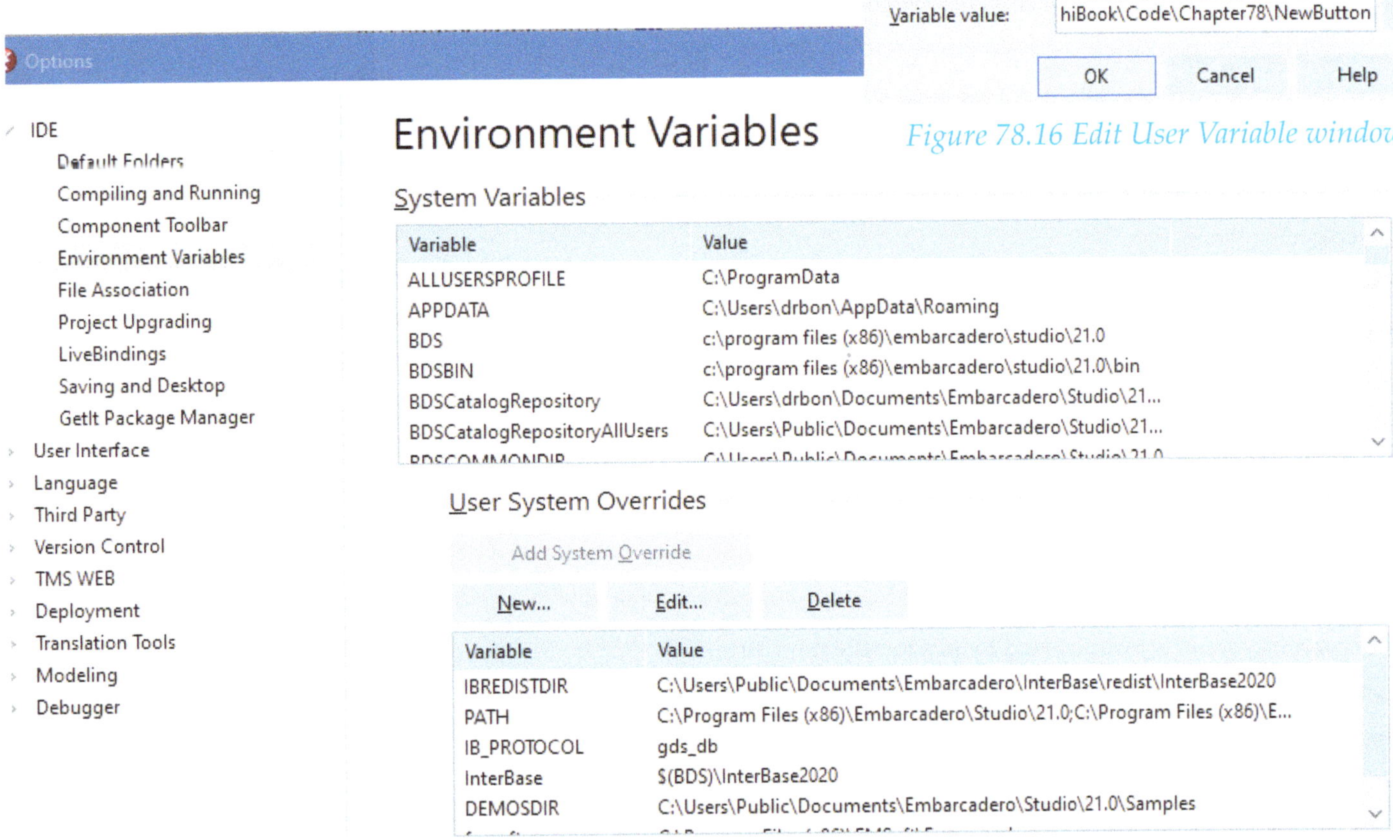

Figure 78.15 Tools|Options|Environment Variables window

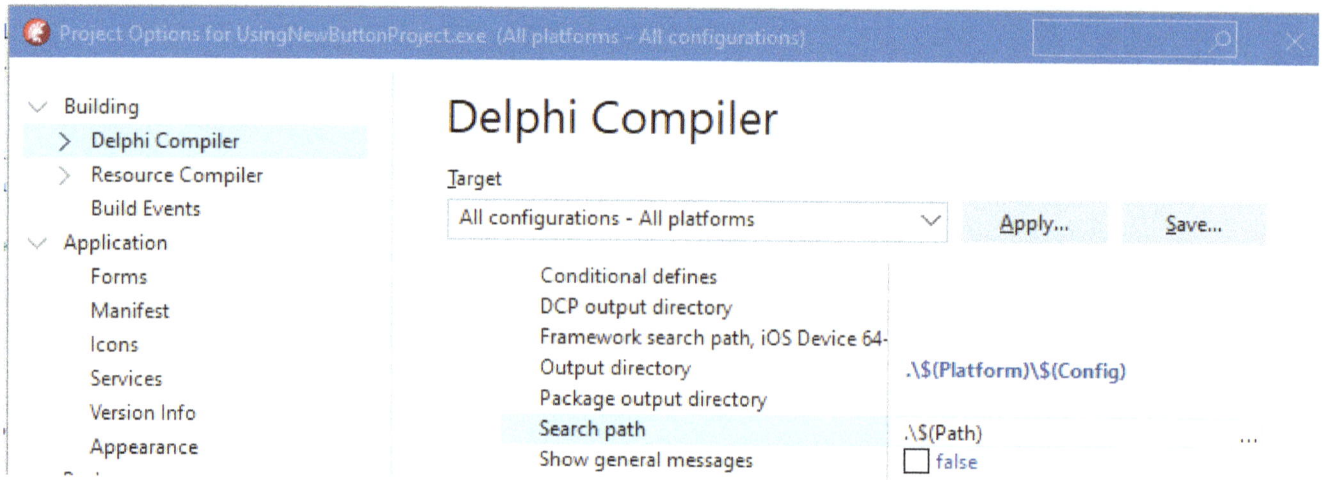

Figure 78.17 Setting Search Path for the Delphi compiler

Using TNewButton in a project

Select File|New|VCL Application - Delphi.

Add a TNewButton component/control from the Samples palette to the form - *Figure 78.18*. Delphi automatically names this control `NewButton1` and adds reference to `NewButton` to the uses clause in the Interface section.

Rename the form `frmNewButton` and its caption `New Button Form`.

Save the project as `UsingNewButtonProject.dproj` and its unit as `UsingNewButtonUnit.Pas`. *Table 78.2* shows the unit `UsingNewButton.Pas`.

Compile and **run** this project (F9). If the compiler reports that it cannot find `NewButton.Pas`, **select** Project|Options|Building|Delphi Compiler and **add** the explicit path to Search Path.

The result is shown in *Figure 78.19*.

The TNewButton control doesn't do very much because it has limited capabilities.

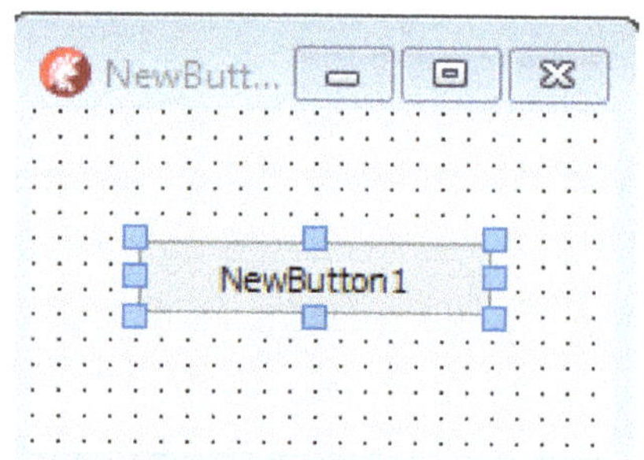

Figure 78.18 Design view of form with TNewButton control, NewButton1

```
Unit UsingNewButtonUnit;
Interface
Uses
  Winapi.Windows, Winapi.Messages, System.SysUtils,
  System.Variants, System.Classes, Vcl.Graphics,
  Vcl.Controls, Vcl.Forms, Vcl.Dialogs, Vcl.
StdCtrls,
  NewButton;
Type
  TfrmNewButton = Class(TForm)
                    NewButton1 : TNewButton;
                    Private
                      { Private declarations }
                    Public
                      { Public declarations }
                  End;
Var
  frmNewButton : TfrmNewButton;
Implementation
{$R *.dfm}
End.
```

Table 78.2 UsingNewButtonUnit.pas

Using TCustomisedButton in a project

We need to create a new button type which does more than TNewButton in order to show what Delphi can leverage.

Repeat the process that was followed to create a unit for the new component but this time **name** the component TCustomisedButton and **store** its unit with the filename `CustomisedButton.Pas` in folder `CustomisedButton`.

Table 78.3 shows `CustomisedButton.Pas`.

It has a private field `fNewTag` of type Integer (create this first).

The property `NewTag` was created by placing the template name propgs in the Published part of the class and then pressing Ctrl + J to expand the template - see *Chapter 54*.

Install this component into the package `dclusr.dpk` which was used for TNewButton.

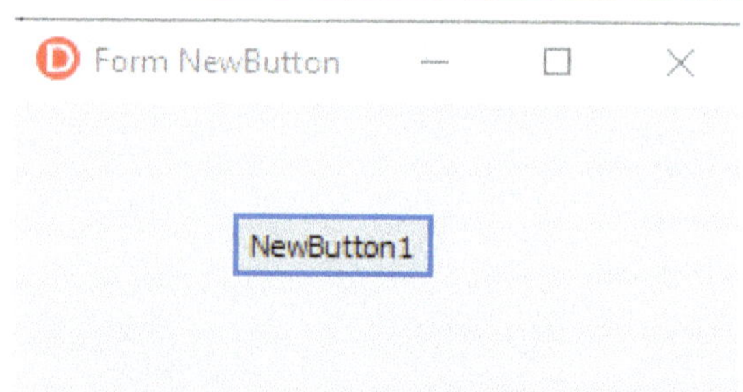

Figure 78.19 UsingNewButtonProject in execution

Copy CustomisedButton.Pas to a folder on a local drive, e.g. D:\CustomisedButton\Source (use as short a path as possible as Delphi and Windows **Path** can be problematic when the latter is near its capacity). **Select** **Tools|Options|Environment Variables** then **Path** in the **User System Overrides** window. **Select** the **Edit** option and then append to the **Variable value** the path to the folder on the local drive containing CustomisedButton.pas. **Close All**.

```
Unit CustomisedButton;
Interface
Uses
  System.SysUtils, System.Classes, Vcl.Controls, Vcl.StdCtrls;
Type
  TCustomisedButton = Class(TButton)
                        Private
                          fNewTag : Integer;
                          Function GetNewTag : Integer;
                          Procedure SetNewTag(Const Value : Integer);
                          { Private declarations }
                        Protected
                          { Protected declarations }
                        Public
                          { Public declarations }
                        Published
                          Property NewTag : Integer Read GetNewTag Write SetNewTag;
                        End;
Procedure Register;

Implementation
  Procedure Register;
  Begin
    RegisterComponents('Samples', [TCustomisedButton]);
  End;
  { TCustomisedButton }
  Function TCustomisedButton.GetNewTag : Integer;
  Begin
    Result := fNewTag;
  End;
  Procedure TCustomisedButton.SetNewTag(const Value : Integer);
  Begin
    fNewTag := Value;
  End;
End.
```

Table 78.3 CustomisedButton.Pas

Select **File|New|VCL Application - Delphi**.

Add a **TCustomisedButton** component/control from the **Samples** palette and a **TButton** control to the form - *Figure 78.20*. Delphi automatically names the first control CustomisedButton1 and adds CustomisedButton to the uses clause of the interface section. **Select** CustomisedButton1 and **inspect** the **Object Inspector**. **Note** that there is a property NewTag as shown in *Figure 78.21*. **Compare** with Button1 and **note** the absence of such a property. **Rename** the form frmCustomisedButton and its caption Customised Button Form.

Double click button CustomisedButton1 on the form to create an event handler, CustomisedButton1Click.

Double click button Button1 on the form to create an event handler, Button1Click.

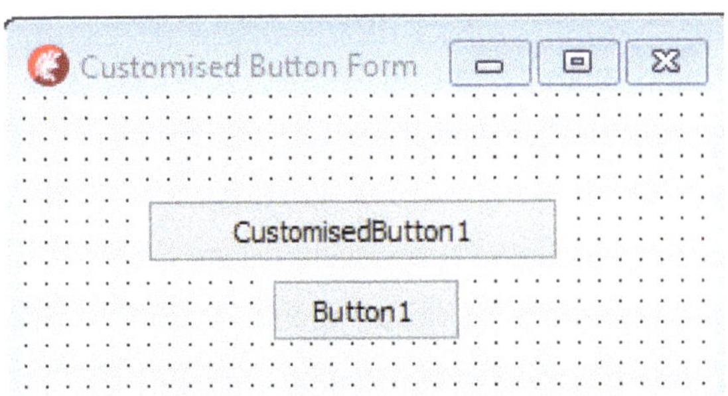

Figure 78.20 Design view of form with TCustomisedButton control, CustomisedButton1 and TButton control, Button1

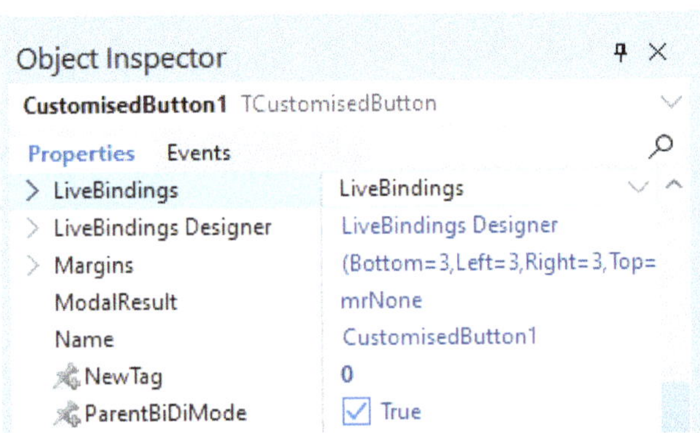

Figure 78.21 New property NewTag

Add the code shown in *Table 78.4* to the body of the corresponding handler.

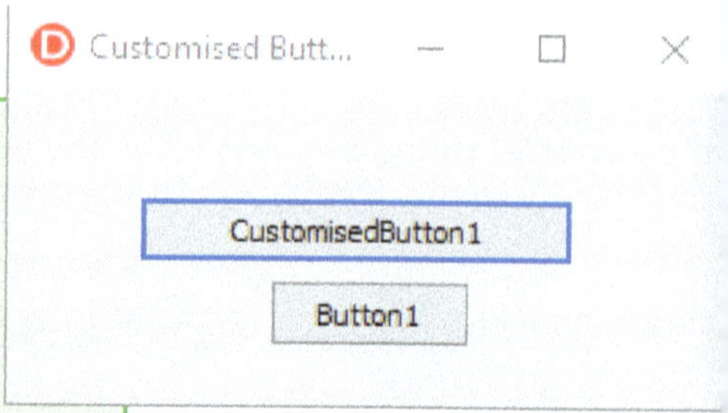

Figure 78.22 UsingCustomisedButtonProject in execution

Figure 78.23 UsingCustomisedButtonProject in execution, Button1 clicked

Figure 78.24 UsingCustomisedButtonProject in execution, CustomisedButton1 clicked then Button1 clicked

```
Unit UsingCustomisedButtonUnit;
Interface
Uses
  Winapi.Windows, Winapi.Messages, System.SysUtils, System.Variants,
  System.Classes, Vcl.Graphics, Vcl.Controls, Vcl.Forms, Vcl.Dialogs,
  Vcl.StdCtrls, CustomisedButton;
Type
  TfrmCustomisedButton = Class(TForm)
                           CustomisedButton1 : TCustomisedButton;
                           Button1 : TButton;
                           Procedure CustomisedButton1Click(Sender : TObject);
                           Procedure Button1Click(Sender: TObject);
                           Private
                            { Private declarations }
                           Public
                            { Public declarations }
                          End;
Var
  frmCustomisedButton : TfrmCustomisedButton;
Implementation
{$R *.dfm}
  Procedure TfrmCustomisedButton.Button1Click(Sender : TObject);
    Begin
      ShowMessage(IntToStr(CustomisedButton1.NewTag));
    End;
  Procedure TfrmCustomisedButton.CustomisedButton1Click(Sender : TObject);
    Begin
      CustomisedButton1.NewTag := 6;
    End;
End.
```

Table 78.4 UsingCustomisedButton.Pas

Save the project as `UsingCustomisedButtonProject.dproj` and its unit as `UsingCustomisedButtonUnit.Pas`. *Table 78.4* shows the unit `UsingCustomisedButton.Pas`.

Compile and **run** this project (F9). If the compiler reports that it cannot find `CustomisedButton.Pas`, **select** **Project|Options|Building|Delphi Compiler** and **add** the explicit path to **Search Path**.

The result is shown in *Figure 78.22*.

Click `Button1` - *Figure 78.23*.

Click `CustomisedButton1` then `Button1` - *Figure 78.24*.

Placing the property **NewTag** below the access specifier **Published** in the class definition of **TCustomisedButton** exposes this property in the Object Inspector. The **Published** access specifier is is a special kind of public that has meaning for the component streaming service which allows a form's controls and settings to be saved and restored without any code having to be explicitly written. In VCL Forms applications, **Published** is the default in the absence of any access specifiers.

Hopefully, this chapter has given the reader an appreciation of how packages are used to build the component palette of the IDE. *Table 78.5* shows the contents of the package that was used in this chapter for the two components/controls added to the **Samples** component palette. *Figure 78.25* shows Delphi in its launch phase where it loads the packages it needs for design time, i.e. the components/controls which go into the component palette and the runtime packages which are need when an application executes.

```
Package dclusr;

{$R *.res}
{$IFDEF IMPLICITBUILDING This IFDEF should not be used by users}
{$ALIGN 8}
{$ASSERTIONS ON}
{$BOOLEVAL OFF}
{$DEBUGINFO OFF}
{$EXTENDEDSYNTAX ON}
{$IMPORTEDDATA ON}
{$IOCHECKS ON}
{$LOCALSYMBOLS ON}
{$LONGSTRINGS ON}
{$OPENSTRINGS ON}
{$OPTIMIZATION OFF}
{$OVERFLOWCHECKS OFF}
{$RANGECHECKS OFF}
{$REFERENCEINFO ON}
{$SAFEDIVIDE OFF}
{$STACKFRAMES ON}
{$TYPEDADDRESS OFF}
{$VARSTRINGCHECKS ON}
{$WRITEABLECONST OFF}
{$MINENUMSIZE 1}
{$IMAGEBASE $400000}
{$DEFINE DEBUG}
{$ENDIF IMPLICITBUILDING}
{$DESCRIPTION 'Customised Button'}
{$IMPLICITBUILD ON}

Requires
  rtl,
  designide,
  vcl,
  vclactnband,
  vclx,
  xmlrtl;

Contains
  NewButton in 'NewButton.pas',
  CustomisedButton in '..\CustomisedButton\CustomisedButton.pas';
End.
```

Table 78.5 Package dclusr.dpk

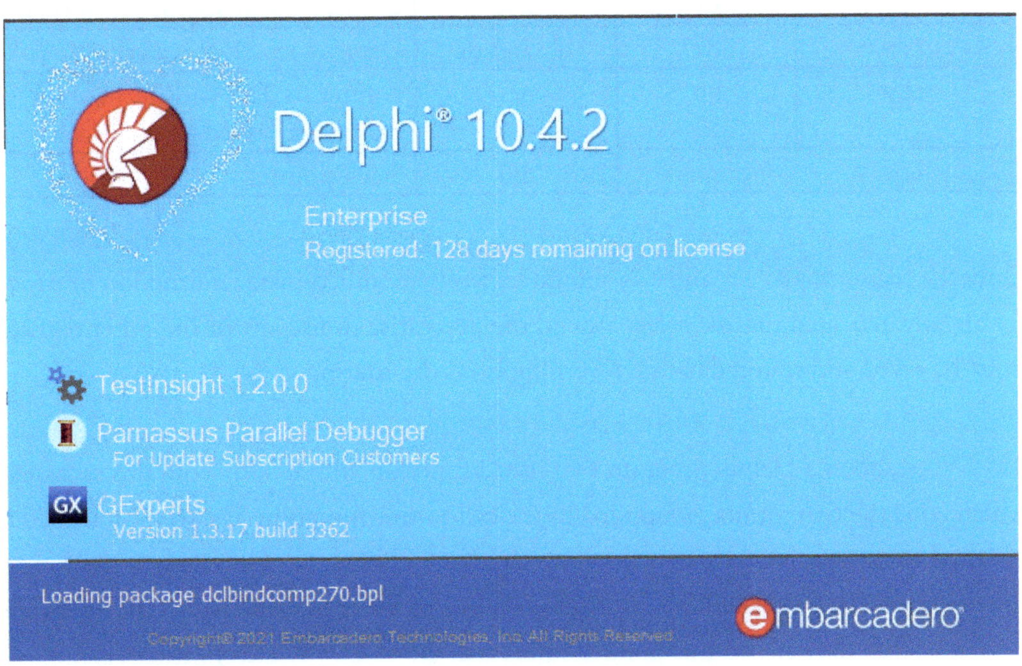

Figure 78.25 Delphi in the launch phase which loads design and runtime packages

79 Incorporating assembly language

Incorporating assembly language

Purpose: To learn how to include assembly language inline, in a Delphi program

Delphi supports a built-in assembler which allows assembly code to be included within a Delphi program.
All instructions found in the Intel Pentium 4, Intel MMX extensions, Streaming SIMD Extensions (SSE), and the AMD Athlon (including 3D) are supported. The Intel 64 architecture is supported with some limitations.
The use of Delphi identifiers, such as constants, types, and variables in assembly statements is supported.
Delphi uses the **asm** statement to indicate the beginning of an assembler block. The end of the block is indicated by an **end** statement - *Table 79.2*. Assembler code should be isolated inside a separate function or procedure.
The number of pages that can be devoted to this topic is limited, nevertheless the inclusion of this topic serves to illustrate that Delphi provides access down to the 'bare metal'. Therefore, it can be used to illustrate machine architecture down to the register and stack level. For the professional programmer, assembly language is used where (a) speed is important e.g. in cryptographic applications or where bit manipulation is involved (b) where memory is limited such as in IOT peripherals/devices.
Registers are frequently referenced in assembly language programs. Registers are memory locations internal to the processor that support fast access as well as rapid manipulation of their contents because they are made from the fastest memory technology. Moving data in and out of registers is facilitated by dedicated pathways within the processor. For this purpose, each register has a symbolic name in assembly language and a purpose, e.g. eax - see *Table 79.1* that covers six of the eight general purpose 32-bit registers found in x86 processors. The x64 architecture of x64 processors is a backwards-compatible extension of x86. It provides a legacy 32-bit mode, which is identical to x86 so eax, ebx, etc can still be used.

Register name	16-bit half	8-bit halves	Description
eax	ax	ah and al	Accumulator
ebx	bx	bh and bl	Base
ecx	cx	ch and cl	Counter for string operations and loops
edx	dx	dh and dl	Data
ebp	bp	n/a	Pointer to data within the stack, used by routines to locate parameters saved on the stack
esp	sp	n/a	Stack pointer

Table 79.1 32-bit registers of relevance that may be encountered when programming in assembly language in Delphi

Only the registers **eax**, **ecx** and **edx** should be freely modified inside a function or procedure, as the other registers are already allocated specific roles. Should the need arise to use any of the other registers inside the routine, they must be saved and restored before returning from the routine.

Adding two numbers in assembly language

Table 79.2 shows a Delphi program that uses a function whose body contains an assembly language code block which adds the two numbers supplied in the call to this function. The result returned from a function must be assigned to the special variable **@Result** as shown in *Table 79.2*. On entry to the function, the **ebp** register points to the current stack frame and the **esp** register points to the top of the stack (the operation of pushing an item of data onto the stack decrements this pointer - the stack grows downwards in memory).

```
Program AddTwoNumbersProject;
{$APPTYPE CONSOLE}
{$R *.res}
Uses
  System.SysUtils;
Var
  No1, No2 : Integer;
Function Add(FirstNo, SecondNo : Integer) : Integer;  stdcall;
  Begin
    asm
      mov eax, FirstNo //Copies FirstNo to the eax register
      add eax, SecondNo //Adds the SecondNo to the eax register storing the result in eax
      mov @Result, eax //Copies the contents of the eax register to the Result variable
    end;
  End;
Begin
  Write('Input first integer: ');
  Readln(No1);
  Write('Input second integer: ');
  Readln(No2);
  Writeln('Sum = ', Add(No1, No2));
  Readln;
End.
```

Table 79.2 Mixing assembly language and high level language in Delphi

Performing a loop in assembly language

Table 79.3 shows a Delphi program that uses a function `DoFastAdd`[1] to add the value supplied in function argument variable `x`, by the number of times stored in function argument `y`. Its body, written in assembly language, performs this addition. It uses a label `@loop` to faciliate a loop operation over three assembly language statements. The function `DoFastAdd` is called with values supplied in `No1` and `No2` from the main block. The mechanism for returning a result from a function via a block of assembly language code relies on the special variable `@Result`. Therefore, the last assembly language statement copies the value in the accumulator register `eax` to `@Result`.

```
Program LoopingProject;
{$APPTYPE CONSOLE}
{$R *.res}
Uses
  System.SysUtils;
Var
  No1, No2 : Integer;
Function DoFastAdd(x, y : Integer): Integer; stdcall;
  Begin
    asm
      mov ecx, y //use ecx as a loop control counter, initialise to y
      mov eax, 0 //set eax to zero - accumulator
      mov edx, x //use edx as the data register which is initialised to x
      @loop: //defining a labelled point in the program - @loop is the symbolic name of the label
      add eax,edx //accumulate x, y number of times in eax
      dec ecx //decrement the loop control register (using decrement operation saves using a comparison instruction)
      jnz @loop //jump on eax not zero to label @loop
      mov @Result, eax //transfer accumulated result, x added to y times, to special variable @Result
    end;
  End;
Begin
  Write('Input first number: ');
  Readln(No1);
  Write('Input first number: ');
  Readln(No2);
  Writeln('Result = ', DoFastAdd(No1, No2));
  Readln;
End.
```

Table 79.3 Looping in assembly language

1 This is a trivial example to illustrate principes and so does not significantly outperform a loop encoded entirely at high level

Using assembly language to investigate the stack on a 64-bit machine

Table 79.4 shows a Delphi program that uses a function `ShowStackVariables` to investigate where the integer arguments, `First` and `Second`, passed to the function and the value for the local variable `LocalVar` are stored on the stack for a 64-bit machine (register size is 64 bits). *Figure 79.1* shows a schematic of the area of the stack of interest. The contents of the `ebp` register point to the base memory cell of the stack that stores the first byte of an eight byte value which is the address in the program to return to once the function has finished executing (return address). The two function arguments, `First` and `Second`, which are each four bytes in length are located using the `ebp` register by adding 8 and 12 respectively to the `ebp` register contents. The number 8 is used because the return address occupies 8 bytes and the number 8 + 4 = 12 because the `First` argument occupies 4 bytes.

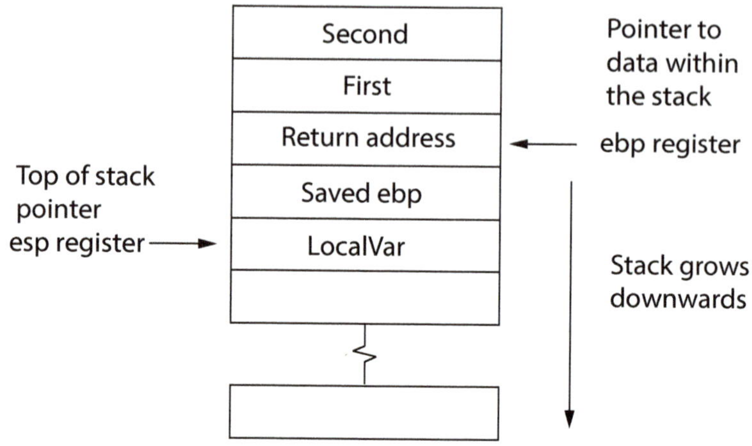

Figure 79.4 Schematic of section of stack on a 64-bit machine (register size is 64 bits)

The previous value of the `ebp` register is stored on the stack so that when the function finishes executing, the `ebp` register may be restored to its previous value. The function's local variable `LocalVar`, occupies the first free slot on the stack after the saved `ebp` slot. To get to the start of the stack memory block of cells that store the value for `LocalVar`, 8 must be substracted from `ebp` because the saved `ebp` value occupies 8 bytes. Alternatively, the stack pointer `esp` may be used as shown in *Table 79.4* - `mov eax, [esp]`. The stack may also be used to store other values temporarily using the `push` operation. The program does this with `push eax` to store the contents of the `eax` register on the stack. The `pop eax` code retrieves the stored value from the stack, and places it back in the `eax` register.

Compile and **run** the program.

Remove and **restore** the single line comments as needed to test each operation.

```
Program ShowStackVariablesProject;
{$APPTYPE CONSOLE}
{$R *.res}
Uses
  System.SysUtils;
Var
  No1, No2 : Integer;
Function ShowStackVariables(First, Second : Integer) : Integer; stdcall;
  Var
    LocalVar : Integer;
  Begin
    LocalVar := 6;
    asm
    // mov eax, [ebp + 12] // ebp + 12 points to Second
    // push eax //Pushes the value stored in eax onto the stack
      mov eax, [ebp + 8] // ebp + 8 points to First
    // mov eax, [ebp -8] // Accesses the value stored in local variable LocalVar
    // pop eax //Retrieves the value at the top of the stack, placing it in eax
    // mov eax, [esp] //Copies the value stored at the top of stack
      mov @Result, eax //Copies the value in eax to the special varible @Result
    end;
  End;
Begin
  Write('Input first no: ');
  Readln(No1);
  Write('Input second no: ');
  Readln(No2);
  Writeln('Result = ', ShowStackVariables(No1, No2));
  Readln;
End.
```

Table 79.4 Exposing the stack on a 64-bit machine

https://pythongui.org/6-best-python-gui-frameworks-in-2021/

Python4Delphi

Purpose: To become familiar with the use of Python4Delphi

Information

Why use Python4Delphi?

Python4Delphi combines the strengths of Delphi and Python. It supports Python-based data analytics in Delphi applications and Python GUI development using the VCL.

What is Python4Delphi?

Python[1] for Delphi (**Python4Delphi**) is a set of free components that wrap up the **Python dll** so that Python scripts can be executed from Delphi.

Figure 80.1 shows a simple demonstration in which a Python script **BubbleSort.py** is loaded and executed from a Delphi program **Demo1Project.exe**.

The upper window shows the version of python being used (**Python 3.8**), then the output, [0, 1, 2, 3, 5, 8, 9], from the execution of the python script, **BubbleSort.py**, shown in the lower window, acting on the unsorted list, [5, 1, 2, 3, 9, 8, 0].

Information

The programs in this chapter rely on Python4Delphi software, inspiration being derived from the software demos provided with Python4Delphi.

For licensing see https://github.com/pyscripter/python4delphi/blob/master/LICENSE

Information

Six best Python GUI frameworks in 2021:

https://pythongui.org/6-best-python-gui-frameworks-in-2021/

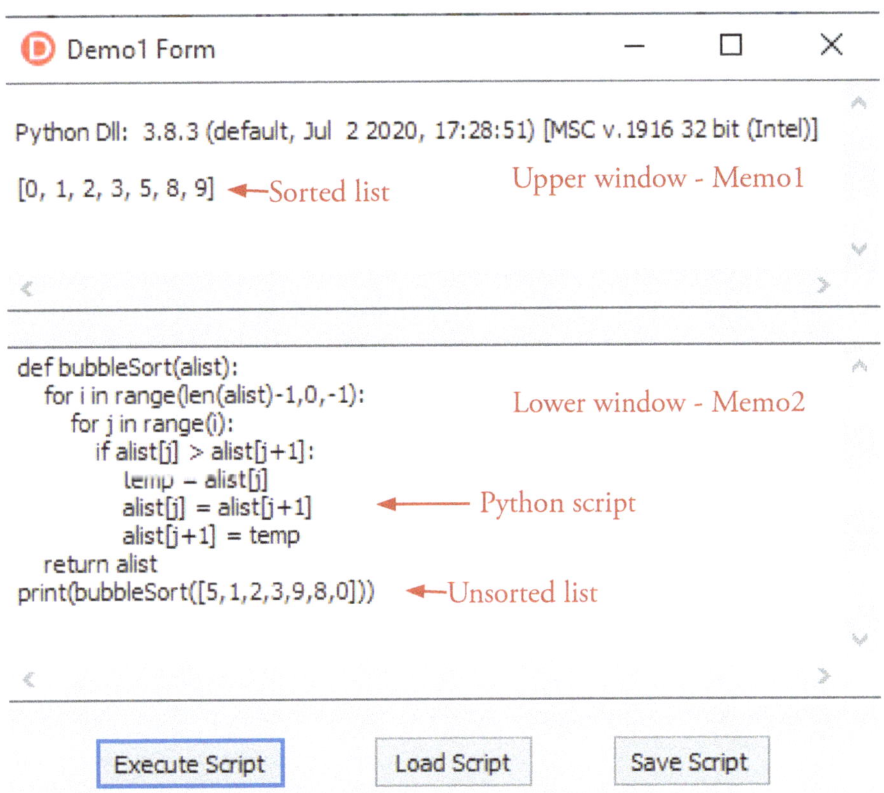

Figure 80.1 Demo1Project.exe executing Python script BubbleSort.py

www.educational-computing.com/DelphiBook/Code/Chapter80/Demo1Project.zip

1 "Python" is a registered trademark of the Python Software Foundation

Setting up Python4Delphi

Download **python4delphi** code, **python4delphi-master.zip**, or clone this code from the GitHub repository at github.com/pyscripter/python4delphi. Unzip it to create a **python4delphi-master** folder with the contents shown in *Figure 80.2* (September 2020).

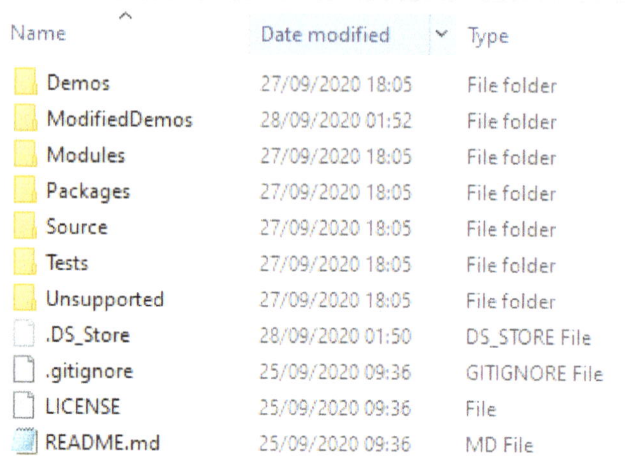

Figure 80.2 python4delphi_master folder contents

1. Start **RAD Studio.**
2. Add the source subdirectory (e.g., **C:\Users\drbond\python4delphi-master\Source**) to the IDE's library path for the targets you are planning to use (**Tools|Options|Language|Delphi|Library**) - *Figure 80.3*.
3. Open the **Python4Delphi** package specific to the version of Delphi being used. For **Delphi 10.4.1** and later, use the package in the **Packages\Delphi\Delphi 10.4+** directory. For earlier versions including **Delphi 10.4** (version before **10.4.1**) use the package in the **Packages\Delphi\Delphi 10.3-** directory - *Figure 80.4*. This will need editing for **Delphi 10.4**. Remove all the **{$IFDEF ....}{$LIBSUFFIX ....} {$ENDIF}** statements and replace with **{$LIBSUFFIX '270'}**. *Figure 80.5* shows the **Projects** pane in the Delphi IDE after opening the the package for **Delphi 10.4**.

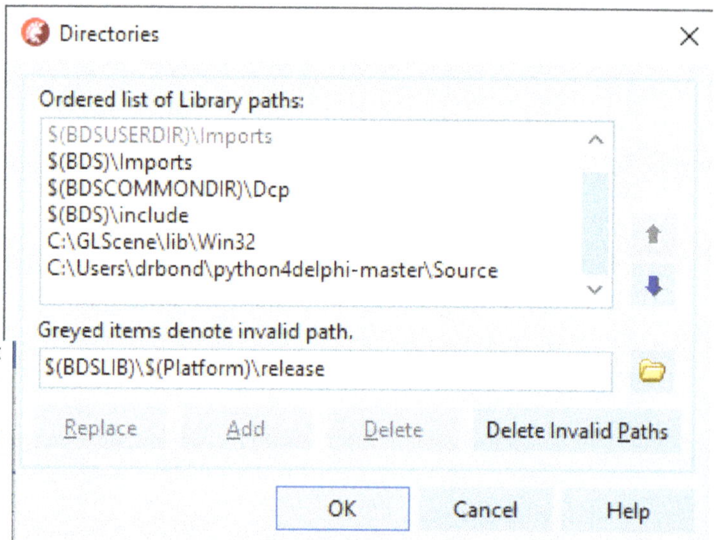

Figure 80.3 Setting Library path

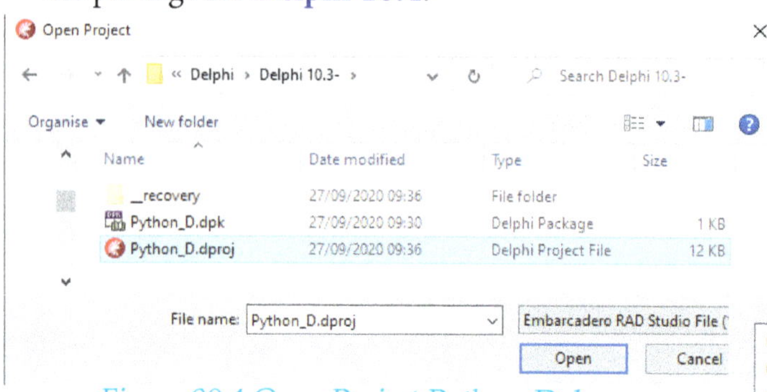

Figure 80.4 Open Project Python_D.dprog

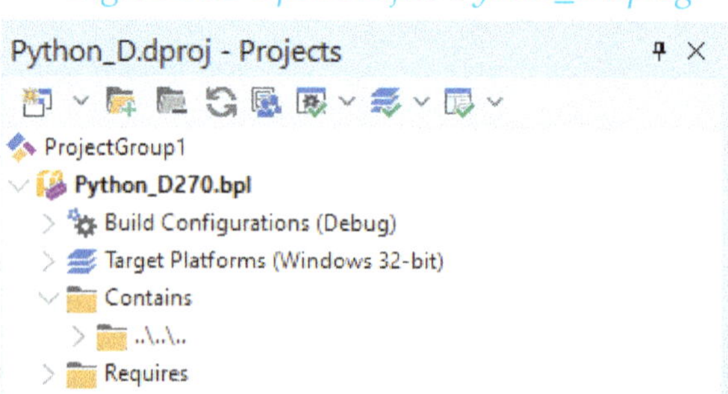

Figure 80.5 Projects pane after opening Python_D.dproj

4. Python was installed as a part of an Anaconda distribution (32-bit), **Anaconda3,** but Python can also be installed directly from Python.org. You must also add the **\Library\bin** path of the Anaconda distribution to the system environment variable - *Figure 80.6* (**Tools|Options|Environment Variables**).

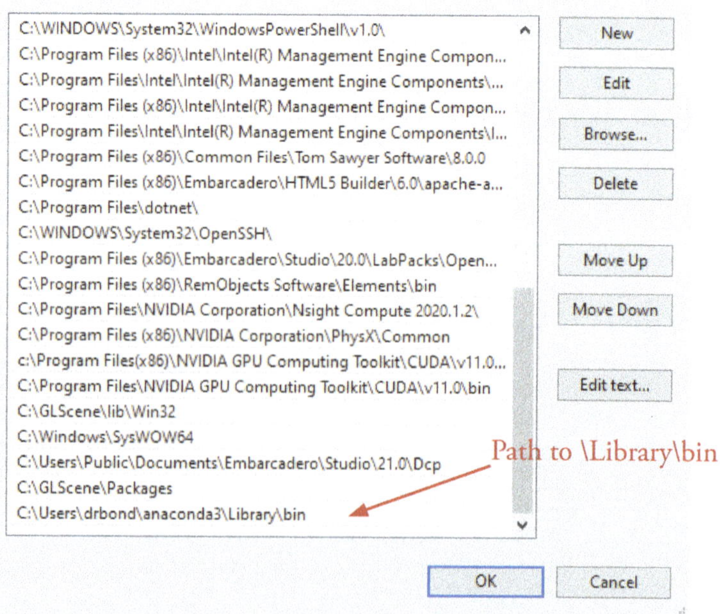

Figure 80.6 System environment variable

www.educational-computing.com/DelphiBook/Code/Chapter80/FirstExample.zip

5. Right click on **Python_D270.bpl** to bring up the menu shown in *Figure 80.7*. Click on **Install** to install the python components. If successful, the component palette should now contain a **Python palette** of components as shown in *Figure 80.8*.

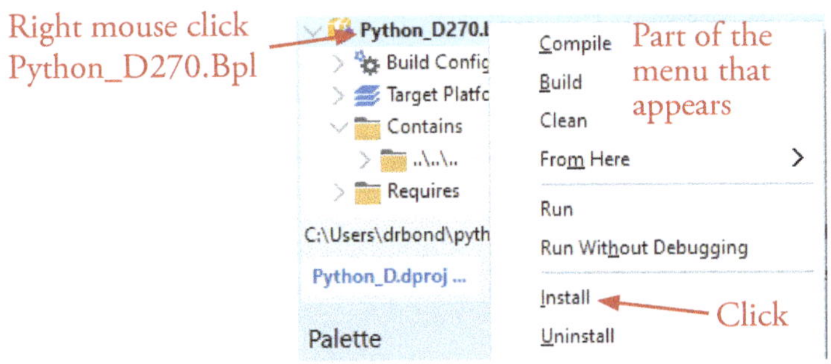

Figure 80.7 Install components from here

First project

1. Create a new **Windows VCL Application for Delphi**.
2. Drop a **TPanel** component on the form and set its **Align** property to **alTop** in the **Object Inspector**. Change its **Caption** property to `Python Source Code`.
3. Drop a **TMemo** component (`Memo1`) on the form and set its **Align** property to **alTop**. Open its **Lines** property and delete `Memo1` string to leave the memo box empty. Set **ScrollBars** to **ssBoth**.
4. Drop a **TSplitter** component from the **Additional** palette on the form and set its **Align** property to **alTop** and its **Height** property to 2.
5. Drop a **TPanel** component on the form and set its **Align** property to **alTop** in the **Object Inspector**. Change its **Caption** property to `Python Output`.
6. Drop a **TPanel** component on the form and set its **Align** property to **alBottom** in the **Object Inspector**. Empty its **Caption** property.
7. Drop a **TMemo** component (`Memo2`) on the form and set its **Align** property to **alClient** so that it fills the gap between the bottom panel and the **TSplitter** component. Open its **Lines** property and delete `Memo2` string to leave the memo box empty. Set **ScrollBars** to **ssBoth**.
8. Select the bottom panel and then drop a **TButton** component (`Button1`) onto this panel. Set its caption to `Execute`. Set its **Anchors** property to **[akTop,akRight, akBottom]**.

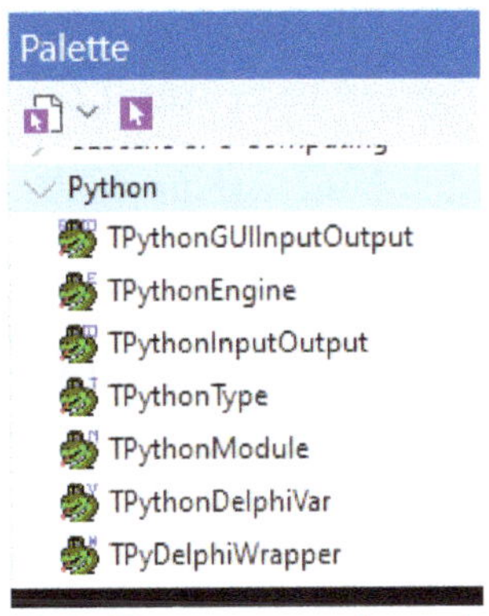

Figure 80.8 Component palette showing installed Python components

The user interface's appearance in the design window should now be as shown in *Figure 80.9*.

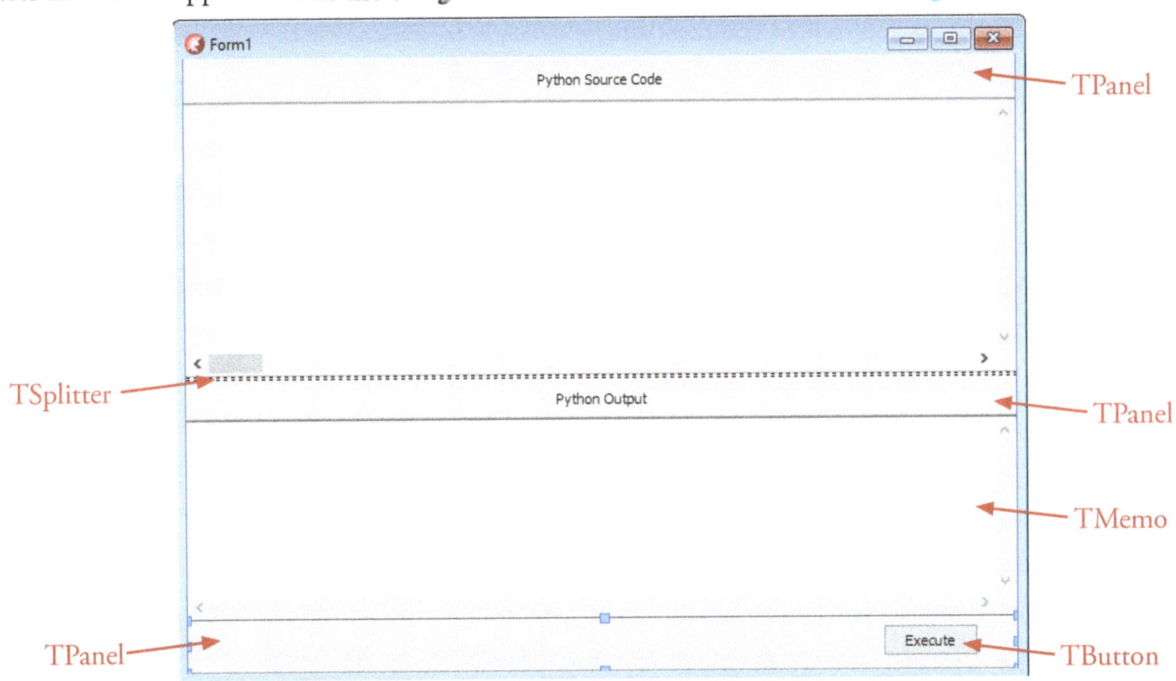

Figure 80.9 Design of the user interface

9. Drop a **TPythonEngine** component from the **Python** palette on the form. This component provides the connection to **Python** or rather the **Python API**. Its default name is **PythonEngine1**.

10. Drop a **TPythonGUIInputOutput** component on the form. Its default name is **PythonGUIInputOutput1**. This component provides a conduit for routing input and output between the Graphical User Interface (GUI) and the currently executing Python script.

11. As this project uses an **Anaconda** distribution (see later for the same project implemented with Python from www.Python.org) **PythonEngine1**'s properties are required to be set up as follows

- Set property **DllName** to `python38.dll` (because **Python 3.8** is installed) or the version that you have installed.
- Set property **DllPath** to the Anaconda distribution, e.g. `c:\users\drbond\anaconda3`.
- Set property **AutoLoad** to `False`.
- Set **UseLastKnownVersion** to `False`.
- Set **PythonEngine1**'s property **IO** to **PythonGUIInputOutput1**.

12. Set **PythonGUIInputOutput1**'s property **Output** to **Memo2**.

13. As this Delphi application relies on an Anaconda distribution, we are required to set up a **Form Create** event handler with the following two lines of code (this is unnecessary with Python from Python.org)

```
Procedure TForm1.FormCreate(Sender: TObject);
  Begin
    PythonEngine1.SetPythonHome('c:\drbond\users\anaconda3');
    PythonEngine1.LoadDll;
  End;
```

14. Double click **Button1** and add the line of code to the event handler

```
PythonEngine1.ExecStrings(Memo1.Lines);
```

15. Save the project and its unit in folder `FirstExample`. Name project `FirstExampleProject` and its unit `FirstExampleUnit`.

16. Now compile, link and run (**F9**) the executable.

17. Write `print(2 + 2)` in the `Python Source Code` window then click **Execute**. *Figure 80.10* shows the result. The executable calls up the **Python** interpreter which executes the `print` function with the given argument `2 + 2` returning the result `4`. This result is passed to the Delphi executable which then displays it in the `Python Output` window.

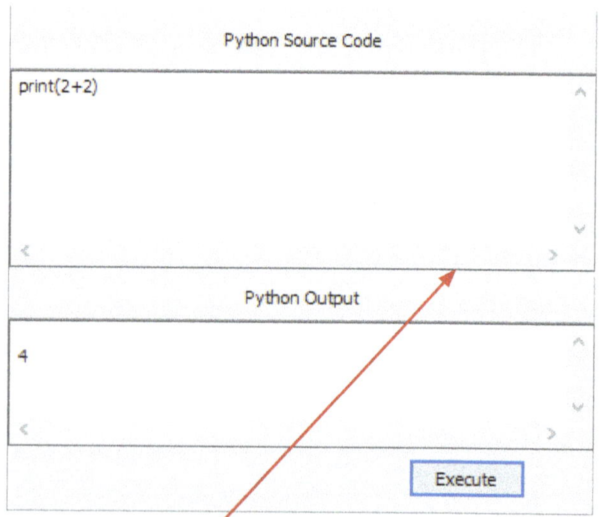

Figure 80.10 FirstExampleProject.exe in execution

The **TSplitter** component allows the sizes of the two windows to be adjusted together so that as one is enlarged the other is reduced in size accordingly seamlessly - *Figure 80.11*.

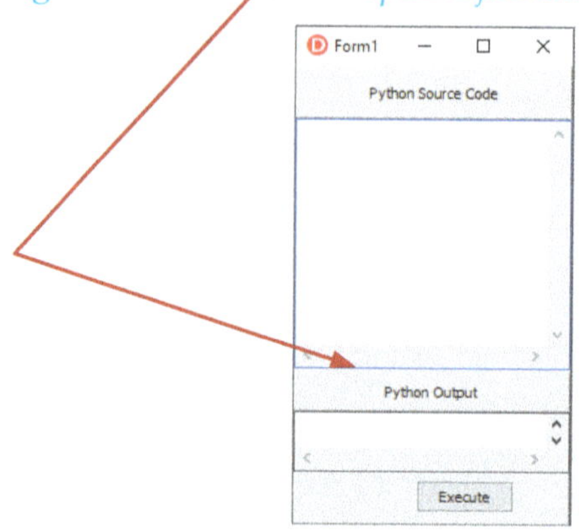

Figure 80.11

In order to be able to load and save Python scripts for execution by `FirstExampleProject.exe`, two more **TButton** components need to be added to the bottom panel as shown in *Figure 80.12*.

18. Select the bottom panel then add two **TButton** components to this panel, **Button2** and **Button3**. Set the **Caption** property of **Button2** to `Save` and the **Caption** property of **Button3** to `Load`. Position these two buttons as shown in *Figure 80.12*.
19. Set the **Anchors** property of **Button3** to **[akLeft, akTop, akBottom]**.
20. Set the **Anchors** property of **Button2** to **[akTop, akBottom]**.

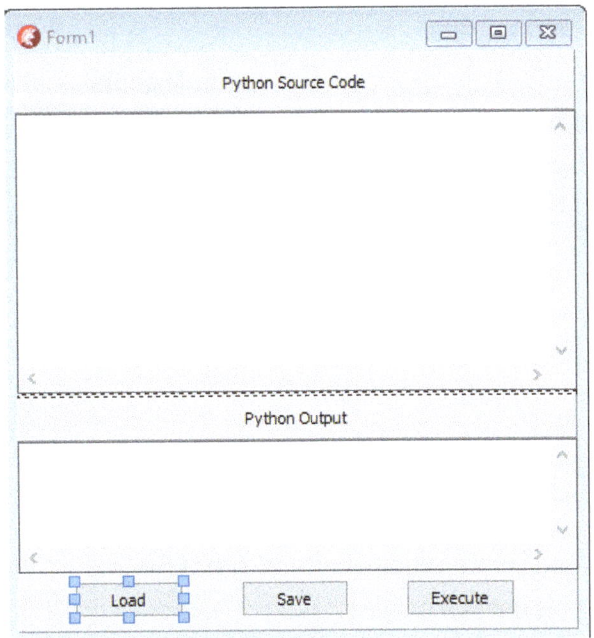

Figure 80.12 FirstExampleProject with two additional buttons Open and Save

When the application's window is resized, **Button3** (`Load`) will remain anchored at the same distance from the left, top and bottom edges of the bottom panel. **Button 2** (`Save`) will remain anchored at the same distance from the top and bottom edges of the bottom panel but it will move to the right or to the left, respectively, if the application's window is resized in either of these directions. **Button1** (`Execute`) will remain anchored at the same distance from the right, top and bottom edges of the bottom panel.

21. Add a **TOpenDialog** and a **TSaveDialog** to the form.
22. Double click **Button2** (`Save`) and add the following lines of code to the event handler

```
With SaveDialog1
  Do
    Begin
      If Execute
        Then Memo1.Lines.SaveToFile(FileName);
    End;
```

Property of SaveDialog1

23. Double click **Button3** (`Load`) and add the following lines of code to the event handler

```
With OpenDialog1
  Do
    Begin
      If Execute
        Then Memo1.Lines.LoadFromFile(FileName);
    End;
```

Property of OpenDialog1

24. Save project and unit in folder `FirstExample`.
25. Now compile, link and run (**F9**) the executable.
26. Click **Load** and select `BubbleSort.py`.
27. Click **Execute**.

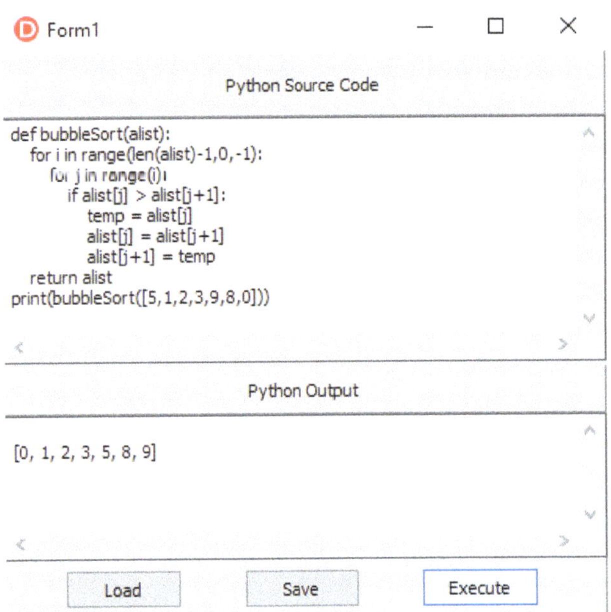

Figure 80.13 FirstExampleProject.exe in execution and with Python script BubbleSort.py loaded

Figure 80.13 shows the result.

www.educational-computing.com/DelphiBook/Code/Chapter80/SecondExample.zip

Second project

Save project `FirstExampleProject.dproj` in a new folder, `SecondExample`, rename the project `SecondExampleProject.dproj` (**Save Project As**).

Save unit `FirstExampleUnit.pas` in new folder `SecondExample`, rename the unit `SecondExampleUnit.pas` (**Save As**).

1. Select bottom panel and add a **TButton** component to this panel. Change its **Caption** property to `Show Var`. Position as shown in *Figure 80.14*.
2. Add a **TPythonDelphiVar** component from the **Python** palette. Change its **VarName** property to `test`. Set its **Engine** property to **PythonEngine1** if this doesn't happen automatically.
3. Double click `Show Var` and add the following line of code to the event handler

```
ShowMessage('Value = ' +
PythonDelphiVar1.ValueAsString);
```

4. Save project and unit.
5. Now compile, link and run (**F9**) the executable.
6. Enter the following **Python** code into the `Python Source Code` window

```
test.value = 5
print(test, test.value)
```

   as shown in *Figure 80.15*.
7. Click `Execute`. The line `<PythonDelphiVar: 5> 5` appears in the `Python Output` window. Python function `print` copies the numeric value 5 stored in the Python variable `test.value` and then sends it to Delphi to handle via **PythonGUIInputOutput1** which is also connected to `Memo2`.
8. Now click `Show Var` to execute some Delphi code. The window shown in *Figure 80.15* should appear displaying the string '`Value = 5`'. This occurs because the identifiers `PythonDelphiVar1` and `test` are aliases for the same variable.

The fact that these identify the same variable means it is possible to read and write the variable's content in both Python and Delphi!

Information

The identifiers ***test*** and ***PythonDelphiVar1*** operate as aliases for the same variable. It makes better sense therefore to use the same identifier name for each. ***PythonDelphiVar1*** is the property value of property **Name** for a ***TPythonDelphiVar*** object and the other, ***test,*** is the property value of property **VarName**. The latter is the variable name that is accessible to a Python script.

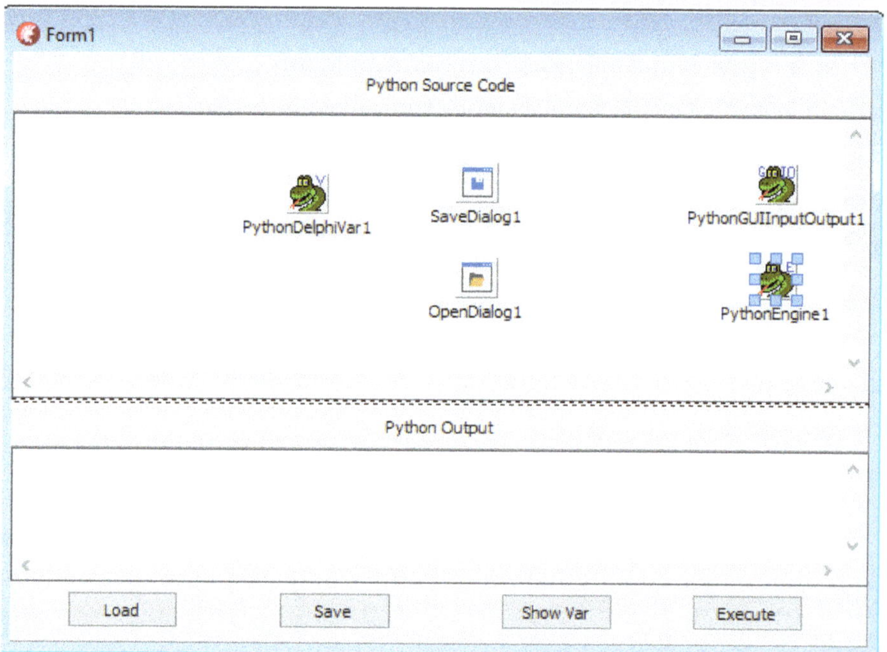

Figure 80.14 SecondExampleProject user interface design

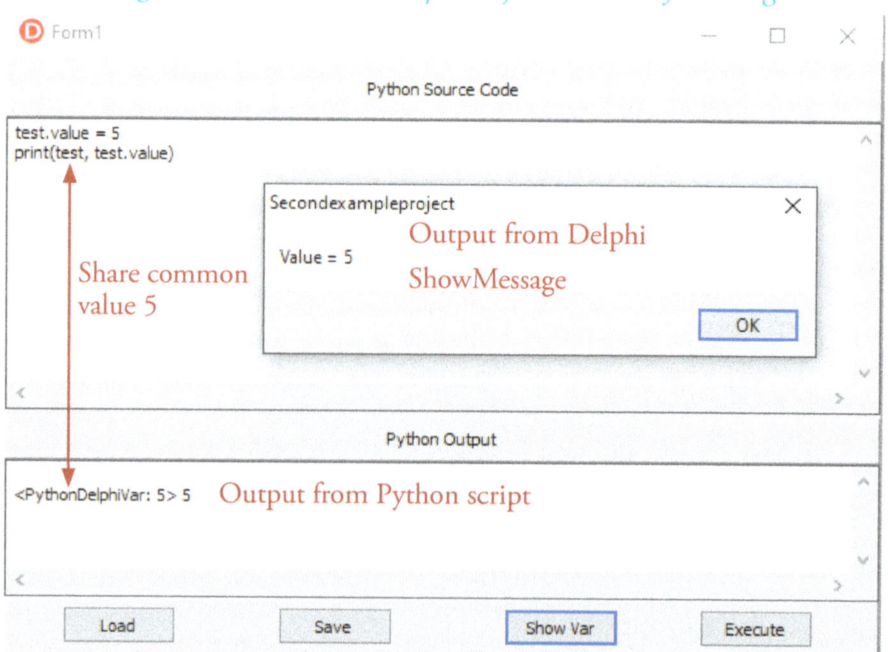

Figure 80.15 SecondExampleProject.exe in execution

www.educational-computing.com/DelphiBook/Code/Chapter80/ThirdExample.zip

Third project

Save project `SecondExampleProject.dproj` in a new folder, `ThirdExample`, renaming the project `ThirdExampleProject.dproj` (**Save Project As**).

Save unit `SecondExampleUnit.pas` in new folder `ThirdExample` renaming the unit `ThirdExampleUnit.pas` (**Save As**).

1. Select bottom panel and add a **TEdit** component, **Edit1**, to this panel as shown in *Figure 80.16*. Set its **Text** property to `0`.
2. Click on **PythonDelphiVar1** and in the **Object Inspector** switch to the **Events** tab.
3. Double-click on attribute **OnGetData** to create its event handler. Add the following line of code to this event handler: `Data := Edit1.Text;`
4. Double-click on attribute **OnSetData**, and add the following line of code to this event handler:

```
Edit1.Text := Data;
```

5. Double-click on the **OnChange** attribute, and add the following line of code to this event handler:

```
With Sender As TPythonDelphiVar
  Do ShowMessage('Var test changed: ' + PythonDelphiVar.ValueAsString);
```

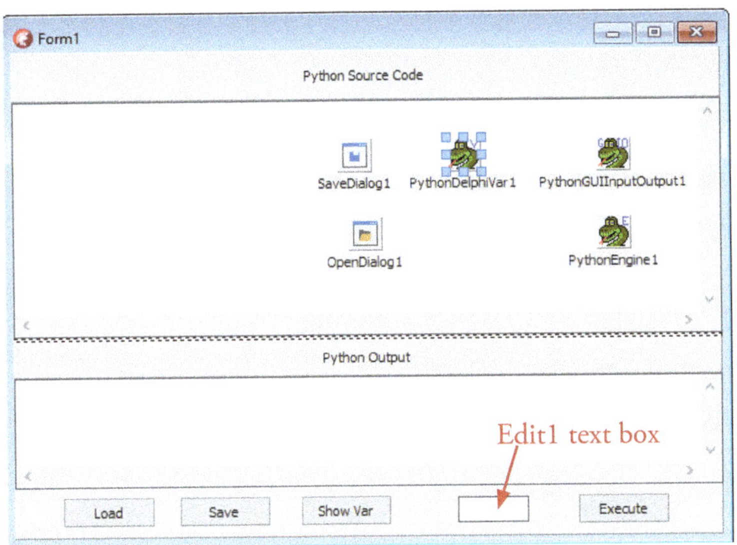

Figure 80.16 ThirdExampleProject user interface design

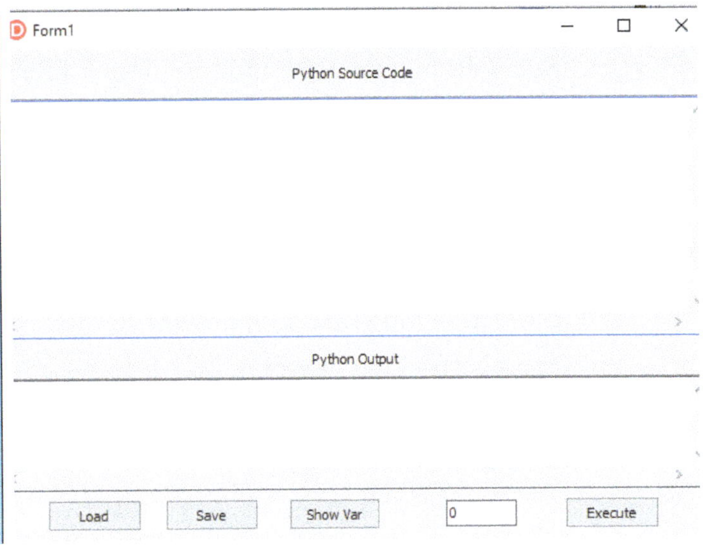

Figure 80.17 ThirdExampleProject just launched

6. Save project and unit.
7. Now compile, link and run (**F9**) the executable - *Figure 80.17*.
8. Write the Python script `test.value=45` in the `Python Source Code` window.
9. Click `Execute`. The value shown in the text box **Edit1** will change from its default value 0 to new value 45 as a consequence of executing the given Python script. The outcome demonstrates that Python variable `test` is associated with the variable `Edit1` in the Delphi program.

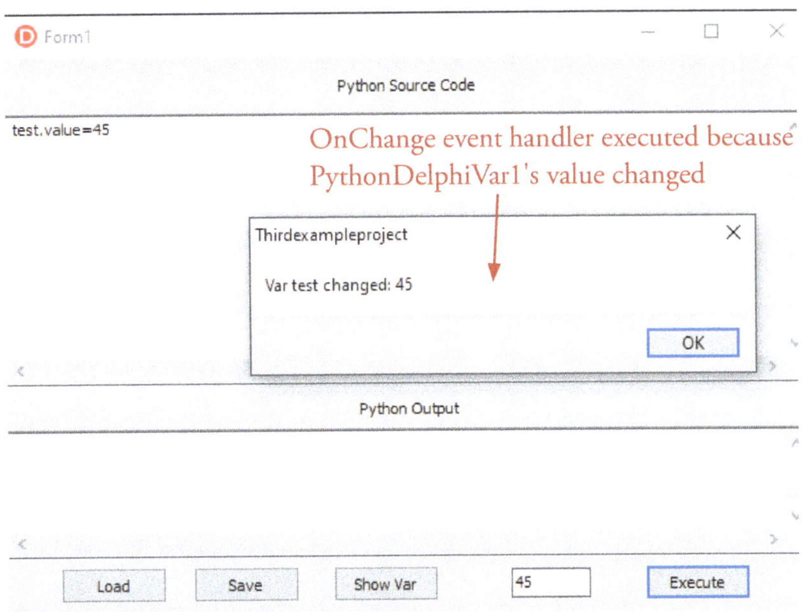

Figure 80.18 ThirdExampleProject executing script test.value=45

10. Click **OK** to close the popup window.
11. Delete `test.value=45` in the `Python Source Code window`.
12. Write `print(test.value)` in the blank `Python Source Code` window
13. Change the contents of text box `Edit1` to 30.
14. Click `Execute`. The value 30 now appears in the `Python Output` window reflecting the fact that the value assigned to Python variable `test` has been updated to the value of Delphi text box, `Edit1`.

This exercise has demonstrated that it is possible using components from the Python palette to create two-way communication between a Delphi program in execution and a Python script in execution.

Fourth project www.educational-computing.com/DelphiBook/Code/Chapter80/FourthExample.zip

1. Create a new **Windows VCL Application for Delphi**.
2. Drop a **TPanel** component on the form and set its **Align** property to **alTop** in the **Object Inspector**. Change its **Caption** property to `Python Source Code`.
3. Drop a **TPanel** component on the form and set its **Align** property to **alBottom** in the **Object Inspector**. Empty its **Caption** property.
4. Select the bottom panel and then drop a T**Button** component (`Button1`) onto this panel. Set its caption to `Execute`. Set its **Anchors** property to **[akTop,akRight, akBottom]**.
5. Drop a **TMemo** component (`Memo1`) on the form and set its **Align** property to **alClient**. Open its **Lines** property and delete `Memo1` string to leave the memo box empty. Set **ScrollBars** to **ssBoth**.
6. Drop a **TPythonEngine** component from the **Python** palette on the form. This component provides the connection to **Python** or rather the **Python API**. Its default name is **PythonEngine1**.
7. Drop a **TPythonInputOutput** component on the form. Its default name is **PythonInputOutput1**. This component provides a conduit for routing input and output between a console window and the currently executing Python script.

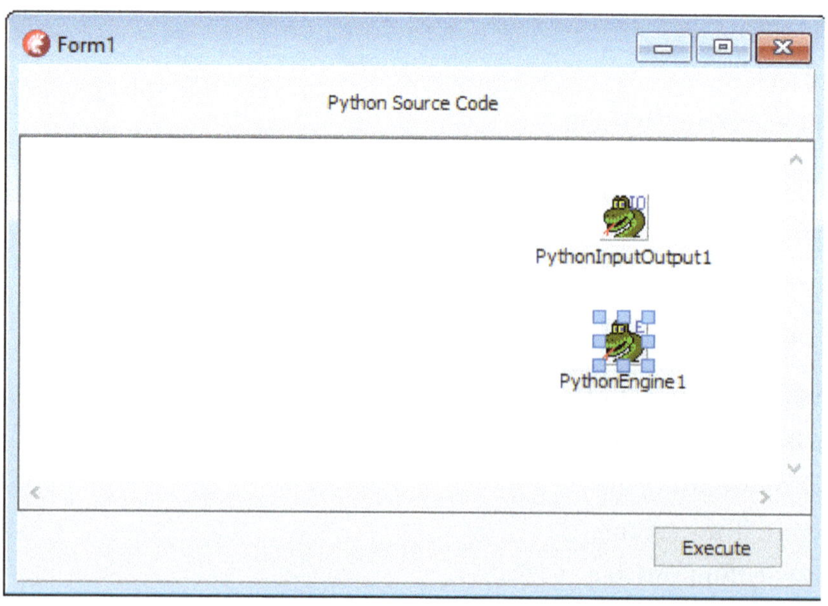

Figure 80.19 FourthExampleProject GUI design

The user interface's appearance in the design window should now be as shown in *Figure 80.19*. As this project uses an **Anaconda** distribution (see later for the same project implemented with Python from www.Python.org) **PythonEngine1**'s properties are required to be set up as follows

- Set property **DllName** to `python38.dll` (because **Python 3.8** is installed) or the version that you have installed).
- Set property **DllPath** to the Anaconda distribution, e.g. `c:\users\drbond\anaconda3`.
- Set property **AutoLoad** to `False`.
- Set **UseLastKnownVersion** to `False`.
- Set **PythonEngine1**'s property **IO** to **PythonInputOutput1**.

8. Select **PythonInputOutput1** and its **Events** page. Double click **OnReceiveData** to create event handler **PythonInputOutputReceiveData**.
9. Select **PythonInputOutput1** and its **Events** page. Double click **OnSendData** to create event handler **PythonInputOutputSendData**.
10. Add the line of code to **PythonInputOutputReceiveData**

```
Readln(Data);
```

11. Add the line of code to **PythonInputOutputSendData**

```
Writeln(Data);
```

12. In order to read from and write to the console we need to create a console at run time. Click **Project|View Source** to bring up the application's source code. Add the following directive to the application's source code as shown in *Figure 80.20*

```
Program FourthExampleProject;
{$APPTYPE CONSOLE}          <-- Creates Console window
Uses
  Vcl.Forms,
  FourthExampleUnit in 'FourthExampleUnit.pas' {Form1};

{$R *.res}

Begin
  Application.Initialize;
  Application.MainFormOnTaskbar := True;
  Application.CreateForm(TForm1, Form1);   <-- Creates GUI window
  Application.Run;
End.
```

Figure 80.20 Program FourthExampleProject

```
{$APPTYPE CONSOLE}
```

13. Save the project using filename `FourthExampleProject.dproj` (**Save Project As**) in a folder `FourthExample`.
14. Save its unit using filename `FourthExampleUnit.pas` in the same folder `FourthExample`.

15. Now compile, link and run (**F9**) the executable. Two windows should appear: a console window and an application window as shown in *Figure 80.21*.
16. Enter the following Python script in the `Python Source Code` window and click `Execute`

```
value = input("Please enter a string\n")
print(f'You entered {value}')
```

17. The prompt `Please enter a string` should appear in the console window as shown in *Figure 80.21*.
18. Click the console window and enter `Hello World!` then press return.

    The string `You entered Hello world!` shown in *Figure 80.21* should be echoed to the console window.

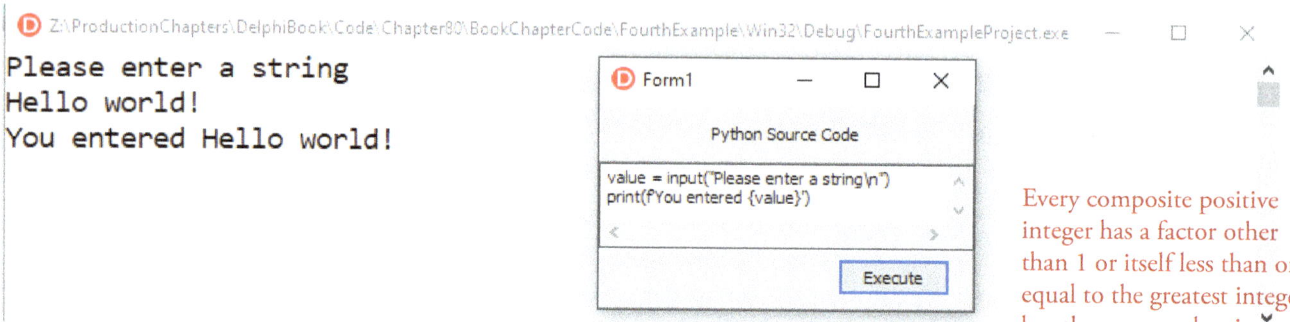

Figure 80.21 FourthExampleProject in execution

Every composite positive integer has a factor other than 1 or itself less than or equal to the greatest integer less than or equal to its square root.

www.educational-computing.com/DelphiBook/Code/Chapter80/FifthExample.zip

Fifth project - this project was inspired by Kiriakos Vlahos (aka PyScripter)

Open project `FirstExampleProject.dproj` and save in a new folder, `FifthExample`, whilst renaming it `FifthExampleProject.dproj` (**Save Project As**).

Save unit `FirstExampleUnit.pas` in folder `FifthExample` renaming it `FifthExampleUnit.pas` (**Save As**).

1. Add a **TPythonModule** to the form (the form should already contain a **TPythonEngine** and a **TPythonGUIInputOutput** component).
2. Add the function `IsPrime` shown in *Figure 80.22* to the implementation section of `FifthExampleUnit.pas`.

```
Function IsPrime(No : Integer) : Boolean;
  Begin
    If (No <= 1) Then Exit(False);
    Var UpperLimit := Floor(Sqrt(No));
    For Var i := 2 To UpperLimit
      Do If (No Mod i = 0) Then Exit(False);
    Exit(True);
  End;
```

Figure 80.22 Function IsPrime

3. Select **PythonModule1** and in the Object Inspector click the ellipsis (*Figure 80.23*) to bring up the **Events editor** shown in *Figure 80.24*.

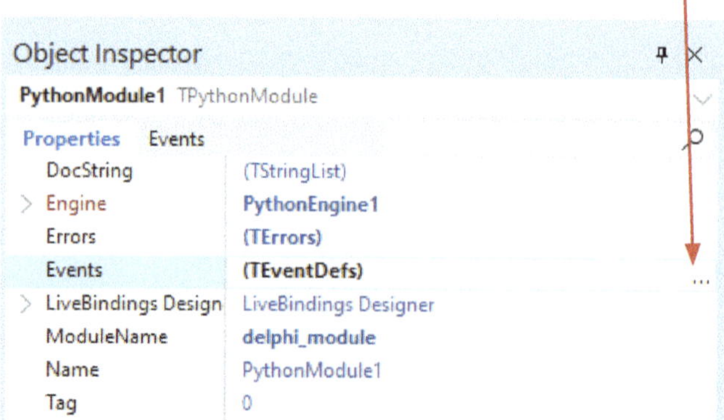

Figure 80.23 Events property PythonModule1

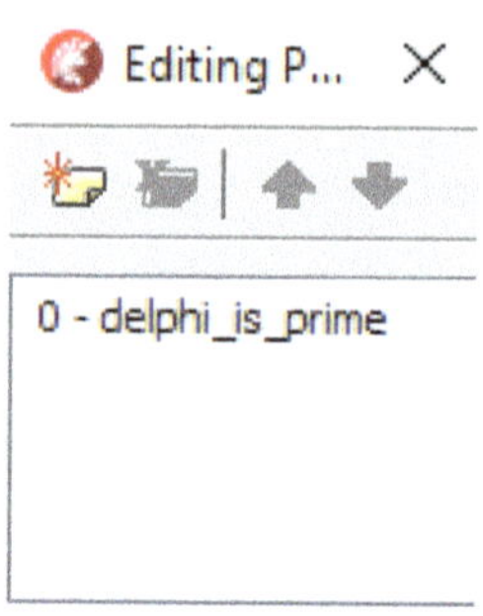

Figure 80.24 delphi_is_prime event

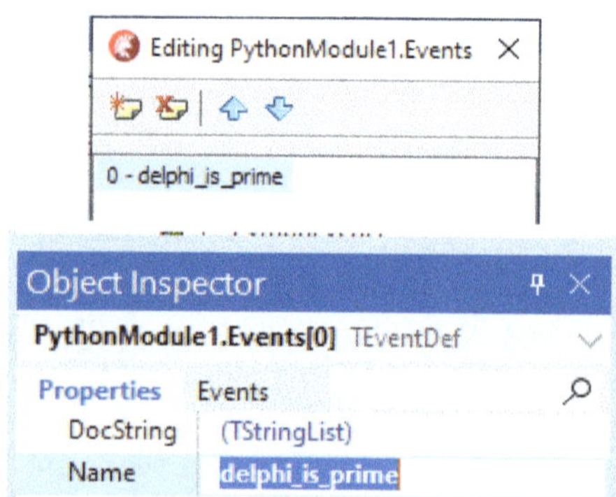

Figure 80.25 delphi_is_prime event

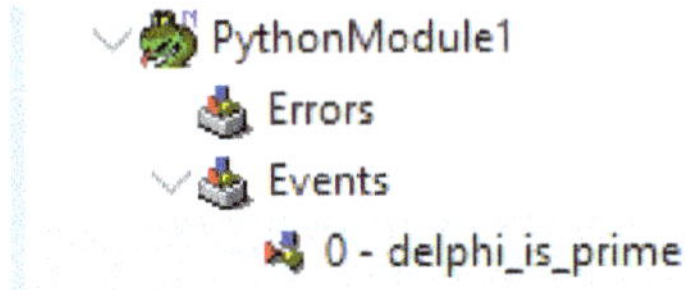

Figure 80.26

4. Click [icon] in the **Events editor** to add a new event named `delphi_is_prime`. *Figure 80.24* already shows that a new event has already been added and then named `delphi_is_prime`. This naming is done by highlighting the default name of this new event in the **Events editor** and then in the Object Inspector, changing the events **Name** property to `delphi_is_prime` - *Figure 80.25*.
5. In the **Structure pane** select **Events** and `0 - delphi_is_prime` - *Figure 80.26.*
6. Switch to the **Events** page for `PythonModule1.Events[0]` and double click the field for the **OnExecute** event to create the event handler `PythonModule1Events0Execute` - *Figure 80.27*.
7. Switch to the source code view of `FifthExampleUnit.pas` and add the lines of source code shown in *Figure 80.28* to the event handler `PythonModule1Events0Execute`.
8. Select **PythonModule1** in the Object Inspector and set its **ModuleName** property to `delphi_module`.
9. Save all (**Shift+Ctrl+S**).
10. Now compile, link and run (**Shift+Ctrl+F9**) the executable.

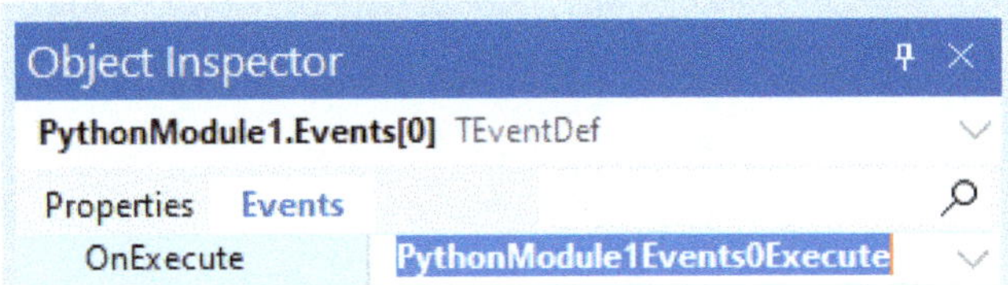

Figure 80.27 Creating OnExecute event handler

```
Procedure TForm1.PythonModule1Events0Execute(Sender: TObject; PSelf,
                                             Args: PPyObject;
                                             Var Result: PPyObject);

  Var
    N : Integer;
  Begin
    With GetPythonEngine
      Do
        Begin
          If PyArg_ParseTuple(Args, 'i:delphi_is_prime', @N) <> 0
            Then
              Begin
                If IsPrime(N)
                  Then Result := PPyObject(Py_True)
                  Else Result := PPyObject(Py_False);
                Py_INCREF(Result);
              End
            Else Result := Nil;
        End;
  End;
```

Figure 80.28 Event handler PythonModule1Events0Execute

The following exercise was inspired by a Webinar given by Kiriakos Vlahos (aka PyScripter):

11. Click `Load` and open `countofprimesinpythononly.py` (*Figure 80.29*).
12. Click `Execute` to run `countofprimesinpythononly.py`. Repeat this two more times.
13. The Python program counts the number of primes between 0 and 1000000, measures the time that elapses and then prints both results - *Figure 80.30*. The elapsed time is approximately 6.5 seconds.
14. Click `Load` and open `pythondelphiprime.py` - see *Figure 80.31*. This script uses a function, `delphi_is_prime`, linked to `PythonModule1` via module `delphi_module`, to test for primality in place of the Python `is_prime` function in `countofprimesinpythononly.py`. *Figure 80.28* shows that `delphi_is_prime` in turn relies on function `IsPrime` written in Delphi. When the Python script is run it invokes the event handler `PythonModule1Events0Execute` which in turn calls the Delphi function `IsPrime`.

```
from timeit import Timer
import math
def is_prime(n):
    if n <= 1:
        return False
    upperlimit = math.floor(math.sqrt(n))
    for i in range(2, upperlimit + 1):
        if (n % i== 0):
            return False
    return True
def count_primes(max_n):
    result = 0
    for i in range(2, max_n + 1):
        if is_prime(i):
            result += 1
    return result
def test():
    max_n= 1000000
    print(f'Numberof primes between 0 and {max_n} = {count_primes(max_n)}')
def main():
    print(f'Elapsedtime: {Timer(stmt=test).timeit(1)} secs')
if __name__ == '__main__':
    main()
```

Figure 80.29 countofprimesinpythononly.py

PythonEngine1 and **PythonModule1** provide the "wiring" between the Python script and the Delphi event handler `PythonModule1Events0Execute`. The remainder of the code of the latter packs and unpacks the communication between Python script and the Delphi program.

15. Click `Execute` to run `pythondelphiprime.py`. Repeat this two more times.
16. The Python program counts the number of primes between 0 and 1000000, measures the time that elapses and then prints both results - *Figure 80.32*. The elapsed time is approximately 0.32 seconds. Twenty times faster than script `countofprimesinpythononly.py`.

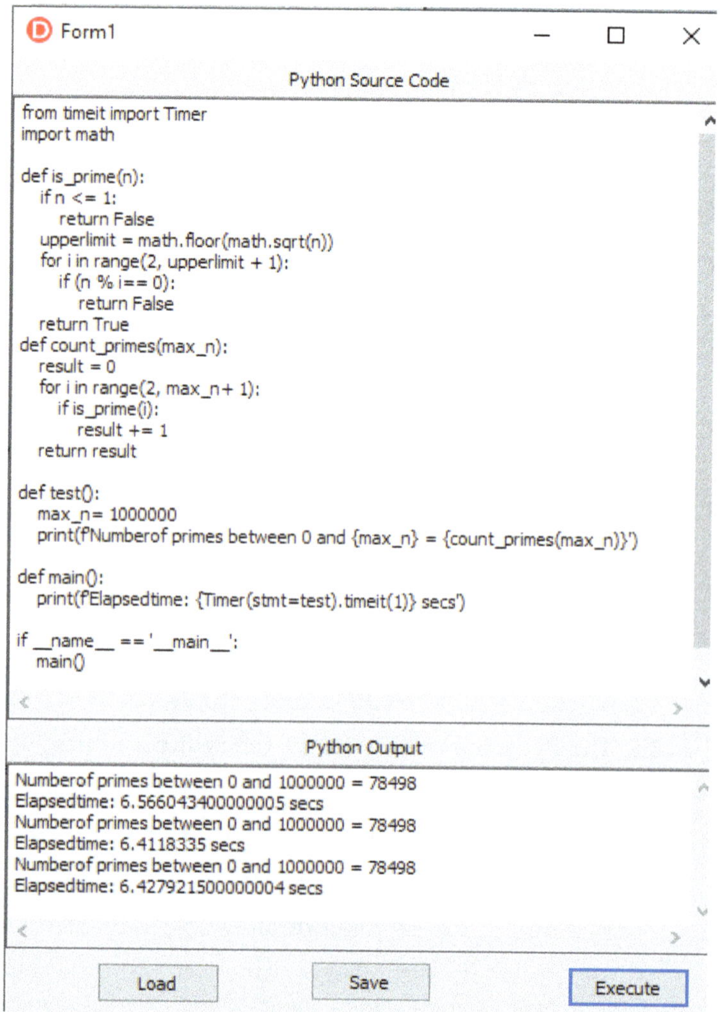

Figure 80.30 countofprimesinpythononly.py executed three times

```
from delphi_module import delphi_is_prime
from timeit import Timer
import math

def count_primes(max_n):
    result=0
    for i in range(2,max_n+1):
        if delphi_is_prime(i):
            result +=1
    return result
def test():
    max_n=1000000
    print(f'Number of primes between 0 and {max_n}={count_primes(max_n)}')
def main():
    print(f'Elapsed time:{Timer(stmt=test).timeit(1)}secs')
if __name__=='__main__':
    main()
```

Figure 80.31 pythondelphiprime.py

Information

Threading issue in Python

Python is not suitable for parallelising computationally intensive Python code because threaded Python code is locked to one thread executing at a time. However, C extensions and I/O (e.g.PIL or numpy operations), and any C code can run in parallel with one active Python thread. One solution is to delegate to a dedicated external library.

Sixth project

www.educational-computing.com/DelphiBook/Code/Chapter80/SixthExample.zip

This project was inspired by Kiriakos Vlahos (aka PyScripter):

1. Save project `FifthExampleProject.dproj` in a new folder, `SixthExample`, renaming it `SixthExampleProject.dproj` (**Save Project As**). Save unit `FifthExampleUnit.pas` in folder `SixthExample` renaming it `SixthExampleUnit.pas` (**Save As**).
2. Select **PythonModule1** and in the Object Inspector click the ellipsis (*Figure 80.23*) to bring up the **Events editor**.
3. Click [icon] in the **Events editor** to add a new event `delphi_count_primes` - *Figure 80.33*.
4. In the **Structure pane** select **Events** and `1 - delphi_count_primes`.
5. Switch to the **Events** page for `PythonModule1.Events[1]` and double click the field for the **OnExecute** event to create the event handler `PythonModule1Events1Execute`.
6. Switch to the source code view of `SixthExampleUnit.pas` and add the function `CountPrimes` - *Figure 80.34*.
7. Add the lines of source code shown in *Figure 80.35* to the event handler `PythonModule1Events1Execute`.
8. Save all (**Shift+Ctrl+S**).
9. Now compile, link and run (**Shift+Ctrl+F9**) the executable.
10. Click `Load` and open `CountoPrimesParallel.py` (*Figure 80.36*).

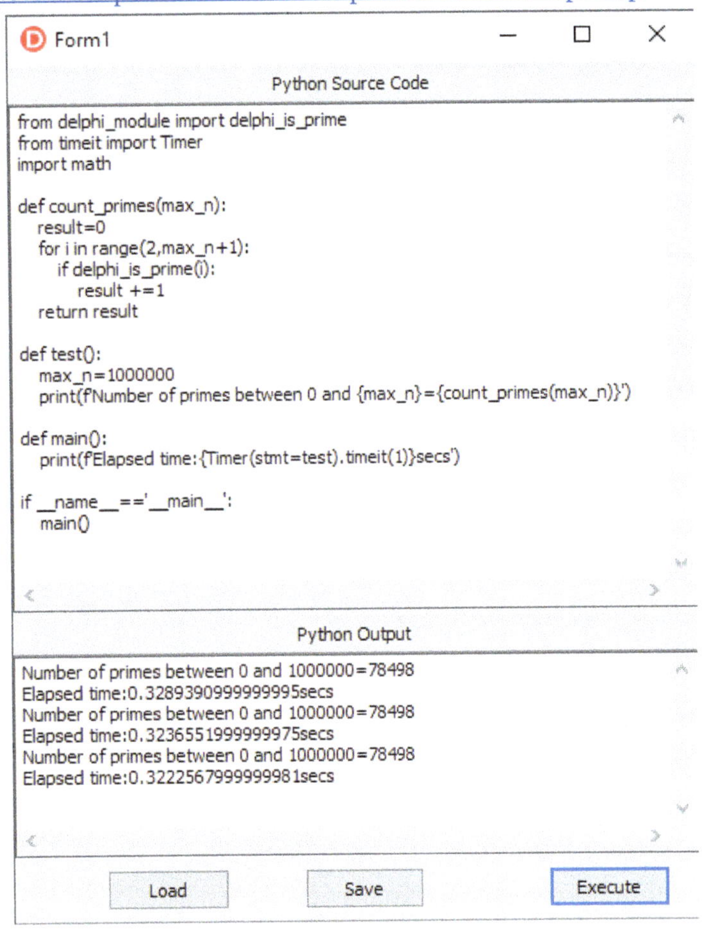

Figure 80.32 pythondelphiprime.py executed three times

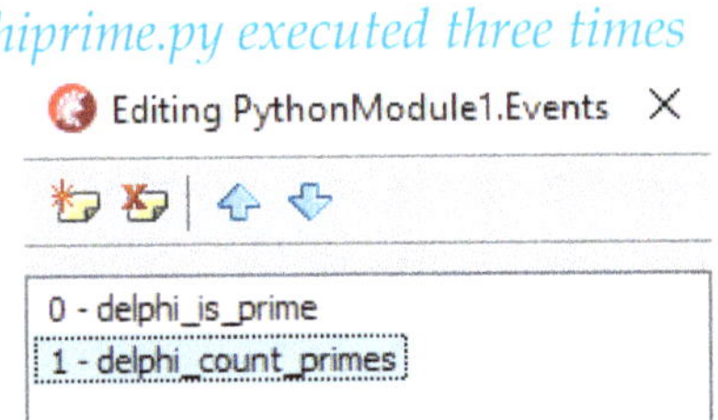

Figure 80.33 Events editor, new event delphi_count_primes

11. Click `Execute` to run `CountoPrimesParallel.py`. Repeat this two more times.
12. The Python program counts the number of primes between 0 and 1000000, measures the time that elapses and then prints both results - *Figure 80.37*. The elapsed time is approximately 0.06 seconds which is 100 times faster than the python script `countofprimesinpythononly.py`.

TParallel provides a class for-loop, **&For**, which makes efficient use of all the CPU cores in the system.

```
Function CountPrimes(MaxN : Integer): Integer;
  Begin
    Var Count := 0;
    TParallel.&For(2, MaxN, Procedure(i : Integer)
                                      Begin
                                        If IsPrime(i)
                                          Then AtomicIncrement(Count);
                                       End
                          );
    Result := Count;
  End;
```

Figure 80.34 Function CountPrimes

```
Procedure TForm1.PythonModule1Events1Execute(Sender: TObject; PSelf,
                                             Args: PPyObject;
                                             Var Result: PPyObject);
  Var
    N : Integer;
  Begin
    With GetPythonEngine
      Do
        Begin
          If PyArg_ParseTuple(Args, 'i:delphi_count_primes', @N) <> 0
            Then
              Begin
                Result := PyLong_FromLong(CountPrimes(N));
                Py_INCREF(Result);
              End
            Else Result := Nil;
        End;
  End;
```

Figure 80.35 Event handler PythonModule1Events1Execute

```
from delphi_module import delphi_count_primes
from timeit import Timer
import math
def test():
    max_n = 1000000
    print(f'Number of primes between 0 and {max_n} = {delphi_count_primes(max_n)}')
def main():
    print(f'Elapsed time:{Timer(stmt=test).timeit(1)}secs')
if __name__=='__main__':
    main()
```

Figure 80.36 CountPrimesParallel.py

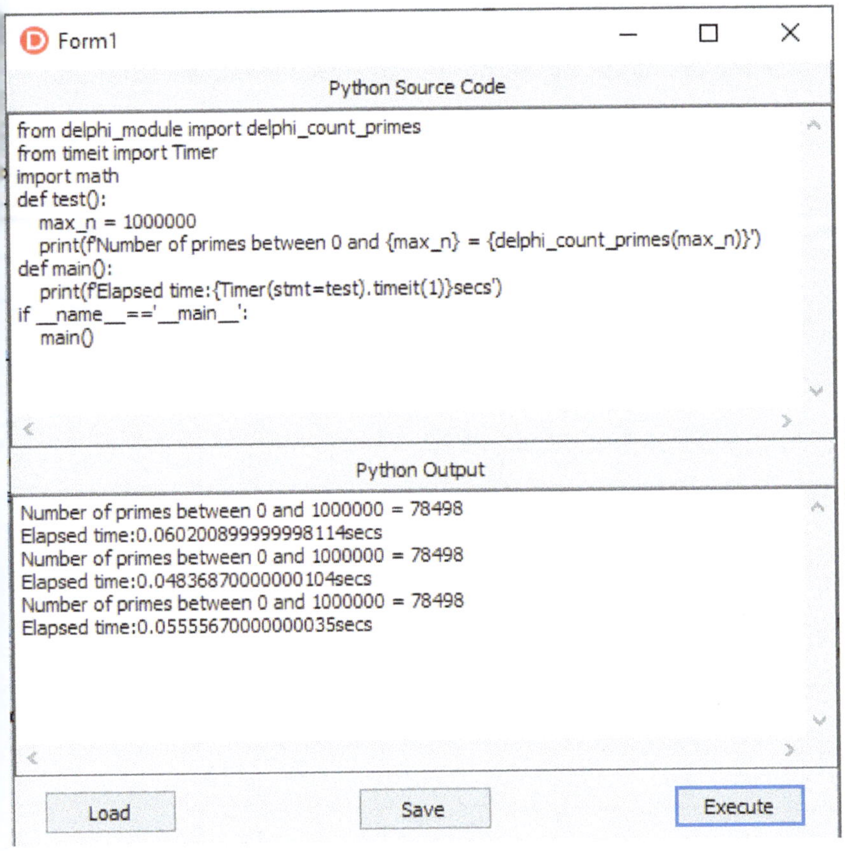

Figure 80.37 CountPrimesParallel.py

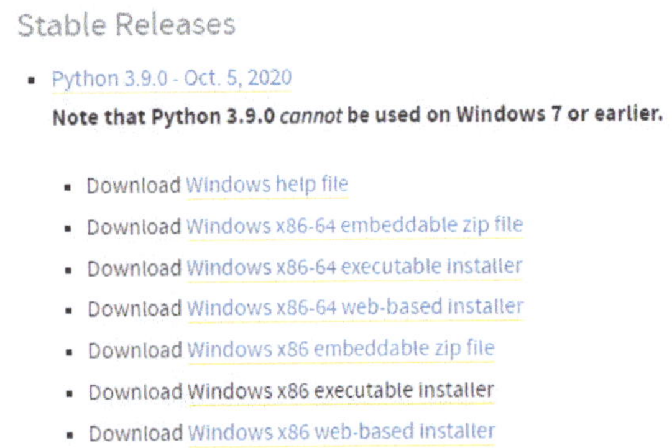

Figure 80.38 Python 3.9 download versions

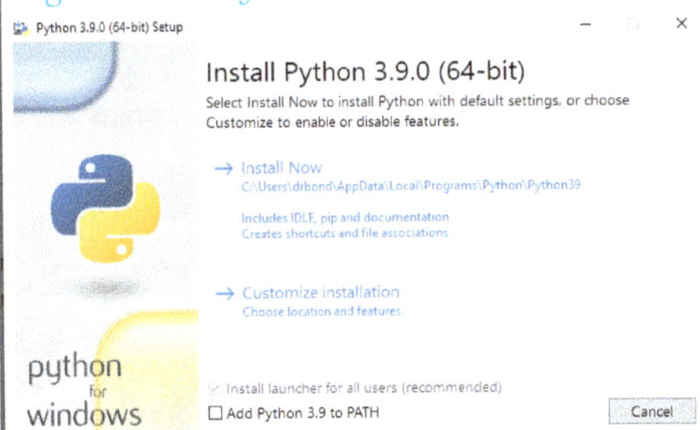

Figure 80.39 Python 3.9.0(64-bit) install

Using Python4Delphi with a version of Python installed from Python.org

Download **Windows x86-64 executable installer** for Python from python.org/downloads/windows - *Figure 80.38*.

Click on **python-3.9.0-amd64.exe** (or the version that you downloaded) to launch the install window. Tick **Add Python 3.9 to PATH** then click **Install Now** to install **Python 3.9** - *Figure 80.39*.

Python4Delphi should find **Python39.dll** automatically.

Create a new VCL application and add a **TPythonEngine** component to the form. *Figure 80.40* shows the Object Inspector pane for **PythonEngine1**. For this version of **Python4Delphi** the default settings of interest for **DelphiPython1** are

- **UseLastKnownVersion** = **True**
- **DllName** = **python39.dll**
- **AutoLoad** = **True**.

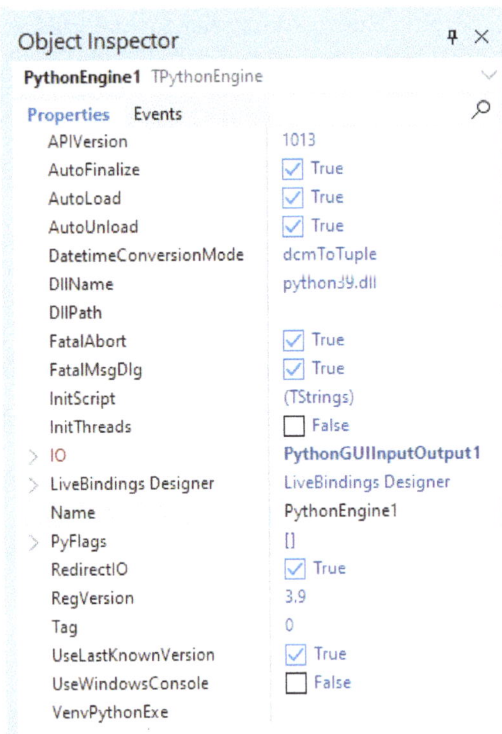

Figure 80.40 Objector Inspector

When earlier in this chapter we worked with an Anaconda installation of Python - **Python 3.8** we needed the application to initialise **PythonEngine1** as follows

```
PythonEngine1.SetPythonHome('c:\Users\drbond\anaconda3');
PythonEngine1.LoadDll;
```

Using **AutoLoad** set to **True** takes care of this automatically.

When Python is installed in Windows, the user has the option to register it, either for all users or just for this user. Registration involves writing information to the registry about the location of the installation, the name and location of the help file etc.

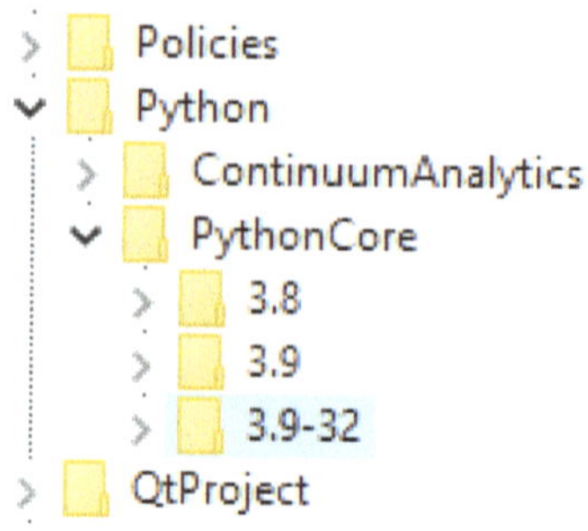

Figure 80.41 Registry entry for Computer\HKEY_CURRENT_USER\SOFTWARE\Python\PythonCore

Setting **UseLastKnownVersion** = **True** forces Delphi to use the latest **registered** version of Python.

If the programmer requires a different **registered**[2] version then they need to set the following properties:

- **DLLName** e.g. python38.dll
- **RegVersion** e.g 3.8
- Set **UseLastKnownVersion** property to **False**.

A little more work needs to be done to use a specific **unregistered** version:

Set

- **DLLName** e.g. python38.dll
- **RegVersion** e.g 3.8
- Set **UseLastKnownVersion** property to **False**
- Set **DLLPath** to the path where the DLL is located, e.g. `C:\Users\drbond\anaconda3`
- Set **AutoLoad** property to False
- The event handler for the **OnCreate** event of **Form1** (or whatever the form launched by the application is called), or in another suitable place, must contain the following code (assuming that **PythonEngine1** is the name of the component)

```
PythonEngine1.SetPythonHome('Python installation directory');
PythonEngine1.LoadDLL;
```

32-bit Delphi applications only work with 32-versions of Python and 64-bit Delphi applications only work with 64-bit versions of Python.

The project **FirstExampleProject** created using the Anaconda installed Python may now be recreated in Python 3.9 downloaded directly from www.python.org.

2 Anaconda distributions require that **SetPythonHome** is called as shown above even if they are registered.

Seventh project

www.educational-computing.com/DelphiBook/Code/Chapter80/SeventhExample.zip

This project manipulates images in Python which are loaded, displayed and saved using Delphi.

The Python side of things requires a module called pillow (PIL). The easiest way to install pillow is automatically as an integral part of an Anaconda installation, installing it directly is quite tricky because it depends on other modules being pre- installed. Anaconda automatically takes care of everything. For this reason, the Anaconda installation of Python - Python 3.8 - is used in this project. It will therefore be necessary to set up the Python Engine as per the instructions for unregistered versions of Python - see previous page.

1. Create a new **Windows VCL Application for Delphi** and save in a new folder `SeventhExample` with filenames `SeventhExampleProject.dproj` and `SeventhExampleUnit.pas`.
2. Drop a **TPanel** component on the form and set its **Align** property to **alBottom** in the **Object Inspector**. Set its **Height** property to 41 and clear its **Caption** property.
3. With this panel selected drop three buttons on the panel and set the **Top** property of each to 8. Position the buttons as shown in *Figure 80.42*.
4. Label the buttons `Load Image`, `Save Image` and `Execute` according to *Figure 80.42* adjusting the width of each accordingly.
5. Set the **Anchors** property of `Load Image` to **[akLeft, akTop, akBottom]**.
6. Set the **Anchors** property of `Save Image` to **[akTop, akBottom]**.
7. Set the **Anchors** property of `Execute` to **[akTop, akRight, akBottom]**.

Figure 80.42 SeventhExampleProject in execution

8. Drop a **TMemo** component (change **Name** to `Memo2`) on the form and set its **Align** property to **alBottom**. Open its **Lines** property and delete `Memo2` string to leave the memo box empty for the moment. Set **ScrollBars** to **ssBoth**.
9. Drop a **TSplitter** component from the **Additional** palette on the form and set its **Align** property to **alBottom** and its **Height** property to 2.
10. Drop a **TPanel** component on the form and set its **Align** property to **alBottom** in the **Object Inspector**. Change its **Caption** property to `Python Script`.
11. Drop a **TMemo** component (`Memo1`) on the form and set its **Align** property to **alBottom**. Open its **Lines** property and delete `Memo1` string to leave the memo box empty. Set **ScrollBars** to **ssBoth**.
12. Drop a **TPanel** component on the form and set its **Align** property to **alBottom** in the **Object Inspector**. Set its **Caption** property to `Image information (Don't exceed 2.5 MB)`.
13. Drop a **TImage** component and set its **Align** property to **alClient** and its **Proportional** property to **True**.
14. Drop a **TPythonEngine** and a **TPythonGUIInputOutput** component on the form.

15. As the author's Python installation was done via Anaconda, **PythonEngine1** needs to be set up as follows
    - **DLLName** e.g. python38.dll
    - **RegVersion** e.g 3.8
    - Set **UseLastKnownVersion** property to **False**
    - Set **DLLPath** to the path where the DLL is located, e.g. `C:\Users\drbond\anaconda3`
    - Set **AutoLoad** property to False
    - The event handler for the **OnCreate** event of **Form1** (or whatever the form launched by the application is called), or in another suitable place, must contain the following code (assuming that **PythonEngine1** is the name of the component)

```
PythonEngine1.SetPythonHome('Python installation directory');
PythonEngine1.LoadDLL;
```

16. Set **PythonEngine1**'s **IO** property to **PythonGUIInputOutput1**.
17. Set **PythonGUIInputOutput1**'s **Output** property to Memo1.
18. Add a **TOpenDialog** and a `T`**SaveDialog** component to the form.
19. Double click `Save Image` button and add the following lines of code to the event handler

```
With SaveDialog1
  Do
    Begin
      If Execute
        Then Memo1.Lines.SaveToFile(FileName);
    End;
```

Property of SaveDialog1 (FileName)

20. Double click `Load Image` button and add the following lines of code to the event handler

```
With OpenDialog1
  Do
    Begin
      If Execute
        Then Memo1.Lines.LoadFromFile(FileName);
    End;
```

Property of OpenDialog1 (FileName)

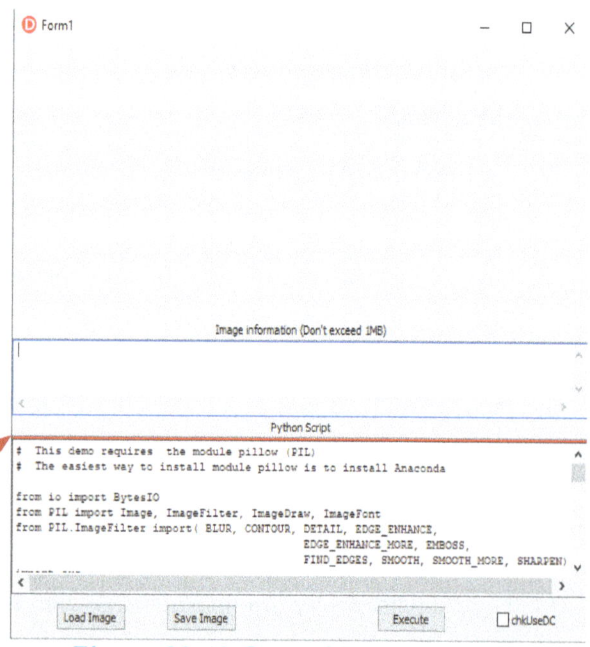

Figure 80.43 SeventhExampleProject in execution

21. Save project and unit in folder `SeventhExample`.
22. Select `Memo2` and open its **Lines** property so that the contents of script `ImageProcessingScript.py` shown in *Figure 80.45* can be pasted into the **String List Editor**.
23. Add a **Uses** clause to the **Implementation** section (place below **{R *.dfm}**) as follows

```
Uses
  VarPyth,
  Math,
  jpeg;
```

24. Add the source code shown in *Figure 80.46* to the implementation section.
25. Save all (**Shift+Ctrl+S**).
26. Now compile, link and run (**Shift+Ctrl+F9**) the executable.
27. The form shown in *Figure 80.43* should show.
28. Use the splitter bar to enlarge the Python script window.
29. The default setting of Python script is `new_im = im.convert('L')`. This Python statement when executed converts an RGB image to a black and white image one.

30. Click `Load Image` and select from the images folder `BorneoOrangUtan1SmallRes1.jpg` and open - *Figure 80.42*.
31. Click `Execute` to convert the image to a black and white one - *Figure 80.44*.
32. Comment out `new_im = im.convert('L')` in the Python Script window and uncomment

    `new_im = im.rotate(90, expand=True)`.
33. Click `Load Image` and select from the images folder `FarmPortDicksonLowResSmall.jpg` and open.
34. Click `Execute` to rotate this image through 90° counterclockwise. *Figure 80.47* shows the rotated image.
35. Click `Load Image` and select from the images folder `CockatooSmallLowRes.jpg` and open.
36. Comment out `new_im = im.rotate(90, expand=True)` in the Python Script window and uncomment `new_im = im.filter(FIND_EDGES)`.
37. Click `Execute` to find the images edges - *Figure 80.48*.

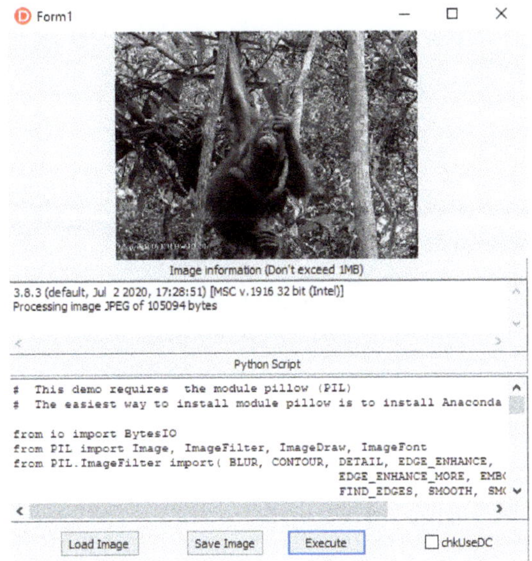

Figure 80.44 Black & white conversion

```
#  This demo requires  the module pillow (PIL)
#  The easiest way to install module pillow is to install Anaconda
from io import BytesIO
from PIL import Image, ImageFilter, ImageDraw, ImageFont
from PIL.ImageFilter import( BLUR, CONTOUR, DETAIL, EDGE_ENHANCE,
                             EDGE_ENHANCE_MORE, EMBOSS,
                             FIND_EDGES,SMOOTH, SMOOTH_MORE, SHARPEN)
import sys
def ProcessImage(data):
    print(sys.version)
    stream = BytesIO(data)
    im = Image.open(stream)
    print ("Processing image %s of %d bytes" % (im.format, len(data)))
    # new_im = im.rotate(90, expand=True)
    # new_im = im.filter(ImageFilter.BLUR)
    # new_im = im.filter(ImageFilter.BoxBlur(5))
    # new_im = im.filter(ImageFilter.GaussianBlur(5))
    # new_im = im.crop((100,200,400,500))
    # new_im = im.transpose(Image.FLIP_LEFT_RIGHT)
    # new_im = im.transpose(Image.FLIP_TOP_BOTTOM)
    # new_im = im.transpose(Image.ROTATE_90)
    # new_im = im.resize(round(im.size[0]*0.5), round(im.size[1]*0.5))
    # width, height = im.size
    # draw = ImageDraw.Draw(im)
    # text = "sample watermark"
    # font = ImageFont.truetype('arial.ttf', 36)
    # textwidth, textheight = draw.textsize(text, font)
    # calculate the x,y coordinates of the text
    # margin = 10
    # x = width - textwidth - margin
    # y = height - textheight - margin
    # draw watermark in the bottom right corner
    # draw.text((x, y), text, font=font)
    new_im = im.convert('L')
    # new_im = im.filter(CONTOUR)
    # new_im = im.filter(EMBOSS)
    # new_im = im.filter(FIND_EDGES)
    new_im.format = im.format
    return new_im
def ImageToString(image):
    stream = BytesIO()
    image.save(stream, image.format)
    return stream.getvalue()
```

Figure 80.45 ImageProcessingScript.py

```
Function ImageToPyStr(AGraphic : TGraphic) : Variant;
  Var
    _Stream : TMemoryStream;
    _Str : PPyObject;
  Begin
    _Stream := TMemoryStream.Create();
    Try
       AGraphic.SaveToStream(_Stream);
      _Str := GetPythonEngine.PyString_FromStringAndSize(_Stream.Memory, _Stream.Size);
      Result := VarPythonCreate(_Str);
      GetPythonEngine.Py_DECREF(_Str);
    Finally
      _Stream.Free;
    End;
  End;
Procedure TForm1.Button1Click(Sender: TObject);
  Var
    _im : Variant;
    _Stream : TMemoryStream;
    _dib : Variant;
    pargs: PPyObject;
    presult :PPyObject;
    P : PAnsiChar;
    Len : NativeInt;
  Begin
    If (Image1.Picture.Graphic = nil) or Image1.Picture.Graphic.Empty
      Then Raise Exception.Create('You must first select an image');
    PythonEngine1.ExecStrings(Memo2.Lines);
    _im := MainModule.ProcessImage(ImageToPyStr(Image1.Picture.Graphic));
    If Not chkUseDC.Checked
      Then
        Begin
         // We have to call PyString_AsStringAndSize because the image may contain zeros
          With GetPythonEngine
            Do
              Begin
                pargs := MakePyTuple([ExtractPythonObjectFrom(_im)]);
                Try
                  Try
                   presult := PyEval_CallObjectWithKeywords(ExtractPythonObjectFrom(MainModule.ImageToString),
                                                            pargs, nil);
                    If (PyString_AsStringAndSize(presult, P, Len) < 0) or (P = nil)
                      Then
                        Begin
                          ShowMessage('This does not work and needs fixing');
                          Abort;
                        End;
                  Finally
                    Py_XDECREF(pResult);
                  End;
                Finally
                  Py_DECREF(pargs);
                End;
              End;
          _Stream := TMemoryStream.Create();
          Try
            _Stream.Write(P^, Len);
            _Stream.Position := 0;
            Image1.Picture.Graphic.LoadFromStream(_stream);
          Finally
            _Stream.Free;
          End;
        End
      Else
        Begin
          Image1.Picture.Bitmap.SetSize(Image1.Width, Image1.Height);
          _dib := Import('PIL.ImageWin').Dib(_im);
          Image1.Picture.Bitmap.SetSize(Image1.Height, Image1.Width);
          _dib.expose(NativeInt(Image1.Picture.Bitmap.Canvas.Handle));
        End;
```

Figure 80.46 Source code from Python4Delphi Demo 29

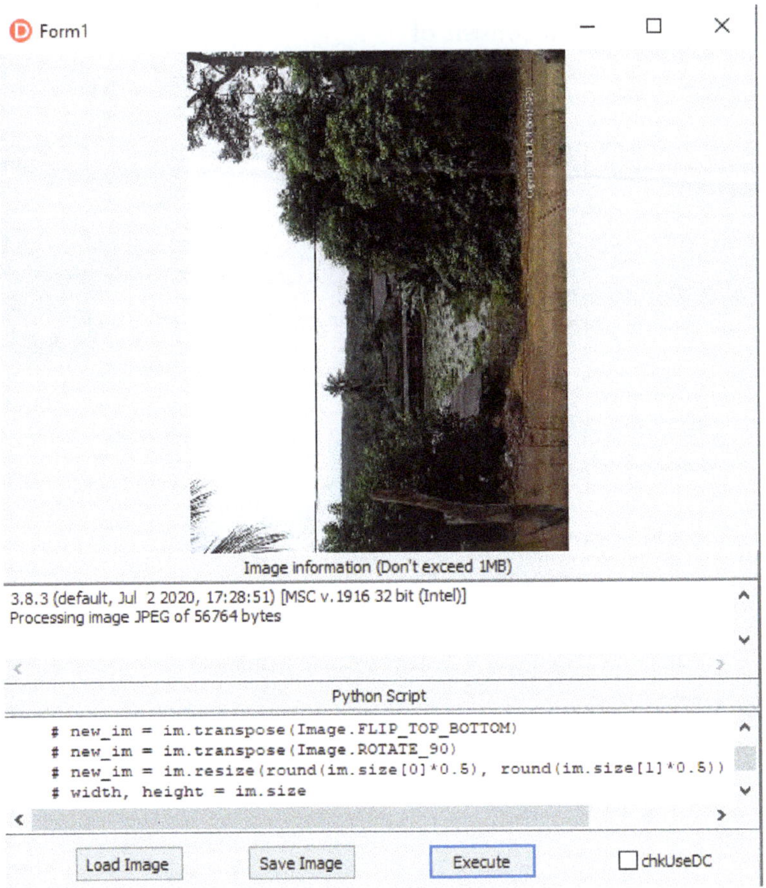

Figure 80.47 Rotated image

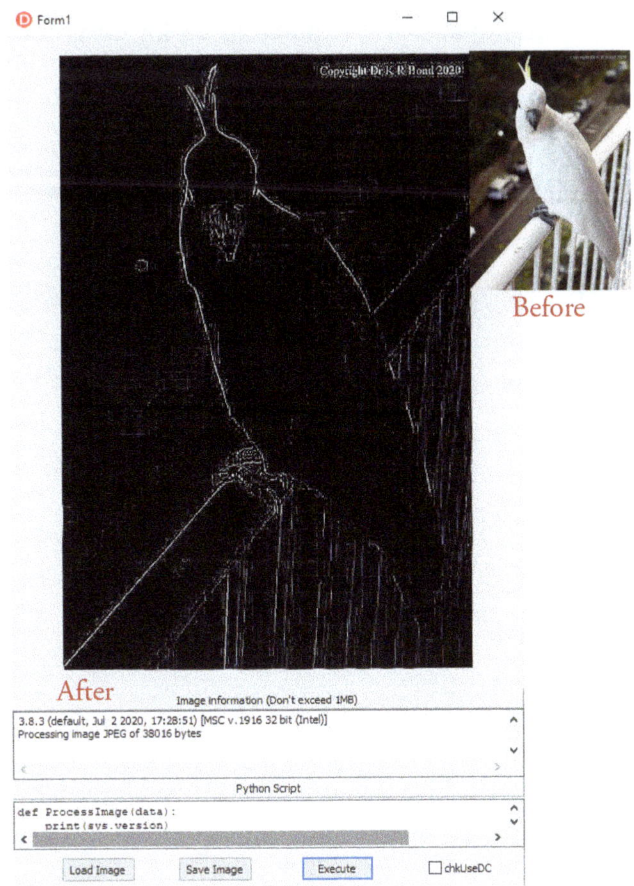

Figure 80.48 Finding edges

Programming Task

1. Create a new VCL application which implements image processing based on the Python script shown in *Figure 80.45*.

The user interface should enable a user to

- load an image
- save an image
- select and apply a particular image processing effect, e.g. convert a coloured image to monochrome (black and white). The application should then automatically execute the corresponding Python code to achieve this effect. No visible reference to this Python code should appear in the user interface when operating normally.

The application should

- check that an image is loaded before attempting to apply any image processing
- prevent images from loading that are above 1MB in size.

Deploying Python4Delphi Application

The minimum that is required to deploy a **Python4Delphi** application consists of

1. the application's exe, e.g. `FirstExampleProject.exe`
2. The dll of the version of Python that was used when developing the application, e.g. `python38.dll`.

Information

Download Inno Setup QuickStart pack - it is much easier to use because it uses a wizard to guide you through setting up an installer.

Figure 80.49 and *Figure 80.50* show the first two stages of creating a software installer for the two files mentioned above. A free Microsoft Windows® installer **Inno SetUp** by JRSoftware.org was used to create an installer `setup.exe` for `FirstExampleProject`.

Figure 80.51 shows that `FirstExampleProject` has been added to the **Start Menu** after running its installer `setup.exe`.

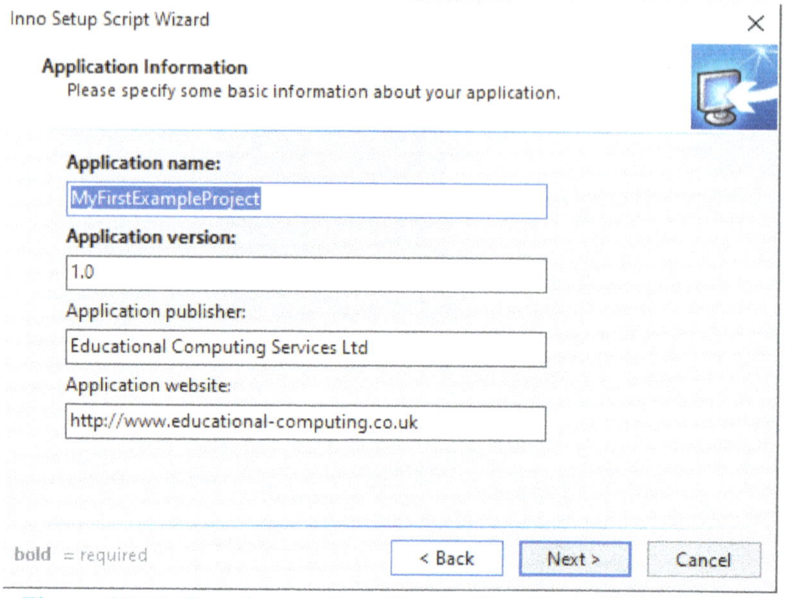

Figure 80.49 Creating an installer for FirstExampleProject.exe using Inno Script Studio Community edition

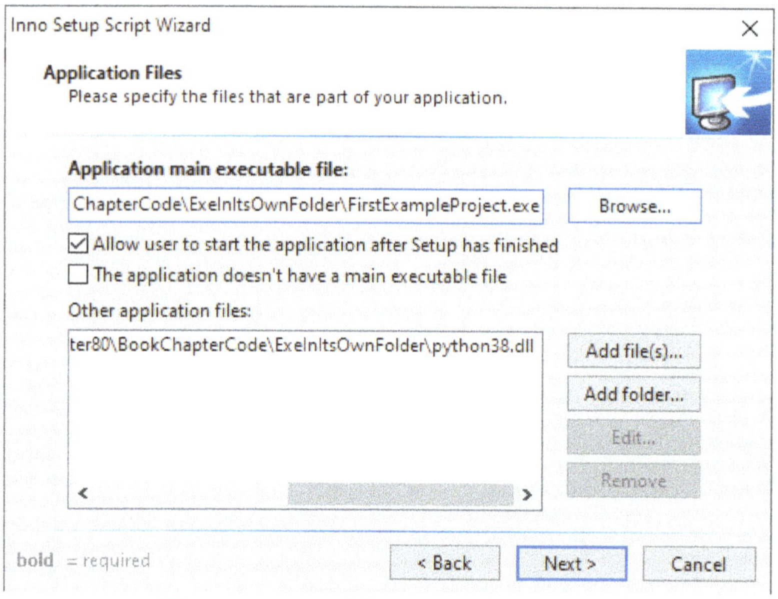

Figure 80.50 Adding the application files

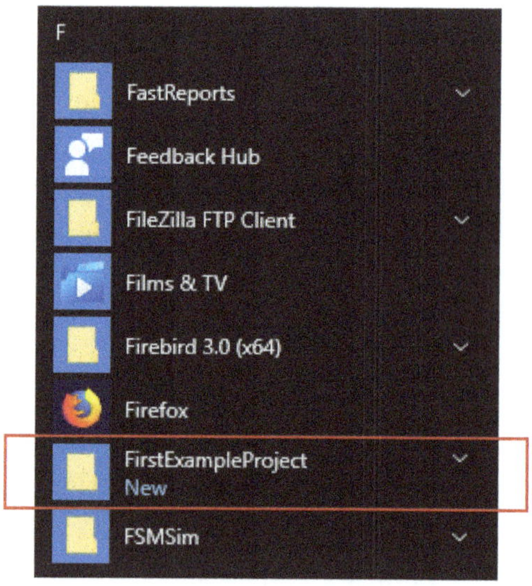

Figure 80.51 Start menu showing FirstExampleProject

TPythonEngine InitScript

TPythonEngine has a property called **InitScript** of type **TStrings** - *Figure 80.52*. Valid Python source code assigned to this property is executed when the application is launched as shown in *Figure 80.53*. In this example, the Python source code assigned to **InitScript** is the string

```
print ("This FirstExampleProject enables
Python scripts in the window\r\n above to be
executed with output appearing here.")
```

`\r` is the escape code for carriage return.

`\n` is the escape code for new line.

www.educational-computing.com/DelphiBook/Code/Chapter80/EighthExample.zip

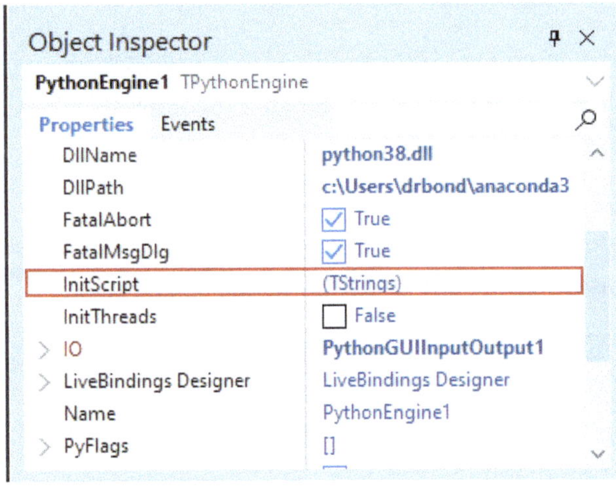

Figure 80.52 Object Inspectator view of PythonEngine1 in FirstExampleProject

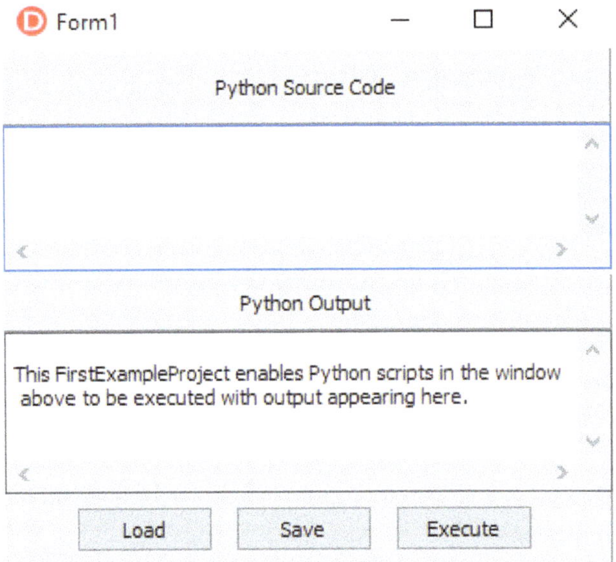

Figure 80.53 FirstExampleProject in execution

Eighth project

This project makes use of the package **SynEdit** which provides syntax highlighting. The package may be downloaded:

1. As a zip file from https://github.com/SynEdit/SynEdit.
2. Or using **Tools|GetIt Package Manager**.
3. Or from within Delphi - **File|Open From Version Control...** if you have installed git (https://gitforwindows.org) on your computer.

Figure 80.54 shows the expanded **SynEdit** download.

Open **SynEdit.groupproj** from the **Packages** folder in the Delphi IDE choosing the version corresponding to your version of Delphi, e.g. **104S** for **Delphi 10.4 Sydney**.

Highlight the runtime package **SynEdit_R104S.bpl** in the **Projects** pane (or highlight your particular version of **SynEdit**) and click the right mouse button to bring up the menu to use to build the package. Select **From Here|Build All From Here.**

Do the same for the design time package **SynEdit_D104S.bpl**. Once built, click the right mouse button over **SynEdit_D104S.bpl** to bring up the menu again. Select the **Install** option to install the **SynEdit** components.

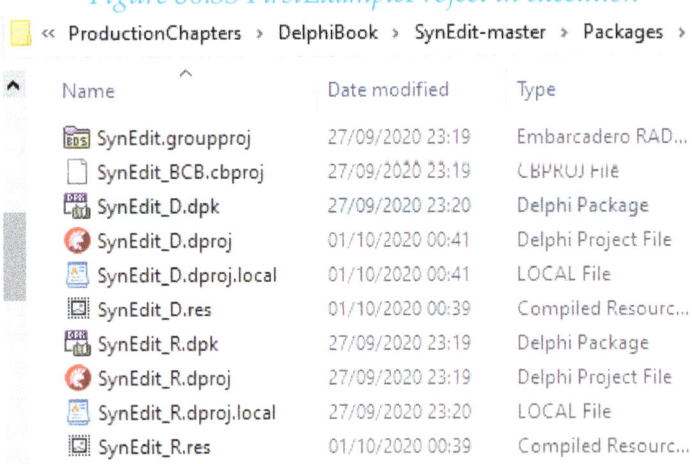

Figure 80.54 Expanded SynEdit download

Figure 80.55 shows that menus for the installed **SynEdit** and **SynEdit Highlighters** components have been installed in the **Component Palette**.

Open project `FirstExampleProject.dproj` and save in a new folder, `EighthExample`, rename the project `EighthExampleProject.dproj` (**Save Project As**).

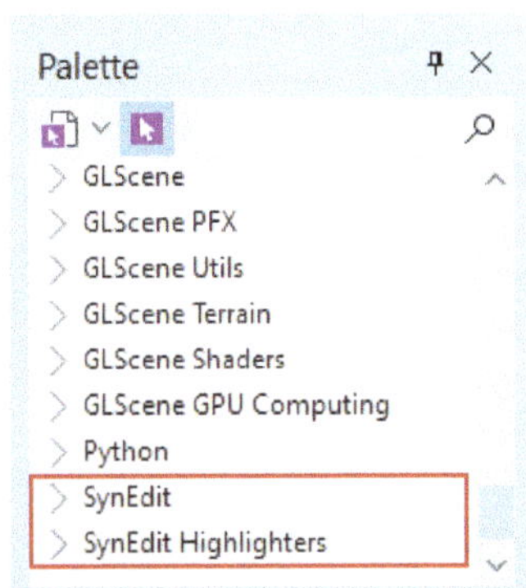

Figure 80.55 Component Palette

Save unit `FirstExampleUnit.pas` in new folder `EighthExample`, rename the unit `EighthExampleUnit.pas` (**Save As**).

Add a **TSynEdit** component from the **SynEdit Palette** to the form. Set it **Align** property to **alTop**. Now move it so that it is immediately below the panel with caption `Python Source Code`.

Select `Memo1` in the **Structure** pane and click the right mouse button and select from **Edit** from the popup menu then **Delete**. The form should look similar to that shown in *Figure 80.56*.

Open the **Lines** property of `SynEdit1` in **Object Inspector** and delete the line `SynEdit1`.

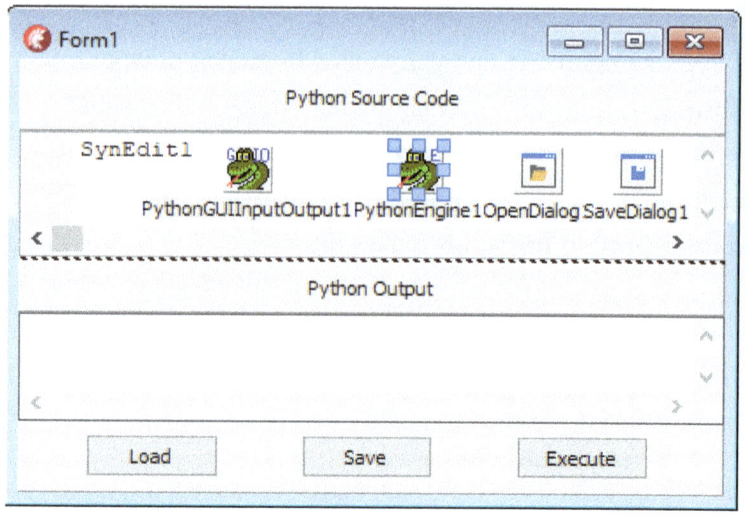

Figure 80.56 Form design for EighthExampleProject

Add a **TSynEditPythonBehaviour** component from the **SynEdit Palette** to the form. Set its **Editor** property to `SynEdit1`.

Add a **TSynPythonSyn** component from the **SynEdit Highlighters Palette** to the form. Set the **Highlighter** property of the **Editor** property of `SynEditPythonBehaviour1` to `SynPythonSyn1`.

Change the event handler for the button labelled `Execute` to

`PythonEngine1.ExecStrings(UTF8Encode(SynEdit1.Text)).`

Replace `Memo1` in the event handler for the button labelled `Load` with `SynEdit1`.

Replace `Memo1` in the event handler for the button labelled `Save` with `SynEdit1`.

Select `SynPythonSyn1` in the **Object Inspector** and change the **ForeGround** of **KeyAttri** property to **clRed** - *Figure 80.57*.

Change the **ForeGround** of **IndentifierAttri** property to **clHighlight**.

Save project and unit in folder `EighthExample`.

Now compile, link and run (**Shift+Ctrl+F9**) the executable.

Click **Load** and select `BubbleSort.py`.

Click **Execute**.

Figure 80.58 shows the result.

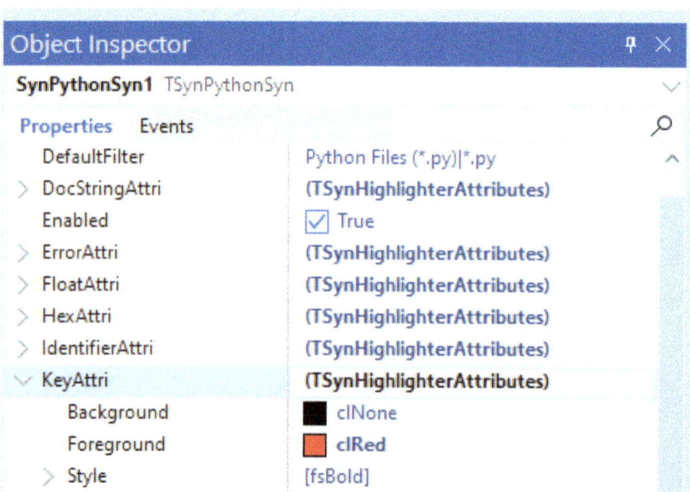

Figure 80.57 Section of Object Inspector showing how to change attribute colour

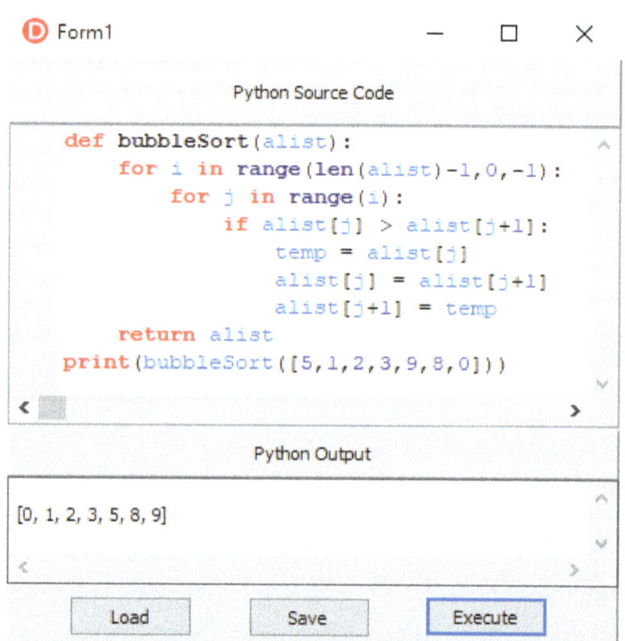

Figure 80.58 EighthExampleProject in execution with BubbleSort.py loaded and run

www.educational-computing.com/DelphiBook/Code/Chapter80/NinthExample.zip

Ninth project

Save project `EighthExampleProject.dproj` in a new folder, `NinthExample`, rename the project `NinthExampleProject.dproj` (**Save Project As**).

Save unit `EighthExampleUnit.pas` in new folder `NinthExample`, rename the unit `NinthExampleUnit.pas` (**Save As**).

1. Add a **TPyDelphiWrapper** from the **Python Palette** to the form.
2. Check in Object Inspector that **Engine** property of `PyDelphiWrapper1` (default identifier of **TPyDelphiWrapper component**) is set to `PythonEngine1` and **Module** property is set to `PythonModule1`.
3. Add the additional source code shown in *Figure 80.59* to the **FormCreate** event handler in `NinthExampleUnit.Pas`.

```
Procedure TForm1.FormCreate(Sender: TObject);
  Begin
    PythonEngine1.SetPythonHome('c:\Users\drbond\Anaconda3');
    PythonEngine1.LoadDll;
    Var Py := PyDelphiWrapper1.WrapRecord(@DelphiFunctions,
                TRttiContext.Create.GetType(TypeInfo(TDelphiFunctions))
                  As TRttiStructuredType);
    PythonModule1.SetVar('delphi_functions', Py);
    PythonEngine1.Py_DecRef(Py);
  End;
```

Required because Anaconda3 was used to install Python 3.8

@ means use address of

Figure 80.59 Event handler TForm1.FormCreate

The properties and events displayed at design time in the **Object Inspector** for an instance of a class have the scope **published**. **Published** means that runtime type information (**RTTI**) is generated about these through the application's published interface. External applications can also access this **RTTI** to get information that enables each application to determine the fields, methods, and properties an otherwise indeterminate object has at runtime.

4. Add the following to the **Implementation** section

```
Uses
  System.Rtti,
  System.Threading
  System.Math

Type
  TDelphiFunctions = Record
                       Class Function count_primes(MaxN : Integer) : Integer; Static;
                     End;
Var
  DelphiFunctions : TDelphiFunctions;
```

For a Python program to access a type defined in a Delphi program we need to supply a published interface, i.e. an **RTTI** structure.

The inline variable declaration(introduced in Delphi 10.3):

```
Var Py := PyDelphiWrapper1.WrapRecord(@DelphiFunctions,
            TRttiContext.Create.GetType(TypeInfo(TDelphiFunctions))
              As TRttiStructuredType);
```

wraps up the published type information in variable `Py` which

```
PythonModule1.SetVar('delphi_functions', Py);
```

associates with the class variable `delphi_functions`, the identifier to be used in the Python program side of things as follows

```
from delphi_module import delphi_functions
```

Check that the **ModuleName** property of `PythonModule1` is `delphi_module`.

The final added line of source code shown in *Figure 80.59* frees the object reference stored in `Py` by calling `Py_DecRef`

```
PythonEngine1.Py_DecRef(Py);
```

5. Add the source code shown in *Figure 80.60* to the end of `NinthExampleUnit.pas`.

A class method is a method (other than a constructor) that operates on classes instead of objects. To be able to access the function `count_primes` independently of any object reference, it is made a **static** class function.

A **class static method** therefore has no **Self** parameter. The **Self** parameter identifies the object to which the method call applies or is to operate on but there won't be one in this example.

```
Function IsPrime(x : Integer) : Boolean;
  Begin
    If (x <= 1) Then Exit(False);
    Var UpperLimit := Floor(Sqrt(x));
    For Var i := 2 To UpperLimit
      Do If (x Mod i = 0) Then Exit(False);
    Exit(True);
  End;

Class Function TDelphiFunctions.count_primes(MaxN : Integer) : Integer;
  Begin
    Var Count := 0;
    TParallel.&For(2, MaxN, Procedure(i : Integer)
                              Begin
                                If IsPrime(i) Then AtomicIncrement(Count);
                              End);
    Result := Count;
  End;
```

Count accessible by more than one thread so must ensure that transaction is atomic

Figure 80.60 More Source code for NinthExampleUnit.Pas

6. Save project and unit in folder `NinthExample`.
7. Now compile, link (**Shift + F9**) to build the project.
8. Create the Python script `NinthExample.py` as shown in *Figure 80.61*.

```
from delphi_module import delphi_functions
from timeit import Timer
import math
def test():
    max_n = 1000000
    print(f'Number of primes between 0 and {max_n} = {delphi_functions.count_primes(max_n)}')
def main():
    print(f'Elapsed time: {Timer(stmt=test).timeit(1)} secs')
if __name__ == '__main__':
    main()
```

Figure 80.61 NinthExample.py

9. Press **Shift + Ctrl + F9** to run `NinthExampleProject` without debugging.
10. Click `Load` and open `NinthExample.py`
11. Click `Execute`.

12. The outcome from `NinthExample.py` when run from Delphi `NinthExampleProject` is shown in *Figure 80.62* - `delphi_functions.count_primes` with multiple threads takes to five sig. figs only 0.042383 seconds.

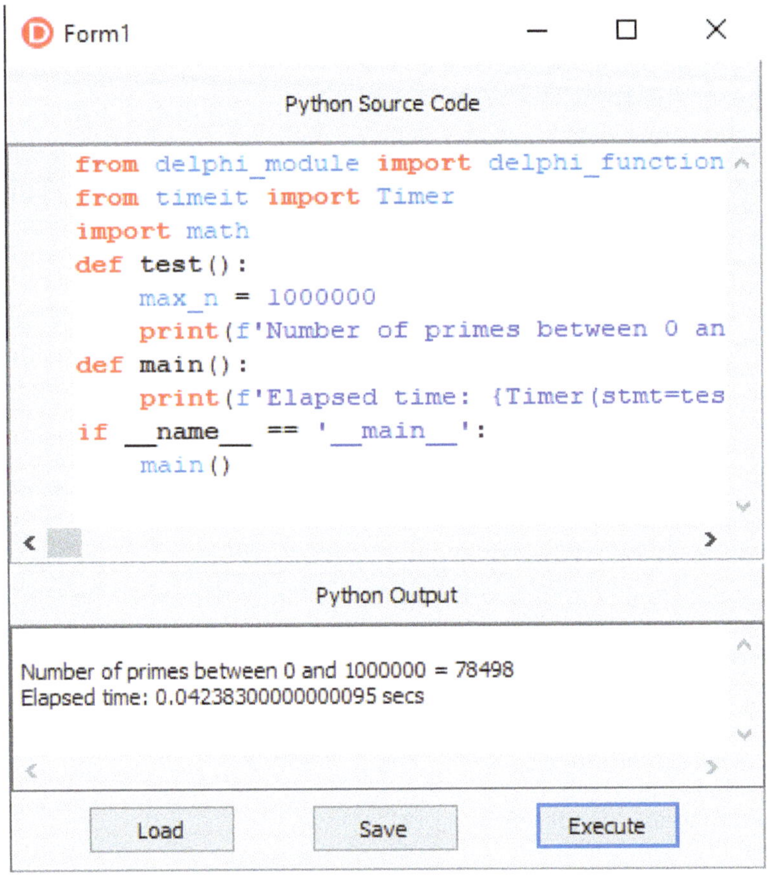

Figure 80.62 NinthExampleProject in execution

Tenth project

www.educational-computing.com/DelphiBook/Code/Chapter80/TenthExample.zip

NumPy is a Python programming language library which adds support for large, multi-dimensional arrays and matrices, as well as a large collection of high-level mathematical functions to operate on these arrays.

NumPy can be installed by using the installer **pip** from the command line. However installing some of the larger Python libraries, particularly those such as **NumPy** which depend on complex low-level C and Fortran packages, is made easier with **Anaconda**. **Anaconda** does all the dependency checking and binary installs that are required. **Anaconda** is free to download and install from https://www.anaconda.com/products/individual.

Information

Modules are individual .py files from which we can import functions and objects. Packages are collections of such modules.

Once the **NumPy** library is installed, an array, for example, is created after importing the numpy module (alias **np**) in Python as follow:

```
import numpy as np
vector = np.array([0, 1, 2, 3])
```

Python list [0, 1, 2, 3] is converted and returned by function **np.array**. Python has no native array construct so we rely on libraries such as **NumPy** for array support.

The module **numpy** can be imported into Delphi as follows

```
Var np := Import('numpy');
```

For this statement to compile the **VarPyth** unit from **Python4Delphi** must appear in the **Uses** clause.

A delphi array is created and returned by Delphi function `np.array` is as follows

```
Var np_array : Variant := np.array(VarPythonCreate([1,2,3,4,5,6,7,8,9,10])
```

The variable `np_array` is a variant data structure. A variant data structure is one that allows types that cannot be determined at compile time or whose data structure values can change their type at run time. In this example, `TenthExample`, using a variant for the variable `np_array` allows it to work in both Delphi and Python. We need a **TPythonModule**, `PythonModule1`, with which to set up shared access to `np_array` for Delphi and Python as follows

```
PythonModule1.SetVar('np_array', ExtractPythonObjectFrom(np_array));
```

This setting up may be done in the `FormCreate` event handler as shown in *Figure 80.63*.

```
Procedure TForm1.FormCreate(Sender : TObject);
  Begin
    PythonEngine1.SetPythonHome('c:\Users\drbond\Anaconda3');
    PythonEngine1.LoadDll;
    Var np := Import('numpy');
    Var np_array : Variant := np.array(VarPythonCreate([1,2,3,4,5,6,7,8,9,10]));
    PythonModule1.SetVar('np_array', ExtractPythonObjectFrom(np_array));
  End;
```

These two statements needed because Anaconda installed Python 3.8 which is used for the Python program.

Figure 80.63 TenthExampleUnit.pas

With the **ModuleName** property `delphi_module` assigned to `PythonModule1`, the Delphi constructed array `np_array` may be imported into the Python program `np_array.py` as shown in *Figure 80.64*.

`np_array` may then be accessed in Python, e.g. `print("np_array = ", np_array)`

In order to use what has been described, a graphical user interface is needed.

```
from delphi_module import np_array
print("type(np_array) = ", type(np_array))
print("len(np_array) = ", len(np_array))
print("np_array = ", np_array)
res_array = np_array.copy()
for i in range(len(np_array)):
    res_array[i] *= np_array[i]
print("res_array = ", res_array)
```

Figure 80.64 np_array.py

Save project `NinthExampleProject.dproj` in a new folder, `TenthExample`, rename the project `TenthExampleProject.dproj` (**Save Project As**).

Save unit `NinthExampleUnit.pas` in new folder `TenthExample`, rename the unit `TenthExampleUnit.pas` (**Save As**).

1. Delete `PyDelphiWrapper1`, `Function IsPrime` and `Class Function TDelphiFunctions.count_primes`.
2. Edit `FormCreate` so that it conforms to *Figure 80.63*.
3. Edit the **Uses** clause under **Implementation** as follows

```
Uses
  System.Threading,
  System.Math,
  VarPyth;
```

4. Drop a **TListBox** component on the form and set its **Align** property to **alRight** in the **Object Inspector** so it aligns between the `Python Output` panel and the bottom panel.
5. Drop a **TSplitter** component on the form and set its **Align** property to **alRight** so it aligns to the left of the **TListBox** component.

The user interface at design time should look similar to *Figure 80.65*.

6. Edit `Button1Click` so that its body now is as shown in *Figure 80.66*.

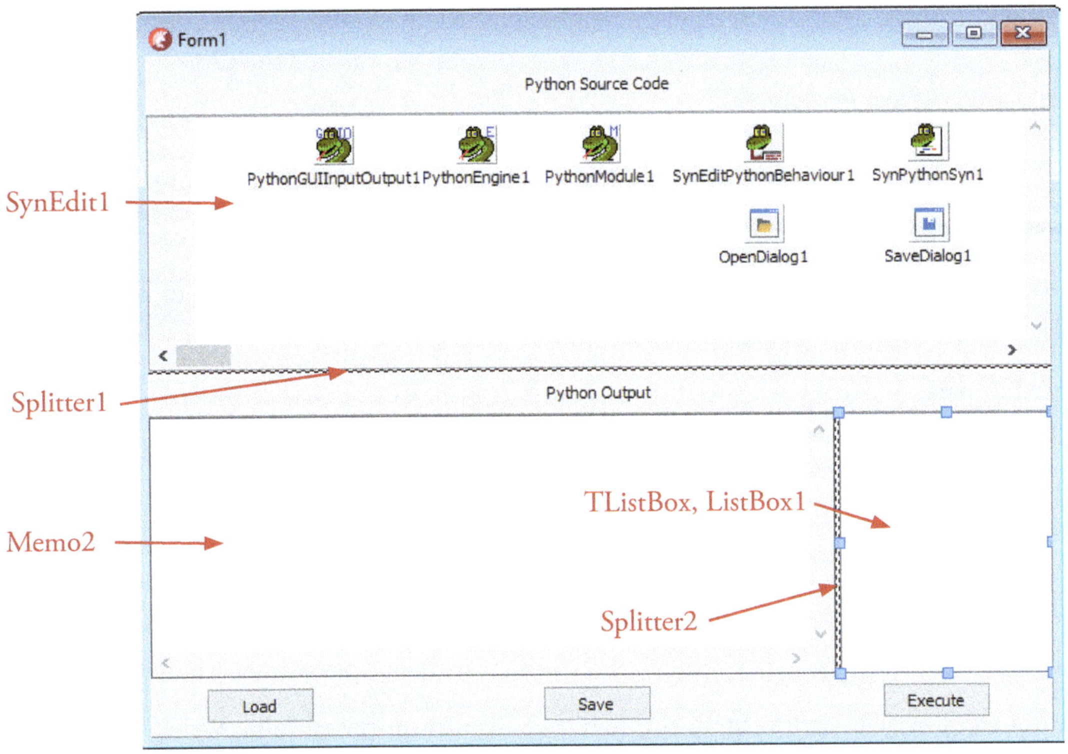

Figure 80.65 TenthExampleProject user interface at design time

Information

FPU Exception mask

Delphi's default FPU Exception mask is different from most other Windows apps. It is incompatible with Python libraries written in C or C++. It is necessary to match the FPU mask that numpy, scipy, tensorflow, etc expect to operate with. PythonEngine.pas provides a function for doing that, MaskFPUExceptions, which needs to be called - MaskFPUExceptions(True) - before Python is loaded. The Initialization section of the main Delphi form can be used to do this.

```
Procedure TForm1.Button1Click(Sender : TObject);
  Begin
   // PythonEngine1.ExecStrings(SynEdit1.Lines);
    GetPythonEngine.ExecString(UTF8Encode(SynEdit1.Text));
    For Var V In VarPyIterate(MainModule.res_array)
      Do ListBox1.Items.Add(V);
  End;
```

Alternative way of executing the contents of SynEdit1

MainModule always refers to a Python module, in this case np_array.py

Figure 80.66 TenthExampleUnit.pas Button1Click event handler

7. Add at the end of `TenthExampleUnit.Pas`

   ```
   Initialization
     MaskFPUExceptions(True);
     ReportMemoryLeaksOnShutdown := True;
   ```

   just before final **End**.
8. Save project and unit in folder `TenthExample`.
9. Create the Python script `numpy_array.py` as shown in *Figure 80.64*.
10. Now build and run the project without debugging (**Shift+Ctrl+F9**).
11. Click `Load` and open `numpy_array.py`.
12. Click `Execute`.

Figure 80.67 shows the outcome. The array of integers submitted to the Python script are returned squared. The returned result is displayed in the **TMemo** window `Memo2` and in the **TListBox** window `ListBox1`.

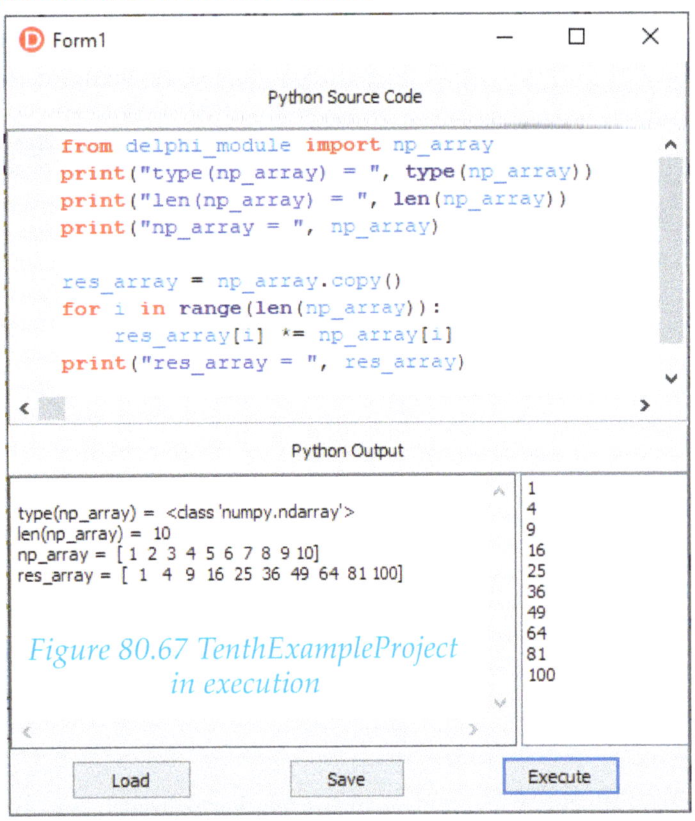

Figure 80.67 TenthExampleProject in execution

Eleventh project www.educational-computing.com/DelphiBook/Code/Chapter80/EleventhExample.zip

Save project `TenthExampleProject.dproj` in a new folder, `EleventhExample`, rename the project `EleventhExampleProject.dproj` (**Save Project As**).

Save unit `TenthExampleUnit.pas` in new folder `EleventhExample`, rename the unit `EleventhExampleUnit.pas` (**Save As**).

1. Add two **TPanel** components to the form, `Panel4` and `Panel5`, clear the **Caption** property of each.
2. Set **Align** property of `Panel4` to **alLeft** and adjust its **Width** property so that it occupies less than half of a wide form - see *Figure 80.69*.
3. In this order in the **Structure** pane, move `Panel3` to `Panel4`, move `Memo2` to `Panel4`, move `Splitter1` to `Panel4`, move `Panel2` to `Panel4`, move `SynEdit1` to `Panel4`, finally move `Panel1` to `Panel4`.
4. Delete `ListBox1`.
5. **Align** property of `Panel5` to **alClient**.
6. Set `Splitter2`'s **Align** property to **alLeft**.
7. Add a **TEdgeBrowser** component, `EdgeBrowser1`, to `Panel5` and set its **Align** property to **alClient**.

Support in VCL applications for working with web content through the **Chromium-based Edge WebView2** browser control is now present in Delphi 10.4 via the new **TEdgeBrowser** component.

TEdgeBrowser replaces **TWebBrowser**, which uses the **Internet Explorer WebBrowser** browser control. **TWebBrowser** is still available in the VCL component set, with some notable changes.

TWebBrowser uses the Operating System-supplied **Internet Explorer WebBrowser browser control** so there is no preparation required; it will work wherever Windows has the Internet Explorer control available.

As **Microsoft Edge** is not an Operating System component at the time of writing this book, it is necessary to install **EdgeView2 SDK 0.9.488** by Microsoft® before the **TEdgeBrowser** component can work in Delphi applications.

The easiest way to do this is to use **GetIt Package Manager** - **Tools|GetIt Package Manager...**, type **Edge** in search box then return. *Figure 80.68* shows the currently available **EdgeView2 SDK**. Click this to select, then click the install button to install the package. This is shown as done in *Figure 80.68* by **Installed** being ticked.

Figure 80.68 GetIt Package Manager EdgeView2 SDK

For the **TEdgeBrowser** component to work at runtime, the corresponding **WebView2Loader.dll** - x86 or x64 - must be placed in the project's output directory, i.e. `EleventhExample\Win32\Debug` or `EleventhExample\Win64\Debug`. Locate the folder containing the relevant **WebView2Loader.dll** (where Delphi 10.4 is installed, use **Redist** folder) and copy this dll.

8. Add a **TPyDelphiWrapper** component, `PyDelphiWrapper1`, to the form.
9. The **Engine** property of `PyDelphiWrapper1` should be set to `PythonEngine1` and its **Module** property set to `PythonModule1`.
10. Edit the `FormCreate` event handler so that it is as shown in *Figure 80.70*.

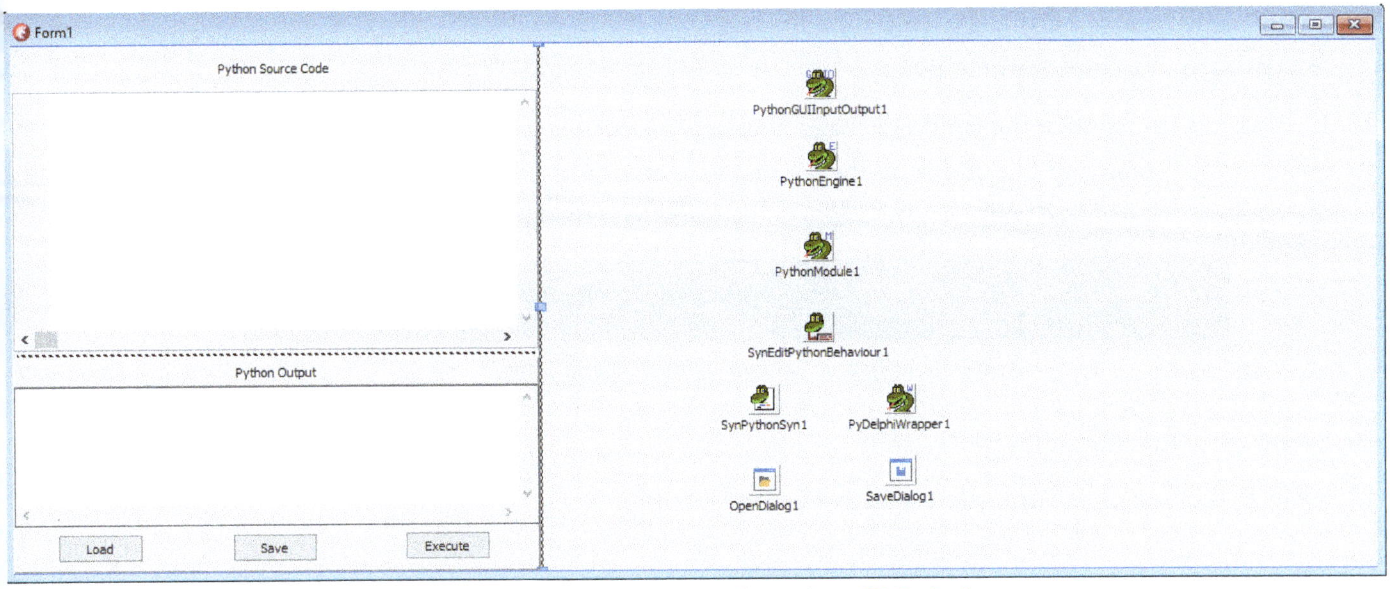

Figure 80.69 EleventhExampleProject GUI design

11. Edit the `Button1Click` event handler so that it is as shown in *Figure 80.71*.

12. Delete the **Uses** clause in the **Implementation** section.

Object reference variable Py assigned reference to wrapped EdgeBrowser1

```
Procedure TForm1.FormCreate(Sender : TObject);
  Begin
    PythonEngine1.SetPythonHome('c:\Users\drbond\Anaconda3');
    PythonEngine1.LoadDll;
    Var Py := PyDelphiWrapper1.Wrap(EdgeBrowser1, soReference);
    PythonModule1.SetVar('edge_browser', Py);
    GetPythonEngine.Py_DECREF(Py);
  End;
```

Enumerated type defined in WrapDelphi.pas

Setting name that Python script will use to refer to the object referenced by Py

Figure 80.70 EleventhExampleUnit.pas FormCreate event handler

```
Procedure TForm1.Button1Click(Sender : TObject);
  Begin
    PythonEngine1.ExecStrings(SynEdit1.Lines);
  End;
```

Figure 80.71 EleventhExampleUnit.pas Button1Click event handler

13. Change **ReportMemoryLeaksOnShutdown** in the Initialization section to **False**. There is a very small memory leak.

14. This example project and others require the following python modules:

numpy - supports large, multi-dimensional arrays and matrices, and high-level mathematical functions to operate on these arrays.

pandas - supports data manipulation and analysis, includes data structures and operations for manipulating numerical tables and time series.

matplotlib - plotting library.

seaborn - data visualization library based on matplotlib, providing a high-level interface for drawing attractive and informative statistical graphics.

mpld3 - brings together matplotlib and the JavaScript library for creating interactive data visualizations for the web, **D3js**. The result is a simple API for exporting your matplotlib graphics to HTML code which can be used within the browser.

bokeh - an interactive visualization library for modern web browsers.

altair - a declarative statistical visualization library.

scikit-learn - machine learning library.

15. If Anaconda is used then the **conda package manager** is available to install any required packages. Switch to the command line and enter the command as shown in *Figure 80.72*, replacing package-name with the name of the required package. Anaconda will already have installed some of the required packages.

```
conda install package-name
```

Figure 80.72 Command line use of conda

16. Save project and unit in folder `EleventhExample`.
17. Three Python example scripts have already been prepared:
    - `EleventhExampleMatPlotlib.py`
    - `EleventhExampleBokeh.py`
    - `EleventhExampleAltair.py`
18. Now build (**Shift+F9**) the project.
19. Paste **WebView2Loader.dll** in `Win32\Debug` or `Win64\Debug` folder depending on target.
20. Click Run Without Debugging (**Shift+Ctrl+F9**).
21. Click `Load` and open `EleventhExampleBokeh.py`.
22. Click `Execute` - *Figure 80.73* shows the outcome.
23. Use the sliders in the righthand window to interact with the Python script and alter the sine wave drawn by Delphi in the righthand window.

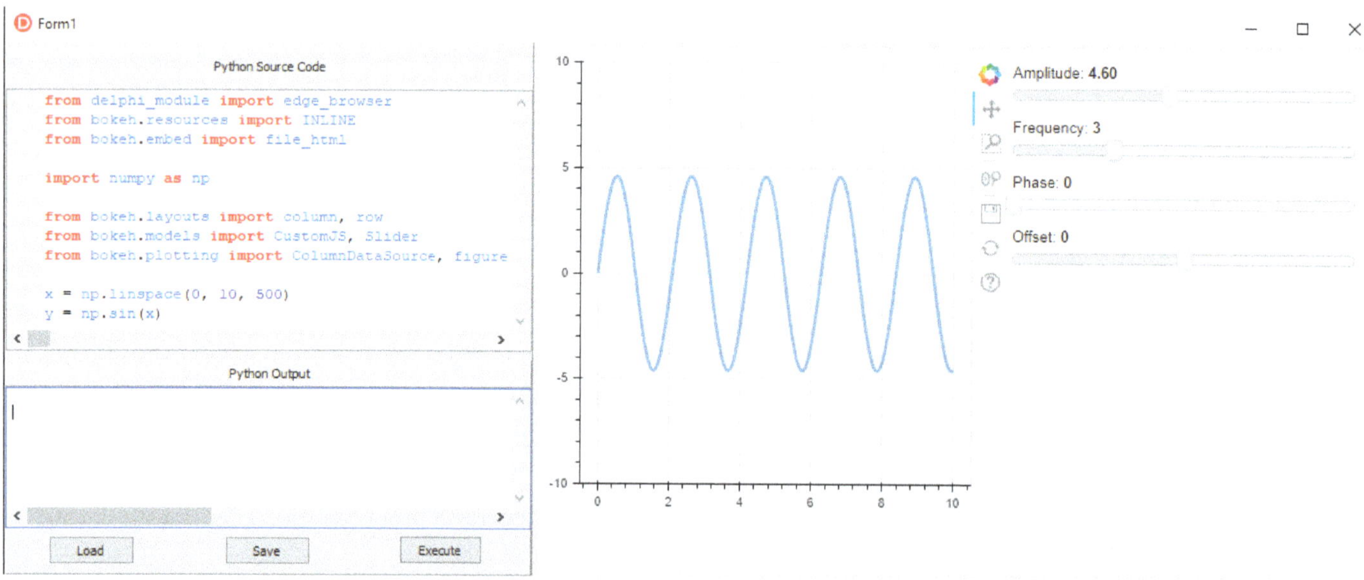

Figure 80.73 EleventhExampleProject in execution with script EleventhExampleBokeh.py loaded

www.educational-computing.com/DelphiBook/Code/Chapter80/TwelfthExample.zip

Twelfth project - uses Python libraries to create charts which are saved in SVG format and then plotted in Delphi

Save project `EleventhExampleProject.dproj` in a new folder, `TwelfthExample`, rename the project `TwelfthExampleProject.dproj` (**Save Project As**).

Save unit `EleventhExampleUnit.pas` in new folder `TwelfthExample`, rename the unit `TwelfthExampleUnit.pas` (**Save As**).

We need to install the package **SVGIconImageList VCL & FMX** (*Figure 80.74*) using GetIt Package Manager - **Tools|GetIt Package Manager**. Use of the components in this package simplifies manipulating SVG images.

Figure 80.74 View in GetIt Package Manager of SVGIconImageList VCL and FMX

Once installed the components can be found in the component palette under **Ethea**.

1. Delete `EdgeBrowser1` component from `Panel5`.
2. Add a **TSVGIconImage** component, `SVGIconImage1` to `Panel5`.
3. Edit `FormCreate` so that it is as shown in *Figure 80.75*.

```
Procedure TForm1.FormCreate(Sender : TObject);
  Begin
    PythonEngine1.SetPythonHome('c:\Users\drbond\Anaconda3');
    PythonEngine1.LoadDll;
    Var Py := PyDelphiWrapper1.Wrap(SVGIconImage1, soReference);
    PythonModule1.SetVar('svg_image', Py);
    GetPythonEngine.Py_DECREF(Py);
  End;
```

Setting name that Python script will use to refer to the object referenced by Py

Figure 80.75 TwelfthExampleUnit.pas FormCreate event handler

4. Save project and unit in folder `TwelfthExample`.
5. A Python example script has already been prepared `TwelfthExamplePenguins.py` - *Figure 80.76*.
6. Now run (**Shift+Ctrl+F9**) the project.
7. Click `Load` and open `TwelfthExamplePenguins.py`.
8. Click `Execute` - *Figure 80.77* shows the outcome.

```
from delphi_module import svg_image
from io import StringIO
import seaborn as sns
import matplotlib.pyplot as plt
df = sns.load_dataset("penguins")
sns.pairplot(df, hue="species")
figfile = StringIO()
plt.savefig(figfile, format='svg')
figdata_svg = figfile.getvalue()
svg_image.SvgText = figdata_svg
```

Figure 80.76 TwelfthExamplePenguins.py

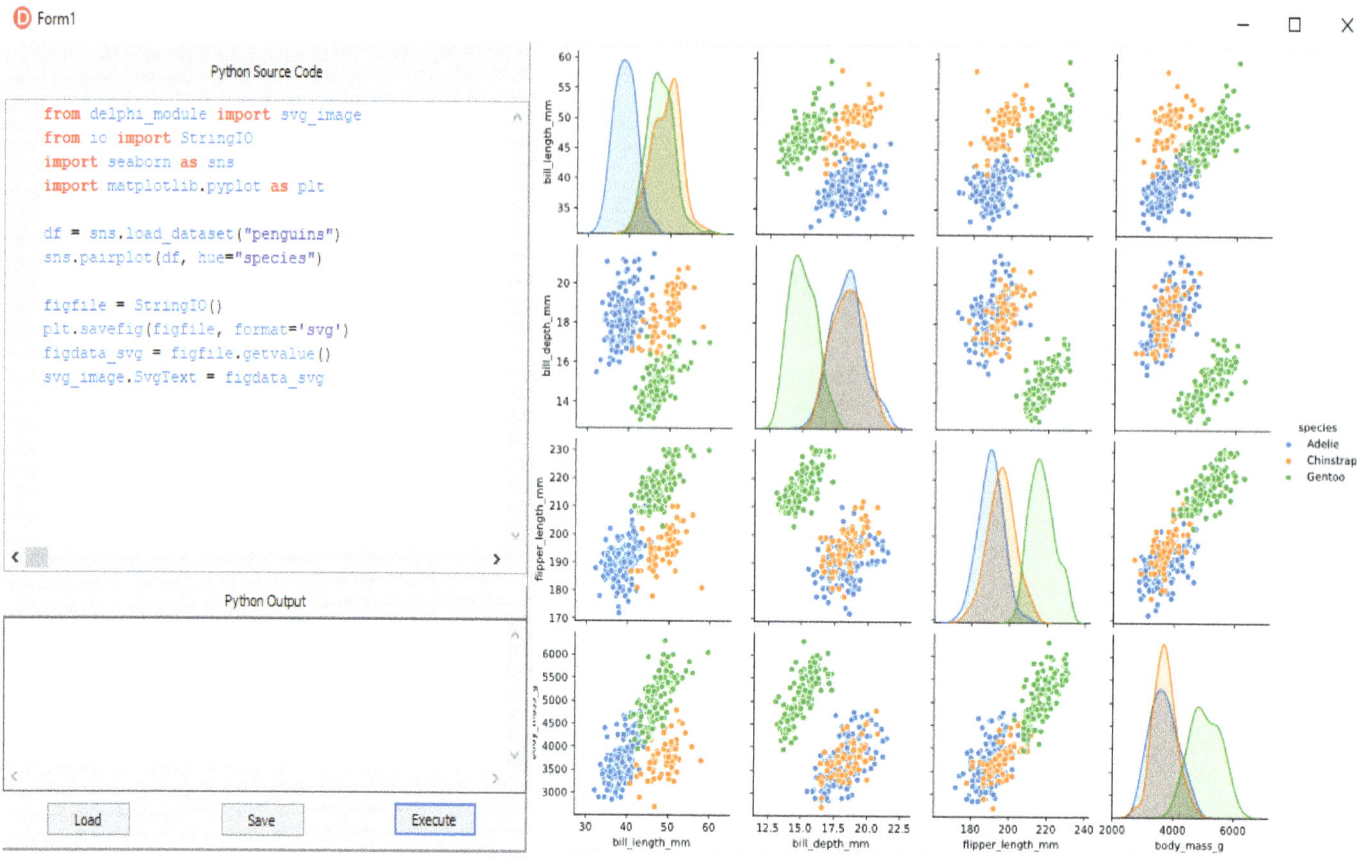

Figure 80.77 TwelfthExampleProject in execution

Thirteenth project

www.educational-computing.com/DelphiBook/Code/Chapter80/ThirteenthExample.zip

Load project `NinthExampleProject.dproj` and then save in a new folder, `ThirteenthExample`, rename the project `ThirteenthExampleProject.dproj` (**Save Project As**).

Save unit `NinthExampleUnit.pas` in new folder `ThirteenthExample`, rename the unit `ThirteenthExampleUnit.pas` (**Save As**).

1. Delete `PythonWrapper1`.
2. Replace **Uses** clause in the **Implementation** section with

```
Uses
  TypInfo, VarPyth, WrapDelphiVCL
```

3. Delete **Type** and **Var** statements in the **Implementation** section.
4. Delete **Function** `IsPrime` in the **Implementation** section.
5. Delete **Class Function** `TDelphiFunctions.count_primes` in the **Implementation** section.
6. Insert just before **End** keyword of `TForm1 Class` definition

```
Public
  PyDelphiWrapper1 : TPyDelphiWrapper;
```

7. Delete body of event handler `FormCreate` and replace with

```
PythonEngine1.SetPythonHome('c:\Users\drbond\Anaconda3');
PythonEngine1.LoadDll;
PyDelphiWrapper1 := TPyDelphiWrapper.Create(Self);
PyDelphiWrapper1.Engine := PythonEngine1;
PyDelphiWrapper1.Module := PythonModule1;
PyDelphiWrapper1.Initialize; //Use only if PyDelphiWrapper1 created at run time
```

8. Replace event handler `Button1Click` with

```
Procedure TForm1.Button1Click(Sender : TObject);
  Var
    PyObjectRef : PPyObject;
  Begin
    PyObjectRef := PyDelphiWrapper1.Wrap(Form1);
    PythonModule1.SetVar('MainForm', PyObjectRef);
    PythonEngine1.Py_DECREF(PyObjectRef);
    PythonEngine1.CheckError;
    PythonEngine1.ExecStrings(SynEdit1.Lines);
  End;
```

9. Rename **ModuleName** property of `PythonModule1`, `delphi_controls.`
10. Set `Form1`'s **Width** property to 980.
11. Set `Form1`'s **Height** property to 690.
12. Set `SynEdit`'s **RightEdge** property to 120.
13. Add to the end of the unit

```
Initialization
  ReportMemoryLeaksOnShutdown := DebugHoook <> 0;
```

14. Save project and unit in folder `ThirteenthExample`.
15. A Python example script has already been prepared, `ThirteenthExample.py` - *Figure 80.79*.
16. Now run (**Shift+Ctrl+ F9**) the project.
17. Click `Load` and open `ThirteenthExample.py`.
18. Click `Execute` - *Figure 80.78* shows the outcome.

The design of the Python-generated form may be prototyped first in Delphi. Once the form design is complete in Delphi, the property values may be read from the corresponding `.dfm` file and used in the Python script.

Output from Python script ThirteenthExample.py

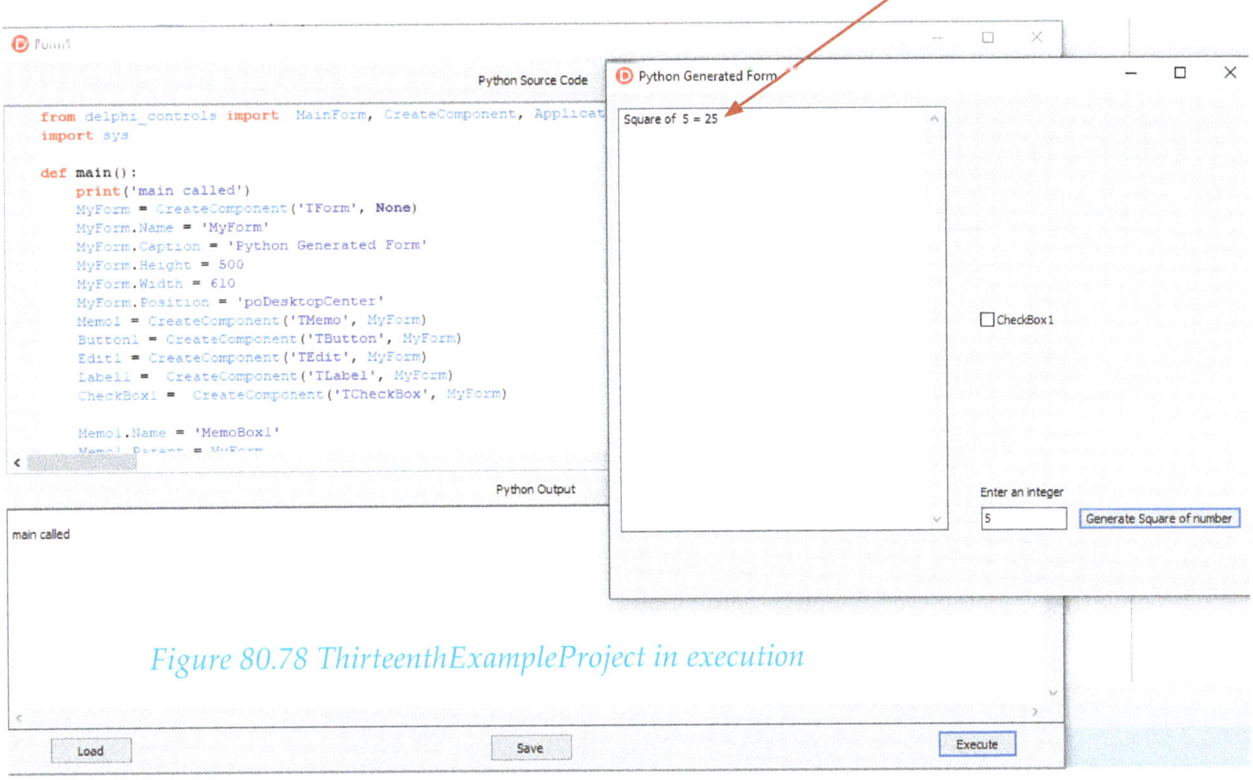

Figure 80.78 ThirteenthExampleProject in execution

```
from delphi_controls import MainForm, CreateComponent, Application, Screen, Form, Button, CheckBox, Label, Memo
import sys

def main():
    print('main called')
    MyForm = CreateComponent('TForm', None)
    MyForm.Name = 'MyForm'
    MyForm.Caption = 'Python Generated Form'
    MyForm.Height = 500
    MyForm.Width = 610
    MyForm.Position = 'poDesktopCenter'
    Memo1 = CreateComponent('TMemo', MyForm)
    Button1 = CreateComponent('TButton', MyForm)
    Edit1 = CreateComponent('TEdit', MyForm)
    Label1 =  CreateComponent('TLabel', MyForm)
    CheckBox1 =  CreateComponent('TCheckBox', MyForm)

    Memo1.Name = 'MemoBox1'
    Memo1.Parent = MyForm
    Memo1.Top = 14
    Memo1.Width = 300
    Memo1.Height = 387
    Memo1.Left = 10
    Memo1.Text = ''
    Memo1.TabOrder = 0
    Memo1.ScrollBars = 'ssVertical'
    Button1.Name = 'Button1'
    Button1.Parent = MyForm
    Button1.Left = 430
    Button1.Top = 380
    Button1.Width = 150
    Button1.Height = 21
    Button1.Caption = 'Generate Square of number'
    Button1.TabOrder = 1
    def ClickHandler(Sender):
        if CheckBox1.Checked:
            print(Sender.Name, ' was clicked')
        Memo1.Lines.Add( 'Square of  ' + Edit1.Text + ' = ' +  str(int(Edit1.Text) * int(Edit1.Text)))

    Button1.OnClick = ClickHandler
    Edit1.Name = 'Edit1'
    Edit1.Parent = MyForm
    Edit1.Left = 340
    Edit1.Top = 380
    Edit1.Width = 80
    Edit1.Height = 21
    Edit1.NumbersOnly = True
    Edit1.TabOrder = 2
    Edit1.Text = ''

    def KeyPressHandler(Sender, Key):
        print('non-numeric value')

    def KeyUpHandler(Sender, Key, Shift):
        if not (Key.Value  in range(48, 59)) :
            a = Edit1.Text
            Edit1.Text = a[:len(a)-1]
            Edit1.SelStart = len(a)
            print('UP:non-numeric value')

    Edit1.OnKeyUp = KeyUpHandler
    Label1.Name = 'Label1'
    Label1.Parent = MyForm
    Label1.Left = 340
    Label1.Top = 359
    Label1.Width = 121
    Label1.Height = 21
    Label1.Caption = 'Enter an integer'
    CheckBox1.Name = 'CheckBox1'
    CheckBox1.Parent = MyForm
    CheckBox1.Left = 340
    CheckBox1.Top = 200
    CheckBox1.Width = 97
    CheckBox1.Height = 17

    MyForm.ShowModal()

if __name__ == '__main__':
    main()
```

Figure 80.79 ThirteenExample.py

www.educational-computing.com/DelphiBook/Code/Chapter80/FourteenthExample.zip

Fourteenth project

Figure 80.80 FourteenthExampleProject form design

1. Create a new **Windows VCL Application for Delphi**.
2. Drop a **TPythonEngine** component on the form, `PythonEngine1`.
3. Drop a **TPythonModule** component on the form, `PythonModule1` - *Figure 80.80*.
4. Set `Form1`'s **Width** property to 136, its **Height** property to 198 and **BorderIcons** property to to **[biSystemMenu]**.
5. Set properties of `PythonEngine1` and `PythonModule1` in Object Inspector as for `ThirteenthExample`.
6. Create event handler `FormCreate` with body as shown in *Figure 80.81*.
7. Add `PyDelphiWrapper1` to `TForm1`, a **Uses** clause to the **Implementation** section and variable `PythonProgram` as shown in *Figure 80.81*.
8. Rename the project `FourteenExampleProject.dproj` (**Save Project As**) and save in new folder `FourteenExample`.
9. Save unit as `FourteenExampleUnit.pas` in new folder `FourteenExample` (**Save As**).
10. Now build (**Shift+F9**) the project.
11. Place a copy of `FourteenthExample.py` (*Figure 80.82*) in the `Windows32\Debug` folder of FourteenthExample.
12. Now run (**Shift+Ctrl+F9**) the project. *Figure 80.83* shows the outcome.

```
Unit FourteenthExampleUnit;
 Interface
 Uses
   Winapi.Windows, Winapi.Messages, System.SysUtils, System.Variants,
   System.Classes, Vcl.Graphics,
   Vcl.Controls, Vcl.Forms, Vcl.Dialogs, Vcl.StdCtrls, Vcl.ExtCtrls,
   PythonEngine, WrapDelphi;
 Type
   TForm1 = Class(TForm)
              PythonEngine1 : TPythonEngine;
              PythonModule1 : TPythonModule;
              Procedure FormCreate(Sender : TObject);
              Public
                PyDelphiWrapper1 : TPyDelphiWrapper;
            End;
 Var
   Form1 : TForm1;
 Implementation
 {$R *.dfm}
 Uses
   TypInfo, VarPyth, WrapDelphiVCL;
 Var
   PythonProgram : TStringList;
 Procedure TForm1.FormCreate(Sender : TObject);
   Var
     PyObjectRef : PPyObject;
   Begin
     Form1.Position:= poDesktopCenter;
     Form1.Width := 0;
     Form1.Height := 0;
     Form1.BorderIcons := [biSystemMenu];
     PythonEngine1.SetPythonHome('c:\Users\drbond\Anaconda3');
     PythonEngine1.LoadDll;
     PyDelphiWrapper1 := TPyDelphiWrapper.Create(Self);
     PyDelphiWrapper1.Engine := PythonEngine1;
     PyDelphiWrapper1.Module := PythonModule1;
     PyDelphiWrapper1.Initialize;
     PyObjectRef := PyDelphiWrapper1.Wrap(Form1);
     PythonModule1.SetVar('MainForm', PyObjectRef);
     PythonEngine1.Py_DECREF(PyObjectRef);
     PythonEngine1.CheckError;
     PythonProgram := TStringList.Create;
     PythonProgram.LoadFromFile('ThirteenthExample.py', TEncoding.UTF8);
     PythonEngine1.ExecString(PythonProgram.Text);
   End;
End.
```

Figure 80.81 FourteenthExampleUnit.pas

```
from delphi_controls import MainForm, CreateComponent, Application, Screen, Form, Button, Label,
Memo
import sys
def main():
    print('main called')
    MyForm = CreateComponent('TForm', None)
    MyForm.Name = 'MyForm'
    MyForm.Caption = 'Python Generated Form'
    MyForm.Height = 500
    MyForm.Width = 610
    MyForm.Position = 'poDesktopCenter'
    Memo1 = CreateComponent('TMemo', MyForm)
    Button1 = CreateComponent('TButton', MyForm)
    Edit1 = CreateComponent('TEdit', MyForm)
    Label1 =  CreateComponent('TLabel', MyForm)
    Memo1.Name = 'MemoBox1'
    Memo1.Parent = MyForm
    Memo1.Top = 14
    Memo1.Width = 300
    Memo1.Height = 387
    Memo1.Left = 10
    Memo1.Text = ''
    Memo1.TabOrder = 0
    Memo1.ScrollBars = 'ssVertical'
    Button1.Name = 'Button1'
    Button1.Parent = MyForm
    Button1.Left = 430
    Button1.Top = 380
    Button1.Width = 150
    Button1.Height = 21
    Button1.Caption = 'Generate Square of number'
    Button1.TabOrder = 1
    def ClickHandler(Sender):
        Memo1.Lines.Add( 'Square of  ' + Edit1.Text + ' = ' +  str(int(Edit1.Text) * int(Edit1.Text)))
    Button1.OnClick = ClickHandler
    Edit1.Name = 'Edit1'
    Edit1.Parent = MyForm
    Edit1.Left = 340
    Edit1.Top = 380
    Edit1.Width = 80
    Edit1.Height = 21
    Edit1.NumbersOnly = True
    Edit1.TabOrder = 2
    Edit1.Text = ''
    def KeyUpHandler(Sender, Key, Shift):
        if not (Key.Value  in range(48, 59)):
            a = Edit1.Text
            Edit1.Text = a[:len(a)-1]
            Edit1.SelStart = len(a)

    Edit1.OnKeyUp = KeyUpHandler
    Label1.Name = 'Label1'
    Label1.Parent = MyForm
    Label1.Left = 340
    Label1.Top = 359
    Label1.Width = 121
    Label1.Height = 21
    Label1.Caption = 'Enter an integer'
    MyForm.ShowModal()
if __name__ == '__main__':
    main()
```

Figure 80.82 FourteenthExample.py

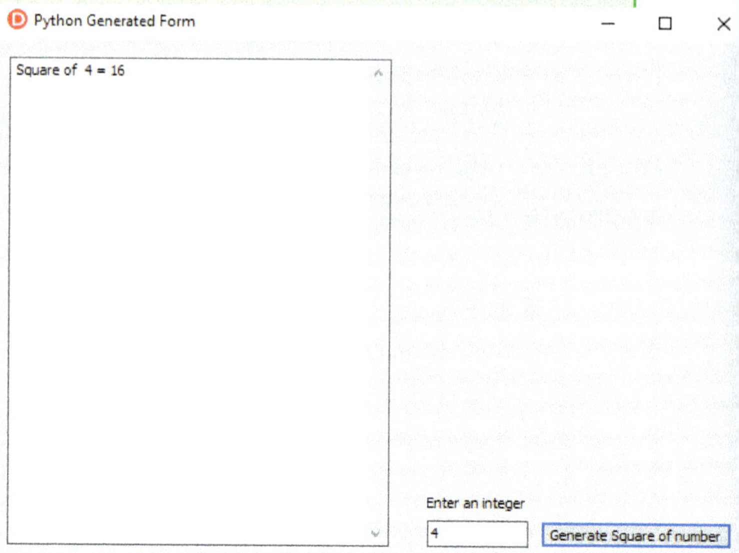

Figure 80.83 FourteenthExampleProject in execution

Information

Python for Delphi

With Python for Delphi it is possible to leverage the best of both Python and Delphi.

With Python for Delphi:

1. It is very easy to integrate Python into Delphi applications in a RAD way, thus providing access to a vast range of Python libraries.
2. Expose Delphi functions/procedures, objects, records and types to Python using low-or high-level interfaces.
3. Create/access/use Python objects/modules in Delphi code using a high-level interface (VarPyth).
4. Run Python code in threads.
5. Create Python extension modules.
6. Wrap VCL as a Python extension module to create GUIs with Python.

Fifteenth project www.educational-computing.com/DelphiBook/Code/Chapter80/FifteenthExample.zip

This project was inspired by Kiriakos Vlahos's Webinar

https://github.com/pyscripter/python4delphi/tree/master/Tutorials/Webinar%20I

Python's excellent library support for data science and machine learning has led to it dominating these two areas.

Delphi is renowned for its support for Rapid Application Development(RAD) - the first version of Skype to be created used a Delphi-programmed front end and a C-programmed back end.

It therefore makes sense to leverage the strengths of each to create a usable machine learning application.

This project is dependent on the Python library scikit-learn (**sklearn**), a free software machine learning library for the Python Programming Language. This machine learning library forms the core of the Python back end whilst the front end, written in Delphi, reports on and displays an output graph that shows the closeness of the predicted world-wide figures for the total number of Covid-19 cases over a ten day period at the end of data range. The front and back ends are connected by Python for Delphi.

Use the **conda package manager** from Anaconda or **pip** to install the Python machine learning library **sklearn**.

Also make sure that **numpy**, **pandas**, **matplotlib** and **io** are also installed.

This project uses COVID-19 time-series data for every country in the world reporting the total number of Covid-19 cases to-date. This data is available in comma separated value(**csv**) format from the Center(sic) for Systems Science and Engineering (CSSE) at John Hopkins University:

https://raw.githubusercontent.com/CSSEGISandData/COVID-19/master/csse_covid_19_data/csse_covid_19_time_series/time_series_covid19_confirmed_global.csv

The format is *Province/State, Country/Region, Latitude, Longitude, total recorded number of cases to date* (dates range from 22/1/2020 to 25/10/2020, inclusive for the day that this project was run).

For example,

, United Kingdom, 55.3781, -3.4336, 0, 0, ..., 873800

The first field is empty because the figures are not broken down in the UK's case by area.

The Python back end program is trained and confirmed on a subset of this data. The evolved statistical model is then tested on a ten day subset of this data and the result plotted and saved as an SVG image. This image is then exported for display by the Delphi program. Python for Delphi connects the front and back ends.

The machine learning model uses Bayesian Ridge Regression hybridized with an n-degree Polynomial. Probabilistic distribution is used to estimate the value of the dependent variable instead of relying on traditional methods.

The initial values of the parameters to be fine-tuned are

tol = [1e-4, 1e-3, 1e-2]
alpha_1 = [1e-7, 1e-6, 1e-5, 1e-4]
alpha_2 = [1e-7, 1e-6, 1e-5, 1e-4]
lambda_1 = [1e-7, 1e-6, 1e-5, 1e-4]
lambda_2 = [1e-7, 1e-6, 1e-5, 1e-4]

The **pandas**("panel data") is ideal for for importing and extracting data from csv files. **Pandas** enables data to be represented as a virtual spreadsheet and as such shares many features with Microsoft® Excel:

```
confirmed_df = pd.read_csv('https://raw.githubusercontent.com/CSSEGISandData/COVID-19/master/csse_covid_19_
data/csse_covid_19_time_series/time_series_covid19_confirmed_global.csv')
```

The Bayesian ridge polynomial regression model expressed in Python 3.8 is as follows

bayesian_grid = {'tol': tol, 'alpha_1': alpha_1, 'alpha_2': alpha_2, 'lambda_1': lambda_1, 'lambda_2': lambda_2}

bayesian = BayesianRidge(fit_intercept = False, normalize = True)

bayesian_search = RandomizedSearchCV(bayesian, bayesian_grid, scoring = 'neg_mean_squared_error', cv = 3, return_train_score = True, n_jobs = −1, n_iter = 40, verbose = 1)

bayesian_search.fit(poly_X_train_confirmed, y_train_confirmed)

1. Load `TwelfthExampleProject.dproj` into Delphi.
1. Save project `TwelfthExampleProject.dproj` in a new folder, `FifteenthExample`, rename the project `FifteenthExampleProject.dproj` (**Save Project As**).
2. Save unit `TwelfthExampleUnit.pas` in new folder `FifteenthExample`, rename the unit `FifteenthExampleUnit.pas` (**Save As**).
3. If the package **SVGIconImageList VCL & FMX** is not already installed then install it as per `TwelfthExampleProject`.
4. Compile, link and run (**Shift+Ctrl+F9**) the project.
5. *Figure 80.85* shows `FifteenthExample.py` which is the Python program which performs Bayesian ridge polynomial regression. It takes about 15 seconds to produce output so be patient.
6. Click `Load` button and open `FifteenthExample.py`.
7. Click `Execute` button. The output produced is shown in *Figure 80.84*.

On 26th October 2020 the number of worldwide confirmed Covid-19 cases was 43, 446, 557.

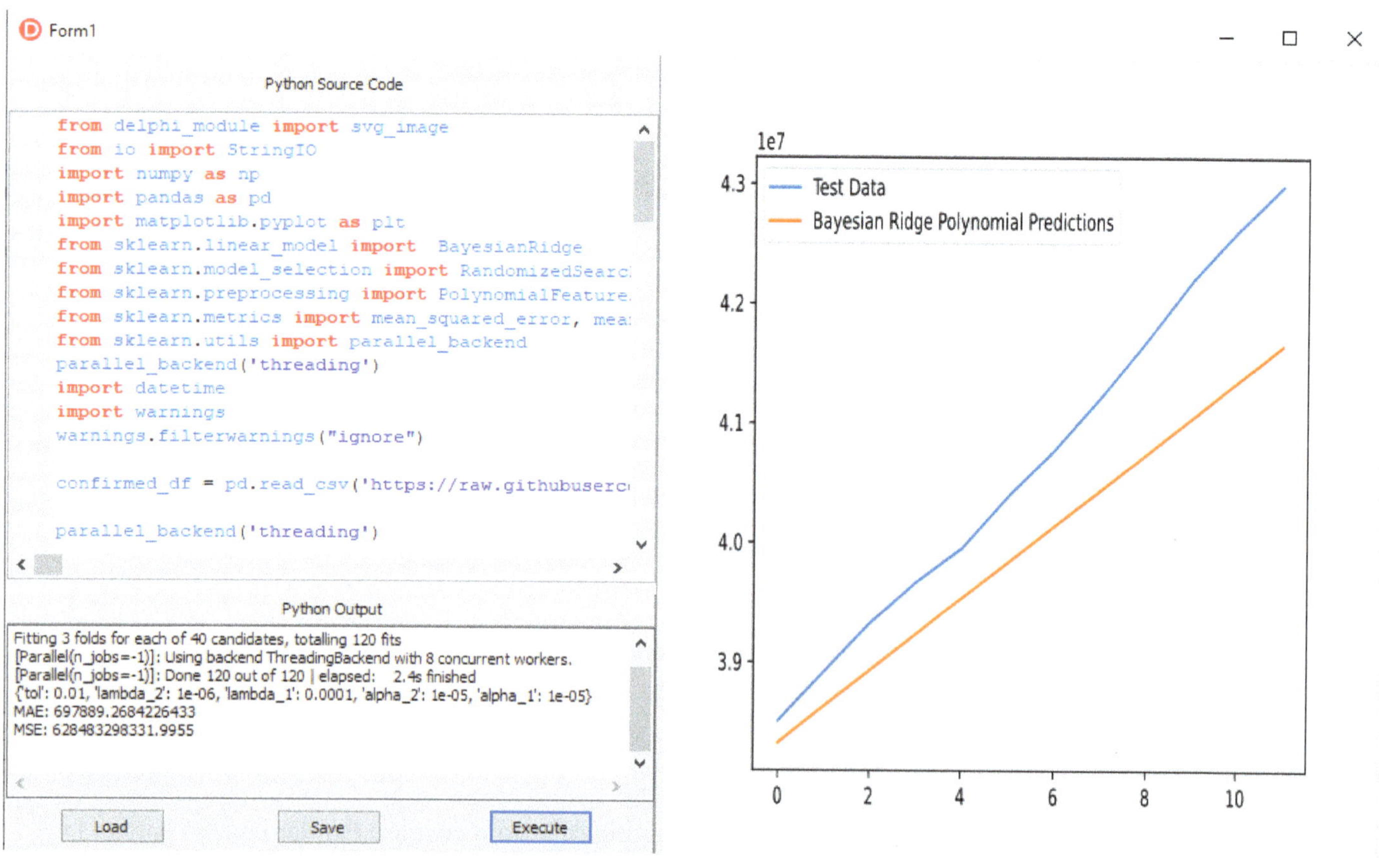

Figure 80.84 FifteenthExampleProject in execution

```
from delphi_module import svg_image
from io import StringIO
import numpy as np
import pandas as pd
import matplotlib.pyplot as plt
from sklearn.linear_model import  BayesianRidge
from sklearn.model_selection import RandomizedSearchCV, train_test_split
from sklearn.preprocessing import PolynomialFeatures
from sklearn.metrics import mean_squared_error, mean_absolute_error
from sklearn.utils import parallel_backend
parallel_backend('threading')
import datetime
import warnings
warnings.filterwarnings("ignore")
confirmed_df = pd.read_csv('https://raw.githubusercontent.com/CSSEGISandData/COVID-19/master/csse_
covid_19_data/csse_covid_19_time_series/time_series_covid19_confirmed_global.csv')
parallel_backend('threading')
cols = confirmed_df.keys()
confirmed = confirmed_df.loc[:, cols[4]:cols[-1]]
dates = confirmed.keys()
world_cases = []
for i in dates:
    confirmed_sum = confirmed[i].sum()
    world_cases.append(confirmed_sum)
# window size
window = 7
days_since_1_22 = np.array([i for i in range(len(dates))]).reshape(-1, 1)
world_cases = np.array(world_cases).reshape(-1, 1)
days_in_future = 10
future_forcast = np.array([i for i in range(len(dates)+days_in_future)]).reshape(-1, 1)
start = '1/22/2020'
start_date = datetime.datetime.strptime(start, '%m/%d/%Y')
future_forcast_dates = []
for i in range(len(future_forcast)):
    future_forcast_dates.append((start_date + datetime.timedelta(days=i)).strftime('%m/%d/%Y'))
X_train_confirmed, X_test_confirmed, y_train_confirmed, y_test_confirmed = train_test_split(days_
since_1_22[50:], world_cases[50:], test_size=0.05, shuffle=False)
# transform the data for polynomial regression
bayesian_poly = PolynomialFeatures(degree=5)
bayesian_poly_X_train_confirmed = bayesian_poly.fit_transform(X_train_confirmed)
bayesian_poly_X_test_confirmed = bayesian_poly.fit_transform(X_test_confirmed)
bayesian_poly_future_forcast = bayesian_poly.fit_transform(future_forcast)
# bayesian ridge polynomial regression
tol=[1e-4, 1e-3, 1e-2]
alpha_1=[1e-7, 1e-6, 1e-5, 1e-4]
alpha_2=[1e-7, 1e-6, 1e-5, 1e-4]
lambda_1=[1e-7, 1e-6, 1e-5, 1e-4]
lambda_2=[1e-7, 1e-6, 1e-5, 1e-4]
normalize = [True, False]
bayesian_grid = {'tol': tol, 'alpha_1': alpha_1, 'alpha_2' : alpha_2, 'lambda_1': lambda_1,
'lambda_2' : lambda_2}
bayesian = BayesianRidge(fit_intercept=False, normalize=True)
bayesian_search = RandomizedSearchCV(bayesian, bayesian_grid, scoring='neg_mean_squared_error',
cv=3, return_train_score=True, n_jobs=-1, n_iter=40, verbose=1)
bayesian_search.fit(bayesian_poly_X_train_confirmed, y_train_confirmed)
print(bayesian_search.best_params_)
bayesian_confirmed = bayesian_search.best_estimator_
test_bayesian_pred = bayesian_confirmed.predict(bayesian_poly_X_test_confirmed)
bayesian_pred = bayesian_confirmed.predict(bayesian_poly_future_forcast)
print('MAE:', mean_absolute_error(test_bayesian_pred, y_test_confirmed))
print('MSE:',mean_squared_error(test_bayesian_pred, y_test_confirmed))
plt.plot(y_test_confirmed)
plt.plot(test_bayesian_pred)
plt.legend(['Test Data', 'Bayesian Ridge Polynomial Predictions'])
figfile = StringIO()
plt.savefig(figfile, format='svg')
figdata_svg = figfile.getvalue()
svg_image.SvgText = figdata_svg
```

Figure 80.85 FifteenthExample.py

81 Delphi to Javascript

Quartex Pascal

Purpose: To consider an overview of Quartex Pascal in preparation for its release

Traditionally, the go to language for web development has been Javascript. However, Javascript was never designed for large-scale application development, a fact which modern website development has exposed. Increasingly website development has turned to alternatives, in particular Webassembly which supports programming in a traditional programming language, C/C++. Webassembly is a bytecode binary format consisting of low-level instructions, similar to assembly code for x86 processors. These instructions are translated into real machine code by the browser. As a consequence the performance of Webassembly is close to native code. But Webassembly has its own set of restrictions and challenges, in particular when manipulating the DOM (the document object model, the elements that make up a HTML document). Quartex Pascal, developed by Jon Aasenden, provides a solution that overcomes these challenges and restrictions whilst supporting a traditional high level language approach at the same time. Quartex Pascal's approach is a compiler that parses Object Pascal code to an abstract symbol tree model of the entire program, which is then converted to optimised and high-speed Javascript. The development of Quartex Pascal was a collobarative effort between Jon Aasenden and Eric Grange from Creative IT, the maintainer of Delphi Web Script (DWScript). DWScript is an object-oriented scripting language based on Delphi. Its scripts may be executed from Delphi applications (in a safe, sand-boxed fashion), but it is also possible to compile and execute with tools such as Smart Mobile Studio.

Jon had to develop a whole new RTL (runtime-library) in order that the traditional components of Delphi would be compatible with HTML. However, the interface with HTML5 required the development of a new IDE, one that would deal with web technology exclusively. Jon wrote this IDE entirely with Delphi. The IDE is highly modular with everything isolated in classes thus providing an excellent foundation for future expansion, if desired.

Quartex Pascal supports full stack development by supporting client and server creation within the IDE. The IDE also provides tools for async network programming and comes with the Ragnarok message framework which facilitates simplifying communication between servers, services or clients. To support this the IDE includes a visual protocol designer for designing messages and complex datatypes for communications.

Object Pascal brings the clarity to web development that is lacking in Javascript and TypeScript. It has been adapted to include what is needed to embrace the web language paradigm by including elements such as partial classes, lambdas, inline variables, anonymous procedures, records, async and await keywords for working with promises (its event loop is based on the Javascript event loop). But more than this, it brings to web development the solidity of a strongly-typed object-oriented language that does inheritance in the Delphi and C++ way with abstract and virtual methods. Quartex Pascal is scheduled for release at the end of 2021 and will be free to use in education and freeware/open source projects. A modest charge for use in commercial projects will apply ($300 as of October 6th 2021) - see https://jonlennartaasenden.wordpress.com/2021/10/05/quartex-pascal-nearing-completion/.

Figure 81.1 shows the **Quartex Pascal IDE**. *Figure 81.2* shows the **Assets** window for a project opened in the Quartex Pascal IDE. *Figure 81.3* shows this project prepared for the Web in the Quartex Pascal IDE, copied to a Web server and then displayed in a Web browser - www.educational-computing.com/CS/Book/Australia/index.html. *Figure 81.4* shows the possible project types. *Figure 81.5* shows the **Ragnarok Protocol Generator** window.

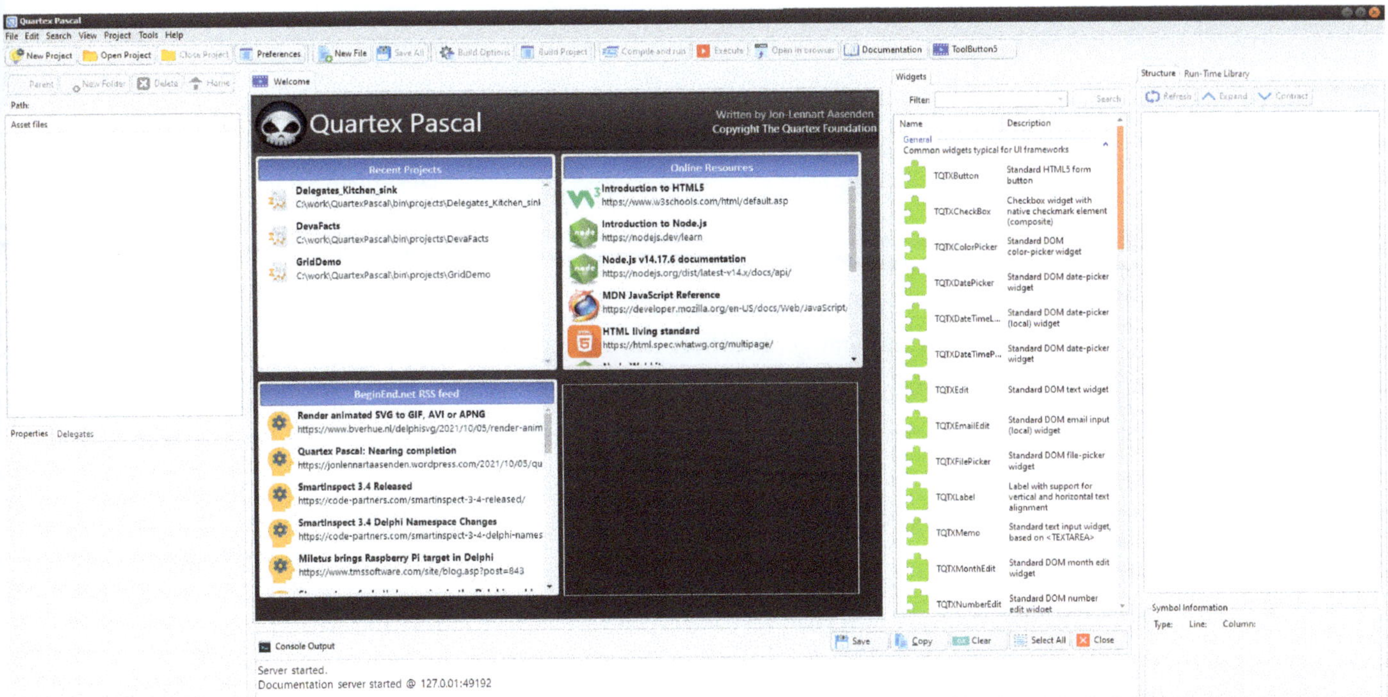

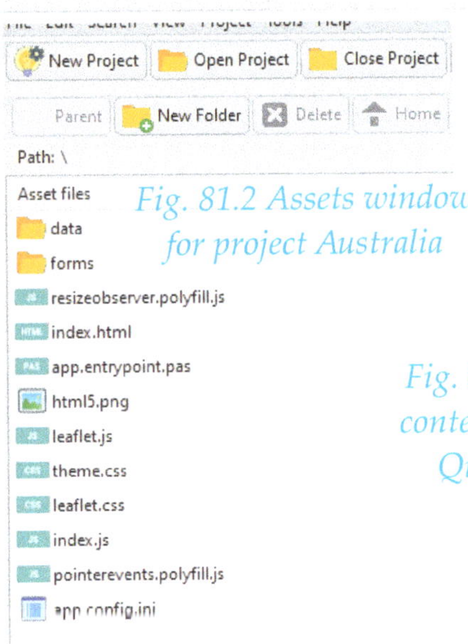

Fig. 81.2 Assets window for project Australia

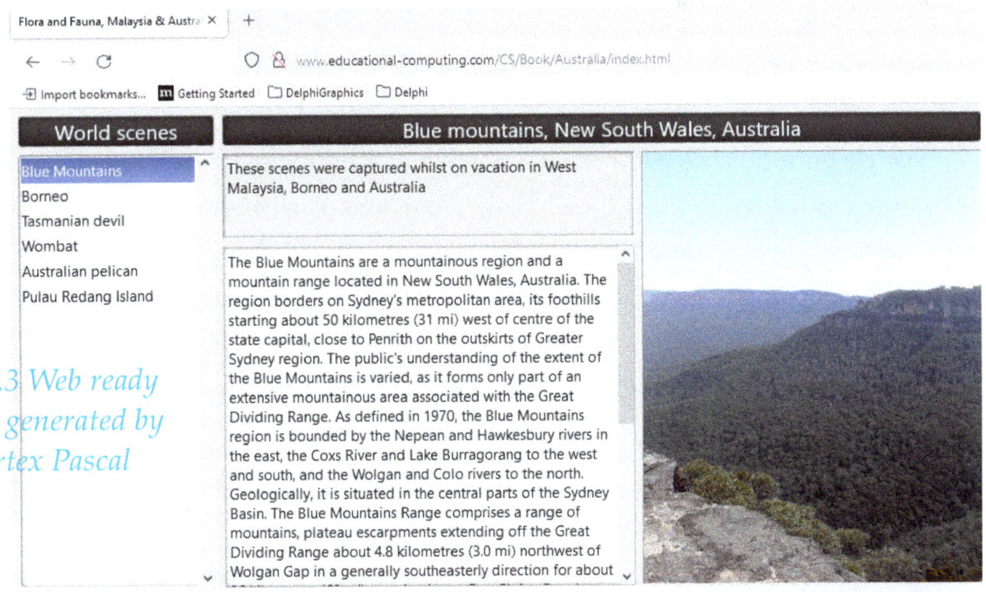

Fig. 81.3 Web ready content generated by Quartex Pascal

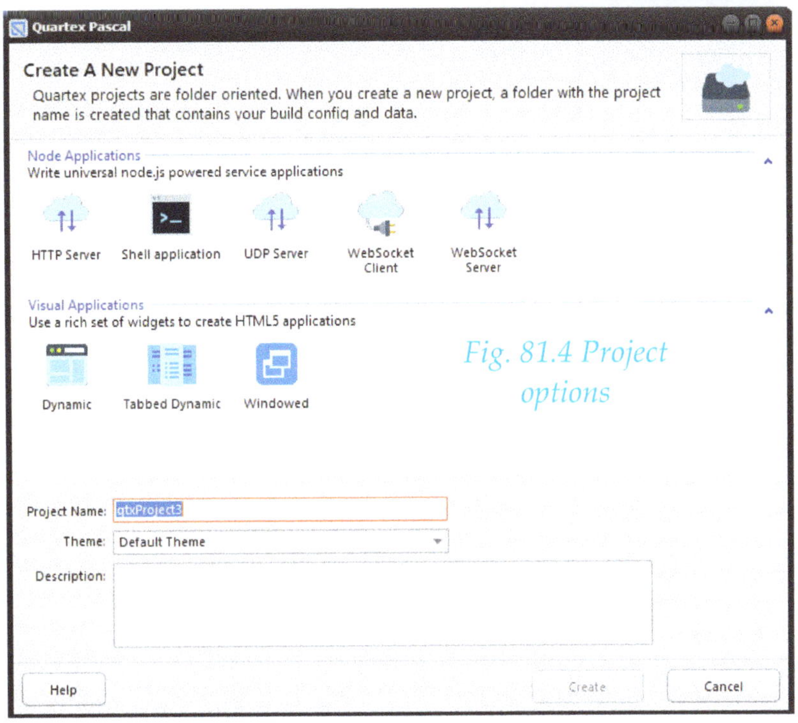

Fig. 81.4 Project options

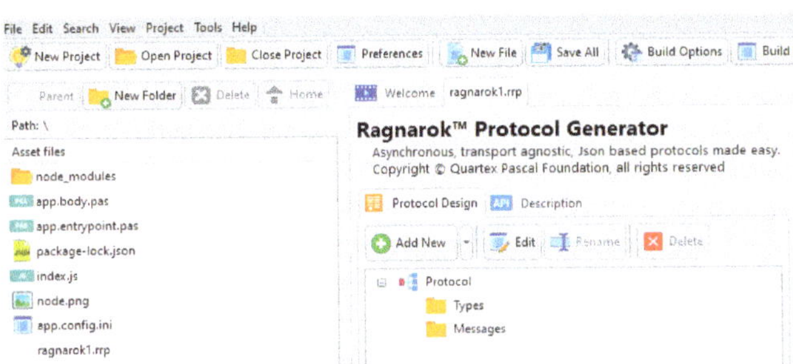

Fig. 81.5 Ragnarok Protocol Generator

Smart Pascal

Purpose: To become familiar with Smart Pascal

Smart Pascal is a dialect of Object Pascal derived from Delphi Web Script and adapted and enhanced for **Smart Mobile Studio**, a commercial development suite[1] that generates **JavaScript**.

Smart Mobile Studio is an **HTML5** development and programming platform created by Jon Aasenden and Eric Grange. It differs from Quartex Pascal in that Quartex Pascal is being created as a Delphi equivalent of Java's Eclipse IDE and as such is intended by design to be a generic IDE capable of supporting different compilers. Quartex Pascal is not a replacement for Smart Mobile Studio IDE. Smart Mobile Studio was designed to interface with and to absorb the document object model (DOM) and Javascript completely. Smart Mobile Studio provides access to the web browser with the same fine grain detail relationship that the VCL has with WinAPI. The runtime library of Quartex Pascal, on the other hand, is designed to be generic so that it is capable of working with any platform.

Key concept

Document Object Model (DOM)

The Document Object Model (DOM) is the data representation of the objects that comprise the structure and content of a document on the web. The Document Object Model (DOM) representation allows a web page (a document) to be manipulated via a programming interface. To allow manipulation the DOM provides an object-oriented representation of the web page, so that it can be modified with a scripting language such as JavaScript.

Figure 81.6 shows the **Smart Mobile Studio IDE** and a new project `Memo.sproj1` consisting of a single form with a single button, label, edit box and memo box. This compiles to Javscript and HTML5 so that when the contents of the created folder `www` (World Wide Web) are uploaded to a web server or just accessed locally, the web page `index.html` is rendered in a web browser as shown in *Figure 81.7*. The web page is interactive because of the JavaScript that lies under the hood which allow new names to be added to the memo box. `Save` and `Load` buttons with functionality are now required to complete the project. This is left as an exercise for the reader.

Table 81.1 shows the unit that contains the button's on click event handler which adds the name in the edit box to the memo box. *Figure 81.8* shows the unit's structure.

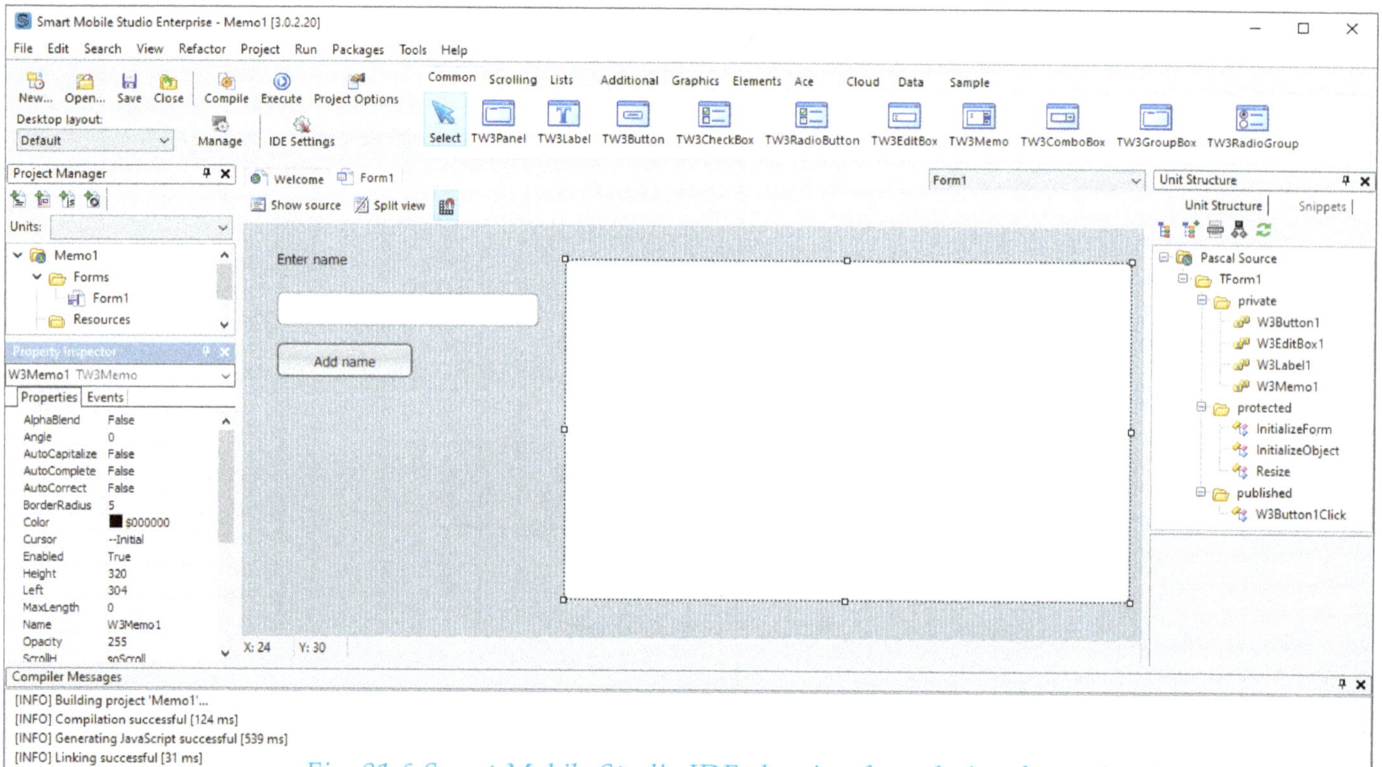

Fig. 81.6 Smart Mobile Studio IDE showing form design for project Memo1.sproj

1 Smart Mobile Studio is free for education

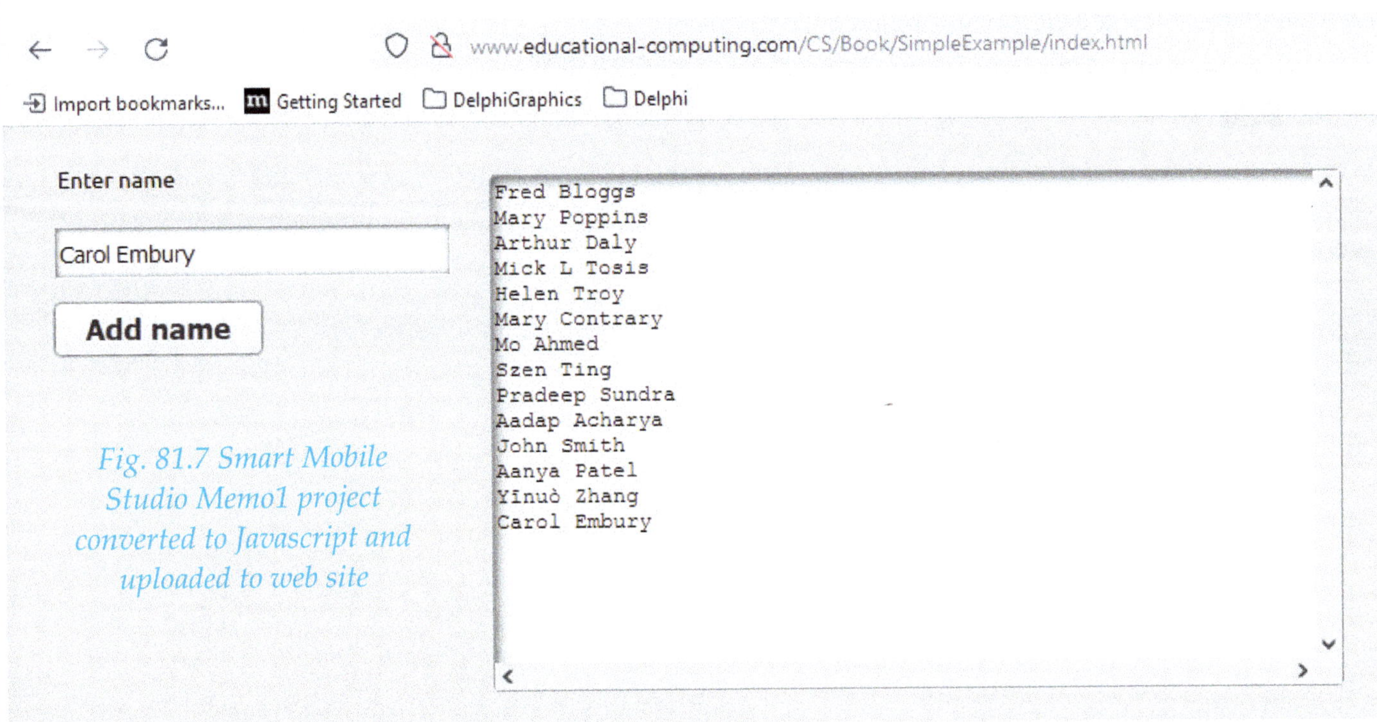

Fig. 81.7 Smart Mobile Studio Memo1 project converted to Javascript and uploaded to web site

```
Unit Form1;
interface
uses
  System.Types, System.Types.Convert, System.Objects, System.Time, System.IOUtils, System.Device.Storage,
  SmartCL.System, SmartCL.Time, SmartCL.Graphics, SmartCL.Components, SmartCL.FileUtils, SmartCL.Device.
Storage, SmartCL.Forms, SmartCL.Fonts, SmartCL.Theme, SmartCL.Borders, SmartCL.Application,
  SmartCL.Controls.Button,
  SmartCL.Controls.Memo, SmartCL.Controls.EditBox, SmartCL.Controls.Label;
type
  TForm1 = class(TW3Form)
    procedure W3Button1Click(Sender: TObject);
  private
    {$I 'Form1:intf'}
  protected
    procedure InitializeForm; override;
    procedure InitializeObject; override;
    procedure Resize; override;
  end;
implementation
{ TForm1 }
procedure TForm1.W3Button1Click(Sender: TObject);
begin
  W3Memo1.Add(W3EditBox1.Text);
  W3Memo1.Add(#13#10);
end;
procedure TForm1.InitializeForm;
begin
  inherited;
  // this is a good place to initialize components
end;
procedure TForm1.InitializeObject;
begin
  inherited;
  {$I 'Form1:impl'}
end;
procedure TForm1.Resize;
begin
  inherited;
end;
 initialization
  Forms.RegisterForm({$I %FILE%}, TForm1);
end.
```

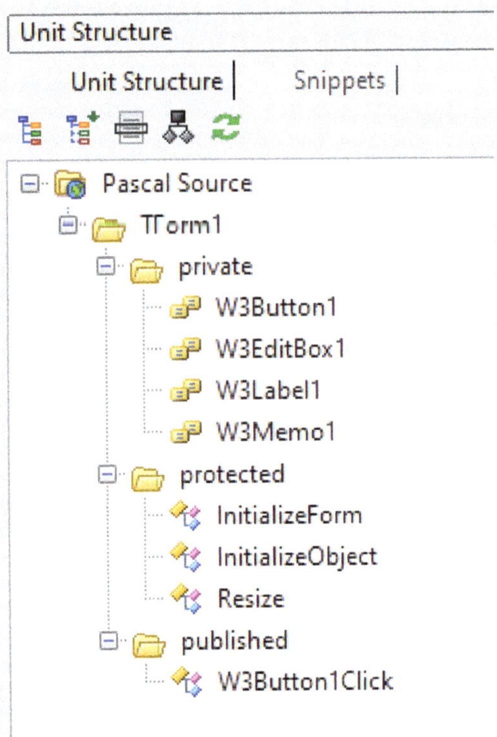

Fig. 81.8 Smart Mobile Studio Unit Structure window showing TForm1

Table 81.1 Form1 of Memo1.sproj project

Smart Mobile Studio comes with a large number of example projects.
Figure 81.9 shows one such project, `LSystem Fiddle.sproj` from folder
`C:\Users\`[redacted]`\Documents\Smart Mobile Projects\Demos\Featured Demos\Forms & Components\LSystem Fiddle`

Figure 81.10 shows a browser rendering of www.educational-computing.com/CS/Book/LSystems/, after uploading the `www` folder to this site.

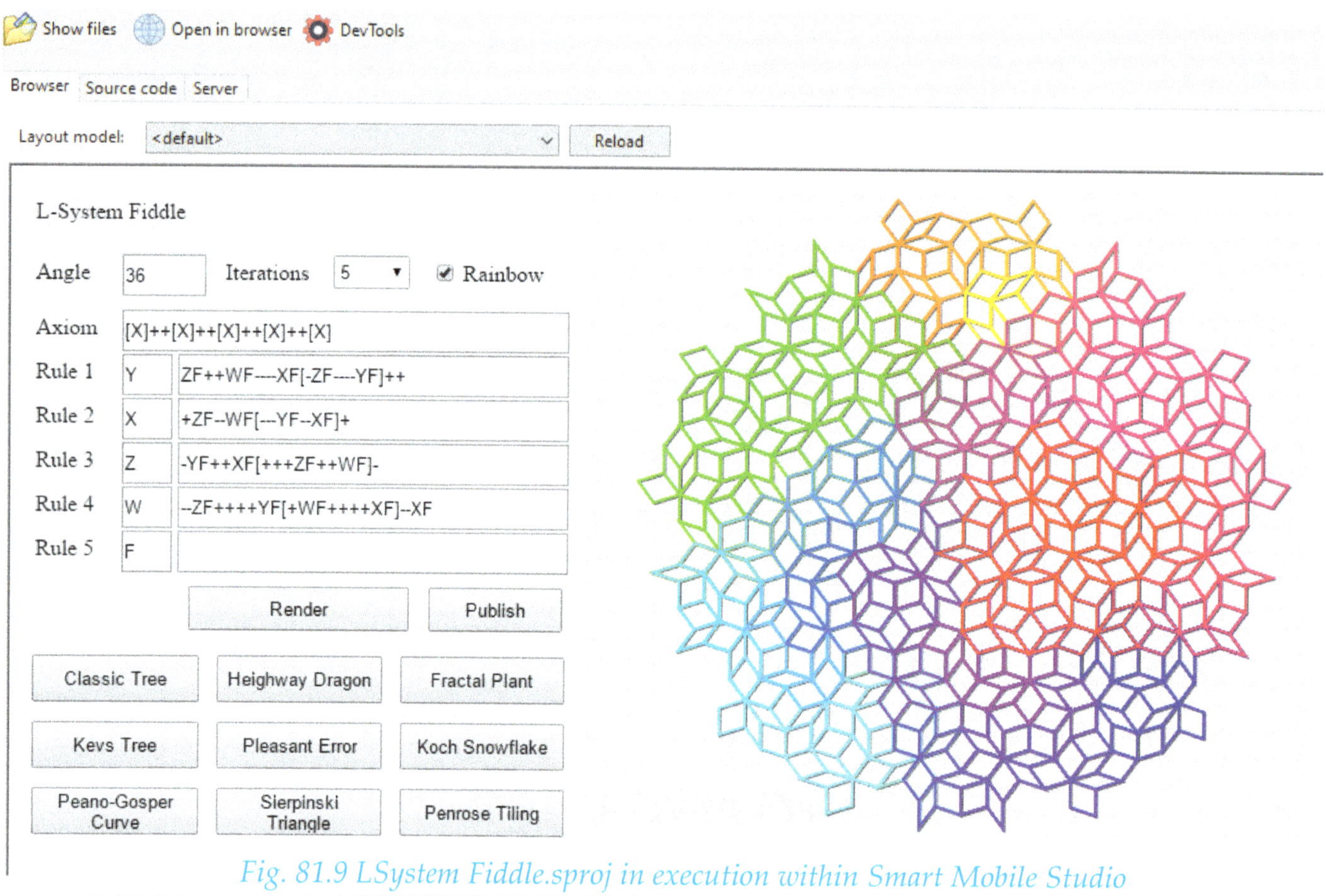

Fig. 81.9 LSystem Fiddle.sproj in execution within Smart Mobile Studio

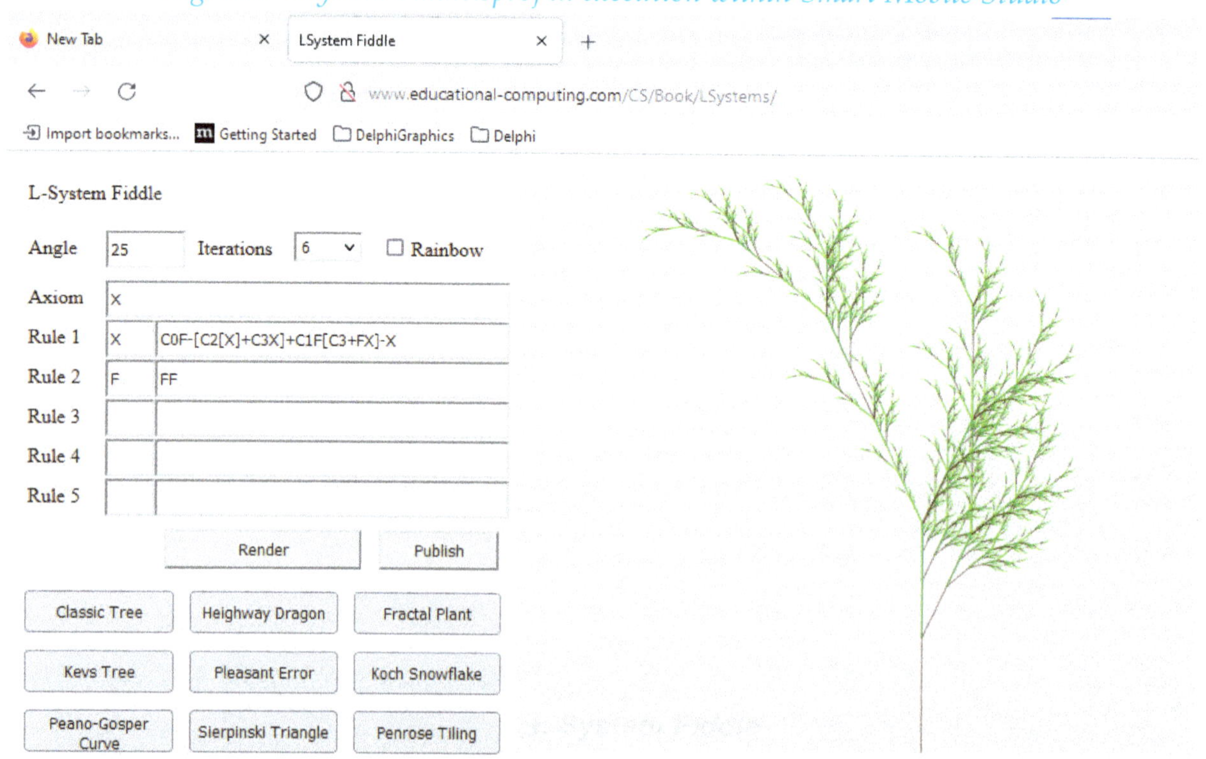

Fig. 81.10 LSystem Fiddle www folder uploaded to web server and accessed via web browser as shown

TMS WEB Core

Purpose: To briefly revisit TMS WEB Core components

We have seen in *Chapter 73* how **TMS WEB Core** makes it possible to develop web(client) applications with Delphi. A Delphi application uses **TMS WEB Core** components to build form-based projects which are then converted into JavaScript when the project is compiled and linked. Applications created in this way must be executed in a web browser.

TMS provide a series of training videos which are accessible from **TMS WEBACADEMY** (https://www.tmswebacademy.com/)and **YouTube**. For example, the DIY Navigation system summer project video is available from https://www.youtube.com/watch?v=5vwSoxuLYkM&t=41s and

https://www.tmswebacademy.com/replay/ with introduction video accessible from https://www.tmssoftware.com/site/videos.asp?v=241.

82 Using Delphi with Arduino

Information

dpk: The source file for a Delphi package. When compiled, produces a .bpl file.

Information

You may need to open CPortLibDXE.dpk in the Samples folder or the dpk for your version of Delphi and then build this package before opening DsgnCPortDXE.dpk or the dpk for your version of Delphi and installing this package.

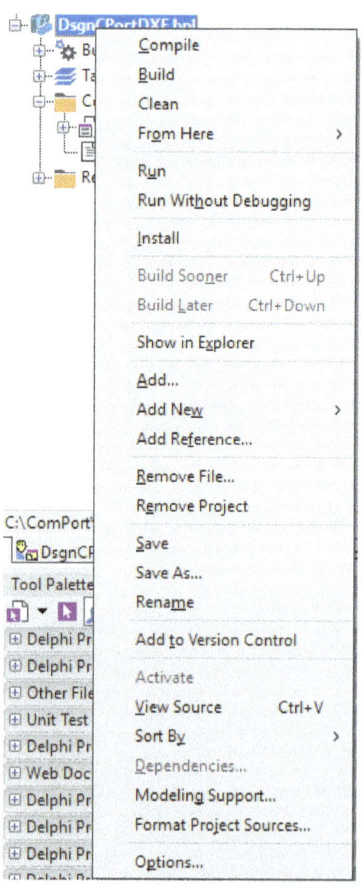

Fig. 82.2 Dropdown menu

Installing ComPort components

Purpose: To learn how to install the Delphi Comport package

Download the library of components for serial communication - **ComPort** from https://sourceforge.net/projects/comport.

Create folder **Comport** on your local drive.

Unzip the downloaded zip file comport411f.zip (or later version, if available) to this folder **Comport**.

Open folder **Comport** and then **open** folder **Source**.

Find the design package for the version of Delphi you are using, e.g. **DsgnCPort7.dpk** for **Delphi 7**.

For this demonstration, we will be using **DsgnCPortDXE.dpk** which is the package for the **XE** versions of Delphi including **Delphi Community Edition**.

Launch Delphi Community Edition and **select File|Open Project.**

Select DsgnCPortDXE.dprog from the **Source** folder within **ComPort** and **click** on **Open**.

The **Project Manager** should change to that shown in *Figure 82.1*.

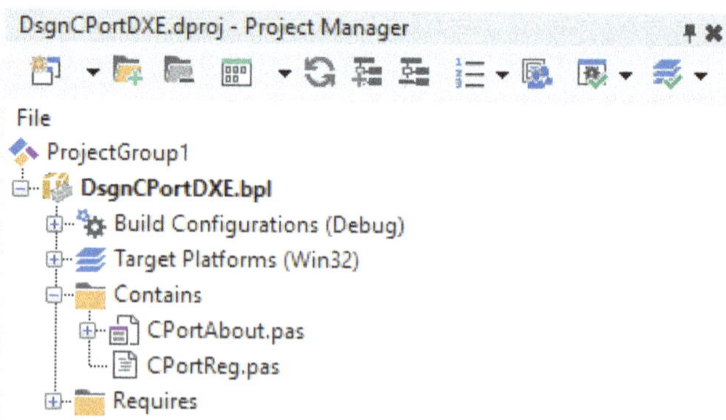

Fig. 82.1 Project Manager.

Right click on **DsgnCPortDXE.bpl** and from the **dropdown menu** - *Figure 82.2* - **select** the **Install** option. This will install the package and on successful completion the dialogue box shown in *Figure 82.3* should appear.

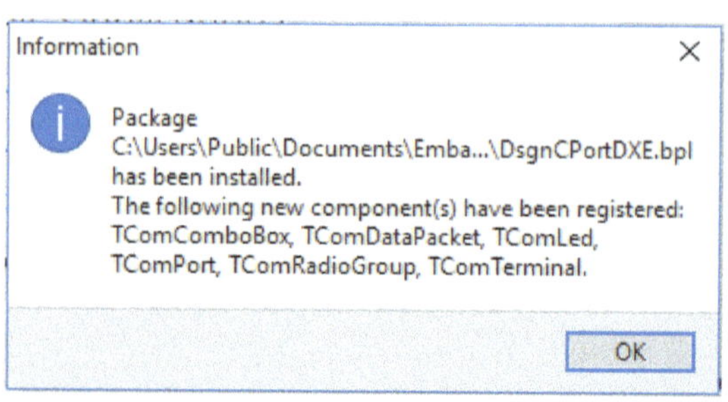

Fig. 82.3 Dialogue box confirming that the compiled design package DsgnCPortDXE.bpl has been successfully installed

Select File|Close All and **click** on OK to save.

Select File|New VCL Forms Application.

Scroll down the Tool Palette, at the bottom of the Palette you should see the **CPortLib** page - *Figure 82.4*.

Open the page and you should see the serial communication components shown in *Figure 82.5*.

Information

A package is a special dynamic-link library used by applications, the IDE, or both. Run-time packages provide functionality when a user runs an application. Design-time packages are used to install components in the IDE and to create special property editors for custom components. To distinguish them from other DLLs, package libraries are stored in files that end with the .bpl (Borland package library) extension.

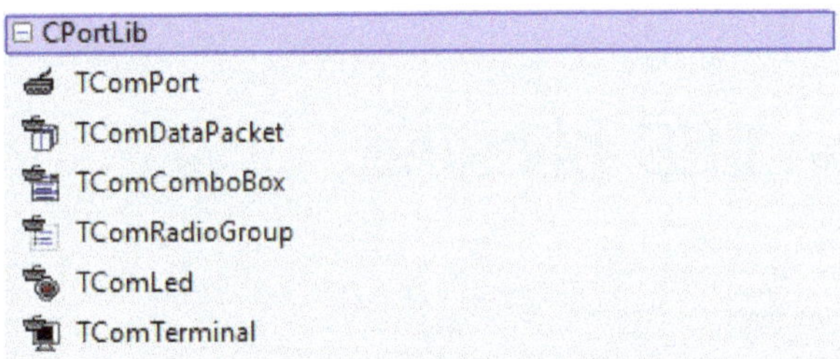

Fig. 82.5 Tool Palette CPortLib page

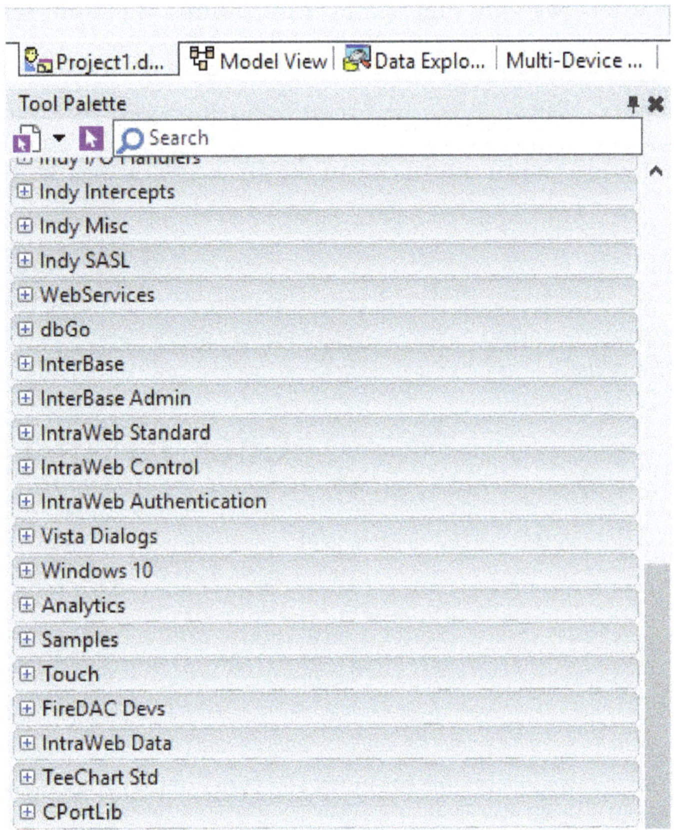

Fig. 82.4 Tool Palette

Communicating with the Arduino® Uno

Purpose: To learn how to communicate with an Arduino over USB

Select File|New VCL Forms Application (Delphi Community Edition).

Click File|Save All and, **save** unit as **ArduinoSimpleBlinkUnit** and **save** project as **ArduinoSimpleBlink** in folder **ArduinoSimpleBlink**.

Place on the form one TComport component from the CPortLib page of the Tool palette, two buttons, one label, from the Standard page and one SpeedButton component from the Additonal page.

Arrange these components as shown in *Figure 82.6* - at this stage the components will still have their original captions, Button1, Button2, etc, and their original names.

Change the Form's **Caption** property in the Object Inspector to **Arduino Simple Blink**.

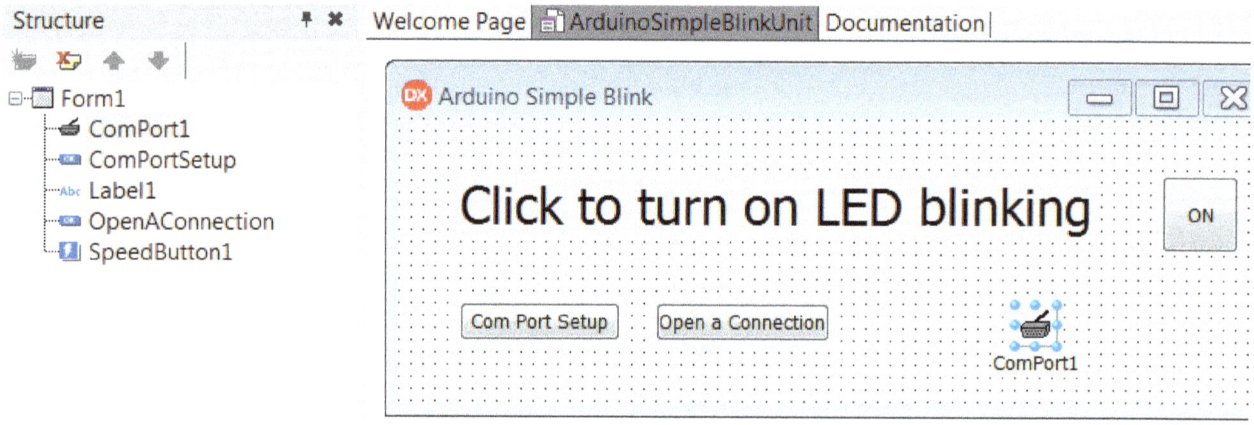

Fig. 82.6 Tool Palette Arduino Simple Blink project main form

Change the first button's **Name** property to **ComPortSetup**. Change its caption to **Com Port Setup**.

Change the second button's **Name** property to **OpenAConnection**. **Change** its caption to **Open a Connection**.

Change **OpenAConnection Enabled** property to **False**.

Change **Label1**'s **Caption** property to **Click to turn on LED blinking**.

Change **SpeedButton1**'s **Caption** property to **ON**.

Change **SpeedButton1**'s **Enable** property to **True**.

Double click button **ComPortSetup** to create the event handler **TForm1.ComPortSetupClick(Sender: TObject)**.

Add the code shown in *Table 82.1* to the body of this event handler.

```
ComPort1.ShowSetupDialog;
If Comport1.Port <> ''
  Then OpenAConnection.Enabled := True
  Else OpenAConnection.Enabled := False;
```

Table 82.1 Event handling code for TForm1.ComPortSetupClick(Sender: TObject)

Double click button **OpenAConnection** to create the event handler **TForm1.OpenAConnectionClick(Sender: TObject);**.

Add the code shown in *Table 82.2* to the body of this event handler. **UpdateState** is a procedure that will be created later.

```
If ComPort1.Connected
    Then ComPort1.Close
    Else Comport1.Open;
  UpdateState;
```

Table 82.2 Event handling code for TForm1.OpenAConnectionClick(Sender: TObject)

Double click button **SpeedButton1** to create the event handler **TForm1.SpeedButton1Click(Sender: TObject)**.

Add the code shown in *Table 82.3* to the body of this event handler.

```
If SpeedButton1.Down
    Then
      Begin
        ComPort1.WriteStr('BLINK_ON');
        SpeedButton1.Caption := 'OFF';
        Label1.Caption := 'Click to turn off LED blinking';
      End
    Else
      Begin
        ComPort1.WriteStr('BLINK_OFF');
        SpeedButton1.Caption := 'ON';
        Label1.Caption := 'Click to turn on LED blinking';
      End;
```

Table 82.3 Event handling code for TForm1.SpeedButton1Click(Sender: TObject)

Add the code for procedure **TForm1.Update** shown in *Table 82.4* to the **Implementation** section before the event handlers.

Add procedure **TForm1.Update;** to the class definition for **TForm1**.

```
Procedure TForm1.UpdateState;
  Begin
    SpeedButton1.Enabled := ComPort1.Connected;
    Label1.Enabled := ComPort1.Connected;
    If ComPort1.Connected
      Then OpenAConnection.Caption := 'Close connection'
      Else OpenAConnection.Caption := 'Open connection';
  End;
```

Table 82.4 Procedure TForm1.UpdateState

Select **Form1** in the **Object Inspector** and click on the **Events** tab.

Find the **OnDestroy** property and **double click** the blank space to create the event handler stub for **Procedure TForm1.FormDestroy(Sender: TObject).**

Add the code from *Table 82.5* to complete this event handler.

Select **Form1** in the **Object Inspector** and click on the **Events** tab.

Find the **OnShow** property and **double click** the blank space to create the event handler stub for **Procedure TForm1.FormShow(Sender: TObject).**

Add the code from *Table 82.5* to complete this event handler.

```
Procedure TForm1.FormDestroy(Sender: TObject);
  Begin
    If ComPort1.Connected
      Then ComPort1.Close;
  End;

Procedure TForm1.FormShow(Sender: TObject);
  Begin
    UpdateState;
  End;
```

Table 82.5 Procedure TForm1.FormDestroy(Sender: TObject) and procedure TForm1.FormDestroy(Sender: TObject)

Click **File|Save** to save the unit.

Now **click** **Project|Build ArduinoSimpleBlink** to compile and build the project.

If you haven't done so already **download** the latest version of the Arduino IDE from ardunio.cc/download and install.

Connect your Arduino using a USB cable to your computer. The board will automatically draw power from the USB connection of the computer and the green LED (labelled ON) will turn on.

Windows initiates its driver installation process when the board is plugged in. You may have to help Windows find the driver on your computer. The driver is located in the **Drivers** folder in the **Arduino** folder.

Launch the Arduino IDE - *Figure 82.7* - and enter the code shown in *Table 82.6*.

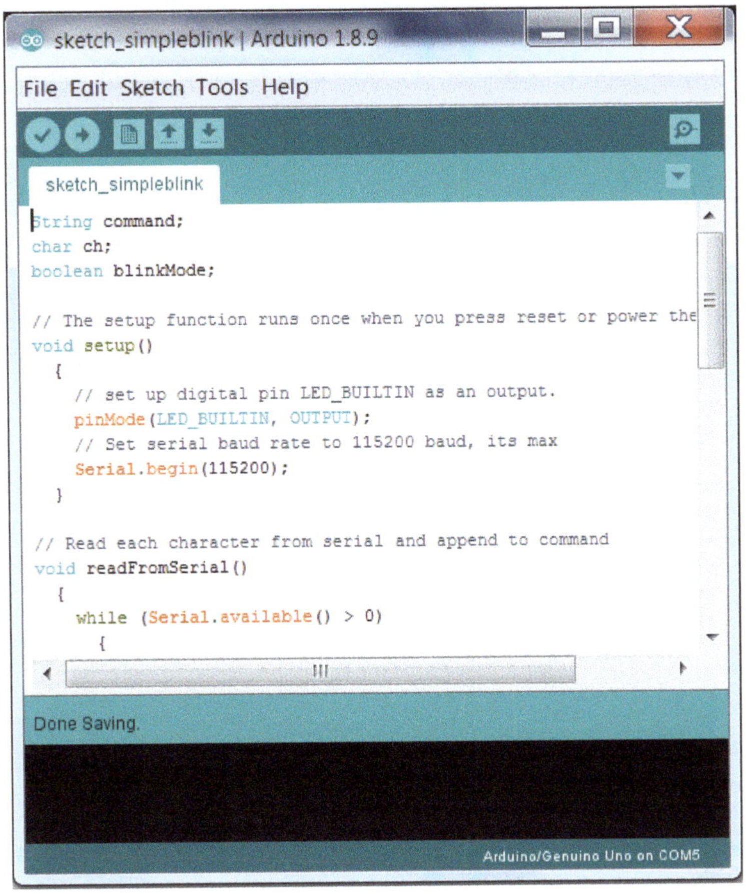

Fig. 82.7 Arduino IDE

Click on Sketch|Verify/Compile to check that you have entered the program correctly and if this is the case compile the program.

Click on the Upload symbol to upload the compiled code to the Arduino device via the USB connection.

Now **return** to the Delphi IDE and **click** on Run|Run or press F9.

The application launches as shown in *Figure 82.8*.

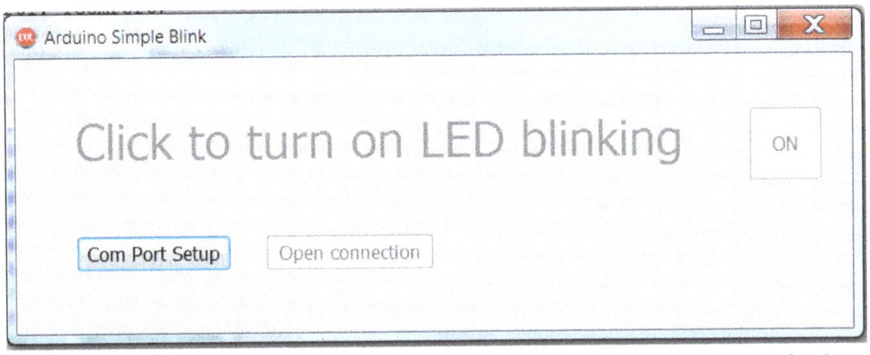

Fig. 82.8 Arduino Simple Blink application when first launched

```
String command;
char receivedChar;
boolean blinkMode;
// the setup function runs once when you press reset or power the board
void setup() {
  // initialize digital pin LED_BUILTIN as an output.
  pinMode(LED_BUILTIN, OUTPUT);
  // initialize Serial to max data rate
  Serial.begin(115200); // Port serial 115200 baud.
}
// read from serial and concat it to command
void readFromSerial() {
  while (Serial.available() > 0) {
    receivedChar = Serial.read();
    command.concat(receivedChar);
    delay(10);
  }
}
// do the led blink
void doBlink() {
  digitalWrite(LED_BUILTIN, HIGH); // turn the LED on (HIGH is the voltage level)
  delay(1000); // wait for a second
  digitalWrite(LED_BUILTIN, LOW); // turn the LED off by making the voltage LOW
  delay(1000); // wait for a second
}
// the loop function runs over and over again forever
void loop() {
  readFromSerial();
  if (command.equals("BLINK_ON") == true) {
    blinkMode = true;
  } else if (command.equals("BLINK_OFF") == true) {
    blinkMode = false;
  }
  if (blinkMode) {
    doBlink();
  }
  // Clean the command to receive the next
  command = "";
}
```

Table 82.6 Arduino Sketch code

Click on the button **Com Port Setup**.

The popup window shown in *Figure 82.9* should appear.

Click on the **Port** listbox down arrow to check that a **COM** port has been assigned. *Figure 82.10* shows that for this exercise, **COM5** serial port of the computer has been reserved for the connection to the **Arduino**.

Select **Baud rate 115200** from the listbox.

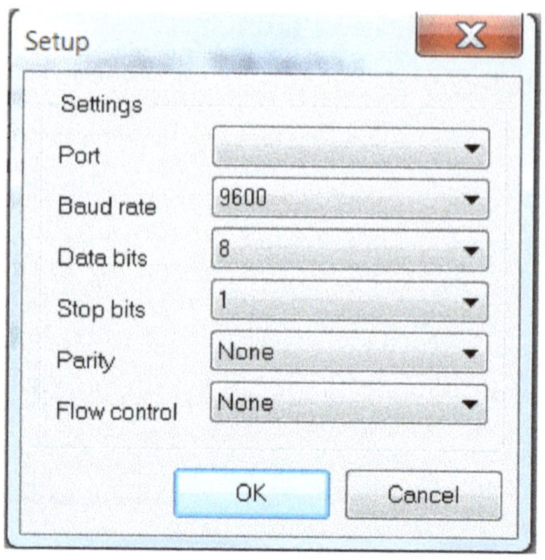

Fig. 82.9 Com Port Setup popup window

Click OK on the Setup popup window to close it.

If everything is successful, the button **Open Connection** should now be enabled as shown in *Figure 82.11*.

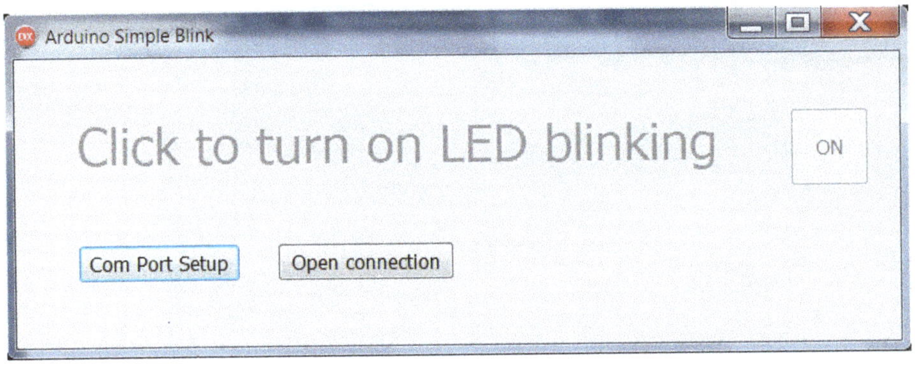

Fig. 82.11 Arduino Simple Blink application after Com Port set up successfully

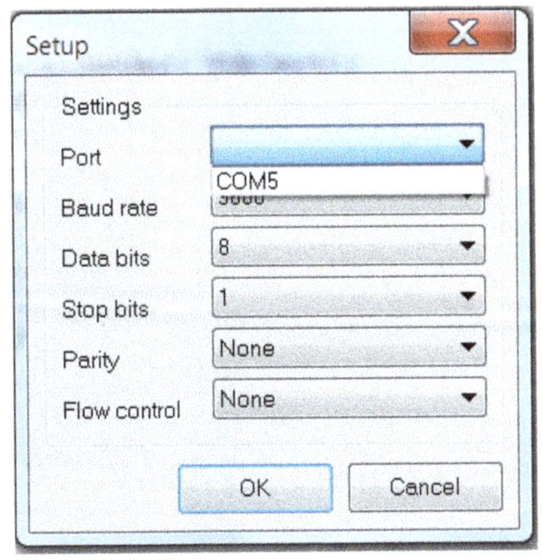

Fig. 82.10 Com Port Setup popup window showing Port COM5 is available for selection

Click on the **Open connection** button.If successful, the label **Click to turn on LED blinking** and the **ON** button will be enabled as shown in *Figure 82.12*.

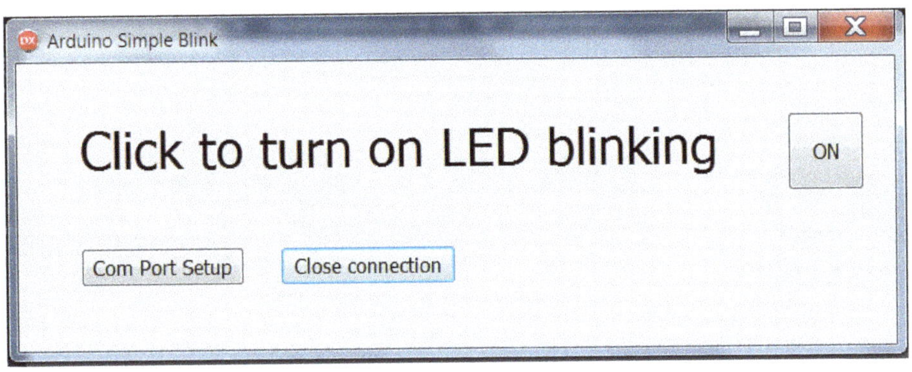

Fig. 82.12 Arduino Simple Blink application after connection opened successfully

Click the **ON** button to turn on **LED** blinking on the **Arduino**. The **ON** button caption will change to **OFF** as shown in *Figure 82.13*.

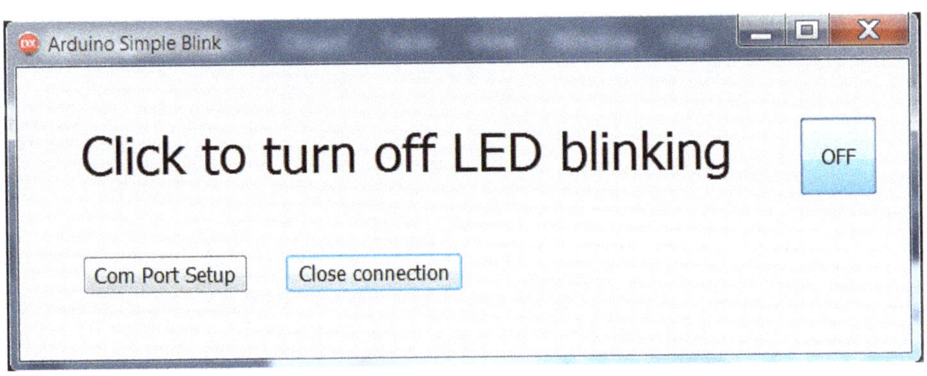

Fig. 82.13 Arduino Simple Blink application after ON button clicked

Figure 82.14 shows the **Arduino Uno** used in this exercise.

Fig. 82.14 Arduino Uno showing LED controlled by application

The **Arduino Uno** used in this exercise came from the **Arduino Starter Kit** shown in *Figure 82.*

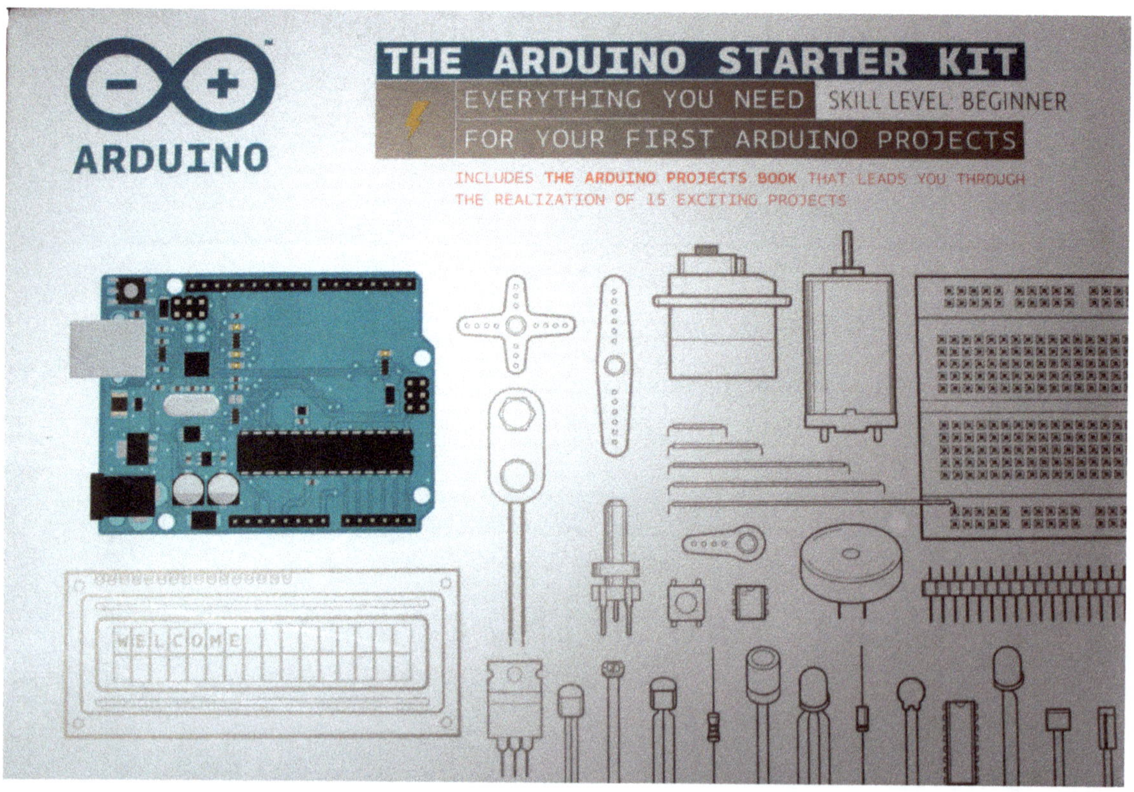

Fig. 82.15 The Arduino Starter Kit comprising an Arduino Uno, a breadboard and various components and wires for wiring LEDs, switches, temperature sensors, etc to the Arduino Uno.

Serial data communication

Purpose: To understand serial data communication

Serial data transmission

In serial data transmission, **single bits (binary digits) are sent one after another along a single wire** by varying the voltage on the wire.

Figure 83.1 shows a simple electrical circuit for sending single bits coded as 0 volts and 5 volts. When the switch is in position A the lamp bulb is connected to 5 volts. When the switch is in position B the lamp bulb is connected to 0 volts. We need to decide what the signal lamp on and the signal lamp off represent.

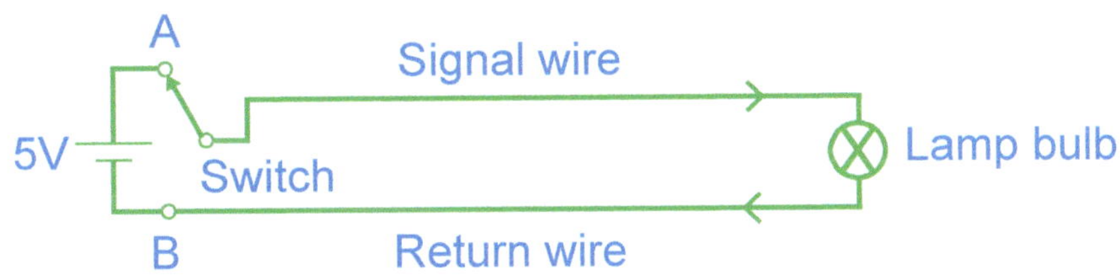

Fig. 83.1 Simple circuit for sending binary digits serially

Key principle

Serial data transmission:
In serial data transmission, single bits (binary digits) are sent one after another along a single wire.

Information

In Figure 83.1 the current travels along a single wire loop. The moving electric charge picks up electrical energy in the battery and delivers this energy to the lamp bulb.

If single bits are being sent along the wire, then we have one of two possible binary digit values to represent at any moment, 0 or 1. We may choose to let the state *lamp on* represent binary digit 1 and the state *lamp off* represent binary digit 0. In which case, the equivalent signals travelling along the signal wire represent binary digit 1 by 5 volts and binary digit 0 by 0 volts. The binary digits represent data and the voltages 0 volts and 5 volts their signal equivalent. *Figure 83.2* shows the transmission of a sequence of data bits using signals of 0 volts and 5 volts.

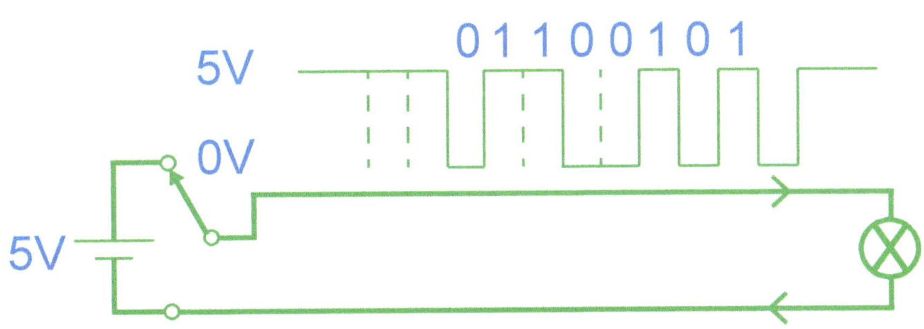

Fig. 83.2 Serial data transmission of a sequence of data bits sent as electrical signals

Key fact

Serial interfaces:
Serial interfaces are divided into two groups: synchronous or asynchronous.

Key concept

Synchronous serial data transmission:
Synchronous serial data transmission is a form of serial communication in which the communicating endpoints' interfaces are continuously synchronized by a common clock.

Synchronous and asynchronous data transmission

Serial interfaces are divided into two groups: synchronous or asynchronous.

Synchronous serial data transmission is a form of serial communication in which the communicating endpoints' interfaces are continuously synchronized by a common clock. Synchronisation may take the form of special synchronising bit patterns that are sent periodically or which are attached to a block of data. It may also take the form of a special clock line as shown in Figure 83.3 which is an I2C or I^2C interface.

In the Inter-Integrated Circuit (I2C, pronounced I-two-C) synchronous serial interface, used by microcontroller-based systems such as the Raspberry Pi, the clock signal requires its own wire and so adds to the total number of wires that connect the communicating devices.

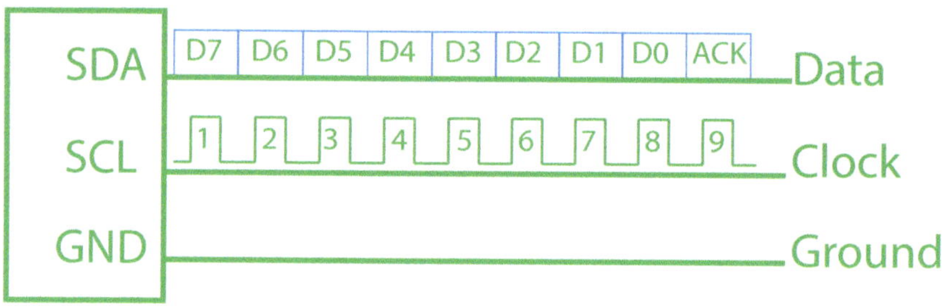

Fig. 83.3 Synchronous serial data transmission for an I2C interface

Figure 83.3 shows the three pin and three wire interface for I2C. The data bits D7 to D0 are individually clocked into the receiving interface by 8 clock pulses. The receiving I2C interface places an acknowledgement bit onto the data wire on receipt of the 9th clock pulse.

Whatever the type of synchronous serial interface, a clock signal is associated with its data line(s) and this clock signal is used by all the devices connected to the serial bus to synchronise all data transfers.

Another example of a synchronous interface used by embedded microcontroller systems is the Serial Peripheral Interface bus (SPI).

Synchronous serial communication is used in telecommunication systems which the Internet relies upon. These are time-division systems which continuously send frames of bits between nodes. The nodes are kept in sync by synchronisation frames which are sent periodically and which distribute the common clock signal derived from an atomic clock. This enables very high data transfer rates not achievable with asynchronous data transfer.

Asynchronous means that data is transferred without support from an external clock signal. No clock wire is required so reducing the number of wires by one and the number of connecting pins in each interface by one as well.

Figure 83.4 shows a serial interface A connected to another serial interface B by a serial bus consisting of three wires, one to transmit from interface A to interface B and one to transmit from interface B to interface A. Both interfaces share a common ground wire.

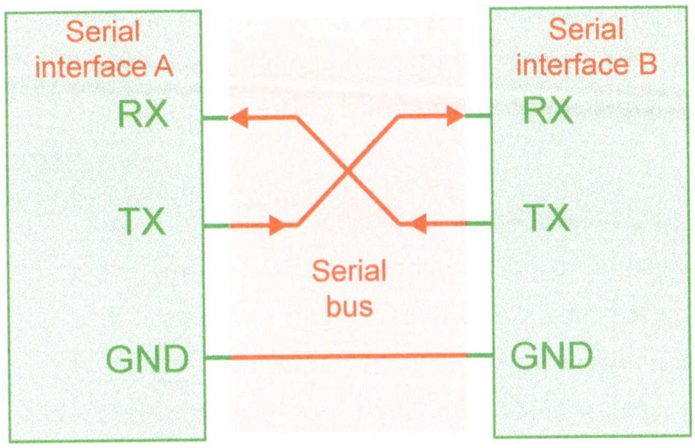

Fig. 83.4 Asynchronous serial data transmission between two interfaces supporting transmit (TX) and receive (RX) in both directions simultaneously.

Asynchronous serial data transmission sends 7 or 8 data bits at a time and an optional parity bit framed by start and stop bits in the RS232/RS422 protocol as shown in *Figure 83.5*. These 7 or 8 bits often represent character data from the ASCII character data set.

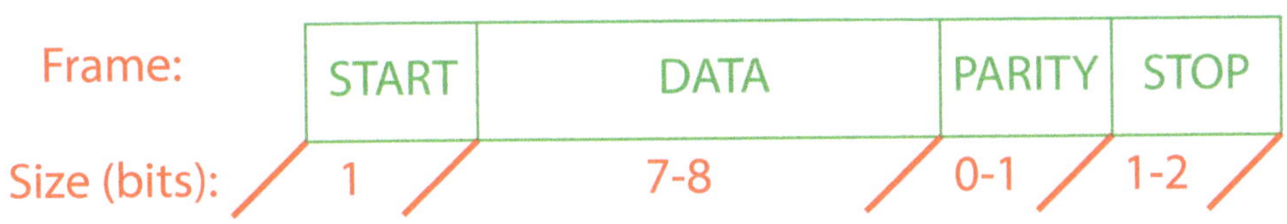

Fig. 83.5 Asynchronous serial data transmission frame.

The serial interface is usually a part of an integrated circuit called a **UART** (Universal Asynchronous Receiver Transmitter) that buffers a serially received data byte before placing it on an internal 8-bit bus as shown in *Figure 83.6*. The UART buffers a byte from the 8-bit data bus before clocking it out onto the serial TX wire framed in start and stop bits. The UART performs serial to parallel conversion and vice versa. If the parity bit system is being used, it also generates a parity bit as well as checking the received data for parity errors.

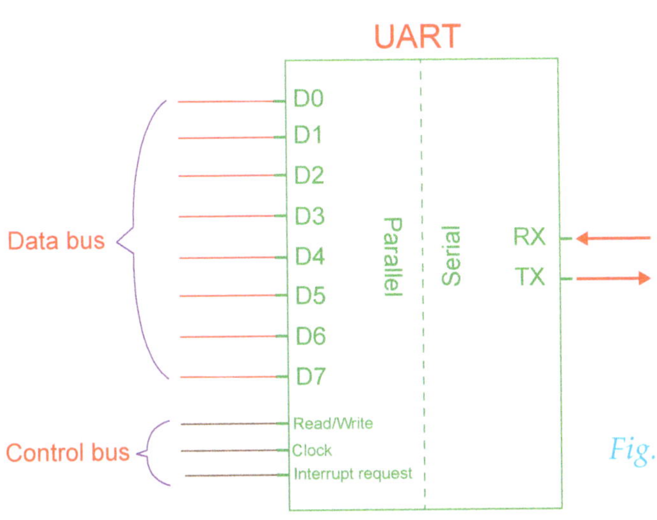

Fig. 83.6 UART

Information

Serial ports:

Desktop PCs used to have at least one serial port called the COM port but the advent of USB meant manufacturers stopped supplying PCs with serial ports. They are absent from tablets and smart phones where the space for ports is limited. However, the demise of serial ports is greatly exaggerated. Serial ports are everywhere, in everything from industrial automation systems to scientific instrumentation and in Internet of Things (IoT) devices. The Arduino has at least one TTL serial port for transmitting and receiving serial data.

Operating systems in computers without serial ports allow programs that communicate with serial ports to achieve this via virtual serial ports created in software. This allows applications to read from and write to serial ports whilst the actual data transfer takes place via a USB connection.

Key concept

Asynchronous data transmission:

Asynchronous means that data is transferred without support from an external clock signal. No clock wire is required.

Information

Ethernet and USB:

These are serial data transmission protocols that both encode timing information in the communication symbols, i.e. the bit patterns or codes that they use. This coding therefore delivers both a clock signal and data, so both can be classified as synchronous.

Comparison of synchronous and asynchronous data transmission

RS232/RS422 asynchronous serial data transmission is relatively cheap because it requires less hardware than synchronous serial data transmission and is appropriate in situations where messages are generated at irregular intervals, for example from embedded systems used in scientific instruments as initiation of a transfer is relatively quick. However, two in nine or ten bits are control bits thus a significant proportion of the data transmission conveys no information.

Synchronous data transmissions requires the distribution of a stable clock signal. In parallel synchronous data transmission this limits the distance and clock speed. This can also limit serial synchronous data transmission if a separate clock wire is used. However, in time-division multiplexed synchronous serial data transmission, this is less of a problem because all clocks are kept in synchronisation with a master clock by periodically sending synchronising frames and thus doing away with the need for a separate clock wire. High speed data transmission is achievable with this method.

The purpose of start and stop bits

In asynchronous serial data communication such as RS232 the data are words of a certain word length, for example, a byte, each word is delimited by **start** and **stop bits** as shown in *Figure 83.5*. In asynchronous serial data transmission the transmitter and receiver are not kept synchronised between transmissions. Instead, the receiver is synchronised with the transmitter only at the time of transmission. This allows data to be transmitted intermittently such as when typing characters on a keyboard.

Start bit

The arrival of data at the receiver is signalled by a special bit called a **start bit**. As the arrival of data cannot be predicted by the receiver, the transmission is called **asynchronous**.

The start bit is used to wake up the receiver. The receiver's clock is set ticking by the start bit. The clock is just a circuit that is designed to generate a preset number of pulses at fixed intervals which are used to sample the data bits as they arrive one after another. The signal changes in the serial data transmission take place at regular time intervals so the receiver must operate a timing device **set at the same rate as the transmitter**, so the received bits can be read at the same regular time intervals.

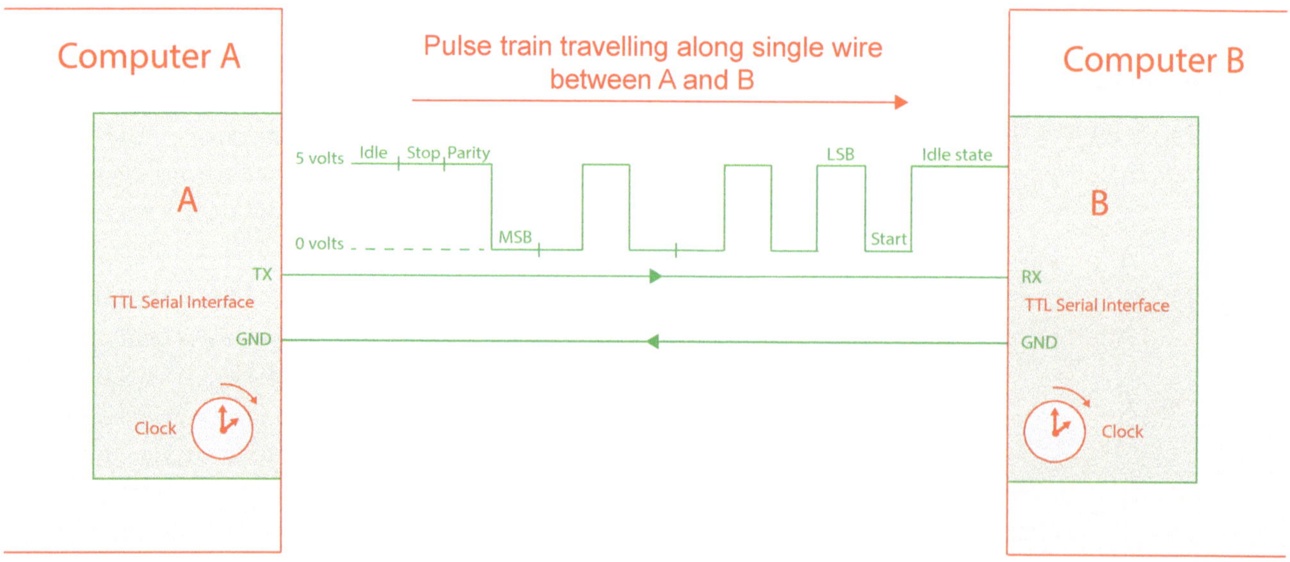

Fig. 83.7 Asynchronous serial data transmission between the TTL serial interface of two computers, A and B.

The transmitter also operates a timing device, a clock, that is set at a rate determined by the baud rate (see later in this chapter for an explanation of baud rate). Again this can be as simple a circuit to generate a preset number of pulses at fixed intervals of time.

It is important that the receiver reads each bit during the time that it is not changing, i.e. in the time interval between when changes can take place. This is why the receiver's timing device needs to be brought in step or synchronism with the transmission's timing.

Figure 83.7 shows two computers, A and B, with a TTL serial connection between their serial ports. TTL is Transistor-Transistor Logic and is a logic that operates between 0 volts and 5 or 3.3 volts. TTL relies on circuits built from bipolar transistors to achieve switching and maintain logic states.

For the link from computer A to computer B, the data wire is kept at the voltage level corresponding to a binary digit 1 when not sending – the **idle state**. A data transmission is started by changing the voltage level to the level for binary digit 0. This is the **start bit**. The transmitter (TX) then follows the start bit with 7 or 8 data bits depending on how the serial port has been configured. The least significant data bit (LSB) is sent first and the most significant data bit (MSB) last. If parity is enabled, the last data bit is followed by a parity bit.

Stop bit

Finally, the transmitter attaches a **stop bit.** The voltage level chosen for the stop bit is the level for binary digit 1. The time interval for the stop bit allows the receiver (RX) to deal with the received bits, i.e. transfer them into the RAM of the computer, before receiving and processing the next serial frame as shown in *Figure 83.8*. Two stop bits are used if the receiver needs more time to deal with the received bits.

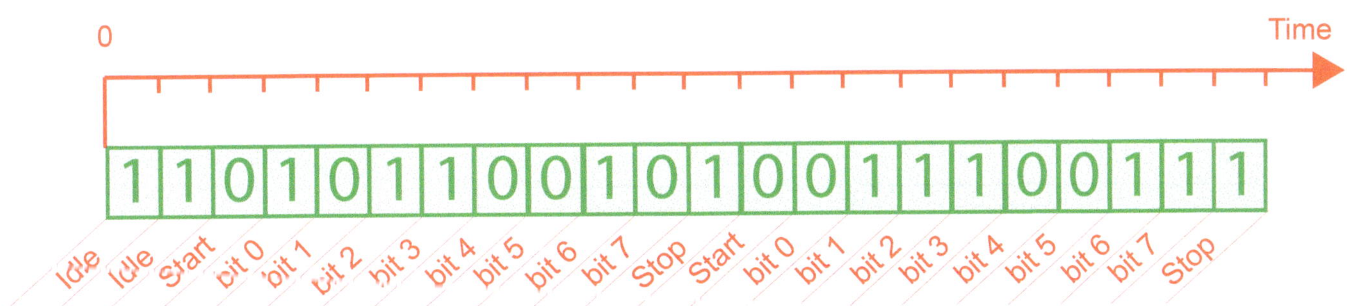

Fig. 83.8 Asynchronous serial data transmission frame showing transmission of two bytes without parity.

Baud rate

The **baud rate sets the maximum frequency at which signals may change**. To understand the meaning of baud rate consider the following simplified switching system shown in *Figure 83.9*. Switch A operates at the baud rate. For example if the baud rate is 1 baud then the switch remains connected to one of the four electrical voltages for one second. At the end of each second, the switch can switch the connection to any one of the four possible voltages. The changeover happens in a time period very much smaller than one second (theoretically, it happens instantaneously). Thus, the output signal that appears on the signal wire may change every one second but no quicker. If the baud rate is 10 baud then the switch can change position every tenth of a second.

Key concept

Baud rate: The maximum rate at which signals on a wire or line may change.

1 baud: One signal change per second.

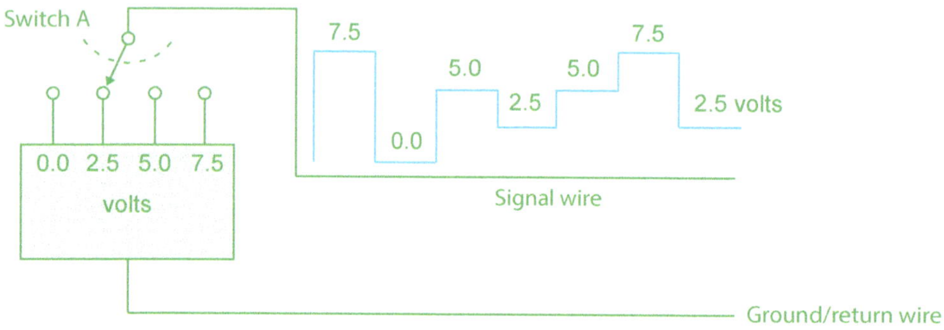

Fig. 83.9 Simplified switching system illustrating baud rate

For example, a computer's serial port may be set to send at 1 baud, the signal sent out by the computer can change only at the end of each elapsed second.

Table 83.1 shows the rates of signal change for some baud rates.

Baud rate	Time between signal changes (s)	Rate of signal changes (changes per second)
1	1	1
2	0.5	2
4	0.25	4
1000	0.001	1000
10000	0.0001	10000

Table 83.1 Relationship between baud rate and rate of signal changes

Key concept

Bit rate: The number of bits transmitted per second.

Bit rate

Bit rate is measured in bits per second. It is the **number of bits transmitted per second**. The bit rate is the same as the baud rate when one bit is sent between consecutive signal changes. However, it is possible to send more than one bit between signal changes if more than two voltage levels are used to encode bits. If the voltages 0 volts, 2.5 volts, 5 volts and 7.5 volts are used, then the decimal numbers in *Table 83.2* can be encoded.

Signal level (volts)	Decimal number	Binary number
0	0	00
2.5	1	01
5	2	10
7.5	3	11

Table 83.2 Linking signal levels and number of bits they encode

Fig. 83.10 shows how two bits of data can be encoded per time slot on a 1 baud line, giving a bit rate of 2 bits per second.

From this we may conclude that the relationship between bit rate and baud rate is

bit rate = baud rate x the no of bits per signal (voltage)

Key fact

bit rate = baud rate x the no of bits per signal (voltage)

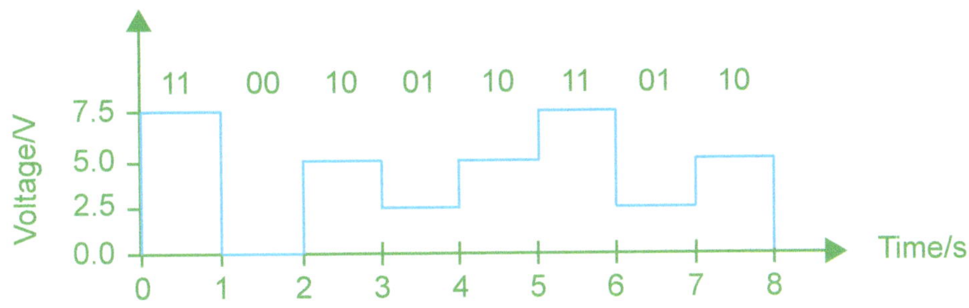

Figure 83.10 Sending data along a 1 baud line using four levels of voltage to encode bits

Protocol

A communication protocol is a set of pre-agreed signals, codes and rules used to ensure successful communication between computers or a computer and a peripheral device such as a printer.

Key concept

Communication protocol:
A set of pre-agreed signals, codes and rules to be used for data and information exchange between computers, or a computer and a peripheral device such as a printer, that ensure that the communication is successful.

A protocol will govern such things as:

- Physical connections – e.g. RS423 serial
- Data format – packet/frame size
- Error detection and correction
- Cabling – Cat 5, Optical fibre
- Speed – baud rate, bit rate
- Flow control
- How data is to be sent

Information

Handshaking protocol:
The sending and receiving devices exchange signals to establish that the receiving device is connected and ready to receive. Then the sending device coordinates the sending of the data, informing the receiver that it is sending. Finally, the receiver indicates it has received the data and is ready to receive again.

For example, serial data communication, uses a handshaking protocol to control the flow of data - *Table 83.3*.

C	→	Are you ready?	→	P
C	←	Yes I am	←	P
C	→	Here it is (Start bit)	→	P
C	←	Busy	←	P
C	→	That's it (Stop bit)	→	P
C	←	I'm ready again	←	P

Table 83.3 Handshaking protocol: computer = C, printer = P

In a handshaking protocol, the sending device checks first to see if the receiving device is present. If it is present, the sending device then enquires if the receiving device is ready to receive. The sending device waits for a response which indicates that the receiving device is ready to receive. On receipt of this signal, the sending device coordinates the sending of the data and informs the receiver that it is sending the data. The sender then waits for the receiver to become ready to receive more data.

Figure 83.11 shows the **COMPort Setup pop up window** from the exercise in *Chapter 82*. The pop up window shows that the default baud rate is 9600 Baud , the default number of data bits is 8, the default number of stop bits is one, the default is to not use a parity bit, and to not use flow control.

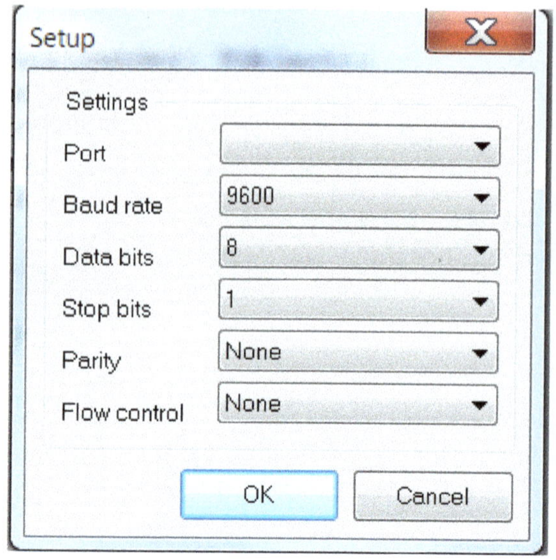

Fig. 83.11 Com Port Setup pop up window

Arduino Uno

Purpose: To become more familiar with the Arduino Uno

Arduino Uno development board

The **Arduino Uno** is a development board comprising a programmable microcontroller, an **Atmega 328P**, and other electronic circuits that allow the board to be connected to electronic output devices or input devices through its digital input/output pins and analogue input pins, and a host computer via **USB**. The **Arduino Uno** is shown with its main components labelled in *Figure 84.1*.

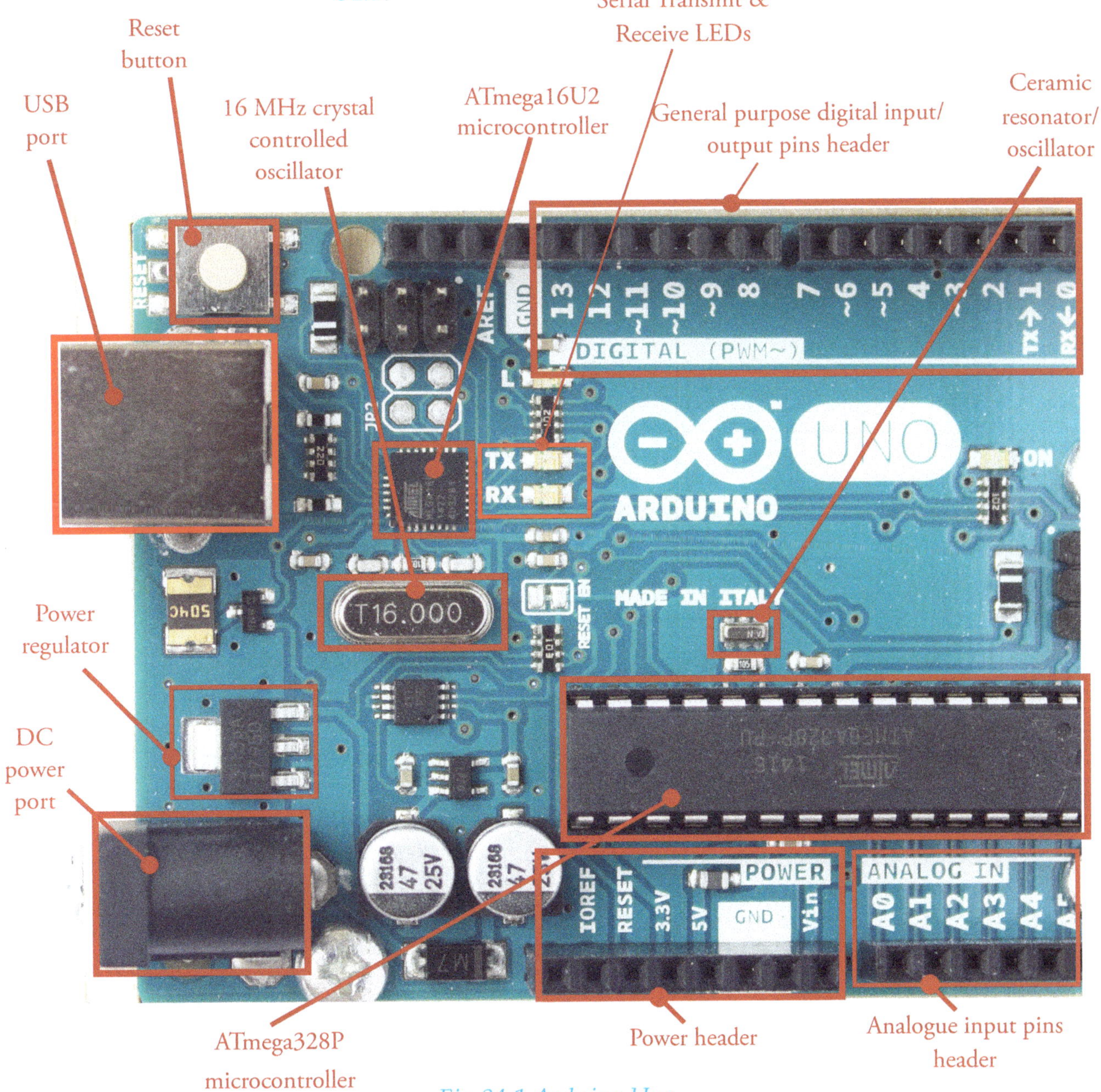

Fig.84.1 Arduino Uno

A secondary microcontroller, ATmega 16U2, is used as a **USB/serial signal converter** and is necessary because the ATmega 328P has a traditional **serial (COM) port** but no **USB port**. The ATmega 328P uses the ATmega16U2 to convert the serial signals sent from **ATmega 328P COM port** to **ATmega16U2 COM port**, to signals suitable for communication by **USB** from **ATmega16U2 USB port** to **host computer USB port**.

The host computer needs to be configured with a **virtual serial (COM) communications port** if it has no physical traditonal **serial (COM) port**, e.g. RS232 port.

In the reverse direction from host computer to Arduino Uno, **USB** signals received by the ATmega 16U2 on its **USB port** are converted to **serial (COM) port** signals that can be sent to the **ATmega328P's serial (COM) port.**

The end-to-end communication between a program running in the host computer and a program running in the ATmega328P microcontroller can thus exchange data as if they were connected directly via traditional serial ports governed by a traditional serial data communication protocol such as RS232- *Figure 84.2*.

The ATmega328P has firmware that intercepts serial data from the ATmega16U2 and allocates program memory to store it.

A **16MHz crystal controlled oscillator** is connected to the ATmega16U2 to provide precise timing signals for synchronising serial communication.

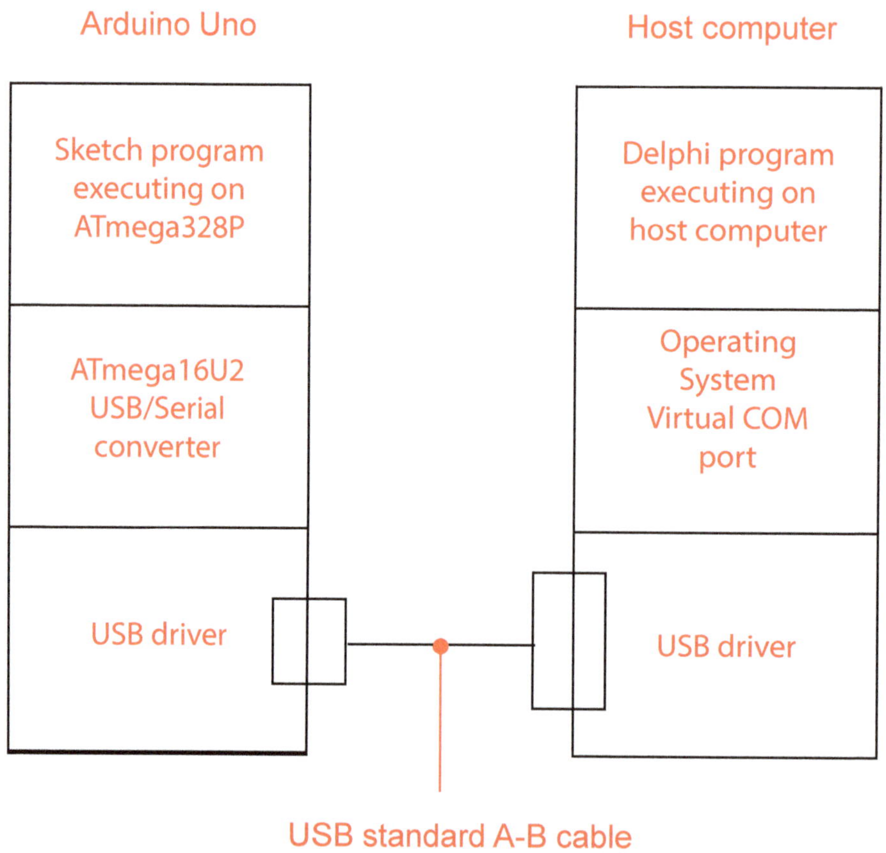

Fig. 84.2 Communication pathway between program executing on an Arduino Uno and a program executing on a host computer

The ATmega328P has its own oscillators driven by a ceramic resonator instead of a crystal oscillator as shown in *Figure 84.1*. These provide timing signals for the processor for its execution cycle and for various other timing operations such as when a **LED**s made to flash on and off periodically.

The host computer provides via the **USB** connection to the **Uno**, 500mA at 5V for an enumerated device (one that properly identifies itself to the **USB** host) and 100mA of current at 5V for an unenumerated device. This current is enough for small projects, but is insufficient for larger loads like motors, relays, etc. An advantage of **USB** over the previous serial communication standard, **RS232**, is that **USB** provides a regulated 5V supply.

To provide more power requires a separate power supply in the range 7-20V that connects via a barrel connector shown in *Figure 84.1*. It is a circular port, 2.1mm in diameter. The center pin is positive, and the outer sleeve is ground (GND).

In addition to powering up the **Arduino Uno** hardware, the power supplied via the barrel connector can be accessed at **Vin** to power up components on the breadboard[1] or shields.

Shields are additional boards that usually follow the form factor of the **Arduino Uno** and can be attached to the **Arduino** to add different functionalities, e.g. WiFi capability.

All the general purpose **I/O pins** on the **Arduino** can be used as **digital I/O pins**. Digital input pins read digital inputs, and digital output pins write digital outputs.

The six analogue pins on the **Arduino Uno** are analogue input pins only.

Analogue electrical signals are electrical signals that vary in a continuous manner in a particular range.

Data sensed by analogue sensors are converted into an equivalent analogue signal by a transducer, e.g. air temperatures are converted by a thermocouple sensor into an equivalent analogue electrical signal. The analogue electrical signals are voltages that vary over some range. The analogue input pins of an **Arduino Uno** can measure such voltages (or signals) in the range 0-5V.

Digital data are discrete values, e.g. 0 or 5. The corresponding electrical signals could be 0 volts and 5 volts. **Analogue data** encompasses all the values between these two discrete values, 0 and 5, for the given example.

Sensors usually output analogue signals. The **ATmega 328P** cannot process analogue signals directly but it is able to use a special electronic component called an **Analogue to Digital Converter (ADC)** to convert the analogue signal into an equivalent digital value represented in 1024 bits.

Virtual COM port

Software drivers that create a Virtual COM Port are installed when the Arduino IDE software is installed on the host computer.

A Virtual COM Port is a setting within the Windows Operating System that allows software applications to "talk" to USB devices connected to the host's USB connector as if the ost and USB device were connected using traditional serial (COM Port) connections.

A driver is a piece of software that installs into the Windows Operating System that allows all applications to communicate with the connected device. Without a driver, a device can not be used.

1 See later in this chapter for a description of breadboard.

Determining the COM Port Number of a Virtual COM Port

Once the Arduino Uno driver is installed, you can check that a Virtual COM Port has been set up as follows:

1. Open Device Manager:
   Click: Start > Control Panel > Hardware and Sound > Device Manager (under "Devices and Printers")
2. In the Device Manager list, look in Ports and find the Virtual COM Port, which was created by the USB driver, e.g. Arduino Uno (COM5) - see *Figure 84.3*.

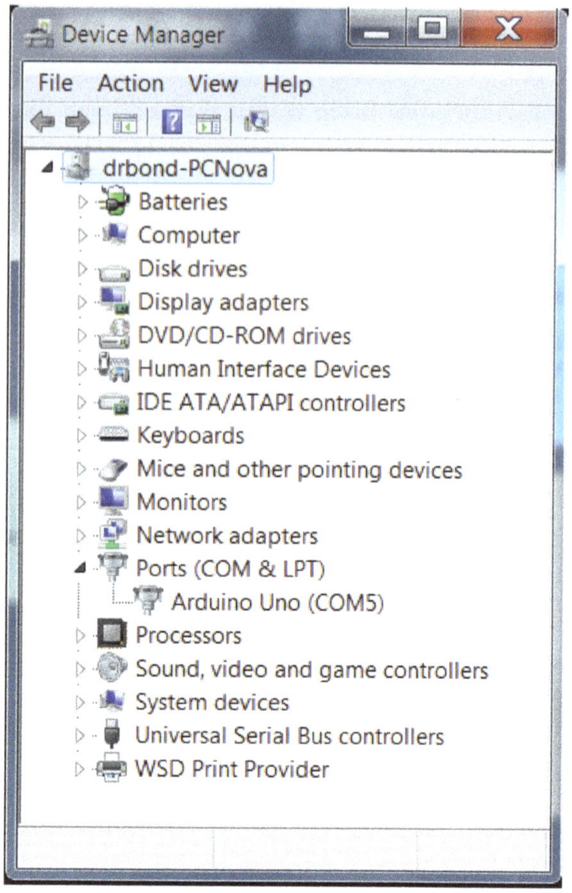

Fig. 84.3 Windows 7 Device Manager window showing that a virtual port COM5 has been set up for the Arduino Uno

Arduino Serial library functions

The full list of **Serial library functions** and their descriptions can be found at https://www.arduino.cc/reference/en/language/functions/communication/serial/.

We use the **Arduino IDE** running on the host computer to prepare programs which will be uploaded and run in the **Arduino Uno**. Arduino provides several software libraries of functions, one of which is the **Serial library**. Functions from the **Serial library** run in the **Arduino Uno** and enable serial communications between the **Arduino** and the host computer. *Table 84.1* shows a list of the most important functions from this library.

Serial library functions	Description
`Serial.begin()`	Sets the data rate in bits per second (baud) for serial data transmission, e.g. `Serial.begin(9600);`

`Serial.print()`	Prints data to the serial port as human-readable ASCII text. Numbers are printed using an ASCII character for each digit. Floats are similarly printed as ASCII digits, defaulting to two decimal places. Bytes are sent as a single character. Characters and strings are sent as is. For example-
	`Serial.print(78); gives "78"`
	`Serial.print(1.23456); gives "1.23"`
	`Serial.print('N'); gives "N"`
	`Serial.print("Hello world."); gives "Hello world."`

`Serial.println`	Prints data to the serial port as human-readable ASCII text followed by a carriage return character (ASCII 13, or '\r') and a newline character (ASCII 10, or '\n'). This command takes the same forms as `Serial.print()`.
`Serial.read()`	Reads incoming serial data. Returns the first byte of incoming serial data available (or -1 if no data is available, e.g. `incomingByte = Serial.read();`

`Serial.available()`	Gets the number of bytes (characters) available for reading from the serial port. This is data that's already arrived and stored in the serial receive buffer (which holds 64 bytes).
	`if (Serial.available() > 0) {`
	`// read the incoming byte:`
	`incomingByte = Serial.read();}`

Table 84.1 Some useful functions from the Arduino Serial library

Arduino programming language

The Arduino IDE allows users to write programs in a simplified version of C/C++.

Arduino uses the name **sketch** for a program. A **compiled sketch program** is the unit of code that is uploaded to and run on an Arduino board.

Reading voltages from a temperature sensor

Table 84.2 shows a program that reads the output from a temperature sensor, **TMP326,** continually.

The special functions `setup()` and `loop()` are a part of every Arduino sketch

The function `setup()` is called once, when the sketch starts executing.

Function `setup()` is the place to do setup tasks like setting pin modes or stablishing a serial connection with `Serial.begin(9600)`.

The function `loop()` runs its body over and over again.

The function call `analogRead(sensorPin)` reads the value from the specified analogue pin, **A1**.

The Arduino Uno contains a multichannel, 10-bit analog to digital converter that services 6 analogue pins.

It maps input voltages between 0 and the operating voltage(5V or 3.3V) into integer values between 0 and 1023.

The integer value is assigned to an int varibale sensorVal as follows

```
int sensorVal = analogRead(sensorPin);
```

The resolution between readings is 5 volts / 1024 units or, 0.0049 volts (4.9 mV) per unit.

Therefore, to calculate the voltage equivalent of the sensor reading we use

```
float voltage = sensorVal * 5.0 / 1024.0;
```

The result is a number with a fractional part so we assign the result to a floating point variable, `voltage`.

The float datatype stores 32 bits (4 bytes) of information. The statement `Serial.print(voltage);` sends these four bytes as four ASCII digits, defaulting to two decimal places - see *Table 84.1*. A one second delay before the next voltage is sent is achieved by `delay(1000)`.

```
// named constant for the pin the sensor is connected to
const int sensorPin = A1;
void setup()
  {
    // open a serial connection at 9600 Baud
    Serial.begin(9600);
  }
void loop()
  {
    // read the value on AnalogIn pin 1 and store it in variable sensorVal
    int sensorVal = analogRead(sensorPin);
    // convert the ADC reading to voltage
    float voltage = (sensorVal * 5.0 / 1024.0);
    /*
      The sensor changes 10 mV per degree
      A 500 mV offset is required according to the datasheet
      which states temperature should be calculated as follows
      Temperature =((voltage in mV - 500 mV)/10)
      Conversion will be done in Delphi program
    */
    // Send the voltage level through serial port to host computer
    Serial.print(voltage);
    // Send voltage at one second intervals using delay of 1000 milliseconds
    delay(1000);
  }
```

Table 84.2 Arduino reading temperatures program

Delphi program to read temperatures

Select File|New VCL Forms Application (Delphi Community Edition).

Click File|Save All and, **save** unit as ArduinoTemperatureSensorUnit and **save** project as ArduinoTemperatureSensor in folder ArduinoTemperatureSensor.

Place on the form one TComPort component from the CPortLib page of the Tool palette, two buttons, one label, from the Standard page.

Arrange these components as shown in *Figure 84.4* - at this stage the components will still have their original captions, Button1, Button2, etc, and their original names.

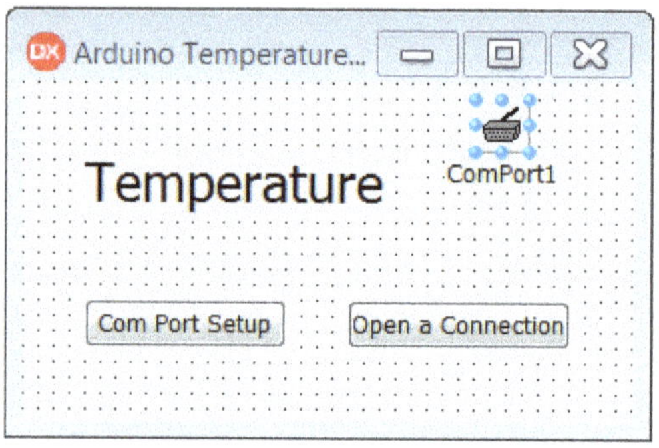

Fig.84.4 Delphi Community Edition design window for temperature program

Change the Form's Caption property in the Object Inspector to Arduino Temperature Sensor Application.

Change the first button's Name property to ComPortSetup. **Change** its Caption property to Com Port Setup.

Change the second button's Name property to OpenAConnection. **Change** its caption to Open a Connection.

Change OpenAConnection Enabled property to False.

Change Label1's Caption property to Temperature.

Double click button ComPortSetup to create the event handler TForm1.ComPortSetupClick(Sender: TObject).

Add the code shown in *Table 84.3* to the body of this event handler.

```
ComPort1.ShowSetupDialog;
If Comport1.Port <> ''
  Then OpenAConnection.Enabled := True
  Else OpenAConnection.Enabled := False;
```

Table 84.3 Event handling code for TForm1.ComPortSetupClick(Sender: TObject)

Double click button OpenAConnection to create the event handler TForm1.OpenAConnectionClick(Sender: TObject);.

Add the code shown in *Table 84.4* to the body of this event handler. UpdateState is a procedure that will be created later.

```
If ComPort1.Connected
  Then
    Begin
      ComPort1.Close;
      Label1.Caption := '';
    End
  Else Comport1.Open;
UpdateState;
```

Table 84.4 Event handling code for TForm1.OpenAConnectionClick(Sender: TObject)

Add the code for procedure **TForm1.UpdateState** shown in *Table 84.5* to the **Implementation** section before the event handlers.

Add procedure **TForm1.UpdateState;** to the class definition for **TForm1**.

```
Procedure TForm1.UpdateState;
  Begin
    SpeedButton1.Enabled := ComPort1.Connected;
    Label1.Enabled := ComPort1.Connected;
    If ComPort1.Connected
      Then OpenAConnection.Caption := 'Close connection'
      Else OpenAConnection.Caption := 'Open connection';
  End;
```

Table 84.5 Procedure TForm1.UpdateState

Select **Form1** in the **Object Inspector** and click on the **Events** tab.

Find the **OnDestroy** property and **double click** the blank space to create the event handler stub for **Procedure TForm1.FormDestroy(Sender: TObject).**

Add the code from *Table 84.6* to complete this event handler.

Select **Form1** in the **Object Inspector** and click on the **Events** tab.

Find the **OnShow** property and **double click** the blank space to create the event handler stub for **Procedure TForm1.FormShow(Sender: TObject).**

Add the code from *Table 82.6* to complete this event handler.

```
Procedure TForm1.FormDestroy(Sender: TObject);
  Begin
    If ComPort1.Connected
      Then ComPort1.Close;
  End;

Procedure TForm1.FormShow(Sender: TObject);
  Begin
    UpdateState;
  End;
```

Table 84.6 Procedure TForm1.FormDestroy(Sender: TObject) and procedure TForm1.FormDestroy(Sender: TObject)

Click File|Save to save the unit.

Now **click** Project|Build ArduinoTemperatureSensor to compile and build the project.

Wiring the temperature sensor TMP36 to breadboard and Arduino Uno

Figure 84.5 shows the temperature sensor **TMP36** wired to breadboard as follows:

Plug the **TMP36** into the breadboard, columns 14, 15 and 16 as shown with flatside facing Arduino.

Connect Arduino power rails to Arduino, red rail to Arduino 5V and black rail to Arduino **GND** as shown in *Figure 84.6*.

Connect column 16 to the **5V** power rail and column 14 to the **GND** power rail.

Connect column 15 to **Analogue pin 1** on the Arduino Uno as shown in *Figure 84.6*.

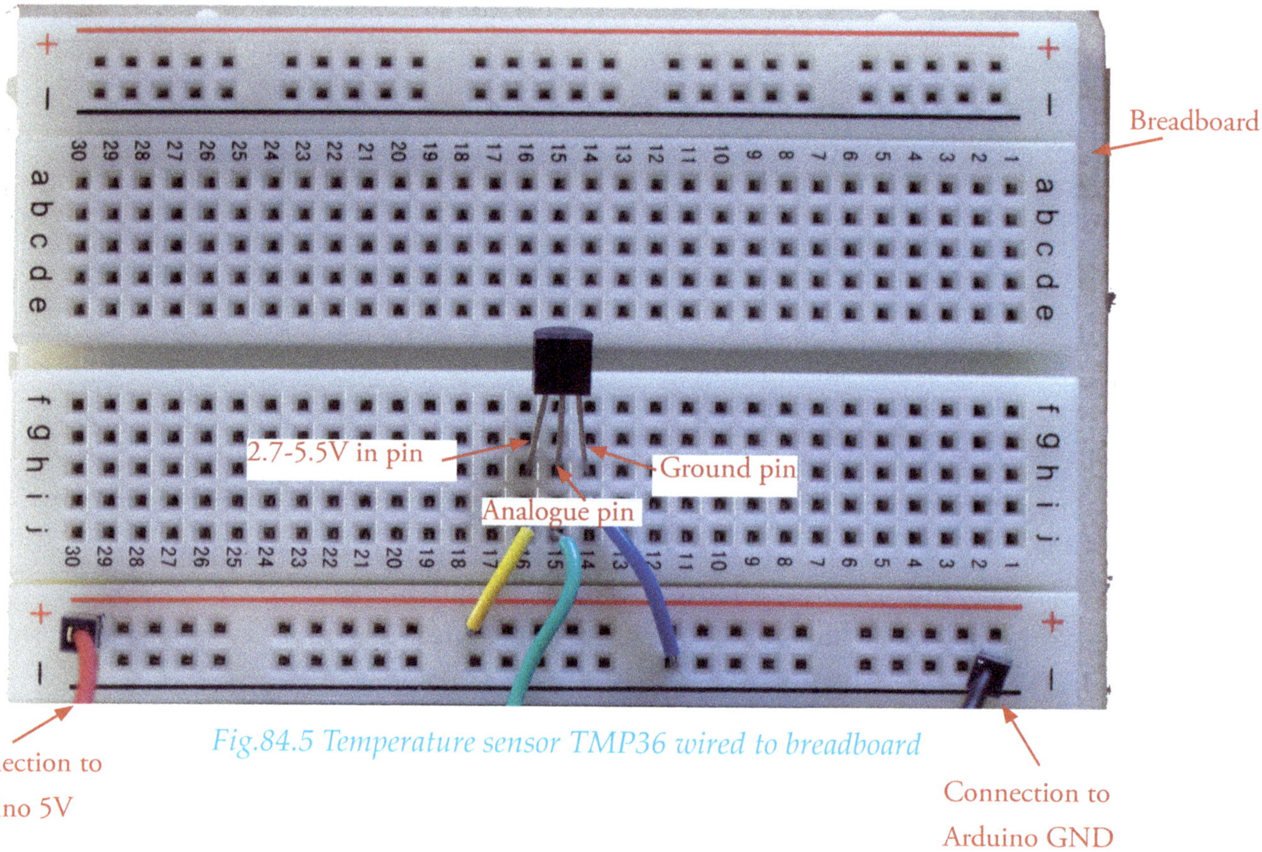

Fig.84.5 Temperature sensor TMP36 wired to breadboard

Plug the USB cable into the Arduino Uno and **connect** this cable to the computer.

Upload the Arduino program shown in *Table 84.2* to the Arduino Uno.

Run the ArduinoTemperatureSensor program.

Click on **Com Port Setup** button.

Select the **Com Port** - see *Figure 84.7* where it is **COM5**.

Select Baud rate 9600.

Click OK.

Click Open connection button. The current temperature should now display as shown in *Figure 84.8*.

The displayed temperature will refresh every one second.

Fig.84.6 Arduino Uno connected to breadboard

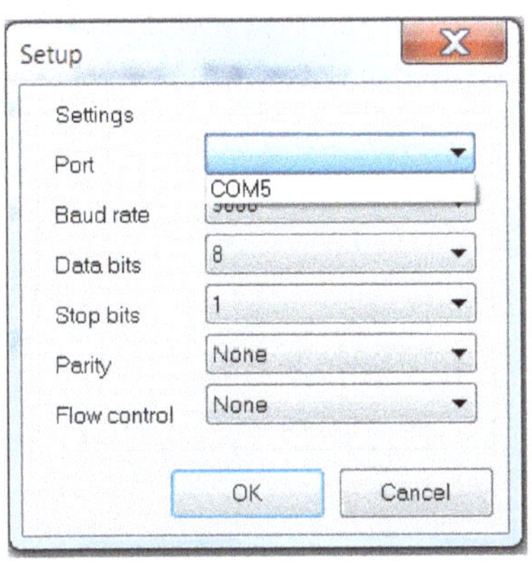

Fig.84.7 Com Port Setup window

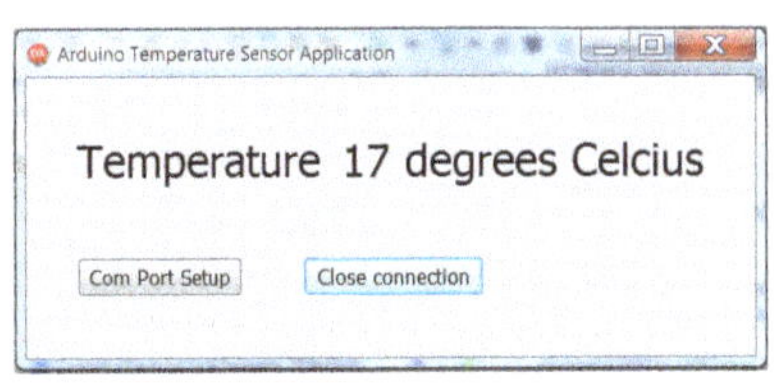

Fig.84.8 Arduino temperature sensor program in execution

Index

V

W

X

www.ingramcontent.com/pod-product-compliance
Ingram Content Group UK Ltd.
Pitfield, Milton Keynes, MK11 3LW, UK
UKHW061506081026
15590UKWH00024B/2049

9 780992 753603